HISPANIC AMERICAN PERIODICALS INDEX

An adjunct to the

UCLA LATIN AMERICAN CENTER PUBLICATIONS

Reference Series

BARBARA G. VALK

General Editor

Hapi

HISPANIC AMERICAN PERIODICALS INDEX

1993

EDITOR: BARBARA G. VALK
ASSOCIATE EDITOR: MAJ-BRITT V. NILSSON

UCLA LATIN AMERICAN CENTER PUBLICATIONS
UNIVERSITY OF CALIFORNIA, LOS ANGELES

Hispanic American Periodicals Index

UCLA Latin American Center

University of California, Los Angeles

CONTENTS

INTRODUCTION

The *Hispanic American Periodicals Index* lists annually by subject and author articles, documents, reviews, bibliographies, original literary works, and other items appearing in nearly two hundred fifty journals published throughout the world which regularly contain information on Latin America. Also indexed are leading journals treating the United States-Mexico border region and Hispanics in the United States. All materials relevant to the region are indexed.

The journals to be indexed were selected with the assistance of the Committee on Bibliography of the Seminar on the Acquisition of Latin American Library Materials (SALALM) and an international panel of indexers on the basis of scholarly value and representative coverage of editorial viewpoint, subject matter, and geographical area. Included are leading journals in all major disciplines of the social sciences and the humanities: archaeology and anthropology; art; economics, development, and finance; education; folklore; film; geography; history; language and linguistics; literature; music; philosophy; political science; sociology; and others. Only the pure and technical sciences have been excluded.

Every effort is made to index the same journals each year, and significant new titles are added as they appear. The journals indexed for this volume were published in 1993, although some bear earlier dates because of delayed or irregular publication schedules.

The index is divided into Subject, Book Review, and Author sections. Headings in the Subject section are selected from the *HAPI Thesaurus and Name Authority, 1970-1989* and its updates. The *Thesaurus* is based on the Library of Congress' *Subject Headings*, 12th edition, adapted to meet the specialized requirements of research on Latin America. Although most headings are in English, exceptions include proper names and concepts, such as "Indigenismo," for which no commonly accepted translation has been established. Form headings provide access to drama and film reviews and to archaeological site reports. Spanish and Portuguese translations of all primary level English language subject headings, excluding proper names and equivalent terms, precede the Subject section.

Cross references guide the reader to proper headings and tie together related articles. References are also used extensively under the names of countries to indicate the presence of information about that country listed under other major headings.

Book reviews are listed in a separate section under the author of the book. Reviews of nonfiction books also appear under pertinent headings in the Subject section. Poems, short stories, and other original literary works are listed only in the Author section under the author's name.

The Author section contains in a single alphabetical listing entries for personal, joint, and corporate authors and editors of articles and original literary works. Names have been verified whenever possible in authoritative bibliographic sources. They do not, however, always conform to AACR2 regulations for using the most simplified form of the name. More extensive forms are used when needed to distinguish one individual from another.

Complete bibliographic information is given for each entry: author(s), full article title, short journal title (followed by country of origin if necessary for clarification), volume and/or issue number, abbreviated date, inclusive page numbers, and appropriate bibliographic notes.

The Key to Periodicals lists variant forms of journal titles, the subscription address of the publishers, and, when available, International Standard Serial Numbers. Journals indexed in previous volumes that have ceased or suspended publication during the year are also noted.

In addition to the printed volumes, HAPI is available for online searching through the UCLA Latin American Center and the Research Libraries Group's CitaDel Citation and Delivery Service. The index is also published on CD-ROM by National Information Services Corporation (NISC), Baltimore, Maryland.

The publication of the *Hispanic American Periodicals Index* depends upon the combined efforts of many contributors. Among these, the editor particularly wishes to thank the international panel of indexers for their volunteer service in supplying the basic data on the articles, the Seminar on the Acquisition of Latin American Library Materials for its institutional support and advice, and Colleen Trujillo of the UCLA Latin American Center for her invaluable aid in the operational tasks of preparing the index for publication. Most of all we owe thanks to the National Endowment for the Humanities for the financial support that launched HAPI.

Barbara G. Valk
Editor

KEY TO PERIODICALS

The key lists the short form of the journal title as it appears in the index; the complete title and/or variant forms of the title; the subscription address of the publisher; and when available, the International Standard Serial Number of the journal.

Afro-Hispanic Review

Editor
143 Arts and Science Building
University of Missouri-Columbia
Columbia, Missouri 65211

ISSN: 0278-8969

Aisthesis

Aisthesis; Revista Chilena de Investigaciones Estéticas

Instituto de Estética
Facultad de Filosofía
Pontificia Universidad Católica de Chile
Casilla 114-D
Santiago, Chile

ISSN: 0568-3939

Allpanchis

Instituto de Pastoral Andina
Apartado 1018
Cusco, Peru

Amazonia Indígena

Amazonia Indígena; Boletín de Análisis

COPAL
Apartado 502
Iquitos, Peru

(No issues received in 1993)

Amazonía Peruana

Centro Amazónico de Antropología y Aplicación
Práctica
Programa de Difusión
Apartado 14-0166
Lima 14, Peru

ISSN: 0252-886X

América Indígena

Instituto Indigenista Interamericano
Calle Nubes 232
Colonia Pedregal de San Angel
01900 México, D.F., Mexico

ISSN: 0185-1179

América Latina (USSR)

EBSCO Industries, Inc.
1st Avenue, North at 13th Street
Birmingham, Alabama 35203

ISSN: 0207-7116

(Ceased: no. 2, February 1992)

Américas

Subscription Service
P.O. Box 2103
Knoxville, Iowa 50197-2103

ISSN: 0379-0940

The Americas

Americas; Quarterly Review of Inter-American Cultural History

Journals Division, CUA Press
303 Administration Building
The Catholic University of America
620 Michigan Avenue, N.E.
Washington, D.C. 20064

ISSN: 0003-1615

The Americas Review

The Americas Review; A Review of Hispanic Literature and Art of the U.S.A

(Formerly: *Revista Chicano-Riqueña*)

University of Houston
Houston, Texas 77204-2090

ISSN: 1042-6213

Anales de Antropología

Juan Comas, Editor
Instituto de Investigaciones Antropológicas
Universidad Nacional Autónoma de México
Ciudad Universitaria
Delegación Coyoacán
04510 México, D.F., Mexico

ISSN: 0020-3947

(No issues received in 1993)

Anales de Literatura Hispanoamericana

Editorial Complutense
Donoso Cortés, 65
28015 Madrid, Spain

ISSN: 0210-4547

(No issues received in 1993)

Anales del Instituto de Investigaciones Estéticas

Mexico (City). Universidad Nacional. Instituto de Investigaciones Estéticas. Anales

Instituto de Investigaciones Estéticas
Circuito Exterior Oriente
Zona Cultural
Ciudad Universitaria
04510 México, D.F., Mexico

ISSN: 0185-1276

Ancient Mesoamerica

Cambridge University Press
40 West 20th Street
New York, New York 10011

ISSN: 0956-5361

Antropológica

Fundación La Salle
Instituto Caribe de Antropología y Sociología
Apartado 1930
Caracas 1010-A, Venezuela

ISSN: 0003-6110

(No issues received in 1993)

Anuario Colombiano de Historia Social y de la Cultura

Departamento de Historia
Facultad de Ciencias Humanas
Universidad Nacional de Colombia
Apartado Aéreo 14490
Bogotá, D.E., Colombia

ISSN: 0066-5045

Anuario de Estudios Americanos

Escuela de Estudios Hispano-Americanos
Alfonso XII, 16
41002 Sevilla, Spain

ISSN: 0210-5810

Anuario de Estudios Centroamericanos

Editorial de la Universidad de Costa Rica
Apartado Postal 75
2600 Ciudad Universitaria "Rodrigo Facio"
San José, Costa Rica

ISSN: 0377-7316

Anuario de Geografía (Mexico)

Mexico (City). Universidad Nacional. Facultad de Filosofía y Letras. Anuario de Geografía

Editor
Dirección General de Publicaciones
Universidad Nacional Autónoma de México
Ciudad Universitaria
04510 México, D.F., Mexico

ISSN: 0185-1322

(No issues published in 1993)

Anuario de Letras (Mexico)

Mexico (City). Universidad Nacional. Facultad de Filosofía y Letras. Anuario de Letras

Ciudad de la Investigación en Humanidades
Circuito Mario de la Cueva
Ciudad Universitaria
04510 México, D.F., Mexico

ISSN: 0185-1373

Anuario Indigenista

Editor
Instituto Indigenista Interamericano
Calle Nubes 232
Colonia Pedregal de San Angel
01900 México, D.F., Mexico

ISSN: 0185-5441

Anuario Interamericano de Archivos

(Formerly: *Boletín Interamericano de Archivos*)

Centro Interamericano de Desarrollo de Archivos
Avenida Hipólito Irigoyen 174
5000 Córdoba, Argentina

ISSN: 0326-842X

(Presumed suspended: v. 13, 1989)

Apuntes

Librería de la Universidad del Pacífico
Apartado Postal 4683
Lima 100, Peru

ISSN: 0252-1865

Archivo Ibero-Americano

Joaquín Costa, 36
28002 Madrid, Spain

ISBN: 84-86379-22-9

Art Nexus

Apartado Aéreo 90193
Bogotá, D.E., Colombia

ISSN: 0121-5639

Artes de México

Plaza Río de Janeiro 52
Colonia Roma
06700 México, D.F., Mexico

ISSN: 0300-4953

Atenea (Chile)

Atenea; Revista de Ciencia, Arte y Literatura

Universidad de Concepción
Biblioteca Central, Campus Universitario
Casilla 1557
Concepción, Chile

ISSN: 0716-1840

Aztlán

Aztlán; A Journal of Chicano Studies

(Formerly: *Aztlán; International Journal of Chicano Studies Research*)

Chicano Studies Research Center
University of California, Los Angeles
405 Hilgard Avenue
Los Angeles, California 90024-1447

ISSN 0005-2604

Belizean Studies

P.O. Box 548
St. John's College
Belize City, Belize

ISSN 0250-6831

Bilingual Review/Revista Bilingüe

Hispanic Research Center
Arizona State University
Tempe, Arizona 85287-2702

ISSN: 0094-5366

Boletín Americanista

Edicions de la Universitat de Barcelona
Gran Via de les Corts Catalanes, 585
08007 Barcelona, Spain

ISSN 0520-4100

Boletín de Antropología Americana

Instituto Panamericano de Geografía e Historia
Secretaría General
Apartado Postal 18879
11870 México, D.F., Mexico

ISSN 0252-841X

Boletín de Historia y Antigüedades

Academia Colombiana de Historia
Calle 10, No. 8-95
Apartado Aéreo 14428
Bogotá, D.E., Colombia

ISSN 0006-6303

Boletín de la Academia Chilena de la Historia

Academia Chilena de la Historia
Clasificador 245 – Correo Central
Santiago, Chile

ISSN: 0716-5439

Boletín de la Academia Hondureña de la Lengua

Academia Hondureña de la Lengua. Boletín

Academia Hondureña de la Lengua
Apartado Postal 38
Tegucigalpa, D.C., Honduras

ISSN: 0065-0471

(No issues published in 1993)

Boletín de la Academia Nacional de la Historia (Venezuela)

Academia Nacional de la Historia, Caracas. Boletín

Academia Nacional de la Historia
Palacio de las Academias
Antigua Universidad Central
Caracas, Venezuela

ISSN: 0001-382X

Brasil/Cultura

Sector Cultural de la Embajada del Brasil
Cerrito No. 1350
Caja Postal 1010
Buenos Aires, Argentina

(No issues received in 1993)

Bulletin de l'Institut Français d'Etudes Andines

Institut Français d'Etudes Andines. Bulletin

(Formerly: *Institut Français d'Etudes Andines. Travaux*)

Institut Français d'Etudes Andines
Casilla 18-1217
Lima 18, Peru

ISSN: 0303-7495

Bulletin of Latin American Research

Pergamom Press, Inc.
660 White Plains Road
Tarrytown, New York 10591-5153

ISSN: 0261-3050

Business Mexico

American Chamber of Commerce of Mexico, A.C.
Lucerna 78
Colonia Juárez
Delegación Cuauhtemoc
06600 México, D.F., Mexico

ISSN: 0187-1455

CEPAL Review (English version)

(Formerly: *Economic Bulletin for Latin America*)

United Nations Publications
Sales Section
Office DC-2-866
United Nations
New York, New York 10017

ISSN: 0251-2920

Cahiers des Amériques Latines

Editions de ITHEAL
Institut des Hautes Etudes de l'Amérique Latine
28 rue Saint-Guillaume
75007 Paris, France

ISSN 0008-0020

Canadian Journal of Latin American and Caribbean Studies

NS: Canadian Journal of Latin American and Caribbean Studies/ Revue Canadienne des Etudes Latino-Américaines et Caraïbes

(Formerly: *NS/NorthSouth; Canadian Journal of Latin American Studies*)

José del Pozo, Managing Editor, CJLACS
Department of History
Université du Quebec à Montréal
P.O. Box 8888
Station "A"
Montréal, Canada H3C3P8

ISSN: 0826-3663

Caravelle

(Formerly: *Cahiers du Monde Hispanique et Luso-Brésilien*

Régisseur des Presses Universitaires du Mirail
56 rue du Taur
31069 Toulouse, France

ISSN: 0008-0152

Caribbean Geography

University of the West Indies Publishers' Association
P.O. Box 42
Kingston 7, Jamaica

ISSN: 0252-9939

Caribbean Quarterly

The Editor
School of Continuing Studies
University of the West Indies
Mona, Kingston 7, Jamaica

ISSN: 0008-6495

Caribbean Studies

Estudios del Caribe/Caribbean Studies/Estudes des Caraïbes

Institute of Caribbean Studies
University of Puerto Rico
P.O. Box 23361
University Station
Río Piedras, Puerto Rico 00931-3361

ISSN: 0008-6533

El Caribe Contemporáneo

Centro de Estudios Latinoamericanos – Area del Caribe
Facultad de Ciencias Políticas y Sociales
Universidad Nacional Autónoma de México
Ciudad Universitaria
Delegación Coyoacán
04510 México, D.F., Mexico

ISSN: 0185-2426

(No issues received in 1993)

Casa de las Américas

Empresa "Ediciones Cubanas"
Vice-Dirección de Exportación
Obispo 461
Apartado 605
La Habana, Cuba

ISSN: 0008-7157

Chasqui

Howard M. Fraser
Department of Modern Languages
College of William and Mary
Williamsburg, Virginia 23185

ISSN: 0145-8973

Colonial Latin American Historical Review

Editor
Spanish Colonial Research Center
Zimmerman Library
University of New Mexico
Albuquerque, New Mexico 87131

ISSN: 1063-5769

Colonial Latin American Review

Raquel Chang-Rodríguez, General Editor
Department of Romance Languages (NAC 5/223)
Convent Avenue at 138th Street
The City College, CUNY
New York, New York 10031

ISSN: 1060-9164

Comercio Exterior

Banco Nacional de Comercio Exterior, S.N.C.
Gerencia de Publicaciones
Apartado Postal 21-258
Cerrada de Malintzin 28
Colonia del Carmen
Delegación Coyocacán
04100 México, D.F., Mexico

ISSN: 0185-0601

Confluencia

Confluencia; Revista Hispánica de Cultura y Literatura

Department of Hispanic Studies
University of Northern Colorado
Greeley, Colorado 80639

ISSN: 0888-6091

Conjunto

Empresa "Ediciones Cubanas"
Vice-Dirección de Exportación
Obispo 461
Apartado 605
La Habana, Cuba

ISSN: 0010-5937

Convivium

Convivium; Revista Bimestral de Investigação e Cultura

Alameda Eduardo Prado 705
01218 São Paulo, SP, Brazil

ISSN: 0589-6185

El Cotidiano

Universidad Autónoma Metropolitana
Unidad Azcapotzalco. División de Ciencias Sociales y Humanidades
Edificio E, Cubículo 004
Avenida San Pablo 180
Colonia Reynosa Tamaulipas
02200 México, D.F., Mexico

ISSN: 0186-1840

Cristianismo y Sociedad

Apartado Postal 15067
Guayaquil, Ecuador

ISSN: 0011-1457

Cuadernos Americanos

Cuadernos Americanos; La Revista del Nuevo Mundo

Torre I de Humanidades, Planta Baja
Ciudad Universitaria
04510 México, D.F., Mexico

ISSN: 0185-156X

Cuadernos de Economía (Chile)

Instituto de Economía
Universidad Católica de Chile
Oficina de Publicaciones
Casilla 274-V, Correo 21
Santiago, Chile

ISSN: 0716-0046

Cuadernos de Historia (Chile)

Departamento de Ciencias Históricas
Facultad de Filosofía, Humanidades y Educación
Universidad de Chile
Capitán Ignacio Carrera Pinto 1025
Santiago, Chile

ISSN: 0716-1832

Cuadernos del CLAEH

Centro Latinoamericano de Economía Humana

Centro Latinoamericano de Economía Humana
Zelmar Michelini 1220
Casilla de Correo 5021
11100 Montevideo, Uruguay

ISSN: 0797-6062

Cuadernos Hispanoamericanos

Instituto de Cooperación Iberoamericana
Avenida de los Reyes Católicos, 4
28040 Madrid, Spain

ISSN: 0011-250X

Cuban Studies/Estudios Cubanos

Center for Latin American Studies
4E04 Forbes Quadrangle
University of Pittsburgh
Pittsburgh, Pennsylvania 15260

ISSN: 0361-4441

Dados

Dados; Revista de Ciências Sociais

    IUPERJ
Rua da Matriz No. 82
Botafogo
22260-100 Rio de Janeiro, RJ, Brazil

    ISSN: 0011-5258

Debate

    Rocío Guzmán
Apoyo, S.A.
Apartado 671
Lima 100, Peru

Derecho y Reforma Agraria

Derecho y Reforma Agraria; Revista

    Instituto Iberoamericano de Derecho Agrario y
Reforma Agraria
Facultad de Ciencias Jurídicas y Políticas
Universidad de los Andes
Mérida, Venezuela

    ISSN: 0304-2820

Desarrollo Económico

Desarrollo Económico; Revista de Ciencias Sociales

    Instituto de Desarrollo Económico y Social
Aráoz 2838
1425 Buenos Aires, Argentina

    ISSN: 0046-001X

Desarrollo Indoamericano

    Carrera 54, No. 58-132
Apartado Aéreo 50122
Barranquilla, Colombia

    ISSN: 0418-7547

Deslindes

Deslindes; Revista de la Biblioteca Nacional

(Formerly: *Revista de la Biblioteca Nacional*)

    Hemeroteca
Biblioteca Nacional
Avenida 18 de Julio 1790
Casilla de Correos 452
Montevideo, Uruguay

(No issues published in 1993)

Diálogos (Puerto Rico)

    EDUPR
P.O. Box 23322
U.P.R. Station
San Juan, Puerto Rico 00931

    ISSN: 0012-2122

ECA; Estudios Centroamericanos

(Formerly: *Estudios Centroamericanos*)

    Revista Estudios Centroamericanos
Distribuidora de Publicaciones
Universidad Centroamericana José Simeón Cañas
Apartado 01-575
San Salvador, El Salvador

    ISSN: 0014-1445

EURE

*Revista Latinoamericana de Estudios Urbano Regionales;
E.U.R.E.*

(Formerly: *Cuadernos de Desarrollo Urbano y Regional*)

    El Comendador 1916
Casilla 16.002, Correo 9
Santiago, Chile

    ISSN: 0250-7161

Economía de América Latina

    Centro de Investigación y Docencia Económicas
Carretera México – Toluca, Km. 16.5
Lomas de Santa Fe
Delegación Alvaro Obregón
Apartado Postal 10-883
01210 México, D.F., Mexico

    ISSN: 0815-0504

(No issues received in 1993)

Economic Development and Cultural Change

    The University of Chicago Press
Journals Division
P.O. Box 37005
Chicago, Illinois 60637

    ISSN: 0013-0079

La Educación

*Organization of American States. General Secretariat. La
Educación*

(Formerly: *Pan American Union. La Educación*)

    Editorial Center "La Educación"
Department of Educational Affairs
1889 "F" Street, N.W., 2nd Floor
Washington, D.C. 20006

    ISSN: 0013-1059

Encuentro

Encuentro; Revista Trimestral

    Universidad Centroamericana
Apartado Postal 69
70352 Managua, Nicaragua

    ISSN: 0424-9674

(No issues published in 1993)

Escritura

Escritura; Teoría y Crítica Literarias

    Dr. Rafael Di Prisco
Apartado de Correos 65603
Caracas 1066-A, Venezuela

    ISSN: 1011-7989

Estado y Sociedad

    Facultad Latinoamericana de Ciencias Sociales
(FLACSO)
Casilla No. 9914
La Paz, Bolivia

Estudios de Cultura Maya

    Centro de Estudios Mayas
Ciudad de la Investigación en Humanidades
Ciudad Universitaria
04510 México, D.F., Mexico

    ISSN: 0185-2574 or 0185-5271

(No issues published in 1993)

Estudios de Cultura Náhuatl

Instituto de Investigaciones Históricas
Ciudad de la Investigación en Humanidades
Tercer Circuito Cultural Universitario
Ciudad Universitaria
04510 México, D.F., Mexico

ISSN: 0071-1675

Estudios de Historia Moderna y Contemporánea de México

Instituto de Investigaciones Históricas
Universidad Nacional Autónoma de México
Ciudad Universitaria
04510 México, D.F., Mexico

ISSN: 0185-2620

(No issues received in 1993)

Estudios Demográficos y Urbanos

(Formerly: *Demografía y Economía*)

El Colegio de México
Departamento de Publicaciones
Camino al Ajusco 20
10740 México, D.F., Mexico

ISSN: 0186-7210

Estudios Fronterizos

Instituto de Investigaciones Sociales
Universidad Autónoma de Baja California
P.O. Box 3280
Calexico, California 92231

ISSN: 0187-697X

Estudios Interdisciplinarios de América Latina y el Caribe

Tzvi Medin
Aranne School of History
University of Tel Aviv
Ramat Aviv 69978
Tel Aviv, Israel
ISSN: 0792-7061

Estudios Internacionales (Chile)

Revista de Estudios Internacionales

Instituto de Estudios Internacionales de la
    Universidad de Chile
Condell 249
Casilla 14187, Sucursal 21
Santiago 9, Chile

ISSN: 0716-0240

Estudios Paraguayos

Universidad Católica "Nuestra Señora de la
    Asunción"
Casilla de Correo 1718
Asunción, Paraguay

ISSN: 0251-2483

Estudios Públicos

Centro de Estudios Públicos
Monseñor Sótero Sanz No. 175
Santiago 9, Chile

ISSN: 0716-1115

Estudios Rurales Latinoamericanos

Apartado Aéreo 11386
Bogotá, D.E., Colombia

ISSN: 0120-0747

Estudios Sociales (Chile)

Corporación de Promoción Universitaria
Avenida Miguel Claro No. 1460
Casilla 42, Correo 22
Santiago, Chile

ISSN: 0716-0321

Estudios Sociales (Dominican Republic)

Estudios Sociales. Santo Domingo

Centro de Investigación y Acción Social (CIAS)
Apartado 1004
Santo Domingo, Dominican Republic

Estudios Sociales Centroamericanos

Confederación Universitaria Centro-Americana
Apartado Postal 37
2060 Ciudad Universitaria "Rodrigo Facio"
San José, Costa Rica

ISSN: 0303-9676

(No issues received in 1993)

Estudios Sociológicos (Mexico)

El Colegio de México
Camino al Ajusco 20
Pedregal de Santa Teresa
10740 México, D.F., Mexico

ISSN: 0185-4186

Estudos Econômicos

Fundação Instituto de Pesquisas Econômicas
a/c Departamento de Publicações
Caixa Postal 11474
05422-970 São Paulo, SP, Brazil

ISSN: 0101-4161

Estudos Feministas

CIEC/ECO/UFRJ
Avenida Pasteur, 250
Urca
22290-240, Rio de Janeiro, RJ, Brazil

ISSN: 0104-026Y

Estudos Históricos

Centro de Pesquisa e Documentação de História
    Contempôranea do Brasil da Fundação Gétulio
    Vargas (CPDOC/FGV)
Praia de Botafogo, 190 12º Andar
22253 Rio de Janeiro, RJ, Brazil

ISSN: 0103-2186

Estudos Ibero-Americanos

Departamento de História
Pós-Graduação em História
Pontifícia Universidade Católica do Rio Grande do
    Sul
Caixa Postal 1429
Avenida Ipiranga No. 6681, Prédio 33
90001-970 Pôrto Alegre, RS, Brasil

ISSN: 0101-4064

European Review of Latin American and Caribbean Studies

(Formerly: *Boletín de Estudios Latinoamericanos y del Caribe*)

(Formerly: *Boletín de Estudios Latinoamericanos*)

Centro de Estudios y Documentación
Latinoamericanos
Keizergracht 395-397
1016 EK, Amsterdam, Netherlands

ISSN: 0924-0608

Explicación de Textos Literarios

Department of Foreign Languages
California State University, Sacramento
6000 J Street
Sacramento, California 95819

ISSN: 0361-9621

Fem

Difusión Cultural Feminista, A.C.
Avenida Insurgentes Sur 598-302
Colonia del Valle
03100 México, D.F., Mexico

ISSN: 0185-4666

Feminaria

Andrés Avellaneda
Department of Romance Languages and Literatures
University of Florida
Gainesville, Florida 32611

Folklore Americano

Instituto Panamericano de Geografía e Historia
Secretaría General
Apartado Postal 18879
11870 México, D.F., Mexico

ISSN: 0071-6774

Foro Internacional

El Colegio de México, A.C.
Camino al Ajusco No. 20
Colonia Pedregal de Santa Teresa
10740 México, D.F., Mexico

ISSN: 0185-013X

Frontera Norte

El Colegio de la Frontera Norte
Departamento de Publicaciones
Blvd. Abelardo L. Rodríguez, No. 21
Zona del Río
22320 Tijuana, BC, Mexico

ISSN: 0187-7372

Geographical Review

The American Geographical Society
156 5th Avenue, Suite 600
New York, New York 10010-7002

ISSN: 0016-7428

Grassroots Development (English edition)

Inter-American Foundation
901 N. Stuart Street, 10th Floor
Arlington, Virginia 22203

ISSN: 0733-6608

Hemisphere

Hemisphere; A Magazine of Latin American and Caribbean Affairs

Latin American and Caribbean Center
Florida International University
University Park
Miami, Florida 33199

ISSN: 0898-3038

Hispamérica

c/o Saúl Sosnowski, Editor
5 Pueblo Court
Gaithersburg, Maryland 20878

ISSN: 0363-0471

Hispania (United States)

James R. Chatham
Mississippi State University
Lee Hall 218
P.O. Box 6349
Mississippi State, Mississippi 39762-6349

ISSN: 0018-2133

Hispanic American Historical Review

Duke University Press
P.O. Box 90660
Brightleaf Square, 905 W. Main Street 18-B
Durham, North Carolina 27708-0660

ISSN: 0018-2168

Hispanic Journal

Department of Spanish and Classical Languages
462 Sutton Hall
Indiana University of Pennsylvania
Indiana, Pennsylvania 15705

ISSN: 0271-0986

Hispanic Journal of Behavioral Sciences

Sage Publications, Inc.
2455 Teller Road
Thousand Oaks, California 91320

ISSN: 0739-9863

Hispanic Review

Erika Sutherland
512 Williams Hall
University of Pennsylvania
Philadelphia, Pennsylvania 19104-6305

ISSN: 0018-2176

Historia (Chile)

Pontificia Universidad Católica de Chile
Instituto de Historia
Casilla 6277
Santiago 22, Chile

ISSN: 0073-2435

Historia Mexicana

El Colegio de México, A.C.
Camino al Ajusco 20
Colonia Pedregal de Santa Teresa
10740 México, D.F., Mexico

ISSN: 0185-0172

Historia y Cultura (Peru)

> Museo Nacional de Historia
> Plaza Bolívar, Magdalena Vieja (Pueblo Libre)
> Apartado 1992
> Lima 21, Peru
>
> ISSN: 0073-2486

Homines

> *Revista Homines*
>
> Recinto Metropolitano
> División de Ciencias Sociales
> Apartado 1293
> Hato Rey, Puerto Rico 00919
>
> ISSN: 0252-8908

Hoy Es Historia

> Casilla de Correo No. 6311
> Montevideo, Uruguay

Hueso Húmero

> Camino Real 1286
> Lima 27, Peru

Humboldt (Spanish Edition)

> F. Bruckmann Verlag
> Postfach 27
> D-8 München 20, Germany
>
> ISSN: 0018-7615

IMR; International Migration Review

> (Formerly: *International Migration Review*)
>
> Center for Migration Studies of New York, Inc.
> 209 Flagg Place
> Staten Island, New York 10304-1199
>
> ISSN: 0197-9183

Ibero Americana

> *Ibero Americana; Nordic Journal of Latin American Studies*
>
> NOSALF
> Latinamerika-Institutet
> S-10691, Stockholm, Sweden
>
> ISSN: 0046-8444

Iberoamericana

> Vervuert Verlagsgessellschaft
> Wielandstrasse 40
> D-60318 Frankfurt, Germany
>
> ISSN: 0342-1864

Ibero-Amerikanisches Archiv

> Ibero-Amerikanisches Institut Preussischer
>   Kulturbesitz
> Potsdamerstrasse 37
> 10785 Berlin, Germany
>
> ISSN: 0340-3068

Insula

> Librería, Ediciones y Publicaciones
> Carretera de Irún, KM 12,200 (Variante de
>   Fuencarral)
> 28049 Madrid, Spain
>
> ISSN: 0020-4536

Integración Latinoamericana

> Banco Interamericano de Desarrollo
> Instituto para la Integración de América Latina
> Esmeralda No. 130
> 1035 Buenos Aires, Argentina
>
> ISSN: 0325-1675

Inter-American Music Review

> Theodore Front Musical Literature
> 16122 Cohasset Street
> Van Nuys, California 91406
>
> ISSN: 0195-6655

Interciencia

> Apartado Postal 51842
> Caracas 1050-A, Venezuela
>
> ISSN: 0378-1844

Inti

> Department of Modern Languages
> Providence College
> Providence, Rhode Island 02918
>
> ISSN: 0732-6750

Investigaciones y Ensayos

> Academia Nacional de la Historia
> Balcarce 139
> 1064 Buenos Aires, Argentina
>
> ISSN: 0539-242X

Islas (Cuba)

> C. Dr. Olga Cortijo Jacomino
> Centro de Documentación e Información Científico-
>   Técnica
> Universidad Central de las Villas
> Santa Clara, 54830 Villa Clara, Cuba
>
> ISSN: 0047-1542

Jahrbuch für Geschichte von Staat, Wirtschaft und Gesellschaft Lateinamerikas

> Iberische und Lateinamerikanische Abteilung des
>   Historischen Seminars der Universität zu Köln
> Albertus-Magnus-Platz
> D-5000 Köln 41, Germany
>
> ISSN: 0075-2673

Jamaica Journal

> The Institute of Jamaica Publications, Ltd.
> 2A Suthermere Road
> Kingston 10, Jamaica
>
> ISSN: 0021-4124

Journal de la Société des Américanistes

> *Société des Américanistes de Paris. Journal*
>
> Musée de l'Homme
> 17 Place du Trocadéro
> 75116 Paris, France
>
> ISSN: 0037-9174
>
> (No issues published in 1993)

Journal of Borderlands Studies

> Department of Economics
> Box 30001
> New Mexico State University
> Las Cruces, New Mexico 88003
>
> ISSN: 0886-5655

Journal of Caribbean Studies

Association of Caribbean Studies
P.O. Box 22202
Lexington, Kentucky 40522-2202

ISSN: 0190-2008

Journal of Developing Areas

Business Manager
232 Morgan Hall
Western Illinois University
900 West Adams Street
Macomb, Illinois 61455

ISSN: 0022-037X

Journal of Inter-American Studies and World Affairs

University of Miami
P.O. Box 248205
Coral Gables, Florida 33124-3027

ISSN: 0022-1937

Journal of Latin American Lore

UCLA Latin American Center
University of California
Los Angeles, California 90024-1447

ISSN: 0360-1927

(No issues published in 1993)

Journal of Latin American Studies

Cambridge University Press
Journals Department
40 W. 20th Street
New York, New York 10011-4211

ISSN: 0022-216X

Káñina

Káñina; Revista de Artes y Letras de la Universidad de Costa Rica

Editorial Universitaria
Universidad de Costa Rica
Apartado 75
San José, Coasta Rica

ISSN: 0378-0473

Lateinamerika

Wilhelm-Pieck-Universität Rostock
Universitätsbibliothek
Universitätsplatz 5
2500 Rostock, Germany

ISSN: 0458-7944

(Ceased: v. 25, no. 2, 1990)

Lateinamerika Nachrichten

Institut für Lateinamerikaforschung und
   Entwicklungszusammenarbeit (ILE)
An der Hochschule St. Gallen
Bereich Lateinamerikaforschung (LAC)
Tigerbergstrasse 2
CH-9000 St. Gallen, Switzerland

ISSN: 0174-6324

(No issues received in 1993)

Latin American Antiquity

Society for American Archaeology
900 Second Street, N.E.
Suite 12
Washington, D.C. 20002

ISSN: 1045-6635

Latin American Art

Latin American Art Magazine, Inc.
P.O. Box 9888
Scottsdale, Arizona 85252-3888

ISSN: 1042-9808

Latin American Indian Literatures Journal

Latin American Indian Literatures Journal; A Review of American Indian Texts and Studies

(Formerly: *Latin American Indian Literatures*)

Pennsylvania State University
University Drive
McKeesport, Pennsylvania 15231-7698

ISSN: 0888-5613

Latin American Literary Review

121 Edgewood Avenue
Pittsburgh, Pennsylvania 15218

ISSN: 0047-4134

Latin American Music Review

Revista de Música Latino Americana/Latin American Music Review

Journals Department
University of Texas Press
Box 7819
Austin, Texas 78713

ISSN: 0163-0350

Latin American Perspectives

Sage Publications, Inc.
2455 Teller Road
Thousand Oaks, California 91320

ISSN: 0094-582X

Latin American Research Review

801 Yale, N.E.
University of New Mexico
Albuquerque, New Mexico 87131-1016

ISSN: 0023-8791

Latin American Theatre Review

The Center of Latin American Studies
The University of Kansas
Lawrence, Kansas 66045-2168

ISSN: 0023-8813

Latino América

Latino América; Anuario de Estudios Latinoamericanos

Facultad de Filosofía y Letras
Universidad Nacional Autónoma de Méxcio
Ciudad Universitaria
04510 México, D.F., Mexico

ISSN: 0185-0385

(No issues received in 1993)

Lenguaje y Ciencias

Ernesto Zierer
Departamento de Idiomas y Lingüística
Universidad Nacional de Trujillo
Trujillo, Peru

ISSN: 0024-0796

(No issues received in 1993)

Letras Femeninas

Department of Modern Languages
University of Nebraska-Lincoln
Lincoln, Nebraska 68588-0315

ISSN: 0277-4356

Luso-Brazilian Review

Journals Department
University of Wisconsin Press
114 North Murray Street
Madison, Wisconsin 53715

ISSN: 0024-7413

Mensaje

Almirante Barroso 24
Casilla 10445
Santiago, Chile

ISSN: 0716-0062

Mesoamérica

Plumsock Mesoamerican Studies
P.O. Box 38
South Woodstock, Vermont 05071

ISSN: 0252-9963

Mexican Studies/Estudios Mexicanos

Subscription Manager
University of California Press
2120 Berkeley Way
Berkeley, California 94720

ISSN: 0742-9797

Momento Económico

*Momento Económico: Información y Análisis de la
Coyuntura Económica*

Rubén Monroy
Torre II de Humanidades, Primer Piso
Apartado Postal 20-721
Ciudad Universitaria
04510 México, D.F., Mexico

ISSN: 0186-2901

Montalbán

Universidad Católica "Andrés Bello"
Apartado 29068
Caracas 1021, Venezuela

ISSN: 0252-9086

Mundo Nuevo

Instituto de Altos Estudios de América Latina
Universidad Simón Bolívar
Apartado Postal 17.271
El Conde
Caracas 1015-A, Venezuela

ISSN: 0379-6922

(No issues received in 1993)

NACLA Report on the Americas

(Formerly: *Report on the Americas*)

(Formerly: *NACLA's Latin America and Empire Report*)

North American Congress on Latin America (NACLA)
P.O. Box 77
Hopewell, Pennsylvania 16650-0077

ISSN: 1071-4839

Nexos

Mazatlán No. 119
Colonia Condesa
06140 México, D.F., Mexico

ISSN: 0185-1535

Nueva Antropología

Nueva Antropología; Revista de Ciencias Sociales

Avenida Popocatépetl No. 510
03330 México, D.F., Mexico

ISSN: 0185-0636

Nueva Revista de Filología Hispánica

El Colegio de México
Camino al Ajusco No. 20
Colonia Pedregal de Santa Teresa
10740 México, D.F., Mexico

ISSN: 0185-0121

Nueva Sociedad

Apartado 61.712, Chacao
Caracas 1060-A, Venezuela

ISSN: 0251-3552

Nuevo Texto Crítico

Department of Spanish and Portuguese
Stanford University
Stanford, California 94305-2014

ISSN: 1048-6380

Op. Cit.

*Op. Cit.; Boletín del Centro de Investigaciones Históricas
(Puerto Rico)*

Editorial de la Universidad de Puerto Rico
Apartado 23322
UPR Station
San Juan, Puerto Rico 00931-3322

La Palabra y el Hombre

Apartado Postal 97
91000 Xalapa, Veracruz, Mexico

ISSN: 0185-5527

Pensamiento Iberoamericano

*Pensamiento Iberoamericano; Revista de Economía
Política*

Agencia Española de Cooperación Internacional
Avenida de los Reyes Católicos No. 4
28040 Madrid, Spain

ISSN: 0212-0208

Pesquisa e Planejamento Econômico

IPEA
Avenida Presidente Antônio Carlos 51, 14° Andar
20020-010 Rio de Janeiro, RJ, Brazil

ISSN: 0100-0551

El Pez y la Serpiente

El Pez y la Serpiente; Revista de Cultura

Apartado Postal 192
Managua, Nicaragua

ISSN: 0031-6652

(No issues received in 1993)

Planeación y Desarrollo

(Formerly: *Revista de Planeación y Desarrollo*)

Departamento Nacional de Planeación. Biblioteca
Calle 26, No. 13-19, 2° Piso
Edificio Seguros Colombia
Bogotá, D.E., Colombia

ISSN: 0034-8686

Plural

Departamento de Subscripciones
Reforma No. 18, Primer Piso, Centro
Delegación Cuauhtémoc
06600 México, D.F., Mexico

ISSN: 0185-4925

Política e Estratégia

*Política e Estratégia; Revista Trimestral do Centro de
Estudos Estratégicos do CONVIVIO – Sociedade
Brasileira de Cultura*

Alameda Eduardo Prado 705
01218-010 São Paulo, SP, Brazil

ISSN: 0102-2636

Problemas Brasileiros

Avenida Paulista, 119 5° Andar
01311-903 São Paulo, SP, Brazil

Problemas del Desarrollo

*Problemas del Desarrollo; Revista Latinoamericana de
Economía*

Instituto de Investigaciones Económicas
Apartado Postal 20-721
Ciudad Universitaria
01000 México, D.F., Mexico

ISSN: 0301-7036

Quaderni Ibero-Americani

ARCSAL Palazzo dell'Università
Via Montebello 21
10124 Torino, Italy

ISSN: 0033-4960

RAE

RAE; Revista de Administração de Empresas

Avenida Nove de Julho, 2029
Caixa Postal 5.534
01313-902 São Paulo, SP, Brazil

ISSN: 0034-7590

Realidad Económica

Instituto Argentino para el Desarrollo Económico
Hipólito Yrigoyen 1116, 4° Piso
1086 Buenos Aires, Argentina

ISSN: 0325-1926

Relaciones Internacionales

Centro de Relaciones Internacionales
Facultad de Ciencias Políticas y Sociales
Universidad Nacional Autónoma de México
Ciudad Universitaria
Delegación Coyoacán
04510 México, D.F., Mexico

ISSN: 0185-0814

Report on the Americas

Title changed in 1993: See **NACLA Report on the
Americas**

Review

Review; Latin American Literature and Arts

Subscription Department
P.O. Box 3000
Denville, New Jersey 07834-9481

ISSN: 0890-5762

Review of Latin American Studies

(Formerly: *Proceedings of the Pacific Coast Council on
Latin American Studies*)

Secretariat
Pacific Coast Council on Latin American Studies
San Diego State University, Imperial Valley Campus
720 Heber Avenue
Calexico, California 92231

(Ceased: v. 4, no. 2, 1991)

Revista Andina

Revista Andina, Administración
CBC – Centro "Bartolomé de las Casas"
Apartado 14-0087
Lima 14, Peru

ISSN: 0259-9600

Revista Argentina de Estudios Estratégicos

(Formerly: *Estrategia*)

OLCESE Editores
Viamonte 494, 3° Piso, Oficina 11
1053 Buenos Aires, Argentina

ISSN: 0326-6427

(No issues received in 1993)

Revista Brasileira de Ciências Sociais

Sra. Guita Debert
Secretaria Adjunta
ANPOCS
Avenida Prof. Luciano Gualberto 315-Sala 116
05508-900 São Paulo, SP, Brazil

ISSN: 0102-6909

Revista Brasileira de Economia

Fundação Getúlio Vargas/Editora
Caixa Postal 62591
22257-970 Rio de Janeiro, RJ, Brazil

ISSN: 0034-7140

Revista Brasileira de Estudos Pedagógicos

INEP
Campus da UnB-Acesso Sul
Caixa Postal 04662
70312 Brasília, DF, Brazil

ISSN: 0034-7183

Revista Brasileira de Estudos Políticos

Faculdade de Direito da Universidade Federal de
  Minas Gerais
Caixa Postal 1621
31270 Belo Horizonte, MG, Brazil

ISSN: 0034-7191

Revista Brasileira de Geografia

Centro de Documentação e Disseminação de
Informações
Avenida Beira Mar 436, 8° Andar
20021 Rio de Janeiro, RJ, Brazil

ISSN: 0034-723X

Revista Canadiense de Estudios Hispánicos

(Formerly: *Reflexión)*

C. A. Marsden
Department of Spanish
Carleton University
Ottawa K1S 5B6, Canada

ISSN: 0384-8167

Revista Chilena de Historia y Geografía

Sociedad Chilena de Historia y Geografía
Londres 65
Casilla 1386
Santiago, Chile

ISSN: 0176-2812

(No issues received in 1993)

Revista Chilena de Literatura

Universidad de Chile
Facultad de Filosofía, Humanidades y Educación
Departamento de Literatura
Casilla 10136
Santiago, Chile

ISSN: 0048-7651

Revista Colombiana de Antropología

Instituto Colombiano de Antropología
Apartado Aéreo 407
Calle 8, No. 8-87
Bogotá, D.E., Colombia

ISSN: 0486-6525

Revista Cultural Lotería

(Formerly: *Lotería)*

(Formerly: *Revista Lotería)*

Lotería Nacional de Beneficiencia
Departamento Cultural
Apartado 21
Panamá 1, Panama

ISSN: 0024-662X

Revista de Antropologia

Departamento de Ciências Sociais da Faculdade de
Filosofia, Letras e Ciências Humanas da
Universidade de São Paulo
Caixa Postal 8105
01000 São Paulo, SP, Brazil

ISSN: 0034-7701

Revista de Ciencias Sociales (Costa Rica)

Editorial de la Universidad de Costa Rica
Apartado Postal 75
2060 Ciudad Universitaria "Rodrigo Facio"
San José, Costa Rica

ISSN: 0482-5276

Revista de Ciencias Sociales (Puerto Rico)

Editor
Revista de Ciencias Sociales
Universidad de Puerto Rico
Río Piedras, Puerto Rico 00931

ISSN: 0034-7817

(No issues received in 1993)

Revista de Crítica Literaria Latinoamericana

University of Pittsburgh
1309 C. of L.
Pittsburgh, Pennsylvania 15260

ISSN: 0252-8843

Revista de Economia Política

Centro de Economia Política
Avenida Jorge João Saad, 104
05618-000 São Paulo, SP, Brazil

ISSN: 0101-3157

Revista de Economia e Sociologia Rural

(Formerly: *Revista de Economia Rural)*

SRTN – Avenida W/3 Norte – Quadra 702
Ed. Brasília Rádio Center, Salas 1049/50
70719-900 Brasília, DF, Brazil

ISSN: 0103-2003

**Revista de Estudios Colombianos y
Latinoamericanos**

(Formerly: *Revista de Estudios Colombianos)*

James Alstrum, Secretary
Department of Foreign Languages
Illinois State University
Normal, Illinois 61761

ISSN: 0121-2117

(No issues received in 1993)

**Revista de Filosofía de la Universidad de Costa
Rica**

Editorial de la Universidad de Costa Rica
Apartado Postal 75
2060 Ciudad Universitaria "Rodrigo Facio"
San José, Costa Rica

ISSN: 0034-8252

Revista de Historia (Costa Rica)

Escuela de Historia
Universidad Nacional
Apartado 86
Heredia, Costa Rica
ISSN: 1012-9790

Revista de Historia de América

Instituto Panamericano de Geografía e Historia
Secretaría General
Apartado Postal 18879
11870 México, D.F., Mexico

ISSN: 0034-8325

Revista de Historia de las Ideas (Ecuador)

Casa de la Cultura Ecuatoriana
Centro de Estudios Latinoamericanos
Pontificia Universidad Católica del Ecuador
Quito, Ecuador

ISSN: 0556-5987

(Presumed suspended: no. 10, Nueva época, 1990)

Revista de Indias

Departamento de Historia de América
Centro de Estudios Históricos, CSIC
Duque de Medinaceli 6
28014 Madrid, Spain

ISSN: 0034-8341

Revista de la Biblioteca Nacional José Martí

Havana. Biblioteca Nacional José Martí. Revista

Biblioteca Nacional José Martí
Plaza de la Revolución
La Habana, Cuba

ISSN: 0006-1727

(No issues published in 1993)

Revista de Letras (Brazil)

Faculdade de Ciências e Letras
Caixa Postal 335
19800 Assis, SP, Brazil

ISSN: 0101-3505

Revista do Instituto de Estudos Brasileiros

São Paulo, Brazil (City). Universidade. Instituto de Estudos Brasileiros. Revista

Instituto de Estudos Brasileiros (USP)
Avenida Professor Mello Moraes 1.235 – Bloco D, 1°
Andar
Cidade Universitária "Armando de Salles Oliveira"
05508-900 São Paulo, SP, Brazil

ISSN: 0020-3874

(No issues received in 1993)

Revista do Instituto Histórico e Geográfico Brasileiro

Instituto Histórico e Geográfico Brasileiro. Revista

Avenida Augusto Severo 8
20021 Rio de Janeiro, RJ, Brazil

ISSN: 0101-4366

Revista Española de Antropología Americana

Editorial Complutense
Donoso Cortés 65
28015 Madrid, Spain

ISSN: 0556-6533

Revista Geográfica (Mexico)

Instituto Panamericano de Geografía e Historia
Secretaría General
Apartado Postal 18879
Delegación Miguel Hidalgo
11870 México, D.F., Mexico

ISSN: 0556-6630

Revista Iberoamericana

Instituto Internacional de Literatura Iberoamericana
Erika Braga
1312 C.L.
University of Pittsburgh
Pittsburgh, Pennsylvania 15260

ISSN: 0034-9631

Revista Interamericana de Bibliografía

Organization of American States. Interamerican Review of Bibliography/Revista Interamericana de Bibliografía

(Formerly: *Pan American Union. Interamerican Review of Bibliography/Revista Interamericana de Bibliografía*)

Sales and Promotion Unit
Office of Public Information
General Secretariat of the OAS
Washington, D.C. 20006

ISSN: 0250-6262

Revista Interamericana de Planificación

Sociedad Interamericana de Planificación
P.O. Box 1566
San Antonio, Texas 78296

ISSN: 0579-3718

Revista Javeriana

Revista Javeriana; El Pensamiento Cristiano en Díalogo con el Mundo

Distribuidoras Unidas
Transversal 93, No. 52-03
Bogotá, D.E., Colombia

ISSN: 0120-3088

Revista Latinoamericana de Estudios Educativos

(Formerly: *Revista del Centro de Estudios Educativos*)

Centro de Estudios Educativos, A.C.
Avenida Revolución No. 1291
01040 México, D.F., Mexico

ISSN: 0185-1284

Revista Mexicana de Ciencias Políticas y Sociales

(Formerly: *Revista Mexicana de Ciencia Política*)

Facultad de Ciencias Políticas y Sociales
Circuito Cultural UNAM
Edificio "C", 2° Piso
Ciudad Universitaria
Departamento de Publicaciones
04510 México, D.F., Mexico

ISSN: 0185-1918

Revista Mexicana de Sociología

Laura Chaho Vega
Torre II de Humanidades, 7° Piso
Apartado Postal 70-401
Ciudad Universitaria
04510 México, D.F., Mexico

ISSN: 0188-2503

Revista Musical Chilena

Facultad de Artes
Universidad de Chile
Compañía 1264
Casilla 2100
Santiago, Chile

ISSN: 0716-2790

Revista Musical de Venezuela

Instituto Latinoamericano de Investigaciones y
Estudios Musicales Vicente Emilio Sojo
Consejo Nacional de la Cultura (CONAC)
Apartado Postal 70537
Caracas 1071, Venezuela

Revista Nacional de Cultura (Venezuela)

Consejo Nacional de la Cultura
Avenida Araure, Quinta Mery
Urbanización Chuao
Apartado de Correos 50995
Caracas, Venezuela

ISSN: 0035-0230

Revista Paraguaya de Sociología

Centro Paraguayo de Estudios Sociológicos
Eligio Ayala 973
Casilla No. 2.157
Asunción, Paraguay

ISSN: 0035-0354

Revista/Review Interamericana

Inter American University of Puerto Rico
San Germán Campus
Call Box 5100
San Germán, Puerto Rico 00683

ISSN: 0360-7917

Runa

Runa; Archivo para las Ciencias del Hombre

Universidad de Buenos Aires
Facultad de Filosofía y Letras
Museo Etnográfico "Juan B. Ambrosetti"
Moreno 350 (1091)
Buenos Aires, Argentina

ISSN: 0325-1217

SALALM Papers

*Papers of the Thirty-Fourth and Thirty-Sixth Meetings of
the Seminar on the Acquisition of Latin American
Library Materials*

SALALM Secretariat
General Library
University of New Mexico
Albuquerque, New Mexico 87131

ISBN: 0-917617-32-X (Vol. 34)

ISBN: 0-917617-38-X (Vol. 36)

Sapientia

Facultad de Filosofía y Letras UCA
Bartolomé Mitre 1869
1039 Buenos Aires, Argentina

ISSN: 0036-4703

Siglo XIX; Cuadernos de Historia

Universidad Autónoma de Nuevo León
Apartado Postal 3024
64000 Monterrey, Nuevo León, Mexico

Siglo XIX; Revista de Historia

Instituto de Investigaciones Dr. José María Luis Mora
Plaza Valentín Gómez Farías 12
San Juan Mixcoac, Argentina

ISSN: 0187-8550

Signo

Signo; Cuadernos Bolivianos de Cultura

Editorial Don Bosco
Casilla 1913
La Paz, Bolivia

ISSN: 0258-2112

Social and Economic Studies

Institute of Social and Economic Research
University of the West Indies
Mona, Kingston 7, Jamaica

ISSN 0037-7651

Studi di Letteratura Ispano-Americana

Cattedra di Lingua e Letteratura Ispano-Americana
Istituto di Lingue e Letterature Iberiche e
Iberoamericane
Facoltà di Lettere e Filosofia
Università degli Studi di Milano
Via Albricci 9
20122 Milano, Italy

ISSN: 0585-4776

Studies in Comparative International Development

Transactions Periodicals Consortium, Dept. 4010
Rutgers University
New Brunswick, New Jersey 08903

ISSN: 0039-3606

Studies in Latin American Popular Culture

Charles M. Tatum, Co-Editor
Faculty of Humanities
University of Arizona
Tucson, Arizona 85721

ISSN: 0730-9139

Sur

Revista Sur

Tucumán 677, 5° Piso "D"
1049 Capital Federal
Buenos Aires, Argentina

ISSN: 0035-0478

(Presumed ceased: no. 360-361, January-December
1987)

Thesaurus

Thesaurus; Boletín del Instituto Caro y Cuervo

Instituto Caro y Cuervo
Apartado Aéreo 51502
Bogotá, D.E., Colombia

ISSN: 0040-604X

Tiers Monde

Revue Tiers Monde

Presses Universitaires de France
Département des Revues
14, avenue du Bois-de-l'Epine
B.P. 90
91003 Evry Cedex, France

ISSN: 0040-7356

Todo Es Historia

Viamonte 773, 3° Piso
Caja Postal 1053
Buenos Aires, Argentina

ISSN: 0040-8611

La Tradición Popular

Centro de Estudios Folklóricos
Universidad de San Carlos de Guatemala
Avenida La Reforma 0-09, Zona 10
Guatemala City, Guatemala

El Trimestre Económico

Subgerencia de Economía y Dirección de *El Trimestre Económico*
Carretera Picacho Ajusco, No. 227
Colonia Bosques del Pedregal
Delegación Tlalpan
04200 México, D.F., Mexico

ISSN: 0041-3011

USAC

USAC; Revista de la Universidad de San Carlos

Universidad de San Carlos de Guatemala
Edificio de Rectoría
Tercer Nivel, Oficina 307
Ciudad Universitaria, Zona 12
Guatemala City, Guatemala

Vínculos

Departamento de Administración y Finanzas
Museo Nacional de Costa Rica
Apartado 749-1000
San José, Costa Rica

ISSN 0304-3703

Vozes

Vozes; Revista de Cultura

Rua Frei Luís 100
Caixa Postal 90023
25689 Petrópolis, RJ, Brazil

ISSN: 0100-707

Vuelta

Presidente Carranza No. 210
Colonia Coyoacán
Delegación Coyoacán
04000 México, D.F., Mexico

ISSN: 0185-1586

World Literature Today

(Formerly: *Books Abroad*)

Editorial Office
110 Monnet Hall
University of Oklahoma
Norman, Oklahoma 73069

ISSN: 0196-3570

Zeitschrift für Lateinamerika Wien

Österreichisches Lateinamerika-Institut
Schmerlingplatz 8
A-1010 Vienna, Austria

ISSN: 0049-8645

MAIN SUBJECT HEADINGS
SPANISH

Abogados
Lawyers

Aborto
Abortion

Abuso infantil
Child abuse

Acero (Industria y comercio)
Steel industry and trade

Actores y actrices
Actors and actresses

Actuación
Acting

Aculturación
Acculturation

Administración
Management

Administración pública
Public administration

Aduanas (Aranceles)
Tariff

Afiches
Posters

Agricultura
Agriculture

Agricultura y estado
Agriculture and state

Agua
Water

Agustinos
Augustinians

Ahorro e inversiones
Saving and investment

Alcohol
Alcohol

Alemanes
Germans

Algodón
Cotton

Alienación (Psicología social)
Alienation

Alimentación (Hábitos)
Food habits

Alimentos (Abastecimiento)
Food supply

Alimentos (Industria y comercio)
Food industry and trade

Aluminio (Industria y comercio)
Aluminum industry and trade

América en la literatura
America in literature

América Latina en el arte
Latin America in art

América Latina en la cinematografía
Latin America in motion pictures

América Latina en la literatura
Latin America in literature

Americanos
Americans

Amor en la literatura
Love in literature

Analfabetismo
Illiteracy

Análisis funcional (Matemática)
Functional analysis (Mathematics)

Análisis lingüístico (Literatura)
Linguistic analysis (Literature)

Anarquismo
Anarchism and anarchists

Añil
> Indigo

Animales
> Animals

Animales y plantas (Distribución geográfica)
> Geographical distribution of plants and animals

Antillanos
> West Indians

Antisemitismo
> Antisemitism

Antropofagia
> Cannibalism

Antropología
> Anthropology

Antropología filosófica
> Philosophical anthropology

Antropología médica
> Medical anthropology

Antropólogos
> Anthropologists

Arabes
> Arabs

Archivos
> Archives

Areas naturales
> Natural areas

Argentina en la literatura
> Argentina in literature

Argentinos
> Argentines

Armamentos
> Armaments

Armas atómicas y desarme
> Atomic weapons and disarmament

Armas de fuego
> Firearms

Arqueología
> Archaeology

Arquitectura
> Architecture

Arquitectura colonial
> Architecture, Colonial

Arquitectura religiosa
> Church architecture

Arroz
> Rice

Arte
> Art

Arte colonial
> Art, Colonial

Arte cristiano
> Christian art and symbolism

Arte popular
> Folk art

Arte y literatura
> Art and literature

Arte y religión
> Art and religion

Arte y sociedad
> Art and society

Artesanía
> Handicraft

Artesanos
> Artisans

Artistas (Artes plásticas)
> Artists

Artistas hispanoamericanos (EE.UU.)
> Hispanic American artists (U.S.)

Artistas méxico-americanos
> Mexican American artists

Asistencia agrícola extranjera
> Agricultural assistance, Foreign

Asistencia económica
> Economic assistance

Asistencia económica extranjera
> Economic assistance, Foreign

Asistencia educativa
> Educational assistance

Asistencia militar extranjera
> Military assistance, Foreign

Asistencia social
> Social service

Asociaciones de beneficio mutuo
> Mutual benefit associations

Atlas
> Atlases

Automatización
> Automation

Automóviles (Industria y comercio)
> Automobile industry and trade

Autoras
> Women authors

Autores
> Authors

Autoritarismo
> Authoritarianism

Aves
> Birds

Avicultura
> Poultry industry

Aviones (Industria y comercio)
> Airplane industry and trade

Azúcar
> Sugar

Balanza de pagos
> Balance of payments

Bancos
> Banks and banking

Bandoleros
> Bandits and banditry

Barrios bajos
> Slums

Barroco
> Baroque

Basura y eliminación de basura
> Refuse and refuse disposal

Bauxita
> Bauxite

Beneficiencia
> Charities

Biblia
> Bible

Bibliotecas y bibliotecarios
> Libraries and librarians

Bienes raíces
> Real property

Bilingüismo
> Bilingualism

Biografía
> Biography (as a literary form)

Biotecnología
> Biotechnology

Bolsa de valores
> Stock exchange

Bosques
> Forests

Botánica
> Botany

Brasil en la literatura
> Brazil in literature

Brasileños
> Brazilians

Brujería
> Witchcraft

Caciquismo
> Caciquism

Café
> Coffee

Cambio exterior
> Foreign exchange problem

Cambio social
> Social change

Caminos
> Roads

Campesinos
> Peasantry

Canciones
> Songs

Canciones infantiles
> Children's songs

Capital (Productividad de)
Capital productivity

Capital humano
Human capital

Capitalismo
Capitalism

Capitalismo estatal
State capitalism

Capitalistas
Capitalists and financiers

Capuchinos
Capuchins

Carbón (Minas y minería)
Coal mines and mining

El Caribe en la literatura
Caribbean area in literature

Caricaturas y dibujos animados
Caricatures and cartoons

Carne (Industria y comercio)
Meat industry and trade

Carreteras
Highways

Carteles
Cartels and commodity agreements

Cartografía
Cartography

Caucho (Industria y comercio)
Rubber industry and trade

Caza
Hunting

Censura
Censorship

Centroamericanos
Central Americans

Centros comunales
Community centers

Cerveza
Beer

Chamanismo
Shamanism

Chilam Balam, Libros del
Chilam Balam books

Chinos
Chinese

Chocolate y cacao
Chocolate and cacao

Ciencia
Science

Ciencia ficción
Science fiction

Ciencia militar
Military art and science

Ciencia política
Political science

Ciencia y civilización
Science and civilization

Ciencia y estado
Science and state

Ciencias sociales
Social sciences

Ciencias sociales (Investigaciones)
Social science research

Cimarrones
Maroons

Cine (Crítica)
Film reviews

Cinematografía
Motion pictures

Cinematografía y literatura
Motion pictures and literature

Circo
Circus

Cítricos
Citrus fruits

Ciudadanía
Citizenship

Ciudades y pueblos
Cities and towns

Ciudades y pueblos en la literatura
Cities and towns in literature

Civilización

Civilization

Civilización moderna

Civilization, Modern

Clase media

Middle classes

Clases sociales

Social classes

Cobre (Industria y comercio)

Copper industry and trade

Coca y cocaína

Coca and cocaine

Cocina

Cookery

Comercio exterior (Control)

Foreign trade regulation

Comercio exterior (Promoción)

Foreign trade promotion

Competencia

Competition

Compositores

Composers

Computadores (Industria y comercio)

Computer industry

Comunicación de masas

Mass media

Comunicación de masas y las artes

Mass media and the arts

Comunidad (Desarrollo)

Community development

Comunidad (Organización)

Community organization

Comunidad Europea

European Community

Comunismo

Communism

Concesiones (Negocios)

Franchises (Retail trade

Condecoraciones

Decorations of honor

Condiciones de vida

Quality of life

Conducta sexual

Sexual behavior

Conocimiento (Teoría de)

Knowledge, Theory of

Conservadurismo

Conservatism

Construcción naval

Ship building

Consumo (Economía)

Consumption (Economics)

Contaminación

Pollution

Contrabando

Smuggling

Control social

Social control

Conventos

Convents and nunneries

Cooperación intelectual

Intellectual cooperation

Cooperativas

Cooperatives

Cooperativismo agrícola

Agriculture, Cooperative

Corporativismo

Corporate state

Corridas de toros

Bull fights

Corrupción política

Corruption (in politics)

Cosmología

Cosmology

Costas

Coasts

Costo y nivel de vida

Cost and standard of living

Creación (Literaria, artística, etc.)

Creation (Literary, artistic, etc.)

Crédito

Credit

Crédito agrícola

Agricultural credit

Crímenes contra la mujer

Crimes against women

Crítica literaria

Literary criticism

Crítica teatral

Drama reviews

Cuarteles militares

Military posts

Cuba en la literatura

Cuba in literature

Cubanos

Cubans

Cuentos

Véase la sección de **Autores** *bajo el nombre del cuentista*

Cuestión monetaria

Currency question

Cultura popular

Popular culture

Danza

Dancing

Danzas populares y nacionales

Folk dancing

Delincuencia juvenil

Juvenile delinquency

Delitos y delincuentes

Crime and criminals

Democracia

Democracy

Deportes

Sports

Derecho

Law

Derecho de aguas

Water rights

Derecho internacional

International law

Derecho laboral

Labor laws and legislation

Derecho penal

Criminal law

Derechos de autor

Copyright

Derechos humanos

Human rights

Dermatoglífica

Dermatoglyphics

Desarrollo económico

Economic development

Desastres naturales

Natural disasters

Descentralización administrativa

Decentralization in government

Desempleo

Unemployment

Desiertos

Deserts

Deuda pública

Debts, Public

Dialectos creole

Creole dialects

Diarios

Newspapers

Dibujo esgrafiado

Graffiti

Dictadores

Dictators

Dientes

Teeth

Discriminación racial

Race discrimination

Discriminación sexual

Sexism

División del trabajo

Division of labor

Divorcio

Divorce

Dominicanos (República Dominicana)

Dominicans (Dominican Republic)

Donación de tierras

Land grants

Dramas

Véase la sección de **Autores** *bajo el nombre del dramaturgo*

Drogas ilegales

Drugs, Illegal

Ecología

Ecology

Ecología y desarrollo

Ecology and development

Economía

Economics

Economía forestal

Forestry

Economía marxista

Marxian economics

Editoriales

Publishers and publishing

Educación

Education

Educación (Aspectos sociales)

Educational sociology

Educación (Evaluación)

Educational accountability

Educación (Investigaciones)

Educational research

Educación (Tecnología)

Educational technology

Educación bilingüe

Education, Bilingual

Educación de adultos

Adult education

Educación preescolar

Education, Preschool

Educación primaria

Education, Primary

Educación religiosa

Religious education

Educación secundaria

Education, Secondary

Educación superior

Education, Higher

Educación técnica

Technical education

Educación vocacional

Vocational education

Educación y estado

Education and state

Elecciones

Elections

Elecciones locales

Local elections

Electrónica

Electronics

Elite (Ciencias sociales)

Elite (Social sciences)

Embarazo

Pregnancy

Emblemas nacionales

Emblems, National

Empleados (Participación en la administración de empresas)

Employees' representation in management

Empleo

Employment

Empresas comerciales

Business enterprises

Empresas estatales

Government ownership of business enterprises

Empresas internacionales

International business enterprises

Energía (Política)

Energy policy

Energía atómica (Industria)
    Atomic power industry

Energía eléctrica
    Electric power

Energía hidráulica
    Water power

Enfermedades
    Diseases

Enfermedades mentales
    Mental illness

Enfermedades venéreas
    Venereal diseases

Enfermeras
    Nurses

Ensayo
    Essay

Ensayos
    Véase la sección de **Autores** *bajo el nombre del ensayista*

Enseñanza audiovisual
    Audiovisual education

Enseñanza programada
    Programmed instruction

Enseñanza y maestros
    Teaching and teachers

Entomología
    Entomology

Epigramas
    Epigrams

Erosión
    Erosion

Escepticismo
    Skepticism

Esclavitud
    Slavery

Escritura
    Writing

Escuelas (Administración y organización)
    School management and organization

Escultura
    Sculpture

Espacio en la literatura
    Space in literature

Espacio en la sociología
    Space in sociology

España en la literatura
    Spain in literature

Español (Idioma)
    Spanish language

Españoles
    Spaniards

Espejos en la literatura
    Mirrors in literature

Espionaje
    Espionage

Espiritualismo
    Spiritualism

Estado
    State, The

Estela (Arqueología)
    Stele (Archaeology)

Estética
    Aesthetics

Estructura social
    Social structure

Estudiantes
    Students

Estudios latinoamericanos
    Latin American studies

Etica
    Ethics

Etica médica
    Medical ethics

Etnicidad
    Ethnicity

Etnobotánica
    Ethnobotany

Etnomusicología
    Ethnomusicology

Europeos
  Europeans

Evangelismo
  Evangelicalism

Evolución
  Evolution

Excavaciones arqueológicas
  Archaeological site reports

Exiliados
  Exiles

Existencialismo
  Existentialism

Expediciones científicas
  Scientific expeditions

Familia
  Family

Farmacia
  Pharmacy

Fascismo
  Fascism

Fecundidad humana
  Fertility, Human

Feminismo
  Women's rights

Ferrocarriles
  Railroads

Fertilizantes (Industria)
  Fertilizer industry

Festivales teatrales
  Drama festivals

Ficción
  Fiction

Fiestas populares
  Folk festivals

Filosofía
  Philosophy

Filosofía y política
  Philosophy and politics

Finanzas
  Finance

Finanzas internacionales
  International finance

Finanzas públicas
  Finance, Public

Física
  Physics

Folklore
  Folk lore

Fondos de pensiones
  Pension trusts

Fotografía aérea
  Photography, Aerial

Fotografía y fotógrafos
  Photography and photographers

Fotografías
  Photographs

Francés (Idioma)
  French language

Franceses
  French

Franciscanos
  Franciscans

Francmasones
  Freemasons

Frontera méxico – americana
  Mexican – American Border Region

Frontera y exploradores (Vida)
  Frontier and pioneer life

Fronteras
  Boundaries

Frutas (Comercio)
  Fruit trade

Fuego (Religión, folklore, etc.)
  Fire (in religion, folk lore, etc.)

Fuentes de energía
  Power resources

Fuga de cerebros
  Brain drain

Funcionalismo (Ciencias sociales)
  Functional analysis (Social sciences)

Fútbol

    Soccer

Gamines

    Street children

Ganado porcino

    Swine

Ganado vacuno (Comercio)

    Cattle trade

Gauchos en la literatura

    Gauchos in literature

Geografía

    Geography

Geografía económica

    Geography, Economic

Geografía histórica

    Geography, Historical

Geografía humana

    Anthropo-geography

Geología

    Geology

Geomorfología

    Geomorphology

Geopolítica

    Geopolitics

Gobierno local

    Local government

Gobierno militar

    Military in government

Golpes de estado

    Coups d'état

Grabadoras y grabaciones

    Tape recorders and recordings

Granos (Comercio)

    Grain trade

Grotesco en la literatura

    Grotesque in literature

Grupos de presión

    Pressure groups

Guerra

    War

Guerra Mundial I, 1914 – 1918

    World War, 1914 – 1918

Guerra Mundial II, 1939 – 1945

    World War, 1939 – 1945

Guerrilleros

    Guerrillas

Guiones cinematográficos

    Screenplays

Haciendas

    Haciendas

Haití en la literatura

    Haiti in literature

Haitianos

    Haitians

Hierro (Industria y comercio)

    Iron industry and trade

Hinduismo

    Hinduism

Hindus

    East Indians

Hispanoamericanos (EE.UU.)

    Hispanic Americans (U.S.)

Hispanoamericanos como consumidores (EE.UU.)

    Hispanic Americans as consumers (U.S.)

Hispanoamericanos en la literatura (EE.UU.)

    Hispanic Americans in literature (U.S.)

Historia

    History

Historia natural

    Natural history

Historia oral

    Oral history

Historiadores

    Historians

Holandeses

    Dutch

Hombre

    Man

Hombre prehistórico

    Man, Prehistoric

Homosexualidad

    Homosexuality

Horticultura

    Horticulture

Hospitales

    Hospitals

Huelgas y paros patronales

    Strikes and lockouts

Humanismo

    Humanism

Humorismo

    Wit and humor

Ideología

    Ideology

Idiomas indígenas

    Véase las siguientes categorías de entrada:
    (1) *El nombre del idioma particular: v.g.,* Pipil
        language, Nahuatl language, *etc.*
    (2) *La subdivisión* Languages *bajo la categoría*
        geográfica pertinente: v.g., Indians of Mexico —
        Languages, *etc.*

Iglesia Católica

    Catholic Church

Iglesia y educación

    Church and education

Iglesia y estado

    Church and state

Iglesia y problemas sociales

    Church and social problems

Ilegitimidad

    Illegitimacy

Ilustración

    Enlightenment

Imperialismo

    Imperialism

Imperialismo cultural

    Cultural imperialism

Imprenta y grabado

    Printing and engraving

Impuestos

    Taxation

Indicadores sociales

    Social indicators

Indios

    Hay dos categorías de entrada:
    (1) *Bajo el nombre de la tribu particular, v.g.,* Mayas,
        Incas, Otomi Indians, *etc.*
    (2) *Bajo la región geográfica pertinente: v.g.,* Indians
        of Argentina, Indians of the Caribbean area,
        Indians of South America, *etc.*

Indios, Trato de los

    Indians, Treatment of

Indios en la literatura

    Indians in literature

Industria (Productividad)

    Industrial productivity

Industria (Promoción)

    Industrial promotion

Industria (Ubicación)

    Industries, Location of

Industria, organización

    Industrial organization

Industria de la construcción

    Construction industry

Industria lechera

    Dairying

Industria y estado

    Industry and state

Industrias (Tamaño)

    Industries, Size of

Inflación (Finanzas)

    Inflation (Finance)

Información (Servicios de)

    Information services

Ingeniería

    Engineering

Inglés (Idioma)

    English language

Ingleses

    British

Ingreso nacional

    National income

Ingresos (Distribución de)
Income distribution

Inquisición
Inquisition

Insecticidas
Pesticides

Instrumentos de piedra
Stone implements

Instrumentos musicales
Musical instruments

Integración económica internacional
International economic integration

Inundaciones
Floods

Inversiones de capital
Capital investments

Inversiones extranjeras
Investments, Foreign

Investigación (Institutos de)
Research institutes

Investigación científica
Scientific research

Investigaciones
Research

Ironía en la literatura
Irony in literature

Islam
Islam

Italianos
Italians

Jamaica en la literatura
Jamaica in literature

Japoneses
Japanese

Jesuitas
Jesuits

Judíos
Jews

Judíos en la literatura
Jews in literature

Juegos
Games

Juguetes
Toys

Jurisprudencia sociológica
Sociological jurisprudence

Justicia distributiva
Distributive justice

Juventud
Youth

Juventud hispanoamericana (EE.UU)
Hispanic American youth (U.S.)

Juventud méxico-americana
Mexican American youth

Lana (Industria y comercio)
Wool industry and trade

Latín (Idioma)
Latin language

Latinoamericanos
Latin Americans

Lectura (Intereses)
Reading interests

Lenguaje y lenguas
Language and languages

Leyenda negra
Black legend

Leyendas
Legends

Libaneses
Lebanese

Liberalismo
Liberalism

Libertad
Freedom

Libertad de prensa
Freedom of the press

Libreros y librerías
Booksellers and bookselling

Libros
Books

Libros de texto

   Textbooks

Lingüística

   Linguistics

Literatura

   Literature

Literatura

   Literature. *Véase también la categoría geográfica pertinente, v.g., French literature, Nicaraguan literature, etc.*

Literatura e historia

   Literature and history

Literatura erótica

   Erotica

Literatura fantástica

   Fantastic literature

Literatura folklórica

   Folk literature

Literatura hebrea

   Jewish literature

Literatura hispanoamericana (EE.UU.)

   Hispanic American literature (U.S.)

Literatura infantil

   Children's literature

Literatura méxico-americana

   Mexican American literature

Literatura revolucionaria

   Revolutionary literature

Literatura y ciencia

   Literature and science

Literatura y sociedad

   Literature and society

Lucha de clases

   Social conflict

Maestros (Formación profesional)

   Teachers, Training of

Magia

   Magic

Maíz

   Corn

Mandioca

   Manioc

Manuscritos

   Manuscripts

Marcas registradas

   Trade marks

Marginalidad

   Marginalization

Mártires

   Martyrs

Marxismo

   Marxism

Matemática

   Mathematics

Matrimonio

   Marriage

Medicina

   Medicine

Medicina popular

   Folk medicine

Médicos

   Physicians

Mercadeo

   Marketing

Mercados y comerciantes

   Markets and merchants

Mesianismo

   Messianism

Metros

   Subways

Mexicanos

   Mexicans

México-americanos

   Mexican Americans

México-americanos en la literatura

   Mexican Americans in literature

México-americanos y comunicación de masas

   Mexican Americans and mass media

México en la literatura

   Mexico in literature

Microfilmes
> Microforms

Migración interna
> Migration, Internal

Milagros
> Miracles

Militares en la literatura
> Military in literature

Mimo
> Mime

Minas y recursos minerales
> Mines and mineral resources

Minería (Industria y finanzas)
> Mining industry and finance

Misiones
> Missions

Mito
> Myth

Mito en la literatura
> Myth in literature

Mitología
> Mythology

Mitología en la literatura
> Mythology in literature

Moblaje
> Furniture

Modernismo (Literatura)
> Modernism (Literature)

Momias
> Mummies

Monasticismo y órdenes religiosas
> Monasticism and religious orders

Mortalidad infantil
> Infant mortality

Movilidad social
> Social mobility

Movimientos sociales
> Social movements

Muerte
> Death

Muerte en la literatura
> Death in literature

Mujeres
> Women

Mujeres (Artistas)
> Women artists

Mujeres en la comunicación de masas
> Women in mass media

Mujeres en la literatura
> Women in literature

Mujeres hispanoamericanas (EE.UU.)
> Hispanic American women (U.S.)

Mujeres méxico-americanas
> Mexican American women

Mujeres y religión
> Women and religion

Murales
> Mural painting and decoration

Museos
> Museums

Música
> Music

Música folklórica
> Folk music

Música popular
> Popular music

Música sacra
> Church music

Música y literatura
> Music and literature

Música y sociedad
> Music and society

Musicología
> Musicology

Músicos
> Musicians

Nacionalismo
> Nationalism

Nacionalismo en la literatura
> Nationalism in literature

Natalidad (Control de la)
Birth control

Naturaleza en la literatura
Nature in literature

Naturalización
Naturalization

Navegación
Navigation

Navegación interior
Inland water transportation

Negros
Blacks

Negros en la literatura
Blacks in literature

Nicaragüenses
Nicaraguans

Niños
Children

Niños excepcionales
Exceptional children

Nitratos
Nitrates

Nombres geográficos
Names, Geographical

Nombres personales
Names, Personal

Novelas
Véase la sección de **Autores** *bajo el nombre del novelista*

Novelas policíacas
Detective and mystery stories

Nueces (Industria y comercio)
Nut industry

Números índices (Economía)
Index numbers (Economics)

Nutrición
Nutrition

Obras de arte (Hurtos)
Art thefts

Obsidiana
Obsidian

Oferta de mano de obra
Labor supply

Oferta monetaria
Money and money supply

Oligarquía
Oligarchy

Opinión pública
Public opinion

Oración
Prayer

Organizaciones no-gubermentales
Non-governmental organizations

Oriente Medio
Middle East

Oro
Gold

Oro (Minas y minería)
Gold mines and mining

Ovejas (Cría de)
Sheep ranches

Pacífico (Región)
Pacific Area

Padres e hijos
Parent and child

Padres y maestros
Parent – teacher relationships

Países en desarrollo
Developing countries

Paleobotánica
Paleobotany

Paleontología
Paleontology

Palmas
Palms

Panamericanismo
Pan-Americanism

Paraguayos
Paraguayans

Parásitos

    Parasites

Parentesco

    Kinship

Parques

    Parks

Participación política

    Political participation

Partidos políticos

    Political parties

Parto

    Childbirth

Patatas

    Potatoes

Patrimonio cultural

    Cultural property

Patronato político

    Patronage, Political

Paz

    Peace

Pentecostés (Secta)

    Pentecostalism

Peregrinos y peregrinaciones

    Pilgrims and pilgrimages

Periodismo

    Journalism

Peronismo

    Peronism

Perú en la literatura

    Peru in literature

Peruanos

    Peruvians

Pesca

    Fishing

Petroglifos

    Petroglyphs

Petróleo (Industria y comercio)

    Petroleum industry and trade

Piezas de teatro

    Véase la sección de **Autores** *bajo el nombre del dramaturgo*

Piratas

    Pirates

Planificación regional

    Regional planning

Plata (Minas y minería)

    Silver mines and mining

Plátanos (Comercio)

    Banana trade

Plateros

    Silversmiths

Población

    Population

Pobreza

    Poverty

Poder (Ciencias sociales)

    Power (Social sciences)

Poder ejecutivo

    Executive power

Poder judicial

    Judiciary

Poder legislativo

    Legislative power

Poemas, Poemas concretos *y* **Poemas en prosa**

    Véase la sección de **Autores** *bajo el nombre del poeta*

Poesía

    Poetry

Poesía

    Poetry. *Véase también la categoría geográfica pertinente: v.g., Brazilian poetry, French poetry, etc.*

Poesía épica

    Epic poetry

Poesía méxico-americana

    Mexican American poetry

Poesía religiosa

    Religious poetry

Poesía revolucionaria

    Revolutionary poetry

Poetas
Poets

Poética
Poetics

Policía
Police

Política ambiental
Environmental policy

Política en la literatura
Politics in literature

Portugal en la literatura
Portugal in literature

Portugués (Idioma)
Portuguese language

Portugueses
Portuguese

Positivismo
Positivism

Postmodernismo
Postmodernism

Precios
Prices

Precios (Control)
Price regulation

Premios literarios
Literary prizes

Prendas de vestir
Clothing and dress

Prensa
Press

Prensa y política
Press and politics

Presos politicos
Political prisoners

Prisioneros de guerra
Prisoners of war

Prisiones
Prisons

Privatización
Privatization

Producción (Teoría económica)
Production (Economic theory)

Productos sintéticos
Synthetic products

Pronósticos económicos
Economic forecasting

Propiedad
Property

Propiedad intelectual
Intellectual property

Prostitución
Prostitution

Protestantismo
Protestantism

Proverbios
Proverbs

Pruebas y evaluaciones en educación
Educational tests and measurements

Psicoanálisis en la literatura
Psychoanalysis in literature

Psicología adolescente
Adolescent psychology

Psicología del aprendizaje
Learning, Psychology of

Psicología educacional
Educational psychology

Psicología infantil
Child psychology

Psicología social
Social psychology

Psiquiatría
Psychiatry

Publicidad
Advertising

Puerto Rico en la literatura
Puerto Rico in literature

Puertorriqueños
Puerto Ricans

Puertorriqueños en la literatura
Puerto Ricans in literature

Puertos

Harbors

Química

Chemistry

Radiodifusión

Radio broadcasting

Realismo en la literatura

Realism in literature

Realismo mágico (Literatura)

Magical realism (Literature)

Recursos marinos

Marine resources

Recursos naturales

Natural resources

Reforma agraria

Land reform

Regionalismo

Regionalism

Regionalismo en la literatura

Regionalism in literature

Relaciones económicas internacionales

International economic relations

Relaciones internacionales

International relations

Relaciones laborales

Labor relations

Relaciones pan-pacíficas

Pan-Pacific relations

Religión

Religion

Religión y economía

Religion and economics

Religión y literatura

Religion and literature

Religión y política

Religion and politics

Religión y sociología

Religion and sociology

Represas

Dams and reservoirs

La República Dominicana en la literatura

Dominican Republic in literature

Retórica

Rhetoric

Revistas

Periodicals

Revoluciones

Revolutions

Ríos

Rivers

Ritos y ceremonias

Rites and ceremonies

Rutas comerciales

Trade routes

Sacrificios

Sacrifice

Sal (Industria y comercio)

Salt industry and trade

Salarios

Wages

Salud pública

Public health

Sangre

Blood

Santuarios

Shrines

Sátira

Satire

Sector de servicios

Service industries

Sector informal (Economía)

Informal sector (Economics)

Seguridad nacional

National security

Seguro social

Social security

Seguros

Insurance

Semiótica

Semiotics

Sequías

Droughts

Servicios ambientales

Environmental services

Servicios públicos

Public utilities

Servicios sociales

Social services

Sexo (Papeles masculinos y femeninos)

Sex role

Sexo (Papeles masculinos y femininos) en la literatura

Sex role in literature

SIDA (Enfermedad)

AIDS (Disease)

Simbolismo en la literatura

Symbolism in literature

Sincretismo (Religión)

Syncretism (Religion)

Sindicatos

Trade unions

Sindicatos de maestros

Teachers' unions

Sisal

Sisal hemp

Sistemas de Información Geográfica

Geographic Information Systems

Socialismo

Socialism

Socialismo e Iglesia Católica

Socialism and Catholic Church

Socialización

Socialization

Sociobiología

Sociobiology

Sociolingüística

Sociolinguistics

Sociología

Sociology

Sociología industrial

Industrial sociology

Sociología política

Political sociology

Sociología rural

Sociology, Rural

Sociología urbana

Sociology, Urban

Soya

Soybean

Subcontratación

Subcontracting

Suelos

Soils

Sueños

Dreams

Suicidio

Suicide

Suizos

Swiss

Superstición

Superstition

Surrealismo

Surrealism

Sustancias peligrosas

Hazardous substances

Tabaco

Tobacco

Tabú

Taboo

Tacna y Arica (Cuestión de)

Tacna – Arica question

Tasas de interés

Interest rates

Té

Tea

Teatro

Drama

Teatro

Theater

Teatro

Drama *y* Theater. *Véase también la categoría geográfica pertinente: v.g.,* Argentine drama, Cuban drama, Spanish drama, *etc.*

Teatro experimental

Experimental theater

Teatro folklórico

Folk drama

Teatro hispanoamericano (EE.UU.)

Hispanic American drama (U.S.)

Teatro infantil

Children's theater

Teatro méxico-americano

Mexican American drama

Teatro religioso

Religious drama

Teatros

Theaters

Tecnología

Technology

Tecnología médica

Technology, Medical

Tecnología y civilización

Technology and civilization

Tecnología y estado

Technology and state

Telecomunicación

Telecommunication

Teléfono

Telephone

Televisión

Television

Televisión infantil

Children's television

Tenencia de la tierra

Land tenure

Tensión (Fisiología)

Stress (Physiology)

Teología

Theology

Teología de la liberación

Liberation theology

Terremotos

Earthquakes

Terrenos de la iglesia

Church lands

Terrorismo

Terrorism

Tesis académicas

Dissertations, Academic

Textiles (Industria)

Textile industry and fabrics

Texto visual (Arte)

Visual text

Tiempo de trabajo

Time allocation

Tiempo en la literatura

Time in literature

Tierras (Colonización)

Land settlement

Tiras cómicas

Comic books, strips, etc.

Títeres y teatro de títeres

Puppets and puppet-plays

Trabajadores agrícolas

Agricultural laborers

Trabajadores indocumentados

Undocumented workers

Trabajo (Productividad)

Labor productivity

Trabajo y trabajadores

Labor and laboring classes

Tradición oral

Oral tradition

Traducción e interpretación

Translating and interpreting

Tráfico de drogas

Drug trade

Transferencia de tecnología

Technology transfer

Transporte
> Transportation

Transporte marítimo
> Transportation, Maritime

Trata de esclavos
> Slave trade

Tratado de Libre Comercio
> North American Free Trade Agreement

Trigo
> Wheat

Turismo
> Tourist trade

Universidades
> Universities and colleges

Universidades católicas
> Catholic universities and colleges

Urbanización
> Urbanization

Uso de la tierra
> Land use

Utopías
> Utopias

Vascos
> Basques

Vegetación y clima
> Vegetation and climate

Vejez
> Old age

Venezuela en la literatura
> Venezuela in literature

Vida cristiana
> Christian life

Video-tape
> Video tape recorders and recording

Vinicultura
> Wine and wine making

Violencia
> Violence

Violencia en la literatura
> Violence in literature

Visión
> Vision

Vivienda
> Housing

Voduísmo
> Voodooism

Volcanismo
> Volcanism

Zoología
> Zoology

MAIN SUBJECT HEADINGS
PORTUGUESE

Abôrto

    Abortion

Abuso infantil

    Child abuse

Aço (Indústria e comércio)

    Steel industry and trade

Açúcar

    Sugar

Aculturação

    Acculturation

Administração

    Management

Administração pública

    Public administration

Advogados

    Lawyers

Agostinianos

    Augustinians

Agricultura

    Agriculture

Agricultura e estado

    Agriculture and state

Agua

    Water

Alcool

    Alcohol

Alemães

    Germans

Algodão

    Cotton

Alienação (Psicologia social)

    Alienation

Alimentação (Hábitos)

    Food habits

Alimentos (Abastecimento)

    Food supply

Alimentos (Indústria e comércio)

    Food industry and trade

Alojamento

    Housing

Alumínio (Indústria e comércio)

    Aluminum industry and trade

América Latina na arte

    Latin America in art

América Latina na cinematografia

    Latin America in motion pictures

América Latina na literatura

    Latin America in literature

América na literatura

    America in literature

Americanos

    Americans

Amor na literatura

    Love in literature

Analfabetismo

    Illiteracy

Análise funcional (Matemática)

    Functional analysis (Mathematics)

Análise lingüística (Literatura)

    Linguistic analysis (Literature)

Anarquismo

    Anarchism and anarchists

Anil

    Indigo

Animais

    Animals

Animais e plantas (Distribuição geográfica)

    Geographical distribution of plants and animals

Anti-semitismo
  Antisemitism

Antilhanos
  West Indians

Antropologia
  Anthropology

Antropologia filosófica
  Philosophical anthropology

Antropologia médica
  Medical anthropology

Antropólogos
  Anthropologists

Arabes
  Arabs

Areas naturais
  Natural areas

Argentina na literatura
  Argentina in literature

Argentinos
  Argentines

Armamentos
  Armaments

Armas atômicas e desarmamento
  Atomic weapons and disarmament

Armas de fogo
  Firearms

Arqueologia
  Archaeology

Arquitetura
  Architecture

Arquitetura colonial
  Architecture, Colonial

Arquitetura religiosa
  Church architecture

Arquivos
  Archives

Arroz
  Rice

Arte
  Art

Arte colonial
  Art, Colonial

Arte cristã
  Christian art and symbolism

Arte e literatura
  Art and literature

Arte e religião
  Art and religion

Arte e sociedade
  Art and society

Arte popular
  Folk art

Artesania
  Handicraft

Artesões
  Artisans

Artistas (Artes plásticas)
  Artists

Artistas hispano-americanos (E.U.A.)
  Hispanic American artists (U.S.)

Artistas mexicano-americanos
  Mexican American artists

Assistência agrícola estrangeira
  Agricultural assistance, Foreign

Assistência econômica
  Economic assistance

Assistência econômica estrangeira
  Economic assistance, Foreign

Assistência educativa
  Educational assistance

Assistência militar estrangeira
  Military assistance, Foreign

Associações de benefício mútuo
  Mutual benefit associations

Atlas
  Atlases

Atores e atrizes
  Actors and actresses

Automação
  Automation

Automóveis (Indústria e comércio)
  Automobile industry and trade

Autoras
  Women authors

Autores
  Authors

Autoritarismo
  Authoritarianism

Aves
  Birds

Avicultura
  Poultry industry

Aviões (Indústria e comércio)
  Airplane industry and trade

Balança de pagamentos
  Balance of payments

Bananas (Comércio)
  Banana trade

Bancos
  Banks and banking

Bandoleiros
  Bandits and banditry

Barroco
  Baroque

Bascos
  Basques

Batatas
  Potatoes

Bauxita
  Bauxite

Bens de raiz
  Real property

Bíblia
  Bible

Bibliotecas e bibliotecários
  Libraries and librarians

Bilingüismo
  Bilingualism

Biografia
  Biography (as a literary form)

Biotecnologia
  Biotechnology

Bôlsa de valôres
  Stock exchange

Borracha (Indústria e comércio)
  Rubber industry and trade

Bosques
  Forests

Botânica
  Botany

Brasil na literatura
  Brazil in literature

Brasileiros
  Brazilians

Brinquedos
  Toys

Bruxaria
  Witchcraft

Caça
  Hunting

Caciquismo
  Caciquism

Café
  Coffee

Câmbio exterior
  Foreign exchange problem

Caminhos
  Roads

Camponeses
  Peasantry

Canções
  Songs

Canções infantis
  Children's songs

Canibalismo
  Cannibalism

Capital (Produtividade de)
  Capital productivity

Capital humano
  Human capital

Capitalismo
    Capitalism

Capitalismo estatal
    State capitalism

Capitalistas
    Capitalists and financiers

Capuchinhos
    Capuchins

O Caribe na literatura
    Caribbean area in literature

Caricaturas e desenhos animados
    Caricatures and cartoons

Caridade (Instituições)
    Charities

Carne (Indústria e comércio)
    Meat industry and trade

Cartazes
    Posters

Cartéis
    Cartels and commodity agreements

Cartografia
    Cartography

Carvão (Minas e mineração)
    Coal mines and mining

Casamento
    Marriage

Censura
    Censorship

Centro-americanos
    Central Americans

Centros de comunidade
    Community centers

Cepticismo
    Skepticism

Cereais (Comércio)
    Grain trade

Cerveja
    Beer

Chá
    Tea

Chilan Balam, Libros do
    Chilam Balam books

Chineses
    Chinese

Chocolate e cacau
    Chocolate and cacao

Cidadania
    Citizenship

Cidades e municípios
    Cities and towns

Cidades e municípios na literatura
    Cities and towns in literature

Ciência
    Science

Ciência e civilização
    Science and civilization

Ciência e estado
    Science and state

Ciência militar
    Military art and science

Ciência política
    Political science

Ciências sociais
    Social sciences

Ciências sociais (Pesquisas)
    Social science research

Cinema (Crítica)
    Film reviews

Cinematografia
    Motion pictures

Cinematografia e literatura
    Motion pictures and literature

Circo
    Circus

Cítricos
    Citrus fruits

Civilização
    Civilization

Civilização moderna
    Civilization, Modern

Classe média
  Middle classes

Classes sociais
  Social classes

Cobre (Indústria e comércio)
  Copper industry and trade

Coca e cocaína
  Coca and cocaine

Comércio exterior (Promoção)
  Foreign trade promotion

Comércio exterior (Regulamento)
  Foreign trade regulation

Competição
  Competition

Compositores
  Composers

Computadores (Indústria e comércio)
  Computer industry

Comunicações de massa
  Mass media

Comunicações de massa e as artes
  Mass media and the arts

Comunidade (Desenvolvimento)
  Community development

Comunidade (Organização)
  Community organization

Comunidade Européia
  European Community

Comunismo
  Communism

Concessões (Negócios)
  Franchises (Retail trade

Condecorações
  Decorations of honor

Condições de vida
  Quality of life

Conduta sexual
  Sexual behavior

Conhecimento (Teoria do)
  Knowledge, Theory of

Conservatismo
  Conservatism

Construção naval
  Ship building

Consumo (Economia)
  Consumption (Economics)

Contos
  Veja a seção de **Autores** *baixo o nome do contista*

Contrabando
  Smuggling

Contrôle social
  Social control

Conventos
  Convents and nunneries

Cooperação intelectual
  Intellectual cooperation

Cooperativas
  Cooperatives

Cooperativismo agrícola
  Agriculture, Cooperative

Corporativismo
  Corporate state

Corrupção política
  Corruption (in politics)

Cosmologia
  Cosmology

Costas
  Coasts

Cozinha
  Cookery

Crédito
  Credit

Crédito agrícola
  Agricultural credit

Criação (Literária, artística, etc.)
  Creation (Literary, artistic, etc.)

Crianças
  Children

Crianças excepcionais
  Exceptional children

Crime e criminosos
　　Crime and criminals

Crimes contra a mulher
　　Crimes against women

Crítica literária
　　Literary criticism

Crítica teatral
　　Drama reviews

Cuba na literatura
　　Cuba in literature

Cubanos
　　Cubans

Cultura popular
　　Popular culture

Custo e padrão de vida
　　Cost and standard of living

Dança
　　Dancing

Danças populares e nacionais
　　Folk dancing

Decentralização administrativa
　　Decentralization in government

Delinqüência juvenil
　　Juvenile delinquency

Democracia
　　Democracy

Dentes
　　Teeth

Dermatoglífica
　　Dermatoglyphics

Desastres naturais
　　Natural disasters

Desempenho
　　Acting

Desemprêgo
　　Unemployment

Desenvolvimento econômico
　　Economic development

Desertos
　　Deserts

Dialetos creole
　　Creole dialects

Direito
　　Law

Direito de águas
　　Water rights

Direito do trabalho
　　Labor laws and legislation

Direito internacional
　　International law

Direito penal
　　Criminal law

Direitos autorais
　　Copyright

Direitos humanos
　　Human rights

Discriminação racial
　　Race discrimination

Discriminação sexual
　　Sexism

Ditadores
　　Dictators

Dívida pública
　　Debts, Public

Divisão do trabalho
　　Division of labor

Divórcio
　　Divorce

Doenças
　　Diseases

Doenças mentais
　　Mental illness

Doenças venéreas
　　Venereal diseases

Dominicanos (República Dominicana)
　　Dominicans (Dominican Republic)

Dramas
　　Veja a seção de **Autores** *baixo o nome do dramaturgo*

Drogas ilegais

Drugs, Illegal

Ecologia

Ecology

Ecologia e desenvolvimento

Ecology and development

Economia

Economics

Economia florestal

Forestry

Economia marxista

Marxian economics

Editôras

Publishers and publishing

Educação

Education

Educação (Aspectos sociais)

Educational sociology

Educação (Avaliação)

Educational accountability

Educação (Pesquisas)

Educational research

Educação (Tecnologia)

Educational technology

Educação bilíngüe

Education, Bilingual

Educação de adultos

Adult education

Educação e estado

Education and state

Educação pré-escolar

Education, Preschool

Educação primária

Education, Primary

Educação religiosa

Religious education

Educação secundária

Education, Secondary

Educação superior

Education, Higher

Educacão técnica

Technical education

Educação vocacional

Vocational education

Eleições

Elections

Eleições locais

Local elections

Eletrônica

Electronics

Elite (Ciências sociais)

Elite (Social sciences)

Emblemas nacionais

Emblems, National

Empregados (Participação na administração de emprêsas)

Employees' representation in management

Emprêgo

Employment

Emprêsas comerciais

Business enterprises

Emprêsas estatais

Government ownership of business enterprises

Emprêsas internacionais

International business enterprises

Energia (Política)

Energy policy

Energia atômica (Indústria)

Atomic power industry

Energia elétrica

Electric power

Energia hidráulica

Water power

Enfermeiras

Nurses

Engenharia

Engineering

Ensaio

Essay

Ensaios

Veja a seção de **Autores** *baixo o nome do ensaista*

Ensino audiovisual

Audiovisual education

Ensino e professores

Teaching and teachers

Entomologia

Entomology

Epigramas

Epigrams

Erosão

Erosion

Escavações arqueológicas

Archaeological site reports

Escolas (Administração e organização)

School management and organization

Escravidão

Slavery

Escrita

Writing

Escultura

Sculpture

Espaço na literatura

Space in literature

Espaço na sociologia

Space in sociology

Espanha na literatura

Spain in literature

Espanhóis

Spaniards

Espanhol (Língua)

Spanish language

Espelhos na literatura

Mirrors in literature

Espionagem

Espionage

Espiritismo

Spiritualism

Esportes

Sports

Estado

State, The

Estela (Arqueologia)

Stele (Archaeology)

Estética

Aesthetics

Estrutura social

Social structure

Estudantes

Students

Estudos latino-americanos

Latin American studies

Etica

Ethics

Etica médica

Medical ethics

Etnicidade

Ethnicity

Etnobotânica

Ethnobotany

Etnomusicologia

Ethnomusicology

Europeus

Europeans

Evangelismo

Evangelicalism

Evolução

Evolution

Exilados

Exiles

Existencialismo

Existentialism

Expedições científicas

Scientific expeditions

Família

Family

Farmácia

Pharmacy

Fascismo

Fascism

Favelas
    Slums

Fazendas
    Haciendas

Fecundidade humana
    Fertility, Human

Feminismo
    Women's rights

Ferro (Indústria e comércio)
    Iron industry and trade

Ferrovias
    Railroads

Fertilizantes (Indústria)
    Fertilizer industry

Festivais populares
    Folk festivals

Festivais teatrais
    Drama festivals

Ficção
    Fiction

Ficção científica
    Science fiction

Filosofia
    Philosophy

Filosofia e política
    Philosophy and politics

Finanças
    Finance

Finanças internacionais
    International finance

Finanças públicas
    Finance, Public

Física
    Physics

Fogo (Religião, folclore, etc.)
    Fire (in religion, folk lore, etc.)

Folclore
    Folk lore

Fontes de energia
    Power resources

Força de trabalho
    Labor supply

Fotografia aérea
    Photography, Aerial

Fotografia e fotógrafos
    Photography and photographers

Fotografias
    Photographs

Francês (Língua)
    French language

Franceses
    French

Franciscanos
    Franciscans

Fronteira meicana – americana
    Mexican – American Border Region

Fronteiras
    Boundaries

Frutas (Comércio)
    Fruit trade

Fuga de cérebros
    Brain drain

Funcionalismo (Ciências sociais)
    Functional analysis (Social sciences)

Fundos de pensões
    Pension trusts

Futebol
    Soccer

Gado porcino
    Swine

Gado vacum (Comércio)
    Cattle trade

Gaúchos na literatura
    Gauchos in literature

Geografia
    Geography

Geografia econômica
    Geography, Economic

Geografia histórica
    Geography, Historical

Geografia humana
  Anthropo-geography

Geologia
  Geology

Geomorfologia
  Geomorphology

Geopolítica
  Geopolitics

Golpes de estado
  Coups d'état

Govêrno local
  Local government

Govêrno militar
  Military in government

Grafito
  Graffiti

Gravadores de fita e gravações
  Tape recorders and recordings

Gravidez
  Pregnancy

Greves
  Strikes and lockouts

Grotesco na literatura
  Grotesque in literature

Grupos de pressão
  Pressure groups

Guerra
  War

Guerra Mundial I, 1914 – 1918
  World War, 1914 – 1918

Guerra Mundial II, 1939 – 1945
  World War, 1939 – 1945

Guerrilhas
  Guerrillas

Haiti na literatura
  Haiti in literature

Haitianos
  Haitians

Hinduísmo
  Hinduism

Hindus
  East Indians

Hispano-americanos (E.U.A.)
  Hispanic Americans (U.S.)

Hispano-americanos como consumidores (E.U.A.)
  Hispanic Americans as consumers (U.S.)

Hispano-americanos na literatura (E.U.A.)
  Hispanic Americans in literature (U.S.)

História
  History

História natural
  Natural history

História oral
  Oral history

Historiadores
  Historians

Holandeses
  Dutch

Homem
  Man

Homem pré-histórico
  Man, Prehistoric

Homossexualismo
  Homosexuality

Horticultura
  Horticulture

Hospitais
  Hospitals

Humanismo
  Humanism

Humor
  Wit and humor

Ideologia
  Ideology

Igreja Católica
  Catholic Church

Igreja e educação
  Church and education

Igreja e estado
  Church and state

Igreja e problemas sociais

    Church and social problems

Ilegitimidade

    Illegitimacy

Iluminismo

    Enlightenment

Imperialismo

    Imperialism

Imperialismo cultural

    Cultural imperialism

Impôstos

    Taxation

Imprensa

    Press

Imprensa e política

    Press and politics

Indicadores sociais

    Social indicators

Indios

    Tem duas categorias de entrada:
    (1) *Baixo o nome da tribo particular: p.e.,*
    Araucanians, Navajo Indians, Quichés, *etc.*
    (2) *Baixo a região geográfica pertinente: p.e.,*
    Indians of Argentina, Indians of the Caribbean
    area, Indians of South America, *etc.*

Indios, Tratamento dos

    Indians, Treatment of

Indios na literatura

    Indians in literature

Indústria (Localização)

    Industries, Location of

Indústria (Produtividade)

    Industrial productivity

Indústria (Promoção)

    Industrial promotion

Indústria, organização

    Industrial organization

Indústria da construção

    Construction industry

Indústria e estado

    Industry and state

Indústria lacticínia

    Dairying

Indústrias (Tamanho)

    Industries, Size of

Inflação (Finanças)

    Inflation (Finance)

Informacão (Serviços de)

    Information services

Inglês (Língua)

    English language

Inglêses

    British

Inquisição

    Inquisition

Insecticidas

    Pesticides

Instrução programada

    Programmed instruction

Instrumentos de pedra

    Stone implements

Instrumentos musicais

    Musical instruments

Integração econômica internacional

    International economic integration

Inundações

    Floods

Investimentos de capital

    Capital investments

Investimentos estrangeiros

    Investments, Foreign

Ironia na literatura

    Irony in literature

Islame

    Islam

Italianos

    Italians

Jamaica na literatura

    Jamaica in literature

Japonês (Língua)

    Japanese

Jesuítas

Jesuits

Jogos

Games

Jornais

Newspapers

Jornalismo

Journalism

Judeus

Jews

Judeus na literatura

Jews in literature

Jurisprudência sociológica

Sociological jurisprudence

Justiça distributiva

Distributive justice

Juventude

Youth

Juventude hispano-americana (E.U.A.)

Hispanic American youth (U.S.)

Juventude mexicana-americana

Mexican American youth

Lã (Indústria e comércio)

Wool industry and trade

Latim (Língua)

Latin language

Latino-americanos

Latin Americans

Leitura (Interêsses)

Reading interests

Lenda negra

Black legend

Lendas

Legends

Libaneses

Lebanese

Liberalismo

Liberalism

Liberdade

Freedom

Liberdade de imprensa

Freedom of the press

Linguagem e línguas

Language and languages

Línguas indígenas

Veja as seguintes categorias de entrada:
(1) *O nome da língua particular: p.e.,* Chibcha
language, Nahuatl language, *etc.*
(2) *A subdivisão* Languages *baixo a categoria
geográfica pertinente: p.e.,* Indians of Mexico –
Languages, *etc.*

Lingüística

Linguistics

Literatura

Literature

Literatura

Literature. *Veja também a categoria geográfica
pertinente: p.e.,* French literature, Nicaraguan
literature, *etc.*

Literatura e ciência

Literature and science

Literatura e história

Literature and history

Literatura e sociedade

Literature and society

Literatura erótica

Erotica

Literatura fantástica

Fantastic literature

Literatura folclórica

Folk literature

Literatura hebréia

Jewish literature

Literatura hispano-americana (E.U.A.)

Hispanic American literature (U.S.)

Literatura infantil

Children's literature

Literatura mexicana-americana

Mexican American literature

Literatura revolucionária

Revolutionary literature

Livreiros e livrarias

Booksellers and bookselling

Livros
> Books

Livros escolares
> Textbooks

Lixo e remoção de lixo
> Refuse and refuse disposal

Luta de classes
> Social conflict

Maçons
> Freemasons

Magia
> Magic

Mandioca
> Manioc

Manuscritos
> Manuscripts

Marcas registradas
> Trade marks

Marginalização
> Marginalization

Marionetes e teatro de marionetes
> Puppets and puppet-plays

Mártires
> Martyrs

Marxismo
> Marxism

Matemática
> Mathematics

Medicina
> Medicine

Medicina popular
> Folk medicine

Médicos
> Physicians

Meninos de rua
> Street children

Mercadologia
> Marketing

Mercados e comerciantes
> Markets and merchants

Messianismo
> Messianism

Metros
> Subways

Mexicano-americanos
> Mexican Americans

Mexicano-americanos e comunicações de massa
> Mexican Americans and mass media

Mexicano-americanos na literatura
> Mexican Americans in literature

Mexicanos
> Mexicans

México na literatura
> Mexico in literature

Microfilmes
> Microforms

Migração interna
> Migration, Internal

Milagres
> Miracles

Milho
> Corn

Militares na literatura
> Military in literature

Mimo
> Mime

Minas e recursos minerais
> Mines and mineral resources

Mineração (Indústria e finanças)
> Mining industry and finance

Missões
> Missions

Mito
> Myth

Mito na literatura
> Myth in literature

Mitologia
> Mythology

Mitologia na literatura
> Mythology in literature

Mobília
    Furniture

Mobilidade social
    Social mobility

Modernismo (Literatura)
    Modernism (Literature)

Monasticismo e ordens religiosas
    Monasticism and religious orders

Mortalidade infantil
    Infant mortality

Morte
    Death

Morte na literatura
    Death in literature

Movimentos sociais
    Social movements

Mudança social
    Social change

Mulheres
    Women

Mulheres (Artistas)
    Women artists

Mulheres e religião
    Women and religion

Mulheres hispano-americanas (E.U.A.)
    Hispanic American women (U.S.)

Mulheres mexicana-americanas
    Mexican American women

Mulheres na literatura
    Women in literature

Mulheres nas comunicações de massa
    Women in mass media

Múmias
    Mummies

Murais
    Mural painting and decoration

Museus
    Museums

Música
    Music

Música e literatura
    Music and literature

Música e sociedade
    Music and society

Música folclórica
    Folk music

Música popular
    Popular music

Música sacra
    Church music

Musicologia
    Musicology

Músicos
    Musicians

Nacionalismo
    Nationalism

Nacionalismo na literatura
    Nationalism in literature

Natalidade (Contrôle da)
    Birth control

Naturalização
    Naturalization

Natureza na literatura
    Nature in literature

Navegação
    Navigation

Navegação interior
    Inland water transportation

Negros
    Blacks

Negros na literatura
    Blacks in literature

Nicaraguanos
    Nicaraguans

Nitratos
    Nitrates

Nomes geográficos
    Names, Geographical

Nomes pessoais
    Names, Personal

Novelas policiais
   Detective and mystery stories

Nozes (Indústria e comércio)
   Nut industry

Números índices (Economia)
   Index numbers (Economics)

Nutrição
   Nutrition

Obras de arte (Furtos)
   Art thefts

Obsidiana
   Obsidian

Oferta monetária
   Money and money supply

Oligarquia
   Oligarchy

Opinião pública
   Public opinion

Oração
   Prayer

Organizações não-governamentais
   Non-governmental organizations

Oriente Médio
   Middle East

Ouro
   Gold

Ouro (Minas e mineração)
   Gold mines and mining

Ovelhas (Criação de)
   Sheep ranches

Pacífico (Região)
   Pacific Area

Pais e filhos
   Parent and child

Pais e professores
   Parent – teacher relationships

Países em desenvolvimento
   Developing countries

Paleobotânica
   Paleobotany

Paleontologia
   Paleontology

Palmas
   Palms

Pan-americanismo
   Pan-Americanism

Paraguaios
   Paraguayans

Parasitos
   Parasites

Parentesco
   Kinship

Parques
   Parks

Participação política
   Political participation

Partidos políticos
   Political parties

Parto
   Childbirth

Patrimônio cultural
   Cultural property

Patronato político
   Patronage, Political

Paz
   Peace

Peças de teatro
   Veja a seção de **Autores** *baixo o nome do dramaturgo*

Pentecostalismo
   Pentecostalism

Peregrinos e peregrinações
   Pilgrims and pilgrimages

Peronismo
   Peronism

Peru na literatura
   Peru in literature

Peruanos
   Peruvians

Pescaria

Fishing

Pesquisa (Institutos de)

Research institutes

Pesquisa científica

Scientific research

Pesquisas

Research

Petroglifos

Petroglyphs

Petroleo (Indústria e comércio)

Petroleum industry and trade

Piratas

Pirates

Planejamento regional

Regional planning

Pobreza

Poverty

Poder (Ciências sociais)

Power (Social sciences)

Poder executivo

Executive power

Poder judicial

Judiciary

Poder legislativo

Legislative power

Poemas, Poemas concretos *e* **Poemas em prosa**

Veja a seção de **Autores** *baixo o nome do poeta*

Poesia

Poetry

Poesia

Poetry. *Veja também a categoria geográfica pertinente: p.e.,* Brazilian poetry, French poetry, *etc.*

Poesia épica

Epic poetry

Poesia mexicana-americana

Mexican American poetry

Poesia religiosa

Religious poetry

Poesia revolucionária

Revolutionary poetry

Poetas

Poets

Poética

Poetics

Polícia

Police

Política ambiental

Environmental policy

Política na literatura

Politics in literature

Poluição

Pollution

População

Population

Pôrto-riquenhos

Puerto Ricans

Pôrto-riquenhos na literatura

Puerto Ricans in literature

Pôrtos

Harbors

Portugal na literatura

Portugal in literature

Português (Língua)

Portuguese language

Portuguêses

Portuguese

Pós-modernismo

Postmodernism

Positivismo

Positivism

Posse da terra

Land tenure

Poupança e inversões

Saving and investment

Prata (Minas e mineração)

Silver mines and mining

Prateiros

Silversmiths

Preços
  Prices

Preços (Contrôle)
  Price regulation

Prêmios literários
  Literary prizes

Prêsos políticos
  Political prisoners

Previdência social
  Social security

Prisioneiros de guerra
  Prisoners of war

Prisões
  Prisons

Privatização
  Privatization

Produção (Teoria econômica)
  Production (Economic theory)

Produtos sintéticos
  Synthetic products

Professores (Formação profissional)
  Teachers, Training of

Prognósticos econômicos
  Economic forecasting

Propiedade
  Property

Propriedade intelectual
  Intellectual property

Prostituição
  Prostitution

Protestantismo
  Protestantism

Provas e avaliações na educação
  Educational tests and measurements

Provérbios
  Proverbs

Psicanálise na literatura
  Psychoanalysis in literature

Psicologia adolescente
  Adolescent psychology

Psicologia do aprendizado
  Learning, Psychology of

Psicologia educacional
  Educational psychology

Psicologia infantil
  Child psychology

Psicologia social
  Social psychology

Psiquiatria
  Psychiatry

Publicidade
  Advertising

Puerto Rico na literatura
  Puerto Rico in literature

Quadrinhos (Histórias em)
  Comic books, strips, etc.

Quartéis militares
  Military posts

Questão monetária
  Currency question

Quilombos
  Maroons

Química
  Chemistry

Rádiodifusão
  Radio broadcasting

Realismo mágico (Literatura)
  Magical realism (Literature)

Realismo na literatura
  Realism in literature

Recursos do mar
  Marine resources

Recursos naturais
  Natural resources

Reforma agrária
  Land reform

Regionalismo
  Regionalism

Regionalismo na literatura
  Regionalism in literature

Relações de trabalho
Labor relations

Relações econômicas internacionais
International economic relations

Relações internacionais
International relations

Relações pan-pacíficas
Pan-Pacific relations

Religião
Religion

Religião e economia
Religion and economics

Religião e literatura
Religion and literature

Religião e política
Religion and politics

Religião e sociologia
Religion and sociology

Renda (Distribuição de)
Income distribution

Renda nacional
National income

Reprêsas
Dams and reservoirs

A República Dominicana na literatura
Dominican Republic in literature

Retórica
Rhetoric

Revistas
Periodicals

Revoluções
Revolutions

Rios
Rivers

Ritos e ceremônias
Rites and ceremonies

Rodovias
Highways

Romances
Veja a seção de **Autores** *baixo o nome do romancista*

Rotas comerciais
Trade routes

Roteiros cinematográficos
Screenplays

Roupas e vestidos
Clothing and dress

Sacrifícios
Sacrifice

Sal (Indústria e comércio)
Salt industry and trade

Salários
Wages

Sangue
Blood

Santuários
Shrines

Sátira
Satire

Saúde pública
Public health

Sêcas
Droughts

Segurança nacional
National security

Seguros
Insurance

Semiótica
Semiotics

Sertão (Exploração e vida)
Frontier and pioneer life

Serviço social
Social service

Serviços ambientais
Environmental services

Serviços públicos
Public utilities

Serviços sociais
Social services

Sesmarias
Land grants

Setor de serviços
Service industries

Setor informal (Economia)
Informal sector (Economics)

Sexo (Papéis masculinos e femininos)
Sex role

Sexo (Papéis masculinos e femininos) na literatura
Sex role in literature

SIDA (Doença)
AIDS (Disease)

Simbolismo na literatura
Symbolism in literature

Sincretismo (Religião)
Syncretism (Religion)

Sindicatos
Trade unions

Sindicatos de professores
Teachers' unions

Sisal
Sisal hemp

Sistemas de Informação Geográfica
Geographic Information Systems

Socialismo
Socialism

Socialismo e Igreja Católica
Socialism and Catholic Church

Socialização
Socialization

Sociobiologia
Sociobiology

Sociolingüística
Sociolinguistics

Sociologia
Sociology

Sociologia industrial
Industrial sociology

Sociologia política
Political sociology

Sociologia rural
Sociology, Rural

Sociologia urbana
Sociology, Urban

Soja
Soybean

Solos
Soils

Sonhos
Dreams

Subcontratação
Subcontracting

Substâncias perigosas
Hazardous substances

Suicídio
Suicide

Suiços
Swiss

Superstição
Superstition

Surrealismo
Surrealism

Tabaco
Tobacco

Tabu
Taboo

Tacna e Arica (Questão de)
Tacna – Arica question

Tarifas
Tariff

Taxas de juros
Interest rates

Teatro
Drama

Teatro
Theater

Teatro

Drama e Theater. *Veja também a categoria geográfica pertinente: p.e.,* Argentine drama, Cuban drama, Spanish drama, *etc.*

Teatro experimental

Experimental theater

Teatro folclórico

Folk drama

Teatro hispano-americano (E.U.A.)

Hispanic American drama (U.S.)

Teatro infantil

Children's theater

Teatro mexicano-americano

Mexican American drama

Teatro religioso

Religious drama

Teatros

Theaters

Tecidos (Indústria)

Textile industry and fabrics

Tecnologia

Technology

Tecnologia e civilização

Technology and civilization

Tecnologia e estado

Technology and state

Tecnologia médica

Technology, Medical

Telecomunicação

Telecommunication

Telefone

Telephone

Televisão

Television

Televisão infantil

Children's television

Tempo de trabalho

Time allocation

Tempo na literatura

Time in literature

Tensão (Fisiologia)

Stress (Physiology)

Teologia

Theology

Teologia da libertação

Liberation theology

Terras (Colonização)

Land settlement

Terras da igreja

Church lands

Terremotos

Earthquakes

Terrorismo

Terrorism

Tesis de doutoramento

Dissertations, Academic

Texto visível (Arte)

Visual text

Tipografia e gravação

Printing and engraving

Touradas

Bull fights

Trabalhadores rurais

Agricultural laborers

Trabalhadores sem documentação

Undocumented workers

Trabalho (Produtividade)

Labor productivity

Trabalho e trabalhadores

Labor and laboring classes

Tradição oral

Oral tradition

Tradução e interpretação

Translating and interpreting

Tráfico de drogas

Drug trade

Tráfico de escravos

Slave trade

Transferência de tecnologia

Technology transfer

Transporte

Transportation

Transporte marítimo

Transportation, Maritime

Tratado de Comércio Livre

North American Free Trade Agreement

Trigo

Wheat

Turismo

Tourist trade

Universidades

Universities and colleges

Universidades católicas

Catholic universities and colleges

Urbanização

Urbanization

Uso da terra

Land use

Utopias

Utopias

Vegetação e clima

Vegetation and climate

Velhice

Old age

Venezuela na literatura

Venezuela in literature

Vida cristã

Christian life

Video-teipe

Video tape recorders and recording

Vinicultura

Wine and wine making

Violência

Violence

Violência na literatura

Violence in literature

Visão

Vision

Vodu

Voodooism

Vulcanismo

Volcanism

Xamanismo

Shamanism

Zoologia

Zoology

SUBJECTS

SUBJECTS

ABOLITION OF SLAVERY
See
Slavery

ABORTION
Brazil
Araújo, Maria José de Oliveira. Aborto legal no hospital do Jabaquara. *Estudos Feministas,* v. 1, no. 2 (1993), pp. 424 – 428.

Silva, Rebeca de Souza e. Cegonhas indesejadas: aborto provocado. *Estudos Feministas,* v. 1, no. 1 (1993), pp. 123 – 134. Bibl.

Law and legislation
Barsted, Leila de Andrade Linhares. Legalização e descriminalização do aborto no Brazil: 10 anos de luta feminista (Accompanied by an English translation by Christopher Peterson). *Estudos Feministas,* v. 0, no. 0 (1992), pp. 104 – 130. Bibl.

Blay, Eva Alterman. Projeto de lei sobre o aborto. *Estudos Feministas,* v. 1, no. 2 (1993), pp. 430 – 434.

Mexico
Charlas en la cocina: mi experiencia de aborto. *Fem,* v. 17, no. 126 (Aug 93), p. 31.

Tarrés Barraza, María Luisa. El movimiento de mujeres y el sistema político mexicano: análisis de la lucha por la liberación del aborto, 1976 – 1990. *Estudios Sociológicos,* v. 11, no. 32 (May – Aug 93), pp. 365 – 397. Bibl, tables.

Law and legislation
Begné, Patricia. El derecho a la salud y el aborto en el sistema legal mexicano. *Fem,* v. 17, no. 129 (Nov 93), pp. 12 – 14.

Leal, Luisa María. Pocas perspectivas de despenalización del aborto (Excerpt from *Estrategias en salud y derechos reproductivos: la legalización del aborto en América Latina).* *Fem,* v. 17, no. 129 (Nov 93), pp. 10 – 11.

ABREU, JOÃO CAPISTRANO DE
Wehling, Arno. Capistrano de Abreu e Sílvio Romero: um paralelo cientificista. *Revista do Instituto Histórico e Geográfico Brasileiro,* no. 370 (Jan – Mar 91), pp. 265 – 274.

ABREU, JOSÉ VICENTE
Criticism of specific works
Palabreus
Freytez Arrieche, Gustavo A. *Palabreus:* una (re)visión del llano venezolano. *Revista Nacional de Cultura (Venezuela),* v. 53, no. 286 (July – Sept 92), pp. 50 – 63. Bibl, il.

ABREU GÓMEZ, ERMILO
Correspondence, reminiscences, etc.
Jiménez, Juan Ramón. Buzón de fantasmas: de Juan Ramón Jiménez a Ermilo Abreu Gómez. *Vuelta,* v. 17, no. 205 (Dec 93), pp. 87 – 88.

Torres Bodet, Jaime. Buzón de fantasmas: de Jaime Torres Bodet a Ermilo Abreu Gómez. *Vuelta,* v. 17, no. 204 (Nov 93), pp. 68 – 69.

Valle-Arizpe, Artemio de. Buzón de fantasmas: de Artemio de Valle-Arizpe a Ermilo Abreu Gómez. *Vuelta,* v. 17, no. 202 (Sept 93), pp. 71 – 72.

ACADEMIA COLOMBIANA DE HISTORIA
Velandia, Roberto. Informe de labores. *Boletín de Historia y Antigüedades,* v. 79, no. 779 (Oct – Dec 92), pp. 871 – 886.

ACADEMIA NACIONAL DE LA HISTORIA (VENEZUELA)
Academia Nacional de la Historia: memoria y cuenta, octubre 1991 – septiembre 1992. *Boletín de la Academia Nacional de la Historia (Venezuela),* v. 76, no. 301 (Jan – Mar 93), pp. 151 – 194.

Bossio Penso, Bertalibia. Guía del Archivo Histórico de la Academia Nacional de la Historia. *Boletín de la Academia Nacional de la Historia (Venezuela),* v. 75, no. 299 (July – Sept 92), pp. 150 – 156.

Suárez, Santiago Gerardo. Informe 1990 – 1991 del Departamento de Investigaciones Históricas de la Academia Nacional de la Historia. *Boletín de la Academia Nacional de la Historia (Venezuela),* v. 75, no. 297 (Jan – Mar 92), pp. 147 – 168.

— Informe 1991 – 1992 del Departamento de Investigaciones Históricas de la Academia Nacional de la Historia. *Boletín de la Academia Nacional de la Historia (Venezuela),* v. 75, no. 300 (Oct – Dec 92), pp. 197 – 222.

Catalogs
Jiménez Emán, Gabriel. Notas bibliográficas del catálogo de publicaciones de la Academia Nacional de la Historia. *Boletín de la Academia Nacional de la Historia (Venezuela),* v. 75, no. 298 (Apr – June 92), pp. 99 – 107.

ACAPULCO, MEXICO
Denton, Dan. Acapulco Renaissance. *Business Mexico,* v. 3, no. 3 (Mar 93), pp. 15 – 16. Il.

McCarthy, William J. Between Policy and Prerogative: Malfeasance in the Inspection of the Manila Galleons at Acapulco, 1637. *Colonial Latin American Historical Review,* v. 2, no. 2 (Spring 93), pp. 163 – 183. Bibl, maps.

ACCIÓN DEMOCRÁTICA (VENEZUELA)
Conde Tudanca, Rodrigo. Un incidente olvidado del trienio adeco: la creación de la iglesia católica, apostólica, venezolana. *Boletín de la Academia Nacional de la Historia (Venezuela),* v. 76, no. 302 (Apr – June 93), pp. 87 – 117. Bibl.

ACCULTURATION
See also
Socialization
Subdivision *Government relations* under names of Indian groups

Chile
Larraín Barros, Horacio. Identidad cultural indígena tras quinientos años de aculturación: desafío y destino. *Estudios Sociales (Chile),* no. 76 (Apr – June 93), pp. 135 – 148. Bibl.

Mexico
Alberro, Solange Behocaray de. *Del gachupín al criollo: o de cómo los españoles de México dejaron de serlo* reviewed by Patricia Schraer. *La Educación (USA),* v. 37, no. 115 (1993), pp. 411 – 412.

— *Les espagnols dans le Mexique colonial: histoire d'une acculturation* reviewed by Frédérique Lanque. *Caravelle,* no. 60 (1993), pp. 141 – 143.

León-Portilla, Miguel. *Endangered Cultures* reviewed by Susan Shattuck Benson. *La Educación (USA),* v. 37, no. 114 (1993), p. 162.

Offutt, Leslie S. Levels of Acculturation in Northeastern New Spain: San Esteban Testaments of the Seventeenth and Eighteenth Centuries. *Estudios de Cultura Náhuatl,* v. 22 (1992), pp. 409 – 443.

Zimmermann, Klaus. *Sprachkontakt, ethnische Identität und Identitätsbeschädigung: Aspekte der Assimilation der Otomí-Indianer an die hispanophone mexikanische Kultur* reviewed by Eva Gugenberger. *Iberoamericana,* v. 17, no. 49 (1993), pp. 84 – 86.

Nicaragua

Gould, Jeffrey L. "¡Vana ilusión!": The Highlands Indians and the Myth of Nicaragua Mestiza, 1880 – 1925. *Hispanic American Historical Review,* v. 73, no. 3 (Aug 93), pp. 393 – 429. Bibl, maps.

United States

Flores-Ortiz, Yvette G. Levels of Acculturation, Marital Satisfaction, and Depression among Chicana Workers: A Psychological Perspective. *Aztlán,* v. 20, no. 1 – 2 (Spring – Fall 91), pp. 151 – 175. Bibl, tables.

ACEVEDO, ARTURO

Alcorta, Rodrigo. Arturo Acevedo, un hombre de acero. *Todo Es Historia,* v. 26, no. 307 (Feb 93), pp. 50 – 53. Il.

ACHUALE INDIANS

See
   Jívaro Indians

ACOSTA, AGUSTÍN

Criticism of specific works

El apóstol y su isla

Febles, Jorge M. "Un pueblo": *Menosprecio de corte y alabanza de aldea* en la poesía de Agustín Acosta. *Anuario de Letras (Mexico),* v. 30 (1992), pp. 133 – 152. Bibl.

ACOSTA, OSCAR ZETA

Criticism of specific works

Autobiography of a Brown Buffalo

Thwaites, Jeanne. The Use of Irony in Oscar Zeta Acosta's *Autobiography of a Brown Buffalo. The Americas Review,* v. 20, no. 1 (Spring 92), pp. 73 – 82. Bibl.

ACTING

Antunes Filho. Confesiones de un fingidor. *Conjunto,* no. 93 (Jan – June 93), pp. 38 – 43. Il.

ACTORS AND ACTRESSES

Argentina

Manso, Leonor. Los actores en las décadas del '70 y del '80. *Cuadernos Hispanoamericanos,* no. 517 – 519 (July – Sept 93), pp. 538 – 540.

Méndez Avellaneda, Juan María. La vida privada de Trinidad Guevara. *Todo Es Historia,* v. 27, no. 311 (June 93), pp. 26 – 40. Il, facs.

Seibel, Beatriz. Mujer, teatro y sociedad en el siglo XIX. *Conjunto,* no. 92 (July – Dec 92), pp. 54 – 57. Bibl, il.

Mexico

Arana, Auxiliadora and Philip C. Kloin. An Interview with Wolf Ruvinskis: The First Mexican Stanley Kowalski. *Latin American Theatre Review,* v. 26, no. 2 (Spring 93), pp. 158 – 165. Il.

Infiesta, Jesús. Al humanismo, a la ternura y a la caridad por el humor (Originally published in *Ecclesia). Mensaje,* v. 42, no. 423 (Oct 93), pp. 499 – 500. Il.

Venezuela

Giménez, Carlos. Homenaje a Pepe Tejera: palabras del director de Rajatabla a su actor galardonado. *Conjunto,* no. 90 – 91 (Jan – June 92), pp. 40 – 42. Il.

Pepe Tejera: Premio Simón Bolívar. *Conjunto,* no. 90 – 91 (Jan – June 92), p. 39.

ACUERDO DE CARTAGENA

See
   Andean Common Market

ACUÑA, LUIS ALBERTO

Obituaries

Acuña Cañas, Alonso. Semblanza del maestro Acuña. *Boletín de Historia y Antigüedades,* v. 80, no. 781 (Apr – June 93), pp. 357 – 358.

Gallo, Lylia. Evocación de Luis Alberto Acuña (1904 – 1993). *Boletín de Historia y Antigüedades,* v. 80, no. 781 (Apr – June 93), pp. 365 – 367.

Medina Flórez, Enrique. Ante el féretro del maestro Acuña. *Boletín de Historia y Antigüedades,* v. 80, no. 781 (Apr – June 93), pp. 355 – 356.

Ocampo López, Javier. El maestro Luis Alberto Acuña y el nacionalismo artístico. *Boletín de Historia y Antigüedades,* v. 80, no. 781 (Apr – June 93), pp. 343 – 354.

Santa, Eduardo. Luis Alberto Acuña, pintor de América. *Boletín de Historia y Antigüedades,* v. 80, no. 781 (Apr – June 93), pp. 359 – 363.

Serrano, Eduardo. Acuña y el nacionalismo. *Boletín de Historia y Antigüedades,* v. 80, no. 781 (Apr – June 93), pp. 369 – 372.

ADÁN, MARTÍN

See
   Fuente Benavides, Rafael de la

ADOLESCENT PSYCHOLOGY

Cánepa, María Angela. Recuerdos, olvidos y desencuentros: aproximaciones a la subjetividad de los jóvenes andinos. *Allpanchis,* v. 25, no. 41 (Jan – June 93), pp. 11 – 37. Bibl.

Degregori, Carlos Iván et al. Comentarios y réplica (to the article "Recuerdos, olvidos y desencuentros" by María Angela Cánepa). *Allpanchis,* v. 25, no. 41 (Jan – June 93), pp. 38 – 73.

Romero C., Paulino. Vida familiar y adolescencia. *Revista Cultural Lotería,* v. 50, no. 385 (Sept – Oct 91), pp. 73 – 82. Bibl.

ADOPTION

See
   Parent and child

ADRIANI, ALBERTO

Rojas Guardia, Armando. Palabras pronunciadas en el acto de inauguración de un busto del dr. Alberto Adriani en Caracas el día 14 de junio de 1991. *Boletín de la Academia Nacional de la Historia (Venezuela),* v. 75, no. 297 (Jan – Mar 92), pp. 43 – 46.

ADULT EDUCATION

Chile

Von Baer, Heinrich. Extensión universitaria: reflexiones para la acción. *Estudios Sociales (Chile),* no. 74 (Oct – Dec 92), pp. 159 – 166.

Mexico

López Rodríguez, Ramón. A Different Solution. *Business Mexico,* v. 3, no. 6 (June 93), pp. 16 – 18. Il.

ADVERTISING

See also
   Marketing

Baena Paz, Guillermina. Perspectivas de la comunicación en los noventa. *Revista Mexicana de Ciencias Políticas y Sociales,* v. 38, Nueva época, no. 154 (Oct – Dec 93), pp. 103 – 114.

Costa Rica

Sandoval García, Carlos. Programas de ajuste estructural e industria de la publicidad en Costa Rica. *Revista de Ciencias Sociales (Costa Rica),* no. 57 (Sept 92), pp. 17 – 29. Bibl, tables.

Latin America

Montecino, Marcelo. Signs That Sell (Photographs by the author). *Américas,* v. 45, no. 5 (Sept – Oct 93), pp. 40 – 41. Il.

Paxman, Andrew. Selling in a Second Language. *Business Mexico,* v. 3, no. 6 (June 93), pp. 36 – 37.

Mexico

Lepri, Jean-Pierre. *Images de la femme dans les annonces publicitaires des quotidiens au Mexique* reviewed by Héctor Ruiz Rivas. *Caravelle,* no. 59 (1992), pp. 313 – 314.

AERONAUTICS

See
Airplane industry and trade

AESTHETICS

Acha, Juan. El arte contemporáneo y la estética latinoamericana. *Plural (Mexico),* v. 22, no. 257 (Feb 93), pp. 60 – 67.

Sánchez Vázquez, Adolfo. Prólogo a *Obra estética. Casa de las Américas,* no. 190 (Jan – Mar 93), pp. 136 – 140.

AFRICA

See also
Missions – Africa
Slavery – Africa

Oliveira, Henrique Altemani de. Política externa independente: fundamentos da política africana do Brasil. *Política e Estratégica,* v. 8, no. 2 – 4 (Apr – Dec 90), pp. 268 – 284. Bibl, tables.

AFRO-AMERICAN LITERATURE

See
Blacks in literature
Subdivision *Black authors* under names of specific national literatures

AFRO-HISPANIC REVIEW (PERIODICAL)

Indexes

Davis, James J. Index of *Afro-Hispanic Review,* Volumes 8 – 12. *Afro-Hispanic Review,* v. 12, no. 2 (Fall 93), pp. 48 – 53.

AGING

See
Old age

AGOSÍN, MARJORIE

Criticism and interpretation

Mujica, Barbara Kaminar de. Marjorie Agosín Weaves Magic with Social Vision (Photographs by Ted Polumbaum). *Américas,* v. 45, no. 1 (Jan – Feb 93), pp. 44 – 49. Il.

AGRARIAN REFORM

See
Land reform

AGRARIAN UNIONS

See
Subdivision *Political activity* under *Agricultural laborers* and *Peasantry*

AGRIBUSINESS

See
Agriculture and state
Food industry and trade

AGRICULTURAL ASSISTANCE, FOREIGN

Central America

Barry, Tom and Rachel Garst. *Feeding the Crisis: U.S. Food Aid and Farm Policy in Central America* reviewed by Melvin G. Blase. *Journal of Developing Areas,* v. 27, no. 4 (July 93), pp. 566 – 567.

AGRICULTURAL CREDIT

Latin America

Cebreros, Alfonso and Carlos Pomareda. Mecanismos financieros para la modernización de la agricultura. *Comercio Exterior,* v. 43, no. 4 (Apr 93), pp. 328 – 335. Bibl, tables, charts.

AGRICULTURAL LABORERS

See also
Migration, Internal
Peasantry
Undocumented workers

Amazon Valley

Chibnik, Michael and Wil de Jong. Organización de la mano de obra agrícola en las comunidades ribereñas de la Amazonía peruana. *Amazonía Peruana,* v. 11, no. 21 (Sept 92), pp. 181 – 215. Bibl.

Argentina

Caravaglia, Juan Carlos. Los labradores de San Isidro, siglos XVIII – XIX. *Desarrollo Económico (Argentina),* v. 32, no. 128 (Jan – Mar 93), pp. 513 – 542. Bibl, tables, charts.

Eizykovicz, José. Los peones rurales después de la revolución, 1815 – 1823. *Todo Es Historia,* v. 27, no. 312 (July 93), pp. 28 – 42. Bibl, il, facs.

Guy, Donna Jane. "Oro Blanco": Cotton, Technology, and Family Labor in Nineteenth-Century Argentina. *The Americas,* v. 49, no. 4 (Apr 93), pp. 457 – 478. Bibl.

Brazil

Kohlhepp, Gerd. Mudanças estruturais na agropecuária e mobilidade da população rural no norte do Paraná (Brasil). *Revista Brasileira de Geografia,* v. 53, no. 2 (Apr – June 91), pp. 79 – 94. Bibl, il, tables, maps.

Chile

Political activity

Gómez, Sergio. Grupos sociales, organizaciones representativas y movilizaciones políticas: las dos caras de la modernización de la agricultura chilena. *Estudios Sociales (Chile),* no. 76 (Apr – June 93), pp. 9 – 66. Tables.

Dominican Republic

Murphy, Martin Francis. *Dominican Sugar Plantations: Production and Foreign Labor Integration* reviewed by Michel-Rolph Trouillot. *Hispanic American Historical Review,* v. 73, no. 3 (Aug 93), pp. 535 – 536.

— *Dominican Sugar Plantations: Production and Foreign Labor Integration* reviewed by Tom Spencer-Walters. *Journal of Caribbean Studies,* v. 9, no. 1 – 2 (Winter 92 – Spring 93), pp. 140 – 142.

Pou, Francis. Inmigración de agricultores españoles a la República Dominicana en el período Franco – Trujillo, 1939 – 1961. *Revista de Indias,* v. 53, no. 198 (May – Aug 93), pp. 563 – 582. Bibl, tables, charts.

Ruiz, Marta. Migración entre Haití y la República Dominicana. *Cuadernos Hispanoamericanos,* no. 522 (Dec 93), pp. 77 – 86.

Ecuador

Lentz, Carola. *Buscando la vida: trabajadores temporales en una plantación de azúcar* reviewed by Alberto Cheng Hurtado. *América Indígena,* v. 51, no. 4 (Oct – Dec 91), pp. 219 – 222.

Martínez Valle, Luciano. Cambios en la fuerza de trabajo y conflicto social en el agro ecuatoriano. *Revista Paraguaya de Sociología,* v. 29, no. 84 (May – Aug 92), pp. 101 – 113. Bibl.

— El empleo en economías campesinas productoras para el mercado interno: el caso de la sierra ecuatoriana. *European Review of Latin American and Caribbean Studies,* no. 53 (Dec 92), pp. 83 – 93. Bibl, tables.

Latin America

Cartón de Grammont, Hubert. Algunas reflexiones en torno al mercado de trabajo en el campo latinoamericano. *Revista Mexicana de Sociología,* v. 54, no. 1 (Jan – Mar 92), pp. 49 – 58. Bibl.

Klein, Emilio. El mundo de trabajo rural. *Nueva Sociedad,* no. 124 (Mar – Apr 93), pp. 72 – 81. Bibl, tables.

Mexico

Henderson, Peter V. N. Modernization and Change in Mexico: La Zacualpa Rubber Plantation, 1890 – 1920. *Hispanic American Historical Review,* v. 73, no. 2 (May 93), pp. 235 – 260. Bibl, tables.

Lara Flores, Sara María. La flexibilidad del mercado de trabajo rural: una propuesta que involucra a las mujeres. *Revista Mexicana de Sociología,* v. 54, no. 1 (Jan – Mar 92), pp. 29 – 48. Bibl.

Loete, Sylvia K. Aspects of Modernization on a Mexican Hacienda: Labour on San Nicolás del Moral (Chalco) at the End of the Nineteenth Century. *European Review of Latin American and Caribbean Studies,* no. 54 (June 93), pp. 45 – 64. Bibl, charts.

Puig, Juan Carlos. *Entre el río Perla y el Nazas: la China decimonónica y sus braceros emigrantes. Vuelta,* v. 17, no. 202 (Sept 93), p. 53.

Nicaragua

Quandt, Midge. Nicaragua: Unbinding the Ties; Popular Movements and the FSLN. *Report on the Americas,* v. 26, no. 4 (Feb 93), pp. 11 – 14. Il.

United States
Law and legislation

Calavita, Kitty. *Inside the State: The Bracero Program, Immigration, and the I.N.S.* reviewed by Rodolfo O. de la Garza. *International Migration Review,* v. 27, no. 4 (Winter 93), pp. 895 – 896.

AGRICULTURE

See also
- Ayllus
- Banana trade
- Beans
- Chocolate and cacao
- Citrus fruits
- Coffee
- Corn
- Cotton
- Dairying
- Ejidos
- Encomiendas
- Fertilizer industry
- Food industry and trade
- Food supply
- Fruit trade
- Grain trade
- Haciendas
- Horticulture
- Land reform
- Land settlement
- Land tenure
- Land use
- Manioc
- Palms
- Peasantry
- Pesticides
- Potatoes
- Rice
- Rubber industry and trade
- Sisal hemp
- Soybean
- Sugar
- Tea
- Tobacco
- Wheat
- Subdivision *Agriculture* under names of Indian groups

Di Girólamo, Giovanni. The World Agricultural Outlook in the 1990s. *CEPAL Review,* no. 47 (Aug 92), pp. 95 – 114. Bibl, tables, charts.

Perea Dallos, Margarita. Biotecnología y agricultura. *Revista Javeriana,* v. 61, no. 591 (Jan – Feb 93), pp. 35 – 40. Bibl, charts.

Smith, Nigel J. H. et al. *Tropical Forests and Their Crops* reviewed by David M. Kummer. *Geographical Review,* v. 83, no. 3 (July 93), pp. 339 – 341.

Congresses

Angulo Carrera, Alejandro and Salvador Rodríguez y Rodríguez. Agricultura orgánica, desarrollo sustentable y comercio justo. *Problemas del Desarrollo,* v. 24, no. 94 (July – Sept 93), pp. 265 – 274.

Delgado Martínez, Irma. XII Seminario de Economía Agrícola del Tercer Mundo. *Problemas del Desarrollo,* v. 24, no. 93 (Apr – June 93), pp. 221 – 226.

VI Congreso Internacional de Derecho Agrario. *Derecho y Reforma Agraria,* no. 23 (1992), pp. 207 – 211.

Law and legislation

Gelsi Bidart, Adolfo. Individualización del derecho agrario. *Derecho y Reforma Agraria,* no. 24 (1993), pp. 53 – 62.

Congresses

Congreso Internacional e Iberoamericano de Derecho Agrario. *Derecho y Reforma Agraria,* no. 24 (1993), pp. 173 – 174.

America

Río Moreno, Justo L. del. *Los inicios de la agricultura europea en el Nuevo Mundo, 1492 – 1542* reviewed by María del Carmen Morales García. *Anuario de Estudios Americanos,* v. 49, Suppl. 1 (1992), pp. 260 – 261.

Argentina

Gilberti, Horacio. Cambios en las estructuras agrarias. *Realidad Económica,* no. 113 (Jan – Feb 93), pp. 87 – 89.

Marco, Miguel Angel de. Pellegrini contra la langosta, 1891 – 1892. *Todo Es Historia,* v. 27, no. 311 (June 93), pp. 62 – 73. Il.

Posada, Marcelo Germán. Crisis estatal y nuevo entramado social: la emergencia de las organizaciones no gubernamentales; el rol de las ONGs en el agro argentino. *Revista Paraguaya de Sociología,* v. 29, no. 85 (Sept – Dec 92), pp. 99 – 131. Bibl.

Law and legislation

Brebbia, Fernando P. *Manual de derecho agrario* reviewed by Arnaldo Gómez A. *Derecho y Reforma Agraria,* no. 24 (1993), pp. 205 – 206.

Carrera, Rodolfo Ricardo. *El problema de la tierra en el derecho agrario* reviewed by Arnaldo Gómez A. *Derecho y Reforma Agraria,* no. 24 (1993), pp. 203 – 204.

Belize

Bliss, Elaine. Adaptation to Agricultural Change among Garifuna Women in Hopkins, Belize. *Caribbean Geography,* v. 3, no. 3 (Mar 92), pp. 160 – 174. Bibl, tables, maps.

Brazil

O campo se moderniza. *Problemas Brasileiros,* v. 30, no. 295 (Jan – Feb 93), pp. 29 – 31. Il, charts.

Font, Mauricio A. City and the Countryside in the Onset of Brazilian Industrialization. *Studies in Comparative International Development,* v. 27, no. 3 (Fall 92), pp. 26 – 56. Bibl, tables, charts.

Grabois, José and Mauro José da Silva. O breja de Natuba: estudo da organização de um espaço periférico. *Revista Brasileira de Geografia,* v. 53, no. 2 (Apr – June 91), pp. 33 – 62. Bibl, il, tables, maps.

Kohlhepp, Gerd. Mudanças estruturais na agropecuária e mobilidade da população rural no norte do Paraná (Brasil). *Revista Brasileira de Geografia,* v. 53, no. 2 (Apr – June 91), pp. 79 – 94. Bibl, il, tables, maps.

Laroche, Rose Claire. Ecossistemas e impactos ambientais da modernização agrícola do vale São Francisco. *Revista Brasileira de Geografia,* v. 53, no. 2 (Apr – June 91), pp. 63 – 77. Bibl, il, charts.

Salles Filho, Sérgio L. M. et al. Estratégias empresariais em agrobiotecnologia no Brasil: um estudo de casos relevantes. *Revista de Economia e Sociologia Rural,* v. 30, no. 3 (July – Sept 92), pp. 203 – 224. Bibl, tables.

Mathematical models

Bacha, Carlos José Caetano. Alguns aspectos dos modelos de análise dos impactos de mudança tecnológica no comportamento do setor agrícola. *Revista de Economia e Sociologia Rural,* v. 30, no. 1 (Jan – Mar 92), pp. 41 – 62. Bibl, charts.

Hoffmann, Rodolfo. A dinâmica da modernização da agricultura em 157 microrregiões homogêneas do Brasil. *Revista de Economia e Sociologia Rural,* v. 30, no. 4 (Oct – Dec 92), pp. 271 – 290. Bibl, tables, charts.

Santana, Antônio Cordeiro de. Análise econômica da produção agrícola sob condições de risco numa comunidade amazônica. *Revista de Economia e Sociologia Rural,* v. 30, no. 2 (Apr – June 92), pp. 159 – 170. Bibl, tables.

Methodology

Souza, Jaimeval Caetano de et al. Combinações agrícolas no estado da Bahia, 1970 – 1980: uma contribuição metodológica. *Revista Brasileira de Geografia,* v. 53, no. 2 (Apr – June 91), pp. 95 – 112. Bibl, tables, maps.

Study and teaching

Capdeville, Guy. O ensino superior agrícola no Brasil. *Revista Brasileira de Estudos Pedagógicos,* v. 72, no. 172 (Sept – Dec 91), pp. 229 – 261. Bibl, tables, charts.

Chile

Byé, Pascal and Jean-Pierre Frey. Le modèle chilien à la lumière de l'expérience des pays agro-exportateurs de l'ASEAN. *Cahiers des Amériques Latines,* no. 14 (1992), pp. 37 – 49. Bibl, tables.

Gómez, Sergio. Grupos sociales, organizaciones representativas y movilizaciones políticas: las dos caras de la modernización de la agricultura chilena. *Estudios Sociales (Chile),* no. 76 (Apr – June 93), pp. 9 – 66. Tables.

Mujica Ateaga, Rodrigo. El desempeño del sector agrícola entre 1991 y 1993. *Estudios Sociales (Chile),* no. 75 (Jan – Mar 93), pp. 129 – 139. Tables.

Norambuena Carrasco, Carmen. Inmigración, agricultura y ciudades intermedias, 1880 – 1930. *Cuadernos de Historia (Chile),* no. 11 (Dec 91), pp. 105 – 123. Bibl, tables.

Síntesis agro-regional reviewed by Fernando Riveros R. *EURE,* v. 19, no. 56 (Mar 93), p. 118.

Colombia

La apertura económica y el sector agrícola colombiano. *Revista Javeriana,* v. 61, no. 591 (Jan – Feb 93), pp. 11 – 19. Charts.

Guatemala

Alarcón, Jorge A. and Maarten Dirk Cornelis Immink. Household Income, Food Availability, and Commercial Crop Production by Smallholder Farmers in the Western Highlands of Guatemala. *Economic Development and Cultural Change,* v. 41, no. 2 (Jan 93), pp. 319 – 342. Bibl, tables.

Jamaica

Meikle, Paulette. Spatio-Temporal Trends in Root Crop Production and Marketing in Jamaica. *Caribbean Geography,* v. 3, no. 4 (Sept 92), pp. 223 – 235. Bibl, tables, maps, charts.

Latin America

Cebreros, Alfonso. La competitividad agropecuaria en condiciones de apertura económica. *Comercio Exterior,* v. 43, no. 10 (Oct 93), pp. 946 – 953. Bibl.

Guerra E., Guillermo A. América Latina: la empresa agropecuaria ante la modernización. *Comercio Exterior,* v. 43, no. 4 (Apr 93), pp. 344 – 352. Bibl, tables, charts.

Iokoi, Zilda Márcia Gricoli. Questão agrária e meio ambiente: 500 anos de destruição. *Vozes,* v. 86, no. 5 (Sept – Oct 92), pp. 12 – 20.

Law and legislation

Brebbia, Fernando P. Tendencias de la doctrina agrarista. *Derecho y Reforma Agraria,* no. 23 (1992), pp. 17 – 32.

Casanova, Ramón Vicente. El derecho agrario iberoamericano: su vocación regional. *Derecho y Reforma Agraria,* no. 24 (1993), pp. 11 – 26.

"De Aragón partió nuestro agrarismo": palabras pronunciadas en acto de instalación del Congreso, 28 – 9 – 92. *Derecho y Reforma Agraria,* no. 24 (1993), pp. 175 – 179.

Duque Corredor, Ramón José. El derecho agrario y su vocación regional: sentido y principios funcionales. *Derecho y Reforma Agraria,* no. 24 (1993), pp. 27 – 31.

Mexico

Freebairn, Donald K. Posibles pérdidas y ganancias en el sector agrícola bajo un Tratado de Libre Comercio entre Estados Unidos y México. *Revista Mexicana de Sociología,* v. 54, no. 1 (Jan – Mar 92), pp. 3 – 28. Bibl, tables.

García, Arturo. Reality in the "Campo." *Business Mexico,* v. 3, no. 8 (Aug 93), pp. 30 – 31. Il.

González Herrera, Carlos. La agricultura en el proyecto económico de Chihuahua durante el porfiriato. *Siglo XIX: Cuadernos,* v. 2, no. 5 (Feb 93), pp. 9 – 37. Bibl, tables, maps.

López Gallardo, Julio. The Potential of Mexican Agriculture and Options for the Future. *CEPAL Review,* no. 47 (Aug 92), pp. 137 – 148. Tables.

Pepin Lehalleur, Marielle and Marie-France Prévôt-Schapira. Cuclillos en un nido de gorrión: espacio municipal y poder local en Altamira, Tamaulipas. *Estudios Sociológicos,* v. 10, no. 30 (Sept – Dec 92), pp. 583 – 617. Bibl, maps.

Solleiro, José Luis et al. La innovación tecnológica en la agricultura mexicana. *Comercio Exterior,* v. 43, no. 4 (Apr 93), pp. 353 – 369. Bibl, charts.

Bibliography

Tutino, John. Historias del México agrario (Translated by Mario A. Zamudio Vega). *Historia Mexicana,* v. 42, no. 2 (Oct – Dec 92), pp. 177 – 220.

Law and legislation

Calva, José Luis. La reforma neoliberal del régimen agrario: en el cuarto año de gobierno de C. S. G. *Problemas del Desarrollo,* v. 24, no. 92 (Jan – Mar 93), pp. 31 – 39. Tables.

Research

Bellon, Mauricio R. and J. Edward Taylor. "Folk" Soil Taxonomy and the Partial Adoption of New Seed Varieties. *Economic Development and Cultural Change,* v. 41, no. 4 (July 93), pp. 763 – 786. Bibl, tables.

Statistics

Cabello Naranjo, Elena. El censo agropecuario de 1991: un retrato del campo mexicano. *Comercio Exterior,* v. 43, no. 4 (Apr 93), pp. 392 – 394. Tables, charts.

Torres Torres, Felipe. Los desequilibrios de la balanza comercial agropecuaria. *Momento Económico,* no. 66 (Mar – Apr 93), pp. 9 – 13. Tables.

Panama

Castillo Galástica, Adán. Cuestiones del desarrollo: la modernización en el agro-panameño. *Revista Cultural Lotería,* v. 50, no. 386 (Nov – Dec 91), pp. 25 – 46. Bibl.

Paraguay

Kleinpenning, Jan M. G. *Rural Paraguay, 1870 – 1932* reviewed by Jerry W. Cooney. *Hispanic American Historical Review,* v. 73, no. 4 (Nov 93), pp. 710 – 711.

— *Rural Paraguay, 1870 – 1932* reviewed by R. Andrew Nickson. *Bulletin of Latin American Research,* v. 12, no. 2 (May 93), pp. 220 – 221.

— *Rural Paraguay, 1870 – 1932* reviewed by Vera Blinn Reber. *Journal of Latin American Studies,* v. 25, no. 2 (May 93), pp. 398 – 399.

Peru

Amat y León, Carlos. La competitividad del sector agrícola. *Apuntes (Peru),* no. 30 (Jan – June 92), pp. 3 – 11.

Congresses

Bey, Marguerite. La cinquième Séminaire Permanent de Recherche Agraire. *Tiers Monde,* v. 34, no. 136 (Oct – Dec 93), pp. 937 – 938.

Puerto Rico

Tannenbaum, Frank. Los últimos treinta años, 1898 – 1928 (Translated by Sara Irizarry). *Op. Cit.,* no. 7 (1992), pp. 165 – 207. Il, tables.

Río de la Plata region

Gelman, Jorge Daniel. Los caminos del mercado: campesinos, estancieros y pulperos en una región del Río de la Plata colonial. *Latin American Research Review,* v. 28, no. 2 (1993), pp. 89 – 118. Bibl, tables.

Venezuela

Finol Urdaneta, Hermán. Propuesta de nueva estrategia para la producción agropecuaria y forestal sobre una base ecológica. *Derecho y Reforma Agraria,* no. 23 (1992), pp. 73 – 82.

Law and legislation

Portocarrero de Guzmán, Blancanieve. El derecho agrario iberoamericano: su vocación regional. *Derecho y Reforma Agraria,* no. 24 (1993), pp. 43 – 52. Bibl.

XXX años de jurisprudencia agraria en Venezuela reviewed by Arnaldo Gómez A. *Derecho y Reforma Agraria,* no. 23 (1992), p. 217.

AGRICULTURE, COOPERATIVE
Amazon Valley
Chibnik, Michael and Wil de Jong. Organización de la mano de obra agrícola en las comunidades ribereñas de la Amazonía peruana. *Amazonía Peruana*, v. 11, no. 21 (Sept 92), pp. 181 – 215. Bibl.

Brazil
Mathematical models
Barni, Euclides João and Sérgio Alberto Brandt. Descentralização, diversificação e tamanho de cooperativas agropecuárias. *Revista de Economia e Sociologia Rural*, v. 30, no. 1 (Jan – Mar 92), pp. 1 – 10. Bibl, tables.

Chile
Rosenfeld, Stephanie. Comunero Democracy Endures in Chile. *NACLA Report on the Americas*, v. 27, no. 2 (Sept – Oct 93), pp. 29 – 34.

Haiti
Maguire, Robert et al. Food Security and Development in Haiti. *Grassroots Development*, v. 16, no. 2 (1992), pp. 35 – 39. Il.

Mexico
Bibliography
Stanford, Lois. The "Organization" of Mexican Agriculture: Conflicts and Compromises (Review article). *Latin American Research Review*, v. 28, no. 1 (1993), pp. 188 – 201. Bibl.

Nicaragua
Ton, Giel and Gerda Zijm. Matrimonio conflictivo: cooperativas en un proyecto agroindustrial; el caso de Sébaco, Nicaragua. *Estudios Rurales Latinoamericanos*, v. 15, no. 2 – 3 (May – Dec 92), pp. 121 – 138. Bibl, tables.

Paraguay
Rengifo V., Grimaldo and Marcos Sánchez. *Hacia una agricultura sostenible: el caso de Coronel Oviedo*. *Revista Paraguaya de Sociología*, v. 29, no. 85 (Sept – Dec 92), pp. 190 – 191.

Venezuela
Denis, Paul-Yves and José Ismael Jaspe Alvarez. Estudio de la distribución espacial del sistema cooperativo de "Ferias de Consumo Familiar" (FCF) y de su papel en el abastecimiento alimentario en la región centro-occidental de Venezuela. *Revista Geográfica (Mexico)*, no. 114 (July – Dec 91), pp. 5 – 36. Bibl, maps, charts.

AGRICULTURE AND STATE
See also
Land reform

Argentina
Giarracca, Norma. Campesinos y agroindustrias en los tiempos del "ajuste": algunas reflexiones para pensar la relación, con especial referencia a México y la Argentina. *Realidad Económica*, no. 114 – 115 (Feb – May 93), pp. 13 – 28. Bibl.

Girbal de Blacha, Noemí M. Tradición y modernización en la agricultura cerealera argentina, 1910 – 1930: comportamiento y propuestas de los ingenieros agrónomos. *Jahrbuch für Geschichte von Staat, Wirtschaft und Gesellschaft Lateinamerikas*, v. 29 (1992), pp. 369 – 395. Bibl.

Supplee, Joan E. Vitivinicultura, recursos públicos y ganancias privadas en Mendoza, 1880 – 1914. *Siglo XIX: Cuadernos*, v. 2, no. 5 (Feb 93), pp. 81 – 94. Bibl.

Bolivia
Paz Ballivián, Danilo. Cuestión agraria y campesina en Bolivia. *Revista Paraguaya de Sociología*, v. 29, no. 84 (May – Aug 92), pp. 115 – 133.

Brazil
Beaney, Peter W. The Irrigated Eldorado: State-Managed Rural Development, Redemocratisation, and Popular Participation in the Brazilian Northeast. *Bulletin of Latin American Research*, v. 12, no. 3 (Sept 93), pp. 249 – 272. Bibl.

Brito, Maria Socorro. O Programa Nacional de Irrigação: uma avaliação prévia dos resultados. *Revista Brasileira de Geografia*, v. 53, no. 2 (Apr – June 91), pp. 113 – 125. Bibl, tables.

Carvalho, Maria Auxiliadora de and César Roberto Leite da Silva. Preços mínimos e estabilização de preços agrícolas. *Revista de Economia Política (Brazil)*, v. 13, no. 1 (Jan – Mar 93), pp. 52 – 63. Bibl, tables.

Ferreira, Ignez Costa Barbosa. Gestão do espaço agrário. *Revista Brasileira de Geografia*, v. 53, no. 3 (July – Sept 91), pp. 149 – 159. Bibl, tables, maps.

Pereira, Laércio Barbosa. O estado e o desempenho da agricultura paranaense no período de 1975 – 1985. *Revista de Economia e Sociologia Rural*, v. 30, no. 2 (Apr – June 92), pp. 115 – 133. Bibl, tables.

Veiga, Alberto. Agricultura e processo político: o caso brasileiro. *Revista de Economia e Sociologia Rural*, v. 29, no. 4 (Oct – Dec 91), pp. 285 – 334. Bibl, tables.

Mathematical models
Teixeira, Erly Cardoso et al. A política de investimentos agrícolas e seu efeito sobre a distribuição de renda. *Revista de Economia e Sociologia Rural*, v. 30, no. 4 (Oct – Dec 92), pp. 291 – 303. Bibl, tables, charts.

Chile
Gómez, Sergio. ¿Cosas nuevas en la agricultura? *Estudios Sociales (Chile)*, no. 75 (Jan – Mar 93), pp. 141 – 153. Tables.

Hojman A., David E., ed. *Change in the Chilean Countryside: From Pinochet to Aylwin and Beyond; The Proceedings of the 46th International Congress of Americanists, Amsterdam* reviewed by Walter Belik. *Journal of Latin American Studies*, v. 25, no. 3 (Oct 93), pp. 679 – 680.

Costa Rica
Jiménez Arce, Ana Cecilia et al. La agricultura de cambio en el contexto del ajuste estructural. *Revista de Ciencias Sociales (Costa Rica)*, no. 60 (June 93), pp. 27 – 38. Bibl, tables.

Li Kam, Sui Moy. Costa Rica ante la internacionalización de la agricultura. *Revista de Ciencias Sociales (Costa Rica)*, no. 57 (Sept 92), pp. 87 – 96. Bibl.

Developing countries
Utting, Peter. *Economic Reform and Third-World Socialism* reviewed by S. P. Chakravarty. *Bulletin of Latin American Research*, v. 12, no. 1 (Jan 93), pp. 122 – 124.

— *Economic Reform and Third-World Socialism: A Political Economy of Food Policy in Post-Revolutionary Societies* reviewed by Kenneth P. Jameson. *Journal of Developing Areas*, v. 27, no. 4 (July 93), pp. 543 – 544.

Guatemala
Bell, John Patrick. La Asociación General de Agricultores frente a la reforma agraria en la Guatemala revolucionaria, 1944 – 1954. *Anuario de Estudios Centroamericanos*, v. 18, no. 1 (1992), pp. 17 – 28. Bibl.

Berger, Susan A. *Political and Agrarian Development in Guatemala* reviewed by Kenneth J. Grieb. *Hispanic American Historical Review*, v. 73, no. 3 (Aug 93), pp. 530 – 531.

Latin America
Bibliography
Grindle, Merilee Serrill. Agrarian Class Structures and State Policies: Past, Present, and Future (Review article). *Latin American Research Review*, v. 28, no. 1 (1993), pp. 174 – 187.

Mexico
Azpeitia Gómez, Hugo et al. *Los tiempos de la crisis, 1970 – 1982, partes 1 y 2: Historia de la cuestión agraria mexicana* reviewed by David W. Walker. *Hispanic American Historical Review*, v. 73, no. 3 (Aug 93), pp. 529 – 530.

Cervantes Herrera, Joel and César Ramírez Miranda. México: del imperio del maíz al maíz del imperio. *Problemas del Desarrollo*, v. 24, no. 94 (July – Sept 93), pp. 97 – 112. Tables.

Giarracca, Norma. Campesinos y agroindustrias en los tiempos del "ajuste": algunas reflexiones para pensar la relación, con especial referencia a México y la Argentina. *Realidad Económica*, no. 114 – 115 (Feb – May 93), pp. 13 – 28. Bibl.

Hank González, Carlos. El Procampo: estrategia de apoyos al productor del agro. *Comercio Exterior*, v. 43, no. 10 (Oct 93), pp. 982 – 984.

Bibliography

Stanford, Lois. The "Organization" of Mexican Agriculture: Conflicts and Compromises (Review article). *Latin American Research Review*, v. 28, no. 1 (1993), pp. 188 – 201. Bibl.

Mathematical models

Levy, Santiago and Sweder van Wijnbergen. Mercados de trabajo, migración y bienestar: la agricultura en el Tratado de Libre Comercio entre México y los Estados Unidos (Translated by Carlos Villegas). *El Trimestre Económico*, v. 60, no. 238 (Apr – June 93), pp. 371 – 411. Bibl, tables.

Robinson, Sherman et al. Las políticas agrícolas y la migración en un área de libre comercio de los Estados Unidos y México: un análisis de equilibrio general computable (Translated by Carlos Villegas). *El Trimestre Económico*, v. 60, no. 237 (Jan – Mar 93), pp. 53 – 89. Bibl, tables, charts.

Nicaragua

Enríquez, Laura Jean. *Harvesting Change: Labor and Agrarian Reform in Nicaragua, 1979 – 1990* reviewed by Elizabeth Dore. *Journal of Latin American Studies*, v. 25, no. 1 (Feb 93), pp. 211 – 212.

Spoor, Max. La política de precios agrícolas en Nicaragua durante el régimen sandinista, 1979 – 1990 (Translated by Carlos Villegas). *El Trimestre Económico*, v. 60, no. 239 (July – Sept 93), pp. 601 – 641. Bibl, tables, charts.

Paraguay

Rengifo V., Grimaldo and Marcos Sánchez. *Hacia una agricultura sostenible: el caso de Coronel Oviedo*. *Revista Paraguaya de Sociología*, v. 29, no. 85 (Sept – Dec 92), pp. 190 – 191.

Venezuela

Gutiérrez M., Alejandro and Raúl León Palencia P. Lineamientos de política científica y tecnológica para el estado Mérida: área agrícola agroalimentaria; ideas para la discusión. *Derecho y Reforma Agraria*, no. 23 (1992), pp. 141 – 160. Bibl.

Sources

El IIDARA ante la crisis agraria. *Derecho y Reforma Agraria*, no. 24 (1993), pp. 195 – 196.

Soto, Oscar David. (Letter from Oscar David Soto, Ex-President of the IAN, to the Agricultural Commission of the Chamber of Deputies). *Derecho y Reforma Agraria*, no. 24 (1993), pp. 197 – 200.

AGRUPACIÓN SIERRA MADRE
Criticism of specific works
Lacandonia

Pallares, Eugenia. Lacandonia: el último refugio. *Artes de México*, no. 19 (Spring 93), pp. 114 – 115. Il.

AGUASCALIENTES, MEXICO (STATE)

Geyer, Anne. Chronicles of Success. *Business Mexico*, v. 3, no. 5 (May 93), pp. 32 – 35. Il.

Gutiérrez, José Luis. Aguascalientes: A Model of Development. *Business Mexico*, v. 3, no. 5 (May 93), pp. 26 – 28. Tables.

Russell, Joel. Governing for Growth. *Business Mexico*, v. 3, no. 5 (May 93), pp. 29 – 30. Il.

AGUDO FREITES, RAÚL
Criticism and interpretation

Lizardo, Pedro Francisco. Raúl Agudo Freites: periodismo y novela como afirmación y destino. *Revista Nacional de Cultura (Venezuela)*, v. 54, no. 287 (Oct – Dec 92), pp. 162 – 176. Il.

AGUIAR, MANOEL PINTO DE
Obituaries

Tavares, Luís Henrique Dias. In memoriam: Pinto de Aguiar, Alagoinhas (7.3.1910 – Rio de Janeiro, 24.11.1991). *Revista do Instituto Histórico e Geográfico Brasileiro*, no. 373 (Oct – Dec 91), pp. 1204 – 1205.

AGUILA, MIGUEL DEL

Holston, Mark. The Composer's Muse as Master. *Américas*, v. 45, no. 3 (May – June 93), pp. 56 – 57. Il.

AGUILAR, LUIS MIGUEL
Correspondence, reminiscences, etc.

Aguilar, Luis Miguel. *Suerte con las mujeres* reviewed by José Ricardo Chaves. *Vuelta*, v. 17, no. 200 (July 93), pp. 59 – 60.

Criticism of specific works
Suerte con las mujeres

Mastretta, Angeles and Rafael Pérez Gay. Días de parque, futbol y confesiones. *Nexos*, v. 16, no. 181 (Jan 93), pp. 17 – 20.

AGUILAR CAMÍN, HÉCTOR
Criticism of specific works
Guerra de galio

Trujillo Muñoz, Gabriel. Dos guerras paralelas, dos novelas complementarias. *La Palabra y el Hombre*, no. 84 (Oct – Dec 92), pp. 296 – 298. Il.

Morir en el golfo

De Beer, Gabriella. Narrativa y periodismo en *Morir en el golfo* de Héctor Aguilar Camín. *Revista Interamericana de Bibliografía*, v. 42, no. 2 (1992), pp. 215 – 221. Bibl.

AGUILAR Y BASTIDA, CRISTÓBAL DE
Criticism and interpretation

Martini, Mónica Patricia and Daisy Rípodas Ardanaz. Aportes sobre el voseo en Córdoba a horcajadas de los siglos XVIII y XIX: sus modalidades en la obra de Cristóbal de Aguilar. *Investigaciones y Ensayos*, no. 41 (Jan – Dec 91), pp. 139 – 151. Bibl.

AGUIRRE, LOPE DE

Rodríguez, Aleida Anselma. *Arqueología de Omagua y Dorado* reviewed by Ligia Rodríguez. *Colonial Latin American Review*, v. 2, no. 1 – 2 (1993), pp. 277 – 279.

— *Arqueología de Omagua y Dorado* reviewed by Amelia Mondragón. *Revista de Crítica Literaria Latinoamericana*, v. 19, no. 37 (Jan – June 93), pp. 383 – 386.

Fiction

Triviños, Gilberto. *Ramón J. Sender: mito y contramito de Lope de Aguirre* reviewed by Berta López Morales. *Atenea (Chile)*, no. 465 – 466 (1992), pp. 379 – 382.

AGUIRRE BELTRÁN, GONZALO

Medina Cárdenas, Eduardo. El modelo "región de refugio" de Aguirre Beltrán: teoría, aplicaciones y perspectivas. *Siglo XIX: Cuadernos*, v. 2, no. 4 (Oct 92), pp. 61 – 82. Bibl.

AGUIRRE LAVAYÉN, JOAQUÍN
Criticism of specific works
Guano maldito

Muñoz Cadima, Willy Oscar. Joaquín Aguirre Lavayén: la escatología política en *Guano maldito*. *Latin American Theatre Review*, v. 26, no. 2 (Spring 93), pp. 131 – 142. Bibl.

AIDS (DISEASE)

Agüero, Abel Luis. Desde Colón y la sífilis al hombre contemporáneo y el SIDA. *Todo Es Historia*, v. 26, no. 306 (Jan 93), pp. 74 – 85. Il.

Barbosa, Regina Helena Simões. AIDS, gênero e reprodução. *Estudos Feministas*, v. 1, no. 2 (1993), pp. 418 – 423. Bibl.

Chacón Echeverría, Laura. La mujer prostituta: cuerpo de suciedad, fermento de muerte; reflexiones en torno a algunos rituales de purificación. *Revista de Ciencias Sociales (Costa Rica)*, no. 58 (Dec 92), pp. 23 – 34. Bibl, il.

Dinechin, Olivier de. SIDA: educar, acompañar . . . . *Mensaje*, v. 42, no. 422 (Sept 93), pp. 427 – 431.

Fellay, Jean-Blaise. SIDA, preservativos y continencia. *Mensaje*, v. 42, no. 419 (June 93), pp. 211 – 212.

Flores, Mercedes and Roxana Hidalgo Xirinachs. El autoritarismo en la vida cotidiana: SIDA, homofobia y moral sexual. *Revista de Ciencias Sociales (Costa Rica)*, no. 58 (Dec 92), pp. 35 – 44. Bibl.

Frajman, Mauricio. Aspectos sociales de SIDA. *Revista de Ciencias Sociales (Costa Rica)*, no. 58 (Dec 92), pp. 7 – 10. Bibl.

Grmek, Mirko Drazen. *Historia del SIDA* reviewed by Mario Bronfman and Héctor Gómez Dantés. *Plural (Mexico),* v. 22, no. 265 (Oct 93), pp. 76 – 77.

Mujer y SIDA reviewed by Beatriz Jiménez Carrillo. *El Cotidiano,* v. 9, no. 53 (Mar – Apr 93), p. 119.

Mujer y SIDA reviewed by Nelson Minello. *Estudios Sociológicos,* v. 10, no. 30 (Sept – Dec 92), pp. 825 – 830.

Caribbean area

Hamm, Lyta. Archipelago Lessons: AIDS in the Islands; A Comparative Study of Cuba, Haiti, and Hawaii. *Interciencia,* v. 18, no. 4 (July – Aug 93), pp. 184 – 189. Bibl, tables.

Costa Rica

Céspedes Castro, Cristina and Sonia León Montoya. Terapia de grupo no directiva con pacientes seropositivos y con SIDA. *Revista de Ciencias Sociales (Costa Rica),* no. 58 (Dec 92), pp. 45 – 54. Bibl, charts.

López Subirós, Marta Eugenia. Costa Rica: la opinión pública y el SIDA, 1989 – 1991. *Revista de Ciencias Sociales (Costa Rica),* no. 58 (Dec 92), pp. 55 – 64. Bibl, tables.

Ramírez Quirós, Ileana. Mujer y SIDA: la exclusión de la mujer de las campañas comunicacionales. *Revista de Ciencias Sociales (Costa Rica),* no. 58 (Dec 92), pp. 11 – 22. Bibl.

Latin America

Asís, Enrique and James N. Green. Gays and Lesbians: The Closet Door Swings Open. *Report on the Americas,* v. 26, no. 4 (Feb 93), pp. 4 – 7. Il.

Mexico

González Block, Miguel A. and Ana Luisa Liguori. El SIDA en los de abajo. *Nexos,* v. 16, no. 185 (May 93), pp. 15 – 20.

Peru

SIDA: vida compartida. *Debate (Peru),* v. 16, no. 74 (Sept – Oct 93), pp. 46 – 48. Il, tables.

Puerto Rico

Cunningham, Ineke et al, eds. *El SIDA en Puerto Rico: acercamientos multidisciplinarios* reviewed by Víctor I. García Toro. *Caribbean Studies,* v. 25, no. 1 – 2 (Jan – July 92), pp. 162 – 163.

AIRPLANE INDUSTRY AND TRADE

Argentina

Schvarzer, Jorge. El proceso de privatizaciones en la Argentina: implicaciones preliminares sobre sus efectos en la gobernabilidad del sistema. *Realidad Económica,* no. 120 (Nov – Dec 93), pp. 79 – 143. Bibl.

Thwaites Rey, Mabel. La política de privatizaciones en la Argentina: consideraciones a partir del caso de Aerolíneas. *Realidad Económica,* no. 116 (May – June 93), pp. 46 – 75. Bibl, tables.

Weiss, Osvaldo and Eduardo Yurevich. *En la universidad del aire* reviewed by Pedro A. González Bofil. *Realidad Económica,* no. 113 (Jan – Feb 93), pp. 142 – 143.

Brazil

Drouvot, Hubert. Libéralisme et politique nationale de développement technologique: l'industrie aéronautique au Brésil. *Cahiers des Amériques Latines,* no. 14 (1992), pp. 95 – 118. Bibl, tables, charts.

Hong Kong

Geyer, Anne. Jet-Set Capitalism. *Business Mexico,* v. 3, no. 9 (Sept 93), pp. 20 – 22. Il.

Mexico

Geyer, Anne. Jet-Set Capitalism. *Business Mexico,* v. 3, no. 9 (Sept 93), pp. 20 – 22. Il.

Ruiz, Gabriela. To Go or Not to Go. *Business Mexico,* v. 3, no. 10 (Oct 93), pp. 20 – 22.

ALABAU, MAGALY

Criticism and interpretation

Martínez, Elena M. Two Poetry Books of Magali Alabau. *Confluencia,* v. 8, no. 1 (Fall 92), pp. 155 – 158.

Interviews

Martínez, Elena M. Conversación con Magali Alabau. *Fem,* v. 17, no. 119 (Jan 93), pp. 22 – 23.

ALADI

See

Latin American Integration Association

ALAS, LEOPOLDO

Criticism and interpretation

Sotelo Vázquez, Adolfo. Leopoldo Alas "Clarín" en Nueva York, 1894 – 1897: las novedades de Hispanoamérica. *Cuadernos Hispanoamericanos,* no. 511 (Jan 93), pp. 115 – 123. Bibl, il.

ALBA DE LISTE, LUIS HENRÍQUEZ DE GUZMÁN, CONDE DE

See

Enríquez de Guzmán, Luis, conde de Alba de Liste

ALBERDI, JUAN BAUTISTA

Biography

Stefanich Irala, Juan. Alberdi, Latinoamérica y el Paraguay. *Estudios Paraguayos,* v. 17, no. 1 – 2 (1989 – 1993), pp. 107 – 119.

Criticism and interpretation

Rodríguez Pérsico, Adriana C. *Un huracán llamado progreso: utopía y autobiografía en Sarmiento y Alberdi* reviewed by Carlos E. Paldao. *La Educación (USA),* v. 37, no. 115 (1993), pp. 435 – 437.

—— Sarmiento y Alberdi: una práctica legitimante. *La Educación (USA),* v. 36, no. 111 – 113 (1992), pp. 177 – 192. Bibl.

ALCOHOL

See also

Beer
Wine and wine making

Costa Rica

Badilla, Beatriz B. et al. Consumo de sustancias sicotrópicas en los estudiantes de la Facultad de Farmacia de la Universidad de Costa Rica. *Revista de Ciencias Sociales (Costa Rica),* no. 60 (June 93), pp. 63 – 72. Bibl, tables, charts.

Mexican – American Border Region

Croston, Kendel. Women's Activities during the Prohibition Era along the U.S. – Mexico Border. *Journal of Borderlands Studies,* v. 8, no. 1 (Spring 93), pp. 99 – 113. Bibl.

Mexico

Research

Menéndez, Eduardo L. Investigación antropológica, biografía y controles artesanales. *Nueva Antropología,* v. 13, no. 43 (Nov 92), pp. 23 – 37. Bibl.

United States

Dassori, Albana M. et al. Ethnic and Gender Differences in the Diagnostic Profiles of Substance Abusers. *Hispanic Journal of Behavioral Sciences,* v. 15, no. 3 (Aug 93), pp. 382 – 390. Bibl.

Marín, Gerardo et al. Alcohol Expectancies among Hispanic and Non-Hispanic Whites: Role of Drinking Status and Acculturation. *Hispanic Journal of Behavioral Sciences,* v. 15, no. 3 (Aug 93), pp. 373 – 381. Bibl, tables.

Morrissey, Laverne and Amado M. Padilla. Place of Last Drink by Repeat DUI Offenders: A Retrospective Study of Gender and Ethnic Group Differences. *Hispanic Journal of Behavioral Sciences,* v. 15, no. 3 (Aug 93), pp. 357 – 372. Bibl, tables.

ALCOHOLISM

See

Alcohol

ALCOLEA GARCÍA, GABRIEL

Recio Ferreras, Eloy. Diario inédito escrito por un soldado español en la guerra de Cuba, 1896 – 1899. *Revista de Historia de América,* no. 112 (July – Dec 91), pp. 21 – 42. Facs.

ALDANA, LORENZO DE

Torres, Angel. Aldana, un capitán de la conquista. *Signo,* no. 38, Nueva época (Jan – Apr 93), pp. 63 – 72.

ALEGRÍA, CIRO

Biography

Delgado Aparicio, Vielka R. and Jézer González Picado. Introducción al estudio de *Huasipungo* y de *Los perros hambrientos. Revista Cultural Lotería,* v. 51, no. 392 (Nov – Dec 93), pp. 41 – 54. Bibl.

Criticism of specific works
Los perros hambrientos

Delgado Aparicio, Vielka R. and Jézer González Picado. Introducción al estudio de *Huasipungo* y de *Los perros hambrientos. Revista Cultural Lotería,* v. 51, no. 392 (Nov – Dec 93), pp. 41 – 54. Bibl.

ALEGRÍA, CLARIBEL

Criticism of specific works
Luisa en el país de la realidad

McGowan, Marcia P. Mapping a New Territory: *Luisa in Realityland. Letras Femeninas,* v. 19, no. 1 – 2 (Spring – Fall 93), pp. 84 – 99. Bibl.

ALEMÁN, MIGUEL

Medin, Tzvi. *El sexenio alemanista: ideología y praxis política de Miguel Alemán* reviewed by Errol D. Jones. *Hispanic American Historical Review,* v. 73, no. 1 (Feb 93), pp. 182 – 183.

ALFARO, GLORIA G. DE

See
Guardia de Alfaro, Gloria

ALFARO SIQUEIROS, DAVID

See
Siqueiros, David Alfaro

ALFÍNGER, AMBROSIO

Piqueras Céspedes, Ricardo. Alfínger y Portolá: dos modelos de frontera. *Boletín Americanista,* v. 33, no. 42 – 43 (1992 – 1993), pp. 107 – 121. Bibl.

ALIANZA POPULAR REVOLUCIONARIA AMERICANA

Graham, Carol. *Peru's APRA: Parties, Politics, and the Elusive Quest for Democracy* reviewed by Fredrick B. Pike. *Hispanic American Historical Review,* v. 73, no. 3 (Aug 93), pp. 518 – 519.

— *Peru's APRA: Parties, Politics, and the Elusive Quest for Democracy* reviewed by Giorgio Alberti. *Journal of Latin American Studies,* v. 25, no. 2 (May 93), pp. 414 – 415.

— *Peru's APRA: Parties, Politics, and the Elusive Quest for Democracy* reviewed by Henry Dietz. *Revista Interamericana de Bibliografía,* v. 42, no. 3 (1992), pp. 504 – 505.

Melgar Bao, Ricardo. Militancia aprista en el Caribe: la sección cubana. *Cuadernos Americanos,* no. 37, Nueva época (Jan – Feb 93), pp. 208 – 226. Bibl.

Taracena Arriola, Arturo. El APRA, Haya de la Torre y la crisis del liberalismo guatemalteco en 1928 – 1929. *Cuadernos Americanos,* no. 37, Nueva época (Jan – Feb 93), pp. 183 – 197. Bibl.

— El APRA, Haya de La Torre y la crisis del liberalismo guatemalteco en 1928 – 1929. *Revista de Historia (Costa Rica),* no. 25 (Jan – June 92), pp. 9 – 25. Bibl.

Tísoc Lindley, Hilda. De los orígenes del APRA en Cuba: el testimonio de Enrique de la Osa. *Cuadernos Americanos,* no. 37, Nueva época (Jan – Feb 93), pp. 198 – 207. Bibl.

ALIENATION

Beltrán-Vocal, María Antonia. Soledad, aislamiento y búsqueda de identidad en Nash Candelaria y Juan Goytisolo. *The Americas Review,* v. 21, no. 1 (Spring 93), pp. 103 – 111.

Varela, José R. El tema de la alienación en *La rosa separada* de Pablo Neruda. *Revista Canadiense de Estudios Hispánicos,* v. 17, no. 1 (Fall 92), pp. 177 – 206. Bibl.

ALLENDE, ISABEL

Criticism and interpretation

Aguirre Rehbein, Edna and Sonia Riquelme, eds. *Critical Approaches to Isabel Allende's Novels* reviewed by Edward W. Hook. *World Literature Today,* v. 67, no. 1 (Winter 93), pp. 163 – 164.

Dölz-Blackburn, Inés and Violeta Sulsona. Isabel Allende a través de sus entrevistas. *Revista Interamericana de Bibliografía,* v. 42, no. 3 (1992), pp. 421 – 430. Bibl.

Criticism of specific works
Eva Luna

Arguedas Chaverri, María Eugenia. *Eva Luna:* algunas de sus posibilidades significativas. *Káñina,* v. 16, no. 2 (July – Dec 92), pp. 105 – 108. Bibl.

Aronson, Stacey L. Parker and Cristina Enríquez de Salamanca. La textura del exilio: *Querido Diego, te abraza Quiela; Eva Luna; Crónica de una muerte anunciada. Chasqui,* v. 22, no. 2 (Nov 93), pp. 3 – 14. Bibl.

Cabrera, Vicente. Refracciones del cuerpo y la palabra de *Eva Luna. Revista Interamericana de Bibliografía,* v. 42, no. 4 (1992), pp. 591 – 615. Bibl.

Taggart, Kenneth M. *Eva Luna:* la culminación del neofeminismo de Isabel Allende. *Fem,* v. 17, no. 126 (Aug 93), pp. 43 – 45. Bibl.

ALLENDE, SALVADOR

Rodríguez Elizondo, José. Salvador Allende: el tabú y el mito. *Debate (Peru),* v. 16, no. 74 (Sept – Oct 93), pp. 53 – 56. Il.

— Salvador Allende: el tabú y el mito. *Nueva Sociedad,* no. 128 (Nov – Dec 93), pp. 24 – 28.

ALMARAZ, CARLOS DAVID

Nieto, Margarita. Carlos Almaraz: Genesis of a Chicano Painter. *Latin American Art,* v. 5, no. 1 (Spring 93), pp. 37 – 39. Bibl, il.

ALTAMIRANO, IGNACIO MANUEL

Biography

Girón, Nicole. Altamirano, diplomático. *Mexican Studies,* v. 9, no. 2 (Summer 93), pp. 161 – 185.

Correspondence, reminiscences, etc.

Altamirano, Ignacio Manuel. *Diarios: obras completas, XX* reviewed by Julián Andrade Jardí (Review entitled "Radiografía cotidiana"). *Nexos,* v. 16, no. 181 (Jan 93), p. 76. Il.

Bibliography

Domínguez Michael, Christopher. Altamirano íntimo y sentimental (Review article). *Vuelta,* v. 17, no. 200 (July 93), pp. 60 – 61.

ALTAR PIECES

See
Christian art and symbolism

ALTHUSSER, LOUIS

Correspondence, reminiscences, etc.

Althusser, Louis. Louis Althusser: ante la muerte de Ernesto Che Guevara. *Casa de las Américas,* no. 190 (Jan – Mar 93), pp. 59 – 64.

ALUMINUM INDUSTRY AND TRADE

See also
Bauxite

Mexico

Fuentes Aguilar, Luis and Consuelo Soto Mora. La industria del aluminio en el Tratado de Libre Comercio. *Problemas del Desarrollo,* v. 24, no. 93 (Apr – June 93), pp. 75 – 93. Bibl, tables, maps.

ALVAREZ, MARÍA AUXILIADORA

Criticism and interpretation

Chacón, Alfredo. María Auxiliadora Alvarez: Cuerpo y Ca(z)a de palabras. *Inti,* no. 37 – 38 (Spring – Fall 93), pp. 207 – 214.

Ramírez Quintero, Gonzalo. La poesía venezolana actual: tres ejemplos. *Inti,* no. 37 – 38 (Spring – Fall 93), pp. 187 – 195.

ALVAREZ, MARTA

Arteaga Llona, José. Marta Alvarez: "Estar cerca de Dios, estar cerca de los hombres." *Mensaje,* v. 42, no. 421 (Aug 93), pp. 359 – 360. Il.

ALVAREZ BRAVO, LOLA

Obituaries

González Rodríguez, Sergio. Lola Alvarez Bravo: la luz en el espejo. *Nexos,* v. 16, no. 190 (Oct 93), pp. 16 – 20.

ALVAREZ MURENA, HÉCTOR

See

Murena, Héctor Alvarez

ALVEAR, ENRIQUE

Salinas Campos, Maximiliano A. Don Enrique Alvear: la solidaridad como unión mística entre Jesús y los pobres. *Mensaje,* v. 42, no. 421 (Aug 93), pp. 350 – 352. Il.

ALVES, ANTÔNIO DE CASTRO

Criticism of specific works

O navio negreiro

Kothe, Flávio R. Heine, Nerval, Castro Alves: "o negreiro." *Iberoamericana,* v. 17, no. 49 (1993), pp. 42 – 63.

AMACURO, VENEZUELA

Burguera, Magaly. Macuro: vigía de boca de dragos. *Revista de Historia de América,* no. 113 (Jan – June 92), pp. 65 – 102. Bibl, il, charts.

AMADO, JORGE

Correspondence, reminiscences, etc.

Amado, Jorge. Sailing the Shore: Notes for Memoirs I'll Never Write (Translated by Alfred MacAdam). *Review,* no. 47 (Fall 93), pp. 32 – 38.

Criticism and interpretation

Chamberlain, Bobby J. *Jorge Amado* reviewed by John Gledson. *Hispanic Review,* v. 61, no. 2 (Spring 93), pp. 308 – 310.

Societies, etc.

Ribeiro, Simone. A Casa de Jorge Amado. *Vozes,* v. 87, no. 3 (May – June 93), pp. 41 – 47. Il.

AMARAL, TARSILA DO

Amaral, Aracy A. Tarsila: modernidade entre a racionalidade e o onírico. *Vozes,* v. 87, no. 4 (July – Aug 93), pp. 53 – 59. Il.

AMAZON VALLEY

See also

Agricultural laborers – Amazon Valley
Agriculture, Cooperative – Amazon Valley
Botany – Amazon Valley
Ecology – Amazon Valley
Ecology and development – Amazon Valley
Entomology – Amazon Valley
Environmental policy – Amazon Valley
Forestry – Amazon Valley
Forests – Amazon Valley
Frontier and pioneer life – Amazon Valley
Geographical distribution of plants and animals – Amazon Valley
Geomorphology – Amazon Valley
Geopolitics – Amazon Valley
Land use – Amazon Valley
Motion pictures – Amazon Valley
Natural resources – Amazon Valley
Non-governmental organizations – Amazon Valley
Regional planning – Amazon Valley
Soils – Amazon Valley

Civilization

Bibliography

Vickers, William T. The Anthropology of Amazonia (Review article). *Latin American Research Review,* v. 28, no. 1 (1993), pp. 111 – 127. Bibl.

Congresses

Declaración de Santa Cruz de la Sierra. *Anuario Indigenista,* v. 30 (Dec 91), pp. 335 – 337.

Description and travel

Ribeiro, Darcy. A Amazônia. *Vozes,* v. 86, no. 4 (July – Aug 92), pp. 42 – 52.

Methodology

Day, Douglas. Humboldt and the Casiquiare: Modes of Travel Writing. *Review,* no. 47 (Fall 93), pp. 4 – 8. Il.

Discovery and exploration

Amate Blanco, Juan José. El realismo mágico en la expedición amazónica de Orellana. *Cuadernos Hispanoamericanos,* no. 510 (Dec 92), pp. 61 – 72. Bibl.

Rodríguez, Aleida Anselma. *Arqueología de Omagua y Dorado* reviewed by Ligia Rodríguez. *Colonial Latin American Review,* v. 2, no. 1 – 2 (1993), pp. 277 – 279.

— *Arqueología de Omagua y Dorado* reviewed by Amelia Mondragón. *Revista de Crítica Literaria Latinoamericana,* v. 19, no. 37 (Jan – June 93), pp. 383 – 386.

Economic conditions

Barclay, Federica et al. *Amazonía, 1940 – 1990* reviewed by Nicole Bernex. *Amazonía Peruana,* v. 11, no. 21 (Sept 92), pp. 240 – 242.

Brack Egg, Antonio. La Amazonía: problemas y posibilidades. *Amazonía Peruana,* v. 11, no. 21 (Sept 92), pp. 9 – 22. Il.

Schmink, Marianne and Charles Howard Wood. *Contested Frontiers in Amazonia* reviewed by Philip A. Dennis. *Journal of Developing Areas,* v. 28, no. 1 (Oct 93), pp. 111 – 113.

Economic policy

Cleary, David. After the Frontier: Problems with Political Economy in the Modern Brazilian Amazon. *Journal of Latin American Studies,* v. 25, no. 2 (May 93), pp. 331 – 349. Bibl.

Dourojeanni, Marc J. *Amazonia: ¿Qué hacer?* reviewed by Richard Bustamante M. *Amazonía Peruana,* v. 11, no. 21 (Sept 92), pp. 238 – 239.

Social policy

Dourojeanni, Marc J. *Amazonia: ¿Qué hacer?* reviewed by Richard Bustamante M. *Amazonía Peruana,* v. 11, no. 21 (Sept 92), pp. 238 – 239.

AMAZONAS, BRAZIL (STATE)

Chaves, Omar Emir. A Amazônia brasileira. *Revista do Instituto Histórico e Geográfico Brasileiro,* no. 370 (Jan – Mar 91), pp. 196 – 216.

Reis, Arthur Cézar Ferreira. O conde dos Arcos na Amazôna. *Revista do Instituto Histórico e Geográfico Brasileiro,* no. 370 (Jan – Mar 91), pp. 134 – 139. Bibl.

Silva, Jorge Xavier da. Um banco de dados ambientais para a Amazônia. *Revista Brasileira de Geografia,* v. 53, no. 3 (July – Sept 91), pp. 91 – 124. Bibl, il, tables, maps.

AMERICA

See also

Agriculture – America
Automobile industry and trade – America
Blacks – America
Catholic Church – America
Christian art and symbolism – America
Cookery – America
Drug trade – America
Education, Higher – America
Environmental policy – America
Europeans – America
Evangelicalism – America
Folk medicine – America
Food habits – America
Franciscans – America
Geography, Historical – America
Geopolitics – America
Indians, Treatment of – America
Journalism – America
Labor laws and legislation – America
Literature and society – America
Missions – America
Musicians – America
Natural history – America

Population – America
Public administration – America
Refuse and refuse disposal – America
Religion – America
Roads – America
Sexual behavior – America
Slavery – America
Spanish language – America
Taxation – America
Theater – America
Universities and colleges – America
Women authors – America
Women's rights – America

Antiquities

Fiedel, Stuart J. *Prehistory of the Americas*, 2d edition, reviewed by Gary M. Feinman. *Hispanic American Historical Review*, v. 73, no. 4 (Nov 93), pp. 679 – 680.

— *Prehistory of the Americas*, 2d edition, reviewed by Aaron Segal. *Interciencia*, v. 18, no. 3 (May – June 93), pp. 163 – 164.

Bibliography

América en la bibliografía española: reseñas informativas. *Anuario de Estudios Americanos*, v. 49, Suppl. 1, 2 (1992), All issues.

Antichi libri d'America: censimento romano, 1493 – 1701 reviewed by Fernando I. Ortiz Crespo (Review entitled "Antiguos libros de America en Roma"). *Interciencia*, v. 18, no. 3 (May – June 93), pp. 164 – 165.

Boundaries

Herzog, Lawrence Arthur, ed. *Changing Boundaries in the Americas: New Perspectives on the U.S. – Mexican, Central American, and South American Borders* reviewed by Elizabeth Méndez Mungaray. *Frontera Norte*, v. 4, no. 8 (July – Dec 92), pp. 173 – 176.

— *Changing Boundaries in the Americas: New Perspectives on the U.S. – Mexican, Central American, and South American Borders* reviewed by Michael G. Ellis. *Journal of Borderlands Studies*, v. 8, no. 1 (Spring 93), pp. 125 – 127. Bibl.

Centennial celebrations, etc.

Arciniegas, Germán. Los 500 años de América. *Boletín de Historia y Antigüedades*, v. 79, no. 779 (Oct – Dec 92), pp. 865 – 870.

Arrieta, María Stella. La conquista española cuestionada. *Hoy Es Historia*, v. 10, no. 57 (Apr – May 93), pp. 22 – 32. Bibl.

Bernecker, Walther L. El aniversario del "descubrimiento" de América en el conflicto de opiniones (Translated by Verónica Jaffé). *Ibero-Amerikanisches Archiv*, v. 18, no. 3 – 4 (1992), pp. 501 – 520. Bibl.

Borrat, Héctor. Autocelebración de España: ¿Potenciación de Latinoamérica? *Cuadernos del CLAEH*, v. 17, no. 63 – 64 (Oct 92), pp. 117 – 123.

Fernández-Shaw, Félix. Cinco quintos centenarios: entre pasado y futuro. *Cuadernos del CLAEH*, v. 17, no. 63 – 64 (Oct 92), pp. 21 – 33. Bibl.

García Godoy, Cristián. A 500 años del descubrimiento de un nuevo mundo: Colón en Estados Unidos. *Revista de Historia de América*, no. 112 (July – Dec 91), pp. 63 – 84. Bibl, il.

Manzino, Leonardo. La música uruguaya en los festejos de 1892 con motivo del IV centenario del encuentro de dos mundos. *Latin American Music Review*, v. 14, no. 1 (Spring – Summer 93), pp. 102 – 130. Bibl, facs.

Ortega, José. Conmemoración del genocidio de las Indias. *La Palabra y el Hombre*, no. 81 (Jan – Mar 92), pp. 11 – 19. Bibl.

Roitman Rosenmann, Marcos. España y América Latina en el contexto del quinto centenario. *Boletín de Antropología Americana*, no. 23 (July 91), pp. 83 – 98. Bibl, il.

Santos Pires, Manuel. El IVº centenario en Mercedes. *Hoy Es Historia*, v. 9, no. 54 (Nov – Dec 92), pp. 60 – 68. Il.

Taviani, Paolo Emilio. Programas conmemorativos del quinto centenario en Italia. *Atenea (Chile)*, no. 467 (1993), pp. 223 – 236. Bibl.

Civilization

Aínsa Amigues, Fernando. *Necesidad de la utopía* reviewed by Edgar Montiel (Review entitled "Fernando Aínsa: expedición a utopía"). *Plural (Mexico)*, v. 22, no. 261 (June 93), pp. 91 – 92.

Angulo Barturén, Carmelo. La conmemoración de los 500 años: una visión constructiva. *Signo*, no. 36 – 37, Nueva época (May – Dec 92), pp. 279 – 298.

Ansaldi, Waldo. América, la cuestión de la alteridad y la hipótesis de la culpabilidad del caballo. *Cuadernos del CLAEH*, v. 17, no. 63 – 64 (Oct 92), pp. 53 – 66. Bibl.

Campos Harriet, Fernando. 1492 – 1992: la más gigantesca fusión vital. *Boletín de la Academia Chilena de la Historia*, v. 58 – 59, no. 102 (1991 – 1992), pp. 239 – 268. Bibl, il.

Cerutti Guldberg, Horacio V. Hacia la utopía de nuestra América. *Ibero-Amerikanisches Archiv*, v. 18, no. 3 – 4 (1992), pp. 455 – 465. Bibl.

Cueva, Agustín. Falacias y coartadas del quinto centenario. *Boletín de Antropología Americana*, no. 23 (July 91), pp. 5 – 12. Bibl, il.

Díaz Gómez, Floriberto. Las celebraciones de los 500 años. *Caravelle*, no. 59 (1992), pp. 33 – 37.

Edwards, Jorge. El encuentro y el desencuentro. *Atenea (Chile)*, no. 465 – 466 (1992), pp. 35 – 37.

Fernández Retamar, Roberto. *Nuestra América*: cien años. *Nueva Revista de Filología Hispánica*, v. 40, no. 2 (July – Dec 92), pp. 791 – 806.

Gargantini, Ricardo. *Paralelas divergentes* reviewed by Arnaldo Gómez A. *Derecho y Reforma Agraria*, no. 24 (1993), pp. 207 – 208.

Lewis, Rupert. The Contemporary Significance of the African Diaspora in the Americas. *Caribbean Quarterly*, v. 38, no. 2 – 3 (June – Sept 92), pp. 73 – 80. Bibl.

Morón Montero, Guillermo. Palabras del director de la Academia Nacional de la Historia, dr. Guillermo Morón. *Boletín de la Academia Nacional de la Historia (Venezuela)*, v. 75, no. 300 (Oct – Dec 92), pp. 11 – 16.

Ochoa Antich, Fernando. Sesión solemne de las academias nacionales con motivo de la conmemoración del V centenario del descubrimiento de América: palabras del ministro de relaciones exteriores, general Fernando Ochoa Antich. *Boletín de la Academia Nacional de la Historia (Venezuela)*, v. 75, no. 300 (Oct – Dec 92), pp. 5 – 9.

Pérez Antón, Romeo and Carlos Pareja. América y Europa: asimetrías e inmadurez. *Cuadernos del CLAEH*, v. 17, no. 63 – 64 (Oct 92), pp. 81 – 98.

Salcedo-Bastardo, José Luis. En los comienzos de América. *Boletín de la Academia Nacional de la Historia (Venezuela)*, v. 75, no. 300 (Oct – Dec 92), pp. 120 – 126.

Sobrino, Jon. Relectura cristiana del quinto centenario. *ECA; Estudios Centroamericanos*, v. 47, no. 528 (Oct 92), pp. 855 – 866. Il.

Velasco Toro, José. América: voz de múltiples raíces. *La Palabra y el Hombre*, no. 84 (Oct – Dec 92), pp. 256 – 258.

Vidales, Raúl. Fin de la historia: "¿Fin de la utopía?"; frente a los 500 años. *Cristianismo y Sociedad*, v. 30, no. 113 (1992), pp. 53 – 84. Bibl.

Zea, Leopoldo. Emigración igual a conquista y ocupación. *Cuadernos Americanos*, no. 37, Nueva época (Jan – Feb 93), pp. 13 – 22.

— Lo mexicano en la universalidad. *Cuadernos Americanos*, no. 41, Nueva época (Sept – Oct 93), pp. 193 – 203.

— Vasconcelos y la utopía de la raza cósmica. *Cuadernos Americanos*, no. 37, Nueva época (Jan – Feb 93), pp. 23 – 36. Bibl.

Foreign influences

Bellegarde-Smith, Patrick. "Pawol la pale": Reflections of an Initiate (Introduction to the special issue entitled "Traditional Spirituality in the African Diaspora"). *Journal of Caribbean Studies*, v. 9, no. 1 – 2 (Winter 92 – Spring 93), pp. 3 – 9. Bibl.

Costa, Octavio R. *El impacto creador de España sobre el Nuevo Mundo, 1492 – 1592* reviewed by William Mejías López. *Hispania (USA)*, v. 76, no. 2 (May 93), pp. 282 – 284.

Discovery and exploration

Anghiera, Pietro Martire d'. *De Orbe Novo Decades* reviewed by Keith Ellis. *Revista Canadiense de Estudios Hispánicos,* v. 17, no. 1 (Fall 92), pp. 221 – 223.

Angulo Barturén, Carmelo. La conmemoración de los 500 años: una visión constructiva. *Signo,* no. 36 – 37, Nueva época (May – Dec 92), pp. 279 – 298.

Arrieta, María Stella. La conquista española cuestionada. *Hoy Es Historia,* v. 10, no. 57 (Apr – May 93), pp. 22 – 32. Bibl.

Bennassar, Bartolomé and Lucile Bennassar. *1492: un monde nouveau?* reviewed by Marie Cécile Bénassy-Berling (Review entitled "Notas sobre el quinto centenario en Francia"). *Colonial Latin American Review,* v. 2, no. 1 – 2 (1993), pp. 269 – 272.

Bensen, Robert. Columbus at the Abyss: The Genesis of New World Literature. *Jamaica Journal,* v. 24, no. 3 (Feb 93), pp. 48 – 54. Bibl, il.

Campos Harriet, Fernando. 1492 – 1992: la más gigantesca fusión vital. *Boletín de la Academia Chilena de la Historia,* v. 58 – 59, no. 102 (1991 – 1992), pp. 239 – 268. Bibl, il.

Castro, Sílvio. Europa America Americhe: la geometria asimmetrica. *Quaderni Ibero-Americani,* no. 72 (Dec 92), pp. 732 – 742. Bibl.

Cristobal Colón y el descubrimiento en los cronistas: el arribo al Nuevo Mundo (Excerpts from the writings of several chroniclers). *Boletín de la Academia Nacional de la Historia (Venezuela),* v. 75, no. 300 (Oct – Dec 92), pp. 127 – 152.

Cuesta Domingo, Mariano. Descubrimientos geográficos durante el siglo XVIII: acción franciscana en la ampliación de fronteras. *Archivo Ibero-Americano,* v. 52, no. 205 – 208 (Jan – Dec 92), pp. 293 – 342. Bibl, il, maps.

Deckers, Daniel. La justicia de la conquista de América: consideraciones en torno a la cronología y a los protagonistas de una controversia del siglo XVI muy actual. *Ibero-Amerikanisches Archiv,* v. 18, no. 3 – 4 (1992), pp. 331 – 366. Bibl.

La "découverte" de l'Amérique?: les regards sur l'autre à travers les manuels scolaires du monde reivewed by Pierre Ragon. *Cahiers des Amériques Latines,* no. 14 (1992), pp. 159 – 160.

Díaz I., Gloria. La celebración del quinto centenario del descubrimiento de América. *Revista Cultural Lotería,* v. 51, no. 391 (Sept – Oct 92), pp. 7 – 12.

Fernández Retamar, Roberto. En la Casa de América, hacia la casa del futuro. *Casa de las Américas,* no. 190 (Jan – Mar 93), pp. 75 – 81.

Gannon, Michael. Primeros encuentros en el Nuevo Mundo. *Atenea (Chile),* no. 465 – 466 (1992), pp. 45 – 52.

Gil Fernández, Juan. *Mitos y utopías del descubrimiento* reviewed by Fernando Aínsa. *Colonial Latin American Review,* v. 2, no. 1 – 2 (1993), pp. 286 – 288.

— *Mitos y utopías del descubrimiento,* vol. III, reviewed by Juha Pekka Helminen. *Ibero Americana (Sweden),* v. 22, no. 2 (Dec 92), pp. 86 – 87.

Gómez, Thomas. *L'invention de l'Amérique: rêve et réalités de la conquête* reviewed by Janny Chenu. *Caravelle,* no. 59 (1992), pp. 304 – 306.

Gómez Tabanera, José Manuel. Reencuentro desde la otra orilla: utopía europea, utopía indiana y utopía del Pacífico. *Boletín de la Academia Nacional de la Historia (Venezuela),* v. 75, no. 297 (Jan – Mar 92), pp. 5 – 20. Bibl.

Greenblatt, Stephen Jay, ed. *New World Encounters* reviewed by Lee A. Daniel. *Hispania (USA),* v. 76, no. 4 (Dec 93), pp. 738 – 739.

Kadir, Djelal. *Columbus and the Ends of the Earth: Europe's Prophetic Rhetoric as Conquering Ideology* reviewed by Margarita Zamora (Review entitled "Searching for Columbus in the Quincentennial: Three Recent Books on the Discovery"). *Colonial Latin American Review,* v. 2, no. 1 – 2 (1993), pp. 261 – 267.

— *Columbus and the Ends of the Earth: Europe's Prophetic Rhetoric as Conquering Ideology* reviewed by John Incledon. *Hispania (USA),* v. 76, no. 2 (May 93), pp. 288 – 289.

— *Columbus and the Ends of the Earth: Europe's Prophetic Rhetoric as Conquering Ideology* reviewed by Martin Torodash. *Hispanic American Historical Review,* v. 73, no. 1 (Feb 93), p. 147.

León de D'Empaire, Arleny. El gran viaje de descubrimiento: las crónicas americanas. *Montalbán,* no. 24 (1992), pp. 85 – 97. Bibl.

León-Portilla, Miguel. Encuentro de dos mundos. *Estudios de Cultura Náhuatl,* v. 22 (1992), pp. 15 – 27.

López Bohórquez, Alí Enrique and Alberto Rodríguez C. Visión americanista de la conquista española: el reverso del descubrimiento. *Boletín de la Academia Nacional de la Historia (Venezuela),* v. 75, no. 300 (Oct – Dec 92), pp. 69 – 77. Bibl.

Luigi Lemus, Juan de. Amerigo Vespucci (Includes reproductions of paintings by Enrique Boccaletti G. from his book entitled *América, el Nuevo Mundo y los navegantes italianos,* co-authored by Juan de Luigi Lemus). *Atenea (Chile),* no. 465 – 466 (1992), pp. 177 – 186 +. Il.

Marino, Ruggiero. Innocenzo VIII, il papa di Cristoforo Colombo. *Quaderni Ibero-Americani,* no. 72 (Dec 92), pp. 595 – 602. Bibl.

Martinell Gifre, Emma. *Aspectos lingüísticos del descubrimiento y de la conquista* reviewed by Ma. Angeles Soler Arechalde. *Estudios de Cultura Náhuatl,* v. 22 (1992), pp. 505 – 508.

Martínez G., Miguel A. Recursos tecno-científicos que se conjugan en el descubrimiento de América. *Boletín de la Academia Nacional de la Historia (Venezuela),* v. 75, no. 300 (Oct – Dec 92), pp. 79 – 88.

Mason, Peter, ed. *Indianen en Nederlanders, 1492 – 1992* reviewed by Menno Oostra. *European Review of Latin American and Caribbean Studies,* no. 54 (June 93), pp. 145 – 147.

Milton, Heloisa Costa. O *Diário* de Cristóvão Colombo: discurso da "maravilha" americana. *Revista de Letras (Brazil),* v. 32 (1992), pp. 169 – 183.

Moreno Casamitjana, Antonio. Descubrimiento y evangelización de América. *Atenea (Chile),* no. 465 – 466 (1992), pp. 53 – 66. Bibl.

Pérez de Tudela y Bueso, Juan. El descubrimiento: historia de secretos y de secretismos rigurosos. *Boletín de Historia y Antigüedades,* v. 80, no. 780 (Jan – Mar 93), pp. 31 – 70. Bibl.

Pérez Tenreiro, Tomás. 12 de octubre de 1492 – 12 de octubre de 1992. *Boletín de la Academia Nacional de la Historia (Venezuela),* v. 75, no. 300 (Oct – Dec 92), pp. 116 – 117.

Pérez Tomás, Eduardo E. Nuevo aporte al esclarecimiento de un punto relativo a la "cuestión vespuciana." *Revista de Historia de América,* no. 113 (Jan – June 92), pp. 103 – 138. Bibl, tables, charts.

Phillips, Carla Rahn and William D. Phillips, Jr. *The Worlds of Christopher Columbus* reviewed by Peter T. Bradley. *Bulletin of Latin American Research,* v. 12, no. 1 (Jan 93), pp. 109 – 110.

Piqueras Céspedes, Ricardo. Alfínger y Portolá: dos modelos de frontera. *Boletín Americanista,* v. 33, no. 42 – 43 (1992 – 1993), pp. 107 – 121. Bibl.

Pronunciamiento de la Universidad Centroamericana "José Simeón Cañas": quinientos años de injusticia y utopía. *ECA; Estudios Centroamericanos,* v. 47, no. 528 (Oct 92), pp. 835 – 840.

Rivera Ramos, José Antonio. El descubrimiento de América. *Revista Cultural Lotería,* v. 51, no. 391 (Sept – Oct 92), pp. 13 – 21. Bibl.

Rodríguez Fernández, Mario et al. Opinan profesores de la Universidad de Concepción. *Atenea (Chile),* no. 465 – 466 (1992), pp. 39 – 44.

Rojas Guardia, Armando. El deslumbramiento del Almirante. *Boletín de la Academia Nacional de la Historia (Venezuela),* v. 75, no. 300 (Oct – Dec 92), pp. 118 – 120.

— El deslumbramiento del Almirante. *Revista Nacional de Cultura (Venezuela),* v. 54, no. 287 (Oct – Dec 92), pp. 234 – 236.

Sale, Kirkpatrick. *The Conquest of Paradise: Christopher Columbus and the Columbian Legacy* reviewed by Stelio Cro. *Revista de Indias*, v. 53, no. 197 (Jan – Apr 93), pp. 119 – 121.

Sievernich, Michael. Visiones teológicas en torno al quinto centenario. *Ibero-Amerikanisches Archiv*, v. 18, no. 3 – 4 (1992), pp. 367 – 385. Bibl.

Sten, María. Cristóbal Colón en Polonia. *Plural (Mexico)*, v. 22, no. 266 (Nov 93), pp. 63 – 67.

Tapajós, Vicente Costa Santos. Cristovão Colombo: o homem e o mito. *Revista do Instituto Histórico e Geográfico Brasileiro*, no. 371 (Apr – June 91), pp. 470 – 488. Bibl.

Taviani, Paolo Emilio. Fecha inolvidable: 12 de octubre de 1492; lugar: isla Guanahaní. *Atenea (Chile)*, no. 465 – 466 (1992), pp. 23 – 34. Il.

Tisnés Jiménez, Roberto María. La "leyenda negra" de los criminales descubridores. *Boletín de Historia y Antigüedades*, v. 79, no. 779 (Oct – Dec 92), pp. 1019 – 1035. Bibl.

Verne, Jules. *Les conquistadores* reviewed by Claude Castro. *Caravelle*, no. 60 (1993), pp. 175 – 176.

Vincent, Bernard. *1492: l'année admirable* reviewed by Bernadette Alvarez-Ferrandiz. *Caravelle*, no. 59 (1992), pp. 302 – 304.

— *1492: l'année admirable* reviewed by Marie Cécile Bénassy-Berling (Review entitled "Notas sobre el quinto centenario en Francia"). *Colonial Latin American Review*, v. 2, no. 1 – 2 (1993), pp. 269 – 272.

Weddle, Robert S. *The French Thorn: Rival Explorers in the Spanish Sea, 1682 – 1762* reviewed by Gwendolyn Hall. *Hispanic American Historical Review*, v. 73, no. 2 (May 93), p. 319.

Bibliography

Bertrand, Michel. Un regard sur les publications françaises à l'occasion du Ve centenaire de la rencontre des deux mondes (Review article). *Caravelle*, no. 59 (1992), pp. 256 – 266.

Huhle, Rainer. El V centenario a través de los libros en Alemania. *Ibero-Amerikanisches Archiv*, v. 18, no. 3 – 4 (1992), pp. 543 – 557. Bibl.

López Bohórquez, Alí Enrique. El descubrimiento de América en el *Boletín de la Academia Nacional de la Historia*. *Boletín de la Academia Nacional de la Historia (Venezuela)*, v. 75, no. 300 (Oct – Dec 92), pp. 166 – 171.

Maura, Juan Francisco. En busca de la verdad: algunas mujeres excepcionales de la conquista. *Hispania (USA)*, v. 76, no. 4 (Dec 93), pp. 904 – 910.

Congresses

Comella, Beatriz, ed. *América, siglos XVIII – XX: III Simposio sobre el V Centenario del Descubrimiento de América celebrado en el Colegio Mayor Zurbarán, Madrid, 1989 – 1990* reviewed by Osvaldo Chiareno. *Quaderni Ibero-Americani*, no. 72 (Dec 92), pp. 751 – 755.

Exhibitions

Domnick, Heinz-Joachim. América, 1492 – 1992: nuevos mundos, nuevas realidades (Translated by Ricardo Barra). *Humboldt*, no. 109 (1993), pp. 76 – 83. Il.

Sources

Columbus, Christopher. *The 'Diario' of Christopher Columbus' First Voyage to America, 1492 – 1493* abstracted by Fray Bartolomé de las Casas; transcribed and translated by Oliver Dunn and James E. Kelley, Jr. Reviewed by Aaron P. Mahr. *Colonial Latin American Historical Review*, v. 1, no. 1 (Fall 92), pp. 122 – 124.

Henige, David P. *In Search of Columbus: The Sources for the First Voyage* reviewed by Rosalind Z. Rock. *Colonial Latin American Historical Review*, v. 1, no. 1 (Fall 92), pp. 117 – 118.

— *In Search of Columbus: The Sources for the First Voyage* reviewed by Margarita Zamora (Review entitled "Searching for Columbus in the Quincentennial: Three Recent Books on the Discovery"). *Colonial Latin American Review*, v. 2, no. 1 – 2 (1993), pp. 261 – 267.

Rumeu de Armas, Antonio. *Libro copiador de Cristóbal Colón: correspondencia inédita con los reyes católicos sobre los viajes a América* reviewed by Margarita Zamora (Review entitled "Searching for Columbus in the Quincentennial: Three Recent Books on the Discovery"). *Colonial Latin American Review*, v. 2, no. 1 – 2 (1993), pp. 261 – 267.

Study and teaching

Mueller, RoseAnna M. Teaching beyond the Quincentennial. *Hispania (USA)*, v. 76, no. 3 (Sept 93), pp. 586 – 592.

Economic integration

Bouzas, Roberto and Nora Lustig, eds. *Liberalización comercial e integración regional: de NAFTA a MERCOSUR* (Review). *Integración Latinoamericana*, v. 18, no. 187 – 188 (Mar – Apr 93), p. 69.

Chudnovsky, Daniel. El futuro de la integración hemisférica: el MERCOSUR y la Iniciativa para las Américas. *Desarrollo Económico (Argentina)*, v. 32, no. 128 (Jan – Mar 93), pp. 483 – 511. Bibl, tables.

Cruz, Justino de la. Integración económica del hemisferio occidental. *Integración Latinoamericana*, v. 18, no. 193 (Sept 93), pp. 53 – 54. Charts.

Hurrell, Andrew. Os blocos regionais nas Américas (Translated by João Roberto Martins Filho). *Revista Brasileira de Ciências Sociais*, v. 8, no. 22 (June 93), pp. 98 – 118. Bibl.

Mace, Gordon et al. Regionalism in the Americas and the Hierarchy of Power. *Journal of Inter-American Studies and World Affairs*, v. 35, no. 2 (Summer 93), pp. 115 – 157. Bibl, tables, maps.

Mateo y Sousa, Eligio de. De la geopolítica a la geoeconomía: una lectura del siglo XX. *Comercio Exterior*, v. 43, no. 10 (Oct 93), pp. 974 – 978.

Bibliography

Frohmann, Alicia. Hacia una integración comercial hemisférica? (Review article). *Pensamiento Iberoamericano*, no. 22 – 23, tomo I (July 92 – June 93), pp. 347 – 356. Tables, charts.

Congresses

Berglund, Susan. Las Migraciones en el Proceso de Integración de las Américas: Seminario Internacional/Migration in the Integration Process in the Americas: International Seminar. *International Migration Review*, v. 27, no. 1 (Spring 93), pp. 182 – 190.

Emigration and immigration

Altman, Ida and James J. Horn. *"To Make America": European Emigration in the Early Modern Period* reviewed by Alan L. Karras. *The Americas*, v. 49, no. 3 (Jan 93), pp. 402 – 404.

— *"To Make America": European Emigration in the Early Modern Period* reviewed by Magnus Mörner. *Hispanic American Historical Review*, v. 73, no. 1 (Feb 93), pp. 130 – 132.

Congresses

Berglund, Susan. Las Migraciones en el Proceso de Integración de las Américas: Seminario Internacional/Migration in the Integration Process in the Americas: International Seminar. *International Migration Review*, v. 27, no. 1 (Spring 93), pp. 182 – 190.

Foreign economic relations

Segal, Aaron. Opciones comerciales del Caribe: las cartas de Europa, América del Norte y América Latina. *Comercio Exterior*, v. 43, no. 11 (Nov 93), pp. 1019 – 1030. Bibl, tables, charts.

Congresses

Cohen, Joshua A. and Joel Russell. A New Dynamic in the Americas. *Business Mexico*, v. 3, no. 12 (Dec 93), pp. 43 – 45. Il.

Foreign opinion

Amodio, Emanuele. El otro americano: construcción y difusión de la iconografía del indio americano en Europa en el primer siglo de la conquista (Translated by Francesco Russo). *Montalbán*, no. 24 (1992), pp. 33 – 84. Bibl, il, maps, facs.

Casalla, Mario Carlos. *América en el pensamiento de Hegel: admiración y rechazo* reviewed by Daniel Toribio. *Todo Es Historia*, v. 27, no. 316 (Nov 93), p. 91. Il.

Cury, Maria Zilda Ferreira. O olhar do Papa e o navegador: Leão XIII descobre a América. *Cuadernos del CLAEH*, v. 17, no. 63 – 64 (Oct 92), pp. 35 – 42. Bibl.

La *"découverte" de l'Amérique?: les regards sur l'autre à travers les manuels scolaires du monde* reivewed by Pierre Ragon. *Cahiers des Amériques Latines*, no. 14 (1992), pp. 159 – 160.

Foreign relations
Cuba

Wrobel, Paulo S. Aspectos da política externa independente: a questão do desarmamento e o caso de Cuba (Translated by Dora Rocha). *Estudos Históricos*, v. 6, no. 12 (July – Dec 93), pp. 191 – 209. Bibl.

Historiography

Morón Montero, Guillermo. Un acercamiento a la *Historia general de América. Boletín de la Academia Nacional de la Historia (Venezuela)*, v. 75, no. 300 (Oct – Dec 92), pp. 155 – 166.

Zea, Leopoldo. *The Role of the Americas in History*, a translation of *América en la historia* edited by Amy A. Oliver, translated by Sonja Karsen. Reviewed by Iván Jaksic. *Hispanic American Historical Review*, v. 73, no. 1 (Feb 93), pp. 132 – 133.

History

Fernández Retamar, Roberto. El Golfo y el Caribe a la mesa del mundo. *La Palabra y el Hombre*, no. 82 (Apr – June 92), pp. 5 – 19.

Methol Ferré, Alberto. El fracaso del V centenario. *Cuadernos del CLAEH*, v. 17, no. 63 – 64 (Oct 92), pp. 11 – 20. Bibl.

Premazzi, Javier. La España de la conquista y la América indígena. *Hoy Es Historia*, v. 9, no. 54 (Nov – Dec 92), pp. 27 – 38.

Torres Marín, Manuel. Los dos imperios: la doble herencia de Carlos V. *Boletín de la Academia Chilena de la Historia*, v. 58 – 59, no. 102 (1991 – 1992), pp. 505 – 527. Bibl, il, facs.

Valcárcel Esparza, Carlos Daniel. Histórica contribución integracionista (Introduction to three works on the history of Bolivia, Canada, and Peru published by the Academia Nacional de la Historia de Venezuela within the series "El libro menor"). *Boletín de la Academia Nacional de la Historia (Venezuela)*, v. 76, no. 302 (Apr – June 93), pp. 154 – 155.

Congresses

Gutiérrez Escudero, Antonio. X Coloquio de Historia Canario – Americana. *Anuario de Estudios Americanos*, v. 49, Suppl. 2 (1992), pp. 217 – 221.

Pelegrí Pedrosa, Luis Vicente. XI Jornadas de Andalucía y América: "Huelva y América." *Anuario de Estudios Americanos*, v. 49, Suppl. 1 (1992), pp. 204 – 209.

Laws, statutes, etc.
Bibliography

Suárez, Santiago Gerardo. *Las reales audiencias indianas: fuentes y bibliografía* reviewed by José María Mariluz Urquijo. *Boletín de la Academia Nacional de la Historia (Venezuela)*, v. 75, no. 297 (Jan – Mar 92), pp. 139 – 141.

Maps

Buisseret, David and Arthur Holzheimer. The Enigma of the Jean Bellère Maps of the New World, 1554: A Historical Note. *Colonial Latin American Historical Review*, v. 2, no. 3 (Summer 93), pp. 363 – 367. Maps.

Name

Funes, Patricia. Del "Mundus Novus" al novomundismo: algunas reflexiones sobre el nombre de América Latina. *Cuadernos del CLAEH*, v. 17, no. 63 – 64 (Oct 92), pp. 67 – 79. Bibl.

AMERICA IN LITERATURE

Ahumada Peña, Haydée. Apropiación del espacio americano en *Epitalamio del Prieto Trinidad. Revista Chilena de Literatura*, no. 42 (Aug 93), pp. 7 – 11.

Arellano Ayuso, Ignacio, ed. *Las Indias (América) en la literatura del siglo de oro* reviewed by Teodoro Hampe Martínez. *Anuario de Estudios Americanos*, v. 50, no. 1 (1993), pp. 308 – 310.

Berrettini, Célia. O teatro de Lope de Vega e o descobrimento da América. *Vozes*, v. 86, no. 4 (July – Aug 92), pp. 66 – 71. Il, facs.

Bridges, Christine M. E. El discurso oficial del Nuevo Mundo. *La Palabra y el Hombre*, no. 81 (Jan – Mar 92), pp. 61 – 69. Bibl.

Brioso Sánchez, Máximo and Héctor Brioso Santos. La picaresca y América en los siglos de oro. *Anuario de Estudios Americanos*, v. 49 (1992), pp. 207 – 232. Bibl.

Cirillo, Teresa. Colombo bifronte. *Quaderni Ibero-Americani*, no. 72 (Dec 92), pp. 571 – 594. Bibl.

Fitz, Earl E. *Rediscovering the New World: Inter-American Literature in a Comparative Context* reviewed by Charles B. Moore. *Hispania (USA)*, v. 76, no. 1 (Mar 93), pp. 84 – 85.

Hadzelek, Aleksandra. Imagen de América en la poesía de la generación del '27. *Cuadernos Hispanoamericanos*, no. 514 – 515 (Apr – May 93), pp. 155 – 183. Il.

Martínez, Gustavo. Lo real-maravilloso o el redescubrimiento de América. *Plural (Mexico)*, v. 22, no. 265 (Oct 93), pp. 60 – 69.

Pastor, Beatriz. *The Armature of Conquest: Spanish Accounts of the Discovery of America, 1492 – 1589* reviewed by Patricia Seed. *Journal of Latin American Studies*, v. 25, no. 2 (May 93), pp. 387 – 388.

— Utopía y conquista: dinámica utópica e identidad colonial. *Revista de Crítica Literaria Latinoamericana*, v. 19, no. 38 (July – Dec 93), pp. 105 – 113.

Shannon, Robert M. *Visions of the New World in the Drama of Lope de Vega* reviewed by James Mandrell. *Hispanic Review*, v. 61, no. 1 (Winter 93), pp. 100 – 102.

Varas Reyes, Víctor. América en tres momentos de la lírica rubendariana: miscelánea. *Signo*, no. 36 – 37, Nueva época (May – Dec 92), pp. 433 – 442.

AMERICAN CHAMBER OF COMMERCE OF MEXICO

Kelso, Laura. Mission NAFTA. *Business Mexico*, v. 3, no. 7 (July 93), p. 20 +. Il.

Witoshynsky, Mary. The Essence of Partnership. *Business Mexico*, v. 3, no. 7 (July 93), pp. 28 – 31. Il.

AMERICAN LITERATURE
History and criticism

Fitz, Earl E. *Rediscovering the New World: Inter-American Literature in a Comparative Context* reviewed by Charles B. Moore. *Hispania (USA)*, v. 76, no. 1 (Mar 93), pp. 84 – 85.

Rocard, Marcienne. *The Children of the Sun: Mexican-Americans in the Literature of the United States* reviewed by Chuck Tatum. *The Americas Review*, v. 20, no. 2 (Summer 92), pp. 113 – 115.

Williams, Raymond Leslie, ed. *The Novel in the Americas* reviewed by Edward Waters Hood. *Hispania (USA)*, v. 76, no. 4 (Dec 93), pp. 742 – 743.

— *The Novel in the Americas* reviewed by John L. Brown. *World Literature Today*, v. 67, no. 4 (Fall 93), pp. 908 – 909.

Study and teaching

Candelaria, Cordelia, ed. *Multiethnic Literature of the United States: Critical Introductions and Classroom Resources* reviewed by Genevieve M. Ramírez. *The Americas Review*, v. 19, no. 2 (Summer 91), pp. 107 – 109.

AMERICANS
Mexico

Erlich, Marc I. Making Sense of the Bicultural Workplace. *Business Mexico*, v. 3, no. 8 (Aug 93), pp. 16 – 19.

Peru

Hampe Martínez, Teodoro. Apuntes documentales sobre inmigrantes europeos y norteamericanos en Lima, siglo XIX. *Revista de Indias*, v. 53, no. 198 (May – Aug 93), pp. 459 – 491. Bibl.

THE AMERICAS REVIEW (PERIODICAL)
Indexes

Dicennial Index, 1983 – 1992. *The Americas Review*, v. 20, no. 3 – 4 (Fall – Winter 92), pp. 257 – 271.

AMORÓS, GRIMANESA

Padurano, Dominique. Grimanesa Amorós: Mysteries and Metaphors. *Latin American Art,* v. 5, no. 1 (Spring 93), pp. 67 – 69. Il.

AMUESHA INDIANS

Santos Granero, Fernando. *The Power of Love: The Moral Use of Knowledge amongst the Amuesha of Central Peru* reviewed by Jaime Regan. *Amazonía Peruana,* v. 11, no. 22 (Oct 92), pp. 285 – 288.

— *The Power of Love: The Moral Use of Knowledge amongst the Amuesha of Central Peru* reviewed by Richard. C. Smith. *Bulletin de l'Institut Français d'Etudes Andines,* v. 21, no. 2 (1992), pp. 793 – 797. Bibl.

ANARCHISM AND ANARCHISTS

Argentina

Ciafardo, Eduardo O. and Daniel Espesir. Patología de la acción política anarquista: criminólogos, psiquiatras y conflicto social en Argentina, 1890 – 1910. *Siglo XIX: Revista,* no. 12, 2a época (July – Dec 92), pp. 23 – 40. Bibl.

Reichardt, Dieter. *Humano ardor* por Alberto Ghiraldo: la novela autobiográfica de un anarquista argentino. *Iberoamericana,* v. 17, no. 50 (1993), pp. 79 – 88. Bibl.

Brazil

Seixas, Jacy Alves de. *Mémoire et oubli: anarchisme et syndicalisme révolutionnaire au Brésil, 1890 – 1930* reviewed by Pierre Jarrige. *Cahiers des Amériques Latines,* no. 13 (1992), pp. 180 – 181.

ANDAMARCA, PERU

Ossio Acuña, Juan M. *Parentesco, reciprocidad y jerarquía en los Andes: una aproximación a la organización social de la comunidad de Andamarca* reviewed by Penny Dransart. *Journal of Latin American Studies,* v. 25, no. 3 (Oct 93), pp. 684 – 686.

ANDEAN COMMON MARKET

El arancel externo común en el Grupo Andino. *Integración Latinoamericana,* v. 18, no. 194 (Oct 93), pp. 37 – 39. Tables.

Cáceres, Luis René. Ecuador y la integración andina: experiencias y perspectivas. *Integración Latinoamericana,* v. 18, no. 195 (Nov 93), pp. 31 – 46. Bibl, tables, charts.

Cárdenas, Manuel José. La integración andina: indicio de una nueva etapa. *Revista Javeriana,* v. 61, no. 594 (May 93), pp. 210 – 215.

Fairlie Reinoso, Alan. Crisis, integración y desarrollo en América Latina: la dinámica del Grupo Andino con el MERCOSUR en la década de 1980. *Integración Latinoamericana,* v. 18, no. 192 (Aug 93), pp. 11 – 40. Bibl, tables, charts.

Frambes-Buxeda, Aline. Bolivia: eje vital de la integración económica andina y latinoamericana. *Homines,* v. 15 – 16, no. 2 – 1 (Oct 91 – Dec 92), pp. 187 – 248. Bibl, tables.

González Vigil, Fernando. Crisis andina e integración. *Debate (Peru),* v. 16, no. 72 (Mar – May 93), pp. 49 – 51. Il.

Grupo Andino: Decisión 329; Acuerdo Marco de Cooperación entre la Comunidad Económica Europea y el Acuerdo de Cartagena y Sus Países Miembros; Bolivia, Colombia, Ecuador, Perú, Venezuela. *Integración Latinoamericana,* v. 18, no. 189 – 190 (May – June 93), pp. 46 – 55.

Palacios Maldonado, Carlos. Confusión en el Grupo Andino. *Integración Latinoamericana,* v. 18, no. 194 (Oct 93), pp. 23 – 33.

Portocarrero Maisch, Javier. *Experiencia de la Comunidad Europea y perspectivas del Grupo Andino* (Review). *Integración Latinoamericana,* v. 18, no. 189 – 190 (May – June 93), pp. 57 – 58.

Salgado, Germánico. Integración andina y apertura externa: las nuevas tendencias. *Nueva Sociedad,* no. 125 (May – June 93), pp. 130 – 137.

Salgado, Germánico and Rafael Urriola, eds. *El fin de las barreras: los empresarios y el Pacto Andino en la década de los '90* (Review). *Integración Latinoamericana,* v. 18, no. 189 – 190 (May – June 93), p. 57.

Simons Chirinos, Andrés. La teoría de las uniones aduaneras y el Pacto Andino. *Apuntes (Peru),* no. 31 (July – Dec 92), pp. 41 – 54.

Congresses

Grupo Andino: Primera Reunión Global Andina sobre Servicios. *Integración Latinoamericana,* v. 18, no. 186 (Jan – Feb 93), pp. 73 – 78.

Law and legislation

Grupo Andino: Decisión 313; Regimen Común sobre Propiedad Industrial. *Integración Latinoamericana,* v. 18, no. 187 – 188 (Mar – Apr 93), pp. 55 – 64.

Sources

Andean Common Market. Armonización de políticas macroeconómicas en el Grupo Andino. *Integración Latinoamericana,* v. 18, no. 192 (Aug 93), pp. 41 – 52.

Grupo Andino (Five documents dealing with decisions made between the members of the Andean Group). *Integración Latinoamericana,* v. 18, no. 187 – 188 (Mar – Apr 93), pp. 55 – 68.

ANDEAN REGION

See also

Andean Common Market
Anthropo-geography – Andean region
Caciquism – Andean region
Catholic Church – Andean region
Coca and cocaine – Andean region
Folk dancing – Andean region
Folk music – Andean region
Foreign trade promotion – Andean region
Haciendas – Andean region
Indians, Treatment of – Andean region
Investments, Foreign – Andean region
Land use – Andean region
Legislative power – Andean region
Manuscripts – Andean region
Markets and merchants – Andean region
Migration, Internal – Andean region
Oral tradition – Andean region
Peasantry – Andean region
Photography and photographers – Andean region
Railroads – Andean region
Religion and sociology – Andean region
Service industries – Andean region
Social conflict – Andean region
Sociolinguistics – Andean region
Syncretism (Religion) – Andean region
Tariff – Andean region
Textile industry and fabrics – Andean region
Urbanization – Andean region
Violence – Andean region
Names of specific countries within the region

Antiquities

Burger, Richard Lewis. *Chavín and the Origins of Andean Civilization* reviewed by Thomas Pozorski and Shelia Pozorski. *Latin American Antiquity,* v. 4, no. 4 (Dec 93), pp. 389 – 390.

Shady Solís, Ruth. Del arcaico al formativo en los Andes centrales. *Revista Andina,* v. 11, no. 1 (July 93), pp. 103 – 132. Bibl, tables, maps.

Stanish, Charles. *Ancient Andean Political Economy* reviewed by Penny Dransart. *Journal of Latin American Studies,* v. 25, no. 2 (May 93), pp. 391 – 392.

— *Ancient Andean Political Economy* reviewed by Michael E. Moseley. *Revista Interamericana de Bibliografía,* v. 42, no. 2 (1992), pp. 287 – 288.

Bibliography

MacCormack, Sabine G. Myth, History, and Language in the Andes (Review article). *Colonial Latin American Review,* v. 2, no. 1 – 2 (1993), pp. 247 – 260. Bibl.

Civilization

Millones Santa Gadea, Luis and Hiroyasu Tomoeda. *500 años de mestizaje en los Andes* reviewed by Emma María Sordo. *Hispanic American Historical Review,* v. 73, no. 4 (Nov 93), p. 676.

Climate

Thompson, Lonnie G. Reconstructing the Paleo ENSO Records from Tropical and Subtropical Ice Cores. *Bulletin de l'Institut Français d'Etudes Andines*, v. 22, no. 1 (1993), pp. 65 – 83. Bibl, il, maps, charts.

Economic conditions

Muñoz Portugal, Ismael. Ajuste y desarrollo en América Latina: el contexto de los países andinos. *Cristianismo y Sociedad*, v. 30, no. 113 (1992), pp. 7 – 14. Bibl.

Economic policy

International cooperation

Andean Common Market. Armonización de políticas macroeconómicas en el Grupo Andino. *Integración Latinoamericana*, v. 18, no. 192 (Aug 93), pp. 41 – 52.

Foreign economic relations

European Community

Grupo Andino: Decisión 329; Acuerdo Marco de Cooperación entre la Comunidad Económica Europea y el Acuerdo de Cartagena y Sus Países Miembros; Bolivia, Colombia, Ecuador, Perú, Venezuela. *Integración Latinoamericana*, v. 18, no. 189 – 190 (May – June 93), pp. 46 – 55.

Historiography

Huhle, Rainer. El terremoto de Cajamarca: la derrota del Inca en la memoria colectiva; elementos para un análisis de la resistencia cultural de los pueblos andinos. *Ibero-Amerikanisches Archiv*, v. 18, no. 3 – 4 (1992), pp. 387 – 426. Il, facs.

Rappaport, Joanne. Textos legales e interpretación histórica: una etnografía andina de la lectura. *Iberoamericana*, v. 16, no. 47 – 48 (1992), pp. 67 – 81. Bibl.

History

Lauer, Mirko and Henrique-Osvaldo Urbano, eds. *Poder y violencia en los Andes* reviewed by Kenneth J. Andrien. *Hispanic American Historical Review*, v. 73, no. 1 (Feb 93), pp. 177 – 178.

— *Poder y violencia en los Andes* reviewed by Víctor Peralta Ruiz. *Revista de Indias*, v. 53, no. 197 (Jan – Apr 93), pp. 124 – 126.

O'Phelan Godoy, Scarlett. Rebeliones andinas anticoloniales: Nueva Granada, Perú y Charcas entre el siglo XVIII y el XIX. *Anuario de Estudios Americanos*, v. 49 (1992), pp. 395 – 440. Bibl, maps.

Rural conditions

Glave Testino, Luis Miguel. La sociedad campesina andina a mediados del siglo XVII: estructura social y tendencias de cambio. *Historia y Cultura (Peru)*, no. 20 (1990), pp. 81 – 132. Bibl, tables.

ANDRADE, CARLOS DRUMMOND DE

Translations

Andrade, Carlos Drummond de. El amor natural (Translated by Víctor Sosa). *Vuelta*, v. 17, no. 198 (May 93), pp. 24 – 25.

ANDRADE, MÁRIO DE

Correspondence, reminiscences, etc.

Moraes, Marcos Antônio. Cromos, vilegiatura: cartões-postais de Mário de Andrade. *Vozes*, v. 87, no. 2 (Mar – Apr 93), pp. 63 – 75. Il, facs.

Criticism and interpretation

Gonçalves, João Francisco Franklin. Mário de Andrade e o avô presidente: dois projetos para o Brasil. *Vozes*, v. 87, no. 4 (July – Aug 93), pp. 65 – 69. Il.

Lopez, Telê Porto Ancona. Mário de Andrade: um bailado em prosa. *Vozes*, v. 87, no. 1 (Jan – Feb 93), pp. 84 – 91. Il.

Toni, Flávia Camargo. Memória: Mário de Andrade escreve para as crianças. *Vozes*, v. 87, no. 3 (May – June 93), pp. 67 – 72. Facs.

ANDRÉA, FRANCISCO JOSÉ DE SOUSA SOARES DE

Andréa, José. O marechal Soares Andréa nos relevos da história do Brasil. *Revista do Instituto Histórico e Geográfico Brasileiro*, no. 373 (Oct – Dec 91), pp. 1071 – 1084.

ANDRIÓN, MARTINA

Criticism and interpretation

Sánchez Fuentes, Porfirio. Martina Andrión, ruiseñor coclesano. *Revista Cultural Lotería*, v. 51, no. 390 (July – Aug 92), pp. 58 – 64.

ANGEL, ABRAHAM

Moreno Sánchez, Manuel. *Notas desde Abraham Angel* reviewed by Hugo Hiriart (Review entitled "La flor de mil filosofías"). *Nexos*, v. 16, no. 190 (Oct 93), p. 81.

ANGEL, ALBALUCÍA

Criticism and interpretation

Jaramillo de Velasco, María Mercedes. Por la insubordinación: Albalucía Angel y Fanny Buitrago. *Conjunto*, no. 92 (July – Dec 92), pp. 46 – 54. Bibl.

ANGUITA, EDUARDO

Criticism and interpretation

Warnken, Cristián. Eduardo Anguita en la generación del '38. *Estudios Públicos (Chile)*, no. 52 (Spring 93), pp. 329 – 342.

Obituaries

Lastra, Pedro. Eduardo Anguita. *Inti*, no. 36 (Fall 92), p. 129.

Mueren dos poetas. *Atenea (Chile)*, no. 465 – 466 (1992), pp. 353 – 355. Il.

Uribe, Armando. Eduardo Anguita (1914 – 1992). *Estudios Públicos (Chile)*, no. 49 (Summer 93), pp. 259 – 260.

ANHALT, NEDDA G. DE

Criticism of specific works

Cine

Anhalt, Nedda G. de. A la sombra de una sombrilla: cronología de *Cine: la gran seducción*, a la manera de la cronología de Caín. *La Palabra y el Hombre*, no. 81 (Jan – Mar 92), pp. 372 – 382. Il.

Arredondo, Arturo. La labor de *Scherezada* de Nedda G. de Anhalt. *La Palabra y el Hombre*, no. 81 (Jan – Mar 92), pp. 368 – 369.

González Dueñas, Daniel. Una voz en "off": *Cine: la gran seducción*. *La Palabra y el Hombre*, no. 81 (Jan – Mar 92), pp. 370 – 371.

ANIMALS

See also
Birds
Entomology
Geographical distribution of plants and animals
Sheep ranches
Swine
Zoology

Argentina

Carrazzoni, José Andrés. El caballo del indio del desierto. *Todo Es Historia*, v. 27, no. 315 (Oct 93), pp. 76 – 89. Bibl, il.

Belize

Cohn, Jeffrey P. Keeper of the Wild Side. *Américas*, v. 45, no. 2 (Mar – Apr 93), pp. 34 – 37. Il.

Chile

Ramírez Morales, Fernando. Apuntes para una historia ecológica de Chile. *Cuadernos de Historia (Chile)*, no. 11 (Dec 91), pp. 149 – 196. Bibl, tables.

ANTARCTIC REGIONS

See also
Falkland Islands
Patagonia
Tierra del Fuego

Congresses

Pinochet de la Barra, Oscar. Recuerdos de la Conferencia del Tratado Antártico de 1959. *Estudios Internacionales (Chile)*, v. 26, no. 102 (Apr – June 93), pp. 268 – 274.

ANTHROPO-GEOGRAPHY

See also
Land settlement
Subdivision *Influence of environment* under *Man*

Andean region

Viola Recasens, Andreu. La cara oculta de los Andes: notas para una redefinición de la relación histórica entre sierra y selva. *Boletín Americanista*, v. 33, no. 42 – 43 (1992 – 1993), pp. 7 – 22. Bibl, charts.

ANTHROPOLOGISTS

Argentina

Arenas, Patricia and Elvira Inés Baffi. José Imbelloni: una lectura crítica. *Runa*, v. 20 (1991 – 1992), pp. 167 – 176. Bibl.

Mexico

Sullivan, Paul R. *Conversaciones inconclusas*, a translation of *Unfinished Conversations: Mayas and Foreigners between Two Wars* reviewed by Héctor Tejera Gaona (Review entitled "Antropólogos y mayas: el encuentro de expectativas"). *Nueva Antropología*, v. 13, no. 44 (Aug 93), pp. 147 – 150.

ANTHROPOLOGY

See also
  Acculturation
  Anthropo-geography
  Anthropologists
  Archaeology
  Cannibalism
  Ethnobotany
  Ethnomusicology
  Family
  Folk lore
  Functional analysis (Social sciences)
  Kinship
  Man
  Medical anthropology
  Myth
  Mythology
  Oral tradition
  Philosophical anthropology
  Rites and ceremonies
  Shamanism
  Teeth

Fernández Poncela, Anna M. De la antropología de la mujer a la antropología feminista. *Fem*, v. 17, no. 128 (Oct 93), pp. 6 – 7.

Argentina

Belli, Elena. Recordatorios, biografías y necrológicas: usos y sentidos en la historia de la antropología argentina. *Runa*, v. 20 (1991 – 1992), pp. 151 – 161. Bibl.

Berbeglia, Carlos Enrique, ed. *Propuestas para una antropología argentina*, vol. II, reviewed by Gabriel Genise. *Todo Es Historia*, v. 26, no. 309 (Apr 93), p. 72. Il.

Carnese, Francisco R. et al. Análisis histórico y estado actual de la antropología biológica en la Argentina. *Runa*, v. 20 (1991 – 1992), pp. 35 – 67. Bibl.

Garbulsky, Edgardo O. La antropología social en la Argentina. *Runa*, v. 20 (1991 – 1992), pp. 11 – 33. Bibl.

González, Alberto Rex. A cuatro décadas del comienzo de una etapa: apuntes marginales para la historia de la antropología argentina. *Runa*, v. 20 (1991 – 1992), pp. 91 – 110. Bibl.

Palermo, Miguel Angel. La etnohistoria en la Argentina: antecedentes y estado actual. *Runa*, v. 20 (1991 – 1992), pp. 145 – 150.

Piaggio, Laura Raquel. Fotos, historia, indios y antropólogos. *Runa*, v. 20 (1991 – 1992), pp. 163 – 166. Bibl.

Cuba

Research

Campos Mitjans, Gertrudis and Jesús Guanche Pérez. La antropología cultural en Cuba durante el presente siglo. *Interciencia*, v. 18, no. 4 (July – Aug 93), pp. 176 – 183. Bibl.

Latin America

Steger, Hanns Albert. Antropología cultural histórica (Translated by Elsa Cecilia Frost). *Cuadernos Americanos*, no. 39, Nueva época (May – June 93), pp. 134 – 166. Bibl.

Zarur, George de Cerqueira Leite, ed. *A antropologia na América Latina* reviewed by Bernardo Berdichewsky. *Revista Interamericana de Bibliografía*, v. 42, no. 2 (1992), pp. 291 – 293.

Mexico

Cook, Scott. Toward a New Paradigm for Anthropology in Mexican Studies (Review article). *Mexican Studies*, v. 9, no. 2 (Summer 93), pp. 303 – 336. Bibl.

Congresses

Garma Navarro, Carlos. Enfoques teóricos en la antropología mexicana reciente: tercera reunión anual de *Nueva Antropología*. *Nueva Antropología*, v. 13, no. 43 (Nov 92), pp. 139 – 141.

Krotz, Esteban. Aspectos de la discusión antropológica. *Nueva Antropología*, v. 13, no. 43 (Nov 92), pp. 9 – 22. Bibl.

Methodology

Boege, Eckart. Contradicciones en la identidad étnica mazateca: construyendo un objeto de estudio. *Nueva Antropología*, v. 13, no. 43 (Nov 92), pp. 61 – 81. Bibl.

Peru

Methodology

Ansión, Juan. Acerca de un irritante debate entre antropólogos del norte: comentarios al artículo de O. Starn. *Allpanchis*, v. 23, no. 39 (Jan – June 92), pp. 113 – 122.

Poole, Deborah A. and Gerardo Rénique. Perdiendo de vista al Perú: réplica a Orin Starn. *Allpanchis*, v. 23, no. 39 (Jan – June 92), pp. 73 – 92. Bibl.

Salomon, Frank. "Una polémica de once años de antigüedad": comentarios al artículo de Starn. *Allpanchis*, v. 23, no. 39 (Jan – June 92), pp. 109 – 112.

Seligman, Linda Jane. "Es más fácil destruir que crear": comentarios y respuesta. *Allpanchis*, v. 23, no. 39 (Jan – June 92), pp. 93 – 101.

Starn, Orin. Algunas palabras finales. *Allpanchis*, v. 23, no. 39 (Jan – June 92), pp. 123 – 129. Bibl.

— Antropología andina, "andinismo" y Sendero Luminoso. *Allpanchis*, v. 23, no. 39 (Jan – June 92), pp. 15 – 71. Bibl.

Thurner, Mark. ¿Una conclusión resulta prematura?: comentario a propósito del artículo de O. Starn. *Allpanchis*, v. 23, no. 39 (Jan – June 92), pp. 103 – 108.

ANTIGUA, GUATEMALA

Sanchiz Ochoa, Pilar. Poder y conflictos de autoridad en Santiago de Guatemala durante el siglo XVI. *Anuario de Estudios Americanos*, v. 49 (1992), pp. 21 – 54. Bibl.

ANTILLES

See
  Caribbean area
  Netherlands Antilles

ANTIOQUIA, COLOMBIA (DEPARTMENT)

Ortiz Mesa, Luis Javier. Elites en Antioquia, Colombia, en los inicios de la regeneración, 1886 – 1896. *Anuario Colombiano de Historia Social y de la Cultura*, no. 20 (1992), pp. 27 – 42. Bibl.

Rodríguez Jiménez, Pablo. *Seducción, amancebamiento y abandono en la colonia* reviewed by Frédérique Langue. *Anuario de Estudios Americanos*, v. 49, Suppl. 2 (1992), pp. 261 – 262.

ANTIQUITIES

See
  Subdivision *Antiquities* under names of specific countries

ANTISEMITISM

See also
  Jews

Argentina

Nascimbene, Mario C. G. and Mauricio Isaac Neuman. El nacionalismo católico, el fascismo y la inmigración en la Argentina, 1927 – 1943: una aproximación teórica. *Estudios Interdisciplinarios de América Latina y el Caribe*, v. 4, no. 1 (Jan – June 93), pp. 116 – 140. Bibl.

Senkman, Leonardo. *Argentina, la segunda guerra mundial y los refugiados indeseables, 1933 – 1945* reviewed by Hebe Clementi. *Todo Es Historia,* v. 27, no. 316 (Nov 93), pp. 88 – 89. Il.

Senkman, Leonardo, ed. *El antisemitismo en la Argentina* reviewed by Marguerite Feitlowitz. *Estudios Interdisciplinarios de América Latina y el Caribe,* v. 4, no. 1 (Jan – June 93), pp. 170 – 174.

ANTITRUST LAWS

See
Cartels and commodity agreements
Competition

ANTOFAGASTA, CHILE (PROVINCE)

Gana, Víctor. Jesuitas en la región de Antofagasta. *Mensaje,* v. 42, no. 420 (July 93), p. 297.

ANTUNES FILHO

Antunes Filho. Confesiones de un fingidor. *Conjunto,* no. 93 (Jan – June 93), pp. 38 – 43. Il.

Milaré, Sebastião. Las estaciones poéticas de Antunes Filho. *Conjunto,* no. 93 (Jan – June 93), pp. 26 – 37. Il.

APASA, JULIÁN

Valle de Siles, María Eugenia del. *Historia de la rebelión de Tupac Catari, 1781 – 1782* reviewed by Marie-Danielle Démelas-Bohy. *Caravelle,* no. 59 (1992), pp. 249 – 253.

APPRENTICESHIP

See
Vocational education

APRA

See
Alianza Popular Revolucionaria Americana

ARAB COUNTRIES

See
Middle East

ARABS

See also
Lebanese

Argentina

Klich, Ignacio. Argentine – Ottoman Relations and Their Impact on Immigrants from the Middle East: A History of Unfulfilled Expectations, 1910 – 1915. *The Americas,* v. 50, no. 2 (Oct 93), pp. 177 – 205. Bibl, tables.

Brazil

Campos, Mintaha Alcuri. *Turco pobre, sirio remediado, libanês rico* reviewed by Gabriel Bittencourt. *Revista do Instituto Histórico e Geográfico Brasileiro,* no. 373 (Oct – Dec 91), pp. 1207 – 1208.

Honduras

Gonzalez, Nancie L. Solien. *Dollar, Dove, and Eagle: One Hundred Years of Palestinian Migration to Honduras* reviewed by Caroline B. Brettell. *International Migration Review,* v. 27, no. 4 (Winter 93), pp. 899 – 900.

Paraguay

Hamed Franco, Alejandro. La cultura árabe en el Paraguay. *Plural (Mexico),* v. 22, no. 264 (Sept 93), pp. 115 – 117.

ARANA, FRANCISCO

Gleijeses, Piero. La muerte de Francisco Arana. *Mesoamérica (USA),* v. 13, no. 24 (Dec 92), pp. 385 – 412. Bibl, il.

ARAUCANIAN INDIANS

Bengoa, José. El país del censo. *Mensaje,* v. 42, no. 424 (Nov 93), pp. 543 – 546. Il, tables.

Casanueva Valencia, Fernando. Una peste de viruelas en la región de la frontera de guerra hispano-indígena en el reino de Chile, 1791. *Revista de Historia (Costa Rica),* no. 26 (July – Dec 92), pp. 31 – 65. Bibl, maps, charts.

Larraín Barros, Horacio. Identidad cultural indígena tras quinientos años de aculturación: desafío y destino. *Estudios Sociales (Chile),* no. 76 (Apr – June 93), pp. 135 – 148. Bibl.

Marimán, José. Cuestión mapuche, descentralización del estado y autonomía regional. *Caravelle,* no. 59 (1992), pp. 189 – 205. Bibl.

Silva Galdames, Osvaldo. Acerca de los capitanes de amigos: un documento y un comentario. *Cuadernos de Historia (Chile),* no. 11 (Dec 91), pp. 29 – 45. Bibl.

Silva Galdames, Osvaldo et al. Junta de los pehuenches de Malargüe con el comandante general de armas y frontera de Mendoza, don Francisco José de Amigorena. *Cuadernos de Historia (Chile),* no. 11 (Dec 91), pp. 199 – 209. Bibl, facs.

Triviños, Gilberto. La sombra de los héroes. *Atenea (Chile),* no. 465 – 466 (1992), pp. 67 – 97. Bibl, il.

ARAUCANIAN LANGUAGE

Bibliography

Salas Santana, Adalberto. Lingüística mapuche: guía bibliográfica. *Revista Andina,* v. 10, no. 2 (Dec 92), pp. 473 – 537. Bibl.

ARAWAK INDIANS

Reid, Basil. Arawak Archaeology in Jamaica: New Approaches, New Perspectives. *Caribbean Quarterly,* v. 38, no. 2 – 3 (June – Sept 92), pp. 15 – 20.

ARBELÁEZ GÓMEZ, TULIO

Interviews

Pachón, Efraín. Los invitados del mes. *Revista Javeriana,* v. 61, no. 593 (Apr 93), pp. 170 – 178. Il.

ARBENZ GUZMÁN, JACOBO

Gleijeses, Piero. *Shattered Hope: The Guatemalan Revolution and the United States, 1944 – 1954* reviewed by Jim Handy. *The Americas,* v. 49, no. 4 (Apr 93), pp. 562 – 564.

Fiction

Arce, Manuel José. Arbenz, el coronel de la primavera. *USAC,* no. 13 (Mar 91), pp. 83 – 120.

ARBITRATION

See
Labor relations

ARBOLEDA, JOSÉ RAFAEL

Acuerdo n° 02 de 1993. *Boletín de Historia y Antigüedades,* v. 80, no. 781 (Apr – June 93), pp. 285 – 286. Il.

Obituaries

Brociner de Milewicz, Julia. José Rafael Arboleda, S.J. *Boletín de Historia y Antigüedades,* v. 80, no. 781 (Apr – June 93), pp. 287 – 288.

Gómez Latorre, Armando. Réquiem por cuatro académicos. *Boletín de Historia y Antigüedades,* v. 80, no. 781 (Apr – June 93), pp. 339 – 340.

ARCHAEOLOGICAL SITE REPORTS

See also
Names of specific sites

Colombia

Mora Camargo, Santiago et al. *Cultivars, Anthropic Soils, and Stability: A Preliminary Report of Archaeological Research in Araracuara, Colombian Amazonia* reviewed by Leonor Herrera Angel. *Revista Colombiana de Antropología,* v. 29 (1992), pp. 251 – 253.

Costa Rica

Herrera Villalobos, Anaysy and Felipe Solís del Vecchio. Lomas Entierros: un centro político prehispánico en la cuenca baja del Río Grande de Tárcoles. *Vínculos,* v. 16, no. 1 – 2 (1990), pp. 85 – 110. Bibl, il, tables, maps.

Quintanilla Jiménez, Ifigenia. La Malla: un sitio arqueológico asociado con el uso de recursos del Manglar de Tivives, Pacífico central de Costa Rica. *Vínculos,* v. 16, no. 1 – 2 (1990), pp. 57 – 83. Bibl, il, tables, maps.

Solís Alpízar, Olman E. Jesús María: un sitio con actividad doméstica en el Pacífico central, Costa Rica. *Vínculos*, v. 16, no. 1 – 2 (1990), pp. 31 – 56. Bibl, il.

Mexico

Rivera Dorado, Miguel et al. Trabajos arqueológicos en Oxkintok durante el verano de 1991. *Revista Española de Antropología Americana*, v. 23 (1993), pp. 41 – 65. Bibl, il, tables, maps.

Stark, Barbara L., ed. *Settlement Aｿchaelogy of Cerro de las Mesas, Veracruz, Mexico* reviewed by Ronald W. Webb. *Latin American Antiquity*, v. 4, no. 3 (Sept 93), pp. 299 – 300.

Peru

Browne, David M. et al. A Cache of 48 Nasca Trophy Heads from Cerro Carapo, Peru. *Latin American Antiquity*, v. 4, no. 3 (Sept 93), pp. 274 – 294. Bibl, il, maps.

Canziani Amico, José and Santiago Uceda C. Evidencias de grandes precipitaciones en diversas etapas constructivas de La Huaca de la Luna, costa norte del Perú. *Bulletin de l'Institut Français d'Etudes Andines*, v. 22, no. 1 (1993), pp. 313 – 343. Bibl, il.

ARCHAEOLOGY

See also
   Anthropology
   Archaeological site reports
   Cultural property
   Dermatoglyphics
   Man, Prehistoric
   Mummies
   Obsidian
   Paleobotany
   Paleontology
   Petroglyphs
   Photography, Aerial
   Stele (Archaeology)
   Stone implements
   Subdivision *Antiquities* under names of specific countries

Methodology

Arnold, Philip J., III. *Domestic Ceramic Production and Spatial Organization* reviewed by Dean E. Arnold. *Latin American Antiquity*, v. 4, no. 3 (Sept 93), pp. 297 – 299.

Criado Boado, Felipe. Construcción social del espacio y reconstrucción arqueológica del paisaje. *Boletín de Antropología Americana*, no. 24 (Dec 91), pp. 5 – 30. Bibl, il.

Love, Michael W. Ceramic Chronology and Chronometric Dating: Stratigraphy and Seriation at La Blanca, Guatemala. *Ancient Mesoamerica*, v. 4, no. 1 (Spring 93), pp. 17 – 29. Bibl, il, tables, maps, charts.

Montero, Ignacio and Carmen Varela Torrecilla. Cuantificación y representación gráfica de los materiales cerámicos mayas: una propuesta metodológica. *Revista Española de Antropología Americana*, v. 23 (1993), pp. 83 – 100. Bibl, tables, charts.

Staski, Edward and Livingston Delafield Sutro, eds. *The Ethnoarchaeology of Refuse Disposal* reviewed by María Josefa Iglesias Ponce de León. *Revista Española de Antropología Americana*, v. 23 (1993), pp. 256 – 258.

Webster, David et al. The Obsidian Hydration Dating Project at Copán: A Regional Approach and Why It Works. *Latin American Antiquity*, v. 4, no. 4 (Dec 93), pp. 303 – 324. Bibl, tables, charts.

Argentina

Boschín, María Teresa. Arqueología: categorías, conceptos, unidades de análisis. *Boletín de Antropología Americana*, no. 24 (Dec 91), pp. 79 – 110. Bibl, il.

— Historia de las investigaciones arqueológicas en Pampa y Patagonia. *Runa*, v. 20 (1991 – 1992), pp. 111 – 114. Bibl.

Belize

Pendergast, David Michael et al. Locating Maya Lowlands Spanish Colonial Towns: A Case Study from Belize. *Latin American Antiquity*, v. 4, no. 1 (Mar 93), pp. 59 – 73. Bibl, il, maps.

Jamaica

Reid, Basil. Arawak Archaeology in Jamaica: New Approaches, New Perspectives. *Caribbean Quarterly*, v. 38, no. 2 – 3 (June – Sept 92), pp. 15 – 20.

Latin America

Politis, Gustavo, ed. *Arqueología en América Latina hoy* reviewed by Betty J. Meggars. *Latin American Antiquity*, v. 4, no. 4 (Dec 93), pp. 388 – 389.

Mexico

Barnhart, Katherine. Digging Up Mexico's Past. *Business Mexico*, v. 3, no. 11 (Nov 93), pp. 42 – 44. Il, maps.

Uruguay

Hilbert, Klaus. Aspectos de la arqueología en el Uruguay reviewed by Arno Alvarez Kern (Review entitled "Coleções arqueológicas e aspectos de arqueologia no Uruguai"). *Estudos Ibero-Americanos*, v. 18, no. 1 (July 92), pp. 105 – 108. Bibl.

ARCHITECTURE

See also
   Church architecture
   Cultural property
   Postmodernism
   Subdivision *Art and architecture* under names of Indian groups

Argentina

Cacciatore, Julio. Dos décadas de arquitectura argentina: universalidad e identidad en la arquitectura argentina. *Cuadernos Hispanoamericanos*, no. 517 – 519 (July – Sept 93), pp. 207 – 230. Bibl, il.

Ramos, Jorge Abelardo. *La aventura de La Pampa argentina: arquitectura, ambiente y cultura* reviewed by Alicia Novick. *Todo Es Historia*, v. 27, no. 312 (July 93), p. 77. Il.

Wuellner, Margarita Jerabek. Argentine Architect Julián García Núñez, 1875 – 1944. *SALALM Papers*, v. 34 (1989), pp. 53 – 91. Bibl, il.

Cuba

Coyula, Mario. El veril entre dos siglos: tradición e innovación para un desarollo sustentable. *Casa de las Américas*, no. 189 (Oct – Dec 92), pp. 94 – 101.

Ecuador

Bock Godard, Marie S. *Guayaquil: arquitectura, espacio y sociedad, 1900 – 1940* reviewed by Eduardo Figari Gold. *Bulletin de l'Institut Français d'Etudes Andines*, v. 21, no. 3 (1992), pp. 1082 – 1084.

Latin America

Bibliography

Noelle, Louise. Nueve libros sobre arquitectura latinoamericana (Review article). *Anales del Instituto de Investigaciones Estéticas*, v. 16, no. 62 (1991), pp. 218 – 222.

Sources

Robertson, Jack S. and Margarita Jerabek Wuellner. A Computer Search on Latin American Architecture: Results and Implications. *SALALM Papers*, v. 34 (1989), pp. 92 – 96.

Mexico

Barragán, Luis. *Barragán: Armando Salas Portugal Photographs of the Architecture of Luis Barragán*, essays by Ernest H. Brooks II et al. Reviewed by Max Underwood. *Latin American Art*, v. 4, no. 4 (Winter 92), pp. 94 – 95.

Cordero Espinosa, Sergio. Las flores en la arquitectura de Xochimilco (Accompanied by an English translation). *Artes de México*, no. 20 (Summer 93), pp. 74 – 79. Il.

Cossío Lagarde, Francisco Javier. Notas de un arquitecto (Accompanied by an English translation). *Artes de México*, no. 18 (Winter 92), pp. 37 – 43. Il.

Hiriart, Hugo. Felipe Leal, arquitecto. *Artes de México*, no. 20 (Summer 93), pp. 114 – 115. Il.

Puerto Rico

Rigau, Jorge. *Puerto Rico, 1900: Turn of the Century Architecture in the Hispanic Caribbean, 1890 – 1930* reviewed by Max Underwood. *Latin American Art*, v. 4, no. 4 (Winter 92), p. 94.

Uruguay

Bach, Caleb. Making Bricks Soar (Photographs by Oscar Bonilla). *Américas*, v. 45, no. 2 (Mar – Apr 93), pp. 38 – 45. Il.

Venezuela

Gasparini, Marina, ed. *Obras de arte de la Ciudad Universitaria de Caracas* reviewed by Antonio Rodríguez (Accompanied by an English translation). *Art Nexus*, no. 8 (Apr – June 93), pp. 33 – 34. Il.

ARCHITECTURE, COLONIAL

See also
Church architecture

Latin America

Bayón, Damián Carlos and Murillo Marx. *A History of South American Colonial Art and Architecture: Spanish South America and Brazil* translated by Jennifer A. Blankley, Angela P. Hall, and Richard L. Rees. Reviewed by Marcus B. Burke. *Latin American Art*, v. 5, no. 1 (Spring 93), pp. 94 – 95.

Foreign influences

Aguilar Ponce, Luis. Las influencias de la arquitectura española en el pensamiento del ser latinoamericano. *Revista Cultural Lotería*, v. 51, no. 391 (Sept – Oct 92), pp. 98 – 104.

Mexico

Toscano, Guadalupe. *Testigos de piedra: las hornacinas del centro histórico de la ciudad de México* reviewed by Gustavo Curiel and Yolanda Bravo Saldaña. *Anales del Instituto de Investigaciones Estéticas*, v. 16, no. 62 (1991), pp. 203 – 208. Bibl.

ARCHIVES

See also
Libraries and librarians
Manuscripts

Argentina

Schenkolewski-Kroll, Silvia. Los archivos de S.I.A.M. Di Tella S.A.: primera organización de fuentes en la historia de las empresas argentinas. *Estudios Interdisciplinarios de América Latina y el Caribe*, v. 3, no. 2 (July – Dec 92), pp. 105 – 122. Bibl.

Austria

Hampe Martínez, Teodoro. La recepción del Nuevo Mundo: temas y personajes indianos ante la corte imperial de los Habsburgo, 1530 – 1670. *Revista de Historia de América*, no. 113 (Jan – June 92), pp. 139 – 160. Bibl.

Czech Republic

Binková, Simona and Katerina Kozická. El dominio marítimo español en los materiales cartográficos y náuticos de Praga. *Anuario de Estudios Americanos*, v. 49, Suppl. 1 (1992), pp. 47 – 54. Bibl, maps.

Guatemala

Lovell, William George. Los registros parroquiales de Jacaltenango, Guatemala. *Mesoamérica (USA)*, v. 13, no. 24 (Dec 92), pp. 441 – 453.

Italy

Vázquez Janeiro, Isaac. Documentación americana en el Pontificio Ateneo Antoniano de Roma. *Archivo Ibero-Americano*, v. 52, no. 205 – 208 (Jan – Dec 92), pp. 767 – 809.

Mexico

Boyd-Bowman, Peter. *Indice y extractos del Archivo de Protocolos de Puebla de los Angeles, México, 1538 – 1556* reviewed by Linda Greenow. *Hispanic American Historical Review*, v. 73, no. 3 (Aug 93), pp. 486 – 487.

Soto Pérez, José Luis. Fuentes documentales para la historia de la provincia franciscana de Michoacán en el siglo XVIII. *Archivo Ibero-Americano*, v. 52, no. 205 – 208 (Jan – Dec 92), pp. 81 – 106. Facs.

Peru

Varón Gabai, Rafael. El Archivo Arzobispal de Lima: apuntes históricos y archivísticos. *Historia y Cultura (Peru)*, no. 20 (1990), pp. 351 – 360. Bibl.

Portugal

Leal, Ildefonso. Palabras pronunciadas por el doctor Ildefonso Leal el día 6 de mayo de 1992, con motivo de la exposición de documentos Portugal – Venezuela en el Archivo Nacional de la Torre do Tombo, en la ciudad universitaria de Lisboa. *Boletín de la Academia Nacional de la Historia (Venezuela)*, v. 76, no. 301 (Jan – Mar 93), pp. 41 – 43.

Puerto Rico

Matos Rodríguez, Félix and Marta Villaizán. "Para que vayan y produzcan frutos y ese fruto permanezca": descripción de los fondos documentales del Archivo Eclesiástico de San Juan de Puerto Rico. *Op. Cit.*, no. 7 (1992), pp. 208 – 228. Bibl, il, facs.

Spain

Reyes Ramírez, Rocío de los. Expediciones y viajes de franciscanos en los libros registros del Archivo General de Indias, siglo XVIII. *Archivo Ibero-Americano*, v. 52, no. 205 – 208 (Jan – Dec 92), pp. 811 – 832.

Rueda Iturrate, Carlos José de. Financiación de la Orden de San Francisco en los cedularios del Archivo General de Indias. *Archivo Ibero-Americano*, v. 52, no. 205 – 208 (Jan – Dec 92), pp. 833 – 848.

Sosa Llanos, Pedro Vicente. Pleitos venezolanos en el Archivo Histórico Nacional de Madrid. *Boletín de la Academia Nacional de la Historia (Venezuela)*, v. 75, no. 300 (Oct – Dec 92), pp. 223 – 247.

Catalogs

Tau Anzoátegui, Víctor et al, ed. *Libros registros – cedularios del Río de La Plata, 1534 – 1717: catálogo* reviewed by Sergio Martínez Baeza. *Boletín de la Academia Chilena de la Historia*, v. 58 – 59, no. 102 (1991 – 1992), pp. 557 – 558.

United States

Pérez, Louis A., Jr. *A Guide to Cuban Collections in the United States* reviewed by John M. Kirk. *Revista Interamericana de Bibliografía*, v. 42, no. 2 (1992), p. 287.

Venezuela

Bossio Penso, Bertalibia. Guía del Archivo Histórico de la Academia Nacional de la Historia. *Boletín de la Academia Nacional de la Historia (Venezuela)*, v. 75, no. 299 (July – Sept 92), pp. 150 – 156.

Mörner, Magnus. Breves apuntes sobre nuestro viaje a Ocumare de la costa, del 19 al 20 de julio de 1991. *Boletín de la Academia Nacional de la Historia (Venezuela)*, v. 75, no. 298 (Apr – June 92), pp. 141 – 142.

ARCINIEGAS, GERMÁN

Llorente Martínez, Rodrigo. El maestro Arciniegas y su visión de América. *Boletín de Historia y Antigüedades*, v. 79, no. 779 (Oct – Dec 92), pp. 1061 – 1064.

Awards

Cuervo de Jaramillo, Elvira. Premio Jiménez de Quesada 1992 al doctor Germán Arciniegas. *Boletín de Historia y Antigüedades*, v. 79, no. 779 (Oct – Dec 92), pp. 1053 – 1059.

ARCOS, MARCOS DE NORONHA E BRITO, CONDE DOS

Reis, Arthur Cézar Ferreira. O conde dos Arcos na Amazôna. *Revista do Instituto Histórico e Geográfico Brasileiro*, no. 370 (Jan – Mar 91), pp. 134 – 139. Bibl.

ARDAO, ARTURO

Sasso, Javier. Arturo Ardao, historiador de las ideas. *Hoy Es Historia*, v. 10, no. 59 (Sept – Oct 93), pp. 4 – 12. Bibl, il.

Biobibliography

Arturo Ardao: curriculum vitae. *Hoy Es Historia*, v. 10, no. 59 (Sept – Oct 93), pp. 13 – 15. Il.

ARDILES, OSVALDO A.

Rojas Gómez, Miguel. Del exilio de la razón a la razón de la libertad en Osvaldo Ardiles. *Islas*, no. 99 (May – Aug 91), pp. 112 – 129. Bibl.

ARENAS, REINALDO
Biography

Arenas, Reinaldo. *Antes que anochezca* reviewed by José Homero. *Vuelta*, v. 17, no. 195 (Feb 93), pp. 37 – 38.

Criticism and interpretation

Ette, Ottmar. *La escritura de la memoria: Reinaldo Arenas; textos, estudios y documentación* reviewed by Gudrun Wogatzke-Luckow. *Iberoamericana*, v. 16, no. 47 – 48 (1992), pp. 137 – 140.

Foster, David William. Consideraciones en torno a la sensibilidad "gay" en la narrativa de Reinaldo Arenas. *Revista Chilena de Literatura*, no. 42 (Aug 93), pp. 89 – 94. Bibl.

Soto, Francisco. Reinaldo Arenas: The Pentagonia and the Cuban Documentary Novel. *Cuban Studies/Estudios Cubanos*, v. 23 (1993), pp. 135 – 166. Bibl.

Urbina, Nicasio. La risa como representación del horror en la obra de Reinaldo Arenas. *The Americas Review*, v. 19, no. 2 (Summer 91), pp. 94 – 103.

Criticism of specific works
Arturo, la estrella más brillante

Soto, Francisco. La transfiguración del poder en *La vieja Rosa* y *Arturo, la estrella más brillante*. *Confluencia*, v. 8, no. 1 (Fall 92), pp. 71 – 78. Bibl.

La loma del ángel

García Sánchez, Franklin B. El dionisismo paródico – grotesco de *La loma del ángel* de Reinaldo Arenas. *Revista Canadiense de Estudios Hispánicos*, v. 17, no. 2 (Winter 93), pp. 271 – 279. Bibl.

La vieja Rosa

Soto, Francisco. La transfiguración del poder en *La vieja Rosa* y *Arturo, la estrella más brillante*. *Confluencia*, v. 8, no. 1 (Fall 92), pp. 71 – 78. Bibl.

Interviews

Soto, Francisco. *Conversación con Reinaldo Arenas* reviewed by Elena M. Martínez. *Revista Iberoamericana*, v. 59, no. 162 – 163 (Jan – June 93), pp. 389 – 390.

Torres Fierro, Danubio. Verdades de ayer y verdades de hoy: entrevista con Reinaldo Arenas. *Vuelta*, v. 17, no. 195 (Feb 93), pp. 49 – 52.

ARGENTINA
See also

Actors and actresses – Argentina
Agricultural laborers – Argentina
Agriculture – Argentina
Agriculture and state – Argentina
Airplane industry and trade – Argentina
Anarchism and anarchists – Argentina
Animals – Argentina
Antarctic regions
Anthropologists – Argentina
Anthropology – Argentina
Antisemitism – Argentina
Arabs – Argentina
Archaeology – Argentina
Architecture – Argentina
Archives – Argentina
Art – Argentina
Art and society – Argentina
Artists – Argentina
Authoritarianism – Argentina
Banks and banking – Argentina
Basques – Argentina
Booksellers and bookselling – Argentina
Brazilians – Argentina
Buenos Aires, Argentina (City)
Buenos Aires, Argentina (Province)
Business enterprises – Argentina
Caricatures and cartoons – Argentina
Catholic Church – Argentina
Cattle trade – Argentina
Chaco, Argentina
Children – Argentina
Church and social problems – Argentina
Church and state – Argentina
Cities and towns – Argentina
Communism – Argentina
Composers – Argentina
Conservativism – Argentina

Convents and nunneries – Argentina
Cookery – Argentina
Córdoba, Argentina (City)
Córdoba, Argentina (Province)
Corrientes, Argentina (Province)
Cotton – Argentina
Coups d'état – Argentina
Credit – Argentina
Crime and criminals – Argentina
Cultural property – Argentina
Cuyo, Argentina
Decentralization in government – Argentina
Decorations of honor – Argentina
Democracy – Argentina
Deserts – Argentina
Diseases – Argentina
Ecology – Argentina
Ecology and development – Argentina
Education – Argentina
Education, Higher – Argentina
Education, Primary – Argentina
Education and state – Argentina
Educational accountability – Argentina
Elections – Argentina
Elite (Social sciences) – Argentina
Entre Ríos, Argentina
Ethnomusicology – Argentina
Evangelicalism – Argentina
Exiles – Argentina
Falkland Islands
Fascism – Argentina
Finance – Argentina
Finance, Public – Argentina
Floods – Argentina
Folk art – Argentina
Folk festivals – Argentina
Folk literature – Argentina
Folk lore – Argentina
Food habits – Argentina
Foreign exchange problem – Argentina
Forestry – Argentina
Forests – Argentina
Franciscans – Argentina
Gauchos
Geography – Argentina
Geography, Economic – Argentina
Germans – Argentina
Grain trade – Argentina
Haciendas – Argentina
Handicraft – Argentina
Horticulture – Argentina
Housing – Argentina
Human capital – Argentina
Human rights – Argentina
Indians, Treatment of – Argentina
Industrial organization – Argentina
Industrial productivity – Argentina
Industrial promotion – Argentina
Industry and state – Argentina
Inflation (Finance) – Argentina
Information services – Argentina
Information technology – Argentina
Investments, Foreign – Argentina
Italians – Argentina
Japanese – Argentina
Jews – Argentina
Journalism – Argentina
Labor and laboring classes – Argentina
Labor relations – Argentina
Labor supply – Argentina
Land settlement – Argentina
Land tenure – Argentina
Land use – Argentina
Legends – Argentina
Legislative power – Argentina
Literary criticism – Argentina
Literature and history – Argentina
Literature and society – Argentina
Local government – Argentina
Magellan, Strait of
Mar del Plata, Argentina
Marriage – Argentina
Marxism – Argentina
Mass media – Argentina
Medical anthropology – Argentina
Mendoza, Argentina (Province)
Migration, Internal – Argentina
Military in government – Argentina

Mining industry and finance – Argentina
Misiones, Argentina
Missions – Argentina
Monasticism and religious orders – Argentina
Money and money supply – Argentina
Motion pictures – Argentina
Mural painting and decoration – Argentina
Music – Argentina
Music and society – Argentina
Musical instruments – Argentina
Musicians – Argentina
National income – Argentina
Nationalism – Argentina
Natural areas – Argentina
Natural disasters – Argentina
Neuquén, Argentina (Province)
Newspapers – Argentina
Non-governmental organizations – Argentina
Nutrition – Argentina
Oligarchy – Argentina
Oral tradition – Argentina
Paleontology – Argentina
La Pampa, Argentina
Patagonia
Peasantry – Argentina
Periodicals – Argentina
Peronism
Petroglyphs – Argentina
Petroleum industry and trade – Argentina
Philosophy – Argentina
Philosophy and politics – Argentina
Photography and photographers – Argentina
Police – Argentina
Political participation – Argentina
Political parties – Argentina
Political prisoners – Argentina
Political sociology – Argentina
Politics in literature – Argentina
Popular culture – Argentina
Popular music – Argentina
Population – Argentina
Positivism – Argentina
Postmodernism – Argentina
Press and politics – Argentina
Printing and engraving – Argentina
Privatization – Argentina
Property – Argentina
Prostitution – Argentina
Public administration – Argentina
Public health – Argentina
Publishers and publishing – Argentina
Quality of life – Argentina
Race discrimination – Argentina
Railroads – Argentina
Reading interests – Argentina
Regional planning – Argentina
Religion and politics – Argentina
Religious education – Argentina
Río de la Plata region
Rites and ceremonies – Argentina
Rivers – Argentina
Santa Fe, Argentina (Province)
Santiago del Estero, Argentina (Province)
Science – Argentina
Scientific research – Argentina
Sculpture – Argentina
Sex role – Argentina
Sexual behavior – Argentina
Sheep ranches – Argentina
Shopping malls – Argentina
Soccer – Argentina
Social conflict – Argentina
Social movements – Argentina
Social psychology – Argentina
Social security – Argentina
Socialization – Argentina
Sociolinguistics – Argentina
Sociology – Argentina
Sociology, Rural – Argentina
Spaniards – Argentina
Spanish language – Argentina
Steel industry and trade – Argentina
Strikes and lockouts – Argentina
Students – Argentina
Sugar – Argentina
Swiss – Argentina
Tape recorders and recordings – Argentina
Tea – Argentina

Teachers, Training of – Argentina
Teaching and teachers – Argentina
Technology – Argentina
Telecommunication – Argentina
Telephone – Argentina
Television – Argentina
Terrorism – Argentina
Textile industry and fabrics – Argentina
Theater – Argentina
Theaters – Argentina
Tierra del Fuego
Tobacco – Argentina
Trade unions – Argentina
Transportation – Argentina
Tucumán, Argentina (Province)
Unemployment – Argentina
Universities and colleges – Argentina
Urbanization – Argentina
Video tape recorders and recording – Argentina
Viedma, Argentina
Violence – Argentina
Water rights – Argentina
Wheat – Argentina
Wine and wine making – Argentina
Women – Argentina
Women artists – Argentina
Women authors – Argentina
Women in literature – Argentina
Women's rights – Argentina
Wool industry and trade – Argentina
Youth – Argentina

Antiquities

Boschín, María Teresa. Arqueología: categorías, conceptos, unidades de análisis. *Boletín de Antropología Americana*, no. 24 (Dec 91), pp. 79 – 110. Bibl, il.

Gómez Otero, Julieta. The Function of Small Rock Shelters in the Magallanes IV Phase Settlement System, South Patagonia. *Latin American Antiquity*, v. 4, no. 4 (Dec 93), pp. 325 – 345. Bibl, il, tables, maps, charts.

Poujade, Ruth. Poblamiento prehistórico y colonial de Misiones. *Estudos Ibero-Americanos*, v. 18, no. 1 (July 92), pp. 29 – 70. Bibl, maps.

Armed forces

Fraga, Rosendo M. Las fuerzas armadas y los diez años de democracia. *Todo Es Historia*, v. 27, no. 317 (Dec 93), pp. 20 – 25. Il.

Villalba, Miguel Angel. La revolución radical de 1933 en paso de los libres. *Todo Es Historia*, v. 27, no. 311 (June 93), pp. 8 – 24. Bibl, il, maps.

Zaverucha, Jorge. The Degree of Military Political Autonomy during the Spanish, Argentine, and Brazilian Transitions. *Journal of Latin American Studies*, v. 25, no. 2 (May 93), pp. 283 – 299. Bibl, tables.

Foreign influences

Sahni, Varun. Not Quite British: A Study of External Influences on the Argentine Navy. *Journal of Latin American Studies*, v. 25, no. 3 (Oct 93), pp. 489 – 513. Bibl, tables, charts.

Biography

Correa, Alejandra. La pasión según los Sábato. *Todo Es Historia*, v. 26, no. 305 (Dec 92), pp. 85 – 94. Bibl, il.

Boundaries

Chile

Güenaga de Silva, Rosario and Adriana C. Rodríguez Pérsico. El interés de la diplomacia española por los problemas argentino – chilenos en el seno de Ultima Esperanza. *Revista de Historia de América*, no. 112 (July – Dec 91), pp. 85 – 103. Bibl.

Civilization

Abraham, Tomás. Operación ternura. *Cuadernos Hispanoamericanos*, no. 517 – 519 (July – Sept 93), pp. 27 – 40.

Brocato, Carlos Alberto. Cultura y mitos argentinos. *Cuadernos Hispanoamericanos*, no. 517 – 519 (July – Sept 93), pp. 465 – 470.

Hernández, Raúl Augusto. Correlación y correspondencia en la acción social. *Revista Paraguaya de Sociología*, v. 29, no. 84 (May – Aug 92), pp. 171 – 185. Bibl.

Kovadloff, Santiago. Un oscuro país. *Cuadernos Hispanoamericanos*, no. 517 – 519 (July – Sept 93), pp. 575 – 581.

Ramos, Jorge Abelardo. *La aventura de La Pampa argentina: arquitectura, ambiente y cultura* reviewed by Alicia Novick. *Todo Es Historia*, v. 27, no. 312 (July 93), p. 77. Il.

Shua, Ana María. *El marido argentino promedio* reviewed by Beth Pollack. *Chasqui*, v. 22, no. 1 (May 93), pp. 105 – 107.

Vendimias de tinieblas. *Cuadernos Hispanoamericanos*, no. 517 – 519 (July – Sept 93), pp. 574 – 575.

Climate

Ferpozzi, Luis Humberto and José María Suriano. Los cambios climáticos en la pampa también son historia. *Todo Es Historia*, v. 26, no. 306 (Jan 93), pp. 8 – 25. Bibl, il, maps.

Commerce

Asdrúbal Silva, Hernán and Marcela V. Tejerina. De las Georgias del Sur a Cantón: los norteamericanos en la explotación y tráfico de pieles a fines del siglo XVIII y principios del siglos XIX. *Investigaciones y Ensayos*, no. 41 (Jan – Dec 91), pp. 315 – 327. Bibl.

Constitutional law

Riz, Liliana de and Catalina Smulovitz. Instauración democrática y reforma política en Argentina y Uruguay: un análisis comparado. *Ibero-Amerikanisches Archiv*, v. 18, no. 1 – 2 (1992), pp. 181 – 224. Bibl, tables.

Vanossi, Jorge Reinaldo. Las reformas de la constitución. *Todo Es Historia*, v. 27, no. 316 (Nov 93), pp. 8 – 32. Bibl, il.

Description and travel

De Looze, Laurence and Martha Gil-Montero. On the Tucumán Trail (Photographs by Jorge Provenza). *Américas*, v. 45, no. 5 (Sept – Oct 93), pp. 22 – 33. Il, maps.

Moncaut, Carlos Antonio. *Travesías de antaño: por caminos reales, postas y mensajerías* reviewed by Gregorio A. Caro Figueroa. *Todo Es Historia*, v. 27, no. 315 (Oct 93), pp. 62 – 63. Il.

Padula Perkins, Jorge Eduardo. Ulrico Schmidel: un periodismo sin periódico. *Todo Es Historia*, v. 27, no. 313 (Aug 93), pp. 88 – 91. Bibl, il.

Salvatore, Ricardo Donato. Los viajeros y sus miradas. *Todo Es Historia*, v. 27, no. 315 (Oct 93), pp. 8 – 23. Bibl, il.

Verdicchio, Gastón Pablo. Fondas, hoteles y otras formas de hospedaje en el viejo Buenos Aires. *Todo Es Historia*, v. 27, no. 315 (Oct 93), pp. 24 – 28. Il.

Discovery and exploration

Schillat, Monika. Los gigantes patagónicos: historia de una leyenda. *Todo Es Historia*, v. 26, no. 309 (Apr 93), pp. 60 – 66. Bibl, il.

Economic conditions

Bilder, Ernesto A. La demora. *Realidad Económica*, no. 118 (Aug – Sept 93), pp. 82 – 92. Bibl, tables.

Chiaramonte, José Carlos. *Mercaderes del litoral: economía y sociedad en la provincia de Corrientes, primera mitad del siglo XIX* reviewed by Jerry W. Cooney. *Hispanic American Historical Review*, v. 73, no. 2 (May 93), pp. 322 – 323.

¿Es posible cumplir con las metas del FMI? *Realidad Económica*, no. 114 – 115 (Feb – May 93), pp. 5 – 12.

Repetto, Fabián. La construcción de un nuevo orden, o el final de una época . . . . *Realidad Económica*, no. 120 (Nov – Dec 93), pp. 18 – 40. Bibl, tables.

Congresses

¿Es posible lograr el desarrollo económico con equidad social? (A seminar organized by the Fundación de Investigaciones Sociales y Políticas (FISYP) de Argentina and summarized by Dora Douthat). *Realidad Económica*, no. 119 (Oct – Nov 93), pp. 139 – 144.

Economic policy

Acuña, Carlos H. Argentina: hacia un nuevo modelo. *Nueva Sociedad*, no. 126 (July – Aug 93), pp. 11 – 24.

Barbeito, Alberto C. and Rubén M. Lo Vuolo. *La modernización excluyente: transformación económica y estado de bienestar en Argentina* reviewed by Mauricio Tenewicki. *Realidad Económica*, no. 118 (Aug – Sept 93), pp. 142 – 144.

Batista Júnior, Paulo Nogueira. Dolarização, âncora cambial e reservas internacionais. *Revista de Economia Política (Brazil)*, v. 13, no. 3 (July – Sept 93), pp. 5 – 20. Bibl, tables.

Bouzas, Roberto. ¿Más allá de la estabilización y la reforma?: un ensayo sobre la economía argentina a comienzos de los '90. *Desarrollo Económico (Argentina)*, v. 33, no. 129 (Apr – June 93), pp. 3 – 28. Bibl, tables.

Castillo, José. Qué legitimidad para qué crisis: opciones de políticas. *Realidad Económica*, no. 114 – 115 (Feb – May 93), pp. 86 – 98. Bibl.

Castro Escudero, Alfredo. Inflación en Argentina: ¿Un problema resuelto? *Comercio Exterior*, v. 43, no. 10 (Oct 93), pp. 954 – 964. Bibl.

Cuattromo, Oscar Julio et al. Argentina en crecimiento, 1993 – 1995: proyecciones oficiales. *Realidad Económica*, no. 117 (July – Aug 93), pp. 8 – 23. Charts.

Himelfarb, Célia. Convertibilité, stabilisation et dérégulation en Argentine. *Cahiers des Amériques Latines*, no. 14 (1992), pp. 51 – 66. Bibl, tables.

Lavergne, Néstor. Argentina, 1993: estabilidad económica, democracia y estado-nación. *Realidad Económica*, no. 116 (May – June 93), pp. 5 – 20.

Sánchez, Marcelo and Pablo Sirlin. Elementos de una propuesta transformadora para el desarrollo económico argentino. *Realidad Económica*, no. 117 (July – Aug 93), pp. 36 – 160. Bibl.

Sikkink, Kathryn. *Ideas and Institutions: Developmentalism in Brazil and Argentina* reviewed by Laura A. Hastings. *Journal of Latin American Studies*, v. 25, no. 1 (Feb 93), pp. 216 – 217.

Emigration and immigration

Espínola, Julio César. La inmigración brasileña en el este misionero argentino: nuevo examen de un antiguo problema. *Revista Paraguaya de Sociología*, v. 29, no. 85 (Sept – Dec 92), pp. 133 – 155. Bibl, tables, maps, charts.

Higa, Jorge. La Argentina vista con ojos oblicuos. *Todo Es Historia*, v. 27, no. 316 (Nov 93), pp. 60 – 80. Il, maps.

Meding, Holger M. German Emigration to Argentina and the Illegal Brain Drain to the Plate, 1945 – 1955. *Jahrbuch für Geschichte von Staat, Wirtschaft und Gesellschaft Lateinamerikas*, v. 29 (1992), pp. 397 – 419. Bibl, tables.

Padula Perkins, Jorge Eduardo. Los valesanos tras la esperanza americana: de Suiza a la Confederación Argentina. *Todo Es Historia*, v. 27, no. 316 (Nov 93), pp. 82 – 85. Il.

Rocamora, Joan. *Catalanes en la Argentina: centenario del Casal de Catalunya* reviewed by Alicia Vidaurreta. *Revista de Indias*, v. 53, no. 197 (Jan – Apr 93), pp. 117 – 119.

Sánchez Alonso, Blanca. *La inmigración española en Argentina, siglos XIX y XX* reviewed by Hebe Clementi. *Todo Es Historia*, v. 26, no. 310 (May 93), p. 80. Il.

Siegrist de Gentile, Nora L. *Inmigración vasca en la ciudad de Buenos Aires, 1830 – 1855* reviewed by Oscar Alvarez Gila. *Revista de Indias*, v. 53, no. 197 (Jan – Apr 93), pp. 121 – 124.

Bibliography

Viglione de Arrastía, Hebe. Población e inmigración: producción historiográfica en la provincia de Santa Fe, Argentina. *Revista Interamericana de Bibliografía*, v. 42, no. 3 (1992), pp. 489 – 500. Bibl.

Law and legislation

Castro, Donald S. *The Development and Politics of Argentine Immigration Policy, 1852 – 1914: "To Govern Is to Populate"* reviewed by Samuel L. Baily. *International Migration Review*, v. 27, no. 1 (Spring 93), pp. 214 – 215.

Quijada Mauriño, Mónica. De Perón a Alberdi: selectividad étnica y construcción nacional en la política inmigratoria argentina. *Revista de Indias*, v. 52, no. 195 – 196 (May – Dec 92), pp. 867 – 888. Bibl.

Senkman, Leonardo. *Argentina, la segunda guerra mundial y los refugiados indeseables, 1933 – 1945* reviewed by Hebe Clementi. *Todo Es Historia*, v. 27, no. 316 (Nov 93), pp. 88 – 89. Il.

— Etnicidad e inmigración durante el primer peronismo. *Estudios Interdisciplinarios de América Latina y el Caribe*, v. 3, no. 2 (July – Dec 92), pp. 5 – 38. Bibl.

Sources

Anasagasti, Iñaki, ed. *Homenaje al Comité Pro-Inmigación Vasca en la Argentina, 1940* reviewed by Oscar Alvarez Gila. *Revista de Indias,* v. 53, no. 197 (Jan – Apr 93), pp. 99 – 101.

Foreign economic relations

Brazil

ALADI: Acuerdo de Complementación Económica n° 14 concertado entre la República Argentina y la república federativa del Brasil. *Integración Latinoamericana,* v. 18, no. 193 (Sept 93), pp. 68 – 70.

Anales del I Seminario de Universidades por la Integración Brasil y Argentina (Review). *Integración Latinoamericana,* v. 18, no. 192 (Aug 92), p. 98.

Barbosa, Rubens Antonio. Liberalização do comércio, integração regional e Mercado Comum do Sul: o papel do Brasil. *Revista de Economia Política (Brazil),* v. 13, no. 1 (Jan – Mar 93), pp. 64 – 81.

Bekerman, Marta. O setor petroquímico e a integração Argentina – Brasil. *Pesquisa e Planejamento Econômico,* v. 22, no. 2 (Aug 92), pp. 369 – 398. Bibl, tables.

Czar de Zalduendo, Susana. Empresas binacionales: el estatuto argentino – brasileño. *Integración Latinoamericana,* v. 17, no. 184 (Nov 92), pp. 16 – 25. Bibl.

Stülp, Valter José and Bartholomeu E. Stein Neto. A vitivinicultura do Rio Grande do Sul e a integração econômica Brasil – Argentina. *Revista de Economia e Sociologia Rural,* v. 29, no. 4 (Oct – Dec 91), pp. 387 – 400. Bibl, tables.

Ecuador

Acuerdo de Alcance Parcial de Complementación Económica concertado con la república del Ecuador y la República Argentina. *Integración Latinoamericana,* v. 18, no. 194 (Oct 93), pp. 61 – 64.

Paraguay

Argentina – Paraguay: Tratado para el Establecimiento de un Estatuto de Empresas Binacionales Argentino – Paraguayas. *Integración Latinoamericana,* v. 17, no. 184 (Nov 92), pp. 75 – 78.

Peru

Acuerdo de Alcance Parcial de Complementación Económica n° 9 concertado entre Argentina y Perú. *Integración Latinoamericana,* v. 18, no. 193 (Sept 93), pp. 70 – 74.

Foreign opinion

Figallo, Beatriz J. Yrigoyen y su segundo gobierno vistos por Ramiro de Maeztu. *Todo Es Historia,* v. 27, no. 312 (July 93), pp. 80 – 93. Bibl, il.

Foreign relations

Brancato, Sandra Maria Lubisco. A conexão EUA/Brasil e a "questão argentina," 1943 – 1944. *Estudos Ibero-Americanos,* v. 18, no. 1 (July 92), pp. 89 – 101. Bibl.

Brazil

Argentina – Brasil: Acuerdo de Alcance Parcial de Cooperación e Intercambio de Bienes Utilizados en la Defensa y Protección del Medio Ambiente. *Integración Latinoamericana,* v. 17, no. 184 (Nov 92), pp. 74 – 75.

Great Britain

Altamirano Toledo, Carlos. Lecciones de una guerra. *Cuadernos Hispanoamericanos,* no. 517 – 519 (July – Sept 93), pp. 586 – 590.

Middle East

Klich, Ignacio. Argentine – Ottoman Relations and Their Impact on Immigrants from the Middle East: A History of Unfulfilled Expectations, 1910 – 1915. *The Americas,* v. 50, no. 2 (Oct 93), pp. 177 – 205. Bibl, tables.

Paraguay

Argentina – Paraguay (Six documents dealing with relations between Argentina and Paraguay). *Integración Latinoamericana,* v. 17, no. 185 (Dec 92), pp. 72 – 79.

Spain

Rein, Raanan. El antifranquismo durante el régimen peronista. *Cuadernos Americanos,* no. 37, Nueva época (Jan – Feb 93), pp. 90 – 114. Bibl.

Historiography

Saguier, Eduardo Ricardo. La crisis de un estado colonial: balance de la cuestión rioplatense. *Anuario de Estudios Americanos,* v. 49, Suppl. 2 (1992), pp. 65 – 91. Bibl.

Bibliography

Tandeter, Enrique. El período colonial en la historiografía argentina reciente. *Historia Mexicana,* v. 42, no. 3 (Jan – Mar 93), pp. 789 – 819.

Foreign influences

Pelosi, Carmen. *Historiografía y sociedad: las fuentes de 'Annales' y su recepción en la historiografía argentina* reviewed by Hebe Clementi. *Todo Es Historia,* v. 27, no. 311 (June 93), pp. 58 – 59. Il.

History

Bazán, Armando Raúl. *El noroeste y la Argentina contemporánea, 1853 – 1992* reviewed by Gastón Carranza. *Todo Es Historia,* v. 26, no. 308 (Mar 93), pp. 73 – 74. Il.

Benarós, León. El desván de Clío: personajes, hechos, anécdotas y curiosidades de la historia. *Todo Es Historia,* v. 26 – 27 (Dec 92 – Dec 93), All issues. Il.

Pictorial works

Luna, Felicitas. La fotohistoria del mes (A regular feature that presents historical photographs along with a brief biography or description). *Todo Es Historia,* v. 26 – 27 (Dec 92 – Dec 93), All issues.

Sources

Tau Anzoátegui, Víctor et al, ed. *Libros registros – cedularios del Río de La Plata, 1534 – 1717: catálogo* reviewed by Sergio Martínez Baeza. *Boletín de la Academia Chilena de la Historia,* v. 58 – 59, no. 102 (1991 – 1992), pp. 557 – 558.

19th century

Duarte, María Amalia. La ley de amnistía de 1875 y el proceder del jordanismo. *Investigaciones y Ensayos,* no. 41 (Jan – Dec 91), pp. 171 – 213. Bibl.

García Godoy, Cristián. *Tomás Godoy Cruz: su tiempo, su vida, su drama* reviewed by Mario Luis Descotte. *Revista Interamericana de Bibliografía,* v. 42, no. 3 (1992), p. 503.

Leguizamón, Martiniano. La república de Entre Ríos. *Hoy Es Historia,* v. 10, no. 60 (Nov – Dec 93), pp. 82 – 83.

Mazzuchi, Silvia and Héctor Sambuceti. Santos Pérez: alegato y ejecución. *Todo Es Historia,* v. 26, no. 308 (Mar 93), pp. 26 – 35. Il.

Quiroga Micheo, Ernesto. Los mazorqueros: ¿Gente decente o asesinos? *Todo Es Historia,* v. 26, no. 308 (Mar 93), pp. 38 – 55. Bibl, il, facs.

1943 –

Castillo, Abelardo. La década vacía. *Cuadernos Hispanoamericanos,* no. 517 – 519 (July – Sept 93), pp. 604 – 611.

Fumarola, Eduardo V. 1992: hechos que han hecho historia. *Todo Es Historia,* v. 26, no. 306 (Jan 93), pp. 86 – 98. Il.

Industries

Alcorta, Rodrigo. "El Henry Ford argentino": Torquato di Tella; de los Apeninos a los Andes. *Todo Es Historia,* v. 26, no. 310 (May 93), pp. 64 – 67. Il.

Basualdo, Eduardo M. and Miguel Khavisse. El nuevo poder terrateniente (Excerpt from the forthcoming book of the same title). *Realidad Económica,* no. 113 (Jan – Feb 93), pp. 90 – 99.

Schvarzer, Jorge. Expansión, maduración y perspectivas de las ramas básicas de procesos en la industria argentina: una mirada "ex post" desde la economía política. *Desarrollo Económico (Argentina),* v. 33, no. 131 (Oct – Dec 93), pp. 377 – 402. Bibl, tables, charts.

Intellectual life

Anglade, Roberto. Tiempo de no morir. *Cuadernos Hispanoamericanos,* no. 517 – 519 (July – Sept 93), pp. 474 – 477.

Biagini, Hugo Edgardo. *Historia ideológica y poder social* reviewed by Daniel Omar de Lucia. *Todo Es Historia,* v. 27, no. 311 (June 93), pp. 56 – 58. Il.

Ciria, Alberto. *Treinta años de política y cultura: recuerdos y ensayos* reviewed by Andrés Avellaneda. *Hispamérica,* v. 21, no. 62 (Aug 92), pp. 138 – 140.

Goloboff, Gerardo Mario. Algunos antecedentes de la narrativa arltiana. *Cuadernos Hispanoamericanos,* no. Special issue, 11 (July 93), pp. 47 – 51.

Maresca, Silvio Juan. Por qué Nietzsche en la Argentina no es (solamente) posmoderno. *Cuadernos Hispanoamericanos,* no. 517 – 519 (July – Sept 93), pp. 477 – 483.

Martínez, Guillermo. Consideraciones de un ex-político. *Cuadernos Hispanoamericanos,* no. 517 – 519 (July – Sept 93), pp. 495 – 498.

Pino, Diego A. del. José González Castillo y el mundo literario de Boedo. *Todo Es Historia,* v. 27, no. 311 (June 93), pp. 84 – 92. Bibl, il, maps.

Rozitchner, León. Marxismo, crisis e intelectuales. *Cuadernos Hispanoamericanos,* no. 517 – 519 (July – Sept 93), pp. 483 – 494.

Shumway, Nicolás Standifird. *La invención de la Argentina: historia de una idea,* a translation of *The Invention of Argentina.* Reviewed by Alejandro Herrero. *Todo Es Historia,* v. 27, no. 315 (Oct 93), pp. 63 – 64. Il.

— *The Invention of Argentina* reviewed by Paula Alonso. *Bulletin of Latin American Research,* v. 12, no. 2 (May 93), pp. 231 – 232.

— *The Invention of Argentina* reviewed by Thomas L. Whigham. *The Americas,* v. 49, no. 3 (Jan 93), pp. 409 – 410.

Terán, Oscar. El fin de siglo argentino: democracia y nación. *Cuadernos Hispanoamericanos,* no. 517 – 519 (July – Sept 93), pp. 41 – 50. Bibl.

— Representaciones intelectuales de la nación. *Realidad Económica,* no. 118 (Aug – Sept 93), pp. 94 – 96.

Warley, Jorge. Revistas culturales de dos décadas, 1970 – 1990. *Cuadernos Hispanoamericanos,* no. 517 – 519 (July – Sept 93), pp. 195 – 207. Bibl.

Foreign influences

Satas, Hugo Raúl. El pensamiento italiano del siglo XIX en la sociedad argentina. *Todo Es Historia,* v. 26, no. 305 (Dec 92), pp. 40 – 44. Il.

Maps

Barba, Fernando Enrique. El río Santa Ana. *Investigaciones y Ensayos,* no. 41 (Jan – Dec 91), pp. 261 – 268. Bibl.

Politics and government

Manzetti, Luigi and Peter G. Snow. *Political Forces in Argentina,* 3d edition, reviewed by Robert J. Alexander. *Hispanic American Historical Review,* v. 73, no. 4 (Nov 93), pp. 703 – 705.

19th century

Alonso, Paula. Politics and Elections in Buenos Aires, 1890 – 1898: The Performance of the Radical Party. *Journal of Latin American Studies,* v. 25, no. 3 (Oct 93), pp. 465 – 487. Bibl, tables, charts.

Segreti, Carlos S. A. *El unitarismo argentino: notas para su estudio en la etapa 1810 – 1819* reviewed by Aurora Ravina. *Revista de Historia de América,* no. 112 (July – Dec 91), pp. 183 – 185.

1943 –

Cheresky, Isidoro. Argentina: una democracia a la búsqueda de su institución. *European Review of Latin American and Caribbean Studies,* no. 53 (Dec 92), pp. 7 – 45.

Waldmann, Peter. "Was ich mache, ist Justicialismus, nicht Liberalismus": Menems Peronismus und Peróns Peronismus; Ein vorläufiger Vergleich. *Ibero-Amerikanisches Archiv,* v. 18, no. 1 – 2 (1992), pp. 5 – 29. Bibl.

1955 –

Jordán, Alberto R. Cámpora: siete semanas de gobierno. *Todo Es Historia,* v. 26, no. 310 (May 93), pp. 8 – 36. Bibl, il.

Larriqueta, Daniel E. El "pacto social" como yo lo viví. *Todo Es Historia,* v. 26, no. 310 (May 93), pp. 38 – 42. Il.

Loreti, Miguel. Cronología social y política de la Argentina, 1970 – 1990. *Cuadernos Hispanoamericanos,* no. 517 – 519 (July – Sept 93), pp. 15 – 24.

Sikkink, Kathryn. Las capacidades y la autonomía del estado en Brasil y la Argentina: un enfoque neoinstitucionalista (Translated by Leandro Wolfson). *Desarrollo Económico (Argentina),* v. 32, no. 128 (Jan – Mar 93), pp. 543 – 574. Bibl, charts.

Smulovitz, Catalina. La eficacia como crítica y utopía: notas sobre la caída de Illia. *Desarrollo Económico (Argentina),* v. 33, no. 131 (Oct – Dec 93), pp. 403 – 423. Bibl.

1983 –

Acuña, Carlos H. Argentina: hacia un nuevo modelo. *Nueva Sociedad,* no. 126 (July – Aug 93), pp. 11 – 24.

Alonso, María Ernestina. 1983 – 1993: el nuevo poder político. *Realidad Económica,* no. 120 (Nov – Dec 93), pp. 61 – 68.

Castello, Antonio Emilio. Entrevista al ex-vicepresidente de la república, dr. Víctor Martínez. *Todo Es Historia,* v. 27, no. 317 (Dec 93), pp. 84 – 95. Il.

Castillo, José. Qué legitimidad para qué crisis: opciones de políticas. *Realidad Económica,* no. 114 – 115 (Feb – May 93), pp. 86 – 98. Bibl.

Epstein, Edward C., ed. *The New Argentine Democracy: The Search for a Successful Formula* reviewed by David Rock. *Revista Interamericana de Bibliografía,* v. 42, no. 4 (1992), p. 656.

García Costa, Víctor O. Como viví estos diez años de democracia. *Todo Es Historia,* v. 27, no. 317 (Dec 93), pp. 30 – 37. Il.

Sebreli, Juan José. La dolorosa transición. *Todo Es Historia,* v. 27, no. 317 (Dec 93), pp. 26 – 29. Il.

Unamuno, Miguel. El acuerdo político: una asignatura pendiente. *Todo Es Historia,* v. 27, no. 317 (Dec 93), pp. 10 – 15. Il.

20th century

Bra, Gerardo. ¿Nacionalismo, nazionalismo o nacionalismo frontal? *Todo Es Historia,* v. 26, no. 308 (Mar 93), pp. 82 – 91. Bibl, il, facs.

Figallo, Beatriz J. Yrigoyen y su segundo gobierno vistos por Ramiro de Maeztu. *Todo Es Historia,* v. 27, no. 312 (July 93), pp. 80 – 93. Bibl, il.

Fraga, Rosendo M. *El general Justo* reviewed by Félix Luna. *Todo Es Historia,* v. 27, no. 312 (July 93), p. 74. Il.

Race question

Plá León, Rafael. La idea del mestizaje en representantes del positivismo en Argentina y México en el siglo XIX. *Islas,* no. 98 (Jan – Apr 91), pp. 135 – 142. Bibl.

Quijada Mauriño, Mónica. De Perón a Alberdi: selectividad étnica y construcción nacional en la política inmigratoria argentina. *Revista de Indias,* v. 52, no. 195 – 196 (May – Dec 92), pp. 867 – 888. Bibl.

Rural conditions

Bixio, Beatriz and Luis D. Heredia. *Distancia cultural y lingüística: el fracaso escolar en poblaciones rurales del oeste de la provincia de Córdoba* (Review). *La Educación (USA),* v. 36, no. 111 – 113 (1992), pp. 296 – 298.

Calvo, Bernardino S. Nicolás Repetto y Juan B. Justo, pioneros de la educación rural. *Todo Es Historia,* v. 27, no. 315 (Oct 93), pp. 50 – 53. Il.

Eizykovicz, José. Los peones rurales después de la revolución, 1815 – 1823. *Todo Es Historia,* v. 27, no. 312 (July 93), pp. 28 – 42. Bibl, il, facs.

Forni, Floreal H. et al. *Empleo, estrategias de vida y reproducción: hogares rurales en Santiago del Estero* (Review). *La Educación (USA),* v. 37, no. 114 (1993), p. 156.

Giarracca, Norma and Miguel Teubal. El día en que la Plaza de Mayo se vistió de campo (Includes interviews with six agricultural producers). *Realidad Económica,* no. 118 (Aug – Sept 93), pp. 5 – 17. Tables.

Moreno, Carlos. *Patrimonio de la producción rural en el antiguo partido de Cañuelas* reviewed by Silvina Ruiz Moreno de Bunge. *Todo Es Historia,* v. 26, no. 308 (Mar 93), p. 72. Il.

Que no sea demasiado tarde . . . . *Realidad Económica,* no. 117 (July – Aug 93), pp. 27 – 29.

Social conditions

Lesser, Ricardo. El cuerpo de la democracia: la crónica de las condiciones de vida de los sectores populares en esta democracia renovada . . . . *Todo Es Historia,* v. 27, no. 317 (Dec 93), pp. 50 – 56. Il.

Medina, Enrique. *Deuda de honor* reviewed by David William Foster. *World Literature Today*, v. 67, no. 2 (Spring 93), pp. 339 – 340.

ARGENTINA IN LITERATURE

Morales Toro, Leonidas. Misiones y las macrofiguras narrativas hispanoamericanas. *Hispamérica*, v. 21, no. 63 (Dec 92), pp. 25 – 34.

Verdesio, Gustavo. La *Argentina*: tipología textual y construcción de los referentes. *Revista de Crítica Literaria Latinoamericana*, v. 19, no. 38 (July – Dec 93), pp. 345 – 360. Bibl.

ARGENTINE DRAMA
History and criticism

Pellettieri, Osvaldo. El teatro argentino en su período finisecular, 1700 – 1930: un sistema teatral y sus intertextos. *Conjunto*, no. 89 (Oct – Dec 91), pp. 2 – 6. Bibl.

ARGENTINE LITERATURE
See also
Gauchos in literature
Foreign influences

Babini, Pablo. Los italianos en las letras argentinas. *Todo Es Historia*, v. 26, no. 305 (Dec 92), pp. 66 – 69. Bibl, il.

History and criticism
20th century

Berg, Egdardo H. Las poéticas narrativas actuales de la Argentina: líneas de reflexión crítica. *Escritura (Venezuela)*, v. 17, no. 33 – 34 (Jan – Dec 92), pp. 115 – 125.

Borello, Rodolfo A. *El peronismo (1943 – 1955) en la narrativa argentina* reviewed by Raúl Ianes. *Hispanic Review*, v. 61, no. 4 (Fall 93), pp. 590 – 592.

— *El peronismo (1943 – 1955) en la narrativa argentina* reviewed by Nicolas Shumway. *Revista Interamericana de Bibliografía*, v. 42, no. 2 (1992), pp. 282 – 283.

Chitarroni, Luis. Narrativa: nuevas tendencias; relato de los márgenes. *Cuadernos Hispanoamericanos*, no. 517 – 519 (July – Sept 93), pp. 437 – 444. Il.

Gimbernat de González, Ester. *Aventuras del desacuerdo: novelistas argentinas de los '80* reviewed by David William Foster. *Chasqui*, v. 22, no. 1 (May 93), pp. 83 – 84.

Longoni, Ana. Vanguardia artística y vanguardia política en la Argentina de los sesenta: una primera aproximación. *Revista Chilena de Literatura*, no. 42 (Aug 93), pp. 107 – 114.

Piglia, Ricardo. Ficción y política en la literatura argentina. *Cuadernos Hispanoamericanos*, no. 517 – 519 (July – Sept 93), pp. 514 – 516.

Piña, Cristina. La narrativa argentina de los años setenta y ochenta. *Cuadernos Hispanoamericanos*, no. 517 – 519 (July – Sept 93), pp. 121 – 138. Bibl.

Reati, Fernando. *Nombrar lo innombrable: violencia política y novela argentina, 1975 – 1985* reviewed by David William Foster. *World Literature Today*, v. 67, no. 2 (Spring 93), pp. 341 – 342.

Rodríguez Pérsico, Adriana C. Las fronteras de la identidad: la pregunta por la identidad nacional. *Hispamérica*, v. 22, no. 64 – 65 (Apr – Aug 93), pp. 23 – 48. Bibl.

Rosa, Nicolás. Veinte años después o la "novela familiar" de la crítica literaria. *Cuadernos Hispanoamericanos*, no. 517 – 519 (July – Sept 93), pp. 161 – 186.

Spiller, Roland, ed. *La novela argentina de los años ochenta* reviewed by Andrés Avellaneda. *Hispamérica*, v. 21, no. 63 (Dec 92), pp. 108 – 112.

ARGENTINE POETRY

Feldman, Lila María et al. Tres poetas jóvenes (Lila María Feldman, Verónica Parcellis, Gisela K. Szneiberg). *Feminaria*, v. 6, no. 10, Suppl. (Apr 93), p. 18.

History and criticism

Freidemberg, Daniel. Poesía argentina de los años '70 y '80: la palabra a prueba. *Cuadernos Hispanoamericanos*, no. 517 – 519 (July – Sept 93), pp. 139 – 160.

Perlongher, Néstor. Introducción a la poesía neobarroca cubana y rioplatense. *Revista Chilena de Literatura*, no. 41 (Apr 93), pp. 47 – 57. Bibl.

ARGENTINES
Spain

Grande, Félix. Con octubre en los hombros. *Cuadernos Hispanoamericanos*, no. 517 – 519 (July – Sept 93), pp. 562 – 568.

ARGENTINO PAOLETTI, MARIO
See
Paoletti, Mario Argentino

ARGUEDAS, ALCIDES
Criticism and interpretation

Irurozqui Victoriano, Marta. ¿Qué hacer con el indio?: un análisis de las obras de Franz Tamayo y Alcides Arguedas. *Revista de Indias*, v. 52, no. 195 – 196 (May – Dec 92), pp. 559 – 587.

Rovira, José Carlos. Dos novelas de Alcides Arguedas. *Cuadernos Hispanoamericanos*, no. 512 (Feb 93), pp. 103 – 106.

ARGUEDAS, JOSÉ MARÍA
Criticism and interpretation

Lastra, Pedro. Imágenes de José María Arguedas. *Escritura (Venezuela)*, v. 17, no. 33 – 34 (Jan – Dec 92), pp. 47 – 59.

Criticism of specific works
Los ríos profundos

Fornet, Jorge. Dos novelas peruanas: entre sapos y halcones. *Plural (Mexico)*, v. 22, no. 263 (Aug 93), pp. 57 – 62.

ARGÜELLES, HUGO

Partida Tayzán, Armando. El año editorial de Hugo Argüelles. *Plural (Mexico)*, v. 22, no. 260 (May 93), pp. 69 – 70.

ARIAS, ABELARDO
Biography

Spinetto, Horacio Julio. Abelardo Arias: de *Alamos talados* a *El, Juan Facundo*. *Todo Es Historia*, v. 27, no. 313 (Aug 93), pp. 74 – 87. Il.

ARIAS, CARLOS

Tejada, Roberto. Carlos Arias: delirios de la figura. *Artes de México*, no. 20 (Summer 93), pp. 122 – 124. Il.

ARICA, CHILE

Marshall, Santiago. Una misión de la Santa Sede: Arica. *Mensaje*, v. 42, no. 420 (July 93), pp. 287 – 289.

ARINOS, AFONSO
See
Franco, Afonso Arinos de Melo

ARISMENDI, RODNEY

Figueroa Casas, Vilma and Israel López Pino. Rodney Arismendi: su posición político – ideológica. *Islas*, no. 96 (May – Aug 90), pp. 71 – 77.

ARISTIDE, JEAN-BERTRAND

Pires, Nielsen de Paula. Escollos a la democracia: Haití y Perú. *Mensaje*, v. 42, no. 425 (Dec 93), pp. 646 – 648. Il.

ARISTOCRACY
See
Elite (Social sciences)

ARIZTÍA, FERNANDO
Correspondence, reminiscences, etc.

Ariztía, Fernando. *25 años acompañando a su pueblo: testimonio vivo de una época dolorosa* reviewed by Mariano Arroyo. *Mensaje*, v. 42, no. 418 (May 93), p. 168. Il.

ARLT, ROBERTO
Criticism and interpretation

Aínsa Amigues, Fernando. La provocación como antiutopía en Roberto Arlt. *Cuadernos Hispanoamericanos*, no. Special issue, 11 (July 93), pp. 15 – 22.

Capdevila, Analía. Sobre la teatralidad en la narrativa de Arlt. *Cuadernos Hispanoamericanos*, no. Special issue, 11 (July 93), pp. 53 – 57. Facs.

Goloboff, Gerardo Mario. Algunos antecedentes de la narrativa arltiana. *Cuadernos Hispanoamericanos*, no. Special issue, 11 (July 93), pp. 47 – 51.

Jarkowski, Aníbal. La colección Arlt: modelos para cada temporada. *Cuadernos Hispanoamericanos*, no. Special issue, 11 (July 93), pp. 23 – 36. Bibl, il.

Rodríguez Pérsico, Adriana C. Arlt: sacar las palabras de todos los ángulos. *Cuadernos Hispanoamericanos*, no. Special issue, 11 (July 93), pp. 5 – 14. Bibl, il.

Saítta, Sylvia. Roberto Arlt y las nuevas formas periodísticas. *Cuadernos Hispanoamericanos*, no. Special issue, 11 (July 93), pp. 59 – 69. Bibl.

Criticism of specific works
Las fieras

Crisafio, Raúl. Roberto Arlt: el lenguaje negado. *Cuadernos Hispanoamericanos*, no. Special issue, 11 (July 93), pp. 37 – 46. Bibl.

Los lanzallamas

Matamoro, Blas. El Astrólogo y la muerte. *Cuadernos Hispanoamericanos*, no. Special issue, 11 (July 93), pp. 95 – 102. II.

Ortega, José. La visión del mundo de Arlt: *Los siete locos/Los lanzallamas. Cuadernos Hispanoamericanos*, no. Special issue, 11 (July 93), pp. 71 – 76. II.

Los siete locos

Gilman, Claudia. *Los siete locos:* novela sospechosa de Roberto Arlt. *Cuadernos Hispanoamericanos*, no. Special issue, 11 (July 93), pp. 77 – 94. II.

Matamoro, Blas. El Astrólogo y la muerte. *Cuadernos Hispanoamericanos*, no. Special issue, 11 (July 93), pp. 95 – 102. II.

Ortega, José. La visión del mundo de Arlt: *Los siete locos/Los lanzallamas. Cuadernos Hispanoamericanos*, no. Special issue, 11 (July 93), pp. 71 – 76. II.

ARMAMENTS
See also
Atomic weapons and disarmament
Military assistance, Foreign
Brazil

Dagnino, Renato Peixoto. A indústria de armamentos brasileira e a segurança comum na América do Sul. *Política e Estratégica,* v. 8, no. 2 – 4 (Apr – Dec 90), pp. 383 – 399. Charts.

El Salvador

Arsenales de armas: grave incumplimiento de los acuerdos de paz. *ECA; Estudios Centroamericanos,* v. 48, no. 536 (June 93), pp. 577 – 581. II.

Latin America

Larue, J. William. Some Observations on a Model 1799 Infantry Officer's Short Saber. *Colonial Latin American Historical Review,* v. 2, no. 4 (Fall 93), pp. 441 – 448. Bibl, il.

ARMANDO ROJAS, RAFAEL
See
Rojas Guardia, Armando

ARMAS CHITTY, JOSÉ ANTONIO DE
Criticism of specific works
Vida del general Carlos Soublette

Pérez Tenreiro, Tomás. Presentación del libro *Vida del general Carlos Soublette, 1789 – 1870,* escrito por el académico profesor J. A. Armas Chitty y editado por la Comisión Nacional Bicentenario general en jefe, Carlos Soublette. *Boletín de la Academia Nacional de la Historia (Venezuela),* v. 75, no. 299 (July – Sept 92), pp. 27 – 28.

ARMED FORCES
See
Armaments
Military art and science
Military assistance, Foreign

Military in government
Military posts
National security
Police
Subdivision *Armed forces* under names of specific countries

ARMELLA, PEDRO ASPE
See
Aspe Armella, Pedro

ARMENIA, COLOMBIA

Glick, Curtis R. Parámetros sociales para la planificación en Colombia. *Revista Interamericana de Planificación,* v. 26, no. 101 – 102 (Jan – June 93), pp. 95 – 111. Bibl.

ARMS CONTROL
See
Armaments
Atomic weapons and disarmament

ARRÁIZ, RAFAEL CLEMENTE
Criticism of specific works
Multitud secreta

Yarza, Pálmenes. Otros comentarios acerca de *Multitud secreta. Revista Nacional de Cultura (Venezuela),* v. 53, no. 285 (Apr – June 92), pp. 227 – 232.

ARRÁIZ LUCCA, RAFAEL
Criticism of specific works
Pesadumbre en Bridgetown

Flores, María Antonieta. La inevitable visión sombría. *Inti,* no. 37 – 38 (Spring – Fall 93), pp. 253 – 255.

ART
See also
Aesthetics
Architecture
Architecture, Colonial
Artisans
Artists
Baroque
Christian art and symbolism
Church architecture
Creation (Literary, artistic, etc.)
Cultural property
Folk art
Handicraft
Latin America in art
Mass media and the arts
Mural painting and decoration
Museums
Photographs
Photography and photographers
Posters
Postmodernism
Sculpture
Silversmiths
Surrealism
Subdivision *Art and architecture* under names of Indian groups

Gazzolo, Ana María. El cubismo y la poética vallejiana. *Cuadernos Hispanoamericanos*, no. 510 (Dec 92), pp. 31 – 42. II.

Vale, Vanda Arantes do. Pintores estrangeiros no Brasil: Museu Mariano Procópio. *Vozes,* v. 87, no. 2 (Mar – Apr 93), pp. 55 – 62. Bibl, il.

Collectors and collecting

Bargellini, Clara. Frederic Edwin Church, Sor Pudenciana y Andrés López. *Anales del Instituto de Investigaciones Estéticas,* v. 16, no. 62 (1991), pp. 123 – 138. Bibl, il.

Damian, Carol. The Latin American Art Scene in South Florida. *Latin American Art,* v. 4, no. 4 (Winter 92), pp. 65 – 68. II.

Nader, Gary. *Latin American Price Guide: Auction Records, May 1977 – May 1993* reviewed by Andrés Salgado R. (Accompanied by an English translation). *Art Nexus,* no. 10 (Sept – Dec 93), p. 42.

Pau-Llosa, Ricardo. Conversation with Art Dealer César Segnini. *Latin American Art,* v. 5, no. 2 (Summer 93), pp. 31 – 32. II.

Santiago, Chiori. Conversation with Art Collector Robert Marcus. *Latin American Art,* v. 4, no. 4 (Winter 92), pp. 38 – 39. Il.

Seggerman, Helen-Louise. Arte latinoamericano en Christie's y Sotheby's (Accompanied by the English original, translated by Magdalena Holguín). *Art Nexus,* no. 10 (Sept – Dec 93), pp. 104 – 106. Il.

Sokoloff Gutiérrez, Ana. El arte latinoamericano en Christie's y Sotheby's (Accompanied by an English translation). *Art Nexus,* no. 8 (Apr – June 93), pp. 105 – 107. Tables.

Methodology

Balby, Claudia Negrão. Bibliographic Control of Art Materials: The Experience of the Universidade de São Paulo. *SALALM Papers,* v. 34 (1989), pp. 401 – 413. Bibl.

Maddox, Brent F. Visual Research Cataloging at the Getty Center for the History of Art and the Humanities. *SALALM Papers,* v. 34 (1989), pp. 391 – 400. Bibl.

Exhibitions

Bartl, Johanna. Artistas latinoamericanos buscan mitos en Salzwedel. *Humboldt,* no. 110 (1993), p. 102. Il.

Benko, Susana. FIA '93: Caracas (Accompanied by an English translation). *Art Nexus,* no. 10 (Sept – Dec 93), pp. 110 – 112. Il.

Birbragher, Celia S. de. Chicago 1993 (Accompanied by an English translation). *Art Nexus,* no. 10 (Sept – Dec 93), pp. 108 – 109. Il.

Blanc, Giulio V. Art Miami '93 (Accompanied by the English original, translated by Andrés Salgado). *Art Nexus,* no. 8 (Apr – June 93), pp. 108 – 109. Il.

Blanco, Alberto. Doce maestros latinoamericanos. *Artes de México,* no. 19 (Spring 93), pp. 100 – 101. Il.

Breton, André. El arte de México (Translated by Fabienne Bradu). *Vuelta,* v. 17, no. 205 (Dec 93), pp. 37 – 39.

Bucher, Bernadette et al. *America: Bride of the Sun; 500 Years Latin America and the Low Countries* reviewed by Peter Mason. *European Review of Latin American and Caribbean Studies,* no. 53 (Dec 92), pp. 114 – 117.

Calendario de exposiciones. *Artes de México,* n.v. (1992, 1993), All issues.

Camnitzer, Luis. La 45ª Bienal de Venecia. *Art Nexus,* no. 10 (Sept – Dec 93), pp. 58 – 63. Il.

Camnitzer, Luis et al. XXXIV Salón Nacional de Artistas (Accompanied by an English translation). *Art Nexus,* no. 7 (Jan – Mar 93), pp. 140 – 144. Il.

Cresswell, Peter. Insiders and Outsiders: The Annual National Exhibition 1991 and "Homage to John Dunkley." *Jamaica Journal,* v. 24, no. 3 (Feb 93), pp. 29 – 35. Il.

Crónica (Brief reports on exhibits by Latin American artists throughout the world, accompanied by English translations). *Art Nexus,* no. 7 – 10 (1993), All issues. Il.

Damian, Carol. Art Miami '93. *Latin American Art,* v. 5, no. 1 (Spring 93), pp. 82 – 84. Il.

Fletcher, Valerie J., ed. *Crosscurrents of Modernism: Four Latin American Pioneers* reviewed by Carol Damian. *Hispanic American Historical Review,* v. 73, no. 4 (Nov 93), pp. 671 – 672.

Goldman, Shifra M. Artistas latinoamericanos del siglo XX: MOMA (Accompanied by the English original, translated by Magalena Holguín). *Art Nexus,* no. 10 (Sept – Dec 93), pp. 84 – 89. Il.

Guía de la estación. *Artes de México,* n.v. (1992, 1993), All issues.

Haase, Amine. La magia colorista de un continente: la mayor muestra de arte latinoamericana en el siglo XX. *Humboldt,* no. 109 (1993), pp. 60 – 65. Il.

Haupt, Gerhard. Latinoamérica y el surrealismo en Bochum (Includes several pages of colored art reproductions, translated by José García). *Humboldt,* no. 110 (1993), pp. 82 – 89. Il.

Jiménez, Carlos. ARCO '93 (Accompanied by an English translation). *Art Nexus,* no. 8 (Apr – June 93), pp. 110 – 111. Il.

— Bienal de Venecia. *Art Nexus,* no. 10 (Sept – Dec 93), pp. 56 – 58.

— Indian Summer (Accompanied by an English translation). *Art Nexus,* no. 7 (Jan – Mar 93), pp. 48 – 51. Il.

— Voces de ultramar: arte en América Latina y Canarias, 1910 – 1960 (Accompanied by an English translation). *Art Nexus,* no. 8 (Apr – June 93), pp. 48 – 49. Il.

Luza, Mónica and Ricardo Zamora. Exposición de arte contemporáneo de artistas latinoamericanos en Berlín. *Humboldt,* no. 108 (1993), pp. 100 – 101. Il.

Medina, Alvaro. Quien mucho abarca poco aprieta (Accompanied by an English translation). *Art Nexus,* no. 9 (June – Aug 93), pp. 62 – 64. Il.

Pérez Oramas, Luis. Cuadros en una exposición (Accompanied by an English translation). *Art Nexus,* no. 9 (June – Aug 93), pp. 59 – 61. Il.

Pini, Ivonne. Ante América (Accompanied by an English translation). *Art Nexus,* no. 7 (Jan – Mar 93), pp. 60 – 64. Il.

Recent Exhibitions. *Latin American Art,* v. 4 – 5 (Winter 92 – Summer 93), All issues. Il.

Rodríguez, Bélgica. Un re-descubrimiento (Accompanied by an English translation). *Art Nexus,* no. 9 (June – Aug 93), pp. 56 – 58. Il.

Rubiano Caballero, Germán. I Bienal de Pintura del Caribe y Centroamérica (Accompanied by an English translation). *Art Nexus,* no. 7 (Jan – Mar 93), pp. 81 – 82. Il.

Scott, Nadine Althea Theda. 1992: The Annual National Exhibition, National Gallery of Jamaica. *Jamaica Journal,* v. 25, no. 1 (Oct 93), pp. 45 – 53. Il.

Sichel, Berta. Artistas latinoamericanos del siglo XX (Accompanied by an English translation). *Art Nexus,* no. 9 (June – Aug 93), pp. 52 – 56. Il.

Steinmetz, Klauss. El Caribe en Santo Domingo (Accompanied by an English translation). *Art Nexus,* no. 7 (Jan – Mar 93), pp. 83 – 85. Il.

Argentina

Buccelato, Laura. Acentos y reseñas de los '90. *Cuadernos Hispanoamericanos,* no. 517 – 519 (July – Sept 93), pp. 383 – 387. Il.

Fèvre, Fermín. Una mirada al arte argentino. *Cuadernos Hispanoamericanos,* no. 517 – 519 (July – Sept 93), pp. 230 – 244. Il.

Garsd, Marta S. The Broken Mirror: Argentine Art in the 1980s. *SALALM Papers,* v. 34 (1989), pp. 33 – 39. Bibl.

Klitenik, Carlos Espartaco. La pintura de los ochenta: el eclecticismo como estilo. *Cuadernos Hispanoamericanos,* no. 517 – 519 (July – Sept 93), pp. 371 – 381. Il.

Noé, Luis Felipe. Artes Plásticas Argentinas, Sociedad Anónima. *Cuadernos Hispanoamericanos,* no. 517 – 519 (July – Sept 93), pp. 245 – 268. Il.

Bolivia

Gisbert de Mesa, Teresa. *Arte y desacralización* reviewed by María Elena Alzérreca Barbery (Review entitled "Resacralización del sincretismo cultural"). *Homines,* v. 15 – 16, no. 2 – 1 (Oct 91 – Dec 92), pp. 358 – 360.

Bibliography

Guttentag Tichauer, Werner. El arte pictórico en la bibliografía boliviana. *SALALM Papers,* v. 34 (1989), pp. 261 – 268. Bibl.

Brazil

Klintowitz, Jacob. Multiplicidade de estilos. *Problemas Brasileiros,* v. 30, no. 295 (Jan – Feb 93), pp. 57 – 58. Il.

Canary Islands

Jiménez, Carlos. Voces de ultramar: arte en América Latina y Canarias, 1910 – 1960 (Accompanied by an English translation). *Art Nexus,* no. 8 (Apr – June 93), pp. 48 – 49. Il.

Voces de ultramar: arte en América Latina y Canarias, 1910 – 1960 reviewed by Ivonne Pini (Accompanied by an English translation). *Art Nexus,* no. 7 (Jan – Mar 93), p. 40. Il.

Caribbean area

Rubiano Caballero, Germán. I Bienal de Pintura del Caribe y Centroamérica (Accompanied by an English translation). *Art Nexus,* no. 7 (Jan – Mar 93), pp. 81 – 82. Il.

Steinmetz, Klauss. El Caribe en Santo Domingo (Accompanied by an English translation). *Art Nexus,* no. 7 (Jan – Mar 93), pp. 83 – 85. Il.

Sources

Moss, Alan. Art Publishing in the Contemporary Caribbean. *SALALM Papers,* v. 34 (1989), pp. 269 – 274. Bibl.

Central America

Flores Zúñiga, Juan Carlos, ed. *Magic and Realism: Central American Contemporary Art/Magia y realismo: arte contemporáneo centroamericano* reviewed by Ivonne Pini (Accompanied by an English translation). *Art Nexus,* no. 9 (June – Aug 93), p. 33. Il.

Bibliography

Vijil, Alfonso. Central American Art Publications, 1986 – 1989: A Brief Survey and Bibliography. *SALALM Papers,* v. 34 (1989), pp. 307 – 315. Bibl.

Chile

Bibliography

Domínguez Díaz, Marta Silvia. Arte chileno: una contribución bibliográfica. *SALALM Papers,* v. 34 (1989), pp. 369 – 388.

Colombia

Camnitzer, Luis et al. XXXIV Salón Nacional de Artistas (Accompanied by an English translation). *Art Nexus,* no. 7 (Jan – Mar 93), pp. 140 – 144. Il.

Herrera C., J. Noé. Colombia: ¿Atenas suramericana . . . o apenas suramericana? *SALALM Papers,* v. 34 (1989), pp. 275 – 306. Bibl.

Cuba

Goldman, Shifra M. La década crítica de la vanguardia cubana (Accompanied by the English original, translated by Ignacio Zuleta Lleras). *Art Nexus,* no. 7 (Jan – Mar 93), pp. 52 – 57. Bibl, il.

Martínez, Juan A. Cuban Vanguardia Painting in the 1930s. *Latin American Art,* v. 5, no. 2 (Summer 93), pp. 36 – 38. Bibl, il.

Foreign influences

Quirós, Oscar E. Values and Aesthetics in Cuban Arts and Cinema. *SALALM Papers,* v. 34 (1989), pp. 151 – 171. Bibl.

Haiti

Alexis Fils, Gerald. Haitian Art in the Twentieth Century. *SALALM Papers,* v. 34 (1989), pp. 40 – 47.

Jamaica

Cresswell, Peter. Insiders and Outsiders: The Annual National Exhibition 1991 and "Homage to John Dunkley." *Jamaica Journal,* v. 24, no. 3 (Feb 93), pp. 29 – 35. Il.

Scott, Nadine Althea Theda. 1992: The Annual National Exhibition, National Gallery of Jamaica. *Jamaica Journal,* v. 25, no. 1 (Oct 93), pp. 45 – 53. Il.

Latin America

Bayón, Damián Carlos. Arte latinoamericano en el MOMA: una ocasión perdida. *Vuelta,* v. 17, no. 201 (Aug 93), pp. 60 – 62.

Blanc, Giulio V. Art Miami '93 (Accompanied by the English original, translated by Andrés Salgado). *Art Nexus,* no. 8 (Apr – June 93), pp. 108 – 109. Il.

Haupt, Gerhard. Latinoamérica y el surrealismo en Bochum (Includes several pages of colored art reproductions, translated by José García). *Humboldt,* no. 110 (1993), pp. 82 – 89. Il.

Horton, Anne. Conversation with Curator Waldo Rasmussen. *Latin American Art,* v. 5, no. 1 (Spring 93), pp. 40 – 41. Il.

Jiménez, Carlos. ARCO '93 (Accompanied by an English translation). *Art Nexus,* no. 8 (Apr – June 93), pp. 110 – 111. Il.

— Indian Summer (Accompanied by an English translation). *Art Nexus,* no. 7 (Jan – Mar 93), pp. 48 – 51. Il.

— Voces de ultramar: arte en América Latina y Canarias, 1910 – 1960 (Accompanied by an English translation). *Art Nexus,* no. 8 (Apr – June 93), pp. 48 – 49. Il.

Medina, Alvaro. Quien mucho abarca poco aprieta (Accompanied by an English translation). *Art Nexus,* no. 9 (June – Aug 93), pp. 62 – 64. Il.

Noticias (Brief reports on awards, exhibits, and workshops of Latin American art and artists appearing in all issues, accompanied by English translations). *Art Nexus,* no. 7 – 10 (1993), All issues.

Pau-Llosa, Ricardo. Conversation with Art Dealer César Segnini. *Latin American Art,* v. 5, no. 2 (Summer 93), pp. 31 – 32. Il.

Pérez Oramas, Luis. Cuadros en una exposición (Accompanied by an English translation). *Art Nexus,* no. 9 (June – Aug 93), pp. 59 – 61. Il.

Pini, Ivonne. Ante América (Accompanied by an English translation). *Art Nexus,* no. 7 (Jan – Mar 93), pp. 60 – 64. Il.

Rodríguez, Bélgica. Un re-descubrimiento (Accompanied by an English translation). *Art Nexus,* no. 9 (June – Aug 93), pp. 56 – 58. Il.

Seggerman, Helen-Louise. Arte latinoamericano en Christie's y Sotheby's (Accompanied by the English original, translated by Magdalena Holguín). *Art Nexus,* no. 10 (Sept – Dec 93), pp. 104 – 106. Il.

Sichel, Berta. Artistas latinoamericanos del siglo XX (Accompanied by an English translation). *Art Nexus,* no. 9 (June – Aug 93), pp. 52 – 56. Il.

Sokoloff Gutiérrez, Ana. El arte latinoamericano en Christie's y Sotheby's (Accompanied by an English translation). *Art Nexus,* no. 8 (Apr – June 93), pp. 105 – 107. Tables.

Bibliography

Delpar, Helen. Art in Latin America: Recent Writings (Review article). *Studies in Latin American Popular Culture,* v. 12 (1993), pp. 229 – 234. Bibl.

Joy-Karno, Beverly. Latin American Government Documents on the Arts: Introductory Guide. *SALALM Papers,* v. 34 (1989), pp. 239 – 260. Bibl.

Catalogs

Bucher, Bernadette et al. *America: Bride of the Sun; 500 Years Latin America and the Low Countries* reviewed by Peter Mason. *European Review of Latin American and Caribbean Studies,* no. 53 (Dec 92), pp. 114 – 117.

Fletcher, Valerie J., ed. *Crosscurrents of Modernism: Four Latin American Pioneers* reviewed by Carol Damian. *Hispanic American Historical Review,* v. 73, no. 4 (Nov 93), pp. 671 – 672.

Voces de ultramar: arte en América Latina y Canarias, 1910 – 1960 reviewed by Ivonne Pini (Accompanied by an English translation). *Art Nexus,* no. 7 (Jan – Mar 93), p. 40. Il.

Congresses

Hulick, Diana Emery. Modernism in Latin America: Fact, Fiction, or Fabrication? *Latin American Art,* v. 5, no. 2 (Summer 93), pp. 64 – 65.

Cost

Nader, Gary. *Latin American Price Guide: Auction Records, May 1977 – May 1993* reviewed by Andrés Salgado R. (Accompanied by an English translation). *Art Nexus,* no. 10 (Sept – Dec 93), p. 42.

Sources

Barberena Blásquez, Elsa. Investigación sobre arte latinoamericano: acceso a través de material publicado. *SALALM Papers,* v. 34 (1989), pp. 345 – 362. Bibl.

Bustamante, Jorge I. Optical Disk Possibilities in the Distribution of Information on Latin American Art. *SALALM Papers,* v. 34 (1989), pp. 316 – 322. Tables.

Leyva, María. The Museum of Modern Art of Latin America: A Guide to Its Resources. *SALALM Papers,* v. 34 (1989), pp. 417 – 427.

Sorensen, Lee R. Art Reference: Visual Information and Sources for Latin America. *SALALM Papers,* v. 34 (1989), pp. 325 – 333. Bibl.

Stegmann, Wilhelm. Artistic Representation of German Book Collections and Picture Archives. *SALALM Papers,* v. 34 (1989), pp. 428 – 438.

Mexico

Bargellini, Clara. Frederic Edwin Church, Sor Pudenciana y Andrés López. *Anales del Instituto de Investigaciones Estéticas,* v. 16, no. 62 (1991), pp. 123 – 138. Bibl, il.

Blanco, Alberto. Arte contemporáneo de Oaxaca: la semilla de la visión. *Nexos,* v. 16, no. 186 (June 93), pp. 15 – 19.

— Arte de Oaxaca (Accompanied by an English translation). *Artes de México,* no. 21 (Fall 93), pp. 68 – 83. Il.

Breton, André. El arte de México (Translated by Fabienne Bradu). *Vuelta,* v. 17, no. 205 (Dec 93), pp. 37 – 39.

Gas, Gelsen. El grupo Tlalpuente. *Plural (Mexico),* v. 22, no. 258 (Mar 93), pp. 41 – 44. Il.

Juan, Adelaida de. José Martí y el arte mexicano. *La Palabra y el Hombre,* no. 82 (Apr – June 92), pp. 45 – 56. Bibl.

Ocharán, Leticia. Las artes plásticas frente al TLC. *Plural (Mexico),* v. 22, no. 258 (Mar 93), pp. 72 – 73.

Paz, Octavio. *Essays on Mexican Art* translated by Helen Lane. Reviewed by Margarita Nieto. *Latin American Art,* v. 5, no. 2 (Summer 93), p. 71.

Bibliography

Moyssén Echeverría, Xavier. Bibliografía mexicana de arte, 1990. *Anales del Instituto de Investigaciones Estéticas,* v. 16, no. 62 (1991), pp. 223 – 229. Bibl.

Spain

Sources

Gates, Thomas P. Meadows Museum of Spanish Art Book Collection: An Overview. *SALALM Papers,* v. 34 (1989), pp. 439 – 451. Bibl.

United States

Damian, Carol. The Latin American Art Scene in South Florida. *Latin American Art,* v. 4, no. 4 (Winter 92), pp. 65 – 68. Il.

Venezuela

Gasparini, Marina, ed. *Obras de arte de la Ciudad Universitaria de Caracas* reviewed by Antonio Rodríguez (Accompanied by an English translation). *Art Nexus,* no. 8 (Apr – June 93), pp. 33 – 34. Il.

Ramos, María Elena. *Pistas para quedar mirando: fragmentos sobre arte* reviewed by Ivonne Pini (Accompanied by an English translation). *Art Nexus,* no. 8 (Apr – June 93), p. 33. Il.

Societies, etc.

Calzadilla, Juan. El Círculo de Bellas Artes y los paisajistas de la luz, 1912 – 1992. *Revista Nacional de Cultura (Venezuela),* v. 53, no. 286 (July – Sept 92), pp. 95 – 105. Il.

ART, COLONIAL

See also
Architecture, Colonial
Christian art and symbolism

Exhibitions

Westbrook, Leslie A. "Cambios": The Spirit of Transformation in Spanish Colonial Art. *Latin American Art,* v. 5, no. 1 (Spring 93), pp. 54 – 57. Il.

Bolivia

Von Barghahn, Barbara. The Colonial Paintings of Leonardo Flores. *Latin American Art,* v. 5, no. 2 (Summer 93), pp. 47 – 49. Bibl, il.

Latin America

Bayón, Damián Carlos and Murillo Marx. *A History of South American Colonial Art and Architecture: Spanish South America and Brazil* translated by Jennifer A. Blankley, Angela P. Hall, and Richard L. Rees. Reviewed by Marcus B. Burke. *Latin American Art,* v. 5, no. 1 (Spring 93), pp. 94 – 95.

Kaye, Susan. A Living Venue for Cultural Crossroads. *Américas,* v. 45, no. 3 (May – June 93), pp. 48 – 51. Il.

ART AND LITERATURE

Bracho, Coral and Irma Palacios. *Tierra de entraña ardiente* reviewed by Jacobo Sefamí. *Vuelta,* v. 17, no. 200 (July 93), pp. 58 – 59.

Matorell, Antonio. Imalabra. *Conjunto,* no. 92 (July – Dec 92), pp. 95 – 97. Il.

Paz, Octavio. *Al paso* reviewed by George R. McMurray. *World Literature Today,* v. 67, no. 2 (Spring 93), p. 340.

Peterson, Gabriela and Víctor Valembois. Los epígrafes en *El siglo de las luces:* su interpretación; de Goya a Carpentier. *Káñina,* v. 16, no. 2 (July – Dec 92), pp. 89 – 100. Bibl, il, tables.

— Los epígrafes en *El siglo de las luces:* su ubicación; de Goya a Carpentier. *Káñina,* v. 16, no. 1 (Jan – June 92), pp. 79 – 89. Bibl, il.

Sahakián, Carlos. Plástica y poética. *Plural (Mexico),* v. 22, no. 260 (May 93), pp. 40 – 48.

Unruh, Vicky Wolff. Art's "Disorderly Humanity" in Torres Bodet's *La educación sentimental. Revista Canadiense de Estudios Hispánicos,* v. 17, no. 1 (Fall 92), pp. 123 – 136. Bibl.

Vélez, Julio. Estética del trabajo y la modernidad autóctona. *Casa de las Américas,* no. 189 (Oct – Dec 92), pp. 71 – 80.

Young, Richard A. "Verano" de Julio Cortázar, *The Nightmare* de John Henry Fuseli y "the judicious adoption of figures in art." *Revista Canadiense de Estudios Hispánicos,* v. 17, no. 2 (Winter 93), pp. 373 – 382. Bibl.

ART AND RELIGION

See also
Christian art and symbolism

Haiti

Scalora, Sal. A Salute to the Spirits. *Américas,* v. 45, no. 2 (Mar – Apr 93), pp. 27 – 33. Il.

Foreign influences

Benson, LeGrace. Some Observations on West African Islamic Motifs and Haitian Religious Art. *Journal of Caribbean Studies,* v. 9, no. 1 – 2 (Winter 92 – Spring 93), pp. 59 – 66. Bibl.

ART AND SOCIETY

Exhibitions

Mosquera, Gerardo. Encuentros/Desplazamientos: arte conceptual y política; Luis Caminitzer, Alfredo Jaar y Cildo Meireles (Accompanied by an English translation). *Art Nexus,* no. 8 (Apr – June 93), pp. 88 – 91. Il.

Weiss, Raquel. Los colores unidos del Whitney (Accompanied by the English original, translated by Magdalena Holguín). *Art Nexus,* no. 10 (Sept – Dec 93), pp. 98 – 102. Il.

Argentina

Facio, Sara. Fotografía: la memoria cuestionada. *Cuadernos Hispanoamericanos,* no. 517 – 519 (July – Sept 93), pp. 269 – 279. Il.

Austria

Foreign influences

Hampe Martínez, Teodoro. VII Simposio Hispano – Austriaco "España, Austria e Iberoamérica, 1492 – 1992." *Anuario de Estudios Americanos,* v. 49, Suppl. 1 (1992), pp. 209 – 213.

Chile

Domínguez Díaz, Marta Silvia. El arte popular chileno. *SALALM Papers,* v. 34 (1989), pp. 9 – 16. Bibl.

Colombia

Merewether, Charles. Comunidad y continuidad: Doris Salcedo; nombrando la violencia (Accompanied by the English original, translated by Magdalena Holguín). *Art Nexus,* no. 9 (June – Aug 93), pp. 104 – 109. Bibl, il.

Cuba

Stern, Peter A. Art and the State in Post-Revolutionary Mexico and Cuba. *SALALM Papers,* v. 34 (1989), pp. 17 – 32. Bibl.

Latin America

Acha, Juan. El arte contemporáneo y la estética latinoamericana. *Plural (Mexico),* v. 22, no. 257 (Feb 93), pp. 60 – 67.

Foreign influences

Mosquera, Gerardo. Plástico afroamericana (Accompanied by an English translation). *Art Nexus,* no. 9 (June – Aug 93), pp. 100 – 102. Il.

Mexico

Zúñiga, Víctor. Promover el arte en una ciudad del norte de México: los proyectos artísticos en Monterrey, 1940 – 1960. *Estudios Sociológicos,* v. 11, no. 31 (Jan – Apr 93), pp. 155 – 181. Bibl, tables.

ART MUSEUMS

See
Museums

ART THEFTS

Meyer, Karl Ernest. *El saqueo del pasado: historia del tráfico internacional ilegal de obras de arte* translated by Roberto Ramón Reyes Mazzoni. Reviewed by Jorge Luján Muñoz. *Mesoamérica (USA),* v. 13, no. 24 (Dec 92), pp. 492 – 494.

Reynales, Trish. The Looting of the Royal Tombs of Sipán. *Latin American Art,* v. 5, no. 2 (Summer 93), pp. 50 – 52. Il.

ARTISANS

See also
   Handicraft

Colombia
Political activity

Sowell, David Lee. *The Early Colombian Labor Movement: Artisans and Politics in Bogotá, 1832 – 1919* reviewed by Jane M. Rausch. *Hispanic American Historical Review,* v. 73, no. 4 (Nov 93), pp. 715 – 716.

Guatemala

Dary Fuentes, Claudia. Los artesanos de la Nueva Guatemala de la Asunción, 1871 – 1898 (Photographs by Jorge Estuardo Molina L.). *La Tradición Popular,* no. 78 – 79 (1990), Issue. Bibl, il, tables, facs.

Dary Fuentes, Claudia and Aracely Esquivel. Los artesanos de la piedra: estudio sobre la cantería de San Luis Jilotepeque. *La Tradición Popular,* no. 85 (1991), Issue. Bibl, il.

Mexico

Jiménez López, Lexa. "Como la luna nos enseñó a tejer" (Translated by Ambar Past). *Artes de México,* no. 19 (Spring 93), pp. 40 – 41. Il.

Peru

Krüggeler, Thomas. Los artesanos del Cusco, la crisis regional y el régimen republicano, 1824 – 1869. *Siglo XIX: Revista,* no. 11, 2a época (Jan – June 92), pp. 111 – 148. Bibl, tables.

United States

Harris, Patricia and David Lyon. Memory's Persistence: The Living Art. *Américas,* v. 45, no. 6 (Nov – Dec 93), pp. 26 – 37. Il.

ARTISTS

See also
   Creation (Literary, artistic, etc.)
   Hispanic American artists (U.S.)
   Mexican American artists
   Mural painting and decoration
   Sculpture
   Women artists

Argentina

Jiménez, Carlos. Guillermo Kuitca, un pintor teatral (Accompanied by an English translation). *Art Nexus,* no. 9 (June – Aug 93), pp. 48 – 51. Il.

Un libro sobre Guillermo Kuitca reviewed by Ivonne Pini (Accompanied by an English translation). *Art Nexus,* no. 9 (June – Aug 93), p. 32. Il.

Perazzo, Nelly. Xul Solar: la imaginación desenfrenada (Accompanied by an English translation). *Art Nexus,* no. 8 (Apr – June 93), pp. 96 – 100. Il.

Pérez Celis. Through the Eyes of the Heart. *Américas,* v. 45, no. 2 (Mar – Apr 93), pp. 56 – 59. Il.

Brazil

Brenken, Anna. El artista Carybé de Salvador da Bahía (Translated by Mónica Perne). *Humboldt,* no. 109 (1993), pp. 70 – 75. Il.

Tieppo, Marcelo. Caderno de artista. *Vozes,* v. 87, no. 3 (May – June 93), pp. 83 – 84. Facs.

Pictorial works

Esteves, Juan. Ensaio fotográfico: portraits. *Vozes,* v. 87, no. 2 (Mar – Apr 93), pp. 76 – 83. Il.

Chile

Crumlish, Rebecca. Stepping into the Picture with Raimundo Rubio. *Américas,* v. 45, no. 1 (Jan – Feb 93), pp. 52 – 53. Il.

Tejada, Roberto. Carlos Arias: delirios de la figura. *Artes de México,* no. 20 (Summer 93), pp. 122 – 124. Il.

Valdés, Adriana. *Roser Bru* reviewed by Ivonne Pini (Accompanied by an English translation). *Art Nexus,* no. 7 (Jan – Mar 93), p. 41. Il.

Colombia

Acuña Cañas, Alonso. Semblanza del maestro Acuña. *Boletín de Historia y Antigüedades,* v. 80, no. 781 (Apr – June 93), pp. 357 – 358.

Gallo, Lylia. Evocación de Luis Alberto Acuña (1904 – 1993). *Boletín de Historia y Antigüedades,* v. 80, no. 781 (Apr – June 93), pp. 365 – 367.

Guevara, Roberto. Manuel Hernández: el espacio otro en la pintura. *Art Nexus,* no. 10 (Sept – Dec 93), pp. 92 – 95. Il.

Iriarte, María Elvira. Fernando Botero: la corrida (Accompanied by an English translation). *Art Nexus,* no. 9 (June – Aug 93), pp. 92 – 93. Il.

Medina Flórez, Enrique. Ante el féretro del maestro Acuña. *Boletín de Historia y Antigüedades,* v. 80, no. 781 (Apr – June 93), pp. 355 – 356.

Ocampo López, Javier. El maestro Luis Alberto Acuña y el nacionalismo artístico. *Boletín de Historia y Antigüedades,* v. 80, no. 781 (Apr – June 93), pp. 343 – 354.

Santa, Eduardo. Luis Alberto Acuña, pintor de América. *Boletín de Historia y Antigüedades,* v. 80, no. 781 (Apr – June 93), pp. 359 – 363.

Serrano, Eduardo. Acuña y el nacionalismo. *Boletín de Historia y Antigüedades,* v. 80, no. 781 (Apr – June 93), pp. 369 – 372.

Costa Rica

Chase, Alfonso. "Puertas abiertas": pasos a la pintura de José Luis López Escarré. *Káñina,* v. 16, no. 1 (Jan – June 92), pp. 225 – 227. Il.

Cuba

Blanc, Giulio V. Tomás Sánchez: obra reciente (Accompanied by the English original, translated by Magdalena Holguín). *Art Nexus,* no. 10 (Sept – Dec 93), pp. 51 – 53.

Goldman, Shifra M. La década crítica de la vanguardia cubana (Accompanied by the English original, translated by Ignacio Zuleta Lleras). *Art Nexus,* no. 7 (Jan – Mar 93), pp. 52 – 57. Bibl, il.

Mosquera, Gerardo. Tomás Sánchez: mística del paisaje (Accompanied by an English translation). *Art Nexus,* no. 10 (Sept – Dec 93), pp. 48 – 51. Il.

Dominican Republic

David, León. Tito Cánepa. *Latin American Art,* v. 4, no. 4 (Winter 92), pp. 69 – 71. Bibl, il.

Ecuador

Fernández Vilches, Antonio. Guayasamín y su visión del Nuevo Mundo. *Atenea (Chile),* no. 467 (1993), pp. 237 – 258. Il.

Europe

Tuchman, Maurice. *Parallel Visions: Modern Artists and Outsider Art* reviewed by Andrés Salgado R. (Accompanied by an English translation). *Art Nexus,* no. 9 (June – Aug 93), p. 33. Il.

France

Barnes, Julian. El fusilamiento de Maximiliano (Translated by Ana Becerril). *Nexos,* v. 16, no. 187 (July 93), pp. 39 – 47. Il.

Wilson-Bareau, Juliet. *Manet: 'The Execution of Maximilian'; Painting, Politics, and Censorship* reviewed by Paul J. Vanderwood. *Hispanic American Historical Review,* v. 73, no. 2 (May 93), p. 331.

Guatemala

Herner de Larrea, Irene. Carlos Mérida y la realidad auténtica. *Nexos,* v. 16, no. 182 (Feb 93), pp. 13 – 15. Il.

Ireland

Bayón, Damián Carlos. Francis Bacon en Buenos Aires. *Cuadernos Hispanoamericanos,* no. 510 (Dec 92), pp. 97 – 100. Il.

Latin America

Crónica (Brief reports on exhibits by Latin American artists throughout the world, accompanied by English translations). *Art Nexus,* no. 7 – 10 (1993), All issues. Il.

Goldman, Shifra M. Artistas latinoamericanos del siglo XX: MOMA (Accompanied by the English original, translated by Magalena Holguín). *Art Nexus,* no. 10 (Sept – Dec 93), pp. 84 – 89. Il.

Mosquera, Gerardo. Encuentros/Desplazamientos: arte conceptual y política; Luis Caminitzer, Alfredo Jaar y Cildo Meireles (Accompanied by an English translation). *Art Nexus,* no. 8 (Apr – June 93), pp. 88 – 91. Il.

Mexico

Agosín, Marjorie. A Dreamy Oaxacan Fantasy (Translated by Ruth Morales). *Américas,* v. 45, no. 6 (Nov – Dec 93), pp. 44 – 45. Il.

Azuela, Alicia. La presencia de Diego Rivera en los Estados Unidos: dos versiones de la historia. *Anales del Instituto de Investigaciones Estéticas,* v. 16, no. 62 (1991), pp. 175 – 180.

Blanco, Alberto. Manual de sología fantástica de Rodolfo Nieto. *Vuelta,* v. 17, no. 200 (July 93), pp. 80 – 82.

— La música de la retina. *Nexos,* v. 16, no. 192 (Dec 93), pp. 9 – 15.

Blas Galindo, Carlos. *Enrique Guzmán, transformador y víctima* reviewed by José Manuel Springer (Accompanied by an English translation). *Art Nexus,* no. 10 (Sept – Dec 93), p. 41. Il.

Conde, Teresa del. Diálogo con Roberto Parodi. *Plural (Mexico),* v. 22, no. 257 (Feb 93), p. 45.

Cuevas, José Luis. Roberto Parodi, transvanguardista. *Plural (Mexico),* v. 22, no. 257 (Feb 93), pp. 41 – 44. Il.

Gómez Haro, Germaine. Krzysztof Augustín: la pintura; poesía silenciosa. *Artes de México,* no. 19 (Spring 93), pp. 98 – 99. Il.

Herner de Larrea, Irene. Erika Billeter y el arte mexicano en Europa. *Nexos,* v. 16, no. 183 (Mar 93), pp. 10 – 12. Il.

Labastida, Jaime. De la serenidad (Includes reproductions of *Chalma, La bruma, Tlalmanalco, Iztaccíhuatl, Xilitla, San Luis Potosí,* and *La recua, Xochitlán, Puebla). Plural (Mexico),* v. 22, no. 262 (July 93), pp. 40 – 45. Il.

Lara de la Fuente, Leonor. Arturo Rivera: una pasión renacentista. *Artes de México,* no. 21 (Fall 93), pp. 100 – 101.

León González, Francisco. Entrevista con Juan Soriano. *Artes de México,* no. 19 (Spring 93), pp. 104 – 105. Il.

Martínez Duarte, Margarita. Los hombres – instrumento de "Guardaes de los ídolos." *Plural (Mexico),* v. 22, no. 263 (Aug 93), p. 68.

Martínez Quijano, Ana. El mítico mural de Siqueiros en la Argentina (Accompanied by an English translation). *Art Nexus,* no. 9 (June – Aug 93), pp. 110 – 112. Il.

Moreno Toscano, Alejandra. López Castro y la función del sol. *Nexos,* v. 16, no. 188 (Aug 93), pp. 8 – 10.

Nieto, Margarita. Vladimir Cora. *Latin American Art,* v. 4, no. 4 (Winter 92), pp. 80 – 81. Il.

Ortiz Flores, Carlos Iván. Efraín Castro: "Revisión de lo invisible." *Nexos,* v. 16, no. 185 (May 93), pp. 86 – 87. Il.

Pitol, Sergio. Julio Galán: la lección del sí y el no. *Vuelta,* v. 17, no. 204 (Nov 93), pp. 21 – 25.

Ramírez, Fermín. José Luis Cuevas, ave de tempestades. *Plural (Mexico),* v. 22, no. 265 (Oct 93), pp. 42 – 48. Il.

— Moreno Capdevila, un boceto vespertino (Includes reproductions by the artist). *Plural (Mexico),* v. 22, no. 264 (Sept 93), pp. 66 – 75. Il.

— El paisaje de Jesús Martínez. *Plural (Mexico),* v. 22, no. 261 (June 93), pp. 48 – 54. Il.

Rebollar, Juan L. Jorge Rosano: una aseveración plástica sin alardes. *Artes de México,* no. 19 (Spring 93), p. 117. Il.

Rivera, José María. Aarón Cruz: el laberinto en el universo. *Plural (Mexico),* v. 22, no. 263 (Aug 93), pp. 40 – 45. Il.

Rocha, Paulina. Huellas del humo: Gerardo Lartigue. *Artes de México,* no. 18 (Winter 92), p. 97. Il.

Samperio, Guillermo. Libertad y sujeción en Sigfrido Walter Aguilar. *Artes de México,* no. 20 (Summer 93), pp. 120 – 121. Il.

Law and legislation

Benavides, Pedro. "Declarándome por exento y libre de pagar la dicha alcabala." *Vuelta,* v. 17, no. 196 (Mar 93), pp. 38 – 39.

MacDonald, Christine. Artists against Taxes. *Business Mexico,* v. 3, no. 4 (Apr 93), p. 44.

Zaid, Gabriel. Razones para la exención. *Vuelta,* v. 17, no. 196 (Mar 93), pp. 43 – 47.

Sources

Batista, Marta Rossetti. Da passagem meteórica de Siqueiros pelo Brasil, 1933 (Includes reproductions of a text and an interview published in 1933 – 1934 after the artist's visit to Brazil). *Vozes,* v. 86, no. 5 (Sept – Oct 92), pp. 81 – 94. Il.

Peru

Cisneros, Luis Jaime. De Atahualpa al Museo de la Nación: entrevista a Fernando de Szyszlo. *Debate (Peru),* v. 16, no. 75 (Dec 93 – Jan 94), pp. 70 – 73. Il.

Switzerland

Young, Richard A. "Verano" de Julio Cortázar, *The Nightmare* de John Henry Fuseli y "the judicious adoption of figures in art." *Revista Canadiense de Estudios Hispánicos,* v. 17, no. 2 (Winter 93), pp. 373 – 382. Bibl.

United States

Butler, Ron. The Colors between Earth and Sky. *Américas,* v. 45, no. 2 (Mar – Apr 93), pp. 14 – 21. Il.

Uruguay

Haber, Alicia. Carlos Capelán: una formulación antropológica (Accompanied by an English translation). *Art Nexus,* no. 7 (Jan – Mar 93), pp. 92 – 96. Bibl, il.

Palomero, Federica. Ignacio Iturria (Accompanied by an English translation). *Art Nexus,* no. 7 (Jan – Mar 93), pp. 88 – 90. Il.

Pérez Oramas, Luis. José Gamarra: después del Edén (Accompanied by an English translation). *Art Nexus,* no. 8 (Apr – June 93), pp. 92 – 94. Il.

Rosso, Walter Betbeder. Alberto Schunk: A Canvas for Contemplation (Translated by Kathleen Forrester). *Américas,* v. 45, no. 4 (July – Aug 93), pp. 54 – 55. Il.

Venezuela

Amor E., Mónica. Meyer Vaisman, explorador de significados (Accompanied by an English translation). *Art Nexus,* no. 7 (Jan – Mar 93), pp. 129 – 131. Il.

Arocha Vargas, Arnaldo. Acto de presentación de los libros *José Antonio Páez* y *Cristóbal Rojas, un pintor venezolano,* pertenecientes a la Biblioteca de Autores y Temas Mirandinos. *Boletín de la Academia Nacional de la Historia (Venezuela),* v. 75, no. 299 (July – Sept 92), pp. 5 – 8.

Calzadilla, Juan. Angel Peña: el calmo y brillante acontecer del trópico. *Revista Nacional de Cultura (Venezuela),* v. 54, no. 287 (Oct – Dec 92), pp. 157 – 160.

— El Círculo de Bellas Artes y los paisajistas de la luz, 1912 – 1992. *Revista Nacional de Cultura (Venezuela),* v. 53, no. 286 (July – Sept 92), pp. 95 – 105. Il.

— Marcos Castillo o cómo rehacer la naturaleza en el taller. *Revista Nacional de Cultura (Venezuela),* v. 53, no. 285 (Apr – June 92), pp. 219 – 223. Il.

Medina, Alvaro. Milton Becerra: piedras atadas y geometría desatada (Accompanied by an English translation). *Art Nexus,* no. 8 (Apr – June 93), pp. 64 – 68. Il.

Rodríguez, Antonio. Milton Becerra, la voz milenaria del hombre (Accompanied by an English translation). *Art Nexus,* no. 8 (Apr – June 93), pp. 68 – 70. Il.

Sichel, Berta. Carlos Zerpa. *Latin American Art,* v. 5, no. 2 (Summer 93), pp. 33 – 35. Bibl, il.

Viloria Vera, Enrique. *Ender Cepeda: la recreación de una identidad* reviewed by María Clara Martínez R. (Accompanied by an English translation). *Art Nexus,* no. 8 (Apr – June 93), p. 33. Il.

ASEAN

See

Association of South East Asian Nations

ASHÁNINKA INDIANS

See
Campa Indians

ASIA

See also
China
Foreign trade promotion – Asia
Hinduism
Human capital – Asia
Islam
Korea
Labor supply – Asia
Philippine Islands

Choi, Dae Won. Las nuevas relaciones económicas entre los "tigres" asiáticos y América Latina. *Comercio Exterior,* v. 43, no. 5 (May 93), pp. 457 – 462. Tables.

Dijck, Pitou van. The Empty Box Syndrome. *CEPAL Review,* no. 47 (Aug 92), pp. 21 – 36. Bibl, tables, charts.

Lande, Stephen. Think Globally, Trade Locally. *Business Mexico,* v. 3, no. 11 (Nov 93), pp. 8 – 11.

ASOCIACIÓN LATINOAMERICANA DE INTEGRACIÓN

See
Latin American Integration Association

ASPE ARMELLA, PEDRO

"Realista y prudente" la propuesta fiscal para 1994: Pedro Aspe. *Fem,* v. 17, no. 130 (Dec 93), p. 48. Il.

ASSIMILATION

See
Acculturation

ASSOCIATION OF AMERICAN CHAMBERS OF COMMERCE IN LATIN AMERICA

Congresses

Cohen, Joshua A. and Joel Russell. A New Dynamic in the Americas. *Business Mexico,* v. 3, no. 12 (Dec 93), pp. 43 – 45. Il.

ASSOCIATION OF SOUTH EAST ASIAN NATIONS

Byé, Pascal and Jean-Pierre Frey. Le modèle chilien à la lumière de l'expérience des pays agro-exportateurs de l'ASEAN. *Cahiers des Amériques Latines,* no. 14 (1992), pp. 37 – 49. Bibl, tables.

ASTORGA, FRANCISCO

Huneeus, Virginia. Un auténtico poeta popular. *Mensaje,* v. 42, no. 416 (Jan – Feb 93), pp. 49 – 50. Il.

ASTRONOMY

See
Subdivision *Astronomy* under names of Indian groups

ASTURIAS, MIGUEL ANGEL

Criticism of specific works

Sábado de gloria

Taracena Arriola, Arturo. *Sábado de gloria:* fuente literaria de *El señor presidente. Studi di Letteratura Ispano-Americana,* v. 24 (1993), pp. 37 – 46.

El señor presidente

Taracena Arriola, Arturo. *Sábado de gloria:* fuente literaria de *El señor presidente. Studi di Letteratura Ispano-Americana,* v. 24 (1993), pp. 37 – 46.

Week-end en Guatemala

Arguedas Chaverri, María Eugenia. Week-end en Guatemala. *Káñina,* v. 16, no. 1 (Jan – June 92), pp. 53 – 59. Bibl.

ASTURIAS, SPAIN

Díaz-Jove Blanco, Santiago. *Gijoneses en Indias: notas sobre emigración e índice geobiográfico* reviewed by José Ramón García López. *Revista de Indias,* v. 53, no. 197 (Jan – Apr 93), pp. 102 – 103.

ATACAMA, CHILE

Zapata, Francisco. *Atacama: desierto de la discordia; minería y política internacional en Bolivia, Chile y Perú* reviewed by Andrea Ostrov. *La Educación (USA),* v. 37, no. 114 (1993), pp. 175 – 176.

ATAHUALPA, INCA OF PERU

Benso, Silvia. Il silenzio e la voce di Atahualpa. *Quaderni Ibero-Americani,* no. 72 (Dec 92), pp. 649 – 660. Bibl.

Bermúdez-Gallegos, Marta. Oralidad y escritura: Atahualpa; ¿Traidor or traicionado? *Revista de Crítica Literaria Latinoamericana,* v. 19, no. 38 (July – Dec 93), pp. 331 – 344. Bibl.

Huhle, Rainer. El terremoto de Cajamarca: la derrota del Inca en la memoria colectiva; elementos para un análisis de la resistencia cultural de los pueblos andinos. *Ibero-Amerikanisches Archiv,* v. 18, no. 3 – 4 (1992), pp. 387 – 426. Il, facs.

Oleszkiewicz, Malgorzata. El ciclo de la muerte de Atahualpa: de la fiesta popular a la representación teatral. *Allpanchis,* v. 23, no. 39 (Jan – June 92), pp. 185 – 220. Bibl.

ATAHUALPA, JUAN SANTOS

Mateos Fernández-Maquieira, B. Sara. Juan Santos Atahualpa: un movimiento milenarista en la selva. *Amazonía Peruana,* v. 11, no. 22 (Oct 92), pp. 47 – 60. Bibl.

Regan, Jaime. En torno a la entrevista de los jesuitas con Juan Santos Atahualpa. *Amazonía Peruana,* v. 11, no. 22 (Oct 92), pp. 61 – 92. Bibl, maps.

ATHLETES

See
Sports

ATLASES

See also
Subdivision *Maps* under names of specific countries

Sources

Binková, Simona and Katerina Kozická. El dominio marítimo español en los materiales cartográficos y náuticos de Praga. *Anuario de Estudios Americanos,* v. 49, Suppl. 1 (1992), pp. 47 – 54. Bibl, maps.

Mexico

Lope Blanch, Juan M., ed. *Atlas lingüístico de México, vol. 1: Fonética* reviewed by Klaus Zimmermann. *Iberoamericana,* v. 16, no. 47 – 48 (1992), pp. 111 – 112.

ATOMIC POWER INDUSTRY

Mexico

Johnson, Jessica. Whatever Happened to Laguna Verde? *Business Mexico,* v. 3, no. 5 (May 93), pp. 20 – 22. Il.

ATOMIC WEAPONS AND DISARMAMENT

Leventhal, Paul L. and Sharon Tanzer, eds. *Averting a Latin American Nuclear Arms Race: New Prospects and Challenges for Argentine – Brazil Nuclear Cooperation* reviewed by Mónica Serrano. *Journal of Latin American Studies,* v. 25, no. 2 (May 93), pp. 426 – 429.

Wrobel, Paulo S. Aspectos da política externa independente: a questão do desarmamento e o caso de Cuba (Translated by Dora Rocha). *Estudos Históricos,* v. 6, no. 12 (July – Dec 93), pp. 191 – 209. Bibl.

AUDIOVISUAL EDUCATION

See also
Educational technology
Tape recorders and recordings
Video tape recorders and recording

Bibliography

Milstein, Renée and Richard A. Raschio. Bibliografía anotada de logicales, videodiscos y discos compactos para la enseñanza del español o para el uso en cursos bilingües. *Hispania (USA),* v. 76, no. 4 (Dec 93), pp. 683 – 720.

Latin America

Río Reynaga, Julio del. Desarrollo y tendencias de la enseñanza en comunicación colectiva. *Revista Mexicana de Ciencias Políticas y Sociales,* v. 37, Nueva época, no. 149 (July – Sept 92), pp. 153 – 176. Bibl.

AUGUSTÍN, KRZYSZTOF

Gómez Haro, Germaine. Krzysztof Augustín: la pintura; poesía silenciosa. *Artes de México,* no. 19 (Spring 93), pp. 98 – 99. Il.

AUGUSTINIANS

Venezuela

Campo del Pozo, Fernando. Los mártires agustinos en la misión de Aricagua, Venezuela. *Boletín de la Academia Nacional de la Historia (Venezuela),* v. 76, no. 302 (Apr – June 93), pp. 119 – 129. Bibl.

AUSTRALIA

Cabrera Infante, Guillermo. Alice in Wondercontinent (Translated by Alfred MacAdam). *Review,* no. 47 (Fall 93), pp. 14 – 15.

AUSTRIA

See also
 Archives – Austria
 Art and society – Austria
 Exiles – Austria

Anderle, Adám and Monika Kozári. Koloman von Kánya: Ein österreichisch-ungarischer Botschafter in Mexiko. *Zeitschrift für Lateinamerika Wien,* no. 43 (1992), pp. 63 – 80. Bibl.

Silva, Geraldo Eulálio do Nascimento e. As relações diplomáticas entre o Brasil e a Austria. *Revista do Instituto Histórico e Geográfico Brasileiro,* no. 372 (July – Sept 91), pp. 665 – 676.

Winkelbauer, Waltraud. Osterreich-Ungarns Handelsvertragsprojekte mit Lateinamerika nach 1870. *Zeitschrift für Lateinamerika Wien,* no. 43 (1992), pp. 7 – 62. Bibl.

Congresses

Hampe Martínez, Teodoro. VII Simposio Hispano – Austriaco "España, Austria e Iberoamérica, 1492 – 1992." *Anuario de Estudios Americanos,* v. 49, Suppl. 1 (1992), pp. 209 – 213.

AUTHORITARIANISM

See also
 Corporate state
 Dictators
 Fascism
 Military in government

Argentina

Rock, David P. *La Argentina autoritaria: los nacionalistas; su historia y su influencia en la vida pública* reviewed by Rosana Guber (Review entitled "Bandos y trincheras"). *Desarrollo Económico (Argentina),* v. 33, no. 131 (Oct – Dec 93), pp. 453 – 456. Bibl.

— *Authoritarian Argentina: The Nationalist Movement; Its History, and Its Impact* reviewed by Jeremy Adelman. *Hispanic American Historical Review,* v. 73, no. 4 (Nov 93), pp. 705 – 706.

Chile

Drake, Paul Winter and Ivan Jaksic, eds. *The Struggle for Democracy in Chile, 1982 – 1990* reviewed by Tom Wright. *The Americas,* v. 49, no. 4 (Apr 93), pp. 568 – 569.

— *The Struggle for Democracy in Chile, 1982 – 1990* reviewed by Robert H. Dix. *Journal of Developing Areas,* v. 28, no. 1 (Oct 93), pp. 115 – 116.

Lowden, Pamela. The Ecumenical Committee for Peace in Chile, 1973 – 1975: The Foundation of Moral Opposition to Authoritarian Rule in Chile. *Bulletin of Latin American Research,* v. 12, no. 2 (May 93), pp. 189 – 203. Bibl.

Tironi B., Eugenio. *Autoritarismo, modernización y marginalidad: el caso de Chile* reviewed by Felipe Cabello (Review entitled "Don Andrés Bello: iCon cuánta nostalgia lo recordamos y cuánta falta nos hace!"). *Interciencia,* v. 18, no. 6 (Nov – Dec 93), pp. 329 – 333.

Latin America

Sznajder, Mario. Legitimidad y poder políticos frente a las herencias autoritarias: transición y consolidación democrática en América Latina. *Estudios Interdisciplinarios de América Latina y el Caribe,* v. 4, no. 1 (Jan – June 93), pp. 27 – 55. Bibl.

AUTHORS

See also
 Copyright
 Creation (Literary, artistic, etc.)
 Poets
 Women authors

Interviews

Costa, Marithelma and Adelaida López. *Las dos caras de la escritura* reviewed by Gustavo Fares. *Revista Iberoamericana,* v. 59, no. 162 – 163 (Jan – June 93), pp. 380 – 382.

Brazil

Guzik, Alberto. Un ejercicio de la memoria: dramaturgia de los '80. *Conjunto,* no. 93 (Jan – June 93), pp. 8 – 12. Il.

Caribbean area
Bibliography

Fenwick, Mary Jane. *Writers of the Caribbean and Central America: A Bibliography* reviewed by Richard D. Woods. *Hispania (USA),* v. 76, no. 4 (Dec 93), pp. 734 – 735.

Central America
Bibliography

Fenwick, Mary Jane. *Writers of the Caribbean and Central America: A Bibliography* reviewed by Richard D. Woods. *Hispania (USA),* v. 76, no. 4 (Dec 93), pp. 734 – 735.

Cuba
Interviews

Bejel, Emilio F. *Escribir en Cuba: entrevistas con escritores cubanos, 1979 – 1989* reviewed by José Otero. *Chasqui,* v. 22, no. 1 (May 93), pp. 104 – 105.

— *Escribir en Cuba: entrevistas con escritores cubanos, 1979 – 1989* reviewed by William Luis. *Cuban Studies/ Estudios Cubanos,* v. 23 (1993), pp. 228 – 231.

— *Escribir en Cuba: entrevistas con escritores cubanos, 1979 – 1989* reviewed by Antonio Lobos. *Revista Chilena de Literatura,* no. 40 (Nov 92), pp. 161 – 162.

Latin America
Biobibliography

Flores, Angel. *Spanish American Authors: The Twentieth Century* reviewed by Barbara Mujica (Review entitled "Wanderers and References"). *Américas,* v. 45, no. 2 (Mar – Apr 93), p. 63.

— *Spanish American Authors: The Twentieth Century* reviewed by Warren L. Meinhardt. *Chasqui,* v. 22, no. 1 (May 93), pp. 101 – 102.

— *Spanish American Authors: The Twentieth Century* reviewed by David William Foster. *Chasqui,* v. 22, no. 1 (May 93), pp. 82 – 83.

Interviews

Espacios y fronteras del texto en América Latina. *Conjunto,* no. 93 (Jan – June 93), pp. 101 – 112. Il.

Mexico
Law and legislation

Aspe Armella, Pedro and Gabriel Zaid. De la esquina. *Vuelta,* v. 17, no. 197 (Apr 93), pp. 82 – 84.

MacDonald, Christine. Artists against Taxes. *Business Mexico,* v. 3, no. 4 (Apr 93), p. 44.

Zaid, Gabriel. Razones para la exención. *Vuelta,* v. 17, no. 196 (Mar 93), pp. 43 – 47.

Southern Cone of South America
Congresses

Staudacher, Cornelia. Autores de Río de la Plata en la Casa de Culturas del Mundo (Translated by José Luis Gómez y Patiño). *Humboldt,* no. 110 (1993), p. 96. Il.

AUTOBIOGRAPHY

See
 Biography (as a literary form)

AUTOMATION

See also
Computer industry
Information services
Information technology

Serrano, Juan F. Computer Acquisition Policy. *Business Mexico*, v. 3, no. 9 (Sept 93), pp. 7 – 8.

Brazil

Frischtak, Claudio R. Automação bancária e mudança na produtividade: a experiência brasileira. *Pesquisa e Planejamento Econômico*, v. 22, no. 2 (Aug 92), pp. 197 – 239. Bibl, tables.

AUTOMOBILE INDUSTRY AND TRADE

America

Womack, James P. Awaiting NAFTA. *Business Mexico*, v. 3, no. 4 (Apr 93), pp. 4 – 7. Il.

Brazil

Andando em círculos. *Problemas Brasileiros*, v. 30, no. 295 (Jan – Feb 93), pp. 32 – 34. Il, charts.

Bedê, Marco Aurélio. Evolução tecnológica na indústria de autopeças: resultados de estudos de caso. *Estudos Econômicos*, v. 22, no. 3 (Sept – Dec 92), pp. 409 – 428. Bibl, tables, charts.

Buarque de Hollanda Filho, Sérgio. A crise da indústria automobilística brasileira sob a perspectiva da evolução mundial do setor. *Estudos Econômicos*, v. 23, no. 1 (Jan – Apr 93), pp. 67 – 124. Bibl, tables.

Corrêa, Henrique Luiz. Flexibilidade nos sistemas de produção. *RAE; Revista de Administração de Empresas*, v. 33, no. 3 (May – June 93), pp. 22 – 35. Bibl.

Chile

Autopartes y vehículos: oportunidades en el mercado chileno. *Comercio Exterior*, v. 43, no. 10 (Oct 93), pp. 925 – 926. Tables.

Great Britain

Corrêa, Henrique Luiz. Flexibilidade nos sistemas de produção. *RAE; Revista de Administração de Empresas*, v. 33, no. 3 (May – June 93), pp. 22 – 35. Bibl.

Mexico

Guzmán Pineda, Jesús Ignacio. Industria automotriz y medio ambiente. *El Cotidiano*, v. 8, no. 52 (Jan – Feb 93), pp. 70 – 75. Il.

Herrera Lima, Fernando Francisco. Dina: del enfrentamiento a la negociación. *El Cotidiano*, v. 9, no. 56 (July 93), pp. 69 – 73. Il.

Herrera Toledano, Salvador. Strategies for a Dynamic Market. *Business Mexico*, v. 3, no. 4 (Apr 93), pp. 11 – 14. Il.

Lazaroff, León. Auto Workers Seek Quality Wages. *Business Mexico*, v. 3, no. 4 (Apr 93), pp. 20 – 21 +. Il.

Méndez, Luis and José Othón Quiroz Trejo. El conflicto de la Volkswagen: crónica de una muerte inesperada. *El Cotidiano*, v. 8, no. 51 (Nov – Dec 92), pp. 81 – 94. Bibl, il, tables, charts.

Paxman, Andrew. Truck Market Picks Up. *Business Mexico*, v. 3, no. 4 (Apr 93), pp. 8 – 10. Tables.

Sotomayor Yalán, Maritza. La producción automotriz en México y el Tratado de Libre Comercio México – Estados Unidos – Canadá. *Frontera Norte*, v. 4, no. 8 (July – Dec 92), pp. 165 – 172.

Werner, Johannes. Plastics Mold into Auto Boom. *Business Mexico*, v. 3, no. 4 (Apr 93), pp. 16 – 19.

AVANZA, JULIO CÉSAR

Ciarnello, Nicolás. *Julio César Avanza: un homenaje demorado* reviewed by F. L. *Todo Es Historia*, v. 27, no. 311 (June 93), p. 60. Il.

AVÉ LALLEMANT, GERMÁN

Chávez, Fermín. Un marxista alemán en San Luis. *Todo Es Historia*, v. 26, no. 310 (May 93), pp. 48 – 52. Il.

AVIATION

See
Airplane industry and trade

AVILA, SILVIA MERCEDES

Obituaries

Colaboraciones póstumas. *Signo*, no. 35, Nueva época (Jan – Apr 92), p. 157.

AVILA C., JOSÉ A.

Obituaries

Sánchez Fuentes, Porfirio. Recordando a José Avila. *Revista Cultural Lotería*, v. 51, no. 387 (Feb 92), pp. 72 – 75.

AVILA MARTEL, ALAMIRO DE

Obituaries

Guzmán Brito, Alejandro. Don Alamiro de Avila Martel. *Boletín de la Academia Chilena de la Historia*, v. 58 – 59, no. 102 (1991 – 1992), pp. 25 – 32.

AWARDS

See
Decorations of honor
Literary prizes
Subdivision *Awards* under specific names and topics

AYACUCHO, BATTLE OF, 1824

Martínez G., Miguel A. Ayacucho. *Boletín de la Academia Nacional de la Historia (Venezuela)*, v. 75, no. 298 (Apr – June 92), pp. 90 – 93.

AYACUCHO, PERU (DEPARTMENT)

Gamarra, Jefrey. Estado, modernidad y sociedad regional: Ayacucho, 1920 – 1940. *Apuntes (Peru)*, no. 31 (July – Dec 92), pp. 103 – 114. Bibl.

AYLLUS

See also
Agriculture, Cooperative

Salazar Mostajo, Carlos. La *"Taika"*: teoría y práctica de la escuela – *ayllu* reviewed by Carlos Coello Vila. *Signo*, no. 38, Nueva época (Jan – Apr 93), pp. 256 – 257.

AYLWIN AZÓCAR, ANDRÉS

Verdugo, Patricia. Andrés Aylwin: "Hay situaciones que claman a Dios." *Mensaje*, v. 42, no. 421 (Aug 93), pp. 382 – 383. Il.

AYLWIN AZÓCAR, PATRICIO

Infante Caffi, María Teresa and Manfred Wilhelmy von Wolff. La política exterior chilena en los años '90: el gobierno del presidente Aylwin y algunas proyecciones. *Estudios Sociales (Chile)*, no. 75 (Jan – Mar 93), pp. 97 – 112.

Rabkin, Rhoda Pearl. The Aylwin Government and "Tutelary" Democracy: A Concept in Search of a Case? *Journal of Inter-American Studies and World Affairs*, v. 34, no. 4 (Winter 92 – 93), pp. 119 – 194. Bibl, tables.

Rehren, Alfredo J. La presidencia en el gobierno de la concertación. *Estudios Sociales (Chile)*, no. 75 (Jan – Mar 93), pp. 15 – 38. Bibl.

AYMARA INDIANS

Albó, Xavier. Bolivia: La Paz/Chukiyawu; las dos caras de una ciudad. *América Indígena*, v. 51, no. 4 (Oct – Dec 91), pp. 107 – 158. Bibl, tables, maps.

Albó, Xavier and Matías Preiswerk. El Gran Poder: fiesta del aimara urbano. *América Indígena*, v. 51, no. 2 – 3 (Apr – Sept 91), pp. 293 – 352. Bibl, tables, maps.

Arnold, Denise Y. et al. *Hacia un orden andino de las cosas: tres pistas de los Andes meridionales* reviewed by Jan Szeminski. *Estudios Interdisciplinarios de América Latina y el Caribe*, v. 4, no. 1 (Jan – June 93), pp. 175 – 176.

— *Hacia un orden andino de las cosas: tres pistas de los Andes meridionales* reviewed by Javier Albó. *Signo*, no. 38, Nueva época (Jan – Apr 93), pp. 220 – 224.

Encinas Cueto, Ives and Wigberto Rivero Pinto. La presencia aimara en la ciudad de La Paz: Chuquiyawu Marka; entre la participación y la sobrevivencia. *América Indígena*, v. 51, no. 2 – 3 (Apr – Sept 91), pp. 273 – 292.

Irurozqui Victoriano, Marta. La guerra de razas en Bolivia: la (re)invención de una tradición. *Revista Andina,* v. 11, no. 1 (July 93), pp. 163 – 200. Bibl.

Kessel, Juan J. M. M. van. El pago a la tierra: porque el desarrollo lo exige. *Allpanchis,* v. 23, no. 40 (July – Dec 92), pp. 201 – 217. Bibl.

Langevin, André. Las zampoñas del conjunto de kantu y el debate sobre la función de la segunda hilera de tubos: datos etnográficos y análisis semiótico. *Revista Andina,* v. 10, no. 2 (Dec 92), pp. 405 – 440. Bibl, tables.

Música autóctona del norte de Potosí reviewed by Honoria Arredondo Calderón. *Revista Musical Chilena,* v. 46, no. 178 (July – Dec 92), pp. 127 – 128.

Valle de Siles, María Eugenia del. *Historia de la rebelión de Tupac Catari, 1781 – 1782* reviewed by Marie-Danielle Démelas-Bohy. *Caravelle,* no. 59 (1992), pp. 249 – 253.

AZAMBUJA, MARCOS CASTRIOTO DE

Scarabôtolo, Hélio Antônio. Saudação ao honorário Marcos Castrioto de Azambuja (Speech given in honor of Marcos Azambuja's induction into the Instituto Histórico e Geográfico Brasileiro). *Revista do Instituto Histórico e Geográfico Brasileiro,* no. 371 (Apr – June 91), pp. 489 – 491.

AZEVEDO, ALUÍZIO

Criticism of specific works

Philomena Borges

Ribeiro, Luís Filipe. O sexo e o poder no império: *Philomena Borges. Luso-Brazilian Review,* v. 30, no. 1 (Summer 93), pp. 7 – 20. Bibl.

AZEVEDO, LUIZ HEITOR CORRÊA DE

See
Corrêa de Azevedo, Luiz Heitor

AZOFEIFA, ISAAC FELIPE

Criticism of specific works

Vigilia en pie de muerte

Herra, Mayra. *Vigilia en pie de muerte:* una lectura. *Káñina,* v. 16, no. 1 (Jan – June 92), pp. 23 – 28. Bibl.

AZORÍN

See
Martínez Ruiz, José

AZTEC LANGUAGE

See
Nahuatl language

AZTEC LITERATURE

See
Nahuatl literature

AZTECS

See also
Nahuas

Commerce

Berdan, Frances F. Economic Dimensions of Precious Metals, Stones, and Feathers: The Aztec State Society. *Estudios de Cultura Náhuatl,* v. 22 (1992), pp. 291 – 323. Bibl, tables, maps.

Mathematical models

Cowgill, George L. Comments on Andrew Sluyter: "Long Distance Staple Transport in Western Mesoamerica; Insights through Quantitative Modeling." *Ancient Mesoamerica,* v. 4, no. 2 (Fall 93), pp. 201 – 203. Bibl.

Sluyter, Andrew. Long-Distance Staple Transport in Western Mesoamerica: Insights through Quantitative Modeling. *Ancient Mesoamerica,* v. 4, no. 2 (Fall 93), pp. 193 – 199. Bibl, tables, maps, charts.

Costume and adornment

Otis Charlton, Cynthia L. Obsidian as Jewelry: Lapidary Production in Aztec Otumba, Mexico. *Ancient Mesoamerica,* v. 4, no. 2 (Fall 93), pp. 231 – 243. Bibl, il, tables, maps.

Culture

León-Portilla, Miguel. *The Aztec Image of Self and Society: An Introduction to Nahua Culture* reviewed by Frances Karttunen. *Latin American Indian Literatures Journal,* v. 9, no. 1 (Spring 93), pp. 85 – 92.

— *The Aztec Image of Self and Society,* a translation of *Los antiguos mexicanos a través de sus crónicas y cantares* edited by José Jorge Klor de Alva. Reviewed by Inga Clendinnen. *Hispanic American Historical Review,* v. 73, no. 1 (Feb 93), pp. 142 – 143.

Olmos, Andrés de. *Tratado de hechicerías y sortilegios* edited and translated by Georges Baudot. Reviewed by Jacqueline de Durand-Forest. *Caravelle,* no. 59 (1992), pp. 300 – 302.

Food

Cowgill, George L. Comments on Andrew Sluyter: "Long Distance Staple Transport in Western Mesoamerica; Insights through Quantitative Modeling." *Ancient Mesoamerica,* v. 4, no. 2 (Fall 93), pp. 201 – 203. Bibl.

Sluyter, Andrew. Long-Distance Staple Transport in Western Mesoamerica: Insights through Quantitative Modeling. *Ancient Mesoamerica,* v. 4, no. 2 (Fall 93), pp. 193 – 199. Bibl, tables, maps, charts.

History

Carrasco, David and Eduardo Matos Moctezuma. *Moctezuma's México: Visions of the Aztec World* reviewed by James N. Corbridge, Jr. *La Educación (USA),* v. 37, no. 115 (1993), pp. 413 – 414.

Gillespie, Susan D. *The Aztec Kings: The Construction of Rulership in Mexica History* reviewed by Frances Karttunen. *Latin American Indian Literatures Journal,* v. 9, no. 1 (Spring 93), pp. 85 – 92.

Townsend, Richard F. *The Aztecs* reviewed by Arturo Dell'Acqua. *Colonial Latin American Historical Review,* v. 1, no. 1 (Fall 92), pp. 127 – 128.

— *The Aztecs* reviewed by Susan Toby Evans. *Hispanic American Historical Review,* v. 73, no. 4 (Nov 93), pp. 680 – 681.

Sources

Baudot, Georges and Tzvetan Todorov. *Récits aztèques de la conquête* reviewed by Guilhem Olivier. *Caravelle,* no. 59 (1992), pp. 241 – 249.

Legends

Cordero López, Rodolfo. Leyenda de Ahuejote (Accompanied by an English translation). *Artes de México,* no. 20 (Summer 93), pp. 48 – 49. Il.

Graulich, Michel. Las brujas de las peregrinaciones aztecas. *Estudios de Cultura Náhuatl,* v. 22 (1992), pp. 87 – 98. Bibl.

Pottery

Hodge, Mary G. et al. Black-on-Orange Ceramic Production in the Aztec Empire's Heartland. *Latin American Antiquity,* v. 4, no. 2 (June 93), pp. 130 – 157. Bibl, il, tables, maps.

Taube, Karl Andreas. The Bilimek Pulque Vessel: Starlore, Calendrics, and Cosmology of Late Postclassic Central Mexico. *Ancient Mesoamerica,* v. 4, no. 1 (Spring 93), pp. 1 – 15. Bibl, il.

Religion and mythology

Bellini, Giuseppe. Il dramma del mondo azteca e i "Dodici Apostoli." *Quaderni Ibero-Americani,* no. 72 (Dec 92), pp. 640 – 648. Bibl.

Carrasco, David, ed. *To Change Place: Aztec Ceremonial Landscapes* reviewed by Michael E. Smith. *Latin American Antiquity,* v. 4, no. 2 (June 93), p. 200.

Covarrubias, Javier. La tecnología del sacrificio: la idea del "calor" y otros mitos encontrados. *Plural (Mexico),* v. 22, no. 258 (Mar 93), pp. 18 – 28. Bibl.

González de Guebara, Ruby Cecilia. El mito y su influencia en la sociedad actual. *Revista Cultural Lotería,* v. 51, no. 388 (Mar – Apr 92), pp. 85 – 92.

Hassler, Peter. *Menschenopfer bei den Azteken?: Eine quellen- und ideologiekritische Studie* reviewed by Norbert Rehrmann. *Iberoamericana,* v. 17, no. 49 (1993), pp. 95 – 96.

Kendall, Jonathan. The Thirteen Volatiles: Representation and Symbolism. *Estudios de Cultura Náhuatl,* v. 22 (1992), pp. 99 – 131. Bibl.

Taube, Karl Andreas. The Bilimek Pulque Vessel: Starlore, Calendrics, and Cosmology of Late Postclassic Central Mexico. *Ancient Mesoamerica,* v. 4, no. 1 (Spring 93), pp. 1 – 15. Bibl, il.

Social life and customs

Clendinnen, Inga. *Aztecs: An Interpretation* reviewed by María J. Rodríguez Shadow. *Mesoamérica (USA),* v. 13, no. 24 (Dec 92), pp. 480 – 487.

— *Aztecs: An Interpretation* reviewed by Sarah Cline. *The Americas,* v. 49, no. 3 (Jan 93), pp. 395 – 396.

Women

Burkhart, Louise M. Mujeres mexicas en "el frente" del hogar: trabajo doméstico y religión en el México azteca. *Mesoamérica (USA),* v. 13, no. 23 (June 92), pp. 23 – 54. Bibl, il.

Writing

Batalla Rosado, Juan José. La perspectiva planigráfica precolombina y el *Códice Borbónico:* página 31; escena central. *Revista Española de Antropología Americana,* v. 23 (1993), pp. 113 – 134. Bibl, il.

AZUELA, MARIANO

Criticism of specific works

Los de abajo

Jiménez de Báez, Yvette. *Los de abajo* de Mariano Azuela: escritura y punto de partida. *Nueva Revista de Filología Hispánica,* v. 40, no. 2 (July – Dec 92), pp. 843 – 874. Bibl.

BABEL (PERIODICAL)

Caparrós, Martín. Mientras *Babel. Cuadernos Hispanoamericanos,* no. 517 – 519 (July – Sept 93), pp. 525 – 528.

BACA, JIMMY-SANTIAGO

Interviews

Meléndez, Gabriel. Carrying the Magic of His People's Heart: An Interview with Jimmy Santiago Baca. *The Americas Review,* v. 19, no. 3 – 4 (Winter 91), pp. 64 – 86.

BACCINO PONCE DE LEÓN, NAPOLEÓN

Criticism of specific works

Maluco

Cordones-Cook, Juanamaría. Contexto y proceso creador de *Maluco: la novela de los conquistadores. Chasqui,* v. 22, no. 2 (Nov 93), pp. 103 – 108.

Interviews

Cordones-Cook, Juanamaría. Contexto y proceso creador de *Maluco: la novela de los conquistadores. Chasqui,* v. 22, no. 2 (Nov 93), pp. 103 – 108.

BACON, FRANCIS

Bayón, Damián Carlos. Francis Bacon en Buenos Aires. *Cuadernos Hispanoamericanos,* no. 510 (Dec 92), pp. 97 – 100. Il.

BÁEZ-JORGE, FÉLIX

Criticism of specific works

En el nombre de América

Velasco Toro, José. América: voz de múltiples raíces. *La Palabra y el Hombre,* no. 84 (Oct – Dec 92), pp. 256 – 258.

Las voces del agua

Capetillo Hernández, Juan. Las voces del agua. *La Palabra y el Hombre,* no. 82 (Apr – June 92), pp. 301 – 305.

Díaz Infante, Fernando. Las voces del agua. *La Palabra y el Hombre,* no. 81 (Jan – Mar 92), pp. 388 – 390.

Ramos, Luis Arturo. El agua y su lenguaje. *La Palabra y el Hombre,* no. 82 (Apr – June 92), pp. 306 – 309.

Williams García, Roberto. Las voces del agua. *La Palabra y el Hombre,* no. 81 (Jan – Mar 92), pp. 386 – 387.

BAHAMAS

Craton, Michael and Gail Saunders. *Islanders in the Stream: A History of the Bahamian People* reviewed by William F. Keegan. *Hispanic American Historical Review,* v. 73, no. 4 (Nov 93), pp. 702 – 703.

Haagen, Victor. The Abaco Cays: Anchors of Tradition. *Américas,* v. 45, no. 1 (Jan – Feb 93), pp. 36 – 43. Il, maps.

Lewis, James Allen. *The Final Campaign of the American Revolution: Rise and Fall of the Spanish Bahamas* reviewed by Francisco Castillo Meléndez. *Anuario de Estudios Americanos,* v. 49, Suppl. 2 (1992), pp. 249 – 250.

BAHIA, BRAZIL

Agier, Michel, ed. *Cantos e toques: etnografias do espaço negro na Bahia* reviewed by Fernando Costa Conceição. *Revista de Antropologia (Brazil),* v. 34 (1991), pp. 223 – 227.

Bastos, Eni Santana Barreto et al. Guia de fontes de documentação para a história da educação na Bahia. *Revista Brasileira de Estudos Pedagógicos,* v. 72, no. 172 (Sept – Dec 91), pp. 385 – 387.

Borges, Dain Edward. *The Family in Bahia, Brazil, 1870 – 1945* reviewed by Sandra Lauderdale Graham. *Journal of Latin American Studies,* v. 25, no. 2 (May 93), pp. 399 – 401.

— *The Family in Bahia, Brazil, 1870 – 1945* reviewed by Robert M. Levine. *Luso-Brazilian Review,* v. 30, no. 1 (Summer 93), pp. 146 – 147.

Cabrera Infante, Guillermo. Oh Bahia (Translated by Alfred MacAdam). *Review,* no. 47 (Fall 93), pp. 16 – 19.

Guimarães, Antônio Sérgio Alfredo. Operários e mobilidade social na Bahia: análise de uma trajetória individual. *Revista Brasileira de Ciências Sociais,* v. 8, no. 22 (June 93), pp. 81 – 97. Bibl, tables.

Ribeiro, Simone. A Casa de Jorge Amado. *Vozes,* v. 87, no. 3 (May – June 93), pp. 41 – 47. Il.

Robben, Antonius C. G. M. *Sons of the Sea Goddess: Economic Practice and Discursive Conflict in Brazil* reviewed by Paul Cammack. *Journal of Latin American Studies,* v. 25, no. 3 (Oct 93), pp. 686 – 687.

Silva, Barbara-Christine Nentwig. Análise comparativa da posição de Salvador e do estado da Bahia no cenário nacional. *Revista Brasileira de Geografia,* v. 53, no. 4 (Oct – Dec 91), pp. 49 – 79. Bibl, tables, maps, charts.

Silva, Sylvio Carlos Bandeira de Mello e and Jaimeval Caetano de Souza. Análise da hierarquia urbana do estado da Bahia. *Revista Brasileira de Geografia,* v. 53, no. 1 (Jan – Mar 91), pp. 51 – 79. Bibl, tables, maps, charts.

Souza, Jaimeval Caetano de et al. Combinações agrícolas no estado da Bahia, 1970 – 1980: uma contribuição metodológica. *Revista Brasileira de Geografia,* v. 53, no. 2 (Apr – June 91), pp. 95 – 112. Bibl, tables, maps.

Walger, Christian. "Nova música baiana": Musikszene Bahia; Kultursoziologische Betrachtungen zur schwarzen Musik Brasiliens. *Zeitschrift für Lateinamerika Wien,* no. 42 (1992), pp. 27 – 51. Bibl.

BAJA CALIFORNIA, MEXICO

Espinoza Valle, Víctor Alejandro and Tania Hernández Vicencio. Tendencias de cambio en la estructura corporativa mexicana: Baja California, 1989 – 1992. *El Cotidiano,* v. 8, no. 52 (Jan – Feb 93), pp. 25 – 29.

— Las transformaciones del corporativismo regional: relaciones estado – sindicato en el sector público de Baja California. *Frontera Norte,* v. 4, no. 8 (July – Dec 92), pp. 79 – 110.

Estrella Valenzuela, Gabriel. Dinámica de los componentes demográficos de Baja California durante el período 1985 – 1990. *Estudios Fronterizos,* no. 26 (Sept – Dec 91), pp. 39 – 53.

Johnstone, Nick. Comparative Advantage, Transfrontier Pollution, and the Environmental Degradation of a Border Region: The Case of the Californias. *Journal of Borderlands Studies,* v. 7, no. 2 (Fall 92), pp. 33 – 52. Bibl.

Valenzuela Arce, José Manuel. *Empapados de sereno: el movimiento urbano popular en Baja California, 1928 – 1988* reviewed by Miguel Angel Vite Pérez. *Estudios Sociológicos,* v. 11, no. 31 (Jan – Apr 93), pp. 285 – 288.

Waller, Thomas. Southern California Water Politics and U.S. –
Mexican Relations: Lining the All-American Canal. *Journal
of Borderlands Studies,* v. 7, no. 2 (Fall 92), pp. 1 – 32. Bibl,
maps.

BALANCE OF PAYMENTS

See also
Debts, Public
Finance, Public
Foreign exchange problem
International finance
National income

Brazil

Nabão, Márcia. Os efeitos de variações cambiais sobre o déficit público. *Revista de Economia Política (Brazil),* v. 13, no.
1 (Jan – Mar 93), pp. 37 – 51. Bibl, tables.

A passo de cágado. *Problemas Brasileiros,* v. 30, no. 295
(Jan – Feb 93), pp. 25 – 27. Il, tables.

Mathematical models

Ferreira, Afonso Henriques Borges. Testes de cointegração e
um modelo de correção de erro para a balança comercial
brasileira. *Estudos Econômicos,* v. 23, no. 1 (Jan – Apr 93),
pp. 35 – 65. Bibl, tables.

— Testes de Granger-causalidade a balança comercial brasileira. *Revista Brasileira de Economia,* v. 47, no. 1 (Jan –
Mar 93), pp. 83 – 95. Bibl, tables.

Martner Fanta, Ricardo. Efeitos macroeconômicos de uma
desvalorização cambial: análise de simulações para o Brasil. *Pesquisa e Planejamento Econômico,* v. 22, no. 1 (Apr
92), pp. 35 – 72. Bibl, tables, charts.

Guatemala

Calderón González, Arnoldo. El sector externo antes de la
flotación del quetzal: capacidad de pagos internacionales
de Guatemala, 1970 – 1988. *USAC,* no. 12 (Dec 90), pp.
66 – 75. Tables.

Guyana

Bennett, Karl M. Exchange Rate Management in a Balance of
Payments Crisis: The Guyana and Jamaica Experience.
Social and Economic Studies, v. 41, no. 4 (Dec 92), pp.
113 – 131. Bibl, tables.

Jamaica

Bennett, Karl M. Exchange Rate Management in a Balance of
Payments Crisis: The Guyana and Jamaica Experience.
Social and Economic Studies, v. 41, no. 4 (Dec 92), pp.
113 – 131. Bibl, tables.

Latin America

Statistics

Compensación multilateral de saldos y líneas de crédito recí-
proco: primer cuatrimestre de 1993. *Integración Latinoamericana,* v. 18, no. 194 (Oct 93), pp. 78 – 81. Tables, charts.

Mexico

Ortiz Wadgymar, Arturo. El desequilibrio externo: talón de
Aquiles del salinismo. *Problemas del Desarrollo,* v. 24, no.
92 (Jan – Mar 93), pp. 24 – 30. Tables.

Torres Torres, Felipe. Los desequilibrios de la balanza comercial agropecuaria. *Momento Económico,* no. 66 (Mar –
Apr 93), pp. 9 – 13. Tables.

Mathematical models

Alfaro Desentis, Samuel and Javier Salas Martín del Campo.
Evolución de la balanza comercial del sector privado en
México: evaluacíon con un modelo econométrico. *El Trimestre Económico,* v. 59, no. 236 (Oct – Dec 92), pp. 773 –
797. Bibl, tables, charts.

BALBOA, VASCO NUÑEZ DE

Escarreola Palacio, Rommel. El conquistador Nuñez de Balboa. *Revista Cultural Lotería,* v. 51, no. 391 (Sept – Oct 92),
pp. 22 – 46. Bibl.

BALLADS

See
Folk music

BALLET

Ballet. *Revista Musical Chilena,* v. 46, no. 178 (July – Dec 92),
pp. 121 – 122.

Durbin, Pamela. Transcultural Steps with a Flair. *Américas,* v.
45, no. 3 (May – June 93), pp. 18 – 23. Il.

Ferri, Olga. La danza y el Teatro Colón: mi pasión y mi vida.
Cuadernos Hispanoamericanos, no. 517 – 519 (July – Sept
93), pp. 541 – 543.

BALTIC STATES

See
Europe, Eastern

BALZA, JOSÉ

Biography

Balza, José. El delta del relato: confesiones en Brown University. *Inti,* no. 37 – 38 (Spring – Fall 93), pp. 17 – 21.

Criticism and interpretation

Noguera, Carlos. La convergencia múltiple: una aproximación
a la narrativa de José Balza. *Inti,* no. 37 – 38 (Spring – Fall
93), pp. 179 – 185. Bibl.

Zacklin, Lyda. Escritura, exactitud y fascinación en la narrativa
de José Balza. *Inti,* no. 37 – 38 (Spring – Fall 93), pp. 171 –
177. Bibl.

BANANA TRADE

Loyola Campos, Alicia. El mercado mundial del banano: nuevas realidades e incertidumbres. *Comercio Exterior,* v. 43,
no. 2 (Feb 93), pp. 163 – 170. Tables.

Costa Rica

Aguilar Hernández, Marielos. Las libertades sindicales en los
ochentas: el caso de las organizaciones bananeras costarricenses. *Revista de Ciencias Sociales (Costa Rica),* no.
58 (Dec 92), pp. 85 – 94. Bibl.

Latin America

Sources

Países exportadores de banano: declaración de Santiago de
Guayaquil. *Integración Latinoamericana,* v. 18, no. 191
(July 93), p. 73.

Windward Islands

Derné, Marie-Claude et al. Business Opportunities in Caribbean Cooperation. *Social and Economic Studies,* v. 41, no.
3 (Sept 92), pp. 65 – 100. Bibl, tables.

BANCHS, ENRIQUE

Foreign influences

Meo Zilio, Giovanni. A propósito de ecos petrarquistas en el
argentino Enrique Banchs. *Nueva Revista de Filología Hispánica,* v. 40, no. 2 (July – Dec 92), pp. 909 – 920.

BANDEIRA, MANUEL

Biography

Mariz, Vasco. Perigrinação a Clavadel. *Revista do Instituto
Histórico e Geográfico Brasileiro,* no. 370 (Jan – Mar 91),
pp. 140 – 150.

BANDITS AND BANDITRY

See also
Crime and criminals

Mexican – American Border Region

Darío Murrieta, Rubén and María Rosa Palazón Mayoral. Las
verdaderas leyendas de Joaquín Murrieta. *Casa de las
Américas,* no. 191 (Apr – June 93), pp. 37 – 49. Bibl.

Peru

Aguirre, Carlos and Charles Walker, eds. *Bandoleros, abigeos
y montoneros: criminalidad y violencia en el Perú, siglos
XVIII – XX* reviewed by Vincent Peloso. *The Americas,* v.
50, no. 2 (Oct 93), pp. 283 – 285.

— *Bandoleros, abigeos y montoneros: criminalidad y vio-
lencia en el Perú, siglos XVIII – XX* reviewed by Scarlett
O'Phelan Godoy. *Anuario de Estudios Americanos,* v. 49,
Suppl. 2 (1992), pp. 243 – 244.

BANKS AND BANKING

See also
Finance
Inter-American Development Bank
International finance
Money and money supply

Zahler, Roberto. Monetary Policy and an Open Capital Account. *CEPAL Review*, no. 48 (Dec 92), pp. 157 – 166. Bibl.

Argentina

Junio, Juan Carlos. Participación democrática. *Realidad Económica*, no. 116 (May – June 93), pp. 29 – 31.

Brazil

Carvalho, Carlos Eduardo Vieira de. Liquidez dos haveres financeiros e zeragem automática do mercado. *Revista de Economia Política (Brazil)*, v. 13, no. 1 (Jan – Mar 93), pp. 25 – 36.

Frischtak, Claudio R. Automação bancária e mudança na produtividade: a experiência brasileira. *Pesquisa e Planejamento Econômico*, v. 22, no. 2 (Aug 92), pp. 197 – 239. Bibl, tables.

Lees, Francis A. et al. *Banking and Financial Deepening in Brazil* reviewed by Arnold W. Sametz. *Economic Development and Cultural Change*, v. 41, no. 3 (Apr 93), pp. 686 – 690.

Pellegrini, Josué Alfredo. As funções do Banco Central do Brasil e o contrôle monetário. *Estudos Econômicos*, v. 22, no. 2 (May – Aug 92), pp. 221 – 252. Bibl, tables.

Chile

Eyzaguirre, Nicolás and Rodrigo Vergara M. Reflexiones en torno a la experiencia de autonomía del Banco Central de Chile. *Cuadernos de Economía (Chile)*, v. 30, no. 91 (Dec 93), pp. 327 – 347. Bibl, tables.

Hernández T., Leonardo and Eduardo Walker H. Estructura de financiamiento corporativo en Chile, 1978 – 1990: evidencia a partir de datos contables. *Estudios Públicos (Chile)*, no. 51 (Winter 93), pp. 87 – 156. Bibl, tables, charts.

Rosende Ramírez, Francisco. La autonomía del Banco Central de Chile: una evaluación preliminar. *Cuadernos de Economía (Chile)*, v. 30, no. 91 (Dec 93), pp. 293 – 326. Bibl, tables.

Tapia de la Puente, Daniel. Experiencia del Banco Central autónomo. *Cuadernos de Economía (Chile)*, v. 30, no. 91 (Dec 93), pp. 349 – 355. Tables.

Law and legislation

Reinstein A., Andrés and Rodrigo Vergara M. Hacia una regulación y supervisión más eficiente del sistema bancario. *Estudios Públicos (Chile)*, no. 49 (Summer 93), pp. 99 – 136. Bibl, tables.

Colombia

Sowell, David Lee. La Caja de Ahorros de Bogotá, 1846 – 1865: Artisans, Credit, Development, and Savings in Early National Colombia. *Hispanic American Historical Review*, v. 73, no. 4 (Nov 93), pp. 615 – 638. Bibl, tables.

Cuba

Collazo Pérez, Enrique. *Cuba, banca y crédito, 1950 – 1958* reviewed by Jorge Salazar-Carrillo. *Hispanic American Historical Review*, v. 73, no. 4 (Nov 93), pp. 725 – 726.

Germany

Young, George F. W. German Banking and German Imperialism in Latin America in the Wilhelmine Era. *Ibero-Amerikanisches Archiv*, v. 18, no. 1 – 2 (1992), pp. 31 – 66. Bibl, tables.

Guadeloupe

Buffon, Alain. La Banque de la Guadeloupe en 1895: le rapport Chaudie. *Revista/Review Interamericana*, v. 22, no. 1 – 2 (Spring – Summer 92), pp. 191 – 207. Bibl.

Latin America

Laks, Jacobo. La banca cooperativa en períodos de ajuste. *Realidad Económica*, no. 116 (May – June 93), pp. 21 – 29.

Mexico

González García, Juan Francisco. El desafío de la banca mexicana frente a la cuenca del Pacífico. *Comercio Exterior*, v. 43, no. 12 (Dec 93), pp. 1173 – 1180. Bibl, tables.

León G., Ricardo. La banca chihuahuense durante el porfiriato. *Siglo XIX: Cuadernos*, v. 1, no. 2 (Feb 92), pp. 9 – 47. Bibl, tables, maps.

Olivier, Michele. Global Finance for Mexican Corporations. *Business Mexico*, v. 3, no. 7 (July 93), p. 27 +. Tables.

Government ownership

White, Russell N. *State, Class, and the Nationalization of the Mexican Banks* reviewed by Terry McKinley and Diana Alarcón (Review entitled "Mexican Bank Nationalization"). *Latin American Perspectives*, v. 20, no. 3 (Summer 93), pp. 80 – 82.

Mathematical models

Bouchain Galicia, Rafael. Análisis sobre concentración y economías de escala en la industria bancaria dentro de la literatura económica: el caso de la banca mexicana. *Problemas del Desarrollo*, v. 24, no. 92 (Jan – Mar 93), pp. 171 – 196. Bibl, tables.

Pacific Area

González García, Juan Francisco. El desafío de la banca mexicana frente a la cuenca del Pacífico. *Comercio Exterior*, v. 43, no. 12 (Dec 93), pp. 1173 – 1180. Bibl, tables.

BAQUERO, GASTÓN

Criticism and interpretation

Shimose Kawamura, Pedro. Homenaje a un cubano universal. *Signo*, no. 38, Nueva época (Jan – Apr 93), pp. 193 – 197.

BARANDA, BENITO J.

Delfau, Antonio. Benito Baranda y Lorena Cornejo: una vida solidaria. *Mensaje*, v. 42, no. 421 (Aug 93), pp. 374 – 375. Il.

BARATA, MANUEL

Barata, Mário. Manuel Barata, republicano histórico. *Revista do Instituto Histórico e Geográfico Brasileiro*, no. 373 (Oct – Dec 91), pp. 1008 – 1021.

BARBA, ENRIQUE M.

Criticism of specific works

Iberoamérica

Corzo Ramírez, Ricardo. Catálogo de la Biblioteca Quinto Centenario y comentario al libro *Iberoamérica: una comunidad*. *La Palabra y el Hombre*, no. 83 (July – Sept 92), pp. 322 – 346. Bibl.

BARBADOS

See
Electronics – Barbados
Subcontracting – Barbados

BARBOSA, OROZIMBO

Martínez Baeza, Sergio. El general don Orozimbo Barbosa y la revolución de 1891. *Boletín de la Academia Chilena de la Historia*, v. 58 – 59, no. 102 (1991 – 1992), pp. 459 – 479. Il.

BARBOSA, RUY

Meira, Sílvio Augusto de Bastos. Um parecer inédito de Rui Barbosa (Includes Rui Barbosa's text regarding the rejection by the city of Belém, Pará, of an electrical transportation contract in the late 19th century). *Revista do Instituto Histórico e Geográfico Brasileiro*, no. 372 (July – Sept 91), pp. 647 – 658.

BARBOZA, MÁRIO GIBSON

Teixeira, Jorge Leão. Reliquias diplomáticas. *Problemas Brasileiros*, v. 30, no. 296 (Mar – Apr 93), pp. 17 – 23. Il.

BARCO CENTENERA, MARTÍN DEL

Criticism of specific works

Argentina y conquista del Río de la Plata

Manzotti, Vilma. Del Barco Centenera y su poema como justicia en una hazaña desventurada. *Revista Interamericana de Bibliografía*, v. 42, no. 3 (1992), pp. 453 – 462. Bibl.

Verdesio, Gustavo. La *Argentina:* tipología textual y construcción de los referentes. *Revista de Crítica Literaria Latinoamericana,* v. 19, no. 38 (July – Dec 93), pp. 345 – 360. Bibl.

BARINAS, VENEZUELA (STATE)

Gómez Grillo, Elio. Sucedió en Barinas. *Boletín de la Academia Nacional de la Historia (Venezuela),* v. 76, no. 301 (Jan – Mar 93), pp. 127 – 128.

Tosta, Virgilio. Huella y presencia de médicos europeos en el estado Barinas. *Boletín de la Academia Nacional de la Historia (Venezuela),* v. 75, no. 297 (Jan – Mar 92), pp. 69 – 95.

BARNET, MIGUEL
Criticism of specific works
Biografía de un cimarrón

Nofal, Rossana. *Biografía de un cimarrón* de Miguel Barnet: "la construcción de una voz." *Revista Chilena de Literatura,* no. 40 (Nov 92), pp. 35 – 39. Bibl.

BARNSTONE, WILLIS
Correspondence, reminiscences, etc.

Barnstone, Willis. *With Borges on an Ordinary Evening in Buenos Aires: A Memoir* reviewed by Naomi Lindstrom. *World Literature Today,* v. 67, no. 4 (Fall 93), p. 787.

BAROQUE

Báez-Jorge, Félix. La afición arqueológica de Alejo Carpentier. *Plural (Mexico),* v. 22, no. 262 (July 93), pp. 46 – 50.

— Mitla y el barroco: notas sobre la afición arqueológica de Alejo Carpentier. *La Palabra y el Hombre,* no. 82 (Apr – June 92), pp. 57 – 73. Il.

Cruz Ovalle de Amenábar, Isabel. Arte jesuita en Chile: la huella del barroco bávaro. *Mensaje,* v. 42, no. 420 (July 93), pp. 234 – 238. Il.

Godoy Urzúa, Hernán. La hegemonía cultural jesuita y el barroco. *Mensaje,* v. 42, no. 420 (July 93), pp. 228 – 233. Il.

Mejías Alvarez, María Jesús. Muerte regia en cuatro ciudades peruanas del barroco. *Anuario de Estudios Americanos,* v. 49 (1992), pp. 189 – 205. Bibl, il.

Perlongher, Néstor. Introducción a la poesía neobarroca cubana y rioplatense. *Revista Chilena de Literatura,* no. 41 (Apr 93), pp. 47 – 57. Bibl.

Ribeiro, João Roberto Inácio. O gongorismo na poesia latina de Manuel Botelho de Oliveira. *Revista de Letras (Brazil),* v. 32 (1992), pp. 199 – 206. Bibl.

Stawicka, Bárbara. La selva en flor: Alejo Carpentier y el diálogo entre las vanguardias europeas del siglo XX y el barroco latinoamericano. *La Palabra y el Hombre,* no. 81 (Jan – Mar 92), pp. 193 – 199. Bibl.

Torres, Daniel. Indagación sobre la técnica escritural "diferente" en la lírica barroca colonial. *Hispanic Journal,* v. 13, no. 2 (Fall 92), pp. 281 – 287. Bibl.

BARRA, EMMA DE LA
Criticism and interpretation

Sosa de Newton, Lily. César Duayen, una mujer que se adelantó a su tiempo. *Todo Es Historia,* v. 27, no. 311 (June 93), pp. 46 – 48. Bibl, il.
Criticism of specific works
Stella

Nari, Marcela M. Alejandra. Alejandra: maternidad e independencia femenina. *Feminaria,* v. 6, no. 10, Suppl. (Apr 93), pp. 7 – 9.

BARRAGÁN, LUIS

Barragán, Luis. *Barragán: Armando Salas Portugal Photographs of the Architecture of Luis Barragán,* essays by Ernest H. Brooks II et al. Reviewed by Max Underwood. *Latin American Art,* v. 4, no. 4 (Winter 92), pp. 94 – 95.

BARRAL, BASILIO MARÍA DE
Obituaries

Díaz Alvarez, Manuel. In memoriam: Basilio de Barral, misionero y antropólogo. *Montalbán,* no. 24 (1992), pp. 21 – 24.

BARRAL, LUÍSA MARGARIDA PORTUGAL DE BARROS

Sena, Consuelo Pondé de. A condessa de Barral, a grande dama do segundo reinado. *Revista do Instituto Histórico e Geográfico Brasileiro,* no. 372 (July – Sept 91), pp. 677 – 684. Bibl.

BARRENECHEA, ANA MARÍA
Interviews

Rodríguez Pérsico, Adriana C. Entrevista con Ana María Barrenechea. *La Educación (USA),* v. 36, no. 111 – 113 (1992), pp. 237 – 243. Il.

BARRENECHEA Y ALBIS, JUAN DE
Criticism of specific works
Restauración de la imperial

Arbea G., Antonio. El fromato centonario en la *Restauración de la imperial* de Juan de Barrenechea y Albis. *Revista Chilena de Literatura,* no. 42 (Aug 93), pp. 31 – 39.

BARRETO, LIMA
See
Lima Barreto, Alfonso Henrique de

BARROS, PÍA
Criticism of specific works
A horcajadas

Agosín, Marjorie. A horcajadas. *Fem,* v. 17, no. 127 (Sept 93), pp. 47 – 48.

BARRY, JAMES MIRANDA STEUART

Kerdel Vegas, Francisco. El inspector general doctor James Barry. *Boletín de la Academia Nacional de la Historia (Venezuela),* v. 75, no. 299 (July – Sept 92), pp. 157 – 162.

BASQUES
Argentina

Siegrist de Gentile, Nora L. *Inmigración vasca en la ciudad de Buenos Aires, 1830 – 1855* reviewed by Oscar Alvarez Gila. *Revista de Indias,* v. 53, no. 197 (Jan – Apr 93), pp. 121 – 124.

Sources

Anasagasti, Iñaki, ed. *Homenaje al Comité Pro-Inmigación Vasca en la Argentina, 1940* reviewed by Oscar Alvarez Gila. *Revista de Indias,* v. 53, no. 197 (Jan – Apr 93), pp. 99 – 101.

Mexican – American Border Region

Garate, Donald T. Basque Names, Nobility, and Ethnicity on the Spanish Frontier. *Colonial Latin American Historical Review,* v. 2, no. 1 (Winter 93), pp. 77 – 104. Bibl, facs.

BASTIDAS, ARÍSTIDES

Beltrán Guerrero, Luis. Un gran mestizo. *Boletín de la Academia Nacional de la Historia (Venezuela),* v. 76, no. 302 (Apr – June 93), pp. 139 – 140.

BATISTA, CÍCERO ROMÃO

Slater, Candace. *Trail of Miracles: Stories from a Pilgrimage in Northeast Brazil* reviewed by David T. Haberly. *Hispanic Review,* v. 61, no. 3 (Summer 93), pp. 449 – 451.

BATTISTA, VICENTE
Correspondence, reminiscences, etc.

Battista, Vicente. El difícil arte de volver. *Cuadernos Hispanoamericanos,* no. 517 – 519 (July – Sept 93), pp. 560 – 562.

BAUXITE
Jamaica

Auty, Richard M. Intensified Dependence on a Maturing Mining Sector: The Jamaican Bauxite Levy. *Caribbean Geography,* v. 3, no. 3 (Mar 92), pp. 143 – 159. Bibl, tables.

BEALS, CARLETON
Criticism of specific works
Banana Gold
Pailler, Claire. El reportaje del guerillero: una narrativa ambigua. *Studi di Letteratura Ispano-Americana,* v. 24 (1993), pp. 67 – 82. Tables.

BEANS
Aguiar, José Vangeliso de and José de Jesus Sousa Lemos. Produção do caupi irrigado em Bragança, Pará. *Revista de Economia e Sociologia Rural,* v. 30, no. 3 (July – Sept 92), pp. 239 – 252. Bibl, tables, charts.

Janssen, Willem et al. Adoção de cultivares melhoradas de feijão em estados selecionados no Brasil. *Revista de Economia e Sociologia Rural,* v. 30, no. 4 (Oct – Dec 92), pp. 321 – 338. Bibl, tables, charts.

BECERRA, MILTON
Medina, Alvaro. Milton Becerra: piedras atadas y geometría desatada (Accompanied by an English translation). *Art Nexus,* no. 8 (Apr – June 93), pp. 64 – 68. Il.

Rodríguez, Antonio. Milton Becerra, la voz milenaria del hombre (Accompanied by an English translation). *Art Nexus,* no. 8 (Apr – June 93), pp. 68 – 70. Il.

BECKFORD, GEORGE L.
Best, Lloyd. The Contribution of George Beckford. *Social and Economic Studies,* v. 41, no. 3 (Sept 92), pp. 5 – 23.

BÉCQUER, GUSTAVO ADOLFO
Criticism and interpretation
Campo, Angel Esteban-P. del. Bécquer y Martí: una audiencia especial con el sentimiento. *Anuario de Letras (Mexico),* v. 30 (1992), pp. 177 – 189. Bibl.

BEEF INDUSTRY
See
Cattle trade
Meat industry and trade

BEER
Brazil
Mandioca vira cerveja. *Problemas Brasileiros,* v. 30, no. 296 (Mar – Apr 93), pp. 26 – 27. Il.

BEHAVIOR
See
Sexual behavior

BEKER, ANA
Medrano, Carmen. Ana Beker. *Todo Es Historia,* v. 27, no. 313 (Aug 93), pp. 48 – 49. Il.

BELAUSTEGUIGOITIA, RAMÓN DE
Criticism of specific works
Con Sandino en Nicaragua
Pailler, Claire. El reportaje del guerillero: una narrativa ambigua. *Studi di Letteratura Ispano-Americana,* v. 24 (1993), pp. 67 – 82. Tables.

BELÉM, BRAZIL
Meira, Sílvio Augusto de Bastos. Um parecer inédito de Rui Barbosa (Includes Rui Barbosa's text regarding the rejection by the city of Belém, Pará, of an electrical transportation contract in the late 19th century). *Revista do Instituto Histórico e Geográfico Brasileiro,* no. 372 (July – Sept 91), pp. 647 – 658.

BELGIUM
See
Periodicals – Belgium

BELIZE
See also
Agriculture – Belize
Animals – Belize
Archaeology – Belize
Central Americans – Belize
Cooperatives – Belize
Cuello site, Belize
Ecology and development – Belize
Fishing – Belize
Geomorphology – Belize
Obsidian – Belize
Parks – Belize
Population – Belize
Publishers and publishing – Belize
Stone implements – Belize
Television – Belize
Tourist trade – Belize
Water – Belize

Antiquities
Hammond, Norman, ed. *Cuello: An Early Maya Community in Belize* reviewed by Paul F. Healy. *Latin American Antiquity,* v. 4, no. 3 (Sept 93), pp. 295 – 297.

Kelly, Thomas C. Preceramic Projectile-Point Typology in Belize. *Ancient Mesoamerica,* v. 4, no. 2 (Fall 93), pp. 205 – 227. Bibl, il, tables, maps.

Pendergast, David Michael et al. Locating Maya Lowlands Spanish Colonial Towns: A Case Study from Belize. *Latin American Antiquity,* v. 4, no. 1 (Mar 93), pp. 59 – 73. Bibl, il, maps.

History
Ashdown, Peter D. Alan Burns and Sidney Turton: Two Views of the Public Good. *Belizean Studies,* v. 21, no. 1 (May 93), pp. 21 – 24. Bibl.

Race question
Humphreys, Francis. Afro-Belizean Cultural Heritage: Its Role in Combating Recolonization. *Belizean Studies,* v. 20, no. 3 (Dec 92), pp. 11 – 16. Bibl.

Social conditions
Palacio, Joseph O. Social and Cultural Implications of Recent Demographic Changes in Belize (The Fourth Annual Signa L. Yorke Memorial Lecture). *Belizean Studies,* v. 21, no. 1 (May 93), pp. 3 – 12. Bibl, tables.

BELIZEAN LITERATURE
Bibliography
Ergood, Bruce. Belize as Presented in Her Literature. *Belizean Studies,* v. 21, no. 2 (Oct 93), pp. 3 – 14. Bibl, tables.

History and criticism
Ruiz, David. Belize's Literary Heritage: A 500-Year Perspective. *Belizean Studies,* v. 21, no. 2 (Oct 93), pp. 28 – 33.

BELLÈRE, JEAN
Buisseret, David and Arthur Holzheimer. The Enigma of the Jean Bellère Maps of the New World, 1554: A Historical Note. *Colonial Latin American Historical Review,* v. 2, no. 3 (Summer 93), pp. 363 – 367. Maps.

BELLESSI, DIANA
Criticism and interpretation
Ortega, Eliana. Travesías bellessianas. *Revista Chilena de Literatura,* no. 42 (Aug 93), pp. 183 – 191.

BELLI, GIOCONDA
Criticism and interpretation
Moyano, Pilar. La transformación de la mujer y la nación en la poesía comprometida de Gioconda Belli. *Revista Canadiense de Estudios Hispánicos,* v. 17, no. 2 (Winter 93), pp. 319 – 331. Bibl.

BELLO, ANDRÉS
Biography
Jaramillo Lyon, Armando. Don Andrés Bello en Santiago. *Boletín de Historia y Antigüedades,* v. 79, no. 779 (Oct – Dec 92), pp. 1037 – 1051.

Primer rector de la Universidad de Chile. *Atenea (Chile),* no. 465 – 466 (1992), pp. 301 – 302. Il.

Criticism and interpretation

Cussen, Antonio. *Bello and Bolívar: Poetry and Politics in the Spanish American Revolution* reviewed by Fernando Cervantes. *Bulletin of Latin American Research*, v. 12, no. 1 (Jan 93), pp. 114 – 115.

— *Bello and Bolívar: Poetry and Politics in the Spanish American Revolution* reviewed by Myron I. Lichtblau. *Hispania (USA)*, v. 76, no. 2 (May 93), p. 285.

Criticism of specific works

Gramática de la lengua castellana . . .

Mendoza, José G. Bello y los verbos abstractos en el análisis de los modos. *Signo*, no. 35, Nueva época (Jan – Apr 92), pp. 83 – 97. Bibl.

BELTRÁN, EDUARDO

La mina. *Hoy Es Historia*, v. 10, no. 59 (Sept – Oct 93), p. 100. II.

BELTRÁN GUERRERO, LUIS

Biography

Bermúdez, Manuel. Luis Beltrán Guerrero. *Boletín de la Academia Nacional de la Historia (Venezuela)*, v. 76, no. 302 (Apr – June 93), pp. 151 – 152.

BELTRÃO, MARIA DA CONCEICÃO DE M. C.

Madeira, Marcos Almir. Uma senhora em sua casa (Speech given in honor of Maria Beltrão's induction into the Instituto Histórico e Geográfico Brasileiro). *Revista do Instituto Histórico e Geográfico Brasileiro*, no. 372 (July – Sept 91), pp. 800 – 805.

Addresses, essays, lectures

Beltrão, Maria da Conceição de M. C. A coleção egípcia do Museu Nacional (Speech given at the occasion of her induction into the Instituto Histórico e Geográfico Brasileiro). *Revista do Instituto Histórico e Geográfico Brasileiro*, no. 372 (July – Sept 91), pp. 806 – 811.

BENCOMO BARRIOS, HÉCTOR

Criticism of specific works

Campañas libertadoras suramericanas

Eljuri, José Ramón. *Campañas libertadoras suramericanas* del general de brigada Héctor Bencomo Barrios. *Boletín de la Academia Nacional de la Historia (Venezuela)*, v. 76, no. 301 (Jan – Mar 93), pp. 130 – 131.

BENEDETTO, ANTONIO DI

Criticism of specific works

Zama

Corro, Gaspar Pío del. *'Zama': zona de contacto* reviewed by Gloria Videla de Rivero. *Revista Chilena de Literatura*, no. 41 (Apr 93), pp. 134 – 135.

BENEDICTIS, SAVINO DE

Toni, Flávia Camargo. Memória: Mário de Andrade escreve para as crianças. *Vozes*, v. 87, no. 3 (May – June 93), pp. 67 – 72. Facs.

BENET GOITIA, JUAN

Compitello, Malcolm Alan. Reflexiones sobre el acto de narrar: Benet, Vargas Llosa y Euclides da Cunha. *Insula*, no. 559 – 560 (July – Aug 93), pp. 19 – 22.

BENEVIDES, MARIA VICTORIA DE MESQUITA

Criticism of specific works

A cidadania ativa

Barretto, Vicente. Democracia, participação e cidadania. *Revista Brasileira de Estudos Políticos*, no. 76 (Jan 93), pp. 141 – 145.

BENJAMIN, WALTER

Gutiérrez Girardot, Rafael. César Vallejo y Walter Benjamin. *Cuadernos Hispanoamericanos*, no. 520 (Oct 93), pp. 55 – 72. Bibl, il.

BERGQUIST, CHARLES WYLIE

Flórez Gallego, Lenín. Historias nacionales, historias de los trabajadores y el problema de la democracia en la obra de Charles Bergquist. *Anuario Colombiano de Historia Social y de la Cultura*, no. 20 (1992), pp. 73 – 88. Bibl, tables.

BERISTÁIN DE SOUZA, JOSÉ MARIANO

Zayas de Lille, Gabriela. Los sermones políticos de José Mariano Beristáin de Souza. *Nueva Revista de Filología Hispánica*, v. 40, no. 2 (July – Dec 92), pp. 719 – 759. Bibl.

BERNABÓ, HÉCTOR

Brenken, Anna. El artista Carybé de Salvador da Bahía (Translated by Mónica Perne). *Humboldt*, no. 109 (1993), pp. 70 – 75. Il.

BERNAL, IGNACIO

Obituaries

Báez-Jorge, Félix. Ignacio Bernal (1910 – 1992). *La Palabra y el Hombre*, no. 81 (Jan – Mar 92), pp. 258 – 259. Il.

Ballesteros Gaibrois, Manuel. Ignacio Bernal: in memoriam. *Revista Española de Antropología Americana*, v. 23 (1993), pp. 242 – 243.

BERNARDES, LYSIA M. C.

Obituaries

Geiger, Pedro Pinchas. In memoriam: Nilo e Lysia Bernardes. *Revista Geográfica (Mexico)*, no. 114 (July – Dec 91), pp. 111 – 118.

BERNARDES, NILO

Obituaries

Geiger, Pedro Pinchas. In memoriam: Nilo e Lysia Bernardes. *Revista Geográfica (Mexico)*, no. 114 (July – Dec 91), pp. 111 – 118.

BERTOLOZZI DE OYUELA, MARÍA C.

Biography

Solís Tolosa, Lucía S. María Bertolozzi: de la narración histórica a la historia social. *Todo Es Historia*, v. 26, no. 309 (Apr 93), pp. 56 – 59. Il.

BESTARD VÁZQUEZ, JOAQUÍN

Criticism of specific works

Sol de la guacamaya de fuego

Morris, Robert J. *Sol de la guacamaya de fuego:* novela pionera maya por Joaquín Bestard Vázquez. *Confluencia*, v. 8, no. 1 (Fall 92), pp. 165 – 171. Bibl.

BETANCOURT, RÓMULO

Dávila, Luis Ricardo. Rómulo Betancourt and the Development of Venezuelan Nationalism, 1930 – 1945. *Bulletin of Latin American Research*, v. 12, no. 1 (Jan 93), pp. 49 – 63. Bibl.

BETANZOS, JUAN DE

Criticism of specific works

Suma y narración de los incas

Hurtado, Liliana R. de. *La sucesión incaica: aproximación al mando y poder entre los incas a partir de la crónica de Betanzos* reviewed by Nicanor Domínguez Faura. *Revista Andina*, v. 11, no. 1 (July 93), pp. 250 – 251.

Martín Rubio, María del Carmen. El Cuzco incaico, según Juan de Betanzos. *Cuadernos Hispanoamericanos*, no. 511 (Jan 93), pp. 7 – 23. Bibl, il.

BEVERAGES

See

Alcohol

Tea

BIANCO, JOSÉ

Biobibliography

Cobo Borda, Juan Gustavo. Páginas dispersas de José Bianco (1908 – 1986). *Cuadernos Hispanoamericanos*, no. 516 (June 93), pp. 7 – 9. Il.

BIBLE

Criticism, interpretation, etc.

Barrera, Pablo. Religiosidad y resistencia andina: la fe de los no creyentes. *Cristianismo y Sociedad,* v. 30, no. 113 (1992), pp. 15 – 34. Bibl.

Camps Cruell, Carlos M. Fe, responsabilidad, democracia: desde una perspectiva de una historia de la creación; un desafío para América Latina hoy. *Cristianismo y Sociedad,* v. 30, no. 113 (1992), pp. 35 – 44.

Tamez, Elsa. Que la mujer no calle en la congregación: pautas hermenéuticas para comprender *Gá.* 3.28 y 1 *Co.* 14.23. *Cristianismo y Sociedad,* v. 30, no. 113 (1992), pp. 45 – 52. Bibl.

BIBLIOGRAPHY

See

Agriculture – Mexico – Bibliography
Agriculture, Cooperative – Mexico – Bibliography
Agriculture and state – Latin America – Bibliography
Agriculture and state – Mexico – Bibliography
America – Bibliography
Andean region – Bibliography
Araucanian language – Bibliography
Architecture – Latin America – Bibliography
Art – Bolivia – Bibliography
Art – Central America – Bibliography
Art – Chile – Bibliography
Art – Latin America – Bibliography
Art – Mexico – Bibliography
Audiovisual education – Bibliography
Authors – Caribbean area – Bibliography
Authors – Central America – Bibliography
Belizean literature – Bibliography
Blacks – Brazil – Bibliography
Books
Books – Germany – Bibliography
Books – Italy – Bibliography
Brazilian literature – Bibliography
Brazilian literature – Black authors – Bibliography
Catholic Church – Central America – Bibliography
Chiapas, Mexico – Bibliography
Chile – Bibliography
Chilean literature – Bibliography
Church music – Mexico – Bibliography
Cities and towns – Mexico – Bibliography
El Cojo Ilustrado (Periodical) – Bibliography
Columbus, Christopher – Bibliography
Comic books, strips, etc. – Mexico – Bibliography
Communism – Latin America – Bibliography
Condé, Maryse – Bibliography
Cruz Ovalle de Amenábar, Isabel – Bibliography
Cuba – Bibliography
Decentralization in government – Mexico – Bibliography
Democracy – Colombia – Bibliography
Democracy – Guatemala – Bibliography
Democracy – Latin America – Bibliography
Dougnac Rodríguez, Antonio – Bibliography
Drug trade – Mexico – Bibliography
Earle, Peter G. – Bibliography
Ecology – Bibliography
Ecology – Chile – Bibliography
Economics – Latin America – Bibliography
Economics – Spain – Bibliography
Education, Higher – America – Bibliography
Education, Primary – Mexico – Bibliography
Family – Brazil – Bibliography
Family – Latin America – Bibliography
Ferré, Rosario – Bibliography
Folk lore – Mexico – Bibliography
Franciscans – America – Bibliography
García Márquez, Gabriel – Bibliography
Geography, Historical – Peru – Bibliography
Guyana – Bibliography
Human rights – Chile – Bibliography
Humanism – Bibliography
Incas – Bibliography
Indians, Treatment of – Bibliography
Indians of South America – Bibliography
Indigenismo – Bibliography
International economic integration – Bibliography
International relations – Bibliography
Israel – Bibliography
Journalism – Mexico – Bibliography

Labor and laboring classes – Latin America – Bibliography
Lange, Francisco Curt – Bibliography
Latin America – Bibliography
Latin American fiction – Bibliography
Latin American literature – Bibliography
Latin American poetry – Bibliography
Literature and history – Chile – Bibliography
Literature and society – Latin America – Bibliography
Malaspina, Alessandro – Bibliography
Manuscripts
Marcano, Vicente – Bibliography
Marqués, René – Bibliography
Mayas – Bibliography
Mexican literature – Spain – Bibliography
Mexican poetry – Bibliography
Mexico (City) – Bibliography
Military assistance, Foreign – Latin America – Bibliography
Military in government – Chile – Bibliography
Millar Carvacho, René – Bibliography
Mining industry and finance – Mexico – Bibliography
Motion pictures – Latin America – Bibliography
Music – Latin America – Bibliography
Music – Mexico – Bibliography
Music – Puerto Rico – Bibliography
Musicology – Bibliography
Nahuatl language – Bibliography
Nahuatl literature – Bibliography
Netherlands Antilles – Bibliography
North American Free Trade Agreement – Bibliography
Oaxaca, Mexico (City) – Bibliography
Pacific Area – Bibliography
Paraguay – Bibliography
Peasantry – Latin America – Bibliography
Periodicals – Brazil – Bibliography
Periodicals – Latin America – Bibliography
Periodicals – Venezuela – Bibliography
Peruvian literature – Bibliography
Photography and photographers – Latin America – Bibliography
Picón Salas, Mariano – Bibliography
Political parties – Mexico – Bibliography
Popular culture – Caribbean area – Bibliography
Press and politics – Mexico – Bibliography
Pressure groups – Mexico – Bibliography
Privatization – Latin America – Bibliography
Public health – Latin America – Bibliography
Religion and politics – Latin America – Bibliography
Retamal Favereau, Julio – Bibliography
Revolutions – Mexico – Bibliography
Revolutions – Nicaragua – Bibliography
Río, Eduardo del – Bibliography
San Luis Potosí, Mexico (City) – Bibliography
Scientific expeditions – Bibliography
Scorza, Manuel – Bibliography
Sex role – Latin America – Bibliography
Sexual behavior – Brazil – Bibliography
Slave trade – Bibliography
Slavery – Bibliography
Social classes – Mexico – Bibliography
Social conflict – Andean region – Bibliography
Social movements – Brazil – Bibliography
Social movements – Mexico – Bibliography
Social sciences – Bibliography
Social security – Latin America – Bibliography
Socialism – Latin America – Bibliography
Sociolinguistics – Bibliography
Soils – Brazil – Bibliography
Spanish language – Mexico – Bibliography
Spanish literature – Bibliography
Surinam – Bibliography
Taxation – Latin America – Bibliography
Technology and state – Latin America – Bibliography
Textile industry and fabrics – Andean region – Bibliography
Theater – Latin America – Bibliography
Toledo, Francisco de – Bibliography
Torriente-Brau, Pablo de la – Bibliography
Trade unions – Latin America – Bibliography
United Nations. Economic Commission for Latin America and the Caribbean – Bibliography
Uruguayan poetry – Bibliography
Walcott, Derek – Bibliography
Women – Brazil – Bibliography
Women – Latin America – Bibliography
Women authors – Caribbean area – Bibliography
Women authors – Latin America – Bibliography

Xochimilco, Mexico – Bibliography
Subdivisions *Bibliography* and *Biobibliography* under
names of individuals

BID

See
Inter-American Development Bank

BILINGUALISM

See also
Education, Bilingual

Hamel, Rainer Enrique. Derechos lingüísticos. *Nueva Antropología*, v. 13, no. 44 (Aug 93), p. 71 +.

Mexico

Coronado Suzán, Gabriela. Entre la homogeneidad y la diferencia en los pueblos indohablantes de México. *Revista Latinoamericana de Estudios Educativos*, v. 22, no. 4 (Oct – Dec 92), pp. 37 – 62. Bibl, tables, charts.

Paraguay

Granda, Germán de. *Sociedad, historia y lengua en el Paraguay* reviewed by Rafael Rodríguez Marín. *Anuario de Letras (Mexico)*, v. 30 (1992), pp. 265 – 269.

United States

Pearson, Barbara Z. Predictive Validity of the Scholastic Aptitude Test (SAT) for Hispanic Bilingual Students. *Hispanic Journal of Behavioral Sciences*, v. 15, no. 3 (Aug 93), pp. 342 – 356. Bibl, tables.

BILLETER, ERIKA

Herner de Larrea, Irene. Erika Billeter y el arte mexicano en Europa. *Nexos*, v. 16, no. 183 (Mar 93), pp. 10 – 12. Il.

BIOGRAPHY (AS A LITERARY FORM)

Barnet, Miguel. La novela testimonio: alquimia de la memoria. *La Palabra y el Hombre*, no. 82 (Apr – June 92), pp. 75 – 78.

Stolley, Karen. Sins of the Father: Hernando Colón's *Life of the Admiral*. *Latin American Literary Review*, v. 21, no. 41 (Jan – June 93), pp. 53 – 64. Bibl.

Brazil

Franconi, Rodolfo A. The Fictionalization of a Diary (Translated by Barbara Meza). *Américas*, v. 45, no. 6 (Nov – Dec 93), pp. 60 – 63. Il.

Gárate, Miriam Viviana. El diario de Helena Morley o de la vida de las mujeres en la Diamantina finisecular. *Escritura (Venezuela)*, v. 16, no. 31 – 32 (Jan – Dec 91), pp. 65 – 80. Bibl.

Chile

Hunsaker, Steven V. The Problematics of the Representative Self: The Case of *Tejas verdes*. *Hispanic Journal*, v. 13, no. 2 (Fall 92), pp. 353 – 361. Bibl.

Lemogodeuc, Jean-Marie. Las máscaras y las marcas de la autobiografía: la cuestión del narrador en *El jardín de al lado* de José Donoso. *Revista de Crítica Literaria Latinoamericana*, v. 19, no. 38 (July – Dec 93), pp. 383 – 392. Bibl.

Narváez, Jorge E., ed. *La invención de la memoria* reviewed by Domnita Dumitrescu. *Nuevo Texto Crítico*, v. 6, no. 11 (1993), pp. 268 – 270.

El Salvador

McGowan, Marcia P. Mapping a New Territory: *Luisa in Realityland*. *Letras Femeninas*, v. 19, no. 1 – 2 (Spring – Fall 93), pp. 84 – 99. Bibl.

Guatemala

Costa, Cláudia de Lima. Rigoberta Menchú: a história de um depoimento. *Estudos Feministas*, v. 1, no. 2 (1993), pp. 306 – 320.

Trejos Montero, Elisa. Conversación con Rigoberta Menchú. *Káñina*, v. 16, no. 2 (July – Dec 92), pp. 65 – 71.

— *Me llamo Rigoberta Menchú y así me nació la conciencia*: un texto de literatura testimonial. *Káñina*, v. 16, no. 2 (July – Dec 92), pp. 53 – 63. Bibl.

Latin America

Lavrin, Asunción. La vida femenina como experiencia religiosa: biografía y hagiografía en Hispanoamérica colonial. *Colonial Latin American Review*, v. 2, no. 1 – 2 (1993), pp. 27 – 51. Bibl.

Melis, Antonio et al. Debate (on the second session of the symposium "Latinoamérica: Nuevas Direcciones en Teoría y Crítica Literarias, III"). *Revista de Crítica Literaria Latinoamericana*, v. 19, no. 38 (July – Dec 93), pp. 91 – 101.

Molloy, Sylvia. *At Face Value: Autobiographical Writing in Spanish America* reviewed by Robert A. Parsons. *Hispania (USA)*, v. 76, no. 2 (May 93), pp. 290 – 291.

— *At Face Value: Autobiographical Writing in Spanish America* reviewed by Kathleen Ross. *Hispanic Review*, v. 61, no. 4 (Fall 93), pp. 596 – 598.

— *At Face Value: Autobiographical Writing in Spanish America* reviewed by John Walker. *Revista Canadiense de Estudios Hispánicos*, v. 17, no. 2 (Winter 93), pp. 404 – 407.

Sklodowska, Elzbieta. Testimonio mediatizado: ¿Ventriloquia o heteroglosia?; Barnet/Montejo; Burgos/Menchú. *Revista de Crítica Literaria Latinoamericana*, v. 19, no. 38 (July – Dec 93), pp. 81 – 90. Bibl.

Williams, Gareth. Translation and Mourning: The Cultural Challenge of Latin American Testimonial Autobiography. *Latin American Literary Review*, v. 21, no. 41 (Jan – June 93), pp. 79 – 99. Bibl.

— Translation and Mourning: The Cultural Challenge of Latin American Testimonial Autobiography. *Latin American Literary Review*, v. 21, no. 41 (Jan – June 93), pp. 79 – 99. Bibl.

Mexico

McDonald, Robert. An Incredible Graph: Sor Juana's *Respuesta*. *Revista Canadiense de Estudios Hispánicos*, v. 17, no. 2 (Winter 93), pp. 297 – 318. Bibl.

Meyer, Jean A., ed. *Egohistorias: el amor a Clío* reviewed by Jorge F. Hernández. *Vuelta*, v. 17, no. 204 (Nov 93), pp. 38 – 40.

Peru

Ribeyro, Julio Ramón. La tentación de la memoria. *Debate (Peru)*, v. 15, no. 70 (Sept – Oct 92), pp. 56 – 59. Il.

Puerto Rico

Cruz, Arnaldo. Para virar al macho: la autobiografía como subversión en la cuentística de Manuel Ramos Otero. *Revista Iberoamericana*, v. 59, no. 162 – 163 (Jan – June 93), pp. 239 – 263. Bibl.

Venezuela

Lizardo, Pedro Francisco. La pasión biográfica en Tomás Polanco Alcántara. *Revista Nacional de Cultura (Venezuela)*, v. 53, no. 286 (July – Sept 92), pp. 188 – 202. Il.

Rondón de Sansó, Hildegard. Tomás Polanco Alcántara o el hombre que venció los tabúes impuestos al biógrafo contemporáneo. *Boletín de la Academia Nacional de la Historia (Venezuela)*, v. 75, no. 298 (Apr – June 92), pp. 29 – 31.

BIOLOGY

See
Biotechnology
Evolution
Sociobiology

BIOMBO NEGRO (PERIODICAL)

Martínez Duarte, Margarita. *Biombo Negro:* lo que nos faltaba. *Plural (Mexico)*, v. 22, no. 265 (Oct 93), pp. 86 – 87.

BIOTECHNOLOGY

Peritore, N. Patrick. El surgimiento del cártel biotecnológico. *Revista Mexicana de Sociología*, v. 54, no. 2 (Apr – June 92), pp. 101 – 131. Bibl, tables.

Wildes, Kevin. Tecnología médica y el surgimiento de la bioética. *Mensaje*, v. 42, no. 418 (May 93), pp. 129 – 132. Il.

International cooperation

Casas Castañeda, Fernando. Política exterior en el campo de los recursos genéticos, el medio ambiente y la economía internacional. *Revista Javeriana*, v. 61, no. 594 (May 93), pp. 277 – 282. Bibl.

Brazil

Salles Filho, Sérgio L. M. et al. Estratégias empresariais em agrobiotecnologia no Brasil: um estudo de casos relevantes. *Revista de Economia e Sociologia Rural,* v. 30, no. 3 (July – Sept 92), pp. 203 – 224. Bibl, tables.

Chile

Law and legislation

Moraga-Rojel, Jubel R. et al. La biotecnología agrícola y la privatización del conocimiento en la transferencia tecnológica universidad – empresa. *Estudios Sociales (Chile),* no. 77 (July – Sept 93), pp. 117 – 137. Bibl.

Colombia

Perea Dallos, Margarita. Biotecnología y agricultura. *Revista Javeriana,* v. 61, no. 591 (Jan – Feb 93), pp. 35 – 40. Bibl, charts.

Cuba

Feinsilver, Julie M. Can Biotechnology Save the Revolution? *NACLA Report on the Americas,* v. 26, no. 5 (May 93), pp. 7 – 10. Il.

Montalvo Arriete, Luis F. Biotecnología en Cuba como una ventana de oportunidad. *Interciencia,* v. 18, no. 6 (Nov – Dec 93), pp. 295 – 299. Bibl.

Mexico

Casas Guerrero, Rosalba et al, eds. *La biotecnología y sus repercusiones socioeconómicas y políticas* reviewed by Eugenia J. Olguín. *Revista Mexicana de Sociología,* v. 55, no. 2 (Apr – June 93), pp. 397 – 404. Bibl.

Venezuela

Sayago, Luis Rodrigo. Biotecnología, agricultura y ecología: un dilema para el futuro. *Derecho y Reforma Agraria,* no. 24 (1993), pp. 159 – 165.

BIOY CASARES, ADOLFO

Biography

Bach, Caleb. The Inventions of Adolfo Bioy Casares (Photographs by Lisl Steiner). *Américas,* v. 45, no. 6 (Nov – Dec 93), pp. 14 – 19. Il.

Criticism and interpretation

Monmany, Mercedes. Las mujeres imposibles en Bioy Casares. *Cuadernos Hispanoamericanos,* no. 513 (Mar 93), pp. 117 – 122.

Morán, Carlos Roberto. Adolfo Bioy Casares o la aventura de imaginar. *Revista Nacional de Cultura (Venezuela),* v. 54, no. 287 (Oct – Dec 92), pp. 222 – 230. Il.

Criticism of specific works

El sueño de los héroes

Navascués, Javier de. *El sueño de los héroes:* un conflicto trágico entre dos lealtades. *Revista Canadiense de Estudios Hispánicos,* v. 17, no. 3 (Spring 93), pp. 453 – 463. Bibl.

Interviews

Sorrentino, Fernando. *Siete conversaciones con Adolfo Bioy Casares* reviewed by Ted Lyon. *Chasqui,* v. 22, no. 2 (Nov 93), pp. 168 – 170.

— *Siete conversaciones con Adolfo Bioy Casares* reviewed by Ilán Stavans. *World Literature Today,* v. 67, no. 3 (Summer 93), pp. 592 – 593.

BIRDS

Guatemala

Girón Mena, Manuel Antonio. Meditaciones frente al quetzal. *USAC,* no. 14 (June 91), pp. 74 – 82. Bibl, il.

BIRTH CONTROL

See also
Abortion
Population

Dacach, Solange and Giselle Israel. *As rotas do Norplant: desvios da contracepção* reviewed by Angela Regina Cunha (Review entitled "Risco de vida"). *Estudos Feministas,* v. 1, no. 2 (1993), pp. 489 – 491.

Guevara, Nancy. Fábricas de bebés: ¿Fantasía o profecía? (Translated by Victoria Zamudio Jasso). *Fem,* v. 17, no. 121 (Mar 93), pp. 4 – 8. Bibl.

Brazil

Berquó, Elza Salvatori. Brasil: um caso exemplar; anticoncepção e parto cirúrgicos; à espera de uma ação exemplar (Accompanied by an English translation by Christopher Peterson). *Estudos Feministas,* v. 1, no. 2 (1993), pp. 366 – 381. Bibl, tables.

Mexico

Ramírez, Socorro. Sujetos y no objetos de las políticas de población. *Fem,* v. 17, no. 121 (Mar 93), pp. 13 – 14.

Zúñiga Herrera, Elena. Cambios en el nivel de fecundidad deseada en las mujeres mexicanas, 1976 – 1986. *Revista Mexicana de Sociología,* v. 55, no. 1 (Jan – Mar 93), pp. 83 – 96. Bibl, tables, charts.

BITITA

See
Jesus, Carolina Maria de

BLACK AUTHORS

See
Brazilian literature – Black authors
Ecuadorian literature – Black authors
Latin American literature – Black authors
Puerto Rican poetry – Black authors
Venezuelan literature – Black authors

BLACK CARIBS

See
Carib Indians

BLACK LEGEND

See also
Casas, Bartolomé de las
Indians, Treatment of

García Cárcel, Ricardo. *La leyenda negra: historia y opinión* reviewed by Blas Matamoro. *Cuadernos Hispanoamericanos,* no. 511 (Jan 93), p. 137.

Izard, Miquel. Elegir lo posible y escoger lo mejor. *Boletín Americanista,* v. 33, no. 42 – 43 (1992 – 1993), pp. 141 – 182. Bibl.

Tisnés Jiménez, Roberto María. La "leyenda negra" de los criminales descubridores. *Boletín de Historia y Antigüedades,* v. 79, no. 779 (Oct – Dec 92), pp. 1019 – 1035. Bibl.

BLACKS

See also
Carib Indians
Maroons
Race discrimination
Slavery
Subdivision *Race question* under names of specific countries

America

Bonnett, Aubrey W. and G. Llewellyn Watson, eds. *Emerging Perspectives on the Black Diaspora* reviewed by Harry Goulbourne. *Caribbean Quarterly,* v. 38, no. 2 – 3 (June – Sept 92), pp. 115 – 116.

Lewis, Rupert. The Contemporary Significance of the African Diaspora in the Americas. *Caribbean Quarterly,* v. 38, no. 2 – 3 (June – Sept 92), pp. 73 – 80. Bibl.

Brazil

Agier, Michel, ed. *Cantos e toques: etnografias do espaço negro na Bahia* reviewed by Fernando Costa Conceição. *Revista de Antropologia (Brazil),* v. 34 (1991), pp. 223 – 227.

Andrews, George Reid. *Blacks and Whites in São Paulo, Brazil, 1888 – 1988* reviewed by Michael Hanchard. *The Américas,* v. 50, no. 1 (July 93), pp. 134 – 136.

— *Blacks and Whites in São Paulo, Brazil, 1888 – 1988* reviewed by Joseph P. Love. *Hispanic American Historical Review,* v. 73, no. 1 (Feb 93), pp. 167 – 168.

— *Blacks and Whites in São Paulo, Brazil, 1888 – 1988* reviewed by Robert M. Levine. *Revista Interamericana de Bibliografía,* v. 42, no. 2 (1992), p. 282.

Desch, T. J. Capoeira: Martial Art as Spiritual Discipline. *Journal of Caribbean Studies,* v. 9, no. 1 – 2 (Winter 92 – Spring 93), pp. 87 – 98. Bibl.

Dunn, Christopher. Afro-Bahian Carnival: A Stage for Protest. *Afro-Hispanic Review*, v. 11, no. 1 – 3 (1992), pp. 11 – 20. Bibl.

Lima, Magali Alonso de and Roberto Kant de Lima. Capoeira e cidadania: negritude e identidade no Brasil republicano. *Revista de Antropologia (Brazil)*, v. 34 (1991), pp. 143 – 182. Bibl.

Piratininga Júnior, Luiz Gonzaga. *Dietário dos negros de São Bento* reviewed by Maria de Lourdes Beldi de Alcântara. *Revista de Antropologia (Brazil)*, v. 34 (1991), pp. 227 – 228.

Ricci, Maria Lúcia de Souza Rangel. A problemática do negro no Brasil. *Hoy Es Historia*, v. 10, no. 55 (Jan – Feb 93), pp. 82 – 87.

Turner, Doris J. The "Teatro Experimental do Negro" and Its Black Beauty Contests. *Afro-Hispanic Review*, v. 11, no. 1 – 3 (1992), pp. 76 – 81. Bibl.

Walger, Christian. "Nova música baiana": Musikszene Bahia; Kultursoziologische Betrachtungen zur schwarzen Musik Brasiliens. *Zeitschrift für Lateinamerika Wien*, no. 42 (1992), pp. 27 – 51. Bibl.

Bibliography

Igel, Regina. Reavaliação de estudos sobre o negro brasileiro. *Iberoamericana*, v. 17, no. 49 (1993), pp. 16 – 32. Bibl.

Societies, etc.

Fischer, Tânia et al. Olodum: a arte e o negócio. *RAE; Revista de Administração de Empresas*, v. 33, no. 2 (Mar – Apr 93), pp. 90 – 99. Bibl.

Smith, E. Valerie. The Sisterhood of Nossa Senhora da Boa Morte and the Brotherhood of Nossa Senhora do Rosario: African-Brazilian Cultural Adaptations to Antebellum Restrictions. *Afro-Hispanic Review*, v. 11, no. 1 – 3 (1992), pp. 58 – 69. Bibl, tables.

Caribbean area

Castañeda Fuertes, Digna. Presencia africana en la identidad cultural de las sociedades caribeñas. *Boletín de la Academia Nacional de la Historia (Venezuela)*, v. 75, no. 299 (July – Sept 92), pp. 77 – 90. Bibl.

Central America

Rodino Pierri, Ana María. Language Rights and Education for the Afro-Caribbean, English-Speaking Minorities in Central America: Contributions to the Discussion on Bilingual Education in Costa Rica. *La Educación (USA)*, v. 36, no. 111 – 113 (1992), pp. 137 – 154. Bibl.

Costa Rica

Harpelle, Ronald N. The Social and Political Integration of West Indians in Costa Rica, 1930 – 1950. *Journal of Latin American Studies*, v. 25, no. 1 (Feb 93), pp. 103 – 120. Bibl.

Cuba

Castellanos, Isabel Mercedes and Jorge Castellanos. *Cultura afrocubana, III: Las religiones y las lenguas* reviewed by Luis A. Jiménez. *Hispania (USA)*, v. 76, no. 2 (May 93), pp. 281 – 282.

Ocasio, Rafael. "Babalú Ayé": Santería and Contemporary Cuban Literature. *Journal of Caribbean Studies*, v. 9, no. 1 – 2 (Winter 92 – Spring 93), pp. 29 – 40. Bibl.

Palmié, Stephan. *Das Exil der Götter: Geschichte und Vorstellungswelt einer afrokubanischen Religion* reviewed by Matthias Perl. *Iberoamericana*, v. 17, no. 49 (1993), pp. 101 – 102.

Sáenz, Carmen María and María Elena Vinueza. El aporte africano en la formación de la cultura musical cubana. *Folklore Americano*, no. 53 (Jan – June 92), pp. 55 – 80. Bibl.

Societies, etc.

Howard, Philip A. The Spanish Colonial Government's Responses to the Pan-Nationalist Agenda of the Afro-Cuban Mutual Aid Societies, 1868 – 1895. *Revista/Review Interamericana*, v. 22, no. 1 – 2 (Spring – Summer 92), pp. 151 – 167. Bibl.

Guatemala

Ruz, Mario Humberto. Sebastiana de la Cruz, alias "La Polilla": mulata de Petapa y madre del hijo de Dios. *Mesoamérica (USA)*, v. 13, no. 23 (June 92), pp. 55 – 66. Bibl.

Haiti

Garrigus, John D. Blue and Brown: Contraband Indigo and the Rise of a Free Colored Planter Class in French Saint-Domingue. *The Americas*, v. 50, no. 2 (Oct 93), pp. 233 – 263. Bibl, tables, maps, charts.

— Catalyst or Catastrophe?: Saint-Domingue's Free Men of Color and the Battle of Savannah, 1779 – 1782. *Revista/Review Interamericana*, v. 22, no. 1 – 2 (Spring – Summer 92), pp. 109 – 125. Bibl.

Martin, Michel L. and Alain Yacou, eds. *Mourir pour les Antilles: indépendance nègre ou esclavage, 1802 – 1804* reviewed by Frédérique Langue. *Caravelle*, no. 60 (1993), pp. 157 – 159.

Jamaica

Aborampah, Osei-Mensah. Religious Sanction and Social Order in Traditional Akan Communities of Ghana and Jamaica. *Journal of Caribbean Studies*, v. 9, no. 1 – 2 (Winter 92 – Spring 93), pp. 41 – 58. Bibl, charts.

Latin America

Mosquera, Gerardo. Plástico afroamericana (Accompanied by an English translation). *Art Nexus*, no. 9 (June – Aug 93), pp. 100 – 102. Il.

Tardieu, Jean-Pierre. Las vistas de un arbitrista sobre la aparición de un hombre nuevo en las Indias Occidentales, mitad del siglo XVII. *Anuario de Estudios Americanos*, v. 50, no. 1 (1993), pp. 235 – 249. Bibl.

Mexico

Carroll, Patrick James. *Blacks in Colonial Veracruz: Race, Ethnicity, and Regional Development* reviewed by Linda A. Newson. *Journal of Latin American Studies*, v. 25, no. 1 (Feb 93), pp. 192 – 193.

Panama

Pastor Núñez, Aníbal. Medicina popular y creencias mágico – religiosas de la población negra del Darién. *Revista Cultural Lotería*, v. 51, no. 387 (Feb 92), pp. 61 – 68. Bibl.

Peru

Hünefeldt, Christine. *Lasmanuelos: vida cotidiana de una familia negra en la Lima del s. XIX* reviewed by Sara Mateos (Review entitled "Esclavitud urbana"). *Debate (Peru)*, v. 15, no. 70 (Sept – Oct 92), pp. 67 – 68.

Puerto Rico

Quintero Rivera, Angel Guillermo. El tambor oculto en el cuatro: la melodización de ritmos y la etnicidad cimarroneada en la caribeña cultura de la contraplantación. *Boletín Americanista*, v. 33, no. 42 – 43 (1992 – 1993), pp. 87 – 106. Bibl, facs.

United States

Dassori, Albana M. et al. Ethnic and Gender Differences in the Diagnostic Profiles of Substance Abusers. *Hispanic Journal of Behavioral Sciences*, v. 15, no. 3 (Aug 93), pp. 382 – 390. Bibl.

Edwards, Jack E. et al. Willingness to Relocate for Employment: A Survey of Hispanics, Non-Hispanic Whites, and Blacks. *Hispanic Journal of Behavioral Sciences*, v. 15, no. 1 (Feb 93), pp. 121 – 133. Bibl, tables.

Massey, Douglas S. Latinos, Poverty, and the Underclass: A New Agenda for Research. *Hispanic Journal of Behavioral Sciences*, v. 15, no. 4 (Nov 93), pp. 449 – 475. Bibl.

Uruguay

Díaz, José Enrique. Los descendientes de africanos en el Uruguay. *Afro-Hispanic Review*, v. 12, no. 2 (Fall 93), pp. 24 – 25.

Ruiz, Rosa. El aporte de la cultura negra en el departamento de Cerro Largo. *Hoy Es Historia*, v. 10, no. 55 (Jan – Feb 93), pp. 72 – 75.

Venezuela

Rodríguez, Manuel Alfredo. Los pardos libres en la colonia y la independencia. *Boletín de la Academia Nacional de la Historia (Venezuela)*, v. 75, no. 299 (July – Sept 92), pp. 33 – 62. Bibl.

BLACKS IN LITERATURE

Ferguson, Moira. *Subject to Others: British Women Writers and Colonial Slavery, 1670 – 1834* reviewed by Karen Mead. *Hispanic American Historical Review*, v. 73, no. 4 (Nov 93), p. 675.

Kothe, Flávio R. Heine, Nerval, Castro Alves: "o negreiro." *Iberoamericana*, v. 17, no. 49 (1993), pp. 42 – 63.

Brazil

Durham, Carolyn Richardson. Sônia Fátima da Conceição's Literature for Social Change. *Afro-Hispanic Review*, v. 11, no. 1 – 3 (1992), pp. 21 – 25. Bibl.

Lima, Robert. Xangô and Other Yoruba Deities in the Plays of Zora Seljan. *Afro-Hispanic Review*, v. 11, no. 1 – 3 (1992), pp. 26 – 33. Bibl.

Platt, Kamala. Race and Gender Representation in Clarice Lispector's "A menor mulher do mundo" and Carolina Maria de Jesus' *Quarto de despejo*. *Afro-Hispanic Review*, v. 11, no. 1 – 3 (1992), pp. 51 – 57. Bibl.

Caribbean area

Dukats, Mara L. A Narrative of Violated Maternity: *Moi, Tituba, sorcière . . . noire de Salem*. *World Literature Today*, v. 67, no. 4 (Fall 93), pp. 745 – 750. Bibl.

Manzor-Coats, Lillian. Of Witches and Other Things: Maryse Condé's Challenges to Feminist Discourse. *World Literature Today*, v. 67, no. 4 (Fall 93), pp. 737 – 744. Bibl, il.

Williams, Claudette Rose-Green. The Myth of Black Female Sexuality in Spanish Caribbean Poetry: A Deconstructive Critical View. *Afro-Hispanic Review*, v. 12, no. 1 (Spring 93), pp. 16 – 23. Bibl.

Colombia

Prescott, Laurence E. "Negro nací": Authorship and Voice in Verses Attributed to Candelario Obeso. *Afro-Hispanic Review*, v. 12, no. 1 (Spring 93), pp. 3 – 15. Bibl.

Cuba

Araújo, Nara. La Avellaneda, la Merlin: una manera de ver y sentir. *Iberoamericana*, v. 17, no. 49 (1993), pp. 33 – 41. Bibl.

— Raza y género en *Sab*. *Casa de las Américas*, no. 190 (Jan – Mar 93), pp. 42 – 49. Bibl.

González Bolaños, Aimée. El arte narrativo de Lino Novás Calvo en *El negrero*. *Islas*, no. 98 (Jan – Apr 91), pp. 87 – 97.

Guicharnaud-Tollis, Michèle. *L'émergence du noir dans le roman cubain du XIXe siècle* reviewed by Paul Estrade. *Caravelle*, no. 59 (1992), pp. 278 – 280.

— *L'émergence du noir dans le roman cubain du XIXe siècle* reviewed by Paul Estrade. *Revista de Indias*, v. 53, no. 197 (Jan – Apr 93), pp. 108 – 109.

Luis, William. *Literary Bondage: Slavery in Cuban Narrative* reviewed by Antonio Benítez-Rojo. *Hispanic Review*, v. 61, no. 1 (Winter 93), pp. 125 – 127.

Phaf, Ineke. La introducción emblemática de la nación mulata: el contrapunteo híbrido en las culturas de Suriname y Cuba. *Revista de Crítica Literaria Latinoamericana*, v. 19, no. 38 (July – Dec 93), pp. 195 – 215. Bibl.

Sommer, Doris. Cecilia no sabe o los bloqueos que blanquean. *Revista de Crítica Literaria Latinoamericana*, v. 19, no. 38 (July – Dec 93), pp. 239 – 248. Bibl.

Williams, Lorna Valerie. The Representation of the Female Slave in Villaverde's *Cecilia Valdés*. *Hispanic Journal*, v. 14, no. 1 (Spring 93), pp. 73 – 89. Bibl.

Ecuador

Handelsman, Michael Howard. Ubicando la literatura afroecuatoriana en el contexto nacional: ¿Ilusión o realidad? *Afro-Hispanic Review*, v. 12, no. 1 (Spring 93), pp. 42 – 47. Bibl.

Latin America

Ramos, Julio. Cuerpo, lengua, subjetividad. *Revista de Crítica Literaria Latinoamericana*, v. 19, no. 38 (July – Dec 93), pp. 225 – 237. Bibl.

Martinique

Burton, Richard D. E. Créolité, Négritude, and Metropolis. *Hemisphere*, v. 5, no. 3 (Summer – Fall 93), pp. 10 – 12. Il.

Surinam

Phaf, Ineke. La introducción emblemática de la nación mulata: el contrapunteo híbrido en las culturas de Suriname y Cuba. *Revista de Crítica Literaria Latinoamericana*, v. 19, no. 38 (July – Dec 93), pp. 195 – 215. Bibl.

Uruguay

Cordones-Cook, Juanamaría. Surgimiento y desaparición del Teatro Negro Uruguayo: entrevista con Andrés Castillo. *Afro-Hispanic Review*, v. 12, no. 2 (Fall 93), pp. 31 – 36.

Venezuela

Lewis, Marvin A. *Ethnicity and Identity in Contemporary Afro-Venezuelan Literature: A Culturalist Approach* reviewed by Jorge J. Rodríguez-Florido. *Hispania (USA)*, v. 76, no. 2 (May 93), p. 289.

LA BLANCA SITE, GUATEMALA

Love, Michael W. Ceramic Chronology and Chronometric Dating: Stratigraphy and Seriation at La Blanca, Guatemala. *Ancient Mesoamerica*, v. 4, no. 1 (Spring 93), pp. 17 – 29. Bibl, il, tables, maps, charts.

BLEST, CLOTARIO

Echeverría, Mónica. *Antihistoria de un luchador: Clotario Blest, 1823 – 1990* reviewed by G. A. C. *Mensaje*, v. 42, no. 424 (Nov 93), pp. 597 – 599. Il.

BLOOD

Research

Sanz, Mónica et al. Blood Group Frequencies and the Question of Race Mixture in Uruguay. *Interciencia*, v. 18, no. 1 (Jan – Feb 93), pp. 29 – 32. Bibl, tables.

BOCANEGRA, MATÍAS DE

Criticism of specific works

Comedia de San Francisco de Borja

Luciani, Frederick William. The *Comedia de San Francisco de Borja* (1640): The Mexican Jesuits and the "Education of the Prince." *Colonial Latin American Review*, v. 2, no. 1 – 2 (1993), pp. 121 – 141. Bibl.

BODY, HUMAN

See

    Blood

    Pregnancy

    Teeth

BOGOTÁ, COLOMBIA

Bernal Leongómez, Jaime and José Joaquín Montes Giraldo. El verbo en el habla culta de Bogotá: frecuencia de categorías tradicionales y creación de otras nuevas. *Thesaurus*, v. 45, no. 3 (Sept – Dec 90), pp. 732 – 742. Bibl, tables.

COMPENSAR: Centro Urbano de Recreación (CUR). *Revista Javeriana*, v. 61, no. 592 (Mar 93), pp. 98 – 100. Il.

Díaz, Jairo et al. Determinantes del precio de los inmuebles en Bogotá. *Planeación y Desarrollo*, v. 24, no. 2 (May – Aug 93), pp. 315 – 327. Tables, charts.

— Elementos del mercado del suelo urbano. *Planeación y Desarrollo*, v. 24, no. 2 (May – Aug 93), pp. 329 – 338. Tables.

Gouëset, Vincent and Fabio Zambrano Pantoja. Géopolitique du district spécial de Bogotá et du Haut-Sumapaz, 1900 – 1990. *Bulletin de l'Institut Français d'Etudes Andines*, v. 21, no. 3 (1992), pp. 1053 – 1071. Bibl, maps.

Pastrana Arango, Andrés. En busca de una Bogotá más humana (Previously published in this journal, no. 566, 1990). *Revista Javeriana*, v. 61, no. 596 (July 93), pp. 95 – 101.

Silva Téllez, Armando. *Punto de vista ciudadano: focalización visual y puesta en escena del graffiti* reviewed by Maurice P. Brungardt (Review entitled "Readings on Colombia?"). *Studies in Latin American Popular Culture*, v. 12 (1993), pp. 235 – 242.

Sowell, David Lee. *The Early Colombian Labor Movement: Artisans and Politics in Bogotá, 1832 – 1919* reviewed by Jane M. Rausch. *Hispanic American Historical Review*, v. 73, no. 4 (Nov 93), pp. 715 – 716.

BOHR, JOSÉ

Vega Alfaro, Eduardo de la. *José Bohr* reviewed by Beatriz Valdés Lagunes (Review entitled "Pioneros del cine sonoro III"). *Revista Mexicana de Ciencias Políticas y Sociales*, v. 37, Nueva época, no. 150 (Oct – Dec 92), pp. 191 – 192.

BOLERO (DANCE)

Gómez García, Zoila. Siempre el bolero. *Plural (Mexico)*, v. 22, no. 263 (Aug 93), pp. 71 – 72.

BOLETÍN DE LA ACADEMIA NACIONAL DE LA HISTORIA (VENEZUELA) (PERIODICAL)

Indexes

López Bohórquez, Alí Enrique. El descubrimiento de América en el *Boletín de la Academia Nacional de la Historia. Boletín de la Academia Nacional de la Historia (Venezuela)*, v. 75, no. 300 (Oct – Dec 92), pp. 166 – 171.

BOLÍVAR, GREGORIO DE

Gato Castaño, Purificación. *El informe del p. Gregorio de Bolívar a la Congregación de Propaganda Fide de 1623* reviewed by Pedro de Anasagasti. *Signo*, no. 35, Nueva época (Jan – Apr 92), pp. 214 – 216.

BOLÍVAR, SIMÓN

Biography

Cacua Prada, Antonio. *Los hijos secretos de Bolívar* reviewed by Alfonso Gómez Gómez. *Boletín de Historia y Antigüedades*, v. 79, no. 779 (Oct – Dec 92), pp. 1071 – 1083.

— *Los hijos secretos de Bolívar* reviewed by Manuel Drezner (Review entitled "Tres nuevos libros del académico Cacua Prada"). *Boletín de Historia y Antigüedades*, v. 80, no. 781 (Apr – June 93), pp. 479 – 480.

Mejía Gutiérrez, Carlos. Esbozos para un estudio psicológico del Libertador. *Boletín de Historia y Antigüedades*, v. 80, no. 781 (Apr – June 93), pp. 443 – 462. Bibl.

Ramos Pérez, Demetrio. *Simón Bolívar, el Libertador* reviewed by R. J. Lovera De-Sola (Review entitled "El Bolívar de Demetrio Ramos Pérez"). *Boletín de la Academia Nacional de la Historia (Venezuela)*, v. 75, no. 298 (Apr – June 92), pp. 108 – 109.

Criticism and interpretation

Carrera Damas, Germán. *El culto a Bolívar: esbozo para un estudio de la historia de las ideas en Venezuela* reviewed by Frédérique Langue. *Cahiers des Amériques Latines*, no. 13 (1992), p. 184.

Cussen, Antonio. *Bello and Bolívar: Poetry and Politics in the Spanish American Revolution* reviewed by Fernando Cervantes. *Bulletin of Latin American Research*, v. 12, no. 1 (Jan 93), pp. 114 – 115.

— *Bello and Bolívar: Poetry and Politics in the Spanish American Revolution* reviewed by Myron I. Lichtblau. *Hispania (USA)*, v. 76, no. 2 (May 93), p. 285.

Díaz, María Eugenia. Liberación en las luchas latinoamericanas. *Islas*, no. 98 (Jan – Apr 91), pp. 167 – 176. Charts.

Torrealba Lossi, Mario et al. Bibliográficas. *Boletín de la Academia Nacional de la Historia (Venezuela)*, v. 76, no. 301 (Jan – Mar 93), pp. 121 – 127.

Fiction

Alvarez-Borland, Isabel. The Task of the Historian in *El general en su laberinto. Hispania (USA)*, v. 76, no. 3 (Sept 93), pp. 439 – 445. Bibl.

Matarrita M., Estébana. La polifuncionalidad en *El general en su laberinto. Káñina*, v. 16, no. 2 (July – Dec 92), pp. 109 – 113. Bibl.

Monuments, etc.

Bruni Celli, Blas. Palabras pronunciadas por el doctor Blas Bruni Celli ante la estatua del Libertador Simón Bolívar en Lisboa el 6 de mayo de 1992, con motivo del I Encuentro de las Academias de Historia de Portugal y Venezuela. *Boletín de la Academia Nacional de la Historia (Venezuela)*, v. 76, no. 301 (Jan – Mar 93), pp. 39 – 40.

Poetry

Briceño Perozo, Mario, ed. *Sonetos a Bolívar* reviewed by Luis Gustavo Acuña Luco (Review entitled "Homenaje sonetístico a Simón Bolívar"). *Boletín de la Academia Nacional de la Historia (Venezuela)*, v. 75, no. 298 (Apr – June 92), pp. 112 – 114.

Societies, etc.

En la Sociedad Bolivariana de París. *Boletín de Historia y Antigüedades*, v. 80, no. 781 (Apr – June 93), pp. 487 – 489.

BOLIVIA

See also
    Agriculture and state – Bolivia
    Art – Bolivia
    Art, Colonial – Bolivia
    Botany – Bolivia
    Chaco War, 1932 – 1935
    Christian art and symbolism – Bolivia
    Chuquisaca, Bolivia
    Coca and cocaine – Bolivia
    Cochabamba, Bolivia (Department)
    Communism – Bolivia
    Diseases – Bolivia
    Drug trade – Bolivia
    Education – Bolivia
    Elections – Bolivia
    Ethnicity – Bolivia
    Evangelicalism – Bolivia
    Finance, Public – Bolivia
    Folk art – Bolivia
    Folk dancing – Bolivia
    Folk festivals – Bolivia
    Folk lore – Bolivia
    Folk music – Bolivia
    Franciscans – Bolivia
    Guerrillas – Bolivia
    Indians, Treatment of – Bolivia
    Informal sector (Economics) – Bolivia
    Jesuits – Bolivia
    Journalism – Bolivia
    Labor supply – Bolivia
    Libraries and librarians – Bolivia
    Literary criticism – Bolivia
    Literature and history – Bolivia
    Literature and society – Bolivia
    Medical anthropology – Bolivia
    Military in government – Bolivia
    Missions – Bolivia
    Motion pictures – Bolivia
    Music and society – Bolivia
    Musical instruments – Bolivia
    National security – Bolivia
    Nationalism – Bolivia
    Non-governmental organizations – Bolivia
    Oral tradition – Bolivia
    Oruro, Bolivia
    La Paz, Bolivia (City)
    Peasantry – Bolivia
    Periodicals – Bolivia
    Philosophy – Bolivia
    Political participation – Bolivia
    Political sociology – Bolivia
    Politics in literature – Bolivia
    Potosí, Bolivia (Department)
    Press and politics – Bolivia
    Protestantism – Bolivia
    Public opinion – Bolivia
    Regional planning – Bolivia
    Regionalism – Bolivia
    Religion and politics – Bolivia
    Silver mines and mining – Bolivia
    Social change – Bolivia
    Social classes – Bolivia
    Sociolinguistics – Bolivia
    Spanish language – Bolivia
    Tacna – Arica question
    Tarija, Bolivia (Department)
    Taxation – Bolivia
    Television – Bolivia
    Tiahuanacu, Bolivia
    Titicaca, Lake
    Trade unions – Bolivia
    Women – Bolivia
    Women authors – Bolivia
    Yungas, Bolivia

Antiquities

Schávelzon, Daniel. La arqueología como ciencia o como ficción. *Todo Es Historia,* v. 26, no. 309 (Apr 93), pp. 32 – 49. Bibl, il.

Armed forces

Barrios Morón, J. Raúl. La política contra las drogas en Bolivia: interdicción y guerra de baja intensidad. *Nueva Sociedad,* no. 123 (Jan – Feb 93), pp. 35 – 49. Bibl.

Boundaries

Chile

Padilla, Mario. *Mar para Bolivia* reviewed by Raúl Rivadeneira Prada. *Signo,* no. 38, Nueva época (Jan – Apr 93), pp. 247 – 248.

Southern Cone of South America

Jordán Sandoval, Santiago. Coincidentes y respuestas alarmantes a una pregunta sobre *Bolivia y el equilibrio del Cono Sur. Signo,* no. 35, Nueva época (Jan – Apr 92), pp. 37 – 41. Bibl.

Civilization

Flores López, Domingo. Conversaciones sobre el destino de Bolivia. *Signo,* no. 36 – 37, Nueva época (May – Dec 92), pp. 147 – 167.

Teixidó, Raúl. *Autores y personajes* reviewed by Carlos Castañón Barrientos. *Signo,* no. 38, Nueva época (Jan – Apr 93), pp. 257 – 258.

Description and travel

Castañón Barrientos, Carlos. Escritores extranjeros en Bolivia (Segunda parte). *Signo,* no. 38, Nueva época (Jan – Apr 93), pp. 15 – 25.

Ferrufino Coqueugniot, Claudio. Ayopaya: el mundo perdido. *Signo,* no. 35, Nueva época (Jan – Apr 92), pp. 3 – 4.

Gottret Baldivieso, Augusto. *Imágenes y vivencias* reviewed by Raúl Rivadeneira Prada. *Signo,* no. 35, Nueva época (Jan – Apr 92), pp. 217 – 221.

Economic conditions

Toranzo Roca, Carlos F. Bolivia: tedios, desafíos y sorpresas. *Nueva Sociedad,* no. 124 (Mar – Apr 93), pp. 11 – 16. Bibl.

Economic policy

Gallego, Ferran. La política económica del "socialismo militar" boliviano. *Anuario de Estudios Americanos,* v. 50, no. 1 (1993), pp. 213 – 234. Bibl, tables.

Foreign economic relations

Andean region

Frambes-Buxeda, Aline. Bolivia: eje vital de la integración económica andina y latinoamericana. *Homines,* v. 15 – 16, no. 2 – 1 (Oct 91 – Dec 92), pp. 187 – 248. Bibl, tables.

Chile

ALADI: Acuerdo de Complementación Económica entre Bolivia y Chile. *Integración Latinoamericana,* v. 18, no. 194 (Oct 93), pp. 56 – 60.

Pizarro, Roberto. Las negociaciones comerciales Chile – Bolivia: vacilaciones chilenas y sensibilidades bolivianas. *Mensaje,* v. 42, no. 417 (Mar – Apr 93), pp. 99 – 100.

Foreign relations

America

Espada, Joaquín. *Bolivia en la interamericanidad* reviewed by Pedro de Anasagasti. *Signo,* no. 38, Nueva época (Jan – Apr 93), pp. 236 – 237.

History

Anasagasti, Pedro de. El mariscal Andrés de Santa Cruz, gran pacificador. *Signo,* no. 38, Nueva época (Jan – Apr 93), pp. 95 – 104. Bibl.

Ascarrunz, Eduardo. Ideología política y comunicación social en el proceso histórico de la colonia a la independencia. *Signo,* no. 35, Nueva época (Jan – Apr 92), pp. 59 – 76. Bibl.

Irurozqui Victoriano, Marta. La guerra de razas en Bolivia: la (re)invención de una tradición. *Revista Andina,* v. 11, no. 1 (July 93), pp. 163 – 200. Bibl.

Morales, Waltraud Queiser. *Bolivia: Land of Struggle* reviewed by Christopher Mitchell. *Studies in Comparative International Development,* v. 27, no. 3 (Fall 92), pp. 124 – 125.

— *Bolivia: Land of Struggle* reviewed by Erick D. Langer. *Hispanic American Historical Review,* v. 73, no. 1 (Feb 93), p. 173.

— *Bolivia: Land of Struggle* reviewed by Robert H. Jackson. *The Americas,* v. 50, no. 1 (July 93), pp. 145 – 146.

Reque Terán, Luis. *La campaña de Ñancahuazu* reviewed by René López Murillo. *Signo,* no. 35, Nueva época (Jan – Apr 92), pp. 245 – 247.

Politics and government

Lavaud, Jean-Pierre. *L'instabilité politique de l'Amérique Latine: le cas de la Bolivie* reviewed by Frédérique Langue. *Cahiers des Amériques Latines,* no. 13 (1992), pp. 179 – 180.

Toranzo Roca, Carlos F. Bolivia: tedios, desafíos y sorpresas. *Nueva Sociedad,* no. 124 (Mar – Apr 93), pp. 11 – 16. Bibl.

Race question

Boero Rojo, Hugo. Orígenes de la polémica Franz Tamayo – Fernando Díez de Medina. *Signo,* no. 36 – 37, Nueva época (May – Dec 92), pp. 43 – 69.

Rural conditions

Paz Ballivián, Danilo. Cuestión agraria y campesina en Bolivia. *Revista Paraguaya de Sociología,* v. 29, no. 84 (May – Aug 92), pp. 115 – 133.

BOLIVIAN LITERATURE

Soriano Badani, Armando, ed. *Antología del cuento boliviano,* 2d ed., reviewed by Melvin S. Arrington, Jr. *World Literature Today,* v. 67, no. 1 (Winter 93), pp. 161 – 162.

History and criticism

Quirós, Juan. *Fronteras movedizas* reviewed by Carlos Coello Vila (Review entitled *"Fronteras movedizas:* 35 años de crítica literaria"). *Signo,* no. 36 – 37, Nueva época (May – Dec 92), pp. 227 – 231.

BOLIVIAN POETRY

History and criticism

Dávalos Arze, Gladys. La mujer poeta y la sociedad: cocinan tan bien como escriben. *Signo,* no. 38, Nueva época (Jan – Apr 93), pp. 105 – 111. Bibl.

Morales Cavero, Hugo. Apuntes para un estudio de la poesía revolucionaria. *Signo,* no. 35, Nueva época (Jan – Apr 92), pp. 163 – 195. Bibl.

Quiroga, Giancarla de. La mujer poeta en la sociedad. *Signo,* no. 38, Nueva época (Jan – Apr 93), pp. 123 – 130.

Congresses

Wiethüchter, Blanca. Primer Encuentro Nacional de Mujeres Poetas: surtidores de enigmas. *Signo,* no. 38, Nueva época (Jan – Apr 93), pp. 113 – 121.

BOLLA, LUIS

Interviews

Entrevista al padre Luis Bolla. *Amazonía Peruana,* v. 11, no. 22 (Oct 92), pp. 255 – 272.

BOLOÑA BEHR, CARLOS ALBERTO

Interviews

Alvarez Rodrich, Augusto and Pilar Dávila. Entrevista a Carlos Boloña. *Debate (Peru),* v. 15, no. 70 (Sept – Oct 92), pp. 8 – 14. Il.

BOMBAL, MARÍA LUISA

Criticism of specific works

La última niebla

Guerra-Cunningham, Lucía. La marginalidad subversiva del deseo en *La última niebla* de María Luisa Bombal. *Hispamérica,* v. 21, no. 62 (Aug 92), pp. 53 – 63.

Tolliver, Joyce. "Otro modo de ver": The Gaze in *La última niebla. Revista Canadiense de Estudios Hispánicos,* v. 17, no. 1 (Fall 92), pp. 105 – 121. Bibl.

BONFÁ, LUIZ

Holston, Mark. Playing the Heartstrings. *Américas,* v. 45, no. 5 (Sept – Oct 93), pp. 58 – 59. Il.

BONFIL BATALLA, GUILLERMO

Dauzier, Martine. Tous des indiens?: la "réindianisation"; force ou fiction: débats autour des essais de Guillermo Bonfil Batalla. *Cahiers des Amériques Latines*, no. 13 (1992), pp. 147 – 158. Bibl.

Obituaries

Bartolomé, Miguel Alberto and Salomón Nahmad Sittón. Semblanza. *América Indígena*, v. 51, no. 2 – 3 (Apr – Sept 91), pp. 417 – 418.

Davis, Shelton H. Guillermo Bonfil Batalla y el movimiento indio latinoamericano (Translated by Alvaro González R.). *América Indígena*, v. 51, no. 2 – 3 (Apr – Sept 91), pp. 411 – 416.

Nahmad Sittón, Salomón. Guillermo Bonfil, un visionario de la sociedad multiétnica mexicana. *América Indígena*, v. 51, no. 2 – 3 (Apr – Sept 91), pp. 403 – 409. Il.

BONIFAZ NUÑO, RUBÉN

Criticism of specific works

Los demonios y los días

Buye-Goyri Minter, Rafael. En torno a *Los demonios y los días*. La Palabra y el Hombre, no. 84 (Oct – Dec 92), pp. 240 – 245. Bibl.

BONITO OLIVA, ACHILLE

Interviews

Jiménez, Carlos. Bienal de Venecia. *Art Nexus*, no. 10 (Sept – Dec 93), pp. 56 – 58.

BOOK TRADE

See
   Booksellers and bookselling
   Publishers and publishing

BOOKS

See also
   Manuscripts
   Microforms
   Printing and engraving
   Publishers and publishing
   Reading interests
   Textbooks

Collectors and collecting

Deal, Carl W. A Survey of Latin American Collections. *SALALM Papers*, v. 36 (1991), pp. 315 – 324. Tables.

Gardner, Jeffrey J. Scholarship, Research Libraries, and Foreign Publishing in the 1990s. *SALALM Papers*, v. 36 (1991), pp. 277 – 293.

Methodology

Hazen, Dan C. The Latin American Conspectus: Panacea or Pig in a Poke? *SALALM Papers*, v. 36 (1991), pp. 235 – 247. Bibl.

Noble, Patricia E. Collection Evaluation Techniques: A British Pilot Study. *SALALM Papers*, v. 36 (1991), pp. 248 – 257. Tables.

Wade, Ann E. European Approaches to the Conspectus. *SALALM Papers*, v. 36 (1991), pp. 258 – 264.

Chile

Subercaseaux S., Bernardo. *Historia del libro en Chile: alma y cuerpo* reviewed by G. A. C. *Mensaje*, v. 42, no. 419 (June 93), p. 218.

Costa Rica

Molina Jiménez, Iván and Arnaldo Moya Gutiérrez. Leyendo "lecturas": documentos para la historia del libro en Costa Rica a comienzos del siglo XIX. *Revista de Historia (Costa Rica)*, no. 26 (July – Dec 92), pp. 241 – 262.

Germany

Bibliography

Huhle, Rainer. El V centenario a través de los libros en Alemania. *Ibero-Amerikanisches Archiv*, v. 18, no. 3 – 4 (1992), pp. 543 – 557. Bibl.

Italy

Bibliography

Antichi libri d'America: censimento romano, 1493 – 1701 reviewed by Fernando I. Ortiz Crespo (Review entitled "Antiguos libros de America en Roma"). *Interciencia*, v. 18, no. 3 (May – June 93), pp. 164 – 165.

Latin America

Cost

Block, David. Latin American Book Prices: The Trends of Two Decades. *SALALM Papers*, v. 36 (1991), pp. 305 – 314. Tables, charts.

Mexico

Blanco, Hugo Diego. La biblioteca sitiada. *Vuelta*, v. 17, no. 198 (May 93), pp. 67 – 71. Bibl, tables.

Peru

Collectors and collecting

Hampe Martínez, Teodoro. The Diffusion of Books and Ideas in Colonial Peru: A Study of Private Libraries in the Sixteenth and Seventeenth Centuries. *Hispanic American Historical Review*, v. 73, no. 2 (May 93), pp. 211 – 233. Bibl, tables.

Uruguay

Sources

Retta, Luis A. Publicaciones uruguayas incluidas en LATBOOK. *SALALM Papers*, v. 36 (1991), pp. 435 – 437.

BOOKSELLERS AND BOOKSELLING

See also
   Publishers and publishing

Argentina

Yánover, Héctor. La librería: escenas domésticas. *Cuadernos Hispanoamericanos*, no. 517 – 519 (July – Sept 93), pp. 521 – 524.

BORDER INDUSTRIES

See
   Subcontracting
   Subdivision *Industries* under *Mexican-American Border Region*

BORDERS

See
   Boundaries
   Mexican – American Border Region
   Subdivision *Boundaries* under names of specific countries and regions

BORGES, FRANCISCO

Barrenechea, Ana María. Jorge Luis Borges y la ambivalente mitificación de su abuelo paterno. *Nueva Revista de Filología Hispánica*, v. 40, no. 2 (July – Dec 92), pp. 1005 – 1024. Bibl.

BORGES, JORGE LUIS

Biography

Barnstone, Willis. *With Borges on an Ordinary Evening in Buenos Aires: A Memoir* reviewed by Naomi Lindstrom. *World Literature Today*, v. 67, no. 4 (Fall 93), p. 787.

Criticism and interpretation

Barrenechea, Ana María. Jorge Luis Borges y la ambivalente mitificación de su abuelo paterno. *Nueva Revista de Filología Hispánica*, v. 40, no. 2 (July – Dec 92), pp. 1005 – 1024. Bibl.

Gorodischer, Angélica. Borges y los judíos. *Confluencia*, v. 8, no. 1 (Fall 92), pp. 9 – 18.

Kluback, William. Our Gentile Guides: Jorge Luis Borges and Franz Kafka. *Confluencia*, v. 8, no. 1 (Fall 92), pp. 19 – 27.

Kushigian, Julia A. *Orientalism in the Hispanic Tradition: In Dialogue with Borges, Paz, and Sarduy* reviewed by John Incledon. *Hispania (USA)*, v. 76, no. 3 (Sept 93), pp. 483 – 484.

Lindstrom, Naomi. *Jorge Luis Borges: A Study of the Short Fiction* reviewed by Adriana J. Bergero. *Hispanic Review*, v. 61, no. 1 (Winter 93), pp. 131 – 133.

Marcos, Juan Manuel. Jorge Luis Borges y el museo imaginario: en torno al debate conceptual sobre postboom y post modernidad. *Estudios Paraguayos,* v. 17, no. 1 – 2 (1989 – 1993), pp. 151 – 166. Bibl.

Merrell, Floyd Fenly. *Unthinking Thinking: Jorge Luis Borges, Mathematics, and the New Physics* reviewed by Harley D. Oberhelman. *Hispania (USA),* v. 76, no. 2 (May 93), pp. 289 – 290.

Ortega, Julio. El arte de la lectura: encuentros con Borges. *Nexos,* v. 16, no. 182 (Feb 93), pp. 41 – 50.

Planells, Antonio. Borges y Narciso: dos espejos enfrentados. *Hispanic Journal,* v. 13, no. 2 (Fall 92), pp. 213 – 239. Bibl.

Quesada, Uriel. El juego de la ruta definitiva. *La Palabra y el Hombre,* no. 82 (Apr – June 92), pp. 258 – 259.

Rodríguez-Luis, Julio. *The Contemporary Praxis of the Fantastic: Borges and Cortázar* reviewed by John Incledon. *Hispania (USA),* v. 76, no. 1 (Mar 93), p. 89.

— *The Contemporary Praxis of the Fantastic: Borges and Cortázar* reviewed by John Incledon. *Revista de Crítica Literaria Latinoamericana,* v. 19, no. 38 (July – Dec 93), pp. 403 – 404.

Shaw, Donald Leslie. *Borges' Narrative Strategy* reviewed by Didier T. Jaén. *Revista Interamericana de Bibliografía,* v. 42, no. 3 (1992), pp. 509 – 510.

Stabb, Martin S. *Borges Revisited* reviewed by Bruno Bosteels. *Hispanic Review,* v. 61, no. 4 (Fall 93), pp. 594 – 596.

Stavans, Ilán. El arte de la memoria. *La Palabra y el Hombre,* no. 81 (Jan – Mar 92), pp. 241 – 253. Bibl.

Tyler, Joseph, ed. *Borges' Craft of Fiction: Selected Essays on His Writing* reviewed by Donald A. Yates. *World Literature Today,* v. 67, no. 2 (Spring 93), p. 343.

Urraca, Beatriz. Wor(l)ds through the Looking-Glass: Borges' Mirrors and Contemporary Theory. *Revista Canadiense de Estudios Hispánicos,* v. 17, no. 1 (Fall 92), pp. 153 – 176. Bibl.

Criticism of specific works
La biblioteca de Babel
Martínez Morales, Manuel. Entropía y complejidad en *La biblioteca de Babel. La Palabra y el Hombre,* no. 82 (Apr – June 92), pp. 249 – 257. Bibl.

Pierre Ménard, autor del Quijote
Rabell, Carmen R. Cervantes y Borges: relaciones intertextuales en "Pierre Ménard, autor del Quijote." *Revista Chilena de Literatura,* no. 42 (Aug 93), pp. 201 – 207. Bibl.

Rodríguez-Luis, Julio. Los borradores de Pierre Ménard. *Nueva Revista de Filología Hispánica,* v. 40, no. 2 (July – Dec 92), pp. 1025 – 1045. Bibl.

Sueña Alonso Quijano
Nallim, Carlos Orlando. Borges y Cervantes: *Don Quijote* y "Alonso Quijano." *Nueva Revista de Filología Hispánica,* v. 40, no. 2 (July – Dec 92), pp. 1047 – 1056. Bibl.

Interviews
Brögger, Suzanne. El primer tango (Excerpt from *Kvaelstof* translated by Sergio Peña). *Plural (Mexico),* v. 22, no. 262 (July 93), pp. 10 – 13.

BORORO INDIANS
Fabian, Stephen Michael. *Space – Time of the Bororo of Brazil* reviewed by Gary Urton. *Hispanic American Historical Review,* v. 73, no. 3 (Aug 93), pp. 496 – 498.

BOTANY
See also
Biotechnology
Ethnobotany
Geographical distribution of plants and animals
Horticulture
Paleobotany
Parks
Vegetation and climate

Amazon Valley
Listabarth, Christian. A Survey of Pollination Strategies in the "Bactridinae" (Palmae). *Bulletin de l'Institut Français d'Etudes Andines,* v. 21, no. 2 (1992), pp. 699 – 714. Bibl, il, tables.

Bolivia
Moraes R., Mónica and Jaime Sarmiento. Contribución al estudio de biología reproductiva de una especia de "Bactris" (Palmae) en el bosque de galería, depto. Beni, Bolivia. *Bulletin de l'Institut Français d'Etudes Andines,* v. 21, no. 2 (1992), pp. 685 – 698. Bibl, il, tables, maps.

Brazil
Orlandi, Eni Pulcinelli. O discurso dos naturalistas. *Vozes,* v. 87, no. 1 (Jan – Feb 93), pp. 62 – 76.

Mexico
Field, Christopher B. and Carlos Vázquez-Yanes. Species of the Genus "Piper" Provide a Model to Study How Plants Can Grow in Different Kinds of Rainforest Habitats. *Interciencia,* v. 18, no. 5 (Sept – Oct 93), pp. 230 – 236. Bibl, il.

Franco, Miguel and Ana Mendoza. Integración clonal en una palma tropical. *Bulletin de l'Institut Français d'Etudes Andines,* v. 21, no. 2 (1992), pp. 623 – 635. Bibl, il, tables, charts.

Ibarra-Manríquez, Guillermo. Fenología de las palmas de una selva cálido húmeda de México. *Bulletin de l'Institut Français d'Etudes Andines,* v. 21, no. 2 (1992), pp. 669 – 683. Bibl, tables, charts.

Orellana, Roger. Síndromes morfológicos y funcionales de las palmas de la península de Yucatán. *Bulletin de l'Institut Français d'Etudes Andines,* v. 21, no. 2 (1992), pp. 651 – 667. Bibl, tables, maps, charts.

Puerto Rico
Fitzmaurice, Sylvia. *Field Guide to the Plants of Inter American University of Puerto Rico, San Germán Campus* reviewed by Juan G. González Lagoa. *Homines,* v. 15 – 16, no. 2 – 1 (Oct 91 – Dec 92), p. 371. Il.

Venezuela
Texera Arnal, Yolanda. *La exploración botánica en Venezuela, 1754 – 1950* reviewed by Stuart McCook. *Interciencia,* v. 18, no. 6 (Nov – Dec 93), pp. 328 – 329.

BOTANY, MEDICAL
See
Ethnobotany

BOTERO, FERNANDO
Iriarte, María Elvira. Fernando Botero: la corrida (Accompanied by an English translation). *Art Nexus,* no. 9 (June – Aug 93), pp. 92 – 93. Il.

BOUNDARIES
González Aguayo, Leopoldo Augusto. Notas sobre la geopolítica de las fronteras. *Relaciones Internacionales (Mexico),* v. 14, Nueva época, no. 55 (July – Sept 92), pp. 23 – 30. Bibl.

BOUNDARY DISPUTES
See
Subdivision *Boundaries* under names of specific countries

BOXER, CHARLES RALPH
Correspondence, reminiscences, etc.
Boxer, Charles Ralph and José Honório Rodrigues. Correspondência de José Honório Rodrigues: a correspondência com Charles R. Boxer (Organized and annotated by Lêda Boechat Rodrigues). *Revista do Instituto Histórico e Geográfico Brasileiro,* no. 372 (July – Sept 91), pp. 828 – 907. Tables.

BOYTLER ROSOSBKY, ARCADY
Vega Alfaro, Eduardo de la. *Arcady Boytler Rososbky, 1895 – 1965* reviewed by Sonia Hernández Briseño (Review entitled "Pioneros del cine sonoro II"). *Revista Mexicana de Ciencias Políticas y Sociales,* v. 37, Nueva época, no. 150 (Oct – Dec 92), pp. 189 – 190.

BRACHO, CORAL
Criticism and interpretation
Castañón, Adolfo. Dos voces mujeres. *Vuelta,* v. 17, no. 202 (Sept 93), pp. 60 – 63.

BRAIN DRAIN

Meding, Holger M. German Emigration to Argentina and the Illegal Brain Drain to the Plate, 1945 – 1955. *Jahrbuch für Geschichte von Staat, Wirtschaft und Gesellschaft Lateinamerikas*, v. 29 (1992), pp. 397 – 419. Bibl, tables.

BRANT, ALICE DAYRELL CALDEIRA
Criticism of specific works
Minha vida de menina

Gárate, Miriam Viviana. El diario de Helena Morley o de la vida de las mujeres en la Diamantina finisecular. *Escritura (Venezuela)*, v. 16, no. 31 – 32 (Jan – Dec 91), pp. 65 – 80. Bibl.

BRAVO, ABEL

Dr. Abel Bravo: conflictos y convulsiones políticas en el siglo XIX. *Revista Cultural Lotería*, v. 51, no. 389 (May – June 93), pp. 38 – 49.

BRAVO DEL RIVERO Y CORREA, JUAN

Larraín Mira, Paz and René Millar Carvacho. Notas para la historia de la cultura en el período indiano: la biblioteca del obispo de Santiago, Juan Bravo del Rivero y Correa, 1685 – 1752. *Historia (Chile)*, no. 26 (1991 – 1992), pp. 173 – 211. Bibl.

BRAZIL

See also
Abortion – Brazil
Agricultural laborers – Brazil
Agriculture – Brazil
Agriculture, Cooperative – Brazil
Agriculture and state – Brazil
Airplane industry and trade – Brazil
Amazon Valley
Amazonas, Brazil (State)
Anarchism and anarchists – Brazil
Arabs – Brazil
Armaments – Brazil
Art – Brazil
Artists – Brazil
Authors – Brazil
Automation – Brazil
Automobile industry and trade – Brazil
Bahia, Brazil
Balance of payments – Brazil
Banks and banking – Brazil
Beer – Brazil
Belém, Brazil
Biography (as a literary form) – Brazil
Biotechnology – Brazil
Birth control – Brazil
Blacks – Brazil
Blacks in literature – Brazil
Botany – Brazil
Canudos, Brazil
Capital – Brazil
Capital productivity – Brazil
Capitalism – Brazil
Capitalists and financiers – Brazil
Caricatures and cartoons – Brazil
Catholic Church – Brazil
Ceará, Brazil
Censorship – Brazil
Children – Brazil
Christian art and symbolism – Brazil
Church and social problems – Brazil
Church music – Brazil
Cities and towns – Brazil
Citizenship – Brazil
Coffee – Brazil
Communism – Brazil
Community centers – Brazil
Community development – Brazil
Competition – Brazil
Composers – Brazil
Computer industry – Brazil
Convents and nunneries – Brazil
Cooperatives – Brazil
Corn – Brazil
Corruption (in politics) – Brazil
Cotton – Brazil
Coups d'état – Brazil
Crime and criminals – Brazil
Criminal law – Brazil

Curitiba, Brazil
Dairying – Brazil
Dams and reservoirs – Brazil
Debts, Public – Brazil
Decentralization in government – Brazil
Democracy – Brazil
Diseases – Brazil
Dissertations, Academic – Brazil
Droughts – Brazil
Ecology – Brazil
Ecology and development – Brazil
Economics – Brazil
Education – Brazil
Education, Higher – Brazil
Education and state – Brazil
Educational research – Brazil
Educational technology – Brazil
Elections – Brazil
Electronics – Brazil
Elite (Social sciences) – Brazil
Emblems, National – Brazil
Employment – Brazil
Environmental policy – Brazil
Environmental services – Brazil
Espírito Santo, Brazil
Ethnomusicology – Brazil
Family – Brazil
Fascism – Brazil
Fertility, Human – Brazil
Finance – Brazil
Finance, Public – Brazil
Fishing – Brazil
Folk art – Brazil
Folk festivals – Brazil
Folk literature – Brazil
Folk lore – Brazil
Food industry and trade – Brazil
Food supply – Brazil
Foreign exchange problem – Brazil
Foreign trade promotion – Brazil
Foreign trade regulation – Brazil
Forestry – Brazil
Forests – Brazil
Fortaleza, Brazil
Franchises (Retail trade) – Brazil
French – Brazil
Frontier and pioneer life – Brazil
Fruit trade – Brazil
Gas, Natural – Brazil
Geographic Information Systems – Brazil
Geography, Economic – Brazil
Geography, Historical – Brazil
Geology – Brazil
Germans – Brazil
Government ownership of business enterprises – Brazil
Handicraft – Brazil
Highways – Brazil
Historians – Brazil
Horticulture – Brazil
Hospitals – Brazil
Housing – Brazil
Human capital – Brazil
Human rights – Brazil
Illiteracy – Brazil
Income distribution – Brazil
Indians, Treatment of – Brazil
Industrial organization – Brazil
Industrial productivity – Brazil
Industrial sociology – Brazil
Industries, Location of – Brazil
Industry and state – Brazil
Infant mortality – Brazil
Inflation (Finance) – Brazil
Information services – Brazil
Information technology – Brazil
Inland water transportation – Brazil
Investments, Foreign – Brazil
Italians – Brazil
Jewish literature – Brazil
Jews – Brazil
Journalism – Brazil
Labor and laboring classes – Brazil
Labor laws and legislation – Brazil
Labor relations – Brazil
Labor supply – Brazil
Land reform – Brazil
Land use – Brazil
Law – Brazil

Lawyers – Brazil
Legends – Brazil
Legislative power – Brazil
Liberalism – Brazil
Libraries and librarians – Brazil
Literary criticism – Brazil
Literature and history – Brazil
Literature and society – Brazil
Local government – Brazil
Management – Brazil
Maranhão, Brazil
Marine resources – Brazil
Marketing – Brazil
Marriage – Brazil
Mato Grosso, Brazil
Meat industry and trade – Brazil
Medicine – Brazil
Messianism – Brazil
Middle classes – Brazil
Migration, Internal – Brazil
Military in government – Brazil
Minas Gerais, Brazil
Mines and mineral resources – Brazil
Money and money supply – Brazil
Motion pictures – Brazil
Museums – Brazil
Music – Brazil
Music and society – Brazil
Musicians – Brazil
Mutual benefit associations – Brazil
National income – Brazil
National security – Brazil
Nationalism – Brazil
Natural areas – Brazil
Natural history – Brazil
Newspapers – Brazil
Non-governmental organizations – Brazil
Nut industry – Brazil
Oligarchy – Brazil
Opera – Brazil
Oral history – Brazil
Oral tradition – Brazil
Pará, Brazil
Paraguayans – Brazil
Paraíba, Brazil
Paraná, Brazil
Peasantry – Brazil
Periodicals – Brazil
Pernambuco, Brazil
Petroglyphs – Brazil
Petroleum industry and trade – Brazil
Pharmacy – Brazil
Philosophy – Brazil
Photography and photographers – Brazil
Pilgrims and pilgrimages – Brazil
Political participation – Brazil
Political parties – Brazil
Political sociology – Brazil
Politics in literature – Brazil
Pollution – Brazil
Popular culture – Brazil
Popular music – Brazil
Population – Brazil
Portuguese – Brazil
Portuguese language – Brazil
Posters – Brazil
Poultry industry – Brazil
Poverty – Brazil
Power resources – Brazil
Pregnancy – Brazil
Presidente Prudente, Brazil
Press – Brazil
Press and politics – Brazil
Price regulation – Brazil
Prices – Brazil
Prisoners of war – Brazil
Privatization – Brazil
Prostitution – Brazil
Public administration – Brazil
Public health – Brazil
Publishers and publishing – Brazil
Race discrimination – Brazil
Radio broadcasting – Brazil
Railroads – Brazil
Real property – Brazil
Recife, Brazil
Refuse and refuse disposal – Brazil
Regional planning – Brazil

Regionalism – Brazil
Regionalism in literature – Brazil
Religion and politics – Brazil
Religion and sociology – Brazil
Research institutes – Brazil
Rio de Janeiro, Brazil (City)
Rio de Janeiro, Brazil (State)
Rio Grande do Norte, Brazil
Rio Grande do Sul, Brazil
Rites and ceremonies – Brazil
Roraima, Brazil
Salvador, Brazil
Santa Catarina, Brazil
São Luís, Brazil
São Paulo, Brazil (City)
São Paulo, Brazil (State)
Science – Brazil
Science and state – Brazil
Scientific research – Brazil
Sex role – Brazil
Sexual behavior – Brazil
Shamanism – Brazil
Slavery – Brazil
Smuggling – Brazil
Sobradinho, Brazil
Social change – Brazil
Social classes – Brazil
Social conflict – Brazil
Social mobility – Brazil
Social movements – Brazil
Social security – Brazil
Social services – Brazil
Socialism – Brazil
Socialization – Brazil
Sociolinguistics – Brazil
Sociology, Rural – Brazil
Sociology, Urban – Brazil
Soils – Brazil
Soybean – Brazil
Spaniards – Brazil
Street children – Brazil
Tariff – Brazil
Taubaté, Brazil
Taxation – Brazil
Teaching and teachers – Brazil
Technical education – Brazil
Technology – Brazil
Technology and state – Brazil
Technology transfer – Brazil
Television – Brazil
Theater – Brazil
Tocantins, Brazil
Trade unions – Brazil
Transportation – Brazil
Undocumented workers – Brazil
Universities and colleges – Brazil
Urbanization – Brazil
Video tape recorders and recording – Brazil
Violence – Brazil
Wages – Brazil
Water – Brazil
Water power – Brazil
Wine and wine making – Brazil
Wit and humor – Brazil
Women – Brazil
Women artists – Brazil
Women authors – Brazil
Women in literature – Brazil
Women's rights – Brazil
Youth – Brazil

Armed forces

Bento, Cláudio Moreira. Participação das forças armadas e da marinha mercante do Brasil na segunda guerra mundial, 1942 – 1945. *Revista do Instituto Histórico e Geográfico Brasileiro,* no. 372 (July – Sept 91), pp. 685 – 745. Bibl, maps.

Costa, Thomaz Guedes da. Cooperação e conflito nas intera-ções estratégicas do Brasil: os desafios da nova década. *Política e Estratégica,* v. 8, no. 2 – 4 (Apr – Dec 90), pp. 141 – 152. Bibl.

Guedes, Max Justo, ed. *História naval brasileira, vol. II: As guerras holandesas no mar* reviewed by Ramón Ezquerra Abadía. *Revista de Indias,* v. 53, no. 197 (Jan – Apr 93), pp. 110 – 111.

Santos, Murillo. *O caminho da profissionalização das forças armadas* reviewed by José Augusto Vaz Sampaio Neto. *Revista do Instituto Histórico e Geográfico Brasileiro,* no. 370 (Jan – Mar 91), pp. 333 – 335.

Waak, William. *As duas faces da glória* reviewed by Cláudio Moreira Bento. *Revista do Instituto Histórico e Geográfico Brasileiro,* no. 372 (July – Sept 91), pp. 930 – 932.

Zaverucha, Jorge. The Degree of Military Political Autonomy during the Spanish, Argentine, and Brazilian Transitions. *Journal of Latin American Studies,* v. 25, no. 2 (May 93), pp. 283 – 299. Bibl, tables.

Biography

Lacombe, Américo Jacobina. Estudos cariocas. *Revista do Instituto Histórico e Geográfico Brasileiro,* no. 370 (Jan – Mar 91), pp. 310 – 329.

Boundaries

Mattos, Carlos de Meira. *Geopolítica e teoria de fronteiras: fronteiras do Brasil* reviewed by Vicente Tapajós. *Revista do Instituto Histórico e Geográfico Brasileiro,* no. 370 (Jan – Mar 91), p. 340.

Moyano Bazzani, Eduardo L. Aportaciones de la historiografía portuguesa a la problemática fronteriza luso – española en América meridional, 1750 – 1778. *Revista de Indias,* v. 52, no. 195 – 196 (May – Dec 92), pp. 723 – 747. Bibl, maps.

Peru

Scarabôtolo, Hélio Antônio. Rio Branco, Euclides da Cunha e o tratado de limites com o Peru. *Revista do Instituto Histórico e Geográfico Brasileiro,* no. 370 (Jan – Mar 91), pp. 82 – 93.

Civilization

Borges, Dain Edward. Salvador's 1890s: Paternalism and Its Discontents. *Luso-Brazilian Review,* v. 30, no. 2 (Winter 93), pp. 47 – 57. Bibl.

Calligaris, Contardo. Brasil: país do futuro de quem? *Vozes,* v. 86, no. 6 (Nov – Dec 92), pp. 21 – 29.

Funari, Pedro Paulo Abreu. El mito candeirante: élite brasileña, cultura material e identidad. *Boletín de Antropología Americana,* no. 24 (Dec 91), pp. 111 – 122. Bibl, il.

Greenfield, Gerald Michael. "Sertão" and "Sertanejo": An Interpretive Context for Canudos. *Luso-Brazilian Review,* v. 30, no. 2 (Winter 93), pp. 35 – 46. Bibl.

Moreira Neto, Carlos and Darcy Ribeiro. *A fundação do Brasil: testemunhos, 1500 – 1700* reviewed by José Carlos Sebe Bohn Meihy. *Vozes,* v. 87, no. 3 (May – June 93), pp. 90 – 91.

Sevcenko, Nicolau. *Orfeu extático na metrópole: São Paulo; sociedade e cultura nos frementes anos '20* reviewed by Elias Thomé Saliba (Review entitled "Cultura modernista em São Paulo"). *Estudos Históricos,* v. 6, no. 11 (Jan – June 93), pp. 128 – 132.

— *Orfeu extático na metrópole: São Paulo; sociedade e cultura nos frementes anos '20* (Review). *Vozes,* v. 87, no. 1 (Jan – Feb 93), pp. 102 – 104.

Exhibitions

Pesavento, Sandra Jatahy. Exposições universais: palcos de exibição do mundo burguês; em cena: Brasil e Estados Unidos. *Siglo XIX: Revista,* no. 12, 2a época (July – Dec 92), pp. 63 – 85. Bibl.

Commerce

Fujii Gambero, Gerardo and Noemí Levy. Composición de las exportaciones de Brasil, Corea, España y México. *Comercio Exterior,* v. 43, no. 9 (Sept 93), pp. 844 – 851. Tables.

History

Santamaría, Daniel J. La guerra Guaykurú: expansión colonial y conflicto interétnico en la cuenca del alto Paraguay, siglo XVIII. *Jahrbuch für Geschichte von Staat, Wirtschaft und Gesellschaft Lateinamerikas,* v. 29 (1992), pp. 121 – 148. Bibl.

Mathematical models

Hidalgo, Alvaro Barrantes. O intercâmbio comercial brasileiro intra-indústria: uma análise entre indústrias e entre países. *Revista Brasileira de Economia,* v. 47, no. 2 (Apr – June 93), pp. 243 – 264. Bibl, tables.

Constitutional law

Artigos da constituição do Brasil referentes à questão ambiental (Introduced by Marilson Alves Gonçalves). *RAE; Revista de Administração de Empresas,* v. 33, no. 3 (May – June 93), pp. 66 – 67.

Coeli, Jaime Collier. MP 312: iníqua e inócua. *Problemas Brasileiros,* v. 30, no. 296 (Mar – Apr 93), pp. 29 – 34. Il.

González Encinar, José Juan et al. El proceso constituyente: enseñanzas a partir de cuatro casos recientes: España, Portugal, Brasil y Chile. *Ibero-Amerikanisches Archiv,* v. 18, no. 1 – 2 (1992), pp. 151 – 179. Tables.

Lamounier, Bolivar. O modelo institucional brasileiro: a presente crise e propostas de reforma. *Ibero-Amerikanisches Archiv,* v. 18, no. 1 – 2 (1992), pp. 225 – 244. Bibl, tables.

Monclaire, Stéphane, ed. *A constituição desejada: SAIC; as 72.719 sugestões enviadas pelos brasileiros à Assembléia Nacional Constituinte* reviewed by Carlos Schmidt Arturi. *Cahiers des Amériques Latines,* no. 14 (1992), pp. 153 – 156.

Serra, José. As vicissitudes do orçamento. *Revista de Economia Política (Brazil),* v. 13, no. 4 (Oct – Dec 93), pp. 143 – 149.

Souza, Washington Peluso Albino de. Constituição e direito cultural: uma "revisita" aos conceitos básicos. *Revista Brasileira de Estudos Políticos,* no. 76 (Jan 93), pp. 117 – 130.

Cultural policy

Augras, Monique. A ordem na desordem: a regulamentação do desfile das escolas de samba e a exigência de "motivos nacionais." *Revista Brasileira de Ciências Sociais,* v. 8, no. 21 (Feb 93), pp. 90 – 103. Bibl.

Sevcenko, Nicolau. Transformações da linguagem e advento da cultura modernista no Brasil (Translated by Dora Rocha). *Estudos Históricos,* v. 6, no. 11 (Jan – June 93), pp. 78 – 88.

Souza, Washington Peluso Albino de. Constituição e direito cultural: uma "revisita" aos conceitos básicos. *Revista Brasileira de Estudos Políticos,* no. 76 (Jan 93), pp. 117 – 130.

Description and travel

Cherpak, Evelyn M. A Diplomat's Lady in Brazil: Selections from the Diary of Mary Robinson Hunter, 1834 – 1848. *Revista Interamericana de Bibliografía,* v. 42, no. 4 (1992), pp. 617 – 634. Bibl.

Léry, Jean de. *History of a Voyage to the Land of Brazil, Otherwise Called America* translated by Janet Whatley. Reviewed by Maria Laura Bettencourt Pires. *Colonial Latin American Review,* v. 2, no. 1 – 2 (1993), pp. 279 – 281.

Economic conditions

Barrôs, Alexandre Rands. A Periodization of the Business Cycles in the Brazilian Economy, 1856 – 1985. *Revista Brasileira de Economia,* v. 47, no. 1 (Jan – Mar 93), pp. 53 – 82. Bibl, tables, charts.

Becker, Bertha Koiffman and Claudio Antonio G. Egler. *Brasil: uma nova potência regional na economia-mundo* reviewed by Oscar D'Ambrosio (Review entitled "Uma potência regional"). *Problemas Brasileiros,* v. 30, no. 297 (May – June 93), pp. 54 – 55. Il.

Mathematical models

Lima, Elcyon Caiado Rocha et al. Efeitos dinâmicos dos choques de oferta e demanda agregadas sobre o nível de atividade econômica do Brasil. *Revista Brasileira de Economia,* v. 47, no. 2 (Apr – June 93), pp. 177 – 204. Bibl, tables, charts.

19th century

Rangel, Armênio de Souza. A economia do município de Taubaté, 1798 a 1835. *Estudos Econômicos,* v. 23, no. 1 (Jan – Apr 93), pp. 149 – 179. Bibl, tables, charts.

20th century

Faria, José Eduardo. O Brasil no MERCOSUL. *Problemas Brasileiros,* v. 30, no. 297 (May – June 93), pp. 30 – 35. Il.

Fritsch, Winston. 1922: a crise econômica. *Estudos Históricos,* v. 6, no. 11 (Jan – June 93), pp. 3 – 8.

Furtado, Celso. *Brasil: a construção interrompida* reviewed by Rosa Maria Vieira. *RAE; Revista de Administração de Empresas,* v. 33, no. 1 (Jan – Feb 93), pp. 122 – 123.

Mazzali, Leonel. A crise do estado. *Revista de Economia Política (Brazil),* v. 13, no. 3 (July – Sept 93), pp. 139 – 143. Bibl.

Moisés, José Alvaro, ed. *O futuro do Brasil: a América Latina e o fim da guerra fria* reviewed by Bernardo Kucinski. *Journal of Latin American Studies,* v. 25, no. 2 (May 93), pp. 410 – 411.

Nítolo, Miguel Roberto. Um grande laboratório. *Problemas Brasileiros,* v. 30, no. 295 (Jan – Feb 93), pp. 19 – 21. Il.

Vidal, José Walter Bautista. *Soberania e dignidade: raízes da sobrevivência* (Review). *Vozes,* v. 86, no. 4 (July – Aug 92), pp. 89 – 90.

Economic policy

Almonacid, Ruben Dario. Os dois pilares. *Problemas Brasileiros,* v. 30, no. 296 (Mar – Apr 93), pp. 13 – 14.

Aragão, José Maria. El Arancel Externo Común del MERCOSUR: reflexiones a partir de aspectos parciales de la realidad brasileña. *Integración Latinoamericana,* v. 18, no. 187 – 188 (Mar – Apr 93), pp. 3 – 12.

Barbosa, Fernando de Holanda. Hiperinflação e estabilização. *Revista de Economia Política (Brazil),* v. 13, no. 4 (Oct – Dec 93), pp. 5 – 15. Bibl, charts.

Batista Júnior, Paulo Nogueira. Dolarização, âncora cambial e reservas internacionais. *Revista de Economia Política (Brazil),* v. 13, no. 3 (July – Sept 93), pp. 5 – 20. Bibl, tables.

Buffet, Jacky. Le Brésil: du "miracle" à la difficile gestion de l'"après-miracle." *Cahiers des Amériques Latines,* no. 14 (1992), pp. 67 – 93. Bibl.

Cleary, David. After the Frontier: Problems with Political Economy in the Modern Brazilian Amazon. *Journal of Latin American Studies,* v. 25, no. 2 (May 93), pp. 331 – 349. Bibl.

Fiori, José Luís. The Political Economy of the Developmentalist State in Brazil. *CEPAL Review,* no. 47 (Aug 92), pp. 173 – 186. Bibl.

Franco, Gustavo Henrique Barroso. Alternativas de estabilização: gradualismo, dolarização e populismo. *Revista de Economia Política (Brazil),* v. 13, no. 2 (Apr – June 93), pp. 28 – 45. Bibl, tables, charts.

Mattos, César Costa Alves de. Prefixação, expectativas e inflação. *Revista Brasileira de Economia,* v. 47, no. 1 (Jan – Mar 93), pp. 131 – 144. Bibl.

Meyer, Arno. Apoio financeiro externo e estabilização econômica. *Revista de Economia Política (Brazil),* v. 13, no. 1 (Jan – Mar 93), pp. 135 – 148. Tables.

Nylen, William R. Selling Neoliberalism: Brazil's Instituto Liberal. *Journal of Latin American Studies,* v. 25, no. 2 (May 93), pp. 301 – 311. Bibl.

Pena, Maria Valéria Junho. O surgimento do imposto de renda: um estudo sobre a relação entre estado e mercado no Brasil. *Dados,* v. 35, no. 3 (1992), pp. 337 – 370. Bibl.

Pereira, Luiz Carlos Bresser. Estabilização em um ambiente adverso: a experiência brasileira de 1987. *Revista de Economia Política (Brazil),* v. 13, no. 4 (Oct – Dec 93), pp. 16 – 36. Bibl.

Rossetti, José Paschoal. *Política e programação econômicas* reviewed by Anita Kon. *RAE; Revista de Administração de Empresas,* v. 33, no. 2 (Mar – Apr 93), pp. 124 – 126.

Sikkink, Kathryn. *Ideas and Institutions: Developmentalism in Brazil and Argentina* reviewed by Laura A. Hastings. *Journal of Latin American Studies,* v. 25, no. 1 (Feb 93), pp. 216 – 217.

Law and legislation

Coeli, Jaime Collier. A defesa da concorrência. *Problemas Brasileiros,* v. 30, no. 297 (May – June 93), pp. 41 – 53. Il.

Emigration and immigration

Bellotto, Manoel Lelo. A imigração espanhola no Brasil: estado do fluxo migratório para o estado de São Paulo, 1931 – 1936. *Estudios Interdisciplinarios de América Latina y el Caribe,* v. 3, no. 2 (July – Dec 92), pp. 59 – 73. Bibl, tables.

Campos, Mintaha Alcuri. *Turco brasileiro, sirio remediado, libanês rico* reviewed by Gabriel Bittencourt. *Revista do Instituto Histórico e Geográfico Brasileiro,* no. 373 (Oct – Dec 91), pp. 1207 – 1208.

González Martínez, Elda Evangelina. Los españoles en un país más allá del océano: Brasil; notas acerca de las etapas de la emigración. *Revista de Indias,* v. 52, no. 195 – 196 (May – Dec 92), pp. 515 – 527. Bibl, tables, charts.

Lorenzo Alcalá, May. El utopismo en Brasil: una experiencia fourierista. *Todo Es Historia,* v. 27, no. 313 (Aug 93), pp. 56 – 68. Bibl, il.

Wilcox, Robert. Paraguayans and the Making of the Brazilian Far West, 1870 – 1935. *The Americas,* v. 49, no. 4 (Apr 93), pp. 479 – 512. Bibl, tables, maps.

Foreign economic relations

Becker, Bertha Koiffman and Claudio Antonio G. Egler. *Brasil: uma nova potência regional na economia-mundo* reviewed by Oscar D'Ambrosio (Review entitled "Uma potência regional"). *Problemas Brasileiros,* v. 30, no. 297 (May – June 93), pp. 54 – 55. Il.

Furtado, Celso. A ordem mundial emergente e o Brasil. *Vozes,* v. 86, no. 5 (Sept – Oct 92), pp. 21 – 25.

Sarmento, Walney Moraes. Política externa no contexto do subdesenvolvimento: o exemplo do Brasil. *Política e Estratégica,* v. 8, no. 2 – 4 (Apr – Dec 90), pp. 241 – 267. Bibl, tables.

Silva, Vera Alice Cardoso. A política externa brasileira na década de '90: possibilidades de acomodação à nova fase do capitalismo internacional. *Política e Estratégica,* v. 8, no. 2 – 4 (Apr – Dec 90), pp. 224 – 240. Bibl.

Africa

Oliveira, Henrique Altemani de. Política externa independente: fundamentos da política africana do Brasil. *Política e Estratégica,* v. 8, no. 2 – 4 (Apr – Dec 90), pp. 268 – 284. Bibl, tables.

Argentina

ALADI: Acuerdo de Complementación Económica n° 14 concertado entre la República Argentina y la república federativa del Brasil. *Integración Latinoamericana,* v. 18, no. 193 (Sept 93), pp. 68 – 70.

Anales del I Seminario de Universidades por la Integración Brasil y Argentina (Review). *Integración Latinoamericana,* v. 18, no. 192 (Aug 92), p. 98.

Barbosa, Rubens Antonio. Liberalização do comércio, integração regional e Mercado Comum do Sul: o papel do Brasil. *Revista de Economia Política (Brazil),* v. 13, no. 1 (Jan – Mar 93), pp. 64 – 81.

Bekerman, Marta. O setor petroquímico e a integração Argentina – Brasil. *Pesquisa e Planejamento Econômico,* v. 22, no. 2 (Aug 92), pp. 369 – 398. Bibl, tables.

Czar de Zalduendo, Susana. Empresas binacionales: el estatuto argentino – brasileño. *Integración Latinoamericana,* v. 17, no. 184 (Nov 92), pp. 16 – 25. Bibl.

Stülp, Valter José and Bartholomeu E. Stein Neto. A vitivinicultura do Rio Grande do Sul e a integração econômica Brasil – Argentina. *Revista de Economia e Sociologia Rural,* v. 29, no. 4 (Oct – Dec 91), pp. 387 – 400. Bibl, tables.

European Community

Fritsch, Winston and João Roberto Teixeira. Fatores determinantes das exportações brasileiras para a CE: uma análise prospectiva dos impactos da ampliação do espaço econômico. *Revista de Economia Política (Brazil),* v. 13, no. 3 (July – Sept 93), pp. 82 – 101. Bibl, tables, charts.

Southern Cone of South America

Hirst, Mónica. Brasil en el MERCOSUR: costos y beneficios. *Integración Latinoamericana,* v. 18, no. 186 (Jan – Feb 93), pp. 3 – 11. Bibl.

Uruguay

Acuerdo de Complementación Económica concertado entre la república federativa del Brasil y la república oriental del Uruguay. *Integración Latinoamericana,* v. 18, no. 194 (Oct 93), pp. 64 – 65.

Foreign relations

Barboza, Mário Gibson. *Na diplomacia: o traço todo da vida* reviewed by Alexandra de Mello e Silva (Review entitled "História e histórias da política externa brasileira"). *Estudos Históricos,* v. 6, no. 12 (July – Dec 93), pp. 285 – 290.

Brancato, Sandra Maria Lubisco. A conexão EUA/Brasil e a "questão argentina," 1943 – 1944. *Estudos Ibero-Americanos,* v. 18, no. 1 (July 92), pp. 89 – 101. Bibl.

Carneiro, Maria Cecília Ribas. A política externa do Brasil e a segunda guerra mundial. *Revista do Instituto Histórico e Geográfico Brasileiro,* no. 373 (Oct – Dec 91), pp. 1032 – 1051. Bibl.

Cavagnari Filho, Geraldo Lesbat. Introdução à estratégia brasileira. *Política e Estratégica,* v. 8, no. 2 – 4 (Apr – Dec 90), pp. 347 – 351.

Costa, Thomaz Guedes da. Cooperação e conflito nas interações estratégicas do Brasil: os desafios da nova década. *Política e Estratégica,* v. 8, no. 2 – 4 (Apr – Dec 90), pp. 141 – 152. Bibl.

Cruz Júnior, Ademar Seabra de et al. Brazil's Foreign Policy under Collor. *Journal of Inter-American Studies and World Affairs,* v. 35, no. 1 (1993), pp. 119 – 144. Bibl.

Gonçalves, Williams da Silva and Shiguenoli Miyamoto. Os militares na política externa brasileira, 1964 – 1984. *Estudos Históricos,* v. 6, no. 12 (July – Dec 93), pp. 211 – 246. Bibl.

Guerreiro, Ramiro Elysio Saraiva. *Lembranças de um empregado do Itamaraty* reviewed by Alexandra de Mello e Silva (Review entitled "História e histórias da política externa brasileira"). *Estudos Históricos,* v. 6, no. 12 (July – Dec 93), pp. 285 – 290.

Mello, Celso Duvivier de Albuquerque. O Brasil e o direito internacional na nova ordem mundial. *Revista Brasileira de Estudos Políticos,* no. 76 (Jan 93), pp. 7 – 26. Bibl.

Moisés, José Alvaro, ed. *O futuro do Brasil: a América Latina e o fim da guerra fria* reviewed by Bernardo Kucinski. *Journal of Latin American Studies,* v. 25, no. 2 (May 93), pp. 410 – 411.

Moura, Gerson. Neutralidade dependente: o caso do Brasil, 1939 – 1942. *Estudos Históricos,* v. 6, no. 12 (July – Dec 93), pp. 177 – 189. Bibl.

Pereira, Antônio Carlos. As transformações na Europa e o Brasil. *Política e Estratégica,* v. 8, no. 2 – 4 (Apr – Dec 90), pp. 168 – 191.

Silva, Alexandra de Mello e and Paulo S. Wrobel. Entrevista com Celso Lafer. *Estudos Históricos,* v. 6, no. 12 (July – Dec 93), pp. 271 – 284.

Teixeira, Jorge Leão. Relíquias diplomáticas. *Problemas Brasileiros,* v. 30, no. 296 (Mar – Apr 93), pp. 17 – 23. Il.

Vinhosa, Francisco Luiz Teixeira. *O Brasil e a 1ª guerra mundial: a diplomacia brasileira e as grandes potências* reviewed by Claudio Moreira Bento. *Revista do Instituto Histórico e Geográfico Brasileiro,* no. 370 (Jan – Mar 91), pp. 338 – 339.

— Torre de Londres, 19 de outubro de 1915: as carabinas Mauser e o fuzilamento de Fernando Buschmann. *Revista do Instituto Histórico e Geográfico Brasileiro,* no. 371 (Apr – June 91), pp. 460 – 469. Bibl.

Wrobel, Paulo S. Aspectos da política externa independente: a questão do desarmamento e o caso de Cuba (Translated by Dora Rocha). *Estudos Históricos,* v. 6, no. 12 (July – Dec 93), pp. 191 – 209. Bibl.

Bibliography

Cervo, Amado Luiz. A historiografia brasileira das relações internacionais. *Revista Interamericana de Bibliografía,* v. 42, no. 3 (1992), pp. 393 – 409. Bibl.

Argentina

Argentina – Brasil: Acuerdo de Alcance Parcial de Cooperación e Intercambio de Bienes Utilizados en la Defensa y Protección del Medio Ambiente. *Integración Latinoamericana,* v. 17, no. 184 (Nov 92), pp. 74 – 75.

Austria

Silva, Geraldo Eulálio do Nascimento e. As relações diplomáticas entre o Brasil e a Austria. *Revista do Instituto Histórico e Geográfico Brasileiro,* no. 372 (July – Sept 91), pp. 665 – 676.

Chile

Meira, Sílvio Augusto de Bastos. Relacionamento histórico entre o Brasil e o Chile. *Revista do Instituto Histórico e Geográfico Brasileiro,* no. 370 (Jan – Mar 91), pp. 102 – 126.

China

Pinheiro, Letícia. Restabelecimento de relações diplomáticas com a República Popular da China: uma análise do processo de tomada de decisão. *Estudos Históricos,* v. 6, no. 12 (July – Dec 93), pp. 247 – 270. Bibl.

United States

Leacock, Ruth. *Requiem for Revolution: The United States and Brazil, 1961 – 1969* reviewed by John W. F. Dulles. *The Americas,* v. 49, no. 4 (Apr 93), pp. 564 – 566.

Smith, Joseph. *Unequal Giants: Diplomatic Relations between the United States and Brazil, 1889 – 1930* reviewed by Stanley E. Hilton. *The Americas,* v. 50, no. 1 (July 93), pp. 131 – 133.

Historiography

Guimarães, Manoel Luiz Lima Salgado. A historiografia brasileira do século XX: os anos '30. *Revista do Instituto Histórico e Geográfico Brasileiro,* no. 370 (Jan – Mar 91), pp. 275 – 288.

Lacombe, Américo Jacobina. A construção da historiografia brasileira: o IHGB e a obra de Varnhagen. *Revista do Instituto Histórico e Geográfico Brasileiro,* no. 370 (Jan – Mar 91), pp. 245 – 264.

Martinière, Guy. A propos de l'histoire de l'historiographie brésilienne. *Cahiers des Amériques Latines,* no. 14 (1992), pp. 119 – 148. Bibl.

Pérez Ochoa, Eduardo. El problema de guerra irregular referido en los congresos del Instituto Histórico y Geográfico del Brasil, IHGB. *Estudos Ibero-Americanos,* v. 18, no. 1 (July 92), pp. 71 – 88. Bibl.

Sanches, Marcos Guimarães. História e desenvolvimento: um problema na historiografia brasileira nos anos '50. *Revista do Instituto Histórico e Geográfico Brasileiro,* no. 370 (Jan – Mar 91), pp. 289 – 299. Bibl.

Santos, Myrian S. Objetos, memória e história: observação e análise de um museu histórico brasileiro. *Dados,* v. 35, no. 2 (1992), pp. 217 – 237. Bibl.

Tapajós, Vicente Costa Santos. A historiografia colonial. *Revista do Instituto Histórico e Geográfico Brasileiro,* no. 370 (Jan – Mar 91), pp. 232 – 244.

Wehling, Arno. Capistrano de Abreu e Sílvio Romero: um paralelo cientificista. *Revista do Instituto Histórico e Geográfico Brasileiro,* no. 370 (Jan – Mar 91), pp. 265 – 274.

History

Lopes, Luís Carlos and Mário José Maestri Filho. *Storia del Brasile* reviewed by Silvio Castro. *Quaderni Ibero-Americani,* no. 72 (Dec 92), pp. 745 – 746.

Wanderley Pinho, José. *Coletânea de textos históricos* reviewed by José Gomes Bezerra Câmara. *Revista do Instituto Histórico e Geográfico Brasileiro,* no. 372 (July – Sept 91), pp. 932 – 933.

Sources

Lacombe, Américo Jacobina. Papéis velhos. *Revista do Instituto Histórico e Geográfico Brasileiro,* no. 371 (Apr – June 91), pp. 596 – 604.

1763 – 1821

Graham, Richard, ed. *Brazil and the World System* reviewed by Nancy Priscilla S. Naro. *The Americas,* v. 50, no. 2 (Oct 93), pp. 286 – 287.

— *Brazil and the World System* reviewed by Kees de Groot. *European Review of Latin American and Caribbean Studies,* no. 53 (Dec 92), pp. 117 – 118.

1822 – 1889

Andréa, José. O marechal Soares Andréa nos relevos da história do Brasil. *Revista do Instituto Histórico e Geográfico Brasileiro,* no. 373 (Oct – Dec 91), pp. 1071 – 1084.

Nunes, Antonietta de Aguiar. O processo brasileiro da independência. *Revista do Instituto Histórico e Geográfico Brasileiro,* no. 373 (Oct – Dec 91), pp. 942 – 947.

Silveira, Maria Dutra da. Mauá e a revolução farroupilha. *Hoy Es Historia,* v. 10, no. 59 (Sept – Oct 93), pp. 75 – 81. Il.

1889 – 1930

Madden, Lori. The Canudos War in History. *Luso-Brazilian Review,* v. 30, no. 2 (Winter 93), pp. 5 – 22. Bibl.

Mathias, Herculano Gomes. O primeiro decênio da república no Brasil, 1889 – 1899. *Revista do Instituto Histórico e Geográfico Brasileiro,* no. 370 (Jan – Mar 91), pp. 7 – 64. Bibl.

Saliba, Elias Thomé. A dimensão cômica do dilema brasileiro. *Vozes,* v. 87, no. 1 (Jan – Feb 93), pp. 46 – 54. Bibl.

Sampaio, Consuelo Novais. Repensando Canudos: o jogo das oligarquias. *Luso-Brazilian Review,* v. 30, no. 2 (Winter 93), pp. 97 – 113. Bibl, tables.

Sena, Davis Ribeiro de. A guerra das caatingas. *Revista do Instituto Histórico e Geográfico Brasileiro,* no. 373 (Oct – Dec 91), pp. 954 – 1007. Bibl, il.

Industries

Estevão, Marcello. Employment Level, Hours of Work, and Labor Adjustment Cost in the Brazilian Industry. *Revista Brasileira de Economia,* v. 47, no. 2 (Apr – June 93), pp. 205 – 242. Bibl, tables, charts.

Font, Mauricio A. City and the Countryside in the Onset of Brazilian Industrialization. *Studies in Comparative International Development,* v. 27, no. 3 (Fall 92), pp. 26 – 56. Bibl, tables, charts.

Nítolo, Miguel Roberto. Retrato áspero. *Problemas Brasileiros,* v. 30, no. 296 (Mar – Apr 93), pp. 7 – 12. Il.

Souza, Maria Tereza Saraiva de. Rumo à prática empresarial sustentável. *RAE; Revista de Administração de Empresas,* v. 33, no. 4 (July – Aug 93), pp. 40 – 52. Bibl.

Versiani, Flávio Rabelo. Imigrantes, trabalho qualificado e industrialização: Rio e São Paulo no início do século. *Revista de Economia Política (Brazil),* v. 13, no. 4 (Oct – Dec 93), pp. 77 – 96. Bibl, tables.

Mathematical models

Clements, Benedict J. and José W. Rossi. Ligações interindustriais e setores-chave na economia brasileira. *Pesquisa e Planejamento Econômico,* v. 22, no. 1 (Apr 92), pp. 101 – 123. Bibl, tables.

Hidalgo, Alvaro Barrantes. O intercâmbio comercial brasileiro intra-indústria: uma análise entre indústrias e entre países. *Revista Brasileira de Economia,* v. 47, no. 2 (Apr – June 93), pp. 243 – 264. Bibl, tables.

Statistics

Façanha, Luís Otávio de Figueiredo and Denise A. Rodrigues. Indústria brasileira na década de '70: interpretação de resultados de estatística multivariada e de aspectos da dinâmica concorrencial. *Revista Brasileira de Economia,* v. 46, no. 4 (Oct – Dec 92), pp. 447 – 476. Bibl, tables.

Intellectual life

Borges, Dain Edward. "Puffy, Ugly, Slothful, and Inert": Degeneration in Brazilian Social Thought, 1880 – 1940. *Journal of Latin American Studies,* v. 25, no. 2 (May 93), pp. 235 – 256. Bibl.

Glezer, Raquel. São Paulo e a elite letrada brasileira no século XIX. *Siglo XIX: Revista,* no. 11, 2a época (Jan – June 92), pp. 149 – 160. Bibl.

Gomes, Angela Maria de Castro. Essa gente do Rio . . . : os intelectuais cariocas e o modernismo. *Estudos Históricos,* v. 6, no. 11 (Jan – June 93), pp. 62 – 77.

Gomes, Eustáquio. *Os rapazes d'"a Onda" e outros rapazes* reviewed by Elias Thomé Saliba. *Vozes,* v. 86, no. 6 (Nov – Dec 92), pp. 101 – 103.

Macedo, Ubiratan Borges de. Presença de Miguel Reale na cultura brasileira. *Convivium,* v. 34, no. 2 (July – Dec 91), pp. 127 – 137.

Menezes, Geraldo Bezerra de. A presença dos intelectuais brasileiros na campanha abolicionista. *Revista do Instituto Histórico e Geográfico Brasileiro,* no. 370 (Jan – Mar 91), pp. 226 – 230.

Schwarz, Roberto. *Misplaced Ideas: Essays on Brazilian Culture* translated by John Gledson. Reviewed by Lisa Jesse. *Bulletin of Latin American Research,* v. 12, no. 3 (Sept 93), pp. 343 – 344.

— *Misplaced Ideas: Essays on Brazilian Culture* reviewed by T. F. Earle. *Journal of Latin American Studies,* v. 25, no. 3 (Oct 93), pp. 696 – 697.

Maps

Horch, Rosemarie Erika. Os primeiros mapas do Brasil. *Vozes,* v. 86, no. 4 (July – Aug 92), pp. 8 – 15. Il.

Name

Guimarães, Eduardo Augusto de Almeida. Terra de Vera Cruz, Brasil. *Vozes,* v. 86, no. 4 (July – Aug 92), pp. 16 – 21.

Officials and public employees

Hochman, Gilberto. Os cardeais da previdência social: gênese e consolidação de uma elite burocrática. *Dados,* v. 35, no. 3 (1992), pp. 371 – 401. Bibl.

Uma saga sinistra. *Problemas Brasileiros,* v. 30, no. 295 (Jan – Feb 93), pp. 17 – 18. Il.

Politics and government

Dulles, John W. F. *Carlos Lacerda, Brazilian Crusader, Vol. I: The Years 1914 – 1960* reviewed by Thomas E. Skidmore. *The Americas,* v. 49, no. 3 (Jan 93), pp. 416 – 417.

Lamounier, Bolivar. O modelo institucional brasileiro: a presente crise e propostas de reforma. *Ibero-Amerikanisches Archiv,* v. 18, no. 1 – 2 (1992), pp. 225 – 244. Bibl, tables.

Schneider, Ronald M. *"Order and Progress": A Political History of Brazil* reviewed by Neale J. Pearson. *Journal of Developing Areas,* v. 27, no. 4 (July 93), pp. 564 – 566.

1889 – 1930

Ferreira, Marieta de Moraes. A reação republicana e a crise política dos anos '20. *Estudos Históricos,* v. 6, no. 11 (Jan – June 93), pp. 9 – 23. Bibl.

Hochman, Gilberto. Regulando os efeitos da interdependência: sobre as relações entre saúde pública e construção do estado; Brasil, 1910 – 1930. *Estudos Históricos,* v. 6, no. 11 (Jan – June 93), pp. 40 – 61. Bibl.

Meirinho, Jali. O governo federalista em Santa Catarina. *Hoy Es Historia,* v. 10, no. 60 (Nov – Dec 93), pp. 43 – 49. Bibl.

Moraes, Maria Célia Marcondes de. Francisco Campos: o caminho de uma definição ideológica; anos '20 e '30. *Dados,* v. 35, no. 2 (1992), pp. 239 – 265. Bibl.

1930 – 1954

Nascimento, Benedicto Heloiz. Pensamento e atuação de Vargas. *Vozes,* v. 86, no. 4 (July – Aug 92), pp. 22 – 28.

1954 –

Alexander, Robert Jackson. *Juscelino Kubitschek and the Development of Brazil* reviewed by Peter Flynn. *Bulletin of Latin American Research,* v. 12, no. 3 (Sept 93), pp. 348 – 349.

— *Juscelino Kubitschek and the Development of Brazil* reviewed by John W. F. Dulles. *Hispanic American Historical Review,* v. 73, no. 1 (Feb 93), pp. 168 – 169.

Lamounier, Bolivar. Empresarios, partidos y democratización en Brasil, 1974 – 1990. *Revista Mexicana de Sociología,* v. 54, no. 1 (Jan – Mar 92), pp. 77 – 97. Bibl.

Moraes, Dênis de. *A esquerda e o golpe de '64: vinte e cinco anos depois, as forças populares repensam seus mitos, sonhos, e ilusões* reviewed by Cliff Welch. *Hispanic American Historical Review,* v. 73, no. 1 (Feb 93), p. 170.

Sikkink, Kathryn. Las capacidades y la autonomía del estado en Brasil y la Argentina: un enfoque neoinstitucionalista (Translated by Leandro Wolfson). *Desarrollo Económico (Argentina),* v. 32, no. 128 (Jan – Mar 93), pp. 543 – 574. Bibl, charts.

Teixeira, Jorge Leão. Da queda de Jango à renúncia de Collor. *Problemas Brasileiros,* v. 30, no. 295 (Jan – Feb 93), pp. 10 – 16. Il.

1985 –

Carvalho, Carlos Eduardo Vieira de. Brasil: la caída de Collor. *Nueva Sociedad,* no. 124 (Mar – Apr 93), pp. 22 – 26.

Flynn, Peter. Collor, Corruption, and Crisis: Time for Reflection. *Journal of Latin American Studies,* v. 25, no. 2 (May 93), pp. 351 – 371. Bibl.

Pires, Nielsen de Paula. Brasil: transición, crisis y triunfo de la democracia. *Mensaje,* v. 42, no. 417 (Mar – Apr 93), pp. 79 – 81. Il.

Weyland, Kurt. The Rise and Fall of President Collor and Its Impact on Brazilian Democracy. *Journal of Inter-American Studies and World Affairs,* v. 35, no. 1 (1993), pp. 1 – 37. Bibl.

Race question

Andrews, George Reid. *Blacks and Whites in São Paulo, Brazil, 1888 – 1988* reviewed by Michael Hanchard. *The Americas,* v. 50, no. 1 (July 93), pp. 134 – 136.

— *Blacks and Whites in São Paulo, Brazil, 1888 – 1988* reviewed by Joseph P. Love. *Hispanic American Historical Review,* v. 73, no. 1 (Feb 93), pp. 167 – 168.

— *Blacks and Whites in São Paulo, Brazil, 1888 – 1988* reviewed by Robert M. Levine. *Revista Interamericana de Bibliografía,* v. 42, no. 2 (1992), p. 282.

Borges, Dain Edward. "Puffy, Ugly, Slothful, and Inert": Degeneration in Brazilian Social Thought, 1880 – 1940. *Journal of Latin American Studies,* v. 25, no. 2 (May 93), pp. 235 – 256. Bibl.

Chalhoub, Sidney. The Politics of Disease Control: Yellow Fever and Race in Nineteenth Century Rio de Janeiro. *Journal of Latin American Studies,* v. 25, no. 3 (Oct 93), pp. 441 – 463. Bibl.

Lima, Magali Alonso de and Roberto Kant de Lima. Capoeira e cidadania: negritude e identidade no Brasil republicano. *Revista de Antropologia (Brazil),* v. 34 (1991), pp. 143 – 182. Bibl.

Maio, Marcos Chor. "A nação no microscópio": intelectuais médicos e ordem social no Brasil. *Siglo XIX: Revista,* no. 12, 2a época (July – Dec 92), pp. 41 – 62. Bibl.

Ricci, Maria Lúcia de Souza Rangel. A problemática do negro no Brasil. *Hoy Es Historia,* v. 10, no. 55 (Jan – Feb 93), pp. 82 – 87.

Skidmore, Thomas E. Bi-Racial U.S.A. vs. Multi-Racial Brazil: Is the Contrast Still Valid? *Journal of Latin American Studies,* v. 25, no. 2 (May 93), pp. 373 – 386. Bibl.

Telles, Edward E. Racial Distance and Region in Brazil: Intermarriage in Brazilian Urban Areas. *Latin American Research Review,* v. 28, no. 2 (1993), pp. 141 – 162. Bibl, tables.

Bibliography

Igel, Regina. Reavaliação de estudos sobre o negro brasileiro. *Iberoamericana,* v. 17, no. 49 (1993), pp. 16 – 32. Bibl.

Rural conditions

Hoffmann, Rodolfo. Vinte anos de desigualdade e pobreza na agricultura brasileira. *Revista de Economia e Sociologia Rural,* v. 30, no. 2 (Apr – June 92), pp. 97 – 113. Bibl, tables, charts.

Navarro, Zander. Reclaiming the Land: Rural Poverty and the Promise of Small Farmers in Brazil (Photographs by Jofre Masceno from his book *Imagem reflexa).* *Grassroots Development,* v. 17, no. 1 (1993), pp. 20 – 24. Il.

Mathematical models

Buvinich, Manuel J. Rojas. The Evaluation of Rural Development Projects Using the Social Accounting Matrix Approach. *Revista Brasileira de Economia,* v. 46, no. 4 (Oct – Dec 92), pp. 555 – 593. Bibl, tables.

Social policy

Melo, Marcus André Barreto Campelo de. Anatomia do fracasso: intermediação de interesses e a reforma das políticas sociais na nova república. *Dados,* v. 36, no. 1 (1993), pp. 119 – 163. Bibl, tables.

BRAZIL IN LITERATURE

Vieira, Nelson H. *Brasil e Portugal: a imagem recíproca; o mito e a realidade na expressão literária* reviewed by Bobby J. Chamberlain. *Hispania (USA),* v. 76, no. 1 (Mar 93), pp. 90 – 92.

BRAZILIAN DRAMA

History and criticism

Magaldi, Sábato. Atos heróicos. *Problemas Brasileiros,* v. 30, no. 295 (Jan – Feb 93), p. 64.

BRAZILIAN LITERATURE

Sadlier, Darlene J., ed. *One Hundred Years after Tomorrow: Brazilian Women's Fiction in the 20th Century* translated by the editor. Reviewed by Candace Slater. *Letras Femeninas,* v. 19, no. 1 – 2 (Spring – Fall 93), pp. 163 – 164.

Bibliography

Schwartz, Jorge. ¡Abajo Tordesillas! *Casa de las Américas,* no. 191 (Apr – June 93), pp. 26 – 35. Bibl.

Black authors

Bibliography

Igel, Regina. Reavaliação de estudos sobre o negro brasileiro. *Iberoamericana,* v. 17, no. 49 (1993), pp. 16 – 32. Bibl.

History and criticism

Reis, Roberto. *The Pearl Necklace: Toward an Archaeology of Brazilian Transition Discourse* translated by Aparecida de Godoy Johnson. Reviewed by Nelson H. Vieira. *Hispanic American Historical Review,* v. 73, no. 3 (Aug 93), pp. 484 – 485.

Ventura, Roberto. *Estilo tropical: história cultural e polêmicas literárias no Brasil* reviewed by Geraldo de Menezes. *Revista do Instituto Histórico e Geográfico Brasileiro,* no. 372 (July – Sept 91), pp. 933 – 935.

Vieira, Nelson H. *Brasil e Portugal: a imagem recíproca; o mito e a realidade na expressão literária* reviewed by Bobby J. Chamberlain. *Hispania (USA),* v. 76, no. 1 (Mar 93), pp. 90 – 92.

Colonial period

Narváez, Jorge E. El estatuto de los textos coloniales y el canon literario: algunos antecedentes en el sistema literario del Brasil-colonia, s. XVI y XVII. *Revista Chilena de Literatura,* no. 40 (Nov 92), pp. 17 – 33. Bibl.

20th century

Abdala Júnior, Benjamin. Do Brasil a Portugal: imagens na ação política. *Revista de Letras (Brazil),* v. 32 (1992), pp. 15 – 30. Bibl.

D'Ambrosio, Oscar. Décadas produtivas. *Problemas Brasileiros,* v. 30, no. 295 (Jan – Feb 93), pp. 59 – 61.

George, David. Socio-Criticism and Brazilian Literature: Changing Perspectives. *Chasqui,* v. 22, no. 2 (Nov 93), pp. 49 – 56.

Johnson, John Randal, ed. *Tropical Paths: Essays on Modern Brazilian Literature* reviewed by Malcolm Silverman. *Hispania (USA),* v. 76, no. 4 (Dec 93), pp. 739 – 740.

Ring, Ano. La narrativa brasileña después de 1964: escribir como alternativa. *Islas,* no. 97 (Sept – Dec 90), pp. 20 – 25.

Vieira, Nelson H. "Closing the Gap" between High and Low: Intimation on the Brazilian Novel of the Future. *Latin American Literary Review,* v. 20, no. 40 (July – Dec 92), pp. 109 – 119. Bibl.

BRAZILIANS

Argentina

Espínola, Julio César. La inmigración brasileña en el este misionero argentino: nuevo examen de un antiguo problema. *Revista Paraguaya de Sociología,* v. 29, no. 85 (Sept – Dec 92), pp. 133 – 155. Bibl, tables, maps, charts.

United States

Forjaz, Maria Cecília Spina. Os exilados da década de '80: imigrantes brasileiros nos Estados Unidos. *RAE; Revista de Administração de Empresas,* v. 33, no. 1 (Jan – Feb 93), pp. 66 – 83. Bibl.

BRIBRI INDIANS

Cervantes Gamboa, Laura. La función social de la música en el ritual fúnebre bribrí. *Káñina,* v. 16, no. 1 (Jan – June 92), pp. 245 – 265. Bibl, il, tables.

Pailler, Claire. Severiano Fernández, pueblo bribrí: "el rescate de ser indígena"; entretien réalisé le 16 avril 1992 à San José, par Claire Pailler. *Caravelle,* no. 59 (1992), pp. 49 – 58.

BRICEÑO GUERRERO, JOSÉ M.

Criticism and interpretation

Páez Monzón, Charles R. Discursos y senderos de Briceño Guerrero. *Revista Nacional de Cultura (Venezuela),* v. 53, no. 285 (Apr – June 92), pp. 115 – 129. Il.

BRICEÑO JÁUREGUI, MANUEL

Acuerdo n° 03 de 1993. *Boletín de Historia y Antigüedades,* v. 80, no. 781 (Apr – June 93), pp. 289 – 292. Il.

Obituaries

Abella Rodríguez, Arturo. La muerte del padre Briceño Jáuregui. *Boletín de Historia y Antigüedades,* v. 80, no. 781 (Apr – June 93), pp. 323 – 325.

Briceño Perozo, Mario. Manuel Briceño Jáuregui, humanista de América. *Boletín de Historia y Antigüedades,* v. 80, no. 781 (Apr – June 93), pp. 327 – 330.

— Manuel Briceño Jáuregui, humanista de América. *Boletín de la Academia Nacional de la Historia (Venezuela),* v. 76, no. 301 (Jan – Mar 93), pp. 110 – 112.

Chávez, Ignacio. In memoriam: Manuel Briceño Jáuregui, humanista integral. *Boletín de Historia y Antigüedades,* v. 80, no. 781 (Apr – June 93), pp. 321 – 322.

Gómez Latorre, Armando. Réquiem por cuatro académicos. *Boletín de Historia y Antigüedades,* v. 80, no. 781 (Apr – June 93), pp. 339 – 340.

Ocampo López, Javier. El padre Manuel Briceño Jáuregui, S.J. y el humanismo clásico. *Boletín de Historia y Antigüedades,* v. 80, no. 781 (Apr – June 93), pp. 293 – 318. Bibl.

Socarrás, José Francisco. Manuel Briceño Jáuregui, S.J. *Boletín de Historia y Antigüedades,* v. 80, no. 781 (Apr – June 93), pp. 319 – 320.

BRINDIS DE SALAS, VIRGINIA

Criticism of specific works

Pregón de Marimorena

Young, Caroll Mills. Virginia Brindis de Salas vs. Julio Guadalupe: A Question of Authorship. *Afro-Hispanic Review,* v. 12, no. 2 (Fall 93), pp. 26 – 30. Bibl.

BRITISH

Caribbean area

Games, Alison F. Survival Strategies in Early Bermuda and Barbados. *Revista/Review Interamericana,* v. 22, no. 1 – 2 (Spring – Summer 92), pp. 55 – 71. Bibl, tables.

BRITISH GUIANA

See
Guyana

BRITISH HONDURAS

See
Belize

BRITO FIGUEROA, FEDERICO

Beltrán Guerrero, Luis. Meritocracia: Federico Brito Figueroa. *Revista Nacional de Cultura (Venezuela),* v. 53, no. 286 (July – Sept 92), pp. 129 – 132.

BRITTO GARCÍA, LUIS

Criticism of specific works

Abrapalabra

Hidalgo de Jesús, Amarilis. *Abrapalabra:* el discurso desmitificador de la historia colonial venezolana. *Inti,* no. 37 – 38 (Spring – Fall 93), pp. 163 – 169. Bibl.

BROWN, RONALD

Witoshynsky, Mary. "An Extraordinary Visit." *Business Mexico,* v. 3, no. 4 (Apr 93), pp. 40 – 41. Il.

BRU, ROSER

Madrid Letelier, Alberto. Roser Bru: iconografía de la memoria. *Cuadernos Hispanoamericanos,* no. 510 (Dec 92), pp. 7 – 12. Il.

Valdés, Adriana. *Roser Bru* reviewed by Ivonne Pini (Accompanied by an English translation). *Art Nexus,* no. 7 (Jan – Mar 93), p. 41. Il.

BRUNET, MARTA

Biography

Montes Brunet, Hugo. Evocación de Marta Brunet. *Atenea (Chile),* no. 465 – 466 (1992), pp. 291 – 297. Facs.

BRYCE ECHENIQUE, ALFREDO

Correspondence, reminiscences, etc.

Bryce Echenique, Alfredo. *Permiso para vivir* reviewed by Marco Martos (Review entitled "Las memorias de tres novelistas peruanos"). *Debate (Peru),* v. 16, no. 73 (June – Aug 93), pp. 68 – 72. Il.

Criticism of specific works

La última mudanza de Felipe Carrillo

Ferreira, César. Bryce Echenique y la novela del posboom: lectura de La última mudanza de Felipe Carrillo. *Chasqui,* v. 22, no. 2 (Nov 93), pp. 34 – 48. Bibl.

Gutiérrez Mouat, Ricardo. Travesía y regresos de Alfredo Bryce: La última mudanza de Felipe Carrillo. *Hispamérica,* v. 21, no. 63 (Dec 92), pp. 73 – 79.

La vida exagerada de Martín Romaña

Ortega, Julio. Alfredo Bryce Echenique y la estética de la exageración. *Cuadernos Hispanoamericanos,* no. 521 (Nov 93), pp. 71 – 86. Il.

BUENOS AIRES, ARGENTINA (CITY)

Adelman, Jeremy. State and Labour in Argentina: The Portworkers of Buenos Aires, 1910 – 1921. *Journal of Latin American Studies,* v. 25, no. 1 (Feb 93), pp. 73 – 102. Bibl, maps.

Alonso, Paula. Politics and Elections in Buenos Aires, 1890 – 1898: The Performance of the Radical Party. *Journal of Latin American Studies,* v. 25, no. 3 (Oct 93), pp. 465 – 487. Bibl, tables, charts.

Arango de Maglio, Aída. Descentralización y tiempo y espacio newtonianos: un análisis de la descentralización "real" en la Argentina. *Realidad Económica,* no. 119 (Oct – Nov 93), pp. 73 – 102. Bibl.

Baer, James. Tenant Mobilization and the 1907 Rent Strike in Buenos Aires. *The Americas,* v. 49, no. 3 (Jan 93), pp. 343 – 368. Bibl, tables, maps.

Barrancos, Dora. La modernidad redentora: difusión de las ciencias entre los trabajadores de Buenos Aires, 1890 – 1920. *Siglo XIX: Revista,* no. 12, 2a época (July – Dec 92), pp. 5 – 21. Bibl, tables.

Bevilacqua, Claudia. Transformaciones territoriales en el marco de las políticas del estado en la región metropolitana de Buenos Aires: el caso del municipio de Marcos Paz, 1945 – 1990. *Revista Interamericana de Planificación,* v. 26, no. 101 – 102 (Jan – June 93), pp. 154 – 182. Bibl, tables, maps.

Carretero, Andrés M. Las prostitutas en Buenos Aires. *Todo Es Historia,* v. 27, no. 315 (Oct 93), pp. 46 – 49.

Ciafardo, Eduardo O. *Los niños en la ciudad de Buenos Aires, 1850 – 1910* reviewed by Sergio A. Pujol. *Todo Es Historia,* v. 27, no. 311 (June 93), p. 58. Il.

Korn, Francis. Il popolo minuto: La Boca, 1895. *Todo Es Historia,* v. 26, no. 305 (Dec 92), pp. 46 – 49. Il.

Krantzer, Guillermo and Jorge Sánchez. Regulaciones en el transporte urbano: el caso de Buenos Aires. *EURE,* v. 19, no. 56 (Mar 93), pp. 41 – 53. Bibl.

Malatesta, Parisina. Mega Shoppings: Playgrounds for Today's Porteños (Translated by Ruth Morales, photographs by Jorge Provenza). *Américas,* v. 45, no. 4 (July – Aug 93), pp. 14 – 19. Il.

Mayo, Carlos Alberto and Jaime Antonio Peire. Iglesia y crédito colonial: la política crediticia de los conventos de Buenos Aires, 1767 – 1810. *Revista de Historia de América,* no. 112 (July – Dec 91), pp. 147 – 157. Bibl.

Newland, Carlos. *Buenos Aires no es pampa: la educación elemental porteña, 1820 – 1860* reviewed by Mariano Narodowski. *Todo Es Historia,* v. 26, no. 308 (Mar 93), pp. 72 – 73. Il.

Pino, Diego A. del. El barrio porteño de Boedo. *Todo Es Historia,* v. 26, no. 310 (May 93), pp. 84 – 94. Il.

— José González Castillo y el mundo literario de Boedo. *Todo Es Historia,* v. 27, no. 311 (June 93), pp. 84 – 92. Bibl, il, maps.

Sábato, Hilda. Ciudadanía, participación política y formación en una esfera pública en Buenos Aires, 1850 – 1880. *Siglo XIX: Revista,* no. 11, 2a época (Jan – June 92), pp. 46 – 73. Bibl.

Siegrist de Gentile, Nora L. *Inmigración vasca en la ciudad de Buenos Aires, 1830 – 1855* reviewed by Oscar Alvarez Gila. *Revista de Indias,* v. 53, no. 197 (Jan – Apr 93), pp. 121 – 124.

Sweeney, Judith L. Las lavanderas de Buenos Aires en la segunda mitad del siglo XIX. *Todo Es Historia,* v. 27, no. 314 (Sept 93), pp. 46 – 48. Bibl, il.

Verdicchio, Gastón Pablo. Fondas, hoteles y otras formas de hospedaje en el viejo Buenos Aires. *Todo Es Historia,* v. 27, no. 315 (Oct 93), pp. 24 – 28. Il.

BUENOS AIRES, ARGENTINA (PROVINCE)

Birocco, Carlos María and Gabriela Gresores. *Arrendamientos, desalojos y subordinación campesina: Buenos Aires, siglo XVIII* reviewed by Carlos G. A. Bulcourf. *Todo Es Historia,* v. 27, no. 313 (Aug 93), p. 71. Il.

Infesta, María Elena and Marla Valencia. Los criterios legales en la revisión de la política rosista de tierras públicas: Buenos Aires, 1852 – 1864. *Investigaciones y Ensayos,* no. 41 (Jan – Dec 91), pp. 407 – 421. Bibl.

Mayo, Carlos Alberto. *Los betlemitas en Buenos Aires: convento, economía y sociedad, 1748 – 1822* reviewed by Angela Fernández. *Todo Es Historia,* v. 26, no. 309 (Apr 93), pp. 70 – 71. Il.

Posada, Marcelo Germán. La conformación del perfil del empresariado pecuario: el caso del partido de Mercedes (Buenos Aires, Argentina), 1850 – 1890. *Revista de Historia de América,* no. 112 (July – Dec 91), pp. 159 – 177. Bibl, tables, charts.

Romero, Luis Alberto and Hilda Sábato. *Los trabajadores de Buenos Aires: la experiencia del mercado, 1850 – 1880* reviewed by María Cecilia Cangiano (Review entitled "¿Clase obrera o trabajadores?"). *Desarrollo Económico (Argentina),* v. 33, no. 131 (Oct – Dec 93), pp. 445 – 448.

— *Los trabajadores de Buenos Aires: la experiencia del mercado, 1850 – 1880* reviewed by Susan Migden Socolow. *Hispanic American Historical Review,* v. 73, no. 2 (May 93), pp. 323 – 324.

— *Los trabajadores de Buenos Aires: la experiencia del mercado, 1850 – 1880* reviewed by Paula Alonso. *Journal of Latin American Studies,* v. 25, no. 2 (May 93), pp. 396 – 397.

— *Los trabajadores de Buenos Aires: la experiencia del mercado, 1850 – 1880* reviewed by Hobart A. Spalding. *Revista Interamericana de Bibliografía,* v. 42, no. 4 (1992), pp. 663 – 664.

Slatta, Richard W. *Gauchos and the Vanishing Frontier* reviewed by Jeremy Adelman. *Journal of Latin American Studies,* v. 25, no. 2 (May 93), pp. 401 – 402.

BUITRAGO, FANNY

Criticism and interpretation

Jaramillo de Velasco, María Mercedes. Por la insubordinación: Albalucía Angel y Fanny Buitrago. *Conjunto,* no. 92 (July – Dec 92), pp. 46 – 54. Bibl.

BULL FIGHTS

Cáceres Vega, Baldomero. Toros: balance ferial. *Debate (Peru),* v. 16, no. 75 (Dec 93 – Jan 94), p. 69. Il.

Iwasaki Cauti, Fernando A. Toros y sociedad en Lima colonial. *Anuario de Estudios Americanos,* v. 49 (1992), pp. 311 – 333. Bibl.

BUÑUEL, LUIS

Paz, Octavio. Buzón entre dos mundos: de Octavio Paz a Luis Buñuel. *Vuelta,* v. 17, no. 201 (Aug 93), pp. 72 – 73.

BUREAUCRACY

See

Public administration
Subdivision *Officials and public employees* under names of specific countries

BURGOS, JULIA DE

Criticism of specific works

Canción de la verdad sencilla

Caulfield, Carlota. *Canción de la verdad sencilla:* Julia de Burgos y su diálogo erótico – místico con la naturaleza. *Revista Iberoamericana,* v. 59, no. 162 – 163 (Jan – June 93), pp. 119 – 126. Bibl.

BURNS, ALAN

Ashdown, Peter D. Alan Burns and Sidney Turton: Two Views of the Public Good. *Belizean Studies,* v. 21, no. 1 (May 93), pp. 21 – 24. Bibl.

BUSCH BECERRA, GERMÁN

Gallego, Ferran. *Ejército, nacionalismo y reformismo en América Latina: la gestión de Germán Busch en Bolivia* reviewed by Marta Irurozqui Victoriano. *Revista Andina,* v. 11, no. 1 (July 93), pp. 246 – 247.

BUSCHMANN, FERNANDO

Vinhosa, Francisco Luiz Teixeira. Torre de Londres, 19 de outubro de 1915: as carabinas Mauser e o fuzilamento de Fernando Buschmann. *Revista do Instituto Histórico e Geográfico Brasileiro,* no. 371 (Apr – June 91), pp. 460 – 469. Bibl.

BUSES

See

Transportation

BUSINESS ADMINISTRATION

See

Management

BUSINESS AND POLITICS

See

Industry and state

BUSINESS ENTERPRISES

See also

Cooperatives
Franchises (Retail trade)
Government ownership of business enterprises
Informal sector (Economics)
International business enterprises
Privatization
Shopping malls
Subdivision *Industries* under names of specific countries

Garretón, Oscar Guillermo. Seis comentarios sobre la empresa del siglo XXI. *Mensaje,* v. 42, no. 422 (Sept 93), pp. 432 – 439. Il.

International cooperation

Cortelesse, Claudio. Competitividad de los sistemas productivos y las empresas pequeñas y medianas: campo para la cooperación internacional. *Comercio Exterior,* v. 43, no. 6 (June 93), pp. 519 – 524.

Czar de Zalduendo, Susana. Empresas binacionales: el estatuto argentino – brasileño. *Integración Latinoamericana,* v. 17, no. 184 (Nov 92), pp. 16 – 25. Bibl.

Sources

Argentina – Paraguay: Tratado para el Establecimiento de un Estatuto de Empresas Binacionales Argentino – Paraguayas. *Integración Latinoamericana,* v. 17, no. 184 (Nov 92), pp. 75 – 78.

Argentina

Sources

Schenkolewski-Kroll, Silvia. Los archivos de S.I.A.M. Di Tella S.A.: primera organización de fuentes en la historia de las empresas argentinas. *Estudios Interdisciplinarios de América Latina y el Caribe,* v. 3, no. 2 (July – Dec 92), pp. 105 – 122. Bibl.

Chile

Henríquez Amestoy, Lysette. Chile: experiencia exportadora de las empresas pequeñas y medianas. *Comercio Exterior,* v. 43, no. 6 (June 93), pp. 547 – 552.

Colombia

Dávila L. de Guevara, Carlos. *Historia empresarial de Colombia: estudios, problemas y perspectivas* reviewed by Luis Aurelio Ordóñez B. (Review entitled "Un balance historiográfico exhaustivo y sugestivo"). *Anuario Colombiano de Historia Social y de la Cultura*, no. 20 (1992), pp. 147 – 152.

Latin America

Mattos, Carlos António de. Nuevas estrategias empresariales y mutaciones territoriales en los procesos de reestructuración en América Latina. *Revista Paraguaya de Sociología*, v. 29, no. 84 (May – Aug 92), pp. 145 – 170. Bibl.

Congresses

Las micro, pequeñas y medianas empresas ante las nuevas realidades económicas. *Comercio Exterior*, v. 43, no. 6 (June 93), pp. 572 – 584.

Mexican – American Border Region

Curtis, James R. Central Business Districts of the Two Laredos. *Geographical Review*, v. 83, no. 1 (Jan 93), pp. 54 – 65. Bibl, tables, charts.

Mexico

Holt, Douglas. Aftershocks in Guadalajara. *Business Mexico*, v. 3, no. 5 (May 93), pp. 39 – 40. Il.

— Guadalajara Gambles with Expansion. *Business Mexico*, v. 3, no. 6 (June 93), pp. 30 – 31. Il.

Keenan, Joe. Corporate Mexico Goes for the Green. *Business Mexico*, v. 3, no. 1 (Jan – Feb 93), pp. 31 – 32. Il.

Lazaroff, León. A Tight Squeeze in Sonora. *Business Mexico*, v. 3, no. 3 (Mar 93), pp. 8 – 9.

Riner, Deborah L. A Third-Quarter Perspective. *Business Mexico*, v. 3, no. 9 (Sept 93), pp. 32 – 35. Charts.

Ruiz Durán, Clemente. México: crecimiento e innovación en las micro y pequeñas empresas. *Comercio Exterior*, v. 43, no. 6 (June 93), pp. 525 – 529.

Salas Porras Soule, Alejandra. Globalización y proceso corporativo de los grandes grupos económicos en México. *Revista Mexicana de Sociología*, v. 54, no. 2 (Apr – June 92), pp. 133 – 162. Bibl, tables.

Sánchez-Ugarte, Fernando J. Acciones en favor de las micro, pequeñas y medianas industrias en México. *Comercio Exterior*, v. 43, no. 6 (June 93), pp. 539 – 543.

Silverstein, Jeffrey. Banking on the Future. *Business Mexico*, v. 3, no. 3 (Mar 93), pp. 10 – 11.

Terrones López, Víctor Manuel. Las micro, pequeñas y medianas empresas en el proceso de globalización. *Comercio Exterior*, v. 43, no. 6 (June 93), pp. 544 – 546.

Waitling, John. Small Businesses in a Big-Time Economy. *Business Mexico*, v. 3, no. 3 (Mar 93), pp. 4 – 7. Tables.

Zabludovsky, Gina. Hacia un perfil de la mujer empresaria en México. *El Cotidiano*, v. 9, no. 53 (Mar – Apr 93), pp. 54 – 59 +. Tables.

Charitable contributions

Paxman, Andrew. Art for Sale's Sake. *Business Mexico*, v. 3, no. 3 (Mar 93), pp. 17 – 19. Il.

Cost

Cohen, Joshua A. Caught in the Squeeze. *Business Mexico*, v. 3, no. 9 (Sept 93), pp. 28 – 30. Charts.

Societies, etc.

Castillo, Alejandro. Industrial Chambers: A Continuing Saga (Translated by Robert Brackney). *Business Mexico*, v. 3, no. 8 (Aug 93), pp. 10 – 13.

Paraguay

Borda, Dionisio. Empresariado y transición a la democracia en el Paraguay. *Revista Paraguaya de Sociología*, v. 30, no. 86 (Jan – Apr 93), pp. 31 – 66. Tables.

BUSINESS MEXICO (PERIODICAL)

Fleischman, Cristopher and Joel Russell. The Company You Keep. *Business Mexico*, v. 3, no. 5 (May 93), pp. 42 – 43. Charts.

BUSINESSMEN

See

    Capitalists and financiers
    Markets and merchants

BUSTAMANTE, CALIXTO CARLOS

See

    Carrió de la Vandera, Alonso

CABEZA DE VACA

See

    Núñez Cabeza de Vaca, Alvar

CABEZAS LACAYO, OMAR

Biography

Cabezas Lacayo, Omar. Testimonio de mis testimonios: sobre preguntas de Edward Waters Hood. *Hispamérica*, v. 22, no. 64 – 65 (Apr – Aug 93), pp. 111 – 120.

CABRERA INFANTE, GUILLERMO

Criticism of specific works

Mea Cuba

Torres Fierro, Danubio. Memoria, historia, desmemoria. *Vuelta*, v. 17, no. 201 (Aug 93), pp. 55 – 56.

Interviews

Levine, Suzanne Jill. El traductor en la guarida del escritor: entrevista con Guillermo Cabrera Infante (Translated by Mario Ojeda Revah). *Vuelta*, v. 17, no. 198 (May 93), pp. 59 – 63.

Torres Fierro, Danubio. El "apartheid" cubano: entrevista con Guillermo Cabrera Infante. *Vuelta*, v. 17, no. 198 (May 93), pp. 58 – 59.

CACAO

See

    Chocolate and cacao

CACIQUISM

Andean region

Pease G. Y., Franklin. *Curacas: reciprocidad y riqueza* reviewed by Thomas Abercrombie. *Hispanic American Historical Review*, v. 73, no. 4 (Nov 93), pp. 698 – 699.

Latin America

Hamill, Hugh M., Jr., ed. *Caudillos: Dictators in Spanish America*, revised edition. Reviewed by Stuart F. Voss. *Hispanic American Historical Review*, v. 73, no. 2 (May 93), pp. 321 – 322.

Lynch, John. *Caudillos in Spanish America, 1800 – 1850* reviewed by Charles Walker. *Bulletin of Latin American Research*, v. 12, no. 1 (Jan 93), pp. 115 – 116.

— *Caudillos in Spanish America, 1800 – 1850* reviewed by Frank Safford. *Journal of Latin American Studies*, v. 25, no. 1 (Feb 93), pp. 188 – 190.

Peru

Sources

Fernández Villegas, Oswaldo. La desestructuración de los curacazgos andinos: conflictos por la residencia del curaca de Colán, costa norte. *Allpanchis*, v. 23, no. 40 (July – Dec 92), pp. 97 – 115. Bibl.

Río de la Plata region

Pedoja Riet, Eduardo. El caudillaje en Hispanoamérica. *Hoy Es Historia*, v. 10, no. 56 (Mar – Apr 93), pp. 61 – 68.

Venezuela

Chacón, Zully. Clío y Siquis o una visión del caudillismo en Venezuela. *Boletín de la Academia Nacional de la Historia (Venezuela)*, v. 75, no. 299 (July – Sept 92), pp. 135 – 144. Bibl.

CAJAMARCA, PERU

Deere, Carmen Diana. *Household and Class Relations: Peasants and Landlords in Northern Peru* reviewed by William Roseberry. *Hispanic American Historical Review*, v. 73, no. 1 (Feb 93), pp. 174 – 175.

Julien, Daniel G. Late Pre-Inkaic Ethnic Groups in Highland Peru: An Archaeological – Ethnohistorical Model of the Political Geography of the Cajamarca Region. *Latin American Antiquity*, v. 4, no. 3 (Sept 93), pp. 246 – 273. Bibl, il, tables, maps, charts.

Remy S., Pilar and María Rostworowski Tovar de Diez Canseco, eds. *Las visitas a Cajamarca, 1571/72 – 1578* reviewed by Pedro Guibovich. *Apuntes (Peru),* no. 31 (July – Dec 92), pp. 119 – 121.

— *Las visitas a Cajamarca, 1571/72 – 1578* reviewed by Jorge Montenegro. *Bulletin de l'Institut Français d'Etudes Andines,* v. 21, no. 3 (1992), pp. 1073 – 1074.

— *Las visitas a Cajamarca, 1571/72 – 1578* reviewed by Noble David Cook. *Hispanic American Historical Review,* v. 73, no. 2 (May 93), pp. 313 – 314.

— *Las visitas a Cajamarca, 1571/72 – 1578* reviewed by Carmen Beatriz Loza. *Revista Andina,* v. 10, no. 2 (Dec 92), pp. 548 – 550.

CAJAR ESCALA, JOSÉ AGUSTÍN

Criticism of specific works

El cabecilla

Delgado Aparicio, Vielka R. La perspectiva en la novela *El cabecilla* de José Agustín Cajar Escala. *Revista Cultural Lotería,* v. 50, no. 385 (Sept – Oct 91), pp. 83 – 87.

CAJATAMBO, PERU (PROVINCE)

Itier, César. La tradición oral quechua antigua en los procesos de idolatrías de Cajatambo. *Bulletin de l'Institut Français d'Etudes Andines,* v. 21, no. 3 (1992), pp. 1009 – 1051. Bibl.

CALABOZO, VENEZUELA

Pérez, Tibisay and Eugenio Sanhueza. Concentraciones atmosféricas y estimación de las emisiones H2S en la saba de Trachypogon, Calabozo, estado Guárico, Venezuela. *Interciencia,* v. 18, no. 2 (Mar – Apr 93), pp. 83 – 87. Bibl, il, tables, maps, charts.

CALDERÓN DE LA BARCA, PEDRO

Criticism of specific works

La aurora en Copacabana

White Navarro, Gladys. El drama americano de Calderón: mesianismo oficial y estrategias de dominación. *Revista de Crítica Literaria Latinoamericana,* v. 19, no. 38 (July – Dec 93), pp. 115 – 122.

CALENDARS

See

Subdivision *Calendars* under names of Indian groups

CALIFORNIA

See also

Los Angeles, California

Bernabéu Albert, Salvador. El "virrey de California" Gaspar de Portolá y la problemática de la primera gobernación californiana, 1767 – 1769. *Revista de Indias,* v. 52, no. 195 – 196 (May – Dec 92), pp. 271 – 295. Bibl.

Cutter, Donald C., ed. *California in 1792: A Spanish Naval Visit* reviewed by Donald T. Garate. *Colonial Latin American Historical Review,* v. 2, no. 1 (Winter 93), pp. 117 – 118.

Jackson, Robert H. The Impact of Liberal Policy on Mexico's Northern Frontier: Mission Secularization and the Development of Alta California, 1812 – 1846. *Colonial Latin American Historical Review,* v. 2, no. 2 (Spring 93), pp. 195 – 225. Bibl, tables.

Johnstone, Nick. Comparative Advantage, Transfrontier Pollution, and the Environmental Degradation of a Border Region: The Case of the Californias. *Journal of Borderlands Studies,* v. 7, no. 2 (Fall 92), pp. 33 – 52. Bibl.

Russell, Craig H. Newly Discovered Treasures from Colonial California: The Masses at San Fernando. *Inter-American Music Review,* v. 13, no. 1 (Fall – Winter 92), pp. 5 – 9. Bibl.

Székely, Gabriel. California Sunrise. *Nexos,* v. 16, no. 185 (May 93), pp. 13 – 15.

Waller, Thomas. Southern California Water Politics and U.S. – Mexican Relations: Lining the All-American Canal. *Journal of Borderlands Studies,* v. 7, no. 2 (Fall 92), pp. 1 – 32. Bibl, maps.

Fiction

Morton, Carlos. Rewriting Southwestern History: A Playwright's Perspective. *Mexican Studies,* v. 9, no. 2 (Summer 93), pp. 225 – 239. Il.

CALLAO, PERU (CITY)

Bradley, Peter T. The Defence of Peru, 1648 – 1700. *Jahrbuch für Geschichte von Staat, Wirtschaft und Gesellschaft Lateinamerikas,* v. 29 (1992), pp. 90 – 120. Bibl, tables.

CALMON, PEDRO

Boaventura, Edivaldo M. A contribuição de Pedro Calmon para a biografia de Castro Alves. *Revista do Instituto Histórico e Geográfico Brasileiro,* no. 370 (Jan – Mar 91), pp. 65 – 77. Bibl.

Ipanema, Cybelle Moreira de and Marcello Moreira de Ipanema. Pedro Calmon no cinqüentenário e no centenário dos cursos jurídicos no Rio de Janeiro. *Revista do Instituto Histórico e Geográfico Brasileiro,* no. 370 (Jan – Mar 91), pp. 78 – 81.

CALVO, NOVÁS

See

Novás Calvo, Lino

CAMACHO SOLÍS, MANUEL

Geyer, Anne. Challenges for the Modern Metropolis. *Business Mexico,* v. 3, no. 10 (Oct 93), pp. 48 – 49.

CAMBACÉRÈS, EUGENIO

Criticism of specific works

Sin rumbo

Fernández, Nancy P. Violencia, risa y parodia: "El niño proletario" de O. Lamborghini y *Sin rumbo* de E. Cambacérès. *Escritura (Venezuela),* v. 17, no. 33 – 34 (Jan – Dec 92), pp. 159 – 164.

CAMEJO, JOSEFA

Troconis de Veracoechea, Ermila. Josefa Camejo, una mujer en la historia. *Boletín de la Academia Nacional de la Historia (Venezuela),* v. 75, no. 297 (Jan – Mar 92), pp. 21 – 31. Bibl.

CAMPA INDIANS

Brown, Michael F. *War of Shadows: The Struggle for Utopia in the Peruvian Amazon* reviewed by Oscar Espinoza. *Amazonía Peruana,* v. 11, no. 22 (Oct 92), pp. 278 – 284.

Hvalkof, Sören. La naturaleza del desarrollo: perspectivas de los nativos y de los colonos en el gran pajonal. *Amazonía Peruana,* v. 11, no. 21 (Sept 92), pp. 145 – 173. Bibl.

Renard-Casevitz, France-Marie. Les guerriers du sel: chronique '92. *Cahiers des Amériques Latines,* no. 13 (1992), pp. 107 – 118.

Rojas Zolezzi, Enrique Carlos. Concepciones sobre la relación entre géneros: mitos, ritual y organización del trabajo en la unidad doméstica campa – asháninka. *Amazonía Peruana,* v. 11, no. 22 (Oct 92), pp. 175 – 220. Bibl.

CÁMPORA, HÉCTOR J.

Jordán, Alberto R. Cámpora: siete semanas de gobierno. *Todo Es Historia,* v. 26, no. 310 (May 93), pp. 8 – 36. Bibl, il.

CAMPOS, FRANCISCO LUÍS DA SILVA

Moraes, Maria Célia Marcondes de. Francisco Campos: o caminho de uma definição ideológica; anos '20 e '30. *Dados,* v. 35, no. 2 (1992), pp. 239 – 265. Bibl.

CAMPOS, GREGORIO FRANCISCO DE

Valle de Siles, María Eugenia del. Gregorio Francisco de Campos, un obispo ilustrado que presiente la independencia. *Boletín de la Academia Nacional de la Historia (Venezuela),* v. 76, no. 302 (Apr – June 93), pp. 71 – 86. Il.

CAMPOS, JULIETA
Criticism of specific works
Tiene los cabellos rojizos y se llama Sabina
Bilbija, Ksenija. Tiene los cabellos rojizos y se llama Sabina. *La Palabra y el Hombre,* no. 84 (Oct – Dec 92), pp. 228 – 239. Bibl.

CAMPRUBÍ DE JIMÉNEZ, ZENOBIA
Correspondence, reminiscences, etc.
Camprubí de Jiménez, Zenobia. *Diario, 1: Cuba, 1937 – 1939* introduced and translated by Graciela Palau de Nemes. Reviewed by Aleksandra Hadzelek. *Revista Iberoamericana,* v. 59, no. 162 – 163 (Jan – June 93), pp. 385 – 387.

CAMUS, ALBERT
Criticism of specific works
L'homme révolté
Gutiérrez Mouat, Ricardo. Vargas Llosa's Poetics of the Novel and Camus' *Rebel. World Literature Today,* v. 67, no. 2 (Spring 93), pp. 283 – 290. Bibl, il.

CANADA
Foreign economic relations
Mexico
Castro Martínez, Pedro Fernando. Comercio e inversiones México – Canadá: un asunto trilateral. *Comercio Exterior,* v. 43, no. 5 (May 93), pp. 498 – 506. Bibl, tables.
United States
Rosas González, María Cristina. El TLC entre México, Estados Unidos y Canadá: semejanzas y diferencias con el ALC entre Canadá y Estados Unidos. *Relaciones Internacionales (Mexico),* v. 15, Nueva época, no. 57 (Jan – Mar 93), pp. 55 – 62. Charts.
Stewart, Hamish. El Acuerdo de Libre Comercio entre Estados Unidos y Canadá: algunas lecciones. *Estudios Internacionales (Chile),* v. 26, no. 102 (Apr – June 93), pp. 187 – 203. Bibl, tables.
Watson, Hilbourne Alban. The U.S. – Canada Free Trade Agreement and the Caribbean, with a Case Study of Electronics Assembly in Barbados. *Social and Economic Studies,* v. 41, no. 3 (Sept 92), pp. 37 – 64. Bibl.
Foreign relations
Latin America
McKenna, Peter. Canada – OAS Relations during the Trudeau Years. *Revista Interamericana de Bibliografía,* v. 42, no. 3 (1992), pp. 373 – 391. Bibl.
Ventosa del Campo, Andrés. La política exterior de Canadá y la América Latina. *Relaciones Internacionales (Mexico),* v. 14, Nueva época, no. 55 (July – Sept 92), pp. 51 – 59. Bibl.

CANADIAN LITERATURE
Foreign influences
Pratt, Mary Louise. La liberación de los márgenes: literaturas canadiense y latinoamericana en el contexto de la dependencia. *Casa de las Américas,* no. 190 (Jan – Mar 93), pp. 25 – 33. Bibl.

CANALES, MARIO
Interviews
Téllez A., Isabel. Colegio San Lorenzo: cuando la solidaridad es contagiosa. *Mensaje,* v. 42, no. 421 (Aug 93), pp. 402 – 403. Il.

CAÑARI INDIANS
Dean, Carolyn Sue. Ethnic Conflict and Corpus Christi in Colonial Cuzco. *Colonial Latin American Review,* v. 2, no. 1 – 2 (1993), pp. 93 – 120. Bibl, il.

CANARY ISLANDS
See also
Art – Canary Islands
Paz Sánchez, Manuel de. *Wangüemert y Cuba,* vols. I y II, reviewed by Louis A. Pérez, Jr. *Journal of Latin American Studies,* v. 25, no. 3 (Oct 93), pp. 658 – 659.

Congresses
Gutiérrez Escudero, Antonio. X Coloquio de Historia Canario – Americana. *Anuario de Estudios Americanos,* v. 49, Suppl. 2 (1992), pp. 217 – 221.

CANDELARIA, NASH
Criticism of specific works
Memories of the Alhambra
Beltrán-Vocal, María Antonia. Soledad, aislamiento y búsqueda de identidad en Nash Candelaria y Juan Goytisolo. *The Americas Review,* v. 21, no. 1 (Spring 93), pp. 103 – 111.

CANDOMBLÉ (CULT)
See
Umbanda (Cultus)

CANELONES, URUGUAY (DEPARTMENT)
Mieres, Pablo. Canelones, 1989: el fin del bipartidismo. *Cuadernos del CLAEH,* v. 18, no. 67 (Nov 93), pp. 121 – 131. Tables.

CÁNEPA, TITO ENRIQUE
David, León. Tito Cánepa. *Latin American Art,* v. 4, no. 4 (Winter 92), pp. 69 – 71. Bibl, il.

CANFIELD, D. LINCOLN
Obituaries
Beardsley, Theodore S. Necrology: Delos Lincoln Canfield (1903 – 1991). *Hispanic Review,* v. 61, no. 1 (Winter 93), pp. 135 – 137.

CANNIBALISM
Chacón, Zully. Antropofagia y resistencia caribe: armas jurídicas de la corona española. *Boletín de la Academia Nacional de la Historia (Venezuela),* v. 75, no. 300 (Oct – Dec 92), pp. 89 – 107. Bibl, maps.
Villaça, Aparecida Maria Neiva. *Comendo como gente: formas de canibalismo wari' (pakaa nova)* reviewed by Robin M. Wright. *Revista Brasileira de Ciências Sociais,* v. 8, no. 23 (Oct 93), pp. 146 – 148.

CANTINFLAS
See
Moreno, Mario

CANTÚ, AGOSTINO
Translations
Toni, Flávia Camargo. Memória: Mário de Andrade escreve para as crianças. *Vozes,* v. 87, no. 3 (May – June 93), pp. 67 – 72. Facs.

CANUDOS, BRAZIL
Borges, Dain Edward. Salvador's 1890s: Paternalism and Its Discontents. *Luso-Brazilian Review,* v. 30, no. 2 (Winter 93), pp. 47 – 57. Bibl.
Greenfield, Gerald Michael. "Sertão" and "Sertanejo": An Interpretive Context for Canudos. *Luso-Brazilian Review,* v. 30, no. 2 (Winter 93), pp. 35 – 46. Bibl.
Levine, Robert M. *Vale of Tears: Revisiting the Canudos Massacre in Northeastern Brazil, 1893 – 1897* reviewed by Francis Lambert. *Bulletin of Latin American Research,* v. 12, no. 3 (Sept 93), pp. 353 – 354.
— *Vale of Tears: Revisiting the Canudos Massacre in Northeastern Brazil, 1893 – 1897* reviewed by Dain Borges. *Hispanic American Historical Review,* v. 73, no. 3 (Aug 93), pp. 515 – 516.
— *Vale of Tears: Revisiting the Canudos Massacre in Northeastern Brazil, 1893 – 1897* reviewed by Jeff Lesser. *Journal of Latin American Studies,* v. 25, no. 2 (May 93), pp. 397 – 398.
— *Vale of Tears: Revisiting the Canudos Massacre in Northeastern Brazil, 1893 – 1897* reviewed by Steven C. Topik. *Luso-Brazilian Review,* v. 30, no. 2 (Winter 93), pp. 115 – 116.

Madden, Lori. The Canudos War in History. *Luso-Brazilian Review,* v. 30, no. 2 (Winter 93), pp. 5 – 22. Bibl.

Meihy, José Carlos Sebe Bom. "Meu empenho foi ser o tradutor do universo sertanejo": entrevista com José Calazans (Interviewed and transcribed by José Carlos Sebe Bom Meihy). *Luso-Brazilian Review,* v. 30, no. 2 (Winter 93), pp. 23 – 33.

Otten, Alexandre H. A influência do ideário religioso na construção da comunidade de Belo Monte. *Luso-Brazilian Review,* v. 30, no. 2 (Winter 93), pp. 71 – 95. Bibl.

Sampaio, Consuelo Novais. Repensando Canudos: o jogo das oligarquias. *Luso-Brazilian Review,* v. 30, no. 2 (Winter 93), pp. 97 – 113. Bibl, tables.

Sena, Davis Ribeiro de. A guerra das caatingas. *Revista do Instituto Histórico e Geográfico Brasileiro,* no. 373 (Oct – Dec 91), pp. 954 – 1007. Bibl, il.

CAPELÁN, CARLOS

Haber, Alicia. Carlos Capelán: una formulación antropológica (Accompanied by an English translation). *Art Nexus,* no. 7 (Jan – Mar 93), pp. 92 – 96. Bibl, il.

CAPITAL

See also
   Human capital

Brazil

Welch, John H. *Capital Markets in the Development Process: The Case of Brazil* reviewed by David E. Hojman. *Bulletin of Latin American Research,* v. 12, no. 3 (Sept 93), pp. 350 – 351.

— *Capital Markets in the Development Process: The Case of Brazil* reviewed by Tomás Bruginski de Paula. *Journal of Latin American Studies,* v. 25, no. 3 (Oct 93), pp. 677 – 678.

Chile

Morandé Lavín, Felipe Guillermo. La dinámica de los precios de los activos reales y el tipo de cambio real: las reformas al comercio exterior y las entradas de capital extranjero; Chile, 1976 – 1989. *El Trimestre Económico,* v. 59, Special issue (Dec 92), pp. 141 – 186. Bibl, tables, charts.

Colombia

Langebaek, Andrés. Colombia y los flujos de capital privado a América Latina, 1970 – 1991. *Planeación y Desarrollo,* v. 24, no. 2 (May – Aug 93), pp. 401 – 425. Bibl, tables, charts.

Mathematical models

López Mejía, Alejandro. La teoría del ingreso permanente en un mercado de capitales imperfecto: el caso colombiano. *Planeación y Desarrollo,* v. 24, no. 1 (Jan – Apr 93), pp. 385 – 423. Bibl, tables.

Latin America

Griffith-Jones, Stephany et al. El retorno de capital a América Latina. *Comercio Exterior,* v. 43, no. 1 (Jan 93), pp. 37 – 50. Bibl, tables.

Langebaek, Andrés. Colombia y los flujos de capital privado a América Latina, 1970 – 1991. *Planeación y Desarrollo,* v. 24, no. 2 (May – Aug 93), pp. 401 – 425. Bibl, tables, charts.

Welch, John H. The New Face of Latin America: Financial Flows, Markets, and Institutions in the 1990s. *Journal of Latin American Studies,* v. 25, no. 1 (Feb 93), pp. 1 – 24. Bibl, tables.

Mexico

Delgado, Dora. The Search for Capital. *Business Mexico,* v. 3, no. 11 (Nov 93), pp. 12 – 14.

CAPITAL INVESTMENTS

See also
   Investments, Foreign
   Saving and investment
   State capitalism

Chile

Daher, Antonio. Infraestructuras: regiones estatales y privadas en Chile. *Estudios Públicos (Chile),* no. 49 (Summer 93), pp. 137 – 173. Bibl, tables.

Méndez G., Juan Carlos. Análisis de las fuentes de financiamiento de CODELCO. *Estudios Públicos (Chile),* no. 50 (Fall 93), pp. 281 – 343. Bibl, tables, charts.

Mexican – American Border Region

Anguiano Téllez, María Eugenia. Irrigación y capital para transformar el desierto: la formación social del valle de Mexicali a principios del siglo XX. *Frontera Norte,* v. 4, no. 8 (July – Dec 92), pp. 125 – 147. Bibl.

CAPITAL PRODUCTIVITY

See also
   Industrial productivity

Brazil

Poli, Beatriz Trois Cunha and Jairo Laser Procianoy. A política de dividendos como geradora de economia fiscal e do desenvolvimento do mercado de capitais: uma proposta criativa. *RAE; Revista de Administração de Empresas,* v. 33, no. 4 (July – Aug 93), pp. 6 – 15. Bibl, tables.

Chile

Hernández T., Leonardo and Eduardo Walker H. Estructura de financiamiento corporativo en Chile, 1978 – 1990: evidencia a partir de datos contables. *Estudios Públicos (Chile),* no. 51 (Winter 93), pp. 87 – 156. Bibl, tables, charts.

Colombia

Mathematical models

Olivera, Mauricio. El costo de uso del capital en Colombia: una nueva estimación. *Planeación y Desarrollo,* v. 24, no. 2 (May – Aug 93), pp. 373 – 400. Bibl, tables, charts.

Latin America

United Nations. Economic Commission for Latin America and the Caribbean. *Equidad y transformación productiva: un enfoque integrado* reviewed by Gloria González Salazar. *Problemas del Desarrollo,* v. 24, no. 92 (Jan – Mar 93), pp. 233 – 236.

— *Equity and Changing Production Patterns: An Integrated Approach* (Review). *CEPAL Review,* no. 47 (Aug 92), pp. 190 – 191.

CAPITAL PUNISHMENT

See
   Criminal law

CAPITALISM

See also
   Competition
   Distributive justice
   Privatization
   State capitalism

Castellanos Guerrero, Alicia and Gilberto López y Rivas. Grupos étnicos y procesos nacionalitarios en el capitalismo neoliberal. *Nueva Antropología,* v. 13, no. 44 (Aug 93), pp. 27 – 41. Bibl.

Piñón A., Rosa María. América Latina y el Caribe en el nuevo orden capitalista mundial: Estados Unidos, Japón y Comunidad Europea. *Relaciones Internacionales (Mexico),* v. 14, Nueva época, no. 56 (Oct – Dec 92), pp. 7 – 18. Tables.

Repetto, Fabián. La construcción de un nuevo orden, o el final de una época . . . . *Realidad Económica,* no. 120 (Nov – Dec 93), pp. 18 – 40. Bibl, tables.

Salvat Monguillot, Manuel. Francisco de Vitoria y el nacimiento del capitalismo. *Boletín de la Academia Chilena de la Historia,* v. 58 – 59, no. 102 (1991 – 1992), pp. 329 – 347. Bibl.

Silva, Vera Alice Cardoso. A política externa brasileira na década de '90: possibilidades de acomodação à nova fase do capitalismo internacional. *Política e Estratégica,* v. 8, no. 2 – 4 (Apr – Dec 90), pp. 224 – 240. Bibl.

Brazil

Paim, Antônio. Perspectivas do capitalismo no Brasil. *Convivium,* v. 34, no. 2 (July – Dec 91), pp. 34 – 40.

Latin America

Alzate Montoya, Rubelia. Por un reencuentro latinoamericano. *Estudios Rurales Latinoamericanos,* v. 15, no. 2 – 3 (May – Dec 92), pp. 113 – 120.

Windward Islands

Trouillot, Michel-Rolph. *Peasants and Capital: Dominica in the World Economy* reviewed by Michael H. Allen (Review entitled "Rethinking Political Economy and Praxis in the Caribbean"). *Latin American Perspectives*, v. 20, no. 2 (Spring 93), pp. 111 – 119.

CAPITALISTS AND FINANCIERS
Brazil

Boschi, Renato Raul and Eli Diniz. Lideranças empresariais e problemas da estratégia liberal no Brasil. *Revista Brasileira de Ciências Sociais*, v. 8, no. 23 (Oct 93), pp. 101 – 119. Bibl.

Lamounier, Bolivar. Empresarios, partidos y democratización en Brasil, 1974 – 1990. *Revista Mexicana de Sociología*, v. 54, no. 1 (Jan – Mar 92), pp. 77 – 97. Bibl.

Societies, etc.

Nylen, William R. Selling Neoliberalism: Brazil's Instituto Liberal. *Journal of Latin American Studies*, v. 25, no. 2 (May 93), pp. 301 – 311. Bibl.

Chile
Interviews

Etcheberry, Blanca. Empresarios formados por la Compañía de Jesús: un acercamiento de este último tiempo. *Mensaje*, v. 42, no. 420 (July 93), pp. 322 – 325. Il.

Colombia

Dávila L. de Guevara, Carlos. *Historia empresarial de Colombia: estudios, problemas y perspectivas* reviewed by Luis Aurelio Ordóñez B. (Review entitled "Un balance historiográfico exhaustivo y sugestivo"). *Anuario Colombiano de Historia Social y de la Cultura*, no. 20 (1992), pp. 147 – 152.

Mexico

Geyer, Anne. Chronicles of Success. *Business Mexico*, v. 3, no. 5 (May 93), pp. 32 – 35. Il.

Luna, Matilde and Cristina Puga. Modernización en México: la propuesta empresarial. *Revista Mexicana de Ciencias Políticas y Sociales*, v. 38, Nueva época, no. 151 (Jan – Mar 93), pp. 35 – 49. Bibl.

Luna, Matilde and Ricardo Tirado. Los empresarios en el escenario del cambio: trayectoria y tendencias de sus estrategias de acción colectiva. *Revista Mexicana de Sociología*, v. 55, no. 2 (Apr – June 93), pp. 243 – 271. Bibl, tables, charts.

Mizrahi, Yemile. La nueva oposición conservadora en México: la radicalización política de los empresarios norteños. *Foro Internacional*, v. 32, no. 5 (Oct – Dec 92), pp. 744 – 771. Bibl, tables.

Walker, David Wayne. *Parentescos, negocios y política: la familia Martínez del Río en México, 1823 – 1867* reviewed by María del Carmen Collado Herrera. *Historia Mexicana*, v. 42, no. 1 (July – Sept 92), pp. 133 – 138.

CAPOEIRA (DANCE)

Desch, T. J. Capoeira: Martial Art as Spiritual Discipline. *Journal of Caribbean Studies*, v. 9, no. 1 – 2 (Winter 92 – Spring 93), pp. 87 – 98. Bibl.

Dossar, Kenneth. Capoeira Angola: Dancing between Two Worlds. *Afro-Hispanic Review*, v. 11, no. 1 – 3 (1992), pp. 5 – 10. Bibl.

Lima, Magali Alonso de and Roberto Kant de Lima. Capoeira e cidadania: negritude e identidade no Brasil republicano. *Revista de Antropologia (Brazil)*, v. 34 (1991), pp. 143 – 182. Bibl.

CAPUCHINS
Venezuela

Díaz Alvarez, Manuel. Palabras del r.p. Manuel Díaz Alvarez con motivo de los 100 años del reingreso a Venezuela de los rr.pp. capuchinos. *Boletín de la Academia Nacional de la Historia (Venezuela)*, v. 76, no. 302 (Apr – June 93), pp. 15 – 19.

CARACAS, VENEZUELA

Ferry, Robert James. *The Colonial Elite of Early Caracas: Formation and Crisis, 1567 – 1767* reviewed by John Lynch. *Journal of Latin American Studies*, v. 25, no. 1 (Feb 93), pp. 191 – 192.

Fuentes Bajo, María Dolores. Amor y desamor en la Venezuela hispánica: Caracas, 1701 – 1791. *Boletín de la Academia Nacional de la Historia (Venezuela)*, v. 75, no. 298 (Apr – June 92), pp. 49 – 62. Bibl.

Gasparini, Marina, ed. *Obras de arte de la Ciudad Universitaria de Caracas* reviewed by Antonio Rodríguez (Accompanied by an English translation). *Art Nexus*, no. 8 (Apr – June 93), pp. 33 – 34. Il.

Jiménez Arraiz, Francisco. Antiguallas: orígenes caraqueños (Previously published in this journal vol. 1, no. 1, 1912). *Boletín de la Academia Nacional de la Historia (Venezuela)*, v. 75, no. 300 (Oct – Dec 92), pp. 262 – 273.

Langue, Frédérique. Antagonismos y solidaridades en un cabildo colonial: Caracas, 1750 – 1810. *Anuario de Estudios Americanos*, v. 49 (1992), pp. 371 – 393. Bibl.

Lucena Salmoral, Manuel. *Características del comercio exterior de la provincia de Caracas durante el sexenio revolucionario, 1807 – 1812* reviewed by Adriana Rodríguez. *Revista de Historia de América*, no. 113 (Jan – June 92), pp. 173 – 174.

Palabras pronunciadas por González Lander en la ocasión de recibir la colección de obras de la Academia. *Boletín de la Academia Nacional de la Historia (Venezuela)*, v. 75, no. 298 (Apr – June 92), pp. 21 – 25.

Rotker, Susana. Crónica y cultura urbana: Caracas, la última década. *Inti*, no. 37 – 38 (Spring – Fall 93), pp. 233 – 242. Bibl.

CARDENAL, ERNESTO
Criticism and interpretation

Pailler, Claire. Avatares del tiempo histórico en dos poetas nicaragüenses de hoy: Ernesto Cardenal y Pablo Antonio Cuadra. *Caravelle*, no. 60 (1993), pp. 85 – 99. Bibl.

Criticism of specific works
El estrecho dudoso

Minard, Evelyne. Un example d'utilisation de l'histoire par Ernesto Cardenal: *El estrecho dudoso*. *Caravelle*, no. 60 (1993), pp. 101 – 121. Bibl.

Interviews

Salmon, Russell. El proceso poético: entrevista con Ernesto Cardenal. *Cuadernos Americanos*, no. 40, Nueva época (July – Aug 93), pp. 99 – 109.

CÁRDENAS, LÁZARO

Cárdenas de la Peña, Enrique. La política económica en la época de Cárdenas. *El Trimestre Económico*, v. 60, no. 239 (July – Sept 93), pp. 675 – 697. Bibl, tables.

Semo, Ilán. El cardenismo revisado: la tercera vía y otras utopías inciertas. *Revista Mexicana de Sociología*, v. 55, no. 2 (Apr – June 93), pp. 197 – 223. Bibl.

CARDOZA Y ARAGÓN, LUIS
Criticism and interpretation

Rodríguez, Francisco. Luis Cardoza y Aragón: las paradojas de la escritura. *Plural (Mexico)*, v. 22, no. 264 (Sept 93), pp. 52 – 55. Bibl.

CARGO SYSTEM
See
Community organization

CARIB INDIANS

Beckles, Hilary. Kalinago (Carib) Resistance to European Colonisation of the Caribbean. *Caribbean Quarterly*, v. 38, no. 2 – 3 (June – Sept 92), pp. 1 – 14. Bibl.

Bliss, Elaine. Adaptation to Agricultural Change among Garifuna Women in Hopkins, Belize. *Caribbean Geography*, v. 3, no. 3 (Mar 92), pp. 160 – 174. Bibl, tables, maps.

Boucher, Philip Paul. *Cannibal Encounters: Europeans and Island Caribs, 1492 – 1763* reviewed by Irving Rouse. *Hispanic American Historical Review,* v. 73, no. 3 (Aug 93), pp. 495 – 496.

Hulme, Peter and Neil L. Whitehead, eds. *Wild Majesty: Encounters with Caribs from Columbus to the Present Day; An Anthology* reviewed by Peter T. Bradley. *Bulletin of Latin American Research,* v. 12, no. 1 (Jan 93), pp. 111 – 112.

Humphreys, Francis. Afro-Belizean Cultural Heritage: Its Role in Combating Recolonization. *Belizean Studies,* v. 20, no. 3 (Dec 92), pp. 11 – 16. Bibl.

CARIBAN LANGUAGES

Alvarado, Lisandro. Ensayo sobre el caribe venezolano (Previously published in this journal vol. 1, no. 1, 1912). *Boletín de la Academia Nacional de la Historia (Venezuela),* v. 75, no. 300 (Oct – Dec 92), pp. 295 – 319.

CARIBBEAN AREA

See also

AIDS (Disease) – Caribbean area
Art – Caribbean area
Authors – Caribbean area
Bahamas
Blacks – Caribbean area
Blacks in literature – Caribbean area
British – Caribbean area
Cost and standard of living – Caribbean area
Creole dialects – Caribbean area
Cuba
Democracy – Caribbean area
Dominica
Dominican Republic
Ecology – Caribbean area
Ecology and development – Caribbean area
Economic assistance – Caribbean area
Economic assistance, Foreign – Caribbean area
Economics – Caribbean area
Educational sociology – Caribbean area
Employment – Caribbean area
Ethnicity – Caribbean area
Ethnomusicology – Caribbean area
Europeans – Caribbean area
Federation of the West Indies
Finance, Public – Caribbean area
Food habits – Caribbean area
Foreign trade promotion – Caribbean area
Frontier and pioneer life – Caribbean area
Furniture – Caribbean area
Geography – Caribbean area
Geopolitics – Caribbean area
Government ownership of business enterprises – Caribbean area
Haiti
Hospitals – Caribbean area
Indians, Treatment of – Caribbean area
Jamaica
Journalism – Caribbean area
Literature and society – Caribbean area
Mass media – Caribbean area
Money and money supply – Caribbean area
Museums – Caribbean area
Music and society – Caribbean area
Netherlands Antilles
Nevis, West Indies
Non-governmental organizations – Caribbean area
Nutrition – Caribbean area
Popular culture – Caribbean area
Popular music – Caribbean area
Postmodernism – Caribbean area
Press – Caribbean area
Privatization – Caribbean area
Public health – Caribbean area
Publishers and publishing – Caribbean area
Puerto Rico
Saint Kitts, West Indies
Saint Vincent, West Indies
Sex role – Caribbean area
Slave trade – Caribbean area
Slavery – Caribbean area
Social psychology – Caribbean area
Sociolinguistics – Caribbean area
Spanish language – Caribbean area
Subcontracting – Caribbean area
Sugar – Caribbean area

Tourist trade – Caribbean area
Transportation, Maritime – Caribbean area
Trinidad and Tobago
Turks and Caicos Islands
Unemployment – Caribbean area
Universities and colleges – Caribbean area
Volcanism – Caribbean area
West Indians
Women – Caribbean area
Women authors – Caribbean area
Women in literature – Caribbean area

Civilization

Castañeda Fuertes, Digna. Presencia africana en la identidad cultural de las sociedades caribeñas. *Boletín de la Academia Nacional de la Historia (Venezuela),* v. 75, no. 299 (July – Sept 92), pp. 77 – 90. Bibl.

Cummins, Alissandra. Exhibiting Culture: Museums and National Identity in the Caribbean. *Caribbean Quarterly,* v. 38, no. 2 – 3 (June – Sept 92), pp. 33 – 53. Bibl.

Nettleford, Rex. Surviving Columbus: Caribbean Achievements in the Encounter of Worlds, 1492 – 1992. *Caribbean Quarterly,* v. 38, no. 2 – 3 (June – Sept 92), pp. 97 – 112. Bibl.

Pierre-Charles, Gérard. El Caribe en el mundo. *Cuadernos Americanos,* no. 40, Nueva época (July – Aug 93), pp. 78 – 83.

Rojas Osorio, Carlos. Hostos y la identidad caribeña. *Caribbean Studies,* v. 25, no. 1 – 2 (Jan – July 92), pp. 133 – 145. Bibl.

Santana, Adalberto. Visiones del área del litoral mediterráneo latinoamericano continental. *Cuadernos Americanos,* no. 37, Nueva época (Jan – Feb 93), pp. 65 – 75. Bibl.

Walcott, Derek. The Antilles: Fragments of Epic Memory; The 1992 Nobel Lecture. *World Literature Today,* v. 67, no. 2 (Spring 93), pp. 260 – 267. Il.

Bibliography

Duff, Ernest A. Attack and Counterattack: Dynamics of Transculturation in the Caribbean (Review article). *Studies in Latin American Popular Culture,* v. 12 (1993), pp. 195 – 202.

Commerce

History

Carrington, Selwyn H. H. The American Revolution, British Policy, and the West Indian Economy, 1775 – 1808. *Revista/Review Interamericana,* v. 22, no. 1 – 2 (Spring – Summer 92), pp. 72 – 108. Bibl, tables.

López y Sebastián, Lorenzo Eladio and Justo L. del Río Moreno. Comercio y transporte en la economía del azúcar antillano durante el siglo XVI. *Anuario de Estudios Americanos,* v. 49 (1992), pp. 55 – 87. Bibl, maps.

Discovery and exploration

Sauer, Carl Ortwin. *The Early Spanish Main* reviewed by Peter T. Bradley. *Bulletin of Latin American Research,* v. 12, no. 1 (Jan 93), pp. 110 – 111.

Economic conditions

Fletcher, G. Richard and Robert A. Pastor. El Caribe en el siglo XXI. *Integración Latinoamericana,* v. 18, no. 187 – 188 (Mar – Apr 93), pp. 13 – 22. Bibl.

Harker, Trevor. Caribbean Economic Performance: An Overview. *Social and Economic Studies,* v. 41, no. 3 (Sept 92), pp. 101 – 143. Tables.

Pierre-Charles, Gérard. El Caribe en el mundo. *Cuadernos Americanos,* no. 40, Nueva época (July – Aug 93), pp. 78 – 83.

Ramsaran, Ramesh. Growth, Employment, and the Standard of Living in Selected Commonwealth Caribbean Countries. *Caribbean Studies,* v. 25, no. 1 – 2 (Jan – July 92), pp. 103 – 122. Tables.

Economic integration

Derné, Marie-Claude et al. Business Opportunities in Caribbean Cooperation. *Social and Economic Studies,* v. 41, no. 3 (Sept 92), pp. 65 – 100. Bibl, tables.

Hart, Richard. Federation: An Ill-Fated Design. *Jamaica Journal,* v. 25, no. 1 (Oct 93), pp. 10 – 16. Bibl, il.

Maríñez, Pablo A. Procesos de integración e identidad cultural en el Caribe. *Integración Latinoamericana,* v. 17, no. 185 (Dec 92), pp. 23 – 32. Bibl.

Serbín, Andrés. El Grupo de los Tres y el proceso de regionalización en la cuenca del Caribe. *Nueva Sociedad,* no. 125 (May – June 93), pp. 120 – 129. Bibl.

Economic policy

McAfee, Kathy. *Storm Signals: Structural Adjustment and Development Alternatives in the Caribbean* reviewed by Peter Meel. *European Review of Latin American and Caribbean Studies,* no. 54 (June 93), pp. 128 – 131.

Ramsaran, Ramesh. *The Challenge of Structural Adjustment in the Commonwealth Caribbean* reviewed by Vicente Galbis. *Journal of Developing Areas,* v. 27, no. 4 (July 93), pp. 575 – 576.

Thomas, Clive Yolande. *The Poor and Powerless: Economic Policy and Change in the Caribbean* reviewed by Michael H. Allen (Review entitled "Rethinking Political Economy and Praxis in the Caribbean"). *Latin American Perspectives,* v. 20, no. 2 (Spring 93), pp. 111 – 119.

Bibliography

Dew, Edward. Caribbean Paths in the Dark (Review article). *Latin American Research Review,* v. 28, no. 1 (1993), pp. 162 – 173. Bibl.

Emigration and immigration

Domenach, Hervé and Michel Picouet. *La dimension migratoire des Antilles* reviewed by Guy Caire. *Tiers Monde,* v. 34, no. 135 (July – Sept 93), pp. 716 – 718.

Duany, Jorge. Más allá de la válvula de escape: tendencias recientes en la migración caribeña. *Nueva Sociedad,* no. 127 (Sept – Oct 93), pp. 80 – 99. Bibl.

Foreign economic relations

Erisman, H. Michael. *Pursuing Postdependency Politics: South – South Relations in the Caribbean* reviewed by Thomas D. Anderson. *Revista Interamericana de Bibliografía,* v. 42, no. 4 (1992), p. 657.

Gill, Henry S. The Caribbean in a World of Economic Blocks. *Social and Economic Studies,* v. 41, no. 3 (Sept 92), pp. 25 – 36.

Payne, Anthony John and Paul K. Sutton. The Commonwealth Caribbean in the New World Order: Between Europe and North America? *Journal of Inter-American Studies and World Affairs,* v. 34, no. 4 (Winter 92 – 93), pp. 39 – 75. Bibl.

Rosenberg, Mark B. Whither the Caribbean?: Whither Florida? *Hemisphere,* v. 5, no. 2 (Winter – Spring 93), pp. 9 – 11.

Segal, Aaron. Opciones comerciales del Caribe: las cartas de Europa, América del Norte y América Latina. *Comercio Exterior,* v. 43, no. 11 (Nov 93), pp. 1019 – 1030. Bibl, tables, charts.

United States

Deere, Carmen Diana et al. *In the Shadows of the Sun: Caribbean Development Alternatives and U.S. Policy* reviewed by Georges A. Fauriol. *Studies in Comparative International Development,* v. 27, no. 2 (Summer 92), pp. 110 – 112.

Venezuela

Comunidad del Caribe: Acuerdo sobre Comercio e Inversiones entre el Gobierno de la República de Venezuela y la Comunidad del Caribe (CARICOM). *Integración Latinoamericana,* v. 18, no. 186 (Jan – Feb 93), pp. 69 – 73.

Foreign relations

Central America

I Conferencia Ministerial de los Países del Istmo Centroamericano y de la Comunidad del Caribe. *Integración Latinoamericana,* v. 17, no. 185 (Dec 92), pp. 71 – 72.

Mexico

Martínez Vara, Gerardo. México y el Caribe: un encuentro necesario en la problemática regional. *Relaciones Internacionales (Mexico),* v. 14, Nueva época, no. 56 (Oct – Dec 92), pp. 129 – 132.

History

Craton, Michael and Gail Saunders. *Islanders in the Stream: A History of the Bahamian People* reviewed by William F. Keegan. *Hispanic American Historical Review,* v. 73, no. 4 (Nov 93), pp. 702 – 703.

Garciga Garciga, Orestes. El estudio de la conquista castellana de las Antillas en un libro inédito de Fernando Ortiz. *Anuario de Estudios Americanos,* v. 49, Suppl. 2 (1992), pp. 253 – 256.

Maríñez, Pablo A. Democracia y descolonización en el Caribe. *Estudios Sociales (Dominican Republic),* v. 26, no. 92 (Apr – June 93), pp. 5 – 20. Bibl, tables.

— Procesos de integración e identidad cultural en el Caribe. *Integración Latinoamericana,* v. 17, no. 185 (Dec 92), pp. 23 – 32. Bibl.

Industries

Green, Cecilia. *The World Market Factory: A Study of Enclave Industrialization in the Eastern Caribbean and Its Impact on Women Workers* reviewed by Nan Wiegersma. *Journal of Developing Areas,* v. 27, no. 2 (Jan 93), pp. 269 – 270.

Politics

Bibliography

Dew, Edward. Caribbean Paths in the Dark (Review article). *Latin American Research Review,* v. 28, no. 1 (1993), pp. 162 – 173. Bibl.

Study and teaching

Dietz, James L. Reviewing and Renewing Puerto Rican and Caribbean Studies: From Dependency to What? *Caribbean Studies,* v. 25, no. 1 – 2 (Jan – July 92), pp. 27 – 48. Bibl.

CARIBBEAN AREA IN LITERATURE

González, Aníbal. Ana Lydia Pluravega: unidad y multiplicidad caribeñas en la obra de Ana Lydia Vega. *Revista Iberoamericana,* v. 59, no. 162 – 163 (Jan – June 93), pp. 289 – 300. Bibl.

Sánchez, Luis Rafael. Voyage to Caribbean Identity: The Caribbean Sounds, the Caribbean Resounds (Translated by Alfred MacAdam). *Review,* no. 47 (Fall 93), pp. 20 – 22.

CARIBBEAN COMMUNITY

Gill, Henry S. CARICOM: origen, objetivos y perspectivas de integración en el Caribe. *Integración Latinoamericana,* v. 18, no. 191 (July 93), pp. 37 – 44. Bibl, tables.

Congresses

I Conferencia Ministerial de los Países del Istmo Centroamericano y de la Comunidad del Caribe. *Integración Latinoamericana,* v. 17, no. 185 (Dec 92), pp. 71 – 72.

Sources

Comunidad del Caribe: Acuerdo sobre Comercio e Inversiones entre el Gobierno de la República de Venezuela y la Comunidad del Caribe (CARICOM). *Integración Latinoamericana,* v. 18, no. 186 (Jan – Feb 93), pp. 69 – 73.

CARIBBEAN LITERATURE

Esteves, Carmen C. and Lizabeth Paravisini-Gebert. *Green Cane and Juicy Flotsam: Short Stories by Caribbean Women* reviewed by Ivette Romero. *Letras Femeninas,* v. 19, no. 1 – 2 (Spring – Fall 93), pp. 154 – 155.

History and criticism

Bensen, Robert. Columbus at the Abyss: The Genesis of New World Literature. *Jamaica Journal,* v. 24, no. 3 (Feb 93), pp. 48 – 54. Bibl, il.

Gikandi, Simon. *Writing in Limbo: Modernism and Caribbean Literature* reviewed by Bruce King. *World Literature Today,* v. 67, no. 2 (Spring 93), p. 426.

Ndiaye, Christiane. Le réalisme merveilleux au féminin. *Canadian Journal of Latin American and Caribbean Studies,* v. 17, no. 34 (1992), pp. 115 – 117.

Rohlehr, F. Gordon. *My Strangled City and Other Essays* reviewed by Rupert Lewis. *Social and Economic Studies,* v. 41, no. 3 (Sept 92), pp. 169 – 173.

Study and teaching

Benítez Rojo, Antonio. La literatura caribeña y la teoría de caos. *Latin American Literary Review,* v. 20, no. 40 (July – Dec 92), pp. 16 – 18.

CARIBBEAN POETRY
History and criticism
Williams, Claudette Rose-Green. The Myth of Black Female Sexuality in Spanish Caribbean Poetry: A Deconstructive Critical View. *Afro-Hispanic Review,* v. 12, no. 1 (Spring 93), pp. 16 – 23. Bibl.

CARICATURES AND CARTOONS
See also
Comic books, strips, etc.
Satire
Wit and humor
Argentina
Fontanarrosa, Roberto. Nos tocó hacer reír. *Cuadernos Hispanoamericanos,* no. 517 – 519 (July – Sept 93), pp. 353 – 360. Il.

Loiseau, Carlos. A través de la ventana. *Cuadernos Hispanoamericanos,* no. 517 – 519 (July – Sept 93), pp. 361 – 368. Il.

Brazil
Saliba, Elias Thomé. A dimensão cômica do dilema brasileiro. *Vozes,* v. 87, no. 1 (Jan – Feb 93), pp. 46 – 54. Bibl.

Chile
Cruz Ovalle de Amenábar, Isabel. Reseña de una sonrisa: los comienzos de la caricatura en Chile decimonónico, 1858 – 1868. *Boletín de la Academia Chilena de la Historia,* v. 58 – 59, no. 102 (1991 – 1992), pp. 107 – 138. Bibl, il.

Mexico
Molina, Silvia. El discurso escéptico: su expresión en la caricatura política. *Revista Mexicana de Ciencias Políticas y Sociales,* v. 38, Nueva época, no. 154 (Oct – Dec 93), pp. 79 – 89. Bibl.

CARICOM
See
Caribbean Community

CARNIVALESQUE LITERATURE
See
Magical realism (Literature)

CARNIVALS
See
Folk festivals

CARO COPETE, JORGE
Obituaries
Cacua Prada, Antonio. Jorge Caro Copete. *Boletín de Historia y Antigüedades,* v. 80, no. 781 (Apr – June 93), pp. 373 – 375.

CARPENTIER, ALEJO
Criticism and interpretation
Báez-Jorge, Félix. La afición arqueológica de Alejo Carpentier. *Plural (Mexico),* v. 22, no. 262 (July 93), pp. 46 – 50.

— Mitla y el barroco: notas sobre la afición arqueológica de Alejo Carpentier. *La Palabra y el Hombre,* no. 82 (Apr – June 92), pp. 57 – 73. Il.

Díaz Ruiz, Ignacio. El recurso de la historia: a propósito de Carpentier. *Nueva Revista de Filología Hispánica,* v. 40, no. 2 (July – Dec 92), pp. 1073 – 1086. Bibl.

Perilli de Garmendia, Carmen. *Imágenes de la mujer en Carpentier y García Márquez* reviewed by Rita Gnutzmann. *Revista Interamericana de Bibliografía,* v. 42, no. 3 (1992), p. 507.

Stawicka, Bárbara. La selva en flor: Alejo Carpentier y el diálogo entre las vanguardias europeas del siglo XX y el barroco latinoamericano. *La Palabra y el Hombre,* no. 81 (Jan – Mar 92), pp. 193 – 199. Bibl.

Criticism of specific works
El arpa y la sombra
Pérez Villacampa, Gilberto. Enjuiciamiento advertido de la sombra de Colón. *Islas,* no. 98 (Jan – Apr 91), pp. 98 – 118.

Los pasos perdidos
Klüppelholz, Heinz. Alejo Carpentiers orphische Beschwörung. *Zeitschrift für Lateinamerika Wien,* no. 42 (1992), pp. 17 – 25. Bibl.

El siglo de las luces
Basile, María Teresa. La naturaleza como discurso sobre la identidad latinoamericana. *La Educación (USA),* v. 36, no. 111 – 113 (1992), pp. 75 – 88. Bibl.

Peterson, Gabriela and Víctor Valembois. Los epígrafes en *El siglo de las luces:* su interpretación; de Goya a Carpentier. *Káñina,* v. 16, no. 2 (July – Dec 92), pp. 89 – 100. Bibl, il, tables.

— Los epígrafes en *El siglo de las luces:* su ubicación; de Goya a Carpentier. *Káñina,* v. 16, no. 1 (Jan – June 92), pp. 79 – 89. Bibl, il.

Translations
Carpentier, Alejo. Prologue to *The Kingdom of This World* (Translated by Alfred MacAdam). *Review,* no. 47 (Fall 93), pp. 28 – 31.

CARRILLO PUERTO, FELIPE
Sarkisyanz, Manuel. *Vom Wirken und Sterben des Felipe Carrillo Puerto, des "Roten" Apostels der Maya-Indianer: Zur politischen Heiligenlegende im revolutionären Mexiko* reviewed by Jürgen Buchenau. *Hispanic American Historical Review,* v. 73, no. 2 (May 93), pp. 332 – 333.

CARRIÓ DE LA VANDERA, ALONSO
Díaz-Jove Blanco, Santiago. Alonso Carrió de Lavandera, "Concoloncorvo": el contexto migratorio de su época y lugar de origen. *Revista de Indias,* v. 53, no. 198 (May – Aug 93), pp. 639 – 649.

CARRIÓN, BENJAMÍN
Criticism and interpretation
Handelsman, Michael Howard. *Ideario de Benjamín Carrión* reviewed by José Otero. *Chasqui,* v. 22, no. 1 (May 93), p. 105.

CARRIZO, JUAN ALFONSO
Alcorta, Rodrigo. Juan Alfonso Carriza y medio siglo del Instituto Nacional de Antropología. *Todo Es Historia,* v. 27, no. 312 (July 93), pp. 62 – 65. Il.

CARTAGENA, COLOMBIA
Mora de Tovar, Gilma Lucía. El deber de vivir ordenadamente para obedecer al rey. *Anuario Colombiano de Historia Social y de la Cultura,* no. 20 (1992), pp. 109 – 131.

CARTELS AND COMMODITY AGREEMENTS
See also
Competition
Price regulation
Peritore, N. Patrick. El surgimiento del cártel biotecnológico. *Revista Mexicana de Sociología,* v. 54, no. 2 (Apr – June 92), pp. 101 – 131. Bibl, tables.

Portillo, Luis. El Convenio Internacional de Café y la crisis del mercado. *Comercio Exterior,* v. 43, no. 4 (Apr 93), pp. 378 – 391. Bibl, tables.

Law and legislation
Orozco, Claudia. Marco legal para la promoción de la competencia en derecho comparado y en Colombia. *Planeación y Desarrollo,* v. 24, no. 2 (May – Aug 93), pp. 95 – 144. Bibl.

CARTOGRAPHY
See also
Atlases
Subdivision *Maps* under names of specific countries and regions
Donís Ríos, Manuel Alberto. Venezuela: topónimo afortunado en la cartografía auroral de América. *Montalbán,* no. 24 (1992), pp. 99 – 118. Bibl, maps.

Hardoy, Jorge Enrique. *Cartografía urbana colonial de América Latina y el Caribe* reviewed by María Elena Ducci. *EURE,* v. 19, no. 58 (Oct 93), pp. 87 – 88.

Horch, Rosemarie Erika. Os primeiros mapas do Brasil. *Vozes*, v. 86, no. 4 (July – Aug 92), pp. 8 – 15. Il.

CARTOONS

See
Caricatures and cartoons
Comic books, strips, etc.

CARÚPANO, VENEZUELA

Salcedo-Bastardo, José Luis. En el 170° aniversario de la municipalidad de Carúpano. *Boletín de la Academia Nacional de la Historia (Venezuela)*, v. 75, no. 297 (Jan – Mar 92), pp. 33 – 42.

CARVALHO, RONALD DE

Criticism of specific works

Toda a América

Paro, Maria Clara Bonetti. Ronald de Carvalho e Walt Whitman. *Revista de Letras (Brazil)*, v. 32 (1992), pp. 141 – 151.

CARYBÉ

See
Bernabó, Héctor

CASA DE LAS AMÉRICAS

Pizarro, Ana. Para ser jóvenes en cien años más. *Casa de las Américas*, no. 191 (Apr – June 93), pp. 5 – 7.

CASADO DE ALISAL, CARLOS

Marco, Miguel Angel de. *Carlos Casado de Alisal y el progreso argentino* reviewed by F. L. *Todo Es Historia*, v. 27, no. 311 (June 93), p. 60. Il.

CASALLA, MARIO CARLOS

Alsina Gutiérrez, Rogelio and Xiomara García Machado. Un nuevo estilo de filosofar: polémica con Mario Casalla desde la alteridad. *Islas*, no. 96 (May – Aug 90), pp. 111 – 120. Bibl.

García Machado, Xiomara. Notas críticas para la "transcendencia" de un proyecto liberador: Mario Casalla y Silvio Maresca. *Islas*, no. 99 (May – Aug 91), pp. 15 – 20. Bibl.

CASAS, BARTOLOMÉ DE LAS

Correspondence, reminiscences, etc.

Borello, Rodolfo A. Los diarios de Colón y el padre Las Casas. *Cuadernos Hispanoamericanos*, no. 512 (Feb 93), pp. 7 – 22. Bibl, il.

Criticism and interpretation

Benítez, Fernando. *1992: ¿Qué celebramos, qué lamentamos?* reviewed by Alvaro Ruiz Abreu (Review entitled "En lengua propia"). *Nexos*, v. 16, no. 181 (Jan 93), pp. 70 – 72.

Castilla Urbano, Francisco. Juan Ginés de Sepúlveda: en torno a una idea de civilización. *Revista de Indias*, v. 52, no. 195 – 196 (May – Dec 92), pp. 329 – 348. Bibl.

Durán Luzio, Juan. *Bartolomé de las Casas ante la conquista de América: las voces del historiador* reviewed by Juan Adolfo Vázquez. *Latin American Indian Literatures Journal*, v. 9, no. 1 (Spring 93), pp. 79 – 83.

— *Bartolomé de las Casas ante la conquista de América: las voces del historiador* reviewed by Lilian Uribe. *Revista de Crítica Literaria Latinoamericana*, v. 19, no. 37 (Jan – June 93), pp. 377 – 380.

— *Bartolomé de las Casas ante la conquista de América: las voces del historiador* reviewed by Danuta Teresa Mosejko. *Revista de Historia (Costa Rica)*, no. 26 (July – Dec 92), pp. 209 – 216.

Feijóo Seguín, María Luisa. El polémico fray Bartolomé de las Casas. *Hoy Es Historia*, v. 10, no. 60 (Nov – Dec 93), pp. 22 – 33. Il.

Fernández Buey, Francisco. La controversia entre Ginés de Sepúlveda y Bartolomé de las Casas: una revisión. *Boletín Americanista*, v. 33, no. 42 – 43 (1992 – 1993), pp. 301 – 347. Bibl.

Gutiérrez, Gustavo. *En busca de los pobres de Jesuscristo* reviewed by Carlos Garatea Grau (Review entitled "Por la vida y la libertad"). *Debate (Peru)*, v. 16, no. 72 (Mar – May 93), p. 63. Il.

— *En busca de los pobres de Jesuscristo: el pensamiento de Bartolomé de las Casas* reviewed by Aníbal Edwards. *Mensaje*, v. 42, no. 417 (Mar – Apr 93), pp. 109 – 110.

Helminen, Juha Pekka. Las Casas, los judíos, los moros y los negros. *Cuadernos Hispanoamericanos*, no. 512 (Feb 93), pp. 23 – 28. Bibl.

Ortega, José. Las Casas, un reformador social "por abajo." *Cuadernos Hispanoamericanos*, no. 512 (Feb 93), pp. 29 – 38. Bibl, il.

Soria, Giuliano Oreste. Echi della conquista nella Torino del '600: Valerio Fulvio Savoiano e Bartolomé de Las Casas. *Quaderni Ibero-Americani*, no. 72 (Dec 92), pp. 721 – 731. Bibl.

Criticism of specific works

En defensa de los indios

Himmerich y Valencia, Robert. Historical Objectivity and the Persistence of Fray Bartolomé de las Casas: A Commentary. *Colonial Latin American Historical Review*, v. 2, no. 1 (Winter 93), pp. 105 – 108. Il.

Memorial

Baptiste, Victor N. *Bartolomé de las Casas and Thomas More's Utopia: Connections and Similarities; A Translation and Study* reviewed by Juan Durán Luzio. *Latin American Indian Literatures Journal*, v. 9, no. 1 (Spring 93), pp. 83 – 85.

Obras completas

Alcina Franch, José. Las *Obras completas* de Las Casas. *Cuadernos Hispanoamericanos*, no. 520 (Oct 93), pp. 93 – 97. Bibl, il.

CASAS, MYRNA

Criticism of specific works

La trampa

Aguilú de Murphy, Raquel. Hacia un teorización del absurdo en el teatro de Myrna Casas. *Revista Iberoamericana*, v. 59, no. 162 – 163 (Jan – June 93), pp. 169 – 176. Bibl.

CASOY, BORIS

Squirra, S. Boris Casoy, o âncora brasileiro e o modelo norte-americano. *Vozes*, v. 87, no. 4 (July – Aug 93), pp. 3 – 12. Bibl, il.

CASSAVA

See
Manioc

CASTELLANOS, ROSARIO

Criticism of specific works

El eterno femenino

Pulido Jiménez, Juan José. El humor satírico en *El eterno femenino* de Rosario Castellanos. *Revista Canadiense de Estudios Hispánicos*, v. 17, no. 3 (Spring 93), pp. 483 – 494. Bibl.

Oficio de tinieblas

Lavou, Victorien. El juego de los programas narrativos en *Oficio de tinieblas* de Rosario Castellanos. *Revista de Crítica Literaria Latinoamericana*, v. 19, no. 37 (Jan – June 93), pp. 319 – 332.

CASTELLI, JUAN JOSÉ

Fiction

Delgado, Josefina. Andrés Rivera y el sueño eterno de Castelli. *Todo Es Historia*, v. 27, no. 315 (Oct 93), pp. 56 – 59. Il.

CASTILHOS, JÚLIO DE

Isaia, Artur Cesar. Catolicismo, regeneração social e castilhismo na república velha gaúcha. *Estudos Ibero-Americanos*, v. 18, no. 1 (July 92), pp. 5 – 18. Bibl.

CASTILLO, ANA

Criticism and interpretation

Yarbro-Bejarano, Ivonne. The Multiple Subject in the Writing of Ana Castillo. *The Americas Review*, v. 20, no. 1 (Spring 92), pp. 65 – 72. Bibl.

CASTILLO, ANDRÉS

Interviews

Cordones-Cook, Juanamaría. Surgimiento y desaparición del Teatro Negro Uruguayo: entrevista con Andrés Castillo. *Afro-Hispanic Review*, v. 12, no. 2 (Fall 93), pp. 31 – 36.

CASTILLO, DIEGO DEL

Rubial García, Antonio. Un mercader de plata andaluz en Nueva España: Diego del Castillo, 161? – 1683. *Anuario de Estudios Americanos*, v. 49 (1992), pp. 143 – 170. Bibl, il.

CASTILLO, FRANCISCO DEL

Nieto Vélez, Armando. *Francisco del Castillo, el apóstol de Lima* reviewed by Pedro Guibovich. *Apuntes (Peru)*, no. 30 (Jan – June 92), pp. 109 – 110.

CASTILLO, GERMÁN

Criticism of specific works

De piedra ardiendo, de sangre helada

Partida Tayzán, Armando. ¡Jaque al peón! *Plural (Mexico)*, v. 22, no. 257 (Feb 93), p. 80.

CASTILLO, GUIDO

Interviews

Rebollo, Eduardo. 500 años de historia universal: con Guido Castillo en Barcelona. *Cuadernos del CLAEH*, v. 17, no. 63 – 64 (Oct 92), pp. 43 – 52.

CASTILLO, MARCOS

Calzadilla, Juan. Marcos Castillo o cómo rehacer la naturaleza en el taller. *Revista Nacional de Cultura (Venezuela)*, v. 53, no. 285 (Apr – June 92), pp. 219 – 223. Il.

CASTILLO LARA, LUCAS GUILLERMO

Paredes, Pedro Pablo. Lucas Guillermo Castillo Lara. *Boletín de la Academia Nacional de la Historia (Venezuela)*, v. 76, no. 301 (Jan – Mar 93), pp. 128 – 130.

Criticism of specific works

San Sebastián de los Reyes y sus ilustres próceres

Alvarez, Luis. Discurso pronunciado por el profesor Luis Alvarez con motivo de la presentación del libro *San Sebastián de los Reyes y sus ilustres próceres* en la Escuela de Música de San Sebastián de los Reyes, el 20 de enero de 1993. *Boletín de la Academia Nacional de la Historia (Venezuela)*, v. 76, no. 301 (Jan – Mar 93), pp. 51 – 54.

CASTILLO MÉNDEZ, LUIS FERNANDO

Conde Tudanca, Rodrigo. Un incidente olvidado del trienio adeco: la creación de la iglesia católica, apostólica, venezolana. *Boletín de la Academia Nacional de la Historia (Venezuela)*, v. 76, no. 302 (Apr – June 93), pp. 87 – 117. Bibl.

CASTILLO VELASCO, FERNANDO

Téllez A., Isabel. Fernando Castillo Velasco: la solidaridad implica confianza. *Mensaje*, v. 42, no. 421 (Aug 93), pp. 383 – 384. Il.

CASTRO, CARLO ANTONIO

Criticism of specific works

Los hombres verdaderos

Morosini, Francisco. Y seguirán siendo hombres verdaderos. *La Palabra y el Hombre*, no. 81 (Jan – Mar 92), pp. 383 – 385.

CASTRO, CIPRIANO

Cipriano Castro y su época reviewed by Pascual Venegas Filardo. *Revista Nacional de Cultura (Venezuela)*, v. 53, no. 286 (July – Sept 92), pp. 255 – 256.

CASTRO, EFRAÍN

Ortiz Flores, Carlos Iván. Efraín Castro: "Revisión de lo invisible." *Nexos*, v. 16, no. 185 (May 93), pp. 86 – 87. Il.

CASTRO, FIDEL

Berástegui, Rafael. La Cuba de Fidel: algunas claves de interpretación. *Estudios Públicos (Chile)*, no. 52 (Spring 93), pp. 309 – 328.

Montaner, Carlos Alberto. *Fidel Castro and the Cuban Revolution: Age, Position, Character, Destiny, Personality, and Ambition* reviewed by Rhoda P. Rabkin. *Cuban Studies/Estudios Cubanos*, v. 23 (1993), pp. 235 – 238.

Oppenheimer, Andrés. *Castro's Final Hour: The Secret Story behind the Coming Downfall of Communist Cuba* reviewed by Harold Dana Sims. *Cuban Studies/Estudios Cubanos*, v. 23 (1993), pp. 240 – 242.

— *Castro's Final Hour: The Secret Story behind the Coming Downfall of Communist Cuba* reviewed by Damián Fernández (Review entitled "The Theater of Cuban Politics"). *Hemisphere*, v. 5, no. 2 (Winter – Spring 93), pp. 46 – 48.

— *La hora final de Castro* reviewed by Ernesto Hernández Busto (Review entitled "Fin del siglo con Castro"). *Vuelta*, v. 17, no. 200 (July 93), pp. 55 – 56.

Schulz, Donald E. Can Castro Survive? *Journal of Inter-American Studies and World Affairs*, v. 35, no. 1 (1993), pp. 89 – 117. Bibl.

CASTRO ALVES, ANTÔNIO DE

Biography

Boaventura, Edivaldo M. A contribuição de Pedro Calmon para a biografia de Castro Alves. *Revista do Instituto Histórico e Geográfico Brasileiro*, no. 370 (Jan – Mar 91), pp. 65 – 77. Bibl.

CASTRO MONSALVO, PEDRO

Castro Socarras, Alvaro. Pedro Castro Monsalvo. *Desarrollo Indoamericano*, v. 23, no. 91 (June 93), pp. 54 – 61. Il.

CATALANS

See
Spaniards

CATECHETICS

See
Religious education

CATHOLIC CHURCH

See also
Catholic universities and colleges
Charities
Christian art and symbolism
Church and education
Church and social problems
Church and state
Church architecture
Church lands
Church music
Convents and nunneries
Evangelicalism
Liberation theology
Missions
Monasticism and religious orders
Pilgrims and pilgrimages
Prayer
Religion and politics
Religion and sociology
Religious education
Shrines
Socialism and Catholic Church
Syncretism (Religion)
Theology
Names of Popes

Ceremonies and practices

Harrison, Regina. Confesando el pecado en los Andes: del siglo XVI hacia nuestros días. *Revista de Crítica Literaria Latinoamericana*, v. 19, no. 37 (Jan – June 93), pp. 169 – 184. Bibl.

Clergy

Bruno, Cayetano. La recia personalidad de fray Juan Capistrano Tissera, obispo de Córdoba. *Investigaciones y Ensayos*, no. 41 (Jan – Dec 91), pp. 107 – 137. Bibl.

Errázuriz Edwards, Aníbal. Juan Francisco Fresno: una ecle-siología cordial. *Mensaje,* v. 42, no. 419 (June 93), p. 182. II.

Fortique, José Rafael. El primer obispo de Maracaibo y su médico personal. *Boletín de la Academia Nacional de la Historia (Venezuela),* v. 76, no. 302 (Apr – June 93), pp. 133 – 139.

Langue, Frédérique. De moralista a arbitrista: don Francisco de Ibarra, obispo de Venezuela, 1798 – 1806; recopilación documental. *Anuario de Estudios Americanos,* v. 49, Suppl. 1 (1992), pp. 55 – 84. Bibl.

McGlone, Mary H. The King's Surprise: The Mission Method-ology of Toribio de Mogrovejo. *The Americas,* v. 50, no. 1 (July 93), pp. 65 – 83. Bibl.

Montes M., Fernando. Alberto Hurtado, signo y apóstol de la solidaridad. *Mensaje,* v. 42, no. 421 (Aug 93), pp. 353 – 357. II.

Olmedo Jiménez, Manuel. *Jerónimo de Loaysa, O.P., pacifi-cador de españoles y protector de indios* reviewed by Xi-mena Sosa-Buchholz. *Colonial Latin American Historical Review,* v. 2, no. 3 (Summer 93), pp. 371 – 372.

Salinas Campos, Maximiliano A. Don Enrique Alvear: la soli-daridad como unión mística entre Jesús y los pobres. *Men-saje,* v. 42, no. 421 (Aug 93), pp. 350 – 352. II.

Urquiza, Fernando Carlos. Iglesia y revolución: un estudio acerca de la actuación política del clero porteño en la dé-cada 1810 – 1820. *Anuario de Estudios Americanos,* v. 49 (1992), pp. 441 – 495. Bibl, tables.

Valle de Siles, María Eugenia del. Gregorio Francisco de Cam-pos, un obispo ilustrado que presiente la independencia. *Boletín de la Academia Nacional de la Historia (Venezuela),* v. 76, no. 302 (Apr – June 93), pp. 71 – 86. II.

Zilli Mánica, José Benigno. *Frailes, curas y laicos* reviewed by Carmen Blázquez Domínguez. *La Palabra y el Hombre,* no. 83 (July – Sept 92), pp. 350 – 352.

Catalogs

Maldonado Toro, Francisco Armando. Expediente de órdenes del seminario interdiocesano de Caracas, 1613 – 1923, obispado y después arzobispado de Caracas. *Boletín de la Academia Nacional de la Historia (Venezuela),* v. 76, no. 302 (Apr – June 93), pp. 185 – 216.

Diplomatic relations

Brazil

Della Cava, Ralph. Thinking about Current Vatican Policy in Central and East Europe and the Utility of the "Brazilian Paradigm." *Journal of Latin American Studies,* v. 25, no. 2 (May 93), pp. 257 – 281. Bibl.

Europe

Della Cava, Ralph. Thinking about Current Vatican Policy in Central and East Europe and the Utility of the "Brazilian Paradigm." *Journal of Latin American Studies,* v. 25, no. 2 (May 93), pp. 257 – 281. Bibl.

Venezuela

Querales, Juan Bautista. Relaciones de Venezuela con la Santa Sede, 1830 – 1835. *Boletín de la Academia Nacional de la Historia (Venezuela),* v. 75, no. 298 (Apr – June 92), pp. 93 – 95.

Finance

Mayo, Carlos Alberto and Jaime Antonio Peire. Iglesia y cré-dito colonial: la política crediticia de los conventos de Bue-nos Aires, 1767 – 1810. *Revista de Historia de América,* no. 112 (July – Dec 91), pp. 147 – 157. Bibl.

Sala i Vila, Nuria. Gobierno colonial, iglesia y poder en Perú, 1784 – 1814. *Revista Andina,* v. 11, no. 1 (July 93), pp. 133 – 161. Bibl.

Sources

Rueda Iturrate, Carlos José de. Financiación de la Orden de San Francisco en los cedularios del Archivo General de Indias. *Archivo Ibero-Americano,* v. 52, no. 205 – 208 (Jan – Dec 92), pp. 833 – 848.

Mission

Schreiter, Robert J. Inculturación: opción por el otro. *Amazonía Peruana,* v. 11, no. 22 (Oct 92), pp. 9 – 46.

Sermons

Schubert, Guilherme. Homilia pronunciada pelo sócio monsen-hor Guilherme Schubert na missa pelo centenário da morte de dom Pedro II. *Revista do Instituto Histórico e Geográfico Brasileiro,* no. 373 (Oct – Dec 91), pp. 1183 – 1187.

Societies, etc.

Pedoja Riet, Eduardo. Monseñor Escrivá y el Opus Dei. *Hoy Es Historia,* v. 9, no. 54 (Nov – Dec 92), pp. 6 – 10.

America

Lippy, Charles H. et al. *Christianity Comes to the Americas, 1492 – 1776* reviewed by Susan E. Ramírez. *The Americas,* v. 50, no. 1 (July 93), pp. 124 – 125.

Luque Alcaide, Elisa and José Ignacio Saranyana. *La iglesia católica y América* reviewed by Carmen J. Alejos-Grau. *Anuario de Estudios Americanos,* v. 50, no. 1 (1993), pp. 322 – 323.

Sievernich, Michael. Visiones teológicas en torno al quinto centenario. *Ibero-Amerikanisches Archiv,* v. 18, no. 3 – 4 (1992), pp. 367 – 385. Bibl.

Andean region

Harrison, Regina. Confesando el pecado en los Andes: del siglo XVI hacia nuestros días. *Revista de Crítica Literaria Latinoamericana,* v. 19, no. 37 (Jan – June 93), pp. 169 – 184. Bibl.

Argentina

Bruno, Cayetano. La recia personalidad de fray Juan Capis-trano Tissera, obispo de Córdoba. *Investigaciones y Ensa-yos,* no. 41 (Jan – Dec 91), pp. 107 – 137. Bibl.

Brazil

Terra, J. Evangelista Martins. Motivação religiosa dos desco-brimentos. *Revista do Instituto Histórico e Geográfico Bra-sileiro,* no. 373 (Oct – Dec 91), pp. 1145 – 1175.

Societies, etc.

Smith, E. Valerie. The Sisterhood of Nossa Senhora da Boa Morte and the Brotherhood of Nossa Senhora do Rosario: African-Brazilian Cultural Adaptations to Antebellum Re-strictions. *Afro-Hispanic Review,* v. 11, no. 1 – 3 (1992), pp. 58 – 69. Bibl, tables.

Central America

Bibliography

Brett, Edward T. The Impact of Religion in Central America: A Bibliographical Essay. *The Americas,* v. 49, no. 3 (Jan 93), pp. 297 – 341. Bibl.

Chile

Montes M., Fernando. Iglesia en Chile, 1973 – 1993: veinte años anunciando el evangelio. *Mensaje,* v. 42, no. 422 (Sept 93), pp. 419 – 424.

Congresses

Silva G., Sergio. La iglesia interpelada. *Mensaje,* v. 42, no. 417 (Mar – Apr 93), pp. 100 – 102.

Colombia

Levine, Daniel H. *Popular Voices in Latin American Catholi-cism* reviewed by John Hillman. *Bulletin of Latin American Research,* v. 12, no. 3 (Sept 93), pp. 354 – 355.

— *Popular Voices in Latin American Catholicism* reviewed by W. E. Hewitt. *Journal of Developing Areas,* v. 27, no. 4 (July 93), pp. 550 – 552.

Societies, etc.

Sotomayor, María Lucía. Organización socio-política de las co-fradías. *Revista Colombiana de Antropología,* v. 29 (1992), pp. 155 – 189. Bibl, tables.

Cuba

Congresses

Barredo, Lázaro et al. Cuban Responses to the Bishops (Ed-ited excerpts of original statements gathered and translated by the Foreign Broadcast Information Service). *Hemi-sphere,* v. 5, no. 3 (Summer – Fall 93), pp. 5 – 6.

Voices from Within: Cuba Must Change; A Historic Message from the Cuban Conference of Bishops. (Edited excerpts from the pastoral message). *Hemisphere,* v. 5, no. 3 (Summer – Fall 93), pp. 2 – 4.

Guatemala
Sources

García Añoveros, Jesús María. Discrepancias del obispo y de los doctrineros con la Audiencia y los indígenas de Guatemala, 1687. *Revista de Indias,* v. 52, no. 195 – 196 (May – Dec 92), pp. 385 – 441.

Haiti

La iglesia de Haití hoy. *Cristianismo y Sociedad,* v. 30, no. 114 (1992), pp. 41 – 45.

Latin America

Cleary, Edward L. and Hannah W. Stewart-Gambino, eds. *Conflict and Competition: The Latin American Church in a Changing Environment* reviewed by Michael LaRosa (Review entitled "Religion in a Changing Latin America: A Review"). *Journal of Inter-American Studies and World Affairs,* v. 34, no. 4 (Winter 92 – 93), pp. 245 – 255. Bibl.

— *Conflict and Competition: The Latin American Church in a Changing Environment* reviewed by Carl Elliott Meacham. *Revista Interamericana de Bibliografía,* v. 42, no. 2 (1992), pp. 284 – 285.

Montes M., Fernando. El documento final de Santo Domingo. *Mensaje,* v. 42, no. 416 (Jan – Feb 93), pp. 8 – 13. Il.

Pazos, Antón. *La iglesia en la América del IV centenario* reviewed by John Lynch. *Journal of Latin American Studies,* v. 25, no. 3 (Oct 93), pp. 659 – 660.

Schreiter, Robert J. Inculturación: opción por el otro. *Amazonía Peruana,* v. 11, no. 22 (Oct 92), pp. 9 – 46.

Mexico

Zilli Mánica, José Benigno. *Frailes, curas y laicos* reviewed by Carmen Blázquez Domínguez. *La Palabra y el Hombre,* no. 83 (July – Sept 92), pp. 350 – 352.

— Una reflexión sobre la religiosidad mexicana. *La Palabra y el Hombre,* no. 81 (Jan – Mar 92), pp. 147 – 158. Bibl.

Peru

McGlone, Mary H. The King's Surprise: The Mission Methodology of Toribio de Mogrovejo. *The Americas,* v. 50, no. 1 (July 93), pp. 65 – 83. Bibl.

Nguyen, Thai Hop, ed. *Evangelización y teología en el Perú* reviewed by Wilfredo Ardito Vega. *Amazonía Peruana,* v. 11, no. 22 (Oct 92), pp. 273 – 277.

Sánchez, Ana. *Amancebados, hechiceros y rebeldes: Chancay, siglo XVII* reviewed by Irene Silverblatt. *Hispanic American Historical Review,* v. 73, no. 1 (Feb 93), pp. 157 – 159.

Puerto Rico
Sources

Matos Rodríguez, Félix and Marta Villaizán. "Para que vayan y produzcan frutos y ese fruto permanezca": descripción de los fondos documentales del Archivo Eclesiástico de San Juan de Puerto Rico. *Op. Cit.,* no. 7 (1992), pp. 208 – 228. Bibl, il, facs.

Uruguay

Benítez Burgos, Wilson Andrés. La presencia religiosa en la historia de Melo. *Hoy Es Historia,* v. 10, no. 57 (Apr – May 93), pp. 61 – 68.

Venezuela

Levine, Daniel H. *Popular Voices in Latin American Catholicism* reviewed by John Hillman. *Bulletin of Latin American Research,* v. 12, no. 3 (Sept 93), pp. 354 – 355.

— *Popular Voices in Latin American Catholicism* reviewed by W. E. Hewitt. *Journal of Developing Areas,* v. 27, no. 4 (July 93), pp. 550 – 552.

CATHOLIC CHURCH. CONFERENCIA GENERAL DEL EPISCOPADO LATINOAMERICANO

Alliende Luco, Joaquín. *Santo Domingo: una moción del espíritu para América Latina* reviewed by Alejandro Sifri. *Mensaje,* v. 42, no. 422 (Sept 93), p. 470.

Alvarez Gándara, Miguel. Santo Domingo: doloroso avance de la iglesia latinoamericana. *Cristianismo y Sociedad,* v. 30, no. 114 (1992), pp. 25 – 39.

Codina, Víctor. Crónica de Santo Domingo. *ECA; Estudios Centroamericanos,* v. 47, no. 529 – 530 (Nov – Dec 92), pp. 1057 – 1065.

García Ahumada, Enrique. La promoción humana en la Conferencia de Santo Domingo. *Estudios Sociales (Chile),* no. 78 (Oct – Dec 93), pp. 245 – 257.

CATHOLIC UNIVERSITIES AND COLLEGES
Chile

Arriagada, Eduardo. La política a la manera de Ignacio de Loyola. *Mensaje,* v. 42, no. 420 (July 93), pp. 317 – 321. Il.

Barrios V., Marciano. Jesuitas en la Facultad de Teología de la Universidad Católica. *Mensaje,* v. 42, no. 420 (July 93), pp. 293 – 296. Il.

Etcheberry, Blanca. Empresarios formados por la Compañía de Jesús: un acercamiento de este último tiempo. *Mensaje,* v. 42, no. 420 (July 93), pp. 322 – 325. Il.

Galecio, Jorge. El trabajo de los jesuitas en la educación. *Mensaje,* v. 42, no. 420 (July 93), pp. 275 – 279. Il.

Soto Sandoval, Andrés. INFOCAP: en la senda de Ignacio y de Alberto Hurtado. *Mensaje,* v. 42, no. 420 (July 93), pp. 280 – 282. Il.

Téllez A., Isabel. ILADES: instituto de postgrado con acento en lo social. *Mensaje,* v. 42, no. 420 (July 93), pp. 283 – 284. Il.

Zegers A., Cristián. El carisma de San Ignacio está vigente. *Mensaje,* v. 42, no. 420 (July 93), pp. 335 – 336. Il.

Mexico

González Rodríguez, Jaime. La cátedra de Escoto en México en el siglo XVIII. *Archivo Ibero-Americano,* v. 52, no. 205 – 208 (Jan – Dec 92), pp. 561 – 584. Bibl, tables.

CATTLE TRADE

See also
> Dairying
> Meat industry and trade

Argentina

Carrazzoni, José Andrés. De ganaderos y veterinarios. *Todo Es Historia,* v. 26, no. 306 (Jan 93), pp. 28 – 38. Bibl, il.

Colombia

Visbal Martelo, Jorge. Producción y política ganadera en Colombia. *Revista Javeriana,* v. 61, no. 591 (Jan – Feb 93), pp. 20 – 24.

CAUDILLISMO

See
> Caciquism

CAYAPO INDIANS

Giannini, Isabelle Vidal. Os dominios cósmicos: um dos aspectos da construção da categoria humana kayapó – xikrin. *Revista de Antropologia (Brazil),* v. 34 (1991), pp. 35 – 58. Bibl.

CEARÁ, BRAZIL

Khan, Ahmad Saeed and Lúcia Maria Ramos Silva. Características sócio-econômicas de produtores rurais, conservação do solo e produtividade agrícola. *Revista de Economia e Sociologia Rural,* v. 30, no. 3 (July – Sept 92), pp. 225 – 237. Bibl, tables.

CEMENT INDUSTRIES

See
> Construction industry

CENSORSHIP

See also
> Freedom of the press
> Press and politics

Brazil

Magaldi, Sábato. Atos heróicos. *Problemas Brasileiros,* v. 30, no. 295 (Jan – Feb 93), p. 64.

Cuba

Moussong, Lazlo. Revolución y libre expresión. *Plural (Mexico),* v. 22, no. 259 (Apr 93), p. 68.

Vargas Lozano, Gabriel. Cuba, el socialismo y la crisis de nuestro tiempo (Response to articles on Cuba in *Plural,* no. 250). *Plural (Mexico),* v. 22, no. 259 (Apr 93), pp. 66 – 68.

CENSUS

See
Population
Subdivision *Statistics* under specific topics

CENTRAL AMERICA

See also
Agricultural assistance, Foreign – Central America
Art – Central America
Authors – Central America
Blacks – Central America
Catholic Church – Central America
Church and state – Central America
Corn – Central America
Debts, Public – Central America
Democracy – Central America
Drug trade – Central America
Ecology – Central America
Ecology and development – Central America
Elections – Central America
Elite (Social sciences) – Central America
English language – Central America
Environmental policy – Central America
Food supply – Central America
Foreign trade promotion – Central America
Foreign trade regulation – Central America
Forestry – Central America
Industry and state – Central America
Informal sector (Economics) – Central America
Judiciary – Central America
Land use – Central America
Medicine – Central America
Obsidian – Central America
Oligarchy – Central America
Parasites – Central America
Political parties – Central America
Politics in literature – Central America
Public administration – Central America
Religion and politics – Central America
Social change – Central America
Social conflict – Central America
Social psychology – Central America
Socialism – Central America
Sports – Central America
Women – Central America
Women's rights – Central America

Antiquities
Bove, Frederick Joseph and Lynette Heller, eds. *New Frontiers in the Archaeology of the Pacific Coast of Southern Mesoamerica* reviewed by Molly R. Mignon. *Latin American Antiquity,* v. 4, no. 1 (Mar 93), pp. 98 – 99.

Bibliography
Ashmore, Wendy. The Theme "Is" Variation: Recent Publications on the Archaeology of Southern Mesoamerica (Review article). *Latin American Research Review,* v. 28, no. 1 (1993), pp. 128 – 140. Bibl.

Biography
Stone, Samuel Z. *The Heritage of the Conquistadors: Ruling Classes in Central America from the Conquest to the Sandinistas* reviewed by Carlos M. Vilas. *Journal of Latin American Studies,* v. 25, no. 3 (Oct 93), pp. 660 – 662.

Discovery and exploration
Cardenal Chamorro, Rodolfo. La expansión imperial española en Centroamérica. *ECA; Estudios Centroamericanos,* v. 47, no. 528 (Oct 92), pp. 841 – 854. Il.

Economic conditions
Castillo G., Manuel Angel. La economía centroamericana y la inmigración a México. *Comercio Exterior,* v. 43, no. 8 (Aug 93), pp. 763 – 773. Bibl, tables.

Informe sobre la situación económica de los países centroamericanos en 1992 (Review). *Integración Latinoamericana,* v. 18, no. 193 (Sept 93), p. 76.

Economic integration
Caballeros Otero, Rómulo. Reflexiones sobre la integración centroamericana en la década de 1990. *Integración Latinoamericana,* v. 17, no. 185 (Dec 92), pp. 17 – 22.

Guerra Borges, Alfredo. Integración centroamericana en los noventa: de la crisis a las perspectivas. *Revista Mexicana de Sociología,* v. 54, no. 3 (July – Sept 92), pp. 115 – 127.

León M., José Luis. Propuestas, retos y alternativas hacia el futuro. *Relaciones Internacionales (Mexico),* v. 14, Nueva época, no. 56 (Oct – Dec 92), pp. 107 – 116. Bibl.

Prospects for the Processes of Sub-Regional Integration in Central and South America (Review). *Integración Latinoamericana,* v. 18, no. 189 – 190 (May – June 93), pp. 58 – 59.

Congresses
América Central: XIII Reunión Cumbre de Presidentes. *Integración Latinoamericana,* v. 18, no. 186 (Jan – Feb 93), pp. 65 – 69.

Sources
Acuerdo de Managua. *Integración Latinoamericana,* v. 18, no. 191 (July 93), pp. 71 – 72.

Economic policy
Pérez Jérez, Cristóbal. Políticas de ajuste estructural y reforma del estado. *USAC,* no. 14 (June 91), pp. 56 – 70. Bibl.

Emigration and immigration
Pacheco O., Gilda. Migraciones forzadas en Centroamérica: evolución psicosocial. *Nueva Sociedad,* no. 127 (Sept – Oct 93), pp. 114 – 125. Bibl.

Foreign economic relations
Colombia
Acuerdo sobre Comercio e Inversión entre las Repúblicas de Colombia y Venezuela y las Repúblicas de Costa Rica, El Salvador, Guatemala, Honduras y Nicaragua. *Integración Latinoamericana,* v. 18, no. 191 (July 93), pp. 67 – 71.

Mexico
Tratado América Central – México: acuerdo marco multilateral para el programa de liberalización comercial entre los gobiernos de Costa Rica, El Salvador, Guatemala, Honduras, México y Nicaragua. *Integración Latinoamericana,* v. 17, no. 184 (Nov 92), pp. 72 – 74.

United States
United Nations. Economic Commission for Latin America and the Caribbean. *A Collection of Documents on Economic Relations between the United States and Central America, 1906 – 1956* (Review). *CEPAL Review,* no. 47 (Aug 92), p. 189.

Venezuela
Acuerdo sobre Comercio e Inversión entre las Repúblicas de Colombia y Venezuela y las Repúblicas de Costa Rica, El Salvador, Guatemala, Honduras y Nicaragua. *Integración Latinoamericana,* v. 18, no. 191 (July 93), pp. 67 – 71.

Foreign relations
Jauberth, H. Rodrigo et al. *The Difficult Triangle: Mexico, Central America, and the United States,* a translation of *La triangulación Centroamérica – México – EUA.* Reviewed by Robert H. Holden. *Hispanic American Historical Review,* v. 73, no. 1 (Feb 93), pp. 192 – 194.

International cooperation
Harto de Vera, Fernando. La resolución del proceso de negociaciones de paz. *ECA; Estudios Centroamericanos,* v. 48, no. 531 – 532 (Jan – Feb 93), pp. 27 – 38. Bibl, il.

Caribbean area
I Conferencia Ministerial de los Países del Istmo Centroamericano y de la Comunidad del Caribe. *Integración Latinoamericana,* v. 17, no. 185 (Dec 92), pp. 71 – 72.

Spain
Rosenberg, Robin L. *Spain and Central America: Democracy and Foreign Policy* reviewed by Paul C. Sondrol. *Hispanic American Historical Review,* v. 73, no. 4 (Nov 93), pp. 731 – 732.

— *Spain and Central America: Democracy and Foreign Policy* reviewed by Joan Font. *Revista Interamericana de Bibliografía,* v. 42, no. 4 (1992), pp. 662 – 663.

United States
Coleman, Kenneth M. and George C. Herring, eds. *Understanding the Central American Crisis: Sources of Conflict, U.S. Policy, and Options for Peace* reviewed by Orlando Peña. *Canadian Journal of Latin American and Caribbean Studies,* v. 17, no. 34 (1992), pp. 129 – 130.

Eguizábal, Cristina. De Contadora a Esquipulas: Washington y Centroamérica en un mundo cambiante. *Anuario de Estudios Centroamericanos,* v. 18, no. 1 (1992), pp. 5 – 15. Bibl.

Leonard, Thomas Michael. Central America and the United States: Overlooked Foreign Policy Objectives. *The Americas,* v. 50, no. 1 (July 93), pp. 1 – 30. Bibl.

History

Palmer, Steven. Central American Union or Guatemalan Republic?: The National Question in Liberal Guatemala, 1871 – 1885. *The Americas,* v. 49, no. 4 (Apr 93), pp. 513 – 530. Bibl.

Politics

Arnaud, Hélène and Alain Rouquié, eds. *Les forces politiques en Amérique Centrale* reviewed by Rodolfo Cerdas-Cruz. *Journal of Latin American Studies,* v. 25, no. 2 (May 93), pp. 416 – 417.

Casaus Arzú, Marta Elena. La metamorfosis de las oligarquías centroamericanas. *Revista Mexicana de Sociología,* v. 54, no. 3 (July – Sept 92), pp. 69 – 114. Bibl, tables, charts.

Goodman, Louis Wolf et al, eds. *Political Parties and Democracy in Central America* reviewed by James Dunkerley. *Bulletin of Latin American Research,* v. 12, no. 2 (May 93), pp. 233 – 234.

Torres-Rivas, Edelberto. Escenarios y lecciones de las elecciones centroamericanas, 1980 – 1991. *Revista Mexicana de Sociología,* v. 54, no. 3 (July – Sept 92), pp. 45 – 67. Tables.

CENTRAL AMERICAN COMMON MARKET

Guerra Borges, Alfredo. La reestructuración del Mercado Común Centroamericano: notas para una evaluación crítica. *Integración Latinoamericana,* v. 18, no. 195 (Nov 93), pp. 3 – 9. Bibl.

CENTRAL AMERICAN LITERATURE

History and criticism

Acevedo, Ramón Luis. Rumbos de la narrativa centroamericana actual. *Káñina,* v. 16, no. 2 (July – Dec 92), pp. 39 – 51. Bibl.

CENTRAL AMERICAN POETRY

History and criticism

Beverley, John and Marc Zimmerman. *Literature and Politics in the Central American Revolutions* reviewed by Antony Higgins. *Revista de Crítica Literaria Latinoamericana,* v. 19, no. 37 (Jan – June 93), pp. 380 – 382.

CENTRAL AMERICANS

Belize

Palacio, Joseph O. Social and Cultural Implications of Recent Demographic Changes in Belize (The Fourth Annual Signa L. Yorke Memorial Lecture). *Belizean Studies,* v. 21, no. 1 (May 93), pp. 3 – 12. Bibl, tables.

Mexican – American Border Region

Sánchez Munguía, Vicente. Matamoros-sur de Texas: el tránsito de los migrantes de América Central por la frontera México – Estados Unidos. *Estudios Sociológicos,* v. 11, no. 31 (Jan – Apr 93), pp. 183 – 207. Bibl, tables.

Mexico

Castillo G., Manuel Angel. La economía centroamericana y la inmigración a México. *Comercio Exterior,* v. 43, no. 8 (Aug 93), pp. 763 – 773. Bibl, tables.

United States

Palacio, Joseph O. Garifuna Immigrants in Los Angeles: Attempts at Self-Improvements. *Belizean Studies,* v. 20, no. 3 (Dec 92), pp. 17 – 26. Bibl.

Self, Robert. Intimidate First, Ask Questions Later: The INS and Immigration Rights. *NACLA Report on the Americas,* v. 26, no. 5 (May 93), pp. 11 – 14. Il.

CENTRO DE ESTUDIOS EDUCATIVOS

Informe de actividades académicas del Centro de Estudios Educativos, 1992. *Revista Latinoamericana de Estudios Educativos,* v. 23, no. 1 (Jan – Mar 93), pp. 97 – 109. Bibl.

CEPEDA, ENDER

Viloria Vera, Enrique. *Ender Cepeda: la recreación de una identidad* reviewed by María Clara Martínez R. (Accompanied by an English translation). *Art Nexus,* no. 8 (Apr – June 93), p. 33. Il.

CEREZO ARÉVALO, VINICIO

Manz, Beatriz. Elections without Change: The Human Rights Record of Guatemala. *SALALM Papers,* v. 36 (1991), pp. 191 – 200. Bibl.

CERNUDA, LUIS

Criticism and interpretation

Matamoro, Blas. Villaurrutia y Cernuda: Eros y cosmos. *Cuadernos Hispanoamericanos,* no. 514 – 515 (Apr – May 93), pp. 209 – 213. Il.

Criticism of specific works

Quetzalcóatl

Amor y Vázquez, José. Máscaras mexicanas en la poesía de Cernuda y Moreno Villa: Quetzalcóatl y Xochipilli (Includes the poem "Quetzalcóatl"). *Nueva Revista de Filología Hispánica,* v. 40, no. 2 (July – Dec 92), pp. 1057 – 1072.

CERRO DE LAS MESAS SITE, MEXICO

Stark, Barbara L., ed. *Settlement Archaelogy of Cerro de las Mesas, Veracruz, Mexico* reviewed by Ronald W. Webb. *Latin American Antiquity,* v. 4, no. 3 (Sept 93), pp. 299 – 300.

CERUTTI GULDBERG, HORACIO V.

Pérez Villacampa, Gilberto. Horacio Cerutti y el problema del fin de la filosofía clásica de la liberación. *Islas,* no. 99 (May – Aug 91), pp. 168 – 172.

CERVANTES DE SALAZAR, FRANCISCO

Criticism of specific works

Diálogo de la dignidad del hombre

Bono, Diane M. *Cultural Diffusion of Spanish Humanism in New Spain: Francisco Cervantes de Salazar's 'Diálogo de la dignidad del hombre'* reviewed by William Mejías López. *Hispania (USA),* v. 76, no. 2 (May 93), pp. 282 – 284.

CERVANTES SAAVEDRA, MIGUEL DE

Criticism of specific works

Don Quixote

Beltrán Guerrero, Luis. La edición del *Quijote* de la Academia Nacional de la Historia. *Boletín de la Academia Nacional de la Historia (Venezuela),* v. 75, no. 299 (July – Sept 92), pp. 187 – 189.

Lapuente, Felipe-Antonio. Cervantes en la perspectiva de Fuentes. *Cuadernos Americanos,* no. 39, Nueva época (May – June 93), pp. 228 – 242. Bibl.

Nallim, Carlos Orlando. Borges y Cervantes: *Don Quijote* y "Alonso Quijano." *Nueva Revista de Filología Hispánica,* v. 40, no. 2 (July – Dec 92), pp. 1047 – 1056. Bibl.

Rabell, Carmen R. Cervantes y Borges: relaciones intertextuales en "Pierre Ménard, autor del Quijote." *Revista Chilena de Literatura,* no. 42 (Aug 93), pp. 201 – 207. Bibl.

CÉSAR, CORNELIO ADRIÁN

Segovia, Francisco. Juan Pascoe y Cornelio Adrián César, impresores de México. *Artes de México,* no. 19 (Spring 93), pp. 111 – 113. Il.

CHACO, ARGENTINA

Foschiatti de dell'Orto, Ana María H. El desarrollo urbano y las particularidades demográficas del Chaco y su capital entre 1960 y 1990. *Revista Geográfica (Mexico),* no. 115 (Jan – June 92), pp. 37 – 54. Bibl, tables, maps, charts.

CHACO WAR, 1932 – 1935

Sources

Montero Mallo, Benicio. Diario de la campaña del Chaco. *Signo,* no. 36 – 37, Nueva época (May – Dec 92), pp. 171 – 195.

CHACÓN, JOAQUÍN ARMANDO
Criticism of specific works
Los largos días
Pratt, Dale J. Feminine Freedom/Metafictional Autonomy in *Los largos días. Chasqui,* v. 22, no. 2 (Nov 93), pp. 94 – 102. Bibl.

CHALCATZINGO, MEXICO
Guillén, Ann Cyphers. Women, Rituals, and Social Dynamics at Ancient Chalcatzingo. *Latin American Antiquity,* v. 4, no. 3 (Sept 93), pp. 209 – 224. Bibl, il.

CHALLE, ROBERTO
Zapata Saldaña, Eduardo E. El personaje que se le olvidó a Ribeyro: Roberto Challe. *Debate (Peru),* v. 15, no. 70 (Sept – Oct 92), pp. 60 – 62. Il.

CHAMBI, MARTÍN
Heredia, Jorge. Avatares de la obra del fotógrafo peruano Martín Chambi (1891 – 1973) y reseña de dos monografías recientes. *Hueso Húmero,* no. 29 (May 93), pp. 144 – 173. Bibl.

CHAMOISEAU, PATRICK
Criticism of specific works
Texaco
Burton, Richard D. E. Créolité, Négritude, and Metropolis. *Hemisphere,* v. 5, no. 3 (Summer – Fall 93), pp. 10 – 12. Il.

CHAPARRO, OMAR
Interviews
Pachón, Efraín. Los invitados del mes. *Revista Javeriana,* v. 61, no. 593 (Apr 93), pp. 170 – 178. Il.

CHAPBOOKS
See
Folk literature

CHARITIES
Cárdenas Gueudinot, Mario. Grupos marginados en los inicios de la era republicana: vagabundos, mendigos e indigentes. *Cuadernos de Historia (Chile),* no. 11 (Dec 91), pp. 47 – 61. Bibl, tables.

CHARLES V, EMPEROR OF THE HOLY ROMAN EMPIRE
Torres Marín, Manuel. Los dos imperios: la doble herencia de Carlos V. *Boletín de la Academia Chilena de la Historia,* v. 58 – 59, no. 102 (1991 – 1992), pp. 505 – 527. Bibl, il, facs.

CHATHAM, JAMES R.
Homenaje a/Homenagem a: James R. Chatham. *Hispania (USA),* v. 76, no. 2 (May 93), pp. 182 – 188.

CHAUNU, PIERRE
Saignes, Thierry. Pierre Chaunu, l'Amérique et nous: essai d'égo-histoire. *Cahiers des Amériques Latines,* no. 13 (1992), pp. 7 – 24. Bibl.

CHAVARRÍA, DANIEL
Criticism and interpretation
Ramírez, Fermín. Daniel Chavarría: al mundo clásico vía Macondo. *Plural (Mexico),* v. 22, no. 260 (May 93), pp. 23 – 26.

CHAVES MENDOZA, ALVARO
Obituaries
Morales Gómez, Jorge. Alvaro Chaves Mendoza (1930 – 1992). *Revista Colombiana de Antropología,* v. 29 (1992), pp. 265 – 266.

CHÁVEZ GARCÍA, JOSÉ INÉS
Cardozo-Freeman, Inez. José Inés Chávez García: Hero or Villain of the Mexican Revolution? (Includes the text of two corridos). *Bilingual Review/Revista Bilingüe,* v. 18, no. 1 (Jan – Apr 93), pp. 3 – 13. Bibl.

CHAVÍN CULTURE
Burger, Richard Lewis. *Chavín and the Origins of Andean Civilization* reviewed by Thomas Pozorski and Shelia Pozorski. *Latin American Antiquity,* v. 4, no. 4 (Dec 93), pp. 389 – 390.

CHAYANOV, ALEXANDER VASILIEVICH
Cortés C., Fernando and Oscar Cuéllar Saavedra, eds. *Crisis y reproducción social: los comerciantes del sector informal* reviewed by José Antonio Alonso. *Estudios Sociológicos,* v. 10, no. 30 (Sept – Dec 92), pp. 819 – 822.

CHEMISTRY
Research
Cagnin, Maria Aparecida H. The State of Scientific Research in Chemistry: A View from the Brazilian Community. *Interciencia,* v. 18, no. 3 (May – June 93), pp. 146 – 154. Bibl, tables.

CHIAPAS, MEXICO
Alfaro, Alfonso. Elogio de la opulencia, la distancia y el cordero (Accompanied by an English translation). *Artes de México,* no. 19 (Spring 93), pp. 31 – 38. Il.

Fábregas Puig, Andrés A. El textil como resistencia cultural (Accompanied by an English translation). *Artes de México,* no. 19 (Spring 93), pp. 25 – 27. Il.

Falquet, France-Jules. Les femmes indiennes et la reproduction culturelle: réalités, mythes, enjeux; le cas des femmes indiennes au Chiapas, Mexique. *Cahiers des Amériques Latines,* no. 13 (1992), pp. 135 – 146. Bibl.

Morris, Walter F., Jr. Simbolismo de un huipil ceremonial (Accompanied by the English original, translated by Ana Rosa González Matute). *Artes de México,* no. 19 (Spring 93), pp. 65 – 71. Il.

Orellana, Margarita de. Voces entretejidas: testimonios del arte textil (Accompanied by an English translation). *Artes de México,* no. 19 (Spring 93), pp. 43 – 59. Il.

Pellizzi, Francesco. La colección Pellizzi de textiles de Chiapas (Accompanied by an English translation). *Artes de México,* no. 19 (Spring 93), pp. 75 – 79. Il.

El proceso de tejido visto por los niños de Tenejapa. *Artes de México,* no. 19 (Spring 93), pp. 60 – 61.

Rodríguez Rivera, Oscar. Derechos políticos y autonomía regional. *Nueva Antropología,* v. 13, no. 44 (Aug 93), pp. 137 – 141.

Steele, Cynthia. Indigenismo y posmodernidad: narrativa indigenista, testimonio, teatro campesino y video en el Chiapas finisecular. *Iberoamericana,* v. 16, no. 47 – 48 (1992), pp. 82 – 94. Bibl.

— Indigenismo y posmodernidad: narrativa indigenista, testimonio, teatro campesino y video en el Chiapas finisecular. *Revista de Crítica Literaria Latinoamericana,* v. 19, no. 38 (July – Dec 93), pp. 249 – 260. Bibl.

Vachon, Michael. Onchocerciasis in Chiapas, Mexico. *Geographical Review,* v. 83, no. 2 (Apr 93), pp. 141 – 149. Bibl, il, maps.

Bibliography
Bibliografía (to the articles on textiles from Chiapas appearing in this issue). *Artes de México,* no. 19 (Spring 93), pp. 81 – 82. Il.

CHIBÁS, EDUARDO
Salwen, Michael Brian. "Eddie" Chibás, the "Magic Bullet" of Radio. *Studies in Latin American Popular Culture,* v. 12 (1993), pp. 113 – 126. Bibl.

CHIBCHA INDIANS
Bermúdez Páez, Alvaro E. Etnohistoria de Subachoque, siglos XVI – XVIII. *Revista Colombiana de Antropología,* v. 29 (1992), pp. 81 – 117. Bibl, tables, maps.

Sotomayor, María Lucía. Organización socio-política de las cofradías. *Revista Colombiana de Antropología,* v. 29 (1992), pp. 155 – 189. Bibl, tables.

CHICANOS

See
Mexican Americans

CHIHUAHUA, MEXICO (STATE)

Almada, Sergio. Chihuahua Redefines Success. *Business Mexico*, v. 3, no. 12 (Dec 93), pp. 22 – 23. Tables.

Fournier G., Patricia and Andrea K. L. Freeman. El razonamiento analógico en etnoarqueología: el caso de la tradición alfarera de Mata Ortiz, Chihuahua, México. *Boletín de Antropología Americana*, no. 23 (July 91), pp. 109 – 118. Bibl, il.

González Herrera, Carlos. La agricultura en el proyecto económico de Chihuahua durante el porfiriato. *Siglo XIX: Cuadernos*, v. 2, no. 5 (Feb 93), pp. 9 – 37. Bibl, tables, maps.

León G., Ricardo. La banca chihuahuense durante el porfiriato. *Siglo XIX: Cuadernos*, v. 1, no. 2 (Feb 92), pp. 9 – 47. Bibl, tables, maps.

Saborit, Antonio. Tomóchic (Excerpt from the forthcoming book entitled *Los doblados de Tomóchic*). *Nexos*, v. 16, no. 185 (May 93), pp. 69 – 75.

CHILAM BALAM BOOKS

Heaven Born Mérida and Its Destiny: 'The Book of Chilam Balam of Chumayel' edited and translated by Munro S. Edmonson. Reviewed by Enrique Sam Colop. *Mesoamérica (USA)*, v. 13, no. 23 (June 92), pp. 194 – 196.

CHILD ABUSE

Bonilla, Flory Stella. Orientación de poblaciones abusadas. *Revista de Ciencias Sociales (Costa Rica)*, no. 59 (Mar 93), pp. 53 – 62. Bibl.

Costa Rica

Obando Hidalgo, Iris María and Ana Isabel Ruiz Rojas. Epidemiología del abuso físico y sexual en niños atendidos en el Hospital de Niños, 1988 – 1990. *Revista de Ciencias Sociales (Costa Rica)*, no. 59 (Mar 93), pp. 63 – 70. Bibl, tables, charts.

Mexico

Acosta, Mariclaire. Fabricación de culpables por discriminación de minorías: caso de Flor Melo. *Fem*, v. 17, no. 122 (Apr 93), pp. 18 – 19.

Peru

Basili D., Francisco. *Crisis y comercio sexual de menores en el Perú* (Review). *La Educación (USA)*, v. 36, no. 111 – 113 (1992), pp. 283 – 284.

CHILD PSYCHOLOGY

See also
Adolescent psychology
Learning, Psychology of

Núñez, Blanca. *El niño sordo y su familia: apontes desde la psicología clínica* reviewed by Aurora Pérez T. *La Educación (USA)*, v. 37, no. 114 (1993), pp. 166 – 167.

CHILDBIRTH

Costa Rica

Study and teaching

Chaves Araya, Mariana. Impacto de los cursos de parto sin temor en el área de salud de San Ramón. *Revista de Ciencias Sociales (Costa Rica)*, no. 60 (June 93), pp. 39 – 50. Bibl, tables, charts.

CHILDREN

See also
Child abuse
Child psychology
Exceptional children
Hispanic American youth (U.S.)
Infant mortality
Mexican American youth
Parent and child
Street children
Youth

Grizzolle Gómez, Juan. *La creación literaria en los niños: cómo estimular la creatividad* reviewed by Alberto Gómez Martínez. *La Educación (USA)*, v. 36, no. 111 – 113 (1992), pp. 294 – 295.

Employment

Amador Debernardi, Rocío and Laura González Hernández. Características de las familias y de los niños trabajadores de la calle. *Revista de Ciencias Sociales (Costa Rica)*, no. 59 (Mar 93), pp. 19 – 26. Bibl, tables, charts.

Lezama, José Luis. Trabajo, familia e infancia en la ciudad de México: convergencias y divergencias. *Comercio Exterior*, v. 43, no. 7 (July 93), pp. 677 – 687. Bibl, tables.

Health and hygiene

Arango Montoya, Marta. La niñez y la juventud en riesgo: el gran desafío para América Latina y el Caribe. *La Educación (USA)*, v. 36, no. 111 – 113 (1992), pp. 1 – 24. Bibl.

Language

Barriga Villanueva, Rebeca. De "Cenicienta" a "Amor en silencio": un estudio sobre narraciones infantiles. *Nueva Revista de Filología Hispánica*, v. 40, no. 2 (July – Dec 92), pp. 673 – 697. Bibl.

Argentina

Ciafardo, Eduardo O. *Los niños en la ciudad de Buenos Aires, 1850 – 1910* reviewed by Sergio A. Pujol. *Todo Es Historia*, v. 27, no. 311 (June 93), p. 58. Il.

Brazil

Dimenstein, Gilberto. *Meninas da noite: a prostituição de meninas-escravas no Brasil* reviewed by Jenny K. Pilling. *Luso-Brazilian Review*, v. 30, no. 1 (Summer 93), pp. 148 – 149.

Chile

Saavedra, Gonzalo. La familia grande de Rosario y Manuel. *Mensaje*, v. 42, no. 419 (June 93), pp. 214 – 215. Il.

Latin America

Arango Montoya, Marta. La niñez y la juventud en riesgo: el gran desafío para América Latina y el Caribe. *La Educación (USA)*, v. 36, no. 111 – 113 (1992), pp. 1 – 24. Bibl.

Fernández Poncela, Anna M. Yo juego, tú estudias, ellos sobreviven: ser niño en América Latina. *Fem*, v. 17, no. 121 (Mar 93), pp. 25 – 27.

Mexico

Lezama, José Luis. Trabajo, familia e infancia en la ciudad de México: convergencias y divergencias. *Comercio Exterior*, v. 43, no. 7 (July 93), pp. 677 – 687. Bibl, tables.

Peru

Zuloaga, E. et al. *Prácticas de crianza* (Review). *Revista Paraguaya de Sociología*, v. 30, no. 86 (Jan – Apr 93), p. 209.

CHILDREN'S LITERATURE

Bortolussi, Marisa. *El cuento infantil cubano: un estudio crítico* reviewed by Antonio Benítez-Rojo. *Hispanic Review*, v. 61, no. 4 (Fall 93), pp. 592 – 594.

Fernández de Carrasco, Rosa. *Caracola: cuentos para niños* reviewed by Jaime Martínez Salguero. *Signo*, no. 38, Nueva época (Jan – Apr 93), pp. 237 – 238.

Fraser, Howard M. *La Edad de Oro* and José Martí's Modernist Ideology for Children. *Revista Interamericana de Bibliografía*, v. 42, no. 2 (1992), pp. 223 – 232. Bibl.

López, Ricardo and Isidora Mena, eds. *Las ovejas y el infinito: contribución al estudio de la creatividad y la formulación de propuestas para el sistema educacional* reviewed by Luis Weinstein (Review entitled *"Para saber y contar* sobre *Las ovejas y el infinito"*). *Estudios Sociales (Chile)*, no. 78 (Oct – Dec 93), pp. 284 – 290.

Mena, Isidora and Mario Salazar, eds. *Para saber y contar: narraciones sobre niños, viejos y viejísimos* reviewed by Luis Weinstein (Review entitled *"Para saber y contar* sobre *Las ovejas y el infinito"*). *Estudios Sociales (Chile)*, no. 78 (Oct – Dec 93), pp. 284 – 290.

Vásquez, Magdalena. Adela Ferreto: un sujeto histórico particular en una época de transición. *Káñina*, v. 16, no. 1 (Jan – June 92), pp. 37 – 49. Bibl.

Dictionaries and encyclopedias

Villalón-Galdames, Alberto. *Thesauro de literatura infantil* (Review). *La Educación (USA),* v. 36, no. 111 – 113 (1992), pp. 305 – 306.

Handbooks, manuals, etc.

Mena, Isidora and Mario Salazar, eds. *Para saber y contar: manual metodológico* reviewed by Luis Weinstein (Review entitled *"Para saber y contar* sobre *Las ovejas y el infinito").* *Estudios Sociales (Chile),* no. 78 (Oct – Dec 93), pp. 284 – 290.

CHILDREN'S SONGS

Toni, Flávia Camargo. Memória: Mário de Andrade escreve para as crianças. *Vozes,* v. 87, no. 3 (May – June 93), pp. 67 – 72. Facs.

CHILDREN'S TELEVISION

Fuenzalida F., Valerio. La TV infantil vista desde la televisión. *Estudios Sociales (Chile),* no. 76 (Apr – June 93), pp. 95 – 110. Bibl.

CHILDREN'S THEATER

See also

Puppets and puppet-plays

Suárez Durán, Esther. El teatro: un mundo para el hombre. *Conjunto,* no. 93 (Jan – June 93), pp. 119 – 125. Il.

CHILE

See also

Acculturation – Chile
Adult education – Chile
Agricultural laborers – Chile
Agriculture – Chile
Agriculture, Cooperative – Chile
Agriculture and state – Chile
Animals – Chile
Antofagasta, Chile (Province)
Arica, Chile
Art – Chile
Art and society – Chile
Artists – Chile
Atacama, Chile
Authoritarianism – Chile
Automobile industry and trade – Chile
Banks and banking – Chile
Biography (as a literary form) – Chile
Biotechnology – Chile
Books – Chile
Business enterprises – Chile
Capital – Chile
Capital investments – Chile
Capital productivity – Chile
Capitalists and financiers – Chile
Caricatures and cartoons – Chile
Catholic Church – Chile
Catholic universities and colleges – Chile
Children – Chile
Chiloé, Chile
Christian art and symbolism – Chile
Church and education – Chile
Church and social problems – Chile
Church and state – Chile
Church lands – Chile
Cities and towns – Chile
Community development – Chile
Competition – Chile
Concepción, Chile (City)
Las Condes, Chile
Conservatism – Chile
Copper industry and trade – Chile
Corruption (in politics) – Chile
Debts, Public – Chile
Decentralization in government – Chile
Democracy – Chile
Diseases – Chile
Drama festivals – Chile
Ecology – Chile
Education – Chile
Education, Higher – Chile
Education, Secondary – Chile
Education and state – Chile
Educational accountability – Chile
Elections – Chile

Electric power – Chile
Elite (Social sciences) – Chile
Employees' representation in management – Chile
Engineering – Chile
Evangelicalism – Chile
Experimental theater – Chile
Family – Chile
Finance – Chile
Finance, Public – Chile
Food industry and trade – Chile
Foreign exchange problem – Chile
Foreign trade promotion – Chile
Forestry – Chile
Forests – Chile
Frontier and pioneer life – Chile
Germans – Chile
Haciendas – Chile
Human rights – Chile
Hunting – Chile
Illiteracy – Chile
Income distribution – Chile
Indians, Treatment of – Chile
Industrial productivity – Chile
Industrial sociology – Chile
Industry and state – Chile
Information technology – Chile
Investments, Foreign – Chile
Jesuits – Chile
Judiciary – Chile
Labor productivity – Chile
Labor relations – Chile
Land reform – Chile
Land settlement – Chile
Libraries and librarians – Chile
Literary criticism – Chile
Literature and history – Chile
Literature and society – Chile
Local government – Chile
Magellan, Strait of
Marginalization – Chile
Markets and merchants – Chile
Medicine – Chile
Migration, Internal – Chile
Military in government – Chile
Mines and mineral resources – Chile
Mining industry and finance – Chile
Missions – Chile
Money and money supply – Chile
Music – Chile
Natural disasters – Chile
Newspapers – Chile
Nitrates – Chile
Non-governmental organizations – Chile
Opera – Chile
Oral tradition – Chile
Patagonia
Peasantry – Chile
Pension trusts – Chile
Periodicals – Chile
Philosophy – Chile
Poets – Chile
Political parties – Chile
Political sociology – Chile
Politics in literature – Chile
Popular culture – Chile
Population – Chile
Poverty – Chile
Press – Chile
Press and politics – Chile
Prisons – Chile
Privatization – Chile
Public administration – Chile
Public health – Chile
Puerto Montt, Chile
Quality of life – Chile
Reading interests – Chile
Real property – Chile
Regional planning – Chile
Regionalism in literature – Chile
Religion and politics – Chile
Religious education – Chile
Roads – Chile
Santiago de Chile
Scientific research – Chile
La Serena, Chile
Shopping malls – Chile
Social change – Chile
Social conflict – Chile

Social movements – Chile
Social services – Chile
Sociology, Rural – Chile
Spaniards – Chile
Spanish poetry – Chile
Tacna – Arica question
Tarapacá, Chile (Province)
Teachers, Training of – Chile
Teaching and teachers – Chile
Technical education – Chile
Technology and civilization – Chile
Technology transfer – Chile
Television – Chile
Theater – Chile
Theology – Chile
Tierra del Fuego
Trade unions – Chile
Transportation – Chile
Universities and colleges – Chile
Urbanization – Chile
Valparaíso, Chile (City)
Vocational education – Chile
Wages – Chile
Water – Chile
Women – Chile
Women artists – Chile
Women authors – Chile
Women in literature – Chile
Women's rights – Chile
Youth – Chile

Armed forces

Rabkin, Rhoda Pearl. The Aylwin Government and "Tutelary" Democracy: A Concept in Search of a Case? *Journal of Inter-American Studies and World Affairs*, v. 34, no. 4 (Winter 92 – 93), pp. 119 – 194. Bibl, tables.

Vargas Cariola, Juan Eduardo. Estilo de vida en el ejército de Chile durante el siglo XVII. *Revista de Indias*, v. 53, no. 198 (May – Aug 93), pp. 425 – 457. Bibl.

Bibliography

Couyoumdjian Bergamil, Juan Ricardo. Fichero bibliográfico, 1989 – 1991. *Historia (Chile)*, no. 26 (1991 – 1992), pp. 385 – 459. Bibl.

Biography

Retamal Favereau, Julio et al. *Familias fundadoras de Chile, 1540 – 1600* reviewed by Narciso Binayán Carmona. *Todo Es Historia*, v. 27, no. 312 (July 93), pp. 75 – 77. Il.

Boundaries

Argentina

Güenaga de Silva, Rosario and Adriana C. Rodríguez Pérsico. El interés de la diplomacia española por los problemas argentino – chilenos en el seno de Ultima Esperanza. *Revista de Historia de América*, no. 112 (July – Dec 91), pp. 85 – 103. Bibl.

Bolivia

Padilla, Mario. *Mar para Bolivia* reviewed by Raúl Rivadeneira Prada. *Signo*, no. 38, Nueva época (Jan – Apr 93), pp. 247 – 248.

Civilization

Garretón Merino, Manuel Antonio. El tupido velo. *Mensaje*, v. 42, no. 425 (Dec 93), pp. 619 – 625. Il.

Silva, Patricio. La historia, la política y el futuro. *Mensaje*, v. 42, no. 423 (Oct 93), pp. 495 – 499.

Commerce

Great Britain

Mayo, John K. British Merchants in Chile and on Mexico's West Coast in the Mid-Nineteenth Century: The Age of Isolation. *Historia (Chile)*, no. 26 (1991 – 1992), pp. 144 – 171. Bibl.

Constitutional law

González Encinar, José Juan et al. El proceso constituyente: enseñanzas a partir de cuatro casos recientes: España, Portugal, Brasil y Chile. *Ibero-Amerikanisches Archiv*, v. 18, no. 1 – 2 (1992), pp. 151 – 179. Tables.

Cultural policy

Domínguez Díaz, Marta Silvia. El arte popular chileno. *SALALM Papers*, v. 34 (1989), pp. 9 – 16. Bibl.

Garretón Merino, Manuel Antonio. Avances, límites y perspectivas de una política cultural. *Estudios Sociales (Chile)*, no. 75 (Jan – Mar 93), pp. 113 – 128.

— El Festival Mundial de Teatro y Política. *Mensaje*, v. 42, no. 419 (June 93), pp. 175 – 177. Il.

Subercaseaux S., Bernardo. Las industrias culturales: desafíos para una política cultural. *Cuadernos Hispanoamericanos*, no. 510 (Dec 92), pp. 100 – 104. Bibl.

Economic conditions

Daher, Antonio. Santiago estatal, Chile liberal. *Revista Interamericana de Planificación*, v. 26, no. 101 – 102 (Jan – June 93), pp. 43 – 62. Bibl, tables.

Foxley R., Alejandro. Entrando a una nueva fase. *Mensaje*, v. 42, no. 422 (Sept 93), pp. 448 – 451.

Garcés Durán, Mario. *Crisis social y motines populares en el 1900* reviewed by Ricardo López (Review entitled "Buscar la historia y reconstruirla"). *Casa de las Américas*, no. 189 (Oct – Dec 92), pp. 142 – 145.

Schneider, Cathy. Chile: The Underside of the Miracle. *Report on the Americas*, v. 26, no. 4 (Feb 93), pp. 30 – 31 +. Bibl, il.

Bibliography

Cariola Sutter, Carmen and Osvaldo Sunkel. *Un siglo de historia económica de Chile, 1830 – 1930* reviewed by Juan Ricardo Couyoumdjian. *Boletín de la Academia Chilena de la Historia*, v. 58 – 59, no. 102 (1991 – 1992), pp. 561 – 562.

Economic policy

Büchi Buc, Hernán. Reactivación económica en tiempos de recesión. *Apuntes (Peru)*, no. 30 (Jan – June 92), pp. 91 – 103.

Celedón, Carmen and Oscar Muñoz Gomá. La política económica durante la transición a la democracia en Chile, 1990 – 1992. *Estudios Sociales (Chile)*, no. 75 (Jan – Mar 93), pp. 77 – 95. Bibl.

Fontaine T., Juan Andrés. Transición económica y política en Chile, 1970 – 1990. *Estudios Públicos (Chile)*, no. 50 (Fall 93), pp. 230 – 279. Bibl, tables.

Larraín Arroyo, Luis et al. ¿Un neoliberalismo en declinación?: debates. *Mensaje*, v. 42, no. 418 (May 93), pp. 142 – 151. Il.

Mattos, Carlos António de. Modernización y reestructuración global en Chile: de la génesis autoritaria a la consolidación democrática. *Revista Paraguaya de Sociología*, v. 30, no. 86 (Jan – Apr 93), pp. 7 – 30. Bibl, tables.

Rosende Ramírez, Francisco. La economía chilena en el gobierno de la concertación: una evaluación preliminar. *Estudios Sociales (Chile)*, no. 75 (Jan – Mar 93), pp. 57 – 76. Tables.

Silva, Patricio. Intelectuales, tecnócratas y cambio social en Chile: pasado, presente y perspectivas futuras. *Revista Mexicana de Sociología*, v. 54, no. 1 (Jan – Mar 92), pp. 130 – 166. Bibl.

Sunkel, Osvaldo. La consolidación de la democracia y del desarrollo en Chile: desafíos y tareas *El Trimestre Económico*, v. 59, no. 236 (Oct – Dec 92), pp. 816 – 830.

— Consolidating Democracy and Development in Chile. *CEPAL Review*, no. 47 (Aug 92), pp. 37 – 46.

Vergara, Pilar. Ruptura y continuidad en la política social del gobierno democrático. *Estudios Sociales (Chile)*, no. 78 (Oct – Dec 93), pp. 105 – 144. Bibl, tables.

Volk, Steven S. Mine Owners, Money Lenders, and the State in Mid-Nineteenth Century Chile: Transitions and Conflicts. *Hispanic American Historical Review*, v. 73, no. 1 (Feb 93), pp. 67 – 98. Bibl, tables.

Emigration and immigration

Norambuena Carrasco, Carmen. Inmigración, agricultura y ciudades intermedias, 1880 – 1930. *Cuadernos de Historia (Chile)*, no. 11 (Dec 91), pp. 105 – 123. Bibl, tables.

Salinas Meza, René. Una comunidad inmigrante: los alemanes en Valparaíso, 1860 – 1960; estudio demográfico. *Jahrbuch für Geschichte von Staat, Wirtschaft und Gesellschaft Lateinamerikas*, v. 29 (1992), pp. 309 – 342. Bibl, tables, charts.

Foreign economic relations

Tokman, Marcelo and Andrés Velasco. Opciones para la política comercial chilena en los '90. *Estudios Públicos (Chile)*, no. 52 (Spring 93), pp. 53 – 99. Bibl, tables.

America

Agosin, Manuel Roberto. Beneficios y costos potenciales para Chile de los acuerdos de libre comercio. *Estudios Públicos (Chile)*, no. 52 (Spring 93), pp. 101 – 126. Bibl, tables.

Stewart, Hamish. El Acuerdo de Libre Comercio entre Estados Unidos y Canadá: algunas lecciones. *Estudios Internacionales (Chile)*, v. 26, no. 102 (Apr – June 93), pp. 187 – 203. Bibl, tables.

Bolivia

ALADI: Acuerdo de Complementación Económica entre Bolivia y Chile. *Integración Latinoamericana*, v. 18, no. 194 (Oct 93), pp. 56 – 60.

Pizarro, Roberto. Las negociaciones comerciales Chile – Bolivia: vacilaciones chilenas y sensibilidades bolivianas. *Mensaje*, v. 42, no. 417 (Mar – Apr 93), pp. 99 – 100.

United States

Fermandois Huerta, Joaquín. Del unilateralismo a la negociación: Chile, Estados Unidos y la deuda de largo plazo, 1934 – 1938. *Historia (Chile)*, no. 26 (1991 – 1992), pp. 71 – 115. Bibl.

Foreign opinion

Corfield M., Isabel. Hacia la creación intelectual del Nuevo Mundo. *Hoy Es Historia*, v. 10, no. 57 (Apr – May 93), pp. 69 – 75. Bibl.

Foreign relations

Infante Caffi, María Teresa and Manfred Wilhelmy von Wolff. La política exterior chilena en los años '90: el gobierno del presidente Aylwin y algunas proyecciones. *Estudios Sociales (Chile)*, no. 75 (Jan – Mar 93), pp. 97 – 112.

Sources

Donoso Letelier, Crescente. Libro copiador de telegramas del presidente Carlos Ibáñez, 1928 – 1931. *Historia (Chile)*, no. 26 (1991 – 1992), pp. 297 – 383. Bibl.

Brazil

Meira, Sílvio Augusto de Bastos. Relacionamento histórico entre o Brasil e o Chile. *Revista do Instituto Histórico e Geográfico Brasileiro*, no. 370 (Jan – Mar 91), pp. 102 – 126.

Italy

Martinic Drpic, Zvonimir. El tribunal arbitral italo – chileno y las reclamaciones italianas de los poseedores de certificados salitreros: evolución histórica de la problemática. *Cuadernos de Historia (Chile)*, no. 11 (Dec 91), pp. 71 – 104. Bibl, tables.

Peru

Macera dall'Orso, Pablo. Los acuerdos Perú – Chile. *Debate (Peru)*, v. 16, no. 73 (June – Aug 93), pp. 49 – 51. Il.

Valdivieso Belaunde, Felipe. Un acuerdo mezquino. *Debate (Peru)*, v. 16, no. 73 (June – Aug 93), pp. 51 – 56. Il.

Vidal Ramírez, Fernando. El camino del porvenir. *Debate (Peru)*, v. 16, no. 73 (June – Aug 93), pp. 56 – 60. Il.

United States

Sater, William F. *Chile and the United States: Empires in Conflict* reviewed by David Sheinin. *The Americas*, v. 50, no. 1 (July 93), pp. 133 – 134.

— *Chile and the United States: Empires in Conflict* reviewed by Juan Ricardo Couyoumdjian. *Historia (Chile)*, no. 26 (1991 – 1992), pp. 461 – 464.

History

Brezzo, Liliana M. El general Guillermo Miller después de Ayacucho. *Investigaciones y Ensayos*, no. 41 (Jan – Dec 91), pp. 395 – 406. Bibl.

Jaramillo Lyon, Armando. Don Andrés Bello en Santiago. *Boletín de Historia y Antigüedades*, v. 79, no. 779 (Oct – Dec 92), pp. 1037 – 1051.

Martínez Baeza, Sergio. El general don Orozimbo Barbosa y la revolución de 1891. *Boletín de la Academia Chilena de la Historia*, v. 58 – 59, no. 102 (1991 – 1992), pp. 459 – 479. Il.

Rodríguez Elizondo, José. Salvador Allende: el tabú y el mito. *Debate (Peru)*, v. 16, no. 74 (Sept – Oct 93), pp. 53 – 56. Il.

— Salvador Allende: el tabú y el mito. *Nueva Sociedad*, no. 128 (Nov – Dec 93), pp. 24 – 28.

Sources

Actas del Cabildo de Santiago, 1795 – 1809 reviewed by Fernando Campos Harriet. *Boletín de la Academia Chilena de la Historia*, v. 58 – 59, no. 102 (1991 – 1992), pp. 531 – 533.

Industries

Ortega, Luis. El proceso de industrialización en Chile, 1850 – 1930. *Historia (Chile)*, no. 26 (1991 – 1992), pp. 213 – 246. Bibl.

Intellectual life

Bascuñán, Carlos and Sol Serrano. La idea de América en los exiliados españoles en Chile (Excerpt from *El pensamiento español contemporáneo y la idea de América* edited by José Luis Abellán and Antonio Monclús Estella). *Atenea (Chile)*, no. 465 – 466 (1992), pp. 99 – 149. Bibl, tables.

Caiceo E., Jaime. El planteamiento filosófico – político de Maritain aplicado en Chile. *Estudios Sociales (Chile)*, no. 76 (Apr – June 93), pp. 205 – 210. Bibl.

Cristi, Renato and Carlos Ruiz. *El pensamiento conservador en Chile* reviewed by Simon Collier. *Hispanic American Historical Review*, v. 73, no. 4 (Nov 93), pp. 708 – 709.

— *El pensamiento conservador en Chile* reviewed by Patricio Silva. *Journal of Latin American Studies*, v. 25, no. 2 (May 93), pp. 429 – 430.

Cristoffanini, Pablo Rolando. *Dominación y legitimidad política en Hispanoamérica: un estudio de la historia de las ideas políticas en la experiencia colonial y la formación del estado nacional en Chile* reviewed by Marcello Carmagnani. *Hispanic American Historical Review*, v. 73, no. 2 (May 93), pp. 328 – 329.

Gazmuri Riveros, Cristián. *El "48" chileno: igualitarios, reformistas, radicales, masones y bomberos* reviewed by Ricardo Krebs. *Historia (Chile)*, no. 26 (1991 – 1992), pp. 464 – 469.

Godoy Urzúa, Hernán. La hegemonía cultural jesuita y el barroco. *Mensaje*, v. 42, no. 420 (July 93), pp. 228 – 233. Il.

Sources

Larraín Mira, Paz and René Millar Carvacho. Notas para la historia de la cultura en el período indiano: la biblioteca del obispo de Santiago, Juan Bravo del Rivero y Correa, 1685 – 1752. *Historia (Chile)*, no. 26 (1991 – 1992), pp. 173 – 211. Bibl.

Politics and government

Sources

Fontaine Aldunate, Arturo. La historia reciente de Chile a través de "La semana política" (Part IV, introduced by Miguel González Pino). *Estudios Públicos (Chile)*, no. 49 (Summer 93), pp. 305 – 419.

1970 –

Almeyda Medina, Clodomiro et al. 20 años después: ¿Qué aprendimos del golpe militar?; debates (Introduced by G. Arroyo). *Mensaje*, v. 42, no. 422 (Sept 93), pp. 440 – 447.

Drake, Paul Winter and Ivan Jaksic, eds. *The Struggle for Democracy in Chile, 1982 – 1990* reviewed by Tom Wright. *The Americas*, v. 49, no. 4 (Apr 93), pp. 568 – 569.

— *The Struggle for Democracy in Chile, 1982 – 1990* reviewed by Robert H. Dix. *Journal of Developing Areas*, v. 28, no. 1 (Oct 93), pp. 115 – 116.

Espinoza, Malva and Manuel Antonio Garretón Merino. ¿Reforma del estado o cambio en la matriz socio-política? *Estudios Sociales (Chile)*, no. 74 (Oct – Dec 92), pp. 7 – 37. Bibl.

Fontaine T., Juan Andrés. Transición económica y política en Chile, 1970 – 1990. *Estudios Públicos (Chile)*, no. 50 (Fall 93), pp. 230 – 279. Bibl, tables.

Godoy Arcaya, Oscar. A veinte años de la crisis de la democracia chilena. *Mensaje*, v. 42, no. 422 (Sept 93), pp. 415 – 418.

Montecinos, Verónica. Economic Policy Elites and Democratization. *Studies in Comparative International Development*, v. 28, no. 1 (Spring 93), pp. 25 – 53. Bibl.

Silva, Eduardo. Capitalist Regime Loyalties and Redemocratization in Chile. *Journal of Inter-American Studies and World Affairs,* v. 34, no. 4 (Winter 92 – 93), pp. 77 – 117. Bibl.

Tagle Domínguez, Matías. *La crisis de la democracia en Chile: antecendentes y causas* reviewed by Joaquín Fermandois. *Historia (Chile),* no. 26 (1991 – 1992), pp. 469 – 477.

1990 –

Garretón Merino, Manuel Antonio. La redemocratización política en Chile: transición, inauguración y evolución. *Estudios Interdisciplinarios de América Latina y el Caribe,* v. 4, no. 1 (Jan – June 93), pp. 5 – 25. Bibl.

Rabkin, Rhoda Pearl. The Aylwin Government and "Tutelary" Democracy: A Concept in Search of a Case? *Journal of Inter-American Studies and World Affairs,* v. 34, no. 4 (Winter 92 – 93), pp. 119 – 194. Bibl, tables.

Rehren, Alfredo J. La presidencia en el gobierno de la concertación. *Estudios Sociales (Chile),* no. 75 (Jan – Mar 93), pp. 15 – 38. Bibl.

Tomassini, Luciano. Decidiendo el futuro. *Mensaje,* v. 42, no. 417 (Mar – Apr 93), pp. 61 – 63.

Wolter, Matilde. Chile renueva su democracia. *Nueva Sociedad,* no. 128 (Nov – Dec 93), pp. 6 – 11.

Public works

Daher, Antonio. Infraestructuras: regiones estatales y privadas en Chile. *Estudios Públicos (Chile),* no. 49 (Summer 93), pp. 137 – 173. Bibl, tables.

Rural conditions

Busquet I., Jaime. INPROA: treinta años presente en el mundo rural. *Mensaje,* v. 42, no. 418 (May 93), pp. 154 – 156. Il.

Hojman A., David E., ed. *Change in the Chilean Countryside: From Pinochet to Aylwin and Beyond; The Proceedings of the 46th International Congress of Americanists, Amsterdam* reviewed by Walter Belik. *Journal of Latin American Studies,* v. 25, no. 3 (Oct 93), pp. 679 – 680.

Kay, Cristóbal and Patricio Silva, eds. *Development and Social Change in the Chilean Countryside: From the Pre-Land Reform Period to the Democratic Transition* reviewed by Chris Scott. *Journal of Latin American Studies,* v. 25, no. 2 (May 93), p. 407.

Social conditions

Análisis de la situación y proyecciones del país. *Mensaje,* v. 42, no. 419 (June 93), pp. 220 – 224.

Tironi B., Eugenio. *Autoritarismo, modernización y marginalidad: el caso de Chile* reviewed by Felipe Cabello (Review entitled "Don Andrés Bello: ¡Con cuánta nostalgia lo recordamos y cuánta falta nos hace!"). *Interciencia,* v. 18, no. 6 (Nov – Dec 93), pp. 329 – 333.

Social policy

Atria Benaprés, Raúl. Contribuciones para una discusión sobre la ruta de cambio de la sociedad chilena. *Estudios Sociales (Chile),* no. 75 (Jan – Mar 93), pp. 155 – 182.

Camhi P., Rosa and Patricia Matte Larraín. Pobreza en la década de los '90 y desafíos futuros. *Estudios Sociales (Chile),* no. 75 (Jan – Mar 93), pp. 39 – 56. Tables.

Ruiz-Tagle P., Jaime. ONG y políticas públicas: nuevas formas de solidaridad institucionalizada. *Mensaje,* v. 42, no. 421 (Aug 93), pp. 378 – 381. Il, tables.

Sunkel, Osvaldo. La consolidación de la democracia y del desarrollo en Chile: desafíos y tareas. *El Trimestre Económico,* v. 59, no. 236 (Oct – Dec 92), pp. 816 – 830.

— Consolidating Democracy and Development in Chile. *CEPAL Review,* no. 47 (Aug 92), pp. 37 – 46.

Vergara, Pilar. Ruptura y continuidad en la política social del gobierno democrático. *Estudios Sociales (Chile),* no. 78 (Oct – Dec 93), pp. 105 – 144. Bibl, tables.

Methodology

Figueroa, Víctor et al. Un modelo de bienestar social. *Estudios Sociales (Chile),* no. 77 (July – Sept 93), pp. 139 – 147. Bibl.

CHILEAN DRAMA
History and criticism

Flores, Arturo C. Chile: acerca de la relación teatro – sociedad. *La Palabra y el Hombre,* no. 81 (Jan – Mar 92), pp. 73 – 84. Bibl.

CHILEAN LITERATURE

Kappatos, Rigas and Pedro Lastra, eds. *Antología del cuento chileno* reviewed by Marina Catzaras. *Revista de Crítica Literaria Latinoamericana,* v. 19, no. 37 (Jan – June 93), pp. 392 – 396.

Bibliography

Blume, Jaime. 1992 y sus libros. *Mensaje,* v. 42, no. 416 (Jan – Feb 93), pp. 53 – 55.

Echevarría, Evelio A. La novela histórica de Chile: deslinde y bibliografía, 1852 – 1990. *Revista Interamericana de Bibliografía,* v. 42, no. 4 (1992), pp. 643 – 650. Bibl.

History and criticism

Alegría, Fernando. La novela chilena del exilio interior. *Revista Chilena de Literatura,* no. 42 (Aug 93), pp. 13 – 17.

Avaria, Antonio. Nunca en punto muerto: la novela chilena. *Mensaje,* v. 42, no. 425 (Dec 93), pp. 654 – 655.

Brintrup H., Lilianet. El libro móvil: viaje y escritura en algunos viajeros chilenos del siglo XIX. *Revista Chilena de Literatura,* no. 42 (Aug 93), pp. 57 – 64.

Godoy Gallardo, Eduardo. *La generación del '50 en Chile: historia de un movimiento literario* reviewed by Lon Pearson. *Chasqui,* v. 22, no. 2 (Nov 93), pp. 177 – 179.

Loyola Goich, Lorena. Las sociedades campesinas: un retrato de cambios y permanencias a través de la literatura criollista chilena, 1920 – 1950. *Cuadernos de Historia (Chile),* no. 11 (Dec 91), pp. 127 – 148. Bibl.

Nordenflycht, Adolfo. Historización literaria y architextualidad: el cuento chileno (1888 – 1938); formaciones y transformaciones. *Revista Chilena de Literatura,* no. 42 (Aug 93), pp. 73 – 80.

Osses Moya, Darío. La fundación de una literatura nacional y la Universidad de Chile. *Atenea (Chile),* no. 465 – 466 (1992), pp. 337 – 347. Bibl.

Piña, Juan Andrés. *Conversaciones con la narrativa chilena* reviewed by Guillermo García-Corales. *Chasqui,* v. 22, no. 2 (Nov 93), pp. 164 – 165.

Roa de la Carrera, Cristián. El discurso de la guerra en los textos chilenos del siglo XVI. *Revista Chilena de Literatura,* no. 42 (Aug 93), pp. 217 – 221.

Saldes Báez, Sergio. Narrativa chilena, 1966 – 1991: en busca de continuidad e integración. *Aisthesis,* no. 24 (1991), pp. 67 – 78. Bibl.

Sánchez Durán, Fernando. *Narrativa chilena ultrarrealista* reviewed by Antonio Campaña. *Atenea (Chile),* no. 465 – 466 (1992), pp. 382 – 384.

Subercaseaux, Benjamín. Lo masculino y lo femenino en el imaginario colectivo de comienzos de siglo. *Revista Chilena de Literatura,* no. 42 (Aug 93), pp. 245 – 249.

Teitelboim, Volodia. Sobre la antología del '35 y la generación del '38. *Revista Chilena de Literatura,* no. 42 (Aug 93), pp. 251 – 263.

CHILEAN POETRY
History and criticism

Agosín, Marjorie. Un paisaje silencioso: las mujeres en la poesía chilena. *Fem,* v. 17, no. 125 (July 93), pp. 40 – 42.

Merino, Carolina. Entre la cohesión y la diáspora: 25 años de poesía chilena. *Aisthesis,* no. 24 (1991), pp. 9 – 19. Bibl.

Montes Brunet, Hugo. Poesía chilena de hoy. *Aisthesis,* no. 24 (1991), pp. 21 – 27. Bibl.

Morales, Andrés. Poesía chilena y poesía española: convergencias y divergencias. *Revista Chilena de Literatura,* no. 42 (Aug 93), pp. 139 – 141.

Nómez, Naín. Literatura, cultura y sociedad: el modernismo y la génesis de la poesía chilena contemporánea. *Revista Chilena de Literatura,* no. 42 (Aug 93), pp. 157 – 164. Bibl.

Rodríguez Fernández, Mario. De Neruda a Lihn: tres oposiciones complementarias en la poesía chilena contemporánea. *Atenea (Chile),* no. 465 – 466 (1992), pp. 261 – 268.

Verba, Ericka Kim. "Las hojas sueltas" (Broadsides): Nineteenth-Century Chilean Popular Poetry as a Source for the Historian. *Studies in Latin American Popular Culture*, v. 12 (1993), pp. 141 – 158. Bibl.

White, Steven F. La traducción y la poesía chilena de post-golpe: historicidad e identidad de género. *Revista Chilena de Literatura*, no. 42 (Aug 93), pp. 275 – 279.

CHILES, LAWTON

Witoshynsky, Mary. Florida Governor Puts Trade Focus on Mexico. *Business Mexico*, v. 3, no. 7 (July 93), p. 50. Il.

CHILLIDA, EDUARDO

Chacón, Katherine. Chillida: el cuerpo, el espacio. *Art Nexus*, no. 8 (Apr – June 93), pp. 80 – 81. Il.

CHILOÉ, CHILE

Tampe, Eduardo. Chiloé: misión circular. *Mensaje*, v. 42, no. 420 (July 93), pp. 224 – 227. Il.

Vázquez de Acuña, Isidoro. Evolución de la población de Chiloé, siglos XVI – XX. *Boletín de la Academia Chilena de la Historia*, v. 58 – 59, no. 102 (1991 – 1992), pp. 403 – 457. Bibl, tables.

CHIMALPAHIN CUAUHTLEHUANITZIN, DOMINGO FRANCISCO

Schroeder, Susan. *Chimalpahin and the Kingdoms of Chalco* reviewed by J. Benedict Warren. *The Americas*, v. 49, no. 3 (Jan 93), pp. 396 – 398.

CHINA

See also
  Latin American studies – China

Pinheiro, Letícia. Restabelecimento de relações diplomáticas com a República Popular da China: uma análise do processo de tomada de decisão. *Estudos Históricos*, v. 6, no. 12 (July – Dec 93), pp. 247 – 270. Bibl.

CHINANDEGA, NICARAGUA

Gould, Jeffrey L. *To Lead as Equals: Rural Protest and Political Consciousness in Chinandega, Nicaragua, 1912 – 1979* reviewed by Daniel Little. *Economic Development and Cultural Change*, v. 41, no. 4 (July 93), pp. 894 – 898.

— *To Lead as Equals: Rural Protest and Political Consciousness in Chinandega, Nicaragua, 1912 – 1979* reviewed by Michael F. Jiménez. *Hispanic American Historical Review*, v. 73, no. 1 (Feb 93), pp. 186 – 188.

CHINESE

Mexico

Puig, Juan Carlos. *Entre el río Perla y el Nazas: la China decimonónica y sus braceros emigrantes. Vuelta*, v. 17, no. 202 (Sept 93), p. 53.

Peru

Lausent Herrera, Isabelle. La cristianización de los chinos en el Perú: integración, sumisión y resistencia. *Bulletin de l'Institut Français d'Etudes Andines*, v. 21, no. 3 (1992), pp. 977 – 1007. Bibl, il.

CHIRIBOGA, LUZ ARGENTINA

Interviews

Beane, Carol. Entrevista con Luz Argentina Chiriboga. *Afro-Hispanic Review*, v. 12, no. 2 (Fall 93), pp. 17 – 23.

Feal, Rosemary Geisdorfer. Entrevista con Luz Argentina Chiriboga (Followed by poems from her *La contraportada del deseo* translated by Rosemary Geisforfer Feal). *Afro-Hispanic Review*, v. 12, no. 2 (Fall 93), pp. 12 – 16.

CHIRIBOGA DE ORDÓÑEZ, MERCEDES ANDRADE

Cueva Jaramillo, Juan. Aquí entre nos: madame Paul Rivet. *Cahiers des Amériques Latines*, no. 13 (1992), pp. 161 – 162.

CHIRIGUANO INDIANS

Combès, Isabelle and Thierry Saignes. *Alter ego: naissance de l'identité chiriguano* reviewed by Marie-Danielle Demélas-Bohy. *Caravelle*, no. 60 (1993), pp. 166 – 170.

Hurtado, Liliana R. de. Santiago entre los chiriguanos: una caso de aculturación y resistencia. *Amazonía Peruana*, v. 11, no. 22 (Oct 92), pp. 147 – 173. Bibl.

Mingo de la Concepción, Manuel. *Historia de las misiones franciscanas de Tarija entre chiriguanos* reviewed by Pedro de Anasagasti. *Signo*, no. 35, Nueva época (Jan – Apr 92), pp. 237 – 239.

CHIRINOS SOTO, ENRIQUE

Interviews

Cisneros, Luis Jaime. Entrevista a Enrique Chirinos Soto. *Debate (Peru)*, v. 16, no. 73 (June – Aug 93), pp. 8 – 16. Il.

CHOCÓ, COLOMBIA

Camargo Pérez, Gabriel. Los descubridores del Chocó. *Boletín de Historia y Antigüedades*, v. 79, no. 779 (Oct – Dec 92), pp. 1007 – 1018. Bibl.

CHOCOLATE AND CACAO

Harwich Vallenilla, Nikita. *Histoire du chocolat* reviewed by Teodoro Hampe Martínez. *Cuadernos Americanos*, no. 41, Nueva época (Sept – Oct 93), pp. 235 – 237.

Venezuela

Piñero, Eugenio. Accounting Practices in a Colonial Economy: A Case Study of Cacao Haciendas in Venezuela, 1700 – 1770. *Colonial Latin American Historical Review*, v. 1, no. 1 (Fall 92), pp. 37 – 66. Bibl, tables.

CHOCRÓN, ISAAC

Addresses, essays, lectures

Chalbaud, Román. Pequeño Chocrón ilustrado. *Conjunto*, no. 90 – 91 (Jan – June 92), p. 47. Il.

Criticism and interpretation

Irausquin, Rossi and Barbara Younoszai. Not Establishing Limits: The Writing of Isaac Chocrón. *Inti*, no. 37 – 38 (Spring – Fall 93), pp. 155 – 161. Bibl.

Criticism of specific works

Solimán, el Magnífico

Ulive, Ugo. Solimán, el Magnífico en la obra de Chocrón. *Conjunto*, no. 90 – 91 (Jan – June 92), pp. 43 – 45. Il.

CHOL INDIANS

See
  Mayas

CHORTI INDIANS

See
  Mayas

CHRISTIAN ART AND SYMBOLISM

Exhibitions

Westbrook, Leslie A. "Cambios": The Spirit of Transformation in Spanish Colonial Art. *Latin American Art*, v. 5, no. 1 (Spring 93), pp. 54 – 57. Il.

America

Myers, Joan et al. *Santiago: Saint of Two Worlds*. Photographs by Joan Myers. Reviewed by Jeffrey Klaiber. *Hispanic American Historical Review*, v. 73, no. 3 (Aug 93), p. 492.

Bolivia

Von Barghahn, Barbara. The Colonial Paintings of Leonardo Flores. *Latin American Art*, v. 5, no. 2 (Summer 93), pp. 47 – 49. Bibl, il.

Brazil

Pfeiffer, Wolfgang. Exvotos en Brasil (Translated by Ricardo Barda). *Humboldt*, no. 110 (1993), pp. 90 – 93. Il.

Chile

Cruz Ovalle de Amenábar, Isabel. Arte jesuita en Chile: la huella del barroco bávaro. *Mensaje*, v. 42, no. 420 (July 93), pp. 234 – 238. Il.

Ecuador

Grizzard, Mary Faith Mitchell. The "Retablos Mayores" of the Cantuña Chapel of San Francisco in Quito, Ecuador. *Anales del Instituto de Investigaciones Estéticas*, v. 16, no. 62 (1991), pp. 103 – 110. Bibl.

Latin America

Von Barghahn, Barbara. Colonial Statuary of New Spain. *Latin American Art,* v. 4, no. 4 (Winter 92), pp. 77 – 79. Bibl, il.

Mexico

Giffords, Gloria Fraser, ed. *The Art of Private Devotion: Retablo Painting of Mexico* reviewed by Luis Cerda. *Hispanic American Historical Review,* v. 73, no. 1 (Feb 93), pp. 125 – 126.

Maza, Francisco de la. San Bernardino de Xochimilco: caciques domésticos (Accompanied by an English translation). *Artes de México,* no. 20 (Summer 93), pp. 67 – 73.

Vargas Lugo, Elisa. Comentarios acerca de la construcción de retablos en México, 1687 – 1713. *Anales del Instituto de Investigaciones Estéticas,* v. 16, no. 62 (1991), pp. 93 – 101. Bibl.

— Un retablo de encaje (Accompanied by an English translation). *Artes de México,* no. 21 (Fall 93), pp. 54 – 59. Il.

Peru

Rodríguez-Camilloni, Humberto. The "Retablo-Façade" as Transparency: A Study of the Frontispiece of San Francisco, Lima. *Anales del Instituto de Investigaciones Estéticas,* v. 16, no. 62 (1991), pp. 111 – 122. Bibl, il.

Spain

Myers, Joan et al. *Santiago: Saint of Two Worlds.* Photographs by Joan Myers. Reviewed by Jeffrey Klaiber. *Hispanic American Historical Review,* v. 73, no. 3 (Aug 93), p. 492.

United States

Harris, Patricia and David Lyon. Memory's Persistence: The Living Art. *Américas,* v. 45, no. 6 (Nov – Dec 93), pp. 26 – 37. Il.

CHRISTIAN BASE COMMUNITIES

See
Church and social problems

CHRISTIAN LIFE

Arteaga Llona, José. Marta Alvarez: "Estar cerca de Dios, estar cerca de los hombres." *Mensaje,* v. 42, no. 421 (Aug 93), pp. 359 – 360. Il.

Delfau, Antonio. Benito Baranda y Lorena Cornejo: una vida solidaria. *Mensaje,* v. 42, no. 421 (Aug 93), pp. 374 – 375. Il.

Pérez Yoma, Marisi. Hugo Yaconi: solidaridad entre empresarios. *Mensaje,* v. 42, no. 421 (Aug 93), pp. 376 – 377. Il.

Pescador C., Juan Javier. *De bautizados a fieles difuntos: familia y mentalidades en una parroquia urbana; Santa Catarina de México, 1568 – 1820* reviewed by Patricia Schraer. *La Educación (USA),* v. 37, no. 115 (1993), pp. 431 – 433.

Saavedra, Gonzalo. Mercedes Echeñique: la tía Pin tocó "la verdad de Chile." *Mensaje,* v. 42, no. 421 (Aug 93), pp. 361 – 362. Il.

Téllez A., Isabel. Fernando Castillo Velasco: la solidaridad implica confianza. *Mensaje,* v. 42, no. 421 (Aug 93), pp. 383 – 384. Il.

Societies, etc.

Ochagavía Larraín, Juan. La Compañía de Jesús y la formación de los laicos. *Mensaje,* v. 42, no. 420 (July 93), pp. 311 – 316.

CHRISTIANIZATION OF INDIANS

See
Evangelicalism
Religious education
Subdivision *Religion and mythology* under names of Indian groups

CHUQUISACA, BOLIVIA

Langer, Erick Detlef. *Economic Change and Rural Resistance in Southern Bolivia, 1880 – 1930* reviewed by Marie-Danielle Démelas-Bohy. *Caravelle,* no. 59 (1992), pp. 309 – 311.

CHURCH AND EDUCATION

See also
Religious education

Chile

Contreras, Juan Pablo. Trabajos de Verano: formando en la solidaridad. *Mensaje,* v. 42, no. 421 (Aug 93), pp. 404 – 407.

Galecio, Jorge. El trabajo de los jesuitas en la educación. *Mensaje,* v. 42, no. 420 (July 93), pp. 275 – 279. Il.

Téllez A., Isabel. Colegio San Lorenzo: cuando la solidaridad es contagiosa. *Mensaje,* v. 42, no. 421 (Aug 93), pp. 402 – 403. Il.

Colombia

Clemente B., Isabel. Un caso de conflicto cultural en el Caribe: de la imposición al reconocimiento. *Nueva Sociedad,* no. 127 (Sept – Oct 93), pp. 32 – 45. Bibl.

CHURCH AND SOCIAL PROBLEMS

See also
Liberation theology
Religion and politics

Díaz-Salazar, Rafael. La crítica cristiana a la civilización del capital: aportaciones de la doctrina social de la iglesia a la construcción de un nuevo socialismo. *ECA; Estudios Centroamericanos,* v. 47, no. 529 – 530 (Nov – Dec 92), pp. 999 – 1014. Bibl, il.

Dinechin, Olivier de. SIDA: educar, acompañar . . . . *Mensaje,* v. 42, no. 422 (Sept 93), pp. 427 – 431.

Fellay, Jean-Blaise. SIDA, preservativos y continencia. *Mensaje,* v. 42, no. 419 (June 93), pp. 211 – 212.

John Paul II, Pope. "Si quieres la paz, sal al encuentro del pobre": mensaje de su santidad Juan Pablo II para la celebración de la Jornada Mundial de la Paz, 1 de enero de 1993. *ECA; Estudios Centroamericanos,* v. 48, no. 531 – 532 (Jan – Feb 93), pp. 18 – 26.

Mensaje de Juan Pablo para la Jornada Mundial de la Paz: "Si quieres la paz, sal al encuentro del pobre" (Commentary on the Pope's speech transcribed on pp. 18 – 26 of this issue). *ECA; Estudios Centroamericanos,* v. 48, no. 531 – 532 (Jan – Feb 93), pp. 96 – 99.

Mifsud, Tony. Juan Pablo II: "Si quieres la paz, sal al encuentro del pobre." *Mensaje,* v. 42, no. 417 (Mar – Apr 93), pp. 96 – 98.

Pell, George. *Rerum Novarum:* cien años después. *Estudios Públicos (Chile),* no. 50 (Fall 93), pp. 177 – 200. Bibl.

Stella, Aldo. ¿Padre, puedo casarme de nuevo? *Revista Javeriana,* v. 61, no. 599 (Oct 93), pp. 305 – 318.

Argentina

Amado Aguirre, José. La primera década divorcista argentina. *Todo Es Historia,* v. 27, no. 317 (Dec 93), pp. 42 – 44. Il.

Brazil

Carvalho, José Geraldo Vidigal de. A influencia da igreja na política social do Brasil: uma visão histórica. *Convivium,* v. 34, no. 2 (July – Dec 91), pp. 138 – 145. Bibl.

Hewitt, Warren Edward. *Base Christian Communities and Social Change in Brazil* reviewed by Joan B. Anderson. *Journal of Developing Areas,* v. 27, no. 4 (July 93), pp. 573 – 574.

— *Base Christian Communities and Social Change in Brazil* reviewed by Michael LaRosa (Review entitled "Religion in a Changing Latin America: A Review"). *Journal of Inter-American Studies and World Affairs,* v. 34, no. 4 (Winter 92 – 93), pp. 245 – 255. Bibl.

Chile

Arroyo, Gonzalo. ?Es posible ser solidarios en un mundo competitivo? *Mensaje,* v. 42, no. 421 (Aug 93), pp. 368 – 373. Il.

Garretón Merino, Manuel Antonio. Los jesuitas y el pensamiento social de los sesenta en Chile. *Mensaje,* v. 42, no. 420 (July 93), pp. 298 – 303. Il.

Loyola, Alberto. Los jesuitas y la cuestión social. *Mensaje,* v. 42, no. 420 (July 93), pp. 304 – 307. Il.

Poblete B., Renato. El Hogar de Cristo. *Mensaje,* v. 42, no. 420 (July 93), pp. 290 – 291. Il, tables.

Stragier, Julio. Hogar de Cristo Viviendas. *Mensaje,* v. 42, no. 420 (July 93), p. 292. Il.

Swope, John. Anita Goossens: "Llorar con los que lloran y gozar con los que gozan." *Mensaje,* v. 42, no. 424 (Nov 93), pp. 590 – 591. Il.

Vives Pérez-Cotapos, Cristián. Iglesia y pastoral social: un camino de solidaridad. *Mensaje,* v. 42, no. 421 (Aug 93), pp. 363 – 366. Il.

Congresses

El reencuentro que anhelamos. *Mensaje,* v. 42, no. 423 (Oct 93), pp. 533 – 536.

Study and teaching

Téllez A., Isabel. ILADES: instituto de postgrado con acento en lo social. *Mensaje,* v. 42, no. 420 (July 93), pp. 283 – 284. Il.

Costa Rica

Miller, Eugene D. Labour and the War-Time Alliance in Costa Rica, 1943 – 1948. *Journal of Latin American Studies,* v. 25, no. 3 (Oct 93), pp. 515 – 541. Bibl, tables.

Cuba

"El amor todo lo espera" (I Cor. 13, 7). *Mensaje,* v. 42, no. 424 (Nov 93), pp. 587 – 589. Il.

"El amor todo lo espera" (I Cor. 13, 7): mensaje de la Conferencia de Obispos Católicos de Cuba. *Revista Javeriana,* v. 61, no. 599 (Oct 93), pp. 319 – 332.

Congresses

Barredo, Lázaro et al. Cuban Responses to the Bishops (Edited excerpts of original statements gathered and translated by the Foreign Broadcast Information Service). *Hemisphere,* v. 5, no. 3 (Summer – Fall 93), pp. 5 – 6.

Voices from Within: Cuba Must Change; A Historic Message from the Cuban Conference of Bishops. (Edited excerpts from the pastoral message). *Hemisphere,* v. 5, no. 3 (Summer – Fall 93), pp. 2 – 4.

Dominican Republic

Thomas, Luis. La crisis social del pueblo. *Cristianismo y Sociedad,* v. 30, no. 114 (1992), pp. 47 – 48.

Latin America

Alliende Luco, Joaquín. *Santo Domingo: una moción del espíritu para América Latina* reviewed by Alejandro Sifri. *Mensaje,* v. 42, no. 422 (Sept 93), p. 470.

Montes M., Fernando. El documento final de Santo Domingo. *Mensaje,* v. 42, no. 416 (Jan – Feb 93), pp. 8 – 13. Il.

Mexico

Baldeón Larrea, Eduardo. CEBs: vivir y luchar en común. *El Cotidiano,* v. 10, no. 57 (Aug – Sept 93), pp. 11 – 16. Il, tables.

Venezuela

Sources

Langue, Frédérique. De moralista a arbitrista: don Francisco de Ibarra, obispo de Venezuela, 1798 – 1806; recopilación documental. *Anuario de Estudios Americanos,* v. 49, Suppl. 1 (1992), pp. 55 – 84. Bibl.

CHURCH AND STATE

See also
Religion and politics
Socialism and Catholic Church

Argentina

Bianchi, Susana. Iglesia católica y peronismo: la cuestión de la enseñanza religiosa, 1946 – 1955. *Estudios Interdisciplinarios de América Latina y el Caribe,* v. 3, no. 2 (July – Dec 92), pp. 89 – 103. Bibl.

Laguna, Justo. La iglesia y diez años de democracia. *Todo Es Historia,* v. 27, no. 317 (Dec 93), pp. 8 – 9. Il.

Urquiza, Fernando Carlos. Etiquetas y conflictos: el obispo, el virrey y el cabildo en el Río de la Plata en la segunda mitad del siglo XVIII. *Anuario de Estudios Americanos,* v. 50, no. 1 (1993), pp. 55 – 100. Bibl.

— Iglesia y revolución: un estudio acerca de la actuación política del clero porteño en la década 1810 – 1820. *Anuario de Estudios Americanos,* v. 49 (1992), pp. 441 – 495. Bibl, tables.

Central America

Sagastume Fajardo, Alejandro S. El papel de la iglesia de Centroamérica en la guerra contra William Walker, 1856 – 1860. *Revista de Indias,* v. 53, no. 198 (May – Aug 93), pp. 529 – 544.

Chile

Arenas, José. El retorno de los jesuitas en el siglo XIX: el no-restablecimiento de la Compañía de Jesús en Chile. *Mensaje,* v. 42, no. 420 (July 93), pp. 253 – 258. Il, facs.

Dougnac Rodríguez, Antonio. Algunas manifestaciones del regalismo borbónico a fines del siglo XVIII. *Boletín de la Academia Chilena de la Historia,* v. 58 – 59, no. 102 (1991 – 1992), pp. 43 – 94. Bibl.

Lowden, Pamela. The Ecumenical Committee for Peace in Chile, 1973 – 1975: The Foundation of Moral Opposition to Authoritarian Rule in Chile. *Bulletin of Latin American Research,* v. 12, no. 2 (May 93), pp. 189 – 203. Bibl.

Colombia

Gómez Betancur, Rafael. En que quedamos por fin: ¿Concordato sí o concordato no?; ?De qué y para qué sirven los pactos si no hay voluntad previa de cumplirlos? *Revista Javeriana,* v. 61, no. 599 (Oct 93), pp. 354 – 356.

Mora Gaitán, Alvaro. Lo que usted debe saber sobre la personería jurídica eclesiástica y su tratamiento legal en Colombia. *Revista Javeriana,* v. 61, no. 599 (Oct 93), pp. 357 – 364.

Suescún Mutis, Fabio. Intervención ante la Comisión II de la Honorable Cámara de Representantes. *Revista Javeriana,* v. 61, no. 599 (Oct 93), pp. 293 – 303.

Costa Rica

Vargas Arias, Claudio Antonio. *El liberalismo, la iglesia y el estado en Costa Rica* reviewed by Miguel Picado G. *Revista de Historia (Costa Rica),* no. 26 (July – Dec 92), pp. 203 – 208.

Latin America

Sánchez Bella, Ismael. *Iglesia y estado en la América española,* 2d ed., reviewed by Teodoro Hampe Martínez. *Revista Interamericana de Bibliografía,* v. 42, no. 4 (1992), p. 664.

Mexico

García Ugarte, Marta Eugenia. El estado y la iglesia católica: balance y perspectivas de una relación. *Revista Mexicana de Sociología,* v. 55, no. 2 (Apr – June 93), pp. 225 – 242. Bibl.

Jackson, Robert H. The Impact of Liberal Policy on Mexico's Northern Frontier: Mission Secularization and the Development of Alta California, 1812 – 1846. *Colonial Latin American Historical Review,* v. 2, no. 2 (Spring 93), pp. 195 – 225. Bibl, tables.

Morales, Francisco. Secularización de doctrinas: ¿Fin de un modelo evangelizador en la Nueva España? *Archivo Ibero-Americano,* v. 52, no. 205 – 208 (Jan – Dec 92), pp. 465 – 495. Bibl.

Orozco H., María Angélica. Los franciscanos y el caso del Real Colegio Seminario de México, 1749. *Archivo Ibero-Americano,* v. 52, no. 205 – 208 (Jan – Dec 92), pp. 497 – 512.

Pérez-Rayón, Nora. Iglesia y estado ante el desafío de la credibilidad. *El Cotidiano,* v. 10, no. 58 (Oct – Nov 93), pp. 79 – 85. Bibl, il.

Nicaragua

Kirk, John M. *Politics and the Catholic Church in Nicaragua* reviewed by Daniel H. Levine. *Hispanic American Historical Review,* v. 73, no. 4 (Nov 93), pp. 722 – 724.

— *Politics and the Catholic Church in Nicaragua* reviewed by Laura Nuzzi O'Shaughnessy. *Journal of Latin American Studies,* v. 25, no. 3 (Oct 93), pp. 674 – 675.

Peru

Bronner, Fred. Church, Crown, and Commerce in Seventeenth-Century Lima: A Synoptic Interpretation. *Jahrbuch für Geschichte von Staat, Wirtschaft und Gesellschaft Lateinamerikas,* v. 29 (1992), pp. 75 – 89. Bibl.

García Jordán, Pilar. *Iglesia y poder en el Perú contemporáneo, 1821 – 1919* reviewed by Patricia B. McRae. *The Americas,* v. 50, no. 1 (July 93), pp. 144 – 145.

— *Iglesia y poder en el Perú contemporáneo, 1821 – 1919* reviewed by Alfonso W. Quiroz. *Hispanic American Historical Review,* v. 73, no. 3 (Aug 93), pp. 522 – 523.

— *Iglesia y poder en el Perú contemporáneo, 1821 – 1919* reviewed by Nils Jacobsen. *Revista Andina,* v. 10, no. 2 (Dec 92), pp. 541 – 545.

Sala i Vila, Nuria. Gobierno colonial, iglesia y poder en Perú, 1784 – 1814. *Revista Andina,* v. 11, no. 1 (July 93), pp. 133 – 161. Bibl.

Venezuela

Conde Tudanca, Rodrigo. Un incidente olvidado del trienio adeco: la creación de la iglesia católica, apostólica, venezolana. *Boletín de la Academia Nacional de la Historia (Venezuela),* v. 76, no. 302 (Apr – June 93), pp. 87 – 117. Bibl.

Querales, Juandemaro. El Decreto 321: la iglesia como factor aglutinador de la oposición a los gobiernos de Betancourt y Gallegos. *Boletín de la Academia Nacional de la Historia (Venezuela),* v. 75, no. 299 (July – Sept 92), pp. 180 – 183. Bibl.

CHURCH ARCHITECTURE

Mexico

Chávez G., Gerardo. Las ceremonias sincretas de San Juan Chamula. *Hoy Es Historia,* v. 10, no. 58 (July – Aug 93), pp. 77 – 79.

Flores Marini, Carlos. El arte religioso de Xochimilco: un recorrido (Accompanied by an English translation). *Artes de México,* no. 20 (Summer 93), pp. 55 – 65. Il.

Meade, Joaquín. Breve descripción del templo de Carmen. *Artes de México,* no. 18 (Winter 92), pp. 53 – 61. Il.

Morales Bocardo, Rafael. El Convento de San Francisco (Accompanied by an English translation). *Artes de México,* no. 18 (Winter 92), pp. 45 – 51. Il.

Perea, Héctor. Arte escondido de Oaxaca (Accompanied by an English translation). *Artes de México,* no. 21 (Fall 93), pp. 48 – 53. Il.

Perry, Richard and Rosalind Perry. *Maya Missions: Exploring the Spanish Colonial Churches of Yucatán* reviewed by Miguel A. Bretos. *Hispanic American Historical Review,* v. 73, no. 1 (Feb 93), pp. 134 – 136.

Sources

Ramírez Montes, Mina. Un ensamblador poblano en Querétaro: Luis Ramos Franco. *Anales del Instituto de Investigaciones Estéticas,* v. 16, no. 62 (1991), pp. 151 – 161. Bibl.

Paraguay

Conservation and restoration

Pusineri Scala, Carlos Alberto. Oratorio de San Carlos en la estancia de Olivares. *Estudios Paraguayos,* v. 17, no. 1 – 2 (1989 – 1993), pp. 121 – 147. Il, tables.

Peru

Sources

San Cristóbal, Antonio. Reconversión de la iglesia del Convento de Santo Domingo (Lima) durante el siglo XVII. *Anuario de Estudios Americanos,* v. 49 (1992), pp. 233 – 270. Bibl.

CHURCH ART

See
  Christian art and symbolism

CHURCH LANDS

Chile

Valdés Bunster, Gustavo. Las riquezas de los antiguos jesuitas de Chile. *Mensaje,* v. 42, no. 420 (July 93), pp. 243 – 246. Charts.

CHURCH MUSIC

Brazil

Diniz, Jaime C. *Mestres de Capela de Misericórdia da Bahía, 1647 – 1810* (Review). *Inter-American Music Review,* v. 13, no. 2 (Spring – Summer 93), pp. 159 – 160.

Latin America

Sources

Araujo, Juan de. *Juan de Araujo: antología* compiled and transcribed by Carmen García Muñoz (Review). *Inter-American Music Review,* v. 13, no. 1 (Fall – Winter 92), pp. 119 – 120.

— *Juan de Araujo: antología* compiled and transcribed by Carmen García Muñoz (Review). *Inter-American Music Review,* v. 13, no. 2 (Spring – Summer 93), p. 155.

Mexico

Guerrero Guerrero, Raúl. Cantos populares mexicanos de Navidad en el estado de Hidalgo. *Revista Musical de Venezuela,* no. 28 (May – Dec 89), pp. 148 – 165. Facs.

Russell, Craig H. Musical Life in Baroque Mexico: Rowdy Musicians, Confraternities, and the Holy Office. *Inter-American Music Review,* v. 13, no. 1 (Fall – Winter 92), pp. 11 – 14. Bibl, facs.

Bibliography

Lemmon, Alfred E. Colonial Discography. *The Americas,* v. 49, no. 3 (Jan 93), pp. 388 – 390.

Paraguay

Nawrot, Piotr. *Vespers Music in the Paraguay Reductions* reviewed by James Radomski. *Inter-American Music Review,* v. 13, no. 2 (Spring – Summer 93), pp. 157 – 159. Bibl.

United States

Russell, Craig H. Newly Discovered Treasures from Colonial California: The Masses at San Fernando. *Inter-American Music Review,* v. 13, no. 1 (Fall – Winter 92), pp. 5 – 9. Bibl.

CÍBOLA, SEVEN CITIES OF

Mora Valcárcel, Carmen de. *Las siete ciudades de Cíbola: textos y testimonios sobre la expedición de Vázquez Coronado* reviewed by Francisco Noguerol Jiménez. *Anuario de Estudios Americanos,* v. 50, no. 1 (1993), pp. 323 – 324.

CICALESE, VICENTE

Interviews

Gandolfo, Elvio E. El legado de una lengua plena. *Cuadernos del CLAEH,* v. 17, no. 63 – 64 (Oct 92), pp. 137 – 139.

CIMARRONES

See
  Maroons

CINEMA

See
  Film reviews
  Motion pictures
  Motion pictures and literature

CIRCUS

Page, Joseph A. A Leap for Life. *Américas,* v. 45, no. 4 (July – Aug 93), pp. 34 – 41. Il.

Seibel, Beatriz. *Historia del circo* reviewed by María Rosa Figari. *Todo Es Historia,* v. 27, no. 313 (Aug 93), p. 73. Il.

CISNEROS VIZQUERRA, LUIS F.

Interviews

Cisneros, Luis Jaime. Entrevista al general Luis Cisneros. *Debate (Peru),* v. 15, no. 71 (Nov 92 – Jan 93), pp. 8 – 16. Il.

CITIES AND TOWNS

See also
  Sociology, Urban
  Urbanization
  Names of specific cities

Planning

Portella, Eduardo. La reconstrucción de la ciudad hacia la nueva sociedad. *Cuadernos Americanos,* no. 39, Nueva época (May – June 93), pp. 74 – 76.

Puente Lafoy, Patricio de la et al. Familia, vecindario y comunidad: un modelo sistémico para la interpretación del desarrollo progresivo. *Estudios Sociales (Chile),* no. 76 (Apr – June 93), pp. 149 – 167. Bibl.

Argentina

Brailovsky, Antonio Elio. Viedma: la capital inundable. *Todo Es Historia*, v. 26, no. 306 (Jan 93), pp. 60 – 71. Bibl, il.

Ríos, Javier Enrique de los. La huelga de Campana de 1915: conflicto olvido. *Todo Es Historia*, v. 27, no. 314 (Sept 93), pp. 56 – 69. Bibl, il.

Scobie, James Ralston. *Secondary Cities of Argentina: The Social History of Corrientes, Salta, and Mendoza, 1850 – 1910* completed and edited by Samuel L. Baily. Reviewed by Roy Hora. *Todo Es Historia*, v. 26, no. 309 (Apr 93), pp. 68 – 69. Il.

Urquiza Almandoz, Oscar F. El traslado de la capital entre-rriana, 1883. *Investigaciones y Ensayos*, no. 41 (Jan – Dec 91), pp. 329 – 347. Bibl.

Planning

Bevilacqua, Claudia. Transformaciones territoriales en el marco de las políticas del estado en la región metropolitana de Buenos Aires: el caso del municipio de Marcos Paz, 1945 – 1990. *Revista Interamericana de Planificación*, v. 26, no. 101 – 102 (Jan – June 93), pp. 154 – 182. Bibl, tables, maps.

Brazil

Cabrera Infante, Guillermo. Oh Bahia (Translated by Alfred MacAdam). *Review*, no. 47 (Fall 93), pp. 16 – 19.

Glezer, Raquel. São Paulo e a elite letrada brasileira no século XIX. *Siglo XIX: Revista*, no. 11, 2a época (Jan – June 92), pp. 149 – 160. Bibl.

Levine, Robert M. The Singular Brazilian City of Salvador. *Luso-Brazilian Review*, v. 30, no. 2 (Winter 93), pp. 59 – 69. Bibl.

Silva, Sylvio Carlos Bandeira de Mello e and Jaimeval Caetano de Souza. Análise da hierarquia urbana do estado da Bahia. *Revista Brasileira de Geografia*, v. 53, no. 1 (Jan – Mar 91), pp. 51 – 79. Bibl, tables, maps, charts.

Planning

Davidovich, Fany Rachel. Gestão do território: um tema em questão. *Revista Brasileira de Geografia*, v. 53, no. 3 (July – Sept 91), pp. 7 – 31. Bibl.

Lerner, Jaime. La ciudad optimista. *Nexos*, v. 16, no. 189 (Sept 93), pp. 13 – 15.

Meira, Sílvio Augusto de Bastos. Um parecer inédito de Rui Barbosa (Includes Rui Barbosa's text regarding the rejec-tion by the city of Belém, Pará, of an electrical transporta-tion contract in the late 19th century). *Revista do Instituto Histórico e Geográfico Brasileiro*, no. 372 (July – Sept 91), pp. 647 – 658.

Chile

Acuña Casas, Ricardo and Tulio González Abuter. *Los Ange-les durante la colonia* reviewed by Fernando Campos Ha-rriet (Review entitled "Dos estudios sobre Los Angeles"). *Boletín de la Academia Chilena de la Historia*, v. 58 – 59, no. 102 (1991 – 1992), pp. 553 – 554.

Norambuena Carrasco, Carmen. Inmigración, agricultura y ciudades intermedias, 1880 – 1930. *Cuadernos de Historia (Chile)*, no. 11 (Dec 91), pp. 105 – 123. Bibl, tables.

Varas Bordeu, María Teresa. *Villa de Nuestra Señora de Los Angeles: época fundacional* reviewed by Fernando Campos Harriet (Review entitled "Dos estudios sobre Los Angeles"). *Boletín de la Academia Chilena de la Historia*, v. 58 – 59, no. 102 (1991 – 1992), pp. 553 – 554.

Planning

Barros Franco, José Miguel. Rey Don Felipe: plano de una fundación hispana en el estrecho de Magallanes. *Boletín de la Academia Chilena de la Historia*, v. 58 – 59, no. 102 (1991 – 1992), pp. 387 – 401. Il, facs.

Figueroa Sala, Jonas. Las ciudades lineales chilenas, 1910 – 1930. *Revista de Indias*, v. 53, no. 198 (May – Aug 93), pp. 651 – 662. Il, maps.

Gross Fuentes, Patricio. Bases para una futura planificación de la ciudad chilena. *EURE*, v. 19, no. 57 (July 93), pp. 117 – 123.

Lavín Infante, Joaquín. Las Condes: un nuevo plan regulador. *EURE*, v. 19, no. 57 (July 93), pp. 132 – 133.

Ossandón Widow, María Eugenia. Proyecto para un plano de Valparaíso, 1675 – 1700. *Historia (Chile)*, no. 26 (1991 – 1992), pp. 247 – 258. Bibl.

Colombia

Bedoya Ramírez, Josué. Fundación de la ciudad de "El Gua-mo," Tolima. *Boletín de Historia y Antigüedades*, v. 80, no. 780 (Jan – Mar 93), pp. 205 – 210.

Santa, Eduardo. Honda: ciudad clave en la historia de Colom-bia. *Boletín de Historia y Antigüedades*, v. 79, no. 779 (Oct – Dec 92), pp. 975 – 991. Bibl.

Planning

Glick, Curtis R. Parámetros sociales para la planificación en Colombia. *Revista Interamericana de Planificación*, v. 26, no. 101 – 102 (Jan – June 93), pp. 95 – 111. Bibl.

Pastrana Arango, Andrés. En busca de una Bogotá más hu-mana (Previously published in this journal, no. 566, 1990). *Revista Javeriana*, v. 61, no. 596 (July 93), pp. 95 – 101.

Costa Rica

Fernández González, Alvaro. Todo empezó en el '53: historia oral de un distrito liberacionista. *Revista de Historia (Costa Rica)*, no. 26 (July – Dec 92), pp. 97 – 142. Bibl.

Loáiciga G., María Elena and Rosa Rosales O. La población anciana de Liberia: condición socioeconómica precaria. *Re-vista de Ciencias Sociales (Costa Rica)*, no. 59 (Mar 93), pp. 95 – 106. Bibl, tables.

Dominican Republic

Robertiello, Jack. Dominican Chutzpah: The Story of Sosua. *Américas*, v. 45, no. 4 (July – Aug 93), pp. 20 – 25. Il, maps.

Ecuador

Bock Godard, Marie S. *Guayaquil: arquitectura, espacio y so-ciedad, 1900 – 1940* reviewed by Eduardo Figari Gold. *Bul-letin de l'Institut Français d'Etudes Andines*, v. 21, no. 3 (1992), pp. 1082 – 1084.

Guatemala

Piel, Jean. *Sajcabajá: muerte y resurrección de un pueblo de Guatemala, 1500 – 1970* reviewed by David McCreery. *Me-soamérica (USA)*, v. 13, no. 24 (Dec 92), pp. 458 – 459.

Korea

Gutman, Pablo. La Habana y Seul: ejemplos de metropoliza-ción. *EURE*, v. 19, no. 57 (July 93), pp. 103 – 115. Bibl, tables.

Latin America

Hoberman, Louisa Schell and Susan Migden Socolow, eds. *Cities and Society in Colonial Latin America* reviewed by Arij Ouweneel. *European Review of Latin American and Caribbean Studies*, no. 54 (June 93), pp. 125 – 126.

Romero, José Luis. La ciudad latinoamericana y los movimien-tos políticos. *Siglo XIX: Revista*, no. 11, 2a época (Jan – June 92), pp. 15 – 27.

Maps

Hardoy, Jorge Enrique. *Cartografía urbana colonial de Amé-rica Latina y el Caribe* reviewed by María Elena Ducci. *EURE*, v. 19, no. 58 (Oct 93), pp. 87 – 88.

Planning

Rivera, Jorge B. "Dameros": la utopía urbanística de la ciudad de Indias. *Cuadernos del CLAEH*, v. 17, no. 63 – 64 (Oct 92), pp. 149 – 154. Bibl.

Mexican – American Border Region

Curtis, James R. Central Business Districts of the Two Lare-dos. *Geographical Review*, v. 83, no. 1 (Jan 93), pp. 54 – 65. Bibl, tables, charts.

Mexico

Aguilar, Adrián Guillermo. Las ciudades medias en México: hacia una diferenciación de sus atributos. *Revista Intera-mericana de Planificación*, v. 26, no. 101 – 102 (Jan – June 93), pp. 129 – 153. Bibl, tables, charts.

Aubry, Andrés. *San Cristóbal de las Casas: su historia urbana, demográfica y monumental, 1528 – 1990* reviewed by Sid-ney David Markman. *Mesoamérica (USA)*, v. 13, no. 23 (June 92), p. 183.

Bayón, Damián Carlos. Reencuentro con Oaxaca (Accompa-nied by an English translation). *Artes de México*, no. 21 (Fall 93), pp. 36 – 39. Il.

Calvillo, Tomás. Una paradoja en el corazón de México (Accompanied by an English translation). *Artes de México, no.* 18 (Winter 92), pp. 26 – 27. Il.

Contreras Cruz, Carlos. Urbanización y modernidad en el porfiriato: el caso de la ciudad de Puebla. *La Palabra y el Hombre,* no. 83 (July – Sept 92), pp. 167 – 188. Bibl.

Durán, Ana María and María Concepción Huerta Trujillo. Cambios de usos del suelo y despoblamiento en la colonia Roma. *El Cotidiano,* v. 10, no. 57 (Aug – Sept 93), pp. 73 – 77. Il, tables.

Florescano Mayet, Sergio. Xalapa y su región durante el siglo XIX: las principales vertientes de su desarrollo económico, social y político. *La Palabra y el Hombre,* no. 83 (July – Sept 92), pp. 135 – 165. Bibl, tables.

Fuentes Aguilar, Luis and Juan Vargas González. La articulación espacial de la ciudad colonial de Puebla, México. *Revista de Historia de América,* no. 112 (July – Dec 91), pp. 43 – 62. Bibl, il, maps.

García de Fuentes, Ana. Comercio, modernización y procesos territoriales: el caso de Mérida, Yucatán. *Problemas del Desarrollo,* v. 24, no. 94 (July – Sept 93), pp. 133 – 163. Bibl, tables, maps, charts.

Haskett, Robert Stephen. Visions of Municipal Glory Undimmed: The Nahuatl Town Histories of Colonial Cuernavaca. *Colonial Latin American Historical Review,* v. 1, no. 1 (Fall 92), pp. 1 – 36. Bibl, il.

Hiriart, Hugo. Impresión de Xochimilco (Accompanied by an English translation). *Artes de México,* no. 20 (Summer 93), pp. 27 – 32.

Manrique, Jorge Alberto and Hipólito Rodríguez. *Veracruz: la ciudad hecha de mar, 1519 – 1821* (Review). *La Palabra y el Hombre,* no. 83 (July – Sept 92), pp. 347 – 349.

Montejano y Aguiñaga, Rafael. Orígenes de San Luis Potosí (Accompanied by an English translation). *Artes de México,* no. 18 (Winter 92), pp. 29 – 35. Il, facs.

Müller, Gabriele et al. *Pátzcuaro, Romantik und Kommerzialität* reviewed by Thomas D. Schoonover. *Hispanic American Historical Review,* v. 73, no. 2 (May 93), pp. 338 – 339.

Vargas Uribe, Guillermo. Geografía histórica de la ciudad de Morelia, Michoacán, México: su evolución demográfica. *Islas,* no. 98 (Jan – Apr 91), pp. 58 – 70. Bibl, tables, maps, charts.

Weinberger, Eliot. El zócalo: centro del universo (Accompanied by the English original, translated by Magali Tercero). *Artes de México,* no. 21 (Fall 93), pp. 26 – 31. Il, maps.

Widmer S., Rolf. La ciudad de Veracruz en el último siglo colonial, 1680 – 1820: algunos aspectos de la historia demográfica de una ciudad portuaria. *La Palabra y el Hombre,* no. 83 (July – Sept 92), pp. 121 – 134. Bibl, tables.

Bibliography

Bibliografía (to the articles on Oaxaca appearing in this issue). *Artes de México,* no. 21 (Fall 93), p. 84.

Bibliografía (to the articles on San Luis Potosí appearing in this issue). *Artes de México,* no. 18 (Winter 92), p. 81.

Bibliografía (to the articles on Xochimilco appearing in this issue). *Artes de México,* no. 20 (Summer 93), p. 93.

Pictorial works

Stephan-Otto, Erwin. Xochimilco: fuente de historias (Accompanied by an English translation). *Artes de México,* no. 20 (Summer 93), pp. 33 – 35.

Planning

Astudillo Moya, Marcela and Alejandro Méndez Rodríguez. Planes urbanos sin descentralización financiera en México. *Problemas del Desarrollo,* v. 24, no. 93 (Apr – June 93), pp. 153 – 174. Bibl, tables, charts.

Denton, Dan. Acapulco Renaissance. *Business Mexico,* v. 3, no. 3 (Mar 93), pp. 15 – 16. Il.

Duhau, Emilio and Alejandro Suárez Pareyón. Sistemas de planeación y política de desarrollo urbano en la ciudad de México. *El Cotidiano,* v. 9, no. 54 (May 93), pp. 3 – 9. Bibl, il.

García Zambrano, Angel Julián. El poblamiento de México en la época del contacto, 1520 – 1540. *Mesoamérica (USA),* v. 13, no. 24 (Dec 92), pp. 239 – 296. Bibl, il, facs, charts.

Lipsett-Rivera, Sonya. Water and Bureaucracy in Colonial Puebla de los Angeles. *Journal of Latin American Studies,* v. 25, no. 1 (Feb 93), pp. 25 – 44. Bibl, tables, maps.

Pérez Morales, Constantino Alberto. Fortalecimiento municipal para el desarrollo regional en Oaxaca. *Problemas del Desarrollo,* v. 24, no. 92 (Jan – Mar 93), pp. 137 – 169. Tables.

Pradilla Cobos, Emilio, ed. *Planeación urbana y bienestar social, vol. II: Democracia y desarrollo de la ciudad de México* reviewed by J. Verónica Ramírez Rangel. *El Cotidiano,* v. 9, no. 54 (May 93), p. 118. Il.

Rébora Togno, Alberto. Los planificadores urbanos ante el cambio. *EURE,* v. 19, no. 57 (July 93), pp. 31 – 40.

Sources

Boyd-Bowman, Peter. *Indice y extractos del Archivo de Protocolos de Puebla de los Angeles, México, 1538 – 1556* reviewed by Linda Greenow. *Hispanic American Historical Review,* v. 73, no. 3 (Aug 93), pp. 486 – 487.

Panama

Osorio Osorio, Alberto. Natá de los caballeros, madre de pueblos. *Revista Cultural Lotería,* v. 51, no. 387 (Feb 92), pp. 26 – 30.

Peru

Barnes, Monica and Daniel J. Slive. El puma de Cuzco: ¿Plano de la ciudad ynga o noción europea? *Revista Andina,* v. 11, no. 1 (July 93), pp. 70 – 102. Bibl, maps, facs.

Uruguay

Benítez Burgos, Wilson Andrés. La presencia religiosa en la historia de Melo. *Hoy Es Historia,* v. 10, no. 57 (Apr – May 93), pp. 61 – 68.

Venezuela

Alvarez, Luis. Discurso pronunciado por el profesor Luis Alvarez con motivo de la presentación del libro *San Sebastián de los Reyes y sus ilustres próceres* en la Escuela de Música de San Sebastián de los Reyes, el 20 de enero de 1993. *Boletín de la Academia Nacional de la Historia (Venezuela),* v. 76, no. 301 (Jan – Mar 93), pp. 51 – 54.

Castillo Lara, Lucas Guillermo. San Juan Bautista de Colón, de Ayacucho y Sucre, Almirante de Lejanías, mariscal de voluntades. *Boletín de la Academia Nacional de la Historia (Venezuela),* v. 75, no. 300 (Oct – Dec 92), pp. 43 – 67. Bibl.

Salcedo-Bastardo, José Luis. En el 170º aniversario de la municipalidad de Carúpano. *Boletín de la Academia Nacional de la Historia (Venezuela),* v. 75, no. 297 (Jan – Mar 92), pp. 33 – 42.

Santos Urriola, José. Discurso de orden pronunciado por el profesor José Santos Urriola, el día 16 de enero de 1992, en la sesión especial con que la Academia Nacional de la Historia conmemoró los cuatrocientos años de la fundación de Guanare. *Boletín de la Academia Nacional de la Historia (Venezuela),* v. 76, no. 301 (Jan – Mar 93), pp. 19 – 26.

CITIES AND TOWNS IN LITERATURE

See also
Name of country in literature; e.g., Chile in literature

Andreu, Alicia G. *Habla la ciudad:* poética de la migración. *Revista Chilena de Literatura,* no. 42 (Aug 93), pp. 19 – 24.

Elmore, Peter. *Los muros invisibles: Lima y la modernidad en la novela del siglo XX* reviewed by Rodrigo Quijano (Review entitled "Experiencia urbana"). *Debate (Peru),* v. 16, no. 73 (June – Aug 93), p. 74. Il.

Gomes, Miguel. El lenguaje de las destrucciones: Caracas y la novela urbana. *Inti,* no. 37 – 38 (Spring – Fall 93), pp. 217 – 224. Bibl.

Hernández, Consuelo. La arquitectura poética de Eugenio Montejo. *Inti,* no. 37 – 38 (Spring – Fall 93), pp. 133 – 143. Bibl.

Segre, Roberto. La poesía ambiental como proyecto de vida: la obra de Fernando Salinas (1930 – 1992). *Casa de las Américas,* no. 189 (Oct – Dec 92), pp. 107 – 108.

Tarn, Nathaniel. Santo Domingo de Guzmán, Oaxaca: origen del orden (Accompanied by the English original, translated by Osvaldo Sánchez and Roberto Tejada). *Artes de México,* no. 21 (Fall 93), pp. 40 – 41.

CITIZENSHIP

See also
Naturalization

Brazil

Barretto, Vicente. Democracia, participação e cidadania. *Revista Brasileira de Estudos Políticos*, no. 76 (Jan 93), pp. 141 – 145.

Duarte, Luiz Fernando Dias et al. Vicissitudes e limites da conversão à cidadania nas classes populares brasileiras. *Revista Brasileira de Ciências Sociais*, v. 8, no. 22 (June 93), pp. 5 – 19. Bibl.

Fischer, Nilton Bueno. A história de Rose: classes populares, mulheres e cidadania. *Vozes*, v. 86, no. 6 (Nov – Dec 92), pp. 38 – 44.

Lopez, Luiz Roberto. As transfigurações da cidadania no Brasil. *Vozes*, v. 86, no. 6 (Nov – Dec 92), pp. 92 – 95.

Latin America

O'Donnell, Guillermo A. Estado, democratización y ciudadanía. *Nueva Sociedad*, no. 128 (Nov – Dec 93), pp. 62 – 87.

CITRUS FRUITS

Mexico

Olvera Sandoval, José Antonio. Agricultura, riego y conflicto social en la región citrícola de Nuevo León, 1860 – 1910. *Siglo XIX: Cuadernos*, v. 2, no. 5 (Feb 93), pp. 59 – 78.

CIUDAD JUÁREZ, MEXICO

Jones, Robert W. A Content Comparison of Daily Newspapers in the El Paso – Juárez Circulation Area. *Journal of Borderlands Studies*, v. 7, no. 2 (Fall 92), pp. 93 – 100. Bibl, tables.

Woo Morales, Ofelia. La migración internacional desde una perspectiva regional: el caso de Tijuana y Ciudad Juárez. *Relaciones Internacionales (Mexico)*, v. 15, Nueva época, no. 57 (Jan – Mar 93), pp. 87 – 94. Charts.

CIVIL RIGHTS

See
Human rights

CIVIL SERVICE

See
Public administration
Subdivision *Officials and public employees* under names of specific countries

CIVILIZATION

See also
Baroque
Enlightenment
Humanism
Science and civilization
Technology and civilization

Zea, Leopoldo. Filosofía de las relaciones de América Latina con el mundo. *Cuadernos Americanos*, no. 41, Nueva época (Sept – Oct 93), pp. 93 – 100.

Study and teaching

Beverley, John. Cultural Studies. *Latin American Literary Review*, v. 20, no. 40 (July – Dec 92), pp. 19 – 22. Bibl.

CIVILIZATION, MODERN

See also
Popular culture
Subdivision *Culture* under *Hispanic Americans (U.S.)* and names of Indian groups
Subdivisions *Civilization* and *Intellectual life* under names of specific countries

Amoretti Hurtado, María. El discurso político y el discurso religioso en el apocalipsis de la modernidad. *Káñina*, v. 16, no. 1 (Jan – June 92), pp. 111 – 116.

Corbisier, Margarida. Drogas e educação. *Convivium*, v. 34, no. 2 (July – Dec 91), pp. 154 – 156.

Madrid Hurtado, Miguel de la. Notas sobre democracia y cultura. *Cuadernos Americanos*, no. 39, Nueva época (May – June 93), pp. 34 – 41.

Marras, Sergio. América en plural y en singular, II: Los nacionalismos y otros bemoles; entrevista con Octavio Paz (Fragment from the book *América Latina: marca registrada*). *Vuelta*, v. 17, no. 195 (Feb 93), pp. 26 – 30.

Ordóñez, Andrés. El fin de una historia: la comunicación intercultural y el nuevo orden internacional en formación. *Cuadernos Americanos*, no. 42, Nueva época (Nov – Dec 93), pp. 101 – 111. Bibl.

Portella, Eduardo. La reconstrucción de la ciudad hacia la nueva sociedad. *Cuadernos Americanos*, no. 39, Nueva época (May – June 93), pp. 74 – 76.

Tironi B., Eugenio. Las vueltas de la historia. *Mensaje*, v. 42, no. 424 (Nov 93), pp. 563 – 566. Il.

CLARÍN

See
Alas, Leopoldo

CLASTRES, PIERRE

Cappelletti, Angel J. Pierre Clastres: la sociedad contra el estado. *Revista de Filosofía de la Universidad de Costa Rica*, v. 30, no. 72 (Dec 92), pp. 145 – 151.

CLAVIJERO, FRANCISCO JAVIER

Micheli, Alfredo de. Un mexicano en la Italia del siglo de las luces. *La Palabra y el Hombre*, no. 81 (Jan – Mar 92), pp. 85 – 93. Bibl, il.

Stoetzer, Otto Carlos. Tradition and Progress in the Late Eighteenth-Century Jesuit Rediscovery of America: Francisco Javier Clavijero's Philosophy and History. *Colonial Latin American Historical Review*, v. 2, no. 3 (Summer 93), pp. 289 – 324. Bibl.

CLEVELAND, GROVER

Consalvi, Simón Alberto. *Grover Cleveland y la controversia Venezuela – Gran Bretaña* reviewed by H. Michael Tacver. *Hispanic American Historical Review*, v. 73, no. 4 (Nov 93), pp. 727 – 728.

CLIENTELISM

See
Patronage, Political

CLIMATE

See
Droughts
Vegetation and climate
Subdivision *Climate* under names of specific countries
Subdivision *Influence of climate* under *Man*

CLINTON, WILLIAM JEFFERSON

Burbach, Roger. Clinton's Latin American Policy: A Look at Things to Come. *NACLA Report on the Americas*, v. 26, no. 5 (May 93), pp. 16 – 22+. Bibl, il.

Landau, Saul. Clinton's Cuba Policy: A Low-Priority Dilemma. *NACLA Report on the Americas*, v. 26, no. 5 (May 93), pp. 35 – 37+.

Levine, Elaine. Significado del programa de Bill Clinton para México y América Latina. *Problemas del Desarrollo*, v. 24, no. 93 (Apr – June 93), pp. 22 – 26.

Mercado Celis, Alejandro. El déficit, los impuestos, solidaridad y Clinton. *Problemas del Desarrollo*, v. 24, no. 93 (Apr – June 93), pp. 27 – 33. Bibl.

Pozzi, Pablo Alejandro. Estados Unidos entre la crisis y la legitimidad. *Realidad Económica*, no. 113 (Jan – Feb 93), pp. 103 – 121. Bibl, tables.

Rangel Díaz, José. La "Clintonomics": ¿Nuevas señales para la economía mundial? *Problemas del Desarrollo*, v. 24, no. 93 (Apr – June 93), pp. 15 – 21.

Vargas, Rocío. El proyecto económico de Clinton: posibles repercusiones para México y América Latina. *Problemas del Desarrollo*, v. 24, no. 93 (Apr – June 93), pp. 34 – 38.

CLOTHING AND DRESS

See also
Textile industry and fabrics
Subdivision *Costume and adornment* under names of Indian groups

Peru

Cortés, Laia. Paloma La Hoz: Made in Perú. *Debate (Peru),* v. 16, no. 75 (Dec 93 – Jan 94), pp. 57 – 58. Il.

COAHUILA, MEXICO

Cárdenas, Fe Esperanza and Vincent Redonnet. Modernización de la empresa AHMSA en Monclova, Coahuila y su impacto sobre la población. *Estudios Demográficos y Urbanos,* v. 6, no. 3 (Sept – Dec 91), pp. 677 – 716. Bibl, tables.

González Chávez, Gerardo. Monclova: algunos efectos del neoliberalismo. *Momento Económico,* no. 66 (Mar – Apr 93), pp. 18 – 22.

COAL MINES AND MINING

Mexico

Chávez Martínez, Luis and Jorge E. Ordóñez. Fueling Industry. *Business Mexico,* v. 3, no. 12 (Dec 93), pp. 10 – 11.

Venezuela

Escobar Navarro, Marcos Eligio and Manuel Martínez Santana. Características geoquímicas y petrográficas de los principales yacimientos carboníferos venezolanos. *Interciencia,* v. 18, no. 2 (Mar – Apr 93), pp. 62 – 70. Bibl, tables, maps, charts.

— Los depósitos de carbón en Venezuela. *Interciencia,* v. 18, no. 5 (Sept – Oct 93), pp. 224 – 229. Bibl, tables, maps, charts.

COASTS

Mexico

Sources

Moncada Maya, J. Omar. Miguel Constanzó y el reconocimiento geográfico de la costa de Veracruz de 1797. *Anuario de Estudios Americanos,* v. 49, Suppl. 2 (1992), pp. 31 – 64. Bibl.

Venezuela

Statistics

Almeida, Yajaida. Estudio preliminar sobre la variabilidad del nivel del mar en las costas de Venezuela. *Revista Geográfica (Mexico),* no. 115 (Jan – June 92), pp. 5 – 26. Tables, maps, charts.

COBO, BERNABÉ

Criticism of specific works

Historia del Nuevo Mundo

Olmo Pintado, Margarita del. La historia natural en la *Historia del Nuevo Mundo* del p. Cobo. *Revista de Indias,* v. 52, no. 195 – 196 (May – Dec 92), pp. 795 – 823. Maps, charts.

COCA AND COCAINE

Andean region

Paz Zamora, Jaime. La diplomacia de la coca. *Nueva Sociedad,* no. 124 (Mar – Apr 93), pp. 168 – 172.

Bolivia

Bruzonic, Erika. Erythroxylum Coca L. *Signo,* no. 38, Nueva época (Jan – Apr 93), pp. 61 – 62.

Hargreaves, Clare. *Snowfields: The War on Cocaine in the Andes* reviewed by Madeleine Barbara Léons. *Journal of Latin American Studies,* v. 25, no. 2 (May 93), pp. 422 – 423.

Léons, Madeline Barbara. Risk and Opportunity in the Coca/Cocaine Economy of the Bolivian Yungas. *Journal of Latin American Studies,* v. 25, no. 1 (Feb 93), pp. 121 – 157. Bibl, charts.

Malamud Goti, Jaime E. *Smoke and Mirrors: The Paradox of the Drug Wars* reviewed by Kevin Healy. *Journal of Latin American Studies,* v. 25, no. 3 (Oct 93), pp. 688 – 689.

Colombia

Betancourt Echeverry, Darío. Tendencias de las mafias colombianas de la cocaína y la amapola. *Nueva Sociedad,* no. 128 (Nov – Dec 93), pp. 38 – 47.

COCHABAMBA, BOLIVIA (DEPARTMENT)

Lagos, María L. The Politics of Representation: Class and Ethnic Identities in Cochabamba, Bolivia. *Boletín de Antropología Americana,* no. 24 (Dec 91), pp. 143 – 150. Bibl, il.

CODEX BORBONICUS

Batalla Rosado, Juan José. La perspectiva planigráfica precolombina y el *Códice Borbónico:* página 31; escena central. *Revista Española de Antropología Americana,* v. 23 (1993), pp. 113 – 134. Bibl, il.

CODEX BORGIA

Kendall, Jonathan. The Thirteen Volatiles: Representation and Symbolism. *Estudios de Cultura Náhuatl,* v. 22 (1992), pp. 99 – 131. Bibl.

CODEX CHIMALPOPOCA

History and Mythology of the Aztecs: The 'Codex Chimalpopoca' translated by John Bierhorst. Reviewed by David Johnson. *Colonial Latin American Historical Review,* v. 2, no. 1 (Winter 93), pp. 112 – 113.

COE, MICHAEL D.

Interviews

Rodríguez Ochoa, Patricia. El desciframiento de la escritura maya: una historia. *Vuelta,* v. 17, no. 203 (Oct 93), pp. 21 – 22.

COELHO, PAULO

Criticism and interpretation

Fischer, Luís Augusto. As sete razões do sucesso de Paulo Coelho. *Vozes,* v. 86, no. 5 (Sept – Oct 92), pp. 58 – 61.

COELHO NETTO, HENRIQUE

Criticism and interpretation

Daniel, Mary L. Coelho Neto revisitado. *Luso-Brazilian Review,* v. 30, no. 1 (Summer 93), pp. 175 – 180.

COFFEE

Portillo, Luis. El Convenio Internacional de Café y la crisis del mercado. *Comercio Exterior,* v. 43, no. 4 (Apr 93), pp. 378 – 391. Bibl, tables.

Romero Polanco, Emilio. Crisis internacional del café: impactos y perspectivas. *Problemas del Desarrollo,* v. 24, no. 94 (July – Sept 93), pp. 75 – 95. Bibl, tables.

Brazil

Homem de Melo, Fernando Bento. Café brasileiro: não a um novo acordo internacional. *Revista de Economia Política (Brazil),* v. 13, no. 4 (Oct – Dec 93), pp. 37 – 46. Bibl, tables, charts.

Rangel, Armênio de Souza. A economia do município de Taubaté, 1798 a 1835. *Estudos Econômicos,* v. 23, no. 1 (Jan – Apr 93), pp. 149 – 179. Bibl, tables, charts.

Costa Rica

Herrera Balharry, Eugenio. *Los alemanes y el estado cafetalero* reviewed by Gertrud Peters Solórzano (Review entitled "Café, familia y política"). *Revista de Historia (Costa Rica),* no. 25 (Jan – June 92), pp. 239 – 242.

Molina Jiménez, Iván and Eugenia Rodríguez Sáenz. Compraventas de cafetales y haciendas de café en el valle central de Costa Rica, 1834 – 1850. *Anuario de Estudios Centroamericanos,* v. 18, no. 1 (1992), pp. 29 – 50. Bibl, tables, maps, charts.

El Salvador

Paige, Jeffrey M. Coffee and Power in El Salvador. *Latin American Research Review,* v. 28, no. 3 (1993), pp. 7 – 40. Bibl.

Mexico

Anderson, L. Susan. The Nature of Good Business. *Business Mexico,* v. 3, no. 1 (Jan – Feb 93), p. 66. Il.

Hoffmann, Odile. Renovación de los actores sociales en el campo: un ejemplo en el sector cafetalero en Veracruz. *Estudios Sociológicos,* v. 10, no. 30 (Sept – Dec 92), pp. 523 – 554. Bibl, tables, maps.

Romero Polanco, Emilio. Comercialización del café y el sector social en México. *Momento Económico,* no. 66 (Mar – Apr 93), pp. 14 – 17. Tables.

Nicaragua

Craipeau, Carine. El café en Nicaragua. *Anuario de Estudios Centroamericanos,* v. 18, no. 2 (1992), pp. 41 – 69. Bibl, tables, maps, charts.

COFRADÍAS

See

Subdivision *Societies, etc.* under *Catholic Church*

COGHLAN, EDGARDO

Art reproductions

Labastida, Jaime. De la serenidad (Includes reproductions of *Chalma, La bruma, Tlalmanalco, Iztaccíhuatl, Xilitla, San Luis Potosí,* and *La recua, Xochitlán, Puebla). Plural (Mexico),* v. 22, no. 262 (July 93), pp. 40 – 45. Il.

COHEN, LAURA

Ferrer, Elizabeth. Laura Cohen (Translated by Francisco Martínez Negrete). *Artes de México,* no. 19 (Spring 93), pp. 106 – 109. Il.

EL COJO ILUSTRADO (PERIODICAL)

Alcibíades, Mirla. De cómo una tabacalera devinó en revista cultural. *Revista Nacional de Cultura (Venezuela),* v. 53, no. 286 (July – Sept 92), pp. 167 – 174. Il.

Rivas Rivas, José. Una insólita misión cultural. *Revista Nacional de Cultura (Venezuela),* v. 53, no. 286 (July – Sept 92), pp. 159 – 166. Il.

Ruiz Chataing, David. La revista *El Cojo Ilustrado* y el antiimperialismo. *Revista Nacional de Cultura (Venezuela),* v. 53, no. 286 (July – Sept 92), pp. 177 – 186. Bibl, il.

Bibliography

Alcibíades, Mirla. Bibliografía selecta sobre *El Cojo Ilustrado. Revista Nacional de Cultura (Venezuela),* v. 53, no. 286 (July – Sept 92), pp. 175 – 176.

COLDWELL, PEDRO JOAQUÍN

Addresses, essays, lectures

Coldwell, Pedro Joaquín. Service for Survival (Excerpt from a speech given by the Secretary of Tourism). *Business Mexico,* v. 3, no. 10 (Oct 93), pp. 16 – 17. Il.

EL COLEGIO DE MÉXICO

Staples, Anne. Los últimos diez años de historia regional en el Colegio de México. *La Palabra y el Hombre,* no. 83 (July – Sept 92), pp. 299 – 303. Bibl.

COLLADO MARTELL, ALFREDO

Criticism of specific works

Un hombre bueno que fue un hombre malo

Rosa, William. Ciencia y literatura en Alfredo Collado Martell: un primer caso de inseminación artificial. *Revista Iberoamericana,* v. 59, no. 162 – 163 (Jan – June 93), pp. 111 – 118. Bibl.

COLLECTIVE BARGAINING

See

Labor relations

COLLOR DE MELLO, FERNANDO AFFONSO

Carvalho, Carlos Eduardo Vieira de. Brasil: la caída de Collor. *Nueva Sociedad,* no. 124 (Mar – Apr 93), pp. 22 – 26.

Cruz Júnior, Ademar Seabra de et al. Brazil's Foreign Policy under Collor. *Journal of Inter-American Studies and World Affairs,* v. 35, no. 1 (1993), pp. 119 – 144. Bibl.

Flynn, Peter. Collor, Corruption, and Crisis: Time for Reflection. *Journal of Latin American Studies,* v. 25, no. 2 (May 93), pp. 351 – 371. Bibl.

Pires, Nielsen de Paula. Brasil: transición, crisis y triunfo de la democracia. *Mensaje,* v. 42, no. 417 (Mar – Apr 93), pp. 79 – 81. Il.

Santos, Theotonio dos. Brazil's Controlled Purge: The Impeachment of Fernando Collor (Translated by Phillip Berryman). *NACLA Report on the Americas,* v. 27, no. 3 (Nov – Dec 93), pp. 17 – 21. Il.

Weyland, Kurt. The Rise and Fall of President Collor and Its Impact on Brazilian Democracy. *Journal of Inter-American Studies and World Affairs,* v. 35, no. 1 (1993), pp. 1 – 37. Bibl.

COLOMBIA

See also

Agriculture – Colombia
Antioquia, Colombia (Department)
Archaeological site reports – Colombia
Armenia, Colombia
Art – Colombia
Art and society – Colombia
Artists – Colombia
Banks and banking – Colombia
Biotechnology – Colombia
Blacks in literature – Colombia
Bogotá, Colombia
Business enterprises – Colombia
Capital – Colombia
Capital productivity – Colombia
Capitalists and financiers – Colombia
Cartagena, Colombia
Catholic Church – Colombia
Cattle trade – Colombia
Chocó, Colombia
Church and education – Colombia
Church and state – Colombia
Cities and towns – Colombia
Coca and cocaine – Colombia
Community centers – Colombia
Competition – Colombia
Construction industry – Colombia
Credit – Colombia
Decentralization in government – Colombia
Democracy – Colombia
Diseases – Colombia
Drug trade – Colombia
Ecology – Colombia
Education – Colombia
Education and state – Colombia
Elite (Social sciences) – Colombia
Employment – Colombia
Energy policy – Colombia
Ethnobotany – Colombia
Evangelicalism – Colombia
Experimental theater – Colombia
Finance, Public – Colombia
Folk medicine – Colombia
Food supply – Colombia
Foreign trade promotion – Colombia
Franciscans – Colombia
Freedom of the press – Colombia
Gas, Natural – Colombia
Geographical distribution of plants and animals – Colombia
Germans – Colombia
Government ownership of business enterprises – Colombia
El Guamo, Colombia
Guerrillas – Colombia
Historians – Colombia
Honda, Colombia
Human capital – Colombia
Human rights – Colombia
Indians, Treatment of – Colombia
Industrial organization – Colombia
Industries, Size of – Colombia
Industry and state – Colombia
Jesuits – Colombia
Journalism – Colombia
Judiciary – Colombia
Labor and laboring classes – Colombia
Labor laws and legislation – Colombia
Land reform – Colombia
Liberalism – Colombia
Libraries and librarians – Colombia
Literature and history – Colombia
Local government – Colombia
Marine resources – Colombia
Markets and merchants – Colombia
Marriage – Colombia

Medellín, Colombia
Mining industry and finance – Colombia
Missions – Colombia
Money and money supply – Colombia
National income – Colombia
National security – Colombia
Neiva, Colombia (Department)
Peasantry – Colombia
Periodicals – Colombia
Petroleum industry and trade – Colombia
Philosophy – Colombia
Photography and photographers – Colombia
Political parties – Colombia
Popular culture – Colombia
Prices – Colombia
Printing and engraving – Colombia
Privatization – Colombia
Providencia Island, Colombia
Public administration – Colombia
Public health – Colombia
Quality of life – Colombia
Real property – Colombia
Research institutes – Colombia
San Andrés Island, Colombia
Saving and investment – Colombia
Science – Colombia
Scientific expeditions – Colombia
Social conflict – Colombia
Social psychology – Colombia
Social security – Colombia
Social service – Colombia
Spanish language – Colombia
Subcontracting – Colombia
Taxation – Colombia
Technology – Colombia
Textile industry and fabrics – Colombia
Trade marks – Colombia
Tunja, Colombia
Unemployment – Colombia
Universities and colleges – Colombia
Violence – Colombia
Wages – Colombia
Women – Colombia
Women artists – Colombia

Administrative and political divisions

Gouëset, Vincent and Fabio Zambrano Pantoja. Géopolitique du district spécial de Bogotá et du Haut-Sumapaz, 1900 – 1990. *Bulletin de l'Institut Français d'Etudes Andines*, v. 21, no. 3 (1992), pp. 1053 – 1071. Bibl, maps.

Antiquities

Bermúdez Páez, Alvaro E. Reconstrucción de un conjunto funerario en el Alto de las Piedras (Isnos). *Revista Colombiana de Antropología*, v. 29 (1992), pp. 257 – 264. Bibl, il.

Correal Urrego, Gonzalo. *Aguazuque: evidencias de cazadores, recolectores y plantadores en la altaplanicie de la cordillera oriental* reviewed by Marianne Cardale de Schrimpff. *Revista Colombiana de Antropología*, v. 29 (1992), pp. 235 – 238.

Mora Camargo, Santiago et al. *Cultivars, Anthropic Soils, and Stability: A Preliminary Report of Archaeological Research in Araracuara, Colombian Amazonia* reviewed by Leonor Herrera Angel. *Revista Colombiana de Antropología*, v. 29 (1992), pp. 251 – 253.

Patiño Castaño, Diógenes. Arqueología del Bajo Patía: fases y correlaciones en la costa pacífica de Colombia y Ecuador. *Latin American Antiquity*, v. 4, no. 2 (June 93), pp. 180 – 199. Bibl, il, tables, maps.

Peña León, Germán Alberto. *Exploraciones arqueológicas en la cuenca media del río Bogotá* reviewed by Mónika Therrien. *Revista Colombiana de Antropología*, v. 29 (1992), pp. 247 – 250. Bibl.

Armed forces

Velandia, Roberto. El Batallón Guarda Presidencial. *Boletín de Historia y Antigüedades*, v. 80, no. 780 (Jan – Mar 93), pp. 109 – 120. Bibl.

Biography

Díaz del Castillo Z., Emiliano. *Gutiérrez de Caviedes: una familia de próceres* reviewed by Hernán Díaz del Castillo Guerrero. *Boletín de Historia y Antigüedades*, v. 79, no. 779 (Oct – Dec 92), pp. 1065 – 1070.

Díaz Granados, José Luis. Los míos. *Boletín de Historia y Antigüedades*, v. 80, no. 780 (Jan – Mar 93), pp. 243 – 246.

Civilization

Camacho Guizado, Alvaro, ed. *La Colombia de hoy: sociología y sociedad* reviewed by Maurice P. Brungardt (Review entitled "Readings on Colombia?"). *Studies in Latin American Popular Culture*, v. 12 (1993), pp. 235 – 242.

Deveny, John J., Jr. and Peter C. Rollins, eds. *Culture and Development in Colombia: Study of Changes in Social Roles, Religion, Literature* . . . Special issue of *Journal of Popular Culture*, 22:1 (Summer 88), reviewed by Maurice P. Brungardt (Review entitled "Readings on Colombia?"). *Studies in Latin American Popular Culture*, v. 12 (1993), pp. 235 – 242.

Uribe Celis, Carlos. *La mentalidad del colombiano* reviewed by Gonzalo Serrano Escallón. *Anuario Colombiano de Historia Social y de la Cultura*, no. 20 (1992), pp. 159 – 162.

Climate

Castillo, Francisco A. and Zenaida Vizcaino Bravo. Observación del fitoplancton del Pacífico colombiano durante 1991 – 1992 en condiciones El Niño. *Bulletin de l'Institut Français d'Etudes Andines*, v. 22, no. 1 (1993), pp. 179 – 190. Bibl, il, maps.

Commerce

History

Dávila L. de Guevara, Carlos. *El empresariado colombiano: una perspectiva histórica* reviewed by Luis Aurelio Ordóñez B. (Review entitled "Un balance historiográfico exhaustivo y sugestivo"). *Anuario Colombiano de Historia Social y de la Cultura*, no. 20 (1992), pp. 147 – 152.

Statistics

Colombia. Departamento Nacional de Planeación. Sector externo. *Planeación y Desarrollo*, v. 24 (1993), All issues.

Constitutional law

Aja, Eliseo. El Proyecto de Ley colombiano visto por un español. *Planeación y Desarrollo*, v. 24, no. 1 (Jan – Apr 93), pp. 191 – 197.

Bolaño Movilla, Rafael. Apuntes sobre la constitución colombiana de 1991. *Desarrollo Indoamericano*, v. 23, no. 91 (June 93), pp. 24 – 25. Il.

Buenahora Febres-Cordero, Jaime. Reglamentación y desarrollo de la constitución del '91. *Revista Javeriana*, v. 61, no. 597 (Aug 93), pp. 183 – 189.

Cáceres Corrales, Pablo. La tutela: procesos, resultados, consecuencias y limitaciones. *Revista Javeriana*, v. 61, no. 598 (Sept 93), pp. 237 – 245.

Colombia: dispositivos constitucionales sobre pueblos indígenas, sus culturas y territorios. *Anuario Indigenista*, v. 30 (Dec 91), pp. 473 – 480.

Gros, Christian. Atention!: un indien peut en cacher un autre; droits indigènes et nouvelle constitution en Colombie. *Caravelle*, no. 59 (1992), pp. 139 – 160. Bibl.

Jaramillo Gómez, William. Legislación de prensa a la luz de la nueva constitución. *Revista Javeriana*, v. 61, no. 595 (June 93), pp. 292 – 297.

Lloreda Caicedo, Rodrigo. La acción de tutela. *Revista Javeriana*, v. 61, no. 595 (June 93), pp. 299 – 305.

Pastrana Borrero, Misael. Memorial de agravios a la constituyente y a la constitución. *Revista Javeriana*, v. 61, no. 598 (Sept 93), pp. 215 – 225.

Pérez González-Rubio, Jesús. Casi no reconozco la constitución que aprobé. *Revista Javeriana*, v. 61, no. 597 (Aug 93), pp. 175 – 181.

Sánchez, Ricardo. Constitución y vida social. *Revista Javeriana*, v. 61, no. 597 (Aug 93), pp. 169 – 173.

Vallejo Mejía, Jesús. Responsabilidad social del periodista frente a los nuevos derechos que ha consagrado la constitución: fundamentalmente el derecho a la vida privada. *Revista Javeriana*, v. 61, no. 595 (June 93), pp. 307 – 316.

Discovery and exploration

Camargo Pérez, Gabriel. Los descubridores del Chocó. *Boletín de Historia y Antigüedades*, v. 79, no. 779 (Oct – Dec 92), pp. 1007 – 1018. Bibl.

Economic conditions

Sanín, Noemí. Discurso de la señora ministro de relaciones exteriores de Colombia en la Universidad de Sofía. *Revista Javeriana*, v. 60, no. 590 (Nov – Dec 92), pp. 339 – 343.

Sevilla Soler, María Rosario. Capital y mercado interno en Colombia, 1880 – 1930. *Anuario de Estudios Americanos*, v. 49 (1992), pp. 585 – 599. Bibl.

Vida nacional. *Revista Javeriana*, v. 60 – 61, no. 590 – 599 (Dec 92 – Oct 93), All issues.

Economic policy

García Echeverría, Luis. La economía durante el gobierno Gaviria. *Revista Javeriana*, v. 61, no. 597 (Aug 93), pp. 143 – 152. Charts.

Thorp, Rosemary. *Economic Management and Economic Development in Peru and Colombia* reviewed by Eva A. Paus. *Hispanic American Historical Review*, v. 73, no. 1 (Feb 93), pp. 176 – 177.

Urrutia Montoya, Miguel. El Consejo Nacional de Política Económica y Social y la planeación en Colombia. *Planeación y Desarrollo*, v. 24, no. 1 (Jan – Apr 93), pp. 349 – 364.

Foreign economic relations

Sanín, Noemí. Discurso de la señora ministro de relaciones exteriores de Colombia en la Universidad de Sofía. *Revista Javeriana*, v. 60, no. 590 (Nov – Dec 92), pp. 339 – 343.

Central America

Acuerdo sobre Comercio e Inversión entre las Repúblicas de Colombia y Venezuela y las Repúblicas de Costa Rica, El Salvador, Guatemala, Honduras y Nicaragua. *Integración Latinoamericana*, v. 18, no. 191 (July 93), pp. 67 – 71.

Ecuador

Castro Guerrero, Gustavo. Evolución de las relaciones colombo – ecuatorianas durante el gobierno del señor presidente César Gaviria. *Revista Javeriana*, v. 61, no. 594 (May 93), pp. 217 – 223. Tables, charts.

European Community

Niño Guarín, Juan Enrique. El Plan Especial de Cooperación (P.E.C.) de la CE: balance satisfactorio pero no suficiente. *Revista Javeriana*, v. 61, no. 594 (May 93), pp. 263 – 269. Bibl, tables.

United States

Espriella, Andrés de la. Hacia una integración comercial con los Estados Unidos. *Revista Javeriana*, v. 61, no. 593 (Apr 93), pp. 148 – 154. Tables.

Foreign relations

Escudero de Paz, Angel. Participación de Colombia en el sistema de las Naciones Unidas. *Revista Javeriana*, v. 61, no. 594 (May 93), pp. 238 – 245.

Sanín, Javier. Editorial: Noemí en el torbellino mundial. *Revista Javeriana*, v. 61, no. 594 (May 93), pp. 199 – 200.

Vázquez Carrizosa, Alfredo. La política internacional de Colombia hasta la época neoliberal. *Revista Javeriana*, v. 61, no. 594 (May 93), pp. 202 – 208.

Asia

García, Pío. Asia y el Pacífico: la dimensión promisoria. *Revista Javeriana*, v. 61, no. 594 (May 93), pp. 271 – 276. Bibl.

Germany

García Pombo, Pablo. Alemania y Colombia: trayectoria de una larga amistad. *Boletín de Historia y Antigüedades*, v. 80, no. 780 (Jan – Mar 93), pp. 79 – 108.

Pacific Area

García, Pío. Asia y el Pacífico: la dimensión promisoria. *Revista Javeriana*, v. 61, no. 594 (May 93), pp. 271 – 276. Bibl.

Spain

Samper Pizano, Ernesto. Balance de actividades de la embajada de Colombia en España durante el año de 1992 y primer trimestre de 1993. *Revista Javeriana*, v. 61, no. 594 (May 93), pp. 256 – 262.

United States

Randall, Stephen J. *Colombia and the United States: Hegemony and Interdependence* reviewed by Frank Safford. *Hispanic American Historical Review*, v. 73, no. 1 (Feb 93), pp. 190 – 191.

— *Colombia and the United States: Hegemony and Interdependence* reviewed by Diana Pardo. *Journal of Inter-American Studies and World Affairs*, v. 35, no. 2 (Summer 93), pp. 163 – 166.

Venezuela

Bermúdez Merizalde, Jaime. Por la senda de la integración: balance. *Revista Javeriana*, v. 61, no. 594 (May 93), pp. 225 – 237.

History

Caro Copete, Jorge. Las Ciudades Amigas y Confederadas del Valle. *Boletín de Historia y Antigüedades*, v. 80, no. 781 (Apr – June 93), pp. 377 – 386.

Mantilla Ruiz, Luis Carlos. La búsqueda de la verdad (Commentary on the speech by Alfonso María Pinilla Cote). *Boletín de Historia y Antigüedades*, v. 80, no. 780 (Jan – Mar 93), pp. 23 – 30.

Minaudier, Jean-Pierre. *Histoire de la Colombie: de la conquête à nos jours* reviewed by Scarlett O'Phelan Godoy. *Anuario de Estudios Americanos*, v. 49, Suppl. 1 (1992), p. 257.

— *Histoire de la Colombie: de la conquête à nos jours* reviewed by Frédérique Langue. *Caravelle*, no. 60 (1993), pp. 162 – 165.

O'Phelan Godoy, Scarlett. Rebeliones andinas anticoloniales: Nueva Granada, Perú y Charcas entre el siglo XVIII y el XIX. *Anuario de Estudios Americanos*, v. 49 (1992), pp. 395 – 440. Bibl, maps.

Parejo, Antonio. Historia de Colombia (Previously published in this journal vol. 1, no. 1, 1912). *Boletín de la Academia Nacional de la Historia (Venezuela)*, v. 75, no. 300 (Oct – Dec 92), pp. 335 – 348.

Ruiz Churión, Jairo. *Mexa, Grameta, Metacuyá, el Meta: recopilación, cronistas e historiadores, 1530 – 1830* reviewed by Jorge Morales Gómez (Review entitled "Historia del Meta"). *Boletín de Historia y Antigüedades*, v. 80, no. 781 (Apr – June 93), pp. 481 – 482.

Societies, etc.

Ruiz Martínez, Eduardo. ¿Qué es la "Sociedad Nariñista de Colombia"? *Boletín de Historia y Antigüedades*, v. 80, no. 780 (Jan – Mar 93), pp. 247 – 249.

Sources

Guerrero Rincón, Amado A. La provincia de Muzo en 1754: informe presentado al rey. *Anuario Colombiano de Historia Social y de la Cultura*, no. 20 (1992), pp. 133 – 145.

Mora de Tovar, Gilma Lucía. El deber de vivir ordenadamente para obedecer al rey. *Anuario Colombiano de Historia Social y de la Cultura*, no. 20 (1992), pp. 109 – 131.

Study and teaching

Cacua Prada, Antonio. 30 años del Instituto Universitario de Historia de Colombia. *Boletín de Historia y Antigüedades*, v. 80, no. 780 (Jan – Mar 93), pp. 121 – 203. Bibl.

Tres décadas del Instituto Universitario de Historia de Colombia. *Boletín de Historia y Antigüedades*, v. 80, no. 781 (Apr – June 93), pp. 491 – 517. Il.

Industries

Echeverri, Clara. Maquila o diseño. *Revista Javeriana*, v. 61, no. 593 (Apr 93), pp. 160 – 162.

Politics and government

Bergquist, Charles Wylie et al, eds. *Violence in Colombia: The Contemporary Crisis in Historical Perspective* reviewed by Mary Roldán. *The Americas*, v. 50, no. 1 (July 93), pp. 142 – 144.

— *Violence in Colombia: The Contemporary Crisis in Historical Perspective* reviewed by Víctor Peralta Ruiz. *Revista Andina*, v. 11, no. 1 (July 93), pp. 244 – 245.

Colombia: fragilidades y promesas de la doble transición. *Nueva Sociedad*, no. 128 (Nov – Dec 93), pp. 12 – 17.

Bibliography

Gold-Biss, Michael. Colombia: Understanding Recent Democratic Transformations in a Violent Polity (Review article). *Latin American Research Review*, v. 28, no. 1 (1993), pp. 215 – 234. Bibl.

1822 –

Ortiz Mesa, Luis Javier. Procesos de descentralización en Colombia durante el período federal, 1850 – 1886. *Planeación y Desarrollo*, v. 24, no. 1 (Jan – Apr 93), pp. 199 – 231. Bibl, tables.

1946 –

Ayala Diago, César Augusto. El Movimiento de Acción Nacional (MAN): movilización y confluencia de idearios políticos durante el gobierno de Gustavo Rojas Pinilla. *Anuario Colombiano de Historia Social y de la Cultura*, no. 20 (1992), pp. 44 – 70. Bibl.

Barbosa Estepa, Reinaldo. *Guadalupe y sus centauros: memorias de la insurrección llanera* reviewed by Hermes Tovar Pinzón. *Anuario Colombiano de Historia Social y de la Cultura*, no. 20 (1992), pp. 169 – 172.

García Duarte, Ricardo. La paz esquiva: negociaciones, desencuentros y rediseño de estrategias. *Revista Javeriana*, v. 60, no. 590 (Nov – Dec 92), pp. 316 – 322.

Leal Buitrago, Francisco. La guerra y la paz en Colombia. *Nueva Sociedad*, no. 125 (May – June 93), pp. 157 – 161.

Noriega, Carlos Augusto. Las innovaciones políticas del gobierno Gaviria. *Revista Javeriana*, v. 61, no. 597 (Aug 93), pp. 129 – 142.

Vida nacional. *Revista Javeriana*, v. 60 – 61, no. 590 – 599 (Dec 92 – Oct 93), All issues.

Public works

Lucena Giraldo, Manuel. ¿Filántropos u oportunistas?: ciencia y política en los proyectos de obras públicas del Consulado de Cartagena de Indias, 1795 – 1810. *Revista de Indias*, v. 52, no. 195 – 196 (May – Dec 92), pp. 627 – 646. Bibl, maps.

Race question

La literatura y la medicina. *Desarrollo Indoamericano*, v. 23, no. 91 (June 93), pp. 20 – 21. Il.

Rural conditions

Ramírez Vallejo, Jorge. Una nueva mirada a la reforma agraria colombiana. *Planeación y Desarrollo*, v. 24, no. 1 (Jan – Apr 93), pp. 425 – 461. Bibl, tables, charts.

Social conditions

Clavijo, Sergio. Variaciones en el criterio sobre necesidades básicas: aplicación al caso colombiano. *Planeación y Desarrollo*, v. 24, no. 1 (Jan – Apr 93), pp. 367 – 382. Bibl, tables.

Escobar Herrán, Guillermo León. Tres años de confusión social. *Revista Javeriana*, v. 61, no. 597 (Aug 93), pp. 166 – 168.

Social policy

Cost

Castañeda, Tarcisio. Descentralización de los sectores sociales: riesgos y oportunidades. *Planeación y Desarrollo*, v. 24, no. 1 (Jan – Apr 93), pp. 97 – 115. Tables, charts.

COLOMBIAN LITERATURE

History and criticism

Cobo Borda, Juan Gustavo. Poesía y novela colombiana: años '80. *Revista Nacional de Cultura (Venezuela)*, v. 53, no. 285 (Apr – June 92), pp. 40 – 71. Bibl.

Tittler, Jonathan, ed. *Violencia y literatura en Colombia* reviewed by Hans Paschen. *Iberoamericana*, v. 17, no. 49 (1993), pp. 99 – 101.

Williams, Raymond Leslie. *The Colombian Novel, 1844 – 1987* reviewed by Gilberto Gómez Ocampo (Review entitled "Novela y poder en Colombia"). *La Palabra y el Hombre*, no. 81 (Jan – Mar 92), pp. 358 – 361.

COLOMBIAN POETRY

History and criticism

Cobo Borda, Juan Gustavo. Poesía y novela colombiana: años '80. *Revista Nacional de Cultura (Venezuela)*, v. 53, no. 285 (Apr – June 92), pp. 40 – 71. Bibl.

COLÓN, FERNANDO

Criticism and interpretation

Stolley, Karen. Sins of the Father: Hernando Colón's *Life of the Admiral*. *Latin American Literary Review*, v. 21, no. 41 (Jan – June 93), pp. 53 – 64. Bibl.

COLONIALISM

See

Imperialism

COLONIES

See

France – Colonies
Great Britain – Colonies
Portugal – Colonies
Spain – Colonies

COLONIZATION

See

Frontier and pioneer life
Land settlement

COLUMBUS, CHRISTOPHER

Andrade Rives, Santiago. La mentira de Cristóbal Colón. *La Palabra y el Hombre*, no. 81 (Jan – Mar 92), pp. 23 – 44. Bibl.

Anghiera, Pietro Martire d'. *De Orbe Novo Decades* reviewed by Keith Ellis. *Revista Canadiense de Estudios Hispánicos*, v. 17, no. 1 (Fall 92), pp. 221 – 223.

Barreto, Mascarenhas. *The Portuguese Columbus: Secret Agent of King John II* translated by Reginald A. Brown. Reviewed by Robert Kern. *Colonial Latin American Historical Review*, v. 2, no. 1 (Winter 93), pp. 114 – 117.

— *The Portuguese Columbus: Secret Agent of King John II* reviewed by David Henige. *Hispanic American Historical Review*, v. 73, no. 3 (Aug 93), pp. 505 – 506.

Briceño Perozo, Mario. La hazaña de Colón. *Boletín de la Academia Nacional de la Historia (Venezuela)*, v. 75, no. 300 (Oct – Dec 92), pp. 111 – 113.

Cristobal Colón y el descubrimiento en los cronistas: el arribo al Nuevo Mundo (Excerpts from the writings of several chroniclers). *Boletín de la Academia Nacional de la Historia (Venezuela)*, v. 75, no. 300 (Oct – Dec 92), pp. 127 – 152.

García Godoy, Cristián. A 500 años del descubrimiento de un nuevo mundo: Colón en Estados Unidos. *Revista de Historia de América*, no. 112 (July – Dec 91), pp. 63 – 84. Bibl, il.

Henige, David P. *In Search of Columbus: The Sources for the First Voyage* reviewed by Rosalind Z. Rock. *Colonial Latin American Historical Review*, v. 1, no. 1 (Fall 92), pp. 117 – 118.

— *In Search of Columbus: The Sources for the First Voyage* reviewed by Margarita Zamora (Review entitled "Searching for Columbus in the Quincentennial: Three Recent Books on the Discovery"). *Colonial Latin American Review*, v. 2, no. 1 – 2 (1993), pp. 261 – 267.

Kadir, Djelal. *Columbus and the Ends of the Earth: Europe's Prophetic Rhetoric as Conquering Ideology* reviewed by Margarita Zamora (Review entitled "Searching for Columbus in the Quincentennial: Three Recent Books on the Discovery"). *Colonial Latin American Review*, v. 2, no. 1 – 2 (1993), pp. 261 – 267.

— *Columbus and the Ends of the Earth: Europe's Prophetic Rhetoric as Conquering Ideology* reviewed by John Incledon. *Hispania (USA)*, v. 76, no. 2 (May 93), pp. 288 – 289.

— *Columbus and the Ends of the Earth: Europe's Prophetic Rhetoric as Conquering Ideology* reviewed by Martin Torodash. *Hispanic American Historical Review*, v. 73, no. 1 (Feb 93), p. 147.

Knight, Franklin W. Columbus and Slavery in the New World and Africa. *Revista/Review Interamericana*, v. 22, no. 1 – 2 (Spring – Summer 92), pp. 18 – 35. Bibl.

Marino, Ruggiero. Innocenzo VIII, il papa di Cristoforo Colombo. *Quaderni Ibero-Americani*, no. 72 (Dec 92), pp. 595 – 602. Bibl.

Martinengo, Alessandro. La utopía de Cristóbal Colón. *Quaderni Ibero-Americani*, no. 72 (Dec 92), pp. 554 – 563. Bibl.

Pérez de Tudela y Bueso, Juan. El descubrimiento: historia de secretos y de secretismos rigurosos. *Boletín de Historia y Antigüedades*, v. 80, no. 780 (Jan – Mar 93), pp. 31 – 70. Bibl.

Phillips, Carla Rahn and William D. Phillips, Jr. *The Worlds of Christopher Columbus* reviewed by Peter T. Bradley. *Bulletin of Latin American Research*, v. 12, no. 1 (Jan 93), pp. 109 – 110.

Proust, Marcel. El eclipse (Introduced and translated by Javier García Méndez). *Plural (Mexico)*, v. 22, no. 264 (Sept 93), pp. 40 – 42.

Rojas Guardia, Armando. El deslumbramiento del Almirante. *Boletín de la Academia Nacional de la Historia (Venezuela)*, v. 75, no. 300 (Oct – Dec 92), pp. 118 – 120.

— El deslumbramiento del Almirante. *Revista Nacional de Cultura (Venezuela)*, v. 54, no. 287 (Oct – Dec 92), pp. 234 – 236.

Sale, Kirkpatrick. *The Conquest of Paradise: Christopher Columbus and the Columbian Legacy* reviewed by Stelio Cro. *Revista de Indias*, v. 53, no. 197 (Jan – Apr 93), pp. 119 – 121.

Sten, María. Cristóbal Colón en Polonia. *Plural (Mexico)*, v. 22, no. 266 (Nov 93), pp. 63 – 67.

Tapajós, Vicente Costa Santos. Cristovão Colombo: o homem e o mito. *Revista do Instituto Histórico e Geográfico Brasileiro*, no. 371 (Apr – June 91), pp. 470 – 488. Bibl.

Taviani, Paolo Emilio. Fecha inolvidable: 12 de octubre de 1492; lugar: isla Guanahaní. *Atenea (Chile)*, no. 465 – 466 (1992), pp. 23 – 34. Il.

Thiemer-Sachse, Ursula. Un autógrafo de Cristóbal Colón (Cristóforo Colombo) en la colección especial de la biblioteca de la Universidad de Rostock. *Ibero-Amerikanisches Archiv*, v. 18, no. 3 – 4 (1992), pp. 523 – 541. Bibl, facs.

Tisnés Jiménez, Roberto María. La "leyenda negra" de los criminales descubridores. *Boletín de Historia y Antigüedades*, v. 79, no. 779 (Oct – Dec 92), pp. 1019 – 1035. Bibl.

Zherdinovskaya, Margarita. Colón en la polémica. *Plural (Mexico)*, v. 22, no. 262 (July 93), pp. 77 – 78.

Bibliography

Anastasia, Luis Víctor. Colón en la historiografía uruguaya. *Revista de Historia de América*, no. 113 (Jan – June 92), pp. 21 – 64.

Correspondence, reminiscences, etc.

Borello, Rodolfo A. Los diarios de Colón y el padre Las Casas. *Cuadernos Hispanoamericanos*, no. 512 (Feb 93), pp. 7 – 22. Bibl, il.

Martínez G., Miguel A. Recursos tecno-científicos que se conjugan en el descubrimiento de América. *Boletín de la Academia Nacional de la Historia (Venezuela)*, v. 75, no. 300 (Oct – Dec 92), pp. 79 – 88.

Rumeu de Armas, Antonio. *Libro copiador de Cristóbal Colón: correspondencia inédita con los reyes católicos sobre los viajes a América* reviewed by Margarita Zamora (Review entitled "Searching for Columbus in the Quincentennial: Three Recent Books on the Discovery"). *Colonial Latin American Review*, v. 2, no. 1 – 2 (1993), pp. 261 – 267.

Criticism of specific works

Diario

Bensen, Robert. Columbus at the Abyss: The Genesis of New World Literature. *Jamaica Journal*, v. 24, no. 3 (Feb 93), pp. 48 – 54. Bibl, il.

Diario de primera navegación

Chiareno, Osvaldo. Altre postille linguistiche al testo del *Libro de la primera navegación*. *Quaderni Ibero-Americani*, no. 72 (Dec 92), pp. 564 – 570.

Columbus, Christopher. *The 'Diario' of Christopher Columbus' First Voyage to America, 1492 – 1493* abstracted by Fray Bartolomé de las Casas; transcribed and translated by Oliver Dunn and James E. Kelley, Jr. Reviewed by Aaron P. Mahr. *Colonial Latin American Historical Review*, v. 1, no. 1 (Fall 92), pp. 122 – 124.

Milton, Heloisa Costa. O *Diário* de Cristóvão Colombo: discurso da "maravilha" americana. *Revista de Letras (Brazil)*, v. 32 (1992), pp. 169 – 183.

Fiction

Berrettini, Célia. O teatro de Lope de Vega e o descobrimento da América. *Vozes*, v. 86, no. 4 (July – Aug 92), pp. 66 – 71. Il, facs.

Cirillo, Teresa. Colombo bifronte. *Quaderni Ibero-Americani*, no. 72 (Dec 92), pp. 571 – 594. Bibl.

Martínez, Herminio. *Las puertas del mundo: una autobiografía hipócrita del Almirante* reviewed by Rafael H. Mojica. *World Literature Today*, v. 67, no. 2 (Spring 93), p. 336.

Minard, Evelyne. Un example d'utilisation de l'histoire par Ernesto Cardenal: El estrecho dudoso. *Caravelle*, no. 60 (1993), pp. 101 – 121. Bibl.

Ortega, José. Verdad poética e histórica en *Vigilia del Almirante*. *Cuadernos Hispanoamericanos*, no. 513 (Mar 93), pp. 108 – 111.

Pérez Villacampa, Gilberto. Enjuiciamiento advertido de la sombra de Colón. *Islas*, no. 98 (Jan – Apr 91), pp. 98 – 118.

Roa Bastos, Augusto Antonio. *Vigilia del Almirante* reviewed by Diego F. Barros. *Todo Es Historia*, v. 26, no. 310 (May 93), p. 82. Il.

— *Vigilia del Almirante* reviewed by Fabrizio Mejía Madrid (Review entitled "Al deseo por mar"). *Nexos*, v. 16, no. 185 (May 93), p. 81. Il.

— *Vigilia del Almirante* reviewed by Milagros Ezquerro (Review entitled "Don Quijote de la mar oceana"). *Cuadernos Hispanoamericanos*, no. 522 (Dec 93), pp. 128 – 134.

— *Vigilia del Almirante* reviewed by Sealtiel Alatriste (Review entitled "El mercado literario"). *Nexos*, v. 16, no. 182 (Feb 93), pp. 78 – 79.

— Vigilia del Almirante (Excerpt from the novel of the same title). *Nexos*, v. 16, no. 182 (Feb 93), pp. 53 – 58.

Stavans, Ilán. *Imagining Columbus: The Literary Voyage* reviewed by Elena M. Martínez. *Chasqui*, v. 22, no. 2 (Nov 93), pp. 170 – 171.

Monuments, etc.

Destéfani, Laurio Hedelvio. La Argentina y Colón. *Revista de Historia de América*, no. 113 (Jan – June 92), pp. 7 – 19. Bibl.

Poetry

Nava L., E. Fernando and Judith Orozco. El "Sistema de Cristóbal Colón" y la "Biografía de Colón": una muestra de poesía popular mexicana (Includes the two texts). *Cuadernos Americanos*, no. 42, Nueva época (Nov – Dec 93), pp. 203 – 241.

COLUMBUS, FERNANDO

See
   Colón, Fernando

COLUNGA, ALEJANDRO

Gómez Haco, Claudia. El "mysterium maximum" en la obra de Alejandro Colunga. *Artes de México*, no. 20 (Summer 93), pp. 117 – 119. Il.

COMECON COUNTRIES

See
   Europe, Eastern

COMIC BOOKS, STRIPS, ETC.

See also
   Caricatures and cartoons

Latin America

Birmajer, Marcelo. *Historieta: la imaginación al cuadrado* reviewed by Carlos Salá. *La Educación (USA)*, v. 36, no. 111 – 113 (1992), pp. 284 – 285.

Mexico

Hinds, Harold E., Jr. and Charles M. Tatum. *Not Just for Children: The Mexican Comic Book in the Late 1960s and 1970s* reviewed by Helen Delpar. *Hispanic American Historical Review,* v. 73, no. 4 (Nov 93), pp. 670 – 671.

— *Not Just for Children: The Mexican Comic Book in the Late 1960s and 1970s* reviewed by Cornelia Butler Flora. *Revista Interamericana de Bibliografía,* v. 42, no. 4 (1992), pp. 657 – 658.

Bibliography

Jones, Errol D. Ríus: Still a Thorn in the Side of the Mexican Establishment (Review article). *Studies in Latin American Popular Culture,* v. 12 (1993), pp. 221 – 227. Bibl.

United States

Barceló Aspeitia, Axel Arturo. Comics de amor y cohetes. *Nexos,* v. 16, no. 185 (May 93), pp. 88 – 89.

COMISIÓN NACIONAL DE DERECHOS HUMANOS (MEXICO)

Criticism of specific works

La contaminación atmosférica en México

Farquharson, Mary. Is It Safe to Breathe? *Business Mexico,* v. 3, no. 3 (Mar 93), pp. 32 – 35.

COMMERCE

See
    Foreign trade promotion
    Foreign trade regulation
    Trade routes
    Subdivision *Commerce* under names of Indian groups
    Subdivisions *Commerce* and *Foreign economic relations* under names of specific countries

COMMODITY AGREEMENTS

See
    Cartels and commodity agreements

COMMUNICATION

See
    Information services
    Information technology
    Mass media
    Rhetoric
    Telecommunication
    Telephone
    Writing

COMMUNISM

See also
    Marxism
    Socialism

Argentina

Korzeniewicz, Roberto P. Labor Unrest in Argentina, 1930 – 1943. *Latin American Research Review,* v. 28, no. 1 (1993), pp. 7 – 40. Bibl, tables.

Bolivia

García Fernández, Irsa Teresa. Aproximaciones para un estudio del trotskismo en Bolivia. *Islas,* no. 96 (May – Aug 90), pp. 78 – 82. Bibl.

Brazil

Prestes, Anita Leocadia. Luiz Carlos Prestes e a revolução socialista. *Vozes,* v. 87, no. 2 (Mar – Apr 93), pp. 11 – 17. Il.

Prestes, Maria. *Meu companheiro: 40 anos ao lado de Luiz Carlos Prestes* reviewed by Maurício Tragtemberg. *Vozes,* v. 87, no. 2 (Mar – Apr 93), pp. 97 – 101.

Costa Rica

Longley, Kyle. Peaceful Costa Rica: The First Battleground; The United States and the Costa Rican Revolution of 1948. *The Americas,* v. 50, no. 2 (Oct 93), pp. 149 – 175. Bibl.

Cuba

Cardoso, Eliana Anastasia and Ann Helwege. *Cuba after Communism* reviewed by Nicolás Sánchez. *Cuban Studies/Estudios Cubanos,* v. 23 (1993), pp. 210 – 213.

Fitzgerald, Frank T. *Managing Socialism: From Old Cadres to New Professionals in Revolutionary Cuba* reviewed by Linda Fuller (Review entitled "Cuba's 'Middle Class' "). *Latin American Perspectives,* v. 20, no. 1 (Winter 93), pp. 44 – 46.

Fleites-Lear, Marisela and Enrique Patterson. Teoría y praxis de la revolución cubana: apuntes críticos. *Nueva Sociedad,* no. 123 (Jan – Feb 93), pp. 50 – 64.

Developing countries

Utting, Peter. *Economic Reform and Third-World Socialism* reviewed by S. P. Chakravarty. *Bulletin of Latin American Research,* v. 12, no. 1 (Jan 93), pp. 122 – 124.

— *Economic Reform and Third-World Socialism: A Political Economy of Food Policy in Post-Revolutionary Societies* reviewed by Kenneth P. Jameson. *Journal of Developing Areas,* v. 27, no. 4 (July 93), pp. 543 – 544.

Latin America

Martínez Heredia, Fernando. El Che y el socialismo de hoy. *Casa de las Américas,* no. 189 (Oct – Dec 92), pp. 111 – 120.

Bibliography

Angell, Alan. The Left in Latin America since 1930: A Bibliographical Essay. *Historia (Chile),* no. 26 (1991 – 1992), pp. 61 – 70. Bibl.

Mexico

Carr, Barry. *Marxism and Communism in Twentieth-Century Mexico* reviewed by George Philip. *Bulletin of Latin American Research,* v. 12, no. 2 (May 93), pp. 230 – 231.

COMMUNITY CENTERS

Brazil

Miranda, Danilo Santos de. Descobertas em tom de aventura. *Problemas Brasileiros,* v. 30, no. 297 (May – June 93), pp. 26 – 29.

— No ritmo da mudança. *Problemas Brasileiros,* v. 30, no. 295 (Jan – Feb 93), pp. 69 – 70. Il.

Um palco de qualidade. *Problemas Brasileiros,* v. 30, no. 295 (Jan – Feb 93), p. 66. Il.

Colombia

COMPENSAR: Centro Urbano de Recreación (CUR). *Revista Javeriana,* v. 61, no. 592 (Mar 93), pp. 98 – 100. Il.

Panama

Pastor Núñez, Aníbal. Los centros comunales urbanos: una alternativa de extensión educativa y recreación social. *Revista Cultural Lotería,* v. 51, no. 390 (July – Aug 92), pp. 44 – 52. Bibl, il.

COMMUNITY DEVELOPMENT

See also
    Cooperatives
    Mutual benefit associations
    Non-governmental organizations

Brazil

Assies, Willem. *To Get out of the Mud: Neighborhood Associativism in Recife, 1964 – 1988* reviewed by Joe Foweraker. *Bulletin of Latin American Research,* v. 12, no. 3 (Sept 93), pp. 345 – 346.

— *To Get Out of the Mud: Neighborhood Associativism in Recife, 1964 – 1988* reviewed by Martine Droulers. *Cahiers des Amériques Latines,* no. 14 (1992), pp. 157 – 158.

— *To Get out of the Mud: Neighborhood Associativism in Recife, 1964 – 1988* reviewed by Vania Salles and João Francisco Souza. *Revista Mexicana de Sociología,* v. 54, no. 4 (Oct – Dec 92), pp. 251 – 257.

Chile

Arroyo, Gonzalo. Fundación Rodelillo: profesionales se sensibilizan en la ayuda de familias de sectores populares. *Mensaje,* v. 42, no. 421 (Aug 93), pp. 387 – 388. Il.

Dominican Republic

Douzant Rosenfeld, Denise and Laura Faxas. Equipements urbains et services de remplacement: le cas de Santo Domingo, République Dominicaine. *Tiers Monde,* v. 34, no. 133 (Jan – Mar 93), pp. 139 – 151.

Ecuador

Bebbington, Anthony et al. From Protest to Productivity: The Evolution of Indigenous Federations in Ecuador. *Grassroots Development,* v. 16, no. 2 (1992), pp. 11 – 21. Il.

El Salvador

La vida en la Comunidad Segundo Montes: prototipo de la nueva economía popular. *ECA; Estudios Centroamericanos,* v. 48, no. 534 – 535 (Apr – May 93), pp. 437 – 444.

Jamaica

Societies, etc.

Hart, Pansy Rae. Out to Build a New Jamaica. *Jamaica Journal,* v. 25, no. 1 (Oct 93), pp. 29 – 37. Il.

Latin America

Linares Pontón, María Eugenia, ed. *Del hecho al dicho hay menos trecho: ¿Qué hemos aprendido en los programas de apoyo a la familia para la crianza de los niños?* reviewed by María Bertha Fortoul O. *Revista Latinoamericana de Estudios Educativos,* v. 23, no. 1 (Jan – Mar 93), pp. 134 – 138. Il.

La nueva economía popular: realismo y utopía. *ECA; Estudios Centroamericanos,* v. 48, no. 539 (Sept 93), pp. 877 – 883. Il.

Mexico

Alonso, Claudio. La participación de las mujeres en el combate a la pobreza. *Fem,* v. 17, no. 120 (Feb 93), p. 44.

Herrasti Aguirre, María Emilia. La promoción inmobiliaria popular autogestiva: ¿Tendrá futuro? *El Cotidiano,* v. 10, no. 57 (Aug – Sept 93), pp. 17 – 22. Il.

Martínez Anaya, Efraín. San Miguel Teotongo: a contrapelo del neoliberalismo. *El Cotidiano,* v. 10, no. 57 (Aug – Sept 93), pp. 23 – 27. Tables.

Peru

Pásara, Luis H. et al. *La otra cara de la luna: nuevos actores sociales en el Perú* reviewed by Romeo Grompone (Review entitled "Nuevos actores"). *Debate (Peru),* v. 15, no. 70 (Sept – Oct 92), pp. 69 – 70.

United States

Pardo, Mary Santoli. Creating Community: Mexican American Women in Eastside Los Angeles. *Aztlán,* v. 20, no. 1 – 2 (Spring – Fall 91), pp. 39 – 71. Bibl.

COMMUNITY ORGANIZATION

Mexico

Miller, Simon and Arij Ouweneel, eds. *The Indian Community of Colonial Mexico: Fifteen Essays on Land Tenure, Corporate Organizations, Ideology, and Village Politics* reviewed by Margarita Menegus Bornemann. *Historia Mexicana,* v. 42, no. 1 (July – Sept 92), pp. 138 – 144.

Moctezuma Barragán, Pedro. El espejo desenterrado. *El Cotidiano,* v. 9, no. 54 (May 93), pp. 49 – 54. Il.

Peru

Diez Hurtado, Alejandro. El poder de las varas: los cabildos en Piura a fines de la colonia. *Apuntes (Peru),* no. 30 (Jan – June 92), pp. 81 – 90. Bibl, tables.

COMPADRINAZGO

See
Kinship

COMPETITION

Cortelesse, Claudio. Competitividad de los sistemas productivos y las empresas pequeñas y medianas: campo para la cooperación internacional. *Comercio Exterior,* v. 43, no. 6 (June 93), pp. 519 – 524.

Garretón, Oscar Guillermo. Seis comentarios sobre la empresa del siglo XXI. *Mensaje,* v. 42, no. 422 (Sept 93), pp. 432 – 439. Il.

Brazil

Barbosa, Margareth L. and Rosa M. O. Fontes. Efeitos da integração econômica do MERCOSUL e da Europa na competitividade das exportações brasileiras de soja. *Revista de Economia e Sociologia Rural,* v. 29, no. 4 (Oct – Dec 91), pp. 335 – 351. Bibl, tables.

Statistics

Façanha, Luís Otávio de Figueiredo and Denise A. Rodrigues. Indústria brasileira na década de '70: interpretação de resultados de estatística multivariada e de aspectos da dinâmica concorrencial. *Revista Brasileira de Economia,* v. 46, no. 4 (Oct – Dec 92), pp. 447 – 476. Bibl, tables.

Chile

Messner, Dirk. Shaping Competitiveness in the Chilean Wood-Processing Industry. *CEPAL Review,* no. 49 (Apr 93), pp. 117 – 137. Bibl, charts.

Colombia

Bonilla Muñoz, Guillermo and Horacio Osorio Velosa. Estructura de mercado y prácticas comerciales en los sectores industrial, minero – energético y de servicios públicos en Colombia. *Planeación y Desarrollo,* v. 24, no. 2 (May – Aug 93), pp. 191 – 256. Tables, charts.

González, Humberto. La industria de confecciones o la competitividad amenazada. *Revista Javeriana,* v. 61, no. 593 (Apr 93), pp. 163 – 166.

Urrutia Montoya, Miguel. Competencia y desarrollo económico. *Planeación y Desarrollo,* v. 24, no. 2 (May – Aug 93), pp. 49 – 72. Bibl, charts.

Law and legislation

Normas de 1992 sobre Competencia (Dec. 2153 del 30/dic/ 92). *Planeación y Desarrollo,* v. 24, no. 2 (May – Aug 93), pp. 145 – 190.

Orozco, Claudia. Marco legal para la promoción de la competencia en derecho comparado y en Colombia. *Planeación y Desarrollo,* v. 24, no. 2 (May – Aug 93), pp. 95 – 144. Bibl.

Latin America

Cebreros, Alfonso. La competitividad agropecuaria en condiciones de apertura económica. *Comercio Exterior,* v. 43, no. 10 (Oct 93), pp. 946 – 953. Bibl.

Quijano, José Manuel. Integración competitiva para los nuevos países industrializados en América Latina. *Integración Latinoamericana,* v. 18, no. 193 (Sept 93), pp. 3 – 11. Bibl, tables.

Law and legislation

Ibarra Pardo, Gabriel. Políticas de competencia en la integración en América Latina. *Integración Latinoamericana,* v. 18, no. 193 (Sept 93), pp. 45 – 51. Bibl.

Mexico

Delgado, Dora. Taking a Bite Out of Competition. *Business Mexico,* v. 3, no. 11 (Nov 93), pp. 23 – 26. Il.

Law and legislation

A Level Playing Field (Excerpts from *The New Federal Law of Economic Competition* published by the Secretariat of Commerce and Industrial Development/SECOFI, introduced by Joel Russell). *Business Mexico,* v. 3, no. 8 (Aug 93), pp. 4 – 7.

Mathematical models

Casar Pérez, José I. La competitividad de la industria manufacturera mexicana, 1980 – 1990. *El Trimestre Económico,* v. 60, no. 237 (Jan – Mar 93), pp. 113 – 183. Bibl, tables, charts.

Sources

Castañeda, Gabriel et al. Antecedentes económicos para una ley federal de competencia económica. *El Trimestre Económico,* v. 60, no. 237 (Jan – Mar 93), pp. 230 – 268. Bibl.

Peru

Amat y León, Carlos. La competitividad del sector agrícola. *Apuntes (Peru),* no. 30 (Jan – June 92), pp. 3 – 11.

Southern Cone of South America

Law and legislation

Halperín, Marcelo. Lealtad competitiva y dilemas de la integración: el caso del MERCOSUR. *Integración Latinoamericana,* v. 17, no. 184 (Nov 92), pp. 36 – 43.

COMPOSERS

Argentina

Helguera, Luis Ignacio. Astor Piazzolla. *Vuelta,* v. 17, no. 204 (Nov 93), pp. 64 – 65.

— Ginastera a diez años de su muerte. *Vuelta,* v. 17, no. 202 (Sept 93), pp. 67 – 69.

Herbort, Heinz Josef. "Jungla de silencio": una semblanza de la compositora Silvia Fómina (Translated by Carlos Caramés). *Humboldt,* no. 110 (1993), pp. 56 – 59. Il, facs.

Brazil

Holston, Mark. Playing the Heartstrings. *Américas,* v. 45, no. 5 (Sept – Oct 93), pp. 58 – 59. Il.

Magaldi, Cristina. Mozart Camargo Guarnieri (1907 – 1993). *Inter-American Music Review,* v. 13, no. 2 (Spring – Summer 93), pp. 168 – 170.

Peppercorn, Lisa M. *Villa-Lobos: The Music; An Analysis of His Style,* a translation of *Heitor Villa-Lobos: Leben und Werk des brasilianischen Komponist,* translated by Stefan de Haan (Review). *Inter-American Music Review,* v. 13, no. 2 (Spring – Summer 93), pp. 162 – 163. Bibl.

Reis, Sandra Loureiro de Freitas. A *Opera Tiradentes* de Manuel Joaquim de Macedo e Augusto de Lima. *Latin American Music Review,* v. 14, no. 1 (Spring – Summer 93), pp. 131 – 144. Bibl.

Toni, Flávia Camargo. Quatro concertos "progressistas" de Villa-Lobos. *Vozes,* v. 86, no. 6 (Nov – Dec 92), pp. 69 – 81. Il, facs.

Wright, Simon J. *Villa-Lobos* (Review). *Inter-American Music Review,* v. 13, no. 2 (Spring – Summer 93), p. 162.

— *Villa-Lobos* reviewed by E. Bradford Burns. *Hispanic American Historical Review,* v. 73, no. 4 (Nov 93), pp. 672 – 673.

— *Villa-Lobos* reviewed by Gerard Béhague. *Latin American Music Review,* v. 14, no. 2 (Fall – Winter 93), pp. 294 – 297.

Cuba

Cabrera Infante, Guillermo. Guantanamerías: sobre un emblema musical de los años '60. *Vuelta,* v. 17, no. 203 (Oct 93), pp. 11 – 13.

Mexico

Enríquez, Manuel. Blas Galindo Dimas (1910 – 1993). *Inter-American Music Review,* v. 13, no. 2 (Spring – Summer 93), pp. 171 – 172.

Peru

Estenssoro Fuchs, Juan Carlos. El mulato José Onofre de la Cadena: didáctica, estética musical y modernismo en el Perú del siglo XVIII. *Historia y Cultura (Peru),* no. 20 (1990), pp. 201 – 220.

Yep, Virginia. El vals peruano. *Latin American Music Review,* v. 14, no. 2 (Fall – Winter 93), pp. 268 – 280. Bibl, facs.

Interviews

Campos, José Carlos et al. Estado de la música en el Perú (An interview with five Peruvian composers). *Hueso Húmero,* no. 29 (May 93), pp. 93 – 104.

Uruguay

Aharonián, Coriún. Músicos uruguayos en el exterior (Segunda parte). *Hoy Es Historia,* v. 10, no. 59 (Sept – Oct 93), pp. 44 – 55. Bibl.

— Valores notables de la cultura uruguaya: músicos uruguayos en el exterior (Primera parte). *Hoy Es Historia,* v. 10, no. 55 (Jan – Feb 93), pp. 45 – 47.

Holston, Mark. The Composer's Muse as Master. *Américas,* v. 45, no. 3 (May – June 93), pp. 56 – 57. Il.

Manzino, Leonardo. La música uruguaya en los festejos de 1892 con motivo del IV centenario del encuentro de dos mundos. *Latin American Music Review,* v. 14, no. 1 (Spring – Summer 93), pp. 102 – 130. Bibl, facs.

COMPUTER INDUSTRY

See also
Automation
Information technology

Brazil

Cassiolato, José Eduardo and Hubert Schmitz, eds. *Hi-tech for Industrial Development: Lessons from the Brazilian Experience in Electronics and Automation* reviewed by Rhys Jenkins. *Bulletin of Latin American Research,* v. 12, no. 3 (Sept 93), pp. 349 – 350.

Fernandes, Rosângela. A informática nas relações internacionais. *Revista Brasileira de Estudos Políticos,* no. 76 (Jan 93), pp. 147 – 162. Bibl.

Profecias não concretizadas. *Problemas Brasileiros,* v. 30, no. 295 (Jan – Feb 93), pp. 35 – 36. Il.

Tonooka, Eduardo Kiyoshi. Política nacional de informática: vinte anos de intervenção governamental. *Estudos Econômicos,* v. 22, no. 2 (May – Aug 92), pp. 273 – 297. Bibl.

Mexico

Ayre, Shirley. Bobbing for Apples. *Business Mexico,* v. 3, no. 9 (Sept 93), pp. 12 – 15. Il.

Delgado, Dora. Taking a Bite Out of Competition. *Business Mexico,* v. 3, no. 11 (Nov 93), pp. 23 – 26. Il.

MacDonald, Christine. Duel of the Desk-Top Computers. *Business Mexico,* v. 3, no. 9 (Sept 93), pp. 4 – 6. Il.

Olvera Pomar, Daniel. The Information Trade. *Business Mexico,* v. 3, no. 11 (Nov 93), p. 38.

Serrano, Juan F. Computer Acquisition Policy. *Business Mexico,* v. 3, no. 9 (Sept 93), pp. 7 – 8.

COMUNERO REVOLUTION, 1779 – 1781

See
Subdivision *History* under *Colombia* and *Venezuela*

COMUNIDAD SEGUNDO MONTES, EL SALVADOR

La vida en la Comunidad Segundo Montes: prototipo de la nueva economía popular. *ECA; Estudios Centroamericanos,* v. 48, no. 534 – 535 (Apr – May 93), pp. 437 – 444.

CONCEIÇÃO, SÔNIA FÁTIMA DA
Criticism and interpretation

Durham, Carolyn Richardson. Sônia Fátima da Conceição's Literature for Social Change. *Afro-Hispanic Review,* v. 11, no. 1 – 3 (1992), pp. 21 – 25. Bibl.

CONCEPCIÓN, CHILE (CITY)

Campos Harriet, Fernando. La Real Audiencia de Concepción. *Atenea (Chile),* no. 465 – 466 (1992), pp. 151 – 156.

— La Real Audiencia de Concepción, 1565 – 1573. *Boletín de la Academia Chilena de la Historia,* v. 58 – 59, no. 102 (1991 – 1992), pp. 534 – 538.

CONCOLORCORVO

See
Carrió de la Vandera, Alonso

CONDÉ, MARYSE
Addresses, essays, lectures

Condé, Maryse. The Role of the Writer. *World Literature Today,* v. 67, no. 4 (Fall 93), pp. 697 – 699. Il.

Bibliography

Maryse Condé in *Books Abroad/World Literature Today,* 1973 – 1992. *World Literature Today,* v. 67, no. 4 (Fall 93), p. 710. Il.

Selected Bibliography (Maryse Condé). *World Literature Today,* v. 67, no. 4 (Fall 93), p. 709. Il.

Biography

Chronology (Maryse Condé). *World Literature Today,* v. 67, no. 4 (Fall 93), pp. 704 – 708. Il.

Criticism and interpretation

Arnold, Albert James. The Novelist as Critic. *World Literature Today,* v. 67, no. 4 (Fall 93), pp. 711 – 716. Il.

Herndon, Gerise. Gender Construction and Neocolonialism. *World Literature Today,* v. 67, no. 4 (Fall 93), pp. 731 – 736. Bibl, il.

Shelton, Marie-Denise. Condé: The Politics of Gender and Identity. *World Literature Today,* v. 67, no. 4 (Fall 93), pp. 717 – 722. Bibl, il.

Spear, Thomas C. Individual Quests and Collective History. *World Literature Today,* v. 67, no. 4 (Fall 93), pp. 723 – 730. Il.

Wylie, Harold A. The Cosmopolitan Condé, or, Unscrambling the Worlds. *World Literature Today,* v. 674, no. 4 (Fall 93), pp. 763 – 768. Il.

Criticism of specific works
Les derniers rois mages

Mortimer, Mildred P. A Sense of Place and Space in Maryse Condé's *Les derniers rois mages. World Literature Today,* v. 67, no. 4 (Fall 93), pp. 757 – 762. Bibl.

Moi, Tituba, sorcière . . . noire de Salem

Dukats, Mara L. A Narrative of Violated Maternity: *Moi, Tituba, sorcière . . . noire de Salem. World Literature Today,* v. 67, no. 4 (Fall 93), pp. 745 – 750. Bibl.

Manzor-Coats, Lillian. Of Witches and Other Things: Maryse Condé's Challenges to Feminist Discourse. *World Literature Today,* v. 67, no. 4 (Fall 93), pp. 737 – 744. Bibl, il.

Mudimbé-Boyi, Elizabeth. Giving Voice to Tituba: The Death of the Author? *World Literature Today,* v. 67, no. 4 (Fall 93), pp. 751 – 756. II.

LAS CONDES, CHILE

Lavín Infante, Joaquín. Las Condes: un nuevo plan regulador. *EURE,* v. 19, no. 57 (July 93), pp. 132 – 133.

CONFRATERNITIES
See
Subdivision *Societies, etc.* under *Catholic Church*

CONSEJO NACIONAL DE POLÍTICA ECONÓMICA Y SOCIAL (COLOMBIA)

Urrutia Montoya, Miguel. El Consejo Nacional de Política Económica y Social y la planeación en Colombia. *Planeación y Desarrollo,* v. 24, no. 1 (Jan – Apr 93), pp. 349 – 364.

CONSELHEIRO, ANTÔNIO
See
Maciel, Antônio Vicente Mendes

CONSERVATION OF NATURAL RESOURCES
See
Ecology
Energy policy
Forests
Marine resources
Natural resources
Power resources
Water

CONSERVATISM
Chile

Cristi, Renato and Carlos Ruiz. *El pensamiento conservador en Chile* reviewed by Simon Collier. *Hispanic American Historical Review,* v. 73, no. 4 (Nov 93), pp. 708 – 709.

— *El pensamiento conservador en Chile* reviewed by Patricio Silva. *Journal of Latin American Studies,* v. 25, no. 2 (May 93), pp. 429 – 430.

Latin America

Rachum, Ilan. Intellectuals and the Emergence of the Latin American Political Right, 1917 – 1936. *European Review of Latin American and Caribbean Studies,* no. 54 (June 93), pp. 95 – 110. Bibl.

Mexico

Mizrahi, Yemile. La nueva oposición conservadora en México: la radicalización política de los empresarios norteños. *Foro Internacional,* v. 32, no. 5 (Oct – Dec 92), pp. 744 – 771. Bibl, tables.

Venezuela

Pino Iturrieta, Elías. *Pensamiento conservador del siglo XIX* reviewed by Amaya Llebot Cazalis. *Revista Nacional de Cultura (Venezuela),* v. 54, no. 287 (Oct – Dec 92), pp. 262 – 264. II.

CONSERVATIVISM
Argentina

Deutsch, Sandra F. McGee and Ronald H. Dolkart, eds. *The Argentine Right: Its History and Intellectual Origins, 1910 to the Present* reviewed by Alberto Spektorowski. *Estudios Interdisciplinarios de América Latina y el Caribe,* v. 4, no. 1 (Jan – June 93), pp. 166 – 170.

CONSTANZÓ, MIGUEL

Moncada Maya, J. Omar. Miguel Constanzó y el reconocimiento geográfico de la costa de Veracruz de 1797. *Anuario de Estudios Americanos,* v. 49, Suppl. 2 (1992), pp. 31 – 64. Bibl.

CONSTITUTIONAL LAW
See
Subdivision *Constitutional law* under names of specific countries

CONSTRUCTION INDUSTRY
See also
Housing
Colombia
Statistics

Díaz, Jairo et al. Dinámica de la construcción entre 1950 y 1991. *Planeación y Desarrollo,* v. 24, no. 2 (May – Aug 93), pp. 263 – 313. Tables, charts.

Mexico

Barragán, Juan Ignacio. Cemento, vidrio y explosivos: empresarios del norte e importación de tecnología a principios del siglo XX. *Siglo XIX: Cuadernos,* v. 3, no. 6 (June 93), pp. 9 – 21.

Ziccardi, Alicia. *Las obras públicas de la ciudad de México, 1976 – 1982: política urbana e industria de la construcción* reviewed by Matilde Luna. *Revista Mexicana de Sociología,* v. 54, no. 4 (Oct – Dec 92), pp. 259 – 261.

CONSUMERS
See
Consumption (Economics)
Hispanic Americans as consumers (U.S.)

CONSUMPTION (ECONOMICS)

Chacón Vargas, Ramón Vicente. La sociedad de consumo, 1945 – 1960. *Boletín de la Academia Nacional de la Historia (Venezuela),* v. 75, no. 299 (July – Sept 92), pp. 109 – 133. Bibl.

Mathematical models

López Mejía, Alejandro. La teoría del ingreso permanente en un mercado de capitales imperfecto: el caso colombiano. *Planeación y Desarrollo,* v. 24, no. 1 (Jan – Apr 93), pp. 385 – 423. Bibl, tables.

CONTEMPORÁNEOS (PERIODICAL)

Garza Cuarón, Beatriz. La poética de José Gorostiza y "el grupo sin grupo" de la revista *Contemporáneos. Nueva Revista de Filología Hispánica,* v. 40, no. 2 (July – Dec 92), pp. 891 – 907. Bibl.

CONTINUING EDUCATION
See
Adult education

CONVENTS AND NUNNERIES
See also
Monasticism and religious orders
Congresses

Paniagua Pérez, Jesús. Congreso Internacional de Monacato Femenino en España, Portugal y América, 1492 – 1992. *Anuario de Estudios Americanos,* v. 49, Suppl. 1 (1992), pp. 213 – 215.

Argentina

Mayo, Carlos Alberto and Jaime Antonio Peire. Iglesia y crédito colonial: la política crediticia de los conventos de Buenos Aires, 1767 – 1810. *Revista de Historia de América,* no. 112 (July – Dec 91), pp. 147 – 157. Bibl.

Brazil

Dantas, Maria Teresa do Menino Jesus da Costa Pinto. *O Convento de Nossa Senhora das Mercês* reviewed by Raul Lima. *Revista do Instituto Histórico e Geográfico Brasileiro,* no. 373 (Oct – Dec 91), pp. 1208 – 1210.

Latin America

Arenal, Electa and Stacey Schlau, eds. *Untold Sisters: Hispanic Nuns in Their Own Works* translated by Amanda Powell. Reviewed by Noël Valis. *Colonial Latin American Review,* v. 2, no. 1 – 2 (1993), pp. 304 – 308.

Mexico

López García, Guadalupe. Los ángeles que habitan el claustro. *Fem,* v. 17, no. 122 (Apr 93), p. 43.

Reyes Valerio, Constantino. *El pintor de conventos: los murales del siglo XVI en la Nueva España* reviewed by Rogelio Ruiz Gomar. *Anales del Instituto de Investigaciones Estéticas,* v. 16, no. 62 (1991), pp. 208 – 215.

Spain

Arenal, Electa and Stacey Schlau, eds. *Untold Sisters: Hispanic Nuns in Their Own Works* translated by Amanda Powell. Reviewed by Noël Valis. *Colonial Latin American Review,* v. 2, no. 1 – 2 (1993), pp. 304 – 308.

COOKERY

See also
    Food habits

America

Robertiello, Jack. Pecan/Pacana/Nogueira Americana (Includes recipes). *Américas,* v. 45, no. 2 (Mar – Apr 93), pp. 54 – 55. Il.

Argentina

Elichondo, Margarita. *La comida criolla* reviewed by Félix Coluccio. *Folklore Americano,* no. 53 (Jan – June 92), p. 180.

Dominican Republic

Robertiello, Jack. It's Mealtime in Santo Domingo (Includes recipes). *Américas,* v. 45, no. 6 (Nov – Dec 93), pp. 58 – 59. Il.

El Salvador

Gross, Liza. Pupusas and Potpourri (Includes recipes). *Américas,* v. 45, no. 5 (Sept – Oct 93), p. 49. Il.

Guatemala

Robertiello, Jack. The Quest for Maya Meals (Includes recipes). *Américas,* v. 45, no. 3 (May – June 93), pp. 58 – 59. Il.

Mexico

Stoopen, María. *El universo de la cocina mexicana* reviewed by Susan N. Masuoka (Review entitled "Mexican Eating: The Work and the Haute Cuisine"). *Studies in Latin American Popular Culture,* v. 12 (1993), pp. 189 – 194.

COOPERATIVES

See also
    Agriculture, Cooperative

Belize

Selbert, Pamela. Pooling Forces on a Belizean Caye. *Américas,* v. 45, no. 6 (Nov – Dec 93), pp. 20 – 25. Il, maps.

Brazil

Souza, Maria Tereza Saraiva de. Uma estratégia de "marketing" para cooperativas de artesanato: o caso do Rio Grande do Norte. *RAE; Revista de Administração de Empresas,* v. 33, no. 1 (Jan – Feb 93), pp. 30 – 38. Bibl, tables, charts.

El Salvador

Montoya, Aquiles. El sector cooperativo: elemento clave para una estrategia de desarrollo popular. *ECA; Estudios Centroamericanos,* v. 48, no. 539 (Sept 93), pp. 855 – 873. Bibl, il, tables.

Paraguay

Law and legislation

Carbonell de Masy, Rafael. Análisis crítico de la ley vigente de cooperativas en el Paraguay. *Estudios Paraguayos,* v. 17, no. 1 – 2 (1989 – 1993), pp. 91 – 103.

COPÁN, HONDURAS

Webster, David et al. The Obsidian Hydration Dating Project at Copán: A Regional Approach and Why It Works. *Latin American Antiquity,* v. 4, no. 4 (Dec 93), pp. 303 – 324. Bibl, tables, charts.

COPPER INDUSTRY AND TRADE

Chile

Government ownership

Méndez G., Juan Carlos. Análisis de las fuentes de financiamiento de CODELCO. *Estudios Públicos (Chile),* no. 50 (Fall 93), pp. 281 – 343. Bibl, tables, charts.

COPYRIGHT

See also
    Intellectual property
    Trade marks

United States

Levy, David L. Use and Reproduction of Photographs: Copyright Issues. *SALALM Papers,* v. 34 (1989), pp. 135 – 140.

CORA, VLADIMIR

Nieto, Margarita. Vladimir Cora. *Latin American Art,* v. 4, no. 4 (Winter 92), pp. 80 – 81. Il.

CORDIS, ROSA, MADRE

See
    Erickson, Dorothy

CÓRDOBA, ARGENTINA (CITY)

Arcondo, Aníbal B. Mortalidad general, mortalidad epidémica y comportamiento de la población de Córdoba durante el siglo XVIII. *Desarrollo Económico (Argentina),* v. 33, no. 129 (Apr – June 93), pp. 67 – 85. Bibl, tables, charts.

Barros, Enrique F. et al. 75 años de la reforma universitaria: manifiesto liminar de la reforma universitaria. *Realidad Económica,* no. 118 (Aug – Sept 93), pp. 117 – 122.

Dellaferrera, Nelson C. *Catálogo de causas matrimoniales: obispado de Córdoba, 1688 – 1810* reviewed by Jesús María García Añoveros. *Revista de Indias,* v. 53, no. 197 (Jan – Apr 93), p. 101.

CÓRDOBA, ARGENTINA (PROVINCE)

Bixio, Beatriz and Luis D. Heredia. *Distancia cultural y lingüística: el fracaso escolar en poblaciones rurales del oeste de la provincia de Córdoba* (Review). *La Educación (USA),* v. 36, no. 111 – 113 (1992), pp. 296 – 298.

CÓRDOBA, MEXICO

Naveda Chávez-Hita, Adriana. Consideraciones sobre comercio y crédito en la villa de Córdoba, siglo XVIII. *La Palabra y el Hombre,* no. 83 (July – Sept 92), pp. 109 – 120. Bibl.

CÓRDOVA ITURREGUI, FÉLIX

Criticism of specific works

El momento divino de Caruso Llompart

Vázquez Arce, Carmen. Los desastres de la guerra: sobre la articulación de la ironía en los cuentos "La recién nacida sangre," de Luis Rafael Sánchez y "El momento divino de Caruso Llompart," de Félix Córdova Iturregui. *Revista Iberoamericana,* v. 59, no. 162 – 163 (Jan – June 93), pp. 187 – 201. Bibl.

CORN

Brazil

Silva, Gabriel Luiz Seraphico Peixoto da et al. Mudança tecnológica e produtividade do milho e da soja no Brasil. *Revista Brasileira de Economia,* v. 47, no. 2 (Apr – June 93), pp. 281 – 303. Bibl, tables.

Mathematical models

Carvalhais, Jane Noronha and João Eustáquio da Lima. Distribuição dos ganhos com inovação tecnológica na produção de milho entre categorias de pequenos produtores em Minas Gerais. *Revista de Economia e Sociologia Rural,* v. 29, no. 4 (Oct – Dec 91), pp. 373 – 385. Bibl.

Central America

Sluyter, Andrew. Long-Distance Staple Transport in Western Mesoamerica: Insights through Quantitative Modeling. *Ancient Mesoamerica,* v. 4, no. 2 (Fall 93), pp. 193 – 199. Bibl, tables, maps, charts.

Mexico

Cervantes Herrera, Joel and César Ramírez Miranda. México: del imperio del maíz al maíz del imperio. *Problemas del Desarrollo,* v. 24, no. 94 (July – Sept 93), pp. 97 – 112. Tables.

Hibon, Albéric et al. El maíz de temporal en México: tendencias, restricciones y retos. *Comercio Exterior,* v. 43, no. 4 (Apr 93), pp. 311 – 327. Bibl, tables, charts.

Salcedo, Salomón et al. Política agrícola y maíz en México: hacia el libre comercio norteamericano. *Comercio Exterior,* v. 43, no. 4 (Apr 93), pp. 302 – 310. Bibl, tables, charts.

CORNEJO M., LORENA

Delfau, Antonio. Benito Baranda y Lorena Cornejo: una vida solidaria. *Mensaje,* v. 42, no. 421 (Aug 93), pp. 374 – 375. Il.

CORONA, BERT

Correspondence, reminiscences, etc.

García, Mario T. Working for the Union. *Mexican Studies,* v. 9, no. 2 (Summer 93), pp. 241 – 257. Il.

CORONADO, FRANCISCO VÁZQUEZ DE

See
Vázquez de Coronado, Francisco

CORPORATE CULTURE

See
Industrial sociology

CORPORATE STATE

Castro Martínez, Pedro Fernando. Corporativismo y TLC: las viejas y nuevas alianzas del estado. *Plural (Mexico),* v. 22, no. 261 (June 93), pp. 63 – 73. Bibl.

Espinoza Valle, Víctor Alejandro and Tania Hernández Vicencio. Tendencias de cambio en la estructura corporativa mexicana: Baja California, 1989 – 1992. *El Cotidiano,* v. 8, no. 52 (Jan – Feb 93), pp. 25 – 29.

— Las transformaciones del corporativismo regional: relaciones estado – sindicato en el sector público de Baja California. *Frontera Norte,* v. 4, no. 8 (July – Dec 92), pp. 79 – 110.

Garza Toledo, Enrique de la. Reestructuración del corporativismo en México: siete tesis. *El Cotidiano,* v. 9, no. 56 (July 93), pp. 47 – 53. Il.

Salas Porras Soule, Alejandra. Globalización y proceso corporativo de los grandes grupos económicos en México. *Revista Mexicana de Sociología,* v. 54, no. 2 (Apr – June 92), pp. 133 – 162. Bibl, tables.

Semo, Ilán. El cardenismo revisado: la tercera vía y otras utopías inciertas. *Revista Mexicana de Sociología,* v. 55, no. 2 (Apr – June 93), pp. 197 – 223. Bibl.

CORPORATIONS

See
Business enterprises
International business enterprises
Names of specific corporations
Subdivision *Industries* under names of specific countries

CORRALES QUESADA, JORGE

Criticism of specific works

De la pobreza a la abundancia en Costa Rica

Irías, Jorge et al. De la pobreza a la abundancia o la abundancia de la pobreza. *Revista de Ciencias Sociales (Costa Rica),* no. 57 (Sept 92), pp. 79 – 86. Bibl.

CORREA, JUAN

Vargas Lugo, Elisa. Comentarios acerca de la construcción de retablos en México, 1687 – 1713. *Anales del Instituto de Investigaciones Estéticas,* v. 16, no. 62 (1991), pp. 93 – 101. Bibl.

CORRÊA DE AZEVEDO, LUIZ HEITOR

Obituaries

Béhague, Gerard. Luiz Heitor Corrêa de Azevedo (13 December 1905 – 10 November 1992). *Latin American Music Review,* v. 14, no. 1 (Spring – Summer 93), n.p. Il.

Luiz Heitor Corrêa de Azevedo (1905 – 1992). *Inter-American Music Review,* v. 13, no. 2 (Spring – Summer 93), pp. 166 – 167.

CORREAS, EDMUNDO

Obituaries

Campos Harriet, Fernando. Dr. Edmundo Correas, historiador de Cuyo: réquiem para un gran señor. *Boletín de la Academia Chilena de la Historia,* v. 58 – 59, no. 102 (1991 – 1992), pp. 39 – 40.

EL CORREO ESPAÑOL (NEWSPAPER)

Herrero Rubio, Alejandro and Fabián Herrero. A propósito de la prensa española en Buenos Aires: el estudio de un caso: *El Correo Español,* 1872 – 1875. *Anuario de Estudios Americanos,* v. 49, Suppl. 1 (1992), pp. 107 – 120.

CORRIDOS

See
Folk music

CORRIENTES, ARGENTINA (PROVINCE)

Chiaramonte, José Carlos. *Mercaderes del litoral: economía y sociedad en la provincia de Corrientes, primera mitad del siglo XIX* reviewed by Jerry W. Cooney. *Hispanic American Historical Review,* v. 73, no. 2 (May 93), pp. 322 – 323.

CORRUPTION (IN POLITICS)

See also
Patronage, Political

La corrupción: ¡No nos quedemos en la periferia! *Mensaje,* v. 42, no. 418 (May 93), pp. 115 – 116.

Brazil

Carvalho, Carlos Eduardo Vieira de. Brasil: la caída de Collor. *Nueva Sociedad,* no. 124 (Mar – Apr 93), pp. 22 – 26.

Flynn, Peter. Collor, Corruption, and Crisis: Time for Reflection. *Journal of Latin American Studies,* v. 25, no. 2 (May 93), pp. 351 – 371. Bibl.

Pires, Nielsen de Paula. Brasil: transición, crisis y triunfo de la democracia. *Mensaje,* v. 42, no. 417 (Mar – Apr 93), pp. 79 – 81. Il.

Santos, Theotonio dos. Brazil's Controlled Purge: The Impeachment of Fernando Collor (Translated by Phillip Berryman). *NACLA Report on the Americas,* v. 27, no. 3 (Nov – Dec 93), pp. 17 – 21. Il.

Weyland, Kurt. The Rise and Fall of President Collor and Its Impact on Brazilian Democracy. *Journal of Inter-American Studies and World Affairs,* v. 35, no. 1 (1993), pp. 1 – 37. Bibl.

Chile

Orrego Larraín, Claudio. ¿Corrupción en Chile? *Mensaje,* v. 42, no. 418 (May 93), p. 159.

Guyana

Brana-Shute, Gary. Guyana '92: It's About Time. *Hemisphere,* v. 5, no. 2 (Winter – Spring 93), pp. 40 – 44. Maps.

Latin America

Andreas, Peter. Profits, Poverty, and Illegality: The Logic of Drug Corruption. *NACLA Report on the Americas,* v. 27, no. 3 (Nov – Dec 93), pp. 22 – 28 + . Bibl.

Bell, Daniel. La corrupción y la política de la reforma (Translated by Rubén Gallo). *Vuelta,* v. 17, no. 202 (Sept 93), pp. 41 – 43.

Bravo Lira, Bernardino. Democracia: ¿Antídoto frente a la corrupción? *Estudios Públicos (Chile),* no. 52 (Spring 93), pp. 299 – 308.

Perelli, Carina. Corruption and Democracy. *Hemisphere,* v. 5, no. 2 (Winter – Spring 93), pp. 31 – 32. Il.

Peru

Brenot, Anne-Marie. *Pouvoirs et profits au Pérou colonial au XVIIIᵉ siècle: gouverneurs, clientèles et ventes forcées* reviewed by Pierre Ragon. *Cahiers des Amériques Latines*, no. 14 (1992), pp. 152 – 153.

Río de la Plata region

Saguier, Eduardo Ricardo. La corrupción de la burocracia colonial borbónica y los orígenes del federalismo: el caso del virreinato del Río de la Plata. *Jahrbuch für Geschichte von Staat, Wirtschaft und Gesellschaft Lateinamerikas*, v. 29 (1992), pp. 149 – 177. Bibl.

United States

Byrne, Malcolm and Peter R. Kornbluh. Iran – Contra: A Postmortem. *NACLA Report on the Americas*, v. 27, no. 3 (Nov – Dec 93), pp. 29 – 34 +. Il.

Venezuela

Ellner, Steven B. A Tolerance Worn Thin: Corruption in the Age of Austerity. *NACLA Report on the Americas*, v. 27, no. 3 (Nov – Dec 93), pp. 13 – 16 +. Bibl, il.

CORTÁZAR, AUGUSTO RAÚL

Coluccio, Félix. Augusto Raúl Cortázar a dieciocho años de su muerte. *Folklore Americano*, no. 53 (Jan – June 92), pp. 153 – 155.

CORTÁZAR, JULIO

Criticism and interpretation

Elbanowski, Adam. El espacio y lo fantástico en la cuentística de Cortázar. *La Palabra y el Hombre*, no. 81 (Jan – Mar 92), pp. 273 – 278. Bibl.

Peavler, Terry J. *Julio Cortázar* reviewed by Alfred MacAdam. *Hispanic Review*, v. 61, no. 2 (Spring 93), pp. 310 – 312.

Rodríguez-Luis, Julio. *The Contemporary Praxis of the Fantastic: Borges and Cortázar* reviewed by John Incledon. *Hispania (USA)*, v. 76, no. 1 (Mar 93), p. 89.

— *The Contemporary Praxis of the Fantastic: Borges and Cortázar* reviewed by John Incledon. *Revista de Crítica Literaria Latinoamericana*, v. 19, no. 38 (July – Dec 93), pp. 403 – 404.

Vargas Llosa, Mario. La trompeta de Deyá. *Vuelta*, v. 17, no. 195 (Feb 93), pp. 10 – 14.

Criticism of specific works

Apocalipsis de Solentiname

Pons, María Cristina. Compromiso político y ficción en "Segunda vez" y "Apocalipsis de Solentiname" de Julio Cortázar. *Revista Mexicana de Sociología*, v. 54, no. 4 (Oct – Dec 92), pp. 183 – 203. Bibl.

Las babas del diablo

Báez Báez, Edith María. Versiones de la realidad en "Las babas del diablo" de Cortázar. *Hispanic Journal*, v. 14, no. 1 (Spring 93), pp. 47 – 61. Bibl.

Continuidad de los parques

Isava, Luis Miguel. La escritura, la lectura, lo fantástico: análisis de "Continuidad de los parques" de Julio Cortázar. *Revista Nacional de Cultura (Venezuela)*, v. 54, no. 287 (Oct – Dec 92), pp. 72 – 82. Bibl, il.

Juan-Navarro, Santiago. 79 ó 99/modelos para desarmar: claves para una lectura morelliana de "Continuidad de los parques" de Julio Cortázar. *Hispanic Journal*, v. 13, no. 2 (Fall 92), pp. 241 – 249. Bibl.

La noche boca arriba

Vallejo, Catharina Vanderplaats de. *La noche boca arriba* de Julio Cortázar: la estética como síntesis entre dos cosmovisiones. *Káñina*, v. 16, no. 2 (July – Dec 92), pp. 115 – 120. Bibl.

Rayuela

Cruz, Jacqueline. Reflexiones y reflejos: *Rayuela* como una novela de espejos. *Chasqui*, v. 22, no. 2 (Nov 93), pp. 24 – 33. Bibl.

Sicard, Alain. Poder de la escritura: ¿El crepúsculo de los chamanes? *Revista de Crítica Literaria Latinoamericana*, v. 19, no. 38 (July – Dec 93), pp. 155 – 162.

Segunda vez

Pons, María Cristina. Compromiso político y ficción en "Segunda vez" y "Apocalipsis de Solentiname" de Julio Cortázar. *Revista Mexicana de Sociología*, v. 54, no. 4 (Oct – Dec 92), pp. 183 – 203. Bibl.

Verano

Young, Richard A. "Verano" de Julio Cortázar, *The Nightmare* de John Henry Fuseli y "the judicious adoption of figures in art." *Revista Canadiense de Estudios Hispánicos*, v. 17, no. 2 (Winter 93), pp. 373 – 382. Bibl.

Interviews

Fuentes, José Lorenzo. Cortázar habla de las manos en la máquina de escribir. *Plural (Mexico)*, v. 22, no. 258 (Mar 93), pp. 48 – 49.

CORTEN, ANDRÉ

Criticism of specific works

El estado débil

Yunén, Rafael Emilio. André Corten y la debilidad del estado. *Estudios Sociales (Dominican Republic)*, v. 26, no. 93 (July – Sept 93), pp. 41 – 60.

CORTÉS, BENJAMÍN ALFONSO

Espinosa López, Elia. Gramática y lenguaje del orden y el caos. *Anales del Instituto de Investigaciones Estéticas*, v. 16, no. 62 (1991), pp. 139 – 150. Bibl, il.

CORTEZ, HERNANDO

Martínez, José Luis. *Hernán Cortés* reviewed by Bernard Grunberg. *Caravelle*, no. 60 (1993), pp. 138 – 139.

— *Hernán Cortés* reviewed by María Justina Sarabia Viejo. *Anuario de Estudios Americanos*, v. 49, Suppl. 2 (1992), pp. 252 – 253.

Morino, Angelo. Hernán Cortés e la regina Calafia. *Quaderni Ibero-Americani*, no. 72 (Dec 92), pp. 603 – 620. Bibl.

Correspondence, reminiscences, etc.

Axer, Jersy. Una carta: correspondencia de Hernán Cortés con Jan Dantyszek (Includes the reproduction of one letter by Hernando Cortez). *Plural (Mexico)*, v. 22, no. 266 (Nov 93), pp. 68 – 72. Bibl.

Sources

Baudot, Georges. Malintzin, imagen y discurso de mujer en el primer México virreinal. *Cuadernos Americanos*, no. 40, Nueva época (July – Aug 93), pp. 181 – 207. Bibl.

COSMOLOGY

Covarrubias, Javier. La tecnología del sacrificio: la idea del "calor" y otros mitos encontrados. *Plural (Mexico)*, v. 22, no. 258 (Mar 93), pp. 18 – 28. Bibl.

Dover, Robert V. H. *Andean Cosmologies through Time: Persistence and Emergence* reviewed by Jean-Jacques Decoster. *Latin American Indian Literatures Journal*, v. 9, no. 1 (Spring 93), pp. 73 – 78.

Fabian, Stephen Michael. *Space – Time of the Bororo of Brazil* reviewed by Gary Urton. *Hispanic American Historical Review*, v. 73, no. 3 (Aug 93), pp. 496 – 498.

Lienhard, Martín. La cosmología poética en los waynos quechuas tradicionales. *Revista de Crítica Literaria Latinoamericana*, v. 19, no. 37 (Jan – June 93), pp. 87 – 103. Bibl.

Pinto, Márnio Teixeira. Corpo, morte e sociedade: um ensaio a partir da forma e da razão de se esquartejar um inimigo. *Revista Brasileira de Ciências Sociais*, v. 8, no. 21 (Feb 93), pp. 52 – 67. Bibl, charts.

COSSA, ROBERTO M.

Criticism of specific works

Angelito

Ciria, Alberto. La historia argentina en el teatro de Roberto Cossa: a propósito de *Angelito*. *Revista Interamericana de Bibliografía*, v. 42, no. 4 (1992), pp. 577 – 583. Bibl.

Gris de ausencia

Giella, Miguel Angel. Inmigración y exilio: el limbo del lenguaje. *Latin American Theatre Review*, v. 26, no. 2 (Spring 93), pp. 111 – 121. Bibl.

COST AND STANDARD OF LIVING

See also
Inflation (Finance)
Quality of life
Subdivision *Social conditions* under names of specific
countries

Caribbean area

Ramsaran, Ramesh. Growth, Employment, and the Standard
of Living in Selected Commonwealth Caribbean Countries.
Caribbean Studies, v. 25, no. 1 – 2 (Jan – July 92), pp.
103 – 122. Tables.

Cuba

Aldereguía Henriques, Jorge. Cuba: orientación humanista de
su desarrollo económico – social. *Problemas del Desarrollo,*
v. 24, no. 94 (July – Sept 93), pp. 191 – 207. Tables, charts.

Mexico

Cohen, Joshua A. Filling the Basket. *Business Mexico,* v. 3,
no. 12 (Dec 93), pp. 19 – 20. Tables, charts.

— The Myth of "Economical" Mexico. *Business Mexico,* v. 3,
no. 7 (July 93), pp. 38 – 39. Tables.

Márquez, Viviane Brachet de and Margaret Sherraden. Austeridad fiscal, el estado de bienestar y el cambio político: los
casos de la salud y la alimentación en México, 1970 – 1990
(Translated by Armando Castellanos). *Estudios Sociológicos,* v. 11, no. 32 (May – Aug 93), pp. 331 – 364. Bibl, tables.

Peru

Davies, Thomas M., Jr. Disintegration of a Culture: Peru into
the 1990s. *SALALM Papers,* v. 36 (1991), pp. 42 – 48.

COSTA, OLGA

Obituaries

Martínez, Jesús. Olga Costa: "in memoriam." *Plural (Mexico),*
v. 22, no. 263 (Aug 93), pp. 68 – 69.

COSTA RICA

See also
Advertising – Costa Rica
Agriculture and state – Costa Rica
AIDS (Disease) – Costa Rica
Alcohol – Costa Rica
Archaeological site reports – Costa Rica
Artists – Costa Rica
Banana trade – Costa Rica
Blacks – Costa Rica
Books – Costa Rica
Child abuse – Costa Rica
Childbirth – Costa Rica
Church and social problems – Costa Rica
Church and state – Costa Rica
Cities and towns – Costa Rica
Coffee – Costa Rica
Communism – Costa Rica
Crime and criminals – Costa Rica
Democracy – Costa Rica
Drugs, Illegal – Costa Rica
Ecology – Costa Rica
Ecology and development – Costa Rica
Economic assistance, Foreign – Costa Rica
Education, Bilingual – Costa Rica
Education, Secondary – Costa Rica
Education and state – Costa Rica
Elections – Costa Rica
Environmental policy – Costa Rica
Ethnicity – Costa Rica
Family – Costa Rica
Fertilizer industry – Costa Rica
Food industry and trade – Costa Rica
Forests – Costa Rica
Germans – Costa Rica
Gold – Costa Rica
Guanacaste, Costa Rica
Haciendas – Costa Rica
Harbors – Costa Rica
Industrial promotion – Costa Rica
Journalism – Costa Rica
Labor laws and legislation – Costa Rica
Land tenure – Costa Rica
Liberalism – Costa Rica
Liberia, Costa Rica
Limón, Costa Rica

Literary criticism – Costa Rica
Literature and society – Costa Rica
Marriage – Costa Rica
Medicine – Costa Rica
Mural painting and decoration – Costa Rica
Musicians – Costa Rica
Nationalism – Costa Rica
Natural resources – Costa Rica
Papagayo site, Costa Rica
Parks – Costa Rica
Peasantry – Costa Rica
Petroleum industry and trade – Costa Rica
Philosophy – Costa Rica
Political parties – Costa Rica
Political sociology – Costa Rica
Press – Costa Rica
Press and politics – Costa Rica
Public health – Costa Rica
Public opinion – Costa Rica
Publishers and publishing – Costa Rica
Railroads – Costa Rica
Regional planning – Costa Rica
San José, Costa Rica
Science – Costa Rica
Sexual behavior – Costa Rica
Social conflict – Costa Rica
Social movements – Costa Rica
Social services – Costa Rica
Socialization – Costa Rica
Sociology – Costa Rica
Sociology, Urban – Costa Rica
Street children – Costa Rica
Students – Costa Rica
Tariff – Costa Rica
Teaching and teachers – Costa Rica
Television – Costa Rica
Tourist trade – Costa Rica
Trade unions – Costa Rica
Universities and colleges – Costa Rica
Wages – Costa Rica
West Indians – Costa Rica
Women – Costa Rica
Women artists – Costa Rica
Women authors – Costa Rica
Women in literature – Costa Rica

Antiquities

Baudez, Claude-François et al. *Papagayo: un hameau précolombien du Costa Rica* reviewed by Frederick W. Lange.
Latin American Antiquity, v. 4, no. 4 (Dec 93), pp. 390 –
392.

Corrales Ulloa, Francisco. Investigaciones arqueológicas en el
Pacífico central de Costa Rica. *Vínculos,* v. 16, no. 1 – 2
(1990), pp. 1 – 29. Bibl, il, tables, maps.

Corrales Ulloa, Francisco and Ifigenia Quintanilla Jiménez. El
Pacífico central de Costa Rica y el intercambio regional.
Vínculos, v. 16, no. 1 – 2 (1990), pp. 111 – 126. Bibl, tables,
maps.

Guerrero Miranda, Juan Vicente et al. Entierros secundarios y
restos orgánicos de ca. 500 a.c. preservados en una área
de inundación marina, golfo de Nicoya, Costa Rica. *Vínculos,* v. 17, no. 1 – 2 (1991), pp. 17 – 51. Bibl, il, tables,
maps.

Herrera Villalobos, Anaysy and Felipe Solís del Vecchio. Lomas Entierros: un centro político prehispánico en la cuenca
baja del Río Grande de Tárcoles. *Vínculos,* v. 16, no. 1 – 2
(1990), pp. 85 – 110. Bibl, il, tables, maps.

Odio Orozco, Eduardo. La Pochota: un complejo cerámico
temprano en las tierras bajas del Guanacaste, Costa Rica.
Vínculos, v. 17, no. 1 – 2 (1991), pp. 1 – 16. Bibl, il, tables,
maps.

Quintanilla Jiménez, Ifigenia. La Malla: un sitio arqueológico
asociado con el uso de recursos del Manglar de Tivives,
Pacífico central de Costa Rica. *Vínculos,* v. 16, no. 1 – 2
(1990), pp. 57 – 83. Bibl, il, tables, maps.

Solís Alpízar, Olman E. Jesús María: un sitio con actividad
doméstica en el Pacífico central, Costa Rica. *Vínculos,* v.
16, no. 1 – 2 (1990), pp. 31 – 56. Bibl, il.

Cultural policy

Cuevas Molina, Rafael. Estado y cultura en Guatemala y
Costa Rica. *Anuario de Estudios Centroamericanos,* v. 18,
no. 2 (1992), pp. 25 – 39. Bibl.

Discovery and exploration

Solórzano Fonseca, Juan Carlos. La búsqueda de oro y la resistencia indígena: campañas de exploración y conquista de Costa Rica, 1502 – 1610. *Mesoamérica (USA)*, v. 13, no. 24 (Dec 92), pp. 313 – 363. Bibl.

Economic conditions

Rivera, Rolando and David Smith. Organización, movilización popular y desarrollo regional en el Atlántico costarricense. *Estudios Rurales Latinoamericanos*, v. 15, no. 2 – 3 (May – Dec 92), pp. 79 – 110. Tables.

Economic policy

Calvo Coin, Luis Alberto. Las políticas económicas aplicadas en Costa Rica y los orígenes y bases de la política económica neoliberal o neoclásica. *Revista de Ciencias Sociales (Costa Rica)*, no. 60 (June 93), pp. 101 – 115. Bibl.

Edelman, Marc and Rodolfo Monge Oviedo. Costa Rica: The Non-Market Roots of Market Success. *Report on the Americas*, v. 26, no. 4 (Feb 93), pp. 22 – 29 +. Bibl, il.

Sandoval García, Carlos. Programas de ajuste estructural e industria de la publicidad en Costa Rica. *Revista de Ciencias Sociales (Costa Rica)*, no. 57 (Sept 92), pp. 17 – 29. Bibl, tables.

Foreign relations

United States

Longley, Kyle. Peaceful Costa Rica: The First Battleground; The United States and the Costa Rican Revolution of 1948. *The Americas*, v. 50, no. 2 (Oct 93), pp. 149 – 175. Bibl.

Historiography

Gil Zúñiga, José Daniel. Nuestra historia: un intento de popularizar la historia. *Revista de Historia (Costa Rica)*, no. 25 (Jan – June 92), pp. 229 – 233.

Palmer, Steven. Getting to Know the Unknown Soldier: Offical Nationalism in Liberal Costa Rica, 1880 – 1900. *Journal of Latin American Studies*, v. 25, no. 1 (Feb 93), pp. 45 – 72. Bibl, maps.

Quesada Monge, Rodrigo. El paraíso perdido: nueva historia y utopía en Costa Rica. *Revista de Historia (Costa Rica)*, no. 26 (July – Dec 92), pp. 187 – 200. Bibl.

History

Lehoucq, Fabrice Edouard. Conflicto de clases, crisis política y destrucción de las prácticas democráticas en Costa Rica: reevaluando los orígenes de la guerra civil de 1948. *Revista de Historia (Costa Rica)*, no. 25 (Jan – June 92), pp. 65 – 96. Bibl.

Dictionaries and encyclopedias

Creedman, Theodore S. *Historical Dictionary of Costa Rica* reviewed by Kenneth J. Grieb. *The Americas*, v. 49, no. 3 (Jan 93), pp. 426 – 427.

— *Historical Dictionary of Costa Rica*, 2d edition, reviewed by Lowell Gudmundson. *Mesoamérica (USA)*, v. 13, no. 23 (June 92), p. 178.

Sources

Ibarra Rojas, Eugenia. Documentos para el estudio de la participación indígena en la campaña nacional de 1856. *Revista de Historia (Costa Rica)*, no. 25 (Jan – June 92), pp. 245 – 250. Bibl, tables.

Politics and government

Chinchilla Coto, José Carlos. Estado y democracia en la sociedad costarricense contemporánea. *Anuario de Estudios Centroamericanos*, v. 18, no. 2 (1992), pp. 101 – 114. Bibl.

Salazar Mora, Orlando. *El apogeo de la república liberal en Costa Rica, 1870 – 1914* reviewed by Fernando González Davidson. *Mesoamérica (USA)*, v. 13, no. 23 (June 92), pp. 179 – 182.

Social policy

Miller, Eugene D. Labour and the War-Time Alliance in Costa Rica, 1943 – 1948. *Journal of Latin American Studies*, v. 25, no. 3 (Oct 93), pp. 515 – 541. Bibl, tables.

COSTA RICAN LITERATURE

Berrón, Linda, ed. *Relatos de mujeres: antología de narradoras de Costa Rica* reviewed by Judy Berry-Bravo. *Chasqui*, v. 22, no. 2 (Nov 93), pp. 153 – 154.

Jaramillo Levi, Enrique, ed. *When New Flowers Bloomed: Short Stories by Women Writers from Costa Rica and Panama* reviewed by Cynthia Tompkins. *World Literature Today*, v. 67, no. 1 (Winter 93), pp. 164 – 165. Il.

History and criticism

Chaverri, Amalia. Génesis y evolución de los títulos de la novelística costarricense. *Canadian Journal of Latin American and Caribbean Studies*, v. 17, no. 34 (1992), pp. 73 – 95. Bibl, tables.

Quesada Soto, Alvaro. Identidad nacional y literatura nacional en Costa Rica: la "generación del Olimpo." *Canadian Journal of Latin American and Caribbean Studies*, v. 17, no. 34 (1992), pp. 97 – 113. Bibl.

COTTON

Argentina

Guy, Donna Jane. "Oro Blanco": Cotton, Technology, and Family Labor in Nineteenth-Century Argentina. *The Americas*, v. 49, no. 4 (Apr 93), pp. 457 – 478. Bibl.

Brazil

Mathematical models

Carvalho, Flávio Condé de and Samira Aóun Marques. Concentração municipal do beneficiamento de algodão no estado do Paraná nos anos oitenta. *Revista de Economia e Sociologia Rural*, v. 30, no. 2 (Apr – June 92), pp. 149 – 157. Bibl, tables.

Mexico

Aguirre Anaya, Carmen. Industria y tecnología: motricidad en los textiles de algodón en el XIX. *Siglo XIX: Cuadernos*, v. 3, no. 6 (June 93), pp. 23 – 33. Bibl.

Echanove Huacuja, Flavia. El mercado del algodón: políticas de Estados Unidos y México y el Tratado de Libre Comercio. *Comercio Exterior*, v. 43, no. 11 (Nov 93), pp. 1046 – 1051. Bibl, tables.

United States

Echanove Huacuja, Flavia. El mercado del algodón: políticas de Estados Unidos y México y el Tratado de Libre Comercio. *Comercio Exterior*, v. 43, no. 11 (Nov 93), pp. 1046 – 1051. Bibl, tables.

COUPS D'ÉTAT

See also
  Military in government
  Revolutions

Argentina

Villalba, Miguel Angel. La revolución radical de 1933 en paso de los libres. *Todo Es Historia*, v. 27, no. 311 (June 93), pp. 8 – 24. Bibl, il, maps.

Brazil

Moraes, Dênis de. *A esquerda e o golpe de '64: vinte e cinco anos depois, as forças populares repensam seus mitos, sonhos, e ilusões* reviewed by Cliff Welch. *Hispanic American Historical Review*, v. 73, no. 1 (Feb 93), p. 170.

Guatemala

Berger, Susan A. Guatemala: Coup and Countercoup. *NACLA Report on the Americas*, v. 27, no. 1 (July – Aug 93), pp. 4 – 7. Il.

Hernández Pico, Juan. Guatemala: ¿Fructificará la democracia? *ECA; Estudios Centroamericanos*, v. 48, no. 536 (June 93), pp. 545 – 562. Il.

Osorio Paz, Saúl. Golpe de estado y situación socioeconómica en Guatemala. *Momento Económico*, no. 69 (Sept – Oct 93), pp. 20 – 23.

COURTS

See
  Judiciary

COUVE, ADOLFO

Criticism and interpretation

Cecereu Lagos, Luis Enrique. A propósito de Couve y Hagel, narradores. *Aisthesis*, no. 24 (1991), pp. 79 – 102. Bibl.

COWBOYS

See
Frontier and pioneer life
Gauchos

CREATION (LITERARY, ARTISTIC, ETC.)

See also
Fiction
Poetry
Writing

Garmendia, Salvador. Por qué escribo. *Inti,* no. 37 – 38 (Spring – Fall 93), pp. 263 – 272.

Grizzolle Gómez, Juan. *La creación literaria en los niños: cómo estimular la creatividad* reviewed by Alberto Gómez Martínez. *La Educación (USA),* v. 36, no. 111 – 113 (1992), pp. 294 – 295.

Heker, Liliana. Los talleres literarios. *Cuadernos Hispanoamericanos,* no. 517 – 519 (July – Sept 93), pp. 187 – 194.

Laviery, Ricardo. La añorada trampa del estímulo para el escritor. *Revista Cultural Lotería,* v. 50, no. 383 (May – June 91), pp. 43 – 51.

Lorenzo Fuentes, José. García Márquez: un concepto obrero de la inspiración. *Plural (Mexico),* v. 22, no. 259 (Apr 93), pp. 52 – 55.

Morábito, Fabio. El escritor en busca de una lengua. *Vuelta,* v. 17, no. 195 (Feb 93), pp. 22 – 24.

Pomer, León. El animal que imagina. *Revista de Letras (Brazil),* v. 32 (1992), pp. 153 – 167. Bibl.

Ruiz, Bernardo. José Juan Tablada escribe un poema. *Nexos,* v. 16, no. 192 (Dec 93), pp. 89 – 90.

Sahakián, Carlos. Plástica y poética. *Plural (Mexico),* v. 22, no. 260 (May 93), pp. 40 – 48.

Vargas Llosa, Mario. *A Writer's Reality* edited by Myron I. Lichtblau. Reviewed by Alfred MacAdam. *Hispanic Review,* v. 61, no. 3 (Summer 93), pp. 454 – 456.

— *A Writer's Reality* reviewed by Barbara Mujica (Review entitled "The Creative Subtext of Life"). *Américas,* v. 45, no. 3 (May – June 93), pp. 62 – 63. Il.

CREDIT

See also
Agricultural credit

Argentina

Junio, Juan Carlos. Participación democrática. *Realidad Económica,* no. 116 (May – June 93), pp. 29 – 31.

Mayo, Carlos Alberto and Jaime Antonio Peire. Iglesia y crédito colonial: la política crediticia de los conventos de Buenos Aires, 1767 – 1810. *Revista de Historia de América,* no. 112 (July – Dec 91), pp. 147 – 157. Bibl.

Colombia

Sowell, David Lee. La Caja de Ahorros de Bogotá, 1846 – 1865: Artisans, Credit, Development, and Savings in Early National Colombia. *Hispanic American Historical Review,* v. 73, no. 4 (Nov 93), pp. 615 – 638. Bibl, tables.

Cuba

Collazo Pérez, Enrique. *Cuba, banca y crédito, 1950 – 1958* reviewed by Jorge Salazar-Carrillo. *Hispanic American Historical Review,* v. 73, no. 4 (Nov 93), pp. 725 – 726.

Mexico

Alford, Annika E. K. The Automation of Money. *Business Mexico,* v. 3, no. 9 (Sept 93), pp. 24 – 27. Il.

Blears, James. Measuring Risk. *Business Mexico,* v. 3, no. 11 (Nov 93), pp. 15 – 16.

Lazaroff, León. A Tight Squeeze in Sonora. *Business Mexico,* v. 3, no. 3 (Mar 93), pp. 8 – 9.

Naveda Chávez-Hita, Adriana. Consideraciones sobre comercio y crédito en la villa de Córdoba, siglo XVIII. *La Palabra y el Hombre,* no. 83 (July – Sept 92), pp. 109 – 120. Bibl.

Silverstein, Jeffrey. Banking on the Future. *Business Mexico,* v. 3, no. 3 (Mar 93), pp. 10 – 11.

CREOLE DIALECTS

Caribbean area

Berrouët-Oriol, Robert and Robert Fournier. Créolophonie et francophonie nord – sud: transcontinuum. *Canadian Journal of Latin American and Caribbean Studies,* v. 17, no. 34 (1992), pp. 13 – 25. Bibl.

Mexico

Zimmermann, Klaus. Zur Sprache der afrohispanischen Bevölkerung im Mexiko der Kolonialzeit. *Iberoamericana,* v. 17, no. 50 (1993), pp. 89 – 111. Bibl.

CRESPO, JOSÉ DANIEL

Doctor José Daniel Crespo. *Revista Cultural Lotería,* v. 51, no. 389 (May – June 93), pp. 66 – 87. Il.

CRESPO, LUIS ALBERTO

Criticism and interpretation

Guzmán, Patricia. El lugar como absoluto: Vicente Gerbasi, Ramón Palomares y Luis Alberto Crespo. *Inti,* no. 37 – 38 (Spring – Fall 93), pp. 107 – 115. Bibl.

CRIME AND CRIMINALS

See also
Art thefts
Bandits and banditry
Crimes against women
Criminal law
Juvenile delinquency
Pirates
Prisons
Smuggling
Violence

Argentina

Johnson, Lyman L., ed. *The Problem of Order in Changing Societies: Essays on Crime and Policing in Argentina and Uruguay* reviewed by Carlos A. Mayo. *Revista de Indias,* v. 53, no. 197 (Jan – Apr 93), pp. 111 – 112.

Vallejos, Marcelo. Los crímenes del Petiso Orejudo. *Todo Es Historia,* v. 27, no. 312 (July 93), pp. 8 – 19. Bibl, il.

Brazil

Zaluar, Alba. Mulher de bandido: crônica de uma cidade menos musical (Accompanied by an English translation). *Estudos Feministas,* v. 1, no. 1 (1993), pp. 135 – 142. Bibl.

Costa Rica

Bejarano Orozco, Julio and Hannia Carvajal Morera. Abuso de drogas y conducta delictiva. *Revista de Ciencias Sociales (Costa Rica),* no. 60 (June 93), pp. 51 – 62. Bibl, tables, charts.

El Salvador

Documento especial: la delincuencia urbana; encuesta explorativa. *ECA; Estudios Centroamericanos,* v. 48, no. 534 – 535 (Apr – May 93), pp. 471 – 479. Tables.

Uruguay

Johnson, Lyman L., ed. *The Problem of Order in Changing Societies: Essays on Crime and Policing in Argentina and Uruguay* reviewed by Carlos A. Mayo. *Revista de Indias,* v. 53, no. 197 (Jan – Apr 93), pp. 111 – 112.

Venezuela

Sources

Expediente no. 14, año 1813. *Boletín de la Academia Nacional de la Historia (Venezuela),* v. 75, no. 298 (Apr – June 92), pp. 145 – 146.

CRIMES AGAINST WOMEN

Dowdeswell, Jane. *La violación: hablan las mujeres* (Review). *Homines,* v. 15 – 16, no. 2 – 1 (Oct 91 – Dec 92), p. 383. Il.

Fernández Poncela, Anna M. Un delito social: la violencia contra la mujer. *Fem,* v. 17, no. 126 (Aug 93), pp. 34 – 35.

— El torbellino de la violencia alcanza a las mujeres nicaragüenses. *Fem,* v. 17, no. 119 (Jan 93), pp. 9 – 12.

Gargallo, Francesca. ¿Las calles también son nuestras? *Fem,* v. 17, no. 122 (Apr 93), pp. 4 – 5. Il.

— Derechos humanos y trabajo doméstico asalariado. *Fem,* v. 17, no. 130 (Dec 93), pp. 4 – 6. Bibl.

González, Lucero. Derechos humanos de las mujeres y la filantropía. *Fem,* v. 17, no. 126 (Aug 93), p. 4.

Gregori, Maria Filomena. *Cenas e queixas: um estudo sobre mulheres, relações violentas e a prática feminista* reviewed by Danielle Ardaillon (Review entitled "Facetas do feminino"). *Estudos Feministas,* v. 1, no. 2 (1993), pp. 487 – 489.

— *Cenas e queixas: um estudo sobre mulheres, relações violentas e a prática feminista* reviewed by Wânia Pasinato Izumino. *Revista Brasileira de Ciências Sociais,* v. 8, no. 22 (June 93), pp. 145 – 146.

— *Cenas e queixas: um estudo sobre mulheres, relações violentas e a prática feminista* (Review). *Vozes,* v. 87, no. 4 (July – Aug 93), p. 99.

— As desventuras do vitimismo (Accompanied by an English translation). *Estudos Feministas,* v. 1, no. 1 (1993), pp. 143 – 149. Bibl.

Grossi, Miriam Pillar. De Angela Diniz a Daniela Perez: a trajetória da impunidade. *Estudos Feministas,* v. 1, no. 1 (1993), pp. 166 – 168.

Hernández Téllez, Josefina. Servicios a la comunidad de la PGJDF: por el trato humano en la impartición de justicia. *Fem,* v. 17, no. 119 (Jan 93), p. 30.

Oliveira, Eleonora Menicucci de and Lucila Amaral Carneiro Vianna. Violência conjugal na gravidez. *Estudos Feministas,* v. 1, no. 1 (1993), pp. 162 – 165.

Pitanguy, Jacqueline. Um estudo americano sobre violência no Brazil. *Estudos Feministas,* v. 1, no. 1 (1993), pp. 150 – 151.

Poole, Linda J. CIM: Making Women's Rights Human Rights. *Américas,* v. 45, no. 2 (Mar – Apr 93), pp. 48 – 49.

Romany, Celina. Hacia una crítica feminista del derecho internacional en materia de derechos humanos. *Fem,* v. 17, no. 126 (Aug 93), pp. 19 – 22.

Saucedo, Irma. Violencia doméstica: hecho y espacio de desestructuración de la subordinación de la mujer. *Fem,* v. 17, no. 122 (Apr 93), pp. 16 – 17. Il.

Terán, Matilde. Violencia intrafamiliar: trabajo con hombres agresores. *Fem,* v. 17, no. 126 (Aug 93), p. 42.

Law and legislation

Caulfield, Sueann and Martha de Abreu Esteves. 50 Years of Virginity in Rio de Janeiro: Sexual Politics and Gender Roles in Juridical and Popular Discourse, 1890 – 1940. *Luso-Brazilian Review,* v. 30, no. 1 (Summer 93), pp. 47 – 74. Bibl, tables.

Manifesto das Mulheres: propostas de alteração do código penal brasileiro (Accompanied by an English translation). *Estudos Feministas,* v. 1, no. 1 (1993), pp. 159 – 161.

Pierro, Maria Inês Valente and Sílvia Pimentel. Proposta de lei contra a violência familiar. *Estudos Feministas,* v. 1, no. 1 (1993), pp. 169 – 175.

Societies, etc.

Atención a víctimas de delitos sexuales. *Fem,* v. 17, no. 124 (June 93), p. 42.

Statistics

Fernández Poncela, Anna M. Una lacra mundial: la violencia contra la mujer. *Fem,* v. 17, no. 125 (July 93), pp. 27 – 29.

CRIMINAL LAW

See also
Crime and criminals

Adorno, Sérgio and Túlio Kahn. Pena de morte: para que e para quem serve esse debate? *Vozes,* v. 87, no. 3 (May – June 93), pp. 14 – 30. Tables, charts.

Brazil

Caulfield, Sueann and Martha de Abreu Esteves. 50 Years of Virginity in Rio de Janeiro: Sexual Politics and Gender Roles in Juridical and Popular Discourse, 1890 – 1940. *Luso-Brazilian Review,* v. 30, no. 1 (Summer 93), pp. 47 – 74. Bibl, tables.

Manifesto das Mulheres: propostas de alteração do código penal brasileiro (Accompanied by an English translation). *Estudos Feministas,* v. 1, no. 1 (1993), pp. 159 – 161.

Pierro, Maria Inês Valente and Sílvia Pimentel. Proposta de lei contra a violência familiar. *Estudos Feministas,* v. 1, no. 1 (1993), pp. 169 – 175.

El Salvador

Las reformas penales y los derechos humanos. *ECA; Estudios Centroamericanos,* v. 47, no. 528 (Oct 92), pp. 883 – 888. Il.

Venezuela
Sources

Ley Penal del Ambiente. *Derecho y Reforma Agraria,* no. 23 (1992), pp. 185 – 203.

CRISTERO REBELLION, 1926 – 1929

Fiction

Chao Ebergenyi, Guillermo. De los altos reviewed by Raymundo León (Review entitled *"De los altos:* la verdadera guerra cristera"). *La Palabra y el Hombre,* no. 81 (Jan – Mar 92), pp. 339 – 340.

CROSS, ELSA

Criticism of specific works
Canto malabar y otros poemas

Castañón, Adolfo. Dos voces mujeres. *Vuelta,* v. 17, no. 202 (Sept 93), pp. 60 – 63.

CRUZ, AARÓN

Rivera, José María. Aarón Cruz: el laberinto en el universo. *Plural (Mexico),* v. 22, no. 263 (Aug 93), pp. 40 – 45. Il.

CRUZ OVALLE DE AMENÁBAR, ISABEL

González Echenique, Javier. Discurso de recepción de doña Isabel Cruz Ovalle de Amenábar. *Boletín de la Academia Chilena de la Historia,* v. 58 – 59, no. 102 (1991 – 1992), pp. 139 – 144.

Bibliography

Bibliografía de doña Isabel Cruz Ovalle de Amenábar. *Boletín de la Academia Chilena de la Historia,* v. 58 – 59, no. 102 (1991 – 1992), pp. 145 – 146.

CUADERNOS AMERICANOS (PERIODICAL)

Awards

Finisterre, Alejandro. El premio León Felipe 1993. *Cuadernos Americanos,* no. 41, Nueva época (Sept – Oct 93), pp. 183 – 186.

Weinberg, Liliana Irene. León Felipe y *Cuadernos Americanos. Cuadernos Americanos,* no. 41, Nueva época (Sept – Oct 93), pp. 187 – 189.

CUADERNOS DE ECONOMÍA (PERIODICAL)

Indexes

Cuadernos de Economía: clasificación de artículos por materia, volúmenes 26 – 31, números 77 – 91, años 1989 – 1993. *Cuadernos de Economía (Chile),* v. 30, no. 91 (Dec 93), pp. 407 – 413.

Indice alfabético por autores de *Cuadernos de Economía,* años 1989 a 1993: simbología utilizada; volumen, número, página, año. *Cuadernos de Economía (Chile),* v. 30, no. 91 (Dec 93), pp. 395 – 406.

CUADERNOS DE HISTORIA (CHILE) (PERIODICAL)

Indexes

Fuchslocher Arancibia, Luz María. Indice: *Cuadernos de Historia,* desde no. 1 (diciembre, 1981) al no. 10 (diciembre, 1990). *Cuadernos de Historia (Chile),* no. 11 (Dec 91), pp. 211 – 226.

CUADRA, PABLO ANTONIO

Criticism and interpretation

Arellano, Jorge Eduardo. *Pablo Antonio Cuadra: aproximaciones a su vida y obra* reviewed by Amelia Mondragón. *Hispamérica,* v. 21, no. 63 (Dec 92), pp. 91 – 93.

Cobo Borda, Juan Gustavo. Pablo Antonio Cuadra. *Cuadernos Hispanoamericanos,* no. 522 (Dec 93), pp. 7 – 17. Il.

Pailler, Claire. Avatares del tiempo histórico en dos poetas nicaragüenses de hoy: Ernesto Cardenal y Pablo Antonio Cuadra. *Caravelle,* no. 60 (1993), pp. 85 – 99. Bibl.

Criticism of specific works
Canto temporal

Palacios, Conny. Acercamiento al "Canto temporal" de Pablo Antonio Cuadra. *Confluencia*, v. 8, no. 1 (Fall 92), pp. 51 – 59.

CUARÓN, CARLOS
Interviews

Pliego, Roberto. Don Juan en calzoncillos: una entrevista a Carlos Cuarón. *Nexos*, v. 16, no. 183 (Mar 93), pp. 62 – 63.

CUBA

See also

Anthropology – Cuba
Architecture – Cuba
Art – Cuba
Art and society – Cuba
Artists – Cuba
Authors – Cuba
Banks and banking – Cuba
Biotechnology – Cuba
Blacks – Cuba
Blacks in literature – Cuba
Catholic Church – Cuba
Censorship – Cuba
Church and social problems – Cuba
Communism – Cuba
Composers – Cuba
Cost and standard of living – Cuba
Credit – Cuba
Cultural imperialism – Cuba
Dancing – Cuba
Education – Cuba
Education, Primary – Cuba
Elections – Cuba
Employees' representation in management – Cuba
Energy policy – Cuba
Exiles – Cuba
Experimental theater – Cuba
Family – Cuba
Food industry and trade – Cuba
Foreign exchange problem – Cuba
Geography, Economic – Cuba
Germans – Cuba
Government ownership of business enterprises – Cuba
Handicraft – Cuba
Havana, Cuba
Housing – Cuba
Human rights – Cuba
Labor supply – Cuba
Land settlement – Cuba
Literature and history – Cuba
Literature and society – Cuba
Markets and merchants – Cuba
Marriage – Cuba
Mass media and the arts – Cuba
Matanzas, Cuba
Middle classes – Cuba
Motion pictures – Cuba
Music – Cuba
Musicians – Cuba
Mutual benefit associations – Cuba
Nationalism – Cuba
Oral history – Cuba
Periodicals – Cuba
Philosophy – Cuba
Political participation – Cuba
Political prisoners – Cuba
Politics in literature – Cuba
Popular music – Cuba
Population – Cuba
Power resources – Cuba
Press and politics – Cuba
Publishers and publishing – Cuba
Radio broadcasting – Cuba
Real property – Cuba
Regionalism – Cuba
Religion – Cuba
Revolutions – Cuba
Science – Cuba
Slavery – Cuba
Social conflict – Cuba
Social science research – Cuba
Sociology – Cuba
Spaniards – Cuba
Spanish language – Cuba
Sugar – Cuba
Technology – Cuba
Textile industry and fabrics – Cuba
Theater – Cuba
Tourist trade – Cuba
Trade unions – Cuba
Women – Cuba
Women artists – Cuba
Women in literature – Cuba
Women's rights – Cuba

Administrative and political divisions

Roman, Peter. Representative Government in Socialist Cuba. *Latin American Perspectives*, v. 20, no. 1 (Winter 93), pp. 7 – 27.

Armed forces

Domingo Acebrón, María Dolores. La participación de españoles en el ejército libertador en Cuba, 1895 – 1898. *Revista de Indias*, v. 52, no. 195 – 196 (May – Dec 92), pp. 349 – 363. Bibl, tables.

Bibliography

Bibliografía: Cuba. *Estudios Internacionales (Chile)*, v. 26, no. 103 (July – Sept 93), pp. 565 – 568.

Pérez-López, René. Recent Work in Cuban Studies. *Cuban Studies/Estudios Cubanos*, v. 23 (1993), pp. 245 – 275.

Civilization

Cabrera Infante, Guillermo. *Mea Cuba* reviewed by Aurelio Asiaín. *Vuelta*, v. 17, no. 201 (Aug 93), pp. 43 – 45.

— *Mea Cuba* reviewed by Fabienne Bradu. *Vuelta*, v. 17, no. 198 (May 93), pp. 48 – 49.

— *Mea Cuba* reviewed by Juan Goytisolo (Review entitled "Una memoria de Cuba"). *Nexos*, v. 16, no. 184 (Apr 93), pp. 65 – 66.

— *Mea Cuba* reviewed by Will H. Corral. *World Literature Today*, v. 67, no. 2 (Spring 93), pp. 342 – 343.

Fogel, Jean-François and Bertrand Rosenthal. *Fin de siècle à la Havane: les secrets du pouvoir cubain* reviewed by Ernesto Hernández Busto (Review entitled "Fin de siglo con Castro"). *Vuelta*, v. 17, no. 200 (July 93), pp. 55 – 56.

Ibargoyen Islas, Saúl. Encuentros y desencuentros con la revolución cubana. *Plural (Mexico)*, v. 22, no. 256 (Jan 93), pp. 77 – 78.

Portuondo Zúñiga, Olga. Criollidad y patria local en campo geométrico. *Islas*, no. 98 (Jan – Apr 91), pp. 40 – 46.

Torres Fierro, Danubio. Memoria, historia, desmemoria. *Vuelta*, v. 17, no. 201 (Aug 93), pp. 55 – 56.

Foreign influences

Vega Suñol, José. *Presencia norteamericana en el área nororiental de Cuba* reviewed by Lawrence A. Glasco. *Cuban Studies/Estudios Cubanos*, v. 23 (1993), pp. 227 – 228.

Constitutional law

Charlone, Silvana and Carlos Varela Nestier. Cuba: ¿Democratización y legitimidad?; los cambios en el sistema político cubano. *Hoy Es Historia*, v. 10, no. 59 (Sept – Oct 93), pp. 56 – 66. Il.

Cultural policy

Quirós, Oscar E. Values and Aesthetics in Cuban Arts and Cinema. *SALALM Papers*, v. 34 (1989), pp. 151 – 171. Bibl.

Reed, Roger. *The Cultural Revolution in Cuba* reviewed by James Maraniss. *Cuban Studies/Estudios Cubanos*, v. 23 (1993), pp. 225 – 227.

Stern, Peter A. Art and the State in Post-Revolutionary Mexico and Cuba. *SALALM Papers*, v. 34 (1989), pp. 17 – 32. Bibl.

Description and travel

Paporov, Yuri. *Hemingway en Cuba* reviewed by Martí Soler (Review entitled "Ernest y Yuri"). *Plural (Mexico)*, v. 22, no. 263 (Aug 93), pp. 78 – 79.

Sources

Pérez, Louis A., Jr., ed. *Slaves, Sugar, and Colonial Society: Travel Accounts of Cuba, 1801 – 1899* reviewed by Laurence A. Glasco. *Cuban Studies/Estudios Cubanos*, v. 23 (1993), pp. 219 – 220.

Economic conditions

Cardoso, Eliana Anastasia. Cuba: un caso único de reforma anti-mercado; comentarios al artículo de Carmelo Mesa-Lago. *Pensamiento Iberoamericano,* no. 22 – 23, tomo II (July 92 – June 93), pp. 101 – 107. Tables.

García Reyes, Miguel. El pueblo de Cuba: entre el drama y la esperanza, V; La crisis económica en Cuba. *Hoy Es Historia,* v. 10, no. 58 (July – Aug 93), pp. 54 – 58. II, tables.

Mesa-Lago, Carmelo. Efectos económicos en Cuba del derrumbe del socialismo en la Unión Soviética y Europa Oriental. *Estudios Internacionales (Chile),* v. 26, no. 103 (July – Sept 93), pp. 341 – 414. Bibl, tables.

Morales, Josefina. Cuba '93. *Problemas del Desarrollo,* v. 24, no. 93 (Apr – June 93), pp. 211 – 220. Bibl.

Ritter, Archibald R. M. Cuba en los noventa: reorientación económica y reintegración internacional. *Estudios Internacionales (Chile),* v. 26, no. 103 (July – Sept 93), pp. 454 – 479. Bibl, tables.

Rodríguez, José Luis. Cuba en la economía internacional: nuevos mercados y desafíos de los años noventa. *Estudios Internacionales (Chile),* v. 26, no. 103 (July – Sept 93), pp. 415 – 453. Bibl, tables.

— The Cuban Economy in a Changing International Environment. *Cuban Studies/Estudios Cubanos,* v. 23 (1993), pp. 33 – 47. Bibl, tables.

Sánchez, Antulio. El pueblo de Cuba: entre el drama y la esperanza, IV: Cuba en la opción cero; situación actual de la economía cubana. *Hoy Es Historia,* v. 10, no. 57 (Apr – May 93), pp. 49 – 53.

Zimbalist, Andrew S. Cuba in the Age of "Perestroika" (Review article). *Latin American Perspectives,* v. 20, no. 1 (Winter 93), pp. 47 – 57. Bibl.

Economic policy

Díaz-Briquets, Sergio. "Dollarization": Castro's Latest Economic Miracle? *Hemisphere,* v. 5, no. 3 (Summer – Fall 93), pp. 8 – 9.

Espino, María Dolores. Tourism in Cuba: A Development Strategy for the 1990s? *Cuban Studies/Estudios Cubanos,* v. 23 (1993), pp. 49 – 69. Bibl, tables.

Mesa-Lago, Carmelo. Cuba: un caso único de reforma anti-mercado; retrospectiva y perspectivas. *Pensamiento Iberoamericano,* no. 22 – 23, tomo II (July 92 – June 93), pp. 65 – 100. Bibl, tables.

Ritter, Archibald R. M. Exploring Cuba's Alternate Economic Futures. *Cuban Studies/Estudios Cubanos,* v. 23 (1993), pp. 3 – 31. Bibl, tables.

Emigration and immigration

Núñez Seixas, Xosé M. Inmigración y galleguismo en Cuba, 1879 – 1930. *Revista de Indias,* v. 53, no. 197 (Jan – Apr 93), pp. 53 – 95. Bibl.

Statistics

Naranjo Orovio, V. Consuelo. Trabajo libre e inmigración española en Cuba, 1880 – 1930. *Revista de Indias,* v. 52, no. 195 – 196 (May – Dec 92), pp. 749 – 794. Bibl, charts.

Foreign economic relations

García Reyes, Miguel. El pueblo de Cuba: entre el drama y la esperanza, V; La crisis económica en Cuba. *Hoy Es Historia,* v. 10, no. 58 (July – Aug 93), pp. 54 – 58. II, tables.

Ritter, Archibald R. M. Cuba en los noventa: reorientación económica y reintegración internacional. *Estudios Internacionales (Chile),* v. 26, no. 103 (July – Sept 93), pp. 454 – 479. Bibl, tables.

Rodríguez, José Luis. Cuba en la economía internacional: nuevos mercados y desafíos de los años noventa. *Estudios Internacionales (Chile),* v. 26, no. 103 (July – Sept 93), pp. 415 – 453. Bibl, tables.

— The Cuban Economy in a Changing International Environment. *Cuban Studies/Estudios Cubanos,* v. 23 (1993), pp. 33 – 47. Bibl, tables.

Research

Roca, Sergio G. Evolución del pensamiento cubano sobre Cuba y la economía mundial a través de las revistas económicas. *Estudios Internacionales (Chile),* v. 26, no. 103 (July – Sept 93), pp. 537 – 564. Bibl, tables.

Latin America

Monreal González, Pedro. Cuba y América Latina y el Caribe: apuntes sobre un caso de inserción económica. *Estudios Internacionales (Chile),* v. 26, no. 103 (July – Sept 93), pp. 500 – 536. Bibl, tables.

United States

Carriazo Moreno, George. Las relaciones económicas Cuba – Estados Unidos: una mirada al futuro. *Estudios Internacionales (Chile),* v. 26, no. 103 (July – Sept 93), pp. 480 – 499. Bibl, tables.

Maingot, Anthony Peter. Quid Pro Quo with Cuba. *Hemisphere,* v. 5, no. 3 (Summer – Fall 93), pp. 22 – 25.

Ritter, Archibald R. M. Seized Properties vs. Embargo Losses. *Hemisphere,* v. 5, no. 3 (Summer – Fall 93), pp. 31 – 35. Tables.

Zanetti Lecuona, Oscar. *Los cautivos de la reciprocidad: la burguesía cubana y la dependencia comercial* reviewed by Antonio Santamaría García. *Revista de Indias,* v. 53, no. 197 (Jan – Apr 93), pp. 129 – 132.

Foreign opinion

Moussong, Lazlo. Revolución y libre expresión. *Plural (Mexico),* v. 22, no. 259 (Apr 93), p. 68.

Núñez Florencio, Rafael. Los republicanos españoles ante el problema colonial: la cuestión cubana. *Revista de Indias,* v. 53, no. 198 (May – Aug 93), pp. 545 – 561.

Vargas Lozano, Gabriel. Cuba, el socialismo y la crisis de nuestro tiempo (Response to articles on Cuba in *Plural,* no. 250). *Plural (Mexico),* v. 22, no. 259 (Apr 93), pp. 66 – 68.

Foreign relations

¡Cuba libre . . . ! *Fem,* v. 17, no. 125 (July 93), p. 33.

Mesa-Lago, Carmelo. Efectos económicos en Cuba del derrumbe del socialismo en la Unión Soviética y Europa Oriental. *Estudios Internacionales (Chile),* v. 26, no. 103 (July – Sept 93), pp. 341 – 414. Bibl, tables.

Bibliography

Goslinga, Marian. The US, Cuba, and Puerto Rico. *Hemisphere,* v. 5, no. 3 (Summer – Fall 93), pp. 54 – 56.

Central America

Carranza Valdés, Julio. New Challenges for Cuban Policy toward Central America (Translated by Lucía Rayas). *Latin American Perspectives,* v. 20, no. 1 (Winter 93), pp. 58 – 63.

Israel

Metz, Allan Sheldon. Cuban – Israeli Relations: From the Cuban Revolution to the New World Order. *Cuban Studies/ Estudios Cubanos,* v. 23 (1993), pp. 113 – 134. Bibl.

Soviet Union

Blasier, Cole. El fin de la asociación soviético – cubana. *Estudios Internacionales (Chile),* v. 26, no. 103 (July – Sept 93), pp. 296 – 340. Bibl, tables.

United States

Cardoso, Eliana Anastasia and Ann Helwege. *Cuba after Communism* reviewed by Nicolás Sánchez. *Cuban Studies/ Estudios Cubanos,* v. 23 (1993), pp. 210 – 213.

Fernández Cabrelli, Alfonso. El pueblo de Cuba: entre el drama y la esperanza. *Hoy Es Historia,* v. 9, no. 54 (Nov – Dec 92), pp. 69 – 76.

Hernández, José M. *Cuba and the United States: Intervention and Militarism, 1868 – 1933* reviewed by Jules R. Benjamin. *Cuban Studies/Estudios Cubanos,* v. 23 (1993), pp. 213 – 215.

Hernández, Rafael and Joseph S. Tulchin, eds. *Cuba and the United States: Will the Cold War in the Caribbean End?* reviewed by Jorge I. Domínguez. *Cuban Studies/Estudios Cubanos,* v. 23 (1993), pp. 215 – 217.

Huidobro, Vicente. Defendamos la revolución de Cuba: los Estados Unidos no tienen ningún derecho para meterse en los asuntos de Cuba. *Casa de las Américas,* no. 191 (Apr – June 93), pp. 10 – 11.

Murphy, Douglas. Teeing Off: Dwight, JFK, and Fidel. *Hemisphere,* v. 5, no. 2 (Winter – Spring 93), pp. 18 – 21. II.

Opatrny, Josef. *U.S. Expansionism and Cuban Annexationism in the 1850s* reviewed by Allan J. Kuethe. *Hispanic American Historical Review,* v. 73, no. 4 (Nov 93), pp. 724 – 725.

Pérez, Louis A., Jr. *Cuba and the United States: Ties of a Singular Intimacy* reviewed by Thomas Schoonover. *The Americas*, v. 50, no. 1 (July 93), pp. 130 – 131.

Suchlicki, Jaime. Myths and Realities in US – Cuban Relations. *Journal of Inter-American Studies and World Affairs*, v. 35, no. 2 (Summer 93), pp. 103 – 113.

Vega Suñol, José. *Presencia norteamericana en el área nororiental de Cuba* reviewed by Lawrence A. Glasco. *Cuban Studies/Estudios Cubanos*, v. 23 (1993), pp. 227 – 228.

Historiography

García Blanco, Rolando. Perspectivas de la historia regional en Cuba. *Islas*, no. 98 (Jan – Apr 91), pp. 3 – 12. Bibl.

Maldonado Jiménez, Rubén. Algunas reflexiones sobre la historiografía cubana y puertorriqueña en torno a la abolición de la esclavitud. *Homines*, v. 15 – 16, no. 2 – 1 (Oct 91 – Dec 92), pp. 31 – 38. Bibl.

Yglesia Martínez, Teresita. The History of Cuba and Its Interpreters, 1898 – 1935 (Translated by Néstor Capote). *The Americas*, v. 49, no. 3 (Jan 93), pp. 369 – 385. Bibl.

History

Niess, Frank. *20mal Kuba* reviewed by Martin Franzbach. *Iberoamericana*, v. 16, no. 47 – 48 (1992), pp. 142 – 143.

Sources

Hernández González, Pablo J. La comarca de Vuelta Abajo, isla de Cuba, en 1755: recuento de un obispo ilustrado. *Anuario de Estudios Americanos*, v. 50, no. 1 (1993), pp. 251 – 268. Bibl, maps.

Pérez, Louis A., Jr. *A Guide to Cuban Collections in the United States* reviewed by John M. Kirk. *Revista Interamericana de Bibliografía*, v. 42, no. 2 (1992), p. 287.

Study and teaching

Morales, Salvador. El reto de la historia regional en la enseñanza de la historia. *Islas*, no. 98 (Jan – Apr 91), pp. 22 – 27.

To 1895

González García, Juan Francisco. Matanzas: su historia, 1868 – 1878. *Islas*, no. 97 (Sept – Dec 90), pp. 64 – 78. Bibl.

— Matanzas: su historia; los tiempos de tregua, 1878 – 1895. *Islas*, no. 98 (Jan – Apr 91), pp. 47 – 57. Bibl.

Howard, Philip A. The Spanish Colonial Government's Responses to the Pan-Nationalist Agenda of the Afro-Cuban Mutual Aid Societies, 1868 – 1895. *Revista/Review Interamericana*, v. 22, no. 1 – 2 (Spring – Summer 92), pp. 151 – 167. Bibl.

1895 –

Paz Sánchez, Manuel de. *Wangüemert y Cuba*, vols. I y II, reviewed by Louis A. Pérez, Jr. *Journal of Latin American Studies*, v. 25, no. 3 (Oct 93), pp. 658 – 659.

Robles Muñoz, Cristóbal. Triunfar en Washington: España ante Baire. *Anuario de Estudios Americanos*, v. 49 (1992), pp. 563 – 584. Bibl.

Rojas, Rafael. La memoria de un patricio. *Op. Cit.*, no. 7 (1992), pp. 121 – 144. Il.

1895 – 1898, Revolution

Domingo Acebrón, María Dolores. La participación de españoles en el ejército libertador en Cuba, 1895 – 1898. *Revista de Indias*, v. 52, no. 195 – 196 (May – Dec 92), pp. 349 – 363. Bibl, tables.

Núñez Florencio, Rafael. Los republicanos españoles ante el problema colonial: la cuestión cubana. *Revista de Indias*, v. 53, no. 198 (May – Aug 93), pp. 545 – 561.

Offner, John L. *An Unwanted War: The Diplomacy of the United States and Spain over Cuba, 1895 – 1898* reviewed by Jules R. Benjamin. *Hispanic American Historical Review*, v. 73, no. 3 (Aug 93), pp. 539 – 540.

Recio Ferreras, Eloy. Diario inédito escrito por un soldado español en la guerra de Cuba, 1896 – 1899. *Revista de Historia de América*, no. 112 (July – Dec 91), pp. 21 – 42. Facs.

Robles Muñoz, Cristóbal. Negociar la paz en Cuba, 1896 – 1897. *Revista de Indias*, v. 53, no. 198 (May – Aug 93), pp. 493 – 527. Bibl.

1959 –

Prada Oropeza, Renato. Los condenados de la tierra. *Plural (Mexico)*, v. 22, no. 262 (July 93), pp. 63 – 70.

Intellectual life

Barquet, Jesús J. El grupo "Orígenes" y España. *Cuadernos Hispanoamericanos*, no. 513 (Mar 93), pp. 31 – 48. Bibl, il.

Manzoni, Celina. Vanguardia y nacionalismo: itinerario de la *Revista de Avance*. *Iberoamericana*, v. 17, no. 49 (1993), pp. 5 – 15. Bibl.

Masiello, Francine Rose. Rethinking Neocolonial Esthetics: Literature, Politics, and Intellectual Community in Cuba's *Revista de Avance*. *Latin American Research Review*, v. 28, no. 2 (1993), pp. 3 – 31. Bibl, facs.

Reed, Roger. *The Cultural Revolution in Cuba* reviewed by James Maraniss. *Cuban Studies/Estudios Cubanos*, v. 23 (1993), pp. 225 – 227.

Languages

Castellanos, Isabel Mercedes and Jorge Castellanos. *Cultura afrocubana, III: Las religiones y las lenguas* reviewed by Luis A. Jiménez. *Hispania (USA)*, v. 76, no. 2 (May 93), pp. 281 – 282.

Politics and government
1899 – 1959

Melgar Bao, Ricardo. Militancia aprista en el Caribe: la sección cubana. *Cuadernos Americanos*, no. 37, Nueva época (Jan – Feb 93), pp. 208 – 226. Bibl.

Tísoc Lindley, Hilda. De los orígenes del APRA en Cuba: el testimonio de Enrique de la Osa. *Cuadernos Americanos*, no. 37, Nueva época (Jan – Feb 93), pp. 198 – 207. Bibl.

1959 –

Aguila, Juan M. del. The Party, the Fourth Congress, and the Process of Counter-Reform. *Cuban Studies/Estudios Cubanos*, v. 23 (1993), pp. 71 – 90. Bibl, tables.

Berástegui, Rafael. La Cuba de Fidel: algunas claves de interpretación. *Estudios Públicos (Chile)*, no. 52 (Spring 93), pp. 309 – 328.

Cuba in Transition reviewed by Nicolás Sánchez. *Cuban Studies/Estudios Cubanos*, v. 23 (1993), pp. 210 – 213.

Fleites-Lear, Marisela and Enrique Patterson. Teoría y praxis de la revolución cubana: apuntes críticos. *Nueva Sociedad*, no. 123 (Jan – Feb 93), pp. 50 – 64.

Geldof, Lynn. *Cubans: Voices of Change* reviewed by Rubén Berríos. *Cuban Studies/Estudios Cubanos*, v. 23 (1993), pp. 243 – 244.

Halebsky, Sandor and John M. Kirk, eds. *Cuba in Transition: Crisis and Transformation* reviewed by Nicolás Sánchez. *Cuban Studies/Estudios Cubanos*, v. 23 (1993), pp. 210 – 213.

— *Cuba in Transition: Crisis and Transformation* reviewed by Frank T. Fitzgerald. *Journal of Latin American Studies*, v. 25, no. 1 (Feb 93), pp. 219 – 220.

Montaner, Carlos Alberto. La revolución cubana y sus últimos alabarderos. *Vuelta*, v. 17, no. 205 (Dec 93), pp. 74 – 80.

Oppenheimer, Andrés. *Castro's Final Hour: The Secret Story behind the Coming Downfall of Communist Cuba* reviewed by Harold Dana Sims. *Cuban Studies/Estudios Cubanos*, v. 23 (1993), pp. 240 – 242.

— *Castro's Final Hour: The Secret Story behind the Coming Downfall of Communist Cuba* reviewed by Damián Fernández (Review entitled "The Theater of Cuban Politics"). *Hemisphere*, v. 5, no. 2 (Winter – Spring 93), pp. 46 – 48.

— *La hora final de Castro* reviewed by Ernesto Hernández Busto (Review entitled "Fin del siglo con Castro"). *Vuelta*, v. 17, no. 200 (July 93), pp. 55 – 56.

Rabkin, Rhoda Pearl. *Cuban Politics: The Revolutionary Experiment* reviewed by H. Michael Erisman. *Cuban Studies/Estudios Cubanos*, v. 23 (1993), pp. 231 – 233.

— *Cuban Politics: The Revolutionary Experiment* reviewed by Damián Fernández (Review entitled "The Theater of Cuban Politics"). *Hemisphere*, v. 5, no. 2 (Winter – Spring 93), pp. 46 – 48.

Roman, Peter. Representative Government in Socialist Cuba. *Latin American Perspectives*, v. 20, no. 1 (Winter 93), pp. 7 – 27.

Schulz, Donald E. Can Castro Survive? *Journal of Inter-American Studies and World Affairs*, v. 35, no. 1 (1993), pp. 89 – 117. Bibl.

Torres Fierro, Danubio. El "apartheid" cubano: entrevista con Guillermo Cabrera Infante. *Vuelta*, v. 17, no. 198 (May 93), pp. 58 – 59.

Zimbalist, Andrew S. Cuba in the Age of "Perestroika" (Review article). *Latin American Perspectives*, v. 20, no. 1 (Winter 93), pp. 47 – 57. Bibl.

Research

Fernández, Damián J., ed. *Cuban Studies since the Revolution* reviewed by Martin Weinstein. *Hispanic American Historical Review*, v. 73, no. 3 (Aug 93), pp. 533 – 534.

— *Cuban Studies since the Revolution* reviewed by John M. Kirk. *Journal of Latin American Studies*, v. 25, no. 2 (May 93), p. 424.

Rural conditions

Bergad, Laird W. *Cuban Rural Society in the Nineteenth Century: The Social and Economic History of Monoculture in Matanzas* reviewed by Gert Oostindie. *European Review of Latin American and Caribbean Studies*, no. 53 (Dec 92), pp. 111 – 112.

Social conditions

Benítez Pérez, María Elena. La familia cubana: principales rasgos sociodemográficos que han caracterizado su desarrollo y dinámica. *Estudios Demográficos y Urbanos*, v. 7, no. 2 – 3 (May – Dec 92), pp. 479 – 492. Bibl, tables.

Geldof, Lynn. *Cubans: Voices of Change* reviewed by Rubén Berríos. *Cuban Studies/Estudios Cubanos*, v. 23 (1993), pp. 243 – 244.

Grass, Günter Wilhelm. Compasión hacia Cuba (Translated by Julio Colón Gómez). *Nexos*, v. 16, no. 188 (Aug 93), pp. 10 – 13.

Mesa-Lago, Carmelo. The Social Safety Net Unravels. *Hemisphere*, v. 5, no. 3 (Summer – Fall 93), pp. 26 – 30. Charts.

Michelena, Alejandro Daniel. El pueblo de Cuba, entre el drama y la esperanza, III; Cuba: las auténticas "permanencias." *Hoy Es Historia*, v. 10, no. 56 (Mar – Apr 93), pp. 69 – 74.

CUBA IN LITERATURE

Araújo, Nara. La Avellaneda, la Merlin: una manera de ver y sentir. *Iberoamericana*, v. 17, no. 49 (1993), pp. 33 – 41. Bibl.

Cuadra, Angel. El tema de lo cubano en el escritor exiliado. *Plural (Mexico)*, v. 22, no. 262 (July 93), pp. 32 – 39.

CUBAN AMERICANS

See
Subdivision *United States* under *Cubans*

CUBAN DRAMA

United States

Colecchia, Francesca and Luis F. González-Cruz, eds. *Cuban Theater in the United States: A Criticial Anthology* translated by the editors. Reviewed by Luis A. Jiménez. *Hispania (USA)*, v. 76, no. 4 (Dec 93), pp. 737 – 738.

Cortina, Rodolfo J., ed. *Cuban American Theater* reviewed by José A. Escarpanter. *Latin American Theatre Review*, v. 26, no. 2 (Spring 93), pp. 203 – 204.

CUBAN LITERATURE

Foreign influences

Santí, Enrico-Mario. El tronco y la rama: literatura cubana y legado español. *Vuelta*, v. 17, no. 195 (Feb 93), pp. 53 – 55.

History and criticism

Bortolussi, Marisa. *El cuento infantil cubano: un estudio crítico* reviewed by Antonio Benítez-Rojo. *Hispanic Review*, v. 61, no. 4 (Fall 93), pp. 592 – 594.

Fornet, Ambrosio. Las máscaras del tiempo en la novela de la revolución cubana. *Casa de las Américas*, no. 191 (Apr – June 93), pp. 12 – 24. Bibl.

Guicharnaud-Tollis, Michèle. *L'émergence du noir dans le roman cubain du XIXe siècle* reviewed by Paul Estrade. *Caravelle*, no. 59 (1992), pp. 278 – 280.

— *L'émergence du noir dans le roman cubain du XIXe siècle* reviewed by Paul Estrade. *Revista de Indias*, v. 53, no. 197 (Jan – Apr 93), pp. 108 – 109.

Luis, William. *Literary Bondage: Slavery in Cuban Narrative* reviewed by Antonio Benítez-Rojo. *Hispanic Review*, v. 61, no. 1 (Winter 93), pp. 125 – 127.

United States

Duany, Jorge. Neither Golden Exile Nor Dirty Worm: Ethnic Identity in Recent Cuban-American Novels. *Cuban Studies/Estudios Cubanos*, v. 23 (1993), pp. 167 – 183. Bibl.

CUBAN POETRY

Alonso Yodú, Odette. Poesía joven de Cuba. *La Palabra y el Hombre*, no. 84 (Oct – Dec 92), pp. 5 – 19.

Anhalt, Nedda G. de et al. *La fiesta innombrable: trece poetas cubanos* reviewed by José Homero (Review entitled "Isla, historia y fiesta de la lengua"). *Vuelta*, v. 17, no. 194 (Jan 93), pp. 48 – 49.

Suardíaz, Luis, ed. *No me dan pena los burgueses vencidos* reviewed by Silvia Yáñez (Review entitled "Poesía y lucha social"). *Plural (Mexico)*, v. 22, no. 260 (May 93), p. 70.

Foreign influences

Barquet, Jesús J. El grupo "Orígenes" y España. *Cuadernos Hispanoamericanos*, no. 513 (Mar 93), pp. 31 – 48. Bibl, il.

History and criticism

Barquet, Jesús J. Tres apuntes para el futuro: poesía cubana posterior a 1959. *Plural (Mexico)*, v. 22, no. 262 (July 93), pp. 51 – 56. Bibl.

Cuadra, Angel. El tema de lo cubano en el escritor exiliado. *Plural (Mexico)*, v. 22, no. 262 (July 93), pp. 32 – 39.

Perlongher, Néstor. Introducción a la poesía neobarroca cubana y rioplatense. *Revista Chilena de Literatura*, no. 41 (Apr 93), pp. 47 – 57. Bibl.

CUBANS

United States

Fernández Cabrelli, Alfonso. El pueblo de Cuba: entre el drama y la esperanza. *Hoy Es Historia*, v. 9, no. 54 (Nov – Dec 92), pp. 69 – 76.

Manuel, Peter, ed. *Essays on Cuban Music: North American and Cuban Perspectives* reviewed by Lucy Durán. *Latin American Music Review*, v. 14, no. 2 (Fall – Winter 93), pp. 281 – 288.

Nodal, Roberto. The Concept of "Ebbo" (Sacrifice) as a Healing Mechanism in Santería. *Journal of Caribbean Studies*, v. 9, no. 1 – 2 (Winter 92 – Spring 93), pp. 113 – 124. Bibl.

Schulman, Iván A. ¿Más allá de la literatura?: un álbum de Cayo Hueso, 1891 – 1892. *Casa de las Américas*, no. 190 (Jan – Mar 93), pp. 50 – 55. Bibl.

Varela, Beatriz. *El español cubano-americano* reviewed by Thomas M. Stephens. *Hispania (USA)*, v. 76, no. 4 (Dec 93), pp. 745 – 746.

CUBEO INDIANS

Kaplan, Joanna Overing. A estética da produção: o senso de comunidade entre os cubeo e os piaroa. *Revista de Antropologia (Brazil)*, v. 34 (1991), pp. 7 – 33. Bibl.

CUELLO SITE, BELIZE

Hammond, Norman, ed. *Cuello: An Early Maya Community in Belize* reviewed by Paul F. Healy. *Latin American Antiquity*, v. 4, no. 3 (Sept 93), pp. 295 – 297.

CUERNAVACA, MEXICO

Haskett, Robert Stephen. *Indigenous Rulers: An Ethnohistory of Town Government in Colonial Cuernavaca* reviewed by Eric Van Young. *Journal of Latin American Studies*, v. 25, no. 3 (Oct 93), pp. 653 – 654.

— *Visions of Municipal Glory Undimmed: The Nahuatl Town Histories of Colonial Cuernavaca*. *Colonial Latin American Historical Review*, v. 1, no. 1 (Fall 92), pp. 1 – 36. Bibl, il.

CUERVO, RUFINO JOSÉ

Rodríguez-Izquierdo y Gavala, Fernando. Aspectos de la personalidad de Rufino José Cuervo. *Thesaurus*, v. 45, no. 3 (Sept – Dec 90), pp. 747 – 757.

Correspondence, reminiscences, etc.

Quesada Pacheco, Miguel Angel. Correspondencia de Carlos Gagini con Rufino José Cuervo y Ricardo Palma. *Káñina*, v. 16, no. 1 (Jan – June 92), pp. 197 – 206.

CUESTA, JORGE

Criticism and interpretation

Domínguez Michael, Christopher. Jorge Cuesta o la crítica del demonio (Chapter from the book *Tiros en el concierto*). *Vuelta*, v. 17, no. 194 (Jan 93), pp. 28 – 36. Bibl.

Fiction

Volpi Escalante, Jorge. *A pesar del oscuro silencio* reviewed by Christopher Domínguez (Review entitled "De envidia a envidia"). *Vuelta*, v. 17, no. 195 (Feb 93), pp. 40 – 41.

CUEVAS, JOSÉ LUIS

Interviews

Ramírez, Fermín. José Luis Cuevas, ave de tempestades. *Plural (Mexico)*, v. 22, no. 265 (Oct 93), pp. 42 – 48. Il.

CUGAT, DELIA

Escallón, Ana María. Delia Cugat: la atmósfera de la condición humana (Accompanied by an English translation). *Art Nexus*, no. 9 (June – Aug 93), pp. 88 – 90. Il.

CULTURAL CHANGE

See
Acculturation
Civilization, Modern
Social change
Socialization

CULTURAL COOPERATION

See
Intellectual cooperation

CULTURAL GEOGRAPHY

See
Anthropo-geography

CULTURAL IDENTITY

See
Ethnicity
Indigenismo
Subdivision *Civilization* under names of specific countries
Subdivision *Ethnic identity* under *Blacks, Hispanic Americans (U.S.)*, and names of Indian groups

CULTURAL IMPERIALISM

See also
Imperialism
Mass media

Cuba

Ocasio, Rafael. "Babalú Ayé": Santería and Contemporary Cuban Literature. *Journal of Caribbean Studies*, v. 9, no. 1 – 2 (Winter 92 – Spring 93), pp. 29 – 40. Bibl.

Latin America

Bohórquez, Carmen L. Colonialismo escolar-izado. *Islas*, no. 96 (May – Aug 90), pp. 121 – 126.

Pérez-Yglesias, María. Entre lo escolar y los medios informativos: políticas neoliberales y educación. *Revista de Ciencias Sociales (Costa Rica)*, no. 57 (Sept 92), pp. 41 – 55. Bibl.

CULTURAL PROPERTY

See also
Archaeological site reports
Archives
Art thefts
Shrines

Messenger, Phyllis Mauch, ed. *The Ethics of Collecting Cultural Property: Whose Culture? Whose Property?* reviewed by Jorge Luján Muñoz. *Mesoamérica (USA)*, v. 13, no. 24 (Dec 92), pp. 492 – 494.

Meyer, Karl Ernest. *El saqueo del pasado: historia del tráfico internacional ilegal de obras de arte* translated by Roberto Ramón Reyes Mazzoni. Reviewed by Jorge Luján Muñoz. *Mesoamérica (USA)*, v. 13, no. 24 (Dec 92), pp. 492 – 494.

Argentina

Devincenzi, Roberto Marcos. Los estribos de la conquista. *Todo Es Historia*, v. 26, no. 309 (Apr 93), pp. 85 – 95. Bibl, il, tables.

Mexico

Abundis Canales, Jaime. A Mansion in the City of Palaces. *Business Mexico*, v. 3, no. 12 (Dec 93), pp. 34 – 36. Il.

Peru

Preservation

Bouchard, Jean-François et al. Machu Picchu: problemas de conservación de un sitio inca de ceja de selva. *Bulletin de l'Institut Français d'Etudes Andines*, v. 21, no. 3 (1992), pp. 905 – 927. Bibl, il, maps.

Puerto Rico

Preservation

Harrison Flores, Joseph. ¿Caos de preservación histórica o preservación histórica del caos?: el caso de Puerto Rico. *Homines*, v. 15 – 16, no. 2 – 1 (Oct 91 – Dec 92), pp. 262 – 264.

CULTURAL RELATIVISM

See
Anthropology

CULTURE

See
Civilization
Civilization, Modern
Popular culture
Subdivisions *Civilization, Cultural policy*, and *Intellectual life* under names of specific countries
Subdivisions *Culture* and *History* under *Hispanic Americans (U.S.)* and names of Indian groups

CUMANÁ, VENEZUELA

Vetancourt Vigas, F. C. El pendón español en el ayuntamiento de Cumaná (Previously published in this journal vol. 1, no. 1, 1912). *Boletín de la Academia Nacional de la Historia (Venezuela)*, v. 75, no. 300 (Oct – Dec 92), pp. 279 – 293.

CUNA INDIANS

Rivera Domínguez, Juan Antonio. Relato de un viaje a San Blas. *Revista Cultural Lotería*, v. 50, no. 385 (Sept – Oct 91), pp. 88 – 92.

CUNHA, EUCLYDES DA

Scarabôtolo, Hélio Antônio. Rio Branco, Euclides da Cunha e o tratado de limites com o Peru. *Revista do Instituto Histórico e Geográfico Brasileiro*, no. 370 (Jan – Mar 91), pp. 82 – 93.

Criticism and interpretation

Compitello, Malcolm Alan. Reflexiones sobre el acto de narrar: Benet, Vargas Llosa y Euclides da Cunha. *Insula*, no. 559 – 560 (July – Aug 93), pp. 19 – 22.

Criticism of specific works

Os sertões

Bernucci, Leopoldo M. *Historia de un malentendido: un estudio transtextual de 'La guerra del fin del mundo' de Mario Vargas Llosa* reviewed by Sara Castro-Klarén. *Hispanic Review*, v. 61, no. 1 (Winter 93), pp. 133 – 134.

CURANDERISMO

See
Folk medicine

CURITIBA, BRAZIL

Lerner, Jaime. La ciudad optimista. *Nexos*, v. 16, no. 189 (Sept 93), pp. 13 – 15.

CURRENCY QUESTION

See also
Foreign exchange problem
Money and money supply

Baldinelli, Elvio. Políticas monetarias y fiscales en la integración regional. *Integración Latinoamericana,* v. 18, no. 189 – 190 (May – June 93), pp. 28 – 37. Bibl, tables.

CUSI YUPANQUI, TITO

Correspondence, reminiscences, etc.

Yupanqui, Titu Cusi. *Instrucción al licenciado don Lope García de Castro, 1750* edited by Liliana Regalado de Hurtado. Reviewed by Raquel Chang-Rodríguez. *Hispanic American Historical Review,* v. 73, no. 4 (Nov 93), pp. 699 – 700.

CUSTOMS ADMINISTRATION

See
Tariff

CUYO, ARGENTINA

Terbeck, C. Augusto. La promoción minera intentada por Rivadavia: las minas de Cuyo y "The River Plate Mining Association." *Investigaciones y Ensayos,* no. 41 (Jan – Dec 91), pp. 423 – 455. Bibl.

CUZCO, PERU (CITY)

Barnes, Monica and Daniel J. Slive. El puma de Cuzco: ¿Plano de la ciudad ynga o noción europea? *Revista Andina,* v. 11, no. 1 (July 93), pp. 70 – 102. Bibl, maps, facs.

Krüggeler, Thomas. Los artesanos del Cusco, la crisis regional y el régimen republicano, 1824 – 1869. *Siglo XIX: Revista,* no. 11, 2a época (Jan – June 92), pp. 111 – 148. Bibl, tables.

Martín Rubio, María del Carmen. El Cuzco incaico, según Juan de Betanzos. *Cuadernos Hispanoamericanos,* no. 511 (Jan 93), pp. 7 – 23. Bibl, il.

CUZCO, PERU (DEPARTMENT)

Mesclier, Evelyne. Cusco: espacios campesinos en un contexto de inestabilidad económica y retracción del estado (With several commentaries and a response by the authoress). *Revista Andina,* v. 11, no. 1 (July 93), pp. 7 – 53. Bibl, maps.

Peralta Ruiz, Víctor. *En pos del tributo: burocracia estatal, élite regional y comunidades indígenas en el Cusco rural, 1826 – 1854* reviewed by Paul Gootenberg. *Revista Andina,* v. 10, no. 2 (Dec 92), pp. 547 – 548.

— *En pos del tributo: burocracia estatal, élite regional y comunidades indígenas en el Cusco rural, 1826 – 1854* reviewed by Serena Fernández Alonso. *Revista de Indias,* v. 53, no. 197 (Jan – Apr 93), pp. 116 – 117.

CYPESS, SANDRA MESSINGER

Correspondence, reminiscences, etc.

Cypess, Sandra Messinger. Otro monólogo más (D'après Oscar Villegas' *Un señor y una señora*). *Latin American Theatre Review,* v. 26, no. 2 (Spring 93), pp. 89 – 92.

CZECH REPUBLIC

See
Archives – Czech Republic

DAIRYING

Brazil

Fornetti, Marco et al. Desenvolvimento e uso de modelos computacionais no planejamento da produção em indústrias laticinistas de pequeno porte: um estudo de caso. *Revista de Economia e Sociologia Rural,* v. 29, no. 4 (Oct – Dec 91), pp. 401 – 410. Bibl, charts.

Silva, Maurício Corrêa da et al. Rentabilidade e risco no produção de leite numa região de Santa Catarina. *Revista de Economia e Sociologia Rural,* v. 30, no. 1 (Jan – Mar 92), pp. 63 – 81. Bibl, tables.

DAMS AND RESERVOIRS

See also
Water
Water power

Brazil

Arcifa, Marlene Sofia and Adriana Jorge Meschiatti. Distribution and Feeding Ecology of Fishes in a Brazilian Reservoir: Lake Monte Alegre. *Interciencia,* v. 18, no. 6 (Nov – Dec 93), pp. 302 – 313. Bibl, tables, charts.

Assunção, Luiz Márcio and Ian Livingstone. Desenvolvimento inadequado: construção de açudes e secas no sertão do Nordeste. *Revista Brasileira de Economia,* v. 47, no. 3 (July – Sept 93), pp. 425 – 448. Bibl, tables, charts.

Beaney, Peter W. The Irrigated Eldorado: State-Managed Rural Development, Redemocratisation, and Popular Participation in the Brazilian Northeast. *Bulletin of Latin American Research,* v. 12, no. 3 (Sept 93), pp. 249 – 272. Bibl.

Jamaica

Miller, Learie A. A Preliminary Assessment of the Economic Cost of Land Degradation: The Hermitage Catchment, Jamaica. *Caribbean Geography,* v. 3, no. 4 (Sept 92), pp. 244 – 252. Bibl, tables, maps.

Peru

Martínez, Héctor. Perú: la irrigación Jequetepeque – Zana; impacto de la presa de Gallito Ciego. *Estudios Rurales Latinoamericanos,* v. 15, no. 2 – 3 (May – Dec 92), pp. 3 – 27. Bibl, tables.

Venezuela

Cova, Maritza and Teresa Vegas Vilarrubia. Estudio sobre la distribución y ecología de macrofitos acuáticos en el embalse de Guri. *Interciencia,* v. 18, no. 2 (Mar – Apr 93), pp. 77 – 82. Bibl, tables, maps, charts.

DANCING

See also
Ballet
Bolero (Dance)
Capoeira (Dance)
Folk dancing
Habanera (Dance)
Merengue (Dance)
Samba (Dance)
Tango (Dance)

Cuba

Hernández García, Lissette. Entrevista con Ramiro Guerra. *La Palabra y el Hombre,* no. 82 (Apr – June 92), pp. 285 – 290.

Latin America

Sources

Van Jacob, Scott. Basic Reference Sources for Latin American Dramatic Arts. *SALALM Papers,* v. 34 (1989), pp. 334 – 344. Bibl.

Mexico

Vázquez Hall, Patricia. Concurso de INBA: premios inexplicables. *Plural (Mexico),* v. 22, no. 261 (June 93), pp. 88 – 89.

— Danza: de todo en un día. *Plural (Mexico),* v. 22, no. 263 (Aug 93), p. 80.

— Palabras con Rodolfo Lastra. *Plural (Mexico),* v. 22, no. 257 (Feb 93), pp. 75 – 76.

— Pilar Medina, un águila mestiza. *Plural (Mexico),* v. 22, no. 258 (Mar 93), p. 72.

— Waldeen, pensadora y maestra de la danza. *Plural (Mexico),* v. 22, no. 265 (Oct 93), p. 85.

DANTYSZEK, JAN

Axer, Jersy. Una carta: correspondencia de Hernán Cortés con Jan Dantyszek (Includes the reproduction of one letter by Hernando Cortez). *Plural (Mexico),* v. 22, no. 266 (Nov 93), pp. 68 – 72. Bibl.

DARIÉN, PANAMA

Pastor Núñez, Aníbal. Medicina popular y creencias mágico – religiosas de la población negra del Darién. *Revista Cultural Lotería,* v. 51, no. 387 (Feb 92), pp. 61 – 68. Bibl.

DARÍO, RUBÉN

Biography

Darío, Rubén. *Autobiografía; Ora de Mallorca* reviewed by Graciela Montaldo. *Revista de Crítica Literaria Latinoamericana,* v. 19, no. 38 (July – Dec 93), pp. 411 – 413.

Criticism and interpretation

Hauser, Rex. Settings and Connections: Darío's Poetic "Engarce." *Revista Canadiense de Estudios Hispánicos,* v. 17, no. 3 (Spring 93), pp. 437 – 451. Bibl.

Lloreda, Waldo César. La transformación de Rubén Darío en Chile. *La Palabra y el Hombre,* no. 84 (Oct – Dec 92), pp. 93 – 109. Bibl.

Varas Reyes, Víctor. América en tres momentos de la lírica rubendariana: miscelánea. *Signo,* no. 36 – 37, Nueva época (May – Dec 92), pp. 433 – 442.

Criticism of specific works

Azul

Mattalía Alonso, Sonia. El canto del "aura": autonomía y mercado literario en los cuentos de *Azul* . . . . *Revista de Crítica Literaria Latinoamericana,* v. 19, no. 38 (July – Dec 93), pp. 279 – 292.

Zimmermann Martí, María. Estudio paralelo de *Azul* y *Versos sencillos. Revista Cultural Lotería,* v. 51, no. 390 (July – Aug 92), pp. 65 – 84. Bibl.

DARWIN, CHARLES ROBERT

Ayala, Francisco J. and Rosaura Ruiz Gutiérrez. Darwinismo y sociedad en México. *Siglo XIX: Revista,* no. 12, 2a época (July – Dec 92), pp. 87 – 104. Bibl.

DEATH

Barriga Calle, Irma. La experiencia de la muerte en Lima, siglo XVII. *Apuntes (Peru),* no. 31 (July – Dec 92), pp. 81 – 102. Bibl.

Carmichael, Elizabeth and Chloë Sayer. *The Skeleton and the Feast: The Day of the Dead in Mexico* reviewed by Ward S. Albro III. *Hispanic American Historical Review,* v. 73, no. 1 (Feb 93), p. 127.

Garscha, Karsten. Das Leben, nur eine kurze Reise: Der mexikanische Totenkult. *Iberoamericana,* v. 17, no. 50 (1993), pp. 16 – 37. Bibl.

Martínez, Ronald. La posición horizontal. *Signo,* no. 38, Nueva época (Jan – Apr 93), pp. 177 – 179.

Szászdi León-Borja, István. Un tabú de la muerte: la innominación de los vivos y los difuntos como norma jurídica prehispánica. *Anuario de Estudios Americanos,* v. 49 (1992), pp. 3 – 20. Bibl.

DEATH IN LITERATURE

Canfield, Martha L. Muerte y redención en la poesía de César Vallejo. *Inti,* no. 36 (Fall 92), pp. 39 – 44. Bibl.

Garabedian, Martha Ann. Visión fantástica de la muerte en algunos poemas de Oscar Hahn. *Revista Chilena de Literatura,* no. 41 (Apr 93), pp. 71 – 78. Bibl.

González, Eduardo. *The Monstered Self: Narratives of Death and Performance in Latin American Fiction* reviewed by Ana Eire. *Hispania (USA),* v. 76, no. 2 (May 93), pp. 286 – 287.

Oliveira, Ana Maria Domingues de. A temática da morte em Cecília Meireles e Gabriela Mistral. *Revista de Letras (Brazil),* v. 32 (1992), pp. 127 – 139. Bibl.

Zacklin, Lyda. Escritura, exactitud y fascinación en la narrativa de José Balza. *Inti,* no. 37 – 38 (Spring – Fall 93), pp. 171 – 177. Bibl.

DEBT-FOR-NATURE SWAPS

See
Debts, Public
Ecology

DEBTS, PUBLIC

Brazil

Giambiagi, Fábio and Alvaro Antônio Zini Júnior. Renegociação da dívida interna mobiliária: uma proposta. *Revista de Economia Política (Brazil),* v. 13, no. 2 (Apr – June 93), pp. 5 – 27. Bibl, tables, charts.

Meyer, Arno. Apoio financeiro externo e estabilização econômica. *Revista de Economia Política (Brazil),* v. 13, no. 1 (Jan – Mar 93), pp. 135 – 148. Tables.

Central America

Cáceres, Luis René. Elementos para una estrategia centroamericana de renegociación de la deuda externa y captación de recursos. *ECA; Estudios Centroamericanos,* v. 48, no. 537 – 538 (July – Aug 93), pp. 693 – 709. Bibl, tables.

Chile

Fermandois Huerta, Joaquín. Del unilateralismo a la negociación: Chile, Estados Unidos y la deuda de largo plazo, 1934 – 1938. *Historia (Chile),* no. 26 (1991 – 1992), pp. 71 – 115. Bibl.

Developing countries

Ahmed, Masood and Lawrence Summers. Informe sobre la crisis de la deuda en su décimo aniversario. *Comercio Exterior,* v. 43, no. 1 (Jan 93), pp. 74 – 78. Tables.

Latin America

Castro Escudero, Alfredo. Deuda externa: avances y sinsabores del esfuerzo regional. *Comercio Exterior,* v. 43, no. 1 (Jan 93), pp. 58 – 66. Bibl, tables.

Devlin, Robert T. Canje de deuda por naturaleza: la necesidad de una nueva agenda. *Revista de Economia Política (Brazil),* v. 13, no. 3 (July – Sept 93), pp. 69 – 81. Tables.

Devlin, Robert T. and Ricardo Ffrench-Davis. Diez años de crisis de la deuda latinoamericana. *Comercio Exterior,* v. 43, no. 1 (Jan 93), pp. 4 – 20. Bibl, tables.

Ffrench-Davis, Ricardo. Los desafíos de la deuda externa y el desarrollo: a diez años del inicio de la crisis. *Estudios Internacionales (Chile),* v. 26, no. 102 (Apr – June 93), pp. 155 – 156. Tables.

Guimarães, Roberto Pereira. Deuda externa y desarrollo sustentable en América Latina: una perspectiva sociopolítica. *Revista Interamericana de Planificación,* v. 26, no. 101 – 102 (Jan – June 93), pp. 7 – 42. Bibl.

Larraín B., Felipe and Marcelo Selowsky, eds. *The Public Sector and the Latin American Crisis* reviewed by Christian Anglade. *Journal of Latin American Studies,* v. 25, no. 2 (May 93), pp. 404 – 405.

Martínez, Osvaldo. Debt and Foreign Capital: The Origin of the Crisis (Translated by Luis Fierro). *Latin American Perspectives,* v. 20, no. 1 (Winter 93), pp. 64 – 82. Bibl, tables.

Osorio Paz, Saúl. ¿Está resuelta el problema de la deuda? *Momento Económico,* no. 66 (Mar – Apr 93), pp. 28 – 30.

Pietschmann, Horst. Entstehung und innere Auswirkungen der lateinamerikanischen Schuldenkrise. *Jahrbuch für Geschichte von Staat, Wirtschaft und Gesellschaft Lateinamerikas,* v. 29 (1992), pp. 421 – 444. Bibl, tables.

Mexico

Phillips, Fred P., IV and Steven M. Rubin. Debt for Nature: Swap Meet for the '90s. *Business Mexico,* v. 3, no. 1 (Jan – Feb 93), pp. 46 – 47.

Mathematical models

Armendáriz de Aghion, Beatriz. El precio de los bonos, las razones deuda – exportación y las moratorias en el servicio de la deuda exterior de un país: el caso de México. *El Trimestre Económico,* v. 60, no. 237 (Jan – Mar 93), pp. 185 – 202. Bibl, tables, charts.

Werner, Martín. La solvencia del sector público: el caso de México in 1988 (Translated by Carlos Villegas). *El Trimestre Económico,* v. 59, no. 236 (Oct – Dec 92), pp. 751 – 772. Bibl, tables, charts.

DECENTRALIZATION IN GOVERNMENT

Argentina

Arango de Maglio, Aída. Descentralización y tiempo y espacio newtonianos: un análisis de la descentralización "real" en la Argentina. *Realidad Económica,* no. 119 (Oct – Nov 93), pp. 73 – 102. Bibl.

Prévôt-Schapira, Marie-France. Argentine: fédéralisme et territoires. *Cahiers des Amériques Latines,* no. 14 (1992), pp. 4 – 32. Bibl, tables, maps.

Brazil

Ferreira, Marieta de Moraes. A reação republicana e a crise política dos anos '20. *Estudos Históricos*, v. 6, no. 11 (Jan – June 93), pp. 9 – 23. Bibl.

Lopez, Luiz Roberto. Brasil: o federalismo mal costurado. *Vozes*, v. 87, no. 3 (May – June 93), pp. 79 – 82.

Melo, Marcus André Barreto Campelo de. Municipalismo, "Nation-Building" e a modernização do estado no Brasil. *Revista Brasileira de Ciências Sociais*, v. 8, no. 23 (Oct 93), pp. 85 – 100. Bibl.

Chile

Irarrázaval Llona, Ignacio. Autonomía municipal: un proyecto político perdiente. *EURE*, v. 19, no. 57 (July 93), pp. 79 – 94. Bibl, tables.

Letelier S., Leonardo. La teoría del federalismo fiscal y su relevancia en el caso municipal chileno. *Cuadernos de Economía (Chile)*, v. 30, no. 90 (Aug 93), pp. 199 – 224. Bibl, tables.

Colombia

Gaviria Trujillo, César. Palabras del presidente de la república, César Gaviria Trujillo, en el acto de instalación. *Planeación y Desarrollo*, v. 24, no. 1 (Jan – Apr 93), pp. 17 – 25.

Ortiz Mesa, Luis Javier. Procesos de descentralización en Colombia durante el período federal, 1850 – 1886. *Planeación y Desarrollo*, v. 24, no. 1 (Jan – Apr 93), pp. 199 – 231. Bibl, tables.

Wiesner Durán, Eduardo. *Colombia: descentralización y federalismo fiscal* reviewed by César Vargas. *Planeación y Desarrollo*, v. 24, no. 1 (Jan – Apr 93), pp. 465 – 471.

Cost

Castañeda, Tarcisio. Descentralización de los sectores sociales: riesgos y oportunidades. *Planeación y Desarrollo*, v. 24, no. 1 (Jan – Apr 93), pp. 97 – 115. Tables, charts.

Montenegro Trujillo, Armando. Descentralización en Colombia: una perspectiva internacional. *Planeación y Desarrollo*, v. 24, no. 1 (Jan – Apr 93), pp. 279 – 307. Bibl.

Vargas, César et al. Financiamiento del desarrollo regional: situación actual y perspectivas. *Planeación y Desarrollo*, v. 24, no. 1 (Jan – Apr 93), pp. 311 – 346. Tables, charts.

Law and legislation

Aja, Eliseo. El Proyecto de Ley colombiano visto por un español. *Planeación y Desarrollo*, v. 24, no. 1 (Jan – Apr 93), pp. 191 – 197.

Latin America

Ahumada Pacheco, Jaime. Descentralización, desarrollo local y municipios en América Latina. *Revista Paraguaya de Sociología*, v. 29, no. 85 (Sept – Dec 92), pp. 73 – 94. Bibl.

Campbell, Tim et al. Descentralización hacia los gobiernos locales en América Latina y el Caribe. *Planeación y Desarrollo*, v. 24, no. 1 (Jan – Apr 93), pp. 27 – 95. Tables, charts.

Curbelo Ranero, José Luis. Positive Adjustment in Latin America: On Decentralization and Development Planning. *European Review of Latin American and Caribbean Studies*, no. 54 (June 93), pp. 25 – 44. Bibl.

Navarro, Juan Carlos. *Descentralización: una alternativa de política educativa* reviewed by Emil Alvarado Vera. *La Educación (USA)*, v. 36, no. 111 – 113 (1992), p. 301.

Palma, Eduardo and Dolores María Rufián Lizana. La descentralización de los servicios sociales. *Estudios Sociales (Chile)*, no. 77 (July – Sept 93), pp. 73 – 116. Bibl.

Methodology

Sili, Marcelo Enrique. Desarrollo local: entre la realidad y la utopía. *Revista Interamericana de Planificación*, v. 26, no. 101 – 102 (Jan – June 93), pp. 63 – 77. Bibl, charts.

Mexico

Massolo, Alejandra. Descentralización y reforma municipal: ¿Fracaso anunciado y sorpresas inesperadas? *Revista Interamericana de Planificación*, v. 26, no. 101 – 102 (Jan – June 93), pp. 196 – 230. Bibl, tables.

Rodríguez, Victoria Elizabeth. The Politics of Decentralisation in Mexico: From "Municipio Libre" to "Solidaridad." *Bulletin of Latin American Research*, v. 12, no. 2 (May 93), pp. 133 – 145. Bibl.

Rodríguez Rivera, Oscar. Derechos políticos y autonomía regional. *Nueva Antropología*, v. 13, no. 44 (Aug 93), pp. 137 – 141.

Bibliography

Vázquez, Josefina Zoraida. Un viejo tema: el federalismo y el centralismo. *Historia Mexicana*, v. 42, no. 3 (Jan – Mar 93), pp. 621 – 631.

Peru

Cipriani, Juan Luis et al. ¿Qué quiere el peruano común y corriente? *Debate (Peru)*, v. 16, no. 75 (Dec 93 – Jan 94), pp. 15 – 18. Il.

DECORATIONS OF HONOR

Argentina

Facciolo, Osvaldo Adolfo. Los 50 años de la "Orden del Libertador General San Martín." *Todo Es Historia*, v. 27, no. 315 (Oct 93), pp. 90 – 94. Il.

DEFENSE

See
  Armaments
  Atomic weapons and disarmament
  Military art and science
  Military posts
  National security
  Subdivision *Armed forces* under names of specific countries

DE FIORI, ERNESTO

Laudanna, Mayra. Ernesto de Fiori. *Vozes*, v. 86, no. 4 (July – Aug 92), pp. 59 – 65. Il.

DE GRAZIA, ETTORE

Butler, Ron. The Colors between Earth and Sky. *Américas*, v. 45, no. 2 (Mar – Apr 93), pp. 14 – 21. Il.

DELGADO, ANTONIO

Interviews

Hernández Téllez, Josefina. ¿Cómo funciona y para qué sirve la participacíon en la Procuraduría General de Justicia del D.F.? *Fem*, v. 17, no. 123 (May 93), p. 43.

DELGADO, HONORIO F.

Chiappo, Leopoldo. La concepción del hombre en Honorio Delgado. *Apuntes (Peru)*, no. 31 (July – Dec 92), pp. 55 – 62.

DEMOCRACY

See also
  Elections
  Political participation

Ballesteros, Carlos. El problema de la legitimidad democrática ante las transformaciones políticas. *Revista Mexicana de Ciencias Políticas y Sociales*, v. 38, Nueva época, no. 151 (Jan – Mar 93), pp. 103 – 116.

Escobar Herrán, Guillermo León. Participación, legitimidad y gobernabilidad. *Cuadernos Americanos*, no. 39, Nueva época (May – June 93), pp. 53 – 56.

Fernández-Baca, Jorge. La importancia de la democracia para los economistas. *Apuntes (Peru)*, no. 29 (July – Dec 91), pp. 9 – 16. Bibl, charts.

Fernández Santillán, José F. Democracia y liberalismo: ensayo de filosofía política. *Revista Mexicana de Ciencias Políticas y Sociales*, v. 38, Nueva época, no. 151 (Jan – Mar 93), pp. 157 – 183. Bibl.

Gandolfo, Carlos. El régimen parlamentario y la estabilidad democrática. *Apuntes (Peru)*, no. 29 (July – Dec 91), pp. 17 – 25.

Gunther, Richard and John Higley, eds. *Elites and Democratic Consolidation in Latin America and Southern Europe* reviewed by Richard Gillespie. *Bulletin of Latin American Research*, v. 12, no. 2 (May 93), pp. 235 – 236.

— *Elites and Democratic Consolidation in Latin America and Southern Europe* reviewed by Eric Hershberg. *Hispanic American Historical Review*, v. 73, no. 2 (May 93), pp. 298 – 299.

— *Elites and Democratic Consolidation in Latin America and Southern Europe* reviewed by Troy M. Bollinger. *Journal of Inter-American Studies and World Affairs,* v. 35, no. 1 (1993), pp. 158 – 166.

— *Elites and Democratic Consolidation in Latin America and Southern Europe* reviewed by Laura A. Hastings. *Journal of Latin American Studies,* v. 25, no. 1 (Feb 93), pp. 212 – 214.

Ipola, Emilio de. La democracia en el amanecer de la sociología. *Revista Mexicana de Sociología,* v. 54, no. 2 (Apr – June 92), pp. 215 – 232. Bibl.

Madrid Hurtado, Miguel de la. Notas sobre democracia y cultura. *Cuadernos Americanos,* no. 39, Nueva época (May – June 93), pp. 34 – 41.

Quer Antich, Santiago. Conspiremos por la democracia o la democracia "a la Maturana." *Estudios Sociales (Chile),* no. 76 (Apr – June 93), pp. 197 – 203.

Argentina

Aftalión, Marcelo E. Que diez años no es nada. *Todo Es Historia,* v. 27, no. 317 (Dec 93), pp. 58 – 60. II.

Alonso, María Ernestina. 1983 – 1993: el nuevo poder político. *Realidad Económica,* no. 120 (Nov – Dec 93), pp. 61 – 68.

Cheresky, Isidoro. Argentina: una democracia a la búsqueda de su institución. *European Review of Latin American and Caribbean Studies,* no. 53 (Dec 92), pp. 7 – 45.

Gorlier, Juan Carlos. Democratización en América del Sur: una reflexión sobre el potencial de los movimientos sociales en Argentina y Brasil. *Revista Mexicana de Sociología,* v. 54, no. 4 (Oct – Dec 92), pp. 119 – 151. Bibl.

Marrero Fente, Raúl and Mirta Yordi. El tema de la democracia en pensadores políticos argentinos. *Islas,* no. 96 (May – Aug 90), pp. 67 – 70. Bibl.

Rabanal, Rodolfo. Reflexiones sobre una realidad objetable. *Todo Es Historia,* v. 27, no. 317 (Dec 93), pp. 62 – 65. II.

Riz, Liliana de and Catalina Smulovitz. Instauración democrática y reforma política en Argentina y Uruguay: un análisis comparado. *Ibero-Amerikanisches Archiv,* v. 18, no. 1 – 2 (1992), pp. 181 – 224. Bibl, tables.

Brazil

Gorlier, Juan Carlos. Democratización en América del Sur: una reflexión sobre el potencial de los movimientos sociales en Argentina y Brasil. *Revista Mexicana de Sociología,* v. 54, no. 4 (Oct – Dec 92), pp. 119 – 151. Bibl.

Moisés, José Alvaro. Democratización y cultura política de masas en Brasil. *Revista Mexicana de Sociología,* v. 54, no. 1 (Jan – Mar 92), pp. 167 – 203. Bibl, tables.

Pécaut, Daniel and Bernardo Sorj, eds. *Métamorphoses de la représentation politique au Brésil et en Europe* reviewed by Stéphane Monclaire (Review entitled "Partis et représentations politiques au Brésil"). *Cahiers des Amériques Latines,* no. 13 (1992), pp. 173 – 177.

Weffort, Francisco Corrêa. *Qual democracia?* reviewed by José de Arimateia da Cruz (Review entitled "Review Essay: Democratic Consolidation and the Socio-Economic Crisis of Latin America"). *Journal of Inter-American Studies and World Affairs,* v. 35, no. 1 (1993), pp. 145 – 152. Bibl, tables.

Caribbean area

Maríñez, Pablo A. Democracia y descolonización en el Caribe. *Estudios Sociales (Dominican Republic),* v. 26, no. 92 (Apr – June 93), pp. 5 – 20. Bibl, tables.

Central America

Vilas, Carlos María. Después de la revolución: democratización y cambio social en Centroamérica. *Revista Mexicana de Sociología,* v. 54, no. 3 (July – Sept 92), pp. 3 – 44. Bibl.

Chile

Garretón Merino, Manuel Antonio. Aprendizaje y gobernabilidad en la redemocratización chilena. *Nueva Sociedad,* no. 128 (Nov – Dec 93), pp. 148 – 157.

— La redemocratización política en Chile: transición, inauguración y evolución. *Estudios Interdisciplinarios de América Latina y el Caribe,* v. 4, no. 1 (Jan – June 93), pp. 5 – 25. Bibl.

Godoy Arcaya, Oscar. A veinte años de la crisis de la democracia chilena. *Mensaje,* v. 42, no. 422 (Sept 93), pp. 415 – 418.

Hojman A., David E. Non-Governmental Organisations (NGOs) and the Chilean Transition to Democracy. *European Review of Latin American and Caribbean Studies,* no. 54 (June 93), pp. 7 – 24. Bibl.

Rabkin, Rhoda Pearl. The Aylwin Government and "Tutelary" Democracy: A Concept in Search of a Case? *Journal of Inter-American Studies and World Affairs,* v. 34, no. 4 (Winter 92 – 93), pp. 119 – 194. Bibl, tables.

Sunkel, Guillermo and Eugenio Tironi B. Modernización de las comunicaciones y democratización de la política: los medios en la transición a la democracia en Chile. *Estudios Públicos (Chile),* no. 52 (Spring 93), pp. 215 – 246. Bibl, tables.

Sunkel, Osvaldo. La consolidación de la democracia y del desarrollo en Chile: desafíos y tareas. *El Trimestre Económico,* v. 59, no. 236 (Oct – Dec 92), pp. 816 – 830.

— Consolidating Democracy and Development in Chile. *CEPAL Review,* no. 47 (Aug 92), pp. 37 – 46.

Wolter, Matilde. Chile renueva su democracia. *Nueva Sociedad,* no. 128 (Nov – Dec 93), pp. 6 – 11.

Colombia
Bibliography

Gold-Biss, Michael. Colombia: Understanding Recent Democratic Transformations in a Violent Polity (Review article). *Latin American Research Review,* v. 28, no. 1 (1993), pp. 215 – 234. Bibl.

Costa Rica

Barrantes Araya, Trino. Democracia y modernización en Costa Rica: proceso electoral y bipartidismo, 1983 – 1991. *Revista de Ciencias Sociales (Costa Rica),* no. 60 (June 93), pp. 17 – 26. Bibl, tables.

Dabène, Olivier. *Costa Rica: juicio a la democracia* reviewed by Manuel A. Solís. *Anuario de Estudios Centroamericanos,* v. 18, no. 2 (1992), pp. 117 – 121.

Zeledón Cambronero, Mario. Periodismo, historia y democracia. *Revista de Ciencias Sociales (Costa Rica),* no. 57 (Sept 92), pp. 7 – 16. Bibl.

Developing countries

Berat, Lynn and Yossi Shain. Evening the Score: Layered Legacies of the Interregnum. *Estudios Interdisciplinarios de América Latina y el Caribe,* v. 4, no. 1 (Jan – June 93), pp. 57 – 91. Bibl.

Dominican Republic

Maríñez, Pablo A. El proceso democrático en República Dominicana: algunos rasgos fundamentales. *Estudios Sociales (Dominican Republic),* v. 26, no. 93 (July – Sept 93), pp. 27 – 39. Bibl.

Europe

Pécaut, Daniel and Bernardo Sorj, eds. *Métamorphoses de la représentation politique au Brésil et en Europe* reviewed by Stéphane Monclaire (Review entitled "Partis et représentations politiques au Brésil"). *Cahiers des Amériques Latines,* no. 13 (1992), pp. 173 – 177.

Europe, Eastern

Przeworski, Adam. *Democracy and the Market: Political and Economic Reforms in Eastern Europe and Latin America* reviewed by Carlos Maya Ambía. *El Trimestre Económico,* v. 60, no. 239 (July – Sept 93), pp. 733 – 744.

Guatemala
Bibliography

Trudeau, Robert H. Understanding Transitions to Democracy: Recent Work on Guatemala (Review article). *Latin American Research Review,* v. 28, no. 1 (1993), pp. 235 – 247.

Guyana

Ramharack, Baytoram. Consociational Democracy: A Democratic Option for Guyana. *Caribbean Studies,* v. 25, no. 1 – 2 (Jan – July 92), pp. 75 – 101. Bibl.

Latin America

Alcántara Sáez, Manuel. ¿Democracias inciertas o democracias consolidadas en América Latina? *Revista Mexicana de Sociología,* v. 54, no. 1 (Jan – Mar 92), pp. 205 – 223.

Benítez Manaut, Raúl. Identity Crisis: The Military in Changing Times (Translated by Kent Klineman). *NACLA Report on the Americas*, v. 27, no. 2 (Sept – Oct 93), pp. 15 – 19.

Bravo Lira, Bernardino. Democracia: ¿Antidoto frente a la corrupción? *Estudios Públicos (Chile)*, no. 52 (Spring 93), pp. 299 – 308.

Carpizo, Jorge. América Latina y sus problemas. *Cuadernos Americanos*, no. 42, Nueva época (Nov – Dec 93), pp. 28 – 42.

Couffignal, Georges, ed. *Réinventer la démocratie: le défi latino-américain* reviewed by Giorgio Alberti. *Journal of Latin American Studies*, v. 25, no. 2 (May 93), pp. 409 – 410.

Flórez Gallego, Lenín. Historias nacionales, historias de los trabajadores y el problema de la democracia en la obra de Charles Bergquist. *Anuario Colombiano de Historia Social y de la Cultura*, no. 20 (1992), pp. 73 – 88. Bibl, tables.

Franco, Carlos. Visión de la democracia y crisis del régimen. *Nueva Sociedad*, no. 128 (Nov – Dec 93), pp. 50 – 61.

Nun, José. Democracy and Modernization Thirty Years Later. *Latin American Perspectives*, v. 20, no. 4 (Fall 93), pp. 7 – 27. Bibl.

O'Donnell, Guillermo A. Acerca del estado, la democratización y algunos problemas conceptuales: una perspectiva latinoamericana con referencias a países poscomunistas (Translated by Leandro Wolfson). *Desarrollo Económico (Argentina)*, v. 33, no. 130 (July – Sept 93), pp. 163 – 184. Bibl.

— Estado, democratización y ciudadanía. *Nueva Sociedad*, no. 128 (Nov – Dec 93), pp. 62 – 87.

Przeworski, Adam. *Democracy and the Market: Political and Economic Reforms in Eastern Europe and Latin America* reviewed by Carlos Maya Ambía. *El Trimestre Económico*, v. 60, no. 239 (July – Sept 93), pp. 733 – 744.

Remmer, Karen L. The Process of Democratization in Latin America. *Studies in Comparative International Development*, v. 27, no. 4 (Winter 92 – 93), pp. 3 – 24. Bibl.

Roitman Rosenmann, Marcos. Democracia y estado multiétnico en América Latina. *Boletín de Antropología Americana*, no. 24 (Dec 91), pp. 63 – 78. Bibl, il.

Sánchez Agesta, Luis. *La democracia en Hispanoamérica: un balance histórico* reviewed by Frédérique Langue. *Cahiers des Amériques Latines*, no. 13 (1992), pp. 178 – 179.

Sznajder, Mario. Legitimidad y poder políticos frente a las herencias autoritarias: transición y consolidación democrática en América Latina. *Estudios Interdisciplinarios de América Latina y el Caribe*, v. 4, no. 1 (Jan – June 93), pp. 27 – 55. Bibl.

Torres-Rivas, Edelberto. América Latina: gobernabilidad y democracia en sociedades en crisis. *Nueva Sociedad*, no. 128 (Nov – Dec 93), pp. 88 – 101.

Woldenberg, José. ¿Un nuevo animal? *Nexos*, v. 16, no. 185 (May 93), pp. 61 – 65.

Bibliography

Panizza, Francisco E. Democracy's Lost Treasure (Review article). *Latin American Research Review*, v. 28, no. 3 (1993), pp. 251 – 266.

International cooperation

Declaración del Comité Político. *Nueva Sociedad*, no. 123 (Jan – Feb 93), p. 160.

Mexico

Camou, Antonio N. Gobernabilidad y democracia en Mexico: avantares de una transición incierta. *Nueva Sociedad*, no. 128 (Nov – Dec 93), pp. 102 – 119.

Flores Olea, Víctor Manuel. Los sistemas políticos y su crisis, parte II: La articulación democrática y el caso de México. *Revista Mexicana de Ciencias Políticas y Sociales*, v. 38, Nueva época, no. 152 (Apr – June 93), pp. 143 – 160.

Gordillo, Gustavo. Ayudando a la mano invisible: el compromiso democrático. *Nexos*, v. 16, no. 189 (Sept 93), pp. 41 – 43.

Loaeza, Soledad. La incertidumbre política mexicana. *Nexos*, v. 16, no. 186 (June 93), pp. 47 – 59. Bibl.

Merino Huerta, Mauricio. Democracia, después. *Nexos*, v. 16, no. 185 (May 93), pp. 51 – 60. Bibl.

Romero, Jorge Javier. La política de mañana: la futura forma institucional. *Nexos*, v. 16, no. 192 (Dec 93), pp. 53 – 67. Bibl.

Schmidt, Samuel. Lo tortuoso de la democratización mexicana. *Estudios Interdisciplinarios de América Latina y el Caribe*, v. 4, no. 1 (Jan – June 93), pp. 93 – 114. Bibl.

Nicaragua

Serra, Luis. Democracy in Times of War and Socialist Crisis: Reflections Stemming from the Sandinista Revolution. *Latin American Perspectives*, v. 20, no. 2 (Spring 93), pp. 21 – 44. Bibl.

Peru

Hernández, Max and Francisco R. Sagasti. La crisis de gobernabilidad democrática en el Perú. *Debate (Peru)*, v. 16, no. 75 (Dec 93 – Jan 94), pp. 24 – 28. Il.

Rodríguez Rabanal, César. La cultura del diálogo. *Debate (Peru)*, v. 16, no. 73 (June – Aug 93), pp. 27 – 30. Il.

Southern Cone of South America

Caro Figueroa, Gregorio A. Oleada democratizadora en el Cono Sur. *Todo Es Historia*, v. 27, no. 317 (Dec 93), pp. 78 – 81. Il.

Uruguay

Achard, Diego. *La transición en Uruguay* reviewed by Fernando Errandonea. *Cuadernos del CLAEH*, v. 18, no. 67 (Nov 93), pp. 147 – 155.

Riz, Liliana de and Catalina Smulovitz. Instauración democrática y reforma política en Argentina y Uruguay: un análisis comparado. *Ibero-Amerikanisches Archiv*, v. 18, no. 1 – 2 (1992), pp. 181 – 224. Bibl, tables.

DEMOGRAPHY

See
Population

DENIZ, GERARDO

Criticism and interpretation

Casado, Miguel. Pistas para llegar a Gerardo Deniz. *Vuelta*, v. 17, no. 198 (May 93), pp. 63 – 64.

DEREGULATION

See
Foreign trade regulation
Subdivision *Deregulation* under names of specific industries

DERMATOGLYPHICS

Vidal, Lux et al, eds. *Grafismo indígena: ensaios de antropologia estética* reviewed by Clarice Cohn. *Revista de Antropologia (Brazil)*, v. 34 (1991), pp. 230 – 232.

DESERTS

See also
Droughts

Argentina

Malatesta, Parisina. Tracing Evolution in the Land of the Sand (Translated by Barbara Meza, photographs by Jorge Provenza). *Américas*, v. 45, no. 4 (July – Aug 93), pp. 6 – 13. Il, maps.

DETECTIVE AND MYSTERY STORIES

Ludmer, Josefina. El delito: ficciones de exclusión y sueños de justicia. *Revista de Crítica Literaria Latinoamericana*, v. 19, no. 38 (July – Dec 93), pp. 145 – 153.

Prieto Taboada, Antonio. El caso de las pistas culturales en *Partners in Crime*. *The Americas Review*, v. 19, no. 3 – 4 (Winter 91), pp. 117 – 132. Bibl.

Saravia Quiroz, Leobardo, ed. *En la línea de fuego: relatos policíacos de frontera* (Review). *La Palabra y el Hombre*, no. 81 (Jan – Mar 92), pp. 324 – 325.

Simpson, Amelia S., ed. *New Tales of Mystery and Crime from Latin America* reviewed by John Gledson. *Bulletin of Latin American Research*, v. 12, no. 1 (Jan 93), pp. 130 – 131.

DEVALUATION

See
Foreign exchange problem

DEVELOPING COUNTRIES

See also
Agriculture and state – Developing countries
Communism – Developing countries
Debts, Public – Developing countries
Democracy – Developing countries
Ecology and development – Developing countries
Education – Developing countries
Education and state – Developing countries
Food supply – Developing countries
Income distribution – Developing countries
International business enterprises – Developing
countries
Investments, Foreign – Developing countries
Land reform – Developing countries
Pollution – Developing countries
Population – Developing countries
Privatization – Developing countries
Public administration – Developing countries
Public health – Developing countries
Regional planning – Developing countries
School management and organization – Developing
countries
Slums – Developing countries
Subcontracting – Developing countries
Urbanization – Developing countries
Women – Developing countries

Commerce

Bourguignon, François and Christian Morrisson, eds. *External
Trade and Income Distribution* reviewed by Jaime de Melo.
Economic Development and Cultural Change, v. 42, no. 1
(Oct 93), pp. 198 – 200.

Edwards, Sebastián. Orientación del comercio exterior, deformaciones y crecimiento en los países en desarrollo. *El Trimestre Económico*, v. 59, Special issue (Dec 92), pp. 41 –
74. Bibl, tables.

Economic conditions

Santos, Wanderley Guilherme dos. *Razões da desordem* reviewed by Cláudio Gonçalves Couto. *Revista Brasileira de
Ciências Sociais*, v. 8, no. 23 (Oct 93), pp. 153 – 155.

Sen, Amartya Kumar. A economia da vida e da morte (Translated by Heloisa Jahn). *Revista Brasileira de Ciências Sociais*, v. 8, no. 23 (Oct 93), pp. 138 – 145.

Economic policy

Akyüz, Yilmaz. Intervención del estado y crecimiento económico. *Pensamiento Iberoamericano*, no. 22 – 23, tomo II
(July 92 – June 93), pp. 251 – 253.

Birdsall, Nancy. Ajuste y reformas económicas: la necesidad
de gestionar la transición al crecimiento. *Pensamiento Iberoamericano*, no. 22 – 23, tomo II (July 92 – June 93), pp.
255 – 258. Charts.

Bruno, Michael et al, eds. *Lessons of Economic Stabilization
and Its Aftermath* reviewed by Peter Winglee. *Journal of
Developing Areas*, v. 27, no. 2 (Jan 93), pp. 248 – 250.

Haggard, Stephan. *Pathways from the Periphery* reviewed by
Henry J. Bruton. *Economic Development and Cultural
Change*, v. 41, no. 4 (July 93), pp. 883 – 886.

Uribe-Echeverría, J. Francisco. Problemas regionales en las
economías abiertas del Tercer Mundo. *EURE*, v. 19, no. 58
(Oct 93), pp. 7 – 17. Bibl.

Foreign economic relations

Agosin, Manuel Roberto and Diana A. Tussie de Federman.
Globalización, regionalización y nuevos dilemas en la polí-
tica de comercio exterior para el desarrollo (Translated by
Carlos Villegas). *El Trimestre Económico*, v. 60, no. 239
(July – Sept 93), pp. 559 – 599. Bibl, tables.

Raghavan, Chakravarthi. *Recolonization: GATT, the Uruguay
Round, and the Third World* (Review entitled "Un libro para
despertar al Tercer Mundo"). *Homines*, v. 15 – 16, no. 2 – 1
(Oct 91 – Dec 92), pp. 384 – 385.

Sarmento, Walney Moraes. Política externa no contexto do
subdesenvolvimento: o exemplo do Brasil. *Política e Estratégica*, v. 8, no. 2 – 4 (Apr – Dec 90), pp. 241 – 267. Bibl,
tables.

Industries

Alvarez Icaza, Pablo. Marco teórico de la industria maquiladora de exportación. *Comercio Exterior*, v. 43, no. 5 (May
93), pp. 415 – 429. Bibl.

Batou, Jean, ed. *Between Development and Underdevelopment: The Precocious Attempts at Industrialization of the
Periphery, 1800 – 1870/Entre développement et sous-
développement: les tentatives précoces d'industrialisation
de la périphérie, 1800 – 1870* reviewed by Colin M. Lewis.
Journal of Latin American Studies, v. 25, no. 2 (May 93), pp.
395 – 396.

Politics

Berat, Lynn and Yossi Shain. Evening the Score: Layered Legacies of the Interregnum. *Estudios Interdisciplinarios de
América Latina y el Caribe*, v. 4, no. 1 (Jan – June 93), pp.
57 – 91. Bibl.

DEVELOPMENT BANKS

See
Banks and banking
International economic relations

DÍAZ, PORFIRIO

Castello, Antonio Emilio. El porfiriato en México. *Todo Es Historia*, v. 26, no. 307 (Feb 93), pp. 9 – 34. Il.

Tello Díaz, Carlos. Porfirio Díaz: album de familia. *Nexos*, v.
16, no. 182 (Feb 93), pp. 69 – 74. Il, facs.

DÍAZ-CASANUEVA, HUMBERTO
Obituaries

Mueren dos poetas. *Atenea (Chile)*, no. 465 – 466 (1992), pp.
353 – 355. Il.

DÍAZ DEL CASTILLO, BERNAL
Criticism of specific works
Historia verdadera de la conquista de la Nueva España

Cortínez, Verónica. "Yo, Bernal Díaz del Castillo": ¿Soldado de
a pie o idiota sin letras? *Revista Chilena de Literatura*, no.
41 (Apr 93), pp. 59 – 69. Bibl.

DÍAZ-DIOCARETZ, MYRIAM
Criticism and interpretation

Klein, Carol Ebersole. The Social Text in Writing by Hispanic
Women: Critical Perspectives of Myriam Díaz-Diocaretz.
The Americas Review, v. 21, no. 1 (Spring 93), pp. 79 – 90.
Bibl.

DÍAZ HERRERA, JORGE
Criticism of specific works
Por qué morimos tanto

Cabrera, Miguel. Las capitulaciones de una derrota. *Cuadernos Hispanoamericanos*, no. 513 (Mar 93), pp. 149 – 155.
Bibl.

DÍAZ MIRÓN, SALVADOR
Criticism and interpretation

El amor y la pasión: la verdad y la poesía de Salvador Díaz
Mirón. *La Palabra y el Hombre*, no. 81 (Jan – Mar 92), pp.
302 – 305. Il.

DÍAZ RODRÍGUEZ, JESÚS
Criticism of specific works
Las iniciales de la tierra

Vera-León, Antonio. Jesús Díaz: Politics of Self-Narration in
Revolutionary Cuba. *Latin American Literary Review*, v. 21,
no. 41 (Jan – June 93), pp. 65 – 78. Bibl.

DÍAZ VALCÁRCEL, EMILIO
Criticism of specific works
Harlem todos los días

Béjar, Eduardo C. *Harlem todos los días:* el exilio del
nombre/el nombre del exilio. *Revista Iberoamericana*, v. 59,
no. 162 – 163 (Jan – June 93), pp. 329 – 343. Bibl.

DICTATORS

See also
Authoritarianism
Caciquism
Military in government

Hamill, Hugh M., Jr., ed. *Caudillos: Dictators in Spanish America,* revised edition. Reviewed by Stuart F. Voss. *Hispanic American Historical Review,* v. 73, no. 2 (May 93), pp. 321 – 322.

Fiction

Sabugo Abril, Amancio. Historia, biografía, ficción en *Yo el Supremo. Hoy Es Historia,* v. 10, no. 57 (Apr – May 93), pp. 5 – 14. Bibl, il.

DIEGO, ELISEO
Criticism and interpretation

Ramírez, Fermín. Un poeta de luz: Eliseo Diego. *Plural (Mexico),* v. 22, no. 263 (Aug 93), pp. 66 – 67.

DIEGO, GERARDO
Criticism of specific works
Imagen

Neghme Echeverría, Lidia. Análisis comparado de *Imagen* de Gerardo Diego y de *Poemas árticos* de Vicente Huidobro. *Revista Chilena de Literatura,* no. 41 (Apr 93), pp. 99 – 112. Bibl.

DIESTE, ELADIO

Bach, Caleb. Making Bricks Soar (Photographs by Oscar Bonilla). *Américas,* v. 45, no. 2 (Mar – Apr 93), pp. 38 – 45. Il.

DÍEZ DE MEDINA, FERNANDO

Boero Rojo, Hugo. Orígenes de la polémica Franz Tamayo – Fernando Díez de Medina. *Signo,* no. 36 – 37, Nueva época (May – Dec 92), pp. 43 – 69.

DISARMAMENT

See
Armaments
Atomic weapons and disarmament

DISCÉPOLO, ARMANDO
Criticism of specific works
Mustafá

Giella, Miguel Angel. Inmigración y exilio: el limbo del lenguaje. *Latin American Theatre Review,* v. 26, no. 2 (Spring 93), pp. 111 – 121. Bibl.

DISCRIMINATION

See
Antisemitism
Race discrimination
Sexism
Subdivision *Civil rights* under *Hispanic Americans (U.S.)*

DISEASES

See also
AIDS (Disease)
Medicine
Parasites
Public health
Venereal diseases

Argentina

Arcondo, Aníbal B. Mortalidad general, mortalidad epidémica y comportamiento de la población de Córdoba durante el siglo XVIII. *Desarrollo Económico (Argentina),* v. 33, no. 129 (Apr – June 93), pp. 67 – 85. Bibl, tables, charts.

Bolivia

Renshaw, John and Daniel Rivas. Un programa integrado para combatir el mal de Chagas: el Proyecto Boliviano – Británico "Cardenal Maurer." *Estudios Paraguayos,* v. 17, no. 1 – 2 (1989 – 1993), pp. 323 – 344.

Brazil

Chalhoub, Sidney. The Politics of Disease Control: Yellow Fever and Race in Nineteenth Century Rio de Janeiro. *Journal of Latin American Studies,* v. 25, no. 3 (Oct 93), pp. 441 – 463. Bibl.

Universo deprimente. *Problemas Brasileiros,* v. 30, no. 295 (Jan – Feb 93), pp. 51 – 52. Il.

Research

Gonçalves, Aguinaldo et al. Avaliação e perspectivas de ciência e tecnologia nas endemias infecciosas brasileiras. *Interciencia,* v. 18, no. 3 (May – June 93), pp. 142 – 145. Bibl.

Chile

Casanueva Valencia, Fernando. Una peste de viruelas en la región de la frontera de guerra hispano-indígena en el reino de Chile, 1791. *Revista de Historia (Costa Rica),* no. 26 (July – Dec 92), pp. 31 – 65. Bibl, maps, charts.

Jiménez de la Jara, Jorge. Cambio y salud: adaptaciones de los sistemas de salud al cambio epidemiológico, socioeconómico y políticocultural. *Estudios Sociales (Chile),* no. 77 (July – Sept 93), pp. 49 – 59.

Colombia

Frías Núñez, Marcelo. *Enfermedad y sociedad en la crisis colonial del antiguo régimen: Nueva Granada en el tránsito del siglo XVIII al XIX; las epidemias de viruelas* reviewed by Juan A. Villamarín. *Hispanic American Historical Review,* v. 73, no. 4 (Nov 93), pp. 693 – 694.

Dominican Republic

Cook, Noble David. Disease and the Depopulation of Hispaniola, 1492 – 1518. *Colonial Latin American Review,* v. 2, no. 1 – 2 (1993), pp. 213 – 245. Bibl, tables.

Ecuador

Alchon, Suzanne Austin. *Native Society and Disease in Colonial Ecuador* reviewed by Linda A. Newson. *Bulletin of Latin American Research,* v. 12, no. 1 (Jan 93), pp. 112 – 113.

— *Native Society and Disease in Colonial Ecuador* reviewed by Robert H. Jackson. *Colonial Latin American Historical Review,* v. 2, no. 3 (Summer 93), pp. 375 – 377.

— *Native Society and Disease in Colonial Ecuador* reviewed by Susan M. Deeds. *Colonial Latin American Review,* v. 2, no. 1 – 2 (1993), pp. 284 – 285.

— *Native Society and Disease in Colonial Ecuador* reviewed by Karen M. Powers. *Hispanic American Historical Review,* v. 73, no. 4 (Nov 93), pp. 694 – 695.

Guatemala

Menéndez Martínez, Otto R. Alimentación – nutrición y salud – enfermedad estomatológica: revisión de literatura. *USAC,* no. 13 (Mar 91), pp. 61 – 75. Bibl, charts.

Latin America

Aguiar Estrada, Eliene. Cólera. *Revista Cultural Lotería,* v. 51, no. 390 (July – Aug 92), pp. 17 – 26. Bibl.

Cook, Noble David and William George Lovell, eds. *"Secret Judgments of God": Old World Disease in Colonial Spanish America* reviewed by Ronn F. Pineo. *The Americas,* v. 50, no. 1 (July 93), pp. 126 – 127.

— *"Secret Judgments of God": Old World Disease in Colonial Spanish America* reviewed by Cynthia Radding. *Hispanic American Historical Review,* v. 73, no. 2 (May 93), pp. 309 – 311.

Mexican – American Border Region

Reff, Daniel T. *Disease, Depopulation, and Culture Change in Northwestern New Spain, 1518 – 1764* reviewed by Cynthia Radding. *The Americas,* v. 49, no. 3 (Jan 93), pp. 399 – 401.

Mexico

Corzo Ramírez, Ricardo and Soledad García Morales. Políticas, instituciones públicas de salud y enfermedades en Veracruz: fines del siglo XIX y principios del siglo XX. *La Palabra y el Hombre,* no. 83 (July – Sept 92), pp. 275 – 298. Bibl, tables.

García Quintanilla, Alejandra. Salud y progreso en Yucatán en el XIX: Mérida; el sarampión de 1882. *Siglo XIX: Cuadernos,* v. 1, no. 3 (June 92), pp. 29 – 53. Bibl, tables.

Márquez Morfín, Lourdes. El cólera en la ciudad de México en el siglo XIX. *Estudios Demográficos y Urbanos,* v. 7, no. 1 (Jan – Apr 92), pp. 77 – 93. Bibl, tables, maps, charts.

Thompson, Angela T. To Save the Children: Smallpox Inoculation, Vaccination, and Public Health in Guanajuato, Mexico, 1797 – 1840. *The Americas,* v. 49, no. 4 (Apr 93), pp. 431 – 455. Bibl, tables.

Vachon, Michael. Onchocerciasis in Chiapas, Mexico. *Geographical Review*, v. 83, no. 2 (Apr 93), pp. 141 – 149. Bibl, il, maps.

Velasco M. L., María del Pilar. La epidemia de cólera de 1833 y la mortalidad en la ciudad de México. *Estudios Demográficos y Urbanos*, v. 7, no. 1 (Jan – Apr 92), pp. 95 – 135. Bibl, tables, charts.

Whitmore, Thomas M. *Disease and Death in Early Colonial Mexico: Simulating Amerindian Depopulation* reviewed by Susan Austin Anchon. *Hispanic American Historical Review*, v. 73, no. 4 (Nov 93), pp. 695 – 696.

Statistics

Martínez Salgado, Carolina. Recursos sociodemográficos y daños a la salud en unidades domésticas campesinas del estado de México. *Estudios Demográficos y Urbanos*, v. 7, no. 2 – 3 (May – Dec 92), pp. 451 – 463. Bibl, tables.

Puerto Rico

Camuñas Madera, Ricardo R. El progreso material y las epidemias de 1856 en Puerto Rico. *Jahrbuch für Geschichte von Staat, Wirtschaft und Gesellschaft Lateinamerikas*, v. 29 (1992), pp. 241 – 277. Bibl.

Venezuela

Briceño, José de and Pedro Vicente Sosa Llanos. El "Cólera morbus" en la Venezuela de 1854. *Boletín de la Academia Nacional de la Historia (Venezuela)*, v. 76, no. 301 (Jan – Mar 93), pp. 197 – 208.

DISSERTATIONS, ACADEMIC

Moore, Robin. Directory of Latin American and Caribbean Music Theses and Dissertations since 1988. *Latin American Music Review*, v. 14, no. 1 (Spring – Summer 93), pp. 145 – 171.

Tesis doctorales recientes/Recent Dissertations. *Revista Interamericana de Bibliografía*, v. 42 (1992), All issues.

Brazil

Resumos de teses e dissertações/Summary of Ph.D. and Master Theses. *Revista de Letras (Brazil)*, v. 32 (1992), pp. 271 – 291.

United States

Fraser, Howard M. Dissertations, 1992. *Hispania (USA)*, v. 76, no. 2 (May 93), pp. 324 – 348.

Venezuela

Miranda Bastidas, Haidée and David Ruiz Chataing. El antiimperialismo en la prensa de la época de Cipriano Castro, 1899 – 1908 reviewed by Julián Rodríguez Barazarte. *Boletín de la Academia Nacional de la Historia (Venezuela)*, v. 76, no. 302 (Apr – June 93), pp. 152 – 153.

DISTRIBUTIVE JUSTICE

Angulo, Alejandro. Prólogo para una ética social. *Revista Javeriana*, v. 61, no. 599 (Oct 93), pp. 366 – 370.

Friszman, Marcos. Globalidad de los derechos humanos. *Realidad Económica*, no. 113 (Jan – Feb 93), pp. 40 – 44. II.

Rey Romay, Benito. Comentarios al libro *Pobreza y desigualdad en América Latina* de Pedro Vuskovic. *Problemas del Desarrollo*, v. 24, no. 94 (July – Sept 93), pp. 258 – 263.

Teixeira, Jorge Leão. O país do desperdício. *Problemas Brasileiros*, v. 30, no. 297 (May – June 93), pp. 6 – 9. II.

Villagrán Kramer, Francisco. La integración económica y la justicia. *Integración Latinoamericana*, v. 18, no. 187 – 188 (Mar – Apr 93), pp. 35 – 47. Bibl.

DI TELLA, TORCUATO S.

Alcorta, Rodrigo. "El Henry Ford argentino": Torquato di Tella; de los Apeninos a los Andes. *Todo Es Historia*, v. 26, no. 310 (May 93), pp. 64 – 67. II.

DIVISION OF LABOR

See also
   Subcontracting

Rubalcava, Rosa María and Vania Salles. Hogares de trabajadoras y percepciones femeninas. *El Cotidiano*, v. 9, no. 53 (Mar – Apr 93), pp. 40 – 46. Tables.

Saffioti, Heleieth Iara Bongiovani. Reminiscências, releituras, reconceituações. *Estudos Feministas*, v. 0, no. 0 (1992), pp. 97 – 103. Bibl.

DIVORCE

Amado Aguirre, José. La primera década divorcista argentina. *Todo Es Historia*, v. 27, no. 317 (Dec 93), pp. 42 – 44. II.

Law and legislation

Medina Perdomo, Alvaro. El segundo matrimonio: matrimonio de segunda. *Revista Javeriana*, v. 61, no. 599 (Oct 93), pp. 349 – 350.

Rojas Beltrán, Fabio Augusto. El divorcio. *Revista Javeriana*, v. 61, no. 599 (Oct 93), pp. 351 – 353.

Sources

Cerdas Bokhan, Dora. Las fuentes eclesiásticas como develadoras de la vida cotidiana de los fieles. *Revista de Historia (Costa Rica)*, no. 25 (Jan – June 92), pp. 251 – 259.

DOBLES, FABIÁN

Criticism of specific works

Historias de Tata Mundo

Solano Jiménez, Ronald. Crítica literaria en Costa Rica: de las *Historias de Tata Mundo. Anuario de Estudios Centroamericanos*, v. 18, no. 1 (1992), pp. 85 – 95. Bibl.

DOMESTIC SERVICE

See
   Subdivision *Employment* under *Women*

DOMÍNGUEZ BASTIDA, GUSTAVO ADOLFO

See
   Bécquer, Gustavo Adolfo

DOMÍNGUEZ CABALLERO, DIEGO

Moreno Davis, Julio César. Diego Domínguez Caballero, o las facetas de un educador. *Revista Cultural Lotería*, v. 51, no. 392 (Nov – Dec 93), pp. 31 – 40.

DOMÍNGUEZ MALDONADO, GENARO

Interviews

Baudot, Georges. Genaro Domínguez Maldonado: entrevista realizada el 15 de agosto de 1991 en la ciudad de México por Georges Baudot. *Caravelle*, no. 59 (1992), pp. 39 – 47.

DOMINICA

Hulme, Peter and Neil L. Whitehead, eds. *Wild Majesty: Encounters with Caribs from Columbus to the Present Day; An Anthology* reviewed by Peter T. Bradley. *Bulletin of Latin American Research*, v. 12, no. 1 (Jan 93), pp. 111 – 112.

Trouillot, Michel-Rolph. *Peasants and Capital: Dominica in the World Economy* reviewed by Michael H. Allen (Review entitled "Rethinking Political Economy and Praxis in the Caribbean"). *Latin American Perspectives*, v. 20, no. 2 (Spring 93), pp. 111 – 119.

DOMINICAN POETRY

History and criticism

Bankay, Anne-Maria. Contemporary Women Poets of the Dominican Republic: Perspectives on Race and Other Social Issues. *Afro-Hispanic Review*, v. 12, no. 1 (Spring 93), pp. 34 – 41. Bibl.

DOMINICAN REPUBLIC

See also
   Agricultural laborers – Dominican Republic
   Artists – Dominican Republic
   Church and social problems – Dominican Republic
   Cities and towns – Dominican Republic
   Community development – Dominican Republic
   Cookery – Dominican Republic
   Democracy – Dominican Republic
   Diseases – Dominican Republic
   Foreign trade promotion – Dominican Republic
   Frontier and pioneer life – Dominican Republic
   Geopolitics – Dominican Republic
   Haitians – Dominican Republic
   Jews – Dominican Republic
   Literature and society – Dominican Republic

Marginalization – Dominican Republic
Music and society – Dominican Republic
Musicians – Dominican Republic
Periodicals – Dominican Republic
Political participation – Dominican Republic
Popular music – Dominican Republic
Race discrimination – Dominican Republic
Rice – Dominican Republic
Santo Domingo, Dominican Republic
Slavery – Dominican Republic
Sociology, Urban – Dominican Republic
Sosua, Dominican Republic
Spaniards – Dominican Republic
Sugar – Dominican Republic
Television – Dominican Republic
Textile industry and fabrics – Dominican Republic
Women – Dominican Republic
Women authors – Dominican Republic

Armed forces

Gascón, Margarita. The Military of Santo Domingo, 1720 – 1764. *Hispanic American Historical Review*, v. 73, no. 3 (Aug 93), pp. 431 – 452. Bibl.

Boundaries

Haiti

Baud, Michiel. Una frontera – refugio: dominicanos y haitianos contra el estado, 1870 – 1930 (Translated by Montserrat Planas Alberti). *Estudios Sociales (Dominican Republic)*, v. 26, no. 92 (Apr – June 93), pp. 39 – 64. Bibl.

Gewecke, Frauke. "El corte" oder "Les vêpres dominicaines": Trujillos "dominicanización de la frontera" und ihr Reflex in der dominikanischen und haitianischen Literatur. *Iberoamericana*, v. 17, no. 50 (1993), pp. 38 – 62. Bibl.

Civilization

San Miguel, Pedro Luis. Discurso racial e identidad nacional en la República Dominicana. *Op. Cit.*, no. 7 (1992), pp. 67 – 120. Bibl, il.

Emigration and immigration

Grasmuck, Sherri and Patricia R. Pessar. *Between Two Islands: Dominican International Migration* reviewed by André Corten. *Canadian Journal of Latin American and Caribbean Studies*, v. 17, no. 34 (1992), pp. 138 – 141.

Pou, Francis. Inmigración de agricultores españoles a la República Dominicana en el período Franco – Trujillo, 1939 – 1961. *Revista de Indias*, v. 53, no. 198 (May – Aug 93), pp. 563 – 582. Bibl, tables, charts.

Ruiz, Marta. Migración entre Haití y la República Dominicana. *Cuadernos Hispanoamericanos*, no. 522 (Dec 93), pp. 77 – 86.

Foreign economic relations

Haiti

Baud, Michiel. Una fortuna para cruzar: la sociedad rural a través de la frontera domínico – haitiana, 1870 – 1930 (Translated by Eugenio Rivas). *Estudios Sociales (Dominican Republic)*, v. 26, no. 94 (Oct – Dec 93), pp. 5 – 28. Bibl.

Foreign relations

Haiti

Vega, Bernardo. Etnicidad y el futuro de las relaciones domínico – haitianas. *Estudios Sociales (Dominican Republic)*, v. 26, no. 94 (Oct – Dec 93), pp. 29 – 43.

United States

Nelson, William Javier. *Almost a Territory: America's Attempt to Annex the Dominican Republic* reviewed by Mu-Kien Adriana Sang. *Afro-Hispanic Review*, v. 12, no. 1 (Spring 93), pp. 55 – 56.

History

Cordero Michel, Emilio. Gregorio Luperón y Haití. *Anuario de Estudios Americanos*, v. 49 (1992), pp. 497 – 528. Bibl.

Martínez Fernández, Luis N. El anexionismo dominicano y la lucha entre imperios durante la primera republica, 1844 – 1861. *Revista/Review Interamericana*, v. 22, no. 1 – 2 (Spring – Summer 92), pp. 168 – 190. Bibl.

Public works

Douzant Rosenfeld, Denise and Laura Faxas. Equipements urbains et services de remplacement: le cas de Santo Domingo, République Dominicaine. *Tiers Monde*, v. 34, no. 133 (Jan – Mar 93), pp. 139 – 151.

Race question

San Miguel, Pedro Luis. Discurso racial e identidad nacional en la República Dominicana. *Op. Cit.*, no. 7 (1992), pp. 67 – 120. Bibl, il.

Rural conditions

Rodríguez Morel, Genaro. Esclavitud y vida rural en las plantaciones azucareras de Santo Domingo, siglo XVI. *Anuario de Estudios Americanos*, v. 49 (1992), pp. 89 – 117. Bibl.

Social conditions

Thomas, Luis. La crisis social del pueblo. *Cristianismo y Sociedad*, v. 30, no. 114 (1992), pp. 47 – 48.

DOMINICAN REPUBLIC IN LITERATURE

Gewecke, Frauke. "El corte" oder "Les vêpres dominicaines": Trujillos "dominicanización de la frontera" und ihr Reflex in der dominikanischen und haitianischen Literatur. *Iberoamericana*, v. 17, no. 50 (1993), pp. 38 – 62. Bibl.

DOMINICANS (DOMINICAN REPUBLIC)

United States

Grasmuck, Sherri and Patricia R. Pessar. *Between Two Islands: Dominican International Migration* reviewed by André Corten. *Canadian Journal of Latin American and Caribbean Studies*, v. 17, no. 34 (1992), pp. 138 – 141.

DONOSO, JOSÉ

Criticism and interpretation

Borinsky, Alicia. Donoso: perros y apuesta sexual. *Estudios Públicos (Chile)*, no. 49 (Summer 93), pp. 279 – 294.

Magnarelli, Sharon Dishaw. *Understanding José Donoso* reviewed by Pamela Finnegan. *World Literature Today*, v. 67, no. 3 (Summer 93), pp. 595 – 596.

Criticism of specific works

El jardín del al lado

Lemogodeuc, Jean-Marie. Las máscaras y las marcas de la autobiografía: la cuestión del narrador en *El jardín de al lado* de José Donoso. *Revista de Crítica Literaria Latinoamericana*, v. 19, no. 38 (July – Dec 93), pp. 383 – 392. Bibl.

El obsceno pájaro de la noche

Browning, Richard L. La arquitectura de la memoria: los edificios y sus significados en *El obsceno pájaro de la noche* de José Donoso. *Chasqui*, v. 22, no. 2 (Nov 93), pp. 15 – 23. Bibl.

Finnegan-Smith, Pamela May. *The Tension of Paradox: José Donoso's 'The Obscene Bird of Night' as Spiritual Exercises* reviewed by George R. McMurray. *Chasqui*, v. 22, no. 1 (May 93), pp. 98 – 99.

— *The Tension of Paradox: José Donoso's 'The Obscene Bird of Night' as Spiritual Exercises* reviewed by Ricardo Gutiérrez Mouat. *World Literature Today*, v. 67, no. 2 (Spring 93), pp. 343 – 344.

Taratuta

González, Flora M. Masking History in Donoso's *Taratuta*. *Revista Canadiense de Estudios Hispánicos*, v. 17, no. 1 (Fall 92), pp. 47 – 62. Bibl.

Interviews

Encuentro con José Donoso. *La Palabra y el Hombre*, no. 81 (Jan – Mar 92), pp. 260 – 264. Il.

DORFMAN, ARIEL

Criticism and interpretation

Oropesa, Salvador A. *La obra de Ariel Dorfman: ficción y crítica* reviewed by Charles A. Piano. *World Literature Today*, v. 67, no. 3 (Summer 93), p. 592.

DOUGNAC RODRÍGUEZ, ANTONIO

Salvat Monguillot, Manuel. Discurso de recepción de don Antonio Dougnac Rodríguez. *Boletín de la Academia Chilena de la Historia*, v. 58 – 59, no. 102 (1991 – 1992), pp. 95 – 99.

Bibliography

Bibliografía de don Antonio Dougnac Rodríguez. *Boletín de la Academia Chilena de la Historia*, v. 58 – 59, no. 102 (1991 – 1992), pp. 100 – 103.

DOVIDJENKO, DARKO

Carrasco, Sergio. Jugar en pared. *Debate (Peru)*, v. 16, no. 72 (Mar – May 93), p. 57. Il.

DRAGÚN, OSVALDO

Criticism and interpretation

Gladhart, Amalia. Narrative Foregrounding in the Plays of Osvaldo Dragún. *Latin American Theatre Review*, v. 26, no. 2 (Spring 93), pp. 93 – 109. Bibl.

DRAMA

See also
Folk drama
Motion pictures
Religious drama
Screenplays
Theater

Technique

Garzón Céspedes, Francisco. *El arte escénico de contar cuentos* reviewed by Fernando Rodríguez Sosa (Review entitled "Sobre la narración oral escénica"). *Conjunto*, no. 90 – 91 (Jan – June 92), pp. 103 – 105. Il.

DRAMA FESTIVALS

Chile

Di Girólamo, Claudio. Festival Mundial Teatro de las Naciones: saliendo de la isla. *Mensaje*, v. 42, no. 418 (May 93), pp. 164 – 165. Il.

Garretón Merino, Manuel Antonio. El Festival Mundial de Teatro y Política. *Mensaje*, v. 42, no. 419 (June 93), pp. 175 – 177. Il.

Iñiguez A., Ignacio. A Stage for International Fraternity (Translated by Kathleen Forrester, photographs by Claudio Pérez R.). *Américas*, v. 45, no. 4 (July – Aug 93), pp. 48 – 51. Il.

Mexico

Beverido Duhalt, Francisco. Notas de un espectador en la XII Muestra Nacional de Teatro. *La Palabra y el Hombre*, no. 81 (Jan – Mar 92), pp. 362 – 367.

Spain

Boudet, Rosa Ileana. Inventario de Cádiz. *Conjunto*, no. 93 (Jan – June 93), pp. 113 – 115. Il.

Krebs, Brenda. Festival Iberoamericano de Teatro, Santiago de Compostela. *Latin American Theatre Review*, v. 26, no. 2 (Spring 93), pp. 183 – 186.

Reverte Bernal, Concepción. VII Festival Iberoamericano de Teatro de Cádiz, 1992. *Latin American Theatre Review*, v. 26, no. 2 (Spring 93), pp. 171 – 182. Il.

United States

Rizk, Beatriz J. TENAZ XVI: la muestra de un teatro en transición. *Latin American Theatre Review*, v. 26, no. 2 (Spring 93), pp. 187 – 190.

Unruh, Vicky Wolff and George W. Woodyard. Latin American Theatre Today: A 1992 Conference in Kansas. *Latin American Theatre Review*, v. 26, no. 2 (Spring 93), pp. 6 – 8. Il.

DRAMA REVIEWS

El hilo de Ariadna

Vargas, Enrique. *El hilo de Ariadna (o la máquina de imaginar)* reviewed by Nora Eidelberg. *Latin American Theatre Review*, v. 26, no. 2 (Spring 93), pp. 201 – 202.

La increíble y triste historia de la cándida Eréndira

García Márquez, Gabriel. *La cándida Eréndira* reviewed by Ileana Azor Hernández (Review entitled "La cándida Eréndira: relato y espectáculo"). *Conjunto*, no. 93 (Jan – June 93), pp. 91 – 100. Il.

Lo que cala son los filos

Jiménez, Mauricio. *Lo que cala son los filos* reviewed by Armando Partido (Review entitled "Camino real de Comala"). *Plural (Mexico)*, v. 22, no. 258 (Mar 93), pp. 79 – 80.

Malinche

Stranger, Inés. *Malinche* reviewed by Juan Andres Piña. *Mensaje*, v. 42, no. 422 (Sept 93), p. 468.

Roberto Zucco

Koltès, Bernard-Marie. *Roberto Zucco* reviewed by Carlos B. Ossandón. *Mensaje*, v. 42, no. 417 (Mar – Apr 93), p. 107.

DRAMAS

See
Author Index under names of specific playwrights

DREAMS

Kane, Connie M. et al. Differences in the Manifest Dream Content of Mexican, Mexican American, and Anglo American College Women: A Research Note. *Hispanic Journal of Behavioral Sciences*, v. 15, no. 1 (Feb 93), pp. 134 – 139. Bibl, tables.

DRESDEN CODEX

Martin, Frederick. A *Dresden Codex* Eclipse Sequence: Projections for the Years 1970 – 1992. *Latin American Antiquity*, v. 4, no. 1 (Mar 93), pp. 74 – 93. Bibl, il, tables.

DROUGHTS

See also
Deserts

Brazil

Assunção, Luiz Márcio and Ian Livingstone. Desenvolvimento inadequado: construção de açudes e secas no sertão do Nordeste. *Revista Brasileira de Economia*, v. 47, no. 3 (July – Sept 93), pp. 425 – 448. Bibl, tables, charts.

DRUG TRADE

America

Doyle, Kate. Drug War: A Quietly Escalating Failure. *NACLA Report on the Americas*, v. 26, no. 5 (May 93), pp. 29 – 34 +. Bibl, il.

Kaplan, Marcos. La internacionalización del narcotráfico latinoamericano y Estados Unidos. *Relaciones Internacionales (Mexico)*, v. 15, Nueva época, no. 57 (Jan – Mar 93), pp. 75 – 86. Bibl.

Smith, Peter H., ed. *Drug Policy in the Americas* reviewed by Mariana Mould de Pease. *Hispanic American Historical Review*, v. 73, no. 4 (Nov 93), pp. 732 – 733.

Bolivia

Barrios Morón, J. Raúl. La política contra las drogas en Bolivia: interdicción y guerra de baja intensidad. *Nueva Sociedad*, no. 123 (Jan – Feb 93), pp. 35 – 49. Bibl.

Hargreaves, Clare. *Snowfields: The War on Cocaine in the Andes* reviewed by Madeleine Barbara Léons. *Journal of Latin American Studies*, v. 25, no. 2 (May 93), pp. 422 – 423.

Malamud Goti, Jaime E. *Smoke and Mirrors: The Paradox of the Drug Wars* reviewed by Kevin Healy. *Journal of Latin American Studies*, v. 25, no. 3 (Oct 93), pp. 688 – 689.

Sources

Coca: cronología; Bolivia, 1986 – 1992 reviewed by M. A. *Nueva Sociedad*, no. 124 (Mar – Apr 93), p. 173.

Central America

Marshall, Jonathan and Peter Dale Scott. *Cocaine Politics: Drugs, Armies, and the CIA in Central America* reviewed by Donald J. Mabry. *Hispanic American Historical Review*, v. 73, no. 2 (May 93), p. 353.

Colombia

Betancourt Echeverry, Darío. Tendencias de las mafias colombianas de la cocaína y la amapola. *Nueva Sociedad*, no. 128 (Nov – Dec 93), pp. 38 – 47.

Gouëset, Vincent. L'impact du "narcotrafic" à Médellin. *Cahiers des Amériques Latines*, no. 13 (1992), pp. 27 – 52. Bibl, tables.

Latin America

Andreas, Peter. Profits, Poverty, and Illegality: The Logic of Drug Corruption. *NACLA Report on the Americas,* v. 27, no. 3 (Nov – Dec 93), pp. 22 – 28 +. Bibl.

Kaplan, Marcos. La crisis del estado y el narcotráfico latinoamericano. *Cuadernos Americanos,* no. 40, Nueva época (July – Aug 93), pp. 11 – 34. Bibl.

Suárez Salazar, Luis. "Drug Trafficking" and Social and Political Conflicts in Latin America: Some Hypotheses (Translated by Luis Fierro). *Latin American Perspectives,* v. 20, no. 1 (Winter 93), pp. 83 – 98. Bibl, tables.

Mexico

Vargas Uribe, Guillermo. Michoacán en la red internacional del narcotráfico. *El Cotidiano,* v. 8, no. 52 (Jan – Feb 93), pp. 38 – 50. Tables, maps, charts.

Bibliography

Ochoa Méndez, Jacqueline. Orientación bibliográfica sobre narcotráfico. *El Cotidiano,* v. 8, no. 52 (Jan – Feb 93), p. 120.

DRUGS, ILLEGAL

See also
Coca and cocaine

Drug-Producing Plants: From Use to Abuse. *Jamaica Journal,* v. 24, no. 3 (Feb 93), pp. 62 – 63. Il.

Costa Rica

Bejarano Orozco, Julio and Hannia Carvajal Morera. Abuso de drogas y conducta delictiva. *Revista de Ciencias Sociales (Costa Rica),* no. 60 (June 93), pp. 51 – 62. Bibl, tables, charts.

Palmer, Steven. El consumo de heroína entre los artesanos de San José y el pánico moral de 1929. *Revista de Historia (Costa Rica),* no. 25 (Jan – June 92), pp. 29 – 63. Bibl.

Mexico

Tenorio Tagle, Fernando. *El control social de las drogas en México: una aproximación a las imágenes que han proyectado sus discursos* reviewed by Horacio Cerutti Guldberg. *Cuadernos Americanos,* no. 40, Nueva época (July – Aug 93), pp. 235 – 237.

United States

Dassori, Albana M. et al. Ethnic and Gender Differences in the Diagnostic Profiles of Substance Abusers. *Hispanic Journal of Behavioral Sciences,* v. 15, no. 3 (Aug 93), pp. 382 – 390. Bibl.

Smith, Peter H., ed. *Drug Policy in the Americas* reviewed by Mariana Mould de Pease. *Hispanic American Historical Review,* v. 73, no. 4 (Nov 93), pp. 732 – 733.

Law and legislation

Kaplan, Marcos. La internacionalización del narcotráfico latinoamericano y Estados Unidos. *Relaciones Internacionales (Mexico),* v. 15, Nueva época, no. 57 (Jan – Mar 93), pp. 75 – 86. Bibl.

DRUGS, PHARMACEUTICAL

See
Pharmacy

DUAYEN, CÉSAR

See
Barra, Emma de la

DUMONT, ALBERTO DOS SANTOS

See
Santos-Dumont, Alberto

DUNKLEY, JOHN

Cresswell, Peter. Insiders and Outsiders: The Annual National Exhibition 1991 and "Homage to John Dunkley." *Jamaica Journal,* v. 24, no. 3 (Feb 93), pp. 29 – 35. Il.

DUPUY, BEN

Interviews

Orenstein, Catherine. An Interview with Ben Dupuy. *NACLA Report on the Americas,* v. 27, no. 1 (July – Aug 93), pp. 12 – 15. Il.

DURANGO, MEXICO (CITY)

Leal F., Gustavo and Martha Singer S. Gobernando desde la oposición: ayuntamiento de Durango, 1992 – 1995. *El Cotidiano,* v. 9, no. 54 (May 93), pp. 90 – 100. Bibl, il, tables.

DUSSEL, ENRIQUE D.

Pérez Villacampa, Gilberto. Enrique Dussel: ¿De la metafísica de la alteridad al humanismo real? *Islas,* no. 99 (May – Aug 91), pp. 160 – 167.

Rosell Gómez, Eunice et al. Dussel: dependencia y liberación en los marcos de la teoría económica. *Islas,* no. 99 (May – Aug 91), pp. 155 – 159.

Criticism of specific works
Filosofía de la liberación

Pérez Villacampa, Gilberto. *Filosofía de la liberación* de Enrique Dussel: apuntes sobre un diario íntimo. *Islas,* no. 97 (Sept – Dec 90), pp. 52 – 63. Bibl.

DUTCH

Mexico

Marley, David F. *Pirates and Engineers* reviewed by Joel Russell (Review entitled "Swashbuckler's Paradise"). *Business Mexico,* v. 3, no. 4 (Apr 93), p. 52.

— *Pirates and Engineers: Dutch and Flemish Adventurers in New Spain, 1607 – 1697* reviewed by Peter T. Bradley. *Bulletin of Latin American Research,* v. 12, no. 2 (May 93), pp. 219 – 220.

EARLE, PETER G.

Aponte, Bárbara Bockus et al. Tributes to Peter G. Earle (A collection of 24 tributes in English and Spanish honoring Peter G. Earle). *Hispanic Review,* v. 61, no. 2 (Spring 93), pp. 149 – 165.

Lloyd, Paul M. Peter Guyon Earle. *Hispanic Review,* v. 61, no. 2 (Spring 93), pp. 145 – 148.

Bibliography

Publications of Peter G. Earle. *Hispanic Review,* v. 61, no. 2 (Spring 93), pp. 167 – 173.

EARTH SUMMIT '92

See
Subdivision *International cooperation - Congresses* under *Ecology*

EARTHQUAKES

Ecuador
Methodology

Argudo R., Jaime et al. Metodología para la reducción de la vulnerabilidad sísmica de escuelas y bibliotecas en Guayaquil (noviembre 1992). *La Educación (USA),* v. 37, no. 115 (1993), pp. 333 – 352. Bibl, il, tables, charts.

Mexico

Lomnitz, Cinna. De pilones y poemas. *Nexos,* v. 16, no. 192 (Dec 93), pp. 15 – 16.

— Violines y sismos de otoño. *Nexos,* v. 16, no. 191 (Nov 93), pp. 12 – 14.

Venezuela

Díaz, José Domingo. El terremoto del año de 1812 y nuestra independencia (Previously published in this journal vol. 1, no. 1, 1912). *Boletín de la Academia Nacional de la Historia (Venezuela),* v. 75, no. 300 (Oct – Dec 92), pp. 321 – 326.

EAST INDIANS

Trinidad and Tobago

De Verteuil, Anthony. *Eight East Indian Immigrants* reviewed by F. Birbalsingh. *Caribbean Quarterly,* v. 38, no. 2 – 3 (June – Sept 92), pp. 119 – 122.

Vertovec, Steven. *Hindu Trinidad: Religion, Ethnicity, and Socio-Economic Change* reviewed by William A. Harris (Review entitled "Ethnicity and Development"). *Social and Economic Studies,* v. 41, no. 4 (Dec 92), pp. 225 – 230.

EC

See
European Community

ECA; ESTUDIOS CENTROAMERICANOS (PERIODICAL)

Gómez Díez, Francisco Javier. El reformismo jesuítico en Centroamérica: La revista *ECA* en los años de la guerra fría, 1946 – 1965. *Anuario de Estudios Americanos*, v. 49, Suppl. 1 (1992), pp. 85 – 105. Tables.

ECHEÑIQUE, MERCEDES

Saavedra, Gonzalo. Mercedes Echeñique: la tía Pin tocó "la verdad de Chile." *Mensaje*, v. 42, no. 421 (Aug 93), pp. 361 – 362. Il.

ECHEVERRÍA, RAÚL

Statland de López, Rhona. Profile of an Entrepreneur. *Business Mexico*, v. 3, no. 3 (Mar 93), pp. 12 – 14.

ECOLOGY

See also

Environmental policy
Environmental services
Forests
Hazardous substances
Marine resources
Natural areas
Pesticides
Pollution
Refuse and refuse disposal

Salazar Ramírez, Hilda. Mujer y medio ambiente. *Fem*, v. 17, no. 128 (Oct 93), pp. 11 – 15.

Zea, Leopoldo. Naturaleza y cultura. *Cuadernos Americanos*, no. 39, Nueva época (May – June 93), pp. 91 – 95.

Bibliography

Landeo, Liliam. Bibliografía sobre ecología. *Amazonía Peruana*, v. 11, no. 21 (Sept 92), pp. 223 – 237.

Congresses

Declaración de La Paz. *Anuario Indigenista*, v. 30 (Dec 91), pp. 339 – 342.

Handbooks, manuals, etc.

Ham, Sam H. *Environmental Interpretation: A Practical Guide for People with Big Ideas and Small Budgets/Interpretación ambiental: una guía práctica* . . . reviewed by Martin Groebel. *La Educación (USA)*, v. 37, no. 115 (1993), pp. 422 – 423.

International cooperation

Congresses

Garrison, John W., II. UNCED and the Greening of Brazilian NGOs. *Grassroots Development*, v. 17, no. 1 (1993), pp. 2 – 11. Bibl, il.

Oliveira, Rosiska Darcy de. Memórias do Planeta Fêmea. *Estudos Feministas*, v. 0, no. 0 (1992), pp. 131 – 142.

Vasconcelos, Naumi A. de. Ecos femininos na Eco '92. *Estudos Feministas*, v. 0, no. 0 (1992), pp. 151 – 154.

Sources

Argentina – Brasil: Acuerdo de Alcance Parcial de Cooperación e Intercambio de Bienes Utilizados en la Defensa y Protección del Medio Ambiente. *Integración Latinoamericana*, v. 17, no. 184 (Nov 92), pp. 74 – 75.

Amazon Valley

Acosta-Solís, Misael. Por la conservación de la Amazonia. *Revista Geográfica (Mexico)*, no. 115 (Jan – June 92), pp. 77 – 84.

Aragón, Luis E., ed. *A desordem ecológica na Amazônia* (Review). *La Educación (USA)*, v. 37, no. 115 (1993), pp. 439 – 440.

Encarnación, Filomeno. Conservación en la Amazonía. *Amazonía Peruana*, v. 11, no. 21 (Sept 92), pp. 49 – 72. Bibl.

Medio ambiente: "Una sublevación con hachas y sierras de cadena" (From *Der Spiegel*). *Amazonía Peruana*, v. 11, no. 21 (Sept 92), pp. 23 – 48. Il, maps.

Argentina

Brailovsky, Antonio Elio and Dina Foguelman. *Memoria verde: historia ecológica de la Argentina* reviewed by Adrián Gustavo Zarrilli. *Revista de Historia de América*, no. 113 (Jan – June 92), pp. 174 – 177.

Colombres, Diego and Jorge Gavilán. El daño ecológico y social que provocó La Forestal. *Todo Es Historia*, v. 26, no. 306 (Jan 93), pp. 42 – 47. Il.

Brazil

Delgado, Maria Berenice Godinho and Maria Margareth Lopes. Mulheres trabalhadoras e meio ambiente: um olhar feminista no sindicalismo. *Estudos Feministas*, v. 0, no. 0 (1992), pp. 155 – 162.

Cost

Azzoni, Carlos Roberto and João Yo Isai. Custo da proteção de áreas com interesse ambiental no estado de São Paulo. *Estudos Econômicos*, v. 22, no. 2 (May – Aug 92), pp. 253 – 271. Bibl, tables, charts.

Sources

Muricy, Carmen Meurer. Environment in Brazil: A Checklist of Current Serials. *SALALM Papers*, v. 36 (1991), pp. 88 – 104.

Caribbean area

Study and teaching

Howell, Calvin A. Trends in Environmental Education in the English-Speaking Caribbean. *La Educación (USA)*, v. 37, no. 115 (1993), pp. 303 – 316. Bibl.

Central America

Chapin, Mac. The View from the Shore: Central America's Indians Encounter the Quincentenary. *Grassroots Development*, v. 16, no. 2 (1992), pp. 2 – 10. Bibl, il, maps.

Chile

Gestión ambiental en Chile: aportes del IVº Encuentro Científico sobre el Medio Ambiente reviewed by Ricardo Jordán Fuchs. *EURE*, v. 19, no. 56 (Mar 93), pp. 119 – 120.

Bibliography

Domínguez Díaz, Marta Silvia. El medio ambiente en Chile hoy: informe y bibliografía. *SALALM Papers*, v. 36 (1991), pp. 130 – 156.

Colombia

Study and teaching

Torres Carrasco, Maritza. Colombia: dimensión ambiental en la escuela y la formación docente. *La Educación (USA)*, v. 37, no. 115 (1993), pp. 317 – 330. Bibl, charts.

Costa Rica

Morgner, Fred G. Poisoning the Garden: Costa Rica's Ecological Crisis. *SALALM Papers*, v. 36 (1991), pp. 77 – 87. Bibl.

Honduras

Study and teaching

Ham, Sam H. and Richard A. Meganck. The Transferability of U.S. Environmental Education Programs in Rural Central America: A Case Study from Honduras. *La Educación (USA)*, v. 37, no. 115 (1993), pp. 289 – 301. Bibl, tables.

Jamaica

Cost

Miller, Learie A. A Preliminary Assessment of the Economic Cost of Land Degradation: The Hermitage Catchment, Jamaica. *Caribbean Geography*, v. 3, no. 4 (Sept 92), pp. 244 – 252. Bibl, tables, maps.

Latin America

Devlin, Robert T. Canje de deuda por naturaleza: la necesidad de una nueva agenda. *Revista de Economia Política (Brazil)*, v. 13, no. 3 (July – Sept 93), pp. 69 – 81. Tables.

Valenzuela Fuenzalida, Rafael. Pérdida y degradación de suelos en América Latina y el Caribe. *EURE*, v. 19, no. 58 (Oct 93), pp. 61 – 72. Bibl.

Study and teaching

Edwards, Beatrice. Linking the Social and Natural Worlds: Environmental Education in the Hemisphere. *La Educación (USA)*, v. 37, no. 115 (1993), pp. 231 – 256. Bibl.

Mexico

Goebel, J. Martin. Mexico: The Natural Factory. *Business Mexico*, v. 3, no. 1 (Jan – Feb 93), pp. 6 – 8. Il, tables, charts.

Phillips, Fred P., IV and Steven M. Rubin. Debt for Nature: Swap Meet for the '90s. *Business Mexico*, v. 3, no. 1 (Jan – Feb 93), pp. 46 – 47.

Ruge S., Tiahoga. It's Not Nice to Fool Mother Nature. *Business Mexico*, v. 3, no. 1 (Jan – Feb 93), pp. 63 – 64. Il.

Tabasco: Yumká; 30 años adelante en la protección ecológica. *Plural (Mexico)*, v. 22, no. 262 (July 93), Insert. Il.

Societies, etc.

Elmendorf, George F. and Joan A. Quillen. Mexico's Environmental and Ecological Organizations and Movements. *SALALM Papers*, v. 36 (1991), pp. 123 – 129.

Study and teaching

Valenzuela, Lucia. Cultural Ecology. *Business Mexico*, v. 3, no. 3 (Mar 93), p. 36.

Saint Vincent, West Indies

Grossman, Lawrence S. Pesticides, People, and the Environment in St. Vincent. *Caribbean Geography*, v. 3, no. 3 (Mar 92), pp. 175 – 186. Bibl, tables, maps.

ECOLOGY AND DEVELOPMENT

See also
Environmental policy

Haq, Mahbubul and Jan Pronk. Desarrollo sostenible: del concepto a la acción. *El Trimestre Económico*, v. 59, no. 236 (Oct – Dec 92), pp. 799 – 815.

Hume, Patricia. ¿Por qué población, medio ambiente y desarrollo y no mujer, naturaleza y desarrollo? *Fem*, v. 17, no. 128 (Oct 93), pp. 26 – 29. Tables, charts.

Morales, Orlando M. Participación sobre derechos ecológicos. *Cuadernos Americanos*, no. 39, Nueva época (May – June 93), pp. 72 – 73.

Morton, Colleen S. Economic Instruments Protect the Earth. *Business Mexico*, v. 3, no. 1 (Jan – Feb 93), pp. 40 – 43. Il.

Ruiz-Giménez, Guadalupe. Un nuevo orden internacional para el desarrollo sostenible. *Cuadernos Americanos*, no. 39, Nueva época (May – June 93), pp. 81 – 87.

Congresses

Angulo Carrera, Alejandro and Salvador Rodríguez y Rodríguez. Agricultura orgánica, desarrollo sustentable y comercio justo. *Problemas del Desarrollo*, v. 24, no. 94 (July – Sept 93), pp. 265 – 274.

Pérez Calderón, Luis Jorge. Medio ambiente y desarrollo: el Decenio Internacional para la Reducción de los Desastres Naturales. *Amazonía Peruana*, v. 11, no. 21 (Sept 92), pp. 175 – 180.

United Nations. Conference on Environment and Development. Propuestas para la Conferencia de Naciones Unidas sobre el Medio Ambiente y el Desarrollo. *Anuario Indigenista*, v. 30 (Dec 91), pp. 331 – 333.

International cooperation

Brown, Janet Welsh and Arnoldo José Gabaldón. Moving the Americas toward Sustainable Development. *La Educación (USA)*, v. 37, no. 115 (1993), pp. 273 – 288. Bibl.

Caldwell, Lynton Keith. Strategies in Hemispheric Cooperation for Environmentally Sustainable Development. *La Educación (USA)*, v. 37, no. 115 (1993), pp. 257 – 272. Bibl.

Research

Varela Barraza, Hilda. Nuevos temas de investigación en relaciones internacionales: la ecología. *Relaciones Internacionales (Mexico)*, v. 14, Nueva época, no. 55 (July – Sept 92), pp. 31 – 41. Bibl.

Sources

Declaração do Rio sobre meio ambiente e desenvolvimento. *RAE; Revista de Administração de Empresas*, v. 33, no. 6 (Nov – Dec 93), pp. 48 – 49.

Amazon Valley

Hvalkof, Sören. La naturaleza del desarrollo: perspectivas de los nativos y de los colonos en el gran pajonal. *Amazonía Peruana*, v. 11, no. 21 (Sept 92), pp. 145 – 173. Bibl.

Margolis, Mac. *The Last New World: The Conquest of the Amazon Frontier* reviewed by Gordon MacMillan. *Bulletin of Latin American Research*, v. 12, no. 3 (Sept 93), pp. 352 – 353.

Pavan, Crodowaldo et al, eds. *Uma estratégia latino-americana para a Amazônia* reviewed by John Dickenson. *Bulletin of Latin American Research*, v. 12, no. 3 (Sept 93), pp. 351 – 352.

Peluso, Daniela. Conservation and Indigenismo. *Hemisphere*, v. 5, no. 2 (Winter – Spring 93), pp. 6 – 8.

Argentina

Durán, Diana. El desarrollo sustentable: ¿Un nuevo modelo? (Excerpts from *Convivir en la tierra* by Diana Durán and Albina L. Lara). *Realidad Económica*, no. 113 (Jan – Feb 93), pp. 31 – 39. Bibl.

Belize

Higinio, Egbert and Ian Munt. Belize: Eco Tourism Gone Awry. *Report on the Americas*, v. 26, no. 4 (Feb 93), pp. 8 – 10. Il.

Brazil

Guimarães, Roberto Pereira. Development Pattern and Environment in Brazil. *CEPAL Review*, no. 47 (Aug 92), pp. 47 – 62. Bibl.

Laroche, Rose Claire. Ecossistemas e impactos ambientais da modernização agrícola do vale São Francisco. *Revista Brasileira de Geografia*, v. 53, no. 2 (Apr – June 91), pp. 63 – 77. Bibl, il, charts.

Lerner, Jaime. La ciudad optimista. *Nexos*, v. 16, no. 189 (Sept 93), pp. 13 – 15.

Randall, Laura Regina Rosenbaum. Petróleo, economía y medio ambiente en Brasil. *Revista Mexicana de Sociología*, v. 54, no. 2 (Apr – June 92), pp. 185 – 211. Tables.

Souza, Maria Tereza Saraiva de. Rumo à prática empresarial sustentável. *RAE; Revista de Administração de Empresas*, v. 33, no. 4 (July – Aug 93), pp. 40 – 52. Bibl.

Velloso, João Paulo dos Reis, ed. *A ecologia e o novo patrão de desenvolvimento no Brasil* reviewed by Euridson de Sá Jr. *Revista de Economia Política (Brazil)*, v. 13, no. 2 (Apr – June 93), pp. 155 – 156.

Societies, etc.

Lins Ribeiro, Gustavo. Ambientalismo e desenvolvimento sustentado: nova ideologia/utopia do desenvolvimento. *Revista de Antropologia (Brazil)*, v. 34 (1991), pp. 59 – 101. Bibl, tables.

Caribbean area

Potter, Robert B. Caribbean Views on Environment and Development: A Cognitive Perspective. *Caribbean Geography*, v. 3, no. 4 (Sept 92), pp. 236 – 243. Bibl, tables.

Singh, Naresh Charan. Sustainable Development: Its Meaning for the Caribbean. *Social and Economic Studies*, v. 41, no. 3 (Sept 92), pp. 145 – 167. Bibl.

International cooperation

Wilken, Gene C. Future Caribbean Donor Landscapes: A Geographic Interpretation of Contemporary Trends. *Caribbean Geography*, v. 3, no. 4 (Sept 92), pp. 215 – 222. Bibl.

Central America

Barzetti, Valerie and Yanina Rovinski, eds. *Towards a Green Central America: Integrating Conservation and Development*, a translation of *Hacia una Centroamérica verde*. Reviewed by L. Alan Eyre. *Caribbean Geography*, v. 3, no. 4 (Sept 92), pp. 277 – 278.

Costa Rica

Girot, Pascal-Olivier. Parcs nationaux et développement rural au Costa Rica: mythes et réalités. *Tiers Monde*, v. 34, no. 134 (Apr – June 93), pp. 405 – 421. Bibl, tables, maps, charts.

Developing countries

Stone, Roger D. *The Nature of Development* reviewed by David Barton Bray. *Grassroots Development*, v. 17, no. 1 (1993), pp. 44 – 45. Il.

Ecuador

Meyer, Carrie A. Environmental NGOs in Ecuador: An Economic Analysis of Institutional Change. *Journal of Developing Areas*, v. 27, no. 2 (Jan 93), pp. 191 – 210. Bibl.

Latin America

Ferrer, Aldo. Nuevos paradigmas tecnológicos y desarrollo sostenible: perspectiva latinoamericana. *Comercio Exterior*, v. 43, no. 9 (Sept 93), pp. 807 – 813. Bibl.

Goodman, David Edwin and Michael R. Redclift, eds. *Environment and Development in Latin America: The Politics of Sustainability* reviewed by Margaret E. Keck. *Studies in Comparative International Development*, v. 27, no. 3 (Fall 92), pp. 120 – 122.

Guimarães, Roberto Pereira. Deuda externa y desarrollo sustentable en América Latina: una perspectiva sociopolítica. *Revista Interamericana de Planificación*, v. 26, no. 101 – 102 (Jan – June 93), pp. 7 – 42. Bibl.

Leriche, Christian E. La propuesta cepalina del desarrollo sustentable latinoamericano y medio ambiente. *El Cotidiano*, v. 8, no. 52 (Jan – Feb 93), pp. 109 – 111. Il.

Reilly, Charles A. The Road from Rio: NGO Policy Makers and the Social Ecology of Development. *Grassroots Development*, v. 17, no. 1 (1993), pp. 25 – 35. Bibl, il.

Rudman, Andrew I. and Joseph S. Tulchin, eds. *Economic Development and Environmental Protection in Latin America* reviewed by Steve Ellner. *Journal of Developing Areas*, v. 27, no. 3 (Apr 93), p. 441.

— *Economic Development and Environmental Protection in Latin America* reviewed by Margaret E. Keck. *Studies in Comparative International Development*, v. 27, no. 3 (Fall 92), pp. 120 – 122.

Tomic, Tonci. Participation and the Environment. *CEPAL Review*, no. 48 (Dec 92), pp. 107 – 115. Bibl.

Tudela, Fernando. Población y sustentabilidad del desarrollo: los desafíos de la complejidad. *Comercio Exterior*, v. 43, no. 8 (Aug 93), pp. 698 – 707. Bibl, charts.

Mexican – American Border Region

Johnstone, Nick. Comparative Advantage, Transfrontier Pollution, and the Environmental Degradation of a Border Region: The Case of the Californias. *Journal of Borderlands Studies*, v. 7, no. 2 (Fall 92), pp. 33 – 52. Bibl.

Mexico

Anderson, L. Susan. The Nature of Good Business. *Business Mexico*, v. 3, no. 1 (Jan – Feb 93), p. 66. Il.

Cochet, Hubert. Agriculture sur brûlis, élevage extensif et dégradation de l'environnement en Amérique Latine: un exemple en Sierra Madre del Sur, au Mexique. *Tiers Monde*, v. 34, no. 134 (Apr – June 93), pp. 281 – 303. Maps, charts.

Kamp, Dick. Mexico's Mines: Source of Wealth or Woe? *Business Mexico*, v. 3, no. 1 (Jan – Feb 93), pp. 29 – 30. Il.

Keenan, Joe. Corporate Mexico Goes for the Green. *Business Mexico*, v. 3, no. 1 (Jan – Feb 93), pp. 31 – 32. Il.

Long, Veronica H. Monkey Business: Mixing Tourism with Ecology. *Business Mexico*, v. 3, no. 1 (Jan – Feb 93), pp. 23 – 26. Il.

March, Ignacio J. and Rosa María Vidal. The Road to Success. *Business Mexico*, v. 3, no. 1 (Jan – Feb 93), pp. 10 – 12. Il, maps.

Savage, Melissa. Ecological Disturbance and Nature Tourism. *Geographical Review*, v. 83, no. 3 (July 93), pp. 290 – 300. Bibl, il, maps.

Cost

Sands, Benjamin. Financing Compliance. *Business Mexico*, v. 3, no. 1 (Jan – Feb 93), pp. 34 – 35 +.

Panama

Heckadon Moreno, Stanley. Impact of Development on the Panama Canal Environment (Translated by Jane Marchi). *Journal of Inter-American Studies and World Affairs*, v. 35, no. 3 (Fall 93), pp. 129 – 149. Bibl.

Paraguay

Dietze, Rolando et al. *Los caminos de la diversidad: condiciones y potenciales para un desarrollo sostenible en el Paraguay* (Review). *Revista Paraguaya de Sociología*, v. 29, no. 85 (Sept – Dec 92), pp. 189 – 190.

Peru

Yepes del Castillo, Ernesto. Un balance 500 años después: ciencia, biodiversidad y futuro. *Debate (Peru)*, v. 16, no. 74 (Sept – Oct 93), pp. 57 – 60.

Venezuela

Sayago, Luis Rodrigo. Biotecnología, agricultura y ecología: un dilema para el futuro. *Derecho y Reforma Agraria*, no. 24 (1993), pp. 159 – 165.

ECONOMÍA Y DESARROLLO (PERIODICAL)

Roca, Sergio G. A Critical Review of *Economía y Desarrollo*. *Cuban Studies/Estudios Cubanos*, v. 23 (1993), pp. 205 – 210. Bibl, tables.

ECONOMIC ASSISTANCE

Caribbean area

Wilken, Gene C. Future Caribbean Donor Landscapes: A Geographic Interpretation of Contemporary Trends. *Caribbean Geography*, v. 3, no. 4 (Sept 92), pp. 215 – 222. Bibl.

Latin America

Sources

World Bank. Directiva operacional concerniente a pueblos indígenas. *Anuario Indigenista*, v. 30 (Dec 91), pp. 255 – 266. Bibl.

ECONOMIC ASSISTANCE, FOREIGN

See also
    Agricultural assistance, Foreign
    Educational assistance
    Military assistance, Foreign

Caribbean area

DeMar, Margaretta. Constraints on Constrainers: Limits on External Economic Policy Affecting Nutritional Vulnerability in the Caribbean. *Latin American Perspectives*, v. 20, no. 2 (Spring 93), pp. 54 – 73. Bibl.

Costa Rica

Edelman, Marc and Rodolfo Monge Oviedo. Costa Rica: The Non-Market Roots of Market Success. *Report on the Americas*, v. 26, no. 4 (Feb 93), pp. 22 – 29 +. Bibl, il.

El Salvador

Cuenca, Breny. *El poder intangible: la AID y el estado salvadoreño en los años ochenta* reviewed by Rachel Sieder. *Journal of Latin American Studies*, v. 25, no. 3 (Oct 93), p. 670.

Curtis, Cynthia and Danielle Yariv. Después de la guerra: una mirada preliminar al papel de la ayuda militar de EE.UU. en la reconstrucción postguerra en El Salvador. *ECA; Estudios Centroamericanos*, v. 48, no. 531 – 532 (Jan – Feb 93), pp. 61 – 74. Il.

Latin America

Serafino, Nina M. et al. Latin American Indigenous Peoples and Considerations for U.S. Assistance. *Anuario Indigenista*, v. 30 (Dec 91), pp. 11 – 144. Bibl.

ECONOMIC CONDITIONS

See
    Cost and standard of living
    Quality of life
    Subdivision *Economic conditions* under names of
      specific countries

ECONOMIC DEVELOPMENT

See also
    Ecology and development
    International economic relations
    Subdivisions *Economic conditions* and *Economic policy*
      under names of specific countries

Cardoso, Fernando Henrique. *As idéias e seu lugar* (Review). *Vozes*, v. 87, no. 3 (May – June 93), pp. 91 – 92.

Santos, Theotonio dos. Globalización financiera y estrategias de desarrollo. *Nueva Sociedad*, no. 126 (July – Aug 93), pp. 98 – 109.

Sprout, Ronald V. A. La economía política de Prebisch. *Pensamiento Iberoamericano*, no. 22 – 23, tomo I (July 92 – June 93), pp. 315 – 343. Bibl, tables.

Congresses

¿Es posible lograr el desarrollo económico con equidad social? (A seminar organized by the Fundación de Investigaciones Sociales y Políticas (FISYP) de Argentina and summarized by Dora Douthat). *Realidad Económica*, no. 119 (Oct – Nov 93), pp. 139 – 144.

ECONOMIC FORECASTING

Cuattromo, Oscar Julio et al. Argentina en crecimiento, 1993 – 1995: proyecciones oficiales. *Realidad Económica*, no. 117 (July – Aug 93), pp. 8 – 23. Charts.

Damill, Mario et al. Crecimiento económico en América Latina: experiencia reciente y perspectivas (Translated by Leandro Wolfson). *Desarrollo Económico (Argentina)*, v. 33, no. 130 (July – Sept 93), pp. 237 – 264. Bibl, tables.

Elías, Víctor Jorge. *Sources of Growth: A Study of Seven Latin American Economies* reviewed by David E. Hojman. *Journal of Latin American Studies*, v. 25, no. 3 (Oct 93), pp. 675 – 677.

Fletcher, G. Richard and Robert A. Pastor. El Caribe en el siglo XXI. *Integración Latinoamericana*, v. 18, no. 187 – 188 (Mar – Apr 93), pp. 13 – 22. Bibl.

Riner, Deborah L. A Third-Quarter Perspective. *Business Mexico*, v. 3, no. 9 (Sept 93), pp. 32 – 35. Charts.

Ritter, Archibald R. M. Exploring Cuba's Alternate Economic Futures. *Cuban Studies/Estudios Cubanos*, v. 23 (1993), pp. 3 – 31. Bibl, tables.

ECONOMIC GEOGRAPHY

See

Geography, Economic

ECONOMIC INTEGRATION

See

International economic integration
Names of specific regional organizations
Subdivision *Economic integration* under names of specific regions

ECONOMIC POLICY

See

Economics
Subdivision *Economic policy* under names of specific countries

ECONOMIC ZONING

See

Geography, Economic
Industries, Location of
Regional planning

ECONOMICS

See also

Balance of payments
Banks and banking
Capital
Capital investments
Capital productivity
Capitalism
Capitalists and financiers
Cartels and commodity agreements
Consumption (Economics)
Cost and standard of living
Credit
Currency question
Debts, Public
Distributive justice
Division of labor
Economic forecasting
Employment
Finance
Finance, Public
Foreign exchange problem
Foreign trade promotion
Foreign trade regulation
Geography, Economic
Income distribution
Index numbers (Economics)
Industrial organization
Industrial promotion
Inflation (Finance)

Informal sector (Economics)
Interest rates
International economic relations
International finance
Labor and laboring classes
Labor productivity
Marxian economics
Money and money supply
National income
Price regulation
Prices
Privatization
Production (Economic theory)
Religion and economics
Saving and investment
Socialism
Subcontracting
Tariff
Taxation
Wages
Subdivision *Economic aspects* under specific topics
Subdivisions *Economic conditions* and *Economic policy* under names of specific countries

Bledel, Rodolfo. Epistemología económica y crisis de los sistemas. *Realidad Económica*, no. 116 (May – June 93), pp. 98 – 110. Bibl.

Sáenz, Josué. Diálogo con Adam Smith. *Vuelta*, v. 17, no. 197 (Apr 93), pp. 27 – 31.

Awards

Mancera Aguayo, Miguel. Discurso de Miguel Mancera en la recepción del premio de economía rey Juan Carlos (Introduced by Luis Angel Rojo). *El Trimestre Económico*, v. 60, no. 237 (Jan – Mar 93), pp. 212 – 229.

Mathematical models

Fernández-Baca, Jorge. La importancia de la democracia para los economistas. *Apuntes (Peru)*, no. 29 (July – Dec 91), pp. 9 – 16. Bibl, charts.

Brazil

Pereira, Luiz Carlos Bresser and José Márcio Rego. Um mestre da economia brasileira: Ignácio Rangel. *Revista de Economia Política (Brazil)*, v. 13, no. 2 (Apr – June 93), pp. 98 – 119.

Rocha, Antônio Penalves. A difusão da economia política no Brasil entre os fins do século XVIII e início do XIX. *Revista de Economia Política (Brazil)*, v. 13, no. 4 (Oct – Dec 93), pp. 47 – 57. Bibl.

Caribbean area

Best, Lloyd. The Contribution of George Beckford. *Social and Economic Studies*, v. 41, no. 3 (Sept 92), pp. 5 – 23.

Latin America

Bibliography

Revista de revistas iberoamericanas. *Pensamiento Iberoamericano*, no. 22 – 23, tomo II (July 92 – June 93), pp. 271 – 405.

Spain

Bibliography

Revista de revistas iberoamericanas. *Pensamiento Iberoamericano*, no. 22 – 23, tomo II (July 92 – June 93), pp. 271 – 405.

ECUADOR

See also

Agricultural laborers – Ecuador
Architecture – Ecuador
Artists – Ecuador
Blacks in literature – Ecuador
Christian art and symbolism – Ecuador
Cities and towns – Ecuador
Community development – Ecuador
Diseases – Ecuador
Earthquakes – Ecuador
Ecology and development – Ecuador
Education, Bilingual – Ecuador
Fertility, Human – Ecuador
Finance, Public – Ecuador
Forestry – Ecuador
Guayaquil, Ecuador
Infant mortality – Ecuador
Informal sector (Economics) – Ecuador

Jews – Ecuador
Labor supply – Ecuador
Literature and society – Ecuador
Migration, Internal – Ecuador
Music – Ecuador
Non-governmental organizations – Ecuador
Paleobotany – Ecuador
Philosophy – Ecuador
Quito, Ecuador
Regional planning – Ecuador
Religion and politics – Ecuador
Social conflict – Ecuador
Social services – Ecuador
Sociology, Urban – Ecuador
Taxation – Ecuador

Antiquities

Patiño Castaño, Diógenes. Arqueología del Bajo Patía: fases y correlaciones en la costa pacífica de Colombia y Ecuador. *Latin American Antiquity*, v. 4, no. 2 (June 93), pp. 180 – 199. Bibl, il, tables, maps.

Stothert, Karen Elizabeth. *La prehistoria temprana de la península de Santa Elena: cultura Las Vegas* reviewed by Michael Malpass. *Latin American Antiquity*, v. 4, no. 4 (Dec 93), pp. 392 – 393.

Villalba O., Marcelo. *Cotocollao: una aldea formativa del valle de Quito* reviewed by Tamara L. Bray. *Latin American Antiquity*, v. 4, no. 1 (Mar 93), pp. 96 – 97.

Boundaries
Peru

Bustamante Ponce, Fernando. Ecuador: Putting an End to Ghosts of the Past? (Translated by Jane Marchi). *Journal of Inter-American Studies and World Affairs*, v. 34, no. 4 (Winter 92 – 93), pp. 195 – 224. Bibl.

Civilization

Salcedo-Bastardo, José Luis. Sobre el civismo y la solidaridad: por Montalvo de Venezuela a Ecuador. *Revista Nacional de Cultura (Venezuela)*, v. 53, no. 286 (July – Sept 92), pp. 11 – 18.

Climate

Pourrut, Pierre. L'effet "ENSO" sur les précipitations et les écoulements au XXème siècle: exemple de l'Equateur. *Bulletin de l'Institut Français d'Etudes Andines*, v. 22, no. 1 (1993), pp. 85 – 98. Bibl, tables, maps, charts.

Steinitz-Kannan, Miriam et al. The Fossil Diatoms of Lake Yambo, Ecuador: A Possible Record of El Niño Events. *Bulletin de l'Institut Français d'Etudes Andines*, v. 22, no. 1 (1993), pp. 227 – 241. Bibl, il, maps, charts.

Economic policy

Báez, René. La quimera de la modernización. *Desarrollo Indoamericano*, v. 23, no. 91 (June 93), pp. 33 – 35. Il.

Foreign economic relations
Andean region

Cáceres, Luis René. Ecuador y la integración andina: experiencias y perspectivas. *Integración Latinoamericana*, v. 18, no. 195 (Nov 93), pp. 31 – 46. Bibl, tables, charts.

Argentina

Acuerdo de Alcance Parcial de Complementación Económica concertado con la república del Ecuador y la República Argentina. *Integración Latinoamericana*, v. 18, no. 194 (Oct 93), pp. 61 – 64.

Colombia

Castro Guerrero, Gustavo. Evolución de las relaciones colombo – ecuatorianas durante el gobierno del señor presidente César Gaviria. *Revista Javeriana*, v. 61, no. 594 (May 93), pp. 217 – 223. Tables, charts.

Foreign relations

Bustamante Ponce, Fernando. Ecuador: Putting an End to Ghosts of the Past? (Translated by Jane Marchi). *Journal of Inter-American Studies and World Affairs*, v. 34, no. 4 (Winter 92 – 93), pp. 195 – 224. Bibl.

Hey, Jeanne A. K. Foreign Policy Options under Dependence: A Theoretical Evaluation with Evidence from Ecuador. *Journal of Latin American Studies*, v. 25, no. 3 (Oct 93), pp. 543 – 574. Bibl.

History
Sources

Ortiz de la Tabla Ducasse, Javier et al, eds. *Cartas de cabildos hispanoamericanos: Audiencia de Quito* reviewed by Frédérique Langue. *Caravelle*, no. 60 (1993), pp. 147 – 148.

Politics and government

Sánchez Parga, José. Ecuador: en el engranaje neoliberal. *Nueva Sociedad*, no. 123 (Jan – Feb 93), pp. 12 – 17. Tables.

Rural conditions

Martínez Valle, Luciano. Cambios en la fuerza de trabajo y conflicto social en el agro ecuatoriano. *Revista Paraguaya de Sociología*, v. 29, no. 84 (May – Aug 92), pp. 101 – 113. Bibl.

ECUADORIAN LITERATURE

Primera bienal del cuento ecuatoriano: obras premiadas reviewed by Barbara Mujica (Review entitled "A Roundup of Stories"). *Américas*, v. 45, no. 1 (Jan – Feb 93), pp. 60 – 61. Il.

Black authors

Handelsman, Michael Howard. Ubicando la literatura afroecuatoriana en el contexto nacional: ¿Ilusión o realidad? *Afro-Hispanic Review*, v. 12, no. 1 (Spring 93), pp. 42 – 47. Bibl.

History and criticism

Chanady, Amaryll. La ambivalencia del discurso indigenista en la nueva narrativa ecuatoriana. *Canadian Journal of Latin American and Caribbean Studies*, v. 17, no. 34 (1992), pp. 53 – 71. Bibl.

Jaramillo Buendía, Gladys et al, eds. *Indice de la narrativa ecuatoriana* reviewed by Carlos Orihuela. *Revista de Crítica Literaria Latinoamericana*, v. 19, no. 38 (July – Dec 93), pp. 413 – 415.

Sacoto, Antonio. *El ensayo equatoriano* reviewed by Gerardo Sáenz. *Revista Interamericana de Bibliografía*, v. 42, no. 3 (1992), p. 508.

LA EDAD DE ORO (PERIODICAL)

Fraser, Howard M. *La Edad de Oro* and José Martí's Modernist Ideology for Children. *Revista Interamericana de Bibliografía*, v. 42, no. 2 (1992), pp. 223 – 232. Bibl.

EDGELL, ZEE
Criticism of specific works
Beka Lamb

Parham, Mary Helene. Why Toycie Bruk Down: A Study of Zee Edgell's *Beka Lamb*. *Belizean Studies*, v. 21, no. 2 (Oct 93), pp. 15 – 22. Bibl.

LA EDUCACIÓN (PERIODICAL)

Paldao, Carlos E. Spreading the Word on Education. *Américas*, v. 45, no. 3 (May – June 93), pp. 54 – 55. Il.

EDUCATION
See also
Adult education
Audiovisual education
Bilingualism
Catholic universities and colleges
Church and education
Illiteracy
Learning, Psychology of
Parent – teacher relationships
Programmed instruction
Reading interests
Religious education
Research institutes
School management and organization
Socialization
Students
Teacher – student relationships
Teachers, Training of
Teachers' unions
Teaching and teachers
Technical education
Textbooks
Universities and colleges

Vocational education
Subdivision *Education* under *Hispanic Americans (U.S.)*, *Women*, and names of Indian groups

Aims and objectives

Gallegos, Carlos. Pensamiento y acción política de José Vasconcelos. *Revista Mexicana de Ciencias Políticas y Sociales*, v. 37, Nueva época, no. 149 (July – Sept 92), pp. 125 – 138. Bibl.

Latapí, Pablo. El pensamiento educativo de Torres Bodet: una apreciación crítica. *Revista Latinoamericana de Estudios Educativos*, v. 22, no. 3 (July – Sept 92), pp. 13 – 44. Bibl.

Levin, Henry M. and Marlaine E. Lockheed, eds. *Effective Schools in Developing Countries* reviewed by Maria Valéria Junho Pena. *La Educación (USA)*, v. 37, no. 115 (1993), pp. 437 – 439.

Mejía, Marco Raúl. Educación popular: una fuerza creativa desde los sectores populares. *Estudios Sociales (Dominican Republic)*, v. 26, no. 93 (July – Sept 93), pp. 61 – 82.

Mueses de Molina, Carolina. Educación popular en salud y nutrición: revisión de bibliografía. *Estudios Sociales (Dominican Republic)*, v. 26, no. 93 (July – Sept 93), pp. 83 – 108. Bibl.

Rondinelli, Dennis A. et al. *Planning Education Reforms in Developing Countries* reviewed by Maria Valéria Junho Pena. *La Educación (USA)*, v. 37, no. 115 (1993), pp. 437 – 439.

Ruz Ruz, Juan D. Lo instrumental y lo valórico en la educación chilena: aportes para la discusión sobre los objetivos fundamentales y los contenidos mínimos de la educación. *Estudios Sociales (Chile)*, no. 74 (Oct – Dec 92), pp. 167 – 175.

Samour, Héctor. Universidad y derechos humanos. *ECA; Estudios Centroamericanos*, v. 47, no. 528 (Oct 92), pp. 894 – 900. Bibl, il.

Sánchez Gamboa, Silvio Ancísar. La concepción del hombre en la investigación educativa: algunas consideraciones. *Islas*, no. 96 (May – Aug 90), pp. 34 – 41. Bibl.

Schiefelbein, Ernesto. *En busca de la escuela del siglo XXI* reviewed by Marta Llames Murúa. *La Educación (USA)*, v. 37, no. 114 (1993), pp. 170 – 171.

Tovar López, Ramón Adolfo. Proposición para una organización de la función social: educación en una sociedad masificada. *Boletín de la Academia Nacional de la Historia (Venezuela)*, v. 76, no. 302 (Apr – June 93), pp. 226 – 234.

Urquidi, Víctor L. La educación: eje para el futuro desarrollo de la potencialidad latinoamericana. *Revista Latinoamericana de Estudios Educativos*, v. 22, no. 3 (July – Sept 92), pp. 123 – 131.

Congresses

Arroyo, Gonzalo and Joaquín Silva Soler. Mesa redonda: educando para la solidaridad. *Mensaje*, v. 42, no. 421 (Aug 93), pp. 392 – 401. Il.

Economic aspects

Carlsen, Laura. A Failure to Educate. *Business Mexico*, v. 3, no. 6 (June 93), pp. 10 – 13. Il, tables, charts.

Díaz-Briquets, Sergio. Collision Course: Labor Force and Educational Trends in Cuba. *Cuban Studies/Estudios Cubanos*, v. 23 (1993), pp. 91 – 112. Bibl, tables.

Fajnzylber, Fernando. Education and Changing Production Patterns with Social Equity. *CEPAL Review*, no. 47 (Aug 92), pp. 7 – 19. Tables, charts.

López Rodríguez, Ramón. A Different Solution. *Business Mexico*, v. 3, no. 6 (June 93), pp. 16 – 18. Il.

Ormeño Ortíz, Eugenio et al. *Educación para los desarrollos locales: macrocomunas y sustrato material en la IX región de la Araucanía* (Review). *La Educación (USA)*, v. 36, no. 111 – 113 (1992), pp. 302 – 303.

Paredes, Cándido A. Relaciones de la agricultura tradicional con el ausentismo y la deserción escolar: el referente empírico del piedemonte barinés. *Derecho y Reforma Agraria*, no. 24 (1993), pp. 63 – 71.

Patrinos, Harry Anthony and George Psacharopoulos. The Cost of Being Indigenous in Bolivia: An Empirical Analysis of Educational Attainments and Outcomes. *Bulletin of Latin American Research*, v. 12, no. 3 (Sept 93), pp. 293 – 309. Bibl, tables, charts.

Trahtemberg Siederer, León. Juventud, educación, empleo y empresa. *Debate (Peru)*, v. 16, no. 74 (Sept – Oct 93), pp. 34 – 36. Il.

United Nations. Economic Commission for Latin America and the Caribbean. *Educación y conocimiento: eje de la transformación productiva con equidad* reviewed by Gloria González Salazar. *Problemas del Desarrollo*, v. 24, no. 94 (July – Sept 93), pp. 286 – 290.

— *Education and Knowledge: Basic Pillars of Changing Production Patterns with Social Equity* (Review). *CEPAL Review*, no. 47 (Aug 92), pp. 191 – 193.

Congresses

Swope, John. Un foro internacional: educación media como estrategia de desarrollo con equidad. *Mensaje*, v. 42, no. 419 (June 93), pp. 208 – 210. Il.

Experimental methods

Contreras, Juan Pablo. Trabajos de Verano: formando en la solidaridad. *Mensaje*, v. 42, no. 421 (Aug 93), pp. 404 – 407.

Llanos Zuloaga, Martha. Programas de intervención temprana en América Latina: modelo Portage con base en el hogar; una experiencia peruana. *Revista Latinoamericana de Estudios Educativos*, v. 22, no. 3 (July – Sept 92), pp. 89 – 107. Bibl, tables.

Muñoz Valenzuela, Josefina. Experiencia alfabetizadora del Taller de Acción Cultura, TAC: oralidad y escritura colectiva en Curacaví. *Revista Chilena de Literatura*, no. 42 (Aug 93), pp. 143 – 148. Bibl.

Oliveira, João Batista Araújo e and Greville Rumble, eds. *Educación a distancia en América Latina: análisis de costo-efectividad* reviewed by Aaron Segal. *Interciencia*, v. 18, no. 6 (Nov – Dec 93), pp. 327 – 328.

La promoción de los derechos humanos y la educación no formal. *ECA; Estudios Centroamericanos*, v. 48, no. 531 – 532 (Jan – Feb 93), pp. 100 – 104. Il.

Reimers A., Fernando. Fe y Alegría: una innovación educativa para proporcionar educación básica con calidad y equidad. *Revista Paraguaya de Sociología*, v. 29, no. 85 (Sept – Dec 92), pp. 41 – 58. Bibl, tables.

Rojas Orozco, Rodrigo. Reinserción y educación: el programa piloto-experimental de pedagogía para la paz y la reconciliación nacional. *Revista Javeriana*, v. 60, no. 590 (Nov – Dec 92), pp. 325 – 329.

Romero C., Paulino. Pedagogía experimental y política. *Revista Cultural Lotería*, v. 50, no. 384 (July – Aug 91), pp. 68 – 75.

Salinas Amescua, Bertha. Descripción de cinco modelos de "pedagogía de la organización" prevalecientes en el movimiento de educación popular en América Latina. *Revista Latinoamericana de Estudios Educativos*, v. 22, no. 3 (July – Sept 92), pp. 45 – 87. Bibl.

Sánchez de Irarrázabal, Elena. Manuel y Carolina, anfitriones del choque entre dos mundos. *Mensaje*, v. 42, no. 418 (May 93), pp. 161 – 162. Il.

Finance

Melchior, José Carlos de Araújo. Financiamento da educação: gestão democrática dos recursos financeiros públicos em educação. *Revista Brasileira de Estudos Pedagógicos*, v. 72, no. 172 (Sept – Dec 91), pp. 262 – 290. Bibl.

Muñoz Izquierdo, Carlos. Comentarios a la propuesta que hace el dr. Pablo Latapí en el artículo "Reflexiones sobre la justicia en la educación." *Revista Latinoamericana de Estudios Educativos*, v. 23, no. 2 (Apr – June 93), pp. 43 – 53.

— Tendencias observadas en las investigaciones y en las políticas relacionadas con el financiamiento de la educación técnica y vocacional en América Latina. *Revista Latinoamericana de Estudios Educativos*, v. 23, no. 1 (Jan – Mar 93), pp. 9 – 41. Bibl, tables.

Argentina

Bixio, Beatriz and Luis D. Heredia. *Distancia cultural y lingüística: el fracaso escolar en poblaciones rurales del oeste de la provincia de Córdoba* (Review). *La Educación (USA)*, v. 36, no. 111 – 113 (1992), pp. 296 – 298.

De Lella Allevato, Cayetano and Carlos P. Krotsch, eds. *Congreso Pedagógico Nacional: evaluación y perspectivas* reviewed by Carlos Salá. *La Educación (USA),* v. 36, no. 111 – 113 (1992), pp. 285 – 291.

Congresses

Revolución científico – técnica, educación y área laboral (A seminar organized by the Fundación de Investigaciones Sociales y Políticas (FISYP) de Argentina and summarized by Dora Douthat). *Realidad Económica,* no. 119 (Oct – Nov 93), pp. 134 – 138.

Bolivia

Patrinos, Harry Anthony and George Psacharopoulos. The Cost of Being Indigenous in Bolivia: An Empirical Analysis of Educational Attainments and Outcomes. *Bulletin of Latin American Research,* v. 12, no. 3 (Sept 93), pp. 293 – 309. Bibl, tables, charts.

Brazil

Melchior, José Carlos de Araújo. Financiamento da educação: gestão democrática dos recursos financeiros públicos em educação. *Revista Brasileira de Estudos Pedagógicos,* v. 72, no. 172 (Sept – Dec 91), pp. 262 – 290. Bibl.

Pfromm Netto, Samuel. Caminhamos para trás. *Problemas Brasileiros,* v. 30, no. 295 (Jan – Feb 93), pp. 45 – 47. Il.

Sampaio Neto, José Augusto Vaz. O ensino na corte e na província. *Revista do Instituto Histórico e Geográfico Brasileiro,* no. 373 (Oct – Dec 91), pp. 1115 – 1144. Bibl.

Sources

Almeida, Stela Borges de and Luiz Felippe Perret Serpa. Guia de fontes fotográficas para a história da educação. *Revista Brasileira de Estudos Pedagógicos,* v. 72, no. 172 (Sept – Dec 91), pp. 392 – 394.

Antoniazzi, Maria Regina Filgueiras. Guia de fontes literárias para o estudo da história da educação na Bahia. *Revista Brasileira de Estudos Pedagógicos,* v. 72, no. 172 (Sept – Dec 91), pp. 388 – 391.

Bastos, Eni Santana Barreto et al. Guia de fontes de documentação para a história da educação na Bahia. *Revista Brasileira de Estudos Pedagógicos,* v. 72, no. 172 (Sept – Dec 91), pp. 385 – 387.

Chile

Muñoz Valenzuela, Josefina. Experiencia alfabetizadora del Taller de Acción Cultura, TAC: oralidad y escritura colectiva en Curacaví. *Revista Chilena de Literatura,* no. 42 (Aug 93), pp. 143 – 148. Bibl.

Ormeño Ortíz, Eugenio et al. *Educación para los desarrollos locales: macrocomunas y sustrato material en la IX región de la Araucanía* (Review). *La Educación (USA),* v. 36, no. 111 – 113 (1992), pp. 302 – 303.

Ruz Ruz, Juan D. Lo instrumental y lo valórico en la educación chilena: aportes para la discusión sobre los objetivos fundamentales y los contenidos mínimos de la educación. *Estudios Sociales (Chile),* no. 74 (Oct – Dec 92), pp. 167 – 175.

Sánchez de Irarrázabal, Elena. Manuel y Carolina, anfitriones del choque entre dos mundos. *Mensaje,* v. 42, no. 418 (May 93), pp. 161 – 162. Il.

Schiefelbein, Ernesto. *En busca de la escuela del siglo XXI* reviewed by Marta Llames Murúa. *La Educación (USA),* v. 37, no. 114 (1993), pp. 170 – 171.

Colombia

Rojas Orozco, Rodrigo. Reinserción y educación: el programa piloto-experimental de pedagogía para la paz y la reconciliación nacional. *Revista Javeriana,* v. 60, no. 590 (Nov – Dec 92), pp. 325 – 329.

Cuba

Díaz-Briquets, Sergio. Collision Course: Labor Force and Educational Trends in Cuba. *Cuban Studies/Estudios Cubanos,* v. 23 (1993), pp. 91 – 112. Bibl, tables.

Developing countries

Levin, Henry M. and Marlaine E. Lockheed, eds. *Effective Schools in Developing Countries* reviewed by Maria Valéria Junho Pena. *La Educación (USA),* v. 37, no. 115 (1993), pp. 437 – 439.

El Salvador

La promoción de los derechos humanos y la educación no formal. *ECA; Estudios Centroamericanos,* v. 48, no. 531 – 532 (Jan – Feb 93), pp. 100 – 104. Il.

Latin America

Actividades del PREDE. *La Educación (USA),* v. 36, 37 (1992, 1992), All issues. Il.

Aguerrondo, Inés. *El planeamiento educativo como instrumento de cambio* (Review). *La Educación (USA),* v. 36, no. 111 – 113 (1992), pp. 277 – 279.

Bohórquez, Carmen L. Colonialismo escolar-izado. *Islas,* no. 96 (May – Aug 90), pp. 121 – 126.

Fajnzylber, Fernando. Education and Changing Production Patterns with Social Equity. *CEPAL Review,* no. 47 (Aug 92), pp. 7 – 19. Tables, charts.

Reimers A., Fernando. Fe y Alegría: una innovación educativa para proporcionar educación básica con calidad y equidad. *Revista Paraguaya de Sociología,* v. 29, no. 85 (Sept – Dec 92), pp. 41 – 58. Bibl, tables.

Salinas Amescua, Bertha. Descripción de cinco modelos de "pedagogía de la organización" prevalecientes en el movimiento de educación popular en América Latina. *Revista Latinoamericana de Estudios Educativos,* v. 22, no. 3 (July – Sept 92), pp. 45 – 87. Bibl.

United Nations. Economic Commission for Latin America and the Caribbean. *Educación y conocimiento: eje de la transformación productiva con equidad* reviewed by Gloria González Salazar. *Problemas del Desarrollo,* v. 24, no. 94 (July – Sept 93), pp. 286 – 290.

— *Education and Knowledge: Basic Pillars of Changing Production Patterns with Social Equity* (Review). *CEPAL Review,* no. 47 (Aug 92), pp. 191 – 193.

United Nations Educational, Scientific and Cultural Organization. *Situación educativa de América Latina y el Caribe, 1980 – 1990* reviewed by M. Dino Carelli. *Estudios Sociales (Chile),* no. 78 (Oct – Dec 93), pp. 232 – 234.

— *Situación educativa de América Latina y el Caribe, 1980 – 1990* reviewed by Dino Carelli. *Revista Latinoamericana de Estudios Educativos,* v. 23, no. 2 (Apr – June 93), pp. 127 – 129.

Urquidi, Víctor L. La educación: eje para el futuro desarrollo de la potencialidad latinoamericana. *Revista Latinoamericana de Estudios Educativos,* v. 22, no. 3 (July – Sept 92), pp. 123 – 131.

Congresses

Leal, Ildefonso. Bajo los auspicios de la Universidad Pedagógica Nacional de Bogotá, Colombia, se celebró el I Congreso Iberoamericano de Docentes e Investigadores en Historia de la Educación Latinoamericana, del 2 al 5 de septiembre del año 1992. *Boletín de la Academia Nacional de la Historia (Venezuela),* v. 76, no. 302 (Apr – June 93), pp. 179 – 180.

Mexico

Carlsen, Laura. A Failure to Educate. *Business Mexico,* v. 3, no. 6 (June 93), pp. 10 – 13. Il, tables, charts.

García Canclini, Néstor and Gilberto Guevara Niebla, eds. *La educación y la cultura ante el Tratado de Libre Comercio* reviewed by Fernando de Mateo (Review entitled "El jalón del TLC"). *Nexos,* v. 16, no. 189 (Sept 93), pp. 66 – 67.

Las necesidades educativas de las mayorías mexicanas ante el Tratado de Libre Comercio. *Revista Latinoamericana de Estudios Educativos,* v. 23, no. 1 (Jan – Mar 93), pp. 5 – 8.

Vázquez, Josefina Zoraida, ed. *La educación en la historia de México* reviewed by Carlos Salá. *La Educación (USA),* v. 37, no. 114 (1993), pp. 174 – 175.

Zúñiga Molina, Leonel. Entrevista con Margarita Gómez-Palacio Muñoz. *La Educación (USA),* v. 37, no. 115 (1993), pp. 381 – 394.

Law and legislation

Nicolás, Juan Antonio. ¿Por qué una nueva ley federal de educación? *Plural (Mexico),* v. 22, no. 262 (July 93), pp. 81 – 83.

Statistics

Díaz Covarrubias, José. *La instrucción pública en México: estado que guardan la instrucción primaria, la secundaria y la profesional en la república; progresos realizados, mejoras que deben introducirse* reviewed by Pablo Latapí. *Revista Latinoamericana de Estudios Educativos*, v. 23, no. 1 (Jan – Mar 93), pp. 129 – 133.

Hayashi Martínez, Laureano. *La educación mexicana en cifras* reviewed by Norma Ilse Veloz Avila. *El Cotidiano*, v. 8, no. 51 (Nov – Dec 92), pp. 115 – 116.

Peru

Palomino Thompson, Eduardo. *Educación peruana: historia, análisis y propuestas* reviewed by Marta Llames Murúa. *La Educación (USA)*, v. 37, no. 115 (1993), pp. 429 – 431.

Trahtemberg Siederer, León. Juventud, educación, empleo y empresa. *Debate (Peru)*, v. 16, no. 74 (Sept – Oct 93), pp. 34 – 36. Il.

Venezuela

Paredes, Cándido A. Relaciones de la agricultura tradicional con el ausentismo y la deserción escolar: el referente empírico del piedemonte barinés. *Derecho y Reforma Agraria*, no. 24 (1993), pp. 63 – 71.

EDUCATION, BILINGUAL

See also
Bilingualism

Costa Rica

Rodino Pierri, Ana María. Language Rights and Education for the Afro-Caribbean, English-Speaking Minorities in Central America: Contributions to the Discussion on Bilingual Education in Costa Rica. *La Educación (USA)*, v. 36, no. 111 – 113 (1992), pp. 137 – 154. Bibl.

Ecuador

Torre, Luis Alberto de la. Una experiencia educativa bilingüe en el Ecuador. *Revista Latinoamericana de Estudios Educativos*, v. 22, no. 4 (Oct – Dec 92), pp. 89 – 110. Bibl.

Mexico

Calvo Pontón, Beatriz and Laura Donnadieu Aguado. *Una educación ¿indígena, bilingüe o bicultural?* reviewed by Salvador Martínez. *Revista Latinoamericana de Estudios Educativos*, v. 22, no. 4 (Oct – Dec 92), pp. 123 – 125.

Francis, Norbert and Rainer Enrique Hamel. La redacción en dos lenguas: escritura y narrativa en tres escuelas bilingües del valle del Mezquital. *Revista Latinoamericana de Estudios Educativos*, v. 22, no. 4 (Oct – Dec 92), pp. 11 – 35. Bibl, tables.

Nicaragua

Rodino Pierri, Ana María. Language Rights and Education for the Afro-Caribbean, English-Speaking Minorities in Central America: Contributions to the Discussion on Bilingual Education in Costa Rica. *La Educación (USA)*, v. 36, no. 111 – 113 (1992), pp. 137 – 154. Bibl.

United States

Dicker, Susan J. Examining the Myths of Language and Cultural Diversity: A Response to Rosalie Pedalino Porter's *Forked Tongue: The Politics of Bilingual Education*. *Bilingual Review/Revista Bilingüe*, v. 17, no. 3 (Sept – Dec 92), pp. 210 – 230. Bibl.

Escamilla, Kathy Cogburn and Marcello Medina. English and Spanish Acquisition by Limited-Language-Proficient Mexican Americans in a Three-Year Maintenance Bilingual Program. *Hispanic Journal of Behavioral Sciences*, v. 15, no. 1 (Feb 93), pp. 108 – 120. Bibl, tables.

EDUCATION, HIGHER

See also
Catholic universities and colleges
Universities and colleges

Aims and objectives

Atria Benaprés, Raúl. La educación superior desde el mundo de la vida. *Estudios Sociales (Chile)*, no. 78 (Oct – Dec 93), pp. 159 – 177. Bibl.

Fuenzalida Faivovich, Edmundo. Internacionalización de la educación superior en América Latina. *Estudios Sociales (Chile)*, no. 74 (Oct – Dec 92), pp. 39 – 73. Bibl.

Luque, Mónica G. The Idea of the University in Newman, Ortega y Gasset, and Jaspers: A Point of Departure for Analyses of the Current Problems Facing Latin American Universities. *La Educación (USA)*, v. 37, no. 114 (1993), pp. 115 – 118.

Economic aspects

Holguín Quiñones, Fernando. Encuesta a egresados de la Facultad de Ciencias Políticas y Sociales: I parte. *Revista Mexicana de Ciencias Políticas y Sociales*, v. 38, Nueva época, no. 153 (July – Sept 93), pp. 137 – 210. Tables, charts.

Villegas, Abelardo, ed. *Posgrado y desarrollo en América Latina* reviewed by Ana Lilia Delgadillo Ibarra. *Revista Mexicana de Ciencias Políticas y Sociales*, v. 38, Nueva época, no. 151 (Jan – Mar 93), pp. 213 – 216.

Statistics

Lorey, David E. *The Rise of the Professions in Twentieth-Century Mexico: University Graduates and Occupational Change since 1929* reviewed by Roderic A. Camp. *Journal of Latin American Studies*, v. 25, no. 2 (May 93), pp. 412 – 413.

Finance

Salinas, Augusto. La primera década de FONDECYT: un balance positivo. *Estudios Sociales (Chile)*, no. 74 (Oct – Dec 92), pp. 177 – 189. Bibl.

International cooperation

Aboites, Hugo. Internacionalización de la educación superior: los probables beneficiarios en el marco de la integración económico. *El Cotidiano*, v. 8, no. 52 (Jan – Feb 93), pp. 84 – 91. Bibl, il, tables.

Standards

Delhumeau Arrecillas, Antonio. El maestro: dignidad y deterioro. *Revista Mexicana de Ciencias Políticas y Sociales*, v. 38, Nueva época, no. 151 (Jan – Mar 93), pp. 205 – 210.

America

Bibliography

Ochoa Méndez, Jacqueline. Orientación bibliográfica sobre educación superior en Canadá, E.U.A. y México. *El Cotidiano*, v. 9, no. 55 (June 93), p. 120.

Argentina

Mollis, Marcela. Evaluación de la calidad universitaria: elementos para su discusión. *Realidad Económica*, no. 118 (Aug – Sept 93), pp. 97 – 116. Bibl, tables.

Sigal, Víctor. El acceso a la educación superior: el ingreso irrestricto; ¿Una falacia? *Desarrollo Económico (Argentina)*, v. 33, no. 130 (July – Sept 93), pp. 265 – 280. Bibl, tables.

Brazil

Candotti, Ennio. O sistema federal de ensino superior: problemas das alternativas (Comment on the article of the same title by Eunice Ribeiro Durham). *Revista Brasileira de Ciências Sociais*, v. 8, no. 23 (Oct 93), pp. 38 – 41.

Capdeville, Guy. O ensino superior agrícola no Brasil. *Revista Brasileira de Estudos Pedagógicos*, v. 72, no. 172 (Sept – Dec 91), pp. 229 – 261. Bibl, tables, charts.

Durham, Eunice Ribeiro. O sistema federal de ensino superior: problemas e alternativas. *Revista Brasileira de Ciências Sociais*, v. 8, no. 23 (Oct 93), pp. 5 – 37. Bibl, tables.

Guimarães, Jorge A. Perspectivas para as instituições federais de ensino superior (Comment on the article "O sistema federal de ensino superior: problemas e alternativas" by Eunice Ribeiro Durham). *Revista Brasileira de Ciências Sociais*, v. 8, no. 23 (Oct 93), pp. 42 – 47. Bibl.

Martins, Carlos Benedito. Caminhos e descaminhos das universidades federais (Comment on the article "O sistema federal de ensino superior: problemas e alternativas" by Eunice Ribeiro Durham). *Revista Brasileira de Ciências Sociais*, v. 8, no. 23 (Oct 93), pp. 48 – 54. Bibl.

Chile

Allende, Jorge E. Presentación del libro *La investigación universitaria en Chile: reflexiones críticas* de Manuel Krauskopf. *Estudios Sociales (Chile)*, no. 75 (Jan – Mar 93), pp. 231 – 238.

Letelier Sotomayor, Mario. Posibilidades efectivas de innovación en la docencia universitaria chilena: problemas y perspectivas. *Estudios Sociales (Chile),* no. 74 (Oct – Dec 92), pp. 191 – 199.

Lorca A., Carlos. Presentación del libro: *Los estudios de postgrado y el desarrollo universitario en Chile. Estudios Sociales (Chile),* no. 74 (Oct – Dec 92), pp. 201 – 211. Tables.

Ramírez Gatica, Soledad. *Estado de la docencia universitaria de pregrado en Chile* reviewed by Ricardo López P. *Estudios Sociales (Chile),* no. 78 (Oct – Dec 93), pp. 227 – 231.

Salinas, Augusto. La primera década de FONDECYT: un balance positivo. *Estudios Sociales (Chile),* no. 74 (Oct – Dec 92), pp. 177 – 189. Bibl.

Von Baer, Heinrich. Extensión universitaria: reflexiones para la acción. *Estudios Sociales (Chile),* no. 74 (Oct – Dec 92), pp. 159 – 166.

Law and legislation

González P., María Teresa and Rolando Mellafe Rojas. La Ley Orgánica de Instrucción Secundaria y Superior de 1879. *Cuadernos de Historia (Chile),* no. 11 (Dec 91), pp. 63 – 69. Bibl.

Latin America

Cataño, Gonzalo. De la publicación oral a la publicación impresa: estrategias para desarrollar la producción intelectual en la universidad. *Revista Paraguaya de Sociología,* v. 29, no. 84 (May – Aug 92), pp. 7 – 23. Bibl.

Luque, Mónica G. The Idea of the University in Newman, Ortega y Gasset, and Jaspers: A Point of Departure for Analyses of the Current Problems Facing Latin American Universities. *La Educación (USA),* v. 37, no. 114 (1993), pp. 115 – 118.

Parra M., Augusto. La universidad en un contexto de cambio. *Estudios Sociales (Chile),* no. 75 (Jan – Mar 93), pp. 211 – 223.

Pérez-Yglesias, María. Entre lo escolar y los medios informativos: políticas neoliberales y educación. *Revista de Ciencias Sociales (Costa Rica),* no. 57 (Sept 92), pp. 41 – 55. Bibl.

Villegas, Abelardo, ed. *Posgrado y desarrollo en América Latina* reviewed by Ana Lilia Delgadillo Ibarra. *Revista Mexicana de Ciencias Políticas y Sociales,* v. 38, Nueva época, no. 151 (Jan – Mar 93), pp. 213 – 216.

International cooperation

Aboites, Hugo. Internacionalización de la educación superior: los probables beneficiarios en el marco de la integración económico. *El Cotidiano,* v. 8, no. 52 (Jan – Feb 93), pp. 84 – 91. Bibl, il, tables.

Fuenzalida Faivovich, Edmundo. Internacionalización de la educación superior en América Latina. *Estudios Sociales (Chile),* no. 74 (Oct – Dec 92), pp. 39 – 73. Bibl.

García Guadilla, Carmen. Integración académica y nuevo valor del conocimiento. *Nueva Sociedad,* no. 126 (July – Aug 93), pp. 156 – 168. Bibl.

Mexico

Aboites, Hugo. La relación universidad – industria en el marco del Tratado de Libre Comercio. *El Cotidiano,* v. 9, no. 55 (June 93), pp. 78 – 84. Charts.

La diferencia es la excelencia sé gente CONALEP reviewed by Luis Miguel Bascones. *El Cotidiano,* v. 9, no. 55 (June 93), p. 118. Il.

Gil Antón, Manuel, ed. *Académicos: un botón de muestra* reviewed by Quetzalcóatl Gutiérrez Granados. *El Cotidiano,* v. 9, no. 55 (June 93), p. 119.

González Ruiz, José Enrique and Francisco Navarrete González. México: educación superior y nación hacia el siglo XXI. *Problemas del Desarrollo,* v. 24, no. 93 (Apr – June 93), pp. 175 – 194.

Lomnitz, Cinna. Gloria y el TLC. *Nexos,* v. 16, no. 189 (Sept 93), pp. 8 – 13.

Morales Hernández, Liliana. Mujer que sabe latín: la mujer en la educación superior de México. *El Cotidiano,* v. 9, no. 53 (Mar – Apr 93), pp. 71 – 77. Il, tables.

Statistics

Lorey, David E. *The Rise of the Professions in Twentieth-Century Mexico: University Graduates and Occupational Change since 1929* reviewed by Roderic A. Camp. *Journal of Latin American Studies,* v. 25, no. 2 (May 93), pp. 412 – 413.

Panama

Campos Flores, Nivia. Consideraciones para la evaluación de los estudiantes en la enseñanza superior. *Revista Cultural Lotería,* v. 51, no. 388 (Mar – Apr 92), pp. 48 – 61. Bibl.

Romero C., Paulino. La planificación de la educación superior. *Revista Cultural Lotería,* v. 51, no. 387 (Feb 92), pp. 52 – 60.

Southern Cone of South America

Espínola, Blanca Rosa Humberto de. El rol de las universidades regionales en el contexto del MERCOSUR: la educación superior del nordeste argentino y áreas de fronteras de países limítrofes. *Revista Paraguaya de Sociología,* v. 30, no. 86 (Jan – Apr 93), pp. 83 – 112. Bibl, tables, charts.

Saravia, Enrique J. *Los sistemas de educación superior en los países del MERCOSUR: elementos fundamentales y bases para su integración* reviewed by Antônio Octávio Cintra. *La Educación (USA),* v. 37, no. 114 (1993), pp. 168 – 169.

EDUCATION, PRESCHOOL

Mexico

Villanueva Villanueva, Nancy Beatriz. La práctica docente en la educación preescolar: ¿Autonomía o control? *Nueva Antropología,* v. 13, no. 44 (Aug 93), pp. 103 – 117. Bibl.

Peru

Llanos Zuloaga, Martha. Programas de intervención temprana en América Latina: modelo Portage con base en el hogar; una experiencia peruana. *Revista Latinoamericana de Estudios Educativos,* v. 22, no. 3 (July – Sept 92), pp. 89 – 107. Bibl, tables.

EDUCATION, PRIMARY

Experimental methods

Garduño E., León and Magdalena Lorandi T. Desarrollo y evaluación del proyecto educativo Ixtliyollotl. *Revista Latinoamericana de Estudios Educativos,* v. 22, no. 3 (July – Sept 92), pp. 109 – 121. Bibl, tables.

Finance

Noriega, Margarita. La equidad y el financiamiento educativo: problemas clave de la federalización. *El Cotidiano,* v. 8, no. 51 (Nov – Dec 92), pp. 34 – 38. Il, tables.

Argentina

Newland, Carlos. *Buenos Aires no es pampa: la educación elemental porteña, 1820 – 1860* reviewed by Mariano Narodowski. *Todo Es Historia,* v. 26, no. 308 (Mar 93), pp. 72 – 73. Il.

Cuba

Huerta Martínez, Angel. *La enseñanza primaria en Cuba en el siglo XIX, 1812 – 1868* reviewed by Francisco Castillo Meléndez. *Anuario de Estudios Americanos,* v. 49, Suppl. 2 (1992), pp. 247 – 248.

Latin America

Arango Montoya, Marta. La niñez y la juventud en riesgo: el gran desafío para América Latina y el Caribe. *La Educación (USA),* v. 36, no. 111 – 113 (1992), pp. 1 – 24. Bibl.

Mexico

Corona Martínez, Eduardo. Las insuficiencias del Acuerdo Nacional para la Modernización de la Educación Básica. *El Cotidiano,* v. 8, no. 51 (Nov – Dec 92), pp. 23 – 26. Il, tables.

Garduño E., León and Magdalena Lorandi T. Desarrollo y evaluación del proyecto educativo Ixtliyollotl. *Revista Latinoamericana de Estudios Educativos,* v. 22, no. 3 (July – Sept 92), pp. 109 – 121. Bibl, tables.

Gordillo, Elba Esther. El SNTE ante la modernización de la educación básica. *El Cotidiano,* v. 8, no. 51 (Nov – Dec 92), pp. 12 – 16. Il.

Loyo Brambila, Aurora. Actores y tiempos políticos en la modernización educativa. *El Cotidiano*, v. 8, no. 51 (Nov – Dec 92), pp. 17 – 22. Bibl, il.

— ¿Modernización educativa o modernización del aparato educativo? *Revista Mexicana de Sociología*, v. 55, no. 2 (Apr – June 93), pp. 339 – 349. Bibl.

Martin, Christopher James. The Dynamics of School Relations on the Urban Periphery of Guadalajara, Western Mexico. *European Review of Latin American and Caribbean Studies*, no. 53 (Dec 92), pp. 61 – 81.

Mora Heredia, Juan. Educación y política: un acercamiento al ANMEB. *El Cotidiano*, v. 8, no. 52 (Jan – Feb 93), pp. 76 – 83. Il, tables.

Noriega, Margarita. La equidad y el financiamiento educativo: problemas clave de la federalización. *El Cotidiano*, v. 8, no. 51 (Nov – Dec 92), pp. 34 – 38. Il, tables.

Pescador Osuna, José Angel. Acuerdo Nacional para la Modernización de la Educación Básica: una visión integral. *El Cotidiano*, v. 8, no. 51 (Nov – Dec 92), pp. 3 – 11. Il, tables.

Sandoval Flores, Etelvina. La educación básica y la posibilidad de cambios. *El Cotidiano*, v. 8, no. 51 (Nov – Dec 92), pp. 27 – 30.

Bibliography

Ochoa Méndez, Jacqueline. Orientación bibliográfica sobre educación básica. *El Cotidiano*, v. 8, no. 51 (Nov – Dec 92), p. 117.

Uruguay

Piotti Núñez, Diosma Elena. La escuela primaria como generadora y reproductora de contenidos sexistas en la sociedad uruguaya. *La Educación (USA)*, v. 36, no. 111 – 113 (1992), pp. 97 – 110.

Venezuela

Arroyo Alvarez, Eduardo. Don Simón Rodríguez, el maestro. *Revista Nacional de Cultura (Venezuela)*, v. 53, no. 286 (July – Sept 92), pp. 142 – 147. Il.

EDUCATION, SECONDARY
Aims and objectives

Gil, Francisco Javier. Ponderar mejor la enseñanza media: una experiencia de la Universidad de Chile. *Mensaje*, v. 42, no. 425 (Dec 93), pp. 637 – 639. Il.

Curricula

Negrín Fajardo, Olegario. Krausismo, positivismo y currículum científico en el bachillerato costarricense. *Siglo XIX: Revista*, no. 12, 2a época (July – Dec 92), pp. 105 – 118. Bibl.

Economic aspects

Bobenrieth H., Eugenio H. and Carlos Cáceres Sandoval. Determinantes del salario de los egresados de la enseñanza media técnico profesional en Chile. *Cuadernos de Economía (Chile)*, v. 30, no. 89 (Apr 93), pp. 111 – 129. Bibl, tables.

Rittershaussen, Silvia and Judith Scharager, eds. *Análisis y proyecciones en torno a la educación media y el trabajo* reviewed by María José Lemaitre. *Estudios Sociales (Chile)*, no. 78 (Oct – Dec 93), pp. 279 – 283.

Chile

Gil, Francisco Javier. Ponderar mejor la enseñanza media: una experiencia de la Universidad de Chile. *Mensaje*, v. 42, no. 425 (Dec 93), pp. 637 – 639. Il.

Rittershaussen, Silvia and Judith Scharager, eds. *Análisis y proyecciones en torno a la educación media y el trabajo* reviewed by María José Lemaitre. *Estudios Sociales (Chile)*, no. 78 (Oct – Dec 93), pp. 279 – 283.

Schiefelbein, Ernesto. La calidad de la enseñanza media chilena en el contexto internacional: VI Jornadas del Seminario de Evaluación, Universidad de Playa Ancha. *Estudios Sociales (Chile)*, no. 78 (Oct – Dec 93), pp. 291 – 299.

Law and legislation

González P., María Teresa and Rolando Mellafe Rojas. La Ley Orgánica de Instrucción Secundaria y Superior de 1879. *Cuadernos de Historia (Chile)*, no. 11 (Dec 91), pp. 63 – 69. Bibl.

Costa Rica

Negrín Fajardo, Olegario. Krausismo, positivismo y currículum científico en el bachillerato costarricense. *Siglo XIX: Revista*, no. 12, 2a época (July – Dec 92), pp. 105 – 118. Bibl.

Jamaica

Miller, Errol L. *Jamaican Society and High Schooling* reviewed by J. Edward Greene. *La Educación (USA)*, v. 36, no. 111 – 113 (1992), pp. 300 – 301.

Panama

Reseña histórica de la Escuela Angel María Herrera. *Revista Cultural Lotería*, v. 51, no. 389 (May – June 93), pp. 22 – 37. Bibl.

Reseña histórica del Colegio Abel Bravo. *Revista Cultural Lotería*, v. 51, no. 389 (May – June 93), pp. 50 – 65. Bibl.

Reseña histórica del Colegio José Daniel Crespo. *Revista Cultural Lotería*, v. 51, no. 389 (May – June 93), pp. 88 – 97. Bibl.

Reseña histórica del Colegio Manuel María Tejada Roca. *Revista Cultural Lotería*, v. 51, no. 389 (May – June 93), pp. 112 – 124. Bibl.

Congresses

Las bodas de oro del Colegio Manuel María Tejada Roca. *Revista Cultural Lotería*, v. 51, no. 389 (May – June 93), pp. 125 – 126.

EDUCATION AND EMPLOYMENT
See
  Subdivision *Economic aspects* under *Education*

EDUCATION AND STATE

Romero C., Paulino. Pedagogía experimental y política. *Revista Cultural Lotería*, v. 50, no. 384 (July – Aug 91), pp. 68 – 75.

Argentina

Escudé, Carlos. *El fracaso del proyecto argentino: educación e ideología* reviewed by Aurora Ravina. *Revista de Historia de América*, no. 113 (Jan – June 92), pp. 177 – 179.

Newland, Carlos. *Buenos Aires no es pampa: la educación elemental porteña, 1820 – 1860* reviewed by Mariano Narodowski. *Todo Es Historia*, v. 26, no. 308 (Mar 93), pp. 72 – 73. Il.

Brazil

Bohemy, Helena. Novos talentos, vícios antigos: os renovadores e a política educacional. *Estudos Históricos*, v. 6, no. 11 (Jan – June 93), pp. 24 – 39. Bibl.

Candotti, Ennio. O sistema federal de ensino superior: problemas das alternativas (Comment on the article of the same title by Eunice Ribeiro Durham). *Revista Brasileira de Ciências Sociais*, v. 8, no. 23 (Oct 93), pp. 38 – 41.

Durham, Eunice Ribeiro. O sistema federal de ensino superior: problemas e alternativas. *Revista Brasileira de Ciências Sociais*, v. 8, no. 23 (Oct 93), pp. 5 – 37. Bibl, tables.

Guimarães, Jorge A. Perspectivas para as instituições federais de ensino superior (Comment on the article "O sistema federal de ensino superior: problemas e alternativas" by Eunice Ribeiro Durham). *Revista Brasileira de Ciências Sociais*, v. 8, no. 23 (Oct 93), pp. 42 – 47. Bibl.

Martins, Carlos Benedito. Caminhos e descaminhos das universidades federais (Comment on the article "O sistema federal de ensino superior: problemas e alternativas" by Eunice Ribeiro Durham). *Revista Brasileira de Ciências Sociais*, v. 8, no. 23 (Oct 93), pp. 48 – 54. Bibl.

Santos, Maria Madalena Rodrigues dos. The Challenge of Educational Reforms in Brazil. *La Educación (USA)*, v. 37, no. 114 (1993), pp. 59 – 75. Bibl.

Research

Dall'igna, Maria Antonieta. Políticas públicas de educação: a (des)articulação entre a união, o estado e os municípios. *Revista Brasileira de Estudos Pedagógicos*, v. 72, no. 172 (Sept – Dec 91), pp. 394 – 397.

Chile

Martínez K., Marcelo. Calidad de la educación y redefinición del rol del estado en Chile, en el contexto de los proyectos de modernización. *Estudios Sociales (Chile)*, no. 77 (July – Sept 93), pp. 171 – 196. Bibl.

— Calidad de la educación y redefinición del rol del estado en Chile, en el contexto de los proyectos de modernización. *Revista Paraguaya de Sociología*, v. 30, no. 86 (Jan – Apr 93), pp. 139 – 159. Bibl, tables.

Colombia

Clemente B., Isabel. Un caso de conflicto cultural en el Caribe: de la imposición al reconocimiento. *Nueva Sociedad*, no. 127 (Sept – Oct 93), pp. 32 – 45. Bibl.

Vallejo M., César. Descentralización de la educación en Colombia: antecedentes históricos. *Planeación y Desarrollo*, v. 24, no. 1 (Jan – Apr 93), pp. 233 – 277. Bibl.

Costa Rica

Chaves Salas, Ana Lupita. Reseña histórica de la regionalización de la Universidad de Costa Rica. *Revista de Ciencias Sociales (Costa Rica)*, no. 60 (June 93), pp. 7 – 16. Bibl.

Developing countries

Rondinelli, Dennis A. et al. *Planning Education Reforms in Developing Countries* reviewed by Maria Valéria Junho Pena. *La Educación (USA)*, v. 37, no. 115 (1993), pp. 437 – 439.

France

Noriega, Margarita. La descentralización educativa: los casos de Francia y México. *Revista Latinoamericana de Estudios Educativos*, v. 23, no. 1 (Jan – Mar 93), pp. 43 – 74. Bibl, tables.

Guatemala

Fuentes Soria, Alfonso et al. Estado, universidad y sociedad: panel-foro. *USAC*, no. 13 (Mar 91), pp. 5 – 18.

Latin America

Malo, Salvador. Las nuevas políticas y las estrategias en materia de ciencia y tecnología. *Revista Latinoamericana de Estudios Educativos*, v. 22, no. 3 (July – Sept 92), pp. 133 – 139.

Navarro, Juan Carlos. *Descentralización: una alternativa de política educativa* reviewed by Emil Alvarado Vera. *La Educación (USA)*, v. 36, no. 111 – 113 (1992), p. 301.

Mexico

Corona Martínez, Eduardo. Las insuficiencias del Acuerdo Nacional para la Modernización de la Educación Básica. *El Cotidiano*, v. 8, no. 51 (Nov – Dec 92), pp. 23 – 26. Il, tables.

Gallegos, Carlos. Pensamiento y acción política de José Vasconcelos. *Revista Mexicana de Ciencias Políticas y Sociales*, v. 37, Nueva época, no. 149 (July – Sept 92), pp. 125 – 138. Bibl.

González Ruiz, José Enrique and Francisco Navarrete González. México: educación superior y nación hacia el siglo XXI. *Problemas del Desarrollo*, v. 24, no. 93 (Apr – June 93), pp. 175 – 194.

Gordillo, Elba Esther. El SNTE ante la modernización de la educación básica. *El Cotidiano*, v. 8, no. 51 (Nov – Dec 92), pp. 12 – 16. Il.

Latapí, Pablo. El pensamiento educativo de Torres Bodet: una apreciación crítica. *Revista Latinoamericana de Estudios Educativos*, v. 22, no. 3 (July – Sept 92), pp. 13 – 44. Bibl.

López Angel, Carlos. El sindicalismo universitario de hoy y su futuro. *El Cotidiano*, v. 9, no. 56 (July 93), pp. 75 – 85. Il.

Loyo Brambila, Aurora. Actores y tiempos políticos en la modernización educativa. *El Cotidiano*, v. 8, no. 51 (Nov – Dec 92), pp. 17 – 22. Bibl, il.

— ¿Modernización educativa o modernización del aparato educativo? *Revista Mexicana de Sociología*, v. 55, no. 2 (Apr – June 93), pp. 339 – 349. Bibl.

Miranda López, Francisco. Descentralización educativa y modernización del estado. *Revista Mexicana de Sociología*, v. 54, no. 2 (Apr – June 92), pp. 19 – 44. Bibl, tables.

Mora Heredia, Juan. Educación y política: un acercamiento al ANMEB. *El Cotidiano*, v. 8, no. 52 (Jan – Feb 93), pp. 76 – 83. Il, tables.

Noriega, Margarita. La descentralización educativa: los casos de Francia y México. *Revista Latinoamericana de Estudios Educativos*, v. 23, no. 1 (Jan – Mar 93), pp. 43 – 74. Bibl, tables.

— La equidad y el financiamiento educativo: problemas clave de la federalización. *El Cotidiano*, v. 8, no. 51 (Nov – Dec 92), pp. 34 – 38. Il, tables.

Pescador Osuna, José Angel. Acuerdo Nacional para la Modernización de la Educación Básica: una visión integral. *El Cotidiano*, v. 8, no. 51 (Nov – Dec 92), pp. 3 – 11. Il, tables.

Reséndiz García, Ramón. Reforma educativa y conflicto inter-burocrático en México, 1978 – 1988. *Revista Mexicana de Sociología*, v. 54, no. 2 (Apr – June 92), pp. 3 – 18. Bibl.

Sandoval Flores, Etelvina. La educación básica y la posibilidad de cambios. *El Cotidiano*, v. 8, no. 51 (Nov – Dec 92), pp. 27 – 30.

— Maestras y modernización educativa. *El Cotidiano*, v. 9, no. 53 (Mar – Apr 93), pp. 78 – 82. Tables, charts.

Street, Susan L. *Maestros en movimiento: transformaciones en la burocracia estatal, 1978 – 1982* reviewed by Sylvia Schmelkes. *El Cotidiano*, v. 8, no. 51 (Nov – Dec 92), pp. 114 – 115.

— El SNTE Y la política educativa, 1970 – 1990. *Revista Mexicana de Sociología*, v. 54, no. 2 (Apr – June 92), pp. 45 – 72. Bibl.

Suárez Zozaya, María Herlinda. Equidad en una sociedad desigual: reto de la modernización educativa. *Revista Mexicana de Ciencias Políticas y Sociales*, v. 38, Nueva época, no. 154 (Oct – Dec 93), pp. 137 – 158. Bibl, tables.

Villaseñor García, Guillermo. El gobierno y la conducción en las universidades públicas: situación reciente y tendencias actuales. *El Cotidiano*, v. 9, no. 55 (June 93), pp. 85 – 90. Il.

Congresses

Conclusiones y recomendaciones (regarding the education of the indigenous population of Mexico). *Anuario Indigenista*, v. 30 (Dec 91), pp. 303 – 316.

Zedillo Ponce de León, Ernesto. Palabras de Ernesto Zedillo Ponce de León, secretario de educación pública, en la inauguración de la reunión "La Reforma del Estado y las Nuevas Aristas de la Democracia en Iberoamérica," organizada por El Colegio de México, el 17 de marzo de 1992. *Foro Internacional*, v. 32, no. 5 (Oct – Dec 92), pp. 772 – 776.

Panama

Romero C., Paulino. La planificación de la educación superior. *Revista Cultural Lotería*, v. 51, no. 387 (Feb 92), pp. 52 – 60.

Peru

Cisneros, Luis Jaime et al. La educación: ¿Reforma con futuro? *Debate (Peru)*, v. 16, no. 72 (Mar – May 93), pp. 20 – 27. Il, charts.

Southern Cone of South America

Piñón, Francisco José. Educación y procesos de integración económica: el caso del MERCOSUR. *La Educación (USA)*, v. 37, no. 114 (1993), pp. 19 – 32. Bibl, tables.

United States

Reyes, Pedro and Richard R. Valencia. Educational Policy and the Growing Latino Student Population: Problems and Prospects. *Hispanic Journal of Behavioral Sciences*, v. 15, no. 2 (May 93), pp. 258 – 283. Bibl.

Uruguay

Monestier, Jaime. *El combate laico: bajorrelieve de la reforma valeriana* reviewed by Alfonso Fernández Cabrelli. *Hoy Es Historia*, v. 10, no. 57 (Apr – May 93), p. 80.

EDUCATIONAL ACCOUNTABILITY

Menéndez Menéndez, Libertad. Investigación y evaluación en pedagogía. *Revista Mexicana de Ciencias Políticas y Sociales*, v. 37, Nueva época, no. 149 (July – Sept 92), pp. 139 – 152. Bibl.

Argentina

Mollis, Marcela. Evaluación de la calidad universitaria: elementos para su discusión. *Realidad Económica*, no. 118 (Aug – Sept 93), pp. 97 – 116. Bibl, tables.

Chile

Schiefelbein, Ernesto. La calidad de la enseñanza media chilena en el contexto internacional: VI Jornadas del Seminario de Evaluación, Universidad de Playa Ancha. *Estudios Sociales (Chile),* no. 78 (Oct – Dec 93), pp. 291 – 299.

Latin America

Lafourcade, Pedro D. *La autoevaluación institucional* reviewed by Luis O. Roggi. *La Educación (USA),* v. 37, no. 114 (1993), pp. 159 – 160.

Mexico

Garduño E., León and Magdalena Lorandi T. Desarrollo y evaluación del proyecto educativo Ixtliyollotl. *Revista Latinoamericana de Estudios Educativos,* v. 22, no. 3 (July – Sept 92), pp. 109 – 121. Bibl, tables.

Martínez Rizo, Felipe. Las desigualdades de la oferta y la demanda educativa: pasado, presente y futuro de las políticas compensatorias. *Revista Latinoamericana de Estudios Educativos,* v. 23, no. 2 (Apr – June 93), pp. 55 – 70. Bibl.

Panama

Campos Flores, Nivia. Consideraciones para la evaluación de los estudiantes en la enseñanza superior. *Revista Cultural Lotería,* v. 51, no. 388 (Mar – Apr 92), pp. 48 – 61. Bibl.

EDUCATIONAL ADMINISTRATION

See

School management and organization
Subdivision *Administration* under *Universities and colleges*

EDUCATIONAL ASSISTANCE

United States

Merkx, Gilbert W. The Progress of Alliance: Confronting the Crisis in Resources for Foreign Area Studies in the United States. *SALALM Papers,* v. 36 (1991), pp. 294 – 302. Bibl.

EDUCATIONAL PLANNING

See

Education and state

EDUCATIONAL PSYCHOLOGY

See

Learning, Psychology of
Parent and child
Parent – teacher relationships
Teacher – student relationships

EDUCATIONAL RESEARCH

Menéndez Menéndez, Libertad. Investigación y evaluación en pedagogía. *Revista Mexicana de Ciencias Políticas y Sociales,* v. 37, Nueva época, no. 149 (July – Sept 92), pp. 139 – 152. Bibl.

International cooperation

Linhares, Célia Frazão. A ANPEd e a cooperação latinoamericana em pesquisa educational. *Revista Brasileira de Estudos Pedagógicos,* v. 72, no. 172 (Sept – Dec 91), pp. 405 – 408.

Brazil

Gama, Elizabeth Maria Pinheiro. As percepções sobre a causalidade do fracasso escolar no discurso descontente do magistério. *Revista Brasileira de Estudos Pedagógicos,* v. 72, no. 172 (Sept – Dec 91), pp. 356 – 384. Bibl, tables.

Sánchez Gamboa, Silvio Ancísar. La concepción del hombre en la investigación educativa: algunas consideraciones. *Islas,* no. 96 (May – Aug 90), pp. 34 – 41. Bibl.

Valente, Edna Fátima Barros. Os filhos pródigos da educação pública: um estudo sobre os evadidos da escola pública num bairro periférico do município de Santarém. *Revista Brasileira de Estudos Pedagógicos,* v. 72, no. 172 (Sept – Dec 91), pp. 397 – 400.

Latin America

Propuesta para una agenda de la investigación educacional latinoamericana de cara al año 2000. *Revista Latinoamericana de Estudios Educativos,* v. 23, no. 2 (Apr – June 93), pp. 117 – 125.

Mexico

Díaz Sustaeta, Federico and Sumie Prado Arai. Estudio de las actitudes de los estudiantes de posgrado de la Universidad Iberoamericana ante las metas de la institución. *Revista Latinoamericana de Estudios Educativos,* v. 23, no. 2 (Apr – June 93), pp. 71 – 85. Bibl, tables.

Informe de actividades académicas del Centro de Estudios Educativos, 1992. *Revista Latinoamericana de Estudios Educativos,* v. 23, no. 1 (Jan – Mar 93), pp. 97 – 109. Bibl.

Congresses

II Congreso Nacional de Investigación Educativa: la investigación educativa en los '80s; perspectiva para los noventa (México). *Revista Latinoamericana de Estudios Educativos,* v. 23, no. 1 (Jan – Mar 93), pp. 111 – 127.

EDUCATIONAL SOCIOLOGY

Latapí, Pablo. Reflexiones sobre la justicia en la educación. *Revista Latinoamericana de Estudios Educativos,* v. 23, no. 2 (Apr – June 93), pp. 9 – 41. Bibl.

Muñoz Izquierdo, Carlos. Comentarios a la propuesta que hace el dr. Pablo Latapí en el artículo "Reflexiones sobre la justicia en la educación." *Revista Latinoamericana de Estudios Educativos,* v. 23, no. 2 (Apr – June 93), pp. 43 – 53.

Caribbean area

Edwards, Beatrice. Interview with Errol Miller. *La Educación (USA),* v. 37, no. 114 (1993), pp. 125 – 134.

Jamaica

Miller, Errol L. *Jamaican Society and High Schooling* reviewed by J. Edward Greene. *La Educación (USA),* v. 36, no. 111 – 113 (1992), pp. 300 – 301.

Mexico

Díaz Sustaeta, Federico and Sumie Prado Arai. Estudio de las actitudes de los estudiantes de posgrado de la Universidad Iberoamericana ante las metas de la institución. *Revista Latinoamericana de Estudios Educativos,* v. 23, no. 2 (Apr – June 93), pp. 71 – 85. Bibl, tables.

Martínez Rizo, Felipe. Las desigualdades de la oferta y la demanda educativa: pasado, presente y futuro de las políticas compensatorias. *Revista Latinoamericana de Estudios Educativos,* v. 23, no. 2 (Apr – June 93), pp. 55 – 70. Bibl.

Suárez Zozaya, María Herlinda. Equidad en una sociedad desigual: reto de la modernización educativa. *Revista Mexicana de Ciencias Políticas y Sociales,* v. 38, Nueva época, no. 154 (Oct – Dec 93), pp. 137 – 158. Bibl, tables.

Research

Muñoz García, Humberto. Los valores educativos en México. *Revista Mexicana de Ciencias Políticas y Sociales,* v. 38, Nueva época, no. 154 (Oct – Dec 93), pp. 159 – 184. Bibl, tables.

Peru

Céspedes Aguirre, Patricia. Universidad, deporte y agresividad juvenil: apuntes en torno a la Olimpiada UNSAAC, 1991. *Allpanchis,* v. 25, no. 41 (Jan – June 93), pp. 159 – 174.

EDUCATIONAL TECHNOLOGY

See also

Audiovisual education
Programmed instruction

Brazil

Litto, Fredric M. A "escola do futuro" da Universidade de São Paulo: um laboratório de tecnologia-de-ponta para a educação. *Revista Brasileira de Estudos Pedagógicos,* v. 72, no. 172 (Sept – Dec 91), pp. 409 – 412.

Mayrink, Paulo Tarcísio. School Libraries in Brazil Facing the Twenty-First Century: New Formats. *SALALM Papers,* v. 36 (1991), pp. 357 – 390.

EDUCATIONAL TESTS AND MEASUREMENTS

Barker, David. The UWI Scholarship Examination in Geography: An Analysis of the 1992 Results. *Caribbean Geography,* v. 3, no. 4 (Sept 92), pp. 270 – 274. Tables.

Pearson, Barbara Z. Predictive Validity of the Scholastic Aptitude Test (SAT) for Hispanic Bilingual Students. *Hispanic Journal of Behavioral Sciences*, v. 15, no. 3 (Aug 93), pp. 342 – 356. Bibl, tables.

EDWARDS, JORGE
Interviews
Mujica, Barbara Kaminar de. Persona Gratissima. *Américas*, v. 45, no. 3 (May – June 93), pp. 24 – 29. Il.

EEC
See
European Community

EGERTON, DANIEL THOMAS
MacAdam, Alfred J. Daniel Thomas Egerton, the Unfortunate Traveler. *Review*, no. 47 (Fall 93), pp. 9 – 13. Il.

EJIDOS
See also
Agriculture, Cooperative

Gledhill, John. *"Casi nada": A Study of Agrarian Reform in the Homeland of Cardenismo* reviewed by Alan Knight. *Hispanic American Historical Review*, v. 73, no. 1 (Feb 93), pp. 181 – 182.

Thompson, Gary D. and Paul N. Wilson. Common Property and Uncertainy: Compensating Coalitions by Mexico's Pastoral "Ejidatarios." *Economic Development and Cultural Change*, v. 41, no. 2 (Jan 93), pp. 301 – 318. Bibl, tables, charts.

Law and legislation
Cruz Rodríguez, María Soledad. La nueva ley agraria y su impacto en la periferia ejidal de la ciudad de México. *El Cotidiano*, v. 10, no. 57 (Aug – Sept 93), pp. 54 – 59. Bibl, il, tables.

Durand Alcántara, Carlos Humberto. Las reformas y adicionales al Artículo 27 constitucional, 1857 – 1992. *Derecho y Reforma Agraria*, no. 24 (1993), pp. 139 – 157. Bibl.

Salinas de Gortari, Carlos. Iniciativa para la reforma del régimen ejidal: Artículo 27 de la constitución mexicana. *Anuario Indigenista*, v. 30 (Dec 91), pp. 155 – 184.

— México: decreto por el que se reforma el Artículo 27 de la constitución política de los Estados Unidos Mexicanos. *Anuario Indigenista*, v. 30 (Dec 91), pp. 489 – 496.

Societies, etc.
Heuzé de Icaza, Patricia. La Coalición de Ejidos Colectivos de los valles de Yaqui y Mayo: una experiencia de autonomía campesina en México. *Estudios Rurales Latinoamericanos*, v. 15, no. 2 – 3 (May – Dec 92), pp. 65 – 77. Bibl.

EJUTLA, MEXICO
Feinman, Gary M. and Linda M. Nicholas. Shell-Ornament Production in Ejutla: Implications for Highland – Coastal Interaction in Ancient Oaxaca. *Ancient Mesoamerica*, v. 4, no. 1 (Spring 93), pp. 103 – 119. Bibl, il, tables, maps, charts.

EL SALVADOR
See also
Armaments – El Salvador
Biography (as a literary form) – El Salvador
Coffee – El Salvador
Community development – El Salvador
Comunidad Segundo Montes, El Salvador
Cookery – El Salvador
Cooperatives – El Salvador
Crime and criminals – El Salvador
Criminal law – El Salvador
Economic assistance, Foreign – El Salvador
Education – El Salvador
Elections – El Salvador
Elite (Social sciences) – El Salvador
Human rights – El Salvador
Jesuits – El Salvador
Labor laws and legislation – El Salvador
Land settlement – El Salvador
Liberalism – El Salvador
Libraries and librarians – El Salvador
Martyrs – El Salvador
Military assistance, Foreign – El Salvador

Oligarchy – El Salvador
Periodicals – El Salvador
Political participation – El Salvador
Political parties – El Salvador
Press and politics – El Salvador
Protestantism – El Salvador
Public opinion – El Salvador
Religion and politics – El Salvador
Social conflict – El Salvador
Social psychology – El Salvador
Socialism – El Salvador
Strikes and lockouts – El Salvador
Trade unions – El Salvador
Violence – El Salvador
Women in literature – El Salvador

Armed forces
Cardenal Chamorro, Rodolfo. Las crisis del proceso de pacificación. *ECA; Estudios Centroamericanos*, v. 47, no. 529 – 530 (Nov – Dec 92), pp. 963 – 981. Il.

"La depuración de la fuerza armada no es negociable": pronunciación del Consejo Superior Universitario. *ECA; Estudios Centroamericanos*, v. 47, no. 529 – 530 (Nov – Dec 92), pp. 955 – 961.

Los desafíos de la paz. *ECA; Estudios Centroamericanos*, v. 48, no. 531 – 532 (Jan – Feb 93), pp. 5 – 17. Il.

Militarismo y democratización. *ECA; Estudios Centroamericanos*, v. 47, no. 529 – 530 (Nov – Dec 92), pp. 1015 – 1020. Il.

La sociedad civil y el reto de la democratización. *ECA; Estudios Centroamericanos*, v. 48, no. 536 (June 93), pp. 507 – 525. Il.

Walter, Knut and Philip J. Williams. El ejército y la democratización en El Salvador. *ECA; Estudios Centroamericanos*, v. 48, no. 539 (Sept 93), pp. 813 – 839. Bibl, il, tables.

— The Military and Democratization in El Salvador. *Journal of Inter-American Studies and World Affairs*, v. 35, no. 1 (1993), pp. 39 – 88. Bibl, tables.

Constitutional law
Consideraciones sobre la ley de amnistía. *ECA; Estudios Centroamericanos*, v. 48, no. 534 – 535 (Apr – May 93), pp. 414 – 419. Il.

Huertas Bartolomé, Tebelia. Libertad sindical, tratados internacionales y constitución. *ECA; Estudios Centroamericanos*, v. 48, no. 537 – 538 (July – Aug 93), pp. 657 – 675. Bibl, il.

Economic conditions
Lindo Fuentes, Héctor. *Weak Foundations: The Economy of El Salvador in the Nineteenth Century, 1821 – 1898* reviewed by E. Bradford Burns. *Mesoamérica (USA)*, v. 13, no. 23 (June 92), pp. 184 – 186.

Economic policy
Arriola Palomares, Joaquín and David Amílcar Mena. La transición: los proyectos en disputa. *ECA; Estudios Centroamericanos*, v. 48, no. 536 (June 93), pp. 527 – 544. Bibl, il, tables.

Montoya, Aquiles. ¿Qué cabría esperar en materia económica y social, si un gobierno "progresista" accediera al poder en el '94? *ECA; Estudios Centroamericanos*, v. 48, no. 536 (June 93), pp. 582 – 587. Il.

Los salvadoreños ante las medidas de política fiscal y opiniones sobre la coyuntura política. *ECA; Estudios Centroamericanos*, v. 47, no. 529 – 530 (Nov – Dec 92), pp. 1071 – 1082. Tables.

Sources
Documentación: foro de concertación económico social. *ECA; Estudios Centroamericanos*, v. 47, no. 528 (Oct 92), pp. 937 – 942.

Foreign relations
Honduras
Ciarnello, Nicolás. "La guerra del futbol": Honduras – El Salvador. *Todo Es Historia*, v. 26, no. 307 (Feb 93), pp. 36 – 45. Bibl, il, maps.

Laws, statutes, etc.
Sources
Leyendo el *Diario Oficial*. *ECA; Estudios Centroamericanos*, v. 47 – 48 (1992 – 1993), All issues.

Officials and public employees

La aleccionadora huelga en el Ministerio de Salud. *ECA; Estudios Centroamericanos,* v. 48, no. 539 (Sept 93), pp. 890 – 894. Il.

Sindicalización y huelga de los trabajadores del gobierno e instituciones autónomas. *ECA; Estudios Centroamericanos,* v. 48, no. 536 (June 93), pp. 588 – 593. Il.

Politics and government

Benítez Manaut, Raúl. El Salvador: paz conflictiva, democracia frágil. *Nueva Sociedad,* no. 126 (July – Aug 93), pp. 6 – 11.

Cardenal Chamorro, Rodolfo. Las crisis del proceso de pacificación. *ECA; Estudios Centroamericanos,* v. 47, no. 529 – 530 (Nov – Dec 92), pp. 963 – 981. Il.

Crónica del mes. *ECA; Estudios Centroamericanos,* v. 47 – 48 (1992 – 1993), All issues.

"La depuración de la fuerza armada no es negociable": pronunciación del Consejo Superior Universitario. *ECA; Estudios Centroamericanos,* v. 47, no. 529 – 530 (Nov – Dec 92), pp. 955 – 961.

Los desafíos de la paz. *ECA; Estudios Centroamericanos,* v. 48, no. 531 – 532 (Jan – Feb 93), pp. 5 – 17. Il.

Holiday, David and William Deane Stanley. La construcción de la paz: las lecciones preliminares de El Salvador. *ECA; Estudios Centroamericanos,* v. 48, no. 531 – 532 (Jan – Feb 93), pp. 39 – 59. Il.

Insulza, José Miguel. El Salvador: el más exitoso proceso de paz. *Mensaje,* v. 42, no. 416 (Jan – Feb 93), p. 48.

Lazo M., José Francisco. El Salvador: de la locura a la esperanza. *Nueva Sociedad,* no. 127 (Sept – Oct 93), pp. 158 – 162.

Militarismo y democratización. *ECA; Estudios Centroamericanos,* v. 47, no. 529 – 530 (Nov – Dec 92), pp. 1015 – 1020. Il.

Los principales problemas: lo que debe hacer el próximo gobierno; una encuesta de opinión pública. *ECA; Estudios Centroamericanos,* v. 48, no. 539 (Sept 93), pp. 841 – 854. Tables, charts.

Pronunciamiento de la Universidad Centroamericana "José Simeón Cañas": "Es hora de cumplir con el pueblo salvadoreño." *ECA; Estudios Centroamericanos,* v. 47, no. 528 (Oct 92), pp. 827 – 833.

Los salvadoreños ante las medidas de política fiscal y opiniones sobre la coyuntura política. *ECA; Estudios Centroamericanos,* v. 47, no. 529 – 530 (Nov – Dec 92), pp. 1071 – 1082. Tables.

¿Son históricas las elecciones de 1994? *ECA; Estudios Centroamericanos,* v. 48, no. 537 – 538 (July – Aug 93), pp. 641 – 656. Il.

Walter, Knut and Philip J. Williams. El ejército y la democratización en El Salvador. *ECA; Estudios Centroamericanos,* v. 48, no. 539 (Sept 93), pp. 813 – 839. Bibl, il, tables.

— The Military and Democratization in El Salvador. *Journal of Inter-American Studies and World Affairs,* v. 35, no. 1 (1993), pp. 39 – 88. Bibl, tables.

Sources

Documentación (regarding socio-economic, human rights, and political issues). *ECA; Estudios Centroamericanos,* v. 47 – 48 (1992 – 1993), All issues.

Leyendo el *Diario Oficial. ECA; Estudios Centroamericanos,* v. 47 – 48 (1992 – 1993), All issues.

Social conditions

Argueta, Manlio. An Exile's Return. *NACLA Report on the Americas,* v. 26, no. 5 (May 93), pp. 4 – 6. Il.

Los principales problemas: lo que debe hacer el próximo gobierno; una encuesta de opinión pública. *ECA; Estudios Centroamericanos,* v. 48, no. 539 (Sept 93), pp. 841 – 854. Tables, charts.

La sociedad civil y el reto de la democratización. *ECA; Estudios Centroamericanos,* v. 48, no. 536 (June 93), pp. 507 – 525. Il.

Social policy

Montoya, Aquiles. ¿Qué cabría esperar en materia económica y social, si un gobierno "progresista" accediera al poder en el '94? *ECA; Estudios Centroamericanos,* v. 48, no. 536 (June 93), pp. 582 – 587. Il.

Sources

Documentación: foro de concertación económico social. *ECA; Estudios Centroamericanos,* v. 47, no. 528 (Oct 92), pp. 937 – 942.

ELECTIONS

See also
Local elections

Antezana Villegas, Mauricio. Epílogo y prefacio. *Estado y Sociedad,* v. 8, no. 9 (Jan – June 92), pp. 99 – 105.

Argentina

Alonso, Paula. Politics and Elections in Buenos Aires, 1890 – 1898: The Performance of the Radical Party. *Journal of Latin American Studies,* v. 25, no. 3 (Oct 93), pp. 465 – 487. Bibl, tables, charts.

Cabrera, Ernesto. La cuestión de la proporcionalidad y las elecciones legislativas en la República Argentina. *Revista Mexicana de Sociología,* v. 54, no. 4 (Oct – Dec 92), pp. 153 – 182. Bibl.

Echegaray, Fabián. Elecciones y partidos provinciales en la Argentina. *Nueva Sociedad,* no. 124 (Mar – Apr 93), pp. 46 – 52. Tables.

Pastoriza, Elisa. Dirigentes obreros y política en el marco de la gestación de un peronismo periférico: Mar del Plata, 1935 – 1948. *Todo Es Historia,* v. 27, no. 314 (Sept 93), pp. 32 – 43. Il, tables.

Research

Cabrera, Ernesto. Magnitud de distrito y fórmula electoral en la representación proporcional. *Desarrollo Económico (Argentina),* v. 33, no. 130 (July – Sept 93), pp. 281 – 294. Bibl, tables.

Bolivia

Cortez, Roger. El impacto de los medios en la política. *Estado y Sociedad,* v. 8, no. 9 (Jan – June 92), pp. 81 – 90.

Laserna, Roberto. Integración y gobernabilidad: los nuevos desafíos de la democracia en Bolivia. *Nueva Sociedad,* no. 128 (Nov – Dec 93), pp. 120 – 131.

Mesa Gisbert, Carlos D. Televisión y elecciones: ¿El poder total? *Estado y Sociedad,* v. 8, no. 9 (Jan – June 92), pp. 39 – 52.

Brazil

Araújo, Maria Celina d' and Gláucio Ary Dillon Soares. A imprensa, os mitos e os votos nas eleições de 1990. *Revista Brasileira de Estudos Políticos,* no. 76 (Jan 93), pp. 163 – 189. Tables, charts.

Kinzo, Maria d'Alva Gil. The 1989 Presidential Election: Electoral Behaviour in a Brazilian City. *Journal of Latin American Studies,* v. 25, no. 2 (May 93), pp. 313 – 330. Bibl, tables.

Lavareda, José Antônio. A democracia nas urnas reviewed by Glória Diógenes. *Revista Brasileira de Ciências Sociais,* v. 8, no. 22 (June 93), pp. 156 – 157.

— A democracia nas urnas: o processo partidário eleitoral brasileiro reviewed by Stéphane Monclaire (Review entitled "Partis et représentations politiques au Brésil"). *Cahiers des Amériques Latines,* no. 13 (1992), pp. 173 – 177.

— A democracia nas urnas: o processo partidário eleitoral brasileiro reviewed by Paul Cammack. *Journal of Latin American Studies,* v. 25, no. 3 (Oct 93), pp. 665 – 666.

Lima Júnior, Olavo Brasil de. A reforma das instituições políticas: a experiência brasileira e o aperfeiçoamento democrático. *Dados,* v. 36, no. 1 (1993), pp. 89 – 117. Bibl, tables.

Moisés, José Alvaro. Elections, Political Parties, and Political Culture in Brazil: Changes and Continuities. *Journal of Latin American Studies,* v. 25, no. 3 (Oct 93), pp. 575 – 611. Bibl, tables, charts.

Sader, Emir and Ken Silverstein. *Without Fear of Being Happy: Lula, the Workers Party, and Brazil* reviewed by Joel Wolfe. *The Americas,* v. 49, no. 4 (Apr 93), pp. 566 – 568.

— *Without Fear of Being Happy: Lula, the Workers Party, and Brazil* reviewed by John Humphrey. *Bulletin of Latin American Research*, v. 12, no. 3 (Sept 93), p. 347.

— *Without Fear of Being Happy: Lula, the Workers Party, and Brazil* reviewed by Paul Cammack. *Journal of Latin American Studies*, v. 25, no. 3 (Oct 93), pp. 666 – 667.

Central America

Krennerich, Michael. Die Kompetitivität der Wahlen in Nicaragua, El salvador und Guatemala in historisch – vergleichender Perspektive. *Ibero-Amerikanisches Archiv*, v. 18, no. 1 – 2 (1992), pp. 245 – 290. Bibl.

Torres-Rivas, Edelberto. Escenarios y lecciones de las elecciones centroamericanas, 1980 – 1991. *Revista Mexicana de Sociología*, v. 54, no. 3 (July – Sept 92), pp. 45 – 67. Tables.

Chile

Análisis de la situación y proyecciones del país. *Mensaje*, v. 42, no. 419 (June 93), pp. 220 – 224.

Araya P., Marilu et al. ?Cómo votarán los católicos?: debates (Introduced by G. Arroyo). *Mensaje*, v. 42, no. 424 (Nov 93), pp. 569 – 576. Il.

Caviedes L., César N. *Elections in Chile: The Road toward Redemocratization* reviewed by Paul E. Sigmund. *Hispanic American Historical Review*, v. 73, no. 3 (Aug 93), pp. 517 – 518.

— *Elections in Chile: The Road toward Redemocratization* reviewed by William W. Culver. *Revista Interamericana de Bibliografía*, v. 42, no. 4 (1992), p. 655.

Fuentes, José María. La alternativa proporcional con barreras de entrada: un sistema electoral adecuado para Chile. *Estudios Públicos (Chile)*, no. 51 (Winter 93), pp. 269 – 301. Bibl, tables.

Godoy Arcaya, Oscar. Un año electoral. *Mensaje*, v. 42, no. 416 (Jan – Feb 93), pp. 5 – 7.

Guzmán A., Eugenio. Reflexiones sobre el sistema binomial. *Estudios Públicos (Chile)*, no. 51 (Winter 93), pp. 303 – 324. Bibl, charts.

Scully, Timothy R. and J. Samuel Valenzuela. De la democracia a la democracia: continuidad y variaciones en las preferencias del electorado y en el sistema de partidos en Chile. *Estudios Públicos (Chile)*, no. 51 (Winter 93), pp. 195 – 228. Bibl, tables.

Siavelis, Peter. Nuevos argumentos y viejos supuestos: simulaciones de sistemas electorales alternativos para las elecciones parlamentarias chilenas. *Estudios Públicos (Chile)*, no. 51 (Winter 93), pp. 229 – 267. Tables, charts.

Tagle, Andrés. Comentario en torno a los trabajos de José María Fuentes y Peter Siavelis. *Estudios Públicos (Chile)*, no. 51 (Winter 93), pp. 325 – 330.

Colombia

Law and legislation

Calle Lombana, Humberto de la. Proyecto de reforma electoral (Previously published in this journal, no. 507, 1984). *Revista Javeriana*, v. 61, no. 596 (July 93), pp. 105 – 108.

Costa Rica

Barrantes Araya, Trino. Democracia y modernización en Costa Rica: proceso electoral y bipartidismo, 1983 – 1991. *Revista de Ciencias Sociales (Costa Rica)*, no. 60 (June 93), pp. 17 – 26. Bibl, tables.

Cuba

Law and legislation

Charlone, Silvana and Carlos Varela Nestier. Cuba: ¿Democratización y legitimidad?; los cambios en el sistema político cubano. *Hoy Es Historia*, v. 10, no. 59 (Sept – Oct 93), pp. 56 – 66. Il.

El Salvador

La Comisión de la Verdad y el proceso electoral en la opinión pública salvadoreña. *ECA; Estudios Centroamericanos*, v. 48, no. 537 – 538 (July – Aug 93), pp. 711 – 734. Tables, charts.

O'Donnell, Madalene T. El Salvador: The Electoral Test. *Hemisphere*, v. 5, no. 3 (Summer – Fall 93), pp. 13 – 15.

¿Son históricas las elecciones de 1994? *ECA; Estudios Centroamericanos*, v. 48, no. 537 – 538 (July – Aug 93), pp. 641 – 656. Il.

¿Son libres las elecciones de 1994? *ECA; Estudios Centroamericanos*, v. 48, no. 539 (Sept 93), pp. 801 – 812. Il.

Guyana

Brana-Shute, Gary. Guyana '92: It's About Time. *Hemisphere*, v. 5, no. 2 (Winter – Spring 93), pp. 40 – 44. Maps.

Honduras

Molina Chocano, Guillermo. Honduras: ¿Del ajuste neoliberal al liberalismo social? *Nueva Sociedad*, no. 128 (Nov – Dec 93), pp. 18 – 23.

Latin America

Couffignal, Georges, ed. *Réinventer la démocratie: le défi latino-américain* reviewed by Giorgio Alberti. *Journal of Latin American Studies*, v. 25, no. 2 (May 93), pp. 409 – 410.

Mexico

Alvarado Mendoza, Arturo and Nelson Minello. Política y elecciones en Tamaulipas: la relación entre lo local y lo nacional. *Estudios Sociológicos*, v. 10, no. 30 (Sept – Dec 92), pp. 619 – 647. Charts.

Arroyo Alejandre, Jesús and Stephen D. Morris. The Electoral Recovery of the PRI in Guadalajara, Mexico, 1988 – 1992. *Bulletin of Latin American Research*, v. 12, no. 1 (Jan 93), pp. 91 – 102. Bibl, tables.

Galve-Peritore, Ana Karina and N. Patrick Peritore. Cleavage and Polarization in Mexico's Ruling Party: A Field Study of the 1988 Presidential Election. *Journal of Developing Areas*, v. 28, no. 1 (Oct 93), pp. 67 – 88. Bibl, tables.

Gómez Tagle, Silvia. Balance de las elecciones de 1991 en México. *Revista Mexicana de Sociología*, v. 54, no. 1 (Jan – Mar 92), pp. 253 – 287. Charts.

Graizbord, Boris. Geografías electorales: cambio y participación en el voto de diputados federales de 1988 y 1991. *Estudios Sociológicos*, v. 11, no. 32 (May – Aug 93), pp. 497 – 514. Bibl, tables, maps.

Klesner, Joseph L. Modernization, Economic Crisis, and Electoral Realignment in Mexico. *Mexican Studies*, v. 9, no. 2 (Summer 93), pp. 187 – 223. Bibl, tables.

Kuschick, Murilo. Sucesión presidencial: sondeo de opinión. *El Cotidiano*, v. 10, no. 58 (Oct – Nov 93), pp. 54 – 58. Il, charts.

Merino Huerta, Mauricio. Democracia, después. *Nexos*, v. 16, no. 185 (May 93), pp. 51 – 60. Bibl.

Peschard, Jacqueline. El fin del sistema de partido hegemónico. *Revista Mexicana de Sociología*, v. 55, no. 2 (Apr – June 93), pp. 97 – 117. Bibl, tables.

La sucesión presidencial de 1994 (A collection of thirteen brief articles on the upcoming presidential elections in Mexico). *Nexos*, v. 16, no. 188 (Aug 93), pp. 27 – 70.

Congresses

Guillén López, Tonatiuh. Relatoría de la mesa redonda "La Estadística Electoral, el Nuevo Patrón y la Dinámica Demográfica en Mexico." *Estudios Demográficos y Urbanos*, v. 6, no. 3 (Sept – Dec 91), pp. 745 – 755.

Law and legislation

Bolívar Espinoza, Augusto et al. Partido sin competencia, luego competencia de partidos. *El Cotidiano*, v. 10, no. 57 (Aug – Sept 93), pp. 60 – 72. Il, tables.

Reyes del Campillo, Juan. La legitimidad de la sucesión presidencial. *El Cotidiano*, v. 10, no. 58 (Oct – Nov 93), pp. 34 – 38. Il.

Valdés Zurita, Leonardo. La sucesión presidencial: "Back to the Basics." *El Cotidiano*, v. 10, no. 58 (Oct – Nov 93), pp. 29 – 33. Il.

Valenzuela, Georgette José. *Legislación electoral mexicana, 1812 – 1921: cambios y continuidades* reviewed by Josefina MacGregor. *Revista Mexicana de Sociología*, v. 55, no. 1 (Jan – Mar 93), pp. 251 – 255.

Nicaragua

Anderson, Leslie Elin. Surprises and Secrets: Lessons from the 1990 Nicaragua Election. *Studies in Comparative International Development,* v. 27, no. 3 (Fall 92), pp. 93 – 119. Bibl, tables.

Dodd, Thomas Joseph. *Managing Democracy in Central America: A Case Study of United States Election Supervision in Nicaragua, 1927 – 1933* reviewed by Neill Macaulay. *Hispanic American Historical Review,* v. 73, no. 4 (Nov 93), pp. 730 – 731.

Robinson, William I. *A Faustian Bargain: U.S. Intervention in the Nicaraguan Elections and American Foreign Policy in the Post-Cold War Era* reviewed by Thomas P. Anderson. *Hispanic American Historical Review,* v. 73, no. 3 (Aug 93), pp. 541 – 542.

Panama

Scranton, Margaret E. Consolidation after Imposition: Panama's 1992 Referendum. *Journal of Inter-American Studies and World Affairs,* v. 35, no. 3 (Fall 93), pp. 65 – 102. Bibl, tables.

Paraguay

Black, Jan Knippers. Almost Free, Almost Fair: Paraguay's Ambiguous Election. *NACLA Report on the Americas,* v. 27, no. 2 (Sept – Oct 93), pp. 26 – 28. Il.

Peru

Protzel, Javier. Industrias electorales y culturas políticas. *Estado y Sociedad,* v. 8, no. 9 (Jan – June 92), pp. 1 – 12.

Puerto Rico

Barreto Márquez, Amílcar A. The Debate over Puerto Rican Statehood: Language and the "Super-Majority." *Homines,* v. 15 – 16, no. 2 – 1 (Oct 91 – Dec 92), pp. 135 – 141. Bibl.

Berríos Martínez, Rubén. Independencia y plebiscito. *Homines,* v. 15 – 16, no. 2 – 1 (Oct 91 – Dec 92), pp. 118 – 125.

García-Passalacqua, Juan M. El regreso de Babel. *Homines,* v. 15 – 16, no. 2 – 1 (Oct 91 – Dec 92), pp. 132 – 134.

El plebiscito: una contestación a Rubén Berríos. *Homines,* v. 15 – 16, no. 2 – 1 (Oct 91 – Dec 92), pp. 126 – 131.

Uruguay

Mieres, Pablo. Canelones, 1989: el fin del bipartidismo. *Cuadernos del CLAEH,* v. 18, no. 67 (Nov 93), pp. 121 – 131. Tables.

Pedoja Riet, Eduardo. Algunas causas que determinaron la derrota del Partido Nacional en 1966. *Hoy Es Historia,* v. 10, no. 60 (Nov – Dec 93), pp. 34 – 38. Il.

ELECTRIC POWER

See also
Water power

Chile

Cost

Fierro, Gabriel and Pablo J. Serra. Un modelo de estimación del costo de falla: el caso de Chile. *Cuadernos de Economía (Chile),* v. 30, no. 90 (Aug 93), pp. 247 – 259. Bibl, tables.

Mexico

Pérez Pérez, Gabriel. El SME ante el reto de la modernización del sector eléctrico. *El Cotidiano,* v. 10, no. 58 (Oct – Nov 93), pp. 98 – 102. Il.

Sheinbaum Pardo, Claudia. Políticas de conservación de electricidad en México: costos sociales y alternativos. *Momento Económico,* no. 67 (May – June 93), pp. 7 – 14. Bibl, tables, charts.

Sturm, Russell and Michael Totten. Bright Ideas. *Business Mexico,* v. 3, no. 1 (Jan – Feb 93), pp. 55 – 57. Il.

ELECTRONICS

See also
Automation
Computer industry
Telecommunication

Barbados

Watson, Hilbourne Alban. The U.S. – Canada Free Trade Agreement and the Caribbean, with a Case Study of Electronics Assembly in Barbados. *Social and Economic Studies,* v. 41, no. 3 (Sept 92), pp. 37 – 64. Bibl.

Brazil

Campos, Nauro and João Carlos Ferraz. Uma discussão sobre o padrão de concorrência no complexo eletrônico brasileiro. *Estudos Econômicos,* v. 23, no. 1 (Jan – Apr 93), pp. 125 – 147. Bibl, tables.

Cassiolato, José Eduardo and Hubert Schmitz, eds. *Hi-tech for Industrial Development: Lessons from the Brazilian Experience in Electronics and Automation* reviewed by Rhys Jenkins. *Bulletin of Latin American Research,* v. 12, no. 3 (Sept 93), pp. 349 – 350.

Uruguay

Snoeck, Michele et al. Tecnología de punta en un pequeño país subdesarrollado: la industria electrónica en el Uruguay. *Desarrollo Económico (Argentina),* v. 33, no. 129 (Apr – June 93), pp. 87 – 107. Bibl, tables.

ELIADE, MIRCEA

Criticism of specific works

Traité d'histoire des religions

Chinchilla Sánchez, Kattia. Mircea Eliade, una clave para la interpretación del pensamiento mítico. *Káñina,* v. 16, no. 1 (Jan – June 92), pp. 207 – 218. Bibl.

ELITE (SOCIAL SCIENCES)

See also
Capitalists and financiers
Oligarchy
Social classes

Gunther, Richard and John Higley, eds. *Elites and Democratic Consolidation in Latin America and Southern Europe* reviewed by Richard Gillespie. *Bulletin of Latin American Research,* v. 12, no. 2 (May 93), pp. 235 – 236.

— *Elites and Democratic Consolidation in Latin America and Southern Europe* reviewed by Eric Hershberg. *Hispanic American Historical Review,* v. 73, no. 2 (May 93), pp. 298 – 299.

— *Elites and Democratic Consolidation in Latin America and Southern Europe* reviewed by Troy M. Bollinger. *Journal of Inter-American Studies and World Affairs,* v. 35, no. 1 (1993), pp. 158 – 166.

— *Elites and Democratic Consolidation in Latin America and Southern Europe* reviewed by Laura A. Hastings. *Journal of Latin American Studies,* v. 25, no. 1 (Feb 93), pp. 212 – 214.

Argentina

Lacoste, Pablo Alberto. Lucha de élites en Argentina: la Unión Cívica Radical en Mendoza, 1890 – 1905. *Anuario de Estudios Americanos,* v. 50, no. 1 (1993), pp. 181 – 212. Bibl, tables.

Urquiza, Fernando Carlos. Etiquetas y conflictos: el obispo, el virrey y el cabildo en el Río de la Plata en la segunda mitad del siglo XVIII. *Anuario de Estudios Americanos,* v. 50, no. 1 (1993), pp. 55 – 100. Bibl.

Brazil

Funari, Pedro Paulo Abreu. El mito candeirante: élite brasileña, cultura material e identidad. *Boletín de Antropología Americana,* no. 24 (Dec 91), pp. 111 – 122. Bibl, il.

Central America

Stone, Samuel Z. *The Heritage of the Conquistadors: Ruling Classes in Central America from the Conquest to the Sandinistas* reviewed by Carlos M. Vilas. *Journal of Latin American Studies,* v. 25, no. 3 (Oct 93), pp. 660 – 662.

Chile

Silva, Eduardo. Capitalist Regime Loyalties and Redemocratization in Chile. *Journal of Inter-American Studies and World Affairs,* v. 34, no. 4 (Winter 92 – 93), pp. 77 – 117. Bibl.

Colombia

Ortiz Mesa, Luis Javier. Elites en Antioquia, Colombia, en los inicios de la regeneración, 1886 – 1896. *Anuario Colombiano de Historia Social y de la Cultura*, no. 20 (1992), pp. 27 – 42. Bibl.

El Salvador

Paige, Jeffrey M. Coffee and Power in El Salvador. *Latin American Research Review*, v. 28, no. 3 (1993), pp. 7 – 40. Bibl.

Guatemala

Casaus Arzú, Marta Elena. *Guatemala: linaje y racismo* reviewed by Carlos M. Vilas. *Journal of Latin American Studies*, v. 25, no. 3 (Oct 93), pp. 662 – 663.

Latin America

Langue, Frédérique. Las élites en América Española: actitudes y mentalidades. *Boletín Americanista*, v. 33, no. 42 – 43 (1992 – 1993), pp. 123 – 139. Bibl.

Peire, Jaime Antonio. La manipulación de los capítulos provinciales, las élites y el imaginario socio-político colonial tardío. *Anuario de Estudios Americanos*, v. 50, no. 1 (1993), pp. 13 – 54.

Congresses

Castañeda García, Carmen. Informe del simposio: "Las Elites Hispanoamericanas en el Período Colonial." *Anuario de Estudios Americanos*, v. 49, Suppl. 1 (1992), pp. 175 – 181.

Mexico

Suárez Farías, Francisco. Familias y dinastías políticas de los presidentes del PNR – PRM – PRI. *Revista Mexicana de Ciencias Políticas y Sociales*, v. 38, Nueva época, no. 151 (Jan – Mar 93), pp. 51 – 79. Bibl.

Walker, David Wayne. *Parentescos, negocios y política: la familia Martínez del Río en México, 1823 – 1867* reviewed by María del Carmen Collado Herrera. *Historia Mexicana*, v. 42, no. 1 (July – Sept 92), pp. 133 – 138.

Panama

Lasso de Paulis, Marixa. La mentalidad en la sociedad colonial: la importancia de la etiqueta y de la ceremonia en los conflictos políticos del siglo XVII panameño. *Revista Cultural Lotería*, v. 51, no. 391 (Sept – Oct 92), pp. 105 – 111. Bibl.

Venezuela

Ferry, Robert James. *The Colonial Elite of Early Caracas: Formation and Crisis, 1567 – 1767* reviewed by John Lynch. *Journal of Latin American Studies*, v. 25, no. 1 (Feb 93), pp. 191 – 192.

Gerdes, Claudia. *Eliten und Fortschritt: Zur Geschichte der Lebensstile in Venezuela, 1908 – 1915* reviewed by Nikita Harwich Vallenilla. *Iberoamericana*, v. 17, no. 49 (1993), pp. 96 – 97.

ELIZONDO, SALVADOR

Criticism and interpretation

Graniela-Rodríguez, Magda. *El papel del lector en la novela mexicana contemporánea: José Emilio Pacheco y Salvador Elizondo* reviewed by Roberto Bravo. *Hispania (USA)*, v. 76, no. 2 (May 93), pp. 287 – 288.

Criticism of specific works

Farabeuf

Cadena, Agustín. *Farabeuf:* el espacio como metáforo del tiempo. *Plural (Mexico)*, v. 22, no. 258 (Mar 93), pp. 50 – 56. Bibl.

ELLACURÍA, IGNACIO

Domínguez Miranda, Manuel. Ignacio Ellacuría, filósofo de la realidad latinoamericana. *ECA; Estudios Centroamericanos*, v. 47, no. 529 – 530 (Nov – Dec 92), pp. 983 – 998.

EL PASO, TEXAS

Jones, Robert W. A Content Comparison of Daily Newspapers in the El Paso – Juárez Circulation Area. *Journal of Borderlands Studies*, v. 7, no. 2 (Fall 92), pp. 93 – 100. Bibl, tables.

ELTIT, DIAMELA

Criticism and interpretation

Olea, Raquel. El cuerpo-mujer: un recorte de lectura en la narrativa de Diamela Eltit. *Revista Chilena de Literatura*, no. 42 (Aug 93), pp. 165 – 171. Bibl.

Interviews

Garabano, Sandra and Guillermo García-Corales. Diamela Eltit. *Hispamérica*, v. 21, no. 62 (Aug 92), pp. 65 – 75.

EMAR, JUAN

See
Yáñez, Alvaro

EMBARGO

Sábato, Ernesto R. Críticas al bloqueo norteamericano a Cuba. *Realidad Económica*, no. 117 (July – Aug 93), pp. 33 – 34.

EMBLEMS, NATIONAL

Brazil

Law and legislation

Projeto de lei: altera a Lei no. 5700 de setembro de 1971, que dispõe sobre a forma e a apresentação dos símbolos nacionais (Includes three letters regarding this law). *Revista do Instituto Histórico e Geográfico Brasileiro*, no. 370 (Jan – Mar 91), pp. 303 – 309. Il.

Panama

Berrío-Lemm, Vladimir. En torno a los símbolos patrios tradicionales de Panamá. *Revista Cultural Lotería*, v. 51, no. 392 (Nov – Dec 93), pp. 55 – 77. Bibl, il.

Venezuela

Bencomo Barrios, Héctor. El cuartel San Carlos de Caracas y la bandera nacional. *Boletín de la Academia Nacional de la Historia (Venezuela)*, v. 76, no. 302 (Apr – June 93), pp. 140 – 141.

Vetancourt Vigas, F. C. El pendón español en el ayuntamiento de Cumaná (Previously published in this journal vol. 1, no. 1, 1912). *Boletín de la Academia Nacional de la Historia (Venezuela)*, v. 75, no. 300 (Oct – Dec 92), pp. 279 – 293.

EMIGRATION AND IMMIGRATION

See
Brain drain
Exiles
Migration, Internal
Naturalization
Undocumented workers
Names of specific national groups
Subdivision *Emigration and immigration* under names of specific countries
Subdivision *Migrations* under Man

EMPLOYEES' REPRESENTATION IN MANAGEMENT

Chile

Anwandter P., Jorge. Una empresa de trabajadores para la economía solidaria. *Mensaje*, v. 42, no. 423 (Oct 93), pp. 504 – 505. Il.

Cuba

Fuller, Linda. *Work and Democracy in Socialist Cuba* reviewed by Samuel Farber. *Cuban Studies/Estudios Cubanos*, v. 23 (1993), pp. 238 – 240.

— *Work and Democracy in Socialist Cuba* reviewed by Jean Stubbs. *Journal of Latin American Studies*, v. 25, no. 2 (May 93), pp. 424 – 425.

— *Work and Democracy in Socialist Cuba* reviewed by Ronald H. Chilcote (Review entitled "Participation and the Workplace in Socialist Cuba"). *Latin American Perspectives*, v. 20, no. 1 (Winter 93), pp. 40 – 43.

EMPLOYMENT

See also
Labor supply
Unemployment
Subdivision *Employment* under *Children, Hispanic Americans (U.S.),* and *Women*

Brazil
Mathematical models
Estevão, Marcello. Employment Level, Hours of Work, and Labor Adjustment Cost in the Brazilian Industry. *Revista Brasileira de Economia,* v. 47, no. 2 (Apr – June 93), pp. 205 – 242. Bibl, tables, charts.

Caribbean area
Ramsaran, Ramesh. Growth, Employment, and the Standard of Living in Selected Commonwealth Caribbean Countries. *Caribbean Studies,* v. 25, no. 1 – 2 (Jan – July 92), pp. 103 – 122. Tables.

Colombia
Statistics
Colombia. Departamento Nacional de Planeación. Indicadores del sector rural. *Planeación y Desarrollo,* v. 24 (1993), All issues.

Mexico
Pries, Ludger. Movilidad en el empleo: una comparación de trabajo asalariado y por cuenta propia en Puebla. *Estudios Sociológicos,* v. 11, no. 32 (May – Aug 93), pp. 475 – 496. Bibl, charts.

Statistics
García Guzmán, Brígida. La ocupación en México en los años ochenta: hechos y datos. *Revista Mexicana de Sociología,* v. 55, no. 1 (Jan – Mar 93), pp. 137 – 153. Bibl, tables.

Lorey, David E. *The Rise of the Professions in Twentieth-Century Mexico: University Graduates and Occupational Change since 1929* reviewed by Roderic A. Camp. *Journal of Latin American Studies,* v. 25, no. 2 (May 93), pp. 412 – 413.

Rendón, Teresa and Carlos Salas Páez. El empleo en México en los ochenta: tendencias y cambios. *Comercio Exterior,* v. 43, no. 8 (Aug 93), pp. 717 – 730. Bibl, tables, charts.

Rueda Peiró, Isabel. Deterioro y mayor desigualdad en el empleo y los salarios de los trabajadores mexicanos. *Momento Económico,* no. 69 (Sept – Oct 93), pp. 6 – 9. Tables.

Peru
Hurtado, Isabel. Importancia del empleo estatal en los mercados de trabajo regionales: el caso del sur peruano entre 1961 y 1981. *Revista Andina,* v. 11, no. 1 (July 93), pp. 55 – 78. Bibl, tables, maps, charts.

Puerto Rico
Muschkin, Clara G. Consequences of Return Migrant Status for Employment in Puerto Rico. *International Migration Review,* v. 27, no. 1 (Spring 93), pp. 79 – 102. Bibl, tables, charts.

ENCOMIENDAS
See also
Subdivision *Government relations* under names of Indian groups

Mexico
Himmerich y Valencia, Robert. *The Encomenderos of New Spain, 1521 – 1555* reviewed by J. Benedict Warren. *The Americas,* v. 50, no. 2 (Oct 93), pp. 272 – 273.

— *The Encomenderos of New Spain, 1521 – 1555* reviewed by Bernard Grunberg. *Caravelle,* no. 60 (1993), pp. 139 – 140.

— *The Encomenderos of New Spain, 1521 – 1555* reviewed by Robert McGeagh. *Colonial Latin American Historical Review,* v. 2, no. 1 (Winter 93), pp. 118 – 120.

— *The Encomenderos of New Spain, 1521 – 1555* reviewed by Murdo J. Macleod. *Hispanic American Historical Review,* v. 73, no. 1 (Feb 93), pp. 149 – 150.

Puerto Rico
Moscoso, Francisco. Encomendero y esclavista: Francisco Manuel de Lando. *Anuario de Estudios Americanos,* v. 49 (1992), pp. 119 – 142. Bibl.

ENERGY CONSERVATION
See
Energy policy
Power resources

ENERGY POLICY
See also
Atomic power industry
Electric power
Gas, Natural
Petroleum industry and trade
Power resources
Water power

Colombia
Bonilla Muñoz, Guillermo and Horacio Osorio Velosa. Estructura de mercado y prácticas comerciales en los sectores industrial, minero – energético y de servicios públicos en Colombia. *Planeación y Desarrollo,* v. 24, no. 2 (May – Aug 93), pp. 191 – 256. Tables, charts.

Cuba
Pichs Madruga, Ramón. Problemas y opciones del sector energético cubano. *Problemas del Desarrollo,* v. 24, no. 92 (Jan – Mar 93), pp. 197 – 208. Bibl.

Mexico
Baker, George. Does Modernization at PEMEX Meet Consumer Needs? *Business Mexico,* v. 3, no. 5 (May 93), pp. 4 – 7+. Il, tables.

Sheinbaum Pardo, Claudia. Políticas de conservación de electricidad en México: costos sociales y alternativos. *Momento Económico,* no. 67 (May – June 93), pp. 7 – 14. Bibl, tables, charts.

Sturm, Russell and Michael Totten. Delivering the Goods. *Business Mexico,* v. 3, no. 5 (May 93), pp. 15 – 18. Il.

ENGINEERING
Chile
Guarda Geywitz, Gabriel. Obras hidráulicas en el reino de Chile. *Boletín de la Academia Chilena de la Historia,* v. 58 – 59, no. 102 (1991 – 1992), pp. 269 – 289. Bibl.

Awards
Zahler, Roberto. Palabras de agradecimiento (for the "premio de la Asociación de Egresados de Ingeniería Comercial de la Universidad de Chile al ingeniero comercial más destacado del año 1992"). *Estudios Sociales (Chile),* no. 77 (July – Sept 93), pp. 197 – 202.

ENGLISH LANGUAGE
Martinell Gifre, Emma. El uso de las formas "un," "uno," "una," "unos," "unas," en español y de sus equivalentes en inglés. *Anuario de Letras (Mexico),* v. 30 (1992), pp. 29 – 45. Bibl.

Central America
Rodino Pierri, Ana María. Language Rights and Education for the Afro-Caribbean, English-Speaking Minorities in Central America: Contributions to the Discussion on Bilingual Education in Costa Rica. *La Educación (USA),* v. 36, no. 111 – 113 (1992), pp. 137 – 154. Bibl.

Mexico
Baker, George. Know Your Vowels. *Business Mexico,* v. 3, no. 8 (Aug 93), pp. 20 – 22. Il.

ENGRAVING
See
Printing and engraving

ENLIGHTENMENT
Aceves, Patricia. La ilustración novohispana en el área farmacéutica, química y metalúrgica. *Cuadernos Americanos,* no. 38, Nueva época (Mar – Apr 93), pp. 92 – 120. Bibl.

Quintero Esquivel, Jorge Eliécer. Ergotismo, ilustración y utilitarismo en Colombia: siglos XVIII y XIX. *Islas,* no. 96 (May – Aug 90), pp. 53 – 66. Bibl, tables, charts.

ENRÍQUEZ DE GUZMÁN, LUIS, CONDE DE ALBA DE LISTE
Bradley, Peter T. *Society, Economy, and Defence in Seventeenth-Century Peru: The Administration of the Count of Alba de Liste, 1655 – 1661* reviewed by Teodoro Hampe Martínez. *Colonial Latin American Review,* v. 2, no. 1 – 2 (1993), pp. 298 – 300.

— *Society, Economy, and Defence in Seventeenth-Century Peru: The Administration of the Count of Alba de Liste, 1655 – 1661* reviewed by Stephen J. Homick. *Hispanic American Historical Review,* v. 73, no. 2 (May 93), pp. 314 – 315.

— *Society, Economy, and Defence in Seventeenth-Century Peru: The Administration of the Count of Alba de Liste, 1655 – 1661* reviewed by Mark A. Burkholder. *Revista Interamericana de Bibliografía,* v. 42, no. 2 (1992), pp. 283 – 284.

ENTOMOLOGY

Amazon Valley

Couturier, Guy and Francis Kahn. Notes on the Insect Fauna of Two Species of "Astrocaryum" (Palmae, Cocoeae, Bactridinae) in Peruvian Amazonia, with Emphasis on Potential Pests of Cultivated Palms. *Bulletin de l'Institut Français d'Etudes Andines,* v. 21, no. 2 (1992), pp. 715 – 725. Bibl, il, tables, maps.

ENTRE RÍOS, ARGENTINA

Leguizamón, Martiniano. La república de Entre Ríos. *Hoy Es Historia,* v. 10, no. 60 (Nov – Dec 93), pp. 82 – 83.

Urquiza Almandoz, Oscar F. El traslado de la capital entrerriana, 1883. *Investigaciones y Ensayos,* no. 41 (Jan – Dec 91), pp. 329 – 347. Bibl.

ENVIRONMENTAL MOVEMENTS

See

Pressure groups
Social movements
Subdivision *Societies, etc.* under *Ecology*

ENVIRONMENTAL POLICY

See also

Ecology and development

Galarza, Elsa and Roberto Urrunaga. La economía de los recursos naturales: políticas extractivas y ambientales. *Apuntes (Peru),* no. 30 (Jan – June 92), pp. 45 – 61. Bibl.

González, Anabel. Comercio internacional y medio ambiente. *Comercio Exterior,* v. 43, no. 9 (Sept 93), pp. 827 – 835. Bibl.

International cooperation

Casas Castañeda, Fernando. Política exterior en el campo de los recursos genéticos, el medio ambiente y la economía internacional. *Revista Javeriana,* v. 61, no. 594 (May 93), pp. 277 – 282. Bibl.

Much Ado about Nothing . . . Hopefully. *Business Mexico,* v. 3, no. 8 (Aug 93), pp. 23 – 24.

Ranger, Edward M., Jr. The Environment and NAFTA. *Business Mexico,* v. 3, no. 1 (Jan – Feb 93), pp. 78 – 79.

Research

Varela Barraza, Hilda. Nuevos temas de investigación en relaciones internacionales: la ecología. *Relaciones Internacionales (Mexico),* v. 14, Nueva época, no. 55 (July – Sept 92), pp. 31 – 41. Bibl.

Amazon Valley

Dourado, Maria Cristina, ed. *Direito ambiental e a questão amazônica* (Review). *La Educación (USA),* v. 37, no. 115 (1993), pp. 439 – 440.

America

Muñoz Valenzuela, Heraldo, ed. *Environment and Diplomacy in the Americas* reviewed by Joan Martínez Alier. *Hispanic American Historical Review,* v. 73, no. 3 (Aug 93), pp. 536 – 537.

Stoub, Jeffrey. NAFTA's "Green" Thumb. *Business Mexico,* v. 3, no. 10 (Oct 93), pp. 35 – 36.

Brazil

Artigos da constituição do Brasil referentes à questão ambiental (Introduced by Marilson Alves Gonçalves). *RAE; Revista de Administração de Empresas,* v. 33, no. 3 (May – June 93), pp. 66 – 67.

Câmara, Ibsen de Gusmão. Gestão do território: uma perspectiva conservacionista. *Revista Brasileira de Geografia,* v. 53, no. 3 (July – Sept 91), pp. 161 – 168. Bibl.

Carneiro, José Mário et al. Meio ambiente, empresário e governo: conflitos ou parceria? *RAE; Revista de Administração de Empresas,* v. 33, no. 3 (May – June 93), pp. 68 – 75. Bibl.

Guimarães, Paulo César Vaz. Instrumentos econômicos para gerenciamento ambiental: a cobrança pelo uso da água no estado de São Paulo. *RAE; Revista de Administração de Empresas,* v. 33, no. 5 (Sept – Oct 93), pp. 88 – 97.

Guimarães, Roberto Pereira. *The Ecopolitics of Development in the Third World: Politics and Environment in Brazil* reviewed by Margaret E. Keck. *Hispanic American Historical Review,* v. 73, no. 1 (Feb 93), p. 171.

Leite, Cristina Maria Costa. Uma análise sobre o processo de organização do território: o caso do zoneamento ecológico – econômico. *Revista Brasileira de Geografia,* v. 53, no. 3 (July – Sept 91), pp. 67 – 90. Bibl.

Machado, Rosa Maria de Oliveira and Ana Lúcia Magyar. A regulamentação da lei de recursos hídricos do estado de São Paulo: desafios e perspectivas. *RAE; Revista de Administração de Empresas,* v. 33, no. 6 (Nov – Dec 93), pp. 42 – 47. Bibl.

Central America

Weinberg, William J. *War on the Land: Ecology and Politics in Central America* reviewed by Anthony Bebbington. *Bulletin of Latin American Research,* v. 12, no. 2 (May 93), p. 242.

Costa Rica

Vargas Ulate, Gilberto. La protección de los recursos naturales en un país subdesarrollado: caso de Costa Rica. *Revista de Ciencias Sociales (Costa Rica),* no. 59 (Mar 93), pp. 81 – 93. Bibl, maps.

Europe

Summerer, Stefan. La política ambiental de la Comunidad Europea: ¿Un ejemplo para otros hemisferios? (Translated by Raquel García de Sanjurjo). *Cuadernos del CLAEH,* v. 18, no. 65 – 66 (May 93), pp. 123 – 134.

Latin America

Ballesteros, Carlos. La política ambiental en América Latina después de la cumbre de Río. *Relaciones Internacionales (Mexico),* v. 14, Nueva época, no. 56 (Oct – Dec 92), pp. 103 – 106.

Mexican – American Border Region

Rosas, Alan L. et al. NAFTA's Environmental Issues and Opportunities. *Business Mexico,* v. 3, no. 9 (Sept 93), pp. 42 – 45.

Mexico

Alfie Cohen, Miriam. Las transformaciones de la política gubernamental en materia ecológica. *El Cotidiano,* v. 8, no. 52 (Jan – Feb 93), pp. 51 – 56. Il, tables, charts.

Alfie Cohen, Miriam and Godofredo Vidal de la Rosa. Hacia los acuerdos paralelos: el medio ambiente. *El Cotidiano,* v. 9, no. 56 (July 93), pp. 104 – 111. Bibl, il, tables.

Ballesteros, Carlos. El concepto de seguridad ambiental y la integración del mercado norteamericano. *Relaciones Internacionales (Mexico),* v. 15, Nueva época, no. 58 (Apr – June 93), pp. 63 – 68.

Cardoso Frías, Joaquín. When the Inspector Calls . . . Be Prepared! *Business Mexico,* v. 3, no. 1 (Jan – Feb 93), p. 87.

Elmendorf, George F. and Joan A. Quillen. Mexico's Environmental and Ecological Organizations and Movements. *SALALM Papers,* v. 36 (1991), pp. 123 – 129.

Fernandez, Adolfo and Melanie Treviño. The Maquiladora Industry, Adverse Environmental Impact, and Proposed Solutions. *Journal of Borderlands Studies,* v. 7, no. 2 (Fall 92), pp. 53 – 72. Bibl.

McCurry, Patrick. Starting at the Top. *Business Mexico,* v. 3, no. 1 (Jan – Feb 93), pp. 80 – 82. Il.

Newman, Gray. Laying Down the Law. *Business Mexico,* v. 3, no. 1 (Jan – Feb 93), pp. 75 – 77.

Olivier, Michele. Shared Responsibility. *Business Mexico,* v. 3, no. 6 (June 93), pp. 43 – 45. Tables, charts.

Ranger, Edward M., Jr. A Compliance Checklist. *Business Mexico,* v. 3, no. 1 (Jan – Feb 93), p. 86.

— The High Cost of Noncompliance. *Business Mexico,* v. 3, no. 7 (July 93), p. 44 + .

Rivera de los Reyes, Julio M. Plant Shutdown?: Here's What to Do. *Business Mexico*, v. 3, no. 1 (Jan – Feb 93), p. 88.

Stern, Marc A. A Critique of Eco-Strategies. *Business Mexico*, v. 3, no. 10 (Oct 93), pp. 40 – 43.

Stoub, Jeffrey. De-Fossilizing the Fuel Industry. *Business Mexico*, v. 3, no. 1 (Jan – Feb 93), pp. 16 – 18. Il.

— Sustainable Policies. *Business Mexico*, v. 3, no. 8 (Aug 93), pp. 46 – 47. Il.

Venezuela

Law and legislation

Ley Penal del Ambiente. *Derecho y Reforma Agraria*, no. 23 (1992), pp. 185 – 203.

Pérez, Carlos Andrés. Venezuela: Decreto 1633 que crea la reserva de biosfera Delta del Orinoco. *Anuario Indigenista*, v. 30 (Dec 91), pp. 497 – 502.

— Venezuela: Decreto 1635 que declara reserva de biosfera el sector sureste del territorio federal Amazonas. *Anuario Indigenista*, v. 30 (Dec 91), pp. 503 – 508.

— Venezuela: Decreto 1636 que crea el parque nacional Parima – Tapirapeco en el alto Orinoco. *Anuario Indigenista*, v. 30 (Dec 91), pp. 509 – 512.

ENVIRONMENTAL SERVICES

Brazil

Silva, Jorge Xavier da. Um banco de dados ambientais para a Amazônia. *Revista Brasileira de Geografia*, v. 53, no. 3 (July – Sept 91), pp. 91 – 124. Bibl, il, tables, maps.

Mexico

Corporate Sources (A directory of member companies of the Chamber of Commerce of Mexico, A.C. that offer services in the field of environmental planning, protection, and remediation). *Business Mexico*, v. 3, no. 1 (Jan – Feb 93), pp. 93 – 95.

Jones, Robert S. and David Robinson. Protection + Environment = Future Growth. *Business Mexico*, v. 3, no. 1 (Jan – Feb 93), pp. 37 – 39. Il.

Smith, Morgan. Lifting the "Brown Cloud." *Business Mexico*, v. 3, no. 9 (Sept 93), pp. 39 – 40.

United States

Smith, Morgan. Lifting the "Brown Cloud." *Business Mexico*, v. 3, no. 9 (Sept 93), pp. 39 – 40.

EPIC POETRY

Manzotti, Vilma. Del Barco Centenera y su poema como justicia en una hazaña desventurada. *Revista Interamericana de Bibliografía*, v. 42, no. 3 (1992), pp. 453 – 462. Bibl.

Verdesio, Gustavo. La *Argentina*: tipología textual y construcción de los referentes. *Revista de Crítica Literaria Latinoamericana*, v. 19, no. 38 (July – Dec 93), pp. 345 – 360. Bibl.

EPIGRAMS

Huidobro, Vicente. Greguerías y paradojas (Excerpt from the book *Vientos contrarios*). *Atenea (Chile)*, no. 467 (1993), pp. 143 – 144.

EPISTEMOLOGY

See
Knowledge, Theory of

ERCILLA Y ZÚÑIGA, ALONSO DE

Criticism of specific works

La araucana

Moore, Charles B. Las influencias clásicas en la descripción del desierto en el canto XXXV de *La araucana*. *Confluencia*, v. 8, no. 1 (Fall 92), pp. 99 – 107. Bibl.

ERICKSON, DOROTHY

Obituaries

Montejo, Víctor Dionicio. Sirviendo al pueblo: la vida ejemplar de madre Rosa Cordis. *Mesoamérica (USA)*, v. 13, no. 23 (June 92), pp. 219 – 220.

EROSION

See also
Deserts
Geology
Water

Haiti

Brochet, Michel. Les stratégies de lutte contre l'érosion et l'aménagement des bassins versants en Haïti. *Tiers Monde*, v. 34, no. 134 (Apr – June 93), pp. 423 – 436.

Peru

Teves Rivas, Néstor. Erosion and Accretion Processes during El Niño Phenomenon of 1982 – 1983 and Its Relation to Previous Events. *Bulletin de l'Institut Français d'Etudes Andines*, v. 22, no. 1 (1993), pp. 99 – 110. Bibl, tables, maps, charts.

Research

Loker, William M. et al. Identification of Areas of Land Degradation in the Peruvian Amazon Using a Geographic Information System. *Interciencia*, v. 18, no. 3 (May – June 93), pp. 133 – 141. Bibl, tables, maps, charts.

EROTICA

Fernández Olmos, Margarite and Lizabeth Paravisini-Gebert. *El placer de la palabra: literatura erótica femenina de América Latina; antología crítica* reviewed by Mónica Zapata. *Canadian Journal of Latin American and Caribbean Studies*, v. 17, no. 34 (1992), pp. 135 – 138.

Riccio, Alessandra. Eros y poder en *Informe bajo llave* de Marta Lynch. *Escritura (Venezuela)*, v. 16, no. 31 – 32 (Jan – Dec 91), pp. 223 – 229. Bibl.

ESCARDÓ, FLORENCIO

Correspondence, reminiscences, etc.

Escardó, Florencio. Florencio Escardó. *Realidad Económica*, no. 119 (Oct – Nov 93), pp. 69 – 72.

ESCOBEDO Y ALARCÓN, JORGE

Fernández Alonso, Serena. Perfil biográfico y acción de gobierno de don Jorge Escobedo y Alarcón. *Revista de Indias*, v. 52, no. 195 – 196 (May – Dec 92), pp. 365 – 383. Bibl.

ESCRIVÁ DE BALAGUER, JOSÉ MARÍA

Pedoja Riet, Eduardo. Monseñor Escrivá y el Opus Dei. *Hoy Es Historia*, v. 9, no. 54 (Nov – Dec 92), pp. 6 – 10.

ESPINOSA, ALEJANDRO

Martínez Duarte, Margarita. Los hombres – instrumento de "Guardaos de los ídolos." *Plural (Mexico)*, v. 22, no. 263 (Aug 93), p. 68.

ESPINOSA, ALFREDO

Criticism and interpretation

En todas partes la utopía. *La Palabra y el Hombre*, no. 81 (Jan – Mar 92), pp. 328 – 329.

ESPINOSA, AMPARO

Interviews

Velázquez, Carolina. "Soy optimista . . . ahora tenemos más opciones": Amparo Espinosa. *Fem*, v. 17, no. 130 (Dec 93), pp. 26 – 27. Il.

ESPIONAGE

United States

Caruso, Brooke A. *The Mexican Spy Company: United States Covert Actions in Mexico, 1845 – 1848* reviewed by Daniela Spenser. *Hispanic American Historical Review*, v. 73, no. 1 (Feb 93), p. 189.

ESPÍRITO SANTO, BRAZIL

Bittencourt, Gabriel Augusto de Mello. A imprensa no Espírito Santo. *Revista do Instituto Histórico e Geográfico Brasileiro*, no. 373 (Oct – Dec 91), pp. 1022 – 1031.

ESPY, MIKE

Witoshynsky, Mary. "The Final Steps." *Business Mexico*, v. 3, no. 10 (Oct 93), p. 47. Il.

ESQUINEA, JORGE
Criticism and interpretation
Trujillo Muñoz, Gabriel. La alquimia de la voz. *La Palabra y el Hombre,* no. 81 (Jan – Mar 92), pp. 330 – 331.

ESSAY
Rodríguez Castro, María Elena. Las casas del porvenir: nación y narración en el ensayo puertorriqueño. *Revista Iberoamericana,* v. 59, no. 162 – 163 (Jan – June 93), pp. 33 – 54. Bibl.

ESSAYS
See
Author Index under names of specific essayists

ESTORINO, ABELARDO
Criticism of specific works
El robo del cochino
Bejel, Emilio F. La transferencia dialéctica en *El robo del cochino* de Estorino. *La Palabra y el Hombre,* no. 84 (Oct – Dec 92), pp. 291 – 295.

Vagos rumores
Martínez Tabares, Vivian. *Vagos rumores:* reafirmación de cubanía. *Conjunto,* no. 92 (July – Dec 92), pp. 63 – 66. Il.

ESTRADA, GENARO
Correspondence, reminiscences, etc.
Reyes, Alfonso. Buzón de fantasmas: de Alfonso Reyes a Genaro Estrada. *Vuelta,* v. 17, no. 196 (Mar 93), pp. 76 – 77.

Tablada, José Juan. Buzón de fantasmas: de José Juan Tablada a Genaro Estrada. *Vuelta,* v. 17, no. 197 (Apr 93), pp. 76 – 77.

Zaitzeff, Serge Ivan. Cartas de Gabriela Mistral a Genaro Estrada (Includes four letters). *Cuadernos Americanos,* no. 37, Nueva época (Jan – Feb 93), pp. 115 – 131.

ESTRELLA, ULÍSES
Biography
Beltrán Salmón, Ramiro. Ulíses Estrella, "peatón de Quito" y amigo de Bolivia. *Signo,* no. 38, Nueva época (Jan – Apr 93), pp. 143 – 145.

ESTUDIOS INTERNACIONALES (PERIODICAL)
Indexes
Indice general: *Estudios Internacionales,* nos. 1 – 99. *Estudios Internacionales (Chile),* v. 25, no. 100 (Oct – Dec 92), Issue.

ESTUDIOS PÚBLICOS (PERIODICAL)
Vial Correa, Juan de Dios. Cincuenta números de revista *Estudios Públicos. Estudios Públicos (Chile),* no. 51 (Winter 93), pp. 331 – 335.

Indexes
Indice por temas y autores: *Estudios Públicos,* nos. 1 al 50, 1980 – 1993. *Estudios Públicos (Chile),* no. 50 (Fall 93), pp. 415 – 492.

ESTUDIOS SOCIALES (PERIODICAL)
Celebración de los veinte años de la revista *Estudios Sociales* (Includes several letters of congratulations). *Estudios Sociales (Chile),* no. 78 (Oct – Dec 93), pp. 259 – 278.

Zaglul, Jesús M. Documento: *Estudios Sociales;* 25 años de reflexión y análisis. *Estudios Sociales (Dominican Republic),* v. 26, no. 92 (Apr – June 93), pp. 93 – 99.

Indexes
Contenidos y autores de los números anteriores de la revista *Estudios Sociales,* nos. 1 – 77. *Estudios Sociales (Chile),* no. 78 (Oct – Dec 93), pp. 307 – 351.

ETCHEPARE DE HENESTROSA, ARMONÍA
See
Somers, Armonía

ETHICS
See also
Medical ethics

Arruda, Maria Cecília Coutinho de. A ética no "marketing" das indústrias de bens de consumo no Brasil. *RAE; Revista de Administração de Empresas,* v. 33, no. 1 (Jan – Feb 93), pp. 16 – 28. Bibl, tables, charts.

Benedetti, Mario. Etica de amplio espectro. *Nexos,* v. 16, no. 187 (July 93), pp. 13 – 15.

Deckers, Daniel. La justicia de la conquista de América: consideraciones en torno a la cronología y a los protagonistas de una controversia del siglo XVI muy actual. *Ibero-Amerikanisches Archiv,* v. 18, no. 3 – 4 (1992), pp. 331 – 366. Bibl.

Heath, Hilarie J. British Merchant Houses in Mexico, 1821 – 1860: Conforming Business Practices and Ethics. *Hispanic American Historical Review,* v. 73, no. 2 (May 93), pp. 261 – 290. Bibl.

Langue, Frédérique. De moralista a arbitrista: don Francisco de Ibarra, obispo de Venezuela, 1798 – 1806; recopilación documental. *Anuario de Estudios Americanos,* v. 49, Suppl. 1 (1992), pp. 55 – 84. Bibl.

Lasaga, Ignacio. La eticidad del pobre. *Estudios Sociales (Dominican Republic),* v. 26, no. 91 (Jan – Mar 93), pp. 61 – 76.

Lince, Ricardo A. and Roberto Núñez Escobar. Aporte para una legislación de prensa. *Revista Cultural Lotería,* v. 50, no. 386 (Nov – Dec 91), pp. 5 – 24.

MacGregor, Felipe E. La ética periodística ante la información de la violencia. *Apuntes (Peru),* no. 29 (July – Dec 91), pp. 27 – 34. Tables.

Olguín Pérez, Palmira. Las reglas del juego: moralidad y moraleja en la telenovela. *Fem,* v. 17, no. 130 (Dec 93), pp. 22 – 23.

Salmón Jordán, Jorge. *Entre la vanidad y el poder: memoria y testimonio* reviewed by Oscar Malca (Review entitled "Contra la corriente"). *Debate (Peru),* v. 16, no. 72 (Mar – May 93), pp. 65 – 66. Il.

Santos Granero, Fernando. *The Power of Love: The Moral Use of Knowledge amongst the Amuesha of Central Peru* reviewed by Jaime Regan. *Amazonía Peruana,* v. 11, no. 22 (Oct 92), pp. 285 – 288.

— *The Power of Love: The Moral Use of Knowledge amongst the Amuesha of Central Peru* reviewed by Richard. C. Smith. *Bulletin de l'Institut Français d'Etudes Andines,* v. 21, no. 2 (1992), pp. 793 – 797. Bibl.

ETHNICITY
See also
Indigenismo
Subdivision *Ethnic identity* under *Blacks, Hispanic Americans (U.S.),* and names of Indian groups

Castellanos Guerrero, Alicia and Gilberto López y Rivas. Grupos étnicos y procesos nacionalitarios en el capitalismo neoliberal. *Nueva Antropología,* v. 13, no. 44 (Aug 93), pp. 27 – 41. Bibl.

Conciencia étnica y modernidad: etnias de Oriente y Occidente reviewed by Alberto Cheng Hurtado. *América Indígena,* v. 51, no. 2 – 3 (Apr – Sept 91), pp. 353 – 356.

Bolivia
Abercrombie, Thomas Alan. La fiesta del carnaval postcolonial en Oruro: clase, etnicidad y nacionalismo en la danza folklórica (With commentaries by seven historians and a response by the author). *Revista Andina,* v. 10, no. 2 (Dec 92), pp. 279 – 352. Bibl, il.

Lagos, María L. The Politics of Representation: Class and Ethnic Identities in Cochabamba, Bolivia. *Boletín de Antropología Americana,* no. 24 (Dec 91), pp. 143 – 150. Bibl, il.

Caribbean area
Giacalone de Romero, Rita. Condicionamientos étnicos en la conformación de estereotipos femeninos en el Caribe hispánico y Caribe angloparlante. *Homines,* v. 15 – 16, no. 2 – 1 (Oct 91 – Dec 92), pp. 289 – 297. Bibl.

Costa Rica
Hernández Cruz, Omar. Historias de vida e identidades étnicas: la visión de los maestros del Atlántico costarricense. *Revista de Ciencias Sociales (Costa Rica),* no. 58 (Dec 92), pp. 75 – 83. Bibl.

Latin America

Diaz, Harry P. et al. *Forging Identities and Patterns of Development* reviewed by William A. Harris (Review entitled "Ethnicity and Development"). *Social and Economic Studies,* v. 41, no. 4 (Dec 92), pp. 225 – 230.

Roitman Rosenmann, Marcos. Democracia y estado. multiétnico en América Latina. *Boletín de Antropología Americana,* no. 24 (Dec 91), pp. 63 – 78. Bibl, il.

ETHNOBOTANY

See also
    Folk medicine

Colombia

Weiskopf, Jimmy. Healing Secrets in a Shaman's Garden. *Américas,* v. 45, no. 4 (July – Aug 93), pp. 42 – 47. Il.

Uruguay

Soiza Larrosa, Augusto. Medicina popular. *Hoy Es Historia,* v. 10, no. 59 (Sept – Oct 93), pp. 98 – 99.

ETHNOHISTORY

See
    Anthropology
    Subdivision *History* under names of Indian groups

ETHNOLINGUISTICS

See
    Sociolinguistics

ETHNOLOGY

See
    Acculturation
    Blacks
    Hispanic Americans (U.S.) – Ethnic identity

ETHNOMUSICOLOGY

See also
    Folk music

Argentina

Alcorta, Rodrigo. Juan Alfonso Carriza y medio siglo del Instituto Nacional de Antropología. *Todo Es Historia,* v. 27, no. 312 (July 93), pp. 62 – 65. Il.

Brazil

Carvalho, José Jorge de. Aesthetics of Opacity and Transparence: Myth, Music, and Ritual in the Xangô Cult and in the Western Art Tradition. *Latin American Music Review,* v. 14, no. 2 (Fall – Winter 93), pp. 202 – 231. Bibl, tables, facs.

Segato, Rita Laura. Okarilé: Yemoja's Icon Tune. *Latin American Music Review,* v. 14, no. 1 (Spring – Summer 93), pp. 1 – 19. Bibl, facs.

Vidal, Lux. As pesquisas mais freqüentes em etnologia e historia indígena na Amazônia: uma abordagem musical. *Revista de Antropologia (Brazil),* v. 34 (1991), pp. 183 – 196.

Caribbean area

Thompson, Donald. The "Cronistas de Indias" Revisited: Historical Reports, Archaeological Evidence, and Literary and Artistic Traces of Indigenous Music and Dance in the Greater Antilles at the Time of the "Conquista." *Latin American Music Review,* v. 14, no. 2 (Fall – Winter 93), pp. 181 – 201. Bibl.

Latin America

Aretz de Ramón y Rivera, Isabel. *Historia de la etnomusicología en América Latina: desde la época precolombina hasta nuestros días* reviewed by Irma Poletti. *La Educación (USA),* v. 36, no. 111 – 113 (1992), pp. 280 – 281.

EUROPE

See also
    Artists – Europe
    Austria
    Democracy – Europe
    Environmental policy – Europe
    Europe, Eastern
    European Community
    Exiles – Europe
    Food habits – Europe
    Food industry and trade – Europe
    France
    Germany
    Great Britain
    Imperialism – Europe
    Information services – Europe
    Italy
    Latin Americans – Europe
    Netherlands
    Popular music – Europe
    Portugal
    Scandinavia
    Science – Europe
    Spain
    Sweden

Civilization

Pérez Antón, Romeo and Carlos Pareja. América y Europa: asimetrías e inmadurez. *Cuadernos del CLAEH,* v. 17, no. 63 – 64 (Oct 92), pp. 81 – 98.

Zea, Leopoldo. Emigración igual a conquista y ocupación. *Cuadernos Americanos,* no. 37, Nueva época (Jan – Feb 93), pp. 13 – 22.

— Vasconcelos y la utopía de la raza cósmica. *Cuadernos Americanos,* no. 37, Nueva época (Jan – Feb 93), pp. 23 – 36. Bibl.

Foreign economic relations

Latin America

Secchi, Carlo. Europe et Amérique Latine: Quelles relations pour les années '90? *Tiers Monde,* v. 34, no. 136 (Oct – Dec 93), pp. 781 – 806. Bibl, tables.

Foreign relations

Pereira, Antônio Carlos. As transformações na Europa e o Brasil. *Política e Estratégica,* v. 8, no. 2 – 4 (Apr – Dec 90), pp. 168 – 191.

Latin America

Klaveren, Alberto van. Europa – Lateinamerika: Zwischen Illusion und Realismus, auch nach 1992. *Zeitschrift für Lateinamerika Wien,* no. 43 (1992), pp. 95 – 119. Bibl.

EUROPE, EASTERN

See also
    Democracy – Europe, Eastern
    Hungary
    Nationalism – Europe, Eastern
    Philosophy – Europe, Eastern
    Poland
    Romania
    Soviet Union

Economic integration

Arroyo Pichardo, Graciela. Factores históricos y fuerzas mundiales en la interacción entre sistemas regionales: América Latina y Europa del Este. *Relaciones Internacionales (Mexico),* v. 14, Nueva época, no. 56 (Oct – Dec 92), pp. 19 – 29. Bibl.

Economic policy

Coatsworth, John Henry. Pax (norte) americana: América Latina después de la guerra fría (Translated by Marcela Pineda Camacho). *Revista Mexicana de Sociología,* v. 55, no. 2 (Apr – June 93), pp. 293 – 314. Bibl.

Przeworski, Adam. *Democracy and the Market: Political and Economic Reforms in Eastern Europe and Latin America* reviewed by Carlos Maya Ambía. *El Trimestre Económico,* v. 60, no. 239 (July – Sept 93), pp. 733 – 744.

Ramos, Joseph R. Reformas económicas en América Latina: lecciones para Europa oriental: comentarios a los artículos de Patricio Meller y Carmelo Mesa-Lago. *Pensamiento Iberoamericano,* no. 22 – 23, tomo II (July 92 – June 93), pp. 109 – 118.

Solimano, Andrés. Diversidad en la reforma económica: experiencias recientes en economías de mercado y economías socialistas. *Pensamiento Iberoamericano,* no. 22 – 23, tomo I (July 92 – June 93), pp. 59 – 100. Bibl, tables, charts.

Szlajfer, Henryk, ed. *Economic Nationalism in East-Central Europe and South America, 1918 – 1939* reviewed by Joseph L. Love. *Journal of Latin American Studies,* v. 25, no. 1 (Feb 93), pp. 206 – 208.

Foreign relations

Dávila Aldás, Francisco Rafael and Edgar Ortiz. Del antagonismo a la cooperación entre el Este y el Oeste para la búsqueda de un mundo más humano. *Revista Mexicana de Ciencias Políticas y Sociales,* v. 37, Nueva época, no. 149 (July – Sept 92), pp. 49 – 81.

EUROPEAN COMMUNITY

Conroy, Michael E. and Amy K. Glasmeier. Unprecedented Disparities, Unparalleled Adjustment Needs: Winners and Losers on the NAFTA "Fast Track." *Journal of Inter-American Studies and World Affairs,* v. 34, no. 4 (Winter 92 – 93), pp. 1 – 37. Bibl, tables, charts.

González, Florencia. Solución de conflictos en un sistema de integración: los casos del MERCOSUR y la CEE. *Integración Latinoamericana,* v. 17, no. 185 (Dec 92), pp. 33 – 44. Bibl.

Grabendorff, Wolf. La integración europea: consecuencias para América Latina. *Nueva Sociedad,* no. 126 (July – Aug 93), pp. 122 – 143. Bibl.

Gutiérrez, Miguel Angel, ed. *Integración: experiencia en Europa y América Latina* (Review). *Integración Latinoamericana,* v. 18, no. 193 (Sept 93), p. 75.

Linkohr, Rolf. Los procedimientos institucionales de decisión de la Comunidad Europea (Translated by Sandra Carreras). *Cuadernos del CLAEH,* v. 18, no. 65 – 66 (May 93), pp. 111 – 121.

Portocarrero Maisch, Javier. *Experiencia de la Comunidad Europea y perspectivas del Grupo Andino* (Review). *Integración Latinoamericana,* v. 18, no. 189 – 190 (May – June 93), pp. 57 – 58.

Foreign economic relations
Andean region

Grupo Andino: Decisión 329; Acuerdo Marco de Cooperación entre la Comunidad Económica Europea y el Acuerdo de Cartagena y Sus Países Miembros; Bolivia, Colombia, Ecuador, Perú, Venezuela. *Integración Latinoamericana,* v. 18, no. 189 – 190 (May – June 93), pp. 46 – 55.

Brazil

Fritsch, Winston and João Roberto Teixeira. Fatores determinantes das exportações brasileiras para a CE: uma análise prospectiva dos impactos da ampliação do espaço econômico. *Revista de Economia Política (Brazil),* v. 13, no. 3 (July – Sept 93), pp. 82 – 101. Bibl, tables, charts.

Colombia

Niño Guarín, Juan Enrique. El Plan Especial de Cooperación (P.E.C.) de la CE: balance satisfactorio pero no suficiente. *Revista Javeriana,* v. 61, no. 594 (May 93), pp. 263 – 269. Bibl, tables.

Latin America

Estay Reino, Jaime and Héctor Sotomayor, eds. *América Latina y México ante la Unión Europea de 1992* reviewed by Gilberto A. Cardoso Vargas. *Problemas del Desarrollo,* v. 24, no. 92 (Jan – Mar 93), pp. 236 – 238.

El Mercado Unico Europeo y su impacto en América Latina reviewed by A. L. R. *Comercio Exterior,* v. 43, no. 11 (Nov 93), pp. 1095 – 1096.

Trein, Franklin. A Europa '92 e a América Latina. *Política e Estratégica,* v. 8, no. 2 – 4 (Apr – Dec 90), pp. 213 – 223. Bibl, tables.

Mexico

Estay Reino, Jaime and Héctor Sotomayor, eds. *América Latina y México ante la Unión Europea de 1992* reviewed by Gilberto A. Cardoso Vargas. *Problemas del Desarrollo,* v. 24, no. 92 (Jan – Mar 93), pp. 236 – 238.

Peru

Mathews, Juan Carlos and Carlos Parodi Zevallos. El comercio exterior del Perú con la Comunidad Económica Europea. *Apuntes (Peru),* no. 31 (July – Dec 92), pp. 29 – 39. Tables.

Southern Cone of South America

Bizzozero, Lincoln J. La relación entre el MERCOSUR y la Comunidad Europa: ¿Un nuevo parametro de vinculación? *Estudios Internacionales (Chile),* v. 26, no. 101 (Jan – Mar 93), pp. 37 – 56. Bibl.

Gratius, Susanne. *El MERCOSUR y la Comunidad Europea: una guía para la investigación* (Review). *Integración Latinoamericana,* v. 18, no. 195 (Nov 93), pp. 57 – 58.

Foreign relations
Latin America

Bieber, León Enrique. Las relaciones entre la Comunidad Europea y América Latina: problemas y perspectivas. *Homines,* v. 15 – 16, no. 2 – 1 (Oct 91 – Dec 92), pp. 13 – 30. Bibl.

L'Europe et l'Amérique Latine: processus d'intégration et nouveaux rapports. *Cahiers des Amériques Latines,* no. 14 (1992), pp. 149 – 150.

EUROPEANS

America

Altman, Ida and James J. Horn. *"To Make America": European Emigration in the Early Modern Period* reviewed by Alan L. Karras. *The Americas,* v. 49, no. 3 (Jan 93), pp. 402 – 404.

— *"To Make America": European Emigration in the Early Modern Period* reviewed by Magnus Mörner. *Hispanic American Historical Review,* v. 73, no. 1 (Feb 93), pp. 130 – 132.

Caribbean area

Boucher, Philip Paul. *Cannibal Encounters: Europeans and Island Caribs, 1492 – 1763* reviewed by Irving Rouse. *Hispanic American Historical Review,* v. 73, no. 3 (Aug 93), pp. 495 – 496.

Latin America

Rodríguez Ozán, María Elena. Las ideologías de los inmigrantes europeos en América Latina. *Cuadernos Americanos,* no. 41, Nueva época (Sept – Oct 93), pp. 122 – 130. Bibl.

— La inmigración europea en Latinoamérica. *Cuadernos Americanos,* no. 37, Nueva época (Jan – Feb 93), pp. 37 – 47. Bibl.

Sources

Martínez, José Luis. *El mundo privado de los emigrantes en Indias* reviewed by Antonio Saborit (Review entitled "Cartas de llamada"). *Nexos,* v. 16, no. 184 (Apr 93), pp. 67 – 68.

— *El mundo privado de los emigrantes en Indias* reviewed by Jorge F. Hernández (Review entitled "Correspondencias con el pasado"). *Vuelta,* v. 17, no. 198 (May 93), pp. 55 – 57.

Otte, Enrique, ed. *Cartas privadas de emigrantes a Indias, 1540 – 1616* reviewed by Jorge F. Hernández (Review entitled "Correspondencias con el pasado"). *Vuelta,* v. 17, no. 198 (May 93), pp. 55 – 57.

Mexico

Gardner, David Skerritt. Colonización y modernización del campo en el centro de Veracruz, siglo XIX. *Siglo XIX: Cuadernos,* v. 2, no. 5 (Feb 93), pp. 39 – 57. Bibl, tables.

Peru

Hampe Martínez, Teodoro. Apuntes documentales sobre inmigrantes europeos y norteamericanos en Lima, siglo XIX. *Revista de Indias,* v. 53, no. 198 (May – Aug 93), pp. 459 – 491. Bibl.

Venezuela

Tosta, Virgilio. Huella y presencia de médicos europeos en el estado Barinas. *Boletín de la Academia Nacional de la Historia (Venezuela),* v. 75, no. 297 (Jan – Mar 92), pp. 69 – 95.

EVALUATION RESEARCH

See
Educational accountability

EVANGELICALISM

See also
Protestantism

America

Moreno Casamitjana, Antonio. Descubrimiento y evangelización de América. *Atenea (Chile),* no. 465 – 466 (1992), pp. 53 – 66. Bibl.

Sobrino, Jon. Relectura cristiana del quinto centenario. *ECA; Estudios Centroamericanos*, v. 47, no. 528 (Oct 92), pp. 855 – 866. Il.

Argentina

Videla, Horacio. La evangelización del Nuevo Mundo. *Investigaciones y Ensayos*, no. 41 (Jan – Dec 91), pp. 65 – 75. Bibl.

Bolivia

Ströbele-Gregor, Juliana. Las comunidades religiosas fundamentalistas en Bolivia: sobre el éxito misionero de los Adventistas del Séptimo Día. *Allpanchis*, v. 23, no. 40 (July – Dec 92), pp. 219 – 253. Bibl.

Chile

Ariztía, Fernando. La Compañía de Jesús en la nueva evangelización. *Mensaje*, v. 42, no. 420 (July 93), p. 329.

Colombia

Díaz del Castillo Z., Emiliano. La cultura en la evangelización del Nuevo Reino de Granada. *Boletín de Historia y Antigüedades*, v. 80, no. 781 (Apr – June 93), pp. 415 – 434.

Guatemala

García Ruiz, Jesús F. El misionero, las lenguas mayas y la traducción de los conceptos del catolicismo ibérico en Guatemala. *Folklore Americano*, no. 53 (Jan – June 92), pp. 103 – 131. Bibl.

Latin America

Dixon, David and Richard Dixon. Culturas e identidades populares y el surgimiento de los evangélicos en América Latina. *Cristianismo y Sociedad*, v. 30, no. 114 (1992), pp. 61 – 74. Bibl.

Robles Robles, J. Amando. La evangelización imposible. *Revista de Historia (Costa Rica)*, no. 25 (Jan – June 92), pp. 207 – 219. Bibl.

Saranyana, José Ignacio. *Teología profética americana: diez estudios sobre la evangelización fundante* reviewed by Pilar Gonzalbo Aizpuru. *Historia Mexicana*, v. 42, no. 1 (July – Sept 92), pp. 129 – 133.

Congresses

García Ahumada, Enrique. La promoción humana en la Conferencia de Santo Domingo. *Estudios Sociales (Chile)*, no. 78 (Oct – Dec 93), pp. 245 – 257.

Mexico

Bellini, Giuseppe. Il dramma del mondo azteca e i "Dodici Apostoli." *Quaderni Ibero-Americani*, no. 72 (Dec 92), pp. 640 – 648. Bibl.

Peru

Nguyen, Thai Hop, ed. *Evangelización y teología en el Perú* reviewed by Wilfredo Ardito Vega. *Amazonía Peruana*, v. 11, no. 22 (Oct 92), pp. 273 – 277.

EVOLUTION

Ayala, Francisco J. and Rosaura Ruiz Gutiérrez. Darwinismo y sociedad en México. *Siglo XIX: Revista*, no. 12, 2a época (July – Dec 92), pp. 87 – 104. Bibl.

EXCAVATIONS (ARCHAEOLOGY)

See

Archaeological site reports
Subdivision *Antiquities* under names of specific countries

EXCÉLSIOR (NEWSPAPER)

Texas Weekly: presencia de *Excélsior* en Estados Unidos. *Plural (Mexico)*, v. 22, no. 259 (Apr 93), pp. 64 – 65. Il.

EXCEPTIONAL CHILDREN

Núñez, Blanca. *El niño sordo y su familia: apontes desde la psicología clínica* reviewed by Aurora Pérez T. *La Educación (USA)*, v. 37, no. 114 (1993), pp. 166 – 167.

EXECUTIVE POWER

See also

Subdivision *Presidents* under names of specific countries

Gandolfo, Carlos. El régimen parlamentario y la estabilidad democrática. *Apuntes (Peru)*, no. 29 (July – Dec 91), pp. 17 – 25.

Guatemala

Hernández Pico, Juan. Guatemala: ¿Fructificará la democracia? *ECA; Estudios Centroamericanos*, v. 48, no. 536 (June 93), pp. 545 – 562. Il.

Mexico

Leff Zimmerman, Gloria. *Los pactos obreros y la institución presidencial en México, 1915 – 1938* reviewed by Mónica García Suárez. *El Cotidiano*, v. 9, no. 56 (July 93), p. 117.

Meyer, Lorenzo. El presidencialismo: del populismo al neoliberalismo. *Revista Mexicana de Sociología*, v. 55, no. 2 (Apr – June 93), pp. 57 – 81. Bibl.

Philip, George D. E. *The Presidency in Mexican Politics* reviewed by Roderic Ai Camp. *The Americas*, v. 49, no. 3 (Jan 93), p. 425.

Southern Cone of South America

Thibaut, Bernhard. Präsidentialismus, Parlamentarismus und das Problem der Konsolidierung der Demokratie in Lateinamerika. *Ibero-Amerikanisches Archiv*, v. 18, no. 1 – 2 (1992), pp. 107 – 150. Bibl.

— Presidencialismo, parlamentarismo y el problema de la consolidación democrática en América Latina. *Estudios Internacionales (Chile)*, v. 26, no. 102 (Apr – June 93), pp. 216 – 252. Bibl.

Uruguay

Caetano, Gerardo, ed. *La alternativa parlamentarista* reviewed by Carlos Filgueira. *Cuadernos del CLAEH*, v. 18, no. 67 (Nov 93), pp. 135 – 140.

Lanzaro, Jorge Luis. La "doble transición" en el Uruguay: gobierno de partidos y neo-presidencialismo. *Nueva Sociedad*, no. 128 (Nov – Dec 93), pp. 132 – 147.

EXILES

Argentina

Battista, Vicente. El difícil arte de volver. *Cuadernos Hispanoamericanos*, no. 517 – 519 (July – Sept 93), pp. 560 – 562.

Cortázar, Julio and Liliana Heker. Polémica sobre el exilio (Debate between Julio Cortázar and Liliana Heker on the subject of exiles). *Cuadernos Hispanoamericanos*, no. 517 – 519 (July – Sept 93), pp. 590 – 604.

Grande, Félix. Con octubre en los hombros. *Cuadernos Hispanoamericanos*, no. 517 – 519 (July – Sept 93), pp. 562 – 568.

Liberman, Arnoldo. Rememoración del exilio. *Cuadernos Hispanoamericanos*, no. 517 – 519 (July – Sept 93), pp. 544 – 552.

Martini, Juan Carlos. Naturaleza del exilio. *Cuadernos Hispanoamericanos*, no. 517 – 519 (July – Sept 93), pp. 552 – 555.

Salas, Horacio. Duro oficio el exilio. *Cuadernos Hispanoamericanos*, no. 517 – 519 (July – Sept 93), pp. 555 – 559.

Austria

Furtado Kestler, Izabela María. Stefan Zweig, Brasil e o holocausto. *Estudios Interdisciplinarios de América Latina y el Caribe*, v. 3, no. 2 (July – Dec 92), pp. 123 – 126. Bibl.

Cuba

Cuadra, Angel. El tema de lo cubano en el escritor exiliado. *Plural (Mexico)*, v. 22, no. 262 (July 93), pp. 32 – 39.

Europe

Senkman, Leonardo. *Argentina, la segunda guerra mundial y los refugiados indeseables, 1933 – 1945* reviewed by Hebe Clementi. *Todo Es Historia*, v. 27, no. 316 (Nov 93), pp. 88 – 89. Il.

Italy

Fanesi, Pietro Rinaldo. El exilio antifascista en América Latina: el caso mexicano; Mario Montagnana y la "Garibaldi," 1941 – 1945. *Estudios Interdisciplinarios de América Latina y el Caribe*, v. 3, no. 2 (July – Dec 92), pp. 39 – 57. Bibl.

Latin America

Alegría, Fernando and Jorge Ruffinelli, eds. *Paradise Lost or Gained?: The Literature of Hispanic Exile* reviewed by Barbara Mujica (Review entitled "The Creative Subtext of Life"). *Américas*, v. 45, no. 3 (May – June 93), pp. 60 – 61.

— *Paradise Lost or Gained?: The Literature of Hispanic Exile* reviewed by Joseph F. Vélez. *Hispania (USA),* v. 76, no. 1 (Mar 93), pp. 80 – 82.

Schumm, Petra. *Exilerfahrung und Literatur: Lateinamerikanische Autoren in Spanien* reviewed by Monika Wehrheim-Peuker. *Iberoamericana,* v. 16, no. 47 – 48 (1992), pp. 135 – 137.

Mexico

Tello Díaz, Carlos. *El exilio: un relato de familia* reviewed by Adolfo Castañón. *Vuelta,* v. 17, no. 204 (Nov 93), pp. 36 – 38.

Southern Cone of South America

Bolzman, Claudio. Los exiliados del Cono Sur: dos décadas más tarde. *Nueva Sociedad,* no. 127 (Sept – Oct 93), pp. 126 – 135. Bibl.

Spain

Bascuñán, Carlos and Sol Serrano. La idea de América en los exiliados españoles en Chile (Excerpt from *El pensamiento español contemporáneo y la idea de América* edited by José Luis Abellán and Antonio Monclús Estella). *Atenea (Chile),* no. 465 – 466 (1992), pp. 99 – 149. Bibl, tables.

Camprubí de Jiménez, Zenobia. *Diario, 1: Cuba, 1937 – 1939* introduced and translated by Graciela Palau de Nemes. Reviewed by Aleksandra Hadzelek. *Revista Iberoamericana,* v. 59, no. 162 – 163 (Jan – June 93), pp. 385 – 387.

Naharro-Calderón, José María, ed. *El exilio de las Españas de 1939 en las Américas: "¿Adónde fue la canción?"* reviewed by Nancy Vosburg. *Hispania (USA),* v. 76, no. 2 (May 93), pp. 277 – 278.

EXISTENTIALISM

Pérez Leyva, Leonardo. Algunas consideraciones sobre la filosofía existencialista de Ernesto Mayz Vallenilla. *Islas,* no. 96 (May – Aug 90), pp. 27 – 33.

Silva, Carlos da. A narrativa como expressão e conhecimento do ser: *Insônia* de Graciliano Ramos. *Revista de Letras (Brazil),* v. 32 (1992), pp. 51 – 67. Bibl.

EXPERIMENTAL THEATER

Chile

Piga T., Domingo. Homenaje al medio siglo de TEUCH. *Latin American Theatre Review,* v. 26, no. 2 (Spring 93), pp. 197 – 198.

Colombia

Cajamarca Castro, Orlando. Esquina Latina: dos décadas de teatro. *Latin American Theatre Review,* v. 26, no. 2 (Spring 93), pp. 167 – 170.

Gutiérrez, Natalia. *El hilo de Ariadna:* laberinto de oscuridad (Accompanied by an English translation). *Art Nexus,* no. 8 (Apr – June 93), pp. 102 – 104. Il.

Cuba

Hernández, Esther María. Machurrucutu en seis tiempos: crónica de septiembre. *Conjunto,* no. 90 – 91 (Jan – June 92), pp. 79 – 84. Il.

Herrero, Ramiro. Machurrucutu. *Conjunto,* no. 90 – 91 (Jan – June 92), pp. 85 – 91. Il.

EXPLORERS

See
  Scientific expeditions
  Names of specific explorers
  Subdivision *Discovery and exploration* under names of specific countries and regions

EXPORTS AND IMPORTS

See
  Balance of payments
  Foreign exchange problem
  Foreign trade promotion
  Foreign trade regulation
  International economic relations
  Tariff
  Subdivisions *Commerce* and *Foreign economic relations* under names of specific countries

EYZAGUIRRE Y ARECHAVALA, MIGUEL DE

Chassin, Joëlle. Protecteur d'indiens contre vice-roi: la lutte de Miguel de Eyzaguirre pour l'abolition du tribut au Pérou. *Cahiers des Amériques Latines,* no. 13 (1992), pp. 61 – 74. Bibl.

FALKLAND ISLANDS

Altamirano Toledo, Carlos. Lecciones de una guerra. *Cuadernos Hispanoamericanos,* no. 517 – 519 (July – Sept 93), pp. 586 – 590.

Ballester, Horacio P. Proyecciones geopolíticas hacia el tercer milenio: el dramático futuro latinoamericano caribeño (A chapter from Horacio P. Ballester's book of the same title, introduced by Fermín Chávez). *Realidad Económica,* no. 116 (May – June 93), pp. 137 – 141.

Moreno Alonso, Manuel. Las cosas de España y la política americana de Carlos III en Inglaterra. *Hoy Es Historia,* v. 9, no. 54 (Nov – Dec 92), pp. 44 – 59. Il.

FALLA, RICARDO

Criticism of specific works

Masacre de la selva

Vinos derramados: el libro de Ricardo Falla sobre los masacres de Ixcán, Guatemala. *ECA; Estudios Centroamericanos,* v. 47, no. 529 – 530 (Nov – Dec 92), pp. 1037 – 1044. Il.

FALLAS, CARLOS LUIS

Criticism of specific works

Mamita Yunai

Ortiz O., María Salvadora. *Mamita Yunai:* novela de la plantación bananera. *Káñina,* v. 16, no. 1 (Jan – June 92), pp. 9 – 17. Bibl.

FAMILY

See also
  Child abuse
  Divorce
  Kinship
  Marriage
  Parent and child
  Population
  Women
  Subdivision *Kinship* under names of Indian groups

Reyes, Carmen et al. Matrimonios: la ardua búsqueda de felicidad; debates (Introduced by G. Arroyo). *Mensaje,* v. 42, no. 425 (Dec 93), pp. 629 – 636.

Brazil

Borges, Dain Edward. *The Family in Bahia, Brazil, 1870 – 1945* reviewed by Sandra Lauderdale Graham. *Journal of Latin American Studies,* v. 25, no. 2 (May 93), pp. 399 – 401.

— *The Family in Bahia, Brazil, 1870 – 1945* reviewed by Robert M. Levine. *Luso-Brazilian Review,* v. 30, no. 1 (Summer 93), pp. 146 – 147.

Metcalf, Alida C. *Family and Frontier in Colonial Brazil: Santana de Paranaíba, 1580 – 1822* reviewed by Susan Migden Socolow. *The Americas,* v. 50, no. 2 (Oct 93), pp. 279 – 280.

Nazzari, Muriel. *Disappearance of the Dowry: Women, Families, and Social Change in São Paulo, Brazil, 1600 – 1900* reviewed by Susan M. Socolow. *The Americas,* v. 49, no. 3 (Jan 93), pp. 414 – 415.

— *Disappearance of the Dowry: Women, Families, and Social Change in São Paulo, Brazil, 1600 – 1900* reviewed by John E. Kicza. *Colonial Latin American Review,* v. 2, no. 1 – 2 (1993), pp. 308 – 311.

— *Disappearance of the Dowry: Women, Families, and Social Change in São Paulo, Brazil, 1600 – 1900* reviewed by Sandra Lauderdale Graham. *Journal of Latin American Studies,* v. 25, no. 1 (Feb 93), pp. 193 – 194.

— *Disappearance of the Dowry: Women, Families, and Social Change in São Paulo, Brazil, 1600 – 1900* reviewed by Dain Borges. *Luso-Brazilian Review,* v. 30, no. 1 (Summer 93), pp. 141 – 142.

Ramos, Donald. From Minho to Minas: The Portuguese Roots of the Mineiro Family. *Hispanic American Historical Review,* v. 73, no. 4 (Nov 93), pp. 639 – 662. Bibl, tables.

Bibliography

Kuznesof, Elizabeth Anne. Sexuality, Gender, and the Family in Colonial Brazil (Review article). *Luso-Brazilian Review,* v. 30, no. 1 (Summer 93), pp. 119 – 132. Bibl.

Statistics

Oliveira, Maria Coleta F. A. de. Condición femenina y alternativas de organización doméstica: las mujeres sin pareja en São Paulo. *Estudios Demográficos y Urbanos,* v. 7, no. 2 – 3 (May – Dec 92), pp. 511 – 537. Bibl, tables, charts.

Chile .

Bilbao, María Josefina. La familia chilena hoy: ¿A qué conclusiones llegó la Comisión Nacional de la Familia? *Mensaje,* v. 42, no. 425 (Dec 93), pp. 626 – 628. Il, tables.

Edwards, Marta. Percepción de la familia y de la formación de los hijos. *Estudios Públicos (Chile),* no. 52 (Spring 93), pp. 191 – 214. Tables, charts.

Irarrázaval Llona, Ignacio and Juan Pablo Valenzuela. La ilegitimidad en Chile: ¿Hacia un cambio en la conformación de la familia? *Estudios Públicos (Chile),* no. 52 (Spring 93), pp. 145 – 190. Bibl, tables, charts.

Costa Rica

Amador Debernardi, Rocío and Laura González Hernández. Características de las familias y de los niños trabajadores de la calle. *Revista de Ciencias Sociales (Costa Rica),* no. 59 (Mar 93), pp. 19 – 26. Bibl, tables, charts.

Rodríguez Sáenz, Eugenia. Historia de la familia en América Latina: balance de las principales tendencias. *Revista de Historia (Costa Rica),* no. 26 (July – Dec 92), pp. 145 – 183. Bibl.

Cuba

Statistics

Benítez Pérez, María Elena. La familia cubana: principales rasgos sociodemográficos que han caracterizado su desarrollo y dinámica. *Estudios Demográficos y Urbanos,* v. 7, no. 2 – 3 (May – Dec 92), pp. 479 – 492. Bibl, tables.

Latin America

Gonzalbo Aizpuru, Pilar, ed. *Familias novohispanas, siglos XVI al XIX* reviewed by María Luisa Pérez-González. *Colonial Latin American Historical Review,* v. 2, no. 4 (Fall 93), pp. 479 – 480.

Linares Pontón, María Eugenia, ed. *Del hecho al dicho hay menos trecho: ¿Qué hemos aprendido en los programas de apoyo a la familia para la crianza de los niños?* reviewed by María Bertha Fortoul O. *Revista Latinoamericana de Estudios Educativos,* v. 23, no. 1 (Jan – Mar 93), pp. 134 – 138. Il.

Núñez Sánchez, Jorge, ed. *Historia de la mujer y la familia* reviewed by Gilma Mora de Tovar. *Anuario Colombiano de Historia Social y de la Cultura,* no. 20 (1992), pp. 164 – 167.

Rodríguez Sáenz, Eugenia. Historia de la familia en América Latina: balance de las principales tendencias. *Revista de Historia (Costa Rica),* no. 26 (July – Dec 92), pp. 145 – 183. Bibl.

Bibliography

Arrom, Silvia Marina. Historia de la mujer y de la familia latinoamericanas. *Historia Mexicana,* v. 42, no. 2 (Oct – Dec 92), pp. 379 – 418.

Mexico

García González, Francisco. Los muros de la vida privada y la familia: casa y tamaño familiar en Zacatecas; primeras décadas del siglo XIX. *Estudios Demográficos y Urbanos,* v. 7, no. 1 (Jan – Apr 92), pp. 35 – 52. Bibl, tables.

Gonzalbo Aizpuru, Pilar. "La familia" y las familias en el México colonial. *Estudios Sociológicos,* v. 10, no. 30 (Sept – Dec 92), pp. 693 – 711. Bibl.

Myers, Kathleen Ann. A Glimpse of Family Life in Colonial Mexico: A Nun's Account. *Latin American Research Review,* v. 28, no. 2 (1993), pp. 63 – 87. Bibl, il.

Tuirán Gutiérrez, Rodolfo A. Vivir en familias: hogares y estructura familiar en México, 1976 – 1987. *Comercio Exterior,* v. 43, no. 7 (July 93), pp. 662 – 676. Bibl, tables, charts.

Statistics

Levine, Ruth E. and Rebeca Wong. Estructura del hogar como respuesta a los ajustes económicos: evidencia del México urbano de los ochenta. *Estudios Demográficos y Urbanos,* v. 7, no. 2 – 3 (May – Dec 92), pp. 493 – 509. Bibl, tables, charts.

Panama

Coriat R., Carola and Mario de Obaldía A. La influencia de la abuela en la percepción familiar del niño bajo su cuidado. *Revista Cultural Lotería,* v. 50, no. 383 (May – June 91), pp. 74 – 93. Bibl, tables.

United States

Flores-Ortiz, Yvette G. Levels of Acculturation, Marital Satisfaction, and Depression among Chicana Workers: A Psychological Perspective. *Aztlán,* v. 20, no. 1 – 2 (Spring – Fall 91), pp. 151 – 175. Bibl, tables.

Segura, Denise Anne. Ambivalence or Continuity?: Motherhood and Employment among Chicanas and Mexican Immigrant Women Workers. *Aztlán,* v. 20, no. 1 – 2 (Spring – Fall 91), pp. 119 – 150. Bibl, charts.

Venezuela

Fuentes Bajo, María Dolores. Amor y desamor en la Venezuela hispánica: Caracas, 1701 – 1791. *Boletín de la Academia Nacional de la Historia (Venezuela),* v. 75, no. 298 (Apr – June 92), pp. 49 – 62. Bibl.

FANTASTIC LITERATURE

See also
Magical realism (Literature)
Surrealism

Dezotti, Maria Celeste Consolin, ed. *A tradição da fábula* reviewed by João Décio. *Revista de Letras (Brazil),* v. 32 (1992), pp. 268 – 270.

Elbanowski, Adam. El espacio y lo fantástico en la cuentística de Cortázar. *La Palabra y el Hombre,* no. 81 (Jan – Mar 92), pp. 273 – 278. Bibl.

Garabedian, Martha Ann. Visión fantástica de la muerte en algunos poemas de Oscar Hahn. *Revista Chilena de Literatura,* no. 41 (Apr 93), pp. 71 – 78. Bibl.

Isava, Luis Miguel. La escritura, la lectura, lo fantástico: análisis de "Continuidad de los parques" de Julio Cortázar. *Revista Nacional de Cultura (Venezuela),* v. 54, no. 287 (Oct – Dec 92), pp. 72 – 82. Bibl, il.

Neghme Echeverría, Lidia. Lo fantástico y algunos datos intertextuales en *Poema de Chile* de Gabriela Mistral. *Revista Interamericana de Bibliografía,* v. 42, no. 2 (1992), pp. 241 – 250. Bibl.

Rodríguez-Luis, Julio. *The Contemporary Praxis of the Fantastic: Borges and Cortázar* reviewed by John Incledon. *Hispania (USA),* v. 76, no. 1 (Mar 93), p. 89.

— *The Contemporary Praxis of the Fantastic: Borges and Cortázar* reviewed by John Incledon. *Revista de Crítica Literaria Latinoamericana,* v. 19, no. 38 (July – Dec 93), pp. 403 – 404.

Terrón de Bellomo, Herminia. Literatura fantástica y denuncia social: Juana Manuela Gorriti. *Letras Femeninas,* v. 19, no. 1 – 2 (Spring – Fall 93), pp. 113 – 116. Bibl.

FARMERS

See
Agricultural laborers
Agriculture
Peasantry

FASCISM

Argentina

Newton, Ronald C. *The "Nazi Menace" in Argentina, 1931 – 1947* reviewed by Joel Horowitz. *The Americas,* v. 50, no. 1 (July 93), pp. 140 – 141.

— *The "Nazi Menace" in Argentina, 1931 – 1947* reviewed by Walter Little. *Bulletin of Latin American Research,* v. 12, no. 1 (Jan 93), pp. 117 – 118.

— *The "Nazi Menace" in Argentina, 1931 – 1947* reviewed by Jeff Lesser. *European Review of Latin American and Caribbean Studies,* no. 54 (June 93), pp. 136 – 137.

— *The "Nazi Menace" in Argentina, 1931 – 1947* reviewed by Stanley E. Hilton. *Hispanic American Historical Review,* v. 73, no. 4 (Nov 93), pp. 706 – 707.

— *The "Nazi Menace" in Argentina, 1931 – 1947* reviewed by Celia Szusterman. *Journal of Latin American Studies,* v. 25, no. 1 (Feb 93), pp. 202 – 205.

— *The "Nazi Menace" in Argentina, 1931 – 1947* reviewed by Mario Rapoport. *Revista Interamericana de Bibliografía,* v. 42, no. 4 (1992), pp. 659 – 660.

Brazil

Lopez, Luiz Roberto. Neonazismo, estilo tropical. *Vozes,* v. 87, no. 1 (Jan – Feb 93), pp. 97 – 101.

FEBRES CORDERO, ELOY
Obituaries

Rojas Gil, Rogelio. Eloy Febres Cordero. *Boletín de la Academia Nacional de la Historia (Venezuela),* v. 76, no. 302 (Apr – June 93), pp. 144 – 145.

FEDERALISM
See
   Decentralization in government

FEDERATION OF THE WEST INDIES

Hart, Richard. Federation: An Ill-Fated Design. *Jamaica Journal,* v. 25, no. 1 (Oct 93), pp. 10 – 16. Bibl, il.

FEM (PERIODICAL)

López García, Guadalupe. *Fem* y sus colaboradoras. *Fem,* v. 17, no. 119 (Jan 93), p. 26. Il.

FEMINISM
See
   Sex role
   Sex role in literature
   Women in literature
   Women's rights

FERNÁNDEZ, EMILIO

Tuñón Pablos, Julia. Between the Nation and Utopia: The Image of Mexico in the Films of Emilio "Indio" Fernández. *Studies in Latin American Popular Culture,* v. 12 (1993), pp. 159 – 174. Bibl.

FERNÁNDEZ, ROBERTA
Criticism of specific works
Intaglio

Gómez-Vega, Ibis. La mujer como artista en *Intaglio. Bilingual Review/Revista Bilingüe,* v. 18, no. 1 (Jan – Apr 93), pp. 14 – 22. Bibl.

FERNÁNDEZ, ROBERTO G.
Criticism of specific works
La montaña rusa

Febles, Jorge M. En torno al personaje degradado en *La montaña rusa:* vigencia del doble paródico dentro de un espacio carnavalesco. *The Americas Review,* v. 19, no. 3 – 4 (Winter 91), pp. 101 – 115. Bibl.

Raining Backwards

Deaver, William O., Jr. *Raining Backwards:* Colonization and the Death of a Culture. *The Americas Review,* v. 21, no. 1 (Spring 93), pp. 112 – 118.

FERNÁNDEZ, SEVERIANO
Interviews

Pailler, Claire. Severiano Fernández, pueblo bribrí: "el rescate de ser indígena"; entretien réalisé le 16 avril 1992 à San José, par Claire Pailler. *Caravelle,* no. 59 (1992), pp. 49 – 58.

FERNÁNDEZ DE LEÓN, ESTEBAN

Andreo García, Juan. *La Intendencia en Venezuela: don Esteban Fernández de León, intendente de Caracas, 1791 – 1803* reviewed by Jean-Christian Tulet. *Caravelle,* no. 59 (1992), pp. 307 – 308.

FERNÁNDEZ DE LIZARDI, JOSÉ JOAQUÍN
Criticism and interpretation

Meyer-Minnemann, Klaus. Apropiaciones de realidad en las novelas de José Joaquín Fernández de Lizardi. *Iberoamericana,* v. 17, no. 50 (1993), pp. 63 – 78. Bibl.

FERNÁNDEZ DE OVIEDO Y VALDÉS, GONZALO
See
   Oviedo y Valdés, Gonzalo Fernández de

FERNÁNDEZ FONT, MARCELO

Halperin, Maurice. Return to Havana: Portrait of a Loyalist. *Cuban Studies/Estudios Cubanos,* v. 23 (1993), pp. 187 – 193.

FERNÁNDEZ RETAMAR, ROBERTO
Correspondence, reminiscences, etc.

Althusser, Louis. Louis Althusser: ante la muerte de Ernesto Che Guevara. *Casa de las Américas,* no. 190 (Jan – Mar 93), pp. 59 – 64.

Criticism of specific works
Calibán

Fernández Retamar, Roberto. Adiós a Calibán. *Casa de las Américas,* no. 191 (Apr – June 93), pp. 116 – 122. Bibl.

FERRÉ, ROSARIO
Bibliography

Cook, Jacqueline. Bibliography on Rosario Ferré. *Chasqui,* v. 22, no. 2 (Nov 93), pp. 129 – 149.

Criticism and interpretation

Cragnolino, Aída Apter. De sitios y asedios: la escritura de Rosario Ferré. *Revista Chilena de Literatura,* no. 42 (Aug 93), pp. 25 – 30. Bibl.

Roses, Lorraine Elena. Las esperanzas de Pandora: prototipos femeninos de la obra de Rosario Ferré. *Revista Iberoamericana,* v. 59, no. 162 – 163 (Jan – June 93), pp. 279 – 287.

FERREIRA, VERGÍLIO
Criticism of specific works
O fantasma

Iannone, Carlos Alberto. Variações sobre um conto de Vergílio Ferreira. *Revista de Letras (Brazil),* v. 32 (1992), pp. 185 – 189.

FERRETO, ADELA
Criticism of specific works
Las palabras perdidas y otros cuentos

Vásquez, Magdalena. Adela Ferreto: un sujeto histórico particular en una época de transición. *Káñina,* v. 16, no. 1 (Jan – June 92), pp. 37 – 49. Bibl.

FERRUFINO COQUEUGNIOT, CLAUDIO
Correspondence, reminiscences, etc.

Ferrufino Coqueugniot, Claudio. Apuntes para dos soledades. *Signo,* no. 36 – 37, Nueva época (May – Dec 92), pp. 13 – 22.

FERTILITY, HUMAN
See also
   Birth control

Peláez, Jorge Humberto. El invitado del mes: interrogantes éticos de la reproducción asistida. *Revista Javeriana,* v. 61, no. 595 (June 93), pp. 337 – 344. Il.

Brazil

Avila, Maria Betânia. Modernidade e cidadania reprodutiva. *Estudos Feministas,* v. 1, no. 2 (1993), pp. 382 – 393.

Ecuador
Statistics

Juárez, Fátima. Intervención de las instituciones en la reducción de la fecundidad y la mortalidad infantil. *Estudios Demográficos y Urbanos,* v. 7, no. 2 – 3 (May – Dec 92), pp. 377 – 405. Bibl, tables, charts.

Latin America

Azeredo, Sandra and Verena Stolcke, eds. *Direitos reproductivos* (Review). *Estudos Feministas,* v. 0, no. 0 (1992), p. 230.

Mexico

Suárez López, Leticia. Trayectorias laborales y reproductivas: una comparación entre México y España. *Estudios Demográficos y Urbanos,* v. 7, no. 2 – 3 (May – Dec 92), pp. 359 – 375. Bibl, tables, charts.

Statistics

Gómez de León, José and Virgilio Partida Bush. Niveles de mortalidad infantil y fecundidad en México, por entidad federativa, 1990. *Revista Mexicana de Sociología,* v. 55, no. 1 (Jan – Mar 93), pp. 97 – 135. Bibl, tables, charts.

Mier y Terán, Marta and Cecilia Andrea Rabell Romero. Inicio de la transición de la fecundidad en México: descendencias de mujeres nacidas en la primera mitad del siglo XX. *Revista Mexicana de Sociología,* v. 55, no. 1 (Jan – Mar 93), pp. 41 – 81. Bibl, tables, charts.

Zúñiga Herrera, Elena. Cambios en el nivel de fecundidad deseada en las mujeres mexicanas, 1976 – 1986. *Revista Mexicana de Sociología,* v. 55, no. 1 (Jan – Mar 93), pp. 83 – 96. Bibl, tables, charts.

Peru

Statistics

Fort, Alfredo L. Fecundidad y comportamiento reproductivo en la sierra y selva del Perú. *Estudios Demográficos y Urbanos,* v. 7, no. 2 – 3 (May – Dec 92), pp. 327 – 357. Bibl, tables, maps, charts.

Spain

Suárez López, Leticia. Trayectorias laborales y reproductivas: una comparación entre México y España. *Estudios Demográficos y Urbanos,* v. 7, no. 2 – 3 (May – Dec 92), pp. 359 – 375. Bibl, tables, charts.

FERTILIZER INDUSTRY

Costa Rica

Government ownership

Muñoz García, Ileana and Claudio Antonio Vargas Arias. La producción de fertilizantes en Costa Rica y el modelo estatal costarricense: el caso Fertica. *Anuario de Estudios Centroamericanos,* v. 18, no. 1 (1992), pp. 61 – 83. Bibl, tables, charts.

FESTIVALS

See
Drama festivals
Folk festivals
Subdivision *Festivals* under *Motion pictures* and *Music*

FICTION

See also
Creation (Literary, artistic, etc.)

Compitello, Malcolm Alan. Reflexiones sobre el acto de narrar: Benet, Vargas Llosa y Euclides da Cunha. *Insula,* no. 559 – 560 (July – Aug 93), pp. 19 – 22.

Costa, Marithelma and Adelaida López. *Las dos caras de la escritura* reviewed by Gustavo Fares. *Revista Iberoamericana,* v. 59, no. 162 – 163 (Jan – June 93), pp. 380 – 382.

Vallejo, Catharina Vanderplaats de. *Teoría cuentística del siglo XX* reviewed by Marisa Bortolussi. *Revista Canadiense de Estudios Hispánicos,* v. 17, no. 1 (Fall 92), pp. 228 – 229.

FIELDS, THOMAS

McGeagh, Robert. Thomas Fields and the Precursor of the Guaraní "Reducciones." *Colonial Latin American Historical Review,* v. 2, no. 1 (Winter 93), pp. 35 – 55. Bibl.

FIGUEIREDO, JACKSON DE

Carvalho, José Geraldo Vidigal de. Atualidade de Jackson de Figueiredo. *Convivium,* v. 34, no. 2 (July – Dec 91), pp. 150 – 153.

Rios, José Arthur. Jackson de Figueiredo: perfil e formação de um pensador. *Revista do Instituto Histórico e Geográfico Brasileiro,* no. 373 (Oct – Dec 91), pp. 1085 – 1106. Bibl.

FIGUEROA, MARÍA EUGENIA

Interviews

Ramírez, Fermín. María Eugenia Figueroa, pintora de luz y tierra (Includes reproductions of her paintings). *Plural (Mexico),* v. 22, no. 267 (Dec 93), pp. 41 – 48. Il.

FILM REVIEWS

Amelia Lopes O'Neill

Amelia Lopes O'Neill reviewed by Filma Canales. *Mensaje,* v. 42, no. 423 (Oct 93), pp. 528 – 529.

El bulto

El bulto reviewed by Fabrizo Prada (Review entitled *"El bulto: la historia ineludible").* *Plural (Mexico),* v. 22, no. 257 (Feb 93), pp. 76 – 77.

El mariachi

Rodríguez, Robert. *El mariachi* reviewed by Terrence Rafferty (Review entitled "Una guitarra sin nombre," translated by Katia Rheault). *Nexos,* v. 16, no. 184 (Apr 93), pp. 77 – 79.

Palomita blanca

Palomita blanca reviewed by Filma Canales. *Mensaje,* v. 42, no. 416 (Jan – Feb 93), p. 51.

El viaje

El viaje reviewed by Hans Günther Pflaum (Review entitled "La película *El viaje* de Fernando E. Solanas," review translated by José Luis Gómez y Patiño). *Humboldt,* no. 109 (1993), p. 98. Il.

FILMS

See
Motion pictures

FINANCE

See also
Balance of payments
Banks and banking
Capital
Capital investments
Capital productivity
Capitalists and financiers
Credit
Currency question
Debts, Public
Economics
Foreign exchange problem
Inflation (Finance)
Interest rates
International economic relations
International finance
Investments, Foreign
Money and money supply
National income
Prices
Saving and investment
Stock exchange
Tariff
Taxation
Subdivision *Finance* under *Education* and *Education, Higher*
Subdivisions *Commerce* and *Industries* under names of specific countries

Argentina

García, Alfredo T. Las transformaciones del sector financiero en los últimos diez años. *Realidad Económica,* no. 120 (Nov – Dec 93), pp. 41 – 60. Tables, charts.

Brazil

Lees, Francis A. et al. *Banking and Financial Deepening in Brazil* reviewed by Arnold W. Sametz. *Economic Development and Cultural Change,* v. 41, no. 3 (Apr 93), pp. 686 – 690.

Welch, John H. *Capital Markets in the Development Process: The Case of Brazil* reviewed by David E. Hojman. *Bulletin of Latin American Research,* v. 12, no. 3 (Sept 93), pp. 350 – 351.

— *Capital Markets in the Development Process: The Case of Brazil* reviewed by Tomás Bruginski de Paula. *Journal of Latin American Studies,* v. 25, no. 3 (Oct 93), pp. 677 – 678.

Chile

Hernández T., Leonardo and Eduardo Walker H. Estructura de financiamiento corporativo en Chile, 1978 – 1990: evidencia a partir de datos contables. *Estudios Públicos (Chile)*, no. 51 (Winter 93), pp. 87 – 156. Bibl, tables, charts.

Latin America

Correa Vázquez, Eugenia. *Los mercados financieros y la crisis en América Latina* reviewed by Rafael Bouchain Galicia. *Problemas del Desarrollo*, v. 24, no. 93 (Apr – June 93), pp. 236 – 239.

Welch, John H. The New Face of Latin America: Financial Flows, Markets, and Institutions in the 1990s. *Journal of Latin American Studies*, v. 25, no. 1 (Feb 93), pp. 1 – 24. Bibl, tables.

FINANCE, PUBLIC

See also
Balance of payments
Banks and banking
Debts, Public
Foreign exchange problem
International finance
National income
Price regulation
Taxation

Argentina

Tolosa, Fernando. El sistema financiero, el financiamiento del desarrollo y la reforma previsional. *Realidad Económica*, no. 113 (Jan – Feb 93), pp. 13 – 17.

Bolivia

Gallo, Carmenza. *Taxes and State Power: Political Instability in Bolivia, 1900 – 1950* reviewed by Eduardo A. Gamarra. *Hispanic American Historical Review*, v. 73, no. 3 (Aug 93), pp. 523 – 526.

Gierhake, Klaus-Ulrich. La inversión pública como instrumento de evaluación del proceso de planificación regional en Bolivia, 1987 – 1990. *Revista Interamericana de Planificación*, v. 26, no. 101 – 102 (Jan – June 93), pp. 112 – 128. Bibl, tables, maps, charts.

Brazil

Barbosa, Fernando de Holanda. A indexação dos ativos financeiros: a experiência brasileira. *Revista Brasileira de Economia*, v. 47, no. 3 (July – Sept 93), pp. 373 – 397. Bibl, tables, charts.

Giambiagi, Fábio and Alvaro Antônio Zini Júnior. Renegociação da dívida interna mobiliária: uma proposta. *Revista de Economia Política (Brazil)*, v. 13, no. 2 (Apr – June 93), pp. 5 – 27. Bibl, tables, charts.

Melchior, José Carlos de Araújo. Financiamento da educação: gestão democrática dos recursos financeiros públicos em educação. *Revista Brasileira de Estudos Pedagógicos*, v. 72, no. 172 (Sept – Dec 91), pp. 262 – 290. Bibl.

Rocha, Carlos Henrique. Sobre a reforma fiscal. *Revista de Economia Política (Brazil)*, v. 13, no. 2 (Apr – June 93), pp. 144 – 145.

Villela, Luis. Sistema tributario y relaciones financieras intergubernamentales: la experiencia brasileña. *Planeación y Desarrollo*, v. 24, no. 1 (Jan – Apr 93), pp. 171 – 188. Tables.

Law and legislation

Cysne, Rubens Penha. Reforma financeira: aspectos gerais e análise do projeto de lei complementar. *Revista de Economia Política (Brazil)*, v. 13, no. 3 (July – Sept 93), pp. 21 – 40. Bibl.

Serra, José. As vicissitudes do orçamento. *Revista de Economia Política (Brazil)*, v. 13, no. 4 (Oct – Dec 93), pp. 143 – 149.

Mathematical models

Giambiagi, Fábio. Financiamento do governo através de senhoriagem em condições de equilíbrio: algumas simulações. *Revista Brasileira de Economia*, v. 47, no. 2 (Apr – June 93), pp. 265 – 279. Bibl, tables.

Caribbean area

Theodore, Karl. Privatization: Conditions for Success and Fiscal Policy Implications. *Social and Economic Studies*, v. 41, no. 4 (Dec 92), pp. 133 – 148. Bibl.

Chile

Letelier S., Leonardo. La teoría del federalismo fiscal y su relevancia en el caso municipal chileno. *Cuadernos de Economía (Chile)*, v. 30, no. 90 (Aug 93), pp. 199 – 224. Bibl, tables.

Mathematical models

Cifuentes, María Cecilia. Impacto fiscal de la privatización en Chile, 1985 – 1990. *Estudios Públicos (Chile)*, no. 51 (Winter 93), pp. 157 – 193. Bibl.

Colombia

Gaviria Trujillo, César. La política y la crisis fiscal (Previously published in this journal, no. 508, 1984). *Revista Javeriana*, v. 61, no. 596 (July 93), pp. 111 – 113.

Perfetti, Mauricio. Algunas precisiones en cuanto a la reforma de la seguridad social. *Revista Javeriana*, v. 61, no. 592 (Mar 93), pp. 102 – 100. Bibl, tables.

Vargas, César et al. Financiamiento del desarrollo regional: situación actual y perspectivas. *Planeación y Desarrollo*, v. 24, no. 1 (Jan – Apr 93), pp. 311 – 346. Tables, charts.

Wiesner Durán, Eduardo. *Colombia: descentralización y federalismo fiscal* reviewed by César Vargas. *Planeación y Desarrollo*, v. 24, no. 1 (Jan – Apr 93), pp. 465 – 471.

Law and legislation

García Hurtado, Jorge. La acción de la Veeduría del Tesoro. *Revista Javeriana*, v. 61, no. 598 (Sept 93), pp. 259 – 268.

Ecuador

Jara, Alvaro and John Jay TePaske. *The Royal Treasuries of the Spanish Empire in America, Vol. IV: Eighteenth-Century Ecuador* reviewed by Franklin Pease G. Y. *Colonial Latin American Review*, v. 2, no. 1 – 2 (1993), pp. 311 – 312.

Latin America

Larraín B., Felipe and Marcelo Selowsky, eds. *The Public Sector and the Latin American Crisis* reviewed by Christian Anglade. *Journal of Latin American Studies*, v. 25, no. 2 (May 93), pp. 404 – 405.

Mexico

Astudillo Moya, Marcela. La política fiscal en el IV Informe de Gobierno. *Momento Económico*, no. 65 (Jan – Feb 93), pp. 16 – 19. Tables.

Astudillo Moya, Marcela and Alejandro Méndez Rodríguez. Planes urbanos sin descentralización financiera en México. *Problemas del Desarrollo*, v. 24, no. 93 (Apr – June 93), pp. 153 – 174. Bibl, tables, charts.

Cabello Naranjo, Elena. La política presupuestaria para 1993. *Comercio Exterior*, v. 43, no. 1 (Jan 93), pp. 21 – 29. Tables.

"Realista y prudente" la propuesta fiscal para 1994: Pedro Aspe. *Fem*, v. 17, no. 130 (Dec 93), p. 48. Il.

Peru

TePaske, John Jay. The Costs of Empire: Spending Patterns and Priorities in Colonial Peru, 1581 – 1820. *Colonial Latin American Historical Review*, v. 2, no. 1 (Winter 93), pp. 1 – 33. Tables, charts.

Venezuela

Research

Mendoza, Héctor and Fabricio Vivas. Informe 1990 – 1991: estadísticas históricas de Venezuela; historia de las finanzas públicas en Venezuela. *Boletín de la Academia Nacional de la Historia (Venezuela)*, v. 75, no. 297 (Jan – Mar 92), pp. 169 – 176.

FIRE (IN RELIGION, FOLK LORE, ETC.)

Passafari de Gutiérrez, Clara. El dominio del fuego y la noche en San Juan: tradiciones populares de la Argentina. *Folklore Americano*, no. 53 (Jan – June 92), pp. 141 – 150.

FISHING

See also
Marine resources

Belize

Selbert, Pamela. Pooling Forces on a Belizean Caye. *Américas*, v. 45, no. 6 (Nov – Dec 93), pp. 20 – 25. Il, maps.

Brazil

Robben, Antonius C. G. M. *Sons of the Sea Goddess: Economic Practice and Discursive Conflict in Brazil* reviewed by Paul Cammack. *Journal of Latin American Studies,* v. 25, no. 3 (Oct 93), pp. 686 – 687.

Mexico

Compean, Guillermo and Rafael Girón Botello. La pesca en la cuenca del Pacífico: el caso del atún en México. *Comercio Exterior,* v. 43, no. 12 (Dec 93), pp. 1195 – 1201. Bibl, tables, charts.

Neumann, Holly. Tales from the Deep. *Business Mexico,* v. 3, no. 6 (June 93), p. 28 +. Il, tables, maps.

Pesca y mercado de atún. *Comercio Exterior,* v. 43, no. 5 (May 93), pp. 443 – 448. Tables, charts.

Venezuela

Gutiérrez M., Alejandro and Raúl León Palencia P. Lineamientos de política científica y tecnológica para el estado Mérida: área agrícola agroalimentaria; ideas para la discusión. *Derecho y Reforma Agraria,* no. 23 (1992), pp. 141 – 160. Bibl.

FLAGS

See

Emblems, National

FLOODS

Argentina

Brailovsky, Antonio Elio. Viedma: la capital inundable. *Todo Es Historia,* v. 26, no. 306 (Jan 93), pp. 60 – 71. Bibl, il.

Río de la Plata region

Giddings, Lorrain Eugene. Visión por satélite de las inundaciones extraordinarias de la cuenca del Río de la Plata. *Interciencia,* v. 18, no. 1 (Jan – Feb 93), pp. 16 – 23. Bibl, il, tables, charts.

FLORA AND FAUNA

See

Animals
Birds
Botany
Entomology
Ethnobotany
Geographical distribution of plants and animals
Horticulture
Vegetation and climate
Zoology

FLORES, LEONARDO

Von Barghahn, Barbara. The Colonial Paintings of Leonardo Flores. *Latin American Art,* v. 5, no. 2 (Summer 93), pp. 47 – 49. Bibl, il.

FLORES LÓPEZ, DOMINGO

Correspondence, reminiscences, etc.

Flores López, Domingo. Conversaciones sobre el destino de Bolivia. *Signo,* no. 36 – 37, Nueva época (May – Dec 92), pp. 147 – 167.

FLORIDA

See also

Miami, Florida

Alonso de Jesús, Francisco. 1630 Memorial of Fray Francisco Alonso de Jesús on Spanish Florida's Missions and Natives (Introduced and translated by John H. Hann). *The Americas,* v. 50, no. 1 (July 93), pp. 85 – 105.

García B., Pantaleón. La adquisición de las Floridas por los Estados Unidos en 1819. *Revista Cultural Lotería,* v. 51, no. 387 (Feb 92), pp. 37 – 42. Bibl.

Griffin, Patricia C. *Mullet on the Beach: The Minorcans of Florida, 1768 – 1788* reviewed by Amy Turner Bushnell. *The Americas,* v. 49, no. 4 (Apr 93), pp. 550 – 551.

Hann, John H., ed. *Missions to the Calusa* reviewed by Amy Turner Bushnell. *The Americas,* v. 49, no. 4 (Apr 93), pp. 548 – 549.

Matter, Robert Allen. *Pre-Seminole Florida: Spanish Soldiers, Friars, and Indian Missions, 1513 – 1763* reviewed by Amy Turner Bushnell. *The Americas,* v. 49, no. 4 (Apr 93), pp. 547 – 548.

Rosenberg, Mark B. Whither the Caribbean?: Whither Florida? *Hemisphere,* v. 5, no. 2 (Winter – Spring 93), pp. 9 – 11.

FLOWERS

See

Botany

FMLN

See

Frente Farabundo Martí para la Liberación Nacional (El Salvador)

FOLK ART

See also

Artisans
Handicraft

Exhibitions

Gross, Liza. Humble Art of Life. *Américas,* v. 45, no. 1 (Jan – Feb 93), pp. 14 – 23. Il.

Argentina

Gramajo de Martínez Moreno, Amalia and Hugo N. Martínez Moreno. *Rasgos del folklore de Santiago del Estero* reviewed by Félix Coluccio. *Folklore Americano,* no. 53 (Jan – June 92), pp. 179 – 180.

Bolivia

Arnold, Denise Y. At the Heart of the Woven Dance-Floor: The Wayñu in Qaqachaka. *Iberoamericana,* v. 16, no. 47 – 48 (1992), pp. 21 – 66. Bibl, il, tables.

Brazil

Peregrino, Umberto. Discurso do sócio-benemérito general Umberto Peregrino Seabra Fagundes, na inauguração do Museu de Arte Popular, em 23 de outubro de 1991. *Revista do Instituto Histórico e Geográfico Brasileiro,* no. 373 (Oct – Dec 91), pp. 1201 – 1203.

Pfeiffer, Wolfgang. Exvotos en Brasil (Translated by Ricardo Barda). *Humboldt,* no. 110 (1993), pp. 90 – 93. Il.

Latin America

Gross, Liza. Humble Art of Life. *Américas,* v. 45, no. 1 (Jan – Feb 93), pp. 14 – 23. Il.

Mexico

Poniatowska, Elena. El otro gran arte. *Nexos,* v. 16, no. 183 (Mar 93), pp. 31 – 38. Il.

FOLK DANCING

Andean region

Estenssoro Fuchs, Juan Carlos. Los bailes de los indios y el proyecto colonial (With commentaries by T. Abercrombie, J. Flores Espinoza, C. Itier, and S. E. Ramírez and a response by the author). *Revista Andina,* v. 10, no. 2 (Dec 92), pp. 353 – 404. Bibl.

Poole, Deborah A. Adaptación y resistencia en la danza ritual andina. *Conjunto,* no. 89 (Oct – Dec 91), pp. 13 – 27. Bibl, il.

Bolivia

Arnold, Denise Y. At the Heart of the Woven Dance-Floor: The Wayñu in Qaqachaka. *Iberoamericana,* v. 16, no. 47 – 48 (1992), pp. 21 – 66. Bibl, il, tables.

Guyana

Gibson, Kean. An African Work: The Guyanese Comfa Dance. *Journal of Caribbean Studies,* v. 9, no. 1 – 2 (Winter 92 – Spring 93), pp. 99 – 111. Bibl.

Mexico

Vázquez Hall, Patricia. Danza folklórica hoy. *Plural (Mexico),* v. 22, no. 259 (Apr 93), pp. 72 – 73.

Panama

Villarreal, José B. La danza de los diablos cucúas. *Revista Cultural Lotería,* v. 51, no. 387 (Feb 92), pp. 7 – 25. Bibl.

Peru

Núñez Rebaza, Lucy. *Los dansaq* reviewed by Gérard Borras. *Caravelle,* no. 59 (1992), pp. 311 – 313.

Venezuela

Salazar M., Rafael. *Del joropo y sus andanzas* (Review). *Inter-American Music Review*, v. 13, no. 2 (Spring – Summer 93), p. 160.

FOLK DRAMA

Guatemala

García Escobar, Carlos René. Historia antigua: historia y etnografía del *Rabinal Achí*. *La Tradición Popular*, no. 81 (1991), Issue. Bibl, il.

Padial Guerchoux, Anita Louise and Angel Manuel Vázquez-Bigi. *Quiche Vinak: tragedia; nueva versión española y estudio histórico – literario del llamado 'Rabinal-Achí'* reviewed by Enrique Sam Colop. *Mesoamérica (USA)*, v. 13, no. 24 (Dec 92), pp. 465 – 473.

Latin America

Ares Queija, Berta. Representaciones dramáticas de la conquista: el pasado al servicio del presente. *Revista de Indias*, v. 52, no. 195 – 196 (May – Dec 92), pp. 231 – 250. Bibl.

González Cajiao, Fernando. El teatro precolombino siempre fue callejero. *Conjunto*, no. 92 (July – Dec 92), pp. 7 – 11. Il.

Foreign influences

Gómez García, Pedro. Moros y cristianos, indios y españoles: esquema de la conquista del otro. *Allpanchis*, v. 23, no. 39 (Jan – June 92), pp. 221 – 261. Bibl.

Mexico

Steele, Cynthia. Indigenismo y posmodernidad: narrativa indigenista, testimonio, teatro campesino y video en el Chiapas finisecular. *Iberoamericana*, v. 16, no. 47 – 48 (1992), pp. 82 – 94. Bibl.

— Indigenismo y posmodernidad: narrativa indigenista, testimonio, teatro campesino y video en el Chiapas finisecular. *Revista de Crítica Literaria Latinoamericana*, v. 19, no. 38 (July – Dec 93), pp. 249 – 260. Bibl.

Peru

Oleszkiewicz, Malgorzata. El ciclo de la muerte de Atahualpa: de la fiesta popular a la representación teatral. *Allpanchis*, v. 23, no. 39 (Jan – June 92), pp. 185 – 220. Bibl.

Spain

Gómez García, Pedro. Moros y cristianos, indios y españoles: esquema de la conquista del otro. *Allpanchis*, v. 23, no. 39 (Jan – June 92), pp. 221 – 261. Bibl.

Venezuela

Rodríguez B., Orlando. Venezuela: mestizaje y teatro. *Conjunto*, no. 92 (July – Dec 92), pp. 2 – 6. Il.

FOLK FESTIVALS

Argentina

Cazón, Sandra. Las fiestas populares en Hispanoamérica: el carnaval en la Argentina a principios del siglo XX. *Jahrbuch für Geschichte von Staat, Wirtschaft und Gesellschaft Lateinamerikas*, v. 29 (1992), pp. 343 – 367. Bibl.

Bolivia

Abercrombie, Thomas Alan. La fiesta del carnaval postcolonial en Oruro: clase, etnicidad y nacionalismo en la danza folklórica (With commentaries by seven historians and a response by the author). *Revista Andina*, v. 10, no. 2 (Dec 92), pp. 279 – 352. Bibl, il.

Albó, Xavier and Matías Preiswerk. El Gran Poder: fiesta del aimara urbano. *América Indígena*, v. 51, no. 2 – 3 (Apr – Sept 91), pp. 293 – 352. Bibl, tables, maps.

Brazil

Dunn, Christopher. Afro-Bahian Carnival: A Stage for Protest. *Afro-Hispanic Review*, v. 11, no. 1 – 3 (1992), pp. 11 – 20. Bibl.

Linger, Daniel Touro. *Dangerous Encounters: Meanings of Violence in a Brazilian City* reviewed by David Cleary. *Bulletin of Latin American Research*, v. 12, no. 3 (Sept 93), pp. 344 – 345.

Queiroz, Maria Isaura Pereira de. *Carnaval brasileiro: o vivido e o mito* reviewed by Oscar D'Ambrosio (Review entitled "O mito do carnaval"). *Problemas Brasileiros*, v. 30, no. 296 (Mar – Apr 93), pp. 40 – 41. Il.

— *Carnaval brasileiro: o vivido e o mito* reviewed by Rita de Cássia Amaral. *Revista Brasileira de Ciências Sociais*, v. 8, no. 21 (Feb 93), pp. 118 – 119.

Sales, Fernando. Uma visão do folclore nacional. *Convivium*, v. 34, no. 2 (July – Dec 91), pp. 75 – 90. Bibl.

Guatemala

Déleon Meléndez, Ofelia Columba and Brenda Ninette Mayol Baños. Aproximación a la cultura popular tradicional de los municipios de Ciudad Flores, San José y la aldea Santa Eleana del departamento de Petén, Guatemala. *La Tradición Popular*, no. 76 – 77 (1990), Issue. Il, facs.

Mexico

Carmichael, Elizabeth and Chloë Sayer. *The Skeleton and the Feast: The Day of the Dead in Mexico* reviewed by Ward S. Albro III. *Hispanic American Historical Review*, v. 73, no. 1 (Feb 93), p. 127.

Garscha, Karsten. Das Leben, nur eine kurze Reise: Der mexikanische Totenkult. *Iberoamericana*, v. 17, no. 50 (1993), pp. 16 – 37. Bibl.

Gonzalbo Aizpuru, Pilar. Las fiestas novohispanas: espectáculo y ejemplo. *Mexican Studies*, v. 9, no. 1 (Winter 93), pp. 19 – 45. Bibl.

Peru

Dean, Carolyn Sue. Ethnic Conflict and Corpus Christi in Colonial Cuzco. *Colonial Latin American Review*, v. 2, no. 1 – 2 (1993), pp. 93 – 120. Bibl, il.

Oleszkiewicz, Malgorzata. El ciclo de la muerte de Atahualpa: de la fiesta popular a la representación teatral. *Allpanchis*, v. 23, no. 39 (Jan – June 92), pp. 185 – 220. Bibl.

Zecenarro Villalobos, Bernardino. De fiestas, ritos y batallas: algunos comportamientos folk de la sociedad andina de los k'anas y ch'umpiwillcas. *Allpanchis*, v. 23, no. 40 (July – Dec 92), pp. 147 – 172. Bibl.

Uruguay

Casaravilla, Diego. La cultura política uruguaya desde el carnaval: heroísmo antimilitar, crisis del socialismo real y MERCOSUR. *Cuadernos del CLAEH*, v. 18, no. 65 – 66 (May 93), pp. 151 – 165. Bibl.

Venezuela

Foreign influences

Pollak-Eltz, Angelina. Aportes españoles a la cultura popular venezolana. *Montalbán*, no. 24 (1992), pp. 167 – 219. Bibl.

FOLK LITERATURE

See also
Legends
Mythology
Oral tradition

Cazzaniga, Néstor J. Historias de vampiros y hombres lobo. *Todo Es Historia*, v. 26, no. 309 (Apr 93), pp. 8 – 26. Bibl, il, maps.

Argentina

Rojas, Elena M., ed. *Acerca de los relatos orales en la provincia de Tucumán* reviewed by Félix Coluccio. *Folklore Americano*, no. 53 (Jan – June 92), pp. 180 – 181.

Brazil

Breguêz, Sebastião Geraldo. Literatura de cordel em Minas Gerais, Brasil. *Folklore Americano*, no. 52 (July – Dec 91), pp. 145 – 148. Bibl.

McCarthy, Cavan Michael. Recent Political Events in Brazil as Reflected in Popular Poetry Pamphlets: "Literatura de Cordel." *SALALM Papers*, v. 34 (1989), pp. 491 – 513. Bibl.

Guatemala

Lara Figueroa, Celso A. Cuentos maravillosos de tradición oral del oriente guatemalteco. *La Tradición Popular*, no. 83 – 84 (1991), Issue. Il, maps.

— Cuentos populares del "Aprendiz de brujo" en Guatemala. *La Tradición Popular*, no. 80 (1990), Issue. Bibl, il, maps.

— Presencia del cuento popular en Guatemala: estudio histórico – etnográfico del tipo AT 325. *Folklore Americano*, no. 52 (July – Dec 91), pp. 7 – 37. Bibl, maps.

Peñalosa, Fernando. El cuento popular: patrimonio del pueblo maya del sur de Mesoamérica. *Folklore Americano,* no. 52 (July – Dec 91), pp. 39 – 92. Bibl.

Foreign influences

Lara Figueroa, Celso A. El cuento popular de raíz europea en el oriente de Guatemala. *Folklore Americano,* no. 53 (Jan – June 92), pp. 37 – 53.

Latin America

Lienhard, Martín. Kulturelle Heterogenität und Literatur in Lateinamerika. *Iberoamericana,* v. 16, no. 47 – 48 (1992), pp. 95 – 110. Bibl.

Mexican – American Border Region

García, Nasario. *Abuelitos: Stories of the Río Puerco Valley* reviewed by Enrique R. Lamadrid. *Confluencia,* v. 8, no. 1 (Fall 92), p. 175.

Mexico

Nava L., E. Fernando and Judith Orozco. El "Sistema de Cristóbal Colón" y la "Biografía de Colón": una muestra de poesía popular mexicana (Includes the two texts). *Cuadernos Americanos,* no. 42, Nueva época (Nov – Dec 93), pp. 203 – 241.

Panama

Villarreal, José B. La danza de los diablos cucúas. *Revista Cultural Lotería,* v. 51, no. 387 (Feb 92), pp. 7 – 25. Bibl.

FOLK LORE

See also
Fire (in religion, folk lore, etc.)
Legends
Mythology
Oral tradition
Rites and ceremonies
Superstition
Taboo
Subdivisions *Legends* and *Religion and mythology* under names of Indian groups

Carvalho-Neto, Paulo de. Folklore extraterrestre II: los caminos y las bases. *Folklore Americano,* no. 53 (Jan – June 92), pp. 11 – 36. Bibl.

Argentina

Befán, José. *Las supersticiones, conjuros, ritos, espíritus nefastos* reviewed by Félix Coluccio. *Folklore Americano,* no. 52 (July – Dec 91), pp. 165 – 166.

Blache, Martha Teresa. Folklore y nacionalismo en la Argentina: su vinculación de origen y su desvinculación actual. *Runa,* v. 20 (1991 – 1992), pp. 69 – 89. Bibl.

Coluccio, Félix. Creencias populares del nordeste argentino. *Folklore Americano,* no. 52 (July – Dec 91), pp. 149 – 161. Bibl.

Gramajo de Martínez Moreno, Amalia and Hugo N. Martínez Moreno. *Rasgos del folklore de Santiago del Estero* reviewed by Félix Coluccio. *Folklore Americano,* no. 53 (Jan – June 92), pp. 179 – 180.

Passafari de Gutiérrez, Clara. El dominio del fuego y la noche en San Juan: tradiciones populares de la Argentina. *Folklore Americano,* no. 53 (Jan – June 92), pp. 141 – 150.

Bolivia

Martínez Salguero, Jaime. Sociedad y folklore. *Signo,* no. 38, Nueva época (Jan – Apr 93), pp. 137 – 142.

Brazil

Sales, Fernando. Uma visão do folclore nacional. *Convivium,* v. 34, no. 2 (July – Dec 91), pp. 75 – 90. Bibl.

Guatemala

Déleon Meléndez, Ofelia Columba and Brenda Ninette Mayol Baños. Aproximación a la cultura popular tradicional de los municipios de Ciudad Flores, San José y la aldea Santa Eleana del departamento de Petén, Guatemala. *La Tradición Popular,* no. 76 – 77 (1990), Issue. ll, facs.

Italy

Carvalho-Neto, Paulo de. La universalidad de Italia según la memoria popular: ensayo metódico sobre la confluencia tradicional entre Italia y el Nuevo Mundo, basado en 294 hechos folklóricos. *Folklore Americano,* no. 53 (Jan – June 92), pp. 133 – 140. Bibl.

Latin America

Capetillo Hernández, Juan. Las voces del agua. *La Palabra y el Hombre,* no. 82 (Apr – June 92), pp. 301 – 305.

Carvalho, José Jorge de. As duas faces da tradição: o clássico e o popular na modernidade latinoamericana. *Dados,* v. 35, no. 3 (1992), pp. 403 – 434.

Díaz Infante, Fernando. Las voces del agua. *La Palabra y el Hombre,* no. 81 (Jan – Mar 92), pp. 388 – 390.

Ramos, Luis Arturo. El agua y su lenguaje. *La Palabra y el Hombre,* no. 82 (Apr – June 92), pp. 306 – 309.

Santana, Jorge A. La adivinanza a través de quinientos años de cultura hispánica: antología histórica. *Explicación de Textos Literarios,* v. 21, no. 1 – 2 (1992), Issue. Bibl.

Williams García, Roberto. Las voces del agua. *La Palabra y el Hombre,* no. 81 (Jan – Mar 92), pp. 386 – 387.

Foreign influences

Carvalho-Neto, Paulo de. La universalidad de Italia según la memoria popular: ensayo metódico sobre la confluencia tradicional entre Italia y el Nuevo Mundo, basado en 294 hechos folklóricos. *Folklore Americano,* no. 53 (Jan – June 92), pp. 133 – 140. Bibl.

Mexico

Bibliography

Hinds, Harold E., Jr. Boundaries and Popular Culture Theory: Recent Works on Folklore and Mexican Folkways (Review article). *Studies in Latin American Popular Culture,* v. 12 (1993), pp. 243 – 249.

Spain

Santana, Jorge A. La adivinanza a través de quinientos años de cultura hispánica: antología histórica. *Explicación de Textos Literarios,* v. 21, no. 1 – 2 (1992), Issue. Bibl.

FOLK MEDICINE

See also
Ethnobotany
Medical anthropology

America

Foreign influences

Voeks, Robert. African Medicine and Magic in the Americas. *Geographical Review,* v. 83, no. 1 (Jan 93), pp. 66 – 78. Bibl, maps.

Colombia

Urrea Giraldo, Fernando and Diego Zapata Ortega. El síndrome de los nervios en el imaginario popular en una población urbana de Cali. *Revista Colombiana de Antropología,* v. 29 (1992), pp. 207 – 232. Bibl.

Honduras

Flores Andino, Francisco A. Medicina tradicional, magia y mitos entre los miskitos de Honduras. *Folklore Americano,* no. 52 (July – Dec 91), pp. 131 – 144.

Panama

Pastor Núñez, Aníbal. Medicina popular y creencias mágico – religiosas de la población negra del Darién. *Revista Cultural Lotería,* v. 51, no. 387 (Feb 92), pp. 61 – 68. Bibl.

FOLK MUSIC

See also
Ethnomusicology
Songs

Andean region

Nagy, Silvia. *Historia de la canción folkórica en los Andes* reviewed by Juan Zevallos Aguilar. *Revista de Crítica Literaria Latinoamericana,* v. 19, no. 37 (Jan – June 93), pp. 370 – 372.

Bolivia

Wara Céspedes, Gilka. "Huayño," "Saya," and "Chuntunqui": Bolivan Identity in the Music of "Los Kjarkas." *Latin American Music Review,* v. 14, no. 1 (Spring – Summer 93), pp. 52 – 101. Bibl, il, facs.

Guatemala

Arrivillaga Cortés, Alfonso. Marimbas, bandas y conjuntos orquestales de Petén. *La Tradición Popular,* no. 82 (1991), Issue. Bibl, il.

Latin America

Gómez García, Zoila. El folklore: antes y ahora. *Plural (Mexico),* v. 22, no. 264 (Sept 93), pp. 119 – 120.

Mexico

Barriga Villanueva, Rebeca. Tintes de subjetividad en las coplas de amor: *Cancionero folklórico de México. Caravelle,* no. 60 (1993), pp. 59 – 83.

Cardozo-Freeman, Inez. José Inés Chávez García: Hero or Villain of the Mexican Revolution? (Includes the text of two corridos). *Bilingual Review/Revista Bilingüe,* v. 18, no. 1 (Jan – Apr 93), pp. 3 – 13. Bibl.

Guerrero Guerrero, Raúl. Cantos populares mexicanos de Navidad en el estado de Hidalgo. *Revista Musical de Venezuela,* no. 28 (May – Dec 89), pp. 148 – 165. Facs.

Peru

Turino, Thomas. Del esencialismo a lo esencial: pragmática y significado de la interpretación de los sikuri puneños en Lima. *Revista Andina,* v. 10, no. 2 (Dec 92), pp. 441 – 456. Bibl.

Puerto Rico

Hernández, Prisco. "Décima," "Seis," and the Art of the Puertorican "Trovador" within the Modern Social Context. *Latin American Music Review,* v. 14, no. 1 (Spring – Summer 93), pp. 20 – 51. Bibl, il, facs.

Foreign influences

Quintero Rivera, Angel Guillermo. El tambor oculto en el cuatro: la melodización de ritmos y la etnicidad cimarroneada en la caribeña cultura de la contraplantación. *Boletín Americanista,* v. 33, no. 42 – 43 (1992 – 1993), pp. 87 – 106. Bibl, facs.

FÓMINA, SILVIA

Criticism of specific works

Bajo la penumbra

Herbort, Heinz Josef. "Jungla de silencio": una semblanza de la compositora Silvia Fómina (Translated by Carlos Caramés). *Humboldt,* no. 110 (1993), pp. 56 – 59. Il, facs.

FONSECA, GONZALO

Bach, Caleb. Chiseler of Timeless Forms. *Américas,* v. 45, no. 4 (July – Aug 93), pp. 26 – 33. Il.

FONSECA, JOÃO SEVERIANO DA

Criticism of specific works

Serafim Moreira da Silva Júnior

Silva, Alberto Martins da. Um inédito de João Severiano da Fonseca: *Serafim Moreira da Silva Júnior, um herói de Diamantina, 1850 – 1868* (Includes the previously unpublished text). *Revista do Instituto Histórico e Geográfico Brasileiro,* no. 371 (Apr – June 91), pp. 518 – 532. Bibl.

FONSECA, RUBEM

Criticism of specific works

Vastas emoções e pensamentos imperfeitos

Oviedo, José Miguel. El mundo vertiginoso de Rubem Fonseca. *Cuadernos Hispanoamericanos,* no. 512 (Feb 93), pp. 143 – 145.

Translations

Fonseca, Rubem. El campeonato (Translated by Marco Tulio Aguilera Garramuño). *La Palabra y el Hombre,* no. 82 (Apr – June 92), pp. 239 – 245.

FOOD HABITS

See also
Cookery
Nutrition
Subdivision *Food* under names of Indian groups

America

Foreign influences

Puglia, Sergio. El choque y la mezcla de los sabores (Excerpts from a transcribed interview by Elvio E. Gandolfo). *Cuadernos del CLAEH,* v. 17, no. 63 – 64 (Oct 92), pp. 155 – 160.

Argentina

Alcorta, Rodrigo. Artesanos del pan de Navidad. *Todo Es Historia,* v. 26, no. 305 (Dec 92), pp. 50 – 53. Il.

Vidal Buzzi, Fernando. De pizzas y ravioles. *Todo Es Historia,* v. 26, no. 305 (Dec 92), pp. 22 – 26. Il.

Caribbean area

Adams, John E. Fish Lovers of the Caribbean. *Caribbean Studies,* v. 25, no. 1 – 2 (Jan – July 92), pp. 1 – 10. Tables.

Europe

Foreign influences

Puglia, Sergio. El choque y la mezcla de los sabores (Excerpts from a transcribed interview by Elvio E. Gandolfo). *Cuadernos del CLAEH,* v. 17, no. 63 – 64 (Oct 92), pp. 155 – 160.

Jamaica

Foreign influences

Rashford, John H. Arawak, Spanish, and African Contributions to Jamaica's Settlement Vegetation. *Jamaica Journal,* v. 24, no. 3 (Feb 93), pp. 17 – 23. Bibl, il.

Latin America

Cordell, Linda S. and Nelson Foster, eds. *Chilies to Chocolate: Food the Americas Gave the World* reviewed by John C. Super. *Hispanic American Historical Review,* v. 73, no. 3 (Aug 93), p. 487.

Mexico

Arana, Federico. *Comer insectos* reviewed by Susan N. Masuoka (Review entitled "Mexican Eating: The Work and the Haute Cuisine"). *Studies in Latin American Popular Culture,* v. 12 (1993), pp. 189 – 194. Bibl.

Castelló Yturbide, Teresa. *Presencia de la comida prehispánica* reviewed by Susan N. Masuoka (Review entitled "Mexican Eating: The Work and the Haute Cuisine"). *Studies in Latin American Popular Culture,* v. 12 (1993), pp. 189 – 194.

Stoopen, María. *El universo de la cocina mexicana* reviewed by Susan N. Masuoka (Review entitled "Mexican Eating: The Work and the Haute Cuisine"). *Studies in Latin American Popular Culture,* v. 12 (1993), pp. 189 – 194.

Pacific Area

Cisneros, Antonio. Homenaje a lo crudo: contra Claude Lévi-Strauss. *Debate (Peru),* v. 15, no. 71 (Nov 92 – Jan 93), pp. 58 – 59. Il.

FOOD INDUSTRY AND TRADE

See also
Agriculture
Dairying
Meat industry and trade
Nut industry

Brazil

Mathematical models

Vicente, José R. Modelos estruturais para previsão das produções brasileiras de carne de frango e ovos. *Revista de Economia e Sociologia Rural,* v. 30, no. 4 (Oct – Dec 92), pp. 305 – 319. Bibl, tables, charts.

Chile

Byé, Pascal and Jean-Pierre Frey. Le modèle chilien à la lumière de l'expérience des pays agro-exportateurs de l'ASEAN. *Cahiers des Amériques Latines,* no. 14 (1992), pp. 37 – 49. Bibl, tables.

Costa Rica

Li Kam, Sui Moy. Costa Rica ante la internacionalización de la agricultura. *Revista de Ciencias Sociales (Costa Rica),* no. 57 (Sept 92), pp. 87 – 96. Bibl.

Cuba

Aguilar Gómez, Javier de J. Cuba: comercialización de productos agrícolas. *Momento Económico,* no. 69 (Sept – Oct 93), pp. 24 – 28. Bibl.

Europe

Green, Raúl H. Economía industrial alimentaria: reflexiones en torno de América Latina. *Realidad Económica,* no. 119 (Oct – Nov 93), pp. 15 – 33.

Latin America

Green, Raúl H. Economía industrial alimentaria: reflexiones en torno de América Latina. *Realidad Económica,* no. 119 (Oct – Nov 93), pp. 15 – 33.

Guerra E., Guillermo A. América Latina: la empresa agropecuaria ante la modernización. *Comercio Exterior,* v. 43, no. 4 (Apr 93), pp. 344 – 352. Bibl, tables, charts.

Mexico

Carlsen, Laura. Feeding Mexico. *Business Mexico,* v. 3, no. 7 (July 93), pp. 11 – 15. Il.

Dutrénit, Gabriela. Las agroindustrias exportadoras: su penetración en Estados Unidos. *Comercio Exterior,* v. 43, no. 4 (Apr 93), pp. 336 – 343. Tables.

González Pacheco, Cuauhtémoc and Felipe Torres Torres, eds. *Los retos de la soberanía alimentaria en México* reviewed by Argelia Salinas Ontiveros. *Problemas del Desarrollo,* v. 24, no. 93 (Apr – June 93), pp. 239 – 241.

Recipes for Higher Profits. *Business Mexico,* v. 3, no. 10 (Oct 93), pp. 27 – 28 +. Tables.

Russell, Joel. Pass the Chips. *Business Mexico,* v. 3, no. 8 (Aug 93), pp. 39 – 41. Il.

Nicaragua

Ton, Giel and Gerda Zijm. Matrimonio conflictivo: cooperativas en un proyecto agroindustrial; el caso de Sébaco, Nicaragua. *Estudios Rurales Latinoamericanos,* v. 15, no. 2 – 3 (May – Dec 92), pp. 121 – 138. Bibl, tables.

Uruguay

Fernández Cabrelli, Alfonso. Las panaderías montevideanas en 1774. *Hoy Es Historia,* v. 10, no. 60 (Nov – Dec 93), pp. 84 – 85. Facs.

Venezuela

Cardozo Galué, Germán. El circuito agroexportador marabino a mediados del siglo XIX. *Boletín Americanista,* v. 33, no. 42 – 43 (1992 – 1993), pp. 367 – 393. Bibl, maps, charts.

— *Maracaibo y su región histórica: el circuito agroexportador, 1830 – 1860* reviewed by Frédérique Langue. *Cahiers des Amériques Latines,* no. 13 (1992), pp. 184 – 185.

FOOD SUPPLY

Brazil

Marques, Pedro V. Integração vertical da avicultura de corte no estado de São Paulo. *Revista de Economia e Sociologia Rural,* v. 30, no. 3 (July – Sept 92), pp. 189 – 202. Bibl, tables.

Teixeira, Jorge Leão. O país do desperdício. *Problemas Brasileiros,* v. 30, no. 297 (May – June 93), pp. 6 – 9. Il.

Congresses

Coeli, Jaime Collier. O desafio do abastecimento. *Problemas Brasileiros,* v. 30, no. 297 (May – June 93), pp. 15 – 24. Il.

Central America

Barry, Tom and Rachel Garst. *Feeding the Crisis: U.S. Food Aid and Farm Policy in Central America* reviewed by Melvin G. Blase. *Journal of Developing Areas,* v. 27, no. 4 (July 93), pp. 566 – 567.

Ferguson, Anne E. and Scott Whiteford, eds. *Harvest of Want: Hunger and Food Security in Central America and Mexico* reviewed by LaMond Tullis. *Journal of Developing Areas,* v. 27, no. 2 (Jan 93), pp. 253 – 254.

Colombia

Gómez Jiménez, Alcides. Seguridad alimentaria: problemas grandes y políticas pobres. *Revista Javeriana,* v. 61, no. 591 (Jan – Feb 93), pp. 26 – 33. Bibl, tables.

Developing countries

Barraclough, Solon Lovett. *An End to Hunger?: The Social Origins of Food Strategies* reviewed by Michaeline Crichlow. *Social and Economic Studies,* v. 41, no. 4 (Dec 92), pp. 234 – 239.

Utting, Peter. *Economic Reform and Third-World Socialism* reviewed by S. P. Chakravarty. *Bulletin of Latin American Research,* v. 12, no. 1 (Jan 93), pp. 122 – 124.

— *Economic Reform and Third-World Socialism: A Political Economy of Food Policy in Post-Revolutionary Societies* reviewed by Kenneth P. Jameson. *Journal of Developing Areas,* v. 27, no. 4 (July 93), pp. 543 – 544.

Guatemala

Alarcón, Jorge A. and Maarten Dirk Cornelis Immink. Household Income, Food Availability, and Commercial Crop Production by Smallholder Farmers in the Western Highlands of Guatemala. *Economic Development and Cultural Change,* v. 41, no. 2 (Jan 93), pp. 319 – 342. Bibl, tables.

Fernández Molina, José Antonio. Producción indígena y mercado urbano a finales del período colonial: la provisión de alimentos a la ciudad de Guatemala, 1787 – 1822. *Revista de Historia (Costa Rica),* no. 26 (July – Dec 92), pp. 9 – 30. Bibl, tables, maps, charts.

Haiti

Maguire, Robert et al. Food Security and Development in Haiti. *Grassroots Development,* v. 16, no. 2 (1992), pp. 35 – 39. Il.

Latin America

Super, John Clay. *Food, Conquest, and Colonization in Sixteenth-Century Spanish America* reviewed by Jorge Luján Muñoz. *Mesoamérica (USA),* v. 13, no. 24 (Dec 92), pp. 463 – 464.

Mexico

Ferguson, Anne E. and Scott Whiteford, eds. *Harvest of Want: Hunger and Food Security in Central America and Mexico* reviewed by LaMond Tullis. *Journal of Developing Areas,* v. 27, no. 2 (Jan 93), pp. 253 – 254.

González Pacheco, Cuauhtémoc and Felipe Torres Torres, eds. *Los retos de la soberanía alimentaria en México* reviewed by Argelia Salinas Ontiveros. *Problemas del Desarrollo,* v. 24, no. 93 (Apr – June 93), pp. 239 – 241.

Venezuela

Denis, Paul-Yves and José Ismael Jaspe Alvarez. Estudio de la distribución espacial del sistema cooperativo de "Ferias de Consumo Familiar" (FCF) y de su papel en el abastecimiento alimentario en la región centro-occidental de Venezuela. *Revista Geográfica (Mexico),* no. 114 (July – Dec 91), pp. 5 – 36. Bibl, maps, charts.

FOOTBALL

See
Soccer

FORCED LABOR

See
Encomiendas
Indians, Treatment òf
Labor supply
Slavery

FOREIGN AID

See
Agricultural assistance, Foreign
Economic assistance, Foreign
Educational assistance
Military assistance, Foreign

FOREIGN DEBT

See
Debts, Public

FOREIGN EXCHANGE PROBLEM

See also
Balance of payments
Currency question
Finance, Public

Argentina

Batista Júnior, Paulo Nogueira. Dolarização, âncora cambial e reservas internacionais. *Revista de Economia Política (Brazil),* v. 13, no. 3 (July – Sept 93), pp. 5 – 20. Bibl, tables.

Deregulation

Himelfarb, Célia. Convertibilité, stabilisation et dérégulation en Argentine. *Cahiers des Amériques Latines,* no. 14 (1992), pp. 51 – 66. Bibl, tables.

Brazil

Batista Júnior, Paulo Nogueira. Dolarização, âncora cambial e reservas internacionais. *Revista de Economia Política (Brazil),* v. 13, no. 3 (July – Sept 93), pp. 5 – 20. Bibl, tables.

Nabão, Márcia. Os efeitos de variações cambiais sobre o déficit público. *Revista de Economia Política (Brazil)*, v. 13, no. 1 (Jan – Mar 93), pp. 37 – 51. Bibl, tables.

Mathematical models

Martner Fanta, Ricardo. Efeitos macroeconômicos de uma desvalorização cambial: análise de simulações para o Brasil. *Pesquisa e Planejamento Econômico*, v. 22, no. 1 (Apr 92), pp. 35 – 72. Bibl, tables, charts.

Varga, Gyorgy. Estratégias de proteção no mercado futuro do dólar. *Revista Brasileira de Economia*, v. 47, no. 3 (July – Sept 93), pp. 449 – 466. Bibl, tables.

Chile

Licandro, José Antonio. Análisis de la zona objetivo para el tipo de cambio en Chile. *Cuadernos de Economía (Chile)*, v. 30, no. 90 (Aug 93), pp. 179 – 198. Bibl, tables, charts.

Mathematical models

Morandé Lavín, Felipe Guillermo. La dinámica de los precios de los activos reales y el tipo de cambio real: las reformas al comercio exterior y las entradas de capital extranjero; Chile, 1976 – 1989. *El Trimestre Económico*, v. 59, Special issue (Dec 92), pp. 141 – 186. Bibl, tables, charts.

Cuba

Díaz-Briquets, Sergio. "Dollarization": Castro's Latest Economic Miracle? *Hemisphere*, v. 5, no. 3 (Summer – Fall 93), pp. 8 – 9.

Guyana

Bennett, Karl M. Exchange Rate Management in a Balance of Payments Crisis: The Guyana and Jamaica Experience. *Social and Economic Studies*, v. 41, no. 4 (Dec 92), pp. 113 – 131. Bibl, tables.

Jamaica

Bennett, Karl M. Exchange Rate Management in a Balance of Payments Crisis: The Guyana and Jamaica Experience. *Social and Economic Studies*, v. 41, no. 4 (Dec 92), pp. 113 – 131. Bibl, tables.

Mexico

Riner, Deborah L. Is Maxi-Devaluation upon the Peso? *Business Mexico*, v. 3, no. 6 (June 93), pp. 22 – 23 +. Tables.

FOREIGN INVESTMENT

See
International business enterprises
Investments, Foreign

FOREIGN RELATIONS

See
Espionage
Geopolitics
Intellectual cooperation
International relations
War
Subdivision *Foreign relations* under names of specific countries
Subdivision *International cooperation* under specific topics

FOREIGN TRADE PROMOTION

Di Girólamo, Giovanni. The World Agricultural Outlook in the 1990s. *CEPAL Review*, no. 47 (Aug 92), pp. 95 – 114. Bibl, tables, charts.

Vieira Posada, Edgar. Promoción de exportaciones: reflexiones para una nueva política. *Integración Latinoamericana*, v. 18, no. 189 – 190 (May – June 93), pp. 35 – 37.

Andean region

Salgado, Germánico and Rafael Urriola, eds. *El fin de las barreras: los empresarios y el Pacto Andino en la década de los '90* (Review). *Integración Latinoamericana*, v. 18, no. 189 – 190 (May – June 93), p. 57.

Asia

Agosin, Manuel Roberto. Política comercial en los países dinámicos de Asia: aplicaciones a América Latina. *Desarrollo Económico (Argentina)*, v. 33, no. 131 (Oct – Dec 93), pp. 355 – 375. Bibl, tables.

Mathematical models

Gouvea Neto, Raul de and Geraldo M. Vasconcellos. La diversificación de las exportaciones y la eficiencia de la cartera de exportación: estudio comparativo de los países del sureste de Asia y de la América Latina (Translated by Carlos Villegas). *El Trimestre Económico*, v. 60, no. 237 (Jan – Mar 93), pp. 29 – 52. Bibl, tables, charts.

Brazil

Amadeo Swaelen, Edward Joaquim and José Márcio Camargo. Liberalização comercial, distribuição e emprego. *Revista de Economia Política (Brazil)*, v. 13, no. 4 (Oct – Dec 93), pp. 58 – 76. Bibl, tables.

Bonelli, Regis. Crecimiento y productividad en las industrias brasileñas: efectos de la orientación del comercio exterior. *El Trimestre Económico*, v. 59, Special issue (Dec 92), pp. 109 – 140. Bibl, tables, charts.

Mathematical models

Amadeo Swaelen, Edward Joaquim and José Márcio Camargo. Política comercial e distribuição funcional da renda. *Pesquisa e Planejamento Econômico*, v. 22, no. 1 (Apr 92), pp. 73 – 100. Bibl, tables, charts.

Barbosa, Margareth L. and Rosa M. O. Fontes. Efeitos da integração econômica do MERCOSUL e da Europa na competitividade das exportações brasileiras de soja. *Revista de Economia e Sociologia Rural*, v. 29, no. 4 (Oct – Dec 91), pp. 335 – 351. Bibl, tables.

Caribbean area

Segal, Aaron. Opciones comerciales del Caribe: las cartas de Europa, América del Norte y América Latina. *Comercio Exterior*, v. 43, no. 11 (Nov 93), pp. 1019 – 1030. Bibl, tables, charts.

Central America

Willmore, Larry N. Industrial Policy in Central America. *CEPAL Review*, no. 48 (Dec 92), pp. 95 – 105. Bibl, tables.

Chile

Byé, Pascal and Jean-Pierre Frey. Le modèle chilien à la lumière de l'expérience des pays agro-exportateurs de l'ASEAN. *Cahiers des Amériques Latines*, no. 14 (1992), pp. 37 – 49. Bibl, tables.

Gwynne, Robert N. Non-Traditional Export Growth and Economic Development: The Chilean Forestry Sector since 1974. *Bulletin of Latin American Research*, v. 12, no. 2 (May 93), pp. 147 – 169. Bibl, maps, charts.

Hachette, Dominique. Estrategias de globalización del comercio. *Estudios Públicos (Chile)*, no. 51 (Winter 93), pp. 45 – 85. Bibl, tables, charts.

Henríquez Amestoy, Lysette. Chile: experiencia exportadora de las empresas pequeñas y medianas. *Comercio Exterior*, v. 43, no. 6 (June 93), pp. 547 – 552.

Messner, Dirk. Shaping Competitiveness in the Chilean Wood-Processing Industry. *CEPAL Review*, no. 49 (Apr 93), pp. 117 – 137. Bibl, charts.

Rosales, Osvaldo. La segunda fase exportadora en Chile. *Comercio Exterior*, v. 43, no. 9 (Sept 93), pp. 859 – 864.

Ruiz-Tagle P., Jaime. La CUT acepta el modelo exportador. *Mensaje*, v. 42, no. 418 (May 93), pp. 117 – 119. Tables.

Colombia

La apertura económica y el sector agrícola colombiano. *Revista Javeriana*, v. 61, no. 591 (Jan – Feb 93), pp. 11 – 19. Charts.

Dominican Republic

Nanita-Kennett, Milagros. Industrial Free Zones in the Dominican Republic. *Caribbean Geography*, v. 3, no. 3 (Mar 92), pp. 200 – 204. Tables.

Latin America

Agosin, Manuel Roberto. Política comercial en los países dinámicos de Asia: aplicaciones a América Latina. *Desarrollo Económico (Argentina)*, v. 33, no. 131 (Oct – Dec 93), pp. 355 – 375. Bibl, tables.

Ander-Egg, Ezequiel et al. El porvenir de América Latina (Question – answer forum by Latin American intellectuals on Latin America's economic future). *Desarrollo Indoamericano*, v. 23, no. 91 (June 93), pp. 7 – 16.

Barbosa, Rubens Antonio. Liberalização do comércio, integração regional e Mercado Comum do Sul: o papel do Brasil. *Revista de Economia Política (Brazil)*, v. 13, no. 1 (Jan – Mar 93), pp. 64 – 81.

Cebreros, Alfonso. La competitividad agropecuaria en condiciones de apertura económica. *Comercio Exterior*, v. 43, no. 10 (Oct 93), pp. 946 – 953. Bibl.

Consuegra Higgins, José and Hernán Echavarría Olozaga. Tres cartas, dos opiniones. *Desarrollo Indoamericano*, v. 23, no. 91 (June 93), pp. 17 – 19. Il.

Peña Guerrero, Roberto. Los proyectos latinoamericanos: ¿Libre comercio o integración fragmentada? *Relaciones Internacionales (Mexico)*, v. 14, Nueva época, no. 56 (Oct – Dec 92), pp. 55 – 61.

Ventosa del Campo, Andrés. Hacia una zona continental de libre comercio. *Relaciones Internacionales (Mexico)*, v. 14, Nueva época, no. 56 (Oct – Dec 92), pp. 87 – 96. Bibl, tables, maps.

Mathematical models

Gouvea Neto, Raul de and Geraldo M. Vasconcellos. La diversificación de las exportaciones y la eficiencia de la cartera de exportación: estudio comparativo de los países del sureste de Asia y de la América Latina (Translated by Carlos Villegas). *El Trimestre Económico*, v. 60, no. 237 (Jan – Mar 93), pp. 29 – 52. Bibl, tables, charts.

Mexico

Ocampo Sigüenza, Daniel. Los puertos y las ciudades costeras ante la apertura comercial de México. *Comercio Exterior*, v. 43, no. 8 (Aug 93), pp. 731 – 742. Bibl, tables.

Ortiz Wadgymar, Arturo. La pequeña y mediana industrias ante la apertura comercial y el Tratado de Libre Comercio: los costos de la desprotección industrial en México, 1985 – 1992. *Problemas del Desarrollo*, v. 24, no. 93 (Apr – June 93), pp. 55 – 74. Bibl, tables.

Ramírez, Miguel D. Stabilization and Trade Reform in Mexico, 1983 – 1989. *Journal of Developing Areas*, v. 27, no. 2 (Jan 93), pp. 173 – 190. Bibl, tables, charts.

Russell, Joel. Quiet Revolution. *Business Mexico*, v. 3, no. 6 (June 93), p. 27. Il.

Nicaragua

Craipeau, Carine. El café en Nicaragua. *Anuario de Estudios Centroamericanos*, v. 18, no. 2 (1992), pp. 41 – 69. Bibl, tables, maps, charts.

Peru

García Belaúnde, José Antonio. Promoción, imagen, diplomacia. *Debate (Peru)*, v. 16, no. 72 (Mar – May 93), pp. 46 – 48. Il.

Southern Cone of South America

Bekerman, Marta. Apertura importadora e integración en el Cono Sur. *Comercio Exterior*, v. 43, no. 11 (Nov 93), pp. 1040 – 1045. Bibl.

Bouzas, Roberto. Apertura comercial e integración en el Cono Sur. *Nueva Sociedad*, no. 125 (May – June 93), pp. 112 – 119.

United States

Russell, Joel. Stating Their Case. *Business Mexico*, v. 3, no. 12 (Dec 93), pp. 24 – 28.

Wilson, Michael. Hacia la próxima centuria americana: construyendo una nueva asociación con América Latina. *Relaciones Internacionales (Mexico)*, v. 15, Nueva época, no. 57 (Jan – Mar 93), pp. 17 – 30. Bibl.

FOREIGN TRADE REGULATION

See also
Embargo
Tariff

Baldinelli, Elvio. La protección contra el comercio desleal. *Integración Latinoamericana*, v. 17, no. 184 (Nov 92), pp. 26 – 35.

Brazil

Amadeo Swaelen, Edward Joaquim and José Márcio Camargo. Liberalização comercial, distribuição e emprego. *Revista de Economia Política (Brazil)*, v. 13, no. 4 (Oct – Dec 93), pp. 58 – 76. Bibl, tables.

Central America

Reglamento Centroamericano sobre Prácticas de Comercio Desleal y Cláusula de Salvaguardia. *Integración Latinoamericana*, v. 18, no. 191 (July 93), pp. 60 – 66.

Latin America

González Rubí, Rafael. América Latina y las barreras no arancelarias de los gigantes económicos. *Comercio Exterior*, v. 43, no. 3 (Mar 93), pp. 248 – 253. Bibl.

Mexico

Delgado, Dora. Resolving Conflicts Out of Court. *Business Mexico*, v. 3, no. 12 (Dec 93), p. 30.

Legislación comercial para las nuevas circunstancias. *Comercio Exterior*, v. 43, no. 9 (Sept 93), pp. 814 – 816.

Mexico. Secretaría de Comercio y Fomento Industrial. Ley de Comercio Exterior. *Comercio Exterior*, v. 43, no. 9 (Sept 93), pp. 870 – 884.

United States

Chisholm, Patrick D. Steel Wars. *Business Mexico*, v. 3, no. 4 (Apr 93), pp. 34 – 37. Il.

Marshall, Timon L. and William E. Perry. Defending Antidumping Actions. *Business Mexico*, v. 3, no. 8 (Aug 93), pp. 26 – 28.

Olmedo Carranza, Bernardo. Ofensiva proteccionista norteamericana: el acero. *Relaciones Internacionales (Mexico)*, v. 15, Nueva época, no. 58 (Apr – June 93), pp. 89 – 91.

FORESTRY

Amazon Valley

Anderson, Anthony B. et al. *The Subsidy from Nature: Palm Forests, Peasantry, and Development on an Amazon Frontier* reviewed by Kathryn Smith Pyle. *Grassroots Development*, v. 17, no. 1 (1993), pp. 45 – 46. Il.

— *The Subsidy from Nature: Palm Forests, Peasantry, and Development on an Amazon Frontier* reviewed by Emilio F. Moran. *Journal of Developing Areas*, v. 28, no. 1 (Oct 93), pp. 116 – 117.

Argentina

Colombres, Diego and Jorge Gavilán. El daño ecológico y social que provocó La Forestal. *Todo Es Historia*, v. 26, no. 306 (Jan 93), pp. 42 – 47. Il.

Brazil

Santana, Antônio Cordeiro de. Custo social da depredação florestal no Pará: o caso da castanha-do-Brasil. *Revista de Economia e Sociologia Rural*, v. 30, no. 3 (July – Sept 92), pp. 253 – 269. Bibl, tables, charts.

Central America

Panorama de la deseconomía forestal en Centroamérica. *Comercio Exterior*, v. 43, no. 11 (Nov 93), pp. 1031 – 1035. Bibl, tables.

Chile

Gwynne, Robert N. Non-Traditional Export Growth and Economic Development: The Chilean Forestry Sector since 1974. *Bulletin of Latin American Research*, v. 12, no. 2 (May 93), pp. 147 – 169. Bibl, maps, charts.

Messner, Dirk. Shaping Competitiveness in the Chilean Wood-Processing Industry. *CEPAL Review*, no. 49 (Apr 93), pp. 117 – 137. Bibl, charts.

Ecuador

Borgtaft Pederson, Henrick. Uses and Management of "Aphandra Natalia" (Palmae) in Ecuador. *Bulletin de l'Institut Français d'Etudes Andines*, v. 21, no. 2 (1992), pp. 741 – 753. Bibl, il, tables, maps.

Haiti

Brochet, Michel. Les stratégies de lutte contre l'érosion et l'aménagement des bassins versants en Haïti. *Tiers Monde*, v. 34, no. 134 (Apr – June 93), pp. 423 – 436.

Mexico

Cortez Ruiz, Carlos. El sector forestal mexicano: ¿Entre la economía y la ecología? *Comercio Exterior*, v. 43, no. 4 (Apr 93), pp. 370 – 377. Bibl.

Ortega Escalona, Fernando. El recurso madera desde la conquista hasta principios del siglo XX. *La Palabra y el Hombre*, no. 81 (Jan – Mar 92), pp. 45 – 60. Bibl, il.

Law and legislation

Chapela, Francisco. ¿Podrá la nueva ley forestal detener la deforestación? *El Cotidiano,* v. 8, no. 52 (Jan – Feb 93), pp. 57 – 59 +. Bibl.

Peru

Mejía, Kember. Las palmeras en los mercados de Iquitos. *Bulletin de l'Institut Français d'Etudes Andines,* v. 21, no. 2 (1992), pp. 755 – 769. Bibl, il, tables, maps.

Venezuela

Finol Urdaneta, Hermán. Propuesta de nueva estrategia para la producción agropecuaria y forestal sobre una base ecológica. *Derecho y Reforma Agraria,* no. 23 (1992), pp. 73 – 82.

FORESTS

Defensa de las selvas: tarea de todos. *Amazonía Peruana,* v. 11, no. 21 (Sept 92), pp. 217 – 222.

Smith, Nigel J. H. et al. *Tropical Forests and Their Crops* reviewed by David M. Kummer. *Geographical Review,* v. 83, no. 3 (July 93), pp. 339 – 341.

Amazon Valley

Anderson, Anthony B., ed. *Alternatives to Deforestation: Steps toward Sustained Use of the Amazon Rain Forest* reviewed by David Cleary. *Journal of Latin American Studies,* v. 25, no. 2 (May 93), pp. 408 – 409.

Braga, Ricardo Forin Lisboa and Luiz Góes-Filho. A vegetação do Brasil: desmatamento e queimadas. *Revista Brasileira de Geografia,* v. 53, no. 2 (Apr – June 91), pp. 135 – 141. Bibl, tables, maps.

Guerra, Francisco. A problemática floresta amazônica. *Revista Brasileira de Geografia,* v. 53, no. 3 (July – Sept 91), pp. 125 – 132.

Jordan, Carl F., ed. *An Amazonian Rain Forest* reviewed by H. Tiessen (Review entitled "Amazonia"). *Interciencia,* v. 18, no. 4 (July – Aug 93), pp. 208 – 209.

Meira, Alcyr Boris de Souza. Amazônia: gestão do território. *Revista Brasileira de Geografia,* v. 53, no. 3 (July – Sept 91), pp. 133 – 147.

Argentina

Burkart, Rodolfo. Nuestros bosques norteños: desvaloración y deterioro. *Realidad Económica,* no. 114 – 115 (Feb – May 93), pp. 54 – 73. Bibl, tables, charts.

Brazil

Nedel, João Carlos. Florestas nacionais. *Revista Brasileira de Geografia,* v. 53, no. 3 (July – Sept 91), pp. 205 – 227. Bibl, il.

Chile

Quintanilla, Víctor G. Problemas y consecuencias ambientales sobre el bosque de Alerce, "Fitzroya Cupressoides (Mol) Johnst," debido a la explotación de la cordillera costera de Chile austral. *Revista Geográfica (Mexico),* no. 114 (July – Dec 91), pp. 54 – 72. Bibl, il, maps, charts.

Costa Rica

Bolaños Arquín, Margarita. Los indígenas y la conservación de la biodiversidad: 500 años de resistencia. *Revista de Historia (Costa Rica),* no. 25 (Jan – June 92), pp. 165 – 180. Bibl, il, maps, charts.

Jamaica

McDonald, M. A. et al. The Effects of Forest Clearance on Soil Conservation: Preliminary Findings from the Yallahs Valley, Jamaican Blue Mountains. *Caribbean Geography,* v. 3, no. 4 (Sept 92), pp. 253 – 260. Bibl.

Latin America

Padoch, Christine and Kent H. Redford, eds. *Conservation of Neotropical Forests: Working from Traditional Resource Use* reviewed by Mahesh Rangarajan. *Journal of Latin American Studies,* v. 25, no. 3 (Oct 93), pp. 687 – 688.

Steen, Harold K. and Richard P. Tucker, eds. *Changing Tropical Forests: Historical Perspectives on Today's Challenges in Central and South America* reviewed by Rick B. Smith. *Colonial Latin American Historical Review,* v. 2, no. 3 (Summer 93), pp. 373 – 375.

Mexico

Cochet, Hubert. Agriculture sur brûlis, élevage extensif et dégradation de l'environnement en Amérique Latine: un exemple en Sierra Madre del Sur, au Mexique. *Tiers Monde,* v. 34, no. 134 (Apr – June 93), pp. 281 – 303. Maps, charts.

Field, Christopher B. and Carlos Vázquez-Yanes. Species of the Genus "Piper" Provide a Model to Study How Plants Can Grow in Different Kinds of Rainforest Habitats. *Interciencia,* v. 18, no. 5 (Sept – Oct 93), pp. 230 – 236. Bibl, il.

Pallares, Eugenia. Lacandonia: el último refugio. *Artes de México,* no. 19 (Spring 93), pp. 114 – 115. Il.

Peru

Echavarría, Fernando R. Cuantificación de la deforestación en el valle del Huallaga, Perú. *Revista Geográfica (Mexico),* no. 114 (July – Dec 91), pp. 37 – 53. Bibl, tables, maps, charts.

Venezuela

Law and legislation

Silva, José David. Entrega o recuperación de la reserva forestal de Ticoporo. *Derecho y Reforma Agraria,* no. 24 (1993), pp. 183 – 193. Tables.

FORMER SOVIET REPUBLICS

See
Russia

FORTALEZA, BRAZIL

Barreira, Irlys Alencar Firmo. *O reverso das vitrines: conflitos urbanos e cultura política em construção* reviewed by Glória Diógenes. *Revista Brasileira de Ciências Sociais,* v. 8, no. 23 (Oct 93), pp. 156 – 157.

FOSSILS

See
Man, Prehistoric
Paleobotany
Paleontology

FRANCE

See also
Artists – France
Education and state – France
Periodicals – France

Colonies

Boucher, Philip Paul and Patricia Galloway, eds. *Proceedings of the Fifteenth Meeting of the French Colonial Historical Society, Martinique and Guadeloupe, May 1989* reviewed by Paul Lachance. *Hispanic American Historical Review,* v. 73, no. 3 (Aug 93), pp. 502 – 503.

Foreign relations

Caribbean area

Aldridge, Robert and John Connell. *France's Overseas Frontier: départements et territoires d'outremer* reviewed by W. Marvin Will. *Social and Economic Studies,* v. 41, no. 4 (Dec 92), pp. 243 – 246. Bibl.

Mexico

Rolland, Denis. *Vichy et la France libre au Mexique: guerre, cultures et propagande pendant la deuxième guerre mondiale* reviewed by Thomas D. Schoonover. *Hispanic American Historical Review,* v. 73, no. 4 (Nov 93), pp. 726 – 727.

FRANCHISES (RETAIL TRADE)

Brazil

Bernard, Daniel Alberto. "Franchising" estratégico: como obter alavancagens e sinergias por meio da taxa inicial e dos "royalties." *RAE; Revista de Administração de Empresas,* v. 33, no. 4 (July – Aug 93), pp. 18 – 31. Tables.

Mexico

Barnhart, Katherine. Pumping Out a New Image. *Business Mexico,* v. 3, no. 5 (May 93), pp. 8 – 12 +. Il, maps.

Farver, Deena. Franchising Frenzy. *Business Mexico,* v. 3, no. 8 (Aug 93), pp. 34 – 36.

FRANCIA, JOSÉ GASPAR RODRÍGUEZ DE
Fiction

Osorio, Manuel. Conversación con Roa Bastos: *Yo el Supremo; la contrahistoria. Plural (Mexico),* v. 22, no. 263 (Aug 93), pp. 29 – 31.

FRANCISCANS
America

Arenas Frutos, Isabel. Expediciones franciscanas a Indias, 1700 – 1725. *Archivo Ibero-Americano,* v. 52, no. 205 – 208 (Jan – Dec 92), pp. 157 – 185. Tables.

Castro y Castro, Manuel de. Lenguas indígenas americanas transmitidas por los franciscanos del siglo XVIII. *Archivo Ibero-Americano,* v. 52, no. 205 – 208 (Jan – Dec 92), pp. 585 – 628. Bibl.

Cebrián González, Carmen. Expediciones franciscanas a Indias, 1725 – 1750. *Archivo Ibero-Americano,* v. 52, no. 205 – 208 (Jan – Dec 92), pp. 187 – 207. Bibl, tables.

Cuesta Domingo, Mariano. Descubrimientos geográficos durante el siglo XVIII: acción franciscana en la ampliación de fronteras. *Archivo Ibero-Americano,* v. 52, no. 205 – 208 (Jan – Dec 92), pp. 293 – 342. Bibl, il, maps.

Bibliography

Mota Murillo, Rafael. Fuentes para la historia franciscano – americana del siglo XVIII: esbozo de bibliografía. *Archivo Ibero-Americano,* v. 52, no. 205 – 208 (Jan – Dec 92), pp. 1 – 80.

Zamora Jambrina, Hermenegildo. Escritos franciscanos americanos del siglo XVIII. *Archivo Ibero-Americano,* v. 52, no. 205 – 208 (Jan – Dec 92), pp. 691 – 766.

Law and legislation

García, Sebastián. América en la legislación general de la orden franciscana, siglo XVIII. *Archivo Ibero-Americano,* v. 52, no. 205 – 208 (Jan – Dec 92), pp. 629 – 689. Bibl, facs.

Sources

Reyes Ramírez, Rocío de los. Expediciones y viajes de franciscanos en los libros registros del Archivo General de Indias, siglo XVIII. *Archivo Ibero-Americano,* v. 52, no. 205 – 208 (Jan – Dec 92), pp. 811 – 832.

Rueda Iturrate, Carlos José de. Financiación de la Orden de San Francisco en los cedularios del Archivo General de Indias. *Archivo Ibero-Americano,* v. 52, no. 205 – 208 (Jan – Dec 92), pp. 833 – 848.

Vázquez Janeiro, Isaac. Documentación americana en el Pontificio Ateneo Antoniano de Roma. *Archivo Ibero-Americano,* v. 52, no. 205 – 208 (Jan – Dec 92), pp. 767 – 809.

Statistics

Abad Pérez, Antolín. Estadística franciscano – misionera en ultramar del siglo XVIII: un intento de aproximación. *Archivo Ibero-Americano,* v. 52, no. 205 – 208 (Jan – Dec 92), pp. 125 – 156. Bibl, tables.

Argentina

Gullón Abao, Alberto José. Las reducciones del este de la provincia del Tucumán en la segunda mitad del siglo XVIII bajo la administración franciscana. *Archivo Ibero-Americano,* v. 52, no. 205 – 208 (Jan – Dec 92), pp. 255 – 276. Bibl, tables, maps, charts.

Maeder, Ernesto J. A. La segunda evangelización del Chaco: las misiones franciscanas de Propaganda Fide, 1854 – 1900. *Investigaciones y Ensayos,* no. 41 (Jan – Dec 91), pp. 227 – 247. Bibl.

Bolivia

Abad Pérez, Antolín. *Las misiones de Apolobamba, Bolivia* reviewed by Pedro de Anasagasti. *Signo,* no. 35, Nueva época (Jan – Apr 92), pp. 199 – 200.

Anasagasti, Pedro de. *Los franciscanos en Bolivia* reviewed by Lorenzo Calzavarini. *Signo,* no. 38, Nueva época (Jan – Apr 93), pp. 147 – 153.

— La labor humanizadora de los franciscanos en Bolivia. *Signo,* no. 36 – 37, Nueva época (May – Dec 92), pp. 89 – 108. Bibl.

Torres, Angel. *José Zampa, pionero social – cristiano en Bolivia* reviewed by Pedro de Anasagasti. *Signo,* no. 35, Nueva época (Jan – Apr 92), pp. 250 – 252.

Sources

Comajuncosa, Antonio. *Manifiesto histórico, geográfico, topográfico, apostólico y político de los misioneros franciscanos de Tarija* reviewed by Pedro de Anasagasti. *Signo,* no. 38, Nueva época (Jan – Apr 93), pp. 231 – 233.

Gato Castaño, Purificación. *El informe del p. Gregorio de Bolívar a la Congregación de Propaganda Fide de 1623* reviewed by Pedro de Anasagasti. *Signo,* no. 35, Nueva época (Jan – Apr 92), pp. 214 – 216.

Colombia

Duque Gómez, Luis. La orden seráfica en América y en Colombia. *Boletín de Historia y Antigüedades,* v. 79, no. 779 (Oct – Dec 92), pp. 919 – 923.

Mantilla Ruiz, Luis Carlos. Las últimas expediciones de franciscanos españoles que vinieron a Colombia, 1759 y 1784. *Archivo Ibero-Americano,* v. 52, no. 205 – 208 (Jan – Dec 92), pp. 403 – 443. Bibl.

— El último cronista franciscano de la época colonial en el Nuevo Reino de Granada: fray Juan de Santa Gertrudis Serra. *Boletín de Historia y Antigüedades,* v. 79, no. 779 (Oct – Dec 92), pp. 889 – 917. Bibl.

Mexican – American Border Region

Almaráz, Félix D., Jr. Franciscan Evangelization in Spanish Frontier Texas: Apex of Social Contact, Conflict, and Confluence, 1751 – 1761. *Colonial Latin American Historical Review,* v. 2, no. 3 (Summer 93), pp. 253 – 287. Bibl, il, maps.

Marchena Fernández, Juan. De franciscanos, apaches y ministros ilustrados en los pasos perdidos del norte de Nueva España. *Archivo Ibero-Americano,* v. 52, no. 205 – 208 (Jan – Dec 92), pp. 513 – 559. Bibl, tables.

Sheridan, Thomas E. et al, eds. *The Franciscan Missions of Northern Mexico* reviewed by Robert H. Jackson. *Hispanic American Historical Review,* v. 73, no. 2 (May 93), pp. 312 – 313.

Mexico

Bellini, Giuseppe. Il dramma del mondo azteca e i "Dodici Apostoli." *Quaderni Ibero-Americani,* no. 72 (Dec 92), pp. 640 – 648. Bibl.

Escandón, Patricia. Los problemas de la administración franciscana en las misiones sonorenses, 1768 – 1800. *Archivo Ibero-Americano,* v. 52, no. 205 – 208 (Jan – Dec 92), pp. 277 – 291.

González Rodríguez, Jaime. La cátedra de Escoto en México en el siglo XVIII. *Archivo Ibero-Americano,* v. 52, no. 205 – 208 (Jan – Dec 92), pp. 561 – 584. Bibl, tables.

Heredia Correa, Roberto. Fray Juan Agustín Morfi, humanista y crítico de su tiempo. *Archivo Ibero-Americano,* v. 52, no. 205 – 208 (Jan – Dec 92), pp. 107 – 124. Bibl.

Luna Moreno, Carmen de. Alternativa en el siglo XVIII: franciscanos de la provincia del Santo Evangelio de México. *Archivo Ibero-Americano,* v. 52, no. 205 – 208 (Jan – Dec 92), pp. 343 – 371.

Morales, Francisco. Secularización de doctrinas: ¿Fin de un modelo evangelizador en la Nueva España? *Archivo Ibero-Americano,* v. 52, no. 205 – 208 (Jan – Dec 92), pp. 465 – 495. Bibl.

Orozco H., María Angélica. Los franciscanos y el caso del Real Colegio Seminario de México, 1749. *Archivo Ibero-Americano,* v. 52, no. 205 – 208 (Jan – Dec 92), pp. 497 – 512.

Sánchez Fuertes, Cayetano. México: puente franciscano entre España y Filipinas. *Archivo Ibero-Americano,* v. 52, no. 205 – 208 (Jan – Dec 92), pp. 373 – 401. Bibl.

Torre Villar, Ernesto de la. Discurso del dr. Ernesto de la Torre Villar sobre fray Vicente de Santa María. *Archivo Ibero-Americano,* v. 52, no. 205 – 208 (Jan – Dec 92), pp. 849 – 856.

Sources

Soto Pérez, José Luis. Fuentes documentales para la historia de la provincia franciscana de Michoacán en el siglo XVIII. *Archivo Ibero-Americano,* v. 52, no. 205 – 208 (Jan – Dec 92), pp. 81 – 106. Facs.

Peru

Domínguez I., Manuel F. El Colegio Franciscano de Propaganda Fide de Moquegua, 1775 – 1825. *Archivo Ibero-Americano,* v. 52, no. 205 – 208 (Jan – Dec 92), pp. 221 – 254. Bibl.

Heras, Julián. Significado y extensión de la obra misionera de Ocopa en el siglo XVIII. *Archivo Ibero-Americano,* v. 52, no. 205 – 208 (Jan – Dec 92), pp. 209 – 220. Bibl, il.

Philippine Islands

Sánchez Fuertes, Cayetano. México: puente franciscano entre España y Filipinas. *Archivo Ibero-Americano,* v. 52, no. 205 – 208 (Jan – Dec 92), pp. 373 – 401. Bibl.

FRANCO, AFONSO ARINOS DE MELO

Venâncio Filho, Alberto. Lembrança de Afonso Arinos. *Revista do Instituto Histórico e Geográfico Brasileiro,* no. 372 (July – Sept 91), pp. 762 – 765.

FREE MARKET ECONOMY

See
 Capitalism
 Competition
 Privatization

FREE PORTS AND ZONES

See
 Foreign trade promotion
 Names of specific zones

FREEDOM

Alsina Gutiérrez, Rogelio. Filosofía de la liberación en Brasil: aproximación inicial al tema. *Islas,* no. 99 (May – Aug 91), pp. 30 – 37.

Cano, Lidia and Pablo M. Guadarrama González. Filosofía de la liberación en Colombia. *Islas,* no. 99 (May – Aug 91), pp. 51 – 74. Bibl.

Castro Leiva, Luis. The Dictatorship of Virtue or Opulence of Commerce. *Jahrbuch für Geschichte von Staat, Wirtschaft und Gesellschaft Lateinamerikas,* v. 29 (1992), pp. 195 – 240. Bibl.

Figueroa Casas, Vilma and Israel López Pino. Hacia una filosofía de la liberación uruguaya. *Islas,* no. 99 (May – Aug 91), pp. 38 – 44.

García Fernández, Irsa Teresa. El pensamiento boliviano: ¿Hacia una filosofía de la liberación? *Islas,* no. 99 (May – Aug 91), pp. 45 – 50. Bibl.

García Machado, Xiomara. Notas críticas para la "transcendencia" de un proyecto liberador: Mario Casalla y Silvio Maresca. *Islas,* no. 99 (May – Aug 91), pp. 15 – 20. Bibl.

Gómez-Martínez, José Luis. El pensamiento de la liberación: hacia una posición dialógica. *Cuadernos Americanos,* no. 40, Nueva época (July – Aug 93), pp. 53 – 61. Bibl.

Guadarrama González, Pablo M. Las alternativas sociales en América Latina y la filosofía de la liberación. *Islas,* no. 96 (May – Aug 90), pp. 89 – 102. Bibl.

Guadarrama González, Pablo M. et al. El humanismo en la filosofía latinoamericana de la liberación. *Islas,* no. 99 (May – Aug 91), pp. 173 – 199. Bibl.

León del Río, Yohanka. La historia de las ideas como una de las problemáticas de la filosofía de la liberación en el Ecuador. *Islas,* no. 99 (May – Aug 91), pp. 75 – 86. Bibl.

Pérez Villacampa, Gilberto. Enrique Dussel: ¿De la metafísica de la alteridad al humanismo real? *Islas,* no. 99 (May – Aug 91), pp. 160 – 167.

— Horacio Cerutti y el problema del fin de la filosofía clásica de la liberación. *Islas,* no. 99 (May – Aug 91), pp. 168 – 172.

Rojas Gómez, Miguel. Del exilio de la razón a la razón de la libertad en Osvaldo Ardiles. *Islas,* no. 99 (May – Aug 91), pp. 112 – 129. Bibl.

— Identidad cultural y liberación en la filosofía latinoamericana de la liberación. *Islas,* no. 96 (May – Aug 90), pp. 103 – 110.

Valdés García, Félix and María Teresa Vila Bormey. La filosofía de la liberación en Perú: de Augusto Salazar Bondy a Francisco Miró Quesada. *Islas,* no. 99 (May – Aug 91), pp. 21 – 29. Bibl.

Vetter, Ulrich. La "nueva metafísica" latinoamericana y las "filosofías para la liberación": dimensiones del término "liberación." *Islas,* no. 96 (May – Aug 90), pp. 127 – 131.

Pictorial works

Beramendi Usera, Fernando. Intimate Openings through Prison Walls (Photographs by Oscar Bonilla). *Américas,* v. 45, no. 1 (Jan – Feb 93), pp. 30 – 35. Il.

FREEDOM OF THE PRESS

See also
 Censorship
 Press and politics

Conejeros A., Senén et al. ¿En qué fallan los periodistas y los medios de comunicación?: debates. *Mensaje,* v. 42, no. 419 (June 93), pp. 194 – 201. Il.

Leturia M., Juan Miguel. Información: derecho y dignidad. *Mensaje,* v. 42, no. 419 (June 93), pp. 210 – 211.

Colombia

Jaramillo Gómez, William. Legislación de prensa a la luz de la nueva constitución. *Revista Javeriana,* v. 61, no. 595 (June 93), pp. 292 – 297.

Mexico

Adler, Ilya. Press – Government Relations in Mexico: A Study of Freedom of the Mexican Press and Press Criticism of Government Institutions. *Studies in Latin American Popular Culture,* v. 12 (1993), pp. 1 – 30. Bibl, tables.

Venezuela

Arellano, Homero. La libertad de las libertades. *Revista Nacional de Cultura (Venezuela),* v. 53, no. 286 (July – Sept 92), pp. 19 – 28.

FREEMASONS

Combes, André. Las logias del gran oriente de Francia en América Latina, 1842 – 1870. *Hoy Es Historia,* v. 10, no. 60 (Nov – Dec 93), pp. 14 – 21. Bibl, facs.

Fernández Cabrelli, Alfonso. Institucionalización y desarrollo de la masonería uruguaya, 1830 – 1885. *Hoy Es Historia,* v. 10, no. 56 (Mar – Apr 93), pp. 20 – 32. Bibl, facs.

FRENCH

Brazil

Pianzola, Maurice. *Des français à la conquête du Brésil, XVIIᵉ siècle: les perroquets jaunes* reviewed by Pierre Ragon. *Cahiers des Amériques Latines,* no. 14 (1992), pp. 156 – 157.

Mexico

Skerritt, David A. Una historia dinámica entre la sierra y la costa. *La Palabra y el Hombre,* no. 83 (July – Sept 92), pp. 5 – 25. Bibl, tables, maps.

FRENCH ANTILLES

See
 Caribbean area

FRENCH GUIANA

Lezy, Emmanuel. *Guyane de l'autre côté des images* reviewed by Pierre Ragon. *Cahiers des Amériques Latines,* no. 14 (1992), pp. 151 – 152.

FRENCH LANGUAGE

Berrouët-Oriol, Robert and Robert Fournier. Créolophonie et francophonie nord – sud: transcontinuum. *Canadian Journal of Latin American and Caribbean Studies,* v. 17, no. 34 (1992), pp. 13 – 25. Bibl.

FRENTE FARABUNDO MARTÍ PARA LA LIBERACIÓN NACIONAL (EL SALVADOR)

Arsenales de armas: grave incumplimiento de los acuerdos de paz. *ECA; Estudios Centroamericanos,* v. 48, no. 536 (June 93), pp. 577 – 581. Il.

"La depuración de la fuerza armada no es negociable": pronunciación del Consejo Superior Universitario. *ECA; Estudios Centroamericanos,* v. 47, no. 529 – 530 (Nov – Dec 92), pp. 955 – 961.

Sources
Documentación: FMLN. *ECA; Estudios Centroamericanos,* v. 47, no. 528 (Oct 92), pp. 936 – 937.

FRENTE SANDINISTA DE LIBERACIÓN NACIONAL (NICARAGUA)
Cardenal, Ernesto. Vénganos a la tierra la república de los cielos. *Cuadernos Americanos,* no. 40, Nueva época (July – Aug 93), pp. 35 – 52.

Walker, Thomas W., ed. *Revolution and Counterrevolution in Nicaragua* reviewed by Roland Ebel. *Hispanic American Historical Review,* v. 73, no. 1 (Feb 93), pp. 185 – 186.

— *Revolution and Counterrevolution in Nicaragua* reviewed by Elizabeth Dore. *Journal of Latin American Studies,* v. 25, no. 1 (Feb 93), pp. 220 – 221.

— *Revolution and Counterrevolution in Nicaragua* reviewed by D. Neil Snarr. *Revista Interamericana de Bibliografía,* v. 42, no. 2 (1992), pp. 290 – 291.

Pictorial works
Morgner, Fred G. Posters and the Sandinista Revolution (Accompanied by a descriptive list of posters). *SALALM Papers,* v. 34 (1989), pp. 183 – 213. Il.

FRESNO LARRAÍN, JUAN FRANCISCO
Errázuriz Edwards, Aníbal. Juan Francisco Fresno: una eclesiología cordial. *Mensaje,* v. 42, no. 419 (June 93), p. 182. Il.

FRÍAS, HERIBERTO
Saborit, Antonio. Tomóchic (Excerpt from the forthcoming book entitled *Los doblados de Tomóchic). Nexos,* v. 16, no. 185 (May 93), pp. 69 – 75.

FROLDI, WALTER
Translations
Froldi, Walter. La llegada de los cangaceiros (Translated by Saúl Ibargoyen). *Plural (Mexico),* v. 22, no. 265 (Oct 93), pp. 39 – 41.

FRONTIER AND PIONEER LIFE
See also
Land settlement

Amazon Valley
Cleary, David. After the Frontier: Problems with Political Economy in the Modern Brazilian Amazon. *Journal of Latin American Studies,* v. 25, no. 2 (May 93), pp. 331 – 349. Bibl.

Brazil
Metcalf, Alida C. *Family and Frontier in Colonial Brazil: Santana de Paranaíba, 1580 – 1822* reviewed by Susan Migden Socolow. *The Americas,* v. 50, no. 2 (Oct 93), pp. 279 – 280.

Pianzola, Maurice. *Des français à la conquête du Brésil, XVIIe siècle: les perroquets jaunes* reviewed by Pierre Ragon. *Cahiers des Amériques Latines,* no. 14 (1992), pp. 156 – 157.

Caribbean area
Games, Alison F. Survival Strategies in Early Bermuda and Barbados. *Revista/Review Interamericana,* v. 22, no. 1 – 2 (Spring – Summer 92), pp. 55 – 71. Bibl, tables.

Chile
Vargas Cariola, Juan Eduardo. Estilo de vida en el ejército de Chile durante el siglo XVII. *Revista de Indias,* v. 53, no. 198 (May – Aug 93), pp. 425 – 457. Bibl.

Dominican Republic
Baud, Michiel. Una frontera – refugio: dominicanos y haitianos contra el estado, 1870 – 1930 (Translated by Montserrat Planas Alberti). *Estudios Sociales (Dominican Republic),* v. 26, no. 92 (Apr – June 92), pp. 39 – 64. Bibl.

Mexican – American Border Region
Marchena Fernández, Juan. De franciscanos, apaches y ministros ilustrados en los pasos perdidos del norte de Nueva España. *Archivo Ibero-Americano,* v. 52, no. 205 – 208 (Jan – Dec 92), pp. 513 – 559. Bibl, tables.

FRUIT TRADE
See also
Names of specific fruits

Brazil
Mathematical models
Campos, José Ribamar Silva and José de Jesus Sousa Lemos. Fundamentação dinâmica para a produção e comercialização de hortifrutigranjeiros. *Revista de Economia e Sociologia Rural,* v. 30, no. 1 (Jan – Mar 92), pp. 11 – 20. Bibl, tables.

Dutton, John C., Jr. and Orlando Monteiro da Silva. O mercado internacional de suco de laranja concentrado congelado: um modelo com produtos diferenciados. *Revista de Economia e Sociologia Rural,* v. 29, no. 4 (Oct – Dec 91), pp. 353 – 371. Bibl, tables.

Silva, Orlando Monteiro da. Elasticidade de substituição para o suco de laranja no mercado internacional. *Revista de Economia e Sociologia Rural,* v. 30, no. 2 (Apr – June 92), pp. 135 – 147. Bibl, tables.

Mexico
La industria de la naranja en México (Includes appendices on world production and trade). *Comercio Exterior,* v. 43, no. 3 (Mar 93), pp. 222 – 247. Tables, charts.

Rodríguez, María de los Angeles. Las frutas y legumbres en el comercio exterior de México. *La Palabra y el Hombre,* no. 82 (Apr – June 92), pp. 199 – 227. Bibl, tables.

Statland de López, Rhona. Cross Over Dreams. *Business Mexico,* v. 3, no. 5 (May 93), pp. 23 – 24 + . Il.

FUENMAYOR, JUAN BAUTISTA
Criticism of specific works
Historia de la Venezuela política contemporánea
Fuenmayor, Juan Bautista. Palabras del dr. Juan Bautista Fuenmayor, premio nacional de historia Francisco González Guinán, 1991. *Boletín de la Academia Nacional de la Historia (Venezuela),* v. 75, no. 299 (July – Sept 92), pp. 29 – 32.

FUENTE BENAVIDES, RAFAEL DE LA
Criticism of specific works
De lo barroco en el Perú
Lauer, Mirko. La mentira cordial. *Debate (Peru),* v. 16, no. 74 (Sept – Oct 93), pp. 41 – 45. Bibl.

FUENTES, CARLOS
Criticism and interpretation
Mastretta, Angeles. Fuentes: la edad de su tiempo. *Nexos,* v. 16, no. 186 (June 93), pp. 27 – 28.

Criticism of specific works
Cristóbal Nonato
Llano, Aymara de. El lector: ¿Un lector que elige o que es elegido? *Escritura (Venezuela),* v. 17, no. 33 – 34 (Jan – Dec 92), pp. 149 – 157.

Gringo viejo
Portal, Marta. *Gringo viejo:* diálogo de culturas. *Cuadernos Americanos,* no. 39, Nueva época (May – June 93), pp. 217 – 227. Bibl.

Terra nostra
García Gutiérrez, Georgina. *Terra nostra:* crónica universal del orbe; apuntes sobre intertextualidad. *Nueva Revista de Filología Hispánica,* v. 40, no. 2 (July – Dec 92), pp. 1135 – 1148.

Foreign influences
Lapuente, Felipe-Antonio. Cervantes en la perspectiva de Fuentes. *Cuadernos Americanos,* no. 39, Nueva época (May – June 93), pp. 228 – 242. Bibl.

Interviews

Torres Fierro, Danubio. La fortaleza latinoamericana: conversación con Carlos Fuentes. *Cuadernos Hispanoamericanos,* no. 510 (Dec 92), pp. 104 – 107.

FUJIMORI, ALBERTO

Bustamante Belaúnde, Alberto et al. Pensando en la reelección. *Debate (Peru),* v. 16, no. 72 (Mar – May 93), pp. 14 – 18. II, charts.

Cotler, Julio C. Golpe a golpe . . . . *Debate (Peru),* v. 15, no. 71 (Nov 92 – Jan 93), pp. 18 – 19. II.

Gonzales de Olarte, Efraín. Economic Stabilization and Structural Adjustment under Fujimori. *Journal of Inter-American Studies and World Affairs,* v. 35, no. 2 (Summer 93), pp. 51 – 80. Bibl, tables.

Pires, Nielsen de Paula. Escollos a la democracia: Haití y Perú. *Mensaje,* v. 42, no. 425 (Dec 93), pp. 646 – 648. II.

FUKUYAMA, FRANCIS

Criticism of specific works

The End of History and the Last Man

Fragoso, José Manoel. O Atlântico e o mundo de língua portuguesa. *Revista do Instituto Histórico e Geográfico Brasileiro,* no. 373 (Oct – Dec 91), pp. 1107 – 1114.

FUNCTIONAL ANALYSIS (MATHEMATICS)

Ordorica Mellado, Manuel. Desarrollo y aplicación de una función expologística para el análisis de congruencia de las fuentes demográficas entre 1940 y 1990: el caso de México. *Revista Mexicana de Sociología,* v. 55, no. 1 (Jan – Mar 93), pp. 3 – 16. Tables, charts.

FUNCTIONAL ANALYSIS (SOCIAL SCIENCES)

Hernández, Raúl Augusto. Correlación y correspondencia en la acción social. *Revista Paraguaya de Sociología,* v. 29, no. 84 (May – Aug 92), pp. 171 – 185. Bibl.

FUNDACIÓN SALVADOREÑA PARA EL DESARROLLO ECONÓMICO Y SOCIAL

Martínez, Julia Evelyn. Neoliberalismo y derechos humanos. *ECA; Estudios Centroamericanos,* v. 47, no. 529 – 530 (Nov – Dec 92), pp. 1028 – 1036. II.

FUNERAL RITES AND CEREMONIES

See

> Mummies
> Subdivision *Ceremonies and practices* under *Catholic Church*
> Subdivision *Mortuary customs* under names of Indian groups

FURNITURE

Caribbean area

Derné, Marie-Claude et al. Business Opportunities in Caribbean Cooperation. *Social and Economic Studies,* v. 41, no. 3 (Sept 92), pp. 65 – 100. Bibl, tables.

FUSELI, JOHN HENRY

Criticism of specific works

The Nightmare

Young, Richard A. "Verano" de Julio Cortázar, *The Nightmare* de John Henry Fuseli y "the judicious adoption of figures in art." *Revista Canadiense de Estudios Hispánicos,* v. 17, no. 2 (Winter 93), pp. 373 – 382. Bibl.

GABRIEL, JUAN

Geirola, Gustavo. Juan Gabriel: cultura popular y sexo de los ángeles. *Latin American Music Review,* v. 14, no. 2 (Fall – Winter 93), pp. 232 – 267. Bibl.

GAGINI, CARLOS

Correspondence, reminiscences, etc.

Quesada Pacheco, Miguel Angel. Correspondencia de Carlos Gagini con Rufino José Cuervo y Ricardo Palma. *Káñina,* v. 16, no. 1 (Jan – June 92), pp. 197 – 206.

GALÁN, JULIO

Pitol, Sergio. Julio Galán: la lección del sí y el no. *Vuelta,* v. 17, no. 204 (Nov 93), pp. 21 – 25.

GALEANA, BENITA

Interviews

Díaz Castellanos, Guadalupe. Desde su cotidianidad . . . : Benita Galeana y su lucha (Part I). *Fem,* v. 17, no. 124 (June 93), pp. 18 – 20. II.

— Desde su cotidianidad . . . : Benita Galeana y su lucha (Part II). *Fem,* v. 17, no. 125 (July 93), pp. 21 – 23. II.

GALINDO, BLAS

Obituaries

Enríquez, Manuel. Blas Galindo Dimas (1910 – 1993). *Inter-American Music Review,* v. 13, no. 2 (Spring – Summer 93), pp. 171 – 172.

GALINDO, SERGIO

Criticism and interpretation

Ruiz Abreu, Alvaro. Sergio Galindo: las letras solitarias. *Nexos,* v. 16, no. 182 (Feb 93), pp. 11 – 13.

GALLEGOS, RÓMULO

Criticism of specific works

El forastero

Bastardo Casañas, Antonio. A 50 años de una novela galleguiana: *El forastero;* sus dos versiones. *Revista Nacional de Cultura (Venezuela),* v. 53, no. 286 (July – Sept 92), pp. 154 – 155.

GALVÁN, KYRA

Criticism and interpretation

Gartner, Bruce S. and Anita M. Hart. A Space of One's Own: Mexican Poets Kyra Galván and Perla Schwartz. *Confluencia,* v. 8, no. 1 (Fall 92), pp. 79 – 89. Bibl.

GALVE, GELVIRA DE TOLEDO, CONDESA DE

Correspondence, reminiscences, etc.

Galve, Gelvira de Toledo, condesa de. *Two Hearts, One Soul: The Correspondence of the Condesa de Galve, 1688 – 1696* edited, annotated, and translated by Meredith D. Dodge and Rick Hendricks. Reviewed by John E. Kicza. *Colonial Latin American Historical Review,* v. 2, no. 4 (Fall 93), pp. 475 – 477.

GÁLVEZ, MARIANO

Taracena Arriola, Arturo. Un testimonio francés del triunfo liberal de 1829: el papel del doctor Mariano Gálvez. *Mesoamérica (USA),* v. 13, no. 23 (June 92), pp. 143 – 156. Bibl.

GAMARRA, JOSÉ

Pérez Oramas, Luis. José Gamarra: después del Edén (Accompanied by an English translation). *Art Nexus,* no. 8 (Apr – June 93), pp. 92 – 94. II.

GAMES

See also

> Toys

Baratti, Abel and Eduardo Casali. *Del juego al deporte, I: Actividades para nivel primero* reviewed by Cora Céspedes. *La Educación (USA),* v. 36, no. 111 – 113 (1992), pp. 282 – 283.

GAMONET DE LOS HEROS, JIMMY

Durbin, Pamela. Transcultural Steps with a Flair. *Américas,* v. 45, no. 3 (May – June 93), pp. 18 – 23. II.

GANGOTENA, ALFREDO

Criticism and interpretation

Castillo de Berchenko, Adriana. *Alfredo Gangotena, poète équatorien, 1904 – 1944, ou, l'écriture partagée* reviewed by Rogelio Arenas. *Caravelle,* no. 60 (1993), pp. 170 – 172.

GARCÍA, ALAN

See

García Pérez, Alan

GARCIA, ELISABETH SOUZA-LOBO

See

Souza-Lobo, Elizabeth

GARCÍA, HÉCTOR

Coronel Rivera, Juan. Héctor García. *Artes de México,* no. 19 (Spring 93), p. 116. Il.

GARCÍA, MANUEL DEL PÓPULO VICENTE

Radomski, James. Manuel García in Mexico: Part II. *Inter-American Music Review,* v. 13, no. 1 (Fall – Winter 92), pp. 15 – 20. Facs.

GARCÍA, SANTIAGO

Criticism of specific works

Maravilla estar

Duque Mesa, Fernando. *Maravilla estar* en el laberinto de la postmodernidad. *Conjunto,* no. 93 (Jan – June 93), pp. 84 – 90. Bibl.

GARCÍA AGUILAR, EDUARDO

Correspondence, reminiscences, etc.

García Aguilar, Eduardo. *Urbes luminosas* reviewed by José Ricardo Chaves. *Vuelta,* v. 17, no. 195 (Feb 93), p. 42.

GARCÍA APONTE, ISAÍAS

Criticism and interpretation

Moreno Davis, Julio César. El estro poético de Isaías García Aponte: filosofía y poesía. *Revista Cultural Lotería,* v. 50, no. 385 (Sept – Oct 91), pp. 46 – 72. Bibl.

GARCÍA BACCA, JUAN DAVID

Bruni Celli, Blas. García Bacca: dos discursos en su presencia. *Boletín de la Academia Nacional de la Historia (Venezuela),* v. 75, no. 299 (July – Sept 92), pp. 164 – 173. Bibl.

Obituaries

In memoriam: Juan David García Bacca. *Revista Nacional de Cultura (Venezuela),* v. 53, no. 286 (July – Sept 92), pp. 203 – 205. Il.

GARCÍA GALLÓ, GASPAR M. JORGE

Morales Hernández, Xiomara et al. Gaspar Jorge García Galló y su labor de divulgación de la filosofía marxista – leninista. *Islas,* no. 98 (Jan – Apr 91), pp. 128 – 134. Bibl.

GARCÍA MÁRQUEZ, GABRIEL

Bibliography

Cobo Borda, Juan Gustavo. *Cien años de soledad:* un cuarto de siglo; creación y crítica. *Revista Interamericana de Bibliografía,* v. 42, no. 3 (1992), pp. 411 – 420.

Criticism and interpretation

Amoretti Hurtado, María. El discurso político y el discurso religioso en el apocalipsis de la modernidad. *Káñina,* v. 16, no. 1 (Jan – June 92), pp. 111 – 116.

Oberhelman, Harley D. *Gabriel García Márquez: A Study of the Short Fiction* reviewed by R. A. Kerr. *Hispania (USA),* v. 76, no. 2 (May 93), pp. 291 – 292.

Perilli de Garmendia, Carmen. *Imágenes de la mujer en Carpentier y García Márquez* reviewed by Rita Gnutzmann. *Revista Interamericana de Bibliografía,* v. 42, no. 3 (1992), p. 507.

Rodríguez-Vergara, Isabel. *El mundo satírico de Gabriel García Márquez* reviewed by Francisca Noguerol Jiménez. *Anuario de Estudios Americanos,* v. 49, Suppl. 1 (1992), pp. 261 – 262.

Criticism of specific works

El amor en los tiempos del cólera

Lemus, Silvia. El barco donde estaba el paraíso: una entrevista con Gabriel García Márquez. *Nexos,* v. 16, no. 192 (Dec 93), pp. 32 – 39. Il.

Cien años de soledad

Alzugarat, Alfredo J. *Cien años de soledad:* veinticinco años de diálogo con América Latina. *Cuadernos del CLAEH,* v. 17, no. 63 – 64 (Oct 92), pp. 175 – 181. Bibl.

Chamberlain, Daniel Frank. *Narrative Perspective in Fiction: A Phenomenological Mediation of Reader, Text, and World* reviewed by Lois Parkinson Zamora. *Revista Canadiense de Estudios Hispánicos,* v. 17, no. 1 (Fall 92), pp. 211 – 213.

Cobo Borda, Juan Gustavo. *Cien años de soledad:* un cuarto de siglo; creación y crítica. *Revista Interamericana de Bibliografía,* v. 42, no. 3 (1992), pp. 411 – 420.

Pera, Cristóbal. Alienación (europeización) o introversión (incesto): Latinoamérica y Europa en *Cien años de soledad. Chasqui,* v. 22, no. 2 (Nov 93), pp. 85 – 93. Bibl.

Urbina, Nicasio. *Cien años de soledad:* un texto lúdico con implicaciones muy serias. *Revista Canadiense de Estudios Hispánicos,* v. 17, no. 1 (Fall 92), pp. 137 – 152. Bibl.

Crónica de una muerte anunciada

Aronson, Stacey L. Parker and Cristina Enríquez de Salamanca. La textura del exilio: *Querido Diego, te abraza Quiela; Eva Luna; Crónica de una muerte anunciada. Chasqui,* v. 22, no. 2 (Nov 93), pp. 3 – 14. Bibl.

Christie, John S. Fathers and Virgins: García Márquez's Faulknerian *Chronicle of a Death Foretold. Latin American Literary Review,* v. 21, no. 41 (Jan – June 93), pp. 21 – 29. Bibl.

Eyzaguirre, Luis B. Rito y sacrificio en *Crónica de una muerte anunciada. Revista Chilena de Literatura,* no. 42 (Aug 93), pp. 81 – 87.

Doce cuentos peregrinos

Triviño Anzola, Consuelo. La escritura errante. *Cuadernos Hispanoamericanos,* no. 513 (Mar 93), pp. 140 – 144. Bibl.

Entre cachacos

Cruz Pérez, Francisco José. García Márquez: la realidad sin mediaciones. *Cuadernos Hispanoamericanos,* no. 512 (Feb 93), pp. 115 – 120.

El general en su laberinto

Alvarez-Borland, Isabel. The Task of the Historian in *El general en su laberinto. Hispania (USA),* v. 76, no. 3 (Sept 93), pp. 439 – 445. Bibl.

Matarrita M., Estébana. La polifuncionalidad en *El general en su laberinto. Káñina,* v. 16, no. 2 (July – Dec 92), pp. 109 – 113. Bibl.

El otoño del patriarca

Holdsworth, Carole A. Two Contemporary Versions of the Persephone Myth. *Revista Interamericana de Bibliografía,* v. 42, no. 4 (1992), pp. 571 – 576. Bibl.

Interviews

Lemus, Silvia. El barco donde estaba el paraíso: una entrevista con Gabriel García Márquez. *Nexos,* v. 16, no. 192 (Dec 93), pp. 32 – 39. Il.

Lorenzo Fuentes, José. García Márquez: un concepto obrero de la inspiración. *Plural (Mexico),* v. 22, no. 259 (Apr 93), pp. 52 – 55.

GARCÍA NÚÑEZ, JULIÁN

Wuellner, Margarita Jerabek. Argentine Architect Julián García Núñez, 1875 – 1944. *SALALM Papers,* v. 34 (1989), pp. 53 – 91. Bibl, il.

GARCÍA PÉREZ, ALAN

Crabtree, John. *Peru under García: An Opportunity Lost* reviewed by Alfonso W. Quiroz. *Hispanic American Historical Review,* v. 73, no. 4 (Nov 93), pp. 713 – 714.

— *Peru under García: An Opportunity Lost* reviewed by Carol Graham. *Journal of Latin American Studies,* v. 25, no. 2 (May 93), pp. 413 – 414.

GARCÍA PIEDRAHITA, EVARISTO

Borrero Garcés, Luis Enrique. Evaristo García Piedrahita, un varón epónimo. *Boletín de Historia y Antigüedades,* v. 80, no. 780 (Jan – Mar 93), pp. 223 – 231.

GARCÍA PONCE, JUAN
Criticism and interpretation
Moreno Uscanga, Ivonne. Juan García Ponce: la bifurcación del amor. *La Palabra y el Hombre,* no. 81 (Jan – Mar 92), pp. 313 – 315.

GARCÍA RAMIS, MAGALI
Criticism of specific works
Felices días, tío Sergio
Sotomayor Miletti, Aurea María. Si un nombre convoca un mundo . . . : *Felices días, tío Sergio* en la narrativa puertorriqueña contemporánea. *Revista Iberoamericana,* v. 59, no. 162 – 163 (Jan – June 93), pp. 317 – 327. Bibl.
Interviews
Negrón-Muntaner, Frances. Magali García Ramis. *Hispamérica,* v. 22, no. 64 – 65 (Apr – Aug 93), pp. 89 – 104.

GARCÍA TASSARA, GABRIEL
Jou, Maite. Gabriel García y Tassara: del nacionalismo romántico al concepto de raza hispana. *Anuario de Estudios Americanos,* v. 49 (1992), pp. 529 – 562. Bibl.

GARCILASO DE LA VEGA, EL INCA
Criticism and interpretation
Cornejo Polar, Antonio. El discurso de la armonía imposible: el Inca Garcilaso de la Vega; discurso y recepción social. *Revista de Crítica Literaria Latinoamericana,* v. 19, no. 38 (July – Dec 93), pp. 73 – 80.
Hilton, Sylvia-Lyn and Amancio Labandeira Fernández. La sensibilidad cromática y estética del Inca Garcilaso. *Revista de Indias,* v. 52, no. 195 – 196 (May – Dec 92), pp. 529 – 558. Bibl.
Criticism of specific works
Comentarios reales de los incas
Fernández Ariza, María Guadalupe. Los *Comentarios reales* del Inca Garcilaso y el humanismo renacentista. *Studi di Letteratura Ispano-Americana,* v. 24 (1993), pp. 23 – 35.

GARIBAY, RICARDO
Correspondence, reminiscences, etc.
Garibay, Ricardo. *Cómo se gana la vida* reviewed by Roberto Pliego (Review entitled "Garibay para sí mismo"). *Nexos,* v. 16, no. 185 (May 93), pp. 79 – 80.

GARIBAY KINTANA, ANGEL MARÍA
Archives
Herr Solé, Alberto. El Archivo Angel María Garibay Kintana de la Biblioteca Nacional. *Estudios de Cultura Náhuatl,* v. 22 (1992), pp. 181 – 222.
Biography
León-Portilla, Miguel. Angel Ma. Garibay K. (1892 – 1992): en el centenario de su nacimiento. *Estudios de Cultura Náhuatl,* v. 22 (1992), pp. 167 – 180.

GARIF INDIANS
See
Carib Indians

GARMENDIA, JULIO
Criticism and interpretation
Barrera Linares, Luis. Julio Garmendia: mito y realidad/ ambigüedad e ironía. *Escritura (Venezuela),* v. 17, no. 33 – 34 (Jan – Dec 92), pp. 21 – 46. Bibl.

GARMENDIA, SALVADOR
Biography
Garmendia, Salvador. Por qué escribo. *Inti,* no. 37 – 38 (Spring – Fall 93), pp. 263 – 272.

GARRO, ELENA
Correspondence, reminiscences, etc.
Garro, Elena. *Memorias de España 1937* reviewed by Federico Alvarez. *Plural (Mexico),* v. 22, no. 259 (Apr 93), pp. 69 – 71.

GAS, NATURAL
Brazil
Guerra, Sinclair Mallet-Guy et al. Perspectivas y estrategias para el gas natural en la América Latina: Brasil y Venezuela. *Interciencia,* v. 18, no. 1 (Jan – Feb 93), pp. 24 – 28. Bibl, tables, maps.
Colombia
Vásquez Rodríguez, Raúl. Petróleo y gas en el gobierno Gaviria. *Revista Javeriana,* v. 61, no. 597 (Aug 93), pp. 153 – 158.
Mexican – American Border Region
Nabers, Mary Scott. A Growing Love Affair. *Business Mexico,* v. 3, no. 5 (May 93), pp. 13 – 14. Charts.
Mexico
Baker, George and Bart Van Aardenne. CNG: A Fuel for the Future. *Business Mexico,* v. 3, no. 1 (Jan – Feb 93), pp. 48 – 50.
United States
Baker, George and Bart Van Aardenne. CNG: A Fuel for the Future. *Business Mexico,* v. 3, no. 1 (Jan – Feb 93), pp. 48 – 50.
Venezuela
Guerra, Sinclair Mallet-Guy et al. Perspectivas y estrategias para el gas natural en la América Latina: Brasil y Venezuela. *Interciencia,* v. 18, no. 1 (Jan – Feb 93), pp. 24 – 28. Bibl, tables, maps.

GATT
See
General Agreement on Tariffs and Trade

GAUCHOS
Lopez, Luiz Roberto. A quem serviu o mito do gaúcho. *Vozes,* v. 86, no. 5 (Sept – Oct 92), pp. 99 – 101.
Quevedo, Raul. Realidade e mitos do Rio Grande antigo. *Vozes,* v. 87, no. 4 (July – Aug 93), pp. 86 – 90. Il.
Slatta, Richard W. *Gauchos and the Vanishing Frontier* reviewed by Jeremy Adelman. *Journal of Latin American Studies,* v. 25, no. 2 (May 93), pp. 401 – 402.

GAUCHOS IN LITERATURE
Aguiar, Flávio. Cultura de contrabando: estudo sobre os contos de Simões Lopes Neto. *Vozes,* v. 86, no. 6 (Nov – Dec 92), pp. 13 – 20.

LOS GAVILANES, PERU
Bonavia, Duccio and John G. Jones. Análisis de coprolitos de llama (Lama glama) del precerámico tardío de la costa nor central del Perú. *Bulletin de l'Institut Français d'Etudes Andines,* v. 21, no. 3 (1992), pp. 835 – 852. Bibl, tables.

GAVIRIA TRUJILLO, CÉSAR
Escobar Herrán, Guillermo León. Tres años de confusión social. *Revista Javeriana,* v. 61, no. 597 (Aug 93), pp. 166 – 168.
Noriega, Carlos Augusto. Las innovaciones políticas del gobierno Gaviria. *Revista Javeriana,* v. 61, no. 597 (Aug 93), pp. 129 – 142.
Addresses, essays, lectures
Gaviria Trujillo, César. Palabras del presidente de la república, César Gaviria Trujillo, en el acto de instalación. *Planeación y Desarrollo,* v. 24, no. 1 (Jan – Apr 93), pp. 17 – 25.

GAZETA DO RIO DE JANEIRO (NEWSPAPER)
Cardoso, Tereza Maria R. Fachada Levy. A *Gazeta do Rio de Janeiro:* subsídios para a história da cidade, 1808 – 1821. *Revista do Instituto Histórico e Geográfico Brasileiro,* no. 371 (Apr – June 91), pp. 341 – 436. Bibl, il, tables, maps.

GÊ INDIANS
Giannini, Isabelle Vidal. Os dominios cósmicos: um dos aspectos da construção da categoria humana kayapó – xikrin. *Revista de Antropologia (Brazil),* v. 34 (1991), pp. 35 – 58. Bibl.

GELMAN, JUAN

Interviews

Dimo, Edith. Una voz nacida del silencio: conversación con Juan Gelman. *Chasqui*, v. 22, no. 2 (Nov 93), pp. 109 – 113.

GENDER ROLES

See
Sex role

GENEALOGY

See
Subdivision *Biography* under names of specific countries

GENERAL AGREEMENT ON TARIFFS AND TRADE

Baldinelli, Elvio. La protección contra el comercio desleal. *Integración Latinoamericana*, v. 17, no. 184 (Nov 92), pp. 26 – 35.

Corona Guzmán, Roberto. El entorno actual de la negociación comercial de América Latina. *Relaciones Internacionales (Mexico)*, v. 14, Nueva época, no. 56 (Oct – Dec 92), pp. 63 – 86. Tables.

González, Anabel. Comercio internacional y medio ambiente. *Comercio Exterior*, v. 43, no. 9 (Sept 93), pp. 827 – 835. Bibl.

Raghavan, Chakravarthi. *Recolonization: GATT, the Uruguay Round, and the Third World* (Review entitled "Un libro para despertar al Tercer Mundo"). *Homines*, v. 15 – 16, no. 2 – 1 (Oct 91 – Dec 92), pp. 384 – 385.

Watkins, Kevin. El GATT y el Tercer Mundo: como establecer las normas (Excerpt from *Fixing the Rules: North – South Issues in International Trade and the GATT Uruguay Round*, translated by Cecilia M. Mata). *Realidad Económica*, no. 113 (Jan – Feb 93), pp. 122 – 141.

Woss W., Herfreid. Calculating Customs Valuation. *Business Mexico*, v. 3, no. 6 (June 93), pp. 38 – 39.

GENETICS

See
Biotechnology

GEOGRAPHIC INFORMATION SYSTEMS

Brazil

Silva, Jorge Xavier da. Um banco de dados ambientais para a Amazônia. *Revista Brasileira de Geografia*, v. 53, no. 3 (July – Sept 91), pp. 91 – 124. Bibl, il, tables, maps.

Peru

Loker, William M. et al. Identification of Areas of Land Degradation in the Peruvian Amazon Using a Geographic Information System. *Interciencia*, v. 18, no. 3 (May – June 93), pp. 133 – 141. Bibl, tables, maps, charts.

GEOGRAPHICAL DISTRIBUTION OF PLANTS AND ANIMALS

See also
Vegetation and climate

Amazon Valley

Kahn, Francis and Betty Millán. "Astrocaryum" (Palmae) in Amazonia: A Preliminary Treatment. *Bulletin de l'Institut Français d'Etudes Andines*, v. 21, no. 2 (1992), pp. 459 – 531. Bibl, il, tables.

Kahn, Francis et al. Datos preliminares a la actualización de la flora de palamae del Perú: intensidad de herborización y riqueza de las colecciones. *Bulletin de l'Institut Français d'Etudes Andines*, v. 21, no. 2 (1992), pp. 549 – 563. Bibl, tables, maps.

Moussa, Farana et al. Las palmeras en los valles principales de la Amazonia peruana. *Bulletin de l'Institut Français d'Etudes Andines*, v. 21, no. 2 (1992), pp. 565 – 597. Maps.

Colombia

Galeano Garcés, Gloria. Patrones de distribución de las palmas de Colombia. *Bulletin de l'Institut Français d'Etudes Andines*, v. 21, no. 2 (1992), pp. 599 – 607. Bibl, maps, charts.

Guyana

Granville, Jean-Jacques de. Life Forms and Growth Strategies of Guianan Palms as Related to Their Ecology. *Bulletin de l'Institut Français d'Etudes Andines*, v. 21, no. 2 (1992), pp. 533 – 548. Bibl, il, tables.

Jamaica

Rashford, John H. Arawak, Spanish, and African Contributions to Jamaica's Settlement Vegetation. *Jamaica Journal*, v. 24, no. 3 (Feb 93), pp. 17 – 23. Bibl, il.

Latin America

Hodel, Donald R. "Chamaedorea": Diverse Species in Diverse Habitats. *Bulletin de l'Institut Français d'Etudes Andines*, v. 21, no. 2 (1992), pp. 433 – 458. Bibl, il.

Mexico

Durán, Rafael and Miguel Franco. Estudio demográfico de "Pseudophoenix sargentii." *Bulletin de l'Institut Français d'Etudes Andines*, v. 21, no. 2 (1992), pp. 609 – 621. Bibl, maps, charts.

GEOGRAPHY

See also
Anthropo-geography
Cartography
Coasts
Deserts
Geographic information systems
Natural history
Soils
Vegetation and climate

Argentina

Study and teaching

Dodds, Klaus-John. Geography, Identity, and the Creation of the Argentine State. *Bulletin of Latin American Research*, v. 12, no. 3 (Sept 93), pp. 311 – 331. Bibl.

Caribbean area

Study and teaching

Barker, David. The UWI Scholarship Examination in Geography: An Analysis of the 1992 Results. *Caribbean Geography*, v. 3, no. 4 (Sept 92), pp. 270 – 274. Tables.

Hart, Graham and Mike Morrissey. *Practical Skills in Caribbean Geography, Book 1: Grade 8 – Basic CXC and Book 2: Grade 10 – General CXC* reviewed by Laurence Neuville. *Caribbean Geography*, v. 3, no. 4 (Sept 92), pp. 279 – 280.

Latin America

Bataillon, Claude et al. *Amérique Latine* reviewed by Evelyne Mesclier. *Bulletin de l'Institut Français d'Etudes Andines*, v. 21, no. 2 (1992), pp. 789 – 792.

— *Amérique Latine, vol. III: Géographie universelle* reviewed by Isabel Hurtado. *Revista Andina*, v. 11, no. 1 (July 93), pp. 243 – 244.

Venezuela

Solano y Pérez-Lila, Francisco de, ed. *Relaciones topográficas de Venezuela, 1815 – 1819* reviewed by María del Carmen Mena García. *Anuario de Estudios Americanos*, v. 49, Suppl. 1 (1992), pp. 258 – 260.

GEOGRAPHY, ECONOMIC

See also
Industries, Location of
Regional planning

Argentina

Prévôt-Schapira, Marie-France. Argentine: fédéralisme et territoires. *Cahiers des Amériques Latines*, no. 14 (1992), pp. 4 – 32. Bibl, tables, maps.

Brazil

Ajara, Cesar et al. O estado do Tocantins: reinterpretação de um espaço de fronteira. *Revista Brasileira de Geografia*, v. 53, no. 4 (Oct – Dec 91), pp. 5 – 48. Bibl, maps.

Cardoso, Maria Francisca Thereza. Organização e reorganização do espaço no vale do Paraíba do sul: uma análise geográfica até 1940. *Revista Brasileira de Geografia*, v. 53, no. 1 (Jan – Mar 91), pp. 81 – 135. Bibl, maps.

Grabois, José and Mauro José da Silva. O breja de Natuba: estudo da organização de um espaço periférico. *Revista Brasileira de Geografia*, v. 53, no. 2 (Apr – June 91), pp. 33 – 62. Bibl, il, tables, maps.

Grabois, José et al. A organização do espaço no baixo vale do Taperoá: uma ocupação extensiva em mudança. *Revista Brasileira de Geografia*, v. 53, no. 4 (Oct – Dec 91), pp. 81 – 114. Bibl, il, tables, maps.

Silva, Barbara-Christine Nentwig. Análise comparativa da posição de Salvador e do estado da Bahia no cenário nacional. *Revista Brasileira de Geografia*, v. 53, no. 4 (Oct – Dec 91), pp. 49 – 79. Bibl, tables, maps, charts.

Cuba

García Negrete, Gloria. Problemas de la regionalización económica de Cuba en la primera mitad del siglo XIX. *Islas*, no. 98 (Jan – Apr 91), pp. 28 – 39. Tables.

Mexico

Graizbord, Boris. Estructura y posibilidades de crecimiento de 22 ciudades industriales mexicanas. *Comercio Exterior*, v. 43, no. 2 (Feb 93), pp. 149 – 158. Bibl, tables.

Marchal, Jean-Ives. Municipios vecinos, hermanos enemigos: esbozo de dos desarrollos divergentes; Tuxpan y Alamo, Veracruz. *Estudios Sociológicos*, v. 10, no. 30 (Sept – Dec 92), pp. 555 – 581. Bibl, maps.

Wilson, Patricia Ann. *Exports and Local Development: Mexico's New Maquiladoras* reviewed by Alfredo Hualde. *Estudios Sociológicos*, v. 11, no. 32 (May – Aug 93), pp. 569 – 573.

— *Exports and Local Development: Mexico's New Maquiladoras* reviewed by Helen Icken Saja. *Hispanic American Historical Review*, v. 73, no. 4 (Nov 93), pp. 719 – 720.

— *Exports and Local Development: Mexico's New Maquiladoras* reviewed by David J. Molina. *Journal of Borderlands Studies*, v. 7, no. 2 (Fall 92), pp. 106 – 108.

Pacific Area

Wong González, Pablo. La región norte de México en la triangulación comercial y productiva del Pacífico. *Comercio Exterior*, v. 43, no. 12 (Dec 93), pp. 1153 – 1163. Bibl, tables.

Southern Cone of South America

Schvarzer, Jorge. El MERCOSUR: la geografía a la espera de actores. *Nueva Sociedad*, no. 126 (July – Aug 93), pp. 72 – 83.

Uruguay

Wettstein, Germán. La producción y valorización del espacio en un país estancado: interpretación geográfica del caso uruguayo. *Derecho y Reforma Agraria*, no. 23 (1992), pp. 51 – 72. Bibl.

GEOGRAPHY, HISTORICAL

America

Cuesta Domingo, Mariano. Descubrimientos geográficos durante el siglo XVIII: acción franciscana en la ampliación de fronteras. *Archivo Ibero-Americano*, v. 52, no. 205 – 208 (Jan – Dec 92), pp. 293 – 342. Bibl, il, maps.

Brazil

Cardoso, Maria Francisca Thereza. Organização e reorganização do espaço no vale do Paraíba do sul: uma análise geográfica até 1940. *Revista Brasileira de Geografia*, v. 53, no. 1 (Jan – Mar 91), pp. 81 – 135. Bibl, maps.

Chacón, Vamireh. A civilização do planalto. *Revista do Instituto Histórico e Geográfico Brasileiro*, no. 372 (July – Sept 91), pp. 613 – 646. Bibl.

Guatemala

Lovell, William George. *Conquest and Survival in Colonial Guatemala: A Historical Geography of the Cuchumatán Highlands, 1500 – 1821* reviewed by Rob de Ridder. *European Review of Latin American and Caribbean Studies*, no. 54 (June 93), pp. 118 – 120. Bibl.

— *Conquest and Survival in Colonial Guatemala: A Historical Geography of the Cuchumatán Highlands, 1500 – 1821* reviewed by Raymond Buvé. *Journal of Latin American Studies*, v. 25, no. 1 (Feb 93), pp. 197 – 198.

— *Conquista y cambio cultural: la sierra de los Cuchumatanes de Guatemala, 1500 – 1821*, a translation of *Conquest and Survival in Colonial Guatemala*, translated by Eddy Gaytán. Reviewed by María Milagros Ciudad Suárez. *Anuario de Estudios Americanos*, v. 49, Suppl. 2 (1992), pp. 250 – 252.

Latin America

Venegas Delgado, Hernán. Acerca del concepto de región histórica. *Islas*, no. 98 (Jan – Apr 91), pp. 13 – 21. Bibl.

Mexico

Aranda Romero, José Luis and Agustín Grajales Porras. Perfil sociodemográfico de Tehuacán durante el virreinato. *Estudios Demográficos y Urbanos*, v. 7, no. 1 (Jan – Apr 92), pp. 53 – 76. Bibl, tables, maps, charts.

Musset, Alain. *De l'eau vive à l'eau morte: enjeux techniques et culturels dans la vallée de Mexico, XVIe – XIXe siècles* reviewed by Marie-Danielle Démelas-Bohy. *Caravelle*, no. 59 (1992), p. 307.

Vargas Uribe, Guillermo. Geografía histórica de la ciudad de Morelia, Michoacán, México: su evolución demográfica. *Islas*, no. 98 (Jan – Apr 91), pp. 58 – 70. Bibl, tables, maps, charts.

— Geografía histórica de la población de Michoacán, siglo XVIII. *Estudios Demográficos y Urbanos*, v. 7, no. 1 (Jan – Apr 92), pp. 193 – 222. Bibl, tables, maps, charts.

Sources

Moncada Maya, J. Omar. Miguel Constanzó y el reconocimiento geográfico de la costa de Veracruz de 1797. *Anuario de Estudios Americanos*, v. 49, Suppl. 2 (1992), pp. 31 – 64. Bibl.

Peru

Bibliography

Domínguez Faura, Nicanor. La conformación de la imagen del espacio andino: geografía e historia en el Perú colonial, 1530 – 1820; crónica bibliográfica. *Revista Andina*, v. 11, no. 1 (July 93), pp. 201 – 237. Bibl.

Uruguay

Díaz de Guerra, María A. La zona de José Ignacio en el departamento de Maldonado y su incidencia en la evolución regional. *Hoy Es Historia*, v. 10, no. 58 (July – Aug 93), pp. 27 – 53. Bibl, il, facs.

GEOLOGY

See also
Coasts
Earthquakes
Erosion
Geomorphology
Natural disasters
Soils
Volcanism

Brazil

Figueroa, Sílvia Fernanda de Mendonça. Las ciencias geológicas en Brasil en el siglo XIX (Translated by Hernán G. H. Taboada). *Cuadernos Americanos*, no. 38, Nueva época (Mar – Apr 93), pp. 180 – 204. Bibl.

GEOMORPHOLOGY

Amazon Valley

Dumont, Jean-François. Rasgos morfoestructurales de la llanura amazónica del Perú: efecto de la neotectónica sobre los cambios fluviales y la delimitación de las provincias morfológicas. *Bulletin de l'Institut Français d'Etudes Andines*, v. 21, no. 3 (1992), pp. 801 – 833. Bibl, il, maps.

Belize

Day, Michael J. The Geomorphology and Hydrology of the Blue Hole, Caves Branch. *Belizean Studies*, v. 20, no. 3 (Dec 92), pp. 3 – 10. Bibl, maps, charts.

Peru

Mabres, Antonio and Ronald F. Woodman. Formación de un cordón litoral en Máncora, Perú, a raíz de El Niño de 1983. *Bulletin de l'Institut Français d'Etudes Andines*, v. 22, no. 1 (1993), pp. 213 – 226. Bibl, il, maps.

Ortlieb, Luc et al. Beach-Ridge Series in Northern Peru: Chronology, Correlation, and Relationship with Major Late Holocene El Niño Events. *Bulletin de l'Institut Français d'Etudes Andines*, v. 22, no. 1 (1993), pp. 191 – 212. Bibl, il, tables, maps, charts.

GEOPOLITICS

See also
International relations
Subdivisions *Boundaries* and *Foreign relations* under names of specific countries

Aínsa Amigues, Fernando. Nuestro Sur: fragmentos para una nueva geografía. *Plural (Mexico)*, v. 22, no. 260 (May 93), pp. 16 – 22.

Coatsworth, John Henry. Pax (norte) americana: América Latina después de la guerra fría (Translated by Marcela Pineda Camacho). *Revista Mexicana de Sociología*, v. 55, no. 2 (Apr – June 93), pp. 293 – 314. Bibl.

Fragoso, José Manoel. O Atlântico e o mundo de língua portuguesa. *Revista do Instituto Histórico e Geográfico Brasileiro*, no. 373 (Oct – Dec 91), pp. 1107 – 1114.

González Aguayo, Leopoldo Augusto. Notas sobre la geopolítica de las fronteras. *Relaciones Internacionales (Mexico)*, v. 14, Nueva época, no. 55 (July – Sept 92), pp. 23 – 30. Bibl.

Mattos, Carlos de Meira. *Geopolítica e teoria de fronteiras: fronteiras do Brasil* reviewed by Vicente Tapajós. *Revista do Instituto Histórico e Geográfico Brasileiro*, no. 370 (Jan – Mar 91), p. 340.

Silva Herzog, Jesús. Crisis humana y post-guerra. *Hoy Es Historia*, v. 10, no. 58 (July – Aug 93), pp. 59 – 70. Il.

Amazon Valley

Becker, Bertha Koiffman. Geografia política e gestão do território no limiar do século XXI: uma representação a partir do Brasil. *Revista Brasileira de Geografia*, v. 53, no. 3 (July – Sept 91), pp. 169 – 182. Bibl.

America

Mace, Gordon et al. Regionalism in the Americas and the Hierarchy of Power. *Journal of Inter-American Studies and World Affairs*, v. 35, no. 2 (Summer 93), pp. 115 – 157. Bibl, tables, maps.

Caribbean area

Martínez Vara, Gerardo. México y el Caribe: un encuentro necesario en la problemática regional. *Relaciones Internacionales (Mexico)*, v. 14, Nueva época, no. 56 (Oct – Dec 92), pp. 129 – 132.

Richardson, Bonham C. *The Caribbean in the Wider World, 1492 – 1992: A Regional Geography* reviewed by Brian J. Hudson. *Caribbean Geography*, v. 3, no. 3 (Mar 92), pp. 209 – 210.

— *The Caribbean in the Wider World, 1492 – 1992: A Regional Geography* reviewed by David Barker. *Social and Economic Studies*, v. 41, no. 3 (Sept 92), pp. 183 – 186.

Dominican Republic

Martínez Fernández, Luis N. El anexionismo dominicano y la lucha entre imperios durante la primera republica, 1844 – 1861. *Revista/Review Interamericana*, v. 22, no. 1 – 2 (Spring – Summer 92), pp. 168 – 190. Bibl.

Latin America

Ballester, Horacio P. Proyecciones geopolíticas hacia el tercer milenio: el dramático futuro latinoamericano caribeño (A chapter from Horacio P. Ballester's book of the same title, introduced by Fermín Chávez). *Realidad Económica*, no. 116 (May – June 93), pp. 137 – 141.

González Aguayo, Leopoldo Augusto. La geopolítica de América Latina. *Relaciones Internacionales (Mexico)*, v. 14, Nueva época, no. 56 (Oct – Dec 92), pp. 97 – 102. Bibl.

Zapata, Francisco. *Atacama: desierto de la discordia; minería y política internacional en Bolivia, Chile y Perú* reviewed by Andrea Ostrov. *La Educación (USA)*, v. 37, no. 114 (1993), pp. 175 – 176.

Paraguay

Mattos, Carlos de Meira. Geopolítica do Paraguai. *Política e Estratégica*, v. 8, no. 2 – 4 (Apr – Dec 90), pp. 400 – 404.

GÉRARD DE NERVAL, GÉRARD LABRUNIE

Kothe, Flávio R. Heine, Nerval, Castro Alves: "o negreiro." *Iberoamericana*, v. 17, no. 49 (1993), pp. 42 – 63.

GERBASI, VICENTE

Criticism and interpretation

Guzmán, Patricia. El lugar como absoluto: Vicente Gerbasi, Ramón Palomares y Luis Alberto Crespo. *Inti*, no. 37 – 38 (Spring – Fall 93), pp. 107 – 115. Bibl.

Obituaries

Beltrán Guerrero, Luis. Vicente Gerbasi. *Boletín de la Academia Nacional de la Historia (Venezuela)*, v. 76, no. 301 (Jan – Mar 93), pp. 112 – 113.

Osuna, William. Viajes a través de Vicente Gerbasi. *Revista Nacional de Cultura (Venezuela)*, v. 54, no. 287 (Oct – Dec 92), pp. 16 – 17. Il.

Vicente Gerbasi. *Revista Nacional de Cultura (Venezuela)*, v. 54, no. 287 (Oct – Dec 92), pp. 9 – 13. Il.

Poetry

Lizardo, Pedro Francisco. Vicente Gerbasi en Canoabo. *Revista Nacional de Cultura (Venezuela)*, v. 54, no. 287 (Oct – Dec 92), pp. 14 – 15.

GERMANS

Argentina

Meding, Holger M. German Emigration to Argentina and the Illegal Brain Drain to the Plate, 1945 – 1955. *Jahrbuch für Geschichte von Staat, Wirtschaft und Gesellschaft Lateinamerikas*, v. 29 (1992), pp. 397 – 419. Bibl, tables.

Newton, Ronald C. *The "Nazi Menace" in Argentina, 1931 – 1947* reviewed by Joel Horowitz. *The Americas*, v. 50, no. 1 (July 93), pp. 140 – 141.

— *The "Nazi Menace" in Argentina, 1931 – 1947* reviewed by Walter Little. *Bulletin of Latin American Research*, v. 12, no. 1 (Jan 93), pp. 117 – 118.

— *The "Nazi Menace" in Argentina, 1931 – 1947* reviewed by Jeff Lesser. *European Review of Latin American and Caribbean Studies*, no. 54 (June 93), pp. 136 – 137.

— *The "Nazi Menace" in Argentina, 1931 – 1947* reviewed by Stanley E. Hilton. *Hispanic American Historical Review*, v. 73, no. 4 (Nov 93), pp. 706 – 707.

— *The "Nazi Menace" in Argentina, 1931 – 1947* reviewed by Celia Szusterman. *Journal of Latin American Studies*, v. 25, no. 1 (Feb 93), pp. 202 – 205.

— *The "Nazi Menace" in Argentina, 1931 – 1947* reviewed by Mario Rapoport. *Revista Interamericana de Bibliografía*, v. 42, no. 4 (1992), pp. 659 – 660.

Brazil

Gertz, René E. *O perigo alemão* reviewed by Jeff Lesser. *The Americas*, v. 50, no. 1 (July 93), pp. 141 – 142.

— *O perigo alemão* reviewed by Ronald C. Newton. *Hispanic American Historical Review*, v. 73, no. 2 (May 93), pp. 324 – 325.

Chile

Cruz Ovalle de Amenábar, Isabel. Arte jesuita en Chile: la huella del barroco bávaro. *Mensaje*, v. 42, no. 420 (July 93), pp. 234 – 238. Il.

Salinas Meza, René. Una comunidad inmigrante: los alemanes en Valparaíso, 1860 – 1960; estudio demográfico. *Jahrbuch für Geschichte von Staat, Wirtschaft und Gesellschaft Lateinamerikas*, v. 29 (1992), pp. 309 – 342. Bibl, tables, charts.

Tampe, Eduardo. Jesuitas alemanes y la colonización del sur. *Mensaje*, v. 42, no. 420 (July 93), pp. 259 – 263. Il.

Colombia

García Pombo, Pablo. Alemania y Colombia: trayectoria de una larga amistad. *Boletín de Historia y Antigüedades*, v. 80, no. 780 (Jan – Mar 93), pp. 79 – 108.

Costa Rica

Herrera Balharry, Eugenio. *Los alemanes y el estado cafetalero* reviewed by Gertrud Peters Solórzano (Review entitled "Café, familia y política"). *Revista de Historia (Costa Rica)*, no. 25 (Jan – June 92), pp. 239 – 242.

Cuba

Franzbach, Martin. Die beiden Deutschlands auf Kuba: Ein Beitrag zur Geschichte der Auslandsdeutschen in der Karibik. *Iberoamericana,* v. 17, no. 50 (1993), pp. 5 – 15. Bibl.

GERMANY

See also
Banks and banking – Germany
Books – Germany
Latin American studies – Germany
Libraries and librarians – Germany
Manuscripts – Germany
Mexican drama – Germany
Periodicals – Germany
Sculpture – Germany
Women authors – Germany

Commerce
Latin America

Young, George F. W. German Banking and German Imperialism in Latin America in the Wilhelmine Era. *Ibero-Amerikanisches Archiv,* v. 18, no. 1 – 2 (1992), pp. 31 – 66. Bibl, tables.

Foreign relations
Colombia

García Pombo, Pablo. Alemania y Colombia: trayectoria de una larga amistad. *Boletín de Historia y Antigüedades,* v. 80, no. 780 (Jan – Mar 93), pp. 79 – 108.

Latin America

Botet, Violanda. Germany and Latin America. *Hemisphere,* v. 5, no. 2 (Winter – Spring 93), pp. 16 – 17.

Müller, Jürgen. Hitler, Lateinamerika und die Weltherrschaft. *Ibero-Amerikanisches Archiv,* v. 18, no. 1 – 2 (1992), pp. 67 – 101. Bibl.

Silveira, Helder Gordim da. A ofensiva política dos EUA sobre a América Latina na visão alemã: uma face do confronto interimperialista, 1938. *Estudos Ibero-Americanos,* v. 18, no. 1 (July 92), pp. 19 – 27. Bibl.

GHANA

See
Religion and sociology – Ghana

GHIRALDO, ALBERTO

Criticism of specific works
Humano ardor

Reichardt, Dieter. *Humano ardor* por Alberto Ghiraldo: la novela autobiográfica de un anarquista argentino. *Iberoamericana,* v. 17, no. 50 (1993), pp. 79 – 88. Bibl.

GIL, GILBERTO

Sparks, David Hatfield. Gilberto Gil, Praise Singer of the Gods. *Afro-Hispanic Review,* v. 11, no. 1 – 3 (1992), pp. 70 – 75. Bibl.

GIL DE BIEDMA, JAIME

Criticism and interpretation

Alonso Martínez, María Nieves and Mario Rodríguez. Poesía chilena y española: Lihn y Gil de Biedma. *Atenea (Chile),* no. 467 (1993), pp. 197 – 219. Bibl.

GIL DÍAZ, FRANCISCO

MacDonald, Christine. Customs' Unsung Hero? *Business Mexico,* v. 3, no. 4 (Apr 93), pp. 27 – 29. Il.

GIMÉNEZ, CARLOS

Interviews

Rajatabla y Yuyachkani: veinte años. *Conjunto,* no. 90 – 91 (Jan – June 92), pp. 32 – 38. Il.

Obituaries

Kage, Hedda. Carlos Giménez ha muerto (Translated by José Luis Gómez y Patiño). *Humboldt,* no. 109 (1993), p. 99.

GINASTERA, ALBERTO EVARISTO

Helguera, Luis Ignacio. Ginastera a diez años de su muerte. *Vuelta,* v. 17, no. 202 (Sept 93), pp. 67 – 69.

GINÉS DE SEPÚLVEDA, JUAN

See
Sepúlveda, Juan Ginés de

GODFREY, GLENN D.

Criticism of specific works
The Sinners' Bossanova

Glassman, Steve. *The Sinners' Bossanova:* Its Caribbean Roots. *Belizean Studies,* v. 21, no. 2 (Oct 93), pp. 23 – 27.

GODOY ALCAYAGA, LUCILA

See
Mistral, Gabriela

GODOY CRUZ, TOMÁS

García Godoy, Cristián. *Tomás Godoy Cruz: su tiempo, su vida, su drama* reviewed by Mario Luis Descotte. *Revista Interamericana de Bibliografía,* v. 42, no. 3 (1992), p. 503.

GOLD

Costa Rica

Solórzano Fonseca, Juan Carlos. La búsqueda de oro y la resistencia indígena: campañas de exploración y conquista de Costa Rica, 1502 – 1610. *Mesoamérica (USA),* v. 13, no. 24 (Dec 92), pp. 313 – 363. Bibl.

GOLD MINES AND MINING

Mexico

Tegart, Peter F. A Ton of Dirt, a Trickle of Gold. *Business Mexico,* v. 3, no. 12 (Dec 93), pp. 15 – 16.

GOLOBOFF, GERARDO MARIO

Criticism and interpretation

Gutiérrez Girardot, Rafael. La tierra prometida: la trilogía novelística de Gerardo Mario Goloboff. *Hispamérica,* v. 21, no. 62 (Aug 92), pp. 111 – 126.

GOLTE, JÜRGEN

Interviews

Oviedo, Cecilia. Identidad nacional y desarrollo: entrevista a Jürgen Golte. *Debate (Peru),* v. 16, no. 72 (Mar – May 93), pp. 40 – 41. Il.

GÓMEZ, GONZALO

Greenleaf, Richard E. and Janin Benedict Warren. *Gonzalo Gómez, primer poblador español de Guayangareo (Morelia): proceso inquisitorial* translated by Alvaro Ochoa S. Reviewed by Frederick P. Bowser. *The Americas,* v. 49, no. 4 (Apr 93), pp. 544 – 545.

GÓMEZ, JUAN VICENTE

Lovera De-Sola, Roberto J. et al. El Gómez de Tomás Polanco Alcántara (Reprints from Venezuelan newspapers of fifteen reviews of the book *Juan Vicente Gómez* by Tomás Polanco Alcántara). *Boletín de la Academia Nacional de la Historia (Venezuela),* v. 75, no. 298 (Apr – June 92), pp. 116 – 138.

GÓMEZ DE AVELLANEDA Y ARTEAGA, GERTRUDIS

Correspondence, reminiscences, etc.

Volek, Emil. Cartas de amor de la Avellaneda. *Cuadernos Hispanoamericanos,* no. 511 (Jan 93), pp. 103 – 113. Bibl.

Criticism of specific works
Sab

Araújo, Nara. La Avellaneda, la Merlin: una manera de ver y sentir. *Iberoamericana,* v. 17, no. 49 (1993), pp. 33 – 41. Bibl.

— Raza y género en *Sab. Casa de las Américas,* no. 190 (Jan – Mar 93), pp. 42 – 49. Bibl.

Torres-Pou, Joan. La ambigüedad del mensaje feminista de *Sab* de Gertrudis Gómez de Avellaneda. *Letras Femeninas,* v. 19, no. 1 – 2 (Spring – Fall 93), pp. 55 – 64. Bibl.

GÓMEZ MONTERO, SERGIO
Criticism of specific works
Historias de la guerra menor
Trujillo Muñoz, Gabriel. Historias de la guerra menor. *La Palabra y el Hombre,* no. 84 (Oct – Dec 92), pp. 305 – 306.

GÓMEZ MORÍN, MANUEL
Correspondence, reminiscences, etc.
Gómez Morín, Manuel. Buzón de fantasmas: de Manuel Gómez Morín al abate González de Mendoza. *Vuelta,* v. 17, no. 194 (Jan 93), pp. 62 – 64.

GÓMEZ-PALACIO MUÑOZ, MARGARITA
Interviews
Zúñiga Molina, Leonel. Entrevista con Margarita Gómez-Palacio Muñoz. *La Educación (USA),* v. 37, no. 115 (1993), pp. 381 – 394.

GÓMEZ QUEZADA, RUBÉN
Correspondence, reminiscences, etc.
Gómez Quezada, Rubén. *Crónicas pampinas: en busca del tiempo perdido* reviewed by Carlos Hallet C. *Mensaje,* v. 42, no. 424 (Nov 93), p. 599.

GÓMEZ WANGÜMERT, LUIS FELIPE
Paz Sánchez, Manuel de. *Wangüemert y Cuba,* vols. I y II, reviewed by Louis A. Pérez, Jr. *Journal of Latin American Studies,* v. 25, no. 3 (Oct 93), pp. 658 – 659.

GONEZ, ARPAD
Colmenares, Hugo. El presidente de Hungría en Caracas: pocas veces los poetas han regido el destino del mundo. *Boletín de la Academia Nacional de la Historia (Venezuela),* v. 75, no. 297 (Jan – Mar 92), pp. 120 – 121.

GÓNGORA DEL CAMPO, MARIO
Andrade de Labadía, Gabriela. Una aproximación al estudio de la biblioteca privada de Mario Góngora del Campo. *Historia (Chile),* no. 26 (1991 – 1992), pp. 5 – 60. Bibl.

GONZÁLEZ, JOSÉ LUIS
Criticism of specific works
En el fondo del caño hay un negrito
Díaz, Luis Felipe. "En el fondo del caño hay un negrito" de José Luis González: estructura y discurso narcisistas. *Revista Iberoamericana,* v. 59, no. 162 – 163 (Jan – June 93), pp. 127 – 143. Bibl.

GONZÁLEZ, LUIS
See
    González y González, Luis

GONZÁLEZ ACOSTA, ALEJANDRO
Correspondence, reminiscences, etc.
González Acosta, Alejandro. Carta abierta a Dulce María Loynaz. *Plural (Mexico),* v. 22, no. 262 (July 93), pp. 18 – 22.

GONZÁLEZ CASANOVA, PABLO
Criticism of specific works
El estado en América Latina
Martínez Escamilla, Ramón. El estado en América Latina: teoría y práctica. *Problemas del Desarrollo,* v. 24, no. 93 (Apr – June 93), pp. 227 – 233.

GONZÁLEZ CASTILLO, JOSÉ
Criticism and interpretation
Pino, Diego A. del. José González Castillo y el mundo literario de Boedo. *Todo Es Historia,* v. 27, no. 311 (June 93), pp. 84 – 92. Bibl, il, maps.

GONZÁLEZ DE MENDOZA, JOSÉ MARÍA
Correspondence, reminiscences, etc.
Gómez Morín, Manuel. Buzón de fantasmas: de Manuel Gómez Morín al abate González de Mendoza. *Vuelta,* v. 17, no. 194 (Jan 93), pp. 62 – 64.

GONZÁLEZ LLORENTE, JOSÉ MARÍA
Ortega Ricaurte, Carmen. Semblanza de don José González Llorente. *Boletín de Historia y Antigüedades,* v. 80, no. 781 (Apr – June 93), pp. 389 – 405. Il.

GONZÁLEZ PALMA, LUIS
Castro, Fernando. Luis González Palma: los iluminados (Accompanied by an English translation). *Art Nexus,* no. 7 (Jan – Mar 93), pp. 136 – 138. Il.

GONZÁLEZ TUÑÓN, RAÚL
Criticism and interpretation
Sarabia, Rosa. Raúl González Tuñón: poesía ciudadana y tono conversacional. *Hispanic Journal,* v. 13, no. 2 (Fall 92), pp. 323 – 344. Bibl.

GONZÁLEZ Y GONZÁLEZ, LUIS
Interviews
Carreño King, Tania and Angélica Vázquez del Mercado. Crítica de la historia pragmática: una entrevista con Luis González y González. *Nexos,* v. 16, no. 191 (Nov 93), pp. 35 – 39.

GONZÁLEZ YÁÑEZ, ALEJANDRO
Leal F., Gustavo and Martha Singer S. Gobernando desde la oposición: ayuntamiento de Durango, 1992 – 1995. *El Cotidiano,* v. 9, no. 54 (May 93), pp. 90 – 100. Bibl, il, tables.

GOOSSENS, ANITA
Swope, John. Anita Goossens: "Llorar con los que lloran y gozar con los que gozan." *Mensaje,* v. 42, no. 424 (Nov 93), pp. 590 – 591. Il.

GOROSTIZA, JOSÉ
Correspondence, reminiscences, etc.
Gorostiza, José and Carlos Pellicer. *Correspondencia, 1918 – 1928* edited and introduced by Guillermo Sheridan. Reviewed by David Medina Portillo. *Vuelta,* v. 17, no. 202 (Sept 93), pp. 44 – 45.

— *Correspondencia, 1918 – 1928* edited and introduced by Guillermo Sheridan. Reviewed by Rosa Beltrán. *Vuelta,* v. 17, no. 203 (Oct 93), pp. 44 – 45.

Villaurrutia, Xavier. Buzón de fantasmas: de Xavier Villaurrutia a José Gorostiza. *Vuelta,* v. 17, no. 195 (Feb 93), p. 65.
Criticism and interpretation
Garza Cuarón, Beatriz. La poética de José Gorostiza y "el grupo sin grupo" de la revista *Contemporáneos. Nueva Revista de Filología Hispánica,* v. 40, no. 2 (July – Dec 92), pp. 891 – 907. Bibl.

GORRITI, JUANA MANUELA
Criticism and interpretation
Mizraje, Gabriela. El sexo despiadado: sobre Juana Manuela Gorriti. *Feminaria,* v. 6, no. 11, Suppl. (Nov 93), pp. 5 – 7.
Criticism of specific works
El emparedado
Terrón de Bellomo, Herminia. Literatura fantástica y denuncia social: Juana Manuela Gorriti. *Letras Femeninas,* v. 19, no. 1 – 2 (Spring – Fall 93), pp. 113 – 116. Bibl.

GOSSAÍN, JUAN
Criticism of specific works
La mala hierba
Noriega, Teobaldo A. *La mala hierba* de Juan Gossaín: consideraciones estéticas ante una escritura de la nueva violencia colombiana. *Revista Canadiense de Estudios Hispánicos,* v. 17, no. 3 (Spring 93), pp. 465 – 481. Bibl.

GOUVÊA, FERNANDO DA CRUZ
Souza, Luís de Castro. Saudação a Fernando da Cruz Gouvêa. *Revista do Instituto Histórico e Geográfico Brasileiro,* no. 372 (July – Sept 91), pp. 812 – 814.

GOVERNMENT OWNERSHIP OF BUSINESS ENTERPRISES

See also

Privatization

State capitalism

Subdivision *Government ownership* under names of specific industries

Brazil

Giambiagi, Fábio and Armando Castelar Pinheiro. As empresas estatais e o programa de privatização do governo Collor. *Pesquisa e Planejamento Econômico*, v. 22, no. 2 (Aug 92), pp. 241 – 288. Bibl, tables.

Caribbean area

Blackman, Courtney N. An Analytical Framework for the Study of Caribbean Public Enterprise. *Social and Economic Studies*, v. 41, no. 4 (Dec 92), pp. 77 – 93. Bibl.

Colombia

Urrutia Montoya, Miguel. Competencia y desarrollo económico. *Planeación y Desarrollo*, v. 24, no. 2 (May – Aug 93), pp. 49 – 72. Bibl, charts.

Cuba

Mesa-Lago, Carmelo. Cuba: un caso único de reforma antimercado; retrospectiva y perspectivas. *Pensamiento Iberoamericano*, no. 22 – 23, tomo II (July 92 – June 93), pp. 65 – 100. Bibl, tables.

Latin America

Baer, Werner and Melissa H. Birch. La privatización y el rol cambiante del estado en América Latina. *Revista Paraguaya de Sociología*, v. 29, no. 85 (Sept – Dec 92), pp. 7 – 28. Bibl.

GOYA Y LUCIENTES, FRANCISCO JOSÉ DE

Peterson, Gabriela and Víctor Valembois. Los epígrafes en *El siglo de las luces:* su interpretación; de Goya a Carpentier. *Káñina*, v. 16, no. 2 (July – Dec 92), pp. 89 – 100. Bibl, il, tables.

— Los epígrafes en *El siglo de las luces:* su ubicación; de Goya a Carpentier. *Káñina*, v. 16, no. 1 (Jan – June 92), pp. 79 – 89. Bibl, il.

GOYTISOLO, JUAN

Criticism of specific works

La cuarentena

Gimferrer, Pedro. *La cuarentena* de Juan Goytisolo. *Vuelta*, v. 17, no. 197 (Apr 93), pp. 11 – 12.

Señas de identidad

Beltrán-Vocal, María Antonia. Soledad, aislamiento y búsqueda de identidad en Nash Candelaria y Juan Goytisolo. *The Americas Review*, v. 21, no. 1 (Spring 93), pp. 103 – 111.

GRAFFITI

Silva Téllez, Armando. *Punto de vista ciudadano: focalización visual y puesta en escena del graffiti* reviewed by Maurice P. Brungardt (Review entitled "Readings on Colombia?"). *Studies in Latin American Popular Culture*, v. 12 (1993), pp. 235 – 242.

GRAHAM, ROBERT BONTINE CUNNINGHAME

Criticism of specific works

José Antonio Páez

Arocha Vargas, Arnaldo. Acto de presentación de los libros *José Antonio Páez* y *Cristóbal Rojas, un pintor venezolano*, pertenecientes a la Biblioteca de Autores y Temas Mirandinos. *Boletín de la Academia Nacional de la Historia (Venezuela)*, v. 75, no. 299 (July – Sept 92), pp. 5 – 8.

GRAIN TRADE

Argentina

Girbal de Blacha, Noemí M. Tradición y modernización en la agricultura cerealera argentina, 1910 – 1930: comportamiento y propuestas de los ingenieros agrónomos. *Jahrbuch für Geschichte von Staat, Wirtschaft und Gesellschaft Lateinamerikas*, v. 29 (1992), pp. 369 – 395. Bibl.

GRAMSCI, ANTONIO

Alvarez, Federico et al, eds. *Gramsci en América Latina: del silencio al olvido* reviewed by Mario Sznajder. *Estudios Interdisciplinarios de América Latina y el Caribe*, v. 3, no. 2 (July – Dec 92), pp. 133 – 137.

Ramos Serpa, Gerardo. Gramsci: salvación o desacierto del marxismo latinoamericano. *Islas*, no. 98 (Jan – Apr 91), pp. 157 – 166. Bibl.

GRAN COLOMBIA

See

Latin America

Names of specific countries within the region, e.g., Colombia, Ecuador, Venezuela

GRANADOS ROLDÁN, OTTO

Interviews

Russell, Joel. Governing for Growth. *Business Mexico*, v. 3, no. 5 (May 93), pp. 29 – 30. Il.

GRAPES

See

Wine and wine making

GRASSROOTS DEVELOPMENT

See

Community development

Non-governmental organizations

GREAT BRITAIN

See also

Automobile industry and trade – Great Britain

Industrial productivity – Great Britain

Libraries and librarians – Great Britain

Periodicals – Great Britain

Public health – Great Britain

Sculpture – Great Britain

West Indians – Great Britain

Women authors – Great Britain

Colonies

Ashdown, Peter D. Alan Burns and Sidney Turton: Two Views of the Public Good. *Belizean Studies*, v. 21, no. 1 (May 93), pp. 21 – 24. Bibl.

Royle, Stephen A. The Small Island as Colony. *Caribbean Geography*, v. 3, no. 4 (Sept 92), pp. 261 – 269. Bibl, tables, maps.

Commerce

Chile

Mayo, John K. British Merchants in Chile and on Mexico's West Coast in the Mid-Nineteenth Century: The Age of Isolation. *Historia (Chile)*, no. 26 (1991 – 1992), pp. 144 – 171. Bibl.

Mexico

Heath, Hilarie J. British Merchant Houses in Mexico, 1821 – 1860: Conforming Business Practices and Ethics. *Hispanic American Historical Review*, v. 73, no. 2 (May 93), pp. 261 – 290. Bibl.

Mayo, John K. British Merchants in Chile and on Mexico's West Coast in the Mid-Nineteenth Century: The Age of Isolation. *Historia (Chile)*, no. 26 (1991 – 1992), pp. 144 – 171. Bibl.

Puerto Rico

Dávila Ruiz, Emma A. Apuntes sobre el comercio entre Puerto Rico y Gran Bretaña durante el siglo XIX. *Op. Cit.*, no. 7 (1992), pp. 255 – 292. Bibl, il, tables, charts.

Emigration and immigration

Western, John. *A Passage to England: Barbadian Londoners Speak of Home* reviewed by Thomas D. Anderson. *Geographical Review*, v. 83, no. 2 (Apr 93), pp. 219 – 220.

Foreign relations

Argentina

Altamirano Toledo, Carlos. Lecciones de una guerra. *Cuadernos Hispanoamericanos*, no. 517 – 519 (July – Sept 93), pp. 586 – 590.

Caribbean area

Harding, Richard. *Amphibious Warfare in the Eighteenth Century: The British Expedition to the West Indies, 1740 – 1742* reviewed by Christon I. Archer. *Hispanic American Historical Review,* v. 73, no. 2 (May 93), pp. 317 – 319.

Mexico

Meyer, Lorenzo. *Su majestad británica contra la revolución mexicana: el fin de un imperio informal* reviewed by Freidrich Katz. *Historia Mexicana,* v. 42, no. 1 (July – Sept 92), pp. 152 – 157.

Peru

Wu, Celia. *Generals and Diplomats: Great Britain and Peru, 1820 – 1840* reviewed by Betford Betalleluz. *Revista Andina,* v. 11, no. 1 (July 93), pp. 254 – 256.

Spain

Moreno Alonso, Manuel. Las cosas de España y la política americana de Carlos III en Inglaterra. *Hoy Es Historia,* v. 9, no. 54 (Nov – Dec 92), pp. 44 – 59. Il.

Venezuela

Consalvi, Simón Alberto. *Grover Cleveland y la controversia Venezuela – Gran Bretaña* reviewed by H. Michael Tacver. *Hispanic American Historical Review,* v. 73, no. 4 (Nov 93), pp. 727 – 728.

GRIERSON, CECILIA

Cazzaniga, Néstor J. Cecilia Grierson y las aves. *Todo Es Historia,* v. 26, no. 307 (Feb 93), pp. 46 – 47. Bibl, il.

GRONK

See

Nicandro, Glugio Gronk

GROSS NATIONAL PRODUCT

See

National income

GROTESQUE IN LITERATURE

García Sánchez, Franklin B. El dionisismo paródico – grotesco de *La loma del ángel* de Reinaldo Arenas. *Revista Canadiense de Estudios Hispánicos,* v. 17, no. 2 (Winter 93), pp. 271 – 279. Bibl.

GRUPO ANDINO

See

Andean Common Market

GUADALAJARA, MEXICO

Arroyo Alejandre, Jesús and Stephen D. Morris. The Electoral Recovery of the PRI in Guadalajara, Mexico, 1988 – 1992. *Bulletin of Latin American Research,* v. 12, no. 1 (Jan 93), pp. 91 – 102. Bibl, tables.

Doñán, Juan José et al. Carta de Guadalajara (Regular feature appearing in most issues). *Vuelta,* v. 17 (1993), All issues.

Holt, Douglas. Aftershocks in Guadalajara. *Business Mexico,* v. 3, no. 5 (May 93), pp. 39 – 40. Il.

— Guadalajara Gambles with Expansion. *Business Mexico,* v. 3, no. 6 (June 93), pp. 30 – 31. Il.

Martin, Christopher James. The Dynamics of School Relations on the Urban Periphery of Guadalajara, Western Mexico. *European Review of Latin American and Caribbean Studies,* no. 53 (Dec 92), pp. 61 – 81.

Olveda, Jaime. Las viejas oligarquías y la reforma liberal: el caso de Guadalajara. *Siglo XIX: Cuadernos,* v. 2, no. 4 (Oct 92), pp. 9 – 30. Bibl.

GUADALUPE, JULIO

Young, Caroll Mills. Virginia Brindis de Salas vs. Julio Guadalupe: A Question of Authorship. *Afro-Hispanic Review,* v. 12, no. 2 (Fall 93), pp. 26 – 30. Bibl.

GUADALUPE, NUESTRA SEÑORA DE

Nebel, Richard. *Santa María Tonantzin, Virgen de Guadalupe: Religiöse Kontinuität und Transformation in Mexiko* reviewed by Teodoro Hampe Martínez. *Revista de Indias,* v. 53, no. 197 (Jan – Apr 93), pp. 114 – 116.

GUADELOUPE

See

Banks and banking – Guadeloupe

GUAMÁN, JACINTO

Interviews

Santana, Roberto. Jacinto Guamán, ex-vice-presidente de la Confederación de las Nacionalidades Indígenas del Ecuador (CONAIE): entrevista realizada el 23 de noviembre de 1988, por Roberto Santana. *Caravelle,* no. 59 (1992), pp. 59 – 65.

GUAMÁN POMA DE AYALA, FELIPE

See

Poma de Ayala, Felipe Huamán

EL GUAMO, COLOMBIA

Bedoya Ramírez, Josué. Fundación de la ciudad de "El Guamo," Tolima. *Boletín de Historia y Antigüedades,* v. 80, no. 780 (Jan – Mar 93), pp. 205 – 210.

GUANABARA, BRAZIL

See

Rio de Janeiro, Brazil (State)

GUANACASTE, COSTA RICA

Loáiciga G., María Elena. Condiciones psicosociales vinculadas a la atención institucional de los ancianos. *Revista de Ciencias Sociales (Costa Rica),* no. 60 (June 93), pp. 135 – 141.

Odio Orozco, Eduardo. La Pochota: un complejo cerámico temprano en las tierras bajas del Guanacaste, Costa Rica. *Vínculos,* v. 17, no. 1 – 2 (1991), pp. 1 – 16. Bibl, il, tables, maps.

GUANAJUATO, MEXICO (STATE)

Alemán Alemán, Ricardo. *Guanajuato: espejismo electoral* reviewed by Pedro García Rodríguez. *El Cotidiano,* v. 10, no. 58 (Oct – Nov 93), pp. 117 – 118.

Rabell Romero, Cecilia Andrea. Matrimonio y raza en una parroquia rural: San Luis de la Paz, Guanajuato, 1715 – 1810. *Historia Mexicana,* v. 42, no. 1 (July – Sept 92), pp. 3 – 44. Bibl, tables, charts.

Rionda, Jorge I. La industria maquiladora de exportación en Guanajuato. *Comercio Exterior,* v. 43, no. 2 (Feb 93), pp. 132 – 134. Tables.

Sepúlveda Garza, Manola. El este de Guanajuato, 1760 – 1900: microhistoria de alianzas sociales. *Cuadernos Americanos,* no. 37, Nueva época (Jan – Feb 93), pp. 76 – 89. Bibl, tables.

Thompson, Angela T. To Save the Children: Smallpox Inoculation, Vaccination, and Public Health in Guanajuato, Mexico, 1797 – 1840. *The Americas,* v. 49, no. 4 (Apr 93), pp. 431 – 455. Bibl, tables.

GUANARE, VENEZUELA

Santos Urriola, José. Discurso de orden pronunciado por el profesor José Santos Urriola, el día 16 de enero de 1992, en la sesión especial con que la Academia Nacional de la Historia conmemoró los cuatrocientos años de la fundación de Guanare. *Boletín de la Academia Nacional de la Historia (Venezuela),* v. 76, no. 301 (Jan – Mar 93), pp. 19 – 26.

GUARANI INDIANS

Cadogan, León. *Ayvu Rapytá: textos míticos de los mbyá-guaraní del Guairá* (Review). *Revista Paraguaya de Sociología,* v. 29, no. 85 (Sept – Dec 92), pp. 188 – 189.

Carbonell de Masy, Rafael et al. *Estrategias de desarrollo rural en los pueblos guaraníes, 1609 – 1767* reviewed by José Luis Mora Mérida. *Anuario de Estudios Americanos,* v. 50, no. 1 (1993), pp. 311 – 312.

McGeagh, Robert. Thomas Fields and the Precursor of the Guaraní "Reducciones." *Colonial Latin American Historical Review,* v. 2, no. 1 (Winter 93), pp. 35 – 55. Bibl.

Tissera, Ramón. Una alucinante fiesta guaraní: el Tata-Yehesá. *Todo Es Historia,* v. 26, no. 308 (Mar 93), pp. 95 – 96. Il.

GUARDIA DE ALFARO, GLORIA

Criticism and interpretation

Correa Vásquez, Pedro Francisco. Cuando se enferma el amor: a propósito de los cuentos de Gloria Guardia. *Revista Cultural Lotería*, v. 51, no. 387 (Feb 92), pp. 69 – 71.

GUARNIERI, CAMARGO

Obituaries

Magaldi, Cristina. Mozart Camargo Guarnieri (1907 – 1993). *Inter-American Music Review*, v. 13, no. 2 (Spring – Summer 93), pp. 168 – 170.

GUATEMALA

See also

Agriculture – Guatemala
Agriculture and state – Guatemala
Antigua, Guatemala
Archives – Guatemala
Artisans – Guatemala
Artists – Guatemala
Balance of payments – Guatemala
Biography (as a literary form) – Guatemala
Birds – Guatemala
Blacks – Guatemala
La Blanca site, Guatemala
Catholic Church – Guatemala
Cities and towns – Guatemala
Cookery – Guatemala
Coups d'état – Guatemala
Democracy – Guatemala
Diseases – Guatemala
Education and state – Guatemala
Elite (Social sciences) – Guatemala
Evangelicalism – Guatemala
Executive power – Guatemala
Folk drama – Guatemala
Folk festivals – Guatemala
Folk literature – Guatemala
Folk lore – Guatemala
Folk music – Guatemala
Food supply – Guatemala
Geography, Historical – Guatemala
Guatemala (City)
Handicraft – Guatemala
Human rights – Guatemala
Indians, Treatment of – Guatemala
Jacaltenango, Guatemala
Labor supply – Guatemala
Land reform – Guatemala
Migration, Internal – Guatemala
Nakbe site, Guatemala
Nutrition – Guatemala
Oligarchy – Guatemala
Oral tradition – Guatemala
Pacific Islanders – Guatemala
Periodicals – Guatemala
Petén, Guatemala
Photography and photographers – Guatemala
Population – Guatemala
Public health – Guatemala
Religion – Guatemala
Religion and sociology – Guatemala
San Andrés Sajcabajá, Guatemala
Social classes – Guatemala
Social conflict – Guatemala
Social mobility – Guatemala
Stone implements – Guatemala
Subcontracting – Guatemala
Theater – Guatemala
Theaters – Guatemala
Trade unions – Guatemala
Universities and colleges – Guatemala
Violence – Guatemala
Women – Guatemala

Antiquities

Forsyth, Donald W. The Ceramic Sequence at Nakbe, Guatemala. *Ancient Mesoamerica*, v. 4, no. 1 (Spring 93), pp. 31 – 53. Bibl, il, maps.

Hermes, Bernard A. Adiciones tipológicas a los complejos Eb, Tzec y Manik de Tikal, Guatemala. *Revista Española de Antropología Americana*, v. 23 (1993), pp. 9 – 27. Bibl. il.

Laporte, Jean Pierre. Los sitios arqueológicos del valle de Dolores en las montañas mayas de Guatemala. *Mesoamérica (USA)*, v. 13, no. 24 (Dec 92), pp. 413 – 439. Bibl, il, tables, maps.

Love, Michael W. Ceramic Chronology and Chronometric Dating: Stratigraphy and Seriation at La Blanca, Guatemala. *Ancient Mesoamerica*, v. 4, no. 1 (Spring 93), pp. 17 – 29. Bibl, il, tables, maps, charts.

Centennial celebrations, etc.

Pérez Molina de Lara, Olga. Cultura y sociedad: la empresa del V centenario: su significancia para el reino de España y el gobierno de Guatemala. *Folklore Americano*, no. 53 (Jan – June 92), pp. 81 – 90.

Civilization

Girón Mena, Manuel Antonio. Meditaciones frente al quetzal. *USAC*, no. 14 (June 91), pp. 74 – 82. Bibl, il.

Cultural policy

Cuevas Molina, Rafael. Estado y cultura en Guatemala y Costa Rica. *Anuario de Estudios Centroamericanos*, v. 18, no. 2 (1992), pp. 25 – 39. Bibl.

Description and travel

Daniels, Anthony. *Sweet Waist of America: Travels around Guatemala* reviewed by Alan C. Hunsaker (Review entitled "Guatemala: Small Country, Big Problems"). *Hispanic Journal of Behavioral Sciences*, v. 15, no. 3 (Aug 93), pp. 418 – 423.

West, Donnamarie. *Between Two Worlds: The Human Side of Development* reviewed by Alan C. Hunsaker (Review entitled "Guatemala: Small Country, Big Problems"). *Hispanic Journal of Behavioral Sciences*, v. 15, no. 3 (Aug 93), pp. 418 – 423.

Economic conditions

Osorio Paz, Saúl. Golpe de estado y situación socioeconómica en Guatemala. *Momento Económico*, no. 69 (Sept – Oct 93), pp. 20 – 23.

Economic policy

Gerardi Conedera, Juan et al. La alternativa para el desarrollo democrático de Guatemala: panel-foro. *USAC*, no. 14 (June 91), pp. 24 – 43.

History

Breton, André et al, eds. *Vingt études sur le Mexique et le Guatemala réunies à la mémoire de Nicole Percheron* reviewed by Stephen Webre. *Hispanic American Historical Review*, v. 73, no. 2 (May 93), pp. 305 – 306.

Palmer, Steven. Central American Union or Guatemalan Republic?: The National Question in Liberal Guatemala, 1871 – 1885. *The Americas*, v. 49, no. 4 (Apr 93), pp. 513 – 530. Bibl.

Taracena Arriola, Arturo. Un testimonio francés del triunfo liberal de 1829: el papel del doctor Mariano Gálvez. *Mesoamérica (USA)*, v. 13, no. 23 (June 92), pp. 143 – 156. Bibl.

Sources

Suñé Blanco, Beatriz. *La documentación del cabildo secular de Guatemala, siglo XVI: estudio diplomático y valor etnográfico* reviewed by Olga Joya. *Mesoamérica (USA)*, v. 13, no. 24 (Dec 92), pp. 462 – 463.

Industries

Estrada Vásquez, Luis Everardo. La industria maquiladora en Guatemala. *USAC*, no. 13 (Mar 91), pp. 53 – 60. Bibl.

Politics and government

Aguilera Peralta, Gabriel Edgardo. Guatemala: transición sin llegar a ninguna parte. *Nueva Sociedad*, no. 123 (Jan – Feb 93), pp. 6 – 9.

Berger, Susan A. Guatemala: Coup and Countercoup. *NACLA Report on the Americas*, v. 27, no. 1 (July – Aug 93), pp. 4 – 7. Il.

Gerardi Conedera, Juan et al. La alternativa para el desarrollo democrático de Guatemala: panel-foro. *USAC*, no. 14 (June 91), pp. 24 – 43.

Gleijeses, Piero. La muerte de Francisco Arana. *Mesoamérica (USA)*, v. 13, no. 24 (Dec 92), pp. 385 – 412. Bibl, il.

— *Shattered Hope: The Guatemalan Revolution and the United States, 1944 - 1954* reviewed by Jim Handy. *The Americas*, v. 49, no. 4 (Apr 93), pp. 562 – 564.

Hernández Pico, Juan. Guatemala: ¿Fructificará la democracia? *ECA; Estudios Centroamericanos*, v. 48, no. 536 (June 93), pp. 545 – 562. Il.

Jonas, Susanne Leilani. *The Battle for Guatemala: Rebels, Death Squads, and U.S. Power* reviewed by B. H. Barlow. *Canadian Journal of Latin American and Caribbean Studies*, v. 17, no. 34 (1992), pp. 141 – 143.

— *The Battle for Guatemala: Rebels, Death Squads, and U.S. Power* reviewed by Alan C. Hunsaker (Review entitled "Guatemala: Small Country, Big Problems"). *Hispanic Journal of Behavioral Sciences*, v. 15, no. 3 (Aug 93), pp. 418 – 423.

Kit, Wade. The Unionist Experiment in Guatemala, 1920 – 1921: Conciliation, Disintegration, and the Liberal Junta. *The Americas*, v. 50, no. 1 (July 93), pp. 31 – 64.

Taracena Arriola, Arturo. El APRA, Haya de la Torre y la crisis del liberalismo guatemalteco en 1928 – 1929. *Cuadernos Americanos*, no. 37, Nueva época (Jan – Feb 93), pp. 183 – 197. Bibl.

— El APRA, Haya de La Torre y la crisis del liberalismo guatemalteco en 1928 – 1929. *Revista de Historia (Costa Rica)*, no. 25 (Jan – June 92), pp. 9 – 25. Bibl.

Bibliography

Trudeau, Robert H. Understanding Transitions to Democracy: Recent Work on Guatemala (Review article). *Latin American Research Review*, v. 28, no. 1 (1993), pp. 235 – 247.

Race question

Casaus Arzú, Marta Elena. *Guatemala: linaje y racismo* reviewed by Carlos M. Vilas. *Journal of Latin American Studies*, v. 25, no. 3 (Oct 93), pp. 662 – 663.

Social conditions

Osorio Paz, Saúl. Golpe de estado y situación socioeconómica en Guatemala. *Momento Económico*, no. 69 (Sept – Oct 93), pp. 20 – 23.

Paredes, Pedro. Etnicidad, clases sociales, resistencia y participación social en los procesos de cambio en Guatemala. *USAC*, no. 13 (Mar 91), pp. 37 – 52. Bibl.

Social policy

Gerardi Conedera, Juan et al. La alternativa para el desarrollo democrático de Guatemala: panel-foro. *USAC*, no. 14 (June 91), pp. 24 – 43.

GUATEMALA (CITY)

Dary Fuentes, Claudia. Los artesanos de la Nueva Guatemala de la Asunción, 1871 – 1898 (Photographs by Jorge Estuardo Molina L.). *La Tradición Popular*, no. 78 – 79 (1990), Issue. Bibl, il, tables, facs.

Pérez Sáinz, Juan Pablo et al. Trayectorias laborales y constitución de identidades: los trabajadores indígenas en la ciudad de Guatemala. *Estudios Sociológicos*, v. 11, no. 32 (May – Aug 93), pp. 515 – 545. Bibl, tables.

GUAYAQUIL, ECUADOR

Argudo R., Jaime et al. Metodología para la reducción de la vulnerabilidad sísmica de escuelas y bibliotecas en Guayaquil (noviembre 1992). *La Educación (USA)*, v. 37, no. 115 (1993), pp. 333 – 352. Bibl, il, tables, charts.

Bock Godard, Marie S. *Guayaquil: arquitectura, espacio y sociedad, 1900 – 1940* reviewed by Eduardo Figari Gold. *Bulletin de l'Institut Français d'Etudes Andines*, v. 21, no. 3 (1992), pp. 1082 – 1084.

Carrasco, Hernán. Indígenas serranos en Quito y Guayaquil: relaciones interétnicas y urbanización de migrantes. *América Indígena*, v. 51, no. 4 (Oct – Dec 91), pp. 159 – 183. Bibl.

GUAYASAMÍN, OSWALDO

Fernández Vilches, Antonio. Guayasamín y su visión del Nuevo Mundo. *Atenea (Chile)*, no. 467 (1993), pp. 237 – 258. Il.

GUERNICA, SPAIN

Leis, Raúl. Panamá: desactivar la muerte. *Nueva Sociedad*, no. 123 (Jan – Feb 93), pp. 114 – 123.

GUERRA, FRANCOIS-XAVIER

Interviews

Sánchez Rebolledo, Adolfo. La herencia de la revolución mexicana: una entrevista con François-Xavier Guerra. *Nexos*, v. 16, no. 182 (Feb 93), pp. 7 – 9.

GUERRA, JUAN LUIS

Haidar de Maríñez, Julieta. La música como cultura y como poesía: Juan Luis Guerra y el Grupo 4:40. *Homines*, v. 15 – 16, no. 2 – 1 (Oct 91 – Dec 92), pp. 316 – 326. Bibl.

GUERRA, RAMIRO

Interviews

Hernández García, Lissette. Entrevista con Ramiro Guerra. *La Palabra y el Hombre*, no. 82 (Apr – June 92), pp. 285 – 290.

GUERRA Y SÁNCHEZ, RAMIRO

Rojas, Rafael. La memoria de un patricio. *Op. Cit.*, no. 7 (1992), pp. 121 – 144. Il.

Criticism of specific works

Azúcar y población en las Antillas

Díaz Quiñones, Arcadio. El enemigo íntimo: cultura nacional y autoridad en Ramiro Guerra y Sánchez y Antonio S. Pedreira. *Op. Cit.*, no. 7 (1992), pp. 9 – 65. Bibl.

GUERRERO, MEXICO

Fernández Menéndez, Jorge. Las elecciones en Guerrero. *Nexos*, v. 16, no. 182 (Feb 93), pp. 59 – 62.

GUERRILLAS

See also
Social conflict
Terrorism
Violence
Names of specific guerrilla groups

Bolivia

Reque Terán, Luis. *La campaña de Ñancahuazu* reviewed by René López Murillo. *Signo*, no. 35, Nueva época (Jan – Apr 92), pp. 245 – 247.

Colombia

Caballero, Antonio et al. Su lucha no propicia la justicia social (A reprinted letter signed by many Colombian intellectuals objecting to the use of violence and terrorism by the guerrillas). *Nueva Sociedad*, no. 125 (May – June 93), pp. 146 – 147.

García Duarte, Ricardo. La paz esquiva: negociaciones, desencuentros y rediseño de estrategias. *Revista Javeriana*, v. 60, no. 590 (Nov – Dec 92), pp. 316 – 322.

Losada Lora, Rodrigo. La evolución del orden público. *Revista Javeriana*, v. 61, no. 597 (Aug 93), pp. 159 – 165.

Marulanda V., Manuel et al. Estamos comprometidos en la solución política (A reply by members of the Coordinadora Guerrillera Simón Bolívar to the letter by Antonio Caballero et al.). *Nueva Sociedad*, no. 125 (May – June 93), pp. 147 – 148.

Mendoza, Plinio Apuleyo. La guerra que nunca quisimos ver. *Nueva Sociedad*, no. 125 (May – June 93), pp. 149 – 153.

Serpa Uribe, Horacio. La paz primero que la guerra. *Nueva Sociedad*, no. 125 (May – June 93), pp. 153 – 156.

Latin America

Chasteen, John Charles. Fighting Words: The Discourse of Insurgency in Latin American History. *Latin American Research Review*, v. 28, no. 3 (1993), pp. 83 – 111. Bibl, il.

Wickham-Crowley, Timothy P. *Guerrillas and Revolution in Latin America: A Comparative Study of Insurgents and Regimes since 1956* reviewed by Willem Assies. *European Review of Latin American and Caribbean Studies*, no. 54 (June 93), pp. 133 – 136.

— *Guerrillas and Revolution in Latin America: A Comparative Study of Insurgents and Regimes since 1956* reviewed by Brian Loveman. *Hispanic American Historical Review*, v. 73, no. 2 (May 93), pp. 350 – 352.

Venezuela

Zago, Angela. Testimonio y verdad: un testimonio sobre la guerrilla. *Inti*, no. 37 – 38 (Spring – Fall 93), pp. 29 – 35.

GUEVARA, ANTONIO DE

Criticism of specific works

Menosprecio de corte y alabanza de aldea

Febles, Jorge M. "Un pueblo": *Menosprecio de corte y alabanza de aldea* en la poesía de Agustín Acosta. *Anuario de Letras (Mexico)*, v. 30 (1992), pp. 133 – 152. Bibl.

GUEVARA, ERNESTO CHE

Althusser, Louis. Louis Althusser: ante la muerte de Ernesto Che Guevara. *Casa de las Américas*, no. 190 (Jan – Mar 93), pp. 59 – 64.

Martínez Heredia, Fernando. El Che y el socialismo de hoy. *Casa de las Américas*, no. 189 (Oct – Dec 92), pp. 111 – 120.

Pensar al Che reviewed by Luis Suárez Salazar (Review entitled "¿Cómo y para qué releer al Che?"). *Casa de las Américas*, no. 191 (Apr – June 93), pp. 144 – 147.

Reque Terán, Luis. *La campaña de Ñancahuazu* reviewed by René López Murillo. *Signo*, no. 35, Nueva época (Jan – Apr 92), pp. 245 – 247.

GUEVARA, TRINIDAD

Méndez Avellaneda, Juan María. La vida privada de Trinidad Guevara. *Todo Es Historia*, v. 27, no. 311 (June 93), pp. 26 – 40. Il, facs.

GUEVARA NIEBLA, GILBERTO

Correspondence, reminiscences, etc.

Guevara Niebla, Gilberto. Volver al '68 (Interview transcribed and edited by Luis Miguel Aguilar and Rafael Pérez Gay). *Nexos*, v. 16, no. 190 (Oct 93), pp. 31 – 43.

GUIJOSA, MARCELA

Correspondence, reminiscences, etc.

Guijosa, Marcela. Querido diario . . . . *Fem*, v. 17, no. 119 – 130 (Jan – Dec 93), All issues.

GUILDS

See

Artisans
Trade unions

GUILLÉN, JORGE

Correspondence, reminiscences, etc.

Guillén, Jorge and Pedro Salinas. *Pedro Salinas y Jorge Guillén: correspondencia, 1923 – 1951* edited by Andrés Soria Olmedo. Reviewed by Jean Cross Newman. *Revista Canadiense de Estudios Hispánicos*, v. 17, no. 3 (Spring 93), pp. 567 – 569.

Criticism and interpretation

Badano G., Alondra. La poesía de Jorge Guillén. *Revista Cultural Lotería*, v. 50, no. 386 (Nov – Dec 91), pp. 89 – 93.

GUILLÉN, NICOLÁS

Criticism and interpretation

Smart, Ian Isidore. *Nicolás Guillén, Popular Poet of the Caribbean* reviewed by José Quiroga. *Hispanic Review*, v. 61, no. 1 (Winter 93), pp. 129 – 131.

Criticism of specific works

Cerebro y corazón

Rogachevesky, Jorge R. When Does It Snow in Cuba?: Nicolás Guillén and the Poetry of *Cerebro y corazón*. *Afro-Hispanic Review*, v. 12, no. 1 (Spring 93), pp. 24 – 33. Bibl.

Poetry

Campbell, Shirley. A Nicolás Guillén. *Afro-Hispanic Review*, v. 12, no. 1 (Spring 93), p. 48.

GUIMARÃES ROSA, JOÃO

See

Rosa, João Guimarães

GÜIRALDES, RICARDO

Criticism of specific works

Don Segundo Sombra

Spicer, Juan Pablo. *Don Segundo Sombra*: en busca del "otro." *Revista de Crítica Literaria Latinoamericana*, v. 19, no. 38 (July – Dec 93), pp. 361 – 373. Bibl.

GUTIÉRREZ, GUSTAVO

Interviews

Leturia M., Juan Miguel. Hacer teología es como escribir una "carta de amor." *Mensaje*, v. 42, no. 424 (Nov 93), pp. 555 – 558. Il.

GUYANA

See also

Balance of payments – Guyana
Corruption (in politics) – Guyana
Democracy – Guyana
Elections – Guyana
Folk dancing – Guyana
Foreign exchange problem – Guyana
Geographical distribution of plants and animals – Guyana
Rites and ceremonies – Guyana

Dijk, Meine Pieter van. Guyana: Economic Recession and Transition. *European Review of Latin American and Caribbean Studies*, no. 53 (Dec 92), pp. 95 – 110. Bibl, tables.

Premdas, Ralph R. *Ethnic Conflict and Development: The Case of Guyana* reviewed by William A. Harris (Review entitled "Ethnicity and Development"). *Social and Economic Studies*, v. 41, no. 4 (Dec 92), pp. 225 – 230.

Bibliography

Goslinga, Marian. Guyana. *Hemisphere*, v. 5, no. 2 (Winter – Spring 93), pp. 50 – 52.

GUZMÁN, ENRIQUE

Blas Galindo, Carlos. *Enrique Guzmán, transformador y víctima* reviewed by José Manuel Springer (Accompanied by an English translation). *Art Nexus*, no. 10 (Sept – Dec 93), p. 41. Il.

GUZMÁN, SEBASTIÁN DE

Fortique, José Rafael. El primer obispo de Maracaibo y su médico personal. *Boletín de la Academia Nacional de la Historia (Venezuela)*, v. 76, no. 302 (Apr – June 93), pp. 133 – 139.

GUZMÁN REYNOSO, ABIMAEL

Bowen, Sally and Manuel Jesús Orbegozo. 1992: el año que vivimos al galope. *Debate (Peru)*, v. 15, no. 71 (Nov 92 – Jan 93), pp. 22 – 26. Il.

Cisneros Vizquerra, Luis F. Perspectivas después de la detención. *Debate (Peru)*, v. 15, no. 70 (Sept – Oct 92), pp. 21 – 22. Il.

Degregori, Carlos Iván. Guzmán y Sendero: después de la caída. *Nueva Sociedad*, no. 124 (Mar – Apr 93), pp. 53 – 58.

Obando Arbulú, Enrique. Situación de la subversión: después de la caída de Abimael Guzmán. *Debate (Peru)*, v. 15, no. 70 (Sept – Oct 92), pp. 19 – 22. Il.

HABANERA (DANCE)

Febres, Xavier. Primera aproximación a la habanera en Cataluña. *Boletín Americanista*, v. 33, no. 42 – 43 (1992 – 1993), pp. 349 – 365.

HACIENDAS

Andean region

Thurner, Mark. Peasant Politics and Andean Haciendas in the Transition to Capitalism: An Ethnographic History. *Latin American Research Review*, v. 28, no. 3 (1993), pp. 41 – 82. Bibl, charts.

Argentina

Posada, Marcelo Germán. La conformación del perfil del empresariado pecuario: el caso del partido de Mercedes (Buenos Aires, Argentina), 1850 – 1890. *Revista de Historia de América*, no. 112 (July – Dec 91), pp. 159 – 177. Bibl, tables, charts.

Chile

Lorenzo Schiaffino, Santiago. Las estancias de Puchacay, según un catastro predial del año 1779. *Boletín de la Academia Chilena de la Historia*, v. 58 – 59, no. 102 (1991 – 1992), pp. 491 – 504.

Montes M., Fernando. Calera de Tango: evocación de nuestra historia. *Mensaje*, v. 42, no. 420 (July 93), pp. 239 – 242. Il.

Costa Rica

Molina Jiménez, Iván and Eugenia Rodríguez Sáenz. Compraventas de cafetales y haciendas de café en el valle central de Costa Rica, 1834 – 1850. *Anuario de Estudios Centroamericanos*, v. 18, no. 1 (1992), pp. 29 – 50. Bibl, tables, maps, charts.

Mexico

Jiménez Pelayo, Agueda. *Haciendas y comunidades indígenas en el sur de Zacatecas* reviewed by Frédérique Langue. *Cahiers des Amériques Latines*, no. 13 (1992), pp. 182 – 183.

Loete, Sylvia K. Aspects of Modernization on a Mexican Hacienda: Labour on San Nicolás del Moral (Chalco) at the End of the Nineteenth Century. *European Review of Latin American and Caribbean Studies*, no. 54 (June 93), pp. 45 – 64. Bibl, charts.

Peru

Deere, Carmen Diana. *Household and Class Relations: Peasants and Landlords in Northern Peru* reviewed by William Roseberry. *Hispanic American Historical Review*, v. 73, no. 1 (Feb 93), pp. 174 – 175.

Ramírez-Horton, Susan Elizabeth. *Patriarcas provinciales: la tenencia de la tierra y la economía del poder en el Perú colonial* reviewed by Scarlett O'Phelan Godoy. *Anuario de Estudios Americanos*, v. 49, Suppl. 1 (1992), pp. 257 – 258.

Río de la Plata region

Gelman, Jorge Daniel. Mundo rural y mercados: una estancia y las formas de circulación mercantil en la campaña rioplatense tardocolonial. *Revista de Indias*, v. 52, no. 195 – 196 (May – Dec 92), pp. 477 – 514. Bibl, tables.

Venezuela

Piñero, Eugenio. Accounting Practices in a Colonial Economy: A Case Study of Cacao Haciendas in Venezuela, 1700 – 1770. *Colonial Latin American Historical Review*, v. 1, no. 1 (Fall 92), pp. 37 – 66. Bibl, tables.

HAENKE, THADDÄUS
Correspondence, reminiscences, etc.

Ibáñez Montoya, María Victoria, ed. *La expedición Malaspina, 1789 – 1794, tomo IV: Trabajos científicos y correspondencia de Tadeo Haenke* reviewed by Oldrich Kaspar (Review translated by Eva Mánková). *Anuario de Estudios Americanos*, v. 50, no. 1 (1993), pp. 317 – 319. Bibl.

HAGEL, JAIME
Criticism and interpretation

Cecereu Lagos, Luis Enrique. A propósito de Couve y Hagel, narradores. *Aisthesis*, no. 24 (1991), pp. 79 – 102. Bibl.

HAHN, OSCAR ARTURO
Criticism and interpretation

Garabedian, Martha Ann. Visión fantástica de la muerte en algunos poemas de Oscar Hahn. *Revista Chilena de Literatura*, no. 41 (Apr 93), pp. 71 – 78. Bibl.

HAITI
See also
Agriculture, Cooperative – Haiti
Art – Haiti
Art and religion – Haiti
Blacks – Haiti
Catholic Church – Haiti
Erosion – Haiti

Food supply – Haiti
Forestry – Haiti
Literature and society – Haiti
Poverty – Haiti
Religion and politics – Haiti
Sex role – Haiti
Smuggling – Haiti
Social classes – Haiti
Spaniards – Haiti
Women – Haiti

Boundaries
Dominican Republic

Baud, Michiel. Una frontera – refugio: dominicanos y haitianos contra el estado, 1870 – 1930 (Translated by Montserrat Planas Alberti). *Estudios Sociales (Dominican Republic)*, v. 26, no. 92 (Apr – June 93), pp. 39 – 64. Bibl.

Gewecke, Frauke. "El corte" oder "Les vêpres dominicaines": Trujillos "dominicanización de la frontera" und ihr Reflex in der dominikanischen und haitianischen Literatur. *Iberoamericana*, v. 17, no. 50 (1993), pp. 38 – 62. Bibl.

Civilization

Hoffmann, Léon François. *Haïti: lettres et l'être* reviewed by Hal Wylie. *World Literature Today*, v. 67, no. 3 (Summer 93), pp. 657 – 658.

Laroche, Maximilien. *La découverte de l'Amérique par les américains* reviewed by Susanne Crosta. *Canadian Journal of Latin American and Caribbean Studies*, v. 17, no. 34 (1992), pp. 144 – 146.

Economic policy

Fass, Simon M. *Political Economy in Haiti: The Drama of Survival* reviewed by Michael H. Allen (Review entitled "Rethinking Political Economy and Praxis in the Caribbean"). *Latin American Perspectives*, v. 20, no. 2 (Spring 93), pp. 111 – 119.

Foreign economic relations
Dominican Republic

Baud, Michiel. Una fortuna para cruzar: la sociedad rural a través de la frontera domínico – haitiana, 1870 – 1930 (Translated by Eugenio Rivas). *Estudios Sociales (Dominican Republic)*, v. 26, no. 94 (Oct – Dec 93), pp. 5 – 28. Bibl.

Foreign opinion

Lawless, Robert. *Haiti's Bad Press* reviewed by J. Michael Dash. *Social and Economic Studies*, v. 41, no. 4 (Dec 92), pp. 239 – 243.

— *Haiti's Bad Press: Origins, Development, and Consequences* reviewed by A. V. Catanese. *Journal of Developing Areas*, v. 28, no. 1 (Oct 93), pp. 141 – 142.

Foreign relations
Dominican Republic

Vega, Bernardo. Etnicidad y el futuro de las relaciones domínico – haitianas. *Estudios Sociales (Dominican Republic)*, v. 26, no. 94 (Oct – Dec 93), pp. 29 – 43.

United States

Plummer, Brenda Gayle. *Haiti and the United States: The Psychological Moment* reviewed by Brian Weinstein. *Revista Interamericana de Bibliografía*, v. 42, no. 4 (1992), p. 661.

History

Bellegarde-Smith, Patrick. *Haiti: The Breached Citadel* reviewed by Jorge Rodríguez Beruff. *Caribbean Studies*, v. 25, no. 1 – 2 (Jan – July 92), pp. 159 – 161.

Cordero Michel, Emilio. Gregorio Luperón y Haití. *Anuario de Estudios Americanos*, v. 49 (1992), pp. 497 – 528. Bibl.

Fick, Carolyn E. *The Making of Haiti: The Saint Dominique Revolution from Below* reviewed by David Geggus. *Hispanic American Historical Review*, v. 73, no. 2 (May 93), pp. 343 – 345.

Garrigus, John D. Catalyst or Catastrophe?: Saint-Domingue's Free Men of Color and the Battle of Savannah, 1779 – 1782. *Revista/Review Interamericana*, v. 22, no. 1 – 2 (Spring – Summer 92), pp. 109 – 125. Bibl.

Segal, Aaron and Brian Weinstein. *Haiti: The Failure of Politics* reviewed by Patrick Bellegarde-Smith. *Hispanic American Historical Review*, v. 73, no. 2 (May 93), p. 345.

Politics and government

Naudón de la Sotta, Carlos. Haití: ¿Muros o puentes? *Mensaje*, v. 42, no. 418 (May 93), pp. 156 – 157. Il.

Orenstein, Catherine. An Interview with Ben Dupuy. *NACLA Report on the Americas*, v. 27, no. 1 (July – Aug 93), pp. 12 – 15. Il.

HAITI IN LITERATURE

Gewecke, Frauke. "El corte" oder "Les vêpres dominicaines": Trujillos "dominicanización de la frontera" und ihr Reflex in der dominikanischen und haitianischen Literatur. *Iberoamericana*, v. 17, no. 50 (1993), pp. 38 – 62. Bibl.

HAITIAN LITERATURE

Criticism and interpretation

Hoffmann, Léon François. *Haïti: lettres et l'être* reviewed by Hal Wylie. *World Literature Today*, v. 67, no. 3 (Summer 93), pp. 657 – 658.

HAITIANS

Dominican Republic

Derby, Robin L. H. and Richard Turits. Historias de terror y los terrores de la historia: la masacre haitiana de 1937 en la República Dominicana (Translated by Eugenio Rivas and Mario Alberto Torres). *Estudios Sociales (Dominican Republic)*, v. 26, no. 92 (Apr – June 93), pp. 65 – 76. Bibl.

Murphy, Martin Francis. *Dominican Sugar Plantations: Production and Foreign Labor Integration* reviewed by Michel-Rolph Trouillot. *Hispanic American Historical Review*, v. 73, no. 3 (Aug 93), pp. 535 – 536.

— *Dominican Sugar Plantations: Production and Foreign Labor Integration* reviewed by Tom Spencer-Walters. *Journal of Caribbean Studies*, v. 9, no. 1 – 2 (Winter 92 – Spring 93), pp. 140 – 142.

Ruiz, Marta. Migración entre Haití y la República Dominicana. *Cuadernos Hispanoamericanos*, no. 522 (Dec 93), pp. 77 – 86.

Vega, Bernardo. Etnicidad y el futuro de las relaciones domínico – haitianas. *Estudios Sociales (Dominican Republic)*, v. 26, no. 94 (Oct – Dec 93), pp. 29 – 43.

United States

Chaffee, Sue. Haitian Women in Miami. *Hemisphere*, v. 5, no. 2 (Winter – Spring 93), pp. 22 – 23. Il.

McAlister, Elizabeth. Sacred Stories from the Haitian Diaspora: A Collective Biography of Seven Vodou Priestesses in New York City. *Journal of Caribbean Studies*, v. 9, no. 1 – 2 (Winter 92 – Spring 93), pp. 11 – 27. Bibl.

HANDICAPPED

See

Exceptional children

HANDICRAFT

See also

Artisans
Folk art
Subdivision *Textile industry and fabrics* under names of Indian groups

Argentina

Pistone, J. Catalina. *Estudio histórico de las artesanías en Santa Fe* reviewed by Félix Coluccio. *Folklore Americano*, no. 52 (July – Dec 91), pp. 166 – 167.

Brazil

Souza, Maria Tereza Saraiva de. Uma estratégia de "marketing" para cooperativas de artesanato: o caso do Rio Grande do Norte. *RAE; Revista de Administração de Empresas*, v. 33, no. 1 (Jan – Feb 93), pp. 30 – 38. Bibl, tables, charts.

Cuba

Guanche Pérez, Jesús. Proyección contemporánea de la artesanía popular en Cuba: su investigación y perspectivas. *Folklore Americano*, no. 52 (July – Dec 91), pp. 93 – 99. Bibl.

Guatemala

Déleon Meléndez, Ofelia Columba and Brenda Ninette Mayol Baños. Una muestra de juguetes populares de la ciudad de Guatemala. *La Tradición Popular*, no. 86 – 87 (1992), Issue. Bibl, il.

Mexico

Binford, Leigh and Scott Cook. *Obliging Need: Rural Petty Industry in Mexican Capitalism* reviewed by Peter Gregory. *Economic Development and Cultural Change*, v. 42, no. 1 (Oct 93), pp. 210 – 215.

O'Brian, Robin. Un mercado indígena de artesanías en los altos de Chiapas: persistencia y cambio en las vidas de las vendedoras mayas. *Mesoamérica (USA)*, v. 13, no. 23 (June 92), pp. 79 – 84. Bibl.

HANKE, LEWIS

Obituaries

Keen, Benjamin. Lewis Hanke (1905 – 1993). *Hispanic American Historical Review*, v. 73, no. 4 (Nov 93), pp. 663 – 665.

HARBORS

Costa Rica

Deregulation

Botey Sobrado, Ana María. Ferroviarios y portuarios frente al ajuste estructural. *Revista de Ciencias Sociales (Costa Rica)*, no. 60 (June 93), pp. 73 – 84. Bibl.

Jamaica

Issa, Richard. Port Royal Dockyard Repairs in 1789. *Jamaica Journal*, v. 24, no. 3 (Feb 93), pp. 11 – 14. Il, tables, facs.

Latin America

Deregulation

United Nations. Economic Commission for Latin America and the Caribbean. *La reestructuración de empresas públicas: el caso de los puertos de América Latina y el Caribe* (Review). *CEPAL Review*, no. 48 (Dec 92), pp. 171 – 172.

Mexico

Ocampo Sigüenza, Daniel. Los puertos y las ciudades costeras ante la apertura comercial de México. *Comercio Exterior*, v. 43, no. 8 (Aug 93), pp. 731 – 742. Bibl, tables.

Silverstein, Jeffrey. Wave of the Future. *Business Mexico*, v. 3, no. 4 (Apr 93), pp. 38 – 39. Il.

HARCOURT, MARGUERITE BÉCLARD D'

Criticism of specific works

La musique des incas et ses survivances

Bendezú Aybar, Edmundo. Los textos de D'Harcourt. *Revista de Crítica Literaria Latinoamericana*, v. 19, no. 37 (Jan – June 93), pp. 105 – 115.

HARCOURT, RAOUL D'

Criticism of specific works

La musique des incas et ses survivances

Bendezú Aybar, Edmundo. Los textos de D'Harcourt. *Revista de Crítica Literaria Latinoamericana*, v. 19, no. 37 (Jan – June 93), pp. 105 – 115.

HARDOY, JORGE ENRIQUE

Obituaries

Ramón Folch, Armando de et al. En recuerdo de Jorge Enrique Hardoy. *EURE*, v. 19, no. 58 (Oct 93), pp. 92 – 94.

HAVANA, CUBA

Gutman, Pablo. La Habana y Seul: ejemplos de metropolización. *EURE*, v. 19, no. 57 (July 93), pp. 103 – 115. Bibl, tables.

HAYA DE LA TORRE, VÍCTOR RAÚL

Taracena Arriola, Arturo. El APRA, Haya de la Torre y la crisis del liberalismo guatemalteco en 1928 – 1929. *Cuadernos Americanos*, no. 37, Nueva época (Jan – Feb 93), pp. 183 – 197. Bibl.

— El APRA, Haya de La Torre y la crisis del liberalismo guatemalteco en 1928 – 1929. *Revista de Historia (Costa Rica)*, no. 25 (Jan – June 92), pp. 9 – 25. Bibl.

HAZARDOUS SUBSTANCES
Mexican – American Border Region
Fernandez, Adolfo and Melanie Treviño. The Maquiladora Industry, Adverse Environmental Impact, and Proposed Solutions. *Journal of Borderlands Studies,* v. 7, no. 2 (Fall 92), pp. 53 – 72. Bibl.

Mexico
Guerra, Javier and David Robinson. The 6 Million Ton Question. *Business Mexico,* v. 3, no. 9 (Sept 93), pp. 36 – 38. Charts.

Skolnik, Howard B. A Different Drum. *Business Mexico,* v. 3, no. 5 (May 93), pp. 36 – 38. Il.

Law and legislation
Proceed with Caution. *Business Mexico,* v. 3, no. 6 (June 93), p. 46.

United States
Walters, Keith. Waste Not, Want Not. *Business Mexico,* v. 3, no. 12 (Dec 93), pp. 38 – 39. Charts.

HEALTH CARE
See
Public health

HEARNE, JOHN
Criticism and interpretation
Hudson, Brian J. The Landscapes of Cayuna: Jamaica through the Senses of John Hearne. *Caribbean Geography,* v. 3, no. 3 (Mar 92), pp. 187 – 199. Bibl.

HEBRÓN, AURELIO DEL
See
Zum Felde, Alberto

HEGEL, GEORG WILHELM FRIEDRICH
Casalla, Mario Carlos. *América en el pensamiento de Hegel: admiración y rechazo* reviewed by Daniel Toribio. *Todo Es Historia,* v. 27, no. 316 (Nov 93), p. 91. Il.

HEINE, HEINRICH
Kothe, Flávio R. Heine, Nerval, Castro Alves: "o negreiro." *Iberoamericana,* v. 17, no. 49 (1993), pp. 42 – 63.

HEKER, LILIANA
Criticism of specific works
Zona de clivaje
Frouman-Smith, Erica. Women on the Verge of a Breakthrough: Liliana Heker's *Zona de clivaje* as a Female "Bildungsroman." *Letras Femeninas,* v. 19, no. 1 – 2 (Spring – Fall 93), pp. 100 – 112. Bibl.

HEMINGWAY, ERNEST
Paporov, Yuri. *Hemingway en Cuba* reviewed by Martí Soler (Review entitled "Ernest y Yuri"). *Plural (Mexico),* v. 22, no. 263 (Aug 93), pp. 78 – 79.

HENEQUEN
See
Sisal hemp

HENRÍQUEZ UREÑA, PEDRO
Biography
Roggiano, Alfredo A. *Pedro Henríquez Ureña en México* reviewed by Gustavo Fares. *Nuevo Texto Crítico,* v. 6, no. 11 (1993), pp. 266 – 268.

Criticism and interpretation
Weinberg, Liliana Irene. Diálogo sobre España y América. *Nueva Revista de Filología Hispánica,* v. 40, no. 2 (July – Dec 92), pp. 807 – 821. Bibl.

HERMENEUTICS
See
Bible

HERNÁNDEZ, FRANCISCO
Criticism of specific works
De Antiquitatibus Novae Hispaniae
Boruchoff, David A. The Conflict of Natural History and Moral Philosophy in *De Antiquitatibus Novae Hispaniae* of Francisco Hernández. *Revista Canadiense de Estudios Hispánicos,* v. 17, no. 2 (Winter 93), pp. 241 – 258. Bibl.

Bustamante García, Jesús. De la naturaleza y los naturales americanos en el siglo XVI: algunas cuestiones críticas sobre la obra de Francisco Hernández. *Revista de Indias,* v. 52, no. 195 – 196 (May – Dec 92), pp. 297 – 328. Bibl.

HERNÁNDEZ, JOSÉ
Criticism of specific works
Martín Fierro
Vassallo, Marta. Identidad nacional y chivos expiatorios. *Feminaria,* v. 6, no. 10, Suppl. (Apr 93), pp. 9 – 12. Bibl.

Weinberg, Liliana Irene. *Ezequiel Martínez Estrada y la interpretación del 'Martín Fierro'* reviewed by María Andueza. *Cuadernos Americanos,* no. 40, Nueva época (July – Aug 93), pp. 229 – 234.

— *Ezequiel Martínez Estrada y la interpretación del 'Martín Fierro'* reviewed by Carmen Vrljicak-Espaín. *Todo Es Historia,* v. 26, no. 310 (May 93), p. 81. Il.

HERNÁNDEZ, MANUEL
Guevara, Roberto. Manuel Hernández: el espacio otro en la pintura. *Art Nexus,* no. 10 (Sept – Dec 93), pp. 92 – 95. Il.

HERNÁNDEZ, MIGUEL
Criticism and interpretation
Miranda, Julio E. Miguel Hernández en la literatura venezolana. *Cuadernos Hispanoamericanos,* no. 510 (Dec 92), pp. 23 – 29.

Muñoz González, Luis. Noticias de Miguel Hernández en Chile. *Cuadernos Hispanoamericanos,* no. 510 (Dec 92), pp. 13 – 22.

Pictorial works
Madrid Letelier, Alberto. Roser Bru: iconografía de la memoria. *Cuadernos Hispanoamericanos,* no. 510 (Dec 92), pp. 7 – 12. Il.

HERNÁNDEZ CAMPOS, JORGE
Criticism and interpretation
Asiaín, Aurelio. Jorge Hernández Campos. *Vuelta,* v. 17, no. 204 (Nov 93), pp. 58 – 59.

HERNÁNDEZ MARÍN, RAFAEL
Camuñas, Jaime. Dos letras a Rafael Hernández: in memoriam (Includes the poems "Lamento borincano," "Preciosa," "Mañanita campanera," "El cumbanchero," "El buen borincano," and "Mi guajirita"). *Homines,* v. 15 – 16, no. 2 – 1 (Oct 91 – Dec 92), pp. 327 – 337. Bibl.

HERRERA, ANGEL MARÍA
El maestro Angel María Herrera. *Revista Cultural Lotería,* v. 51, no. 389 (May – June 93), pp. 8 – 21. Il.

HERRERA, CARLOS
Kit, Wade. The Unionist Experiment in Guatemala, 1920 – 1921: Conciliation, Disintegration, and the Liberal Junta. *The Americas,* v. 50, no. 1 (July 93), pp. 31 – 64.

HERRERA, FABIO
Fabio Herrera: premio nacional "Aquileo J. Echeverría," 1991. *Káñina,* v. 16, no. 2 (July – Dec 92), pp. 175 – 178.

Art reproductions
Herrera, Fabio. Reproductions of *Humanidad, Mujer, Cardinal, Cristo de Monimbo, Luz, La india,* and *Tres botes. Káñina,* v. 16, no. 2 (July – Dec 92), pp. 179 – 185. Il.

— Reproductions of *Silla, Ventana al futuro, El grabador, Mario, Madre, Arturo, Francisco, Miss Daisy,* and *Alajuelita. Káñina,* v. 16, no. 2 (July – Dec 92), Issue.

HERRERA Y REISSIG, JULIO
Criticism of specific works
Los nuevos charrúas

Trigo, Abril. Un texto antropológico de Julio Herrera y Reissig (Includes a chapter from the text "Los nuevos charrúas" edited by Abril Trigo). *Escritura (Venezuela),* v. 17, no. 33 – 34 (Jan – Dec 92), pp. 127 – 142. Bibl.

HIERRO DE MATTE, GRACIELA
Interviews

Díaz Castellanos, Guadalupe. Graciela Hierro y la filosofía feminista. *Fem,* v. 17, no. 127 (Sept 93), pp. 17 – 19.

HIGH SCHOOLS
See
Education, Secondary

HIGHER EDUCATION
See
Education, Higher

HIGHWAYS
See also
Roads

Brazil
Cost

Sánchez Ruiz, Jorge Ernesto. Privatização de estradas no Brasil: comentário sobre a viabilidade financeira. *Revista de Economia Política (Brazil),* v. 13, no. 3 (July – Sept 93), pp. 41 – 53. Bibl, tables.

Mexico

Denton, Dan. Acapulco Renaissance. *Business Mexico,* v. 3, no. 3 (Mar 93), pp. 15 – 16. Il.

March, Ignacio J. and Rosa María Vidal. The Road to Success. *Business Mexico,* v. 3, no. 1 (Jan – Feb 93), pp. 10 – 12. Il, maps.

Venezuela

Casanova, Ramón Vicente et al. Consideraciones sobre un proyecto vial: carretera Mérida – La Culata – Tucani. *Derecho y Reforma Agraria,* no. 23 (1992), pp. 163 – 183.

HIJUELOS, OSCAR
Criticism of specific works
Mambo Kings Play Songs of Love

Pescador, Alejandro. Un mambo con sabor a bolero. *La Palabra y el Hombre,* no. 81 (Jan – Mar 92), pp. 269 – 272. Il.

HINDUISM

Vertovec, Steven. *Hindu Trinidad: Religion, Ethnicity, and Socio-Economic Change* reviewed by William A. Harris (Review entitled "Ethnicity and Development"). *Social and Economic Studies,* v. 41, no. 4 (Dec 92), pp. 225 – 230.

HINOJOSA-SMITH, ROLANDO R.
Criticism of specific works
Partners in Crime

Prieto Taboada, Antonio. El caso de las pistas culturales en *Partners in Crime. The Americas Review,* v. 19, no. 3 – 4 (Winter 91), pp. 117 – 132. Bibl.

The Valley

Akers, John C. From Translation to Rewriting: Rolando Hinojosa's *The Valley. The Americas Review,* v. 21, no. 1 (Spring 93), pp. 91 – 102. Bibl.

HISPANIC AMERICAN ARTISTS (U.S.)

Kozik, K. K. Julio Larraz: Exile and Reality. *Latin American Art,* v. 4, no. 4 (Winter 92), pp. 35 – 37. Bibl, il.

HISPANIC AMERICAN DRAMA (U.S.)

Cortina, Rodolfo J., ed. *Cuban American Theater* reviewed by José A. Escarpanter. *Latin American Theatre Review,* v. 26, no. 2 (Spring 93), pp. 203 – 204.

Osborn, Elizabeth M., ed. *On Common Ground: Contemporary Hispanic-American Plays* reviewed by Wilma Feliciano. *Latin American Theatre Review,* v. 26, no. 2 (Spring 93), pp. 206 – 208.

History and criticism

Kanellos, Nicholas Charles. *A History of Hispanic Theatre in the United States: Origins to 1940* reviewed by Joshua Al Mora. *Hispania (USA),* v. 76, no. 1 (Mar 93), pp. 87 – 88.

HISPANIC AMERICAN LITERATURE (U.S.)
History and criticism

Horno Delgado, Asunción et al, eds. *Breaking Boundaries: Latina Writings and Critical Readings* reviewed by Miriam Bornstein. *Confluencia,* v. 8, no. 1 (Fall 92), pp. 177 – 179.

HISPANIC AMERICAN WOMEN (U.S.)
Economic conditions

Enchautegui, María E. Geographical Differentials in the Socioeconomic Status of Puerto Ricans: Human Capital Variations and Labor Market Characteristics. *International Migration Review,* v. 26, no. 4 (Winter 92), pp. 1267 – 1290. Bibl, tables.

Employment

Friaz, Guadalupe Mendez. "I Want to Be Treated as an Equal": Testimony from a Latina Union Activist. *Aztlán,* v. 20, no. 1 – 2 (Spring – Fall 91), pp. 195 – 202.

Soldatenko, Maria Angelina. Organizing Latina Garment Workers in Los Angeles. *Aztlán,* v. 20, no. 1 – 2 (Spring – Fall 91), pp. 73 – 96. Bibl.

Stier, Haya and Marta Tienda. Family, Work, and Women: The Labor Supply of Hispanic Immigrant Wives. *International Migration Review,* v. 26, no. 4 (Winter 92), pp. 1291 – 1313. Bibl, tables, charts.

Health and hygiene

McGraw, Sarah A. and Kevin W. Smith. Smoking Behavior of Puerto Rican Women: Evidence from Caretakers of Adolescents in Two Urban Areas. *Hispanic Journal of Behavioral Sciences,* v. 15, no. 1 (Feb 93), pp. 140 – 149. Bibl, tables.

HISPANIC AMERICAN YOUTH (U.S.)

Solberg, V. Scott et al. Development of the College Stress Inventory for Use with Hispanic Populations: A Confirmatory Analytic Approach. *Hispanic Journal of Behavioral Sciences,* v. 15, no. 4 (Nov 93), pp. 490 – 497. Bibl, tables, charts.

— Self-Efficacy and Hispanic College Students: Validation of the College Self-Efficacy Instrument. *Hispanic Journal of Behavioral Sciences,* v. 15, no. 1 (Feb 93), pp. 80 – 95. Bibl, tables.

Sommers, Ira et al. Sociocultural Influences on the Explanation of Delinquency for Puerto Rican Youths. *Hispanic Journal of Behavioral Sciences,* v. 15, no. 1 (Feb 93), pp. 36 – 62. Bibl, tables.

HISPANIC AMERICANS (U.S.)

See also
Education, Bilingual
Mexican Americans
Undocumented workers
Subdivision *United States* under specific topics and national groups; e.g., *Puerto Ricans*

Lowenthal, Abraham F. El hemisferio interdoméstico. *Relaciones Internacionales (Mexico),* v. 15, Nueva época, no. 57 (Jan – Mar 93), pp. 13 – 15.

Culture

Ahmeduzzaman, Mohammad and Jaipaul L. Roopnarine. Puerto Rican Fathers' Involvement with Their Preschool-Age Children. *Hispanic Journal of Behavioral Sciences,* v. 15, no. 1 (Feb 93), pp. 96 – 107. Bibl, tables.

Marín, Gerardo et al. Alcohol Expectancies among Hispanic and Non-Hispanic Whites: Role of Drinking Status and Acculturation. *Hispanic Journal of Behavioral Sciences,* v. 15, no. 3 (Aug 93), pp. 373 – 381. Bibl, tables.

Economic conditions

Chávez, Linda. *Out of the Barrio: Toward a New Politics of Assimilation* reviewed by Cristóbal S. Berry-Cabán. *International Migration Review,* v. 27, no. 1 (Spring 93), pp. 208 – 210.

Education

Chapa, Jorge and Richard R. Valencia. Latino Population Growth, Demographic Characteristics, and Educational Stagnation: An Examination of Recent Trends. *Hispanic Journal of Behavioral Sciences,* v. 15, no. 2 (May 93), pp. 165 – 187. Bibl, tables.

De la Rosa Salazar, Denise and Sonia M. Pérez. Economic, Labor Force, and Social Implications of Latino Educational and Population Trends. *Hispanic Journal of Behavioral Sciences,* v. 15, no. 2 (May 93), pp. 188 – 229. Bibl, tables, charts.

Macías, Reynaldo F. Language and Ethnic Classification of Language Minorities: Chicano and Latino Students in the 1990s. *Hispanic Journal of Behavioral Sciences,* v. 15, no. 2 (May 93), pp. 230 – 257. Bibl, tables, charts.

Meier, Kenneth J. and Joseph Stewart, Jr. *The Politics of Hispanic Education: "un paso pa'lante y dos pa'tras"* reviewed by Francesco Cordasco. *International Migration Review,* v. 26, no. 4 (Winter 92), pp. 1464 – 1465.

Pearson, Barbara Z. Predictive Validity of the Scholastic Aptitude Test (SAT) for Hispanic Bilingual Students. *Hispanic Journal of Behavioral Sciences,* v. 15, no. 3 (Aug 93), pp. 342 – 356. Bibl, tables.

Reyes, Pedro and Richard R. Valencia. Educational Policy and the Growing Latino Student Population: Problems and Prospects. *Hispanic Journal of Behavioral Sciences,* v. 15, no. 2 (May 93), pp. 258 – 283. Bibl.

Solberg, V. Scott et al. Self-Efficacy and Hispanic College Students: Validation of the College Self-Efficacy Instrument. *Hispanic Journal of Behavioral Sciences,* v. 15, no. 1 (Feb 93), pp. 80 – 95. Bibl, tables.

Employment

DeFreitas, Gregory. *Inequality at Work: Hispanics in the U.S. Labor Force* reviewed by Luis M. Falcón. *International Migration Review,* v. 27, no. 1 (Spring 93), pp. 207 – 208.

De la Rosa Salazar, Denise and Sonia M. Pérez. Economic, Labor Force, and Social Implications of Latino Educational and Population Trends. *Hispanic Journal of Behavioral Sciences,* v. 15, no. 2 (May 93), pp. 188 – 229. Bibl, tables, charts.

Edwards, Jack E. et al. Willingness to Relocate for Employment: A Survey of Hispanics, Non-Hispanic Whites, and Blacks. *Hispanic Journal of Behavioral Sciences,* v. 15, no. 1 (Feb 93), pp. 121 – 133. Bibl, tables.

Knouse, Stephen B. et al, eds. *Hispanics in the Workplace* reviewed by Peggy A. Lovell. *Hispanic American Historical Review,* v. 73, no. 2 (May 93), p. 301.

Ethnic identity

Acosta-Belén, Edna. Etnicidad, género y revitalización cultural en la literatura nuyorriqueña. *Homines,* v. 15 – 16, no. 2 – 1 (Oct 91 – Dec 92), pp. 338 – 357. Bibl.

Health and hygiene

Dassori, Albana M. et al. Ethnic and Gender Differences in the Diagnostic Profiles of Substance Abusers. *Hispanic Journal of Behavioral Sciences,* v. 15, no. 3 (Aug 93), pp. 382 – 390. Bibl.

Language

Macías, Reynaldo F. Language and Ethnic Classification of Language Minorities: Chicano and Latino Students in the 1990s. *Hispanic Journal of Behavioral Sciences,* v. 15, no. 2 (May 93), pp. 230 – 257. Bibl, tables, charts.

Music

Boggs, Vernon W. *Salsiology: Afro-Cuban Music and the Evolution of Salsa in New York City* reviewed by Jerma Jackson. *Hispanic American Historical Review,* v. 73, no. 4 (Nov 93), pp. 673 – 674.

— *Salsiology: Afro-Cuban Music and the Evolution of Salsa in New York City* reviewed by Gerard Béhague. *Latin American Music Review,* v. 14, no. 1 (Spring – Summer 93), pp. 172 – 175.

Manuel, Peter, ed. *Essays on Cuban Music: North American and Cuban Perspectives* reviewed by Lucy Durán. *Latin American Music Review,* v. 14, no. 2 (Fall – Winter 93), pp. 281 – 288.

Martínez Saldaña, Jesús. Los Tigres del Norte en Silicon Valley. *Nexos,* v. 16, no. 191 (Nov 93), pp. 77 – 83. Il.

Political activity

Cohen, Isaac. The Rise of the Hispanics. *Ibero Americana (Sweden),* v. 22, no. 2 (Dec 92), pp. 3 – 20. Bibl.

Population

Belanger, Alain and Andrei Rogers. The Internal Migration and Spatial Redistribution of the Foreign-Born Population in the United States: 1965 – 1970 and 1975 – 1980. *International Migration Review,* v. 26, no. 4 (Winter 92), pp. 1342 – 1369. Bibl, tables, charts.

Chapa, Jorge and Richard R. Valencia. Latino Population Growth, Demographic Characteristics, and Educational Stagnation: An Examination of Recent Trends. *Hispanic Journal of Behavioral Sciences,* v. 15, no. 2 (May 93), pp. 165 – 187. Bibl, tables.

De la Rosa Salazar, Denise and Sonia M. Pérez. Economic, Labor Force, and Social Implications of Latino Educational and Population Trends. *Hispanic Journal of Behavioral Sciences,* v. 15, no. 2 (May 93), pp. 188 – 229. Bibl, tables, charts.

Psychology

Eaton, William W. and Roberta Garrison. Mental Health in Mariel Cubans and Haitian Boat People. *International Migration Review,* v. 26, no. 4 (Winter 92), pp. 1395 – 1415. Bibl, tables.

Social conditions

Hayes-Bautista, David E. et al. Latinos and the 1992 Los Angeles Riots: A Behavioral Sciences Perspective. *Hispanic Journal of Behavioral Sciences,* v. 15, no. 4 (Nov 93), pp. 427 – 448. Bibl, charts.

Massey, Douglas S. Latinos, Poverty, and the Underclass: A New Agenda for Research. *Hispanic Journal of Behavioral Sciences,* v. 15, no. 4 (Nov 93), pp. 449 – 475. Bibl.

HISPANIC AMERICANS AS CONSUMERS (U.S.)

Lara M., Carlos. Mexicans outside Mexico. *Business Mexico,* v. 3, no. 7 (July 93), pp. 24 – 26. Il, tables.

HISPANIC AMERICANS IN LITERATURE (U.S.)

Deaver, William O., Jr. *Raining Backwards:* Colonization and the Death of a Culture. *The Americas Review,* v. 21, no. 1 (Spring 93), pp. 112 – 118.

Duany, Jorge. Neither Golden Exile Nor Dirty Worm: Ethnic Identity in Recent Cuban-American Novels. *Cuban Studies/ Estudios Cubanos,* v. 23 (1993), pp. 167 – 183. Bibl.

HISTORIANS

Brazil

Segismundo, Fernando. Professores de história de Colégio Pedro II: esboço. *Revista do Instituto Histórico e Geográfico Brasileiro,* no. 370 (Jan – Mar 91), pp. 151 – 192.

Colombia

Duque Gómez, Luis. Brillante trayectoria de la mujer en la Academia (Commentary on the speech by Carmen Ortega Ricaurte). *Boletín de Historia y Antigüedades,* v. 80, no. 781 (Apr – June 93), pp. 407 – 413.

HISTORIC SITES

See
　Cultural property
　Subdivision *Antiquities* under names of specific countries

HISTORIOGRAPHY

See
　Subdivision *Historiography* under names of specific
　countries

HISTORY

See also
　Literature and history
　Natural history

Oral history
  Subdivision *History* under names of specific countries,
  groups, and topics
Chevalier, François. Los últimos adelantos en el campo de la
  historia (Originally published in *Cuadernos Americanos,* no.
  1, 1955). *Hoy Es Historia,* v. 10, no. 60 (Nov – Dec 93), pp.
  70 – 78. Bibl.
Fukuyama, Francis. El futuro después del fin de la historia
  (Introduced by Arturo Fontaine Talavera). *Estudios Públicos
  (Chile),* no. 52 (Spring 93), pp. 5 – 24.
Plá León, Rafael. Marxismo: ¿Eurocentrismo o universidad?
  Islas, no. 96 (May – Aug 90), pp. 132 – 138. Bibl.

Methodology

Cruz Vergara, Eliseo. Comentarios generales sobre los as-
  pectos metodológicos de la historia como ciencia socioló-
  gica en la obra de Eugenio María de Hostos y Bonilla.
  Diálogos (Puerto Rico), no. 62 (July 93), pp. 87 – 129.
Luna, Félix. Discurso del doctor Félix Luna (On the occasion
  of his induction into the National Academy of History). *Todo
  Es Historia,* v. 27, no. 316 (Nov 93), pp. 50 – 58. Il.
Pinilla Cote, Alfonso María. ¿La historia: alabanza o diatriba?
  Boletín de Historia y Antigüedades, v. 80, no. 780 (Jan –
  Mar 93), pp. 11 – 21.

HITLER, ADOLF

Müller, Jürgen. Hitler, Lateinamerika und die Weltherrschaft.
  Ibero-Amerikanisches Archiv, v. 18, no. 1 – 2 (1992), pp.
  67 – 101. Bibl.

HOLZMANN, RODOLFO

Obituaries

Rodolfo Holzmann (1910 – 1992). *Inter-American Music Review,* v. 13, no. 1 (Fall – Winter 92), pp. 123 – 125. Bibl.

HOMEM, JOAQUIM VICENTE DE TORRES

Ribeiro, Lourival. Conselheiro Jaoquim Vicente de Torres Homem. *Revista do Instituto Histórico e Geográfico Brasileiro,*
  no. 370 (Jan – Mar 91), pp. 94 – 101. Bibl, facs.

HOMERO, JOSÉ

Criticism of specific works

La construcción del amor

Aguilera Garramuño, Marco Tulio. José Homero y *La construcción del amor. La Palabra y el Hombre,* no. 81 (Jan –
  Mar 92), pp. 265 – 268.

HOMOSEXUALITY

Asís, Enrique and James N. Green. Gays and Lesbians: The
  Closet Door Swings Open. *Report on the Americas,* v. 26,
  no. 4 (Feb 93), pp. 4 – 7. Il.
Foster, David William. Consideraciones en torno a la sensibilidad "gay" en la narrativa de Reinaldo Arenas. *Revista Chilena de Literatura,* no. 42 (Aug 93), pp. 89 – 94. Bibl.
  — *Gay and Lesbian Themes in Latin American Writing* reviewed by Donna J. Guy. *Hispanic American Historical Review,* v. 73, no. 1 (Feb 93), p. 137.
González Block, Miguel A. and Ana Luisa Liguori. El SIDA en
  los de abajo. *Nexos,* v. 16, no. 185 (May 93), pp. 15 – 20.
Lumsden, Ian. *Homosexualidad, sociedad y estado en México*
  reviewed by Leticia Santa María Gallegos (Review entitled
  "Ante todo, por la dignidad de ser humano"). *Fem,* v. 17, no.
  119 (Jan 93), pp. 46 – 47.
Martínez, Elena M. Las "otras" voces de mujeres: narrativa y
  poesía. *Fem,* v. 17, no. 121 (Mar 93), pp. 36 – 37.
Muñoz M., Mario. En torno a la narrativa mexicana de tema
  homosexual. *La Palabra y el Hombre,* no. 84 (Oct – Dec
  92), pp. 21 – 37. Bibl.
Rodríguez Rabanal, César. Momento de escozor. *Debate
  (Peru),* v. 16, no. 72 (Mar – May 93), p. 29.
Salazar, Jorge. La coartada del gobierno: homosexualidad y
  sociedad. *Debate (Peru),* v. 16, no. 72 (Mar – May 93), pp.
  28 – 30.
Trujillo, Carla, ed. *Chicana Lesbians: The Girls Our Mothers
  Warned Us About* reviewed by Tamara Parker. *Letras Fe-
  meninas,* v. 19, no. 1 – 2 (Spring – Fall 93), pp. 155 – 157.

Umpierre Herrera, Luz María. Incitaciones lesbianas en "Milagros, calle Mercurio" de Carmen Lugo Filippi. *Revista Iberoamericana,* v. 59, no. 162 – 163 (Jan – June 93), pp.
  309 – 316.

HONDA, COLOMBIA

Santa, Eduardo. Honda: ciudad clave en la historia de Colombia. *Boletín de Historia y Antigüedades,* v. 79, no. 779
  (Oct – Dec 92), pp. 975 – 991. Bibl.

HONDURAS

See also
  Arabs – Honduras
  Copán, Honduras
  Ecology – Honduras
  Elections – Honduras
  Folk medicine – Honduras
  Human rights – Honduras
  Income distribution – Honduras
  Indians, Treatment of – Honduras
  Land tenure – Honduras
  Liberalism – Honduras
  Mining industry and finance – Honduras
  Mosquitia
  Nicaraguans – Honduras
  Obsidian – Honduras
  Peasantry – Honduras
  Poverty – Honduras
  Sociolinguistics – Honduras

Description and travel

Sletto, Bjorn. Crosscurrents to the Mainland (Photographs by
  the author). *Américas,* v. 45, no. 5 (Sept – Oct 93), pp.
  6 – 13. Il, maps.

Emigration and immigration

Gonzalez, Nancie L. Solien. *Dollar, Dove, and Eagle: One
  Hundred Years of Palestinian Migration to Honduras* reviewed by Caroline B. Brettell. *International Migration Review,* v. 27, no. 4 (Winter 93), pp. 899 – 900.

Foreign relations

El Salvador

Ciarnello, Nicolás. "La guerra del futbol": Honduras – El Salvador. *Todo Es Historia,* v. 26, no. 307 (Feb 93), pp. 36 –
  45. Bibl, il, maps.

HONG KONG

See
  Airplane industry and trade – Hong Kong

HORTICULTURE

Argentina

Benencia, Roberto and Javier Souza Casadinho. Alimentos y
  salud: uso y abuso de pesticidas en la horticultura bonaerense. *Realidad Económica,* no. 114 – 115 (Feb – May 93),
  pp. 29 – 53. Bibl, tables.

Brazil

Barros, Henrique de. Just One Foot in the Market: Internal
  Strategies of Small Horticultural Farmers in Northeast Brazil. *Bulletin of Latin American Research,* v. 12, no. 3 (Sept
  93), pp. 273 – 292. Bibl, tables.

Mathematical models

Campos, José Ribamar Silva and José de Jesus Sousa Lemos. Fundamentação dinâmica para a produção e comercialização de hortifrutigranjeiros. *Revista de Economia e
  Sociologia Rural,* v. 30, no. 1 (Jan – Mar 92), pp. 11 – 20.
  Bibl, tables.

Mexico

Rodríguez, María de los Angeles. Las frutas y legumbres en el
  comercio exterior de México. *La Palabra y el Hombre,* no.
  82 (Apr – June 92), pp. 199 – 227. Bibl, tables.

HOSPITALS

Brazil

Ribeiro, Eliane. "Dose unitária": sistema de distribuição de medicamentos em hospitais. *RAE; Revista de Administração
  de Empresas,* v. 33, no. 6 (Nov – Dec 93), pp. 62 – 73. Tables, charts.

Caribbean area
Cost
Lewis, Maureen A. User Fees in Public Hospitals: Comparison of Three Country Case Studies. *Economic Development and Cultural Change*, v. 41, no. 3 (Apr 93), pp. 513 – 532. Bibl, tables.

HOSTOS Y BONILLA, EUGENIO MARÍA DE
Cruz Vergara, Eliseo. Comentarios generales sobre los aspectos metodológicos de la historia como ciencia sociológica en la obra de Eugenio María de Hostos y Bonilla. *Diálogos (Puerto Rico)*, no. 62 (July 93), pp. 87 – 129.

Rojas Osorio, Carlos. Hostos y la identidad caribeña. *Caribbean Studies*, v. 25, no. 1 – 2 (Jan – July 92), pp. 133 – 145. Bibl.

Villanueva Collado, Alfredo. Eugenio María de Hostos ante el conflicto modernismo/modernidad. *Caribbean Studies*, v. 25, no. 1 – 2 (Jan – July 92), pp. 147 – 158.

— Eugenio María de Hostos ante el conflicto modernismo/modernidad. *Revista Iberoamericana*, v. 59, no. 162 – 163 (Jan – June 93), pp. 21 – 32. Bibl.

Criticism of specific works
La peregrinación de Bayoán
Rivera, Angel A. *La peregrinación de Bayoán* de Eugenio María de Hostos: viaje de retorno al caos. *Revista Canadiense de Estudios Hispánicos*, v. 17, no. 3 (Spring 93), pp. 525 – 535. Bibl.

HOUSING
See also
Slums

Subdivision *Dwellings* under names of Indian groups
Argentina
Baer, James. Tenant Mobilization and the 1907 Rent Strike in Buenos Aires. *The Americas*, v. 49, no. 3 (Jan 93), pp. 343 – 368. Bibl, tables, maps.

Brazil
Melo, Marcus André Barreto Campelo de. Anatomia do fracasso: intermediação de interesses e a reforma das políticas sociais na nova república. *Dados*, v. 36, no. 1 (1993), pp. 119 – 163. Bibl, tables.

Cuba
Coyula, Mario. El veril entre dos siglos: tradición e innovación para un desarrollo sustentable. *Casa de las Américas*, no. 189 (Oct – Dec 92), pp. 94 – 101.

Mexico
Bazán, Lucía. *Vivienda para los obreros: reproduccíon de clase y condiciones urbanas* reviewed by Margarita Estrada Iguíniz. *El Cotidiano*, v. 8, no. 52 (Jan – Feb 93), pp. 112 – 113.

Connolly, Priscilla et al. *"Cambiar de casa, pero no de barrio": estudios sobre la reconstrucción en la ciudad de México* reviewed by María Elena Ducci. *EURE*, v. 19, no. 57 (July 93), pp. 126 – 127. Il.

García González, Francisco. Los muros de la vida privada y la familia: casa y tamaño familiar en Zacatecas; primeras décadas del siglo XIX. *Estudios Demográficos y Urbanos*, v. 7, no. 1 (Jan – Apr 92), pp. 35 – 52. Bibl, tables.

Gilbert, Alan G. and Ann Varley. *Landlord and Tenant: Housing the Poor in Urban Mexico* reviewed by Nikki Craske. *Journal of Latin American Studies*, v. 25, no. 2 (May 93), pp. 418 – 419.

Herrasti Aguirre, María Emilia. La promoción inmobiliaria popular autogestiva: ¿Tendrá futuro? *El Cotidiano*, v. 10, no. 57 (Aug – Sept 93), pp. 17 – 22. Il.

Martínez Anaya, Efraín. San Miguel Teotongo: a contrapelo del neoliberalismo. *El Cotidiano*, v. 10, no. 57 (Aug – Sept 93), pp. 23 – 27. Tables.

Massolo, Alejandra, ed. *Mujeres y ciudades* reviewed by Maribel Nicasio González. *El Cotidiano*, v. 10, no. 57 (Aug – Sept 93), p. 110.

Villarreal González, Diana R. *La política de vivienda del gobierno del estado de Nuevo León, 1970 – 1990* reviewed by Gustavo Garza. *Estudios Demográficos y Urbanos*, v. 6, no. 3 (Sept – Dec 91), pp. 773 – 778.

Ziccardi, Alicia. Los organismos de vivienda de los asalariados y la política social. *EURE*, v. 19, no. 57 (July 93), pp. 95 – 102. Bibl, tables.

United States
Alba, Richard D. and John R. Logan. Assimilation and Stratification in the Homeownership Patterns of Racial and Ethnic Groups. *International Migration Review*, v. 26, no. 4 (Winter 92), pp. 1314 – 1341. Bibl, tables.

HOUSTON, TEXAS
Baker, Susan Gonzalez and Jacqueline Maria Hagan. Implementing the U.S. Legalization Program: The Influence of Immigrant Communities and Local Agencies on Immigration Policy Reform. *International Migration Review*, v. 27, no. 3 (Fall 93), pp. 513 – 536. Bibl.

HOY ES HISTORIA (PERIODICAL)
Indexes
Michelena, Alejandro Daniel. Tercer indice trianual: autores y materias, 1990 – 1992. *Hoy Es Historia*, v. 10, no. 55 (Jan – Feb 93), Insert.

HUARI CULTURE, PERU
Isbell, William Harris and Gordon Francis McEwan, ed. *Huari Administrative Structure: Prehistoric Monumental Architecture and State Government* reviewed by Mario A. Rivera. *Latin American Antiquity*, v. 4, no. 1 (Mar 93), pp. 95 – 96.

HUAYHUACA, JOSÉ CARLOS
Criticism of specific works
Martín Chambi, fotógrafo
Heredia, Jorge. Avatares de la obra del fotógrafo peruano Martín Chambi (1891 – 1973) y reseña de dos monografías recientes. *Hueso Húmero*, no. 29 (May 93), pp. 144 – 173. Bibl.

HUDSON, WILLIAM HENRY
Criticism of specific works
Purple Land
Burgos, Nidia. Un documento inédito de Martínez Estrada: la creación de otra *Tierra purpúrea;* una república libertaria, federal y representativa. *Cuadernos Americanos*, no. 42, Nueva época (Nov – Dec 93), pp. 157 – 164. Bibl.

HUERTA, EFRAÍN
Criticism and interpretation
Aguilera Garramuño, Marco Tulio. José Homero y *La construcción del amor*. *La Palabra y el Hombre*, no. 81 (Jan – Mar 92), pp. 265 – 268.

HUEYAPAN, MEXICO
Vargas Lugo, Elisa. Un retablo de encaje (Accompanied by an English translation). *Artes de México*, no. 21 (Fall 93), pp. 54 – 59. Il.

HUGHES, LANGSTON
Mullen, Edward James. Langston Hughes in Mexico and Cuba. *Review*, no. 47 (Fall 93), pp. 23 – 27. Il.

HUICHOL INDIANS
Schaefer, Stacy. Huichol Indian Costumes: A Transforming Tradition. *Latin American Art*, v. 5, no. 1 (Spring 93), pp. 70 – 73. Bibl, il.

HUIDOBRO, VICENTE
Addresses, essays, lectures
Montes Brunet, Hugo. Un discurso inédito de Vicente Huidobro (Includes the transcription of "Discurso leído en Madrid en el Segundo Congreso Internacional de Escritores para la Defensa de la Cultura"). *Revista Chilena de Literatura*, no. 41 (Apr 93), pp. 123 – 129.

Biobibliography
Espinosa V., Ismael. Las ediciones originales de Vicente Huidobro: ensayo de una bio-bibliografía. *Atenea (Chile)*, no. 467 (1993), pp. 103 – 122. Il.

Biography

Anguita, Eduardo. Huidobro y Neruda: final. *Atenea (Chile)*, no. 467 (1993), pp. 145 – 147.

Astorga, Luz María. Rasgos humanos de un gran poeta. *Atenea (Chile)*, no. 467 (1993), pp. 81 – 96. Il, facs.

Castillo, Tito. Gratos recuerdos de Vicente Huidobro y Jacques Lipchitz. *Atenea (Chile)*, no. 467 (1993), pp. 149 – 154. Il, facs.

Montes Brunet, Hugo. La maestría de Huidobro. *Atenea (Chile)*, no. 467 (1993), pp. 137 – 141. Il.

Vicente Huidobro: centenario de su nacimiento (Includes a photograph and two drawings of Huidobro). *Atenea (Chile)*, no. 467 (1993), pp. 17 – 21. Il.

Criticism and interpretation

Aguirre, Mariano. Huidobro narrador. *Atenea (Chile)*, no. 467 (1993), pp. 101 – 102.

Arenas, Braulio. Vicente Huidobro y el creacionismo (A chapter from Braulio Arenas' book *Escritos y escritores chilenos* reproduced as the prologue to *Obras completas de Vicente Huidobro*). *Atenea (Chile)*, no. 467 (1993), pp. 23 – 63. Bibl, il, facs.

Concha, Edmundo. Neruda y Huidobro. *Atenea (Chile)*, no. 467 (1993), pp. 155 – 156.

Hahn, Oscar Arturo. Huidobro, un niño de cien años. *Atenea (Chile)*, no. 467 (1993), pp. 67 – 74. Il.

Milán, Eduardo. Algo de Huidobro ahora. *Vuelta*, v. 17, no. 204 (Nov 93), pp. 59 – 62.

Rojas, Gonzalo. Huidobro de repente. *Atenea (Chile)*, no. 467 (1993), pp. 65 – 66. Il.

Teitelboim, Volodia. *Huidobro: la marcha infinita* reviewed by Antonio Avaria (Review entitled "Crónica de varia lección"). *Mensaje*, v. 42, no. 424 (Nov 93), pp. 596 – 597. Il.

Zonana, Víctor Gustavo. Geografía ocular: elementos para una poética de la visión en la poesía de vanguardia hispanoamericana: Huidobro y Marechal. *Revista Chilena de Literatura*, no. 40 (Nov 92), pp. 57 – 67. Bibl.

Criticism of specific works

Altazor

Espinosa V., Ismael. Significado de *Altazor*. *Atenea (Chile)*, no. 467 (1993), pp. 123 – 125.

Valdovinos, Hernán. Vicente Huidobro y *Altazor* (Includes the author's illustrations for Huidobro's book *Altazor*). *Atenea (Chile)*, no. 467 (1993), pp. 127 – 136. Il.

En la luna

Roa, Natalia. Vicente Huidobro: la luna era mi tierra. *Mensaje*, v. 42, no. 417 (Mar – Apr 93), pp. 77 – 78. Il.

El espejo del agua

Hahn, Oscar Arturo. Vicente Huidobro o las metamorfosis del ruiseñor. *Revista Chilena de Literatura*, no. 40 (Nov 92), pp. 97 – 103.

Poemas árticos

Neghme Echeverría, Lidia. Análisis comparado de *Imagen* de Gerardo Diego y de *Poemas árticos* de Vicente Huidobro. *Revista Chilena de Literatura*, no. 41 (Apr 93), pp. 99 – 112. Bibl.

Poetry

Gómez Rogers, Jaime. El litoral de los poetas (Includes a poem about Vicente Huidobro). *Atenea (Chile)*, no. 467 (1993), pp. 157 – 159.

Rojas, Gonzalo. Carta a Huidobro y otros poemas. *Vuelta*, v. 17, no. 202 (Sept 93), pp. 10 – 12. Il.

HUMAN BEHAVIOR

See
    Sexual behavior

HUMAN CAPITAL

See also
    Subdivision *Economic aspects* under *Education*

Argentina

Congresses

Revolución científico – técnica, educación y área laboral (A seminar organized by the Fundación de Investigaciones Sociales y Políticas (FISYP) de Argentina and summarized by Dora Douthat). *Realidad Económica*, no. 119 (Oct – Nov 93), pp. 134 – 138.

Mathematical models

Ceballos, Marta. Metodología cuantitativa para una caracterización diacrónica de recursos humanos desocupados. *Revista Paraguaya de Sociología*, v. 29, no. 85 (Sept – Dec 92), pp. 157 – 169. Bibl, tables, charts.

Asia

Dijck, Pitou van. The Empty Box Syndrome. *CEPAL Review*, no. 47 (Aug 92), pp. 21 – 36. Bibl, tables, charts.

Brazil

Almeida, Martinho Isnard Ribeiro et al. ¿Por qué administrar estrategicamente recursos humanos? *RAE; Revista de Administração de Empresas*, v. 33, no. 2 (Mar – Apr 93), pp. 12 – 24. Bibl, tables.

Cacciamali, Maria Cristina and Paulo Springer de Freitas. Do capital humano ao salário-eficiência: uma aplicação para analisar os diferenciais de salários em cinco ramos manufatureiros da grande São Paulo. *Pesquisa e Planejamento Econômico*, v. 22, no. 2 (Aug 92), pp. 343 – 367. Bibl, tables.

Colombia

Torres Díaz, Jorge H. Dimensión gerencial del trabajo social laboral. *Desarrollo Indoamericano*, v. 23, no. 91 (June 93), pp. 47 – 53. Il.

Latin America

Dijck, Pitou van. The Empty Box Syndrome. *CEPAL Review*, no. 47 (Aug 92), pp. 21 – 36. Bibl, tables, charts.

United Nations. Economic Commission for Latin America and the Caribbean. *Equidad y transformación productiva: un enfoque integrado* reviewed by Gloria González Salazar. *Problemas del Desarrollo*, v. 24, no. 92 (Jan – Mar 93), pp. 233 – 236.

— *Equity and Changing Production Patterns: An Integrated Approach* (Review). *CEPAL Review*, no. 47 (Aug 92), pp. 190 – 191.

Mexico

Carrillo Viveros, Jorge and Oscar F. Contreras. Calificación en el trabajo: análisis de la industria maquiladora. *Frontera Norte*, v. 4, no. 8 (July – Dec 92), pp. 49 – 78. Bibl, tables, charts.

Hamer, Thurston R. The Hunt for Local Talent. *Business Mexico*, v. 3, no. 6 (June 93), pp. 4 – 6.

López Rodríguez, Ramón. A Different Solution. *Business Mexico*, v. 3, no. 6 (June 93), pp. 16 – 18. Il.

Puerto Rico

Enchautegui, María E. The Value of U.S. Labor Market Experience in the Home Country: The Case of Puerto Rican Return Migrants. *Economic Development and Cultural Change*, v. 42, no. 1 (Oct 93), pp. 168 – 191. Bibl, tables, charts.

United States

Enchautegui, María E. Geographical Differentials in the Socioeconomic Status of Puerto Ricans: Human Capital Variations and Labor Market Characteristics. *International Migration Review*, v. 26, no. 4 (Winter 92), pp. 1267 – 1290. Bibl, tables.

HUMAN RESOURCES

See
    Human capital
    Labor supply
    Subdivision *Economic aspects* under *Education*

HUMAN RIGHTS

See also
    Political prisoners
    Terrorism

Carpizo, Jorge. Los derechos de la tercera generación: paz y desarrollo. *Cuadernos Americanos*, no. 39, Nueva época (May – June 93), pp. 27 – 33.

Chipoco Cáceda, Carlos. *En defensa de la vida: ensayos sobre derechos humanos y derecho internacional humanitario* reviewed by Susana Villarán (Review entitled "Causa tomada"). *Debate (Peru)*, v. 15, no. 71 (Nov 92 – Jan 93), p. 80. Il.

Friszman, Marcos. Globalidad de los derechos humanos. *Realidad Económica*, no. 113 (Jan – Feb 93), pp. 40 – 44. Il.

Galeano, Eduardo H. The Corruption of Memory (Translated by Mark Fried). *NACLA Report on the Americas*, v. 27, no. 3 (Nov – Dec 93), pp. 35 – 38.

Romany, Celina. Hacia una crítica feminista del derecho internacional en materia de derechos humanos. *Fem*, v. 17, no. 126 (Aug 93), pp. 19 – 22.

Sarquís, David J. 10 de diciembre de 1992: 44° aniversario de la Declaración Universal de los Derechos Humanos. *Relaciones Internacionales (Mexico)*, v. 15, Nueva época, no. 57 (Jan – Mar 93), pp. 97 – 100.

Stavenhagen, Rodolfo. Los derechos de los indígenas: algunos problemas conceptuales. *Nueva Antropología*, v. 13, no. 43 (Nov 92), pp. 83 – 99. Bibl.

Villagrán Kramer, Francisco. La integración económica y la justicia. *Integración Latinoamericana*, v. 18, no. 187 – 188 (Mar – Apr 93), pp. 35 – 47. Bibl.

Sources

United Nations. Working Group of Indigenous Populations. Declaración Universal sobre los Derechos de los Pueblos Indígenas. *Revista Latinoamericana de Estudios Educativos*, v. 22, no. 4 (Oct – Dec 92), pp. 111 – 121.

Study and teaching

Samour, Héctor. Universidad y derechos humanos. *ECA; Estudios Centroamericanos*, v. 47, no. 528 (Oct 92), pp. 894 – 900. Bibl, il.

Argentina

Guest, Iain. *Behind the Disappearances: Argentina's Dirty War against Human Rights and the United Nations* reviewed by Erick Bridoux. *Journal of Inter-American Studies and World Affairs*, v. 34, no. 4 (Winter 92 – 93), pp. 257 – 262.

Paoletti, Mario Argentino. Tiempo de desprecio. *Cuadernos Hispanoamericanos*, no. 517 – 519 (July – Sept 93), pp. 581 – 586.

Quiroga, Hugo. Los derechos humanos en la Argentina: entre el realismo político y la ética. *Cuadernos Hispanoamericanos*, no. 517 – 519 (July – Sept 93), pp. 77 – 92. Bibl.

Sábato, Ernesto R. Nunca más (Prologue to the book of the same title). *Cuadernos Hispanoamericanos*, no. 517 – 519 (July – Sept 93), pp. 571 – 573.

Brazil

Trindade, Antônio Augusto Cançado, ed. *A proteção dos direitos humanos nos planos nacional e internacional: perspectivas brasileiras* reviewed by José Filomeno de Morais Filho. *Revista Brasileira de Estudos Políticos*, no. 76 (Jan 93), pp. 197 – 202.

Congresses

Lamego, Valéria. A desonra de uma sociedade patriarcal. *Estudos Feministas*, v. 1, no. 1 (1993), pp. 152 – 154.

Chile

Verdugo, Patricia. Andrés Aylwin: "Hay situaciones que claman a Dios." *Mensaje*, v. 42, no. 421 (Aug 93), pp. 382 – 383. Il.

Bibliography

Jaksic, Ivan. The Legacies of Military Rule in Chile (Review article). *Latin American Research Review*, v. 28, no. 1 (1993), pp. 258 – 269.

Colombia

Vargas Castaño, Alfredo. La suerte de caracol: expatriados, expropiados, desterrados y desplazados en Colombia. *Nueva Sociedad*, no. 123 (Jan – Feb 93), pp. 144 – 155.

Law and legislation

Cáceres Corrales, Pablo. La tutela: procesos, resultados, consecuencias y limitaciones. *Revista Javeriana*, v. 61, no. 598 (Sept 93), pp. 237 – 245.

Sánchez, Ricardo. Constitución y vida social. *Revista Javeriana*, v. 61, no. 597 (Aug 93), pp. 169 – 173.

Cuba

El pueblo de Cuba: entre el drama y la esperanza, II; La situación de los derechos humanos en Cuba. *Hoy Es Historia*, v. 10, no. 55 (Jan – Feb 93), pp. 88 – 96.

El Salvador

Aldunate L., José. Un "Informe Rettig" para El Salvador. *Mensaje*, v. 42, no. 418 (May 93), pp. 153 – 154.

Cardenal Chamorro, Rodolfo. El fracaso del estado salvadoreño. *ECA; Estudios Centroamericanos*, v. 48, no. 534 – 535 (Apr – May 93), pp. 351 – 375. Il.

La Comisión de la Verdad y el proceso electoral en la opinión pública salvadoreña. *ECA; Estudios Centroamericanos*, v. 48, no. 537 – 538 (July – Aug 93), pp. 711 – 734. Tables, charts.

Comisión Interamericana de Derechos Humanos: Organización de Estados Americanos. *ECA; Estudios Centroamericanos*, v. 47, no. 528 (Oct 92), pp. 919 – 925.

La cultura de la muerte. *ECA; Estudios Centroamericanos*, v. 48, no. 539 (Sept 93), pp. 886 – 889. Il.

¿De la locura a la esperanza?: reflexiones a propósito del informe de la verdad. *ECA; Estudios Centroamericanos*, v. 48, no. 534 – 535 (Apr – May 93), pp. 409 – 413. Il.

Derechos humanos en 1992: el derecho a la vida y los derechos de la infancia. *ECA; Estudios Centroamericanos*, v. 48, no. 537 – 538 (July – Aug 93), pp. 677 – 691. Tables, charts.

Esperar contra toda esperanza. *ECA; Estudios Centroamericanos*, v. 48, no. 534 – 535 (Apr – May 93), pp. 333 – 349. Il.

Estados Unidos conocía la violencia de El Salvador. *ECA; Estudios Centroamericanos*, v. 48, no. 534 – 535 (Apr – May 93), pp. 420 – 429. Il.

Hernández Pico, Juan. Significado ético – político del informe de la verdad: "La verdad nos hará libres." *ECA; Estudios Centroamericanos*, v. 48, no. 534 – 535 (Apr – May 93), pp. 377 – 387. Il.

Indicadores actuales de la violencia. *ECA; Estudios Centroamericanos*, v. 48, no. 536 (June 93), pp. 594 – 598. Il.

Un informe increíble sobre El Salvador. *ECA; Estudios Centroamericanos*, v. 48, no. 537 – 538 (July – Aug 93), pp. 750 – 761. Il.

Martínez, Julia Evelyn. Neoliberalismo y derechos humanos. *ECA; Estudios Centroamericanos*, v. 47, no. 529 – 530 (Nov – Dec 92), pp. 1028 – 1036. Il.

Las reformas penales y los derechos humanos. *ECA; Estudios Centroamericanos*, v. 47, no. 528 (Oct 92), pp. 883 – 888. Il.

Sobrino, Jon. Reflexiones teológicas sobre el informe de la Comisión de la Verdad. *ECA; Estudios Centroamericanos*, v. 48, no. 534 – 535 (Apr – May 93), pp. 389 – 408. Il.

Tojeira, José María. Tercer aniversario de los mártires de la UCA: homilia. *ECA; Estudios Centroamericanos*, v. 47, no. 529 – 530 (Nov – Dec 92), pp. 951 – 953.

Law and legislation

Consideraciones sobre la ley de amnistía. *ECA; Estudios Centroamericanos*, v. 48, no. 534 – 535 (Apr – May 93), pp. 414 – 419. Il.

Sources

De la locura a la esperanza: la guerra de doce años en El Salvador; informe de la Comisión de la Verdad para El Salvador (Introduced by the Secretary General of the Commission). *ECA; Estudios Centroamericanos*, v. 48, no. 533 (Mar 93), Issue.

Documentación (regarding socio-economic, human rights, and political issues). *ECA; Estudios Centroamericanos*, v. 47 – 48 (1992 – 1993), All issues.

ONUSAL: Séptimo Informe sobre la Situación de los Derechos Humanos. *ECA; Estudios Centroamericanos*, v. 48, no. 537 – 538 (July – Aug 93), pp. 743 – 749. Il.

Tercer aniversario de los mártires de la UCA (Two documents). *ECA; Estudios Centroamericanos*, v. 47, no. 529 – 530 (Nov – Dec 92), pp. 1085 – 1086.

Study and teaching

La promoción de los derechos humanos y la educación no formal. *ECA; Estudios Centroamericanos*, v. 48, no. 531 – 532 (Jan – Feb 93), pp. 100 – 104. Il.

Guatemala

Manz, Beatriz. Elections without Change: The Human Rights Record of Guatemala. *SALALM Papers*, v. 36 (1991), pp. 191 – 200. Bibl.

Rigoberta Menchú, premio Nobel de la paz: nuevo amanecer para Guatemala. *ECA; Estudios Centroamericanos*, v. 47, no. 528 (Oct 92), pp. 889 – 893. Il.

Vinos derramados: el libro de Ricardo Falla sobre los masacres de Ixcán, Guatemala. *ECA; Estudios Centroamericanos*, v. 47, no. 529 – 530 (Nov – Dec 92), pp. 1037 – 1044. Il.

Honduras

Morgner, Fred G. Cracks in the Mirror: The Nicaraguan War and Human Rights in Honduras. *SALALM Papers*, v. 34 (1989), pp. 475 – 490. Bibl, il, tables.

Latin America

Asís, Enrique and James N. Green. Gays and Lesbians: The Closet Door Swings Open. *Report on the Americas*, v. 26, no. 4 (Feb 93), pp. 4 – 7. Il.

Dorfman, Ariel. Comments (on the panel "Liberty and Justice for All: Human Rights and Democratization in Latin America"). *SALALM Papers*, v. 36 (1991), pp. 209 – 212.

Menchú, Rigoberta. Un homenaje a los pueblos indígenas. *Realidad Económica*, no. 114 – 115 (Feb – May 93), pp. 74 – 85. Il.

Panizza, Francisco E. Human Rights: Global Culture and Social Fragmentation. *Bulletin of Latin American Research*, v. 12, no. 2 (May 93), pp. 205 – 214. Bibl.

Weschler, Lawrence. A Miracle, a Universe: Settling Accounts with Torturers. *SALALM Papers*, v. 36 (1991), pp. 201 – 208.

Wilde, Alexander. Do Human Rights Exist in Latin American Democracies? *SALALM Papers*, v. 36 (1991), pp. 187 – 190.

Zovatto G., Daniel. *Los estados de excepción y los derechos humanos en la América Latina* reviewed by Natan Lerner. *Estudios Interdisciplinarios de América Latina y el Caribe*, v. 3, no. 2 (July – Dec 92), pp. 127 – 129.

Law and legislation

Mattarollo, Rodolfo. Proceso a la impunidad de crímenes de lesa humanidad en América Latina, 1989 – 1991. *ECA; Estudios Centroamericanos*, v. 47, no. 528 (Oct 92), pp. 867 – 882. Bibl, il.

Mexico

Anguiano Téllez, María Eugenia. Migración y derechos humanos: el caso de los mixtecos. *Estudios Fronterizos*, no. 26 (Sept – Dec 91), pp. 55 – 69. Bibl.

Cedillo, Miguel Angel. La Comisión Nacional de Derechos Humanos: ¿Justicia para la democracia? *Revista Mexicana de Ciencias Políticas y Sociales*, v. 37, Nueva época, no. 149 (July – Sept 92), pp. 83 – 108.

Peru

Americas Watch Committee. *Peru under Fire: Human Rights since the Return to Democracy* reviewed by Sarah A. Radcliffe. *Bulletin of Latin American Research*, v. 12, no. 1 (Jan 93), pp. 120 – 121.

— *Peru under Fire: Human Rights since the Return to Democracy* reviewed by Orazio A. Ciccarelli. *Revista Interamericana de Bibliografía*, v. 42, no. 2 (1992), p. 281.

United States

Self, Robert. Intimidate First, Ask Questions Later: The INS and Immigration Rights. *NACLA Report on the Americas*, v. 26, no. 5 (May 93), pp. 11 – 14. Il.

Uruguay

Servicio Paz y Justicia (Uruguay). *"Uruguay nunca más": Human Rights Violations, 1972 – 1985* translated by Elizabeth Hampsten. Reviewed by Marvin Alisky. *Hispanic American Historical Review*, v. 73, no. 4 (Nov 93), pp. 709 – 710.

Venezuela

Cuando la injusticia toca a nuestra puerta. *Nueva Sociedad*, no. 123 (Jan – Feb 93), pp. 161 – 164.

HUMANISM

Bono, Diane M. *Cultural Diffusion of Spanish Humanism in New Spain: Francisco Cervantes de Salazar's 'Diálogo de la dignidad del hombre'* reviewed by William Mejías López. *Hispania (USA)*, v. 76, no. 2 (May 93), pp. 282 – 284.

Casañas Díaz, Mirta. Una variante del humanismo burgués en América Latina. *Islas*, no. 98 (Jan – Apr 91), pp. 143 – 156. Bibl.

Fernández Ariza, María Guadalupe. Los *Comentarios reales* del Inca Garcilaso y el humanismo renacentista. *Studi di Letteratura Ispano-Americana*, v. 24 (1993), pp. 23 – 35.

García Machado, Xiomara. Medardo Vitier en la tradición humanista del pensamiento cubano: ¿Herencia o ruptura? *Islas*, no. 98 (Jan – Apr 91), pp. 119 – 127. Bibl.

Guadarrama González, Pablo M. et al. El humanismo en la filosofía latinoamericana de la liberación. *Islas*, no. 99 (May – Aug 91), pp. 173 – 199. Bibl.

Jaramillo, Diego. El hombre latinoamericano y la transformación social. *Islas*, no. 96 (May – Aug 90), pp. 18 – 26.

Ocampo López, Javier. El padre Manuel Briceño Jáuregui, S.J. y el humanismo clásico. *Boletín de Historia y Antigüedades*, v. 80, no. 781 (Apr – June 93), pp. 293 – 318. Bibl.

Weinberg, Gregorio. Viejo y nuevo humanismo. *Cuadernos Americanos*, no. 38, Nueva época (Mar – Apr 93), pp. 13 – 16.

Bibliography

Garza Mercado, Ario. *Obras de consulta para estudiantes de ciencias sociales y humanidades* reviewed by Enrique Núñez. *La Educación (USA)*, v. 37, no. 114 (1993), pp. 157 – 158.

HUMBOLDT, ALEXANDER, FREIHERR VON

Day, Douglas. Humboldt and the Casiquiare: Modes of Travel Writing. *Review*, no. 47 (Fall 93), pp. 4 – 8. Il.

Veracoechea de Castillo, Luisa. Palabras de la profesora Luisa Veracoechea de Castillo en el acto de presentación de libro *La huella del sabio: el municipio foráneo Alejandro de Humboldt* con motivo de los 193 años de la visita del sabio a Caracas .... *Boletín de la Academia Nacional de la Historia (Venezuela)*, v. 76, no. 301 (Jan – Mar 93), pp. 27 – 31.

HUMBOLDT, WILHELM, FREIHERR VON

Nansen Díaz, Eréndira. Las lenguas americanas y la teoría del tipo lingüístico en Wilhelm von Humboldt. *Estudios de Cultura Náhuatl*, v. 22 (1992), pp. 223 – 233. Bibl.

HUMOR

See

Caricatures and cartoons
Comic books, strips, etc.
Wit and humor

HUNGARY

Anderle, Adám and Monika Kozári. Koloman von Kánya: Ein österreichisch-ungarischer Botschafter in Mexiko. *Zeitschrift für Lateinamerika Wien*, no. 43 (1992), pp. 63 – 80. Bibl.

HUNTER, MARY ROBINSON

Cherpak, Evelyn M. A Diplomat's Lady in Brazil: Selections from the Diary of Mary Robinson Hunter, 1834 – 1848. *Revista Interamericana de Bibliografía*, v. 42, no. 4 (1992), pp. 617 – 634. Bibl.

HUNTING

Chile

Law and legislation

Ramírez Morales, Fernando. Apuntes para una historia ecológica de Chile. *Cuadernos de Historia (Chile)*, no. 11 (Dec 91), pp. 149 – 196. Bibl, tables.

HURTADO CRUCHAGA, ALBERTO

Hevia, Renato. El milagro del padre Hurtado. *Mensaje*, v. 42, no. 424 (Nov 93), pp. 552 – 554. Il.

Montes M., Fernando. Alberto Hurtado, signo y apóstol de la solidaridad. *Mensaje*, v. 42, no. 421 (Aug 93), pp. 353 – 357. Il.

HYDROELECTRIC POWER

See
Water power

IBÁÑEZ DEL CAMPO, CARLOS

Correspondence, reminiscences, etc.

Donoso Letelier, Crescente. Libro copiador de telegramas del presidente Carlos Ibáñez, 1928 – 1931. *Historia (Chile)*, no. 26 (1991 – 1992), pp. 297 – 383. Bibl.

IBARGOYEN ISLAS, SAÚL

Addresses, essays, lectures

Ibargoyen Islas, Saúl. Plurales hacia afuera, plurales hacia adentro. *Plural (Mexico)*, v. 22, no. 262 (July 93), p. 79.

IBARGÜENGOITIA, JORGE

Criticism of specific works

Las muertas

León, Fidel de. Repertorio y estrategias narrativas en *Las muertas*. *La Palabra y el Hombre*, no. 81 (Jan – Mar 92), pp. 316 – 323. Bibl.

IBARRA, ALEJANDRO

Leal, Henry. Alejandro Ibarra: primer tratadista de física experimental en la UCV, 1834 – 1874. *Revista Nacional de Cultura (Venezuela)*, v. 54, no. 287 (Oct – Dec 92), pp. 238 – 258. Bibl, il.

IBARRA, FRANCISCO DE

Langue, Frédérique. De moralista a arbitrista: don Francisco de Ibarra, obispo de Venezuela, 1798 – 1806; recopilación documental. *Anuario de Estudios Americanos*, v. 49, Suppl. 1 (1992), pp. 55 – 84. Bibl.

IBEROAMERICANA (PERIODICAL)

Indexes

Index des Nummern 1/1977 – 49/1993/Indices de los números 1/1977 – 49/1993. *Iberoamericana*, v. 17, no. 50 (1993), pp. 112 – 134.

ICAZA, JORGE

Criticism of specific works

Huasipungo

Delgado Aparicio, Vielka R. and Jézer González Picado. Introducción al estudio de *Huasipungo* y de *Los perros hambrientos*. *Revista Cultural Lotería*, v. 51, no. 392 (Nov – Dec 93), pp. 41 – 54. Bibl.

IDB

See
Inter-American Development Bank

IDEOLOGY

Rodríguez Ozán, María Elena. Las ideologías de los inmigrantes europeos en América Latina. *Cuadernos Americanos*, no. 41, Nueva época (Sept – Oct 93), pp. 122 – 130. Bibl.

Sung, Jung Mo. Crisis de las ideologías: utopías secularizadas versus reino de Dios (Translated by Juan Michel). *Realidad Económica*, no. 118 (Aug – Sept 93), pp. 68 – 81. Bibl.

IDEOLOGY AND LITERATURE

See
Literature and society
Politics in literature

IGNATIUS, OF LOYOLA, SAINT

See
Loyola, Ignacio de

IKANANA, EVARISTO NUGKUAG

Interviews

Morin, Françoise. Evaristo Nugkuag Ikanana, presidente de la Coordinadora de las Organizaciones Indígenas de la Cuenca Amazónica (COICA), Perú: entrevista realizada el 7 de julio de 1992 en Lima por Françoise Morin. *Caravelle*, no. 59 (1992), pp. 67 – 70.

ILLEGAL ALIENS

See
Undocumented workers
Names of specific national groups, subdivided by country of entry; e.g., *Mexicans - United States*

ILLEGITIMACY

Mannarelli, María Emma. *Pecados públicos: la ilegitimidad en Lima, siglo XVII* reviewed by Arturo Ferrari (Review entitled "Un plancito cholifacio"). *Debate (Peru)*, v. 16, no. 75 (Dec 93 – Jan 94), pp. 78 – 79. Il.

Statistics

Irarrázaval Llona, Ignacio and Juan Pablo Valenzuela. La ilegitimidad en Chile: ¿Hacia un cambio en la conformación de la familia? *Estudios Públicos (Chile)*, no. 52 (Spring 93), pp. 145 – 190. Bibl, tables, charts.

ILLIA, ARTURO U.

Smulovitz, Catalina. La eficacia como crítica y utopía: notas sobre la caída de Illia. *Desarrollo Económico (Argentina)*, v. 33, no. 131 (Oct – Dec 93), pp. 403 – 423. Bibl.

ILLITERACY

Kalman L., Judith. En búsqueda de una palabra nueva: la complejidad conceptual y las dimensiones sociales de la alfabetización. *Revista Latinoamericana de Estudios Educativos*, v. 23, no. 1 (Jan – Mar 93), pp. 87 – 95. Bibl.

Brazil

Freire, Ana María Araújo. *Analfabetismo no Brasil* (Review). *La Educación (USA)*, v. 37, no. 114 (1993), p. 151.

Research

Valente, Edna Fátima Barros. Os filhos pródigos da educação pública: um estudo sobre os evadidos da escola pública num bairro periférico do município de Santarém. *Revista Brasileira de Estudos Pedagógicos*, v. 72, no. 172 (Sept – Dec 91), pp. 397 – 400.

Chile

Gajardo, Marcela. Recent Literacy Development in Chilean Society. *La Educación (USA)*, v. 36, no. 111 – 113 (1992), pp. 89 – 95.

Mexico

Majchrzak, Irena. El nombre propio, enlace natural entre un ser iletrado y el universo de la escritura. *Revista Latinoamericana de Estudios Educativos*, v. 22, no. 4 (Oct – Dec 92), pp. 77 – 87.

Rendón Monzón, Juan José. Apuntes en torno a la alfabetización en lenguas indígenas. *Revista Latinoamericana de Estudios Educativos*, v. 22, no. 4 (Oct – Dec 92), pp. 63 – 76.

IMBELLONI, JOSÉ

Arenas, Patricia and Elvira Inés Baffi. José Imbelloni: una lectura crítica. *Runa*, v. 20 (1991 – 1992), pp. 167 – 176. Bibl.

IMPERIALISM

See also
Cultural imperialism

Fernández Retamar, Roberto. *Calibán*: quinientos años más tarde. *Nuevo Texto Crítico*, v. 6, no. 11 (1993), pp. 223 – 244. Bibl.

Galeano, Eduardo H. The Corruption of Memory (Translated by Mark Fried). *NACLA Report on the Americas*, v. 27, no. 3 (Nov – Dec 93), pp. 35 – 38.

Miranda Bastidas, Haidée and David Ruiz Chataing. *El antiimperialismo en la prensa de la época de Cipriano Castro, 1899 – 1908* reviewed by Julián Rodríguez Barazarte. *Boletín de la Academia Nacional de la Historia (Venezuela)*, v. 76, no. 302 (Apr – June 93), pp. 152 – 153.

Royle, Stephen A. The Small Island as Colony. *Caribbean Geography*, v. 3, no. 4 (Sept 92), pp. 261 – 269. Bibl, tables, maps.

Ruiz Chataing, David. La revista *El Cojo Ilustrado* y el antiimperialismo. *Revista Nacional de Cultura (Venezuela)*, v. 53, no. 286 (July – Sept 92), pp. 177 – 186. Bibl, il.

Europe

Beckles, Hilary. Kalinago (Carib) Resistance to European Colonisation of the Caribbean. *Caribbean Quarterly*, v. 38, no. 2 – 3 (June – Sept 92), pp. 1 – 14. Bibl.

León, Aracely de. Doctrinas económicas en el contexto de la expansión europea. *Revista Cultural Lotería*, v. 51, no. 391 (Sept – Oct 92), pp. 47 – 57. Bibl.

Spain

Jou, Maite. Gabriel García y Tassara: del nacionalismo romántico al concepto de raza hispana. *Anuario de Estudios Americanos*, v. 49 (1992), pp. 529 – 562. Bibl.

United States

Broad, Dave. Revolution, Counterrevolution, and Imperialism: "¡La lucha continúa!" *Latin American Perspectives*, v. 20, no. 2 (Spring 93), pp. 6 – 20. Bibl.

Jou, Maite. Gabriel García y Tassara: del nacionalismo romántico al concepto de raza hispana. *Anuario de Estudios Americanos*, v. 49 (1992), pp. 529 – 562. Bibl.

Maríñez, Pablo A. Democracia y descolonización en el Caribe. *Estudios Sociales (Dominican Republic)*, v. 26, no. 92 (Apr – June 93), pp. 5 – 20. Bibl, tables.

Opatrny, Josef. *U.S. Expansionism and Cuban Annexationism in the 1850s* reviewed by Allan J. Kuethe. *Hispanic American Historical Review*, v. 73, no. 4 (Nov 93), pp. 724 – 725.

Schoonover, Thomas David. *The United States in Central America, 1860 – 1911: Episodes of Social Imperialism and Imperial Rivalry in the World System* reviewed by Lester D. Langley. *The Americas*, v. 49, no. 4 (Apr 93), pp. 561 – 562.

— *The United States in Central America, 1860 – 1911: Episodes of Social Imperialism and Imperial Rivalry in the World System* reviewed by Rob van Vuurde. *European Review of Latin American and Caribbean Studies*, no. 54 (June 93), pp. 131 – 133.

— *The United States in Central America, 1860 – 1911: Episodes of Social Imperialism and Imperial Rivalry in the World System* reviewed by Lester D. Langley. *Journal of Latin American Studies*, v. 25, no. 1 (Feb 93), pp. 200 – 201.

Silveira, Helder Gordim da. A ofensiva política dos EUA sobre a América Latina na visão alemã: uma face do confronto interimperialista, 1938. *Estudos Ibero-Americanos*, v. 18, no. 1 (July 92), pp. 19 – 27. Bibl.

INCAS

Agriculture

Junquera, Carlos. Antropología y paleotecnología: ayer y hoy de una situación agraria en Lambayeque (Perú). *Revista Española de Antropología Americana*, v. 23 (1993), pp. 165 – 187. Bibl.

Art and architecture

Barnes, Monica and Daniel J. Slive. El puma de Cuzco: ¿Plano de la ciudad ynga o noción europea? *Revista Andina*, v. 11, no. 1 (July 93), pp. 70 – 102. Bibl, maps, facs.

Paternosto, César. *Piedra abstracta: la escultura inca; una visión contemporánea* reviewed by María Elvira Iriarte (Accompanied by an English translation). *Art Nexus*, no. 9 (June – Aug 93), pp. 32 – 33. Il.

Bibliography

Benson, Elizabeth P. Bibliography (to the articles in this issue entitled "Sacred Space and Its Uses"). *Latin American Indian Literatures Journal*, v. 9, no. 1 (Spring 93), pp. 55 – 65.

MacCormack, Sabine G. Myth, History, and Language in the Andes (Review article). *Colonial Latin American Review*, v. 2, no. 1 – 2 (1993), pp. 247 – 260. Bibl.

Ramírez-Horton, Susan Elizabeth. Recent Writing on the Peoples of the Andes (Review article). *Latin American Research Review*, v. 28, no. 3 (1993), pp. 174 – 182. Bibl.

Culture

Huhle, Rainer. El terremoto de Cajamarca: la derrota del Inca en la memoria colectiva; elementos para un análisis de la resistencia cultural de los pueblos andinos. *Ibero-Amerikanisches Archiv*, v. 18, no. 3 – 4 (1992), pp. 387 – 426. Il, facs.

Drama

Meneses, Georgina. *Tradición oral en el imperio de los incas: historia, religión y teatro* reviewed by Elizabeth Fonseca C. *Revista de Historia (Costa Rica)*, no. 25 (Jan – June 92), pp. 235 – 237.

Ethnic identity

Dean, Carolyn Sue. Ethnic Conflict and Corpus Christi in Colonial Cuzco. *Colonial Latin American Review*, v. 2, no. 1 – 2 (1993), pp. 93 – 120. Bibl, il.

Government relations

Adorno, Rolena and Kenneth James Andrien, eds. *Transatlantic Encounters: Europeans and Andeans in the Sixteenth Century* reviewed by Ann Zulawski. *Colonial Latin American Review*, v. 2, no. 1 – 2 (1993), pp. 273 – 275.

— *Transatlantic Encounters: Europeans and Andeans in the Sixteenth Century* reviewed by Patricia Seed. *Hispanic American Historical Review*, v. 73, no. 1 (Feb 93), pp. 156 – 157.

— *Transatlantic Encounters: Europeans and Andeans in the Sixteenth Century* reviewed by Gabriela Ramos and Natalia Majluf. *Revista Andina*, v. 11, no. 1 (July 93), pp. 239 – 243. Bibl.

History

Bermúdez-Gallegos, Marta. Oralidad y escritura: Atahualpa; ¿Traidor or traicionado? *Revista de Crítica Literaria Latinoamericana*, v. 19, no. 38 (July – Dec 93), pp. 331 – 344. Bibl.

Marmontel, Jean François. *Los incas o la destrucción del imperio del Perú*, a translation of *Les incas ou la destruction de l'empire du Pérou*. Reviewed by Carlos Garatea Grau (Review entitled "Conquista y fanatismo"). *Debate (Peru)*, v. 15, no. 70 (Sept – Oct 92), p. 67. Il.

Martín Rubio, María del Carmen. El Cuzco incaico, según Juan de Betanzos. *Cuadernos Hispanoamericanos*, no. 511 (Jan 93), pp. 7 – 23. Bibl, il.

Moseley, Michael Edward. *The Incas and Their Ancestors: The Archaeology of Peru* reviewed by Richard L. Burger. *Hispanic American Historical Review*, v. 73, no. 4 (Nov 93), pp. 682 – 684.

— *The Incas and Their Ancestors: The Archaeology of Peru* reviewed by Monica Barnes. *Latin American Indian Literatures Journal*, v. 9, no. 1 (Spring 93), pp. 78 – 79.

Nowak, Kerstin and Dagmar Schweitzer. *Die Inka und der Krieg* reviewed by Mónica Ricketts. *Revista Andina*, v. 11, no. 1 (July 93), pp. 249 – 250.

Quijano Guerrero, Alberto. Dos caciques legendarios. *Boletín de Historia y Antigüedades*, v. 80, no. 780 (Jan – Mar 93), pp. 71 – 77.

Reinhard, Johan. Llullaillaco: An Investigation of the World's Highest Archaelogical Site. *Latin American Indian Literatures Journal*, v. 9, no. 1 (Spring 93), pp. 31 – 54. Il, maps.

Sallmann, Jean-Michel, ed. *Visions indiennes, visions baroques: les métissages de l'inconscient* reviewed by Frédérique Langue. *Caravelle*, no. 60 (1993), pp. 154 – 157.

Scaramuzza Vidoni, Mariarosa. La ritrattistica nella *Nueva corónica* de Guamán Poma de Ayala. *Quaderni Ibero-Americani*, no. 72 (Dec 92), pp. 682 – 694. Bibl.

Sources

Yupanqui, Titu Cusi. *Instrucción al licenciado don Lope García de Castro, 1750* edited by Liliana Regalado de Hurtado. Reviewed by Raquel Chang-Rodríguez. *Hispanic American Historical Review*, v. 73, no. 4 (Nov 93), pp. 699 – 700.

Maps

Compendio cartográfico de la región inka reviewed by Jean-Paul Deler. *Revista Andina*, v. 10, no. 2 (Dec 92), pp. 540 – 541.

Music

Bendezú Aybar, Edmundo. Los textos de D'Harcourt. *Revista de Crítica Literaria Latinoamericana*, v. 19, no. 37 (Jan – June 93), pp. 105 – 115.

Religion and mythology

Barrera, Pablo. Religiosidad y resistencia andina: la fe de los no creyentes. *Cristianismo y Sociedad*, v. 30, no. 113 (1992), pp. 15 – 34. Bibl.

Eeckhout, Peter. Le créateur et le devin: à propos de Pachacamac, dieu précolombien de la côte centrale du Pérou. *Revista Española de Antropología Americana*, v. 23 (1993), pp. 135 – 152. Bibl, tables.

Gareis, Iris. Brujos y brujas en el antiguo Perú: apariencia y realidad en las fuentes históricas. *Revista de Indias*, v. 53, no. 198 (May – Aug 93), pp. 583 – 613. Bibl, facs.

Jürth, Max. Plegarias incaicas. *Revista de Crítica Literaria Latinoamericana*, v. 19, no. 37 (Jan – June 93), pp. 159 – 168.

MacCormack, Sabine G. *Religion in the Andes: Vision and Imagination in Early Colonial Peru* reviewed by Susan Ramírez. *The Americas*, v. 50, no. 2 (Oct 93), pp. 271 – 272.

— *Religion in the Andes: Vision and Imagination in Early Colonial Peru* reviewed by Frank Solomon. *Colonial Latin American Review*, v. 2, no. 1 – 2 (1993), pp. 281 – 284.

— *Religion in the Andes: Vision and Imagination in Early Colonial Peru* reviewed by Irene Silverblatt. *Hispanic American Historical Review*, v. 73, no. 1 (Feb 93), pp. 157 – 159.

Meneses, Georgina. *Tradición oral en el imperio de los incas: historia, religión y teatro* reviewed by Elizabeth Fonseca C. *Revista de Historia (Costa Rica)*, no. 25 (Jan – June 92), pp. 235 – 237.

Seminiski, Jan. Manqu Qhapaq Inka: ¿Un poeta religioso? *Revista de Crítica Literaria Latinoamericana*, v. 19, no. 37 (Jan – June 93), pp. 131 – 158. Bibl.

Szeminski, Jan. Manqu Qhapaq Inka según Anello Oliva, S.J., 1631. *Historia y Cultura (Peru)*, no. 20 (1990), pp. 269 – 280.

Urbano, Henrique-Osvaldo. Huayna Cápac y sus enanos: huellas de un ciclo mítico andino prehispano. *Historia y Cultura (Peru)*, no. 20 (1990), pp. 281 – 293. Bibl.

Urton, Gary. *The History of a Myth: Pacariqtambo and the Origin of the Inkas* reviewed by María Benavides. *Bulletin de l'Institut Français d'Etudes Andines*, v. 21, no. 2 (1992), pp. 785 – 787.

Social life and customs

Rostworowski Tovar de Diez Canseco, María. La visita de Urcos de 1652: un kipu pueblerino. *Historia y Cultura (Peru)*, no. 20 (1990), pp. 295 – 317. Bibl, tables.

Tribal government

Alcina Franch, José. Los orígenes del estado inca. *Revista de Indias*, v. 53, no. 197 (Jan – Apr 93), pp. 9 – 22. Bibl, charts.

D'Altroy, Terence Norman. *Provincial Power in the Inka Empire* reviewed by Helaine Silverman. *The Americas*, v. 50, no. 1 (July 93), pp. 119 – 121.

Hurtado, Liliana R. de. *La sucesión incaica: aproximación al mando y poder entre los incas a partir de la crónica de Betanzos* reviewed by Nicanor Domínguez Faura. *Revista Andina*, v. 11, no. 1 (July 93), pp. 250 – 251.

Julien, Catherine Jean. *Condesuyo: The Political Division of Territory under Inca and Spanish Rule* reviewed by Nicanor Domínguez. *Revista Andina*, v. 10, no. 2 (Dec 92), pp. 546 – 547.

Melgar Bao, Ricardo. Nuevo Mundo y área mediterránea en confrontación: sistemas político – culturales en los siglos XV – XIX. *Boletín de Antropología Americana*, no. 23 (July 91), pp. 99 – 108. Bibl, il.

Patterson, Thomas C. *The Inca Empire: The Formation and Disintegration of a Pre-Capitalist State* reviewed by Olivia Harris. *Bulletin of Latin American Research*, v. 12, no. 2 (May 93), pp. 217 – 218.

INCOME DISTRIBUTION

Brazil

Bonelli, Regis and Lauro Roberto Albrecht Ramos. Distribuição de renda no Brasil: avaliação das tendências de longo prazo e mudanças na desigualdade desde meados dos anos '70. *Revista de Economia Política (Brazil)*, v. 13, no. 2 (Apr – June 93), pp. 76 – 97. Bibl, tables, charts.

Cardoso, Eliana Anastasia. Cyclical Variations of Earnings Inequality in Brazil. *Revista de Economia Política (Brazil)*, v. 13, no. 4 (Oct – Dec 93), pp. 112 – 124. Bibl, tables, charts.

Hoffmann, Rodolfo. Vinte anos de desigualdade e pobreza na agricultura brasileira. *Revista de Economia e Sociologia Rural*, v. 30, no. 2 (Apr – June 92), pp. 97 – 113. Bibl, tables, charts.

Lanzana, Antonio. A realidade dos salários. *Problemas Brasileiros*, v. 30, no. 296 (Mar – Apr 93), pp. 15 – 16. Tables, charts.

Mathematical models

Amadeo Swaelen, Edward Joaquim and José Márcio Camargo. Política comercial e distribuição funcional da renda. *Pesquisa e Planejamento Econômico*, v. 22, no. 1 (Apr 92), pp. 73 – 100. Bibl, tables, charts.

Hoffmann, Rodolfo. Sensibilidade das medidas de desigualdade a transferências regressivas. *Pesquisa e Planejamento Econômico*, v. 22, no. 2 (Aug 92), pp. 289 – 304. Bibl, tables, charts.

Teixeira, Erly Cardoso et al. A política de investimentos agrícolas e seu efeito sobre a distribuição de renda. *Revista de Economia e Sociologia Rural*, v. 30, no. 4 (Oct – Dec 92), pp. 291 – 303. Bibl, tables, charts.

Chile

Celedón, Carmen and Oscar Muñoz Gomá. La política económica durante la transición a la democracia en Chile, 1990 – 1992. *Estudios Sociales (Chile)*, no. 75 (Jan – Mar 93), pp. 77 – 95. Bibl.

Ruiz-Tagle P., Jaime. Reducción de la pobreza y distribución de los ingresos en Chile: tareas pendientes. *Mensaje*, v. 42, no. 425 (Dec 93), pp. 640 – 643. Il, tables.

Developing countries

Bourguignon, François and Christian Morrisson, eds. *External Trade and Income Distribution* reviewed by Jaime de Melo. *Economic Development and Cultural Change*, v. 42, no. 1 (Oct 93), pp. 198 – 200.

Honduras

Navarro, Jorge. Poverty and Adjustment: The Case of Honduras. *CEPAL Review*, no. 49 (Apr 93), pp. 91 – 101. Bibl, tables.

Latin America

Sarmiento Palacio, Eduardo. Growth and Income Distribution in Countries at Intermediate Stages of Development. *CEPAL Review*, no. 48 (Dec 92), pp. 141 – 155. Tables, charts.

INDEX NUMBERS (ECONOMICS)

Amadeo Swaelen, Edward Joaquim and Elena Landau. Indexação e dispersão de preços relativos: análise do caso brasileiro, 1975 – 1991. *Revista de Economia Política (Brazil)*, v. 13, no. 3 (July – Sept 93), pp. 130 – 138. Bibl, charts.

Barbosa, Fernando de Holanda. A indexação dos ativos financeiros: a experiência brasileira. *Revista Brasileira de Economia*, v. 47, no. 3 (July – Sept 93), pp. 373 – 397. Bibl, tables, charts.

Carvalho, Carlos Eduardo Vieira de. Liquidez dos haveres financeiros e zeragem automática do mercado. *Revista de Economia Política (Brazil)*, v. 13, no. 1 (Jan – Mar 93), pp. 25 – 36.

Catão, Luís. A New Wholesale Price Index for Brazil during the Period 1870 – 1913. *Revista Brasileira de Economia*, v. 46, no. 4 (Oct – Dec 92), pp. 519 – 533. Bibl, tables, charts.

Landau, Elena and Suzana S. Peixoto. Inflação, indexação e preços relativos: novas evidências para o Brasil. *Pesquisa e Planejamento Econômico*, v. 22, no. 1 (Apr 92), pp. 125 – 167. Bibl, tables, charts.

Mattos, César Costa Alves de. O regime de expectativas e a política salarial: indexação x prefixação. *Revista de Economia Política (Brazil),* v. 13, no. 2 (Apr – June 93), pp. 137 – 143.

INDIANS (INDIA)

See
East Indians

INDIANS, TREATMENT OF

See also
Black legend
Encomiendas
Subdivision *Government relations* under names of Indian groups

Bibliography

Ward, Thomas Butler. Toward a Concept of Unnatural Slavery during the Renaissance: A Review of Primary and Secondary Sources. *Revista Interamericana de Bibliografía,* v. 42, no. 2 (1992), pp. 259 – 279. Bibl.

America

Castilla Urbano, Francisco. Juan Ginés de Sepúlveda: en torno a una idea de civilización. *Revista de Indias,* v. 52, no. 195 – 196 (May – Dec 92), pp. 329 – 348. Bibl.

Deckers, Daniel. La justicia de la conquista de América: consideraciones en torno a la cronología y a los protagonistas de una controversia del siglo XVI muy actual. *Ibero-Amerikanisches Archiv,* v. 18, no. 3 – 4 (1992), pp. 331 – 366. Bibl.

Fernández Buey, Francisco. La controversia entre Ginés de Sepúlveda y Bartolomé de las Casas: una revisión. *Boletín Americanista,* v. 33, no. 42 – 43 (1992 – 1993), pp. 301 – 347. Bibl.

Fernández Cabrelli, Alfonso. El trato al indio en la colonización ibérica y en la anglosajona. *Hoy Es Historia,* v. 9, no. 54 (Nov – Dec 92), pp. 39 – 43. Il.

Gutiérrez, Gustavo. *En busca de los pobres de Jesucristo* reviewed by Carlos Garatea Grau (Review entitled "Por la vida y la libertad"). *Debate (Peru),* v. 16, no. 72 (Mar – May 93), p. 63. Il.

— *En busca de los pobres de Jesuscristo: el pensamiento de Bartolomé de las Casas* reviewed by Aníbal Edwards. *Mensaje,* v. 42, no. 417 (Mar – Apr 93), pp. 109 – 110.

Izard, Miquel. Elegir lo posible y escoger lo mejor. *Boletín Americanista,* v. 33, no. 42 – 43 (1992 – 1993), pp. 141 – 182. Bibl.

— Poca subordinación y menos ambición. *Boletín Americanista,* v. 33, no. 42 – 43 (1992 – 1993), pp. 159 – 182. Bibl.

Llera Esteban, Luis de. Recordando a Francisco de Vitoria en el V centenario. *Quaderni Ibero-Americani,* no. 72 (Dec 92), pp. 661 – 681. Bibl.

Martínez Martín, Jaime J. La defensa del indio americano en un diálogo del renacimiento: *Los coloquios de la verdad* de Pedro Quiroga. *Studi di Letteratura Ispano-Americana,* v. 24 (1993), pp. 7 – 24.

Methol Ferré, Alberto. El fracaso del V centenario. *Cuadernos del CLAEH,* v. 17, no. 63 – 64 (Oct 92), pp. 11 – 20. Bibl.

Ortega, José. Conmemoración del genocidio de las Indias. *La Palabra y el Hombre,* no. 81 (Jan – Mar 92), pp. 11 – 19. Bibl.

Premazzi, Javier. La España de la conquista y la América indígena. *Hoy Es Historia,* v. 9, no. 54 (Nov – Dec 92), pp. 27 – 38.

Salvat Monguillot, Manuel. Francisco de Vitoria y el nacimiento del capitalismo. *Boletín de la Academia Chilena de la Historia,* v. 58 – 59, no. 102 (1991 – 1992), pp. 329 – 347. Bibl.

Seed, Patricia Pauline. "Are These Not Also Men?": The Indians' Humanity and Capacity for Spanish Civilisation. *Journal of Latin American Studies,* v. 25, no. 3 (Oct 93), pp. 629 – 652. Bibl.

Sievernich, Michael. Visiones teológicas en torno al quinto centenario. *Ibero-Amerikanisches Archiv,* v. 18, no. 3 – 4 (1992), pp. 367 – 385. Bibl.

Soria, Giuliano Oreste. Echi della conquista nella Torino del '600: Valerio Fulvio Savoiano e Bartolomé de Las Casas. *Quaderni Ibero-Americani,* no. 72 (Dec 92), pp. 721 – 731. Bibl.

Tau Anzoátegui, Víctor. *Casuísmo y sistema: indagación histórica sobre el espíritu del derecho indiano* reviewed by Nelson Nogueira Saldanha. *Revista Brasileira de Estudos Políticos,* no. 76 (Jan 93), pp. 202 – 203.

Law and legislation

Aspell de Yanzi Ferreira, Marcela. La regulación jurídica de las formas del trabajo forzado (Segunda parte). *Investigaciones y Ensayos,* no. 41 (Jan – Dec 91), pp. 349 – 394. Bibl.

Moreno, Mariano. Sobre el servicio personal de los indios, en general, y sobre el particular de yanaconas y mitayos. *Signo,* no. 36 – 37, Nueva época (May – Dec 92), pp. 455 – 474.

Andean region

Zum Felde, Alberto. La tragedia del indio en Suramérica. *Hoy Es Historia,* v. 10, no. 55 (Jan – Feb 93), pp. 102 – 113. Il.

Argentina

Viñas, David. Nueve apuntes para conjurar el olvido de indios y genocidas (Interview transcribed by Jean Andreu and Claude Castro). *Caravelle,* no. 59 (1992), pp. 71 – 73.

Bolivia

Gato Castaño, Purificación. *El informe del p. Gregorio de Bolívar a la Congregación de Propaganda Fide de 1623* reviewed by Pedro de Anasagasti. *Signo,* no. 35, Nueva época (Jan – Apr 92), pp. 214 – 216.

Brazil

Farage, Nádia. *As muralhas dos sertões: os povos indígenas no rio Branco e a colonização* reviewed by David Cleary. *Journal of Latin American Studies,* v. 25, no. 2 (May 93), pp. 394 – 395.

Caribbean area

Chacón, Zully. Antropofagia y resistencia caribe: armas jurídicas de la corona española. *Boletín de la Academia Nacional de la Historia (Venezuela),* v. 75, no. 300 (Oct – Dec 92), pp. 89 – 107. Bibl, maps.

Chile

Zapater Equioiz, Horacio. El padre Luis de Valdivia y la guerra defensiva. *Mensaje,* v. 42, no. 420 (July 93), pp. 220 – 223. Il.

Colombia

Albónico, Aldo. Un' opera in difesa degli indi nella Milano del seicento: il *Llanto sagrado de la América meridional. Quaderni Ibero-Americani,* no. 72 (Dec 92), pp. 695 – 708. Bibl.

Guatemala

Vinos derramados: el libro de Ricardo Falla sobre los masacres de Ixcán, Guatemala. *ECA; Estudios Centroamericanos,* v. 47, no. 529 – 530 (Nov – Dec 92), pp. 1037 – 1044. Il.

Honduras

Newson, Linda A. Variaciones regionales en el impacto del dominio colonial español en las poblaciones indígenas de Honduras y Nicaragua. *Mesoamérica (USA),* v. 13, no. 24 (Dec 92), pp. 297 – 312. Bibl, tables, maps.

Mexico

Benítez, Fernando. *1992: ¿Qué celebramos, qué lamentamos?* reviewed by Alvaro Ruiz Abreu (Review entitled "En lengua propia"). *Nexos,* v. 16, no. 181 (Jan 93), pp. 70 – 72.

Nicaragua

Newson, Linda A. Variaciones regionales en el impacto del dominio colonial español en las poblaciones indígenas de Honduras y Nicaragua. *Mesoamérica (USA),* v. 13, no. 24 (Dec 92), pp. 297 – 312. Bibl, tables, maps.

Peru

Brenot, Anne-Marie. *Pouvoirs et profits au Pérou colonial au XVIII* siècle: gouverneurs, clientèles et ventes forcées* reviewed by Pierre Ragon. *Cahiers des Amériques Latines,* no. 14 (1992), pp. 152 – 153.

INDIANS IN LITERATURE

Amodio, Emanuele. El otro americano: construcción y difusión de la iconografía del indio americano en Europa en el primer siglo de la conquista (Translated by Francesco Russo). *Montalbán*, no. 24 (1992), pp. 33 – 84. Bibl, il, maps, facs.

Cardenal, Ernesto. *Golden UFOs: The Indian Poems/Los ovnis de oro: poemas indios* edited by Russell O. Salmon, translated by Carlos and Monique Altschul. Reviewed by Marc Zimmerman. *Hispanic American Historical Review*, v. 73, no. 2 (May 93), pp. 295 – 296.

Chanady, Amaryll. La ambivalencia del discurso indigenista en la nueva narrativa ecuatoriana. *Canadian Journal of Latin American and Caribbean Studies*, v. 17, no. 34 (1992), pp. 53 – 71. Bibl.

Cró, Stelio. *The Noble Savage: Allegory of Freedom* reviewed by Dianne M. Bono. *Colonial Latin American Review*, v. 2, no. 1 – 2 (1993), pp. 288 – 290.

Fornet, Jorge. Dos novelas peruanas: entre sapos y halcones. *Plural (Mexico)*, v. 22, no. 263 (Aug 93), pp. 57 – 62.

Lienhard, Martín. *La voz y su huella: escritura y conflicto étnico – social en América Latina, 1492 – 1988* reviewed by Gustavo Fares. *Hispania (USA)*, v. 76, no. 1 (Mar 93), pp. 88 – 89.

— *La voz y su huella: escritura y conflicto étnico – social en América Latina, 1492 – 1988* reviewed by José Prats Sariol. *Iberoamericana*, v. 16, no. 47 – 48 (1992), pp. 113 – 116.

— *La voz y su huella: escritura y conflicto étnico – social en América Latina, 1492 – 1988* reviewed by Antonio Cornejo Polar. *Revista de Crítica Literaria Latinoamericana*, v. 19, no. 38 (July – Dec 93), pp. 395 – 397.

Steele, Cynthia. Indigenismo y posmodernidad: narrativa indigenista, testimonio, teatro campesino y video en el Chiapas finisecular. *Iberoamericana*, v. 16, no. 47 – 48 (1992), pp. 82 – 94. Bibl.

— Indigenismo y posmodernidad: narrativa indigenista, testimonio, teatro campesino y video en el Chiapas finisecular. *Revista de Crítica Literaria Latinoamericana*, v. 19, no. 38 (July – Dec 93), pp. 249 – 260. Bibl.

Triviños, Gilberto. La sombra de los héroes. *Atenea (Chile)*, no. 465 – 466 (1992), pp. 67 – 97. Bibl, il.

Urruela V. de Quezada, María. El indio en la literatura hispanoamericana: un esbozo. *Boletín de la Academia Nacional de la Historia (Venezuela)*, v. 75, no. 299 (July – Sept 92), pp. 91 – 108. Bibl.

INDIANS OF AMERICA

Arms and armor

Salas, Alberto Mario. Armas de la conquista: venenos y gases. *Hoy Es Historia*, v. 10, no. 59 (Sept – Oct 93), pp. 87 – 97. Il.

Art and architecture

Kaye, Susan. A Living Venue for Cultural Crossroads. *Américas*, v. 45, no. 3 (May – June 93), pp. 48 – 51. Il.

Exhibitions

Joralemon, Peter David. Treasures of the New World. *Latin American Art*, v. 4, no. 4 (Winter 92), pp. 40 – 43. Il.

Congresses

Declaración de La Paz. *Anuario Indigenista*, v. 30 (Dec 91), pp. 339 – 342.

Lartigue, François. México '92: les amérindiens dans la ville. *Caravelle*, no. 59 (1992), pp. 99 – 108.

Costume and adornment

Anawalt, Patricia Rieff. Reply to Helen Perlstein Pollard (On her comment on the article "Ancient Cultural Contacts between Ecuador, West Mexico, and the American Southwest" by Patricia Anawalt which appeared in this journal in 1992). *Latin American Antiquity*, v. 4, no. 4 (Dec 93), pp. 386 – 387. Bibl.

Pollard, Helen Perlstein. Merchant Colonies, Semi-Mesoamericans, and the Study of Cultural Contact: A Comment on Anawalt (Comment on the article "Ancient Cultural Contacts between Ecuador, West Mexico, and the American Southwest" by Patricia Anawalt which appeared in this journal in 1992). *Latin American Antiquity*, v. 4, no. 4 (Dec 93), pp. 383 – 385. Bibl.

Culture

Sources

Strosetzki, Christoph, ed. *Der Griff nach der Neuen Welt: Der Untergang der indianischen Kulturen im Spiegel zeitgenössischer Texte* reviewed by Augustín F. Seguí. *Iberoamericana*, v. 17, no. 49 (1993), pp. 87 – 89.

Drama

González Cajiao, Fernando. El teatro precolombino siempre fue callejero. *Conjunto*, no. 92 (July – Dec 92), pp. 7 – 11. Il.

Economic conditions

Padoch, Christine and Kent H. Redford, eds. *Conservation of Neotropical Forests: Working from Traditional Resource Use* reviewed by Mahesh Rangarajan. *Journal of Latin American Studies*, v. 25, no. 3 (Oct 93), pp. 687 – 688.

Ethnic identity

Baudot, Georges. Genaro Domínguez Maldonado: entrevista realizada el 15 de agosto de 1991 en la ciudad de México por Georges Baudot. *Caravelle*, no. 59 (1992), pp. 39 – 47.

Pino Díaz, Fermín del. Indianismo, hispanismo y antropología: acerca de la identidad autóctona de los indios de América. *Revista de Indias*, v. 52, no. 195 – 196 (May – Dec 92), pp. 825 – 838.

Food

Super, John Clay. *Food, Conquest, and Colonization in Sixteenth-Century Spanish America* reviewed by Jorge Luján Muñoz. *Mesoamérica (USA)*, v. 13, no. 24 (Dec 92), pp. 463 – 464.

Foreign opinion

Amodio, Emanuele. El otro americano: construcción y difusión de la iconografía del indio americano en Europa en el primer siglo de la conquista (Translated by Francesco Russo). *Montalbán*, no. 24 (1992), pp. 33 – 84. Bibl, il, maps, facs.

Ragon, Pierre. *Les amours indiennes ou l'imaginaire du conquistador* reviewed by Christian Satge. *Caravelle*, no. 59 (1992), pp. 297 – 300.

Seed, Patricia Pauline. "Are These Not Also Men?": The Indians' Humanity and Capacity for Spanish Civilisation. *Journal of Latin American Studies*, v. 25, no. 3 (Oct 93), pp. 629 – 652. Bibl.

Government relations

Chihuailaf Nahuelpan, Elicura and Pedro Marimán. Reflexions mapuches autour d'un voyage au Mexique et au Guatémala. *Caravelle*, no. 59 (1992), pp. 109 – 126. Il.

Díaz Polanco, Héctor. El quinto centenario y los pueblos indios. *Boletín de Antropología Americana*, no. 23 (July 91), pp. 13 – 29. Bibl, il.

Lienhard, Martín. "Nosotros hemos resuelto y mandamos . . . ": textos indígenas destinados a los extraños, siglos XVIII y XIX. *Revista de Crítica Literaria Latinoamericana*, v. 19, no. 38 (July – Dec 93), pp. 173 – 184. Bibl.

Menchú, Rigoberta. ¿Por qué se discrimina al indígena? *Hoy Es Historia*, v. 10, no. 58 (July – Aug 93), pp. 80 – 83. Il.

Nahmad Sittón, Salomón. Los quinientos años de dominación y colonialismo y los pueblos étnicos de México. *Estudios Sociológicos*, v. 10, no. 30 (Sept – Dec 92), pp. 651 – 675. Bibl, tables.

Stavenhagen, Rodolfo. Los derechos de los indígenas: algunos problemas conceptuales. *Nueva Antropología*, v. 13, no. 43 (Nov 92), pp. 83 – 99. Bibl.

Bibliography

Lázaro Avila, Carlos. Un freno a la conquista: la resistencia de los cacicazgos indígenas americanos en la bibliografía histórico – antropológica. *Revista de Indias*, v. 52, no. 195 – 196 (May – Dec 92), pp. 589 – 609. Bibl.

Congresses

Declaración de Guadalajara. *Anuario Indigenista,* v. 30 (Dec 91), pp. 289 – 298.

History

Cueva, Agustín. Falacias y coartadas del quinto centenario. *Boletín de Antropología Americana,* no. 23 (July 91), pp. 5 – 12. Bibl, il.

Fernández Herrero, Beatriz. El "otro" descubrimiento: la imagen del español en el indio americano. *Cuadernos Hispanoamericanos,* no. 520 (Oct 93), pp. 7 – 35. Bibl.

Mason, Peter, ed. *Indianen en Nederlanders, 1492 – 1992* reviewed by Menno Oostra. *European Review of Latin American and Caribbean Studies,* no. 54 (June 93), pp. 145 – 147.

Menchú, Rigoberta. Un homenaje a los pueblos indígenas. *Realidad Económica,* no. 114 – 115 (Feb – May 93), pp. 74 – 85. Il.

Languages

Hamel, Rainer Enrique. Derechos lingüísticos. *Nueva Antropología,* v. 13, no. 44 (Aug 93), p. 71 + .

Martinell Gifre, Emma. *Aspectos lingüísticos del descubrimiento y de la conquista* reviewed by Ma. Angeles Soler Arechalde. *Estudios de Cultura Náhuatl,* v. 22 (1992), pp. 505 – 508.

Bibliography

Castro y Castro, Manuel de. Lenguas indígenas americanas transmitidas por los franciscanos del siglo XVIII. *Archivo Ibero-Americano,* v. 52, no. 205 – 208 (Jan – Dec 92), pp. 585 – 628. Bibl.

Legal status, laws, etc.

United Nations. Commission on Human Rights. Proyecto de Declaración Universal sobre los Derechos de los Pueblos Indígenas. *Anuario Indigenista,* v. 30 (Dec 91), pp. 513 – 524.

World Council of Indigenous Peoples. Declaración universal de las primeras naciones. *Anuario Indigenista,* v. 30 (Dec 91), pp. 317 – 319.

Literature

Granillo Vázquez, Lilia. Pensamiento indígena. *Fem,* v. 17, no. 125 (July 93), pp. 18 – 20.

Medicine

Fernández, Fiz Antonio. *Antropología cultural, medicina indígena de América y arte rupestre argentino* reviewed by Hebe Clementi. *Todo Es Historia,* v. 26, no. 307 (Feb 93), pp. 75 – 76. Il.

Mortuary customs

Szászdi León-Borja, István. Un tabú de la muerte: la innominación de los vivos y los difuntos como norma jurídica prehispánica. *Anuario de Estudios Americanos,* v. 49 (1992), pp. 3 – 20. Bibl.

Origin

Tapajós, Vicente Costa Santos. O homem que Colombo encontrou nas Indias Ocidentais (I). *Revista do Instituto Histórico e Geográfico Brasileiro,* no. 372 (July – Sept 91), pp. 785 – 799. Bibl.

Population

Cook, Noble David and William George Lovell, eds. *"Secret Judgments of God": Old World Disease in Colonial Spanish America* reviewed by Ronn F. Pineo. *The Americas,* v. 50, no. 1 (July 93), pp. 126 – 127.

— *"Secret Judgments of God": Old World Disease in Colonial Spanish America* reviewed by Cynthia Radding. *Hispanic American Historical Review,* v. 73, no. 2 (May 93), pp. 309 – 311.

Methodology

Henige, David P. Counting the Encounter: The Pernicious Appeal of Verisimilitude. *Colonial Latin American Historical Review,* v. 2, no. 3 (Summer 93), pp. 325 – 361. Bibl, tables, charts.

Religion and mythology

Báez-Jorge, Félix. *Las voces del agua: el simbolismo de las sirenas y las mitologías americanas* reviewed by Mario M. Muñoz (Review entitled "Las seductoras macabras"). *La Palabra y el Hombre,* no. 84 (Oct – Dec 92), pp. 252 – 255. Il.

Caunedo Madrigal, Silvia. *Las entrañas mágicas de América* reviewed by Paloma Lapuerta. *Cuadernos Hispanoamericanos,* no. 520 (Oct 93), pp. 127 – 128.

Women

Congresses

Alberti Manzanares, Pilar. Mujer Indígena y II Encuentro Continental 500 Años de Resistencia Indígena, Negra y Popular, Guatemala, 1991. *Anuario de Estudios Americanos,* v. 49, Suppl. 1 (1992), pp. 186 – 193.

Writing

Lienhard, Martín. "Nosotros hemos resuelto y mandamos . . . ": textos indígenas destinados a los extraños, siglos XVIII y XIX. *Revista de Crítica Literaria Latinoamericana,* v. 19, no. 38 (July – Dec 93), pp. 173 – 184. Bibl.

INDIANS OF ARGENTINA

See also
> Araucanian Indians
> Chiriguano Indians
> Guarani Indians

Argentina: Ley 23.302 sobre política indígena y apoyo a las comunidades aborígenes. *Anuario Indigenista,* v. 30 (Dec 91), pp. 437 – 456.

Carrazzoni, José Andrés. El caballo del indio del desierto. *Todo Es Historia,* v. 27, no. 315 (Oct 93), pp. 76 – 89. Bibl, il.

Carril, Bonifacio del. *Los indios en la Argentina, 1536 – 1845, según la iconografía de la época* reviewed by María Sáenz Quesada. *Todo Es Historia,* v. 27, no. 315 (Oct 93), p. 63. Il.

Levaggi, Abelardo. Muerte y resurrección del derecho indiano sobre el aborigen en la Argentina del siglo XIX. *Jahrbuch für Geschichte von Staat, Wirtschaft und Gesellschaft Lateinamerikas,* v. 29 (1992), pp. 179 – 193. Bibl.

Poujade, Ruth. Poblamiento prehistórico y colonial de Misiones. *Estudos Ibero-Americanos,* v. 18, no. 1 (July 92), pp. 29 – 70. Bibl, maps.

INDIANS OF BELIZE

See also
> Carib Indians
> Kekchi Indians
> Mayas

Bolland, O. Nigel. "Indios Bravos" or "Gentle Savages": 19th Century Views of the "Indians" of Belize and the Miskito Coast. *Revista/Review Interamericana,* v. 22, no. 1 – 2 (Spring – Summer 92), pp. 36 – 54. Bibl.

INDIANS OF BOLIVIA

See also
> Aymara Indians
> Yura Indians

Arnold, Denise Y. At the Heart of the Woven Dance-Floor: The Wayñu in Qaqachaka. *Iberoamericana,* v. 16, no. 47 – 48 (1992), pp. 21 – 66. Bibl, il, tables.

Healy, Kevin. Back to the Future: Ethnodevelopment among the Jalq'a of Bolivia. *Grassroots Development,* v. 16, no. 2 (1992), pp. 22 – 34. Il.

Irurozqui Victoriano, Marta. ¿Qué hacer con el indio?: un análisis de las obras de Franz Tamayo y Alcides Arguedas. *Revista de Indias,* v. 52, no. 195 – 196 (May – Dec 92), pp. 559 – 587.

Patrinos, Harry Anthony and George Psacharopoulos. The Cost of Being Indigenous in Bolivia: An Empirical Analysis of Educational Attainments and Outcomes. *Bulletin of Latin American Research,* v. 12, no. 3 (Sept 93), pp. 293 – 309. Bibl, tables, charts.

Salazar Mostajo, Carlos. *La "Taika": teoría y práctica de la escuela – ayllu* reviewed by Carlos Coello Vila. *Signo,* no. 38, Nueva época (Jan – Apr 93), pp. 256 – 257.

INDIANS OF BRAZIL

See also
Bororo Indians
Cayapo Indians
Cubeo Indians
Gê Indians
Kamaiurá Indians
Yanoama Indians

Pinto, Márnio Teixeira. Corpo, morte e sociedade: um ensaio a partir da forma e da razão de se esquartejar um inimigo. *Revista Brasileira de Ciências Sociais*, v. 8, no. 21 (Feb 93), pp. 52 – 67. Bibl, charts.

Possuelo, Sydney Ferreira. Brasil: Decreto 828/91 que crea la Comisión de Defensa de los Derechos Indígenas. *Anuario Indigenista*, v. 30 (Dec 91), pp. 457 – 459.

Salzano, Francisco M. Color Vision in Four Brazilian Indian Tribes. *Interciencia*, v. 18, no. 4 (July – Aug 93), pp. 195 – 197. Bibl, tables.

Vidal, Lux et al, eds. *Grafismo indígena: ensaios de antropologia estética* reviewed by Clarice Cohn. *Revista de Antropologia (Brazil)*, v. 34 (1991), pp. 230 – 232.

Villaça, Aparecida Maria Neiva. *Comendo como gente: formas de canibalismo wari' (pakaa nova)* reviewed by Robin M. Wright. *Revista Brasileira de Ciências Sociais*, v. 8, no. 23 (Oct 93), pp. 146 – 148.

INDIANS OF CENTRAL AMERICA

See also
Carib Indians
Mayas
Mosquito Indians
Nahuas

Agriculture

Bolaños Arquín, Margarita. Los indígenas y la conservación de la biodiversidad: 500 años de resistencia. *Revista de Historia (Costa Rica)*, no. 25 (Jan – June 92), pp. 165 – 180. Bibl, il, maps, charts.

Art and architecture

Gussinyer i Alfonso, Jordi. Notas para el concepto de espacio en la arquitectura precolombina de Mesoamérica. *Boletín Americanista*, v. 33, no. 42 – 43 (1992 – 1993), pp. 183 – 230. Bibl, il.

Pang, Hildegard Delgado. *Pre-Columbian Art: Investigations and Insights* reviewed by John F. Scott. *Hispanic American Historical Review*, v. 73, no. 1 (Feb 93), pp. 140 – 141.

Commerce

Corrales Ulloa, Francisco and Ifigenia Quintanilla Jiménez. El Pacífico central de Costa Rica y el intercambio regional. *Vínculos*, v. 16, no. 1 – 2 (1990), pp. 111 – 126. Bibl, tables, maps.

Fernández Molina, José Antonio. Producción indígena y mercado urbano a finales del período colonial: la provisión de alimentos a la ciudad de Guatemala, 1787 – 1822. *Revista de Historia (Costa Rica)*, no. 26 (July – Dec 92), pp. 9 – 30. Bibl, tables, maps, charts.

Culture

Chapin, Mac. The View from the Shore: Central America's Indians Encounter the Quincentenary. *Grassroots Development*, v. 16, no. 2 (1992), pp. 2 – 10. Bibl, il, maps.

Houwald, Götz Dieter, Freiherr von. *Mayangna = WIR: Zur Geschichte der Sumu-Indianer in Mittelamerika* reviewed by Wolfgang Haberland. *Mesoamérica (USA)*, v. 13, no. 23 (June 92), pp. 217 – 218.

Dwellings

Solís Alpízar, Olman E. Jesús María: un sitio con actividad doméstica en el Pacífico central, Costa Rica. *Vínculos*, v. 16, no. 1 – 2 (1990), pp. 31 – 56. Bibl, il.

Ethnic identity

García Ruiz, Jesús F. De la identidad aceptada a la identidad elegida: el papel de lo religioso en la politización de las identificaciones étnicas en Guatemala. *Estudios Sociológicos*, v. 10, no. 30 (Sept – Dec 92), pp. 713 – 733. Bibl.

Gould, Jeffrey L. "¡Vana ilusión!": The Highlands Indians and the Myth of Nicaragua Mestiza, 1880 – 1925. *Hispanic American Historical Review*, v. 73, no. 3 (Aug 93), pp. 393 – 429. Bibl, maps.

Humphreys, Francis. Afro-Belizean Cultural Heritage: Its Role in Combating Recolonization. *Belizean Studies*, v. 20, no. 3 (Dec 92), pp. 11 – 16. Bibl.

Food

Andrews, Jean. Diffusion of Mesoamerican Food Complex to Southeastern Europe. *Geographical Review*, v. 83, no. 2 (Apr 93), pp. 194 – 204. Bibl, maps.

Foreign opinion

Bolland, O. Nigel. "Indios Bravos" or "Gentle Savages": 19th Century Views of the "Indians" of Belize and the Miskito Coast. *Revista/Review Interamericana*, v. 22, no. 1 – 2 (Spring – Summer 92), pp. 36 – 54. Bibl.

Government relations

Daza, Patricio. *Ethnies et révolution: Nicaragua, 1979 – 1987* reviewed by Maxime Haubert. *Tiers Monde*, v. 34, no. 134 (Apr – June 93), pp. 471 – 473.

Pailler, Claire. Les indigènes du Costa Rica: éveil d'une conscience? *Caravelle*, no. 59 (1992), pp. 127 – 137. Bibl.

— Severiano Fernández, pueblo bribrí: "el rescate de ser indígena"; entretien réalisé le 16 avril 1992 à San José, par Claire Pailler. *Caravelle*, no. 59 (1992), pp. 49 – 58.

Perera, Víctor. *Unfinished Conquest: The Guatemalan Tragedy* (Review). *NACLA Report on the Americas*, v. 27, no. 3 (Nov – Dec 93), p. 48.

Smith, Carol A., ed. *Guatemalan Indians and the State, 1540 – 1988* reviewed by James Dunkerley. *Mesoamérica (USA)*, v. 13, no. 23 (June 92), pp. 186 – 190.

Solórzano Fonseca, Juan Carlos. La búsqueda de oro y la resistencia indígena: campañas de exploración y conquista de Costa Rica, 1502 – 1610. *Mesoamérica (USA)*, v. 13, no. 24 (Dec 92), pp. 313 – 363. Bibl.

— Conquista, colonización y resistencia indígena en Costa Rica. *Revista de Historia (Costa Rica)*, no. 25 (Jan – June 92), pp. 191 – 205. Bibl.

Thomas, David Hurst, ed. *Columbian Consequences, III: The Spanish Borderlands in Pan-American Perspectives* reviewed by David Henige. *Hispanic Review*, v. 61, no. 3 (Summer 93), pp. 447 – 449.

— *Columbian Consequences, Vol. III: The Spanish Borderlands in Pan-American Perspective* reviewed by Linda A. Watson. *Journal of Latin American Studies*, v. 25, no. 1 (Feb 93), pp. 196 – 197.

— *Columbian Consequences, Vol. III: The Spanish Borderlands in Pan-American Perspective* reviewed by Winifred Creamer. *Latin American Antiquity*, v. 4, no. 1 (Mar 93), pp. 94 – 95.

Bibliography

Dennis, Philip Adams. The Miskito – Sandinista Conflict in Nicaragua in the 1980s (Review article). *Latin American Research Review*, v. 28, no. 3 (1993), pp. 214 – 234.

Sources

García Añoveros, Jesús María. Discrepancias del obispo y de los doctrineros con la Audiencia y los indígenas de Guatemala, 1687. *Revista de Indias*, v. 52, no. 195 – 196 (May – Dec 92), pp. 385 – 441.

Ibarra Rojas, Eugenia. Documentos para el estudio de la participación indígena en la campaña nacional de 1856. *Revista de Historia (Costa Rica)*, no. 25 (Jan – June 92), pp. 245 – 250. Bibl, tables.

History

Cardenal Chamorro, Rodolfo. La expansión imperial española en Centroamérica. *ECA; Estudios Centroamericanos*, v. 47, no. 528 (Oct 92), pp. 841 – 854. Il.

Corrales Ulloa, Francisco. Del oro al vidrio, de la piedra al hierro: la evidencia arqueológica y la desestructuración de la sociedad indígena. *Revista de Historia (Costa Rica)*, no. 25 (Jan – June 92), pp. 181 – 189. Bibl.

Literature

Bricker, Victoria Reifler and Munro S. Edmonson, eds. *Supplement to 'The Handbook of Middle American Indians,' Vol. III: Literatures* reviewed by Jorge F. Travieso. *Mesoamérica (USA)*, v. 13, no. 23 (June 92), pp. 205 – 209.

Medicine

Flores Andino, Francisco A. Medicina tradicional, magia y mitos entre los miskitos de Honduras. *Folklore Americano, no.* 52 (July – Dec 91), pp. 131 – 144.

Mortuary customs

Cervantes Gamboa, Laura. La función social de la música en el ritual fúnebre bribrí. *Káñina,* v. 16, no. 1 (Jan – June 92), pp. 245 – 265. Bibl, il, tables.

Guerrero Miranda, Juan Vicente et al. Entierros secundarios y restos orgánicos de ca. 500 a.c. preservados en una área de inundación marina, golfo de Nicoya, Costa Rica. *Vínculos,* v. 17, no. 1 – 2 (1991), pp. 17 – 51. Bibl, il, tables, maps.

Music

Cervantes Gamboa, Laura. La función social de la música en el ritual fúnebre bribrí. *Káñina,* v. 16, no. 1 (Jan – June 92), pp. 245 – 265. Bibl, il, tables.

Population

Newson, Linda A. Variaciones regionales en el impacto del dominio colonial español en las poblaciones indígenas de Honduras y Nicaragua. *Mesoamérica (USA),* v. 13, no. 24 (Dec 92), pp. 297 – 312. Bibl, tables, maps.

Pottery

Odio Orozco, Eduardo. La Pochota: un complejo cerámico temprano en las tierras bajas del Guanacaste, Costa Rica. *Vínculos,* v. 17, no. 1 – 2 (1991), pp. 1 – 16. Bibl, il, tables, maps.

Religion and mythology

García Ruiz, Jesús F. De la identidad aceptada a la identidad elegida: el papel de lo religioso en la politización de las identificaciones étnicas en Guatemala. *Estudios Sociológicos,* v. 10, no. 30 (Sept – Dec 92), pp. 713 – 733. Bibl.

Social conditions

Brittin, Alice A. and Kenya C. Dworkin. Rigoberta Menchú: "Los indígenas no nos quedamos como bichos aislados, inmunes, desde hace 500 años. No, nosotros hemos sido protagonistas de la historia" (Includes Rigoberta Menchú's poem, "Patria abnegada"). *Nuevo Texto Crítico,* v. 6, no. 11 (1993), pp. 207 – 222.

Obando Obando, William. Repercusiones sociológicas de las exploraciones petroleras en los pueblos shiroles y suretka – talamanca. *Revista de Ciencias Sociales (Costa Rica),* no. 57 (Sept 92), pp. 109 – 119. Bibl, tables.

Social life and customs

Bell, C. Napier. *Tamgweera: Life and Adventures among Gentle Savages* reviewed by Elizabeth Kudin. *América Indígena,* v. 51, no. 2 – 3 (Apr – Sept 91), pp. 357 – 359.

Bletzer, Keith V. Un análisis del rito de vigilia de las mujeres embarazadas entre los indígenas ngawbere, Panamá. *Vínculos,* v. 17, no. 1 – 2 (1991), pp. 53 – 74. Bibl, tables.

Rivera Domínguez, Juan Antonio. Relato de un viaje a San Blas. *Revista Cultural Lotería,* v. 50, no. 385 (Sept – Oct 91), pp. 88 – 92.

Scarborough, Vernon Lee and David R. Wilcox, eds. *The Mesoamerican Ballgame* reviewed by Barbara J. Price. *Hispanic American Historical Review,* v. 73, no. 1 (Feb 93), pp. 144 – 145.

Study and teaching

Quesada Monge, Rodrigo. Quinto centenario y ciencias sociales. *Revista de Historia (Costa Rica),* no. 25 (Jan – June 92), pp. 221 – 226.

INDIANS OF CHILE

See also
Araucanian Indians
Aymara Indians

Bengoa, José. Ley indígena: búsqueda de desarrollo con identidad. *Mensaje,* v. 42, no. 423 (Oct 93), pp. 501 – 503. Il.

INDIANS OF COLOMBIA

See also
Carib Indians
Chibcha Indians
Cuna Indians
Quillacinga Indians

Culture

Díaz del Castillo Z., Emiliano. La cultura en la evangelización del Nuevo Reino de Granada. *Boletín de Historia y Antigüedades,* v. 80, no. 781 (Apr – June 93), pp. 415 – 434.

Economic conditions

Herrera Angel, Marta. El corregidor de naturales y el control económico de las comunidades: cambios y permanencias en la provincia de Santafé siglo XVIII. *Anuario Colombiano de Historia Social y de la Cultura,* no. 20 (1992), pp. 7 – 25. Bibl.

Ethnic identity

Fals Borda, Orlando and Lorenzo Muelas Hurtado. Pueblos indígenas y grupos étnicos. *Anuario Indigenista,* v. 30 (Dec 91), pp. 185 – 212.

Government relations

Gros, Christian. Atention!: un indien peut en cacher un autre; droits indigènes et nouvelle constitution en Colombie. *Caravelle,* no. 59 (1992), pp. 139 – 160. Bibl.

Tattay, Pablo. La reinserción desde la perspectiva indígena. *Revista Javeriana,* v. 60, no. 590 (Nov – Dec 92), pp. 331 – 337.

Valencia Llano, Alonso. *Resistencia indígena a la colonización española: resistencia militar indígena en la gobernación de Popayán* reviewed by Joanne Rappaport. *Hispanic American Historical Review,* v. 73, no. 4 (Nov 93), pp. 690 – 691.

History

Quijano Guerrero, Alberto. Dos caciques legendarios. *Boletín de Historia y Antigüedades,* v. 80, no. 780 (Jan – Mar 93), pp. 71 – 77.

Triana Antorveza, Adolfo. Contribución a la historia de la provincia de Neiva: el caso del Caguán. *Revista Colombiana de Antropología,* v. 29 (1992), pp. 119 – 154. Bibl, tables, maps.

Legal status, laws, etc.

Colombia: dispositivos constitucionales sobre pueblos indígenas, sus culturas y territorios. *Anuario Indigenista,* v. 30 (Dec 91), pp. 473 – 480.

Mortuary customs

Bermúdez Páez, Alvaro E. Reconstrucción de un conjunto funerario en el Alto de las Piedras (Isnos). *Revista Colombiana de Antropología,* v. 29 (1992), pp. 257 – 264. Bibl, il.

Pictorial works

Reichel-Dolmatoff, Gerardo. *Indios de Colombia: momentos vividos, mundos concebidos* reviewed by Jorge Morales Gómez. *Revista Colombiana de Antropología,* v. 29 (1992), pp. 239 – 241.

Religion and mythology

Morales Gómez, Jorge. Cuerpo humano y contexto cultural en el Golfo de Morrosquillo. *Revista Colombiana de Antropología,* v. 29 (1992), pp. 191 – 205. Bibl.

INDIANS OF COSTA RICA

See also
Bribri Indians

Bolaños Arquín, Margarita. Los indígenas y la conservación de la biodiversidad: 500 años de resistencia. *Revista de Historia (Costa Rica),* no. 25 (Jan – June 92), pp. 165 – 180. Bibl, il, maps, charts.

Corrales Ulloa, Francisco. Del oro al vidrio, de la piedra al hierro: la evidencia arqueológica y la desestructuración de la sociedad indígena. *Revista de Historia (Costa Rica),* no. 25 (Jan – June 92), pp. 181 – 189. Bibl.

Corrales Ulloa, Francisco and Ifigenia Quintanilla Jiménez. El Pacífico central de Costa Rica y el intercambio regional. *Vínculos,* v. 16, no. 1 – 2 (1990), pp. 111 – 126. Bibl, tables, maps.

Guerrero Miranda, Juan Vicente et al. Entierros secundarios y restos orgánicos de ca. 500 a.c. preservados en una área de inundación marina, golfo de Nicoya, Costa Rica. *Vínculos,* v. 17, no. 1 – 2 (1991), pp. 17 – 51. Bibl, il, tables, maps.

Ibarra Rojas, Eugenia. Documentos para el estudio de la participación indígena en la campaña nacional de 1856. *Revista de Historia (Costa Rica)*, no. 25 (Jan – June 92), pp. 245 – 250. Bibl, tables.

Obando Obando, William. Repercusiones sociológicas de las exploraciones petroleras en los pueblos shiroles y suretka – talamanca. *Revista de Ciencias Sociales (Costa Rica)*, no. 57 (Sept 92), pp. 109 – 119. Bibl, tables.

Odio Orozco, Eduardo. La Pochota: un complejo cerámico temprano en las tierras bajas del Guanacaste, Costa Rica. *Vínculos*, v. 17, no. 1 – 2 (1991), pp. 1 – 16. Bibl, il, tables, maps.

Pailler, Claire. Les indigènes du Costa Rica: éveil d'une conscience? *Caravelle*, no. 59 (1992), pp. 127 – 137. Bibl.

Quesada Monge, Rodrigo. Quinto centenario y ciencias sociales. *Revista de Historia (Costa Rica)*, no. 25 (Jan – June 92), pp. 221 – 226.

Solórzano Fonseca, Juan Carlos. La búsqueda de oro y la resistencia indígena: campañas de exploración y conquista de Costa Rica, 1502 – 1610. *Mesoamérica (USA)*, v. 13, no. 24 (Dec 92), pp. 313 – 363. Bibl.

— Conquista, colonización y resistencia indígena en Costa Rica. *Revista de Historia (Costa Rica)*, no. 25 (Jan – June 92), pp. 191 – 205. Bibl.

INDIANS OF ECUADOR

See also
   Cañari Indians
   Jívaro Indians
   Quechua Indians

Alchon, Suzanne Austin. *Native Society and Disease in Colonial Ecuador* reviewed by Linda A. Newson. *Bulletin of Latin American Research*, v. 12, no. 1 (Jan 93), pp. 112 – 113.

— *Native Society and Disease in Colonial Ecuador* reviewed by Robert H. Jackson. *Colonial Latin American Historical Review*, v. 2, no. 3 (Summer 93), pp. 375 – 377.

— *Native Society and Disease in Colonial Ecuador* reviewed by Susan M. Deeds. *Colonial Latin American Review*, v. 2, no. 1 – 2 (1993), pp. 284 – 285.

— *Native Society and Disease in Colonial Ecuador* reviewed by Karen M. Powers. *Hispanic American Historical Review*, v. 73, no. 4 (Nov 93), pp. 694 – 695.

Knapp, Gregory Walter. *Andean Ecology: Adaptive Dynamics in Ecuador* reviewed by Marie Price. *Geographical Review*, v. 83, no. 3 (July 93), pp. 341 – 343.

— *Andean Ecology: Adaptive Dynamics in Ecuador* reviewed by Arthur Morris. *Journal of Latin American Studies*, v. 25, no. 1 (Feb 93), p. 224.

Mond, Rebecca Earle. Indian Rebellion and Bourbon Reform in New Granada: Riots in Pasto, 1780 – 1800. *Hispanic American Historical Review*, v. 73, no. 1 (Feb 93), pp. 99 – 124. Bibl.

Naranjo, Marcelo F. Convidados de piedra: los indios en el proceso urbano de Quito. *América Indígena*, v. 51, no. 2 – 3 (Apr – Sept 91), pp. 251 – 272. Bibl.

Puwainchir, Miguel. The Voice of the Ecuadorian Amazon. *Grassroots Development*, v. 16, no. 2 (1992), p. 40.

Santana, Roberto. Actores y escenarios étnicos en Ecuador: el levantamiento de 1990. *Caravelle*, no. 59 (1992), pp. 161 – 188. Bibl.

— *Les indiens d'Equateur: citoyens dans l'ethnicité?* reviewed by Maxime Haubert. *Tiers Monde*, v. 34, no. 134 (Apr – June 93), pp. 471 – 473.

— Trois ans de chronologie indianiste en Equateur. *Caravelle*, no. 59 (1992), pp. 19 – 24.

Villavicencio de Mencías, Gladys. Indígenas en Quito. *América Indígena*, v. 51, no. 2 – 3 (Apr – Sept 91), pp. 223 – 250. Bibl.

INDIANS OF GUATEMALA

See also
   Kekchi Indians
   Mayas
   Quichés

Brittin, Alice A. and Kenya C. Dworkin. Rigoberta Menchú: "Los indígenas no nos quedamos como bichos aislados, inmunes, desde hace 500 años. No, nosotros hemos sido protagonistas de la historia" (Includes Rigoberta Menchú's poem, "Patria abnegada"). *Nuevo Texto Crítico*, v. 6, no. 11 (1993), pp. 207 – 222.

García Añoveros, Jesús María. Discrepancias del obispo y de los doctrineros con la Audiencia y los indígenas de Guatemala, 1687. *Revista de Indias*, v. 52, no. 195 – 196 (May – Dec 92), pp. 385 – 441.

García Ruiz, Jesús F. De la identidad aceptada a la identidad elegida: el papel de lo religioso en la politización de las identificaciones étnicas en Guatemala. *Estudios Sociológicos*, v. 10, no. 30 (Sept – Dec 92), pp. 713 – 733. Bibl.

Perera, Víctor. *Unfinished Conquest: The Guatemalan Tragedy* (Review). *NACLA Report on the Americas*, v. 27, no. 3 (Nov – Dec 93), p. 48.

Pérez Sáinz, Juan Pablo et al. Trayectorias laborales y constitución de identidades: los trabajadores indígenas en la ciudad de Guatemala. *Estudios Sociológicos*, v. 11, no. 32 (May – Aug 93), pp. 515 – 545. Bibl, tables.

Smith, Carol A., ed. *Guatemalan Indians and the State, 1540 – 1988* reviewed by James Dunkerley. *Mesoamérica (USA)*, v. 13, no. 23 (June 92), pp. 186 – 190.

INDIANS OF GUYANA

See
   Cubeo Indians

INDIANS OF HONDURAS

See
   Mayas
   Mosquito Indians

INDIANS OF MEXICO

See also
   Aztecs
   Huichol Indians
   Matlatzinca Indians
   Mayas
   Mayo Indians
   Mazatec Indians
   Mixe Indians
   Mixtec Indians
   Nahuas
   Olmecs
   Otomi Indians
   Tacuate Indians
   Tlascalan Indians
   Toltecs
   Tzeltal Indians
   Tzotzil Indians
   Yaqui Indians
   Zapotec Indians

Agriculture

Alvarez Santiago, Héctor and María Teresa Rodríguez. Estrategias productivas entre los nahuas de Zongolica. *La Palabra y el Hombre*, no. 84 (Oct – Dec 92), pp. 127 – 144. Tables.

Doolittle, William Emery. *Canal Irrigation in Prehistoric Mexico: The Sequence of Technological Change* reviewed by Robert Kuhlken. *Mesoamérica (USA)*, v. 13, no. 24 (Dec 92), pp. 488 – 489.

González Rodrigo, José. Manejo de recursos naturales renovables en una comunidad indígena náhuatl. *Estudios de Cultura Náhuatl*, v. 22 (1992), pp. 445 – 459. Bibl, maps.

Hodges, Denise C. *Agricultural Intensification and Preshistoric Health in the Valley of Oaxaca, Mexico* reviewed by Dale L. Hutchinson. *Latin American Antiquity*, v. 4, no. 2 (June 93), pp. 200 – 201.

Art and architecture

Báez-Jorge, Félix. La afición arqueológica de Alejo Carpentier. *Plural (Mexico)*, v. 22, no. 262 (July 93), pp. 46 – 50.

— Mitla y el barroco: notas sobre la afición arqueológica de Alejo Carpentier. *La Palabra y el Hombre*, no. 82 (Apr – June 92), pp. 57 – 73. Il.

Gruzinski, Serge. *L'Amérique de la conquête peinte par les indiens de Mexique* reviewed by Marie Cécile Bénassy-Berling (Review entitled "Notas sobre el quinto centenario en Francia"). *Colonial Latin American Review*, v. 2, no. 1 – 2 (1993), pp. 269 – 272.

Gussinyer i Alfonso, Jordi. Notas para el concepto de espacio en la arquitectura precolombina de Mesoamérica. *Boletín Americanista*, v. 33, no. 42 – 43 (1992 – 1993), pp. 183 – 230. Bibl, il.

Kristan-Graham, Cynthia. The Business of Narrative at Tula: An Analysis of the Vestibule Frieze, Trade, and Ritual. *Latin American Antiquity*, v. 4, no. 1 (Mar 93), pp. 3 – 21. Bibl, il.

Williams, Eduardo. *Las piedras sagradas: escultura prehispánica del occidente de México* reviewed by Louise I. Paradis. *Latin American Antiquity*, v. 4, no. 4 (Dec 93), pp. 393 – 394.

Methodology

Beyer, Bernd Fahmel. El empleo de una brújula en el diseño de los espacios arquitectónicos en Monte Albán, Oaxaca, México, 400 a.c. – 830 d.c. *Revista Española de Antropología Americana*, v. 23 (1993), pp. 29 – 40. Bibl, il, tables, charts.

Commerce

Arnold, Philip J., III et al. Intensive Ceramic Production and Classic-Period Political Economy in the Sierra de los Tuxtlas, Veracruz, Mexico. *Ancient Mesoamerica*, v. 4, no. 2 (Fall 93), pp. 175 – 191. Bibl, il, tables, maps.

Feinman, Gary M. and Linda M. Nicholas. Shell-Ornament Production in Ejutla: Implications for Highland – Coastal Interaction in Ancient Oaxaca. *Ancient Mesoamerica*, v. 4, no. 1 (Spring 93), pp. 103 – 119. Bibl, il, tables, maps, charts.

Joyce, Arthur A. Interregional Interaction and Social Development on the Oaxaca Coast. *Ancient Mesoamerica*, v. 4, no. 1 (Spring 93), pp. 67 – 84. Bibl, il, maps.

Zeitlin, Robert Norman. Pacific Coastal Laguna Zope: A Regional Center in the Terminal Formative Hinterlands of Monte Albán. *Ancient Mesoamerica*, v. 4, no. 1 (Spring 93), pp. 85 – 101. Bibl, il, maps.

Costume and adornment

Galdemar, Edith. Peintures faciales de la femme mexica: système chromatique des cosmétiques. *Estudios de Cultura Náhuatl*, v. 22 (1992), pp. 143 – 165. Bibl, tables.

Schaefer, Stacy. Huichol Indian Costumes: A Transforming Tradition. *Latin American Art*, v. 5, no. 1 (Spring 93), pp. 70 – 73. Bibl, il.

Culture

Arrieta Fernández, Pedro. Identidades y culturas: su evolución y persistencia. *La Palabra y el Hombre*, no. 82 (Apr – June 92), pp. 163 – 179. Bibl.

Falquet, France-Jules. Les femmes indiennes et la reproduction culturelle: réalités, mythes, enjeux; le cas des femmes indiennes au Chiapas, Mexique. *Cahiers des Amériques Latines*, no. 13 (1992), pp. 135 – 146. Bibl.

Hirabayashi, Lane Ryo. La politización de la cultura regional: zapotecos de la sierra Juárez en la ciudad de México. *América Indígena*, v. 51, no. 4 (Oct – Dec 91), pp. 185 – 218. Bibl.

León-Portilla, Miguel. *Endangered Cultures* reviewed by Susan Shattuck Benson. *La Educación (USA)*, v. 37, no. 114 (1993), p. 162.

Economic conditions

Vargas Montero, Guadalupe. Migraciones mixtecas y relaciones regionales a fines del siglo XIX. *La Palabra y el Hombre*, no. 83 (July – Sept 92), pp. 47 – 57. Bibl.

Education

Calvo Pontón, Beatriz and Laura Donnadieu Aguado. *Una educación ¿indígena, bilingüe o bicultural?* reviewed by Salvador Martínez. *Revista Latinoamericana de Estudios Educativos*, v. 22, no. 4 (Oct – Dec 92), pp. 123 – 125.

Majchrzak, Irena. El nombre propio, enlace natural entre un ser iletrado y el universo de la escritura. *Revista Latinoamericana de Estudios Educativos*, v. 22, no. 4 (Oct – Dec 92), pp. 77 – 87.

Congresses

Conclusiones y recomendaciones (regarding the education of the indigenous population of Mexico). *Anuario Indigenista*, v. 30 (Dec 91), pp. 303 – 316.

Ethnic identity

Hernández Hernández, Natalio. Más allá de los 500 años. *Caravelle*, no. 59 (1992), pp. 25 – 31.

Zimmermann, Klaus. *Sprachkontakt, ethnische Identität und Identitätsbeschädigung: Aspekte der Assimilation der Otomí-Indianer an die hispanophone mexikanische Kultur* reviewed by Eva Gugenberger. *Iberoamericana*, v. 17, no. 49 (1993), pp. 84 – 86.

Bibliography

Mallon, Florencia E. Entre la utopía y la marginalidad: comunidades indígenas y culturas políticas en México y los Andes, 1780 – 1990. *Historia Mexicana*, v. 42, no. 2 (Oct – Dec 92), pp. 473 – 504.

Research

Boege, Eckart. Contradicciones en la identidad étnica mazateca: construyendo un objeto de estudio. *Nueva Antropología*, v. 13, no. 43 (Nov 92), pp. 61 – 81. Bibl.

Food

Castelló Yturbide, Teresa. *Presencia de la comida prehispánica* reviewed by Susan N. Masuoka (Review entitled "Mexican Eating: The Work and the Haute Cuisine"). *Studies in Latin American Popular Culture*, v. 12 (1993), pp. 189 – 194.

Government relations

Anguiano Téllez, María Eugenia. Migración y derechos humanos: el caso de los mixtecos. *Estudios Fronterizos*, no. 26 (Sept – Dec 91), pp. 55 – 69. Bibl.

Baudot, Georges. Chronologie pour l'émergence d'une organisation amérindienne, politique et culturelle, au Mexique. *Caravelle*, no. 59 (1992), pp. 7 – 17.

Calvi, Maria Vittoria. El diálogo entre españoles e indígenas en la *XIII relación* de Fernando de Alva Ixtlilxóchitl. *Quaderni Ibero-Americani*, no. 72 (Dec 92), pp. 621 – 639. Bibl.

Campbell, Howard B. Tradition and the New Social Movements: The Politics of Isthmus Zapotec Culture. *Latin American Perspectives*, v. 20, no. 3 (Summer 93), pp. 83 – 97. Bibl.

Jiménez Pelayo, Agueda. *Haciendas y comunidades indígenas en el sur de Zacatecas* reviewed by Frédérique Langue. *Cahiers des Amériques Latines*, no. 13 (1992), pp. 182 – 183.

Menegus Bornemann, Margarita. *Del señorío a la república de indios: el caso de Toluca, 1500 - 1600* reviewed by Michel Bertrand. *Caravelle*, no. 60 (1993), pp. 143 – 147.

Nahmad Sittón, Salomón. Los quinientos años de dominación y colonialismo y los pueblos étnicos de México. *Estudios Sociológicos*, v. 10, no. 30 (Sept – Dec 92), pp. 651 – 675. Bibl, tables.

Rodríguez Rivera, Oscar. Derechos políticos y autonomía regional. *Nueva Antropología*, v. 13, no. 44 (Aug 93), pp. 137 – 141.

Ruiz Medrano, Ethelia. *Gobierno y sociedad en Nueva España: segunda Audiencia y Antonio de Mendoza* reviewed by Michel Bertrand. *Caravelle*, no. 59 (1992), pp. 270 – 273.

— *Gobierno y sociedad en Nueva España: segunda Audiencia y Antonio de Mendoza* reviewed by Brian R. Hamnett. *Hispanic American Historical Review*, v. 73, no. 3 (Aug 93), pp. 506 – 507.

Salmón, Roberto Mario. *Indian Revolts in Northern New Spain: A Synthesis of Resistance, 1680 - 1786* reviewed by Luis Navarro García. *Hispanic American Historical Review*, v. 73, no. 3 (Aug 93), pp. 508 – 509.

Velasco Toro, José. Autonomía y territorialidad entre los yaquis de Sonora, México. *La Palabra y el Hombre*, no. 82 (Apr – June 92), pp. 147 – 161. Bibl.

Health and hygiene

Hodges, Denise C. *Agricultural Intensification and Preshistoric Health in the Valley of Oaxaca, Mexico* reviewed by Dale L. Hutchinson. *Latin American Antiquity*, v. 4, no. 2 (June 93), pp. 200 – 201.

Whitmore, Thomas M. *Disease and Death in Early Colonial Mexico: Simulating Amerindian Depopulation* reviewed by Susan Austin Anchon. *Hispanic American Historical Review,* v. 73, no. 4 (Nov 93), pp. 695 – 696.

History

García Martínez, Bernardo. Jurisdicción y propiedad: una distinción fundamental en la historia de los pueblos de indios del México colonial. *European Review of Latin American and Caribbean Studies,* no. 53 (Dec 92), pp. 47 – 60. Bibl.

García Martínez, Bernardo, ed. *Los pueblos de indios y las comunidades* reviewed by Woodrow Borah. *Hispanic American Historical Review,* v. 73, no. 3 (Aug 93), pp. 507 – 508.

Grove, David C. and Robert James Sharer, eds. *Regional Perspectives on the Olmec* reviewed by Michael Love. *Mesoamérica (USA),* v. 13, no. 23 (June 92), pp. 209 – 213.

Harvey, Herbert R., ed. *Land and Politics in the Valley of Mexico: A Two Thousand Year Perspective* reviewed by Wayne Osborn. *The Americas,* v. 49, no. 4 (Apr 93), pp. 542 – 544.

— *Land and Politics in the Valley of Mexico: A Two Thousand Year Perspective* reviewed by Jesús Monjarás-Ruiz. *Historia Mexicana,* v. 42, no. 1 (July – Sept 92), pp. 144 – 152.

— *Land and Politics in the Valley of Mexico: A Two Thousand Year Perspective* reviewed by Michael E. Smith. *Latin American Antiquity,* v. 4, no. 1 (Mar 93), pp. 97 – 98.

Hers, Marie-Aretti. Chicomóztoc o el noroeste mesoamericano. *Anales del Instituto de Investigaciones Estéticas,* v. 16, no. 62 (1991), pp. 1 – 22. Bibl.

Lockhart, James Marvin. *The Nahuas after the Conquest: A Social and Cultural History of the Indians of Central Mexico, Sixteenth through Eighteenth Centuries* reviewed by Linda Hall. *Colonial Latin American Historical Review,* v. 2, no. 2 (Spring 93), pp. 233 – 234.

— *The Nahuas after the Conquest: A Social and Cultural History of the Indians of Central Mexico, Sixteenth through Eighteenth Centuries* reviewed by Rik Hoekstra. *European Review of Latin American and Caribbean Studies,* no. 54 (June 93), pp. 120 – 125.

— *The Nahuas after the Conquest: A Social and Cultural History of the Indians of Central Mexico, Sixteenth through Eighteenth Centuries* reviewed by Peter Gerhard. *Hispanic American Historical Review,* v. 73, no. 4 (Nov 93), pp. 697 – 698.

— *The Nahuas after the Conquest: A Social and Cultural History of the Indians of Central Mexico, Sixteenth through Eighteenth Centuries* reviewed by Fernando Cervantes. *Journal of Latin American Studies,* v. 25, no. 2 (May 93), pp. 389 – 391.

— *The Nahuas after the Conquest: A Social and Cultural History of the Indians of Central Mexico; Sixteenth through Eighteenth Centuries* reviewed by David Brading (Review entitled "Los nahuas después de la conquista," translated by Isabel Vericat). *Nexos,* v. 16, no. 186 (June 93), pp. 73 – 74.

— *Nahuas and Spaniards: Postconquest Central Mexican History and Philology* reviewed by Fernando Cervantes. *Journal of Latin American Studies,* v. 25, no. 2 (May 93), pp. 389 – 391.

Morelos García, Noel. Consideraciones teóricas sobre el proceso de urbanización en Mesoamérica. *Boletín de Antropología Americana,* no. 23 (July 91), pp. 137 – 160.

Palerm Vich, Angel. *México prehispánico: evolución y ecología* reviewed by William R. Fowler, Jr. *Hispanic American Historical Review,* v. 73, no. 1 (Feb 93), pp. 145 – 146.

Pardo Pérez, Gastón. Deficiencias de la memoria histórica. *Plural (Mexico),* v. 22, no. 257 (Feb 93), pp. 73 – 75.

Rojas y Gutiérrez de Gandarilla, José Luis de. La sociedad indígena novohispana en el siglo XVI a través del tributo. *Revista Española de Antropología Americana,* v. 23 (1993), pp. 153 – 164. Bibl.

Sallmann, Jean-Michel, ed. *Visions indiennes, visions baroques: les métissages de l'inconscient* reviewed by Frédérique Langue. *Caravelle,* no. 60 (1993), pp. 154 – 157.

Schroeder, Susan. *Chimalpahin and the Kingdoms of Chalco* reviewed by J. Benedict Warren. *The Americas,* v. 49, no. 3 (Jan 93), pp. 396 – 398.

Spores, Ronald. Tututepec: A Postclassic-Period Mixtec Conquest State. *Ancient Mesoamerica,* v. 4, no. 1 (Spring 93), pp. 167 – 174. Bibl, tables, maps, charts.

Weigand, Phil C. Teuchitlán and Central Mexico: Geometry and Cultural Distance. *Anales del Instituto de Investigaciones Estéticas,* v. 16, no. 62 (1991), pp. 23 – 34. Bibl, il, maps.

Wood, Stephanie. The Evolution of the Indian Corporation of the Toluca Region, 1550 – 1810. *Estudios de Cultura Náhuatl,* v. 22 (1992), pp. 381 – 407. Bibl, maps.

Sources

Batalla Rosado, Juan José. Un nuevo códice para el estudio de las culturas mesoamericanas. *Revista Española de Antropología Americana,* v. 23 (1993), pp. 248 – 254. Bibl, il.

León-Portilla, Miguel, ed. *Visión de los vencidos: relaciones indígenas de la conquista* reviewed by Beatriz de la Fuente. *Estudios de Cultura Náhuatl,* v. 22 (1992), pp. 499 – 505.

Lockhart, James Marvin. *Nahuas and Spaniards: Postconquest Central Mexican History and Philology* reviewed by Rik Hoekstra. *European Review of Latin American and Caribbean Studies,* no. 54 (June 93), pp. 120 – 125.

Kinship

Schroeder, Susan. The Noblewomen of Chalco. *Estudios de Cultura Náhuatl,* v. 22 (1992), pp. 45 – 86. Tables, maps, facs.

Languages

Nansen Díaz, Eréndira. Las lenguas americanas y la teoría del tipo lingüístico en Wilhelm von Humboldt. *Estudios de Cultura Náhuatl,* v. 22 (1992), pp. 223 – 233. Bibl.

Zimmermann, Klaus. *Sprachkontakt, ethnische Identität und Identitätsbeschädigung: Aspekte der Assimilation der Otomí-Indianer an die hispanophone mexikanische Kultur* reviewed by Eva Gugenberger. *Iberoamericana,* v. 17, no. 49 (1993), pp. 84 – 86.

Study and teaching

Rendón Monzón, Juan José. Apuntes en torno a la alfabetización en lenguas indígenas. *Revista Latinoamericana de Estudios Educativos,* v. 22, no. 4 (Oct – Dec 92), pp. 63 – 76.

Legal status, laws, etc.

Figueroa Valenzuela, Alejandro. Derechos políticos y organización social: el caso de los yaquis y los mayos. *Nueva Antropología,* v. 13, no. 44 (Aug 93), pp. 43 – 60. Bibl.

Gómez, Magdalena. Hacia una definición del espacio de lo consuetudinario en el medio indígena y de sus posibilidades de ejercicio en el marco de la nueva legalidad. *Nueva Antropología,* v. 13, no. 44 (Aug 93), pp. 9 – 15.

González Rodrigo, José and Regina Leal. Manejo de resursos naturales y derecho consuetudinario. *Nueva Antropología,* v. 13, no. 44 (Aug 93), pp. 61 – 70. Bibl.

Salinas de Gortari, Carlos. Iniciativa para la reforma del Artículo Cuarto de la constitución mexicana. *Anuario Indigenista,* v. 30 (Dec 91), pp. 145 – 154.

— Iniciativa para la reforma del régimen ejidal: Artículo 27 de la constitución mexicana. *Anuario Indigenista,* v. 30 (Dec 91), pp. 155 – 184.

— México: decreto por el que se reforma el Artículo 27 de la constitución política de los Estados Unidos Mexicanos. *Anuario Indigenista,* v. 30 (Dec 91), pp. 489 – 496.

— México: decreto por el que se reforma el Artículo 4 de la constitución política de los Estados Unidos Mexicanos. *Anuario Indigenista,* v. 30 (Dec 91), pp. 487 – 488.

Sierra, María Teresa. Usos y desusos del derecho consuetudinario indígena. *Nueva Antropología,* v. 13, no. 44 (Aug 93), pp. 17 – 26. Bibl.

Research

Chenaut, Victoria and María Teresa Sierra. El campo de investigación de la antropología jurídica. *Nueva Antropología,* v. 13, no. 43 (Nov 92), pp. 101 – 109. Bibl.

Valdivia Dounce, Teresa. ¿Por que hoy una antropología jurídica en México? *Nueva Antropología,* v. 13, no. 43 (Nov 92), pp. 111 – 122. Bibl.

Legends

Bustamante, Juan I. La princesa Donaji (Accompanied by an English translation). *Artes de México*, no. 21 (Fall 93), pp. 34 – 35.

Literature

Bricker, Victoria Reifler and Munro S. Edmonson, eds. *Supplement to 'The Handbook of Middle American Indians,' Vol. III: Literatures* reviewed by Jorge F. Travieso. *Mesoamérica (USA)*, v. 13, no. 23 (June 92), pp. 205 – 209.

Medicine

Lipp, Frank Joseph. *The Mixe of Oaxaca: Religion, Ritual, and Healing* reviewed by James Dow. *The Americas*, v. 49, no. 4 (Apr 93), pp. 545 – 547.

Music

Johansson, Patrick. Yaocuicatl: cantos de guerra y guerra de cantos. *Estudios de Cultura Náhuatl*, v. 22 (1992), pp. 29 – 43.

Population

Reff, Daniel T. *Disease, Depopulation, and Culture Change in Northwestern New Spain, 1518 – 1764* reviewed by Cynthia Radding. *The Americas*, v. 49, no. 3 (Jan 93), pp. 399 – 401.

Pottery

Arnold, Philip J., III. *Domestic Ceramic Production and Spatial Organization* reviewed by Dean E. Arnold. *Latin American Antiquity*, v. 4, no. 3 (Sept 93), pp. 297 – 299.

Arnold, Philip J., III et al. Intensive Ceramic Production and Classic-Period Political Economy in the Sierra de los Tuxtlas, Veracruz, Mexico. *Ancient Mesoamerica*, v. 4, no. 2 (Fall 93), pp. 175 – 191. Bibl, il, tables, maps.

Fournier G., Patricia and Andrea K. L. Freeman. El razonamiento analógico en etnoarqueología: el caso de la tradición alfarera de Mata Ortiz, Chihuahua, México. *Boletín de Antropología Americana*, no. 23 (July 91), pp. 109 – 118. Bibl, il.

Religion and mythology

Alvar, Jaime. Problemas metodológicos sobre el préstamo religioso. *Boletín de Antropología Americana*, no. 24 (Dec 91), pp. 123 – 142. Bibl, il.

Blanco, José Luis et al. El tributo del campo a la ciudad: historias de chaneques y serpientes. *Revista Mexicana de Sociología*, v. 54, no. 3 (July – Sept 92), pp. 131 – 137. Bibl.

Chávez G., Gerardo. Las ceremonias sincretas de San Juan Chamula. *Hoy Es Historia*, v. 10, no. 58 (July – Aug 93), pp. 77 – 79.

Covarrubias, Javier. La tecnología del sacrificio: la idea del "calor" y otros mitos encontrados. *Plural (Mexico)*, v. 22, no. 258 (Mar 93), pp. 18 – 28. Bibl.

Florescano, Enrique. El mito de Quetzalcóatl. *Allpanchis*, v. 23, no. 40 (July – Dec 92), pp. 11 – 93. Bibl, il.

González de Guebara, Ruby Cecilia. El mito y su influencia en la sociedad actual. *Revista Cultural Lotería*, v. 51, no. 388 (Mar – Apr 92), pp. 85 – 92.

Graulich, Michel. *Quetzalcóatl y el espejismo de Tollan* reviewed by Bernadette Alvarez-Ferrandiz. *Caravelle*, no. 59 (1992), pp. 295 – 297.

Kendall, Jonathan. The Thirteen Volatiles: Representation and Symbolism. *Estudios de Cultura Náhuatl*, v. 22 (1992), pp. 99 – 131. Bibl.

López Austin, Alfredo et al. El templo de Quetzalcóatl en Teotihuacán: su posible significado ideológico. *Anales del Instituto de Investigaciones Estéticas*, v. 16, no. 62 (1991), pp. 35 – 52. Bibl, il.

Máynez Vidal, Pilar. *Religión y magia: un problema de transculturación lingüística en la obra de Bernardino de Sahagún* reviewed by María Angeles Soler Arechalde. *Anuario de Letras (Mexico)*, v. 30 (1992), pp. 299 – 303.

Taube, Karl Andreas. The Bilimek Pulque Vessel: Starlore, Calendrics, and Cosmology of Late Postclassic Central Mexico. *Ancient Mesoamerica*, v. 4, no. 1 (Spring 93), pp. 1 – 15. Bibl, il.

Social conditions

Arrieta Fernández, Pedro. Desarrollo social planificado en La Chontalpa, Tabasco. *La Palabra y el Hombre*, no. 81 (Jan – Mar 92), pp. 159 – 175.

Offutt, Leslie S. Levels of Acculturation in Northeastern New Spain: San Esteban Testaments of the Seventeenth and Eighteenth Centuries. *Estudios de Cultura Náhuatl*, v. 22 (1992), pp. 409 – 443.

Social life and customs

Boruchoff, David A. The Conflict of Natural History and Moral Philosophy in *De Antiquitatibus Novae Hispaniae* of Francisco Hernández. *Revista Canadiense de Estudios Hispánicos*, v. 17, no. 2 (Winter 93), pp. 241 – 258. Bibl.

Cline, Sarah. The Spiritual Conquest Reexamined: Baptism and Christian Marriage in early Sixteenth-Century Mexico. *Hispanic American Historical Review*, v. 73, no. 3 (Aug 93), pp. 453 – 480. Bibl, tables.

Coronado Suzán, Gabriela. Entre la homogeneidad y la diferencia en los pueblos indohablantes de México. *Revista Latinoamericana de Estudios Educativos*, v. 22, no. 4 (Oct – Dec 92), pp. 37 – 62. Bibl, tables, charts.

Escalante Gonzalbo, Pablo. El llanto de los antiguos nahuas. *Nexos*, v. 16, no. 186 (June 93), pp. 88 – 91. Bibl.

Figueroa Valenzuela, Alejandro. Derechos políticos y organización social: el caso de los yaquis y los mayos. *Nueva Antropología*, v. 13, no. 44 (Aug 93), pp. 43 – 60. Bibl.

Guillén, Ann Cyphers. Women, Rituals, and Social Dynamics at Ancient Chalcatzingo. *Latin American Antiquity*, v. 4, no. 3 (Sept 93), pp. 209 – 224. Bibl, il.

Scarborough, Vernon Lee and David R. Wilcox, eds. *The Mesoamerican Ballgame* reviewed by Barbara J. Price. *Hispanic American Historical Review*, v. 73, no. 1 (Feb 93), pp. 144 – 145.

Schroeder, Susan. The Noblewomen of Chalco. *Estudios de Cultura Náhuatl*, v. 22 (1992), pp. 45 – 86. Tables, maps, facs.

Vargas Montero, Guadalupe. Espacio físico y espacio sagrado: la territorialidad en una comunidad mixteca, Oaxaca, México. *La Palabra y el Hombre*, no. 84 (Oct – Dec 92), pp. 179 – 189. Bibl.

Zeitlin, Judith Francis. The Politics of Classic-Period Ritual Interaction: Iconography of the Ballgame Cult in Coastal Oaxaca. *Ancient Mesoamerica*, v. 4, no. 1 (Spring 93), pp. 121 – 140. Bibl, il, maps.

Tribal government

Barrera Carranza, Estanislao. Los mayordomía entre los otomíes. *La Palabra y el Hombre*, no. 81 (Jan – Mar 92), pp. 97 – 119. Bibl, il.

Haskett, Robert Stephen. *Indigenous Rulers: An Ethnohistory of Town Government in Colonial Cuernavaca* reviewed by Eric Van Young. *Journal of Latin American Studies*, v. 25, no. 3 (Oct 93), pp. 653 – 654.

León-Portilla, Miguel. Por qué los escribanos y pintores prehispánicos estaban exentos de pagar tributo. *Vuelta*, v. 17, no. 196 (Mar 93), pp. 36 – 37. Il.

Miller, Simon and Arij Ouweneel, eds. *The Indian Community of Colonial Mexico: Fifteen Essays on Land Tenure, Corporate Organizations, Ideology, and Village Politics* reviewed by Margarita Menegus Bornemann. *Historia Mexicana*, v. 42, no. 1 (July – Sept 92), pp. 138 – 144.

Women

Falquet, France-Jules. Les femmes indiennes et la reproduction culturelle: réalités, mythes, enjeux; le cas des femmes indiennes au Chiapas, Mexique. *Cahiers des Amériques Latines*, no. 13 (1992), pp. 135 – 146. Bibl.

Garza Caligaris, Anna María and Juana María Ruiz Ortiz. Madres solteras indígenas. *Mesoamérica (USA)*, v. 13, no. 23 (June 92), pp. 66 – 77. Bibl.

Guillén, Ann Cyphers. Women, Rituals, and Social Dynamics at Ancient Chalcatzingo. *Latin American Antiquity*, v. 4, no. 3 (Sept 93), pp. 209 – 224. Bibl, il.

Morino, Angelo. Hernán Cortés e la regina Calafia. *Quaderni Ibero-Americani*, no. 72 (Dec 92), pp. 603 – 620. Bibl.

Writing

Gruzinski, Serge. *L'Amérique de la conquête peinte par les indiens de Mexique* reviewed by Marie Cécile Bénassy-Berling (Review entitled "Notas sobre el quinto centenario en Francia"). *Colonial Latin American Review*, v. 2, no. 1 – 2 (1993), pp. 269 – 272.

Pascual Soto, Arturo. *Iconografía arqueológica de El Tajín* reviewed by Fernando Winfield Capitaine. *La Palabra y el Hombre*, no. 82 (Apr – June 92), pp. 313 – 314.

Pérez González, Benjamín et al. *Fundamentos para la escritura de las lenguas indígenas* reviewed by Rafael Rodríguez-Ponga. *Anuario de Letras (Mexico)*, v. 30 (1992), pp. 282 – 285.

Urcid Serrano, Javier. The Pacific Coast of Oaxaca and Guerrero: The Westernmost Extent of Zapotec Script. *Ancient Mesoamerica*, v. 4, no. 1 (Spring 93), pp. 141 – 165. Bibl, il, maps.

INDIANS OF NICARAGUA

See also
> Mosquito Indians
> Nahuas
> Sumu Indians

Daza, Patricio. *Ethnies et révolution: Nicaragua, 1979 – 1987* reviewed by Maxime Haubert. *Tiers Monde*, v. 34, no. 134 (Apr – June 93), pp. 471 – 473.

Gould, Jeffrey L. "¡Vana ilusión!": The Highlands Indians and the Myth of Nicaragua Mestiza, 1880 – 1925. *Hispanic American Historical Review*, v. 73, no. 3 (Aug 93), pp. 393 – 429. Bibl, maps.

INDIANS OF PANAMA

See also
> Chibcha Indians
> Cuna Indians

Bletzer, Keith V. Un análisis del rito de vigilia de las mujeres embarazadas entre los indígenas ngawbere, Panamá. *Vínculos*, v. 17, no. 1 – 2 (1991), pp. 53 – 74. Bibl, tables.

Langebaek, Carl Henrik. Competencia por prestigio político y momificación en el norte de Suramérica y el Istmo de Panamá. *Revista Colombiana de Antropología*, v. 29 (1992), pp. 7 – 26. Bibl.

INDIANS OF PARAGUAY

See also
> Guarani Indians

Vysokolán, Oleg. *La traición del Papa Rei* (Review). *Revista Paraguaya de Sociología*, v. 29, no. 84 (May – Aug 92), pp. 208 – 210. Il.

INDIANS OF PERU

See also
> Amuesha Indians
> Arawak Indians
> Aymara Indians
> Campa Indians
> Chavín culture
> Huari culture, Peru
> Incas
> Jívaro Indians
> Machiganga Indians
> Mochica Indians
> Piro Indians
> Quechua Indians
> Sipibo Indians

Art and architecture

Goldstein, Paul. Tiwanaku Temples and State Expansion: A Tiwanaku Sunken-Court Temple in Moquequa, Peru. *Latin American Antiquity*, v. 4, no. 1 (Mar 93), pp. 22 – 47. Bibl, il, tables, maps.

Culture

Huertas Vallejos, Lorenzo. Los chancas: proceso disturbativo en los Andes. *Historia y Cultura (Peru)*, no. 20 (1990), pp. 11 – 48. Bibl, maps.

Mitchell, William P. *Peasants on the Edge: Crop, Cult, and Crisis in the Andes* reviewed by Rodrigo Montoya. *Bulletin of Latin American Research*, v. 12, no. 1 (Jan 93), pp. 121 – 122.

— *Peasants on the Edge: Crop, Cult, and Crisis in the Andes* reviewed by Orin Starn. *Hispanic American Historical Review*, v. 73, no. 1 (Feb 93), pp. 175 – 76.

— *Peasants on the Edge: Crop, Cult, and Crisis in the Andes* reviewed by Thomas M. Davies, Jr. *Journal of Developing Areas*, v. 27, no. 3 (Apr 93), pp. 430 – 432.

Government relations

Chassin, Joëlle. Protecteur d'indiens contre vice-roi: la lutte de Miguel de Eyzaguirre pour l'abolition du tribut au Pérou. *Cahiers des Amériques Latines*, no. 13 (1992), pp. 61 – 74. Bibl.

Husson, Patrick. *De la guerra a la rebelión: Huanta, siglo XIX* reviewed by Jaime Urrutia Ceruti. *Bulletin de l'Institut Français d'Etudes Andines*, v. 21, no. 3 (1992), pp. 1078 – 1082.

Peralta Ruiz, Víctor. *En pos del tributo: burocracia estatal, élite regional y comunidades indígenas en el Cusco rural, 1826 – 1854* reviewed by Paul Gootenberg. *Revista Andina*, v. 10, no. 2 (Dec 92), pp. 547 – 548.

— *En pos del tributo: burocracia estatal, élite regional y comunidades indígenas en el Cusco rural, 1826 – 1854* reviewed by Serena Fernández Alonso. *Revista de Indias*, v. 53, no. 197 (Jan – Apr 93), pp. 116 – 117.

Sala i Vila, Nuria. La constitución de Cádiz y su impacto en el gobierno de las comunidades indígenas en el Virreinato del Perú. *Boletín Americanista*, v. 33, no. 42 – 43 (1992 – 1993), pp. 51 – 70. Bibl.

History

Anders, Martha B. *Historia y etnografía: los mitmaq de Huanuco en las visitas de 1549, 1557 y 1562* translated by Rafael Varón. Reviewed by Nicanor Domínguez Faura. *Historia y Cultura (Peru)*, no. 20 (1990), pp. 379 – 380.

Glave Testino, Luis Miguel. *Vida, símbolos y batallas: creación y recreación de la comunidad indígena, Cusco, siglo XVI – XX* reviewed by Manuel Burga (Review entitled "Los kanas en la historia"). *Debate (Peru)*, v. 16, no. 72 (Mar – May 93), pp. 64 – 65. Il.

Julien, Daniel G. Late Pre-Inkaic Ethnic Groups in Highland Peru: An Archaeological – Ethnohistorical Model of the Political Geography of the Cajamarca Region. *Latin American Antiquity*, v. 4, no. 3 (Sept 93), pp. 246 – 273. Bibl, il, tables, maps, charts.

Implements

Ortiz Sotelo, Jorge. Embarcaciones aborígenes en el área andina. *Historia y Cultura (Peru)*, no. 20 (1990), pp. 49 – 79. Bibl.

Kinship

Ossio Acuña, Juan M. *Parentesco, reciprocidad y jerarquía en los Andes: una aproximación a la organización social de la comunidad de Andamarca* reviewed by Penny Dransart. *Journal of Latin American Studies*, v. 25, no. 3 (Oct 93), pp. 684 – 686.

Population

Sources

Remy S., Pilar and María Rostworowski Tovar de Diez Canseco, eds. *Las visitas a Cajamarca, 1571/72 – 1578* reviewed by Pedro Guibovich. *Apuntes (Peru)*, no. 31 (July – Dec 92), pp. 119 – 121.

— *Las visitas a Cajamarca, 1571/72 – 1578* reviewed by Jorge Montenegro. *Bulletin de l'Institut Français d'Etudes Andines*, v. 21, no. 3 (1992), pp. 1073 – 1074.

— *Las visitas a Cajamarca, 1571/72 – 1578* reviewed by Noble David Cook. *Hispanic American Historical Review*, v. 73, no. 2 (May 93), pp. 313 – 314.

— *Las visitas a Cajamarca, 1571/72 – 1578* reviewed by Carmen Beatriz Loza. *Revista Andina*, v. 10, no. 2 (Dec 92), pp. 548 – 550.

Religion and mythology

Gareis, Iris. Religión popular y etnicidad: la población indígena de Lima colonial. *Allpanchis*, v. 23, no. 40 (July – Dec 92), pp. 117 – 143. Bibl.

Osorio, Alejandra. Una interpretación sobre la extirpación de idolatrías en el Perú: Otuco, Cajatambo, siglo XVII. *Historia y Cultura (Peru)*, no. 20 (1990), pp. 161 – 199. Bibl.

Rostworowski Tovar de Diez Canseco, María. El Dios Con y el misterio de la pampa de Nasca. *Latin American Indian Literatures Journal*, v. 9, no. 1 (Spring 93), pp. 21 – 30.

Sánchez, Ana. *Amancebados, hechiceros y rebeldes: Chancay, siglo XVII* reviewed by Irene Silverblatt. *Hispanic American Historical Review*, v. 73, no. 1 (Feb 93), pp. 157 – 159.

Zecenarro Villalobos, Bernardino. De fiestas, ritos y batallas: algunos comportamientos folk de la sociedad andina de los k'anas y ch'umpiwillcas. *Allpanchis*, v. 23, no. 40 (July – Dec 92), pp. 147 – 172. Bibl.

Sources

Millones Santa Gadea, Luis et al, eds. *El retorno de las huacas: estudios y documentos sobre el Taki Onqoy, siglo XVI* reviewed by Javier Flores Espinoza. *Historia y Cultura (Peru)*, no. 20 (1990), pp. 381 – 382.

Social conditions

Cheng Hurtado, Alberto and José Matos Mar. Comas: lo andino en la modernidad urbana. *América Indígena*, v. 51, no. 2 – 3 (Apr – Sept 91), pp. 35 – 74. Il, tables, maps.

Social life and customs

León Gómez, Miguel. El testamento del licenciado Diego Alvarez. *Historia y Cultura (Peru)*, no. 20 (1990), pp. 319 – 350.

INDIANS OF PUERTO RICO

See
Arawak Indians
Taino Indians

INDIANS OF SOUTH AMERICA

Agriculture

Knapp, Gregory Walter. *Andean Ecology: Adaptive Dynamics in Ecuador* reviewed by Marie Price. *Geographical Review*, v. 83, no. 3 (July 93), pp. 341 – 343.

— *Andean Ecology: Adaptive Dynamics in Ecuador* reviewed by Arthur Morris. *Journal of Latin American Studies*, v. 25, no. 1 (Feb 93), p. 224.

Art and architecture

Goldstein, Paul. Tiwanaku Temples and State Expansion: A Tiwanaku Sunken-Court Temple in Moquequa, Peru. *Latin American Antiquity*, v. 4, no. 1 (Mar 93), pp. 22 – 47. Bibl, il, tables, maps.

Isbell, William Harris and Gordon Francis McEwan, ed. *Huari Administrative Structure: Prehistoric Monumental Architecture and State Government* reviewed by Mario A. Rivera. *Latin American Antiquity*, v. 4, no. 1 (Mar 93), pp. 95 – 96.

Pang, Hildegard Delgado. *Pre-Columbian Art: Investigations and Insights* reviewed by John F. Scott. *Hispanic American Historical Review*, v. 73, no. 1 (Feb 93), pp. 140 – 141.

Reynales, Trish. The Looting of the Royal Tombs of Sipán. *Latin American Art*, v. 5, no. 2 (Summer 93), pp. 50 – 52. Il.

Bibliography

Ramírez-Horton, Susan Elizabeth. Recent Writing on the Peoples of the Andes (Review article). *Latin American Research Review*, v. 28, no. 3 (1993), pp. 174 – 182. Bibl.

Commerce

Harris, Olivia et al, eds. *La participación indígena en los mercados surandinos: estrategias y reproducción social, siglos XVI a XX* reviewed by Richard Warren. *Revista Andina*, v. 10, no. 2 (Dec 92), pp. 545 – 546.

Costume and adornment

Vidal, Lux et al, eds. *Grafismo indígena: ensaios de antropologia estética* reviewed by Clarice Cohn. *Revista de Antropologia (Brazil)*, v. 34 (1991), pp. 230 – 232.

Culture

Albó, Xavier. Bolivia: La Paz/Chukiyawu; las dos caras de una ciudad. *América Indígena*, v. 51, no. 4 (Oct – Dec 91), pp. 107 – 158. Bibl, tables, maps.

Arnold, Denise Y. et al. *Hacia un orden andino de las cosas: tres pistas de los Andes meridionales* reviewed by Jan Szeminski. *Estudios Interdisciplinarios de América Latina y el Caribe*, v. 4, no. 1 (Jan – June 93), pp. 175 – 176.

— *Hacia un orden andino de las cosas: tres pistas de los Andes meridionales* reviewed by Javier Albó. *Signo*, no. 38, Nueva época (Jan – Apr 93), pp. 220 – 224.

Basalisco, Lucio. Culture a confronto: guaraniés y yaros visti da un gesuito alla fine del seicento. *Quaderni Ibero-Americani*, no. 72 (Dec 92), pp. 709 – 720. Bibl.

Díaz del Castillo Z., Emiliano. La cultura en la evangelización del Nuevo Reino de Granada. *Boletín de Historia y Antigüedades*, v. 80, no. 781 (Apr – June 93), pp. 415 – 434.

Huertas Vallejos, Lorenzo. Los chancas: proceso disturbativo en los Andes. *Historia y Cultura (Peru)*, no. 20 (1990), pp. 11 – 48. Bibl, maps.

Mitchell, William P. *Peasants on the Edge: Crop, Cult, and Crisis in the Andes* reviewed by Rodrigo Montoya. *Bulletin of Latin American Research*, v. 12, no. 1 (Jan 93), pp. 121 – 122.

— *Peasants on the Edge: Crop, Cult, and Crisis in the Andes* reviewed by Orin Starn. *Hispanic American Historical Review*, v. 73, no. 1 (Feb 93), pp. 175 – 76.

— *Peasants on the Edge: Crop, Cult, and Crisis in the Andes* reviewed by Thomas M. Davies, Jr. *Journal of Developing Areas*, v. 27, no. 3 (Apr 93), pp. 430 – 432.

Rojas Zolezzi, Enrique Carlos. Concepciones sobre la relación entre géneros: mitos, ritual y organización del trabajo en la unidad doméstica campa – asháninka. *Amazonía Peruana*, v. 11, no. 22 (Oct 92), pp. 175 – 220. Bibl.

Santos Granero, Fernando. *The Power of Love: The Moral Use of Knowledge amongst the Amuesha of Central Peru* reviewed by Jaime Regan. *Amazonía Peruana*, v. 11, no. 22 (Oct 92), pp. 285 – 288.

— *The Power of Love: The Moral Use of Knowledge amongst the Amuesha of Central Peru* reviewed by Richard C. Smith. *Bulletin de l'Institut Français d'Etudes Andines*, v. 21, no. 2 (1992), pp. 793 – 797. Bibl.

Schreiter, Robert J. Inculturación: opción por el otro. *Amazonía Peruana*, v. 11, no. 22 (Oct 92), pp. 9 – 46.

Warren, Patrizio. Mercado, escuelas y proteínas: aspectos históricos, ecológicos y económicos del cambio de modelo de asentamiento entre los achuar meridionales. *Amazonía Peruana*, v. 11, no. 21 (Sept 92), pp. 73 – 107. Bibl, tables.

Bibliography

Vickers, William T. The Anthropology of Amazonia (Review article). *Latin American Research Review*, v. 28, no. 1 (1993), pp. 111 – 127. Bibl.

Economic conditions

Bergman, Roland W. *Economía amazónica* translated by Martha Beinglea. Reviewed by Jaime Regan, S.J. *Amazonía Peruana*, v. 11, no. 21 (Sept 92), pp. 243 – 244.

Herrera Angel, Marta. El corregidor de naturales y el control económico de las comunidades: cambios y permanencias en la provincia de Santafé siglo XVIII. *Anuario Colombiano de Historia Social y de la Cultura*, no. 20 (1992), pp. 7 – 25. Bibl.

Hvalkof, Sören. La naturaleza del desarrollo: perspectivas de los nativos y de los colonos en el gran pajonal. *Amazonía Peruana*, v. 11, no. 21 (Sept 92), pp. 145 – 173. Bibl.

Patrinos, Harry Anthony and George Psacharopoulos. The Cost of Being Indigenous in Bolivia: An Empirical Analysis of Educational Attainments and Outcomes. *Bulletin of Latin American Research*, v. 12, no. 3 (Sept 93), pp. 293 – 309. Bibl, tables, charts.

Pease G. Y., Franklin. *Curacas: reciprocidad y riqueza* reviewed by Thomas Abercrombie. *Hispanic American Historical Review*, v. 73, no. 4 (Nov 93), pp. 698 – 699.

Stanish, Charles. *Ancient Andean Political Economy* reviewed by Penny Dransart. *Journal of Latin American Studies*, v. 25, no. 2 (May 93), pp. 391 – 392.

— *Ancient Andean Political Economy* reviewed by Michael E. Moseley. *Revista Interamericana de Bibliografía*, v. 42, no. 2 (1992), pp. 287 – 288.

Sources

World Bank. Directiva operacional concerniente a pueblos indígenas. *Anuario Indigenista*, v. 30 (Dec 91), pp. 255 – 266. Bibl.

Education

Salazar Mostajo, Carlos. La "Taika": teoría y práctica de la escuela – ayllu reviewed by Carlos Coello Vila. Signo, no. 38, Nueva época (Jan – Apr 93), pp. 256 – 257.

Ethnic identity

Combès, Isabelle and Thierry Saignes. Alter ego: naissance de l'identité chiriguano reviewed by Marie-Danielle Demélas-Bohy. Caravelle, no. 60 (1993), pp. 166 – 170.

Dean, Carolyn Sue. Ethnic Conflict and Corpus Christi in Colonial Cuzco. Colonial Latin American Review, v. 2, no. 1 – 2 (1993), pp. 93 – 120. Bibl, il.

Fals Borda, Orlando and Lorenzo Muelas Hurtado. Pueblos indígenas y grupos étnicos. Anuario Indigenista, v. 30 (Dec 91), pp. 185 – 212.

Gow, Peter. Of Mixed Blood: Kinship and History in Peruvian Amazonia reviewed by Rodrigo Montoya. Journal of Latin American Studies, v. 25, no. 1 (Feb 93), pp. 222 – 224.

Larraín Barros, Horacio. Identidad cultural indígena tras quinientos años de aculturación: desafío y destino. Estudios Sociales (Chile), no. 76 (Apr – June 93), pp. 135 – 148. Bibl.

Naranjo, Marcelo F. Convidados de piedra: los indios en el proceso urbano de Quito. América Indígena, v. 51, no. 2 – 3 (Apr – Sept 91), pp. 251 – 272. Bibl.

Santana, Roberto. Les indiens d'Equateur: citoyens dans l'ethnicité? reviewed by Maxime Haubert. Tiers Monde, v. 34, no. 134 (Apr – June 93), pp. 471 – 473.

Bibliography

Mallon, Florencia E. Entre la utopía y la marginalidad: comunidades indígenas y culturas políticas en México y los Andes, 1780 – 1990. Historia Mexicana, v. 42, no. 2 (Oct – Dec 92), pp. 473 – 504.

Food

Schiavini, Adrián. Los lobos marinos como recurso para cazadores-recolectores marinos: el caso de Tierra del Fuego. Latin American Antiquity, v. 4, no. 4 (Dec 93), pp. 346 – 366. Bibl, tables, maps.

Foreign opinion

Serafino, Nina M. et al. Latin American Indigenous Peoples and Considerations for U.S. Assistance. Anuario Indigenista, v. 30 (Dec 91), pp. 11 – 144. Bibl.

Pictorial works

Carril, Bonifacio del. Los indios en la Argentina, 1536 – 1845, según la iconografía de la época reviewed by María Sáenz Quesada. Todo Es Historia, v. 27, no. 315 (Oct 93), p. 63. Il.

Government relations

Biord Castillo, Horacio. Organización social y resistencia a la conquista europea: los casos teque y cumanagoto. Boletín de la Academia Nacional de la Historia (Venezuela), v. 75, no. 297 (Jan – Mar 92), pp. 51 – 68. Bibl, maps.

Brown, Michael F. War of Shadows: The Struggle for Utopia in the Peruvian Amazon reviewed by Oscar Espinoza. Amazonía Peruana, v. 11, no. 22 (Oct 92), pp. 278 – 284.

Carbonell de Masy, Rafael et al. Estrategias de desarrollo rural en los pueblos guaraníes, 1609 – 1767 reviewed by José Luis Mora Mérida. Anuario de Estudios Americanos, v. 50, no. 1 (1993), pp. 311 – 312.

Chassin, Joëlle. Protecteur d'indiens contre vice-roi: la lutte de Miguel de Eyzaguirre pour l'abolition du tribut au Pérou. Cahiers des Amériques Latines, no. 13 (1992), pp. 61 – 74. Bibl.

El Fondo para el Desarrollo de los Pueblos Indígenas de América Latina y el Caribe. Anuario Indigenista, v. 30 (Dec 91), pp. 7 – 10.

Groot de Mahecha, Ana María and Eva María Hooykaas. Intento de delimitación del territorio de los grupos étnicos pastos y quillacingas en el altiplano nariñense reviewed by María Clemencia Ramírez de Jara. Revista Colombiana de Antropología, v. 29 (1992), pp. 242 – 246. Bibl.

Herrera Angel, Marta. El corregidor de naturales y el control económico de las comunidades: cambios y permanencias en la provincia de Santafé siglo XVIII. Anuario Colombiano de Historia Social y de la Cultura, no. 20 (1992), pp. 7 – 25. Bibl.

Husson, Patrick. De la guerra a la rebelión: Huanta, siglo XIX reviewed by Jaime Urrutia Ceruti. Bulletin de l'Institut Français d'Etudes Andines, v. 21, no. 3 (1992), pp. 1078 – 1082.

Irurozqui Victoriano, Marta. La guerra de razas en Bolivia: la (re)invención de una tradición. Revista Andina, v. 11, no. 1 (July 93), pp. 163 – 200. Bibl.

— ¿Qué hacer con el indio?: un análisis de las obras de Franz Tamayo y Alcides Arguedas. Revista de Indias, v. 52, no. 195 – 196 (May – Dec 92), pp. 559 – 587.

Levaggi, Abelardo. Muerte y resurrección del derecho indiano sobre el aborigen en la Argentina del siglo XIX. Jahrbuch für Geschichte von Staat, Wirtschaft und Gesellschaft Lateinamerikas, v. 29 (1992), pp. 179 – 193. Bibl.

Marimán, José. Cuestión mapuche, descentralización del estado y autonomía regional. Caravelle, no. 59 (1992), pp. 189 – 205. Bibl.

Mond, Rebecca Earle. Indian Rebellion and Bourbon Reform in New Granada: Riots in Pasto, 1780 – 1800. Hispanic American Historical Review, v. 73, no. 1 (Feb 93), pp. 99 – 124. Bibl.

Morin, Françoise. Revendications et stratégies politiques des organisations indigènes amazoniennes. Cahiers des Amériques Latines, no. 13 (1992), pp. 75 – 85. Bibl.

O'Phelan Godoy, Scarlett. Rebeliones andinas anticoloniales: Nueva Granada, Perú y Charcas entre el siglo XVIII y el XIX. Anuario de Estudios Americanos, v. 49 (1992), pp. 395 – 440. Bibl, maps.

Peralta Ruiz, Víctor. En pos del tributo: burocracia estatal, élite regional y comunidades indígenas en el Cusco rural, 1826 – 1854 reviewed by Paul Gootenberg. Revista Andina, v. 10, no. 2 (Dec 92), pp. 547 – 548.

— En pos del tributo: burocracia estatal, élite regional y comunidades indígenas en el Cusco rural, 1826 – 1854 reviewed by Serena Fernández Alonso. Revista de Indias, v. 53, no. 197 (Jan – Apr 93), pp. 116 – 117.

Puwainchir, Miguel. The Voice of the Ecuadorian Amazon. Grassroots Development, v. 16, no. 2 (1992), p. 40.

Rasnake, Roger Neil. Autoridad y poder en los Andes: los kuraqkuna de Yura, a translation of Domination and Cultural Resistance: Authority and Power among an Andean People, translated by Luis Brédow and Luis Huáscar Antezana. Reviewed by Pedro de Anasagasti. Signo, no. 35, Nueva época (Jan – Apr 92), pp. 243 – 244.

Santana, Roberto. Actores y escenarios étnicos en Ecuador: el levantamiento de 1990. Caravelle, no. 59 (1992), pp. 161 – 188. Bibl.

— Trois ans de chronologie indianiste en Equateur. Caravelle, no. 59 (1992), pp. 19 – 24.

Stern, Steve J., ed. Resistencia, rebelión y conciencia campesina de los Andes, siglos XVIII al XX reviewed by Betford Betalleluz. Historia y Cultura (Peru), no. 20 (1990), pp. 369 – 371.

Tattay, Pablo. La reinserción desde la perspectiva indígena. Revista Javeriana, v. 60, no. 590 (Nov – Dec 92), pp. 331 – 337.

Valencia Llano, Alonso. Resistencia indígena a la colonización española: resistencia militar indígena en la gobernación de Popayán reviewed by Joanne Rappaport. Hispanic American Historical Review, v. 73, no. 4 (Nov 93), pp. 690 – 691.

Valle de Siles, María Eugenia del. Historia de la rebelión de Tupac Catari, 1781 – 1782 reviewed by Marie-Danielle Démelas-Bohy. Caravelle, no. 59 (1992), pp. 249 – 253.

Vysokolán, Oleg. La traición del Papa Rei (Review). Revista Paraguaya de Sociología, v. 29, no. 84 (May – Aug 92), pp. 208 – 210. Il.

Bibliography

García B., Pantaleón. Resistencia y rebelión durante el siglo XVIII en la región andina (Review article). Revista Cultural Lotería, v. 51, no. 391 (Sept – Oct 92), pp. 80 – 97. Bibl.

Sources

Silva Galdames, Osvaldo. Acerca de los capitanes de amigos: un documento y un comentario. Cuadernos de Historia (Chile), no. 11 (Dec 91), pp. 29 – 45. Bibl.

Silva Galdames, Osvaldo et al. Junta de los pehuenches de Malargüe con el comandante general de armas y frontera de Mendoza, don Francisco José de Amigorena. *Cuadernos de Historia (Chile)*, no. 11 (Dec 91), pp. 199 – 209. Bibl, facs.

World Bank. Directiva operacional concerniente a pueblos indígenas. *Anuario Indigenista*, v. 30 (Dec 91), pp. 255 – 266. Bibl.

Health and hygiene

Casanueva Valencia, Fernando. Una peste de viruelas en la región de la frontera de guerra hispano-indígena en el reino de Chile, 1791. *Revista de Historia (Costa Rica)*, no. 26 (July – Dec 92), pp. 31 – 65. Bibl, maps, charts.

Salzano, Francisco M. Color Vision in Four Brazilian Indian Tribes. *Interciencia*, v. 18, no. 4 (July – Aug 93), pp. 195 – 197. Bibl, tables.

History

Anders, Martha B. *Historia y etnografía: los mitmaq de Huanuco en las visitas de 1549, 1557 y 1562* translated by Rafael Varón. Reviewed by Nicanor Domínguez Faura. *Historia y Cultura (Peru)*, no. 20 (1990), pp. 379 – 380.

Bermúdez Páez, Alvaro E. Etnohistoria de Subachoque, siglos XVI – XVIII. *Revista Colombiana de Antropología*, v. 29 (1992), pp. 81 – 117. Bibl, tables, maps.

Cárdenas Arroyo, Felipe. Pastos y quillacingas: dos grupos étnicos en busca de identidad arqueológica. *Revista Colombiana de Antropología*, v. 29 (1992), pp. 63 – 79. Bibl, il, tables.

Carrazzoni, José Andrés. El caballo del indio del desierto. *Todo Es Historia*, v. 27, no. 315 (Oct 93), pp. 76 – 89. Bibl, il.

Ferrero-Kellerhoff, Inés Cecilia. *Capacho: un pueblo de indios en la jurisdicción de la villa de San Cristóbal* reviewed by Carlos A. Mayo. *Hispanic American Historical Review*, v. 73, no. 1 (Feb 93), pp. 159 – 160.

Glave Testino, Luis Miguel. *Vida, símbolos y batallas: creación y recreación de la comunidad indígena, Cusco, siglo XVI – XX* reviewed by Manuel Burga (Review entitled "Los kanas en la historia"). *Debate (Peru)*, v. 16, no. 72 (Mar – May 93), pp. 64 – 65. Il.

Julien, Daniel G. Late Pre-Inkaic Ethnic Groups in Highland Peru: An Archaeological – Ethnohistorical Model of the Political Geography of the Cajamarca Region. *Latin American Antiquity*, v. 4, no. 3 (Sept 93), pp. 246 – 273. Bibl, il, tables, maps, charts.

McGeagh, Robert. Thomas Fields and the Precursor of the Guaraní "Reducciones." *Colonial Latin American Historical Review*, v. 2, no. 1 (Winter 93), pp. 35 – 55. Bibl.

Mingo de la Concepción, Manuel. *Historia de las misiones franciscanas de Tarija entre chiriguanos* reviewed by Pedro de Anasagasti. *Signo*, no. 35, Nueva época (Jan – Apr 92), pp. 237 – 239.

Poujade, Ruth. Poblamiento prehistórico y colonial de Misiones. *Estudos Ibero-Americanos*, v. 18, no. 1 (July 92), pp. 29 – 70. Bibl, maps.

Quijano Guerrero, Alberto. Dos caciques legendarios. *Boletín de Historia y Antigüedades*, v. 80, no. 780 (Jan – Mar 93), pp. 71 – 77.

Ramírez de Jara, María Clemencia. Los quillacinga y su posible relación con grupos prehispánicos del oriente ecuatoriano. *Revista Colombiana de Antropología*, v. 29 (1992), pp. 27 – 61. Bibl, maps.

Shady Solís, Ruth. Del arcaico al formativo en los Andes centrales. *Revista Andina*, v. 11, no. 1 (July 93), pp. 103 – 132. Bibl, tables, maps.

Triana Antorveza, Adolfo. Contribución a la historia de la provincia de Neiva: el caso del Caguán. *Revista Colombiana de Antropología*, v. 29 (1992), pp. 119 – 154. Bibl, tables, maps.

Viola Recasens, Andreu. La cara oculta de los Andes: notas para una redefinición de la relación histórica entre sierra y selva. *Boletín Americanista*, v. 33, no. 42 – 43 (1992 – 1993), pp. 7 – 22. Bibl, charts.

Bibliography

Benson, Elizabeth P. Bibliography (to the articles in this issue entitled "Sacred Space and Its Uses"). *Latin American Indian Literatures Journal*, v. 9, no. 1 (Spring 93), pp. 55 – 65.

Congresses

González Rodríguez, Adolfo Luis. II Congreso Internacional de Etnohistoria. *Anuario de Estudios Americanos*, v. 49, Suppl. 1 (1992), pp. 181 – 185.

Pictorial works

Reichel-Dolmatoff, Gerardo. *Indios de Colombia: momentos vividos, mundos concebidos* reviewed by Jorge Morales Gómez. *Revista Colombiana de Antropología*, v. 29 (1992), pp. 239 – 241.

Implements

Ortiz Sotelo, Jorge. Embarcaciones aborígenes en el área andina. *Historia y Cultura (Peru)*, no. 20 (1990), pp. 49 – 79. Bibl.

Kinship

Gow, Peter. *Of Mixed Blood: Kinship and History in Peruvian Amazonia* reviewed by Rodrigo Montoya. *Journal of Latin American Studies*, v. 25, no. 1 (Feb 93), pp. 222 – 224.

Ossio Acuña, Juan M. *Parentesco, reciprocidad y jerarquía en los Andes: una aproximación a la organización social de la comunidad de Andamarca* reviewed by Penny Dransart. *Journal of Latin American Studies*, v. 25, no. 3 (Oct 93), pp. 684 – 686.

Laws, statutes, etc.

Sources

Gómez Rivas, León. Don Francisco de Toledo, comendador de Alcántara, virrey del Perú: guía de fuentes (I). *Anuario de Estudios Americanos*, v. 49, Suppl. 1 (1992), pp. 123 – 171.

— Don Francisco de Toledo, comendador de Alcántara, virrey del Perú: guía de fuentes (II). *Anuario de Estudios Americanos*, v. 49, Suppl. 2 (1992), pp. 95 – 152.

Legal status, laws, etc.

Argentina: Ley 23.302 sobre política indígena y apoyo a las comunidades aborígenes. *Anuario Indigenista*, v. 30 (Dec 91), pp. 437 – 456.

Bengoa, José. Ley indígena: búsqueda de desarrollo con identidad. *Mensaje*, v. 42, no. 423 (Oct 93), pp. 501 – 503. Il.

Brasil: Protaria no. 580 que demarca o território da população indígena yanomami, 15 de novembro de 1991. *Anuario Indigenista*, v. 30 (Dec 91), pp. 461 – 471.

Colombia: dispositivos constitucionales sobre pueblos indígenas, sus culturas y territorios. *Anuario Indigenista*, v. 30 (Dec 91), pp. 473 – 480.

Gros, Christian. Atention!: un indien peut en cacher un autre; droits indigènes et nouvelle constitution en Colombie. *Caravelle*, no. 59 (1992), pp. 139 – 160. Bibl.

Pérez, Carlos Andrés. Venezuela: Decreto 1633 que crea la reserva de biosfera Delta del Orinoco. *Anuario Indigenista*, v. 30 (Dec 91), pp. 497 – 502.

— Venezuela: Decreto 1635 que declara reserva de biosfera el sector sureste del territorio federal Amazonas. *Anuario Indigenista*, v. 30 (Dec 91), pp. 503 – 508.

— Venezuela: Decreto 1636 que crea el parque nacional Parima – Tapirapeco en el alto Orinoco. *Anuario Indigenista*, v. 30 (Dec 91), pp. 509 – 512.

Possuelo, Sydney Ferreira. Brasil: Decreto 828/91 que crea la Comisión de Defensa de los Derechos Indígenas. *Anuario Indigenista*, v. 30 (Dec 91), pp. 457 – 459.

Proyecto preliminar para la creación del Fondo para el Desarrollo de los Pueblos Indígenas de América Latina y el Caribe. *Anuario Indigenista*, v. 30 (Dec 91), pp. 213 – 254. Tables.

Legends

Cadogan, León. *Ayvu Rapytá: textos míticos de los mbyá-guaraní del Guairá* (Review). *Revista Paraguaya de Sociología*, v. 29, no. 85 (Sept – Dec 92), pp. 188 – 189.

Triviños, Gilberto. La sombra de los héroes. *Atenea (Chile)*, no. 465 – 466 (1992), pp. 67 – 97. Bibl, il.

Mortuary customs

Bermúdez Páez, Alvaro E. Reconstrucción de un conjunto funerario en el Alto de las Piedras (Isnos). *Revista Colombiana de Antropología,* v. 29 (1992), pp. 257 – 264. Bibl, il.

Langebaek, Carl Henrik. Competencia por prestigio político y momificación en el norte de Suramérica y el Istmo de Panamá. *Revista Colombiana de Antropología,* v. 29 (1992), pp. 7 – 26. Bibl.

Music

Bastos, Rafael José de Menezes. Musical Cognition and Structure: The Case of the Yawari of the Kamayurá Indians of Central Brazil, Xingu Indian Park, Mato Grosso. *La Educación (USA),* v. 36, no. 111 – 113 (1992), pp. 227 – 233. Bibl.

Langevin, André. Las zampoñas del conjunto de kantu y el debate sobre la función de la segunda hilera de tubos: datos etnográficos y análisis semiótico. *Revista Andina,* v. 10, no. 2 (Dec 92), pp. 405 – 440. Bibl, tables.

Música autóctona del norte de Potosí reviewed by Honoria Arredondo Calderón. *Revista Musical Chilena,* v. 46, no. 178 (July – Dec 92), pp. 127 – 128.

Rowe, William. Dimensiones históricas de la poesía quechua: el caso de las danzas guerreras de Toqroyoq y su relación con la producción poética andina. *Revista de Crítica Literaria Latinoamericana,* v. 19, no. 37 (Jan – June 93), pp. 41 – 62. Bibl.

Population

Alchon, Suzanne Austin. *Native Society and Disease in Colonial Ecuador* reviewed by Linda A. Newson. *Bulletin of Latin American Research,* v. 12, no. 1 (Jan 93), pp. 112 – 113.

— *Native Society and Disease in Colonial Ecuador* reviewed by Robert H. Jackson. *Colonial Latin American Historical Review,* v. 2, no. 3 (Summer 93), pp. 375 – 377.

— *Native Society and Disease in Colonial Ecuador* reviewed by Susan M. Deeds. *Colonial Latin American Review,* v. 2, no. 1 – 2 (1993), pp. 284 – 285.

— *Native Society and Disease in Colonial Ecuador* reviewed by Karen M. Powers. *Hispanic American Historical Review,* v. 73, no. 4 (Nov 93), pp. 694 – 695.

Sources

Remy S., Pilar and María Rostworowski Tovar de Diez Canseco, eds. *Las visitas a Cajamarca, 1571/72 – 1578* reviewed by Pedro Guibovich. *Apuntes (Peru),* no. 31 (July – Dec 92), pp. 119 – 121.

— *Las visitas a Cajamarca, 1571/72 – 1578* reviewed by Jorge Montenegro. *Bulletin de l'Institut Français d'Etudes Andines,* v. 21, no. 3 (1992), pp. 1073 – 1074.

— *Las visitas a Cajamarca, 1571/72 – 1578* reviewed by Noble David Cook. *Hispanic American Historical Review,* v. 73, no. 2 (May 93), pp. 313 – 314.

— *Las visitas a Cajamarca, 1571/72 – 1578* reviewed by Carmen Beatriz Loza. *Revista Andina,* v. 10, no. 2 (Dec 92), pp. 548 – 550.

Statistics

Bengoa, José. El país del censo. *Mensaje,* v. 42, no. 424 (Nov 93), pp. 543 – 546. Il, tables.

Pottery

Blasco, María Concepción and Luis J. Ramos Gómez. Continuidad y cambio: interpretación de la decoración de una vasija nazca. *Revista Andina,* v. 10, no. 2 (Dec 92), pp. 457 – 471. Bibl, il.

Kaulicke, Peter. Moche, Vicús moche y el mochica temprano. *Bulletin de l'Institut Français d'Etudes Andines,* v. 21, no. 3 (1992), pp. 853 – 903. Bibl, il, tables, maps, charts.

Religion and mythology

Columbus, Claudette Kemper. "Pacha": Worlds in a Sacred Word. *Latin American Indian Literatures Journal,* v. 9, no. 1 (Spring 93), pp. 2 – 20.

Dover, Robert V. H. *Andean Cosmologies through Time: Persistence and Emergence* reviewed by Jean-Jacques Decoster. *Latin American Indian Literatures Journal,* v. 9, no. 1 (Spring 93), pp. 73 – 78.

Fabian, Stephen Michael. *Space – Time of the Bororo of Brazil* reviewed by Gary Urton. *Hispanic American Historical Review,* v. 73, no. 3 (Aug 93), pp. 496 – 498.

Gareis, Iris. Religión popular y etnicidad: la población indígena de Lima colonial. *Allpanchis,* v. 23, no. 40 (July – Dec 92), pp. 117 – 143. Bibl.

Giannini, Isabelle Vidal. Os dominios cósmicos: um dos aspectos da construção da categoria humana kayapó – xikrin. *Revista de Antropologia (Brazil),* v. 34 (1991), pp. 35 – 58. Bibl.

Harrison, Regina. Confesando el pecado en los Andes: del siglo XVI hacia nuestros días. *Revista de Crítica Literaria Latinoamericana,* v. 19, no. 37 (Jan – June 93), pp. 169 – 184. Bibl.

Hurtado, Liliana R. de. Santiago entre los chiriguanos: una caso de aculturación y resistencia. *Amazonía Peruana,* v. 11, no. 22 (Oct 92), pp. 147 – 173. Bibl.

Itier, César. La tradición oral quechua antigua en los procesos de idolatrías de Cajatambo. *Bulletin de l'Institut Français d'Etudes Andines,* v. 21, no. 3 (1992), pp. 1009 – 1051. Bibl.

Kessel, Juan J. M. M. van. El pago a la tierra: porque el desarrollo lo exige. *Allpanchis,* v. 23, no. 40 (July – Dec 92), pp. 201 – 217. Bibl.

Lienhard, Martín. La cosmología poética en los waynos quechuas tradicionales. *Revista de Crítica Literaria Latinoamericana,* v. 19, no. 37 (Jan – June 93), pp. 87 – 103. Bibl.

Morales Gómez, Jorge. Cuerpo humano y contexto cultural en el Golfo de Morrosquillo. *Revista Colombiana de Antropología,* v. 29 (1992), pp. 191 – 205. Bibl.

Osorio, Alejandra. Una interpretación sobre la extirpación de idolatrías en el Perú: Otuco, Cajatambo, siglo XVII. *Historia y Cultura (Peru),* no. 20 (1990), pp. 161 – 199. Bibl.

Renard-Casevitz, France-Marie. *Le banquet masqué: une mythologie de l'étranger chez les indiens matsiguenga* reviewed by Edmundo Magaña. *European Review of Latin American and Caribbean Studies,* no. 54 (June 93), pp. 139 – 145.

Rostworowski Tovar de Diez Canseco, María. El Dios Con y el misterio de la pampa de Nasca. *Latin American Indian Literatures Journal,* v. 9, no. 1 (Spring 93), pp. 21 – 30.

Sánchez, Ana. *Amancebados, hechiceros y rebeldes: Chancay, siglo XVII* reviewed by Irene Silverblatt. *Hispanic American Historical Review,* v. 73, no. 1 (Feb 93), pp. 157 – 159.

Zecenarro Villalobos, Bernardino. De fiestas, ritos y batallas: algunos comportamientos folk de la sociedad andina de los k'anas y ch'umpiwillcas. *Allpanchis,* v. 23, no. 40 (July – Dec 92), pp. 147 – 172. Bibl.

Bibliography

Barnes, Monica. Andean Religion (Review article). *Latin American Indian Literatures Journal,* v. 9, no. 1 (Spring 93), pp. 66 – 73.

Benson, Elizabeth P. Bibliography (to the articles in this issue entitled "Sacred Space and Its Uses"). *Latin American Indian Literatures Journal,* v. 9, no. 1 (Spring 93), pp. 55 – 65.

Sources

The Huarochiri Manuscript: A Testament of Ancient and Colonial Andean Religion translated by Frank Solomon and George L. Urioste. Reviewed by Karen Spalding. *The Americas,* v. 49, no. 3 (Jan 93), pp. 398 – 399.

Millones Santa Gadea, Luis et al, eds. *El retorno de las huacas: estudios y documentos sobre el Taki Onqoy, siglo XVI* reviewed by Javier Flores Espinoza. *Historia y Cultura (Peru),* no. 20 (1990), pp. 381 – 382.

Social conditions

Cheng Hurtado, Alberto and José Matos Mar. Comas: lo andino en la modernidad urbana. *América Indígena,* v. 51, no. 2 – 3 (Apr – Sept 91), pp. 35 – 74. Il, tables, maps.

Encinas Cueto, Ives and Wigberto Rivero Pinto. La presencia aimara en la ciudad de La Paz: Chuquiyawu Marka; entre la participación y la sobrevivencia. *América Indígena,* v. 51, no. 2 – 3 (Apr – Sept 91), pp. 273 – 292.

Matos Mar, José. Taquileños, quechuas del lago Titicaca, en Lima. *América Indígena,* v. 51, no. 2 – 3 (Apr – Sept 91), pp. 107 – 166. Il, maps.

Villavicencio de Mencías, Gladys. *Indígenas en Quito. América Indígena*, v. 51, no. 2 – 3 (Apr – Sept 91), pp. 223 – 250. Bibl.

Zum Felde, Alberto. *La tragedia del indio en Suramérica. Hoy Es Historia*, v. 10, no. 55 (Jan – Feb 93), pp. 102 – 113. Il.

Social life and customs

Albó, Xavier and Matías Preiswerk. *El Gran Poder: fiesta del aimara urbano. América Indígena*, v. 51, no. 2 – 3 (Apr – Sept 91), pp. 293 – 352. Bibl, tables, maps.

Arnault, Daniel. *El personaje del pie amputado en la cultura mochica de Perú: un ensayo sobre la arqueología del poder. Latin American Antiquity*, v. 4, no. 3 (Sept 93), pp. 225 – 245. Bibl, il.

Biord Castillo, Horacio. *Organización social y resistencia a la conquista europea: los casos teque y cumanagoto. Boletín de la Academia Nacional de la Historia (Venezuela)*, v. 75, no. 297 (Jan – Mar 92), pp. 51 – 68. Bibl, maps.

Estenssoro Fuchs, Juan Carlos. *Los bailes de los indios y el proyecto colonial* (With commentaries by T. Abercrombie, J. Flores Espinoza, C. Itier, and S. E. Ramírez and a response by the author). *Revista Andina*, v. 10, no. 2 (Dec 92), pp. 353 – 404. Bibl.

Kaplan, Joanna Overing. *A estética da produção: o senso de comunidade entre os cubeo e os piaroa. Revista de Antropologia (Brazil)*, v. 34 (1991), pp. 7 – 33. Bibl.

León Gómez, Miguel. *El testamento del licenciado Diego Alvarez. Historia y Cultura (Peru)*, no. 20 (1990), pp. 319 – 350.

Pinto, Márnio Teixeira. *Corpo, morte e sociedade: um ensaio a partir da forma e da razão de se esquartejar um inimigo. Revista Brasileira de Ciências Sociais*, v. 8, no. 21 (Feb 93), pp. 52 – 67. Bibl, charts.

Sotomayor, María Lucía. *Organización socio-política de las cofradías. Revista Colombiana de Antropología*, v. 29 (1992), pp. 155 – 189. Bibl, tables.

Tissera, Ramón. *Una alucinante fiesta guaraní: el Tata-Yehesá. Todo Es Historia*, v. 26, no. 308 (Mar 93), pp. 95 – 96. Il.

Villaça, Aparecida Maria Neiva. *Comendo como gente: formas de canibalismo wari' (pakaa nova)* reviewed by Robin M. Wright. *Revista Brasileira de Ciências Sociais*, v. 8, no. 23 (Oct 93), pp. 146 – 148.

Textile industry and fabrics

Arnold, Denise Y. *At the Heart of the Woven Dance-Floor: The Wayñu in Qaqachaka. Iberoamericana*, v. 16, no. 47 – 48 (1992), pp. 21 – 66. Bibl, il, tables.

Block, David. *Andean Textiles: Aesthetics, Iconography, and Political Symbolism. SALALM Papers*, v. 34 (1989), pp. 223 – 231. Il.

Healy, Kevin. *Back to the Future: Ethnodevelopment among the Jalq'a of Bolivia. Grassroots Development*, v. 16, no. 2 (1992), pp. 22 – 34. Il.

Bibliography

Block, David. *A Core Bibliography of Andean Weaving. SALALM Papers*, v. 34 (1989), pp. 232 – 233.

Tribal government

Cappelletti, Angel J. *Pierre Clastres: la sociedad contra el estado. Revista de Filosofía de la Universidad de Costa Rica*, v. 30, no. 72 (Dec 92), pp. 145 – 151.

Isbell, William Harris and Gordon Francis McEwan, ed. *Huari Administrative Structure: Prehistoric Monumental Architecture and State Government* reviewed by Mario A. Rivera. *Latin American Antiquity*, v. 4, no. 1 (Mar 93), pp. 95 – 96.

Sala i Vila, Nuria. *La constitución de Cádiz y su impacto en el gobierno de las comunidades indígenas en el Virreinato del Perú. Boletín Americanista*, v. 33, no. 42 – 43 (1992 – 1993), pp. 51 – 70. Bibl.

INDIANS OF THE CARIBBEAN AREA

See also
> Arawak Indians
> Carib Indians
> Taino Indians

Ethnic identity

Palacio, Joseph O. *The Sojourn toward Self Discovery among Indigenous Peoples. Caribbean Quarterly*, v. 38, no. 2 – 3 (June – Sept 92), pp. 55 – 72.

Foreign opinion

Serafino, Nina M. et al. *Latin American Indigenous Peoples and Considerations for U.S. Assistance. Anuario Indigenista*, v. 30 (Dec 91), pp. 11 – 144. Bibl.

Government relations

Beckles, Hilary. *Kalinago (Carib) Resistance to European Colonisation of the Caribbean. Caribbean Quarterly*, v. 38, no. 2 – 3 (June – Sept 92), pp. 1 – 14. Bibl.

El Fondo para el Desarrollo de los Pueblos Indígenas de América Latina y el Caribe. *Anuario Indigenista*, v. 30 (Dec 91), pp. 7 – 10.

History

Boucher, Philip Paul. *Cannibal Encounters: Europeans and Island Caribs, 1492 – 1763* reviewed by Irving Rouse. *Hispanic American Historical Review*, v. 73, no. 3 (Aug 93), pp. 495 – 496.

Cassá, Roberto. *Los indios de las Antillas* reviewed by Genaro Rodríguez Morel. *Anuario de Estudios Americanos*, v. 50, no. 1 (1993), pp. 312 – 314.

Hulme, Peter and Neil L. Whitehead, eds. *Wild Majesty: Encounters with Caribs from Columbus to the Present Day; An Anthology* reviewed by Peter T. Bradley. *Bulletin of Latin American Research*, v. 12, no. 1 (Jan 93), pp. 111 – 112.

Reid, Basil. *Arawak Archaeology in Jamaica: New Approaches, New Perspectives. Caribbean Quarterly*, v. 38, no. 2 – 3 (June – Sept 92), pp. 15 – 20.

Rouse, Irving. *The Tainos: Rise and Decline of the People Who Greeted Columbus* reviewed by Aaron Segal. *Interciencia*, v. 18, no. 1 (Jan – Feb 93), p. 46.

— *The Tainos: Rise and Decline of the People Who Greeted Columbus* reviewed by C. J. M. R. Gullick. *Journal of Latin American Studies*, v. 25, no. 2 (May 93), pp. 388 – 389.

Sauer, Carl Ortwin. *The Early Spanish Main* reviewed by Peter T. Bradley. *Bulletin of Latin American Research*, v. 12, no. 1 (Jan 93), pp. 110 – 111.

Legal status, laws, etc.

Proyecto preliminar para la creación del Fondo para el Desarrollo de los Pueblos Indígenas de América Latina y el Caribe. *Anuario Indigenista*, v. 30 (Dec 91), pp. 213 – 254. Tables.

Music

Thompson, Donald. *The "Cronistas de Indias" Revisited: Historical Reports, Archaeological Evidence, and Literary and Artistic Traces of Indigenous Music and Dance in the Greater Antilles at the Time of the "Conquista". Latin American Music Review*, v. 14, no. 2 (Fall – Winter 93), pp. 181 – 201. Bibl.

Population

Cook, Noble David. *Disease and the Depopulation of Hispaniola, 1492 – 1518. Colonial Latin American Review*, v. 2, no. 1 – 2 (1993), pp. 213 – 245. Bibl, tables.

Women

Bliss, Elaine. *Adaptation to Agricultural Change among Garifuna Women in Hopkins, Belize. Caribbean Geography*, v. 3, no. 3 (Mar 92), pp. 160 – 174. Bibl, tables, maps.

INDIANS OF URUGUAY

Basalisco, Lucio. *Culture a confronto: guaraniés e yaros visti da un gesuito alla fine del seicento. Quaderni Ibero-Americani*, no. 72 (Dec 92), pp. 709 – 720. Bibl.

INDIANS OF VENEZUELA

See also
> Carib Indians
> Piaroa Indians
> Yanoama Indians

Ferrero-Kellerhoff, Inés Cecilia. *Capacho: un pueblo de indios en la jurisdicción de la villa de San Cristóbal* reviewed by Carlos A. Mayo. *Hispanic American Historical Review*, v. 73, no. 1 (Feb 93), pp. 159 – 160.

Pérez, Carlos Andrés. Venezuela: Decreto 1633 que crea la reserva de biosfera Delta del Orinoco. *Anuario Indigenista*, v. 30 (Dec 91), pp. 497 – 502.

— Venezuela: Decreto 1635 que declara reserva de biosfera el sector sureste del territorio federal Amazonas. *Anuario Indigenista*, v. 30 (Dec 91), pp. 503 – 508.

— Venezuela: Decreto 1636 que crea el parque nacional Parima – Tapirapeco en el alto Orinoco. *Anuario Indigenista*, v. 30 (Dec 91), pp. 509 – 512.

INDIGENISMO

See also
Ethnicity
Indians in literature
Subdivisions *Ethnic identity* and *Government relations* under names of Indian groups

Baudot, Georges. Chronologie pour l'émergence d'une organisation amérindienne, politique et culturelle, au Mexique. *Caravelle*, no. 59 (1992), pp. 7 – 17.

Bebbington, Anthony et al. From Protest to Productivity: The Evolution of Indigenous Federations in Ecuador. *Grassroots Development*, v. 16, no. 2 (1992), pp. 11 – 21. Il.

Dauzier, Martine. Comment affronter les 500 ans à venir?: mémoire et projet des indiens du Mexique. *Caravelle*, no. 59 (1992), pp. 87 – 98.

— Tous des indiens?: la "réindianisation"; force ou fiction: débats autour des essais de Guillermo Bonfil Batalla. *Cahiers des Amériques Latines*, no. 13 (1992), pp. 147 – 158. Bibl.

Díaz Polanco, Héctor. El quinto centenario y los pueblos indios. *Boletín de Antropología Americana*, no. 23 (July 91), pp. 13 – 29. Bibl, il.

Favre, Henri. Informe de consultoría. *Anuario Indigenista*, v. 30 (Dec 91), pp. 385 – 403.

Marimán, José. Cuestión mapuche, descentralización del estado y autonomía regional. *Caravelle*, no. 59 (1992), pp. 189 – 205. Bibl.

Matos Mar, José. Informe de actividades, 1991. *Anuario Indigenista*, v. 30 (Dec 91), pp. 347 – 384.

Matute, Mario René. Rigoberta Menchú, premio Nobel de la paz 1992 (Introduced by Alfonso Fernández Cabrelli). *Hoy Es Historia*, v. 10, no. 55 (Jan – Feb 93), pp. 97 – 101. Il.

Morin, Françoise. Evaristo Nugkuag Ikanana, presidente de la Coordinadora de las Organizaciones Indígenas de la Cuenca Amazónica (COICA), Perú: entrevista realizada el 7 de julio de 1992 en Lima por Françoise Morin. *Caravelle*, no. 59 (1992), pp. 67 – 70.

— Revendications et stratégies politiques des organisations indigènes amazoniennes. *Cahiers des Amériques Latines*, no. 13 (1992), pp. 75 – 85. Bibl.

Naranjo, Marcelo F. Convidados de piedra: los indios en el proceso urbano de Quito. *América Indígena*, v. 51, no. 2 – 3 (Apr – Sept 91), pp. 251 – 272. Bibl.

Organization of American States. Resolución sobre el Instituto Indigenista Interamericano. *Anuario Indigenista*, v. 30 (Dec 91), pp. 345 – 346.

Peluso, Daniela. Conservation and Indigenismo. *Hemisphere*, v. 5, no. 2 (Winter – Spring 93), pp. 6 – 8.

Ravines Pérez, Eudocio. El indigenismo como instrumento político: un problema artificial (Excerpt from *La gran promesa*). *Atenea (Chile)*, no. 465 – 466 (1992), pp. 157 – 172. Il.

Renard-Casevitz, France-Marie. Les guerriers du sel: chronique '92. *Cahiers des Amériques Latines*, no. 13 (1992), pp. 107 – 118.

Santana, Roberto. Actores y escenarios étnicos en Ecuador: el levantamiento de 1990. *Caravelle*, no. 59 (1992), pp. 161 – 188. Bibl.

— Les indiens d'Equateur: citoyens dans l'ethnicité? reviewed by Maxime Haubert. *Tiers Monde*, v. 34, no. 134 (Apr – June 93), pp. 471 – 473.

— Jacinto Guamán, ex-vice-presidente de la Confederación de las Nacionalidades Indígenas del Ecuador (CONAIE): entrevista realizada el 23 de noviembre de 1988, por Roberto Santana. *Caravelle*, no. 59 (1992), pp. 59 – 65.

— Trois ans de chronologie indianiste en Equateur. *Caravelle*, no. 59 (1992), pp. 19 – 24.

Tejada de Rivero, David. Informe de consultoría. *Anuario Indigenista*, v. 30 (Dec 91), pp. 405 – 423.

Terena, Marcos. La resistencia indígena: 500 años después. *Nueva Sociedad, no. 123 (Jan – Feb 93)*, pp. 156 – 159.

Bibliography

Mallon, Florencia E. Entre la utopía y la marginalidad: comunidades indígenas y culturas políticas en México y los Andes, 1780 – 1990. *Historia Mexicana*, v. 42, no. 2 (Oct – Dec 92), pp. 473 – 504.

Congresses

Declaración de Chiapas. *Anuario Indigenista*, v. 30 (Dec 91), pp. 299 – 302.

Declaración de Guadalajara. *Anuario Indigenista*, v. 30 (Dec 91), pp. 289 – 298.

Morin, Françoise. Le mythe du 500ème: convergences et divergences. *Caravelle*, no. 59 (1992), pp. 75 – 85. Bibl.

World Council of Indigenous Peoples. Resoluciones del Quinto Encuentro del Parlamento Indígena de América. *Anuario Indigenista*, v. 30 (Dec 91), pp. 321 – 330.

International cooperation

Convenio marco entre la Agencia Española de Cooperación Internacional y el Instituto Indigenista Interamericano. *Anuario Indigenista*, v. 30 (Dec 91), pp. 525 – 528.

Methodology

Medina Cárdenas, Eduardo. El modelo "región de refugio" de Aguirre Beltrán: teoría, aplicaciones y perspectivas. *Siglo XIX: Cuadernos*, v. 2, no. 4 (Oct 92), pp. 61 – 82. Bibl.

INDIGO

Garrigus, John D. Blue and Brown: Contraband Indigo and the Rise of a Free Colored Planter Class in French Saint-Domingue. *The Americas*, v. 50, no. 2 (Oct 93), pp. 233 – 263. Bibl, tables, maps, charts.

INDUSTRIAL ORGANIZATION

Ribeiro, Carlos A. C. A responsabilidade social da empresa: uma nova vantagem competitiva. *RAE; Revista de Administração de Empresas*, v. 33, no. 1 (Jan – Feb 93), p. 46.

Argentina

Schvarzer, Jorge. Expansión, maduración y perspectivas de las ramas básicas de procesos en la industria argentina: una mirada "ex post" desde la economía política. *Desarrollo Económico (Argentina)*, v. 33, no. 131 (Oct – Dec 93), pp. 377 – 402. Bibl, tables, charts.

Brazil

Ferraz, João Carlos et al. Development, Technology, and Flexibility: Brazil Faces the Industrial Divide reviewed by John Humphrey. *Journal of Latin American Studies*, v. 25, no. 3 (Oct 93), pp. 678 – 679.

Fleury, Maria Tereza Leme. Cultura da qualidade e mudança organizacional. *RAE; Revista de Administração de Empresas*, v. 33, no. 2 (Mar – Apr 93), pp. 26 – 34.

Colombia

Bonilla Muñoz, Guillermo and Horacio Osorio Velosa. Estructura de mercado y prácticas comerciales en los sectores industrial, minero – energético y de servicios públicos en Colombia. *Planeación y Desarrollo*, v. 24, no. 2 (May – Aug 93), pp. 191 – 256. Tables, charts.

Mexico

Cárdenas, Fe Esperanza and Vincent Redonnet. Modernización de la empresa AHMSA en Monclova, Coahuila y su impacto sobre la población. *Estudios Demográficos y Urbanos*, v. 6, no. 3 (Sept – Dec 91), pp. 677 – 716. Bibl, tables.

Morales, Josefina, ed. *La reestructuración industrial en México: cinco aspectos fundamentales* reviewed by María Luisa González Marín. *Problemas del Desarrollo*, v. 24, no. 93 (Apr – June 93), pp. 235 – 236.

Salinas Chávez, Antonio. El cambio estructural de PEMEX: más empresa, menos política económica. *Comercio Exterior*, v. 43, no. 11 (Nov 93), pp. 1001 – 1009. Bibl, charts.

Stone, Jeff. The Dating Game. *Business Mexico*, v. 3, no. 9 (Sept 93), p. 46.

Southern Cone of South America

Araújo Júnior, José Tavares de. Reestruturação industrial e integração econômica: as perspectivas do MERCOSUL. *Revista Brasileira de Economia,* v. 47, no. 1 (Jan – Mar 93), pp. 97 – 113. Bibl, tables.

United States

Stone, Jeff. The Dating Game. *Business Mexico,* v. 3, no. 9 (Sept 93), p. 46.

INDUSTRIAL PRODUCTIVITY

See also
    Capital productivity
    Competition

Argentina

Bonano, Luis Marcos and Eduardo Rosenzvaig. Contrapunto azucarero entre relaciones de producción y tecnología: el perfil argentino. *Realidad Económica,* no. 113 (Jan – Feb 93), pp. 52 – 86. Il.

Brazil

Bonelli, Regis. Crecimiento y productividad en las industrias brasileñas: efectos de la orientación del comercio exterior. *El Trimestre Económico,* v. 59, Special issue (Dec 92), pp. 109 – 140. Bibl, tables.

Corrêa, Henrique Luiz. Flexibilidade nos sistemas de produção. *RAE; Revista de Administração de Empresas,* v. 33, no. 3 (May – June 93), pp. 22 – 35. Bibl.

Fornetti, Marco et al. Desenvolvimento e uso de modelos computacionais no planejamento da produção em indústrias laticinistas de pequeno porte: um estudo de caso. *Revista de Economia e Sociologia Rural,* v. 29, no. 4 (Oct – Dec 91), pp. 401 – 410. Bibl, charts.

Frischtak, Claudio R. Automação bancária e mudança na produtividade: a experiência brasileira. *Pesquisa e Planejamento Econômico,* v. 22, no. 2 (Aug 92), pp. 197 – 239. Bibl, tables.

Mathematical models

Moreira, Ajax Reynaldo Bello et al. Um modelo macroeconômico para o nível de atividade: previsões e projeções condicionais. *Revista Brasileira de Economia,* v. 47, no. 3 (July – Sept 93), pp. 349 – 371. Bibl, tables, charts.

Chile

Guajardo Soto, Guillermo. Tecnología y trabajo en Chile, 1850 – 1930. *Cuadernos Americanos,* no. 38, Nueva época (Mar – Apr 93), pp. 155 – 179. Bibl, tables.

Great Britain

Corrêa, Henrique Luiz. Flexibilidade nos sistemas de produção. *RAE; Revista de Administração de Empresas,* v. 33, no. 3 (May – June 93), pp. 22 – 35. Bibl.

Latin America

Mathematical models

Elías, Víctor Jorge. *Sources of Growth: A Study of Seven Latin American Economies* reviewed by David E. Hojman. *Journal of Latin American Studies,* v. 25, no. 3 (Oct 93), pp. 675 – 677.

Mexico

Castro Escudero, Alfredo. Productividad: el gran reto de la industria mexicana. *Comercio Exterior,* v. 43, no. 2 (Feb 93), pp. 125 – 128. Tables.

Cohen, Joshua A. Productivity: A Jump Start to Better Wages. *Business Mexico,* v. 3, no. 6 (June 93), pp. 7 – 8.

Pérez Pérez, Gabriel. El SME ante el reto de la modernización del sector eléctrico. *El Cotidiano,* v. 10, no. 58 (Oct – Nov 93), pp. 98 – 102. Il.

Vera Ferrer, Oscar. Tendencias de la productividad en México: la concepción de las empresas. *Comercio Exterior,* v. 43, no. 11 (Nov 93), pp. 1052 – 1056. Bibl, tables.

INDUSTRIAL PROMOTION

Argentina

Schvarzer, Jorge. Expansión, maduración y perspectivas de las ramas básicas de procesos en la industria argentina: una mirada "ex post" desde la economía política. *Desarrollo Económico (Argentina),* v. 33, no. 131 (Oct – Dec 93), pp. 377 – 402. Bibl, tables, charts.

Costa Rica

Coffey, Brian. Investment Incentives as a Means of Encouraging Tourism Development: The Case of Costa Rica. *Bulletin of Latin American Research,* v. 12, no. 1 (Jan 93), pp. 83 – 90. Bibl, tables, maps.

Mexico

Almada, Sergio. Chihuahua Redefines Success. *Business Mexico,* v. 3, no. 12 (Dec 93), pp. 22 – 23. Tables.

Forde, D. H. One Market for All? *Américas,* v. 45, no. 5 (Sept – Oct 93), pp. 34 – 39. Il, charts.

Ramírez Carrillo, Luis Alfonso. El escenario de la industrialización en Yucatán. *Comercio Exterior,* v. 43, no. 2 (Feb 93), pp. 171 – 177. Bibl, tables.

Sánchez-Ugarte, Fernando J. Acciones en favor de las micro, pequeñas y medianas industrias en México. *Comercio Exterior,* v. 43, no. 6 (June 93), pp. 539 – 543.

Uruguay

Bértola, Luis. *The Manufacturing Industry of Uruguay, 1913 – 1961: A Sectoral Approach to Growth, Fluctuations, and Crisis* reviewed by Mario Zejan. *Ibero Americana (Sweden),* v. 22, no. 2 (Dec 92), pp. 82 – 85. Bibl.

INDUSTRIAL RELATIONS

See
    Industry and state
    Labor relations
    Subdivision *Political activity* under *Trade unions*

INDUSTRIAL SOCIOLOGY

Rangel Martínez, Georgina M. Mujer, trabajo y medio ambiente. *Fem,* v. 17, no. 128 (Oct 93), pp. 22 – 25. Bibl.

Brazil

Fleury, Maria Tereza Leme. Cultura da qualidade e mudança organizacional. *RAE; Revista de Administração de Empresas,* v. 33, no. 2 (Mar – Apr 93), pp. 26 – 34.

Chile

Anwandter P., Jorge. Una empresa de trabajadores para la economía solidaria. *Mensaje,* v. 42, no. 423 (Oct 93), pp. 504 – 505. Il.

Mexico

Aguilar Gómez, J. Eduardo. Mexican Corporate Culture. *Business Mexico,* v. 3, no. 8 (Aug 93), pp. 8 – 9 +.

Alvarez Padilla, Alfredo. La cultura empresarial en el nuevo orden económico internacional. *El Cotidiano,* v. 10, no. 58 (Oct – Nov 93), pp. 112 – 115.

Erlich, Marc I. Making Sense of the Bicultural Workplace. *Business Mexico,* v. 3, no. 8 (Aug 93), pp. 16 – 19.

Congresses

Cornejo Oviedo, Alejandro and Emanuel Orozco. Relatoría del encuentro "Antropología Industrial: Avances de Investigación." *Nueva Antropología,* v. 13, no. 44 (Aug 93), pp. 143 – 145.

Methodology

Matrajt, Miguel. Prevenção de "stress" ocupacional em linha de montagem: um estudo de caso mexicano (Translated by Geni Goldschmidt). *RAE; Revista de Administração de Empresas,* v. 33, no. 5 (Sept – Oct 93), pp. 98 – 108.

INDUSTRIALIZATION

See
    Industrial promotion
    Industry and state
    Technology
    Technology transfer
    Subdivision *Industries* under names of specific countries

INDUSTRIES, LOCATION OF

Brazil

Almeida, Roberto Schmidt de and Miguel Angelo Campos Ribeiro. Os pequenos e medios estabelecimentos industriais nordestinos: padrões de distribuição e fatores condicionantes. *Revista Brasileira de Geografia,* v. 53, no. 1 (Jan – Mar 91), pp. 5 – 49. Bibl, tables, maps.

Corrêa, Roberto Lobato. Corporação e organização espacial: um estudo de caso. *Revista Brasileira de Geografia*, v. 53, no. 3 (July – Sept 91), pp. 33 – 66. Bibl, il, tables, maps.

Egler, Claudio Antonio G. As escalas de economia: uma introdução à dimensão territorial da crise. *Revista Brasileira de Geografia*, v. 53, no. 3 (July – Sept 91), pp. 229 – 245.

Ramires, Julio Cesar Lima. As grandes corporações e a dinâmica socioespacial: a ação da PETROBRAS em Macaé. *Revista Brasileira de Geografia*, v. 53, no. 4 (Oct – Dec 91), pp. 115 – 151. Bibl, tables, maps.

Methodology

Almeida, Roberto Schmidt de and Miguel Angelo Campos Ribeiro. Análise da organização espacial da indústria nordestina através de uma tipologia de centros industriais. *Revista Brasileira de Geografia*, v. 53, no. 2 (Apr – June 91), pp. 5 – 31. Bibl, tables, maps.

Mexico

Garza Villarreal, Gustavo. *Desconcentración, tecnología y localización industrial en México: los parques y ciudades industriales, 1953 – 1988* reviewed by Carlos A. de Mattos. *EURE*, v. 19, no. 58 (Oct 93), pp. 88 – 89.

INDUSTRIES, SIZE OF

Mathematical models

Bouchain Galicia, Rafael. Análisis sobre concentración y economías de escala en la industria bancaria dentro de la literatura económica: el caso de la banca mexicana. *Problemas del Desarrollo*, v. 24, no. 92 (Jan – Mar 93), pp. 171 – 196. Bibl, tables.

Colombia

Rivas, Juan Antonio. Estructura de mercado, innovación y crecimiento. *Planeación y Desarrollo*, v. 24, no. 2 (May – Aug 93), pp. 73 – 93. Bibl.

INDUSTRY

See

Airplane industry and trade
Aluminum industry and trade
Atomic power industry
Automobile industry and trade
Business enterprises
Capital investments
Capital productivity
Computer industry
Construction industry
Employees' representation in management
Fertilizer industry
Fishing
Food industry and trade
Fruit trade
Government ownership of business enterprises
Industrial organization
Industrial productivity
Industries, Location of
Industries, Size of
Insurance
International business enterprises
Labor relations
Management
Marine resources
Marketing
Meat industry and trade
Mining industry and finance
Petroleum industry and trade
Pharmacy
Privatization
Production (Economic theory)
Rubber industry and trade
Salt industry and trade
Service industries
Ship building
Steel industry and trade
Strikes and lockouts
Subcontracting
Synthetic products
Textile industry and fabrics
Tourist trade
Trade marks
Trade unions
Wages
Wine and wine making
Wool industry and trade
Subdivision *Industries* under names of specific countries

INDUSTRY AND STATE

See also

Government ownership of business enterprises
Industrial promotion
State capitalism

Araújo Júnior, José Tavares de. The Scope for Industrial Policy in a Free Trade Environment. *Revista de Economia Política (Brazil)*, v. 13, no. 3 (July – Sept 93), pp. 102 – 113. Bibl, tables.

Argentina

Girbal de Blacha, Noemí M. Azúcar, cambio político y acción empresaria en la Argentina, 1916 – 1930. *Investigaciones y Ensayos*, no. 41 (Jan – Dec 91), pp. 269 – 314. Bibl, tables.

Brazil

Carneiro, José Mário et al. Meio ambiente, empresário e governo: conflitos ou parceria? *RAE; Revista de Administração de Empresas*, v. 33, no. 3 (May – June 93), pp. 68 – 75. Bibl.

Lamounier, Bolivar. Empresarios, partidos y democratización en Brasil, 1974 – 1990. *Revista Mexicana de Sociología*, v. 54, no. 1 (Jan – Mar 92), pp. 77 – 97. Bibl.

Schneider, Ben Ross. *Politics within the State: Elite Bureaucrats and Industrial Policy in Authoritarian Brazil* reviewed by Sonny B. Davis. *Canadian Journal of Latin American and Caribbean Studies*, v. 17, no. 34 (1992), p. 131.

— *Politics within the State: Elite Bureaucrats and Industrial Policy in Authoritarian Brazil* reviewed by John W. Sloan. *Journal of Developing Areas*, v. 27, no. 3 (Apr 93), pp. 424 – 425.

Central America

Willmore, Larry N. Industrial Policy in Central America. *CEPAL Review*, no. 48 (Dec 92), pp. 95 – 105. Bibl, tables.

Chile

Volk, Steven S. Mine Owners, Money Lenders, and the State in Mid-Nineteenth Century Chile: Transitions and Conflicts. *Hispanic American Historical Review*, v. 73, no. 1 (Feb 93), pp. 67 – 98. Bibl, tables.

Colombia

Garay Salamanca, Luis Jorge, ed. *Estrategia industrial e inserción internacional* reviewed by Horacio Osorio. *Planeación y Desarrollo*, v. 24, no. 2 (May – Aug 93), pp. 429 – 435.

Latin America

Esser, Klaus. América Latina: industrialización sin visión (Translated by Friedrich Welsch). *Nueva Sociedad*, no. 125 (May – June 93), pp. 27 – 46. Bibl.

Szlajfer, Henryk, ed. *Economic Nationalism in East-Central Europe and South America, 1918 – 1939* reviewed by Joseph L. Love. *Journal of Latin American Studies*, v. 25, no. 1 (Feb 93), pp. 206 – 208.

Mexico

Alonso, Jorge et al, eds. *El nuevo estado mexicano, tomo III: Estado, actores y movimientos sociales* reviewed by Griselda Martínez Vázquez. *El Cotidiano*, v. 8, no. 52 (Jan – Feb 93), p. 117.

Luna, Matilde and Ricardo Tirado. Los empresarios en el escenario del cambio: trayectoria y tendencias de sus estrategias de acción colectiva. *Revista Mexicana de Sociología*, v. 55, no. 2 (Apr – June 93), pp. 243 – 271. Bibl, tables, charts.

Mizrahi, Yemile. La nueva oposición conservadora en México: la radicalización política de los empresarios norteños. *Foro Internacional*, v. 32, no. 5 (Oct – Dec 92), pp. 744 – 771. Bibl, tables.

Singelmann, Peter Marius. The Sugar Industry in Postrevolutionary Mexico: State Intervention and Private Capital. *Latin American Research Review*, v. 28, no. 1 (1993), pp. 61 – 88. Bibl, tables.

Nicaragua

Dijkstra, Geske. *Industrialization in Sandinista Nicaragua: Policy and Practice in a Mixed Economy* reviewed by Claes Brundenius. *Hispanic American Historical Review*, v. 73, no. 4 (Nov 93), pp. 721 – 722.

Paraguay

Borda, Dionisio. Empresariado y transición a la democracia en el Paraguay. *Revista Paraguaya de Sociología*, v. 30, no. 86 (Jan – Apr 93), pp. 31 – 66. Tables.

INFANT MORTALITY

Brazil

Scheper-Hughes, Nancy. *Death without Weeping: The Violence of Everyday Life in Brazil* reviewed by Bernardo Kucinski. *Journal of Latin American Studies*, v. 25, no. 2 (May 93), pp. 419 – 420.

— *Death without Weeping: The Violence of Everyday Life in Brazil* reviewed by Glenn W. Erickson and Sandra S. Fernandes Erickson. *Luso-Brazilian Review*, v. 30, no. 1 (Summer 93), pp. 142 – 144.

Ecuador

Statistics

Juárez, Fátima. Intervención de las instituciones en la reducción de la fecundidad y la mortalidad infantil. *Estudios Demográficos y Urbanos*, v. 7, no. 2 – 3 (May – Dec 92), pp. 377 – 405. Bibl, tables, charts.

Mexico

Statistics

Gómez de León, José and Virgilio Partida Bush. Niveles de mortalidad infantil y fecundidad en México, por entidad federativa, 1990. *Revista Mexicana de Sociología*, v. 55, no. 1 (Jan – Mar 93), pp. 97 – 135. Bibl, tables, charts.

INFLATION (FINANCE)

Mathematical models

Barbosa, Fernando de Holanda et al. A dinâmica da hiperinflação. *Revista de Economia Política (Brazil)*, v. 13, no. 1 (Jan – Mar 93), pp. 5 – 24. Bibl, tables, charts.

Argentina

Castro Escudero, Alfredo. Inflación en Argentina: ¿Un problema resuelto? *Comercio Exterior*, v. 43, no. 10 (Oct 93), pp. 954 – 964. Bibl.

Lavergne, Néstor. Argentina, 1993: estabilidad económica, democracia y estado-nación. *Realidad Económica*, no. 116 (May – June 93), pp. 5 – 20.

Tavares de Almeida, Maria Hermínia. Sindicatos, crisis económica y alta inflación en Brasil y Argentina. *Revista Mexicana de Sociología*, v. 54, no. 1 (Jan – Mar 92), pp. 99 – 137. Bibl, tables, charts.

Brazil

Amadeo Swaelen, Edward Joaquim and Elena Landau. Indexação e dispersão de preços relativos: análise do caso brasileiro, 1975 – 1991. *Revista de Economia Política (Brazil)*, v. 13, no. 3 (July – Sept 93), pp. 130 – 138. Bibl, charts.

Barbosa, Fernando de Holanda. Hiperinflação e estabilização. *Revista de Economia Política (Brazil)*, v. 13, no. 4 (Oct – Dec 93), pp. 5 – 15. Bibl, charts.

Batista Júnior, Paulo Nogueira and Luiz Gonzaga de Mello Belluzzo, eds. *A luta pela sobrevivência da moeda nacional: ensaios em homenagem a Dilson Funarol* reviewed by Eduardo Refinetti Guardia. *Revista de Economia Política (Brazil)*, v. 13, no. 3 (July – Sept 93), pp. 154 – 155.

Franco, Gustavo Henrique Barroso. Alternativas de estabilização: gradualismo, dolarização e populismo. *Revista de Economia Política (Brazil)*, v. 13, no. 2 (Apr – June 93), pp. 28 – 45. Bibl, tables, charts.

Grandi, Rodolfo and Marcelo Resende. Inflação e variabilidade dos preços relativos no Brasil: a questão da causalidade. *Revista Brasileira de Economia*, v. 46, no. 4 (Oct – Dec 92), pp. 595 – 604. Bibl, tables.

Luque, Carlos António. Observações sobre o processo inflacionário brasileiro, 1986 – 1991. *Revista de Economia Política (Brazil)*, v. 13, no. 2 (Apr – June 93), pp. 46 – 60. Bibl, charts.

Mattos, César Costa Alves de. Prefixação, expectativas e inflação. *Revista Brasileira de Economia*, v. 47, no. 1 (Jan – Mar 93), pp. 131 – 144. Bibl.

Ninguém segura os preços. *Problemas Brasileiros*, v. 30, no. 295 (Jan – Feb 93), pp. 22 – 24. Il, tables.

Pereira, José Maria. Os trinta anos de *A inflação brasileira* de Ignácio Rangel. *Revista de Economia Política (Brazil)*, v. 13, no. 3 (July – Sept 93), pp. 144 – 149. Bibl.

Tavares de Almeida, Maria Hermínia. Sindicatos, crisis económica y alta inflación en Brasil y Argentina. *Revista Mexicana de Sociología*, v. 54, no. 1 (Jan – Mar 92), pp. 99 – 137. Bibl, tables, charts.

Théret, Bruno. Hyperinflation de producteurs et hyperinflation de rentiers: le cas du Brésil. *Tiers Monde*, v. 34, no. 133 (Jan – Mar 93), pp. 37 – 67. Bibl, charts.

Mathematical models

Catão, Luís. A New Wholesale Price Index for Brazil during the Period 1870 – 1913. *Revista Brasileira de Economia*, v. 46, no. 4 (Oct – Dec 92), pp. 519 – 533. Bibl, tables, charts.

Landau, Elena and Suzana S. Peixoto. Inflação, indexação e preços relativos: novas evidências para o Brasil. *Pesquisa e Planejamento Econômico*, v. 22, no. 1 (Apr 92), pp. 125 – 167. Bibl, tables, charts.

Latin America

Salama, Pierre and Jacques Valier. *La economía gangrenada: ensayo sobre la hiperinflación* reviewed by Sebastián Katz and Pablo Sirlin (Review entitled "Las desventuras de un análisis francés sobre la desventura de América Latina"). *Desarrollo Económico (Argentina)*, v. 33, no. 131 (Oct – Dec 93), pp. 449 – 452.

Uruguay

Craven, Carolyn. Wage Determination and Inflation in Uruguay: Regime Changes. *Journal of Developing Areas*, v. 27, no. 4 (July 93), pp. 457 – 468. Bibl, tables, charts.

INFORMAL SECTOR (ECONOMICS)

Bolivia

Mansilla, Hugo Celso Felipe. La economía informal y las modificaciones del movimiento sindical en Bolivia. *Revista Paraguaya de Sociología*, v. 30, no. 86 (Jan – Apr 93), pp. 113 – 126. Bibl.

Central America

Menjívar Larín, Rafael and Juan Pablo Pérez Sáinz, eds. *Informalidad urbana en Centroamérica: entre la acumulación y la subsistencia* reviewed by Stephen Webre. *Hispanic American Historical Review*, v. 73, no. 2 (May 93), pp. 341 – 342.

Ecuador

Pita, Edgar et al. *Informalidad urbana: dinámica y perspectiva en el Ecuador* reviewed by Jose A. Alonso H. *Problemas del Desarrollo*, v. 24, no. 92 (Jan – Mar 93), pp. 238 – 241.

Latin America

Barrantes Alvarado, César A. Del sector informal urbano a la economía popular. *Revista de Ciencias Sociales (Costa Rica)*, no. 57 (Sept 92), pp. 97 – 108. Bibl.

Cortés C., Fernando and Oscar Cuéllar Saavedra, eds. *Crisis y reproducción social: los comerciantes del sector informal* reviewed by José Antonio Alonso. *Estudios Sociológicos*, v. 10, no. 30 (Sept – Dec 92), pp. 819 – 822.

Mattie, Mailer and Dorothea Melcher. Interpretaciones teóricas al sector informal urbano. *Derecho y Reforma Agraria*, no. 23 (1992), pp. 83 – 103. Bibl.

Oliveira, Orlandina de and Bryan R. Roberts. La informalidad urbana en años de expansión, crisis y restructuración económica (Translated by Laura Elena Pulido). *Estudios Sociológicos*, v. 11, no. 31 (Jan – Apr 93), pp. 33 – 58. Bibl, tables.

Wilson, Fiona. Industria informal, talleres y ámbito doméstico. *Revista Mexicana de Sociología*, v. 54, no. 4 (Oct – Dec 92), pp. 91 – 115. Bibl.

Mexico

El comercio en vía pública: la economía informal en la ciudad de México. *El Cotidiano*, v. 9, no. 54 (May 93), pp. 72 – 75. Il, tables.

Lezama, José Luis. Ciudad, mujer y conflicto: el comercio ambulante en el D.F. *Estudios Demográficos y Urbanos*, v. 6, no. 3 (Sept – Dec 91), pp. 649 – 675. Bibl, tables.

Peru

Adams, Norman and Néstor Valdivia. *Los otros empresarios: ética de migrantes y formación de empresas en Lima* reviewed by Orazio A. Ciccarelli. *Hispanic American Historical Review,* v. 73, no. 4 (Nov 93), pp. 714 – 715.

Chávez O'Brien, Eliana. El sector informal urbano: estrategias de vida e identidad. *Nueva Sociedad,* no. 124 (Mar – Apr 93), pp. 82 – 93. Bibl, tables.

Macera dall'Orso, Pablo. Los verdaderos ambulantes. *Debate (Peru),* v. 16, no. 72 (Mar – May 93), pp. 43 – 44. Il.

Saba, Raúl P. Peru's Informal Sector: Hope in the Midst of Crisis. *SALALM Papers,* v. 36 (1991), pp. 35 – 41. Bibl.

INFORMATION SERVICES

See also
Automation
Geographic information systems

Adorno, Sérgio. Ciência, informação, verdade e universalidade: a propósito de "A violência política na América Latina." *Revista Brasileira de Ciências Sociais,* v. 8, no. 21 (Feb 93), pp. 40 – 43.

Caldeira, Teresa Pires do Rio. Comentários a partir do artigo "A violência política na América Latina." *Revista Brasileira de Ciências Sociais,* v. 8, no. 21 (Feb 93), pp. 44 – 47.

Hazen, Dan C. Latin American Studies, Information Resources, and Library Collections: The Contexts of Crisis. *SALALM Papers,* v. 36 (1991), pp. 267 – 271.

Soares, Gláucio Ary Dillon. Comentários adicionais (Response on commentaries to his article "A violência política na América Latina"). *Revista Brasileira de Ciências Sociais,* v. 8, no. 21 (Feb 93), pp. 48 – 51.

— A violência política na América Latina. *Revista Brasileira de Ciências Sociais,* v. 8, no. 21 (Feb 93), pp. 22 – 39. Bibl, tables, charts.

Argentina

García Cambeiro, Marcelo. LATBOOK en CD-ROM: una respuesta profesional de libreros latinoamericanos a las necesidades bibliográficas. *SALALM Papers,* v. 36 (1991), pp. 432 – 434.

Retta, Luis A. Publicaciones uruguayas incluidas en LATBOOK. *SALALM Papers,* v. 36 (1991), pp. 435 – 437.

Brazil

McCarthy, Cavan Michael. A Regional Database for the Brazilian Northeast. *SALALM Papers,* v. 36 (1991), pp. 369 – 386. Bibl, tables.

Europe

International cooperation

Biggins, Alan. Libraries "sans frontières": REDIAL, European Bibliographic Cooperation, and 1992. *SALALM Papers,* v. 36 (1991), pp. 20 – 31.

Latin America

Bustamante, Jorge I. Optical Disk Possibilities in the Distribution of Information on Latin American Art. *SALALM Papers,* v. 34 (1989), pp. 316 – 322. Tables.

Mexico

Bos, Cornelio A. Wanted Now!: Direct Mail. *Business Mexico,* v. 3, no. 3 (Mar 93), pp. 20 – 23.

United States

Sercan, Cecilia S. Preservation Microforms in an RLIN Environment. *SALALM Papers,* v. 36 (1991), pp. 408 – 417.

INFORMATION TECHNOLOGY

See also
Automation
Computer industry
Geographic information systems

Sol, Ricardo. Nuevo orden planetario: comunicación y neoliberalismo. *Revista de Ciencias Sociales (Costa Rica),* no. 57 (Sept 92), pp. 31 – 39.

Argentina

Testa, Julio C. La incidencia del "contexto organizacional" en el análisis de los procesos de incorporación de las nuevas tecnologías informatizadas: acerca de la constitución de los "espacios de aprendizaje." *Revista Paraguaya de Sociología,* v. 30, no. 86 (Jan – Apr 93), pp. 161 – 183. Bibl.

Brazil

Fernandes, Rosângela. A informática nas relações internacionais. *Revista Brasileira de Estudos Políticos,* no. 76 (Jan 93), pp. 147 – 162. Bibl.

Tonooka, Eduardo Kiyoshi. Política nacional de informática: vinte anos de intervenção governamental. *Estudos Econômicos,* v. 22, no. 2 (May – Aug 92), pp. 273 – 297. Bibl.

Study and teaching

Antônio, Iratí and Claudia Negrão Balby. Computer Training in Brazilian Library Schools. *SALALM Papers,* v. 36 (1991), pp. 347 – 368. Bibl, tables.

Chile

Huneeus, Francisco et al. El libro y la irrupción de los medios audiovisuales: debates. *Mensaje,* v. 42, no. 416 (Jan – Feb 93), pp. 29 – 36.

INLAND WATER TRANSPORTATION

Brazil

Estradas líquidas. *Problemas Brasileiros,* v. 30, no. 295 (Jan – Feb 93), pp. 43 – 44.

Southern Cone of South America

Ravina, Arturo Octavio. Algunos aspectos críticos del Acuerdo de Transporte Fluvial por la Hidrovía Paraguay – Paraná (Puerto Cáceres – Nueva Palmira). *Integración Latinoamericana,* v. 17, no. 185 (Dec 92), pp. 45 – 50.

Sanguinetti, Jorge. Conferencia sobre aspectos socio-políticos y económicos de la hidrovía. *Revista Geográfica (Mexico),* no. 114 (July – Dec 91), pp. 73 – 90. Tables.

INNOCENT VIII, POPE

Marino, Ruggiero. Innocenzo VIII, il papa di Cristoforo Colombo. *Quaderni Ibero-Americani,* no. 72 (Dec 92), pp. 595 – 602. Bibl.

INQUISITION

Mexico

Cruz, Anne J. and Mary Elizabeth Perry, eds. *Cultural Encounters: The Impact of the Inquisition in Spain and the New World* reviewed by Teofilo F. Ruiz. *The Americas,* v. 50, no. 1 (July 93), pp. 121 – 123.

— *Cultural Encounters: The Impact of the Inquisition in Spain and the New World* reviewed by Henry Kamen. *Hispanic American Historical Review,* v. 73, no. 1 (Feb 93), p. 146.

González Casanova, Pablo. *La literatura perseguida por la inquisición* reviewed by Solange Alberro (Review entitled "Regreso de un clásico"). *Nexos,* v. 16, no. 189 (Sept 93), pp. 59 – 61.

Greenleaf, Richard E. and Janin Benedict Warren. *Gonzalo Gómez, primer poblador español de Guayangareo (Morelia): proceso inquisitorial* translated by Alvaro Ochoa S. Reviewed by Frederick P. Bowser. *The Americas,* v. 49, no. 4 (Apr 93), pp. 544 – 545.

Peru

Castañeda Delgado, Paulino and Pilar Hernández Aparicio. *La inquisición en Lima, tomo I: 1570 – 1635* reviewed by Hilda Raquel Zapico. *Revista de Historia de América,* no. 113 (Jan – June 92), pp. 161 – 165.

Guibovich Pérez, Pedro. La cultura libresca de un converso procesado por la inquisición de Lima. *Historia y Cultura (Peru),* no. 20 (1990), pp. 133 – 160+. Bibl.

Millar Carvacho, René. Hechicería, marginalidad e inquisición en el distrito del tribunal de Lima. *Boletín de la Academia Chilena de la Historia,* v. 58 – 59, no. 102 (1991 – 1992), pp. 185 – 227.

Spain

Cruz, Anne J. and Mary Elizabeth Perry, eds. *Cultural Encounters: The Impact of the Inquisition in Spain and the New World* reviewed by Teofilo F. Ruiz. *The Americas,* v. 50, no. 1 (July 93), pp. 121 – 123.

— *Cultural Encounters: The Impact of the Inquisition in Spain and the New World* reviewed by Henry Kamen. *Hispanic American Historical Review,* v. 73, no. 1 (Feb 93), p. 146.

INSECTS

See
> Entomology

INSTITUTO GEOGRÁFICO ARGENTINO

Dodds, Klaus-John. Geography, Identity, and the Creation of the Argentine State. *Bulletin of Latin American Research,* v. 12, no. 3 (Sept 93), pp. 311 – 331. Bibl.

INSTITUTO INDIGENISTA INTERAMERICANO

Favre, Henri. Informe de consultoría. *Anuario Indigenista,* v. 30 (Dec 91), pp. 385 – 403.

Matos Mar, José. Informe de actividades, 1991. *Anuario Indigenista,* v. 30 (Dec 91), pp. 347 – 384.

Organization of American States. Resolución sobre el Instituto Indigenista Interamericano. *Anuario Indigenista,* v. 30 (Dec 91), pp. 345 – 346.

Tejada de Rivero, David. Informe de consultoría. *Anuario Indigenista,* v. 30 (Dec 91), pp. 405 – 423.

INSTITUTO UNIVERSITARIO DE HISTORIA DE COLOMBIA

Cacua Prada, Antonio. 30 años del Instituto Universitario de Historia de Colombia. *Boletín de Historia y Antigüedades,* v. 80, no. 780 (Jan – Mar 93), pp. 121 – 203. Bibl.

Tres décadas del Instituto Universitario de Historia de Colombia. *Boletín de Historia y Antigüedades,* v. 80, no. 781 (Apr – June 93), pp. 491 – 517. Il.

INSURANCE

See also
> Pension trusts

Hilbert, Pia. Politically Correct Coverage. *Business Mexico,* v. 3, no. 11 (Nov 93), pp. 18 – 19. Tables.

Mexico

Russell, Joel. Advice for Insurance Shoppers. *Business Mexico,* v. 3, no. 11 (Nov 93), pp. 27 – 28.

INTEGRALISMO

See
> Fascism

INTELLECTUAL COOPERATION

Colmenares, Hugo. El presidente de Hungría en Caracas: pocas veces los poetas han regido el destino del mundo. *Boletín de la Academia Nacional de la Historia (Venezuela),* v. 75, no. 297 (Jan – Mar 92), pp. 120 – 121.

Díaz Martínez, Manuel. La generación del '27 e Hispanoamérica. *Cuadernos Hispanoamericanos,* no. 514 – 515 (Apr – May 93), pp. 143 – 154. Il.

Informe que envía al Ministerio de Relaciones Exteriores el excelentísimo señor Milos Alcalay, embajador de Venezuela en Rumania, acerca de la misión en Rumania del director de la Academia Nacional de la Historia, dr. Guillermo Morón. *Boletín de la Academia Nacional de la Historia (Venezuela),* v. 75, no. 299 (July – Sept 92), pp. 225 – 231.

Morón Montero, Guillermo. Los portugueses en Venezuela: I Encuentro de las Academias de Historia de Portugal y Venezuela en Lisboa, Portugal, mayo de 1992. *Boletín de la Academia Nacional de la Historia (Venezuela),* v. 76, no. 301 (Jan – Mar 93), pp. 33 – 37. Bibl.

Paxman, Andrew. Art for Sale's Sake. *Business Mexico,* v. 3, no. 3 (Mar 93), pp. 17 – 19. Il.

Salcedo-Bastardo, José Luis. Palabras pronunciadas por el dr. José Luis Salcedo Bastardo en el banquete ofrecido por el consejo académico en el Hotel Mundial, Lisboa, 8 de mayo de 1992. *Boletín de la Academia Nacional de la Historia (Venezuela),* v. 76, no. 301 (Jan – Mar 93), pp. 45 – 46.

Sequera Tamayo, Isbelia. Rumania en Venezuela: en las academia nacionales. *Boletín de la Academia Nacional de la Historia (Venezuela),* v. 75, no. 298 (Apr – June 92), pp. 5 – 7.

Sheridan, Guillermo. "Los Contemporáneos" y la generación del '27: documentando un desencuentro. *Cuadernos Hispanoamericanos,* no. 514 – 515 (Apr – May 93), pp. 185 – 194.

INTELLECTUAL PROPERTY

See also
> Copyright

Economic aspects

Rivas, Juan Antonio. Estructura de mercado, innovación y crecimiento. *Planeación y Desarrollo,* v. 24, no. 2 (May – Aug 93), pp. 73 – 93. Bibl.

Law and legislation

Grupo Andino: Decisión 313; Regimen Común sobre Propiedad Industrial. *Integración Latinoamericana,* v. 18, no. 187 – 188 (Mar – Apr 93), pp. 55 – 64.

Moraga-Rojel, Jubel R. et al. La biotecnología agrícola y la privatización del conocimiento en la transferencia tecnológica universidad – empresa. *Estudios Sociales (Chile),* no. 77 (July – Sept 93), pp. 117 – 137. Bibl.

INTELLECTUALS

See
> Brain drain
> Intellectual cooperation
> Subdivision *Intellectual life* under names of specific countries

INTER-AMERICAN COMMISSION ON HUMAN RIGHTS

Comisión Interamericana de Derechos Humanos: Organización de Estados Americanos. *ECA; Estudios Centroamericanos,* v. 47, no. 528 (Oct 92), pp. 919 – 925.

INTER-AMERICAN DEVELOPMENT BANK

Cortelesse, Claudio. Competitividad de los sistemas productivos y las empresas pequeñas y medianas: campo para la cooperación internacional. *Comercio Exterior,* v. 43, no. 6 (June 93), pp. 519 – 524.

A Market Solution for the Americas? *Report on the Americas,* v. 26, no. 4 (Feb 93), pp. 16 – 17. Charts.

INTER-AMERICAN FOUNDATION

Ritchey-Vance, Marion. Grassroots Development Results: Widening the Lens. *Grassroots Development,* v. 17, no. 1 (1993), pp. 42 – 43. Charts.

INTER-AMERICAN INSTITUTE FOR COOPERATION ON AGRICULTURE

Black, David L. IICA Reaps the Seeds of a Half Century. *Américas,* v. 45, no. 4 (July – Aug 93), pp. 56 – 57. Il.

INTEREST RATES

Mexico

Trigueros Legarreta, Ignacio. Programas de estabilización sin credibilidad e intermediación financiera. *El Trimestre Económico,* v. 59, no. 236 (Oct – Dec 92), pp. 641 – 655. Bibl, tables, charts.

Trinidad and Tobago
Mathematical models

Watson, Patrick Kent. Savings, the Rate of Interest, and Growth in a Small Open Economy: The Trinidad and Tobago Experience. *Social and Economic Studies,* v. 41, no. 4 (Dec 92), pp. 1 – 23. Tables, charts.

INTERNATIONAL BUSINESS ENTERPRISES

See also
> Cartels and commodity agreements
> Investments, Foreign
> Names of specific corporations

Baena Paz, Guillermina. Perspectivas de la comunicación en los noventa. *Revista Mexicana de Ciencias Políticas y Sociales*, v. 38, Nueva época, no. 154 (Oct – Dec 93), pp. 103 – 114.

Galloway, Jonathan F. ¿Industrias globales? *Revista Mexicana de Sociología*, v. 54, no. 2 (Apr – June 92), pp. 75 – 100. Bibl, tables, charts.

Mortimore, Michael D. A New International Industrial Order. *CEPAL Review*, no. 48 (Dec 92), pp. 39 – 59. Bibl, tables, charts.

Peritore, N. Patrick. El surgimiento del cártel biotecnológico. *Revista Mexicana de Sociología*, v. 54, no. 2 (Apr – June 92), pp. 101 – 131. Bibl, tables.

Developing countries

Alvarez Icaza, Pablo. Marco teórico de la industria maquiladora de exportación. *Comercio Exterior*, v. 43, no. 5 (May 93), pp. 415 – 429. Bibl.

Mexico

Russell, Joel. Advice for Insurance Shoppers. *Business Mexico*, v. 3, no. 11 (Nov 93), pp. 27 – 28.

— A Worldwide Brand Name. *Business Mexico*, v. 3, no. 10 (Oct 93), pp. 12 – 14. Il.

Sklair, Leslie. Las maquilas en México: una perspectiva global. *Revista Mexicana de Sociología*, v. 54, no. 2 (Apr – June 92), pp. 163 – 183. Bibl.

Handbooks, manuals, etc.

Newman, Gray and Anna Szterenfeld. *Business International's Guide to Doing Business in Mexico* reviewed by Donald McCarthy (Review entitled "Help for Corporate Strategists"). *Business Mexico*, v. 3, no. 3 (Mar 93), p. 52.

INTERNATIONAL BUSINESS MACHINES CORPORATION

Vasconcelos, Isabella Francisca Freitas Gouvêa de. IBM: o desafio da mudança. *RAE; Revista de Administração de Empresas*, v. 33, no. 3 (May – June 93), pp. 84 – 97. Bibl.

INTERNATIONAL ECONOMIC INTEGRATION

Argenti, Gisela et al. *Pequeños países en la integración: oportunidades y riesgos* (Review). *Integración Latinoamericana*, v. 18, no. 187 – 188 (Mar – Apr 93), pp. 69 – 70.

Baldinelli, Elvio. Políticas monetarias y fiscales en la integración regional. *Integración Latinoamericana*, v. 18, no. 189 – 190 (May – June 93), pp. 28 – 37. Bibl, tables.

Barbosa, Margareth L. and Rosa M. O. Fontes. Efeitos da integração econômica do MERCOSUL e da Europa na competitividade das exportações brasileiras de soja. *Revista de Economia e Sociologia Rural*, v. 29, no. 4 (Oct – Dec 91), pp. 335 – 351. Bibl, tables.

Gill, Henry S. The Caribbean in a World of Economic Blocks. *Social and Economic Studies*, v. 41, no. 3 (Sept 92), pp. 25 – 36.

Pelkmans, Jacques. Comparando las integraciones económicas: prerrequisitos, opciones e implicaciones. *Integración Latinoamericana*, v. 18, no. 191 (July 93), pp. 3 – 17. Tables.

Salgado, Germánico. Modelo y políticas de integración. *Integración Latinoamericana*, v. 18, no. 186 (Jan – Feb 93), pp. 12 – 19. Bibl.

Valenciano, Eugenio O. *Disparidades regionales e integración económica* (Review). *Integración Latinoamericana*, v. 18, no. 189 – 190 (May – June 93), pp. 59 – 60.

Villagrán Kramer, Francisco. La integración económica y la justicia. *Integración Latinoamericana*, v. 18, no. 187 – 188 (Mar – Apr 93), pp. 35 – 47. Bibl.

Bibliography

Bibliografía: integración económica. *Estudios Internacionales (Chile)*, v. 26, no. 101 (Jan – Mar 93), pp. 123 – 131.

INTERNATIONAL ECONOMIC RELATIONS

See also
 Andean Common Market
 Caribbean Community
 Central American Common Market
 Currency question
 Embargo
 Foreign trade promotion
 Foreign trade regulation
 General Agreement on Tariffs and Trade
 International business enterprises
 International finance
 Latin American Integration Association
 Pan-Pacific relations
 Subdivision *Foreign economic relations* under names of specific countries

Agosin, Manuel Roberto and Diana A. Tussie de Federman. Nuevos dilemas en la política comercial para el desarrollo (Excerpt from the introduction to the forthcoming book *Trading Places: New Dilemmas in Trade Policy for Development*, edited by Manuel R. Agosin and Diana Tussie, translated by Adriana Hierro). *Comercio Exterior*, v. 43, no. 10 (Oct 93), pp. 899 – 912. Bibl, tables.

Alvarez Padilla, Alfredo. La cultura empresarial en el nuevo orden económico internacional. *El Cotidiano*, v. 10, no. 58 (Oct – Nov 93), pp. 112 – 115.

Benavente, José Miguel and Peter J. West. Globalization and Convergence: Latin America in a Changing World. *CEPAL Review*, no. 47 (Aug 92), pp. 77 – 94. Bibl, charts.

Calcagno, Alfredo Eric. *Estructura y funciones actuales de los organismos internacionales financieros y económicos* (Review). *Integración Latinoamericana*, v. 18, no. 195 (Nov 93), p. 57.

Choi, Dae Won. Globalização na era pacífico. *Vozes*, v. 87, no. 4 (July – Aug 93), pp. 13 – 19.

Dávila Aldás, Francisco Rafael. La revolución científica – técnica, la globalización industrial, la formación de bloques y los nuevos cambios mundiales. *Relaciones Internacionales (Mexico)*, v. 15, Nueva época, no. 58 (Apr – June 93), pp. 15 – 23.

Ferrer, Aldo. Nuevos paradigmas tecnológicos y desarrollo sostenible: perspectiva latinoamericana. *Comercio Exterior*, v. 43, no. 9 (Sept 93), pp. 807 – 813. Bibl.

Frank, André Gunder. América Latina al margen de la historia del sistema mundial (Translated by Hernán G. H. Taboada). *Cuadernos Americanos*, no. 39, Nueva época (May – June 93), pp. 114 – 133. Bibl, tables.

— América Latina al margen del sistema mundial: historia y presente. *Nueva Sociedad*, no. 123 (Jan – Feb 93), pp. 23 – 34. Bibl, tables.

Furtado, Celso. La cosmovisión de Prebisch: una visión actual. *Estudios Internacionales (Chile)*, v. 26, no. 101 (Jan – Mar 93), pp. 89 – 97. Bibl.

— A ordem mundial emergente e o Brasil. *Vozes*, v. 86, no. 5 (Sept – Oct 92), pp. 21 – 25.

González Rubí, Rafael. América Latina y las barreras no arancelarias de los gigantes económicos. *Comercio Exterior*, v. 43, no. 3 (Mar 93), pp. 248 – 253. Bibl.

Guerra Borges, Alfredo. Nuevo contexto mundial para América Latina. *Integración Latinoamericana*, v. 18, no. 192 (Aug 93), pp. 3 – 10. Bibl.

Hachette, Dominique. Estrategias de globalización del comercio. *Estudios Públicos (Chile)*, no. 51 (Winter 93), pp. 45 – 85. Bibl, tables, charts.

Henwood, Doug. Impeccable Logic: Trade, Development, and Free Markets in the Clinton Era. *NACLA Report on the Americas*, v. 26, no. 5 (May 93), pp. 23 – 28 +. Bibl, il.

Ibarra Muñoz, David. Interdependencia y desarrollo (Excerpt from a forthcoming book). *Comercio Exterior*, v. 43, no. 11 (Nov 93), pp. 991 – 1000.

Loría Díaz, Eduardo. La recuperación económica mundial y los ciclos de largo plazo. *Comercio Exterior*, v. 43, no. 10 (Oct 93), pp. 933 – 939. Bibl, tables.

Moneta, Carlos Juan. Alternativas de la integración en el contexto de la globalización. *Nueva Sociedad*, no. 125 (May – June 93), pp. 80 – 97. Bibl, tables.

Smith, Peter H. Latin America and the New World Order. *SALALM Papers*, v. 36 (1991), pp. 3 – 9.

Sol, Ricardo. Nuevo orden planetario: comunicación y neoliberalismo. *Revista de Ciencias Sociales (Costa Rica)*, no. 57 (Sept 92), pp. 31 – 39.

Thurow, Lester C. Estados Unidos y la economía mundial (Translated by Isabel Vericat). *Nexos,* v. 16, no. 187 (July 93), pp. 22 – 24.

Tomassini, Luciano et al. *La política internacional en un mundo post-moderno* (Review). *Integración Latinoamericana,* v. 18, no. 192 (Aug 92), pp. 95 – 96.

Vidal, José Walter Bautista. *Soberania e dignidade: raízes da sobrevivência* (Review). *Vozes,* v. 86, no. 4 (July – Aug 92), pp. 89 – 90.

Watkins, Kevin. El GATT y el Tercer Mundo: como establecer las normas (Excerpt from *Fixing the Rules: North – South Issues in International Trade and the GATT Uruguay Round,* translated by Cecilia M. Mata). *Realidad Económica,* no. 113 (Jan – Feb 93), pp. 122 – 141.

INTERNATIONAL FINANCE

See also
Currency question

Armendáriz de Aghion, Beatriz. El precio de los bonos, las razones deuda – exportación y las moratorias en el servicio de la deuda exterior de un país: el caso de México. *El Trimestre Económico,* v. 60, no. 237 (Jan – Mar 93), pp. 185 – 202. Bibl, tables, charts.

Calcagno, Alfredo Eric. *Estructura y funciones actuales de los organismos internacionales financieros y económicos* (Review). *Integración Latinoamericana,* v. 18, no. 195 (Nov 93), p. 57.

Olivier, Michele. Global Finance for Mexican Corporations. *Business Mexico,* v. 3, no. 7 (July 93), p. 27 +. Tables.

Santos, Theotonio dos. Globalización financiera y estrategias de desarrollo. *Nueva Sociedad,* no. 126 (July – Aug 93), pp. 98 – 109.

INTERNATIONAL LABOR ORGANIZATION
Law and legislation
Huertas Bartolomé, Tebelia. Libertad sindical, tratados internacionales y constitución. *ECA; Estudios Centroamericanos,* v. 48, no. 537 – 538 (July – Aug 93), pp. 657 – 675. Bibl, il.

INTERNATIONAL LAW

América Central: Convenio del Estatuto de la Corte Centroamericana de Justicia. *Integración Latinoamericana,* v. 18, no. 191 (July 93), pp. 57 – 60.

Boggiano, Antonio. Justicia supranacional en América Latina y el Caribe: alternativas para la creación de un sistema. *Integración Latinoamericana,* v. 18, no. 189 – 190 (May – June 93), pp. 18 – 27. Bibl.

Glennon, Michael J. Testimony before the Subcommittee on Civil and Constitutional Rights, Committee on the Judiciary, United States House of Representatives. *Mexican Studies,* v. 9, no. 1 (Winter 93), pp. 1 – 17.

Labariega Villanueva, Pedro Gabriel. La adopción internacional de menores y sus repercusiones en las relaciones internacionales. *Relaciones Internacionales (Mexico),* v. 14, Nueva época, no. 55 (July – Sept 92), pp. 61 – 64. Charts.

Mattarollo, Rodolfo. Proceso a la impunidad de crímenes de lesa humanidad en América Latina, 1989 – 1991. *ECA; Estudios Centroamericanos,* v. 47, no. 528 (Oct 92), pp. 867 – 882. Bibl, il.

Mello, Celso Duvivier de Albuquerque. O Brasil e o direito internacional na nova ordem mundial. *Revista Brasileira de Estudos Políticos,* no. 76 (Jan 93), pp. 7 – 26. Bibl.

Romany, Celina. Hacia una crítica feminista del derecho internacional en materia de derechos humanos. *Fem,* v. 17, no. 126 (Aug 93), pp. 19 – 22.

Tushnet, Mark V. *Central America and the Law: The Constitution, Civil Liberties, and the Courts* reviewed by Jorge Luján Muñoz. *Mesoamérica (USA),* v. 13, no. 24 (Dec 92), pp. 464 – 465.

Villagrán Kramer, Francisco. La integración económica y la justicia. *Integración Latinoamericana,* v. 18, no. 187 – 188 (Mar – Apr 93), pp. 35 – 47. Bibl.

Study and teaching
Caminos, Hugo. Staying on Course with Law (Translated by Willem Daniels). *Américas,* v. 45, no. 5 (Sept – Oct 93), pp. 56 – 57.

INTERNATIONAL RELATIONS

See also
Boundaries
Embargo
Geopolitics
International economic relations
Pan-Americanism
Pan-Pacific relations
War
Subdivision *Foreign relations* under names of specific countries

Broad, Dave. Revolution, Counterrevolution, and Imperialism: "¡La lucha continúa!" *Latin American Perspectives,* v. 20, no. 2 (Spring 93), pp. 6 – 20. Bibl.

Cardoso Vargas, Gilberto A. Iberoamérica ante la agenda internacional de fin de siglo. *Problemas del Desarrollo,* v. 24, no. 94 (July – Sept 93), pp. 275 – 281.

Dávila Aldás, Francisco Rafael and Edgar Ortiz. Del antagonismo a la cooperación entre el Este y el Oeste para la búsqueda de un mundo más humano. *Revista Mexicana de Ciencias Políticas y Sociales,* v. 37, Nueva época, no. 149 (July – Sept 92), pp. 49 – 81.

Declaración final del Consejo de Interacción. *El Trimestre Económico,* v. 60, no. 237 (Jan – Mar 93), pp. 203 – 211.

Faure, Guy Olivier. Teoría de la negociación: el giro interdisciplinario. *Revista Mexicana de Sociología,* v. 54, no. 2 (Apr – June 92), pp. 233 – 242. Bibl.

Fernandes, Rosângela. A informática nas relações internacionais. *Revista Brasileira de Estudos Políticos,* no. 76 (Jan 93), pp. 147 – 162. Bibl.

Hernández Vela Salgado, Edmundo. El Sistema Interamericano ante los cambios mundiales. *Relaciones Internacionales (Mexico),* v. 14, Nueva época, no. 56 (Oct – Dec 92), pp. 31 – 34. Bibl.

Mateo y Sousa, Eligio de. De la geopolítica a la geoeconomía: una lectura del siglo XX. *Comercio Exterior,* v. 43, no. 10 (Oct 93), pp. 974 – 978.

Russell, Roberto G. Reflexiones sobre lo "nuevo" del "nuevo orden mundial." *Estudios Internacionales (Chile),* v. 26, no. 102 (Apr – June 93), pp. 134 – 154. Bibl.

Toro Dávila, Agustín. El espacio en la perspectiva de un nuevo orden político – estratégico internacional. *Estudios Internacionales (Chile),* v. 26, no. 102 (Apr – June 93), pp. 253 – 267. Bibl.

Vidales, Raúl. Fin de la historia: "¿Fin de la utopía?"; frente a los 500 años. *Cristianismo y Sociedad,* v. 30, no. 113 (1992), pp. 53 – 84. Bibl.

Zea, Leopoldo. Filosofía de las relaciones de América Latina con el mundo. *Cuadernos Americanos,* no. 41, Nueva época (Sept – Oct 93), pp. 93 – 100.

Bibliography
Bibliografía: nuevo orden mundial. *Estudios Internacionales (Chile),* v. 26, no. 102 (Apr – June 93), pp. 275 – 281.

INTERNATIONALIZATION OF CAPITAL
See
Capital
International finance

INTERPERSONAL RELATIONS
See
Industrial sociology
Labor relations
Parent and child
Sexual behavior

INVESTMENTS
See
Capital investments
Finance
Saving and investment

INVESTMENTS, FOREIGN

Andean region

Miller, Rory M. Transferencia de técnicas: la construcción y administración de ferrocarriles en la costa occidental de Sudamérica (Translated by Isabel Cristina Mata Velázquez). *Siglo XIX: Cuadernos*, v. 3, no. 7 (Oct 93), pp. 65 – 102. Bibl, maps.

Argentina

Sánchez, Miguel Alberto. Privatizaciones y extranjerización de la economía argentina. *Realidad Económica*, no. 116 (May – June 93), pp. 33 – 45.

Brazil

Cobbs, Elizabeth Anne. *The Rich Neighbor Policy: Rockefeller and Kaiser in Brazil* reviewed by Joel Wolfe. *Hispanic American Historical Review*, v. 73, no. 3 (Aug 93), pp. 538 – 539.

Encanto perdido. *Problemas Brasileiros*, v. 30, no. 295 (Jan – Feb 93), pp. 28 – 29. Il.

Chile

Rojas Flores, Gonzalo. La casa comercial Gibbs y Co. y sus inversiones en Chile entre las décadas de 1920 y 1940. *Historia (Chile)*, no. 26 (1991 – 1992), pp. 259 – 295. Bibl.

Developing countries

Hilbert, Pia. Politically Correct Coverage. *Business Mexico*, v. 3, no. 11 (Nov 93), pp. 18 – 19. Tables.

Latin America

Fuentes, Juan Alberto. European Investment in Latin America: An Overview. *CEPAL Review*, no. 48 (Dec 92), pp. 61 – 81. Bibl, tables, charts.

Kuwayama, Mikio. Nuevas formas de inversión en el comercio entre América Latina y Estados Unidos (Translated by Adriana Hierro). *Comercio Exterior*, v. 43, no. 5 (May 93), pp. 478 – 497. Bibl.

Nuevas modalidades de financiamiento externo de América Latina y el Caribe. *Comercio Exterior*, v. 43, no. 5 (May 93), pp. 474 – 477.

Peres Núñez, Wilson. The Internationalization of Latin American Industrial Firms. *CEPAL Review*, no. 49 (Apr 93), pp. 55 – 74. Bibl, tables.

Young, George F. W. German Banking and German Imperialism in Latin America in the Wilhelmine Era. *Ibero-Amerikanisches Archiv*, v. 18, no. 1 – 2 (1992), pp. 31 – 66. Bibl, tables.

Mexico

Arellanes Jiménez, Paulino E. Crisis capitalista e inversiones extranjeras directas: las norteamericanas en México. *Revista Mexicana de Ciencias Políticas y Sociales*, v. 38, Nueva época, no. 153 (July – Sept 93), pp. 61 – 90. Bibl, tables.

Brown, Jonathan C. *Oil and Revolution in Mexico* reviewed by Rebeca de Gortari Rabiela. *Revista Mexicana de Sociología*, v. 55, no. 2 (Apr – June 93), pp. 389 – 395.

Carlsen, Laura. Making Money in Difficult Times. *Business Mexico*, v. 3, no. 11 (Nov 93), pp. 4 – 7. Tables, charts.

Castro Martínez, Pedro Fernando. Comercio e inversiones México – Canadá: un asunto trilateral. *Comercio Exterior*, v. 43, no. 5 (May 93), pp. 498 – 506. Bibl, tables.

La inversión extranjera en México. *Comercio Exterior*, v. 43, no. 3 (Mar 93), pp. 211 – 216. Tables.

Ortiz, Edgar. TLC e inversión extranjera en México. *Comercio Exterior*, v. 43, no. 10 (Oct 93), pp. 967 – 973. Bibl.

Romero Gil, Juan Manuel. Minería y sociedad en el noroeste porfirista. *Siglo XIX: Cuadernos*, v. 1, no. 1 (Oct 91), pp. 37 – 73. Bibl, tables.

Whiting, Van R., Jr. *The Political Economy of Foreign Investment in Mexico: Nationalism, Liberalism, and Constraints on Choice* reviewed by Sylvia Maxfield. *Journal of Latin American Studies*, v. 25, no. 3 (Oct 93), pp. 682 – 683.

Law and legislation

Rogers, John E. NAFTA Dispute Settlement for the Finance Sector. *Business Mexico*, v. 3, no. 6 (June 93), pp. 40 – 42.

Pacific Area

Palacios L., Juan José. Inversión e integración regional en el Pacífico: entre los acuerdos y los procesos "naturales." *Comercio Exterior*, v. 43, no. 12 (Dec 93), pp. 1128 – 1138. Bibl, tables.

Peru

Boza Dibós, Beatriz. Obstáculo a la inversión extranjera. *Debate (Peru)*, v. 16, no. 75 (Dec 93 – Jan 94), pp. 50 – 51.

IQUITOS, PERU

Chibnik, Michael and Wil de Jong. Organización de la mano de obra agrícola en las comunidades ribereñas de la Amazonía peruana. *Amazonía Peruana*, v. 11, no. 21 (Sept 92), pp. 181 – 215. Bibl.

IRELAND

See

Artists – Ireland

IRISARRI, ANTONIO JOSÉ DE

Criticism of specific works

El cristiano errante

Sanabria, Carolina. *El cristiano errante:* ¿Novela que tiene mucho de historia o historia que contiene mucho de novela?; consideraciones teóricas sobre el discurso crítico contemporáneo. *Káñina*, v. 16, no. 2 (July – Dec 92), pp. 31 – 38. Bibl.

IRON INDUSTRY AND TRADE

Spain

Uriarte Ayo, R. The Hispanic American Market and Iron Production in the Basque Country, 1700 – 1825. *Ibero Americana (Sweden)*, v. 22, no. 2 (Dec 92), pp. 47 – 65. Bibl, tables, charts.

IRONY IN LITERATURE

Thwaites, Jeanne. The Use of Irony in Oscar Zeta Acosta's *Autobiography of a Brown Buffalo*. *The Americas Review*, v. 20, no. 1 (Spring 92), pp. 73 – 82. Bibl.

Vázquez Arce, Carmen. Los desastres de la guerra: sobre la articulación de la ironía en los cuentos "La recién nacida sangre," de Luis Rafael Sánchez y "El momento divino de Caruso Llompart," de Félix Córdova Iturregui. *Revista Iberoamericana*, v. 59, no. 162 – 163 (Jan – June 93), pp. 187 – 201. Bibl.

Zubieta, Ana María. El humor y el problema de narrar las diferencias. *Escritura (Venezuela)*, v. 17, no. 33 – 34 (Jan – Dec 92), pp. 61 – 82.

IRRIGATION

See

Water

Subdivision *Agriculture* under names of Indians groups

ISABEL I, LA CATÓLICA, QUEEN OF SPAIN

Briceño Perozo, Mario. Isabel I de Castilla. *Boletín de la Academia Nacional de la Historia (Venezuela)*, v. 75, no. 300 (Oct – Dec 92), pp. 113 – 115.

ISLAM

Benson, LeGrace. Some Observations on West African Islamic Motifs and Haitian Religious Art. *Journal of Caribbean Studies*, v. 9, no. 1 – 2 (Winter 92 – Spring 93), pp. 59 – 66. Bibl.

ISLAS, CARLOS JUAN

Criticism of specific works

Los recuerdos del tiempo

Peruyero Sánchez, Alfredo. *Los recuerdos del tiempo* de Carlos Juan Islas. *La Palabra y el Hombre*, no. 84 (Oct – Dec 92), pp. 259 – 267. Il.

ISLAS MALVINAS

See

Falkland Islands

ISRAEL

See also

Latin American literature – Israel

Metz, Allan Sheldon. Cuban – Israeli Relations: From the Cuban Revolution to the New World Order. *Cuban Studies/ Estudios Cubanos*, v. 23 (1993), pp. 113 – 134. Bibl.

Bibliography

Metz, Allan Sheldon. Israeli Military Assistance to Latin America (Review article). *Latin American Research Review*, v. 28, no. 2 (1993), pp. 257 – 263.

ISVELBERG, IARA

Patarra, Judith Lieblich. *Iara* reviewed by Marco Aurélio Garcia (Review entitled "Iara: história e cotidiano"). *Estudos Feministas*, v. 1, no. 1 (1993), pp. 210 – 212. Bibl.

ITALIANS

Argentina

Alcorta, Rodrigo. Artesanos del pan de Navidad. *Todo Es Historia*, v. 26, no. 305 (Dec 92), pp. 50 – 53. Il.

Correa, Alejandra. La pasión según los Sábato. *Todo Es Historia*, v. 26, no. 305 (Dec 92), pp. 85 – 94. Bibl, il.

Korn, Francis. Il popolo minuto: La Boca, 1895. *Todo Es Historia*, v. 26, no. 305 (Dec 92), pp. 46 – 49. Il.

Montserrat, Marcelo. La influencia italiana en el desarrollo científico argentino. *Todo Es Historia*, v. 26, no. 305 (Dec 92), pp. 8 – 19. Bibl, il.

Pujol, Sergio Alejandro. Un estilo italiano. *Todo Es Historia*, v. 26, no. 305 (Dec 92), pp. 28 – 33. Bibl, il.

Satas, Hugo Raúl. El pensamiento italiano del siglo XIX en la sociedad argentina. *Todo Es Historia*, v. 26, no. 305 (Dec 92), pp. 40 – 44. Il.

Vidal Buzzi, Fernando. De pizzas y ravioles. *Todo Es Historia*, v. 26, no. 305 (Dec 92), pp. 22 – 26. Il.

Brazil

Silva, Sonia T. Dias Gonçalves da. A colonização italiana no sul do Brasil em "posters." *SALALM Papers*, v. 34 (1989), pp. 177 – 182. Bibl.

Mexico

Fanesi, Pietro Rinaldo. El exilio antifascista en América Latina: el caso mexicano; Mario Montagnana y la "Garibaldi," 1941 – 1945. *Estudios Interdisciplinarios de América Latina y el Caribe*, v. 3, no. 2 (July – Dec 92), pp. 39 – 57. Bibl.

ITALY

See also

Archives – Italy
Books – Italy
Exiles – Italy
Folk lore – Italy
Opera – Italy

Barbano, Filippo et al, eds. *Sociologia, storia, positivismo: Messico, Brasile, Argentina e l'Italia* reviewed by Carlos Strasser (Review entitled "Sobre la formación y ciertas influencias en el desarrollo de las ciencias sociales latinoamericanas: una importante contribución italo-argentina"). *Desarrollo Económico (Argentina)*, v. 32, no. 128 (Jan – Mar 93), pp. 625 – 628.

— *Sociologia, storia, positivismo: Messico, Brasile, Argentina e l'Italia* reviewed by Giorgio Alberti. *Journal of Latin American Studies*, v. 25, no. 2 (May 93), pp. 417 – 418.

Clementi, Hebe. Homenaje a Las Marcas: el país de mis ancestros. *Todo Es Historia*, v. 26, no. 305 (Dec 92), pp. 70 – 80. Bibl, il.

Martinic Drpic, Zvonimir. El tribunal arbitral italo – chileno y las reclamaciones italianas de los poseedores de certificados salitreros: evolución histórica de la problemática. *Cuadernos de Historia (Chile)*, no. 11 (Dec 91), pp. 71 – 104. Bibl, tables.

Micheli, Alfredo de. Un mexicano en la Italia del siglo de las luces. *La Palabra y el Hombre*, no. 81 (Jan – Mar 92), pp. 85 – 93. Bibl, il.

ITURBIDE, GRACIELA

Ferrer, Elizabeth. Manos poderosas: The Photography of Graciela Iturbide. *Review*, no. 47 (Fall 93), pp. 69 – 78. Il.

ITURRIA, IGNACIO

Palomero, Federica. Ignacio Iturria (Accompanied by an English translation). *Art Nexus*, no. 7 (Jan – Mar 93), pp. 88 – 90. Il.

IXTLILXÓCHITL ALVA, FERNANDO DE

Criticism of specific works

Relaciones históricas

Calvi, Maria Vittoria. El diálogo entre españoles e indígenas en la *XIII relación* de Fernando de Alva Ixtlilxóchitl. *Quaderni Ibero-Americani*, no. 72 (Dec 92), pp. 621 – 639. Bibl.

IZQUIERDO FERNÁNDEZ, GONZALO

Obituaries

Krebs Wilckens, Ricardo. Don Gonzalo Izquierdo Fernández. *Boletín de la Academia Chilena de la Historia*, v. 58 – 59, no. 102 (1991 – 1992), pp. 33 – 38.

Silva Galdames, Osvaldo. Gonzalo Izquierdo Fernández (1932 – 1990). *Cuadernos de Historia (Chile)*, no. 11 (Dec 91), pp. 7 – 12. Il.

JACALTENANGO, GUATEMALA

Lovell, William George. Los registros parroquiales de Jacaltenango, Guatemala. *Mesoamérica (USA)*, v. 13, no. 24 (Dec 92), pp. 441 – 453.

JAGAN, CHEDDI

Interviews

Maingot, Anthony Peter. Cheddi Jagan and Democracy: An Interview. *Hemisphere*, v. 5, no. 2 (Winter – Spring 93), pp. 36 – 39. Il.

JALAPA, MEXICO

Blázquez Domínguez, Carmen. Dos años críticos: la expulsión de los españoles en Xalapa y Veracruz, 1827 – 1828. *Siglo XIX: Cuadernos*, v. 2, no. 4 (Oct 92), pp. 31 – 58. Bibl.

Florescano Mayet, Sergio. Xalapa y su región durante el siglo XIX: las principales vertientes de su desarrollo económico, social y político. *La Palabra y el Hombre*, no. 83 (July – Sept 92), pp. 135 – 165. Bibl, tables.

JALISCO, MEXICO

Arroyo Alejandre, Jesús and Luis A. Velázquez Gutiérrez. La transición de los patrones migratorios y las ciudades medias. *Estudios Demográficos y Urbanos*, v. 7, no. 2 – 3 (May – Dec 92), pp. 555 – 574. Bibl, tables.

Jáuregui Moreno, Jesús Manuel. El rancho de Mariachi en 1837. *Plural (Mexico)*, v. 22, no. 261 (June 93), pp. 85 – 93. Bibl.

Rodríguez García, Rubén. *La Cámara Agrícola Nacional Jalisciense: una sociedad de terratenientes en la revolución mexicana* reviewed by Carlos Alba Vega. *Foro Internacional*, v. 32, no. 5 (Oct – Dec 92), pp. 788 – 793.

JAMAICA

See also

Agriculture – Jamaica
Archaeology – Jamaica
Art – Jamaica
Balance of payments – Jamaica
Bauxite – Jamaica
Blacks – Jamaica
Community development – Jamaica
Dams and reservoirs – Jamaica
Ecology – Jamaica
Education, Secondary – Jamaica
Educational sociology – Jamaica
Food habits – Jamaica
Foreign exchange problem – Jamaica
Forests – Jamaica
Geographical distribution of plants and animals – Jamaica
Harbors – Jamaica
Liberation theology – Jamaica
Marketing – Jamaica
Mime – Jamaica
Patronage, Political – Jamaica
Physicians – Jamaica
Port Royal, Jamaica

Public administration – Jamaica
Race discrimination – Jamaica
Ras Tafari movement
Religion and sociology – Jamaica
Soils – Jamaica
Sports – Jamaica
Taxation – Jamaica
Women artists – Jamaica
Zoology – Jamaica

Economic policy

Auty, Richard M. Intensified Dependence on a Maturing Mining Sector: The Jamaican Bauxite Levy. *Caribbean Geography,* v. 3, no. 3 (Mar 92), pp. 143 – 159. Bibl, tables.

Stephens, Evelyne Huber and John D. Stephens. Changing Development Models in Small Economies: The Case of Jamaica from the 1950s to the 1990s. *Studies in Comparative International Development,* v. 27, no. 3 (Fall 92), pp. 57 – 92. Bibl, tables.

History

Bryan, Patrick. Spanish Jamaica. *Caribbean Quarterly,* v. 38, no. 2 – 3 (June – Sept 92), pp. 21 – 31.

Holt, Thomas C. *The Problem of Freedom: Race, Labor, and Politics in Jamaica and Britain, 1832 – 1938* reviewed by Alex Lichtenstein. *Hispanic American Historical Review,* v. 73, no. 2 (May 93), pp. 347 – 349.

Politics and government

Edie, Carlene J. *Democracy by Default: Dependency and Clientelism in Jamaica* reviewed by Tony Thorndike. *Studies in Comparative International Development,* v. 27, no. 2 (Summer 92), pp. 108 – 110.

Jones, Edwin. *Development Administration: Jamaican Adaptation* reviewed by Ian Boxill. *Social and Economic Studies,* v. 41, no. 3 (Sept 92), pp. 180 – 182.

JAMAICA IN LITERATURE

Hudson, Brian J. The Landscapes of Cayuna: Jamaica through the Senses of John Hearne. *Caribbean Geography,* v. 3, no. 3 (Mar 92), pp. 187 – 199. Bibl.

JAMES, DANIEL

Interviews

Hora, Roy and Javier A. Trimboli. Entrevista al historiador Daniel James. *Todo Es Historia,* v. 27, no. 314 (Sept 93), pp. 24 – 30. Il.

JAMES, THE GREATER

Myers, Joan et al. *Santiago: Saint of Two Worlds.* Photographs by Joan Myers. Reviewed by Jeffrey Klaiber. *Hispanic American Historical Review,* v. 73, no. 3 (Aug 93), p. 492.

JAPAN

See
Public administration – Japan

JAPANESE

Argentina

Higa, Jorge. La Argentina vista con ojos oblícuos. *Todo Es Historia,* v. 27, no. 316 (Nov 93), pp. 60 – 80. Il, maps.

Peru

Lausent Herrera, Isabelle. *Pasado y presente de la comunidad japonesa en el Perú* reviewed by Mariana Mould de Pease. *Bulletin de l'Institut Français d'Etudes Andines,* v. 21, no. 2 (1992), pp. 788 – 789.

JARDIM, ANTÔNIO DA SILVA

Wehrs, Carlos. Pelo centenário de morte de Antônio da Silva Jardim, 1891 – 1991. *Revista do Instituto Histórico e Geográfico Brasileiro,* no. 372 (July – Sept 91), pp. 775 – 784. Bibl.

JESUITS

Centro de Espiritualidad Ignaciana. Decálogo de nuestra espiritualidad. *Mensaje,* v. 42, no. 420 (July 93), pp. 196 – 197. Il.

Montes M., Fernando. ¿La Compañía de Jesús sigue siendo la misma? *Mensaje,* v. 42, no. 420 (July 93), pp. 186 – 189. Il, tables.

Bolivia

Arenas Frutos, Isabel and Carmen Cebrián González. Situación de la provincia del Perú a finales del siglo XVI: *La crónica anónima de 1600. Anuario de Estudios Americanos,* v. 49, Suppl. 2 (1992), pp. 11 – 29. Tables.

Romero Romero, Catalina. Tres bibliotecas jesuitas en pueblos de misión: Buenavista, Paila y Santa Rosa en la región de Moxos. *Revista de Indias,* v. 52, no. 195 – 196 (May – Dec 92), pp. 889 – 921.

Brazil

Terra, J. Evangelista Martins. Motivação religiosa dos descobrimentos. *Revista do Instituto Histórico e Geográfico Brasileiro,* no. 373 (Oct – Dec 91), pp. 1145 – 1175.

Chile

Arenas, José. El retorno de los jesuitas en el siglo XIX: el no-restablecimiento de la Compañía de Jesús en Chile. *Mensaje,* v. 42, no. 420 (July 93), pp. 253 – 258. Il, facs.

Ariztía, Fernando. La Compañía de Jesús en la nueva evangelización. *Mensaje,* v. 42, no. 420 (July 93), p. 329.

Arriagada, Eduardo. La política a la manera de Ignacio de Loyola. *Mensaje,* v. 42, no. 420 (July 93), pp. 317 – 321. Il.

Barrios V., Marciano. Jesuitas en la Facultad de Teología de la Universidad Católica. *Mensaje,* v. 42, no. 420 (July 93), pp. 293 – 296. Il.

Contreras, Juan Pablo. La formación de los jóvenes jesuitas hoy. *Mensaje,* v. 42, no. 420 (July 93), pp. 198 – 204. Il.

Cruz Ovalle de Amenábar, Isabel. Arte jesuita en Chile: la huella del barroco bávaro. *Mensaje,* v. 42, no. 420 (July 93), pp. 234 – 238. Il.

Etcheberry, Blanca. Empresarios formados por la Compañía de Jesús: un acercamiento de este último tiempo. *Mensaje,* v. 42, no. 420 (July 93), pp. 322 – 325. Il.

Galecio, Jorge. El trabajo de los jesuitas en la educación. *Mensaje,* v. 42, no. 420 (July 93), pp. 275 – 279. Il.

Gana, Víctor. Jesuitas en la región de Antofagasta. *Mensaje,* v. 42, no. 420 (July 93), p. 297.

Garretón Merino, Manuel Antonio. Los jesuitas y el pensamiento social de los sesenta en Chile. *Mensaje,* v. 42, no. 420 (July 93), pp. 298 – 303. Il.

Godoy Urzúa, Hernán. La hegemonía cultural jesuita y el barroco. *Mensaje,* v. 42, no. 420 (July 93), pp. 228 – 233. Il.

González Cruchaga, Carlos. La Compañía de Jesús y el futuro. *Mensaje,* v. 42, no. 420 (July 93), pp. 330 – 331.

Guarda Geywitz, Gabriel. Las misiones de la Compañía de Jesús en el período español. *Mensaje,* v. 42, no. 420 (July 93), pp. 215 – 219. Il, facs.

Hanisch Espíndola, Walter. Los jesuitas en La Serena, 1672 – 1767. *Boletín de la Academia Chilena de la Historia,* v. 58 – 59, no. 102 (1991 – 1992), pp. 291 – 328. Bibl, tables.

Los jesuitas: cuatro siglos en Chile (Chronology). *Mensaje,* v. 42, no. 420 (July 93), pp. 207 – 208.

Leturia M., Juan Miguel. 1993 - 1593 = 400: itinerario de una aventura. *Mensaje,* v. 42, no. 420 (July 93), pp. 209 – 214. Il.

Lillo, Armando. La expulsión de los jesuitas. *Mensaje,* v. 42, no. 420 (July 93), pp. 247 – 252. Il, facs.

Loyola, Alberto. Los jesuitas y la cuestión social. *Mensaje,* v. 42, no. 420 (July 93), pp. 304 – 307. Il.

Marshall, Santiago. Una misión de la Santa Sede: Arica. *Mensaje,* v. 42, no. 420 (July 93), pp. 287 – 289. Il.

Mercieca, Eddie. Jesuitas en parroquias. *Mensaje,* v. 42, no. 420 (July 93), pp. 285 – 286. Il.

Montes M., Fernando. Calera de Tango: evocación de nuestra historia. *Mensaje,* v. 42, no. 420 (July 93), pp. 239 – 242. Il.

Ochagavía Larraín, Juan. La Compañía de Jesús y la formación de los laicos. *Mensaje,* v. 42, no. 420 (July 93), pp. 311 – 316.

Oviedo Cavada, Carlos. Cuatro siglos de la Compañía de Jesús en Chile. *Mensaje,* v. 42, no. 420 (July 93), pp. 264 – 269. Il.

Precht B., Cristián. Mirando el futuro. *Mensaje,* v. 42, no. 420 (July 93), p. 333.

Puga, Mariano. ¡Corran el riesgo! *Mensaje,* v. 42, no. 420 (July 93), p. 334.

Santos Ascarza, José Manuel. ?Qué espero de los jesuitas? *Mensaje,* v. 42, no. 420 (July 93), p. 332.

Soto Sandoval, Andrés. INFOCAP: en la senda de Ignacio y de Alberto Hurtado. *Mensaje,* v. 42, no. 420 (July 93), pp. 280 – 282. II.

Tampe, Eduardo. Chiloé: misión circular. *Mensaje,* v. 42, no. 420 (July 93), pp. 224 – 227. II.

— Jesuitas alemanes y la colonización del sur. *Mensaje,* v. 42, no. 420 (July 93), pp. 259 – 263. II.

Téllez A., Isabel. ILADES: instituto de postgrado con acento en lo social. *Mensaje,* v. 42, no. 420 (July 93), pp. 283 – 284. II.

Valdés Bunster, Gustavo. Las riquezas de los antiguos jesuitas de Chile. *Mensaje,* v. 42, no. 420 (July 93), pp. 243 – 246. Charts.

Zapater Equioiz, Horacio. El padre Luis de Valdivia y la guerra defensiva. *Mensaje,* v. 42, no. 420 (July 93), pp. 220 – 223. II.

Zegers A., Cristián. El carisma de San Ignacio está vigente. *Mensaje,* v. 42, no. 420 (July 93), pp. 335 – 336. II.

Addresses, essays, lectures

Marshall S., Guillermo. Carta del provincial a los jesuitas de Chile. *Mensaje,* v. 42, no. 420 (July 93), pp. 183 – 185. II.

Biography

Jesuitas de este tiempo. *Mensaje,* v. 42, no. 420 (July 93), pp. 270 – 271. II.

Colombia

Hernández Aparicio, Pilar. Las reducciones jesuíticas de los llanos que pasaron a los franciscanos. *Archivo Ibero-Americano,* v. 52, no. 205 – 208 (Jan – Dec 92), pp. 445 – 463. Bibl, tables.

Rey Fajardo, José del. La presencia científica de la Universidad Javeriana en la Orinoquia. *Boletín de Historia y Antigüedades,* v. 79, no. 779 (Oct – Dec 92), pp. 925 – 952. Bibl.

El Salvador

Gómez Díez, Francisco Javier. El reformismo jesuítico en Centroamérica: La revista *ECA* en los años de la guerra fría, 1946 – 1965. *Anuario de Estudios Americanos,* v. 49, Suppl. 1 (1992), pp. 85 – 105. Tables.

Tojeira, José María. Tercer aniversario de los mártires de la UCA: homilia. *ECA; Estudios Centroamericanos,* v. 47, no. 529 – 530 (Nov – Dec 92), pp. 951 – 953.

Sources

Tercer aniversario de los mártires de la UCA (Two documents). *ECA; Estudios Centroamericanos,* v. 47, no. 529 – 530 (Nov – Dec 92), pp. 1085 – 1086.

Latin America

Arroyo, Gonzalo. La justicia como camino para vivir la fe. *Mensaje,* v. 42, no. 420 (July 93), pp. 190 – 195. II.

Mexico

Dehouve, Danièle. El discípulo de Silo: un aspecto de la literatura náhuatl de los jesuitas del siglo XVIII. *Estudios de Cultura Náhuatl,* v. 22 (1992), pp. 345 – 379. Bibl.

Luciani, Frederick William. The *Comedia de San Francisco de Borja* (1640): The Mexican Jesuits and the "Education of the Prince." *Colonial Latin American Review,* v. 2, no. 1 – 2 (1993), pp. 121 – 141. Bibl.

Monjarás-Ruiz, Jesús. La antigua Sinaloa y Pérez de Ribas. *Plural (Mexico),* v. 22, no. 265 (Oct 93), pp. 70 – 72.

Polzer, Charles W. et al, eds. *The Jesuit Missions of Northern Mexico* reviewed by Robert H. Jackson. *Hispanic American Historical Review,* v. 73, no. 2 (May 93), pp. 312 – 313.

Stoetzer, Otto Carlos. Tradition and Progress in the Late Eighteenth-Century Jesuit Rediscovery of America: Francisco Javier Clavijero's Philosophy and History. *Colonial Latin American Historical Review,* v. 2, no. 3 (Summer 93), pp. 289 – 324. Bibl.

Peru

Ardito Vega, Wilfredo. La estructura de las reducciones de Maynas. *Amazonía Peruana,* v. 11, no. 22 (Oct 92), pp. 93 – 124. Bibl.

Arenas Frutos, Isabel and Carmen Cebrián González. Situación de la provincia del Perú a finales del siglo XVI: *La crónica anónima de 1600. Anuario de Estudios Americanos,* v. 49, Suppl. 2 (1992), pp. 11 – 29. Tables.

Nieto Vélez, Armando. *Francisco del Castillo, el apóstol de Lima* reviewed by Pedro Guibovich. *Apuntes (Peru),* no. 30 (Jan – June 92), pp. 109 – 110.

Tardieu, Jean-Pierre. Los jesuitas y la "lengua de Angola" en Perú, siglo XVII. *Revista de Indias,* v. 53, no. 198 (May – Aug 93), pp. 627 – 637. Bibl.

Venezuela

Goñi, Alejandro. Palabras del r.p. Alejandro Goñi, S.J. *Boletín de la Academia Nacional de la Historia (Venezuela),* v. 75, no. 299 (July – Sept 92), pp. 19 – 24.

JESUS, CAROLINA MARIA DE
Criticism of specific works
Quarto de despejo

Platt, Kamala. Race and Gender Representation in Clarice Lispector's "A menor mulher do mundo" and Carolina Maria de Jesus' *Quarto de despejo. Afro-Hispanic Review,* v. 11, no. 1 – 3 (1992), pp. 51 – 57. Bibl.

LA JEUNE BELGIQUE (PERIODICAL)

Zaid, Gabriel. *La Jeune Belgique* y la poesía mexicana. *Vuelta,* v. 17, no. 200 (July 93), pp. 17 – 18.

JEWELRY

See
Silversmiths
Subdivision *Costume and adornment* under names of Indian groups

JEWISH LITERATURE

Zlotchew, Clark M. Literatura israelí en español: entrevista con Leonardo Senkman. *Confluencia,* v. 8, no. 1 (Fall 92), pp. 111 – 121. Bibl.

History and criticism

Gelman, Juan. Lo judío y la literatura en castellano. *Hispamérica,* v. 21, no. 62 (Aug 92), pp. 83 – 90.

Brazil

Vieira, Nelson H. Simulation and Dissimulation: An Expression of Crypto-Judaism in the Literature of Colonial Brazil. *Colonial Latin American Review,* v. 2, no. 1 – 2 (1993), pp. 143 – 164. Bibl.

JEWS

See also
Antisemitism

Argentina

Grinberg, Samuel. Cuatro grabadores judíos en la confederación argentina. *Todo Es Historia,* v. 27, no. 314 (Sept 93), pp. 50 – 53. II.

Schers, David. Inmigrantes y política: los primeros pasos del Partido Sionista Socialista Poalei Sion en la Argentina, 1910 – 1916. *Estudios Interdisciplinarios de América Latina y el Caribe,* v. 3, no. 2 (July – Dec 92), pp. 75 – 88.

Senkman, Leonardo. *Argentina, la segunda guerra mundial y los refugiados indeseables, 1933 – 1945* reviewed by Hebe Clementi. *Todo Es Historia,* v. 27, no. 316 (Nov 93), pp. 88 – 89. II.

Brazil

Furtado Kestler, Izabela María. Stefan Zweig, Brasil e o holocausto. *Estudios Interdisciplinarios de América Latina y el Caribe,* v. 3, no. 2 (July – Dec 92), pp. 123 – 126. Bibl.

Dominican Republic

Robertiello, Jack. Dominican Chutzpah: The Story of Sosua. *Américas,* v. 45, no. 4 (July – Aug 93), pp. 20 – 25. II, maps.

Ecuador

Varon, Benno Weiser. *Professions of a Lucky Jew* reviewed by Ignacio Klich. *Journal of Latin American Studies,* v. 25, no. 2 (May 93), pp. 430 – 431.

Mexico

Bokser de Liwerant, Judit, ed. *Imágenes de un encuentro: la presencia judía en México durante la primera mitad del siglo XX* reviewed by José María Pérez Gay (Review entitled "La ofrenda, el consuelo, el recuerdo, la admiración"). *Nexos*, v. 16, no. 190 (Oct 93), pp. 77 – 79.

Gardy, Alison. Emerging from the Shadows: A Visit to an Old Jewish Community. *NACLA Report on the Americas*, v. 27, no. 2 (Sept – Oct 93), pp. 10 – 13. Il.

Krauze, Enrique. México en dos abuelos. *Vuelta*, v. 17, no. 202 (Sept 93), pp. 26 – 28.

Río de la Plata region

Saban, Mario Javier. *Los marranos y la economía en el Río de Plata* reviewed by José Federico Lima. *Todo Es Historia*, v. 27, no. 314 (Sept 93), pp. 71 – 72. Il.

JEWS IN LITERATURE

Gorodischer, Angélica. Borges y los judíos. *Confluencia*, v. 8, no. 1 (Fall 92), pp. 9 – 18.

JIMÉNEZ, JUAN RAMÓN

Biography

Camprubí de Jiménez, Zenobia. *Diario, 1: Cuba, 1937 – 1939* introduced and translated by Graciela Palau de Nemes. Reviewed by Aleksandra Hadzelek. *Revista Iberoamericana*, v. 59, no. 162 – 163 (Jan – June 93), pp. 385 – 387.

Correspondence, reminiscences, etc.

Jiménez, Juan Ramón. Buzón de fantasmas: de Juan Ramón Jiménez a Ermilo Abreu Gómez. *Vuelta*, v. 17, no. 205 (Dec 93), pp. 87 – 88.

JIMÉNEZ DE LA ESPADA, MARCOS

López-Ocón Cabrera, Leoncio. Texto y contexto en la obra de Jiménez de la Espada: un modelo interpretativo. *Revista de Indias*, v. 52, no. 195 – 196 (May – Dec 92), pp. 611 – 625. Bibl, charts.

JIMÉNEZ VARELA, LUIS CARLOS

Criticism of specific works

Cartas de infancia

Cedeño Cenci, Diógenes F. Meditaciones sobre "Cartas de infancia:" poemario de Luis Carlos Jiménez Varela. *Revista Cultural Lotería*, v. 51, no. 392 (Nov – Dec 93), pp. 78 – 84.

JÍVARO INDIANS

Warren, Patrizio. Mercado, escuelas y proteínas: aspectos históricos, ecológicos y económicos del cambio de modelo de asentamiento entre los achuar meridionales. *Amazonía Peruana*, v. 11, no. 21 (Sept 92), pp. 73 – 107. Bibl, tables.

JOHN PAUL II, POPE

Addresses, essays, lectures

John Paul II, Pope. "Si quieres la paz, sal al encuentro del pobre": mensaje de su santidad Juan Pablo II para la celebración de la Jornada Mundial de la Paz, 1 de enero de 1993. *ECA; Estudios Centroamericanos*, v. 48, no. 531 – 532 (Jan – Feb 93), pp. 18 – 26.

Mensaje de Juan Pablo para la Jornada Mundial de la Paz: "Si quieres la paz, sal al encuentro del pobre" (Commentary on the Pope's speech transcribed on pp. 18 – 26 of this issue). *ECA; Estudios Centroamericanos*, v. 48, no. 531 – 532 (Jan – Feb 93), pp. 96 – 99.

Mifsud, Tony. Juan Pablo II: "Si quieres la paz, sal al encuentro del pobre." *Mensaje*, v. 42, no. 417 (Mar – Apr 93), pp. 96 – 98.

JORNAL DO BRASIL (NEWSPAPER)

Lima Sobrinho, Alexandre José Barbosa. No centenário do *Jornal do Brasil*. *Revista do Instituto Histórico e Geográfico Brasileiro*, no. 372 (July – Sept 91), pp. 746 – 761.

JOUHANDEAU, MARCEL

Criticism of specific works

Le langage de la tribu

Devoto, Daniel. La lengua de las tribus: de Guéret Chaminadour a Santa María de los Buenos Aires. *Nueva Revista de Filología Hispánica*, v. 40, no. 2 (July – Dec 92), pp. 921 – 958.

JOURNAL OF LATIN AMERICAN STUDIES (PERIODICAL)

Cumulative Index, Volumes 16 – 25 (1984 – 1993). *Journal of Latin American Studies*, n.v. (1993), Issue.

JOURNALISM

See also
Press

Conejeros A., Senén et al. ¿En qué fallan los periodistas y los medios de comunicación?: debates. *Mensaje*, v. 42, no. 419 (June 93), pp. 194 – 201. Il.

Leturia M., Juan Miguel. Información: derecho y dignidad. *Mensaje*, v. 42, no. 419 (June 93), pp. 210 – 211.

Law and legislation

Lince, Ricardo A. and Roberto Núñez Escobar. Aporte para una legislación de prensa. *Revista Cultural Lotería*, v. 50, no. 386 (Nov – Dec 91), pp. 5 – 24.

America

Rotker, Susana. *Fundación de una escritura: las crónicas de José Martí* reviewed by Richard B. Gray. *Hispanic American Historical Review*, v. 73, no. 3 (Aug 93), pp. 483 – 484.

Argentina

Rivera, Jorge B. Periodismo y transición: de la recuperación pluralista al "shopping" comunicacional. *Cuadernos Hispanoamericanos*, no. 517 – 519 (July – Sept 93), pp. 337 – 351. Bibl.

Saítta, Sylvia. Roberto Arlt y las nuevas formas periodísticas. *Cuadernos Hispanoamericanos*, no. Special issue, 11 (July 93), pp. 59 – 69. Bibl.

Vallejos de Llobet, Patricia. El vocabulario científico en la prensa iluminista porteña, 1800 – 1825. *Cuadernos Americanos*, no. 38, Nueva época (Mar – Apr 93), pp. 205 – 224. Bibl.

Bolivia

Rivadeneira Prada, Raúl. Juan Quirós, periodista. *Signo*, no. 36 – 37, Nueva época (May – Dec 92), pp. 201 – 206.

Societies, etc.

Rivadeneira Prada, Raúl. Un fragmento para la historia de la Asociación de Periodistas. *Signo*, no. 35, Nueva época (Jan – Apr 92), pp. 15 – 33.

Salamanca Lafuente, Rodolfo. Memoria de la Asociación de Periodistas de La Paz. *Signo*, no. 38, Nueva época (Jan – Apr 93), pp. 27 – 46.

Brazil

Study and teaching

Sodré, Muniz. Por que uma escola de comunicação? (Originally published in this journal in October 1972). *Vozes*, v. 87, no. 3 (May – June 93), pp. 85 – 89.

Caribbean area

Lent, John A. Mujeres periodistas en el Caribe (Translated by Jimmy Seale Collazo). *Homines*, v. 15 – 16, no. 2 – 1 (Oct 91 – Dec 92), pp. 262 – 272. Bibl.

Colombia

Law and legislation

Vallejo Mejía, Jesús. Responsabilidad social del periodista frente a los nuevos derechos que ha consagrado la constitución: fundamentalmente el derecho a la vida privada. *Revista Javeriana*, v. 61, no. 595 (June 93), pp. 307 – 316.

Costa Rica

Study and teaching

Vega Jiménez, Patricia. Nacimiento y consolidación de la Escuela de Ciencias de la Comunicación Colectiva. *Revista de Ciencias Sociales (Costa Rica)*, no. 57 (Sept 92), pp. 67 – 78. Tables, charts.

Latin America

Moreno Gómez, Luis. Desarrollo latinoamericano y periodismo científico. *Revista Nacional de Cultura (Venezuela)*, v. 53, no. 286 (July – Sept 92), pp. 215 – 244. Bibl, il, tables.

Mexico

Casas Chousal, Xolóxochitl and Sara Lovera. Razones y sinrazones de CIMAC y la población. *Fem*, v. 17, no. 128 (Oct 93), pp. 8 – 10.

Egan, Linda. Entrevistas con periodistas mujeres sobre la prensa mexicana. *Mexican Studies*, v. 9, no. 2 (Summer 93), pp. 275 – 294. Bibl.

— Feminine Perspectives on Journalism: Conversations with Eight Mexican Women. *Studies in Latin American Popular Culture*, v. 12 (1993), pp. 175 – 187.

López García, Guadalupe. Las periodistas y el poder (y en los medios de comunicación). *Fem*, v. 17, no. 129 (Nov 93), pp. 24 – 25.

Bibliography

La France, David G. Politics, Violence, and the Press in Mexico (Review article). *Studies in Latin American Popular Culture*, v. 12 (1993), pp. 215 – 220.

Peru

Bedoya, Jaime. *Ay, qué rico: crónicas periodísticas* reviewed by Luis Jaime Cisneros V. (Review entitled "Oficio febril"). *Debate (Peru)*, v. 15, no. 70 (Sept – Oct 92), p. 70.

Jara, Umberto. Entrevista a Guillermo Thorndike. *Debate (Peru)*, v. 16, no. 72 (Mar – May 93), pp. 6 – 12. Il.

Salmón Jordán, Jorge. *Entre la vanidad y el poder: memoria y testimonio* reviewed by Oscar Malca (Review entitled "Contra la corriente"). *Debate (Peru)*, v. 16, no. 72 (Mar – May 93), pp. 65 – 66. Il.

Venezuela

Pérez, Ana Mercedes. *Entre el cuento y la historia: 50 años del periodismo* reviewed by Pascual Venegas Filardo. *Revista Nacional de Cultura (Venezuela)*, v. 53, no. 286 (July – Sept 92), p. 257.

Rotker, Susana. Crónica y cultura urbana: Caracas, la última década. *Inti*, no. 37 – 38 (Spring – Fall 93), pp. 233 – 242. Bibl.

Sucre, Guillermo. La polvareda y la falacia (Response to the Venezuelan press's reaction to his two earlier articles published in *Vuelta*). *Vuelta*, v. 17, no. 202 (Sept 93), pp. 54 – 55.

JOURNALS

See
　Periodicals

JUAN DE LA CRUZ, SAINT

Andueza, María. *San Juan de la Cruz en México* visto por Alfonso Méndez Plancarte. *Cuadernos Americanos*, no. 37, Nueva época (Jan – Feb 93), pp. 165 – 179. Bibl.

González León, Adriano. Cántico de Jajó. *Plural (Mexico)*, v. 22, no. 262 (July 93), pp. 4 – 9.

JUANA INÉS DE LA CRUZ

Criticism and interpretation

Merrim, Stephanie, ed. *Feminist Perspectives on Sor Juana Inés de la Cruz* reviewed by Noël Valis. *Colonial Latin American Review*, v. 2, no. 1 – 2 (1993), pp. 304 – 308.

Paz, Octavio. *Sor Juana Inés de la Cruz o las trampas de la fe* reviewed by Juan Malpartida (Review entitled "Sor Juana y Paz"). *Cuadernos Hispanoamericanos*, no. 516 (June 93), pp. 131 – 134.

Schmidhuber de la Mora, Guillermo. Hallazgo y significación de un texto en prosa perteneciente a los últimos años de sor Juana Inés de la Cruz. *Hispania (USA)*, v. 76, no. 2 (May 93), pp. 189 – 196. Bibl.

Criticism of specific works

El divino Narciso

Stroud, Matthew D. The Desiring Subject and the Promise of Salvation: A Lacanian Study of Sor Juana's *El divino Narciso*. *Hispania (USA)*, v. 76, no. 2 (May 93), pp. 204 – 212. Bibl.

Los empeños de una casa

Cypess, Sandra Messinger. Los géneros re/velados en *Los empeños de una casa* de sor Juana Inés de la Cruz. *Hispamérica*, v. 22, no. 64 – 65 (Apr – Aug 93), pp. 177 – 185. Bibl.

Respuesta a sor Filotea de la Cruz

McDonald, Robert. An Incredible Graph: Sor Juana's *Respuesta*. *Revista Canadiense de Estudios Hispánicos*, v. 17, no. 2 (Winter 93), pp. 297 – 318. Bibl.

La segunda Celestina

Schmidhuber de la Mora, Guillermo, ed. *'La segunda Celestina': una comedia perdida de sor Juana* reviewed by Francisco Javier Cevallos. *Colonial Latin American Review*, v. 2, no. 1 – 2 (1993), pp. 302 – 304.

El sueño

Hauser, Rex. Two New World Dreamers: Manzano and Sor Juana. *Afro-Hispanic Review*, v. 12, no. 2 (Fall 93), pp. 3 – 11. Bibl.

Nanfito, Jacqueline C. Time as Space in Sor Juana's *El sueño*. *Hispanic Journal*, v. 13, no. 2 (Fall 92), pp. 345 – 352.

JUÁREZ, BENITO PABLO

Correspondence, reminiscences, etc.

Reyes Ramos, Manuel. Juárez a través de su epistolario. *La Palabra y el Hombre*, no. 82 (Apr – June 92), pp. 294 – 300.

Fiction

Pérez Gay, Rafael. Benito Juárez perdido en el norte de México. *Nexos*, v. 16, no. 182 (Feb 93), pp. 21 – 22.

JUÁREZ, RENÉ

Interviews

Custodio, Isabel. Charla con René Juárez, presidente municipal de Acapulco. *Fem*, v. 17, no. 120 (Feb 93), p. 31.

JUDAISM

See
　Jewish literature
　Jews

JUDICIARY

Fernández-Baca, Jorge. Rol judicial en una economía de mercado. *Debate (Peru)*, v. 16, no. 75 (Dec 93 – Jan 94), pp. 51 – 52. Il.

Central America

Rivera Bustamante, Tirza Emilia. Women Judges in Central America. *Hemisphere*, v. 5, no. 3 (Summer – Fall 93), pp. 18 – 19. Charts.

Sources

América Central: Convenio del Estatuto de la Corte Centroamericana de Justicia. *Integración Latinoamericana*, v. 18, no. 191 (July 93), pp. 57 – 60.

Chile

Campos Harriet, Fernando. La Real Audiencia de Concepción. *Atenea (Chile)*, no. 465 – 466 (1992), pp. 151 – 156.

— La Real Audiencia de Concepción, 1565 – 1573. *Boletín de la Academia Chilena de la Historia*, v. 58 – 59, no. 102 (1991 – 1992), pp. 534 – 538.

Colombia

Sintura, Francisco José. La Fiscalía General de la Nación desde la Fiscalía. *Revista Javeriana*, v. 61, no. 598 (Sept 93), pp. 227 – 235.

Yepes Arcila, Hernando. La independencia del poder judicial. *Revista Javeriana*, v. 61, no. 598 (Sept 93), pp. 247 – 257.

Latin America

International cooperation

Boggiano, Antonio. Justicia supranacional en América Latina y el Caribe: alternativas para la creación de un sistema. *Integración Latinoamericana*, v. 18, no. 189 – 190 (May – June 93), pp. 18 – 27. Bibl.

Lavados Montes, Iván and Juan Enrique Vargas. La gestión judicial. *Estudios Sociales (Chile)*, no. 78 (Oct – Dec 93), pp. 203 – 225.

Nicaragua

McConnell, Shelley. Rules of the Game: Nicaragua's Contentious Constitutional Debate. *NACLA Report on the Americas*, v. 27, no. 2 (Sept – Oct 93), pp. 20 – 25. Il.

Peru

Boza Dibós, Beatriz. Obstáculo a la inversión extranjera. *Debate (Peru)*, v. 16, no. 75 (Dec 93 – Jan 94), pp. 50 – 51.

Bullard G., Alfredo. El juez peruano, ¿protagonista o extra? *Debate (Peru)*, v. 16, no. 75 (Dec 93 – Jan 94), pp. 48 – 49.

El poder judicial: encuesta. *Debate (Peru)*, v. 16, no. 75 (Dec 93 – Jan 94), pp. 43 – 47. Il, tables.

Revilla Vergara, Ana Teresa. La justicia informal. *Debate (Peru)*, v. 16, no. 75 (Dec 93 – Jan 94), pp. 49 – 50.

JURISPRUDENCE

See
    Distributive justice
    Law
    Sociological jurisprudence

JUSTO, AGUSTÍN PEDRO

Fraga, Rosendo M. *El general Justo* reviewed by Félix Luna. *Todo Es Historia*, v. 27, no. 312 (July 93), p. 74. Il.

JUSTO, JUAN

Calvo, Bernardino S. Nicolás Repetto y Juan B. Justo, pioneros de la educación rural. *Todo Es Historia*, v. 27, no. 315 (Oct 93), pp. 50 – 53. Il.

JUVENILE DELINQUENCY

See also
    Crime and criminals
    Street children

Mexico

Urteaga Castro-Pozo, Maritza. Identidad y jóvenes urbanos. *Estudios Sociológicos*, v. 11, no. 32 (May – Aug 93), pp. 555 – 568. Bibl.

United States

Moore, Joan W. *Going Down to the Barrio: Homeboys and Homegirls in Change* reviewed by Kathleen Logan. *Hispanic American Historical Review*, v. 73, no. 3 (Aug 93), pp. 488 – 489.

Sommers, Ira et al. Sociocultural Influences on the Explanation of Delinquency for Puerto Rican Youths. *Hispanic Journal of Behavioral Sciences*, v. 15, no. 1 (Feb 93), pp. 36 – 62. Bibl, tables.

KAFKA, FRANZ

Kluback, William. Our Gentile Guides: Jorge Luis Borges and Franz Kafka. *Confluencia*, v. 8, no. 1 (Fall 92), pp. 19 – 27.

KAHLO, FRIDA

Poniatowska, Elena and Carla Stellweg. *Frida Kahlo: la cámara seducida* reviewed by Andrés Salgado R. (Accompanied by an English translation). *Art Nexus*, no. 8 (Apr – June 93), p. 34. Il.

Schaefer-Rodríguez, Claudia. *Textured Lives: Women, Art, and Representation in Modern Mexico* reviewed by Barbara Mujica (Review entitled "A Roundup of Stories"). *Américas*, v. 45, no. 1 (Jan – Feb 93), pp. 61 – 62.

— *Textured Lives: Women, Art, and Representation in Modern Mexico* reviewed by Susan Isabel Stein. *Hispania (USA)*, v. 76, no. 2 (May 93), pp. 292 – 293.

— *Textured Lives: Women, Art, and Representation in Modern Mexico* reviewed by Kathleen Ross. *Hispanic American Historical Review*, v. 73, no. 2 (May 93), pp. 333 – 334.

Exhibitions

Gropp, Rose-Maria. ¡Contra el culto!: Frida Kahlo en Francfort (Translated by Gabriela Fonseca). *Humboldt*, no. 109 (1993), pp. 66 – 69. Il.

KAISER, HENRY

Cobbs, Elizabeth Anne. *The Rich Neighbor Policy: Rockefeller and Kaiser in Brazil* reviewed by Joel Wolfe. *Hispanic American Historical Review*, v. 73, no. 3 (Aug 93), pp. 538 – 539.

KAMAIURÁ INDIANS

Bastos, Rafael José de Menezes. Musical Cognition and Structure: The Case of the Yawari of the Kamayurá Indians of Central Brazil, Xingu Indian Park, Mato Grosso. *La Educación (USA)*, v. 36, no. 111 – 113 (1992), pp. 227 – 233. Bibl.

KAMENSZAIN, TAMARA

Criticism and interpretation

Panesi, Jorge. Banquetes en el living: Tamara Kamenszain. *Hispamérica*, v. 22, no. 64 – 65 (Apr – Aug 93), pp. 167 – 175.

KÁNYA, KÁLMÁN

Anderle, Adám and Monika Kozári. Koloman von Kánya: Ein österreichisch-ungarischer Botschafter in Mexiko. *Zeitschrift für Lateinamerika Wien*, no. 43 (1992), pp. 63 – 80. Bibl.

KAYAPÓ INDIANS

See
    Cayapo Indians

KEKCHI INDIANS

Wilk, Richard R. *Household Ecology: Economic Change and Domestic Life among the Kekchi Maya in Belize* reviewed by Joseph O. Palacio. *Belizean Studies*, v. 21, no. 1 (May 93), pp. 25 – 26.

— *Household Ecology: Economic Change and Domestic Life among the Kekchi Maya in Belize* reviewed by Laura Rival. *Bulletin of Latin American Research*, v. 12, no. 1 (Jan 93), pp. 125 – 126.

— *Household Ecology: Economic Change and Domestic Life among the Kekchi Maya in Belize* reviewed by Norman Ashcraft. *Journal of Developing Areas*, v. 27, no. 3 (Apr 93), pp. 422 – 424.

KELEMEN, PÁL

Obituaries

Fontana, Bernard L. Pál Kelemen (1894 – 1993). *Hispanic American Historical Review*, v. 73, no. 3 (Aug 93), pp. 481 – 482.

KEROUAC, JACK

Fiction

Padrón, Leonardo. El heroe derrotado de la noche occidental (Introduced by María Auxiliadora Alvarez. Article entitled "Voces o seres cercanos"). *Inti*, no. 37 – 38 (Spring – Fall 93), pp. 72 – 75.

KINSHIP

See also
    Family
    Subdivision *Kinship* under names of Indian groups

Ramírez Carrillo, Luis Alfonso. Estratificación, clase y parentesco: empresarios libaneses en el sureste de México. *Nueva Antropología*, v. 13, no. 43 (Nov 92), pp. 123 – 137. Bibl.

KNOWLEDGE, THEORY OF

Maffia, Diana. Feminismo y epistemología: ¿Tiene sexo el sujeto de la ciencia? *Feminaria*, v. 6, no. 10 (Apr 93), pp. 13 – 15. Bibl.

KOREA

See also
    Cities and towns – Korea

Fujii Gambero, Gerardo and Noemí Levy. Composición de las exportaciones de Brasil, Corea, España y México. *Comercio Exterior*, v. 43, no. 9 (Sept 93), pp. 844 – 851. Tables.

KRAUSE, KARL CHRISTIAN FRIEDRICH

Serna Arnáiz, Mercedes. Algunas dilucidaciones sobre el krausismo en José Martí. *Cuadernos Hispanoamericanos*, no. 521 (Nov 93), pp. 137 – 145.

KRAUSKOPF, MANUEL

Criticism of specific works

La investigación universitaria en Chile

Allende, Jorge E. Presentación del libro *La investigación universitaria en Chile: reflexiones críticas* de Manuel Krauskopf. *Estudios Sociales (Chile)*, no. 75 (Jan – Mar 93), pp. 231 – 238.

KRAUZE, ENRIQUE

Correspondence, reminiscences, etc.

Krauze, Enrique. México en dos abuelos. *Vuelta*, v. 17, no. 202 (Sept 93), pp. 26 – 28.

KUBITSCHEK, JUSCELINO

Alexander, Robert Jackson. *Juscelino Kubitschek and the Development of Brazil* reviewed by Peter Flynn. *Bulletin of Latin American Research*, v. 12, no. 3 (Sept 93), pp. 348 – 349.

— *Juscelino Kubitschek and the Development of Brazil* reviewed by John W. F. Dulles. *Hispanic American Historical Review*, v. 73, no. 1 (Feb 93), pp. 168 – 169.

KÜPPERS, GABRIELE

Interviews

Entrevista a Gaby Küppers. *Feminaria*, v. 6, no. 10 (Apr 93), p. 28.

KUITCA, GUILLERMO DAVID

Jiménez, Carlos. Guillermo Kuitca, un pintor teatral (Accompanied by an English translation). *Art Nexus*, no. 9 (June – Aug 93), pp. 48 – 51. Il.

Un libro sobre Guillermo Kuitca reviewed by Ivonne Pini (Accompanied by an English translation). *Art Nexus*, no. 9 (June – Aug 93), p. 32. Il.

KUKULCÁN

See
    Quetzalcóatl

KUNA INDIANS

See
    Cuna Indians

LABASTIDA, JAIME

Criticism of specific works

Dominio de la tarde

Prada Oropeza, Renato. *Dominio de la tarde:* el verbo grave. *Plural (Mexico)*, v. 22, no. 258 (Mar 93), pp. 57 – 63. Bibl.

Interviews

Ramírez, Fermín. Jaime Labastida, poeta en la hora del saber. *Plural (Mexico)*, v. 22, no. 261 (June 93), pp. 16 – 22.

LABOR AND LABORING CLASSES

See also
    Agricultural laborers
    Division of labor
    Employees' representation in management
    Employment
    Human capital
    Labor productivity
    Migration, Internal
    Peasantry
    Strikes and lockouts
    Trade unions
    Undocumented workers
    Unemployment
    Wages
    Subdivision *Employment* under *Children, Hispanic Americans (U.S.),* and *Women*

Argentina

Adelman, Jeremy, ed. *Essays in Argentine Labour History, 1870 – 1930* reviewed by Ronaldo Munck. *Bulletin of Latin American Research*, v. 12, no. 2 (May 93), pp. 229 – 230.

Barrancos, Dora. La modernidad redentora: difusión de las ciencias entre los trabajadores de Buenos Aires, 1890 – 1920. *Siglo XIX: Revista*, no. 12, 2a época (July – Dec 92), pp. 5 – 21. Bibl, tables.

Ranis, Peter. *Argentine Workers: Peronism and Contemporary Class Consciousness* reviewed by Joel Horowitz. *The Americas*, v. 50, no. 2 (Oct 93), pp. 289 – 290.

— *Argentine Workers: Peronism and Contemporary Class Consciousness* reviewed by Walter Little. *Bulletin of Latin American Research*, v. 12, no. 1 (Jan 93), pp. 118 – 119.

Brazil

Castro, Nadya Araújo and Antônio Sérgio Alfredo Guimarães. Trabalhadores afluentes, indústrias recentes: revisitando a tese da aristocracia operária. *Dados*, v. 35, no. 2 (1992), pp. 173 – 191. Bibl.

Duarte, Luiz Fernando Dias et al. Vicissitudes e limites da conversão à cidadania nas classes populares brasileiras. *Revista Brasileira de Ciências Sociais*, v. 8, no. 22 (June 93), pp. 5 – 19. Bibl.

Guimarães, Antônio Sérgio Alfredo. Operários e mobilidade social na Bahia: análise de uma trajetória individual. *Revista Brasileira de Ciências Sociais*, v. 8, no. 22 (June 93), pp. 81 – 97. Bibl, tables.

Colombia

Archila Neira, Mauricio. *Cultura e identidad obrera: Colombia, 1910 – 1945* reviewed by Rocío Londoño B. *Anuario Colombiano de Historia Social y de la Cultura*, no. 20 (1992), pp. 174 – 180.

Latin America

Alzate Montoya, Rubelia. Por un reencuentro latinoamericano. *Estudios Rurales Latinoamericanos*, v. 15, no. 2 – 3 (May – Dec 92), pp. 113 – 120.

Bibliography

Spalding, Hobart A., Jr. New Directions and Themes in Latin American Labor and Working-Class History: A Sampler (Review article). *Latin American Research Review*, v. 28, no. 1 (1993), pp. 202 – 214. Bibl.

Mexican – American Border Region

Heyman, Josiah McConnell. *Life and Labor on the Border: Working People of Northeastern Sonora, Mexico, 1886 – 1986* reviewed by Miguel Tinker Salas. *The Americas*, v. 49, no. 4 (Apr 93), pp. 556 – 558.

— *Life and Labor on the Border: Working People of Northeastern Sonora, Mexico, 1886 – 1986* reviewed by Barry Carr. *Hispanic American Historical Review*, v. 73, no. 3 (Aug 93), pp. 526 – 528.

— *Life and Labor on the Border: Working People of Northeastern Sonora, Mexico, 1886 – 1986* reviewed by Evelyn Hu-Dehart. *International Migration Review*, v. 27, no. 3 (Fall 93), pp. 648 – 649.

Mexico

Bazán, Lucía. *Vivienda para los obreros: reproducción de clase y condiciones urbanas* reviewed by Margarita Estrada Iguíniz. *El Cotidiano*, v. 8, no. 52 (Jan – Feb 93), pp. 112 – 113.

Campos Aragón, Leticia. El TLC y la nueva cultura laboral. *Momento Económico*, no. 65 (Jan – Feb 93), pp. 26 – 30.

Deans-Smith, Susan. Compromise and Conflict: The Tobacco Workers of Mexico City and the Colonial State, 1770 – 1810. *Anuario de Estudios Americanos*, v. 49 (1992), pp. 271 – 309. Bibl.

Flores Clair, Eduardo. Trabajo, salud y muerte: Real del Monte, 1874. *Siglo XIX: Cuadernos*, v. 1, no. 3 (June 92), pp. 9 – 28. Bibl, charts.

Várguez Pasos, Luis A. Cultura obrera en crisis: el caso de los cordeleros de Yucatán. *Estudios Sociológicos*, v. 11, no. 31 (Jan – Apr 93), pp. 93 – 110. Bibl.

Puerto Rico

Santiago, Carlos Enrique. *Labor in the Puerto Rican Economy: Postwar Development and Stagnation* reviewed by William D. Savedoff. *Hispanic American Historical Review*, v. 73, no. 3 (Aug 93), pp. 534 – 535.

LABOR DISPUTES

See
    Labor relations
    Strikes and lockouts

LABOR LAWS AND LEGISLATION
America
Carlsen, Laura. Worker Protection under NAFTA. *Business Mexico*, v. 3, no. 10 (Oct 93), pp. 38 – 39. Il.

Brazil
Araújo, Maria Celina d' and Angela Maria de Castro Gomes. Entrevista com Arnaldo Sussekind. *Estudos Históricos*, v. 6, no. 11 (Jan – June 93), pp. 113 – 127.

Colombia
Quintero, Fernando. Cesantías y pensiones: el reordenamiento laboral. *Revista Javeriana*, v. 61, no. 592 (Mar 93), pp. 81 – 85. Tables.

Sánchez Franco, Germán. Antecedentes de la reforma laboral acerca del tema de las cesantías. *Revista Javeriana*, v. 61, no. 592 (Mar 93), pp. 86 – 89.

Costa Rica
Miller, Eugene D. Labour and the War-Time Alliance in Costa Rica, 1943 – 1948. *Journal of Latin American Studies*, v. 25, no. 3 (Oct 93), pp. 515 – 541. Bibl, tables.

El Salvador
Huertas Bartolomé, Tebelia. Análisis crítico de la legislación laboral en El Salvador. *ECA; Estudios Centroamericanos*, v. 47, no. 529 – 530 (Nov – Dec 92), pp. 1021 – 1027. Il.

Latin America
Aspell de Yanzi Ferreira, Marcela. La regulación jurídica de las formas del trabajo forzado (Segunda parte). *Investigaciones y Ensayos*, no. 41 (Jan – Dec 91), pp. 349 – 394. Bibl.

Mexico
Pérez, Emma Marie. "She Has Served Others in More Intimate Ways": The Domestic Servant Reform in Yucatán, 1915 – 1918. *Aztlán*, v. 20, no. 1 – 2 (Spring – Fall 91), pp. 11 – 37. Bibl.

Peru
Balta Varillas, José. Derecho del trabajo y economía de mercado: ¿Términos compatibles? *Apuntes (Peru)*, no. 29 (July – Dec 91), pp. 57 – 66.

Venezuela
Calero, Fernando and Héctor Lucena R., eds. *Las relaciones de trabajo en los noventa: desafíos y propuestas* reviewed by T. M. van Hettema. *European Review of Latin American and Caribbean Studies*, no. 54 (June 93), pp. 139 – 140.

LABOR PRODUCTIVITY
Chile
Guajardo Soto, Guillermo. Tecnología y trabajo en Chile, 1850 – 1930. *Cuadernos Americanos*, no. 38, Nueva época (Mar – Apr 93), pp. 155 – 179. Bibl, tables.

Mexico
Carrillo Viveros, Jorge and Oscar F. Contreras. Calificación en el trabajo: análisis de la industria maquiladora. *Frontera Norte*, v. 4, no. 8 (July – Dec 92), pp. 49 – 78. Bibl, tables, charts.

Méndez, Luis and José Othón Quiroz Trejo. Productividad, respuesta obrera y sucesión presidencial. *El Cotidiano*, v. 10, no. 58 (Oct – Nov 93), pp. 71 – 78.

Veloz Avila, Norma Ilse. Entre la productividad y el salario: conflictos y concertación obrero – patronal, enero – marzo 1993. *El Cotidiano*, v. 9, no. 54 (May 93), pp. 81 – 89. Il, tables.

Congresses
Cohen, Joshua A. Productivity Goes into Labor. *Business Mexico*, v. 3, no. 11 (Nov 93), pp. 47 – 48.

LABOR RELATIONS
See also
Employees' representation in management
Strikes and lockouts
Trade unions

Argentina
Korzeniewicz, Roberto P. The Labor Politics of Radicalism: The Santa Fe Crisis of 1928. *Hispanic American Historical Review*, v. 73, no. 1 (Feb 93), pp. 1 – 32.

— Labor Unrest in Argentina, 1930 – 1943. *Latin American Research Review*, v. 28, no. 1 (1993), pp. 7 – 40. Bibl, tables.

— Las vísperas del peronismo: los conflictos laborales entre 1930 y 1943. *Desarrollo Económico (Argentina)*, v. 33, no. 131 (Oct – Dec 93), pp. 323 – 354. Bibl, tables.

Brazil
Amadeo Swaelen, Edward Joaquim. Restricciones institucionales a la política económica: negociación salarial y estabilización en el Brasil. *Desarrollo Económico (Argentina)*, v. 33, no. 129 (Apr – June 93), pp. 29 – 47. Bibl, tables, charts.

Leite, Márcia de Paula. Organización del trabajo y relaciones industriales en el Brasil. *Nueva Sociedad*, no. 124 (Mar – Apr 93), pp. 94 – 103. Bibl.

Mathematical models
Pero, Valéria Lúcia. A carteira de trabalho no mercado de trabalho metropolitano brasileiro. *Pesquisa e Planejamento Econômico*, v. 22, no. 2 (Aug 92), pp. 305 – 342. Bibl, tables, charts.

Chile
Díaz Corvalán, Eugenio. Nuevo sindicalismo, viejos problemas: la concertación en Chile. *Nueva Sociedad*, no. 124 (Mar – Apr 93), pp. 114 – 121.

Ruiz-Tagle P., Jaime. La CUT acepta el modelo exportador. *Mensaje*, v. 42, no. 418 (May 93), pp. 117 – 119. Tables.

Latin America
Ermida Uriarte, Oscar. La intervención estatal en las relaciones colectivas de trabajo latinoamericanas. *Nueva Sociedad*, no. 128 (Nov – Dec 93), pp. 29 – 37.

Godio, Julio Félix. Reestructuración del mercado laboral y estrategia sindical. *Nueva Sociedad*, no. 124 (Mar – Apr 93), pp. 104 – 113.

Mexican – American Border Region
Martínez, María Eugenia and Cirila Quintero Ramírez. Sindicalismo y contratación colectiva en las maquiladoras fronterizas: los casos de Tijuana, Ciudad Juárez y Matamoros. *Frontera Norte*, v. 4, no. 8 (July – Dec 92), pp. 7 – 47. Bibl, tables.

Quintero Ramírez, Cirila. Flexibilidad sindical en las maquiladoras: el caso de Agapito González Cavazos. *El Cotidiano*, v. 8, no. 52 (Jan – Feb 93), pp. 92 – 96.

— Tendencias sindicales en la frontera norte de México. *El Cotidiano*, v. 9, no. 56 (July 93), pp. 41 – 46.

Mexico
Aboites A., Jaime and Alenka Guzmán Chávez. Desempeño del sector manufacturero y relaciones laborales: la experiencia reciente de México. *El Cotidiano*, v. 10, no. 58 (Oct – Nov 93), pp. 103 – 111. Il, tables, charts.

Espinoza Valle, Víctor Alejandro. Las transformaciones del corporativismo regional: relaciones estado – sindicato en el sector público de Baja California. *Frontera Norte*, v. 4, no. 8 (July – Dec 92), pp. 79 – 110.

Herrera Lima, Fernando Francisco. Dina: del enfrentamiento a la negociación. *El Cotidiano*, v. 9, no. 56 (July 93), pp. 69 – 73. Il.

Lazaroff, León. Auto Workers Seek Quality Wages. *Business Mexico*, v. 3, no. 4 (Apr 93), pp. 20 – 21 +. Il.

Leff Zimmerman, Gloria. *Los pactos obreros y la institución presidencial en México, 1915 – 1938* reviewed by Mónica García Suárez. *El Cotidiano*, v. 9, no. 56 (July 93), p. 117.

Méndez, Luis and José Othón Quiroz Trejo. El conflicto de la Volkswagen: crónica de una muerte inesperada. *El Cotidiano*, v. 8, no. 51 (Nov – Dec 92), pp. 81 – 94. Bibl, il, tables, charts.

— Productividad, respuesta obrera y sucesión presidencial. *El Cotidiano*, v. 10, no. 58 (Oct – Nov 93), pp. 71 – 78.

Mondragón, Ana Laura. Contratos-ley y sindicatos: huleros y textileros. *El Cotidiano*, v. 9, no. 56 (July 93), pp. 18 – 22. Il, tables.

Montero Tirado, María del Carmen. La industria de la loza y la cerámica: el ascenso de la CROC. *El Cotidiano*, v. 9, no. 56 (July 93), pp. 86 – 88.

Veloz Avila, Norma Ilse. Conflictos y concertación obrero – patronal. *El Cotidiano*, v. 8, no. 51 (Nov – Dec 92), pp. 76 – 80. Il, tables.

— Conflictos y negociación obrero – patronal: septiembre – noviembre de 1992. *El Cotidiano*, v. 8, no. 52 (Jan – Feb 93), pp. 97 – 102. Tables.

— Diecisiete meses de respuesta obrera: conflictos obrero – patronales, 1992 – 1993. *El Cotidiano*, v. 9, no. 56 (July 93), pp. 89 – 103. Il, tables.

— Entre la productividad y el salario: conflictos y concertación obrero – patronal, enero – marzo 1993. *El Cotidiano*, v. 9, no. 54 (May 93), pp. 81 – 89. Il, tables.

Congresses

Cornejo Oviedo, Alejandro and Emanuel Orozco. Relatoría del encuentro "Antropología Industrial: Avances de Investigación." *Nueva Antropología*, v. 13, no. 44 (Aug 93), pp. 143 – 145.

Sources

Langue, Frédérique. El arbitrismo en el gremio minero novohispano o la representación de J. de la Borda y J. L. Lazaga, 1767: documentos. *Anuario de Estudios Americanos*, v. 50, no. 1 (1993), pp. 269 – 302. Bibl.

Venezuela

Calero, Fernando and Héctor Lucena R., eds. *Las relaciones de trabajo en los noventa: desafíos y propuestas* reviewed by T. M. van Hettema. *European Review of Latin American and Caribbean Studies*, no. 54 (June 93), pp. 139 – 140.

LABOR SUPPLY

See also
Employment
Unemployment

Argentina

Romero, Luis Alberto and Hilda Sábato. *Los trabajadores de Buenos Aires: la experiencia del mercado, 1850 – 1880* reviewed by María Cecilia Cangiano (Review entitled "¿Clase obrera o trabajadores?"). *Desarrollo Económico (Argentina)*, v. 33, no. 131 (Oct – Dec 93), pp. 445 – 448.

— *Los trabajadores de Buenos Aires: la experiencia del mercado, 1850 – 1880* reviewed by Susan Migden Socolow. *Hispanic American Historical Review*, v. 73, no. 2 (May 93), pp. 323 – 324.

— *Los trabajadores de Buenos Aires: la experiencia del mercado, 1850 – 1880* reviewed by Paula Alonso. *Journal of Latin American Studies*, v. 25, no. 2 (May 93), pp. 396 – 397.

— *Los trabajadores de Buenos Aires: la experiencia del mercado, 1850 – 1880* reviewed by Hobart A. Spalding. *Revista Interamericana de Bibliografía*, v. 42, no. 4 (1992), pp. 663 – 664.

Asia

Amadeo Swaelen, Edward Joaquim and Tariq Banuri. Mundos dentro del Tercer Mundo: instituciones del mercado de trabajo en Asia y en América Latina (Translated by Carlos Villegas). *El Trimestre Económico*, v. 59, no. 236 (Oct – Dec 92), pp. 657 – 723. Bibl, tables.

Bolivia

Tandeter, Enrique. *Coacción y mercado: la minería de plata en el Potosí colonial, 1692 – 1826* reviewed by Margarita Suárez. *Revista Andina*, v. 11, no. 1 (July 93), pp. 251 – 254.

Brazil

Telles, Edward E. Urban Labor Market Segmentation and Income in Brazil. *Economic Development and Cultural Change*, v. 41, no. 2 (Jan 93), pp. 231 – 249. Bibl, tables.

Versiani, Flávio Rabelo. Imigrantes, trabalho qualificado e industrialização: Rio e São Paulo no início do século. *Revista de Economia Política (Brazil)*, v. 13, no. 4 (Oct – Dec 93), pp. 77 – 96. Bibl, tables.

Cuba

Díaz-Briquets, Sergio. Collision Course: Labor Force and Educational Trends in Cuba. *Cuban Studies/Estudios Cubanos*, v. 23 (1993), pp. 91 – 112. Bibl, tables.

Ecuador

Martínez Valle, Luciano. El empleo en economías campesinas productoras para el mercado interno: el caso de la sierra ecuatoriana. *European Review of Latin American and Caribbean Studies*, no. 53 (Dec 92), pp. 83 – 93. Bibl, tables.

Guatemala

McCreery, David J. and Doug Munro. The Cargo of the *Montserrat*: Gilbertese Labor in Guatemalan Coffee, 1890 – 1908. *The Americas*, v. 49, no. 3 (Jan 93), pp. 271 – 295. Bibl, tables.

Pérez Sáinz, Juan Pablo et al. Trayectorias laborales y constitución de identidades: los trabajadores indígenas en la ciudad de Guatemala. *Estudios Sociológicos*, v. 11, no. 32 (May – Aug 93), pp. 515 – 545. Bibl, tables.

Latin America

Amadeo Swaelen, Edward Joaquim and Tariq Banuri. Mundos dentro del Tercer Mundo: instituciones del mercado de trabajo en Asia y en América Latina (Translated by Carlos Villegas). *El Trimestre Económico*, v. 59, no. 236 (Oct – Dec 92), pp. 657 – 723. Bibl, tables.

Cartón de Grammont, Hubert. Algunas reflexiones en torno al mercado de trabajo en el campo latinoamericano. *Revista Mexicana de Sociología*, v. 54, no. 1 (Jan – Mar 92), pp. 49 – 58. Bibl.

Oliveira, Orlandina de and Bryan R. Roberts. La informalidad urbana en años de expansión, crisis y restructuración económica (Translated by Laura Elena Pulido). *Estudios Sociológicos*, v. 11, no. 31 (Jan – Apr 93), pp. 33 – 58. Bibl, tables.

Mexico

Bustamante, Jorge Agustín et al, eds. *U.S. – Mexico Relations: Labor Market Interdependence* reviewed by Sidney Weintraub. *International Migration Review*, v. 27, no. 3 (Fall 93), p. 646.

— *U.S. – Mexico Relations: Labor Market Interdependence* reviewed by Guillermo Arámburgo Vizcarra. *Journal of Latin American Studies*, v. 25, no. 2 (May 93), pp. 406 – 407.

Cárdenas, Fe Esperanza and Vincent Redonnet. Modernización de la empresa AHMSA en Monclova, Coahuila y su impacto sobre la población. *Estudios Demográficos y Urbanos*, v. 6, no. 3 (Sept – Dec 91), pp. 677 – 716. Bibl, tables.

Gamboa Ojeda, Leticia. Mercado de fuerza de trabajo e industria textil: el centro-oriente de México durante el porfiriato. *Siglo XIX: Cuadernos*, v. 1, no. 1 (Oct 91), pp. 9 – 36. Bibl.

Lara Flores, Sara María. La flexibilidad del mercado de trabajo rural: una propuesta que involucra a las mujeres. *Revista Mexicana de Sociología*, v. 54, no. 1 (Jan – Mar 92), pp. 29 – 48. Bibl.

Pries, Ludger. Aspectos del mercado de trabajo en Puebla: la relación entre trabajo asalariado y por cuenta propia. *El Cotidiano*, v. 8, no. 52 (Jan – Feb 93), pp. 31 – 37. Bibl, il, charts.

Rendón, Teresa and Carlos Salas Páez. El empleo en México en los ochenta: tendencias y cambios. *Comercio Exterior*, v. 43, no. 8 (Aug 93), pp. 717 – 730. Bibl, tables, charts.

Rubin-Kurtzman, Jane R. Los determinantes de la oferta de trabajo femenino en la ciudad de México, 1970. *Estudios Demográficos y Urbanos*, v. 6, no. 3 (Sept – Dec 91), pp. 545 – 582. Bibl, tables.

Research

Cortés C., Fernando and Rosa María Rubalcava. Algunas determinantes de la inserción laboral en la industria maquiladora de exportación de Matamoros. *Estudios Sociológicos*, v. 11, no. 31 (Jan – Apr 93), pp. 59 – 91. Bibl, tables.

Puerto Rico

Enchautegui, María E. The Value of U.S. Labor Market Experience in the Home Country: The Case of Puerto Rican Return Migrants. *Economic Development and Cultural Change*, v. 42, no. 1 (Oct 93), pp. 168 – 191. Bibl, tables, charts.

United States

Borjas, George J. and Richard B. Freeman, eds. *Immigration and the Work Force: Economic Consequences for the United States and Source Areas* reviewed by Jim Thomas. *Journal of Latin American Studies,* v. 25, no. 3 (Oct 93), pp. 683 – 684.

Briggs, Vernon M., Jr. *Mass Immigration and the National Interest* reviewed by Michael Ellis. *Journal of Borderlands Studies,* v. 7, no. 2 (Fall 92), pp. 109 – 111.

Bustamante, Jorge Agustín et al, eds. *U.S. – Mexico Relations: Labor Market Interdependence* reviewed by Sidney Weintraub. *International Migration Review,* v. 27, no. 3 (Fall 93), p. 646.

— *U.S. – Mexico Relations: Labor Market Interdependence* reviewed by Guillermo Arámburgo Vizcarra. *Journal of Latin American Studies,* v. 25, no. 2 (May 93), pp. 406 – 407.

Edwards, Jack E. et al. Willingness to Relocate for Employment: A Survey of Hispanics, Non-Hispanic Whites, and Blacks. *Hispanic Journal of Behavioral Sciences,* v. 15, no. 1 (Feb 93), pp. 121 – 133. Bibl, tables.

Faux, Jeff and Thea Lee. Los efectos del Acuerdo de Libre Comercio de América del Norte en la fuerza de trabajo de Estados Unidos. *Relaciones Internacionales (Mexico),* v. 15, Nueva época, no. 57 (Jan – Mar 93), pp. 37 – 54.

Stier, Haya and Marta Tienda. Family, Work, and Women: The Labor Supply of Hispanic Immigrant Wives. *International Migration Review,* v. 26, no. 4 (Winter 92), pp. 1291 – 1313. Bibl, tables, charts.

LABOR UNIONS

See
Teachers' unions
Trade unions
Subdivision *Political activity* under *Peasantry*

LABRUNIE, GÉRARD

See
Gérard de Nerval, Gérard Labrunie

LACALLE, LUIS ALBERTO

Waksman, Guillermo. Uruguay: la gran derrota de Lacalle. *Nueva Sociedad,* no. 124 (Mar – Apr 93), pp. 17 – 21.

LACAN, JACQUES

Stroud, Matthew D. The Desiring Subject and the Promise of Salvation: A Lacanian Study of Sor Juana's *El divino Narciso. Hispania (USA),* v. 76, no. 2 (May 93), pp. 204 – 212. Bibl.

LACERDA, CARLOS

Dulles, John W. F. *Carlos Lacerda, Brazilian Crusader, Vol. I: The Years 1914 – 1960* reviewed by Thomas E. Skidmore. *The Americas,* v. 49, no. 3 (Jan 93), pp. 416 – 417.

LACUNZA DÍAZ, P. MANUEL

Parra Carrasco, Fredy Omar. *Pensamiento teológico en Chile: contribución a su estudio, tomo V: El reino que ha de venir; historia y esperanza en la obra de Manuel Lacunza* reviewed by José Arteaga. *Mensaje,* v. 42, no. 425 (Dec 93), p. 657. Il.

LAFER, CELSO

Interviews

Silva, Alexandra de Mello e and Paulo S. Wrobel. Entrevista com Celso Lafer. *Estudos Históricos,* v. 6, no. 12 (July – Dec 93), pp. 271 – 284.

LA HOZ, PALOMA

Cortés, Laia. Paloma La Hoz: Made in Perú. *Debate (Peru),* v. 16, no. 75 (Dec 93 – Jan 94), pp. 57 – 58. Il.

LAIA

See
Latin American Integration Association

LAIR, CLARA

See
Negrón Muñoz, Mercedes

LAMBAYEQUE, PERU (DEPARTMENT)

Ramírez-Horton, Susan Elizabeth. *Patriarcas provinciales: la tenencia de la tierra y la economía del poder en el Perú colonial* reviewed by Scarlett O'Phelan Godoy. *Anuario de Estudios Americanos,* v. 49, Suppl. 1 (1992), pp. 257 – 258.

LAMBORGHINI, LEÓNIDAS C.

Correspondence, reminiscences, etc.

Lamborghini, Leónidas C. Digresiones, 1976 – 1993. *Cuadernos Hispanoamericanos,* no. 517 – 519 (July – Sept 93), pp. 498 – 502.

LAMBORGHINI, OSVALDO

Criticism of specific works

El niño proletario

Fernández, Nancy P. Violencia, risa y parodia: "El niño proletario" de O. Lamborghini y *Sin rumbo* de E. Cambacérès. *Escritura (Venezuela),* v. 17, no. 33 – 34 (Jan – Dec 92), pp. 159 – 164.

LAMMING, GEORGE

Addresses, essays, lectures

Lamming, George. Coming, Coming, Coming Home. *Casa de las Américas,* no. 190 (Jan – Mar 93), pp. 65 – 74.

LAND GRANTS

See also
Encomiendas
Real property

Mexico

Haskett, Robert Stephen. Visions of Municipal Glory Undimmed: The Nahuatl Town Histories of Colonial Cuernavaca. *Colonial Latin American Historical Review,* v. 1, no. 1 (Fall 92), pp. 1 – 36. Bibl, il.

LAND REFORM

Sánchez Noguera, Abdón. La reforma agraria: vigencia o caducidad. *Derecho y Reforma Agraria,* no. 23 (1992), pp. 115 – 122.

Brazil

Almeida, Paulo Guillerme de. *Aspectos jurídicos de reforma agraria no Brasil* reviewed by Arnaldo Gómez A. *Derecho y Reforma Agraria,* no. 23 (1992), p. 216.

Gros, Christian. El futuro de la reforma agraria en Brasil. *Revista Mexicana de Sociología,* v. 54, no. 1 (Jan – Mar 92), pp. 59 – 73. Tables.

Chile

Busquet I., Jaime. INPROA: treinta años presente en el mundo rural. *Mensaje,* v. 42, no. 418 (May 93), pp. 154 – 156. Il.

Delahaye, Olivier. Reforma agraria, renta y mercadeo de la tierra agrícola: una reflexión a partir de los casos venezolano y chileno. *Estudios Rurales Latinoamericanos,* v. 15, no. 2 – 3 (May – Dec 92), pp. 29 – 63. Bibl, tables.

Kay, Cristóbal and Patricio Silva, eds. *Development and Social Change in the Chilean Countryside: From the Pre-Land Reform Period to the Democratic Transition* reviewed by Chris Scott. *Journal of Latin American Studies,* v. 25, no. 2 (May 93), p. 407.

Colombia

Ramírez Vallejo, Jorge. Una nueva mirada a la reforma agraria colombiana. *Planeación y Desarrollo,* v. 24, no. 1 (Jan – Apr 93), pp. 425 – 461. Bibl, tables, charts.

Developing countries

Covarrubias M., Isaías. Reflexiones acerca del porqué de la reforma agraria. *Derecho y Reforma Agraria,* no. 23 (1992), pp. 135 – 140.

Guatemala

Bell, John Patrick. La Asociación General de Agricultores frente a la reforma agraria en la Guatemala revolucionaria, 1944 – 1954. *Anuario de Estudios Centroamericanos,* v. 18, no. 1 (1992), pp. 17 – 28. Bibl.

Latin America

Casanova, Ramón Vicente. El derecho agrario iberoamericano: su vocación regional. *Derecho y Reforma Agraria,* no. 24 (1993), pp. 11 – 26.

Pérez Maldonado, Alberto. La reforma agraria: un proceso de transformación social y una política del estado; base de un desarrollo integral del país. *Derecho y Reforma Agraria,* no. 23 (1992), pp. 123 – 133. Bibl.

Mexico

Azpeitia Gómez, Hugo et al. *Los tiempos de la crisis, 1970 – 1982, partes 1 y 2: Historia de la cuestión agraria mexicana* reviewed by David W. Walker. *Hispanic American Historical Review,* v. 73, no. 3 (Aug 93), pp. 529 – 530.

Cruz Rodríguez, María Soledad. La nueva ley agraria y su impacto en la periferia ejidal de la ciudad de México. *El Cotidiano,* v. 10, no. 57 (Aug – Sept 93), pp. 54 – 59. Bibl, il, tables.

Durand Alcántara, Carlos Humberto. Las reformas y adicionales al Artículo 27 constitucional, 1857 – 1992. *Derecho y Reforma Agraria,* no. 24 (1993), pp. 139 – 157. Bibl.

Nicaragua

Enríquez, Laura Jean. *Harvesting Change: Labor and Agrarian Reform in Nicaragua, 1979 – 1990* reviewed by Elizabeth Dore. *Journal of Latin American Studies,* v. 25, no. 1 (Feb 93), pp. 211 – 212.

Peru

Tolentino Tapia, Lorenzo. Perfil para un balance jurídico de la reforma agraria peruana. *Derecho y Reforma Agraria,* no. 24 (1993), pp. 33 – 41.

Venezuela

Casanova, Ramón Vicente. Por qué la reforma agraria. *Derecho y Reforma Agraria,* no. 23 (1992), pp. 11 – 16.

Delahaye, Olivier. Reforma agraria, renta y mercadeo de la tierra agrícola: una reflexión a partir de los casos venezolano y chileno. *Estudios Rurales Latinoamericanos,* v. 15, no. 2 – 3 (May – Dec 92), pp. 29 – 63. Bibl, tables.

LAND SETTLEMENT

See also
Frontier and pioneer life
Geography, Economic

Argentina

Dodds, Klaus-John. Geography, Identity, and the Creation of the Argentine State. *Bulletin of Latin American Research,* v. 12, no. 3 (Sept 93), pp. 311 – 331. Bibl.

Chile

Norambuena Carrasco, Carmen. Inmigración, agricultura y ciudades intermedias, 1880 – 1930. *Cuadernos de Historia (Chile),* no. 11 (Dec 91), pp. 105 – 123. Bibl, tables.

Cuba

Naranjo Orovio, V. Consuelo. Trabajo libre e inmigración española en Cuba, 1880 – 1930. *Revista de Indias,* v. 52, no. 195 – 196 (May – Dec 92), pp. 749 – 794. Bibl, charts.

El Salvador

La vida en la Comunidad Segundo Montes: prototipo de la nueva economía popular. *ECA; Estudios Centroamericanos,* v. 48, no. 534 – 535 (Apr – May 93), pp. 437 – 444.

Mexican – American Border Region

Anguiano Téllez, María Eugenia. Irrigación y capital para transformar el desierto: la formación social del valle de Mexicali a principios del siglo XX. *Frontera Norte,* v. 4, no. 8 (July – Dec 92), pp. 125 – 147. Bibl.

Simmons, Marc. *The Last Conquistador: Juan de Oñate and the Settling of the Far Southwest* reviewed by Adrian Bustamante. *Colonial Latin American Historical Review,* v. 2, no. 2 (Spring 93), pp. 235 – 236.

Sources

El Plan de Pitic de 1789 y las nuevas poblaciones proyectadas en las provincias internas de la Nueva España (Transcribed and edited by Joseph P. Sánchez). *Colonial Latin American Historical Review,* v. 2, no. 4 (Fall 93), pp. 449 – 467. Maps.

Mexico

Arnaiz Burne, Stella M. and Alfredo César Dachary. La frontera caribe de México en el XIX: una historia olvidada. *Siglo XIX: Cuadernos,* v. 3, no. 7 (Oct 93), pp. 33 – 62. Bibl, tables, maps.

García Zambrano, Angel Julián. El poblamiento de México en la época del contacto, 1520 – 1540. *Mesoamérica (USA),* v. 13, no. 24 (Dec 92), pp. 239 – 296. Bibl, il, facs, charts.

Gardner, David Skerritt. Colonización y modernización del campo en el centro de Veracruz, siglo XIX. *Siglo XIX: Cuadernos,* v. 2, no. 5 (Feb 93), pp. 39 – 57. Bibl, tables.

Morelos García, Noel. Consideraciones teóricas sobre el proceso de urbanización en Mesoamérica. *Boletín de Antropología Americana,* no. 23 (July 91), pp. 137 – 160.

Skerritt, David A. Una historia dinámica entre la sierra y la costa. *La Palabra y el Hombre,* no. 83 (July – Sept 92), pp. 5 – 25. Bibl, tables, maps.

LAND TENURE

See also
Haciendas
Land reform
Land use
Real property

Argentina

Basualdo, Eduardo M. and Miguel Khavisse. *El nuevo poder terrateniente* reviewed by Horacio Giberti. *Realidad Económica,* no. 117 (July – Aug 93), pp. 30 – 32.

— El nuevo poder terrateniente (Excerpt from the forthcoming book of the same title). *Realidad Económica,* no. 113 (Jan – Feb 93), pp. 90 – 99.

Birocco, Carlos María and Gabriela Gresores. *Arrendamientos, desalojos y subordinación campesina: Buenos Aires, siglo XVIII* reviewed by Carlos G. A. Bulcourf. *Todo Es Historia,* v. 27, no. 313 (Aug 93), p. 71. Il.

Law and legislation

Infesta, María Elena and Marla Valencia. Los criterios legales en la revisión de la política rosista de tierras públicas: Buenos Aires, 1852 – 1864. *Investigaciones y Ensayos,* no. 41 (Jan – Dec 91), pp. 407 – 421. Bibl.

Costa Rica

Fonseca Corrales, Elizabeth. *Costa Rica colonial: la tierra y el hombre* reviewed by Marvín Barahona. *Mesoamérica (USA),* v. 13, no. 24 (Dec 92), pp. 454 – 457.

Honduras

Fandiño, Mario. Land Titling and Peasant Differentiation in Honduras. *Latin American Perspectives,* v. 20, no. 2 (Spring 93), pp. 45 – 53. Bibl.

Latin America

Bifani, Patricia. Disponibilidad, derecho y gestión del espacio vital. *Nueva Sociedad,* no. 123 (Jan – Feb 93), pp. 84 – 93. Bibl.

Law and legislation

Lira Montt, Luis. La fundación de mayorazgos en Indias: estudio histórico – jurídico. *Boletín de la Academia Chilena de la Historia,* v. 58 – 59, no. 102 (1991 – 1992), pp. 349 – 386. Bibl, il, tables.

Mexico

Brannon, Jeffery T. and Gilbert Michael Joseph, eds. *Land, Labor, and Capital in Modern Yucatán: Essays in Regional History and Political Economy* reviewed by Donald F. Stevens. *The Americas,* v. 49, no. 4 (Apr 93), pp. 558 – 559.

González Rodrigo, José and Regina Leal. Manejo de resursos naturales y derecho consuetudinario. *Nueva Antropología,* v. 13, no. 44 (Aug 93), pp. 61 – 70. Bibl.

Harvey, Herbert R., ed. *Land and Politics in the Valley of Mexico: A Two Thousand Year Perspective* reviewed by Wayne Osborn. *The Americas,* v. 49, no. 4 (Apr 93), pp. 542 – 544.

— *Land and Politics in the Valley of Mexico: A Two Thousand Year Perspective* reviewed by Jesús Monjarás-Ruiz. *Historia Mexicana,* v. 42, no. 1 (July – Sept 92), pp. 144 – 152.

— *Land and Politics in the Valley of Mexico: A Two Thousand Year Perspective* reviewed by Michael E. Smith. *Latin American Antiquity,* v. 4, no. 1 (Mar 93), pp. 97 – 98.

Hoffmann, Odile. *Tierras y territorio en Xico, Veracruz* reviewed by Hipólito Rodríguez. *Estudios Sociológicos,* v. 11, no. 31 (Jan – Apr 93), pp. 274 – 276.

Kanter, Deborah E. Viudas y vecinos, milpas y magueyes: el impacto del auge de la población en el valle de Toluca; el caso de Tenango del Valle en el siglo XVIII. *Estudios Demográficos y Urbanos,* v. 7, no. 1 (Jan – Apr 92), pp. 19 – 33. Bibl, tables.

Martínez Aparicio, Jorge. La tenencia de la tierra, luego de un año de la reforma al 27: nuevos cambios, fenómenos viejos; la tierra caliente. *El Cotidiano,* v. 10, no. 57 (Aug – Sept 93), pp. 86 – 92. Il.

Menegus Bornemann, Margarita. *Del señorío a la república de indios: el caso de Toluca, 1500 – 1600* reviewed by Michel Bertrand. *Caravelle,* no. 60 (1993), pp. 143 – 147.

Law and legislation

García Martínez, Bernardo. Jurisdicción y propiedad: una distinción fundamental en la historia de los pueblos de indios del México colonial. *European Review of Latin American and Caribbean Studies,* no. 53 (Dec 92), pp. 47 – 60. Bibl.

Societies, etc.

Rodríguez García, Rubén. *La Cámara Agrícola Nacional Jalisciense: una sociedad de terratenientes en la revolución mexicana* reviewed by Carlos Alba Vega. *Foro Internacional,* v. 32, no. 5 (Oct – Dec 92), pp. 788 – 793.

Peru

Contreras, Carlos. Mercado de tierras y sociedad campesina: el valle del Mantaro en el siglo XIX. *Historia y Cultura (Peru),* no. 20 (1990), pp. 243 – 265. Bibl.

Ramírez-Horton, Susan Elizabeth. *Patriarcas provinciales: la tenencia de la tierra y la economía del poder en el Perú colonial* reviewed by Scarlett O'Phelan Godoy. *Anuario de Estudios Americanos,* v. 49, Suppl. 1 (1992), pp. 257 – 258.

Sources

Adorno, Rolena. The Genesis of Felipe Guamán Poma de Ayala's *Nueva corónica y buen gobierno. Colonial Latin American Review,* v. 2, no. 1 – 2 (1993), pp. 53 – 92. Bibl, il.

Venezuela
Law and legislation

Soto, Oscar David. Propiedad agraria y desafectación. *Derecho y Reforma Agraria,* no. 23 (1992), pp. 33 – 50.

LAND USE

See also
　Ecology
　Land tenure

Amazon Valley

Anderson, Anthony B., ed. *Alternatives to Deforestation: Steps toward Sustained Use of the Amazon Rain Forest* reviewed by David Cleary. *Journal of Latin American Studies,* v. 25, no. 2 (May 93), pp. 408 – 409.

Andean region

Kessel, Juan J. M. M. van. El pago a la tierra: porque el desarrollo lo exige. *Allpanchis,* v. 23, no. 40 (July – Dec 92), pp. 201 – 217. Bibl.

Argentina

Bonaudo, Marta et al. Ferrocarriles y mercado de tierras en el centro-sur de Santa Fe, 1870 – 1900. *Siglo XIX: Cuadernos,* v. 3, no. 6 (June 93), pp. 37 – 64. Bibl, tables.

Brazil

Ferreira, Ignez Costa Barbosa. Gestão do espaço agrário. *Revista Brasileira de Geografia,* v. 53, no. 3 (July – Sept 91), pp. 149 – 159. Bibl, tables, maps.

Kohlhepp, Gerd. Mudanças estruturais na agropecuária e mobilidade da população rural no norte do Paraná (Brasil). *Revista Brasileira de Geografia,* v. 53, no. 2 (Apr – June 91), pp. 79 – 94. Bibl, il, tables, maps.

Methodology

Souza, Jaimeval Caetano de et al. Combinações agrícolas no estado da Bahia, 1970 – 1980: uma contribuição metodológica. *Revista Brasileira de Geografia,* v. 53, no. 2 (Apr – June 91), pp. 95 – 112. Bibl, tables, maps.

Research

Miranda, Evaristo Eduardo de. Variabilidad espacio-temporal de las quemas en el Brasil. *Interciencia,* v. 18, no. 6 (Nov – Dec 93), pp. 300 – 301. Tables.

Central America

Vargas Ulate, Gilberto. Estudio del uso actual y capacidad de uso de la tierra en América Central. *Anuario de Estudios Centroamericanos,* v. 18, no. 2 (1992), pp. 7 – 23. Bibl, maps.

Weinberg, William J. *War on the Land: Ecology and Politics in Central America* reviewed by Anthony Bebbington. *Bulletin of Latin American Research,* v. 12, no. 2 (May 93), p. 242.

Mexican – American Border Region

Curtis, James R. Central Business Districts of the Two Laredos. *Geographical Review,* v. 83, no. 1 (Jan 93), pp. 54 – 65. Bibl, tables, charts.

Mexico

Durán, Ana María and María Concepción Huerta Trujillo. Cambios de usos del suelo y despoblamiento en la colonia Roma. *El Cotidiano,* v. 10, no. 57 (Aug – Sept 93), pp. 73 – 77. Il, tables.

LANDO, FRANCISCO MANUEL DE

Moscoso, Francisco. Encomendero y esclavista: Francisco Manuel de Lando. *Anuario de Estudios Americanos,* v. 49 (1992), pp. 119 – 142. Bibl.

LANGE, FRANCISCO CURT

Brandão, José Vieira. Curt Lange en Recife. *Revista Musical de Venezuela,* no. 28 (May – Dec 89), pp. 83 – 92.

Oliveira, José Aparecido de et al. Homenaje al doctor Francisco Curt Lange. *Revista Musical de Venezuela,* no. 28 (May – Dec 89), Issue. Bibl, il, facs.

Ruiz, Irma. Un proyecto trunco. *Revista Musical de Venezuela,* no. 28 (May – Dec 89), pp. 98 – 105. Charts.

Velazco, Jorge. La confluencia intelectual y académica en la formación escolástica y la obra de investigación de Francisco Curt Lange. *Revista Musical de Venezuela,* no. 28 (May – Dec 89), pp. 207 – 223.

Bibliography

Bibliografía (Works by and about Francisco Curt Lange). *Revista Musical de Venezuela,* no. 28 (May – Dec 89), pp. 224 – 264.

Indices de las colecciones cooperativas y colectivas publicadas por Francisco Curt Lange, 1935 – 1958 (Indexes to eight journals on Latin American music, introduced by Humberto Sagredo Araya). *Revista Musical de Venezuela,* no. 29 (Jan – June 90), Issue. Il, facs.

LANGE, NORAH

Biography

Miguel, María Esther de. *Norah Lange* reviewed by Eliana C. Hermann. *Chasqui,* v. 22, no. 1 (May 93), pp. 92 – 94.

LANGER, MARIE

Kremlicka, Raimund. Zwei Frauen: Eva Peron und Marie Langer. *Zeitschrift für Lateinamerika Wien,* no. 42 (1992), pp. 53 – 65. Bibl.

LANGUAGE AND LANGUAGES

See also
　Bilingualism
　Linguistics
　Names of specific languages
　Subdivision *Language* under *Children* and *Hispanic*
　　Americans (U.S.)
　Subdivision *Languages* under names of specific
　　countries and Indian groups

Morábito, Fabio. El escritor en busca de una lengua. *Vuelta,* v. 17, no. 195 (Feb 93), pp. 22 – 24.

Study and teaching

Delgado Chinchilla, Carmen. Environment: A Key Factor in Second Language Acquisition. *Káñina,* v. 16, no. 1 (Jan – June 92), pp. 185 – 193. Bibl.

Lerner de Zunino, Delia and Alicia Palacios de Pizani. *El aprendizaje de la lengua escrita en la escuela: reflexiones sobre la propuesta pedagógica constructivista* reviewed by Magaly Muñoz de Pimentel. *La Educación (USA),* v. 37, no. 115 (1993), pp. 426 – 428.

Umaña Chaverri, José Otilio. Una opción teórico – metodológica para la enseñanza de la literatura en programas de aprendizaje de lenguas extranjeras y segundas lenguas. *Káñina,* v. 16, no. 1 (Jan – June 92), pp. 171 – 183. Bibl.

LANGUAGES, INDO-AMERICAN

See
Araucanian language
Cariban languages
Maya languages
Nahuatl language
Quechua language
Subdivision *Languages* under names of specific countries and Indian groups

LARA, AGUSTÍN

Colomé, Delfín. Tres evocaciones de Agustín Lara. *Cuadernos Hispanoamericanos,* no. 521 (Nov 93), pp. 147 – 150. Il.

LARA, JESÚS

Criticism of specific works
Tragedia del fin de Atawallpa

García Pabón, Leonardo. Comunicación, escritura e imaginario social en la *Tragedia del fin de Atahuallpa. Caravelle,* no. 59 (1992), pp. 225 – 240. Bibl.

LARA ZAVALA, HERNÁN

Criticism of specific works
El cantar del pecador

Lara Zavala, Hernán. El cantar del pecador (Text read by the author upon presentation of the newly published book). *Plural (Mexico),* v. 22, no. 265 (Oct 93), pp. 78 – 79.

LARRAZ, JULIO

Kozik, K. K. Julio Larraz: Exile and Reality. *Latin American Art,* v. 4, no. 4 (Winter 92), pp. 35 – 37. Bibl, il.

LARRETA, ENRIQUE RODRÍGUEZ

Criticism of specific works
La gloria de don Ramiro

Saylor-Javaherian, Cheryll. Nietzschean Antagonism, Self-Sacrifice, and Redemption in Enrique Larreta's *La gloria de don Ramiro. Hispanic Journal,* v. 14, no. 1 (Spring 93), pp. 7 – 23. Bibl.

LARTIGUE, GERARDO

Rocha, Paulina. Huellas del humo: Gerardo Lartigue. *Artes de México,* no. 18 (Winter 92), p. 97. Il.

LASTRA, PEDRO

Criticism and interpretation

Gómez, Miguel. Sueños de paraíso y de luz: la poesía de Pedro Lastra. *Revista Chilena de Literatura,* no. 40 (Nov 92), pp. 105 – 113.

LASTRA, RODOLFO

Interviews

Vázquez Hall, Patricia. Palabras con Rodolfo Lastra. *Plural (Mexico),* v. 22, no. 257 (Feb 93), pp. 75 – 76.

LATIFUNDIO

See
Haciendas

LATIN AMERICA

See also
Advertising – Latin America
Agricultural credit – Latin America
Agricultural laborers – Latin America
Agriculture – Latin America
Agriculture and state – Latin America
AIDS (Disease) – Latin America

Anthropology – Latin America
Archaeology – Latin America
Architecture – Latin America
Architecture, Colonial – Latin America
Armaments – Latin America
Art – Latin America
Art, Colonial – Latin America
Art and society – Latin America
Artists – Latin America
Audiovisual education – Latin America
Authoritarianism – Latin America
Authors – Latin America
Balance of payments – Latin America
Banana trade – Latin America
Banks and banking – Latin America
Biography (as a literary form) – Latin America
Blacks – Latin America
Blacks in literature – Latin America
Books – Latin America
Business enterprises – Latin America
Caciquism – Latin America
Capital – Latin America
Capital productivity – Latin America
Capitalism – Latin America
Catholic Church – Latin America
Children – Latin America
Christian art and symbolism – Latin America
Church and social problems – Latin America
Church and state – Latin America
Church music – Latin America
Cities and towns – Latin America
Citizenship – Latin America
Comic books, strips, etc. – Latin America
Communism – Latin America
Community development – Latin America
Competition – Latin America
Conservatism – Latin America
Convents and nunneries – Latin America
Corruption (in politics) – Latin America
Cultural imperialism – Latin America
Dancing – Latin America
Debts, Public – Latin America
Decentralization in government – Latin America
Democracy – Latin America
Diseases – Latin America
Drug trade – Latin America
Ecology – Latin America
Ecology and development – Latin America
Economic assistance – Latin America
Economic assistance, Foreign – Latin America
Economics – Latin America
Education – Latin America
Education, Higher – Latin America
Education, Primary – Latin America
Education and state – Latin America
Educational accountability – Latin America
Educational research – Latin America
Elections – Latin America
Elite (Social sciences) – Latin America
Environmental policy – Latin America
Ethnicity – Latin America
Ethnomusicology – Latin America
Europeans – Latin America
Evangelicalism – Latin America
Exiles – Latin America
Family – Latin America
Fertility, Human – Latin America
Finance – Latin America
Finance, Public – Latin America
Folk art – Latin America
Folk drama – Latin America
Folk literature – Latin America
Folk lore – Latin America
Folk music – Latin America
Food habits – Latin America
Food industry and trade – Latin America
Food supply – Latin America
Foreign trade promotion – Latin America
Foreign trade regulation – Latin America
Forests – Latin America
Geographical distribution of plants and animals – Latin America
Geography – Latin America
Geography, Historical – Latin America
Geopolitics – Latin America
Government ownership of business enterprises – Latin America
Guerrillas – Latin America

Harbors – Latin America
Human capital – Latin America
Human rights – Latin America
Income distribution – Latin America
Industrial productivity – Latin America
Industry and state – Latin America
Inflation (Finance) – Latin America
Informal sector (Economics) – Latin America
Information services – Latin America
Investments, Foreign – Latin America
Jesuits – Latin America
Journalism – Latin America
Judiciary – Latin America
Labor and laboring classes – Latin America
Labor laws and legislation – Latin America
Labor relations – Latin America
Labor supply – Latin America
Land reform – Latin America
Land tenure – Latin America
Legends – Latin America
Liberalism – Latin America
Liberation theology – Latin America
Literary criticism – Latin America
Literature and history – Latin America
Literature and society – Latin America
Local government – Latin America
Marginalization – Latin America
Marriage – Latin America
Marxism – Latin America
Mass media – Latin America
Migration, Internal – Latin America
Military assistance, Foreign – Latin America
Mining industry and finance – Latin America
Monasticism and religious orders – Latin America
Money and money supply – Latin America
Motion pictures – Latin America
Music – Latin America
Musical instruments – Latin America
National income – Latin America
National security – Latin America
Nationalism – Latin America
Natural disasters – Latin America
Natural resources – Latin America
Non-governmental organizations – Latin America
Oral history – Latin America
Oral tradition – Latin America
Paleobotany – Latin America
Patronage, Political – Latin America
Peasantry – Latin America
Periodicals – Latin America
Philosophy – Latin America
Philosophy and politics – Latin America
Photography and photographers – Latin America
Pilgrims and pilgrimages – Latin America
Political participation – Latin America
Political parties – Latin America
Political sociology – Latin America
Politics an literature – Latin America
Politics in literature – Latin America
Popular culture – Latin America
Popular music – Latin America
Population – Latin America
Portuguese – Latin America
Posters – Latin America
Postmodernism – Latin America
Poverty – Latin America
Press – Latin America
Press and politics – Latin America
Pressure groups – Latin America
Privatization – Latin America
Protestantism – Latin America
Public administration – Latin America
Public health – Latin America
Public opinion – Latin America
Public utilities – Latin America
Publishers and publishing – Latin America
Race discrimination – Latin America
Reading interests – Latin America
Regional planning – Latin America
Regionalism – Latin America
Religion and politics – Latin America
Religion and sociology – Latin America
Revolutions – Latin America
Roads – Latin America
Saving and investment – Latin America
School management and organization – Latin America
Science – Latin America
Science and state – Latin America

Scientific expeditions – Latin America
Sculpture – Latin America
Sex role – Latin America
Sexual behavior – Latin America
Slavery – Latin America
Social change – Latin America
Social classes – Latin America
Social conflict – Latin America
Social movements – Latin America
Social sciences – Latin America
Social security – Latin America
Social services – Latin America
Socialism – Latin America
Socialization – Latin America
Sociolinguistics – Latin America
Sociology, Urban – Latin America
Soils – Latin America
Spaniards – Latin America
Spanish language – Latin America
Steel industry and trade – Latin America
Suicide – Latin America
Tariff – Latin America
Taxation – Latin America
Teachers, Training of – Latin America
Technical education – Latin America
Technology – Latin America
Technology and state – Latin America
Television – Latin America
Terrorism – Latin America
Theater – Latin America
Theology – Latin America
Trade unions – Latin America
Transportation – Latin America
Universities and colleges – Latin America
Urbanization – Latin America
Vegetation and climate – Latin America
Violence – Latin America
Vocational education – Latin America
Water – Latin America
Water power – Latin America
Witchcraft – Latin America
Women – Latin America
Women authors – Latin America
Women in literature – Latin America
Women's rights – Latin America

Armed forces

Benítez Manaut, Raúl. Identity Crisis: The Military in Changing Times (Translated by Kent Klineman). *NACLA Report on the Americas*, v. 27, no. 2 (Sept – Oct 93), pp. 15 – 19.

Fitch, John Samuel. The Decline of U.S. Military Influence on Latin America. *Journal of Inter-American Studies and World Affairs*, v. 35, no. 2 (Summer 93), pp. 1 – 49. Bibl, tables, charts.

Moneta, Carlos Juan. As forças armadas latino-americanas nos anos '90. *Política e Estratégica*, v. 8, no. 2 – 4 (Apr – Dec 90), pp. 153 – 167. Bibl.

Nunn, Frederick M. *The Time of the Generals: Latin American Professional Militarism in World Perspective* reviewed by Daniel M. Masterson. *The Americas*, v. 50, no. 1 (July 93), pp. 137 – 139.

— *The Time of the Generals: Latin American Professional Militarism in World Perspective* reviewed by John D. Martz. *Revista Interamericana de Bibliografía*, v. 42, no. 3 (1992), p. 506.

Zagorski, Paul W. *Democracy vs. National Security: Civil – Military Relations in Latin America* reviewed by Gamaliel Perruci. *Journal of Inter-American Studies and World Affairs*, v. 35, no. 1 (1993), pp. 167 – 170.

Bibliography

Artículos recientes/Recent Articles. *Revista Interamericana de Bibliografía*, v. 42 (1992), All issues.

Covington, Paula Hattox, ed. *Latin America and the Caribbean: A Critical Guide to Research Sources* reviewed by Richard D. Woods. *Hispania (USA)*, v. 76, no. 2 (May 93), pp. 284 – 285.

— *Latin America and the Caribbean: A Critical Guide to Research Sources* reviewed by Thomas L. Welch. *Revista Interamericana de Bibliografía*, v. 42, no. 2 (1992), pp. 285 – 286.

Hilton, Sylvia-Lyn and Amancio Labandeira Fernández. El americanismo en España, 1991 – 1992. *Revista de Indias*, v. 53, no. 197 (Jan – Apr 93), pp. 133 – 409.

Publicaciones del Congreso de los Estados Unidos sobre América Latina y el Caribe/Publications of the Congress of the United States about Latin America and the Caribbean. *Revista Interamericana de Bibliografía*, v. 42 (1992), All issues.

Tesis doctorales recientes/Recent Dissertations. *Revista Interamericana de Bibliografía*, v. 42 (1992), All issues.

Boundaries

Sources

Morales, Adolfo de. Tratados de límites de las posesiones americanas entre España y Portugal. *Signo*, no. 36 – 37, Nueva época (May – Dec 92), pp. 387 – 407.

Civilization

Araya Guillén, Victorio. 1492 – 1992: una reflexión desde el reverso de la historia; las víctimas. *Revista de Historia (Costa Rica)*, no. 25 (Jan – June 92), pp. 151 – 156.

Baptista Gumucio, Mariano. *Latinoamericanos y norteamericanos* reviewed by Aída Cometta Manzoni. *Revista Nacional de Cultura (Venezuela)*, v. 53, no. 285 (Apr – June 92), pp. 245 – 247.

Beck, Heinrich. América Latina como encuentro cultural. *Cuadernos Americanos*, no. 41, Nueva época (Sept – Oct 93), pp. 158 – 166.

Briceño Guerrero, José M. La situación cultural y la autoconsciencia de Latinoamérica y el Caribe. *Montalbán*, no. 24 (1992), pp. 25 – 31.

— La situación cultural y la autoconsciencia de Latinoamérica y el Caribe. *Revista Nacional de Cultura (Venezuela)*, v. 53, no. 285 (Apr – June 92), pp. 13 – 21.

Briceño Perozo, Mario. Factores de diferenciación e instancias integradoras en la experiencia del mundo iberoamericano: Bolívar, arquitecto de la unión. *Boletín de la Academia Nacional de la Historia (Venezuela)*, v. 76, no. 302 (Apr – June 93), pp. 21 – 33. Bibl.

Burga, Manuel et al. ¿Por qué seguir discutiendo 1492? (A roundtable of six Peruvian intellectuals). *Hueso Húmero*, no. 29 (May 93), pp. 3 – 67.

Carvalho, José Jorge de. As duas faces da tradição: o clássico e o popular na modernidade latinoamericana. *Dados*, v. 35, no. 3 (1992), pp. 403 – 434.

Dealy, Glen Caudill. *The Latin Americans: Spirit and Ethos* reviewed by S. L. Andreski. *Journal of Latin American Studies*, v. 25, no. 3 (Oct 93), pp. 694 – 695.

Díez Hochleitner, Ricardo. Iberoamérica ante el siglo XXI. *Cuadernos Americanos*, no. 39, Nueva época (May – June 93), pp. 42 – 52. Bibl.

Domingues, José Maurício. A América: intelectuais, interpretações e identidades. *Dados*, v. 35, no. 2 (1992), pp. 267 – 289. Bibl, charts.

Edwards, Jorge. El otro Occidente. *Estudios Públicos (Chile)*, no. 50 (Fall 93), pp. 345 – 351.

Fernández Retamar, Roberto. Adiós a Calibán. *Casa de las Américas*, no. 191 (Apr – June 93), pp. 116 – 122. Bibl.

— *Calibán*: quinientos años más tarde. *Nuevo Texto Crítico*, v. 6, no. 11 (1993), pp. 223 – 244. Bibl.

— Más de cien años de previsión: algunas reflexiones sobre el concepto martiano de *Nuestra América*. *Cuadernos Americanos*, no. 40, Nueva época (July – Aug 93), pp. 65 – 77.

Ferreira de Cassone, Florencia. Arturo Uslar Pietri: historia y pasión de América. *Cuadernos Americanos*, no. 40, Nueva época (July – Aug 93), pp. 125 – 145. Bibl.

Ferrer, Aldo. Iberoamérica: una nueva sociedad. *Cuadernos Americanos*, no. 39, Nueva época (May – June 93), pp. 57 – 64.

Fuentes, Carlos. *The Buried Mirror: Reflections on Spain and the New World* reviewed by John Lynch. *Hispanic American Historical Review*, v. 73, no. 3 (Aug 93), pp. 490 – 491.

— *El espejo enterrado* reviewed by Héctor Aguilar Camín (Review entitled "Por una historia patria para adultos"). *Nexos*, v. 16, no. 184 (Apr 93), pp. 59 – 63.

— *El espejo enterrado* reviewed by Marta Portal (Review entitled "Las tres hispanidades de España"). *Cuadernos Hispanoamericanos*, no. 522 (Dec 93), pp. 143 – 146.

— *El espejo enterrado/The Buried Mirror: Reflections on Spain and the New World* reviewed by John Incledon. *Hispania (USA)*, v. 76, no. 4 (Dec 93), pp. 735 – 737.

Gantiva Silva, Jorge. El conflicto de la identidad en la cultura. *Islas*, no. 97 (Sept – Dec 90), pp. 3 – 6.

García Canclini, Néstor. *Culturas híbridas: estrategias para entrar y salir de la modernidad* reviewed by Ineke Phaf. *Hispamérica*, v. 22, no. 64 – 65 (Apr – Aug 93), pp. 193 – 197.

Guadarrama González, Pablo M. La identidad conflictiva de la cultura. *Islas*, no. 97 (Sept – Dec 90), pp. 7 – 9.

— Urdimbres del pensamiento de Leopoldo Zea frente a la marginación y la barbarie. *Cuadernos Americanos*, no. 37, Nueva época (Jan – Feb 93), pp. 51 – 64. Bibl.

Ianni, Octávio. El laberinto latinoamericano (Translated by Ramón Martínez Escamilla). *Problemas del Desarrollo*, v. 24, no. 92 (Jan – Mar 93), pp. 81 – 101. Bibl.

— O labirinto latino-americano. *Vozes*, v. 87, no. 1 (Jan – Feb 93), pp. 14 – 29. Bibl, il.

Klaveren, Alberto van. América Latina: entre la crisis y la esperanza. *Mensaje*, v. 42, no. 423 (Oct 93), pp. 481 – 483. Il.

Kohut, Karl, ed. *Der eroberte Kontinent: Historische Realität, Rechtfertigung und literarische Darstellung der Kolonisation Amerikas* reviewed by Gernot Stimmer. *Zeitschrift für Lateinamerika Wien*, no. 43 (1992), pp. 123 – 124.

León-Portilla, Miguel. Naturaleza y cultura. *Cuadernos Americanos*, no. 39, Nueva época (May – June 93), pp. 65 – 71.

Mansilla, Hugo Celso Felipe. La crisis de la modernidad en América Latina y lo razonable de la cultura premoderna. *Signo*, no. 36 – 37, Nueva época (May – Dec 92), pp. 299 – 323. Bibl.

Marras, Sergio. América en plural y en singular, I: El baile de los enmascarados; entrevista con Octavio Paz (Fragment from the book *América Latina: marca registrada*). *Vuelta*, v. 17, no. 194 (Jan 93), pp. 11 – 16.

— América en plural y en singular, II: Los nacionalismos y otros bemoles; entrevista con Octavio Paz (Fragment from the book *América Latina: marca registrada*). *Vuelta*, v. 17, no. 195 (Feb 93), pp. 26 – 30.

Mayor Zaragoza, Federico. Las aportaciones de Iberoamérica a la nueva comunidad internacional. *Cuadernos Americanos*, no. 39, Nueva época (May – June 93), pp. 13 – 26.

Ortega, Julio. *El discurso de la abundancia* reviewed by George R. McMurray. *Hispania (USA)*, v. 76, no. 3 (Sept 93), pp. 485 – 486.

Ortiz, Renato. Cultura, modernidade e identidades. *Vozes*, v. 87, no. 2 (Mar – Apr 93), pp. 24 – 30. Bibl.

Pallottini, Michele. Meditación del mestizo: la otra cara del hispanismo. *Cuadernos Americanos*, no. 39, Nueva época (May – June 93), pp. 167 – 214. Bibl.

Rama, Angel. *La crítica de la cultura en América Latina* selected and introduced by Saúl Sosnowski and Tomás Eloy Martínez. Reviewed by Roy Hora. *Todo Es Historia*, v. 26, no. 307 (Feb 93), pp. 74 – 75. Il.

Rojas Gómez, Miguel. Identidad cultural y liberación en la filosofía latinoamericana de la liberación. *Islas*, no. 96 (May – Aug 90), pp. 103 – 110.

Thiercelin-Mejías, Raquel, ed. *Cultures et sociétés: Andes et Méso-Amérique; mélanges en homage à Pierre Duviols* reviewed by Gérard Borras. *Caravelle*, no. 59 (1992), pp. 285 – 289.

— *Cultures et sociétés: Andes et Méso-Amérique*, 2 vols., reviewed by Arnold J. Bauer. *Hispanic American Historical Review*, v. 73, no. 2 (May 93), pp. 306 – 307.

Uslar Pietri, Arturo. *La creación del Nuevo Mundo* reviewed by Luis Franco Ramos (Review entitled "La región mestiza"). *Nexos*, v. 16, no. 181 (Jan 93), p. 77. Il.

Vázquez, Susana. Leopoldo Zea y la conciencia latinoamericana. *Hoy Es Historia*, v. 10, no. 60 (Nov – Dec 93), pp. 4 – 13. Bibl, il.

— El "redescubrimiento," 1492 – 1992. *Hoy Es Historia*, v. 9, no. 54 (Nov – Dec 92), pp. 11 – 26. Bibl, il.

Vitier, Cintio. Latinoamérica: integración y utopía. *Cuadernos Americanos*, no. 42, Nueva época (Nov – Dec 93), pp. 112 – 128.

Weinberg, Liliana Irene. Diálogo sobre España y América. *Nueva Revista de Filología Hispánica*, v. 40, no. 2 (July – Dec 92), pp. 807 – 821. Bibl.

Werz, Nikolaus. Aspectos del pensamiento político y cultural en Latinoamérica (Translated by Irma Lorini). *Ibero-Amerikanisches Archiv*, v. 18, no. 3 – 4 (1992), pp. 429 – 443. Bibl.

Zea, Leopoldo. Conciencia de América (Excerpt from his book entitled *La esencia de lo americano*). *Hoy Es Historia*, v. 10, no. 60 (Nov – Dec 93), pp. 61 – 69. Bibl.

Congresses

Calvo Buezas, Tomás. ¿Hacia una nueva identidad? (Commentary on the Latin American Conferences of Heads of State). *Cuadernos Americanos*, no. 41, Nueva época (Sept – Oct 93), pp. 14 – 75.

Comella, Beatriz, ed. *América, siglos XVIII – XX: III Simposio sobre el V Centenario del Descubrimiento de América celebrado en el Colegio Mayor Zurbarán, Madrid, 1989 – 1990* reviewed by Osvaldo Chiareno. *Quaderni Ibero-Americani*, no. 72 (Dec 92), pp. 751 – 755.

Foreign influences

Aguilar Ponce, Luis. Las influencias de la arquitectura española en el pensamiento del ser latinoamericano. *Revista Cultural Lotería*, v. 51, no. 391 (Sept – Oct 92), pp. 98 – 104.

Climate

Aceituno, Patricio and Aldo Montecinos. Análisis de la estabilidad de la relación entre la oscilación del sur y la precipitación en América del Sur. *Bulletin de l'Institut Français d'Etudes Andines*, v. 22, no. 1 (1993), pp. 53 – 64. Bibl, tables, maps, charts.

Commerce

González Rubí, Rafael. Panorama de la exportación de manufacturas de América Latina. *Comercio Exterior*, v. 43, no. 2 (Feb 93), pp. 141 – 146. Tables.

History

Alemany, Soline and Frédéric Mauro, eds. *Transport et commerce en Amérique Latine* reviewed by Rory Miller. *Journal of Latin American Studies*, v. 25, no. 1 (Feb 93), pp. 208 – 209.

Pérez Herrero, Pedro. *Comercio y mercados en América Latina colonial* reviewed by John Fisher. *Hispanic American Historical Review*, v. 73, no. 4 (Nov 93), pp. 688 – 689.

Statistics

Baumann Neves, Renato. An Appraisal of Recent Intra-Industry Trade for Latin America. *CEPAL Review*, no. 48 (Dec 92), pp. 83 – 94. Tables.

Estadísticas. *Integración Latinoamericana*, v. 18, no. 186 – 194 (1993), All issues. Tables, charts.

Estructura y evolución del comercio intrarregional negociado, 1981 – 1991. *Integración Latinoamericana*, v. 18, no. 194 (Oct 93), pp. 71 – 78. Tables, charts.

Fairlie Reinoso, Alan. Crisis, integración y desarrollo en América Latina: la dinámica del Grupo Andino con el MERCOSUR en la década de 1980. *Integración Latinoamericana*, v. 18, no. 192 (Aug 93), pp. 11 – 40. Bibl, tables, charts.

Constitutional law

Corfield M., Isabel. Constitucionalismo ilustrado en la experiencia poscolonial hispano-americana. *Todo Es Historia*, v. 26, no. 307 (Feb 93), pp. 79 – 83. Il.

Cultural policy

Harvey, Edwin R. *Derecho cultural latinoamericano: Sudamérica y Panamá* reviewed by Juan Carlos Torchia Estrada. *La Educación (USA)*, v. 37, no. 114 (1993), pp. 158 – 159.

Description and travel

Leonard, Irving Albert. *Viajeros por la América Latina colonial* reviewed by Luis Franco Ramos (Review entitled "Viajes sin guía de turistas"). *Nexos*, v. 16, no. 181 (Jan 93), pp. 75 – 76. Il.

Sources

Gregory, Desmond. *Brute New World: The Rediscovery of Latin America in the Early Nineteenth Century* reviewed by Jason Wilson. *Journal of Latin American Studies*, v. 25, no. 3 (Oct 93), pp. 656 – 657.

Santistevan, Miguel de. *Mil leguas por América: de Lima a Caracas, 1740 – 1741; diario de don Miguel de Santisteban* edited by David J. Robinson. Reviewed by Judith E. Villamarin. *Hispanic American Historical Review*, v. 73, no. 4 (Nov 93), pp. 701 – 702.

Economic conditions

Connaughton, Brian F. América Latina, 1700 – 1850: entre el pacto colonial y el imperialismo moderno. *Cuadernos Americanos*, no. 38, Nueva época (Mar – Apr 93), pp. 38 – 66. Bibl.

Bibliography

Cortés Conde, Roberto. El crecimiento de las economías latinoamericanas, 1880 – 1930. *Historia Mexicana*, v. 42, no. 3 (Jan – Mar 93), pp. 633 – 648. Tables.

Ottone, Ernesto. CEPAL: un planteamiento renovado frente a los nuevos desafíos del desarrollo (Review article). *Pensamiento Iberoamericano*, no. 22 – 23, tomo I (July 92 – June 93), pp. 386 – 392. Bibl.

Statistics

Leriche, Christian E. and Sandra Navarrete R. América Latina: problemas actuales en el estilo de crecimiento de la región. *El Cotidiano*, v. 9, no. 54 (May 93), pp. 108 – 113. Il, tables.

20th century

Balance preliminar de la economía de América Latina y el Caribe 1992. *El Trimestre Económico*, v. 60, no. 238 (Apr – June 93), pp. 447 – 555. Tables, charts.

Blomström, Magnus and Patricio Meller, eds. *Trayectorias divergentes* reviewed by Göran G. Lindahl (Review entitled "Commentary and Debate"). *Ibero Americana (Sweden)*, v. 22, no. 2 (Dec 92), pp. 67 – 76.

— *Trayectorias divergentes: comparación de un siglo de desarrollo económico latinoamericano y escandinavo* reviewed by Sérgio Savino Portugal. *Pesquisa e Planejamento Econômico*, v. 22, no. 1 (Apr 92), pp. 189 – 196.

Burgueño Lomelí, Fausto. América Latina: el desarrollo del subdesarrollo. *Problemas del Desarrollo*, v. 24, no. 92 (Jan – Mar 93), pp. 103 – 115. Tables.

Calcagno, Alfredo Eric and Pedro Sáinz. In Search of Another Form of Development. *CEPAL Review*, no. 48 (Dec 92), pp. 7 – 38. Bibl, tables, charts.

Cardoso, Eliana Anastasia and Ann Helwege. *Latin America's Economy: Diversity, Trends, and Conflicts* reviewed by Antonio Jorge and Raúl Moncarz. *Journal of Developing Areas*, v. 27, no. 4 (July 93), pp. 552 – 553.

— *Latin America's Economy: Diversity, Trends, and Conflicts* reviewed by David Hojman. *Journal of Latin American Studies*, v. 25, no. 1 (Feb 93), pp. 209 – 211.

Correa Vázquez, Eugenia. *Los mercados financieros y la crisis en América Latina* reviewed by Rafael Bouchain Galicia. *Problemas del Desarrollo*, v. 24, no. 93 (Apr – June 93), pp. 236 – 239.

Damill, Mario et al. Crecimiento económico en América Latina: experiencia reciente y perspectivas (Translated by Leandro Wolfson). *Desarrollo Económico (Argentina)*, v. 33, no. 130 (July – Sept 93), pp. 237 – 264. Bibl, tables.

Dijck, Pitou van. The Empty Box Syndrome. *CEPAL Review*, no. 47 (Aug 92), pp. 21 – 36. Bibl, tables, charts.

Ffrench-Davis, Ricardo. Los desafíos de la deuda externa y el desarrollo: a diez años del inicio de la crisis. *Estudios Internacionales (Chile)*, v. 26, no. 102 (Apr – June 93), pp. 155 – 156. Tables.

Gregorio, José de. El crecimiento económico en la América Latina. *El Trimestre Económico*, v. 59, Special issue (Dec 92), pp. 75 – 107. Bibl, tables, charts.

Ibarra Muñoz, David. Equidad y desarrollo. *Nexos*, v. 16, no. 184 (Apr 93), pp. 41 – 46.

Mattos, Carlos António de. Nuevas estrategias empresariales y mutaciones territoriales en los procesos de reestructuración en América Latina. *Revista Paraguaya de Sociología*, v. 29, no. 84 (May – Aug 92), pp. 145 – 170. Bibl.

Meller, Patricio. Ajuste y reformas económicas en América Latina: problemas y experiencias recientes. *Pensamiento Iberoamericano,* no. 22 – 23, tomo II (July 92 – June 93), pp. 15 – 58. Bibl, tables, charts.

Muñoz Portugal, Ismael. Ajuste y desarrollo en América Latina: el contexto de los países andinos. *Cristianismo y Sociedad,* v. 30, no. 113 (1992), pp. 7 – 14. Bibl.

Ramírez López, Berenice Patricia. El desempeño de la economía latinoamericana durante 1992. *Momento Económico,* no. 66 (Mar – Apr 93), pp. 23 – 27.

Recuento latinoamericano. *Comercio Exterior,* v. 43 (1993), All issues.

Rosenthal, Gert. Balance preliminar de la economía de América Latina y el Caribe, 1992. *Comercio Exterior,* v. 43, no. 3 (Mar 93), pp. 276 – 298. Tables.

Sánchez Otero, Germán. Neoliberalism and Its Discontents. *Report on the Americas,* v. 26, no. 4 (Feb 93), pp. 18 – 21. II.

Sarmiento Palacio, Eduardo. Growth and Income Distribution in Countries at Intermediate Stages of Development. *CEPAL Review,* no. 48 (Dec 92), pp. 141 – 155. Tables, charts.

Urrutia Montoya, Miguel, ed. *Tendencias a largo plazo en el desarrollo económico de América Latina* (Review). *Integración Latinoamericana,* v. 18, no. 194 (Oct 93), pp. 89 – 91.

Economic integration

Argenti, Gisela et al. *Pequeños países en la integración: oportunidades y riesgos* (Review). *Integración Latinoamericana,* v. 18, no. 187 – 188 (Mar – Apr 93), pp. 69 – 70.

Arroyo Pichardo, Graciela. Factores históricos y fuerzas mundiales en la interacción entre sistemas regionales: América Latina y Europa del Este. *Relaciones Internacionales (Mexico),* v. 14, Nueva época, no. 56 (Oct – Dec 92), pp. 19 – 29. Bibl.

Barbosa, Rubens Antonio. Liberalizaçã do comércio, integração regional e Mercado Comum do Sul: o papel do Brasil. *Revista de Economia Política (Brazil),* v. 13, no. 1 (Jan – Mar 93), pp. 64 – 81.

Carmona Estanga, Pedro. Políticas de convergencia y efectos del ajuste en la integración regional. *Integración Latinoamericana,* v. 18, no. 191 (July 93), pp. 30 – 36.

Cronología: primer semestre de 1993; principales sucesos en materia de integración. *Integración Latinoamericana,* v. 18, no. 192 (Aug 93), pp. 63 – 79.

Daher, Antonio and Guillermo Gisse. América Latina: ambiente y territorio en el cambio de modelo. *Revista Paraguaya de Sociología,* v. 29, no. 84 (May – Aug 92), pp. 25 – 40.

Díaz, Eduardo Alberto. Estrategias empresariales para la integración: el papel de la universidad en su determinación. *Integración Latinoamericana,* v. 18, no. 194 (Oct 93), pp. 15 – 22. Bibl, charts.

Dror, Yehezkel. Conducción del estado hacia la integración. *Integración Latinoamericana,* v. 18, no. 189 – 190 (May – June 93), pp. 3 – 9.

Escobar Sepúlveda, Santiago. La política de la integración. *Nueva Sociedad,* no. 126 (July – Aug 93), pp. 62 – 71.

Fontana Morialdo, Jorge et al. Aprovechamientos hidroeléctricos binacionales: aspectos relacionados con la integración latinoamericana. *Integración Latinoamericana,* v. 17, no. 184 (Nov 92), pp. 44 – 58.

García Belaúnde, José Antonio. El Perú y la América Latina en los '90. *Debate (Peru),* v. 15, no. 71 (Nov 92 – Jan 93), pp. 52 – 57. II.

González Izquierdo, Jorge. Prioridades y opciones para la integración latinoamericana. *Integración Latinoamericana,* v. 18, no. 193 (Sept 93), pp. 13 – 19. Bibl.

Grunwald, Joseph. El escabroso camino hacia la integración económica hemisférica: análisis regional de antecedentes orientado al futuro (Chapter from the book *The Enterprise for the Americas Initiative* translated by Carlos Villegas). *El Trimestre Económico,* v. 60, no. 239 (July – Sept 93), pp. 713 – 732. Bibl, tables.

Gutiérrez, Miguel Angel, ed. *Integración: experiencia en Europa y América Latina* (Review). *Integración Latinoamericana,* v. 18, no. 193 (Sept 93), p. 75.

Ibarra Pardo, Gabriel. Políticas de competencia en la integración en América Latina. *Integración Latinoamericana,* v. 18, no. 193 (Sept 93), pp. 45 – 51. Bibl.

Lahera, Eugenio. Dinámica, restricciones y políticas de la integración. *Integración Latinoamericana,* v. 17, no. 184 (Nov 92), pp. 3 – 15. Bibl.

— Integration Today: Bases and Options. *CEPAL Review,* no. 47 (Aug 92), pp. 63 – 76. Bibl.

Moneta, Carlos Juan. Alternativas de la integración en el contexto de la globalización. *Nueva Sociedad,* no. 125 (May – June 93), pp. 80 – 97. Bibl, tables.

Peña Guerrero, Roberto. Los proyectos latinoamericanos: ¿Libre comercio o integración fragmentada? *Relaciones Internacionales (Mexico),* v. 14, Nueva época, no. 56 (Oct – Dec 92), pp. 55 – 61.

Prospects for the Processes of Sub-Regional Integration in Central and South America (Review). *Integración Latinoamericana,* v. 18, no. 189 – 190 (May – June 93), pp. 58 – 59.

Quijano, José Manuel. Integración competitiva para los nuevos países industrializados en América Latina. *Integración Latinoamericana,* v. 18, no. 193 (Sept 93), pp. 3 – 11. Bibl, tables.

Rodríguez, Juan Manuel. El movimiento sindical ante los procesos de integración. *Nueva Sociedad,* no. 126 (July – Aug 93), pp. 144 – 155.

Rojas Aravena, Francisco. América Latina: el difícil camino de la concertación y la integración. *Nueva Sociedad,* no. 125 (May – June 93), pp. 60 – 69. Bibl.

Rosenthal, Gert. Treinta años de integración en América Latina: un examen crítico. *Estudios Internacionales (Chile),* v. 26, no. 101 (Jan – Mar 93), pp. 74 – 88.

Schaposnik, Eduardo Carlos. La integración en una etapa de confusión. *Desarrollo Indoamericano,* v. 23, no. 91 (June 93), pp. 41 – 46. II.

Sturzenegger, Adolfo C. Encuesta a empresas industriales exportadoras latinoamericanas sobre el proceso de integración regional: informe de resultados. *Nueva Sociedad,* no. 126 (July – Aug 93), pp. 169 – 176.

Thoumi, Francisco E. Estrategias de desarrollo, convergencias de políticas, integración económica. *Nueva Sociedad,* no. 125 (May – June 93), pp. 70 – 79. Bibl.

Vacchino, Juan Mario. La dimensión institucional en la integración latinoamericana. *Integración Latinoamericana,* v. 17, no. 185 (Dec 92), pp. 3 – 16. Bibl.

Ventosa del Campo, Andrés. Hacia una zona continental de libre comercio. *Relaciones Internacionales (Mexico),* v. 14, Nueva época, no. 56 (Oct – Dec 92), pp. 87 – 96. Bibl, tables, maps.

Vieira Posada, Edgar. Una unión aduanera para América Latina. *Integración Latinoamericana,* v. 18, no. 187 – 188 (Mar – Apr 93), pp. 23 – 34. Bibl.

Zea Prado, Irene. El reto de la integración de América Latina: entre Bolívar y Monroe. *Relaciones Internacionales (Mexico),* v. 14, Nueva época, no. 56 (Oct – Dec 92), pp. 49 – 53.

Zemelman Merino, Hugo. Sobre bloqueo histórico y utopía en América Latina. *Estudios Sociológicos,* v. 10, no. 30 (Sept – Dec 92), pp. 809 – 817.

Congresses

América Latina: cronología; segundo semestre de 1992: principales sucesos en materia de integración. *Integración Latinoamericana,* v. 18, no. 186 (Jan – Feb 93), pp. 33 – 51.

VI Cumbre Presidencial del Mecanismo Permanente de Consulta y Concertación Política – Grupo de Río. *Integración Latinoamericana,* v. 17, no. 185 (Dec 92), pp. 68 – 70.

Law and legislation

Barros Charlín, Raymundo. Parámetros jurídico – institucionales de la integración latinoamericana. *Integración Latinoamericana,* v. 18, no. 193 (Sept 93), pp. 29 – 32.

Sources

El Nacional, de Caracas, dedica un número especial al tema de la integración latinoamericana (Quotations on the subject by Latin American heads of state and other notable figures). Integración Latinoamericana, v. 18, no. 194 (Oct 93), pp. 51 – 55.

Economic policy

Ander-Egg, Ezequiel et al. El porvenir de América Latina (Question – answer forum by Latin American intellectuals on Latin America's economic future). Desarrollo Indoamericano, v. 23, no. 91 (June 93), pp. 7 – 16.

Báez, René. La quimera de la modernización. Desarrollo Indoamericano, v. 23, no. 91 (June 93), pp. 33 – 35. Il.

Bradford, Colin I., Jr. Orientación y pertinencia de la política económica en América Latina. Estudios Internacionales (Chile), v. 26, no. 102 (Apr – June 93), pp. 165 – 186. Bibl.

Büchi Buc, Hernán. Reactivación económica en tiempos de recesión. Apuntes (Peru), no. 30 (Jan – June 92), pp. 91 – 103.

Cardoso, Fernando Henrique. As idéias e seu lugar (Review). Vozes, v. 87, no. 3 (May – June 93), pp. 91 – 92.

Coatsworth, John Henry. Pax (norte) americana: América Latina después de la guerra fría (Translated by Marcela Pineda Camacho). Revista Mexicana de Sociología, v. 55, no. 2 (Apr – June 93), pp. 293 – 314. Bibl.

Consuegra Higgins, José and Hernán Echavarría Olozaga. Tres cartas, dos opiniones. Desarrollo Indoamericano, v. 23, no. 91 (June 93), pp. 17 – 19. Il.

Curbelo Ranero, José Luis. Positive Adjustment in Latin America: On Decentralization and Development Planning. European Review of Latin American and Caribbean Studies, no. 54 (June 93), pp. 25 – 44. Bibl.

Daher, Antonio and Guillermo Gisse. América Latina: ambiente y territorio en el cambio de modelo. Revista Paraguaya de Sociología, v. 29, no. 84 (May – Aug 92), pp. 25 – 40.

Devlin, Robert T. and Ricardo Ffrench-Davis. Diez años de crisis de la deuda latinoamericana. Comercio Exterior, v. 43, no. 1 (Jan 93), pp. 4 – 20. Bibl, tables.

Dietz, James L. and Dilmus D. James, eds. Progress toward Development in Latin America: From Prebisch to Technological Autonomy reviewed by Markos J. Mamalakis. Studies in Comparative International Development, v. 27, no. 2 (Summer 92), pp. 106 – 108.

Esser, Klaus. América Latina: industrialización sin visión (Translated by Friedrich Welsch). Nueva Sociedad, no. 125 (May – June 93), pp. 27 – 46. Bibl.

Frenkel, Roberto. Ajuste y reformas económicas en América Latina: problemas y experiencias recientes; comentarios al artículo de Patricio Meller. Pensamiento Iberoamericano, no. 22 – 23, tomo II (July 92 – June 93), pp. 59 – 63.

Frieden, Jeffrey A. Debt, Development, and Democracy: Modern Political Economy and Latin America reviewed by Sidney Weintraub. Studies in Comparative International Development, v. 27, no. 2 (Summer 92), pp. 96 – 98.

Fuentes, Juan Alberto. European Investment in Latin America: An Overview. CEPAL Review, no. 48 (Dec 92), pp. 61 – 81. Bibl, tables, charts.

García Medrano, Renward. Década perdida y planes de ajuste: crecimiento económico y pobreza. Relaciones Internacionales (Mexico), v. 14, Nueva época, no. 56 (Oct – Dec 92), pp. 45 – 48.

González Izquierdo, Jorge. Prioridades y opciones para la integración latinoamericana. Integración Latinoamericana, v. 18, no. 193 (Sept 93), pp. 13 – 19. Bibl.

Iglesias, Enrique V., ed. El legado de Raúl Prebisch (Review). Integración Latinoamericana, v. 18, no. 193 (Sept 93), pp. 77 – 79.

Larraín Arroyo, Luis et al. ¿Un neoliberalismo en declinación?: debates. Mensaje, v. 42, no. 418 (May 93), pp. 142 – 151. Il.

Levine, Barry B., ed. El desafío neoliberal: el fin del tercermundismo en América Latina reviewed by John W. F. Dulles. Hispanic American Historical Review, v. 73, no. 3 (Aug 93), pp. 542 – 543.

A Market Solution for the Americas? Report on the Americas, v. 26, no. 4 (Feb 93), pp. 16 – 17. Charts.

Martín P., Juan and Arturo Núñez del Prado Benavente. Strategic Management, Planning, and Budgets. CEPAL Review, no. 49 (Apr 93), pp. 41 – 54. Bibl.

Meller, Patricio. Ajuste y reformas económicas en América Latina: problemas y experiencias recientes. Pensamiento Iberoamericano, no. 22 – 23, tomo II (July 92 – June 93), pp. 15 – 58. Bibl, tables, charts.

Ozler, Sule and Dani Rodrik. Los choques externos, la política y la inversión privada: algo de teoría y evidencia empírica. El Trimestre Económico, v. 59, Special issue (Dec 92), pp. 187 – 212. Bibl, tables, charts.

Parra Luzardo, Gastón. ¿Hacia dónde nos conduce la política neoliberal? Desarrollo Indoamericano, v. 23, no. 91 (June 93), pp. 36 – 40. Il.

Pinto Santa Cruz, Aníbal. Notas sobre estilos de desarrollo: origen, naturaleza y esquema conceptual. Revista Paraguaya de Sociología, v. 29, no. 84 (May – Aug 92), pp. 91 – 99. Bibl.

Przeworski, Adam. Democracy and the Market: Political and Economic Reforms in Eastern Europe and Latin America reviewed by Carlos Maya Ambía. El Trimestre Económico, v. 60, no. 239 (July – Sept 93), pp. 733 – 744.

Ramos, Joseph R. Reformas económicas en América Latina: lecciones para Europa oriental: comentarios a los artículos de Patricio Meller y Carmelo Mesa-Lago. Pensamiento Iberoamericano, no. 22 – 23, tomo II (July 92 – June 93), pp. 109 – 118.

Ruccio, David F. The Hidden Successes of Failed Economic Policies. Report on the Americas, v. 26, no. 4 (Feb 93), pp. 38 – 43+. Bibl, il, tables.

Sánchez Otero, Germán. Neoliberalism and Its Discontents. Report on the Americas, v. 26, no. 4 (Feb 93), pp. 18 – 21. Il.

Santos, Theotonio dos. Globalización financiera y estrategias de desarrollo. Nueva Sociedad, no. 126 (July – Aug 93), pp. 98 – 109.

Smith, William C. Reestructuración neoliberal y escenarios políticos en América Latina. Nueva Sociedad, no. 126 (July – Aug 93), pp. 25 – 39. Bibl.

Solimano, Andrés. Diversidad en la reforma económica: experiencias recientes en economías de mercado y economías socialistas. Pensamiento Iberoamericano, no. 22 – 23, tomo I (July 92 – June 93), pp. 59 – 100. Bibl, tables, charts.

Szlajfer, Henryk, ed. Economic Nationalism in East-Central Europe and South America, 1918 – 1939 reviewed by Joseph L. Love. Journal of Latin American Studies, v. 25, no. 1 (Feb 93), pp. 206 – 208.

Welch, John H. The New Face of Latin America: Financial Flows, Markets, and Institutions in the 1990s. Journal of Latin American Studies, v. 25, no. 1 (Feb 93), pp. 1 – 24. Bibl, tables.

Bibliography

Ottone, Ernesto. CEPAL: un planteamiento renovado frente a los nuevos desafíos del desarrollo (Review article). Pensamiento Iberoamericano, no. 22 – 23, tomo I (July 92 – June 93), pp. 386 – 392. Bibl.

Congresses

Cabello Naranjo, Elena. III Cumbre Iberoamericana: hacia una agenda de desarrollo. Comercio Exterior, v. 43, no. 9 (Sept 93), pp. 836 – 839.

International cooperation

United Nations. Economic Commission for Latin America and the Caribbean. Ensayos sobre coordinación de políticas macroeconómicas: inferencias para la integración latinoamericana (Review). Integración Latinoamericana, v. 18, no. 194 (Oct 93), pp. 85 – 87.

Emigration and immigration

Díaz-Jove Blanco, Santiago. Gijoneses en Indias: notas sobre emigración e índice geobiográfico reviewed by José Ramón García López. Revista de Indias, v. 53, no. 197 (Jan – Apr 93), pp. 102 – 103.

Hourani, Albert and Nadim Shehadi, eds. *The Lebanese in the World: A Century of Emigration* reviewed by Jorge O. Bestene. *Journal of Latin American Studies*, v. 25, no. 3 (Oct 93), pp. 663 – 664.

Mitchell, Christopher, ed. *Western Hemisphere Immigration and United States Foreign Policy* reviewed by Caroline Thomas. *Bulletin of Latin American Research*, v. 12, no. 2 (May 93), pp. 238 – 239.

Rodríguez Ozán, María Elena. Las ideologías de los inmigrantes europeos en América Latina. *Cuadernos Americanos*, no. 41, Nueva época (Sept – Oct 93), pp. 122 – 130. Bibl.

— La inmigración europea en Latinoamérica. *Cuadernos Americanos*, no. 37, Nueva época (Jan – Feb 93), pp. 37 – 47. Bibl.

Vilar, Juan Bautista. *Los murcianos y América* reviewed by José U. Martínez Carreras. *Revista de Indias*, v. 53, no. 197 (Jan – Apr 93), pp. 126 – 127.

Fiction

Arriaga de Lassel, Adriana. El viaje hacia América: la figura del inmigrante en algunos textos literarios. *Cuadernos Hispanoamericanos*, no. 513 (Mar 93), pp. 93 – 100. Bibl.

Sources

Martínez, José Luis. *El mundo privado de los emigrantes en Indias* reviewed by Antonio Saborit (Review entitled "Cartas de llamada"). *Nexos*, v. 16, no. 184 (Apr 93), pp. 67 – 68.

— *El mundo privado de los emigrantes en Indias* reviewed by Jorge F. Hernández (Review entitled "Correspondencias con el pasado"). *Vuelta*, v. 17, no. 198 (May 93), pp. 55 – 57.

Otte, Enrique, ed. *Cartas privadas de emigrantes a Indias, 1540 – 1616* reviewed by Jorge F. Hernández (Review entitled "Correspondencias con el pasado"). *Vuelta*, v. 17, no. 198 (May 93), pp. 55 – 57.

Foreign economic relations

Corona Guzmán, Roberto. El entorno actual de la negociación comercial de América Latina. *Relaciones Internacionales (Mexico)*, v. 14, Nueva época, no. 56 (Oct – Dec 92), pp. 63 – 86. Tables.

Frank, André Gunder. América Latina al margen de la historia del sistema mundial (Translated by Hernán G. H. Taboada). *Cuadernos Americanos*, no. 39, Nueva época (May – June 93), pp. 114 – 133. Bibl, tables.

— América Latina al margen del sistema mundial: historia y presente. *Nueva Sociedad*, no. 123 (Jan – Feb 93), pp. 23 – 34. Bibl, tables.

Ibarra Muñoz, David. Interdependencia y desarrollo (Excerpt from a forthcoming book). *Comercio Exterior*, v. 43, no. 11 (Nov 93), pp. 991 – 1000.

Piñón A., Rosa María. América Latina y el Caribe en el nuevo orden capitalista mundial: Estados Unidos, Japón y Comunidad Europea. *Relaciones Internacionales (Mexico)*, v. 14, Nueva época, no. 56 (Oct – Dec 92), pp. 7 – 18. Tables.

Sanderson, Steven E. *The Politics of Trade in Latin American Development* reviewed by S. P. Chakravarty. *Bulletin of Latin American Research*, v. 12, no. 2 (May 93), pp. 239 – 240.

Smith, Peter H. Latin America and the New World Order. *SALALM Papers*, v. 36 (1991), pp. 3 – 9.

Tomassini, Luciano et al. *La política internacional en un mundo post-moderno* (Review). *Integración Latinoamericana*, v. 18, no. 192 (Aug 92), pp. 95 – 96.

Asia

Choi, Dae Won. Las nuevas relaciones económicas entre los "tigres" asiáticos y América Latina. *Comercio Exterior*, v. 43, no. 5 (May 93), pp. 457 – 462. Tables.

Austria

Winkelbauer, Waltraud. Osterreich-Ungarns Handelsvertragsprojekte mit Lateinamerika nach 1870. *Zeitschrift für Lateinamerika Wien*, no. 43 (1992), pp. 7 – 62. Bibl.

Cuba

Monreal González, Pedro. Cuba y América Latina y el Caribe: apuntes sobre un caso de inserción económica. *Estudios Internacionales (Chile)*, v. 26, no. 103 (July – Sept 93), pp. 500 – 536. Bibl, tables.

Europe

Grabendorff, Wolf. La integración europea: consequencias para América Latina. *Nueva Sociedad*, no. 126 (July – Aug 93), pp. 122 – 143. Bibl.

Secchi, Carlo. Europe et Amérique Latine: Quelles relations pour les années '90? *Tiers Monde*, v. 34, no. 136 (Oct – Dec 93), pp. 781 – 806. Bibl, tables.

European Community

Estay Reino, Jaime and Héctor Sotomayor, eds. *América Latina y México ante la Unión Europea de 1992* reviewed by Gilberto A. Cardoso Vargas. *Problemas del Desarrollo*, v. 24, no. 92 (Jan – Mar 93), pp. 236 – 238.

Klaveren, Alberto van. Europa – Lateinamerika: Zwischen Illusion und Realismus, auch nach 1992. *Zeitschrift für Lateinamerika Wien*, no. 43 (1992), pp. 95 – 119. Bibl.

El Mercado Unico Europeo y su impacto en América Latina reviewed by A. L. R. *Comercio Exterior*, v. 43, no. 11 (Nov 93), pp. 1095 – 1096.

Trein, Franklin. A Europa '92 e a América Latina. *Política e Estratégica*, v. 8, no. 2 – 4 (Apr – Dec 90), pp. 213 – 223. Bibl, tables.

Viñas, Angel. La política exterior española frente a Iberoamérica: pasado y presente. *Ibero-Amerikanisches Archiv*, v. 18, no. 3 – 4 (1992), pp. 469 – 500. Bibl.

Pacific Area

Choi, Dae Won. The Pacific Basin and Latin America. *CEPAL Review*, no. 49 (Apr 93), pp. 21 – 40. Bibl, tables, charts.

Russia

Sudarev, Vladimir P. Russia and Latin America. *Hemisphere*, v. 5, no. 2 (Winter – Spring 93), pp. 12 – 14.

Sweden

Karlsson, Weine et al, eds. *Suecia – Latinoamérica: relaciones y cooperación* (Review). *Integración Latinoamericana*, v. 18, no. 195 (Nov 93), pp. 59 – 60.

United States

Docampo, César. Iniciativas estadounidenses de la política económica: consecuencias hemisféricas. *Realidad Económica*, no. 119 (Oct – Nov 93), pp. 117 – 132. Bibl.

Grunwald, Joseph. El escabroso camino hacia la integración económica hemisférica: análisis regional de antecedentes orientado al futuro (Chapter from the book *The Enterprise for the Americas Initiative* translated by Carlos Villegas). *El Trimestre Económico*, v. 60, no. 239 (July – Sept 93), pp. 713 – 732. Bibl, tables.

Kuwayama, Mikio. Nuevas formas de inversión en el comercio entre América Latina y Estados Unidos (Translated by Adriana Hierro). *Comercio Exterior*, v. 43, no. 5 (May 93), pp. 478 – 497. Bibl.

Lozano García, Lucrecia. La Iniciativa para las Américas: el comercio hecho estrategia. *Nueva Sociedad*, no. 125 (May – June 93), pp. 98 – 111. Tables.

Osorio, Jaime. Bloque comercial sí, tratados comerciales tal vez. *El Cotidiano*, v. 9, no. 56 (July 93), pp. 113 – 116. Il, tables.

Saxe-Fernández, John. América Latina – Estados Unidos: ¿Hacia una nueva era? *Nueva Sociedad*, no. 125 (May – June 93), pp. 6 – 15. Bibl.

Torres, Víctor. Perspectivas de la Iniciativa para las Américas. *Apuntes (Peru)*, no. 30 (Jan – June 92), pp. 63 – 79. Bibl, tables.

Foreign opinion

Bernecker, Walther L. El aniversario del "descubrimiento" de América en el conflicto de opiniones (Translated by Verónica Jaffé). *Ibero-Amerikanisches Archiv*, v. 18, no. 3 – 4 (1992), pp. 501 – 520. Bibl.

Fernández de Mata, Ignacio. La imagen de América. *Revista Española de Antropología Americana*, v. 23 (1993), pp. 243 – 248. Bibl.

González Pizarro, José Antonio. Imagen e impresiones de América de los integrantes de la armada y de la Comisión de Naturalistas Españoles, 1862 – 1866. *Jahrbuch für Geschichte von Staat, Wirtschaft und Gesellschaft Lateinamerikas*, v. 29 (1992), pp. 279 – 307. Bibl.

Gregory, Desmond. *Brute New World: The Rediscovery of Latin America in the Early Nineteenth Century* reviewed by Jason Wilson. *Journal of Latin American Studies,* v. 25, no. 3 (Oct 93), pp. 656 – 657.

Jou, Maite. Gabriel García y Tassara: del nacionalismo romántico al concepto de raza hispana. *Anuario de Estudios Americanos,* v. 49 (1992), pp. 529 – 562. Bibl.

Pike, Fredrick B. *The United States and Latin America: Myths and Stereotypes of Civilization and Nature* reviewed by Peter Calvert. *Bulletin of Latin American Research,* v. 12, no. 2 (May 93), pp. 232 – 233.

— *The United States and Latin America: Myths and Stereotypes of Civilization and Nature* reviewed by Josef Opatrny. *Hispanic American Historical Review,* v. 73, no. 4 (Nov 93), pp. 667 – 668.

— *The United States and Latin America: Myths and Stereotypes of Civilization and Nature* reviewed by Gordon Connell-Smith. *Journal of Latin American Studies,* v. 25, no. 3 (Oct 93), pp. 689 – 691.

Prizel, Ilya. *Latin America through Soviet Eyes: The Evolution of Soviet Perceptions during the Brezhnev Era* reviewed by Marina Oborotova (Review entitled "Russian Policy in Latin America: Past, Present, and Future"). *Latin American Research Review,* v. 28, no. 3 (1993), pp. 183 – 188.

Santí, Enrico-Mario. Latinamericanism and Restitution. *Latin American Literary Review,* v. 20, no. 40 (July – Dec 92), pp. 88 – 96.

Foreign relations

Cardoso Vargas, Gilberto A. Iberoamérica ante la agenda internacional de fin de siglo. *Problemas del Desarrollo,* v. 24, no. 94 (July – Sept 93), pp. 275 – 281.

Moneta, Carlos Juan. As forças armadas latino-americanas nos anos '90. *Política e Estratégica,* v. 8, no. 2 – 4 (Apr – Dec 90), pp. 153 – 167. Bibl.

Zea, Leopoldo. Filosofía de las relaciones de América Latina con el mundo. *Cuadernos Americanos,* no. 41, Nueva época (Sept – Oct 93), pp. 93 – 100.

Africa

Mourão, Fernando Augusto Albuquerque. O Atlântico Sul e os novos vetores do sistema internacional. *Política e Estratégica,* v. 8, no. 2 – 4 (Apr – Dec 90), pp. 333 – 341.

Canada

McKenna, Peter. Canada – OAS Relations during the Trudeau Years. *Revista Interamericana de Bibliografía,* v. 42, no. 3 (1992), pp. 373 – 391. Bibl.

Europe

Fernández Retamar, Roberto. En la Casa de América, hacia la casa del futuro. *Casa de las Américas,* no. 190 (Jan – Mar 93), pp. 75 – 81.

European Community

Bieber, León Enrique. Las relaciones entre la Comunidad Europea y América Latina: problemas y perspectivas. *Homines,* v. 15 – 16, no. 2 – 1 (Oct 91 – Dec 92), pp. 13 – 30. Bibl.

L'Europe et l'Amérique Latine: processus d'intégration et nouveaux rapports. *Cahiers des Amériques Latines,* no. 14 (1992), pp. 149 – 150.

Germany

Botet, Violanda. Germany and Latin America. *Hemisphere,* v. 5, no. 2 (Winter – Spring 93), pp. 16 – 17.

Silveira, Helder Gordim da. A ofensiva política dos EUA sobre a América Latina na visão alemã: uma face do confronto interimperialista, 1938. *Estudos Ibero-Americanos,* v. 18, no. 1 (July 92), pp. 19 – 27. Bibl.

Israel

Varon, Benno Weiser. *Professions of a Lucky Jew* reviewed by Ignacio Klich. *Journal of Latin American Studies,* v. 25, no. 2 (May 93), pp. 430 – 431.

Mexico

Cabra Ybarra, José G. Las relaciones de México con Latinoamérica durante la última década: ¿Líder, intérprete o interlocutor? *Relaciones Internacionales (Mexico),* v. 14, Nueva época, no. 56 (Oct – Dec 92), pp. 117 – 122.

Romania

Nastase, Adrián. Titulescu y América Latina. *Boletín de la Academia Nacional de la Historia (Venezuela),* v. 75, no. 298 (Apr – June 92), pp. 9 – 14.

Spain

Crespo Martínez, Ismael and Antonia Martínez Rodríguez. Discurso político y realidad económica: las relaciones entre España y la comunidad iberoamericana. *Cuadernos del CLAEH,* v. 17, no. 63 – 64 (Oct 92), pp. 99 – 103. Bibl.

Rebollo, Eduardo. 500 años de incomunicación. *Cuadernos del CLAEH,* v. 17, no. 63 – 64 (Oct 92), pp. 125 – 129.

United States

Cochrane, James D. The Troubled and Misunderstood Relationship: The United States and Latin America (Review article). *Latin American Research Review,* v. 28, no. 2 (1993), pp. 222 – 245.

García B., Pantaleón. La política del buen vecino y Latinoamérica. *Revista Cultural Lotería,* v. 51, no. 388 (Mar – Apr 92), pp. 62 – 77. Bibl.

Hartlyn, Jonathan et al, eds. *The United States and Latin America in the 1990s: Beyond the Cold War* reviewed by David Ryan. *Journal of Latin American Studies,* v. 25, no. 3 (Oct 93), pp. 691 – 692.

Hey, Jeanne A. K. Foreign Policy Options under Dependence: A Theoretical Evaluation with Evidence from Ecuador. *Journal of Latin American Studies,* v. 25, no. 3 (Oct 93), pp. 543 – 574. Bibl.

Shurbutt, Thomas Ray, ed. *United States – Latin American Relations, 1800 – 1850: The Formative Generations* reviewed by Thomas Schoonover. *The Americas,* v. 49, no. 3 (Jan 93), pp. 405 – 407.

Zea, Leopoldo. América Latina: qué hacer con 500 años de historia. *Ibero-Amerikanisches Archiv,* v. 18, no. 3 – 4 (1992), pp. 445 – 453. Bibl.

Zea Prado, Irene. El reto de la integración de América Latina: entre Bolívar y Monroe. *Relaciones Internacionales (Mexico),* v. 14, Nueva época, no. 56 (Oct – Dec 92), pp. 49 – 53.

Government publications
Bibliography

Joy-Karno, Beverly. Latin American Government Documents on the Arts: Introductory Guide. *SALALM Papers,* v. 34 (1989), pp. 239 – 260. Bibl.

Historiography

Arrom, Silvia Marina. Historia de la mujer y de la familia latinoamericanas. *Historia Mexicana,* v. 42, no. 2 (Oct – Dec 92), pp. 379 – 418.

Bravo, Víctor. Poligrafía y consciencia de la escritura. *Boletín de la Academia Nacional de la Historia (Venezuela),* v. 76, no. 301 (Jan – Mar 93), pp. 106 – 108.

Cortés Conde, Roberto. El crecimiento de las economías latinoamericanas, 1880 – 1930. *Historia Mexicana,* v. 42, no. 3 (Jan – Mar 93), pp. 633 – 648. Tables.

Durán Luzio, Juan. Modos de relación en historia y literatura hispanoamericana durante el siglo XIX. *Escritura (Venezuela),* v. 17, no. 33 – 34 (Jan – Dec 92), pp. 83 – 100.

Fernández Herrero, Beatriz. El "otro" descubrimiento: la imagen del español en el indio americano. *Cuadernos Hispanoamericanos,* no. 520 (Oct 93), pp. 7 – 35. Bibl.

Flórez Gallego, Lenín. Historias nacionales, historias de los trabajadores y el problema de la democracia en la obra de Charles Bergquist. *Anuario Colombiano de Historia Social y de la Cultura,* no. 20 (1992), pp. 73 – 88. Bibl, tables.

Klein, Herbert S. Historia fiscal colonial: resultados y perspectivas (Translated by Laura Elena Pulido Varela). *Historia Mexicana,* v. 42, no. 2 (Oct – Dec 92), pp. 261 – 307.

Kohut, Karl, ed. *De conquistadores y conquistados: realidad, justificación, representación* reviewed by Teodoro Hampe Martínez. *European Review of Latin American and Caribbean Studies,* no. 54 (June 93), pp. 116 – 118.

Mallon, Florencia E. Entre la utopía y la marginalidad: comunidades indígenas y culturas políticas en México y los Andes, 1780 – 1990. *Historia Mexicana,* v. 42, no. 2 (Oct – Dec 92), pp. 473 – 504.

Mörner, Magnus. Historia social hispanoamericana de los siglos XVIII y XIX: algunas reflexiones en torno a la historiografía reciente. *Historia Mexicana*, v. 42, no. 2 (Oct – Dec 92), pp. 419 – 471.

Vitale, Luis. *Introducción a una teoría de la historia para América Latina* reviewed by Carmen Urljicak-Espaín. *Todo Es Historia*, v. 26, no. 307 (Feb 93), p. 74. Il.

Bibliography

Rodríguez O., Jaime E. La independencia de la América española: una reinterpretación. *Historia Mexicana*, v. 42, no. 3 (Jan – Mar 93), pp. 571 – 620. Bibl.

History

Bethell, Leslie, ed. *Historia de América Latina* reviewed by Jorge F. Hernández (Review entitled "Para medir la distancia"). *Vuelta*, v. 17, no. 195 (Feb 93), pp. 44 – 45.

Brading, David Anthony. *The First America: The Spanish Monarchy, Creole Patriots, and the Liberal State, 1492 – 1867* reviewed by Marie-Cécile Bénassy-Berling. *Caravelle*, no. 59 (1992), pp. 266 – 270.

— *The First America: The Spanish Monarchy, Creole Patriots, and the Liberal State, 1492 – 1867* reviewed by Eric Van Young. *Colonial Latin American Review*, v. 2, no. 1 – 2 (1993), pp. 291 – 296.

Corzo Ramírez, Ricardo. Catálogo de la Biblioteca Quinto Centenario y comentario al libro *Iberoamérica: una comunidad*. *La Palabra y el Hombre*, no. 83 (July – Sept 92), pp. 322 – 346. Bibl.

Navarro García, Luis, ed. *Historia de las Américas* reviewed by Ana María Cignetti. *Revista de Historia de América*, no. 113 (Jan – June 92), pp. 165 – 170.

Williamson, Edwin. *The Penguin History of Latin America* reviewed by Jorge F. Hernández (Review entitled "Para medir la distancia"). *Vuelta*, v. 17, no. 195 (Feb 93), pp. 44 – 45.

Bibliography

Tisnés Jiménez, Roberto María. Bibliografía (Reviews of books on Latin American history written between 1989 and 1992). *Boletín de Historia y Antigüedades*, v. 80, no. 781 (Apr – June 93), pp. 465 – 475.

Congresses

Ruiz Rivera, Julián Bautista. Congreso internacional: 500 Años de Hispanoamérica; Descubrimiento y Formación de un Mundo Nuevo. *Anuario de Estudios Americanos*, v. 49, Suppl. 2 (1992), pp. 209 – 210.

Dictionaries and encyclopedias

Shavit, David. *The United States in Latin America: A Historical Dictionary* reviewed by Bruce Calder. *Revista Interamericana de Bibliografía*, v. 42, no. 3 (1992), p. 509.

To 1806

Gamarra Durana, Alfonso. La economía realista como provocadora de rebeldías. *Signo*, no. 36 – 37, Nueva época (May – Dec 92), pp. 361 – 378. Bibl.

Lynch, John. *The Hispanic World in Crisis and Change, 1598 – 1700* reviewed by Richard L. Kagan. *Hispanic American Historical Review*, v. 73, no. 3 (Aug 93), pp. 492 – 494.

1806 – 1830, Wars of Independence

Bazán, Armando Raúl. Americanismo y nacionalismo en la emancipación sudamericana. *Revista de Historia de América*, no. 112 (July – Dec 91), pp. 5 – 19.

Eljuri, José Ramón. *Campañas libertadoras suramericanas* del general de brigada Héctor Bencomo Barrios. *Boletín de la Academia Nacional de la Historia (Venezuela)*, v. 76, no. 301 (Jan – Mar 93), pp. 130 – 131.

Gandía, Enrique de. Prolegómenos a la independencia de la América Hispana: Francisco de Miranda y Juan Pablo de Vizcardo y Guzmán. *Investigaciones y Ensayos*, no. 41 (Jan – Dec 91), pp. 15 – 64.

Ramos Pérez, Demetrio et al. *Historia general de España y América, vol. XIII: Emancipación y nacionalidades americanas* reviewed by Luis Navarro García. *Anuario de Estudios Americanos*, v. 49, Suppl. 2 (1992), pp. 257 – 259.

Rodríguez O., Jaime E. La independencia de la América española: una reinterpretación. *Historia Mexicana*, v. 42, no. 3 (Jan – Mar 93), pp. 571 – 620. Bibl.

19th century

Hernández Sánchez-Barba, Mario et al, eds. *Reformismo y progreso en América, 1840 – 1905:* Vol. XV of *Historia general de España y América* reviewed by Antonio Santamaría García. *Anuario de Estudios Americanos*, v. 49, Suppl. 2 (1992), pp. 246 – 247.

20th century

Bethell, Leslie, ed. *The Cambridge History of Latin America, Vol. VIII: Latin America since 1930; Spanish South America* reviewed by Piero Gleijeses. *Journal of Latin American Studies*, v. 25, no. 1 (Feb 93), pp. 187 – 188.

Delgado Martín, Jaime. *Historia general de España y América, vol. XVIII: Hispanoamérica en el siglo XX* reviewed by Luis Navarro García. *Anuario de Estudios Americanos*, v. 49, Suppl. 2 (1992), pp. 245 – 246.

Industries

Batou, Jean. *Cent ans de résistance au sous-développement: l'industrialisation de l'Amérique Latine et du Moyen-Orient face au défi européen, 1770 – 1870* reviewed by Hernán G. H. Taboada. *Cuadernos Americanos*, no. 40, Nueva época (July – Aug 93), pp. 238 – 242.

— *One Hundred Years of Resistance to Underdevelopment, 1770 – 1870* reviewed by Joseph L. Love. *Journal of Latin American Studies*, v. 25, no. 1 (Feb 93), pp. 206 – 208.

Grebe López, Horst. La industrialización latinoamericana: ¿Sólo un recuento de frustraciones? *Nueva Sociedad*, no. 125 (May – June 93), pp. 47 – 57. Bibl.

Intellectual life

Acevedo, Edberto Oscar. San Martín y su ideario hacia 1810. *Investigaciones y Ensayos*, no. 41 (Jan – Dec 91), pp. 89 – 105. Bibl.

Febres, Laura M. Fragmentos para la comprensión de América, 1880 a 1900. *Montalbán*, no. 24 (1992), pp. 253 – 269. Bibl.

Halperín Donghi, Tulio. Hispanoamérica en el espejo: reflexiones hispanoamericanas sobre Hispanoamérica, de Simón Bolívar a Hernando de Soto. *Historia Mexicana*, v. 42, no. 3 (Jan – Mar 93), pp. 745 – 787. Bibl.

Mudrovcic, María Eugenia. *Mundo Nuevo:* hacia la definición de un modelo discursivo. *Nuevo Texto Crítico*, v. 6, no. 11 (1993), pp. 187 – 206. Bibl.

Petras, James F. Una pequeña parte de la lucha (Response to the article "Between Skepticism and Protocol" by Carlos María Vilas). *Nueva Sociedad*, no. 123 (Jan – Feb 93), pp. 165 – 170.

— Reply (to the article "Between Skepticism and Protocol" by Carlos María Vilas). *Latin American Perspectives*, v. 20, no. 2 (Spring 93), pp. 107 – 110.

Rachum, Ilan. Intellectuals and the Emergence of the Latin American Political Right, 1917 – 1936. *European Review of Latin American and Caribbean Studies*, no. 54 (June 93), pp. 95 – 110. Bibl.

Rama, Angel. *La crítica de la cultura en América Latina* selected and introduced by Saúl Sosnowski and Tomás Eloy Martínez. Reviewed by Roy Hora. *Todo Es Historia*, v. 26, no. 307 (Feb 93), pp. 74 – 75. Il.

Shimose Kawamura, Pedro. Homenaje a un cubano universal. *Signo*, no. 38, Nueva época (Jan – Apr 93), pp. 193 – 197.

Vázquez, Susana. El "redescubrimiento," 1492 – 1992. *Hoy Es Historia*, v. 9, no. 54 (Nov – Dec 92), pp. 11 – 26. Bibl, il.

Vilas, Carlos María. Between Skepticism and Protocol: The Defection of the "Critical Intellectuals" (Translated by Sarah Stookey). *Latin American Perspectives*, v. 20, no. 2 (Spring 93), pp. 97 – 106. Bibl.

— Contra el sectarismo (Response to James Petras' article "Los intelectuales en retirada" in *Nueva Sociedad*, no. 107). *Nueva Sociedad*, no. 123 (Jan – Feb 93), pp. 165 – 170.

Werz, Nikolaus. Aspectos del pensamiento político y cultural en Latinoamérica (Translated by Irma Lorini). *Ibero-Amerikanisches Archiv*, v. 18, no. 3 – 4 (1992), pp. 429 – 443. Bibl.

Societies, etc.

Saladino García, Alberto. Función modernizadora de las sociedades económicas de Amigos del País en el Nuevo Mundo. *Cuadernos Americanos,* no. 38, Nueva época (Mar – Apr 93), pp. 225 – 236. Bibl.

Name

Ardao, Arturo. *España en el origen del nombre América Latina* reviewed by Alejandro Daniel Michelena. *Hoy Es Historia,* v. 10, no. 58 (July – Aug 93), p. 86.

Officials and public employees

Rieu de Millán, Marie-Laure. *Los diputados americanos en las Cortes de Cádiz: igualdad o independencia* reviewed by María Lourdes Huarte Cambra. *Anuario de Estudios Americanos,* v. 49, Suppl. 2 (1992), pp. 259 – 261.

— *Los diputados americanos en las Cortes de Cádiz* reviewed by Michel Bertrand. *Caravelle,* no. 60 (1993), pp. 159 – 161.

Pictorial works

Levine, Robert M. *Images of History: Nineteenth and Twentieth Century Latin American Photography as Documents* reviewed by William H. Beezley. *Hispanic American Historical Review,* v. 73, no. 1 (Feb 93), pp. 133 – 134.

Levine, Robert M., ed. *Windows on Latin America: Understanding Society through Photographs* reviewed by William H. Beezley. *Hispanic American Historical Review,* v. 73, no. 1 (Feb 93), pp. 133 – 134.

Politics

Alcántara Sáez, Manuel. ¿Democracias inciertas o democracias consolidadas en América Latina? *Revista Mexicana de Sociología,* v. 54, no. 1 (Jan – Mar 92), pp. 205 – 223.

Broad, Dave. Revolution, Counterrevolution, and Imperialism: "¡La lucha continúa!" *Latin American Perspectives,* v. 20, no. 2 (Spring 93), pp. 6 – 20. Bibl.

Collier, David and Ruth Berins Collier. *Shaping the Political Arena: Critical Junctures, the Labor Movement, and Regime Dynamics in Latin America* reviewed by Francisco Zapata. *Foro Internacional,* v. 32, no. 5 (Oct – Dec 92), pp. 777 – 788.

— *Shaping the Political Arena: Critical Junctures, the Labor Movement, and Regime Dynamics in Latin America* reviewed by David Sowell. *Hispanic American Historical Review,* v. 73, no. 1 (Feb 93), pp. 194 – 195.

Couffignal, Georges, ed. *Réinventer la démocratie: le défi latino-américain* reviewed by Giorgio Alberti. *Journal of Latin American Studies,* v. 25, no. 2 (May 93), pp. 409 – 410.

Dunkerley, James. *Political Suicide in Latin America and Other Essays* reviewed by Walter Little. *Bulletin of Latin American Research,* v. 12, no. 1 (Jan 93), pp. 116 – 117.

Iglesias, Enrique V. América Latina: un decenio dramático. *Mensaje,* v. 42, no. 417 (Mar – Apr 93), pp. 74 – 76. Il.

Jonas, Susanne Leilani and Nancy Stein, eds. *Democracy in Latin America: Visions and Realities* reviewed by Eldon G. Kenworthy. *Hispanic American Historical Review,* v. 73, no. 2 (May 93), pp. 354 – 355.

Kaplan, Marcos. Crisis del estado latinoamericano: decadencia o palingenesia? *Relaciones Internacionales (Mexico),* v. 14, Nueva época, no. 56 (Oct – Dec 92), pp. 35 – 44.

Lavergne, Néstor. Democracia, estado-nación y socialismo en América Latina. *Realidad Económica,* no. 119 (Oct – Nov 93), pp. 47 – 68. Bibl.

Martínez Escamilla, Ramón. El estado en América Latina: teoría y práctica. *Problemas del Desarrollo,* v. 24, no. 93 (Apr – June 93), pp. 227 – 233.

Morley, Morris H. and James F. Petras. Latin America: Poverty and the Democracy of Poverty. *Homines,* v. 15 – 16, no. 2 – 1 (Oct 91 – Dec 92), pp. 75 – 94. Bibl.

— *Latin America in the Time of Cholera: Electoral Politics, Market Economics, and Permanent Crisis* reviewed by Donald F. Stevens. *The Americas,* v. 50, no. 2 (Oct 93), pp. 291 – 292.

Romero, José Luis. La ciudad latinoamericana y los movimientos políticos. *Siglo XIX: Revista,* no. 11, 2a época (Jan – June 92), pp. 15 – 27.

Sánchez Agesta, Luis. *La democracia en Hispanoamérica: un balance histórico* reviewed by Frédérique Langue. *Cahiers des Amériques Latines,* no. 13 (1992), pp. 178 – 179.

Smith, William C. Reestructuración neoliberal y escenarios políticos en América Latina. *Nueva Sociedad,* no. 126 (July – Aug 93), pp. 25 – 39. Bibl.

Wright, Thomas C. *Latin America in the Era of the Cuban Revolution* reviewed by Paul W. Drake. *The Americas,* v. 49, no. 3 (Jan 93), pp. 421 – 422.

— *Latin America in the Era of the Cuban Revolution* reviewed by Brian Loveman. *Hispanic American Historical Review,* v. 73, no. 2 (May 93), pp. 350 – 352.

Zagorski, Paul W. *Democracy vs. National Security: Civil – Military Relations in Latin America* reviewed by Gamaliel Perruci. *Journal of Inter-American Studies and World Affairs,* v. 35, no. 1 (1993), pp. 167 – 170.

Bibliography

Barrios, Harald and Petra Bendel. Los sistemas políticos de América Latina: bibliografía comentada de obras recientes. *Ibero-Amerikanisches Archiv,* v. 18, no. 1 – 2 (1992), pp. 291 – 310. Bibl.

Cicerchia, Ricardo. "O inventamos o erramos": América Latina; ¿La política de la crisis o la crisis de la política? (Review article). *Nueva Sociedad,* no. 128 (Nov – Dec 93), pp. 166 – 171.

Congresses

Lautier, Bruno. Les Nouvelles Politiques d'Ajustement en Amérique Latine: Guadalajara, Mexique, 24 – 27 février 1992. *Cahiers des Amériques Latines,* no. 13 (1992), pp. 171 – 172.

Presidents

Kryzanek, Michael John. *Leaders, Leadership, and U.S. Policy in Latin America* reviewed by Johanna Mendelson-Forman. *Revista Interamericana de Bibliografía,* v. 42, no. 4 (1992), pp. 658 – 659.

Race question

Hollanda, Heloísa Buarque de, ed. *¿Y nosotras latinoamericanas?: estudos sobre gênero e raça* reviewed by Lena Lavinas (Review entitled "Contrapassos da latinidade"). *Estudos Feministas,* v. 1, no. 2 (1993), pp. 501 – 502.

La razón del mestizaje. *ECA; Estudios Centroamericanos,* v. 47, no. 528 (Oct 92), pp. 901 – 904. Il.

Salcedo-Bastardo, José Luis. Día de la Humanidad. *Boletín de la Academia Nacional de la Historia (Venezuela),* v. 75, no. 298 (Apr – June 92), pp. 89 – 90.

Tardieu, Jean-Pierre. Las vistas de un arbitrista sobre la aparición de un hombre nuevo en las Indias Occidentales, mitad del siglo XVII. *Anuario de Estudios Americanos,* v. 50, no. 1 (1993), pp. 235 – 249. Bibl.

Rural conditions

Klein, Emilio. El mundo de trabajo rural. *Nueva Sociedad,* no. 124 (Mar – Apr 93), pp. 72 – 81. Bibl, tables.

Ortega, Emiliano. Evolution of the Rural Dimension in Latin America and the Caribbean. *CEPAL Review,* no. 47 (Aug 92), pp. 115 – 136. Bibl, tables.

Social conditions

Angulo, Alejandro. Prólogo para una ética social. *Revista Javeriana,* v. 61, no. 599 (Oct 93), pp. 366 – 370.

Bibliography

Mörner, Magnus. Historia social hispanoamericana de los siglos XVIII y XIX: algunas reflexiones en torno a la historiografía reciente. *Historia Mexicana,* v. 42, no. 2 (Oct – Dec 92), pp. 419 – 471.

Congresses

Declaración final de la "Cumbre Alternativa: Las Otras Voces de América Latina." *Boletín de Antropología Americana,* no. 24 (Dec 91), p. 179+.

III Encuentro Continental de la Resistencia Indígena, Negra y Popular: declaración de Managua. *Boletín de Antropología Americana,* no. 24 (Dec 91), p. 183+.

Social policy

Barrantes Alvarado, César A. Reflexiones sobre política social. *Revista de Ciencias Sociales (Costa Rica),* no. 58 (Dec 92), pp. 95 – 107. Bibl.

Devlin, Robert T. Privatizations and Social Welfare. *CEPAL Review*, no. 49 (Apr 93), pp. 155 – 180. Bibl, tables.

Kliksberg, Bernardo, ed. *¿Cómo enfrentar la pobreza?: estrategias y experiencias organizacionales innovadoras* reviewed by Michel Mujica Ricardo. *Nueva Sociedad*, no. 124 (Mar – Apr 93), pp. 174 – 175.

Martín P., Juan and Arturo Núñez del Prado Benavente. Strategic Management, Planning, and Budgets. *CEPAL Review*, no. 49 (Apr 93), pp. 41 – 54. Bibl.

Paz Zamora, Jaime et al. *Desarrollo social, democracia y crecimiento económico* (Review). *Integración Latinoamericana*, v. 18, no. 189 – 190 (May – June 93), pp. 56 – 57.

Bibliography

Borzutzky, Silvia. Social Security and Health Policies in Latin America: The Changing Roles of the State and the Private Sector (Review article). *Latin American Research Review*, v. 28, no. 2 (1993), pp. 246 – 256.

Congresses

Cabello Naranjo, Elena. III Cumbre Iberoamericana: hacia una agenda de desarrollo. *Comercio Exterior*, v. 43, no. 9 (Sept 93), pp. 836 – 839.

Cost

Cohen, Ernesto and Rolando Franco. Rationalizing Social Policy: Evaluation and Viability. *CEPAL Review*, no. 47 (Aug 92), pp. 163 – 172. Bibl, charts.

LATIN AMERICA IN ART

Manthorne, Katherine Emma. Up the Andes and Down the Amazon: 19th Century North American Views of South America. *Review*, no. 47 (Fall 93), pp. 39 – 44. Il.

Noé, Luis Felipe. *A Oriente por Occidente* reviewed by Ivonne Pini (Accompanied by an English translation). *Art Nexus*, no. 10 (Sept – Dec 93), pp. 41 – 42. Il.

LATIN AMERICA IN LITERATURE

Alzugarat, Alfredo J. *Cien años de soledad*: veinticinco años de diálogo con América Latina. *Cuadernos del CLAEH*, v. 17, no. 63 – 64 (Oct 92), pp. 175 – 181. Bibl.

Awoonor, Kofi Nyidevu. *The Latin American and Caribbean Notebook* reviewed by Tanure Ojaide. *World Literature Today*, v. 67, no. 4 (Fall 93), pp. 875 – 876.

Basile, María Teresa. La naturaleza como discurso sobre la identidad latinoamericana. *La Educación (USA)*, v. 36, no. 111 – 113 (1992), pp. 75 – 88. Bibl.

Díaz Ruiz, Ignacio. El recurso de la historia: a propósito de Carpentier. *Nueva Revista de Filología Hispánica*, v. 40, no. 2 (July – Dec 92), pp. 1073 – 1086. Bibl.

Ouimette, Victor. Azorín y la América española. *Insula*, no. 556 (Apr 93), pp. 14 – 15.

Pera, Cristóbal. Alienación (europeización) o introversión (incesto): Latinoamérica y Europa en *Cien años de soledad*. *Chasqui*, v. 22, no. 2 (Nov 93), pp. 85 – 93. Bibl.

LATIN AMERICA IN MOTION PICTURES

Godfrey, Brian J. Regional Depiction in Contemporary Film. *Geographical Review*, v. 83, no. 4 (Oct 93), pp. 428 – 440. Bibl, il.

Podalsky, Laura. Disjointed Frames: Melodrama, Nationalism, and Representation in 1940s Mexico. *Studies in Latin American Popular Culture*, v. 12 (1993), pp. 57 – 53. Bibl.

Richard, Alfred Charles, Jr. *The Hispanic Image on the Silver Screen: An Interpretive Filmography from Silents into Sound, 1898 – 1935* reviewed by Paul J. Vanderwood. *Hispanic American Historical Review*, v. 73, no. 2 (May 93), pp. 294 – 295.

— *The Hispanic Image on the Silver Screen: An Interpretive Filmography from Silents into Sound, 1898 – 1935* reviewed by Ana M. Rodríguez-Vivaldi. *Revista Interamericana de Bibliografía*, v. 42, no. 3 (1992), pp. 507 – 508.

Tuñón Pablos, Julia. Between the Nation and Utopia: The Image of Mexico in the Films of Emilio "Indio" Fernández. *Studies in Latin American Popular Culture*, v. 12 (1993), pp. 159 – 174. Bibl.

El viaje reviewed by Hans Günther Pflaum (Review entitled "La película *El viaje* de Fernando E. Solanas," review translated by José Luis Gómez y Patiño). *Humboldt*, no. 109 (1993), p. 98. Il.

Zapiola, Guillermo. Indios y españoles en pantalla grande. *Cuadernos del CLAEH*, v. 17, no. 63 – 64 (Oct 92), pp. 161 – 166.

LATIN AMERICAN DRAMA

See also
Drama festivals
Drama reviews
Experimental theater
Religious drama
Theater

History and criticism

Albuquerque, Severino João Medeiros. *Violent Acts: A Study of Contemporary Latin American Theatre* reviewed by Leslie Damasceno. *Latin American Theatre Review*, v. 26, no. 2 (Spring 93), pp. 210 – 212.

Kronik, John W. Invasions from Outer Space: Narration and Dramatic Art in Spanish America. *Latin American Theatre Review*, v. 26, no. 2 (Spring 93), pp. 25 – 47. Bibl.

Taylor, Diana. *Theatre of Crisis: Drama and Politics in Latin America* reviewed by José Castro-Urioste. *Revista de Crítica Literaria Latinoamericana*, v. 19, no. 38 (July – Dec 93), pp. 405 – 406.

Unruh, Vicky Wolff. Cultural Enactments: Recent Books on Latin American Theatre (Review article). *Latin American Research Review*, v. 28, no. 1 (1993), pp. 141 – 149.

LATIN AMERICAN FICTION

Colchie, Thomas, ed. *A Hammock beneath the Mangoes: Stories from Latin America* reviewed by Barbara Mujica (Review entitled " A Roundup of Stories"). *Américas*, v. 45, no. 1 (Jan – Feb 93), p. 60. Il.

Fernández Olmos, Margarite and Lizabeth Paravisini-Gebert. *El placer de la palabra: literatura erótica femenina de América Latina; antología crítica* reviewed by Mónica Zapata. *Canadian Journal of Latin American and Caribbean Studies*, v. 17, no. 34 (1992), pp. 135 – 138.

Bibliography

Balderston, Daniel, ed. *The Latin American Short Story: An Annotated Guide to Anthologies and Criticism* reviewed by David William Foster. *Chasqui*, v. 22, no. 1 (May 93), pp. 86 – 87.

— *The Latin American Short Story: An Annotated Guide to Anthologies and Criticism* reviewed by Genaro J. Pérez. *Hispania (USA)*, v. 76, no. 3 (Sept 93), pp. 482 – 483.

— *The Latin American Short Story: An Annotated Guide to Anthologies and Criticism* reviewed by Enrique Pupo-Walker. *Revista Interamericana de Bibliografía*, v. 42, no. 3 (1992), p. 501.

— *The Latin American Short Story: An Annotated Guide to Anthologies and Criticism* reviewed by Melvin S. Arrington, Jr. *World Literature Today*, v. 67, no. 3 (Summer 93), pp. 593 – 594.

Libros (Short book reviews). *Plural (Mexico)*, v. 22, no. 263 (Aug 93), pp. 80 – 83.

History and criticism

Fuentes, Carlos. *Le sourire d'Erasme: epopée, utopie et mythe dans le roman hispano-américain*, a translation of *Valiente mundo nuevo: épica, utopía y mito en la novela hispanoamericana*. Reviewed by John L. Brown. *World Literature Today*, v. 67, no. 4 (Fall 93), p. 790.

Bibliography

Peavler, Terry J. After the Boom: The Coming of Age of Latin American Literary Criticism (Review article). *Latin American Research Review*, v. 28, no. 2 (1993), pp. 221 – 231.

19th century

Benítez Rojo, Antonio. Nacionalismo y nacionalización en la novela hispanoamericana del siglo XIX. *Revista de Crítica Literaria Latinoamericana*, v. 19, no. 38 (July – Dec 93), pp. 185 – 193.

Ramos, Julio. Cuerpo, lengua, subjetividad. *Revista de Crítica Literaria Latinoamericana,* v. 19, no. 38 (July – Dec 93), pp. 225 – 237. Bibl.

Sommer, Doris. *Foundational Fictions: The National Romances of Latin America* reviewed by Edgardo C. Krebs. *The Americas,* v. 50, no. 2 (Oct 93), pp. 282 – 283.

— *Foundational Fictions: The National Romances of Latin America* reviewed by Carlos L. Orihuela. *Revista de Crítica Literaria Latinoamericana,* v. 19, no. 38 (July – Dec 93), pp. 399 – 403.

20th century

Brushwood, John Stubbs. Writerly Novels/Readerly Responses. *Latin American Literary Review,* v. 20, no. 40 (July – Dec 92), pp. 23 – 25.

Echavarren Welker, Roberto. *Margen de ficción: poéticas de la narrativa hispanoamericana* reviewed by Thomas E. Case. *World Literature Today,* v. 67, no. 2 (Spring 93), p. 341.

González, Eduardo. *The Monstered Self: Narratives of Death and Performance in Latin American Fiction* reviewed by Ana Eire. *Hispania (USA),* v. 76, no. 2 (May 93), pp. 286 – 287.

Guerra-Cunningham, Lucía. Estrategias discursivas en la narrativa de la mujer latinoamericana. *Escritura (Venezuela),* v. 16, no. 31 – 32 (Jan – Dec 91), pp. 115 – 122.

Kerr, Lucille. *Reclaiming the Author: Figures and Fictions from Spanish America* reviewed by Nicolás Shumway. *Hispanic American Historical Review,* v. 73, no. 2 (May 93), pp. 297 – 298.

— *Reclaiming the Author: Figures and Fictions from Spanish America* reviewed by Pamela Bacarisse. *Revista Iberoamericana,* v. 59, no. 162 – 163 (Jan – June 93), pp. 365 – 368.

Mora, Gabriela. Notas teóricas en torno a las colecciones de cuentos integrados (a veces cíclicos). *Revista Chilena de Literatura,* no. 42 (Aug 93), pp. 131 – 137. Bibl.

Ortega, Julio. *Una poética del cambio* reviewed by George R. McMurray. *Hispania (USA),* v. 76, no. 3 (Sept 93), pp. 485 – 486.

Sklodowska, Elzbieta. *La parodia en la nueva novela hispanoamericana, 1960 – 1985* reviewed by Isabel Rodríguez-Vergara. *La Educación (USA),* v. 36, no. 111 – 113 (1992), pp. 304 – 305.

— *La parodia en la nueva novela hispanoamericana, 1960 – 1985* reviewed by George R. McMurray. *Hispania (USA),* v. 76, no. 2 (May 93), pp. 293 – 294.

— *La parodia en la nueva novela hispanoamericana, 1960 – 1985* reviewed by Donald L. Shaw. *Hispanic Review,* v. 61, no. 2 (Spring 93), pp. 316 – 317.

— *La parodia en la nueva novela hispanoamericana, 1960 – 1985* reviewed by Norman Cheadle. *Revista Canadiense de Estudios Hispánicos,* v. 17, no. 2 (Winter 93), pp. 413 – 414.

— *La parodia en la nueva novela hispanoamericana, 1960 – 1985* reviewed by Brian Evenson. *World Literature Today,* v. 67, no. 1 (Winter 93), p. 161.

Stawicka, Bárbara. La selva en flor: Alejo Carpentier y el diálogo entre las vanguardias europeas del siglo XX y el barroco latinoamericano. *La Palabra y el Hombre,* no. 81 (Jan – Mar 92), pp. 193 – 199. Bibl.

Vallejo, Catharina Vanderplaats de. *Elementos para una semiótica del cuento hispanoamericano del siglo XX* reviewed by R. A. Kerr. *Hispania (USA),* v. 76, no. 3 (Sept 93), p. 482.

Williams, Raymond Leslie, ed. *The Novel in the Americas* reviewed by Edward Waters Hood. *Hispania (USA),* v. 76, no. 4 (Dec 93), pp. 742 – 743.

— *The Novel in the Americas* reviewed by John L. Brown. *World Literature Today,* v. 67, no. 4 (Fall 93), pp. 908 – 909.

LATIN AMERICAN INTEGRATION ASSOCIATION

Congresses

ALADI: Séptima Reunión del Consejo de Ministros de Relaciones Exteriores. *Integración Latinoamericana,* v. 18, no. 186 (Jan – Feb 93), pp. 62 – 65.

Sources

ALADI: acuerdos de cooperación. *Integración Latinoamericana,* v. 17, no. 184 (Nov 92), pp. 69 – 72.

LATIN AMERICAN LITERATURE
See also
America in literature
Argentina in literature
Art and literature
Authors
Baroque
Biography (as a literary form)
Blacks in literature
Brazil in literature
Caribbean area in literature
Children's literature
Cities and towns in literature
Comic books, strips, etc.
Cuba in literature
Death in literature
Detective and mystery stories
Dominican Republic in literature
Fantastic literature
Folk literature
Gauchos in literature
Grotesque in literature
Haiti in literature
Hispanic Americans in literature (U.S.)
Indians in literature
Irony in literature
Jamaica in literature
Jews in literature
Latin America in literature
Linguistic analysis (Literature)
Literary criticism
Literary prizes
Literature and history
Literature and science
Literature and society
Love in literature
Magical realism (Literature)
Mexican Americans in literature
Mexico in literature
Military in literature
Mirrors in literature
Modernism (Literature)
Motion pictures and literature
Music and literature
Myth in literature
Mythology in literature
Nationalism in literature
Nature in literature
Peru in literature
Poets
Politics in literature
Popular culture
Portugal in literature
Postmodernism
Psychoanalysis in literature
Puerto Ricans in literature
Puerto Rico in literature
Realism in literature
Regionalism in literature
Religion and literature
Revolutionary literature
Satire
Science fiction
Semiotics
Sex role in literature
Space in literature
Surrealism
Symbolism in literature
Time in literature
Translating and interpreting
United States in literature
Venezuela in literature
Violence in literature
Visual text
Wit and humor
Women authors
Women in literature
Names of specific authors
Specific genres, specific countries; e.g., *Chilean poetry, Argentine literature,* etc.

Alegría, Fernando and Jorge Ruffinelli, eds. *Paradise Lost or Gained?: The Literature of Hispanic Exile* reviewed by Barbara Mujica (Review entitled "The Creative Subtext of Life"). *Américas,* v. 45, no. 3 (May – June 93), pp. 60 – 61.

— *Paradise Lost or Gained?: The Literature of Hispanic Exile* reviewed by Joseph F. Vélez. *Hispania (USA),* v. 76, no. 1 (Mar 93), pp. 80 – 82.

Castro-Klarén, Sara et al, eds. *Women's Writing in Latin America: An Anthology* reviewed by Lisa Jesse. *Bulletin of Latin American Research*, v. 12, no. 1 (Jan 93), pp. 128 – 129.

— *Women's Writing in Latin America: An Anthology* reviewed by Eva Paulino Bueno. *Revista de Crítica Literaria Latinoamericana*, v. 19, no. 37 (Jan – June 93), pp. 372 – 374.

Santana, Jorge A. La adivinanza a través de quinientos años de cultura hispánica: antología histórica. *Explicación de Textos Literarios*, v. 21, no. 1 – 2 (1992), Issue. Bibl.

Bibliography

Fraser, Howard M. Dissertations, 1992. *Hispania (USA)*, v. 76, no. 2 (May 93), pp. 324 – 348.

Schwartz, Jorge. ¡Abajo Tordesillas! *Casa de las Américas*, no. 191 (Apr – June 93), pp. 26 – 35. Bibl.

Sonntag-Grigera, María Gabriela. Lesser-Known Latin American Women Authors: A Bibliography. *Revista Interamericana de Bibliografía*, v. 42, no. 3 (1992), pp. 463 – 488.

Triviño Anzola, Consuelo. América en los libros (Short book reviews). *Cuadernos Hispanoamericanos*, no. 516, 520 (1993), All issues.

Wentzlaff-Eggebert, Harald. *Las literaturas hispánicas de vanguardia: orientación bibliográfica* reviewed by Hugo Verani (Review entitled "Las vanguardias latinoamericanas"). *Nuevo Texto Crítico*, v. 6, no. 11 (1993), pp. 262 – 263.

Black authors

Miller, Ingrid Watson. *Afro-Hispanic Literature: An Anthology of Hispanic Writers of African Ancestry* reviewed by James J. Davis. *Afro-Hispanic Review*, v. 12, no. 1 (Spring 93), pp. 59 – 60.

Bibliography

Jackson, Richard L. *The Afro-Spanish American Author, II: The 1980s; An Annotated Bibliography of Criticism* reviewed by Donald K. Gordon. *Revista Canadiense de Estudios Hispánicos*, v. 17, no. 2 (Winter 93), pp. 401 – 402.

Study and teaching

Feal, Rosemary Geisdorfer. Bordering Feminism in Afro-Hispanic Studies: Crossroads in the Field. *Latin American Literary Review*, v. 20, no. 40 (July – Dec 92), pp. 41 – 45. Bibl.

Foreign influences

Díaz Martínez, Manuel. La generación del '27 e Hispanoamérica. *Cuadernos Hispanoamericanos*, no. 514 – 515 (Apr – May 93), pp. 143 – 154. Il.

Kushigian, Julia A. *Orientalism in the Hispanic Tradition: In Dialogue with Borges, Paz, and Sarduy* reviewed by John Incledon. *Hispania (USA)*, v. 76, no. 3 (Sept 93), pp. 483 – 484.

Pratt, Mary Louise. La liberación de los márgenes: literaturas canadiense y latinoamericana en el contexto de la dependencia. *Casa de las Américas*, no. 190 (Jan – Mar 93), pp. 25 – 33. Bibl.

Wentzlaff-Eggebert, Harald, ed. *Europäische Avantgarde im lateinamerikanischen Kontext/La vanguardia europea en el contexto latinoamericano* reviewed by Hugo J. Verani (Review entitled "Las vanguardias latinoamericanas"). *Nuevo Texto Crítico*, v. 6, no. 11 (1993), pp. 262 – 263.

History and criticism

Arriaga de Lassel, Adriana. El viaje hacia América: la figura del inmigrante en algunos textos literarios. *Cuadernos Hispanoamericanos*, no. 513 (Mar 93), pp. 93 – 100. Bibl.

Corral, Wilfrido Howard and Norma Klahn, eds. *Los novelistas como críticos*, vol. I, reviewed by Sonia Mattalía. *Nuevo Texto Crítico*, v. 6, no. 11 (1993), pp. 259 – 261.

Fitz, Earl E. *Rediscovering the New World: Inter-American Literature in a Comparative Context* reviewed by Charles B. Moore. *Hispania (USA)*, v. 76, no. 1 (Mar 93), pp. 84 – 85.

Foster, David William. *Gay and Lesbian Themes in Latin American Writing* reviewed by Donna J. Guy. *Hispanic American Historical Review*, v. 73, no. 1 (Feb 93), p. 137.

González Echevarría, Roberto. *Myth and Archives: A Theory of Latin American Narrative* reviewed by Antonio Fama. *Revista Canadiense de Estudios Hispánicos*, v. 17, no. 2 (Winter 93), pp. 399 – 401.

Lienhard, Martín. Kulturelle Heterogenität und Literatur in Lateinamerika. *Iberoamericana*, v. 16, no. 47 – 48 (1992), pp. 95 – 110. Bibl.

Ortega, Julio. *El discurso de la abundancia* reviewed by George R. McMurray. *Hispania (USA)*, v. 76, no. 3 (Sept 93), pp. 485 – 486.

Paz, Octavio. Unidad, modernidad, tradición (Prologue to Volume III of Paz's *Obras completas*). *Vuelta*, v. 17, no. 200 (July 93), pp. 10 – 13.

Urruela V. de Quezada, María. El indio en la literatura hispanoamericana: un esbozo. *Boletín de la Academia Nacional de la Historia (Venezuela)*, v. 75, no. 299 (July – Sept 92), pp. 91 – 108. Bibl.

Bibliography

Montaldo, Graciela R. Imaginación e historia en América Latina (Review article). *Nueva Sociedad*, no. 127 (Sept – Oct 93), pp. 163 – 167.

Colonial period

Barzuna Pérez, Guillermo. Estructura y sentido en la crónica colonial. *Káñina*, v. 16, no. 2 (July – Dec 92), pp. 75 – 79. Bibl.

Cevallos Candau, Francisco Javier, ed. *Narraciones cortas de la América colonial* reviewed by Lee A. Daniel. *Hispania (USA)*, v. 76, no. 3 (Sept 93), pp. 481 – 482.

González Stephan, Beatriz et al. *Crítica y descolonización: el sujeto colonial en la cultura latinoamericana* reviewed by David William Foster. *Chasqui*, v. 22, no. 2 (Nov 93), pp. 162 – 163.

Jara, René and Nicholas Spadaccini, eds. *1492 – 1992: Re/Discovering Colonial Writing* reviewed by David A. Boruchoff. *Revista Canadiense de Estudios Hispánicos*, v. 17, no. 1 (Fall 92), pp. 207 – 209.

Larsen, Neil. En contra de la des-estetización del "discurso" colonial. *Revista de Crítica Literaria Latinoamericana*, v. 19, no. 37 (Jan – June 93), pp. 335 – 342. Bibl.

León de D'Empaire, Arleny. El gran viaje de descubrimiento: las crónicas americanas. *Montalbán*, no. 24 (1992), pp. 85 – 97. Bibl.

Pastor, Beatriz. *The Armature of Conquest: Spanish Accounts of the Discovery of America, 1492 – 1589* reviewed by Patricia Seed. *Journal of Latin American Studies*, v. 25, no. 2 (May 93), pp. 387 – 388.

Promis Ojeda, José M. *The Identity of Hispanoamerica: An Interpretation of Colonial Literature* reviewed by Eric Van Young. *Colonial Latin American Review*, v. 2, no. 1 – 2 (1993), pp. 291 – 296.

19th century

Durán Luzio, Juan. Modos de relación en historia y literatura hispanoamericana durante el siglo XIX. *Escritura (Venezuela)*, v. 17, no. 33 – 34 (Jan – Dec 92), pp. 83 – 100.

20th century

Bassnett, Susan, ed. *Knives and Angels: Women Writers in Latin America* reviewed by Beth E. Jörgensen. *Letras Femeninas*, v. 19, no. 1 – 2 (Spring – Fall 93), pp. 143 – 146.

Castro-Klarén, Sara. Situations. *Latin American Literary Review*, v. 20, no. 40 (July – Dec 92), pp. 26 – 29.

Libertella, Héctor. *Patografía: los juegos desviados de la literatura* reviewed by Jacobo Sefamí. *Revista Chilena de Literatura*, no. 41 (Apr 93), pp. 136 – 137.

Marcos, Juan Manuel. Jorge Luis Borges y el museo imaginario: en torno al debate conceptual sobre postboom y post modernidad. *Estudios Paraguayos*, v. 17, no. 1 – 2 (1989 – 1993), pp. 151 – 166. Bibl.

Mudrovcic, María Eugenia. *Mundo Nuevo*: hacia la definición de un modelo discursivo. *Nuevo Texto Crítico*, v. 6, no. 11 (1993), pp. 187 – 206. Bibl.

Rama, Angel. *La crítica de la cultura en América Latina* selected and introduced by Saúl Sosnowski and Tomás Eloy Martínez. Reviewed by Roy Hora. *Todo Es Historia*, v. 26, no. 307 (Feb 93), pp. 74 – 75. Il.

Richard, Nelly. Alteridad y descentramiento culturales. *Revista Chilena de Literatura*, no. 42 (Aug 93), pp. 209 – 215.

Rivero Potter, Alicia. *Autor/lector: Huidobro, Borges, Fuentes y Sarduy* reviewed by R. A. Kerr. *Hispania (USA)*, v. 76, no. 4 (Dec 93), pp. 741 – 742.

— *Autor/lector: Huidobro, Borges, Fuentes y Sarduy* reviewed by Gustavo Fares. *Revista Iberoamericana*, v. 59, no. 162 – 163 (Jan – June 93), pp. 376 – 379.

Schumm, Petra. *Exilerfahrung und Literatur: Lateinamerikanische Autoren in Spanien* reviewed by Monika Wehrheim-Peuker. *Iberoamericana*, v. 16, no. 47 – 48 (1992), pp. 135 – 137.

Schwartz, Jorge. *Las vanguardias latinoamericanas: textos programáticos y críticos* reviewed by Jacobo Sefamí. *Revista Chilena de Literatura*, no. 40 (Nov 92), pp. 159 – 160.

— *Las vanguardias latinoamericanas: textos programáticos y críticos* reviewed by Djelal Kadir. *World Literature Today*, v. 67, no. 1 (Winter 93), pp. 246 – 247.

Sommer, Doris. Resistant Texts and Incompetent Readers. *Latin American Literary Review*, v. 20, no. 40 (July – Dec 92), pp. 104 – 108.

Welden, Alicia Galaz-Vivar. *Alta marea: introvisión crítica en ocho voces latinoamericanas; Belli, Fuentes, Lagos, Mistral, Neruda, Orrillo, Rojas, Villaurrutia* reviewed by Juvenal López Ruiz. *Revista Nacional de Cultura (Venezuela)*, v. 53, no. 285 (Apr – June 92), pp. 252 – 253.

Periodicals

Vélez, Julio. Revistas hispánicas de vanguardia. *Cuadernos Hispanoamericanos*, no. 514 – 515 (Apr – May 93), pp. 343 – 344.

Study and teaching

Chang-Rodríguez, Raquel. Colonial Connections. *Latin American Literary Review*, v. 20, no. 40 (July – Dec 92), pp. 30 – 31.

González, Aníbal. After 1992: A Latin Americanist Wish List. *Latin American Literary Review*, v. 20, no. 40 (July – Dec 92), pp. 46 – 50.

González Echevarría, Roberto. Reflections on My Crystal Ball. *Latin American Literary Review*, v. 20, no. 40 (July – Dec 92), pp. 51 – 53.

Kerr, Lucille. Frames for the Future: Some Thoughts on Latin American Literary Studies. *Latin American Literary Review*, v. 20, no. 40 (July – Dec 92), pp. 54 – 57.

López-Baralt, Mercedes. Is There Life after 1992?: On the Future of Colonial Studies. *Latin American Literary Review*, v. 20, no. 40 (July – Dec 92), pp. 63 – 65.

Mignolo, Walter D. Second Thoughts on Canon and Corpus. *Latin American Literary Review*, v. 20, no. 40 (July – Dec 92), pp. 66 – 69. Bibl.

Pellón, Gustavo. The Canon, the Boom, and Literary Theory. *Latin American Literary Review*, v. 20, no. 40 (July – Dec 92), pp. 80 – 82.

Pérez Firmat, Gustavo. My Critical Condition. *Latin American Literary Review*, v. 20, no. 40 (July – Dec 92), pp. 83 – 84.

Rodríguez-Luis, Julio. On the Criticism of Latin American Literature. *Latin American Literary Review*, v. 20, no. 40 (July – Dec 92), pp. 85 – 87.

Schulman, Iván A. Critical Crossroads. *Latin American Literary Review*, v. 20, no. 40 (July – Dec 92), pp. 97 – 99.

Translations
Bibliography

Martin, Gerald. *Writers from Latin America* reviewed by Warren L. Meinhardt. *Chasqui*, v. 22, no. 1 (May 93), pp. 99 – 101.

Israel

Zlotchew, Clark M. Literatura israelí en español: entrevista con Leonardo Senkman. *Confluencia*, v. 8, no. 1 (Fall 92), pp. 111 – 121. Bibl.

LATIN AMERICAN POETRY

See also
Modernism (Literature)
Poets
Religious poetry
Revolutionary poetry

Perlongher, Néstor, ed. *Caribe transplatino: poesía neobarroca cubana y rioplatense* reviewed by Bella Jozef. *Hispamérica*, v. 22, no. 64 – 65 (Apr – Aug 93), pp. 204 – 206.

Bibliography

Sefamí, Jacobo, ed. *Contemporary Spanish American Poets: A Bibliography of Primary and Secondary Sources* reviewed by David William Foster. *Chasqui*, v. 22, no. 1 (May 93), pp. 86 – 87.

— *Contemporary Spanish American Poets: A Bibliography of Primary and Secondary Sources* reviewed by Hensley C. Woodbridge. *Hispania (USA)*, v. 76, no. 1 (Mar 93), pp. 89 – 90.

— *Contemporary Spanish American Poets: A Bibliography of Primary and Secondary Sources* reviewed by Miriam Bornstein. *Revista Interamericana de Bibliografía*, v. 42, no. 4 (1992), pp. 665 – 666.

Sosa, Víctor. Poesía y antología (Review article). *Vuelta*, v. 17, no. 199 (June 93), pp. 42 – 44.

History and criticism

Rodríguez-Peralta, Phyllis White. The Modernist Nocturno and the Nocturne in Music. *Hispanic Journal*, v. 14, no. 1 (Spring 93), pp. 143 – 155.

Colonial period

Torres, Daniel. Indagación sobre la técnica escritural "diferente" en la lírica barroca colonial. *Hispanic Journal*, v. 13, no. 2 (Fall 92), pp. 281 – 287. Bibl.

20th century

Madrid, Lelia M. *El estilo del deseo: la poética de Darío, Vallejo, Borges y Paz* reviewed by Martha J. Nandorfy. *Revista Canadiense de Estudios Hispánicos*, v. 17, no. 3 (Spring 93), pp. 562 – 565.

Malpartida Ortega, Juan. La poesía en Hispanoamérica: algunos ejemplos. *Cuadernos Hispanoamericanos*, no. 513 (Mar 93), pp. 73 – 84.

Pérez, Alberto Julián. La poesía de Eduardo Mitre en el contexto de la poesía latinoamericana contemporánea. *Signo*, no. 36 – 37, Nueva época (May – Dec 92), pp. 23 – 42. Bibl.

Rivera-Rodas, Oscar. La modernidad en el lenguaje poético hispánico. *Signo*, no. 36 – 37, Nueva época (May – Dec 92), pp. 109 – 123.

Rodríguez Padrón, Justo Jorge. *Del ocio sagrado: algunos poetas hispanoamericanos* reviewed by Jacobo Sefamí. *Revista Chilena de Literatura*, no. 41 (Apr 93), p. 138.

Videla de Rivero, Gloria. *Direcciones del vanguardismo hispanoamericano, tomo I: Estudios sobre poesía de vanguardia en la década del veinte; tomo II: Documentos* reviewed by Klaus Müller-Bergh. *Hispanic Review*, v. 61, no. 3 (Summer 93), pp. 451 – 454.

LATIN AMERICAN STUDIES

Barradas, Efraín. 1493 también es 1492. *Latin American Literary Review*, v. 20, no. 40 (July – Dec 92), pp. 13 – 15.

Beverley, John. Cultural Studies. *Latin American Literary Review*, v. 20, no. 40 (July – Dec 92), pp. 19 – 22. Bibl.

Earle, Peter G. On Culture and Critical Hangovers. *Latin American Literary Review*, v. 20, no. 40 (July – Dec 92), pp. 32 – 33.

Foster, David William. On Expanding the Base of Latin American Studies. *Latin American Literary Review*, v. 20, no. 40 (July – Dec 92), pp. 34 – 37.

Franco, Jean. Remapping Culture. *Latin American Literary Review*, v. 20, no. 40 (July – Dec 92), pp. 38 – 40.

Larsen, Neil. Latin America and "Cultural Studies." *Latin American Literary Review*, v. 20, no. 40 (July – Dec 92), pp. 58 – 62.

Moreiras, Alberto. The Secret Agency of Disillusionment. *Latin American Literary Review*, v. 20, no. 40 (July – Dec 92), pp. 70 – 74.

Santí, Enrico-Mario. Latinamericanism and Restitution. *Latin American Literary Review*, v. 20, no. 40 (July – Dec 92), pp. 88 – 96.

Williams, Raymond Leslie. After Foucault: On the Future of Indo-Afro-Iberoamerican Studies. *Latin American Literary Review*, v. 20, no. 40 (July – Dec 92), pp. 120 – 124.

Congresses

Langue, Frédérique. Simposio "El Nuevo Mundo – Mundos Nuevos: La Experiencia Americana." *Anuario de Estudios Americanos,* v. 49, Suppl. 1 (1992), pp. 220 – 222.

Ruiz Rivera, Julián Bautista. V Congreso de la Asociación Española de Americanistas. *Anuario de Estudios Americanos,* v. 49, Suppl. 1 (1992), pp. 216 – 219.

Research

Investigaciones en curso/Research in Progress. *Revista Interamericana de Bibliografía,* v. 42 (1992), All issues.

Societies, etc.

Hodgman, Suzanne. SALALM Membership, 1956 – 1990: A Brief Overview. *SALALM Papers,* v. 36 (1991), pp. 215 – 223. Tables.

China

Xu, Wenyuan. El enfoque chino sobre los estudios latinoamericanos. *SALALM Papers,* v. 36 (1991), pp. 15 – 19.

Germany

Steger, Hanns Albert. Antropología cultural histórica (Translated by Elsa Cecilia Frost). *Cuadernos Americanos,* no. 39, Nueva época (May – June 93), pp. 134 – 166. Bibl.

Congresses

Scheerer, Thomas M. Congreso de los hispanistas alemanes en Augsburgo, 1993 (Translated by José Luis Gómez y Patiño). *Humboldt,* no. 109 (1993), p. 97.

Poland

Dembicz, Andrzej. Estudios latinoamericanos en Polonia: retos y proyecciones. *Cuadernos Americanos,* no. 42, Nueva época (Nov – Dec 93), pp. 43 – 47.

Soviet Union

Blasier, Cole. The Impact of Perestroika on Soviet Latin Americanists. *SALALM Papers,* v. 36 (1991), pp. 10 – 14.

Spain

Hilton, Sylvia-Lyn and Amancio Labandeira Fernández. El americanismo en España, 1991 – 1992. *Revista de Indias,* v. 53, no. 197 (Jan – Apr 93), pp. 133 – 409.

Congresses

Malamud, Carlos D. Encuentro de Americanistas Españoles: América Latina; Pasado y Presente. *Anuario de Estudios Americanos,* v. 49, Suppl. 1 (1992), pp. 194 – 195.

United States

Berger, Mark T. Civilising the South: The U.S. Rise to Hegemony in the Americas and the Roots of "Latin American Studies," 1898 – 1945. *Bulletin of Latin American Research,* v. 12, no. 1 (Jan 93), pp. 1 – 48. Bibl.

Deal, Carl W. A Survey of Latin American Collections. *SALALM Papers,* v. 36 (1991), pp. 315 – 324. Tables.

Hazen, Dan C. Latin American Studies, Information Resources, and Library Collections: The Contexts of Crisis. *SALALM Papers,* v. 36 (1991), pp. 267 – 271.

LATIN AMERICANS

Europe

Bolzman, Claudio. Los exiliados del Cono Sur: dos décadas más tarde. *Nueva Sociedad,* no. 127 (Sept – Oct 93), pp. 126 – 135. Bibl.

Puerto Rico

Solano y Pérez-Lila, Francisco de. Inmigración latinoamericana a Puerto Rico, 1800 – 1898. *Revista de Indias,* v. 52, no. 195 – 196 (May – Dec 92), pp. 923 – 957. Tables.

Spain

Herranz Gómez, Yolanda. Latinoamericanos en Madrid: integración en la sociedad española. *Revista Española de Antropología Americana,* v. 23 (1993), pp. 189 – 211. Bibl, tables, charts.

Schumm, Petra. *Exilerfahrung und Literatur: Lateinamerikanische Autoren in Spanien* reviewed by Monika Wehrheim-Peuker. *Iberoamericana,* v. 16, no. 47 – 48 (1992), pp. 135 – 137.

Sweden

Moore, Daniel. Latinoamericanos en Suecia. *Cuadernos Americanos,* no. 41, Nueva época (Sept – Oct 93), pp. 131 – 157. Bibl, tables.

United States

Borjas, George J. and Richard B. Freeman, eds. *Immigration and the Work Force: Economic Consequences for the United States and Source Areas* reviewed by Jim Thomas. *Journal of Latin American Studies,* v. 25, no. 3 (Oct 93), pp. 683 – 684.

Cohen, Isaac. El surgimiento de los hispanos. *Nueva Sociedad,* no. 127 (Sept – Oct 93), pp. 100 – 113. Bibl.

LATIN LANGUAGE

Hanisch Espíndola, Walter. *El latín en Chile* reviewed by Sergio Martínez Baeza. *Boletín de la Academia Chilena de la Historia,* v. 58 – 59, no. 102 (1991 – 1992), pp. 559 – 560.

LAVADOS MONTES, JAIME

Dr. Jaime Lavados, el actual rector. *Atenea (Chile),* no. 465 – 466 (1992), pp. 349 – 351. Il.

LAVARDÉN, MANUEL JOSÉ DE

Carrazzoni, José Andrés. Manuel José de Lavardén: poeta, ganadero y patriota. *Todo Es Historia,* v. 26, no. 310 (May 93), pp. 54 – 62. Bibl, il.

LAW

See also

Copyright
Crime and criminals
Criminal law
Intellectual property
International law
Judiciary
Labor laws and legislation
Lawyers
Sociological jurisprudence
Subdivision *Constitutional law* under names of specific countries
Subdivisions *Law and legislation* and *Legal status, laws, etc.* under specific topics

Brazil

Holston, James. Legalizando o ilegal: propriedade e usurpação no Brasil (A translation of "The Misrule of Law: Land and Usurpation in Brazil," translated by João Vargas. Reprinted from *Comparative Studies in Society and History,* vol. 33, num. 4, 1991). *Revista Brasileira de Ciências Sociais,* v. 8, no. 21 (Feb 93), pp. 68 – 89. Bibl.

Río de la Plata region

Mariluz Urquijo, José María. Roma y su derecho en el Río de la Plata durante la década liberal, 1820 – 1829. *Investigaciones y Ensayos,* no. 41 (Jan – Dec 91), pp. 77 – 88. Bibl.

United States

Compton, Nina H. and Garrett T. Newland. The Functional Border Equivalent. *Journal of Borderlands Studies,* v. 7, no. 2 (Fall 92), pp. 73 – 92. Bibl.

LAW AND SOCIAL CHANGE

See

Sociological jurisprudence

LAWYERS

Brazil

Ipanema, Cybelle Moreira de and Marcello Moreira de Ipanema. Pedro Calmon no cinqüentenário e no centenário dos cursos jurídicos no Rio de Janeiro. *Revista do Instituto Histórico e Geográfico Brasileiro,* no. 370 (Jan – Mar 91), pp. 78 – 81.

Uruguay

Nicoliello, Nelson. Valores notables de la cultura uruguaya: algunos abogados ilustres del Uruguay. *Hoy Es Historia,* v. 10, no. 55 (Jan – Feb 93), pp. 31 – 34.

LAZO, RAIMUNDO
Biography
Loynaz, Dulce María. Imágenes de Raimundo Lazo. *Plural (Mexico),* v. 22, no. 262 (July 93), pp. 16 – 17.

LEAL, FELIPE
Hiriart, Hugo. Felipe Leal, arquitecto. *Artes de México,* no. 20 (Summer 93), pp. 114 – 115. Il.

LEARNING, PSYCHOLOGY OF
Crespo, Leila. Nivel de razonamiento cognoscitivo en una muestra de estudiantes universitarios: sus implicaciones para la docencia. *Homines,* v. 15 – 16, no. 2 – 1 (Oct 91 – Dec 92), pp. 95 – 101. Bibl, tables.

Delgado Chinchilla, Carmen. Environment: A Key Factor in Second Language Acquisition. *Káñina,* v. 16, no. 1 (Jan – June 92), pp. 185 – 193. Bibl.

Lerner de Zunino, Delia and Alicia Palacios de Pizani. *El aprendizaje de la lengua escrita en la escuela: reflexiones sobre la propuesta pedagógica constructivista* reviewed by Magaly Muñoz de Pimentel. *La Educación (USA),* v. 37, no. 115 (1993), pp. 426 – 428.

Research
Náñez, José E. and Raymond V. Padilla. Processing of Simple and Choice Reaction Time Tasks by Chicano Adolescents. *Hispanic Journal of Behavioral Sciences,* v. 15, no. 4 (Nov 93), pp. 498 – 508. Bibl, tables.

LEBANESE
Hourani, Albert and Nadim Shehadi, eds. *The Lebanese in the World: A Century of Emigration* reviewed by Jorge O. Bestene. *Journal of Latin American Studies,* v. 25, no. 3 (Oct 93), pp. 663 – 664.

Mexico
Ramírez Carrillo, Luis Alfonso. Estratificación, clase y parentesco: empresarios libaneses en el sureste de México. *Nueva Antropología,* v. 13, no. 43 (Nov 92), pp. 123 – 137. Bibl.

LEE, RUSSELL
Olivares, Julián. Russell Lee, Photographer. *The Americas Review,* v. 19, no. 3 – 4 (Winter 91), pp. 17 – 19 + . Il.

LEE LÓPEZ, ALBERTO
Acuerdo n° 04 de 1993. *Boletín de Historia y Antigüedades,* v. 80, no. 781 (Apr – June 93), pp. 331 – 332. Il.

Obituaries
Gómez Latorre, Armando. Réquiem por cuatro académicos. *Boletín de Historia y Antigüedades,* v. 80, no. 781 (Apr – June 93), pp. 339 – 340.

Mantilla Ruiz, Luis Carlos. In memoriam: fray Alberto Lee López, O.F.M. (1927 – 1992). *Boletín de Historia y Antigüedades,* v. 80, no. 781 (Apr – June 93), pp. 333 – 337.

LEEWARD ISLANDS
See
Saint Kitts, West Indies

LEGENDS
See also
Black legend
Folk literature
Myth
Mythology
Oral tradition
Subdivision *Legends* under names of Indian groups

Argentina
Quiroga Micheo, Ernesto. El hermano Bernardo, el gran pecador. *Todo Es Historia,* v. 27, no. 312 (July 93), pp. 48 – 59. Bibl, il, facs.

Schillat, Monika. Los gigantes patagónicos: historia de una leyenda. *Todo Es Historia,* v. 26, no. 309 (Apr 93), pp. 60 – 66. Bibl, il.

Brazil
Slater, Candace. *Trail of Miracles: Stories from a Pilgrimage in Northeast Brazil* reviewed by David T. Haberly. *Hispanic Review,* v. 61, no. 3 (Summer 93), pp. 449 – 451.

Latin America
Gil Fernández, Juan. *Mitos y utopías del descubrimiento* reviewed by Fernando Aínsa. *Colonial Latin American Review,* v. 2, no. 1 – 2 (1993), pp. 286 – 288.

— *Mitos y utopías del descubrimiento,* vol. III, reviewed by Juha Pekka Helminen. *Ibero Americana (Sweden),* v. 22, no. 2 (Dec 92), pp. 86 – 87.

Mexico
Darío Murrieta, Rubén and María Rosa Palazón Mayoral. Las verdaderas leyendas de Joaquín Murrieta. *Casa de las Américas,* no. 191 (Apr – June 93), pp. 37 – 49. Bibl.

LEGISLATIVE POWER
Gandolfo, Carlos. El régimen parlamentario y la estabilidad democrática. *Apuntes (Peru),* no. 29 (July – Dec 91), pp. 17 – 25.

Andean region
Sources
Grupo Andino: Parlamento Andino; listado de decisiones y recomendaciones aprobados durante el IV Período Extraordinario de Sesiones. *Integración Latinoamericana,* v. 18, no. 191 (July 93), pp. 55 – 57.

Argentina
Lozada, Salvador María. Dos dictámenes contra la concentración del poder. *Realidad Económica,* no. 113 (Jan – Feb 93), pp. 45 – 51.

Pásara, Luis H. El rol del parlamento: Argentina y Perú. *Desarrollo Económico (Argentina),* v. 32, no. 128 (Jan – Mar 93), pp. 603 – 624. Bibl.

Brazil
Coeli, Jaime Collier. A defesa da concorrência. *Problemas Brasileiros,* v. 30, no. 297 (May – June 93), pp. 41 – 53. Il.

Lima Júnior, Olavo Brasil de. A reforma das instituições políticas: a experiência brasileira e o aperfeiçoamento democrático. *Dados,* v. 36, no. 1 (1993), pp. 89 – 117. Bibl, tables.

Novaes, Ana Dolores and David Rosenblatt. O poder regional no Congresso: uma atualização. *Revista Brasileira de Economia,* v. 47, no. 2 (Apr – June 93), pp. 305 – 312. Bibl, tables.

Vieira, Oldegar Franco. Dom Pedro II e o parlamentarismo. *Convivium,* v. 34, no. 2 (July – Dec 91), pp. 120 – 126.

Peru
Pásara, Luis H. El rol del parlamento: Argentina y Perú. *Desarrollo Económico (Argentina),* v. 32, no. 128 (Jan – Mar 93), pp. 603 – 624. Bibl.

Southern Cone of South America
Thibaut, Bernhard. Präsidentialismus, Parlamentarismus und das Problem der Konsolidierung der Demokratie in Lateinamerika. *Ibero-Amerikanisches Archiv,* v. 18, no. 1 – 2 (1992), pp. 107 – 150. Bibl.

— Presidencialismo, parlamentarismo y el problema de la consolidación democrática en América Latina. *Estudios Internacionales (Chile),* v. 26, no. 102 (Apr – June 93), pp. 216 – 252. Bibl.

Uruguay
Caetano, Gerardo, ed. *La alternativa parlamentarista* reviewed by Carlos Filgueira. *Cuadernos del CLAEH,* v. 18, no. 67 (Nov 93), pp. 135 – 140.

Crisis del parlamento tradicional: entrevista a Francisco Rodríguez Camusso. *Cuadernos del CLAEH,* v. 18, no. 67 (Nov 93), pp. 53 – 67.

Peixoto, Martín. Crisis de la deliberación. *Cuadernos del CLAEH,* v. 18, no. 67 (Nov 93), pp. 69 – 79.

LEITE, CÍLIA C. PEREIRA
Matos, Francisco Gomes de. Amar a Deus e à língua portuguesa. *Vozes,* v. 87, no. 2 (Mar – Apr 93), p. 92.

LEMINSKI, PAULO

Criticism of specific works

Anseios crípticos

Valente, Luiz Fernando. Paulo Leminski e a poética do inútil. *Hispania (USA)*, v. 76, no. 3 (Sept 93), pp. 419 – 427. Bibl.

LEÑERO, VICENTE

Criticism and interpretation

Anderson, Danny J. Retórica de la legitimidad: las exigencias de la crónica en las "novelas sin ficción" de Vicente Leñero. *La Palabra y el Hombre*, no. 84 (Oct – Dec 92), pp. 63 – 80. Bibl.

Criticism of specific works

Los albañiles

Meléndez, Priscilla. Leñero's *Los albañiles:* Assembling the Stage/Dismantling the Theatre. *Latin American Literary Review*, v. 21, no. 41 (Jan – June 93), pp. 39 – 52. Bibl.

LEO XIII, POPE

Cury, Maria Zilda Ferreira. O olhar do Papa e o navegador: Leão XIII descobre a América. *Cuadernos del CLAEH*, v. 17, no. 63 – 64 (Oct 92), pp. 35 – 42. Bibl.

Criticism of specific works

Rerum Novarum

Paupério, Artur Machado. Centenario de *Rerum Novarum*. *Revista do Instituto Histórico e Geográfico Brasileiro*, no. 372 (July – Sept 91), pp. 766 – 774.

Pell, George. *Rerum Novarum:* cien años después. *Estudios Públicos (Chile)*, no. 50 (Fall 93), pp. 177 – 200. Bibl.

LEOPARDI, GIACOMO

Translations

Ramos, Antonio. "Infinito": Giacomo Leopardi. *Vozes*, v. 87, no. 3 (May – June 93), pp. 59 – 63. Il.

LE PLONGEON, ALICE

Desmond, Lawrence Gustave and Phyllis Mauch Messenger. *A Dream of Maya: Augustus and Alice Le Plongeon in Nineteenth-Century Yucatán* reviewed by Kevin Gosner. *Hispanic American Historical Review*, v. 73, no. 3 (Aug 93), pp. 532 – 533.

LE PLONGEON, AUGUSTUS

Desmond, Lawrence Gustave and Phyllis Mauch Messenger. *A Dream of Maya: Augustus and Alice Le Plongeon in Nineteenth-Century Yucatán* reviewed by Kevin Gosner. *Hispanic American Historical Review*, v. 73, no. 3 (Aug 93), pp. 532 – 533.

LESSA, BIA

Süssekind, Maria Flora. La imaginación monológica: Gerald Thomas y Bia Lessa. *Conjunto*, no. 93 (Jan – June 93), pp. 18 – 25. Bibl, il.

LETELIER SOTOMAYOR, MARIO

Criticism of specific works

Los estudios de postgrado y el desarrollo universitario en Chile

Lorca A., Carlos. Presentación del libro: *Los estudios de postgrado y el desarrollo universitario en Chile*. *Estudios Sociales (Chile)*, no. 74 (Oct – Dec 92), pp. 201 – 211. Tables.

LEWIS, C. BERNARD

Obituaries

Farr, Thomas H. and Elaine Fisher. A Tribute to C. Bernard Lewis, OBE (1913 – 1992). *Jamaica Journal*, v. 24, no. 3 (Feb 93), pp. 25 – 26. Il.

LEZAMA LIMA, JOSÉ

Correspondence, reminiscences, etc.

Lezama Lima, José. Diarios. *Vuelta*, v. 17, no. 198 (May 93), pp. 16 – 23.

Rodríguez Feo, José. *Mi correspondencia con Lezama Lima* reviewed by Saïd Benabdelouahed. *Caravelle*, no. 59 (1992), pp. 289 – 293.

Criticism and interpretation

Bravo, Víctor. La realidad del mundo invisible: la poesía de José Lezama Lima. *Revista Nacional de Cultura (Venezuela)*, v. 53, no. 285 (Apr – June 92), pp. 22 – 39. Bibl.

Levinson, Brett. La responsabilidad de Lezama. *Revista Chilena de Literatura*, no. 42 (Aug 93), pp. 101 – 105.

Criticism of specific works

Diario

Sarduy, Severo. Imágenes del tiempo inmóvil. *Vuelta*, v. 17, no. 200 (July 93), pp. 21 – 22.

Paradiso

Marquet, Antonio and Eduardo Ramírez Lozano. El inestable equilibrio del caos. *Plural (Mexico)*, v. 22, no. 262 (July 93), pp. 57 – 62.

LIBERALISM

See also

Subdivision *Economic policy* under names of specific countries

Fernández Santillán, José F. Democracia y liberalismo: ensayo de filosofía política. *Revista Mexicana de Ciencias Políticas y Sociales*, v. 38, Nueva época, no. 151 (Jan – Mar 93), pp. 157 – 183. Bibl.

Parra Luzardo, Gastón. ¿Hacia dónde nos conduce la política neoliberal? *Desarrollo Indoamericano*, v. 23, no. 91 (June 93), pp. 36 – 40. Il.

Brazil

Boschi, Renato Raul and Eli Diniz. Lideranças empresariais e problemas da estratégia liberal no Brasil. *Revista Brasileira de Ciências Sociais*, v. 8, no. 23 (Oct 93), pp. 101 – 119. Bibl.

Colombia

Turbay Ayala, Julio César. La misión del liberalismo como partido moderno (Previously published in this journal, no. 382, 1972). *Revista Javeriana*, v. 61, no. 596 (July 93), pp. 85 – 87.

Costa Rica

Irías, Jorge et al. De la pobreza a la abundancia o la abundancia de la pobreza. *Revista de Ciencias Sociales (Costa Rica)*, no. 57 (Sept 92), pp. 79 – 86. Bibl.

Salazar Mora, Orlando. *El apogeo de la república liberal en Costa Rica, 1870 – 1914* reviewed by Fernando González Davidson. *Mesoamérica (USA)*, v. 13, no. 23 (June 92), pp. 179 – 182.

El Salvador

Martínez, Julia Evelyn. Neoliberalismo y derechos humanos. *ECA; Estudios Centroamericanos*, v. 47, no. 529 – 530 (Nov – Dec 92), pp. 1028 – 1036. Il.

Honduras

Molina Chocano, Guillermo. Honduras: ¿Del ajuste neoliberal al liberalismo social? *Nueva Sociedad*, no. 128 (Nov – Dec 93), pp. 18 – 23.

Latin America

Pérez-Yglesias, María. Entre lo escolar y los medios informativos: políticas neoliberales y educación. *Revista de Ciencias Sociales (Costa Rica)*, no. 57 (Sept 92), pp. 41 – 55. Bibl.

Mexico

Bolívar Espinoza, Augusto et al. Nuevos tiempos de coyuntura: consolidación del cambio y mucho desafío político. *El Cotidiano*, v. 8, no. 52 (Jan – Feb 93), pp. 60 – 66. Il.

Gordillo, Gustavo. Ayudando a la mano invisible: el compromiso democrático. *Nexos*, v. 16, no. 189 (Sept 93), pp. 41 – 43.

Hale, Charles Adams. *La transformación del liberalismo en México a fines del siglo XIX* reviewed by David Aylett. *Vuelta*, v. 17, no. 204 (Nov 93), pp. 41 – 42.

Muñoz, Víctor Manuel. El liberalismo social: propuesta ideológica del salinismo. *Revista Mexicana de Ciencias Políticas y Sociales*, v. 37, Nueva época, no. 149 (July – Sept 92), pp. 29 – 47. Bibl.

Olveda, Jaime. Las viejas oligarquías y la reforma liberal: el caso de Guadalajara. *Siglo XIX: Cuadernos*, v. 2, no. 4 (Oct 92), pp. 9 – 30. Bibl.

Venezuela

Quintero Montiel, Inés Mercedes. *Pensamiento liberal del siglo XIX* reviewed by Amaya Llebot Cazalis. *Revista Nacional de Cultura (Venezuela)*, v. 54, no. 287 (Oct – Dec 92), pp. 264 – 265.

LIBERATION PHILOSOPHY

See
Freedom
Philosophy

LIBERATION THEOLOGY

See also
Catholic Church
Church and social problems
Religion and politics
Theology

Jamaica

Sauve, John. Suggestions for a Jamaican Theology of Psycho-Social Emancipation. *Caribbean Quarterly*, v. 38, no. 2 – 3 (June – Sept 92), pp. 81 – 95. Bibl.

Latin America

Galindo López, Olga. La filosofía inculturada: ¿Una alternativa social para la América Latina? *Islas*, no. 99 (May – Aug 91), pp. 5 – 14. Bibl.

Leturia M., Juan Miguel. Hacer teología es como escribir una "carta de amor." *Mensaje*, v. 42, no. 424 (Nov 93), pp. 555 – 558. Il.

Löwy, Michael. Marxism and Christianity in Latin America (Translated by Claudia Pompan). *Latin American Perspectives*, v. 20, no. 4 (Fall 93), pp. 28 – 42. Bibl.

Smith, Christian. *The Emergence of Liberation Theology: Radical Religion and Social Movement Theory* reviewed by Michael LaRosa. *Journal of Inter-American Studies and World Affairs*, v. 35, no. 2 (Summer 93), pp. 167 – 170.

Nicaragua

Cardenal, Ernesto. Vénganos a la tierra la república de los cielos. *Cuadernos Americanos*, no. 40, Nueva época (July – Aug 93), pp. 35 – 52.

Southern Cone of South America

Lehmann, David. *Democracy and Development in Latin America: Economics, Politics, and Religion in the Post-War Period* reviewed by Ricardo Grinspun and Sally Humphries. *Economic Development and Cultural Change*, v. 41, no. 4 (July 93), pp. 886 – 894. Bibl.

LIBERIA, COSTA RICA

Loáiciga G., María Elena and Rosa Rosales O. La población anciana de Liberia: condición socioeconómica precaria. *Revista de Ciencias Sociales (Costa Rica)*, no. 59 (Mar 93), pp. 95 – 106. Bibl, tables.

LIBERTY

See
Freedom

LIBRARIES AND LIBRARIANS

See also
Archives
Books
Information services
Manuscripts
Microforms

Elliott, Enrique. El bibliotecario profesional. *Revista Cultural Lotería*, v. 50, no. 384 (July – Aug 91), pp. 45 – 55. Bibl.

Methodology

Johnson, Peter T. Guidelines for Collecting Documentation on Marginalized Peoples and Ideas in Latin America. *SALALM Papers*, v. 34 (1989), pp. 455 – 458.

Rêgo, Stella M. de Sá. Access to Photograph Collections. *SALALM Papers*, v. 34 (1989), pp. 123 – 129. Bibl.

Bolivia

Romero Romero, Catalina. Tres bibliotecas jesuitas en pueblos de misión: Buenavista, Paila y Santa Rosa en la región de Moxos. *Revista de Indias*, v. 52, no. 195 – 196 (May – Dec 92), pp. 889 – 921.

Brazil

Mayrink, Paulo Tarcísio. School Libraries in Brazil Facing the Twenty-First Century: New Formats. *SALALM Papers*, v. 36 (1991), pp. 357 – 390.

Methodology

Balby, Claudia Negrão. Bibliographic Control of Art Materials: The Experience of the Universidade de São Paulo. *SALALM Papers*, v. 34 (1989), pp. 401 – 413. Bibl.

Study and teaching

Antônio, Iratí and Claudia Negrão Balby. Computer Training in Brazilian Library Schools. *SALALM Papers*, v. 36 (1991), pp. 347 – 368. Bibl, tables.

Chile

Andrade de Labadía, Gabriela. Una aproximación al estudio de la biblioteca privada de Mario Góngora del Campo. *Historia (Chile)*, no. 26 (1991 – 1992), pp. 5 – 60. Bibl.

Larraín Mira, Paz and René Millar Carvacho. Notas para la historia de la cultura en el período indiano: la biblioteca del obispo de Santiago, Juan Bravo del Rivero y Correa, 1685 – 1752. *Historia (Chile)*, no. 26 (1991 – 1992), pp. 173 – 211. Bibl.

Colombia

Handbooks, manuals, etc.

Mejía, Myriam et al. *La biblioteca pública: manual para su organización y funcionamiento*, vols. I – II (Review). *La Educación (USA)*, v. 36, no. 111 – 113 (1992), pp. 299 – 300.

El Salvador

Study and teaching

Guardado de del Cid, Helen. La carrera de bibliotecología en El Salvador: su nueva orientación curricular. *SALALM Papers*, v. 36 (1991), pp. 441 – 454. Tables.

Europe

Methodology

Wade, Ann E. European Approaches to the Conspectus. *SALALM Papers*, v. 36 (1991), pp. 258 – 264.

Germany

Stegmann, Wilhelm. Artistic Representation of German Book Collections and Picture Archives. *SALALM Papers*, v. 34 (1989), pp. 428 – 438.

Great Britain

Methodology

Noble, Patricia E. Collection Evaluation Techniques: A British Pilot Study. *SALALM Papers*, v. 36 (1991), pp. 248 – 257. Tables.

Mexico

Catalogs

Corzo Ramírez, Ricardo. Catálogo de la Biblioteca Quinto Centenario y comentario al libro *Iberoamérica: una comunidad*. *La Palabra y el Hombre*, no. 83 (July – Sept 92), pp. 322 – 346. Bibl.

Nicaragua

Méndez Rojas, Conny. Algunas reflexiones sobre lo que SALALM podría ofrecer a los bibliotecarios nicaragüenses. *SALALM Papers*, v. 36 (1991), pp. 228 – 232.

Portugal

Polanco Alcántara, Tomás. Palabras del dr. Tomás Polanco Alcántara en la Biblioteca Nacional de Lisboa, 7 de mayo de 1992. *Boletín de la Academia Nacional de la Historia (Venezuela)*, v. 76, no. 301 (Jan – Mar 93), pp. 47 – 49.

United States

Deal, Carl W. A Survey of Latin American Collections. *SALALM Papers*, v. 36 (1991), pp. 315 – 324. Tables.

Esenwein, George and William Ratliff. Latin American Posters at the Hoover Institution: The Lexicons of State and Society. *SALALM Papers*, v. 34 (1989), pp. 214 – 220.

Gardner, Jeffrey J. Scholarship, Research Libraries, and Foreign Publishing in the 1990s. *SALALM Papers*, v. 36 (1991), pp. 277 – 293.

Oliphant, David, ed. *Nahuatl to Rayuela: The Latin American Collection at Texas* reviewed by Deborah L. Jakubs. *Hispanic American Historical Review*, v. 73, no. 2 (May 93), pp. 293 – 294.

Soete, George J. Resource Sharing: The Only Reasonable Whither. *SALALM Papers*, v. 36 (1991), pp. 272 – 276.

Methodology

Hazen, Dan C. The Latin American Conspectus: Panacea or Pig in a Poke? *SALALM Papers*, v. 36 (1991), pp. 235 – 247. Bibl.

Maddox, Brent F. Visual Research Cataloging at the Getty Center for the History of Art and the Humanities. *SALALM Papers*, v. 34 (1989), pp. 391 – 400. Bibl.

Societies, etc.

Herrera, Luis. SALALM and the Public Library. *SALALM Papers*, v. 36 (1991), pp. 224 – 227.

Hodgman, Suzanne. SALALM Membership, 1956 – 1990: A Brief Overview. *SALALM Papers*, v. 36 (1991), pp. 215 – 223. Tables.

Venezuela

Catalogs

Ruiz Chataing, David. Novedades bibliográficas en la Biblioteca Nacional. *Boletín de la Academia Nacional de la Historia (Venezuela)*, no. 297, 299 – 302 (Jan 92 – June 93), All issues.

LIHN, ENRIQUE

Criticism and interpretation

Alonso Martínez, María Nieves and Mario Rodríguez. Poesía chilena y española: Lihn y Gil de Biedma. *Atenea (Chile)*, no. 467 (1993), pp. 197 – 219. Bibl.

Foxley, Carmen. Enrique Lihn y los juegos excéntricos de la imaginación. *Revista Chilena de Literatura*, no. 41 (Apr 93), pp. 15 – 24. Bibl.

Sarmiento, Oscar D. La desconstrucción del autor: Enrique Lihn y Jorge Teillier. *Revista Chilena de Literatura*, no. 42 (Aug 93), pp. 237 – 244.

Criticism of specific works

El paseo ahumada

Favi, Gloria. Las acciones de habla en un texto de Enrique Lihn: *El paseo ahumada*. *Revista Chilena de Literatura*, no. 40 (Nov 92), pp. 91 – 96.

LIMA, AUGUSTO DE

Criticism of specific works

Opera Tiradentes

Reis, Sandra Loureiro de Freitas. A *Opera Tiradentes* de Manuel Joaquim de Macedo e Augusto de Lima. *Latin American Music Review*, v. 14, no. 1 (Spring – Summer 93), pp. 131 – 144. Bibl.

LIMA, FRANCISCA CLOTILDE BARBOSA

Criticism and interpretation

Gotlib, Nádia Battella. Las mujeres y "el otro": tres narradoras brasileñas. *Escritura (Venezuela)*, v. 16, no. 31 – 32 (Jan – Dec 91), pp. 123 – 136. Bibl.

LIMA, PERU

Adams, Norman and Néstor Valdivia. *Los otros empresarios: ética de migrantes y formación de empresas en Lima* reviewed by Orazio A. Ciccarelli. *Hispanic American Historical Review*, v. 73, no. 4 (Nov 93), pp. 714 – 715.

Barriga Calle, Irma. La experiencia de la muerte en Lima, siglo XVII. *Apuntes (Peru)*, no. 31 (July – Dec 92), pp. 81 – 102. Bibl.

Cheng Hurtado, Alberto and José Matos Mar. Comas: lo andino en la modernidad urbana. *América Indígena*, v. 51, no. 2 – 3 (Apr – Sept 91), pp. 35 – 74. Il, tables, maps.

Doughty, Paul L. Perú: . . . y la vida continúa. *América Indígena*, v. 51, no. 4 (Oct – Dec 91), pp. 49 – 79. Bibl, tables, maps.

Durán Montero, María Antonia. Lima en 1613: aspectos urbanos. *Anuario de Estudios Americanos*, v. 49 (1992), pp. 171 – 188. Bibl, maps.

García Ríos, José María and Giulia Tamayo. El escenario como dictador: configuración metropolitana y experiencia cotidiana. *Nueva Sociedad*, no. 123 (Jan – Feb 93), pp. 94 – 103. Bibl.

Gareis, Iris. Religión popular y etnicidad: la población indígena de Lima colonial. *Allpanchis*, v. 23, no. 40 (July – Dec 92), pp. 117 – 143. Bibl.

Hampe Martínez, Teodoro. Apuntes documentales sobre inmigrantes europeos y norteamericanos en Lima, siglo XIX. *Revista de Indias*, v. 53, no. 198 (May – Aug 93), pp. 459 – 491. Bibl.

Hünefeldt, Christine. *Lasmanuelos: vida cotidiana de una familia negra en la Lima del s. XIX* reviewed by Sara Mateos (Review entitled "Esclavitud urbana"). *Debate (Peru)*, v. 15, no. 70 (Sept – Oct 92), pp. 67 – 68.

Iwasaki Cauti, Fernando A. Mujeres al borde de la perfección: Rosa de Santa María y las alumbradas de Lima. *Hispanic American Historical Review*, v. 73, no. 4 (Nov 93), pp. 581 – 613. Bibl.

— Toros y sociedad en Lima colonial. *Anuario de Estudios Americanos*, v. 49 (1992), pp. 311 – 333. Bibl.

Macera dall'Orso, Pablo. Locos, titiriteros y poetas: las opciones limeñas, 1828 – 1840. *Debate (Peru)*, v. 16, no. 72 (Mar – May 93), pp. 42 – 45. Il.

Mannarelli, María Emma. *Pecados públicos: la ilegitimidad en Lima, siglo XVII* reviewed by Arturo Ferrari (Review entitled "Un plancito cholifacio"). *Debate (Peru)*, v. 16, no. 75 (Dec 93 – Jan 94), pp. 78 – 79. Il.

Matos Mar, José. La experiencia popular en Comas: 10 casos. *América Indígena*, v. 51, no. 2 – 3 (Apr – Sept 91), pp. 75 – 105. Tables.

— Taquileños, quechuas del lago Titicaca, en Lima. *América Indígena*, v. 51, no. 2 – 3 (Apr – Sept 91), pp. 107 – 166. Il, maps.

Mossbrucker, Harald. El proceso de migración en el Perú: la revolución clandestina. *América Indígena*, v. 51, no. 2 – 3 (Apr – Sept 91), pp. 167 – 201. Bibl, charts.

Ortiz de Zevallos, Augusto. Carta sobre (o debajo de) Lima. *Debate (Peru)*, v. 15, no. 70 (Sept – Oct 92), pp. 48 – 52. Il.

Pásara, Luis H. Rafael Rabinovich. *Debate (Peru)*, v. 15, no. 70 (Sept – Oct 92), p. 55. Il.

Sánchez León, Abelardo. Perfil del ama de casa limeña. *Debate (Peru)*, v. 16, no. 72 (Mar – May 93), pp. 32 – 38. Il, tables.

Shifter, Michael. Un brindis por Lima. *Debate (Peru)*, v. 15, no. 71 (Nov 92 – Jan 93), pp. 49 – 51. Il.

Turino, Thomas. Del esencialismo a lo esencial: pragmática y significado de la interpretación de los sikuri puneños en Lima. *Revista Andina*, v. 10, no. 2 (Dec 92), pp. 441 – 456. Bibl.

LIMA BARRETO, ALFONSO HENRIQUE DE

Criticism of specific works

Triste fim de Policarpo Quaresma

Martha, Alice Aurea Penteado. Policarpo Quaresma: a história carnavalizada. *Revista de Letras (Brazil)*, v. 32 (1992), pp. 119 – 125.

LIMÓN, COSTA RICA

Harpelle, Ronald N. The Social and Political Integration of West Indians in Costa Rica, 1930 – 1950. *Journal of Latin American Studies*, v. 25, no. 1 (Feb 93), pp. 103 – 120. Bibl.

LINGUISTIC ANALYSIS (LITERATURE)

See also
Semiotics

Bilbija, Ksenija. "La palabra asesino" de Luisa Valenzuela: la entrada en la lengua. *Confluencia*, v. 8, no. 1 (Fall 92), pp. 159 – 164.

Chasteen, John Charles. Fighting Words: The Discourse of Insurgency in Latin American History. *Latin American Research Review*, v. 28, no. 3 (1993), pp. 83 – 111. Bibl, il.

Giella, Miguel Angel. Inmigración y exilio: el limbo del lenguaje. *Latin American Theatre Review*, v. 26, no. 2 (Spring 93), pp. 111 – 121. Bibl.

Ignácio, Sebastião Expedito. Dois aspectos da obra de Graciliano Ramos atestados pela tipologia oracional. *Revista de Letras (Brazil)*, v. 32 (1992), pp. 69 – 78.

Martini, Mónica Patricia and Daisy Rípodas Ardanaz. Aportes sobre el voseo en Córdoba a horcajadas de los siglos XVIII y XIX: sus modalidades en la obra de Cristóbal de Aguilar. *Investigaciones y Ensayos,* no. 41 (Jan – Dec 91), pp. 139 – 151. Bibl.

Motta, Sérgio Vicente. Ser/tão ... somente linguagem. *Revista de Letras (Brazil),* v. 32 (1992), pp. 81 – 99. Bibl.

Underwood, Leticia Iliana. *Octavio Paz and the Language of Poetry: A Psycholinguistic Approach* reviewed by Hugo J. Verani. *Revista Interamericana de Bibliografía,* v. 42, no. 4 (1992), pp. 666 – 667.

Vogeley, Nancy J. Colonial Discourse in a Postcolonial Context: Nineteenth-Century Mexico. *Colonial Latin American Review,* v. 2, no. 1 – 2 (1993), pp. 189 – 212. Bibl.

LINGUISTICS

See also
Language and languages
Semiotics
Sociolinguistics
Translating and interpreting

Guzmán Betancourt, Ignacio. Primeros empleos de la palabra "lingüística" en México. *Plural (Mexico),* v. 22, no. 257 (Feb 93), pp. 52 – 57.

Nansen Díaz, Eréndira. Las lenguas americanas y la teoría del tipo lingüístico en Wilhelm von Humboldt. *Estudios de Cultura Náhuatl,* v. 22 (1992), pp. 223 – 233. Bibl.

LIPCHITZ, JACQUES

Castillo, Tito. Gratos recuerdos de Vicente Huidobro y Jacques Lipchitz. *Atenea (Chile),* no. 467 (1993), pp. 149 – 154. Il, facs.

LIPSCHÜTZ, ALEXANDER

Criticism and interpretation

Manríquez S., Germán. Las relaciones entre literatura y ciencias en el ejemplo de la obra fisiológica de Alejandro Lipschütz y parte de la obra literaria de Thomas Mann (Accompanied by an appendix of texts by the authors). *Revista Chilena de Literatura,* no. 42 (Aug 93), pp. 115 – 121.

LISCANO VELUTINI, JUAN

Criticism of specific works

Nuevo mundo Orinoco

Doudoroff, Michael J. *Nuevo mundo Orinoco* de Juan Liscano: reflexiones sobre sus contextos. *Inti,* no. 37 – 38 (Spring – Fall 93), pp. 81 – 87.

LISPECTOR, CLARICE

Criticism and interpretation

Cixous, Hélène. Retratos: Clarice Lispector/Marina Tsvetaeva (Translated by Esther Levy). *Escritura (Venezuela),* v. 16, no. 31 – 32 (Jan – Dec 91), pp. 45 – 52.

Gotlib, Nádia Battella. Las mujeres y "el otro": tres narradoras brasileñas. *Escritura (Venezuela),* v. 16, no. 31 – 32 (Jan – Dec 91), pp. 123 – 136. Bibl.

Criticism of specific works

A menor mulher do mundo

Platt, Kamala. Race and Gender Representation in Clarice Lispector's "A menor mulher do mundo" and Carolina Maria de Jesus' *Quarto de despejo. Afro-Hispanic Review,* v. 11, no. 1 – 3 (1992), pp. 51 – 57. Bibl.

LITERACY

See
Illiteracy

LITERAL (PERIODICAL)

Aguilera Garramuño, Marco Tulio. Revista *Literal. Plural (Mexico),* v. 22, no. 259 (Apr 93), pp. 75 – 76.

LITERARY CREATION

See
Creation (Literary, artistic, etc.)

LITERARY CRITICISM

See also
Linguistic analysis (Literature)
Literature and society
Semiotics

Benítez Rojo, Antonio. La literatura caribeña y la teoría de caos. *Latin American Literary Review,* v. 20, no. 40 (July – Dec 92), pp. 16 – 18.

Castro-Klarén, Sara. Situations. *Latin American Literary Review,* v. 20, no. 40 (July – Dec 92), pp. 26 – 29.

Chamberlain, Daniel Frank. *Narrative Perspective in Fiction: A Phenomenological Mediation of Reader, Text, and World* reviewed by Lois Parkinson Zamora. *Revista Canadiense de Estudios Hispánicos,* v. 17, no. 1 (Fall 92), pp. 211 – 213.

Chang-Rodríguez, Raquel. Colonial Connections. *Latin American Literary Review,* v. 20, no. 40 (July – Dec 92), pp. 30 – 31.

Costa, Marithelma and Adelaida López. *Las dos caras de la escritura* reviewed by Gustavo Fares. *Revista Iberoamericana,* v. 59, no. 162 – 163 (Jan – June 93), pp. 380 – 382.

Feal, Rosemary Geisdorfer. Bordering Feminism in Afro-Hispanic Studies: Crossroads in the Field. *Latin American Literary Review,* v. 20, no. 40 (July – Dec 92), pp. 41 – 45. Bibl.

George, David. Socio-Criticism and Brazilian Literature: Changing Perspectives. *Chasqui,* v. 22, no. 2 (Nov 93), pp. 49 – 56.

González, Aníbal. After 1992: A Latin Americanist Wish List. *Latin American Literary Review,* v. 20, no. 40 (July – Dec 92), pp. 46 – 50.

González Echevarría, Roberto. Reflections on My Crystal Ball. *Latin American Literary Review,* v. 20, no. 40 (July – Dec 92), pp. 51 – 53.

González Stephan, Beatriz. No sólo para mujeres: el sexismo en los estudios literarios. *Escritura (Venezuela),* v. 16, no. 31 – 32 (Jan – Dec 91), pp. 103 – 113.

Kerr, Lucille. Frames for the Future: Some Thoughts on Latin American Literary Studies. *Latin American Literary Review,* v. 20, no. 40 (July – Dec 92), pp. 54 – 57.

Mignolo, Walter D. Second Thoughts on Canon and Corpus. *Latin American Literary Review,* v. 20, no. 40 (July – Dec 92), pp. 66 – 69. Bibl.

Moussong, Lazlo. La crítica: ¿Objetiva o subjetiva? *Plural (Mexico),* v. 22, no. 261 (June 93), pp. 12 – 15.

Oviedo, José Miguel. La crítica y sus riesgos, hoy. *Latin American Literary Review,* v. 20, no. 40 (July – Dec 92), pp. 75 – 79.

Pellón, Gustavo. The Canon, the Boom, and Literary Theory. *Latin American Literary Review,* v. 20, no. 40 (July – Dec 92), pp. 80 – 82.

Pérez Firmat, Gustavo. My Critical Condition. *Latin American Literary Review,* v. 20, no. 40 (July – Dec 92), pp. 83 – 84.

Rodríguez-Luis, Julio. On the Criticism of Latin American Literature. *Latin American Literary Review,* v. 20, no. 40 (July – Dec 92), pp. 85 – 87.

Schulman, Iván A. Critical Crossroads. *Latin American Literary Review,* v. 20, no. 40 (July – Dec 92), pp. 97 – 99.

Argentina

Rosa, Nicolás. Veinte años después o la "novela familiar" de la crítica literaria. *Cuadernos Hispanoamericanos,* no. 517 – 519 (July – Sept 93), pp. 161 – 186.

Bolivia

Castañón Barrientos, Carlos. La crítica literaria de Juan Quirós. *Signo,* no. 36 – 37, Nueva época (May – Dec 92), pp. 207 – 210.

Martínez Salguero, Jaime. Juan Quirós, crítico literario. *Signo,* no. 36 – 37, Nueva época (May – Dec 92), pp. 215 – 219.

Quirós, Juan. *Fronteras movedizas* reviewed by Carlos Coello Vila (Review entitled *"Fronteras movedizas:* 35 años de crítica literaria"). *Signo,* no. 36 – 37, Nueva época (May – Dec 92), pp. 227 – 231.

Brazil

Narváez, Jorge E. El estatuto de los textos coloniales y el canon literario: algunos antecedentes en el sistema literario del Brasil-colonia, s. XVI y XVII. *Revista Chilena de Literatura,* no. 40 (Nov 92), pp. 17 – 33. Bibl.

Chile

Klein, Carol Ebersole. The Social Text in Writing by Hispanic Women: Critical Perspectives of Myriam Díaz-Diocaretz. *The Americas Review,* v. 21, no. 1 (Spring 93), pp. 79 – 90. Bibl.

Costa Rica

Solano Jiménez, Ronald. Crítica literaria en Costa Rica: de las *Historias de Tata Mundo. Anuario de Estudios Centroamericanos,* v. 18, no. 1 (1992), pp. 85 – 95. Bibl.

Latin America

Adorno, Rolena. Reconsidering Colonial Discourse for Sixteenth- and Seventeenth-Century Spanish America (Response to Patricia Seed's "Colonial and Postcolonial Discourse," LARR, v. 26, no. 3, 1991). *Latin American Research Review,* v. 28, no. 3 (1993), pp. 135 – 145.

Bueno Chávez, Raúl. *Escribir en Hispanoamérica: ensayos sobre teoría y crítica literaria* reviewed by Miguel Angel Huamán. *Revista de Crítica Literaria Latinoamericana,* v. 19, no. 38 (July – Dec 93), pp. 397 – 399.

Bueno Chávez, Raúl et al. Mesa redonda inicial: nuevas direcciones; estado de la cuestión y desarrollos recientes. *Revista de Crítica Literaria Latinoamericana,* v. 19, no. 38 (July – Dec 93), pp. 11 – 33.

Castillo, Debra A. *Talking Back: Toward a Latin American Feminist Literary Criticism* reviewed by Salvador A. Oropesa. *Chasqui,* v. 22, no. 1 (May 93), pp. 102 – 103.

— *Talking Back: Toward a Latin American Feminist Literary Criticism* reviewed by Vicente Cabrera. *Chasqui,* v. 22, no. 2 (Nov 93), pp. 155 – 156.

— *Talking Back: Toward a Latin American Feminist Literary Criticism* reviewed by Rosemary Geisdorfer Feal. *Hispania (USA),* v. 76, no. 1 (Mar 93), pp. 82 – 83.

Gutiérrez Estupiñán, Raquel. Sobre la crítica literaria femenina/feminista en Hispanoamérica. *Fem,* v. 17, no. 129 (Nov 93), pp. 42 – 46. Bibl.

Kaliman, Ricardo J. Sobre la construcción del objeto en la crítica literaria latinoamericana. *Revista de Crítica Literaria Latinoamericana,* v. 19, no. 37 (Jan – June 93), pp. 307 – 317. Bibl.

Mignolo, Walter D. "Colonial and Postcolonial Discourse": Cultural Critique or Academic Colonialism? (Response to Patricia Seed's "Colonial and Postcolonial Discourse," LARR, v. 26, no. 3, 1991). *Latin American Research Review,* v. 28, no. 3 (1993), pp. 121 – 134. Bibl.

Oyarzún, Kemy. Género y etnia: acerca del dialogismo en América Latina. *Revista Chilena de Literatura,* no. 41 (Apr 93), pp. 33 – 45. Bibl.

— Literaturas heterogéneas y dialogismo genérico – sexual. *Revista de Crítica Literaria Latinoamericana,* v. 19, no. 38 (July – Dec 93), pp. 37 – 50. Bibl.

Rama, Angel. *La crítica de la cultura en América Latina* selected and introduced by Saúl Sosnowski and Tomás Eloy Martínez. Reviewed by Roy Hora. *Todo Es Historia,* v. 26, no. 307 (Feb 93), pp. 74 – 75. Il.

Seed, Patricia Pauline. More Colonial and Postcolonial Discourses (Response to previous three responses). *Latin American Research Review,* v. 28, no. 3 (1993), pp. 146 – 152.

Vidal, Hernán. The Concept of Colonial and Postcolonial Discourse: A Perspective from Literary Criticism (Response to Patricia Seed's article "Colonial and Postcolonial Discourse," LARR, v. 26, no 3, 1991), translated by Sharon Kellum. *Latin American Research Review,* v. 28, no. 3 (1993), pp. 113 – 119.

Mexico

Domínguez Michael, Christopher. Jorge Cuesta o la crítica del demonio (Chapter from the book *Tiros en el concierto). Vuelta,* v. 17, no. 194 (Jan 93), pp. 28 – 36. Bibl.

LITERARY PRIZES

Breslow, Stephen P. Derek Walcott, 1992 Nobel Laureate in Literature. *World Literature Today,* v. 67, no. 2 (Spring 93), pp. 267 – 271. Bibl.

Burton, Richard D. E. Créolité, Négritude, and Metropolis. *Hemisphere,* v. 5, no. 3 (Summer – Fall 93), pp. 10 – 12. Il.

González Villarroel, Oscar. Derek Walcott, premio Nobel de literatura 1992. *Atenea (Chile),* no. 465 – 466 (1992), pp. 357 – 359. Il.

Ibargoyen Islas, Saúl. Plurales hacia afuera, plurales hacia adentro. *Plural (Mexico),* v. 22, no. 262 (July 93), p. 79.

Jarque, Fietta and Mauricio Vicent. La poetisa cubana Dulce María Loynaz gana el premio Cervantes. *Humboldt,* no. 108 (1993), p. 104.

Otorgan el Tirso de Molina 1992 a dramaturgo puertorriqueño. *Latin American Theatre Review,* v. 26, no. 2 (Spring 93), p. 110.

Pizarro, Ana. Para ser jóvenes en cien años más. *Casa de las Américas,* no. 191 (Apr – June 93), pp. 5 – 7.

Premios Nobel en el año del quinto centenario. *Casa de las Américas,* no. 190 (Jan – Mar 93), pp. 2 – 12.

Rojas, Gonzalo. Discurso de aceptación del premio Reina Sofía de Poesía Iberoamericana, 1993. *Chasqui,* v. 22, no. 1 (May 93), pp. 4 – 11. Il.

LA LITERATURA ARGENTINA (PERIODICAL)

Fletcher, Lea. El desierto que no es tal: escritoras y escritura. *Feminaria,* v. 6, no. 11, Suppl. (Nov 93), pp. 7 – 13. Bibl.

LITERATURE

See also
Art and literature
Biography (as a literary form)
Children's literature
Creation (Literary, artistic, etc.)
Drama
Essay
Fiction
Latin American literature
Poetics
Poetry
Reading interests
Rhetoric
Satire
Visual text

History and criticism

Domínguez Michael, Christopher. *La utopía de la hospitalidad* reviewed by Fabienne Bradu. *Vuelta,* v. 17, no. 202 (Sept 93), pp. 45 – 46.

Ortega, Julio et al. Las dos orillas: una intervención de Julio Ortega. *Inti,* no. 36 (Fall 92), pp. 113 – 125.

Paz, Octavio. Excursiones a incursiones (Prologue to Volume II of Paz's *Obras completas). Vuelta,* v. 17, no. 199 (June 93), pp. 8 – 12.

Bibliography

Resumos de teses e dissertações/Summary of Ph.D. and Master Theses. *Revista de Letras (Brazil),* v. 32 (1992), pp. 271 – 291.

Study and teaching

Umaña Chaverri, José Otilio. Una opción teórico – metodológica para la enseñanza de la literatura en programas de aprendizaje de lenguas extranjeras y segundas lenguas. *Káñina,* v. 16, no. 1 (Jan – June 92), pp. 171 – 183. Bibl.

LITERATURE AND HISTORY

Argentina

Ciria, Alberto. La historia argentina en el teatro de Roberto Cossa: a propósito de *Angelito. Revista Interamericana de Bibliografía,* v. 42, no. 4 (1992), pp. 577 – 583. Bibl.

Cordones-Cook, Juanamaría. *Una sombra donde sueña Camila O'Gorman:* dimensión poética de la historia. *La Palabra y el Hombre,* no. 84 (Oct – Dec 92), pp. 271 – 276.

Díaz Quiñones, Arcadio. *El entenado:* las palabras de la tribu. *Hispamérica,* v. 21, no. 63 (Dec 92), pp. 3 – 14.

Grandis, Rita de. The First Colonial Encounter in *El entenado* by Juan José Saer: Paratextuality and History in Postmodern Fiction. *Latin American Literary Review*, v. 21, no. 41 (Jan – June 93), pp. 30 – 38. Bibl.

Molinaro, Nina L. Resistance, Gender, and the Mediation of History in Pizarnik's *La condesa sangrienta* and Ortiz's *Urraca*. *Letras Femeninas*, v. 19, no. 1 – 2 (Spring – Fall 93), pp. 45 – 54. Bibl.

Ocampo, Orlando. Interpretando el pasado histórico: el acto referencial en *Una sombra donde sueña Camila O'Gorman*. *Revista Chilena de Literatura*, no. 40 (Nov 92), pp. 83 – 89. Bibl.

Zuccotti, Liliana. Juana Manso: contar historias. *Feminaria*, v. 6, no. 11, Suppl. (Nov 93), pp. 2 – 4.

Bolivia

Aguirre, Nataniel. *Juan de la Rosa: memorias del último hidalgo de la independencia* reviewed by Gaby Vallejo de Bolívar. *Signo*, no. 35, Nueva época (Jan – Apr 92), pp. 201 – 202.

Brazil

Bernucci, Leopoldo M. *Historia de un malentendido: un estudio transtextual de 'La guerra del fin del mundo' de Mario Vargas Llosa* reviewed by Sara Castro-Klarén. *Hispanic Review*, v. 61, no. 1 (Winter 93), pp. 133 – 134.

Martha, Alice Aurea Penteado. Policarpo Quaresma: a história carnavalizada. *Revista de Letras (Brazil)*, v. 32 (1992), pp. 119 – 125.

Valente, Luiz Fernando. Fiction as History: The Case of João Ubaldo Ribeiro. *Latin American Research Review*, v. 28, no. 1 (1993), pp. 41 – 60. Bibl.

Research

Antoniazzi, Maria Regina Filgueiras. Guia de fontes literárias para o estudo da história da educação na Bahia. *Revista Brasileira de Estudos Pedagógicos*, v. 72, no. 172 (Sept – Dec 91), pp. 388 – 391.

Chile

González, Flora M. Masking History in Donoso's *Taratuta*. *Revista Canadiense de Estudios Hispánicos*, v. 17, no. 1 (Fall 92), pp. 47 – 62. Bibl.

Subercaseaux S., Bernardo. *Historia del libro en Chile: alma y cuerpo* reviewed by G. A. C. *Mensaje*, v. 42, no. 419 (June 93), p. 218.

Bibliography

Echevarría, Evelio A. La novela histórica de Chile: deslinde y bibliografía, 1852 – 1990. *Revista Interamericana de Bibliografía*, v. 42, no. 4 (1992), pp. 643 – 650. Bibl.

Colombia

Alvarez-Borland, Isabel. The Task of the Historian in *El general en su laberinto*. *Hispania (USA)*, v. 76, no. 3 (Sept 93), pp. 439 – 445. Bibl.

Cuba

Pérez Villacampa, Gilberto. Enjuiciamiento advertido de la sombra de Colón. *Islas*, no. 98 (Jan – Apr 91), pp. 98 – 118.

Latin America

Díaz Ruiz, Ignacio. El recurso de la historia: a propósito de Carpentier. *Nueva Revista de Filología Hispánica*, v. 40, no. 2 (July – Dec 92), pp. 1073 – 1086. Bibl.

Earle, Peter G. Octavio Paz: poesía e historia. *Nueva Revista de Filología Hispánica*, v. 40, no. 2 (July – Dec 92), pp. 1101 – 1112. Bibl.

Kohut, Karl, ed. *Der eroberte Kontinent: Historische Realität, Rechtfertigung und literarische Darstellung der Kolonisation Amerikas* reviewed by Gernot Stimmer. *Zeitschrift für Lateinamerika Wien*, no. 43 (1992), pp. 123 – 124.

Márquez Rodríguez, Alexis. Historia y ficción en la novela histórica. *Boletín de la Academia Nacional de la Historia (Venezuela)*, v. 75, no. 300 (Oct – Dec 92), pp. 29 – 39. Bibl.

Mexico

García Gutiérrez, Georgina. *Terra nostra:* crónica universal del orbe; apuntes sobre intertextualidad. *Nueva Revista de Filología Hispánica*, v. 40, no. 2 (July – Dec 92), pp. 1135 – 1148.

Jiménez de Báez, Yvette. *Los de abajo* de Mariano Azuela: escritura y punto de partida. *Nueva Revista de Filología Hispánica*, v. 40, no. 2 (July – Dec 92), pp. 843 – 874. Bibl.

Parotti, Phillip. Heroic Conventions in José Antonio Villarreal's *The Fifth Horseman*. *Bilingual Review/Revista Bilingüe*, v. 17, no. 3 (Sept – Dec 92), pp. 237 – 241.

Poot Herrera, Sara. *La hija del judío:* entre la inquisición y la imprenta. *Nueva Revista de Filología Hispánica*, v. 40, no. 2 (July – Dec 92), pp. 761 – 777. Bibl.

Trujillo Muñoz, Gabriel. Historias de la guerra menor. *La Palabra y el Hombre*, no. 84 (Oct – Dec 92), pp. 305 – 306.

Nicaragua

Minard, Evelyne. Un example d'utilisation de l'histoire par Ernesto Cardenal: *El estrecho dudoso. Caravelle*, no. 60 (1993), pp. 101 – 121. Bibl.

Pailler, Claire. Avatares del tiempo histórico en dos poetas nicaragüenses de hoy: Ernesto Cardenal y Pablo Antonio Cuadra. *Caravelle*, no. 60 (1993), pp. 85 – 99. Bibl.

Paraguay

Osorio, Manuel. Conversación con Roa Bastos: *Yo el Supremo;* la contrahistoria. *Plural (Mexico)*, v. 22, no. 263 (Aug 93), pp. 29 – 31.

Peru

García Pabón, Leonardo. Comunicación, escritura e imaginario social en la *Tragedia del fin de Atahuallpa. Caravelle*, no. 59 (1992), pp. 225 – 240. Bibl.

Grandis, Rita de. La problemática del conocimiento histórico en *Historia de Mayta* de M. Vargas Llosa. *Revista de Crítica Literaria Latinoamericana*, v. 19, no. 38 (July – Dec 93), pp. 375 – 382. Bibl.

Montaldo, Graciela R. Vallejo y las formas del pasado. *Revista Nacional de Cultura (Venezuela)*, v. 54, no. 287 (Oct – Dec 92), pp. 178 – 187. Bibl, il.

White Navarro, Gladys. El drama americano de Calderón: mesianismo oficial y estrategias de dominación. *Revista de Crítica Literaria Latinoamericana*, v. 19, no. 38 (July – Dec 93), pp. 115 – 122.

Puerto Rico

Acosta Cruz, María Isabel. Historia y escritura femenina en Olga Nolla, Magali García Ramis, Rosario Ferré y Ana Lydia Vega. *Revista Iberoamericana*, v. 59, no. 162 – 163 (Jan – June 93), pp. 265 – 277. Bibl.

Caballero Wangüemert, María del Milagro. Discurso histórico y carnavalización de la historia: "El juramento" de René Marqués. *Revista Iberoamericana*, v. 59, no. 162 – 163 (Jan – June 93), pp. 145 – 156. Bibl.

Gelpí, Juan E. El clásico y la reescritura: "Insularismo" en las páginas de *La guaracha del macho Camacho. Revista Iberoamericana*, v. 59, no. 162 – 163 (Jan – June 93), pp. 55 – 71. Bibl.

Ríos-Avila, Rubén. La invención de un autor: escritura y poder en Edgardo Rodríguez Juliá. *Revista Iberoamericana*, v. 59, no. 162 – 163 (Jan – June 93), pp. 203 – 219. Bibl.

United States

Morton, Carlos. Rewriting Southwestern History: A Playwright's Perspective. *Mexican Studies*, v. 9, no. 2 (Summer 93), pp. 225 – 239. II.

Uruguay

Trigo, Abril. *Caudillo, estado, nación: literatura, historia e ideología en el Uruguay* reviewed by Gustavo Verdesio. *Nuevo Texto Crítico*, v. 6, no. 11 (1993), pp. 263 – 266.

Venezuela

Hidalgo de Jesús, Amarilis. *Abrapalabra:* el discurso desmitificador de la historia colonial venezolana. *Inti*, no. 37 – 38 (Spring – Fall 93), pp. 163 – 169. Bibl.

Márquez Rodríguez, Alexis. *Historia y ficción en la novela venezolana* reviewed by R. J. Lovera De-Sola. *Revista Nacional de Cultura (Venezuela)*, v. 53, no. 286 (July – Sept 92), pp. 249 – 251.

Osorio Tejeda, Nelson. La historia y las clases en la narrativa de Miguel Otero Silva. *Casa de las Américas*, no. 190 (Jan – Mar 93), pp. 34 – 41. Bibl.

Ríos, Alicia. La época de la independencia en la narrativa venezolana de los ochenta. *Hispamérica*, v. 22, no. 64 – 65 (Apr – Aug 93), pp. 48 – 54.

Strepponi, Blanca. El mal, los verdugos y sus víctimas: acerca de una escritura compartida en *El diario de John Robertson*. *Inti*, no. 37 – 38 (Spring – Fall 93), pp. 61 – 68.

LITERATURE AND SCIENCE

Manríquez S., Germán. Las relaciones entre literatura y ciencias en el ejemplo de la obra fisiológica de Alejandro Lipschütz y parte de la obra literaria de Thomas Mann (Accompanied by an appendix of texts by the authors). *Revista Chilena de Literatura*, no. 42 (Aug 93), pp. 115 – 121.

Rosa, William. Ciencia y literatura en Alfredo Collado Martell: un primer caso de inseminación artificial. *Revista Iberoamericana*, v. 59, no. 162 – 163 (Jan – June 93), pp. 111 – 118. Bibl.

LITERATURE AND SOCIETY

See also
Politics in literature
Revolutionary literature

America

Pratt, Mary Louise. La liberación de los márgenes: literaturas canadiense y latinoamericana en el contexto de la dependencia. *Casa de las Américas*, no. 190 (Jan – Mar 93), pp. 25 – 33. Bibl.

Argentina

Aínsa Amigues, Fernando. La provocación como antiutopía en Roberto Arlt. *Cuadernos Hispanoamericanos*, no. Special issue, 11 (July 93), pp. 15 – 22.

Jarkowski, Aníbal. Sobreviviente en una guerra: enviando tarjetas postales. *Hispamérica*, v. 21, no. 63 (Dec 92), pp. 15 – 24.

Masiello, Francine Rose. *Between Civilization and Barbarism: Women, Nation, and Literary Culture in Modern Argentina* reviewed by Catherine Davies (Review entitled "Women and a Redefinition of Argentinian Nationhood"). *Bulletin of Latin American Research*, v. 12, no. 3 (Sept 93), pp. 333 – 341.

— *Between Civilization and Barbarism: Women, Nation, and Literary Culture in Modern Argentina* reviewed by Myron I. Lichtblau. *Hispania (USA)*, v. 76, no. 3 (Sept 93), pp. 484 – 485.

— *Between Civilization and Barbarism: Women, Nation, and Literary Culture in Modern Argentina* reviewed by Verity Smith. *Journal of Latin American Studies*, v. 25, no. 3 (Oct 93), pp. 695 – 697.

— *Between Civilization and Barbarism: Women, Nation, and Literary Culture in Modern Argentina* reviewed by Naomi Lindstrom. *World Literature Today*, v. 67, no. 2 (Spring 93), p. 344.

Quintero Herencia, Juan Carlos. Los poetas en La Pampa o las "cantidades poéticas" en el *Facundo*. *Hispamérica*, v. 21, no. 62 (Aug 92), pp. 33 – 52.

Vassallo, Marta. Identidad nacional y chivos expiatorios. *Feminaria*, v. 6, no. 10, Suppl. (Apr 93), pp. 9 – 12. Bibl.

Bolivia

Sanjinés C., Javier. Pedro Shimose, poeta rebelde e intelectual letrado. *Signo*, no. 36 – 37, Nueva época (May – Dec 92), pp. 75 – 88. Bibl.

Brazil

Abdala Júnior, Benjamin. Do Brasil a Portugal: imagens na ação política. *Revista de Letras (Brazil)*, v. 32 (1992), pp. 15 – 30. Bibl.

Boyd, Antonio Olliz. The Social and Ethnic Contexts of Machado de Assis' *Dom Casmurro*. *Afro-Hispanic Review*, v. 11, no. 1 – 3 (1992), pp. 34 – 41. Bibl.

Reis, Roberto. *The Pearl Necklace: Toward an Archaeology of Brazilian Transition Discourse* translated by Aparecida de Godoy Johnson. Reviewed by Nelson H. Vieira. *Hispanic American Historical Review*, v. 73, no. 3 (Aug 93), pp. 484 – 485.

Vieira, Nelson H. "Closing the Gap" between High and Low: Intimation on the Brazilian Novel of the Future. *Latin American Literary Review*, v. 20, no. 40 (July – Dec 92), pp. 109 – 119. Bibl.

Caribbean area

Benítez Rojo, Antonio. *The Repeating Island: The Caribbean and the Postmodern Perspective* reviewed by Klaus Müller-Bergh. *Cuban Studies/Estudios Cubanos*, v. 23 (1993), pp. 222 – 225.

— *The Repeating Island: The Caribbean and the Postmodern Perspective*, a translation of *Isla que se repite: el Caribe y la perspectiva posmoderna*, translated by James E. Maraniss. Reviewed by Edna Aizenberg. *Review*, no. 47 (Fall 93), pp. 93 – 95.

Herndon, Gerise. Gender Construction and Neocolonialism. *World Literature Today*, v. 67, no. 4 (Fall 93), pp. 731 – 736. Bibl, il.

Rohlehr, F. Gordon. *My Strangled City and Other Essays* reviewed by Rupert Lewis. *Social and Economic Studies*, v. 41, no. 3 (Sept 92), pp. 169 – 173.

Shelton, Marie-Denise. Condé: The Politics of Gender and Identity. *World Literature Today*, v. 67, no. 4 (Fall 93), pp. 717 – 722. Bibl, il.

Spear, Thomas C. Individual Quests and Collective History. *World Literature Today*, v. 67, no. 4 (Fall 93), pp. 723 – 730. Il.

Chile

Flores, Arturo C. Chile: acerca de la relación teatro – sociedad. *La Palabra y el Hombre*, no. 81 (Jan – Mar 92), pp. 73 – 84. Bibl.

Loyola Goich, Lorena. Las sociedades campesinas: un retrato de cambios y permanencias a través de la literatura criollista chilena, 1920 – 1950. *Cuadernos de Historia (Chile)*, no. 11 (Dec 91), pp. 127 – 148. Bibl.

Narváez, Jorge E., ed. *La invención de la memoria* reviewed by Domnita Dumitrescu. *Nuevo Texto Crítico*, v. 6, no. 11 (1993), pp. 268 – 270.

Nómez, Naín. Literatura, cultura y sociedad: el modernismo y la génesis de la poesía chilena contemporánea. *Revista Chilena de Literatura*, no. 42 (Aug 93), pp. 157 – 164. Bibl.

Verba, Ericka Kim. "Las hojas sueltas" (Broadsides): Nineteenth-Century Chilean Popular Poetry as a Source for the Historian. *Studies in Latin American Popular Culture*, v. 12 (1993), pp. 141 – 158. Bibl.

Vidal, Hernán. *Dictadura militar, trauma social e inauguración de la sociología del teatro en Chile* reviewed by Carlos Alberto Trujillo. *Hispanic Review*, v. 61, no. 3 (Summer 93), pp. 456 – 457.

— *Dictadura militar, trauma social e inauguración de la sociología del teatro en Chile* reviewed by Catherine M. Boyle. *Latin American Theatre Review*, v. 26, no. 2 (Spring 93), pp. 216 – 217.

Costa Rica

Chaverri, Amalia. Génesis y evolución de los títulos de la novelística costarricense. *Canadian Journal of Latin American and Caribbean Studies*, v. 17, no. 34 (1992), pp. 73 – 95. Bibl, tables.

Cuba

Artalejo, Lucrecia. *La máscara y el marañón: la identidad nacional cubana* reviewed by William L. Siemens. *World Literature Today*, v. 67, no. 1 (Winter 93), pp. 160 – 161.

Phaf, Ineke. La introducción emblemática de la nación mulata: el contrapunteo híbrido en las culturas de Suriname y Cuba. *Revista de Crítica Literaria Latinoamericana*, v. 19, no. 38 (July – Dec 93), pp. 195 – 215. Bibl.

Dominican Republic

Bankay, Anne-Maria. Contemporary Women Poets of the Dominican Republic: Perspectives on Race and Other Social Issues. *Afro-Hispanic Review*, v. 12, no. 1 (Spring 93), pp. 34 – 41. Bibl.

Ecuador

Beane, Carol. Entrevista con Luz Argentina Chiriboga. *Afro-Hispanic Review*, v. 12, no. 2 (Fall 93), pp. 17 – 23.

Haiti

Laroche, Maximilien. *La découverte de l'Amérique par les américains* reviewed by Susanne Crosta. *Canadian Journal of Latin American and Caribbean Studies,* v. 17, no. 34 (1992), pp. 144 – 146.

Latin America

Basile, María Teresa. La naturaleza como discurso sobre la identidad latinoamericana. *La Educación (USA),* v. 36, no. 111 – 113 (1992), pp. 75 – 88. Bibl.

Beverley, John. ¿Posliteratura?: sujeto subalterno e impasse de las humanidades. *Casa de las Américas,* no. 190 (Jan – Mar 93), pp. 13 – 24. Bibl.

Hicks, D. Emily. *Border Writing: The Multidimensional Text* reviewed by Kavita Panjabi. *Letras Femeninas,* v. 19, no. 1 – 2 (Spring – Fall 93), pp. 140 – 143.

— *Border Writing: The Multidimensional Text* reviewed by Rafael H. Mojica. *World Literature Today,* v. 67, no. 1 (Winter 93), pp. 243 – 244.

Lienhard, Martín. *La voz y su huella: escritura y conflicto étnico – social en América Latina, 1492 – 1988* reviewed by Gustavo Fares. *Hispania (USA),* v. 76, no. 1 (Mar 93), pp. 88 – 89.

— *La voz y su huella: escritura y conflicto étnico – social en América Latina, 1492 – 1988* reviewed by José Prats Sariol. *Iberoamericana,* v. 16, no. 47 – 48 (1992), pp. 113 – 116.

— *La voz y su huella: escritura y conflicto étnico – social en América Latina, 1492 – 1988* reviewed by Antonio Cornejo Polar. *Revista de Crítica Literaria Latinoamericana,* v. 19, no. 38 (July – Dec 93), pp. 395 – 397.

Ludmer, Josefina. El delito: ficciones de exclusión y sueños de justicia. *Revista de Crítica Literaria Latinoamericana,* v. 19, no. 38 (July – Dec 93), pp. 145 – 153.

Melis, Antonio et al. Debate (on the second session of the symposium "Latinoamérica: Nuevas Direcciones en Teoría y Crítica Literarias, III"). *Revista de Crítica Literaria Latinoamericana,* v. 19, no. 38 (July – Dec 93), pp. 91 – 101.

— Debate (on the sixth session of the symposium "Latinoamérica: Nuevas Direcciones en Teoría y Crítica Literarias, III"). *Revista de Crítica Literaria Latinoamericana,* v. 19, no. 38 (July – Dec 93), pp. 261 – 266.

Pastor, Beatriz et al. Debate (on the fourth session of the symposium "Latinoamérica: Nuevas Direcciones en Teoría y Crítica Literarias, III"). *Revista de Crítica Literaria Latinoamericana,* v. 19, no. 38 (July – Dec 93), pp. 163 – 169.

Pérez V., Carlos. América Latina: marca registrada. *Mensaje,* v. 42, no. 416 (Jan – Feb 93), pp. 20 – 21.

Ramos, Julio et al. Debate (on the fifth session of the symposium "Latinoamérica: Nuevas Direcciones en Teoría y Crítica Literarias, III"). *Revista de Crítica Literaria Latinoamericana,* v. 19, no. 38 (July – Dec 93), pp. 217 – 221.

— Debate (on the seventh session of the symposium "Latinoamérica: Nuevas Direcciones en Teoría y Crítica Literarias, III"). *Revista de Crítica Literaria Latinoamericana,* v. 19, no. 38 (July – Dec 93), pp. 293 – 296.

Sicard, Alain. Poder de la escritura: ¿El crepúsculo de los chamanes? *Revista de Crítica Literaria Latinoamericana,* v. 19, no. 38 (July – Dec 93), pp. 155 – 162.

Sklodowska, Elzbieta. Testimonio mediatizado: ¿Ventriloquia o heteroglosia?; Barnet/Montejo; Burgos/Menchú. *Revista de Crítica Literaria Latinoamericana,* v. 19, no. 38 (July – Dec 93), pp. 81 – 90. Bibl.

Sommer, Doris. *Foundational Fictions: The National Romances of Latin America* reviewed by Edgardo C. Krebs. *The Americas,* v. 50, no. 2 (Oct 93), pp. 282 – 283.

— *Foundational Fictions: The National Romances of Latin America* reviewed by Carlos L. Orihuela. *Revista de Crítica Literaria Latinoamericana,* v. 19, no. 38 (July – Dec 93), pp. 399 – 403.

— Resistant Texts and Incompetent Readers. *Latin American Literary Review,* v. 20, no. 40 (July – Dec 92), pp. 104 – 108.

Taylor, Diana. Negotiating Performance. *Latin American Theatre Review,* v. 26, no. 2 (Spring 93), pp. 49 – 57. Bibl.

Williams, Gareth. Translation and Mourning: The Cultural Challenge of Latin American Testimonial Autobiography. *Latin American Literary Review,* v. 21, no. 41 (Jan – June 93), pp. 79 – 99. Bibl.

Bibliography

Montaldo, Graciela R. Imaginación e historia en América Latina (Review article). *Nueva Sociedad,* no. 127 (Sept – Oct 93), pp. 163 – 167.

Mexico

Meyer-Minnemann, Klaus. Apropiaciones de realidad en las novelas de José Joaquín Fernández de Lizardi. *Iberoamericana,* v. 17, no. 50 (1993), pp. 63 – 78. Bibl.

Nieto-Cadena, Fernando. Mujer, literatura y sociedad en el sureste. *Fem,* v. 17, no. 120 (Feb 93), pp. 21 – 24.

Portal, Marta. *Gringo viejo:* diálogo de culturas. *Cuadernos Americanos,* no. 39, Nueva época (May – June 93), pp. 217 – 227. Bibl.

Peru

Bedoya, Jaime. *Ay, qué rico: crónicas periodísticas* reviewed by Luis Jaime Cisneros V. (Review entitled "Oficio febril"). *Debate (Peru),* v. 15, no. 70 (Sept – Oct 92), p. 70.

Cornejo Polar, Antonio. El discurso de la armonía imposible: el Inca Garcilaso de la Vega; discurso y recepción social. *Revista de Crítica Literaria Latinoamericana,* v. 19, no. 38 (July – Dec 93), pp. 73 – 80.

Díaz, Lisiak-Land. Jerarquía social y económica en *El tungsteno* de César Vallejo. *Inti,* no. 36 (Fall 92), pp. 59 – 71. Bibl, charts.

Portugal

Abdala Júnior, Benjamin. Do Brasil a Portugal: imagens na ação política. *Revista de Letras (Brazil),* v. 32 (1992), pp. 15 – 30. Bibl.

Puerto Rico

Béjar, Eduardo C. *Harlem todos los días:* el exilio del nombre/el nombre del exilio. *Revista Iberoamericana,* v. 59, no. 162 – 163 (Jan – June 93), pp. 329 – 343. Bibl.

Duchesne, Juan Ramón. Multitud y tradición en "El entierro de Cortijo" de Edgardo Rodríguez Juliá. *Revista Iberoamericana,* v. 59, no. 162 – 163 (Jan – June 93), pp. 221 – 237. Bibl.

Rodríguez Castro, María Elena. Las casas del porvenir: nación y narración en el ensayo puertorriqueño. *Revista Iberoamericana,* v. 59, no. 162 – 163 (Jan – June 93), pp. 33 – 54. Bibl.

Surinam

Phaf, Ineke. La introducción emblemática de la nación mulata: el contrapunteo híbrido en las culturas de Suriname y Cuba. *Revista de Crítica Literaria Latinoamericana,* v. 19, no. 38 (July – Dec 93), pp. 195 – 215. Bibl.

United States

Hogue, W. Lawrence. An Unresolved Modern Experience: Richard Rodríguez's *Hunger of Memory. The Americas Review,* v. 20, no. 1 (Spring 92), pp. 52 – 64. Bibl.

Saldívar, José David. *The Dialectics of Our America: Genealogy, Cultural Critique, and Literary History* reviewed by Stephen Minta. *Bulletin of Latin American Research,* v. 12, no. 1 (Jan 93), pp. 129 – 130.

— *The Dialectics of Our America: Genealogy, Cultural Critique, and Literary History* reviewed by John Bruce-Novoa. *Hispania (USA),* v. 76, no. 2 (May 93), pp. 280 – 281.

Saldívar, Ramón David. *Chicano Narrative: The Dialectics of Difference* reviewed by Chuck Tatum (Review entitled "A New Standard for Chicano Literary Scholarship"). *Bilingual Review/Revista Bilingüe,* v. 18, no. 1 (Jan – Apr 93), pp. 64 – 74.

Sánchez, Rosaura. Discourses of Gender, Ethnicity, and Class in Chicano Literature. *The Americas Review,* v. 20, no. 2 (Summer 92), pp. 72 – 88. Bibl.

Venezuela

León, Jesús Alberto. La narrativa de la adolescencia: ¿Signo de crisis social? *Inti,* no. 37 – 38 (Spring – Fall 93), pp. 117 – 122.

Lewis, Marvin A. *Ethnicity and Identity in Contemporary Afro-Venezuelan Literature: A Culturalist Approach* reviewed by Jorge J. Rodríguez-Florido. *Hispania (USA),* v. 76, no. 2 (May 93), p. 289.

Osorio Tejeda, Nelson. La alucinación del petróleo en una obra de César Rengifo. *Hispamérica,* v. 21, no. 63 (Dec 92), pp. 81 – 87.

Rotker, Susana. Crónica y cultura urbana: Caracas, la última década. *Inti,* no. 37 – 38 (Spring – Fall 93), pp. 233 – 242. Bibl.

LIVESTOCK INDUSTRY

See
Cattle trade
Dairying
Meat industry and trade
Poultry industry
Sheep ranches
Swine
Wool industry and trade

LOANS

See
Debts, Public
Economic assistance
Economic assistance, Foreign

LOAYSA, JERÓNIMO DE

Olmedo Jiménez, Manuel. *Jerónimo de Loaysa, O.P., pacificador de españoles y protector de indios* reviewed by Ximena Sosa-Buchholz. *Colonial Latin American Historical Review,* v. 2, no. 3 (Summer 93), pp. 371 – 372.

LOBBIES

See
Pressure groups

LOCAL ELECTIONS

Mexico

Alemán Alemán, Ricardo. *Guanajuato: espejismo electoral* reviewed by Pedro García Rodríguez. *El Cotidiano,* v. 10, no. 58 (Oct – Nov 93), pp. 117 – 118.

Alvarado Mendoza, Arturo and Nelson Minello. Política y elecciones en Tamaulipas: la relación entre lo local y lo nacional. *Estudios Sociológicos,* v. 10, no. 30 (Sept – Dec 92), pp. 619 – 647. Charts.

Fernández Menéndez, Jorge. Las elecciones en Guerrero. *Nexos,* v. 16, no. 182 (Feb 93), pp. 59 – 62.

— San Luis Potosí: ¿Lejos de la estabilidad? *Nexos,* v. 16, no. 184 (Apr 93), pp. 49 – 52.

Santiago Castillo, Javier. Las elecciones locales en 1992. *El Cotidiano,* v. 8, no. 52 (Jan – Feb 93), pp. 19 – 24. Il, tables.

Zamarripa, Roberto. *Sonora '91: historia de políticos y policías* reviewed by Ana Ivonee Rivas García. *El Cotidiano,* v. 10, no. 58 (Oct – Nov 93), p. 117.

Puerto Rico

Benítez, Celeste. ¿Como votaron los caseríos de San Juan?: elecciones de 1988. *Homines,* v. 15 – 16, no. 2 – 1 (Oct 91 – Dec 92), pp. 102 – 105.

Gallisá, Carlos. Análisis electoral, 1988: apuntes preliminares. *Homines,* v. 15 – 16, no. 2 – 1 (Oct 91 – Dec 92), pp. 112 – 115.

LOCAL GOVERNMENT

Argentina

Bonaudo, Marta and Elida Sonzogni. Redes parentales y facciones en la política santafesina, 1850 – 1900. *Siglo XIX: Revista,* no. 11, 2a época (Jan – June 92), pp. 74 – 110. Bibl.

Favaro, Orietta et al. El Neuquén: límites estructurales de una estrategia de distribución, 1958 – 1980. *Realidad Económica,* no. 118 (Aug – Sept 93), pp. 123 – 138. Bibl.

Korzeniewicz, Roberto P. The Labor Politics of Radicalism: The Santa Fe Crisis of 1928. *Hispanic American Historical Review,* v. 73, no. 1 (Feb 93), pp. 1 – 32.

Brazil

Aguiar, Tereza Coni. O papel do poder público municipal e os desafios na criação de políticas para o desenvolvimento integral e harmónico da área rural. *Revista Geográfica (Mexico),* no. 114 (July – Dec 91), pp. 101 – 109.

Davidovich, Fany Rachel. Poder local e município: algumas considerações. *Revista Geográfica (Mexico),* no. 115 (Jan – June 92), pp. 27 – 36. Bibl.

Isaia, Artur Cesar. Catolicismo, regeneração social e castilhismo na república velha gaúcha. *Estudos Ibero-Americanos,* v. 18, no. 1 (July 92), pp. 5 – 18. Bibl.

Melo, Marcus André Barreto Campelo de. Municipalismo, "Nation-Building" e a modernização do estado no Brasil. *Revista Brasileira de Ciências Sociais,* v. 8, no. 23 (Oct 93), pp. 85 – 100. Bibl.

Finance

Villela, Luis. Sistema tributario y relaciones financieras intergubernamentales: la experiencia brasileña. *Planeación y Desarrollo,* v. 24, no. 1 (Jan – Apr 93), pp. 171 – 188. Tables.

Chile

Irarrázaval Llona, Ignacio. Autonomía municipal: un proyecto político perdiente. *EURE,* v. 19, no. 57 (July 93), pp. 79 – 94. Bibl, tables.

Colombia

Finance

Montenegro Trujillo, Armando. Descentralización en Colombia: una perspectiva internacional. *Planeación y Desarrollo,* v. 24, no. 1 (Jan – Apr 93), pp. 279 – 307. Bibl.

Vargas, César et al. Financiamiento del desarrollo regional: situación actual y perspectivas. *Planeación y Desarrollo,* v. 24, no. 1 (Jan – Apr 93), pp. 311 – 346. Tables, charts.

Latin America

Ahumada Pacheco, Jaime. Descentralización, desarrollo local y municipios en América Latina. *Revista Paraguaya de Sociología,* v. 29, no. 85 (Sept – Dec 92), pp. 73 – 94. Bibl.

Campbell, Tim et al. Descentralización hacia los gobiernos locales en América Latina y el Caribe. *Planeación y Desarrollo,* v. 24, no. 1 (Jan – Apr 93), pp. 27 – 95. Tables, charts.

Rufián Lizana, Dolores María. Una nueva administración municipal. *Revista Paraguaya de Sociología,* v. 29, no. 85 (Sept – Dec 92), pp. 59 – 71. Charts.

Mexico

Alvarado Mendoza, Arturo and Nelson Minello. Política y elecciones en Tamaulipas: la relación entre lo local y lo nacional. *Estudios Sociológicos,* v. 10, no. 30 (Sept – Dec 92), pp. 619 – 647. Charts.

Bassols Ricárdez, Mario and Rocio Corona Martínez. Transición institucional y reforma política en el D.F. *El Cotidiano,* v. 10, no. 57 (Aug – Sept 93), pp. 28 – 37. Il, tables.

Bolívar Espinoza, Augusto et al. La competencia de partidos: el que siembra vientos cosecha tempestades. *El Cotidiano,* v. 9, no. 54 (May 93), pp. 60 – 71. Il.

Carrillo, Mario Alejandro et al. Entre la contingencia y la permanencia: los municipios con alternancia del Partido Acción Nacional. *El Cotidiano,* v. 10, no. 58 (Oct – Nov 93), pp. 91 – 97. Il, maps.

Castelazo, José R. *Ciudad de México: reforma posible; escenarios en el porvenir* reviewed by Aída Escamilla Rubio. *El Cotidiano,* v. 9, no. 54 (May 93), p. 115. Il.

Haskett, Robert Stephen. *Indigenous Rulers: An Ethnohistory of Town Government in Colonial Cuernavaca* reviewed by Eric Van Young. *Journal of Latin American Studies,* v. 25, no. 3 (Oct 93), pp. 653 – 654.

Leal F., Gustavo and Martha Singer S. Gobernando desde la oposición: ayuntamiento de Durango, 1992 – 1995. *El Cotidiano,* v. 9, no. 54 (May 93), pp. 90 – 100. Bibl, il, tables.

Linares Zapata, Luis. El plebiscito: un fracaso bien hecho. *El Cotidiano,* v. 9, no. 54 (May 93), pp. 30 – 36. Il, tables.

Massolo, Alejandra. Descentralización y reforma municipal: ¿Fracaso anunciado y sorpresas inesperadas? *Revista Interamericana de Planificación,* v. 26, no. 101 – 102 (Jan – June 93), pp. 196 – 230. Bibl, tables.

Moreno Armella, Florita. Representación vecinal y gestión urbana en el D.F. *El Cotidiano,* v. 10, no. 57 (Aug – Sept 93), pp. 38 – 45. Il.

Pepin Lehalleur, Marielle. Regiones y poder local en el Golfo de México: los andamios de un programa de investigación. *Estudios Sociológicos,* v. 10, no. 30 (Sept – Dec 92), pp. 517 – 522. Maps.

Pepin Lehalleur, Marielle and Marie-France Prévôt-Schapira. Cuclillos en un nido de gorrión: espacio municipal y poder local en Altamira, Tamaulipas. *Estudios Sociológicos,* v. 10, no. 30 (Sept – Dec 92), pp. 583 – 617. Bibl, maps.

Pérez Morales, Constantino Alberto. Fortalecimiento municipal para el desarrollo regional en Oaxaca. *Problemas del Desarrollo,* v. 24, no. 92 (Jan – Mar 93), pp. 137 – 169. Tables.

Peschard, Jacqueline. Una reforma para la ciudad capital. *El Cotidiano,* v. 9, no. 54 (May 93), pp. 37 – 40. Il.

Ramírez Cuellar, Alfonso. La reforma necesaria. *El Cotidiano,* v. 9, no. 54 (May 93), pp. 24 – 29. Il, tables.

Rodríguez, Victoria Elizabeth. The Politics of Decentralisation in Mexico: From "Municipio Libre" to "Solidaridad." *Bulletin of Latin American Research,* v. 12, no. 2 (May 93), pp. 133 – 145. Bibl.

Sánchez-Mejorada F., María Cristina. Las clases medias en la gestión y el gobierno de la ciudad. *El Cotidiano,* v. 10, no. 57 (Aug – Sept 93), pp. 46 – 53. Il, maps.

Trejo Hernández, Raúl et al. *Perfil y semblanza política de la Asamblea de Representantes del Distrito Federal* reviewed by Felipe Solís Acero. *Revista Mexicana de Ciencias Políticas y Sociales,* v. 38, Nueva época, no. 151 (Jan – Mar 93), pp. 220 – 224.

Sources

Elmendorf, George F. and Joan A. Quillen. Serials and Government Documents from the States of Mexico. *SALALM Papers,* v. 36 (1991), pp. 425 – 431.

Peru

Sala i Vila, Nuria. La constitución de Cádiz y su impacto en el gobierno de las comunidades indígenas en el Virreinato del Perú. *Boletín Americanista,* v. 33, no. 42 – 43 (1992 – 1993), pp. 51 – 70. Bibl.

United States

Ortiz, Isidro D. Gloria Molina, líder popular chicana (Translated by Leticia García Cortés). *Plural (Mexico),* v. 22, no. 256 (Jan 93), pp. 63 – 69. Bibl.

Uruguay

Bervejillo, Federico. El nuevo perfil del intendente: un cambio de curso. *Cuadernos del CLAEH,* v. 18, no. 67 (Nov 93), pp. 11 – 18.

Carminatti, Mario and Jorge Larrañaga. De intendentes a gobernadores: coloquio con los intendentes. *Cuadernos del CLAEH,* v. 18, no. 67 (Nov 93), pp. 19 – 34.

Klein, Darío and Fabían Lazovski. Tabaré Vázquez, un líder bien imaginado. *Cuadernos del CLAEH,* v. 18, no. 67 (Nov 93), pp. 37 – 52. Bibl.

Venezuela

Langue, Frédérique. Antagonismos y solidaridades en un cabildo colonial: Caracas, 1750 – 1810. *Anuario de Estudios Americanos,* v. 49 (1992), pp. 371 – 393. Bibl.

Law and legislation

Meza, Robinzon. Bandos de buen gobierno para Mérida durante la colonia y su continuidad en los diversos instrumentos jurídicos del gobierno local de la república. *Boletín de la Academia Nacional de la Historia (Venezuela),* v. 75, no. 299 (July – Sept 92), pp. 174 – 180. Bibl.

LOMBARDI, FRANCISCO

Interviews `

Cisneros, Luis Jaime and Arturo Ferrari. Ni goles, ni milagros: entrevista a Francisco Lombardi. *Debate (Peru),* v. 16, no. 74 (Sept – Oct 93), pp. 14 – 18. Il.

LONG, RUPERTO M.

Interviews

Gliksberg, Isaac. El laboratorio tecnológico de Uruguay: entrevista a su presidente ing. Ruperto M. Long. *Interciencia,* v. 18, no. 6 (Nov – Dec 93), pp. 314 – 316. Il.

LOPE DE VEGA

See

Vega Carpio, Lope Félix de

LOPES NETO, SIMÕES

Criticism of specific works

Contos gauchescos

Aguiar, Flávio. Cultura de contrabando: estudo sobre os contos de Simões Lopes Neto. *Vozes,* v. 86, no. 6 (Nov – Dec 92), pp. 13 – 20.

LÓPEZ, CASTO FULGENCIO

Beltrán Guerrero, Luis. Centenario de Casto Fulgencio López. *Boletín de la Academia Nacional de la Historia (Venezuela),* v. 76, no. 301 (Jan – Mar 93), pp. 114 – 116.

LÓPEZ, ERENIA

Interviews

Caballero, Atilio J. Algo más que un teatro sin historia. *Conjunto,* no. 90 – 91 (Jan – June 92), pp. 92 – 96. Il.

LÓPEZ AVILA, CARLOS

Obituaries

Morales Baranda, Francisco. In Xochitlahtolcuicapihqui Ilnamiquiliz: Carlos López Avila (1922 – 1991). *Estudios de Cultura Náhuatl,* v. 22 (1992), pp. 462 – 465.

LÓPEZ CASTRO, RAFAEL

Moreno Toscano, Alejandra. López Castro y la función del sol. *Nexos,* v. 16, no. 188 (Aug 93), pp. 8 – 10.

LÓPEZ DE SANTA ANNA, ANTONIO

See

Santa Anna, Antonio López de

LÓPEZ ESCARRÉ, JOSÉ LUIS

Chase, Alfonso. "Puertas abiertas": pasos a la pintura de José Luis López Escarré. *Káñina,* v. 16, no. 1 (Jan – June 92), pp. 225 – 227. Il.

LÓPEZ JORDÁN, RICARDO

Duarte, María Amalia. La ley de amnistía de 1875 y el proceder del jordanismo. *Investigaciones y Ensayos,* no. 41 (Jan – Dec 91), pp. 171 – 213. Bibl.

LÓPEZ LLAUSÁS, ANTONIO

Alcorta, Rodrigo. La empresa de editar buenos libros. *Todo Es Historia,* v. 27, no. 311 (June 93), pp. 50 – 53. Il.

LÓPEZ MONDÉJAR, PUBLIO

Criticism of specific works

Martín Chambi, 1920 – 1950

Heredia, Jorge. Avatares de la obra del fotógrafo peruano Martín Chambi (1891 – 1973) y reseña de dos monografías recientes. *Hueso Húmero,* no. 29 (May 93), pp. 144 – 173. Bibl.

LÓPEZ RUIZ, JUVENAL

Obituaries

Franco Marcano, Mercedes. In memoriam: Juvenal López Ruiz. *Revista Nacional de Cultura (Venezuela),* v. 53, no. 286 (July – Sept 92), pp. 206 – 207.

LÓPEZ VELARDE, RAMÓN

Correspondence, reminiscences, etc.

Valle, Rafael Heliodoro. Buzón de fantasmas: páginas de un diario. *Vuelta,* v. 17, no. 200 (July 93), p. 80.

Criticism and interpretation

Chisalita, Ruxandra. El tormentoso goce de la profanación en César Vallejo y Ramón López Velarde. *Casa de las Américas,* no. 189 (Oct – Dec 92), pp. 58 – 64.

LORENZANA, CRISTÓBAL DE

Tardieu, Jean-Pierre. Las vistas de un arbitrista sobre la aparición de un hombre nuevo en las Indias Occidentales, mitad del siglo XVII. *Anuario de Estudios Americanos*, v. 50, no. 1 (1993), pp. 235 – 249. Bibl.

LOS ANGELES, CALIFORNIA

Hayes-Bautista, David E. et al. Latinos and the 1992 Los Angeles Riots: A Behavioral Sciences Perspective. *Hispanic Journal of Behavioral Sciences*, v. 15, no. 4 (Nov 93), pp. 427 – 448. Bibl, charts.

Moore, Joan W. *Going Down to the Barrio: Homeboys and Homegirls in Change* reviewed by Kathleen Logan. *Hispanic American Historical Review*, v. 73, no. 3 (Aug 93), pp. 488 – 489.

Ortiz, Isidro D. Gloria Molina, líder popular chicana (Translated by Leticia García Cortés). *Plural (Mexico)*, v. 22, no. 256 (Jan 93), pp. 63 – 69. Bibl.

Palacio, Joseph O. Garifuna Immigrants in Los Angeles: Attempts at Self-Improvements. *Belizean Studies*, v. 20, no. 3 (Dec 92), pp. 17 – 26. Bibl.

Pardo, Mary Santoli. Creating Community: Mexican American Women in Eastside Los Angeles. *Aztlán*, v. 20, no. 1 – 2 (Spring – Fall 91), pp. 39 – 71. Bibl.

Ríos-Bustamante, Antonio José. *Los Angeles: pueblo y región, 1781 – 1850* reviewed by Aurora Morcillo-Gómez. *Colonial Latin American Historical Review*, v. 2, no. 4 (Fall 93), pp. 473 – 474.

Soldatenko, Maria Angelina. Organizing Latina Garment Workers in Los Angeles. *Aztlán*, v. 20, no. 1 – 2 (Spring – Fall 91), pp. 73 – 96. Bibl.

LOSSADA, JESÚS ENRIQUE
Criticism and interpretation

Delgado Ocando, José Manuel. Relectura posmodernista de Jesús Enrique Lossada. *Revista Nacional de Cultura (Venezuela)*, v. 54, no. 287 (Oct – Dec 92), pp. 37 – 54. Il.

LOUISIANA

Din, Gilbert C. *Francisco Bouligny, a Bourbon Soldier in Spanish Louisiana* reviewed by Thomas E. Chávez. *Colonial Latin American Historical Review*, v. 2, no. 4 (Fall 93), pp. 477 – 478.

LOVE IN LITERATURE

El amor y la pasión: la verdad y la poesía de Salvador Díaz Mirón. *La Palabra y el Hombre*, no. 81 (Jan – Mar 92), pp. 302 – 305. Il.

Barriga Villanueva, Rebeca. Tintes de subjetividad en las coplas de amor: *Cancionero folklórico de México*. *Caravelle*, no. 60 (1993), pp. 59 – 83.

Cluff, Russell M. El motivo del amor en la poesía de Gonzalo Rojas. *Chasqui*, v. 22, no. 1 (May 93), pp. 59 – 69.

Correa Vásquez, Pedro Francisco. Cuando se enferma el amor: a propósito de los cuentos de Gloria Guardia. *Revista Cultural Lotería*, v. 51, no. 387 (Feb 92), pp. 69 – 71.

Escalante, Evodio. Retornar a *Trilce:* hacia una lectura afirmativa de la poesía de César Vallejo. *Casa de las Américas*, no. 189 (Oct – Dec 92), pp. 65 – 70.

Escalante Gutiérrez, Carmen and Ricardo Valderrama Fernández. Canciones de imploración y de amor en los Andes: literatura oral de los quechuas del siglo XX. *Revista de Crítica Literaria Latinoamericana*, v. 19, no. 37 (Jan – June 93), pp. 11 – 39.

León-Portilla, Miguel, ed. *Poésie náhuatl d'amour et d'amitié* translated by Georges Baudot. Reviewed by Patrick Johansson. *Caravelle*, no. 60 (1993), pp. 135 – 138.

Magnarelli, Sharon Dishaw. El significante deseo en *Cambio de armas* de Luisa Valenzuela. *Escritura (Venezuela)*, v. 16, no. 31 – 32 (Jan – Dec 91), pp. 161 – 169.

Mejía Madrid, Fabrizio. Con el corazón en la mano. *Nexos*, v. 16, no. 192 (Dec 93), pp. 21 – 22.

Moreno Uscanga, Ivonne. Juan García Ponce: la bifurcación del amor. *La Palabra y el Hombre*, no. 81 (Jan – Mar 92), pp. 313 – 315.

LOYNAZ, DULCE MARÍA
Awards

Jarque, Fietta and Mauricio Vicent. La poetisa cubana Dulce María Loynaz gana el premio Cervantes. *Humboldt*, no. 108 (1993), p. 104.
Correspondence, reminiscences, etc.

González Acosta, Alejandro. Carta abierta a Dulce María Loynaz. *Plural (Mexico)*, v. 22, no. 262 (July 93), pp. 18 – 22.

Loynaz, Dulce María. Imágenes de Raimundo Lazo. *Plural (Mexico)*, v. 22, no. 262 (July 93), pp. 16 – 17.
Criticism and interpretation

Cámara, Madeline. La dama del jardín. *Plural (Mexico)*, v. 22, no. 262 (July 93), pp. 23 – 24.

LOYOLA, IGNACIO DE

Goñi, Alejandro. Palabras del r.p. Alejandro Goñi, S.J. *Boletín de la Academia Nacional de la Historia (Venezuela)*, v. 75, no. 299 (July – Sept 92), pp. 19 – 24.

Morón Montero, Guillermo. Sesión especial con motivo de los quinientos años del nacimiento de San Ignacio de Loyola: Ignacio de Loyola, 1491 – 1991. *Boletín de la Academia Nacional de la Historia (Venezuela)*, v. 75, no. 299 (July – Sept 92), pp. 9 – 17.

LUGO FILIPPI, CARMEN
Criticism of specific works
Milagros, calle Mercurio

Umpierre Herrera, Luz María. Incitaciones lesbianas en "Milagros, calle Mercurio" de Carmen Lugo Filippi. *Revista Iberoamericana*, v. 59, no. 162 – 163 (Jan – June 93), pp. 309 – 316.
Interviews

Martínez, Elena M. Entrevista con Carmen Lugo Filippi. *Fem*, v. 17, no. 122 (Apr 93), pp. 41 – 42.

LUGONES, LEOPOLDO
Criticism and interpretation

Gramuglio, María Teresa. Literatura y nacionalismo: Leopoldo Lugones y la construcción de imágenes de escritor. *Hispamérica*, v. 22, no. 64 – 65 (Apr – Aug 93), pp. 5 – 22. Bibl.

Neglia, Erminio G. El teatro modernista de Leopoldo Lugones. *Revista Canadiense de Estudios Hispánicos*, v. 17, no. 3 (Spring 93), pp. 549 – 556. Bibl.
Criticism of specific works
Las montañas del oro

Porto Bucciarelli, Lucrecia. *Leopoldo Lugones de parte de los astros: el simbolismo hermético de 'Las montañas del oro'* reviewed by Estrella Ogden. *Hispanic Review*, v. 61, no. 1 (Winter 93), pp. 127 – 129.

LULA
See
   Silva, Luís Inácio da

LUMBER TRADE
See
   Forestry

LUNA, FÉLIX

Bazán, Armando Raúl and Ricardo Zorraquín Becú. La historia y su divulgación (Two speeches on the occasion of Félix Luna's induction into the National Academy of History). *Todo Es Historia*, v. 27, no. 316 (Nov 93), pp. 43 – 49. Il.
Addresses, essays, lectures

Luna, Félix. Discurso del doctor Félix Luna (On the occasion of his induction into the National Academy of History). *Todo Es Historia*, v. 27, no. 316 (Nov 93), pp. 50 – 58. Il.

LUPERÓN, GREGORIO

Cordero Michel, Emilio. Gregorio Luperón y Haití. *Anuario de Estudios Americanos*, v. 49 (1992), pp. 497 – 528. Bibl.

LURTON, H. WILLIAM

Russell, Joel. A Better Neighborhood. *Business Mexico*, v. 3, no. 3 (Mar 93), pp. 46 – 47. Il.

LUZA, MÓNICA

Bartl, Johanna. Artistas latinoamericanos buscan mitos en Salzwedel. *Humboldt,* no. 110 (1993), p. 102. II.

LYNCH, MARTA

Criticism of specific works
Informe bajo llave

Riccio, Alessandra. Eros y poder en *Informe bajo llave* de Marta Lynch. *Escritura (Venezuela),* v. 16, no. 31 – 32 (Jan – Dec 91), pp. 223 – 229. Bibl.

MCCARTHY, MARY

Criticism of specific works
The Company She Keeps

Schmidt, Rita Terezinha. Un juego de máscaras: Nélida Piñon y Mary McCarthy (Translated by Eleonora Cróquer P.). *Escritura (Venezuela),* v. 16, no. 31 – 32 (Jan – Dec 91), pp. 259 – 270.

MACEDO, MANUEL JOAQUIM DE

Criticism of specific works
Opera Tiradentes

Reis, Sandra Loureiro de Freitas. A *Opera Tiradentes* de Manuel Joaquim de Macedo e Augusto de Lima. *Latin American Music Review,* v. 14, no. 1 (Spring – Summer 93), pp. 131 – 144. Bibl.

MACEO, ANTONIO

Briceño Perozo, Mario. *Antonio Maceo, la voz del huracán* reviewed by José Manuel Castañón (Review entitled "El Antonio Maceo de Mario Briceño Perozo"). *Boletín de la Academia Nacional de la Historia (Venezuela),* v. 75, no. 298 (Apr – June 92), pp. 110 – 111.

MACGREGOR, GREGOR

Arends, Tulio. *Sir Gregor MacGregor, un escocés tras la aventura de América* reviewed by Juvenal López Ruiz. *Revista Nacional de Cultura (Venezuela),* v. 53, no. 286 (July – Sept 92), p. 263.

MACHADO, EDUARDO

Criticism of specific works
The Modern Ladies of Guanabacoa

Muñoz, Elías Miguel. Of Small Conquests and Big Victories: Gender Constructs in *The Modern Ladies of Guanabacoa. The Americas Review,* v. 20, no. 2 (Summer 92), pp. 105 – 111. Bibl.

MACHADO DE ASSIS, JOAQUIM MARIA

Wehrs, Carlos. Machado de Assis e a música. *Revista do Instituto Histórico e Geográfico Brasileiro,* no. 373 (Oct – Dec 91), pp. 1057 – 1070. Bibl, il.

Criticism of specific works
Dom Casmurro

Boyd, Antonio Olliz. The Social and Ethnic Contexts of Machado de Assis' *Dom Casmurro. Afro-Hispanic Review,* v. 11, no. 1 – 3 (1992), pp. 34 – 41. Bibl.

MACHIGANGA INDIANS

Renard-Casevitz, France-Marie. *Le banquet masqué: une mythologie de l'étranger chez les indiens matsiguenga* reviewed by Edmundo Magaña. *European Review of Latin American and Caribbean Studies,* no. 54 (June 93), pp. 139 – 145.

MACHU PICCHU, PERU

Bouchard, Jean-François et al. Machu Picchu: problemas de conservación de un sitio inca de ceja de selva. *Bulletin de l'Institut Français d'Etudes Andines,* v. 21, no. 3 (1992), pp. 905 – 927. Bibl, il, maps.

MACIEL, ANTÔNIO VICENTE MENDES

Levine, Robert M. *Vale of Tears: Revisiting the Canudos Massacre in Northeastern Brazil, 1893 – 1897* reviewed by Francis Lambert. *Bulletin of Latin American Research,* v. 12, no. 3 (Sept 93), pp. 353 – 354.

— *Vale of Tears: Revisiting the Canudos Massacre in Northeastern Brazil, 1893 – 1897* reviewed by Dain Borges. *Hispanic American Historical Review,* v. 73, no. 3 (Aug 93), pp. 515 – 516.

— *Vale of Tears: Revisiting the Canudos Massacre in Northeastern Brazil, 1893 – 1897* reviewed by Jeff Lesser. *Journal of Latin American Studies,* v. 25, no. 2 (May 93), pp. 397 – 398.

— *Vale of Tears: Revisiting the Canudos Massacre in Northeastern Brazil, 1893 – 1897* reviewed by Steven C. Topik. *Luso-Brazilian Review,* v. 30, no. 2 (Winter 93), pp. 115 – 116.

Madden, Lori. The Canudos War in History. *Luso-Brazilian Review,* v. 30, no. 2 (Winter 93), pp. 5 – 22. Bibl.

Meihy, José Carlos Sebe Bom. "Meu empenho foi ser o tradutor do universo sertanejo": entrevista com José Calazans (Interviewed and transcribed by José Carlos Sebe Bom Meihy). *Luso-Brazilian Review,* v. 30, no. 2 (Winter 93), pp. 23 – 33.

Otten, Alexandre H. A influência do ideário religioso na construção da comunidade de Belo Monte. *Luso-Brazilian Review,* v. 30, no. 2 (Winter 93), pp. 71 – 95. Bibl.

MADEIRA, MARCOS ALMIR

Addresses, essays, lectures

Madeira, Marcos Almir. Uma senhora em sua casa (Speech given in honor of Maria Beltrão's induction into the Instituto Histórico e Geográfico Brasileiro). *Revista do Instituto Histórico e Geográfico Brasileiro,* no. 372 (July – Sept 91), pp. 800 – 805.

MADERO, FRANCISCO I.

Krauze, Enrique. Madero vivo. *Vuelta,* v. 17, no. 196 (Mar 93), pp. 11 – 14.

MADRAZO, CARLOS A.

Hernández Rodríguez, Rogelio. *La formación del político mexicano: el caso de Carlos A. Madrazo* reviewed by Roderic Ai Camp. *Hispanic American Historical Review,* v. 73, no. 2 (May 93), pp. 334 – 335.

MADRID, ANTONIETA

Criticism of specific works
No es tiempo para rosas

Cunha-Giabbai, Gloria da. La problemática de la mujer hispanoamericana como reflejo del conflicto social: *No es tiempo para rosas* de Antonieta Madrid. *Inti,* no. 37 – 38 (Spring – Fall 93), pp. 145 – 153.

MADRID, SPAIN

Herranz Gómez, Yolanda. Latinoamericanos en Madrid: integración en la sociedad española. *Revista Española de Antropología Americana,* v. 23 (1993), pp. 189 – 211. Bibl, tables, charts.

MAEZTU, RAMIRO DE

Figallo, Beatriz J. Yrigoyen y su segundo gobierno vistos por Ramiro de Maeztu. *Todo Es Historia,* v. 27, no. 312 (July 93), pp. 80 – 93. Bibl, il.

MAGELLAN, STRAIT OF

Barros Franco, José Miguel. Rey Don Felipe: plano de una fundación hispana en el estrecho de Magallanes. *Boletín de la Academia Chilena de la Historia,* v. 58 – 59, no. 102 (1991 – 1992), pp. 387 – 401. Il, facs.

MAGIC

Voeks, Robert. African Medicine and Magic in the Americas. *Geographical Review,* v. 83, no. 1 (Jan 93), pp. 66 – 78. Bibl, maps.

MAGICAL REALISM (LITERATURE)

See also
Fantastic literature

Amate Blanco, Juan José. El realismo mágico en la expedición amazónica de Orellana. *Cuadernos Hispanoamericanos,* no. 510 (Dec 92), pp. 61 – 72. Bibl.

Báez-Jorge, Félix. La afición arqueológica de Alejo Carpentier. *Plural (Mexico),* v. 22, no. 262 (July 93), pp. 46 – 50.

— Mitla y el barroco: notas sobre la afición arqueológica de Alejo Carpentier. *La Palabra y el Hombre,* no. 82 (Apr – June 92), pp. 57 – 73. Il.

Bravo, Víctor. La realidad del mundo invisible: la poesía de José Lezama Lima. *Revista Nacional de Cultura (Venezuela),* v. 53, no. 285 (Apr – June 92), pp. 22 – 39. Bibl.

Martínez, Gustavo. Lo real-maravilloso o el redescubrimiento de América. *Plural (Mexico),* v. 22, no. 265 (Oct 93), pp. 60 – 69.

Ndiaye, Christiane. Le réalisme merveilleux au féminin. *Canadian Journal of Latin American and Caribbean Studies,* v. 17, no. 34 (1992), pp. 115 – 117.

Pratt, Mary Louise. La liberación de los márgenes: literaturas canadienses y latinoamericana en el contexto de la dependencia. *Casa de las Américas,* no. 190 (Jan – Mar 93), pp. 25 – 33. Bibl.

MAINAS, PERU

Ardito Vega, Wilfredo. La estructura de las reducciones de Maynas. *Amazonía Peruana,* v. 11, no. 22 (Oct 92), pp. 93 – 124. Bibl.

MAL-LARA, JUAN DE

Bernal Rodríguez, Manuel. Nota sobre el influjo de la espiritualidad renacentista en la reprobación moral de la emigración a Indias: el camino del infierno. *Anuario de Estudios Americanos,* v. 49, Suppl. 2 (1992), pp. 3 – 9. Bibl.

MALASPINA, ALESSANDRO

Bibliography

Sáiz, Blanca. *Bibliografía sobre Alejandro Malaspina y acerca de la expedición Malaspina y de los marinos y científicos que en ella participaron* reviewed by Oldrich Kaspar (Review translated by Eva Máuková). *Anuario de Estudios Americanos,* v. 50, no. 1 (1993), p. 325.

Criticism of specific works

Axiomas políticos sobre la América

Lucena Giraldo, Manuel and Juan Pimentel Igea, eds. *Los "Axiomas políticos sobre la América" de Alejandro Malaspina* reviewed by O. Carlos Stoetzer. *Hispanic American Historical Review,* v. 73, no. 1 (Feb 93) pp. 160 – 161.

MALDONADO TORO, FRANCISCO ARMANDO

Vélez Boza, Fermín. Introducción al trabajo *Expediente de órdenes, 1613 – 1923* de monseñor dr. F. Maldonado Toro. *Boletín de la Academia Nacional de la Historia (Venezuela),* v. 76, no. 302 (Apr – June 93), pp. 183 – 185.

MALINCHE

Cypess, Sandra Messinger. *La Malinche in Mexican Literature: From History to Myth* reviewed by Salvador A. Oropesa. *Letras Femeninas,* v. 19, no. 1 – 2 (Spring – Fall 93), pp. 146 – 148.

— *La Malinche in Mexican Literature: From History to Myth* reviewed by Julie Greer Johnson. *Revista Interamericana de Bibliografía,* v. 42, no. 3 (1992), p. 502.

— Re-visión de la figura de la Malinche en la dramaturga mexicana contemporánea. *Cuadernos Americanos,* no. 40, Nueva época (July – Aug 93), pp. 208 – 222. Bibl.

Franco, Jean. La Malinche y el primer mundo. *Cuadernos Americanos,* no. 40, Nueva época (July – Aug 93), pp. 170 – 180.

Glantz, Margo. La Malinche, sus padres y sus hijos. *Cuadernos Americanos,* no. 40, Nueva época (July – Aug 93), pp. 167 – 169.

Stranger, Inés. *Malinche* reviewed by Juan Andres Piña. *Mensaje,* v. 42, no. 422 (Sept 93), p. 468.

Wey, Valquiria. La Malinche, sus padres y sus hijos. *Cuadernos Americanos,* no. 40, Nueva época (July – Aug 93), pp. 223 – 226.

Sources

Baudot, Georges. Malintzin, imagen y discurso de mujer en el primer México virreinal. *Cuadernos Americanos,* no. 40, Nueva época (July – Aug 93), pp. 181 – 207. Bibl.

MALLEA, EDUARDO

Criticism of specific works

Todo verdor perecerá

Frankenthaler, Marilyn R. Agata Cruz, prototipo de la "heroína" existencialista. *La Palabra y el Hombre,* no. 84 (Oct – Dec 92), pp. 311 – 320. Bibl, il.

MALNUTRITION

See
Nutrition

MALVINA ISLANDS

See
Falkland Islands

MAN

See also
Children
Old age
Youth

Influence of climate

Ferpozzi, Luis Humberto and José María Suriano. Los cambios climáticos en la pampa también son historia. *Todo Es Historia,* v. 26, no. 306 (Jan 93), pp. 8 – 25. Bibl, il, maps.

Huertas Vallejos, Lorenzo. Anomalías cíclicas de la naturaleza y su impacto en la sociedad: el fenómeno El Niño. *Bulletin de l'Institut Français d'Etudes Andines,* v. 22, no. 1 (1993), pp. 345 – 393. Bibl, il, tables, maps, facs, charts.

Mattos, Carlos de Meira. *Geopolítica e trópicos* reviewed by Sydney Martins Gomes dos Santos. *Revista do Instituto Histórico e Geográfico Brasileiro,* no. 371 (Apr – June 91), pp. 605 – 609.

Influence of environment

León-Portilla, Miguel. Naturaleza y cultura. *Cuadernos Americanos,* no. 39, Nueva época (May – June 93), pp. 65 – 71.

Vitier, Cintio. La tierra adivinada. *Cuadernos Americanos,* no. 39, Nueva época (May – June 93), pp. 88 – 90.

MAN, PREHISTORIC

Correal Urrego, Gonzalo. *Aguazuque: evidencias de cazadores, recolectores y plantadores en la altaplanicie de la cordillera oriental* reviewed by Marianne Cardale de Schrimpff. *Revista Colombiana de Antropología,* v. 29 (1992), pp. 235 – 238.

Fiedel, Stuart J. *Prehistory of the Americas,* 2d edition, reviewed by Gary M. Feinman. *Hispanic American Historical Review,* v. 73, no. 4 (Nov 93), pp. 679 – 680.

— *Prehistory of the Americas,* 2d edition, reviewed by Aaron Segal. *Interciencia,* v. 18, no. 3 (May – June 93), pp. 163 – 164.

Gómez Otero, Julieta. The Function of Small Rock Shelters in the Magallanes IV Phase Settlement System, South Patagonia. *Latin American Antiquity,* v. 4, no. 4 (Dec 93), pp. 325 – 345. Bibl, il, tables, maps, charts.

Schiavini, Adrián. Los lobos marinos como recurso para cazadores-recolectores marinos: el caso de Tierra del Fuego. *Latin American Antiquity,* v. 4, no. 4 (Dec 93), pp. 346 – 366. Bibl, tables, maps.

MAÑACH, JORGE

Criticism of specific works

Martí, el apóstol

Fernández Retamar, Roberto. Sobre la edición cubana de *Martí, el apóstol. Revista de Crítica Literaria Latinoamericana,* v. 19, no. 37 (Jan – June 93), pp. 345 – 351.

MANAGEMENT

See also
Employees' representation in management
Industrial organization
Industrial sociology
Labor relations
Public administration
School management and organization
Time allocation
Subdivision *Administration* under *Universities and colleges*

Brazil

Almeida, Martinho Isnard Ribeiro et al. ¿Por qué administrar estrategicamente recursos humanos? *RAE; Revista de Administração de Empresas,* v. 33, no. 2 (Mar – Apr 93), pp. 12 – 24. Bibl, tables.

Leiria, Jerônimo Souto et al. *Terceirização passo à passo: o caminho para a administração pública e privada* reviewed by Michelle Montone. *RAE; Revista de Administração de Empresas,* v. 33, no. 2 (Mar – Apr 93), pp. 127 – 128.

Vasconcelos, Isabella Francisca Freitas Gouvêa de. IBM: o desafio da mudança. *RAE; Revista de Administração de Empresas,* v. 33, no. 3 (May – June 93), pp. 84 – 97. Bibl.

Mexico

Erlich, Marc I. Making Sense of the Bicultural Workplace. *Business Mexico,* v. 3, no. 8 (Aug 93), pp. 16 – 19.

Hamer, Thurston R. The Hunt for Local Talent. *Business Mexico,* v. 3, no. 6 (June 93), pp. 4 – 6.

Study and teaching

Peñalosa, Raúl. Evaluating Management Seminars. *Business Mexico,* v. 3, no. 7 (July 93), pp. 42 – 43. Il.

MANCERA AGUAYO, MIGUEL

Addresses, essays, lectures

Mancera Aguayo, Miguel. Discurso de Miguel Mancera en la recepción del premio de economía rey Juan Carlos (Introduced by Luis Angel Rojo). *El Trimestre Económico,* v. 60, no. 237 (Jan – Mar 93), pp. 212 – 229.

MANET, EDOUARD

Barnes, Julian. El fusilamiento de Maximiliano (Translated by Ana Becerril). *Nexos,* v. 16, no. 187 (July 93), pp. 39 – 47. Il.

Wilson-Bareau, Juliet. *Manet: 'The Execution of Maximilian'; Painting, Politics, and Censorship* reviewed by Paul J. Vanderwood. *Hispanic American Historical Review,* v. 73, no. 2 (May 93), p. 331.

MANIOC

Uma cultura plebéia. *Problemas Brasileiros,* v. 30, no. 296 (Mar – Apr 93), pp. 27 – 28. Il.

Mandioca vira cerveja. *Problemas Brasileiros,* v. 30, no. 296 (Mar – Apr 93), pp. 26 – 27. Il.

Moura, Demócrito. A revolução da mandioca. *Problemas Brasileiros,* v. 30, no. 296 (Mar – Apr 93), pp. 24 – 25. Il.

Mathematical models

Khan, Ahmad Saeed and José da Silva Souza. Taxa de retorno social do investimento em pesquisa na cultura da mandioca no Nordeste. *Revista de Economia e Sociologia Rural,* v. 29, no. 4 (Oct – Dec 91), pp. 411 – 426. Bibl, tables, charts.

MANLEY, EDNA

Manley, Edna. *Edna Manley: The Diaries* edited by Rachel Manley. Reviewed by Adelaida de Juan (Review entitled "A Woman to Remember"). *Jamaica Journal,* v. 25, no. 1 (Oct 93), pp. 26 – 67. Il.

MANLEY, MICHAEL

Jones, Edwin. *Development Administration: Jamaican Adaptation* reviewed by Ian Boxill. *Social and Economic Studies,* v. 41, no. 3 (Sept 92), pp. 180 – 182.

Levi, Darrell Erville. *Michael Manley: The Making of a Leader* reviewed by Herman McKenzie. *Jamaica Journal,* v. 24, no. 3 (Feb 93), pp. 55 – 57. Il.

MANLEY, NORMAN WASHINGTON

Blake, Vivian. In Pursuit of Excellence. *Jamaica Journal,* v. 25, no. 1 (Oct 93), pp. 2 – 8. Il.

Carnegie, James Alexander. Sporting Hero and More. *Jamaica Journal,* v. 25, no. 1 (Oct 93), pp. 38 – 43. Il.

Hart, Pansy Rae. Out to Build a New Jamaica. *Jamaica Journal,* v. 25, no. 1 (Oct 93), pp. 29 – 37. Il.

Hart, Richard. Federation: An Ill-Fated Design. *Jamaica Journal,* v. 25, no. 1 (Oct 93), pp. 10 – 16. Bibl, il.

O'Gorman, Pamela. Music: A Personal Memoir. *Jamaica Journal,* v. 25, no. 1 (Oct 93), pp. 18 – 24. Bibl, il, facs.

Poetry

Manley, Rachel. Poems ("N.W.M.," "Memory," "Regardless"). *Jamaica Journal,* v. 25, no. 1 (Oct 93), p. 44.

MANN, THOMAS

Manríquez S., Germán. Las relaciones entre literatura y ciencias en el ejemplo de la obra fisiológica de Alejandro Lipschütz y parte de la obra literaria de Thomas Mann (Accompanied by an appendix of texts by the authors). *Revista Chilena de Literatura,* no. 42 (Aug 93), pp. 115 – 121.

MANNS, PATRICIO

Criticism and interpretation

Epple, Juan Armando. *Patricio Manns: actas del cazador en movimiento* reviewed by Arturo C. Flores. *Chasqui,* v. 22, no. 1 (May 93), pp. 81 – 82.

Interviews

Epple, Juan Armando. Post-modernismo: una poética desde el Tercer Mundo; conversación con Patricio Manns. *Confluencia,* v. 8, no. 1 (Fall 92), pp. 123 – 135.

MANPOWER

See

Labor supply

MANQU QHAPAQ, INKA

Seminiski, Jan. Manqu Qhapaq Inka: ¿Un poeta religioso? *Revista de Crítica Literaria Latinoamericana,* v. 19, no. 37 (Jan – June 93), pp. 131 – 158. Bibl.

Szeminski, Jan. Manqu Qhapaq Inka según Anello Oliva, S.J., 1631. *Historia y Cultura (Peru),* no. 20 (1990), pp. 269 – 280.

MANSO, JUANA PAULA

Criticism of specific works

Compendio de la historia de las provincias unidas del Río de la Plata

Zuccotti, Liliana. Juana Manso: contar historias. *Feminaria,* v. 6, no. 11, Suppl. (Nov 93), pp. 2 – 4.

MANUSCRIPTS

See also

Archives
Maya literature
Nahuatl literature
Quechua literature
Names of specific codices and titles of manuscripts

Andean region

The Huarochiri Manuscript: A Testament of Ancient and Colonial Andean Religion translated by Frank Solomon and George L. Urioste. Reviewed by Karen Spalding. *The Americas,* v. 49, no. 3 (Jan 93), pp. 398 – 399.

Germany

Thiemer-Sachse, Ursula. Un autógrafo de Cristóbal Colón (Cristóforo Colombo) en la colección especial de la biblioteca de la Universidad de Rostock. *Ibero-Amerikanisches Archiv,* v. 18, no. 3 – 4 (1992), pp. 523 – 541. Bibl, facs.

Mexico

Máynez Vidal, Pilar. Documentos de Tezcoco: consideraciones sobre tres manuscritos en mexicano del ramo "Tierras." *Estudios de Cultura Náhuatl,* v. 22 (1992), pp. 325 – 343.

MANZANO, JUAN FRANCISCO

Criticism of specific works

Un sueño

Hauser, Rex. Two New World Dreamers: Manzano and Sor Juana. *Afro-Hispanic Review,* v. 12, no. 2 (Fall 93), pp. 3 – 11. Bibl.

MAPS

See

Atlases
Cartography
Subdivision *Maps* under names of specific countries, geographical areas, etc.

MAPUCHE INDIANS

See
Araucanian Indians

MAQUILADORAS

See
Subcontracting

MAR DEL PLATA, ARGENTINA

Pastoriza, Elisa. Dirigentes obreros y política en el marco de la gestación de un peronismo periférico: Mar del Plata, 1935 – 1948. *Todo Es Historia*, v. 27, no. 314 (Sept 93), pp. 32 – 43. Il, tables.

MARACAIBO, VENEZUELA

Cardozo Galué, Germán. El circuito agroexportador marabino a mediados del siglo XIX. *Boletín Americanista*, v. 33, no. 42 – 43 (1992 – 1993), pp. 367 – 393. Bibl, maps, charts.

— *Maracaibo y su región histórica: el circuito agroexportador, 1830 – 1860* reviewed by Frédérique Langue. *Cahiers des Amériques Latines*, no. 13 (1992), pp. 184 – 185.

MARANHÃO, BRAZIL

Campos, José Ribamar Silva and José de Jesus Sousa Lemos. Fundamentação dinâmica para a produção e comercialização de hortifrutigranjeiros. *Revista de Economia e Sociologia Rural*, v. 30, no. 1 (Jan – Mar 92), pp. 11 – 20. Bibl, tables.

MARANHÃO, HAROLDO

Criticism of specific works

Senhoras e senhores

Franconi, Rodolfo A. The Fictionalization of a Diary (Translated by Barbara Meza). *Américas*, v. 45, no. 6 (Nov – Dec 93), pp. 60 – 63. Il.

MARCANO, VICENTE

Bibliography

Pérez Marchelli, Héctor. Bibliografía sobre Vicente Marcano, 1848 – 1891. *Boletín de la Academia Nacional de la Historia (Venezuela)*, v. 75, no. 299 (July – Sept 92), pp. 207 – 212.

Urbani Patat, Franco. Bibliografía de Vicente Marcano, 1848 – 1891. *Boletín de la Academia Nacional de la Historia (Venezuela)*, v. 75, no. 299 (July – Sept 92), pp. 196 – 207.

MARCHA (NEWSPAPER)

Gilman, Claudia. Política y cultura: *Marcha* a partir de los años '60. *Nuevo Texto Crítico*, v. 6, no. 11 (1993), pp. 153 – 186. Bibl.

Rocca, Pablo. 35 años en *Marcha*: escritura y ambiente literario en *Marcha* y en el Uruguay, 1939 – 1974. *Nuevo Texto Crítico*, v. 6, no. 11 (1993), pp. 3 – 151. Bibl, il.

MARCOS, EUGENIA

Orellana, Margarita de. Eugenia Marcos: los frutos prohibidos. *Artes de México*, no. 19 (Spring 93), p. 110. Il.

MARCUS, ROBERT

Interviews

Santiago, Chiori. Conversation with Art Collector Robert Marcus. *Latin American Art*, v. 4, no. 4 (Winter 92), pp. 38 – 39. Il.

MARECHAL, LEOPOLDO

Criticism of specific works

Adán Buenosayres

Vilanova, Angel. Motivo clásico y novela latinoamericana. *Nueva Revista de Filología Hispánica*, v. 40, no. 2 (July – Dec 92), pp. 1087 – 1099. Bibl.

Zonana, Víctor Gustavo. Geografía ocular: elementos para una poética de la visión en la poesía de vanguardia hispanoamericana: Huidobro y Marechal. *Revista Chilena de Literatura*, no. 40 (Nov 92), pp. 57 – 67. Bibl.

Días como flechas

Zonana, Víctor Gustavo. Geografía ocular: elementos para una poética de la visión en la poesía de vanguardia hispanoamericana: Huidobro y Marechal. *Revista Chilena de Literatura*, no. 40 (Nov 92), pp. 57 – 67. Bibl.

MARESCA, SILVIO JUAN

García Machado, Xiomara. Notas críticas para la "transcendencia" de un proyecto liberador: Mario Casalla y Silvio Maresca. *Islas*, no. 99 (May – Aug 91), pp. 15 – 20. Bibl.

MARGINALIZATION

See also
Informal sector (Economics)
Poverty
Slums

Chile

Cárdenas Gueudinot, Mario. Grupos marginados en los inicios de la era republicana: vagabundos, mendigos e indigentes. *Cuadernos de Historia (Chile)*, no. 11 (Dec 91), pp. 47 – 61. Bibl, tables.

Tironi B., Eugenio. *Autoritarismo, modernización y marginalidad: el caso de Chile* reviewed by Felipe Cabello (Review entitled "Don Andrés Bello: ¡Con cuánta nostalgia lo recordamos y cuánta falta nos hace!"). *Interciencia*, v. 18, no. 6 (Nov – Dec 93), pp. 329 – 333.

Dominican Republic

Mejía, Manuel Zacarías and Edmundo Morel. Los impactos de los desalojos: la constitución o reconstitución de las identidades. *Estudios Sociales (Dominican Republic)*, v. 26, no. 94 (Oct – Dec 93), pp. 45 – 74. Bibl.

Latin America

Research

Johnson, Peter T. Guidelines for Collecting Documentation on Marginalized Peoples and Ideas in Latin America. *SALALM Papers*, v. 34 (1989), pp. 455 – 458.

Mexican – American Border Region

Guillén López, Tonatiuh and Gerardo M. Ordóñez B. La marginalidad social en la frontera norte: discrepancias empíricas al concepto de la marginalidad. *Frontera Norte*, v. 4, no. 8 (July – Dec 92), pp. 149 – 163. Tables.

Mexico

Herrero Díaz, Luis F. Desarrollo urbano y estrategias de supervivencia en la periferia de la ciudad de México: Chalco; una aproximación antropológica. *Revista Española de Antropología Americana*, v. 23 (1993), pp. 213 – 232. Bibl, tables.

United States

Murray, Charles. Política social y marginalidad: algunas lecciones de la experiencia norteamericana. *Estudios Públicos (Chile)*, no. 52 (Spring 93), pp. 127 – 143.

MARÍA DE SAN JOSÉ

Myers, Kathleen Ann. A Glimpse of Family Life in Colonial Mexico: A Nun's Account. *Latin American Research Review*, v. 28, no. 2 (1993), pp. 63 – 87. Bibl, il.

MARIÁTEGUI, JOSÉ CARLOS

Löwy, Michael. Los intelectuales latinoamericanos y la crítica social de la modernidad. *Casa de las Américas*, no. 191 (Apr – June 93), pp. 100 – 105. Bibl.

Criticism and interpretation

Jaramillo, Diego. El hombre latinoamericano y la transformación social. *Islas*, no. 96 (May – Aug 90), pp. 18 – 26.

MARINA

See
Malinche

MARINE RESOURCES

See also
Fishing

Brazil

Arcifa, Marlene Sofia and Adriana Jorge Meschiatti. Distribution and Feeding Ecology of Fishes in a Brazilian Reservoir: Lake Monte Alegre. *Interciencia,* v. 18, no. 6 (Nov – Dec 93), pp. 302 – 313. Bibl, tables, charts.

Colombia

Castillo, Francisco A. and Zenaida Vizcaino Bravo. Observación del fitoplancton del Pacífico colombiano durante 1991 – 1992 en condiciones El Niño. *Bulletin de l'Institut Français d'Etudes Andines,* v. 22, no. 1 (1993), pp. 179 – 190. Bibl, il, maps.

Mexico

Neumann, Holly. Tales from the Deep. *Business Mexico,* v. 3, no. 6 (June 93), p. 28 +. Il, tables, maps.

Pacific Area

Shen, Glen T. Reconstruction of El Niño History from Reef Corals. *Bulletin de l'Institut Français d'Etudes Andines,* v. 22, no. 1 (1993), pp. 125 – 158. Bibl, tables, maps, charts.

Peru

Díaz, Amanda and Luc Ortlieb. El fenómeno El Niño y los moluscos de la costa peruana. *Bulletin de l'Institut Français d'Etudes Andines,* v. 22, no. 1 (1993), pp. 159 – 177. Bibl, tables, maps.

Southern Cone of South America

Schiavini, Adrián. Los lobos marinos como recurso para cazadores-recolectores marinos: el caso de Tierra del Fuego. *Latin American Antiquity,* v. 4, no. 4 (Dec 93), pp. 346 – 366. Bibl, tables, maps.

MARITAIN, JACQUES

Caiceo E., Jaime. El planteamiento filosófico – político de Maritain aplicado en Chile. *Estudios Sociales (Chile),* no. 76 (Apr – June 93), pp. 205 – 210. Bibl.

MARITIME TRANSPORTATION

See

Transportation, Maritime

MARIZ, VASCO

Vasco Mariz. *Inter-American Music Review,* v. 13, no. 2 (Spring – Summer 93), pp. iii – iv.

Correspondence, reminiscences, etc.

Mariz, Vasco. Perigrinação a Clavadel. *Revista do Instituto Histórico e Geográfico Brasileiro,* no. 370 (Jan – Mar 91), pp. 140 – 150.

MARKETING

See also

Advertising
Foreign trade promotion
Markets and merchants

Richers, Raimar. A emancipação do executivo de "marketing." *RAE; Revista de Administração de Empresas,* v. 33, no. 1 (Jan – Feb 93), pp. 52 – 65. Bibl.

Brazil

Arruda, Maria Cecília Coutinho de. A ética no "marketing" das indústrias de bens de consumo no Brasil. *RAE; Revista de Administração de Empresas,* v. 33, no. 1 (Jan – Feb 93), pp. 16 – 28. Bibl, tables, charts.

Souza, Maria Tereza Saraiva de. Uma estratégia de "marketing" para cooperativas de artesanato: o caso do Rio Grande do Norte. *RAE; Revista de Administração de Empresas,* v. 33, no. 1 (Jan – Feb 93), pp. 30 – 38. Bibl, tables, charts.

Jamaica

Meikle, Paulette. Spatio-Temporal Trends in Root Crop Production and Marketing in Jamaica. *Caribbean Geography,* v. 3, no. 4 (Sept 92), pp. 223 – 235. Bibl, tables, maps, charts.

Mexico

Bos, Cornelio A. Wanted Now!: Direct Mail. *Business Mexico,* v. 3, no. 3 (Mar 93), pp. 20 – 23.

Lara M., Carlos. Mexicans outside Mexico. *Business Mexico,* v. 3, no. 7 (July 93), pp. 24 – 26. Il, tables.

Romero Polanco, Emilio. Comercialización del café y el sector social en México. *Momento Económico,* no. 66 (Mar – Apr 93), pp. 14 – 17. Tables.

MARKETS AND MERCHANTS

Andean region

Harris, Olivia et al, eds. *La participación indígena en los mercados surandinos: estrategias y reproducción social, siglos XVI a XX* reviewed by Richard Warren. *Revista Andina,* v. 10, no. 2 (Dec 92), pp. 545 – 546.

Chile

Rojas Flores, Gonzalo. La casa comercial Gibbs y Co. y sus inversiones en Chile entre las décadas de 1920 y 1940. *Historia (Chile),* no. 26 (1991 – 1992), pp. 259 – 295. Bibl.

Colombia

Dávila L. de Guevara, Carlos. *El empresariado colombiano: una perspectiva histórica* reviewed by Luis Aurelio Ordóñez B. (Review entitled "Un balance historiográfico exhaustivo y sugestivo"). *Anuario Colombiano de Historia Social y de la Cultura,* no. 20 (1992), pp. 147 – 152.

Cuba

García Alvarez, Alejandro. *La gran burguesía comercial en Cuba, 1899 – 1920* reviewed by Antonio Santamaría García. *Revista de Indias,* v. 53, no. 197 (Jan – Apr 93), pp. 106 – 107.

Mexican – American Border Region

González Quiroga, Miguel. La puerta de México: los comerciantes texanos y el noreste mexicano, 1850 – 1880. *Estudios Sociológicos,* v. 11, no. 31 (Jan – Apr 93), pp. 209 – 236. Bibl, tables, maps.

Mexico

Cerutti, Mario. Españoles, gran comercio y brote fabril en el norte de México, 1850 – 1910. *Siglo XIX: Cuadernos,* v. 1, no. 2 (Feb 92), pp. 49 – 93. Bibl, tables.

Franco Cáceres, Iván. Familias, oligarquía y empresarios en Yucatán, 1879 – 1906. *Siglo XIX: Cuadernos,* v. 3, no. 7 (Oct 93), pp. 9 – 31. Bibl, tables.

Heath, Hilarie J. British Merchant Houses in Mexico, 1821 – 1860: Conforming Business Practices and Ethics. *Hispanic American Historical Review,* v. 73, no. 2 (May 93), pp. 261 – 290. Bibl.

Hoberman, Louisa Schell. *Mexico's Merchant Elite, 1590 – 1660: Silver, State, and Society* reviewed by Stanley J. Stein. *Hispanic American Historical Review,* v. 73, no. 1 (Feb 93), pp. 151 – 152.

— *Mexico's Merchant Elite, 1590 – 1660: Silver, State, and Society* reviewed by Gabriel Haslip-Viera. *Colonial Latin American Review,* v. 2, no. 1 – 2 (1993), pp. 296 – 298.

— *Mexico's Merchant Elite, 1590 – 1660: Silver, State, and Society* reviewed by Richard L. Garner. *Colonial Latin American Historical Review,* v. 2, no. 3 (Summer 93), pp. 369 – 371.

— *Mexico's Merchant Elite, 1590 – 1660: Silver, State, and Society* reviewed by Silvia C. Mallo. *Revista de Historia de América,* no. 113 (Jan – June 92), pp. 170 – 172.

Rubial García, Antonio. Un mercader de plata andaluz en Nueva España: Diego del Castillo, 161? – 1683. *Anuario de Estudios Americanos,* v. 49 (1992), pp. 143 – 170. Bibl, il.

Torales Pacheco, María Cristina. Consideraciones generales sobre los comerciantes de Veracruz en la segunda mitad del s. XVIII. *La Palabra y el Hombre,* no. 83 (July – Sept 92), pp. 314 – 321. Bibl.

Victoria, José Guadalupe. Noticias sobre la antigua plaza y el Mercado del Volador de la ciudad de México. *Anales del Instituto de Investigaciones Estéticas,* v. 16, no. 62 (1991), pp. 69 – 91. Bibl, il.

Yuste, Carmen, ed. *Comerciantes mexicanos en el siglo XVIII* reviewed by Frédérique Langue. *Caravelle,* no. 60 (1993), pp. 151 – 152.

Peru

Bronner, Fred. Church, Crown, and Commerce in Seventeenth-Century Lima: A Synoptic Interpretation. *Jahrbuch für Geschichte von Staat, Wirtschaft und Gesellschaft Lateinamerikas,* v. 29 (1992), pp. 75 – 89. Bibl.

Río de la Plata region

Gelman, Jorge Daniel. Los caminos del mercado: campesinos, estancieros y pulperos en una región del Río de la Plata colonial. *Latin American Research Review*, v. 28, no. 2 (1993), pp. 89 – 118. Bibl, tables.

MAROONS

Yacou, Alain. La insurgencia negra en la isla de Cuba en la primera mitad del siglo XIX. *Revista de Indias*, v. 53, no. 197 (Jan – Apr 93), pp. 23 – 51. Bibl.

MARQUÉS, RENÉ

Bibliography

Torres Ortiz, Víctor F. El teatro de René Marqués: bibliografía anotada. *Revista Interamericana de Bibliografía*, v. 42, no. 2 (1992), pp. 251 – 257.

Criticism of specific works

El juramento

Caballero Wangüemert, María del Milagro. Discurso histórico y carnavalización de la historia: "El juramento" de René Marqués. *Revista Iberoamericana*, v. 59, no. 162 – 163 (Jan – June 93), pp. 145 – 156. Bibl.

Peregrinación

Castillo, Jorge Luis. De la guerra a las sombras: sobre los pasos de *Peregrinación* de René Marqués. *Revista Iberoamericana*, v. 59, no. 162 – 163 (Jan – June 93), pp. 157 – 167. Bibl.

MÁRQUEZ, MIGUEL

Criticism and interpretation

Ramírez Quintero, Gonzalo. La poesía venezolana actual: tres ejemplos. *Inti*, no. 37 – 38 (Spring – Fall 93), pp. 187 – 195.

MARRAS, SERGIO

Criticism of specific works

América Latina

Pérez V., Carlos. América Latina: marca registrada. *Mensaje*, v. 42, no. 416 (Jan – Feb 93), pp. 20 – 21.

MARRIAGE

See also
Divorce
Family
Subdivision *Clergy - Marriage* under *Catholic Church*

Reyes, Carmen et al. Matrimonios: la ardua búsqueda de felicidad; debates (Introduced by G. Arroyo). *Mensaje*, v. 42, no. 425 (Dec 93), pp. 629 – 636.

Stella, Aldo. ¿Padre, puedo casarme de nuevo? *Revista Javeriana*, v. 61, no. 599 (Oct 93), pp. 305 – 318.

Argentina

Dellaferrera, Nelson C. *Catálogo de causas matrimoniales: obispado de Córdoba, 1688 - 1810* reviewed by Jesús María García Añoveros. *Revista de Indias*, v. 53, no. 197 (Jan – Apr 93), p. 101.

Brazil

Nazzari, Muriel. *Disappearance of the Dowry: Women, Families, and Social Change in São Paulo, Brazil, 1600 - 1900* reviewed by Susan M. Socolow. *The Americas*, v. 49, no. 3 (Jan 93), pp. 414 – 415.

— *Disappearance of the Dowry: Women, Families, and Social Change in São Paulo, Brazil, 1600 - 1900* reviewed by John E. Kicza. *Colonial Latin American Review*, v. 2, no. 1 – 2 (1993), pp. 308 – 311.

— *Disappearance of the Dowry: Women, Families, and Social Change in São Paulo, Brazil, 1600 - 1900* reviewed by Sandra Lauderdale Graham. *Journal of Latin American Studies*, v. 25, no. 1 (Feb 93), pp. 193 – 194.

— *Disappearance of the Dowry: Women, Families, and Social Change in São Paulo, Brazil, 1600 - 1900* reviewed by Dain Borges. *Luso-Brazilian Review*, v. 30, no. 1 (Summer 93), pp. 141 – 142.

Telles, Edward E. Racial Distance and Region in Brazil: Intermarriage in Brazilian Urban Areas. *Latin American Research Review*, v. 28, no. 2 (1993), pp. 141 – 162. Bibl, tables.

Colombia

Rodríguez Jiménez, Pablo. *Seducción, amancebamiento y abandono en la colonia* reviewed by Frédérique Langue. *Anuario de Estudios Americanos*, v. 49, Suppl. 2 (1992), pp. 261 – 262.

Costa Rica

Cerdas Bokhan, Dora. Matrimonio y vida cotidiana en el graven central costarricense, 1851 – 1890. *Revista de Historia (Costa Rica)*, no. 26 (July – Dec 92), pp. 69 – 95. Bibl.

Sources

Cerdas Bokhan, Dora. Las fuentes eclesiásticas como develadoras de la vida cotidiana de los fieles. *Revista de Historia (Costa Rica)*, no. 25 (Jan – June 92), pp. 251 – 259.

Cuba

Statistics

Catasús Cervera, Sonia Isabel. La nupcialidad durante la década de los ochenta en Cuba. *Estudios Demográficos y Urbanos*, v. 7, no. 2 – 3 (May – Dec 92), pp. 465 – 477. Bibl, tables.

Latin America

Lavrin, Asunción, ed. *Sexuality and Marriage in Colonial Latin America* reviewed by K. Lynn Stoner (Review entitled "Whores, Witches, and Unwed Mothers: Recent Scholarship on the Control of Sexuality"). *Studies in Latin American Popular Culture*, v. 12 (1993), pp. 207 – 214.

Law and legislation

Pareja Ortiz, María del Carmen. Un aspecto de la vida cotidiana: la mujer ante el matrimonio en la legislación de Indias. *Hoy Es Historia*, v. 10, no. 60 (Nov – Dec 93), pp. 50 – 60. Il.

Mexican – American Border Region

Gutmann, Myron P. et al. Matrimonio y migración en la frontera: patrones de nupcialidad en Texas, 1850 - 1910. *Historia Mexicana*, v. 42, no. 1 (July – Sept 92), pp. 45 – 76. Bibl, tables, charts.

Mexico

Pescador C., Juan Javier. La nupcialidad urbana preindustrial y los límites del mestizaje: características y evolución de los patrones de nupcialidad en la ciudad de México, 1700 – 1850. *Estudios Demográficos y Urbanos*, v. 7, no. 1 (Jan – Apr 92), pp. 137 – 168. Bibl, tables.

Rabell Romero, Cecilia Andrea. Matrimonio y raza en una parroquia rural: San Luis de la Paz, Guanajuato, 1715 – 1810. *Historia Mexicana*, v. 42, no. 1 (July – Sept 92), pp. 3 – 44. Bibl, tables, charts.

Statistics

Quilodrán de Aguirre, Julieta. Cambios y permanencias de la nupcialidad en México. *Revista Mexicana de Sociología*, v. 55, no. 1 (Jan – Mar 93), pp. 17 – 40. Bibl, tables, maps, charts.

Paraguay

Law and legislation

Moreno Ruffinelli, José A. *Régimen patrimonial del matrimonio: Ley no. 1/92 comentada* (Review). *Revista Paraguaya de Sociología*, v. 29, no. 85 (Sept – Dec 92), p. 190.

Peru

Cook, Alexandra Parma and Noble David Cook. *Good Faith and Truthful Ignorance: A Case of Transatlantic Bigamy* reviewed by Meredith Dodge. *Colonial Latin American Historical Review*, v. 1, no. 1 (Fall 92), pp. 124 – 125.

— *Good Faith and Truthful Ignorance: A Case of Transatlantic Bigamy* reviewed by Kenneth J. Andrien. *Colonial Latin American Review*, v. 2, no. 1 – 2 (1993), pp. 275 – 277.

Venezuela

Fuentes Bajo, María Dolores. Amor y desamor en la Venezuela hispánica: Caracas, 1701 - 1791. *Boletín de la Academia Nacional de la Historia (Venezuela)*, v. 75, no. 298 (Apr – June 92), pp. 49 – 62. Bibl.

MARTÍ, JOSÉ

Biography

Fernández Retamar, Roberto. Sobre la edición cubana de *Martí, el apóstol*. *Revista de Crítica Literaria Latinoamericana*, v. 19, no. 37 (Jan – June 93), pp. 345 – 351.

Criticism and interpretation

Campo, Angel Esteban-P. del. Bécquer y Martí: una audiencia especial con el sentimiento. *Anuario de Letras (Mexico)*, v. 30 (1992), pp. 177 – 189. Bibl.

Díaz, María Eugenia. Liberación en las luchas latinoamericanas. *Islas*, no. 98 (Jan – Apr 91), pp. 167 – 176. Charts.

Ette, Ottmar. *José Martí, Teil I: Apostel, Dicther, Revolutinär; Eine Geschichte seiner Rezeption* reviewed by José Morales Saravia. *Revista de Crítica Literaria Latinoamericana*, v. 19, no. 38 (July – Dec 93), pp. 406 – 411.

Fernández Retamar, Roberto. Desde el Martí de Ezequiel Martínez Estrada. *Cuadernos Americanos*, no. 42, Nueva época (Nov – Dec 93), pp. 131 – 147.

Fraser, Howard M. *La Edad de Oro* and José Martí's Modernist Ideology for Children. *Revista Interamericana de Bibliografía*, v. 42, no. 2 (1992), pp. 223 – 232. Bibl.

García González, José. Iteración léxico – semántica en las metáforas de José Martí sobre la patria cubana. *Islas*, no. 96 (May – Aug 90), pp. 139 – 149. Bibl.

Juan, Adelaida de. José Martí y el arte mexicano. *La Palabra y el Hombre*, no. 82 (Apr – June 92), pp. 45 – 56. Bibl.

Rotker, Susana. *Fundación de una escritura: las crónicas de José Martí* reviewed by Richard B. Gray. *Hispanic American Historical Review*, v. 73, no. 3 (Aug 93), pp. 483 – 484.

Schulman, Iván A. ¿Más allá de la literatura?: un álbum de Cayo Hueso, 1891 – 1892. *Casa de las Américas*, no. 190 (Jan – Mar 93), pp. 50 – 55. Bibl.

Vitier, Cintio. La tierra adivinada. *Cuadernos Americanos*, no. 39, Nueva época (May – June 93), pp. 88 – 90.

Criticism of specific works

Nuestra América

Fernández Retamar, Roberto. Más de cien años de previsión: algunas reflexiones sobre el concepto martiano de *Nuestra América*. *Cuadernos Americanos*, no. 40, Nueva época (July – Aug 93), pp. 65 – 77.

— *Nuestra América*: cien años. *Nueva Revista de Filología Hispánica*, v. 40, no. 2 (July – Dec 92), pp. 791 – 806.

Lagmanovich, David. Nueva lectura de *Nuestra América*. *Casa de las Américas*, no. 191 (Apr – June 93), pp. 107 – 110.

Versos sencillos

Zimmermann Martí, María. Estudio paralelo de *Azul* y *Versos sencillos*. *Revista Cultural Lotería*, v. 51, no. 390 (July – Aug 92), pp. 65 – 84. Bibl.

Foreign influences

Serna Arnáiz, Mercedes. Algunas dilucidaciones sobre el krausismo en José Martí. *Cuadernos Hispanoamericanos*, no. 521 (Nov 93), pp. 137 – 145.

MARTÍNEZ, JESÚS

Ramírez, Fermín. El paisaje de Jesús Martínez. *Plural (Mexico)*, v. 22, no. 261 (June 93), pp. 48 – 54. Il.

MARTÍNEZ, VÍCTOR

Interviews

Castello, Antonio Emilio. Entrevista al ex-vicepresidente de la república, dr. Víctor Martínez. *Todo Es Historia*, v. 27, no. 317 (Dec 93), pp. 84 – 95. Il.

MARTÍNEZ CAÑAS, MARÍA

Damian, Carol. María Martínez Cañas: el viaje a casa (Accompanied by the English original, translated by Ignacio Zuleta Ll.). *Art Nexus*, no. 9 (June – Aug 93), pp. 114 – 117. Il.

Turner, Elisa. María Martínez Cañas. *Latin American Art*, v. 5, no. 1 (Spring 93), pp. 85 – 86. Il.

MARTÍNEZ ESTRADA, EZEQUIEL

Criticism and interpretation

Burgos, Nidia. Un documento inédito de Martínez Estrada: la creación de otra *Tierra purpúrea;* una república libertaria, federal y representativa. *Cuadernos Americanos*, no. 42, Nueva época (Nov – Dec 93), pp. 157 – 164. Bibl.

Earle, Peter G. Las soledades de Martínez Estrada. *Cuadernos Americanos*, no. 42, Nueva época (Nov – Dec 93), pp. 148 – 156.

Fernández Retamar, Roberto. Desde el Martí de Ezequiel Martínez Estrada. *Cuadernos Americanos*, no. 42, Nueva época (Nov – Dec 93), pp. 131 – 147.

Weinberg, Liliana Irene. Diálogo sobre España y América. *Nueva Revista de Filología Hispánica*, v. 40, no. 2 (July – Dec 92), pp. 807 – 821. Bibl.

— Ezequiel Martínez Estrada y el universo de la paradoja. *Cuadernos Americanos*, no. 42, Nueva época (Nov – Dec 93), pp. 165 – 199. Bibl.

Criticism of specific works

Muerte y transfiguración de 'Martín Fierro'

Weinberg, Liliana Irene. *Ezequiel Martínez Estrada y la interpretación del 'Martín Fierro'* reviewed by María Andueza. *Cuadernos Americanos*, no. 40, Nueva época (July – Aug 93), pp. 229 – 234.

— *Ezequiel Martínez Estrada y la interpretación del 'Martín Fierro'* reviewed by Carmen Vrljicak-Espaín. *Todo Es Historia*, v. 26, no. 310 (May 93), p. 81. Il.

MARTÍNEZ HERRERA, JUAN

Arnstein, Gustavo. El Quijote querrequerre. *Boletín de la Academia Nacional de la Historia (Venezuela)*, v. 76, no. 301 (Jan – Mar 93), pp. 113 – 114.

MARTÍNEZ RUIZ, JOSÉ

Ouimette, Victor. Azorín y la América española. *Insula*, no. 556 (Apr 93), pp. 14 – 15.

MARTINI, JUAN CARLOS

Criticism and interpretation

Solotorevsky, Myrna. La tetralogía de Martini o la obsesión de la historia. *Hispamérica*, v. 21, no. 62 (Aug 92), pp. 3 – 19. Bibl.

MARTINIQUE

See
  Blacks in literature – Martinique

MARTINS, ANTÔNIO JOSÉ SANTANA

Holston, Mark. Tom Zé: The Conscience of Brazil's Tropicalismo. *Américas*, v. 45, no. 1 (Jan – Feb 93), pp. 58 – 59. Il.

MARTINS, JACKSON DE FIGUEIREDO

See
  Figueiredo, Jackson de

MARTYRS

El Salvador

Tercer aniversario de los mártires de la UCA (Two documents). *ECA; Estudios Centroamericanos*, v. 47, no. 529 – 530 (Nov – Dec 92), pp. 1085 – 1086.

Tojeira, José María. Tercer aniversario de los mártires de la UCA: homilia. *ECA; Estudios Centroamericanos*, v. 47, no. 529 – 530 (Nov – Dec 92), pp. 951 – 953.

Venezuela

Campo del Pozo, Fernando. Los mártires agustinos en la misión de Aricagua, Venezuela. *Boletín de la Academia Nacional de la Historia (Venezuela)*, v. 76, no. 302 (Apr – June 93), pp. 119 – 129. Bibl.

MARXIAN ECONOMICS

Rosell Gómez, Eunice et al. Dussel: dependencia y liberación en los marcos de la teoría económica. *Islas*, no. 99 (May – Aug 91), pp. 155 – 159.

MARXISM
See also
Communism
Socialism

Morales Hernández, Xiomara et al. Gaspar Jorge García Galló y su labor de divulgación de la filosofía marxista – leninista. *Islas,* no. 98 (Jan – Apr 91), pp. 128 – 134. Bibl.

Argentina
Chávez, Fermín. Un marxista alemán en San Luis. *Todo Es Historia,* v. 26, no. 310 (May 93), pp. 48 – 52. Il.

Latin America
Casañas Díaz, Mirta. La recepción del marxismo en la obra de Leopoldo Zea. *Islas,* no. 96 (May – Aug 90), pp. 164 – 176. Bibl.

Figueroa Casas, Vilma and Israel López Pino. Rodney Arismendi: su posición político – ideológica. *Islas,* no. 96 (May – Aug 90), pp. 71 – 77.

Guadarrama González, Pablo M. Balance y perspectivas del marxismo y el antimarxismo en América Latina. *Islas,* no. 98 (Jan – Apr 91), pp. 188 – 200. Bibl.

Harris, Richard L. *Marxism, Socialism, and Democracy in Latin America* reviewed by Carlos M. Vilas. *Journal of Latin American Studies,* v. 25, no. 1 (Feb 93), p. 215.

Löwy, Michael, ed. *Marxism in Latin America from 1909 to the Present: An Anthology* reviewed by Sheldon B. Liss. *Hispanic American Historical Review,* v. 73, no. 4 (Nov 93), pp. 728 – 729.

Pérez Villacampa, Gilberto. Utopía y marxismo: notas para un estudio. *Islas,* no. 96 (May – Aug 90), pp. 83 – 88.

Plá León, Rafael. Marxismo: ¿Eurocentrismo o universidad? *Islas,* no. 96 (May – Aug 90), pp. 132 – 138. Bibl.

Ramos Serpa, Gerardo. Gramsci: salvación o desacierto del marxismo latinoamericano. *Islas,* no. 98 (Jan – Apr 91), pp. 157 – 166. Bibl.

Rojas Gómez, Miguel. Alejandro Serrano Caldera: una nueva filosofía de la conciencia y la libertad. *Islas,* no. 99 (May – Aug 91), pp. 130 – 154. Bibl.

Mexico
Carr, Barry. *Marxism and Communism in Twentieth-Century Mexico* reviewed by George Philip. *Bulletin of Latin American Research,* v. 12, no. 2 (May 93), pp. 230 – 231.

MARY, VIRGIN
Calderón, Gabriela. Amor y tradición en la fiesta de la Virgen de las Peñas. *Mensaje,* v. 42, no. 425 (Dec 93), pp. 617 – 618. Il.

MASONIC MOVEMENT
See
Freemasons

MASS MEDIA
See also
Advertising
Audiovisual education
Censorship
Children's television
Freedom of the press
Mexican Americans and mass media
Motion pictures
Newspapers
Periodicals
Popular culture
Press
Press and politics
Radio broadcasting
Tape recorders and recordings
Television
Video tape recorders and recording
Women in mass media

Baena Paz, Guillermina. Perspectivas de la comunicación en los noventa. *Revista Mexicana de Ciencias Políticas y Sociales,* v. 38, Nueva época, no. 154 (Oct – Dec 93), pp. 103 – 114.

Conejeros A., Senén et al. ¿En qué fallan los periodistas y los medios de comunicación?: debates. *Mensaje,* v. 42, no. 419 (June 93), pp. 194 – 201. Il.

Sarlo Sabajanes, Beatriz. Notas sobre política y cultura. *Cuadernos Hispanoamericanos,* no. 517 – 519 (July – Sept 93), pp. 51 – 64.

Argentina
Lozada, Salvador María. Dos dictámenes contra la concentración del poder. *Realidad Económica,* no. 113 (Jan – Feb 93), pp. 45 – 51.

Caribbean area
Lent, John A. *Mass Communication in the Caribbean* reviewed by Idsa E. Alegría-Ortega. *Caribbean Studies,* v. 25, no. 1 – 2 (Jan – July 92), pp. 164 – 166.

Soderlund, Walter C. and Stuart H. Surlin. *Mass Media and the Caribbean* reviewed by Alan Frizzell. *Canadian Journal of Latin American and Caribbean Studies,* v. 17, no. 34 (1992), pp. 146 – 147.

Latin America
McFadyen, Deidre. Invigorating the Public Debate: Popular Media in the Age of Mass Communications. *NACLA Report on the Americas,* v. 27, no. 2 (Sept – Oct 93), pp. 35 – 37 +. Bibl, il.

Pérez-Yglesias, María. Entre lo escolar y los medios informativos: políticas neoliberales y educación. *Revista de Ciencias Sociales (Costa Rica),* no. 57 (Sept 92), pp. 41 – 55. Bibl.

Study and teaching
Río Reynaga, Julio del. Desarrollo y tendencias de la enseñanza en comunicación colectiva. *Revista Mexicana de Ciencias Políticas y Sociales,* v. 37, Nueva época, no. 149 (July – Sept 92), pp. 153 – 176. Bibl.

Mexico
Barrera Carranza, Estanislao. Prostitución y medios masivos de comunicación social. *La Palabra y el Hombre,* no. 84 (Oct – Dec 92), pp. 39 – 61. Bibl.

Bohmann, Karin. *Medios de comunicación y sistemas informativos en México* reviewed by Susana González Reyna. *Revista Mexicana de Ciencias Políticas y Sociales,* v. 38, Nueva época, no. 154 (Oct – Dec 93), pp. 187 – 191.

García Canclini, Néstor. La cultura visual en la época del posnacionalismo: ¿Quién nos va a contar la identidad? *Nueva Sociedad,* no. 127 (Sept – Oct 93), pp. 23 – 31.

Ruge S., Tiahoga. It's Not Nice to Fool Mother Nature. *Business Mexico,* v. 3, no. 1 (Jan – Feb 93), pp. 63 – 64. Il.

Peru
Law and legislation
MacGregor, Felipe E. La ética periodística ante la información de la violencia. *Apuntes (Peru),* no. 29 (July – Dec 91), pp. 27 – 34. Tables.

Puerto Rico
Subervi-Vélez, Federico A. et al. Los medios de comunicación masiva en Puerto Rico. *Homines,* v. 15 – 16, no. 2 – 1 (Oct 91 – Dec 92), pp. 39 – 60. Bibl.

MASS MEDIA AND THE ARTS
Cuba
Pallottini, Renata. Cuba: os artistas estão vivos. *Vozes,* v. 86, no. 5 (Sept – Oct 92), pp. 32 – 36.

MASTRETTA, ANGELES
Criticism of specific works
Arráncame la vida
Gerendas, Judit. Hacia una problematización de la escritura femenina. *Escritura (Venezuela),* v. 16, no. 31 – 32 (Jan – Dec 91), pp. 91 – 101.

Mujeres de ojos grandes
Cherchi, Grazia. Ponerse la sonrisa (Translated by Aurora Tejeda). *Nexos,* v. 16, no. 183 (Mar 93), p. 59.

Interviews
De Beer, Gabriella. Entre la aventura y el litigio: una entrevista con Angela Mastretta. *Nexos,* v. 16, no. 184 (Apr 93), pp. 33 – 39.

López, Verónica. La penúltima pregunta. *Nexos,* v. 16, no. 184 (Apr 93), pp. 34 – 37.

MATANZAS, CUBA

Bergad, Laird W. *Cuban Rural Society in the Nineteenth Century: The Social and Economic History of Monoculture in Matanzas* reviewed by Gert Oostindie. *European Review of Latin American and Caribbean Studies,* no. 53 (Dec 92), pp. 111 – 112.

González García, Juan Francisco. Matanzas: su historia, 1868 – 1878. *Islas,* no. 97 (Sept – Dec 90), pp. 64 – 78. Bibl.

— Matanzas: su historia; los tiempos de tregua, 1878 – 1895. *Islas,* no. 98 (Jan – Apr 91), pp. 47 – 57. Bibl.

MATE

See
Tea

MATHEMATICS

See also
Functional analysis (Mathematics)

Merrell, Floyd Fenly. *Unthinking Thinking: Jorge Luis Borges, Mathematics, and the New Physics* reviewed by Harley D. Oberhelman. *Hispania (USA),* v. 76, no. 2 (May 93), pp. 289 – 290.

MATLATZINCA INDIANS

Menegus Bornemann, Margarita. *Del señorío a la república de indios: el caso de Toluca, 1500 – 1600* reviewed by Michel Bertrand. *Caravelle,* no. 60 (1993), pp. 143 – 147.

MATO GROSSO, BRAZIL

Wilcox, Robert. Paraguayans and the Making of the Brazilian Far West, 1870 – 1935. *The Americas,* v. 49, no. 4 (Apr 93), pp. 479 – 512. Bibl, tables, maps.

MATOLA, SHARON

Cohn, Jeffrey P. Keeper of the Wild Side. *Américas,* v. 45, no. 2 (Mar – Apr 93), pp. 34 – 37. Il.

MATOS, GREGÓRIO DE

See
Mattos Guerra, Gregório de

MATSIGUENGA INDIANS

See
Machiganga Indians

MATTOS GUERRA, GREGÓRIO DE

Criticism and interpretation

Costigan, Lúcia Helena Santiago. *A sátira e o intelectual criollo na colônia: Gregório de Matos e Juan del Valle y Caviedes* reviewed by Pedro Carlos L. Fonseca. *Colonial Latin American Review,* v. 2, no. 1 – 2 (1993), pp. 300 – 302.

Fiction

Miranda, Ana María. *Bay of All Saints and Every Conceivable Sin,* a translation of *Boca do inferno,* translated by Giovanni Pontiero. Reviewed by Clifford E. Landers. *Review,* no. 47 (Fall 93), pp. 99 – 101.

MATURANA, HUMBERTO R.

Quer Antich, Santiago. Conspiremos por la democracia o la democracia "a la Maturana." *Estudios Sociales (Chile),* no. 76 (Apr – June 93), pp. 197 – 203.

MAUÁ, IRINÊO EVANGELISTA DE SOUZA

Silveira, Maria Dutra da. Mauá e a revolução farroupilha. *Hoy Es Historia,* v. 10, no. 59 (Sept – Oct 93), pp. 75 – 81. Il.

MAXIMILIAN, EMPEROR OF MEXICO

Pictorial works

Barnes, Julian. El fusilamiento de Maximiliano (Translated by Ana Becerril). *Nexos,* v. 16, no. 187 (July 93), pp. 39 – 47. Il.

Wilson-Bareau, Juliet. *Manet: 'The Execution of Maximilian'; Painting, Politics, and Censorship* reviewed by Paul J. Vanderwood. *Hispanic American Historical Review,* v. 73, no. 2 (May 93), p. 331.

MAYA LANGUAGES

García Ruiz, Jesús F. El misionero, las lenguas mayas y la traducción de los conceptos del catolicismo ibérico en Guatemala. *Folklore Americano,* no. 53 (Jan – June 92), pp. 103 – 131. Bibl.

Hanks, William F. *Referential Practice: Language and Lived Space among the Maya* reviewed by John M. Watanabe. *Mesoamérica (USA),* v. 13, no. 23 (June 92), pp. 201 – 205. Charts.

Hanks, William F. and Don Stephen Rice, eds. *Word and Image in Maya Culture: Explorations in Language, Writing, and Representation* reviewed by Stephen D. Houston. *Mesoamérica (USA),* v. 13, no. 23 (June 92), pp. 191 – 193.

— *Word and Image in Maya Culture: Explorations in Language, Writing, and Representation* reviewed by Luis T. Sanz. *Revista Española de Antropología Americana,* v. 23 (1993), pp. 260 – 262.

Hofling, Charles Andrew. *Itza Maya Texts with a Grammatical Overview* reviewed by Barbara Edmonson. *Hispanic American Historical Review,* v. 73, no. 3 (Aug 93), pp. 498 – 499.

— *Itza Maya Texts with a Grammatical Overview* reviewed by Enrique Sam Colop. *Mesoamérica (USA),* v. 13, no. 24 (Dec 92), pp. 489 – 490.

Study and teaching

Tozzer, Alfred M. Una evaluación de los trabajos referentes al lenguaje maya. *La Palabra y el Hombre,* no. 82 (Apr – June 92), pp. 95 – 106. Bibl, maps.

MAYA LITERATURE

See also
Chilam Balam books
Mayas – Writing
Popol Vuh
Names of specific codices

History and criticism

Lara Figueroa, Celso A. Presencia del cuento popular en Guatemala: estudio histórico – etnográfico del tipo AT 325. *Folklore Americano,* no. 52 (July – Dec 91), pp. 7 – 37. Bibl, maps.

Ligorred, Francesc. "Yaax indios yoko cab": pronosticar; una práctica estimulante y poética entre los mayas. *Iberoamericana,* v. 16, no. 47 – 48 (1992), pp. 6 – 20. Bibl, il.

Padial Guerchoux, Anita Louise and Angel Manuel Vázquez-Bigi. *Quiche Vinak: tragedia; nueva versión española y estudio histórico – literario del llamado 'Rabinal-Achí'* reviewed by Enrique Sam Colop. *Mesoamérica (USA),* v. 13, no. 24 (Dec 92), pp. 465 – 473.

Peñalosa, Fernando. El cuento popular: patrimonio del pueblo maya del sur de Mesoamérica. *Folklore Americano,* no. 52 (July – Dec 91), pp. 39 – 92. Bibl.

MAYAS

Art and architecture

Benson, Elizabeth P. and Gillett Good Griffin, eds. *Maya Iconography* reviewed by Martha J. Macri. *Mesoamérica (USA),* v. 13, no. 24 (Dec 92), pp. 490 – 492.

Fernández Marquínez, María Yolanda and Alfonso Muñoz Cosme. Estilos arquitectónicos y estadios constructivos en el Grupo May, Oxkintok, Yucatán. *Revista Española de Antropología Americana,* v. 23 (1993), pp. 67 – 82. Bibl, il.

Maldonado Cárdenas, Rubén. Las pinturas de Sodzil, Yucatán, México. *Revista Española de Antropología Americana,* v. 23 (1993), pp. 101 – 111. Bibl, il.

Millet Cámara, Luis et al. Tecoh, Izamal: nobleza indígena y conquista española. *Latin American Antiquity,* v. 4, no. 1 (Mar 93), pp. 48 – 58. Bibl, il, maps.

Research

Desmond, Lawrence Gustave and Phyllis Mauch Messenger. *A Dream of Maya: Augustus and Alice Le Plongeon in Nineteenth-Century Yucatán* reviewed by Kevin Gosner. *Hispanic American Historical Review,* v. 73, no. 3 (Aug 93), pp. 532 – 533.

Astronomy

Martin, Frederick. A *Dresden Codex* Eclipse Sequence: Projections for the Years 1970 – 1992. *Latin American Antiquity,* v. 4, no. 1 (Mar 93), pp. 74 – 93. Bibl, il, tables.

Bibliography

Ashmore, Wendy. The Theme "Is" Variation: Recent Publications on the Archaeology of Southern Mesoamerica (Review article). *Latin American Research Review*, v. 28, no. 1 (1993), pp. 128 – 140. Bibl.

Cabello, Felipe C. La arqueología y la cultura maya: a propósito del premio Nobel de la paz, 1992 (Review article). *Interciencia*, v. 18, no. 5 (Sept – Oct 93), pp. 272 – 275.

Tedlock, Barbara. Mayans and Mayan Studies from 2000 B.C. to A.D. 1992 (Review article). *Latin American Research Review*, v. 28, no. 3 (1993), pp. 153 – 173. Bibl.

Calendars

Martin, Frederick. A *Dresden Codex* Eclipse Sequence: Projections for the Years 1970 – 1992. *Latin American Antiquity*, v. 4, no. 1 (Mar 93), pp. 74 – 93. Bibl, il, tables.

Costume and adornment

Otzoy, Irma. Identidad y trajes mayas. *Mesoamérica (USA)*, v. 13, no. 23 (June 92), pp. 95 – 112. Bibl, tables.

Culture

García Escobar, Carlos René. Historia antigua: historia y etnografía del *Rabinal Achí*. *La Tradición Popular*, no. 81 (1991), Issue. Bibl, il.

Wilk, Richard R. *Household Ecology: Economic Change and Domestic Life among the Kekchi Maya in Belize* reviewed by Joseph O. Palacio. *Belizean Studies*, v. 21, no. 1 (May 93), pp. 25 – 26.

— *Household Ecology: Economic Change and Domestic Life among the Kekchi Maya in Belize* reviewed by Laura Rival. *Bulletin of Latin American Research*, v. 12, no. 1 (Jan 93), pp. 125 – 126.

— *Household Ecology: Economic Change and Domestic Life among the Kekchi Maya in Belize* reviewed by Norman Ashcraft. *Journal of Developing Areas*, v. 27, no. 3 (Apr 93), pp. 422 – 424.

Dwellings

García Targa, Juan. Unidades habitacionales en el área maya. *Boletín Americanista*, v. 33, no. 42 – 43 (1992 – 1993), pp. 231 – 254. Bibl, il.

Economic conditions

Brannon, Jeffery T. and Gilbert Michael Joseph, eds. *Land, Labor, and Capital in Modern Yucatán: Essays in Regional History and Political Economy* reviewed by Donald F. Stevens. *The Americas*, v. 49, no. 4 (Apr 93), pp. 558 – 559.

Ethnic identity

Otzoy, Irma. Identidad y trajes mayas. *Mesoamérica (USA)*, v. 13, no. 23 (June 92), pp. 95 – 112. Bibl, tables.

Watanabe, John M. *Maya Saints and Souls in a Changing World* reviewed by John Managhan. *Hispanic American Historical Review*, v. 73, no. 4 (Nov 93), pp. 720 – 721.

Food

Robertiello, Jack. The Quest for Maya Meals (Includes recipes). *Américas*, v. 45, no. 3 (May – June 93), pp. 58 – 59. Il.

Government relations

Gosner, Kevin. *Soldiers of the Virgin: The Moral Economy of a Colonial Maya Rebellion* reviewed by Robert M. Hill II. *The Americas*, v. 50, no. 2 (Oct 93), pp. 274 – 276.

— *Soldiers of the Virgin: The Moral Economy of a Colonial Maya Rebellion* reviewed by Kenneth Mills. *Bulletin of Latin American Research*, v. 12, no. 2 (May 93), pp. 223 – 224.

— *Soldiers of the Virgin: The Moral Economy of a Colonial Maya Rebellion* reviewed by Stephen Webre. *Colonial Latin American Historical Review*, v. 2, no. 1 (Winter 93), pp. 109 – 110.

— *Soldiers of the Virgin: The Moral Economy of a Colonial Maya Rebellion* reviewed by Linda A. Newson. *Journal of Latin American Studies*, v. 25, no. 3 (Oct 93), pp. 655 – 656.

Jones, Grant D. *Maya Resistance to Spanish Rule: Time and History on a Colonial Frontier* reviewed by J. C. Cambranes. *Mesoamérica (USA)*, v. 13, no. 23 (June 92), pp. 157 – 177. Bibl.

Le Bot, Yvon. *La guerre en terre maya: communauté, violence et modernité au Guatemala, 1970 – 1992* reviewed by J. P. Pérez Sáinz. *Journal of Latin American Studies*, v. 25, no. 3 (Oct 93), pp. 670 – 672.

— *La guerre en terre maya: communauté, violence et modernité au Guatemala, 1970 – 1992* reviewed by Maxime Haubert. *Tiers Monde*, v. 34, no. 136 (Oct – Dec 93), pp. 952 – 953.

— *Le palimpseste maya: violence, communauté et territoire dans le conflit guatémaltèque. Cahiers des Amériques Latines*, no. 13 (1992), pp. 87 – 105. Bibl, maps.

Millet Cámara, Luis et al. Tecoh, Izamal: nobleza indígena y conquista española. *Latin American Antiquity*, v. 4, no. 1 (Mar 93), pp. 48 – 58. Bibl, il, maps.

Sullivan, Paul R. *Conversaciones inconclusas*, a translation of *Unfinished Conversations: Mayas and Foreigners between Two Wars* reviewed by Héctor Tejera Gaona (Review entitled "Antropólogos y mayas: el encuentro de expectativas"). *Nueva Antropología*, v. 13, no. 44 (Aug 93), pp. 147 – 150.

History

Farriss, Nancy Marguerite. *La sociedad maya bajo el dominio colonial*, a translation of *Maya Society under Colonial Rule* reviewed by Victoria González Muñoz. *Anuario de Estudios Americanos*, v. 49, Suppl. 1 (1992), pp. 252 – 254.

Fields, Virginia M., ed. *Sixth Palenque Round Table, 1986* reviewed by Laura Finsten. *Latin American Antiquity*, v. 4, no. 2 (June 93), pp. 201 – 202.

Freidel, David A. and Linda Schele. *Un bosque de reyes*: la historia no narrada de los antiguos mayas. *La Palabra y el Hombre*, no. 82 (Apr – June 92), pp. 79 – 94. Tables.

Hammond, Norman, ed. *Cuello: An Early Maya Community in Belize* reviewed by Paul F. Healy. *Latin American Antiquity*, v. 4, no. 3 (Sept 93), pp. 295 – 297.

Lovell, William George. *Conquest and Survival in Colonial Guatemala: A Historical Geography of the Cuchumatán Highlands, 1500 – 1821* reviewed by Rob de Ridder. *European Review of Latin American and Caribbean Studies*, no. 54 (June 93), pp. 118 – 120. Bibl.

— *Conquest and Survival in Colonial Guatemala: A Historical Geography of the Cuchumatán Highlands, 1500 – 1821* reviewed by Raymond Buvé. *Journal of Latin American Studies*, v. 25, no. 1 (Feb 93), pp. 197 – 198.

— *Conquista y cambio cultural: la sierra de los Cuchumatanes de Guatemala, 1500 – 1821*, a translation of *Conquest and Survival in Colonial Guatemala*, translated by Eddy Gaytán. Reviewed by María Milagros Ciudad Suárez. *Anuario de Estudios Americanos*, v. 49, Suppl. 2 (1992), pp. 250 – 252.

Pendergast, David Michael et al. Locating Maya Lowlands Spanish Colonial Towns: A Case Study from Belize. *Latin American Antiquity*, v. 4, no. 1 (Mar 93), pp. 59 – 73. Bibl, il, maps.

Implements

Dockall, John Edward and Harry J. Shafer. Testing the Producer – Consumer Model for Santa Rita Corozal, Belize. *Latin American Antiquity*, v. 4, no. 2 (June 93), pp. 158 – 179. Bibl, il, maps.

Pottery

Alvarez Asomoza, Carlos and Luis Casasola García. *Las figurillas de Jonuta, Tabasco* reviewed by Françoise Milhorat. *Caravelle*, no. 59 (1992), pp. 253 – 256.

Forsyth, Donald W. The Ceramic Sequence at Nakbe, Guatemala. *Ancient Mesoamerica*, v. 4, no. 1 (Spring 93), pp. 31 – 53. Bibl, il, maps.

Hermes, Bernard A. Adiciones tipológicas a los complejos Eb, Tzec y Manik de Tikal, Guatemala. *Revista Española de Antropología Americana*, v. 23 (1993), pp. 9 – 27. Bibl, il.

Kerr, Justin. *The Mayas Vase Book, Vol. III: A Corpus of Rollout Photographs of Maya Vases* reviewed by Alfonso Lacadena García-Gallo. *Revista Española de Antropología Americana*, v. 23 (1993), pp. 259 – 260.

Montero, Ignacio and Carmen Varela Torrecilla. Cuantificación y representación gráfica de los materiales cerámicos mayas: una propuesta metodológica. *Revista Española de Antropología Americana*, v. 23 (1993), pp. 83 – 100. Bibl, tables, charts.

Religion and mythology

Florescano, Enrique. Muerte y resurrección del dios del maíz. *Nexos*, v. 16, no. 184 (Apr 93), pp. 21 – 31. Bibl, il.

Fox, John Gerard. The Ballcourt Markers of Tenam Rosario, Chiapas, Mexico. *Ancient Mesoamerica*, v. 4, no. 1 (Spring 93), pp. 55 – 64. Bibl, il.

Ligorred, Francesc. "Yaax indios yoko cab": pronosticar; una práctica estimulante y poética entre los mayas. *Iberoamericana*, v. 16, no. 47 – 48 (1992), pp. 6 – 20. Bibl, il.

Thompson, John Eric Sidney. El papel de las cuevas en la cultura maya (A translation of "The Role of Caves in Maya Culture," originally published in 1959. Introduced, translated, and annotated by Juan Luis Bonon Villarejo and Carolina Martínez Klemm). *Boletín Americanista*, v. 33, no. 42 – 43 (1992 – 1993), pp. 395 – 424. Bibl.

Research

Westphal, Wilfried. *Die Mayaforschung: Geschichte, Methoden, Ergebnisse* reviewed by Andreas Koechert. *Iberoamericana*, v. 17, no. 49 (1993), pp. 89 – 90.

Social conditions

Bizarro Ujpán, Ignacio. *Ignacio: The Diary of a Maya Indian of Guatemala* edited and translated by James D. Sexton. Reviewed by Carol A. Smith. *Hispanic American Historical Review*, v. 73, no. 2 (May 93), pp. 340 – 341.

— *Ignacio: The Diary of a Maya Indian of Guatemala* edited and translated by James D. Sexton. Reviewed by Tracy Ulltveit-Moe. *Journal of Latin American Studies*, v. 25, no. 1 (Feb 93), pp. 221 – 222.

Hanks, William F. *Referential Practice: Language and Lived Space among the Maya* reviewed by John M. Watanabe. *Mesoamérica (USA)*, v. 13, no. 23 (June 92), pp. 201 – 205. Charts.

Social life and customs

Pérez González, María Luisa. La organización socio-política del grupo chol – manché en Guatemala durante el siglo XVII: estudio preliminar. *Colonial Latin American Historical Review*, v. 2, no. 1 (Winter 93), pp. 57 – 75. Bibl.

Textile industry and fabrics

Alfaro, Alfonso. Elogio de la opulencia, la distancia y el cordero (Accompanied by an English translation). *Artes de México*, no. 19 (Spring 93), pp. 31 – 38. Il.

Fábregas Puig, Andrés A. El textil como resistencia cultural (Accompanied by an English translation). *Artes de México*, no. 19 (Spring 93), pp. 25 – 27. Il.

Jiménez López, Lexa. "Como la luna nos enseñó a tejer" (Translated by Ambar Past). *Artes de México*, no. 19 (Spring 93), pp. 40 – 41. Il.

Morris, Walter F., Jr. Simbolismo de un huipil ceremonial (Accompanied by the English original, translated by Ana Rosa González Matute). *Artes de México*, no. 19 (Spring 93), pp. 65 – 71. Il.

Orellana, Margarita de. Voces entretejidas: testimonios del arte textil (Accompanied by an English translation). *Artes de México*, no. 19 (Spring 93), pp. 43 – 59. Il.

Bibliography

Bibliografía (to the articles on textiles from Chiapas appearing in this issue). *Artes de México*, no. 19 (Spring 93), pp. 81 – 82. Il.

Collectors and collecting

Pellizzi, Francesco. La colección Pellizzi de textiles de Chiapas (Accompanied by an English translation). *Artes de México*, no. 19 (Spring 93), pp. 75 – 79. Il.

Pictorial works

(Illustrated map of local garment styles and designs, Chiapas, Mexico). *Artes de México*, no. 19 (Spring 93), pp. 72 – 73. Il, maps.

El proceso de tejido visto por los niños de Tenejapa. *Artes de México*, no. 19 (Spring 93), pp. 60 – 61.

Tribal government

Pérez González, María Luisa. La organización socio-política del grupo chol – manché en Guatemala durante el siglo XVII: estudio preliminar. *Colonial Latin American Historical Review*, v. 2, no. 1 (Winter 93), pp. 57 – 75. Bibl.

Women

O'Brian, Robin. Un mercado indígena de artesanías en los altos de Chiapas: persistencia y cambio en las vidas de las vendedoras mayas. *Mesoamérica (USA)*, v. 13, no. 23 (June 92), pp. 79 – 84. Bibl.

Stephen, Lynn. *Zapotec Women* reviewed by Florence E. Babb. *The Americas*, v. 50, no. 2 (Oct 93), pp. 276 – 277.

Writing

Ayala F., Maricela and Linda Schele. De poesía e historia: el tablero de los glifos de Palenque. *Vuelta*, v. 17, no. 203 (Oct 93), pp. 25 – 27. Charts.

Bricker, Victoria Reifler. *A Grammar of Mayan Hieroglyphs* reviewed by Barbara MacLeod. *Mesoamérica (USA)*, v. 13, no. 23 (June 92), pp. 213 – 216.

Hanks, William F. and Don Stephen Rice, eds. *Word and Image in Maya Culture: Explorations in Language, Writing, and Representation* reviewed by Stephen D. Houston. *Mesoamérica (USA)*, v. 13, no. 23 (June 92), pp. 191 – 193.

— *Word and Image in Maya Culture: Explorations in Language, Writing, and Representation* reviewed by Luis T. Sanz. *Revista Española de Antropología Americana*, v. 23 (1993), pp. 260 – 262.

Knorozov, Yuri V. Los códices jeroglíficos mayas (Translated by Francisco Beverido Pereau). *La Palabra y el Hombre*, no. 82 (Apr – June 92), pp. 189 – 195.

Rodríguez Ochoa, Patricia. Del arte a la escritura, de la visión al desciframiento. *Vuelta*, v. 17, no. 203 (Oct 93), pp. 23 – 24. Il.

— El desciframiento de la escritura maya: una historia. *Vuelta*, v. 17, no. 203 (Oct 93), pp. 21 – 22.

Research

Coe, Michael D. *Breaking the Maya Code* reviewed by Aaron Segal (Review entitled "The Maya Code"). *Interciencia*, v. 18, no. 4 (July – Aug 93), p. 209.

MAYO INDIANS

Figueroa Valenzuela, Alejandro. Derechos políticos y organización social: el caso de los yaquis y los mayos. *Nueva Antropología*, v. 13, no. 44 (Aug 93), pp. 43 – 60. Bibl.

MAYTA, ALEJANDRO

Fiction

Grandis, Rita de. La problemática del conocimiento histórico en *Historia de Mayta* de M. Vargas Llosa. *Revista de Crítica Literaria Latinoamericana*, v. 19, no. 38 (July – Dec 93), pp. 375 – 382. Bibl.

MAYZ VALLENILLA, ERNESTO

Pérez Leyva, Leonardo. Algunas consideraciones sobre la filosofía existencialista de Ernesto Mayz Vallenilla. *Islas*, no. 96 (May – Aug 90), pp. 27 – 33.

MAZATEC INDIANS

Boege, Eckart. Contradicciones en la identidad étnica mazateca: construyendo un objeto de estudio. *Nueva Antropología*, v. 13, no. 43 (Nov 92), pp. 61 – 81. Bibl.

MEAT INDUSTRY AND TRADE

See also
  Cattle trade
  Poultry industry
  Swine

Brazil

Mathematical models

Bacchi, Mirian Rumenos Piedade and Geraldo Sant'Ana de Camargo Barros. Demanda de carne bovina no mercado brasileiro. *Revista de Economia e Sociologia Rural*, v. 30, no. 1 (Jan – Mar 92), pp. 83 – 96. Bibl, tables.

Santana, Antônio Cordeiro de. Estrutura de oferta de carne suína sob condições de risco no Brasil. *Revista de Economia e Sociologia Rural,* v. 30, no. 1 (Jan – Mar 92), pp. 21 – 39. Bibl, tables.

Mexico

Chauvet Sánchez, Michelle. Comida rápida contra comida corrida: repercusiones de la apertura comercial en la producción de cárnicos. *El Cotidiano,* v. 8, no. 52 (Jan – Feb 93), pp. 103 – 108. Bibl, il, tables, charts.

United States

Chauvet Sánchez, Michelle. Comida rápida contra comida corrida: repercusiones de la apertura comercial en la producción de cárnicos. *El Cotidiano,* v. 8, no. 52 (Jan – Feb 93), pp. 103 – 108. Bibl, il, tables, charts.

MEDALS

See
Decorations of honor

MEDELLÍN, COLOMBIA

Gouëset, Vincent. L'impact du "narcotrafic" à Médellin. *Cahiers des Amériques Latines,* no. 13 (1992), pp. 27 – 52. Bibl, tables.

MEDICAL ANTHROPOLOGY

Argentina

Arrúe, Willie and Beatriz Kalinsky. *De "la médica" y el terapeuta: la gestión intercultural de la salud en el sur de la provincia del Neuquén* reviewed by P. Schraer. *La Educación (USA),* v. 36, no. 111 – 113 (1992), pp. 281 – 282.

Bolivia

Crandon-Malamud, Libbet. *From the Fat of Our Souls: Social Change, Political Process, and Medical Pluralism in Bolivia* reviewed by Marcos Cueto. *Hispanic American Historical Review,* v. 73, no. 1 (Feb 93), p. 172.

MEDICAL ETHICS

Boccia Paz, Alfredo et al. *Médicos, ética y tortura en el Paraguay* (Review). *Revista Paraguaya de Sociología,* v. 29, no. 84 (May – Aug 92), pp. 205 – 206. Il.

Peláez, Jorge Humberto. El invitado del mes: interrogantes éticos de la reproducción asistida. *Revista Javeriana,* v. 61, no. 595 (June 93), pp. 337 – 344. Il.

Wildes, Kevin. Tecnología médica y el surgimiento de la bioética. *Mensaje,* v. 42, no. 418 (May 93), pp. 129 – 132. Il.

MEDICINE

See also
Blood
Childbirth
Diseases
Ethnobotany
Folk medicine
Medical anthropology
Medical ethics
Mental illness
Nurses
Pharmacy
Physicians
Public health
Technology, Medical
Subdivision *Medicine* under names of Indian groups

Sources

Escardó, Florencio. Florencio Escardó. *Realidad Económica,* no. 119 (Oct – Nov 93), pp. 69 – 72.

Brazil

Engel, Magali. *Meretrizes e doutores: saber médico e prostituição no Rio de Janeiro, 1840 – 1890* reviewed by Sandra Lauderdale Graham (Review entitled "Dangerous Fantasies: The Altered Vocabulary of Commercial Sex"). *Luso-Brazilian Review,* v. 30, no. 1 (Summer 93), pp. 133 – 139.

Central America

Monroy de Gómez, Carlota. Serología en una población centroamericana infectada con "Trypanosoma Cruzi," "T. Rangeli" y "Leishmania Ssp." *USAC,* no. 13 (Mar 91), pp. 76 – 80. Bibl, tables.

Chile

Study and teaching

Cruz-Coke Madrid, Ricardo. Desarrollo de las ciencias médicas en la U. de Chile. *Atenea (Chile),* no. 465 – 466 (1992), pp. 329 – 336. Bibl.

Costa Rica

Study and teaching

Méndez de Gamboa, Irene. Logro académico estudiantil en el área de salud. *Revista de Ciencias Sociales (Costa Rica),* no. 60 (June 93), pp. 117 – 133. Bibl, tables.

Mexico

Study and teaching

Fuente, Juan Ramón de la. Medical Education in Mexico. *Mexican Studies,* v. 9, no. 2 (Summer 93), pp. 295 – 302. Bibl.

Panama

Study and teaching

Rodríguez, Julio P. Evolución de la medicina familiar y comunitaria en la Facultad de Medicina. *Revista Cultural Lotería,* v. 50, no. 383 (May – June 91), pp. 63 – 73. Bibl.

Peru

Cueto, Marcos. *Excelencia científica en la periferia: actividades científicas e investigaciones biomédicas en el Perú, 1890 – 1950* reviewed by Ricardo Portocarrero Grados. *Historia y Cultura (Peru),* no. 20 (1990), pp. 373 – 377.

Uruguay

Rizzi, Milton. De héroes a encargados: la traqueotomía en el Uruguay. *Hoy Es Historia,* v. 10, no. 58 (July – Aug 93), pp. 71 – 76. Bibl.

Soiza Larrosa, Augusto. Valores notables de la cultura uruguaya: algunos aportes médicos uruguayos a la comunidad científica mundial. *Hoy Es Historia,* v. 10, no. 55 (Jan – Feb 93), pp. 35 – 44. Bibl.

Venezuela

Fortique, José Rafael. *Crónicas médicas* reviewed by Juvenal López Ruiz. *Revista Nacional de Cultura (Venezuela),* v. 53, no. 286 (July – Sept 92), p. 265.

MEDINA, PILAR

Vázquez Hall, Patricia. Pilar Medina, un águila mestiza. *Plural (Mexico),* v. 22, no. 258 (Mar 93), p. 72.

MEIRELES, CECÍLIA

Criticism and interpretation

Oliveira, Ana Maria Domingues de. A temática da morte em Cecília Meireles e Gabriela Mistral. *Revista de Letras (Brazil),* v. 32 (1992), pp. 127 – 139. Bibl.

MELLO, FERNANDO DE COLLOR

See
Collor de Mello, Fernando Affonso

MELO, URUGUAY

Benítez Burgos, Wilson Andrés. La presencia religiosa en la historia de Melo. *Hoy Es Historia,* v. 10, no. 57 (Apr – May 93), pp. 61 – 68.

MELO NETO, JOÃO CABRAL DE

Criticism of specific works

Morte e vida severina

Barbosa, Maria José Somerlate. Nivelamento em *Morte e vida severina.* *Hispania (USA),* v. 76, no. 1 (Mar 93), pp. 30 – 37. Bibl.

MENCHÚ, RIGOBERTA

Escobar, Francisco Andrés. Rigoberta entre nosotros. *ECA; Estudios Centroamericanos,* v. 48, no. 531 – 532 (Jan – Feb 93), pp. 105 – 108. Il.

Addresses, essays, lectures

Menchú, Rigoberta. Un homenaje a los pueblos indígenas. *Realidad Económica,* no. 114 – 115 (Feb – May 93), pp. 74 – 85. Il.

— Mensaje de Rigoberta Menchú Tum, premio Nobel de la paz 1992. *Cuadernos Americanos,* no. 39, Nueva época (May – June 93), pp. 96 – 97.

Awards

Matute, Mario René. Rigoberta Menchú, premio Nobel de la paz 1992 (Introduced by Alfonso Fernández Cabrelli). *Hoy Es Historia,* v. 10, no. 55 (Jan – Feb 93), pp. 97 – 101. Il.

Premios Nobel en el año del quinto centenario. *Casa de las Américas,* no. 190 (Jan – Mar 93), pp. 2 – 12.

Rigoberta Menchú, premio Nobel de la paz: nuevo amanecer para Guatemala. *ECA; Estudios Centroamericanos,* v. 47, no. 528 (Oct 92), pp. 889 – 893. Il.

Criticism of specific works
Me llamo Rigoberta Menchú

Costa, Cláudia de Lima. Rigoberta Menchú: a história de um depoimento. *Estudos Feministas,* v. 1, no. 2 (1993), pp. 306 – 320.

Gerendas, Judit. Hacia una problematización de la escritura femenina. *Escritura (Venezuela),* v. 16, no. 31 – 32 (Jan – Dec 91), pp. 91 – 101.

Trejos Montero, Elisa. *Me llamo Rigoberta Menchú y así me nació la conciencia:* un texto de literatura testimonial. *Káñina,* v. 16, no. 2 (July – Dec 92), pp. 53 – 63. Bibl.

Interviews

Brittin, Alice A. and Kenya C. Dworkin. Rigoberta Menchú: "Los indígenas no nos quedamos como bichos aislados, inmunes, desde hace 500 años. No, nosotros hemos sido protagonistas de la historia" (Includes Rigoberta Menchú's poem, "Patria abnegada"). *Nuevo Texto Crítico,* v. 6, no. 11 (1993), pp. 207 – 222.

Cordera Campos, Rolando. Guatemala: suave tierra; una entrevista con Rigoberta Menchú. *Nexos,* v. 16, no. 186 (June 93), pp. 9 – 15.

Trejos Montero, Elisa. Conversación con Rigoberta Menchú. *Káñina,* v. 16, no. 2 (July – Dec 92), pp. 65 – 71.

MÉNDEZ DÁVILA, LIONEL

Interviews

González López, Waldo. Testimonio de Lionel Méndez D'Avila. *Conjunto,* no. 92 (July – Dec 92), pp. 98 – 99. Il.

Ruiloba C., Rafael. "No me resigno a que el lenguaje pierda su capacidad de alucinar": entrevista con Lionel Méndez D'Avila. *USAC,* no. 12 (Dec 90), pp. 28 – 30.

MÉNDEZ PLANCARTE, ALFONSO

Criticism of specific works
San Juan de la Cruz en México

Andueza, María. *San Juan de la Cruz en México* visto por Alfonso Méndez Plancarte. *Cuadernos Americanos,* no. 37, Nueva época (Jan – Feb 93), pp. 165 – 179. Bibl.

MENDOZA, ANTONIO DE

Ruiz Medrano, Ethelia. *Gobierno y sociedad en Nueva España: segunda Audiencia y Antonio de Mendoza* reviewed by Michel Bertrand. *Caravelle,* no. 59 (1992), pp. 270 – 273.

— *Gobierno y sociedad en Nueva España: segunda Audiencia y Antonio de Mendoza* reviewed by Brian R. Hamnett. *Hispanic American Historical Review,* v. 73, no. 3 (Aug 93), pp. 506 – 507.

MENDOZA, ARGENTINA (PROVINCE)

Furlani de Civit, María Estela and María Josefina Gutiérrez de Manchón. Dinámica agraria en un oasis de especialización vitícola. *Revista Geográfica (Mexico),* no. 115 (Jan – June 92), pp. 85 – 137. Bibl, tables, maps.

Lacoste, Pablo Alberto. Lucha de élites en Argentina: la Unión Cívica Radical en Mendoza, 1890 – 1905. *Anuario de Estudios Americanos,* v. 50, no. 1 (1993), pp. 181 – 212. Bibl, tables.

Supplee, Joan E. Vitivinicultura, recursos públicos y ganancias privadas en Mendoza, 1880 – 1914. *Siglo XIX: Cuadernos,* v. 2, no. 5 (Feb 93), pp. 81 – 94. Bibl.

MENEGHEL, MARIA DA GRAÇA

Simpson, Amelia S. Xuxa and the Politics of Gender. *Luso-Brazilian Review,* v. 30, no. 1 (Summer 93), pp. 95 – 106. Bibl.

MENEM, CARLOS SAÚL

Waldmann, Peter. "Was ich mache, ist Justicialismus, nicht Liberalismus": Menems Peronismus und Peróns Peronismus; Ein vorläufiger Vergleich. *Ibero-Amerikanisches Archiv,* v. 18, no. 1 – 2 (1992), pp. 5 – 29. Bibl.

MENÉNDEZ, MIGUEL

Obituaries

Carvalho, Sílvia M. S. Miguel Angel Menéndez (1949 – 1991). *Revista de Antropologia (Brazil),* v. 34 (1991), pp. 240 – 242. Bibl.

MENÉNDEZ DE AVILÉS, PEDRO

Manucy, Albert. *Menéndez: Pedro Menéndez de Avilés, Captain General of the Ocean Sea* reviewed by Paul E. Hoffman. *Hispanic American Historical Review,* v. 73, no. 2 (May 93), p. 321.

MENTAL ILLNESS

See also
Psychiatry

Eaton, William W. and Roberta Garrison. Mental Health in Mariel Cubans and Haitian Boat People. *International Migration Review,* v. 26, no. 4 (Winter 92), pp. 1395 – 1415. Bibl, tables.

MERCADO, PATRICIA

Interviews

Díaz Castellanos, Guadalupe. Patricia Mercado: feminismo sindical. *Fem,* v. 17, no. 129 (Nov 93), pp. 15 – 17. Il.

MERCADO, TUNUNA

Interviews

Mora, Gabriela. Tununa Mercado. *Hispamérica,* v. 21, no. 62 (Aug 92), pp. 77 – 81.

MERCHANTS

See
Markets and merchants

MERCOSUR

See
Southern Cone of South America – Economic integration

EL MERCURIO (NEWSPAPER)

Fontaine Aldunate, Arturo. La historia reciente de Chile a través de "La semana política" (Part IV, introduced by Miguel González Pino). *Estudios Públicos (Chile),* no. 49 (Summer 93), pp. 305 – 419.

MERENGUE (DANCE)

Pacini Hernandez, Deborah. Dominican Popular Music under the Trujillo Regime. *Studies in Latin American Popular Culture,* v. 12 (1993), pp. 127 – 140. Bibl.

MÉRIDA, CARLOS

Herner de Larrea, Irene. Carlos Mérida y la realidad auténtica. *Nexos,* v. 16, no. 182 (Feb 93), pp. 13 – 15. Il.

MÉRIDA, MEXICO

García de Fuentes, Ana. Comercio, modernización y procesos territoriales: el caso de Mérida, Yucatán. *Problemas del Desarrollo,* v. 24, no. 94 (July – Sept 93), pp. 133 – 163. Bibl, tables, maps, charts.

Ramírez Carrillo, Luis Alfonso. Estratificación, clase y parentesco: empresarios libaneses en el sureste de México. *Nueva Antropología,* v. 13, no. 43 (Nov 92), pp. 123 – 137. Bibl.

Villanueva Villanueva, Nancy Beatriz. La práctica docente en la educación preescolar: ¿Autonomía o control? *Nueva Antropología,* v. 13, no. 44 (Aug 93), pp. 103 – 117. Bibl.

MÉRIDA, VENEZUELA (CITY)

Meza, Robinzon. Bandos de buen gobierno para Mérida durante la colonia y su continuidad en los diversos instrumentos jurídicos del gobierno local de la república. *Boletín de la Academia Nacional de la Historia (Venezuela)*, v. 75, no. 299 (July – Sept 92), pp. 174 – 180. Bibl.

MÉRIDA, VENEZUELA (STATE)

Casanova, Ramón Vicente et al. Consideraciones sobre un proyecto vial: carretera Mérida – La Culata – Tucani. *Derecho y Reforma Agraria*, no. 23 (1992), pp. 163 – 183.

Gutiérrez M., Alejandro and Raúl León Palencia P. Lineamientos de política científica y tecnológica para el estado Mérida: área agrícola agroalimentaria; ideas para la discusión. *Derecho y Reforma Agraria*, no. 23 (1992), pp. 141 – 160. Bibl.

MERLIN, MARÍA DE LAS MERCEDES SANTA CRUZ Y MONTALVO
Criticism and interpretation

Araújo, Nara. La Avellaneda, la Merlin: una manera de ver y sentir. *Iberoamericana*, v. 17, no. 49 (1993), pp. 33 – 41. Bibl.

MESNIER, DESIDERIO

Maza Miquel, Manuel P. Desiderio Mesnier (1852 – 1913): un sacerdote y patriota cubano para todos los tiempos. *Estudios Sociales (Dominican Republic)*, v. 26, no. 92 (Apr – June 93), pp. 77 – 92. Bibl.

MESOAMÉRICA (PERIODICAL)
Indexes

Índice general, 1989 – 1992. *Mesoamérica (USA)*, v. 13, no. 24 (Dec 92), pp. 495 – 512.

MESSIANISM
Brazil

Diacon, Todd Alan. *Millenarian Vision, Capitalist Reality: Brazil's Contestado Rebellion, 1912 – 1916* reviewed by Cliff Welch. *The Americas*, v. 50, no. 2 (Oct 93), pp. 285 – 286.

— *Millenarian Vision, Capitalist Reality: Brazil's Contestado Rebellion, 1912 – 1916* reviewed by Anthony Pereira. *Canadian Journal of Latin American and Caribbean Studies*, v. 17, no. 34 (1992), pp. 132 – 135.

— *Millenarian Vision, Capitalist Reality: Brazil's Contestado Rebellion, 1912 – 1916* reviewed by Kees de Groot. *European Review of Latin American and Caribbean Studies*, no. 53 (Dec 92), pp. 112 – 114.

— *Millenarian Vision, Capitalist Reality: Brazil's Contestado Rebellion, 1912 – 1916* reviewed by Patricia R. Pessar. *Hispanic American Historical Review*, v. 73, no. 1 (Feb 93), pp. 166 – 167.

— *Millenarian Vision, Capitalist Reality: Brazil's Contestado Rebellion, 1912 – 1916* reviewed by Bernardo Kucinski. *Journal of Latin American Studies*, v. 25, no. 1 (Feb 93), pp. 201 – 202.

Levine, Robert M. *Vale of Tears: Revisiting the Canudos Massacre in Northeastern Brazil, 1893 – 1897* reviewed by Francis Lambert. *Bulletin of Latin American Research*, v. 12, no. 3 (Sept 93), pp. 353 – 354.

— *Vale of Tears: Revisiting the Canudos Massacre in Northeastern Brazil, 1893 – 1897* reviewed by Dain Borges. *Hispanic American Historical Review*, v. 73, no. 3 (Aug 93), pp. 515 – 516.

— *Vale of Tears: Revisiting the Canudos Massacre in Northeastern Brazil, 1893 – 1897* reviewed by Jeff Lesser. *Journal of Latin American Studies*, v. 25, no. 2 (May 93), pp. 397 – 398.

— *Vale of Tears: Revisiting the Canudos Massacre in Northeastern Brazil, 1893 – 1897* reviewed by Steven C. Topik. *Luso-Brazilian Review*, v. 30, no. 2 (Winter 93), pp. 115 – 116.

Lorenzo Alcalá, May. El utopismo en Brasil: una experiencia fourierista. *Todo Es Historia*, v. 27, no. 313 (Aug 93), pp. 56 – 68. Bibl, il.

Madden, Lori. The Canudos War in History. *Luso-Brazilian Review*, v. 30, no. 2 (Winter 93), pp. 5 – 22. Bibl.

Peru

Brown, Michael F. *War of Shadows: The Struggle for Utopia in the Peruvian Amazon* reviewed by Oscar Espinoza. *Amazonía Peruana*, v. 11, no. 22 (Oct 92), pp. 278 – 284.

Mateos Fernández-Maquieira, B. Sara. Juan Santos Atahualpa: un movimiento milenarista en la selva. *Amazonía Peruana*, v. 11, no. 22 (Oct 92), pp. 47 – 60. Bibl.

Regan, Jaime. En torno a la entrevista de los jesuitas con Juan Santos Atahualpa. *Amazonía Peruana*, v. 11, no. 22 (Oct 92), pp. 61 – 92. Bibl, maps.

METALLURGY
See
Aluminum industry and trade
Steel industry and trade

METAPHORS
See
Symbolism in literature

METEOROLOGY
See
Droughts
Subdivision *Climate* under names of specific countries

METEPEC, MEXICO

Jarquín Ortega, María Teresa. *Formación y desarrollo de un pueblo novohispano: Metepec en el valle de Toluca.* *Anuario de Estudios Americanos*, v. 49, Suppl. 1 (1992), pp. 254 – 256.

METROPOLITAN AREAS
See
Cities and towns
Urbanization
Names of capital cities

MEXICALI, MEXICO

Guillén López, Tonatiuh and Gerardo M. Ordóñez B. La marginalidad social en la frontera norte: discrepancias empíricas al concepto de la marginalidad. *Frontera Norte*, v. 4, no. 8 (July – Dec 92), pp. 149 – 163. Tables.

MEXICAN AMERICAN ARTISTS

Aguilar Melantzón, Ricardo D. ¡Guache ése! *Plural (Mexico)*, v. 22, no. 256 (Jan 93), pp. 40 – 45. Il.

Anzaldúa, Gloria. Chicana Artists: Exploring "nepantla; el lugar de la frontera." *NACLA Report on the Americas*, v. 27, no. 1 (July – Aug 93), pp. 37 – 42 + . Bibl, il.

Goldman, Shifra M. Voz pública: quince años de carteles chicanos (Translated by Margarita Martínez Duarte). *Plural (Mexico)*, v. 22, no. 256 (Jan 93), pp. 28 – 37. Bibl.

Harris, Patricia and David Lyon. Memory's Persistence: The Living Art. *Américas*, v. 45, no. 6 (Nov – Dec 93), pp. 26 – 37. Il.

Lomelí, Francisco A. Artes y letras chicanas en la actualidad: más allá del barrio y las fronteras. *La Palabra y el Hombre*, no. 84 (Oct – Dec 92), pp. 220 – 227. Il.

Nieto, Margarita. Carlos Almaraz: Genesis of a Chicano Painter. *Latin American Art*, v. 5, no. 1 (Spring 93), pp. 37 – 39. Bibl, il.

MEXICAN – AMERICAN BORDER REGION
See also
Alcohol – Mexican – American Border Region
Bandits and banditry – Mexican – American Border Region
Basques – Mexican – American Border Region
Business enterprises – Mexican – American Border Region
California
Capital investments – Mexican – American Border Region
Central Americans – Mexican – American Border Region
Cities and towns – Mexican – American Border Region
Ciudad Juárez, Mexico
Diseases – Mexican – American Border Region

Civilization

García, José Z. Migración y posmodernidad: efectos culturales; ¿Una nueva ciencia social fronteriza? *Nueva Sociedad,* no. 127 (Sept – Oct 93), pp. 148 – 157. Bibl.

Maril, Robert Lee. *Living on the Edge of America* reviewed by Matt S. Meier. *International Migration Review,* v. 27, no. 4 (Winter 93), pp. 897 – 898.

Commerce

History

González Quiroga, Miguel. La puerta de México: los comerciantes texanos y el noreste mexicano, 1850 – 1880. *Estudios Sociológicos,* v. 11, no. 31 (Jan – Apr 93), pp. 209 – 236. Bibl, tables, maps.

Discovery and exploration

Mora Valcárcel, Carmen de. *Las siete ciudades de Cíbola: textos y testimonios sobre la expedición de Vázquez Coronado* reviewed by Francisco Noguerol Jiménez. *Anuario de Estudios Americanos,* v. 50, no. 1 (1993), pp. 323 – 324.

Economic conditions

Ganster, Paul and Eugenio O. Valenciano, eds. *The Mexican – U.S. Border Region and the Free Trade Agreement* reviewed by Christopher A. Erickson. *Journal of Borderlands Studies,* v. 7, no. 2 (Fall 92), pp. 103 – 105.

Emigration and immigration

Ceballos Ramírez, Manuel and Lawrence D. Taylor. Síntesis histórica del poblamiento de la región fronteriza México – Estados Unidos. *Estudios Fronterizos,* no. 26 (Sept – Dec 91), pp. 9 – 37. Bibl.

Sánchez Munguía, Vicente. Matamoros-sur de Texas: el tránsito de los migrantes de América Central por la frontera México – Estados Unidos. *Estudios Sociológicos,* v. 11, no. 31 (Jan – Apr 93), pp. 183 – 207. Bibl, tables.

Woo Morales, Ofelia. La migración internacional desde una perspectiva regional: el caso de Tijuana y Ciudad Juárez. *Relaciones Internacionales (Mexico),* v. 15, Nueva época, no. 57 (Jan – Mar 93), pp. 87 – 94. Charts.

History

Chipman, Donald E. *Spanish Texas, 1519 – 1821* reviewed by E. A. Mares. *Colonial Latin American Historical Review,* v. 2, no. 4 (Fall 93), pp. 474 – 475.

Din, Gilbert C. *Francisco Bouligny, a Bourbon Soldier in Spanish Louisiana* reviewed by Thomas E. Chávez. *Colonial Latin American Historical Review,* v. 2, no. 4 (Fall 93), pp. 477 – 478.

Ríos-Bustamante, Antonio José. *Los Angeles: pueblo y región, 1781 – 1850* reviewed by Aurora Morcillo-Gómez. *Colonial Latin American Historical Review,* v. 2, no. 4 (Fall 93), pp. 473 – 474.

Thomas, David Hurst, ed. *Columbian Consequences, III: The Spanish Borderlands in Pan-American Perspectives* reviewed by David Henige. *Hispanic Review,* v. 61, no. 3 (Summer 93), pp. 447 – 449.

— *Columbian Consequences, Vol. III: The Spanish Borderlands in Pan-American Perspective* reviewed by Linda A. Watson. *Journal of Latin American Studies,* v. 25, no. 1 (Feb 93), pp. 196 – 197.

— *Columbian Consequences, Vol. III: The Spanish Borderlands in Pan-American Perspective* reviewed by Winifred Creamer. *Latin American Antiquity,* v. 4, no. 1 (Mar 93), pp. 94 – 95.

Weber, David J. *The Spanish Frontier in North America* reviewed by Timothy K. Perttula. *Colonial Latin American Historical Review,* v. 2, no. 1 (Winter 93), pp. 122 – 123.

Industries

Cortés C., Fernando and Rosa María Rubalcava. Algunas determinantes de la inserción laboral en la industria maquiladora de exportación de Matamoros. *Estudios Sociológicos,* v. 11, no. 31 (Jan – Apr 93), pp. 59 – 91. Bibl, tables.

Tamayo, Jesús. The Maquila Industry in Perspective. *Journal of Borderlands Studies,* v. 8, no. 1 (Spring 93), pp. 67 – 76. Bibl, tables.

Intellectual life

Calderón, Héctor and José David Saldívar, eds. *Criticism in the Borderlands: Studies in Chicano Literature, Culture, and Ideology* reviewed by Chuck Tatum (Review entitled "A New Standard for Chicano Literary Scholarship"). *Bilingual Review/Revista Bilingüe,* v. 18, no. 1 (Jan – Apr 93), pp. 64 – 74.

— *Criticism in the Borderlands: Studies in Chicano Literature, Culture, and Ideology* reviewed by Hanny Berkelmans (Review entitled "La literatura chicana de hoy en día"). *European Review of Latin American and Caribbean Studies,* no. 54 (June 93), pp. 111 – 115. Bibl.

— *Criticism in the Borderlands: Studies in Chicano Literature, Culture, and Ideology* reviewed by John Bruce-Novoa. *Hispania (USA),* v. 76, no. 2 (May 93), pp. 280 – 281.

— *Criticism in the Borderlands: Studies in Chicano Literature, Culture, and Ideology* reviewed by Pedro Maligo. *Hispanic American Historical Review,* v. 73, no. 3 (Aug 93), pp. 489 – 490.

Social conditions

Gallegos, Bernardo P. *Literacy, Education, and Society in New Mexico, 1693 – 1821* reviewed by B. Michael Miller. *Colonial Latin American Historical Review,* v. 1, no. 1 (Fall 92), pp. 118 – 119.

— *Literacy, Education, and Society in New Mexico, 1693 – 1821* reviewed by John E. Kicza. *Hispanic American Historical Review,* v. 73, no. 1 (Feb 93), pp. 150 – 151.

MEXICAN AMERICAN DRAMA

History and criticism

Rizk, Beatriz J. TENAZ XVI: la muestra de un teatro en transición. *Latin American Theatre Review,* v. 26, no. 2 (Spring 93), pp. 187 – 190.

MEXICAN AMERICAN LITERATURE

Anaya, Rudolfo A., ed. *Voces: Anthology of New Mexican Writers* reviewed by Salvador Rodríguez del Pino. *The Americas Review,* v. 20, no. 1 (Spring 92), pp. 85 – 87.

History and criticism

Benavides, Rosamel. Cuentos y cuentistas chicanos: perspectiva temática y producción histórica del género, 1947 – 1992. *Revista Chilena de Literatura,* no. 42 (Aug 93), pp. 49 – 56.

Bruce-Novoa, John D. El pensamiento chicano. *Plural (Mexico),* v. 22, no. 256 (Jan 93), pp. 19 – 25. Bibl.

Calderón, Héctor and José David Saldívar, eds. *Criticism in the Borderlands: Studies in Chicano Literature, Culture, and Ideology* reviewed by Chuck Tatum (Review entitled "A New Standard for Chicano Literary Scholarship"). *Bilingual Review/Revista Bilingüe,* v. 18, no. 1 (Jan – Apr 93), pp. 64 – 74.

— *Criticism in the Borderlands: Studies in Chicano Literature, Culture, and Ideology* reviewed by Hanny Berkelmans (Review entitled "La literatura chicana de hoy en día"). *European Review of Latin American and Caribbean Studies,* no. 54 (June 93), pp. 111 – 115. Bibl.

— *Criticism in the Borderlands: Studies in Chicano Literature, Culture, and Ideology* reviewed by John Bruce-Novoa. *Hispania (USA),* v. 76, no. 2 (May 93), pp. 280 – 281.

— *Criticism in the Borderlands: Studies in Chicano Literature, Culture, and Ideology* reviewed by Pedro Maligo. *Hispanic American Historical Review,* v. 73, no. 3 (Aug 93), pp. 489 – 490.

González-Berry, Erlinda, ed. *"Pasó por aquí": Critical Essays on the New Mexican Literary Tradition, 1542 – 1988* reviewed by Arthur Brakel. *The Americas Review,* v. 19, no. 2 (Summer 91), pp. 105 – 107.

Guevara Reyes, Olimpia. Literatura chicana: el sentido de una respuesta histórica. *Plural (Mexico),* v. 22, no. 256 (Jan 93), pp. 46 – 49. Bibl.

Herms, Dieter. *Die zeitgenössische Literatur der Chicanos, 1959 – 1988 (Contemporary Chicano Literature, 1959 – 1988)* reviewed by Horst Tonn. *The Americas Review,* v. 19, no. 3 – 4 (Winter 91), pp. 149 – 150.

Hernández, Guillermo E. *Chicano Satire: A Study in Literary Culture* reviewed by Chuck Tatum (Review entitled "A New Standard for Chicano Literary Scholarship"). *Bilingual Review/Revista Bilingüe,* v. 18, no. 1 (Jan – Apr 93), pp. 64 – 74.

Lomelí, Francisco A. Artes y letras chicanas en la actualidad: más allá del barrio y las fronteras. *La Palabra y el Hombre,* no. 84 (Oct – Dec 92), pp. 220 – 227. Il.

López González, Aralia et al, eds. *Mujer y literatura mexicana y chicana: culturas en contacto* reviewed by Pamela Murray. *Hispanic American Historical Review,* v. 73, no. 3 (Aug 93), p. 490.

Rocard, Marcienne. *The Children of the Sun: Mexican-Americans in the Literature of the United States* reviewed by Chuck Tatum. *The Americas Review,* v. 20, no. 2 (Summer 92), pp. 113 – 115.

Saldívar, José David. *The Dialectics of Our America: Genealogy, Cultural Critique, and Literary History* reviewed by Stephen Minta. *Bulletin of Latin American Research,* v. 12, no. 1 (Jan 93), pp. 129 – 130.

— *The Dialectics of Our America: Genealogy, Cultural Critique, and Literary History* reviewed by John Bruce-Novoa. *Hispania (USA),* v. 76, no. 2 (May 93), pp. 280 – 281.

Saldívar, Ramón David. *Chicano Narrative: The Dialectics of Difference* reviewed by Chuck Tatum (Review entitled "A New Standard for Chicano Literary Scholarship"). *Bilingual Review/Revista Bilingüe,* v. 18, no. 1 (Jan – Apr 93), pp. 64 – 74.

Sánchez, Rosaura. Discourses of Gender, Ethnicity, and Class in Chicano Literature. *The Americas Review,* v. 20, no. 2 (Summer 92), pp. 72 – 88. Bibl.

Translations

Cervantes, Lorna Dee. Bajo de la sombra de la autopista (Translated by Sergio Elizondo and Ricardo Aguilar). *Plural (Mexico),* v. 22, no. 256 (Jan 93), pp. 5 – 7. Il.

MEXICAN AMERICAN POETRY

Gonzalez, Ray, ed. *After Aztlan: Latino Poets of the Nineties* reviewed by Charles Tatum. *World Literature Today,* v. 67, no. 2 (Spring 93), pp. 389 – 390.

History and criticism

Sáenz, Benjamín Alire. Quiero escribir un poema americano: cómo ser un poeta chicano en la América poscolombina (Translated by Aída Espinosa). *Plural (Mexico),* v. 22, no. 256 (Jan 93), pp. 10 – 18.

MEXICAN AMERICAN WOMEN

Culture

Trujillo, Carla, ed. *Chicana Lesbians: The Girls Our Mothers Warned Us About* reviewed by Tamara Parker. *Letras Femeninas,* v. 19, no. 1 – 2 (Spring – Fall 93), pp. 155 – 157.

Employment

Pesquera, Beatriz Margarita. "Work Gave Me a Lot of Confianza": Chicanas' Work Commitment and Work Identity. *Aztlán,* v. 20, no. 1 – 2 (Spring – Fall 91), pp. 97 – 118. Bibl.

Segura, Denise Anne. Ambivalence or Continuity?: Motherhood and Employment among Chicanas and Mexican Immigrant Women Workers. *Aztlán,* v. 20, no. 1 – 2 (Spring – Fall 91), pp. 119 – 150. Bibl, charts.

Political activity

Ortiz, Isidro D. Gloria Molina, líder popular chicana (Translated by Leticia García Cortés). *Plural (Mexico),* v. 22, no. 256 (Jan 93), pp. 63 – 69. Bibl.

Pardo, Mary Santoli. Creating Community: Mexican American Women in Eastside Los Angeles. *Aztlán,* v. 20, no. 1 – 2 (Spring – Fall 91), pp. 39 – 71. Bibl.

Psychology

Flores-Ortiz, Yvette G. Levels of Acculturation, Marital Satisfaction, and Depression among Chicana Workers: A Psychological Perspective. *Aztlán,* v. 20, no. 1 – 2 (Spring – Fall 91), pp. 151 – 175. Bibl, tables.

Pesquera, Beatriz Margarita. "Work Gave Me a Lot of Confianza": Chicanas' Work Commitment and Work Identity. *Aztlán,* v. 20, no. 1 – 2 (Spring – Fall 91), pp. 97 – 118. Bibl.

Social conditions

Romero, Gloria Jean. "No se raje, chicanita": Some Thoughts on Race, Class, and Gender in the Classroom. *Aztlán,* v. 20, no. 1 – 2 (Spring – Fall 91), pp. 203 – 218. Bibl.

MEXICAN AMERICAN YOUTH

Knight, George Preston et al. The Socialization of Cooperative, Competitive, and Individualistic Preferences among Mexican American Children: The Mediating Role of Ethnic Identity. *Hispanic Journal of Behavioral Sciences,* v. 15, no. 3 (Aug 93), pp. 291 – 309. Bibl, tables, charts.

Moore, Joan W. *Going Down to the Barrio: Homeboys and Homegirls in Change* reviewed by Kathleen Logan. *Hispanic American Historical Review,* v. 73, no. 3 (Aug 93), pp. 488 – 489.

Rabow, Jerome and Kathleen A. Rodriguez. Socialization toward Money in Latino Families: An Exploratory Study of Gender Differences. *Hispanic Journal of Behavioral Sciences,* v. 15, no. 3 (Aug 93), pp. 324 – 341. Bibl.

Stoddard, Ellwyn R. Teen-Age Pregnancy in the Texas Borderlands. *Journal of Borderlands Studies,* v. 8, no. 1 (Spring 93), pp. 77 – 98. Bibl, tables, maps.

Valenzuela, Angela. Liberal Gender Role Attitudes and Academic Achievement among Mexican-Origin Adolescents in Two Houston Inner-City Catholic Schools. *Hispanic Journal of Behavioral Sciences,* v. 15, no. 3 (Aug 93), pp. 310 – 323. Bibl, tables.

Research

Náñez, José E. and Raymond V. Padilla. Processing of Simple and Choice Reaction Time Tasks by Chicano Adolescents. *Hispanic Journal of Behavioral Sciences,* v. 15, no. 4 (Nov 93), pp. 498 – 508. Bibl, tables.

MEXICAN AMERICANS

See also

Subdivision *United States* under *Mexicans* and specific topics

Biography

Villaseñor, Víctor. *Rain of Gold* reviewed by Verlene Kelsey (Review entitled "Mining for a Usable Past: Acts of Recovery, Resistance, and Continuity in Víctor Villaseñor's *Rain of Gold*"). *Bilingual Review/Revista Bilingüe*, v. 18, no. 1 (Jan – Apr 93), pp. 79 – 85.

Culture

Bruce-Novoa, John D. El pensamiento chicano. *Plural (Mexico)*, v. 22, no. 256 (Jan 93), pp. 19 – 25. Bibl.

Koegel, John. Calendar of Southern California Amusements (1852 – 1897) Designed for the Spanish-Speaking Public. *Inter-American Music Review*, v. 13, no. 2 (Spring – Summer 93), pp. 115 – 143. Bibl, il.

Lomelí, Francisco A. Artes y letras chicanas en la actualidad: más allá del barrio y las fronteras. *La Palabra y el Hombre*, no. 84 (Oct – Dec 92), pp. 220 – 227. Il.

Meléndez, Gabriel. Carrying the Magic of His People's Heart: An Interview with Jimmy Santiago Baca. *The Americas Review*, v. 19, no. 3 – 4 (Winter 91), pp. 64 – 86.

Una respuesta breve a "El pensamiento chicano" de Juan Bruce-Novoa, publicado en *Plural* de Excelsior, núm. 256, enero de 1993, pp. 19 – 25. *Plural (Mexico)*, v. 22, no. 262 (July 93), pp. 72 – 73.

Sáenz, Benjamín Alire. Quiero escribir un poema americano: cómo ser un poeta chicano en la América poscolombina (Translated by Aída Espinosa). *Plural (Mexico)*, v. 22, no. 256 (Jan 93), pp. 10 – 18.

Education

Escamilla, Kathy Cogburn and Marcello Medina. English and Spanish Acquisition by Limited-Language-Proficient Mexican Americans in a Three-Year Maintenance Bilingual Program. *Hispanic Journal of Behavioral Sciences*, v. 15, no. 1 (Feb 93), pp. 108 – 120. Bibl, tables.

Lopez, Linda C. Mexican-American and Anglo-American Parental Involvement with a Public Elementary School: An Exploratory Study. *Hispanic Journal of Behavioral Sciences*, v. 15, no. 1 (Feb 93), pp. 150 – 155. Bibl, tables.

Valencia, Richard R., ed. *Chicano School Failure and Success: Research and Policy Agendas for the 1990s* reviewed by Maryann Santos de Barona (Review entitled "Chicano Schooling: Ethnic Success or Societal Failure?"). *Bilingual Review/Revista Bilingüe*, v. 17, no. 3 (Sept – Dec 92), pp. 273 – 275.

Valenzuela, Angela. Liberal Gender Role Attitudes and Academic Achievement among Mexican-Origin Adolescents in Two Houston Inner-City Catholic Schools. *Hispanic Journal of Behavioral Sciences*, v. 15, no. 3 (Aug 93), pp. 310 – 323. Bibl, tables.

Employment

Borjas, George J. and Marta Tienda. The Employment and Wages of Legalized Immigrants. *International Migration Review*, v. 27, no. 4 (Winter 93), pp. 712 – 747. Bibl, tables.

Dávila, Alberto E. and Rogelio Sáenz. Chicano Return Migration to the Southwest: An Integrated Human Capital Approach. *International Migration Review*, v. 26, no. 4 (Winter 92), pp. 1248 – 1266. Bibl, tables.

Ethnic identity

Anaya, Rudolfo A. and Francisco A. Lomelí, eds. *Aztlán: Essays on the Chicano Homeland* reviewed by Kirsten F. Nigro (Review entitled "Looking Back to Aztlán from the 1990s"). *Bilingual Review/Revista Bilingüe*, v. 18, no. 1 (Jan – Apr 93), pp. 75 – 78.

García, Mario T. *Mexican Americans: Leadership, Ideology, and Identity, 1930 – 1960* reviewed by Ramón D. Chacón. *Hispanic American Historical Review*, v. 73, no. 1 (Feb 93), pp. 139 – 140.

Knight, George Preston et al. The Socialization of Cooperative, Competitive, and Individualistic Preferences among Mexican American Children: The Mediating Role of Ethnic Identity. *Hispanic Journal of Behavioral Sciences*, v. 15, no. 3 (Aug 93), pp. 291 – 309. Bibl, tables, charts.

Rodríguez del Pino, Salvador. Realidad y mito en las relaciones chicano – mexicanas. *Bilingual Review/Revista Bilingüe*, v. 17, no. 3 (Sept – Dec 92), pp. 231 – 236. Bibl.

Language

Lara, Luis Fernando. Para la historia lingüística del pachuco. *Anuario de Letras (Mexico)*, v. 30 (1992), pp. 75 – 88. Bibl.

Santa Ana A., Otto. Chicano English and the Nature of the Chicano Language Setting. *Hispanic Journal of Behavioral Sciences*, v. 15, no. 1 (Feb 93), pp. 3 – 35. Bibl, tables, charts.

Music

Koegel, John. Mexican and Mexican-American Musical Life in Southern California, 1850 – 1900. *Inter-American Music Review*, v. 13, no. 2 (Spring – Summer 93), pp. 111 – 114. Bibl.

Political activity

García, Mario T. *Mexican Americans: Leadership, Ideology, and Identity, 1930 – 1960* reviewed by Ramón D. Chacón. *Hispanic American Historical Review*, v. 73, no. 1 (Feb 93), pp. 139 – 140.

Goldman, Shifra M. Voz pública: quince años de carteles chicanos (Translated by Margarita Martínez Duarte). *Plural (Mexico)*, v. 22, no. 256 (Jan 93), pp. 28 – 37. Bibl.

Gómez-Quiñones, Juan. *Chicano Politics: Reality and Promise, 1940 – 1990* reviewed by Javier Urbano Reyes (Review entitled "La gran realidad de los Estados Unidos: la comunidad chicana"). *Revista Mexicana de Ciencias Políticas y Sociales*, v. 38, Nueva época, no. 154 (Oct – Dec 93), pp. 193 – 196.

Psychology

Bohon, Lisa M. et al. The Effects of Real-World Status and Manipulated Status on the Self-Esteem and Social Competition of Anglo-Americans and Mexican-Americans. *Hispanic Journal of Behavioral Sciences*, v. 15, no. 1 (Feb 93), pp. 63 – 79. Bibl, tables.

Rabow, Jerome and Kathleen A. Rodriguez. Socialization toward Money in Latino Families: An Exploratory Study of Gender Differences. *Hispanic Journal of Behavioral Sciences*, v. 15, no. 3 (Aug 93), pp. 324 – 341. Bibl.

Public opinion

Rodríguez del Pino, Salvador. Realidad y mito en las relaciones chicano – mexicanas. *Bilingual Review/Revista Bilingüe*, v. 17, no. 3 (Sept – Dec 92), pp. 231 – 236. Bibl.

Social conditions

Garcia, Richard A. *Rise of the Mexican American Middle Class: San Antonio, 1929 – 1941* reviewed by Francesco Cordasco. *International Migration Review*, v. 27, no. 2 (Summer 93), pp. 435 – 436.

Maril, Robert Lee. *Living on the Edge of America* reviewed by Matt S. Meier. *International Migration Review*, v. 27, no. 4 (Winter 93), pp. 897 – 898.

MEXICAN AMERICANS AND MASS MEDIA

Barceló Aspeitia, Axel Arturo. Comics de amor y cohetes. *Nexos*, v. 16, no. 185 (May 93), pp. 88 – 89.

Cortés, Carlos E. Chicanos y medios masivos de comunicación (Translated by Leticia García Cortés). *Plural (Mexico)*, v. 22, no. 256 (Jan 93), pp. 50 – 59.

Lomelí, Francisco A. Artes y letras chicanas en la actualidad: más allá del barrio y las fronteras. *La Palabra y el Hombre*, no. 84 (Oct – Dec 92), pp. 220 – 227. Il.

MEXICAN AMERICANS IN LITERATURE

Martínez, Elena M. El discurso patriarcal y el discurso feminista en *Excepto la muerte* de Carmen Elvira Moreno. *Fem*, v. 17, no. 127 (Sept 93), pp. 6 – 10. Bibl.

Rocard, Marcienne. *The Children of the Sun: Mexican-Americans in the Literature of the United States* reviewed by Chuck Tatum. *The Americas Review*, v. 20, no. 2 (Summer 92), pp. 113 – 115.

MEXICAN DRAMA

Ita, Fernando de, ed. *Antología del teatro mexicano contemporáneo* reviewed by Hugo Gutiérrez Vega. *Cuadernos Hispanoamericanos*, no. 520 (Oct 93), pp. 113 – 118.

History and criticism

Cypess, Sandra Messinger. Re-visión de la figura de la Malinche en la dramaturga mexicana contemporánea. *Cuadernos Americanos,* no. 40, Nueva época (July – Aug 93), pp. 208 – 222. Bibl.

Germany

Paatz, Annette. Reflexiones acerca de la traducción de obras teatrales: un simposio de autores latinoamericanos y traductores (Translated by Gabriela Fonseca). *Humboldt,* no. 108 (1993), pp. 102 – 103.

MEXICAN LITERATURE

Dictionaries and encyclopedias

Cortés, Eladio, ed. *Dictionary of Mexican Literature* reviewed by David William Foster. *World Literature Today,* v. 67, no. 3 (Summer 93), p. 593.

History and criticism

Cypess, Sandra Messinger. *La Malinche in Mexican Literature: From History to Myth* reviewed by Salvador A. Oropesa. *Letras Femeninas,* v. 19, no. 1 – 2 (Spring – Fall 93), pp. 146 – 148.

— *La Malinche in Mexican Literature: From History to Myth* reviewed by Julie Greer Johnson. *Revista Interamericana de Bibliografía,* v. 42, no. 3 (1992), p. 502.

Paz, Octavio. Tránsito y permanencia (Prologue to Volume IV of *Obras completas). Vuelta,* v. 17, no. 201 (Aug 93), pp. 8 – 12.

Colonial period

González Casanova, Pablo. *La literatura perseguida por la inquisición* reviewed by Solange Alberro (Review entitled "Regreso de un clásico"). *Nexos,* v. 16, no. 189 (Sept 93), pp. 59 – 61.

20th century

Castañón, Adolfo. *Arbitrario de literatura mexicana* reviewed by Christopher Domínguez Michael. *Vuelta,* v. 17, no. 203 (Oct 93), pp. 42 – 43.

González, Alfonso. *Euphoria and Crisis: Essays on the Contemporary Mexican Novel* reviewed by George R. McMurray. *Chasqui,* v. 22, no. 2 (Nov 93), pp. 171 – 173.

López González, Aralia et al, eds. *Mujer y literatura mexicana y chicana: culturas en contacto* reviewed by Pamela Murray. *Hispanic American Historical Review,* v. 73, no. 3 (Aug 93), p. 490.

Masoliver Ródenas, Juan Antonio. Paisaje de la narrativa mexicana. *Vuelta,* v. 17, no. 197 (Apr 93), pp. 58 – 62.

Muñoz M., Mario. En torno a la narrativa mexicana de tema homosexual. *La Palabra y el Hombre,* no. 84 (Oct – Dec 92), pp. 21 – 37. Bibl.

Patán, Federico, ed. *Perfiles: ensayos sobre la literatura mexicana reciente* reviewed by Susan Dennis. *Hispania (USA),* v. 76, no. 3 (Sept 93), pp. 486 – 487.

Spain

Bibliography

Rosenzweig, Gabriel. *Autores mexicanos publicados en España, 1879 – 1936* reviewed by Jorge F. Hernández. *Vuelta,* v. 17, no. 196 (Mar 93), pp. 52 – 53.

MEXICAN POETRY

Bibliography

Sánchez Arteche, Alfonso. Letras del estado de México. *Plural (Mexico),* v. 22, no. 258 (Mar 93), pp. 76 – 77.

Foreign influences

Zaid, Gabriel. *La Jeune Belgique* y la poesía mexicana. *Vuelta,* v. 17, no. 200 (July 93), pp. 17 – 18.

Translations

Mexican Poetry Today: A Marginal View (Edited and introduced by Jacobo Sefamí, translated by Roberto Tejada, Edith Grossman, and Suzanne Jill Levine). *Review,* no. 47 (Fall 93), pp. 45 – 68.

MEXICANS

See also
Mexican Americans

Foreign opinion

Richard, Alfred Charles, Jr. *The Hispanic Image on the Silver Screen: An Interpretive Filmography from Silents into Sound, 1898 – 1935* reviewed by Paul J. Vanderwood. *Hispanic American Historical Review,* v. 73, no. 2 (May 93), pp. 294 – 295.

— *The Hispanic Image on the Silver Screen: An Interpretive Filmography from Silents into Sound, 1898 – 1935* reviewed by Ana M. Rodríguez-Vivaldi. *Revista Interamericana de Bibliografía,* v. 42, no. 3 (1992), pp. 507 – 508.

Mexican – American Border Region

Santos, Gilberto de los and Vern Vincent. Tex-Mex Tourism (Excerpt from *Mexican Tourism Market in the Rio Grande Valley of Texas). Business Mexico,* v. 3, no. 3 (Mar 93), pp. 27 – 29. Tables.

United States

Alba-Hernández, Francisco. El Tratado de Libre Comercio y la emigración de mexicanos a Estados Unidos. *Comercio Exterior,* v. 43, no. 8 (Aug 93), pp. 743 – 749. Bibl.

Castillo F., Dídimo. ¿Fin de las fronteras?: la migración indocumentada de México hacia Estados Unidos. *Problemas del Desarrollo,* v. 24, no. 93 (Apr – June 93), pp. 95 – 119. Bibl, tables.

Corona Vázquez, Rodolfo. La migración de mexicanos a los Estados Unidos: cambios en la década de 1980 – 1990. *Revista Mexicana de Sociología,* v. 55, no. 1 (Jan – Mar 93), pp. 213 – 233. Bibl, tables.

Decierdo, Margarita Arce. A Mexican Migrant Family in North Carolina. *Aztlán,* v. 20, no. 1 – 2 (Spring – Fall 91), pp. 183 – 193.

Donato, Katharine M. Current Trends and Patterns of Female Migration: Evidence from Mexico. *International Migration Review,* v. 27, no. 4 (Winter 93), pp. 748 – 771. Bibl, tables.

Koegel, John. Calendar of Southern California Amusements (1852 – 1897) Designed for the Spanish-Speaking Public. *Inter-American Music Review,* v. 13, no. 2 (Spring – Summer 93), pp. 115 – 143. Bibl, il.

— Mexican and Mexican-American Musical Life in Southern California, 1850 – 1900. *Inter-American Music Review,* v. 13, no. 2 (Spring – Summer 93), pp. 111 – 114. Bibl.

Lowenthal, Abraham F. El hemisferio interdoméstico. *Relaciones Internacionales (Mexico),* v. 15, Nueva época, no. 57 (Jan – Mar 93), pp. 13 – 15.

Massey, Douglas S. et al. *Los ausentes: el proceso social de la migración internacional en el occidente de México* reviewed by Janet E. Worrall. *Hispanic American Historical Review,* v. 73, no. 2 (May 93), pp. 337 – 338.

Schmidt, Samuel. Migración o refugio económico: el caso mexicano. *Nueva Sociedad,* no. 127 (Sept – Oct 93), pp. 136 – 147. Bibl.

MEXICO

See also
Abortion – Mexico
Acapulco, Mexico
Acculturation – Mexico
Actors and actresses – Mexico
Adult education – Mexico
Advertising – Mexico
Agricultural laborers – Mexico
Agriculture – Mexico
Agriculture, Cooperative – Mexico
Agriculture and state – Mexico
Aguascalientes, Mexico (State)
AIDS (Disease) – Mexico
Airplane industry and trade – Mexico
Alcohol – Mexico
Aluminum industry and trade – Mexico
Americans – Mexico
Anthropologists – Mexico
Anthropology – Mexico
Archaeological site reports – Mexico
Archaeology – Mexico
Architecture – Mexico
Architecture, Colonial – Mexico
Archives – Mexico
Art – Mexico
Art and society – Mexico
Artisans – Mexico

Artists – Mexico
Atlases – Mexico
Atomic power industry – Mexico
Authors – Mexico
Automobile industry and trade – Mexico
Baja California, Mexico
Balance of payments – Mexico
Banks and banking – Mexico
Bilingualism – Mexico
Biography (as a literary form) – Mexico
Biotechnology – Mexico
Birth control – Mexico
Blacks – Mexico
Books – Mexico
Botany – Mexico
Business enterprises – Mexico
Capital – Mexico
Capitalists and financiers – Mexico
Caricatures and cartoons – Mexico
Catholic Church – Mexico
Catholic universities and colleges – Mexico
Central Americans – Mexico
Cerro de las Mesas site, Mexico
Chalcatzingo, Mexico
Chiapas, Mexico
Chihuahua, Mexico (State)
Child abuse – Mexico
Children – Mexico
Chinese – Mexico
Christian art and symbolism – Mexico
Church and social problems – Mexico
Church and state – Mexico
Church architecture – Mexico
Church music – Mexico
Cities and towns – Mexico
Citrus fruits – Mexico
Ciudad Juárez, Mexico
Coahuila, Mexico
Coal mines and mining – Mexico
Coasts – Mexico
Coffee – Mexico
Comic books, strips, etc. – Mexico
Communism – Mexico
Community development – Mexico
Community organization – Mexico
Competition – Mexico
Composers – Mexico
Computer industry – Mexico
Conservatism – Mexico
Construction industry – Mexico
Convents and nunneries – Mexico
Cookery – Mexico
Córdoba, Mexico
Corn – Mexico
Cost and standard of living – Mexico
Cotton – Mexico
Credit – Mexico
Creole dialects – Mexico
Cristero Rebellion, 1926 – 1929
Cuernavaca, Mexico
Cultural property – Mexico
Dancing – Mexico
Debts, Public – Mexico
Decentralization in government – Mexico
Democracy – Mexico
Diseases – Mexico
Drama festivals – Mexico
Drug trade – Mexico
Drugs, Illegal – Mexico
Durango, Mexico (City)
Dutch – Mexico
Earthquakes – Mexico
Ecology – Mexico
Ecology and development – Mexico
Education – Mexico
Education, Bilingual – Mexico
Education, Higher – Mexico
Education, Preschool – Mexico
Education, Primary – Mexico
Education and state – Mexico
Educational accountability – Mexico
Educational research – Mexico
Educational sociology – Mexico
Ejutla, Mexico
Elections – Mexico
Electric power – Mexico
Elite (Social sciences) – Mexico
Employment – Mexico

Encomiendas – Mexico
Energy policy – Mexico
English language – Mexico
Environmental policy – Mexico
Environmental services – Mexico
Europeans – Mexico
Evangelicalism – Mexico
Executive power – Mexico
Exiles – Mexico
Family – Mexico
Fertility, Human – Mexico
Finance, Public – Mexico
Fishing – Mexico
Folk art – Mexico
Folk dancing – Mexico
Folk drama – Mexico
Folk festivals – Mexico
Folk literature – Mexico
Folk lore – Mexico
Folk music – Mexico
Food habits – Mexico
Food industry and trade – Mexico
Food supply – Mexico
Foreign exchange problem – Mexico
Foreign trade promotion – Mexico
Foreign trade regulation – Mexico
Forestry – Mexico
Forests – Mexico
Franchises (Retail trade) – Mexico
Franciscans – Mexico
Freedom of the press – Mexico
French – Mexico
Fruit trade – Mexico
Gas, Natural – Mexico
Geographical distribution of plants and animals –
    Mexico
Geography, Economic – Mexico
Geography, Historical – Mexico
Gold mines and mining – Mexico
Guadalajara, Mexico
Guanajuato, Mexico (State)
Guerrero, Mexico
Haciendas – Mexico
Handicraft – Mexico
Harbors – Mexico
Hazardous substances – Mexico
Highways – Mexico
Horticulture – Mexico
Housing – Mexico
Hueyapan, Mexico
Human capital – Mexico
Human rights – Mexico
Illiteracy – Mexico
Indians, Treatment of – Mexico
Industrial organization – Mexico
Industrial productivity – Mexico
Industrial promotion – Mexico
Industrial sociology – Mexico
Industries, Location of – Mexico
Industry and state – Mexico
Infant mortality – Mexico
Informal sector (Economics) – Mexico
Information services – Mexico
Inquisition – Mexico
Insurance – Mexico
Interest rates – Mexico
International business enterprises – Mexico
Investments, Foreign – Mexico
Italians – Mexico
Jalapa, Mexico
Jalisco, Mexico
Jesuits – Mexico
Jews – Mexico
Journalism – Mexico
Juvenile delinquency – Mexico
Labor and laboring classes – Mexico
Labor laws and legislation – Mexico
Labor productivity – Mexico
Labor relations – Mexico
Labor supply – Mexico
Land grants – Mexico
Land reform – Mexico
Land settlement – Mexico
Land tenure – Mexico
Land use – Mexico
Lebanese – Mexico
Legends – Mexico
Liberalism – Mexico

Administrative and political divisions

Arnaiz Burne, Stella M. and Alfredo César Dachary. La frontera caribe de México en el XIX: una historia olvidada. *Siglo XIX: Cuadernos,* v. 3, no. 7 (Oct 93), pp. 33 – 62. Bibl, tables, maps.

Téllez Guerrero, Francisco. La segregación de Tuxpan y Chicontepec en 1853. *La Palabra y el Hombre,* no. 83 (July – Sept 92), pp. 27 – 43. Bibl, tables, maps.

Antiquities

Arnold, Philip J., III. *Domestic Ceramic Production and Spatial Organization* reviewed by Dean E. Arnold. *Latin American Antiquity,* v. 4, no. 3 (Sept 93), pp. 297 – 299.

Arnold, Philip J., III et al. Intensive Ceramic Production and Classic-Period Political Economy in the Sierra de los Tuxtlas, Veracruz, Mexico. *Ancient Mesoamerica,* v. 4, no. 2 (Fall 93), pp. 175 – 191. Bibl, il, tables, maps.

Beverido Pereau, Francisco. Estela 16 de Yaxchilán. *La Palabra y el Hombre,* no. 82 (Apr – June 92), pp. 291 – 293.

Beyer, Bernd Fahmel. El empleo de una brújula en el diseño de los espacios arquitectónicos en Monte Albán, Oaxaca, México, 400 a.c. – 830 d.c. *Revista Española de Antropología Americana,* v. 23 (1993), pp. 29 – 40. Bibl, il, tables, charts.

Bove, Frederick Joseph and Lynette Heller, eds. *New Frontiers in the Archaeology of the Pacific Coast of Southern Mesoamerica* reviewed by Molly R. Mignon. *Latin American Antiquity,* v. 4, no. 1 (Mar 93), pp. 98 – 99.

Casimir de Brizuela, Gladys. Proyecto arqueológico Loma Iguana. *La Palabra y el Hombre,* no. 81 (Jan – Mar 92), pp. 348 – 357. Bibl, il, maps, charts.

Dufétel, Dominique. La otra vida en Monte Albán (Accompanied by an English translation). *Artes de México,* no. 21 (Fall 93), pp. 60 – 65. Il.

Fernández Marquínez, María Yolanda and Alfonso Muñoz Cosme. Estilos arquitectónicos y estadios constructivos en el Grupo May, Oxkintok, Yucatán. *Revista Española de Antropología Americana,* v. 23 (1993), pp. 67 – 82. Bibl, il.

Fox, John Gerard. The Ballcourt Markers of Tenam Rosario, Chiapas, Mexico. *Ancient Mesoamerica,* v. 4, no. 1 (Spring 93), pp. 55 – 64. Bibl, il.

González Lauck, Rebecca B. Algunas consideraciones sobre los monumentos 75 y 80 de La Venta, Tabasco. *Anales del Instituto de Investigaciones Estéticas,* v. 16, no. 62 (1991), pp. 163 – 174. Bibl, il.

Kristan-Graham, Cynthia. The Business of Narrative at Tula: An Analysis of the Vestibule Frieze, Trade, and Ritual. *Latin American Antiquity,* v. 4, no. 1 (Mar 93), pp. 3 – 21. Bibl, il.

Maldonado Cárdenas, Rubén. Las pinturas de Sodzil, Yucatán, México. *Revista Española de Antropología Americana,* v. 23 (1993), pp. 101 – 111. Bibl, il.

Matos Moctezuma, Eduardo. Arqueología urbana en el centro de la ciudad de México. *Estudios de Cultura Náhuatl,* v. 22 (1992), pp. 133 – 141.

Millet Cámara, Luis et al. Tecoh, Izamal: nobleza indígena y conquista española. *Latin American Antiquity,* v. 4, no. 1 (Mar 93), pp. 48 – 58. Bibl, il, maps.

Molina Montes, Augusto. Una visión de Xochicalco en el siglo XIX: Dupaix y Castañeda, 1805. *Anales del Instituto de Investigaciones Estéticas,* v. 16, no. 62 (1991), pp. 53 – 68. Bibl, il.

Montero, Ignacio and Carmen Varela Torrecilla. Cuantificación y representación gráfica de los materiales cerámicos mayas: una propuesta metodológica. *Revista Española de Antropología Americana,* v. 23 (1993), pp. 83 – 100. Bibl, tables, charts.

Pascual Soto, Arturo. *Iconografía arqueológica de El Tajín* reviewed by Fernando Winfield Capitaine. *La Palabra y el Hombre,* no. 82 (Apr – June 92), pp. 313 – 314.

Rivera Dorado, Miguel et al. Trabajos arqueológicos en Oxkintok durante el verano de 1991. *Revista Española de Antropología Americana,* v. 23 (1993), pp. 41 – 65. Bibl, il, tables, maps.

Sugiyama, Saburo. Worldview Materialized in Teotihuacán, Mexico. *Latin American Antiquity,* v. 4, no. 2 (June 93), pp. 103 – 129. Bibl, il, maps, charts.

Weigand, Phil C. Teuchitlán and Central Mexico: Geometry and Cultural Distance. *Anales del Instituto de Investigaciones Estéticas,* v. 16, no. 62 (1991), pp. 23 – 34. Bibl, il, maps.

Williams, Eduardo. *Las piedras sagradas: escultura prehispánica del occidente de México* reviewed by Louise I. Paradis. *Latin American Antiquity,* v. 4, no. 4 (Dec 93), pp. 393 – 394.

Conservation and restoration

Ramírez Castilla, Gustavo A. En torno a la restauración de monumentos arqueológicos en México. *La Palabra y el Hombre,* no. 84 (Oct – Dec 92), pp. 165 – 178. Bibl.

Armed forces

Camp, Roderic Ai. *Generals in the Palacio: The Military in Modern Mexico* reviewed by Thomas M. Davies, Jr. *Hispanic American Historical Review,* v. 73, no. 2 (May 93), pp. 335 – 336.

Biography

Franco Cáceres, Iván. Familias, oligarquía y empresarios en Yucatán, 1879 – 1906. *Siglo XIX: Cuadernos,* v. 3, no. 7 (Oct 93), pp. 9 – 31. Bibl, tables.

Himmerich y Valencia, Robert. *The Encomenderos of New Spain, 1521 – 1555* reviewed by J. Benedict Warren. *The Americas,* v. 50, no. 2 (Oct 93), pp. 272 – 273.

— *The Encomenderos of New Spain, 1521 – 1555* reviewed by Bernard Grunberg. *Caravelle,* no. 60 (1993), pp. 139 – 140.

— *The Encomenderos of New Spain, 1521 – 1555* reviewed by Robert McGeagh. *Colonial Latin American Historical Review,* v. 2, no. 1 (Winter 93), pp. 118 – 120.

— *The Encomenderos of New Spain, 1521 – 1555* reviewed by Murdo J. Macleod. *Hispanic American Historical Review,* v. 73, no. 1 (Feb 93), pp. 149 – 150.

Tello Díaz, Carlos. *El exilio: un relato de familia* reviewed by Adolfo Castañón. *Vuelta,* v. 17, no. 204 (Nov 93), pp. 36 – 38.

Walker, David Wayne. *Parentescos, negocios y política: la familia Martínez del Río en México, 1823 – 1867* reviewed by María del Carmen Collado Herrera. *Historia Mexicana,* v. 42, no. 1 (July – Sept 92), pp. 133 – 138.

Boundaries

Belize

Arnaiz Burne, Stella M. and Alfredo César Dachary. La frontera caribe de México en el XIX: una historia olvidada. *Siglo XIX: Cuadernos,* v. 3, no. 7 (Oct 93), pp. 33 – 62. Bibl, tables, maps.

Civilization

Castaingts Teillery, Juan. Las olimpiadas . . . : nación, juego, rito y cultura. *Nueva Antropología,* v. 13, no. 44 (Aug 93), pp. 119 – 136. Bibl.

Labastida, Jaime. El México que quiero. *Plural (Mexico),* v. 22, no. 264 (Sept 93), pp. 23 – 29.

Lomnitz-Adler, Claudio. Hacia una antropología de la nacionalidad mexicana. *Revista Mexicana de Sociología,* v. 55, no. 2 (Apr – June 93), pp. 169 – 195. Bibl.

Mejía Madrid, Fabrizio. El nuevo retorno de los brujos. *Nexos,* v. 16, no. 190 (Oct 93), pp. 53 – 63.

Tovar de Teresa, Guillermo. México entre el fundamentalismo y la globalización. *Vuelta,* v. 17, no. 198 (May 93), pp. 33 – 40.

Vogeley, Nancy J. Colonial Discourse in a Postcolonial Context: Nineteenth-Century Mexico. *Colonial Latin American Review,* v. 2, no. 1 – 2 (1993), pp. 189 – 212. Bibl.

Weinberg, Liliana Irene. Lo mexicano en el México moderno. *Cuadernos Americanos,* no. 41, Nueva época (Sept – Oct 93), pp. 204 – 211. Bibl.

Zea, Leopoldo. Lo mexicano en la universalidad. *Cuadernos Americanos,* no. 41, Nueva época (Sept – Oct 93), pp. 193 – 203.

Commerce

Fujii Gambero, Gerardo and Noemí Levy. Composición de las exportaciones de Brasil, Corea, España y México. *Comercio Exterior,* v. 43, no. 9 (Sept 93), pp. 844 – 851. Tables.

García de Fuentes, Ana. Comercio, modernización y procesos territoriales: el caso de Mérida, Yucatán. *Problemas del Desarrollo,* v. 24, no. 94 (July – Sept 93), pp. 133 – 163. Bibl, tables, maps, charts.

Rodríguez, María de los Angeles. Las frutas y legumbres en el comercio exterior de México. *La Palabra y el Hombre,* no. 82 (Apr – June 92), pp. 199 – 227. Bibl, tables.

History

Blázquez Domínguez, Carmen. Proyectos de comunicación por el Istmo de Tehuantepec, 1842 – 1860. *La Palabra y el Hombre,* no. 83 (July – Sept 92), pp. 199 – 217. Bibl.

Grosso, Juan Carlos. El comercio interregional entre Puebla y Veracruz: de la etapa borbónica al México independiente. *La Palabra y el Hombre,* no. 83 (July – Sept 92), pp. 59 – 91. Bibl, tables, charts.

Juárez Martínez, Abel. España, el Caribe y el puerto de Veracruz en tiempos del libre comercio, 1789 – 1821. *La Palabra y el Hombre,* no. 83 (July – Sept 92), pp. 93 – 108. Bibl.

Naveda Chávez-Hita, Adriana. Consideraciones sobre comercio y crédito en la villa de Córdoba, siglo XVIII. *La Palabra y el Hombre,* no. 83 (July – Sept 92), pp. 109 – 120. Bibl.

Yuste, Carmen, ed. *Comerciantes mexicanos en el siglo XVIII* reviewed by Frédérique Langue. *Caravelle,* no. 60 (1993), pp. 151 – 152.

Statistics

Sumario estadístico. *Comercio Exterior,* v. 43, no. 2, 4, 9, 10 (1993), All issues.

Torres Torres, Felipe. Los desequilibrios de la balanza comercial agropecuaria. *Momento Económico,* no. 66 (Mar – Apr 93), pp. 9 – 13. Tables.

Great Britain

Heath, Hilarie J. British Merchant Houses in Mexico, 1821 – 1860: Conforming Business Practices and Ethics. *Hispanic American Historical Review,* v. 73, no. 2 (May 93), pp. 261 – 290. Bibl.

Mayo, John K. British Merchants in Chile and on Mexico's West Coast in the Mid-Nineteenth Century: The Age of Isolation. *Historia (Chile),* no. 26 (1991 – 1992), pp. 144 – 171. Bibl.

United States

Dávila Flores, Alejandro. *La apertura comercial y la frontera México – Texas* reviewed by David J. Molina. *Journal of Borderlands Studies,* v. 8, no. 1 (Spring 93), pp. 116 – 118. Bibl.

Dutrénit, Gabriela. Las agroindustrias exportadoras: su penetración en Estados Unidos. *Comercio Exterior,* v. 43, no. 4 (Apr 93), pp. 336 – 343. Tables.

Máttar, Jorge and Claudia Schatan. El comercio intraindustrial e intrafirme México – Estados Unidos: autopartes, electrónicos y petroquímicos (Translated by Adriana Hierro). *Comercio Exterior,* v. 43, no. 2 (Feb 93), pp. 103 – 124. Bibl, tables.

Rothstein, Richard. El desarrollo continental y el comercio entre México y Estados Unidos: ¿Por qué los trabajadores estadunidenses necesitan salarios más altos en México? *Relaciones Internacionales (Mexico),* v. 15, Nueva época, no. 57 (Jan – Mar 93), pp. 63 – 74.

Constitutional law

Aprobó la Cámara de Diputados las reformas a los artículos 246 y 18 transitorio del COFIPE. *Fem,* v. 17, no. 128 (Oct 93), p. 41.

Durand Alcántara, Carlos Humberto. Las reformas y adicionales al Artículo 27 constitucional, 1857 – 1992. *Derecho y Reforma Agraria,* no. 24 (1993), pp. 139 – 157. Bibl.

El México nuevo en Mérida y San Lázaro. *Fem,* v. 17, no. 127 (Sept 93), p. 46.

Salinas de Gortari, Carlos. Iniciativa para la reforma del Artículo Cuarto de la constitución mexicana. *Anuario Indigenista,* v. 30 (Dec 91), pp. 145 – 154.

— Iniciativa para la reforma del régimen ejidal: Artículo 27 de la constitución mexicana. *Anuario Indigenista,* v. 30 (Dec 91), pp. 155 – 184.

— México: decreto por el que se reforma el Artículo 27 de la constitución política de los Estados Unidos Mexicanos. *Anuario Indigenista,* v. 30 (Dec 91), pp. 489 – 496.

— México: decreto por el que se reforma el Artículo 4 de la constitución política de los Estados Unidos Mexicanos. *Anuario Indigenista,* v. 30 (Dec 91), pp. 487 – 488.

Cultural policy

García Canclini, Néstor and Gilberto Guevara Niebla, eds. *La educación y la cultura ante el Tratado de Libre Comercio* reviewed by Fernando de Mateo (Review entitled "El jalón del TLC"). *Nexos,* v. 16, no. 189 (Sept 93), pp. 66 – 67.

Magaloni de Bustamante, Ana María. El papel del gobierno mexicano en apoyo del desarrollo cultural. *SALALM Papers,* v. 34 (1989), pp. 3 – 8.

Ocharán, Leticia. Las artes plásticas frente al TLC. *Plural (Mexico),* v. 22, no. 258 (Mar 93), pp. 72 – 73.

Stern, Peter A. Art and the State in Post-Revolutionary Mexico and Cuba. *SALALM Papers,* v. 34 (1989), pp. 17 – 32. Bibl.

Zúñiga, Víctor. Promover el arte en una ciudad del norte de México: los proyectos artísticos en Monterrey, 1940 – 1960. *Estudios Sociológicos,* v. 11, no. 31 (Jan – Apr 93), pp. 155 – 181. Bibl, tables.

Description and travel

Ayre, Shirley. A Rosier Image for the Zona Rosa. *Business Mexico,* v. 3, no. 10 (Oct 93), pp. 4 – 7. Il.

Bayón, Damián Carlos. México, 1947. *Vuelta,* v. 17, no. 196 (Mar 93), pp. 75 – 76.

Sources

Charnay, Désiré. *Le Mexique, 1858 – 1861: souvenirs et impressions de voyage* commentaries by Pascal Mongne. Reviewed by Françoise Milhorat. *Caravelle,* no. 59 (1992), pp. 273 – 277.

Vargas, Diego de. *Letters from the New World: Selected Correspondence of Don Diego de Vargas to His Family, 1675 – 1706* edited and translated by John L. Kessell, Rick Hendricks, and Meredith D. Dodge. Reviewed by Jennifer L. Zimnoch. *The Americas Review,* v. 21, no. 1 (Spring 93), pp. 123 – 124.

— *Letters from the New World: Selected Correspondence of Don Diego de Vargas to His Family, 1675 – 1706* edited and translated by John L. Kessell, Rick Hendricks, and Meredith D. Dodge. Reviewed by Mark A. Burkholder. *Hispanic American Historical Review,* v. 73, no. 3 (Aug 93), pp. 510 – 511.

Discovery and exploration

Morino, Angelo. Hernán Cortés e la regina Calafia. *Quaderni Ibero-Americani,* no. 72 (Dec 92), pp. 603 – 620. Bibl.

Economic conditions

Mancera Aguayo, Miguel. Discurso de Miguel Mancera en la recepción del premio de economía rey Juan Carlos (Introduced by Luis Angel Rojo). *El Trimestre Económico,* v. 60, no. 237 (Jan – Mar 93), pp. 212 – 229.

Bibliography

Miño Grijalva, Manuel. Estructura económica y crecimiento: la historiografía económica colonial mexicana. *Historia Mexicana,* v. 42, no. 2 (Oct – Dec 92), pp. 221 – 260.

Mathematical models

Romero, José and Leslie Young. Crecimiento constante y transición en un modelo dinámico dual del Acuerdo de Libre Comercio de la América del Norte (Translated by Carlos Villegas). *El Trimestre Económico,* v. 60, no. 238 (Apr – June 93), pp. 353 – 370. Bibl.

Research

Puchet Anyul, Martín. La economía durante los '80: notas para un debate sobre sus cambios analíticos y profesionales. *Desarrollo Económico (Argentina),* v. 33, no. 129 (Apr – June 93), pp. 49 – 65. Bibl.

Ruiz Chiapetto, Crescencio. Migración interna y desarrollo económico: tres etapas. *Estudios Demográficos y Urbanos,* v. 6, no. 3 (Sept – Dec 91), pp. 727 – 736.

Statistics

Gutiérrez Lara, Abelardo Aníbal and Luis Rodríguez Medellín. La economía mexicana en la búsqueda de su modernización. *El Cotidiano,* v. 9, no. 55 (June 93), pp. 103 – 110. Tables, charts.

1821 – 1910

Romero Gil, Juan Manuel. Minería y sociedad en el noroeste porfirista. *Siglo XIX: Cuadernos,* v. 1, no. 1 (Oct 91), pp. 37 – 73. Bibl, tables.

1970 –

McCaughan, Edward J. Mexico's Long Crisis: Toward New Regimes of Accumulation and Domination. *Latin American Perspectives,* v. 20, no. 3 (Summer 93), pp. 6 – 31. Bibl.

Sáenz, Josué. Diálogo con Adam Smith. *Vuelta,* v. 17, no. 197 (Apr 93), pp. 27 – 31.

1982 –

Arizcorreta Buchholz, Luis. Interview: Luis Pazos. *Business Mexico,* v. 3, no. 3 (Mar 93), pp. 30 – 31. Il.

Banco de México. Evolución de la economía mexicana en 1992. *Comercio Exterior,* v. 43, no. 6 (June 93), pp. 585 – 593. Tables.

Bernal Sahagún, Víctor Manuel. La coyuntura económica semestral. *Momento Económico,* no. 68 (July – Aug 93), pp. 2 – 7. Bibl.

Bolívar Espinoza, Augusto et al. Se preparan tiempos de coyuntura, vísperas del cambio de gobierno. *El Cotidiano,* v. 9, no. 55 (June 93), pp. 60 – 67. Il.

Carmona de la Peña, Fernando. IV Informe Presidencial: ¿Mayor transnacionalización y más soberanía? *Momento Económico,* no. 65 (Jan – Feb 93), pp. 2 – 7.

Damm Arnal, Arturo. Del porqué de la desaceleración. *Problemas del Desarrollo,* v. 24, no. 94 (July – Sept 93), pp. 32 – 38.

Guillén Romo, Arturo. La desaceleración de la economía mexicana: causas y perspectivas; las dificultades de la actual estrategia del desarrollo. *Problemas del Desarrollo,* v. 24, no. 94 (July – Sept 93), pp. 15 – 19.

Impulso microeconómico. *Comercio Exterior,* v. 43 (1993), All issues. Tables, charts.

Levine, Ruth E. and Rebeca Wong. Estructura del hogar como respuesta a los ajustes económicos: evidencia del México urbano de los ochenta. *Estudios Demográficos y Urbanos,* v. 7, no. 2 – 3 (May – Dec 92), pp. 493 – 509. Bibl, tables, charts.

López Villafañe, Víctor. La integración económica en la cuenca del Pacífico: el reto de la América del Norte. *Comercio Exterior,* v. 43, no. 12 (Dec 93), pp. 1145 – 1152. Bibl, tables.

Loría Díaz, Eduardo. La recuperación económica mundial y los ciclos de largo plazo. *Comercio Exterior,* v. 43, no. 10 (Oct 93), pp. 933 – 939. Bibl, tables.

Ortiz Wadgymar, Arturo. La recesión del '93: neoliberalismo en entredicho. *Momento Económico,* no. 69 (Sept – Oct 93), pp. 2 – 5.

Recuento nacional. *Comercio Exterior,* v. 43 (1993), All issues. Tables.

Saviñón Díez de Sollano, Adalberto. México: identidad y cultura. *Comercio Exterior,* v. 43, no. 10 (Oct 93), pp. 940 – 945. Bibl.

Sotelo Valencia, Adrián. La crisis estructural en México. *El Cotidiano,* v. 9, no. 53 (Mar – Apr 93), pp. 110 – 117. Bibl, tables.

Sousa Vidal, Alejandro. Desaceleración económica: causas y perspectivas. *Problemas del Desarrollo,* v. 24, no. 94 (July – Sept 93), pp. 20 – 24.

Tello Villagrán, Pedro. 1993: el cuadro productivo. *Problemas del Desarrollo,* v. 24, no. 94 (July – Sept 93), pp. 25 – 31.

Zepeda Martínez, Mario Joaquín. La hora de sobreajuste: de la desaceleración hacia . . . ¿la recesión? *Momento Económico,* no. 68 (July – Aug 93), pp. 8 – 15. Tables, charts.

Economic policy

Agostini, Claudio. Liberalización de la economía mexicana. *Estudios Sociales (Chile),* no. 76 (Apr – June 93), pp. 169 – 188. Bibl.

Alonso, Jorge et al, eds. *El nuevo estado mexicano, tomo I: Estado y economía* reviewed by Gonzalo Alejandre Ramos. *El Cotidiano,* v. 8, no. 52 (Jan – Feb 93), p. 114.

Alvarez Bejar, Alejandro and Gabriel Mendoza Pichardo. Mexico, 1988 – 1991: A Successful Economic Adjustment Program? (Translated by John F. Uggen). *Latin American Perspectives,* v. 20, no. 3 (Summer 93), pp. 32 – 45. Bibl.

Barkin, David. *Distorted Development: Mexico in the World Economy* reviewed by Peter Gregory. *Economic Development and Cultural Change,* v. 42, no. 1 (Oct 93), pp. 210 – 215.

— *Distorted Development: Mexico in the World Economy* reviewed by Russell White (Review entitled "Postwar Mexican Development Policy: State and Class Contradictions"). *Latin American Perspectives,* v. 20, no. 3 (Summer 93), pp. 76 – 79.

Cameron, Maxwell A. and Ricardo Grinspun. Mexico: The Wages of Trade. *Report on the Americas,* v. 26, no. 4 (Feb 93), pp. 32 – 37 +. Bibl, il.

Cárdenas de la Peña, Enrique. La política económica en la época de Cárdenas. *El Trimestre Económico,* v. 60, no. 239 (July – Sept 93), pp. 675 – 697. Bibl, tables.

Cypher, James Martin. *State and Capital in Mexico: Development Policy since 1940* reviewed by Russell White (Review entitled "Postwar Mexican Development Policy: State and Class Contradictions"). *Latin American Perspectives,* v. 20, no. 3 (Summer 93), pp. 76 – 79.

Davis, Diane E. The Dialectic of Autonomy: State, Class, and Economic Crisis in Mexico, 1958 – 1982. *Latin American Perspectives,* v. 20, no. 3 (Summer 93), pp. 46 – 75. Bibl, tables, charts.

Favre, Henri. Contra-revolución en México (Translated by Jorge Padín Videla). *Cuadernos Americanos,* no. 39, Nueva época (May – June 93), pp. 101 – 113.

— La contrarrevolución mexicana (Translated by Laia Cortés). *Debate (Peru),* v. 16, no. 74 (Sept – Oct 93), pp. 49 – 52. Il.

Fuentes Aguilar, Luis and Consuelo Soto Mora. El control institucional en el Plan Nacional de Desarrollo en México. *Revista Interamericana de Planificación,* v. 26, no. 101 – 102 (Jan – June 93), pp. 183 – 195. Bibl.

Huerta G., Arturo. Los cambios estructurales de la política salinista: su inviabilidad de alcanzar un crecimiento sostenido. *Problemas del Desarrollo,* v. 24, no. 92 (Jan – Mar 93), pp. 15 – 23.

Loaeza, Soledad. La incertidumbre política mexicana. *Nexos,* v. 16, no. 186 (June 93), pp. 47 – 59. Bibl.

Lustig, Nora. *Mexico: The Remaking of an Economy* reviewed by Luis Felipe Lagos M. *Cuadernos de Economía (Chile),* v. 30, no. 90 (Aug 93), pp. 261 – 263.

— *Mexico: The Remaking of an Economy* reviewed by E. V. K. Fitzgerald. *Journal of Latin American Studies,* v. 25, no. 3 (Oct 93), pp. 680 – 681.

McCaughan, Edward J. Mexico's Long Crisis: Toward New Regimes of Accumulation and Domination. *Latin American Perspectives,* v. 20, no. 3 (Summer 93), pp. 6 – 31. Bibl.

Martínez Escamilla, Ramón. El estado mexicano y la economía en la década 1983 – 1993. *Momento Económico,* no. 68 (July – Aug 93), pp. 16 – 18. Bibl.

Ortiz Wadgymar, Arturo. La política económica de México, 1988 – 1992: hacia una evaluación preliminar. *Relaciones Internacionales (Mexico),* v. 14, Nueva época, no. 56 (Oct – Dec 92), pp. 133 – 141. Bibl, tables, charts.

Pacto para la Estabilidad, la Competitividad y el Empleo: concertación vigente hasta el 31 de diciembre de 1994. *Comercio Exterior,* v. 43, no. 10 (Oct 93), pp. 917 – 920.

Ramírez, Miguel D. Stabilization and Trade Reform in Mexico, 1983 – 1989. *Journal of Developing Areas,* v. 27, no. 2 (Jan 93), pp. 173 – 190. Bibl, tables, charts.

Rodríguez, Flavia. The Mexican Privatization Programme: An Economic Analysis. *Social and Economic Studies,* v. 41, no. 4 (Dec 92), pp. 149 – 171. Bibl, tables, charts.

Rubio F., Luis. El talón de Aquiles de la reforma económica. *Vuelta,* v. 17, no. 200 (July 93), pp. 36 – 39.

Sheahan, John. *Conflict and Change in Mexican Economic Strategy: Implications for Mexico and for Latin America* reviewed by Martin C. Needler (Review entitled "Economic Policy and Political Survival"). *Mexican Studies,* v. 9, no. 1 (Winter 93), pp. 139 – 143.

Soria, Víctor M. Nouvelles politiques d'ajustement et de relégitimation de l'état au Mexique: le rôle du PRONASOL et de la privatisation des entreprises publiques. *Tiers Monde,* v. 34, no. 135 (July – Sept 93), pp. 603 – 623. Bibl, tables.

Stavenhagen, Rodolfo. Democracia, modernización y cambio social en México. *Nueva Sociedad,* no. 124 (Mar – Apr 93), pp. 27 – 45. Bibl.

Trigueros Legarreta, Ignacio. Programas de estabilización sin credibilidad e intermediación financiera. *El Trimestre Económico,* v. 59, no. 236 (Oct – Dec 92), pp. 641 – 655. Bibl, tables, charts.

Valdés Ugalde, Francisco. Concepto y estrategia de la "reforma del estado." *Revista Mexicana de Sociología,* v. 55, no. 2 (Apr – June 93), pp. 315 – 338. Bibl, tables.

Villar, Samuel I. del. El programa económico del PRD. *Nexos,* v. 16, no. 192 (Dec 93), pp. 41 – 45.

Whiting, Van R., Jr. *The Political Economy of Foreign Investment in Mexico: Nationalism, Liberalism, and Constraints on Choice* reviewed by Sylvia Maxfield. *Journal of Latin American Studies,* v. 25, no. 3 (Oct 93), pp. 682 – 683.

Zermeño García, Sergio. La derrota de la sociedad: modernización y modernidad en el México de Norteamérica. *Revista Mexicana de Sociología,* v. 55, no. 2 (Apr – June 93), pp. 273 – 290. Bibl.

Sources

Castañeda, Gabriel et al. Antecedentes económicos para una ley federal de competencia económica. *El Trimestre Económico,* v. 60, no. 237 (Jan – Mar 93), pp. 230 – 268. Bibl.

Salinas de Gortari, Carlos. Quinto Informe de Gobierno. *Comercio Exterior,* v. 43, no. 11 (Nov 93), pp. 1068 – 1094.

— Quinto Informe de Gobierno. *Nexos,* v. 16, no. 192 (Dec 93), Insert.

— V Informe de Gobierno del presidente Carlos Salinas de Gortari. *Fem,* v. 17, no. 129 (Nov 93), p. 41. Il.

Emigration and immigration

Castillo G., Manuel Angel. La economía centroamericana y la inmigración a México. *Comercio Exterior,* v. 43, no. 8 (Aug 93), pp. 763 – 773. Bibl, tables.

Castro Martignoni, Jorge. México: estimación de la migración internacional en el período 1960 – 1980. *Estudios Fronterizos,* no. 26 (Sept – Dec 91), pp. 71 – 122. Bibl, tables.

Corona Vázquez, Rodolfo. Migración permanente interestatal e internacional, 1950 – 1990. *Comercio Exterior,* v. 43, no. 8 (Aug 93), pp. 750 – 762. Bibl, tables.

García Quiñones, Rolando. Análisis comparativo de un tipo singular de retorno: el caso de los mexicanos indocumentados devueltos. *Problemas del Desarrollo,* v. 24, no. 93 (Apr – June 93), pp. 121 – 151. Bibl, tables.

Widmer S., Rolf. La ciudad de Veracruz en el último siglo colonial, 1680 – 1820: algunos aspectos de la historia demográfica de una ciudad portuaria. *La Palabra y el Hombre,* no. 83 (July – Sept 92), pp. 121 – 134. Bibl, tables.

Wilson, Tamar Diana. Theoretical Approaches to Mexican Wage Labor Migration. *Latin American Perspectives,* v. 20, no. 3 (Summer 93), pp. 98 – 129. Bibl.

Law and legislation

Cohen, Joshua A. Requirements for Work Visas. *Business Mexico,* v. 3, no. 8 (Aug 93), pp. 14 – 15.

Foreign economic relations

Barkin, David. *Distorted Development: Mexico in the World Economy* reviewed by Peter Gregory. *Economic Development and Cultural Change,* v. 42, no. 1 (Oct 93), pp. 210 – 215.

— *Distorted Development: Mexico in the World Economy* reviewed by Russell White (Review entitled "Postwar Mexican Development Policy: State and Class Contradictions"). *Latin American Perspectives,* v. 20, no. 3 (Summer 93), pp. 76 – 79.

Gaytán Guzmán, Rosa Isabel. La política exterior mexicana en el marco de los procesos mundiales de integración comercial. *Relaciones Internacionales (Mexico),* v. 15, Nueva época, no. 58 (Apr – June 93), pp. 25 – 37. Bibl, tables.

Urías, Homero. La ofensiva comercial de la diplomacia mexicana. *Comercio Exterior,* v. 43, no. 12 (Dec 93), pp. 1099 – 1106.

Canada

Castro Martínez, Pedro Fernando. Comercio e inversiones México – Canadá: un asunto trilateral. *Comercio Exterior,* v. 43, no. 5 (May 93), pp. 498 – 506. Bibl, tables.

Central America

Tratado América Central – México: acuerdo marco multilateral para el programa de liberalización comercial entre los gobiernos de Costa Rica, El Salvador, Guatemala, Honduras, México y Nicaragua. *Integración Latinoamericana,* v. 17, no. 184 (Nov 92), pp. 72 – 74.

European Community

Estay Reino, Jaime and Héctor Sotomayor, eds. *América Latina y México ante la Unión Europea de 1992* reviewed by Gilberto A. Cardoso Vargas. *Problemas del Desarrollo,* v. 24, no. 92 (Jan – Mar 93), pp. 236 – 238.

Latin America

Dávila Pérez, María del Consuelo. El modelo mexicano: ¿El ejemplo para la región? *Relaciones Internacionales (Mexico),* v. 14, Nueva época, no. 56 (Oct – Dec 92), pp. 123 – 127. Bibl.

United States

Carmona de la Peña, Fernando. IV Informe Presidencial: ¿Mayor transnacionalización y más soberanía? *Momento Económico,* no. 65 (Jan – Feb 93), pp. 2 – 7.

Castro Martínez, Pedro Fernando. Corporativismo y TLC: las viejas y nuevas alianzas del estado. *Plural (Mexico),* v. 22, no. 261 (June 93), pp. 63 – 73. Bibl.

Gaytán Guzmán, Rosa Isabel. *Las relaciones comerciales entre México y Estados Unidos, 1867 – 1876* reviewed by Guadalupe González G. *Relaciones Internacionales (Mexico),* v. 14, Nueva época, no. 55 (July – Sept 92), pp. 79 – 82.

Nabers, Mary Scott. A Growing Love Affair. *Business Mexico,* v. 3, no. 5 (May 93), pp. 13 – 14. Charts.

Székely, Gabriel. California Sunrise. *Nexos,* v. 16, no. 185 (May 93), pp. 13 – 15.

Foreign relations

Abella Armengol, Gloria. La política exterior de México en el gobierno de Carlos Salinas de Gortari: ¿Una nueva concepción? *Revista Mexicana de Ciencias Políticas y Sociales,* v. 37, Nueva época, no. 148 (Apr – June 92), pp. 63 – 76.

Hernández Vela Salgado, Edmundo. La política exterior en México en el umbral del tercer milenio. *Revista Mexicana de Ciencias Políticas y Sociales,* v. 37, Nueva época, no. 148 (Apr – June 92), pp. 77 – 86.

Jauberth, H. Rodrigo et al. *The Difficult Triangle: Mexico, Central America, and the United States,* a translation of *La triangulación Centroamérica – México – EUA.* Reviewed by Robert H. Holden. *Hispanic American Historical Review,* v. 73, no. 1 (Feb 93), pp. 192 – 194.

México y el mundo: historia de sus relaciones exteriores reviewed by Marlene Alcántara Domínguez. *Relaciones Internacionales (Mexico),* v. 14, Nueva época, no. 55 (July – Sept 92), pp. 83 – 84.

Law and legislation

Dávila Pérez, María del Consuelo. La política exterior en la revolución mexicana: bases histórico – jurídicas. *Relaciones Internacionales (Mexico),* v. 14, Nueva época, no. 55 (July – Sept 92), pp. 65 – 73. Bibl.

Austria

Anderle, Adám and Monika Kozári. Koloman von Kánya: Ein österreichisch-ungarischer Botschafter in Mexiko. *Zeitschrift für Lateinamerika Wien,* no. 43 (1992), pp. 63 – 80. Bibl.

Caribbean area

Martínez Vara, Gerardo. México y el Caribe: un encuentro necesario en la problemática regional. *Relaciones Internacionales (Mexico),* v. 14, Nueva época, no. 56 (Oct – Dec 92), pp. 129 – 132.

France

Rolland, Denis. *Vichy et la France libre au Mexique: guerre, cultures et propagande pendant la deuxième guerre mondiale* reviewed by Thomas D. Schoonover. *Hispanic American Historical Review,* v. 73, no. 4 (Nov 93), pp. 726 – 727.

Great Britain

Meyer, Lorenzo. *Su majestad británica contra la revolución mexicana: el fin de un imperio informal* reviewed by Freidrich Katz. *Historia Mexicana,* v. 42, no. 1 (July – Sept 92), pp. 152 – 157.

Latin America

Cabra Ybarra, José G. Las relaciones de México con Latinoamérica durante la última década: ¿Líder, intérprete o interlocutor? *Relaciones Internacionales (Mexico),* v. 14, Nueva época, no. 56 (Oct – Dec 92), pp. 117 – 122.

Nicaragua

Buchenau, Jürgen. Counter-Intervention against Uncle Sam: Mexico's Support for Nicaraguan Nationalism, 1903 – 1910. *The Americas,* v. 50, no. 2 (Oct 93), pp. 207 – 232. Bibl.

Spain

Alizal, Laura del. España en 1992: su integración a Europa y sus relaciones con México. *Revista Mexicana de Ciencias Políticas y Sociales,* v. 37, Nueva época, no. 149 (July – Sept 92), pp. 109 – 122.

United States

Buchenau, Jürgen. Counter-Intervention against Uncle Sam: Mexico's Support for Nicaraguan Nationalism, 1903 – 1910. *The Americas,* v. 50, no. 2 (Oct 93), pp. 207 – 232. Bibl.

Eisenstadt, Todd. Nuevo estilo diplomático: cabildeo y relaciones públicas, 1986 – 1991 (Translated by Martha Elena Venier). *Foro Internacional,* v. 32, no. 5 (Oct – Dec 92), pp. 667 – 702. Bibl, tables, charts.

Glennon, Michael J. Testimony before the Subcommittee on Civil and Constitutional Rights, Committee on the Judiciary, United States House of Representatives. *Mexican Studies,* v. 9, no. 1 (Winter 93), pp. 1 – 17.

Hernández Navarro, Luis. De Washington al Cerro de las Campanas: la exportación de la democracia a la hora del TLC. *El Cotidiano,* v. 9, no. 54 (May 93), pp. 101 – 107. Bibl.

Montaño, Jorge. Una visión desde Washington: México/Estados Unidos en los noventas. *Nexos,* v. 16, no. 187 (July 93), pp. 15 – 19.

Weintraub, Sidney. *A Marriage of Convenience: U.S. – Mexico Relations* reviewed by Lázaro Cárdenas Armenta (Review entitled "Las relaciones México – Estados Unidos: entre el conflicto y la cooperación"). *Relaciones Internacionales (Mexico),* v. 15, Nueva época, no. 57 (Jan – Mar 93), pp. 101 – 103.

Government publications

Sources

Elmendorf, George F. and Joan A. Quillen. Serials and Government Documents from the States of Mexico. *SALALM Papers,* v. 36 (1991), pp. 425 – 431.

Historiography

Carreño King, Tania and Angélica Vázquez del Mercado. Crítica de la historia pragmática: una entrevista con Luis González y González. *Nexos,* v. 16, no. 191 (Nov 93), pp. 35 – 39.

— La disputa por la historia patria: una entrevista con Lorenzo Meyer. *Nexos,* v. 16, no. 191 (Nov 93), pp. 41 – 49.

Covo, Jacqueline. La prensa en la historiografía mexicana: problemas y perspectivas. *Historia Mexicana,* v. 42, no. 3 (Jan – Mar 93), pp. 689 – 710. Bibl.

Florescano, Enrique. *El nuevo pasado mexicano* reviewed by Felícitas López-Portillo Tostado. *Cuadernos Americanos,* no. 38, Nueva época (Mar – Apr 93), pp. 239 – 243.

García Morales, Soledad. Algunas consideraciones sobre la historiografía veracruzana del porfiriato y la revolución en Veracruz. *La Palabra y el Hombre,* no. 83 (July – Sept 92), pp. 304 – 313.

Gonzalbo Aizpuru, Pilar. Hacia una historia de la vida privada en la Nueva España. *Historia Mexicana,* v. 42, no. 2 (Oct – Dec 92), pp. 353 – 377.

González Casasnovas, Ignacio and Guillermo Mira Delli-Zotti. Reflexiones y sugerencias a propósito de la minería colonial. *Historia Mexicana,* v. 42, no. 2 (Oct – Dec 92), pp. 309 – 332.

Haber, Stephen H. La industrialización de México: historiografía y análisis (Translated by Laura Elena Pulido Varela). *Historia Mexicana,* v. 42, no. 3 (Jan – Mar 93), pp. 649 – 688.

Héau de Giménez, Catherine and Enrique Rajchenberg. La leyenda negra y la leyenda rosa en la nueva historiografía de la revolución mexicana. *Revista Mexicana de Sociología,* v. 54, no. 3 (July – Sept 92), pp. 175 – 188. Bibl.

— Región y nación: una antigua polémica resucitada. *Revista Mexicana de Ciencias Políticas y Sociales,* v. 38, Nueva época, no. 154 (Oct – Dec 93), pp. 19 – 34. Bibl.

Mentz de Boege, Brígida M. von. La desigualdad social en México: revisión bibliográfica y propuesta de una visión global. *Historia Mexicana,* v. 42, no. 2 (Oct – Dec 92), pp. 505 – 561.

Miño Grijalva, Manuel. Estructura económica y crecimiento: la historiografía económica colonial mexicana. *Historia Mexicana,* v. 42, no. 2 (Oct – Dec 92), pp. 221 – 260.

Tutino, John. Historias del México agrario (Translated by Mario A. Zamudio Vega). *Historia Mexicana,* v. 42, no. 2 (Oct – Dec 92), pp. 177 – 220.

Vázquez, Josefina Zoraida. Un viejo tema: el federalismo y el centralismo. *Historia Mexicana,* v. 42, no. 3 (Jan – Mar 93), pp. 621 – 631.

History

Aguilar Camín, Héctor. La invención de México. *Nexos,* v. 16, no. 187 (July 93), pp. 49 – 61.

Breton, André et al, eds. *Vingt études sur le Mexique et le Guatemala réunies à la mémoire de Nicole Percheron* reviewed by Stephen Webre. *Hispanic American Historical Review,* v. 73, no. 2 (May 93), pp. 305 – 306.

Carreño King, Tania and Angélica Vázquez del Mercado. La hija de la invención: una entrevista con Edmundo O'Gorman. *Nexos,* v. 16, no. 190 (Oct 93), pp. 45 – 51.

Hernández Chávez, Alicia and Manuel Miño Grijalva, eds. *Cincuenta años de historia en México,* vols. I y II, reviewed by Harold Dana Sims. *Hispanic American Historical Review,* v. 73, no. 4 (Nov 93), pp. 668 – 670.

Bibliography

Anna, Timothy E. Demystifying Early Nineteenth-Century Mexico (Review article). *Mexican Studies*, v. 9, no. 1 (Winter 93), pp. 119 – 137.

Salvucci, Richard J. "La parte más difícil": Recent Works on Nineteenth-Century Mexican History (Review article). *Latin American Research Review*, v. 28, no. 1 (1993), pp. 102 – 110.

Congresses

Sarabia Viejo, María Justina. Primer Congreso Internacional de Historia: "El Mundo Colonial; Examen de una Historia." *Anuario de Estudios Americanos*, v. 49, Suppl. 2 (1992), pp. 210 – 212.

— I Simposio Internacional "España y Nueva España: La Vida Cotidiana." *Anuario de Estudios Americanos*, v. 49, Suppl. 1 (1992), pp. 201 – 203.

Methodology

Pérez Herrero, Pedro, ed. *Región e historia en México, 1700 – 1850* reviewed by Margaret Chowning. *The Americas*, v. 50, no. 2 (Oct 93), pp. 280 – 282.

— *Región e historia en México, 1700 – 1850: métodos de análisis regional* reviewed by Donald F. Stevens. *Hispanic American Historical Review*, v. 73, no. 1 (Feb 93), pp. 154 – 155.

Van Young, Eric. The Cuautla Lazarus: Double Subjectives in Reading Texts on Popular Collective Action. *Colonial Latin American Review*, v. 2, no. 1 – 2 (1993), pp. 3 – 26. Bibl.

Study and teaching

Aguila, Marcos Tonatiuh. Historia, revisionismo y educación: la nueva "revolución pasiva." *El Cotidiano*, v. 8, no. 51 (Nov – Dec 92), pp. 39 – 47. Bibl, il.

Bejarano Martínez, René. Los nexos de la historia. *El Cotidiano*, v. 8, no. 51 (Nov – Dec 92), pp. 48 – 53. Il.

Méndez, Luis et al. Historia y poder. *El Cotidiano*, v. 8, no. 51 (Nov – Dec 92), pp. 60 – 69. Il, tables.

Staples, Anne. Los últimos diez años de historia regional en el Colegio de México. *La Palabra y el Hombre*, no. 83 (July – Sept 92), pp. 299 – 303. Bibl.

Vázquez, Josefina Zoraida. El dilema de la enseñanza de la historia de México. *La Educación (USA)*, v. 37, no. 114 (1993), pp. 77 – 89.

1519 – 1540, Conquest

Baudot, Georges. Malintzin, imagen y discurso de mujer en el primer México virreinal. *Cuadernos Americanos*, no. 40, Nueva época (July – Aug 93), pp. 181 – 207. Bibl.

Baudot, Georges and Tzvetan Todorov. *Récits aztèques de la conquête* reviewed by Guilhem Olivier. *Caravelle*, no. 59 (1992), pp. 241 – 249.

Calvi, Maria Vittoria. El diálogo entre españoles e indígenas en la *XIII relación* de Fernando de Alva Ixtlilxóchitl. *Quaderni Ibero-Americani*, no. 72 (Dec 92), pp. 621 – 639. Bibl.

León-Portilla, Miguel, ed. *Visión de los vencidos: relaciones indígenas de la conquista* reviewed by Beatriz de la Fuente. *Estudios de Cultura Náhuatl*, v. 22 (1992), pp. 499 – 505.

Martínez, José Luis. *Hernán Cortés* reviewed by Bernard Grunberg. *Caravelle*, no. 60 (1993), pp. 138 – 139.

— *Hernán Cortés* reviewed by María Justina Sarabia Viejo. *Anuario de Estudios Americanos*, v. 49, Suppl. 2 (1992), pp. 252 – 253.

1540 – 1810, Spanish colony

Jarquín Ortega, María Teresa. *Formación y desarrollo de un pueblo novohispano: Metepec en el valle de Toluca. Anuario de Estudios Americanos*, v. 49, Suppl. 1 (1992), pp. 254 – 256.

Langue, Frédérique. *Mines, terres et société à Zacatecas (Mexique) de la fin du XVIIe siècle a l'indépendance* reviewed by Manuel Castillo Martos. *Anuario de Estudios Americanos*, v. 50, no. 1 (1993), pp. 319 – 322.

Méndez, Cecilia. ¿Economía moral versus determinismo económico?: dos aproximaciones a la historia colonial hispanoamericana. *Historia y Cultura (Peru)*, no. 20 (1990), pp. 361 – 366.

Wood, Stephanie. The Evolution of the Indian Corporation of the Toluca Region, 1550 – 1810. *Estudios de Cultura Náhuatl*, v. 22 (1992), pp. 381 – 407. Bibl, maps.

1810 –

Escalante Gonzalbo, Fernando. *Ciudadanos imaginarios* reviewed by Rafael Rojas (Review entitled "El riesgo de la imaginación liberal"). *Nexos*, v. 16, no. 187 (July 93), pp. 77 – 78.

Florescano Mayet, Sergio. Xalapa y su región durante el siglo XIX: las principales vertientes de su desarrollo económico, social y político. *La Palabra y el Hombre*, no. 83 (July – Sept 92), pp. 135 – 165. Bibl, tables.

Skerritt, David A. Una historia dinámica entre la sierra y la costa. *La Palabra y el Hombre*, no. 83 (July – Sept 92), pp. 5 – 25. Bibl, tables, maps.

1810 – 1821, Wars of Independence

Boggio de Harasymowicz, Adriana. Movimientos populares e independencia en México y Uruguay. *La Palabra y el Hombre*, no. 82 (Apr – June 92), pp. 107 – 142. Bibl.

Rodríguez O., Jaime E., ed. *The Independence of Mexico and the Creation of the New Nation* reviewed by Pilar Collado de De Bleser. *La Palabra y el Hombre*, no. 83 (July – Sept 92), pp. 353 – 361.

1821 – 1861

Blázquez Domínguez, Carmen. Dos años críticos: la expulsión de los españoles en Xalapa y Veracruz, 1827 – 1828. *Siglo XIX: Cuadernos*, v. 2, no. 4 (Oct 92), pp. 31 – 58. Bibl.

González Pedrero, Enrique. *País de un sólo hombre: el México de Santa Anna* reviewed by Luis Villoro (Review entitled "Santa Anna o la nación sin estado"). *Nexos*, v. 16, no. 190 (Oct 93), pp. 69 – 72.

— *País de un sólo hombre: el México de Santa Anna, vol. I; La ronda de los contrarios* reviewed by Rafael Rojas. *Vuelta*, v. 17, no. 204 (Nov 93), pp. 34 – 36.

— Santa Anna antes de Santa Anna (A chapter from the book *País de un sólo hombre: el México de Santa Anna*). *Vuelta*, v. 17, no. 198 (May 93), pp. 42 – 47. Bibl, tables.

Vázquez Mantecón, Carmen. Espacio social y crisis política: la Sierra Gorda, 1850 – 1855. *Mexican Studies*, v. 9, no. 1 (Winter 93), pp. 47 – 70. Bibl, maps.

1861 – 1867, European intervention

Ridley, Jasper Godwin. *Maximilian and Juárez* reviewed by Timothy E. Anna. *Hispanic American Historical Review*, v. 73, no. 4 (Nov 93), p. 717.

1867 – 1910

Castello, Antonio Emilio. El porfiriato en México. *Todo Es Historia*, v. 26, no. 307 (Feb 93), pp. 9 – 34. Il.

1910 – 1946

Krauze, Enrique. Madero vivo. *Vuelta*, v. 17, no. 196 (Mar 93), pp. 11 – 14.

Industries

Aboites A., Jaime and Alenka Guzmán Chávez. Desempeño del sector manufacturero y relaciones laborales: la experiencia reciente de México. *El Cotidiano*, v. 10, no. 58 (Oct – Nov 93), pp. 103 – 111. Il, tables, charts.

Barragán, Juan Ignacio. Cemento, vidrio y explosivos: empresarios del norte e importación de tecnología a principios del siglo XX. *Siglo XIX: Cuadernos*, v. 3, no. 6 (June 93), pp. 9 – 21.

Capdevielle, Mario and Gabriela Dutrénit. El perfil tecnológico de la industria mexicana y su dinámica innovadora en la década de los ochenta. *El Trimestre Económico*, v. 60, no. 239 (July – Sept 93), pp. 643 – 674. Bibl, tables, charts.

Geyer, Anne. Chronicles of Success. *Business Mexico*, v. 3, no. 5 (May 93), pp. 32 – 35. Il.

Inter-American Development Bank. Las maquiladoras en México en vísperas del TLC (Adapted from the text published in *Progreso Económico y Social en América Latina*). *Comercio Exterior*, v. 43, no. 2 (Feb 93), pp. 159 – 161. Tables.

Luna, Matilde and Cristina Puga. Modernización en México: la propuesta empresarial. *Revista Mexicana de Ciencias Políticas y Sociales*, v. 38, Nueva época, no. 151 (Jan – Mar 93), pp. 35 – 49. Bibl.

Macías V., María de la Luz. Mujeres e industria manufacturera en México. *El Cotidiano,* v. 9, no. 53 (Mar – Apr 93), pp. 33 – 39. Bibl, il, tables.

Máttar, Jorge and Claudia Schatan. El comercio intraindustrial e intrafirme México – Estados Unidos: autopartes, electrónicos y petroquímicos (Translated by Adriana Hierro). *Comercio Exterior,* v. 43, no. 2 (Feb 93), pp. 103 – 124. Bibl, tables.

Ortiz Wadgymar, Arturo. La pequeña y mediana industrias ante la apertura comercial y el Tratado de Libre Comercio: los costos de la desprotección industrial en México, 1985 – 1992. *Problemas del Desarrollo,* v. 24, no. 93 (Apr – June 93), pp. 55 – 74. Bibl, tables.

Reyes Larios, Sandra. Tiempos difíciles en la industria del juguete. *Comercio Exterior,* v. 43, no. 10 (Oct 93), pp. 913 – 916. Bibl, tables.

Rionda, Jorge I. La industria maquiladora de exportación en Guanajuato. *Comercio Exterior,* v. 43, no. 2 (Feb 93), pp. 132 – 134. Tables.

Sklair, Leslie. Las maquilas en México: una perspectiva global. *Revista Mexicana de Sociología,* v. 54, no. 2 (Apr – June 92), pp. 163 – 183. Bibl.

Statland de López, Rhona. Cross Over Dreams. *Business Mexico,* v. 3, no. 5 (May 93), pp. 23 – 24 +. Il.

Tello Villagrán, Pedro. 1993: el cuadro productivo. *Problemas del Desarrollo,* v. 24, no. 94 (July – Sept 93), pp. 25 – 31.

Wilson, Patricia Ann. *Exports and Local Development: Mexico's New Maquiladoras* reviewed by Alfredo Hualde. *Estudios Sociológicos,* v. 11, no. 32 (May – Aug 93), pp. 569 – 573.

— *Exports and Local Development: Mexico's New Maquiladoras* reviewed by Helen Icken Saja. *Hispanic American Historical Review,* v. 73, no. 4 (Nov 93), pp. 719 – 720.

— *Exports and Local Development: Mexico's New Maquiladoras* reviewed by David J. Molina. *Journal of Borderlands Studies,* v. 7, no. 2 (Fall 92), pp. 106 – 108.

Bibliography

Haber, Stephen H. La industrialización de México: historiografía y análisis (Translated by Laura Elena Pulido Varela). *Historia Mexicana,* v. 42, no. 3 (Jan – Mar 93), pp. 649 – 688.

Law and legislation

Cardoso Frías, Joaquín. When the Inspector Calls . . . Be Prepared! *Business Mexico,* v. 3, no. 1 (Jan – Feb 93), p. 87.

Newman, Gray. Laying Down the Law. *Business Mexico,* v. 3, no. 1 (Jan – Feb 93), pp. 75 – 77.

Olivier, Michele. Shared Responsibility. *Business Mexico,* v. 3, no. 6 (June 93), pp. 43 – 45. Tables, charts.

Ranger, Edward M., Jr. A Compliance Checklist. *Business Mexico,* v. 3, no. 1 (Jan – Feb 93), p. 86.

— The High Cost of Noncompliance. *Business Mexico,* v. 3, no. 7 (July 93), p. 44 +.

Rivera de los Reyes, Julio M. Plant Shutdown?: Here's What to Do. *Business Mexico,* v. 3, no. 1 (Jan – Feb 93), p. 88.

Mathematical models

Casar Pérez, José I. La competitividad de la industria manufacturera mexicana, 1980 – 1990. *El Trimestre Económico,* v. 60, no. 237 (Jan – Mar 93), pp. 113 – 183. Bibl, tables, charts.

Statistics

Industrial Hot Spots: A Comparison of 10 Top States. *Business Mexico,* v. 3, no. 8 (Aug 93), pp. 32 – 33. Charts.

Pieza, Ramón. Análisis cuantitativo de la evolución del proceso industrial de septiembre de 1989 a junio de 1992 con datos trimestrales. *Problemas del Desarrollo,* v. 24, no. 92 (Jan – Mar 93), pp. 40 – 48. Tables.

Intellectual life

Ayala, Francisco J. and Rosaura Ruiz Gutiérrez. Darwinismo y sociedad en México. *Siglo XIX: Revista,* no. 12, 2a época (July – Dec 92), pp. 87 – 104. Bibl.

Camp, Roderic Ai et al, eds. *Los intelectuales y el poder en México* reviewed by Carlos Alberto Torres. *Hispanic American Historical Review,* v. 73, no. 2 (May 93), pp. 336 – 337.

Lempérière, Annick. *Intellectuels, état et société au Mexique, XXᵉ siècle: les clercs de la nation* reviewed by Frédérique Langue. *Cahiers des Amériques Latines,* no. 13 (1992), pp. 181 – 182.

Roggiano, Alfredo A. *Pedro Henríquez Ureña en México* reviewed by Gustavo Fares. *Nuevo Texto Crítico,* v. 6, no. 11 (1993), pp. 266 – 268.

Foreign influences

Bono, Diane M. *Cultural Diffusion of Spanish Humanism in New Spain: Francisco Cervantes de Salazar's 'Diálogo de la dignidad del hombre'* reviewed by William Mejías López. *Hispania (USA),* v. 76, no. 2 (May 93), pp. 282 – 284.

Languages

León-Portilla, Ascensión H. de. Nebrija y las lenguas compañeras del imperio. *Cuadernos Americanos,* no. 37, Nueva época (Jan – Feb 93), pp. 135 – 147. Bibl.

Zimmermann, Klaus. Zur Sprache der afrohispanischen Bevölkerung im Mexiko der Kolonialzeit. *Iberoamericana,* v. 17, no. 50 (1993), pp. 89 – 111. Bibl.

Laws, statutes, etc.

Romero Miranda, Miguel Angel et al. Muchos cambios legales que agitan las aguas políticas. *El Cotidiano,* v. 10, no. 58 (Oct – Nov 93), pp. 60 – 70. Il, tables.

Officials and public employees

Chandler, Dewitt Samuel. *Social Assistance and Bureaucratic Politics: The Montepíos of Colonial Mexico, 1767 – 1821* reviewed by Richard J. Salvucci. *The Americas,* v. 49, no. 4 (Apr 93), pp. 551 – 552.

— *Social Assistance and Bureaucratic Politics: The Montepíos of Colonial Mexico, 1767 – 1821* reviewed by Silvia Marina Arrom. *Hispanic American Historical Review,* v. 73, no. 1 (Feb 93), pp. 153 – 154.

— *Social Assistance and Bureaucratic Politics: The Montepíos of Colonial Mexico, 1767 – 1821* reviewed by Eric Van Young. *Journal of Latin American Studies,* v. 25, no. 3 (Oct 93), pp. 653 – 654.

Hernández Rodríguez, Rogelio. Preparación y movilidad de los funcionarios de la administración pública mexicana. *Estudios Sociológicos,* v. 11, no. 32 (May – Aug 93), pp. 445 – 473. Bibl, tables.

Lizalde, Eduardo. La sucesión ministral. *Vuelta,* v. 17, no. 197 (Apr 93), pp. 65 – 67.

Tiburcio Robles, Armando. La FSTSE en el esquema del sindicalismo moderno. *El Cotidiano,* v. 9, no. 56 (July 93), pp. 23 – 32. Il, charts.

Interviews

Gil, Carlos B., ed. *Hope and Frustration: Interviews with Leaders of Mexico's Political Opposition* reviewed by Denis L. Heyck. *Hispania (USA),* v. 76, no. 1 (Mar 93), pp. 86 – 87.

Pictorial works

Coke, Van Deren. *Secular and Sacred: Photographs of Mexico* reviewed by Diana Emery Hulick (Review entitled "Lo secular y lo sagrado: fotografías de México"). *Latin American Art,* v. 5, no. 2 (Summer 93), p. 104.

Politics and government

Romero, Jorge Javier. La política de mañana: la futura forma institucional. *Nexos,* v. 16, no. 192 (Dec 93), pp. 53 – 67. Bibl.

Bibliography

Molinar Horcasitas, Juan. Escuelas de interpretación del sistema político mexicano. *Revista Mexicana de Sociología,* v. 55, no. 2 (Apr – June 93), pp. 3 – 56. Bibl, tables.

Morris, Stephen D. Political Reformism in Mexico: Past and Present (Review article). *Latin American Research Review,* v. 28, no. 2 (1993), pp. 191 – 205. Bibl.

Ochoa Méndez, Jacqueline. Orientación bibliográfica sobre sucesión presidencial y partidos políticos. *El Cotidiano,* v. 10, no. 58 (Oct – Nov 93), pp. 119 – 120.

Vázquez, Josefina Zoraida. Un viejo tema: el federalismo y el centralismo. *Historia Mexicana,* v. 42, no. 3 (Jan – Mar 93), pp. 621 – 631.

Societies, etc.

Guedea, Virginia. La sociedad secreta de los Guadalupes: una nueva forma de organización política. *Siglo XIX: Revista,* no. 11, 2a época (Jan – June 92), pp. 28 – 45. Bibl.

Sources

Salinas de Gortari, Carlos. Quinto Informe de Gobierno. *Comercio Exterior,* v. 43, no. 11 (Nov 93), pp. 1068 – 1094.

— Quinto Informe de Gobierno. *Nexos,* v. 16, no. 192 (Dec 93), Insert.

— V Informe de Gobierno del presidente Carlos Salinas de Gortari. *Fem,* v. 17, no. 129 (Nov 93), p. 41. Il.

19th century

Hale, Charles Adams. *La transformación del liberalismo en México a fines del siglo XIX* reviewed by David Aylett. *Vuelta,* v. 17, no. 204 (Nov 93), pp. 41 – 42.

Stevens, Donald Fithian. *Origins of Instability in Early Republican Mexico* reviewed by Margaret Chowning. *The Americas,* v. 50, no. 1 (July 93), pp. 128 – 130.

— *Origins of Instability in Early Republican Mexico* reviewed by John Jay TePaske. *Hispanic American Historical Review,* v. 73, no. 1 (Feb 93), pp. 179 – 180.

1910 –

Hernández Rodríguez, Rogelio. *La formación del político mexicano: el caso de Carlos A. Madrazo* reviewed by Roderic Ai Camp. *Hispanic American Historical Review,* v. 73, no. 2 (May 93), pp. 334 – 335.

Sánchez Rebolledo, Adolfo. La herencia de la revolución mexicana: una entrevista con François-Xavier Guerra. *Nexos,* v. 16, no. 182 (Feb 93), pp. 7 – 9.

1910 – 1946

Leal, Juan Felipe. Regímenes políticos en el proceso de estructuración del nuevo estado, 1915 – 1928. *Revista Mexicana de Ciencias Políticas y Sociales,* v. 37, Nueva época, no. 148 (Apr – June 92), pp. 11 – 61.

Semo, Ilán. El cardenismo revisado: la tercera vía y otras utopías inciertas. *Revista Mexicana de Sociología,* v. 55, no. 2 (Apr – June 93), pp. 197 – 223. Bibl.

1946 –

Davis, Diane E. The Dialectic of Autonomy: State, Class, and Economic Crisis in Mexico, 1958 – 1982. *Latin American Perspectives,* v. 20, no. 3 (Summer 93), pp. 46 – 75. Bibl, tables, charts.

Medin, Tzvi. *El sexenio alemanista: ideología y praxis política de Miguel Alemán* reviewed by Errol D. Jones. *Hispanic American Historical Review,* v. 73, no. 1 (Feb 93), pp. 182 – 183.

1970 –

Alarcón Olguín, Víctor and César Cancino. La relación gobierno – partido en un régimen semi-competitivo: el caso de México. *Revista Mexicana de Ciencias Políticas y Sociales,* v. 38, Nueva época, no. 151 (Jan – Mar 93), pp. 9 – 33. Bibl.

Alonso, Jorge et al, eds. *El nuevo estado mexicano, tomo II: Estado y política* reviewed by Teresa Rueda Lugo. *El Cotidiano,* v. 8, no. 52 (Jan – Feb 93), pp. 115 – 116.

Craig, Ann L. and Joseph W. Foweraker, eds. *Popular Movements and Political Change in Mexico* reviewed by Daniel C. Levy. *Studies in Comparative International Development,* v. 27, no. 3 (Fall 92), pp. 122 – 124.

Gil, Carlos B., ed. *Hope and Frustration: Interviews with Leaders of Mexico's Political Opposition* reviewed by Denis L. Heyck. *Hispania (USA),* v. 76, no. 1 (Mar 93), pp. 86 – 87.

Gutiérrez Rodríguez, Javier and Miguel Angel Romero Miranda. Síndrome de fin de sexenio. *El Cotidiano,* v. 10, no. 58 (Oct – Nov 93), pp. 8 – 21. Il, tables.

Loaeza, Soledad. La incertidumbre política mexicana. *Nexos,* v. 16, no. 186 (June 93), pp. 47 – 59. Bibl.

Ward, Peter M. Social Welfare Policy and Political Opening in Mexico. *Journal of Latin American Studies,* v. 25, no. 3 (Oct 93), pp. 613 – 628. Bibl, tables.

1988 –

Bolívar Espinoza, Augusto et al. La debilidad de un estado fuerte. *El Cotidiano,* v. 9, no. 53 (Mar – Apr 93), pp. 60 – 68.

— Nuevos tiempos de coyuntura: consolidación del cambio y mucho desafío político. *El Cotidiano,* v. 8, no. 52 (Jan – Feb 93), pp. 60 – 66. Il.

Borja Ochoa, Roberto. La modernización política postergada. *Momento Económico,* no. 65 (Jan – Feb 93), pp. 24 – 25.

Canto Chac, Manuel. Elementos para una agenda de discusión sobre el futuro de la acción gubernamental. *El Cotidiano,* v. 10, no. 58 (Oct – Nov 93), pp. 39 – 46. Bibl.

Favre, Henri. Contra-revolución en México (Translated by Jorge Padín Videla). *Cuadernos Americanos,* no. 39, Nueva época (May – June 93), pp. 101 – 113.

— La contrarrevolución mexicana (Translated by Laia Cortés). *Debate (Peru),* v. 16, no. 74 (Sept – Oct 93), pp. 49 – 52. Il.

Flores Olea, Víctor Manuel. Los sistemas políticos y su crisis, parte II: La articulación democrática y el caso de México. *Revista Mexicana de Ciencias Políticas y Sociales,* v. 38, Nueva época, no. 152 (Apr – June 93), pp. 143 – 160.

Guerrero Orozco, Omar. *El estado en la era de la modernización* reviewed by Gabriel Corona Armenta. *Revista Mexicana de Ciencias Políticas y Sociales,* v. 38, Nueva época, no. 153 (July – Sept 93), pp. 213 – 218.

Meyer, Lorenzo. *La segunda muerte de la revolución mexicana* reviewed by Donald McCarthy (Review entitled "Critiquing the Critic"). *Business Mexico,* v. 3, no. 8 (Aug 93), p. 53.

Rubio F., Luis. Los límites del cambio político. *Nexos,* v. 16, no. 187 (July 93), pp. 63 – 68.

Sánchez Susarrey, Jaime. La escena política (Regular feature appearing in most issues). *Vuelta,* v. 17 (1993), n.p.

Schmidt, Samuel. Lo tortuoso de la democratización mexicana. *Estudios Interdisciplinarios de América Latina y el Caribe,* v. 4, no. 1 (Jan – June 93), pp. 93 – 114. Bibl.

Stavenhagen, Rodolfo. Democracia, modernización y cambio social en México. *Nueva Sociedad,* no. 124 (Mar – Apr 93), pp. 27 – 45. Bibl.

Valdés Ugalde, Francisco. Concepto y estrategia de la "reforma del estado." *Revista Mexicana de Sociología,* v. 55, no. 2 (Apr – June 93), pp. 315 – 338. Bibl, tables.

Presidents

Anguiano, Arturo. Transición política: ¿Hacia dónde? *El Cotidiano,* v. 8, no. 52 (Jan – Feb 93), pp. 3 – 9. Bibl, il.

Constantino, Mario and Rosalía Winocur. Cultura política y elecciones: algunas imágenes de la sucesión presidencial. *El Cotidiano,* v. 10, no. 58 (Oct – Nov 93), pp. 47 – 53. Bibl, tables.

Gutiérrez Rodríguez, Javier and Miguel Angel Romero Miranda. Síndrome de fin de sexenio. *El Cotidiano,* v. 10, no. 58 (Oct – Nov 93), pp. 8 – 21. Il, tables.

Mora Heredia, Juan and Raúl Rodríguez Guillén. El agotamiento del autoritarismo con legitimidad y la sucesión presidencial. *El Cotidiano,* v. 10, no. 58 (Oct – Nov 93), pp. 22 – 28. Il, tables.

Peschard, Jacqueline. Entre lo nuevo y lo viejo: la sucesión de 1994. *El Cotidiano,* v. 10, no. 58 (Oct – Nov 93), pp. 3 – 7. Il.

Reyes del Campillo, Juan. La legitimidad de la sucesión presidencial. *El Cotidiano,* v. 10, no. 58 (Oct – Nov 93), pp. 34 – 38. Il.

— El PRI, el sistema de partidos y la sucesión presidencial. *El Cotidiano,* v. 8, no. 52 (Jan – Feb 93), pp. 10 – 12.

Suárez Farías, Francisco. Familias y dinastías políticas de los presidentes del PNR – PRM – PRI. *Revista Mexicana de Ciencias Políticas y Sociales,* v. 38, Nueva época, no. 151 (Jan – Mar 93), pp. 51 – 79. Bibl.

La sucesión presidencial de 1994 (A collection of thirteen brief articles on the upcoming presidential elections in Mexico). *Nexos,* v. 16, no. 188 (Aug 93), pp. 27 – 70.

Triana Martínez, Azucena, ed. *Sucesión presidencial y transición democrática* reviewed by Raúl Rodríguez Guillén. *El Cotidiano,* v. 10, no. 58 (Oct – Nov 93), p. 116.

Valdés Zurita, Leonardo. La sucesión presidencial: "Back to the Basics." *El Cotidiano,* v. 10, no. 58 (Oct – Nov 93), pp. 29 – 33. Il.

Bibliography

Ochoa Méndez, Jacqueline. Orientación bibliográfica sobre sucesión presidencial y partidos políticos. *El Cotidiano,* v. 10, no. 58 (Oct – Nov 93), pp. 119 – 120.

Public works

Ziccardi, Alicia. *Las obras públicas de la ciudad de México, 1976 – 1982: política urbana e industria de la construcción* reviewed by Matilde Luna. *Revista Mexicana de Sociología,* v. 54, no. 4 (Oct – Dec 92), pp. 259 – 261.

Race question

Carroll, Patrick James. *Blacks in Colonial Veracruz: Race, Ethnicity, and Regional Development* reviewed by Linda A. Newson. *Journal of Latin American Studies,* v. 25, no. 1 (Feb 93), pp. 192 – 193.

Dauzier, Martine. Tous des indiens?: la "réindianisation"; force ou fiction: débats autour des essais de Guillermo Bonfil Batalla. *Cahiers des Amériques Latines,* no. 13 (1992), pp. 147 – 158. Bibl.

Pescador C., Juan Javier. La nupcialidad urbana preindustrial y los límites del mestizaje: características y evolución de los patrones de nupcialidad en la ciudad de México, 1700 – 1850. *Estudios Demográficos y Urbanos,* v. 7, no. 1 (Jan – Apr 92), pp. 137 – 168. Bibl, tables.

Plá León, Rafael. La idea del mestizaje en representantes del positivismo en Argentina y México en el siglo XIX. *Islas,* no. 98 (Jan – Apr 91), pp. 135 – 142. Bibl.

Rural conditions

Baños Ramírez, Othón. Reconfiguración rural – urbana en la zona henequenera de Yucatán. *Estudios Sociológicos,* v. 11, no. 32 (May – Aug 93), pp. 419 – 443. Tables, maps.

Binford, Leigh and Scott Cook. *Obliging Need: Rural Petty Industry in Mexican Capitalism* reviewed by Peter Gregory. *Economic Development and Cultural Change,* v. 42, no. 1 (Oct 93), pp. 210 – 215.

Blanco, José Luis et al. El tributo del campo a la ciudad: historias de chaneques y serpientes. *Revista Mexicana de Sociología,* v. 54, no. 3 (July – Sept 92), pp. 131 – 137. Bibl.

Gledhill, John. *"Casi nada": A Study of Agrarian Reform in the Homeland of Cardenismo* reviewed by Alan Knight. *Hispanic American Historical Review,* v. 73, no. 1 (Feb 93), pp. 181 – 182.

Greenberg, James B. *Blood Ties: Life and Violence in Rural Mexico* reviewed by Richard N. Adams. *Mesoamérica (USA),* v. 13, no. 23 (June 92), pp. 196 – 200.

Robles B., Rosario et al. La mujer campesina en la época de la modernidad. *El Cotidiano,* v. 9, no. 53 (Mar – Apr 93), pp. 25 – 32. Bibl, il, tables.

Bibliography

Tutino, John. Historias del México agrario (Translated by Mario A. Zamudio Vega). *Historia Mexicana,* v. 42, no. 2 (Oct – Dec 92), pp. 177 – 220.

Social conditions

Barrera Carranza, Estanislao. Prostitución y medios masivos de comunicación social. *La Palabra y el Hombre,* no. 84 (Oct – Dec 92), pp. 39 – 61. Bibl.

García Quintanilla, Alejandra. Salud y progreso en Yucatán en el XIX: Mérida; el sarampión de 1882. *Siglo XIX: Cuadernos,* v. 1, no. 3 (June 92), pp. 29 – 53. Bibl, tables.

Garza Toledo, Enrique de la, ed. *Crisis y sujetos sociales en México,* 2 vols., reviewed by Alicia Inés Martínez. *El Cotidiano,* v. 9, no. 54 (May 93), pp. 116 – 117.

Salles, Vania and José Manuel Valenzuela Arce. Ambitos de relaciones sociales de naturaleza íntima e identidades culturales: notas sobre Xochimilco. *Revista Mexicana de Sociología,* v. 54, no. 3 (July – Sept 92), pp. 139 – 173. Bibl.

Bibliography

Gonzalbo Aizpuru, Pilar. Hacia una historia de la vida privada en la Nueva España. *Historia Mexicana,* v. 42, no. 2 (Oct – Dec 92), pp. 353 – 377.

Research

Martínez-Assad, Carlos R. and Sergio Sarmiento, eds. *Nos queda la esperanza: el valle del Mezquital* reviewed by Marta Eugenia García Ugarte. *Revista Mexicana de Sociología,* v. 54, no. 2 (Apr – June 92), pp. 245 – 251.

Statistics

Jarque, Carlos M. La población de México en el último decenio del siglo XX. *Comercio Exterior,* v. 43, no. 7 (July 93), pp. 642 – 651. Tables, charts.

Social policy

Alonso, Jorge et al, eds. *El nuevo estado mexicano, tomo IV: Estado y sociedad* reviewed by Laura Franco Scherer. *El Cotidiano,* v. 8, no. 52 (Jan – Feb 93), pp. 118 – 119.

Bolívar Espinoza, Augusto et al. Nuevos tiempos de coyuntura: consolidación del cambio y mucho desafío político. *El Cotidiano,* v. 8, no. 52 (Jan – Feb 93), pp. 60 – 66. Il.

Cabrera Acevedo, Gustavo. La población y la búsqueda de equilibrios. *Comercio Exterior,* v. 43, no. 7 (July 93), pp. 612 – 617. Bibl.

Contreras Cruz, Carlos. Ciudad y salud en el porfiriato: la política urbana y el saneamiento de Puebla, 1880 – 1906. *Siglo XIX: Cuadernos,* v. 1, no. 3 (June 92), pp. 55 – 76. Bibl, tables.

Cruz Barrera, Nydia E. La higiene y la política sanitaria en el porfiriato: su difusión y ejercicio en Puebla. *La Palabra y el Hombre,* no. 83 (July – Sept 92), pp. 255 – 273. Bibl, maps.

Dresser, Denise. *Neopopulist Solutions to Neoliberal Problems: Mexico's National Solidarity Program* reviewed by Martin C. Needler (Review entitled "Economic Policy and Political Survival"). *Mexican Studies,* v. 9, no. 1 (Winter 93), pp. 139 – 143.

Gordon Rapoport, Sara. La política social y el Programa Nacional de Solidaridad. *Revista Mexicana de Sociología,* v. 55, no. 2 (Apr – June 93), pp. 351 – 366. Bibl, tables.

McCurry, Patrick. Starting at the Top. *Business Mexico,* v. 3, no. 1 (Jan – Feb 93), pp. 80 – 82. Il.

Márquez, Viviane Brachet de and Margaret Sherraden. Austeridad fiscal, el estado de bienestar y el cambio político: los casos de la salud y la alimentación en México, 1970 – 1990 (Translated by Armando Castellanos). *Estudios Sociológicos,* v. 11, no. 32 (May – Aug 93), pp. 331 – 364. Bibl, tables.

Muñoz, Víctor Manuel. El liberalismo social: propuesta ideológica del salinismo. *Revista Mexicana de Ciencias Políticas y Sociales,* v. 37, Nueva época, no. 149 (July – Sept 92), pp. 29 – 47. Bibl.

Pacto para la Estabilidad, la Competitividad y el Empleo: concertación vigente hasta el 31 de diciembre de 1994. *Comercio Exterior,* v. 43, no. 10 (Oct 93), pp. 917 – 920.

Reyna Bernal, Angélica. Políticas de migración y distribución de población en México: ejecución e impactos regionales. *Estudios Demográficos y Urbanos,* v. 6, no. 3 (Sept – Dec 91), pp. 583 – 611. Bibl, tables, charts.

Stoub, Jeffrey. Sustainable Policies. *Business Mexico,* v. 3, no. 8 (Aug 93), pp. 46 – 47. Il.

Villarreal González, Diana R. *La política de vivienda del gobierno del estado de Nuevo León, 1970 – 1990* reviewed by Gustavo Garza. *Estudios Demográficos y Urbanos,* v. 6, no. 3 (Sept – Dec 91), pp. 773 – 778.

Ward, Peter M. Social Welfare Policy and Political Opening in Mexico. *Journal of Latin American Studies,* v. 25, no. 3 (Oct 93), pp. 613 – 628. Bibl, tables.

Ziccardi, Alicia. Los organismos de vivienda de los asalariados y la política social. *EURE,* v. 19, no. 57 (July 93), pp. 95 – 102. Bibl, tables.

Sources

Salinas de Gortari, Carlos. Quinto Informe de Gobierno. *Comercio Exterior,* v. 43, no. 11 (Nov 93), pp. 1068 – 1094.

— Quinto Informe de Gobierno. *Nexos,* v. 16, no. 192 (Dec 93), Insert.

— V Informe de Gobierno del presidente Carlos Salinas de Gortari. *Fem,* v. 17, no. 129 (Nov 93), p. 41. Il.

Statistics

Business Mexico Indicators. *Business Mexico,* v. 3 (1993), All issues. Tables, charts.

MEXICO (CITY)

Aguilar, Luis Miguel. *Suerte con las mujeres* reviewed by José Ricardo Chaves. *Vuelta,* v. 17, no. 200 (July 93), pp. 59 – 60.

Ayre, Shirley. A Rosier Image for the Zona Rosa. *Business Mexico,* v. 3, no. 10 (Oct 93), pp. 4 – 7. Il.

Barnhart, Katherine. Digging Up Mexico's Past. *Business Mexico,* v. 3, no. 11 (Nov 93), pp. 42 – 44. Il, maps.

Barraza, Eduardo and Juan Felipe Leal. Inicios de la reglamentación cinematográfica en la ciudad de México. *Revista Mexicana de Ciencias Políticas y Sociales,* v. 37, Nueva época, no. 150 (Oct – Dec 92), pp. 139 – 175. Bibl, charts.

Bassols Batalla, Angel et al. *Zona metropolitana de la ciudad de México: complejo geográfico, socio-económico y político* reviewed by Alicia Ziccardi. *Problemas del Desarrollo,* v. 24, no. 94 (July – Sept 93), pp. 283 – 286.

Bassols Ricárdez, Mario and Rocio Corona Martínez. Transición institucional y reforma política en el D.F. *El Cotidiano,* v. 10, no. 57 (Aug – Sept 93), pp. 28 – 37. Il, tables.

Benería, Lourdes and Martha Roldán. *Las encrucijadas de clase y género: trabajo a domicilio; subcontratación y dinámica de la unidad doméstica en la ciudad de México* translated by Julio Colón Gómez. Reviewed by Norma Ilse Veloz Avila. *El Cotidiano,* v. 9, no. 53 (Mar – Apr 93), p. 118.

Blanco, José Joaquín. *Se visten novias* reviewed by Julián Andrade Jardí (Review entitled "Toda la ciudad"). *Nexos,* v. 16, no. 189 (Sept 93), pp. 68 – 69.

Bolívar Espinoza, Augusto et al. La competencia de partidos: el que siembra vientos cosecha tempestades. *El Cotidiano,* v. 9, no. 54 (May 93), pp. 60 – 71. Il.

Castelazo, José R. *Ciudad de México: reforma posible; escenarios en el porvenir* reviewed by Aída Escamilla Rubio. *El Cotidiano,* v. 9, no. 54 (May 93), p. 115. Il.

Collins, Charles O. and Steven L. Scott. Air Pollution in the Valley of Mexico. *Geographical Review,* v. 83, no. 2 (Apr 93), pp. 119 – 133. Bibl, charts.

El comercio en vía pública: la economía informal en la ciudad de México. *El Cotidiano,* v. 9, no. 54 (May 93), pp. 72 – 75. Il, tables.

Connolly, Priscilla et al. *"Cambiar de casa, pero no de barrio": estudios sobre la reconstrucción en la ciudad de México* reviewed by María Elena Ducci. *EURE,* v. 19, no. 57 (July 93), pp. 126 – 127. Il.

Corona Cuapio, Reina and José Rodolfo Luque González. Cambios recientes en los patrones migratorios a la zona metropolitana de la ciudad de México. *Estudios Demográficos y Urbanos,* v. 7, no. 2 – 3 (May – Dec 92), pp. 575 – 586. Bibl, tables, charts.

Cruz Rodríguez, María Soledad. La nueva ley agraria y su impacto en la periferia ejidal de la ciudad de México. *El Cotidiano,* v. 10, no. 57 (Aug – Sept 93), pp. 54 – 59. Bibl, il, tables.

Dávila Diez, Enrique. Estos fueron los cines. *Nexos,* v. 16, no. 187 (July 93), pp. 87 – 89. Il.

Deans-Smith, Susan. Compromise and Conflict: The Tobacco Workers of Mexico City and the Colonial State, 1770 – 1810. *Anuario de Estudios Americanos,* v. 49 (1992), pp. 271 – 309. Bibl.

Duhau, Emilio and Alejandro Suárez Pareyón. Sistemas de planeación y política de desarrollo urbano en la ciudad de México. *El Cotidiano,* v. 9, no. 54 (May 93), pp. 3 – 9. Bibl, il.

Durán, Ana María and María Concepción Huerta Trujillo. Cambios de usos del suelo y despoblamiento en la colonia Roma. *El Cotidiano,* v. 10, no. 57 (Aug – Sept 93), pp. 73 – 77. Il, tables.

Esquivel Hernández, María Teresa et al. La zona metropolitana de México: dinámica demográfica y estructura poblacional, 1970 – 1990. *El Cotidiano,* v. 9, no. 54 (May 93), pp. 10 – 17. Bibl, il, tables, charts.

Geyer, Anne. Challenges for the Modern Metropolis. *Business Mexico,* v. 3, no. 10 (Oct 93), pp. 48 – 49.

Herrero Díaz, Luis F. Desarrollo urbano y estrategias de supervivencia en la periferia de la ciudad de México: Chalco; una aproximación antropológica. *Revista Española de Antropología Americana,* v. 23 (1993), pp. 213 – 232. Bibl, tables.

Hirabayashi, Lane Ryo. La politización de la cultura regional: zapotecos de la sierra Juárez en la ciudad de México. *América Indígena,* v. 51, no. 4 (Oct – Dec 91), pp. 185 – 218. Bibl.

Lezama, José Luis. Ciudad, mujer y conflicto: el comercio ambulante en el D.F. *Estudios Demográficos y Urbanos,* v. 6, no. 3 (Sept – Dec 91), pp. 649 – 675. Bibl, tables.

— Trabajo, familia e infancia en la ciudad de México: convergencias y divergencias. *Comercio Exterior,* v. 43, no. 7 (July 93), pp. 677 – 687. Bibl, tables.

Linares Zapata, Luis. El plebiscito: un fracaso bien hecho. *El Cotidiano,* v. 9, no. 54 (May 93), pp. 30 – 36. Il, tables.

Márquez Morfín, Lourdes. El cólera en la ciudad de México en el siglo XIX. *Estudios Demográficos y Urbanos,* v. 7, no. 1 (Jan – Apr 92), pp. 77 – 93. Bibl, tables, maps, charts.

Martínez Anaya, Efraín. San Miguel Teotongo: a contrapelo del neoliberalismo. *El Cotidiano,* v. 10, no. 57 (Aug – Sept 93), pp. 23 – 27. Tables.

Massolo, Alejandra. *Por amor y coraje: mujeres en movimientos urbanos de la ciudad de México* reviewed by Beatriz Almanza. *El Cotidiano,* v. 10, no. 57 (Aug – Sept 93), p. 109.

— *Por amor y coraje: mujeres en movimientos urbanos de la ciudad de México* reviewed by Elena Urrutia. *La Educación (USA),* v. 37, no. 114 (1993), pp. 164 – 165.

Moctezuma Barragán, Pedro. El espejo desenterrado. *El Cotidiano,* v. 9, no. 54 (May 93), pp. 49 – 54. Il.

Moreno Armella, Florita. Representación vecinal y gestión urbana en el D.F. *El Cotidiano,* v. 10, no. 57 (Aug – Sept 93), pp. 38 – 45. Il.

Musset, Alain. *De l'eau vive à l'eau morte: enjeux techniques et culturels dans la vallée de Mexico, XVIe – XIXe siècles* reviewed by Marie-Danielle Démelas-Bohy. *Caravelle,* no. 59 (1992), p. 307.

Navarro Benítez, Bernardo. La ciudad y sus transportes, la metrópoli y sus transportes. *El Cotidiano,* v. 9, no. 54 (May 93), pp. 18 – 23. Il.

Olivera Lozano, Guillermo. Movilidad residencial y expansión física reciente en la ciudad de México. *Revista Geográfica (Mexico),* no. 115 (Jan – June 92), pp. 55 – 76. Bibl, tables, maps.

Pescador C., Juan Javier. *De bautizados a fieles difuntos: familia y mentalidades en una parroquia urbana; Santa Catarina de México, 1568 – 1820* reviewed by Patricia Schraer. *La Educación (USA),* v. 37, no. 115 (1993), pp. 431 – 433.

— La nupcialidad urbana preindustrial y los límites del mestizaje: características y evolución de los patrones de nupcialidad en la ciudad de México, 1700 – 1850. *Estudios Demográficos y Urbanos,* v. 7, no. 1 (Jan – Apr 92), pp. 137 – 168. Bibl, tables.

Peschard, Jacqueline. Una reforma para la ciudad capital. *El Cotidiano,* v. 9, no. 54 (May 93), pp. 37 – 40. Il.

Pradilla Cobos, Emilio, ed. *Planeación urbana y bienestar social, vol. II: Democracia y desarrollo de la ciudad de México* reviewed by J. Verónica Ramírez Rangel. *El Cotidiano,* v. 9, no. 54 (May 93), p. 118. Il.

Ramírez Cuellar, Alfonso. La reforma necesaria. *El Cotidiano,* v. 9, no. 54 (May 93), pp. 24 – 29. Il, tables.

Reyes del Campillo, Juan and Verónica Vázquez Mantecón. ¿Ciudadanos en ciernes?: la cultura política en el distrito XXVII del D.F. *El Cotidiano,* v. 9, no. 54 (May 93), pp. 41 – 48. Il, tables, charts.

Rubin-Kurtzman, Jane R. Los determinantes de la oferta de trabajo femenino en la ciudad de México, 1970. *Estudios Demográficos y Urbanos,* v. 6, no. 3 (Sept – Dec 91), pp. 545 – 582. Bibl, tables.

Ruiz Chiapetto, Crescencio. El desarrollo del México urbano: cambio de protagonista. *Comercio Exterior,* v. 43, no. 8 (Aug 93), pp. 708 – 716. Bibl, tables, maps.

Sánchez-Mejorada F., María Cristina. Las clases medias en la gestión y el gobierno de la ciudad. *El Cotidiano,* v. 10, no. 57 (Aug – Sept 93), pp. 46 – 53. Il, maps.

Schteingart, Martha, ed. *Espacio y vivienda en la ciudad de México* reviewed by Richard Boyer. *Hispanic American Historical Review,* v. 73, no. 3 (Aug 93), pp. 528 – 529.

Sosamontes Herreramoro, Ramón. El reclamo de la seguridad. *El Cotidiano*, v. 9, no. 54 (May 93), pp. 76 – 80. Il.

Toscano, Guadalupe. *Testigos de piedra: las hornacinas del centro histórico de la ciudad de México* reviewed by Gustavo Curiel and Yolanda Bravo Saldaña. *Anales del Instituto de Investigaciones Estéticas*, v. 16, no. 62 (1991), pp. 203 – 208. Bibl.

Trejo Hernández, Raúl et al. *Perfil y semblanza política de la Asamblea de Representantes del Distrito Federal* reviewed by Felipe Solís Acero. *Revista Mexicana de Ciencias Políticas y Sociales*, v. 38, Nueva época, no. 151 (Jan – Mar 93), pp. 220 – 224.

Velasco M. L., María del Pilar. La epidemia de cólera de 1833 y la mortalidad en la ciudad de México. *Estudios Demográficos y Urbanos*, v. 7, no. 1 (Jan – Apr 92), pp. 95 – 135. Bibl, tables, charts.

Velázquez Zárate, Enrique. La contaminación atmosférica en la ciudad de México. *El Cotidiano*, v. 9, no. 54 (May 93), pp. 55 – 59. Il.

Victoria, José Guadalupe. Noticias sobre la antigua plaza y el Mercado del Volador de la ciudad de México. *Anales del Instituto de Investigaciones Estéticas*, v. 16, no. 62 (1991), pp. 69 – 91. Bibl, il.

Ward, Peter M. *México: una mega-ciudad; producción y reproducción de un medio ambiente urbano* reviewed by Eduardo Lozano Ortega. *El Cotidiano*, v. 9, no. 54 (May 93), p. 114.

Zea, Leopoldo. Historia de dos ciudades. *Cuadernos Americanos*, no. 41, Nueva época (Sept – Oct 93), pp. 175 – 179.

Ziccardi, Alicia. *Las obras públicas de la ciudad de México, 1976 – 1982: política urbana e industria de la construcción* reviewed by Matilde Luna. *Revista Mexicana de Sociología*, v. 54, no. 4 (Oct – Dec 92), pp. 259 – 261.

Bibliography

Ochoa Méndez, Jacqueline. Orientación bibliográfica sobre el Distrito Federal. *El Cotidiano*, v. 9, no. 54 (May 93), pp. 119 – 120.

— Orientación bibliográfica sobre el movimiento urbano popular en la ciudad de México. *El Cotidiano*, v. 10, no. 57 (Aug – Sept 93), pp. 111 – 112.

MEXICO (STATE)

Graizbord, Boris. Geografías electorales: cambio y participación en el voto de diputados federales de 1988 y 1991. *Estudios Sociológicos*, v. 11, no. 32 (May – Aug 93), pp. 497 – 514. Bibl, tables, maps.

Kanter, Deborah E. Viudas y vecinos, milpas y magueyes: el impacto del auge de la población en el valle de Toluca; el caso de Tenango del Valle en el siglo XVIII. *Estudios Demográficos y Urbanos*, v. 7, no. 1 (Jan – Apr 92), pp. 19 – 33. Bibl, tables.

Martínez Salgado, Carolina. Recursos sociodemográficos y daños a la salud en unidades domésticas campesinas del estado de México. *Estudios Demográficos y Urbanos*, v. 7, no. 2 – 3 (May – Dec 92), pp. 451 – 463. Bibl, tables.

Sánchez Arteche, Alfonso. Letras del estado de México. *Plural (Mexico)*, v. 22, no. 258 (Mar 93), pp. 76 – 77.

MEXICO, GULF OF

Pepin Lehalleur, Marielle. Regiones y poder local en el Golfo de México: los andamios de un programa de investigación. *Estudios Sociológicos*, v. 10, no. 30 (Sept – Dec 92), pp. 517 – 522. Maps.

MEXICO IN LITERATURE

De Beer, Gabriella. Narrativa y periodismo en *Morir en el golfo* de Héctor Aguilar Camín. *Revista Interamericana de Bibliografía*, v. 42, no. 2 (1992), pp. 215 – 221. Bibl.

Leal, Luis. Sin fronteras: (des)mitificación en las letras norteamericanas y mexicanas. *Mexican Studies*, v. 9, no. 1 (Winter 93), pp. 95 – 118. Bibl.

Peruyero Sánchez, Alfredo. *Los recuerdos del tiempo* de Carlos Juan Islas. *La Palabra y el Hombre*, no. 84 (Oct – Dec 92), pp. 259 – 267. Il.

Sanciprián, Nancy. *B. Traven en México* reviewed by Fermín Ramírez. *Plural (Mexico)*, v. 22, no. 264 (Sept 93), pp. 123 – 124.

Tejada, Roberto, ed. *En algún otro lado: México en la poesía de lengua inglesa* reviewed by Aurelio Major. *Vuelta*, v. 17, no. 194 (Jan 93), pp. 42 – 43.

Zogbaum, Heidi. *B. Traven: A Vision of Mexico* reviewed by Frank Whitehead. *Journal of Latin American Studies*, v. 25, no. 1 (Feb 93), pp. 225 – 226.

MEYER, LORENZO

Interviews

Carreño King, Tania and Angélica Vázquez del Mercado. La disputa por la historia patria: una entrevista con Lorenzo Meyer. *Nexos*, v. 16, no. 191 (Nov 93), pp. 41 – 49.

MEZQUITAL VALLEY, MEXICO

Martínez-Assad, Carlos R. and Sergio Sarmiento, eds. *Nos queda la esperanza: el valle del Mezquital* reviewed by Marta Eugenia García Ugarte. *Revista Mexicana de Sociología*, v. 54, no. 2 (Apr – June 92), pp. 245 – 251.

MIAMI, FLORIDA

Chaffee, Sue. Haitian Women in Miami. *Hemisphere*, v. 5, no. 2 (Winter – Spring 93), pp. 22 – 23. Il.

Durbin, Pamela. Transcultural Steps with a Flair. *Américas*, v. 45, no. 3 (May – June 93), pp. 18 – 23. Il.

MICHOACÁN, MEXICO

Castro Gutiérrez, Felipe. *Movimientos populares en Nueva España: Michoacán, 1766 – 1797* reviewed by Frédérique Langue (Review entitled "Les soulèvements populaires de 1767 en Nouvell-Espagne: le point sur quelques publications récentes"). *Caravelle*, no. 60 (1993), pp. 152 – 154.

Gledhill, John. *"Casi nada": A Study of Agrarian Reform in the Homeland of Cardenismo* reviewed by Alan Knight. *Hispanic American Historical Review*, v. 73, no. 1 (Feb 93), pp. 181 – 182.

Martínez Aparicio, Jorge. La tenencia de la tierra, luego de un año de la reforma al 27: nuevos cambios, fenómenos viejos; la tierra caliente. *El Cotidiano*, v. 10, no. 57 (Aug – Sept 93), pp. 86 – 92. Il.

Vargas Uribe, Guillermo. Geografía histórica de la población de Michoacán, siglo XVIII. *Estudios Demográficos y Urbanos*, v. 7, no. 1 (Jan – Apr 92), pp. 193 – 222. Bibl, tables, maps, charts.

— Michoacán en la red internacional del narcotráfico. *El Cotidiano*, v. 8, no. 52 (Jan – Feb 93), pp. 38 – 50. Tables, maps, charts.

Sources

Soto Pérez, José Luis. Fuentes documentales para la historia de la provincia franciscana de Michoacán en el siglo XVIII. *Archivo Ibero-Americano*, v. 52, no. 205 – 208 (Jan – Dec 92), pp. 81 – 106. Facs.

MICROFORMS

Sercan, Cecilia S. Preservation Microforms in an RLIN Environment. *SALALM Papers*, v. 36 (1991), pp. 408 – 417.

Catalogs

Marshall, Thomas H. OCLC and the Bibliographic Control of Preservation Microform Masters. *SALALM Papers*, v. 36 (1991), pp. 418 – 421.

Bibliography

Graham, Crystal. Microform Cataloging: Current Issues and Selected Bibliography. *SALALM Papers*, v. 36 (1991), pp. 393 – 407.

MIDDLE CLASSES

Brazil

Grün, Roberto. Sindicalismo e anti-sindicalismo e a gênese das novas classes médias brasileiras. *Dados*, v. 35, no. 3 (1992), pp. 435 – 471. Bibl.

Cuba

Fitzgerald, Frank T. *Managing Socialism: From Old Cadres to New Professionals in Revolutionary Cuba* reviewed by Linda Fuller (Review entitled "Cuba's 'Middle Class' "). *Latin American Perspectives*, v. 20, no. 1 (Winter 93), pp. 44 – 46.

Mexico

Sánchez-Mejorada F., María Cristina. Las clases medias en la gestión y el gobierno de la ciudad. *El Cotidiano*, v. 10, no. 57 (Aug – Sept 93), pp. 46 – 53. Il, maps.

MIDDLE EAST

See also
Islam
Israel
Jews

Azambuja, Marcos Castrioto de. O após-guerra no Golfo Pérsico: as lições de guerra e a construção da paz. *Revista do Instituto Histórico e Geográfico Brasileiro*, no. 371 (Apr – June 91), pp. 492 – 508.

Batou, Jean. *Cent ans de résistance au sous-développement: l'industrialisation de l'Amérique Latine et du Moyen-Orient face au défi européen, 1770 – 1870* reviewed by Hernán G. H. Taboada. *Cuadernos Americanos*, no. 40, Nueva época (July – Aug 93), pp. 238 – 242.

— *One Hundred Years of Resistance to Underdevelopment, 1770 – 1870* reviewed by Joseph L. Love. *Journal of Latin American Studies*, v. 25, no. 1 (Feb 93), pp. 206 – 208.

Klich, Ignacio. Argentine – Ottoman Relations and Their Impact on Immigrants from the Middle East: A History of Unfulfilled Expectations, 1910 – 1915. *The Americas*, v. 50, no. 2 (Oct 93), pp. 177 – 205. Bibl, tables.

MIGRANT LABOR

See
Agricultural laborers
Undocumented workers

MIGRATION

See
Migration, Internal
Subdivision *Emigration and immigration* under names of specific countries

MIGRATION, INTERNAL

Andean region

Kingman Garcés, Eduardo, ed. *Ciudades de los Andes: visión histórica y contemporánea* reviewed by Scarlett O'Phelan Godoy. *Anuario de Estudios Americanos*, v. 49, Suppl. 2 (1992), p. 244.

Argentina

Foschiatti de dell'Orto, Ana María H. El desarrollo urbano y las particularidades demográficas del Chaco y su capital entre 1960 y 1990. *Revista Geográfica (Mexico)*, no. 115 (Jan – June 92), pp. 37 – 54. Bibl, tables, maps, charts.

Brazil

Statistics

Cunha, José Marcos Pinto de. Característicos de la movilidad intrametropolitana en el estado de São Paulo, Brasil, 1970 – 1980. *Estudios Demográficos y Urbanos*, v. 7, no. 2 – 3 (May – Dec 92), pp. 587 – 602. Bibl, tables, maps.

Chile

Szasz, Ivonne. Trabajadoras inmigrantes en Santiago de Chile en los años ochenta. *Estudios Demográficos y Urbanos*, v. 7, no. 2 – 3 (May – Dec 92), pp. 539 – 553. Bibl, tables.

Ecuador

Carrasco, Hernán. Indígenas serranos en Quito y Guayaquil: relaciones interétnicas y urbanización de migrantes. *América Indígena*, v. 51, no. 4 (Oct – Dec 91), pp. 159 – 183. Bibl.

Villavicencio de Mencías, Gladys. Indígenas en Quito. *América Indígena*, v. 51, no. 2 – 3 (Apr – Sept 91), pp. 223 – 250. Bibl.

Guatemala

Mathematical models

Morrison, Andrew R. Violence or Economics: What Drives Internal Migration in Guatemala? *Economic Development and Cultural Change*, v. 41, no. 4 (July 93), pp. 817 – 831. Bibl, tables.

Latin America

Altamirano Rúa, Teófilo and Lane Ryo Hirabayashi. Culturas regionales en ciudades de América Latina: un marco conceptual. *América Indígena*, v. 51, no. 4 (Oct – Dec 91), pp. 17 – 48. Bibl, il.

Robinson, David James, ed. *Migration in Colonial Spanish America* reviewed by Ida Altman. *The Americas*, v. 50, no. 2 (Oct 93), pp. 277 – 279.

— *Migration in Colonial Spanish America* reviewed by Martin W. Lewis. *Geographical Review*, v. 83, no. 1 (Jan 93), pp. 106 – 108.

Mexico

Anguiano Téllez, María Eugenia. Migración y derechos humanos: el caso de los mixtecos. *Estudios Fronterizos*, no. 26 (Sept – Dec 91), pp. 55 – 69. Bibl.

Ceballos Ramírez, Manuel and Lawrence D. Taylor. Síntesis histórica del poblamiento de la región fronteriza México – Estados Unidos. *Estudios Fronterizos*, no. 26 (Sept – Dec 91), pp. 9 – 37. Bibl.

Corona Vázquez, Rodolfo. Migración permanente interestatal e internacional, 1950 – 1990. *Comercio Exterior*, v. 43, no. 8 (Aug 93), pp. 750 – 762. Bibl, tables.

Delgadillo Macías, Javier. Economía y migración: la nueva geografía de la movilidad poblacional en México. *Problemas del Desarrollo*, v. 24, no. 94 (July – Sept 93), pp. 113 – 132. Bibl, tables, charts.

Estrella Valenzuela, Gabriel. Dinámica de los componentes demográficos de Baja California durante el período 1985 – 1990. *Estudios Fronterizos*, no. 26 (Sept – Dec 91), pp. 39 – 53.

Olivera Lozano, Guillermo. Movilidad residencial y expansión física reciente en la ciudad de México. *Revista Geográfica (Mexico)*, no. 115 (Jan – June 92), pp. 55 – 76. Bibl, tables, maps.

Reyna Bernal, Angélica. Políticas de migración y distribución de población en México: ejecución e impactos regionales. *Estudios Demográficos y Urbanos*, v. 6, no. 3 (Sept – Dec 91), pp. 583 – 611. Bibl, tables, charts.

Robinson, Sherman et al. Las políticas agrícolas y la migración en un área de libre comercio de los Estados Unidos y México: un análisis de equilibrio general computable (Translated by Carlos Villegas). *El Trimestre Económico*, v. 60, no. 237 (Jan – Mar 93), pp. 53 – 89. Bibl, tables, charts.

Vargas Montero, Guadalupe. Migraciones mixtecas y relaciones regionales a fines del siglo XIX. *La Palabra y el Hombre*, no. 83 (July – Sept 92), pp. 47 – 57. Bibl.

Wilson, Tamar Diana. Theoretical Approaches to Mexican Wage Labor Migration. *Latin American Perspectives*, v. 20, no. 3 (Summer 93), pp. 98 – 129. Bibl.

Research

Ruiz Chiapetto, Crescencio. Migración interna y desarrollo económico: tres etapas. *Estudios Demográficos y Urbanos*, v. 6, no. 3 (Sept – Dec 91), pp. 727 – 736.

Statistics

Arroyo Alejandre, Jesús and Luis A. Velázquez Gutiérrez. La transición de los patrones migratorios y las ciudades medias. *Estudios Demográficos y Urbanos*, v. 7, no. 2 – 3 (May – Dec 92), pp. 555 – 574. Bibl, tables.

Corona Cuapio, Reina and José Rodolfo Luque González. Cambios recientes en los patrones migratorios a la zona metropolitana de la ciudad de México. *Estudios Demográficos y Urbanos*, v. 7, no. 2 – 3 (May – Dec 92), pp. 575 – 586. Bibl, tables, charts.

Partida Bush, Virgilio. Niveles y tendencias de la migración interna en México a partir de las cifras censales, 1970 – 1990. *Revista Mexicana de Sociología*, v. 55, no. 1 (Jan – Mar 93), pp. 155 – 176. Bibl, tables, charts.

Study and teaching

Rodríguez, Hipólito. La antropología urbana y los estudios sobre migración. *La Palabra y el Hombre*, no. 84 (Oct – Dec 92), pp. 145 – 159. Bibl.

Peru

Adams, Norman and Néstor Valdivia. *Los otros empresarios: ética de migrantes y formación de empresas en Lima* reviewed by Orazio A. Ciccarelli. *Hispanic American Historical Review*, v. 73, no. 4 (Nov 93), pp. 714 – 715.

Burt, Jo-Marie. The Dispossessed Look Homeward: Peru's Internal Refugees Organize for Return. *NACLA Report on the Americas*, v. 27, no. 1 (July – Aug 93), pp. 8 – 11. Il.

Doughty, Paul L. Perú: . . . y la vida continúa. *América Indígena*, v. 51, no. 4 (Oct – Dec 91), pp. 49 – 79. Bibl, tables, maps.

Matos Mar, José. El nuevo rostro de la cultura urbana del Perú. *América Indígena*, v. 51, no. 2 – 3 (Apr – Sept 91), pp. 11 – 34. Tables, maps.

— Taquileños, quechuas del lago Titicaca, en Lima. *América Indígena*, v. 51, no. 2 – 3 (Apr – Sept 91), pp. 107 – 166. Il, maps.

Mitchell, William P. Producción campesina y cultura regional. *América Indígena*, v. 51, no. 4 (Oct – Dec 91), pp. 81 – 106. Bibl, tables.

Mossbrucker, Harald. El proceso de migración en el Perú: la revolución clandestina. *América Indígena*, v. 51, no. 2 – 3 (Apr – Sept 91), pp. 167 – 201. Bibl, charts.

United States

Belanger, Alain and Andrei Rogers. The Internal Migration and Spatial Redistribution of the Foreign-Born Population in the United States: 1965 – 1970 and 1975 – 1980. *International Migration Review*, v. 26, no. 4 (Winter 92), pp. 1342 – 1369. Bibl, tables, charts.

Dávila, Alberto E. and Rogelio Sáenz. Chicano Return Migration to the Southwest: An Integrated Human Capital Approach. *International Migration Review*, v. 26, no. 4 (Winter 92), pp. 1248 – 1266. Bibl, tables.

MILITARY ART AND SCIENCE

Study and teaching

Fontes, Arivaldo Silveira. *Vultos do ensino militar* reviewed by Cláudio Moreira Bento. *Revista do Instituto Histórico e Geográfico Brasileiro*, no. 373 (Oct – Dec 91), pp. 1206 – 1207.

MILITARY ASSISTANCE, FOREIGN

El Salvador

Independencia, soberanía y "Fuertes Caminos." *ECA; Estudios Centroamericanos*, v. 48, no. 539 (Sept 93), pp. 875 – 876. Il.

Latin America

Fitch, John Samuel. The Decline of U.S. Military Influence on Latin America. *Journal of Inter-American Studies and World Affairs*, v. 35, no. 2 (Summer 93), pp. 1 – 49. Bibl, tables, charts.

Bibliography

Metz, Allan Sheldon. Israeli Military Assistance to Latin America (Review article). *Latin American Research Review*, v. 28, no. 2 (1993), pp. 257 – 263.

MILITARY IN GOVERNMENT

See also

Subdivision *Armed forces* under names of specific countries

Argentina

Adrogué, Gerardo. Los ex-militares en política: bases sociales y cambios en los patrones de representación política. *Desarrollo Económico (Argentina)*, v. 33, no. 131 (Oct – Dec 93), pp. 425 – 442. Bibl, tables.

Alvarez C., Edwin. Criminalidad y abuso de poder: el caso argentino, 1976 – 1983. *Revista Cultural Lotería*, v. 51, no. 388 (Mar – Apr 92), pp. 5 – 33. Bibl.

Bolivia

Gallego, Ferran. *Ejército, nacionalismo y reformismo en América Latina: la gestión de Germán Busch en Bolivia* reviewed by Marta Irurozqui Victoriano. *Revista Andina*, v. 11, no. 1 (July 93), pp. 246 – 247.

— *Los orígenes del reformismo militar en América Latina: la gestión de David Toro en Bolivia* reviewed by Gary Prado. *Journal of Latin American Studies*, v. 25, no. 1 (Feb 93), pp. 205 – 206.

— *Los orígenes del reformismo militar en América Latina: la gestión de David Toro en Bolivia* reviewed by Marta Irurozqui Victoriano. *Revista Andina*, v. 11, no. 1 (July 93), pp. 246 – 247.

— *Los orígenes del reformismo militar en América Latina: la gestión de David Toro en Bolivia* reviewed by Marta Irurozqui Victoriano. *Revista de Indias*, v. 53, no. 197 (Jan – Apr 93), pp. 104 – 106.

— La política económica del "socialismo militar" boliviano. *Anuario de Estudios Americanos*, v. 50, no. 1 (1993), pp. 213 – 234. Bibl, tables.

Brazil

Gonçalves, Williams da Silva and Shiguenoli Miyamoto. Os militares na política externa brasileira, 1964 – 1984. *Estudos Históricos*, v. 6, no. 12 (July – Dec 93), pp. 211 – 246. Bibl.

Teixeira, Jorge Leão. Da queda de Jango à renúncia de Collor. *Problemas Brasileiros*, v. 30, no. 295 (Jan – Feb 93), pp. 10 – 16. Il.

Chile

Bibliography

Jaksic, Ivan. The Legacies of Military Rule in Chile (Review article). *Latin American Research Review*, v. 28, no. 1 (1993), pp. 258 – 269.

Panama

Gandásegui, Marco A., Jr. The Military Regimes of Panama. *Journal of Inter-American Studies and World Affairs*, v. 35, no. 3 (Fall 93), pp. 1 – 17.

MILITARY IN LITERATURE

Vázquez Arce, Carmen. Los desastres de la guerra: sobre la articulación de la ironía en los cuentos "La recién nacida sangre," de Luis Rafael Sánchez y "El momento divino de Caruso Llompart," de Félix Córdova Iturregui. *Revista Iberoamericana*, v. 59, no. 162 – 163 (Jan – June 93), pp. 187 – 201. Bibl.

MILITARY POSTS

Mexican – American Border Region

Marchena Fernández, Juan. De franciscanos, apaches y ministros ilustrados en los pasos perdidos del norte de Nueva España. *Archivo Ibero-Americano*, v. 52, no. 205 – 208 (Jan – Dec 92), pp. 513 – 559. Bibl, tables.

Peru

Bradley, Peter T. The Defence of Peru, 1648 – 1700. *Jahrbuch für Geschichte von Staat, Wirtschaft und Gesellschaft Lateinamerikas*, v. 29 (1992), pp. 90 – 120. Bibl, tables.

MILK INDUSTRY

See

Dairying

MILLAR CARVACHO, RENÉ

González Echenique, Javier. Discurso de recepción de don René Millar Carvacho. *Boletín de la Academia Chilena de la Historia*, v. 58 – 59, no. 102 (1991 – 1992), pp. 229 – 233.

Bibliography

Bibliografía de don René Millar Carvacho. *Boletín de la Academia Chilena de la Historia*, v. 58 – 59, no. 102 (1991 – 1992), pp. 234 – 235.

MILLENARISM

See

Messianism

MILLER, ERROL L.

Interviews

Edwards, Beatrice. Interview with Errol Miller. *La Educación (USA)*, v. 37, no. 114 (1993), pp. 125 – 134.

MILLER, WILLIAM

Brezzo, Liliana M. El general Guillermo Miller después de Ayacucho. *Investigaciones y Ensayos,* no. 41 (Jan – Dec 91), pp. 395 – 406. Bibl.

MIME

Jamaica

Nettleford, Rex. Fifty Years of the Jamaican Pantomime, 1941 – 1991. *Jamaica Journal,* v. 24, no. 3 (Feb 93), pp. 2 – 9. Il.

MINAS GERAIS, BRAZIL

Breguêz, Sebastião Geraldo. Literatura de cordel em Minas Gerais, Brasil. *Folklore Americano,* no. 52 (July – Dec 91), pp. 145 – 148. Bibl.

Carvalhais, Jane Noronha and João Eustáquio da Lima. Distribuição dos ganhos com inovação tecnológica na produção de milho entre categorias de pequenos produtores em Minas Gerais. *Revista de Economia e Sociologia Rural,* v. 29, no. 4 (Oct – Dec 91), pp. 373 – 385. Bibl.

Costa, Iraci del Nero da and José Flávio Motta. Vila Rica: inconfidência e crise demográfica. *Estudos Econômicos,* v. 22, no. 2 (May – Aug 92), pp. 321 – 346. Bibl, tables, charts.

Ramos, Donald. From Minho to Minas: The Portuguese Roots of the Mineiro Family. *Hispanic American Historical Review,* v. 73, no. 4 (Nov 93), pp. 639 – 662. Bibl, tables.

MINES AND MINERAL RESOURCES

Brazil

Costa, Iraci del Nero da and José Flávio Motta. Vila Rica: inconfidência e crise demográfica. *Estudos Econômicos,* v. 22, no. 2 (May – Aug 92), pp. 321 – 346. Bibl, tables, charts.

Chile

McIntyre, Loren A. Rapture of the Heights (Photographs by the author). *Américas,* v. 45, no. 6 (Nov – Dec 93), pp. 7 – 13. Il.

MINIMUM WAGE

See

Subdivision *Minimum wage* under *Wages*

MINING INDUSTRY AND FINANCE

See also
Bauxite
Coal mines and mining
Copper industry and trade
Gold mines and mining
Iron industry and trade
Nitrates
Obsidian
Salt industry and trade
Silver mines and mining

Argentina

Terbeck, C. Augusto. La promoción minera intentada por Rivadavia: las minas de Cuyo y "The River Plate Mining Association." *Investigaciones y Ensayos,* no. 41 (Jan – Dec 91), pp. 423 – 455. Bibl.

Chile

Volk, Steven S. Mine Owners, Money Lenders, and the State in Mid-Nineteenth Century Chile: Transitions and Conflicts. *Hispanic American Historical Review,* v. 73, no. 1 (Feb 93), pp. 67 – 98. Bibl, tables.

Colombia

Bonilla Muñoz, Guillermo and Horacio Osorio Velosa. Estructura de mercado y prácticas comerciales en los sectores industrial, minero – energético y de servicios públicos en Colombia. *Planeación y Desarrollo,* v. 24, no. 2 (May – Aug 93), pp. 191 – 256. Tables, charts.

Honduras

Fernández Hernández, Bernabé. Crisis de la minería de Honduras a fines de la época colonial. *Mesoamérica (USA),* v. 13, no. 24 (Dec 92), pp. 365 – 383. Bibl, maps, facs.

Latin America

Zapata, Francisco. *Atacama: desierto de la discordia; minería y política internacional en Bolivia, Chile y Perú* reviewed by Andrea Ostrov. *La Educación (USA),* v. 37, no. 114 (1993), pp. 175 – 176.

Mexico

Flores Clair, Eduardo. Trabajo, salud y muerte: Real del Monte, 1874. *Siglo XIX: Cuadernos,* v. 1, no. 3 (June 92), pp. 9 – 28. Bibl, charts.

Hausberger, Bernd. Movimientos estacionales en los registros de oro y plata en las cajas de la Real Hacienda de la Nueva España, 1761 – 1767. *Anuario de Estudios Americanos,* v. 49 (1992), pp. 335 – 369. Bibl, tables, charts.

Hilbert, Pia. Refining Mexican Metal Production. *Business Mexico,* v. 3, no. 12 (Dec 93), pp. 4 – 8. Charts.

Kamp, Dick. Mexico's Mines: Source of Wealth or Woe? *Business Mexico,* v. 3, no. 1 (Jan – Feb 93), pp. 29 – 30. Il.

Langue, Frédérique. *Mines, terres et société à Zacatecas (Mexique) de la fin du XVIIe siècle a l'indépendance* reviewed by Manuel Castillo Martos. *Anuario de Estudios Americanos,* v. 50, no. 1 (1993), pp. 319 – 322.

Monroy, María Isabel. La minería: aventura entrañable (Accompanied by an English translation). *Artes de México,* no. 18 (Winter 92), pp. 71 – 77. Il.

Ramos, Agustín. *La gran cruzada* reviewed by Pablo Mora. *Hispamérica,* v. 21, no. 63 (Dec 92), pp. 106 – 108.

Romero Gil, Juan Manuel. Minería y sociedad en el noroeste porfirista. *Siglo XIX: Cuadernos,* v. 1, no. 1 (Oct 91), pp. 37 – 73. Bibl, tables.

Bibliography

González Casasnovas, Ignacio and Guillermo Mira Delli-Zotti. Reflexiones y sugerencias a propósito de la minería colonial. *Historia Mexicana,* v. 42, no. 2 (Oct – Dec 92), pp. 309 – 332.

Sources

Langue, Frédérique. El arbitrismo en el gremio minero novohispano o la representación de J. de la Borda y J. L. Lazaga, 1767: documentos. *Anuario de Estudios Americanos,* v. 50, no. 1 (1993), pp. 269 – 302. Bibl.

MIR, PEDRO

Criticism and interpretation

Gómez Rosa, Alexis. Salutación a don Pedro Mir. *Plural (Mexico),* v. 22, no. 264 (Sept 93), pp. 43 – 45.

MIRACLES

Hevia, Renato. El milagro del padre Hurtado. *Mensaje,* v. 42, no. 424 (Nov 93), pp. 552 – 554. Il.

Sarignana, Armando. La Soledad (Accompanied by an English translation). *Artes de México,* no. 21 (Fall 93), pp. 44 – 47. Il.

MIRANDA, ALICIA

Criticism of specific works
La huella de abril

Gilard, Jacques. *La huella de abril* de Alicia Miranda. *Káñina,* v. 16, no. 1 (Jan – June 92), pp. 19 – 21.

MIRANDA, FRANCISCO DE

Gandía, Enrique de. Prolegómenos a la independencia de la América Hispana: Francisco de Miranda y Juan Pablo de Vizcardo y Guzmán. *Investigaciones y Ensayos,* no. 41 (Jan – Dec 91), pp. 15 – 64.

Karlsson, Weine. Un estudio sueco sobre Francisco de Miranda. *Boletín de la Academia Nacional de la Historia (Venezuela),* v. 75, no. 299 (July – Sept 92), pp. 189 – 190.

Kerdel Vegas, Francisco. El inspector general doctor James Barry. *Boletín de la Academia Nacional de la Historia (Venezuela),* v. 75, no. 299 (July – Sept 92), pp. 157 – 162.

MIRÓ QUESADA CANTUARIAS, FRANCISCO

Valdés García, Félix and María Teresa Vila Bormey. La filosofía de la liberación en Perú: de Augusto Salazar Bondy a Francisco Miró Quesada. *Islas,* no. 99 (May – Aug 91), pp. 21 – 29. Bibl.

MIRRORS IN LITERATURE

Cruz, Jacqueline. Reflexiones y reflejos: *Rayuela* como una novela de espejos. *Chasqui*, v. 22, no. 2 (Nov 93), pp. 24 – 33. Bibl.

Urraca, Beatriz. Wor(l)ds through the Looking-Glass: Borges' Mirrors and Contemporary Theory. *Revista Canadiense de Estudios Hispánicos*, v. 17, no. 1 (Fall 92), pp. 153 – 176. Bibl.

MISCEGENATION

See
Subdivision *Race question* under names of specific countries

MISIONES, ARGENTINA

Espínola, Julio César. La inmigración brasileña en el este misionero argentino: nuevo examen de un antiguo problema. *Revista Paraguaya de Sociología*, v. 29, no. 85 (Sept – Dec 92), pp. 133 – 155. Bibl, tables, maps, charts.

Poujade, Ruth. Poblamiento prehistórico y colonial de Misiones. *Estudos Ibero-Americanos*, v. 18, no. 1 (July 92), pp. 29 – 70. Bibl, maps.

Sanicky, Cristina Aurora. Los usos y las formas del verbo en Misiones, Argentina. *Hispanic Journal*, v. 14, no. 1 (Spring 93), pp. 25 – 36. Bibl.

MISKITO INDIANS

See
Mosquito Indians

MISSING PERSONS

See
Human rights

MISSIONS

See also
Evangelicalism

Africa

Saavedra, Gonzalo. Para Andrés, la esperanza está en Bitkine. *Mensaje*, v. 42, no. 417 (Mar – Apr 93), pp. 104 – 105. Il.

America

Arenas Frutos, Isabel. Expediciones franciscanas a Indias, 1700 – 1725. *Archivo Ibero-Americano*, v. 52, no. 205 – 208 (Jan – Dec 92), pp. 157 – 185. Tables.

Cebrián González, Carmen. Expediciones franciscanas a Indias, 1725 – 1750. *Archivo Ibero-Americano*, v. 52, no. 205 – 208 (Jan – Dec 92), pp. 187 – 207. Bibl, tables.

Statistics

Abad Pérez, Antolín. Estadística franciscano – misionera en ultramar del siglo XVIII: un intento de aproximación. *Archivo Ibero-Americano*, v. 52, no. 205 – 208 (Jan – Dec 92), pp. 125 – 156. Bibl, tables.

Argentina

Gullón Abao, Alberto José. Las reducciones del este de la provincia del Tucumán en la segunda mitad del siglo XVIII bajo la administración franciscana. *Archivo Ibero-Americano*, v. 52, no. 205 – 208 (Jan – Dec 92), pp. 255 – 276. Bibl, tables, maps, charts.

Maeder, Ernesto J. A. La segunda evangelización del Chaco: las misiones franciscanas de Propaganda Fide, 1854 – 1900. *Investigaciones y Ensayos*, no. 41 (Jan – Dec 91), pp. 227 – 247. Bibl.

Bolivia

Abad Pérez, Antolín. *Las misiones de Apolobamba, Bolivia* reviewed by Pedro de Anasagasti. *Signo*, no. 35, Nueva época (Jan – Apr 92), pp. 199 – 200.

Comajuncosa, Antonio. *Manifiesto histórico, geográfico, topográfico, apostólico y político de los misioneros franciscanos de Tarija* reviewed by Pedro de Anasagasti. *Signo*, no. 38, Nueva época (Jan – Apr 93), pp. 231 – 233.

Mingo de la Concepción, Manuel. *Historia de las misiones franciscanas de Tarija entre chiriguanos* reviewed by Pedro de Anasagasti. *Signo*, no. 35, Nueva época (Jan – Apr 92), pp. 237 – 239.

Romero Romero, Catalina. Tres bibliotecas jesuitas en pueblos de misión: Buenavista, Paila y Santa Rosa en la región de Moxos. *Revista de Indias*, v. 52, no. 195 – 196 (May – Dec 92), pp. 889 – 921.

Chile

Guarda Geywitz, Gabriel. Las misiones de la Compañía de Jesús en el período español. *Mensaje*, v. 42, no. 420 (July 93), pp. 215 – 219. Il, facs.

Tampe, Eduardo. Chiloé: misión circular. *Mensaje*, v. 42, no. 420 (July 93), pp. 224 – 227. Il.

Colombia

Hernández Aparicio, Pilar. Las reducciones jesuíticas de los llanos que pasaron a los franciscanos. *Archivo Ibero-Americano*, v. 52, no. 205 – 208 (Jan – Dec 92), pp. 445 – 463. Bibl, tables.

Mantilla Ruiz, Luis Carlos. Las últimas expediciones de franciscanos españoles que vinieron a Colombia, 1759 y 1784. *Archivo Ibero-Americano*, v. 52, no. 205 – 208 (Jan – Dec 92), pp. 403 – 443. Bibl.

Rey Fajardo, José del. La misión del Airico, 1695 – 1704. *Boletín de la Academia Nacional de la Historia (Venezuela)*, v. 76, no. 302 (Apr – June 93), pp. 49 – 68. Bibl.

Mexican – American Border Region

Almaráz, Félix D., Jr. Franciscan Evangelization in Spanish Frontier Texas: Apex of Social Contact, Conflict, and Confluence, 1751 – 1761. *Colonial Latin American Historical Review*, v. 2, no. 3 (Summer 93), pp. 253 – 287. Bibl, il, maps.

Escandón, Patricia. Los problemas de la administración franciscana en las misiones sonorenses, 1768 – 1800. *Archivo Ibero-Americano*, v. 52, no. 205 – 208 (Jan – Dec 92), pp. 277 – 291.

Jackson, Robert H. The Impact of Liberal Policy on Mexico's Northern Frontier: Mission Secularization and the Development of Alta California, 1812 – 1846. *Colonial Latin American Historical Review*, v. 2, no. 2 (Spring 93), pp. 195 – 225. Bibl, tables.

Marchena Fernández, Juan. De franciscanos, apaches y ministros ilustrados en los pasos perdidos del norte de Nueva España. *Archivo Ibero-Americano*, v. 52, no. 205 – 208 (Jan – Dec 92), pp. 513 – 559. Bibl, tables.

Polzer, Charles W. et al, eds. *The Jesuit Missions of Northern Mexico* reviewed by Robert H. Jackson. *Hispanic American Historical Review*, v. 73, no. 2 (May 93), pp. 312 – 313.

Sheridan, Thomas E. et al, eds. *The Franciscan Missions of Northern Mexico* reviewed by Robert H. Jackson. *Hispanic American Historical Review*, v. 73, no. 2 (May 93), pp. 312 – 313.

Sources

Alonso de Jesús, Francisco. 1630 Memorial of Fray Francisco Alonso de Jesús on Spanish Florida's Missions and Natives (Introduced and translated by John H. Hann). *The Americas*, v. 50, no. 1 (July 93), pp. 85 – 105.

Mexico

Morales, Francisco. Secularización de doctrinas: ¿Fin de un modelo evangelizador en la Nueva España? *Archivo Ibero-Americano*, v. 52, no. 205 – 208 (Jan – Dec 92), pp. 465 – 495. Bibl.

Peru

Ardito Vega, Wilfredo. La estructura de las reducciones de Maynas. *Amazonía Peruana*, v. 11, no. 22 (Oct 92), pp. 93 – 124. Bibl.

Domínguez I., Manuel F. El Colegio Franciscano de Propaganda Fide de Moquegua, 1775 – 1825. *Archivo Ibero-Americano*, v. 52, no. 205 – 208 (Jan – Dec 92), pp. 221 – 254. Bibl.

Entrevista al padre Luis Bolla. *Amazonía Peruana*, v. 11, no. 22 (Oct 92), pp. 255 – 272.

Heras, Julián. Significado y extensión de la obra misionera de Ocopa en el siglo XVIII. *Archivo Ibero-Americano*, v. 52, no. 205 – 208 (Jan – Dec 92), pp. 209 – 220. Bibl, il.

Lausent Herrera, Isabelle. La cristianización de los chinos en el Perú: integración, sumisión y resistencia. *Bulletin de l'Institut Français d'Etudes Andines*, v. 21, no. 3 (1992), pp. 977 – 1007. Bibl, il.

United States

Matter, Robert Allen. *Pre-Seminole Florida: Spanish Soldiers, Friars, and Indian Missions, 1513 – 1763* reviewed by Amy Turner Bushnell. *The Americas,* v. 49, no. 4 (Apr 93), pp. 547 – 548.

Russell, Craig H. Newly Discovered Treasures from Colonial California: The Masses at San Fernando. *Inter-American Music Review,* v. 13, no. 1 (Fall – Winter 92), pp. 5 – 9. Bibl.

Sources

Hann, John H., ed. *Missions to the Calusa* reviewed by Amy Turner Bushnell. *The Americas,* v. 49, no. 4 (Apr 93), pp. 548 – 549.

Venezuela

Burguera, Magaly. Macuro: vigía de boca de dragos. *Revista de Historia de América,* no. 113 (Jan – June 92), pp. 65 – 102. Bibl, il, charts.

Campo del Pozo, Fernando. Los mártires agustinos en la misión de Aricagua, Venezuela. *Boletín de la Academia Nacional de la Historia (Venezuela),* v. 76, no. 302 (Apr – June 93), pp. 119 – 129. Bibl.

MISTRAL, GABRIELA

Correspondence, reminiscences, etc.

Zaitzeff, Serge Ivan. Cartas de Gabriela Mistral a Genaro Estrada (Includes four letters). *Cuadernos Americanos,* no. 37, Nueva época (Jan – Feb 93), pp. 115 – 131.

Criticism and interpretation

Agosín, Marjorie. Gestos y rostros de mujeres: Gabriela Mistral y Violeta Parra. *Plural (Mexico),* v. 22, no. 260 (May 93), pp. 60 – 63.

Arrigoitia, Luis de. *Pensamiento y forma en la prosa de Gabriela Mistral* reviewed by Isabel Silva Aldrete. *Anuario de Letras (Mexico),* v. 30 (1992), pp. 296 – 298.

Cúneo Macchiavello, Ana María. La oralidad como primero elemento de formación de la poética mistraliana. *Revista Chilena de Literatura,* no. 41 (Apr 93), pp. 5 – 13. Bibl.

Mora, Gabriela. La prosa política de Gabriela Mistral. *Escritura (Venezuela),* v. 16, no. 31 – 32 (Jan – Dec 91), pp. 193 – 203.

Oliveira, Ana Maria Domingues de. A temática da morte em Cecília Meireles e Gabriela Mistral. *Revista de Letras (Brazil),* v. 32 (1992), pp. 127 – 139. Bibl.

Ostria González, Mauricio. Gabriela Mistral y César Vallejo: la americanidad como desgarramiento. *Revista Chilena de Literatura,* no. 42 (Aug 93), pp. 193 – 199. Bibl.

Pizarro, Ana. Gabriela Mistral en el discurso cultural. *Escritura (Venezuela),* v. 16, no. 31 – 32 (Jan – Dec 91), pp. 215 – 221. Bibl.

Criticism of specific works

Poema de Chile

Neghme Echeverría, Lidia. Lo fantástico y algunos datos intertextuales en *Poema de Chile* de Gabriela Mistral. *Revista Interamericana de Bibliografía,* v. 42, no. 2 (1992), pp. 241 – 250. Bibl.

MITRE, EDUARDO

Criticism and interpretation

Pérez, Alberto Julián. La poesía de Eduardo Mitre en el contexto de la poesía latinoamericana contemporánea. *Signo,* no. 36 – 37, Nueva época (May – Dec 92), pp. 23 – 42. Bibl.

MIXE INDIANS

Lipp, Frank Joseph. *The Mixe of Oaxaca: Religion, Ritual, and Healing* reviewed by James Dow. *The Americas,* v. 49, no. 4 (Apr 93), pp. 545 – 547.

MIXTEC INDIANS

Anguiano Téllez, María Eugenia. Migración y derechos humanos: el caso de los mixtecos. *Estudios Fronterizos,* no. 26 (Sept – Dec 91), pp. 55 – 69. Bibl.

Spores, Ronald. Tututepec: A Postclassic-Period Mixtec Conquest State. *Ancient Mesoamerica,* v. 4, no. 1 (Spring 93), pp. 167 – 174. Bibl, tables, maps, charts.

Vargas Montero, Guadalupe. Espacio físico y espacio sagrado: la territorialidad en una comunidad mixteca, Oaxaca, México. *La Palabra y el Hombre,* no. 84 (Oct – Dec 92), pp. 179 – 189. Bibl.

— Migraciones mixtecas y relaciones regionales a fines del siglo XIX. *La Palabra y el Hombre,* no. 83 (July – Sept 92), pp. 47 – 57. Bibl.

MOCHE VALLEY, PERU

Canziani Amico, José and Santiago Uceda C. Evidencias de grandes precipitaciones en diversas etapas constructivas de La Huaca de la Luna, costa norte del Perú. *Bulletin de l'Institut Français d'Etudes Andines,* v. 22, no. 1 (1993), pp. 313 – 343. Bibl, il.

MOCHICA INDIANS

Arnault, Daniel. El personaje del pie amputado en la cultura mochica de Perú: un ensayo sobre la arqueología del poder. *Latin American Antiquity,* v. 4, no. 3 (Sept 93), pp. 225 – 245. Bibl, il.

Kaulicke, Peter. Moche, Vicús moche y el mochica temprano. *Bulletin de l'Institut Français d'Etudes Andines,* v. 21, no. 3 (1992), pp. 853 – 903. Bibl, il, tables, maps, charts.

Reynales, Trish. The Looting of the Royal Tombs of Sipán. *Latin American Art,* v. 5, no. 2 (Summer 93), pp. 50 – 52. Il.

MODERNISM (LITERATURE)

Fischer, Luís Augusto. Um modernista extraviado. *Vozes,* v. 86, no. 6 (Nov – Dec 92), pp. 2 – 7.

Gikandi, Simon. *Writing in Limbo: Modernism and Caribbean Literature* reviewed by Bruce King. *World Literature Today,* v. 67, no. 2 (Spring 93), p. 426.

Gomes, Eustáquio. *Os rapazes d'"a Onda" e outros rapazes* reviewed by Elias Thomé Saliba. *Vozes,* v. 86, no. 6 (Nov – Dec 92), pp. 101 – 103.

Larsen, Neil. *Modernism and Hegemony: A Materialist Critique of Aesthetic Agencies* reviewed by Antony Higgins. *Revista de Crítica Literaria Latinoamericana,* v. 19, no. 37 (Jan – June 93), pp. 367 – 370.

Lloreda, Waldo César. La transformación de Rubén Darío en Chile. *La Palabra y el Hombre,* no. 84 (Oct – Dec 92), pp. 93 – 109. Bibl.

Neglia, Erminio G. El teatro modernista de Leopoldo Lugones. *Revista Canadiense de Estudios Hispánicos,* v. 17, no. 3 (Spring 93), pp. 549 – 556. Bibl.

Nómez, Naín. Literatura, cultura y sociedad: el modernismo y la génesis de la poesía chilena contemporánea. *Revista Chilena de Literatura,* no. 42 (Aug 93), pp. 157 – 164. Bibl.

Paro, Maria Clara Bonetti. Ronald de Carvalho e Walt Whitman. *Revista de Letras (Brazil),* v. 32 (1992), pp. 141 – 151.

Rodríguez-Peralta, Phyllis White. The Modernist Nocturno and the Nocturne in Music. *Hispanic Journal,* v. 14, no. 1 (Spring 93), pp. 143 – 155.

Rotker, Susana. *Fundación de una escritura: las crónicas de José Martí* reviewed by Richard B. Gray. *Hispanic American Historical Review,* v. 73, no. 3 (Aug 93), pp. 483 – 484.

Silva Beauregard, Paulette. La narrativa venezolana de la época del modernismo. *Revista Chilena de Literatura,* no. 40 (Nov 92), pp. 41 – 56. Bibl.

Villanueva Collado, Alfredo. Eugenio María de Hostos ante el conflicto modernismo/modernidad. *Caribbean Studies,* v. 25, no. 1 – 2 (Jan – July 92), pp. 147 – 158.

— Eugenio María de Hostos ante el conflicto modernismo/modernidad. *Revista Iberoamericana,* v. 59, no. 162 – 163 (Jan – June 93), pp. 21 – 32. Bibl.

MODOTTI, TINA

Poniatowska, Elena. *Tinísima* reviewed by Carlos Monsiváis (Review entitled "Un cuarto de siglo"). *Nexos,* v. 16, no. 192 (Dec 93), p. 71.

MOGROVEJO, TORIBIO DE

McGlone, Mary H. The King's Surprise: The Mission Methodology of Toribio de Mogrovejo. *The Americas,* v. 50, no. 1 (July 93), pp. 65 – 83. Bibl.

MOLINA, ENRIQUE

Criticism of specific works

Una sombra donde sueña Camila O'Gorman

Cordones-Cook, Juanamaría. *Una sombra donde sueña Camila O'Gorman:* dimensión poética de la historia. *La Palabra y el Hombre,* no. 84 (Oct – Dec 92), pp. 271 – 276.

Ocampo, Orlando. Interpretando el pasado histórico: el acto referencial en *Una sombra donde sueña Camila O'Gorman. Revista Chilena de Literatura,* no. 40 (Nov 92), pp. 83 – 89. Bibl.

MOLINA, GLORIA

Ortiz, Isidro D. Gloria Molina, líder popular chicana (Translated by Leticia García Cortés). *Plural (Mexico),* v. 22, no. 256 (Jan 93), pp. 63 – 69. Bibl.

MONASTICISM AND RELIGIOUS ORDERS

See also
Augustinians
Capuchins
Convents and nunneries
Franciscans
Jesuits

Argentina

Mayo, Carlos Alberto. *Los betlemitas en Buenos Aires: convento, economía y sociedad, 1748 – 1822* reviewed by Angela Fernández. *Todo Es Historia,* v. 26, no. 309 (Apr 93), pp. 70 – 71. Il.

Latin America

Peire, Jaime Antonio. La manipulación de los capítulos provinciales, las élites y el imaginario socio-político colonial tardío. *Anuario de Estudios Americanos,* v. 50, no. 1 (1993), pp. 13 – 54.

MONDRAGÓN VALSECA, MARÍA DEL CARMEN

See
Olín, Nahui

MONETARY POLICY

See
Money and money supply
Subdivision *Economic policy* under names of specific countries

MONEY AND MONEY SUPPLY

See also
Balance of payments
Currency question
Foreign exchange problem

Zahler, Roberto. Monetary Policy and an Open Capital Account. *CEPAL Review,* no. 48 (Dec 92), pp. 157 – 166. Bibl.

Argentina

García, Alfredo T. Las transformaciones del sector financiero en los últimos diez años. *Realidad Económica,* no. 120 (Nov – Dec 93), pp. 41 – 60. Tables, charts.

Brazil

Almonacid, Ruben Dario. Os dois pilares. *Problemas Brasileiros,* v. 30, no. 296 (Mar – Apr 93), pp. 13 – 14.

Batista Júnior, Paulo Nogueira and Luiz Gonzaga de Mello Belluzzo, eds. *A luta pela sobrevivência da moeda nacional: ensaios em homenagem a Dilson Funarol* reviewed by Eduardo Refinetti Guardia. *Revista de Economia Política (Brazil),* v. 13, no. 3 (July – Sept 93), pp. 154 – 155.

Pellegrini, Josué Alfredo. As funções do Banco Central do Brasil e o contrôle monetário. *Estudos Econômicos,* v. 22, no. 2 (May – Aug 92), pp. 221 – 252. Bibl, tables.

Mathematical models

Giambiagi, Fábio. Financiamento do governo através de senhoriagem em condições de equilíbrio: algumas simulações. *Revista Brasileira de Economia,* v. 47, no. 2 (Apr – June 93), pp. 265 – 279. Bibl, tables.

Caribbean area

Mathematical models

Ramsaran, Ramesh. Factors Affecting the Income Velocity of Money in the Commonwealth Caribbean. *Social and Economic Studies,* v. 41, no. 4 (Dec 92), pp. 205 – 223. Bibl, tables.

St. Cyr, Eric B. A. Money in Caribbean Economy: A Theoretical Perspective. *Social and Economic Studies,* v. 41, no. 4 (Dec 92), pp. 95 – 111. Bibl, tables, charts.

Chile

Mathematical models

Martner Fanta, Ricardo and Daniel Titelman Kardonsky. Un análisis de cointegración de las funciones de demanda de dinero: el caso de Chile. *El Trimestre Económico,* v. 60, no. 238 (Apr – June 93), pp. 413 – 446. Bibl, tables, charts.

Rojas Ramos, Patricio. El dinero como un objetivo intermedio de política monetaria en Chile: un análisis empírico. *Cuadernos de Economía (Chile),* v. 30, no. 90 (Aug 93), pp. 139 – 178. Bibl, tables, charts.

Colombia

Statistics

Colombia. Departamento Nacional de Planeación. Agregados monetarios. *Planeación y Desarrollo,* v. 24 (1993), All issues.

Latin America

Vornefeld, Ruth M. *Spanische Geldpolitik in Hispanoamerica, 1750 – 1808: Konzepte und Massnahmen im Rahmen der bourbonischen Reformpolitik* reviewed by Teodoro Hampe Martínez. *Revista de Indias,* v. 53, no. 197 (Jan – Apr 93), pp. 127 – 129.

Mexico

Bouchain Galicia, Rafael. La fortaleza del nuevo peso. *Momento Económico,* no. 66 (Mar – Apr 93), pp. 7 – 8.

Delgado, Dora. A New "Look" for Your Money. *Business Mexico,* v. 3, no. 12 (Dec 93), p. 18.

Jiménez Vázquez, Miguel A. La reforma monetaria de México a la luz de la teoría monetarista. *Momento Económico,* no. 65 (Jan – Feb 93), pp. 11 – 15. Tables.

Law and legislation

Manrique Campos, María Irma. La reforma monetaria en el IV Informe Presidencial. *Momento Económico,* no. 65 (Jan – Feb 93), pp. 8 – 10.

MONOPOLIES

See
Cartels and commodity agreements
Competition

MONTAGNANA, MARIO

Fanesi, Pietro Rinaldo. El exilio antifascista en América Latina: el caso mexicano; Mario Montagnana y la "Garibaldi," 1941 – 1945. *Estudios Interdisciplinarios de América Latina y el Caribe,* v. 3, no. 2 (July – Dec 92), pp. 39 – 57. Bibl.

MONTALVO, JUAN

Salcedo-Bastardo, José Luis. Sobre el civismo y la solidaridad: por Montalvo de Venezuela a Ecuador. *Revista Nacional de Cultura (Venezuela),* v. 53, no. 286 (July – Sept 92), pp. 11 – 18.

MONTE ALBÁN, MEXICO

Beyer, Bernd Fahmel. El empleo de una brújula en el diseño de los espacios arquitectónicos en Monte Albán, Oaxaca, México, 400 a.c. – 830 d.c. *Revista Española de Antropología Americana,* v. 23 (1993), pp. 29 – 40. Bibl, il, tables, charts.

Dufétel, Dominique. La otra vida en Monte Albán (Accompanied by an English translation). *Artes de México,* no. 21 (Fall 93), pp. 60 – 65. Il.

MONTEJO, EUGENIO

Criticism and interpretation

Cruz Pérez, Francisco José. Eugenio Montejo: el viaje hacia atrás. *Revista Nacional de Cultura (Venezuela),* v. 54, no. 287 (Oct – Dec 92), pp. 55 – 71. Bibl, il.

Eyzaguirre, Luis B. Eugenio Montejo, poeta de fin de siglo. *Inti,* no. 37 – 38 (Spring – Fall 93), pp. 123 – 132. Bibl.

Hernández, Consuelo. La arquitectura poética de Eugenio Montejo. *Inti,* no. 37 – 38 (Spring – Fall 93), pp. 133 – 143. Bibl.

MONTEMAYOR, CARLOS
Criticism of specific works
Guerra en el paraíso
Trujillo Muñoz, Gabriel. Dos guerras paralelas, dos novelas complementarias. *La Palabra y el Hombre,* no. 84 (Oct – Dec 92), pp. 296 – 298. Il.

MONTERO MALLO, BENICIO
Correspondence, reminiscences, etc.
Montero Mallo, Benicio. Diario de la campaña del Chaco. *Signo,* no. 36 – 37, Nueva época (May – Dec 92), pp. 171 – 195.

MONTERREY, MEXICO
Zúñiga, Víctor. Promover el arte en una ciudad del norte de México: los proyectos artísticos en Monterrey, 1940 – 1960. *Estudios Sociológicos,* v. 11, no. 31 (Jan – Apr 93), pp. 155 – 181. Bibl, tables.

MONTERROSO, AUGUSTO
Criticism and interpretation
Corral, Wilfrido Howard. ¿Dónde está el chiste en Monterroso? *Studi di Letteratura Ispano-Americana,* v. 24 (1993), pp. 83 – 93. Bibl.
Criticism of specific works
La oveja negra y demás fábulas
Ogno, Lía. Augusto Monterroso, la oveja negra de la literatura hispanoamericana. *Cuadernos Hispanoamericanos,* no. 511 (Jan 93), pp. 33 – 42. Bibl.

MONTES BRUNET, HUGO
Biography
Montes Brunet, Hugo. *De la vida de un profesor* reviewed by Gloria Videla de Rivero. *Revista Chilena de Literatura,* no. 40 (Nov 92), pp. 157 – 158.

MONTES HUIDOBRO, MATÍAS
Criticism of specific works
La navaja de Olofé
González Pérez, Armando. Magia, mito y literatura en *La navaja de Olofé. Revista Interamericana de Bibliografía,* v. 42, no. 4 (1992), pp. 635 – 641. Bibl.

MONTEVIDEO, URUGUAY (CITY)
Fernández Cabrelli, Alfonso. Las panaderías montevideanas en 1774. *Hoy Es Historia,* v. 10, no. 60 (Nov – Dec 93), pp. 84 – 85. Facs.

Solla Olivera, Horacio. Cultos afrobrasileños: un templo de umbanda en la ciudad de Montevideo. *Hoy Es Historia,* v. 10, no. 56 (Mar – Apr 93), pp. 33 – 39. Bibl.

MONTORO Y VALDÉS, RAFAEL
García Mora, Luis Miguel. Un cubano en la corte de la restauración: la labor intelectual de Rafael Montoro, 1875 – 1878. *Revista de Indias,* v. 52, no. 195 – 196 (May – Dec 92), pp. 443 – 475. Bibl.

MONUMENTS
See
Cultural property
Subdivision *Monuments, etc.* under names of specific countries and individuals

MOQUEGUA, PERU
Domínguez I., Manuel F. El Colegio Franciscano de Propaganda Fide de Moquegua, 1775 – 1825. *Archivo Ibero-Americano,* v. 52, no. 205 – 208 (Jan – Dec 92), pp. 221 – 254. Bibl.

MORA, LOLA
Jurcich, Milenko Juan. *Lola Mora: el secreto de su sueño mineral* reviewed by Rodrigo Alcorta. *Todo Es Historia,* v. 26, no. 308 (Mar 93), p. 74. Il.

MORAES, JOAQUIM DE ALMEIDA LEITE
Gonçalves, João Francisco Franklin. Mário de Andrade e o avô presidente: dois projetos para o Brasil. *Vozes,* v. 87, no. 4 (July – Aug 93), pp. 65 – 69. Il.

MORALES BERMÚDEZ, JESÚS
Criticism of specific works
Memorial del tiempo
Steele, Cynthia. Indigenismo y posmodernidad: narrativa indigenista, testimonio, teatro campesino y video en el Chiapas finisecular. *Iberoamericana,* v. 16, no. 47 – 48 (1992), pp. 82 – 94. Bibl.

— Indigenismo y posmodernidad: narrativa indigenista, testimonio, teatro campesino y video en el Chiapas finisecular. *Revista de Crítica Literaria Latinoamericana,* v. 19, no. 38 (July – Dec 93), pp. 249 – 260. Bibl.

MORALES CAVERO, HUGO
Obituaries
Colaboraciones póstumas. *Signo,* no. 35, Nueva época (Jan – Apr 92), p. 157.

MORALES FERNÁNDEZ, JESÚS
Obituaries
Castro, Carlo Antonio. ¡Totazqueh, Teicniuh Chuchotzin! *La Palabra y el Hombre,* no. 81 (Jan – Mar 92), p. 391.

MORALITY
See
Ethics

MORAZÁN QUESADA, FRANCISCO
Meléndez Chaverri, Carlos. El verdadero Morazán. *Revista de Historia (Costa Rica),* no. 26 (July – Dec 92), pp. 219 – 240.

MORE, THOMAS
Criticism of specific works
Utopia
Baptiste, Victor N. *Bartolomé de las Casas and Thomas More's Utopia: Connections and Similarities; A Translation and Study* reviewed by Juan Durán Luzio. *Latin American Indian Literatures Journal,* v. 9, no. 1 (Spring 93), pp. 83 – 85.

MORELIA, MEXICO
Vargas Uribe, Guillermo. Geografía histórica de la ciudad de Morelia, Michoacán, México: su evolución demográfica. *Islas,* no. 98 (Jan – Apr 91), pp. 58 – 70. Bibl, tables, maps, charts.

MORELL DE SANTA CRUZ Y LORA, PEDRO AGUSTÍN
Correspondence, reminiscences, etc.
Hernández González, Pablo J. La comarca de Vuelta Abajo, isla de Cuba, en 1755: recuento de un obispo ilustrado. *Anuario de Estudios Americanos,* v. 50, no. 1 (1993), pp. 251 – 268. Bibl, maps.

MORENO, CARMEN ELVIRA
Criticism of specific works
Excepto la muerte
Martínez, Elena M. El discurso patriarcal y el discurso feminista en *Excepto la muerte* de Carmen Elvira Moreno. *Fem,* v. 17, no. 127 (Sept 93), pp. 6 – 10. Bibl.

MORENO, MARIO
Obituaries
Infiesta, Jesús. Al humanismo, a la ternura y a la caridad por el humor (Originally published in *Ecclesia*). *Mensaje,* v. 42, no. 423 (Oct 93), pp. 499 – 500. Il.

MORENO CAPDEVILA, FRANCISCO
Art reproductions
Ramírez, Fermín. Moreno Capdevila, un boceto vespertino (Includes reproductions by the artist). *Plural (Mexico)*, v. 22, no. 264 (Sept 93), pp. 66 – 75. Il.

MORENO VILLA, JOSÉ
Criticism of specific works
La música que llevaba
Amor y Vázquez, José. Máscaras mexicanas en la poesía de Cernuda y Moreno Villa: Quetzalcóatl y Xochipilli (Includes the poem "Quetzalcóatl"). *Nueva Revista de Filología Hispánica*, v. 40, no. 2 (July – Dec 92), pp. 1057 – 1072.

MORFI, JUAN AGUSTÍN
Heredia Correa, Roberto. Fray Juan Agustín Morfi, humanista y crítico de su tiempo. *Archivo Ibero-Americano*, v. 52, no. 205 – 208 (Jan – Dec 92), pp. 107 – 124. Bibl.

MORLEY, HELENA
See
Brant, Alice Dayrell Caldeira

MORÓN MONTERO, GUILLERMO
Pérez Alencart, Alfredo. Todas las historias de Guillermo Morón, un venezolano en Salamanca. *Boletín de la Academia Nacional de la Historia (Venezuela)*, v. 75, no. 299 (July – Sept 92), pp. 163 – 164.

MORTALITY
See
Infant mortality
Population

MORTON, CARLOS
Correspondence, reminiscences, etc.
Morton, Carlos. Rewriting Southwestern History: A Playwright's Perspective. *Mexican Studies*, v. 9, no. 2 (Summer 93), pp. 225 – 239. Il.

MOSQUITIA
Díaz Polanco, Héctor and Consuelo Sánchez. Cronología de los hechos históricos de la costa atlántica de Nicaragua: primera parte. *Boletín de Antropología Americana*, no. 23 (July 91), pp. 171 – 184. Bibl.
— Cronología de los hechos históricos de la costa atlántica de Nicaragua: segunda parte. *Boletín de Antropología Americana*, no. 24 (Dec 91), pp. 151 – 178. Bibl, il.

MOSQUITO INDIANS
Bell, C. Napier. *Tamgweera: Life and Adventures among Gentle Savages* reviewed by Elizabeth Kudin. *América Indígena*, v. 51, no. 2 – 3 (Apr – Sept 91), pp. 357 – 359.
Flores Andino, Francisco A. Medicina tradicional, magia y mitos entre los miskitos de Honduras. *Folklore Americano*, no. 52 (July – Dec 91), pp. 131 – 144.
Bibliography
Dennis, Philip Adams. The Miskito – Sandinista Conflict in Nicaragua in the 1980s (Review article). *Latin American Research Review*, v. 28, no. 3 (1993), pp. 214 – 234.

MOTION PICTURE REVIEWS
See
Film reviews

MOTION PICTURES
See also
Film reviews
Latin America in motion pictures
Motion pictures and literature
Screenplays
Festivals
Almanza, Iraida América. 20 años de festival internacional de cine en Panamá: un evento que no debió acabarse, 1963 – 1983. *Revista Cultural Lotería*, v. 50, no. 386 (Nov – Dec 91), pp. 70 – 88.

Averbach, Márgara. Festival "Mujer y Cine": entrevista con Anamaría Muchnik. *Feminaria*, v. 6, no. 11 (Nov 93), pp. 23 – 24.
Cockrell, Eddie. Seventh Heaven: The Americas Film Festival. *Américas*, v. 45, no. 6 (Nov – Dec 93), pp. 46 – 49. Il.
Vera-Meiggs, David. Cine en Viña del Mar. *Mensaje*, v. 42, no. 424 (Nov 93), pp. 592 – 593. Il.

History and criticism
Anhalt, Nedda G. de. A la sombra de una sombrilla: cronología de *Cine: la gran seducción*, a la manera de la cronología de *Caín*. *La Palabra y el Hombre*, no. 81 (Jan – Mar 92), pp. 372 – 382. Il.
Arredondo, Arturo. La labor de *Scherezada* de Nedda G. de Anhalt. *La Palabra y el Hombre*, no. 81 (Jan – Mar 92), pp. 368 – 369.
González Dueñas, Daniel. Una voz en "off": *Cine: la gran seducción*. *La Palabra y el Hombre*, no. 81 (Jan – Mar 92), pp. 370 – 371.
Lauretis, Teresa de. Volver a pensar el cine de mujeres: estética y teoría feminista (Excerpt from *Technologies of Gender: Essays on Theory, Film, and Fiction* translated by Beatriz Olivier). *Feminaria*, v. 6, no. 10 (Apr 93), pp. 1 – 12. Bibl.
Mahieu, José Agustín. Cine en tres tiempos. *Cuadernos Hispanoamericanos*, no. 511 (Jan 93), pp. 125 – 133. Il.
Zapiola, Guillermo. Indios y españoles en pantalla grande. *Cuadernos del CLAEH*, v. 17, no. 63 – 64 (Oct 92), pp. 161 – 166.

Production and direction
Millán Moncayo, Márgara. ¿Hacia una estética cinematográfica femenina? *Revista Mexicana de Ciencias Políticas y Sociales*, v. 37, Nueva época, no. 149 (July – Sept 92), pp. 177 – 188.
Patán Tobío, Julio. Ripstein entre nosotros. *Nexos*, v. 16, no. 191 (Nov 93), pp. 73 – 74.
Pliego, Roberto. Los emblemas del metal: una entrevista con Guillermo del Toro. *Nexos*, v. 16, no. 186 (June 93), pp. 85 – 86.
Vega Alfaro, Eduardo de la. *Arcady Boytler Rososbky, 1895 – 1965* reviewed by Sonia Hernández Briseño (Review entitled "Pioneros del cine sonoro II"). *Revista Mexicana de Ciencias Políticas y Sociales*, v. 37, Nueva época, no. 150 (Oct – Dec 92), pp. 189 – 190.
— *Gabriel Soria, 1903 – 1971* reviewed by Beatriz Valdés Lagunes (Review entitled "Pioneros del cine sonoro I"). *Revista Mexicana de Ciencias Políticas y Sociales*, v. 37, Nueva época, no. 150 (Oct – Dec 92), pp. 187 – 188.
— *Gabriel Soria, 1903 – 1971* reviewed by Juan Felipe Leal and Eduardo Barraza (Review entitled "Gabriel Soria y el cine sonoro mexicano"). *Revista Mexicana de Ciencias Políticas y Sociales*, v. 37, Nueva época, no. 150 (Oct – Dec 92), pp. 179 – 186.
— *José Bohr* reviewed by Beatriz Valdés Lagunes (Review entitled "Pioneros del cine sonoro III"). *Revista Mexicana de Ciencias Políticas y Sociales*, v. 37, Nueva época, no. 150 (Oct – Dec 92), pp. 191 – 192.

Amazon Valley
Godfrey, Brian J. Regional Depiction in Contemporary Film. *Geographical Review*, v. 83, no. 4 (Oct 93), pp. 428 – 440. Bibl, il.

Argentina
Alcorta, Rodrigo. Una historia de película. *Todo Es Historia*, v. 26, no. 306 (Jan 93), pp. 50 – 53. Il.
Liev, Daniel. Cine nacional durante el Proceso. *Cuadernos Hispanoamericanos*, no. 517 – 519 (July – Sept 93), pp. 305 – 312.
Mahieu, José Agustín. Cine argentino: las nuevas fronteras. *Cuadernos Hispanoamericanos*, no. 517 – 519 (July – Sept 93), pp. 289 – 304.

Bolivia
Rivadeneira Prada, Raúl. El cine alternativo en Bolivia. *Signo*, no. 38, Nueva época (Jan – Apr 93), pp. 47 – 60. Bibl.

Brazil

Bicalho, Maria Fernanda Baptista. The Art of Seduction: Representation of Women in Brazilian Silent Cinema (Fragment from *Entre a virtude e o pecado* edited by Albertina de Oliveira Costa and Cristina Bruschini, translated by Sueann Caulfield). *Luso-Brazilian Review*, v. 30, no. 1 (Summer 93), pp. 21 – 33. Bibl.

D'Ambrosio, Oscar. Claquete quebrada. *Problemas Brasileiros*, v. 30, no. 295 (Jan – Feb 93), pp. 62 – 64. Il.

Merten, Luiz Carlos. A agonia do cinema nacional. *Vozes*, v. 87, no. 3 (May – June 93), pp. 64 – 66.

Cuba

Quirós, Oscar E. Values and Aesthetics in Cuban Arts and Cinema. *SALALM Papers*, v. 34 (1989), pp. 151 – 171. Bibl.

Latin America

Gil Olivo, Ramón. Nuevo cine latinoamericano, 1955 – 1973: fuentes para un lenguaje. *Plural (Mexico)*, v. 22, no. 263 (Aug 93), pp. 50 – 56. Bibl.

Lenti, Paul. Latin America Takes on Hollywood. *NACLA Report on the Americas*, v. 27, no. 2 (Sept – Oct 93), pp. 4 – 9. Il.

Morris, Barbara. Configuring Women: The Discourse of Empowerment in Latin American Cinema. *SALALM Papers*, v. 34 (1989), pp. 143 – 150. Bibl.

Bibliography

Neugebauer, Rhonda L. Videos and Films Shown at the Conference. *SALALM Papers*, v. 34 (1989), pp. 172 – 174.

Congresses

Martins-Zurhorst, Ida. Restauración y preservación de la historia del cine latinoamericano (Translated by Gabriela Fonseca). *Humboldt*, no. 108 (1993), p. 103. Il.

Mexico

Barraza, Eduardo and Juan Felipe Leal. Inicios de la reglamentación cinematográfica en la ciudad de México. *Revista Mexicana de Ciencias Políticas y Sociales*, v. 37, Nueva época, no. 150 (Oct – Dec 92), pp. 139 – 175. Bibl, charts.

Leal, Juan Felipe. Vistas que no se ven: el cine mexicano anterior a la revolución. *Revista Mexicana de Ciencias Políticas y Sociales*, v. 38, Nueva época, no. 153 (July – Sept 93), pp. 111 – 133.

Patán Tobío, Julio. Ripstein entre nosotros. *Nexos*, v. 16, no. 191 (Nov 93), pp. 73 – 74.

Podalsky, Laura. Disjointed Frames: Melodrama, Nationalism, and Representation in 1940s Mexico. *Studies in Latin American Popular Culture*, v. 12 (1993), pp. 57 – 53. Bibl.

Tuñón Pablos, Julia. Between the Nation and Utopia: The Image of Mexico in the Films of Emilio "Indio" Fernández. *Studies in Latin American Popular Culture*, v. 12 (1993), pp. 159 – 174. Bibl.

Vega Alfaro, Eduardo de la. *Arcady Boytler Rososbky, 1895 – 1965* reviewed by Sonia Hernández Briseño (Review entitled "Pioneros del cine sonoro II"). *Revista Mexicana de Ciencias Políticas y Sociales*, v. 37, Nueva época, no. 150 (Oct – Dec 92), pp. 189 – 190.

— *Gabriel Soria, 1903 – 1971* reviewed by Beatriz Valdés Lagunes (Review entitled "Pioneros del cine sonoro I"). *Revista Mexicana de Ciencias Políticas y Sociales*, v. 37, Nueva época, no. 150 (Oct – Dec 92), pp. 187 – 188.

— *Gabriel Soria, 1903 – 1971* reviewed by Juan Felipe Leal and Eduardo Barraza (Review entitled "Gabriel Soria y el cine sonoro mexicano"). *Revista Mexicana de Ciencias Políticas y Sociales*, v. 37, Nueva época, no. 150 (Oct – Dec 92), pp. 179 – 186.

— *José Bohr* reviewed by Beatriz Valdés Lagunes (Review entitled "Pioneros del cine sonoro III"). *Revista Mexicana de Ciencias Políticas y Sociales*, v. 37, Nueva época, no. 150 (Oct – Dec 92), pp. 191 – 192.

Dictionaries and encyclopedias

García Riera, Emilio. *Historia documental del cine mexicano* reviewed by Luis González y González (Review entitled "Una enciclopedia del cine mexicano"). *Nexos*, v. 16, no. 188 (Aug 93), pp. 85 – 87.

Panama

Almanza, Iraida América. 20 años de festival internacional de cine en Panamá: un evento que no debió acabarse, 1963 – 1983. *Revista Cultural Lotería*, v. 50, no. 386 (Nov – Dec 91), pp. 70 – 88.

United States

Richard, Alfred Charles, Jr. *The Hispanic Image on the Silver Screen: An Interpretive Filmography from Silents into Sound, 1898 – 1935* reviewed by Paul J. Vanderwood. *Hispanic American Historical Review*, v. 73, no. 2 (May 93), pp. 294 – 295.

— *The Hispanic Image on the Silver Screen: An Interpretive Filmography from Silents into Sound, 1898 – 1935* reviewed by Ana M. Rodríguez-Vivaldi. *Revista Interamericana de Bibliografía*, v. 42, no. 3 (1992), pp. 507 – 508.

MOTION PICTURES AND LITERATURE

Cruz Pérez, Francisco José. García Márquez: la realidad sin mediaciones. *Cuadernos Hispanoamericanos*, no. 512 (Feb 93), pp. 115 – 120.

Study and teaching

Dobrian, Walter A. The Dialog of Genres: Hispanic Literature to Film. *Hispania (USA)*, v. 76, no. 1 (Mar 93), pp. 140 – 146. Bibl.

MOVIMIENTO AL SOCIALISMO (VENEZUELA)

Ellner, Steven B. *De la derrota guerrillera a la política innovadora: el Movimiento al Socialismo (MAS)* reviewed by Dick Parker. *Nueva Sociedad*, no. 124 (Mar – Apr 93), p. 174.

MOVIMIENTO DE LIBERACIÓN NACIONAL-TUPAMARO (URUGUAY)

Baeza, Cristina. Mauricio Rosencof: "Ni me bajo de este barco, ni cambio de capitán." *Casa de las Américas*, no. 191 (Apr – June 93), pp. 124 – 131.

MOVIMIENTO REVOLUCIONARIO TUPAC AMARU

Renard-Casevitz, France-Marie. Les guerriers du sel: chronique '92. *Cahiers des Amériques Latines*, no. 13 (1992), pp. 107 – 118.

MOYA PALENCIA, MARIO

Criticism of specific works

El México de Egerton

MacAdam, Alfred J. Daniel Thomas Egerton, the Unfortunate Traveler. *Review*, no. 47 (Fall 93), pp. 9 – 13. Il.

MUCHNIK, ANAMARÍA

Interviews

Averbach, Márgara. Festival "Mujer y Cine": entrevista con Anamaría Muchnik. *Feminaria*, v. 6, no. 11 (Nov 93), pp. 23 – 24.

MUISCAS

See
Chibcha Indians

MUJICA, BARBARA KAMINAR DE

Interviews

Bencastro, Mario. Reviewing Barbara Mujica. *Américas*, v. 45, no. 2 (Mar – Apr 93), pp. 60 – 61. Il.

MULATTOES

See
Blacks
Maroons

MULTICULTURALISM

See
Subdivision *Civilization* under names of specifc countries

MULTINATIONAL CORPORATIONS

See
International business enterprises

MUMMIES

Langebaek, Carl Henrik. Competencia por prestigio político y momificación en el norte de Suramérica y el Istmo de Panamá. *Revista Colombiana de Antropología*, v. 29 (1992), pp. 7 – 26. Bibl.

MUNDO NUEVO (PERIODICAL)

McQuade, Frank. *Mundo Nuevo:* el discurso político en una revista intelectual de los sesenta. *Revista Chilena de Literatura*, no. 42 (Aug 93), pp. 123 – 130.

Mudrovcic, María Eugenia. *Mundo Nuevo:* hacia la definición de un modelo discursivo. *Nuevo Texto Crítico*, v. 6, no. 11 (1993), pp. 187 – 206. Bibl.

MUNICIPAL ELECTIONS

See
Local elections

MUNICIPAL GOVERNMENT

See
Local government

MUNICIPAL SERVICES

See
Public utilities
Social services
Subdivision *Public works* under names of specific countries

MURAL PAINTING AND DECORATION

Argentina

Azuela, Alicia. La presencia de Diego Rivera en los Estados Unidos: dos versiones de la historia. *Anales del Instituto de Investigaciones Estéticas*, v. 16, no. 62 (1991), pp. 175 – 180.

Martínez Quijano, Ana. El mítico mural de Siqueiros en la Argentina (Accompanied by an English translation). *Art Nexus*, no. 9 (June – Aug 93), pp. 110 – 112. Il.

Costa Rica

Macaya T., Emilia. Discurso de la decana dra. Emilia Macaya, con motivo de la inauguración del mural de la Facultad de Letras. *Revista de Filosofía de la Universidad de Costa Rica*, v. 34, no. 74 (July 93), pp. 93 – 94.

Mexico

Maldonado Cárdenas, Rubén. Las pinturas de Sodzil, Yucatán, México. *Revista Española de Antropología Americana*, v. 23 (1993), pp. 101 – 111. Bibl.

Reyes Valerio, Constantino. *El pintor de conventos: los murales del siglo XVI en la Nueva España* reviewed by Rogelio Ruiz Gomar. *Anales del Instituto de Investigaciones Estéticas*, v. 16, no. 62 (1991), pp. 208 – 215.

Stern, Peter A. Art and the State in Post-Revolutionary Mexico and Cuba. *SALALM Papers*, v. 34 (1989), pp. 17 – 32. Bibl.

Peru

Carrasco, Sergio. Jugar en pared. *Debate (Peru)*, v. 16, no. 72 (Mar – May 93), p. 57. Il.

Macera dall'Orso, Pablo. *La pintura mural andina, siglos XVI – XIX* reviewed by Carlos Rodríguez Saavedra (Review entitled "Arte mestizo"). *Debate (Peru)*, v. 16, no. 75 (Dec 93 – Jan 94), p. 77. Il.

MURCIA, SPAIN

Vilar, Juan Bautista. *Los murcianos y América* reviewed by José U. Martínez Carreras. *Revista de Indias*, v. 53, no. 197 (Jan – Apr 93), pp. 126 – 127.

MURENA, HÉCTOR ALVAREZ

Criticism and interpretation

Lagos-Pope, María-Inés. *H. A. Murena en sus ensayos y narraciones: de líder revisionista a marginado* reviewed by Fernando Reati. *Hispamérica*, v. 21, no. 63 (Dec 92), pp. 97 – 99.

MURRIETA, JOAQUÍN

Darío Murrieta, Rubén and María Rosa Palazón Mayoral. Las verdaderas leyendas de Joaquín Murrieta. *Casa de las Américas*, no. 191 (Apr – June 93), pp. 37 – 49. Bibl.

MUSEUMS

Brazil

Barata, Mário. 50 anos de museologia, I: Um fragmento pessoal. *Revista do Instituto Histórico e Geográfico Brasileiro*, no. 371 (Apr – June 91), pp. 554 – 561.

Beltrão, Maria da Conceição de M. C. A coleção egípcia do Museu Nacional (Speech given at the occasion of her induction into the Instituto Histórico e Geográfico Brasileiro). *Revista do Instituto Histórico e Geográfico Brasileiro*, no. 372 (July – Sept 91), pp. 806 – 811.

Costa, Lygia Martins. 50 anos de museologia, II: Significado da homenagem. *Revista do Instituto Histórico e Geográfico Brasileiro*, no. 371 (Apr – June 91), pp. 562 – 567.

Peregrino, Umberto. Discurso do sócio-benemérito general Umberto Peregrino Seabra Fagundes, na inauguração do Museu de Arte Popular, em 23 de outubro de 1991. *Revista do Instituto Histórico e Geográfico Brasileiro*, no. 373 (Oct – Dec 91), pp. 1201 – 1203.

Santos, Myrian S. Objetos, memória e história: observação e análise de um museu histórico brasileiro. *Dados*, v. 35, no. 2 (1992), pp. 217 – 237. Bibl.

Vale, Vanda Arantes do. Pintores estrangeiros no Brasil: Museu Mariano Procópio. *Vozes*, v. 87, no. 2 (Mar – Apr 93), pp. 55 – 62. Bibl, il.

Caribbean area

Cummins, Alissandra. Exhibiting Culture: Museums and National Identity in the Caribbean. *Caribbean Quarterly*, v. 38, no. 2 – 3 (June – Sept 92), pp. 33 – 53. Bibl.

Mexico

Fox, Lorna Scott. Zona: nuevo espacio plástico. *Artes de México*, no. 20 (Summer 93), p. 116. Il.

United States

Barnes, Susan J. Dallas Sheds New Light on Art Treasures. *Américas*, v. 45, no. 5 (Sept – Oct 93), pp. 50 – 53. Il.

Bayón, Damián Carlos. Arte latinoamericano en el MOMA: una ocasión perdida. *Vuelta*, v. 17, no. 201 (Aug 93), pp. 60 – 62.

Gates, Thomas P. Meadows Museum of Spanish Art Book Collection: An Overview. *SALALM Papers*, v. 34 (1989), pp. 439 – 451. Bibl.

Kaye, Susan. A Living Venue for Cultural Crossroads. *Américas*, v. 45, no. 3 (May – June 93), pp. 48 – 51. Il.

Leyva, María. The Museum of Modern Art of Latin America: A Guide to Its Resources. *SALALM Papers*, v. 34 (1989), pp. 417 – 427.

MUSIC

See also
Children's songs
Church music
Composers
Ethnomusicology
Folk music
Musical instruments
Musicians
Musicology
Opera
Popular music
Songs
Subdivision *Music* under names of Indian groups

Festivals

Béjar, Ana María. Cultura, utopía y percepción social: los festivales por la vida y por la paz y la práctica musical juvenil en Sicuani. *Allpanchis*, v. 25, no. 41 (Jan – June 93), pp. 109 – 141. Tables.

Mafra, Antônio. Festival de Inverno de Campos do Jordão. *Vozes*, v. 86, no. 4 (July – Aug 92), pp. 86 – 87. Il.

Argentina

Cabrera, Napoleón. La música argentina entre 1970 y 1990. *Cuadernos Hispanoamericanos*, no. 517 – 519 (July – Sept 93), pp. 280 – 288. Il.

Brazil

Chaves, Celso Loureiro. Como uma placa de trânsito: a música brasileira no meio acadêmico internacional. *Vozes,* v. 86, no. 6 (Nov – Dec 92), pp. 8 – 12.

Grützmacher, Thomas. Salve-se quem souber: lembrando Smetak. *Vozes,* v. 87, no. 1 (Jan – Feb 93), pp. 77 – 83. Il.

Siqueira, Baptista. Características de la música brasileña. *Revista Musical de Venezuela,* no. 28 (May – Dec 89), pp. 197 – 206. Facs.

Chile

Crónica: creación musical en Chile, 1992. *Revista Musical Chilena,* v. 46, no. 178 (July – Dec 92), pp. 109 – 115.

Cuba

Cabrera Infante, Guillermo. La Lupe cantaba: "Con el diablo en el cuerpo y un ángel en la voz." *Vuelta,* v. 17, no. 200 (July 93), pp. 19 – 20.

Manuel, Peter, ed. *Essays on Cuban Music: North American and Cuban Perspectives* reviewed by Lucy Durán. *Latin American Music Review,* v. 14, no. 2 (Fall – Winter 93), pp. 281 – 288.

Foreign influences

Sáenz, Carmen María and María Elena Vinueza. El aporte africano en la formación de la cultura musical cubana. *Folklore Americano,* no. 53 (Jan – June 92), pp. 55 – 80. Bibl.

Ecuador

Guerrero, Juan Agustín. *La música ecuatoriana desde su origen hasta 1875* (Review of a reprint of the 1876 original). *Inter-American Music Review,* v. 13, no. 1 (Fall – Winter 92), pp. 109 – 111. Facs.

Latin America

Franco, Enrique, ed. *Imágenes de la música iberoamericana* (Review). *Inter-American Music Review,* v. 13, no. 1 (Fall – Winter 92), pp. 121 – 122.

Holston, Mark. Everything Old Is New Again. *Américas,* v. 45, no. 6 (Nov – Dec 93), pp. 56 – 57. Il.

— Variations on Themes. *Américas,* v. 45, no. 4 (July – Aug 93), pp. 52 – 53. Il.

Oliveira, José Aparecido de et al. Homenaje al doctor Francisco Curt Lange. *Revista Musical de Venezuela,* no. 28 (May – Dec 89), Issue. Bibl, il, facs.

Bibliography

Bibliografía (Works by and about Francisco Curt Lange). *Revista Musical de Venezuela,* no. 28 (May – Dec 89), pp. 224 – 264.

Latin American Musical Periodicals. *Inter-American Music Review,* v. 13, no. 2 (Spring – Summer 93), pp. 145 – 148. Bibl.

Makuch, Andrew L. From Zarabanda to Salsa: An Overview of Reference Sources on Latin American Music. *SALALM Papers,* v. 34 (1989), pp. 363 – 368.

Moore, Robin. Directory of Latin American and Caribbean Music Theses and Dissertations since 1988. *Latin American Music Review,* v. 14, no. 1 (Spring – Summer 93), pp. 145 – 171.

Congresses

Gómez García, Zoila. ¿Música y aspiraciones humanas? *Plural (Mexico),* v. 22, no. 262 (July 93), p. 75.

Indexes

Indices de las colecciones cooperativas y colectivas publicadas por Francisco Curt Lange, 1935 – 1958 (Indexes to eight journals on Latin American music, introduced by Humberto Sagredo Araya). *Revista Musical de Venezuela,* no. 29 (Jan – June 90), Issue. Il, facs.

Mexico

Helguera, Luis Ignacio. Nuestra música. *Vuelta,* v. 17, no. 197 (Apr 93), pp. 70 – 73.

Herrera y Ogazón, Alba. *El arte musical en México* (Review of a reprint of the 1917 original). *Inter-American Music Review,* v. 13, no. 1 (Fall – Winter 92), p. 111.

Bibliography

Lemmon, Alfred E. Colonial Discography. *The Americas,* v. 49, no. 3 (Jan 93), pp. 388 – 390.

Peru

Campos, José Carlos et al. Estado de la música en el Perú (An interview with five Peruvian composers). *Hueso Húmero,* no. 29 (May 93), pp. 93 – 104.

Yep, Virginia. El vals peruano. *Latin American Music Review,* v. 14, no. 2 (Fall – Winter 93), pp. 268 – 280. Bibl, facs.

Puerto Rico

Bibliography

Thompson, Donald. *Music and Dance in Puerto Rico from the Age of Columbus to Modern Times: An Annotated Bibliography* reviewed by Inés Grandela de Río. *Revista Musical Chilena,* v. 46, no. 178 (July – Dec 92), p. 127.

MUSIC AND LITERATURE

Aparicio, Frances R. Entre la guaracha y el bolero: un ciclo de intertextos musicales en la nueva narrativa puertorriqueña. *Revista Iberoamericana,* v. 59, no. 162 – 163 (Jan – June 93), pp. 73 – 89. Bibl.

Klüppelholz, Heinz. Alejo Carpentiers orphische Beschwörung. *Zeitschrift für Lateinamerika Wien,* no. 42 (1992), pp. 17 – 25. Bibl.

Rodríguez-Peralta, Phyllis White. The Modernist Nocturno and the Nocturne in Music. *Hispanic Journal,* v. 14, no. 1 (Spring 93), pp. 143 – 155.

Wehrs, Carlos. Machado de Assis e a música. *Revista do Instituto Histórico e Geográfico Brasileiro,* no. 373 (Oct – Dec 91), pp. 1057 – 1070. Bibl, il.

MUSIC AND SOCIETY

Argentina

Monteleone, Jorge J. Cuerpo constelado: sobre la poesía de "rock" argentino. *Cuadernos Hispanoamericanos,* no. 517 – 519 (July – Sept 93), pp. 401 – 420.

Pujol, Sergio Alejandro. "Rock" y juventud: de las catacumbas al estrellato. *Todo Es Historia,* v. 27, no. 317 (Dec 93), pp. 70 – 73. Il.

Bolivia

Wara Céspedes, Gilka. "Huayño," "Saya," and "Chuntunqui": Bolivan Identity in the Music of "Los Kjarkas." *Latin American Music Review,* v. 14, no. 1 (Spring – Summer 93), pp. 52 – 101. Bibl, il, facs.

Brazil

Carvalho, Martha de Ulhôa. Musical Style, Migration, and Urbanization: Some Considerations on Brazilian "Música Sertaneja" (Country Music). *Studies in Latin American Popular Culture,* v. 12 (1993), pp. 75 – 94. Bibl, tables.

Cunha, Olívia Maria Gomes da. Fazendo a "coisa certa": reggae, rastas e pentecostais em Salvador. *Revista Brasileira de Ciências Sociais,* v. 8, no. 23 (Oct 93), pp. 120 – 137. Bibl.

Dunn, Christopher. Afro-Bahian Carnival: A Stage for Protest. *Afro-Hispanic Review,* v. 11, no. 1 – 3 (1992), pp. 11 – 20. Bibl.

Moraes, José Geraldo Vinci de. Sonoridades urbanas. *Vozes,* v. 87, no. 3 (May – June 93), pp. 48 – 58. Il.

Walger, Christian. "Nova música baiana": Musikszene Bahia; Kultursoziologische Betrachtungen zur schwarzen Musik Brasiliens. *Zeitschrift für Lateinamerika Wien,* no. 42 (1992), pp. 27 – 51. Bibl.

Caribbean area

Desroches, Monique. Créolisation musicale et identité culturelle aux Antilles françaises. *Canadian Journal of Latin American and Caribbean Studies,* v. 17, no. 34 (1992), pp. 41 – 51. Bibl.

Guilbault, Jocelyne. Sociopolitical, Cultural, and Economic Development through Music: Zouk in the French Antilles. *Canadian Journal of Latin American and Caribbean Studies,* v. 17, no. 34 (1992), pp. 27 – 40. Bibl.

Dominican Republic

Pacini Hernandez, Deborah. Dominican Popular Music under the Trujillo Regime. *Studies in Latin American Popular Culture,* v. 12 (1993), pp. 127 – 140. Bibl.

Peru

Béjar, Ana María. Cultura, utopía y percepción social: los festivales por la vida y por la paz y la práctica musical juvenil en Sicuani. *Allpanchis,* v. 25, no. 41 (Jan – June 93), pp. 109 – 141. Tables.

Cisneros, Luis Jaime. Nosequién y los Nosecuántos. *Debate (Peru),* v. 15, no. 71 (Nov 92 – Jan 93), p. 67. Il.

Cornejo Guinassi, Pedro. Nosequién y los Nosecuántos: ¿Espejo de una generación? *Debate (Peru),* v. 16, no. 74 (Sept – Oct 93), pp. 38 – 40. Il.

United States

Koegel, John. Calendar of Southern California Amusements (1852 – 1897) Designed for the Spanish-Speaking Public. *Inter-American Music Review,* v. 13, no. 2 (Spring – Summer 93), pp. 115 – 143. Bibl, il.

— Mexican and Mexican-American Musical Life in Southern California, 1850 – 1900. *Inter-American Music Review,* v. 13, no. 2 (Spring – Summer 93), pp. 111 – 114. Bibl.

Martínez Saldaña, Jesús. Los Tigres del Norte en Silicon Valley. *Nexos,* v. 16, no. 191 (Nov 93), pp. 77 – 83. Il.

MUSICAL INSTRUMENTS
Study and teaching

Aguilar, Pilar. El maestro Carlos Enrique Vargas y su metodología en la enseñanza del piano. *Káñina,* v. 16, no. 1 (Jan – June 92), pp. 267 – 272. Il.

Argentina

Bach, Caleb. Where Sound Is Born (Photographs by Giancarlo Puppo). *Américas,* v. 45, no. 1 (Jan – Feb 93), pp. 24 – 29. Il.

Bolivia

Langevin, André. Las zampoñas del conjunto de kantu y el debate sobre la función de la segunda hilera de tubos: datos etnográficos y análisis semiótico. *Revista Andina,* v. 10, no. 2 (Dec 92), pp. 405 – 440. Bibl, tables.

Latin America

Olivero, Omar. *El tambor conga: un instrumento musical afroamericano; su función y trascendencia en la música latinoamerica* reviewed by Tulia Bonetti P. *La Educación (USA),* v. 37, no. 115 (1993), pp. 428 – 429.

Peru

Gemert, Hans van. *Organos históricos del Perú* (Review). *Inter-American Music Review,* v. 13, no. 1 (Fall – Winter 92), pp. 114 – 115.

Río de la Plata region

Mazzone, Daniel. Tango y bandoneón: encuentros y tristezas de un doble A. *Cuadernos del CLAEH,* v. 17, no. 63 – 64 (Oct 92), pp. 167 – 173. Bibl.

MUSICIANS
See also
Composers

America

Zavadivker, Ricardo Augusto. *Los primeros músicos en América* (Review). *Inter-American Music Review,* v. 13, no. 2 (Spring – Summer 93), pp. 154 – 155.

Argentina

Persia, Jorge de. Aspectos de la vida y obra de músicos españoles emigrados a Argentina en los años de la guerra civil. *Revista Musical de Venezuela,* no. 28 (May – Dec 89), pp. 165 – 182.

Brazil

Holston, Mark. Tom Zé: The Conscience of Brazil's Tropicalismo. *Américas,* v. 45, no. 1 (Jan – Feb 93), pp. 58 – 59. Il.

Sparks, David Hatfield. Gilberto Gil, Praise Singer of the Gods. *Afro-Hispanic Review,* v. 11, no. 1 – 3 (1992), pp. 70 – 75. Bibl.

Catalogs

As cantoras do rádio: 50 anos de som e imagem da MPB reviewed by Irati Antonio. *Latin American Music Review,* v. 14, no. 2 (Fall – Winter 93), pp. 297 – 299.

Costa Rica

Aguilar, Pilar. El maestro Carlos Enrique Vargas y su metodología en la enseñanza del piano. *Káñina,* v. 16, no. 1 (Jan – June 92), pp. 267 – 272. Il.

Cuba

Aharonián, Coriún. Conversación con César Portillo de la Luz: "Y porque pienso vivo cuando canto." *Casa de las Américas,* no. 190 (Jan – Mar 93), pp. 141 – 146.

Dominican Republic

Haidar de Maríñez, Julieta. La música como cultura y como poesía: Juan Luis Guerra y el Grupo 4:40. *Homines,* v. 15 – 16, no. 2 – 1 (Oct 91 – Dec 92), pp. 316 – 326. Bibl.

Mexico

Colomé, Delfín. Tres evocaciones de Agustín Lara. *Cuadernos Hispanoamericanos,* no. 521 (Nov 93), pp. 147 – 150. Il.

Geirola, Gustavo. Juan Gabriel: cultura popular y sexo de los ángeles. *Latin American Music Review,* v. 14, no. 2 (Fall – Winter 93), pp. 232 – 267. Bibl.

Phillips, Graciela. Para una pianista. *Plural (Mexico),* v. 22, no. 263 (Aug 93), pp. 72 – 73.

Varela-Ruiz, Leticia T. *Zubeldia, maestra maitea* (Review). *Inter-American Music Review,* v. 13, no. 2 (Spring – Summer 93), pp. 163 – 164.

Peru

Campos, José Carlos. Los primeros músicos españoles llegadas al Perú y los siguientes mestizajes musicales producidos en el Perú. *Revista Musical de Venezuela,* no. 28 (May – Dec 89), pp. 127 – 148. Bibl, facs.

Cisneros, Luis Jaime. Nosequién y los Nosecuántos. *Debate (Peru),* v. 15, no. 71 (Nov 92 – Jan 93), p. 67. Il.

Interviews

Cornejo Guinassi, Pedro. Nosequién y los Nosecuántos: ¿Espejo de una generación? *Debate (Peru),* v. 16, no. 74 (Sept – Oct 93), pp. 38 – 40. Il.

Puerto Rico

Camuñas, Jaime. Dos letras a Rafael Hernández: in memoriam (Includes the poems "Lamento borincano," "Preciosa," "Mañanita campanera," "El cumbanchero," "El buen borincano," and "Mi guajirita"). *Homines,* v. 15 – 16, no. 2 – 1 (Oct 91 – Dec 92), pp. 327 – 337. Bibl.

Uruguay

Aharonián, Coriún. Músicos uruguayos en el exterior (Segunda parte). *Hoy Es Historia,* v. 10, no. 59 (Sept – Oct 93), pp. 44 – 55. Bibl.

MUSICOLOGY
See also
Ethnomusicology

Gómez García, Zoila. ¿Sale de la calle o viene de la academia? *Plural (Mexico),* v. 22, no. 265 (Oct 93), pp. 81 – 82.

Ruiz, Irma. Un proyecto trunco. *Revista Musical de Venezuela,* no. 28 (May – Dec 89), pp. 98 – 105. Charts.

Velazco, Jorge. La confluencia intelectual y académica en la formación escolástica y la obra de investigación de Francisco Curt Lange. *Revista Musical de Venezuela,* no. 28 (May – Dec 89), pp. 207 – 223.

Bibliography

Huseby, Gerardo Víctor, ed. Bibliografía musicológica latinoamericana: no. 1, segunda parte (7/01 a 12/04), 1987, 1988, 1989. *Revista Musical Chilena,* v. 46, no. 178 (July – Dec 92), pp. 7 – 89.

Saldívar y Silva, Gabriel. *Bibliografía mexicana de musicología y musicografía* (Review). *Inter-American Music Review,* v. 13, no. 1 (Fall – Winter 92), pp. 116 – 117.

— *Bibliografía mexicana de musicología y musicografía* (Review of a reprint of the 1876 original). *Inter-American Music Review,* v. 13, no. 2 (Spring – Summer 93), pp. 151 – 154.

Congresses

Centrangolo, Aníbal E. La musicología americanista en Europa. *Revista Musical de Venezuela,* no. 28 (May – Dec 89), pp. 112 – 117.

MUTIS, ALVARO

Biography

Quiroz, Fernando. *"El reino que estaba para mí": conversaciones con Alvaro Mutis* reviewed by Fabienne Bradu (Review entitled "Vida y biografía"). *Vuelta,* v. 17, no. 200 (July 93), pp. 54 – 55.

Criticism and interpretation

Castañón, Adolfo. El tesoro de Mutis. *Vuelta,* v. 17, no. 205 (Dec 93), pp. 60 – 63.

Sarduy, Severo. Prólogo para leer como un epílogo. *Hispamérica,* v. 21, no. 63 (Dec 92), pp. 69 – 71.

Interviews

Bradu, Fabienne. Georges Simenon, el inclasificable. *Vuelta,* v. 17, no. 194 (Jan 93), pp. 52 – 55.

MUTUAL BENEFIT ASSOCIATIONS

See also

Community development
Non-governmental organizations

Brazil

Serva, Maurício. O fenômeno das organizações substantivas. *RAE; Revista de Administração de Empresas,* v. 33, no. 2 (Mar – Apr 93), pp. 36 – 43. Bibl.

Cuba

Howard, Philip A. The Spanish Colonial Government's Responses to the Pan-Nationalist Agenda of the Afro-Cuban Mutual Aid Societies, 1868 – 1895. *Revista/Review Interamericana,* v. 22, no. 1 – 2 (Spring – Summer 92), pp. 151 – 167. Bibl.

Mexico

De Diego de Sousa, María Teresa de. Foro internacional sobre derechos humanos y filantropía. *Fem,* v. 17, no. 126 (Aug 93), pp. 8 – 9.

Gómez Cruz, Filiberta. La Sociedad de Fomento en el puerto de Tuxpan, 1841. *La Palabra y el Hombre,* no. 83 (July – Sept 92), pp. 189 – 197. Bibl, tables.

Hoffmann, Odile. Renovación de los actores sociales en el campo: un ejemplo en el sector cafetalero en Veracruz. *Estudios Sociológicos,* v. 10, no. 30 (Sept – Dec 92), pp. 523 – 554. Bibl, tables, maps.

MYTH

Caunedo Madrigal, Silvia. *Las entrañas mágicas de América* reviewed by Paloma Lapuerta. *Cuadernos Hispanoamericanos,* no. 520 (Oct 93), pp. 127 – 128.

González de Guebara, Ruby Cecilia. El mito y su influencia en la sociedad actual. *Revista Cultural Lotería,* v. 51, no. 388 (Mar – Apr 92), pp. 85 – 92.

Methodology

Chinchilla Sánchez, Kattia. Mircea Eliade, una clave para la interpretación del pensamiento mítico. *Káñina,* v. 16, no. 1 (Jan – June 92), pp. 207 – 218. Bibl.

MYTH IN LITERATURE

Amor y Vázquez, José. Máscaras mexicanas en la poesía de Cernuda y Moreno Villa: Quetzalcóatl y Xochipilli (Includes the poem "Quetzalcóatl"). *Nueva Revista de Filología Hispánica,* v. 40, no. 2 (July – Dec 92), pp. 1057 – 1072.

González Echevarría, Roberto. *Myth and Archives: A Theory of Latin American Narrative* reviewed by Antonio Fama. *Revista Canadiense de Estudios Hispánicos,* v. 17, no. 2 (Winter 93), pp. 399 – 401.

González Pérez, Armando. Magia, mito y literatura en *La navaja de Olofé. Revista Interamericana de Bibliografía,* v. 42, no. 4 (1992), pp. 635 – 641. Bibl.

Leal, Luis. Sin fronteras: (des)mitificación en las letras norteamericanas y mexicanas. *Mexican Studies,* v. 9, no. 1 (Winter 93), pp. 95 – 118. Bibl.

MYTHOLOGY

See also

Folk literature
Legends

Quetzalcóatl
Subdivisions *Legends* and *Religion and mythology* under names of Indian groups

Báez-Jorge, Félix. *Las voces del agua: el simbolismo de las sirenas y las mitologías americanas* reviewed by Mario M. Muñoz (Review entitled "Las seductoras macabras"). *La Palabra y el Hombre,* no. 84 (Oct – Dec 92), pp. 252 – 255. Il.

MYTHOLOGY IN LITERATURE

Díaz, Luis Felipe. "En el fondo del caño hay un negrito" de José Luis González: estructura y discurso narcisistas. *Revista Iberoamericana,* v. 59, no. 162 – 163 (Jan – June 93), pp. 127 – 143. Bibl.

Holdsworth, Carole A. Two Contemporary Versions of the Persephone Myth. *Revista Interamericana de Bibliografía,* v. 42, no. 4 (1992), pp. 571 – 576. Bibl.

Vilanova, Angel. Motivo clásico y novela latinoamericana. *Nueva Revista de Filología Hispánica,* v. 40, no. 2 (July – Dec 92), pp. 1087 – 1099. Bibl.

LA NACIÓN (ARGENTINA) (NEWSPAPER)

Sidicaro, Ricardo. *La política mirada desde arriba: las ideas del diario 'La Nación', 1909 – 1989* reviewed by Diego F. Barros. *Todo Es Historia,* v. 27, no. 315 (Oct 93), pp. 65 – 66. Il.

NAFTA

See

North American Free Trade Agreement

NAHUAS

See also

Aztecs

Alvarez Santiago, Héctor and María Teresa Rodríguez. Estrategias productivas entre los nahuas de Zongolica. *La Palabra y el Hombre,* no. 84 (Oct – Dec 92), pp. 127 – 144. Tables.

Boruchoff, David A. The Conflict of Natural History and Moral Philosophy in *De Antiquitatibus Novae Hispaniae* of Francisco Hernández. *Revista Canadiense de Estudios Hispánicos,* v. 17, no. 2 (Winter 93), pp. 241 – 258. Bibl.

Cline, Sarah. The Spiritual Conquest Reexamined: Baptism and Christian Marriage in early Sixteenth-Century Mexico. *Hispanic American Historical Review,* v. 73, no. 3 (Aug 93), pp. 453 – 480. Bibl, tables.

Escalante Gonzalbo, Pablo. El llanto de los antiguos nahuas. *Nexos,* v. 16, no. 186 (June 93), pp. 88 – 91. Bibl.

González Rodrigo, José. Manejo de recursos naturales renovables en una comunidad indígena náhuatl. *Estudios de Cultura Náhuatl,* v. 22 (1992), pp. 445 – 459. Bibl, maps.

González Rodrigo, José and Regina Leal. Manejo de resursos naturales y derecho consuetudinario. *Nueva Antropología,* v. 13, no. 44 (Aug 93), pp. 61 – 70. Bibl.

Haskett, Robert Stephen. *Indigenous Rulers: An Ethnohistory of Town Government in Colonial Cuernavaca* reviewed by Eric Van Young. *Journal of Latin American Studies,* v. 25, no. 3 (Oct 93), pp. 653 – 654.

Johansson, Patrick. Yaocuicatl: cantos de guerra y guerra de cantos. *Estudios de Cultura Náhuatl,* v. 22 (1992), pp. 29 – 43.

Lockhart, James Marvin. *The Nahuas after the Conquest: A Social and Cultural History of the Indians of Central Mexico, Sixteenth through Eighteenth Centuries* reviewed by Linda Hall. *Colonial Latin American Historical Review,* v. 2, no. 2 (Spring 93), pp. 233 – 234.

— *The Nahuas after the Conquest: A Social and Cultural History of the Indians of Central Mexico, Sixteenth through Eighteenth Centuries* reviewed by Rik Hoekstra. *European Review of Latin American and Caribbean Studies,* no. 54 (June 93), pp. 120 – 125.

— *The Nahuas after the Conquest: A Social and Cultural History of the Indians of Central Mexico, Sixteenth through Eighteenth Centuries* reviewed by Peter Gerhard. *Hispanic American Historical Review,* v. 73, no. 4 (Nov 93), pp. 697 – 698.

— *The Nahuas after the Conquest: A Social and Cultural History of the Indians of Central Mexico, Sixteenth through Eighteenth Centuries* reviewed by Fernando Cervantes. *Journal of Latin American Studies,* v. 25, no. 2 (May 93), pp. 389 – 391.

— *The Nahuas after the Conquest: A Social and Cultural History of the Indians of Central Mexico; Sixteenth through Eighteenth Centuries* reviewed by David Brading (Review entitled "Los nahuas después de la conquista," translated by Isabel Vericat). *Nexos,* v. 16, no. 186 (June 93), pp. 73 – 74.

— *Nahuas and Spaniards: Postconquest Central Mexican History and Philology* reviewed by Rik Hoekstra. *European Review of Latin American and Caribbean Studies,* no. 54 (June 93), pp. 120 – 125.

— *Nahuas and Spaniards: Postconquest Central Mexican History and Philology* reviewed by Fernando Cervantes. *Journal of Latin American Studies,* v. 25, no. 2 (May 93), pp. 389 – 391.

Schroeder, Susan. *Chimalpahin and the Kingdoms of Chalco* reviewed by J. Benedict Warren. *The Americas,* v. 49, no. 3 (Jan 93), pp. 396 – 398.

— The Noblewomen of Chalco. *Estudios de Cultura Náhuatl,* v. 22 (1992), pp. 45 – 86. Tables, maps, facs.

Wood, Stephanie. The Evolution of the Indian Corporation of the Toluca Region, 1550 – 1810. *Estudios de Cultura Náhuatl,* v. 22 (1992), pp. 381 – 407. Bibl, maps.

NAHUATL LANGUAGE

Lockhart, James Marvin. *The Nahuas after the Conquest: A Social and Cultural History of the Indians of Central Mexico, Sixteenth through Eighteenth Centuries* reviewed by Linda Hall. *Colonial Latin American Historical Review,* v. 2, no. 2 (Spring 93), pp. 233 – 234.

— *The Nahuas after the Conquest: A Social and Cultural History of the Indians of Central Mexico, Sixteenth through Eighteenth Centuries* reviewed by Rik Hoekstra. *European Review of Latin American and Caribbean Studies,* no. 54 (June 93), pp. 120 – 125.

— *The Nahuas after the Conquest: A Social and Cultural History of the Indians of Central Mexico, Sixteenth through Eighteenth Centuries* reviewed by Peter Gerhard. *Hispanic American Historical Review,* v. 73, no. 4 (Nov 93), pp. 697 – 698.

— *The Nahuas after the Conquest: A Social and Cultural History of the Indians of Central Mexico, Sixteenth through Eighteenth Centuries* reviewed by Fernando Cervantes. *Journal of Latin American Studies,* v. 25, no. 2 (May 93), pp. 389 – 391.

— *The Nahuas after the Conquest: A Social and Cultural History of the Indians of Central Mexico; Sixteenth through Eighteenth Centuries* reviewed by David Brading (Review entitled "Los nahuas después de la conquista," translated by Isabel Vericat). *Nexos,* v. 16, no. 186 (June 93), pp. 73 – 74.

— *Nahuas and Spaniards: Postconquest Central Mexican History and Philology* reviewed by Rik Hoekstra. *European Review of Latin American and Caribbean Studies,* no. 54 (June 93), pp. 120 – 125.

— *Nahuas and Spaniards: Postconquest Central Mexican History and Philology* reviewed by Fernando Cervantes. *Journal of Latin American Studies,* v. 25, no. 2 (May 93), pp. 389 – 391.

Máynez Vidal, Pilar. *Religión y magia: un problema de transculturación lingüística en la obra de Bernardino de Sahagún* reviewed by María Angeles Soler Arechalde. *Anuario de Letras (Mexico),* v. 30 (1992), pp. 299 – 303.

Bibliography

León-Portilla, Ascensión H. de. Algunas publicaciones sobre lengua y literatura nahuas. *Estudios de Cultura Náhuatl,* v. 22 (1992), pp. 468 – 493.

NAHUATL LITERATURE

See also
Names of specific codices

Bibliography

León-Portilla, Ascensión H. de. Algunas publicaciones sobre lengua y literatura nahuas. *Estudios de Cultura Náhuatl,* v. 22 (1992), pp. 468 – 493.

History and criticism

Dehouve, Danièle. El discípulo de Silo: un aspecto de la literatura náhuatl de los jesuitas del siglo XVIII. *Estudios de Cultura Náhuatl,* v. 22 (1992), pp. 345 – 379. Bibl.

León-Portilla, Miguel. *The Aztec Image of Self and Society: An Introduction to Nahua Culture* reviewed by Frances Karttunen. *Latin American Indian Literatures Journal,* v. 9, no. 1 (Spring 93), pp. 85 – 92.

— *The Aztec Image of Self and Society,* a translation of *Los antiguos mexicanos a través de sus crónicas y cantares* edited by José Jorge Klor de Alva. Reviewed by Inga Clendinnen. *Hispanic American Historical Review,* v. 73, no. 1 (Feb 93), pp. 142 – 143.

— A modo de comentario (Response to Amos Segala's commentary on Miguel León-Portilla's review of *Histoire de la littérature náhuatl: sources, identités, répresentations*). *Caravelle,* no. 59 (1992), pp. 221 – 223.

Máynez Vidal, Pilar. Documentos de Tezcoco: consideraciones sobre tres manuscritos en mexicano del ramo "Tierras." *Estudios de Cultura Náhuatl,* v. 22 (1992), pp. 325 – 343.

Segala, Amos. La literatura náhuatl: ¿Un coto privado? (Response to Miguel Léon-Portilla's review of Amos Segala's *Histoire de la littérature náhuatl: sources, identités, représentations*). *Caravelle,* no. 59 (1992), pp. 209 – 219. Bibl.

Translations

History and Mythology of the Aztecs: The 'Codex Chimalpopoca' translated by John Bierhorst. Reviewed by David Johnson. *Colonial Latin American Historical Review,* v. 2, no. 1 (Winter 93), pp. 112 – 113.

León-Portilla, Miguel. *Fifteen Poets of the Aztec World* reviewed by Frances Karttunen. *Hispanic American Historical Review,* v. 73, no. 4 (Nov 93), pp. 681 – 682.

León-Portilla, Miguel, ed. *Poésie náhuatl d'amour et d'amitié* translated by Georges Baudot. Reviewed by Patrick Johansson. *Caravelle,* no. 60 (1993), pp. 135 – 138.

— *Visión de los vencidos: relaciones indígenas de la conquista* reviewed by Beatriz de la Fuente. *Estudios de Cultura Náhuatl,* v. 22 (1992), pp. 499 – 505.

NAIPAUL, VIDIADHAR SURAJPRASAD
Criticism and interpretation

Hedi, Ben Abbes. A Variation on the Theme of Violence and Antagonism in V. S. Naipaul's Fiction. *Caribbean Studies,* v. 25, no. 1 – 2 (Jan – July 92), pp. 49 – 61. Bibl.

NAKBE SITE, GUATEMALA

Forsyth, Donald W. The Ceramic Sequence at Nakbe, Guatemala. *Ancient Mesoamerica,* v. 4, no. 1 (Spring 93), pp. 31 – 53. Bibl, il, maps.

NAMES, GEOGRAPHICAL
Mexico

Jáuregui Moreno, Jesús Manuel. El rancho de Mariachi en 1837. *Plural (Mexico),* v. 22, no. 261 (June 93), pp. 85 – 93. Bibl.

Venezuela

Donís Ríos, Manuel Alberto. Venezuela: topónimo afortunado en la cartografía auroral de América. *Montalbán,* no. 24 (1992), pp. 99 – 118. Bibl, maps.

NAMES, PERSONAL
Mexican – American Border Region

Garate, Donald T. Basque Names, Nobility, and Ethnicity on the Spanish Frontier. *Colonial Latin American Historical Review,* v. 2, no. 1 (Winter 93), pp. 77 – 104. Bibl, facs.

NANDINO, ELÍAS
Interviews

Ramírez, Fermín. Elías Nandino: con el hervor del fuego en llamas. *Plural (Mexico),* v. 22, no. 266 (Nov 93), pp. 78 – 80.

NARCOTICS

See
Drug trade
Drugs, Illegal

NARIÑO, ANTONIO

Posada, Jaime. Don Antonio Nariño, ideólogo de la emancipación. *Boletín de Historia y Antigüedades,* v. 80, no. 781 (Apr – June 93), pp. 435 – 442.

NASCA, PERU

Aveni, Anthony F., ed. *The Lines of Nazca* reviewed by Katharina J. Schreiber. *Latin American Antiquity,* v. 4, no. 2 (June 93), pp. 202 – 203.

Blasco, María Concepción and Luis J. Ramos Gómez. Continuidad y cambio: interpretación de la decoración de una vasija nazca. *Revista Andina,* v. 10, no. 2 (Dec 92), pp. 457 – 471. Bibl, il.

Browne, David M. et al. A Cache of 48 Nasca Trophy Heads from Cerro Carapo, Peru. *Latin American Antiquity,* v. 4, no. 3 (Sept 93), pp. 274 – 294. Bibl, il, maps.

NATÁ, PANAMA

Osorio Osorio, Alberto. Natá de los caballeros, madre de pueblos. *Revista Cultural Lotería,* v. 51, no. 387 (Feb 92), pp. 26 – 30.

NATHAN, VIVIANE

Criticism and interpretation

Ruiloba C., Rafael. Viviane Nathan o la profecía de la ternura. *Revista Cultural Lotería,* v. 51, no. 387 (Feb 92), pp. 43 – 51.

NATIONAL CHARACTERISTICS

See
Subdivision *Civilization* under names of specific countries

NATIONAL IDENTITY

See
Nationalism
Subdivision *Civilization* under names of specific countries

NATIONAL INCOME

See also
Finance, Public

Argentina

Mathematical models

Engle, Robert F. and João Victor Issler. Common Trends and Common Cycles in Latin America. *Revista Brasileira de Economia,* v. 47, no. 2 (Apr – June 93), pp. 149 – 176. Bibl, tables, charts.

Brazil

Desempenho sofrível. *Problemas Brasileiros,* v. 30, no. 295 (Jan – Feb 93), pp. 24 – 25. Il.

Mathematical models

Engle, Robert F. and João Victor Issler. Common Trends and Common Cycles in Latin America. *Revista Brasileira de Economia,* v. 47, no. 2 (Apr – June 93), pp. 149 – 176. Bibl, tables, charts.

Colombia

Statistics

Colombia. Departamento Nacional de Planeación. Indicadores del sector rural. *Planeación y Desarrollo,* v. 24 (1993), All issues.

Latin America

Mathematical models

Elías, Víctor Jorge. *Sources of Growth: A Study of Seven Latin American Economies* reviewed by David E. Hojman. *Journal of Latin American Studies,* v. 25, no. 3 (Oct 93), pp. 675 – 677.

Mexico

Gutiérrez Lara, Abelardo Aníbal and Luis Rodríguez Medellín. La economía mexicana en la búsqueda de su modernización. *El Cotidiano,* v. 9, no. 55 (June 93), pp. 103 – 110. Tables, charts.

Mathematical models

Engle, Robert F. and João Victor Issler. Common Trends and Common Cycles in Latin America. *Revista Brasileira de Economia,* v. 47, no. 2 (Apr – June 93), pp. 149 – 176. Bibl, tables, charts.

NATIONAL PARKS

See
Parks

NATIONAL PATRIMONY

See
Cultural property

NATIONAL SECURITY

Bolivia

Jordán Sandoval, Santiago. Coincidentes y respuestas alarmantes a una pregunta sobre *Bolivia y el equilibrio del Cono Sur. Signo,* no. 35, Nueva época (Jan – Apr 92), pp. 37 – 41. Bibl.

Brazil

Hilton, Stanley Eon. *Brazil and the Soviet Union Challenge, 1917 – 1947* reviewed by John W. F. Dulles. *The Americas,* v. 49, no. 3 (Jan 93), pp. 417 – 418.

Colombia

Catatumbo, Pablo. La doctrina de la seguridad nacional: el principal obstáculo para la paz. *Revista Javeriana,* v. 60, no. 590 (Nov – Dec 92), pp. 303 – 315.

Velandia, Roberto. El Batallón Guarda Presidencial. *Boletín de Historia y Antigüedades,* v. 80, no. 780 (Jan – Mar 93), pp. 109 – 120. Bibl.

Latin America

Dagnino, Renato Peixoto. A indústria de armamentos brasileira e a segurança comum na América do Sul. *Política e Estratégica,* v. 8, no. 2 – 4 (Apr – Dec 90), pp. 383 – 399. Charts.

Panama

Manwaring, Max G. The Security of Panama and the Canal: Now and for the Future. *Journal of Inter-American Studies and World Affairs,* v. 35, no. 3 (Fall 93), pp. 151 – 170.

Puerto Rico

Acosta, Ivonne. Hacia una historia de la persecución política en Puerto Rico. *Homines,* v. 15 – 16, no. 2 – 1 (Oct 91 – Dec 92), pp. 142 – 151.

NATIONAL SOCIALISM

See
Fascism

NATIONALISM

Castellanos Guerrero, Alicia and Gilberto López y Rivas. Grupos étnicos y procesos nacionalitarios en el capitalismo neoliberal. *Nueva Antropología,* v. 13, no. 44 (Aug 93), pp. 27 – 41. Bibl.

Parker, Andrew et al, eds. *Nationalisms and Sexualities* reviewed by Catherine Davies (Review entitled "Women and a Redefinition of Argentinian Nationhood"). *Bulletin of Latin American Research,* v. 12, no. 3 (Sept 93), pp. 333 – 341.

— *Nationalisms and Sexualities* reviewed by Raúl Rodríguez-Hernández. *Letras Femeninas,* v. 19, no. 1 – 2 (Spring – Fall 93), pp. 134 – 135.

Argentina

Blache, Martha Teresa. Folklore y nacionalismo en la Argentina: su vinculación de origen y su desvinculación actual. *Runa,* v. 20 (1991 – 1992), pp. 69 – 89. Bibl.

Bra, Gerardo. ¿Nacionalismo, nazionalismo o nacionalismo frontal? *Todo Es Historia,* v. 26, no. 308 (Mar 93), pp. 82 – 91. Bibl, il, facs.

Dodds, Klaus-John. Geography, Identity, and the Creation of the Argentine State. *Bulletin of Latin American Research,* v. 12, no. 3 (Sept 93), pp. 311 – 331. Bibl.

Nascimbene, Mario C. G. and Mauricio Isaac Neuman. El nacionalismo católico, el fascismo y la inmigración en la Argentina, 1927 – 1943: una aproximación teórica. *Estudios Interdisciplinarios de América Latina y el Caribe,* v. 4, no. 1 (Jan – June 93), pp. 116 – 140. Bibl.

Rock, David P. *La Argentina autoritaria: los nacionalistas; su historia y su influencia en la vida pública* reviewed by Rosana Guber (Review entitled "Bandos y trincheras"). *Desarrollo Económico (Argentina),* v. 33, no. 131 (Oct – Dec 93), pp. 453 – 456. Bibl.

— *Authoritarian Argentina: The Nationalist Movement; Its History, and Its Impact* reviewed by Jeremy Adelman. *Hispanic American Historical Review,* v. 73, no. 4 (Nov 93), pp. 705 – 706.

Shumway, Nicolás Standifird. *La invención de la Argentina: historia de una idea,* a translation of *The Invention of Argentina.* Reviewed by Alejandro Herrero. *Todo Es Historia,* v. 27, no. 315 (Oct 93), pp. 63 – 64. Il.

— *The Invention of Argentina* reviewed by Paula Alonso. *Bulletin of Latin American Research,* v. 12, no. 2 (May 93), pp. 231 – 232.

— *The Invention of Argentina* reviewed by Thomas L. Whigham. *The Americas,* v. 49, no. 3 (Jan 93), pp. 409 – 410.

Terán, Oscar. El fin de siglo argentino: democracia y nación. *Cuadernos Hispanoamericanos,* no. 517 – 519 (July – Sept 93), pp. 41 – 50. Bibl.

— Representaciones intelectuales de la nación. *Realidad Económica,* no. 118 (Aug – Sept 93), pp. 94 – 96.

Tur Donati, Carlos M. Crisis social, xenofobia y nacionalismo en Argentina, 1919. *Cuadernos Americanos,* no. 42, Nueva época (Nov – Dec 93), pp. 48 – 77. Bibl.

Bolivia

Platt, Tristán. Simón Bolívar, the Sun of Justice, and the Amerindian Virgin: Andean Conceptions of the "Patria" in Nineteenth-Century Potosí. *Journal of Latin American Studies,* v. 25, no. 1 (Feb 93), pp. 159 – 185. Bibl.

Brazil

Costa, Marcia Regina da. "Skinheads": carecas do subúrbio. *Vozes,* v. 87, no. 2 (Mar – Apr 93), pp. 2 – 10.

Velloso, Mônica Pimenta. A brasilidade verde – amarela: nacionalismo e regionalismo paulista. *Estudos Históricos,* v. 6, no. 11 (Jan – June 93), pp. 89 – 112. Bibl.

Costa Rica

Palmer, Steven. Getting to Know the Unknown Soldier: Offical Nationalism in Liberal Costa Rica, 1880 – 1900. *Journal of Latin American Studies,* v. 25, no. 1 (Feb 93), pp. 45 – 72. Bibl, maps.

Cuba

Portuondo Zúñiga, Olga. Criollidad y patria local en campo geométrico. *Islas,* no. 98 (Jan – Apr 91), pp. 40 – 46.

Europe, Eastern

Santana, Adalberto. Los nacionalismos de México, Cuba y Centroamérica frente a los de Europa Oriental. *Cuadernos Americanos,* no. 41, Nueva época (Sept – Oct 93), pp. 167 – 174.

Latin America

Bazán, Armando Raúl. Americanismo y nacionalismo en la emancipación sudamericana. *Revista de Historia de América,* no. 112 (July – Dec 91), pp. 5 – 19.

Santana, Adalberto. Los nacionalismos de México, Cuba y Centroamérica frente a los de Europa Oriental. *Cuadernos Americanos,* no. 41, Nueva época (Sept – Oct 93), pp. 167 – 174.

Mexico

Aguilar Camín, Héctor. La invención de México. *Nexos,* v. 16, no. 187 (July 93), pp. 49 – 61.

Lomnitz-Adler, Claudio. Hacia una antropología de la nacionalidad mexicana. *Revista Mexicana de Sociología,* v. 55, no. 2 (Apr – June 93), pp. 169 – 195. Bibl.

Venezuela

Dávila, Luis Ricardo. Rómulo Betancourt and the Development of Venezuelan Nationalism, 1930 – 1945. *Bulletin of Latin American Research,* v. 12, no. 1 (Jan 93), pp. 49 – 63. Bibl.

NATIONALISM IN LITERATURE

Benítez Rojo, Antonio. Nacionalismo y nacionalización en la novela hispanoamericana del siglo XIX. *Revista de Crítica Literaria Latinoamericana,* v. 19, no. 38 (July – Dec 93), pp. 185 – 193.

Díaz Quiñones, Arcadio. El enemigo íntimo: cultura nacional y autoridad en Ramiro Guerra y Sánchez y Antonio S. Pedreira. *Op. Cit.,* no. 7 (1992), pp. 9 – 65. Bibl.

Gramuglio, María Teresa. Literatura y nacionalismo: Leopoldo Lugones y la construcción de imágenes de escritor. *Hispamérica,* v. 22, no. 64 – 65 (Apr – Aug 93), pp. 5 – 22. Bibl.

Moyano, Pilar. La transformación de la mujer y la nación en la poesía comprometida de Gioconda Belli. *Revista Canadiense de Estudios Hispánicos,* v. 17, no. 2 (Winter 93), pp. 319 – 331. Bibl.

Quesada Soto, Alvaro. Identidad nacional y literatura nacional en Costa Rica: la "generación del Olimpo." *Canadian Journal of Latin American and Caribbean Studies,* v. 17, no. 34 (1992), pp. 97 – 113. Bibl.

Rodríguez Pérsico, Adriana C. Las fronteras de la identidad: la pregunta por la identidad nacional. *Hispamérica,* v. 22, no. 64 – 65 (Apr – Aug 93), pp. 23 – 48. Bibl.

Sommer, Doris. *Foundational Fictions: The National Romances of Latin America* reviewed by Edgardo C. Krebs. *The Americas,* v. 50, no. 2 (Oct 93), pp. 282 – 283.

— *Foundational Fictions: The National Romances of Latin America* reviewed by Carlos L. Orihuela. *Revista de Crítica Literaria Latinoamericana,* v. 19, no. 38 (July – Dec 93), pp. 399 – 403.

NATURAL AREAS

Argentina

Winograd, Alejandro. Areas naturales protegidas y desarrollo: perspectivas y restricciones para el manejo de parques y reservas en la Argentina. *SALALM Papers,* v. 36 (1991), pp. 105 – 122. Bibl.

Brazil

Bacha, Carlos José Caetano. As unidades de conservação do Brasil. *Revista de Economia e Sociologia Rural,* v. 30, no. 4 (Oct – Dec 92), pp. 339 – 358. Bibl, tables.

Costa, Nadja Maria Castilho da and Cláudia Rodrigues Segond. Plano de manejo ecológico da reserva particular de Bodoquena. *Revista Geográfica (Mexico),* no. 114 (July – Dec 91), pp. 91 – 100. Bibl, tables, maps.

Cost

Azzoni, Carlos Roberto and João Yo Isai. Custo da proteção de áreas com interesse ambiental no estado de São Paulo. *Estudos Econômicos,* v. 22, no. 2 (May – Aug 92), pp. 253 – 271. Bibl, tables, charts.

NATURAL DISASTERS

See also
Droughts
Earthquakes
Floods
Volcanism

Macías, Jesús Manuel. Significado de la vulnerabilidad social frente a los desastres. *Revista Mexicana de Sociología,* v. 54, no. 4 (Oct – Dec 92), pp. 3 – 10.

Pliego Carrasco, Fernando. Estrategias de desarrollo social en situaciones de desastre. *Revista Mexicana de Sociología,* v. 54, no. 4 (Oct – Dec 92), pp. 11 – 24.

Congresses

Pérez Calderón, Luis Jorge. Medio ambiente y desarrollo: el Decenio Internacional para la Reducción de los Desastres Naturales. *Amazonía Peruana,* v. 11, no. 21 (Sept 92), pp. 175 – 180.

Argentina

Marco, Miguel Angel de. Pellegrini contra la langosta, 1891 – 1892. *Todo Es Historia,* v. 27, no. 311 (June 93), pp. 62 – 73. Il.

Chile

Bertrand S., María. ¿Efímero vedetariado o auténtica preocupación?: reflexiones en torno a un aluvión anunciado. *EURE,* v. 19, no. 57 (July 93), pp. 134 – 135.

Latin America

Lavell Thomas, Allan. Ciencias sociales y desastres naturales en América Latina: un encuentro inconcluso (Chapter from the book entitled *Desastres naturales, sociedad y protección civil). EURE,* v. 19, no. 58 (Oct 93), pp. 73 – 84. Bibl.

Puerto Rico

Hodgson, Michael E. and Risa Palm. Natural Hazards in Puerto Rico. *Geographical Review,* v. 83, no. 3 (July 93), pp. 280 – 289. Bibl, tables.

Venezuela

Bastidas González, Pedro José and Damaris van der Dys. Programa de adaptación del Sistema de Información de la Planta Física Educativa (SIPFE) a los objetivos de reducción de la vulnerabilidad a las amenazas naturales en las escuelas. *La Educación (USA),* v. 37, no. 115 (1993), pp. 365 – 377. Tables.

NATURAL GAS

See
Gas, Natural

NATURAL HISTORY

America

Gerbi, Antonello. *Nature in the New World: From Christopher Columbus to Gonzalo Fernández de Oviedo* translated by Jeremy Moyle. Reviewed by Rick Hendricks. *Colonial Latin American Historical Review,* v. 1, no. 1 (Fall 92), pp. 120 – 121.

Olmo Pintado, Margarita del. La historia natural en la *Historia del Nuevo Mundo* del p. Cobo. *Revista de Indias,* v. 52, no. 195 – 196 (May – Dec 92), pp. 795 – 823. Maps, charts.

Brazil

Orlandi, Eni Pulcinelli. O discurso dos naturalistas. *Vozes,* v. 87, no. 1 (Jan – Feb 93), pp. 62 – 76.

Mexico

Pallares, Eugenia. Lacandonia: el último refugio. *Artes de México,* no. 19 (Spring 93), pp. 114 – 115. Il.

NATURAL RESOURCES

See also
Forests
Marine resources
Mines and mineral resources

Congresses

Declaración de La Paz. *Anuario Indigenista,* v. 30 (Dec 91), pp. 339 – 342.

Economic aspects

Mathematical models

Galarza, Elsa and Roberto Urrunaga. La economía de los recursos naturales: políticas extractivas y ambientales. *Apuntes (Peru),* no. 30 (Jan – June 92), pp. 45 – 61. Bibl.

Amazon Valley

Brack Egg, Antonio. La Amazonía: problemas y posibilidades. *Amazonía Peruana,* v. 11, no. 21 (Sept 92), pp. 9 – 22. Il.

Encarnación, Filomeno. Conservación en la Amazonía. *Amazonía Peruana,* v. 11, no. 21 (Sept 92), pp. 49 – 72. Bibl.

Costa Rica

Law and legislation

Vargas Ulate, Gilberto. La protección de los recursos naturales en un país subdesarrollado: caso de Costa Rica. *Revista de Ciencias Sociales (Costa Rica),* no. 59 (Mar 93), pp. 81 – 93. Bibl, maps.

Latin America

Bifani, Patricia. Disponibilidad, derecho y gestión del espacio vital. *Nueva Sociedad,* no. 123 (Jan – Feb 93), pp. 84 – 93. Bibl.

Mexico

González Rodrigo, José. Manejo de recursos naturales renovables en una comunidad indígena náhuatl. *Estudios de Cultura Náhuatl,* v. 22 (1992), pp. 445 – 459. Bibl, maps.

González Rodrigo, José and Regina Leal. Manejo de resursos naturales y derecho consuetudinario. *Nueva Antropología,* v. 13, no. 44 (Aug 93), pp. 61 – 70. Bibl.

Sarukhán Kermez, José. A Wealth of Life. *Business Mexico,* v. 3, no. 1 (Jan – Feb 93), pp. 60 – 62. Il, tables.

Townsend, John W. Mexico and Its Baby Boom. *Business Mexico,* v. 3, no. 1 (Jan – Feb 93), pp. 58 – 59. Il.

Study and teaching

Bain, Jennifer H. Mexican Rural Women's Knowledge of the Environment. *Mexican Studies,* v. 9, no. 2 (Summer 93), pp. 259 – 274. Bibl.

Venezuela

Cressa, Claudia et al. Aspectos generales de la limnología en Venezuela. *Interciencia,* v. 18, no. 5 (Sept – Oct 93), pp. 237 – 248. Bibl, tables, maps.

NATURALIZATION

See also
Citizenship

United States

Baker, Susan Gonzalez and Jacqueline Maria Hagan. Implementing the U.S. Legalization Program: The Influence of Immigrant Communities and Local Agencies on Immigration Policy Reform. *International Migration Review,* v. 27, no. 3 (Fall 93), pp. 513 – 536. Bibl.

NATURE IN LITERATURE

Andrist, Debra D. Nature Imagery in Sylvia Puentes de Oyenard's *Rosa exigida. Letras Femeninas,* v. 19, no. 1 – 2 (Spring – Fall 93), pp. 117 – 119. Bibl.

Caulfield, Carlota. *Canción de la verdad sencilla:* Julia de Burgos y su diálogo erótico – místico con la naturaleza. *Revista Iberoamericana,* v. 59, no. 162 – 163 (Jan – June 93), pp. 119 – 126. Bibl.

Hernández, Consuelo. La arquitectura poética de Eugenio Montejo. *Inti,* no. 37 – 38 (Spring – Fall 93), pp. 133 – 143. Bibl.

NATURE RESERVES

See
Natural areas

NAVARRO GARCÍA, LUIS

Criticism of specific works

Historia de las Américas

Navarro García, Luis. Presentación de la *Historia de las Américas. Anuario de Estudios Americanos,* v. 49, Suppl. 1 (1992), pp. 242 – 247.

NAVIGATION

See also
Inland water transportation
Trade routes
Transportation, Maritime

Martínez G., Miguel A. Recursos tecno-científicos que se conjugan en el descubrimiento de América. *Boletín de la Academia Nacional de la Historia (Venezuela),* v. 75, no. 300 (Oct – Dec 92), pp. 79 – 88.

Pérez-Mallaína Bueno, Pablo Emilio. *Los hombres del océano* reviewed by Benjamin Keen. *Hispanic American Historical Review,* v. 73, no. 3 (Aug 93), pp. 503 – 504.

Maps

Sources

Binková, Simona and Katerina Kozická. El dominio marítimo español en los materiales cartográficos y náuticos de Praga. *Anuario de Estudios Americanos,* v. 49, Suppl. 1 (1992), pp. 47 – 54. Bibl, maps.

Ringrose, Basil. *A Buccaneer's Atlas: Basil Ringrose's South Seas Waggoner* edited by Derk Howse and Norman J. W. Thrower. Reviewed by Arnold J. Bauer. *Hispanic American Historical Review,* v. 73, no. 4 (Nov 93), pp. 691 – 693.

NAVY
See
Subdivision *Armed forces* under names of specific countries

NAZISM
See
Fascism

NEAR EAST
See
Middle East

NEBRIJA, ELIO ANTONIO DE
León-Portilla, Ascensión H. de. Nebrija y las lenguas compañeras del imperio. *Cuadernos Americanos*, no. 37, Nueva época (Jan – Feb 93), pp. 135 – 147. Bibl.

Criticism of specific works
Gramática de la lengua castellana
Guzmán Betancourt, Ignacio. La lengua: ¿Compañera del imperio?; destino de un "presagio" nebrisense en la Nueva España. *Cuadernos Americanos*, no. 37, Nueva época (Jan – Feb 93), pp. 148 – 164. Bibl.

NEGRISTA LITERATURE
See
Blacks in literature

NEGRÓN MUÑOZ, MERCEDES
Criticism and interpretation
Pieropan, María D. Alfonsina Storni y Clara Lair: de la mujer posmodernista a la mujer "moderna." *Hispania (USA)*, v. 76, no. 4 (Dec 93), pp. 672 – 682. Bibl.

NEGROPONTE, JOHN DIMITRI
Witoshynsky, Mary. Changing of the Guard. *Business Mexico*, v. 3, no. 8 (Aug 93), pp. 42 – 43. Il.

NEIVA, COLOMBIA (DEPARTMENT)
Triana Antorveza, Adolfo. Contribución a la historia de la provincia de Neiva: el caso del Caguán. *Revista Colombiana de Antropología*, v. 29 (1992), pp. 119 – 154. Bibl, tables, maps.

NEJAR, CARLOS
Criticism of specific works
A genealogia da palavra
Coelho, Nelly Novaes. A genealogia da palavra. *Convivium*, v. 34, no. 2 (July – Dec 91), pp. 98 – 104.

NEOLIBERALISM
See
Liberalism
Subdivision *Economic policy* under names of specifc countries

NEPOMUCENO, ERIC
Translations
Nepomuceno, Eric. Coisas da vida (Translated by Francisco Hernández Avilés). *Plural (Mexico)*, v. 22, no. 259 (Apr 93), pp. 14 – 25.

NERUDA, PABLO
Addresses, essays, lectures
Neruda, Pablo. Soy un poeta de utilidad pública. *Hispamérica*, v. 22, no. 64 – 65 (Apr – Aug 93), pp. 105 – 109.

Biography
Anguita, Eduardo. Huidobro y Neruda: final. *Atenea (Chile)*, no. 467 (1993), pp. 145 – 147.

Loyola Guerra, Hernán. Neruda 1923: el año de la encrucijada. *Revista Chilena de Literatura*, no. 40 (Nov 92), pp. 5 – 16.

Teitelboim, Volodia. *Neruda: An Intimate Biography* translated by Beverly J. DeLong-Tonelli. Reviewed by Lucía Guerra Cunningham. *Revista Interamericana de Bibliografía*, v. 42, no. 2 (1992), pp. 289 – 290.

Criticism and interpretation
Concha, Edmundo. Neruda y Huidobro. *Atenea (Chile)*, no. 467 (1993), pp. 155 – 156.

Gutiérrez Revuelta, Pedro. Fernando Villalón, el amigo desconocido de Pablo Neruda. *Cuadernos Hispanoamericanos*, no. 514 – 515 (Apr – May 93), pp. 307 – 311.

Criticism of specific works
Canto general
Rodríguez H., María Elia. Intertextualidad y dialogismo: el funcionamiento paródico del texto poético; análisis de dos series poéticas del *Canto general*. *Káñina*, v. 16, no. 1 (Jan – June 92), pp. 61 – 67.

Discurso de las liras
Paz, Octavio. Pablo Neruda (1904 – 1973). *Vuelta*, v. 17, no. 202 (Sept 93), p. 8.

La rosa separada
Varela, José R. El tema de la alienación en *La rosa separada* de Pablo Neruda. *Revista Canadiense de Estudios Hispánicos*, v. 17, no. 1 (Fall 92), pp. 177 – 206. Bibl.

La última niebla
Garrels, Elizabeth. Ver y ser vista: la mirada fálica en *La última niebla*. *Escritura (Venezuela)*, v. 16, no. 31 – 32 (Jan – Dec 91), pp. 81 – 90. Bibl.

Las uvas y el viento
Melis, Antonio. Poesía y política en *Las uvas y el viento*. *Revista de Crítica Literaria Latinoamericana*, v. 19, no. 38 (July – Dec 93), pp. 123 – 130.

NERVAL, GÉRARD DE
See
Gérard de Nerval, Gérard Labrunie

NETHERLANDS
Mason, Peter, ed. *Indianen en Nederlanders, 1492 – 1992* reviewed by Menno Oostra. *European Review of Latin American and Caribbean Studies*, no. 54 (June 93), pp. 145 – 147.

NETHERLANDS ANTILLES
Bibliography
Brown, Enid. *Suriname and the Netherlands Antilles: An Annotated English-Language Bibliography* reviewed by Gary Brana-Shute. *The Americas*, v. 50, no. 1 (July 93), pp. 123 – 124.

— *Suriname and the Netherlands Antilles: An Annotated English-Language Bibliography* reviewed by Rosemarijn Hoefte. *Hispanic American Historical Review*, v. 73, no. 4 (Nov 93), pp. 677 – 678.

NEUQUÉN, ARGENTINA (PROVINCE)
Arrúe, Willie and Beatriz Kalinsky. *De "la médica" y el terapeuta: la gestión intercultural de la salud en el sur de la provincia del Neuquén* reviewed by P. Schraer. *La Educación (USA)*, v. 36, no. 111 – 113 (1992), pp. 281 – 282.

Bandieri, Susana O. Historia y planificación regional: un encuentro posible. *Revista Interamericana de Planificación*, v. 26, no. 101 – 102 (Jan – June 93), pp. 78 – 94. Bibl.

Favaro, Orietta et al. El Neuquén: límites estructurales de una estrategia de distribución, 1958 – 1980. *Realidad Económica*, no. 118 (Aug – Sept 93), pp. 123 – 138. Bibl.

NEVARES REYES, SALVADOR
Obituaries
Reyes Nevares, Beatriz. Salvador Reyes Nevares. *Cuadernos Americanos*, no. 41, Nueva época (Sept – Oct 93), pp. 212 – 217.

NEVIS, WEST INDIES
Harms, Mike. Nurturing Conservation Naturally in the Twin Isles (Photographs by Michael Ventura). *Américas*, v. 45, no. 2 (Mar – Apr 93), pp. 22 – 25. Il, maps.

NEW GRANADA
See
Colombia

NEW INTERNATIONAL ECONOMIC ORDER (NIEO)

See
International economic relations

NEW MEXICO

Gallegos, Bernardo P. *Literacy, Education, and Society in New Mexico, 1693 – 1821* reviewed by B. Michael Miller. *Colonial Latin American Historical Review*, v. 1, no. 1 (Fall 92), pp. 118 – 119.

— *Literacy, Education, and Society in New Mexico, 1693 – 1821* reviewed by John E. Kicza. *Hispanic American Historical Review*, v. 73, no. 1 (Feb 93), pp. 150 – 151.

García, Nasario. *Abuelitos: Stories of the Río Puerco Valley* reviewed by Enrique R. Lamadrid. *Confluencia*, v. 8, no. 1 (Fall 92), p. 175.

Harris, Patricia and David Lyon. *Memory's Persistence: The Living Art. Américas*, v. 45, no. 6 (Nov – Dec 93), pp. 26 – 37. Il.

Nostrand, Richard L. *The Hispano Homeland* reviewed by Carlos Brazil Ramírez. *Colonial Latin American Historical Review*, v. 2, no. 3 (Summer 93), pp. 379 – 380.

— *The Hispano Homeland* reviewed by Henry F. Dobyns. *Hispanic American Historical Review*, v. 73, no. 2 (May 93), pp. 302 – 303.

— *The Hispano Homeland* reviewed by Martha A. Works. *Geographical Review*, v. 83, no. 2 (Apr 93), pp. 224 – 226.

Simmons, Marc. *The Last Conquistador: Juan de Oñate and the Settling of the Far Southwest* reviewed by Adrian Bustamante. *Colonial Latin American Historical Review*, v. 2, no. 2 (Spring 93), pp. 235 – 236.

Poetry

Villagrá, Gaspar Pérez de. *'Historia de la Nueva México, 1610' by Gaspar Pérez de Villagrá: A Critical and Annotated Spanish/English Edition* edited and translated by Miguel Encinias. Reviewed by Franklin G. Smith. *Colonial Latin American Historical Review*, v. 2, no. 3 (Summer 93), pp. 377 – 379.

— *Historia de Nuevo México.* Critical edition by Mercedes Junquera. Reviewed by Phil Jaramillo (Review entitled "Dispositio Textus: Paleographic or Semipaleographic Edition?"). *Bilingual Review/Revista Bilingüe*, v. 17, no. 3 (Sept – Dec 92), pp. 276 – 278. Bibl.

Sources

Vargas, Diego de. *By Force of Arms: The Journals of Don Diego de Vargas, New Mexico, 1691 – 1693* edited and translated by John L. Kessell and Rick Hendricks. Reviewed by Timothy K. Perttula. *Colonial Latin American Historical Review*, v. 2, no. 3 (Summer 93), pp. 380 – 382.

— *By Force of Arms: The Journals of Don Diego de Vargas, New Mexico, 1691 – 1693* edited and translated by John L. Kessel and Rick Hendricks. Reviewed by Mark A. Burkholder. *Hispanic American Historical Review*, v. 73, no. 3 (Aug 93), pp. 510 – 511.

— *Letters from the New World: Selected Correspondence of Don Diego de Vargas to His Family, 1675 – 1706* edited and translated by John L. Kessell, Rick Hendricks, and Meredith D. Dodge. Reviewed by Jennifer L. Zimnoch. *The Americas Review*, v. 21, no. 1 (Spring 93), pp. 123 – 124.

— *Letters from the New World: Selected Correspondence of Don Diego de Vargas to His Family, 1675 – 1706* edited and translated by John L. Kessel, Rick Hendricks, and Meredith D. Dodge. Reviewed by Mark A. Burkholder. *Hispanic American Historical Review*, v. 73, no. 3 (Aug 93), pp. 510 – 511.

NEW WORLD INFORMATION ORDER

See
Cultural imperialism
Information services
Mass media

NEW YORK (CITY)

Boggs, Vernon W. *Salsiology: Afro-Cuban Music and the Evolution of Salsa in New York City* reviewed by Jerma Jackson. *Hispanic American Historical Review*, v. 73, no. 4 (Nov 93), pp. 673 – 674.

— *Salsiology: Afro-Cuban Music and the Evolution of Salsa in New York City* reviewed by Gerard Béhague. *Latin American Music Review*, v. 14, no. 1 (Spring – Summer 93), pp. 172 – 175.

Grasmuck, Sherri and Patricia R. Pessar. *Between Two Islands: Dominican International Migration* reviewed by André Corten. *Canadian Journal of Latin American and Caribbean Studies*, v. 17, no. 34 (1992), pp. 138 – 141.

Shifter, Michael. Un brindis por Lima. *Debate (Peru)*, v. 15, no. 71 (Nov 92 – Jan 93), pp. 49 – 51. Il.

NEWSPAPERS

See also
Censorship
Journalism
Press
Press and politics
Names of specific newspapers

Argentina

Herrero Rubio, Alejandro and Fabián Herrero. A propósito de la prensa española en Buenos Aires: el estudio de un caso: *El Correo Español*, 1872 – 1875. *Anuario de Estudios Americanos*, v. 49, Suppl. 1 (1992), pp. 107 – 120.

Sidicaro, Ricardo. *La política mirada desde arriba: las ideas del diario 'La Nación', 1909 – 1989* reviewed by Diego F. Barros. *Todo Es Historia*, v. 27, no. 315 (Oct 93), pp. 65 – 66. Il.

Brazil

Cardoso, Tereza Maria R. Fachada Levy. A *Gazeta do Rio de Janeiro*: subsídios para a história da cidade, 1808 – 1821. *Revista do Instituto Histórico e Geográfico Brasileiro*, no. 371 (Apr – June 91), pp. 341 – 436. Bibl, il, tables, maps.

Lima Sobrinho, Alexandre José Barbosa. No centenário do *Jornal do Brasil. Revista do Instituto Histórico e Geográfico Brasileiro*, no. 372 (July – Sept 91), pp. 746 – 761.

Chile

Fontaine Aldunate, Arturo. La historia reciente de Chile a través de "La semana política" (Part IV, introduced by Miguel González Pino). *Estudios Públicos (Chile)*, no. 49 (Summer 93), pp. 305 – 419.

Mexican – American Border Region

Jones, Robert W. A Content Comparison of Daily Newspapers in the El Paso – Juárez Circulation Area. *Journal of Borderlands Studies*, v. 7, no. 2 (Fall 92), pp. 93 – 100. Bibl, tables.

Mexico

Covo, Jacqueline. La prensa en la historiografía mexicana: problemas y perspectivas. *Historia Mexicana*, v. 42, no. 3 (Jan – Mar 93), pp. 689 – 710. Bibl.

Texas Weekly: presencia de *Excélsior* en Estados Unidos. *Plural (Mexico)*, v. 22, no. 259 (Apr 93), pp. 64 – 65. Il.

United States

Texas Weekly: presencia de *Excélsior* en Estados Unidos. *Plural (Mexico)*, v. 22, no. 259 (Apr 93), pp. 64 – 65. Il.

Uruguay

Gilman, Claudia. Política y cultura: *Marcha* a partir de los años '60. *Nuevo Texto Crítico*, v. 6, no. 11 (1993), pp. 153 – 186. Bibl.

Rocca, Pablo. 35 años en *Marcha*: escritura y ambiente literario en *Marcha* y en el Uruguay, 1939 – 1974. *Nuevo Texto Crítico*, v. 6, no. 11 (1993), pp. 3 – 151. Bibl, il.

NGOS

See
Non-governmental organizations

NICANDRO, GLUGIO GRONK

Art reproductions

Nicandro, Glugio Gronk. Reproduction of *Invasion of Dixie(Cup)Series – Hot Vessel* by Gronk. *The Americas Review*, v. 21, no. 1 (Spring 93), p. 77.

NICARAGUA

See also
Acculturation – Nicaragua
Agricultural laborers – Nicaragua

Agriculture, Cooperative – Nicaragua
Agriculture and state – Nicaragua
Chinandega, Nicaragua
Church and state – Nicaragua
Coffee – Nicaragua
Democracy – Nicaragua
Education, Bilingual – Nicaragua
Elections – Nicaragua
Food industry and trade – Nicaragua
Foreign trade promotion – Nicaragua
Indians, Treatment of – Nicaragua
Industry and state – Nicaragua
Judiciary – Nicaragua
Land reform – Nicaragua
Liberation theology – Nicaragua
Libraries and librarians – Nicaragua
Literature and history – Nicaragua
Mosquitia
Peasantry – Nicaragua
Posters – Nicaragua
Price regulation – Nicaragua
Public opinion – Nicaragua
Publishers and publishing – Nicaragua
Regional planning – Nicaragua
Religion and politics – Nicaragua
Revolutions – Nicaragua
Social movements – Nicaragua
Sociology, Rural – Nicaragua
Women – Nicaragua
Women in literature – Nicaragua
Women's rights – Nicaragua

Armed forces

Guzmán, Luis Humberto. *Políticos en uniforme: un balance del poder del EPS* reviewed by Carlos M. Vilas. *Journal of Latin American Studies*, v. 25, no. 3 (Oct 93), pp. 672 – 674.

Constitutional law

Lasaga, Ignacio. La eticidad del pobre. *Estudios Sociales (Dominican Republic)*, v. 26, no. 91 (Jan – Mar 93), pp. 61 – 76.

McConnell, Shelley. Rules of the Game: Nicaragua's Contentious Constitutional Debate. *NACLA Report on the Americas*, v. 27, no. 2 (Sept – Oct 93), pp. 20 – 25. Il.

History

Burns, E. Bradford. *Patriarch and Folk: The Emergence of Nicaragua, 1798 – 1858* reviewed by Thomas M. Leonard. *The Americas*, v. 49, no. 4 (Apr 93), pp. 555 – 556.

— *Patriarch and Folk: The Emergence of Nicaragua, 1798 – 1858* reviewed by Elizabeth Dore. *Journal of Latin American Studies*, v. 25, no. 2 (May 93), pp. 403 – 404.

Díaz Polanco, Héctor and Consuelo Sánchez. Cronología de los hechos históricos de la costa atlántica de Nicaragua: primera parte. *Boletín de Antropología Americana*, no. 23 (July 91), pp. 171 – 184. Bibl.

— Cronología de los hechos históricos de la costa atlántica de Nicaragua: segunda parte. *Boletín de Antropología Americana*, no. 24 (Dec 91), pp. 151 – 178. Bibl, il.

Sagastume Fajardo, Alejandro S. El papel de la iglesia de Centroamérica en la guerra contra William Walker, 1856 – 1860. *Revista de Indias*, v. 53, no. 198 (May – Aug 93), pp. 529 – 544.

Walker, Thomas W. *Nicaragua: The Land of Sandino*, 3d ed., reviewed by Roland Ebel. *Hispanic American Historical Review*, v. 73, no. 1 (Feb 93), pp. 185 – 186.

Politics and government

Quezada, Freddy. Nicaragua: en busca de un nuevo rumbo. *Nueva Sociedad*, no. 123 (Jan – Feb 93), pp. 18 – 22.

NICARAGUANS

Honduras

Morgner, Fred G. Cracks in the Mirror: The Nicaraguan War and Human Rights in Honduras. *SALALM Papers*, v. 34 (1989), pp. 475 – 490. Bibl, il, tables.

NIETO, RODOLFO

Blanco, Alberto. Manual de sología fantástica de Rodolfo Nieto. *Vuelta*, v. 17, no. 200 (July 93), pp. 80 – 82.

NIETZSCHE, FRIEDRICH WILHELM

Saylor-Javaherian, Cheryll. Nietzschean Antagonism, Self-Sacrifice, and Redemption in Enrique Larreta's *La gloria de don Ramiro*. *Hispanic Journal*, v. 14, no. 1 (Spring 93), pp. 7 – 23. Bibl.

NISSEN, BRIAN

Blanco, Alberto. Los jardines flotantes de Brian Nissen (Accompanied by an English translation). *Artes de México, no.* 20 (Summer 93), pp. 52 – 53.

NITRATES

Chile

González Miranda, Sergio. *Hombres y mujeres de la pampa: Tarapacá en el ciclo del salitre: primera parte* reviewed by Juan Ricardo Couyoumdjian. *Boletín de la Academia Chilena de la Historia*, v. 58 – 59, no. 102 (1991 – 1992), pp. 560 – 561.

— *Hombres y mujeres de la pampa: Tarapacá en el ciclo del salitre* reviewed by Carlos A. de Mattos. *EURE*, v. 19, no. 57 (July 93), pp. 129 – 130. Il.

Martinic Drpic, Zvonimir. El tribunal arbitral italo – chileno y las reclamaciones italianas de los poseedores de certificados salitreros: evolución histórica de la problemática. *Cuadernos de Historia (Chile)*, no. 11 (Dec 91), pp. 71 – 104. Bibl, tables.

NIZZA, MARCO DA

Mora Valcárcel, Carmen de. *Las siete ciudades de Cíbola: textos y testimonios sobre la expedición de Vázquez Coronado* reviewed by Francisco Noguerol Jiménez. *Anuario de Estudios Americanos*, v. 50, no. 1 (1993), pp. 323 – 324.

NOBILITY

See
Elite (Social sciences)

NOGUEROL DE ULLOA, FRANCISCO

Cook, Alexandra Parma and Noble David Cook. *Good Faith and Truthful Ignorance: A Case of Transatlantic Bigamy* reviewed by Meredith Dodge. *Colonial Latin American Historical Review*, v. 1, no. 1 (Fall 92), pp. 124 – 125.

— *Good Faith and Truthful Ignorance: A Case of Transatlantic Bigamy* reviewed by Kenneth J. Andrien. *Colonial Latin American Review*, v. 2, no. 1 – 2 (1993), pp. 275 – 277.

NON-ALIGNED COUNTRIES

See
International relations

NON-FORMAL EDUCATION

See
Subdivision *Experimental methods* under *Education*

NON-GOVERNMENTAL ORGANIZATIONS

See also
Community development
Economic assistance

Amazon Valley

Alzate Angel, Beatriz and María T. Ramírez V., eds. *Cinco lustros de actuación institucional nacional e internacional en Amazonia* reviewed by Olga Lucía Turbay. *La Educación (USA)*, v. 36, no. 111 – 113 (1992), pp. 279 – 280.

Argentina

Posada, Marcelo Germán. Crisis estatal y nuevo entramado social: la emergencia de las organizaciones no gubernamentales; el rol de las ONGs en el agro argentino. *Revista Paraguaya de Sociología*, v. 29, no. 85 (Sept – Dec 92), pp. 99 – 131. Bibl.

Bolivia

Renshaw, John and Daniel Rivas. Un programa integrado para combatir el mal de Chagas: el Proyecto Boliviano – Británico "Cardenal Maurer." *Estudios Paraguayos*, v. 17, no. 1 – 2 (1989 – 1993), pp. 323 – 344.

Brazil

Bava, Silvio Caccia and Laura Mullahy. Making Brazil's Cities Livable: NGOs and the Recycling of Human Waste (Adapted chapter from the forthcoming book *Joint Ventures in Urban Policy: NGO – Local Government Collaboration in Democratizing Latin America* edited by Charles A. Reilly). *Grassroots Development,* v. 17, no. 1 (1993), pp. 12 – 19. Bibl, il.

Fischer, Tânia et al. Olodum: a arte e o negócio. *RAE; Revista de Administração de Empresas,* v. 33, no. 2 (Mar – Apr 93), pp. 90 – 99. Bibl.

Garrison, John W., II. UNCED and the Greening of Brazilian NGOs. *Grassroots Development,* v. 17, no. 1 (1993), pp. 2 – 11. Bibl, il.

Landim, Leilah. Can NGOs Help Stitch Together a Safety Net for Brazil's Poor? *Grassroots Development,* v. 17, no. 1 (1993), pp. 36 – 37. Il.

Ribeiro, Mariska. Direitos reprodutivos e políticas descartáveis. *Estudos Feministas,* v. 1, no. 2 (1993), pp. 400 – 407.

Caribbean area

McAfee, Kathy. *Storm Signals: Structural Adjustment and Development Alternatives in the Caribbean* reviewed by Peter Meel. *European Review of Latin American and Caribbean Studies,* no. 54 (June 93), pp. 128 – 131.

Chile

Egaña, María José. De las ollas comunes a microempresarias. *Mensaje,* v. 42, no. 425 (Dec 93), pp. 650 – 653. Il.

Hojman A., David E. Non-Governmental Organisations (NGOs) and the Chilean Transition to Democracy. *European Review of Latin American and Caribbean Studies,* no. 54 (June 93), pp. 7 – 24. Bibl.

Ruiz-Tagle P., Jaime. ONG y políticas públicas: nuevas formas de solidaridad institucionalizada. *Mensaje,* v. 42, no. 421 (Aug 93), pp. 378 – 381. Il, tables.

Ecuador

Meyer, Carrie A. Environmental NGOs in Ecuador: An Economic Analysis of Institutional Change. *Journal of Developing Areas,* v. 27, no. 2 (Jan 93), pp. 191 – 210. Bibl.

Latin America

Reilly, Charles A. The Road from Rio: NGO Policy Makers and the Social Ecology of Development. *Grassroots Development,* v. 17, no. 1 (1993), pp. 25 – 35. Bibl, il.

Ritchey-Vance, Marion. Grassroots Development Results: Widening the Lens. *Grassroots Development,* v. 17, no. 1 (1993), pp. 42 – 43. Charts.

Mexico

Saucedo, Irma. Las ONGs de mujeres en México. *Fem,* v. 17, no. 126 (Aug 93), pp. 10 – 13. Tables.

Peru

Valentín, Isidro. El gusto por la imagen: una vivencia de fotografía social. *Allpanchis,* v. 25, no. 41 (Jan – June 93), pp. 262 – 272. Il.

NORIEGA, MANUEL ANTONIO

Chamorro, Máximo. Retrato de una personalidad antisocial. *Revista Cultural Lotería,* v. 51, no. 392 (Nov – Dec 93), pp. 5 – 21.

NORTH AMERICAN FREE TRADE AGREEMENT

Aboites, Hugo. La relación universidad – industria en el marco del Tratado de Libre Comercio. *El Cotidiano,* v. 9, no. 55 (June 93), pp. 78 – 84. Charts.

Aboites A., Jaime and Alenka Guzmán Chávez. La industria textil mexicana y el Tratado de Libre Comercio. *El Cotidiano,* v. 8, no. 51 (Nov – Dec 92), pp. 102 – 109. Bibl, tables.

Acuerdos paralelos del Tratado de Libre Comercio de América del Norte. *Comercio Exterior,* v. 43, no. 9 (Sept 93), pp. 852 – 858.

Alba-Hernández, Francisco. El Tratado de Libre Comercio y la emigración de mexicanos a Estados Unidos. *Comercio Exterior,* v. 43, no. 8 (Aug 93), pp. 743 – 749. Bibl.

Alfie Cohen, Miriam and Godofredo Vidal de la Rosa. Hacia los acuerdos paralelos: el medio ambiente. *El Cotidiano,* v. 9, no. 56 (July 93), pp. 104 – 111. Bibl, il, tables.

Bailey, Norman A. The No-NAFTA Scenario. *Business Mexico,* v. 3, no. 10 (Oct 93), pp. 29 – 32. Tables, charts.

Ballesteros, Carlos. El concepto de seguridad ambiental y la integración del mercado norteamericano. *Relaciones Internacionales (Mexico),* v. 15, Nueva época, no. 58 (Apr – June 93), pp. 63 – 68.

Blears, James. Mexico in a No-NAFTA Future. *Business Mexico,* v. 3, no. 11 (Nov 93), pp. 32 – 35.

Bolívar Espinoza, Augusto. TLCAN: ganadores y perdedores. *Nueva Sociedad,* no. 126 (July – Aug 93), pp. 110 – 121.

Bolívar Espinoza, Augusto et al. Se preparan tiempos de coyuntura, vísperas del cambio de gobierno. *El Cotidiano,* v. 9, no. 55 (June 93), pp. 60 – 67. Il.

Cameron, Maxwell A. and Ricardo Grinspun. Mexico: The Wages of Trade. *Report on the Americas,* v. 26, no. 4 (Feb 93), pp. 32 – 37 +. Bibl, il.

Campos Aragón, Leticia. El TLC y la nueva cultura laboral. *Momento Económico,* no. 65 (Jan – Feb 93), pp. 26 – 30.

Carlsen, Laura. Worker Protection under NAFTA. *Business Mexico,* v. 3, no. 10 (Oct 93), pp. 38 – 39. Il.

Castañeda, Jorge G. La dinámica de las jerarquías y coaliciones. *Relaciones Internacionales (Mexico),* v. 15, Nueva época, no. 57 (Jan – Mar 93), pp. 95 – 96.

Castañeda, Jorge G. and Carlos Heredia. Hacia otro TLC. *Nexos,* v. 16, no. 181 (Jan 93), pp. 43 – 54.

Castro Martínez, Pedro Fernando. Comercio e inversiones México – Canadá: un asunto trilateral. *Comercio Exterior,* v. 43, no. 5 (May 93), pp. 498 – 506. Bibl, tables.

— Corporativismo y TLC: las viejas y nuevas alianzas del estado. *Plural (Mexico),* v. 22, no. 261 (June 93), pp. 63 – 73. Bibl.

Cohen, Joshua A. Productivity: A Jump Start to Better Wages. *Business Mexico,* v. 3, no. 6 (June 93), pp. 7 – 8.

Conroy, Michael E. and Amy K. Glasmeier. Unprecedented Disparities, Unparalleled Adjustment Needs: Winners and Losers on the NAFTA "Fast Track." *Journal of Inter-American Studies and World Affairs,* v. 34, no. 4 (Winter 92 – 93), pp. 1 – 37. Bibl, tables, charts.

Cornelius, Wayne Armstrong and Philip L. Martin. The Uncertain Connection: Free Trade and Rural Mexican Migration to the United States. *International Migration Review,* v. 27, no. 3 (Fall 93), pp. 484 – 512. Bibl, tables, charts.

Delgado, Dora. Resolving Conflicts Out of Court. *Business Mexico,* v. 3, no. 12 (Dec 93), p. 30.

Docampo, César. Iniciativas estadounidenses de la política económica: consecuencias hemisféricas. *Realidad Económica,* no. 119 (Oct – Nov 93), pp. 117 – 132. Bibl.

Echanove Huacuja, Flavia. El mercado del algodón: políticas de Estados Unidos y México y el Tratado de Libre Comercio. *Comercio Exterior,* v. 43, no. 11 (Nov 93), pp. 1046 – 1051. Bibl, tables.

Eisenstadt, Todd. Nuevo estilo diplomático: cabildeo y relaciones públicas, 1986 – 1991 (Translated by Martha Elena Venier). *Foro Internacional,* v. 32, no. 5 (Oct – Dec 92), pp. 667 – 702. Bibl, tables, charts.

Faux, Jeff and Thea Lee. Los efectos del Acuerdo de Libre Comercio de América del Norte en la fuerza de trabajo de Estados Unidos. *Relaciones Internacionales (Mexico),* v. 15, Nueva época, no. 57 (Jan – Mar 93), pp. 37 – 54.

Forde, D. H. One Market for All? *Américas,* v. 45, no. 5 (Sept – Oct 93), pp. 34 – 39. Il, charts.

Freebairn, Donald K. Posibles pérdidas y ganancias en el sector agrícola bajo un Tratado de Libre Comercio entre Estados Unidos y México. *Revista Mexicana de Sociología,* v. 54, no. 1 (Jan – Mar 92), pp. 3 – 28. Bibl, tables.

Fuentes Aguilar, Luis and Consuelo Soto Mora. La industria del aluminio en el Tratado de Libre Comercio. *Problemas del Desarrollo,* v. 24, no. 93 (Apr – June 93), pp. 75 – 93. Bibl, tables, maps.

Ganster, Paul and Eugenio O. Valenciano, eds. *The Mexican – U.S. Border Region and the Free Trade Agreement* reviewed by Christopher A. Erickson. *Journal of Borderlands Studies,* v. 7, no. 2 (Fall 92), pp. 103 – 105.

García, Arturo. Reality in the "Campo." *Business Mexico,* v. 3, no. 8 (Aug 93), pp. 30 – 31. Il.

García Canclini, Néstor and Gilberto Guevara Niebla, eds. *La educación y la cultura ante el Tratado de Libre Comercio* reviewed by Fernando de Mateo (Review entitled "El jalón del TLC"). *Nexos,* v. 16, no. 189 (Sept 93), pp. 66 – 67.

Hakim, Peter. La empresa para la Iniciativa de las Américas. *Relaciones Internacionales (Mexico),* v. 15, Nueva época, no. 57 (Jan – Mar 93), pp. 31 – 35.

Hernández Navarro, Luis. De Washington al Cerro de las Campanas: la exportación de la democracia a la hora del TLC. *El Cotidiano,* v. 9, no. 54 (May 93), pp. 101 – 107. Bibl.

Hoyt, Edward. Countdown to NAFTA. *Business Mexico,* v. 3, no. 10 (Oct 93), pp. 33 – 34.

Kelso, Laura. Mission NAFTA. *Business Mexico,* v. 3, no. 7 (July 93), p. 20+. Il.

Lande, Stephen. Think Globally, Trade Locally. *Business Mexico,* v. 3, no. 11 (Nov 93), pp. 8 – 11.

López Villafañe, Víctor. La integración económica en la cuenca del Pacífico: el reto de la América del Norte. *Comercio Exterior,* v. 43, no. 12 (Dec 93), pp. 1145 – 1152. Bibl, tables.

Lustig, Nora et al. *North American Free Trade: Assessing the Impact* reviewed by Marlene Alcántara Domínguez (Review entitled "Costos y beneficios del Tratado de Libre Comercio de América del Norte"). *Relaciones Internacionales (Mexico),* v. 15, Nueva época, no. 58 (Apr – June 93), pp. 97 – 98.

Meyer, Lorenzo. *La segunda muerte de la revolución mexicana* reviewed by Donald McCarthy (Review entitled "Critiquing the Critic"). *Business Mexico,* v. 3, no. 8 (Aug 93), p. 53.

Much Ado about Nothing . . . Hopefully. *Business Mexico,* v. 3, no. 8 (Aug 93), pp. 23 – 24.

NAFTA Talking Points: Quick Response to the Inaccuracies about NAFTA. *Business Mexico,* v. 3, no. 11 (Nov 93), pp. 36 – 37.

Las necesidades educativas de las mayorías mexicanas ante el Tratado de Libre Comercio. *Revista Latinoamericana de Estudios Educativos,* v. 23, no. 1 (Jan – Mar 93), pp. 5 – 8.

Ocharán, Leticia. Las artes plásticas frente al TLC. *Plural (Mexico),* v. 22, no. 258 (Mar 93), pp. 72 – 73.

Oelrich, Amy. Marching to the Beat of the Market. *Business Mexico,* v. 3, no. 11 (Nov 93), p. 30. Il.

Olvera Pomar, Daniel. The Information Trade. *Business Mexico,* v. 3, no. 11 (Nov 93), p. 38.

Ortiz, Edgar. TLC e inversión extranjera en México. *Comercio Exterior,* v. 43, no. 10 (Oct 93), pp. 967 – 973. Bibl.

Ortiz Wadgymar, Arturo. La pequeña y mediana industrias ante la apertura comercial y el Tratado de Libre Comercio: los costos de la desprotección industrial en México, 1985 – 1992. *Problemas del Desarrollo,* v. 24, no. 93 (Apr – June 93), pp. 55 – 74. Bibl, tables.

Pastor, Robert A. *Integration with Mexico: Options for the U.S. Policy* reviewed by Robert Domínguez Rivera (Review entitled "Las relaciones México – Estados Unidos: viejos problemas, nuevas opciones"). *Relaciones Internacionales (Mexico),* v. 15, Nueva época, no. 58 (Apr – June 93), pp. 99 – 100.

Pereznieto Castro, Leonel. Algunos aspectos del sistema de solución de controversias en el Tratado Norteamericano de Libre Comercio. *Relaciones Internacionales (Mexico),* v. 15, Nueva época, no. 58 (Apr – June 93), pp. 69 – 77. Bibl.

Prado, Gustavo and Manuel E. Tron. Tri-lateral Taxation. *Business Mexico,* v. 3, no. 3 (Mar 93), pp. 40 – 45.

Randall, Stephen J. et al, eds. *North America without Borders?: Integrating Canada, the United States, and Mexico* reviewed by Benoit Brookens. *Journal of Inter-American Studies and World Affairs,* v. 35, no. 1 (1993), pp. 153 – 158.

Ranger, Edward M., Jr. The Environment and NAFTA. *Business Mexico,* v. 3, no. 1 (Jan – Feb 93), pp. 78 – 79.

La recta final del TLC: una cronología. *Comercio Exterior,* v. 43, no. 12 (Dec 93), pp. 1202 – 1206.

Robinson, Sherman et al. Las políticas agrícolas y la migración en un área de libre comercio de los Estados Unidos y México: un análisis de equilibrio general computable (Translated by Carlos Villegas). *El Trimestre Económico,* v. 60, no. 237 (Jan – Mar 93), pp. 53 – 89. Bibl, tables, charts.

Rogers, John E. NAFTA Dispute Settlement for the Finance Sector. *Business Mexico,* v. 3, no. 6 (June 93), pp. 40 – 42.

Rosas, Alan L. et al. NAFTA's Environmental Issues and Opportunities. *Business Mexico,* v. 3, no. 9 (Sept 93), pp. 42 – 45.

Rosas González, María Cristina. El TLC entre México, Estados Unidos y Canadá: semejanzas y diferencias con el ALC entre Canadá y Estados Unidos. *Relaciones Internacionales (Mexico),* v. 15, Nueva época, no. 57 (Jan – Mar 93), pp. 55 – 62. Charts.

Rubio F., Luis. El TLC y la democracia (Response to the article entitled "Hacia otro TLC" by Jorge G. Castañeda and Carlos Heredia). *Nexos,* v. 16, no. 182 (Feb 93), pp. 63 – 66.

Russell, Joel. A Better Neighborhood. *Business Mexico,* v. 3, no. 3 (Mar 93), pp. 46 – 47. Il.

Salinas de Gortari, Carlos. El libre comercio en Norteamérica: oportunidad de progreso y bienestar. *Comercio Exterior,* v. 43, no. 1 (Jan 93), pp. 32 – 33.

Sotomayor Yalán, Maritza. La producción automotriz en México y el Tratado de Libre Comercio México – Estados Unidos – Canadá. *Frontera Norte,* v. 4, no. 8 (July – Dec 92), pp. 165 – 172.

Stoub, Jeffrey. NAFTA's "Green" Thumb. *Business Mexico,* v. 3, no. 10 (Oct 93), pp. 35 – 36.

Székely, Gabriel. California Sunrise. *Nexos,* v. 16, no. 185 (May 93), pp. 13 – 15.

The Verdict's In (Excerpt from the United States International Trade Commission's report on NAFTA). *Business Mexico,* v. 3, no. 3 (Mar 93), pp. 37 – 39.

Witoshynsky, Mary. A Builder of Bridges. *Business Mexico,* v. 3, no. 4 (Apr 93), p. 42. Charts.

— "An Extraordinary Visit." *Business Mexico,* v. 3, no. 4 (Apr 93), pp. 40 – 41. Il.

— "The Final Steps." *Business Mexico,* v. 3, no. 10 (Oct 93), p. 47. Il.

— The New Politics of NAFTA. *Business Mexico,* v. 3, no. 3 (Mar 93), p. 48. Il.

Womack, James P. Awaiting NAFTA. *Business Mexico,* v. 3, no. 4 (Apr 93), pp. 4 – 7. Il.

Zermeño García, Sergio. La derrota de la sociedad: modernización y modernidad en el México de Norteamérica. *Revista Mexicana de Sociología,* v. 55, no. 2 (Apr – June 93), pp. 273 – 290. Bibl.

Bibliography

Frohmann, Alicia. Hacia una integración comercial hemisférica? (Review article). *Pensamiento Iberoamericano,* no. 22 – 23, tomo I (July 92 – June 93), pp. 347 – 356. Tables, charts.

Mathematical models

Levy, Santiago and Sweder van Wijnbergen. Mercados de trabajo, migración y bienestar: la agricultura en el Tratado de Libre Comercio entre México y los Estados Unidos (Translated by Carlos Villegas). *El Trimestre Económico,* v. 60, no. 238 (Apr – June 93), pp. 371 – 411. Bibl, tables.

Romero, José and Leslie Young. Crecimiento constante y transición en un modelo dinámico dual del Acuerdo de Libre Comercio de la América del Norte (Translated by Carlos Villegas). *El Trimestre Económico,* v. 60, no. 238 (Apr – June 93), pp. 353 – 370. Bibl.

NORTH – SOUTH DIALOGUE

See
   International economic relations

NOVÁS CALVO, LINO
Criticism of specific works
El negrero
González Bolaños, Aimée. El arte narrativo de Lino Novás Calvo en *El negrero. Islas,* no. 98 (Jan – Apr 91), pp. 87 – 97.

NOVELS

See
Fiction
Latin American fiction
Author Index under names of specific novelists

NOVO, SALVADOR

Fiction

Alatriste, Sealtiel. *En defensa de la envidia* reviewed by Christopher Domínquez (Review entitled "De envidia a envidia"). *Vuelta*, v. 17, no. 195 (Feb 93), pp. 40 – 41.

NUCLEAR ENERGY

See
Atomic power industry

NUCLEAR WEAPONS

See
Atomic weapons and disarmament

NUEVO LEÓN, MEXICO

Olvera Sandoval, José Antonio. Agricultura, riego y conflicto social en la región citrícola de Nuevo León, 1860 – 1910. *Siglo XIX: Cuadernos*, v. 2, no. 5 (Feb 93), pp. 59 – 78.

Villarreal González, Diana R. *La política de vivienda del gobierno del estado de Nuevo León, 1970 – 1990* reviewed by Gustavo Garza. *Estudios Demográficos y Urbanos*, v. 6, no. 3 (Sept – Dec 91), pp. 773 – 778.

NUGENT, JOSÉ GUILLERMO

Criticism of specific works

El laberinto de la choledad

Lauer, Mirko. La mentira cordial. *Debate (Peru)*, v. 16, no. 74 (Sept – Oct 93), pp. 41 – 45. Bibl.

NÚÑEZ, ENRIQUE BERNARDO

Criticism of specific works

Cubagua

Vilanova, Angel. Motivo clásico y novela latinoamericana. *Nueva Revista de Filología Hispánica*, v. 40, no. 2 (July – Dec 92), pp. 1087 – 1099. Bibl.

NÚÑEZ, MARÍA CRISTINA

Criticism of specific works

Tuzamapan

Madrazo Miranda, María. Literatura y vida en el testimonio: *Tuzamapan; el poder viene de las cañas*. *Fem*, v. 17, no. 120 (Feb 93), pp. 18 – 20. Il.

NÚÑEZ CABEZA DE VACA, ALVAR

Criticism of specific works

Naufragios

Rivera Martínez, J. Edgardo. Singularidad y carácter de los *Naufragios* de Alvar Núñez Cabeza de Vaca. *Revista de Crítica Literaria Latinoamericana*, v. 19, no. 38 (July – Dec 93), pp. 301 – 315.

Spitta, Silvia. Chamanismo y cristiandad: una lectura de los *Naufragios* de Cabeza de Vaca. *Revista de Crítica Literaria Latinoamericana*, v. 19, no. 38 (July – Dec 93), pp. 317 – 330. Bibl.

NÚÑEZ QUINTERO, JOSÉ MARÍA

Medrano Puyol, Juan A. Dr. José María Núñez Quintero. *Revista Cultural Lotería*, v. 50, no. 383 (May – June 91), pp. 57 – 62.

NUÑO, RUBÉN BONIFAZ

See
Bonifaz Nuño, Rubén

NURSERY SCHOOLS

See
Education, Preschool

NURSES

Panama

Díaz de Alpirez, Magali M. La familia como unidad de atención de la enfermera a través de la visita domiciliaria. *Revista Cultural Lotería*, v. 51, no. 390 (July – Aug 92), pp. 53 – 57.

NUT INDUSTRY

Brazil

Santana, Antônio Cordeiro de. Custo social da depredação florestal no Pará: o caso da castanha-do-Brasil. *Revista de Economia e Sociologia Rural*, v. 30, no. 3 (July – Sept 92), pp. 253 – 269. Bibl, tables, charts.

Mathematical models

Lemos, José de Jesus Sousa and Pedro F. Adeodato de Paula Pessoa. Mercado de exportação e estabilização de preços externos para amêndoas de castanha de caju. *Revista de Economia e Sociologia Rural*, v. 30, no. 2 (Apr – June 92), pp. 171 – 187. Bibl, tables, charts.

NUTRITION

Study and teaching

Mueses de Molina, Carolina. Educación popular en salud y nutrición: revisión de bibliografía. *Estudios Sociales (Dominican Republic)*, v. 26, no. 93 (July – Sept 93), pp. 83 – 108. Bibl.

Argentina

Lesser, Ricardo. El cuerpo de la democracia: la crónica de las condiciones de vida de los sectores populares en esta democracia renovada . . . . *Todo Es Historia*, v. 27, no. 317 (Dec 93), pp. 50 – 56. Il.

Caribbean area

DeMar, Margaretta. Constraints on Constrainers: Limits on External Economic Policy Affecting Nutritional Vulnerability in the Caribbean. *Latin American Perspectives*, v. 20, no. 2 (Spring 93), pp. 54 – 73. Bibl.

Guatemala

Menéndez Martínez, Otto R. Alimentación – nutrición y salud – enfermedad estomatológica: revisión de literatura. *USAC*, no. 13 (Mar 91), pp. 61 – 75. Bibl, charts.

Mexico

Pérez Gil, Sara Elena et al. La salud y la nutrición de las mujeres en México. *El Cotidiano*, v. 9, no. 53 (Mar – Apr 93), pp. 84 – 92. Il, tables.

Study and teaching

Martínez Salgado, Homero and José Romero Keith. La educación nutricional en el medio rural: una propuesta pedagógica. *Revista Latinoamericana de Estudios Educativos*, v. 23, no. 1 (Jan – Mar 93), pp. 75 – 86.

OAS

See
Organization of American States

OAXACA, MEXICO (CITY)

Bayón, Damián Carlos. Reencuentro con Oaxaca (Accompanied by an English translation). *Artes de México*, no. 21 (Fall 93), pp. 36 – 39. Il.

Blanco, Alberto. Arte de Oaxaca (Accompanied by an English translation). *Artes de México*, no. 21 (Fall 93), pp. 68 – 83. Il.

Henestrosa, Andrés. Hechicera Oaxaca (Accompanied by an English translation). *Artes de México*, no. 21 (Fall 93), p. 43. Il.

Murphy, Arthur D. and Alex Stepick. *Social Inequality in Oaxaca: A History of Resistance and Change* reviewed by John K. Chance. *The Americas*, v. 49, no. 4 (Apr 93), pp. 541 – 542.

Perea, Héctor. Arte escondido de Oaxaca (Accompanied by an English translation). *Artes de México*, no. 21 (Fall 93), pp. 48 – 53. Il.

Pérez Morales, Constantino Alberto. Fortalecimiento municipal para el desarrollo regional en Oaxaca. *Problemas del Desarrollo*, v. 24, no. 92 (Jan – Mar 93), pp. 137 – 169. Tables.

Sarignana, Armando. La Soledad (Accompanied by an English translation). *Artes de México,* no. 21 (Fall 93), pp. 44 – 47. Il.

Tarn, Nathaniel. Santo Domingo de Guzmán, Oaxaca: origen del orden (Accompanied by the English original, translated by Osvaldo Sánchez and Roberto Tejada). *Artes de México,* no. 21 (Fall 93), pp. 40 – 41.

Weinberger, Eliot. El zócalo: centro del universo (Accompanied by the English original, translated by Magali Tercero). *Artes de México,* no. 21 (Fall 93), pp. 26 – 31. Il, maps.

Willis, Katie. Women's Work and Social Network Use in Oaxaca City, Mexico. *Bulletin of Latin American Research,* v. 12, no. 1 (Jan 93), pp. 65 – 82. Bibl, tables.

Bibliography

Bibliografía (to the articles on Oaxaca appearing in this issue). *Artes de México,* no. 21 (Fall 93), p. 84.

Maps

Sánchez, Joaquín Ruy. Oaxaca, Oax. *Artes de México,* no. 21 (Fall 93), pp. 32 – 33. Il.

OAXACA, MEXICO (STATE)

Blanco, Alberto. Arte contemporáneo de Oaxaca: la semilla de la visión. *Nexos,* v. 16, no. 186 (June 93), pp. 15 – 19.

Chena R., Rodolfo. La población de una parroquia novohispana del siglo XVIII: Santa María de la Presentación de Chilapa. *Estudios Demográficos y Urbanos,* v. 7, no. 1 (Jan – Apr 92), pp. 169 – 192. Bibl, tables, charts.

Feinman, Gary M. and Linda M. Nicholas. Shell-Ornament Production in Ejutla: Implications for Highland – Coastal Interaction in Ancient Oaxaca. *Ancient Mesoamerica,* v. 4, no. 1 (Spring 93), pp. 103 – 119. Bibl, il, tables, maps, charts.

Hodges, Denise C. *Agricultural Intensification and Preshistoric Health in the Valley of Oaxaca, Mexico* reviewed by Dale L. Hutchinson. *Latin American Antiquity,* v. 4, no. 2 (June 93), pp. 200 – 201.

Joyce, Arthur A. Interregional Interaction and Social Development on the Oaxaca Coast. *Ancient Mesoamerica,* v. 4, no. 1 (Spring 93), pp. 67 – 84. Bibl, il, maps.

Lipp, Frank Joseph. *The Mixe of Oaxaca: Religion, Ritual, and Healing* reviewed by James Dow. *The Americas,* v. 49, no. 4 (Apr 93), pp. 545 – 547.

Rendón Monzón, Juan José. Apuntes en torno a la alfabetización en lenguas indígenas. *Revista Latinoamericana de Estudios Educativos,* v. 22, no. 4 (Oct – Dec 92), pp. 63 – 76.

Spores, Ronald. Tututepec: A Postclassic-Period Mixtec Conquest State. *Ancient Mesoamerica,* v. 4, no. 1 (Spring 93), pp. 167 – 174. Bibl, tables, maps, charts.

Zeitlin, Judith Francis. The Politics of Classic-Period Ritual Interaction: Iconography of the Ballgame Cult in Coastal Oaxaca. *Ancient Mesoamerica,* v. 4, no. 1 (Spring 93), pp. 121 – 140. Bibl, il, maps.

Zeitlin, Robert Norman. Pacific Coastal Laguna Zope: A Regional Center in the Terminal Formative Hinterlands of Monte Albán. *Ancient Mesoamerica,* v. 4, no. 1 (Spring 93), pp. 85 – 101. Bibl, il, maps.

OBESO, CANDELARIO

Criticism and interpretation

Prescott, Laurence E. "Negro nací": Authorship and Voice in Verses Attributed to Candelario Obeso. *Afro-Hispanic Review,* v. 12, no. 1 (Spring 93), pp. 3 – 15. Bibl.

OBITUARIES

See

Acuña, Luis Alberto – Obituaries
Aguiar, Manoel Pinto de – Obituaries
Alvarez Bravo, Lola – Obituaries
Anguita, Eduardo – Obituaries
Avila, Silvia Mercedes – Obituaries
Avila C., José A. – Obituaries
Avila Martel, Alamiro de – Obituaries
Barral, Basilio María de – Obituaries
Bernal, Ignacio – Obituaries
Bernardes, Lysia M. C. – Obituaries
Bernardes, Nilo – Obituaries
Bonfil Batalla, Guillermo – Obituaries

Canfield, D. Lincoln – Obituaries
Caro Copete, Jorge – Obituaries
Chaves Mendoza, Alvaro – Obituaries
Corrêa de Azevedo, Luiz Heitor – Obituaries
Correas, Edmundo – Obituaries
Costa, Olga – Obituaries
Díaz-Casanueva, Humberto – Obituaries
Erickson, Dorothy – Obituaries
Febres Cordero, Eloy – Obituaries
Galindo, Blas – Obituaries
García Bacca, Juan David – Obituaries
Gerbasi, Vicente – Obituaries
Giménez, Carlos – Obituaries
Guarnieri, Camargo – Obituaries
Hanke, Lewis – Obituaries
Hardoy, Jorge Enrique – Obituaries
Holzmann, Rodolfo – Obituaries
Izquierdo Fernández, Gonzalo – Obituaries
Kelemen, Pál – Obituaries
Lee López, Alberto – Obituaries
Lewis, C. Bernard – Obituaries
López Avila, Carlos – Obituaries
López Ruiz, Juvenal – Obituaries
Menéndez, Miguel – Obituaries
Morales Cavero, Hugo – Obituaries
Morales Fernández, Jesús – Obituaries
Moreno, Mario – Obituaries
Nevares Reyes, Salvador – Obituaries
Pardo García, Germán – Obituaries
Pinilla, Enrique – Obituaries
Prado, Caio Graco – Obituaries
Quirós, Juan – Obituaries
Ramos, Julio – Obituaries
Resende, Otto Lara – Obituaries
Reyes Nevares, Salvador – Obituaries
Rocyn-Jones, Susan – Obituaries
Rodríguez, Antonio – Obituaries
Rowe, James William – Obituaries
Ruiz-Tagle, Carlos – Obituaries
Saignes, Thierry – Obituaries
Sanz de Santamaría, Carlos – Obituaries
Sarduy, Severo – Obituaries
Schaden, Egon – Obituaries
Schroeder, Albert H. – Obituaries
Soustelle, Jacques – Obituaries
Tibesar, Antonine S. – Obituaries
Uribe-Echevarría Frey, Bárbara – Obituaries
Valdivieso, Mercedes – Obituaries
Valencia Avaria, Luis – Obituaries
Vuskovic Bravo, Pedro – Obituaries
Wolff, Egon – Obituaries

OBSIDIAN

Belize

Dreiss, Meredith L. et al. Expanding the Role of Trace-Element Studies: Obsidian Use in the Late and Terminal Classic Periods at the Lowland Maya Site of Colha, Belize. *Ancient Mesoamerica,* v. 4, no. 2 (Fall 93), pp. 271 – 283. Bibl, il, maps, charts.

Central America

Freter, Ann Corinne. Obsidian-Hydration Data: Its Past, Present, and Future Application in Mesoamerica. *Ancient Mesoamerica,* v. 4, no. 2 (Fall 93), pp. 285 – 303. Bibl, tables, charts.

Honduras

Webster, David et al. The Obsidian Hydration Dating Project at Copán: A Regional Approach and Why It Works. *Latin American Antiquity,* v. 4, no. 4 (Dec 93), pp. 303 – 324. Bibl, tables, charts.

Mexico

Darling, J. Andrew. Notes on Obsidian Sources of the Southern Sierra Madre Occidental. *Ancient Mesoamerica,* v. 4, no. 2 (Fall 93), pp. 245 – 253. Bibl, il, maps.

Otis Charlton, Cynthia L. Obsidian as Jewelry: Lapidary Production in Aztec Otumba, Mexico. *Ancient Mesoamerica,* v. 4, no. 2 (Fall 93), pp. 231 – 243. Bibl, il, tables, maps.

Trombold, Charles D. et al. Chemical Characteristics of Obsidian from Archaeological Sites in Western Mexico and the Tequila Source Area: Implications for Regional and Pan-Regional Interaction within the Northern Mesoamerican Periphery. *Ancient Mesoamerica,* v. 4, no. 2 (Fall 93), pp. 255 – 270. Bibl, tables, maps, charts.

OCAMPO, VICTORIA

Biography

Vázquez, María Esther. *Victoria Ocampo* reviewed by Eliana C. Hermann. *Chasqui*, v. 22, no. 1 (May 93), pp. 94 – 95.

— *Victoria Ocampo* reviewed by Gustavo Fares and Eliana Hermann (Review entitled "¿Y ahora?: reflexiones acerca de la literatura femenina argentina actual"). *Letras Femeninas*, v. 19, no. 1 – 2 (Spring – Fall 93), pp. 121 – 134. Bibl.

Criticism and interpretation

Meyer, Doris L. Letters and Lines of Correspondence in the Essays of Victoria Ocampo. *Revista Interamericana de Bibliografía*, v. 42, no. 2 (1992), pp. 233 – 240. Bibl.

Criticism of specific works

Autobiografía

Busquets, Loreto. Victoria Ocampo a través de su *Autobiografía*. *Cuadernos Hispanoamericanos*, no. 510 (Dec 92), pp. 121 – 133.

OCCUPATIONAL MOBILITY

See
Social mobility

OCCUPATIONAL TRAINING

See
Technical education
Vocational education

O'DONNELL, GUILLERMO A.

Criticism of specific works

Transiciones desde un gobierno autoritario

Woldenberg, José. ¿Un nuevo animal? *Nexos*, v. 16, no. 185 (May 93), pp. 61 – 65.

O'GORMAN, CAMILA

Fiction

Cordones-Cook, Juanamaría. *Una sombra donde sueña Camila O'Gorman*: dimensión poética de la historia. *La Palabra y el Hombre*, no. 84 (Oct – Dec 92), pp. 271 – 276.

O'GORMAN, EDMUNDO

Interviews

Carreño King, Tania and Angélica Vázquez del Mercado. La hija de la invención: una entrevista con Edmundo O'Gorman. *Nexos*, v. 16, no. 190 (Oct 93), pp. 45 – 51.

O'HIGGINS, BERNARDO

Cayo Córdova, Percy. Santa Cruz y O'Higgins: dos efemérides de 1992. *Apuntes (Peru)*, no. 31 (July – Dec 92), pp. 3 – 18.

OLD AGE

Barros Lezaeta, Carmen. Factores que intervienen en el bienestar de los adultos mayores. *Estudios Sociales (Chile)*, no. 77 (July – Sept 93), pp. 31 – 47. Bibl, charts.

Ham-Chande, Roberto. México: país en proceso de envejecimiento. *Comercio Exterior*, v. 43, no. 7 (July 93), pp. 688 – 696. Bibl, tables.

Hernández Castellón, Raúl. El envejecimiento de la población en Cuba. *Estudios Demográficos y Urbanos*, v. 7, no. 2 – 3 (May – Dec 92), pp. 603 – 617. Bibl, tables.

Loáiciga G., María Elena. Condiciones psicosociales vinculadas a la atención institucional de los ancianos. *Revista de Ciencias Sociales (Costa Rica)*, no. 60 (June 93), pp. 135 – 141.

Loáiciga G., María Elena and Rosa Rosales O. La población anciana de Liberia: condición socioeconómica precaria. *Revista de Ciencias Sociales (Costa Rica)*, no. 59 (Mar 93), pp. 95 – 106. Bibl, tables.

Tamer, Norma Liliana. Possibilities and Conditions of Integral Education for Older Citizens: Pedagogic Proposal. *La Educación (USA)*, v. 37, no. 114 (1993), pp. 119 – 122.

OLIGARCHY

See also
Elite (Social sciences)

Argentina

Saguier, Eduardo Ricardo. La crisis de un estado colonial: balance de la cuestión rioplatense. *Anuario de Estudios Americanos*, v. 49, Suppl. 2 (1992), pp. 65 – 91. Bibl.

Brazil

Gouvêa, Fernando da Cruz. Notas sobre a influência dos senhores rurais na vida política brasileira. *Revista do Instituto Histórico e Geográfico Brasileiro*, no. 372 (July – Sept 91), pp. 815 – 827.

Sampaio, Consuelo Novais. Repensando Canudos: o jogo das oligarquias. *Luso-Brazilian Review*, v. 30, no. 2 (Winter 93), pp. 97 – 113. Bibl, tables.

Central America

Casaus Arzú, Marta Elena. La metamorfosis de las oligarquías centroamericanas. *Revista Mexicana de Sociología*, v. 54, no. 3 (July – Sept 92), pp. 69 – 114. Bibl, tables, charts.

El Salvador

Arriola Palomares, Joaquín and David Amílcar Mena. La transición: los proyectos en disputa. *ECA; Estudios Centroamericanos*, v. 48, no. 536 (June 93), pp. 527 – 544. Bibl, il, tables.

Guatemala

Societies, etc.

Bell, John Patrick. La Asociación General de Agricultores frente a la reforma agraria en la Guatemala revolucionaria, 1944 – 1954. *Anuario de Estudios Centroamericanos*, v. 18, no. 1 (1992), pp. 17 – 28. Bibl.

Mexico

Olveda, Jaime. Las viejas oligarquías y la reforma liberal: el caso de Guadalajara. *Siglo XIX: Cuadernos*, v. 2, no. 4 (Oct 92), pp. 9 – 30. Bibl.

OLIN, NAHUI

Herner de Larrea, Irene. Nahui Olin: años de gato. *Nexos*, v. 16, no. 185 (May 93), pp. 20 – 22. Il.

OLIVEIRA, MANUEL BOTELHO DE

Criticism and interpretation

Chociay, Rogério. Três vertentes métricas na poesia de Manuel Botelho de Oliveira. *Revista de Letras (Brazil)*, v. 32 (1992), pp. 207 – 221. Bibl.

Criticism of specific works

Música de Parnaso

Ribeiro, João Roberto Inácio. O gongorismo na poesia latina de Manuel Botelho de Oliveira. *Revista de Letras (Brazil)*, v. 32 (1992), pp. 199 – 206. Bibl.

OLMECS

Grove, David C. and Robert James Sharer, eds. *Regional Perspectives on the Olmec* reviewed by Michael Love. *Mesoamérica (USA)*, v. 13, no. 23 (June 92), pp. 209 – 213.

OÑATE, JUAN DE

Simmons, Marc. *The Last Conquistador: Juan de Oñate and the Settling of the Far Southwest* reviewed by Adrian Bustamante. *Colonial Latin American Historical Review*, v. 2, no. 2 (Spring 93), pp. 235 – 236.

Poetry

Villagrá, Gaspar Pérez de. *'Historia de la Nueva México, 1610' by Gaspar Pérez de Villagrá: A Critical and Annotated Spanish/English Edition* edited and translated by Miguel Encinias. Reviewed by Franklin G. Smith. *Colonial Latin American Historical Review*, v. 2, no. 3 (Summer 93), pp. 377 – 379.

— *Historia de Nuevo México*. Critical edition by Mercedes Junquera. Reviewed by Phil Jaramillo (Review entitled "Dispositio Textus: Paleographic or Semipaleographic Edition?"). *Bilingual Review/Revista Bilingüe*, v. 17, no. 3 (Sept – Dec 92), pp. 276 – 278. Bibl.

ONETTI, JUAN CARLOS
Criticism of specific works
Los adioses

Méndez Clark, Ronald. *Onetti y la (in)fidelidad a las reglas del juego* reviewed by Harley D. Oberhelman. *Hispania (USA),* v. 76, no. 4 (Dec 93), pp. 740 – 741.

ONOFRE DE LA CADENA, JOSÉ

Estenssoro Fuchs, Juan Carlos. El mulato José Onofre de la Cadena: didáctica, estética musical y modernismo en el Perú del siglo XVIII. *Historia y Cultura (Peru),* no. 20 (1990), pp. 201 – 220.

OPERA
Brazil

Reis, Sandra Loureiro de Freitas. A *Opera Tiradentes* de Manuel Joaquim de Macedo e Augusto de Lima. *Latin American Music Review,* v. 14, no. 1 (Spring – Summer 93), pp. 131 – 144. Bibl.

Chile

Ponce, Gilberto. *Turandot* en el Municipal. *Mensaje,* v. 42, no. 424 (Nov 93), pp. 594 – 595. Il.

Italy

Albónico, Aldo. Un' opera in difesa degli indi nella Milano del seicento: il *Llanto sagrado de la América meridional. Quaderni Ibero-Americani,* no. 72 (Dec 92), pp. 695 – 708. Bibl.

Mexico

Radomski, James. Manuel García in Mexico: Part II. *Inter-American Music Review,* v. 13, no. 1 (Fall – Winter 92), pp. 15 – 20. Facs.

OPINION, PUBLIC
See
Public opinion
Subdivision *Foreign opinion* under names of specific countries
Subdivision *Public opinion* under *Hispanic Americans (U.S.)* and names of Indian groups

ORAL HISTORY
Brazil

Assunção, Matthias Röhrig, ed. *A guerra dos bem-te-vis: a balaiada na memória oral* reviewed by Mary Karasch (Review entitled "A balaiada in Brazil"). *The Americas,* v. 49, no. 3 (Jan 93), pp. 392 – 394.

Cuba

Geldof, Lynn. *Cubans: Voices of Change* reviewed by Rubén Berríos. *Cuban Studies/Estudios Cubanos,* v. 23 (1993), pp. 243 – 244.

Latin America

Lienhard, Martín. *La voz y su huella: escritura y conflicto étnico – social en América Latina, 1492 – 1988* reviewed by Gustavo Fares. *Hispania (USA),* v. 76, no. 1 (Mar 93), pp. 88 – 89.

— *La voz y su huella: escritura y conflicto étnico – social en América Latina, 1492 – 1988* reviewed by José Prats Sariol. *Iberoamericana,* v. 16, no. 47 – 48 (1992), pp. 113 – 116.

— *La voz y su huella: escritura y conflicto étnico – social en América Latina, 1492 – 1988* reviewed by Antonio Cornejo Polar. *Revista de Crítica Literaria Latinoamericana,* v. 19, no. 38 (July – Dec 93), pp. 395 – 397.

Mexico

Madrazo Miranda, María. Literatura y vida en el testimonio: *Tuzamapan; el poder viene de las cañas. Fem,* v. 17, no. 120 (Feb 93), pp. 18 – 20. Il.

Puerto Rico
Societies, etc.

Lugo, Kenneth. Informe académico del Centro de Historia Oral. *Homines,* v. 15 – 16, no. 2 – 1 (Oct 91 – Dec 92), pp. 361 – 363.

ORAL TRADITION
See also
Folk literature
Subdivisions *Legends* and *Religion and mythology* under names of Indian groups

Andean region

Arnold, Denise Y. et al. *Hacia un orden andino de las cosas: tres pistas de los Andes meridionales* reviewed by Jan Szeminski. *Estudios Interdisciplinarios de América Latina y el Caribe,* v. 4, no. 1 (Jan – June 93), pp. 175 – 176.

— *Hacia un orden andino de las cosas: tres pistas de los Andes meridionales* reviewed by Javier Albó. *Signo,* no. 38, Nueva época (Jan – Apr 93), pp. 220 – 224.

Baquerizo, Manuel J. La transición de la visión india a la visión mestiza en la poesía quechua oral. *Revista de Crítica Literaria Latinoamericana,* v. 19, no. 37 (Jan – June 93), pp. 117 – 124. Bibl.

Escalante Gutiérrez, Carmen and Ricardo Valderrama Fernández. Canciones de imploración y de amor en los Andes: literatura oral de los quechuas del siglo XX. *Revista de Crítica Literaria Latinoamericana,* v. 19, no. 37 (Jan – June 93), pp. 11 – 39.

Meneses, Georgina. *Tradición oral en el imperio de los incas: historia, religión y teatro* reviewed by Elizabeth Fonseca C. *Revista de Historia (Costa Rica),* no. 25 (Jan – June 92), pp. 235 – 237.

Rappaport, Joanne. Textos legales e interpretación histórica: una etnografía andina de la lectura. *Iberoamericana,* v. 16, no. 47 – 48 (1992), pp. 67 – 81. Bibl.

Vergara Figueroa, César Abilio. La educación, el trabajo y lo lícito en un relato oral. *Folklore Americano,* no. 52 (July – Dec 91), pp. 109 – 121. Bibl.

Argentina

Rojas, Elena M., ed. *Acerca de los relatos orales en la provincia de Tucumán* reviewed by Félix Coluccio. *Folklore Americano,* no. 53 (Jan – June 92), pp. 180 – 181.

Bolivia

Cáceres Romero, Adolfo. El "jukumari" en la literatura oral de Bolivia. *Revista de Crítica Literaria Latinoamericana,* v. 19, no. 37 (Jan – June 93), pp. 243 – 258.

Brazil

Roazzi, Antonio et al. A arte do repente e as habilidades lingüísticas. *Revista Brasileira de Estudos Pedagógicos,* v. 72, no. 172 (Sept – Dec 91), pp. 291 – 317. Bibl, tables, charts.

Chile

Barraza, Eduardo. La boda como objeto del deseo en cuentos orales de Osorno. *Revista Chilena de Literatura,* no. 42 (Aug 93), pp. 41 – 47.

Guatemala

Lara Figueroa, Celso A. Cuentos maravillosos de tradición oral del oriente guatemalteco. *La Tradición Popular,* no. 83 – 84 (1991), Issue. Il, maps.

— Cuentos populares del "Aprendiz de brujo" en Guatemala. *La Tradición Popular,* no. 80 (1990), Issue. Bibl, il, maps.

Latin America

Carrasco Muñoz, Iván. Literatura etnocultural en Hispanoamérica: concepto y precursores. *Revista Chilena de Literatura,* no. 42 (Aug 93), pp. 65 – 72. Bibl.

Lienhard, Martín. Kulturelle Heterogenität und Literatur in Lateinamerika. *Iberoamericana,* v. 16, no. 47 – 48 (1992), pp. 95 – 110. Bibl.

Slater, Candace. New Directions in Latin American Oral Traditions. *Latin American Literary Review,* v. 20, no. 40 (July – Dec 92), pp. 100 – 103.

Mexico

Mariscal, Beatriz. Mujer y literatura oral. *Escritura (Venezuela),* v. 16, no. 31 – 32 (Jan – Dec 91), pp. 171 – 178.

Peru

Itier, César. La tradición oral quechua antigua en los procesos de idolatrías de Cajatambo. *Bulletin de l'Institut Français d'Etudes Andines,* v. 21, no. 3 (1992), pp. 1009 – 1051. Bibl.

Venezuela

Almoina de Carrera, Pilar. *El héroe en el relato oral venezolano* reviewed by Juvenal López Ruiz. *Revista Nacional de Cultura (Venezuela),* v. 53, no. 286 (July – Sept 92), pp. 263 – 264.

ORBÓN, JULIÁN

Cabrera Infante, Guillermo. Guantanamerías: sobre un emblema musical de los años '60. *Vuelta,* v. 17, no. 203 (Oct 93), pp. 11 – 13.

ORELLANA, FRANCISCO DE

Amate Blanco, Juan José. El realismo mágico en la expedición amazónica de Orellana. *Cuadernos Hispanoamericanos,* no. 510 (Dec 92), pp. 61 – 72. Bibl.

ORFILA REYNAL, ARNALDO

Interviews

Gálvez Cancino, Alejandro. Arnaldo Orfila Reynal, un difundidor cultural. *Plural (Mexico),* v. 22, no. 263 (Aug 93), pp. 32 – 39.

ORGANIZATION OF AMERICAN STATES

Alleyne, Michael H. Approaches to Technical Education and the Evolving Role of the OAS. *La Educación (USA),* v. 36, no. 111 – 113 (1992), pp. 167 – 175.

Democracy in the Americas. *Américas,* v. 45, no. 6 (Nov – Dec 93), pp. 53 – 55. Il.

Hernández Vela Salgado, Edmundo. El Sistema Interamericano ante los cambios mundiales. *Relaciones Internacionales (Mexico),* v. 14, Nueva época, no. 56 (Oct – Dec 92), pp. 31 – 34. Bibl.

Leyva, María. The Museum of Modern Art of Latin America: A Guide to Its Resources. *SALALM Papers,* v. 34 (1989), pp. 417 – 427.

McKenna, Peter. Canada – OAS Relations during the Trudeau Years. *Revista Interamericana de Bibliografía,* v. 42, no. 3 (1992), pp. 373 – 391. Bibl.

Poole, Linda J. CIM: Making Women's Rights Human Rights. *Américas,* v. 45, no. 2 (Mar – Apr 93), pp. 48 – 49.

Ramírez León, José Luis. La OEA en su laberinto. *Revista Javeriana,* v. 61, no. 594 (May 93), pp. 247 – 255. Bibl.

ORÍGENES (PERIODICAL)

Chacón, Alfredo. La experiencia de *Orígenes. Cuadernos Hispanoamericanos,* no. 511 (Jan 93), pp. 25 – 31.

ORINOCO RIVER VALLEY, VENEZUELA

Castañón, Adolfo. Diario del delta. *Vuelta,* v. 17, no. 201 (Aug 93), pp. 35 – 42.

ORTEGA RICAURTE, CARMEN

Duque Gómez, Luis. Brillante trayectoria de la mujer en la Academia (Commentary on the speech by Carmen Ortega Ricaurte). *Boletín de Historia y Antigüedades,* v. 80, no. 781 (Apr – June 93), pp. 407 – 413.

ORTIZ, FERNANDO

Criticism of specific works

La conquista castellana de las Antillas

Garciga Garciga, Orestes. El estudio de la conquista castellana de las Antillas en un libro inédito de Fernando Ortiz. *Anuario de Estudios Americanos,* v. 49, Suppl. 2 (1992), pp. 253 – 256.

ORTIZ, LOURDES

Criticism of specific works

Urraca

Molinaro, Nina L. Resistance, Gender, and the Mediation of History in Pizarnik's *La condesa sangrienta* and Ortiz's *Urraca. Letras Femeninas,* v. 19, no. 1 – 2 (Spring – Fall 93), pp. 45 – 54. Bibl.

ORTIZ COFER, JUDITH

Criticism and interpretation

Bruce-Novoa, John D. Judith Ortiz Cofer's Rituals of Movement. *The Americas Review,* v. 19, no. 3 – 4 (Winter 91), pp. 88 – 99. Bibl.

Criticism of specific works

The Line of the Sun

Bruce-Novoa, John D. Ritual in Judith Ortiz Cofer's *The Line of the Sun. Confluencia,* v. 8, no. 1 (Fall 92), pp. 61 – 69. Bibl.

ORTIZ DE MONTELLANO, BERNARDO R.

Correspondence, reminiscences, etc.

Ortiz de Montellano, Bernardo R. Buzón de fantasmas: de Bernardo Ortiz de Montellano a Emilio Portes Gil. *Vuelta,* v. 17, no. 199 (June 93), pp. 74 – 75.

— Buzón de fantasmas: de Ortiz de Montellano a Torres Bodet. *Vuelta,* v. 17, no. 198 (May 93), pp. 78 – 79.

ORURO, BOLIVIA

Abercrombie, Thomas Alan. La fiesta del carnaval postcolonial en Oruro: clase, etnicidad y nacionalismo en la danza folklórica (With commentaries by seven historians and a response by the author). *Revista Andina,* v. 10, no. 2 (Dec 92), pp. 279 – 352. Bibl, il.

OSA, ENRIQUE DE LA

Interviews

Tísoc Lindley, Hilda. De los orígenes del APRA en Cuba: el testimonio de Enrique de la Osa. *Cuadernos Americanos,* no. 37, Nueva época (Jan – Feb 93), pp. 198 – 207. Bibl.

OSSA, CARLOS DE LA

Criticism of specific works

Obra poética

Goff, Katrina. La imagen de la mujer en la *Obra poética* de Carlos de la Ossa. *Káñina,* v. 16, no. 1 (Jan – June 92), pp. 29 – 35. Bibl.

OTERO, GUSTAVO ADOLFO

Crespo R., Alberto. Gustavo Adolfo Otero: sus años en Quito. *Signo,* no. 38, Nueva época (Jan – Apr 93), pp. 81 – 89.

OTERO, LISANDRO

Criticism of specific works

En ciudad semejante

Marcelo Pérez, Carmen. *En ciudad semejante* de Lisandro Otero. *Islas,* no. 97 (Sept – Dec 90), pp. 32 – 43. Bibl.

OTERO SILVA, MIGUEL

Criticism and interpretation

Osorio Tejeda, Nelson. La historia y las clases en la narrativa de Miguel Otero Silva. *Casa de las Américas,* no. 190 (Jan – Mar 93), pp. 34 – 41. Bibl.

OTOMI INDIANS

Barrera Carranza, Estanislao. Los mayordomía entre los otomíes. *La Palabra y el Hombre,* no. 81 (Jan – Mar 92), pp. 97 – 119. Bibl, il.

Zimmermann, Klaus. *Sprachkontakt, ethnische Identität und Identitätsbeschädigung: Aspekte der Assimilation der Otomí-Indianer an die hispanophone mexikanische Kultur* reviewed by Eva Gugenberger. *Iberoamericana,* v. 17, no. 49 (1993), pp. 84 – 86.

OVIEDO Y VALDÉS, GONZALO FERNÁNDEZ DE

Bolaños Cárdenas, Alvaro Félix. Panegírico y libelo del primer cronista de Indias, Gonzalo Fernández de Oviedo. *Thesaurus,* v. 45, no. 3 (Sept – Dec 90), pp. 577 – 649. Bibl.

Criticism of specific works

Historia general y natural de las Indias

Gerbi, Antonello. *Nature in the New World: From Christopher Columbus to Gonzalo Fernández de Oviedo* translated by Jeremy Moyle. Reviewed by Rick Hendricks. *Colonial Latin American Historical Review,* v. 1, no. 1 (Fall 92), pp. 120 – 121.

OXKINTOK, MEXICO

Fernández Marquínez, María Yolanda and Alfonso Muñoz Cosme. Estilos arquitectónicos y estadios constructivos en el Grupo May, Oxkintok, Yucatán. *Revista Española de Antropología Americana,* v. 23 (1993), pp. 67 – 82. Bibl, il.

Rivera Dorado, Miguel et al. Trabajos arqueológicos en Oxkintok durante el verano de 1991. *Revista Española de Antropología Americana,* v. 23 (1993), pp. 41 – 65. Bibl, il, tables, maps.

PACHECO, CRISTINA
Criticism and interpretation

Valdés, María Elena de. La obra de Cristina Pacheco: ficción testimonial de la mujer mexicana. *Escritura (Venezuela),* v. 16, no. 31 – 32 (Jan – Dec 91), pp. 271 – 279. Bibl.

PACHECO, JOSÉ EMILIO
Criticism and interpretation

Graniela-Rodríguez, Magda. *El papel del lector en la novela mexicana contemporánea: José Emilio Pacheco y Salvador Elizondo* reviewed by Roberto Bravo. *Hispania (USA),* v. 76, no. 2 (May 93), pp. 287 – 288.

Torres, Daniel. *José Emilio Pacheco: poética y poesía del prosaísmo* reviewed by Frank Dauster. *Hispanic Review,* v. 61, no. 2 (Spring 93), pp. 314 – 315.

PACIFIC AREA
See also

Banks and banking – Pacific Area
Food habits – Pacific Area
Geography, Economic – Pacific Area
Investments, Foreign – Pacific Area
Marine resources – Pacific Area
Pan-Pacific relations
Population – Pacific Area
Power resources – Pacific Area
Telecommunication – Pacific Area
Tourist trade – Pacific Area
Transportation – Pacific Area

Choi, Dae Won. Globalização na era pacífico. *Vozes,* v. 87, no. 4 (July – Aug 93), pp. 13 – 19.

Compean, Guillermo and Rafael Girón Botello. La pesca en la cuenca del Pacífico: el caso del atún en México. *Comercio Exterior,* v. 43, no. 12 (Dec 93), pp. 1195 – 1201. Bibl, tables, charts.

Gerhard, Peter. *Pirates in the Pacific, 1575 – 1742* reviewed by Patrick Bryan. *Caribbean Quarterly,* v. 38, no. 2 – 3 (June – Sept 92), pp. 117 – 118.

Shen, Glen T. Reconstruction of El Niño History from Reef Corals. *Bulletin de l'Institut Français d'Etudes Andines,* v. 22, no. 1 (1993), pp. 125 – 158. Bibl, tables, maps, charts.

Bibliography

Miyazaki, Silvio Yoshiro Mizuguchi. Economias do Pacífico asiático: "tigres e dragões" (Includes a bibliography compiled by Heraldo Vasconcellos). *RAE; Revista de Administração de Empresas,* v. 33, no. 2 (Mar – Apr 93), pp. 112 – 123. Bibl, tables, charts.

PACIFIC ISLANDERS
Guatemala

McCreery, David J. and Doug Munro. The Cargo of the *Montserrat:* Gilbertese Labor in Guatemalan Coffee, 1890 – 1908. *The Americas,* v. 49, no. 3 (Jan 93), pp. 271 – 295. Bibl, tables.

PÁEZ, JOSÉ ANTONIO

Arocha Vargas, Arnaldo. Acto de presentación de los libros *José Antonio Páez* y *Cristóbal Rojas, un pintor venezolano,* pertenecientes a la Biblioteca de Autores y Temas Mirandinos. *Boletín de la Academia Nacional de la Historia (Venezuela),* v. 75, no. 299 (July – Sept 92), pp. 5 – 8.

Hernández Carstens, Eduardo. Discurso de orden pronunciado por el doctor Eduardo Hernández Carstens, cronista oficial de la ciudad de Achaguas, . . . en el acto conmemorativo de los 200 años del nacimiento del general en jefe José Antonio Páez . . . . *Boletín de la Academia Nacional de la Historia (Venezuela),* v. 76, no. 302 (Apr – June 93), pp. 41 – 45.

PAIJÁN COMPLEX, PERU

Chauchat, Claude and Jacques Pelegrin. Tecnología y función de las puntas de Paiján: el aporte de la experimentación. *Latin American Antiquity,* v. 4, no. 4 (Dec 93), pp. 367 – 382. Bibl, il, tables, charts.

PAINTERS
See

Artists

PAINTING
See

Art
Mural painting and decoration

PALACIO DE LIBARONA, AGUSTINA

Sáenz Quesada, María. Agustina Palacio de Libarona, heroína del amor conyugal. *Todo Es Historia,* v. 26, no. 310 (May 93), pp. 70 – 72. Il.

PALACIOS, IRMA

López, Gabriela. Irma Palacios: los elementos terrestres. *Nexos,* v. 16, no. 186 (June 93), pp. 89 – 90. Il.

PALACIOS BERRUECOS, JUANA
See

María de San José

PALENQUE, MEXICO

Ayala F., Maricela and Linda Schele. De poesía e historia: el tablero de los glifos de Palenque. *Vuelta,* v. 17, no. 203 (Oct 93), pp. 25 – 27. Charts.

PALEOBOTANY
Ecuador

Steinitz-Kannan, Miriam et al. The Fossil Diatoms of Lake Yambo, Ecuador: A Possible Record of El Niño Events. *Bulletin de l'Institut Français d'Etudes Andines,* v. 22, no. 1 (1993), pp. 227 – 241. Bibl, il, maps, charts.

Latin America

Villagrán M., Carolina. Una interpretación climática del registro palinológico del último ciclo glacial – postglacial en Sudamérica. *Bulletin de l'Institut Français d'Etudes Andines,* v. 22, no. 1 (1993), pp. 243 – 258. Bibl, maps, charts.

Peru

Bonavia, Duccio and John G. Jones. Análisis de coprolitos de llama (Lama glama) del precerámico tardío de la costa nor central del Perú. *Bulletin de l'Institut Français d'Etudes Andines,* v. 21, no. 3 (1992), pp. 835 – 852. Bibl, tables.

PALEONTOLOGY
See also

Man, Prehistoric

Argentina

Malatesta, Parisina. Tracing Evolution in the Land of the Sand (Translated by Barbara Meza, photographs by Jorge Provenza). *Américas,* v. 45, no. 4 (July – Aug 93), pp. 6 – 13. Il, maps.

PALÉS MATOS, LUIS
Criticism of specific works
Tun tun de pasa y griferia

P-Miñambres, Matías. *Tun tun de pasa y griferia:* perpetuación de estereotipos euroetnologocéntricos en el discurso poético afroantillano de Palés Matos. *Chasqui,* v. 22, no. 2 (Nov 93), pp. 73 – 84. Bibl.

PALMA, RICARDO
Correspondence, reminiscences, etc.

Quesada Pacheco, Miguel Angel. Correspondencia de Carlos Gagini con Rufino José Cuervo y Ricardo Palma. *Káñina,* v. 16, no. 1 (Jan – June 92), pp. 197 – 206.

PALMS

Anderson, Anthony B. et al. *The Subsidy from Nature: Palm Forests, Peasantry, and Development on an Amazon Frontier* reviewed by Kathryn Smith Pyle. *Grassroots Development,* v. 17, no. 1 (1993), pp. 45 – 46. Il.

— *The Subsidy from Nature: Palm Forests, Peasantry, and Development on an Amazon Frontier* reviewed by Emilio F. Moran. *Journal of Developing Areas,* v. 28, no. 1 (Oct 93), pp. 116 – 117.

Borgtaft Pederson, Henrick. Uses and Management of "Aphandra Natalia" (Palmae) in Ecuador. *Bulletin de l'Institut Français d'Etudes Andines,* v. 21, no. 2 (1992), pp. 741 – 753. Bibl, il, tables, maps.

Couturier, Guy and Francis Kahn. Notes on the Insect Fauna of Two Species of "Astrocaryum" (Palmae, Cocoeae, Bactridinae) in Peruvian Amazonia, with Emphasis on Potential Pests of Cultivated Palms. *Bulletin de l'Institut Français d'Etudes Andines,* v. 21, no. 2 (1992), pp. 715 – 725. Bibl, il, tables, maps.

Durán, Rafael and Miguel Franco. Estudio demográfico de "Pseudophoenix sargentii." *Bulletin de l'Institut Français d'Etudes Andines,* v. 21, no. 2 (1992), pp. 609 – 621. Bibl, maps, charts.

Franco, Miguel and Ana Mendoza. Integración clonal en una palma tropical. *Bulletin de l'Institut Français d'Etudes Andines,* v. 21, no. 2 (1992), pp. 623 – 635. Bibl, il, tables, charts.

Galeano Garcés, Gloria. Patrones de distribución de las palmas de Colombia. *Bulletin de l'Institut Français d'Etudes Andines,* v. 21, no. 2 (1992), pp. 599 – 607. Bibl, maps, charts.

Granville, Jean-Jacques de. Life Forms and Growth Strategies of Guianan Palms as Related to Their Ecology. *Bulletin de l'Institut Français d'Etudes Andines,* v. 21, no. 2 (1992), pp. 533 – 548. Bibl, il, tables.

Hodel, Donald R. "Chamaedorea": Diverse Species in Diverse Habitats. *Bulletin de l'Institut Français d'Etudes Andines,* v. 21, no. 2 (1992), pp. 433 – 458. Bibl, il.

Ibarra-Manríquez, Guillermo. Fenología de las palmas de una selva cálido húmeda de México. *Bulletin de l'Institut Français d'Etudes Andines,* v. 21, no. 2 (1992), pp. 669 – 683. Bibl, tables, charts.

Kahn, Francis and Betty Millán. "Astrocaryum" (Palmae) in Amazonia: A Preliminary Treatment. *Bulletin de l'Institut Français d'Etudes Andines,* v. 21, no. 2 (1992), pp. 459 – 531. Bibl, il, tables.

Kahn, Francis et al. Datos preliminares a la actualización de la flora de palamae del Perú: intensidad de herborización y riqueza de las colecciones. *Bulletin de l'Institut Français d'Etudes Andines,* v. 21, no. 2 (1992), pp. 549 – 563. Bibl, tables, maps.

Listabarth, Christian. A Survey of Pollination Strategies in the "Bactridinae" (Palmae). *Bulletin de l'Institut Français d'Etudes Andines,* v. 21, no. 2 (1992), pp. 699 – 714. Bibl, il, tables.

Mejía, Kember. Las palmeras en los mercados de Iquitos. *Bulletin de l'Institut Français d'Etudes Andines,* v. 21, no. 2 (1992), pp. 755 – 769. Bibl, il, tables, maps.

Moraes R., Mónica and Jaime Sarmiento. Contribución al estudio de biología reproductiva de una especie de "Bactris" (Palmae) en el bosque de galería, depto. Beni, Bolivia. *Bulletin de l'Institut Français d'Etudes Andines,* v. 21, no. 2 (1992), pp. 685 – 698. Bibl, il, tables, maps.

Moussa, Farana et al. Las palmeras en los valles principales de la Amazonia peruana. *Bulletin de l'Institut Français d'Etudes Andines,* v. 21, no. 2 (1992), pp. 565 – 597. Maps.

Orellana, Roger. Síndromes morfológicos y funcionales de las palmas de la península de Yucatán. *Bulletin de l'Institut Français d'Etudes Andines,* v. 21, no. 2 (1992), pp. 651 – 667. Bibl, tables, maps, charts.

PALOMARES, RAMÓN

Criticism and interpretation

Guzmán, Patricia. El lugar como absoluto: Vicente Gerbasi, Ramón Palomares y Luis Alberto Crespo. *Inti,* no. 37 – 38 (Spring – Fall 93), pp. 107 – 115. Bibl.

LA PAMPA, ARGENTINA

Boschín, María Teresa. Historia de las investigaciones arqueológicas en Pampa y Patagonia. *Runa,* v. 20 (1991 – 1992), pp. 111 – 114. Bibl.

Ramos, Jorge Abelardo. *La aventura de La Pampa argentina: arquitectura, ambiente y cultura* reviewed by Alicia Novick. *Todo Es Historia,* v. 27, no. 312 (July 93), p. 77. Il.

PAN-AMERICANISM

See also
Federation of the West Indies
Organization of American States

Baptista Gumucio, Mariano. Una presencia insoslayable y otros derechos de los latinoamericanos. *Signo,* no. 38, Nueva época (Jan – Apr 93), pp. 91 – 93.

Bazán, Armando Raúl. Americanismo y nacionalismo en la emancipación sudamericana. *Revista de Historia de América,* no. 112 (July – Dec 91), pp. 5 – 19.

Briceño Perozo, Mario. Factores de diferenciación e instancias integradoras en la experiencia del mundo iberoamericano: Bolívar, arquitecto de la unión. *Boletín de la Academia Nacional de la Historia (Venezuela),* v. 76, no. 302 (Apr – June 93), pp. 21 – 33. Bibl.

Díaz, María Eugenia. Liberación en las luchas latinoamericanas. *Islas,* no. 98 (Jan – Apr 91), pp. 167 – 176. Charts.

Febres, Laura M. Fragmentos para la comprensión de América, 1880 a 1900. *Montalbán,* no. 24 (1992), pp. 253 – 269. Bibl.

Fernández Retamar, Roberto. Más de cien años de previsión: algunas reflexiones sobre el concepto martiano de *Nuestra América.* *Cuadernos Americanos,* no. 40, Nueva época (July – Aug 93), pp. 65 – 77.

Hurrell, Andrew. Os blocos regionais nas Américas (Translated by João Roberto Martins Filho). *Revista Brasileira de Ciências Sociais,* v. 8, no. 22 (June 93), pp. 98 – 118. Bibl.

Rivadeneira Vargas, Antonio José. El pensamiento integrador de Carlos Sanz de Santamaría. *Boletín de Historia y Antigüedades,* v. 79, no. 779 (Oct – Dec 92), pp. 953 – 973. Bibl.

PAN-PACIFIC RELATIONS

See also
Pacific Area

Choi, Dae Won. The Pacific Basin and Latin America. *CEPAL Review,* no. 49 (Apr 93), pp. 21 – 40. Bibl, tables, charts.

Cuadra, Héctor. La cuenca del Pacífico en los albores del siglo XXI. *Comercio Exterior,* v. 43, no. 12 (Dec 93), pp. 1107 – 1110. Bibl, tables.

López Villafañe, Víctor. La integración económica en la cuenca del Pacífico: el reto de la América del Norte. *Comercio Exterior,* v. 43, no. 12 (Dec 93), pp. 1145 – 1152. Bibl, tables.

Millán Bojalil, Julio Alfonso. La cuenca del Pacífico: mito o realidad. *Comercio Exterior,* v. 43, no. 12 (Dec 93), pp. 1121 – 1127. Bibl.

Palacios L., Juan José. Inversión e integración regional en el Pacífico: entre los acuerdos y los procesos "naturales." *Comercio Exterior,* v. 43, no. 12 (Dec 93), pp. 1128 – 1138. Bibl, tables.

Ramírez Bonilla, Juan José. ¿Hacia la creación de la comunidad del Pacífico? *Comercio Exterior,* v. 43, no. 12 (Dec 93), pp. 1139 – 1144. Tables.

Congresses

Silva C., Alberto. Una "nueva frontera": el Pacífico. *Mensaje,* v. 42, no. 416 (Jan – Feb 93), pp. 41 – 42.

PANAMA

See also
Agriculture – Panama
Blacks – Panama
Cities and towns – Panama
Community centers – Panama
Darién, Panama
Ecology and development – Panama
Education, Higher – Panama
Education, Secondary – Panama
Education and state – Panama
Educational accountability – Panama

Elections – Panama
Elite (Social sciences) – Panama
Emblems, National – Panama
Family – Panama
Folk dancing – Panama
Folk literature – Panama
Folk medicine – Panama
Medicine – Panama
Military in government – Panama
Motion pictures – Panama
Natá, Panama
National security – Panama
Nurses – Panama
Panama (City)
Panama Canal
Political parties – Panama
Pregnancy – Panama
Public health – Panama
San Blas, Panama
Social classes – Panama
Spanish language – Panama
Students – Panama
Teaching and teachers – Panama
Technology – Panama
Women authors – Panama

Constitutional law

Scranton, Margaret E. Consolidation after Imposition: Panama's 1992 Referendum. *Journal of Inter-American Studies and World Affairs,* v. 35, no. 3 (Fall 93), pp. 65 – 102. Bibl, tables.

Description and travel

Medina A., Gilberto Javier. Exploraciones entre Chagres a Panamá: cartografía de la ciudad. *Revista Cultural Lotería,* v. 50, no. 385 (Sept – Oct 91), pp. 5 – 45. Bibl, tables, maps.

Discovery and exploration

Escarreola Palacio, Rommel. El conquistador Nuñez de Balboa. *Revista Cultural Lotería,* v. 51, no. 391 (Sept – Oct 92), pp. 22 – 46. Bibl.

Medina A., Gilberto Javier. La realidad del descubrimiento de las Indias occidentales. *Revista Cultural Lotería,* v. 51, no. 391 (Sept – Oct 92), pp. 58 – 79. Bibl, maps.

Economic conditions

Weeks, John and Andrew S. Zimbalist. *Panama at the Crossroads: Economic Development and Political Change in the Twentieth Century* reviewed by George Irvin. *Bulletin of Latin American Research,* v. 12, no. 2 (May 93), pp. 236 – 238.

— *Panama at the Crossroads: Economic Development and Political Change in the Twentieth Century* reviewed by Robert Edward Looney. *Revista Interamericana de Bibliografía,* v. 42, no. 2 (1992), pp. 293 – 294.

Foreign relations

Bibliography

Millett, Richard L. Review Essay: Looking beyond the Invasion; A Review of Recent Books on Panama. *Journal of Inter-American Studies and World Affairs,* v. 35, no. 3 (Fall 93), pp. 173 – 180. Bibl.

United States

Conniff, Michael L. *Panama and the United States: The Forced Alliance* reviewed by Walter Lafeber. *Hispanic American Historical Review,* v. 73, no. 1 (Feb 93), pp. 191 – 192.

Krosigk, Friedrich von. Panama und die Grenzen US-amerikanischer Hegemonie: Überlegungen zum Konzept der Gegenmacht. *Zeitschrift für Lateinamerika Wien,* no. 43 (1992), pp. 81 – 93. Bibl, tables.

History

Ruiloba C., Rafael. "No me resigno a que el lenguaje pierda su capacidad de alucinar": entrevista con Lionel Méndez D'Avila. *USAC,* no. 12 (Dec 90), pp. 28 – 30.

Bibliography

Ropp, Steve C. What Have We Learned from the Noriega Crisis? (Review article). *Latin American Research Review,* v. 28, no. 3 (1993), pp. 189 – 196.

Sources

Figueroa Navarro, Alfredo. *Testamento y sociedad en el Istmo de Panamá, siglos XVIII y XIX* reviewed by Christopher Ward. *Hispanic American Historical Review,* v. 73, no. 3 (Aug 93), pp. 509 – 510.

Politics and government

Castro, Nils. Panamá: de movimientos sociales a partidos populares. *Nueva Sociedad,* no. 125 (May – June 93), pp. 15 – 19.

Furlong, William Leon. Panama: The Difficult Transition towards Democracy. *Journal of Inter-American Studies and World Affairs,* v. 35, no. 3 (Fall 93), pp. 19 – 64. Bibl, tables, charts.

Linares, Julio E. Política y moral. *Revista Cultural Lotería,* v. 50, no. 383 (May – June 91), pp. 33 – 42. Bibl.

Weeks, John and Andrew S. Zimbalist. *Panama at the Crossroads: Economic Development and Political Change in the Twentieth Century* reviewed by George Irvin. *Bulletin of Latin American Research,* v. 12, no. 2 (May 93), pp. 236 – 238.

— *Panama at the Crossroads: Economic Development and Political Change in the Twentieth Century* reviewed by Robert Edward Looney. *Revista Interamericana de Bibliografía,* v. 42, no. 2 (1992), pp. 293 – 294.

Bibliography

Millett, Richard L. Review Essay: Looking beyond the Invasion; A Review of Recent Books on Panama. *Journal of Inter-American Studies and World Affairs,* v. 35, no. 3 (Fall 93), pp. 173 – 180. Bibl.

Social conditions

Lasso de Paulis, Marixa. La mentalidad en la sociedad colonial: la importancia de la etiqueta y de la ceremonia en los conflictos políticos del siglo XVII panameño. *Revista Cultural Lotería,* v. 51, no. 391 (Sept – Oct 92), pp. 105 – 111. Bibl.

PANAMA (CITY)

Medina A., Gilberto Javier. Exploraciones entre Chagres a Panamá: cartografía de la ciudad. *Revista Cultural Lotería,* v. 50, no. 385 (Sept – Oct 91), pp. 5 – 45. Bibl, tables, maps.

PANAMA (CITY). CONGRESS, 1826

Illueca Sibauste, Aníbal. El congreso anfictiónico de 1826 como contribución de América al derecho internacional. *Revista Cultural Lotería,* v. 51, no. 388 (Mar – Apr 92), pp. 34 – 47.

PANAMA CANAL

Gandásegui, Marco A., Jr. The Military Regimes of Panama. *Journal of Inter-American Studies and World Affairs,* v. 35, no. 3 (Fall 93), pp. 1 – 17.

Heckadon Moreno, Stanley. Impact of Development on the Panama Canal Environment (Translated by Jane Marchi). *Journal of Inter-American Studies and World Affairs,* v. 35, no. 3 (Fall 93), pp. 129 – 149. Bibl.

Manfredo, Fernando. The Future of the Panama Canal. *Journal of Inter-American Studies and World Affairs,* v. 35, no. 3 (Fall 93), pp. 103 – 128.

Manwaring, Max G. The Security of Panama and the Canal: Now and for the Future. *Journal of Inter-American Studies and World Affairs,* v. 35, no. 3 (Fall 93), pp. 151 – 170.

PANAMANIAN LITERATURE

Jaramillo Levi, Enrique, ed. *When New Flowers Bloomed: Short Stories by Women Writers from Costa Rica and Panama* reviewed by Cynthia Tompkins. *World Literature Today,* v. 67, no. 1 (Winter 93), pp. 164 – 165. Il.

PANI, MARIO

González de León, Teodoro. Mario Pani. *Vuelta,* v. 17, no. 199 (June 93), pp. 58 – 59.

PANTÍN, YOLANDA

Biobibliography

Pantín, Yolanda. De *Casa o lobo* al *Cielo de París:* el futuro imposible. *Inti,* no. 37 – 38 (Spring – Fall 93), pp. 47 – 55.

PÁNUCO, MEXICO

Gamboa Ojeda, Leticia. Historia de una pequeña empresa: la Compañía Petrolera de Puebla en Pánuco, 1916 – 1924. *La Palabra y el Hombre,* no. 83 (July – Sept 92), pp. 219 – 253. Bibl, tables, maps.

PAOLETTI, MARIO ARGENTINO

Correspondence, reminiscences, etc.

Paoletti, Mario Argentino. Tiempo de desprecio. *Cuadernos Hispanoamericanos,* no. 517 – 519 (July – Sept 93), pp. 581 – 586.

PAPAGAYO SITE, COSTA RICA

Baudez, Claude-François et al. *Papagayo: un hameau précolombien du Costa Rica* reviewed by Frederick W. Lange. *Latin American Antiquity,* v. 4, no. 4 (Dec 93), pp. 390 – 392.

PARÁ, BRAZIL

Aguiar, José Vangeliso de and José de Jesus Sousa Lemos. Produção do caupi irrigado em Bragança, Pará. *Revista de Economia e Sociologia Rural,* v. 30, no. 3 (July – Sept 92), pp. 239 – 252. Bibl, tables, charts.

Santana, Antônio Cordeiro de. Custo social da depredação florestal no Pará: o caso da castanha-do-Brasil. *Revista de Economia e Sociologia Rural,* v. 30, no. 3 (July – Sept 92), pp. 253 – 269. Bibl, tables, charts.

Schmink, Marianne and Charles Howard Wood. *Contested Frontiers in Amazonia* reviewed by Philip A. Dennis. *Journal of Developing Areas,* v. 28, no. 1 (Oct 93), pp. 111 – 113.

Valente, Edna Fátima Barros. Os filhos pródigos da educação pública: um estudo sobre os evadidos da escola pública num bairro periférico do município de Santarém. *Revista Brasileira de Estudos Pedagógicos,* v. 72, no. 172 (Sept – Dec 91), pp. 397 – 400.

PARAGUAY

See also

Agriculture – Paraguay
Agriculture, Cooperative – Paraguay
Agriculture and state – Paraguay
Arabs – Paraguay
Bilingualism – Paraguay
Business enterprises – Paraguay
Chaco War, 1932 – 1935
Church architecture – Paraguay
Church music – Paraguay
Cooperatives – Paraguay
Ecology and development – Paraguay
Elections – Paraguay
Geopolitics – Paraguay
Industry and state – Paraguay
Literature and history – Paraguay
Marriage – Paraguay
Regional planning – Paraguay
Religion and politics – Paraguay
Spanish language – Paraguay
State capitalism – Paraguay
Tea – Paraguay
Terrorism – Paraguay
Theater – Paraguay
Tobacco – Paraguay
Trade unions – Paraguay
Undocumented workers – Paraguay
Women – Paraguay
Women authors – Paraguay
Women in literature – Paraguay

Bibliography

Documentación paraguaya. *Revista Paraguaya de Sociología,* v. 29 – 30, no. 84 – 86 (May 92 – Apr 93), All issues.

Civilization

Campos Ruiz Díaz, Daniel, ed. *Desarrollo en el Paraguay: contribuciones a una visión global* (Review). *Revista Paraguaya de Sociología,* v. 29, no. 85 (Sept – Dec 92), pp. 187 – 188.

Commerce

History

Santamaría, Daniel J. La guerra Guaykurú: expansión colonial y conflicto interétnico en la cuenca del alto Paraguay, siglo XVIII. *Jahrbuch für Geschichte von Staat, Wirtschaft und Gesellschaft Lateinamerikas,* v. 29 (1992), pp. 121 – 148. Bibl.

Whigham, Thomas Lyle. *The Politics of River Trade: Tradition and Development in the Upper Plata, 1780 – 1870* reviewed by James Schofield Saeger. *The Americas,* v. 49, no. 4 (Apr 93), pp. 552 – 553.

— *The Politics of River Trade: Tradition and Development in the Upper Plata, 1780 – 1870* reviewed by Jeremy Adelman. *Journal of Latin American Studies,* v. 25, no. 1 (Feb 93), pp. 194 – 196.

Economic conditions

Whigham, Thomas Lyle. La transformación económica del Paraguay: una perspectiva oficial de 1863. *Revista Paraguaya de Sociología,* v. 29, no. 85 (Sept – Dec 92), pp. 95 – 98.

— La transformación económica del Paraguay: una perspectiva oficial de 1863. *Revista Paraguaya de Sociología,* v. 30, no. 86 (Jan – Apr 93), pp. 67 – 70.

Economic policy

Borda, Dionisio. La estatización de la economía y la privatización del estado en el Paraguay, 1954 – 1989. *Estudios Paraguayos,* v. 17, no. 1 – 2 (1989 – 1993), pp. 37 – 89. Bibl, tables.

Foreign economic relations

Argentina

Argentina – Paraguay: Tratado para el Establecimiento de un Estatuto de Empresas Binacionales Argentino – Paraguayas. *Integración Latinoamericana,* v. 17, no. 184 (Nov 92), pp. 75 – 78.

Southern Cone of South America

Achard, Diego et al. MERCOSUR: élites y política en Paraguay y Uruguay. *Integración Latinoamericana,* v. 18, no. 192 (Aug 93), pp. 59 – 61.

Foreign relations

Argentina

Argentina – Paraguay (Six documents dealing with relations between Argentina and Paraguay). *Integración Latinoamericana,* v. 17, no. 185 (Dec 92), pp. 72 – 79.

History

Beraza, Luis Fernando. Perón, Braden y la guerra civil en el Paraguay, 1947. *Todo Es Historia,* v. 26, no. 307 (Feb 93), pp. 84 – 86. Bibl, il.

Cooney, Jerry Wilson. *Economía y sociedad en la Intendencia del Paraguay* reviewed by Edberto Oscar Acevedo. *Revista de Historia de América,* no. 112 (July – Dec 91), pp. 181 – 183.

Raine, Philip. Rebeliones de los comuneros paraguayos. *Hoy Es Historia,* v. 10, no. 57 (Apr – May 93), pp. 54 – 60.

Politics and government

Rodríguez, José Carlos. Paraguay: mansa transición democrática. *Nueva Sociedad,* no. 127 (Sept – Oct 93), pp. 18 – 22.

Bibliography

Sondrol, Paul C. Explaining and Reconceptualizing Underdevelopment: Paraguay and Uruguay (Review article). *Latin American Research Review,* v. 28, no. 3 (1993), pp. 235 – 250. Bibl.

Rural conditions

Kleinpenning, Jan M. G. *Rural Paraguay, 1870 – 1932* reviewed by Jerry W. Cooney. *Hispanic American Historical Review,* v. 73, no. 4 (Nov 93), pp. 710 – 711.

— *Rural Paraguay, 1870 – 1932* reviewed by R. Andrew Nickson. *Bulletin of Latin American Research,* v. 12, no. 2 (May 93), pp. 220 – 221.

— *Rural Paraguay, 1870 – 1932* reviewed by Vera Blinn Reber. *Journal of Latin American Studies,* v. 25, no. 2 (May 93), pp. 398 – 399.

Ocampos, Genoveva. *Mujeres campesinas: estrategias de vida* reviewed by Sylvia Chant. *European Review of Latin American and Caribbean Studies,* no. 54 (June 93), pp. 137 – 138.

PARAGUAYAN POETRY

Fernández, Miguel Angel and Renée Ferrer de Arrellaga, eds. *Poetisas del Paraguay* reviewed by Claude Castro. *Caravelle,* no. 60 (1993), pp. 176 – 178.

PARAGUAYAN WAR, 1865 – 1870

Thompson, George. *La guerra del Paraguay* (Review). *Revista Paraguaya de Sociología,* v. 29, no. 84 (May – Aug 92), p. 205. Il.

PARAGUAYANS

Brazil

Wilcox, Robert. Paraguayans and the Making of the Brazilian Far West, 1870 – 1935. *The Americas,* v. 49, no. 4 (Apr 93), pp. 479 – 512. Bibl, tables, maps.

PARAÍBA, BRAZIL

Buvinich, Manuel J. Rojas. The Evaluation of Rural Development Projects Using the Social Accounting Matrix Approach. *Revista Brasileira de Economia,* v. 46, no. 4 (Oct – Dec 92), pp. 555 – 593. Bibl, tables.

Cardoso, Maria Francisca Thereza. Organização e reorganização do espaço no vale do Paraíba do sul: uma análise geográfica até 1940. *Revista Brasileira de Geografia,* v. 53, no. 1 (Jan – Mar 91), pp. 81 – 135. Bibl, maps.

Grabois, José et al. A organização do espaço no baixo vale do Taperoá: uma ocupação extensiva em mudança. *Revista Brasileira de Geografia,* v. 53, no. 4 (Oct – Dec 91), pp. 81 – 114. Bibl, il, tables, maps.

PARANÁ, BRAZIL

Carvalho, Flávio Condé de and Samira Aóun Marques. Concentração municipal do beneficiamento de algodão no estado do Paraná nos anos oitenta. *Revista de Economia e Sociologia Rural,* v. 30, no. 2 (Apr – June 92), pp. 149 – 157. Bibl, tables.

Pereira, Laércio Barbosa. O estado e o desempenho da agricultura paranaense no período de 1975 – 1985. *Revista de Economia e Sociologia Rural,* v. 30, no. 2 (Apr – June 92), pp. 115 – 133. Bibl, tables.

PARANHOS, JOSÉ MARIA DA SILVA

See
Rio Branco, José Maria da Silva Paranhos

PARASITES

Central America

Monroy de Gómez, Carlota. Serología en una población centroamericana infectada con "Trypanosoma Cruzi," "T. Rangeli" y "Leishmania Ssp." *USAC,* no. 13 (Mar 91), pp. 76 – 80. Bibl, tables.

Mexico

Vachon, Michael. Onchocerciasis in Chiapas, Mexico. *Geographical Review,* v. 83, no. 2 (Apr 93), pp. 141 – 149. Bibl, il, maps.

PARDO GARCÍA, GERMÁN

Obituaries

Páez Escobar, Gustavo. Germán Pardo García: el ocaso del héroe. *Boletín de Historia y Antigüedades,* v. 79, no. 779 (Oct – Dec 92), pp. 1085 – 1091.

PARENT AND CHILD

Acuña, Marlene. La adopción: una alternativa de reubicación del menor abandonado. *Revista de Ciencias Sociales (Costa Rica),* no. 59 (Mar 93), pp. 37 – 46. Bibl, il.

Ahmeduzzaman, Mohammad and Jaipaul L. Roopnarine. Puerto Rican Fathers' Involvement with Their Preschool-Age Children. *Hispanic Journal of Behavioral Sciences,* v. 15, no. 1 (Feb 93), pp. 96 – 107. Bibl, tables.

Coriat R., Carola and Mario de Obaldía A. La influencia de la abuela en la percepción familiar del niño bajo su cuidado. *Revista Cultural Lotería,* v. 50, no. 383 (May – June 91), pp. 74 – 93. Bibl, tables.

Edwards, Marta. Percepción de la familia y de la formación de los hijos. *Estudios Públicos (Chile),* no. 52 (Spring 93), pp. 191 – 214. Tables, charts.

Flores Santamaría, Dunia et al. Reflexiones en torno a la adopción. *Revista de Ciencias Sociales (Costa Rica),* no. 59 (Mar 93), pp. 47 – 51.

Guevara, Nancy. Fábricas de bebés: ¿Fantasía o profecía? (Translated by Victoria Zamudio Jasso). *Fem,* v. 17, no. 121 (Mar 93), pp. 4 – 8. Bibl.

Romero C., Paulino. Vida familiar y adolescencia. *Revista Cultural Lotería,* v. 50, no. 385 (Sept – Oct 91), pp. 73 – 82. Bibl.

Scheper-Hughes, Nancy. *Death without Weeping: The Violence of Everyday Life in Brazil* reviewed by Bernardo Kucinski. *Journal of Latin American Studies,* v. 25, no. 2 (May 93), pp. 419 – 420.

— *Death without Weeping: The Violence of Everyday Life in Brazil* reviewed by Glenn W. Erickson and Sandra S. Fernandes Erickson. *Luso-Brazilian Review,* v. 30, no. 1 (Summer 93), pp. 142 – 144.

Law and legislation

Labariega Villanueva, Pedro Gabriel. La adopción internacional de menores y sus repercusiones en las relaciones internacionales. *Relaciones Internacionales (Mexico),* v. 14, Nueva época, no. 55 (July – Sept 92), pp. 61 – 64. Charts.

PARENT – TEACHER RELATIONSHIPS

Lopez, Linda C. Mexican-American and Anglo-American Parental Involvement with a Public Elementary School: An Exploratory Study. *Hispanic Journal of Behavioral Sciences,* v. 15, no. 1 (Feb 93), pp. 150 – 155. Bibl, tables.

Martin, Christopher James. The Dynamics of School Relations on the Urban Periphery of Guadalajara, Western Mexico. *European Review of Latin American and Caribbean Studies,* no. 53 (Dec 92), pp. 61 – 81.

PARKS

See also
Natural areas

Belize

Day, Michael J. The Geomorphology and Hydrology of the Blue Hole, Caves Branch. *Belizean Studies,* v. 20, no. 3 (Dec 92), pp. 3 – 10. Bibl, maps, charts.

Costa Rica

Girot, Pascal-Olivier. Parcs nationaux et développement rural au Costa Rica: mythes et réalités. *Tiers Monde,* v. 34, no. 134 (Apr – June 93), pp. 405 – 421. Bibl, tables, maps, charts.

Mexico

Tabasco: Yumká; 30 años adelante en la protección ecológica. *Plural (Mexico),* v. 22, no. 262 (July 93), Insert. Il.

Peru

Leo, Mariella. Problemática del parque nacional Río Abiseo. *Amazonía Peruana,* v. 11, no. 21 (Sept 92), pp. 109 – 144. Bibl, il, tables, maps, charts.

Venezuela

Casanova, Ramón Vicente et al. Consideraciones sobre un proyecto vial: carretera Mérida – La Culata – Tucani. *Derecho y Reforma Agraria,* no. 23 (1992), pp. 163 – 183.

Law and legislation

Pérez, Carlos Andrés. Venezuela: Decreto 1636 que crea el parque nacional Parima – Tapirapeco en el alto Orinoco. *Anuario Indigenista,* v. 30 (Dec 91), pp. 509 – 512.

PARODI, ROBERTO

Cuevas, José Luis. Roberto Parodi, transvanguardista. *Plural (Mexico),* v. 22, no. 257 (Feb 93), pp. 41 – 44. Il.

Interviews

Conde, Teresa del. Diálogo con Roberto Parodi. *Plural (Mexico),* v. 22, no. 257 (Feb 93), p. 45.

PARODY

See
Satire

PARRA, NICANOR

Criticism and interpretation

Sepúlveda Llanos, Fidel. Nicanor, Violeta, Roberto Parra: encuentro de tradición y vanguardia. *Aisthesis,* no. 24 (1991), pp. 29 – 42. Bibl.

PARRA, ROBERTO

Sepúlveda Llanos, Fidel. Nicanor, Violeta, Roberto Parra: encuentro de tradición y vanguardia. *Aisthesis,* no. 24 (1991), pp. 29 – 42. Bibl.

PARRA, TERESA DE LA

Criticism of specific works

Las memorias de Mamá Blanca

Bohórquez R., Douglas. Re-escritura de lo oral y de lo rural en *Las memorias de Mamá Blanca. Escritura (Venezuela),* v. 17, no. 33 – 34 (Jan – Dec 92), pp. 3 – 19.

PARRA, VIOLETA

Criticism and interpretation

Agosín, Marjorie. Gestos y rostros de mujeres: Gabriela Mistral y Violeta Parra. *Plural (Mexico),* v. 22, no. 260 (May 93), pp. 60 – 63.

Agosín, Marjorie and Inés Dölz-Blackburn. *Violeta Parra o la expresión inefable: un análisis crítico de su poesía, prosa y pintura* reviewed by Beth Pollack. *Chasqui,* v. 22, no. 2 (Nov 93), pp. 179 – 180.

Sepúlveda Llanos, Fidel. Nicanor, Violeta, Roberto Parra: encuentro de tradición y vanguardia. *Aisthesis,* no. 24 (1991), pp. 29 – 42. Bibl.

PARTIDO APRISTA PERUANA

See
Alianza Popular Revolucionaria Americana

PARTIDO COMUNISTA BRASILEIRO

Hentschke, Jens. Alternativas del desarrollo histórico en el Brasil en los años veinte: contribución a la discusión. *Islas,* no. 97 (Sept – Dec 90), pp. 26 – 31. Bibl.

PARTIDO COMUNISTA DE CUBA

Aguila, Juan M. del. The Party, the Fourth Congress, and the Process of Counter-Reform. *Cuban Studies/Estudios Cubanos,* v. 23 (1993), pp. 71 – 90. Bibl, tables.

Roman, Peter. Representative Government in Socialist Cuba. *Latin American Perspectives,* v. 20, no. 1 (Winter 93), pp. 7 – 27.

PARTIDO COMUNISTA MEXICANO

Carr, Barry. *Marxism and Communism in Twentieth-Century Mexico* reviewed by George Philip. *Bulletin of Latin American Research,* v. 12, no. 2 (May 93), pp. 230 – 231.

PARTIDO DE ACCIÓN NACIONAL (MEXICO)

Carrillo, Mario Alejandro and Miguel Angel Romero Miranda. Un rostro nuevo en una vieja identidad: el Foro Doctrinario y Democrático en la formación de un nuevo partido político. *El Cotidiano,* v. 9, no. 53 (Mar – Apr 93), pp. 105 – 109. Bibl, il.

Córdova, Arnaldo. El PAN: partido gobernante. *Revista Mexicana de Sociología,* v. 54, no. 3 (July – Sept 92), pp. 221 – 240. Bibl.

Cronología: Partido Acción Nacional; rumbo al '94. *El Cotidiano,* v. 10, no. 58 (Oct – Nov 93), pp. 87 – 89.

Reynoso, Víctor Manuel. El Partido Acción Nacional: ¿La oposición hará gobierno? *Revista Mexicana de Sociología,* v. 55, no. 2 (Apr – June 93), pp. 133 – 151.

Romero Miranda, Miguel Angel and Arturo Venegas. Acción Nacional: consolidar espacios de poder regional. *El Cotidiano,* v. 10, no. 57 (Aug – Sept 93), pp. 79 – 85. Il.

PARTIDO DE LA REVOLUCIÓN DEMOCRÁTICA (MEXICO)

Cronología: PRD "en búsqueda de ser partido." *El Cotidiano,* v. 10, no. 58 (Oct – Nov 93), pp. 89 – 90.

Romero Miranda, Miguel Angel. PRD: futuro inmediato. *El Cotidiano,* v. 9, no. 55 (June 93), pp. 99 – 102. Il.

Villar, Samuel I. del. El programa económico del PRD. *Nexos,* v. 16, no. 192 (Dec 93), pp. 41 – 45.

PARTIDO DOS TRABALHADORES (BRAZIL)

Keck, Margaret E. *The Workers' Party and Democratization in Brazil* reviewed by Thomas E. Skidmore. *Hispanic American Historical Review,* v. 73, no. 2 (May 93), pp. 325 – 326.

Sader, Emir and Ken Silverstein. *Without Fear of Being Happy: Lula, the Workers Party, and Brazil* reviewed by Joel Wolfe. *The Americas,* v. 49, no. 4 (Apr 93), pp. 566 – 568.

— *Without Fear of Being Happy: Lula, the Workers Party, and Brazil* reviewed by John Humphrey. *Bulletin of Latin American Research,* v. 12, no. 3 (Sept 93), p. 347.

— *Without Fear of Being Happy: Lula, the Workers Party, and Brazil* reviewed by Paul Cammack. *Journal of Latin American Studies,* v. 25, no. 3 (Oct 93), pp. 666 – 667.

Simões, Júlio Assis. *O dilema da participação popular: a etnografia de um caso* reviewed by Cláudio Novaes Pinto Coelho. *Revista Brasileira de Ciências Sociais,* v. 8, no. 22 (June 93), pp. 154 – 155.

PARTIDO LIBERACIÓN NACIONAL (COSTA RICA)

Solís Avendaño, Manuel. El ascenso de la ideología de la producción en Costa Rica: el Partido Liberación Nacional. *Revista de Ciencias Sociales (Costa Rica),* no. 60 (June 93), pp. 85 – 100. Bibl.

PARTIDO NACIONAL (URUGUAY)

Pedoja Riet, Eduardo. Algunas causas que determinaron la derrota del Partido Nacional en 1966. *Hoy Es Historia,* v. 10, no. 60 (Nov – Dec 93), pp. 34 – 38. Il.

PARTIDO REVOLUCIONARIO INSTITUCIONAL (MEXICO)

Alcocer, Jorge. La tercera refundación del PRI. *Revista Mexicana de Sociología,* v. 55, no. 2 (Apr – June 93), pp. 119 – 131. Bibl.

Arroyo Alejandre, Jesús and Stephen D. Morris. The Electoral Recovery of the PRI in Guadalajara, Mexico, 1988 – 1992. *Bulletin of Latin American Research,* v. 12, no. 1 (Jan 93), pp. 91 – 102. Bibl, tables.

Bolívar Espinoza, Augusto et al. Partido sin competencia, luego competencia de partidos. *El Cotidiano,* v. 10, no. 57 (Aug – Sept 93), pp. 60 – 72. Il, tables.

— Los síntomas de la víspera. *El Cotidiano,* v. 9, no. 56 (July 93), pp. 60 – 68. Il.

Cronología: El PRI en el camino de la refundación y las elecciones de 1994; enero – junio de 1993. *El Cotidiano,* v. 10, no. 58 (Oct – Nov 93), pp. 86 – 87.

Galve-Peritore, Ana Karina and N. Patrick Peritore. Cleavage and Polarization in Mexico's Ruling Party: A Field Study of the 1988 Presidential Election. *Journal of Developing Areas,* v. 28, no. 1 (Oct 93), pp. 67 – 88. Bibl, tables.

Mora Heredia, Juan and Raúl Rodríguez Guillén. El agotamiento del autoritarismo con legitimidad y la sucesión presidencial. *El Cotidiano,* v. 10, no. 58 (Oct – Nov 93), pp. 22 – 28. Il, tables.

Peschard, Jacqueline. Entre lo nuevo y lo viejo: la sucesión de 1994. *El Cotidiano,* v. 10, no. 58 (Oct – Nov 93), pp. 3 – 7. Il.

Reyes del Campillo, Juan. El PRI, el sistema de partidos y la sucesión presidencial. *El Cotidiano,* v. 8, no. 52 (Jan – Feb 93), pp. 10 – 12.

Schmidt, Samuel. Lo tortuoso de la democratización mexicana. *Estudios Interdisciplinarios de América Latina y el Caribe,* v. 4, no. 1 (Jan – June 93), pp. 93 – 114. Bibl.

PASCOE, JUAN
Criticism of specific works
Cornelio Adrián César

Segovia, Francisco. Juan Pascoe y Cornelio Adrián César, impresores de México. *Artes de México,* no. 19 (Spring 93), pp. 111 – 113. Il.

PASTO INDIANS

Cárdenas Arroyo, Felipe. Pastos y quillacingas: dos grupos étnicos en busca de identidad arqueológica. *Revista Colombiana de Antropología,* v. 29 (1992), pp. 63 – 79. Bibl, il, tables.

Groot de Mahecha, Ana María and Eva María Hooykaas. *Intento de delimitación del territorio de los grupos étnicos pastos y quillacingas en el altiplano nariñense* reviewed by María Clemencia Ramírez de Jara. *Revista Colombiana de Antropología,* v. 29 (1992), pp. 242 – 246. Bibl.

PATAGONIA

Boschín, María Teresa. Historia de las investigaciones arqueológicas en Pampa y Patagonia. *Runa,* v. 20 (1991 – 1992), pp. 111 – 114. Bibl.

Gómez Otero, Julieta. The Function of Small Rock Shelters in the Magallanes IV Phase Settlement System, South Patagonia. *Latin American Antiquity,* v. 4, no. 4 (Dec 93), pp. 325 – 345. Bibl, il, tables, maps, charts.

Schillat, Monika. Los gigantes patagónicos: historia de una leyenda. *Todo Es Historia,* v. 26, no. 309 (Apr 93), pp. 60 – 66. Bibl, il.

PATEMAN, CAROLE
Criticism of specific works
Participation and Democratic Theory

Barretto, Vicente. Democracia, participação e cidadania. *Revista Brasileira de Estudos Políticos,* no. 76 (Jan 93), pp. 141 – 145.

PATRONAGE, POLITICAL
Jamaica

Edie, Carlene J. *Democracy by Default: Dependency and Clientelism in Jamaica* reviewed by Tony Thorndike. *Studies in Comparative International Development,* v. 27, no. 2 (Summer 92), pp. 108 – 110.

Latin America

Barbosa Estepa, Reinaldo. Clientelismo y antidemocracia: la acción política en la formación de la conciencia social. *Islas,* no. 96 (May – Aug 90), pp. 5 – 17. Bibl.

PÁTZCUARO, MEXICO

Müller, Gabriele et al. *Pátzcuaro, Romantik und Kommerzialität* reviewed by Thomas D. Schoonover. *Hispanic American Historical Review,* v. 73, no. 2 (May 93), pp. 338 – 339.

PAULS, ALAN
Correspondence, reminiscences, etc.

Pauls, Alan. La retrospectiva intermitente. *Cuadernos Hispanoamericanos,* no. 517 – 519 (July – Sept 93), pp. 470 – 474.

LA PAZ, BOLIVIA (CITY)

Albó, Xavier. Bolivia: La Paz/Chukiyawu; las dos caras de una ciudad. *América Indígena,* v. 51, no. 4 (Oct – Dec 91), pp. 107 – 158. Bibl, tables, maps.

Albó, Xavier and Matías Preiswerk. El Gran Poder: fiesta del aimara urbano. *América Indígena,* v. 51, no. 2 – 3 (Apr – Sept 91), pp. 293 – 352. Bibl, tables, maps.

Encinas Cueto, Ives and Wigberto Rivero Pinto. La presencia aimara en la ciudad de La Paz: Chuquiyawu Marka; entre la participación y la sobrevivencia. *América Indígena,* v. 51, no. 2 – 3 (Apr – Sept 91), pp. 273 – 292.

Marrone, Nila. *El habla de la ciudad de La Paz* reviewed by Carlos Coello Vila. *Signo,* no. 35, Nueva época (Jan – Apr 92), pp. 226 – 229.

PAZ, MARIE JOSÉ

Nieto, Margarita. Marie José Paz. *Latin American Art,* v. 5, no. 2 (Summer 93), pp. 53 – 54. Il.

PAZ, OCTAVIO
Correspondence, reminiscences, etc.

Paz, Octavio. Buzón entre dos mundos: de Octavio Paz a Luis Buñuel. *Vuelta,* v. 17, no. 201 (Aug 93), pp. 72 – 73.

— Excursiones a incursiones (Prologue to Volume II of Paz's *Obras completas*). *Vuelta,* v. 17, no. 199 (June 93), pp. 8 – 12.

Criticism and interpretation

Earle, Peter G. Octavio Paz: poesía e historia. *Nueva Revista de Filología Hispánica,* v. 40, no. 2 (July – Dec 92), pp. 1101 – 1112. Bibl.

Espinoza Orellana, Manuel. Los signos en rotación de Octavio Paz. *Revista Nacional de Cultura (Venezuela),* v. 53, no. 285 (Apr – June 92), pp. 104 – 114.

Jiménez Emán, Gabriel. Octavio Paz: las voces de lo poético. *Revista Nacional de Cultura (Venezuela),* v. 53, no. 285 (Apr – June 92), pp. 233 – 236.

Kushigian, Julia A. *Orientalism in the Hispanic Tradition: In Dialogue with Borges, Paz, and Sarduy* reviewed by John Incledon. *Hispania (USA),* v. 76, no. 3 (Sept 93), pp. 483 – 484.

Pereda, Carlos. *Conversar es humano* reviewed by Isabel Cabrera. *Vuelta,* v. 17, no. 196 (Mar 93), pp. 50 – 51.

Underwood, Leticia Iliana. *Octavio Paz and the Language of Poetry: A Psycholinguistic Approach* reviewed by Hugo J. Verani. *Revista Interamericana de Bibliografía,* v. 42, no. 4 (1992), pp. 666 – 667.

Criticism of specific works
El arco y la lira

Jiménez Emán, Ennio. Tres temas de Octavio Paz en *El arco y la lira*. *Revista Nacional de Cultura (Venezuela),* v. 54, no. 287 (Oct – Dec 92), pp. 83 – 91. Bibl, il.

Stanton, Anthony. Octavio Paz, Alfonso Reyes y el análisis del fenómeno poético. *Hispanic Review,* v. 61, no. 3 (Summer 93), pp. 363 – 378. Bibl.

Topoemas

Meyer-Minnemann, Klaus. Octavio Paz: "Topoemas"; elementos para una lectura. *Nueva Revista de Filología Hispánica,* v. 40, no. 2 (July – Dec 92), pp. 1113 – 1134. Bibl, charts.

Interviews

Marras, Sergio. América en plural y en singular, I: El baile de los enmascarados; entrevista con Octavio Paz (Fragment from the book *América Latina: marca registrada*). *Vuelta,* v. 17, no. 194 (Jan 93), pp. 11 – 16.

— América en plural y en singular, II: Los nacionalismos y otros bemoles; entrevista con Octavio Paz (Fragment from the book *América Latina: marca registrada*). *Vuelta,* v. 17, no. 195 (Feb 93), pp. 26 – 30.

PAZOS, LUIS
Interviews

Arizcorreta Buchholz, Luis. Interview: Luis Pazos. *Business Mexico,* v. 3, no. 3 (Mar 93), pp. 30 – 31. Il.

PEACE

Arias Sánchez, Oscar. Las universidades y la mentalidad armamentista. *La Educación (USA),* v. 36, no. 111 – 113 (1992), pp. 155 – 165.

Awards

Escobar, Francisco Andrés. Rigoberta entre nosotros. *ECA; Estudios Centroamericanos,* v. 48, no. 531 – 532 (Jan – Feb 93), pp. 105 – 108. Il.

Menchú, Rigoberta. Un homenaje a los pueblos indígenas. *Realidad Económica,* no. 114 – 115 (Feb – May 93), pp. 74 – 85. Il.

Rigoberta Menchú, premio Nobel de la paz: nuevo amanecer para Guatemala. *ECA; Estudios Centroamericanos,* v. 47, no. 528 (Oct 92), pp. 889 – 893. Il.

PEASANTRY

See also
Agricultural laborers

Andean region

Glave Testino, Luis Miguel. La sociedad campesina andina a mediados del siglo XVII: estructura social y tendencias de cambio. *Historia y Cultura (Peru)*, no. 20 (1990), pp. 81 – 132. Bibl, tables.

Political activity

Stern, Steve J., ed. *Resistencia, rebelión y conciencia campesina de los Andes, siglos XVIII al XX* reviewed by Betford Betalleluz. *Historia y Cultura (Peru)*, no. 20 (1990), pp. 369 – 371.

Thurner, Mark. Peasant Politics and Andean Haciendas in the Transition to Capitalism: An Ethnographic History. *Latin American Research Review*, v. 28, no. 3 (1993), pp. 41 – 82. Bibl, charts.

Argentina

Birocco, Carlos María and Gabriela Gresores. *Arrendamientos, desalojos y subordinación campesina: Buenos Aires, siglo XVIII* reviewed by Carlos G. A. Bulcourf. *Todo Es Historia*, v. 27, no. 313 (Aug 93), p. 71. Il.

Giarracca, Norma. Campesinos y agroindustrias en los tiempos del "ajuste": algunas reflexiones para pensar la relación, con especial referencia a México y la Argentina. *Realidad Económica*, no. 114 – 115 (Feb – May 93), pp. 13 – 28. Bibl.

Political activity

Giarracca, Norma and Miguel Teubal. El día en que la Plaza de Mayo se vistió de campo (Includes interviews with six agricultural producers). *Realidad Económica*, no. 118 (Aug – Sept 93), pp. 5 – 17. Tables.

Bolivia

Léons, Madeline Barbara. Risk and Opportunity in the Coca/Cocaine Economy of the Bolivian Yungas. *Journal of Latin American Studies*, v. 25, no. 1 (Feb 93), pp. 121 – 157. Bibl, charts.

Paz Ballivián, Danilo. Cuestión agraria y campesina en Bolivia. *Revista Paraguaya de Sociología*, v. 29, no. 84 (May – Aug 92), pp. 115 – 133.

Brazil

Barros, Henrique de. Just One Foot in the Market: Internal Strategies of Small Horticultural Farmers in Northeast Brazil. *Bulletin of Latin American Research*, v. 12, no. 3 (Sept 93), pp. 273 – 292. Bibl, tables.

Political activity

Beaney, Peter W. The Irrigated Eldorado: State-Managed Rural Development, Redemocratisation, and Popular Participation in the Brazilian Northeast. *Bulletin of Latin American Research*, v. 12, no. 3 (Sept 93), pp. 249 – 272. Bibl.

Sources

Assunção, Matthias Röhrig, ed. *A guerra dos bem-te-vis: a balaiada na memória oral* reviewed by Mary Karasch (Review entitled "A balaiada in Brazil"). *The Americas*, v. 49, no. 3 (Jan 93), pp. 392 – 394.

Chile

Dahse, Fernando. Elementos de una metodología participativa para el desarrollo rural. *Estudios Sociales (Chile)*, no. 78 (Oct – Dec 93), pp. 185 – 201. Bibl.

Loyola Goich, Lorena. Las sociedades campesinas: un retrato de cambios y permanencias a través de la literatura criollista chilena, 1920 – 1950. *Cuadernos de Historia (Chile)*, no. 11 (Dec 91), pp. 127 – 148. Bibl.

Colombia

Political activity

Dueñas Vargas, Guiomar. Algunas hipótesis para el estudio de la resistencia campesina en la región central de Colombia, siglo XIX. *Anuario Colombiano de Historia Social y de la Cultura*, no. 20 (1992), pp. 90 – 106. Bibl.

Costa Rica

Political activity

Anderson, Leslie Elin. Bendiciones mezcladas: disrupción y organización entre uniones campesinas en Costa Rica. *Revista de Historia (Costa Rica)*, no. 25 (Jan – June 92), pp. 97 – 143. Bibl.

Honduras

Fandiño, Mario. Land Titling and Peasant Differentiation in Honduras. *Latin American Perspectives*, v. 20, no. 2 (Spring 93), pp. 45 – 53. Bibl.

Latin America

Bibliography

Grindle, Merilee Serrill. Agrarian Class Structures and State Policies: Past, Present, and Future (Review article). *Latin American Research Review*, v. 28, no. 1 (1993), pp. 174 – 187.

Mexico

Giarracca, Norma. Campesinos y agroindustrias en los tiempos del "ajuste": algunas reflexiones para pensar la relación, con especial referencia a México y la Argentina. *Realidad Económica*, no. 114 – 115 (Feb – May 93), pp. 13 – 28. Bibl.

Robles B., Rosario et al. La mujer campesina en la época de la modernidad. *El Cotidiano*, v. 9, no. 53 (Mar – Apr 93), pp. 25 – 32. Bibl, il, tables.

Political activity

Boggio de Harasymowicz, Adriana. Movimientos populares e independencia en México y Uruguay. *La Palabra y el Hombre*, no. 82 (Apr – June 92), pp. 107 – 142. Bibl.

Ramírez Rancaño, Mario. La organización obrera y campesina en Tlaxcala durante el cardenismo. *Revista Mexicana de Sociología*, v. 54, no. 3 (July – Sept 92), pp. 189 – 219. Bibl, tables.

Nicaragua

Houtart, François and Geneviève Lemercinier. *El campesino como actor social: sociología de una comarca de Nicaragua* reviewed by Sergio Sarmiento Silva. *Revista Mexicana de Sociología*, v. 54, no. 3 (July – Sept 92), pp. 263 – 267.

Serra, Luis. Democracy in Times of War and Socialist Crisis: Reflections Stemming from the Sandinista Revolution. *Latin American Perspectives*, v. 20, no. 2 (Spring 93), pp. 21 – 44. Bibl.

Political activity

Gould, Jeffrey L. *To Lead as Equals: Rural Protest and Political Consciousness in Chinandega, Nicaragua, 1912 – 1979* reviewed by Daniel Little. *Economic Development and Cultural Change*, v. 41, no. 4 (July 93), pp. 894 – 898.

— *To Lead as Equals: Rural Protest and Political Consciousness in Chinandega, Nicaragua, 1912 – 1979* reviewed by Michael F. Jiménez. *Hispanic American Historical Review*, v. 73, no. 1 (Feb 93), pp. 186 – 188.

Peru

Contreras, Carlos. Mercado de tierras y sociedad campesina: el valle del Mantaro en el siglo XIX. *Historia y Cultura (Peru)*, no. 20 (1990), pp. 243 – 265. Bibl.

Deere, Carmen Diana. *Household and Class Relations: Peasants and Landlords in Northern Peru* reviewed by William Roseberry. *Hispanic American Historical Review*, v. 73, no. 1 (Feb 93), pp. 174 – 175.

Mesclier, Evelyne. Cusco: espacios campesinos en un contexto de inestabilidad económica y retracción del estado (With several commentaries and a response by the authoress). *Revista Andina*, v. 11, no. 1 (July 93), pp. 7 – 53. Bibl, maps.

Mitchell, William P. *Peasants on the Edge: Crop, Cult, and Crisis in the Andes* reviewed by Rodrigo Montoya. *Bulletin of Latin American Research*, v. 12, no. 1 (Jan 93), pp. 121 – 122.

— *Peasants on the Edge: Crop, Cult, and Crisis in the Andes* reviewed by Orin Starn. *Hispanic American Historical Review*, v. 73, no. 1 (Feb 93), pp. 175 – 76.

— *Peasants on the Edge: Crop, Cult, and Crisis in the Andes* reviewed by Thomas M. Davies, Jr. *Journal of Developing Areas*, v. 27, no. 3 (Apr 93), pp. 430 – 432.

— Producción campesina y cultura regional. *América Indígena,* v. 51, no. 4 (Oct – Dec 91), pp. 81 – 106. Bibl, tables.

Congresses

Bey, Marguerite. La cinquième Séminaire Permanent de Recherche Agraire. *Tiers Monde,* v. 34, no. 136 (Oct – Dec 93), pp. 937 – 938.

Research

Ansión, Juan. Acerca de un irritante debate entre antropólogos del norte: comentarios al artículo de O. Starn. *Allpanchis,* v. 23, no. 39 (Jan – June 92), pp. 113 – 122.

Poole, Deborah A. and Gerardo Rénique. Perdiendo de vista al Perú: réplica a Orin Starn. *Allpanchis,* v. 23, no. 39 (Jan – June 92), pp. 73 – 92. Bibl.

Salomon, Frank. "Una polémica de once años de antigüedad": comentarios al artículo de Starn. *Allpanchis,* v. 23, no. 39 (Jan – June 92), pp. 109 – 112.

Seligman, Linda Jane. "Es más fácil destruir que crear": comentarios y respuesta. *Allpanchis,* v. 23, no. 39 (Jan – June 92), pp. 93 – 101.

Starn, Orin. Algunas palabras finales. *Allpanchis,* v. 23, no. 39 (Jan – June 92), pp. 123 – 129. Bibl.

— Antropología andina, "andinismo" y Sendero Luminoso. *Allpanchis,* v. 23, no. 39 (Jan – June 92), pp. 15 – 71. Bibl.

Thurner, Mark. ¿Una conclusión resulta prematura?: comentario a propósito del artículo de O. Starn. *Allpanchis,* v. 23, no. 39 (Jan – June 92), pp. 103 – 108.

Uruguay

Political activity

Boggio de Harasymowicz, Adriana. Movimientos populares e independencia en México y Uruguay. *La Palabra y el Hombre,* no. 82 (Apr – June 92), pp. 107 – 142. Bibl.

Windward Islands

Trouillot, Michel-Rolph. *Peasants and Capital: Dominica in the World Economy* reviewed by Michael H. Allen (Review entitled "Rethinking Political Economy and Praxis in the Caribbean"). *Latin American Perspectives,* v. 20, no. 2 (Spring 93), pp. 111 – 119.

PEDREIRA, ANTONIO SALVADOR

Criticism of specific works

Insularismo

Díaz Quiñones, Arcadio. El enemigo íntimo: cultura nacional y autoridad en Ramiro Guerra y Sánchez y Antonio S. Pedreira. *Op. Cit.,* no. 7 (1992), pp. 9 – 65. Bibl.

Gelpí, Juan G. El clásico y la reescritura: "Insularismo" en las páginas de *La guaracha del macho Camacho. Revista Iberoamericana,* v. 59, no. 162 – 163 (Jan – June 93), pp. 55 – 71. Bibl.

Rodríguez Castro, María Elena. Las casas del porvenir: nación y narración en el ensayo puertorriqueño. *Revista Iberoamericana,* v. 59, no. 162 – 163 (Jan – June 93), pp. 33 – 54. Bibl.

PEDRO II

Lacombe, Lourenço Luís. Dom Pedro II no centenário de sua morte. *Revista do Instituto Histórico e Geográfico Brasileiro,* no. 373 (Oct – Dec 91), pp. 1176 – 1182. Bibl.

Schubert, Guilherme. Homilia pronunciada pelo sócio monsenhor Guilherme Schubert na missa pelo centenário da morte de dom Pedro II. *Revista do Instituto Histórico e Geográfico Brasileiro,* no. 373 (Oct – Dec 91), pp. 1183 – 1187.

Vieira, Oldegar Franco. Dom Pedro II e o parlamentarismo. *Convivium,* v. 34, no. 2 (July – Dec 91), pp. 120 – 126.

PEHUENCHE INDIANS

See
Araucanian Indians

PELLEGRINI, CARLOS

Marco, Miguel Angel de. Pellegrini contra la langosta, 1891 – 1892. *Todo Es Historia,* v. 27, no. 311 (June 93), pp. 62 – 73. Il.

PELLICER, CARLOS

Correspondence, reminiscences, etc.

Gorostiza, José and Carlos Pellicer. *Correspondencia, 1918 – 1928* edited and introduced by Guillermo Sheridan. Reviewed by David Medina Portillo. *Vuelta,* v. 17, no. 202 (Sept 93), pp. 44 – 45.

— *Correspondencia, 1918 – 1928* edited and introduced by Guillermo Sheridan. Reviewed by Rosa Beltrán. *Vuelta,* v. 17, no. 203 (Oct 93), pp. 44 – 45.

Criticism and interpretation

Reyes Ramos, Manuel. Descubramos a Carlos Pellicer Cámara. *La Palabra y el Hombre,* no. 81 (Jan – Mar 92), pp. 177 – 192. Bibl.

PELUFFO, LUISA

Criticism of specific works

Todo eso oyes

Lorente-Murphy, Silvia. Las voces no-oficiales en *Todo eso oyes* de Luisa Peluffo. *Confluencia,* v. 8, no. 1 (Fall 92), pp. 149 – 153. Bibl.

PEÑA, ANGEL

Calzadilla, Juan. Angel Peña: el calmo y brillante acontecer del trópico. *Revista Nacional de Cultura (Venezuela),* v. 54, no. 287 (Oct – Dec 92), pp. 157 – 160.

PENSION TRUSTS

See also
Social security

Coloma C., Fernando and Viviana Fernández M. Los costos de despido: el efecto de las indemnizaciones por años de servicio. *Cuadernos de Economía (Chile),* v. 30, no. 89 (Apr 93), pp. 77 – 109. Charts.

Chile

Walker H., Eduardo. Desempeño financiero de las carteras accionarias de los fondos de pensiones en Chile: ¿Ha tenido desventajas ser grandes? *Cuadernos de Economía (Chile),* v. 30, no. 89 (Apr 93), pp. 33 – 75. Bibl, tables, charts.

— Desempeño financiero de las carteras de "renta fija" de los fondos de pensiones de Chile: ¿Ha tenido desventajas ser grandes? *Cuadernos de Economía (Chile),* v. 30, no. 89 (Apr 93), pp. 1 – 33. Bibl, tables.

PENTECOSTALISM

Cunha, Olívia Maria Gomes da. Fazendo a "coisa certa": reggae, rastas e pentecostais em Salvador. *Revista Brasileira de Ciências Sociais,* v. 8, no. 23 (Oct 93), pp. 120 – 137. Bibl.

Villamán P., Marcos J. Religión y pobreza: una aproximación a los nuevos movimientos religiosos. *Estudios Sociales (Dominican Republic),* v. 26, no. 94 (Oct – Dec 93), pp. 75 – 96. Bibl, tables.

PEREIRA, LUIZ CARLOS BRESSER

Criticism of specific works

A crise do estado

Mazzali, Leonel. A crise do estado. *Revista de Economia Política (Brazil),* v. 13, no. 3 (July – Sept 93), pp. 139 – 143. Bibl.

PÉREZ, CARLOS ANDRÉS

Ellner, Steven B. A Tolerance Worn Thin: Corruption in the Age of Austerity. *NACLA Report on the Americas,* v. 27, no. 3 (Nov – Dec 93), pp. 13 – 16 + . Bibl, il.

PÉREZ, FÉLIX

Pérez, Félix. Félix Pérez: medio siglo de memoria sindical (A chapter from his autobiography entitled *Hicimos patria trabajando). Todo Es Historia,* v. 27, no. 314 (Sept 93), pp. 84 – 92. Il.

PÉREZ, HÉTEO

Agosín, Marjorie. A Dreamy Oaxacan Fantasy (Translated by Ruth Morales). *Américas,* v. 45, no. 6 (Nov – Dec 93), pp. 44 – 45. Il.

PÉREZ BONALDE, JUAN ANTONIO
Criticism and interpretation
Márquez Rodríguez, Alexis. J. A. Pérez Bonalde y la poesía venezolana del siglo XIX. *Revista Nacional de Cultura (Venezuela)*, v. 54, no. 287 (Oct – Dec 92), pp. 117 – 134. Bibl, il.

PÉREZ CELIS
Pérez Celis. Through the Eyes of the Heart. *Américas*, v. 45, no. 2 (Mar – Apr 93), pp. 56 – 59. Il.

PÉREZ DE RIBAS, ANDRÉS
Criticism of specific works
Historia de los triunfos de nuestra santa fe . . .
Monjarás-Ruiz, Jesús. La antigua Sinaloa y Pérez de Ribas. *Plural (Mexico)*, v. 22, no. 265 (Oct 93), pp. 70 – 72.

PÉREZ FERGUSON, ANITA
Interviews
Marx, Jutta. Construir el poder: entrevista con Anita Pérez Ferguson. *Feminaria*, v. 6, no. 11 (Nov 93), pp. 17 – 19.

PÉREZ RESCANIÈRE, GERÓNIMO
Criticism of specific works
El amor y el interés
Villa Pelayo, José Jesús. Nota crítica sobre la novela *El amor y el interés* de Gerónimo Pérez Rescanière. *Revista Nacional de Cultura (Venezuela)*, v. 53, no. 286 (July – Sept 92), pp. 148 – 150.

PERI ROSSI, CRISTINA
Criticism of specific works
Al ángel caído
Olivera-Williams, María Rosa. *El derrumbamiento* de Armonía Somers y *El ángel caído* de Cristina Peri-Rossi: dos manifestaciones de la narrativa imaginaria. *Revista Chilena de Literatura*, no. 42 (Aug 93), pp. 173 – 181. Bibl.

PERIODICALS
See also
Journalism
Newspapers
Press
Names of specific periodicals

Argentina
Caparrós, Martín. Mientras *Babel*. *Cuadernos Hispanoamericanos*, no. 517 – 519 (July – Sept 93), pp. 525 – 528.

Fletcher, Lea. El desierto que no es tal: escritoras y escritura. *Feminaria*, v. 6, no. 11, Suppl. (Nov 93), pp. 7 – 13. Bibl.

Sáenz Quesada, María. Los 25 años de *Todo Es Historia*. *Revista Interamericana de Bibliografía*, v. 42, no. 4 (1992), pp. 561 – 569. Bibl, il.

Warley, Jorge. Revistas culturales de dos décadas, 1970 – 1990. *Cuadernos Hispanoamericanos*, no. 517 – 519 (July – Sept 93), pp. 195 – 207. Bibl.

Indexes
Indice general, nros. 1/1946 – 186/1992, I: Editoriales y artículos. *Sapientia*, v. 48, no. 187 – 188 (Jan – June 93), Issue.

Belgium
Zaid, Gabriel. *La Jeune Belgique* y la poesía mexicana. *Vuelta*, v. 17, no. 200 (July 93), pp. 17 – 18.

Bolivia
Arze, José Roberto. *Signo* en el contexto de las revistas literarias de Bolivia. *Signo*, no. 36 – 37, Nueva época (May – Dec 93), pp. 11 – 14.

Coello Vila, Carlos. *Signo; Cuadernos Bolivianos de Cultura*, 36 – 37. *Signo*, no. 38, Nueva época (Jan – Apr 93), pp. 7 – 10.

Brazil
Trinta anos de história. *Problemas Brasileiros*, v. 30, no. 295 (Jan – Feb 93), pp. 6 – 9. Il.

Bibliography
Muricy, Carmen Meurer. Environment in Brazil: A Checklist of Current Serials. *SALALM Papers*, v. 36 (1991), pp. 88 – 104.

Chile
Celebración de los veinte años de la revista *Estudios Sociales* (Includes several letters of congratulations). *Estudios Sociales (Chile)*, no. 78 (Oct – Dec 93), pp. 259 – 278.

Vial Correa, Juan de Dios. Cincuenta números de revista *Estudios Públicos*. *Estudios Públicos (Chile)*, no. 51 (Winter 93), pp. 331 – 335.

Indexes
Contenidos y autores de los números anteriores de la revista *Estudios Sociales*, nos. 1 – 77. *Estudios Sociales (Chile)*, no. 78 (Oct – Dec 93), pp. 307 – 351.

Cuadernos de Economía: clasificación de artículos por materia, volúmenes 26 – 31, números 77 – 91, años 1989 – 1993. *Cuadernos de Economía (Chile)*, v. 30, no. 91 (Dec 93), pp. 407 – 413.

Fuchslocher Arancibia, Luz María. Indice: *Cuadernos de Historia*, desde no. 1 (diciembre, 1981) al no. 10 (diciembre, 1990). *Cuadernos de Historia (Chile)*, no. 11 (Dec 91), pp. 211 – 226.

Indice alfabético por autores de *Cuadernos de Economía*, años 1989 a 1993: simbología utilizada; volumen, número, página, año. *Cuadernos de Economía (Chile)*, v. 30, no. 91 (Dec 93), pp. 395 – 406.

Indice general: *Estudios Internacionales*, nos. 1 – 99. *Estudios Internacionales (Chile)*, v. 25, no. 100 (Oct – Dec 92), Issue.

Indice por temas y autores: *Estudios Públicos*, nos. 1 al 50, 1980 – 1993. *Estudios Públicos (Chile)*, no. 50 (Fall 93), pp. 415 – 492.

Sanzana Fuentes, Eva. Indice: *Revista Chilena de Literatura*, desde el n° 1 (otoño 1970) al n° 39 (abril 1992). *Revista Chilena de Literatura*, no. 40 (Nov 92), pp. 139 – 155.

Colombia
Pacheco, Juan Manuel. 15 años más (Previously published in this journal, no. 400, 1973). *Revista Javeriana*, v. 61, no. 596 (July 93), pp. 37 – 40.

Restrepo, Félix. Bajo la insignia de Javier: veinticinco años de historia (Previously published in this journal, no. 51, 1959). *Revista Javeriana*, v. 61, no. 596 (July 93), pp. 17 – 36.

Sanín, Javier. La década ganada. *Revista Javeriana*, v. 61, no. 596 (July 93), pp. 45 – 48.

Vélez Correa, Jaime. Ultimo decenio de *Revista Javeriana* (Previously published in this journal, no. 500, 1983). *Revista Javeriana*, v. 61, no. 596 (July 93), pp. 41 – 43.

Cuba
Chacón, Alfredo. La experiencia de *Orígenes*. *Cuadernos Hispanoamericanos*, no. 511 (Jan 93), pp. 25 – 31.

Fraser, Howard M. *La Edad de Oro* and José Martí's Modernist Ideology for Children. *Revista Interamericana de Bibliografía*, v. 42, no. 2 (1992), pp. 223 – 232. Bibl.

Manzoni, Celina. Vanguardia y nacionalismo: itinerario de la *Revista de Avance*. *Iberoamericana*, v. 17, no. 49 (1993), pp. 5 – 15. Bibl.

Masiello, Francine Rose. Rethinking Neocolonial Esthetics: Literature, Politics, and Intellectual Community in Cuba's *Revista de Avance*. *Latin American Research Review*, v. 28, no. 2 (1993), pp. 3 – 31. Bibl, facs.

Roca, Sergio G. A Critical Review of *Economía y Desarrollo*. *Cuban Studies/Estudios Cubanos*, v. 23 (1993), pp. 205 – 210. Bibl, tables.

— Evolución del pensamiento cubano sobre Cuba y la economía mundial a través de las revistas económicas. *Estudios Internacionales (Chile)*, v. 26, no. 103 (July – Sept 93), pp. 537 – 564. Bibl, tables.

Dominican Republic
Zaglul, Jesús M. Documento: *Estudios Sociales;* 25 años de reflexión y análisis. *Estudios Sociales (Dominican Republic)*, v. 26, no. 92 (Apr – June 93), pp. 93 – 99.

El Salvador

Gómez Díez, Francisco Javier. El reformismo jesuítico en Centroamérica: La revista *ECA* en los años de la guerra fría, 1946 – 1965. *Anuario de Estudios Americanos*, v. 49, Suppl. 1 (1992), pp. 85 – 105. Tables.

France

McQuade, Frank. *Mundo Nuevo:* el discurso político en una revista intelectual de los sesenta. *Revista Chilena de Literatura*, no. 42 (Aug 93), pp. 123 – 130.

Mudrovcic, María Eugenia. *Mundo Nuevo:* hacia la definición de un modelo discursivo. *Nuevo Texto Crítico*, v. 6, no. 11 (1993), pp. 187 – 206. Bibl.

Germany

Indexes

Index des Nummern 1/1977 – 49/1993/Indices de los números 1/1977 – 49/1993. *Iberoamericana*, v. 17, no. 50 (1993), pp. 112 – 134.

Great Britain

Indexes

Cumulative Index, Volumes 16 – 25 (1984 – 1993). *Journal of Latin American Studies*, n.v. (1993), Issue.

Guatemala

Indexes

Indice general, 1989 – 1992. *Mesoamérica (USA)*, v. 13, no. 24 (Dec 92), pp. 495 – 512.

Latin America

Sheridan, Guillermo. "Los Contemporáneos" y la generación del '27: documentando un desencuentro. *Cuadernos Hispanoamericanos*, no. 514 – 515 (Apr – May 93), pp. 185 – 194.

Bibliography

Latin American Musical Periodicals. *Inter-American Music Review*, v. 13, no. 2 (Spring – Summer 93), pp. 145 – 148. Bibl.

Collectors and collecting

González, Nelly S. Stretching the Budget: Developing Latin American and Caribbean Serial Collections for University Libraries. *SALALM Papers*, v. 36 (1991), pp. 325 – 334. Bibl.

Cost

Van Jacob, Scott. Latin American Periodicals Prices Revisited. *SALALM Papers*, v. 36 (1991), pp. 335 – 344. Tables.

Indexes

Indices de las colecciones cooperativas y colectivas publicadas por Francisco Curt Lange, 1935 – 1958 (Indexes to eight journals on Latin American music, introduced by Humberto Sagredo Araya). *Revista Musical de Venezuela*, no. 29 (Jan – June 90), Issue. Il, facs.

Revista de revistas iberoamericanas. *Pensamiento Iberoamericano*, no. 22 – 23, tomo II (July 92 – June 93), pp. 271 – 405.

Mexico

Aguilera Garramuño, Marco Tulio. Revista *Literal*. *Plural (Mexico)*, v. 22, no. 259 (Apr 93), pp. 75 – 76.

Fleischman, Cristopher and Joel Russell. The Company You Keep. *Business Mexico*, v. 3, no. 5 (May 93), pp. 42 – 43. Charts.

Garza Cuarón, Beatriz. La poética de José Gorostiza y "el grupo sin grupo" de la revista *Contemporáneos*. *Nueva Revista de Filología Hispánica*, v. 40, no. 2 (July – Dec 92), pp. 891 – 907. Bibl.

López García, Guadalupe. *Fem* y sus colaboradoras. *Fem*, v. 17, no. 119 (Jan 93), p. 26. Il.

Martínez Duarte, Margarita. *Biombo Negro:* lo que nos faltaba. *Plural (Mexico)*, v. 22, no. 265 (Oct 93), pp. 86 – 87.

Awards

Finisterre, Alejandro. El premio León Felipe 1993. *Cuadernos Americanos*, no. 41, Nueva época (Sept – Oct 93), pp. 183 – 186.

Weinberg, Liliana Irene. León Felipe y *Cuadernos Americanos*. *Cuadernos Americanos*, no. 41, Nueva época (Sept – Oct 93), pp. 187 – 189.

Spain

Indexes

Revista de revistas iberoamericanas. *Pensamiento Iberoamericano*, no. 22 – 23, tomo II (July 92 – June 93), pp. 271 – 405.

United States

Paldao, Carlos E. Spreading the Word on Education. *Américas*, v. 45, no. 3 (May – June 93), pp. 54 – 55. Il.

Indexes

Davis, James J. Index of *Afro-Hispanic Review*, Volumes 8 – 12. *Afro-Hispanic Review*, v. 12, no. 2 (Fall 93), pp. 48 – 53.

Dicennial Index, 1983 – 1992. *The Americas Review*, v. 20, no. 3 – 4 (Fall – Winter 92), pp. 257 – 271.

Uruguay

Indexes

Michelena, Alejandro Daniel. Tercer indice trianual: autores y materias, 1990 – 1992. *Hoy Es Historia*, v. 10, no. 55 (Jan – Feb 93), Insert.

Venezuela

Alcibíades, Mirla. De cómo una tabacalera devinó en revista cultural. *Revista Nacional de Cultura (Venezuela)*, v. 53, no. 286 (July – Sept 92), pp. 167 – 174. Il.

Rivas Rivas, José. Una insólita misión cultural. *Revista Nacional de Cultura (Venezuela)*, v. 53, no. 286 (July – Sept 92), pp. 159 – 166. Il.

Ruiz Chataing, David. La revista *El Cojo Ilustrado* y el antiimperialismo. *Revista Nacional de Cultura (Venezuela)*, v. 53, no. 286 (July – Sept 92), pp. 177 – 186. Bibl, il.

Bibliography

Alcibíades, Mirla. Bibliografía selecta sobre *El Cojo Ilustrado*. *Revista Nacional de Cultura (Venezuela)*, v. 53, no. 286 (July – Sept 92), pp. 175 – 176.

Indexes

López Bohórquez, Alí Enrique. El descubrimiento de América en el *Boletín de la Academia Nacional de la Historia*. *Boletín de la Academia Nacional de la Historia (Venezuela)*, v. 75, no. 300 (Oct – Dec 92), pp. 166 – 171.

PERNAMBUCO, BRAZIL

Barros, Henrique de. Just One Foot in the Market: Internal Strategies of Small Horticultural Farmers in Northeast Brazil. *Bulletin of Latin American Research*, v. 12, no. 3 (Sept 93), pp. 273 – 292. Bibl, tables.

McCarthy, Cavan Michael. A Regional Database for the Brazilian Northeast. *SALALM Papers*, v. 36 (1991), pp. 369 – 386. Bibl, tables.

Motta, Roberto M. C. Transe, sacrifício, comunhão e poder no xangô de Pernambuco. *Revista de Antropologia (Brazil)*, v. 34 (1991), pp. 131 – 142.

PERÓN, EVA DUARTE

Kremlicka, Raimund. Zwei Frauen: Eva Peron und Marie Langer. *Zeitschrift für Lateinamerika Wien*, no. 42 (1992), pp. 53 – 65. Bibl.

Rocha Campos, Adolfo. El patrimonio de Perón. *Todo Es Historia*, v. 27, no. 313 (Aug 93). pp. 26 – 42. Bibl, il.

PERÓN, JUAN DOMINGO

Blasi Brambilla, Alberto. Ezeiza, veinte años después. *Todo Es Historia*, v. 27, no. 311 (June 93), pp. 79 – 83. Il.

García, Marcela A. and Aníbal Iturrieta. Perón en el exilio español: la búsqueda de la legitimidad. *Todo Es Historia*, v. 27, no. 313 (Aug 93), pp. 8 – 25. Bibl, il.

Horowitz, Joel. *Argentine Unions, the State, and the Rise of Perón* reviewed by Daniel J. Greenberg. *Hispanic American Historical Review*, v. 73, no. 1 (Feb 93), pp. 162 – 164.

Rocha Campos, Adolfo. El patrimonio de Perón. *Todo Es Historia*, v. 27, no. 313 (Aug 93), pp. 26 – 42. Bibl, il.

Waldmann, Peter. "Was ich mache, ist Justicialismus, nicht Liberalismus": Menems Peronismus und Peróns Peronismus; Ein vorläufiger Vergleich. *Ibero-Amerikanisches Archiv*, v. 18, no. 1 – 2 (1992), pp. 5 – 29. Bibl.

PERONISM

Bianchi, Susana. Iglesia católica y peronismo: la cuestión de la enseñanza religiosa, 1946 – 1955. *Estudios Interdisciplinarios de América Latina y el Caribe,* v. 3, no. 2 (July – Dec 92), pp. 89 – 103. Bibl.

Franzé, Javier. El peronismo según Sebreli. *Cuadernos Hispanoamericanos,* no. 512 (Feb 93), pp. 127 – 129.

Quevedo, Hugo Orlando. *El partido peronista en La Rioja: crónica y personajes* reviewed by F. L. *Todo Es Historia,* v. 27, no. 311 (June 93), p. 60.

Ranis, Peter. *Argentine Workers: Peronism and Contemporary Class Consciousness* reviewed by Joel Horowitz. *The Americas,* v. 50, no. 2 (Oct 93), pp. 289 – 290.

— *Argentine Workers: Peronism and Contemporary Class Consciousness* reviewed by Walter Little. *Bulletin of Latin American Research,* v. 12, no. 1 (Jan 93), pp. 118 – 119.

Senkman, Leonardo. Etnicidad e inmigración durante el primer peronismo. *Estudios Interdisciplinarios de América Latina y el Caribe,* v. 3, no. 2 (July – Dec 92), pp. 5 – 38. Bibl.

Waldmann, Peter. "Was ich mache, ist Justicialismus, nicht Liberalismus": Menems Peronismus und Peróns Peronismus; Ein vorläufiger Vergleich. *Ibero-Amerikanisches Archiv,* v. 18, no. 1 – 2 (1992), pp. 5 – 29. Bibl.

PERSONNEL MANAGEMENT

See
Human capital

PERU

See also
Agriculture – Peru
AIDS (Disease) – Peru
Americans – Peru
Andamarca, Peru
Anthropology – Peru
Archaeological site reports – Peru
Archives – Peru
Artisans – Peru
Artists – Peru
Ayacucho, Battle of, 1824
Ayacucho, Peru (Department)
Bandits and banditry – Peru
Biography (as a literary form) – Peru
Blacks – Peru
Books – Peru
Caciquism – Peru
Cajamarca, Peru
Cajatambo, Peru (Province)
Callao, Peru (City)
Catholic Church – Peru
Child abuse – Peru
Children – Peru
Chinese – Peru
Christian art and symbolism – Peru
Church and state – Peru
Church architecture – Peru
Cities and towns – Peru
Clothing and dress – Peru
Community development – Peru
Community organization – Peru
Competition – Peru
Composers – Peru
Corruption (in politics) – Peru
Cost and standard of living – Peru
Cultural property – Peru
Cuzco, Peru (City)
Cuzco, Peru (Department)
Dams and reservoirs – Peru
Decentralization in government – Peru
Democracy – Peru
Ecology and development – Peru
Education – Peru
Education, Preschool – Peru
Education and state – Peru
Educational sociology – Peru
Elections – Peru
Employment – Peru
Erosion – Peru
Europeans – Peru
Evangelicalism – Peru
Fertility, Human – Peru
Finance, Public – Peru
Folk dancing – Peru
Folk drama – Peru
Folk festivals – Peru
Folk music – Peru
Foreign trade promotion – Peru
Forestry – Peru
Forests – Peru
Franciscans – Peru
Los Gavilanes, Peru
Geographic Information Systems – Peru
Geography, Historical – Peru
Geomorphology – Peru
Haciendas – Peru
Huari culture, Peru
Human rights – Peru
Indians, Treatment of – Peru
Informal sector (Economics) – Peru
Inquisition – Peru
Investments, Foreign – Peru
Iquitos, Peru
Japanese – Peru
Jesuits – Peru
Journalism – Peru
Judiciary – Peru
Labor laws and legislation – Peru
Lambayeque, Peru (Department)
Land reform – Peru
Land tenure – Peru
Legislative power – Peru
Lima, Peru
Literature and history – Peru
Literature and society – Peru
Local government – Peru
Machu Picchu, Peru
Mainas, Peru
Marine resources – Peru
Markets and merchants – Peru
Marriage – Peru
Mass media – Peru
Medicine – Peru
Messianism – Peru
Migration, Internal – Peru
Military posts – Peru
Missions – Peru
Moche Valley, Peru
Moquegua, Peru
Mural painting and decoration – Peru
Music – Peru
Music and society – Peru
Musical instruments – Peru
Musicians – Peru
Nasca, Peru
Non-governmental organizations – Peru
Oral tradition – Peru
Paiján complex, Peru
Paleobotany – Peru
Parks – Peru
Peasantry – Peru
Petroglyphs – Peru
Philosophy – Peru
Photography, Aerial – Peru
Photography and photographers – Peru
Piura, Peru (Department)
Political parties – Peru
Political sociology – Peru
Politics in literature – Peru
Popular culture – Peru
Popular music – Peru
Population – Peru
Postmodernism – Peru
Press and politics – Peru
Printing and engraving – Peru
Prostitution – Peru
Public opinion – Peru
Puno, Peru (Department)
Quality of life – Peru
Radio broadcasting – Peru
Rites and ceremonies – Peru
Science – Peru
Sex role – Peru
Shamanism – Peru
Silversmiths – Peru
Slavery – Peru
Slums – Peru
Soccer – Peru
Social change – Peru
Social conflict – Peru
Social movements – Peru
Socialism – Peru

Administrative and political divisions

Julien, Catherine Jean. *Condesuyo: The Political Division of Territory under Inca and Spanish Rule* reviewed by Nicanor Domínguez. *Revista Andina*, v. 10, no. 2 (Dec 92), pp. 546 – 547.

Antiquities

Aveni, Anthony F., ed. *The Lines of Nazca* reviewed by Katharina J. Schreiber. *Latin American Antiquity*, v. 4, no. 2 (June 93), pp. 202 – 203.

Chauchat, Claude and Jacques Pelegrin. Tecnología y función de las puntas de Paiján: el aporte de la experimentación. *Latin American Antiquity*, v. 4, no. 4 (Dec 93), pp. 367 – 382. Bibl, il, tables, charts.

Goldstein, Paul. Tiwanaku Temples and State Expansion: A Tiwanaku Sunken-Court Temple in Moquequa, Peru. *Latin American Antiquity*, v. 4, no. 1 (Mar 93), pp. 22 – 47. Bibl, il, tables, maps.

Kaulicke, Peter. Evidencias paleoclimáticas en asentamientos del alto Piura durante el período intermedio temprano. *Bulletin de l'Institut Français d'Etudes Andines*, v. 22, no. 1 (1993), pp. 283 – 311. Bibl, il, maps.

— Moche, Vicús moche y el mochica temprano. *Bulletin de l'Institut Français d'Etudes Andines*, v. 21, no. 3 (1992), pp. 853 – 903. Bibl, il, tables, maps, charts.

Moseley, Michael Edward. *The Incas and Their Ancestors: The Archaeology of Peru* reviewed by Richard L. Burger. *Hispanic American Historical Review*, v. 73, no. 4 (Nov 93), pp. 682 – 684.

— *The Incas and Their Ancestors: The Archaeology of Peru* reviewed by Monica Barnes. *Latin American Indian Literatures Journal*, v. 9, no. 1 (Spring 93), pp. 78 – 79.

Reinhard, Johan. Llullaillaco: An Investigation of the World's Highest Archaeological Site. *Latin American Indian Literatures Journal*, v. 9, no. 1 (Spring 93), pp. 31 – 54. Il, maps.

Armed forces

Bradley, Peter T. The Defence of Peru, 1648 – 1700. *Jahrbuch für Geschichte von Staat, Wirtschaft und Gesellschaft Lateinamerikas*, v. 29 (1992), pp. 90 – 120. Bibl, tables.

Cisneros, Luis Jaime. Entrevista al general Luis Cisneros. *Debate (Peru)*, v. 15, no. 71 (Nov 92), pp. 8 – 16. Il.

Ghersi, Enrique. La ecuación Manuel Prado. *Debate (Peru)*, v. 16, no. 73 (June – Aug 93), pp. 24 – 25. Il.

Masterson, Daniel M. *Militarism and Politics in Latin America: Peru from Sánchez Cerro to Sendero Luminoso* reviewed by Brian Loveman. *The Americas*, v. 49, no. 3 (Jan 93), pp. 422 – 424.

Mercado Jarrín, Edgardo. Fuerzas armadas: constitución y reconversión. *Debate (Peru)*, v. 16, no. 75 (Dec 93 – Jan 94), pp. 31 – 34. Il.

Obando Arbulú, Enrique. Unas fuerzas armadas para el siglo XXI. *Debate (Peru)*, v. 15, no. 71 (Nov 92 – Jan 93), pp. 32 – 36. Il.

Boundaries

Brazil

Scarabôtolo, Hélio Antônio. Rio Branco, Euclides da Cunha e o tratado de limites com o Peru. *Revista do Instituto Histórico e Geográfico Brasileiro*, no. 370 (Jan – Mar 91), pp. 82 – 93.

Ecuador

Bustamante Ponce, Fernando. Ecuador: Putting an End to Ghosts of the Past? (Translated by Jane Marchi). *Journal of Inter-American Studies and World Affairs*, v. 34, no. 4 (Winter 92 – 93), pp. 195 – 224. Bibl.

Civilization

Gamarra, Jefrey. Estado, modernidad y sociedad regional: Ayacucho, 1920 – 1940. *Apuntes (Peru)*, no. 31 (July – Dec 92), pp. 103 – 114. Bibl.

Huertas Vallejos, Lorenzo. Anomalías cíclicas de la naturaleza y su impacto en la sociedad: el fenómeno El Niño. *Bulletin de l'Institut Français d'Etudes Andines*, v. 22, no. 1 (1993), pp. 345 – 393. Bibl, il, tables, maps, facs, charts.

Ortiz de Zevallos, Felipe. *A mitad de camino* reviewed by Alonso Cueto (Review entitled "La mitad del futuro"). *Debate (Peru)*, v. 16, no. 72 (Mar – May 93), pp. 63 – 64. Il.

— *A mitad de camino* reviewed by José Luis Sardón. *Apuntes (Peru)*, no. 31 (July – Dec 92), pp. 117 – 119.

Oviedo, Cecilia. Identidad nacional y desarrollo: entrevista a Jürgen Golte. *Debate (Peru)*, v. 16, no. 72 (Mar – May 93), pp. 40 – 41. Il.

Rudolph, James D. *Peru: The Evolution of a Crisis* reviewed by David P. Werlich. *Hispanic American Historical Review*, v. 73, no. 3 (Aug 93), pp. 519 – 520.

Climate

Canziani Amico, José and Santiago Uceda C. Evidencias de grandes precipitaciones en diversas etapas constructivas de La Huaca de la Luna, costa norte del Perú. *Bulletin de l'Institut Français d'Etudes Andines*, v. 22, no. 1 (1993), pp. 313 – 343. Bibl, il.

Díaz, Amanda and Luc Ortlieb. El fenómeno El Niño y los moluscos de la costa peruana. *Bulletin de l'Institut Français d'Etudes Andines*, v. 22, no. 1 (1993), pp. 159 – 177. Bibl, tables, maps.

Huertas Vallejos, Lorenzo. Anomalías cíclicas de la naturaleza y su impacto en la sociedad: el fenómeno El Niño. *Bulletin de l'Institut Français d'Etudes Andines*, v. 22, no. 1 (1993), pp. 345 – 393. Bibl, il, tables, maps, facs, charts.

Kaulicke, Peter. Evidencias paleoclimáticas en asentamientos del alto Piura durante el período intermedio temprano. *Bulletin de l'Institut Français d'Etudes Andines*, v. 22, no. 1 (1993), pp. 283 – 311. Bibl, il, maps.

Mabres, Antonio and Ronald F. Woodman. Formación de un cordón litoral en Máncora, Perú, a raíz de El Niño de 1983. *Bulletin de l'Institut Français d'Etudes Andines*, v. 22, no. 1 (1993), pp. 213 – 226. Bibl, il, maps.

Mabres, Antonio et al. Algunos apuntes históricos adicionales sobre la cronología de El Niño. *Bulletin de l'Institut Français d'Etudes Andines*, v. 22, no. 1 (1993), pp. 395 – 406. Bibl, tables, charts.

Maché, José and Luc Ortlieb. Registros del fenómeno El Niño en el Perú. *Bulletin de l'Institut Français d'Etudes Andines*, v. 22, no. 1 (1993), pp. 35 – 52. Bibl, tables, charts.

Ortlieb, Luc et al. Beach-Ridge Series in Northern Peru: Chronology, Correlation, and Relationship with Major Late Holocene El Niño Events. *Bulletin de l'Institut Français d'Etudes Andines*, v. 22, no. 1 (1993), pp. 191 – 212. Bibl, il, tables, maps, charts.

Quispe Arce, Juan. Variaciones de la temperatura superficial del mar en Puerto Chicama y del índice de oscilación del sur, 1925 – 1992. *Bulletin de l'Institut Français d'Etudes Andines*, v. 22, no. 1 (1993), pp. 111 – 124. Bibl, tables, charts.

Teves Rivas, Néstor. Erosion and Accretion Processes during El Niño Phenomenon of 1982 – 1983 and Its Relation to Previous Events. *Bulletin de l'Institut Français d'Etudes Andines*, v. 22, no. 1 (1993), pp. 99 – 110. Bibl, tables, maps, charts.

Constitutional law

Chávez, Martha and Francisco R. Sagasti. ¿Hacia un nuevo Perú? *Debate (Peru)*, v. 16, no. 74 (Sept – Oct 93), pp. 10 – 12. Il.

Mercado Jarrín, Edgardo. Fuerzas armadas: constitución y reconversión. *Debate (Peru)*, v. 16, no. 75 (Dec 93 – Jan 94), pp. 31 – 34. Il.

Rubio Correa, Marcial. *Constitución: qué ponerle y qué quitarle* reviewed by José Luis Sardón. *Apuntes (Peru)*, no. 30 (Jan – June 92), pp. 105 – 107.

Description and travel

Denevan, William M. The 1931 Shippee – Johnson Aerial Photography Expedition to Peru. *Geographical Review*, v. 83, no. 3 (July 93), pp. 238 – 251. Bibl, il, maps.

Discovery and exploration

Sánchez-Concha B., Rafael. Las expediciones descubridoras: la entrada al país de los chunchos, 1538 – 1539. *Amazonía Peruana*, v. 11, no. 22 (Oct 92), pp. 125 – 145. Bibl.

Sources

Roldán Fernández de Soldevilla, Francisco. Al señor Marqués de Menahermosa (dn. Joseph de Llamas), brigadier de los Reales Exércitos de S.M. Cabo Principal del Callao, teniente de capitán general de S.E. comandante general de las fronteras de la provincia de Tarma D.O.C. (1751). *Amazonía Peruana*, v. 11, no. 22 (Oct 92), pp. 221 – 254.

Economic conditions

Barclay, Federica et al. *Amazonía, 1940 – 1990* reviewed by Nicole Bernex. *Amazonía Peruana*, v. 11, no. 21 (Sept 92), pp. 240 – 242.

Cáceres, Armando. 1994: el crecimiento debe llegar a todos. *Debate (Peru)*, v. 16, no. 75 (Dec 93 – Jan 94), pp. 20 – 21. Il.

Gonzales de Olarte, Efraín and Julio Velarde F. ¿Es posible el liberalismo en el Perú? *Debate (Peru)*, v. 15, no. 70 (Sept – Oct 92), pp. 15 – 18. Il.

Ortiz de Zevallos, Felipe. El optimismo es frágil. *Debate (Peru)*, v. 16, no. 73 (June – Aug 93), pp. 18 – 21. Il.

Economic policy

Alvarez Rodrich, Augusto and Pilar Dávila. Entrevista a Carlos Boloña. *Debate (Peru)*, v. 15, no. 70 (Sept – Oct 92), pp. 8 – 14. Il.

Béjar, Héctor. Perú: el neoliberalismo realmente existente. *Nueva Sociedad*, no. 127 (Sept – Oct 93), pp. 13 – 18.

Gonzales de Olarte, Efraín. Economic Stabilization and Structural Adjustment under Fujimori. *Journal of Inter-American Studies and World Affairs*, v. 35, no. 2 (Summer 93), pp. 51 – 80. Bibl, tables.

Gonzales de Olarte, Efraín and Julio Velarde F. ¿Es posible el liberalismo en el Perú? *Debate (Peru)*, v. 15, no. 70 (Sept – Oct 92), pp. 15 – 18. Il.

Paredes, Carlos and Jeffrey D. Sachs. *Estabilización y crecimiento en el Perú* reviewed by Martha Rodríguez. *Apuntes (Peru)*, no. 29 (July – Dec 91), pp. 91 – 94.

Thorp, Rosemary. *Economic Management and Economic Development in Peru and Colombia* reviewed by Eva A. Paus. *Hispanic American Historical Review*, v. 73, no. 1 (Feb 93), pp. 176 – 177.

Emigration and immigration

Altamirano Rúa, Teófilo. Un permanente reto. *Debate (Peru)*, v. 15, no. 70 (Sept – Oct 92), pp. 31 – 32.

García Jordán, Pilar. Reflexiones sobre el darwinismo social: inmigración y colonización; mitos de los grupos modernizadores peruanos, 1821 – 1919. *Bulletin de l'Institut Français d'Etudes Andines*, v. 21, no. 3 (1992), pp. 961 – 975. Bibl.

Hampe Martínez, Teodoro. Apuntes documentales sobre inmigrantes europeos y norteamericanos en Lima, siglo XIX. *Revista de Indias*, v. 53, no. 198 (May – Aug 93), pp. 459 – 491. Bibl.

Foreign economic relations

González Vigil, Fernando. Crisis andina e integración. *Debate (Peru)*, v. 16, no. 72 (Mar – May 93), pp. 49 – 51. Il.

Argentina

Acuerdo de Alcance Parcial de Complementación Económica n° 9 concertado entre Argentina y Perú. *Integración Latinoamericana*, v. 18, no. 193 (Sept 93), pp. 70 – 74.

European Community

Mathews, Juan Carlos and Carlos Parodi Zevallos. El comercio exterior del Perú con la Comunidad Económica Europea. *Apuntes (Peru)*, no. 31 (July – Dec 92), pp. 29 – 39. Tables.

Latin America

García Belaúnde, José Antonio. El Perú y la América Latina en los '90. *Debate (Peru)*, v. 15, no. 71 (Nov 92 – Jan 93), pp. 52 – 57. Il.

Foreign opinion

García Belaúnde, José Antonio. Promoción, imagen, diplomacia. *Debate (Peru)*, v. 16, no. 72 (Mar – May 93), pp. 46 – 48. Il.

Foreign relations

Bolivia

Mercado Jarrín, Edgardo et al. *Relaciones del Perú con Chile y Bolivia* (Review). *Integración Latinoamericana*, v. 18, no. 189 – 190 (May – June 93), p. 58.

Chile

Macera dall'Orso, Pablo. Los acuerdos Perú – Chile. *Debate (Peru)*, v. 16, no. 73 (June – Aug 93), pp. 49 – 51. Il.

Mercado Jarrín, Edgardo et al. *Relaciones del Perú con Chile y Bolivia* (Review). *Integración Latinoamericana*, v. 18, no. 189 – 190 (May – June 93), p. 58.

Valdivieso Belaunde, Felipe. Un acuerdo mezquino. *Debate (Peru)*, v. 16, no. 73 (June – Aug 93), pp. 51 – 56. Il.

Vidal Ramírez, Fernando. El camino del porvenir. *Debate (Peru)*, v. 16, no. 73 (June – Aug 93), pp. 56 – 60. Il.

Great Britain

Wu, Celia. *Generals and Diplomats: Great Britain and Peru, 1820 – 1840* reviewed by Betford Betalleluz. *Revista Andina*, v. 11, no. 1 (July 93), pp. 254 – 256.

Historiography

Szeminski, Jan. Manqu Qhapaq Inka según Anello Oliva, S.J., 1631. *Historia y Cultura (Peru)*, no. 20 (1990), pp. 269 – 280.

History

Bibliography

Fernández Alonso, Serena. Selección bibliográfica sobre el Perú virreinal durante el período reformista borbónico. *Anuario de Estudios Americanos*, v. 49, Suppl. 2 (1992), pp. 153 – 205.

To 1548

Marmontel, Jean François. *Los incas o la destrucción del imperio del Perú*, a translation of *Les incas ou la destruction de l'empire du Pérou*. Reviewed by Carlos Garatea Grau (Review entitled "Conquista y fanatismo"). *Debate (Peru)*, v. 15, no. 70 (Sept – Oct 92), p. 67. Il.

Torres, Angel. Aldana, un capitán de la conquista. *Signo*, no. 38, Nueva época (Jan – Apr 93), pp. 63 – 72.

1548 – 1820

Adorno, Rolena and Kenneth James Andrien, eds. *Transatlantic Encounters: Europeans and Andeans in the Sixteenth Century* reviewed by Ann Zulawski. *Colonial Latin American Review*, v. 2, no. 1 – 2 (1993), pp. 273 – 275.

— *Transatlantic Encounters: Europeans and Andeans in the Sixteenth Century* reviewed by Patricia Seed. *Hispanic American Historical Review*, v. 73, no. 1 (Feb 93), pp. 156 – 157.

— *Transatlantic Encounters: Europeans and Andeans in the Sixteenth Century* reviewed by Gabriela Ramos and Natalia Majluf. *Revista Andina*, v. 11, no. 1 (July 93), pp. 239 – 243. Bibl.

Bradley, Peter T. *Society, Economy, and Defence in Seventeenth-Century Peru: The Administration of the Count of Alba de Liste, 1655 – 1661* reviewed by Teodoro Hampe Martínez. *Colonial Latin American Review*, v. 2, no. 1 – 2 (1993), pp. 298 – 300.

— Society, Economy, and Defence in Seventeenth-Century Peru: The Administration of the Count of Alba de Liste, 1655 – 1661 reviewed by Stephen J. Homick. *Hispanic American Historical Review*, v. 73, no. 2 (May 93), pp. 314 – 315.

— Society, Economy, and Defence in Seventeenth-Century Peru: The Administration of the Count of Alba de Liste, 1655 – 1661 reviewed by Mark A. Burkholder. *Revista Interamericana de Bibliografía*, v. 42, no. 2 (1992), pp. 283 – 284.

Hampe Martínez, Teodoro. Hacia una nueva periodificación de la historia del Perú colonial: factores económicos, políticos y sociales. *Jahrbuch für Geschichte von Staat, Wirtschaft und Gesellschaft Lateinamerikas*, v. 29 (1992), pp. 47 – 74. Bibl.

Méndez, Cecilia. ¿Economía moral versus determinismo económico?: dos aproximaciones a la historia colonial hispanoamericana. *Historia y Cultura (Peru)*, no. 20 (1990), pp. 361 – 366.

Pease G. Y., Franklin. *Perú, hombre e historia: entre el siglo XVI y el XVIII* reviewed by Raúl Rivera Serna. *Anuario de Estudios Americanos*, v. 49, Suppl. 2 (1992), pp. 256 – 257.

— *Perú, hombre e historia: entre el siglo XVI y el XVIII* reviewed by Sara Mateos (Review entitled "Invasión y colonia"). *Debate (Peru)*, v. 15, no. 71 (Nov 92 – Jan 93), p. 77. Il.

Sala i Vila, Nuria. Alianzas y enfrentamientos regionales: consideraciones sobre la represión de un ritual andino en Lircay, 1794 – 1814. *Historia y Cultura (Peru)*, no. 20 (1990), pp. 221 – 242. Bibl.

Valle de Siles, María Eugenia del. *Historia de la rebelión de Tupac Catari, 1781 – 1782* reviewed by Marie-Danielle Démelas-Bohy. *Caravelle*, v. 59 (1992), pp. 249 – 253.

1820 – 1929, War of Independence

Brezzo, Liliana M. El general Guillermo Miller después de Ayacucho. *Investigaciones y Ensayos*, no. 41 (Jan – Dec 91), pp. 395 – 406. Bibl.

1830 – 1918

Husson, Patrick. *De la guerra a la rebelión: Huanta, siglo XIX* reviewed by Jaime Urrutia Ceruti. *Bulletin de l'Institut Français d'Etudes Andines*, v. 21, no. 3 (1992), pp. 1078 – 1082.

Intellectual life

Guibovich Pérez, Pedro. La cultura libresca de un converso procesado por la inquisición de Lima. *Historia y Cultura (Peru)*, no. 20 (1990), pp. 133 – 160 +. Bibl.

Hampe Martínez, Teodoro. The Diffusion of Books and Ideas in Colonial Peru: A Study of Private Libraries in the Sixteenth and Seventeenth Centuries. *Hispanic American Historical Review*, v. 73, no. 2 (May 93), pp. 211 – 233. Bibl, tables.

Languages

Tardieu, Jean-Pierre. Los jesuitas y la "lengua de Angola" en Perú, siglo XVII. *Revista de Indias*, v. 53, no. 198 (May – Aug 93), pp. 627 – 637. Bibl.

Pictorial works

Salvaron el año; Los subestimados del '93; Los sobreestimados del '93 (Photographic essays). *Debate (Peru)*, v. 16, no. 75 (Dec 93 – Jan 94), pp. 37 – 41. Il.

Politics and government

Montiel, Edgar. Perú: la construcción política de la nación. *Plural (Mexico)*, v. 22, no. 263 (Aug 93), pp. 16 – 24.

19th century

Fernández Alonso, Serena. Las montoneras como expresión política armada en el camino hacia la constitucionalidad del Perú republicano, siglo XIX. *Anuario de Estudios Americanos*, v. 50, no. 1 (1993), pp. 163 – 180. Bibl.

1919 –

Delpino, Nena. Jóvenes y política, ayer y hoy: carta a mi hija. *Debate (Peru)*, v. 15, no. 70 (Sept – Oct 92), pp. 39 – 44. Il.

Masterson, Daniel M. *Militarism and Politics in Latin America: Peru from Sánchez Cerro to Sendero Luminoso* reviewed by Brian Loveman. *The Americas*, v. 49, no. 3 (Jan 93), pp. 422 – 424.

1968 –

Cisneros, Luis Jaime. Entrevista a Enrique Chirinos Soto. *Debate (Peru)*, v. 16, no. 73 (June – Aug 93), pp. 8 – 16. Il.

Krauze, Enrique. Perú y Vargas Llosa: vidas variopintas. *Vuelta*, v. 17, no. 199 (June 93), pp. 17 – 20.

Vargas Llosa, Mario. *El pez en el agua* reviewed by Carlos Tello Díaz (Review entitled "Un pez fuera del agua"). *Nexos*, v. 16, no. 187 (July 93), pp. 81 – 83.

— *El pez en el agua* reviewed by Fabienne Bradu (Review entitled "Vida y biografía"). *Vuelta*, v. 17, no. 200 (July 93), pp. 54 – 55.

— *El pez en el agua* reviewed by Luis Pásara (Review entitled "Adiós al poder"). *Debate (Peru)*, v. 16, no. 73 (June – Aug 93), pp. 64 – 67. Il.

— *El pez en el agua* reviewed by Marco Martos (Review entitled "Las memorias de tres novelistas peruanos"). *Debate (Peru)*, v. 16, no. 73 (June – Aug 93), pp. 68 – 72. Il.

1980 –

Bowen, Sally and Manuel Jesús Orbegozo. 1992: el año que vivimos al galope. *Debate (Peru)*, v. 15, no. 71 (Nov 92 – Jan 93), pp. 22 – 26. Il.

Bustamante Belaúnde, Alberto et al. Pensando en la reelección. *Debate (Peru)*, v. 16, no. 72 (Mar – May 93), pp. 14 – 18. Il, charts.

Chávez, Martha and Francisco R. Sagasti. ¿Hacia un nuevo Perú? *Debate (Peru)*, v. 16, no. 74 (Sept – Oct 93), pp. 10 – 12. Il.

Cotler, Julio C. Golpe a golpe . . . . *Debate (Peru)*, v. 15, no. 71 (Nov 92 – Jan 93), pp. 18 – 19. Il.

Crabtree, John. *Peru under García: An Opportunity Lost* reviewed by Alfonso W. Quiroz. *Hispanic American Historical Review*, v. 73, no. 4 (Nov 93), pp. 713 – 714.

— *Peru under García: An Opportunity Lost* reviewed by Carol Graham. *Journal of Latin American Studies*, v. 25, no. 2 (May 93), pp. 413 – 414.

Fernández-Baca, Jorge. La importancia de la democracia para los economistas. *Apuntes (Peru)*, no. 29 (July – Dec 91), pp. 9 – 16. Bibl, charts.

Ghersi, Enrique. La ecuación Manuel Prado. *Debate (Peru)*, v. 16, no. 73 (June – Aug 93), pp. 24 – 25. Il.

Guerra García, Francisco. Crisis nacional y crisis de la izquierda. *Debate (Peru)*, v. 16, no. 75 (Dec 93 – Jan 94), pp. 23 – 24. Il.

Hernández, Max and Francisco R. Sagasti. La crisis de gobernabilidad democrática en el Perú. *Debate (Peru)*, v. 16, no. 75 (Dec 93 – Jan 94), pp. 24 – 28. Il.

Pásara, Luis H. El país imprevisible. *Debate (Peru)*, v. 16, no. 74 (Sept – Oct 93), pp. 6 – 9. Il.

— Peru: Into a Black Hole. *Hemisphere*, v. 5, no. 2 (Winter – Spring 93), pp. 26 – 30. Tables, charts.

Pedraglio, Santiago. De Merlín a Popovic. *Debate (Peru)*, v. 16, no. 73 (June – Aug 93), pp. 22 – 24. Il.

El poder en el Perú: XIII encuesta anual. *Debate (Peru)*, v. 16, no. 73 (June – Aug 93), pp. 31 – 47. Il, tables.

Poole, Deborah A. and Gerardo Rénique. *Peru: Time of Fear* reviewed by John Crabtree. *Bulletin of Latin American Research*, v. 12, no. 2 (May 93), pp. 243 – 244.

— *Peru: Time of Fear* reviewed by Lewis Taylor. *Journal of Latin American Studies*, v. 25, no. 3 (Oct 93), pp. 667 – 668.

Romaña, José María de. 1994, ¿decisión o incertidumbre? *Debate (Peru)*, v. 16, no. 75 (Dec 93 – Jan 94), p. 19. Il.

Rospigliosi, Fernando. La ausencia de los jóvenes en la política. *Debate (Peru)*, v. 16, no. 74 (Sept – Oct 93), pp. 32 – 33. Il.

Race question

Cosamalón, Ana Lucía. El lado oculto de lo cholo: presencia de rasgos culturales y afirmación de una identidad. *Allpanchis*, v. 25, no. 41 (Jan – June 93), pp. 211 – 226.

García Jordán, Pilar. Reflexiones sobre el darwinismo social: inmigración y colonización; mitos de los grupos modernizadores peruanos, 1821 – 1919. *Bulletin de l'Institut Français d'Etudes Andines*, v. 21, no. 3 (1992), pp. 961 – 975. Bibl.

Lauer, Mirko. La mentira cordial. *Debate (Peru)*, v. 16, no. 74 (Sept – Oct 93), pp. 41 – 45. Bibl.

Rural conditions

Mesclier, Evelyne. Cusco: espacios campesinos en un contexto de inestabilidad económica y retracción del estado (With several commentaries and a response by the authoress). *Revista Andina*, v. 11, no. 1 (July 93), pp. 7 – 53. Bibl, maps.

Social conditions

Azcueta, Michel et al. ¿Por qué vivir en el Perú de hoy? (Testimonies of various people on why, in light of the present crisis, they choose to live in Peru). *Debate (Peru)*, v. 15, no. 70 (Sept – Oct 92), pp. 29 – 34. Il.

Davies, Thomas M., Jr. Disintegration of a Culture: Peru into the 1990s. *SALALM Papers*, v. 36 (1991), pp. 42 – 48.

Matos Mar, José. El nuevo rostro de la cultura urbana del Perú. *América Indígena*, v. 51, no. 2 – 3 (Apr – Sept 91), pp. 11 – 34. Tables, maps.

Mossbrucker, Harald. El proceso de migración en el Perú: la revolución clandestina. *América Indígena*, v. 51, no. 2 – 3 (Apr – Sept 91), pp. 167 – 201. Bibl, charts.

Pictorial works

Instantes que dejan huella. *Allpanchis*, v. 25, no. 41 (Jan – June 93), pp. 273 – 288. Il.

PERU, UPPER

See
Bolivia

PERU IN LITERATURE

Ferrari, Américo. La presencia del Perú. *Inti*, no. 36 (Fall 92), pp. 29 – 37.

PERUVIAN DRAMA

History and criticism

Beyersdorff, Margot. La "puesta en texto" del primer drama indohispano en los Andes. *Revista de Crítica Literaria Latinoamericana*, v. 19, no. 37 (Jan – June 93), pp. 195 – 221. Bibl, il.

Montoya, Rodrigo. El teatro quechua como lugar de reflexión sobre la historia y la política. *Revista de Crítica Literaria Latinoamericana*, v. 19, no. 37 (Jan – June 93), pp. 223 – 241. Bibl.

PERUVIAN LITERATURE

Kappatos, Rigas and Pedro Lastra, eds. *Antología del cuento peruano* reviewed by Marina Catzaras. *Revista de Crítica Literaria Latinoamericana*, v. 19, no. 37 (Jan – June 93), pp. 392 – 396.

Bibliography

Elmore, Peter. Sobre el volcán: seis novelas peruanas de los '90 (Review article). *Hueso Húmero*, no. 29 (May 93), pp. 125 – 143.

Rodríguez Rea, Miguel Angel. *El Perú y su literatura: guía bibliográfica* reviewed by M. Rozenblat. *Caravelle*, no. 60 (1993), pp. 179 – 180.

— *El Perú y su literatura: guía bibliográfica* reviewed by David William Foster. *Chasqui*, v. 22, no. 1 (May 93), pp. 86 – 87.

History and criticism

Cornejo Polar, Antonio. *La formación de la tradición literaria en el Perú* reviewed by Javier Sanjinés C. *Hispamérica*, v. 21, no. 63 (Dec 92), pp. 93 – 96.

Elmore, Peter. *Los muros invisibles: Lima y la modernidad en la novela del siglo XX* reviewed by Rodrigo Quijano (Review entitled "Experiencia urbana"). *Debate (Peru)*, v. 16, no. 73 (June – Aug 93), p. 74. Il.

PERUVIAN POETRY

Chirinos Arrieta, Eduardo, ed. *Infame turba: poesía en la Universidad Católica, 1917 – 1992* reviewed by Abelardo Oquendo (Review entitled "Pero, ¿existe algo que pueda llamarse un poeta de la Católica?"). *Debate (Peru)*, v. 16, no. 72 (Mar – May 93), pp. 55 – 56. Il.

History and criticism

Millones Santa Gadea, Luis. Poemas y canciones en honor de Santa Rosa: profecías del pasado, voces del presente. *Revista de Crítica Literaria Latinoamericana*, v. 19, no. 37 (Jan – June 93), pp. 185 – 194. Bibl.

PERUVIANS

United States

Altamirano Rúa, Teófilo. Pastores quechuas en el oeste norteamericano. *América Indígena*, v. 51, no. 2 – 3 (Apr – Sept 91), pp. 203 – 222. Maps.

PESTICIDES

Benencia, Roberto and Javier Souza Casadinho. Alimentos y salud: uso y abuso de pesticidas en la horticultura bonaerense. *Realidad Económica*, no. 114 – 115 (Feb – May 93), pp. 29 – 53. Bibl, tables.

Grossman, Lawrence S. Pesticides, People, and the Environment in St. Vincent. *Caribbean Geography*, v. 3, no. 3 (Mar 92), pp. 175 – 186. Bibl, tables, maps.

Morgner, Fred G. Poisoning the Garden: Costa Rica's Ecological Crisis. *SALALM Papers*, v. 36 (1991), pp. 77 – 87. Bibl.

Neumann, Holly. From Pigs to Pesticides. *Business Mexico*, v. 3, no. 1 (Jan – Feb 93), pp. 19 – 22. Il, tables.

PETÉN, GUATEMALA

Arrivillaga Cortés, Alfonso. Marimbas, bandas y conjuntos orquestales de Petén. *La Tradición Popular*, no. 82 (1991), Issue. Bibl, il.

Déleon Meléndez, Ofelia Columba and Brenda Ninette Mayol Baños. Aproximación a la cultura popular tradicional de los municipios de Ciudad Flores, San José y la aldea Santa Eleana del departamento de Petén, Guatemala. *La Tradición Popular*, no. 76 – 77 (1990), Issue. Il, facs.

Laporte, Jean Pierre. Los sitios arqueológicos del valle de Dolores en las montañas mayas de Guatemala. *Mesoamérica (USA)*, v. 13, no. 24 (Dec 92), pp. 413 – 439. Bibl, il, tables, maps.

PETRARCA, FRANCESCO

Meo Zilio, Giovanni. A propósito de ecos petrarquistas en el argentino Enrique Banchs. *Nueva Revista de Filología Hispánica*, v. 40, no. 2 (July – Dec 92), pp. 909 – 920.

PETROCHEMICALS

See
Petroleum industry and trade

PETROGLYPHS

See also
Dermatoglyphics

Argentina

Fernández, Fiz Antonio. *Antropología cultural, medicina indígena de América y arte rupestre argentino* reviewed by Hebe Clementi. *Todo Es Historia*, v. 26, no. 307 (Feb 93), pp. 75 – 76. Il.

Brazil

Vidal, Lux et al, eds. *Grafismo indígena: ensaios de antropologia estética* reviewed by Clarice Cohn. *Revista de Antropologia (Brazil)*, v. 34 (1991), pp. 230 – 232.

Peru

Rostworowski Tovar de Diez Canseco, María. El Dios Con y el misterio de la pampa de Nasca. *Latin American Indian Literatures Journal*, v. 9, no. 1 (Spring 93), pp. 21 – 30.

PETROLEUM INDUSTRY AND TRADE

See also
Gas, Natural

Argentina

Bekerman, Marta. O setor petroquímico e a integração Argentina – Brasil. *Pesquisa e Planejamento Econômico*, v. 22, no. 2 (Aug 92), pp. 369 – 398. Bibl, tables.

Bravo, Víctor. YPF S.A.: ¿Y ahora, qué? *Realidad Económica*, no. 117 (July – Aug 93), pp. 2 – 7.

Gorenstein, Silvia. El complejo petroquímico Bahía Blanca: algunas reflexiones sobre sus implicancias especiales. *Desarrollo Económico (Argentina)*, v. 32, no. 128 (Jan – Mar 93), pp. 575 – 601. Bibl, tables, charts.

Ríos, Javier Enrique de los. La huelga de Campana de 1915: conflicto olvido. *Todo Es Historia*, v. 27, no. 314 (Sept 93), pp. 56 – 69. Bibl, il.

Silenzi de Stagni, Adolfo et al. La privatización de YPF. *Realidad Económica*, no. 118 (Aug – Sept 93), pp. 18 – 67. Tables, charts.

Brazil

Bekerman, Marta. O setor petroquímico e a integração Argentina – Brasil. *Pesquisa e Planejamento Econômico*, v. 22, no. 2 (Aug 92), pp. 369 – 398. Bibl, tables.

Ramires, Julio Cesar Lima. As grandes corporações e a dinâmica socioespacial: a ação da PETROBRAS em Macaé. *Revista Brasileira de Geografia*, v. 53, no. 4 (Oct – Dec 91), pp. 115 – 151. Bibl, tables, maps.

Randall, Laura Regina Rosenbaum. Petróleo, economía y medio ambiente en Brasil. *Revista Mexicana de Sociología*, v. 54, no. 2 (Apr – June 92), pp. 185 – 211. Tables.

Colombia

Vásquez Rodríguez, Raúl. Petróleo y gas en el gobierno Gaviria. *Revista Javeriana*, v. 61, no. 597 (Aug 93), pp. 153 – 158.

Costa Rica

Obando Obando, William. Repercusiones sociológicas de las exploraciones petroleras en los pueblos shiroles y suretka – talamanca. *Revista de Ciencias Sociales (Costa Rica)*, no. 57 (Sept 92), pp. 109 – 119. Bibl, tables.

Mexico

Baker, George. Does Modernization at PEMEX Meet Consumer Needs? *Business Mexico*, v. 3, no. 5 (May 93), pp. 4 – 7 +. Il, tables.

Barbosa, Fabio. Los retos del sindicalismo petrolero. *El Cotidiano*, v. 9, no. 56 (July 93), pp. 33 – 39. Il.

Barnhart, Katherine. Pumping Out a New Image. *Business Mexico*, v. 3, no. 5 (May 93), pp. 8 – 12 +. Il, maps.

Brown, Jonathan C. *Oil and Revolution in Mexico* reviewed by Rebeca de Gortari Rabiela. *Revista Mexicana de Sociología*, v. 55, no. 2 (Apr – June 93), pp. 389 – 395.

Gamboa Ojeda, Leticia. Historia de una pequeña empresa: la Compañía Petrolera de Puebla en Pánuco, 1916 – 1924. *La Palabra y el Hombre*, no. 83 (July – Sept 92), pp. 219 – 253. Bibl, tables, maps.

Novelo, Victoria. *La difícil democracia de los petroleros: historia de un proyecto sindical* reviewed by Aída Escamilla Rubio. *El Cotidiano*, v. 9, no. 56 (July 93), p. 117.

Salinas Chávez, Antonio. El cambio estructural de PEMEX: más empresa, menos política económica. *Comercio Exterior*, v. 43, no. 11 (Nov 93), pp. 1001 – 1009. Bibl, charts.

Stoub, Jeffrey. De-Fossilizing the Fuel Industry. *Business Mexico*, v. 3, no. 1 (Jan – Feb 93), pp. 16 – 18. Il.

Suárez Guevara, Sergio. A 55 de la expropiación petrolera: nuevas y profundas luchas. *Momento Económico*, no. 67 (May – June 93), pp. 2 – 6.

Werner, Johannes. Return of the Gas Crisis Jitters. *Business Mexico*, v. 3, no. 6 (June 93), pp. 32 – 34 +. Tables.

Deregulation

Herrera Toledano, Salvador. Secondary Petrochemicals: Risks and Rewards (Translated by Robert Brackney). *Business Mexico*, v. 3, no. 7 (July 93), pp. 34 – 36. Tables.

Law and legislation

Turcotte, Richard E. Tracing the Pipeline. *Business Mexico*, v. 3, no. 3 (Mar 93), pp. 24 – 26.

Statistics

Pieza, Ramón. PEMEX frente a la nación mexicana: su integración al proceso de desarrollo nacional. *Momento Económico*, no. 68 (July – Aug 93), pp. 23 – 28. Tables.

PHARMACY

Brazil

Arilha, Margareth and Regina Maria Barbosa. A experiência brasileira com o Cytotec. *Estudos Feministas*, v. 1, no. 2 (1993), pp. 408 – 417. Tables, charts.

Ribeiro, Eliane. "Dose unitária": sistema de distribuição de medicamentos em hospitais. *RAE; Revista de Administração de Empresas*, v. 33, no. 6 (Nov – Dec 93), pp. 62 – 73. Tables, charts.

PHILANTHROPY

See
  Charities
  Subdivision *Charitable contributions* under *Business enterprises*

PHILIPPINE ISLANDS

See also
  Franciscans – Philippine Islands

McCarthy, William J. Between Policy and Prerogative: Malfeasance in the Inspection of the Manila Galleons at Acapulco, 1637. *Colonial Latin American Historical Review*, v. 2, no. 2 (Spring 93), pp. 163 – 183. Bibl, maps.

PHILOSOPHICAL ANTHROPOLOGY

Bayardo, Rubens. Acerca de la cuestión postmoderna: una perspectiva antropológica. *Estudios Paraguayos*, v. 17, no. 1 – 2 (1989 – 1993), pp. 23 – 33. Bibl.

Chiappo, Leopoldo. La concepción del hombre en Honorio Delgado. *Apuntes (Peru)*, no. 31 (July – Dec 92), pp. 55 – 62.

Sánchez Gamboa, Silvio Ancísar. La concepción del hombre en la investigación educativa: algunas consideraciones. *Islas*, no. 96 (May – Aug 90), pp. 34 – 41. Bibl.

PHILOSOPHY

See also
  Aesthetics
  Alienation
  Cosmology
  Death
  Ethics
  Existentialism
  Freedom
  Humanism
  Ideology
  Knowledge, Theory of
  Peace
  Philosophical anthropology
  Philosophy and politics
  Positivism
  Skepticism
  Theology
  Utopias
  Names of specific philosophers
  Subdivision *Philosophy* under *History, Language and languages,* and *Science*

Argentina

Castello, Antonio Emilio. Entrevista: Eugenio Pucciarelli. *Todo Es Historia*, v. 26, no. 305 (Dec 92), pp. 58 – 64. Il.

Galindo López, Olga. La filosofía inculturada: ¿Una alternativa social para la América Latina? *Islas*, no. 99 (May – Aug 91), pp. 5 – 14. Bibl.

García Machado, Xiomara. Notas críticas para la "transcendencia" de un proyecto liberador: Mario Casalla y Silvio Maresca. *Islas*, no. 99 (May – Aug 91), pp. 15 – 20. Bibl.

Bolivia

García Fernández, Irsa Teresa. El pensamiento boliviano: ¿Hacia una filosofía de la liberación? *Islas*, no. 99 (May – Aug 91), pp. 45 – 50. Bibl.

Brazil

Alsina Gutiérrez, Rogelio. Filosofía de la liberación en Brasil: aproximación inicial al tema. *Islas*, no. 99 (May – Aug 91), pp. 30 – 37.

Study and teaching

Segismundo, Fernando. A filosofia no Colégio Pedro II. *Revista do Instituto Histórico e Geográfico Brasileiro*, no. 373 (Oct – Dec 91), pp. 948 – 953.

Chile

Ossandón Buljevic, Carlos A. Una historia de la filosofía en Chile: modernidad e institucionalidad. *Estudios Sociales (Chile)*, no. 77 (July – Sept 93), pp. 9 – 15.

Colombia

Cano, Lidia and Pablo M. Guadarrama González. Filosofía de la liberación en Colombia. *Islas*, no. 99 (May – Aug 91), pp. 51 – 74. Bibl.

Quintero Esquivel, Jorge Eliécer. Ergotismo, ilustración y utilitarismo en Colombia: siglos XVIII y XIX. *Islas*, no. 96 (May – Aug 90), pp. 53 – 66. Bibl, tables, charts.

Costa Rica

Study and teaching

Negrín Fajardo, Olegario. Krausismo, positivismo y currículum científico en el bachillerato costarricense. *Siglo XIX: Revista*, no. 12, 2a época (July – Dec 92), pp. 105 – 118. Bibl.

Cuba

Borges Legrá, Félix. Las primeras manifestaciones del pensamiento filosófico en Cuba: la escolástica como teorización dominante en el período del criollismo. *Islas*, no. 96 (May – Aug 90), pp. 150 – 156.

García Mora, Luis Miguel. Un cubano en la corte de la restauración: la labor intelectual de Rafael Montoro, 1875 – 1878. *Revista de Indias*, v. 52, no. 195 – 196 (May – Dec 92), pp. 443 – 475. Bibl.

Ecuador

León del Río, Yohanka. La historia de las ideas como una de las problemáticas de la filosofía de la liberación en el Ecuador. *Islas*, no. 99 (May – Aug 91), pp. 75 – 86. Bibl.

Europe, Eastern

Górski, Eugeniusz. Filosofía y sociedad en el pensamiento europeo oriental y latinoamericano (Translated by Jorge Radín Videla). *Cuadernos Americanos*, no. 41, Nueva época (Sept – Oct 93), pp. 76 – 92. Bibl.

Latin America

Alsina Gutiérrez, Rogelio and Xiomara García Machado. Un nuevo estilo de filosofar: polémica con Mario Casalla desde la alteridad. *Islas*, no. 96 (May – Aug 90), pp. 111 – 120. Bibl.

Ardao, Arturo. El historicismo y la filosofía americana. *Hoy Es Historia*, v. 10, no. 59 (Sept – Oct 93), pp. 81 – 86. Bibl, il.

Biagini, Hugo Edgardo. La filosofía latinoamericana a partir de su historia. *Anuario de Estudios Americanos*, v. 49, Suppl. 1 (1992), pp. 3 – 45. Bibl.

Casañas Díaz, Mirta and Rafael Plá León. La constancia de Leopoldo Zea en la búsqueda de un filosofar autenticamente americano. *Islas*, no. 99 (May – Aug 91), pp. 95 – 111. Bibl.

Domínguez Miranda, Manuel. Ignacio Ellacuría, filósofo de la realidad latinoamericana. *ECA; Estudios Centroamericanos*, v. 47, no. 529 – 530 (Nov – Dec 92), pp. 983 – 998.

Dussel, Enrique D. El proyecto de una filosofía de la historia latinoamericana. *Hoy Es Historia*, v. 10, no. 57 (Apr – May 93), pp. 40 – 48. Bibl.

Gómez-Martínez, José Luis. El pensamiento de la liberación: hacia una posición dialógica. *Cuadernos Americanos*, no. 40, Nueva época (July – Aug 93), pp. 53 – 61. Bibl.

Górski, Eugeniusz. Filosofía y sociedad en el pensamiento europeo oriental y latinoamericano (Translated by Jorge Radín Videla). *Cuadernos Americanos*, no. 41, Nueva época (Sept – Oct 93), pp. 76 – 92. Bibl.

Guadarrama González, Pablo M. Las alternativas sociales en América Latina y la filosofía de la liberación. *Islas*, no. 96 (May – Aug 90), pp. 89 – 102. Bibl.

Guadarrama González, Pablo M. et al. El humanismo en la filosofía latinoamericana de la liberación. *Islas*, no. 99 (May – Aug 91), pp. 173 – 199. Bibl.

Guy, Alain. *Panorama de la philosophie ibéro-américaine* reviewed by Solomon Lipp. *Revista Canadiense de Estudios Hispánicos*, v. 17, no. 1 (Fall 92), pp. 215 – 218.

Kolesov, Mijail. El pensamiento filosófico de América Latina en la búsqueda de su autenticidad. *Islas*, no. 96 (May – Aug 90), pp. 42 – 52.

Pérez Villacampa, Gilberto. Enrique Dussel: ¿De la metafísica de la alteridad al humanismo real? *Islas*, no. 99 (May – Aug 91), pp. 160 – 167.

— Horacio Cerutti y el problema del fin de la filosofía clásica de la liberación. *Islas*, no. 99 (May – Aug 91), pp. 168 – 172.

Rojas Gómez, Miguel. Del exilio de la razón a la razón de la libertad en Osvaldo Ardiles. *Islas*, no. 99 (May – Aug 91), pp. 112 – 129. Bibl.

— Identidad cultural y liberación en la filosofía latinoamericana de la liberación. *Islas*, no. 96 (May – Aug 90), pp. 103 – 110.

Sánchez-Gey Venegas, Juana. El modernismo filosófico en América. *Cuadernos Americanos*, no. 41, Nueva época (Sept – Oct 93), pp. 109 – 121. Bibl.

Vetter, Ulrich. La "nueva metafísica" latinoamericana y las "filosofías para la liberación": dimensiones del término "liberación." *Islas*, no. 96 (May – Aug 90), pp. 127 – 131.

Zea, Leopoldo. Conciencia de América (Excerpt from his book entitled *La esencia de lo americano*). *Hoy Es Historia*, v. 10, no. 60 (Nov – Dec 93), pp. 61 – 69. Bibl.

Mexico

Vargas Lozano, Gabriel. La filosofía mexicana del siglo XX en una nuez. *Plural (Mexico)*, v. 22, no. 257 (Feb 93), pp. 78 – 79.

— Función actual de la filosofía en México. *Plural (Mexico)*, v. 22, no. 265 (Oct 93), pp. 36 – 38.

Peru

Valdés García, Félix and María Teresa Vila Bormey. La filosofía de la liberación en Perú: de Augusto Salazar Bondy a Francisco Miró Quesada. *Islas*, no. 99 (May – Aug 91), pp. 21 – 29. Bibl.

Uruguay

Figueroa Casas, Vilma and Israel López Pino. Hacia una filosofía de la liberación uruguaya. *Islas*, no. 99 (May – Aug 91), pp. 38 – 44.

Michelena, Alejandro Daniel. Vaz Ferreira, filósofo de cercanías. *Hoy Es Historia*, v. 10, no. 58 (July – Aug 93), pp. 4 – 9. Il.

Romero Baró, José María. Ciencia y filosofía en el pensador uruguayo Carlos Vaz Ferreira. *Hoy Es Historia*, v. 10, no. 58 (July – Aug 93), pp. 10 – 14. Bibl.

Sasso, Javier. Arturo Ardao, historiador de las ideas. *Hoy Es Historia*, v. 10, no. 59 (Sept – Oct 93), pp. 4 – 12. Bibl, il.

Venezuela

Nuño Montes, Juan Antonio. *La escuela de la sospecha: nuevos ensayos polémicos* reviewed by Amaya Llebot Cazalis. *Revista Nacional de Cultura (Venezuela)*, v. 54, no. 287 (Oct – Dec 92), pp. 267 – 268.

PHILOSOPHY AND POLITICS

See also
Marxism

Ballesteros, Carlos. El problema de la legitimidad democrática ante las transformaciones políticas. *Revista Mexicana de Ciencias Políticas y Sociales*, v. 38, Nueva época, no. 151 (Jan – Mar 93), pp. 103 – 116.

Caiceo E., Jaime. El planteamiento filosófico – político de Maritain aplicado en Chile. *Estudios Sociales (Chile)*, no. 76 (Apr – June 93), pp. 205 – 210. Bibl.

Fernández Santillán, José F. Democracia y liberalismo: ensayo de filosofía política. *Revista Mexicana de Ciencias Políticas y Sociales*, v. 38, Nueva época, no. 151 (Jan – Mar 93), pp. 157 – 183. Bibl.

Hernández, Raúl Augusto. Indecisión social o crisis de conciencia: los cardinales de la desolación. *Estudios Interdisciplinarios de América Latina y el Caribe*, v. 4, no. 1 (Jan – June 93), pp. 141 – 163. Bibl, tables, charts.

Argentina

Marrero Fente, Raúl and Mirta Yordi. El tema de la democracia en pensadores políticos argentinos. *Islas*, no. 96 (May – Aug 90), pp. 67 – 70. Bibl.

Latin America

Alvarez, Federico et al, eds. *Gramsci en América Latina: del silencio al olvido* reviewed by Mario Sznajder. *Estudios Interdisciplinarios de América Latina y el Caribe*, v. 3, no. 2 (July – Dec 92), pp. 133 – 137.

Baptista Gumucio, Fernando. Orígenes del pensamiento político hispanoamericano. *Signo*, no. 36 – 37, Nueva época (May – Dec 92), pp. 325 – 329.

Barbosa Estepa, Reinaldo. Clientelismo y antidemocracia: la acción política en la formación de la conciencia social. *Islas*, no. 96 (May – Aug 90), pp. 5 – 17. Bibl.

Cornejo Guinassi, Pedro. La ruda sobriedad del realismo. *Debate (Peru)*, v. 15, no. 70 (Sept – Oct 92), pp. 45 – 47. Bibl, il.

Löwy, Michael. Los intelectuales latinoamericanos y la crítica social de la modernidad. *Casa de las Américas*, no. 191 (Apr – June 93), pp. 100 – 105. Bibl.

Stefanich Irala, Juan. Alberdi, Latinoamérica y el Paraguay. *Estudios Paraguayos*, v. 17, no. 1 – 2 (1989 – 1993), pp. 107 – 119.

PHILOSOPHY AND RELIGION

See
Theology

PHOTOGRAPHS

Achutti, Luiz Eduardo Robinson. Ensaio fotográfico: autoretrato de Dina. *Vozes*, v. 86, no. 5 (Sept – Oct 92), pp. 95 – 98. Il.

Beramendi Usera, Fernando. Intimate Openings through Prison Walls (Photographs by Oscar Bonilla). *Américas*, v. 45, no. 1 (Jan – Feb 93), pp. 30 – 35. Il.

Coke, Van Deren. *Secular and Sacred: Photographs of Mexico* reviewed by Diana Emery Hulick (Review entitled "Lo secular y lo sagrado: fotografías de México"). *Latin American Art*, v. 5, no. 2 (Summer 93), p. 104.

Esteves, Juan. Ensaio fotográfico: portraits. *Vozes*, v. 87, no. 2 (Mar – Apr 93), pp. 76 – 83. Il.

Gaiso, Pisco del. Ensaio fotográfico: subjetivismo visual. *Vozes*, v. 87, no. 3 (May – June 93), pp. 73 – 75. Il.

Garduño, Flor. *Witnesses of Time* reviewed by Jerald R. Green. *Latin American Art*, v. 5, no. 1 (Spring 93), p. 95.

Giandalia, Paulo. Ensaio fotográfico: Paris, 1991. *Vozes*, v. 87, no. 4 (July – Aug 93), pp. 70 – 76. Il.

Instantes que dejan huella. *Allpanchis*, v. 25, no. 41 (Jan – June 93), pp. 273 – 288. Il.

López Junqué, Fernando. *Temporada en el ingenio: ensayo fotográfico* introduced by José Lezama Lima. Reviewed by Antonio Santamaría García. *Anuario de Estudios Americanos*, v. 49, Suppl. 1 (1992), p. 256.

Luna, Felicitas. La fotohistoria del mes (A regular feature that presents historical photographs along with a brief biography or description). *Todo Es Historia*, v. 26 – 27 (Dec 92 – Dec 93), All issues.

Plentz, Leopoldo. Ensaio fotográfico: a miséria estética (Includes poems by Nei Duclós, Henrique do Valle, and João Angelo Salvadori). *Vozes*, v. 86, no. 6 (Nov – Dec 92), pp. 82 – 91. Il.

¡Salvaron el '92! (A photographic essay of public and popular Peruvian personalities and current events). *Debate (Peru)*, v. 15, no. 71 (Nov 92 – Jan 93), pp. 27 – 33. Il.

Stephan-Otto, Erwin. Xochimilco: fuente de historias (Accompanied by an English translation). *Artes de México*, no. 20 (Summer 93), pp. 33 – 35.

PHOTOGRAPHY, AERIAL

Peru

Denevan, William M. The 1931 Shippee – Johnson Aerial Photography Expedition to Peru. *Geographical Review*, v. 83, no. 3 (July 93), pp. 238 – 251. Bibl, il, maps.

Echavarría, Fernando R. Cuantificación de la deforestación en el valle del Huallaga, Perú. *Revista Geográfica (Mexico)*, no. 114 (July – Dec 91), pp. 37 – 53. Bibl, tables, maps, charts.

Río de la Plata region

Giddings, Lorrain Eugene. Visión por satélite de las inundaciones extraordinarias de la cuenca del Río de la Plata. *Interciencia*, v. 18, no. 1 (Jan – Feb 93), pp. 16 – 23. Bibl, il, tables, charts.

PHOTOGRAPHY AND PHOTOGRAPHERS

Collectors and collecting

Methodology

Rêgo, Stella M. de Sá. Access to Photograph Collections. *SALALM Papers*, v. 34 (1989), pp. 123 – 129. Bibl.

Exhibitions

Zinkant, Annette. Fotos mexicanas en la Casa de las Culturas (Translated by José Luis Gómez y Patiño). *Humboldt*, no. 109 (1993), p. 96. Il.

Andean region

Indexes

González, Nelly S. Images from Inca Lands: An Index of Photographic Slides from the OAS. *SALALM Papers*, v. 34 (1989), pp. 115 – 122.

Argentina

Alexander, Abel. La magia del daguerrotipo. *Todo Es Historia*, v. 27, no. 311 (June 93), pp. 74 – 77. Il.

El daguerrotipo más curioso de la Argentina: plata y magia. *Hoy Es Historia*, v. 10, no. 60 (Nov – Dec 93), pp. 87 – 88.

Facio, Sara. Fotografía: la memoria cuestionada. *Cuadernos Hispanoamericanos*, no. 517 – 519 (July – Sept 93), pp. 269 – 279. Il.

Kirbus, Federico B. Técnicas y trucos de nuestros fotógrafos. *Todo Es Historia*, v. 26, no. 309 (Apr 93), pp. 74 – 78. Il.

Piaggio, Laura Raquel. Fotos, historia, indios y antropólogos. *Runa*, v. 20 (1991 – 1992), pp. 163 – 166. Bibl.

Congresses

Luna, Felicitas. A ciento cincuenta años de la fotografía: Segundo Congreso de la Fotografía Argentina, 1839 – 1939. *Todo Es Historia*, v. 27, no. 313 (Aug 93), p. 92. Il.

Brazil

Ferrez, Gilberto João Carlos. *Photography in Brazil, 1840 – 1900* translated by Stella de Sá Rêgo. Reviewed by Mary Karasch (Review entitled "Brazilian Photography"). *The Americas*, v. 49, no. 3 (Jan 93), pp. 391 – 392.

Sources

Almeida, Stela Borges de and Luiz Felippe Perret Serpa. Guia de fontes fotográficas para a história da educação. *Revista Brasileira de Estudos Pedagógicos*, v. 72, no. 172 (Sept – Dec 91), pp. 392 – 394.

Colombia

Londoño, Patricia. Visual Images of Urban Colombian Women, 1800 to 1930. *SALALM Papers*, v. 34 (1989), pp. 99 – 114. Bibl.

Exhibitions

Camnitzer, Luis et al. XXXIV Salón Nacional de Artistas (Accompanied by an English translation). *Art Nexus*, no. 7 (Jan – Mar 93), pp. 140 – 144. Il.

Guatemala

Castro, Fernando. Luis González Palma: los iluminados (Accompanied by an English translation). *Art Nexus*, no. 7 (Jan – Mar 93), pp. 136 – 138. Il.

Latin America

Levine, Robert M. *Images of History: Nineteenth and Twentieth Century Latin American Photography as Documents* reviewed by William H. Beezley. *Hispanic American Historical Review*, v. 73, no. 1 (Feb 93), pp. 133 – 134.

Bibliography

Davidson, Martha R. A Bibliography on Photography. *SALALM Papers*, v. 34 (1989), pp. 130 – 134.

Exhibitions

Gutiérrez, Natalia. Cambio de foco (Accompanied by an English translation). *Art Nexus*, no. 9 (June – Aug 93), pp. 96 – 99. Il.

Niño de Guzmán, Guillermo. El desnudo latinoamericano. *Debate (Peru)*, v. 15, no. 71 (Nov 92 – Jan 93), pp. 60 – 63. Il.

Mexico

Coronel Rivera, Juan. Héctor García. *Artes de México,* no. 19 (Spring 93), p. 116. Il.

Ferrer, Elizabeth. Manos poderosas: The Photography of Graciela Iturbide. *Review,* no. 47 (Fall 93), pp. 69 – 78. Il.

González Rodríguez, Sergio. Lola Alvarez Bravo: la luz en el espejo. *Nexos,* v. 16, no. 190 (Oct 93), pp. 16 – 20.

Tejada, Roberto. Eugenia Vargas: el proscenio inevitable (Translated by Paloma Díaz Abreu). *Artes de México,* no. 21 (Fall 93), pp. 98 – 99. Il.

Zinkant, Annette. Fotos mexicanas en la Casa de las Culturas (Translated by José Luis Gómez y Patiño). *Humboldt,* no. 109 (1993), p. 96. Il.

Peru

Hartup, Cheryl. Early Twentieth Century Peruvian Photography. *Latin American Art,* v. 5, no. 2 (Summer 93), pp. 60 – 62. Bibl, il.

Heredia, Jorge. Avatares de la obra del fotógrafo peruano Martín Chambi (1891 – 1973) y reseña de dos monografías recientes. *Hueso Húmero,* no. 29 (May 93), pp. 144 – 173. Bibl.

Study and teaching

Valentín, Isidro. El gusto por la imagen: una vivencia de fotografía social. *Allpanchis,* v. 25, no. 41 (Jan – June 93), pp. 262 – 272. Il.

United States

Damian, Carol. María Martínez Cañas: el viaje a casa (Accompanied by the English original, translated by Ignacio Zuleta Ll.). *Art Nexus,* no. 9 (June – Aug 93), pp. 114 – 117. Il.

Olivares, Julián. Russell Lee, Photographer. *The Americas Review,* v. 19, no. 3 – 4 (Winter 91), pp. 17 – 19 +. Il.

Turner, Elisa. María Martínez Cañas. *Latin American Art,* v. 5, no. 1 (Spring 93), pp. 85 – 86. Il.

Law and legislation

Levy, David L. Use and Reproduction of Photographs: Copyright Issues. *SALALM Papers,* v. 34 (1989), pp. 135 – 140.

PHYSICIANS

Jamaica

Alexander, Philip N. John H. Rapier, Jr. and the Medical Profession in Jamaica, 1861 – 1862 (Part I). *Jamaica Journal,* v. 24, no. 3 (Feb 93), pp. 37 – 46. Bibl, il.

— John H. Rapier, Jr. and the Medical Profession in Jamaica, 1861 – 1862 (Part II). *Jamaica Journal,* v. 25, no. 1 (Oct 93), pp. 55 – 62. Bibl, il, facs.

Uruguay

Soiza Larrosa, Augusto. Valores notables de la cultura uruguaya: algunos aportes médicos uruguayos a la comunidad científica mundial. *Hoy Es Historia,* v. 10, no. 55 (Jan – Feb 93), pp. 35 – 44. Bibl.

Venezuela

Fortique, José Rafael. *Crónicas médicas* reviewed by Juvenal López Ruiz. *Revista Nacional de Cultura (Venezuela),* v. 53, no. 286 (July – Sept 92), p. 265.

— El primer obispo de Maracaibo y su médico personal. *Boletín de la Academia Nacional de la Historia (Venezuela),* v. 76, no. 302 (Apr – June 93), pp. 133 – 139.

Tosta, Virgilio. Huella y presencia de médicos europeos en el estado Barinas. *Boletín de la Academia Nacional de la Historia (Venezuela),* v. 75, no. 297 (Jan – Mar 92), pp. 69 – 95.

PHYSICS

Merrell, Floyd Fenly. *Unthinking Thinking: Jorge Luis Borges, Mathematics, and the New Physics* reviewed by Harley D. Oberhelman. *Hispania (USA),* v. 76, no. 2 (May 93), pp. 289 – 290.

Venezuela

Study and teaching

Leal, Henry. Alejandro Ibarra: primer tratadista de física experimental en la UCV, 1834 – 1874. *Revista Nacional de Cultura (Venezuela),* v. 54, no. 287 (Oct – Dec 92), pp. 238 – 258. Bibl, il.

PIAGUAJE, FRANCISCO

Weiskopf, Jimmy. Healing Secrets in a Shaman's Garden. *Américas,* v. 45, no. 4 (July – Aug 93), pp. 42 – 47. Il.

PIAROA INDIANS

Kaplan, Joanna Overing. A estética da produção: o senso de comunidade entre os cubeo e os piaroa. *Revista de Antropologia (Brazil),* v. 34 (1991), pp. 7 – 33. Bibl.

PIAZZOLLA, ASTOR

Helguera, Luis Ignacio. Astor Piazzolla. *Vuelta,* v. 17, no. 204 (Nov 93), pp. 64 – 65.

PICÓN SALAS, MARIANO

Beltrán Guerrero, Luis. El gran Mariano. *Boletín de la Academia Nacional de la Historia (Venezuela),* v. 76, no. 301 (Jan – Mar 93), pp. 57 – 61.

Bravo, Víctor. Poligrafía y consciencia de la escritura. *Boletín de la Academia Nacional de la Historia (Venezuela),* v. 76, no. 301 (Jan – Mar 93), pp. 106 – 108.

Briceño Ferrigni, Germán. La ciudad y el escritor. *Boletín de la Academia Nacional de la Historia (Venezuela),* v. 76, no. 301 (Jan – Mar 93), pp. 9 – 18.

Liscano, Alirio. El adelantado Mariano Picón Salas. *Boletín de la Academia Nacional de la Historia (Venezuela),* v. 76, no. 301 (Jan – Mar 93), pp. 108 – 109.

Lovera De-Sola, Roberto J. Mariano Picón Salas: sus rasgos vitales. *Boletín de la Academia Nacional de la Historia (Venezuela),* v. 76, no. 301 (Jan – Mar 93), pp. 89 – 92. Bibl.

Márquez Rodríguez, Alexis. Mariano Picón Salas: teoría y práctica del estilo. *Boletín de la Academia Nacional de la Historia (Venezuela),* v. 76, no. 301 (Jan – Mar 93), pp. 79 – 88. Bibl.

— La obra ensayística de Mariano Picón Salas. *Boletín de la Academia Nacional de la Historia (Venezuela),* v. 76, no. 301 (Jan – Mar 93), pp. 63 – 78. Bibl.

Tablante Garrido, Pedro Nicolás. Vuelta a Mérida de don Mariano Picón Salas. *Boletín de la Academia Nacional de la Historia (Venezuela),* v. 76, no. 301 (Jan – Mar 93), pp. 103 – 105.

Bibliography

Rivas Dugarte, Rafael Angel. Cronología de Mariano Picón Salas. *Boletín de la Academia Nacional de la Historia (Venezuela),* v. 76, no. 301 (Jan – Mar 93), pp. 93 – 100.

PIGLIA, RICARDO

Criticism of specific works

Respiración artificial

Grandis, Rita de. La cita como estrategia narrativa en *Respiración artificial. Revista Canadiense de Estudios Hispánicos,* v. 17, no. 2 (Winter 93), pp. 259 – 269. Bibl.

Interviews

Viereck, Roberto. De la tradición a las formas de la experiencia: entrevista a Ricardo Piglia. *Revista Chilena de Literatura,* no. 40 (Nov 92), pp. 129 – 138.

Translations

Piglia, Ricardo. The Absent City (Translated by Alfred MacAdam). *Review,* no. 47 (Fall 93), pp. 83 – 86.

PILGRIMS AND PILGRIMAGES

See also
Shrines

Brazil

Slater, Candace. *Trail of Miracles: Stories from a Pilgrimage in Northeast Brazil* reviewed by David T. Haberly. *Hispanic Review,* v. 61, no. 3 (Summer 93), pp. 449 – 451.

Latin America

Crumrine, N. Ross and E. Alan Morinis, eds. *Pilgrimage in Latin America* reviewed by María J. Rodríguez Shadow and Robert D. Shadow. *Mesoamérica (USA),* v. 13, no. 24 (Dec 92), pp. 473 – 480.

PIMERÍA ALTA, MEXICO

Griffith, James S. *Beliefs and Holy Places: A Spiritual Geography of the Pimería Alta* reviewed by Marth L. Henderson. *Geographical Review*, v. 83, no. 3 (July 93), pp. 334 – 336.

— *Beliefs and Holy Places: A Spiritual Geography of the Pimería Alta* reviewed by Martha L. Henderson (Review entitled "What Is Spiritual Geography?"). *Geographical Review*, v. 83, no. 4 (Oct 93), pp. 469 – 472.

PIÑA, RAMÓN

Criticism and interpretation

Barrio Tosar, Adis. Algunas observaciones sobre las novelas de Piña. *Islas*, no. 98 (Jan – Apr 91), pp. 71 – 82. Bibl.

PINEDA, CECILE

Criticism of specific works

Face

Johnson, David E. Face Value: An Essay on Cecile Pineda's *Face*. *The Americas Review*, v. 19, no. 2 (Summer 91), pp. 73 – 93. Bibl.

PINGLO ALVA, FELIPE

Criticism of specific works

El plebeyo

Yep, Virginia. El vals peruano. *Latin American Music Review*, v. 14, no. 2 (Fall – Winter 93), pp. 268 – 280. Bibl, facs.

PINILLA, ENRIQUE

Obituaries

Enrique Pinilla (1927 – 1989). *Inter-American Music Review*, v. 13, no. 1 (Fall – Winter 92), pp. 126 – 127.

PIÑON, NÉLIDA

Criticism of specific works

O calor das coisas

Schmidt, Rita Terezinha. Un juego de máscaras: Nélida Piñon y Mary McCarthy (Translated by Eleonora Cróquer P.). *Escritura (Venezuela)*, v. 16, no. 31 – 32 (Jan – Dec 91), pp. 259 – 270.

PIPINO, ALBERTO

Interviews

Rozitchner, León. Marxismo, crisis e intelectuales. *Cuadernos Hispanoamericanos*, no. 517 – 519 (July – Sept 93), pp. 483 – 494.

PIRATES

Gerhard, Peter. *Pirates in the Pacific, 1575 – 1742* reviewed by Patrick Bryan. *Caribbean Quarterly*, v. 38, no. 2 – 3 (June – Sept 92), pp. 117 – 118.

Marley, David F. *Pirates and Engineers* reviewed by Joel Russell (Review entitled "Swashbuckler's Paradise"). *Business Mexico*, v. 3, no. 4 (Apr 93), p. 52.

— *Pirates and Engineers: Dutch and Flemish Adventurers in New Spain, 1607 – 1697* reviewed by Peter T. Bradley. *Bulletin of Latin American Research*, v. 12, no. 2 (May 93), pp. 219 – 220.

Ringrose, Basil. *A Buccaneer's Atlas: Basil Ringrose's South Seas Waggoner* edited by Derk Howse and Norman J. W. Thrower. Reviewed by Arnold J. Bauer. *Hispanic American Historical Review*, v. 73, no. 4 (Nov 93), pp. 691 – 693.

PIRO INDIANS

Gow, Peter. *Of Mixed Blood: Kinship and History in Peruvian Amazonia* reviewed by Rodrigo Montoya. *Journal of Latin American Studies*, v. 25, no. 1 (Feb 93), pp. 222 – 224.

PITA RODRÍGUEZ, FÉLIX

Criticism of specific works

Elogio de Marco Polo

Chababo, Rubén Alberto. Félix Pita Rodríguez o el elogio de la literatura. *Islas*, no. 98 (Jan – Apr 91), pp. 83 – 86.

PITOL, SERGIO

Criticism and interpretation

Castañón, Adolfo. Sergio Pitol o la metamorfosis del costumbrismo (Excerpt from the book *Arbitrario*). *Vuelta*, v. 17, no. 199 (June 93), pp. 22 – 23.

PIURA, PERU (DEPARTMENT)

Diez Hurtado, Alejandro. El poder de las varas: los cabildos en Piura a fines de la colonia. *Apuntes (Peru)*, no. 30 (Jan – June 92), pp. 81 – 90. Bibl, tables.

Kaulicke, Peter. Evidencias paleoclimáticas en asentamientos del alto Piura durante el período intermedio temprano. *Bulletin de l'Institut Français d'Etudes Andines*, v. 22, no. 1 (1993), pp. 283 – 311. Bibl, il, maps.

PIZARNIK, FLORA ALEJANDRA

Criticism and interpretation

Cruz Pérez, Francisco José. Alejandra Pizarnik: el extravío en el ser. *Cuadernos Hispanoamericanos*, no. 520 (Oct 93), pp. 105 – 109.

Criticism of specific works

La condesa sangrienta

Molinaro, Nina L. Resistance, Gender, and the Mediation of History in Pizarnik's *La condesa sangrienta* and Ortiz's *Urraca*. *Letras Femeninas*, v. 19, no. 1 – 2 (Spring – Fall 93), pp. 45 – 54. Bibl.

Negroni, María. La dama de estas ruinas: sobre Alejandra Pizarnik. *Feminaria*, v. 6, no. 11, Suppl. (Nov 93), pp. 14 – 17. Bibl.

PIZARRO, EUGENIO

Soto Sandoval, Andrés. La candidatura de Eugenio Pizarro. *Mensaje*, v. 42, no. 417 (Mar – Apr 93), pp. 102 – 103.

PLANNED PARENTHOOD

See

Birth control

PLANNING

See

Cities and towns
Public administration
Regional planning
Subdivision *Planning* under *Cities and towns*

PLANTATIONS

See

Haciendas

PLATH, SYLVIA

Fiction

Guzmán, Patricia. Ese viejo y muerto amor a la muerte (Introduced by María Auxiliadora Alvarez. Article entitled "Voces o seres cercanos"). *Inti*, no. 37 – 38 (Spring – Fall 93), pp. 70 – 72.

PLAYS

See

Puppets and puppet-plays
Screenplays
Author Index under names of specific playwrights

POEMS

See

Author Index under names of specific poets

POETICS

Garza Cuarón, Beatriz. La poética de José Gorostiza y "el grupo sin grupo" de la revista *Contemporáneos*. *Nueva Revista de Filología Hispánica*, v. 40, no. 2 (July – Dec 92), pp. 891 – 907. Bibl.

Madrid, Lelia M. *El estilo del deseo: la poética de Darío, Vallejo, Borges y Paz* reviewed by Martha J. Nandorfy. *Revista Canadiense de Estudios Hispánicos*, v. 17, no. 3 (Spring 93), pp. 562 – 565.

Sánchez Aguilera, Osmar. Del antetexto al texto: transición de normas y permanencia de Vallejo. *Casa de las Américas,* no. 189 (Oct – Dec 92), pp. 82 – 93.

Valente, Luiz Fernando. Paulo Leminski e a poética do inútil. *Hispania (USA),* v. 76, no. 3 (Sept 93), pp. 419 – 427. Bibl.

POETRY

See also
　Epic poetry
　Latin American poetry
　Religious poetry
　Revolutionary poetry

Neruda, Pablo. Soy un poeta de utilidad pública. *Hispamérica,* v. 22, no. 64 – 65 (Apr – Aug 93), pp. 105 – 109.

Paz, Octavio. La casa de la presencia (Prologue to Volume I of Paz's *Obras completas). Vuelta,* v. 17, no. 198 (May 93), pp. 10 – 15.

Ramírez, Fermín. Jaime Labastida, poeta en la hora del saber. *Plural (Mexico),* v. 22, no. 261 (June 93), pp. 16 – 22.

Rojas, Waldo. Motivos, prevenciones y algunas reservas para entrar en materia: o preámbulo evitable a una lectura de poemas. *Revista Chilena de Literatura,* no. 42 (Aug 93), pp. 223 – 236.

Study and teaching

Weiskopf, Jimmy. The Little House of Muses. *Américas,* v. 45, no. 2 (Mar – Apr 93), pp. 50 – 51. Il.

POETS

Chile
Interviews

Piña, Juan Andrés. *Conversaciones con la poesía chilena* reviewed by Judy Berry-Bravo. *Chasqui,* v. 22, no. 1 (May 93), pp. 74 – 76.

POLANCO ALCÁNTARA, TOMÁS

Lizardo, Pedro Francisco. La pasión biográfica en Tomás Polanco Alcántara. *Revista Nacional de Cultura (Venezuela),* v. 53, no. 286 (July – Sept 92), pp. 188 – 202. Il.

Lovera De-Sola, Roberto J. Tomás Polanco Alcántara, el biógrafo. *Boletín de la Academia Nacional de la Historia (Venezuela),* v. 75, no. 299 (July – Sept 92), pp. 191 – 196. Bibl.

Rondón de Sansó, Hildegard. Tomás Polanco Alcántara o el hombre que venció los tabúes impuestos al biógrafo contemporáneo. *Boletín de la Academia Nacional de la Historia (Venezuela),* v. 75, no. 298 (Apr – June 92), pp. 29 – 31.

Awards

Polanco Alcántara, Tomás. Palabras leídas por Tomás Polanco Alcántara. *Boletín de la Academia Nacional de la Historia (Venezuela),* v. 75, no. 298 (Apr – June 92), pp. 35 – 37.

Ramírez Murzi, Marco. Palabras de Marco Ramírez Murzi en la entrega del premio Círculo de Escritores, 1991. *Boletín de la Academia Nacional de la Historia (Venezuela),* v. 75, no. 298 (Apr – June 92), p. 33.

Criticism of specific works
Juan Vicente Gómez

Lovera De-Sola, Roberto J. et al. El Gómez de Tomás Polanco Alcántara (Reprints from Venezuelan newspapers of fifteen reviews of the book *Juan Vicente Gómez* by Tomás Polanco Alcántara). *Boletín de la Academia Nacional de la Historia (Venezuela),* v. 75, no. 298 (Apr – June 92), pp. 116 – 138.

POLAND

See also
　Latin American studies – Poland

Zea, Leopoldo. Historia de dos ciudades. *Cuadernos Americanos,* no. 41, Nueva época (Sept – Oct 93), pp. 175 – 179.

POLETTI, SYRIA

Biography

Medrano, Carmen. Syria Poletti. *Todo Es Historia,* v. 26, no. 305 (Dec 92), pp. 34 – 36. Il.

Criticism of specific works
Extraño oficio

Londero, Renata. La scrittura della marginalità: *Extraño oficio* di Syria Poletti. *Studi di Letteratura Ispano-Americana,* v. 24 (1993), pp. 47 – 65.

POLICE

Argentina

Abregú, Martín. Contra las apologías del "homocidio uniforme": la violencia policial en Argentina. *Nueva Sociedad,* no. 123 (Jan – Feb 93), pp. 68 – 83. Bibl.

Mexico

Sosamontes Herreramoro, Ramón. El reclamo de la seguridad. *El Cotidiano,* v. 9, no. 54 (May 93), pp. 76 – 80. Il.

POLISH LITERATURE

Sten, María. Cristóbal Colón en Polonia. *Plural (Mexico),* v. 22, no. 266 (Nov 93), pp. 63 – 67.

POLITICAL PARTICIPATION

See also
　Community development
　Elections
　Pressure groups
　Social movements

Gyarmati, Gabriel. Notas para una estrategia de participación, II. *Estudios Sociales (Chile),* no. 78 (Oct – Dec 93), pp. 145 – 158. Charts.

Argentina

Sábato, Hilda. Ciudadanía, participación política y formación en una esfera pública en Buenos Aires, 1850 – 1880. *Siglo XIX: Revista,* no. 11, 2a época (Jan – June 92), pp. 46 – 73. Bibl.

Bolivia

Lazarte Rojas, Jorge. Democracia y problemas de representación política. *Estado y Sociedad,* v. 8, no. 9 (Jan – June 92), pp. 13 – 26.

Toranzo Roca, Carlos F. Comentario (on the articles by Javier Protzel and Jorge Lazarte). *Estado y Sociedad,* v. 8, no. 9 (Jan – June 92), pp. 27 – 34.

Brazil

Barretto, Vicente. Democracia, participação e cidadania. *Revista Brasileira de Estudos Políticos,* no. 76 (Jan 93), pp. 141 – 145.

Moisés, José Alvaro. Democratización y cultura política de masas en Brasil. *Revista Mexicana de Sociología,* v. 54, no. 1 (Jan – Mar 92), pp. 167 – 203. Bibl, tables.

Mulher e políticas públicas reviewed by Helena Bocayuva Cunha (Review entitled "Gênero e planejamento"). *Estudos Feministas,* v. 1, no. 1 (1993), pp. 208 – 209.

Simões, Júlio Assis. O dilema da participação popular: a etnografia de um caso reviewed by Cláudio Novaes Pinto Coelho. *Revista Brasileira de Ciências Sociais,* v. 8, no. 22 (June 93), pp. 154 – 155.

Cuba

Fuller, Linda. *Work and Democracy in Socialist Cuba* reviewed by Ronald H. Chilcote (Review entitled "Participation and the Workplace in Socialist Cuba"). *Latin American Perspectives,* v. 20, no. 1 (Winter 93), pp. 40 – 43.

Roa Kourí, Raúl. Gobierno, legitimidad y participación democrática. *Cuadernos Americanos,* no. 39, Nueva época (May – June 93), pp. 77 – 80.

Dominican Republic

Maríñez, Pablo A. El proceso democrático en República Dominicana: algunos rasgos fundamentales. *Estudios Sociales (Dominican Republic),* v. 26, no. 93 (July – Sept 93), pp. 27 – 39. Bibl.

El Salvador

¿Son libres las elecciones de 1994? *ECA; Estudios Centroamericanos,* v. 48, no. 539 (Sept 93), pp. 801 – 812. Il.

Latin America

Nun, José. Democracy and Modernization Thirty Years Later. *Latin American Perspectives,* v. 20, no. 4 (Fall 93), pp. 7 – 27. Bibl.

Vilas, Carlos María. Sociedad civil y pueblo. *Revista Paraguaya de Sociología*, v. 30, no. 86 (Jan – Apr 93), pp. 71 – 82. Bibl.

Mexico

Alonso, Jorge et al, eds. *El nuevo estado mexicano, tomo IV: Estado y sociedad* reviewed by Laura Franco Scherer. *El Cotidiano*, v. 8, no. 52 (Jan – Feb 93), pp. 118 – 119.

Avritzer, Leonardo and Alberto Olvera. El concepto de sociedad civil en el estudio de la transición democrática. *Revista Mexicana de Sociología*, v. 54, no. 4 (Oct – Dec 92), pp. 227 – 248. Bibl.

Crespo, José Antonio. Democratización: el esfuerzo ciudadano. *El Cotidiano*, v. 8, no. 52 (Jan – Feb 93), pp. 13 – 18. Il.

Durand Ponte, Víctor Manuel. La cultura política en nueve ciudades mexicanas. *Revista Mexicana de Sociología*, v. 54, no. 1 (Jan – Mar 92), pp. 289 – 322. Tables, charts.

Linares Zapata, Luis. El plebiscito: un fracaso bien hecho. *El Cotidiano*, v. 9, no. 54 (May 93), pp. 30 – 36. Il, tables.

Millán, René. Orden y cultura política en México. *Revista Mexicana de Sociología*, v. 55, no. 2 (Apr – June 93), pp. 155 – 168.

Moreno Armella, Florita. Representación vecinal y gestión urbana en el D.F. *El Cotidiano*, v. 10, no. 57 (Aug – Sept 93), pp. 38 – 45. Il.

Sánchez-Mejorada F., María Cristina. Las clases medias en la gestión y el gobierno de la ciudad. *El Cotidiano*, v. 10, no. 57 (Aug – Sept 93), pp. 46 – 53. Il, maps.

Congresses

Guillén López, Tonatiuh. Relatoría de la mesa redonda "La Estadística Electoral, el Nuevo Patrón y la Dinámica Demográfica en Mexico." *Estudios Demográficos y Urbanos*, v. 6, no. 3 (Sept – Dec 91), pp. 745 – 755.

POLITICAL PARTIES

See also
Names of specific political parties

Argentina

Alonso, Paula. Politics and Elections in Buenos Aires, 1890 – 1898: The Performance of the Radical Party. *Journal of Latin American Studies*, v. 25, no. 3 (Oct 93), pp. 465 – 487. Bibl, tables, charts.

Echegaray, Fabián. Elecciones y partidos provinciales en la Argentina. *Nueva Sociedad*, no. 124 (Mar – Apr 93), pp. 46 – 52. Tables.

Lacoste, Pablo Alberto. Lucha de élites en Argentina: la Unión Cívica Radical en Mendoza, 1890 – 1905. *Anuario de Estudios Americanos*, v. 50, no. 1 (1993), pp. 181 – 212. Bibl, tables.

Quevedo, Hugo Orlando. *El partido peronista en La Rioja: crónica y personajes* reviewed by F. L. *Todo Es Historia*, v. 27, no. 311 (June 93), p. 60.

Schers, David. Inmigrantes y política: los primeros pasos del Partido Sionista Socialista Poalei Sion en la Argentina, 1910 – 1916. *Estudios Interdisciplinarios de América Latina y el Caribe*, v. 3, no. 2 (July – Dec 92), pp. 75 – 88.

Brazil

Amaral, Roberto and Antônio Houaiss. A via partidária dos socialistas brasileiros. *Vozes*, v. 87, no. 1 (Jan – Feb 93), pp. 2 – 13. Il.

Keck, Margaret E. *The Workers' Party and Democratization in Brazil* reviewed by Thomas E. Skidmore. *Hispanic American Historical Review*, v. 73, no. 2 (May 93), pp. 325 – 326.

Lamounier, Bolivar. Empresarios, partidos y democratización en Brasil, 1974 – 1990. *Revista Mexicana de Sociología*, v. 54, no. 1 (Jan – Mar 92), pp. 77 – 97. Bibl.

Lavareda, José Antônio. *A democracia nas urnas* reviewed by Glória Diógenes. *Revista Brasileira de Ciências Sociais*, v. 8, no. 22 (June 93), pp. 156 – 157.

— *A democracia nas urnas: o processo partidário eleitoral brasileiro* reviewed by Stéphane Monclaire (Review entitled "Partis et représentations politiques au Brésil"). *Cahiers des Amériques Latines*, no. 13 (1992), pp. 173 – 177.

— *A democracia nas urnas: o processo partidário eleitoral brasileiro* reviewed by Paul Cammack. *Journal of Latin American Studies*, v. 25, no. 3 (Oct 93), pp. 665 – 666.

Lima Júnior, Olavo Brasil de. A reforma das instituições políticas: a experiência brasileira e o aperfeiçoamento democrático. *Dados*, v. 36, no. 1 (1993), pp. 89 – 117. Bibl, tables.

Moisés, José Alvaro. Elections, Political Parties, and Political Culture in Brazil: Changes and Continuities. *Journal of Latin American Studies*, v. 25, no. 3 (Oct 93), pp. 575 – 611. Bibl, tables, charts.

Sader, Emir and Ken Silverstein. *Without Fear of Being Happy: Lula, the Workers Party, and Brazil* reviewed by Joel Wolfe. *The Americas*, v. 49, no. 4 (Apr 93), pp. 566 – 568.

— *Without Fear of Being Happy: Lula, the Workers Party, and Brazil* reviewed by John Humphrey. *Bulletin of Latin American Research*, v. 12, no. 3 (Sept 93), p. 347.

— *Without Fear of Being Happy: Lula, the Workers Party, and Brazil* reviewed by Paul Cammack. *Journal of Latin American Studies*, v. 25, no. 3 (Oct 93), pp. 666 – 667.

Simões, Júlio Assis. *O dilema da participação popular: a etnografia de um caso* reviewed by Cláudio Novaes Pinto Coelho. *Revista Brasileira de Ciências Sociais*, v. 8, no. 22 (June 93), pp. 154 – 155.

Central America

Goodman, Louis Wolf et al, eds. *Political Parties and Democracy in Central America* reviewed by James Dunkerley. *Bulletin of Latin American Research*, v. 12, no. 2 (May 93), pp. 233 – 234.

Chile

Scully, Timothy R. *Rethinking the Center: Party Politics in Nineteenth- and Twentieth-Century Chile* reviewed by Iván Jaksic. *Hispanic American Historical Review*, v. 73, no. 2 (May 93), pp. 329 – 330.

— *Rethinking the Center: Party Politics in Nineteenth- and Twentieth-Century Chile* reviewed by Simon Collier. *Journal of Latin American Studies*, v. 25, no. 2 (May 93), pp. 411 – 412.

— *Rethinking the Center: Party Politics in Nineteenth- and Twentieth-Century Chile* reviewed by Peter Winn. *Revista Interamericana de Bibliografía*, v. 42, no. 4 (1992), p. 665.

Scully, Timothy R. and J. Samuel Valenzuela. De la democracia a la democracia: continuidad y variaciones en las preferencias del electorado y en el sistema de partidos en Chile. *Estudios Públicos (Chile)*, no. 51 (Winter 93), pp. 195 – 228. Bibl, tables.

Colombia

Ayala Diago, César Augusto. El Movimiento de Acción Nacional (MAN): movilización y confluencia de idearios políticos durante el gobierno de Gustavo Rojas Pinilla. *Anuario Colombiano de Historia Social y de la Cultura*, no. 20 (1992), pp. 44 – 70. Bibl.

Costa Rica

Solís Avendaño, Manuel. El ascenso de la ideología de la producción en Costa Rica: el Partido Liberación Nacional. *Revista de Ciencias Sociales (Costa Rica)*, no. 60 (June 93), pp. 85 – 100. Bibl.

El Salvador

El ERP se convierte a la socialdemocracia. *ECA; Estudios Centroamericanos*, v. 48, no. 539 (Sept 93), pp. 884 – 885. Il.

Figueroa, Francisco. Opinión política y post-guerra. *ECA; Estudios Centroamericanos*, v. 48, no. 534 – 535 (Apr – May 93), pp. 430 – 436. Il.

Latin America

Di Tella, Torcuato S. *Historia de los partidos políticos en América Latina, siglo XX* (Review). *Revista Paraguaya de Sociología*, v. 30, no. 86 (Jan – Apr 93), pp. 205 – 206.

Mexico

Alcocer, Jorge. La tercera refundación del PRI. *Revista Mexicana de Sociología*, v. 55, no. 2 (Apr – June 93), pp. 119 – 131. Bibl.

Arroyo Alejandre, Jesús and Stephen D. Morris. The Electoral Recovery of the PRI in Guadalajara, Mexico, 1988 – 1992. *Bulletin of Latin American Research*, v. 12, no. 1 (Jan 93), pp. 91 – 102. Bibl, tables.

Bolívar Espinoza, Augusto et al. La competencia de partidos: el que siembra vientos cosecha tempestades. *El Cotidiano*, v. 9, no. 54 (May 93), pp. 60 – 71. Il.

— Partido sin competencia, luego competencia de partidos. *El Cotidiano*, v. 10, no. 57 (Aug – Sept 93), pp. 60 – 72. Il, tables.

— Los síntomas de la víspera. *El Cotidiano*, v. 9, no. 56 (July 93), pp. 60 – 68. Il.

Carrillo, Mario Alejandro and Miguel Angel Romero Miranda. Un rostro nuevo en una vieja identidad: el Foro Doctrinario y Democrático en la formación de un nuevo partido político. *El Cotidiano*, v. 9, no. 53 (Mar – Apr 93), pp. 105 – 109. Bibl, il.

Carrillo, Mario Alejandro et al. Entre la contingencia y la permanencia: los municipios con alternancia del Partido Acción Nacional. *El Cotidiano*, v. 10, no. 58 (Oct – Nov 93), pp. 91 – 97. Il, maps.

Centeno, Miguel Angel. *Mexico in the 1990s: Government and Opposition Speak Out* reviewed by Martin C. Needler (Review entitled "Economic Policy and Political Survival"). *Mexican Studies*, v. 9, no. 1 (Winter 93), pp. 139 – 143.

Córdova, Arnaldo. El PAN: partido gobernante. *Revista Mexicana de Sociología*, v. 54, no. 3 (July – Sept 92), pp. 221 – 240. Bibl.

Klesner, Joseph L. Modernization, Economic Crisis, and Electoral Realignment in Mexico. *Mexican Studies*, v. 9, no. 2 (Summer 93), pp. 187 – 223. Bibl, tables.

Merino Huerta, Mauricio. Democracia, después. *Nexos*, v. 16, no. 185 (May 93), pp. 51 – 60. Bibl.

Peschard, Jacqueline. El fin del sistema de partido hegemónico. *Revista Mexicana de Sociología*, v. 55, no. 2 (Apr – June 93), pp. 97 – 117. Bibl, tables.

Reyes del Campillo, Juan. El PRI, el sistema de partidos y la sucesión presidencial. *El Cotidiano*, v. 8, no. 52 (Jan – Feb 93), pp. 10 – 12.

Reynoso, Víctor Manuel. El Partido Acción Nacional: ¿La oposición hará gobierno? *Revista Mexicana de Sociología*, v. 55, no. 2 (Apr – June 93), pp. 133 – 151.

Romero Miranda, Miguel Angel. PRD: futuro inmediato. *El Cotidiano*, v. 9, no. 55 (June 93), pp. 99 – 102. Il.

Santiago Castillo, Javier. Las elecciones locales en 1992. *El Cotidiano*, v. 8, no. 52 (Jan – Feb 93), pp. 19 – 24. Il, tables.

Suárez Farías, Francisco. Familias y dinastías políticas de los presidentes del PNR – PRM – PRI. *Revista Mexicana de Ciencias Políticas y Sociales*, v. 38, Nueva época, no. 151 (Jan – Mar 93), pp. 51 – 79. Bibl.

Woldenberg, José. Estado y partidos: una periodización. *Revista Mexicana de Sociología*, v. 55, no. 2 (Apr – June 93), pp. 83 – 95. Bibl.

Bibliography

Ochoa Méndez, Jacqueline. Orientación bibliográfica sobre sucesión presidencial y partidos políticos. *El Cotidiano*, v. 10, no. 58 (Oct – Nov 93), pp. 119 – 120.

Interviews

Gil, Carlos B., ed. *Hope and Frustration: Interviews with Leaders of Mexico's Political Opposition* reviewed by Denis L. Heyck. *Hispania (USA)*, v. 76, no. 1 (Mar 93), pp. 86 – 87.

Panama

Castro, Nils. Panamá: de movimientos sociales a partidos populares. *Nueva Sociedad*, no. 125 (May – June 93), pp. 15 – 19.

Peru

Cisneros, Luis Jaime. El porvenir de la izquierda. *Debate (Peru)*, v. 15, no. 71 (Nov 92 – Jan 93), pp. 40 – 43. Il.

Graham, Carol. *Peru's APRA: Parties, Politics, and the Elusive Quest for Democracy* reviewed by Fredrick B. Pike. *Hispanic American Historical Review*, v. 73, no. 3 (Aug 93), pp. 518 – 519.

— *Peru's APRA: Parties, Politics, and the Elusive Quest for Democracy* reviewed by Giorgio Alberti. *Journal of Latin American Studies*, v. 25, no. 2 (May 93), pp. 414 – 415.

— *Peru's APRA: Parties, Politics, and the Elusive Quest for Democracy* reviewed by Henry Dietz. *Revista Interamericana de Bibliografía*, v. 42, no. 3 (1992), pp. 504 – 505.

Guerra García, Francisco. Crisis nacional y crisis de la izquierda. *Debate (Peru)*, v. 16, no. 75 (Dec 93 – Jan 94), pp. 23 – 24. Il.

Puerto Rico

Dávila Santiago, Rubén and Jorge Rodríguez Beruff. Puerto Rico: frente a la nueva época. *Nueva Sociedad*, no. 127 (Sept – Oct 93), pp. 6 – 12.

United States

González-Souza, Luis F. Estados Unidos ante el nuevo milenio: consensos y grilletes bipartidistas. *Relaciones Internacionales (Mexico)*, v. 15, Nueva época, no. 57 (Jan – Mar 93), pp. 7 – 12.

Uruguay

Lanzaro, Jorge Luis. La "doble transición" en el Uruguay: gobierno de partidos y neo-presidencialismo. *Nueva Sociedad*, no. 128 (Nov – Dec 93), pp. 132 – 147.

Mieres, Pablo. Canelones, 1989: el fin del bipartidismo. *Cuadernos del CLAEH*, v. 18, no. 67 (Nov 93), pp. 121 – 131. Tables.

Pedoja Riet, Eduardo. Algunas causas que determinaron la derrota del Partido Nacional en 1966. *Hoy Es Historia*, v. 10, no. 60 (Nov – Dec 93), pp. 34 – 38. Il.

Venezuela

Ellner, Steven B. *De la derrota guerrillera a la política innovadora: el Movimiento al Socialismo (MAS)* reviewed by Dick Parker. *Nueva Sociedad*, no. 124 (Mar – Apr 93), p. 174.

POLITICAL POLLS

See
  Public opinion

POLITICAL PRISONERS

See also
  Human rights
  Prisoners of war

Argentina

Paoletti, Mario Argentino. Tiempo de desprecio. *Cuadernos Hispanoamericanos*, no. 517 – 519 (July – Sept 93), pp. 581 – 586.

Cuba

Brown, Charles J. and Armando M. Lago. *The Politics of Psychiatry in Revolutionary Cuba* reviewed by Roberto Valero. *Cuban Studies/Estudios Cubanos*, v. 23 (1993), pp. 233 – 235.

POLITICAL SCIENCE

Pérez Antón, Romeo. Glosario para la reforma política. *Cuadernos del CLAEH*, v. 18, no. 67 (Nov 93), pp. 113 – 119.

POLITICAL SOCIOLOGY

See also
  Public opinion

Antezana Villegas, Mauricio. Epilogo y prefacio. *Estado y Sociedad*, v. 8, no. 9 (Jan – June 92), pp. 99 – 105.

Ipola, Emilio de. La democracia en el amanecer de la sociología. *Revista Mexicana de Sociología*, v. 54, no. 2 (Apr – June 92), pp. 215 – 232. Bibl.

Argentina

Adrogué, Gerardo. Los ex-militares en política: bases sociales y cambios en los patrones de representación política. *Desarrollo Económico (Argentina)*, v. 33, no. 131 (Oct – Dec 93), pp. 425 – 442. Bibl, tables.

Sarlo Sabajanes, Beatriz. Notas sobre política y cultura. *Cuadernos Hispanoamericanos*, no. 517 – 519 (July – Sept 93), pp. 51 – 64.

Bolivia

Antezana Villegas, Mauricio. La espectacularización de la política y las autoformaciones culturales. *Estado y Sociedad*, v. 8, no. 9 (Jan – June 92), pp. 53 – 68.

Calla Ortega, Ricardo. Comentario (on the article by Roger Cortez). *Estado y Sociedad,* v. 8, no. 9 (Jan – June 92), pp. 91 – 98.

Toranzo Roca, Carlos F. Comentario (on the articles by Javier Protzel and Jorge Lazarte). *Estado y Sociedad,* v. 8, no. 9 (Jan – June 92), pp. 27 – 34.

Brazil

Banck, Geert A. Cultura política brasileira: que tradição é esta? *Revista Brasileira de Estudos Políticos,* no. 76 (Jan 93), pp. 41 – 53. Bibl.

Kinzo, Maria d'Alva Gil. The 1989 Presidential Election: Electoral Behaviour in a Brazilian City. *Journal of Latin American Studies,* v. 25, no. 2 (May 93), pp. 313 – 330. Bibl, tables.

Moisés, José Alvaro. Elections, Political Parties, and Political Culture in Brazil: Changes and Continuities. *Journal of Latin American Studies,* v. 25, no. 3 (Oct 93), pp. 575 – 611. Bibl, tables, charts.

Chile

Scully, Timothy R. and J. Samuel Valenzuela. De la democracia a la democracia: continuidad y variaciones en las preferencias del electorado y en el sistema de partidos en Chile. *Estudios Públicos (Chile),* no. 51 (Winter 93), pp. 195 – 228. Bibl, tables.

Costa Rica

Chinchilla Coto, José Carlos. Estado y democracia en la sociedad costarricense contemporánea. *Anuario de Estudios Centroamericanos,* v. 18, no. 2 (1992), pp. 101 – 114. Bibl.

Latin America

Canelas, Jorge. Comentario (on the articles by Javier Protzel and Jorge Lazarte). *Estado y Sociedad,* v. 8, no. 9 (Jan – June 92), pp. 35 – 37.

Chasteen, John Charles. Fighting Words: The Discourse of Insurgency in Latin American History. *Latin American Research Review,* v. 28, no. 3 (1993), pp. 83 – 111. Bibl, il.

Mexico

Bartra, Roger. *Oficio mexicano* reviewed by Hugo Vargas (Review entitled "El radicalismo posible"). *Nexos,* v. 16, no. 190 (Oct 93), pp. 73 – 75.

Constantino, Mario and Rosalía Winocur. Cultura política y elecciones: algunas imágenes de la sucesión presidencial. *El Cotidiano,* v. 10, no. 58 (Oct – Nov 93), pp. 47 – 53. Bibl, tables.

Durand Ponte, Víctor Manuel. La cultura política en nueve ciudades mexicanas. *Revista Mexicana de Sociología,* v. 54, no. 1 (Jan – Mar 92), pp. 289 – 322. Tables, charts.

Hirabayashi, Lane Ryo. La politización de la cultura regional: zapotecos de la sierra Juárez en la ciudad de México. *América Indígena,* v. 51, no. 4 (Oct – Dec 91), pp. 185 – 218. Bibl.

Kuschick, Murilo. Sucesión presidencial: sondeo de opinión. *El Cotidiano,* v. 10, no. 58 (Oct – Nov 93), pp. 54 – 58. Il, charts.

Martínez F., Alicia. De poder, podemos: diferencias genéricas en la dinámica sociopolítica. *El Cotidiano,* v. 9, no. 53 (Mar – Apr 93), pp. 47 – 52. Tables.

Reyes del Campillo, Juan and Verónica Vázquez Mantecón. ¿Ciudadanos en ciernes?: la cultura política en el distrito XXVII del D.F. *El Cotidiano,* v. 9, no. 54 (May 93), pp. 41 – 48. Il, tables, charts.

Research

Fábregas Puig, Andrés A. Acerca de las relaciones entre sociedad y política. *Nueva Antropología,* v. 13, no. 43 (Nov 92), pp. 53 – 59.

Peru

Lindner, Bernardo. Nadie en quien confiar: actitud política de los jóvenes campesinos del altiplano puneño. *Allpanchis,* v. 25, no. 41 (Jan – June 93), pp. 77 – 108. Bibl, tables.

Protzel, Javier. Industrias electorales y culturas políticas. *Estado y Sociedad,* v. 8, no. 9 (Jan – June 92), pp. 1 – 12.

Tanaka, Martín. Juventud y política en el cambio de una época. *Allpanchis,* v. 25, no. 41 (Jan – June 93), pp. 227 – 261. Bibl.

Uruguay

Casaravilla, Diego. La cultura política uruguaya desde el carnaval: heroísmo antimilitar, crisis del socialismo real y MERCOSUR. *Cuadernos del CLAEH,* v. 18, no. 65 – 66 (May 93), pp. 151 – 165. Bibl.

Venezuela

Carrera Damas, Germán. *El culto a Bolívar: esbozo para un estudio de la historia de las ideas en Venezuela* reviewed by Frédérique Langue. *Cahiers des Amériques Latines,* no. 13 (1992), p. 184.

POLITICS AN LITERATURE

Latin America

Rodríguez Pérsico, Adriana C. Sarmiento y Alberdi: una práctica legitimante. *La Educación (USA),* v. 36, no. 111 – 113 (1992), pp. 177 – 192. Bibl.

POLITICS AND GOVERNMENT

See
  Agriculture and state
  Anarchism and anarchists
  Authoritarianism
  Caciquism
  Capitalism
  Censorship
  Church and state
  Communism
  Conservatism
  Corporate state
  Corruption (in politics)
  Coups d'état
  Decentralization in government
  Democracy
  Dictators
  Education and state
  Elections
  Executive power
  Exiles
  Fascism
  Geopolitics
  Human rights
  Ideology
  Imperialism
  International relations
  Judiciary
  Legislative power
  Liberalism
  Local government
  Martyrs
  Marxism
  Military in government
  Nationalism
  Oligarchy
  Patronage, Political
  Peronism
  Philosophy and politics
  Political participation
  Political parties
  Political prisoners
  Political science
  Political sociology
  Politics in literature
  Power (Social sciences)
  Press and politics
  Pressure groups
  Public administration
  Religion and politics
  Revolutions
  Science and state
  Social control
  Socialism
  Socialism and Catholic Church
  State, The
  State capitalism
  Technology and state
  Terrorism
  Utopias
  Violence
  War
  Subdivision *Politics and government* under names of specific countries

POLITICS IN LITERATURE

See also
Literature and society
Revolutionary literature
Subdivision *Fiction* under *Dictators*

Argentina

Balderston, Daniel. Abel Posse y *Los demonios secretos: ¿Otra vez el nazismo? Nuevo Texto Crítico,* v. 6, no. 11 (1993), pp. 254 – 258. Bibl.

Borello, Rodolfo A. *El peronismo (1943 – 1955) en la narrativa argentina* reviewed by Raúl Ianes. *Hispanic Review,* v. 61, no. 4 (Fall 93), pp. 590 – 592.

— *El peronismo (1943 – 1955) en la narrativa argentina* reviewed by Nicolas Shumway. *Revista Interamericana de Bibliografía,* v. 42, no. 2 (1992), pp. 282 – 283.

Garrels, Elizabeth. Traducir a América: Sarmiento y el proyecto de una literatura nacional. *Revista de Crítica Literaria Latinoamericana,* v. 19, no. 38 (July – Dec 93), pp. 269 – 278. Bibl.

Longoni, Ana. Vanguardia artística y vanguardia política en la Argentina de los sesenta: una primera aproximación. *Revista Chilena de Literatura,* no. 42 (Aug 93), pp. 107 – 114.

Piglia, Ricardo. Ficción y política en la literatura argentina. *Cuadernos Hispanoamericanos,* no. 517 – 519 (July – Sept 93), pp. 514 – 516.

Pons, María Cristina. Compromiso político y ficción en "Segunda vez" y "Apocalipsis de Solentiname" de Julio Cortázar. *Revista Mexicana de Sociología,* v. 54, no. 4 (Oct – Dec 92), pp. 183 – 203. Bibl.

Reati, Fernando. *Nombrar lo innombrable: violencia política y novela argentina, 1975 – 1985* reviewed by David William Foster. *World Literature Today,* v. 67, no. 2 (Spring 93), pp. 341 – 342.

Rodríguez Pérsico, Adriana C. *Un huracán llamado progreso: utopía y autobiografía en Sarmiento y Alberdi* reviewed by Carlos E. Paldao. *La Educación (USA),* v. 37, no. 115 (1993), pp. 435 – 437.

Bolivia

Muñoz Cadima, Willy Oscar. Joaquín Aguirre Lavayén: la escatología política en *Guano maldito. Latin American Theatre Review,* v. 26, no. 2 (Spring 93), pp. 131 – 142. Bibl.

Brazil

Araújo, Arturo Gouveia de. Literatura em cadeia. *Vozes,* v. 86, no. 5 (Sept – Oct 92), pp. 37 – 57.

McCarthy, Cavan Michael. Recent Political Events in Brazil as Reflected in Popular Poetry Pamphlets: "Literatura de Cordel." *SALALM Papers,* v. 34 (1989), pp. 491 – 513. Bibl.

Central America

Beverley, John and Marc Zimmerman. *Literature and Politics in the Central American Revolutions* reviewed by Antony Higgins. *Revista de Crítica Literaria Latinoamericana,* v. 19, no. 37 (Jan – June 93), pp. 380 – 382.

Chile

Melis, Antonio. Poesía y política en *Las uvas y el viento. Revista de Crítica Literaria Latinoamericana,* v. 19, no. 38 (July – Dec 93), pp. 123 – 130.

Mora, Gabriela. La prosa política de Gabriela Mistral. *Escritura (Venezuela),* v. 16, no. 31 – 32 (Jan – Dec 91), pp. 193 – 203.

Roa, Natalia. Vicente Huidobro: la luna era mi tierra. *Mensaje,* v. 42, no. 417 (Mar – Apr 93), pp. 77 – 78. Il.

Cuba

Vera-León, Antonio. Jesús Díaz: Politics of Self-Narration in Revolutionary Cuba. *Latin American Literary Review,* v. 21, no. 41 (Jan – June 93), pp. 65 – 78. Bibl.

Latin America

Cussen, Antonio. *Bello and Bolívar: Poetry and Politics in the Spanish American Revolution* reviewed by Fernando Cervantes. *Bulletin of Latin American Research,* v. 12, no. 1 (Jan 93), pp. 114 – 115.

— *Bello and Bolívar: Poetry and Politics in the Spanish American Revolution* reviewed by Myron I. Lichtblau. *Hispania (USA),* v. 76, no. 2 (May 93), p. 285.

McQuade, Frank. *Mundo Nuevo:* el discurso político en una revista intelectual de los sesenta. *Revista Chilena de Literatura,* no. 42 (Aug 93), pp. 123 – 130.

Ramos, Julio et al. Debate (on the seventh session of the symposium "Latinoamérica: Nuevas Direcciones en Teoría y Crítica Literarias, III"). *Revista de Crítica Literaria Latinoamericana,* v. 19, no. 38 (July – Dec 93), pp. 293 – 296.

Sicard, Alain et al. Debate (on the third session of the symposium "Latinoamérica: Nuevas Direcciones en Teoría y Crítica Literarias, III"). *Revista de Crítica Literaria Latinoamericana,* v. 19, no. 38 (July – Dec 93), pp. 131 – 141.

Taylor, Diana. *Theatre of Crisis: Drama and Politics in Latin America* reviewed by José Castro-Urioste. *Revista de Crítica Literaria Latinoamericana,* v. 19, no. 38 (July – Dec 93), pp. 405 – 406.

Mexico

Luciani, Frederick William. The *Comedia de San Francisco de Borja* (1640): The Mexican Jesuits and the "Education of the Prince." *Colonial Latin American Review,* v. 2, no. 1 – 2 (1993), pp. 121 – 141. Bibl.

Trujillo Muñoz, Gabriel. Dos guerras paralelas, dos novelas complementarias. *La Palabra y el Hombre,* no. 84 (Oct – Dec 92), pp. 296 – 298. Il.

Peru

Delgado Molina, Teresa. Ideología de la expresión en la obra poética de César Vallejo: apuntes al pie de un siglo. *Casa de las Américas,* no. 189 (Oct – Dec 92), pp. 43 – 50.

Gutiérrez Girardot, Rafael. César Vallejo y Walter Benjamin. *Cuadernos Hispanoamericanos,* no. 520 (Oct 93), pp. 55 – 72. Bibl, il.

Paoli, Roberto. Vallejo: herencia ideal y herencia creadora. *Inti,* no. 36 (Fall 92), pp. 51 – 57. Bibl.

Uruguay

Torres, María Inés de. Ideología patriarcal e ideología estatal en el proceso modernizador uruguayo: una lectura de *Tabaré. Cuadernos del CLAEH,* v. 18, no. 65 – 66 (May 93), pp. 167 – 178. Bibl.

Trigo, Abril. *Caudillo, estado, nación: literatura, historia e ideología en el Uruguay* reviewed by Gustavo Verdesio. *Nuevo Texto Crítico,* v. 6, no. 11 (1993), pp. 263 – 266.

Venezuela

Sucre, Guillermo. La polvareda y la falacia (Response to the Venezuelan press's reaction to his two earlier articles published in *Vuelta). Vuelta,* v. 17, no. 202 (Sept 93), pp. 54 – 55.

Torres, Ana Teresa. El escritor ante la realidad política venezolana. *Inti,* no. 37 – 38 (Spring – Fall 93), pp. 37 – 45. Bibl.

POLLUTION

See also
Ecology
Environmental services

Brazil

Randall, Laura Regina Rosenbaum. Petróleo, economía y medio ambiente en Brasil. *Revista Mexicana de Sociología,* v. 54, no. 2 (Apr – June 92), pp. 185 – 211. Tables.

Developing countries

Satterthwaite, David. Problemas sociales y medioambientales asociados a la urbanización acelerada. *EURE,* v. 19, no. 57 (July 93), pp. 7 – 30. Tables.

Mexican – American Border Region

Ballesteros, Carlos. El concepto de seguridad ambiental y la integración del mercado norteamericano. *Relaciones Internacionales (Mexico),* v. 15, Nueva época, no. 58 (Apr – June 93), pp. 63 – 68.

Johnstone, Nick. Comparative Advantage, Transfrontier Pollution, and the Environmental Degradation of a Border Region: The Case of the Californias. *Journal of Borderlands Studies,* v. 7, no. 2 (Fall 92), pp. 33 – 52. Bibl.

Mexico

Ballesteros, Carlos. El concepto de seguridad ambiental y la integración del mercado norteamericano. *Relaciones Internacionales (Mexico),* v. 15, Nueva época, no. 58 (Apr – June 93), pp. 63 – 68.

Bernier F., Richard E. Cutting a New Cloth. *Business Mexico,* v. 3, no. 1 (Jan – Feb 93), pp. 27 – 28. Il.

Collins, Charles O. and Steven L. Scott. Air Pollution in the Valley of Mexico. *Geographical Review,* v. 83, no. 2 (Apr 93), pp. 119 – 133. Bibl, charts.

Farquharson, Mary. Is It Safe to Breathe? *Business Mexico,* v. 3, no. 3 (Mar 93), pp. 32 – 35.

Finn, Patrick J. Treating Water Industrially. *Business Mexico,* v. 3, no. 1 (Jan – Feb 93), pp. 83 – 84. Tables.

Guzmán Pineda, Jesús Ignacio. Industria automotriz y medio ambiente. *El Cotidiano,* v. 8, no. 52 (Jan – Feb 93), pp. 70 – 75. Il.

Neumann, Holly. From Pigs to Pesticides. *Business Mexico,* v. 3, no. 1 (Jan – Feb 93), pp. 19 – 22. Il, tables.

Sánchez, Robert A. Maquila Masquerade. *Business Mexico,* v. 3, no. 1 (Jan – Feb 93), pp. 13 – 15. Il, charts.

Smith, Morgan. Lifting the "Brown Cloud." *Business Mexico,* v. 3, no. 9 (Sept 93), pp. 39 – 40.

Velázquez Zárate, Enrique. La contaminación atmosférica en la ciudad de México. *El Cotidiano,* v. 9, no. 54 (May 93), pp. 55 – 59. Il.

United States

Smith, Morgan. Lifting the "Brown Cloud." *Business Mexico,* v. 3, no. 9 (Sept 93), pp. 39 – 40.

Venezuela

Pérez, Tibisay and Eugenio Sanhueza. Concentraciones atmosféricas y estimación de las emisiones H2S en la saba de Trachypogon, Calabozo, estado Guárico, Venezuela. *Interciencia,* v. 18, no. 2 (Mar – Apr 93), pp. 83 – 87. Bibl, il, tables, maps, charts.

POLO, MARCO

Fiction

Chababo, Rubén Alberto. Félix Pita Rodríguez o el elogio de la literatura. *Islas,* no. 98 (Jan – Apr 91), pp. 83 – 86.

POMA DE AYALA, FELIPE HUAMÁN

Biography

Adorno, Rolena. The Genesis of Felipe Guamán Poma de Ayala's *Nueva corónica y buen gobierno. Colonial Latin American Review,* v. 2, no. 1 – 2 (1993), pp. 53 – 92. Bibl, il.

Criticism and interpretation

Husson, Jean-Phillipe. La poesía quechua prehispánica: sus reglas, sus categorías, sus temas; atravês de los poemas transcritos por Wamán Puma de Ayala. *Revista de Crítica Literaria Latinoamericana,* v. 19, no. 37 (Jan – June 93), pp. 63 – 85. Bibl, il.

Criticism of specific works

Nueva crónica y buen gobierno

Adorno, Rolena. The Genesis of Felipe Guamán Poma de Ayala's *Nueva corónica y buen gobierno. Colonial Latin American Review,* v. 2, no. 1 – 2 (1993), pp. 53 – 92. Bibl, il.

Scaramuzza Vidoni, Mariarosa. La ritrattistica nella *Nueva corónica* de Guamán Poma de Ayala. *Quaderni Ibero-Americani,* no. 72 (Dec 92), pp. 682 – 694. Bibl.

PONCE, MARTHA PATRICIA

Criticism of specific works

Tuzamapan

Madrazo Miranda, María. Literatura y vida en el testimonio: *Tuzamapan; el poder viene de las cañas. Fem,* v. 17, no. 120 (Feb 93), pp. 18 – 20. Il.

PONIATOWSKA, ELENA

Criticism of specific works

La "flor de lis"

Paley de Francescato, Martha. Elena Poniatowska: convergencias en *La "flor de lis". Hispamérica,* v. 21, no. 62 (Aug 92), pp. 127 – 132.

Querido Diego, te abraza Quiela

Aronson, Stacey L. Parker and Cristina Enríquez de Salamanca. La textura del exilio: *Querido Diego, te abraza Quiela; Eva Luna; Crónica de una muerte anunciada. Chasqui,* v. 22, no. 2 (Nov 93), pp. 3 – 14. Bibl.

POPOL VUH

Mosquera Aguilar, Antonio. *Pop Wuj:* el libro de los testimonios y de las tradiciones como recreación popular. *Folklore Americano,* no. 52 (July – Dec 91), pp. 123 – 129. Bibl.

POPOVIC, VLADIMIR

Trelles Aréstegui, Efraín. La química de Popovic. *Debate (Peru),* v. 15, no. 71 (Nov 92 – Jan 93), pp. 64 – 66. Il.

POPULAR CULTURE

See also
Civilization, Modern
Folk literature
Mass media

Argentina

Delfino, Silvia. Educación y democracia: una cultura joven en la Argentina. *La Educación (USA),* v. 37, no. 114 (1993), pp. 47 – 58. Bibl.

Brazil

Dunn, Christopher. It's Forbidden to Forbid. *Américas,* v. 45, no. 5 (Sept – Oct 93), pp. 14 – 21. Il.

Leite, Milu. Antenas diabólicas. *Problemas Brasileiros,* v. 30, no. 295 (Jan – Feb 93), pp. 54 – 56. Il.

McCarthy, Cavan Michael. Recent Political Events in Brazil as Reflected in Popular Poetry Pamphlets: "Literatura de Cordel." *SALALM Papers,* v. 34 (1989), pp. 491 – 513. Bibl.

Simpson, Amelia S. Xuxa and the Politics of Gender. *Luso-Brazilian Review,* v. 30, no. 1 (Summer 93), pp. 95 – 106. Bibl.

Vila, Martinho da. *Kizombas, andanças e festanças* reviewed by Aroldo Souza Silva. *Américas,* v. 45, no. 1 (Jan – Feb 93), pp. 62 – 63.

Caribbean area

Lamming, George. Coming, Coming, Coming Home. *Casa de las Américas,* no. 190 (Jan – Mar 93), pp. 65 – 74.

Bibliography

Duff, Ernest A. Attack and Counterattack: Dynamics of Transculturation in the Caribbean (Review article). *Studies in Latin American Popular Culture,* v. 12 (1993), pp. 195 – 202.

Chile

Aman, Kenneth and Christian Parker Gumucio, eds. *Popular Culture in Chile: Resistance and Survival* reviewed by Ton Salman. *European Review of Latin American and Caribbean Studies,* no. 53 (Dec 92), pp. 120 – 124.

Domínguez Díaz, Marta Silvia. El arte popular chileno. *SALALM Papers,* v. 34 (1989), pp. 9 – 16. Bibl.

Verba, Ericka Kim. "Las hojas sueltas" (Broadsides): Nineteenth-Century Chilean Popular Poetry as a Source for the Historian. *Studies in Latin American Popular Culture,* v. 12 (1993), pp. 141 – 158. Bibl.

Colombia

Deveny, John J., Jr. and Peter C. Rollins, eds. *Culture and Development in Colombia: Study of Changes in Social Roles, Religion, Literature . . .* Special issue of *Journal of Popular Culture,* 22:1 (Summer 88), reviewed by Maurice P. Brungardt (Review entitled "Readings on Colombia?"). *Studies in Latin American Popular Culture,* v. 12 (1993), pp. 235 – 242.

Latin America

Carvalho, José Jorge de. As duas faces da tradição: o clássico e o popular na modernidade latinoamericana. *Dados,* v. 35, no. 3 (1992), pp. 403 – 434.

Rowe, William and Vivian Schelling. *Memory and Modernity: Popular Culture in Latin America* reviewed by Margaret Bullen. *Bulletin of Latin American Research,* v. 12, no. 1 (Jan 93), pp. 126 – 128.

— *Memory and Modernity: Popular Culture in Latin America* reviewed by Ineke Phaf. *Hispamérica*, v. 22, no. 64 – 65 (Apr – Aug 93), pp. 193 – 197.

— *Memory and Modernity: Popular Culture in Latin America* reviewed by David Lehmann. *Journal of Latin American Studies*, v. 25, no. 3 (Oct 93), pp. 692 – 694.

Mexico

Mejía Madrid, Fabrizio. Con el corazón en la mano. *Nexos*, v. 16, no. 192 (Dec 93), pp. 21 – 22.

Peru

Macera dall'Orso, Pablo. Locos, titiriteros y poetas: las opciones limeñas, 1828 – 1840. *Debate (Peru)*, v. 16, no. 72 (Mar – May 93), pp. 42 – 45. Il.

POPULAR MUSIC

Argentina

Monteleone, Jorge J. Cuerpo constelado: sobre la poesía de "rock" argentino. *Cuadernos Hispanoamericanos*, no. 517 – 519 (July – Sept 93), pp. 401 – 420.

Pujol, Sergio Alejandro. Canto y contracanto. *Cuadernos Hispanoamericanos*, no. 517 – 519 (July – Sept 93), pp. 389 – 399. Bibl, il.

— "Rock" y juventud: de las catacumbas al estrellato. *Todo Es Historia*, v. 27, no. 317 (Dec 93), pp. 70 – 73. Il.

Brazil

Avancini, Marta. Na era do ouro das cantoras do rádio. *Luso-Brazilian Review*, v. 30, no. 1 (Summer 93), pp. 85 – 93. Bibl.

Carvalho, Martha de Ulhôa. Musical Style, Migration, and Urbanization: Some Considerations on Brazilian "Música Sertaneja" (Country Music). *Studies in Latin American Popular Culture*, v. 12 (1993), pp. 75 – 94. Bibl, tables.

Geração de ouro. *Problemas Brasileiros*, v. 30, no. 295 (Jan – Feb 93), pp. 67 – 68. Il.

Lenharo, Alcir. Fascínio e solidão: as cantoras do rádio nas ondas sonoras do seu tempo. *Luso-Brazilian Review*, v. 30, no. 1 (Summer 93), pp. 75 – 84. Bibl.

McGowan, Chris and Ricardo Pessanha. *The Brazilian Sound: Samba, Bossa Nova, and the Popular Music of Brazil* reviewed by Randal Johnson. *Hispanic American Historical Review*, v. 73, no. 1 (Feb 93), p. 128.

Walger, Christian. "Nova música baiana": Musikszene Bahia; Kultursoziologische Betrachtungen zur schwarzen Musik Brasiliens. *Zeitschrift für Lateinamerika Wien*, no. 42 (1992), pp. 27 – 51. Bibl.

Foreign influences

Perrone, Charles A. *Axé, Ijexá, Olodum:* The Rise of Afro- and African Currents in Brazilian Popular Music. *Afro-Hispanic Review*, v. 11, no. 1 – 3 (1992), pp. 42 – 50. Bibl.

Caribbean area

Research

Regis, Humphrey A. Three Caribbean Islands' Interest in Popularity of Caribbean Music. *Caribbean Studies*, v. 25, no. 1 – 2 (Jan – July 92), pp. 123 – 132. Bibl, tables.

Cuba

Cabrera Infante, Guillermo. Guantanamerías: sobre un emblema musical de los años '60. *Vuelta*, v. 17, no. 203 (Oct 93), pp. 11 – 13.

Febres, Xavier. Primera aproximación a la habanera en Cataluña. *Boletín Americanista*, v. 33, no. 42 – 43 (1992 – 1993), pp. 349 – 365.

Dominican Republic

Pacini Hernandez, Deborah. Dominican Popular Music under the Trujillo Regime. *Studies in Latin American Popular Culture*, v. 12 (1993), pp. 127 – 140. Bibl.

Europe

Foreign influences

Ostleitner, Elena. Europas Musik zwischen Mambo und Tango: Musikalische Einflüsse Lateinamerikas auf Europa. *Zeitschrift für Lateinamerika Wien*, no. 42 (1992), pp. 7 – 15. Bibl.

Latin America

Holston, Mark. Old Bits, New Beats. *Américas*, v. 45, no. 2 (Mar – Apr 93), pp. 52 – 53. Il.

Ostleitner, Elena. Europas Musik zwischen Mambo und Tango: Musikalische Einflüsse Lateinamerikas auf Europa. *Zeitschrift für Lateinamerika Wien*, no. 42 (1992), pp. 7 – 15. Bibl.

Mexico

Andrade Jardí, Julián. El milenio de Gloria Trevi. *Nexos*, v. 16, no. 183 (Mar 93), pp. 66 – 68.

Blears, James. Star-Crossed Mexico. *Business Mexico*, v. 3, no. 12 (Dec 93), pp. 31 – 33. Il.

Osterroth, María de Jesús. "XX – XXI": música entre los siglos. *Plural (Mexico)*, v. 22, no. 265 (Oct 93), pp. 83 – 84.

Peru

Cisneros, Luis Jaime. Nosequién y los Nosecuántos. *Debate (Peru)*, v. 15, no. 71 (Nov 92 – Jan 93), p. 67. Il.

Cornejo Guinassi, Pedro. Nosequién y los Nosecuántos: ¿Espejo de una generación? *Debate (Peru)*, v. 16, no. 74 (Sept – Oct 93), pp. 38 – 40. Il.

Jáuregui, Eloy. Vorágine de la caja negra. *Debate (Peru)*, v. 16, no. 75 (Dec 93 – Jan 94), pp. 65 – 66. Il.

Puerto Rico

Malavet Vega, Pedro. *Historia de la canción popular en Puerto Rico* reviewed by Donald Thompson. *Latin American Music Review*, v. 14, no. 2 (Fall – Winter 93), pp. 288 – 293.

Spain

Foreign influences

Febres, Xavier. Primera aproximación a la habanera en Cataluña. *Boletín Americanista*, v. 33, no. 42 – 43 (1992 – 1993), pp. 349 – 365.

United States

Boggs, Vernon W. *Salsiology: Afro-Cuban Music and the Evolution of Salsa in New York City* reviewed by Jerma Jackson. *Hispanic American Historical Review*, v. 73, no. 4 (Nov 93), pp. 673 – 674.

— *Salsiology: Afro-Cuban Music and the Evolution of Salsa in New York City* reviewed by Gerard Béhague. *Latin American Music Review*, v. 14, no. 1 (Spring – Summer 93), pp. 172 – 175.

POPULAR RELIGION

See
   Liberation theology
   Religion and sociology
   Syncretism (Religion)

POPULATION

See also
   Abortion
   Birth control
   Family
   Fertility, Human
   Illegitimacy
   Infant mortality
   Marriage
   Migration, Internal
   Subdivision *Emigration and immigration* under names of specific countries
   Subdivision *Population* under *Hispanic Americans (U.S.)* and names of Indian groups

Declaración de las mujeres sobre políticas de población mundial (En preparación a la Conferencia Internacional de Población y Desarrollo de 1994). *Fem*, v. 17, no. 129 (Nov 93), pp. 36 – 39.

Welti Chanes, Carlos. Políticas públicas de población: un tema en debate permanente. *Fem*, v. 17, no. 128 (Oct 93), pp. 16 – 18.

America

Statistics

Arriaga, Eduardo E. Comparación de la mortalidad en las Américas. *Estudios Demográficos y Urbanos*, v. 7, no. 2 – 3 (May – Dec 92), pp. 407 – 449. Tables, charts.

Argentina

Arcondo, Aníbal B. Mortalidad general, mortalidad epidémica y comportamiento de la población de Córdoba durante el siglo XVIII. *Desarrollo Económico (Argentina)*, v. 33, no. 129 (Apr – June 93), pp. 67 – 85. Bibl, tables, charts.

Foschiatti de dell'Orto, Ana María H. El desarrollo urbano y las particularidades demográficas del Chaco y su capital entre 1960 y 1990. *Revista Geográfica (Mexico)*, no. 115 (Jan – June 92), pp. 37 – 54. Bibl, tables, maps, charts.

Belize

Palacio, Joseph O. Social and Cultural Implications of Recent Demographic Changes in Belize (The Fourth Annual Signa L. Yorke Memorial Lecture). *Belizean Studies*, v. 21, no. 1 (May 93), pp. 3 – 12. Bibl, tables.

Brazil

Costa, Iraci del Nero da and José Flávio Motta. Vila Rica: inconfidência e crise demográfica. *Estudos Econômicos*, v. 22, no. 2 (May – Aug 92), pp. 321 – 346. Bibl, tables, charts.

Luna, Francisco Vidal. Características demográficas dos escravos de São Paulo, 1777 – 1829. *Estudos Econômicos*, v. 22, no. 3 (Sept – Dec 92), pp. 443 – 483. Bibl, tables.

Sociedade insalubre. *Problemas Brasileiros*, v. 30, no. 295 (Jan – Feb 93), pp. 52 – 53. Il.

Chile

Salinas Meza, René. Una comunidad inmigrante: los alemanes en Valparaíso, 1860 – 1960; estudio demográfico. *Jahrbuch für Geschichte von Staat, Wirtschaft und Gesellschaft Lateinamerikas*, v. 29 (1992), pp. 309 – 342. Bibl, tables, charts.

Vázquez de Acuña, Isidoro. Evolución de la población de Chiloé, siglos XVI – XX. *Boletín de la Academia Chilena de la Historia*, v. 58 – 59, no. 102 (1991 – 1992), pp. 403 – 457. Bibl, tables.

Cuba

Hernández Castellón, Raúl. El envejecimiento de la población en Cuba. *Estudios Demográficos y Urbanos*, v. 7, no. 2 – 3 (May – Dec 92), pp. 603 – 617. Bibl, tables.

Developing countries

Sen, Amartya Kumar. A economia da vida e da morte (Translated by Heloisa Jahn). *Revista Brasileira de Ciências Sociais*, v. 8, no. 23 (Oct 93), pp. 138 – 145.

Guatemala

Sources

Lovell, William George. Los registros parroquiales de Jacaltenango, Guatemala. *Mesoamérica (USA)*, v. 13, no. 24 (Dec 92), pp. 441 – 453.

Latin America

Benítez Zenteno, Raúl. Visión latinoamericana de la transición demográfica. *Comercio Exterior*, v. 43, no. 7 (July 93), pp. 618 – 624. Bibl.

Tudela, Fernando. Población y sustentabilidad del desarrollo: los desafíos de la complejidad. *Comercio Exterior*, v. 43, no. 8 (Aug 93), pp. 698 – 707. Bibl, charts.

Zlotnik, Hania. América Latina y México ante el panorama de la población mundial. *Comercio Exterior*, v. 43, no. 7 (July 93), pp. 625 – 633. Tables.

Congresses

Conferencia Regional sobre Población y Desarrollo en América Latina y el Caribe. *Comercio Exterior*, v. 43, no. 7, Suppl. (July 93), Issue. Bibl, tables.

Mexican – American Border Region

Ceballos Ramírez, Manuel and Lawrence D. Taylor. Síntesis histórica del poblamiento de la región fronteriza México – Estados Unidos. *Estudios Fronterizos*, no. 26 (Sept – Dec 91), pp. 9 – 37. Bibl.

Ham-Chande, Roberto and John R. Weeks, eds. *Demographic Dynamics of the U.S. – Mexico Border* reviewed by Ellwyn Stoddard. *Journal of Borderlands Studies*, v. 8, no. 1 (Spring 93), pp. 119 – 124. Bibl.

Rubin-Kurtzman, Jane R. La etnia en las políticas de población de la frontera norte: reflexiones sobre un tema poco explorado y una agenda de investigación. *Frontera Norte*, v. 4, no. 8 (July – Dec 92), pp. 111 – 123. Bibl.

Mexico

Aranda Romero, José Luis and Agustín Grajales Porras. Perfil sociodemográfico de Tehuacán durante el virreinato. *Estudios Demográficos y Urbanos*, v. 7, no. 1 (Jan – Apr 92), pp. 53 – 76. Bibl, tables, maps, charts.

Cabrera Acevedo, Gustavo. La población y la búsqueda de equilibrios. *Comercio Exterior*, v. 43, no. 7 (July 93), pp. 612 – 617. Bibl.

Casas Chousal, Xolóxochitl and Sara Lovera. Razones y sinrazones de CIMAC y la población. *Fem*, v. 17, no. 128 (Oct 93), pp. 8 – 10.

Chena R., Rodolfo. La población de una parroquia novohispana del siglo XVIII: Santa María de la Presentación de Chilapa. *Estudios Demográficos y Urbanos*, v. 7, no. 1 (Jan – Apr 92), pp. 169 – 192. Bibl, tables, charts.

Corona Vázquez, Rodolfo. Respuesta al comentario de Arturo Blancas Espejo: "Confiabilidad de la confiabilidad," *Estudios Demográficos y Urbanos*, vol. 6, núm. 2, 1991. *Estudios Demográficos y Urbanos*, v. 6, no. 3 (Sept – Dec 91), pp. 717 – 725.

Cosío, María Eugenia. Los antecedentes de la transición demográfica en México. *Historia Mexicana*, v. 42, no. 1 (July – Sept 92), pp. 103 – 128. Bibl, tables, charts.

Estrella Valenzuela, Gabriel. Dinámica de los componentes demográficos de Baja California durante el período 1985 – 1990. *Estudios Fronterizos*, no. 26 (Sept – Dec 91), pp. 39 – 53.

Ham-Chande, Roberto. México: país en proceso de envejecimiento. *Comercio Exterior*, v. 43, no. 7 (July 93), pp. 688 – 696. Bibl, tables.

Kanter, Deborah E. Viudas y vecinos, milpas y magueyes: el impacto del auge de la población en el valle de Toluca; el caso de Tenango del Valle en el siglo XVIII. *Estudios Demográficos y Urbanos*, v. 7, no. 1 (Jan – Apr 92), pp. 19 – 33. Bibl, tables.

Klein, Herbert S. and Sonia Pérez Toledo. La población de la ciudad de Zacatecas en 1857. *Historia Mexicana*, v. 42, no. 1 (July – Sept 92), pp. 77 – 102. Bibl, tables, charts.

Pescador C., Juan Javier. *De bautizados a fieles difuntos: familia y mentalidades en una parroquia urbana; Santa Catarina de México, 1568 – 1820* reviewed by Patricia Schraer. *La Educación (USA)*, v. 37, no. 115 (1993), pp. 431 – 433.

Ramírez, Socorro. Sujetos y no objetos de las políticas de población. *Fem*, v. 17, no. 121 (Mar 93), pp. 13 – 14.

Reyna Bernal, Angélica. Políticas de migración y distribución de población en México: ejecución e impactos regionales. *Estudios Demográficos y Urbanos*, v. 6, no. 3 (Sept – Dec 91), pp. 583 – 611. Bibl, tables, charts.

Ruiz Chiapetto, Crescencio. El desarrollo del México urbano: cambio de protagonista. *Comercio Exterior*, v. 43, no. 8 (Aug 93), pp. 708 – 716. Bibl, tables, maps.

Sánchez Almanza, Adolfo and Manuel Urbina Fuentes. Distribución de la población y desarrollo en México. *Comercio Exterior*, v. 43, no. 7 (July 93), pp. 652 – 661. Bibl, tables, maps, charts.

Townsend, John W. Mexico and Its Baby Boom. *Business Mexico*, v. 3, no. 1 (Jan – Feb 93), pp. 58 – 59. Il.

Tuirán Gutiérrez, Rodolfo A. Algunos hallazgos recientes de la demografía histórica mexicana. *Estudios Demográficos y Urbanos*, v. 7, no. 1 (Jan – Apr 92), pp. 273 – 312. Bibl, tables.

Vargas Uribe, Guillermo. Geografía histórica de la ciudad de Morelia, Michoacán, México: su evolución demográfica. *Islas*, no. 98 (Jan – Apr 91), pp. 58 – 70. Bibl, tables, maps, charts.

— Geografía histórica de la población de Michoacán, siglo XVIII. *Estudios Demográficos y Urbanos*, v. 7, no. 1 (Jan – Apr 92), pp. 193 – 222. Bibl, tables, maps, charts.

Widmer S., Rolf. La ciudad de Veracruz en el último siglo colonial, 1680 – 1820: algunos aspectos de la historia demográfica de una ciudad portuaria. *La Palabra y el Hombre*, no. 83 (July – Sept 92), pp. 121 – 134. Bibl, tables.

Mathematical models

Ogaz Pierce, Héctor. La función de Gompertz – Makeham en la descripción y proyección de fenómenos demográficos. *Estudios Demográficos y Urbanos*, v. 6, no. 3 (Sept – Dec 91), pp. 485 – 520. Bibl, tables, charts.

Ordorica Mellado, Manuel. Desarrollo y aplicación de una función expologística para el análisis de congruencia de las fuentes demográficas entre 1940 y 1990: el caso de México. *Revista Mexicana de Sociología*, v. 55, no. 1 (Jan – Mar 93), pp. 3 – 16. Tables, charts.

Methodology

Martínez Salgado, Carolina. Métodos cualitativos para los estudios de población: un ejercicio en Xochimilco. *Revista Mexicana de Sociología*, v. 54, no. 3 (July – Sept 92), pp. 243 – 251. Bibl.

Sources

Pescador C., Juan Javier. La demografía histórica mexicana. *Estudios Demográficos y Urbanos*, v. 7, no. 1 (Jan – Apr 92), pp. 7 – 17.

Statistics

Esquivel Hernández, María Teresa et al. La zona metropolitana de la ciudad de México: dinámica demográfica y estructura poblacional, 1970 – 1990. *El Cotidiano*, v. 9, no. 54 (May 93), pp. 10 – 17. Bibl, il, tables, charts.

Jarque, Carlos M. La población de México en el último decenio del siglo XX. *Comercio Exterior*, v. 43, no. 7 (July 93), pp. 642 – 651. Tables, charts.

Ordorica Mellado, Manuel. La población de México en los albores del siglo XXI: ¿Predicción o proyección? *Comercio Exterior*, v. 43, no. 7 (July 93), pp. 634 – 641. Bibl, tables, charts.

Velasco M. L., María del Pilar. La epidemia de cólera de 1833 y la mortalidad en la ciudad de México. *Estudios Demográficos y Urbanos*, v. 7, no. 1 (Jan – Apr 92), pp. 95 – 135. Bibl, tables, charts.

Pacific Area

Morelos, José B. Una mirada a la demografía de los países de la cuenca del Pacífico. *Comercio Exterior*, v. 43, no. 8 (Aug 93), pp. 774 – 786. Bibl, tables.

Peru

Statistics

Fort, Alfredo L. Fecundidad y comportamiento reproductivo en la sierra y selva del Perú. *Estudios Demográficos y Urbanos*, v. 7, no. 2 – 3 (May – Dec 92), pp. 327 – 357. Bibl, tables, maps, charts.

Spain

Margulis, Mario. Población y sociedad en la España imperial. *Estudios Demográficos y Urbanos*, v. 7, no. 1 (Jan – Apr 92), pp. 223 – 272. Bibl, tables.

Uruguay

Filgueira, Nea. Otra vez las mujeres somos culpables: la procreación como una razón de estado. *Fem*, v. 17, no. 121 (Mar 93), pp. 11 – 12.

PORRAS BARRENECHEA, RAÚL

Loayza, Luis. El estilo: arma del conocimiento. *Hueso Húmero*, no. 29 (May 93), pp. 115 – 119.

PORT ROYAL, JAMAICA

Issa, Richard. Port Royal Dockyard Repairs in 1789. *Jamaica Journal*, v. 24, no. 3 (Feb 93), pp. 11 – 14. Il, tables, facs.

PORTER, ROSALIE PEDALINO

Criticism of specific works

Forked Tongue

Dicker, Susan J. Examining the Myths of Language and Cultural Diversity: A Response to Rosalie Pedalino Porter's *Forked Tongue: The Politics of Bilingual Education*. *Bilingual Review/Revista Bilingüe*, v. 17, no. 3 (Sept – Dec 92), pp. 210 – 230. Bibl.

PORTES GIL, EMILIO

Ortiz de Montellano, Bernardo R. Buzón de fantasmas: de Bernardo Ortiz de Montellano a Emilio Portes Gil. *Vuelta*, v. 17, no. 199 (June 93), pp. 74 – 75.

PORTILLA, FERNANDO

Hernández Téllez, Josefina. "Año con año se ha consolidado el trabajo": lic. Fernando Portilla, director gral. de la Supervisión General de Servicios a la Comunidad de la PGJDF. *Fem*, v. 17, no. 125 (July 93), p. 39.

PORTILLO DE LA LUZ, CÉSAR

Interviews

Aharonián, Coriún. Conversación con César Portillo de la Luz: "Y porque pienso vivo cuando canto." *Casa de las Américas*, no. 190 (Jan – Mar 93), pp. 141 – 146.

PORTOLÁ Y DE ROVIRA, GASPAR DE

Bernabéu Albert, Salvador. El "virrey de California" Gaspar de Portolá y la problemática de la primera gobernación californiana, 1767 – 1769. *Revista de Indias*, v. 52, no. 195 – 196 (May – Dec 92), pp. 271 – 295. Bibl.

Piqueras Céspedes, Ricardo. Alfínger y Portolá: dos modelos de frontera. *Boletín Americanista*, v. 33, no. 42 – 43 (1992 – 1993), pp. 107 – 121. Bibl.

PORTS

See

Harbors

PORTUGAL

See also

Archives – Portugal

Libraries and librarians – Portugal

Literature and society – Portugal

Colonies

Administration

Pijning, Ernst. Conflicts in the Portuguese Colonial Administration: Trials and Errors of Luís Lopes Pegado e Serpa, "provedor-mor da fazenda real" in Salvador, Brazil, 1718 – 1721. *Colonial Latin American Historical Review*, v. 2, no. 4 (Fall 93), pp. 403 – 423. Bibl, maps.

Constitutional law

González Encinar, José Juan et al. El proceso constituyente: enseñanzas a partir de cuatro casos recientes: España, Portugal, Brasil y Chile. *Ibero-Amerikanisches Archiv*, v. 18, no. 1 – 2 (1992), pp. 151 – 179. Tables.

Foreign relations

Santos, Milton. Imigração e movimento. *Vozes*, v. 87, no. 3 (May – June 93), pp. 2 – 6.

Spain

Morales, Adolfo de. Tratados de límites de las posesiones americanas entre España y Portugal. *Signo*, no. 36 – 37, Nueva época (May – Dec 92), pp. 387 – 407.

Moyano Bazzani, Eduardo L. Aportaciones de la historiografía portuguesa a la problemática fronteriza luso – española en América meridional, 1750 – 1778. *Revista de Indias*, v. 52, no. 195 – 196 (May – Dec 92), pp. 723 – 747. Bibl, maps.

Monuments, etc.

Bruni Celli, Blas. Palabras pronuciadas por el doctor Blas Bruni Celli ante la estatua del Libertador Simón Bolívar en Lisboa el 6 de mayo de 1992, con motivo del I Encuentro de las Academias de Historia de Portugal y Venezuela. *Boletín de la Academia Nacional de la Historia (Venezuela)*, v. 76, no. 301 (Jan – Mar 93), pp. 39 – 40.

PORTUGAL IN LITERATURE

Vieira, Nelson H. *Brasil e Portugal: a imagem recíproca; o mito e a realidade na expressão literária* reviewed by Bobby J. Chamberlain. *Hispania (USA)*, v. 76, no. 1 (Mar 93), pp. 90 – 92.

PORTUGUESE

Brazil

Ramos, Donald. From Minho to Minas: The Portuguese Roots of the Mineiro Family. *Hispanic American Historical Review*, v. 73, no. 4 (Nov 93), pp. 639 – 662. Bibl, tables.

Latin America

Schwartz, Stuart B. Panic in the Indies: The Portuguese Threat to the Spanish Empire, 1640 – 1650. *Colonial Latin American Review*, v. 2, no. 1 – 2 (1993), pp. 165 – 187. Bibl.

Venezuela

Morón Montero, Guillermo. Los portugueses en Venezuela: I Encuentro de las Academias de Historia de Portugal y Venezuela en Lisboa, Portugal, mayo de 1992. *Boletín de la Academia Nacional de la Historia (Venezuela)*, v. 76, no. 301 (Jan – Mar 93), pp. 33 – 37. Bibl.

PORTUGUESE LANGUAGE

Brazil

Matos, Francisco Gomes de. Amar a Deus e à língua portuguesa. *Vozes*, v. 87, no. 2 (Mar – Apr 93), p. 92.

PORTUGUESE LITERATURE

History and criticism

Abdala Júnior, Benjamin. Do Brasil a Portugal: imagens na ação política. *Revista de Letras (Brazil)*, v. 32 (1992), pp. 15 – 30. Bibl.

Vieira, Nelson H. *Brasil e Portugal: a imagem recíproca; o mito e a realidade na expressão literária* reviewed by Bobby J. Chamberlain. *Hispania (USA)*, v. 76, no. 1 (Mar 93), pp. 90 – 92.

POSADA, JOSÉ GUADALUPE

Carrillo Azpéitia, Rafael. *Posada y el grabado mexicano: desde el famoso grabador de temas populares hasta los artistas contemporáneos* reviewed by J. León Helguera (Review entitled "José Guadalupe Posada Yet Again"). *Studies in Latin American Popular Culture*, v. 12 (1993), pp. 203 – 206.

Haces, Carlos and Marco Antonio Pulido, eds. *José Guadalupe Posada y el amor: para iluminar* reviewed by J. León Helguera (Review entitled "José Guadalupe Posada Yet Again"). *Studies in Latin American Popular Culture*, v. 12 (1993), pp. 203 – 206.

Hiriart, Hugo. *El universo de Posada: estética de la obsolescencia* reviewed by J. León Helguera (Review entitled "José Guadalupe Posada Yet Again"). *Studies in Latin American Popular Culture*, v. 12 (1993), pp. 203 – 206.

POSITIVISM

Argentina

Barrancos, Dora. La modernidad redentora: difusión de las ciencias entre los trabajadores de Buenos Aires, 1890 – 1920. *Siglo XIX: Revista*, no. 12, 2a época (July – Dec 92), pp. 5 – 21. Bibl, tables.

Ciafardo, Eduardo O. and Daniel Espesir. Patología de la acción política anarquista: criminólogos, psiquiatras y conflicto social en Argentina, 1890 – 1910. *Siglo XIX: Revista*, no. 12, 2a época (July – Dec 92), pp. 23 – 40. Bibl.

Plá León, Rafael. La idea del mestizaje en representantes del positivismo en Argentina y México en el siglo XIX. *Islas*, no. 98 (Jan – Apr 91), pp. 135 – 142. Bibl.

Mexico

Plá León, Rafael. La idea del mestizaje en representantes del positivismo en Argentina y México en el siglo XIX. *Islas*, no. 98 (Jan – Apr 91), pp. 135 – 142. Bibl.

POSNANSKY, ARTHUR

Schávelzon, Daniel. La arqueología como ciencia o como ficción. *Todo Es Historia*, v. 26, no. 309 (Apr 93), pp. 32 – 49. Bibl, il.

POSSE, ABEL

Criticism of specific works

Los demonios secretos

Balderston, Daniel. Abel Posse y *Los demonios secretos: ¿Otra vez el nazismo? Nuevo Texto Crítico*, v. 6, no. 11 (1993), pp. 254 – 258. Bibl.

La reina del Plata

Kaplan, Marina E. *La reina del Plata:* pastiche postmoderno. *Chasqui*, v. 22, no. 2 (Nov 93), pp. 57 – 72. Bibl.

Interviews

Pites, Silvia. Entrevista con Abel Posse. *Chasqui*, v. 22, no. 2 (Nov 93), pp. 120 – 128. Bibl.

POSTERS

Brazil

Silva, Sonia T. Dias Gonçalves da. A colonização italiana no sul do Brasil em "posters." *SALALM Papers*, v. 34 (1989), pp. 177 – 182. Bibl.

Latin America

Sources

Esenwein, George and William Ratliff. Latin American Posters at the Hoover Institution: The Lexicons of State and Society. *SALALM Papers*, v. 34 (1989), pp. 214 – 220.

Nicaragua

Morgner, Fred G. Posters and the Sandinista Revolution (Accompanied by a descriptive list of posters). *SALALM Papers*, v. 34 (1989), pp. 183 – 213. Il.

United States

Goldman, Shifra M. Voz pública: quince años de carteles chicanos (Translated by Margarita Martínez Duarte). *Plural (Mexico)*, v. 22, no. 256 (Jan 93), pp. 28 – 37. Bibl.

POSTMODERNISM

Bayardo, Rubens. Acerca de la cuestión postmoderna: una perspectiva antropológica. *Estudios Paraguayos*, v. 17, no. 1 – 2 (1989 – 1993), pp. 23 – 33. Bibl.

Burin, Mabel. Algunos aportes al debate feminismo – posmodernismo. *Feminaria*, v. 6, no. 10 (Apr 93), pp. 21 – 23. Bibl.

Muñoz Cadima, Willy Oscar. Luisa Valenzuela: tautología lingüística y/o realidad nacional. *Revista Canadiense de Estudios Hispánicos*, v. 17, no. 2 (Winter 93), pp. 333 – 342. Bibl.

Valente, Luiz Fernando. Paulo Leminski e a poética do inútil. *Hispania (USA)*, v. 76, no. 3 (Sept 93), pp. 419 – 427. Bibl.

Argentina

Kaplan, Marina E. *La reina del Plata:* pastiche postmoderno. *Chasqui*, v. 22, no. 2 (Nov 93), pp. 57 – 72. Bibl.

Caribbean area

Benítez Rojo, Antonio. *The Repeating Island: The Caribbean and the Postmodern Perspective* reviewed by Klaus Müller-Bergh. *Cuban Studies/Estudios Cubanos*, v. 23 (1993), pp. 222 – 225.

— *The Repeating Island: The Caribbean and the Postmodern Perspective*, a translation of *Isla que se repite: el Caribe y la perspectiva posmoderna*, translated by James E. Maraniss. Reviewed by Edna Aizenberg. *Review*, no. 47 (Fall 93), pp. 93 – 95.

Latin America

Beverley, John. ¿Posliteratura?: sujeto subalterno e impasse de las humanidades. *Casa de las Américas*, no. 190 (Jan – Mar 93), pp. 13 – 24. Bibl.

Cornejo Guinassi, Pedro. La ruda sobriedad del realismo. *Debate (Peru)*, v. 15, no. 70 (Sept – Oct 92), pp. 45 – 47. Bibl, il.

Trevizán, Liliana. Intersecciones: postmodernidad/feminismo/Latinoamérica. *Revista Chilena de Literatura*, no. 42 (Aug 93), pp. 265 – 273.

Peru

Chang-Rodríguez, Eugenio. Las crónicas posmodernistas de César Vallejo. *Inti*, no. 36 (Fall 92), pp. 11 – 22. Bibl.

Venezuela

Delgado Ocando, José Manuel. Relectura posmodernista de Jesús Enrique Lossada. *Revista Nacional de Cultura (Venezuela)*, v. 54, no. 287 (Oct – Dec 92), pp. 37 – 54. Il.

Lasarte Valcárcel, Francisco Javier. Poéticas de la primera contemporaneidad y cambio intelectual en la narrativa venezolana. *Revista Chilena de Literatura*, no. 41 (Apr 93), pp. 79 – 97. Bibl.

POTATOES

Mexico

Russell, Joel. Pass the Chips. *Business Mexico*, v. 3, no. 8 (Aug 93), pp. 39 – 41. Il.

POTOSÍ, BOLIVIA (DEPARTMENT)

Música autóctona del norte de Potosí reviewed by Honoria Arredondo Calderón. *Revista Musical Chilena,* v. 46, no. 178 (July – Dec 92), pp. 127 – 128.

Platt, Tristán. Simón Bolívar, the Sun of Justice, and the Amerindian Virgin: Andean Conceptions of the "Patria" in Nineteenth-Century Potosí. *Journal of Latin American Studies,* v. 25, no. 1 (Feb 93), pp. 159 – 185. Bibl.

Tandeter, Enrique. *Coacción y mercado: la minería de plata en el Potosí colonial, 1692 – 1826* reviewed by Margarita Suárez. *Revista Andina,* v. 11, no. 1 (July 93), pp. 251 – 254.

POTTERY

See
Subdivision *Pottery* under names of Indian groups

POULTRY INDUSTRY

Brazil

Marques, Pedro V. Integração vertical da avicultura de corte no estado de São Paulo. *Revista de Economia e Sociologia Rural,* v. 30, no. 3 (July – Sept 92), pp. 189 – 202. Bibl, tables.

Mathematical models

Vicente, José R. Modelos estruturais para previsão das produções brasileiras de carne de frango e ovos. *Revista de Economia e Sociologia Rural,* v. 30, no. 4 (Oct – Dec 92), pp. 305 – 319. Bibl, tables, charts.

POVERTY

See also
Marginalization
Street children

Brazil

Hoffmann, Rodolfo. Vinte anos de desigualdade e pobreza na agricultura brasileira. *Revista de Economia e Sociologia Rural,* v. 30, no. 2 (Apr – June 92), pp. 97 – 113. Bibl, tables, charts.

Landim, Leilah. Can NGOs Help Stitch Together a Safety Net for Brazil's Poor? *Grassroots Development,* v. 17, no. 1 (1993), pp. 36 – 37. Il.

Navarro, Zander. Reclaiming the Land: Rural Poverty and the Promise of Small Farmers in Brazil (Photographs by Jofre Masceno from his book *Imagem reflexa). Grassroots Development,* v. 17, no. 1 (1993), pp. 20 – 24. Il.

Scheper-Hughes, Nancy. *Death without Weeping: The Violence of Everyday Life in Brazil* reviewed by Bernardo Kucinski. *Journal of Latin American Studies,* v. 25, no. 2 (May 93), pp. 419 – 420.

— *Death without Weeping: The Violence of Everyday Life in Brazil* reviewed by Glenn W. Erickson and Sandra S. Fernandes Erickson. *Luso-Brazilian Review,* v. 30, no. 1 (Summer 93), pp. 142 – 144.

Chile

Análisis de la situación y proyecciones del país. *Mensaje,* v. 42, no. 419 (June 93), pp. 220 – 224.

Camhi P., Rosa and Patricia Matte Larraín. Pobreza en la década de los '90 y desafíos futuros. *Estudios Sociales (Chile),* no. 75 (Jan – Mar 93), pp. 39 – 56. Tables.

Ruiz-Tagle P., Jaime. Reducción de la pobreza y distribución de los ingresos en Chile: tareas pendientes. *Mensaje,* v. 42, no. 425 (Dec 93), pp. 640 – 643. Il, tables.

Zapata, Sonia. La mendicidad y su mundo. *Estudios Sociales (Chile),* no. 76 (Apr – June 93), pp. 67 – 94. Bibl.

Haiti

Fass, Simon M. *Political Economy in Haiti: The Drama of Survival* reviewed by Michael H. Allen (Review entitled "Rethinking Political Economy and Praxis in the Caribbean"). *Latin American Perspectives,* v. 20, no. 2 (Spring 93), pp. 111 – 119.

Honduras

Navarro, Jorge. Poverty and Adjustment: The Case of Honduras. *CEPAL Review,* no. 49 (Apr 93), pp. 91 – 101. Bibl, tables.

Latin America

Bifani, Patricia. Disponibilidad, derecho y gestión del espacio vital. *Nueva Sociedad,* no. 123 (Jan – Feb 93), pp. 84 – 93. Bibl.

Fernández Poncela, Anna M. Yo juego, tú estudias, ellos sobreviven: ser niño en América Latina. *Fem,* v. 17, no. 121 (Mar 93), pp. 25 – 27.

García Medrano, Renward. Década perdida y planes de ajuste: crecimiento económico y pobreza. *Relaciones Internacionales (Mexico),* v. 14, Nueva época, no. 56 (Oct – Dec 92), pp. 45 – 48.

Kliksberg, Bernardo, ed. *¿Cómo enfrentar la pobreza?: estrategias y experiencias organizacionales innovadoras* reviewed by Michel Mujica Ricardo. *Nueva Sociedad,* no. 124 (Mar – Apr 93), pp. 174 – 175.

Rey Romay, Benito. Comentarios al libro *Pobreza y desigualdad en América Latina* de Pedro Vuskovic. *Problemas del Desarrollo,* v. 24, no. 94 (July – Sept 93), pp. 258 – 263.

Mexico

Cohen, Joshua A. Filling the Basket. *Business Mexico,* v. 3, no. 12 (Dec 93), pp. 19 – 20. Tables, charts.

Lustig, Nora. La medición de la pobreza en México (Translated by Carlos Villegas). *El Trimestre Económico,* v. 59, no. 236 (Oct – Dec 92), pp. 725 – 749. Bibl, tables, charts.

United States

Massey, Douglas S. Latinos, Poverty, and the Underclass: A New Agenda for Research. *Hispanic Journal of Behavioral Sciences,* v. 15, no. 4 (Nov 93), pp. 449 – 475. Bibl.

Venezuela

Cariola, Cecilia, ed. *Sobrevivir en la pobreza: el fin de una ilusión* reviewed by María Elena Ducci. *EURE,* v. 19, no. 58 (Oct 93), pp. 86 – 87.

POWER (SOCIAL SCIENCES)

Mace, Gordon et al. Regionalism in the Americas and the Hierarchy of Power. *Journal of Inter-American Studies and World Affairs,* v. 35, no. 2 (Summer 93), pp. 115 – 157. Bibl, tables, maps.

Research

Fábregas Puig, Andrés A. Acerca de las relaciones entre sociedad y política. *Nueva Antropología,* v. 13, no. 43 (Nov 92), pp. 53 – 59.

Varela, Roberto. Reflexiones sobre la expansión de sistemas y las relaciones de poder. *Nueva Antropología,* v. 13, no. 43 (Nov 92), pp. 39 – 43.

POWER RESOURCES

See also
Atomic power industry
Electric power
Energy policy
Gas, Natural
Petroleum industry and trade
Water power

Brazil

Vidal, José Walter Bautista. *Soberania e dignidade: raízes da sobrevivência* (Review). *Vozes,* v. 86, no. 4 (July – Aug 92), pp. 89 – 90.

Cuba

Pichs Madruga, Ramón. Problemas y opciones del sector energético cubano. *Problemas del Desarrollo,* v. 24, no. 92 (Jan – Mar 93), pp. 197 – 208. Bibl.

Pacific Area

Romero Ortiz, María Elena. Energía y desarrollo económico en la cuenca del Pacífico. *Comercio Exterior,* v. 43, no. 12 (Dec 93), pp. 1181 – 1187.

PRADO, CAIO GRACO

Obituaries

Chauí, Marilena de Souza and Olgária Chaim Feres Mattos. Caio Graco Prado. *Vozes,* v. 86, no. 4 (July – Aug 92), pp. 79 – 82. Il.

PRADOS, EMILIO

Valender, James. Emilio Prados y la guerra civil española: dos prosas olvidadas. *Nueva Revista de Filología Hispánica,* v. 40, no. 2 (July – Dec 92), pp. 989 – 1003. Bibl.

PRAYER

Jürth, Max. Plegarias incaicas. *Revista de Crítica Literaria Latinoamericana,* v. 19, no. 37 (Jan – June 93), pp. 159 – 168.

Seminiski, Jan. Manqu Qhapaq Inka: ¿Un poeta religioso? *Revista de Crítica Literaria Latinoamericana,* v. 19, no. 37 (Jan – June 93), pp. 131 – 158. Bibl.

PREBISCH, RAÚL

Furtado, Celso. La cosmovisión de Prebisch: una visión actual. *Estudios Internacionales (Chile),* v. 26, no. 101 (Jan – Mar 93), pp. 89 – 97. Bibl.

Iglesias, Enrique V., ed. *El legado de Raúl Prebisch* (Review). *Integración Latinoamericana,* v. 18, no. 193 (Sept 93), pp. 77 – 79.

Sprout, Ronald V. A. La economía política de Prebisch. *Pensamiento Iberoamericano,* no. 22 – 23, tomo I (July 92 – June 93), pp. 315 – 343. Bibl, tables.

PREDE

See
Programa Regional de Desarrollo Educativo

PREFERENTIAL TRADE AGREEMENTS

See
Foreign trade promotion

PREGNANCY

Peláez, Jorge Humberto. El invitado del mes: interrogantes éticos de la reproducción asistida. *Revista Javeriana,* v. 61, no. 595 (June 93), pp. 337 – 344. Il.

Brazil

Oliveira, Eleonora Menicucci de and Lucila Amaral Carneiro Vianna. Violência conjugal na gravidez. *Estudos Feministas,* v. 1, no. 1 (1993), pp. 162 – 165.

Panama

Bletzer, Keith V. Un análisis del rito de vigilia de las mujeres embarazadas entre los indígenas ngawbere, Panamá. *Vínculos,* v. 17, no. 1 – 2 (1991), pp. 53 – 74. Bibl, tables.

United States

Stoddard, Ellwyn R. Teen-Age Pregnancy in the Texas Borderlands. *Journal of Borderlands Studies,* v. 8, no. 1 (Spring 93), pp. 77 – 98. Bibl, tables, maps.

PRESIDENTE PRUDENTE, BRAZIL

Kinzo, Maria d'Alva Gil. The 1989 Presidential Election: Electoral Behaviour in a Brazilian City. *Journal of Latin American Studies,* v. 25, no. 2 (May 93), pp. 313 – 330. Bibl, tables.

PRESIDENTIAL POWER

See
Executive power
Subdivision *Presidents* under names of specific
countries

PRESS

See also
Freedom of the press
Journalism
Newspapers
Periodicals
Printing and engraving

Brazil

Bittencourt, Gabriel Augusto de Mello. A imprensa no Espírito Santo. *Revista do Instituto Histórico e Geográfico Brasileiro,* no. 373 (Oct – Dec 91), pp. 1022 – 1031.

Taschner, Gisela. *Folhas ao vento: análise de um conglomerado jornalístico no Brasil* reviewed by Maria Luisa Nabinger de Almeida. *RAE; Revista de Administração de Empresas,* v. 33, no. 4 (July – Aug 93), pp. 106 – 107. Il.

Caribbean area

Oreillard, Bernard. Approche sociologique de la presse à Porto Rico et en Guadeloupe/Martinique. *Caribbean Studies,* v. 25, no. 1 – 2 (Jan – July 92), pp. 63 – 73.

Chile

Jaksic, Ivan. Sarmiento y la prensa chilena del siglo XIX. *Historia (Chile),* no. 26 (1991 – 1992), pp. 117 – 144. Bibl.

Costa Rica

Mora Chinchilla, Carolina. Los Estados Unidos: una imagen modelo para Costa Rica, 1880 – 1903. *Anuario de Estudios Centroamericanos,* v. 18, no. 2 (1992), pp. 91 – 101. Bibl.

Latin America

Alvarez, Jesús and Ascensión Martínez Riaza. *Historia de la prensa hispanoamericana* reviewed by Alfonso Braojos Garrido. *Anuario de Estudios Americanos,* v. 50, no. 1 (1993), pp. 307 – 308.

Checa Godoy, Antonio. *Historia de la prensa en Iberoamérica* reviewed by Alfonso Braojos Garrido. *Anuario de Estudios Americanos,* v. 50, no. 1 (1993), pp. 314 – 316.

Mexico

Egan, Linda. Entrevistas con periodistas mujeres sobre la prensa mexicana. *Mexican Studies,* v. 9, no. 2 (Summer 93), pp. 275 – 294. Bibl.

United States

Lawless, Robert. *Haiti's Bad Press* reviewed by J. Michael Dash. *Social and Economic Studies,* v. 41, no. 4 (Dec 92), pp. 239 – 243.

— *Haiti's Bad Press: Origins, Development, and Consequences* reviewed by A. V. Catanese. *Journal of Developing Areas,* v. 28, no. 1 (Oct 93), pp. 141 – 142.

PRESS AND POLITICS

See also
Censorship
Freedom of the press

Antezana Villegas, Mauricio. Epilogo y prefacio. *Estado y Sociedad,* v. 8, no. 9 (Jan – June 92), pp. 99 – 105.

Mansilla, Hugo Celso Felipe. Comentario (on the topic "Industria electoral y comunicación política"). *Estado y Sociedad,* v. 8, no. 9 (Jan – June 92), pp. 77 – 79.

Argentina

Sidicaro, Ricardo. *La política mirada desde arriba: las ideas del diario 'La Nación', 1909 – 1989* reviewed by Diego F. Barros. *Todo Es Historia,* v. 27, no. 315 (Oct 93), pp. 65 – 66. Il.

Bolivia

Antezana Villegas, Mauricio. La espectacularización de la política y las autoformaciones culturales. *Estado y Sociedad,* v. 8, no. 9 (Jan – June 92), pp. 53 – 68.

Calla Ortega, Ricardo. Comentario (on the article by Roger Cortez). *Estado y Sociedad,* v. 8, no. 9 (Jan – June 92), pp. 91 – 98.

Campero, Ana María de. Comentario (on the article by Carlos D. Mesa Gisbert). *Estado y Sociedad,* v. 8, no. 9 (Jan – June 92), pp. 69 – 72.

Cortez, Roger. El impacto de los medios en la política. *Estado y Sociedad,* v. 8, no. 9 (Jan – June 92), pp. 81 – 90.

Cuevas, Roberto. Comentario (on the article by Carlos D. Mesa Gisbert). *Estado y Sociedad,* v. 8, no. 9 (Jan – June 92), pp. 73 – 75.

Mesa Gisbert, Carlos D. Televisión y elecciones: ¿El poder total? *Estado y Sociedad,* v. 8, no. 9 (Jan – June 92), pp. 39 – 52.

Toranzo Roca, Carlos F. Comentario (on the articles by Javier Protzel and Jorge Lazarte). *Estado y Sociedad,* v. 8, no. 9 (Jan – June 92), pp. 27 – 34.

Brazil

Araújo, Maria Celina d' and Gláucio Ary Dillon Soares. A imprensa, os mitos e os votos nas eleições de 1990. *Revista Brasileira de Estudos Políticos,* no. 76 (Jan 93), pp. 163 – 189. Tables, charts.

Chile

Sunkel, Guillermo and Eugenio Tironi B. Modernización de las comunicaciones y democratización de la política: los medios en la transición a la democracia en Chile. *Estudios Públicos (Chile)*, no. 52 (Spring 93), pp. 215 – 246. Bibl, tables.

Costa Rica

Zeledón Cambronero, Mario. Periodismo, historia y democracia. *Revista de Ciencias Sociales (Costa Rica)*, no. 57 (Sept 92), pp. 7 – 16. Bibl.

Cuba

Salwen, Michael Brian. "Eddie" Chibás, the "Magic Bullet" of Radio. *Studies in Latin American Popular Culture*, v. 12 (1993), pp. 113 – 126. Bibl.

El Salvador

Gómez Díez, Francisco Javier. El reformismo jesuítico en Centroamérica: La revista *ECA* en los años de la guerra fría, 1946 – 1965. *Anuario de Estudios Americanos*, v. 49, Suppl. 1 (1992), pp. 85 – 105. Tables.

Latin America

Canelas, Jorge. Comentario (on the articles by Javier Protzel and Jorge Lazarte). *Estado y Sociedad*, v. 8, no. 9 (Jan – June 92), pp. 35 – 37.

Mexico

Adler, Ilya. Press – Government Relations in Mexico: A Study of Freedom of the Mexican Press and Press Criticism of Government Institutions. *Studies in Latin American Popular Culture*, v. 12 (1993), pp. 1 – 30. Bibl, tables.

Bibliography

La France, David G. Politics, Violence, and the Press in Mexico (Review article). *Studies in Latin American Popular Culture*, v. 12 (1993), pp. 215 – 220.

Peru

Protzel, Javier. Industrias electorales y culturas políticas. *Estado y Sociedad*, v. 8, no. 9 (Jan – June 92), pp. 1 – 12.

United States

Silveira, Helder Gordim da. A ofensiva política dos EUA sobre a América Latina na visão alemã: uma face do confronto interimperialista, 1938. *Estudos Ibero-Americanos*, v. 18, no. 1 (July 92), pp. 19 – 27. Bibl.

Uruguay

Gilman, Claudia. Política y cultura: *Marcha* a partir de los años '60. *Nuevo Texto Crítico*, v. 6, no. 11 (1993), pp. 153 – 186. Bibl.

Venezuela

Miranda Bastidas, Haidée and David Ruiz Chataing. *El antiimperialismo en la prensa de la época de Cipriano Castro, 1899 – 1908* reviewed by Julián Rodríguez Barazarte. *Boletín de la Academia Nacional de la Historia (Venezuela)*, v. 76, no. 302 (Apr – June 93), pp. 152 – 153.

PRESSURE GROUPS

See also
   Political participation
   Social movements

Latin America

Frieden, Jeffrey A. *Debt, Development, and Democracy: Modern Political Economy and Latin America* reviewed by Sidney Weintraub. *Studies in Comparative International Development*, v. 27, no. 2 (Summer 92), pp. 96 – 98.

Mexico

Moctezuma Barragán, Pedro. Del movimiento urbano popular a los movimientos comunitarios: el espejo desenterrado. *El Cotidiano*, v. 10, no. 57 (Aug – Sept 93), pp. 3 – 10. Il.

Núñez González, Oscar. *Innovaciones democrático – culturales del movimiento urbano-popular* reviewed by José Javier Gutiérrez Rodríguez. *El Cotidiano*, v. 10, no. 57 (Aug – Sept 93), pp. 107 – 108.

Ramírez Sáiz, Juan Manuel. *¿Son políticos los movimientos urbano-populares?: un planteamiento teórico – metodológico* reviewed by Melchor Negrete Silva. *El Cotidiano*, v. 10, no. 57 (Aug – Sept 93), p. 107.

Bibliography

Ochoa Méndez, Jacqueline. Orientación bibliográfica sobre el movimiento urbano popular en la ciudad de México. *El Cotidiano*, v. 10, no. 57 (Aug – Sept 93), pp. 111 – 112.

United States

Eisenstadt, Todd. Nuevo estilo diplomático: cabildeo y relaciones públicas, 1986 – 1991 (Translated by Martha Elena Venier). *Foro Internacional*, v. 32, no. 5 (Oct – Dec 92), pp. 667 – 702. Bibl, tables, charts.

Landau, Saul. Clinton's Cuba Policy: A Low-Priority Dilemma. *NACLA Report on the Americas*, v. 26, no. 5 (May 93), pp. 35 – 37 + .

PRESTES, LUIS CARLOS

Prestes, Anita Leocadia. Luiz Carlos Prestes e a revolução socialista. *Vozes*, v. 87, no. 2 (Mar – Apr 93), pp. 11 – 17. Il.

Prestes, Maria. *Meu companheiro: 40 anos ao lado de Luiz Carlos Prestes* reviewed by Maurício Tragtemberg. *Vozes*, v. 87, no. 2 (Mar – Apr 93), pp. 97 – 101.

PRICE REGULATION

See also
   Cartels and commodity agreements

Brazil

Carvalho, Maria Auxiliadora de and César Roberto Leite da Silva. Preços mínimos e estabilização de preços agrícolas. *Revista de Economia Política (Brazil)*, v. 13, no. 1 (Jan – Mar 93), pp. 52 – 63. Bibl, tables.

Mathematical models

Lemos, José de Jesus Sousa and Pedro F. Adeodato de Paula Pessoa. Mercado de exportação e estabilização de preços externos para amêndoas de castanha de caju. *Revista de Economia e Sociologia Rural*, v. 30, no. 2 (Apr – June 92), pp. 171 – 187. Bibl, tables, charts.

Nicaragua

Spoor, Max. La política de precios agrícolas en Nicaragua durante el régimen sandinista, 1979 – 1990 (Translated by Carlos Villegas). *El Trimestre Económico*, v. 60, no. 239 (July – Sept 93), pp. 601 – 641. Bibl, tables, charts.

PRICES

See also
   Cost and standard of living
   Inflation (Finance)
   Price regulation

Brazil

Grandi, Rodolfo and Marcelo Resende. Inflação e variabilidade dos preços relativos no Brasil: a questão da causalidade. *Revista Brasileira de Economia*, v. 46, no. 4 (Oct – Dec 92), pp. 595 – 604. Bibl, tables.

Mathematical models

Amadeo Swaelen, Edward Joaquim. Do Relative Wages Move Together with Relative Prices? *Revista Brasileira de Economia*, v. 47, no. 1 (Jan – Mar 93), pp. 33 – 52. Bibl, tables, charts.

— Indexação e dispersão de preços relativos: análise do caso brasileiro, 1975 – 1991. *Revista de Economia Política (Brazil)*, v. 13, no. 3 (July – Sept 93), pp. 130 – 138. Bibl, charts.

Catão, Luís. A New Wholesale Price Index for Brazil during the Period 1870 – 1913. *Revista Brasileira de Economia*, v. 46, no. 4 (Oct – Dec 92), pp. 519 – 533. Bibl, tables, charts.

Landau, Elena and Suzana S. Peixoto. Inflação, indexação e preços relativos: novas evidências para o Brasil. *Pesquisa e Planejamento Econômico*, v. 22, no. 1 (Apr 92), pp. 125 – 167. Bibl, tables, charts.

Colombia

Statistics

Colombia. Departamento Nacional de Planeación. Precios. *Planeación y Desarrollo*, v. 24 (1993), All issues.

PRIMARY PRODUCTS

See
   Natural resources

PRINTING AND ENGRAVING

Badilla, Crisanto. La xilografía (Examples by the author and his students illustrate the issue). *Káñina*, v. 16, no. 1 (Jan – June 92), pp. 221 – 223.

Argentina

Grinberg, Samuel. Cuatro grabadores judíos en la confederación argentina. *Todo Es Historia*, v. 27, no. 314 (Sept 93), pp. 50 – 53. Il.

Colombia

Posada, Jaime. Don Antonio Nariño, ideólogo de la emancipación. *Boletín de Historia y Antigüedades*, v. 80, no. 781 (Apr – June 93), pp. 435 – 442.

Mexico

Carrillo Azpéitia, Rafael. *Posada y el grabado mexicano: desde el famoso grabador de temas populares hasta los artistas contemporáneos* reviewed by J. León Helguera (Review entitled "José Guadalupe Posada Yet Again"). *Studies in Latin American Popular Culture*, v. 12 (1993), pp. 203 – 206.

Haces, Carlos and Marco Antonio Pulido, eds. *José Guadalupe Posada y el amor: para iluminar* reviewed by J. León Helguera (Review entitled "José Guadalupe Posada Yet Again"). *Studies in Latin American Popular Culture*, v. 12 (1993), pp. 203 – 206.

Hiriart, Hugo. *El universo de Posada: estética de la obsolescencia* reviewed by J. León Helguera (Review entitled "José Guadalupe Posada Yet Again"). *Studies in Latin American Popular Culture*, v. 12 (1993), pp. 203 – 206.

Juan, Adelaida de. Pintar sobre piedra. *Casa de las Américas*, no. 189 (Oct – Dec 92), pp. 102 – 106.

Segovia, Francisco. Juan Pascoe y Cornelio Adrián César, impresores de México. *Artes de México*, no. 19 (Spring 93), pp. 111 – 113. Il.

Peru

Medina, José Toribio. *La imprenta en Lima, 1548 – 1824,* tomo IV, reviewed by Sergio Martínez Baeza. *Boletín de la Academia Chilena de la Historia*, v. 58 – 59, no. 102 (1991 – 1992), pp. 558 – 559.

PRISONERS

See
Crime and criminals
Political prisoners
Prisoners of war

PRISONERS OF WAR

See also
Political prisoners

Brazil

Bento, Cláudio Moreira. Campo de prisioneiros de guerra em Pouso Alegre. *Revista do Instituto Histórico e Geográfico Brasileiro*, no. 373 (Oct – Dec 91), pp. 1052 – 1056.

PRISONS

Chile

Etcheberry, Blanca. Capacitación de presos: solidaridad entre rejas. *Mensaje*, v. 42, no. 421 (Aug 93), pp. 390 – 391. Il.

Mexico

Barreda Solórzano, Luis de la. Las condiciones carcelarias de las mujeres. *Fem*, v. 17, no. 127 (Sept 93), pp. 13 – 16. Bibl.

— Mujeres en prisión. *Fem*, v. 17, no. 122 (Apr 93), pp. 20 – 21.

Buffington, Robert. Revolutionary Reform: The Mexican Revolution and the Discourse on Prison Reform. *Mexican Studies*, v. 9, no. 1 (Winter 93), pp. 71 – 93. Bibl.

Cruz Barrera, Nydia E. Reclusión, control social y penitenciaria en Puebla en el siglo XIX. *Siglo XIX: Revista*, no. 12, 2a época (July – Dec 92), pp. 119 – 146.

PRIVATIZATION

Argentina

Bravo, Víctor. YPF S.A.: ¿Y ahora, qué? *Realidad Económica*, no. 117 (July – Aug 93), pp. 2 – 7.

Dinerstein, Ana Cecilia. Privatizaciones y legitimidad: la lógica de la coerción. *Realidad Económica*, no. 113 (Jan – Feb 93), pp. 18 – 30.

Herrera, Alejandra. The Privatization of the Argentine Telephone System. *CEPAL Review*, no. 47 (Aug 92), pp. 149 – 161. Bibl.

Sánchez, Miguel Alberto. Privatizaciones y extranjerización de la economía argentina. *Realidad Económica*, no. 116 (May – June 93), pp. 33 – 45.

Schvarzer, Jorge. El proceso de privatizaciones en la Argentina: implicaciones preliminares sobre sus efectos en la gobernabilidad del sistema. *Realidad Económica*, no. 120 (Nov – Dec 93), pp. 79 – 143. Bibl.

Silenzi de Stagni, Adolfo et al. La privatización de YPF. *Realidad Económica*, no. 118 (Aug – Sept 93), pp. 18 – 67. Tables, charts.

Thwaites Rey, Mabel. La política de privatizaciones en la Argentina: consideraciones a partir del caso de Aerolíneas. *Realidad Económica*, no. 116 (May – June 93), pp. 46 – 75. Bibl, tables.

Brazil

Dourado, Anísio Brasileiro de Freitas. Relaciones contractuales entre los poderes públicos y las empresas privadas de autobuses urbanos en Brasil (Translated by Martín Figueroa). *EURE*, v. 19, no. 56 (Mar 93), pp. 29 – 39. Bibl.

Giambiagi, Fábio and Armando Castelar Pinheiro. As empresas estatais e o programa de privatização do governo Collor. *Pesquisa e Planejamento Econômico*, v. 22, no. 2 (Aug 92), pp. 241 – 288. Bibl, tables.

Henry, Etienne. Autotransporte urbano colectivo en desarrollo: el abanico de las empresas. *EURE*, v. 19, no. 56 (Mar 93), pp. 71 – 78.

Vázquez Trejo, Adela. Consideraciones sobre el proceso de privatización en Brasil y México. *Relaciones Internacionales (Mexico)*, v. 14, Nueva época, no. 55 (July – Sept 92), pp. 75 – 78.

Cost

Sánchez Ruiz, Jorge Ernesto. Privatização de estradas no Brasil: comentário sobre a viabilidade financeira. *Revista de Economia Política (Brazil)*, v. 13, no. 3 (July – Sept 93), pp. 41 – 53. Bibl, tables.

Mathematical models

Menezes, Flávio Marques. Leilões de privatização: uma análise de equilíbrio. *Revista Brasileira de Economia*, v. 47, no. 3 (July – Sept 93), pp. 317 – 348. Bibl.

Caribbean area

Theodore, Karl. Privatization: Conditions for Success and Fiscal Policy Implications. *Social and Economic Studies*, v. 41, no. 4 (Dec 92), pp. 133 – 148. Bibl.

Chile

Opazo, José Luis et al. El descontrol del sistema de buses de Santiago: síntesis de un diagnóstico técnico – institucional. *EURE*, v. 19, no. 56 (Mar 93), pp. 79 – 91. Bibl, tables.

Cost

Cifuentes, María Cecilia. Impacto fiscal de la privatización en Chile, 1985 – 1990. *Estudios Públicos (Chile)*, no. 51 (Winter 93), pp. 157 – 193. Bibl.

Colombia

Ramírez Acuña, Luis Fernando. Privatización en las administraciones tributarias. *Planeación y Desarrollo*, v. 24, no. 2 (May – Aug 93), pp. 341 – 372.

Urrutia Montoya, Miguel. Competencia y desarrollo económico. *Planeación y Desarrollo*, v. 24, no. 2 (May – Aug 93), pp. 49 – 72. Bibl, charts.

Developing countries

Adam, Christopher et al. *Adjusting Privatization: Case Studies from Developing Countries* reviewed by Gladstone Hutchinson. *Social and Economic Studies*, v. 41, no. 4 (Dec 92), pp. 231 – 234.

Latin America

Baer, Werner and Melissa H. Birch. La privatización y el rol cambiante del estado en América Latina. *Revista Paraguaya de Sociología*, v. 29, no. 85 (Sept – Dec 92), pp. 7 – 28. Bibl.

Devlin, Robert T. Privatizations and Social Welfare. *CEPAL Review*, no. 49 (Apr 93), pp. 155 – 180. Bibl, tables.

Minsburg, Naúm. Política privatizadora en América Latina. *Comercio Exterior*, v. 43, no. 11 (Nov 93), pp. 1060 – 1067. Bibl, tables.

— Privatizaciones y reestructuración económica en América Latina. *Realidad Económica*, no. 116 (May – June 93), pp. 76 – 97. Bibl, tables.

Bibliography

Núñez Domingo, Pedro Pablo. Realidad y simbolismo de la privatización (Review article). *Pensamiento Iberoamericano*, no. 22 – 23, tomo I (July 92 – June 93), pp. 357 – 385. Charts.

Mexico

Bautista Romero, Jaime. Al aproximarse a su fin la venta de paraestatales, el gobierno subasta infraestructura y servicios. *Momento Económico*, no. 66 (Mar – Apr 93), pp. 2 – 6. Bibl.

Castillo, Alejandro. The Challenge to Deliver (Translated by Richard Cadena). *Business Mexico*, v. 3, no. 7 (July 93), pp. 4 – 10. Maps, charts.

Cruz Castellanos, Federico. Economía cañero – azucarera: neoliberalismo y crisis. *Momento Económico*, no. 67 (May – June 93), pp. 19 – 22. Tables.

González Chávez, Gerardo. Monclova: algunos efectos del neoliberalismo. *Momento Económico*, no. 66 (Mar – Apr 93), pp. 18 – 22.

Rodríguez, Flavia. The Mexican Privatization Programme: An Economic Analysis. *Social and Economic Studies*, v. 41, no. 4 (Dec 92), pp. 149 – 171. Bibl, tables, charts.

Silverstein, Jeffrey. Wave of the Future. *Business Mexico*, v. 3, no. 4 (Apr 93), pp. 38 – 39. Il.

Soria, Víctor M. Nouvelles politiques d'ajustement et de relégitimation de l'état au Mexique: le rôle du PRONASOL et de la privatisation des entreprises publiques. *Tiers Monde*, v. 34, no. 135 (July – Sept 93), pp. 603 – 623. Bibl, tables.

Vázquez Trejo, Adela. Consideraciones sobre el proceso de privatización en Brasil y México. *Relaciones Internacionales (Mexico)*, v. 14, Nueva época, no. 55 (July – Sept 92), pp. 75 – 78.

Trinidad and Tobago

Forde, Penelope and Kelvin Sergeant. The State Sector and Divestment in Trinidad and Tobago: Some Preliminary Findings. *Social and Economic Studies*, v. 41, no. 4 (Dec 92), pp. 173 – 204. Bibl, tables.

PROBLEMAS BRASILEIROS (PERIODICAL)

Trinta anos de história. *Problemas Brasileiros*, v. 30, no. 295 (Jan – Feb 93), pp. 6 – 9. Il.

PRODUCERS' ASSOCIATIONS

See
Cartels and commodity agreements

PRODUCTION (ECONOMIC THEORY)

See also
Capital productivity
Industrial productivity
Labor productivity
Marxian economics

Santana, Antônio Cordeiro de. Análise econômica da produção agrícola sob condições de risco numa comunidade amazônica. *Revista de Economia e Sociologia Rural*, v. 30, no. 2 (Apr – June 92), pp. 159 – 170. Bibl, tables.

Solís Avendaño, Manuel. El ascenso de la ideología de la producción en Costa Rica: el Partido Liberación Nacional. *Revista de Ciencias Sociales (Costa Rica)*, no. 60 (June 93), pp. 85 – 100. Bibl.

PROGRAMA REGIONAL DE DESARROLLO EDUCATIVO

Actividades del PREDE. *La Educación (USA)*, v. 36, 37 (1992, 1992), All issues. Il.

PROGRAMMED INSTRUCTION

Oliveira, João Batista Araújo e and Greville Rumble, eds. *Educación a distancia en América Latina: análisis de costoefectividad* reviewed by Aaron Segal. *Interciencia*, v. 18, no. 6 (Nov – Dec 93), pp. 327 – 328.

PROJECTILE POINTS

See
Stone implements
Subdivision *Implements* under names of Indian groups

PROPERTY

See also
Intellectual property
Real property

Argentina

Rocha Campos, Adolfo. El patrimonio de Perón. *Todo Es Historia*, v. 27, no. 313 (Aug 93), pp. 26 – 42. Bibl, il.

PROSTITUTION

Chacón Echeverría, Laura. La mujer prostituta: cuerpo de suciedad, fermento de muerte; reflexiones en torno a algunos rituales de purificación. *Revista de Ciencias Sociales (Costa Rica)*, no. 58 (Dec 92), pp. 23 – 34. Bibl, il.

Argentina

Carretero, Andrés M. Las prostitutas en Buenos Aires. *Todo Es Historia*, v. 27, no. 315 (Oct 93), pp. 46 – 49.

Guy, Donna Jane. *Sex and Danger in Buenos Aires: Prostitution, Family, and Nation in Argentina* reviewed by Sandra McGee Deutsch. *The Americas*, v. 49, no. 3 (Jan 93), pp. 411 – 412.

— *Sex and Danger in Buenos Aires: Prostitution, Family, and Nation in Argentina* reviewed by Kristin Ruggiero. *Hispanic American Historical Review*, v. 73, no. 1 (Feb 93), p. 165.

— *Sex and Danger in Buenos Aires: Prostitution, Family, and Nation in Argentina* reviewed by Paula Alonso. *Journal of Latin American Studies*, v. 25, no. 1 (Feb 93), pp. 198 – 200.

— *Sex and Danger in Buenos Aires: Prostitution, Family, and Nation in Argentina* reviewed by K. Lynn Stoner (Review entitled "Whores, Witches, and Unwed Mothers: Recent Scholarship on the Control of Sexuality"). *Studies in Latin American Popular Culture*, v. 12 (1993), pp. 207 – 214.

Brazil

Dimenstein, Gilberto. *Meninas da noite: a prostituição de meninas-escravas no Brasil* reviewed by Jenny K. Pilling. *Luso-Brazilian Review*, v. 30, no. 1 (Summer 93), pp. 148 – 149.

Engel, Magali. *Meretrizes e doutores: saber médico e prostituição no Rio de Janeiro, 1840 – 1890* reviewed by Sandra Lauderdale Graham (Review entitled "Dangerous Fantasies: The Altered Vocabulary of Commercial Sex"). *Luso-Brazilian Review*, v. 30, no. 1 (Summer 93), pp. 133 – 139.

Leite, Gabriela Silva. *Eu, mulher da vida* reviewed by Ana Arruda Callado (Review entitled "Ainda o poder da sedução"). *Estudos Feministas*, v. 0, no. 0 (1992), pp. 228 – 229.

Rago, Margareth. *Prazer e sociabilidade no mundo da prostituição em São Paulo, 1890 – 1930. Luso-Brazilian Review*, v. 30, no. 1 (Summer 93), pp. 35 – 46. Bibl.

— *Os prazeres da noite: prostituição e códigos da sexualidade feminina em São Paulo, 1890 – 1930* reviewed by Sandra Lauderdale Graham (Review entitled "Dangerous Fantasies: The Altered Vocabulary of Commercial Sex"). *Luso-Brazilian Review*, v. 30, no. 1 (Summer 93), pp. 133 – 139.

Soares, Luís Carlos. *Rameiras, ilhoas, polacas: a prostituição do Rio de Janeiro do século XIX* reviewed by Sandra Lauderdale Graham (Review entitled "Dangerous Fantasies: The Altered Vocabulary of Commercial Sex"). *Luso-Brazilian Review*, v. 30, no. 1 (Summer 93), pp. 133 – 139.

Mexican – American Border Region

Croston, Kendel. Women's Activities during the Prohibition Era along the U.S. – Mexico Border. *Journal of Borderlands Studies*, v. 8, no. 1 (Spring 93), pp. 99 – 113. Bibl.

Mexico

Barrera Carranza, Estanislao. Prostitución y medios masivos de comunicación social. *La Palabra y el Hombre*, no. 84 (Oct – Dec 92), pp. 39 – 61. Bibl.

Peru

Basili D., Francisco. *Crisis y comercio sexual de menores en el Perú* (Review). *La Educación (USA)*, v. 36, no. 111 – 113 (1992), pp. 283 – 284.

PROTEST SONGS

See
Music and society

PROTESTANTISM

See also
Names of specific sects

Bolivia

Ströbele-Gregor, Juliana. Las comunidades religiosas fundamentalistas en Bolivia: sobre el éxito misionero de los Adventistas del Séptimo Día. *Allpanchis*, v. 23, no. 40 (July – Dec 92), pp. 219 – 253. Bibl.

— Las comunidades religiosas fundamentalistas en Bolivia: sobre el éxito misionero de los Adventistas del Séptimo Día. *Allpanchis*, v. 23, no. 40 (July – Dec 92), pp. 219 – 253. Bibl.

El Salvador

Aguilar, Edwin Eloy et al. Protestantism in El Salvador: Conventional Wisdom versus Survey Evidence. *Latin American Research Review*, v. 28, no. 2 (1993), pp. 119 – 140. Bibl, tables.

Latin America

Bastian, Jean-Pierre. The Metamorphosis of Latin American Protestant Groups: A Sociohistorical Perspective (Translated by Margaret Caffey-Moquin). *Latin American Research Review*, v. 28, no. 2 (1993), pp. 33 – 61. Bibl, tables.

Gros, Christian. Fondamentalisme protestant et populations indiennes: quelques hypothèses. *Cahiers des Amériques Latines*, no. 13 (1992), pp. 119 – 134.

Stoll, David. *Is Latin America Turning Protestant?: The Politics of Evangelical Growth* reviewed by Michael LaRosa (Review entitled "Religion in a Changing Latin America: A Review"). *Journal of Inter-American Studies and World Affairs*, v. 34, no. 4 (Winter 92 – 93), pp. 245 – 255. Bibl.

Mexico

Meyer, Jean A. Una historia política de la religión en el México contemporáneo. *Historia Mexicana*, v. 42, no. 3 (Jan – Mar 93), pp. 714 – 744. Bibl.

PROVERBS

Devoto, Daniel. La lengua de las tribus: de Guéret Chaminadour a Santa María de los Buenos Aires. *Nueva Revista de Filología Hispánica*, v. 40, no. 2 (July – Dec 92), pp. 921 – 958.

PROVIDENCIA ISLAND, COLOMBIA

Clemente B., Isabel. Un caso de conflicto cultural en el Caribe: de la imposición al reconocimiento. *Nueva Sociedad*, no. 127 (Sept – Oct 93), pp. 32 – 45. Bibl.

PSYCHIATRY

See also
Mental illness

Balán, Jorge. *Cuéntame tu vida: una biografía colectiva del psicoanálisis argentino* reviewed by Thomas F. Glick. *Hispanic American Historical Review*, v. 73, no. 1 (Feb 93), pp. 129 – 130.

— La proyección cultural del psicoanálisis argentino. *Cuadernos Hispanoamericanos*, no. 517 – 519 (July – Sept 93), pp. 105 – 119. Bibl.

Brown, Charles J. and Armando M. Lago. *The Politics of Psychiatry in Revolutionary Cuba* reviewed by Roberto Valero. *Cuban Studies/Estudios Cubanos*, v. 23 (1993), pp. 233 – 235.

Céspedes Castro, Cristina and Sonia León Montoya. Terapia de grupo no directiva con pacientes seropositivos y con SIDA. *Revista de Ciencias Sociales (Costa Rica)*, no. 58 (Dec 92), pp. 45 – 54. Bibl, charts.

Ciafardo, Eduardo O. and Daniel Espesir. Patología de la acción política anarquista: criminólogos, psiquiatras y conflicto social en Argentina, 1890 – 1910. *Siglo XIX: Revista*, no. 12, 2a época (July – Dec 92), pp. 23 – 40. Bibl.

PSYCHOANALYSIS IN LITERATURE

Carvalho, Sônia Maria Rodrigues de. Inscrição e busca. *Revista de Letras (Brazil)*, v. 32 (1992), pp. 41 – 49.

Stroud, Matthew D. The Desiring Subject and the Promise of Salvation: A Lacanian Study of Sor Juana's *El divino Narciso*. *Hispania (USA)*, v. 76, no. 2 (May 93), pp. 204 – 212. Bibl.

PSYCHOLOGY

See
Adolescent psychology
Alienation
Child psychology
Dreams
Learning, Psychology of
Mental illness
Psychiatry
Social psychology
Stress (Physiology)
Suicide

PUBLIC ADMINISTRATION

See also
Local government
Subdivision *Officials and public employees* under names of specific countries

Méndez M., José Luis. La política pública como variable dependiente: hacia un análisis más integral de las políticas públicas. *Foro Internacional*, v. 33, no. 1 (Jan – Mar 93), pp. 111 – 144. Bibl, tables, charts.

America

Hampe Martínez, Teodoro. Los funcionarios de la monarquía española en América: notas para una caracterización política, económica y social. *Revista Interamericana de Bibliografía*, v. 42, no. 3 (1992), pp. 431 – 452. Bibl.

Argentina

Ouellette, Roger. Democracia y reformas administrativas: los casos de Argentina y Uruguay. *Cuadernos del CLAEH*, v. 18, no. 65 – 66 (May 93), pp. 75 – 85. Bibl.

Sánchez, Marcelo and Pablo Sirlin. Elementos de una propuesta transformadora para el desarrollo económico argentino. *Realidad Económica*, no. 117 (July – Aug 93), pp. 36 – 160. Bibl.

Sikkink, Kathryn. Las capacidades y la autonomía del estado en Brasil y la Argentina: un enfoque neoinstitucionalista (Translated by Leandro Wolfson). *Desarrollo Económico (Argentina)*, v. 32, no. 128 (Jan – Mar 93), pp. 543 – 574. Bibl, charts.

Brazil

Hochman, Gilberto. Os cardeais da previdência social: gênese e consolidação de uma elite burocrática. *Dados*, v. 35, no. 3 (1992), pp. 371 – 401. Bibl.

Keinert, Tania Margarete Mezzomo. Reforma administrativa nos anos '90: o caso da prefeitura municipal de São Paulo. *RAE; Revista de Administração de Empresas*, v. 33, no. 4 (July – Aug 93), pp. 66 – 81. Tables, maps, charts.

Leiria, Jerônimo Souto et al. *Terceirização passo à passo: o caminho para a administração pública e privada* reviewed by Michelle Montone. *RAE; Revista de Administração de Empresas*, v. 33, no. 2 (Mar – Apr 93), pp. 127 – 128.

Schneider, Ben Ross. *Politics within the State: Elite Bureaucrats and Industrial Policy in Authoritarian Brazil* reviewed by Sonny B. Davis. *Canadian Journal of Latin American and Caribbean Studies*, v. 17, no. 34 (1992), p. 131.

— *Politics within the State: Elite Bureaucrats and Industrial Policy in Authoritarian Brazil* reviewed by John W. Sloan. *Journal of Developing Areas*, v. 27, no. 3 (Apr 93), pp. 424 – 425.

Sikkink, Kathryn. Las capacidades y la autonomía del estado en Brasil y la Argentina: un enfoque neoinstitucionalista (Translated by Leandro Wolfson). *Desarrollo Económico (Argentina),* v. 32, no. 128 (Jan – Mar 93), pp. 543 – 574. Bibl, charts.

Central America

Pérez Jérez, Cristóbal. Políticas de ajuste estructural y reforma del estado. *USAC,* no. 14 (June 91), pp. 56 – 70. Bibl.

Chile

Garretón Merino, Manuel Antonio. Aprendizaje y gobernabilidad en la redemocratización chilena. *Nueva Sociedad,* no. 128 (Nov – Dec 93), pp. 148 – 157.

Colombia

Losada Lora, Rodrigo. La evolución del orden público. *Revista Javeriana,* v. 61, no. 597 (Aug 93), pp. 159 – 165.

Ramírez Acuña, Luis Fernando. Privatización en las administraciones tributarias. *Planeación y Desarrollo,* v. 24, no. 2 (May – Aug 93), pp. 341 – 372.

Sánchez, Ricardo. Constitución y vida social. *Revista Javeriana,* v. 61, no. 597 (Aug 93), pp. 169 – 173.

Developing countries

Santos, Wanderley Guilherme dos. *Razões da desordem* reviewed by Cláudio Gonçalves Couto. *Revista Brasileira de Ciências Sociais,* v. 8, no. 23 (Oct 93), pp. 153 – 155.

Jamaica

Jones, Edwin. *Development Administration: Jamaican Adaptation* reviewed by Ian Boxill. *Social and Economic Studies,* v. 41, no. 3 (Sept 92), pp. 180 – 182.

Japan

Alvarez, Carmen R. Los cargos políticos y su incidencia en la estabilidad de los proyectos públicos: los casos de Uruguay y Japón. *Cuadernos del CLAEH,* v. 18, no. 65 – 66 (May 93), pp. 61 – 74. Bibl.

Latin America

Rufián Lizana, Dolores María. Una nueva administración municipal. *Revista Paraguaya de Sociología,* v. 29, no. 85 (Sept – Dec 92), pp. 59 – 71. Charts.

Torres-Rivas, Edelberto. América Latina: gobernabilidad y democracia en sociedades en crisis. *Nueva Sociedad,* no. 128 (Nov – Dec 93), pp. 88 – 101.

Mexico

Camou, Antonio N. Gobernabilidad y democracia en Mexico: avantares de una transición incierta. *Nueva Sociedad,* no. 128 (Nov – Dec 93), pp. 102 – 119.

Fuentes Aguilar, Luis and Consuelo Soto Mora. El control institucional en el Plan Nacional de Desarrollo en México. *Revista Interamericana de Planificación,* v. 26, no. 101 – 102 (Jan – June 93), pp. 183 – 195. Bibl.

Hernández Rodríguez, Rogelio. La administración al servicio de la política: la Secretaría de Programación y Presupuesto. *Foro Internacional,* v. 33, no. 1 (Jan – Mar 93), pp. 145 – 173. Bibl, tables.

— Preparación y movilidad de los funcionarios de la administración pública mexicana. *Estudios Sociológicos,* v. 11, no. 32 (May – Aug 93), pp. 445 – 473. Bibl, tables.

Lipsett-Rivera, Sonya. Water and Bureaucracy in Colonial Puebla de los Angeles. *Journal of Latin American Studies,* v. 25, no. 1 (Feb 93), pp. 25 – 44. Bibl, tables, maps.

Study and teaching

Pardo, María del Carmen. La administración pública en México: su desarrollo como disciplina. *Foro Internacional,* v. 33, no. 1 (Jan – Mar 93), pp. 12 – 29. Bibl.

Uruguay

Alvarez, Carmen R. Los cargos políticos y su incidencia en la estabilidad de los proyectos públicos: los casos de Uruguay y Japón. *Cuadernos del CLAEH,* v. 18, no. 65 – 66 (May 93), pp. 61 – 74. Bibl.

Ouellette, Roger. Democracia y reformas administrativas: los casos de Argentina y Uruguay. *Cuadernos del CLAEH,* v. 18, no. 65 – 66 (May 93), pp. 75 – 85. Bibl.

Pérez Piera, Adolfo. Reforma del estado: otra vuelta de tuerca. *Cuadernos del CLAEH,* v. 18, no. 65 – 66 (May 93), pp. 87 – 96.

PUBLIC DEFICIT

See

Finance, Public

PUBLIC HEALTH

See also

Childbirth
Diseases
Food habits
Hospitals
Infant mortality
Medicine
Nurses
Nutrition
Pesticides
Pharmacy
Physicians
Pollution
Refuse and refuse disposal
Subdivision *Health and hygiene* under *Hispanic Americans (U.S.), Women,* and names of Indian groups

Rodríguez Mansilla, Darío. Salud, enfermedad y rol del enfermo. *Estudios Sociales (Chile),* no. 74 (Oct – Dec 92), pp. 75 – 95. Bibl.

Study and teaching

Mueses de Molina, Carolina. Educación popular en salud y nutrición: revisión de bibliografía. *Estudios Sociales (Dominican Republic),* v. 26, no. 93 (July – Sept 93), pp. 83 – 108. Bibl.

Argentina

Benencia, Roberto and Javier Souza Casadinho. Alimentos y salud: uso y abuso de pesticidas en la horticultura bonaerense. *Realidad Económica,* no. 114 – 115 (Feb – May 93), pp. 29 – 53. Bibl, tables.

Brazil

Chalhoub, Sidney. The Politics of Disease Control: Yellow Fever and Race in Nineteenth Century Rio de Janeiro. *Journal of Latin American Studies,* v. 25, no. 3 (Oct 93), pp. 441 – 463. Bibl.

Compromissos desonrados. *Problemas Brasileiros,* v. 30, no. 295 (Jan – Feb 93), pp. 49 – 50. Il.

Guimarães, Paulo César Vaz and Elio Jardanovski. O desafio da eqüidade no setor saúde. *RAE; Revista de Administração de Empresas,* v. 33, no. 3 (May – June 93), pp. 38 – 51.

Hochman, Gilberto. Regulando os efeitos da interdependência: sobre as relações entre saúde pública e construção do estado; Brasil, 1910 – 1930. *Estudos Históricos,* v. 6, no. 11 (Jan – June 93), pp. 40 – 61. Bibl.

Melo, Marcus André Barreto Campelo de. Anatomia do fracasso: intermediação de interesses e a reforma das políticas sociais na nova república. *Dados,* v. 36, no. 1 (1993), pp. 119 – 163. Bibl, tables.

Moura, Demócrito. Problema vital. *Problemas Brasileiros,* v. 30, no. 295 (Jan – Feb 93), pp. 48 – 49. Il.

Sociedade insalubre. *Problemas Brasileiros,* v. 30, no. 295 (Jan – Feb 93), pp. 52 – 53. Il.

Caribbean area

Cost

Lewis, Maureen A. User Fees in Public Hospitals: Comparison of Three Country Case Studies. *Economic Development and Cultural Change,* v. 41, no. 3 (Apr 93), pp. 513 – 532. Bibl, tables.

Chile

Accorsi O., Enrique et al. ¿Hacia qué sistema de salud?: debates. *Mensaje,* v. 42, no. 417 (Mar – Apr 93), pp. 86 – 92. Il.

Jiménez de la Jara, Jorge. Cambio y salud: adaptaciones de los sistemas de salud al cambio epidemiológico, socioeconómico y políticocultural. *Estudios Sociales (Chile),* no. 77 (July – Sept 93), pp. 49 – 59.

Vio, Fernando. La salud está enferma: ¿Es posible su recuperación? *Mensaje,* v. 42, no. 425 (Dec 93), pp. 607 – 611. Il.

Colombia

Cañón Ortegón, Leonardo. La salud en el estado colombiano. *Revista Javeriana,* v. 61, no. 592 (Mar 93), pp. 76 – 80.

Frías Núñez, Marcelo. *Enfermedad y sociedad en la crisis colonial del antiguo régimen: Nueva Granada en el tránsito del siglo XVIII al XIX; las epidemias de viruelas* reviewed by Juan A. Villamarín. *Hispanic American Historical Review,* v. 73, no. 4 (Nov 93), pp. 693 – 694.

Costa Rica

Ramírez Quirós, Ileana. Mujer y SIDA: la exclusión de la mujer de las campañas comunicacionales. *Revista de Ciencias Sociales (Costa Rica),* no. 58 (Dec 92), pp. 11 – 22. Bibl.

Developing countries

Jablonska, Alejandra. La política de salud de la OMS: propuesta para los países en vías de desarrollo. *Revista Mexicana de Ciencias Políticas y Sociales,* v. 38, Nueva época, no. 153 (July – Sept 93), pp. 91 – 107.

Satterthwaite, David. Problemas sociales y medioambientales asociados a la urbanización acelerada. *EURE,* v. 19, no. 57 (July 93), pp. 7 – 30. Tables.

Great Britain

Guimarães, Paulo César Vaz and Elio Jardanovski. O desafio da eqüidade no setor saúde. *RAE; Revista de Administração de Empresas,* v. 33, no. 3 (May – June 93), pp. 38 – 51.

Guatemala

Menéndez Martínez, Otto R. et al. ¿Salud para todos en el año 2000?: panel-foro. *USAC,* no. 14 (June 91), pp. 3 – 23. Bibl.

Latin America

Aguiar Estrada, Eliene. Cólera. *Revista Cultural Lotería,* v. 51, no. 390 (July – Aug 92), pp. 17 – 26. Bibl.

Aldereguía Henriques, Jorge and Jorge Núñez Jover. Aproximaciones al marco conceptual de la sanología. *Interciencia,* v. 18, no. 2 (Mar – Apr 93), pp. 71 – 76. Bibl.

Bibliography

Borzutzky, Silvia. Social Security and Health Policies in Latin America: The Changing Roles of the State and the Private Sector (Review article). *Latin American Research Review,* v. 28, no. 2 (1993), pp. 246 – 256.

Mexico

Contreras Cruz, Carlos. Ciudad y salud en el porfiriato: la política urbana y el saneamiento de Puebla, 1880 – 1906. *Siglo XIX: Cuadernos,* v. 1, no. 3 (June 92), pp. 55 – 76. Bibl, tables.

Corzo Ramírez, Ricardo and Soledad García Morales. Políticas, instituciones públicas de salud y enfermedades en Veracruz: fines del siglo XIX y principios del siglo XX. *La Palabra y el Hombre,* no. 83 (July – Sept 92), pp. 275 – 298. Bibl, tables.

Cruz Barrera, Nydia E. La higiene y la política sanitaria en el porfiriato: su difusión y ejercicio en Puebla. *La Palabra y el Hombre,* no. 83 (July – Sept 92), pp. 255 – 273. Bibl, maps.

Farquharson, Mary. Is It Safe to Breathe? *Business Mexico,* v. 3, no. 3 (Mar 93), pp. 32 – 35.

Flores Clair, Eduardo. Trabajo, salud y muerte: Real del Monte, 1874. *Siglo XIX: Cuadernos,* v. 1, no. 3 (June 92), pp. 9 – 28. Bibl, charts.

López Acuña, Daniel. Para reformar la salud en México. *Nexos,* v. 16, no. 186 (June 93), pp. 20 – 24.

Martínez Salgado, Carolina. Recursos sociodemográficos y daños a la salud en unidades domésticas campesinas del estado de México. *Estudios Demográficos y Urbanos,* v. 7, no. 2 – 3 (May – Dec 92), pp. 451 – 463. Bibl, tables.

Thompson, Angela T. To Save the Children: Smallpox Inoculation, Vaccination, and Public Health in Guanajuato, Mexico, 1797 – 1840. *The Americas,* v. 49, no. 4 (Apr 93), pp. 431 – 455. Bibl, tables.

Congresses

Martínez Salgado, Carolina. Relatoría de la mesa redonda El Programa Nacional de Salud, 1990 – 1994. *Estudios Demográficos y Urbanos,* v. 6, no. 3 (Sept – Dec 91), pp. 756 – 772.

Sources

Declaración de México para una maternidad sin riesgos: Cocoyoc, Morelos, 8 – 11 de febrero de 1993. *Fem,* v. 17, no. 122 (Apr 93), pp. 26 – 31. Il.

Panama

Díaz de Alpirez, Magali M. La familia como unidad de atención de la enfermera a través de la visita domiciliaria. *Revista Cultural Lotería,* v. 51, no. 390 (July – Aug 92), pp. 53 – 57.

Venezuela

Tosta, Virgilio. Huella y presencia de médicos europeos en el estado Barinas. *Boletín de la Academia Nacional de la Historia (Venezuela),* v. 75, no. 297 (Jan – Mar 92), pp. 69 – 95.

PUBLIC OPINION

See also

Subdivision *Foreign opinion* under names of specific countries
Subdivision *Public opinion* under *Hispanic Americans (U.S.)* and names of Indian groups

Bolivia

Frambes-Buxeda, Aline. Bolivia: eje vital de la integración económica andina y latinoamericana. *Homines,* v. 15 – 16, no. 2 – 1 (Oct 91 – Dec 92), pp. 187 – 248. Bibl, tables.

Chile

Edwards, Marta. Percepción de la familia y de la formación de los hijos. *Estudios Públicos (Chile),* no. 52 (Spring 93), pp. 191 – 214. Tables, charts.

Costa Rica

López Subirós, Marta Eugenia. Costa Rica: la opinión pública y el SIDA, 1989 – 1991. *Revista de Ciencias Sociales (Costa Rica),* no. 58 (Dec 92), pp. 55 – 64. Bibl, tables.

Vega Martínez, Mylena. Cultura política y legitimidad: encuesta de opinión entre estudiantes avanzados de la sede central de la Universidad de Costa Rica. *Anuario de Estudios Centroamericanos,* v. 18, no. 2 (1992), pp. 71 – 90. Bibl, tables.

El Salvador

La Comisión de la Verdad y el proceso electoral en la opinión pública salvadoreña. *ECA; Estudios Centroamericanos,* v. 48, no. 537 – 538 (July – Aug 93), pp. 711 – 734. Tables, charts.

Documento especial: la delincuencia urbana; encuesta explorativa. *ECA; Estudios Centroamericanos,* v. 48, no. 534 – 535 (Apr – May 93), pp. 471 – 479. Tables.

Figueroa, Francisco. Opinión política y post-guerra. *ECA; Estudios Centroamericanos,* v. 48, no. 534 – 535 (Apr – May 93), pp. 430 – 436. Il.

Los principales problemas: lo que debe hacer el próximo gobierno; una encuesta de opinión pública. *ECA; Estudios Centroamericanos,* v. 48, no. 539 (Sept 93), pp. 841 – 854. Tables, charts.

Los salvadoreños ante las medidas de política fiscal y opiniones sobre la coyuntura política. *ECA; Estudios Centroamericanos,* v. 47, no. 529 – 530 (Nov – Dec 92), pp. 1071 – 1082. Tables.

Latin America

Sturzenegger, Adolfo C. Encuesta a empresas industriales exportadoras latinoamericanas sobre el proceso de integración regional: informe de resultados. *Nueva Sociedad,* no. 126 (July – Aug 93), pp. 169 – 176.

Mexico

Carrillo Castro, Alejandro and Miguel Angel Romero Miranda. Las preocupaciones públicas: el caso de Tamaulipas. *El Cotidiano,* v. 8, no. 51 (Nov – Dec 92), pp. 95 – 101. Tables.

Constantino, Mario and Rosalía Winocur. Cultura política y elecciones: algunas imágenes de la sucesión presidencial. *El Cotidiano,* v. 10, no. 58 (Oct – Nov 93), pp. 47 – 53. Bibl, tables.

Fleischman, Cristopher and Joel Russell. The Company You Keep. *Business Mexico,* v. 3, no. 5 (May 93), pp. 42 – 43. Charts.

Kuschick, Murilo. Sucesión presidencial: sondeo de opinión. *El Cotidiano,* v. 10, no. 58 (Oct – Nov 93), pp. 54 – 58. II, charts.

Nicaragua

Anderson, Leslie Elin. Surprises and Secrets: Lessons from the 1990 Nicaragua Election. *Studies in Comparative International Development,* v. 27, no. 3 (Fall 92), pp. 93 – 119. Bibl, tables.

Peru

Azcueta, Michel et al. ¿Por qué vivir en el Perú de hoy? (Testimonies of various people on why, in light of the present crisis, they choose to live in Peru). *Debate (Peru),* v. 15, no. 70 (Sept – Oct 92), pp. 29 – 34. II.

Cipriani, Juan Luis et al. ¿Qué quiere el peruano común y corriente? *Debate (Peru),* v. 16, no. 75 (Dec 93 – Jan 94), pp. 15 – 18. II.

Cisneros, Luis Jaime and Arturo Ferrari. Del jardín a la calle: la juventud peruana de los '90s. *Debate (Peru),* v. 16, no. 74 (Sept – Oct 93), pp. 19 – 25. II, tables.

Cisneros C., Luis Fernán. Entre la ira y la paz: encuesta entre jóvenes. *Debate (Peru),* v. 15, no. 70 (Sept – Oct 92), pp. 35 – 38. II, tables.

Pásara, Luis H. Peru: Into a Black Hole. *Hemisphere,* v. 5, no. 2 (Winter – Spring 93), pp. 26 – 30. Tables, charts.

El poder en el Perú: XIII encuesta anual. *Debate (Peru),* v. 16, no. 73 (June – Aug 93), pp. 31 – 47. II, tables.

El poder judicial: encuesta. *Debate (Peru),* v. 16, no. 75 (Dec 93 – Jan 94), pp. 43 – 47. II, tables.

Sánchez León, Abelardo. Perfil del ama de casa limeña. *Debate (Peru),* v. 16, no. 72 (Mar – May 93), pp. 32 – 38. II, tables.

United States

Pike, Fredrick B. *The United States and Latin America: Myths and Stereotypes of Civilization and Nature* reviewed by Peter Calvert. *Bulletin of Latin American Research,* v. 12, no. 2 (May 93), pp. 232 – 233.

— *The United States and Latin America: Myths and Stereotypes of Civilization and Nature* reviewed by Josef Opatrny. *Hispanic American Historical Review,* v. 73, no. 4 (Nov 93), pp. 667 – 668.

— *The United States and Latin America: Myths and Stereotypes of Civilization and Nature* reviewed by Gordon Connell-Smith. *Journal of Latin American Studies,* v. 25, no. 3 (Oct 93), pp. 689 – 691.

PUBLIC SPEAKING

See
  Rhetoric

PUBLIC UTILITIES

Latin America
Cost

Jouravlev, Andrei and Terence R. Lee. Self-Financing Water Supply and Sanitation Services. *CEPAL Review,* no. 48 (Dec 92), pp. 117 – 128. Bibl, tables, charts.

Mexico

Sturm, Russell and Michael Totten. Bright Ideas. *Business Mexico,* v. 3, no. 1 (Jan – Feb 93), pp. 55 – 57. II.

— Delivering the Goods. *Business Mexico,* v. 3, no. 5 (May 93), pp. 15 – 18. II.

PUBLICITY

See
  Advertising

PUBLISHERS AND PUBLISHING

See also
  Books
  Booksellers and bookselling
  Copyright
  Press
  Printing and engraving

Rienner, Lynne. Is the Sky Falling?: Scholarly Publishing in the 1990s. *SALALM Papers,* v. 36 (1991), pp. 159 – 164.

Argentina

Alcorta, Rodrigo. La empresa de editar buenos libros. *Todo Es Historia,* v. 27, no. 311 (June 93), pp. 50 – 53. II.

Divinsky, Daniel. Acerca de la inexistencia de América Latina como uno de los inconvenientes para adquirir material literario a su respecto. *SALALM Papers,* v. 36 (1991), pp. 165 – 170.

— Vicios públicos, virtudes privadas: editar en la Argentina; memorias abreviadas. *Cuadernos Hispanoamericanos,* no. 517 – 519 (July – Sept 93), pp. 516 – 520.

Pichón Rivière, Marcelo. La irrealidad de una literatura y el despertar del mercado. *Cuadernos Hispanoamericanos,* no. 517 – 519 (July – Sept 93), pp. 511 – 513.

Belize

Ergood, Bruce. Belize as Presented in Her Literature. *Belizean Studies,* v. 21, no. 2 (Oct 93), pp. 3 – 14. Bibl, tables.

Brazil

McCarthy, Cavan Michael. A Regional Database for the Brazilian Northeast. *SALALM Papers,* v. 36 (1991), pp. 369 – 386. Bibl, tables.

Biography

Ipanema, Cybelle Moreira de and Marcello Moreira de Ipanema. Indicador bioemerográfico brasileiro: Rio Grande do Norte, 1832 – 1908. *Revista do Instituto Histórico e Geográfico Brasileiro,* no. 371 (Apr – June 91), pp. 437 – 459.

Caribbean area

Moss, Alan. Art Publishing in the Contemporary Caribbean. *SALALM Papers,* v. 34 (1989), pp. 269 – 274. Bibl.

Costa Rica

Molina Jiménez, Iván and Arnaldo Moya Gutiérrez. Leyendo "lecturas": documentos para la historia del libro en Costa Rica a comienzos del siglo XIX. *Revista de Historia (Costa Rica),* no. 26 (July – Dec 92), pp. 241 – 262.

Cuba

Ibargoyen Islas, Saúl. Cuba: crisis editorial, alternativas y esperanzas. *Plural (Mexico),* v. 22, no. 263 (Aug 93), pp. 69 – 70.

Latin America

Cataño, Gonzalo. De la publicación oral a la publicación impresa: estrategias para desarrollar la producción intelectual en la universidad. *Revista Paraguaya de Sociología,* v. 29, no. 84 (May – Aug 92), pp. 7 – 23. Bibl.

Mexico

Castro Escudero, Alfredo. Días de guardar en la industria editorial. *Comercio Exterior,* v. 43, no. 5 (May 93), pp. 430 – 437. Bibl.

Nicaragua

Méndez Rojas, Conny. La situación de la producción bibliográfica nicaragüense. *SALALM Papers,* v. 36 (1991), pp. 171 – 183. Bibl.

PUCCIARELLI, EUGENIO

Interviews

Castello, Antonio Emilio. Entrevista: Eugenio Pucciarelli. *Todo Es Historia,* v. 26, no. 305 (Dec 92), pp. 58 – 64. II.

PUCCINI, GIACOMO

Criticism of specific works
Turandot

Ponce, Gilberto. *Turandot* en el Municipal. *Mensaje,* v. 42, no. 424 (Nov 93), pp. 594 – 595. II.

PUEBLA, MEXICO (CITY)

Contreras Cruz, Carlos. Ciudad y salud en el porfiriato: la política urbana y el saneamiento de Puebla, 1880 – 1906. *Siglo XIX: Cuadernos,* v. 1, no. 3 (June 92), pp. 55 – 76. Bibl, tables.

— Urbanización y modernidad en el porfiriato: el caso de la ciudad de Puebla. *La Palabra y el Hombre,* no. 83 (July – Sept 92), pp. 167 – 188. Bibl.

Cruz Barrera, Nydia E. La higiene y la política sanitaria en el porfiriato: su difusión y ejercicio en Puebla. *La Palabra y el Hombre*, no. 83 (July – Sept 92), pp. 255 – 273. Bibl, maps.

Fuentes Aguilar, Luis and Juan Vargas González. La articulación espacial de la ciudad colonial de Puebla, México. *Revista de Historia de América*, no. 112 (July – Dec 91), pp. 43 – 62. Bibl, il, maps.

Lipsett-Rivera, Sonya. Water and Bureaucracy in Colonial Puebla de los Angeles. *Journal of Latin American Studies*, v. 25, no. 1 (Feb 93), pp. 25 – 44. Bibl, tables, maps.

Pries, Ludger. Aspectos del mercado de trabajo en Puebla: la relación entre trabajo asalariado y por cuenta propia. *El Cotidiano*, v. 8, no. 52 (Jan – Feb 93), pp. 31 – 37. Bibl, il, charts.

Sources

Boyd-Bowman, Peter. *Indice y extractos del Archivo de Protocolos de Puebla de los Angeles, México, 1538 – 1556* reviewed by Linda Greenow. *Hispanic American Historical Review*, v. 73, no. 3 (Aug 93), pp. 486 – 487.

PUEBLA, MEXICO (STATE)

Aranda Romero, José Luis and Agustín Grajales Porras. Perfil sociodemográfico de Tehuacán durante el virreinato. *Estudios Demográficos y Urbanos*, v. 7, no. 1 (Jan – Apr 92), pp. 53 – 76. Bibl, tables, maps, charts.

Cruz Barrera, Nydia E. Reclusión, control social y penitenciaria en Puebla en el siglo XIX. *Siglo XIX: Revista*, no. 12, 2a época (July – Dec 92), pp. 119 – 146.

Gómez Cruz, Filiberta. La Sociedad de Fomento en el puerto de Tuxpan, 1841. *La Palabra y el Hombre*, no. 83 (July – Sept 92), pp. 189 – 197. Bibl, tables.

Grosso, Juan Carlos. El comercio interregional entre Puebla y Veracruz: de la etapa borbónica al México independiente. *La Palabra y el Hombre*, no. 83 (July – Sept 92), pp. 59 – 91. Bibl, tables, charts.

Pries, Ludger. Movilidad en el empleo: una comparación de trabajo asalariado y por cuenta propia en Puebla. *Estudios Sociológicos*, v. 11, no. 32 (May – Aug 93), pp. 475 – 496. Bibl, charts.

Téllez Guerrero, Francisco. La segregación de Tuxpan y Chicontepec en 1853. *La Palabra y el Hombre*, no. 83 (July – Sept 92), pp. 27 – 43. Bibl, tables, maps.

PUENTES DE OYENARD, SYLVIA

Criticism of specific works

Rosa exigida

Andrist, Debra D. Nature Imagery in Sylvia Puentes de Oyenard's *Rosa exigida*. *Letras Femeninas*, v. 19, no. 1 – 2 (Spring – Fall 93), pp. 117 – 119. Bibl.

PUERTO MONTT, CHILE

Quintanilla, Víctor G. Problemas y consecuencias ambientales sobre el bosque de Alerce, "Fitzroya Cupressoides (Mol) Johnst," debido a la explotación de la cordillera costera de Chile austral. *Revista Geográfica (Mexico)*, no. 114 (July – Dec 91), pp. 54 – 72. Bibl, il, maps, charts.

Tampe, Eduardo. Jesuitas alemanes y la colonización del sur. *Mensaje*, v. 42, no. 420 (July 93), pp. 259 – 263. Il.

PUERTO RICAN AMERICAN LITERATURE

History and criticism

Acosta-Belén, Edna. Etnicidad, género y revitalización cultural en la literatura nuyorriqueña. *Homines*, v. 15 – 16, no. 2 – 1 (Oct 91 – Dec 92), pp. 338 – 357. Bibl.

PUERTO RICAN DRAMA

History and criticism

Dávila-López, Grace. Entrevista a Roberto Ramos-Perea. *Latin American Theatre Review*, v. 26, no. 2 (Spring 93), pp. 151 – 157.

Sandoval Sánchez, Alberto. La puesta en escena de la familia inmigrante puertorriqueña. *Revista Iberoamericana*, v. 59, no. 162 – 163 (Jan – June 93), pp. 345 – 359. Bibl.

PUERTO RICAN LITERATURE

History and criticism

Aparicio, Frances R. Entre la guaracha y el bolero: un ciclo de intertextos musicales en la nueva narrativa puertorriqueña. *Revista Iberoamericana*, v. 59, no. 162 – 163 (Jan – June 93), pp. 73 – 89. Bibl.

Ferré, Rosario. *El coloquio de las perras* reviewed by Nara Araújo. *Iberoamericana*, v. 17, no. 49 (1993), pp. 103 – 104.

Solá Márquez, María Magdalena. *Aquí cuentan las mujeres: muestra y estudio de cinco narradoras puertorriqueñas* reviewed by Elena M. Martínez. *Revista Iberoamericana*, v. 59, no. 162 – 163 (Jan – June 93), p. 391.

PUERTO RICAN POETRY

Black authors

P-Miñambres, Matías. *Tun tun de pasa y grifería:* perpetuación de estereotipos euroetnologocéntricos en el discurso poético afroantillano de Palés Matos. *Chasqui*, v. 22, no. 2 (Nov 93), pp. 73 – 84. Bibl.

History and criticism

Román Delgado, Samuel. El atalayismo: innovación y renovación en la literatura puertorriqueña. *Revista Iberoamericana*, v. 59, no. 162 – 163 (Jan – June 93), pp. 93 – 100. Bibl.

PUERTO RICANS

United States

Ahmeduzzaman, Mohammad and Jaipaul L. Roopnarine. Puerto Rican Fathers' Involvement with Their Preschool-Age Children. *Hispanic Journal of Behavioral Sciences*, v. 15, no. 1 (Feb 93), pp. 96 – 107. Bibl, tables.

Chávez, Linda. *Out of the Barrio: Toward a New Politics of Assimilation* reviewed by Cristóbal S. Berry-Cabán. *International Migration Review*, v. 27, no. 1 (Spring 93), pp. 208 – 210.

Enchautegui, María E. Geographical Differentials in the Socioeconomic Status of Puerto Ricans: Human Capital Variations and Labor Market Characteristics. *International Migration Review*, v. 26, no. 4 (Winter 92), pp. 1267 – 1290. Bibl, tables.

McGraw, Sarah A. and Kevin W. Smith. Smoking Behavior of Puerto Rican Women: Evidence from Caretakers of Adolescents in Two Urban Areas. *Hispanic Journal of Behavioral Sciences*, v. 15, no. 1 (Feb 93), pp. 140 – 149. Bibl, tables.

Sommers, Ira et al. Sociocultural Influences on the Explanation of Delinquency for Puerto Rican Youths. *Hispanic Journal of Behavioral Sciences*, v. 15, no. 1 (Feb 93), pp. 36 – 62. Bibl, tables.

Mathematical models

Santiago, Carlos Enrique. The Migratory Impact of Minimum Wage Legislation: Puerto Rico, 1970 – 1987. *International Migration Review*, v. 27, no. 4 (Winter 93), pp. 772 – 795. Bibl, tables, charts.

PUERTO RICANS IN LITERATURE

Béjar, Eduardo C. *Harlem todos los días:* el exilio del nombre/el nombre del exilio. *Revista Iberoamericana*, v. 59, no. 162 – 163 (Jan – June 93), pp. 329 – 343. Bibl.

Cachan, Manuel. *En cuerpo de camisa* de Luis Rafael Sánchez: la antiliteratura alegórica del otro puertorriqueño. *Revista Iberoamericana*, v. 59, no. 162 – 163 (Jan – June 93), pp. 177 – 186. Bibl.

Sandoval Sánchez, Alberto. La puesta en escena de la familia inmigrante puertorriqueña. *Revista Iberoamericana*, v. 59, no. 162 – 163 (Jan – June 93), pp. 345 – 359. Bibl.

PUERTO RICO

See also

Cultural property – Puerto Rico
Diseases – Puerto Rico
Elections – Puerto Rico
Employment – Puerto Rico
Encomiendas – Puerto Rico
Folk music – Puerto Rico
Human capital – Puerto Rico
Labor and laboring classes – Puerto Rico
Labor supply – Puerto Rico
Latin Americans – Puerto Rico
Literature and history – Puerto Rico
Literature and society – Puerto Rico
Local elections – Puerto Rico
Mass media – Puerto Rico
Music – Puerto Rico
Musicians – Puerto Rico
National security – Puerto Rico
Natural disasters – Puerto Rico
Oral history – Puerto Rico
Political parties – Puerto Rico
Popular music – Puerto Rico
Radio broadcasting – Puerto Rico
Sex role – Puerto Rico
Slavery – Puerto Rico
Social conflict – Puerto Rico
Sociolinguistics – Puerto Rico
Spaniards – Puerto Rico
Students – Puerto Rico
Sugar – Puerto Rico
Theater – Puerto Rico
Wages – Puerto Rico
West Indians – Puerto Rico
Wit and humor – Puerto Rico
Women – Puerto Rico
Women authors – Puerto Rico
Women in literature – Puerto Rico

Civilization

González, José R. La cultura de ser y la cultura de tener. *Homines,* v. 15 – 16, no. 2 – 1 (Oct 91 – Dec 92), pp. 185 – 186.

Commerce

Great Britain

Dávila Ruiz, Emma A. Apuntes sobre el comercio entre Puerto Rico y Gran Bretaña durante el siglo XIX. *Op. Cit.,* no. 7 (1992), pp. 255 – 292. Bibl, il, tables, charts.

Economic conditions

Camuñas Madera, Ricardo R. El progreso material y las epidemias de 1856 en Puerto Rico. *Jahrbuch für Geschichte von Staat, Wirtschaft und Gesellschaft Lateinamerikas,* v. 29 (1992), pp. 241 – 277. Bibl.

Cordero Guzmán, Héctor R. Lessons from Operation Bootstrap. *NACLA Report on the Americas,* v. 27, no. 3 (Nov – Dec 93), pp. 7 – 10. Bibl, il.

Santiago, Carlos Enrique. *Labor in the Puerto Rican Economy: Postwar Development and Stagnation* reviewed by William D. Savedoff. *Hispanic American Historical Review,* v. 73, no. 3 (Aug 93), pp. 534 – 535.

Emigration and immigration

Cubano Iguina, Astrid Teresa. La emigración mallorquina a Puerto Rico en el siglo XIX: el caso de los sollerenses. *Op. Cit.,* no. 7 (1992), pp. 229 – 253. Bibl, il, tables, charts.

Funkhouser, Edward and Fernando A. Ramos. The Choice of Migration Destination: Dominican and Cuban Immigrants to the Mainland United States and Puerto Rico. *International Migration Review,* v. 27, no. 3 (Fall 93), pp. 537 – 556. Bibl, tables.

Muschkin, Clara G. Consequences of Return Migrant Status for Employment in Puerto Rico. *International Migration Review,* v. 27, no. 1 (Spring 93), pp. 79 – 102. Bibl, tables, charts.

Solano y Pérez-Lila, Francisco de. Inmigración latinoamericana a Puerto Rico, 1800 – 1898. *Revista de Indias,* v. 52, no. 195 – 196 (May – Dec 92), pp. 923 – 957. Tables.

Foreign relations

Bibliography

Goslinga, Marian. The US, Cuba, and Puerto Rico. *Hemisphere,* v. 5, no. 3 (Summer – Fall 93), pp. 54 – 56.

Historiography

Maldonado Jiménez, Rubén. Algunas reflexiones sobre la historiografía cubana y puertorriqueña en torno a la abolición de la esclavitud. *Homines,* v. 15 – 16, no. 2 – 1 (Oct 91 – Dec 92), pp. 31 – 38. Bibl.

History

García Muñiz, Humberto. "Los últimos treinta años, 1898 – 1928": un manuscripto inédito de Frank Tannenbaum sobre Puerto Rico; ensayo introductorio. *Op. Cit.,* no. 7 (1992), pp. 145 – 164. Bibl, il.

Languages

Barreto Márquez, Amílcar A. The Debate over Puerto Rican Statehood: Language and the "Super-Majority." *Homines,* v. 15 – 16, no. 2 – 1 (Oct 91 – Dec 92), pp. 135 – 141. Bibl.

Delgado Cintrón, Carmelo. La culminación de la lucha por el idioma: el caso de Puerto Rico. *Homines,* v. 15 – 16, no. 2 – 1 (Oct 91 – Dec 92), pp. 179 – 184.

Méndez, José Luis. Puerto Rico: ¿Español o inglés?; un debate sobre su identidad. *Cuadernos Americanos,* no. 40, Nueva época (July – Aug 93), pp. 84 – 96. Bibl.

Politics and government

Dávila Santiago, Rubén and Jorge Rodríguez Beruff. Puerto Rico: frente a la nueva época. *Nueva Sociedad,* no. 127 (Sept – Oct 93), pp. 6 – 12.

Relations

United States

Barreto Márquez, Amílcar A. The Debate over Puerto Rican Statehood: Language and the "Super-Majority." *Homines,* v. 15 – 16, no. 2 – 1 (Oct 91 – Dec 92), pp. 135 – 141. Bibl.

Berríos Martínez, Rubén. Independencia y plebiscito. *Homines,* v. 15 – 16, no. 2 – 1 (Oct 91 – Dec 92), pp. 118 – 125.

Córdova, Gonzalo F. *Luis Sánchez Morales, servidor ejemplar* reviewed by Teresita Martínez-Vergne. *Hispanic American Historical Review,* v. 73, no. 2 (May 93), pp. 346 – 347.

Corrada del Río, Baltasar. The Plebiscite: A Time for Change. *Hemisphere,* v. 5, no. 3 (Summer – Fall 93), pp. 44 – 46.

García-Passalacqua, Juan M. Negotiated Autonomy. *Hemisphere,* v. 5, no. 3 (Summer – Fall 93), pp. 38 – 41. Charts.

— El regreso de Babel. *Homines,* v. 15 – 16, no. 2 – 1 (Oct 91 – Dec 92), pp. 132 – 134.

Laguerre, Enrique Arturo. De espaldas a la historia. *Homines,* v. 15 – 16, no. 2 – 1 (Oct 91 – Dec 92), pp. 116 – 117.

Méndez, José Luis. Puerto Rico: ¿Español o inglés?; un debate sobre su identidad. *Cuadernos Americanos,* no. 40, Nueva época (July – Aug 93), pp. 84 – 96. Bibl.

Ostolaza Bey, Margarita. El bloque histórico colonial de Puerto Rico. *Homines,* v. 15 – 16, no. 2 – 1 (Oct 91 – Dec 92), pp. 152 – 178. Bibl, tables.

El plebiscito: una contestación a Rubén Berríos. *Homines,* v. 15 – 16, no. 2 – 1 (Oct 91 – Dec 92), pp. 126 – 131.

Rigau, Marco Antonio. Mutual Respect: Congress Must Act. *Hemisphere,* v. 5, no. 3 (Summer – Fall 93), pp. 47 – 49. Il.

Rodríguez-Orellana, Manuel. A Chance to Decolonize. *Hemisphere,* v. 5, no. 3 (Summer – Fall 93), pp. 42 – 43.

Weisman, Alan. El futuro de Puerto Rico. *Homines,* v. 15 – 16, no. 2 – 1 (Oct 91 – Dec 92), pp. 106 – 111.

Rural conditions

Tannenbaum, Frank. Los últimos treinta años, 1898 – 1928 (Translated by Sara Irizarry). *Op. Cit.,* no. 7 (1992), pp. 165 – 207. Il, tables.

Study and teaching

Dietz, James L. Reviewing and Renewing Puerto Rican and Caribbean Studies: From Dependency to What? *Caribbean Studies,* v. 25, no. 1 – 2 (Jan – July 92), pp. 27 – 48. Bibl.

PUERTO RICO IN LITERATURE

Gelpí, Juan G. Ana Lydia Vega: ante el debate de la cultura nacional de Puerto Rico. *Revista Chilena de Literatura,* no. 42 (Aug 93), pp. 95 – 99.

PUGA, MARÍA LUISA

Criticism of specific works

Pánico o peligro

Saltz, Joanne. *Pánico o peligro* de María Luisa Puga: reescribiendo la familia. *Káñina*, v. 16, no. 2 (July – Dec 92), pp. 101 – 104. Bibl.

PUIG, MANUEL

Criticism and interpretation

Tittler, Jonathan. *Manuel Puig* reviewed by Ilán Stavans. *World Literature Today*, v. 67, no. 4 (Fall 93), p. 789.

Criticism of specific works

Boquetas pintadas

Márquez, Celina. La nostalgia por la cursilería: a un año yo te recuerdo. *La Palabra y el Hombre*, no. 84 (Oct – Dec 92), pp. 206 – 212.

Maldición eterna a quien lea estas páginas

Herrero-Olaizola, Alejandro. Condenados por leer: lectura y lectores de Puig en *Maldición eterna a quien lea estas páginas*. *Hispanic Review*, v. 61, no. 4 (Fall 93), pp. 483 – 500. Bibl.

PUNO, PERU (DEPARTMENT)

Lindner, Bernardo. Nadie en quien confiar: actitud política de los jóvenes campesinos del altiplano puneño. *Allpanchis*, v. 25, no. 41 (Jan – June 93), pp. 77 – 108. Bibl, tables.

Rodríguez G., Yolanda. Los actores sociales y la violencia política en Puno. *Allpanchis*, v. 23, no. 39 (Jan – June 92), pp. 131 – 154. Bibl.

PUPPETS AND PUPPET-PLAYS

Artiles, Freddy. Títeres en México. *Conjunto*, no. 89 (Oct – Dec 91), pp. 88 – 93. Il.

PYNCHON, THOMAS

Criticism of specific works

Gravity's Rainbow

Holdsworth, Carole A. Two Contemporary Versions of the Persephone Myth. *Revista Interamericana de Bibliografía*, v. 42, no. 4 (1992), pp. 571 – 576. Bibl.

QUALITY OF LIFE

See also
Cost and standard of living

Fortoul V., Freddy. Satisfacción comunitaria: indicador social subjetivo de bienestar. *Estudios Sociales (Chile)*, no. 74 (Oct – Dec 92), pp. 119 – 148. Bibl.

Argentina

Barbeito, Alberto C. and Rubén M. Lo Vuolo. *La modernización excluyente: transformación económica y estado de bienestar en Argentina* reviewed by Mauricio Tenewicki. *Realidad Económica*, no. 118 (Aug – Sept 93), pp. 142 – 144.

Chile

Barros Lezaeta, Carmen. Factores que intervienen en el bienestar de los adultos mayores. *Estudios Sociales (Chile)*, no. 77 (July – Sept 93), pp. 31 – 47. Bibl, charts.

Colombia

Clavijo, Sergio. Variaciones en el criterio sobre necesidades básicas: aplicación al caso colombiano. *Planeación y Desarrollo*, v. 24, no. 1 (Jan – Apr 93), pp. 367 – 382. Bibl, tables.

Peru

Azcueta, Michel et al. ¿Por qué vivir en el Perú de hoy? (Testimonies of various people on why, in light of the present crisis, they choose to live in Peru). *Debate (Peru)*, v. 15, no. 70 (Sept – Oct 92), pp. 29 – 34. Il.

López-Dóriga, Enrique. *Desarrollo humano: estudio general y aplicado al Perú* reviewed by Felipe E. MacGregor. *Apuntes (Peru)*, no. 31 (July – Dec 92), pp. 115 – 117.

Venezuela

Research

Reimel de Carrasquel, Sharon. La calidad de vida del profesorado de la Universidad Simón Bolívar: resultados de una prueba piloto. *La Educación (USA)*, v. 36, no. 111 – 113 (1992), pp. 25 – 45. Bibl, tables, charts.

QUALITY OF WORK LIFE

See
Industrial sociology

QUECHUA INDIANS

Altamirano Rúa, Teófilo. Pastores quechuas en el oeste norteamericano. *América Indígena*, v. 51, no. 2 – 3 (Apr – Sept 91), pp. 203 – 222. Maps.

Estenssoro Fuchs, Juan Carlos. Los bailes de los indios y el proyecto colonial (With commentaries by T. Abercrombie, J. Flores Espinoza, C. Itier, and S. E. Ramírez and a response by the author). *Revista Andina*, v. 10, no. 2 (Dec 92), pp. 353 – 404. Bibl.

Harrison, Regina. Confesando el pecado en los Andes: del siglo XVI hacia nuestros días. *Revista de Crítica Literaria Latinoamericana*, v. 19, no. 37 (Jan – June 93), pp. 169 – 184. Bibl.

Itier, César. La tradición oral quechua antigua en los procesos de idolatrías de Cajatambo. *Bulletin de l'Institut Français d'Etudes Andines*, v. 21, no. 3 (1992), pp. 1009 – 1051. Bibl.

Langevin, André. Las zampoñas del conjunto de kantu y el debate sobre la función de la segunda hilera de tubos: datos etnográficos y análisis semiótico. *Revista Andina*, v. 10, no. 2 (Dec 92), pp. 405 – 440. Bibl, tables.

Matos Mar, José. Taquileños, quechuas del lago Titicaca, en Lima. *América Indígena*, v. 51, no. 2 – 3 (Apr – Sept 91), pp. 107 – 166. Il, maps.

Rasnake, Roger Neil. *Autoridad y poder en los Andes: los kuraqkuna de Yura*, a translation of *Domination and Cultural Resistance: Authority and Power among an Andean People*, translated by Luis Brédow and Luis Huáscar Antezana. Reviewed by Pedro de Anasagasti. *Signo*, no. 35, Nueva época (Jan – Apr 92), pp. 243 – 244.

QUECHUA LANGUAGE

Columbus, Claudette Kemper. "Pacha": Worlds in a Sacred Word. *Latin American Indian Literatures Journal*, v. 9, no. 1 (Spring 93), pp. 2 – 20.

Noriega, Julio E. El quechua: voz y letra en el mundo andino. *Revista de Crítica Literaria Latinoamericana*, v. 19, no. 37 (Jan – June 93), pp. 279 – 301. Bibl.

Study and teaching

Doerflinger, Enrique Ricardo et al. La realidad socio-lingüística del pueblo quechua. *Anuario Indigenista*, v. 30 (Dec 91), pp. 267 – 288.

Congresses

Cheng Hurtado, Alberto. Informe sobre el XVI Curso Interamericano de Observación y Práctica Indigenista: "Lectoescritura computarizada del idioma quechua." *Anuario Indigenista*, v. 30 (Dec 91), pp. 425 – 435.

QUECHUA LITERATURE

History and criticism

Baquerizo, Manuel J. La transición de la visión india a la visión mestiza en la poesía quechua oral. *Revista de Crítica Literaria Latinoamericana*, v. 19, no. 37 (Jan – June 93), pp. 117 – 124. Bibl.

Bendezú Aybar, Edmundo. Los textos de D'Harcourt. *Revista de Crítica Literaria Latinoamericana*, v. 19, no. 37 (Jan – June 93), pp. 105 – 115.

Beyersdorff, Margot. La "puesta en texto" del primer drama indohispano en los Andes. *Revista de Crítica Literaria Latinoamericana*, v. 19, no. 37 (Jan – June 93), pp. 195 – 221. Bibl, il.

Husson, Jean-Phillipe. La poesía quechua prehispánica: sus reglas, sus categorías, sus temas; através de los poemas transcritos por Wamán Puma de Ayala. *Revista de Crítica Literaria Latinoamericana*, v. 19, no. 37 (Jan – June 93), pp. 63 – 85. Bibl, il.

Lienhard, Martín. La cosmología poética en los waynos quechuas tradicionales. *Revista de Crítica Literaria Latinoamericana*, v. 19, no. 37 (Jan – June 93), pp. 87 – 103. Bibl.

Montoya, Rodrigo. El teatro quechua como lugar de reflexión sobre la historia y la política. *Revista de Crítica Literaria Latinoamericana*, v. 19, no. 37 (Jan – June 93), pp. 223 – 241. Bibl.

Rowe, William. Dimensiones históricas de la poesía quechua: el caso de las danzas guerreras de Toqroyoq y su relación con la producción poética andina. *Revista de Crítica Literaria Latinoamericana*, v. 19, no. 37 (Jan – June 93), pp. 41 – 62. Bibl.

Translations

Cinco canciones quechuas contemporáneas (From the collection *Canciones quechuas* compiled by Carmela Morales Lazo, translated by José Víctor Oregón Morales). *Revista de Crítica Literaria Latinoamericana*, v. 19, no. 37 (Jan – June 93), pp. 125 – 130.

Escalante Gutiérrez, Carmen and Ricardo Valderrama Fernández. Canciones de imploración y de amor en los Andes: literatura oral de los quechuas del siglo XX. *Revista de Crítica Literaria Latinoamericana*, v. 19, no. 37 (Jan – June 93), pp. 11 – 39.

Jürth, Max. Plegarias incaicas. *Revista de Crítica Literaria Latinoamericana*, v. 19, no. 37 (Jan – June 93), pp. 159 – 168.

Seminiski, Jan. Manqu Qhapaq Inka: ¿Un poeta religioso? *Revista de Crítica Literaria Latinoamericana*, v. 19, no. 37 (Jan – June 93), pp. 131 – 158. Bibl.

QUEIROZ, RACHEL DE
Criticism and interpretation

Gotlib, Nádia Battella. Las mujeres y "el otro": tres narradoras brasileñas. *Escritura (Venezuela)*, v. 16, no. 31 – 32 (Jan – Dec 91), pp. 123 – 136. Bibl.

Hollanda, Heloísa Buarque de. A roupa da Rachel: um estudo sem importância (Accompanied by an English translation by Christopher Peterson). *Estudos Feministas*, v. 0, no. 0 (1992), pp. 74 – 96.

QUESADA, VICENTE GREGORIO

Vidaurreta de Tjarks, Alicia. Vicente Gregorio Quesada. *Investigaciones y Ensayos*, no. 41 (Jan – Dec 91), pp. 457 – 496. Bibl.

QUETZALCÓATL

Florescano, Enrique. El mito de Quetzalcóatl. *Allpanchis*, v. 23, no. 40 (July – Dec 92), pp. 11 – 93. Bibl, il.

Graulich, Michel. *Quetzalcóatl y el espejismo de Tollan* reviewed by Bernadette Alvarez-Ferrandiz. *Caravelle*, no. 59 (1992), pp. 295 – 297.

López Austin, Alfredo et al. El templo de Quetzalcóatl en Teotihuacán: su posible significado ideológico. *Anales del Instituto de Investigaciones Estéticas*, v. 16, no. 62 (1991), pp. 35 – 52. Bibl, il.

QUICHÉS

García Escobar, Carlos René. Historia antigua: historia y etnografía del *Rabinal Achí*. *La Tradición Popular*, no. 81 (1991), Issue. Bibl, il.

QUILLACINGA INDIANS

Cárdenas Arroyo, Felipe. Pastos y quillacingas: dos grupos étnicos en busca de identidad arqueológica. *Revista Colombiana de Antropología*, v. 29 (1992), pp. 63 – 79. Bibl, il, tables.

Groot de Mahecha, Ana María and Eva María Hooykaas. *Intento de delimitación del territorio de los grupos étnicos pastos y quillacingas en el altiplano nariñense* reviewed by María Clemencia Ramírez de Jara. *Revista Colombiana de Antropología*, v. 29 (1992), pp. 242 – 246. Bibl.

Ramírez de Jara, María Clemencia. Los quillacinga y su posible relación con grupos prehispánicos del oriente ecuatoriano. *Revista Colombiana de Antropología*, v. 29 (1992), pp. 27 – 61. Bibl, maps.

QUIROGA, HORACIO SILVESTRE
Biography

Rosemberg, Fernando. La aventura chaqueña de Horacio Quiroga. *Todo Es Historia*, v. 27, no. 312 (July 93), pp. 66 – 72. Il, facs.

Criticism and interpretation

Morales Toro, Leonidas. Misiones y las macrofiguras narrativas hispanoamericanas. *Hispamérica*, v. 21, no. 63 (Dec 92), pp. 25 – 34.

QUIROGA, PEDRO DE
Criticism of specific works
Los coloquios de la verdad

Martínez Martín, Jaime J. La defensa del indio americano en un diálogo del renacimiento: *Los coloquios de la verdad* de Pedro Quiroga. *Studi di Letteratura Ispano-Americana*, v. 24 (1993), pp. 7 – 24.

QUIRÓS, JUAN
Biography

Rivadeneira Prada, Raúl. Juan Quirós, periodista. *Signo*, no. 36 – 37, Nueva época (May – Dec 92), pp. 201 – 206.

Criticism and interpretation

Camacho, Georgette de. Poesía mística de Juan Quirós. *Signo*, no. 36 – 37, Nueva época (May – Dec 92), pp. 211 – 213.

Castañón Barrientos, Carlos. La crítica literaria de Juan Quirós. *Signo*, no. 36 – 37, Nueva época (May – Dec 92), pp. 207 – 210.

Martínez Salguero, Jaime. Juan Quirós, crítico literario. *Signo*, no. 36 – 37, Nueva época (May – Dec 92), pp. 215 – 219.

Criticism of specific works
Ruta del alba

Anasagasti, Pedro de. La angustia de Juan Quirós. *Signo*, no. 36 – 37, Nueva época (May – Dec 92), pp. 221 – 226.

Obituaries

Salamanca Lafuente, Rodolfo. Juan Quirós, caudal de cultura. *Signo*, no. 36 – 37, Nueva época (May – Dec 92), pp. 197 – 200.

QUITO, ECUADOR

Carrasco, Hernán. Indígenas serranos en Quito y Guayaquil: relaciones interétnicas y urbanización de migrantes. *América Indígena*, v. 51, no. 4 (Oct – Dec 91), pp. 159 – 183. Bibl.

Naranjo, Marcelo F. Convidados de piedra: los indios en el proceso urbano de Quito. *América Indígena*, v. 51, no. 2 – 3 (Apr – Sept 91), pp. 251 – 272. Bibl.

Ponce Leiva, Pilar. Un espacio para la controversia: la Audiencia de Quito en el siglo XVIII. *Revista de Indias*, v. 52, no. 195 – 196 (May – Dec 92), pp. 839 – 865. Bibl.

Villalba O., Marcelo. *Cotocollao: una aldea formativa del valle de Quito* reviewed by Tamara L. Bray. *Latin American Antiquity*, v. 4, no. 1 (Mar 93), pp. 96 – 97.

Villavicencio de Mencías, Gladys. Indígenas en Quito. *América Indígena*, v. 51, no. 2 – 3 (Apr – Sept 91), pp. 223 – 250. Bibl.

RABINOVICH, RAFAEL

Pásara, Luis H. Rafael Rabinovich. *Debate (Peru)*, v. 15, no. 70 (Sept – Oct 92), p. 55. Il.

RACE DISCRIMINATION
See also
Subdivision *Race question* under names of specific countries

Poo, Jorge. Los signos de la barbarie: la búsqueda de culpables en épocas de crisis. *Hoy Es Historia*, v. 10, no. 58 (July – Aug 93), pp. 84 – 85.

Argentina

Senkman, Leonardo. Etnicidad e inmigración durante el primer peronismo. *Estudios Interdisciplinarios de América Latina y el Caribe,* v. 3, no. 2 (July – Dec 92), pp. 5 – 38. Bibl.

Brazil

Statistics

Andrews, George Reid. Desigualdad racial en Brasil y en Estados Unidos: un estudio estadístico comparado. *Desarrollo Económico (Argentina),* v. 33, no. 130 (July – Sept 93), pp. 185 – 216. Bibl, tables, charts.

Dominican Republic

Derby, Robin L. H. and Richard Turits. Historias de terror y los terrores de la historia: la masacre haitiana de 1937 en la República Dominicana (Translated by Eugenio Rivas and Mario Alberto Torres). *Estudios Sociales (Dominican Republic),* v. 26, no. 92 (Apr – June 93), pp. 65 – 76. Bibl.

Jamaica

Holt, Thomas C. *The Problem of Freedom: Race, Labor, and Politics in Jamaica and Britain, 1832 – 1938* reviewed by Alex Lichtenstein. *Hispanic American Historical Review,* v. 73, no. 2 (May 93), pp. 347 – 349.

Latin America

Stepan, Nancy Leys. *The Hour of Eugenics: Race, Gender, and Nation in Latin America* reviewed by Donna J. Guy. *The Americas,* v. 50, no. 1 (July 93), pp. 136 – 137.

— *The Hour of Eugenics: Race, Gender, and Nation in Latin America* reviewed by Aline Helg. *Hispanic American Historical Review,* v. 73, no. 1 (Feb 93), pp. 138 – 139.

— *The Hour of Eugenics: Race, Gender, and Nation in Latin America* reviewed by Francine Masiello. *Letras Femeninas,* v. 19, no. 1 – 2 (Spring – Fall 93), pp. 136 – 138.

United States

Statistics

Andrews, George Reid. Desigualdad racial en Brasil y en Estados Unidos: un estudio estadístico comparado. *Desarrollo Económico (Argentina),* v. 33, no. 130 (July – Sept 93), pp. 185 – 216. Bibl, tables, charts.

RACE PROBLEMS

See
Ethnicity
Indians, Treatment of
Race discrimination
Slavery
Subdivision *Government relations* under names of Indian groups
Subdivision *Race question* under names of specific countries

RADIO BROADCASTING

Brazil

Avancini, Marta. Na era do ouro das cantoras do rádio. *Luso-Brazilian Review,* v. 30, no. 1 (Summer 93), pp. 85 – 93. Bibl.

Lenharo, Alcir. Fascínio e solidão: as cantoras do rádio nas ondas sonoras do seu tempo. *Luso-Brazilian Review,* v. 30, no. 1 (Summer 93), pp. 75 – 84. Bibl.

Cuba

Salwen, Michael Brian. "Eddie" Chibás, the "Magic Bullet" of Radio. *Studies in Latin American Popular Culture,* v. 12 (1993), pp. 113 – 126. Bibl.

Mexico

Fernández Christlieb, Fátima. *La radio mexicana: centro y regiones* reviewed by Guadalupe Cortés (Review entitled "Las desdeñadas fuentes de la radio mexicana"). *Plural (Mexico),* v. 22, no. 258 (Mar 93), pp. 77 – 78.

Hayes, Joy Elizabeth. Early Mexican Radio Broadcasting: Media Imperialism, State Paternalism, or Mexican Nationalism? *Studies in Latin American Popular Culture,* v. 12 (1993), pp. 31 – 55. Bibl.

Osterroth, María de Jesús. "Radio Alicia": el espíritu de los '60. *Plural (Mexico),* v. 22, no. 263 (Aug 93), pp. 73 – 74.

— "XX – XXI": música entre los siglos. *Plural (Mexico),* v. 22, no. 265 (Oct 93), pp. 83 – 84.

Peru

Alvarez Rodrich, Augusto et al. Entrevista a Dennis Vargas Marín. *Debate (Peru),* v. 16, no. 75 (Dec 93 – Jan 94), pp. 6 – 14. Il.

Puerto Rico

Torregrosa, José Luis. *Historia de la radio en Puerto Rico* reviewed by Pedro Zervigón (Review entitled "José Luis Torregrosa y su historia de la radio"). *Homines,* v. 15 – 16, no. 2 – 1 (Oct 91 – Dec 92), pp. 369 – 370. Il.

RAILROADS

Andean region

Miller, Rory M. Transferencia de técnicas: la construcción y administración de ferrocarriles en la costa occidental de Sudamérica (Translated by Isabel Cristina Mata Velázquez). *Siglo XIX: Cuadernos,* v. 3, no. 7 (Oct 93), pp. 65 – 102. Bibl, maps.

Argentina

Bonaudo, Marta et al. Ferrocarriles y mercado de tierras en el centro-sur de Santa Fe, 1870 – 1900. *Siglo XIX: Cuadernos,* v. 3, no. 6 (June 93), pp. 37 – 64. Bibl, tables.

Brazil

Quase fora dos trilhos. *Problemas Brasileiros,* v. 30, no. 295 (Jan – Feb 93), pp. 40 – 42. Il.

Costa Rica

Deregulation

Botey Sobrado, Ana María. Ferroviarios y portuarios frente al ajuste estructural. *Revista de Ciencias Sociales (Costa Rica),* no. 60 (June 93), pp. 73 – 84. Bibl.

RAMÍREZ, MARTÍN

Tuchman, Maurice. *Parallel Visions: Modern Artists and Outsider Art* reviewed by Andrés Salgado R. (Accompanied by an English translation). *Art Nexus,* no. 9 (June – Aug 93), p. 33. Il.

RAMÍREZ, SERGIO

See
Ramírez Mercado, Sergio

RAMÍREZ MERCADO, SERGIO

Correspondence, reminiscences, etc.

Ramírez Mercado, Sergio. Oficios compartidos. *Nuevo Texto Crítico,* v. 6, no. 11 (1993), pp. 245 – 252.

RAMOS, GRACILIANO

Correspondence, reminiscences, etc.

Ramos, Graciliano. Discurso de Graciliano Ramos (Excerpt from *Homenagem a Graciliano Ramos* introduced by Yêdda Dias Lima). *Vozes,* v. 86, no. 4 (July – Aug 92), pp. 72 – 77. Il.

Criticism and interpretation

Ignácio, Sebastião Expedito. Dois aspectos da obra de Graciliano Ramos atestados pela tipologia oracional. *Revista de Letras (Brazil),* v. 32 (1992), pp. 69 – 78.

Criticism of specific works

Angústia

Carvalho, Sônia Maria Rodrigues de. Inscrição e busca. *Revista de Letras (Brazil),* v. 32 (1992), pp. 41 – 49.

Infância

Carvalho, Sônia Maria Rodrigues de. Inscrição e busca. *Revista de Letras (Brazil),* v. 32 (1992), pp. 41 – 49.

Conrado, Regina Fátima de Almeida. Tradição e desvio: a rota do talento. *Revista de Letras (Brazil),* v. 32 (1992), pp. 31 – 39. Bibl.

Insônia

Silva, Carlos da. A narrativa como expressão e conhecimento do ser: *Insônia* de Graciliano Ramos. *Revista de Letras (Brazil),* v. 32 (1992), pp. 51 – 67. Bibl.

Vidas secas

Caetano, Mercy. Graciliano Ramos en la novela del '30. *Hoy Es Historia,* v. 10, no. 60 (Nov – Dec 93), pp. 39 – 42. Bibl.

RAMOS, JULIO

Obituaries

Beltrán Guerrero, Luis. Varones: Julio Ramos. *Boletín de la Academia Nacional de la Historia (Venezuela),* v. 75, no. 297 (Jan – Mar 92), pp. 117 – 118.

RAMOS, LUÍS JOSÉ DA FONSECA

Wehrs, Carlos. Vida e morte do general Fonseca Ramos: escorço biográfico. *Revista do Instituto Histórico e Geográfico Brasileiro,* no. 371 (Apr – June 91), pp. 533 – 553. Bibl, il.

RAMOS DE LORA, JUAN MANUEL ANTONIO

Fortique, José Rafael. El primer obispo de Maracaibo y su médico personal. *Boletín de la Academia Nacional de la Historia (Venezuela),* v. 76, no. 302 (Apr – June 93), pp. 133 – 139.

Porras Cardozo, Baltazar Enrique. Discurso de orden en la sesión solemne de la Academia Nacional de la Historia en homenaje al bicentenario de la muerte de fray Juan Ramos de Lora, Aula Magna de la Universidad de los Andes, 30 de marzo de 1990. *Boletín de la Academia Nacional de la Historia (Venezuela),* v. 76, no. 302 (Apr – June 93), pp. 7 – 14.

RAMOS FRANCO, LUIS

Ramírez Montes, Mina. Un ensamblador poblano en Querétaro: Luis Ramos Franco. *Anales del Instituto de Investigaciones Estéticas,* v. 16, no. 62 (1991), pp. 151 – 161. Bibl.

RAMOS OTERO, MANUEL

Criticism and interpretation

Cruz, Arnaldo. Para virar al macho: la autobiografía como subversión en la cuentística de Manuel Ramos Otero. *Revista Iberoamericana,* v. 59, no. 162 – 163 (Jan – June 93), pp. 239 – 263. Bibl.

RAMOS-PEREA, ROBERTO

Awards

Otorgan el Tirso de Molina 1992 a dramaturgo puertorriqueño. *Latin American Theatre Review,* v. 26, no. 2 (Spring 93), p. 110.

Interviews

Dávila-López, Grace. Entrevista a Roberto Ramos-Perea. *Latin American Theatre Review,* v. 26, no. 2 (Spring 93), pp. 151 – 157.

RANCHING

See

Cattle trade
Sheep ranches

RANGEL, IGNÁCIO DE MOURÃO

Pereira, Luiz Carlos Bresser and José Márcio Rego. Um mestre da economia brasileira: Ignácio Rangel. *Revista de Economia Política (Brazil),* v. 13, no. 2 (Apr – June 93), pp. 98 – 119.

Criticism of specific works

A inflação brasileira

Pereira, José Maria. Os trinta anos de A inflação brasileira de Ignácio Rangel. *Revista de Economia Política (Brazil),* v. 13, no. 3 (July – Sept 93), pp. 144 – 149. Bibl.

RAPE

See

Crimes against women

RAPID TRANSIT

See

Transportation

RAPIER, JOHN H.

Alexander, Philip N. John H. Rapier, Jr. and the Medical Profession in Jamaica, 1861 – 1862 (Part I). *Jamaica Journal,* v. 24, no. 3 (Feb 93), pp. 37 – 46. Bibl, il.

— John H. Rapier, Jr. and the Medical Profession in Jamaica, 1861 – 1862 (Part II). *Jamaica Journal,* v. 25, no. 1 (Oct 93), pp. 55 – 62. Bibl, il, facs.

RARE BOOKS

See

Manuscripts
Printing and engraving

RAS TAFARI MOVEMENT

Cunha, Olívia Maria Gomes da. Fazendo a "coisa certa": reggae, rastas e pentecostais em Salvador. *Revista Brasileira de Ciências Sociais,* v. 8, no. 23 (Oct 93), pp. 120 – 137. Bibl.

RASMUSSEN, WALDO

Interviews

Horton, Anne. Conversation with Curator Waldo Rasmussen. *Latin American Art,* v. 5, no. 1 (Spring 93), pp. 40 – 41. Il.

Sichel, Berta. Artistas latinoamericanos del siglo XX (Accompanied by an English translation). *Art Nexus,* no. 9 (June – Aug 93), pp. 52 – 56. Il.

RAW MATERIALS

See

Natural resources

READING INTERESTS

Brushwood, John Stubbs. Writerly Novels/Readerly Responses. *Latin American Literary Review,* v. 20, no. 40 (July – Dec 92), pp. 23 – 25.

Argentina

Pichón Rivière, Marcelo. La irrealidad de una literatura y el despertar del mercado. *Cuadernos Hispanoamericanos,* no. 517 – 519 (July – Sept 93), pp. 511 – 513.

Chile

Huneeus, Francisco et al. El libro y la irrupción de los medios audiovisuales: debates. *Mensaje,* v. 42, no. 416 (Jan – Feb 93), pp. 29 – 36.

Latin America

Leonard, Irving Albert. *Books of the Brave: Being an Account of Books and of Men in the Spanish Conquest and Settlement of the Sixteenth-Century New World* introduced by Rolena Adorno. Reviewed by Kenneth Mills. *Bulletin of Latin American Research,* v. 12, no. 2 (May 93), pp. 224 – 227.

Spain

Leonard, Irving Albert. *Books of the Brave: Being an Account of Books and of Men in the Spanish Conquest and Settlement of the Sixteenth-Century New World* introduced by Rolena Adorno. Reviewed by Kenneth Mills. *Bulletin of Latin American Research,* v. 12, no. 2 (May 93), pp. 224 – 227.

REAGAN, RONALD

Carothers, Thomas H. *In the Name of Democracy: U.S. Policy toward Latin America in the Reagan Years* reviewed by Rubén M. Perina (Review entitled "La promoción de la democracia en América Latina"). *Estudios Internacionales (Chile),* v. 26, no. 102 (Apr – June 93), pp. 204 – 215.

— *In the Name of Democracy: U.S. Policy toward Latin America in the Reagan Years* reviewed by Dario Moreno. *Hispanic American Historical Review,* v. 73, no. 4 (Nov 93), pp. 729 – 730.

REAL DEL MONTE, MEXICO

Flores Clair, Eduardo. Trabajo, salud y muerte: Real del Monte, 1874. *Siglo XIX: Cuadernos,* v. 1, no. 3 (June 92), pp. 9 – 28. Bibl, charts.

REAL PROPERTY

See also

Church lands
Land tenure

Brazil

Law and legislation

Holston, James. Legalizando o ilegal: propriedade e usurpação no Brasil (A translation of "The Misrule of Law: Land and Usurpation in Brazil," translated by João Vargas. Reprinted from *Comparative Studies in Society and History,* vol. 33, num. 4, 1991). *Revista Brasileira de Ciências Sociais,* v. 8, no. 21 (Feb 93), pp. 68 – 89. Bibl.

Chile

Delahaye, Olivier. Reforma agraria, renta y mercadeo de la tierra agrícola: una reflexión a partir de los casos venezolano y chileno. *Estudios Rurales Latinoamericanos,* v. 15, no. 2 – 3 (May – Dec 92), pp. 29 – 63. Bibl, tables.

Cost

Gutiérrez, Héctor and Dieter Wunder. Determinantes del precio de mercado de los terrenos en el área urbana de Santiago: comentario (on the article by Figueroa and Lever in *Cuadernos de Economía,* v. 29, no. 86). *Cuadernos de Economía (Chile),* v. 30, no. 89 (Apr 93), pp. 131 – 138. Bibl, tables.

Morandé Lavín, Felipe Guillermo. La dinámica de los precios de los activos reales y el tipo de cambio real: las reformas al comercio exterior y las entradas de capital extranjero; Chile, 1976 – 1989. *El Trimestre Económico,* v. 59, Special issue (Dec 92), pp. 141 – 186. Bibl, tables, charts.

Colombia
Cost

Díaz, Jairo et al. Determinantes del precio de los inmuebles en Bogotá. *Planeación y Desarrollo,* v. 24, no. 2 (May – Aug 93), pp. 315 – 327. Tables, charts.

— Elementos del mercado del suelo urbano. *Planeación y Desarrollo,* v. 24, no. 2 (May – Aug 93), pp. 329 – 338. Tables.

Cuba

Ritter, Archibald R. M. Seized Properties vs. Embargo Losses. *Hemisphere,* v. 5, no. 3 (Summer – Fall 93), pp. 31 – 35. Tables.

Venezuela

Delahaye, Olivier. Reforma agraria, renta y mercadeo de la tierra agrícola: una reflexión a partir de los casos venezolano y chileno. *Estudios Rurales Latinoamericanos,* v. 15, no. 2 – 3 (May – Dec 92), pp. 29 – 63. Bibl, tables.

REALE, MIGUEL

Macedo, Ubiratan Borges de. Presença de Miguel Reale na cultura brasileira. *Convivium,* v. 34, no. 2 (July – Dec 91), pp. 127 – 137.

REALISM IN LITERATURE

Anderson, Danny J. Retórica de la legitimidad: las exigencias de la crónica en las "novelas sin ficción" de Vicente Leñero. *La Palabra y el Hombre,* no. 84 (Oct – Dec 92), pp. 63 – 80. Bibl.

Conner, Robert. Contingencia y realidad en la obra de Esther Seligson. *La Palabra y el Hombre,* no. 81 (Jan – Mar 92), pp. 279 – 284. Bibl, il.

Magnarelli, Sharon Dishaw. The Spectacle of Reality in Luisa Valenzuela's *Realidad nacional vista desde la cama. Letras Femeninas,* v. 19, no. 1 – 2 (Spring – Fall 93), pp. 65 – 73. Bibl.

Solano Jiménez, Ronald. Crítica literaria en Costa Rica: de las *Historias de Tata Mundo. Anuario de Estudios Centroamericanos,* v. 18, no. 1 (1992), pp. 85 – 95. Bibl.

RECHY, JOHN
Criticism of specific works
City of Night

Christian, Karen. Will the "Real Chicano" Please Stand Up?: The Challenge of John Rechy and Sheila Ortiz Taylor to Chicano Essentialism. *The Americas Review,* v. 20, no. 2 (Summer 92), pp. 89 – 104. Bibl.

RECIFE, BRAZIL

Assies, Willem. To Get out of the Mud: Neighborhood Associativism in Recife, 1964 – 1988 reviewed by Joe Foweraker. *Bulletin of Latin American Research,* v. 12, no. 3 (Sept 93), pp. 345 – 346.

— To Get Out of the Mud: Neighborhood Associativism in Recife, 1964 – 1988 reviewed by Martine Droulers. *Cahiers des Amériques Latines,* no. 14 (1992), pp. 157 – 158.

— To Get out of the Mud: Neighborhood Associativism in Recife, 1964 – 1988 reviewed by Vania Salles and João Francisco Souza. *Revista Mexicana de Sociología,* v. 54, no. 4 (Oct – Dec 92), pp. 251 – 257.

RECYCLING
See
Refuse and refuse disposal

REFUGEES
See
Exiles

REFUSE AND REFUSE DISPOSAL
America
Research

Staski, Edward and Livingston Delafield Sutro, eds. *The Ethnoarchaeology of Refuse Disposal* reviewed by María Josefa Iglesias Ponce de León. *Revista Española de Antropología Americana,* v. 23 (1993), pp. 256 – 258.

Brazil

Bava, Silvio Caccia and Laura Mullahy. Making Brazil's Cities Livable: NGOs and the Recycling of Human Waste (Adapted chapter from the forthcoming book *Joint Ventures in Urban Policy: NGO – Local Government Collaboration in Democratizing Latin America* edited by Charles A. Reilly). *Grassroots Development,* v. 17, no. 1 (1993), pp. 12 – 19. Bibl, il.

Nítolo, Miguel Roberto. A riqueza vem do lixo. *Problemas Brasileiros,* v. 30, no. 297 (May – June 93), pp. 10 – 14. Il.

Mexico

Corey, Jane. Solutions for the Throw-Away Society. *Business Mexico,* v. 3, no. 8 (Aug 93), pp. 44 – 45. Il.

REGIONAL PLANNING
See also
Geography, Economic
Urbanization

Amazon Valley

Alzate Angel, Beatriz and María T. Ramírez V., eds. *Cinco lustros de actuación institucional nacional e internacional en Amazonia* reviewed by Olga Lucía Turbay. *La Educación (USA),* v. 36, no. 111 – 113 (1992), pp. 279 – 280.

Bant A., Astrid. *Diagnóstico de la vocación de desarrollo y la intervención institucional en la región Loreto* reviewed by Claudia Rohrhirsch. *Apuntes (Peru),* no. 29 (July – Dec 91), pp. 95 – 97.

Becker, Bertha Koiffman. Geografia política e gestão do território no limiar do século XXI: uma representação a partir do Brasil. *Revista Brasileira de Geografia,* v. 53, no. 3 (July – Sept 91), pp. 169 – 182. Bibl.

Meira, Alcyr Boris de Souza. Amazônia: gestão do território. *Revista Brasileira de Geografia,* v. 53, no. 3 (July – Sept 91), pp. 133 – 147.

Argentina
Methodology

Bandieri, Susana O. Historia y planificación regional: un encuentro posible. *Revista Interamericana de Planificación,* v. 26, no. 101 – 102 (Jan – June 93), pp. 78 – 94. Bibl.

Bolivia

Gierhake, Klaus-Ulrich. La inversión pública como instrumento de evaluación del proceso de planificación regional en Bolivia, 1987 – 1990. *Revista Interamericana de Planificación,* v. 26, no. 101 – 102 (Jan – June 93), pp. 112 – 128. Bibl, tables, maps, charts.

Brazil

Aguiar, Tereza Coni. O papel do poder público municipal e os desafios no criação de políticas para o desenvolvimento integral e harmónico da área rural. *Revista Geográfica (Mexico),* no. 114 (July – Dec 91), pp. 101 – 109.

Davidovich, Fany Rachel. Gestão do território: um tema em questão. *Revista Brasileira de Geografia,* v. 53, no. 3 (July – Sept 91), pp. 7 – 31. Bibl.

Leite, Cristina Maria Costa. Uma análise sobre o processo de organização do território: o caso do zoneamento ecológico – econômico. *Revista Brasileira de Geografia,* v. 53, no. 3 (July – Sept 91), pp. 67 – 90. Bibl.

Silberfeld, Jean-Claude. O fator regional. *Problemas Brasileiros,* v. 30, no. 296 (Mar – Apr 93), pp. 35 – 37. Il.

Veiga, Alberto. Agricultura e processo político: o caso brasileiro. *Revista de Economia e Sociologia Rural,* v. 29, no. 4 (Oct – Dec 91), pp. 285 – 334. Bibl, tables.

Mathematical models

Buvinich, Manuel J. Rojas. The Evaluation of Rural Development Projects Using the Social Accounting Matrix Approach. *Revista Brasileira de Economia,* v. 46, no. 4 (Oct – Dec 92), pp. 555 – 593. Bibl, tables.

Chile

Daher, Antonio. Infraestructuras: regiones estatales y privadas en Chile. *Estudios Públicos (Chile),* no. 49 (Summer 93), pp. 137 – 173. Bibl, tables.

— Santiago estatal, Chile liberal. *Revista Interamericana de Planificación,* v. 26, no. 101 – 102 (Jan – June 93), pp. 43 – 62. Bibl, tables.

Costa Rica

Girot, Pascal-Olivier. Parcs nationaux et développement rural au Costa Rica: mythes et réalités. *Tiers Monde,* v. 34, no. 134 (Apr – June 93), pp. 405 – 421. Bibl, tables, maps, charts.

Rosenhek, Zeev. "Desarrollo controlado": la economía política del desarrollo en la región atlántica de Costa Rica. *Ibero Americana (Sweden),* v. 22, no. 2 (Dec 92), pp. 21 – 46. Bibl, tables.

Developing countries

Gilbert, Alan G. Ciudades del Tercer Mundo: la evolución del sistema nacional de asentamientos. *EURE,* v. 19, no. 57 (July 93), pp. 41 – 58. Tables.

Uribe-Echeverría, J. Francisco. Problemas regionales en las economías abiertas del Tercer Mundo. *EURE,* v. 19, no. 58 (Oct 93), pp. 7 – 17. Bibl.

Ecuador

Law and legislation

Van Cott, Donna Lee. Ecuador: Is Modernization Enough? *Hemisphere,* v. 5, no. 3 (Summer – Fall 93), pp. 16 – 17. Il.

Latin America

Boisier E., Sergio. Las transformaciones en el pensamiento regionalista latinoamericano: escenas, discursos y actores. *Estudios Sociales (Chile),* no. 78 (Oct – Dec 93), pp. 69 – 104. Bibl.

Methodology

Sili, Marcelo Enrique. Desarrollo local: entre la realidad y la utopía. *Revista Interamericana de Planificación,* v. 26, no. 101 – 102 (Jan – June 93), pp. 63 – 77. Bibl, charts.

Mexico

Arrieta Fernández, Pedro. Desarrollo social planificado en La Chontalpa, Tabasco. *La Palabra y el Hombre,* no. 81 (Jan – Mar 92), pp. 159 – 175.

Chatterji, Manas and Walter Isard. Ciencia regional: nuevo orden mundial y el desarrollo de México en la era del TLC. *Problemas del Desarrollo,* v. 24, no. 93 (Apr – June 93), pp. 39 – 54. Bibl, charts.

Gutiérrez, José Luis. Aguascalientes: A Model of Development. *Business Mexico,* v. 3, no. 5 (May 93), pp. 26 – 28. Tables.

Research

Pepin Lehalleur, Marielle. Regiones y poder local en el Golfo de México: los andamios de un programa de investigación. *Estudios Sociológicos,* v. 10, no. 30 (Sept – Dec 92), pp. 517 – 522. Maps.

Nicaragua

Wall, David L. Spatial Inequalities in Sandinista Nicaragua. *Geographical Review,* v. 83, no. 1 (Jan 93), pp. 1 – 13. Bibl, maps.

Paraguay

Carbonell de Masy, Rafael et al. *Estrategias de desarrollo rural en los pueblos guaraníes, 1609 – 1767* reviewed by José Luis Mora Mérida. *Anuario de Estudios Americanos,* v. 50, no. 1 (1993), pp. 311 – 312.

REGIONALISM

Bolivia

Romero Pittari, Salvador. Movimientos regionales en Bolivia. *Homines,* v. 15 – 16, no. 2 – 1 (Oct 91 – Dec 92), pp. 61 – 74. Bibl, tables.

Brazil

Teixeira, Jorge Leão. Tudo nos une, muito nos separa. *Problemas Brasileiros,* v. 30, no. 297 (May – June 93), pp. 36 – 40. Il.

Velloso, Mônica Pimenta. A brasilidade verde – amarela: nacionalismo e regionalismo paulista. *Estudos Históricos,* v. 6, no. 11 (Jan – June 93), pp. 89 – 112. Bibl.

Cuba

García Negrete, Gloria. Problemas de la regionalización económica de Cuba en la primera mitad del siglo XIX. *Islas,* no. 98 (Jan – Apr 91), pp. 28 – 39. Tables.

Latin America

Venegas Delgado, Hernán. Acerca del concepto de región histórica. *Islas,* no. 98 (Jan – Apr 91), pp. 13 – 21. Bibl.

Mexico

Sánchez Almanza, Adolfo and Manuel Urbina Fuentes. Distribución de la población y desarrollo en México. *Comercio Exterior,* v. 43, no. 7 (July 93), pp. 652 – 661. Bibl, tables, maps, charts.

Methodology

Pérez Herrero, Pedro, ed. *Región e historia en México, 1700 – 1850* reviewed by Margaret Chowning. *The Americas,* v. 50, no. 2 (Oct 93), pp. 280 – 282.

— *Región e historia en México, 1700 – 1850: métodos de análisis regional* reviewed by Donald F. Stevens. *Hispanic American Historical Review,* v. 73, no. 1 (Feb 93), pp. 154 – 155.

REGIONALISM IN LITERATURE

Brazil

Aguiar, Flávio. Cultura de contrabando: estudo sobre os contos de Simões Lopes Neto. *Vozes,* v. 86, no. 6 (Nov – Dec 92), pp. 13 – 20.

Motta, Sérgio Vicente. Ser/tão . . . somente linguagem. *Revista de Letras (Brazil),* v. 32 (1992), pp. 81 – 99. Bibl.

Chile

Gómez Quezada, Rubén. *Crónicas pampinas: en busca del tiempo perdido* reviewed by Carlos Hallet C. *Mensaje,* v. 42, no. 424 (Nov 93), p. 599.

REIS, ROBERTO

Criticism of specific works

Towards Socio-Criticism

George, David. Socio-Criticism and Brazilian Literature: Changing Perspectives. *Chasqui,* v. 22, no. 2 (Nov 93), pp. 49 – 56.

RELIGION

See also
Art and religion
Bible
Catholic Church
Christian art and symbolism
Christian life
Church and social problems
Church and state
Evangelicalism
Hinduism
Islam
Martyrs
Messianism
Miracles
Myth
Pentecostalism
Pilgrims and pilgrimages
Prayer
Protestantism
Ras Tafari movement
Rites and ceremonies
Shamanism
Shrines
Socialism and Catholic Church

Spiritualism
Syncretism (Religion)
Theology
Umbanda (Cultus)
Voodooism
Witchcraft
Women and religion
Subdivision *Religion and mythology* under names of
    Indian groups
Subdivision *Religion* under *Hispanic Americans (U.S.)*

America
Foreign influences

Bellegarde-Smith, Patrick. "Pawol la pale": Reflections of an Initiate (Introduction to the special issue entitled "Traditional Spirituality in the African Diaspora"). *Journal of Caribbean Studies,* v. 9, no. 1 – 2 (Winter 92 – Spring 93), pp. 3 – 9. Bibl.

Voeks, Robert. African Medicine and Magic in the Americas. *Geographical Review,* v. 83, no. 1 (Jan 93), pp. 66 – 78. Bibl, maps.

Cuba

Castellanos, Isabel Mercedes and Jorge Castellanos. *Cultura afrocubana, III: Las religiones y las lenguas* reviewed by Luis A. Jiménez. *Hispania (USA),* v. 76, no. 2 (May 93), pp. 281 – 282.

Palmié, Stephan. *Das Exil der Götter: Geschichte und Vorstellungswelt einer afrokubanischen Religion* reviewed by Matthias Perl. *Iberoamericana,* v. 17, no. 49 (1993), pp. 101 – 102.

Guatemala

Ruz, Mario Humberto. Sebastiana de la Cruz, alias "La Polilla": mulata de Petapa y madre del hijo de Dios. *Mesoamérica (USA),* v. 13, no. 23 (June 92), pp. 55 – 66. Bibl.

Mexican – American Border Region

Griffith, James S. *Beliefs and Holy Places: A Spiritual Geography of the Pimería Alta* reviewed by Marth L. Henderson. *Geographical Review,* v. 83, no. 3 (July 93), pp. 334 – 336.

— *Beliefs and Holy Places: A Spiritual Geography of the Pimería Alta* reviewed by Martha L. Henderson (Review entitled "What Is Spiritual Geography?"). *Geographical Review,* v. 83, no. 4 (Oct 93), pp. 469 – 472.

Mexico

Cline, Sarah. The Spiritual Conquest Reexamined: Baptism and Christian Marriage in early Sixteenth-Century Mexico. *Hispanic American Historical Review,* v. 73, no. 3 (Aug 93), pp. 453 – 480. Bibl, tables.

Salles, Vania and José Manuel Valenzuela Arce. Ambitos de relaciones sociales de naturaleza íntima e identidades culturales: notas sobre Xochimilco. *Revista Mexicana de Sociología,* v. 54, no. 3 (July – Sept 92), pp. 139 – 173. Bibl.

Trinidad and Tobago

Vertovec, Steven. *Hindu Trinidad: Religion, Ethnicity, and Socio-Economic Change* reviewed by William A. Harris (Review entitled "Ethnicity and Development"). *Social and Economic Studies,* v. 41, no. 4 (Dec 92), pp. 225 – 230.

RELIGION AND ECONOMICS

Sung, Jung Mo. Crisis de las ideologías: utopías secularizadas versus reino de Dios (Translated by Juan Michel). *Realidad Económica,* no. 118 (Aug – Sept 93), pp. 68 – 81. Bibl.

RELIGION AND LITERATURE

Bruce-Novoa, John D. Ritual in Judith Ortiz Cofer's *The Line of the Sun. Confluencia,* v. 8, no. 1 (Fall 92), pp. 61 – 69. Bibl.

Catalá, Rafael. La vanguardia atalayista y la obra de Clemente Soto Vélez. *Revista Iberoamericana,* v. 59, no. 162 – 163 (Jan – June 93), pp. 101 – 109. Bibl.

Lima, Robert. Xangô and Other Yoruba Deities in the Plays of Zora Seljan. *Afro-Hispanic Review,* v. 11, no. 1 – 3 (1992), pp. 26 – 33. Bibl.

Ocasio, Rafael. "Babalú Ayé": Santería and Contemporary Cuban Literature. *Journal of Caribbean Studies,* v. 9, no. 1 – 2 (Winter 92 – Spring 93), pp. 29 – 40. Bibl.

Pérez Zamora, Flor de María. *Al filo del agua:* la modificación de una estructura social. *Káñina,* v. 16, no. 2 (July – Dec 92), pp. 81 – 87.

— La religión: isotopía estructurante en *Al filo del agua. Káñina,* v. 16, no. 1 (Jan – June 92), pp. 69 – 77. Bibl.

Poot Herrera, Sara. *La hija del judío:* entre la inquisición y la imprenta. *Nueva Revista de Filología Hispánica,* v. 40, no. 2 (July – Dec 92), pp. 761 – 777. Bibl.

White Navarro, Gladys. El drama americano de Calderón: mesianismo oficial y estrategias de dominación. *Revista de Crítica Literaria Latinoamericana,* v. 19, no. 38 (July – Dec 93), pp. 115 – 122.

RELIGION AND POLITICS
See also
Church and social problems
Church and state

Argentina

Nascimbene, Mario C. G. and Mauricio Isaac Neuman. El nacionalismo católico, el fascismo y la inmigración en la Argentina, 1927 – 1943: una aproximación teórica. *Estudios Interdisciplinarios de América Latina y el Caribe,* v. 4, no. 1 (Jan – June 93), pp. 116 – 140. Bibl.

Bolivia

Platt, Tristán. Simón Bolívar, the Sun of Justice, and the Amerindian Virgin: Andean Conceptions of the "Patria" in Nineteenth-Century Potosí. *Journal of Latin American Studies,* v. 25, no. 1 (Feb 93), pp. 159 – 185. Bibl.

Brazil

Ireland, Rowan. *Kingdoms Come: Religion and Politics in Brazil* reviewed by Daniel H. Levine. *The Americas,* v. 49, no. 3 (Jan 93), pp. 419 – 421.

— *Kingdoms Come: Religion and Politics in Brazil* reviewed by David Lehmann. *Bulletin of Latin American Research,* v. 12, no. 3 (Sept 93), pp. 356 – 357.

— *Kingdoms Come: Religion and Politics in Brazil* reviewed by W. E. Hewitt. *Hispanic American Historical Review,* v. 73, no. 3 (Aug 93), pp. 516 – 517.

— *Kingdoms Come: Religion and Politics in Brazil* reviewed by Mark L. Grover. *Revista Interamericana de Bibliografía,* v. 42, no. 3 (1992), pp. 505 – 506.

Isaia, Artur Cesar. Catolicismo, regeneração social e castilhismo na república velha gaúcha. *Estudos Ibero-Americanos,* v. 18, no. 1 (July 92), pp. 5 – 18. Bibl.

Central America

Recio Adrados, Juan Luis. Incidencia política de las sectas religiosas: el caso de Centroamérica (Previously published in *Rábida,* no. 12, 1992). *ECA; Estudios Centroamericanos,* v. 48, no. 531 – 532 (Jan – Feb 93), pp. 75 – 91. Bibl, il.

Chile

Araya P., Marilu et al. ?Cómo votarán los católicos?: debates (Introduced by G. Arroyo). *Mensaje,* v. 42, no. 424 (Nov 93), pp. 569 – 576. Il.

Arriagada, Eduardo. La política a la manera de Ignacio de Loyola. *Mensaje,* v. 42, no. 420 (July 93), pp. 317 – 321. Il.

Soto Sandoval, Andrés. La candidatura de Eugenio Pizarro. *Mensaje,* v. 42, no. 417 (Mar – Apr 93), pp. 102 – 103.

Stewart-Gambino, Hannah W. *The Church and Politics in the Chilean Countryside* reviewed by Daniel H. Levine. *Hispanic American Historical Review,* v. 73, no. 2 (May 93), pp. 326 – 328.

Ecuador

Demelas, Danièle and Yves Saint-Geours. *Jerusalén y Babilonia: religión y política en el Ecuador, 1780 – 1880* reviewed by Ana Luz Rodríguez González (Review entitled "Lo particular en el Ecuador del siglo XIX"). *Anuario Colombiano de Historia Social y de la Cultura,* no. 20 (1992), pp. 154 – 157.

El Salvador

Aguilar, Edwin Eloy et al. Protestantism in El Salvador: Conventional Wisdom versus Survey Evidence. *Latin American Research Review,* v. 28, no. 2 (1993), pp. 119 – 140. Bibl, tables.

Sobrino, Jon. Reflexiones teológicas sobre el informe de la Comisión de la Verdad. *ECA; Estudios Centroamericanos,* v. 48, no. 534 – 535 (Apr – May 93), pp. 389 – 408. Il.

Haiti

La iglesia de Haití hoy. *Cristianismo y Sociedad,* v. 30, no. 114 (1992), pp. 41 – 45.

Latin America

Díaz-Salazar, Rafael. Izquierda y cristianismo en América Latina. *ECA; Estudios Centroamericanos,* v. 48, no. 536 (June 93), pp. 563 – 576.

Peire, Jaime Antonio. La manipulación de los capítulos provinciales, las élites y el imaginario socio-político colonial tardío. *Anuario de Estudios Americanos,* v. 50, no. 1 (1993), pp. 13 – 54.

Bibliography

Dodson, Michael. The Changing Spectrum of Religious Activism in Latin America (Review article). *Latin American Perspectives,* v. 20, no. 4 (Fall 93), pp. 61 – 74. Bibl.

Mexico

Meyer, Jean A. Una historia política de la religión en el México contemporáneo. *Historia Mexicana,* v. 42, no. 3 (Jan – Mar 93), pp. 714 – 744. Bibl.

Zayas de Lille, Gabriela. Los sermones políticos de José Mariano Beristáin de Souza. *Nueva Revista de Filología Hispánica,* v. 40, no. 2 (July – Dec 92), pp. 719 – 759. Bibl.

Nicaragua

Cardenal, Ernesto. Vénganos a la tierra la república de los cielos. *Cuadernos Americanos,* no. 40, Nueva época (July – Aug 93), pp. 35 – 52.

Paraguay

Carter, Miguel. *El papel de la iglesia en la caída de Stroessner* reviewed by Jerry W. Cooney. *The Americas,* v. 49, no. 3 (Jan 93), pp. 424 – 425.

— *El papel de la iglesia en la caída de Stroessner* reviewed by W. E. Hewitt. *Hispanic American Historical Review,* v. 73, no. 1 (Feb 93), p. 179.

RELIGION AND SOCIOLOGY

Andean region

Merlino, Rodolfo J. and Mario A. Rabey. Resistencia y hegemonía: cultos locales y religión centralizada en los Andes del sur. *Allpanchis,* v. 23, no. 40 (July – Dec 92), pp. 173 – 200. Bibl.

Brazil

Otten, Alexandre H. A influência do ideário religioso na construção da comunidade de Belo Monte. *Luso-Brazilian Review,* v. 30, no. 2 (Winter 93), pp. 71 – 95. Bibl.

Ghana

Aborampah, Osei-Mensah. Religious Sanction and Social Order in Traditional Akan Communities of Ghana and Jamaica. *Journal of Caribbean Studies,* v. 9, no. 1 – 2 (Winter 92 – Spring 93), pp. 41 – 58. Bibl, charts.

Guatemala

García Ruiz, Jesús F. De la identidad aceptada a la identidad elegida: el papel de lo religioso en la politización de las identificaciones étnicas en Guatemala. *Estudios Sociológicos,* v. 10, no. 30 (Sept – Dec 92), pp. 713 – 733. Bibl.

Jamaica

Aborampah, Osei-Mensah. Religious Sanction and Social Order in Traditional Akan Communities of Ghana and Jamaica. *Journal of Caribbean Studies,* v. 9, no. 1 – 2 (Winter 92 – Spring 93), pp. 41 – 58. Bibl, charts.

Latin America

Bastian, Jean-Pierre. The Metamorphosis of Latin American Protestant Groups: A Sociohistorical Perspective (Translated by Margaret Caffey-Moquin). *Latin American Research Review,* v. 28, no. 2 (1993), pp. 33 – 61. Bibl, tables.

Dixon, David and Richard Dixon. Culturas e identidades populares y el surgimiento de los evangélicos en América Latina. *Cristianismo y Sociedad,* v. 30, no. 114 (1992), pp. 61 – 74. Bibl.

Parker Gumucio, Cristián. *Otra lógica en América Latina: religión popular y modernización capitalista* reviewed by G. A. C. (Review entitled "Religión popular y modernización en América Latina"). *Mensaje,* v. 42, no. 423 (Oct 93), p. 531. Il.

RELIGIOUS ART

See
    Art and religion
    Christian art and symbolism

RELIGIOUS DRAMA

Poole, Deborah A. Adaptación y resistencia en la danza ritual andina. *Conjunto,* no. 89 (Oct – Dec 91), pp. 13 – 27. Bibl, il.

RELIGIOUS EDUCATION

See also
    Church and education

Castillo, José María. El nuevo catecismo y las cuestiones que plantea. *ECA; Estudios Centroamericanos,* v. 48, no. 536 (June 93), pp. 599 – 605. Il.

Argentina

Bianchi, Susana. Iglesia católica y peronismo: la cuestión de la enseñanza religiosa, 1946 – 1955. *Estudios Interdisciplinarios de América Latina y el Caribe,* v. 3, no. 2 (July – Dec 92), pp. 89 – 103. Bibl.

Chile

Contreras, Juan Pablo. La formación de los jóvenes jesuitas hoy. *Mensaje,* v. 42, no. 420 (July 93), pp. 198 – 204. Il.

RELIGIOUS ORDERS

See
    Convents and nunneries
    Missions
    Monasticism and religious orders
    Names of specific orders

RELIGIOUS POETRY

Millones Santa Gadea, Luis. Poemas y canciones en honor de Santa Rosa: profecías del pasado, voces del presente. *Revista de Crítica Literaria Latinoamericana,* v. 19, no. 37 (Jan – June 93), pp. 185 – 194. Bibl.

REMOTE SENSING

See
    Photography, Aerial

RENAULT, DELSO

Madeira, Marcos Almir. Rememorando Delso Renault. *Revista do Instituto Histórico e Geográfico Brasileiro,* no. 370 (Jan – Mar 91), pp. 217 – 222.

RENGIFO, CÉSAR

Criticism of specific works

Las torres y el viento

Osorio Tejeda, Nelson. La alucinación del petróleo en una obra de César Rengifo. *Hispamérica,* v. 21, no. 63 (Dec 92), pp. 81 – 87.

REPETTO, NICOLÁS

Calvo, Bernardino S. Nicolás Repetto y Juan B. Justo, pioneros de la educación rural. *Todo Es Historia,* v. 27, no. 315 (Oct 93), pp. 50 – 53. Il.

REPRODUCTIVE RIGHTS

See
    Birth control
    Fertility, Human
    Women's rights

RESEARCH

See also
    Educational research
    Scientific expeditions
    Scientific research
    Social science research
    Subdivision *Research* under specific topics

Aboites, Hugo. La relación universidad – industria en el marco del Tratado de Libre Comercio. *El Cotidiano,* v. 9, no. 55 (June 93), pp. 78 – 84. Charts.

Cataño, Gonzalo. De la publicación oral a la publicación impresa: estrategias para desarrollar la producción intelectual en la universidad. *Revista Paraguaya de Sociología*, v. 29, no. 84 (May – Aug 92), pp. 7 – 23. Bibl.

RESEARCH INSTITUTES

See also
Names of specific institutions, universities, etc.

Brazil

Souza, Herbert José de. IBASE e os desafios colocados pela situação política. *Vozes*, v. 87, no. 4 (July – Aug 93), pp. 77 – 85.

Colombia

D'Artagnan. Academias sin un pe$$o: su importancia se subestima, ante la falta de prensa y de apoyo oficial. *Boletín de Historia y Antigüedades*, v. 79, no. 779 (Oct – Dec 92), pp. 1097 – 1099.

Socarrás, José Francisco. Las academias al borde del cierre. *Boletín de Historia y Antigüedades*, v. 79, no. 779 (Oct – Dec 92), pp. 1093 – 1095.

Mexico

Minello, Nelson. Entrevistas a Rodolfo Stavenhagen, José Luis Reyna y Claudio Stern. *Estudios Sociológicos*, v. 11, no. 31 (Jan – Apr 93), pp. 19 – 31.

United States

Gannon, Michael. Primeros encuentros en el Nuevo Mundo. *Atenea (Chile)*, no. 465 – 466 (1992), pp. 45 – 52.

Uruguay

Gliksberg, Isaac. El laboratorio tecnológico de Uruguay: entrevista a su presidente ing. Ruperto M. Long. *Interciencia*, v. 18, no. 6 (Nov – Dec 93), pp. 314 – 316. Il.

RESENDE, OTTO LARA

Obituaries

Colasanti, Marina. Ultima conversa com Otto. *Vozes*, v. 87, no. 2 (Mar – Apr 93), pp. 86 – 87.

Sant'Anna, Affonso Romano de. Otto, um moleque adorável (Reprinted from *Jornal do Brasil*, December 30, 1992). *Vozes*, v. 87, no. 2 (Mar – Apr 93), pp. 84 – 86.

RETAMAL FAVEREAU, JULIO

Krebs Wilckens, Ricardo. Discurso de recepción de don Julio Retamal Favereau. *Boletín de la Academia Chilena de la Historia*, v. 58 – 59, no. 102 (1991 – 1992), pp. 173 – 180.

Bibliography

Bibliografía de d. Julio Retamal Favereau. *Boletín de la Academia Chilena de la Historia*, v. 58 – 59, no. 102 (1991 – 1992), pp. 181 – 182.

REVISTA CHILENA DE LITERATURA (PERIODICAL)

Indexes

Sanzana Fuentes, Eva. Indice: *Revista Chilena de Literatura*, desde el n° 1 (otoño 1970) al n° 39 (abril 1992). *Revista Chilena de Literatura*, no. 40 (Nov 92), pp. 139 – 155.

REVISTA DE AVANCE (PERIODICAL)

Manzoni, Celina. Vanguardia y nacionalismo: itinerario de la *Revista de Avance. Iberoamericana*, v. 17, no. 49 (1993), pp. 5 – 15. Bibl.

Masiello, Francine Rose. Rethinking Neocolonial Esthetics: Literature, Politics, and Intellectual Community in Cuba's *Revista de Avance. Latin American Research Review*, v. 28, no. 2 (1993), pp. 3 – 31. Bibl, facs.

REVISTA JAVERIANA (PERIODICAL)

Pacheco, Juan Manuel. 15 años más (Previously published in this journal, no. 400, 1973). *Revista Javeriana*, v. 61, no. 596 (July 93), pp. 37 – 40.

Restrepo, Félix. Bajo la insignia de Javier: veinticinco años de historia (Previously published in this journal, no. 51, 1959). *Revista Javeriana*, v. 61, no. 596 (July 93), pp. 17 – 36.

Sanín, Javier. La década ganada. *Revista Javeriana*, v. 61, no. 596 (July 93), pp. 45 – 48.

Vélez Correa, Jaime. Ultimo decenio de *Revista Javeriana* (Previously published in this journal, no. 500, 1983). *Revista Javeriana*, v. 61, no. 596 (July 93), pp. 41 – 43.

REVOLUTIONARY LITERATURE

See also
Literature and society

Fornet, Ambrosio. Las máscaras del tiempo en la novela de la revolución cubana. *Casa de las Américas*, no. 191 (Apr – June 93), pp. 12 – 24. Bibl.

Marcelo Pérez, Carmen. *En ciudad semejante* de Lisandro Otero. *Islas*, no. 97 (Sept – Dec 90), pp. 32 – 43. Bibl.

REVOLUTIONARY POETRY

Beverley, John and Marc Zimmerman. *Literature and Politics in the Central American Revolutions* reviewed by Antony Higgins. *Revista de Crítica Literaria Latinoamericana*, v. 19, no. 37 (Jan – June 93), pp. 380 – 382.

Morales Cavero, Hugo. Apuntes para un estudio de la poesía revolucionaria. *Signo*, no. 35, Nueva época (Jan – Apr 92), pp. 163 – 195. Bibl.

REVOLUTIONS

See also
Coups d'état
Guerrillas
Social conflict

Cuba

Prada Oropeza, Renato. Los condenados de la tierra. *Plural (Mexico)*, v. 22, no. 262 (July 93), pp. 63 – 70.

Latin America

Demelas, Danièle and François-Xavier Guerra. Un processus révolutionnaire méconnu: l'adoption des formes representatives modernes en Espagne et en Amérique Latine, 1808 – 1810. *Caravelle*, no. 60 (1993), pp. 5 – 57. Bibl.

Vayssière, Pierre. *Les révolutions d'Amérique Latine* reviewed by Claire Pailler. *Caravelle*, no. 59 (1992), pp. 281 – 285.

— *Les révolutions d'Amérique Latine* reviewed by Frank MacDonald Spindler. *Hispanic American Historical Review*, v. 73, no. 2 (May 93), pp. 349 – 350.

— *Les révolutions d'Amérique Latine* reviewed by Pilar Domingo. *Journal of Latin American Studies*, v. 25, no. 1 (Feb 93), p. 214.

Wickham-Crowley, Timothy P. *Guerrillas and Revolution in Latin America: A Comparative Study of Insurgents and Regimes since 1956* reviewed by Willem Assies. *European Review of Latin American and Caribbean Studies*, no. 54 (June 93), pp. 133 – 136.

— *Guerrillas and Revolution in Latin America: A Comparative Study of Insurgents and Regimes since 1956* reviewed by Brian Loveman. *Hispanic American Historical Review*, v. 73, no. 2 (May 93), pp. 350 – 352.

Mexico

Andrews, Gregg. *Shoulder to Shoulder?: The American Federation of Labor, the United States, and the Mexican Revolution, 1910 – 1924* reviewed by Mark T. Gilderhus. *Hispanic American Historical Review*, v. 73, no. 1 (Feb 93), pp. 195 – 196.

Brunk, Samuel. Zapata and the City Boys: In Search of a Piece of the Revolution. *Hispanic American Historical Review*, v. 73, no. 1 (Feb 93), pp. 33 – 65. Bibl.

Héau de Giménez, Catherine and Enrique Rajchenberg. La leyenda negra y la leyenda rosa en la nueva historiografía de la revolución mexicana. *Revista Mexicana de Sociología*, v. 54, no. 3 (July – Sept 92), pp. 175 – 188. Bibl.

Meyer, Lorenzo. *Su majestad británica contra la revolución mexicana: el fin de un imperio informal* reviewed by Freidrich Katz. *Historia Mexicana*, v. 42, no. 1 (July – Sept 92), pp. 152 – 157.

Las mujeres en la revolución mexicana: biografías de mujeres revolucionarias reviewed by Martha Eva Rocha Islas (Review entitled "Más allá del estereotipo"). *Fem*, v. 17, no. 121 (Mar 93), pp. 46 – 48. Bibl.

Bibliography

Salamini, Heather Fowler. The Boom in Regional Studies of the Mexican Revolution: Where Is It Leading? (Review article). *Latin American Research Review*, v. 28, no. 2 (1993), pp. 175 – 190. Bibl.

Nicaragua

Serra, Luis. Democracy in Times of War and Socialist Crisis: Reflections Stemming from the Sandinista Revolution. *Latin American Perspectives*, v. 20, no. 2 (Spring 93), pp. 21 – 44. Bibl.

Walker, Thomas W., ed. *Revolution and Counterrevolution in Nicaragua* reviewed by Roland Ebel. *Hispanic American Historical Review*, v. 73, no. 1 (Feb 93), pp. 185 – 186.

— *Revolution and Counterrevolution in Nicaragua* reviewed by Elizabeth Dore. *Journal of Latin American Studies*, v. 25, no. 1 (Feb 93), pp. 220 – 221.

— *Revolution and Counterrevolution in Nicaragua* reviewed by D. Neil Snarr. *Revista Interamericana de Bibliografía*, v. 42, no. 2 (1992), pp. 290 – 291.

Bibliography

Harris, Richard L. The Nicaraguan Revolution: A Postmortem (Review article). *Latin American Research Review*, v. 28, no. 3 (1993), pp. 197 – 213.

REVUELTAS, JOSÉ

Biography

Ruiz Abreu, Alvaro. *José Revueltas: los muros de la utopía* reviewed by Sergio González Rodríguez (Review entitled "El legado de José Revueltas"). *Nexos*, v. 16, no. 187 (July 93), pp. 73 – 75.

— *José Revueltas: los muros de la utopía* reviewed by Christopher Domínguez. *Vuelta*, v. 17, no. 196 (Mar 93), pp. 49 – 50.

— Revueltas o la fidelidad eterna. *Nexos*, v. 16, no. 183 (Mar 93), pp. 53 – 55.

Criticism of specific works

El cuadrante de la soledad

Huerta, Efraín. El vapuleado *Cuadrante*. *Nexos*, v. 16, no. 183 (Mar 93), pp. 55 – 56.

Los errores

Domínguez Michael, Christopher. Lepra y utopía (Chapter from the book *Tiros en el concierto*). *Vuelta*, v. 17, no. 199 (June 93), pp. 24 – 31. Bibl.

REY FAJARDO, JOSÉ DEL

Criticism of specific works

La pedagogía jesuítica en Venezuela

Rey Fajardo, José del. Palabras pronunciadas por el r.p. José del Rey Fajardo, S.J. en la presentación de la obra *La pedagogía jesuítica en Venezuela, 1628 – 1767*. *Boletín de la Academia Nacional de la Historia (Venezuela)*, v. 75, no. 299 (July – Sept 92), pp. 25 – 26.

REYES, ALFONSO

Biography

Alvar López, Manuel. Alfonso Reyes y España. *Nueva Revista de Filología Hispánica*, v. 40, no. 2 (July – Dec 92), pp. 959 – 987. Bibl.

Correspondence, reminiscences,etc.

Reyes, Alfonso. Buzón de fantasmas: de Alfonso Reyes a Genaro Estrada. *Vuelta*, v. 17, no. 196 (Mar 93), pp. 76 – 77.

Criticism and interpretation

Castañón, Adolfo. *Alfonso Reyes, caballero de la voz errante* reviewed by Sam L. Slick. *World Literature Today*, v. 67, no. 1 (Winter 93), p. 162.

Criticism of specific works

El deslinde

Stanton, Anthony. Octavio Paz, Alfonso Reyes y el análisis del fenómeno poético. *Hispanic Review*, v. 61, no. 3 (Summer 93), pp. 363 – 378. Bibl.

Fiction

Alatriste, Sealtiel. *En defensa de la envidia* reviewed by Christopher Domínquez (Review entitled "De envidia a envidia"). *Vuelta*, v. 17, no. 195 (Feb 93), pp. 40 – 41.

REYES HEROLES, JESÚS

Meyemberg Léycegui, Yolanda. Jesús Reyes Heroles. *Revista Mexicana de Ciencias Políticas y Sociales*, v. 38, Nueva época, no. 151 (Jan – Mar 93), pp. 81 – 99. Bibl.

REYES NEVARES, SALVADOR

Weinberg, Liliana Irene. Lo mexicano en el México moderno. *Cuadernos Americanos*, no. 41, Nueva época (Sept – Oct 93), pp. 204 – 211. Bibl.

Obituaries

Miaja, María Teresa. Salvador Reyes Nevares en mi autobiografía. *Cuadernos Americanos*, no. 41, Nueva época (Sept – Oct 93), pp. 222 – 225.

Reyes, Juan José. Salvador Reyes Nevares, el mejor amigo. *Cuadernos Americanos*, no. 41, Nueva época (Sept – Oct 93), pp. 218 – 221.

REYNA, JOSÉ LUIS

Interviews

Minello, Nelson. Entrevistas a Rodolfo Stavenhagen, José Luis Reyna y Claudio Stern. *Estudios Sociológicos*, v. 11, no. 31 (Jan – Apr 93), pp. 19 – 31.

RHETORIC

Chasteen, John Charles. Fighting Words: The Discourse of Insurgency in Latin American History. *Latin American Research Review*, v. 28, no. 3 (1993), pp. 83 – 111. Bibl, il.

Vogeley, Nancy J. Colonial Discourse in a Postcolonial Context: Nineteenth-Century Mexico. *Colonial Latin American Review*, v. 2, no. 1 – 2 (1993), pp. 189 – 212. Bibl.

RIBEIRO, JOÃO UBALDO

Criticism and interpretation

Valente, Luiz Fernando. Fiction as History: The Case of João Ubaldo Ribeiro. *Latin American Research Review*, v. 28, no. 1 (1993), pp. 41 – 60. Bibl.

RIBEIRO, LEÓN

Manzino, Leonardo. La música uruguaya en los festejos de 1892 con motivo del IV centenario del encuentro de dos mundos. *Latin American Music Review*, v. 14, no. 1 (Spring – Summer 93), pp. 102 – 130. Bibl, facs.

RIBEYRO, JULIO RAMÓN

Correspondence, reminiscences, etc.

Ribeyro, Julio Ramón. *La tentación del fracaso* reviewed by Alonso Cueto (Review entitled "El tesoro escondido"). *Debate (Peru)*, v. 15, no. 70 (Sept – Oct 92), pp. 68 – 69. Il.

— *La tentación del fracaso* reviewed by Marco Martos (Review entitled "Las memorias de tres novelistas peruanos"). *Debate (Peru)*, v. 16, no. 73 (June – Aug 93), pp. 68 – 72. Il.

RICE

Dominican Republic

Inoa, Orlando. El arroz como ejemplo de la producción campesina para el mercado interno en la era de Trujillo. *Estudios Sociales (Dominican Republic)*, v. 26, no. 92 (Apr – June 93), pp. 21 – 38. Bibl, tables.

RÍO, EDUARDO DEL

Bibliography

Jones, Errol D. Ríus: Still a Thorn in the Side of the Mexican Establishment (Review article). *Studies in Latin American Popular Culture*, v. 12 (1993), pp. 221 – 227. Bibl.

RIO BRANCO, JOSÉ MARIA DA SILVA PARANHOS

Scarabôtolo, Hélio Antônio. Rio Branco, Euclides da Cunha e o tratado de limites com o Peru. *Revista do Instituto Histórico e Geográfico Brasileiro*, no. 370 (Jan – Mar 91), pp. 82 – 93.

RIO DE JANEIRO, BRAZIL (CITY)

Cardoso, Tereza Maria R. Fachada Levy. A *Gazeta do Rio de Janeiro:* subsidios para a história da cidade, 1808 – 1821. *Revista do Instituto Histórico e Geográfico Brasileiro,* no. 371 (Apr – June 91), pp. 341 – 436. Bibl, il, tables, maps.

Caulfield, Sueann and Martha de Abreu Esteves. 50 Years of Virginity in Rio de Janeiro: Sexual Politics and Gender Roles in Juridical and Popular Discourse, 1890 – 1940. *Luso-Brazilian Review,* v. 30, no. 1 (Summer 93), pp. 47 – 74. Bibl, tables.

Chalhoub, Sidney. The Politics of Disease Control: Yellow Fever and Race in Nineteenth Century Rio de Janeiro. *Journal of Latin American Studies,* v. 25, no. 3 (Oct 93), pp. 441 – 463. Bibl.

Engel, Magali. *Meretrizes e doutores: saber médico e prostituição no Rio de Janeiro, 1840 – 1890* reviewed by Sandra Lauderdale Graham (Review entitled "Dangerous Fantasies: The Altered Vocabulary of Commercial Sex"). *Luso-Brazilian Review,* v. 30, no. 1 (Summer 93), pp. 133 – 139.

Gomes, Angela Maria de Castro. Essa gente do Rio . . . : os intelectuais cariocas e o modernismo. *Estudos Históricos,* v. 6, no. 11 (Jan – June 93), pp. 62 – 77.

Graham, Sandra Lauderdale. *House and Street: The Domestic World of Servants and Masters in Nineteenth-Century Rio de Janeiro* reviewed by Silvia Marina Arrom. *The Americas,* v. 49, no. 4 (Apr 93), pp. 553 – 555.

Lacombe, Américo Jacobina. Estudos cariocas. *Revista do Instituto Histórico e Geográfico Brasileiro,* no. 370 (Jan – Mar 91), pp. 310 – 329.

Moraes, José Geraldo Vinci de. Sonoridades urbanas. *Vozes,* v. 87, no. 3 (May – June 93), pp. 48 – 58. Il.

Soares, Luís Carlos. *Rameiras, ilhoas, polacas: a prostituição do Rio de Janeiro do século XIX* reviewed by Sandra Lauderdale Graham (Review entitled "Dangerous Fantasies: The Altered Vocabulary of Commercial Sex"). *Luso-Brazilian Review,* v. 30, no. 1 (Summer 93), pp. 133 – 139.

RIO DE JANEIRO, BRAZIL (STATE)

Ramires, Julio Cesar Lima. As grandes corporações e a dinâmica socioespacial: a ação da PETROBRAS em Macaé. *Revista Brasileira de Geografia,* v. 53, no. 4 (Oct – Dec 91), pp. 115 – 151. Bibl, tables, maps.

Versiani, Flávio Rabelo. Imigrantes, trabalho qualificado e industrialização: Rio e São Paulo no início do século. *Revista de Economia Política (Brazil),* v. 13, no. 4 (Oct – Dec 93), pp. 77 – 96. Bibl, tables.

RÍO DE LA PLATA REGION

See also

Agriculture – Río de la Plata region
Caciquism – Río de la Plata region
Corruption (in politics) – Río de la Plata region
Floods – Río de la Plata region
Haciendas – Río de la Plata region
Jews – Río de la Plata region
Law – Río de la Plata region
Markets and merchants – Río de la Plata region
Musical instruments – Río de la Plata region
Photography, Aerial – Río de la Plata region
Smuggling – Río de la Plata region
Spanish language – Río de la Plata region
Wages – Río de la Plata region

Boundaries

Moyano Bazzani, Eduardo L. Aportaciones de la historiografía portuguesa a la problemática fronteriza luso – española en América meridional, 1750 – 1778. *Revista de Indias,* v. 52, no. 195 – 196 (May – Dec 92), pp. 723 – 747. Bibl, maps.

Commerce

History

Gelman, Jorge Daniel. Los caminos del mercado: campesinos, estancieros y pulperos en una región del Río de la Plata colonial. *Latin American Research Review,* v. 28, no. 2 (1993), pp. 89 – 118. Bibl, tables.

Whigham, Thomas Lyle. *The Politics of River Trade: Tradition and Development in the Upper Plata, 1780 – 1870* reviewed by James Schofield Saeger. *The Americas,* v. 49, no. 4 (Apr 93), pp. 552 – 553.

— *The Politics of River Trade: Tradition and Development in the Upper Plata, 1780 – 1870* reviewed by Jeremy Adelman. *Journal of Latin American Studies,* v. 25, no. 1 (Feb 93), pp. 194 – 196.

Zanotti de Medrano, Lilia Inés. Rio Grande do Sul: una provincia brasileña vinculada comercialmente al Plata en el siglo XIX. *Todo Es Historia,* v. 26, no. 307 (Feb 93), pp. 60 – 72. Bibl, il, maps.

Discovery and exploration

Poetry

Manzotti, Vilma. Del Barco Centenera y su poema como justicia en una hazaña desventurada. *Revista Interamericana de Bibliografía,* v. 42, no. 3 (1992), pp. 453 – 462. Bibl.

Economic conditions

Saban, Mario Javier. *Los marranos y la economía en el Río de Plata* reviewed by José Federico Lima. *Todo Es Historia,* v. 27, no. 314 (Sept 93), pp. 71 – 72. Il.

Officials and public employees

Saguier, Eduardo Ricardo. La corrupción de la burocracia colonial borbónica y los orígenes del federalismo: el caso del virreinato del Río de la Plata. *Jahrbuch für Geschichte von Staat, Wirtschaft und Gesellschaft Lateinamerikas,* v. 29 (1992), pp. 149 – 177. Bibl.

RIO GRANDE DO NORTE, BRAZIL

Souza, Maria Tereza Saraiva de. Uma estratégia de "marketing" para cooperativas de artesanato: o caso do Rio Grande do Norte. *RAE; Revista de Administração de Empresas,* v. 33, no. 1 (Jan – Feb 93), pp. 30 – 38. Bibl, tables, charts.

RIO GRANDE DO SUL, BRAZIL

Flores, Hilda Agnes Hübner. Participação da mulher na construção do Rio Grande do Sul. *Hoy Es Historia,* v. 10, no. 59 (Sept – Oct 93), pp. 67 – 74. Bibl.

Gertz, René E. *O perigo alemão* reviewed by Jeff Lesser. *The Americas,* v. 50, no. 1 (July 93), pp. 141 – 142.

— *O perigo alemão* reviewed by Ronald C. Newton. *Hispanic American Historical Review,* v. 73, no. 2 (May 93), pp. 324 – 325.

Isaia, Artur Cesar. Catolicismo, regeneração social e castilhismo na república velha gaúcha. *Estudos Ibero-Americanos,* v. 18, no. 1 (July 92), pp. 5 – 18. Bibl.

Lopez, Luiz Roberto. A quem serviu o mito do gaúcho. *Vozes,* v. 86, no. 5 (Sept – Oct 92), pp. 99 – 101.

Quevedo, Raul. Realidade e mitos do Rio Grande antigo. *Vozes,* v. 87, no. 4 (July – Aug 93), pp. 86 – 90. Il.

Stülp, Valter José and Bartholomeu E. Stein Neto. A vitivinicultura do Rio Grande do Sul e a integração econômica Brasil – Argentina. *Revista de Economia e Sociologia Rural,* v. 29, no. 4 (Oct – Dec 91), pp. 387 – 400. Bibl, tables.

Zanotti de Medrano, Lilia Inés. Rio Grande do Sul: una provincia brasileña vinculada comercialmente al Plata en el siglo XIX. *Todo Es Historia,* v. 26, no. 307 (Feb 93), pp. 60 – 72. Bibl, il, maps.

RÍOS, JUAN

Correspondence, reminiscences, etc.

Ríos, Juan. *Sobre mi propia vida: diario, 1940 – 1991* reviewed by Carlos Garatea Grau (Review entitled "Tiempo de preguntas"). *Debate (Peru),* v. 16, no. 73 (June – Aug 93), pp. 73 – 74. Il.

RIPSTEIN, ARTURO

Patán Tobío, Julio. Ripstein entre nosotros. *Nexos,* v. 16, no. 191 (Nov 93), pp. 73 – 74.

RITES AND CEREMONIES

See also

Sacrifice
Subdivision *Ceremonies and practices* under *Catholic Church*
Subdivisions *Mortuary customs, Religion and mythology,* and *Social life and customs* under Indian groups

Argentina

Urquiza, Fernando Carlos. Etiquetas y conflictos: el obispo, el virrey y el cabildo en el Río de la Plata en la segunda mitad del siglo XVIII. *Anuario de Estudios Americanos,* v. 50, no. 1 (1993), pp. 55 – 100. Bibl.

Brazil

Carvalho, José Jorge de. Aesthetics of Opacity and Transparence: Myth, Music, and Ritual in the Xangô Cult and in the Western Art Tradition. *Latin American Music Review,* v. 14, no. 2 (Fall – Winter 93), pp. 202 – 231. Bibl, tables, facs.

Motta, Roberto M. C. Transe, sacrifício, comunhão e poder no xangô de Pernambuco. *Revista de Antropologia (Brazil),* v. 34 (1991), pp. 131 – 142.

Guyana

Gibson, Kean. An African Work: The Guyanese Comfa Dance. *Journal of Caribbean Studies,* v. 9, no. 1 – 2 (Winter 92 – Spring 93), pp. 99 – 111. Bibl.

Mexico

Aramoni Calderón, Dolores. De diosas y mujeres. *Mesoamérica (USA),* v. 13, no. 23 (June 92), pp. 85 – 94. Bibl.

Clendinnen, Inga. *Aztecs: An Interpretation* reviewed by María J. Rodríguez Shadow. *Mesoamérica (USA),* v. 13, no. 24 (Dec 92), pp. 480 – 487.

— *Aztecs: An Interpretation* reviewed by Sarah Cline. *The Americas,* v. 49, no. 3 (Jan 93), pp. 395 – 396.

Peru

Barriga Calle, Irma. La experiencia de la muerte en Lima, siglo XVII. *Apuntes (Peru),* no. 31 (July – Dec 92), pp. 81 – 102. Bibl.

Mejías Alvarez, María Jesús. Muerte regia en cuatro ciudades peruanas del barroco. *Anuario de Estudios Americanos,* v. 49 (1992), pp. 189 – 205. Bibl, il.

Sala i Vila, Nuria. Alianzas y enfrentamientos regionales: consideraciones sobre la represión de un ritual andino en Lircay, 1794 – 1814. *Historia y Cultura (Peru),* no. 20 (1990), pp. 221 – 242. Bibl.

Zecenarro Villalobos, Bernardino. De fiestas, ritos y batallas: algunos comportamientos folk de la sociedad andina de los k'anas y ch'umpiwillcas. *Allpanchis,* v. 23, no. 40 (July – Dec 92), pp. 147 – 172. Bibl.

RIUS

See
Río, Eduardo del

RIVADAVIA, BERNARDINO

Terbeck, C. Augusto. La promoción minera intentada por Rivadavia: las minas de Cuyo y "The River Plate Mining Association." *Investigaciones y Ensayos,* no. 41 (Jan – Dec 91), pp. 423 – 455. Bibl.

RIVADENEIRA PRADA, RAÚL

Criticism of specific works

Colección de vigilias

Saavedra Pinochet, Rafael. Los rivadeneiros relatos de Rivadeneira Prada. *Signo,* no. 38, Nueva época (Jan – Apr 93), pp. 155 – 160.

El tiempo de lo cotidiano

Pastor Poppe, Ricardo. *El tiempo de lo cotidiano* de Raúl Rivadeneira Prada. *Signo,* no. 35, Nueva época (Jan – Apr 92), pp. 77 – 81. Bibl.

Saavedra Pinochet, Rafael. Los rivadeneiros relatos de Rivadeneira Prada. *Signo,* no. 38, Nueva época (Jan – Apr 93), pp. 155 – 160.

RIVERA, ANDRÉS

Interviews

Delgado, Josefina. Andrés Rivera y el sueño eterno de Castelli. *Todo Es Historia,* v. 27, no. 315 (Oct 93), pp. 56 – 59. Il.

RIVERA, ARTURO

Lara de la Fuente, Leonor. Arturo Rivera: una pasión renacentista. *Artes de México,* no. 21 (Fall 93), pp. 100 – 101.

RIVERA, DIEGO

Azuela, Alicia. La presencia de Diego Rivera en los Estados Unidos: dos versiones de la historia. *Anales del Instituto de Investigaciones Estéticas,* v. 16, no. 62 (1991), pp. 175 – 180.

RIVERA, JOSÉ EUSTASIO

Criticism of specific works

La vorágine

Ordóñez Vila, Montserrat. La loba insaciable de *La vorágine.* *Escritura (Venezuela),* v. 16, no. 31 – 32 (Jan – Dec 91), pp. 205 – 213.

Schulman, Iván A. *La vorágine:* contrapuntos y textualizaciones de la modernidad. *Nueva Revista de Filología Hispánica,* v. 40, no. 2 (July – Dec 92), pp. 875 – 890. Bibl.

RIVERA-RODAS, OSCAR

Criticism and interpretation

Calderón, Fina de. Repaso de la poesía boliviana: dos poetas en Madrid: Oscar Rivera-Rodas y Pedro Shimose. *Signo,* no. 35, Nueva época (Jan – Apr 92), pp. 5 – 13.

RIVERS

See also
Amazon Valley
Dams and reservoirs
Inland water transportation
Orinoco River Valley, Venezuela
Tuy River Valley, Venezuela

Argentina

Barba, Fernando Enrique. El río Santa Ana. *Investigaciones y Ensayos,* no. 41 (Jan – Dec 91), pp. 261 – 268. Bibl.

Venezuela

Mogollón, José Luis et al. Uso de los parámetros físico – químicos de las aguas fluviales como indicadores de influencias naturales y antrópicas. *Interciencia,* v. 18, no. 5 (Sept – Oct 93), pp. 249 – 254. Bibl, tables, maps.

ROA BASTOS, AUGUSTO ANTONIO

Correspondence, reminiscences, etc.

Roa Bastos, Augusto Antonio. Augusto Roa Bastos: dos cartas. *Casa de las Américas,* no. 190 (Jan – Mar 93), pp. 134 – 135.

Criticism and interpretation

Calviño Iglesias, Julio. Augusto Roa Bastos y la gran melopea de lo mismo. *Insula,* no. 562 (Oct 93), pp. 19 – 20. Il.

Criticism of specific works

Vigilia del Almirante

Ortega, José. Verdad poética e histórica en *Vigilia del Almirante.* *Cuadernos Hispanoamericanos,* no. 513 (Mar 93), pp. 108 – 111.

Yo el Supremo

Caisso, Claudia. "El zumo del secreto se esfumara": algunas aventuras verbales en *Yo el Supremo. Escritura (Venezuela),* v. 17, no. 33 – 34 (Jan – Dec 92), pp. 143 – 148.

Osorio, Manuel. Conversación con Roa Bastos: *Yo el Supremo;* la contrahistoria. *Plural (Mexico),* v. 22, no. 263 (Aug 93), pp. 29 – 31.

Sabugo Abril, Amancio. Historia, biografía, ficción en *Yo el Supremo. Hoy Es Historia,* v. 10, no. 57 (Apr – May 93), pp. 5 – 14. Bibl, il.

Sicard, Alain. Poder de la escritura: ¿El crepúsculo de los chamanes? *Revista de Crítica Literaria Latinoamericana,* v. 19, no. 38 (July – Dec 93), pp. 155 – 162.

Interviews

Osorio, Manuel. Conversación con Roa Bastos: *Yo el Supremo;* la contrahistoria. *Plural (Mexico),* v. 22, no. 263 (Aug 93), pp. 29 – 31.

ROADS

See also
Highways

America

Trombold, Charles D., ed. *Ancient Road Networks and Settlement Hierarchies in the New World* reviewed by David R. Ringrose. *Hispanic American Historical Review*, v. 73, no. 1 (Feb 93), pp. 141 – 142.

Chile

Fernández Koprich, Daniel. Vías elevadas para Santiago: ¿Una opción válida? (With commentaries by Jorge Heine, Oscar Figueroa, Juan de Dios Ortúzar, Víctor Basauri, and Daniel Fernández). *EURE*, v. 19, no. 56 (Mar 93), pp. 95 – 115. Charts.

Latin America

United Nations. Economic Commission for Latin America and the Caribbean. *Caminos: un nuevo enfoque para la gestión y conservación de redes viales* (Review). *CEPAL Review*, no. 48 (Dec 92), pp. 169 – 171.

ROCK PAINTINGS

See
Dermatoglyphics
Petroglyphs

ROCKEFELLER, NELSON A.

Cobbs, Elizabeth Anne. *The Rich Neighbor Policy: Rockefeller and Kaiser in Brazil* reviewed by Joel Wolfe. *Hispanic American Historical Review*, v. 73, no. 3 (Aug 93), pp. 538 – 539.

ROCYN-JONES, SUSAN

Obituaries

Dodsworth, Mark. Susan Rocyn-Jones (1940 – 1992): An Appreciation. *Bulletin of Latin American Research*, v. 12, no. 2 (May 93), pp. 215 – 216.

RODÓ, JOSÉ ENRIQUE

Criticism and interpretation

Castro Morales, María Belén. *José E. Rodó, modernista: utopía y regeneración* reviewed by Julio Ricci. *Hispamérica*, v. 22, no. 64 – 65 (Apr – Aug 93), pp. 191 – 192.

Sánchez-Gey Venegas, Juana. El modernismo filosófico en América. *Cuadernos Americanos*, no. 41, Nueva época (Sept – Oct 93), pp. 109 – 121. Bibl.

RODRIGUES, JOSÉ HONÓRIO

Correspondence, reminiscences, etc.

Boxer, Charles Ralph and José Honório Rodrigues. Correspondência de José Honório Rodrigues: a correspondência com Charles R. Boxer (Organized and annotated by Lêda Boechat Rodrigues). *Revista do Instituto Histórico e Geográfico Brasileiro*, no. 372 (July – Sept 91), pp. 828 – 907. Tables.

RODRÍGUEZ, ANTONIO

Obituaries

Martínez, Jesús. Don Antonio Rodríguez. *Plural (Mexico)*, v. 22, no. 267 (Dec 93), pp. 74 – 75.

RODRÍGUEZ, MANUEL ALFREDO

Tovar López, Ramón Adolfo. Contestación al discurso de incorporación a la Academia Nacional de la Historia del dr. Manuel Alfredo Rodríguez . . . . *Boletín de la Academia Nacional de la Historia (Venezuela)*, v. 75, no. 299 (July – Sept 92), pp. 63 – 65.

RODRÍGUEZ, RICHARD

Criticism of specific works

Hunger of Memory

Hogue, W. Lawrence. An Unresolved Modern Experience: Richard Rodríguez's *Hunger of Memory*. *The Americas Review*, v. 20, no. 1 (Spring 92), pp. 52 – 64. Bibl.

RODRÍGUEZ, SIMÓN

Arroyo Alvarez, Eduardo. Don Simón Rodríguez, el maestro. *Revista Nacional de Cultura (Venezuela)*, v. 53, no. 286 (July – Sept 92), pp. 142 – 147. Il.

Rotker, Susana. Simón Rodríguez: utopía y transgresión. *Casa de las Américas*, no. 191 (Apr – June 93), pp. 51 – 57. Bibl.

RODRÍGUEZ CAMUSSO, FRANCISCO

Interviews

Crisis del parlamento tradicional: entrevista a Francisco Rodríguez Camusso. *Cuadernos del CLAEH*, v. 18, no. 67 (Nov 93), pp. 53 – 67.

RODRÍGUEZ FEO, JOSÉ

Correspondence, reminiscences, etc.

Rodríguez Feo, José. *Mi correspondencia con Lezama Lima* reviewed by Saïd Benabdelouahed. *Caravelle*, no. 59 (1992), pp. 289 – 293.

RODRÍGUEZ JULIÁ, EDGARDO

Criticism and interpretation

Ríos-Avila, Rubén. La invención de un autor: escritura y poder en Edgardo Rodríguez Juliá. *Revista Iberoamericana*, v. 59, no. 162 – 163 (Jan – June 93), pp. 203 – 219. Bibl.

Criticism of specific works

El entierro de Cortijo

Duchesne, Juan Ramón. Multitud y tradición en "El entierro de Cortijo" de Edgardo Rodríguez Juliá. *Revista Iberoamericana*, v. 59, no. 162 – 163 (Jan – June 93), pp. 221 – 237. Bibl.

RODRÍGUEZ LARRETA, ENRIQUE

See
Larreta, Enrique Rodríguez

ROIG, ARTURO ANDRÉS

Pérez Leyva, Leonardo. Arturo Andrés Roig: algunas consideraciones sobre su pensamiento filosófico. *Islas*, no. 99 (May – Aug 91), pp. 87 – 94. Bibl.

ROJAS, CRISTÓBAL

Arocha Vargas, Arnaldo. Acto de presentación de los libros *José Antonio Páez* y *Cristóbal Rojas, un pintor venezolano*, pertenecientes a la Biblioteca de Autores y Temas Mirandinos. *Boletín de la Academia Nacional de la Historia (Venezuela)*, v. 75, no. 299 (July – Sept 92), pp. 5 – 8.

ROJAS, GONZALO

Addresses, essays, lectures

Rojas, Gonzalo. Discurso de aceptación del premio Reina Sofía de Poesía Iberoamericana, 1993. *Chasqui*, v. 22, no. 1 (May 93), pp. 4 – 11. Il.

Criticism and interpretation

Cluff, Russell M. El motivo del amor en la poesía de Gonzalo Rojas. *Chasqui*, v. 22, no. 1 (May 93), pp. 59 – 69.

Coddou Peebles, Marcelo. Proyección de Vallejo en la poesía de Gonzalo Rojas. *Revista Chilena de Literatura*, no. 41 (Apr 93), pp. 113 – 118. Bibl.

Forster, Merlin H. El concepto del "Ars Poética" en la poesía de Gonzalo Rojas. *Chasqui*, v. 22, no. 1 (May 93), pp. 51 – 58.

Giordano, Jaime. Más allá de las palabras: Gonzalo Rojas. *Atenea (Chile)*, no. 467 (1993), pp. 187 – 196.

— Más allá de las palabras: Gonzalo Rojas. *Chasqui*, v. 22, no. 1 (May 93), pp. 31 – 37.

Mestre, Juan Carlos. El discurso de la utopía en la poética de Gonzalo Rojas. *Chasqui*, v. 22, no. 1 (May 93), pp. 42 – 46.

Quackenbush, Louis Howard. La realidad detrás de la realidad: Gonzalo Rojas y lo numinoso. *Chasqui*, v. 22, no. 1 (May 93), pp. 23 – 30.

Rodríguez Padrón, Justo Jorge. La palabra en Atacama. *Chasqui*, v. 22, no. 1 (May 93), pp. 19 – 22.

Criticism of specific works

Alabanza y repetición de Eloísa

May, Hilda R. El tiempo como kairós en la poética de Gonzalo Rojas. *Chasqui*, v. 22, no. 1 (May 93), pp. 37 – 41.

Cinco visiones

Ruiz Barrionuevo, Carmen. *Cinco visiones* de Gonzalo Rojas. *Chasqui*, v. 22, no. 1 (May 93), pp. 12 – 18.

Materia de testamento

Sáinz de Medrano Arce, Luis. *Materia de testamento* como etopeya. *Chasqui*, v. 22, no. 1 (May 93), pp. 47 – 51.

Tabla de aire

May, Hilda R. El tiempo como kairós en la poética de Gonzalo Rojas. *Chasqui*, v. 22, no. 1 (May 93), pp. 37 – 41.

Interviews

Araya G., Juan Gabriel. Conversaciones con Gonzalo Rojas. *Atenea (Chile)*, no. 465 – 466 (1992), pp. 269 – 280. Bibl, il.

ROJAS, ISAAC FRANCISCO

González-Crespo, Jorge L. *Memorias del almirante Isaac F. Rojas: conversaciones con Jorge González-Crespo* reviewed by Carmen Vrljicak-Espaín. *Todo Es Historia*, v. 27, no. 315 (Oct 93), p. 66. Il.

ROJAS, RAFAEL ARMANDO

See

Rojas Guardia, Armando

ROJAS GUARDIA, ARMANDO

Criticism and interpretation

Ramírez Quintero, Gonzalo. La poesía venezolana actual: tres ejemplos. *Inti*, no. 37 – 38 (Spring – Fall 93), pp. 187 – 195.

Criticism of specific works

Bolívar, paradigma de la estirpe

Torrealba Lossi, Mario et al. Bibliográficas. *Boletín de la Academia Nacional de la Historia (Venezuela)*, v. 76, no. 301 (Jan – Mar 93), pp. 121 – 127.

ROJAS PINILLA, GUSTAVO

Ayala Diago, César Augusto. El Movimiento de Acción Nacional (MAN): movilización y confluencia de idearios políticos durante el gobierno de Gustavo Rojas Pinilla. *Anuario Colombiano de Historia Social y de la Cultura*, no. 20 (1992), pp. 44 – 70. Bibl.

ROJO, VICENTE

Blanco, Alberto. La música de la retina. *Nexos*, v. 16, no. 192 (Dec 93), pp. 9 – 15.

ROMÁN, JOSÉ

Criticism of specific works

Maldito país

Pailler, Claire. El reportaje del guerillero: una narrativa ambigua. *Studi di Letteratura Ispano-Americana*, v. 24 (1993), pp. 67 – 82. Tables.

ROMANCE LANGUAGES

See

Language and languages
Names of specific languages

ROMANIA

Informe que envía al Ministerio de Relaciones Exteriores el excelentísimo señor Milos Alcalay, embajador de Venezuela en Rumania, acerca de la misión en Rumania del director de la Academia Nacional de la Historia, dr. Guillermo Morón. *Boletín de la Academia Nacional de la Historia (Venezuela)*, v. 75, no. 299 (July – Sept 92) pp. 225 – 231.

Nastase, Adrián. Titulescu y América Latina. *Boletín de la Academia Nacional de la Historia (Venezuela)*, v. 75, no. 298 (Apr – June 92), pp. 9 – 14.

Sequera Tamayo, Isbelia. Rumania en Venezuela: en las academia nacionales. *Boletín de la Academia Nacional de la Historia (Venezuela)*, v. 75, no. 298 (Apr – June 92), pp. 5 – 7.

ROMERO, FRANCISCO

Criticism of specific works

Llanto sagrado de la América meridional

Albónico, Aldo. Un' opera in difesa degli indi nella Milano del seicento: il *Llanto sagrado de la América meridional*. *Quaderni Ibero-Americani*, no. 72 (Dec 92), pp. 695 – 708. Bibl.

ROMERO, SÍLVIO

Wehling, Arno. Capistrano de Abreu e Sílvio Romero: um paralelo cientificista. *Revista do Instituto Histórico e Geográfico Brasileiro*, no. 370 (Jan – Mar 91), pp. 265 – 274.

ROMERO DE TERREROS, PEDRO, CONDE DE REGLA

Ramos, Agustín. *La gran cruzada* reviewed by Pablo Mora. *Hispamérica*, v. 21, no. 63 (Dec 92), pp. 106 – 108.

RORAIMA, BRAZIL

Farage, Nádia. *As muralhas dos sertões: os povos indígenas no rio Branco e a colonização* reviewed by David Cleary. *Journal of Latin American Studies*, v. 25, no. 2 (May 93), pp. 394 – 395.

ROSA, JOÃO GUIMARÃES

Criticism of specific works

Conversa de bois

Esteves, Antônio Roberto. Em torno de uma "Conversa de bois": alguns elementos de teoria da narrativa. *Revista de Letras (Brazil)*, v. 32 (1992), pp. 109 – 117.

A menina de lá

Motta, Sérgio Vicente. Ser/tão . . . somente linguagem. *Revista de Letras (Brazil)*, v. 32 (1992), pp. 81 – 99. Bibl.

Nenhum, nenhuma

Carlos, Ana Maria. De roca e fuso. *Revista de Letras (Brazil)*, v. 32 (1992), pp. 101 – 107. Bibl.

ROSA, JUAN DE LA

Fiction

Aguirre, Nataniel. *Juan de la Rosa: memorias del último hidalgo de la independencia* reviewed by Gaby Vallejo de Bolívar. *Signo*, no. 35, Nueva época (Jan – Apr 92), pp. 201 – 202.

ROSA OF LIMA, SAINT

Poetry

Millones Santa Gadea, Luis. Poemas y canciones en honor de Santa Rosa: profecías del pasado, voces del presente. *Revista de Crítica Literaria Latinoamericana*, v. 19, no. 37 (Jan – June 93), pp. 185 – 194. Bibl.

ROSANO, JORGE

Rebollar, Juan L. Jorge Rosano: una aseveración plástica sin alardes. *Artes de México*, no. 19 (Spring 93), p. 117. Il.

ROSAS, JUAN MANUEL JOSÉ DOMINGO ORTIZ DE

Infesta, María Elena and Marla Valencia. Los criterios legales en la revisión de la política rosista de tierras públicas: Buenos Aires, 1852 – 1864. *Investigaciones y Ensayos*, no. 41 (Jan – Dec 91), pp. 407 – 421. Bibl.

Quiroga Micheo, Ernesto. Los mazorqueros: ¿Gente decente o asesinos? *Todo Es Historia*, v. 26, no. 308 (Mar 93), pp. 38 – 55. Bibl, il, facs.

Tenenbaum, León. Los dientes de Rosas. *Todo Es Historia*, v. 26, no. 308 (Mar 93), pp. 8 – 21. Il, facs.

ROSAS DE GALÍNDEZ, NICANORA

Los recuerdos de una hija de Rosas. *Todo Es Historia*, v. 26, no. 308 (Mar 93), pp. 62 – 67. Il.

ROSENCOF, MAURICIO

Interviews

Baeza, Cristina. Mauricio Rosencof: "Ni me bajo de este barco, ni cambio de capitán." *Casa de las Américas*, no. 191 (Apr – June 93), pp. 124 – 131.

ROSSI, ALEJANDRO

Biography

Krauze, Enrique. Zonas de Rossi. *Vuelta,* v. 17, no. 200 (July 93), pp. 62 – 63.

Criticism and interpretation

Castañón, Adolfo. Aproximaciones a Rossi. *Vuelta,* v. 17, no. 200 (July 93), pp. 64 – 66.

ROUCO BUELA, JUANA

Nari, Marcela M. Alejandra. Milagros y Juana. *Todo Es Historia,* v. 27, no. 312 (July 93), pp. 44 – 45.

ROWE, JAMES WILLIAM

Obituaries

Rieser, Leonard M. James W. Rowe (1929 – 1993). *Interciencia,* v. 18, no. 4 (July – Aug 93), p. 202.

RUBBER INDUSTRY AND TRADE

Mexico

Henderson, Peter V. N. Modernization and Change in Mexico: La Zacualpa Rubber Plantation, 1890 – 1920. *Hispanic American Historical Review,* v. 73, no. 2 (May 93), pp. 235 – 260. Bibl, tables.

Mondragón, Ana Laura. Contratos-ley y sindicatos: huleros y textileros. *El Cotidiano,* v. 9, no. 56 (July 93), pp. 18 – 22. Il, tables.

RUBÍN DE LA BORBOLLA, DANIEL FERNANDO

Chamorro, Inés G. Dr. Daniel F. Rubín de la Borbolla: una visión de su obra latinoamericana. *Folklore Americano,* no. 53 (Jan – June 92), pp. 169 – 175.

RUBIO, MIGUEL

Interviews

Rajatabla y Yuyachkani: veinte años. *Conjunto,* no. 90 – 91 (Jan – June 92), pp. 32 – 38. Il.

RUBIO, RAIMUNDO

Crumlish, Rebecca. Stepping into the Picture with Raimundo Rubio. *Américas,* v. 45, no. 1 (Jan – Feb 93), pp. 52 – 53. Il.

RUCCI, JOSÉ IGNACIO

Senén González, Santiago. José Ignacio Rucci, "el soldado de Perón." *Todo Es Historia,* v. 27, no. 314 (Sept 93), pp. 8 – 22. Bibl, il, facs.

RUIZ DE ALARCÓN, JUAN

King, Willard Fahrenkamp. *Juan Ruiz de Alarcón, letrado y dramaturgo: su mundo mexicano y español* reviewed by Charlotte Stein. *Hispanic Review,* v. 61, no. 2 (Spring 93), pp. 288 – 290.

RUIZ-FONTANORROSA, BLANCA

Macaya T., Emilia. Lo inefable en Blanca Ruiz-Fontanorrosa (Includes reproductions of 12 paintings from her series "Puertas y ventanas"). *Káñina,* v. 16, no. 1 (Jan – June 92), pp. 229 – 241. Il.

RUIZ-TAGLE, CARLOS

Obituaries

Guerrero Yoacham, Cristián. Carlos Ruiz-Tagle Gandarillas (1932 – 1991). *Cuadernos de Historia (Chile),* no. 11 (Dec 91), pp. 13 – 25. Il.

RULFO, JUAN

Criticism and interpretation

Antolín, Francisco, ed. *Los espacios en Juan Rulfo* reviewed by Susan Dennis. *Hispania (USA),* v. 76, no. 4 (Dec 93), pp. 733 – 734.

Elizondo, Salvador. Juan Rulfo. *Vuelta,* v. 17, no. 203 (Oct 93), pp. 8 – 9.

Fuentes, Carlos. Lectura derridiana de Juan Rulfo. *Nexos,* v. 16, no. 188 (Aug 93), pp. 7 – 8.

Jiménez de Báez, Yvette. *Juan Rulfo: del Páramo a la esperanza; una lectura crítica de su obra* reviewed by Luis Leal. *Hispanic Review,* v. 61, no. 2 (Spring 93), pp. 312 – 314.

Criticism of specific works

Pedro Páramo

Preble-Niemi, Oralia. *Pedro Páramo* and the Anima Archetype. *Hispanic Journal,* v. 13, no. 2 (Fall 92), pp. 363 – 373. Bibl.

Vilanova, Angel. Motivo clásico y novela latinoamericana. *Nueva Revista de Filología Hispánica,* v. 40, no. 2 (July – Dec 92), pp. 1087 – 1099. Bibl.

RUNAWAY SLAVES

See

Maroons

RURAL CONDITIONS

See

Agricultural laborers
Agriculture, Cooperative
Community development
Community organization
Land reform
Peasantry
Sociology, Rural
Subdivision *Rural conditions* under names of specific countries

RURAL DEVELOPMENT

See

Regional planning

RURAL – URBAN MIGRATION

See

Migration, Internal

RUSSIA

See also

Soviet Union

Description and travel

Amado, Jorge. Sailing the Shore: Notes for Memoirs I'll Never Write (Translated by Alfred MacAdam). *Review,* no. 47 (Fall 93), pp. 32 – 38.

Foreign economic relations

Latin America

Sudarev, Vladimir P. Russia and Latin America. *Hemisphere,* v. 5, no. 2 (Winter – Spring 93), pp. 12 – 14.

RUVINSKIS, WOLF

Interviews

Arana, Auxiliadora and Philip C. Kloin. An Interview with Wolf Ruvinskis: The First Mexican Stanley Kowalski. *Latin American Theatre Review,* v. 26, no. 2 (Spring 93), pp. 158 – 165. Il.

SÁBATO, ERNESTO R.

Biography

Correa, Alejandra. La pasión según los Sábato. *Todo Es Historia,* v. 26, no. 305 (Dec 92), pp. 85 – 94. Bibl, il.

Criticism and interpretation

Urbina, Nicasio. *La significación del género: estudio semiótico de las novelas y ensayos de Ernesto Sábato* reviewed by Amelia Mondragón. *Chasqui,* v. 22, no. 2 (Nov 93), pp. 173 – 174.

SACKETT, THEODORE ALAN

Homenaje a/Homenagem a: Theodore Alan Sackett, Editor of *Hispania,* 1984 – 1992. *Hispania (USA),* v. 76, no. 1 (Mar 93), pp. 12 – 19.

SACRIFICE

Covarrubias, Javier. La tecnología del sacrificio: la idea del "calor" y otros mitos encontrados. *Plural (Mexico),* v. 22, no. 258 (Mar 93), pp. 18 – 28. Bibl.

Hassler, Peter. *Menschenopfer bei den Azteken?: Eine quellen- und ideologiekritische Studie* reviewed by Norbert Rehrmann. *Iberoamericana,* v. 17, no. 49 (1993), pp. 95 – 96.

Nodal, Roberto. The Concept of "Ebbo" (Sacrifice) as a Healing Mechanism in Santería. *Journal of Caribbean Studies,* v. 9, no. 1 – 2 (Winter 92 – Spring 93), pp. 113 – 124. Bibl.

SADA, MARÍA

Lozoya, Jorge Alberto and Jan M. William. María Sada: sonatina en gris mayor. *Artes de México*, no. 21 (Fall 93), p. 102. Il.

SAER, JUAN JOSÉ

Criticism of specific works
El entenado

Díaz Quiñones, Arcadio. *El entenado:* las palabras de la tribu. *Hispamérica*, v. 21, no. 63 (Dec 92), pp. 3 – 14.

Grandis, Rita de. The First Colonial Encounter in *El entenado* by Juan José Saer: Paratextuality and History in Postmodern Fiction. *Latin American Literary Review*, v. 21, no. 41 (Jan – June 93), pp. 30 – 38. Bibl.

SAGEL, JIM

Interviews

Rodríguez, Pilar. Living the Spanglish Way: A Conversation with Jim Sagel. *Confluencia*, v. 8, no. 1 (Fall 92), pp. 137 – 146.

SAHAGÚN, BERNARDINO DE

Biography

León-Portilla, Ascensión H. de. Las primeras biografías de Bernardino de Sahagún. *Estudios de Cultura Náhuatl*, v. 22 (1992), pp. 235 – 252.

Criticism and interpretation

León-Portilla, Ascensión H. de, ed. *Bernardino de Sahagún: diez estudios acerca de su obra* reviewed by Pilar Maynez. *Estudios de Cultura Náhuatl*, v. 22 (1992), pp. 497 – 498.

Criticism of specific works
Historia general de las cosas de Nueva España

Máynez Vidal, Pilar. *Religión y magia: un problema de transculturación lingüística en la obra de Bernardino de Sahagún* reviewed by María Angeles Soler Arechalde. *Anuario de Letras (Mexico)*, v. 30 (1992), pp. 299 – 303.

SAHLIN, GUNNAR

Criticism of specific works
Francisco de Miranda i Sverige 1787

Karlsson, Weine. Un estudio sueco sobre Francisco de Miranda. *Boletín de la Academia Nacional de la Historia (Venezuela)*, v. 75, no. 299 (July – Sept 92), pp. 189 – 190.

SAIGNES, THIERRY

Biography

Saignes, Thierry. Pierre Chaunu, l'Amérique et nous: essai d'égo-histoire. *Cahiers des Amériques Latines*, no. 13 (1992), pp. 7 – 24. Bibl.

Obituaries

Bouysse-Cassagne, Thérèse. En souvenir de Thierry Saignes (27/09/1946 – 24/08/1992). *Bulletin de l'Institut Français d'Etudes Andines*, v. 21, no. 3 (1992), pp. 1085 – 1092. Il.

Revel-Mouroz, Jean François. Thierry Saignes (27 septembre 1946 – 24 ao + A0t 1992). *Cahiers des Amériques Latines*, no. 13 (1992), pp. 5 – 6.

SAINT-DOMINGUE

See
Science – Saint-Domingue

SAINT KITTS, WEST INDIES

Harms, Mike. Nurturing Conservation Naturally in the Twin Isles (Photographs by Michael Ventura). *Américas*, v. 45, no. 2 (Mar – Apr 93), pp. 22 – 25. Il, maps.

SAINT VINCENT, WEST INDIES

See also
Ecology – Saint Vincent, West Indies

Hulme, Peter and Neil L. Whitehead, eds. *Wild Majesty: Encounters with Caribs from Columbus to the Present Day; An Anthology* reviewed by Peter T. Bradley. *Bulletin of Latin American Research*, v. 12, no. 1 (Jan 93), pp. 111 – 112.

SÁINZ, GUSTAVO

Criticism and interpretation

Careaga, Gabriel. Gustavo Sáinz: una literatura incandescente. *Nexos*, v. 16, no. 184 (Apr 93), pp. 69 – 71.

SALARIES

See
Wages

SALAS, HORACIO

Correspondence, reminiscences, etc.

Salas, Horacio. Duro oficio el exilio. *Cuadernos Hispanoamericanos*, no. 517 – 519 (July – Sept 93), pp. 555 – 559.

SALAS PORTUGAL, ARMANDO

Barragán, Luis. *Barragán: Armando Salas Portugal Photographs of the Architecture of Luis Barragán*, essays by Ernest H. Brooks II et al. Reviewed by Max Underwood. *Latin American Art*, v. 4, no. 4 (Winter 92), pp. 94 – 95.

SALAS RIVERA, JOSÉ EUSTASIO

See
Rivera, José Eustasio

SALAZAR BONDY, AUGUSTO

Valdés García, Félix and María Teresa Vila Bormey. La filosofía de la liberación en Perú: de Augusto Salazar Bondy a Francisco Miró Quesada. *Islas*, no. 99 (May – Aug 91), pp. 21 – 29. Bibl.

SALAZAR Y TORRES, AGUSTÍN DE

Criticism of specific works
La segunda Celestina

Schmidhuber de la Mora, Guillermo, ed. *'La segunda Celestina': una comedia perdida de sor Juana* reviewed by Francisco Javier Cevallos. *Colonial Latin American Review*, v. 2, no. 1 – 2 (1993), pp. 302 – 304.

SALCEDO, DORIS

Merewether, Charles. Comunidad y continuidad: Doris Salcedo; nombrando la violencia (Accompanied by the English original, translated by Magdalena Holguín). *Art Nexus*, no. 9 (June – Aug 93), pp. 104 – 109. Bibl, il.

SALIAS, FRANCISCO

Expediente no. 14, año 1813. *Boletín de la Academia Nacional de la Historia (Venezuela)*, v. 75, no. 298 (Apr – June 92), pp. 145 – 146.

SALINAS, FERNANDO

Criticism and interpretation

Segre, Roberto. La poesía ambiental como proyecto de vida: la obra de Fernando Salinas (1930 – 1992). *Casa de las Américas*, no. 189 (Oct – Dec 92), pp. 107 – 108.

SALINAS, PEDRO

Correspondence, reminiscences, etc.

Guillén, Jorge and Pedro Salinas. *Pedro Salinas y Jorge Guillén: correspondencia, 1923 – 1951* edited by Andrés Soria Olmedo. Reviewed by Jean Cross Newman. *Revista Canadiense de Estudios Hispánicos*, v. 17, no. 3 (Spring 93), pp. 567 – 569.

SALINAS DE GORTARI, CARLOS

Abella Armengol, Gloria. La política exterior de México en el gobierno de Carlos Salinas de Gortari: ¿Una nueva concepción? *Revista Mexicana de Ciencias Políticas y Sociales*, v. 37, Nueva época, no. 148 (Apr – June 92), pp. 63 – 76.

Calva, José Luis. La reforma neoliberal del régimen agrario: en el cuarto año de gobierno de C. S. G. *Problemas del Desarrollo*, v. 24, no. 92 (Jan – Mar 93), pp. 31 – 39. Tables.

Huerta G., Arturo. Los cambios estructurales de la política salinista: su inviabilidad de alcanzar un crecimiento sostenido. *Problemas del Desarrollo*, v. 24, no. 92 (Jan – Mar 93), pp. 15 – 23.

Muñoz, Víctor Manuel. El liberalismo social: propuesta ideológica del salinismo. *Revista Mexicana de Ciencias Políticas y Sociales*, v. 37, Nueva época, no. 149 (July – Sept 92), pp. 29 – 47. Bibl.

Ortiz Wadgymar, Arturo. El desequilibrio externo: talón de Aquiles del salinismo. *Problemas del Desarrollo*, v. 24, no. 92 (Jan – Mar 93), pp. 24 – 30. Tables.

Addresses, essays, lectures

Salinas de Gortari, Carlos. El libre comercio en Norteamérica: oportunidad de progreso y bienestar. *Comercio Exterior*, v. 43, no. 1 (Jan 93), pp. 32 – 33.

SALT INDUSTRY AND TRADE

Mexico

Leytón Ovando, Rubén and Juan Carlos Reyes Garza. Cuyutlán: una cultura salinera. *La Palabra y el Hombre*, no. 81 (Jan – Mar 92), pp. 120 – 146. Bibl, il.

SALVADOR, BRAZIL

Borges, Dain Edward. Salvador's 1890s: Paternalism and Its Discontents. *Luso-Brazilian Review*, v. 30, no. 2 (Winter 93), pp. 47 – 57. Bibl.

Castro, Mary Garcia. Alquimia de categorias sociais na produção dos sujeitos políticos: gênero, raça e geração entre líderes do Sindicato de Trabalhadores Domésticos em Salvador. *Estudos Feministas*, v. 0, no. 0 (1992), pp. 57 – 73. Bibl.

Cunha, Olívia Maria Gomes da. Fazendo a "coisa certa": reggae, rastas e pentecostais em Salvador. *Revista Brasileira de Ciências Sociais*, v. 8, no. 23 (Oct 93), pp. 120 – 137. Bibl.

Levine, Robert M. The Singular Brazilian City of Salvador. *Luso-Brazilian Review*, v. 30, no. 2 (Winter 93), pp. 59 – 69. Bibl.

Nishida, Mieko. Manumission and Ethnicity in Urban Slavery: Salvador, Brazil, 1808 – 1888. *Hispanic American Historical Review*, v. 73, no. 3 (Aug 93), pp. 361 – 391. Bibl, tables, charts.

Pijning, Ernst. Conflicts in the Portuguese Colonial Administration: Trials and Errors of Luís Lopes Pegado e Serpa, "provedor-mor da fazenda real" in Salvador, Brazil, 1718 – 1721. *Colonial Latin American Historical Review*, v. 2, no. 4 (Fall 93), pp. 403 – 423. Bibl, maps.

Silva, Barbara-Christine Nentwig. Análise comparativa da posição de Salvador e do estado da Bahia no cenário nacional. *Revista Brasileira de Geografia*, v. 53, no. 4 (Oct – Dec 91), pp. 49 – 79. Bibl, tables, maps, charts.

Silva, Sylvio Carlos Bandeira de Mello e and Jaimeval Caetano de Souza. Análise da hierarquia urbana do estado da Bahia. *Revista Brasileira de Geografia*, v. 53, no. 1 (Jan – Mar 91), pp. 51 – 79. Bibl, tables, maps, charts.

SALVADOR, EL

See

El Salvador

SAMBA (DANCE)

Law and legislation

Augras, Monique. A ordem na desordem: a regulamentação do desfile das escolas de samba e a exigência de "motivos nacionais." *Revista Brasileira de Ciências Sociais*, v. 8, no. 21 (Feb 93), pp. 90 – 103. Bibl.

SAN ANDRÉS ISLAND, COLOMBIA

Clemente B., Isabel. Un caso de conflicto cultural en el Caribe: de la imposición al reconocimiento. *Nueva Sociedad*, no. 127 (Sept – Oct 93), pp. 32 – 45. Bibl.

SAN ANDRÉS SAJCABAJÁ, GUATEMALA

Piel, Jean. *Sajcabajá: muerte y resurrección de un pueblo de Guatemala, 1500 – 1970* reviewed by David McCreery. *Mesoamérica (USA)*, v. 13, no. 24 (Dec 92), pp. 458 – 459.

SAN BLAS, PANAMA

Rivera Domínguez, Juan Antonio. Relato de un viaje a San Blas. *Revista Cultural Lotería*, v. 50, no. 385 (Sept – Oct 91), pp. 88 – 92.

SAN CRISTÓBAL DE LAS CASAS, MEXICO

Aubry, Andrés. *San Cristóbal de las Casas: su historia urbana, demográfica y monumental, 1528 – 1990* reviewed by Sidney David Markman. *Mesoamérica (USA)*, v. 13, no. 23 (June 92), p. 183.

O'Brian, Robin. Un mercado indígena de artesanías en los altos de Chiapas: persistencia y cambio en las vidas de las vendedoras mayas. *Mesoamérica (USA)*, v. 13, no. 23 (June 92), pp. 79 – 84. Bibl.

Rus, Diane L. La vida y el trabajo en Ciudad Real: conversaciones con las "coletas." *Mesoamérica (USA)*, v. 13, no. 23 (June 92), pp. 113 – 133. Il.

SAN JOSÉ, COSTA RICA

Fernández González, Alvaro. Todo empezó en el '53: historia oral de un distrito liberacionista. *Revista de Historia (Costa Rica)*, no. 26 (July – Dec 92), pp. 97 – 142. Bibl.

SAN JUAN DE COLÓN, VENEZUELA

Castillo Lara, Lucas Guillermo. San Juan Bautista de Colón, de Ayacucho y Sucre, Almirante de Lejanías, mariscal de voluntades. *Boletín de la Academia Nacional de la Historia (Venezuela)*, v. 75, no. 300 (Oct – Dec 92), pp. 43 – 67. Bibl.

SAN LUIS POTOSÍ, MEXICO (CITY)

Calvillo, Tomás. Una paradoja en el corazón de México (Accompanied by an English translation). *Artes de México*, no. 18 (Winter 92), pp. 26 – 27. Il.

Cossío Lagarde, Francisco Javier. Notas de un arquitecto (Accompanied by an English translation). *Artes de México*, no. 18 (Winter 92), pp. 37 – 43. Il.

Espinosa y Pitman, Alejandro. Huellas de plata (Accompanied by an English translation). *Artes de México*, no. 18 (Winter 92), pp. 63 – 67. Il.

Meade, Joaquín. Breve descripción del templo de Carmen. *Artes de México*, no. 18 (Winter 92), pp. 53 – 61. Il.

Monroy, María Isabel. La minería: aventura entrañable (Accompanied by an English translation). *Artes de México*, no. 18 (Winter 92), pp. 71 – 77. Il.

Montejano y Aguiñaga, Rafael. Orígenes de San Luis Potosí (Accompanied by an English translation). *Artes de México*, no. 18 (Winter 92), pp. 29 – 35. Il, facs.

Morales Bocardo, Rafael. El Convento de San Francisco (Accompanied by an English translation). *Artes de México*, no. 18 (Winter 92), pp. 45 – 51. Il.

Bibliography

Bibliografía (to the articles on San Luis Potosí appearing in this issue). *Artes de México*, no. 18 (Winter 92), p. 81.

Maps

Sánchez, Joaquín Ruy. San Luis Potosí. *Artes de México*, no. 18 (Winter 92), pp. 78 – 79. Il.

SAN LUIS POTOSÍ, MEXICO (STATE)

Fernández Menéndez, Jorge. San Luis Potosí: ¿Lejos de la estabilidad? *Nexos*, v. 16, no. 184 (Apr 93), pp. 49 – 52.

SAN MARTÍN, JOSÉ DE

Acevedo, Edberto Oscar. San Martín y su ideario hacia 1810. *Investigaciones y Ensayos*, no. 41 (Jan – Dec 91), pp. 89 – 105. Bibl.

SAN SEBASTIÁN DE LOS REYES, VENEZUELA

Alvarez, Luis. Discurso pronunciado por el profesor Luis Alvarez con motivo de la presentación del libro *San Sebastián de los Reyes y sus ilustres próceres* en la Escuela de Música de San Sebastián de los Reyes, el 20 de enero de 1993. *Boletín de la Academia Nacional de la Historia (Venezuela)*, v. 76, no. 301 (Jan – Mar 93), pp. 51 – 54.

SÁNCHEZ, CECILIA

Criticism of specific works

Una disciplina de la distancia

Ossandón Buljevic, Carlos A. Una historia de la filosofía en Chile: modernidad e institucionalidad. *Estudios Sociales (Chile)*, no. 77 (July – Sept 93), pp. 9 – 15.

SÁNCHEZ, LUIS RAFAEL
Criticism and interpretation
Figueroa, Alvin Joaquín. *La prosa de Luis Rafael Sánchez: texto y contexto* reviewed by Guada Martí-Peña. *Hispamérica,* v. 22, no. 64 – 65 (Apr – Aug 93), pp. 192 – 193.
Criticism of specific works
En cuerpo de camisa
Cachan, Manuel. *En cuerpo de camisa* de Luis Rafael Sánchez: la antiliteratura alegórica del otro puertorriqueño. *Revista Iberoamericana,* v. 59, no. 162 – 163 (Jan – June 93), pp. 177 – 186. Bibl.
La guaracha del macho Camacho
Gelpí, Juan G. El clásico y la reescritura: "Insularismo" en las páginas de *La guaracha del macho Camacho. Revista Iberoamericana,* v. 59, no. 162 – 163 (Jan – June 93), pp. 55 – 71. Bibl.
La recién nacida sangre
Vázquez Arce, Carmen. Los desastres de la guerra: sobre la articulación de la ironía en los cuentos "La recién nacida sangre," de Luis Rafael Sánchez y "El momento divino de Caruso Llompart," de Félix Córdova Iturregui. *Revista Iberoamericana,* v. 59, no. 162 – 163 (Jan – June 93), pp. 187 – 201. Bibl.

SÁNCHEZ, TOMÁS
Blanc, Giulio V. Tomás Sánchez: obra reciente (Accompanied by the English original, translated by Magdalena Holguín). *Art Nexus,* no. 10 (Sept – Dec 93), pp. 51 – 53.

Mosquera, Gerardo. Tomás Sánchez: mística del paisaje (Accompanied by an English translation). *Art Nexus,* no. 10 (Sept – Dec 93), pp. 48 – 51. Il.

SÁNCHEZ MORALES, LUIS
Córdova, Gonzalo F. *Luis Sánchez Morales, servidor ejemplar* reviewed by Teresita Martínez-Vergne. *Hispanic American Historical Review,* v. 73, no. 2 (May 93), pp. 346 – 347.

SANDERLIN, GEORGE
Criticism of specific works
Witness: Writings of Bartolomé de las Casas
Himmerich y Valencia, Robert. Historical Objectivity and the Persistence of Fray Bartolomé de las Casas: A Commentary. *Colonial Latin American Historical Review,* v. 2, no. 1 (Winter 93), pp. 105 – 108. Il.

SANDINISTAS
See
Frente Sandinista de Liberación Nacional (Nicaragua)

SANDINO, AUGUSTO CÉSAR
Pailler, Claire. El reportaje del guerillero: una narrativa ambigua. *Studi di Letteratura Ispano-Americana,* v. 24 (1993), pp. 67 – 82. Tables.

SANDOVAL, ALONSO DE
Mattos, Tomás de. Alonso de Sandoval (1576 – 1652), jesuita de esclavos. *Cuadernos del CLAEH,* v. 17, no. 63 – 64 (Oct 92), pp. 141 – 147.

SANGUINETTI, FLORENTINO V.
Barrera, José F. El centenario de Florentino V. Sanguinetti. *Todo Es Historia,* v. 27, no. 312 (July 93), pp. 20 – 26. Il.

SANÍN, NOEMÍ
Sanín, Javier. Editorial: Noemí en el torbellino mundial. *Revista Javeriana,* v. 61, no. 594 (May 93), pp. 199 – 200.

SANITATION
See
Public health
Public utilities

SANTA ANNA, ANTONIO LÓPEZ DE
González Pedrero, Enrique. *País de un sólo hombre: el México de Santa Anna* reviewed by Luis Villoro (Review entitled "Santa Anna o la nación sin estado"). *Nexos,* v. 16, no. 190 (Oct 93), pp. 69 – 72.

— *País de un sólo hombre: el México de Santa Anna, vol. I; La ronda de los contrarios* reviewed by Rafael Rojas. *Vuelta,* v. 17, no. 204 (Nov 93), pp. 34 – 36.

— Santa Anna antes de Santa Anna (A chapter from the book *País de un sólo hombre: el México de Santa Anna). Vuelta,* v. 17, no. 198 (May 93), pp. 42 – 47. Bibl, tables.

SANTA CATARINA, BRAZIL
Meirinho, Jali. O governo federalista em Santa Catarina. *Hoy Es Historia,* v. 10, no. 60 (Nov – Dec 93), pp. 43 – 49. Bibl.

Silva, Maurício Corrêa da et al. Rentabilidade e risco no produção de leite numa região de Santa Catarina. *Revista de Economia e Sociologia Rural,* v. 30, no. 1 (Jan – Mar 92), pp. 63 – 81. Bibl, tables.

SANTA CRUZ, ANDRÉS DE
Anasagasti, Pedro de. El mariscal Andrés de Santa Cruz, gran pacificador. *Signo,* no. 38, Nueva época (Jan – Apr 93), pp. 95 – 104. Bibl.

Cayo Córdova, Percy. Santa Cruz y O'Higgins: dos efemérides de 1992. *Apuntes (Peru),* no. 31 (July – Dec 92), pp. 3 – 18.

SANTA CRUZ, NICOMEDES
Interviews
Maríñez, Pablo A. Entrevista con Nicomedes Santa Cruz, poeta afroamericano. *Cuadernos Americanos,* no. 40, Nueva época (July – Aug 93), pp. 110 – 124.

SANTA CRUZ Y MONTALVO, MERCEDES
See
Merlin, María de las Mercedes Santa Cruz y Montalvo

SANTA FE, ARGENTINA (PROVINCE)
Bonaudo, Marta and Elida Sonzogni. Redes parentales y facciones en la política santafesina, 1850 – 1900. *Siglo XIX: Revista,* no. 11, 2a época (Jan – June 92), pp. 74 – 110. Bibl.

Korzeniewicz, Roberto P. The Labor Politics of Radicalism: The Santa Fe Crisis of 1928. *Hispanic American Historical Review,* v. 73, no. 1 (Feb 93), pp. 1 – 32.

Pistone, J. Catalina. *Estudio histórico de las artesanías en Santa Fe* reviewed by Félix Coluccio. *Folklore Americano,* no. 52 (July – Dec 91), pp. 166 – 167.

Viglione de Arrastía, Hebe. Población e inmigración: producción historiográfica en la provincia de Santa Fe, Argentina. *Revista Interamericana de Bibliografía,* v. 42, no. 3 (1992), pp. 489 – 500. Bibl.

SANTA MARÍA, ROSA DE
Iwasaki Cauti, Fernando A. Mujeres al borde de la perfección: Rosa de Santa María y las alumbradas de Lima. *Hispanic American Historical Review,* v. 73, no. 4 (Nov 93), pp. 581 – 613. Bibl.

SANTA MARÍA, VICENTE DE
Torre Villar, Ernesto de la. Discurso del dr. Ernesto de la Torre Villar sobre fray Vicente de Santa María. *Archivo Ibero-Americano,* v. 52, no. 205 – 208 (Jan – Dec 92), pp. 849 – 856.

SANTA MARÍA GALLEGOS, LETICIA E.
Correspondence, reminiscences, etc.
Santa María Gallegos, Leticia E. De soledades. *Fem,* v. 17, no. 122 (Apr 93), pp. 44 – 45.

SANTAMARÍA, JUAN
Palmer, Steven. Getting to Know the Unknown Soldier: Offical Nationalism in Liberal Costa Rica, 1880 – 1900. *Journal of Latin American Studies,* v. 25, no. 1 (Feb 93), pp. 45 – 72. Bibl, maps.

SANTERÍA
See
Spiritualism

SANTIAGO DE CHILE

Daher, Antonio. Santiago estatal, Chile liberal. *Revista Interamericana de Planificación*, v. 26, no. 101 – 102 (Jan – June 93), pp. 43 – 62. Bibl, tables.

Fernández Koprich, Daniel. Vías elevadas para Santiago: ¿Una opción válida? (With commentaries by Jorge Heine, Oscar Figueroa, Juan de Dios Ortúzar, Víctor Basauri, and Daniel Fernández). *EURE*, v. 19, no. 56 (Mar 93), pp. 95 – 115. Charts.

Gutiérrez, Héctor and Dieter Wunder. Determinantes del precio de mercado de los terrenos en el área urbana de Santiago: comentario (on the article by Figueroa and Lever in *Cuadernos de Economía*, v. 29, no. 86). *Cuadernos de Economía (Chile)*, v. 30, no. 89 (Apr 93), pp. 131 – 138. Bibl, tables.

Heine, Jorge. En defensa de Santiago: la ciudad que queremos. *EURE*, v. 19, no. 56 (Mar 93), pp. 127 – 128.

Hohmann B., Claudio. La encrucijada del transporte urbano de Santiago. *EURE*, v. 19, no. 56 (Mar 93), pp. 9 – 27.

Opazo, José Luis et al. El descontrol del sistema de buses de Santiago: síntesis de un diagnóstico técnico – institucional. *EURE*, v. 19, no. 56 (Mar 93), pp. 79 – 91. Bibl, tables.

Ortúzar S., Juan de Dios. Congestión y transporte público: una relación mal entendida. *EURE*, v. 19, no. 56 (Mar 93), pp. 124 – 126. Tables.

Zapata, Sonia. La mendicidad y su mundo. *Estudios Sociales (Chile)*, no. 76 (Apr – June 93), pp. 67 – 94. Bibl.

Sources

Actas del Cabildo de Santiago, 1795 – 1809 reviewed by Fernando Campos Harriet. *Boletín de la Academia Chilena de la Historia*, v. 58 – 59, no. 102 (1991 – 1992), pp. 531 – 533.

SANTIAGO DEL ESTERO, ARGENTINA (PROVINCE)

Avila, Elvio Arnoldo. *Cómo habla el santiagueño . . . y el argentino: diccionario de voces usuales que el 'Diccionario oficial' no registra; adhesión al V centenario del descubrimiento de América* reviewed by Félix Coluccio. *Folklore Americano*, no. 52 (July – Dec 91), pp. 167 – 168.

Forni, Floreal H. et al. Empleo, estrategias de vida y reproducción: hogares rurales en Santiago del Estero (Review). *La Educación (USA)*, v. 37, no. 114 (1993), p. 156.

Gramajo de Martínez Moreno, Amalia and Hugo N. Martínez Moreno. *Rasgos del folklore de Santiago del Estero* reviewed by Félix Coluccio. *Folklore Americano*, no. 53 (Jan – June 92), pp. 179 – 180.

SANTISTEVAN, MIGUEL DE

Correspondence, reminiscences, etc.

Santistevan, Miguel de. *Mil leguas por América: de Lima a Caracas, 1740 – 1741; diario de don Miguel de Santisteban* edited by David J. Robinson. Reviewed by Judith E. Villamarin. *Hispanic American Historical Review*, v. 73, no. 4 (Nov 93), pp. 701 – 702.

SANTO DOMINGO, DOMINICAN REPUBLIC

Douzant Rosenfeld, Denise and Laura Faxas. Equipements urbains et services de remplacement: le cas de Santo Domingo, République Dominicaine. *Tiers Monde*, v. 34, no. 133 (Jan – Mar 93), pp. 139 – 151.

Villamán P., Marcos J. Religión y pobreza: una aproximación a los nuevos movimientos religiosos. *Estudios Sociales (Dominican Republic)*, v. 26, no. 94 (Oct – Dec 93), pp. 75 – 96. Bibl, tables.

SANTOS-DUMONT, ALBERTO

Page, Joseph A. Brazil's Daredevil of the Air. *Américas*, v. 45, no. 2 (Mar – Apr 93), pp. 6 – 13. Il.

SANZ DE SANTAMARÍA, CARLOS

Acuerdo nº 01 de 1993. *Boletín de Historia y Antigüedades*, v. 80, no. 781 (Apr – June 93), pp. 267 – 268. Il.

Rivadeneira Vargas, Antonio José. El pensamiento integrador de Carlos Sanz de Santamaría. *Boletín de Historia y Antigüedades*, v. 79, no. 779 (Oct – Dec 92), pp. 953 – 973. Bibl.

Obituaries

Arango Londoño, Gilberto. Carlos Sanz de Santamaría, un colombiano de múltiples virtudes. *Boletín de Historia y Antigüedades*, v. 80, no. 781 (Apr – June 93), pp. 283 – 284.

Arciniegas, Germán. El que no fue presidente. *Boletín de Historia y Antigüedades*, v. 80, no. 781 (Apr – June 93), pp. 277 – 278.

— Señora muerte que se va llevando. *Boletín de Historia y Antigüedades*, v. 80, no. 781 (Apr – June 93), pp. 273 – 275.

Duque Escobar, Iván. Carlos Sanz de Santamaría. *Boletín de Historia y Antigüedades*, v. 80, no. 781 (Apr – June 93), pp. 281 – 282.

Gómez Latorre, Armando. Réquiem por cuatro académicos. *Boletín de Historia y Antigüedades*, v. 80, no. 781 (Apr – June 93), pp. 339 – 340.

López Michelsen, Alfonso. El gran ciudadano Carlos Sanz de Santamaría. *Boletín de Historia y Antigüedades*, v. 80, no. 781 (Apr – June 93), pp. 269 – 272.

Mallarino Botero, Gonzalo. In memoriam C. S. de S. *Boletín de Historia y Antigüedades*, v. 80, no. 781 (Apr – June 93), pp. 279 – 280.

SÃO LUÍS, BRAZIL

Linger, Daniel Touro. *Dangerous Encounters: Meanings of Violence in a Brazilian City* reviewed by David Cleary. *Bulletin of Latin American Research*, v. 12, no. 3 (Sept 93), pp. 344 – 345.

SÃO PAULO, BRAZIL (CITY)

Araújo, Maria José de Oliveira. Aborto legal no hospital do Jabaquara. *Estudos Feministas*, v. 1, no. 2 (1993), pp. 424 – 428.

Cacciamali, Maria Cristina and Paulo Springer de Freitas. Do capital humano ao salário-eficiência: uma aplicação para analisar os diferenciais de salários em cinco ramos manufatureiros da grande São Paulo. *Pesquisa e Planejamento Econômico*, v. 22, no. 2 (Aug 92), pp. 343 – 367. Bibl, tables.

Costa, Marcia Regina da. "Skinheads": carecas do subúrbio. *Vozes*, v. 87, no. 2 (Mar – Apr 93), pp. 2 – 10.

Font, Mauricio A. City and the Countryside in the Onset of Brazilian Industrialization. *Studies in Comparative International Development*, v. 27, no. 3 (Fall 92), pp. 26 – 56. Bibl, tables, charts.

Glezer, Raquel. São Paulo e a elite letrada brasileira no século XIX. *Siglo XIX: Revista*, no. 11, 2a época (Jan – June 92), pp. 149 – 160. Bibl.

Keinert, Tania Margarete Mezzomo. Reforma administrativa nos anos '90: o caso da prefeitura municipal de São Paulo. *RAE; Revista de Administração de Empresas*, v. 33, no. 4 (July – Aug 93), pp. 66 – 81. Tables, maps, charts.

Moraes, José Geraldo Vinci de. Sonoridades urbanas. *Vozes*, v. 87, no. 3 (May – June 93), pp. 48 – 58. Il.

Page, Joseph A. A Leap for Life. *Américas*, v. 45, no. 4 (July – Aug 93), pp. 34 – 41. Il.

Prandi, José Reginaldo. *Os candomblés de São Paulo: a velha magia na metrópole nova* reviewed by Luciana Ferreira Moura Mendonça. *Revista de Antropologia (Brazil)*, v. 34 (1991), pp. 228 – 230.

Rago, Margareth. Prazer e sociabilidade no mundo da prostituição em São Paulo, 1890 – 1930. *Luso-Brazilian Review*, v. 30, no. 1 (Summer 93), pp. 35 – 46. Bibl.

— Os prazeres da noite: prostituição e códigos da sexualidade feminina em São Paulo, 1890 – 1930 reviewed by Sandra Lauderdale Graham (Review entitled "Dangerous Fantasies: The Altered Vocabulary of Commercial Sex"). *Luso-Brazilian Review*, v. 30, no. 1 (Summer 93), pp. 133 – 139.

Sevcenko, Nicolau. *Orfeu extático na metrópole: São Paulo; sociedade e cultura nos frementes anos '20* reviewed by Elias Thomé Saliba (Review entitled "Cultura modernista em São Paulo"). *Estudos Históricos*, v. 6, no. 11 (Jan – June 93), pp. 128 – 132.

— Orfeu extático na metrópole: São Paulo; sociedade e cultura nos frementes anos '20 (Review). *Vozes*, v. 87, no. 1 (Jan – Feb 93), pp. 102 – 104.

— Transformações da linguagem e advento da cultura modernista no Brasil (Translated by Dora Rocha). *Estudos Históricos*, v. 6, no. 11 (Jan – June 93), pp. 78 – 88.

SÃO PAULO, BRAZIL (STATE)

Andrews, George Reid. *Blacks and Whites in São Paulo, Brazil, 1888 – 1988* reviewed by Michael Hanchard. *The Americas*, v. 50, no. 1 (July 93), pp. 134 – 136.

— *Blacks and Whites in São Paulo, Brazil, 1888 – 1988* reviewed by Joseph P. Love. *Hispanic American Historical Review*, v. 73, no. 1 (Feb 93), pp. 167 – 168.

— *Blacks and Whites in São Paulo, Brazil, 1888 – 1988* reviewed by Robert M. Levine. *Revista Interamericana de Bibliografía*, v. 42, no. 2 (1992), p. 282.

Azzoni, Carlos Roberto and João Yo Isai. Custo da proteção de áreas com interesse ambiental no estado de São Paulo. *Estudos Econômicos*, v. 22, no. 2 (May – Aug 92), pp. 253 – 271. Bibl, tables, charts.

Bellotto, Manoel Lelo. A imigração espanhola no Brasil: estado do fluxo migratório para o estado de São Paulo, 1931 – 1936. *Estudios Interdisciplinarios de América Latina y el Caribe*, v. 3, no. 2 (July – Dec 92), pp. 59 – 73. Bibl, tables.

Cunha, José Marcos Pinto de. Carácterístics de la movilidad intrametropolitana en el estado de São Paulo, Brasil, 1970 – 1980. *Estudios Demográficos y Urbanos*, v. 7, no. 2 – 3 (May – Dec 92), pp. 587 – 602. Bibl, tables, maps.

Font, Mauricio A. City and the Countryside in the Onset of Brazilian Industrialization. *Studies in Comparative International Development*, v. 27, no. 3 (Fall 92), pp. 26 – 56. Bibl, tables, charts.

French, John David. *The Brazilian Workers' ABC: Class Conflict and Alliances in Modern São Paulo* reviewed by Peter Ranis. *Hispanic American Historical Review*, v. 73, no. 4 (Nov 93), pp. 707 – 708.

Gomes, Eustáquio. *Os rapazes d'"a Onda" e outros rapazes* reviewed by Elias Thomé Saliba. *Vozes*, v. 86, no. 6 (Nov – Dec 92), pp. 101 – 103.

Guimarães, Paulo César Vaz. Instrumentos econômicos para gerenciamento ambiental: a cobrança pelo uso da água no estado de São Paulo. *RAE; Revista de Administração de Empresas*, v. 33, no. 5 (Sept – Oct 93), pp. 88 – 97.

Luna, Francisco Vidal. Características demográficas dos escravos de São Paulo, 1777 – 1829. *Estudos Econômicos*, v. 22, no. 3 (Sept – Dec 92), pp. 443 – 483. Bibl, tables.

Machado, Rosa Maria de Oliveira and Ana Lúcia Magyar. A regulamentação da lei de recursos hídricos do estado de São Paulo: desafios e perspectivas. *RAE; Revista de Administração de Empresas*, v. 33, no. 6 (Nov – Dec 93), pp. 42 – 47. Bibl.

Marques, Pedro V. Integração vertical da avicultura de corte no estado de São Paulo. *Revista de Economia e Sociologia Rural*, v. 30, no. 3 (July – Sept 92), pp. 189 – 202. Bibl, tables.

Nazzari, Muriel. *Disappearance of the Dowry: Women, Families, and Social Change in São Paulo, Brazil, 1600 – 1900* reviewed by Susan M. Socolow. *The Americas*, v. 49, no. 3 (Jan 93), pp. 414 – 415.

— *Disappearance of the Dowry: Women, Families, and Social Change in São Paulo, Brazil, 1600 – 1900* reviewed by John E. Kicza. *Colonial Latin American Review*, v. 2, no. 1 – 2 (1993), pp. 308 – 311.

— *Disappearance of the Dowry: Women, Families, and Social Change in São Paulo, Brazil, 1600 – 1900* reviewed by Sandra Lauderdale Graham. *Journal of Latin American Studies*, v. 25, no. 1 (Feb 93), pp. 193 – 194.

— *Disappearance of the Dowry: Women, Families, and Social Change in São Paulo, Brazil, 1600 – 1900* reviewed by Dain Borges. *Luso-Brazilian Review*, v. 30, no. 1 (Summer 93), pp. 141 – 142.

Oliveira, Maria Coleta F. A. de. Condición femenina y alternativas de organización doméstica: las mujeres sin pareja en São Paulo. *Estudios Demográficos y Urbanos*, v. 7, no. 2 – 3 (May – Dec 92), pp. 511 – 537. Bibl, tables, charts.

Velloso, Mônica Pimenta. A brasilidade verde – amarela: nacionalismo e regionalismo paulista. *Estudos Históricos*, v. 6, no. 11 (Jan – June 93), pp. 89 – 112. Bibl.

Versiani, Flávio Rabelo. Imigrantes, trabalho qualificado e industrialização: Rio e São Paulo no início do século. *Revista de Economia Política (Brazil)*, v. 13, no. 4 (Oct – Dec 93), pp. 77 – 96. Bibl, tables.

SAPIENTIA (PERIODICAL)

Indexes

Indice general, nros. 1/1946 – 186/1992, I: Editoriales y artículos. *Sapientia*, v. 48, no. 187 – 188 (Jan – June 93), Issue.

SARDUY, SEVERO

Criticism and interpretation

Kushigian, Julia A. *Orientalism in the Hispanic Tradition: In Dialogue with Borges, Paz, and Sarduy* reviewed by John Incledon. *Hispania (USA)*, v. 76, no. 3 (Sept 93), pp. 483 – 484.

Obituaries

Bianciotti, Héctor. El vértigo de los carnavales (Translated by Aurelio Asiaín). *Vuelta*, v. 17, no. 201 (Aug 93), pp. 28 – 29.

Cabrera Infante, Guillermo. Sobre una tumba una rumba. *Vuelta*, v. 17, no. 201 (Aug 93), pp. 22 – 23.

Edwards, Jorge. Una vida cubana. *Vuelta*, v. 17, no. 201 (Aug 93), pp. 26 – 27.

Goytisolo, Juan. Severo Sarduy: "in memoriam." *Vuelta*, v. 17, no. 201 (Aug 93), pp. 24 – 25.

— Si no existiera Sarduy. *Vuelta*, v. 17, no. 201 (Aug 93), p. 25.

Haubrich, Walter. Un vate de la noche tropical con motivo del fallecimiento del escritor cubano Severo Sarduy (Translated by José Luis Gómez y Patiño). *Humboldt*, no. 110 (1993), p. 98. Il.

Lizalde, Eduardo. Severo Sarduy (1937 – 1993). *Vuelta*, v. 17, no. 201 (Aug 93), p. 30.

Milán, Eduardo. Sarduy. *Vuelta*, v. 17, no. 201 (Aug 93), pp. 31 – 32.

SARMIENTO, DOMINGO FAUSTINO

Biography

Jaksic, Ivan. Sarmiento y la prensa chilena del siglo XIX. *Historia (Chile)*, no. 26 (1991 – 1992), pp. 117 – 144. Bibl.

Criticism and interpretation

Cúneo, Dardo. Sarmiento y Unamuno: Sarmiento, el hombre de carne y hueso de Unamuno. *Hoy Es Historia*, v. 10, no. 56 (Mar – Apr 93), pp. 75 – 86. Il.

Rodríguez Pérsico, Adriana C. *Un huracán llamado progreso: utopía y autobiografía en Sarmiento y Alberdi* reviewed by Carlos E. Paldao. *La Educación (USA)*, v. 37, no. 115 (1993), pp. 435 – 437.

— Sarmiento y Alberdi: una práctica legitimante. *La Educación (USA)*, v. 36, no. 111 – 113 (1992), pp. 177 – 192. Bibl.

Criticism of specific works

Facundo

Concha, Jaime. En el umbral del *Facundo*. *Hispamérica*, v. 21, no. 62 (Aug 92), pp. 21 – 31. Bibl.

Garrels, Elizabeth. Traducir a América: Sarmiento y el proyecto de una literatura nacional. *Revista de Crítica Literaria Latinoamericana*, v. 19, no. 38 (July – Dec 93), pp. 269 – 278. Bibl.

Quintero Herencia, Juan Carlos. Los poetas en La Pampa o las "cantidades poéticas" en el *Facundo*. *Hispamérica*, v. 21, no. 62 (Aug 92), pp. 33 – 52.

SATELLITES

See

Photography, Aerial

SATIRE

Caballero Wangüemert, María del Milagro. Discurso histórico y carnavalización de la historia: "El juramento" de René Marqués. *Revista Iberoamericana*, v. 59, no. 162 – 163 (Jan – June 93), pp. 145 – 156. Bibl.

Costigan, Lúcia Helena Santiago. *A sátira e o intelectual criollo na colônia: Gregório de Matos e Juan del Valle y Caviedes* reviewed by Pedro Carlos L. Fonseca. *Colonial Latin American Review*, v. 2, no. 1 – 2 (1993), pp. 300 – 302.

Febles, Jorge M. En torno al personaje degradado en *La montaña rusa*: vigencia del doble paródico dentro de un espacio carnavalesco. *The Americas Review*, v. 19, no. 3 – 4 (Winter 91), pp. 101 – 115. Bibl.

García Sánchez, Franklin B. El dionisismo paródico – grotesco de *La loma del ángel* de Reinaldo Arenas. *Revista Canadiense de Estudios Hispánicos*, v. 17, no. 2 (Winter 93), pp. 271 – 279. Bibl.

Hernández, Guillermo E. *Chicano Satire: A Study in Literary Culture* reviewed by Chuck Tatum (Review entitled "A New Standard for Chicano Literary Scholarship"). *Bilingual Review/Revista Bilingüe*, v. 18, no. 1 (Jan – Apr 93), pp. 64 – 74.

Rodríguez H., María Elia. Intertextualidad y dialogismo: el funcionamiento paródico del texto poético; análisis de dos series poéticas del *Canto general*. *Káñina*, v. 16, no. 1 (Jan – June 92), pp. 61 – 67.

Rodríguez-Vergara, Isabel. *El mundo satírico de Gabriel García Márquez* reviewed by Francisca Noguerol Jiménez. *Anuario de Estudios Americanos*, v. 49, Suppl. 1 (1992), pp. 261 – 262.

Romano, Eduardo. Parodia televisiva y sobre otros géneros discursivos populares. *Cuadernos Hispanoamericanos*, no. 517 – 519 (July – Sept 93), pp. 323 – 335. Bibl.

Schmidt, Heide. La risa: etapas en la narrativa femenina en México y Alemania; una aproximación. *Escritura (Venezuela)*, v. 16, no. 31 – 32 (Jan – Dec 91), pp. 247 – 257. Bibl.

Schmidt, Samuel. Humor y política en México. *Revista Mexicana de Sociología*, v. 54, no. 1 (Jan – Mar 92), pp. 225 – 250. Bibl.

Sklodowska, Elzbieta. *La parodia en la nueva novela hispanoamericana, 1960 – 1985* reviewed by Isabel Rodríguez-Vergara. *La Educación (USA)*, v. 36, no. 111 – 113 (1992), pp. 304 – 305.

— *La parodia en la nueva novela hispanoamericana, 1960 – 1985* reviewed by George R. McMurray. *Hispania (USA)*, v. 76, no. 2 (May 93), pp. 293 – 294.

— *La parodia en la nueva novela hispanoamericana, 1960 – 1985* reviewed by Donald L. Shaw. *Hispanic Review*, v. 61, no. 2 (Spring 93), pp. 316 – 317.

— *La parodia en la nueva novela hispanoamericana, 1960 – 1985* reviewed by Norman Cheadle. *Revista Canadiense de Estudios Hispánicos*, v. 17, no. 2 (Winter 93), pp. 413 – 414.

— *La parodia en la nueva novela hispanoamericana, 1960 – 1985* reviewed by Brian Evenson. *World Literature Today*, v. 67, no. 1 (Winter 93), p. 161.

Wanderley Pinho, José. Humoristas no parlamento do império: notas esparsas. *Revista do Instituto Histórico e Geográfico Brasileiro*, no. 372 (July – Sept 91), pp. 908 – 929.

SAVING AND INVESTMENT

See also
Banks and banking
Capital
Capital investments
Pension trusts
Stock exchange

Colombia

Sowell, David Lee. La Caja de Ahorros de Bogotá, 1846 – 1865: Artisans, Credit, Development, and Savings in Early National Colombia. *Hispanic American Historical Review*, v. 73, no. 4 (Nov 93), pp. 615 – 638. Bibl, tables.

Latin America
Mathematical models

Cardoso, Eliana Anastasia. Private Investment in Latin America. *Economic Development and Cultural Change*, v. 41, no. 4 (July 93), pp. 833 – 848. Bibl, tables, charts.

Ozler, Sule and Dani Rodrik. Los choques externos, la política y la inversión privada: algo de teoría y evidencia empírica. *El Trimestre Económico*, v. 59, Special issue (Dec 92), pp. 187 – 212. Bibl, tables, charts.

Mexico
Mathematical models

Trigueros Legarreta, Ignacio. Programas de estabilización sin credibilidad e intermediación financiera. *El Trimestre Económico*, v. 59, no. 236 (Oct – Dec 92), pp. 641 – 655. Bibl, tables, charts.

Trinidad and Tobago
Mathematical models

Watson, Patrick Kent. Savings, the Rate of Interest, and Growth in a Small Open Economy: The Trinidad and Tobago Experience. *Social and Economic Studies*, v. 41, no. 4 (Dec 92), pp. 1 – 23. Tables, charts.

SAVOIANO, VALERIO FULVIO

Soria, Giuliano Oreste. Echi della conquista nella Torino del '600: Valerio Fulvio Savoiano e Bartolomé de Las Casas. *Quaderni Ibero-Americani*, no. 72 (Dec 92), pp. 721 – 731. Bibl.

SCANDINAVIA

See also
Sweden

Blomström, Magnus and Patricio Meller, eds. *Trayectorias divergentes* reviewed by Göran G. Lindahl (Review entitled "Commentary and Debate"). *Ibero Americana (Sweden)*, v. 22, no. 2 (Dec 92), pp. 67 – 76.

— *Trayectorias divergentes: comparación de un siglo de desarrollo económico latinoamericano y escandinavo* reviewed by Sérgio Savino Portugal. *Pesquisa e Planejamento Econômico*, v. 22, no. 1 (Apr 92), pp. 189 – 196.

SCARABÔTOLO, HÉLIO ANTÔNIO
Addresses, essays, lectures

Scarabôtolo, Hélio Antônio. Saudação ao honorário Marcos Castrioto de Azambuja (Speech given in honor of Marcos Azambuja's induction into the Instituto Histórico e Geográfico Brasileiro). *Revista do Instituto Histórico e Geográfico Brasileiro*, no. 371 (Apr – June 91), pp. 489 – 491.

SCHADEN, EGON
Obituaries

Carvalho, Fernando. Egon Schaden: Aavanimondyiá (1913 – 1991). *Revista de Antropologia (Brazil)*, v. 34 (1991), pp. 239 – 240.

SCHELE, LINDA
Criticism of specific works
A Forest of Kings

Freidel, David A. and Linda Schele. *Un bosque de reyes*: la historia no narrada de los antiguos mayas. *La Palabra y el Hombre*, no. 82 (Apr – June 92), pp. 79 – 94. Tables.

Interviews

Rodríguez Ochoa, Patricia. Del arte a la escritura, de la visión al desciframiento. *Vuelta*, v. 17, no. 203 (Oct 93), pp. 23 – 24. Il.

SCHENDEL, MIRA

Iriarte, María Elvira. Mira Schendel (Accompanied by an English translation). *Art Nexus*, no. 8 (Apr – June 93), pp. 83 – 87. Il.

SCHMIDEL, ULRICH

Padula Perkins, Jorge Eduardo. Ulrico Schmidel: un periodismo sin periódico. *Todo Es Historia*, v. 27, no. 313 (Aug 93), pp. 88 – 91. Bibl, il.

SCHOOL MANAGEMENT AND ORGANIZATION

See also

Subdivision *Administration* under *Universities and colleges*

Developing countries

Levin, Henry M. and Marlaine E. Lockheed, eds. *Effective Schools in Developing Countries* reviewed by Maria Valéria Junho Pena. *La Educación (USA)*, v. 37, no. 115 (1993), pp. 437 – 439.

Latin America

Ezpeleta, Justa and Alfredo Furlan, eds. *La gestión pedagógica en la escuela* reviewed by Luis M. Flores. *La Educación (USA)*, v. 37, no. 115 (1993), p. 420.

Mexico

Martin, Christopher James. The "Shadow Economy" of Local School Management in Contemporary West Mexico. *Bulletin of Latin American Research*, v. 12, no. 2 (May 93), pp. 171 – 188. Bibl.

Venezuela

Bastidas González, Pedro José and Damaris van der Dys. Programa de adaptación del Sistema de Información de la Planta Física Educativa (SIPFE) a los objetivos de reducción de la vulnerabilidad a las amenazas naturales en las escuelas. *La Educación (USA)*, v. 37, no. 115 (1993), pp. 365 – 377. Tables.

SCHROEDER, ALBERT H.

Obituaries

Sánchez, Joseph P. In Memoriam: Albert H. Schroeder (1914 – 1993). *Colonial Latin American Historical Review*, v. 2, no. 4 (Fall 93), pp. 401 – 402. Il.

SCHULZ SOLARI, OSCAR AGUSTÍN ALEJANDRO

See

Solar, Xul

SCHUNK, ALBERTO

Rosso, Walter Betbeder. Alberto Schunk: A Canvas for Contemplation (Translated by Kathleen Forrester). *Américas*, v. 45, no. 4 (July – Aug 93), pp. 54 – 55. Il.

SCHWARTZ, PERLA

Criticism and interpretation

Gartner, Bruce S. and Anita M. Hart. A Space of One's Own: Mexican Poets Kyra Galván and Perla Schwartz. *Confluencia*, v. 8, no. 1 (Fall 92), pp. 79 – 89. Bibl.

SCHWARZ, MAURICIO-JOSÉ

Criticism and interpretation

Trujillo Muñoz, Gabriel. La ciencia ficción que llegó quedarse. *La Palabra y el Hombre*, no. 84 (Oct – Dec 92), pp. 303 – 304.

SCIENCE

See also

Names of specific sciences

Methodology

López-Ocón Cabrera, Leoncio. Texto y contexto en la obra de Jiménez de la Espada: un modelo interpretativo. *Revista de Indias*, v. 52, no. 195 – 196 (May – Dec 92), pp. 611 – 625. Bibl, charts.

Argentina

Study and teaching

Barrancos, Dora. La modernidad redentora: difusión de las ciencias entre los trabajadores de Buenos Aires, 1890 – 1920. *Siglo XIX: Revista*, no. 12, 2a época (July – Dec 92), pp. 5 – 21. Bibl, tables.

Brazil

Schwartzman, Simon. *A Space for Science: The Development of the Scientific Community in Brazil* reviewed by Marcos Cueto. *The Americas*, v. 49, no. 3 (Jan 93), pp. 418 – 419.

— *A Space for Science: The Development of the Scientific Community in Brazil* reviewed by Pedro Turina U. *La Educación (USA)*, v. 37, no. 114 (1993), p. 171.

Societies, etc.

44ª reunião anual do SBPC. *Vozes*, v. 86, no. 4 (July – Aug 92), pp. 82 – 84.

Study and teaching

Oliveira, Renato José de. Análise epistemológica da visão de ciência dos professores de química e física do município do Rio de Janeiro. *Revista Brasileira de Estudos Pedagógicos*, v. 72, no. 172 (Sept – Dec 91), pp. 335 – 355. Bibl, tables.

Colombia

Quintero Esquivel, Jorge Eliécer. Ergotismo, ilustración y utilitarismo en Colombia: siglos XVIII y XIX. *Islas*, no. 96 (May – Aug 90), pp. 53 – 66. Bibl, tables, charts.

Costa Rica

Camacho Naranjo, Luis A. Tradición, modernidad y tendencias contemporáneas en la cultura científica en Costa Rica. *Cuadernos Americanos*, no. 38, Nueva época (Mar – Apr 93), pp. 121 – 134. Bibl.

Cuba

García Capote, Emilio and Tirso W. Sáenz. El desarrollo de la ciencia y la tecnología en Cuba: algunas cuestiones actuales. *Interciencia*, v. 18, no. 6 (Nov – Dec 93), pp. 289 – 294. Bibl, tables.

Europe

Planchart, Alfredo. Bases científicas del descubrimiento de América. *Boletín de la Academia Nacional de la Historia (Venezuela)*, v. 75, no. 297 (Jan – Mar 92), pp. 97 – 109. Bibl.

Latin America

Internoticias/Internews/Internotícias. *Interciencia*, v. 18 (1993), All issues.

Saldaña, Juan José. Nuevas tendencias en la historia latinoamericana de las ciencias. *Cuadernos Americanos*, no. 38, Nueva época (Mar – Apr 93), pp. 69 – 91. Bibl.

Congresses

Castillo Martos, Manuel. III Congreso Latinoamericano de Historia de la Ciencia y la Tecnología. *Anuario de Estudios Americanos*, v. 49, Suppl. 1 (1992), pp. 196 – 201.

Mexico

Aceves, Patricia. La ilustración novohispana en el área farmacéutica, química y metalúrgica. *Cuadernos Americanos*, no. 38, Nueva época (Mar – Apr 93), pp. 92 – 120. Bibl.

Chimal, Carlos. Mirar en el jardín mexicano: paisaje de la ciencia; entrevista con Elías Trabulse. *Vuelta*, v. 17, no. 194 (Jan 93), pp. 50 – 52.

Pérez Tamayo, Ruy. *Ciencia, paciencia y conciencia* reviewed by Antonia González Barranco. *Revista Mexicana de Ciencias Políticas y Sociales*, v. 38, Nueva época, no. 151 (Jan – Mar 93), pp. 217 – 219.

Peru

Cueto, Marcos. *Excelencia científica en la periferia: actividades científicas e investigaciones biomédicas en el Perú, 1890 – 1950* reviewed by Ricardo Portocarrero Grados. *Historia y Cultura (Peru)*, no. 20 (1990), pp. 373 – 377.

Saint-Domingue

McClellan, James Edward, III. *Colonialism and Science: Saint Domingue in the Old Regime* reviewed by Michiel Baud. *European Review of Latin American and Caribbean Studies*, no. 53 (Dec 92), pp. 118 – 119.

SCIENCE AND CIVILIZATION

Mathurin B., José Antonio. Filosofía, ciencia y tecnología. *Revista Cultural Lotería*, v. 50, no. 384 (July – Aug 91), pp. 32 – 37.

Congresses

Revolución científico – técnica, educación y área laboral (A seminar organized by the Fundación de Investigaciones Sociales y Políticas (FISYP) de Argentina and summarized by Dora Douthat). *Realidad Económica*, no. 119 (Oct – Nov 93), pp. 134 – 138.

SCIENCE AND STATE
Brazil
Sobral, Fernanda Antônia da Fonseca. La politique scientifique et technologique du Brésil et la conception du développement national. *Cahiers des Amériques Latines*, no. 13 (1992), pp. 163 – 170. Bibl, tables.

Latin America
Malo, Salvador. Las nuevas políticas y las estrategias en materia de ciencia y tecnología. *Revista Latinoamericana de Estudios Educativos*, v. 22, no. 3 (July – Sept 92), pp. 133 – 139.

Mexico
Lomnitz, Cinna. La ciencia al paso. *Nexos*, v. 16, no. 187 (July 93), pp. 24 – 26.

United States
Lomnitz, Cinna. La ciencia al paso. *Nexos*, v. 16, no. 187 (July 93), pp. 24 – 26.

SCIENCE FICTION
Carvalho-Neto, Paulo de. Folklore extraterrestre II: los caminos y las bases. *Folklore Americano*, no. 53 (Jan – June 92), pp. 11 – 36. Bibl.

Trujillo Muñoz, Gabriel. La ciencia ficción que llegó quedarse. *La Palabra y el Hombre*, no. 84 (Oct – Dec 92), pp. 303 – 304.

SCIENTIFIC EXPEDITIONS
Bibliography
Sáiz, Blanca. *Bibliografía sobre Alejandro Malaspina y acerca de la expedición Malaspina y de los marinos y científicos que en ella participaron* reviewed by Oldrich Kaspar (Review translated by Eva Máuková). *Anuario de Estudios Americanos*, v. 50, no. 1 (1993), p. 325.

Colombia
Rey Fajardo, José del. La presencia científica de la Universidad Javeriana en la Orinoquia. *Boletín de Historia y Antigüedades*, v. 79, no. 779 (Oct – Dec 92), pp. 925 – 952. Bibl.

Latin America
González Pizarro, José Antonio. Imagen e impresiones de América de los integrantes de la armada y de la Comisión de Naturalistas Españoles, 1862 – 1866. *Jahrbuch für Geschichte von Staat, Wirtschaft und Gesellschaft Lateinamerikas*, v. 29 (1992), pp. 279 – 307. Bibl.

Mexico
Bustamante García, Jesús. De la naturaleza y los naturales americanos en el siglo XVI: algunas cuestiones críticas sobre la obra de Francisco Hernández. *Revista de Indias*, v. 52, no. 195 – 196 (May – Dec 92), pp. 297 – 328. Bibl.

Venezuela
Texera Arnal, Yolanda. *La exploración botánica en Venezuela, 1754 – 1950* reviewed by Stuart McCook. *Interciencia*, v. 18, no. 6 (Nov – Dec 93), pp. 328 – 329.

SCIENTIFIC RESEARCH
Argentina
Foreign influences
Montserrat, Marcelo. La influencia italiana en el desarrollo científico argentino. *Todo Es Historia*, v. 26, no. 305 (Dec 92), pp. 8 – 19. Bibl, il.

Brazil
Cagnin, Maria Aparecida H. The State of Scientific Research in Chemistry: A View from the Brazilian Community. *Interciencia*, v. 18, no. 3 (May – June 93), pp. 146 – 154. Bibl, tables.

Chile
Allende, Jorge E. Presentación del libro *La investigación universitaria en Chile: reflexiones críticas* de Manuel Krauskopf. *Estudios Sociales (Chile)*, no. 75 (Jan – Mar 93), pp. 231 – 238.

Salinas, Augusto. La primera década de FONDECYT: un balance positivo. *Estudios Sociales (Chile)*, no. 74 (Oct – Dec 92), pp. 177 – 189. Bibl.

Mexico
Peña, Antonio. La ciencia y los salarios. *Nexos*, v. 16, no. 190 (Oct 93), pp. 12 – 16.

Uruguay
Gliksberg, Isaac. El laboratorio tecnológico de Uruguay: entrevista a su presidente ing. Ruperto M. Long. *Interciencia*, v. 18, no. 6 (Nov – Dec 93), pp. 314 – 316. Il.

Venezuela
Awards
Freites, Yajaira. Ciencia y honor en Venezuela: concepciones y cambios. *Cuadernos Americanos*, no. 38, Nueva época (Mar – Apr 93), pp. 135 – 154. Bibl, tables.

SCORZA, MANUEL
Bibliography
Escorza, Cecilia. Suplemento a la bibliografía sobre Manuel Scorza. *Revista de Crítica Literaria Latinoamericana*, v. 19, no. 37 (Jan – June 93), pp. 361 – 364.

Schmidt, Friedhelm. Bibliografía de y sobre Manuel Scorza: nuevas aportaciones. *Revista de Crítica Literaria Latinoamericana*, v. 19, no. 37 (Jan – June 93), pp. 355 – 359.

SCOTT, JAMES C.
Gutmann, Matthew C. Rituals of Resistance: A Critique of the Theory of Everyday Forms of Resistance. *Latin American Perspectives*, v. 20, no. 2 (Spring 93), pp. 74 – 92. Bibl.

SCREENPLAYS
Garrido, Consuelo. Mi querido Tom Mix. *Nexos*, v. 16, no. 189 (Sept 93), pp. 75 – 76.

SCULPTORS
See
Sculpture

SCULPTURE
See also
Subdivision *Monuments, etc.* under names of specific individuals

Argentina
Jurcich, Milenko Juan. *Lola Mora: el secreto de su sueño mineral* reviewed by Rodrigo Alcorta. *Todo Es Historia*, v. 26, no. 308 (Mar 93), p. 74. Il.

Germany
Laudanna, Mayra. Ernesto de Fiori. *Vozes*, v. 86, no. 4 (July – Aug 92), pp. 59 – 65. Il.

Great Britain
Blanco, Alberto. Los jardines flotantes de Brian Nissen (Accompanied by an English translation). *Artes de México*, no. 20 (Summer 93), pp. 52 – 53.

Latin America
Von Barghahn, Barbara. Colonial Statuary of New Spain. *Latin American Art*, v. 4, no. 4 (Winter 92), pp. 77 – 79. Bibl, il.

Mexico
Arteaga, Agustín. Terra incognita. *Artes de México*, no. 18 (Winter 92), pp. 98 – 100.

Espinosa López, Elia. Gramática y lenguaje del orden y el caos. *Anales del Instituto de Investigaciones Estéticas*, v. 16, no. 62 (1991), pp. 139 – 150. Bibl, il.

Gómez Haco, Claudia. El "mysterium maximum" en la obra de Alejandro Colunga. *Artes de México*, no. 20 (Summer 93), pp. 117 – 119. Il.

Huerta, David. La novela órfica del escultor Juan Soriano. *Nexos*, v. 16, no. 181 (Jan 93), pp. 35 – 38. Il.

Spain
Exhibitions
Chacón, Katherine. Chillida: el cuerpo, el espacio. *Art Nexus*, no. 8 (Apr – June 93), pp. 80 – 81. Il.

Uruguay
Bach, Caleb. Chiseler of Timeless Forms. *Américas*, v. 45, no. 4 (July – Aug 93), pp. 26 – 33. Il.

SEBRELI, JUAN JOSÉ
Criticism of specific works
Los deseos imaginarios del peronismo
Franzé, Javier. El peronismo según Sebreli. *Cuadernos Hispanoamericanos,* no. 512 (Feb 93), pp. 127 – 129.

SEDIMENT TRANSPORT
See
Erosion

SEGALA, AMOS
Criticism of specific works
Literatura náhuatl
León-Portilla, Miguel. A modo de comentario (Response to Amos Segala's commentary on Miguel León-Portilla's review of *Histoire de la littérature náhuatl: sources, identités, réprésentations). Caravelle,* no. 59 (1992), pp. 221 – 223.

Segala, Amos. La literatura náhuatl: ¿Un coto privado? (Response to Miguel León-Portilla's review of Amos Segala's *Histoire de la littérature náhuatl: sources, identités, représentations). Caravelle,* no. 59 (1992), pp. 209 – 219. Bibl.

SEGNINI, CÉSAR
Interviews
Pau-Llosa, Ricardo. Conversation with Art Dealer César Segnini. *Latin American Art,* v. 5, no. 2 (Summer 93), pp. 31 – 32. Il.

SEGOVIA, TOMÁS
Criticism of specific works
Noticia natural
Sabugo Abril, Amancio. Descenso a la cotidianidad. *Insula,* no. 564 (Dec 93), pp. 21 – 23. Il.

SELIGSON, ESTHER
Criticism and interpretation
Conner, Robert. Contingencia y realidad en la obra de Esther Seligson. *La Palabra y el Hombre,* no. 81 (Jan – Mar 92), pp. 279 – 284. Bibl, il.

SELJAN, ZORA
Criticism and interpretation
Lima, Robert. Xangô and Other Yoruba Deities in the Plays of Zora Seljan. *Afro-Hispanic Review,* v. 11, no. 1 – 3 (1992), pp. 26 – 33. Bibl.

SELSER, GREGORIO
Biobibliography
Roitman Rosenmann, Marcos. Gregorio Selser: "Maestro artesano del pensamiento latinoamericano." *Revista Española de Antropología Americana,* v. 23 (1993), pp. 233 – 242.

SEMANTICS
See
Subdivision *Semantics* under *Spanish language*

SEMINAR ON THE ACQUISITION OF LATIN AMERICAN LIBRARY MATERIALS
Herrera, Luis. SALALM and the Public Library. *SALALM Papers,* v. 36 (1991), pp. 224 – 227.

Hodgman, Suzanne. SALALM Membership, 1956 – 1990: A Brief Overview. *SALALM Papers,* v. 36 (1991), pp. 215 – 223. Tables.

Méndez Rojas, Conny. Algunas reflexiones sobre lo que SALALM podría ofrecer a los bibliotecarios nicaragüenses. *SALALM Papers,* v. 36 (1991), pp. 228 – 232.

SEMIOTICS
See also
Symbolism in literature
Vallejo, Catharina Vanderplaats de. *Elementos para una semiótica del cuento hispanoamericano del siglo XX* reviewed by R. A. Kerr. *Hispania (USA),* v. 76, no. 3 (Sept 93), p. 482.

SENDER, RAMÓN J.
Criticism of specific works
La aventura equinoccial de Lope de Aguirre
Triviños, Gilberto. *Ramón J. Sender: mito y contramito de Lope de Aguirre* reviewed by Berta López Morales. *Atenea (Chile),* no. 465 – 466 (1992), pp. 379 – 382.
Epitalamio del Prieto Trinidad
Ahumada Peña, Haydée. Apropiación del espacio americano en *Epitalamio del Prieto Trinidad. Revista Chilena de Literatura,* no. 42 (Aug 93), pp. 7 – 11.

SENDERO LUMINOSO (PERU)
"Asi me engañaron . . . ": testimonio de un arrepentido. *Debate (Peru),* v. 15, no. 70 (Sept – Oct 92), pp. 23 – 26. Il.

Bowen, Sally and Manuel Jesús Orbegozo. 1992: el año que vivimos al galope. *Debate (Peru),* v. 15, no. 71 (Nov 92 – Jan 93), pp. 22 – 26. Il.

Burt, Jo-Marie. The Dispossessed Look Homeward: Peru's Internal Refugees Organize for Return. *NACLA Report on the Americas,* v. 27, no. 1 (July – Aug 93), pp. 8 – 11. Il.

Cisneros Vizquerra, Luis F. Perspectivas después de la detención. *Debate (Peru),* v. 15, no. 70 (Sept – Oct 92), pp. 21 – 22. Il.

Degregori, Carlos Iván. Guzmán y Sendero: después de la caída. *Nueva Sociedad,* no. 124 (Mar – Apr 93), pp. 53 – 58.

Eyzaguirre, Graciela. Los escenarios de la guerra en la región Cáceres. *Allpanchis,* v. 23, no. 39 (Jan – June 92), pp. 155 – 180. Bibl, tables, maps.

Kent, Robert B. Geographical Dimensions of the Shining Path Insurgency in Peru. *Geographical Review,* v. 83, no. 4 (Oct 93), pp. 441 – 454. Bibl, maps.

Obando Arbulú, Enrique. Situación de la subversión: después de la caída de Abimael Guzmán. *Debate (Peru),* v. 15, no. 70 (Sept – Oct 92), pp. 19 – 22. Il.

Palmer, David Scott, ed. *The Shining Path of Peru* reviewed by Florencia E. Mallon. *Hispanic American Historical Review,* v. 73, no. 3 (Aug 93), pp. 520 – 522.

— *The Shining Path of Peru* reviewed by James Dunkerley. *Journal of Latin American Studies,* v. 25, no. 2 (May 93), pp. 421 – 422.

— *The Shining Path of Peru* reviewed by Peter F. Klarén. *The Americas,* v. 50, no. 2 (Oct 93), pp. 287 – 289.

Poole, Deborah A. and Gerardo Rénique. *Peru: Time of Fear* reviewed by John Crabtree. *Bulletin of Latin American Research,* v. 12, no. 2 (May 93), pp. 243 – 244.

— *Peru: Time of Fear* reviewed by Lewis Taylor. *Journal of Latin American Studies,* v. 25, no. 3 (Oct 93), pp. 667 – 668.

Renard-Casevitz, France-Marie. Les guerriers du sel: chronique '92. *Cahiers des Amériques Latines,* no. 13 (1992), pp. 107 – 118.

Rodríguez G., Yolanda. Los actores sociales y la violencia política en Puno. *Allpanchis,* v. 23, no. 39 (Jan – June 92), pp. 131 – 154. Bibl.

Stern, Peter A. Origins and Trajectory of the Shining Path. *SALALM Papers,* v. 36 (1991), pp. 49 – 74. Bibl.

Strong, Simon. *Sendero Luminoso: el movimiento subversivo más letal del mundo* reviewed by Felipe Portocarrero S. *Apuntes (Peru),* no. 29 (July – Dec 91), pp. 89 – 91.

— *Shining Path: The World's Deadliest Revolutionary Force* reviewed by Orin Starn. *Bulletin of Latin American Research,* v. 12, no. 2 (May 93), pp. 244 – 246.

— *Shining Path: The World's Deadliest Revolutionary Force* reviewed by James Dunkerley. *Journal of Latin American Studies,* v. 25, no. 2 (May 93), pp. 421 – 422.

Research
Ansión, Juan. Acerca de un irritante debate entre antropólogos del norte: comentarios al artículo de O. Starn. *Allpanchis,* v. 23, no. 39 (Jan – June 92), pp. 113 – 122.

Seligman, Linda Jane. "Es más fácil destruir que crear": comentarios y respuesta. *Allpanchis,* v. 23, no. 39 (Jan – June 92), pp. 93 – 101.

Starn, Orin. Algunas palabras finales. *Allpanchis,* v. 23, no. 39 (Jan – June 92), pp. 123 – 129. Bibl.

— Antropología andina, "andinismo" y Sendero Luminoso. *Allpanchis,* v. 23, no. 39 (Jan – June 92), pp. 15 – 71. Bibl.

SENKMAN, LEONARDO
Interviews
Zlotchew, Clark M. Literatura israelí en español: entrevista con Leonardo Senkman. *Confluencia,* v. 8, no. 1 (Fall 92), pp. 111 – 121. Bibl.

SEPP, ANTONIO
Criticism of specific works
Relación de viaje a las misiones jesuíticas
Basalisco, Lucio. Culture a confronto: guaraniés e yaros visti da un gesuito alla fine del seicento. *Quaderni Ibero-Americani,* no. 72 (Dec 92), pp. 709 – 720. Bibl.

SEPÚLVEDA, JUAN GINÉS DE
Castilla Urbano, Francisco. Juan Ginés de Sepúlveda: en torno a una idea de civilización. *Revista de Indias,* v. 52, no. 195 – 196 (May – Dec 92), pp. 329 – 348. Bibl.

Fernández Buey, Francisco. La controversia entre Ginés de Sepúlveda y Bartolomé de las Casas: una revisión. *Boletín Americanista,* v. 33, no. 42 – 43 (1992 – 1993), pp. 301 – 347. Bibl.

Stam, Juan. La *Biblia* en la teología colonialista de Juan Ginés de Sepúlveda. *Revista de Historia (Costa Rica),* no. 25 (Jan – June 92), pp. 157 – 164. Bibl.

LA SERENA, CHILE
Hanisch Espíndola, Walter. Los jesuitas en La Serena, 1672 – 1767. *Boletín de la Academia Chilena de la Historia,* v. 58 – 59, no. 102 (1991 – 1992), pp. 291 – 328. Bibl, tables.

SERPA, LUÍS LOPES PEGADO E
Pijning, Ernst. Conflicts in the Portuguese Colonial Administration: Trials and Errors of Luís Lopes Pegado e Serpa, "provedor-mor da fazenda real" in Salvador, Brazil, 1718 – 1721. *Colonial Latin American Historical Review,* v. 2, no. 4 (Fall 93), pp. 403 – 423. Bibl, maps.

SERRA, JUAN DE SANTA GERTRUDIS
Mantilla Ruiz, Luis Carlos. El último cronista franciscano de la época colonial en el Nuevo Reino de Granada: fray Juan de Santa Gertrudis Serra. *Boletín de Historia y Antigüedades,* v. 79, no. 779 (Oct – Dec 92), pp. 889 – 917. Bibl.

SERRANO CALDERA, ALEJANDRO
Rojas Gómez, Miguel. Alejandro Serrano Caldera: una nueva filosofía de la conciencia y la libertad. *Islas,* no. 99 (May – Aug 91), pp. 130 – 154. Bibl.

SERVICE INDUSTRIES
See also
　Environmental services
　Social service
Andean region
Congresses
Grupo Andino: Primera Reunión Global Andina sobre Servicios. *Integración Latinoamericana,* v. 18, no. 186 (Jan – Feb 93), pp. 73 – 78.

SEX ROLE
See also
　Homosexuality
　Women
Charles C., Mercedes. De la denuncia a la creación de alternativas. *Fem,* v. 17, no. 125 (July 93), pp. 4 – 5.

Díaz Castellanos, Guadalupe. Graciela Hierro y la filosofía feminista. *Fem,* v. 17, no. 127 (Sept 93), pp. 17 – 19.

Flores, Mercedes and Roxana Hidalgo Xirinachs. El autoritarismo en la vida cotidiana: SIDA, homofobia y moral sexual. *Revista de Ciencias Sociales (Costa Rica),* no. 58 (Dec 92), pp. 35 – 44. Bibl.

Parker, Andrew et al, eds. *Nationalisms and Sexualities* reviewed by Catherine Davies (Review entitled "Women and a Redefinition of Argentinian Nationhood"). *Bulletin of Latin American Research,* v. 12, no. 3 (Sept 93), pp. 333 – 341.

— *Nationalisms and Sexualities* reviewed by Raúl Rodríguez-Hernández. *Letras Femeninas,* v. 19, no. 1 – 2 (Spring – Fall 93), pp. 134 – 135.
Argentina
Salessi, Jorge. La invasión de sirenas. *Feminaria,* v. 6, no. 10, Suppl. (Apr 93), pp. 2 – 7. Bibl.
Brazil
Caulfield, Sueann and Martha de Abreu Esteves. 50 Years of Virginity in Rio de Janeiro: Sexual Politics and Gender Roles in Juridical and Popular Discourse, 1890 – 1940. *Luso-Brazilian Review,* v. 30, no. 1 (Summer 93), pp. 47 – 74. Bibl, tables.

Del Priore, Mary. *Ao sul do corpo: condição feminina, maternidades e mentalidades no Brasil-colônia* reviewed by Maria Odila Silva Dias (Review entitled "A condição feminina e suas historicidades"). *Estudos Feministas,* v. 1, no. 2 (1993), pp. 481 – 485.

Deutsch, Sandra F. McGee. Afterword (to the issue entitled "Changing Images of the Brazilian Woman: Studies of Female Sexuality in Literature, Mass Media, and Criminal Trials, 1884 – 1992"). *Luso-Brazilian Review,* v. 30, no. 1 (Summer 93), pp. 107 – 117. Bibl.
Caribbean area
Miller, Errol L. *Men at Risk* reviewed by Adam Jones. *Caribbean Studies,* v. 25, no. 1 – 2 (Jan – July 92), pp. 167 – 170.

— *Men at Risk* reviewed by Barry Chavannes. *Social and Economic Studies,* v. 41, no. 3 (Sept 92), pp. 186 – 192.
Haiti
Bellegarde-Smith, Patrick. *Haiti: The Breached Citadel* reviewed by Jorge Rodríguez Beruff. *Caribbean Studies,* v. 25, no. 1 – 2 (Jan – July 92), pp. 159 – 161.
Latin America
Hollanda, Heloísa Buarque de, ed. *¿Y nosotras latinoamericanas?: estudos sobre gênero e raça* reviewed by Lena Lavinas (Review entitled "Contrapassos da latinidade"). *Estudos Feministas,* v. 1, no. 2 (1993), pp. 501 – 502.
Bibliography
Nash, June. Estudios de género en Latinoamérica. *Mesoamérica (USA),* v. 13, no. 23 (June 92), pp. 1 – 22. Bibl.
Mexican – American Border Region
Rubalcava, Rosa María and Vania Salles. Hogares de trabajadoras y percepciones femeninas. *El Cotidiano,* v. 9, no. 53 (Mar – Apr 93), pp. 40 – 46. Tables.
Mexico
Study and teaching
Hierro de Matte, Graciela. Historia del PUEG. *Fem,* v. 17, no. 121 (Mar 93), p. 32.
Peru
Ochoa Rivero, Silvia. Algunas percepciones sobre lo femenino y lo masculino: hablan los jóvenes. *Allpanchis,* v. 25, no. 41 (Jan – June 93), pp. 143 – 158. Bibl.

Rojas Zolezzi, Enrique Carlos. Concepciones sobre la relación entre géneros: mitos, ritual y organización del trabajo en la unidad doméstica campa – asháninka. *Amazonía Peruana,* v. 11, no. 22 (Oct 92), pp. 175 – 220. Bibl.
Puerto Rico
De Leon, Brunilda. Sex Role Identity among College Students: A Cross-Cultural Analysis. *Hispanic Journal of Behavioral Sciences,* v. 15, no. 4 (Nov 93), pp. 476 – 489. Bibl, tables.
United States
De Leon, Brunilda. Sex Role Identity among College Students: A Cross-Cultural Analysis. *Hispanic Journal of Behavioral Sciences,* v. 15, no. 4 (Nov 93), pp. 476 – 489. Bibl, tables.

Valenzuela, Angela. Liberal Gender Role Attitudes and Academic Achievement among Mexican-Origin Adolescents in Two Houston Inner-City Catholic Schools. *Hispanic Journal of Behavioral Sciences,* v. 15, no. 3 (Aug 93), pp. 310 – 323. Bibl, tables.

SEX ROLE IN LITERATURE
See also
　Women in literature

Cypess, Sandra Messinger. Los géneros re/velados en *Los empeños de una casa* de sor Juana Inés de la Cruz. *Hispamérica*, v. 22, no. 64 – 65 (Apr – Aug 93), pp. 177 – 185. Bibl.

Martínez, Elena M. El discurso patriarcal y el discurso feminista en *Excepto la muerte* de Carmen Elvira Moreno. *Fem*, v. 17, no. 127 (Sept 93), pp. 6 – 10. Bibl.

Minkler, Julie A. Helen's Calibans: A Study of Gender Hierarchy in Derek Walcott's *Omeros*. *World Literature Today*, v. 67, no. 2 (Spring 93), pp. 272 – 276. Bibl.

Muñoz, Elías Miguel. Of Small Conquests and Big Victories: Gender Constructs in *The Modern Ladies of Guanabacoa*. *The Americas Review*, v. 20, no. 2 (Summer 92), pp. 105 – 111. Bibl.

Subercaseaux, Benjamín. Lo masculino y lo femenino en el imaginario colectivo de comienzos de siglo. *Revista Chilena de Literatura*, no. 42 (Aug 93), pp. 245 – 249.

SEXISM

González Stephan, Beatriz. No sólo para mujeres: el sexismo en los estudios literarios. *Escritura (Venezuela)*, v. 16, no. 31 – 32 (Jan – Dec 91), pp. 103 – 113.

Mexico

González Ascencio, Gerardo. Políticas públicas y hostigamiento sexual. *Nueva Sociedad*, no. 123 (Jan – Feb 93), pp. 104 – 113.

Magaña Sánchez, Margarita Elena. Clasismo, racismo y sexismo en el discurso escolar de México. *Fem*, v. 17, no. 123 (May 93), pp. 13 – 15.

Nieto-Cadena, Fernando. Mujer, literatura y sociedad en el sureste. *Fem*, v. 17, no. 120 (Feb 93), pp. 21 – 24.

United States

Romero, Gloria Jean. "No se raje, chicanita": Some Thoughts on Race, Class, and Gender in the Classroom. *Aztlán*, v. 20, no. 1 – 2 (Spring – Fall 91), pp. 203 – 218. Bibl.

Uruguay

Piotti Núñez, Diosma Elena. La escuela primaria como generadora y reproductora de contenidos sexistas en la sociedad uruguaya. *La Educación (USA)*, v. 36, no. 111 – 113 (1992), pp. 97 – 110.

SEXUAL BEHAVIOR

See also
    Homosexuality
    Pregnancy
    Prostitution

Fellay, Jean-Blaise. SIDA, preservativos y continencia. *Mensaje*, v. 42, no. 419 (June 93), pp. 211 – 212.

Garza, Alejandro de la. Cinco minutos de sexo al milenio. *Nexos*, v. 16, no. 185 (May 93), pp. 83 – 85.

America

Ragon, Pierre. *Les amours indiennes ou l'imaginaire du conquistador* reviewed by Christian Satge. *Caravelle*, no. 59 (1992), pp. 297 – 300.

Argentina

Lesser, Ricardo. El cuerpo de la democracia: la crónica de las condiciones de vida de los sectores populares en esta democracia renovada . . . . *Todo Es Historia*, v. 27, no. 317 (Dec 93), pp. 50 – 56. Il.

Brazil

Bibliography

Kuznesof, Elizabeth Anne. Sexuality, Gender, and the Family in Colonial Brazil (Review article). *Luso-Brazilian Review*, v. 30, no. 1 (Summer 93), pp. 119 – 132. Bibl.

Study and teaching

Leite, Miriam Lifchitz Moreira. Fontes históricas e estilo acadêmico. *Estudos Feministas*, v. 1, no. 1 (1993), pp. 83 – 95. Bibl.

Costa Rica

Obando Hidalgo, Iris María and Ana Isabel Ruiz Rojas. Epidemiología del abuso físico y sexual en niños atendidos en el Hospital de Niños, 1988 – 1990. *Revista de Ciencias Sociales (Costa Rica)*, no. 59 (Mar 93), pp. 63 – 70. Bibl, tables, charts.

Latin America

Lavrin, Asunción, ed. *Sexuality and Marriage in Colonial Latin America* reviewed by K. Lynn Stoner (Review entitled "Whores, Witches, and Unwed Mothers: Recent Scholarship on the Control of Sexuality"). *Studies in Latin American Popular Culture*, v. 12 (1993), pp. 207 – 214.

Mexico

Baird, Traci L. Mexican Adolescent Sexuality: Attitudes, Knowledge, and Sources of Information. *Hispanic Journal of Behavioral Sciences*, v. 15, no. 3 (Aug 93), pp. 402 – 417. Bibl, tables.

SEXUALITY

See
    Sexual behavior

SHAKESPEARE, WILLIAM

Translations

González Padilla, María Enriqueta. La traducción de Shakespeare: comentario de una experiencia. *Plural (Mexico)*, v. 22, no. 259 (Apr 93), pp. 56 – 63. Bibl.

SHAMANISM

Brazil

Giannini, Isabelle Vidal. Os domínios cósmicos: um dos aspectos da construção da categoria humana kayapó – xikrin. *Revista de Antropologia (Brazil)*, v. 34 (1991), pp. 35 – 58. Bibl.

Mexico

Lipp, Frank Joseph. *The Mixe of Oaxaca: Religion, Ritual, and Healing* reviewed by James Dow. *The Americas*, v. 49, no. 4 (Apr 93), pp. 545 – 547.

Peru

Junquera, Carlos. *El chamanismo en el Amazonas* reviewed by Manuel Cerezo Lasne, Penélope Ranera Sánchez, and Javier Rubio Swift. *Revista Española de Antropología Americana*, v. 23 (1993), pp. 255 – 256.

SHEEP RANCHES

Argentina

Sábato, Hilda. *Agrarian Capitalism and the World Market: Buenos Aires in the Pastoral Age, 1840 – 1890* reviewed by Samuel Amaral. *Hispanic American Historical Review*, v. 73, no. 1 (Feb 93), pp. 161 – 162.

United States

Altamirano Rúa, Teófilo. Pastores quechuas en el oeste norteamericano. *América Indígena*, v. 51, no. 2 – 3 (Apr – Sept 91), pp. 203 – 222. Maps.

SHIMOSE KAWAMURA, PEDRO

Criticism and interpretation

Calderón, Fina de. Repaso de la poesía boliviana: dos poetas en Madrid: Oscar Rivera-Rodas y Pedro Shimose. *Signo*, no. 35, Nueva época (Jan – Apr 92), pp. 5 – 13.

Sanjinés C., Javier. Pedro Shimose, poeta rebelde e intelectual letrado. *Signo*, no. 36 – 37, Nueva época (May – Dec 92), pp. 75 – 88. Bibl.

SHIP BUILDING

Marco, Miguel Angel de. Repercusiones del invento y construcción del submarino *Peral* en la Argentina. *Investigaciones y Ensayos*, no. 41 (Jan – Dec 91), pp. 215 – 225. Bibl.

SHIPIBO INDIANS

See
    Sipibo Indians

SHOPPING MALLS

Argentina

Malatesta, Parisina. Mega Shoppings: Playgrounds for Today's Porteños (Translated by Ruth Morales, photographs by Jorge Provenza). *Américas*, v. 45, no. 4 (July – Aug 93), pp. 14 – 19. Il.

Chile

Piña, Juan Andrés. Estética del "mall." *Mensaje,* v. 42, no. 424 (Nov 93), pp. 567 – 568. Il.

Mexico

Ayre, Shirley. A Rosier Image for the Zona Rosa. *Business Mexico,* v. 3, no. 10 (Oct 93), pp. 4 – 7. Il.

SHORT STORIES

See

Author Index under names of specific writers

SHRINES

Calderón, Gabriela. Amor y tradición en la fiesta de la Virgen de las Peñas. *Mensaje,* v. 42, no. 425 (Dec 93), pp. 617 – 618. Il.

Griffith, James S. *Beliefs and Holy Places: A Spiritual Geography of the Pimería Alta* reviewed by Marth L. Henderson. *Geographical Review,* v. 83, no. 3 (July 93), pp. 334 – 336.

— *Beliefs and Holy Places: A Spiritual Geography of the Pimería Alta* reviewed by Martha L. Henderson (Review entitled "What Is Spiritual Geography?"). *Geographical Review,* v. 83, no. 4 (Oct 93), pp. 469 – 472.

Mexico

Sarignana, Armando. La Soledad (Accompanied by an English translation). *Artes de México,* no. 21 (Fall 93), pp. 44 – 47. Il.

SHUARA INDIANS

See

Jívaro Indians

SIERRA, JUSTO

Zavala, Silvio Arturo. Justo Sierra Méndez, educador. *Hoy Es Historia,* v. 10, no. 55 (Jan – Feb 93), pp. 76 – 81. Il.

SIERRA O'REILLY, JUSTO

Criticism of specific works

La hija del judío

Poot Herrera, Sara. *La hija del judío:* entre la inquisición y la imprenta. *Nueva Revista de Filología Hispánica,* v. 40, no. 2 (July – Dec 92), pp. 761 – 777. Bibl.

SIGNO (PERIODICAL)

Arze, José Roberto. *Signo* en el contexto de las revistas literarias de Bolivia. *Signo,* no. 36 – 37, Nueva época (May – Dec 93), pp. 11 – 14.

Coello Vila, Carlos. *Signo; Cuadernos Bolivianos de Cultura,* 36 – 37. *Signo,* no. 38, Nueva época (Jan – Apr 93), pp. 7 – 10.

SILVA, ALBERTO MARTINS DA

Souza, Luís de Castro. Saudação ao sócio honorário Alberto Martins da Silva: os médicos militares no Instituto Histórico e Geográfico Brasileiro (Speech given in honor of Dr. Silva's induction into the Instituto Histórico e Geográfico Brasileiro). *Revista do Instituto Histórico e Geográfico Brasileiro,* no. 371 (Apr – June 91), pp. 509 – 517. Bibl.

SILVA, JOSÉ ASUNCIÓN

Biography

Cano Gaviria, Ricardo. *José Asunción Silva: una vida en clave de sombra* reviewed by José Ricardo Chaves. *Vuelta,* v. 17, no. 201 (Aug 93), pp. 53 – 54.

SILVA, JOSÉ CALAZANS BRANDÃO DA

Interviews

Meihy, José Carlos Sebe Bom. "Meu empenho foi ser o tradutor do universo sertanejo": entrevista com José Calazans (Interviewed and transcribed by José Carlos Sebe Bom Meihy). *Luso-Brazilian Review,* v. 30, no. 2 (Winter 93), pp. 23 – 33.

SILVA, LUÍS INÁCIO DA

Sader, Emir and Ken Silverstein. *Without Fear of Being Happy: Lula, the Workers Party, and Brazil* reviewed by Joel Wolfe. *The Americas,* v. 49, no. 4 (Apr 93), pp. 566 – 568.

— *Without Fear of Being Happy: Lula, the Workers Party, and Brazil* reviewed by John Humphrey. *Bulletin of Latin American Research,* v. 12, no. 3 (Sept 93), p. 347.

— *Without Fear of Being Happy: Lula, the Workers Party, and Brazil* reviewed by Paul Cammack. *Journal of Latin American Studies,* v. 25, no. 3 (Oct 93), pp. 666 – 667.

Addresses, essays, lectures

Silva, Luís Inácio da. Discurso de Luís Inácio "Lula" da Silva (given at the IV Encuentro del Foro de São Paulo). *Nueva Sociedad,* no. 128 (Nov – Dec 93), pp. 162 – 165.

SILVA HERZOG, JESÚS

Aguilar Monteverde, Alonso. Jesús Silva Herzog como economista. *Problemas del Desarrollo,* v. 24, no. 92 (Jan – Mar 93), pp. 209 – 217. Bibl.

Campos Aragón, Leticia. Economía y humanismo: un modesto homenaje al maestro Jesús Silva Herzog. *Problemas del Desarrollo,* v. 24, no. 92 (Jan – Mar 93), pp. 221 – 225.

Sarukhán Kermez, José. Intervención del dr. José Sarukhán, rector de la UNAM, en la clausura del acto de homenaje al maestro Jesús Silva Herzog en su centenario. *Problemas del Desarrollo,* v. 24, no. 92 (Jan – Mar 93), pp. 218 – 220.

SILVA JÚNIOR, SERAFIM MOREIRA DA

Silva, Alberto Martins da. Um inédito de João Severiano da Fonseca: *Serafim Moreira da Silva Júnior, um herói de Diamantina, 1850 – 1868* (Includes the previously unpublished text). *Revista do Instituto Histórico e Geográfico Brasileiro,* no. 371 (Apr – June 91), pp. 518 – 532. Bibl.

SILVER MINES AND MINING

Bolivia

Saguier, Eduardo Ricardo. La crisis minera en el Alto Perú en su fase extractiva: la producción de plata del cerro de Potosí en la luz de ocho visitas ignoradas de minas, 1778 – 1803. *Colonial Latin American Historical Review,* v. 1, no. 1 (Fall 92), pp. 67 – 100. Bibl, tables.

Tandeter, Enrique. *Coacción y mercado: la minería de plata en el Potosí colonial, 1692 – 1826* reviewed by Margarita Suárez. *Revista Andina,* v. 11, no. 1 (July 93), pp. 251 – 254.

Mexico

Barnhart, Katherine. Silver through the Centuries. *Business Mexico,* v. 3, no. 12 (Dec 93), pp. 12 – 14. Tables.

Hoberman, Louisa Schell. *Mexico's Merchant Elite, 1590 – 1660: Silver, State, and Society* reviewed by Stanley J. Stein. *Hispanic American Historical Review,* v. 73, no. 1 (Feb 93), pp. 151 – 152.

— *Mexico's Merchant Elite, 1590 – 1660: Silver, State, and Society* reviewed by Gabriel Haslip-Viera. *Colonial Latin American Review,* v. 2, no. 1 – 2 (1993), pp. 296 – 298.

— *Mexico's Merchant Elite, 1590 – 1660: Silver, State, and Society* reviewed by Richard L. Garner. *Colonial Latin American Historical Review,* v. 2, no. 3 (Summer 93), pp. 369 – 371.

— *Mexico's Merchant Elite, 1590 – 1660: Silver, State, and Society* reviewed by Silvia C. Mallo. *Revista de Historia de América,* no. 113 (Jan – June 92), pp. 170 – 172.

SILVERSMITHS

Mexico

Espinosa y Pitman, Alejandro. Huellas de plata (Accompanied by an English translation). *Artes de México,* no. 18 (Winter 92), pp. 63 – 67. Il.

Peru

Exhibitions

Sanjurjo de Casciero, Annick. The Sterling Legacy of Peru. *Américas,* v. 45, no. 1 (Jan – Feb 93), pp. 50 – 51. Il.

SIMENON, GEORGES

Bradu, Fabienne. Georges Simenon, el inclasificable. *Vuelta,* v. 17, no. 194 (Jan 93), pp. 52 – 55.

SIPIBO INDIANS

Bergman, Roland W. *Economía amazónica* translated by Martha Beingolea. Reviewed by Jaime Regan, S.J. *Amazonía Peruana,* v. 11, no. 21 (Sept 92), pp. 243 – 244.

SIQUEIROS, DAVID ALFARO

Batista, Marta Rossetti. Da passagem meteórica de Siqueiros pelo Brasil, 1933 (Includes reproductions of a text and an interview published in 1933 – 1934 after the artist's visit to Brazil). *Vozes*, v. 86, no. 5 (Sept – Oct 92), pp. 81 – 94. Il.

Martínez Quijano, Ana. El mítico mural de Siqueiros en la Argentina (Accompanied by an English translation). *Art Nexus*, no. 9 (June – Aug 93), pp. 110 – 112. Il.

SISAL HEMP

Mexico

Baños Ramírez, Othón. Reconfiguración rural – urbana en la zona henequenera de Yucatán. *Estudios Sociológicos*, v. 11, no. 32 (May – Aug 93), pp. 419 – 443. Tables, maps.

Joseph, Gilbert Michael. *Revolución desde afuera: Yucatán, México y Estados Unidos, 1880 – 1924* translated by Eduardo L. Suárez. Reviewed by Othón Baños. *Estudios Sociológicos*, v. 11, no. 31 (Jan – Apr 93), pp. 265 – 270.

Keenan, Joe. Is There Life after Henequen? *Business Mexico*, v. 3, no. 4 (Apr 93), pp. 22 – 23. Il.

Várguez Pasos, Luis A. Cultura obrera en crisis: el caso de los cordeleros de Yucatán. *Estudios Sociológicos*, v. 11, no. 31 (Jan – Apr 93), pp. 93 – 110. Bibl.

SKÁRMETA, ANTONIO

Criticism of specific works

Ardiente paciencia

Bumas, Ethan Shaskan. Metaphor's Exile: The Poets and Postmen of Antonio Skármeta. *Latin American Literary Review*, v. 21, no. 41 (Jan – June 93), pp. 9 – 20. Bibl.

Interviews

García-Corales, Guillermo. Entrevista con Antonio Skármeta: de *El entusiasmo* a *Match ball*. *Chasqui*, v. 22, no. 2 (Nov 93), pp. 114 – 119.

SKEPTICISM

Molina, Silvia. El discurso escéptico: su expresión en la caricatura política. *Revista Mexicana de Ciencias Políticas y Sociales*, v. 38, Nueva época, no. 154 (Oct – Dec 93), pp. 79 – 89. Bibl.

SLAVE TRADE

Bibliography

Murray, David R. Slavery and the Slave Trade: New Comparative Approaches (Review article). *Latin American Research Review*, v. 28, no. 1 (1993), pp. 150 – 161.

Caribbean area

Munford, Clarence J. *The Black Ordeal of Slavery and Slave Trading in the French West Indies, 1625 – 1715* reviewed by David Eltis. *Hispanic American Historical Review*, v. 73, no. 2 (May 93), pp. 316 – 317.

SLAVERY

Bibliography

Murray, David R. Slavery and the Slave Trade: New Comparative Approaches (Review article). *Latin American Research Review*, v. 28, no. 1 (1993), pp. 150 – 161.

Ward, Thomas Butler. Toward a Concept of Unnatural Slavery during the Renaissance: A Review of Primary and Secondary Sources. *Revista Interamericana de Bibliografía*, v. 42, no. 2 (1992), pp. 259 – 279. Bibl.

Congresses

Boucher, Philip Paul and Patricia Galloway, eds. *Proceedings of the Fifteenth Meeting of the French Colonial Historical Society, Martinique and Guadeloupe, May 1989* reviewed by Paul Lachance. *Hispanic American Historical Review*, v. 73, no. 3 (Aug 93), pp. 502 – 503.

Africa

Knight, Franklin W. Columbus and Slavery in the New World and Africa. *Revista/Review Interamericana*, v. 22, no. 1 – 2 (Spring – Summer 92), pp. 18 – 35. Bibl.

Thornton, John K. *Africa and the Africans in the Making of the Atlantic World, 1400 – 1680* reviewed by Stuart B. Schwartz. *Hispanic American Historical Review*, v. 73, no. 3 (Aug 93), pp. 500 – 502.

America

Knight, Franklin W. Columbus and Slavery in the New World and Africa. *Revista/Review Interamericana*, v. 22, no. 1 – 2 (Spring – Summer 92), pp. 18 – 35. Bibl.

Mattos, Tomás de. Alonso de Sandoval (1576 – 1652), jesuita de esclavos. *Cuadernos del CLAEH*, v. 17, no. 63 – 64 (Oct 92), pp. 141 – 147.

Maura, Juan Francisco. Esclavas españolas en el Nuevo Mundo. *Colonial Latin American Historical Review*, v. 2, no. 2 (Spring 93), pp. 185 – 194. Bibl.

Solow, Barbara L., ed. *Slavery and the Rise of the Atlantic System* reviewed by Johannes M. Postma. *The Americas*, v. 49, no. 3 (Jan 93), pp. 404 – 405.

Thornton, John K. *Africa and the Africans in the Making of the Atlantic World, 1400 – 1680* reviewed by Stuart B. Schwartz. *Hispanic American Historical Review*, v. 73, no. 3 (Aug 93), pp. 500 – 502.

Law and legislation

Sala-Molins, Louis. *L'Afrique aux Amériques: le code noir espagnol* reviewed by Germán A. de la Raza. *Ibero Americana (Sweden)*, v. 22, no. 2 (Dec 92), pp. 77 – 81.

Brazil

Luna, Francisco Vidal. Características demográficas dos escravos de São Paulo, 1777 – 1829. *Estudos Econômicos*, v. 22, no. 3 (Sept – Dec 92), pp. 443 – 483. Bibl, tables.

Menezes, Geraldo Bezerra de. A presença dos intelectuais brasileiros na campanha abolicionista. *Revista do Instituto Histórico e Geográfico Brasileiro*, no. 370 (Jan – Mar 91), pp. 226 – 230.

Monteiro, Mário Ypiranga. Da capacidade ociosa do escravo negro libertado. *Revista do Instituto Histórico e Geográfico Brasileiro*, no. 370 (Jan – Mar 91), pp. 223 – 225.

Nishida, Mieko. Manumission and Ethnicity in Urban Slavery: Salvador, Brazil, 1808 – 1888. *Hispanic American Historical Review*, v. 73, no. 3 (Aug 93), pp. 361 – 391. Bibl, tables, charts.

Piratininga Júnior, Luiz Gonzaga. *Dietário dos negros de São Bento* reviewed by Maria de Lourdes Beldi de Alcântara. *Revista de Antropologia (Brazil)*, v. 34 (1991), pp. 227 – 228.

Caribbean area

Beckles, Hilary and Verene A. Sheperd, eds. *Caribbean Slave Society and Economy* reviewed by Paul Lachance. *Hispanic American Historical Review*, v. 73, no. 2 (May 93), pp. 315 – 316.

— *Caribbean Slave Society and Economy: A Student Reader* reviewed by Gert Oostindie. *European Review of Latin American and Caribbean Studies*, no. 54 (June 93), pp. 126 – 127.

Munford, Clarence J. *The Black Ordeal of Slavery and Slave Trading in the French West Indies, 1625 – 1715* reviewed by David Eltis. *Hispanic American Historical Review*, v. 73, no. 2 (May 93), pp. 316 – 317.

Cuba

Maldonado Jiménez, Rubén. Algunas reflexiones sobre la historiografía cubana y puertorriqueña en torno a la abolición de la esclavitud. *Homines*, v. 15 – 16, no. 2 – 1 (Oct 91 – Dec 92), pp. 31 – 38. Bibl.

Yacou, Alain. La insurgencia negra en la isla de Cuba en la primera mitad del siglo XIX. *Revista de Indias*, v. 53, no. 197 (Jan – Apr 93), pp. 23 – 51. Bibl.

Dominican Republic

Cassá, Roberto and Genaro Rodríguez Morel. Consideraciones alternativas acerca de las rebeliones de esclavos en Santo Domingo. *Anuario de Estudios Americanos*, v. 50, no. 1 (1993), pp. 101 – 131. Bibl.

Rodríguez Morel, Genaro. Esclavitud y vida rural en las plantaciones azucareras de Santo Domingo, siglo XVI. *Anuario de Estudios Americanos*, v. 49 (1992), pp. 89 – 117. Bibl.

Latin America

Law and legislation

Mallo, Silvia. La libertad en el discurso del estado, de amos y esclavos, 1780 – 1830. *Revista de Historia de América*, no. 112 (July – Dec 91), pp. 121 – 146. Bibl.

Peru

Aguirre, Carlos. Agentes de su propia emancipación: manumisión de esclavos en Lima, 1821 – 1854. *Apuntes (Peru)*, no. 29 (July – Dec 91), pp. 35 – 56. Bibl, tables.

Blanchard, Peter. *Slavery and Abolition in Early Republican Peru* reviewed by Charles Walker. *Bulletin of Latin American Research*, v. 12, no. 2 (May 93), pp. 227 – 228.

— *Slavery and Abolition in Early Republican Peru* reviewed by Sandra Lauderdale Graham. *Colonial Latin American Historical Review*, v. 2, no. 2 (Spring 93), pp. 230 – 231.

— *Slavery and Abolition in Early Republican Peru* reviewed by Christine Hunefeldt. *Hispanic American Historical Review*, v. 73, no. 4 (Nov 93), pp. 711 – 713.

— *Slavery and Abolition in Early Republican Peru* reviewed by Michael J. Gonzales. *Journal of Latin American Studies*, v. 25, no. 3 (Oct 93), pp. 657 – 658.

Hünefeldt, Christine. *Lasmanuelos: vida cotidiana de una familia negra en la Lima del s. XIX* reviewed by Sara Mateos (Review entitled "Esclavitud urbana"). *Debate (Peru)*, v. 15, no. 70 (Sept – Oct 92), pp. 67 – 68.

Tardieu, Jean-Pierre. Los jesuitas y la "lengua de Angola" en Perú, siglo XVII. *Revista de Indias*, v. 53, no. 198 (May – Aug 93), pp. 627 – 637. Bibl.

Puerto Rico

Maldonado Jiménez, Rubén. Algunas reflexiones sobre la historiografía cubana y puertorriqueña en torno a la abolición de la esclavitud. *Homines*, v. 15 – 16, no. 2 – 1 (Oct 91 – Dec 92), pp. 31 – 38. Bibl.

Moscoso, Francisco. Encomendero y esclavista: Francisco Manuel de Lando. *Anuario de Estudios Americanos*, v. 49 (1992), pp. 119 – 142. Bibl.

Surinam

Stedman, John Gabriel. *Stedman's Surinam: Life in an Eighteenth-Century Slave Society* edited by Richard and Sally Price. Reviewed Jerry Gurulé. *Colonial Latin American Historical Review*, v. 1, no. 1 (Fall 92), pp. 121 – 122.

— *Stedman's Surinam: Life in an Eighteenth-Century Slave Society* edited by Richard and Sally Price. Reviewed by Michael Craton. *Hispanic American Historical Review*, v. 73, no. 3 (Aug 93), pp. 511 – 513.

Virgin Islands of the United States

Hall, Neville A. T. *Slave Society in the Danish West Indies: St. Thomas, St. John, and St. Croix* edited by Barry W. Higman with a foreword by Kamau Brathwaite. Reviewed by Keith Mason. *Bulletin of Latin American Research*, v. 12, no. 2 (May 93), pp. 218 – 219.

— *Slave Society in the Danish West Indies: St. Thomas, St. John, and St. Croix* edited by Barry W. Higman with a foreword by Kamau Brathwaite. Reviewed by Bonham C. Richardson. *Caribbean Geography*, v. 3, no. 4 (Sept 92), pp. 275 – 276.

— *Slave Society in the Danish West Indies: St. Thomas, St. John, and St. Croix* reviewed by William A. Harris. *Social and Economic Studies*, v. 41, no. 3 (Sept 92), pp. 174 – 179.

SLAVERY IN LITERATURE

See

    Blacks in literature

SLUMS

Developing countries

Bolívar, Teolinda. Declaración de Caracas sobre la rehabilitación de los barrios del Tercer Mundo. *Revista Interamericana de Planificación*, v. 26, no. 101 – 102 (Jan – June 93), pp. 231 – 241.

Peru

Matos Mar, José. La experiencia popular en Comas: 10 casos. *América Indígena*, v. 51, no. 2 – 3 (Apr – Sept 91), pp. 75 – 105. Tables.

SMALL BUSINESS

See

    Business enterprises
    Informal sector (Economics)

SMETAK, WALTER

Grützmacher, Thomas. Salve-se quem souber: lembrando Smetak. *Vozes*, v. 87, no. 1 (Jan – Feb 93), pp. 77 – 83. Il.

SMITH, JOHN F.

Oelrich, Amy. Marching to the Beat of the Market. *Business Mexico*, v. 3, no. 11 (Nov 93), p. 30. Il.

SMUGGLING

Brazil

Pijning, Ernst. Conflicts in the Portuguese Colonial Administration: Trials and Errors of Luís Lopes Pegado e Serpa, "provedor-mor da fazenda real" in Salvador, Brazil, 1718 – 1721. *Colonial Latin American Historical Review*, v. 2, no. 4 (Fall 93), pp. 403 – 423. Bibl, maps.

Haiti

Garrigus, John D. Blue and Brown: Contraband Indigo and the Rise of a Free Colored Planter Class in French Saint-Domingue. *The Americas*, v. 50, no. 2 (Oct 93), pp. 233 – 263. Bibl, tables, maps, charts.

Mexican – American Border Region

Croston, Kendel. Women's Activities during the Prohibition Era along the U.S. – Mexico Border. *Journal of Borderlands Studies*, v. 8, no. 1 (Spring 93), pp. 99 – 113. Bibl.

Río de la Plata region

Zanotti de Medrano, Lilia Inés. Rio Grande do Sul: una provincia brasileña vinculada comercialmente al Plata en el siglo XIX. *Todo Es Historia*, v. 26, no. 307 (Feb 93), pp. 60 – 72. Bibl, il, maps.

SOAP OPERAS

See

    Television

SOBRADINHO, BRAZIL

Beaney, Peter W. The Irrigated Eldorado: State-Managed Rural Development, Redemocratisation, and Popular Participation in the Brazilian Northeast. *Bulletin of Latin American Research*, v. 12, no. 3 (Sept 93), pp. 249 – 272. Bibl.

SOCCER

Argentina

Ramírez, Pablo A. La extraordinaria popularidad de Boca Juniors. *Todo Es Historia*, v. 26, no. 310 (May 93), pp. 74 – 78. Il.

Mexico

Aguilar, Luis Miguel. Cómo salvar al futbol mexicano. *Nexos*, v. 16, no. 185 (May 93), pp. 23 – 27.

Peru

Cisneros, Luis Jaime and Arturo Ferrari. Ni goles, ni milagros: entrevista a Francisco Lombardi. *Debate (Peru)*, v. 16, no. 74 (Sept – Oct 93), pp. 14 – 18. Il.

Trelles Aréstegui, Efraín. La química de Popovic. *Debate (Peru)*, v. 15, no. 71 (Nov 92 – Jan 93), pp. 64 – 66. Il.

SOCIAL CHANGE

See also

    Church and social problems
    Pressure groups
    Social mobility
    Social movements
    Sociological jurisprudence

Bolivia

Langer, Erick Detlef. *Economic Change and Rural Resistance in Southern Bolivia, 1880 – 1930* reviewed by Marie-Danielle Démelas-Bohy. *Caravelle*, no. 59 (1992), pp. 309 – 311.

Brazil

Leite, Milu. Antenas diabólicas. *Problemas Brasileiros*, v. 30, no. 295 (Jan – Feb 93), pp. 54 – 56. Il.

Central America

Vilas, Carlos María. Después de la revolución: democratización y cambio social en Centroamérica. *Revista Mexicana de Sociología*, v. 54, no. 3 (July – Sept 92), pp. 3 – 44. Bibl.

Chile

Atria Benaprés, Raúl. Contribuciones para una discusión sobre la ruta de cambio de la sociedad chilena. *Estudios Sociales (Chile)*, no. 75 (Jan – Mar 93), pp. 155 – 182.

Silva, Patricio. Intelectuales, tecnócratas y cambio social en Chile: pasado, presente y perspectivas futuras. *Revista Mexicana de Sociología*, v. 54, no. 1 (Jan – Mar 92), pp. 130 – 166. Bibl.

Latin America

Ferrer, Aldo. Iberoamérica: una nueva sociedad. *Cuadernos Americanos*, no. 39, Nueva época (May – June 93), pp. 57 – 64.

Hopenhayn, Martín. The Social Sciences without Planning or Revolution? *CEPAL Review*, no. 48 (Dec 92), pp. 129 – 140. Bibl.

Krawczyk, Miriam. Women in the Region: Major Changes. *CEPAL Review*, no. 49 (Apr 93), pp. 7 – 19. Bibl.

Mexico

Martínez Vázquez, Griselda. La mujer en el proceso de modernización en México. *El Cotidiano*, v. 9, no. 53 (Mar – Apr 93), pp. 17 – 24. Bibl, tables.

Peru

Gamarra, Jefrey. Estado, modernidad y sociedad regional: Ayacucho, 1920 – 1940. *Apuntes (Peru)*, no. 31 (July – Dec 92), pp. 103 – 114. Bibl.

SOCIAL CLASSES

See also
  Capitalists and financiers
  Elite (Social sciences)
  Labor and laboring classes
  Marginalization
  Middle classes
  Oligarchy
  Peasantry
  Social structure

Bolivia

Abercrombie, Thomas Alan. La fiesta del carnaval postcolonial en Oruro: clase, etnicidad y nacionalismo en la danza folklórica (With commentaries by seven historians and a response by the author). *Revista Andina*, v. 10, no. 2 (Dec 92), pp. 279 – 352. Bibl, il.

Lagos, María L. The Politics of Representation: Class and Ethnic Identities in Cochabamba, Bolivia. *Boletín de Antropología Americana*, no. 24 (Dec 91), pp. 143 – 150. Bibl, il.

Brazil

Costa, Iraci del Nero da. *Arraia-miúda: um estudo sobre os não-proprietários de escravos no Brasil* reviewed by José Flávio Motta. *Estudos Econômicos*, v. 22, no. 3 (Sept – Dec 92), pp. 485 – 487.

Guatemala

Sanchiz Ochoa, Pilar. Poder y conflictos de autoridad en Santiago de Guatemala durante el siglo XVI. *Anuario de Estudios Americanos*, v. 49 (1992), pp. 21 – 54. Bibl.

Haiti

Garrigus, John D. Blue and Brown: Contraband Indigo and the Rise of a Free Colored Planter Class in French Saint-Domingue. *The Americas*, v. 50, no. 2 (Oct 93), pp. 233 – 263. Bibl, tables, maps, charts.

Latin America

Hoberman, Louisa Schell and Susan Migden Socolow, eds. *Cities and Society in Colonial Latin America* reviewed by Arij Ouweneel. *European Review of Latin American and Caribbean Studies*, no. 54 (June 93), pp. 125 – 126.

Vilas, Carlos María. Sociedad civil y pueblo. *Revista Paraguaya de Sociología*, v. 30, no. 86 (Jan – Apr 93), pp. 71 – 82. Bibl.

Mexico

Murphy, Arthur D. and Alex Stepick. *Social Inequality in Oaxaca: A History of Resistance and Change* reviewed by John K. Chance. *The Americas*, v. 49, no. 4 (Apr 93), pp. 541 – 542.

Bibliography

Mentz de Boege, Brígida M. von. La desigualdad social en México: revisión bibliográfica y propuesta de una visión global. *Historia Mexicana*, v. 42, no. 2 (Oct – Dec 92), pp. 505 – 561.

Panama

Méndez Dávila, Lionel. Acerca del público latrocinio de las "lumpen burguesías" y las tropelías del poder bajo las clases residuales. *USAC*, no. 12 (Dec 90), pp. 31 – 35.

SOCIAL CONFLICT

See also
  Guerrillas
  Revolutions
  Terrorism
  Violence

Gilly, Adolfo. 1968: la ruptura en los bordes. *Nexos*, v. 16, no. 191 (Nov 93), pp. 25 – 33.

Andean region
Bibliography

García B., Pantaleón. Resistencia y rebelión durante el siglo XVIII en la región andina (Review article). *Revista Cultural Lotería*, v. 51, no. 391 (Sept – Oct 92), pp. 80 – 97. Bibl.

Argentina

Blasi Brambilla, Alberto. Ezeiza, veinte años después. *Todo Es Historia*, v. 27, no. 311 (June 93), pp. 79 – 83. Il.

Tur Donati, Carlos M. Crisis social, xenofobia y nacionalismo en Argentina, 1919. *Cuadernos Americanos*, no. 42, Nueva época (Nov – Dec 93), pp. 48 – 77. Bibl.

Brazil

Diacon, Todd Alan. *Millenarian Vision, Capitalist Reality: Brazil's Contestado Rebellion, 1912 – 1916* reviewed by Cliff Welch. *The Americas*, v. 50, no. 2 (Oct 93), pp. 285 – 286.

— *Millenarian Vision, Capitalist Reality: Brazil's Contestado Rebellion, 1912 – 1916* reviewed by Anthony Pereira. *Canadian Journal of Latin American and Caribbean Studies*, v. 17, no. 34 (1992), pp. 132 – 135.

— *Millenarian Vision, Capitalist Reality: Brazil's Contestado Rebellion, 1912 – 1916* reviewed by Kees de Groot. *European Review of Latin American and Caribbean Studies*, no. 53 (Dec 92), pp. 112 – 114.

— *Millenarian Vision, Capitalist Reality: Brazil's Contestado Rebellion, 1912 – 1916* reviewed by Patricia R. Pessar. *Hispanic American Historical Review*, v. 73, no. 1 (Feb 93), pp. 166 – 167.

— *Millenarian Vision, Capitalist Reality: Brazil's Contestado Rebellion, 1912 – 1916* reviewed by Bernardo Kucinski. *Journal of Latin American Studies*, v. 25, no. 1 (Feb 93), pp. 201 – 202.

Pérez Ochoa, Eduardo. El problema de guerra irregular referido en los congresos del Instituto Histórico y Geográfico del Brasil, IHGB. *Estudos Ibero-Americanos*, v. 18, no. 1 (July 92), pp. 71 – 88. Bibl.

Sources

Assunção, Matthias Röhrig, ed. *A guerra dos bem-te-vis: a balaiada na memória oral* reviewed by Mary Karasch (Review entitled "A balaiada in Brazil"). *The Americas*, v. 49, no. 3 (Jan 93), pp. 392 – 394.

Central America

Coleman, Kenneth M. and George C. Herring, eds. *Understanding the Central American Crisis: Sources of Conflict, U.S. Policy, and Options for Peace* reviewed by Orlando Peña. *Canadian Journal of Latin American and Caribbean Studies*, v. 17, no. 34 (1992), pp. 129 – 130.

Harto de Vera, Fernando. La resolución del proceso de negociaciones de paz. *ECA; Estudios Centroamericanos*, v. 48, no. 531 – 532 (Jan – Feb 93), pp. 27 – 38. Bibl, il.

Rouquié, Alain. *Guerres et paix en Amérique Centrale* reviewed by Edelberto Torres-Rivas. *Journal of Latin American Studies*, v. 25, no. 3 (Oct 93), pp. 668 – 669.

Chile

Garcés Durán, Mario. *Crisis social y motines populares en el 1900* reviewed by Ricardo López (Review entitled "Buscar la historia y reconstruirla"). *Casa de las Américas*, no. 189 (Oct – Dec 92), pp. 142 – 145.

Colombia

Barbosa Estepa, Reinaldo. *Guadalupe y sus centauros: memorias de la insurrección llanera* reviewed by Hermes Tovar Pinzón. *Anuario Colombiano de Historia Social y de la Cultura*, no. 20 (1992), pp. 169 – 172.

Catatumbo, Pablo. La doctrina de la seguridad nacional: el principal obstáculo para la paz. *Revista Javeriana*, v. 60, no. 590 (Nov – Dec 92), pp. 303 – 315.

Dueñas Vargas, Guiomar. Algunas hipótesis para el estudio de la resistencia campesina en la región central de Colombia, siglo XIX. *Anuario Colombiano de Historia Social y de la Cultura*, no. 20 (1992), pp. 90 – 106. Bibl.

García Duarte, Ricardo. La paz esquiva: negociaciones, desencuentros y rediseño de estrategias. *Revista Javeriana*, v. 60, no. 590 (Nov – Dec 92), pp. 316 – 322.

Leal Buitrago, Francisco. La guerra y la paz en Colombia. *Nueva Sociedad*, no. 125 (May – June 93), pp. 157 – 161.

Mendoza, Plinio Apuleyo. La guerra que nunca quisimos ver. *Nueva Sociedad*, no. 125 (May – June 93), pp. 149 – 153.

Ocampo López, Javier. La rebelión de las alcabalas. *Boletín de Historia y Antigüedades*, v. 79, no. 779 (Oct – Dec 92), pp. 993 – 1005. Bibl.

Samper Pizano, Ernesto. Democracia y paz (Previously published in this journal, no. 549, 1988). *Revista Javeriana*, v. 61, no. 596 (July 93), pp. 89 – 94.

Serpa Uribe, Horacio. La paz primero que la guerra. *Nueva Sociedad*, no. 125 (May – June 93), pp. 153 – 156.

Vargas Castaño, Alfredo. La suerte de caracol: expatriados, expropriados, desterrados y desplazados en Colombia. *Nueva Sociedad*, no. 123 (Jan – Feb 93), pp. 144 – 155.

Costa Rica

Lehoucq, Fabrice Edouard. Conflicto de clases, crisis política y destrucción de las prácticas democráticas en Costa Rica: reevaluando los orígenes de la guerra civil de 1948. *Revista de Historia (Costa Rica)*, no. 25 (Jan – June 92), pp. 65 – 96. Bibl.

Cuba

Yacou, Alain. La insurgencia negra en la isla de Cuba en la primera mitad del siglo XIX. *Revista de Indias*, v. 53, no. 197 (Jan – Apr 93), pp. 23 – 51. Bibl.

Ecuador

Lavallé, Bernard. *Quito et la crise de l'alcabala, 1580 – 1600* reviewed by Michel Bertrand. *Caravelle*, no. 60 (1993), pp. 148 – 150.

Mond, Rebecca Earle. Indian Rebellion and Bourbon Reform in New Granada: Riots in Pasto, 1780 – 1800. *Hispanic American Historical Review*, v. 73, no. 1 (Feb 93), pp. 99 – 124. Bibl.

El Salvador

Sources

De la locura a la esperanza: la guerra de doce años en El Salvador; informe de la Comisión de la Verdad para El Salvador (Introduced by the Secretary General of the Commission). *ECA; Estudios Centroamericanos*, v. 48, no. 533 (Mar 93), Issue.

Guatemala

Carmack, Robert Marin, ed. *Guatemala: cosecha de violencias* reviewed by Manuel Angel Castillo G. *Revista Mexicana de Sociología*, v. 54, no. 1 (Jan – Mar 92), pp. 331 – 334.

Le Bot, Yvon. *La guerre en terre maya: communauté, violence et modernité au Guatemala, 1970 – 1992* reviewed by J. P. Pérez Sáinz. *Journal of Latin American Studies*, v. 25, no. 3 (Oct 93), pp. 670 – 672.

— *La guerre en terre maya: communauté, violence et modernité au Guatemala, 1970 – 1992* reviewed by Maxime Haubert. *Tiers Monde*, v. 34, no. 136 (Oct – Dec 93), pp. 952 – 953.

— Le palimpseste maya: violence, communauté et territoire dans le conflit guatémaltèque. *Cahiers des Amériques Latines*, no. 13 (1992), pp. 87 – 105. Bibl, maps.

Perera, Víctor. *Unfinished Conquest: The Guatemalan Tragedy* (Review). *NACLA Report on the Americas*, v. 27, no. 3 (Nov – Dec 93), p. 48.

Latin America

Suárez Salazar, Luis. "Drug Trafficking" and Social and Political Conflicts in Latin America: Some Hypotheses (Translated by Luis Fierro). *Latin American Perspectives*, v. 20, no. 1 (Winter 93), pp. 83 – 98. Bibl, tables.

Mexico

Castro Gutiérrez, Felipe. *Movimientos populares en Nueva España: Michoacán, 1766 – 1797* reviewed by Frédérique Lanque (Review entitled "Les soulèvements populaires de 1767 en Nouvell-Espagne: le point sur quelques publications récentes"). *Caravelle*, no. 60 (1993), pp. 152 – 154.

Gálvez, José de. *Informe sobre las rebeliones populares en 1767* reviewed by Frédérique Langue (Review entitled "Les soulèvements populaires de 1767 en Nouvell-Espagne: le point sur quelques publications récentes"). *Caravelle*, no. 60 (1993), pp. 152 – 154.

Gosner, Kevin. *Soldiers of the Virgin: The Moral Economy of a Colonial Maya Rebellion* reviewed by Robert M. Hill II. *The Americas*, v. 50, no. 2 (Oct 93), pp. 274 – 276.

— *Soldiers of the Virgin: The Moral Economy of a Colonial Maya Rebellion* reviewed by Kenneth Mills. *Bulletin of Latin American Research*, v. 12, no. 2 (May 93), pp. 223 – 224.

— *Soldiers of the Virgin: The Moral Economy of a Colonial Maya Rebellion* reviewed by Stephen Webre. *Colonial Latin American Historical Review*, v. 2, no. 1 (Winter 93), pp. 109 – 110.

— *Soldiers of the Virgin: The Moral Economy of a Colonial Maya Rebellion* reviewed by Linda A. Newson. *Journal of Latin American Studies*, v. 25, no. 3 (Oct 93), pp. 655 – 656.

Joseph, Gilbert Michael. *Revolución desde afuera: Yucatán, México y Estados Unidos, 1880 – 1924* translated by Eduardo L. Suárez. Reviewed by Othón Baños. *Estudios Sociológicos*, v. 11, no. 31 (Jan – Apr 93), pp. 265 – 270.

Peru

Eyzaguirre, Graciela. Los escenarios de la guerra en la región Cáceres. *Allpanchis*, v. 23, no. 39 (Jan – June 92), pp. 155 – 180. Bibl, tables, maps.

Hernández, Max. La piel dura. *Debate (Peru)*, v. 15, no. 71 (Nov 92 – Jan 93), pp. 20 – 21. Il.

Rodríguez G., Yolanda. Los actores sociales y la violencia política en Puno. *Allpanchis*, v. 23, no. 39 (Jan – June 92), pp. 131 – 154. Bibl.

Puerto Rico

Navarro García, Jesús Raúl. Grupos de poder y tensiones sociales en Puerto Rico durante la crisis del imperio, 1815 – 1837: un intento de síntesis. *Anuario de Estudios Americanos*, v. 50, no. 1 (1993), pp. 133 – 162. Bibl.

United States

Hayes-Bautista, David E. et al. Latinos and the 1992 Los Angeles Riots: A Behavioral Sciences Perspective. *Hispanic Journal of Behavioral Sciences*, v. 15, no. 4 (Nov 93), pp. 427 – 448. Bibl, charts.

SOCIAL CONTROL

Alvarez C., Edwin. Criminalidad y abuso de poder: el caso argentino, 1976 – 1983. *Revista Cultural Lotería*, v. 51, no. 388 (Mar – Apr 92), pp. 5 – 33. Bibl.

Cruz Barrera, Nydia E. Reclusión, control social y penitenciaria en Puebla en el siglo XIX. *Siglo XIX: Revista*, no. 12, 2a época (July – Dec 92), pp. 119 – 146.

Lima, Magali Alonso de and Roberto Kant de Lima. Capoeira e cidadania: negritude e identidade no Brasil republicano. *Revista de Antropologia (Brazil)*, v. 34 (1991), pp. 143 – 182. Bibl.

Losada Lora, Rodrigo. La evolución del orden público. *Revista Javeriana*, v. 61, no. 597 (Aug 93), pp. 159 – 165.

SOCIAL DOCTRINE (CATHOLIC CHURCH)

See

Church and social problems

SOCIAL INDICATORS

Business Mexico Indicators. *Business Mexico*, v. 3 (1993), All issues. Tables, charts.

Fortoul V., Freddy. Satisfacción comunitaria: indicador social subjetivo de bienestar. *Estudios Sociales (Chile)*, no. 74 (Oct – Dec 92), pp. 119 – 148. Bibl.

Jarque, Carlos M. La población de México en el último decenio del siglo XX. *Comercio Exterior*, v. 43, no. 7 (July 93), pp. 642 – 651. Tables, charts.

SOCIAL JUSTICE

See
Distributive justice
Sociological jurisprudence
Subdivision *Social policy* under names of specific countries

SOCIAL MOBILITY

Brazil

Guimarães, Antônio Sérgio Alfredo. Operários e mobilidade social na Bahia: análise de uma trajetória individual. *Revista Brasileira de Ciências Sociais*, v. 8, no. 22 (June 93), pp. 81 – 97. Bibl, tables.

Guatemala

Pérez Sáinz, Juan Pablo et al. Trayectorias laborales y constitución de identidades: los trabajadores indígenas en la ciudad de Guatemala. *Estudios Sociológicos*, v. 11, no. 32 (May – Aug 93), pp. 515 – 545. Bibl, tables.

Mexico

Hernández Rodríguez, Rogelio. Preparación y movilidad de los funcionarios de la administración pública mexicana. *Estudios Sociológicos*, v. 11, no. 32 (May – Aug 93), pp. 445 – 473. Bibl, tables.

Pries, Ludger. Movilidad en el empleo: una comparación de trabajo asalariado y por cuenta propia en Puebla. *Estudios Sociológicos*, v. 11, no. 32 (May – Aug 93), pp. 475 – 496. Bibl, charts.

Ramírez Carrillo, Luis Alfonso. Estratificación, clase y parentesco: empresarios libaneses en el sureste de México. *Nueva Antropología*, v. 13, no. 43 (Nov 92), pp. 123 – 137. Bibl.

SOCIAL MOVEMENTS

See also
Political participation
Pressure groups
Social change

Argentina

Gorlier, Juan Carlos. Democratización en América del Sur: una reflexión sobre el potencial de los movimientos sociales en Argentina y Brasil. *Revista Mexicana de Sociología*, v. 54, no. 4 (Oct – Dec 92), pp. 119 – 151. Bibl.

Brazil

Barreira, Irlys Alencar Firmo. O reverso das vitrines: conflitos urbanos e cultura política em construção reviewed by Glória Diógenes. *Revista Brasileira de Ciências Sociais*, v. 8, no. 23 (Oct 93), pp. 156 – 157.

Gorlier, Juan Carlos. Democratización en América del Sur: una reflexión sobre el potencial de los movimientos sociales en Argentina y Brasil. *Revista Mexicana de Sociología*, v. 54, no. 4 (Oct – Dec 92), pp. 119 – 151. Bibl.

Bibliography

Wolfe, Joel. Social Movements and the State in Brazil (Review article). *Latin American Research Review*, v. 28, no. 1 (1993), pp. 248 – 257. Bibl.

Chile

Sources

Domínguez Díaz, Marta Silvia. Transición política en Chile: documentación y fuentes. *SALALM Papers*, v. 34 (1989), pp. 459 – 474. Bibl.

Costa Rica

Rivera, Rolando and David Smith. Organización, movilización popular y desarrollo regional en el Atlántico costarricense. *Estudios Rurales Latinoamericanos*, v. 15, no. 2 – 3 (May – Dec 92), pp. 79 – 110. Tables.

Latin America

Gutmann, Matthew C. Rejoinder (to James C. Scott's commentaries in "Reply" on Gutmann's original article entitled "Rituals of Resistance"). *Latin American Perspectives*, v. 20, no. 2 (Spring 93), pp. 95 – 96.

— Rituals of Resistance: A Critique of the Theory of Everyday Forms of Resistance. *Latin American Perspectives*, v. 20, no. 2 (Spring 93), pp. 74 – 92. Bibl.

Radcliffe, Sarah A. and Sallie Westwood, eds. *"Viva": Women and Popular Protest in Latin America* reviewed by Tessa Cubitt. *Bulletin of Latin American Research*, v. 12, no. 2 (May 93), pp. 242 – 243.

Scott, James C. Reply (to the article "Rituals of Resistance" by Matthew C. Gutmann). *Latin American Perspectives*, v. 20, no. 2 (Spring 93), pp. 93 – 94.

Vilas, Carlos María. América Latina: la hora de la sociedad civil (Originally published in *NACLA: Report on the Americas*, Sept – Oct 93). *Realidad Económica*, no. 120 (Nov – Dec 93), pp. 7 – 17. Bibl.

— The Hour of Civil Society (Translated by Mark Fried). *NACLA Report on the Americas*, v. 27, no. 2 (Sept – Oct 93), pp. 38 – 42 + . Bibl, il.

Mexico

Alonso, Jorge et al, eds. *El nuevo estado mexicano, tomo III: Estado, actores y movimientos sociales* reviewed by Griselda Martínez Vázquez. *El Cotidiano*, v. 8, no. 52 (Jan – Feb 93), p. 117.

Campbell, Howard B. Tradition and the New Social Movements: The Politics of Isthmus Zapotec Culture. *Latin American Perspectives*, v. 20, no. 3 (Summer 93), pp. 83 – 97. Bibl.

Craig, Ann L. and Joseph W. Foweraker, eds. *Popular Movements and Political Change in Mexico* reviewed by Daniel C. Levy. *Studies in Comparative International Development*, v. 27, no. 3 (Fall 92), pp. 122 – 124.

Moctezuma Barragán, Pedro. Del movimiento urbano popular a los movimientos comunitarios: el espejo desenterrado. *El Cotidiano*, v. 10, no. 57 (Aug – Sept 93), pp. 3 – 10. Il.

— El espejo desenterrado. *El Cotidiano*, v. 9, no. 54 (May 93), pp. 49 – 54. Il.

Núñez González, Oscar. *Innovaciones democrático – culturales del movimiento urbano-popular* reviewed by José Javier Gutiérrez Rodríguez. *El Cotidiano*, v. 10, no. 57 (Aug – Sept 93), pp. 107 – 108.

Ramírez Sáiz, Juan Manuel. *¿Son políticos los movimientos urbano-populares?: un planteamiento teórico – metodológico* reviewed by Melchor Negrete Silva. *El Cotidiano*, v. 10, no. 57 (Aug – Sept 93), p. 107.

Sepúlveda Garza, Manola. El este de Guanajuato, 1760 – 1900: microhistoria de alianzas sociales. *Cuadernos Americanos*, no. 37, Nueva época (Jan – Feb 93), pp. 76 – 89. Bibl, tables.

Valenzuela Arce, José Manuel. *Empapados de sereno: el movimiento urbano popular en Baja California, 1928 – 1988* reviewed by Miguel Angel Vite Pérez. *Estudios Sociológicos*, v. 11, no. 31 (Jan – Apr 93), pp. 285 – 288.

Bibliography

Ochoa Méndez, Jacqueline. Orientación bibliográfica sobre el movimiento urbano popular en la ciudad de México. *El Cotidiano*, v. 10, no. 57 (Aug – Sept 93), pp. 111 – 112.

Nicaragua

Quandt, Midge. Nicaragua: Unbinding the Ties; Popular Movements and the FSLN. *Report on the Americas*, v. 26, no. 4 (Feb 93), pp. 11 – 14. Il.

Peru

Rodríguez Rabanal, César. La cultura del diálogo. *Debate (Peru)*, v. 16, no. 73 (June – Aug 93), pp. 27 – 30. Il.

Southern Cone of South America

Lehmann, David. *Democracy and Development in Latin America: Economics, Politics, and Religion in the Post-War Period* reviewed by Ricardo Grinspun and Sally Humphries. *Economic Development and Cultural Change*, v. 41, no. 4 (July 93), pp. 886 – 894. Bibl.

SOCIAL POLICY

See
Subdivision *Social policy* under names of specific
countries

SOCIAL PSYCHOLOGY

Flores, Mercedes and Roxana Hidalgo Xirinachs. El autoritarismo en la vida cotidiana: SIDA, homofobia y moral sexual. *Revista de Ciencias Sociales (Costa Rica), no.* 58 (Dec 92), pp. 35 – 44. Bibl.

Hernández, Raúl Augusto. Indecisión social o crisis de conciencia: los cardinales de la desolación. *Estudios Interdisciplinarios de América Latina y el Caribe,* v. 4, no. 1 (Jan – June 93), pp. 141 – 163. Bibl, tables, charts.

Pomer, León. El animal que imagina. *Revista de Letras (Brazil),* v. 32 (1992), pp. 153 – 167. Bibl.

Remus Araico, José. La angustia social y el nacimiento de dos mitos modernos. *Revista Mexicana de Ciencias Políticas y Sociales,* v. 38, Nueva época, no. 154 (Oct – Dec 93), pp. 65 – 78.

Argentina

Graziano, Frank. *Divine Violence: Spectacle, Psychosexuality, and Radical Christianity in the Argentine "Dirty War"* reviewed by Ronaldo Munck. *Bulletin of Latin American Research,* v. 12, no. 1 (Jan 93), pp. 119 – 120.

— *Divine Violence: Spectacle, Psychosexuality, and Radical Christianity in the Argentine "Dirty War"* reviewed by Donald C. Hodges. *Hispanic American Historical Review,* v. 73, no. 3 (Aug 93), pp. 513 – 514.

— *Divine Violence: Spectacle, Psychosexuality, and Radical Christianity in the Argentine "Dirty War"* reviewed by Alberto Ciria. *Revista Interamericana de Bibliografía,* v. 42, no. 3 (1992), pp. 503 – 504.

Tamer, Norma Liliana. Possibilities and Conditions of Integral Education for Older Citizens: Pedagogic Proposal. *La Educación (USA),* v. 37, no. 114 (1993), pp. 119 – 122.

Caribbean area

Potter, Robert B. Caribbean Views on Environment and Development: A Cognitive Perspective. *Caribbean Geography,* v. 3, no. 4 (Sept 92), pp. 236 – 243. Bibl, tables.

Central America

Pacheco O., Gilda. Migraciones forzadas en Centroamérica: evolución psicosocial. *Nueva Sociedad, no.* 127 (Sept – Oct 93), pp. 114 – 125. Bibl.

Colombia

Urrea Giraldo, Fernando and Diego Zapata Ortega. El síndrome de los nervios en el imaginario popular en una población urbana de Cali. *Revista Colombiana de Antropología,* v. 29 (1992), pp. 207 – 232. Bibl.

El Salvador

Argueta, Manlio. An Exile's Return. *NACLA Report on the Americas,* v. 26, no. 5 (May 93), pp. 4 – 6. Il.

United States

Bohon, Lisa M. et al. The Effects of Real-World Status and Manipulated Status on the Self-Esteem and Social Competition of Anglo-Americans and Mexican-Americans. *Hispanic Journal of Behavioral Sciences,* v. 15, no. 1 (Feb 93), pp. 63 – 79. Bibl, tables.

Solberg, V. Scott et al. Self-Efficacy and Hispanic College Students: Validation of the College Self-Efficacy Instrument. *Hispanic Journal of Behavioral Sciences,* v. 15, no. 1 (Feb 93), pp. 80 – 95. Bibl, tables.

SOCIAL SCIENCE RESEARCH

See also
Research institutes

Cuba

León Tejera, Francisco. Crisis Challenges Social Researchers. *Hemisphere,* v. 5, no. 3 (Summer – Fall 93), pp. 36 – 37.

Mexico

Methodology

Menéndez, Eduardo L. Investigación antropológica, biografía y controles artesanales. *Nueva Antropología,* v. 13, no. 43 (Nov 92), pp. 23 – 37. Bibl.

Novelo, Victoria. Las tentaciones de doña Victoria. *Nueva Antropología,* v. 13, no. 43 (Nov 92), pp. 45 – 51.

Varela, Roberto. Reflexiones sobre la expansión de sistemas y las relaciones de poder. *Nueva Antropología,* v. 13, no. 43 (Nov 92), pp. 39 – 43.

SOCIAL SCIENCES

See also
Functional analysis (Social sciences)

Bibliography

Garza Mercado, Ario. *Obras de consulta para estudiantes de ciencias sociales y humanidades* reviewed by Enrique Núñez. *La Educación (USA),* v. 37, no. 114 (1993), pp. 157 – 158.

Latin America

Hopenhayn, Martín. The Social Sciences without Planning or Revolution? *CEPAL Review, no.* 48 (Dec 92), pp. 129 – 140. Bibl.

Lavell Thomas, Allan. Ciencias sociales y desastres naturales en América Latina: un encuentro inconcluso (Chapter from the book entitled *Desastres naturales, sociedad y protección civil). EURE,* v. 19, no. 58 (Oct 93), pp. 73 – 84. Bibl.

Foreign influences

Barbano, Filippo et al, eds. *Sociologia, storia, positivismo: Messico, Brasile, Argentina e l'Italia* reviewed by Carlos Strasser (Review entitled "Sobre la formación y ciertas influencias en el desarrollo de las ciencias sociales latinoamericanas: una importante contribución italo-argentina"). *Desarrollo Económico (Argentina),* v. 32, no. 128 (Jan – Mar 93), pp. 625 – 628.

— *Sociologia, storia, positivismo: Messico, Brasile, Argentina e l'Italia* reviewed by Giorgio Alberti. *Journal of Latin American Studies,* v. 25, no. 2 (May 93), pp. 417 – 418.

Mexico

Arizpe Schlosser, Lourdes. Los desafíos intelectuales en las ciencias sociales. *Momento Económico, no.* 69 (Sept – Oct 93), pp. 29 – 30.

Lomnitz, Cinna. Gloria y el TLC. *Nexos,* v. 16, no. 189 (Sept 93), pp. 8 – 13.

SOCIAL SECURITY

See also
Pension trusts

Argentina

Lozano, Claudio. La reforma previsional. *Realidad Económica, no.* 113 (Jan – Feb 93), pp. 6 – 11. Tables.

Tolosa, Fernando. El sistema financiero, el financiamiento del desarrollo y la reforma previsional. *Realidad Económica, no.* 113 (Jan – Feb 93), pp. 13 – 17.

Brazil

Hochman, Gilberto. Os cardeais da previdência social: gênese e consolidação de uma elite burocrática. *Dados,* v. 35, no. 3 (1992), pp. 371 – 401. Bibl.

Colombia

Obando Arboleda, María Cecilia. Una propuesta de reforma pensional: ¿Qué falló? *Revista Javeriana,* v. 61, no. 592 (Mar 93), pp. 91 – 96.

Perfetti, Mauricio. Algunas precisiones en cuanto a la reforma de la seguridad social. *Revista Javeriana,* v. 61, no. 592 (Mar 93), pp. 102 – 100. Bibl, tables.

Quintero, Fernando. Cesantías y pensiones: el reordenamiento laboral. *Revista Javeriana,* v. 61, no. 592 (Mar 93), pp. 81 – 85. Tables.

Robledo Quijano, Fernando and Germán Sánchez Franco. El doble carácter de las administradoras. *Revista Javeriana,* v. 61, no. 592 (Mar 93), pp. 112 – 116.

Sánchez Franco, Germán. Antecedentes de la reforma laboral acerca del tema de las cesantías. *Revista Javeriana,* v. 61, no. 592 (Mar 93), pp. 86 – 89.

Santamaría Tavera, Fanny. La reforma de ISS: los colombianos tienen la palabra. *Revista Javeriana,* v. 61, no. 592 (Mar 93), pp. 69 – 75. Il.

Latin America
Bibliography

Borzutzky, Silvia. Social Security and Health Policies in Latin America: The Changing Roles of the State and the Private Sector (Review article). *Latin American Research Review,* v. 28, no. 2 (1993), pp. 246 – 256.

Mexico

Chandler, Dewitt Samuel. *Social Assistance and Bureaucratic Politics: The Montepíos of Colonial Mexico, 1767 – 1821* reviewed by Richard J. Salvucci. *The Americas,* v. 49, no. 4 (Apr 93), pp. 551 – 552.

— *Social Assistance and Bureaucratic Politics: The Montepíos of Colonial Mexico, 1767 – 1821* reviewed by Silvia Marina Arrom. *Hispanic American Historical Review,* v. 73, no. 1 (Feb 93), pp. 153 – 154.

— *Social Assistance and Bureaucratic Politics: The Montepíos of Colonial Mexico, 1767 – 1821* reviewed by Eric Van Young. *Journal of Latin American Studies,* v. 25, no. 3 (Oct 93), pp. 653 – 654.

Cohen, Joshua A. Reforming the Reforms. *Business Mexico,* v. 3, no. 10 (Oct 93), pp. 44 – 45. Tables.

Olmedo Carranza, Bernardo. Crisis de la seguridad social: el caso de México. *Momento Económico,* no. 69 (Sept – Oct 93), pp. 13 – 15.

Pozas Horcasitas, Ricardo. El desarrollo de la seguridad social en México. *Revista Mexicana de Sociología,* v. 54, no. 4 (Oct – Dec 92), pp. 27 – 63.

SOCIAL SERVICE

See also
   Charities

Colombia

Torres Díaz, Jorge H. Dimensión gerencial del trabajo social laboral. *Desarrollo Indoamericano,* v. 23, no. 91 (June 93), pp. 47 – 53. Il.

SOCIAL SERVICES

See also
   Community development
   Public health
   Subdivisions *Public works* and *Social policy* under names of specific countries

Brazil

Gregori, Maria Filomena. *Cenas e queixas: um estudo sobre mulheres, relações violentas e a prática feminista* reviewed by Danielle Ardaillon (Review entitled "Facetas do feminino"). *Estudos Feministas,* v. 1, no. 2 (1993), pp. 487 – 489.

— *Cenas e queixas: um estudo sobre mulheres, relações violentas e a prática feminista* reviewed by Wânia Pasinato Izumino. *Revista Brasileira de Ciências Sociais,* v. 8, no. 22 (June 93), pp. 145 – 146.

— *Cenas e queixas: um estudo sobre mulheres, relações violentas e a prática feminista* (Review). *Vozes,* v. 87, no. 4 (July – Aug 93), p. 99.

Chile

Poblete B., Renato. El Hogar de Cristo. *Mensaje,* v. 42, no. 420 (July 93), pp. 290 – 291. Il, tables.

Stragier, Julio. Hogar de Cristo Viviendas. *Mensaje,* v. 42, no. 420 (July 93), p. 292. Il.

Costa Rica

Benavides Montoya, Thelma et al. El menor deambulante en Costa Rica. *Revista de Ciencias Sociales (Costa Rica),* no. 59 (Mar 93), pp. 27 – 35. Bibl, charts.

Ecuador

Juárez, Fátima. Intervención de las instituciones en la reducción de la fecundidad y la mortalidad infantil. *Estudios Demográficos y Urbanos,* v. 7, no. 2 – 3 (May – Dec 92), pp. 377 – 405. Bibl, tables, charts.

Latin America

Devlin, Robert T. Privatizations and Social Welfare. *CEPAL Review,* no. 49 (Apr 93), pp. 155 – 180. Bibl, tables.

Palma, Eduardo and Dolores María Rufián Lizana. La descentralización de los servicios sociales. *Estudios Sociales (Chile),* no. 77 (July – Sept 93), pp. 73 – 116. Bibl.

Cost

Cohen, Ernesto and Rolando Franco. Rationalizing Social Policy: Evaluation and Viability. *CEPAL Review,* no. 47 (Aug 92), pp. 163 – 172. Bibl, charts.

Mexico

Apoyo y orientación legal a la medida de nuestras necesidades. *Fem,* v. 17, no. 120 (Feb 93), p. 40.

Atención a víctimas de delitos sexuales. *Fem,* v. 17, no. 124 (June 93), p. 42.

Carrillo Castro, Alejandro and Miguel Angel Romero Miranda. Las preocupaciones públicas: el caso de Tamaulipas. *El Cotidiano,* v. 8, no. 51 (Nov – Dec 92), pp. 95 – 101. Tables.

Hernández Téllez, Josefina. "Año con año se ha consolidado el trabajo": lic. Fernando Portilla, director gral. de la Supervisión General de Servicios a la Comunidad de la PGJDF. *Fem,* v. 17, no. 125 (July 93), p. 39.

— ¿Cómo funciona y para qué sirve la participacíon en la Procuraduría General de Justicia del D.F.? *Fem,* v. 17, no. 123 (May 93), p. 43.

— Dirección de Atención a Víctimas de la SGSC – PGJDF. *Fem,* v. 17, no. 121 (Mar 93), p. 38.

— Servicios a la comunidad de la PGJDF: por el trato humano en la impartición de justicia. *Fem,* v. 17, no. 119 (Jan 93), p. 30.

— 24 horas captando quejas . . . . *Fem,* v. 17, no. 122 (Apr 93), p. 40.

Torres Salcido, Gerardo. Pobreza y organización social: acceso a programas sociales de abasto. *Momento Económico,* no. 68 (July – Aug 93), pp. 19 – 22. Bibl.

Sources

Declaración de México para una maternidad sin riesgos: Cocoyoc, Morelos, 8 – 11 de febrero de 1993. *Fem,* v. 17, no. 122 (Apr 93), pp. 26 – 31. Il.

SOCIAL STRUCTURE

See also
   Social classes
   Subdivisions *Social conditions* and *Social policy* under names of specific countries

Criado Boado, Felipe. Construcción social del espacio y reconstrucción arqueológica del paisaje. *Boletín de Antropología Americana,* no. 24 (Dec 91), pp. 5 – 30. Bibl, il.

Hernández, Raúl Augusto. Correlación y correspondencia en la acción social. *Revista Paraguaya de Sociología,* v. 29, no. 84 (May – Aug 92), pp. 171 – 185. Bibl.

SOCIAL WORK

See
   Social service

SOCIALISM

See also
   Anarchism and anarchists
   Communism
   Marxism

Gilly, Adolfo. ¿Dónde pintar la raya del socialismo? *Nexos,* v. 16, no. 183 (Mar 93), pp. 39 – 46.

Brazil

Amaral, Roberto and Antônio Houaiss. A via partidária dos socialistas brasileiros. *Vozes,* v. 87, no. 1 (Jan – Feb 93), pp. 2 – 13. Il.

Dacanal, José Hildebrando. A alternativa social-democrata. *Vozes,* v. 86, no. 6 (Nov – Dec 92), pp. 45 – 52.

Hentschke, Jens. Alternativas del desarrollo histórico en el Brasil en los años veinte: contribución a la discusión. *Islas,* no. 97 (Sept – Dec 90), pp. 26 – 31. Bibl.

Central America

Hándal, Schafik Jorge and Carlos María Vilas. *The Socialist Option in Central America: Two Reassessments* (Review). *NACLA Report on the Americas,* v. 27, no. 3 (Nov – Dec 93), p. 48.

El Salvador

El ERP se convierte a la socialdemocracia. *ECA; Estudios Centroamericanos*, v. 48, no. 539 (Sept 93), pp. 884 – 885. Il.

Latin America

Castañeda, Jorge G. *Utopia Unarmed: The Latin American Left after the Cold War* reviewed by Nicolás Shumway (Review entitled "La esperanza postdiluviana," translated by Pedro Garland). *Nexos*, v. 16, no. 192 (Dec 93), pp. 76 – 77.

Guadarrama González, Pablo M. Las alternativas sociales en América Latina y la filosofía de la liberación. *Islas*, no. 96 (May – Aug 90), pp. 89 – 102. Bibl.

Harris, Richard L. *Marxism, Socialism, and Democracy in Latin America* reviewed by Carlos M. Vilas. *Journal of Latin American Studies*, v. 25, no. 1 (Feb 93), p. 215.

Peraza Martell, Elina and Tomás Amadeo Vasconi B. Social Democracy and Latin America (Translated by Fred Murphy). *Latin American Perspectives*, v. 20, no. 1 (Winter 93), pp. 99 – 113. Bibl.

Silva, Luís Inácio da. Discurso de Luís Inácio "Lula" da Silva (given at the IV Encuentro del Foro de São Paulo). *Nueva Sociedad*, no. 128 (Nov – Dec 93), pp. 162 – 165.

Bibliography

Angell, Alan. The Left in Latin America since 1930: A Bibliographical Essay. *Historia (Chile)*, no. 26 (1991 – 1992), pp. 61 – 70. Bibl.

Congresses

IV Encuentro del Foro de São Paulo: declaración final. *Nueva Sociedad*, no. 128 (Nov – Dec 93), pp. 158 – 161.

Peru

Cisneros, Luis Jaime. El porvenir de la izquierda. *Debate (Peru)*, v. 15, no. 71 (Nov 92 – Jan 93), pp. 40 – 43. Il.

Venezuela

Ellner, Steven B. *De la derrota guerrillera a la política innovadora: el Movimiento al Socialismo (MAS)* reviewed by Dick Parker. *Nueva Sociedad*, no. 124 (Mar – Apr 93), p. 174.

SOCIALISM AND CATHOLIC CHURCH

See also
Church and social problems
Religion and politics

Díaz-Salazar, Rafael. La crítica cristiana a la civilización del capital: aportaciones de la doctrina social de la iglesia a la construcción de un nuevo socialismo. *ECA; Estudios Centroamericanos*, v. 47, no. 529 – 530 (Nov – Dec 92), pp. 999 – 1014. Bibl, il.

— Izquierda y cristianismo en América Latina. *ECA; Estudios Centroamericanos*, v. 48, no. 536 (June 93), pp. 563 – 576.

Löwy, Michael. Marxism and Christianity in Latin America (Translated by Claudia Pompan). *Latin American Perspectives*, v. 20, no. 4 (Fall 93), pp. 28 – 42. Bibl.

— Marxism and Christianity in Latin America (Translated by Claudia Pompan). *Latin American Perspectives*, v. 20, no. 4 (Fall 93), pp. 28 – 42. Bibl.

SOCIALIST INTERNATIONAL

Peraza Martell, Elina and Tomás Amadeo Vasconi B. Social Democracy and Latin America (Translated by Fred Murphy). *Latin American Perspectives*, v. 20, no. 1 (Winter 93), pp. 99 – 113. Bibl.

SOCIALIZATION

See also
Acculturation
Education and state

Argentina

Escudé, Carlos. *El fracaso del proyecto argentino: educación e ideología* reviewed by Aurora Ravina. *Revista de Historia de América*, no. 113 (Jan – June 92), pp. 177 – 179.

Gómez, Marcelo Flavio. Los problemas de la reproducción cultural en el capitalismo argentino: el caso de la anomia disciplinaria en las escuelas de sectores marginados. *La Educación (USA)*, v. 36, no. 111 – 113 (1992), pp. 195 – 225. Bibl.

Brazil

Duarte, Luiz Fernando Dias et al. Vicissitudes e limites da conversão à cidadania nas classes populares brasileiras. *Revista Brasileira de Ciências Sociais*, v. 8, no. 22 (June 93), pp. 5 – 19. Bibl.

Costa Rica

Lobo, Isaura et al. Televisión: ideología y socialización. *Revista de Ciencias Sociales (Costa Rica)*, no. 57 (Sept 92), pp. 57 – 66. Bibl.

Latin America

Gajardo, Marcela. *La concientización en América Latina* reviewed by Orlando Fals Borda. *La Educación (USA)*, v. 36, no. 111 – 113 (1992), pp. 291 – 294.

Mexico

Vogeley, Nancy J. Colonial Discourse in a Postcolonial Context: Nineteenth-Century Mexico. *Colonial Latin American Review*, v. 2, no. 1 – 2 (1993), pp. 189 – 212. Bibl.

Peru

Vega-Centeno B., Imelda. Ser joven en el Perú: socialización, integración, corporalidad y cultura. *Allpanchis*, v. 25, no. 41 (Jan – June 93), pp. 177 – 210. Bibl, tables.

United States

Knight, George Preston et al. The Socialization of Cooperative, Competitive, and Individualistic Preferences among Mexican American Children: The Mediating Role of Ethnic Identity. *Hispanic Journal of Behavioral Sciences*, v. 15, no. 3 (Aug 93), pp. 291 – 309. Bibl, tables, charts.

SOCIOBIOLOGY

Borges, Dain Edward. "Puffy, Ugly, Slothful, and Inert": Degeneration in Brazilian Social Thought, 1880 – 1940. *Journal of Latin American Studies*, v. 25, no. 2 (May 93), pp. 235 – 256. Bibl.

Stepan, Nancy Leys. *The Hour of Eugenics: Race, Gender, and Nation in Latin America* reviewed by Donna J. Guy. *The Americas*, v. 50, no. 1 (July 93), pp. 136 – 137.

— *The Hour of Eugenics: Race, Gender, and Nation in Latin America* reviewed by Aline Helg. *Hispanic American Historical Review*, v. 73, no. 1 (Feb 93), pp. 138 – 139.

— *The Hour of Eugenics: Race, Gender, and Nation in Latin America* reviewed by Francine Masiello. *Letras Femeninas*, v. 19, no. 1 – 2 (Spring – Fall 93), pp. 136 – 138.

SOCIOLINGUISTICS

Berrouët-Oriol, Robert and Robert Fournier. Créolophonie et francophonie nord – sud: transcontinuum. *Canadian Journal of Latin American and Caribbean Studies*, v. 17, no. 34 (1992), pp. 13 – 25. Bibl.

López Morales, Humberto. *Sociolingüística* reviewed by Dora Pellicer. *Anuario de Letras (Mexico)*, v. 30 (1992), pp. 251 – 262.

Magaña Sánchez, Margarita Elena. Feminolecto y Masculinolecto: II° Encuentro Feminista de la UAM, Unidad Xochimilco de la UAM, julio de 1992. *Fem*, v. 17, no. 125 (July 93), pp. 14 – 17. Bibl.

Bibliography

Medina López, Javier. Esbozo de una guía bibliográfica del tratamiento. *Anuario de Letras (Mexico)*, v. 30 (1992), pp. 233 – 248.

Andean region

Doerflinger, Enrique Ricardo et al. La realidad socio-lingüística del pueblo quechua. *Anuario Indigenista*, v. 30 (Dec 91), pp. 267 – 288.

Argentina

Bixio, Beatriz and Luis D. Heredia. *Distancia cultural y lingüística: el fracaso escolar en poblaciones rurales del oeste de la provincia de Córdoba* (Review). *La Educación (USA)*, v. 36, no. 111 – 113 (1992), pp. 296 – 298.

Martini, Mónica Patricia and Daisy Rípodas Ardanaz. Aportes sobre el voseo en Córdoba a horcajadas de los siglos XVIII y XIX: sus modalidades en la obra de Cristóbal de Aguilar. *Investigaciones y Ensayos*, no. 41 (Jan – Dec 91), pp. 139 – 151. Bibl.

Bolivia

Plaza Martínez, Pedro. Tendencias sociolingüísticas en Bolivia. *Signo*, no. 35, Nueva época (Jan – Apr 92), pp. 117 – 138. Bibl, tables.

Brazil

Roazzi, Antonio et al. A arte do repente e as habilidades lingüísticas. *Revista Brasileira de Estudos Pedagógicos*, v. 72, no. 172 (Sept – Dec 91), pp. 291 – 317. Bibl, tables, charts.

Caribbean area

Lamming, George. Coming, Coming, Coming Home. *Casa de las Américas*, no. 190 (Jan – Mar 93), pp. 65 – 74.

Honduras

Castro-Mitchell, Amanda. Autoridad y poder social de la mujer en Honduras: un estudio sociolingüístico de los pronombres de tratamiento. *Fem*, v. 17, no. 127 (Sept 93), pp. 42 – 45. Tables.

Latin America

Lastra de Suárez, Yolanda. *Sociolingüística para hispanoamericanos: una introducción* reviewed by John Baugh. *La Educación (USA)*, v. 37, no. 114 (1993), pp. 160 – 161.

Mexico

Coronado Suzán, Gabriela. Entre la homogeneidad y la diferencia en los pueblos indohablantes de México. *Revista Latinoamericana de Estudios Educativos*, v. 22, no. 4 (Oct – Dec 92), pp. 37 – 62. Bibl, tables, charts.

Magaña Sánchez, Margarita Elena. Clasismo, racismo y sexismo en el discurso escolar de México. *Fem*, v. 17, no. 123 (May 93), pp. 13 – 15.

Puerto Rico

García del Toro, Antonio. La jerga teatral puertorriqueña (Includes a basic glossary). *Homines*, v. 15 – 16, no. 2 – 1 (Oct 91 – Dec 92), pp. 298 – 308.

SOCIOLOGICAL JURISPRUDENCE

See also
Distributive justice

Lasaga, Ignacio. La eticidad del pobre. *Estudios Sociales (Dominican Republic)*, v. 26, no. 91 (Jan – Mar 93), pp. 61 – 76.

Lavados Montes, Iván and Juan Enrique Vargas. La gestión judicial. *Estudios Sociales (Chile)*, no. 78 (Oct – Dec 93), pp. 203 – 225.

SOCIOLOGY

See also
Acculturation
Alienation
Church and social problems
Community organization
Educational sociology
Family
Industrial sociology
Marginalization
Old age
Political sociology
Quality of life
Religion and sociology
Social change
Social classes
Social conflict
Social indicators
Social mobility
Social psychology
Socialization
Sociobiology
Sociolinguistics
Sociological jurisprudence
Space in sociology
Violence
Youth

Congresses

Girón González, Alicia. Sociología entre dos mundos. *Problemas del Desarrollo*, v. 24, no. 92 (Jan – Mar 93), pp. 227 – 231.

Argentina
Study and teaching

Sidicaro, Ricardo. Reflexiones sobre la accidentada trayectoria de la sociología en la Argentina. *Cuadernos Hispanoamericanos*, no. 517 – 519 (July – Sept 93), pp. 65 – 76. Bibl.

Costa Rica
Study and teaching

Rodríguez Solera, Carlos Rafael. Problemas y perspectivas de la sociología costarricense contemporánea. *Anuario de Estudios Centroamericanos*, v. 18, no. 1 (1992), pp. 51 – 59. Bibl.

Cuba

Armas Vásquez, Antonio. Aspectos pragmáticos en la sociologia contemporánea latinoamericana. *Islas*, no. 98 (Jan – Apr 91), pp. 177 – 187. Bibl.

Mexico
Study and teaching

Vega Shiota, Gustavo de la. Reflexiones en torno al posgrado de sociología en la Facultad de Ciencias Políticas y Sociales de la UNAM. *Revista Mexicana de Ciencias Políticas y Sociales*, v. 38, Nueva época, no. 151 (Jan – Mar 93), pp. 195 – 203.

Southern Cone of South America

Osorio Urbina, Jaime. La democracia ordenada: análisis crítico de la nueva sociología del Cono Sur latinoamericano. *Estudios Sociológicos*, v. 11, no. 31 (Jan – Apr 93), pp. 111 – 132. Bibl.

SOCIOLOGY, RURAL

See also
Subdivision *Rural conditions* under names of specific countries

Argentina

Forni, Floreal H. et al. *Empleo, estrategias de vida y reproducción: hogares rurales en Santiago del Estero* (Review). *La Educación (USA)*, v. 37, no. 114 (1993), p. 156.

Moreno, Carlos. *Patrimonio de la producción rural en el antiguo partido de Cañuelas* reviewed by Silvina Ruiz Moreno de Bunge. *Todo Es Historia*, v. 26, no. 308 (Mar 93), p. 72. Il.

Brazil

Banck, Geert A. and Kees den Boer, eds. *Sowing the Whirlwind: Soya Expansion and Social Change in Southern Brazil* reviewed by Martine Droulers. *Cahiers des Amériques Latines*, no. 14 (1992), pp. 158 – 159.

Gouvêa, Fernando da Cruz. Notas sobre a influência dos senhores rurais na vida política brasileira. *Revista do Instituto Histórico e Geográfico Brasileiro*, no. 372 (July – Sept 91), pp. 815 – 827.

Khan, Ahmad Saeed and Lúcia Maria Ramos Silva. Características sócio-econômicas de produtores rurais, conservação do solo e produtividade agrícola. *Revista de Economia e Sociologia Rural*, v. 30, no. 3 (July – Sept 92), pp. 225 – 237. Bibl, tables.

Khan, Ahmad Saeed and José da Silva Souza. Taxa de retorno social do investimento em pesquisa na cultura da mandioca no Nordeste. *Revista de Economia e Sociologia Rural*, v. 29, no. 4 (Oct – Dec 91), pp. 411 – 426. Bibl, tables, charts.

Chile

Dahse, Fernando. Elementos de una metodología participativa para el desarrollo rural. *Estudios Sociales (Chile)*, no. 78 (Oct – Dec 93), pp. 185 – 201. Bibl.

Nicaragua

Houtart, François and Geneviève Lemercinier. *El campesino como actor social: sociología de una comarca de Nicaragua* reviewed by Sergio Sarmiento Silva. *Revista Mexicana de Sociología*, v. 54, no. 3 (July – Sept 92), pp. 263 – 267.

Peru

Mitchell, William P. Producción campesina y cultura regional. *América Indígena*, v. 51, no. 4 (Oct – Dec 91), pp. 81 – 106. Bibl, tables.

SOCIOLOGY, URBAN

See also
Urbanization

Oszlak, Oscar. *Merecer la ciudad: las pobres y el derecho al espacio urbano* reviewed by Gustavo de la Vega Shiota. *Revista Mexicana de Ciencias Políticas y Sociales*, v. 37, Nueva época, no. 148 (Apr – June 92), pp. 191 – 194.

Puente Lafoy, Patricio de la et al. Familia, vecindario y comunidad: un modelo sistémico para la interpretación del desarrollo progresivo. *Estudios Sociales (Chile)*, no. 76 (Apr – June 93), pp. 149 – 167. Bibl.

Brazil

Telles, Edward E. Racial Distance and Region in Brazil: Intermarriage in Brazilian Urban Areas. *Latin American Research Review*, v. 28, no. 2 (1993), pp. 141 – 162. Bibl, tables.

Costa Rica

Fernández González, Alvaro. Todo empezó en el '53: historia oral de un distrito liberacionista. *Revista de Historia (Costa Rica)*, no. 26 (July – Dec 92), pp. 97 – 142. Bibl.

Palmer, Steven. El consumo de heroína entre los artesanos de San José y el pánico moral de 1929. *Revista de Historia (Costa Rica)*, no. 25 (Jan – June 92), pp. 29 – 63. Bibl.

Dominican Republic

Mejía, Manuel Zacarías and Edmundo Morel. Los impactos de los desalojos: la constitución o reconstitución de las identidades. *Estudios Sociales (Dominican Republic)*, v. 26, no. 94 (Oct – Dec 93), pp. 45 – 74. Bibl.

Ecuador

Carrasco, Hernán. Indígenas serranos en Quito y Guayaquil: relaciones interétnicas y urbanización de migrantes. *América Indígena*, v. 51, no. 4 (Oct – Dec 91), pp. 159 – 183. Bibl.

Latin America

Altamirano Rúa, Teófilo and Lane Ryo Hirabayashi. Culturas regionales en ciudades de América Latina: un marco conceptual. *América Indígena*, v. 51, no. 4 (Oct – Dec 91), pp. 17 – 48. Bibl, il.

Mexico

Herrero Díaz, Luis F. Desarrollo urbano y estrategias de supervivencia en la periferia de la ciudad de México: Chalco; una aproximación antropológica. *Revista Española de Antropología Americana*, v. 23 (1993), pp. 213 – 232. Bibl, tables.

Murphy, Arthur D. and Alex Stepick. *Social Inequality in Oaxaca: A History of Resistance and Change* reviewed by John K. Chance. *The Americas*, v. 49, no. 4 (Apr 93), pp. 541 – 542.

Willis, Katie. Women's Work and Social Network Use in Oaxaca City, Mexico. *Bulletin of Latin American Research*, v. 12, no. 1 (Jan 93), pp. 65 – 82. Bibl, tables.

Research

Damián, Araceli. La investigación urbana en México, 1980 – 1990. *Estudios Demográficos y Urbanos*, v. 6, no. 3 (Sept – Dec 91), pp. 613 – 648. Bibl.

Study and teaching

Rodríguez, Hipólito. La antropología urbana y los estudios sobre migración. *La Palabra y el Hombre*, no. 84 (Oct – Dec 92), pp. 145 – 159. Bibl.

Peru

Cheng Hurtado, Alberto and José Matos Mar. Comas: lo andino en la modernidad urbana. *América Indígena*, v. 51, no. 2 – 3 (Apr – Sept 91), pp. 35 – 74. Il, tables, maps.

García Ríos, José María and Giulia Tamayo. El escenario como dictador: configuración metropolitana y experiencia cotidiana. *Nueva Sociedad*, no. 123 (Jan – Feb 93), pp. 94 – 103. Bibl.

Matos Mar, José. El nuevo rostro de la cultura urbana del Perú. *América Indígena*, v. 51, no. 2 – 3 (Apr – Sept 91), pp. 11 – 34. Tables, maps.

SOILS

See also
Erosion

Amazon Valley

Research

Loker, William M. et al. Identification of Areas of Land Degradation in the Peruvian Amazon Using a Geographic Information System. *Interciencia*, v. 18, no. 3 (May – June 93), pp. 133 – 141. Bibl, tables, maps, charts.

Brazil

Bibliography

Marinho, Mara de Andrade et al. Bibliografia brasileira de levantamento e de interpretação de levantamento de solos para fins agrícolas (com mapa-índice). *Revista Brasileira de Geografia*, v. 53, no. 1 (Jan – Mar 91), pp. 147 – 172. Bibl, maps.

Mathematical models

Khan, Ahmad Saeed and Lúcia Maria Ramos Silva. Características sócio-econômicas de produtores rurais, conservação do solo e produtividade agrícola. *Revista de Economia e Sociologia Rural*, v. 30, no. 3 (July – Sept 92), pp. 225 – 237. Bibl, tables.

Jamaica

McDonald, M. A. et al. The Effects of Forest Clearance on Soil Conservation: Preliminary Findings from the Yallahs Valley, Jamaican Blue Mountains. *Caribbean Geography*, v. 3, no. 4 (Sept 92), pp. 253 – 260. Bibl.

Latin America

Valenzuela Fuenzalida, Rafael. Pérdida y degradación de suelos en América Latina y el Caribe. *EURE*, v. 19, no. 58 (Oct 93), pp. 61 – 72. Bibl.

Mexico

Research

Bellon, Mauricio R. and J. Edward Taylor. "Folk" Soil Taxonomy and the Partial Adoption of New Seed Varieties. *Economic Development and Cultural Change*, v. 41, no. 4 (July 93), pp. 763 – 786. Bibl, tables.

SOLAR, XUL

Perazzo, Nelly. Xul Solar: la imaginación desenfrenada (Accompanied by an English translation). *Art Nexus*, no. 8 (Apr – June 93), pp. 96 – 100. Il.

SOMERS, ARMONÍA

Criticism of specific works

El derrumbamiento

Olivera-Williams, María Rosa. *El derrumbamiento* de Armonía Somers y *El ángel caído* de Cristina Peri-Rossi: dos manifestaciones de la narrativa imaginaria. *Revista Chilena de Literatura*, no. 42 (Aug 93), pp. 173 – 181. Bibl.

La mujer desnuda

Agosín, Marjorie. *La mujer desnuda* o el viaje decapitado: un texto de Armonía Somers. *Revista Interamericana de Bibliografía*, v. 42, no. 4 (1992), pp. 585 – 589.

SONGS

See also
Children's songs
Folk music
Music
Author Index under names of specific composers

Camuñas, Jaime. Dos letras a Rafael Hernández: in memoriam (Includes the poems "Lamento borincano," "Preciosa," "Mañanita campanera," "El cumbanchero," "El buen borincano," and "Mi guajirita"). *Homines*, v. 15 – 16, no. 2 – 1 (Oct 91 – Dec 92), pp. 327 – 337. Bibl.

Johansson, Patrick. Yaocuicatl: cantos de guerra y guerra de cantos. *Estudios de Cultura Náhuatl*, v. 22 (1992), pp. 29 – 43.

SONORA, MEXICO

Escandón, Patricia. Los problemas de la administración franciscana en las misiones sonorenses, 1768 – 1800. *Archivo Ibero-Americano*, v. 52, no. 205 – 208 (Jan – Dec 92), pp. 277 – 291.

Heyman, Josiah McConnell. *Life and Labor on the Border: Working People of Northeastern Sonora, Mexico, 1886 – 1986* reviewed by Miguel Tinker Salas. *The Americas*, v. 49, no. 4 (Apr 93), pp. 556 – 558.

— *Life and Labor on the Border: Working People of Northeastern Sonora, Mexico, 1886 – 1986* reviewed by Barry Carr. *Hispanic American Historical Review*, v. 73, no. 3 (Aug 93), pp. 526 – 528.

— *Life and Labor on the Border: Working People of Northeastern Sonora, Mexico, 1886 – 1986* reviewed by Evelyn Hu-Dehart. *International Migration Review*, v. 27, no. 3 (Fall 93), pp. 648 – 649.

El Plan de Pitic de 1789 y las nuevas poblaciones proyectadas en las provincias internas de la Nueva España (Transcribed and edited by Joseph P. Sánchez). *Colonial Latin American Historical Review*, v. 2, no. 4 (Fall 93), pp. 449 – 467. Maps.

Zamarripa, Roberto. *Sonora '91: historia de políticos y policías* reviewed by Ana Ivonee Rivas García. *El Cotidiano*, v. 10, no. 58 (Oct – Nov 93), p. 117.

SORIA, CECILIA
Interviews

Phillips, Graciela. Para una pianista. *Plural (Mexico)*, v. 22, no. 263 (Aug 93), pp. 72 – 73.

SORIA, GABRIEL

Vega Alfaro, Eduardo de la. *Gabriel Soria, 1903 – 1971* reviewed by Beatriz Valdés Lagunes (Review entitled "Pioneros del cine sonoro I"). *Revista Mexicana de Ciencias Políticas y Sociales*, v. 37, Nueva época, no. 150 (Oct – Dec 92), pp. 187 – 188.

— *Gabriel Soria, 1903 – 1971* reviewed by Juan Felipe Leal and Eduardo Barraza (Review entitled "Gabriel Soria y el cine sonoro mexicano"). *Revista Mexicana de Ciencias Políticas y Sociales*, v. 37, Nueva época, no. 150 (Oct – Dec 92), pp. 179 – 186.

SORIA, MILAGROS DE

Nari, Marcela M. Alejandra. Milagros y Juana. *Todo Es Historia*, v. 27, no. 312 (July 93), pp. 44 – 45.

SORIA Y MATA, ARTURO

Figueroa Sala, Jonas. Las ciudades lineales chilenas, 1910 – 1930. *Revista de Indias*, v. 53, no. 198 (May – Aug 93), pp. 651 – 662. Il, maps.

SORIANO, JUAN

Huerta, David. La novela órfica del escultor Juan Soriano. *Nexos*, v. 16, no. 181 (Jan 93), pp. 35 – 38. Il.

Interviews

León González, Francisco. Entrevista con Juan Soriano. *Artes de México*, no. 19 (Spring 93), pp. 104 – 105. Il.

SORIANO, OSVALDO
Translations

Soriano, Osvaldo. The Eye of the Fatherland (Translated by Alfred MacAdam). *Review*, no. 47 (Fall 93), pp. 79 – 82.

SOSUA, DOMINICAN REPUBLIC

Robertiello, Jack. Dominican Chutzpah: The Story of Sosua. *Américas*, v. 45, no. 4 (July – Aug 93), pp. 20 – 25. Il, maps.

SOTO VÉLEZ, CLEMENTE
Criticism and interpretation

Catalá, Rafael. La vanguardia atalayista y la obra de Clemente Soto Vélez. *Revista Iberoamericana*, v. 59, no. 162 – 163 (Jan – June 93), pp. 101 – 109. Bibl.

Interviews

Costa, Marithelma and Alvin Joaquín Figueroa. *Kaligrafiando: conversaciones con Clemente Soto Vélez* reviewed by Evelyn Uhrhan Irving. *World Literature Today*, v. 67, no. 1 (Winter 93), p. 163.

SOUSTELLE, JACQUES
Obituaries

Pascual Soto, Arturo. Jacques Soustelle (1912 – 1990). *Anales del Instituto de Investigaciones Estéticas*, v. 16, no. 62 (1991), pp. 200 – 202.

SOUTH ATLANTIC NATIONS

Brigagão, Clóvis. Atlântico Sul: Zona de Paz e Cooperação. *Política e Estratégica*, v. 8, no. 2 – 4 (Apr – Dec 90), pp. 342 – 346. Bibl.

Mourão, Fernando Augusto Albuquerque. O Atlântico Sul e os novos vetores do sistema internacional. *Política e Estratégica*, v. 8, no. 2 – 4 (Apr – Dec 90), pp. 333 – 341.

SOUTHERN CONE OF SOUTH AMERICA
See also

Authors – Southern Cone of South America
Competition – Southern Cone of South America
Democracy – Southern Cone of South America
Education, Higher – Southern Cone of South America
Education and state – Southern Cone of South America
Executive power – Southern Cone of South America
Exiles – Southern Cone of South America
Foreign trade promotion – Southern Cone of South America
Geography, Economic – Southern Cone of South America
Industrial organization – Southern Cone of South America
Inland water transportation – Southern Cone of South America
Legislative power – Southern Cone of South America
Liberation theology – Southern Cone of South America
Marine resources – Southern Cone of South America
Social movements – Southern Cone of South America
Sociology – Southern Cone of South America
Tariff – Southern Cone of South America
Women – Southern Cone of South America

Cultural policy

Achugar Ferrari, Hugo, ed. *Cultura MERCOSUR: políticas e industrias culturales* (Review). *Integración Latinoamericana*, v. 18, no. 195 (Nov 93), pp. 58 – 59.

Economic integration

Araújo Júnior, José Tavares de. Reestruturação industrial e integração econômica: as perspectivas do MERCOSUL. *Revista Brasileira de Economia*, v. 47, no. 1 (Jan – Mar 93), pp. 97 – 113. Bibl, tables.

Bekerman, Marta. Apertura importadora e integración en el Cono Sur. *Comercio Exterior*, v. 43, no. 11 (Nov 93), pp. 1040 – 1045. Bibl.

Bekerman, Marta, ed. *MERCOSUR: la oportunidad y el desafío* (Review). *Integración Latinoamericana*, v. 18, no. 194 (Oct 93), pp. 87 – 88.

Berretta, Nora et al. *En el umbral de la integración* (Review). *Integración Latinoamericana*, v. 18, no. 191 (July 93), pp. 76 – 77.

Bouzas, Roberto. Apertura comercial e integración en el Cono Sur. *Nueva Sociedad*, no. 125 (May – June 93), pp. 112 – 119.

Fairlie Reinoso, Alan. Crisis, integración y desarrollo en América Latina: la dinámica del Grupo Andino con el MERCOSUR en la década de 1980. *Integración Latinoamericana*, v. 18, no. 192 (Aug 93), pp. 11 – 40. Bibl, tables, charts.

Faria, José Angelo Estrella. *O MERCOSUL: princípios, finalidade e alcance do Tratado de Assunção* (Review). *Integración Latinoamericana*, v. 18, no. 192 (Aug 92), pp. 96 – 97.

Faria, José Eduardo. O Brasil no MERCOSUL. *Problemas Brasileiros*, v. 30, no. 297 (May – June 93), pp. 30 – 35. Il.

Franco, Albano. Towards a Common Frontier for Trade (Translated by Barbara Meza). *Américas*, v. 45, no. 1 (Jan – Feb 93), pp. 56 – 57. Il.

Garré Copello, Belter. *Solución de controversias en el MERCOSUR* (Review). *Integración Latinoamericana,* v. 18, no. 194 (Oct 93), pp. 88 – 89.

— *Solución de controversias en el MERCOSUR: protocolo de Brasil* (Review). *Integración Latinoamericana,* v. 18, no. 194 (Oct 93), pp. 88 – 89.

González, Florencia. Solución de conflictos en un sistema de integración: los casos del MERCOSUR y la CEE. *Integración Latinoamericana,* v. 17, no. 185 (Dec 92), pp. 33 – 44. Bibl.

Halperín, Marcelo. Lealtad competitiva y dilemas de la integración: el caso del MERCOSUR. *Integración Latinoamericana,* v. 17, no. 184 (Nov 92), pp. 36 – 43.

Hirst, Mónica. Brasil en el MERCOSUR: costos y beneficios. *Integración Latinoamericana,* v. 18, no. 186 (Jan – Feb 93), pp. 3 – 11. Bibl.

Imaz, José Luis de. MERCOSUR y matrícula primaria para el año 2000. *Integración Latinoamericana,* v. 18, no. 194 (Oct 93), pp. 35 – 36.

Lescano, Oscar et al. Las centrales sindicales frente al MERCOSUR. *Nueva Sociedad,* no. 126 (July – Aug 93), pp. 176 – 178.

Linkohr, Rolf. Los procedimientos institucionales de decisión de la Comunidad Europea (Translated by Sandra Carreras). *Cuadernos del CLAEH,* v. 18, no. 65 – 66 (May 93), pp. 111 – 121.

Magariños, Gustavo. *Uruguay en el MERCOSUR* (Review). *Integración Latinoamericana,* v. 18, no. 192 (Aug 92), pp. 97 – 98.

Mandelli, Luiz Carlos. Cambios geopolíticos e integración. *Nueva Sociedad,* no. 126 (July – Aug 93), pp. 178 – 180.

Olivar Jimenez, Martha Lucia. Integración en el Cono Sur: realidad y perspectivas. *Vozes,* v. 86, no. 6 (Nov – Dec 92), pp. 62 – 68.

Olivar Jimenez, Martha Lucia et al. *O regime comum de origem no MERCOSUL* (Review). *Integración Latinoamericana,* v. 18, no. 192 (Aug 92), pp. 98 – 99.

Piñón, Francisco José. Educación y procesos de integración económica: el caso del MERCOSUR. *La Educación (USA),* v. 37, no. 114 (1993), pp. 19 – 32. Bibl, tables.

Realidades y perspectivas del MERCOSUR (Review). *Integración Latinoamericana,* v. 18, no. 191 (July 93), pp. 75 – 76.

Rofman, Alejandro Boris. Estrategias frente al desafío MERCOSUR. *Realidad Económica,* no. 114 – 115 (Feb – May 93), pp. 130 – 189. Bibl, il, tables.

Schvarzer, Jorge. El MERCOSUR: la geografía a la espera de actores. *Nueva Sociedad,* no. 126 (July – Aug 93), pp. 72 – 83.

Stolovich, Luis. Los empresarios, la apertura y los procesos de integración regional: contradicciones y estrategias; el caso de Uruguay en el MERCOSUR. *Revista Paraguaya de Sociología,* v. 29, no. 84 (May – Aug 92), pp. 53 – 90. Bibl, tables.

Zeballos, Carlos A. El protocolo de Brasilia. *Integración Latinoamericana,* v. 17, no. 185 (Dec 92), pp. 51 – 54.

Congresses

IV Reunión del Consejo del Mercado Común. *Integración Latinoamericana,* v. 18, no. 192 (Aug 92), pp. 92 – 94.

MERCOSUR: III Reunión del Consejo del Mercado Común. *Integración Latinoamericana,* v. 17, no. 185 (Dec 92), pp. 70 – 71.

Sources

Comunicado de los presidentes de la República Argentina, de la república federativa del Brasil, de la república del Paraguay y de la república oriental del Uruguay. *Integración Latinoamericana,* v. 18, no. 192 (Aug 93), pp. 91 – 92.

Statistics

MERCOSUL: sinopsis estatística/MERCOSUR: sinopsis estadística (Review). *Integración Latinoamericana,* v. 18, no. 194 (Oct 93), p. 89.

Economic policy

Achard, Diego et al. MERCOSUR: élites y política en Paraguay y Uruguay. *Integración Latinoamericana,* v. 18, no. 192 (Aug 93), pp. 59 – 61.

Antía, Fernando. El MERCOSUR dos años después. *Cuadernos del CLAEH,* v. 18, no. 65 – 66 (May 93), pp. 101 – 110. Bibl, tables.

Aragão, José Maria. *La armonización de políticas macroeconómicas en el MERCOSUR: la construcción de un mercado común* (Review). *Integración Latinoamericana,* v. 18, no. 191 (July 93), pp. 79 – 80.

Lehmann, David. *Democracy and Development in Latin America: Economics, Politics, and Religion in the Post-War Period* reviewed by Ricardo Grinspun and Sally Humphries. *Economic Development and Cultural Change,* v. 41, no. 4 (July 93), pp. 886 – 894. Bibl.

Foreign economic relations

European Community

Bizzozero, Lincoln J. La relación entre el MERCOSUR y la Comunidad Europa: ¿Un nuevo parametro de vinculación? *Estudios Internacionales (Chile),* v. 26, no. 101 (Jan – Mar 93), pp. 37 – 56. Bibl.

Gratius, Susanne. *El MERCOSUR y la Comunidad Europea: una guía para la investigación* (Review). *Integración Latinoamericana,* v. 18, no. 195 (Nov 93), pp. 57 – 58.

Latin America

Halperín, Marcelo. Discriminación y no discriminación en los esquemas de integración económica: el caso de MERCOSUR. *Integración Latinoamericana,* v. 18, no. 195 (Nov 93), pp. 23 – 29.

United States

Rojas Aravena, Francisco. El Cono Sur latinoamericano y la Iniciativa para las Américas. *Estudios Internacionales (Chile),* v. 26, no. 101 (Jan – Mar 93), pp. 98 – 122. Bibl.

Foreign opinion

Fifer, J. Valerie. South of Capricorn: A Review Revisited (Rebuttal of a review of her *United States' Perceptions of Latin America, 1850 – 1930: A "New West" South of Capricorn?*). *Bulletin of Latin American Research,* v. 12, no. 1 (Jan 93), pp. 103 – 107.

— *United States Perceptions of Latin America, 1850 – 1930: A "New West" South of Capricorn* reviewed by Thomas L. Whigham. *The Americas,* v. 49, no. 4 (Apr 93), pp. 559 – 561.

Politics

Thibaut, Bernhard. Präsidentialismus, Parlamentarismus und das Problem der Konsolidierung der Demokratie in Lateinamerika. *Ibero-Amerikanisches Archiv,* v. 18, no. 1 – 2 (1992), pp. 107 – 150. Bibl.

— Presidencialismo, parlamentarismo y el problema de la consolidación democrática en América Latina. *Estudios Internacionales (Chile),* v. 26, no. 102 (Apr – June 93), pp. 216 – 252. Bibl.

SOUZA, IRINEU EVANGELISTA DE

See

Mauá, Irinêo Evangelista de Souza

SOUZA, LUÍS DE CASTRO

Addresses, essays, lectures

Souza, Luís de Castro. Saudação a Fernando da Cruz Gouvêa. *Revista do Instituto Histórico e Geográfico Brasileiro,* no. 372 (July – Sept 91), pp. 812 – 814.

— Saudação ao sócio honorário Alberto Martins da Silva: os médicos militares no Instituto Histórico e Geográfico Brasileiro (Speech given in honor of Dr. Silva's induction into the Instituto Histórico e Geográfico Brasileiro). *Revista do Instituto Histórico e Geográfico Brasileiro,* no. 371 (Apr – June 91), pp. 509 – 517. Bibl.

SOUZA, LUIZA ERUNDINA DE

Penna, Maura. *O que faz ser nordestino?* reviewed by Rita Laura Segato (Review entitled "O que faz ser paulista?"). *Estudos Feministas,* v. 1, no. 1 (1993), pp. 213 – 214.

SOUZA-LOBO, ELIZABETH

Saffioti, Heleieth Iara Bongiovani. Reminiscências, releituras, reconceituações. *Estudos Feministas,* v. 0, no. 0 (1992), pp. 97 – 103. Bibl.

SOUZA SILVA, JOAQUIM NORBERTO DE

Barreto, Dalmo Freire. Centenário de morte de Joaquim Norberto de Souza Silva. *Revista do Instituto Histórico e Geográfico Brasileiro*, no. 373 (Oct – Dec 91), pp. 937 – 941.

SOVIET UNION

See also
    Latin American studies – Soviet Union
    Russia

Foreign relations

Brazil

Hilton, Stanley Eon. *Brazil and the Soviet Union Challenge, 1917 – 1947* reviewed by John W. F. Dulles. *The Americas*, v. 49, no. 3 (Jan 93), pp. 417 – 418.

Cuba

Blasier, Cole. El fin de la asociación soviético – cubana. *Estudios Internacionales (Chile)*, v. 26, no. 103 (July – Sept 93), pp. 296 – 340. Bibl, tables.

Mesa-Lago, Carmelo. Efectos económicos en Cuba del derrumbe del socialismo en la Unión Soviética y Europa Oriental. *Estudios Internacionales (Chile)*, v. 26, no. 103 (July – Sept 93), pp. 341 – 414. Bibl, tables.

Latin America

Miller, Nicola. *Soviet Relations with Latin America, 1959 – 1987* reviewed by Marina Oborotova (Review entitled "Russian Policy in Latin America: Past, Present, and Future"). *Latin American Research Review*, v. 28, no. 3 (1993), pp. 183 – 188.

Prizel, Ilya. *Latin America through Soviet Eyes: The Evolution of Soviet Perceptions during the Brezhnev Era* reviewed by Marina Oborotova (Review entitled "Russian Policy in Latin America: Past, Present, and Future"). *Latin American Research Review*, v. 28, no. 3 (1993), pp. 183 – 188.

Smith, Wayne S., ed. *The Russians Aren't Coming: New Soviet Policy in Latin America* reviewed by Lynn-Darrell Bender. *Cuban Studies/Estudios Cubanos*, v. 23 (1993), pp. 217 – 218.

— *The Russians Aren't Coming: New Soviet Policy in Latin America* reviewed by Marina Oborotova (Review entitled "Russian Policy in Latin America: Past, Present, and Future"). *Latin American Research Review*, v. 28, no. 3 (1993), pp. 183 – 188.

SOYBEAN

Brazil

Banck, Geert A. and Kees den Boer, eds. *Sowing the Whirlwind: Soya Expansion and Social Change in Southern Brazil* reviewed by Martine Droulers. *Cahiers des Amériques Latines*, no. 14 (1992), pp. 158 – 159.

Silva, Gabriel Luiz Seraphico Peixoto da et al. Mudança tecnológica e produtividade do milho e da soja no Brasil. *Revista Brasileira de Economia*, v. 47, no. 2 (Apr – June 93), pp. 281 – 303. Bibl, tables.

Mathematical models

Barbosa, Margareth L. and Rosa M. O. Fontes. Efeitos da integração econômica do MERCOSUL e da Europa na competitividade das exportações brasileiras de soja. *Revista de Economia e Sociologia Rural*, v. 29, no. 4 (Oct – Dec 91), pp. 335 – 351. Bibl, tables.

SPACE IN ECONOMICS

See
    Geography, Economic

SPACE IN LITERATURE

Ahumada Peña, Haydée. Apropiación del espacio americano en *Epitalamio del Prieto Trinidad*. *Revista Chilena de Literatura*, no. 42 (Aug 93), pp. 7 – 11.

Cadena, Agustín. *Farabeuf:* el espacio como metáforo del tiempo. *Plural (Mexico)*, v. 22, no. 258 (Mar 93), pp. 50 – 56. Bibl.

Mortimer, Mildred P. A Sense of Place and Space in Maryse Condé's *Les derniers rois mages*. *World Literature Today*, v. 67, no. 4 (Fall 93), pp. 757 – 762. Bibl.

SPACE IN SOCIOLOGY

Wettstein, Germán. La producción y valorización del espacio en un país estancado: interpretación geográfica del caso uruguayo. *Derecho y Reforma Agraria*, no. 23 (1992), pp. 51 – 72. Bibl.

SPAIN

See also
    Archives – Spain
    Argentines – Spain
    Art – Spain
    Asturias, Spain
    Black legend
    Canary Islands
    Christian art and symbolism – Spain
    Convents and nunneries – Spain
    Drama festivals – Spain
    Economics – Spain
    Exiles – Spain
    Fertility, Human – Spain
    Folk drama – Spain
    Folk lore – Spain
    Guernica, Spain
    Imperialism – Spain
    Inquisition – Spain
    Iron industry and trade – Spain
    Latin American studies – Spain
    Latin Americans – Spain
    Madrid, Spain
    Mexican literature – Spain
    Murcia, Spain
    Periodicals – Spain
    Popular music – Spain
    Population – Spain
    Reading interests – Spain
    Sculpture – Spain
    Spain in literature
    Universities and colleges – Spain
    Women – Spain
    Women authors – Spain

Armed forces

Bradley, Peter T. The Defence of Peru, 1648 – 1700. *Jahrbuch für Geschichte von Staat, Wirtschaft und Gesellschaft Lateinamerikas*, v. 29 (1992), pp. 90 – 120. Bibl, tables.

Zaverucha, Jorge. The Degree of Military Political Autonomy during the Spanish, Argentine, and Brazilian Transitions. *Journal of Latin American Studies*, v. 25, no. 2 (May 93), pp. 283 – 299. Bibl, tables.

Centennial celebrations, etc.

Borrat, Héctor. Autocelebración de España: ¿Potenciación de Latinoamérica? *Cuadernos del CLAEH*, v. 17, no. 63 – 64 (Oct 92), pp. 117 – 123.

Pérez Molina de Lara, Olga. Cultura y sociedad: la empresa del V centenario: su significancia para el reino de España y el gobierno de Guatemala. *Folklore Americano*, no. 53 (Jan – June 92), pp. 81 – 90.

Roitman Rosenmann, Marcos. España y América Latina en el contexto del quinto centenario. *Boletín de Antropología Americana*, no. 23 (July 91), pp. 83 – 98. Bibl, il.

Civilization

Fuentes, Carlos. *The Buried Mirror: Reflections on Spain and the New World* reviewed by John Lynch. *Hispanic American Historical Review*, v. 73, no. 3 (Aug 93), pp. 490 – 491.

— *El espejo enterrado* reviewed by Héctor Aguilar Camín (Review entitled "Por una historia patria para adultos"). *Nexos*, v. 16, no. 184 (Apr 93), pp. 59 – 63.

— *El espejo enterrado* reviewed by Marta Portal (Review entitled "Las tres hispanidades de España"). *Cuadernos Hispanoamericanos*, no. 522 (Dec 93), pp. 143 – 146.

— *El espejo enterrado/The Buried Mirror: Reflections on Spain and the New World* reviewed by John Incledon. *Hispania (USA)*, v. 76, no. 4 (Dec 93), pp. 735 – 737.

Colonies

Bernal Rodríguez, Manuel. Nota sobre el influjo de la espiritualidad renacentista en la reprobación moral de la emigración a Indias: el camino del infierno. *Anuario de Estudios Americanos*, v. 49, Suppl. 2 (1992), pp. 3 – 9. Bibl.

Bryan, Patrick. Spanish Jamaica. *Caribbean Quarterly*, v. 38, no. 2 – 3 (June – Sept 92), pp. 21 – 31.

Pérez-Mallaína Bueno, Pablo Emilio. *Los hombres del océano* reviewed by Benjamin Keen. *Hispanic American Historical Review*, v. 73, no. 3 (Aug 93), pp. 503 – 504.

Administration

Andreo García, Juan. *La Intendencia en Venezuela: don Esteban Fernández de León, intendente de Caracas, 1791 – 1803* reviewed by Jean-Christian Tulet. *Caravelle*, no. 59 (1992), pp. 307 – 308.

Bernabéu Albert, Salvador. El "virrey de California" Gaspar de Portolá y la problemática de la primera gobernación californiana, 1767 – 1769. *Revista de Indias*, v. 52, no. 195 – 196 (May – Dec 92), pp. 271 – 295. Bibl.

Bradley, Peter T. *Society, Economy, and Defence in Seventeenth-Century Peru: The Administration of the Count of Alba de Liste, 1655 – 1661* reviewed by Teodoro Hampe Martínez. *Colonial Latin American Review*, v. 2, no. 1 – 2 (1993), pp. 298 – 300.

— *Society, Economy, and Defence in Seventeenth-Century Peru: The Administration of the Count of Alba de Liste, 1655 – 1661* reviewed by Stephen J. Homick. *Hispanic American Historical Review*, v. 73, no. 2 (May 93), pp. 314 – 315.

— *Society, Economy, and Defence in Seventeenth-Century Peru: The Administration of the Count of Alba de Liste, 1655 – 1661* reviewed by Mark A. Burkholder. *Revista Interamericana de Bibliografía*, v. 42, no. 2 (1992), pp. 283 – 284.

Bronner, Fred. Church, Crown, and Commerce in Seventeenth-Century Lima: A Synoptic Interpretation. *Jahrbuch für Geschichte von Staat, Wirtschaft und Gesellschaft Lateinamerikas*, v. 29 (1992), pp. 75 – 89. Bibl.

Campos Harriet, Fernando. La Real Audiencia de Concepción. *Atenea (Chile)*, no. 465 – 466 (1992), pp. 151 – 156.

— La Real Audiencia de Concepción, 1565 – 1573. *Boletín de la Academia Chilena de la Historia*, v. 58 – 59, no. 102 (1991 – 1992), pp. 534 – 538.

Cardenal Chamorro, Rodolfo. La expansión imperial española en Centroamérica. *ECA; Estudios Centroamericanos*, v. 47, no. 528 (Oct 92), pp. 841 – 854. Il.

Cooney, Jerry Wilson. *Economía y sociedad en la Intendencia del Paraguay* reviewed by Edberto Oscar Acevedo. *Revista de Historia de América*, no. 112 (July – Dec 91), pp. 181 – 183.

Coromoto Nava Santana, Mayela. Un conflicto entre la Real Audiencia y el Ayuntamiento de Caracas: el nombramiento del Fiel Ejecutor, 1793 – 1797. *Boletín de la Academia Nacional de la Historia (Venezuela)*, v. 75, no. 298 (Apr – June 92), pp. 77 – 85.

Deans-Smith, Susan. Compromise and Conflict: The Tobacco Workers of Mexico City and the Colonial State, 1770 – 1810. *Anuario de Estudios Americanos*, v. 49 (1992), pp. 271 – 309. Bibl.

Demelas, Danièle and François-Xavier Guerra. Un processus révolutionnaire méconnu: l'adoption des formes representatives modernes en Espagne et en Amérique Latine, 1808 – 1810. *Caravelle*, no. 60 (1993), pp. 5 – 57. Bibl.

Fernández Alonso, Serena. Perfil biográfico y acción de gobierno de don Jorge Escobedo y Alarcón. *Revista de Indias*, v. 52, no. 195 – 196 (May – Dec 92), pp. 365 – 383. Bibl.

Fisher, John Robert et al, eds. *Reform and Insurrection in Bourbon New Granada and Peru* reviewed by Scarlett O'Phelan Godoy. *Anuario de Estudios Americanos*, v. 50, no. 1 (1993), pp. 316 – 317.

— *Reform and Insurrection in Bourbon New Granada and Peru* reviewed by Lawrence A. Clayton. *Colonial Latin American Historical Review*, v. 2, no. 4 (Fall 93), pp. 470 – 473.

— *Reform and Insurrection in Bourbon New Granada and Peru* reviewed by Caroline A. Williams. *Journal of Latin American Studies*, v. 25, no. 2 (May 93), pp. 392 – 394.

Gamarra Durana, Alfonso. La economía realista como provocadora de rebeldías. *Signo*, no. 36 – 37, Nueva época (May – Dec 92), pp. 361 – 378. Bibl.

Gascón, Margarita. The Military of Santo Domingo, 1720 – 1764. *Hispanic American Historical Review*, v. 73, no. 3 (Aug 93), pp. 431 – 452. Bibl.

Gómez Rivas, León. Don Francisco de Toledo, comendador de Alcántara, virrey del Perú: guía de fuentes (I). *Anuario de Estudios Americanos*, v. 49, Suppl. 1 (1992), pp. 123 – 171.

— Don Francisco de Toledo, comendador de Alcántara, virrey del Perú: guía de fuentes (II). *Anuario de Estudios Americanos*, v. 49, Suppl. 2 (1992), pp. 95 – 152.

Gonzalbo Aizpuru, Pilar. Las fiestas novohispanas: espectáculo y ejemplo. *Mexican Studies*, v. 9, no. 1 (Winter 93), pp. 19 – 45. Bibl.

Groof, Bard de and Thomas Werner, eds. *Rebelión y resistencia en el mundo hispánico del siglo XVII: actos del Coloquio Internacional Lovaina, 20 – 23 de noviembre de 1991* reviewed by Clara López Beltrán. *Hispanic American Historical Review*, v. 73, no. 4 (Nov 93), pp. 689 – 690.

Hampe Martínez, Teodoro. Los funcionarios de la monarquía española en América: notas para una caracterización política, económica y social. *Revista Interamericana de Bibliografía*, v. 42, no. 3 (1992), pp. 431 – 452. Bibl.

Langue, Frédérique. Antagonismos y solidaridades en un cabildo colonial: Caracas, 1750 – 1810. *Anuario de Estudios Americanos*, v. 49 (1992), pp. 371 – 393. Bibl.

Lucena Giraldo, Manuel. ¿Filántropos u oportunistas?: ciencia y política en los proyectos de obras públicas del Consulado de Cartagena de Indias, 1795 – 1810. *Revista de Indias*, v. 52, no. 195 – 196 (May – Dec 92), pp. 627 – 646. Bibl, maps.

Lucena Giraldo, Manuel and Juan Pimentel Igea, eds. *Los "Axiomas políticos sobre la América" de Alejandro Malaspina* reviewed by O. Carlos Stoetzer. *Hispanic American Historical Review*, v. 73, no. 1 (Feb 93), pp. 160 – 161.

Martínez Riaza, Ascensión. Las diputaciones provinciales americanas en el sistema liberal español. *Revista de Indias*, v. 52, no. 195 – 196 (May – Dec 92), pp. 647 – 691. Bibl.

Mond, Rebecca Earle. Indian Rebellion and Bourbon Reform in New Granada: Riots in Pasto, 1780 – 1800. *Hispanic American Historical Review*, v. 73, no. 1 (Feb 93), pp. 99 – 124. Bibl.

Ortiz de la Tabla Ducasse, Javier et al, eds. *Cartas de cabildos hispanoamericanos: Audiencia de Quito* reviewed by Frédérique Langue. *Caravelle*, no. 60 (1993), pp. 147 – 148.

Ponce Leiva, Pilar. Un espacio para la controversia: la Audiencia de Quito en el siglo XVIII. *Revista de Indias*, v. 52, no. 195 – 196 (May – Dec 92), pp. 839 – 865. Bibl.

Rieu de Millán, Marie-Laure. *Los diputados americanos en las Cortes de Cádiz: igualdad o independencia* reviewed by María Lourdes Huarte Cambra. *Anuario de Estudios Americanos*, v. 49, Suppl. 2 (1992), pp. 259 – 261.

— *Los diputados americanos en las Cortes de Cádiz* reviewed by Michel Bertrand. *Caravelle*, no. 60 (1993), pp. 159 – 161.

Ruiz Medrano, Ethelia. *Gobierno y sociedad en Nueva España: segunda Audiencia y Antonio de Mendoza* reviewed by Michel Bertrand. *Caravelle*, no. 59 (1992), pp. 270 – 273.

— *Gobierno y sociedad en Nueva España: segunda Audiencia y Antonio de Mendoza* reviewed by Brian R. Hamnett. *Hispanic American Historical Review*, v. 73, no. 3 (Aug 93), pp. 506 – 507.

Saguier, Eduardo Ricardo. La corrupción de la burocracia colonial borbónica y los orígenes del federalismo: el caso del virreinato del Río de la Plata. *Jahrbuch für Geschichte von Staat, Wirtschaft und Gesellschaft Lateinamerikas*, v. 29 (1992), pp. 149 – 177. Bibl.

Suárez, Santiago Gerardo. *Las reales audiencias indianas: fuentes y bibliografía* reviewed by José María Mariluz Urquijo. *Boletín de la Academia Nacional de la Historia (Venezuela)*, v. 75, no. 297 (Jan – Mar 92), pp. 139 – 141.

Suñé Blanco, Beatriz. *La documentación del cabildo secular de Guatemala, siglo XVI: estudio diplomático y valor etnográfico* reviewed by Olga Joya. *Mesoamérica (USA)*, v. 13, no. 24 (Dec 92), pp. 462 – 463.

Vargas, Diego de. *By Force of Arms: The Journals of Don Diego de Vargas, New Mexico, 1691 – 1693* edited and translated by John L. Kessell and Rick Hendricks. Reviewed by Timothy K. Perttula. *Colonial Latin American Historical Review*, v. 2, no. 3 (Summer 93), pp. 380 – 382.

— *By Force of Arms: The Journals of Don Diego de Vargas, New Mexico, 1691 – 1693* edited and translated by John L. Kessel and Rick Hendricks. Reviewed by Mark A. Burkholder. *Hispanic American Historical Review*, v. 73, no. 3 (Aug 93), pp. 510 – 511.

Commerce

Brenot, Anne-Marie. *Pouvoirs et profits au Pérou colonial au XVIIIᵉ siècle: gouverneurs, clientèles et ventes forcées* reviewed by Pierre Ragon. *Cahiers des Amériques Latines*, no. 14 (1992), pp. 152 – 153.

Cooney, Jerry Wilson. "La Dirección General de la Real Renta de Tabacos" and the Decline of the Royal Tobacco Monopoly in Paraguay, 1779 – 1800. *Colonial Latin American Historical Review*, v. 1, no. 1 (Fall 92), pp. 101 – 115. Bibl.

— Fraude y burócratas: tabaco y Paraguay, 1789 – 1790. *Revista Paraguaya de Sociología*, v. 29, no. 85 (Sept – Dec 92), pp. 29 – 40. Bibl.

Fisher, John Robert. *Relaciones económicas entre España y América hasta la independencia* reviewed by Kendall W. Brown. *Hispanic American Historical Review*, v. 73, no. 3 (Aug 93), pp. 494 – 495.

— *Trade, War, and Revolution: Exports from Spanish America, 1797 – 1820* reviewed by James Schofield Saeger. *The Americas*, v. 50, no. 1 (July 93), pp. 127 – 128.

— *Trade, War, and Revolution: Exports from Spanish America, 1797 – 1820* reviewed by Richard Garner. *European Review of Latin American and Caribbean Studies*, no. 54 (June 93), pp. 138 – 139.

León, Aracely de. Doctrinas económicas en el contexto de la expansión europea. *Revista Cultural Lotería*, v. 51, no. 391 (Sept – Oct 92), pp. 47 – 57. Bibl.

McCarthy, William J. Between Policy and Prerogative: Malfeasance in the Inspection of the Manila Galleons at Acapulco, 1637. *Colonial Latin American Historical Review*, v. 2, no. 2 (Spring 93), pp. 163 – 183. Bibl, maps.

Pérez Herrero, Pedro. *Comercio y mercados en América Latina colonial* reviewed by John Fisher. *Hispanic American Historical Review*, v. 73, no. 4 (Nov 93), pp. 688 – 689.

Uriarte Ayo, R. The Hispanic American Market and Iron Production in the Basque Country, 1700 – 1825. *Ibero Americana (Sweden)*, v. 22, no. 2 (Dec 92), pp. 47 – 65. Bibl, tables, charts.

Congresses

Pelegrí Pedrosa, Luis Vicente. XI Jornadas de Andalucía y América: "Huelva y América." *Anuario de Estudios Americanos*, v. 49, Suppl. 1 (1992), pp. 204 – 209.

Finance

Chandler, Dewitt Samuel. *Social Assistance and Bureaucratic Politics: The Montepíos of Colonial Mexico, 1767 – 1821* reviewed by Richard J. Salvucci. *The Americas*, v. 49, no. 4 (Apr 93), pp. 551 – 552.

— *Social Assistance and Bureaucratic Politics: The Montepíos of Colonial Mexico, 1767 – 1821* reviewed by Silvia Marina Arrom. *Hispanic American Historical Review*, v. 73, no. 1 (Feb 93), pp. 153 – 154.

— *Social Assistance and Bureaucratic Politics: The Montepíos of Colonial Mexico, 1767 – 1821* reviewed by Eric Van Young. *Journal of Latin American Studies*, v. 25, no. 3 (Oct 93), pp. 653 – 654.

Hausberger, Bernd. Movimientos estacionales en los registros de oro y plata en las cajas de la Real Hacienda de la Nueva España, 1761 – 1767. *Anuario de Estudios Americanos*, v. 49 (1992), pp. 335 – 369. Bibl, tables, charts.

Jara, Alvaro and John Jay TePaske. *The Royal Treasuries of the Spanish Empire in America, Vol. IV: Eighteenth-Century Ecuador* reviewed by Franklin Pease G. Y. *Colonial Latin American Review*, v. 2, no. 1 – 2 (1993), pp. 311 – 312.

Klein, Herbert S. Historia fiscal colonial: resultados y perspectivas (Translated by Laura Elena Pulido Varela). *Historia Mexicana*, v. 42, no. 2 (Oct – Dec 92), pp. 261 – 307.

Lavallé, Bernard. *Quito et la crise de l'alcabala, 1580 – 1600* reviewed by Michel Bertrand. *Caravelle*, no. 60 (1993), pp. 148 – 150.

Sala i Vila, Nuria. Gobierno colonial, iglesia y poder en Perú, 1784 – 1814. *Revista Andina*, v. 11, no. 1 (July 93), pp. 133 – 161. Bibl.

TePaske, John Jay. The Costs of Empire: Spending Patterns and Priorities in Colonial Peru, 1581 – 1820. *Colonial Latin American Historical Review*, v. 2, no. 1 (Winter 93), pp. 1 – 33. Tables, charts.

Vornefeld, Ruth M. *Spanische Geldpolitik in Hispanoamerica, 1750 – 1808: Konzepte und Massnahmen im Rahmen der bourbonischen Reformpolitik* reviewed by Teodoro Hampe Martínez. *Revista de Indias*, v. 53, no. 197 (Jan – Apr 93), pp. 127 – 129.

Law

Díaz I., Gloria. La celebración del quinto centenario del descubrimiento de América. *Revista Cultural Lotería*, v. 51, no. 391 (Sept – Oct 92), pp. 7 – 12.

Sala-Molins, Louis. *L'Afrique aux Amériques: le code noir espagnol* reviewed by Germán A. de la Raza. *Ibero Americana (Sweden)*, v. 22, no. 2 (Dec 92), pp. 77 – 81.

Sánchez Bella, Ismael. *Derecho indiano; estudios, vol. I: Las visitas generales en la América española, siglos XVI – XVII; vol. II: Fuentes; literatura jurídica, derecho público* reviewed by Benjamin Keen. *Hispanic American Historical Review*, v. 73, no. 1 (Feb 93), p. 148.

Tau Anzoátegui, Víctor. *Casuísmo y sistema: indagación histórica sobre el espíritu del derecho indiano* reviewed by Nelson Nogueira Saldanha. *Revista Brasileira de Estudos Políticos*, no. 76 (Jan 93), pp. 202 – 203.

— *La ley en América Hispana: del descubrimiento a la emancipación* reviewed by Rubén Darío Salas. *Revista de Historia de América*, no. 113 (Jan – June 92), pp. 179 – 182.

Sources

Hampe Martínez, Teodoro. La recepción del Nuevo Mundo: temas y personajes indianos ante la corte imperial de los Habsburgo, 1530 – 1670. *Revista de Historia de América*, no. 113 (Jan – June 92), pp. 139 – 160. Bibl.

Commerce

Fujii Gambero, Gerardo and Noemí Levy. Composición de las exportaciones de Brasil, Corea, España y México. *Comercio Exterior*, v. 43, no. 9 (Sept 93), pp. 844 – 851. Tables.

Constitutional law

González Encinar, José Juan et al. El proceso constituyente: enseñanzas a partir de cuatro casos recientes: España, Portugal, Brasil y Chile. *Ibero-Amerikanisches Archiv*, v. 18, no. 1 – 2 (1992), pp. 151 – 179. Tables.

Foreign opinion

Rein, Raanan. El antifranquismo durante el régimen peronista. *Cuadernos Americanos*, no. 37, Nueva época (Jan – Feb 93), pp. 90 – 114. Bibl.

Foreign relations

Central America

Rosenberg, Robin L. *Spain and Central America: Democracy and Foreign Policy* reviewed by Paul C. Sondrol. *Hispanic American Historical Review*, v. 73, no. 4 (Nov 93), pp. 731 – 732.

— *Spain and Central America: Democracy and Foreign Policy* reviewed by Joan Font. *Revista Interamericana de Bibliografía*, v. 42, no. 4 (1992), pp. 662 – 663.

Cuba

Robles Muñoz, Cristóbal. Triunfar en Washington: España ante Baire. *Anuario de Estudios Americanos*, v. 49 (1992), pp. 563 – 584. Bibl.

European Community

Alizal, Laura del. España en 1992: su integración a Europa y sus relaciones con México. *Revista Mexicana de Ciencias Políticas y Sociales*, v. 37, Nueva época, no. 149 (July – Sept 92), pp. 109 – 122.

Great Britain

Moreno Alonso, Manuel. Las cosas de España y la política americana de Carlos III en Inglaterra. *Hoy Es Historia*, v. 9, no. 54 (Nov – Dec 92), pp. 44 – 59. Il.

Latin America

Barreiro Cavestany, Fernando. La cooperación española con Latinoamérica a la hora del quinto centenario. *Cuadernos del CLAEH*, v. 17, no. 63 – 64 (Oct 92), pp. 105 – 110. Bibl.

Crespo Martínez, Ismael and Antonia Martínez Rodríguez. Discurso político y realidad económica: las relaciones entre España y la comunidad iberoamericana. *Cuadernos del CLAEH*, v. 17, no. 63 – 64 (Oct 92), pp. 99 – 103. Bibl.

Güenaga de Silva, Rosario and Adriana C. Rodríguez Pérsico. El interés de la diplomacia española por los problemas argentino – chilenos en el seno de Ultima Esperanza. *Revista de Historia de América*, no. 112 (July – Dec 91), pp. 85 – 103. Bibl.

Rebollo, Eduardo. 500 años de incomunicación. *Cuadernos del CLAEH*, v. 17, no. 63 – 64 (Oct 92), pp. 125 – 129.

Viñas, Angel. La política exterior española frente a Iberoamérica: pasado y presente. *Ibero-Amerikanisches Archiv*, v. 18, no. 3 – 4 (1992), pp. 469 – 500. Bibl.

Mexico

Alizal, Laura del. España en 1992: su integración a Europa y sus relaciones con México. *Revista Mexicana de Ciencias Políticas y Sociales*, v. 37, Nueva época, no. 149 (July – Sept 92), pp. 109 – 122.

Portugal

Morales, Adolfo de. Tratados de límites de las posesiones americanas entre España y Portugal. *Signo*, no. 36 – 37, Nueva época (May – Dec 92), pp. 387 – 407.

Moyano Bazzani, Eduardo L. Aportaciones de la historiografía portuguesa a la problemática fronteriza luso – española en América meridional, 1750 – 1778. *Revista de Indias*, v. 52, no. 195 – 196 (May – Dec 92), pp. 723 – 747. Bibl, maps.

Schwartz, Stuart B. Panic in the Indies: The Portuguese Threat to the Spanish Empire, 1640 – 1650. *Colonial Latin American Review*, v. 2, no. 1 – 2 (1993), pp. 165 – 187. Bibl.

History

Dictionaries and encyclopedias

Olson, James Stuart, ed. *Historical Dictionary of the Spanish Empire, 1402 – 1975* reviewed by J. Benedict Warren. *Revista Interamericana de Bibliografía*, v. 42, no. 2 (1992), p. 286.

To 1806

Lynch, John. *The Hispanic World in Crisis and Change, 1598 – 1700* reviewed by Richard L. Kagan. *Hispanic American Historical Review*, v. 73, no. 3 (Aug 93), pp. 492 – 494.

— *Spain, 1516 – 1598: From Nation State to World Empire* reviewed by Richard L. Kagan. *Hispanic American Historical Review*, v. 73, no. 3 (Aug 93), pp. 492 – 494.

Margulis, Mario. Población y sociedad en la España imperial. *Estudios Demográficos y Urbanos*, v. 7, no. 1 (Jan – Apr 92), pp. 223 – 272. Bibl, tables.

Torres Marín, Manuel. Los dos imperios: la doble herencia de Carlos V. *Boletín de la Academia Chilena de la Historia*, v. 58 – 59, no. 102 (1991 – 1992), pp. 505 – 527. Bibl, il, facs.

Vincent, Bernard. *1492: l'année admirable* reviewed by Bernadette Alvarez-Ferrandiz. *Caravelle*, no. 59 (1992), pp. 302 – 304.

— *1492: l'année admirable* reviewed by Marie Cécile Bénassy-Berling (Review entitled "Notas sobre el quinto centenario en Francia"). *Colonial Latin American Review*, v. 2, no. 1 – 2 (1993), pp. 269 – 272.

1936 – 1939, Civil War

Garro, Elena. *Memorias de España 1937* reviewed by Federico Alvarez. *Plural (Mexico)*, v. 22, no. 259 (Apr 93), pp. 69 – 71.

Intellectual life

Alvar López, Manuel. Alfonso Reyes y España. *Nueva Revista de Filología Hispánica*, v. 40, no. 2 (July – Dec 92), pp. 959 – 987. Bibl.

SPAIN IN LITERATURE

Llebot Cazalis, Amaya. César Vallejo y la guerra civil española. *Revista Nacional de Cultura (Venezuela)*, v. 54, no. 287 (Oct – Dec 92), pp. 206 – 216. Bibl, il.

SPANIARDS

Argentina

Persia, Jorge de. Aspectos de la vida y obra de músicos españoles emigrados a Argentina en los años de la guerra civil. *Revista Musical de Venezuela*, no. 28 (May – Dec 89), pp. 165 – 182.

Sánchez Alonso, Blanca. *La inmigración española en Argentina, siglos XIX y XX* reviewed by Hebe Clementi. *Todo Es Historia*, v. 26, no. 310 (May 93), p. 80. Il.

Societies, etc.

Rocamora, Joan. *Catalanes en la Argentina: centenario del Casal de Catalunya* reviewed by Alicia Vidaurreta. *Revista de Indias*, v. 53, no. 197 (Jan – Apr 93), pp. 117 – 119.

Brazil

Bellotto, Manoel Lelo. A imigração espanhola no Brasil: estado do fluxo migratório para o estado de São Paulo, 1931 – 1936. *Estudios Interdisciplinarios de América Latina y el Caribe*, v. 3, no. 2 (July – Dec 92), pp. 59 – 73. Bibl, tables.

González Martínez, Elda Evangelina. Los españoles en un país más allá del océano: Brasil; notas acerca de las etapas de la emigración. *Revista de Indias*, v. 52, no. 195 – 196 (May – Dec 92), pp. 515 – 527. Bibl, tables, charts.

Chile

Bascuñán, Carlos and Sol Serrano. La idea de América en los exiliados españoles en Chile (Excerpt from *El pensamiento español contemporáneo y la idea de América* edited by José Luis Abellán and Antonio Monclús Estella). *Atenea (Chile)*, no. 465 – 466 (1992), pp. 99 – 149. Bibl, tables.

Cuba

Domingo Acebrón, María Dolores. La participación de españoles en el ejército libertador en Cuba, 1895 – 1898. *Revista de Indias*, v. 52, no. 195 – 196 (May – Dec 92), pp. 349 – 363. Bibl, tables.

Núñez Seixas, Xosé M. Inmigración y galleguismo en Cuba, 1879 – 1930. *Revista de Indias*, v. 53, no. 197 (Jan – Apr 93), pp. 53 – 95. Bibl.

Statistics

Naranjo Orovio, V. Consuelo. Trabajo libre e inmigración española en Cuba, 1880 – 1930. *Revista de Indias*, v. 52, no. 195 – 196 (May – Dec 92), pp. 749 – 794. Bibl, charts.

Dominican Republic

Pou, Francis. Inmigración de agricultores españoles a la República Dominicana en el período Franco – Trujillo, 1939 – 1961. *Revista de Indias*, v. 53, no. 198 (May – Aug 93), pp. 563 – 582. Bibl, tables, charts.

Haiti

Szászdi León-Borja, István. Españolas en Haití: la condición jurídica de las primeras pobladoras europeas del Nuevo Mundo. *Revista de Indias*, v. 53, no. 198 (May – Aug 93), pp. 617 – 626. Bibl.

Latin America

Díaz-Jove Blanco, Santiago. *Gijoneses en Indias: notas sobre emigración e índice geobiográfico* reviewed by José Ramón García López. *Revista de Indias*, v. 53, no. 197 (Jan – Apr 93), pp. 102 – 103.

Naharro-Calderón, José María, ed. *El exilio de las Españas de 1939 en las Américas: "¿Adónde fue la canción?"* reviewed by Nancy Vosburg. *Hispania (USA)*, v. 76, no. 2 (May 93), pp. 277 – 278.

Vilar, Juan Bautista. *Los murcianos y América* reviewed by José U. Martínez Carreras. *Revista de Indias*, v. 53, no. 197 (Jan – Apr 93), pp. 126 – 127.

Mexico

Alberro, Solange Behocaray de. *Del gachupín al criollo: o de cómo los españoles de México dejaron de serlo* reviewed by Patricia Schraer. *La Educación (USA)*, v. 37, no. 115 (1993), pp. 411 – 412.

— *Les espagnols dans le Mexique colonial: histoire d'une acculturation* reviewed by Frédérique Langue. *Caravelle*, no. 60 (1993), pp. 141 – 143.

Blázquez Domínguez, Carmen. Dos años críticos: la expulsión de los españoles en Xalapa y Veracruz, 1827 – 1828. *Siglo XIX: Cuadernos*, v. 2, no. 4 (Oct 92), pp. 31 – 58. Bibl.

Cerutti, Mario. Españoles, gran comercio y brote fabril en el norte de México, 1850 – 1910. *Siglo XIX: Cuadernos,* v. 1, no. 2 (Feb 92), pp. 49 – 93. Bibl, tables.

Peru

Campos, José Carlos. Los primeros músicos españoles llegadas al Perú y los siguientes mestizajes musicales producidos en el Perú. *Revista Musical de Venezuela,* no. 28 (May – Dec 89), pp. 127 – 148. Bibl, facs.

Díaz-Jove Blanco, Santiago. Alonso Carrió de Lavandera, "Concoloncorvo": el contexto migratorio de su época y lugar de origen. *Revista de Indias,* v. 53, no. 198 (May – Aug 93), pp. 639 – 649.

Puerto Rico

Cubano Iguina, Astrid Teresa. La emigración mallorquina a Puerto Rico en el siglo XIX: el caso de los sollerenses. *Op. Cit.,* no. 7 (1992), pp. 229 – 253. Bibl, il, tables, charts.

United States

Griffin, Patricia C. *Mullet on the Beach: The Minorcans of Florida, 1768 – 1788* reviewed by Amy Turner Bushnell. *The Americas,* v. 49, no. 4 (Apr 93), pp. 550 – 551.

Venezuela

Margalies de Gasparini, Luisa. Canarias – Venezuela – Canarias: proceso dinámico de migración y retorno en el siglo XX. *Montalbán,* no. 24 (1992), pp. 271 – 290. Bibl.

SPANISH-AMERICAN WAR

See

Subdivision *History - 1898, War of* under *United States*

SPANISH LANGUAGE

See also
Bilingualism

Dialects

Cuartas, Juan Manuel. En torno al concepto de "koiné" o interdialecto. *Thesaurus,* v. 45, no. 3 (Sept – Dec 90), pp. 743 – 746. Bibl.

Lope Blanch, Juan M. *Investigaciones sobre dialectología mexicana,* 2d ed., reviewed by Isabel Silva Aldrete. *Anuario de Letras (Mexico),* v. 30 (1992), pp. 262 – 265.

Moreno de Alba, José G. Léxico de las capitales hispanoamericanas: propuesta de zonas dialectales. *Nueva Revista de Filología Hispánica,* v. 40, no. 2 (July – Dec 92), pp. 575 – 597. Bibl.

Foreign elements

Coello Vila, Carlos. Nuestras lenguas nativas y los bolivianismos. *Signo,* no. 36 – 37, Nueva época (May – Dec 92), pp. 379 – 386. Bibl.

Granda, Germán de. Estudios lingüísticos sobre el español paraguayo. *Estudios Paraguayos,* v. 17, no. 1 – 2 (1989 – 1993), pp. 169 – 319. Bibl.

Jamieson Villiers, Martín. Africanismos en el español de Panamá. *Revista Cultural Lotería,* v. 50, no. 384 (July – Aug 91), pp. 5 – 31. Bibl.

Lope Blanch, Juan M. Mex. "-che, -i(n)che": ¿Nahuatlismo? *Nueva Revista de Filología Hispánica,* v. 40, no. 2 (July – Dec 92), pp. 623 – 636. Bibl.

Meo Zilio, Giovanni. *Estudios hispanoamericanos: temas lingüísticos* reviewed by Joel Rini. *Hispanic Review,* v. 61, no. 2 (Spring 93), pp. 271 – 273.

Schwegler, Armin. "Abrakabraka," "suebbesuebbe" y otras voces palenqueras: sus orígenes e importancia para el estudio de dialectos afrohispanocaribeños. *Thesaurus,* v. 45, no. 3 (Sept – Dec 90), pp. 690 – 731. Bibl.

Grammar

Arze, José Roberto. De Nebrija a Alonso: cinco siglos de gramática castellana. *Signo,* no. 36 – 37, Nueva época (May – Dec 92), pp. 443 – 452.

Guzmán Betancourt, Ignacio. La lengua: ¿Compañera del imperio?; destino de un "presagio" nebrisense en la Nueva España. *Cuadernos Americanos,* no. 37, Nueva época (Jan – Feb 93), pp. 148 – 164. Bibl.

Mendoza, José G. *Gramática castellana* reviewed by Carlos Coello Vila. *Signo,* no. 35, Nueva época (Jan – Apr 92), pp. 232 – 237.

Montes Brunet, Hugo. *Por nuestro idioma* reviewed by Julio Orlandi. *Revista Chilena de Literatura,* no. 41 (Apr 93), p. 140.

Múgica de Fignoni, Nora and Zulema Solana. *La gramática modular* reviewed by Andrea Ostrov. *La Educación (USA),* v. 37, no. 114 (1993), pp. 165 – 166.

History

Avila, Raúl. La lengua española en América cinco siglos después. *Estudios Sociológicos,* v. 10, no. 30 (Sept – Dec 92), pp. 677 – 692. Bibl.

López Estrada, Francisco. Los olvidados: Juan del Valle y Caviedes. *Insula,* no. 563 (Nov 93), p. 3. Il.

Mendoza, José G. El castellano del siglo XVI en el Alto Perú, hoy Bolivia. *Signo,* no. 36 – 37, Nueva época (May – Dec 92), pp. 409 – 432. Bibl.

Sucre Figarella, José Francisco. El español: la palabra solidaria; permanencia y transformación. *Revista Nacional de Cultura (Venezuela),* v. 54, no. 287 (Oct – Dec 92), pp. 21 – 31.

Lexicography

Boyd-Bowman, Peter. *Léxico hispanoamericano del siglo XVI* reviewed by Linda Greenow. *Hispanic American Historical Review,* v. 73, no. 3 (Aug 93), pp. 486 – 487.

Haensch, Günther. La lexicografía del español de América en el umbral del siglo XXI. *Signo,* no. 36 – 37, Nueva época (May – Dec 92), pp. 331 – 360. Bibl.

Pérez Hernández, Francisco Javier. Cinco siglos de lexicografía del español en Venezuela. *Montalbán,* no. 24 (1992), pp. 119 – 166. Bibl.

Sources

Quesada Pacheco, Miguel Angel. Correspondencia de Carlos Gagini con Rufino José Cuervo y Ricardo Palma. *Káñina,* v. 16, no. 1 (Jan – June 92), pp. 197 – 206.

Morphology and syntax

Arjona, Marina and Fernando Rodríguez Guerra. Las oraciones objetivas en el habla popular de la ciudad de México. *Anuario de Letras (Mexico),* v. 30 (1992), pp. 61 – 74. Tables.

Avila, Raúl. Ortografía española: estratificación social y alternativas. *Nueva Revista de Filología Hispánica,* v. 40, no. 2 (July – Dec 92), pp. 649 – 672. Bibl, tables, charts.

Bernal Leongómez, Jaime and José Joaquín Montes Giraldo. El verbo en el habla culta de Bogotá: frecuencia de categorías tradicionales y creación de otras nuevas. *Thesaurus,* v. 45, no. 3 (Sept – Dec 90), pp. 732 – 742. Bibl, tables.

De Mello, George. "-Ra" vs. "-se" Subjunctive: A New Look at an Old Topic. *Hispania (USA),* v. 76, no. 2 (May 93), pp. 235 – 244. Bibl, tables.

López González, Eneyda. Sinonimia y antonimia en unidades fraseológicas usadas por estudiantes de Santa Clara. *Islas,* no. 97 (Sept – Dec 90), pp. 79 – 84. Bibl.

Mendoza, José G. Bello y los verbos abstractos en el análisis de los modos. *Signo,* no. 35, Nueva época (Jan – Apr 92), pp. 83 – 97. Bibl.

Olza Zubiri, Jesús. Homenaje a Nebrija: el genitivo subjectivo determinado con predicativo. *Montalbán,* no. 24 (1992), pp. 11 – 19.

Sanicky, Cristina Aurora. Los usos y las formas del verbo en Misiones, Argentina. *Hispanic Journal,* v. 14, no. 1 (Spring 93), pp. 25 – 36. Bibl.

Phonology

Guitarte, Guillermo L. Sobre la generalidad del yeísmo porteño en el siglo XIX. *Nueva Revista de Filología Hispánica,* v. 40, no. 2 (July – Dec 92), pp. 547 – 574. Bibl.

Quesada Pacheco, Jorge Arturo. La neutralización fonética: más acá del Caribe. *Káñina,* v. 16, no. 1 (Jan – June 92), pp. 165 – 169. Bibl.

Semantics

De Mello, George. "Hasta = no hasta/hasta no = hasta" en el español hablado de once ciudades. *Anuario de Letras (Mexico),* v. 30 (1992), pp. 5 – 28. Bibl, tables.

García, Erica C. Por qué "como" o "porque." *Nueva Revista de Filología Hispánica,* v. 40, no. 2 (July – Dec 92), pp. 599 – 621. Bibl.

Martinell Gifre, Emma. El uso de las formas "un," "uno," "una," "unos," "unas," en español y de sus equivalentes en inglés. *Anuario de Letras (Mexico)*, v. 30 (1992), pp. 29 – 45. Bibl.

Morera Pérez, Marcial. La preposición española "contra": su evolución semántica. *Thesaurus*, v. 45, no. 3 (Sept – Dec 90), pp. 650 – 689. Bibl.

Study and teaching

Marqués, Sarah. *La lengua que heredamos: curso de español para bilingües* reviewed by Jack B. Jelinski. *Hispania (USA)*, v. 76, no. 4 (Dec 93), pp. 747 – 748.

Bibliography

Milstein, Renée and Richard A. Raschio. Bibliografía anotada de logicales, videodiscos y discos compactos para la enseñanza del español o para el uso en cursos bilingües. *Hispania (USA)*, v. 76, no. 4 (Dec 93), pp. 683 – 720.

America

Avila, Raúl. La lengua española en América cinco siglos después. *Estudios Sociológicos*, v. 10, no. 30 (Sept – Dec 92), pp. 677 – 692. Bibl.

Balsas, Héctor. Una lengua favorable. *Cuadernos del CLAEH*, v. 17, no. 63 – 64 (Oct 92), pp. 131 – 135.

Gandolfo, Elvio E. El legado de una lengua plena. *Cuadernos del CLAEH*, v. 17, no. 63 – 64 (Oct 92), pp. 137 – 139.

Haensch, Günther. La lexicografía del español de América en el umbral del siglo XXI. *Signo*, no. 36 – 37, Nueva época (May – Dec 92), pp. 331 – 360. Bibl.

Pastori, Luis. Palabras del presidente de la Academia Venezolana de la Lengua, correspondiente de la Real Española, dr. Luis Pastori. *Boletín de la Academia Nacional de la Historia (Venezuela)*, v. 75, no. 300 (Oct – Dec 92), pp. 17 – 19.

Argentina

Guitarte, Guillermo L. Sobre la generalidad del yeísmo porteño en el siglo XIX. *Nueva Revista de Filología Hispánica*, v. 40, no. 2 (July – Dec 92), pp. 547 – 574. Bibl.

Sanicky, Cristina Aurora. Los usos y las formas del verbo en Misiones, Argentina. *Hispanic Journal*, v. 14, no. 1 (Spring 93), pp. 25 – 36. Bibl.

Vallejos de Llobet, Patricia. El vocabulario científico en la prensa iluminista porteña, 1800 – 1825. *Cuadernos Americanos*, no. 38, Nueva época (Mar – Apr 93), pp. 205 – 224. Bibl.

Dictionaries

Avila, Elvio Arnoldo. *Cómo habla el santiagueño . . . y el argentino: diccionario de voces usuales que el 'Diccionario oficial' no registra; adhesión al V centenario del descubrimiento de América* reviewed by Félix Coluccio. *Folklore Americano*, no. 52 (July – Dec 91), pp. 167 – 168.

Bolivia

Coello Vila, Carlos. Caracterización del castellano boliviano. *Signo*, no. 35, Nueva época (Jan – Apr 92), pp. 47 – 57. Bibl.

— Nuestras lenguas nativas y los bolivianismos. *Signo*, no. 36 – 37, Nueva época (May – Dec 92), pp. 379 – 386. Bibl.

Marrone, Nila. *El habla de la ciudad de La Paz* reviewed by Carlos Coello Vila. *Signo*, no. 35, Nueva época (Jan – Apr 92), pp. 226 – 229.

Mendoza, José G. El castellano del siglo XVI en el Alto Perú, hoy Bolivia. *Signo*, no. 36 – 37, Nueva época (May – Dec 92), pp. 409 – 432. Bibl.

— *Gramática castellana* reviewed by Carlos Coello Vila. *Signo*, no. 35, Nueva época (Jan – Apr 92), pp. 232 – 237.

Varas Reyes, Víctor. *El castellano popular en Tarija* reviewed by Carlos Coello Vila. *Signo*, no. 38, Nueva época (Jan – Apr 93), pp. 260 – 262.

Vargas de Saavedra, Alicia. *Hablemos con propiedad* reviewed by Raúl Rivadeneira Prada. *Signo*, no. 38, Nueva época (Jan – Apr 93), pp. 262 – 263.

Caribbean area

Quesada Pacheco, Jorge Arturo. La neutralización fonética: más acá del Caribe. *Káñina*, v. 16, no. 1 (Jan – June 92), pp. 165 – 169. Bibl.

Schwegler, Armin. "Abrakabraka," "suebbesuebbe" y otras voces palenqueras: sus orígenes e importancia para el estudio de dialectos afrohispanocaribeños. *Thesaurus*, v. 45, no. 3 (Sept – Dec 90), pp. 690 – 731. Bibl.

Colombia

Bernal Leongómez, Jaime and José Joaquín Montes Giraldo. El verbo en el habla culta de Bogotá: frecuencia de categorías tradicionales y creación de otras nuevas. *Thesaurus*, v. 45, no. 3 (Sept – Dec 90), pp. 732 – 742. Bibl, tables.

Cuba

López González, Eneyda. Sinonimia y antonimia en unidades fraseológicas usadas por estudiantes de Santa Clara. *Islas*, no. 97 (Sept – Dec 90), pp. 79 – 84. Bibl.

Latin America

Arze, José Roberto. De Nebrija a Alonso: cinco siglos de gramática castellana. *Signo*, no. 36 – 37, Nueva época (May – Dec 92), pp. 443 – 452.

Boyd-Bowman, Peter. *Léxico hispanoamericano del siglo XVI* reviewed by Linda Greenow. *Hispanic American Historical Review*, v. 73, no. 3 (Aug 93), pp. 486 – 487.

De Mello, George. "-Ra" vs. "-se" Subjunctive: A New Look at an Old Topic. *Hispania (USA)*, v. 76, no. 2 (May 93), pp. 235 – 244. Bibl, tables.

— "Hasta = no hasta/hasta no = hasta" en el español hablado de once ciudades. *Anuario de Letras (Mexico)*, v. 30 (1992), pp. 5 – 28. Bibl, tables.

López Estrada, Francisco. Los olvidados: Juan del Valle y Caviedes. *Insula*, no. 563 (Nov 93), p. 3. Il.

Mendoza, José G. Bello y los verbos abstractos en el análisis de los modos. *Signo*, no. 35, Nueva época (Jan – Apr 92), pp. 83 – 97. Bibl.

Moreno de Alba, José G. Léxico de las capitales hispanoamericanas: propuesta de zonas dialectales. *Nueva Revista de Filología Hispánica*, v. 40, no. 2 (July – Dec 92), pp. 575 – 597. Bibl.

Olza Zubiri, Jesús. Homenaje a Nebrija: el genitivo subjectivo determinado con predicativo. *Montalbán*, no. 24 (1992), pp. 11 – 19.

Rivarola, José Luis. *La formación lingüística de Hispanoamérica: diez estudios* reviewed by Klaus Zimmermann. *Iberoamericana*, v. 17, no. 49 (1993), pp. 90 – 94.

Mexico

Arjona, Marina and Fernando Rodríguez Guerra. Las oraciones objetivas en el habla popular de la ciudad de México. *Anuario de Letras (Mexico)*, v. 30 (1992), pp. 61 – 74. Tables.

Avila, Raúl. Ortografía española: estratificación social y alternativas. *Nueva Revista de Filología Hispánica*, v. 40, no. 2 (July – Dec 92), pp. 649 – 672. Bibl, tables, charts.

Guzmán Betancourt, Ignacio. La lengua: ¿Compañera del imperio?; destino de un "presagio" nebrisense en la Nueva España. *Cuadernos Americanos*, no. 37, Nueva época (Jan – Feb 93), pp. 148 – 164. Bibl.

Lope Blanch, Juan M. *Investigaciones sobre dialectología mexicana*, 2d ed., reviewed by Isabel Silva Aldrete. *Anuario de Letras (Mexico)*, v. 30 (1992), pp. 262 – 265.

— Mex. "-che, -i(n)che": ¿Nahuatlismo? *Nueva Revista de Filología Hispánica*, v. 40, no. 2 (July – Dec 92), pp. 623 – 636. Bibl.

Bibliography

Fulk, Randal C. The Spanish of Mexico: A Partially Annotated Bibliography for 1970 – 1990 (Part I). *Hispania (USA)*, v. 76, no. 2 (May 93), pp. 245 – 270.

— The Spanish of Mexico: A Partially Annotated Bibliography for 1970 – 1990 (Part II). *Hispania (USA)*, v. 76, no. 3 (Sept 93), pp. 446 – 468.

Dictionaries

Moreno de Alba, José G. Revisión de mexicanismos en el *Diccionario* de la Academia. *Anuario de Letras (Mexico)*, v. 30 (1992), pp. 165 – 172. Bibl.

Maps

Lope Blanch, Juan M., ed. *Atlas lingüístico de México, vol. 1: Fonética* reviewed by Klaus Zimmermann. *Iberoamericana*, v. 16, no. 47 – 48 (1992), pp. 111 – 112.

Panama

Jamieson Villiers, Martín. Africanismos en el español de Panamá. *Revista Cultural Lotería*, v. 50, no. 384 (July – Aug 91), pp. 5 – 31. Bibl.

Paraguay

Granda, Germán de. Estudios lingüísticos sobre el español paraguayo. *Estudios Paraguayos*, v. 17, no. 1 – 2 (1989 – 1993), pp. 169 – 319. Bibl.

Río de la Plata region

Meo Zilio, Giovanni. *Estudios hispanoamericanos: temas lingüísticos* reviewed by Joel Rini. *Hispanic Review*, v. 61, no. 2 (Spring 93), pp. 271 – 273.

United States

Lara, Luis Fernando. Para la historia lingüística del pachuco. *Anuario de Letras (Mexico)*, v. 30 (1992), pp. 75 – 88. Bibl.

Lope Blanch, Juan M. *El español hablado en el suroeste de los Estados Unidos: materiales para su estudio* reviewed by Jerry. R. Craddock. *Hispanic Review*, v. 61, no. 1 (Winter 93), pp. 88 – 90.

Varela, Beatriz. *El español cubano-americano* reviewed by Thomas M. Stephens. *Hispania (USA)*, v. 76, no. 4 (Dec 93), pp. 745 – 746.

Venezuela

Pérez Hernández, Francisco Javier. Cinco siglos de lexicografía del español en Venezuela. *Montalbán*, no. 24 (1992), pp. 119 – 166. Bibl.

Tejera, María Josefina. Venezolano y caraqueño: el nacimiento de los gentilicios y la nacionalidad. *Boletín de la Academia Nacional de la Historia (Venezuela)*, v. 75, no. 299 (July – Sept 92), pp. 69 – 76. Bibl.

SPANISH LITERATURE

Santana, Jorge A. La adivinanza a través de quinientos años de cultura hispánica: antología histórica. *Explicación de Textos Literarios*, v. 21, no. 1 – 2 (1992), Issue. Bibl.

Bibliography

Fraser, Howard M. Dissertations, 1992. *Hispania (USA)*, v. 76, no. 2 (May 93), pp. 324 – 348.

Wentzlaff-Eggebert, Harald. *Las literaturas hispánicas de vanguardia: orientación bibliográfica* reviewed by Hugo Verani (Review entitled "Las vanguardias latinoamericanas"). *Nuevo Texto Crítico*, v. 6, no. 11 (1993), pp. 262 – 263.

Foreign influences

Díaz Martínez, Manuel. La generación del '27 e Hispanoamérica. *Cuadernos Hispanoamericanos*, no. 514 – 515 (Apr – May 93), pp. 143 – 154. Il.

History and criticism

Arellano Ayuso, Ignacio, ed. *Las Indias (América) en la literatura del siglo de oro* reviewed by Teodoro Hampe Martínez. *Anuario de Estudios Americanos*, v. 50, no. 1 (1993), pp. 308 – 310.

Brioso Sánchez, Máximo and Héctor Brioso Santos. La picaresca y América en los siglos de oro. *Anuario de Estudios Americanos*, v. 49 (1992), pp. 207 – 232. Bibl.

Hadzelek, Aleksandra. Imagen de América en la poesía de la generación del '27. *Cuadernos Hispanoamericanos*, no. 514 – 515 (Apr – May 93), pp. 155 – 183. Il.

Paz, Octavio. Unidad, modernidad, tradición (Prologue to Volume III of Paz's *Obras completas*). *Vuelta*, v. 17, no. 200 (July 93), pp. 10 – 13.

SPANISH POETRY

History and criticism

Morales, Andrés. Poesía chilena y poesía española: convergencias y divergencias. *Revista Chilena de Literatura*, no. 42 (Aug 93), pp. 139 – 141.

Periodicals

Sheridan, Guillermo. "Los Contemporáneos" y la generación del '27: documentando un desencuentro. *Cuadernos Hispanoamericanos*, no. 514 – 515 (Apr – May 93), pp. 185 – 194.

Chile

Muñoz González, Luis. Noticias de Miguel Hernández en Chile. *Cuadernos Hispanoamericanos*, no. 510 (Dec 92), pp. 13 – 22.

Venezuela

Miranda, Julio E. Miguel Hernández en la literatura venezolana. *Cuadernos Hispanoamericanos*, no. 510 (Dec 92), pp. 23 – 29.

SPIRITUALISM

Bellegarde-Smith, Patrick. "Pawol la pale": Reflections of an Initiate (Introduction to the special issue entitled "Traditional Spirituality in the African Diaspora"). *Journal of Caribbean Studies*, v. 9, no. 1 – 2 (Winter 92 – Spring 93), pp. 3 – 9. Bibl.

Nodal, Roberto. The Concept of "Ebbo" (Sacrifice) as a Healing Mechanism in Santería. *Journal of Caribbean Studies*, v. 9, no. 1 – 2 (Winter 92 – Spring 93), pp. 113 – 124. Bibl.

Ocasio, Rafael. "Babalú Ayé": Santería and Contemporary Cuban Literature. *Journal of Caribbean Studies*, v. 9, no. 1 – 2 (Winter 92 – Spring 93), pp. 29 – 40. Bibl.

SPORTS

See also
Bull fights
Hunting
Soccer

Baratti, Abel and Eduardo Casali. *Del juego al deporte, I: Actividades para nivel primero* reviewed by Cora Céspedes. *La Educación (USA)*, v. 36, no. 111 – 113 (1992), pp. 282 – 283.

Castaingts Teillery, Juan. Las olimpiadas . . . : nación, juego, rito y cultura. *Nueva Antropología*, v. 13, no. 44 (Aug 93), pp. 119 – 136. Bibl.

Murphy, Douglas. Teeing Off: Dwight, JFK, and Fidel. *Hemisphere*, v. 5, no. 2 (Winter – Spring 93), pp. 18 – 21. Il.

Central America

Scarborough, Vernon Lee and David R. Wilcox, eds. *The Mesoamerican Ballgame* reviewed by Barbara J. Price. *Hispanic American Historical Review*, v. 73, no. 1 (Feb 93), pp. 144 – 145.

Jamaica

Carnegie, James Alexander. Sporting Hero and More. *Jamaica Journal*, v. 25, no. 1 (Oct 93), pp. 38 – 43. Il.

Mexico

Fox, John Gerard. The Ballcourt Markers of Tenam Rosario, Chiapas, Mexico. *Ancient Mesoamerica*, v. 4, no. 1 (Spring 93), pp. 55 – 64. Bibl, il.

Lencioni, Vincent. The Pro Sports Money Game. *Business Mexico*, v. 3, no. 7 (July 93), p. 32.

Zeitlin, Judith Francis. The Politics of Classic-Period Ritual Interaction: Iconography of the Ballgame Cult in Coastal Oaxaca. *Ancient Mesoamerica*, v. 4, no. 1 (Spring 93), pp. 121 – 140. Bibl, il, maps.

Peru

Céspedes Aguirre, Patricia. Universidad, deporte y agresividad juvenil: apuntes en torno a la Olimpiada UNSAAC, 1991. *Allpanchis*, v. 25, no. 41 (Jan – June 93), pp. 159 – 174.

United States

Lencioni, Vincent. The Pro Sports Money Game. *Business Mexico*, v. 3, no. 7 (July 93), p. 32.

STANDARD OF LIVING

See
Cost and standard of living

STATE, THE

Cappelletti, Angel J. Pierre Clastres: la sociedad contra el estado. *Revista de Filosofía de la Universidad de Costa Rica*, v. 30, no. 72 (Dec 92), pp. 145 – 151.

Castro Leiva, Luis. The Dictatorship of Virtue or Opulence of Commerce. *Jahrbuch für Geschichte von Staat, Wirtschaft und Gesellschaft Lateinamerikas*, v. 29 (1992), pp. 195 – 240. Bibl.

Dror, Yehezkel. Conducción del estado hacia la integración. *Integración Latinoamericana,* v. 18, no. 189 – 190 (May – June 93), pp. 3 – 9.

Espinoza, Malva and Manuel Antonio Garretón Merino. ¿Reforma del estado o cambio en la matriz socio-política? *Estudios Sociales (Chile),* no. 74 (Oct – Dec 92), pp. 7 – 37. Bibl.

Fiori, José Luís. The Political Economy of the Developmentalist State in Brazil. *CEPAL Review,* no. 47 (Aug 92), pp. 173 – 186. Bibl.

Guerrero Orozco, Omar. *El estado en la era de la modernización* reviewed by Gabriel Corona Armenta. *Revista Mexicana de Ciencias Políticas y Sociales,* v. 38, Nueva época, no. 153 (July – Sept 93), pp. 213 – 218.

Kaplan, Marcos. Crisis del estado latinoamericano: decadencia o palingenesia? *Relaciones Internacionales (Mexico),* v. 14, Nueva época, no. 56 (Oct – Dec 92), pp. 35 – 44.

Lavergne, Néstor. Democracia, estado-nación y socialismo en América Latina. *Realidad Económica,* no. 119 (Oct – Nov 93), pp. 47 – 68. Bibl.

Leal, Juan Felipe. Regímenes políticos en el proceso de estructuración del nuevo estado, 1915 – 1928. *Revista Mexicana de Ciencias Políticas y Sociales,* v. 37, Nueva época, no. 148 (Apr – June 92), pp. 11 – 61.

Martínez Escamilla, Ramón. El estado en América Latina: teoría y práctica. *Problemas del Desarrollo,* v. 24, no. 93 (Apr – June 93), pp. 227 – 233.

O'Donnell, Guillermo A. Acerca del estado, la democratización y algunos problemas conceptuales: una perspectiva latinoamericana con referencias a países poscomunistas (Translated by Leandro Wolfson). *Desarrollo Económico (Argentina),* v. 33, no. 130 (July – Sept 93), pp. 163 – 184. Bibl.

— Estado, democratización y ciudadanía. *Nueva Sociedad,* no. 128 (Nov – Dec 93), pp. 62 – 87.

Rodríguez Pérsico, Adriana C. Sarmiento y Alberdi: una práctica legitimante. *La Educación (USA),* v. 36, no. 111 – 113 (1992), pp. 177 – 192. Bibl.

Yunén, Rafael Emilio. André Corten y la debilidad del estado. *Estudios Sociales (Dominican Republic),* v. 26, no. 93 (July – Sept 93), pp. 41 – 60.

Zedillo Ponce de León, Ernesto. Palabras de Ernesto Zedillo Ponce de León, secretario de educación pública, en la inauguración de la reunión "La Reforma del Estado y las Nuevas Aristas de la Democracia en Iberoamérica," organizada por El Colegio de México, el 17 de marzo de 1992. *Foro Internacional,* v. 32, no. 5 (Oct – Dec 92), pp. 772 – 776.

STATE CAPITALISM

See also

Capital investments
Government ownership of business enterprises
Privatization
Subdivision *Economic policy* under names of specific countries
Subdivision *Government ownership* under names of specific industries

Mexico

Alonso, Jorge et al, eds. *El nuevo estado mexicano, tomo I: Estado y economía* reviewed by Gonzalo Alejandre Ramos. *El Cotidiano,* v. 8, no. 52 (Jan – Feb 93), p. 114.

Bautista Romero, Jaime. Al aproximarse a su fin la venta de paraestatales, el gobierno subasta infraestructura y servicios. *Momento Económico,* no. 66 (Mar – Apr 93), pp. 2 – 6. Bibl.

Paraguay

Borda, Dionisio. La estatización de la economía y la privatización del estado en el Paraguay, 1954 – 1989. *Estudios Paraguayos,* v. 17, no. 1 – 2 (1989 – 1993), pp. 37 – 89. Bibl, tables.

Peru

Hurtado, Isabel. Importancia del empleo estatal en los mercados de trabajo regionales: el caso del sur peruano entre 1961 y 1981. *Revista Andina,* v. 11, no. 1 (July 93), pp. 55 – 78. Bibl, tables, maps, charts.

STATE ELECTIONS

See

Local elections

STATE GOVERNMENT

See

Local government

STATISTICS

See

Subdivision *Statistics* under specific topics

STATUES

See

Cultural property
Sculpture
Stele (Archaeology)
Subdivision *Monuments, etc.* under names of specific individuals

STAVENHAGEN, RODOLFO

Interviews

Minello, Nelson. Entrevistas a Rodolfo Stavenhagen, José Luis Reyna y Claudio Stern. *Estudios Sociológicos,* v. 11, no. 31 (Jan – Apr 93), pp. 19 – 31.

STEDMAN, JOHN GABRIEL

Correspondence, reminiscences, etc.

Stedman, John Gabriel. *Stedman's Surinam: Life in an Eighteenth-Century Slave Society* edited by Richard and Sally Price. Reviewed Jerry Gurulé. *Colonial Latin American Historical Review,* v. 1, no. 1 (Fall 92), pp. 121 – 122.

— *Stedman's Surinam: Life in an Eighteenth-Century Slave Society* edited by Richard and Sally Price. Reviewed by Michael Craton. *Hispanic American Historical Review,* v. 73, no. 3 (Aug 93), pp. 511 – 513.

STEEL INDUSTRY AND TRADE

Argentina

Alcorta, Rodrigo. Arturo Acevedo, un hombre de acero. *Todo Es Historia,* v. 26, no. 307 (Feb 93), pp. 50 – 53. Il.

Latin America

Cabello Naranjo, Elena. La siderurgia: ¿Una señal equivocada? *Comercio Exterior,* v. 43, no. 5 (May 93), pp. 463 – 469. Tables.

Mexico

Cárdenas, Fe Esperanza and Vincent Redonnet. Modernización de la empresa AHMSA en Monclova, Coahuila y su impacto sobre la población. *Estudios Demográficos y Urbanos,* v. 6, no. 3 (Sept – Dec 91), pp. 677 – 716. Bibl, tables.

Castro Escudero, Alfredo. Días de temple para la siderurgia. *Comercio Exterior,* v. 43, no. 3 (Mar 93), pp. 201 – 206. Bibl, tables.

Chisholm, Patrick D. Steel Wars. *Business Mexico,* v. 3, no. 4 (Apr 93), pp. 34 – 37. Il.

González Chávez, Gerardo. Monclova: algunos efectos del neoliberalismo. *Momento Económico,* no. 66 (Mar – Apr 93), pp. 18 – 22.

Gutiérrez Romero, Elizabeth. El dilema del acero mexicano: apertura o proteccionismo. *Momento Económico,* no. 67 (May – June 93), pp. 15 – 18. Bibl.

United States

Olmedo Carranza, Bernardo. Ofensiva proteccionista norteamericana: el acero. *Relaciones Internacionales (Mexico),* v. 15, Nueva época, no. 58 (Apr – June 93), pp. 89 – 91.

STELE (ARCHAEOLOGY)

Beverido Pereau, Francisco. Estela 16 de Yaxchilán. *La Palabra y el Hombre,* no. 82 (Apr – June 92), pp. 291 – 293.

González Lauck, Rebecca B. Algunas consideraciones sobre los monumentos 75 y 80 de La Venta, Tabasco. *Anales del Instituto de Investigaciones Estéticas,* v. 16, no. 62 (1991), pp. 163 – 174. Bibl, il.

STERN, CLAUDIO

Interviews

Minello, Nelson. Entrevistas a Rodolfo Stavenhagen, José Luis Reyna y Claudio Stern. *Estudios Sociológicos*, v. 11, no. 31 (Jan – Apr 93), pp. 19 – 31.

STIMSON, HENRY LEWIS

Stimson, Henry Lewis. *Henry L. Stimson's American Policy in Nicaragua: The Lasting Legacy* reviewed by Thomas W. Walker. *Hispanic American Historical Review*, v. 73, no. 3 (Aug 93), pp. 540 – 541.

STOCK EXCHANGE

Mexico

Cancelada, Gregory D. et al. Market Moves. *Business Mexico*, v. 3 (1993), All issues.

Carlsen, Laura. Making Money in Difficult Times. *Business Mexico*, v. 3, no. 11 (Nov 93), pp. 4 – 7. Tables, charts.

Low, Ann M. Bolstering the "Bolsa." *Business Mexico*, v. 3, no. 6 (June 93), pp. 24 – 26. Tables.

Mathematical models

Arellano Cadena, Rogelio. Relación de largo plazo del mercado bursátil mexicano con el estadunidense: un análisis de cointegración. *El Trimestre Económico*, v. 60, no. 237 (Jan – Mar 93), pp. 91 – 112. Bibl, tables, charts.

Peru

Wong, David. La bolsa de valores de Lima, 1980 a 1990: un análisis de liquidez, rentabilidad y riesgo. *Apuntes (Peru)*, no. 29 (July – Dec 91), pp. 67 – 87. Bibl, tables.

United States

Mathematical models

Arellano Cadena, Rogelio. Relación de largo plazo del mercado bursátil mexicano con el estadunidense: un análisis de cointegración. *El Trimestre Económico*, v. 60, no. 237 (Jan – Mar 93), pp. 91 – 112. Bibl, tables, charts.

STONE IMPLEMENTS

See also
Obsidian

Belize

Dockall, John Edward and Harry J. Shafer. Testing the Producer – Consumer Model for Santa Rita Corozal, Belize. *Latin American Antiquity*, v. 4, no. 2 (June 93), pp. 158 – 179. Bibl, il, maps.

Kelly, Thomas C. Preceramic Projectile-Point Typology in Belize. *Ancient Mesoamerica*, v. 4, no. 2 (Fall 93), pp. 205 – 227. Bibl, il, tables, maps.

Guatemala

Dary Fuentes, Claudia and Aracely Esquivel. Los artesanos de la piedra: estudio sobre la cantería de San Luis Jilotepeque. *La Tradición Popular*, no. 85 (1991), Issue. Bibl, il.

Peru

Chauchat, Claude and Jacques Pelegrin. Tecnología y función de las puntas de Paiján: el aporte de la experimentación. *Latin American Antiquity*, v. 4, no. 4 (Dec 93), pp. 367 – 382. Bibl, il, tables, charts.

STORNI, ALFONSINA

Criticism and interpretation

Pieropan, María D. Alfonsina Storni y Clara Lair: de la mujer posmodernista a la mujer "moderna." *Hispania (USA)*, v. 76, no. 4 (Dec 93), pp. 672 – 682. Bibl.

STREET CHILDREN

Valverde Obando, Luis Alberto. La sociedad y los niños de la calle. *Revista de Ciencias Sociales (Costa Rica)*, no. 59 (Mar 93), pp. 9 – 17. Bibl.

Brazil

Page, Joseph A. A Leap for Life. *Américas*, v. 45, no. 4 (July – Aug 93), pp. 34 – 41. Il.

Costa Rica

Amador Debernardi, Rocío and Laura González Hernández. Características de las familias y de los niños trabajadores de la calle. *Revista de Ciencias Sociales (Costa Rica)*, no. 59 (Mar 93), pp. 19 – 26. Bibl, tables, charts.

Benavides Montoya, Thelma et al. El menor deambulante en Costa Rica. *Revista de Ciencias Sociales (Costa Rica)*, no. 59 (Mar 93), pp. 27 – 35. Bibl, charts.

STREPPONI, BLANCA

Criticism of specific works

El diario de John Robertson

Strepponi, Blanca. El mal, los verdugos y sus víctimas: acerca de una escritura compartida en *El diario de John Robertson. Inti*, no. 37 – 38 (Spring – Fall 93), pp. 61 – 68.

STRESS (PHYSIOLOGY)

Matrajt, Miguel. Prevenção de "stress" ocupacional em linha de montagem: um estudo de caso mexicano (Translated by Geni Goldschmidt). *RAE; Revista de Administração de Empresas*, v. 33, no. 5 (Sept – Oct 93), pp. 98 – 108.

Solberg, V. Scott et al. Development of the College Stress Inventory for Use with Hispanic Populations: A Confirmatory Analytic Approach. *Hispanic Journal of Behavioral Sciences*, v. 15, no. 4 (Nov 93), pp. 490 – 497. Bibl, tables, charts.

STRIKES AND LOCKOUTS

See also
Labor relations
Trade unions

Argentina

Adelman, Jeremy. State and Labour in Argentina: The Portworkers of Buenos Aires, 1910 – 1921. *Journal of Latin American Studies*, v. 25, no. 1 (Feb 93), pp. 73 – 102. Bibl, maps.

Baer, James. Tenant Mobilization and the 1907 Rent Strike in Buenos Aires. *The Americas*, v. 49, no. 3 (Jan 93), pp. 343 – 368. Bibl, tables, maps.

Korzeniewicz, Roberto P. The Labor Politics of Radicalism: The Santa Fe Crisis of 1928. *Hispanic American Historical Review*, v. 73, no. 1 (Feb 93), pp. 1 – 32.

Ríos, Javier Enrique de los. La huelga de Campana de 1915: conflicto olvido. *Todo Es Historia*, v. 27, no. 314 (Sept 93), pp. 56 – 69. Bibl, il.

El Salvador

La aleccionadora huelga en el Ministerio de Salud. *ECA; Estudios Centroamericanos*, v. 48, no. 539 (Sept 93), pp. 890 – 894. Il.

Sindicalización y huelga de los trabajadores del gobierno e instituciones autónomas. *ECA; Estudios Centroamericanos*, v. 48, no. 536 (June 93), pp. 588 – 593. Il.

Mexico

Veloz Avila, Norma Ilse. Conflictos y concertación obrero – patronal. *El Cotidiano*, v. 8, no. 51 (Nov – Dec 92), pp. 76 – 80. Il, tables.

Statistics

Veloz Avila, Norma Ilse. Diecisiete meses de respuesta obrera: conflictos obrero – patronales, 1992 – 1993. *El Cotidiano*, v. 9, no. 56 (July 93), pp. 89 – 103. Il, tables.

Uruguay

Porrini Beracochea, Rodolfo. ¿Mitin contra la dictadura o huelga contra la burguesía? *Hoy Es Historia*, v. 10, no. 58 (July – Aug 93), pp. 19 – 26. Bibl, il.

STRUCTURALISM (SOCIAL SCIENCES)

See
Functional analysis (Social sciences)

STUDENTS

See also
Hispanic American youth (U.S.)
Mexican American youth
Youth

Argentina

Political activity

Barros, Enrique F. et al. 75 años de la reforma universitaria: manifiesto liminar de la reforma universitaria. *Realidad Económica,* no. 118 (Aug – Sept 93), pp. 117 – 122.

Costa Rica

Badilla, Beatriz B. et al. Consumo de sustancias sicotrópicas en los estudiantes de la Facultad de Farmacia de la Universidad de Costa Rica. *Revista de Ciencias Sociales (Costa Rica),* no. 60 (June 93), pp. 63 – 72. Bibl, tables, charts.

Vega Martínez, Mylena. Cultura política y legitimidad: encuesta de opinión entre estudiantes avanzados de la sede central de la Universidad de Costa Rica. *Anuario de Estudios Centroamericanos,* v. 18, no. 2 (1992), pp. 71 – 90. Bibl, tables.

Mexico

Díaz Sustaeta, Federico and Sumie Prado Arai. Estudio de las actitudes de los estudiantes de posgrado de la Universidad Iberoamericana ante las metas de la institución. *Revista Latinoamericana de Estudios Educativos,* v. 23, no. 2 (Apr – June 93), pp. 71 – 85. Bibl, tables.

Holguín Quiñones, Fernando. Análisis comparativo de los egresados de las carreras de la FCPyS con otros similares. *Revista Mexicana de Ciencias Políticas y Sociales,* v. 37, Nueva época, no. 148 (Apr – June 92), pp. 143 – 184. Tables, charts.

Employment

Holguín Quiñones, Fernando. Encuesta a egresados de la Facultad de Ciencias Políticas y Sociales: I parte. *Revista Mexicana de Ciencias Políticas y Sociales,* v. 38, Nueva época, no. 153 (July – Sept 93), pp. 137 – 210. Tables, charts.

Political activity

González de Alba, Luis. 1968: la fiesta y la tragedia. *Nexos,* v. 16, no. 189 (Sept 93), pp. 23 – 31.

Guevara Niebla, Gilberto. Volver al '68 (Interview transcribed and edited by Luis Miguel Aguilar and Rafael Pérez Gay). *Nexos,* v. 16, no. 190 (Oct 93), pp. 31 – 43.

Panama

Castro S., Claudio de. El papel del estudiante universitario en el desarrollo científico y tecnológico. *Revista Cultural Lotería,* v. 50, no. 386 (Nov – Dec 91), pp. 58 – 66.

Puerto Rico

Crespo, Leila. Nivel de razonamiento cognoscitivo en una muestra de estudiantes universitarios: sus implicaciones para la docencia. *Homines,* v. 15 – 16, no. 2 – 1 (Oct 91 – Dec 92), pp. 95 – 101. Bibl, tables.

De Leon, Brunilda. Sex Role Identity among College Students: A Cross-Cultural Analysis. *Hispanic Journal of Behavioral Sciences,* v. 15, no. 4 (Nov 93), pp. 476 – 489. Bibl, tables.

United States

De Leon, Brunilda. Sex Role Identity among College Students: A Cross-Cultural Analysis. *Hispanic Journal of Behavioral Sciences,* v. 15, no. 4 (Nov 93), pp. 476 – 489. Bibl, tables.

Macías, Reynaldo F. Language and Ethnic Classification of Language Minorities: Chicano and Latino Students in the 1990s. *Hispanic Journal of Behavioral Sciences,* v. 15, no. 2 (May 93), pp. 230 – 257. Bibl, tables, charts.

Pearson, Barbara Z. Predictive Validity of the Scholastic Aptitude Test (SAT) for Hispanic Bilingual Students. *Hispanic Journal of Behavioral Sciences,* v. 15, no. 3 (Aug 93), pp. 342 – 356. Bibl, tables.

Reyes, Pedro and Richard R. Valencia. Educational Policy and the Growing Latino Student Population: Problems and Prospects. *Hispanic Journal of Behavioral Sciences,* v. 15, no. 2 (May 93), pp. 258 – 283. Bibl.

Solberg, V. Scott et al. Development of the College Stress Inventory for Use with Hispanic Populations: A Confirmatory Analytic Approach. *Hispanic Journal of Behavioral Sciences,* v. 15, no. 4 (Nov 93), pp. 490 – 497. Bibl, tables, charts.

— Self-Efficacy and Hispanic College Students: Validation of the College Self-Efficacy Instrument. *Hispanic Journal of Behavioral Sciences,* v. 15, no. 1 (Feb 93), pp. 80 – 95. Bibl, tables.

Uruguay

Bosch Vinelli, Julia Beatriz. Estudiantes norteños en el Colegio del Uruguay. *Investigaciones y Ensayos,* no. 41 (Jan – Dec 91), pp. 153 – 169. Bibl.

SUBCONTRACTING

Barbados

Watson, Hilbourne Alban. The U.S. – Canada Free Trade Agreement and the Caribbean, with a Case Study of Electronics Assembly in Barbados. *Social and Economic Studies,* v. 41, no. 3 (Sept 92), pp. 37 – 64. Bibl.

Caribbean area

Green, Cecilia. *The World Market Factory: A Study of Enclave Industrialization in the Eastern Caribbean and Its Impact on Women Workers* reviewed by Nan Wiegersma. *Journal of Developing Areas,* v. 27, no. 2 (Jan 93), pp. 269 – 270.

Colombia

Echeverri, Clara. Maquila o diseño. *Revista Javeriana,* v. 61, no. 593 (Apr 93), pp. 160 – 162.

Developing countries

Alvarez Icaza, Pablo. Marco teórico de la industria maquiladora de exportación. *Comercio Exterior,* v. 43, no. 5 (May 93), pp. 415 – 429. Bibl.

Guatemala

Estrada Vásquez, Luis Everardo. La industria maquiladora en Guatemala. *USAC,* no. 13 (Mar 91), pp. 53 – 60. Bibl.

Mexico

Benería, Lourdes and Martha Roldán. *Las encrucijadas de clase y género: trabajo a domicilio; subcontratación y dinámica de la unidad doméstica en la ciudad de México* translated by Julio Colón Gómez. Reviewed by Norma Ilse Veloz Avila. *El Cotidiano,* v. 9, no. 53 (Mar – Apr 93), p. 118.

Carrillo Viveros, Jorge and Oscar F. Contreras. Calificación en el trabajo: análisis de la industria maquiladora. *Frontera Norte,* v. 4, no. 8 (July – Dec 92), pp. 49 – 78. Bibl, tables, charts.

Fernandez, Adolfo and Melanie Treviño. The Maquiladora Industry, Adverse Environmental Impact, and Proposed Solutions. *Journal of Borderlands Studies,* v. 7, no. 2 (Fall 92), pp. 53 – 72. Bibl.

Inter-American Development Bank. Las maquiladoras en México en vísperas del TLC (Adapted from the text published in *Progreso Económico y Social en América Latina*). *Comercio Exterior,* v. 43, no. 2 (Feb 93), pp. 159 – 161. Tables.

Martínez, María Eugenia and Cirila Quintero Ramírez. Sindicalismo y contratación colectiva en las maquiladoras fronterizas: los casos de Tijuana, Ciudad Juárez y Matamoros. *Frontera Norte,* v. 4, no. 8 (July – Dec 92), pp. 7 – 47. Bibl, tables.

Passe-Smith, John T. and Edward J. Williams. *The Unionization of the Maquiladora Industry: The Tamaulipan Case in National Context* reviewed by Heather Fowler-Salamini. *Hispanic American Historical Review,* v. 73, no. 4 (Nov 93), pp. 718 – 719.

Quintero Ramírez, Cirila. Flexibilidad sindical en las maquiladoras: el caso de Agapito González Cavazos. *El Cotidiano,* v. 8, no. 52 (Jan – Feb 93), pp. 92 – 96.

Rionda, Jorge I. La industria maquiladora de exportación en Guanajuato. *Comercio Exterior,* v. 43, no. 2 (Feb 93), pp. 132 – 134. Tables.

Sánchez, Robert A. Maquila Masquerade. *Business Mexico,* v. 3, no. 1 (Jan – Feb 93), pp. 13 – 15. Il, charts.

Sklair, Leslie. Las maquilas en México: una perspectiva global. *Revista Mexicana de Sociología,* v. 54, no. 2 (Apr – June 92), pp. 163 – 183. Bibl.

Tamayo, Jesús. The Maquila Industry in Perspective. *Journal of Borderlands Studies,* v. 8, no. 1 (Spring 93), pp. 67 – 76. Bibl, tables.

Wilson, Patricia Ann. *Exports and Local Development: Mexico's New Maquiladoras* reviewed by Alfredo Hualde. *Estudios Sociológicos*, v. 11, no. 32 (May – Aug 93), pp. 569 – 573.

— *Exports and Local Development: Mexico's New Maquiladoras* reviewed by Helen Icken Saja. *Hispanic American Historical Review*, v. 73, no. 4 (Nov 93), pp. 719 – 720.

— *Exports and Local Development: Mexico's New Maquiladoras* reviewed by David J. Molina. *Journal of Borderlands Studies*, v. 7, no. 2 (Fall 92), pp. 106 – 108.

Wong González, Pablo. La región norte de México en la triangulación comercial y productiva del Pacífico. *Comercio Exterior*, v. 43, no. 12 (Dec 93), pp. 1153 – 1163. Bibl, tables.

Research

Cortés C., Fernando and Rosa María Rubalcava. Algunas determinantes de la inserción laboral en la industria maquiladora de exportación de Matamoros. *Estudios Sociológicos*, v. 11, no. 31 (Jan – Apr 93), pp. 59 – 91. Bibl, tables.

SUBWAYS

Mexico

Barnhart, Katherine. Digging Up Mexico's Past. *Business Mexico*, v. 3, no. 11 (Nov 93), pp. 42 – 44. Il, maps.

Venezuela

Palabras pronunciadas por González Lander en la ocasión de recibir la colección de obras de la Academia. *Boletín de la Academia Nacional de la Historia (Venezuela)*, v. 75, no. 298 (Apr – June 92), pp. 21 – 25.

SUCRE, ANTONIO JOSÉ DE

Gil-Montero, Martha. The Liberator's Noble Match (Photographs by Jorge Provenza). *Américas*, v. 45, no. 3 (May – June 93), pp. 6 – 17. Il.

SUCRE, GUILLERMO

Criticism and interpretation

Liscano Velutini, Juan. Polémica venezolana en México. *Vuelta*, v. 17, no. 203 (Oct 93), pp. 53 – 55.

SUGAR

Argentina

Bonano, Luis Marcos and Eduardo Rosenzvaig. Contrapunto azucarero entre relaciones de producción y tecnología: el perfil argentino. *Realidad Económica*, no. 113 (Jan – Feb 93), pp. 52 – 86. Il.

Campi, Daniel, ed. *Estudios sobre la historia de la industria azucarera argentina* reviewed by Federico Torres Quevedo. *Todo Es Historia*, v. 26, no. 306 (Jan 93), pp. 56 – 57.

Girbal de Blacha, Noemí M. Azúcar, cambio político y acción empresaria en la Argentina, 1916 – 1930. *Investigaciones y Ensayos*, no. 41 (Jan – Dec 91), pp. 269 – 314. Bibl, tables.

León, Carlos A. El desarrollo agrario de Tucumán en el período de transición de la economía de capitalismo incipiente a la expansión azucarera. *Desarrollo Económico (Argentina)*, v. 33, no. 130 (July – Sept 93), pp. 217 – 236. Bibl, tables.

Caribbean area

Carrington, Selwyn H. H. The American Revolution, British Policy, and the West Indian Economy, 1775 – 1808. *Revista/Review Interamericana*, v. 22, no. 1 – 2 (Spring – Summer 92), pp. 72 – 108. Bibl, tables.

López y Sebastián, Lorenzo Eladio and Justo L. del Río Moreno. Comercio y transporte en la economía del azúcar antillano durante el siglo XVI. *Anuario de Estudios Americanos*, v. 49 (1992), pp. 55 – 87. Bibl, maps.

Cuba

Bergad, Laird W. *Cuban Rural Society in the Nineteenth Century: The Social and Economic History of Monoculture in Matanzas* reviewed by Gert Oostindie. *European Review of Latin American and Caribbean Studies*, no. 53 (Dec 92), pp. 111 – 112.

Pérez-López, Jorge F. *The Economics of Cuban Sugar* reviewed by Mieke Meurs. *Hispanic American Historical Review*, v. 73, no. 1 (Feb 93), p. 184.

Zanetti Lecuona, Oscar. *Los cautivos de la reciprocidad: la burguesía cubana y la dependencia comercial* reviewed by Antonio Santamaría García. *Revista de Indias*, v. 53, no. 197 (Jan – Apr 93), pp. 129 – 132.

Pictorial works

López Junqué, Fernando. *Temporada en el ingenio: ensayo fotográfico* introduced by José Lezama Lima. Reviewed by Antonio Santamaría García. *Anuario de Estudios Americanos*, v. 49, Suppl. 1 (1992), p. 256.

Dominican Republic

Murphy, Martin Francis. *Dominican Sugar Plantations: Production and Foreign Labor Integration* reviewed by Michel-Rolph Trouillot. *Hispanic American Historical Review*, v. 73, no. 3 (Aug 93), pp. 535 – 536.

— *Dominican Sugar Plantations: Production and Foreign Labor Integration* reviewed by Tom Spencer-Walters. *Journal of Caribbean Studies*, v. 9, no. 1 – 2 (Winter 92 – Spring 93), pp. 140 – 142.

Rodríguez Morel, Genaro. Esclavitud y vida rural en las plantaciones azucareras de Santo Domingo, siglo XVI. *Anuario de Estudios Americanos*, v. 49 (1992), pp. 89 – 117. Bibl.

Mexico

Cruz Castellanos, Federico. Economía cañero – azucarera: neoliberalismo y crisis. *Momento Económico*, no. 67 (May – June 93), pp. 19 – 22. Tables.

Singelmann, Peter Marius. The Sugar Industry in Postrevolutionary Mexico: State Intervention and Private Capital. *Latin American Research Review*, v. 28, no. 1 (1993), pp. 61 – 88. Bibl, tables.

Puerto Rico

Martínez Vergne, Teresita. *Capitalism in Colonial Puerto Rico: Central San Vicente in the Late Nineteenth Century* reviewed by Martin F. Murphy. *Hispanic American Historical Review*, v. 73, no. 2 (May 93), pp. 320 – 321.

SUICIDE

Latin America

Dunkerley, James. *Political Suicide in Latin America and Other Essays* reviewed by Walter Little. *Bulletin of Latin American Research*, v. 12, no. 1 (Jan 93), pp. 116 – 117.

SUMU INDIANS

Houwald, Götz Dieter, Freiherr von. *Mayangna = WIR: Zur Geschichte der Sumu-Indianer in Mittelamerika* reviewed by Wolfgang Haberland. *Mesoamérica (USA)*, v. 13, no. 23 (June 92), pp. 217 – 218.

SUPERSTITION

Befán, José. *Las supersticiones, conjuros, ritos, espíritus nefastos* reviewed by Félix Coluccio. *Folklore Americano*, no. 52 (July – Dec 91), pp. 165 – 166.

SURINAM

See also

Blacks in literature – Surinam
Literature and society – Surinam
Slavery – Surinam
Theater – Surinam

Bibliography

Brown, Enid. *Suriname and the Netherlands Antilles: An Annotated English-Language Bibliography* reviewed by Gary Brana-Shute. *The Americas*, v. 50, no. 1 (July 93), pp. 123 – 124.

— *Suriname and the Netherlands Antilles: An Annotated English-Language Bibliography* reviewed by Rosemarijn Hoefte. *Hispanic American Historical Review*, v. 73, no. 4 (Nov 93), pp. 677 – 678.

SURREALISM

Báez Báez, Edith María. Versiones de la realidad en "Las babas del diablo" de Cortázar. *Hispanic Journal*, v. 14, no. 1 (Spring 93), pp. 47 – 61. Bibl.

Haupt, Gerhard. Latinoamérica y el surrealismo en Bochum (Includes several pages of colored art reproductions, translated by José García). *Humboldt*, no. 110 (1993), pp. 82 – 89. Il.

Sánchez Durán, Fernando. *Narrativa chilena ultrarrealista* reviewed by Antonio Campaña. *Atenea (Chile),* no. 465 – 466 (1992), pp. 382 – 384.

Vélez, Julio. Estética del trabajo y la modernidad autóctona. *Casa de las Américas,* no. 189 (Oct – Dec 92), pp. 71 – 80.

SURVEY RESEARCH
See
　Public opinion

SUSSEKIND, ARNALDO
Interviews
Araújo, Maria Celina d' and Angela Maria de Castro Gomes. Entrevista com Arnaldo Sussekind. *Estudos Históricos,* v. 6, no. 11 (Jan – June 93), pp. 113 – 127.

SUSTAINABLE DEVELOPMENT
See
　Ecology and development

SWEDEN
See also
　Latin Americans – Sweden
Karlsson, Weine et al, eds. *Suecia – Latinoamérica: relaciones y cooperación* (Review). *Integración Latinoamericana,* v. 18, no. 195 (Nov 93), pp. 59 – 60.

SWINE
Neumann, Holly. From Pigs to Pesticides. *Business Mexico,* v. 3, no. 1 (Jan – Feb 93), pp. 19 – 22. Il, tables.

Santana, Antônio Cordeiro de. Estrutura de oferta de carne suína sob condições de risco no Brasil. *Revista de Economia e Sociologia Rural,* v. 30, no. 1 (Jan – Mar 92), pp. 21 – 39. Bibl, tables.

SWISS
Argentina
Padula Perkins, Jorge Eduardo. Los valesanos tras la esperanza americana: de Suiza a la Confederación Argentina. *Todo Es Historia,* v. 27, no. 316 (Nov 93), pp. 82 – 85. Il.

SWITZERLAND
See
　Artists – Switzerland

SYMBOLISM IN LITERATURE
See also
　Semiotics
Arguedas Chaverri, María Eugenia. *Eva Luna:* algunas de sus posibilidades significativas. *Káñina,* v. 16, no. 2 (July – Dec 92), pp. 105 – 108. Bibl.

Bilbija, Ksenija. Tiene los cabellos rojizos y se llama Sabina. *La Palabra y el Hombre,* no. 84 (Oct – Dec 92), pp. 228 – 239. Bibl.

Browning, Richard L. La arquitectura de la memoria: los edificios y sus significados en *El obsceno pájaro de la noche* de José Donoso. *Chasqui,* v. 22, no. 2 (Nov 93), pp. 15 – 23. Bibl.

Bumas, Ethan Shaskan. Metaphor's Exile: The Poets and Postmen of Antonio Skármeta. *Latin American Literary Review,* v. 21, no. 41 (Jan – June 93), pp. 9 – 20. Bibl.

Capetillo Hernández, Juan. Las voces del agua. *La Palabra y el Hombre,* no. 82 (Apr – June 92), pp. 301 – 305.

Díaz Infante, Fernando. Las voces del agua. *La Palabra y el Hombre,* no. 81 (Jan – Mar 92), pp. 388 – 390.

García González, José. Iteración léxico – semántica en las metáforas de José Martí sobre la patria cubana. *Islas,* no. 96 (May – Aug 90), pp. 139 – 149. Bibl.

Gerendas, Judit. Imágenes y símbolos en algunos textos poéticos de César Vallejo. *Revista Nacional de Cultura (Venezuela),* v. 54, no. 287 (Oct – Dec 92), pp. 188 – 196. Il.

Planells, Antonio. Borges y Narciso: dos espejos enfrentados. *Hispanic Journal,* v. 13, no. 2 (Fall 92), pp. 213 – 239. Bibl.

Ramos, Luis Arturo. El agua y su lenguaje. *La Palabra y el Hombre,* no. 82 (Apr – June 92), pp. 306 – 309.

Spicer, Juan Pablo. *Don Segundo Sombra:* en busca del "otro." *Revista de Crítica Literaria Latinoamericana,* v. 19, no. 38 (July – Dec 93), pp. 361 – 373. Bibl.

Williams García, Roberto. Las voces del agua. *La Palabra y el Hombre,* no. 81 (Jan – Mar 92), pp. 386 – 387.

SYMBOLISM IN POLITICS
See
　Political sociology

SYNCRETISM (RELIGION)
Andean region
Merlino, Rodolfo J. and Mario A. Rabey. Resistencia y hegemonía: cultos locales y religión centralizada en los Andes del sur. *Allpanchis,* v. 23, no. 40 (July – Dec 92), pp. 173 – 200. Bibl.

Mexico
Alvar, Jaime. Problemas metodológicos sobre el préstamo religioso. *Boletín de Antropología Americana,* no. 24 (Dec 91), pp. 123 – 142. Bibl, il.

Chávez G., Gerardo. Las ceremonias sincretas de San Juan Chamula. *Hoy Es Historia,* v. 10, no. 58 (July – Aug 93), pp. 77 – 79.

Garscha, Karsten. Das Leben, nur eine kurze Reise: Der mexikanische Totenkult. *Iberoamericana,* v. 17, no. 50 (1993), pp. 16 – 37. Bibl.

Peru
Hurtado, Liliana R. de. Santiago entre los chiriguanos: una caso de aculturación y resistencia. *Amazonía Peruana,* v. 11, no. 22 (Oct 92), pp. 147 – 173. Bibl.

Lausent Herrera, Isabelle. La cristianización de los chinos en el Perú: integración, sumisión y resistencia. *Bulletin de l'Institut Français d'Etudes Andines,* v. 21, no. 3 (1992), pp. 977 – 1007. Bibl, il.

SYNDICALISM
See
　Corporate state
　Trade unions

SYNTHETIC PRODUCTS
Werner, Johannes. Plastics Mold into Auto Boom. *Business Mexico,* v. 3, no. 4 (Apr 93), pp. 16 – 19.

SZYSZLO, FERNANDO DE
Interviews
Cisneros, Luis Jaime. De Atahualpa al Museo de la Nación: entrevista a Fernando de Szyszlo. *Debate (Peru),* v. 16, no. 75 (Dec 93 – Jan 94), pp. 70 – 73. Il.

TABASCO, MEXICO
Alvarez Asomoza, Carlos and Luis Casasola García. *Las figurillas de Jonuta, Tabasco* reviewed by Françoise Milhorat. *Caravelle,* no. 59 (1992), pp. 253 – 256.

Arrieta Fernández, Pedro. Desarrollo social planificado en La Chontalpa, Tabasco. *La Palabra y el Hombre,* no. 81 (Jan – Mar 92), pp. 159 – 175.

TABLADA, JOSÉ JUAN
Correspondence, reminiscences, etc.
Tablada, José Juan. Buzón de fantasmas: de José Juan Tablada a Genaro Estrada. *Vuelta,* v. 17, no. 197 (Apr 93), pp. 76 – 77.

—— Buzón de fantasmas: de José Juan Tablada a Julio Torri. *Vuelta,* v. 17, no. 203 (Oct 93), pp. 73 – 74.

Criticism of specific works
Diario
Sheridan, Guillermo. José Juan Tablada en su *Diario. Vuelta,* v. 17, no. 198 (May 93), pp. 28 – 31.

TABOO
Szászdi León-Borja, István. Un tabú de la muerte: la innominación de los vivos y los difuntos como norma jurídica prehispánica. *Anuario de Estudios Americanos,* v. 49 (1992), pp. 3 – 20. Bibl.

TÁCHIRA, VENEZUELA

Castillo Lara, Lucas Guillermo. San Juan Bautista de Colón, de Ayacucho y Sucre, Almirante de Lejanías, mariscal de voluntades. *Boletín de la Academia Nacional de la Historia (Venezuela)*, v. 75, no. 300 (Oct – Dec 92), pp. 43 – 67. Bibl.

Ferrero-Kellerhoff, Inés Cecilia. *Capacho: un pueblo de indios en la jurisdicción de la villa de San Cristóbal* reviewed by Carlos A. Mayo. *Hispanic American Historical Review*, v. 73, no. 1 (Feb 93), pp. 159 – 160.

Paredes, Pedro Pablo. Lucas Guillermo Castillo Lara. *Boletín de la Academia Nacional de la Historia (Venezuela)*, v. 76, no. 301 (Jan – Mar 93), pp. 128 – 130.

TACNA – ARICA QUESTION

Macera dall'Orso, Pablo. Los acuerdos Perú – Chile. *Debate (Peru)*, v. 16, no. 73 (June – Aug 93), pp. 49 – 51. Il.

Valdivieso Belaunde, Felipe. Un acuerdo mezquino. *Debate (Peru)*, v. 16, no. 73 (June – Aug 93), pp. 51 – 56. Il.

Vidal Ramírez, Fernando. El camino del porvenir. *Debate (Peru)*, v. 16, no. 73 (June – Aug 93), pp. 56 – 60. Il.

TACUATE INDIANS

Arrieta Fernández, Pedro. Identidades y culturas: su evolución y persistencia. *La Palabra y el Hombre*, no. 82 (Apr – June 92), pp. 163 – 179. Bibl.

TAINO INDIANS

Cook, Noble David. Disease and the Depopulation of Hispaniola, 1492 – 1518. *Colonial Latin American Review*, v. 2, no. 1 – 2 (1993), pp. 213 – 245. Bibl, tables.

Rouse, Irving. *The Tainos: Rise and Decline of the People Who Greeted Columbus* reviewed by Aaron Segal. *Interciencia*, v. 18, no. 1 (Jan – Feb 93), p. 46.

— *The Tainos: Rise and Decline of the People Who Greeted Columbus* reviewed by C. J. M. R. Gullick. *Journal of Latin American Studies*, v. 25, no. 2 (May 93), pp. 388 – 389.

EL TAJÍN, MEXICO

Pascual Soto, Arturo. *Iconografía arqueológica de El Tajín* reviewed by Fernando Winfield Capitaine. *La Palabra y el Hombre*, no. 82 (Apr – June 92), pp. 313 – 314.

TAMAULIPAS, MEXICO

Alvarado Mendoza, Arturo and Nelson Minello. Política y elecciones en Tamaulipas: la relación entre lo local y lo nacional. *Estudios Sociológicos*, v. 10, no. 30 (Sept – Dec 92), pp. 619 – 647. Charts.

Carrillo Castro, Alejandro and Miguel Angel Romero Miranda. Las preocupaciones públicas: el caso de Tamaulipas. *El Cotidiano*, v. 8, no. 51 (Nov – Dec 92), pp. 95 – 101. Tables.

Cortés C., Fernando and Rosa María Rubalcava. Algunas determinantes de la inserción laboral en la industria maquiladora de exportación de Matamoros. *Estudios Sociológicos*, v. 11, no. 31 (Jan – Apr 93), pp. 59 – 91. Bibl, tables.

Passe-Smith, John T. and Edward J. Williams. *The Unionization of the Maquiladora Industry: The Tamaulipan Case in National Context* reviewed by Heather Fowler-Salamini. *Hispanic American Historical Review*, v. 73, no. 4 (Nov 93), pp. 718 – 719.

Pepin Lehalleur, Marielle and Marie-France Prévôt-Schapira. Cuclillos en un nido de gorrión: espacio municipal y poder local en Altamira, Tamaulipas. *Estudios Sociológicos*, v. 10, no. 30 (Sept – Dec 92), pp. 583 – 617. Bibl, maps.

Sánchez Munguía, Vicente. Matamoros-sur de Texas: el tránsito de los migrantes de América Central por la frontera México – Estados Unidos. *Estudios Sociológicos*, v. 11, no. 31 (Jan – Apr 93), pp. 183 – 207. Bibl, tables.

TAMAYO, FRANZ

Biography

Martínez Salguero, Jaime. *Tamayo, el hombre, la obra* reviewed by Rodolfo Salamanca L. *Signo*, no. 35, Nueva época (Jan – Apr 92), pp. 224 – 225.

Criticism and interpretation

Boero Rojo, Hugo. Orígenes de la polémica Franz Tamayo – Fernando Díez de Medina. *Signo*, no. 36 – 37, Nueva época (May – Dec 92), pp. 43 – 69.

Criticism of specific works

Creación de la pedagogía nacional

Irurozqui Victoriano, Marta. ¿Qué hacer con el indio?: un análisis de las obras de Franz Tamayo y Alcides Arguedas. *Revista de Indias*, v. 52, no. 195 – 196 (May – Dec 92), pp. 559 – 587.

TANGO (DANCE)

Mazzone, Daniel. Tango y bandoneón: encuentros y tristezas de un doble A. *Cuadernos del CLAEH*, v. 17, no. 63 – 64 (Oct 92), pp. 167 – 173. Bibl.

TANNENBAUM, FRANK

Criticism of specific works

Los últimos treinta años

García Muñiz, Humberto. "Los últimos treinta años, 1898 – 1928": un manuscripto inédito de Frank Tannenbaum sobre Puerto Rico; ensayo introductorio. *Op. Cit.*, no. 7 (1992), pp. 145 – 164. Bibl, il.

TAPE RECORDERS AND RECORDINGS

See also
Video tape recorders and recording

Argentina

Castrillón, Ernesto G. Panorama del audio y el video histórico en la Argentina. *Todo Es Historia*, v. 27, no. 315 (Oct 93), p. 61. Il.

TAPIA, ELENA

Interviews

Díaz Castellanos, Guadalupe. Elena Tapia . . . feminismo . . . Mujeres en Acción Sindical. *Fem*, v. 17, no. 128 (Oct 93), pp. 30 – 32.

TARAPACÁ, CHILE (PROVINCE)

González Miranda, Sergio. *Hombres y mujeres de la pampa: Tarapacá en el ciclo del salitre: primera parte* reviewed by Juan Ricardo Couyoumdjian. *Boletín de la Academia Chilena de la Historia*, v. 58 – 59, no. 102 (1991 – 1992), pp. 560 – 561.

— *Hombres y mujeres de la pampa: Tarapacá en el ciclo del salitre* reviewed by Carlos A. de Mattos. *EURE*, v. 19, no. 57 (July 93), pp. 129 – 130. Il.

TARIFF

See also
Foreign trade promotion
Foreign trade regulation
General Agreement on Tariffs and Trade
Taxation
Subdivisions *Commerce, Economic policy,* and *Foreign economic relations* under names of specific countries

Andean region

El arancel externo común en el Grupo Andino. *Integración Latinoamericana*, v. 18, no. 194 (Oct 93), pp. 37 – 39. Tables.

Cárdenas, Manuel José. La integración andina: indicio de una nueva etapa. *Revista Javeriana*, v. 61, no. 594 (May 93), pp. 210 – 215.

Simons Chirinos, Andrés. La teoría de las uniones aduaneras y el Pacto Andino. *Apuntes (Peru)*, no. 31 (July – Dec 92), pp. 41 – 54.

Brazil

Mathematical models

Sousa, Maria da Conceição Sampaio de. Reforma tarifária no Brasil: uma abordagem de "second best." *Revista Brasileira de Economia*, v. 47, no. 1 (Jan – Mar 93), pp. 3 – 31. Bibl, tables.

Costa Rica

Reinert, Kenneth A. Discriminatory Export Taxation in Costa Rica: A Counterfactual History. *Journal of Developing Areas*, v. 28, no. 1 (Oct 93), pp. 39 – 48. Bibl, tables, charts.

Latin America

Vieira Posada, Edgar. Una unión aduanera para América Latina. *Integración Latinoamericana*, v. 18, no. 187 – 188 (Mar – Apr 93), pp. 23 – 34. Bibl.

Mexican – American Border Region

Lazaroff, León. Border Blues. *Business Mexico*, v. 3, no. 4 (Apr 93), pp. 24 – 26.

Mexico

Lencioni, Vincent. The Chinese Tariff Tactic. *Business Mexico*, v. 3, no. 7 (July 93), p. 22. Tables.

MacDonald, Christine. Customs' Unsung Hero? *Business Mexico*, v. 3, no. 4 (Apr 93), pp. 27 – 29. Il.

Law and legislation

Woss W., Herfreid. Calculating Customs Valuation. *Business Mexico*, v. 3, no. 6 (June 93), pp. 38 – 39.

Southern Cone of South America

Aragão, José Maria. El Arancel Externo Común del MERCOSUR: reflexiones a partir de aspectos parciales de la realidad brasileña. *Integración Latinoamericana*, v. 18, no. 187 – 188 (Mar – Apr 93), pp. 3 – 12.

EL Arancel Externo Común (AEC) del MERCOSUR: los conflictos (Review). *Integración Latinoamericana*, v. 18, no. 187 – 188 (Mar – Apr 93), pp. 70 – 71.

United States

Gutiérrez Romero, Elizabeth. El dilema del acero mexicano: apertura o proteccionismo. *Momento Económico*, no. 67 (May – June 93), pp. 15 – 18. Bibl.

TARIJA, BOLIVIA (DEPARTMENT)

Comajuncosa, Antonio. *Manifiesto histórico, geográfico, topográfico, apostólico y político de los misioneros franciscanos de Tarija* reviewed by Pedro de Anasagasti. *Signo*, no. 38, Nueva época (Jan – Apr 93), pp. 231 – 233.

Mingo de la Concepción, Manuel. *Historia de las misiones franciscanas de Tarija entre chiriguanos* reviewed by Pedro de Anasagasti. *Signo*, no. 35, Nueva época (Jan – Apr 92), pp. 237 – 239.

Varas Reyes, Víctor. *El castellano popular en Tarija* reviewed by Carlos Coello Vila. *Signo*, no. 38, Nueva época (Jan – Apr 93), pp. 260 – 262.

TAUBATÉ, BRAZIL

Rangel, Armênio de Souza. A economia do município de Taubaté, 1798 a 1835. *Estudos Econômicos*, v. 23, no. 1 (Jan – Apr 93), pp. 149 – 179. Bibl, tables, charts.

TAVIRA NORIEGA, LUIS DE

Interviews

Olguín, David. La mano ausente: una entrevista con Luis de Tavira. *Nexos*, v. 16, no. 186 (June 93), pp. 86 – 88.

TAXATION

See also
Finance, Public
Tariff
Subdivision *Economic policy* under names of specific countries

America

International cooperation

Prado, Gustavo and Manuel E. Tron. Tri-lateral Taxation. *Business Mexico*, v. 3, no. 3 (Mar 93), pp. 40 – 45.

Bolivia

Gallo, Carmenza. *Taxes and State Power: Political Instability in Bolivia, 1900 – 1950* reviewed by Eduardo A. Gamarra. *Hispanic American Historical Review*, v. 73, no. 3 (Aug 93), pp. 523 – 526.

Brazil

Albuquerque, Marcos Cintra Cavalcanti de, ed. *Imposto único sobre transações: prós e contras* reviewed by Eduardo Lundberg. *Revista de Economia Política (Brazil)*, v. 13, no. 2 (Apr – June 93), pp. 153 – 154.

Bernard, Daniel Alberto. "Franchising" estratégico: como obter alavancagens e sinergias por meio da taxa inicial e dos "royalties." *RAE; Revista de Administração de Empresas*, v. 33, no. 4 (July – Aug 93), pp. 18 – 31. Tables.

Longo, Carlos Alberto. A tributação da renda no sistema federativo. *Estudos Econômicos*, v. 22, no. 2 (May – Aug 92), pp. 157 – 219. Bibl, tables, charts.

Pena, Maria Valéria Junho. O surgimento do imposto de renda: um estudo sobre a relação entre estado e mercado no Brasil. *Dados*, v. 35, no. 3 (1992), pp. 337 – 370. Bibl.

Villela, Luis. Sistema tributario y relaciones financieras intergubernamentales: la experiencia brasileña. *Planeación y Desarrollo*, v. 24, no. 1 (Jan – Apr 93), pp. 171 – 188. Tables.

Colombia

Ocampo López, Javier. La rebelión de las alcabalas. *Boletín de Historia y Antigüedades*, v. 79, no. 779 (Oct – Dec 92), pp. 993 – 1005. Bibl.

Ramírez Acuña, Luis Fernando. Privatización en las administraciones tributarias. *Planeación y Desarrollo*, v. 24, no. 2 (May – Aug 93), pp. 341 – 372.

Vargas, César et al. Financiamiento del desarrollo regional: situación actual y perspectivas. *Planeación y Desarrollo*, v. 24, no. 1 (Jan – Apr 93), pp. 311 – 346. Tables, charts.

Ecuador

Lavallé, Bernard. *Quito et la crise de l'alcabala, 1580 – 1600* reviewed by Michel Bertrand. *Caravelle*, no. 60 (1993), pp. 148 – 150.

Jamaica

Auty, Richard M. Intensified Dependence on a Maturing Mining Sector: The Jamaican Bauxite Levy. *Caribbean Geography*, v. 3, no. 3 (Mar 92), pp. 143 – 159. Bibl, tables.

Latin America

Bibliography

Klein, Herbert S. Historia fiscal colonial: resultados y perspectivas (Translated by Laura Elena Pulido Varela). *Historia Mexicana*, v. 42, no. 2 (Oct – Dec 92), pp. 261 – 307.

Mexico

Aspe Armella, Pedro and Gabriel Zaid. De la esquina. *Vuelta*, v. 17, no. 197 (Apr 93), pp. 82 – 84.

Benavides, Pedro. "Declarándome por exento y libre de pagar la dicha alcabala." *Vuelta*, v. 17, no. 196 (Mar 93), pp. 38 – 39.

León-Portilla, Miguel. Por qué los escribanos y pintores prehispánicos estaban exentos de pagar tributo. *Vuelta*, v. 17, no. 196 (Mar 93), pp. 36 – 37. Il.

MacDonald, Christine. Artists against Taxes. *Business Mexico*, v. 3, no. 4 (Apr 93), p. 44.

Riner, Deborah L. A Pact for All Seasons. *Business Mexico*, v. 3, no. 11 (Nov 93), p. 20. Charts.

Zaid, Gabriel. Razones para la exención. *Vuelta*, v. 17, no. 196 (Mar 93), pp. 43 – 47.

Peru

Peralta Ruiz, Víctor. *En pos del tributo: burocracia estatal, élite regional y comunidades indígenas en el Cusco rural, 1826 – 1854* reviewed by Paul Gootenberg. *Revista Andina*, v. 10, no. 2 (Dec 92), pp. 547 – 548.

— *En pos del tributo: burocracia estatal, élite regional y comunidades indígenas en el Cusco rural, 1826 – 1854* reviewed by Serena Fernández Alonso. *Revista de Indias*, v. 53, no. 197 (Jan – Apr 93), pp. 116 – 117.

Sala i Vila, Nuria. Gobierno colonial, iglesia y poder en Perú, 1784 – 1814. *Revista Andina*, v. 11, no. 1 (July 93), pp. 133 – 161. Bibl.

TAYLOR, SHEILA ORTIZ

Criticism of specific works

Faultline

Christian, Karen. Will the "Real Chicano" Please Stand Up?: The Challenge of John Rechy and Sheila Ortiz Taylor to Chicano Essentialism. *The Americas Review*, v. 20, no. 2 (Summer 92), pp. 89 – 104. Bibl.

TEA

Argentina

Alcorta, Rodrigo. Del arte de producir el buen mate y el buen té. *Todo Es Historia,* v. 26, no. 309 (Apr 93), pp. 50 – 53. Il.

Paraguay

Whigham, Thomas Lyle. *La yerba mate del Paraguay, 1780 – 1870* reviewed by Jeremy Adelman. *Journal of Latin American Studies,* v. 25, no. 1 (Feb 93), pp. 194 – 196.

TEACHER – STUDENT RELATIONSHIPS

Mexico

Vega Shiota, Gustavo de la. Reflexiones en torno al posgrado de sociología en la Facultad de Ciencias Políticas y Sociales de la UNAM. *Revista Mexicana de Ciencias Políticas y Sociales,* v. 38, Nueva época, no. 151 (Jan – Mar 93), pp. 195 – 203.

TEACHERS, TRAINING OF

Santos, Lucíola Licínio de C. P. Problemas e alternativas no campo da formação de professores. *Revista Brasileira de Estudos Pedagógicos,* v. 72, no. 172 (Sept – Dec 91), pp. 318 – 334. Bibl.

Argentina

Pascual, Liliana. Exitos y fracasos de una innovación educativa en el marco de las instituciones escolares. *Revista Latinoamericana de Estudios Educativos,* v. 23, no. 2 (Apr – June 93), pp. 87 – 104. Bibl.

Chile

Letelier Sotomayor, Mario. Posibilidades efectivas de innovación en la docencia universitaria chilena: problemas y perspectivas. *Estudios Sociales (Chile),* no. 74 (Oct – Dec 92), pp. 191 – 199.

Latin America

Ormeño O., Alejandro. Las universidades pedagógicas y el desafío de la formación de profesores. *Estudios Sociales (Chile),* no. 75 (Jan – Mar 93), pp. 225 – 230.

Mexico

Díaz Barriga, Angel. Investigación en la formación de profesores: relaciones particulares y contradictorias. *Revista Latinoamericana de Estudios Educativos,* v. 23, no. 2 (Apr – June 93), pp. 105 – 116. Bibl, tables.

Hernández Palacios, Aureliano. Orígenes de la formación docente en la Universidad Veracruzana. *La Palabra y el Hombre,* no. 81 (Jan – Mar 92), pp. 292 – 301. Il.

TEACHERS' UNIONS

Mexico

Campos Castañeda, Jesús Martín del. El SNTE después del acuerdo. *El Cotidiano,* v. 8, no. 51 (Nov – Dec 92), pp. 71 – 75. Il.

Corona Martínez, Eduardo. Las insuficiencias del Acuerdo Nacional para la Modernización de la Educación Básica. *El Cotidiano,* v. 8, no. 51 (Nov – Dec 92), pp. 23 – 26. Il, tables.

Gordillo, Elba Esther. El SNTE ante la modernización de la educación básica. *El Cotidiano,* v. 8, no. 51 (Nov – Dec 92), pp. 12 – 16. Il.

Hernández Navarro, Luis. SNTE: la transición difícil. *El Cotidiano,* v. 8, no. 51 (Nov – Dec 92), pp. 54 – 59 +. Bibl, il.

López Angel, Carlos. El sindicalismo universitario de hoy y su futuro. *El Cotidiano,* v. 9, no. 56 (July 93), pp. 75 – 85. Il.

Loyo Brambila, Aurora. Actores y tiempos políticos en la modernización educativa. *El Cotidiano,* v. 8, no. 51 (Nov – Dec 92), pp. 17 – 22. Bibl, il.

Miranda López, Francisco. Descentralización educativa y modernización del estado. *Revista Mexicana de Sociología,* v. 54, no. 2 (Apr – June 92), pp. 19 – 44. Bibl, tables.

Reséndiz García, Ramón. Reforma educativa y conflicto interburocrático en México, 1978 – 1988. *Revista Mexicana de Sociología,* v. 54, no. 2 (Apr – June 92), pp. 3 – 18. Bibl.

Street, Susan L. SNTE: ¿Proyecto de quién? *El Cotidiano,* v. 9, no. 56 (July 93), pp. 54 – 59. Il.

— El SNTE Y la política educativa, 1970 – 1990. *Revista Mexicana de Sociología,* v. 54, no. 2 (Apr – June 92), pp. 45 – 72. Bibl.

TEACHING AND TEACHERS

See also

Parent – teacher relationships

Delhumeau Arrecillas, Antonio. El maestro: dignidad y deterioro. *Revista Mexicana de Ciencias Políticas y Sociales,* v. 38, Nueva época, no. 151 (Jan – Mar 93), pp. 205 – 210.

Argentina

Calvo, Bernardino S. Nicolás Repetto y Juan B. Justo, pioneros de la educación rural. *Todo Es Historia,* v. 27, no. 315 (Oct 93), pp. 50 – 53. Il.

Gómez, Marcelo Flavio. Los problemas de la reproducción cultural en el capitalismo argentino: el caso de la anomia disciplinaria en las escuelas de sectores marginados. *La Educación (USA),* v. 36, no. 111 – 113 (1992), pp. 195 – 225. Bibl.

Brazil

Segismundo, Fernando. Professores de história de Colégio Pedro II: esboço. *Revista do Instituto Histórico e Geográfico Brasileiro,* no. 370 (Jan – Mar 91), pp. 151 – 192.

Research

Oliveira, Renato José de. Análise epistemológica da visão de ciência dos professores de química e física do município do Rio de Janeiro. *Revista Brasileira de Estudos Pedagógicos,* v. 72, no. 172 (Sept – Dec 91), pp. 335 – 355. Bibl, tables.

Chile

Gómez Figueroa, Carlos. Situación de los profesores: un problema nacional. *Mensaje,* v. 42, no. 423 (Oct 93), pp. 491 – 494. Il, tables.

Letelier Sotomayor, Mario. Posibilidades efectivas de innovación en la docencia universitaria chilena: problemas y perspectivas. *Estudios Sociales (Chile),* no. 74 (Oct – Dec 92), pp. 191 – 199.

Ramírez Gatica, Soledad. *Estado de la docencia universitaria de pregrado en Chile* reviewed by Ricardo López P. *Estudios Sociales (Chile),* no. 78 (Oct – Dec 93), pp. 227 – 231.

Costa Rica

Hernández Cruz, Omar. Historias de vida e identidades étnicas: la visión de los maestros del Atlántico costarricense. *Revista de Ciencias Sociales (Costa Rica),* no. 58 (Dec 92), pp. 75 – 83. Bibl.

Mexico

Bueno Rodríguez, Luis and Salvador T. Porras Duarte. Deshomologación salarial: ¿Cuánto por punto? *El Cotidiano,* v. 9, no. 55 (June 93), pp. 91 – 98. Tables, charts.

Gil Antón, Manuel, ed. *Académicos: un botón de muestra* reviewed by Quetzalcóatl Gutiérrez Granados. *El Cotidiano,* v. 9, no. 55 (June 93), p. 119.

Góngora Soberanes, Janette. ¿Carrera magisterial emergente? o el magisterio a la carrera. *El Cotidiano,* v. 8, no. 51 (Nov – Dec 92), pp. 31 – 33.

Sandoval Flores, Etelvina. Maestras y modernización educativa. *El Cotidiano,* v. 9, no. 53 (Mar – Apr 93), pp. 78 – 82. Tables, charts.

Villanueva Villanueva, Nancy Beatriz. La práctica docente en la educación preescolar: ¿Autonomía o control? *Nueva Antropología,* v. 13, no. 44 (Aug 93), pp. 103 – 117. Bibl.

Zavala, Silvio Arturo. Justo Sierra Méndez, educador. *Hoy Es Historia,* v. 10, no. 55 (Jan – Feb 93), pp. 76 – 81. Il.

Panama

Moreno Davis, Julio César. Diego Domínguez Caballero, o las facetas de un educador. *Revista Cultural Lotería,* v. 51, no. 392 (Nov – Dec 93), pp. 31 – 40.

Reflexiones finales. *Revista Cultural Lotería,* v. 51, no. 389 (May – June 93), pp. 127 – 134. Bibl.

Venezuela

Arroyo Alvarez, Eduardo. Don Simón Rodríguez, el maestro. *Revista Nacional de Cultura (Venezuela),* v. 53, no. 286 (July – Sept 92), pp. 142 – 147. Il.

Research

Reimel de Carrasquel, Sharon. La calidad de vida del profesorado de la Universidad Simón Bolívar: resultados de una prueba piloto. *La Educación (USA)*, v. 36, no. 111 – 113 (1992), pp. 25 – 45. Bibl, tables, charts.

TEATRO ABIERTO (ARGENTINA)

Cossa, Roberto M. Teatro Abierto: un fenómeno antifascista. *Cuadernos Hispanoamericanos*, no. 517 – 519 (July – Sept 93), pp. 529 – 532.

Dragún, Osvaldo. Cómo lo hicimos. *Cuadernos Hispanoamericanos*, no. 517 – 519 (July – Sept 93), pp. 532 – 535.

Giella, Miguel Angel. *Teatro Abierto, 1981: teatro argentino bajo vigilancia*, vol. I, reviewed by Claudia Ferman. *Latin American Theatre Review*, v. 26, no. 2 (Spring 93), pp. 212 – 214.

Kartun, Mauricio O. Los ciclos del final. *Cuadernos Hispanoamericanos*, no. 517 – 519 (July – Sept 93), pp. 535 – 538.

TEATRO ESQUINA LATINA (COLOMBIA)

Cajamarca Castro, Orlando. Esquina Latina: dos décadas de teatro. *Latin American Theatre Review*, v. 26, no. 2 (Spring 93), pp. 167 – 170.

TEATRO EXPERIMENTAL DE LA UNIVERSIDAD DE CHILE

Piga T., Domingo. Homenaje al medio siglo de TEUCH. *Latin American Theatre Review*, v. 26, no. 2 (Spring 93), pp. 197 – 198.

TEATRO EXPERIMENTAL DO NEGRO (BRAZIL)

Turner, Doris J. The "Teatro Experimental do Negro" and Its Black Beauty Contests. *Afro-Hispanic Review*, v. 11, no. 1 – 3 (1992), pp. 76 – 81. Bibl.

TECHNICAL EDUCATION

See also
Vocational education

Brazil

Salgado, Luiz Francisco de Assis. Em dia com o futuro. *Problemas Brasileiros*, v. 30, no. 295 (Jan – Feb 93), pp. 71 – 72.

Chile
Economic aspects

Bobenrieth H., Eugenio H. and Carlos Cáceres Sandoval. Determinantes del salario de los egresados de la enseñanza media técnico profesional en Chile. *Cuadernos de Economía (Chile)*, v. 30, no. 89 (Apr 93), pp. 111 – 129. Bibl, tables.

Latin America

Alleyne, Michael H. Approaches to Technical Education and the Evolving Role of the OAS. *La Educación (USA)*, v. 36, no. 111 – 113 (1992), pp. 167 – 175.

Cost

Muñoz Izquierdo, Carlos. Tendencias observadas en las investigaciones y en las políticas relacionadas con el financiamiento de la educación técnica y vocacional en América Latina. *Revista Latinoamericana de Estudios Educativos*, v. 23, no. 1 (Jan – Mar 93), pp. 9 – 41. Bibl, tables.

TECHNOLOGY

See also
Biotechnology
Information technology

Ferrer, Aldo. Nuevos paradigmas tecnológicos y desarrollo sostenible: perspectiva latinoamericana. *Comercio Exterior*, v. 43, no. 9 (Sept 93), pp. 807 – 813. Bibl.

Congresses

Castillo Martos, Manuel. III Congreso Latinoamericano de Historia de la Ciencia y la Tecnología. *Anuario de Estudios Americanos*, v. 49, Suppl. 1 (1992), pp. 196 – 201.

Mira Delli-Zotti, Guillermo and Julio C. Sánchez. III Curso de Historia de la Técnica: Procesos de Industrialización en América y la Península Ibérica. *Anuario de Estudios Americanos*, v. 49, Suppl. 1 (1992), pp. 215 – 216.

Argentina

Bonano, Luis Marcos and Eduardo Rosenzvaig. Contrapunto azucarero entre relaciones de producción y tecnología: el perfil argentino. *Realidad Económica*, no. 113 (Jan – Feb 93), pp. 52 – 86. Il.

Brazil

Bedê, Marco Aurélio. Evolução tecnológica na indústria de autopeças: resultados de estudos de caso. *Estudos Econômicos*, v. 22, no. 3 (Sept – Dec 92), pp. 409 – 428. Bibl, tables, charts.

Khan, Ahmad Saeed and José da Silva Souza. Taxa de retorno social do investimento em pesquisa na cultura da mandioca no Nordeste. *Revista de Economia e Sociologia Rural*, v. 29, no. 4 (Oct – Dec 91), pp. 411 – 426. Bibl, tables, charts.

Silva, Maurício Corrêa da et al. Rentabilidade e risco no produção de leite numa região de Santa Catarina. *Revista de Economia e Sociologia Rural*, v. 30, no. 1 (Jan – Mar 92), pp. 63 – 81. Bibl, tables.

Mathematical models

Carvalhais, Jane Noronha and João Eustáquio da Lima. Distribuição dos ganhos com inovação tecnológica na produção de milho entre categorias de pequenos produtores em Minas Gerais. *Revista de Economia e Sociologia Rural*, v. 29, no. 4 (Oct – Dec 91), pp. 373 – 385. Bibl.

Hoffmann, Rodolfo. A dinâmica da modernização da agricultura em 157 microrregiões homogêneas do Brasil. *Revista de Economia e Sociologia Rural*, v. 30, no. 4 (Oct – Dec 92), pp. 271 – 290. Bibl, tables, charts.

Colombia

Rivas, Juan Antonio. Estructura de mercado, innovación y crecimiento. *Planeación y Desarrollo*, v. 24, no. 2 (May – Aug 93), pp. 73 – 93. Bibl.

Cuba

García Capote, Emilio and Tirso W. Sáenz. El desarrollo de la ciencia y la tecnología en Cuba: algunas cuestiones actuales. *Interciencia*, v. 18, no. 6 (Nov – Dec 93), pp. 289 – 294. Bibl, tables.

Latin America

Internoticias/Internews/Internotícias. *Interciencia*, v. 18 (1993), All issues.

Sutz, Judith. Innovación e integración en América Latina. *Nueva Sociedad*, no. 126 (July – Aug 93), pp. 84 – 97. Bibl.

Mexico

Capdevielle, Mario and Gabriela Dutrénit. El perfil tecnológico de la industria mexicana y su dinámica innovadora en la década de los ochenta. *El Trimestre Económico*, v. 60, no. 239 (July – Sept 93), pp. 643 – 674. Bibl, tables, charts.

Olivares, Enrique. *México: crisis y dependencia tecnológica* reviewed by Irma Portos. *Problemas del Desarrollo*, v. 24, no. 94 (July – Sept 93), pp. 290 – 292.

Solleiro, José Luis et al. La innovación tecnológica en la agricultura mexicana. *Comercio Exterior*, v. 43, no. 4 (Apr 93), pp. 353 – 369. Bibl, charts.

Panama

Castillo Galástica, Adán. Cuestiones del desarrollo: la modernización en el agro-panameño. *Revista Cultural Lotería*, v. 50, no. 386 (Nov – Dec 91), pp. 25 – 46. Bibl.

Castro S., Claudio de. El papel del estudiante universitario en el desarrollo científico y tecnológico. *Revista Cultural Lotería*, v. 50, no. 386 (Nov – Dec 91), pp. 58 – 66.

TECHNOLOGY, MEDICAL

Statland de López, Rhona. Profile of an Entrepreneur. *Business Mexico*, v. 3, no. 3 (Mar 93), pp. 12 – 14.

Wildes, Kevin. Tecnología médica y el surgimiento de la bioética. *Mensaje*, v. 42, no. 418 (May 93), pp. 129 – 132. Il.

TECHNOLOGY AND CIVILIZATION

Mathurin B., José Antonio. Filosofía, ciencia y tecnología. *Revista Cultural Lotería*, v. 50, no. 384 (July – Aug 91), pp. 32 – 37.

Sabrovsky, Eduardo, ed. *Tecnología y modernidad en Latinoamérica: ética, política y cultura* reviewed by Felipe Cabello (Review entitled "Don Andrés Bello: ¡Con cuánta nostalgia lo recordamos y cuánta falta nos hace!"). *Interciencia,* v. 18, no. 6 (Nov – Dec 93), pp. 329 – 333.

Sala, Mariella. Tecnologías invisibles: seis estudios de casos develan papel de la mujer latinoamericana como innovadora de tecnologías en procesos productivos. *Fem,* v. 17, no. 126 (Aug 93), pp. 32 – 33.

Congresses

Revolución científico – técnica, educación y área laboral (A seminar organized by the Fundación de Investigaciones Sociales y Políticas (FISYP) de Argentina and summarized by Dora Douthat). *Realidad Económica,* no. 119 (Oct – Nov 93), pp. 134 – 138.

Chile

Guajardo Soto, Guillermo. Tecnología y trabajo en Chile, 1850 – 1930. *Cuadernos Americanos,* no. 38, Nueva época (Mar – Apr 93), pp. 155 – 179. Bibl, tables.

TECHNOLOGY AND STATE

Brazil

Drouvot, Hubert. Libéralisme et politique nationale de développement technologique: l'industrie aéronautique au Brésil. *Cahiers des Amériques Latines,* no. 14 (1992), pp. 95 – 118. Bibl, tables, charts.

Sobral, Fernanda Antônia da Fonseca. La politique scientifique et technologique du Brésil et la conception du développement national. *Cahiers des Amériques Latines,* no. 13 (1992), pp. 163 – 170. Bibl, tables.

Latin America

Malo, Salvador. Las nuevas políticas y las estrategias en materia de ciencia y tecnología. *Revista Latinoamericana de Estudios Educativos,* v. 22, no. 3 (July – Sept 92), pp. 133 – 139.

Bibliography

James, Dilmus D. Technology Policy and Technological Change: A Latin American Emphasis (Review article). *Latin American Research Review,* v. 28, no. 1 (1993), pp. 89 – 101. Bibl.

Mexico

Garza Villarreal, Gustavo. *Desconcentración, tecnología y localización industrial en México: los parques y ciudades industriales, 1953 – 1988* reviewed by Carlos A. de Mattos. *EURE,* v. 19, no. 58 (Oct 93), pp. 88 – 89.

Venezuela

Gutiérrez M., Alejandro and Raúl León Palencia P. Lineamientos de política científica y tecnológica para el estado Mérida: área agrícola agroalimentaria; ideas para la discusión. *Derecho y Reforma Agraria,* no. 23 (1992), pp. 141 – 160. Bibl.

TECHNOLOGY TRANSFER

See also
International economic relations

Dávila Aldás, Francisco Rafael. La revolución científica – técnica, la globalización industrial, la formación de bloques y los nuevos cambios mundiales. *Relaciones Internacionales (Mexico),* v. 15, Nueva época, no. 58 (Apr – June 93), pp. 15 – 23.

Brazil

Bacha, Carlos José Caetano. Alguns aspectos dos modelos de análise dos impactos da mudança tecnológica no comportamento do setor agrícola. *Revista de Economia e Sociologia Rural,* v. 30, no. 1 (Jan – Mar 92), pp. 41 – 62. Bibl, charts.

Silva, Gabriel Luiz Seraphico Peixoto da et al. Mudança tecnológica e produtividade do milho e da soja no Brasil. *Revista Brasileira de Economia,* v. 47, no. 2 (Apr – June 93), pp. 281 – 303. Bibl, tables.

Law and legislation

Barbieri, José Carlos and Walter Delazaro. Nova regulamentação da transferência de tecnologia no Brasil. *RAE; Revista de Administração de Empresas,* v. 33, no. 3 (May – June 93), pp. 6 – 19. Bibl, tables.

Chile

Moraga-Rojel, Jubel R. et al. La biotecnología agrícola y la privatización del conocimiento en la transferencia tecnológica universidad – empresa. *Estudios Sociales (Chile),* no. 77 (July – Sept 93), pp. 117 – 137. Bibl.

Mexico

Barragán, Juan Ignacio. Cemento, vidrio y explosivos: empresarios del norte e importación de tecnología a principios del siglo XX. *Siglo XIX: Cuadernos,* v. 3, no. 6 (June 93), pp. 9 – 21.

TEETH

Tenenbaum, León. Los dientes de Rosas. *Todo Es Historia,* v. 26, no. 308 (Mar 93), pp. 8 – 21. Il, facs.

TEHUANTEPEC, ISTHMUS OF

Blázquez Domínguez, Carmen. Proyectos de comunicación por el Istmo de Tehuantepec, 1842 – 1860. *La Palabra y el Hombre,* no. 83 (July – Sept 92), pp. 199 – 217. Bibl.

TEILLIER SANDOVAL, JORGE

Criticism and interpretation

Llanos Melussa, Eduardo. Jorge Teillier, poeta fronterizo. *Casa de las Américas,* no. 191 (Apr – June 93), pp. 112 – 115.

Sarmiento, Oscar D. La desconstrucción del autor: Enrique Lihn y Jorge Teillier. *Revista Chilena de Literatura,* no. 42 (Aug 93), pp. 237 – 244.

TEITELBOIM, CLAUDIO

Interviews

Valdivieso, Jaime. Poesía, lenguaje y universo: una conversación. *Estudios Públicos (Chile),* no. 52 (Spring 93), pp. 343 – 466.

TEIXEIRA, BENTO

Criticism of specific works

Prosopopea

Vieira, Nelson H. Simulation and Dissimulation: An Expression of Crypto-Judaism in the Literature of Colonial Brazil. *Colonial Latin American Review,* v. 2, no. 1 – 2 (1993), pp. 143 – 164. Bibl.

TEJADA ROCA, MANUEL MARÍA

Manuel María Tejada Roca. *Revista Cultural Lotería,* v. 51, no. 389 (May – June 93), pp. 100 – 111. Il.

TEJERA, PEPE

Giménez, Carlos. Homenaje a Pepe Tejera: palabras del director de Rajatabla a su actor galardonado. *Conjunto,* no. 90 – 91 (Jan – June 92), pp. 40 – 42. Il.

Pepe Tejera: Premio Simón Bolívar. *Conjunto,* no. 90 – 91 (Jan – June 92), p. 39.

TELECOMMUNICATION

See also
Information services
Mass media
Radio broadcasting
Telephone
Television

Argentina

Schvarzer, Jorge. El proceso de privatizaciones en la Argentina: implicaciones preliminares sobre sus efectos en la gobernabilidad del sistema. *Realidad Económica,* no. 120 (Nov – Dec 93), pp. 79 – 143. Bibl.

Pacific Area

Rivas Mira, Fernando Alonso. Transporte, telecomunicaciones y turismo: el Proyecto Triple T. *Comercio Exterior,* v. 43, no. 12 (Dec 93), pp. 1188 – 1194.

TELEPHONE

Argentina

Herrera, Alejandra. The Privatization of the Argentine Telephone System. *CEPAL Review,* no. 47 (Aug 92), pp. 149 – 161. Bibl.

Mexico

Velázquez, Carolina. Las operadoras de TELMEX. *Fem*, v. 17, no. 128 (Oct 93), pp. 19 – 21.

TELEVISION

See also
Children's television
Video tape recorders and recording

Charles C., Mercedes. Modelo globalizador e imágenes femeninas. *Fem*, v. 17, no. 126 (Aug 93), pp. 29 – 30.

— Televisión y estereotipos sexuales. *Fem*, v. 17, no. 129 (Nov 93), pp. 20 – 21.

Mansilla, Hugo Celso Felipe. Comentario (on the topic "Industria electoral y comunicación política"). *Estado y Sociedad*, v. 8, no. 9 (Jan – June 92), pp. 77 – 79.

Congresses

Los estereotipos y clichés en las telenovelas son un obstáculo para la credibilidad de las mujeres (Translated by Victoria E. Zamudio J.). *Fem*, v. 17, no. 130 (Dec 93), pp. 14 – 15.

Argentina

Romano, Eduardo. Parodia televisiva y sobre otros géneros discursivos populares. *Cuadernos Hispanoamericanos*, no. 517 – 519 (July – Sept 93), pp. 323 – 335. Bibl.

Belize

Weaver, Dion. The History of Television in Belize, 1980 – Present. *Belizean Studies*, v. 21, no. 1 (May 93), pp. 13 – 20. Bibl.

Bolivia

Campero, Ana María de. Comentario (on the article by Carlos D. Mesa Gisbert). *Estado y Sociedad*, v. 8, no. 9 (Jan – June 92), pp. 69 – 72.

Cuevas, Roberto. Comentario (on the article by Carlos D. Mesa Gisbert). *Estado y Sociedad*, v. 8, no. 9 (Jan – June 92), pp. 73 – 75.

Mesa Gisbert, Carlos D. Televisión y elecciones: ¿El poder total? *Estado y Sociedad*, v. 8, no. 9 (Jan – June 92), pp. 39 – 52.

Brazil

Squirra, S. Boris Casoy, o âncora brasileiro e o modelo norteamericano. *Vozes*, v. 87, no. 4 (July – Aug 93), pp. 3 – 12. Bibl, il.

Chile

Congresses

Contreras, Juan Pablo. Desde dentro. *Mensaje*, v. 42, no. 418 (May 93), p. 160.

Costa Rica

Lobo, Isaura et al. Televisión: ideología y socialización. *Revista de Ciencias Sociales (Costa Rica)*, no. 57 (Sept 92), pp. 57 – 66. Bibl.

Dominican Republic

Menéndez Alarcón, Antonio V. Television Culture: The Dominican Case. *Studies in Latin American Popular Culture*, v. 12 (1993), pp. 95 – 112. Bibl.

Latin America

Zarattini, María. Las telenovelas y la imagen de la mujer. *Fem*, v. 17, no. 130 (Dec 93), pp. 18 – 19.

Mexico

Bracho, Diana. La buena-buena y la mala-mala. *Fem*, v. 17, no. 130 (Dec 93), pp. 16 – 17.

Bustos Romero, Olga. Mujeres y telenovelas: audiencia cautiva; ¿Sumisa o crítica? *Fem*, v. 17, no. 130 (Dec 93), pp. 20 – 21.

Charles C., Mercedes. Televisión y proyecto de mujer. *Fem*, v. 17, no. 127 (Sept 93), pp. 4 – 5.

Crovi Druetta, Delia María. Libre comercio en TV . . . : fantasía de diversidad. *Revista Mexicana de Ciencias Políticas y Sociales*, v. 38, Nueva época, no. 154 (Oct – Dec 93), pp. 91 – 107.

Olguín Pérez, Palmira. Las reglas del juego: moralidad y moraleja en la telenovela. *Fem*, v. 17, no. 130 (Dec 93), pp. 22 – 23.

Paxman, Andrew. The New TV Azteca. *Business Mexico*, v. 3, no. 11 (Nov 93), pp. 39 – 41. Il, tables.

United States

Charles C., Mercedes. Televisión y proyecto de mujer. *Fem*, v. 17, no. 127 (Sept 93), pp. 4 – 5.

— Violencia, televisión y niños. *Fem*, v. 17, no. 128 (Oct 93), pp. 4 – 5.

Squirra, S. Boris Casoy, o âncora brasileiro e o modelo norteamericano. *Vozes*, v. 87, no. 4 (July – Aug 93), pp. 3 – 12. Bibl, il.

TENAM ROSARIO SITE, MEXICO

Fox, John Gerard. The Ballcourt Markers of Tenam Rosario, Chiapas, Mexico. *Ancient Mesoamerica*, v. 4, no. 1 (Spring 93), pp. 55 – 64. Bibl, il.

TENOCHTITLÁN, MEXICO

Matos Moctezuma, Eduardo. Arqueología urbana en el centro de la ciudad de México. *Estudios de Cultura Náhuatl*, v. 22 (1992), pp. 133 – 141.

TEOTIHUACÁN, MEXICO

López Austin, Alfredo et al. El templo de Quetzalcóatl en Teotihuacán: su posible significado ideológico. *Anales del Instituto de Investigaciones Estéticas*, v. 16, no. 62 (1991), pp. 35 – 52. Bibl, il.

Sugiyama, Saburo. Worldview Materialized in Teotihuacán, Mexico. *Latin American Antiquity*, v. 4, no. 2 (June 93), pp. 103 – 129. Bibl, il, maps, charts.

TERESA DE LOS ANDES, SAINT

García Ahumada, Enrique. Crecimiento hacia la santidad en Teresa de los Andes. *Mensaje*, v. 42, no. 417 (Mar – Apr 93), pp. 64 – 68. Il.

Parker Gumucio, Christián. Primera santa chilena. *Mensaje*, v. 42, no. 418 (May 93), pp. 158 – 159.

TERRORISM

See also
Guerrillas
Violence

Argentina

Alvarez C., Edwin. Criminalidad y abuso de poder: el caso argentino, 1976 – 1983. *Revista Cultural Lotería*, v. 51, no. 388 (Mar – Apr 92), pp. 5 – 33. Bibl.

Graziano, Frank. *Divine Violence: Spectacle, Psychosexuality, and Radical Christianity in the Argentine "Dirty War"* reviewed by Ronaldo Munck. *Bulletin of Latin American Research*, v. 12, no. 1 (Jan 93), pp. 119 – 120.

— *Divine Violence: Spectacle, Psychosexuality, and Radical Christianity in the Argentine "Dirty War"* reviewed by Donald C. Hodges. *Hispanic American Historical Review*, v. 73, no. 3 (Aug 93), pp. 513 – 514.

— *Divine Violence: Spectacle, Psychosexuality, and Radical Christianity in the Argentine "Dirty War"* reviewed by Alberto Ciria. *Revista Interamericana de Bibliografía*, v. 42, no. 3 (1992), pp. 503 – 504.

Quiroga Micheo, Ernesto. Los mazorqueros: ¿Gente decente o asesinos? *Todo Es Historia*, v. 26, no. 308 (Mar 93), pp. 38 – 55. Bibl, il, facs.

Sábato, Ernesto R. Nunca más (Prologue to the book of the same title). *Cuadernos Hispanoamericanos*, no. 517 – 519 (July – Sept 93), pp. 571 – 573.

Latin America

Weschler, Lawrence. A Miracle, a Universe: Settling Accounts with Torturers. *SALALM Papers*, v. 36 (1991), pp. 201 – 208.

Paraguay

Boccia Paz, Alfredo et al. *Médicos, ética y tortura en el Paraguay* (Review). *Revista Paraguaya de Sociología*, v. 29, no. 84 (May – Aug 92), pp. 205 – 206. Il.

Peru

García Ríos, José María and Giulia Tamayo. El escenario como dictador: configuración metropolitana y experiencia cotidiana. *Nueva Sociedad,* no. 123 (Jan – Feb 93), pp. 94 – 103. Bibl.

Obando Arbulú, Enrique. Situación de la subversión: después de la caída de Abimael Guzmán. *Debate (Peru),* v. 15, no. 70 (Sept – Oct 92), pp. 19 – 22. Il.

TERTIARY SECTOR

See
> Service industries

TESTIMONIAL NOVELS

See
> Biography (as a literary form)
> Literature and society

TEXAS

See also
> El Paso, Texas
> Houston, Texas

Almaráz, Félix D., Jr. Franciscan Evangelization in Spanish Frontier Texas: Apex of Social Contact, Conflict, and Confluence, 1751 – 1761. *Colonial Latin American Historical Review,* v. 2, no. 3 (Summer 93), pp. 253 – 287. Bibl, il, maps.

Caruso, Brooke A. *The Mexican Spy Company: United States Covert Actions in Mexico, 1845 – 1848* reviewed by Daniela Spenser. *Hispanic American Historical Review,* v. 73, no. 1 (Feb 93), p. 189.

Chipman, Donald E. *Spanish Texas, 1519 – 1821* reviewed by E. A. Mares. *Colonial Latin American Historical Review,* v. 2, no. 4 (Fall 93), pp. 474 – 475.

González Quiroga, Miguel. La puerta de México: los comerciantes texanos y el noreste mexicano, 1850 – 1880. *Estudios Sociológicos,* v. 11, no. 31 (Jan – Apr 93), pp. 209 – 236. Bibl, tables, maps.

Gutmann, Myron P. et al. Matrimonio y migración en la frontera: patrones de nupcialidad en Texas, 1850 – 1910. *Historia Mexicana,* v. 42, no. 1 (July – Sept 92), pp. 45 – 76. Bibl, tables, charts.

Santos, Gilberto de los and Vern Vincent. Tex-Mex Tourism (Excerpt from *Mexican Tourism Market in the Rio Grande Valley of Texas). Business Mexico,* v. 3, no. 3 (Mar 93), pp. 27 – 29. Tables.

Stoddard, Ellwyn R. Teen-Age Pregnancy in the Texas Borderlands. *Journal of Borderlands Studies,* v. 8, no. 1 (Spring 93), pp. 77 – 98. Bibl, tables, maps.

TEXCOCO, MEXICO

Máynez Vidal, Pilar. Documentos de Tezcoco: consideraciones sobre tres manuscritos en mexicano del ramo "Tierras." *Estudios de Cultura Náhuatl,* v. 22 (1992), pp. 325 – 343.

TEXTBOOKS

Aguila, Marcos Tonatiuh. Historia, revisionismo y educación: la nueva "revolución pasiva." *El Cotidiano,* v. 8, no. 51 (Nov – Dec 92), pp. 39 – 47. Bibl, il.

Bejarano Martínez, René. Los nexos de la historia. *El Cotidiano,* v. 8, no. 51 (Nov – Dec 92), pp. 48 – 53. Il.

Hart, Graham and Mike Morrissey. *Practical Skills in Caribbean Geography, Book 1: Grade 8 – Basic CXC and Book 2: Grade 10 – General CXC* reviewed by Laurence Neuville. *Caribbean Geography,* v. 3, no. 4 (Sept 92), pp. 279 – 280.

Marqués, Sarah. *La lengua que heredamos: curso de español para bilingües* reviewed by Jack B. Jelinski. *Hispania (USA),* v. 76, no. 4 (Dec 93), pp. 747 – 748.

Méndez, Luis et al. Historia y poder. *El Cotidiano,* v. 8, no. 51 (Nov – Dec 92), pp. 60 – 69. Il, tables.

TEXTILE INDUSTRY AND FABRICS

See also
> Clothing and dress
> Indigo
> Wool industry and trade
> Subdivisions *Costume and adornment* and *Textile industry and fabrics* under names of Indian groups

Andean region

Block, David. Andean Textiles: Aesthetics, Iconography, and Political Symbolism. *SALALM Papers,* v. 34 (1989), pp. 223 – 231. Il.

Bibliography

Block, David. A Core Bibliography of Andean Weaving. *SALALM Papers,* v. 34 (1989), pp. 232 – 233.

Argentina

Di Tella, Torcuato S. La unión obrera textil, 1930 – 1945. *Desarrollo Económico (Argentina),* v. 33, no. 129 (Apr – June 93), pp. 109 – 136. Bibl, tables.

Guy, Donna Jane. "Oro Blanco": Cotton, Technology, and Family Labor in Nineteenth-Century Argentina. *The Americas,* v. 49, no. 4 (Apr 93), pp. 457 – 478. Bibl.

Colombia

Adarve, Luz Helena. La importancia de las marcas en la industria de la confección: nuevo enfoque. *Revista Javeriana,* v. 61, no. 593 (Apr 93), pp. 156 – 158.

Arango R., Sol Beatriz. La industria textil colombiana. *Revista Javeriana,* v. 61, no. 593 (Apr 93), pp. 143 – 146. Tables.

Echeverri, Clara. Maquila o diseño. *Revista Javeriana,* v. 61, no. 593 (Apr 93), pp. 160 – 162.

Espriella, Andrés de la. Hacia una integración comercial con los Estados Unidos. *Revista Javeriana,* v. 61, no. 593 (Apr 93), pp. 148 – 154. Tables.

Feria H., Eduardo. Situación actual potencial a nivel nacional e internacional: informe de prensa. *Revista Javeriana,* v. 61, no. 593 (Apr 93), pp. 168 – 169.

González, Humberto. La industria de confecciones o la competitividad amenazada. *Revista Javeriana,* v. 61, no. 593 (Apr 93), pp. 163 – 166.

Moreno Mejía, Luis Alberto. La apertura en el sector textil. *Revista Javeriana,* v. 61, no. 593 (Apr 93), pp. 141 – 142.

Pachón, Efraín. Los invitados del mes. *Revista Javeriana,* v. 61, no. 593 (Apr 93), pp. 170 – 178. Il.

Cuba

Lindenberg, Gail. The Labor Union in the Cuban Workplace. *Latin American Perspectives,* v. 20, no. 1 (Winter 93), pp. 28 – 39.

Dominican Republic

Guerrero, María Angustias. Costureras y producción mercantil en la sociedad dominicana: los orígenes. *Anuario de Estudios Americanos,* v. 49 (1992), pp. 601 – 614. Bibl, tables.

Mexico

Aboites A., Jaime and Alenka Guzmán Chávez. La industria textil mexicana y el Tratado de Libre Comercio. *El Cotidiano,* v. 8, no. 51 (Nov – Dec 92), pp. 102 – 109. Bibl, tables.

Aguirre Anaya, Carmen. Industria y tecnología: motricidad en los textiles de algodón en el XIX. *Siglo XIX: Cuadernos,* v. 3, no. 6 (June 93), pp. 23 – 33. Bibl.

Bernier F., Richard E. Cutting a New Cloth. *Business Mexico,* v. 3, no. 1 (Jan – Feb 93), pp. 27 – 28. Il.

Gamboa Ojeda, Leticia. Mercado de fuerza de trabajo e industria textil: el centro-oriente de México durante el porfiriato. *Siglo XIX: Cuadernos,* v. 1, no. 1 (Oct 91), pp. 9 – 36. Bibl.

García Díaz, Bernardo. *Textiles del valle de Orizaba, 1880 – 1925* reviewed by Patricia Arias. *La Palabra y el Hombre,* no. 82 (Apr – June 92), pp. 310 – 312.

Mondragón, Ana Laura. Contratos-ley y sindicatos: huleros y textileros. *El Cotidiano,* v. 9, no. 56 (July 93), pp. 18 – 22. Il, tables.

Portos, Irma. Notas sobre textiles en Estados Unidos y México. *Momento Económico,* no. 69 (Sept – Oct 93), pp. 10 – 12. Tables.

Wilson, Fiona. *De la casa al taller: mujeres, trabajo y clase social en la industria textil y del vestido* reviewed by Soledad González Montes. *Estudios Sociológicos,* v. 11, no. 31 (Jan – Apr 93), pp. 288 – 290. Bibl.

— *Sweaters: Gender, Class, and Workshop-Based Industry in Mexico* reviewed by Tessa Cubitt. *Bulletin of Latin American Research,* v. 12, no. 1 (Jan 93), pp. 124 – 125.

Statistics

Pieza, Ramón. Análisis coyuntural de la industria textil mexicana. *Momento Económico,* no. 65 (Jan – Feb 93), pp. 31 – 34. Tables.

United States

Portos, Irma. Notas sobre textiles en Estados Unidos y México. *Momento Económico,* no. 69 (Sept – Oct 93), pp. 10 – 12. Tables.

THEATER

See also
Acting
Actors and actresses
Ballet
Children's theater
Drama
Drama festivals
Experimental theater
Folk drama
Mime
Opera
Puppets and puppet-plays
Religious drama

Production and direction

Bravo-Elizondo, Pedro. Teatro en el Cono Sur: Carlos Manuel Varela (Uruguay). *Latin American Theatre Review,* v. 26, no. 2 (Spring 93), pp. 143 – 150.

Labaki, Aimar. Nueve comentarios sobre los directores teatrales. *Conjunto,* no. 93 (Jan – June 93), pp. 13 – 17. Il.

Milaré, Sebastião. Las estaciones poéticas de Antunes Filho. *Conjunto,* no. 93 (Jan – June 93), pp. 26 – 37. Il.

Olguín, David. La mano ausente: una entrevista con Luis de Tavira. *Nexos,* v. 16, no. 186 (June 93), pp. 86 – 88.

Süssekind, Maria Flora. La imaginación monológica: Gerald Thomas y Bia Lessa. *Conjunto,* no. 93 (Jan – June 93), pp. 18 – 25. Bibl, il.

Stage setting and scenery

Lima, Mariângela Alves de. Teatro brasileño de hoy: tendencias actuales de la puesta en escena. *Conjunto,* no. 93 (Jan – June 93), pp. 3 – 7. Il.

America

Pianca, Marina. *El teatro de nuestra América: un proyecto continental, 1959 – 1989* reviewed by Pedro Bravo-Elizondo. *Latin American Theatre Review,* v. 26, no. 2 (Spring 93), pp. 214 – 216.

Argentina

Cossa, Roberto M. Teatro Abierto: un fenómeno antifascista. *Cuadernos Hispanoamericanos,* no. 517 – 519 (July – Sept 93), pp. 529 – 532.

Dragún, Osvaldo. Cómo lo hicimos. *Cuadernos Hispanoamericanos,* no. 517 – 519 (July – Sept 93), pp. 532 – 535.

Dubatti, Jorge A. El nuevo teatro de Buenos Aires, 1983 – 1992. *Cuadernos Hispanoamericanos,* no. 517 – 519 (July – Sept 93), pp. 445 – 462. Bibl.

Giella, Miguel Angel. *Teatro Abierto, 1981: teatro argentino bajo vigilancia,* vol. I, reviewed by Claudia Ferman. *Latin American Theatre Review,* v. 26, no. 2 (Spring 93), pp. 212 – 214.

Kartun, Mauricio O. Los ciclos del final. *Cuadernos Hispanoamericanos,* no. 517 – 519 (July – Sept 93), pp. 535 – 538.

Pellettieri, Osvaldo. Actualidad del sainete en el teatro argentino. *Cuadernos Hispanoamericanos,* no. 517 – 519 (July – Sept 93), pp. 421 – 436. Bibl, il.

— Los '80: el teatro porteño entre la dictadura y la democracia. *Cuadernos Hispanoamericanos,* no. 517 – 519 (July – Sept 93), pp. 313 – 322.

Seibel, Beatriz. *De ninfas a capitanas* reviewed by Ileana Azor. *Conjunto,* no. 92 (July – Dec 92), pp. 100 – 101.

— Mujer, teatro y sociedad en el siglo XIX. *Conjunto,* no. 92 (July – Dec 92), pp. 54 – 57. Bibl, il.

Brazil

Antunes Filho. Confesiones de un fingidor. *Conjunto,* no. 93 (Jan – June 93), pp. 38 – 43. Il.

George, David. *The Modern Brazilian Stage* reviewed by Frank Dauster. *World Literature Today,* v. 67, no. 2 (Spring 93), p. 348.

Guzik, Alberto. Un ejercicio de la memoria: dramaturgia de los '80. *Conjunto,* no. 93 (Jan – June 93), pp. 8 – 12. Il.

Labaki, Aimar. Nueve comentarios sobre los directores teatrales. *Conjunto,* no. 93 (Jan – June 93), pp. 13 – 17. Il.

Lima, Mariângela Alves de. Teatro brasileño de hoy: tendencias actuales de la puesta en escena. *Conjunto,* no. 93 (Jan – June 93), pp. 3 – 7. Il.

Milaré, Sebastião. Las estaciones poéticas de Antunes Filho. *Conjunto,* no. 93 (Jan – June 93), pp. 26 – 37. Il.

Um palco de qualidade. *Problemas Brasileiros,* v. 30, no. 295 (Jan – Feb 93), p. 66. Il.

Süssekind, Maria Flora. La imaginación monológica: Gerald Thomas y Bia Lessa. *Conjunto,* no. 93 (Jan – June 93), pp. 18 – 25. Bibl, il.

O talento do teatro. *Problemas Brasileiros,* v. 30, no. 295 (Jan – Feb 93), p. 65.

Chile

Guerrero del Río, Eduardo. Teatro chileno contemporáneo: una visión panorámica de las dos últimas décadas. *Aisthesis,* no. 24 (1991), pp. 55 – 63. Bibl.

— El teatro chileno contemporáneo: una visión panorámica de las dos últimas décadas. *Conjunto,* no. 89 (Oct – Dec 91), pp. 33 – 39. Il.

Lagos, María Soledad. El teatro chileno de creación colectiva desde sus orígenes hasta fines de la década de los '80: algunas reflexiones. *Aisthesis,* no. 24 (1991), pp. 45 – 53. Bibl.

Piña, Juan Andrés. Modos y temas del teatro chileno: la voz de los ochenta. *Conjunto,* no. 89 (Oct – Dec 91), pp. 28 – 32. Il.

Vidal, Hernán. *Dictadura militar, trauma social e inauguración de la sociología del teatro en Chile* reviewed by Carlos Alberto Trujillo. *Hispanic Review,* v. 61, no. 3 (Summer 93), pp. 456 – 457.

— *Dictadura militar, trauma social e inauguración de la sociología del teatro en Chile* reviewed by Catherine M. Boyle. *Latin American Theatre Review,* v. 26, no. 2 (Spring 93), pp. 216 – 217.

Cuba

Study and teaching

Hernández, Esther María. Machurrucutu en seis tiempos: crónica de septiembre. *Conjunto,* no. 90 – 91 (Jan – June 92), pp. 79 – 84. Il.

Herrero, Ramiro. Machurrucutu. *Conjunto,* no. 90 – 91 (Jan – June 92), pp. 85 – 91. Il.

Guatemala

Barrios y Barrios, Catalina. Manifestaciones teatrales en Guatemala durante el siglo XIX. *USAC,* no. 12 (Dec 90), pp. 76 – 90. Bibl.

Latin America

Dauster, Frank N. Hacia la historia del teatro hispanoamericano. *Latin American Theatre Review,* v. 26, no. 2 (Spring 93), pp. 9 – 15. Il.

Entreactos (Brief reviews of Latin American theater groups and productions throughout the world). *Conjunto,* no. 89 – 93 (1992 – 1993), All issues.

Gené, Juan Carlos. Atavismos y teatro. *Conjunto,* no. 93 (Jan – June 93), pp. 116 – 117. Il.

La mujer y la escena latinoamericana actual (A summary of four productions: *Medea húngara* by Arpad Göncz, *Naira Yawiña* by Isidora Aguirre, *O marinheiro* by Fernando Pessoa, and *Las ruinas circulares* by Raquel Carrió). *Conjunto,* no. 92 (July – Dec 92), pp. 58 – 62. Il.

Nigro, Kirsten F. Textualidad, historia y sujetividad: género y género. *Latin American Theatre Review,* v. 26, no. 2 (Spring 93), pp. 17 – 24.

Rojo, Grínor. El teatro latinoamericano moderno: notas para una nueva historia, primer movimiento. *Conjunto,* no. 90 – 91 (Jan – June 92), pp. 2 – 9. Bibl.

Taylor, Diana. Negotiating Performance. *Latin American Theatre Review,* v. 26, no. 2 (Spring 93), pp. 49 – 57. Bibl.

Bibliography

Unruh, Vicky Wolff. Cultural Enactments: Recent Books on Latin American Theatre (Review article). *Latin American Research Review*, v. 28, no. 1 (1993), pp. 141 – 149.

Congresses

Unruh, Vicky Wolff and George W. Woodyard. Latin American Theatre Today: A 1992 Conference in Kansas. *Latin American Theatre Review*, v. 26, no. 2 (Spring 93), pp. 6 – 8. Il.

Sources

Van Jacob, Scott. Basic Reference Sources for Latin American Dramatic Arts. *SALALM Papers*, v. 34 (1989), pp. 334 – 344. Bibl.

Mexico

Olguín, David. La mano ausente: una entrevista con Luis de Tavira. *Nexos*, v. 16, no. 186 (June 93), pp. 86 – 88.

— Tradición y novedad. *Nexos*, v. 16, no. 187 (July 93), pp. 90 – 91.

Paraguay

Caballero, Atilio J. Algo más que un teatro sin historia. *Conjunto*, no. 90 – 91 (Jan – June 92), pp. 92 – 96. Il.

Peru

Eidelberg, Nora. El teatro en Lima en 1991 y 1992. *Latin American Theatre Review*, v. 26, no. 2 (Spring 93), pp. 191 – 195.

Rajatabla y Yuyachkani: veinte años. *Conjunto*, no. 90 – 91 (Jan – June 92), pp. 32 – 38. Il.

Puerto Rico

García del Toro, Antonio. La jerga teatral puertorriqueña (Includes a basic glossary). *Homines*, v. 15 – 16, no. 2 – 1 (Oct 91 – Dec 92), pp. 298 – 308.

Matorell, Antonio. Imalabra. *Conjunto*, no. 92 (July – Dec 92), pp. 95 – 97. Il.

Surinam

Ganga, Sharda. Suriname: testimonio teatral de una práctica. *Conjunto*, no. 90 – 91 (Jan – June 92), pp. 97 – 100. Il.

United States

Kanellos, Nicholas Charles. *A History of Hispanic Theatre in the United States: Origins to 1940* reviewed by Joshua Al Mora. *Hispania (USA)*, v. 76, no. 1 (Mar 93), pp. 87 – 88.

Woodyard, George W. El teatro hispánico en Estados Unidos: ¿Cruce o choque de culturas? *Conjunto*, no. 89 (Oct – Dec 91), pp. 7 – 12. Bibl, il.

Uruguay

Bravo-Elizondo, Pedro. Teatro en el Cono Sur: Carlos Manuel Varela (Uruguay). *Latin American Theatre Review*, v. 26, no. 2 (Spring 93), pp. 143 – 150.

Cordones-Cook, Juanamaría. Surgimiento y desaparición del Teatro Negro Uruguayo: entrevista con Andrés Castillo. *Afro-Hispanic Review*, v. 12, no. 2 (Fall 93), pp. 31 – 36.

Venezuela

Azparrén Giménez, Leonardo. El teatro en Venezuela: una historia para ser construida. *Revista Nacional de Cultura (Venezuela)*, v. 53, no. 285 (Apr – June 92), pp. 179 – 198.

León, Idalia de. Abrirse paso ante lo adverso: el teatro universitario en Venezuela. *Conjunto*, no. 89 (Oct – Dec 91), pp. 105 – 111. Il.

Rajatabla y Yuyachkani: veinte años. *Conjunto*, no. 90 – 91 (Jan – June 92), pp. 32 – 38. Il.

THEATER REVIEWS

See
Drama reviews

THEATERS

Argentina

Page, Carlos A. Los cien años del Teatro Mayor de Córdoba. *Todo Es Historia*, v. 26, no. 308 (Mar 93), pp. 56 – 59. Bibl, il.

Guatemala

Barrios y Barrios, Catalina. Manifestaciones teatrales en Guatemala durante el siglo XIX. *USAC*, no. 12 (Dec 90), pp. 76 – 90. Bibl.

Mexico

Dávila Diez, Enrique. Estos fueron los cines. *Nexos*, v. 16, no. 187 (July 93), pp. 87 – 89. Il.

Law and legislation

Barraza, Eduardo and Juan Felipe Leal. Inicios de la reglamentación cinematográfica en la ciudad de México. *Revista Mexicana de Ciencias Políticas y Sociales*, v. 37, Nueva época, no. 150 (Oct – Dec 92), pp. 139 – 175. Bibl, charts.

THEOLOGY

See also
Bible
Catholic Church
Christian life
Death
Ethics
Evangelicalism
Existentialism
Liberation theology
Prayer

Chile

Parra Carrasco, Fredy Omar. *Pensamiento teológico en Chile: contribución a su estudio, tomo V: El reino que ha de venir; historia y esperanza en la obra de Manuel Lacunza* reviewed by José Arteaga. *Mensaje*, v. 42, no. 425 (Dec 93), p. 657. Il.

Study and teaching

Barrios V., Marciano. Jesuitas en la Facultad de Teología de la Universidad Católica. *Mensaje*, v. 42, no. 420 (July 93), pp. 293 – 296. Il.

Latin America

Parentelli, Gladys. Teología feminista en América Latina. *Fem*, v. 17, no. 130 (Dec 93), pp. 7 – 12. Bibl.

Saranyana, José Ignacio. *Teología profética americana: diez estudios sobre la evangelización fundante* reviewed by Pilar Gonzalbo Aizpuru. *Historia Mexicana*, v. 42, no. 1 (July – Sept 92), pp. 129 – 133.

Mexico

Stam, Juan. La *Biblia* en la teología colonialista de Juan Ginés de Sepúlveda. *Revista de Historia (Costa Rica)*, no. 25 (Jan – June 92), pp. 157 – 164. Bibl.

Peru

Nguyen, Thai Hop, ed. *Evangelización y teología en el Perú* reviewed by Wilfredo Ardito Vega. *Amazonía Peruana*, v. 11, no. 22 (Oct 92), pp. 273 – 277.

THOMAS, DOROTHY

Criticism of specific works

Criminal Injustice

Pitanguy, Jacqueline. Um estudo americano sobre violência no Brazil. *Estudos Feministas*, v. 1, no. 1 (1993), pp. 150 – 151.

THOMAS, GERALD

Süssekind, Maria Flora. La imaginación monológica: Gerald Thomas y Bia Lessa. *Conjunto*, no. 93 (Jan – June 93), pp. 18 – 25. Bibl, il.

THORNDIKE, GUILLERMO

Interviews

Jara, Umberto. Entrevista a Guillermo Thorndike. *Debate (Peru)*, v. 16, no. 72 (Mar – May 93), pp. 6 – 12. Il.

TIAHUANACU, BOLIVIA

Goldstein, Paul. Tiwanaku Temples and State Expansion: A Tiwanaku Sunken-Court Temple in Moquequa, Peru. *Latin American Antiquity*, v. 4, no. 1 (Mar 93), pp. 22 – 47. Bibl, il, tables, maps.

Schávelzon, Daniel. La arqueología como ciencia o como ficción. *Todo Es Historia*, v. 26, no. 309 (Apr 93), pp. 32 – 49. Bibl, il.

TIBESAR, ANTONINE S.
Obituaries
Morales, Francisco. Antonine Tibesar, O.F.M. (1901 – 1992): in memoriam. *Estudios de Cultura Náhuatl*, v. 22 (1992), pp. 495 – 496.

TIERRA DEL FUEGO
Schiavini, Adrián. Los lobos marinos como recurso para cazadores-recolectores marinos: el caso de Tierra del Fuego. *Latin American Antiquity*, v. 4, no. 4 (Dec 93), pp. 346 – 366. Bibl, tables, maps.

TIJUANA, MEXICO
Guillén López, Tonatiuh and Gerardo M. Ordóñez B. La marginalidad social en la frontera norte: discrepancias empíricas al concepto de la marginalidad. *Frontera Norte*, v. 4, no. 8 (July – Dec 92), pp. 149 – 163. Tables.

Woo Morales, Ofelia. La migración internacional desde una perspectiva regional: el caso de Tijuana y Ciudad Juárez. *Relaciones Internacionales (Mexico)*, v. 15, Nueva época, no. 57 (Jan – Mar 93), pp. 87 – 94. Charts.

TIME ALLOCATION
Garrocho, Carlos. De la casa al hospital: un enfoque espacio – temporal. *Estudios Sociológicos*, v. 11, no. 32 (May – Aug 93), pp. 547 – 554. Bibl, charts.

TIME IN LITERATURE
Cadena, Agustín. *Farabeuf:* el espacio como metáforo del tiempo. *Plural (Mexico)*, v. 22, no. 258 (Mar 93), pp. 50 – 56. Bibl.

May, Hilda R. El tiempo como kairós en la poética de Gonzalo Rojas. *Chasqui*, v. 22, no. 1 (May 93), pp. 37 – 41.

Nanfito, Jacqueline C. Time as Space in Sor Juana's *El sueño*. *Hispanic Journal*, v. 13, no. 2 (Fall 92), pp. 345 – 352.

TIÓ, SALVADOR
Criticism of specific works
Desde el tuétano
Hernández Agosto, Miguel A. Mensaje del presidente de la Comisión Puertorriqueña para la Celebración del Quinto Centenario del Descubrimiento de América y Puerto Rico, en ocasión de la presentación del libro – periódico *Desde el tuétano*, de don Salvador Tió. *Homines*, v. 15 – 16, no. 2 – 1 (Oct 91 – Dec 92), pp. 372 – 373.

TISSERA, JUAN CAPISTRANO
Bruno, Cayetano. La recia personalidad de fray Juan Capistrano Tissera, obispo de Córdoba. *Investigaciones y Ensayos*, no. 41 (Jan – Dec 91), pp. 107 – 137. Bibl.

TITICACA, LAKE
Dejoux, Claude and André Iltis, eds. *El lago Titicaca: síntesis del conocimiento limnológico actual* reviewed by Néstor Teves. *Bulletin de l'Institut Français d'Etudes Andines*, v. 21, no. 3 (1992), pp. 1075 – 1078.

TITU CUSI
See
Yupanqui, Titu Cusi

TITULESCU, NICOLAE
Nastase, Adrián. Titulescu y América Latina. *Boletín de la Academia Nacional de la Historia (Venezuela)*, v. 75, no. 298 (Apr – June 92), pp. 9 – 14.

TIZÓN, HÉCTOR
Correspondence, reminiscences, etc.
Tizón, Héctor. Las palabras que narran. *Cuadernos Hispanoamericanos*, no. 517 – 519 (July – Sept 93), pp. 506 – 511.

TLASCALAN INDIANS
Offutt, Leslie S. Levels of Acculturation in Northeastern New Spain: San Esteban Testaments of the Seventeenth and Eighteenth Centuries. *Estudios de Cultura Náhuatl*, v. 22 (1992), pp. 409 – 443.

TLAXCALA, MEXICO (STATE)
Ramírez Rancaño, Mario. La organización obrera y campesina en Tlaxcala durante el cardenismo. *Revista Mexicana de Sociología*, v. 54, no. 3 (July – Sept 92), pp. 189 – 219. Bibl, tables.

TLC
See
North American Free Trade Agreement

TOBACCO
Argentina
Alcorta, Rodrigo. Con títulos de Nobleza: hacia un siglo de historia. *Todo Es Historia*, v. 27, no. 313 (Aug 93), pp. 50 – 53. Il.

Mexico
Government ownership
Alvarez de Castrillón, Anes and Guillermo Céspedes del Castillo. *El tabaco en Nueva España* reviewed by Dawn Keremitsis. *Hispanic American Historical Review*, v. 73, no. 2 (May 93), pp. 311 – 312.

Deans-Smith, Susan. *Bureaucrats, Planters, and Workers: The Making of the Tobacco Monopoly in Bourbon Mexico* reviewed by Michael P. Costeloe. *Bulletin of Latin American Research*, v. 12, no. 2 (May 93), pp. 221 – 222.

— *Bureaucrats, Planters, and Workers: The Making of the Tobacco Monopoly in Bourbon Mexico* reviewed by Mark A. Buckholder. *Colonial Latin American Historical Review*, v. 2, no. 2 (Spring 93), pp. 227 – 228.

— Compromise and Conflict: The Tobacco Workers of Mexico City and the Colonial State, 1770 – 1810. *Anuario de Estudios Americanos*, v. 49 (1992), pp. 271 – 309. Bibl.

Paraguay
Cooney, Jerry Wilson. "La Dirección General de la Real Renta de Tabacos" and the Decline of the Royal Tobacco Monopoly in Paraguay, 1779 – 1800. *Colonial Latin American Historical Review*, v. 1, no. 1 (Fall 92), pp. 101 – 115. Bibl.

— Fraude y burócratas: tabaco y Paraguay, 1789 – 1790. *Revista Paraguaya de Sociología*, v. 29, no. 85 (Sept – Dec 92), pp. 29 – 40. Bibl.

United States
McGraw, Sarah A. and Kevin W. Smith. Smoking Behavior of Puerto Rican Women: Evidence from Caretakers of Adolescents in Two Urban Areas. *Hispanic Journal of Behavioral Sciences*, v. 15, no. 1 (Feb 93), pp. 140 – 149. Bibl, tables.

TOBAGO
See
Trinidad and Tobago

TOCANTINS, BRAZIL
Ajara, Cesar et al. O estado do Tocantins: reinterpretação de um espaço de fronteira. *Revista Brasileira de Geografia*, v. 53, no. 4 (Oct – Dec 91), pp. 5 – 48. Bibl, maps.

TODO ES HISTORIA (PERIODICAL)
Sáenz Quesada, María. Los 25 años de *Todo Es Historia*. *Revista Interamericana de Bibliografía*, v. 42, no. 4 (1992), pp. 561 – 569. Bibl, il.

TOLEDO, FRANCISCO DE
Bibliography
Gómez Rivas, León. Don Francisco de Toledo, comendador de Alcántara, virrey del Perú: guía de fuentes (I). *Anuario de Estudios Americanos*, v. 49, Suppl. 1 (1992), pp. 123 – 171.

— Don Francisco de Toledo, comendador de Alcántara, virrey del Perú: guía de fuentes (II). *Anuario de Estudios Americanos*, v. 49, Suppl. 2 (1992), pp. 95 – 152.

TOLTECS
Graulich, Michel. *Quetzalcóatl y el espejismo de Tollan* reviewed by Bernadette Alvarez-Ferrandiz. *Caravelle*, no. 59 (1992), pp. 295 – 297.

Kristan-Graham, Cynthia. The Business of Narrative at Tula: An Analysis of the Vestibule Frieze, Trade, and Ritual. *Latin American Antiquity*, v. 4, no. 1 (Mar 93), pp. 3 – 21. Bibl, il.

TOLUCA VALLEY, MEXICO

Menegus Bornemann, Margarita. *Del señorío a la república de indios: el caso de Toluca, 1500 – 1600* reviewed by Michel Bertrand. *Caravelle*, no. 60 (1993), pp. 143 – 147.

TOMÁS, CONSUELO
Criticism and interpretation
Ruiloba C., Rafael. Consuelo Tomás o la nueva mirada. *Revista Cultural Lotería*, v. 51, no. 390 (July – Aug 92), pp. 27 – 32.

TORO, DAVID
Gallego, Ferran. *Los orígenes del reformismo militar en América Latina: la gestión de David Toro en Bolivia* reviewed by Gary Prado. *Journal of Latin American Studies*, v. 25, no. 1 (Feb 93), pp. 205 – 206.

— *Los orígenes del reformismo militar en América Latina: la gestión de David Toro en Bolivia* reviewed by Marta Irurozqui Victoriano. *Revista Andina*, v. 11, no. 1 (July 93), pp. 246 – 247.

— *Los orígenes del reformismo militar en América Latina: la gestión de David Toro en Bolivia* reviewed by Marta Irurozqui Victoriano. *Revista de Indias*, v. 53, no. 197 (Jan – Apr 93), pp. 104 – 106.

TORO, GUILLERMO DEL
Interviews
Pliego, Roberto. Los emblemas del metal: una entrevista con Guillermo del Toro. *Nexos*, v. 16, no. 186 (June 93), pp. 85 – 86.

TORRES, JUAN
Criticism of specific works
Peralillo
Muñoz, Silverio Baltazar. Vivir y escribir en los Estados Unidos: sobre la novela *Peralillo: desde USA con amor* de Juan Torres. *Revista Chilena de Literatura*, no. 42 (Aug 93), pp. 149 – 156.

TORRES BODET, JAIME
Latapí, Pablo. El pensamiento educativo de Torres Bodet: una apreciación crítica. *Revista Latinoamericana de Estudios Educativos*, v. 22, no. 3 (July – Sept 92), pp. 13 – 44. Bibl.

Correspondence, reminiscences, etc.
Ortiz de Montellano, Bernardo R. Buzón de fantasmas: de Ortiz de Montellano a Torres Bodet. *Vuelta*, v. 17, no. 198 (May 93), pp. 78 – 79.

Torres Bodet, Jaime. Buzón de fantasmas: de Jaime Torres Bodet a Ermilo Abreu Gómez. *Vuelta*, v. 17, no. 204 (Nov 93), pp. 68 – 69.

Criticism of specific works
La educación sentimental
Unruh, Vicky Wolff. Art's "Disorderly Humanity" in Torres Bodet's *La educación sentimental*. *Revista Canadiense de Estudios Hispánicos*, v. 17, no. 1 (Fall 92), pp. 123 – 136. Bibl.

TORRES GARCÍA, JOAQUÍN
Art reproductions
Torres García, Joaquín. (Reproduction of an untitled graphic text by Joaquín Torres García). *Nexos*, v. 16, no. 183 (Mar 93), pp. 66 – 69.

TORRI, JULIO
Correspondence, reminiscences, etc.
Tablada, José Juan. Buzón de fantasmas: de José Juan Tablada a Julio Torri. *Vuelta*, v. 17, no. 203 (Oct 93), pp. 73 – 74.

TORRIENTE-BRAU, PABLO DE LA
Bibliography
Toro González, Aída Julia de. Pablo de la Torriente Brau: bibliografía pasiva. *Islas*, no. 97 (Sept – Dec 90), pp. 44 – 51.

TORTURE
See
>Human rights
>Political prisoners
>Terrorism

TOSTA, VIRGILIO
Criticism of specific works
Historia de Barinas
Gómez Grillo, Elio. Sucedió en Barinas. *Boletín de la Academia Nacional de la Historia (Venezuela)*, v. 76, no. 301 (Jan – Mar 93), pp. 127 – 128.

TOURIST TRADE
Belize
Higinio, Egbert and Ian Munt. Belize: Eco Tourism Gone Awry. *Report on the Americas*, v. 26, no. 4 (Feb 93), pp. 8 – 10. Il.

Caribbean area
Derné, Marie-Claude et al. Business Opportunities in Caribbean Cooperation. *Social and Economic Studies*, v. 41, no. 3 (Sept 92), pp. 65 – 100. Bibl, tables.

Harms, Mike. Nurturing Conservation Naturally in the Twin Isles (Photographs by Michael Ventura). *Américas*, v. 45, no. 2 (Mar – Apr 93), pp. 22 – 25. Il, maps.

Walvin, James. Selling the Sun: Tourism and Material Consumption. *Revista/Review Interamericana*, v. 22, no. 1 – 2 (Spring – Summer 92), pp. 208 – 225. Bibl.

Weaver, David B. Model of Urban Tourism for Small Caribbean Islands. *Geographical Review*, v. 83, no. 2 (Apr 93), pp. 134 – 140. Bibl, charts.

Costa Rica
Coffey, Brian. Investment Incentives as a Means of Encouraging Tourism Development: The Case of Costa Rica. *Bulletin of Latin American Research*, v. 12, no. 1 (Jan 93), pp. 83 – 90. Bibl, tables, maps.

Cuba
Espino, María Dolores. Tourism in Cuba: A Development Strategy for the 1990s? *Cuban Studies/Estudios Cubanos*, v. 23 (1993), pp. 49 – 69. Bibl, tables.

Mexican – American Border Region
Santos, Gilberto de los and Vern Vincent. Tex-Mex Tourism (Excerpt from *Mexican Tourism Market in the Rio Grande Valley of Texas*). *Business Mexico*, v. 3, no. 3 (Mar 93), pp. 27 – 29. Tables.

Law and legislation
Lazaroff, León. Border Blues. *Business Mexico*, v. 3, no. 4 (Apr 93), pp. 24 – 26.

Mexico
Ayre, Shirley. A Rosier Image for the Zona Rosa. *Business Mexico*, v. 3, no. 10 (Oct 93), pp. 4 – 7. Il.

Blears, James. The Show Goes On. *Business Mexico*, v. 3, no. 10 (Oct 93), pp. 8 – 11. Il.

Coldwell, Pedro Joaquín. Service for Survival (Excerpt from a speech given by the Secretary of Tourism). *Business Mexico*, v. 3, no. 10 (Oct 93), pp. 16 – 17. Il.

Galindo Blanco, Adán. Tourism in a Trap. *Business Mexico*, v. 3, no. 10 (Oct 93), pp. 18 – 19. Il.

Holt, Douglas. Guadalajara Gambles with Expansion. *Business Mexico*, v. 3, no. 6 (June 93), pp. 30 – 31. Il.

Long, Veronica H. Monkey Business: Mixing Tourism with Ecology. *Business Mexico*, v. 3, no. 1 (Jan – Feb 93), pp. 23 – 26. Il.

Megaprojects in Progress. *Business Mexico*, v. 3, no. 10 (Oct 93), p. 15. Tables.

Ruiz, Gabriela. To Go or Not to Go. *Business Mexico*, v. 3, no. 10 (Oct 93), pp. 20 – 22.

Russell, Joel. A Worldwide Brand Name. *Business Mexico,* v. 3, no. 10 (Oct 93), pp. 12 – 14. Il.

Savage, Melissa. Ecological Disturbance and Nature Tourism. *Geographical Review,* v. 83, no. 3 (July 93), pp. 290 – 300. Bibl, il, maps.

Pacific Area

Rivas Mira, Fernando Alonso. Transporte, telecomunicaciones y turismo: el Proyecto Triple T. *Comercio Exterior,* v. 43, no. 12 (Dec 93), pp. 1188 – 1194.

TOVAR LÓPEZ, RAMÓN ADOLFO

Curriculum vitae (Ramón Tovar López). *Boletín de la Academia Nacional de la Historia (Venezuela),* v. 76, no. 302 (Apr – June 93), pp. 221 – 226. Il.

TOYS

See also
Games

Déleon Meléndez, Ofelia Columba and Brenda Ninette Mayol Baños. Una muestra de juguetes populares de la ciudad de Guatemala. *La Tradición Popular,* no. 86 – 87 (1992), Issue. Bibl, il.

Reyes Larios, Sandra. Tiempos difíciles en la industria del juguete. *Comercio Exterior,* v. 43, no. 10 (Oct 93), pp. 913 – 916. Bibl, tables.

TRABA, MARTA

Criticism of specific works
Homérica latina

Thompkins, Cynthia. La construcción del subalterno en *Homérica latina* de Marta Traba y *Libro que no muerde* y *Donde viven las águilas* de Luisa Valenzuela. *Confluencia,* v. 8, no. 1 (Fall 92), pp. 31 – 37. Bibl.

TRABULSE A., ELÍAS

Interviews

Chimal, Carlos. Mirar en el jardín mexicano: paisaje de la ciencia; entrevista con Elías Trabulse. *Vuelta,* v. 17, no. 194 (Jan 93), pp. 50 – 52.

TRADE

See
Cartels and commodity agreements
Foreign trade promotion
Foreign trade regulation
Markets and merchants
Price regulation
Tariff
Trade routes
Subdivision *Commerce* under names of Indian groups
Subdivisions *Commerce* and *Foreign economic relations* under names of specific countries

TRADE MARKS

Colombia

Adarve, Luz Helena. La importancia de las marcas en la industria de la confección: nuevo enfoque. *Revista Javeriana,* v. 61, no. 593 (Apr 93), pp. 156 – 158.

TRADE REGULATION

See
Foreign trade regulation

TRADE ROUTES

Andrews, Jean. Diffusion of Mesoamerican Food Complex to Southeastern Europe. *Geographical Review,* v. 83, no. 2 (Apr 93), pp. 194 – 204. Bibl, maps.

Asdrúbal Silva, Hernán and Marcela V. Tejerina. De las Georgias del Sur a Cantón: los norteamericanos en la explotación y tráfico de pieles a fines del siglo XVIII y principios del siglos XIX. *Investigaciones y Ensayos,* no. 41 (Jan – Dec 91), pp. 315 – 327. Bibl.

TRADE UNIONS

See also
Anarchism and anarchists
Labor and laboring classes
Labor relations

Strikes and lockouts
Teachers' unions
Subdivision *Political activity* under *Agricultural laborers* and *Peasantry*

Blanco B., Gustavo. El movimiento: nuevos panoramas. *Nueva Sociedad,* no. 124 (Mar – Apr 93), pp. 134 – 145.

Argentina

Adelman, Jeremy, ed. *Essays in Argentine Labour History, 1870 – 1930* reviewed by Ronaldo Munck. *Bulletin of Latin American Research,* v. 12, no. 2 (May 93), pp. 229 – 230.

Bunel, Jean. Sindicalismo, democracia y desarrollo (Translated by Francisco Zapata). *Estudios Sociológicos,* v. 11, no. 31 (Jan – Apr 93), pp. 133 – 153. Bibl.

Di Tella, Torcuato S. La unión obrera textil, 1930 – 1945. *Desarrollo Económico (Argentina),* v. 33, no. 129 (Apr – June 93), pp. 109 – 136. Bibl, tables.

Hora, Roy and Javier A. Trimboli. Entrevista al historiador Daniel James. *Todo Es Historia,* v. 27, no. 314 (Sept 93), pp. 24 – 30. Il.

Korzeniewicz, Roberto P. Labor Unrest in Argentina, 1930 – 1943. *Latin American Research Review,* v. 28, no. 1 (1993), pp. 7 – 40. Bibl, tables.

Pérez, Félix. Félix Pérez: medio siglo de memoria sindical (A chapter from his autobiography entitled *Hicimos patria trabajando*). *Todo Es Historia,* v. 27, no. 314 (Sept 93), pp. 84 – 92. Il.

Senén González, Santiago. Diez años de sindicalismo en democracia. *Todo Es Historia,* v. 27, no. 317 (Dec 93), pp. 66 – 69. Il.

Tavares de Almeida, Maria Hermínia. Sindicatos, crisis económica y alta inflación en Brasil y Argentina. *Revista Mexicana de Sociología,* v. 54, no. 1 (Jan – Mar 92), pp. 99 – 137. Bibl, tables, charts.

Political activity

Adelman, Jeremy. State and Labour in Argentina: The Portworkers of Buenos Aires, 1910 – 1921. *Journal of Latin American Studies,* v. 25, no. 1 (Feb 93), pp. 73 – 102. Bibl, maps.

Ferrari Etcheberry, Alberto. Sindicalistas en la bancada conservadora. *Todo Es Historia,* v. 27, no. 314 (Sept 93), pp. 74 – 83. Il.

Horowitz, Joel. *Argentine Unions, the State, and the Rise of Perón* reviewed by Daniel J. Greenberg. *Hispanic American Historical Review,* v. 73, no. 1 (Feb 93), pp. 162 – 164.

Pastoriza, Elisa. Dirigentes obreros y política en el marco de la gestación de un peronismo periférico: Mar del Plata, 1935 – 1948. *Todo Es Historia,* v. 27, no. 314 (Sept 93), pp. 32 – 43. Il, tables.

Senén González, Santiago. José Ignacio Rucci, "el soldado de Perón." *Todo Es Historia,* v. 27, no. 314 (Sept 93), pp. 8 – 22. Bibl, il, facs.

Bolivia

Political activity

Mansilla, Hugo Celso Felipe. La economía informal y las modificaciones del movimiento sindical en Bolivia. *Revista Paraguaya de Sociología,* v. 30, no. 86 (Jan – Apr 93), pp. 113 – 126. Bibl.

Brazil

Amadeo Swaelen, Edward Joaquim. Restricciones institucionales a la política económica: negociación salarial y estabilización en el Brasil. *Desarrollo Económico (Argentina),* v. 33, no. 129 (Apr – June 93), pp. 29 – 47. Bibl, tables, charts.

Delgado, Maria Berenice Godinho and Maria Margareth Lopes. Mulheres trabalhadoras e meio ambiente: um olhar feminista no sindicalismo. *Estudos Feministas,* v. 0, no. 0 (1992), pp. 155 – 162.

French, John David. *The Brazilian Workers' ABC: Class Conflict and Alliances in Modern São Paulo* reviewed by Peter Ranis. *Hispanic American Historical Review,* v. 73, no. 4 (Nov 93), pp. 707 – 708.

Grün, Roberto. Sindicalismo e anti-sindicalismo e a gênese das novas classes médias brasileiras. *Dados,* v. 35, no. 3 (1992), pp. 435 – 471. Bibl.

Seixas, Jacy Alves de. *Mémoire et oubli: anarchisme et syndicalisme révolutionnaire au Brésil, 1890 – 1930* reviewed by Pierre Jarrige. *Cahiers des Amériques Latines,* no. 13 (1992), pp. 180 – 181.

Tavares de Almeida, Maria Hermínia. Sindicatos, crisis económica y alta inflación en Brasil y Argentina. *Revista Mexicana de Sociología,* v. 54, no. 1 (Jan – Mar 92), pp. 99 – 137. Bibl, tables, charts.

Political activity

Castro, Mary Garcia. Alquimia de categorias sociais na produção dos sujeitos políticos: gênero, raça e geração entre líderes do Sindicato de Trabalhadores Domésticos em Salvador. *Estudos Feministas,* v. 0, no. 0 (1992), pp. 57 – 73. Bibl.

Chile

Díaz Corvalán, Eugenio. Nuevo sindicalismo, viejos problemas: la concertación en Chile. *Nueva Sociedad,* no. 124 (Mar – Apr 93), pp. 114 – 121.

Echeverría, Mónica. *Antihistoria de un luchador: Clotario Blest, 1823 – 1990* reviewed by G. A. C. *Mensaje,* v. 42, no. 424 (Nov 93), pp. 597 – 599. Il.

Ruiz-Tagle P., Jaime. La CUT acepta el modelo exportador. *Mensaje,* v. 42, no. 418 (May 93), pp. 117 – 119. Tables.

Political activity

Zapata, Francisco. Transición democrática y sindicalismo en Chile. *Foro Internacional,* v. 32, no. 5 (Oct – Dec 92), pp. 703 – 721. Bibl, tables.

Costa Rica

Aguilar Hernández, Marielos. Costa Rica: democracia y libertades sindicales, 1980 – 1989. *Revista de Ciencias Sociales (Costa Rica),* no. 59 (Mar 93), pp. 71 – 80. Bibl, tables.

— Las libertades sindicales en los ochentas: el caso de las organizaciones bananeras costarricenses. *Revista de Ciencias Sociales (Costa Rica),* no. 58 (Dec 92), pp. 85 – 94. Bibl.

Miller, Eugene D. Labour and the War-Time Alliance in Costa Rica, 1943 – 1948. *Journal of Latin American Studies,* v. 25, no. 3 (Oct 93), pp. 515 – 541. Bibl, tables.

Cuba

Fuller, Linda. *Work and Democracy in Socialist Cuba* reviewed by Samuel Farber. *Cuban Studies/Estudios Cubanos,* v. 23 (1993), pp. 238 – 240.

— *Work and Democracy in Socialist Cuba* reviewed by Jean Stubbs. *Journal of Latin American Studies,* v. 25, no. 2 (May 93), pp. 424 – 425.

Lindenberg, Gail. The Labor Union in the Cuban Workplace. *Latin American Perspectives,* v. 20, no. 1 (Winter 93), pp. 28 – 39.

El Salvador

Los avances del foro de concertación. *ECA; Estudios Centroamericanos,* v. 48, no. 537 – 538 (July – Aug 93), pp. 735 – 742.

Law and legislation

Huertas Bartolomé, Tebelia. Libertad sindical, tratados internacionales y constitución. *ECA; Estudios Centroamericanos,* v. 48, no. 537 – 538 (July – Aug 93), pp. 657 – 675. Bibl, il.

Sources

Problemática laboral (Five documents regarding Salvadoran labor unions, their stands, and their rights). *ECA; Estudios Centroamericanos,* v. 48, no. 531 – 532 (Jan – Feb 93), pp. 137 – 147.

Guatemala

Witzel de Ciudad, Renate, ed. *Más de cien años de movimiento obrero urbano en Guatemala, tomo I: Artesanos y obreros en el período liberal, 1877 – 1944* reviewed by Ana Lorena Carrillo. *Mesoamérica (USA),* v. 13, no. 24 (Dec 92), pp. 459 – 462.

Latin America

Calderón Gutiérrez, Fernando. The Trade Union System: Its Background and Future Prospects. *CEPAL Review,* no. 49 (Apr 93), pp. 103 – 115. Bibl.

Ermida Uriarte, Oscar. La intervención estatal en las relaciones colectivas de trabajo latinoamericanas. *Nueva Sociedad,* no. 128 (Nov – Dec 93), pp. 29 – 37.

Flórez Gallego, Lenín. Historias nacionales, historias de los trabajadores y el problema de la democracia en la obra de Charles Bergquist. *Anuario Colombiano de Historia Social y de la Cultura,* no. 20 (1992), pp. 73 – 88. Bibl, tables.

Kofas, Jon V. *The Struggle for Legitimacy: Latin American Labor and the United States, 1930 – 1960* reviewed by Henry W. Berger. *Hispanic American Historical Review,* v. 73, no. 1 (Feb 93), pp. 196 – 197.

Lescano, Oscar et al. Las centrales sindicales frente al MERCOSUR. *Nueva Sociedad,* no. 126 (July – Aug 93), pp. 176 – 178.

Rodríguez, Juan Manuel. El movimiento sindical ante los procesos de integración. *Nueva Sociedad,* no. 126 (July – Aug 93), pp. 144 – 155.

Bibliography

Korzeniewicz, Roberto P. Contested Arenas: Recent Studies on Politics and Labor (Review article). *Latin American Research Review,* v. 28, no. 2 (1993), pp. 206 – 220.

Spalding, Hobart A., Jr. New Directions and Themes in Latin American Labor and Working-Class History: A Sampler (Review article). *Latin American Research Review,* v. 28, no. 1 (1993), pp. 202 – 214. Bibl.

Political activity

Collier, David and Ruth Berins Collier. *Shaping the Political Arena: Critical Junctures, the Labor Movement, and Regime Dynamics in Latin America* reviewed by Francisco Zapata. *Foro Internacional,* v. 32, no. 5 (Oct – Dec 92), pp. 777 – 788.

— *Shaping the Political Arena: Critical Junctures, the Labor Movement, and Regime Dynamics in Latin America* reviewed by David Sowell. *Hispanic American Historical Review,* v. 73, no. 1 (Feb 93), pp. 194 – 195.

Mexican – American Border Region

Martínez, María Eugenia and Cirila Quintero Ramírez. Sindicalismo y contratación colectiva en las maquiladoras fronterizas: los casos de Tijuana, Ciudad Juárez y Matamoros. *Frontera Norte,* v. 4, no. 8 (July – Dec 92), pp. 7 – 47. Bibl, tables.

Passe-Smith, John T. and Edward J. Williams. *The Unionization of the Maquiladora Industry: The Tamaulipan Case in National Context* reviewed by Heather Fowler-Salamini. *Hispanic American Historical Review,* v. 73, no. 4 (Nov 93), pp. 718 – 719.

Quintero Ramírez, Cirila. Flexibilidad sindical en las maquiladoras: el caso de Agapito González Cavazos. *El Cotidiano,* v. 8, no. 52 (Jan – Feb 93), pp. 92 – 96.

— Tendencias sindicales en la frontera norte de México. *El Cotidiano,* v. 9, no. 56 (July 93), pp. 41 – 46.

Mexico

Barbosa, Fabio. Los retos del sindicalismo petrolero. *El Cotidiano,* v. 9, no. 56 (July 93), pp. 33 – 39. Il.

Carlsen, Laura. Reflexiones sobre un proyecto sindical feminista: el Sindicato "19 de Septiembre" siete años después del sismo. *El Cotidiano,* v. 9, no. 53 (Mar – Apr 93), pp. 93 – 98. Bibl, tables, charts.

Díaz Castellanos, Guadalupe. Elena Tapia . . . feminismo . . . Mujeres en Acción Sindical. *Fem,* v. 17, no. 128 (Oct 93), pp. 30 – 32.

Espinoza Valle, Víctor Alejandro and Tania Hernández Vicencio. Tendencias de cambio en la estructura corporativa mexicana: Baja California, 1989 – 1992. *El Cotidiano,* v. 8, no. 52 (Jan – Feb 93), pp. 25 – 29.

— Las transformaciones del corporativismo regional: relaciones estado – sindicato en el sector público de Baja California. *Frontera Norte,* v. 4, no. 8 (July – Dec 92), pp. 79 – 110.

Garza Toledo, Enrique de la. Reestructuración del corporativismo en México: siete tesis. *El Cotidiano,* v. 9, no. 56 (July 93), pp. 47 – 53. Il.

Herrera Lima, Fernando Francisco. Dina: del enfrentamiento a la negociación. *El Cotidiano,* v. 9, no. 56 (July 93), pp. 69 – 73. Il.

Lazaroff, León. Auto Workers Seek Quality Wages. *Business Mexico,* v. 3, no. 4 (Apr 93), pp. 20 – 21 +. Il.

Leff Zimmerman, Gloria. *Los pactos obreros y la institución presidencial en México, 1915 – 1938* reviewed by Mónica García Suárez. *El Cotidiano,* v. 9, no. 56 (July 93), p. 117.

Méndez, Luis and José Othón Quiroz Trejo. Productividad, respuesta obrera y sucesión presidencial. *El Cotidiano,* v. 10, no. 58 (Oct – Nov 93), pp. 71 – 78.

— El proyecto cetemista y la modernidad laboral. *El Cotidiano,* v. 9, no. 56 (July 93), pp. 8 – 17. Il.

— El sindicalismo mexicano en los noventas: los sectores y las perspectivas. *El Cotidiano,* v. 9, no. 56 (July 93), pp. 3 – 7. Il.

Middlebrook, Kevin J. Estructuras del estado y política de registro sindical en el México posrevolucionario. *Revista Mexicana de Sociología,* v. 54, no. 4 (Oct – Dec 92), pp. 65 – 90.

Mondragón, Ana Laura. Contratos-ley y sindicatos: huleros y textileros. *El Cotidiano,* v. 9, no. 56 (July 93), pp. 18 – 22. Il, tables.

Montero Tirado, María del Carmen. La industria de la loza y la cerámica: el ascenso de la CROC. *El Cotidiano,* v. 9, no. 56 (July 93), pp. 86 – 88.

Novelo, Victoria. *La difícil democracia de los petroleros: historia de un proyecto sindical* reviewed by Aída Escamilla Rubio. *El Cotidiano,* v. 9, no. 56 (July 93), p. 117.

Pérez Pérez, Gabriel. El SME ante el reto de la modernización del sector eléctrico. *El Cotidiano,* v. 10, no. 58 (Oct – Nov 93), pp. 98 – 102. Il.

Ravelo Blancas, Patricia. Breve balance del movimiento de costureras del Sindicato "19 de Septiembre." *El Cotidiano,* v. 9, no. 53 (Mar – Apr 93), pp. 99 – 104. Il, tables.

Tiburcio Robles, Armando. La FSTSE en el esquema del sindicalismo moderno. *El Cotidiano,* v. 9, no. 56 (July 93), pp. 23 – 32. Il, charts.

Veloz Avila, Norma Ilse. Entre la productividad y el salario: conflictos y concertación obrero – patronal, enero – marzo 1993. *El Cotidiano,* v. 9, no. 54 (May 93), pp. 81 – 89. Il, tables.

Bibliography

Ochoa Méndez, Jacqueline. Orientación bibliográfica sobre sindicalismo en México. *El Cotidiano,* v. 9, no. 56 (July 93), pp. 119 – 120.

Political activity

Middlebrook, Kevin J., ed. *Unions, Workers, and the State in Mexico* reviewed by John A. Britton. *Hispanic American Historical Review,* v. 73, no. 1 (Feb 93), pp. 183 – 184.

Ramírez Rancaño, Mario. La organización obrera y campesina en Tlaxcala durante el cardenismo. *Revista Mexicana de Sociología,* v. 54, no. 3 (July – Sept 92), pp. 189 – 219. Bibl, tables.

Research

Novelo, Victoria. Las tentaciones de doña Victoria. *Nueva Antropología,* v. 13, no. 43 (Nov 92), pp. 45 – 51.

Paraguay
Political activity

Cardozo Rodas, Victorino. *Lucha sindical y transición política en Paraguay* (Review). *Revista Paraguaya de Sociología,* v. 29, no. 84 (May – Aug 92), pp. 206 – 207. Il.

Peru

Balbi, Carmen Rosa. Miseria del sindicalismo. *Debate (Peru),* v. 15, no. 71 (Nov 92 – Jan 93), pp. 37 – 39. Il.

United States

Andrews, Gregg. *Shoulder to Shoulder?: The American Federation of Labor, the United States, and the Mexican Revolution, 1910 – 1924* reviewed by Mark T. Gilderhus. *Hispanic American Historical Review,* v. 73, no. 1 (Feb 93), pp. 195 – 196.

Friaz, Guadalupe Mendez. "I Want to Be Treated as an Equal": Testimony from a Latina Union Activist. *Aztlán,* v. 20, no. 1 – 2 (Spring – Fall 91), pp. 195 – 202.

García, Mario T. Working for the Union. *Mexican Studies,* v. 9, no. 2 (Summer 93), pp. 241 – 257. Il.

Soldatenko, Maria Angelina. Organizing Latina Garment Workers in Los Angeles. *Aztlán,* v. 20, no. 1 – 2 (Spring – Fall 91), pp. 73 – 96. Bibl.

Uruguay
Political activity

Chiesa, Blanca and Ana María Reyes. El Congreso del Pueblo y su significación en el proceso de lucha, movilización y unificación sindical, años 1950 – 1966. *Hoy Es Historia,* v. 10, no. 56 (Mar – Apr 93), pp. 40 – 60. Bibl, il.

Dutrénit, Silvia. Visiones de la crisis nacional que influyeron en el programa del movimiento obrero-popular uruguayo, 1958 – 1965. *Cuadernos Americanos,* no. 42, Nueva época (Nov – Dec 93), pp. 78 – 100. Bibl.

TRANSLATING AND INTERPRETING
See also
Subdivision *Translations* under names of specific authors and literary genres

Akers, John C. From Translation to Rewriting: Rolando Hinojosa's *The Valley. The Americas Review,* v. 21, no. 1 (Spring 93), pp. 91 – 102. Bibl.

Aparicio, Frances R. *Versiones, interpretaciones y creaciones: instancias de la traducción literaria en Hispanoamérica en el siglo veinte* reviewed by László Scholz. *Revista de Crítica Literaria Latinoamericana,* v. 19, no. 37 (Jan – June 93), pp. 375 – 377.

Chaves, Celso Loureiro. Como uma placa de trânsito: a música brasileira no meio acadêmico internacional. *Vozes,* v. 86, no. 6 (Nov – Dec 92), pp. 8 – 12.

González Padilla, María Enriqueta. La traducción de Shakespeare: comentario de una experiencia. *Plural (Mexico),* v. 22, no. 259 (Apr 93), pp. 56 – 63. Bibl.

Levine, Suzanne Jill. El traductor en la guarida del escritor: entrevista con Guillermo Cabrera Infante (Translated by Mario Ojeda Revah). *Vuelta,* v. 17, no. 198 (May 93), pp. 59 – 63.

Paxman, Andrew. Selling in a Second Language. *Business Mexico,* v. 3, no. 6 (June 93), pp. 36 – 37.

Ramos, Antonio. "Infinito": Giacomo Leopardi. *Vozes,* v. 87, no. 3 (May – June 93), pp. 59 – 63. Il.

Congresses

Paatz, Annette. Reflexiones acerca de la traducción de obras teatrales: un simposio de autores latinoamericanos y traductores (Translated by Gabriela Fonseca). *Humboldt,* no. 108 (1993), pp. 102 – 103.

TRANSNATIONAL CORPORATIONS
See
International business enterprises

TRANSPORTATION
See also
Airplane industry and trade
Automobile industry and trade
Highways
Inland water transportation
Railroads
Roads
Subways
Transportation, Maritime

Argentina

Salas, Andrés Alberto. La carreta. *Todo Es Historia,* v. 27, no. 315 (Oct 93), pp. 30 – 43. Il.

Sartelli, Eduardo. Barcos en la pradera: los carreros pampeanos; de la colonia al "granero del mundo." *Todo Es Historia,* v. 27, no. 315 (Oct 93), pp. 68 – 75. Bibl, il, tables.

Law and legislation

Krantzer, Guillermo and Jorge Sánchez. Regulaciones en el transporte urbano: el caso de Buenos Aires. *EURE,* v. 19, no. 56 (Mar 93), pp. 41 – 53. Bibl.

Brazil

Cascudo, Luís da Câmara. Jangada e carro de bois (Originally published in this journal in May 1941). *Vozes,* v. 87, no. 4 (July – Aug 93), pp. 91 – 96.

Henry, Etienne. Autotransporte urbano colectivo en desarrollo: el abanico de las empresas. *EURE*, v. 19, no. 56 (Mar 93), pp. 71 – 78.

Meira, Sílvio Augusto de Bastos. Um parecer inédito de Rui Barbosa (Includes Rui Barbosa's text regarding the rejection by the city of Belém, Pará, of an electrical transportation contract in the late 19th century). *Revista do Instituto Histórico e Geográfico Brasileiro*, no. 372 (July – Sept 91), pp. 647 – 658.

Morrison, Allen. *The Tramways of Brazil: A 130-Year Survey* reviewed by Carlos Wehrs. *Revista do Instituto Histórico e Geográfico Brasileiro*, no. 371 (Apr – June 91), pp. 609 – 610.

Pompeu, Paulo de Tarso. Nas malhas da rodovia. *Problemas Brasileiros*, v. 30, no. 295 (Jan – Feb 93), pp. 37 – 39. Il.

Law and legislation

Dourado, Anísio Brasileiro de Freitas. Relaciones contractuales entre los poderes públicos y las empresas privadas de autobuses urbanos en Brasil (Translated by Martín Figueroa). *EURE*, v. 19, no. 56 (Mar 93), pp. 29 – 39. Bibl.

Chile

Fernández Koprich, Daniel. Vías elevadas para Santiago: ¿Una opción válida? (With commentaries by Jorge Heine, Oscar Figueroa, Juan de Dios Ortúzar, Víctor Basauri, and Daniel Fernández). *EURE*, v. 19, no. 56 (Mar 93), pp. 95 – 115. Charts.

Heine, Jorge. En defensa de Santiago: la ciudad que queremos. *EURE*, v. 19, no. 56 (Mar 93), pp. 127 – 128.

Ortúzar S., Juan de Dios. Congestión y transporte público: una relación mal entendida. *EURE*, v. 19, no. 56 (Mar 93), pp. 124 – 126. Tables.

Deregulation

Opazo, José Luis et al. El descontrol del sistema de buses de Santiago: síntesis de un diagnóstico técnico – institucional. *EURE*, v. 19, no. 56 (Mar 93), pp. 79 – 91. Bibl, tables.

Law and legislation

Hohmann B., Claudio. La encrucijada del transporte urbano de Santiago. *EURE*, v. 19, no. 56 (Mar 93), pp. 9 – 27.

Latin America

Alemany, Soline and Frédéric Mauro, eds. *Transport et commerce en Amérique Latine* reviewed by Rory Miller. *Journal of Latin American Studies*, v. 25, no. 1 (Feb 93), pp. 208 – 209.

Thomson, Ian. Improving Urban Transport for the Poor. *CEPAL Review*, no. 49 (Apr 93), pp. 139 – 153. Bibl, tables.

Law and legislation

Acuerdo sobre Reglamentación Básica Unificada de Tránsito. *Integración Latinoamericana*, v. 18, no. 194 (Oct 91), pp. 65 – 71.

Thomson, Ian. Un análisis de la institucionalidad del transporte colectivo urbano latinoamericano: reformas para mejorarla. *EURE*, v. 19, no. 56 (Mar 93), pp. 55 – 70. Tables, charts.

Mexico

Blázquez Domínguez, Carmen. Proyectos de comunicación por el Istmo de Tehuantepec, 1842 – 1860. *La Palabra y el Hombre*, no. 83 (July – Sept 92), pp. 199 – 217. Bibl.

Blears, James. Getting Down to Bus-ness. *Business Mexico*, v. 3, no. 10 (Oct 93), pp. 23 – 26.

Castillo, Alejandro. The Challenge to Deliver (Translated by Richard Cadena). *Business Mexico*, v. 3, no. 7 (July 93), pp. 4 – 10. Maps, charts.

Navarro Benítez, Bernardo. La ciudad y sus transportes, la metrópoli y sus transportes. *El Cotidiano*, v. 9, no. 54 (May 93), pp. 18 – 23. Il.

Pacific Area

Rivas Mira, Fernando Alonso. Transporte, telecomunicaciones y turismo: el Proyecto Triple T. *Comercio Exterior*, v. 43, no. 12 (Dec 93), pp. 1188 – 1194.

Venezuela

Palabras pronunciadas por González Lander en la ocasión de recibir la colección de obras de la Academia. *Boletín de la Academia Nacional de la Historia (Venezuela)*, v. 75, no. 298 (Apr – June 92), pp. 21 – 25.

TRANSPORTATION, MARITIME

See also
　Harbors
　Inland water transportation
　Trade routes

Caribbean area

López y Sebastián, Lorenzo Eladio and Justo L. del Río Moreno. Comercio y transporte en la economía del azúcar antillano durante el siglo XVI. *Anuario de Estudios Americanos*, v. 49 (1992), pp. 55 – 87. Bibl, maps.

Peru

Ortiz Sotelo, Jorge. Embarcaciones aborígenes en el área andina. *Historia y Cultura (Peru)*, no. 20 (1990), pp. 49 – 79. Bibl.

TRATADO DE LIBRE COMERCIO

See
　North American Free Trade Agreement

TRAVELERS

See
　Pilgrims and pilgrimages
　Tourist trade
　Subdivision *Description and travel* under names of specific countries

TRAVEN, BRUNO

Sanciprián, Nancy. *B. Traven en México* reviewed by Fermín Ramírez. *Plural (Mexico)*, v. 22, no. 264 (Sept 93), pp. 123 – 124.

Zogbaum, Heidi. *B. Traven: A Vision of Mexico* reviewed by Frank Whitehead. *Journal of Latin American Studies*, v. 25, no. 1 (Feb 93), pp. 225 – 226.

TREATIES

See
　Names of specific treaties

TREJO, OSWALDO

Criticism and interpretation

Barrera Linares, Luis. La narrativa breve de Oswaldo Trejo: más allá del textualismo. *Inti*, no. 37 – 38 (Spring – Fall 93), pp. 97 – 106. Bibl.

TREVI, GLORIA

Andrade Jardí, Julián. El milenio de Gloria Trevi. *Nexos*, v. 16, no. 183 (Mar 93), pp. 66 – 68.

TRINIDAD AND TOBAGO

See also
　East Indians – Trinidad and Tobago
　Interest rates – Trinidad and Tobago
　Privatization – Trinidad and Tobago
　Religion – Trinidad and Tobago
　Saving and investment – Trinidad and Tobago

Economic policy

Forde, Penelope and Kelvin Sergeant. The State Sector and Divestment in Trinidad and Tobago: Some Preliminary Findings. *Social and Economic Studies*, v. 41, no. 4 (Dec 92), pp. 173 – 204. Bibl, tables.

TRUJILLO, VENEZUELA (STATE)

Sambrano Urdaneta, Oscar. Lo trascendental trujillano en sus letras. *Revista Nacional de Cultura (Venezuela)*, v. 53, no. 286 (July – Sept 92), pp. 39 – 49. Il.

TRUJILLO AMPUERO, CARLOS ALBERTO

Criticism and interpretation

Brooks, Zelda Irene. *Carlos Alberto Trujillo, un poeta del sur de Sudamérica* reviewed by Alberto Gutiérrez de la Solana. *Chasqui*, v. 22, no. 2 (Nov 93), pp. 167 – 168.

TRUJILLO MOLINA, RAFAEL LEONIDAS

Pacini Hernandez, Deborah. Dominican Popular Music under the Trujillo Regime. *Studies in Latin American Popular Culture*, v. 12 (1993), pp. 127 – 140. Bibl.

TSVETAEVA, MARINA IVANOVA EFRON

Cixous, Hélène. Retratos: Clarice Lispector/Marina Tsvetaeva (Translated by Esther Levy). *Escritura (Venezuela),* v. 16, no. 31 – 32 (Jan – Dec 91), pp. 45 – 52.

TUCUMÁN, ARGENTINA (PROVINCE)

De Looze, Laurence and Martha Gil-Montero. On the Tucumán Trail (Photographs by Jorge Provenza). *Américas,* v. 45, no. 5 (Sept – Oct 93), pp. 22 – 33. Il, maps.

Gullón Abao, Alberto José. Las reducciones del este de la provincia del Tucumán en la segunda mitad del siglo XVIII bajo la administración franciscana. *Archivo Ibero-Americano,* v. 52, no. 205 – 208 (Jan – Dec 92), pp. 255 – 276. Bibl, tables, maps, charts.

León, Carlos A. El desarrollo agrario de Tucumán en el período de transición de la economía de capitalismo incipiente a la expansión azucarera. *Desarrollo Económico (Argentina),* v. 33, no. 130 (July – Sept 93), pp. 217 – 236. Bibl, tables.

Rojas, Elena M., ed. *Acerca de los relatos orales en la provincia de Tucumán* reviewed by Félix Coluccio. *Folklore Americano,* no. 53 (Jan – June 92), pp. 180 – 181.

TUNJA, COLOMBIA

Ocampo López, Javier. La rebelión de las alcabalas. *Boletín de Historia y Antigüedades,* v. 79, no. 779 (Oct – Dec 92), pp. 993 – 1005. Bibl.

TÚPAC KATARI

See
Apasa, Julián

TUPAMAROS

See
Movimiento de Liberación Nacional-Tupamaro (Uruguay)

TURKS AND CAICOS ISLANDS

Royle, Stephen A. The Small Island as Colony. *Caribbean Geography,* v. 3, no. 4 (Sept 92), pp. 261 – 269. Bibl, tables, maps.

TURTON, ROBERT SYDNEY

Ashdown, Peter D. Alan Burns and Sidney Turton: Two Views of the Public Good. *Belizean Studies,* v. 21, no. 1 (May 93), pp. 21 – 24. Bibl.

TUY RIVER VALLEY, VENEZUELA

Mogollón, José Luis et al. Uso de los parámetros físico – químicos de las aguas fluviales como indicadores de influencias naturales y antrópicas. *Interciencia,* v. 18, no. 5 (Sept – Oct 93), pp. 249 – 254. Bibl, tables, maps.

TZELTAL INDIANS

Gosner, Kevin. *Soldiers of the Virgin: The Moral Economy of a Colonial Maya Rebellion* reviewed by Robert M. Hill II. *The Americas,* v. 50, no. 2 (Oct 93), pp. 274 – 276.

— *Soldiers of the Virgin: The Moral Economy of a Colonial Maya Rebellion* reviewed by Kenneth Mills. *Bulletin of Latin American Research,* v. 12, no. 2 (May 93), pp. 223 – 224.

— *Soldiers of the Virgin: The Moral Economy of a Colonial Maya Rebellion* reviewed by Stephen Webre. *Colonial Latin American Historical Review,* v. 2, no. 1 (Winter 93), pp. 109 – 110.

— *Soldiers of the Virgin: The Moral Economy of a Colonial Maya Rebellion* reviewed by Linda A. Newson. *Journal of Latin American Studies,* v. 25, no. 3 (Oct 93), pp. 655 – 656.

TZOTZIL INDIANS

Chávez G., Gerardo. Las ceremonias sincretas de San Juan Chamula. *Hoy Es Historia,* v. 10, no. 58 (July – Aug 93), pp. 77 – 79.

UMBANDA (CULTUS)

Carvalho, José Jorge de. Aesthetics of Opacity and Transparence: Myth, Music, and Ritual in the Xangô Cult and in the Western Art Tradition. *Latin American Music Review,* v. 14, no. 2 (Fall – Winter 93), pp. 202 – 231. Bibl, tables, facs.

Motta, Roberto M. C. Transe, sacrifício, comunhão e poder no xangô de Pernambuco. *Revista de Antropologia (Brazil),* v. 34 (1991), pp. 131 – 142.

Prandi, José Reginaldo. *Os candomblés de São Paulo: a velha magia na metrópole nova* reviewed by Luciana Ferreira Moura Mendonça. *Revista de Antropologia (Brazil),* v. 34 (1991), pp. 228 – 230.

Segato, Rita Laura. Okarilé: Yemoja's Icon Tune. *Latin American Music Review,* v. 14, no. 1 (Spring – Summer 93), pp. 1 – 19. Bibl, facs.

Severino, Francisca E. S. O candomblé visto de fora. *Vozes,* v. 87, no. 4 (July – Aug 93), pp. 41 – 45. Il.

Solla Olivera, Horacio. Cultos afrobrasileños: un templo de umbanda en la ciudad de Montevideo. *Hoy Es Historia,* v. 10, no. 56 (Mar – Apr 93), pp. 33 – 39. Bibl.

UNAMUNO Y JUGO, MIGUEL DE

Cúneo, Dardo. Sarmiento y Unamuno: Sarmiento, el hombre de carne y hueso de Unamuno. *Hoy Es Historia,* v. 10, no. 56 (Mar – Apr 93), pp. 75 – 86. Il.

UNDERDEVELOPED AREAS

See
Developing countries

UNDOCUMENTED WORKERS

See also
Names of specific national groups

Brazil

Gamboa, Aldo Horacio. The "Brasiguayos": People in Search of a Country (Translated by NACLA). *NACLA Report on the Americas,* v. 27, no. 3 (Nov – Dec 93), pp. 4 – 6. Il, maps.

Mexican – American Border Region

Sánchez Munguía, Vicente. Matamoros-sur de Texas: el tránsito de los migrantes de América Central por la frontera México – Estados Unidos. *Estudios Sociológicos,* v. 11, no. 31 (Jan – Apr 93), pp. 183 – 207. Bibl, tables.

Paraguay

Gamboa, Aldo Horacio. The "Brasiguayos": People in Search of a Country (Translated by NACLA). *NACLA Report on the Americas,* v. 27, no. 3 (Nov – Dec 93), pp. 4 – 6. Il, maps.

United States

Castillo F., Dídimo. ¿Fin de las fronteras?: la migración indocumentada de México hacia Estados Unidos. *Problemas del Desarrollo,* v. 24, no. 93 (Apr – June 93), pp. 95 – 119. Bibl, tables.

Chavez, Leo R. *Shadowed Lives: Undocumented Immigrants in American Society* reviewed by Susan González Baker. *International Migration Review,* v. 27, no. 1 (Spring 93), pp. 206 – 207.

Cornelius, Wayne Armstrong and Philip L. Martin. The Uncertain Connection: Free Trade and Rural Mexican Migration to the United States. *International Migration Review,* v. 27, no. 3 (Fall 93), pp. 484 – 512. Bibl, tables, charts.

Deciderio, Margarita Arce. A Mexican Migrant Family in North Carolina. *Aztlán,* v. 20, no. 1 – 2 (Spring – Fall 91), pp. 183 – 193.

García Quiñones, Rolando. Análisis comparativo de un tipo singular de retorno: el caso de los mexicanos indocumentados devueltos. *Problemas del Desarrollo,* v. 24, no. 93 (Apr – June 93), pp. 121 – 151. Bibl, tables.

UNEMPLOYMENT

See also
Employment
Labor supply

Argentina

Mathematical models

Ceballos, Marta. Metodología cuantitativa para una caracterización diacrónica de recursos humanos desocupados. *Revista Paraguaya de Sociología,* v. 29, no. 85 (Sept – Dec 92), pp. 157 – 169. Bibl, tables, charts.

Caribbean area
Mathematical models

Clarke, Christopher Martin. Unemployment Theory in the LDCs: A Test of the Generalized Segmentation Hypothesis. *Social and Economic Studies,* v. 41, no. 4 (Dec 92), pp. 25 – 51. Bibl.

Colombia

Quintero, Fernando. Cesantías y pensiones: el reordenamiento laboral. *Revista Javeriana,* v. 61, no. 592 (Mar 93), pp. 81 – 85. Tables.

Sánchez Franco, Germán. Antecedentes de la reforma laboral acerca del tema de las cesantías. *Revista Javeriana,* v. 61, no. 592 (Mar 93), pp. 86 – 89.

UNIÓN CÍVICA RADICAL (ARGENTINA)

Lacoste, Pablo Alberto. Lucha de élites en Argentina: la Unión Cívica Radical en Mendoza, 1890 – 1905. *Anuario de Estudios Americanos,* v. 50, no. 1 (1993), pp. 181 – 212. Bibl, tables.

UNITED NATIONS

Escudero de Paz, Angel. Participación de Colombia en el sistema de las Naciones Unidas. *Revista Javeriana,* v. 61, no. 594 (May 93), pp. 238 – 245.

Guest, Iain. *Behind the Disappearances: Argentina's Dirty War against Human Rights and the United Nations* reviewed by Erick Bridoux. *Journal of Inter-American Studies and World Affairs,* v. 34, no. 4 (Winter 92 – 93), pp. 257 – 262.

UNITED NATIONS. COMMISSION ON THE TRUTH FOR EL SALVADOR

See
Subdivision *El Salvador* under *Human rights*

UNITED NATIONS. CONFERENCE ON ENVIRONMENT AND DEVELOPMENT, 1992

See
Subdivision *International cooperation - Congresses* under *Ecology*

UNITED NATIONS. ECONOMIC COMMISSION FOR LATIN AMERICA AND THE CARIBBEAN

Leriche, Christian E. La propuesta cepalina del desarrollo sustentable latinoamericano y medio ambiente. *El Cotidiano,* v. 8, no. 52 (Jan – Feb 93), pp. 109 – 111. Il.

Malo, Salvador. Las nuevas políticas y las estrategias en materia de ciencia y tecnología. *Revista Latinoamericana de Estudios Educativos,* v. 22, no. 3 (July – Sept 92), pp. 133 – 139.

Urquidi, Víctor L. La educación: eje para el futuro desarrollo de la potencialidad latinoamericana. *Revista Latinoamericana de Estudios Educativos,* v. 22, no. 3 (July – Sept 92), pp. 123 – 131.

Bibliography

Ottone, Ernesto. CEPAL: un planteamiento renovado frente a los nuevos desafíos del desarrollo (Review article). *Pensamiento Iberoamericano,* no. 22 – 23, tomo I (July 92 – June 93), pp. 386 – 392. Bibl.

UNITED NATIONS. SECURITY COUNCIL

Holiday, David and William Deane Stanley. La construcción de la paz: las lecciones preliminares de El Salvador. *ECA; Estudios Centroamericanos,* v. 48, no. 531 – 532 (Jan – Feb 93), pp. 39 – 59. Il.

ONUSAL: Séptimo Informe sobre la Situación de los Derechos Humanos. *ECA; Estudios Centroamericanos,* v. 48, no. 537 – 538 (July – Aug 93), pp. 743 – 749. Il.

UNITED STATES

See also
Acculturation – United States
Agricultural laborers – United States
Alcohol – United States
Archives – United States
Art – United States
Artisans – United States
Artists – United States
Bilingualism – United States

Blacks – United States
Brazilians – United States
California
Central Americans – United States
Christian art and symbolism – United States
Church music – United States
Comic books, strips, etc. – United States
Community development – United States
Copyright – United States
Corruption (in politics) – United States
Cotton – United States
Cuban drama – United States
Cuban literature – United States
Cubans – United States
Dissertations, Academic – United States
Dominicans (Dominican Republic) – United States
Drama festivals – United States
Drugs, Illegal – United States
Education, Bilingual – United States
Education and state – United States
Educational assistance – United States
Environmental services – United States
Espionage – United States
Family – United States
Florida
Foreign trade promotion – United States
Foreign trade regulation – United States
Gas, Natural – United States
Haitians – United States
Hazardous substances – United States
Housing – United States
Human capital – United States
Human rights – United States
Imperialism – United States
Industrial organization – United States
Information services – United States
Juvenile delinquency – United States
Labor supply – United States
Latin American studies – United States
Latin Americans – United States
Law – United States
Libraries and librarians – United States
Literature and history – United States
Literature and society – United States
Local government – United States
Louisiana
Marginalization – United States
Meat industry and trade – United States
Mexican – American Border Region
Mexicans – United States
Migration, Internal – United States
Missions – United States
Motion pictures – United States
Museums – United States
Music and society – United States
Naturalization – United States
New Mexico
Newspapers – United States
Periodicals – United States
Peruvians – United States
Photography and photographers – United States
Political parties – United States
Pollution – United States
Popular music – United States
Posters – United States
Poverty – United States
Pregnancy – United States
Press – United States
Press and politics – United States
Pressure groups – United States
Public opinion – United States
Puerto Ricans – United States
Race discrimination – United States
Research institutes – United States
Science and state – United States
Sex role – United States
Sexism – United States
Sheep ranches – United States
Social conflict – United States
Social psychology – United States
Socialization – United States
Spaniards – United States
Spanish language – United States
Sports – United States
Steel industry and trade – United States
Stock exchange – United States
Students – United States
Tariff – United States

Television – United States
Texas
Textile industry and fabrics – United States
Theater – United States
Tobacco – United States
Trade unions – United States
Undocumented workers – United States
Vocational education – United States
Wages – United States
Water rights – United States
West Indians – United States
Women – United States
Women authors – United States
Women in literature – United States
Women's rights – United States
Youth – United States
Names of specific cities

Boundaries

Law and legislation

Compton, Nina H. and Garrett T. Newland. The Functional Border Equivalent. *Journal of Borderlands Studies*, v. 7, no. 2 (Fall 92), pp. 73 – 92. Bibl.

Civilization

Baptista Gumucio, Mariano. *Latinoamericanos y norteamericanos* reviewed by Aída Cometta Manzoni. *Revista Nacional de Cultura (Venezuela)*, v. 53, no. 285 (Apr – June 92), pp. 245 – 247.

Commerce

Mexico

Máttar, Jorge and Claudia Schatan. El comercio intraindustrial e intrafirme México – Estados Unidos: autopartes, electrónicos y petroquímicos (Translated by Adriana Hierro). *Comercio Exterior*, v. 43, no. 2 (Feb 93), pp. 103 – 124. Bibl, tables.

Rothstein, Richard. El desarrollo continental y el comercio entre México y Estados Unidos: ¿Por qué los trabajadores estadunidenses necesitan salarios más altos en México? *Relaciones Internacionales (Mexico)*, v. 15, Nueva época, no. 57 (Jan – Mar 93), pp. 63 – 74.

Discovery and exploration

Cutter, Donald C., ed. *California in 1792: A Spanish Naval Visit* reviewed by Donald T. Garate. *Colonial Latin American Historical Review*, v. 2, no. 1 (Winter 93), pp. 117 – 118.

Economic conditions

López Villafañe, Víctor. La integración económica en la cuenca del Pacífico: el reto de la América del Norte. *Comercio Exterior*, v. 43, no. 12 (Dec 93), pp. 1145 – 1152. Bibl, tables.

Economic policy

Mercado Celis, Alejandro. El déficit, los impuestos, solidaridad y Clinton. *Problemas del Desarrollo*, v. 24, no. 93 (Apr – June 93), pp. 27 – 33. Bibl.

Rangel Díaz, José. La "Clintonomics": ¿Nuevas señales para la economía mundial? *Problemas del Desarrollo*, v. 24, no. 93 (Apr – June 93), pp. 15 – 21.

Vargas, Rocío. El proyecto económico de Clinton: posibles repercusiones para México y América Latina. *Problemas del Desarrollo*, v. 24, no. 93 (Apr – June 93), pp. 34 – 38.

Emigration and immigration

Alba-Hernández, Francisco. El Tratado de Libre Comercio y la emigración de mexicanos a Estados Unidos. *Comercio Exterior*, v. 43, no. 8 (Aug 93), pp. 743 – 749. Bibl.

Borjas, George J. and Richard B. Freeman, eds. *Immigration and the Work Force: Economic Consequences for the United States and Source Areas* reviewed by Jim Thomas. *Journal of Latin American Studies*, v. 25, no. 3 (Oct 93), pp. 683 – 684.

Castillo F., Dídimo. ¿Fin de las fronteras?: la migración indocumentada de México hacia Estados Unidos. *Problemas del Desarrollo*, v. 24, no. 93 (Apr – June 93), pp. 95 – 119. Bibl, tables.

Chavez, Leo R. *Shadowed Lives: Undocumented Immigrants in American Society* reviewed by Susan González Baker. *International Migration Review*, v. 27, no. 1 (Spring 93), pp. 206 – 207.

Cohen, Isaac. El surgimiento de los hispanos. *Nueva Sociedad*, no. 127 (Sept – Oct 93), pp. 100 – 113. Bibl.

Cornelius, Wayne Armstrong and Philip L. Martin. The Uncertain Connection: Free Trade and Rural Mexican Migration to the United States. *International Migration Review*, v. 27, no. 3 (Fall 93), pp. 484 – 512. Bibl, tables, charts.

Corona Vázquez, Rodolfo. La migración de mexicanos a los Estados Unidos: cambios en la década de 1980 – 1990. *Revista Mexicana de Sociología*, v. 55, no. 1 (Jan – Mar 93), pp. 213 – 233. Bibl, tables.

Donato, Katharine M. Current Trends and Patterns of Female Migration: Evidence from Mexico. *International Migration Review*, v. 27, no. 4 (Winter 93), pp. 748 – 771. Bibl, tables.

Forjaz, Maria Cecília Spina. Os exilados da década de '80: imigrantes brasileiros nos Estados Unidos. *RAE; Revista de Administração de Empresas*, v. 33, no. 1 (Jan – Feb 93), pp. 66 – 83. Bibl.

Funkhouser, Edward and Fernando A. Ramos. The Choice of Migration Destination: Dominican and Cuban Immigrants to the Mainland United States and Puerto Rico. *International Migration Review*, v. 27, no. 3 (Fall 93), pp. 537 – 556. Bibl, tables.

Massey, Douglas S. et al. *Los ausentes: el proceso social de la migración internacional en el occidente de México* reviewed by Janet E. Worrall. *Hispanic American Historical Review*, v. 73, no. 2 (May 93), pp. 337 – 338.

Palacio, Joseph O. Garifuna Immigrants in Los Angeles: Attempts at Self-Improvements. *Belizean Studies*, v. 20, no. 3 (Dec 92), pp. 17 – 26. Bibl.

Robinson, Sherman et al. Las políticas agrícolas y la migración en un área de libre comercio de los Estados Unidos y México: un análisis de equilibrio general computable (Translated by Carlos Villegas). *El Trimestre Económico*, v. 60, no. 237 (Jan – Mar 93), pp. 53 – 89. Bibl, tables, charts.

Schmidt, Samuel. Migración o refugio económico: el caso mexicano. *Nueva Sociedad*, no. 127 (Sept – Oct 93), pp. 136 – 147. Bibl.

Law and legislation

Baker, Susan Gonzalez and Jacqueline Maria Hagan. Implementing the U.S. Legalization Program: The Influence of Immigrant Communities and Local Agencies on Immigration Policy Reform. *International Migration Review*, v. 27, no. 3 (Fall 93), pp. 513 – 536. Bibl.

Briggs, Vernon M., Jr. *Mass Immigration and the National Interest* reviewed by Michael Ellis. *Journal of Borderlands Studies*, v. 7, no. 2 (Fall 92), pp. 109 – 111.

Calavita, Kitty. *Inside the State: The Bracero Program, Immigration, and the I.N.S.* reviewed by Rodolfo O. de la Garza. *International Migration Review*, v. 27, no. 4 (Winter 93), pp. 895 – 896.

Cohen, Joshua A. Requirements for Work Visas. *Business Mexico*, v. 3, no. 8 (Aug 93), pp. 14 – 15.

Mitchell, Christopher, ed. *Western Hemisphere Immigration and United States Foreign Policy* reviewed by Caroline Thomas. *Bulletin of Latin American Research*, v. 12, no. 2 (May 93), pp. 238 – 239.

Muñoz, Cecilia. Immigration Policy: A Tricky Business. *NACLA Report on the Americas*, v. 26, no. 5 (May 93), pp. 38 – 41 +. Bibl, il.

Self, Robert. Intimidate First, Ask Questions Later: The INS and Immigration Rights. *NACLA Report on the Americas*, v. 26, no. 5 (May 93), pp. 11 – 14. Il.

Mathematical models

Santiago, Carlos Enrique. The Migratory Impact of Minimum Wage Legislation: Puerto Rico, 1970 – 1987. *International Migration Review*, v. 27, no. 4 (Winter 93), pp. 772 – 795. Bibl, tables, charts.

Foreign economic relations

Rangel Díaz, José. La "Clintonomics": ¿Nuevas señales para la economía mundial? *Problemas del Desarrollo*, v. 24, no. 93 (Apr – June 93), pp. 15 – 21.

Canada

Rosas González, María Cristina. El TLC entre México, Estados Unidos y Canadá: semejanzas y diferencias con el ALC entre Canadá y Estados Unidos. *Relaciones Internacionales (Mexico)*, v. 15, Nueva época, no. 57 (Jan – Mar 93), pp. 55 – 62. Charts.

Stewart, Hamish. El Acuerdo de Libre Comercio entre Estados Unidos y Canadá: algunas lecciones. *Estudios Internacionales (Chile),* v. 26, no. 102 (Apr – June 93), pp. 187 – 203. Bibl, tables.

Watson, Hilbourne Alban. The U.S. – Canada Free Trade Agreement and the Caribbean, with a Case Study of Electronics Assembly in Barbados. *Social and Economic Studies,* v. 41, no. 3 (Sept 92), pp. 37 – 64. Bibl.

Caribbean area

Deere, Carmen Diana et al. *In the Shadows of the Sun: Caribbean Development Alternatives and U.S. Policy* reviewed by Georges A. Fauriol. *Studies in Comparative International Development,* v. 27, no. 2 (Summer 92), pp. 110 – 112.

Central America

United Nations. Economic Commission for Latin America and the Caribbean. *A Collection of Documents on Economic Relations between the United States and Central America, 1906 – 1956* (Review). *CEPAL Review,* no. 47 (Aug 92), p. 189.

Chile

Fermandois Huerta, Joaquín. Del unilateralismo a la negociación: Chile, Estados Unidos y la deuda de largo plazo, 1934 – 1938. *Historia (Chile),* no. 26 (1991 – 1992), pp. 71 – 115. Bibl.

Cuba

Cardoso, Eliana Anastasia. Cuba: un caso único de reforma anti-mercado; comentarios al artículo de Carmelo Mesa-Lago. *Pensamiento Iberoamericano,* no. 22 – 23, tomo II (July 92 – June 93), pp. 101 – 107. Tables.

Carriazo Moreno, George. Las relaciones económicas Cuba – Estados Unidos: una mirada al futuro. *Estudios Internacionales (Chile),* v. 26, no. 103 (July – Sept 93), pp. 480 – 499. Bibl, tables.

Maingot, Anthony Peter. Quid Pro Quo with Cuba. *Hemisphere,* v. 5, no. 3 (Summer – Fall 93), pp. 22 – 25.

Ritter, Archibald R. M. Seized Properties vs. Embargo Losses. *Hemisphere,* v. 5, no. 3 (Summer – Fall 93), pp. 31 – 35. Tables.

Sábato, Ernesto R. Críticas al bloqueo norteamericano a Cuba. *Realidad Económica,* no. 117 (July – Aug 93), pp. 33 – 34.

Zanetti Lecuona, Oscar. *Los cautivos de la reciprocidad: la burguesía cubana y la dependencia comercial* reviewed by Antonio Santamaría García. *Revista de Indias,* v. 53, no. 197 (Jan – Apr 93), pp. 129 – 132.

El Salvador

Cuenca, Breny. *El poder intangible: la AID y el estado salvadoreño en los años ochenta* reviewed by Rachel Sieder. *Journal of Latin American Studies,* v. 25, no. 3 (Oct 93), p. 670.

Latin America

Docampo, César. Iniciativas estadounidenses de la política económica: consecuencias hemisféricas. *Realidad Económica,* no. 119 (Oct – Nov 93), pp. 117 – 132. Bibl.

Grunwald, Joseph. El escabroso camino hacia la integración económica hemisférica: análisis regional de antecedentes orientado al futuro (Chapter from the book *The Enterprise for the Americas Initiative* translated by Carlos Villegas). *El Trimestre Económico,* v. 60, no. 239 (July – Sept 93), pp. 713 – 732. Bibl, tables.

Hakim, Peter. La empresa para la Iniciativa de las Américas. *Relaciones Internacionales (Mexico),* v. 15, Nueva época, no. 57 (Jan – Mar 93), pp. 31 – 35.

Kuwayama, Mikio. Nuevas formas de inversión en el comercio entre América Latina y Estados Unidos (Translated by Adriana Hierro). *Comercio Exterior,* v. 43, no. 5 (May 93), pp. 478 – 497. Bibl.

Levine, Elaine. Significado del programa de Bill Clinton para México y América Latina. *Problemas del Desarrollo,* v. 24, no. 93 (Apr – June 93), pp. 22 – 26.

Lozano García, Lucrecia. La Iniciativa para las Américas: el comercio hecho estrategia. *Nueva Sociedad,* no. 125 (May – June 93), pp. 98 – 111. Tables.

Osorio, Jaime. Bloque comercial sí, tratados comerciales tal vez. *El Cotidiano,* v. 9, no. 56 (July 93), pp. 113 – 116. Il, tables.

Saxe-Fernández, John. América Latina – Estados Unidos: ¿Hacia una nueva era? *Nueva Sociedad,* no. 125 (May – June 93), pp. 6 – 15. Bibl.

Torres, Víctor. Perspectivas de la Iniciativa para las Américas. *Apuntes (Peru),* no. 30 (Jan – June 92), pp. 63 – 79. Bibl, tables.

Mexico

Bolívar Espinoza, Augusto et al. La debilidad de un estado fuerte. *El Cotidiano,* v. 9, no. 53 (Mar – Apr 93), pp. 60 – 68.

Chauvet Sánchez, Michelle. Comida rápida contra comida corrida: repercusiones de la apertura comercial en la producción de cárnicos. *El Cotidiano,* v. 8, no. 52 (Jan – Feb 93), pp. 103 – 108. Bibl, il, tables, charts.

Gaytán Guzmán, Rosa Isabel. *Las relaciones comerciales entre México y Estados Unidos, 1867 – 1876* reviewed by Guadalupe González G. *Relaciones Internacionales (Mexico),* v. 14, Nueva época, no. 55 (July – Sept 92), pp. 79 – 82.

Levine, Elaine. Significado del programa de Bill Clinton para México y América Latina. *Problemas del Desarrollo,* v. 24, no. 93 (Apr – June 93), pp. 22 – 26.

Marshall, Timon L. and William E. Perry. Defending Antidumping Actions. *Business Mexico,* v. 3, no. 8 (Aug 93), pp. 26 – 28.

Nabers, Mary Scott. A Growing Love Affair. *Business Mexico,* v. 3, no. 5 (May 93), pp. 13 – 14. Charts.

Russell, Joel. Stating Their Case. *Business Mexico,* v. 3, no. 12 (Dec 93), pp. 24 – 28.

Witoshynsky, Mary. Florida Governor Puts Trade Focus on Mexico. *Business Mexico,* v. 3, no. 7 (July 93), p. 50. Il.

Southern Cone of South America

Fifer, J. Valerie. South of Capricorn: A Review Revisited (Rebuttal of a review of her *United States' Perceptions of Latin America, 1850 – 1930: A "New West" South of Capricorn?*). *Bulletin of Latin American Research,* v. 12, no. 1 (Jan 93), pp. 103 – 107.

Rojas Aravena, Francisco. El Cono Sur latinoamericano y la Iniciativa para las Américas. *Estudios Internacionales (Chile),* v. 26, no. 101 (Jan – Mar 93), pp. 98 – 122. Bibl.

Foreign opinion

Mora Chinchilla, Carolina. Los Estados Unidos: una imagen modelo para Costa Rica, 1880 – 1903. *Anuario de Estudios Centroamericanos,* v. 18, no. 2 (1992), pp. 91 – 101. Bibl.

Sources

Schoonover, Ebba and Thomas David Schoonover, eds. *A Mexican View of America in the 1860s: A Foreign Diplomat Describes the Civil War and Reconstruction* reviewed by John A. Britton. *The Americas,* v. 49, no. 3 (Jan 93), pp. 407 – 409.

Foreign relations

Consalvi, Simón Alberto. *Grover Cleveland y la controversia Venezuela – Gran Bretaña* reviewed by H. Michael Tacver. *Hispanic American Historical Review,* v. 73, no. 4 (Nov 93), pp. 727 – 728.

González-Souza, Luis F. Estados Unidos ante el nuevo milenio: consensos y grilletes bipartidistas. *Relaciones Internacionales (Mexico),* v. 15, Nueva época, no. 57 (Jan – Mar 93), pp. 7 – 12.

Jauberth, H. Rodrigo et al. *The Difficult Triangle: Mexico, Central America, and the United States,* a translation of *La triangulación Centroamérica – México – EUA.* Reviewed by Robert H. Holden. *Hispanic American Historical Review,* v. 73, no. 1 (Feb 93), pp. 192 – 194.

Bibliography

Goslinga, Marian. The US, Cuba, and Puerto Rico. *Hemisphere,* v. 5, no. 3 (Summer – Fall 93), pp. 54 – 56.

Dictionaries and encyclopedias

Shavit, David. *The United States in Latin America: A Historical Dictionary* reviewed by Bruce Calder. *Revista Interamericana de Bibliografía,* v. 42, no. 3 (1992), p. 509.

Bolivia

Barrios Morón, J. Raúl. La política contra las drogas en Bolivia: interdicción y guerra de baja intensidad. *Nueva Sociedad*, no. 123 (Jan – Feb 93), pp. 35 – 49. Bibl.

Brazil

Leacock, Ruth. *Requiem for Revolution: The United States and Brazil, 1961 – 1969* reviewed by John W. F. Dulles. *The Americas*, v. 49, no. 4 (Apr 93), pp. 564 – 566.

Smith, Joseph. *Unequal Giants: Diplomatic Relations between the United States and Brazil, 1889 – 1930* reviewed by Stanley E. Hilton. *The Americas*, v. 50, no. 1 (July 93), pp. 131 – 133.

Central America

Coleman, Kenneth M. and George C. Herring, eds. *Understanding the Central American Crisis: Sources of Conflict, U.S. Policy, and Options for Peace* reviewed by Orlando Peña. *Canadian Journal of Latin American and Caribbean Studies*, v. 17, no. 34 (1992), pp. 129 – 130.

Eguizábal, Cristina. De Contadora a Esquipulas: Washington y Centroamérica en un mundo cambiante. *Anuario de Estudios Centroamericanos*, v. 18, no. 1 (1992), pp. 5 – 15. Bibl.

Leonard, Thomas Michael. Central America and the United States: Overlooked Foreign Policy Objectives. *The Americas*, v. 50, no. 1 (July 93), pp. 1 – 30. Bibl.

Marshall, Jonathan and Peter Dale Scott. *Cocaine Politics: Drugs, Armies, and the CIA in Central America* reviewed by Donald J. Mabry. *Hispanic American Historical Review*, v. 73, no. 2 (May 93), p. 353.

Schoonover, Thomas David. *The United States in Central America, 1860 – 1911: Episodes of Social Imperialism and Imperial Rivalry in the World System* reviewed by Lester D. Langley. *The Americas*, v. 49, no. 4 (Apr 93), pp. 561 – 562.

— *The United States in Central America, 1860 – 1911: Episodes of Social Imperialism and Imperial Rivalry in the World System* reviewed by Rob van Vuurde. *European Review of Latin American and Caribbean Studies*, no. 54 (June 93), pp. 131 – 133.

— *The United States in Central America, 1860 – 1911: Episodes of Social Imperialism and Imperial Rivalry in the World System* reviewed by Lester D. Langley. *Journal of Latin American Studies*, v. 25, no. 1 (Feb 93), pp. 200 – 201.

Tushnet, Mark V. *Central America and the Law: The Constitution, Civil Liberties, and the Courts* reviewed by Jorge Luján Muñoz. *Mesoamérica (USA)*, v. 13, no. 24 (Dec 92), pp. 464 – 465.

Chile

Sater, William F. *Chile and the United States: Empires in Conflict* reviewed by David Sheinin. *The Americas*, v. 50, no. 1 (July 93), pp. 133 – 134.

— *Chile and the United States: Empires in Conflict* reviewed by Juan Ricardo Couyoumdijan. *Historia (Chile)*, no. 26 (1991 – 1992), pp. 461 – 464.

Colombia

Randall, Stephen J. *Colombia and the United States: Hegemony and Interdependence* reviewed by Frank Safford. *Hispanic American Historical Review*, v. 73, no. 1 (Feb 93), pp. 190 – 191.

— *Colombia and the United States: Hegemony and Interdependence* reviewed by Diana Pardo. *Journal of Inter-American Studies and World Affairs*, v. 35, no. 2 (Summer 93), pp. 163 – 166.

Costa Rica

Longley, Kyle. Peaceful Costa Rica: The First Battleground; The United States and the Costa Rican Revolution of 1948. *The Americas*, v. 50, no. 2 (Oct 93), pp. 149 – 175. Bibl.

Cuba

Cardoso, Eliana Anastasia and Ann Helwege. *Cuba after Communism* reviewed by Nicolás Sánchez. *Cuban Studies/Estudios Cubanos*, v. 23 (1993), pp. 210 – 213.

Fernández Cabrelli, Alfonso. El pueblo de Cuba: entre el drama y la esperanza. *Hoy Es Historia*, v. 9, no. 54 (Nov – Dec 92), pp. 69 – 76.

Hernández, José M. *Cuba and the United States: Intervention and Militarism, 1868 – 1933* reviewed by Jules R. Benjamin. *Cuban Studies/Estudios Cubanos*, v. 23 (1993), pp. 213 – 215.

Hernández, Rafael and Joseph S. Tulchin, eds. *Cuba and the United States: Will the Cold War in the Caribbean End?* reviewed by Jorge I. Domínguez. *Cuban Studies/Estudios Cubanos*, v. 23 (1993), pp. 215 – 217.

Huidobro, Vicente. Defendamos la revolución de Cuba: los Estados Unidos no tienen ningún derecho para meterse en los asuntos de Cuba. *Casa de las Américas*, no. 191 (Apr – June 93), pp. 10 – 11.

Landau, Saul. Clinton's Cuba Policy: A Low-Priority Dilemma. *NACLA Report on the Americas*, v. 26, no. 5 (May 93), pp. 35 – 37 +.

Murphy, Douglas. Teeing Off: Dwight, JFK, and Fidel. *Hemisphere*, v. 5, no. 2 (Winter – Spring 93), pp. 18 – 21. Il.

Opatrny, Josef. *U.S. Expansionism and Cuban Annexationism in the 1850s* reviewed by Allan J. Kuethe. *Hispanic American Historical Review*, v. 73, no. 4 (Nov 93), pp. 724 – 725.

Pérez, Louis A., Jr. *Cuba and the United States: Ties of a Singular Intimacy* reviewed by Thomas Schoonover. *The Americas*, v. 50, no. 1 (July 93), pp. 130 – 131.

Schulz, Donald E. The United States and Cuba: From a Strategy of Conflict to Constructive Engagement. *Journal of Inter-American Studies and World Affairs*, v. 35, no. 2 (Summer 93), pp. 81 – 102. Bibl.

Suchlicki, Jaime. Myths and Realities in US – Cuban Relations. *Journal of Inter-American Studies and World Affairs*, v. 35, no. 2 (Summer 93), pp. 103 – 113.

Vega Suñol, José. *Presencia norteamericana en el área nororiental de Cuba* reviewed by Lawrence A. Glasco. *Cuban Studies/Estudios Cubanos*, v. 23 (1993), pp. 227 – 228.

Dominican Republic

Nelson, William Javier. *Almost a Territory: America's Attempt to Annex the Dominican Republic* reviewed by Mu-Kien Adriana Sang. *Afro-Hispanic Review*, v. 12, no. 1 (Spring 93), pp. 55 – 56.

Palmer, Bruce. *Intervention in the Caribbean: The Dominican Crisis of 1965* reviewed by G. Pope Atkins. *Hispanic American Historical Review*, v. 73, no. 1 (Feb 93), pp. 188 – 189.

El Salvador

Estados Unidos conocía la violencia de El Salvador. *ECA; Estudios Centroamericanos*, v. 48, no. 534 – 535 (Apr – May 93), pp. 420 – 429. Il.

Independencia, soberanía y "Fuertes Caminos." *ECA; Estudios Centroamericanos*, v. 48, no. 539 (Sept 93), pp. 875 – 876. Il.

Un informe increíble sobre El Salvador. *ECA; Estudios Centroamericanos*, v. 48, no. 537 – 538 (July – Aug 93), pp. 750 – 761. Il.

Guatemala

Gleijeses, Piero. *Shattered Hope: The Guatemalan Revolution and the United States, 1944 – 1954* reviewed by Jim Handy. *The Americas*, v. 49, no. 4 (Apr 93), pp. 562 – 564.

Haiti

Plummer, Brenda Gayle. *Haiti and the United States: The Psychological Moment* reviewed by Brian Weinstein. *Revista Interamericana de Bibliografía*, v. 42, no. 4 (1992), p. 661.

Latin America

Brancato, Sandra Maria Lubisco. A conexão EUA/Brasil e a "questão argentina," 1943 – 1944. *Estudos Ibero-Americanos*, v. 18, no. 1 (July 92), pp. 89 – 101. Bibl.

Burbach, Roger. Clinton's Latin American Policy: A Look at Things to Come. *NACLA Report on the Americas*, v. 26, no. 5 (May 93), pp. 16 – 22 +. Bibl, il.

Carothers, Thomas H. *In the Name of Democracy: U.S. Policy toward Latin America in the Reagan Years* reviewed by Rubén M. Perina (Review entitled "La promoción de la democracia en América Latina"). *Estudios Internacionales (Chile)*, v. 26, no. 102 (Apr – June 93), pp. 204 – 215.

— *In the Name of Democracy: U.S. Policy toward Latin America in the Reagan Years* reviewed by Dario Moreno. *Hispanic American Historical Review*, v. 73, no. 4 (Nov 93), pp. 729 – 730.

Coatsworth, John Henry. Pax (norte) americana: América Latina después de la guerra fría (Translated by Marcela Pineda Camacho). *Revista Mexicana de Sociología,* v. 55, no. 2 (Apr – June 93), pp. 293 – 314. Bibl.

Cochrane, James D. The Troubled and Misunderstood Relationship: The United States and Latin America (Review article). *Latin American Research Review,* v. 28, no. 2 (1993), pp. 222 – 245.

Doyle, Kate. Drug War: A Quietly Escalating Failure. *NACLA Report on the Americas,* v. 26, no. 5 (May 93), pp. 29 – 34 +. Bibl, il.

García B., Pantaleón. La política del buen vecino y Latinoamérica. *Revista Cultural Lotería,* v. 51, no. 388 (Mar – Apr 92), pp. 62 – 77. Bibl.

Hartlyn, Jonathan et al, eds. *The United States and Latin America in the 1990s: Beyond the Cold War* reviewed by David Ryan. *Journal of Latin American Studies,* v. 25, no. 3 (Oct 93), pp. 691 – 692.

Kryzanek, Michael John. *Leaders, Leadership, and U.S. Policy in Latin America* reviewed by Johanna Mendelson-Forman. *Revista Interamericana de Bibliografía,* v. 42, no. 4 (1992), pp. 658 – 659.

Lowenthal, Abraham F. El hemisferio interdoméstico. *Relaciones Internacionales (Mexico),* v. 15, Nueva época, no. 57 (Jan – Mar 93), pp. 13 – 15.

Mitchell, Christopher, ed. *Western Hemisphere Immigration and United States Foreign Policy* reviewed by Caroline Thomas. *Bulletin of Latin American Research,* v. 12, no. 2 (May 93), pp. 238 – 239.

Moneta, Carlos Juan. As forças armadas latino-americanas nos anos '90. *Política e Estratégica,* v. 8, no. 2 – 4 (Apr – Dec 90), pp. 153 – 167. Bibl.

Pastor, Robert A. *Whirlpool: U.S. Foreign Policy toward Latin America and the Caribbean* reviewed by Joseph S. Tulchin (Review entitled "A New Course in Foreign Affairs?"). *Hemisphere,* v. 5, no. 3 (Summer – Fall 93), pp. 50 – 52. Il.

— *Whirlpool: U.S. Foreign Policy toward Latin America and the Caribbean* reviewed by Javier Urbano Reyes (Review entitled "América Latina y el Caribe en la mira de Estados Unidos"). *Relaciones Internacionales (Mexico),* v. 15, Nueva época, no. 57 (Jan – Mar 93), pp. 105 – 106.

Pike, Fredrick B. *The United States and Latin America: Myths and Stereotypes of Civilization and Nature* reviewed by Peter Calvert. *Bulletin of Latin American Research,* v. 12, no. 2 (May 93), pp. 232 – 233.

— *The United States and Latin America: Myths and Stereotypes of Civilization and Nature* reviewed by Josef Opatrny. *Hispanic American Historical Review,* v. 73, no. 4 (Nov 93), pp. 667 – 668.

— *The United States and Latin America: Myths and Stereotypes of Civilization and Nature* reviewed by Gordon Connell-Smith. *Journal of Latin American Studies,* v. 25, no. 3 (Oct 93), pp. 689 – 691.

Shurbutt, Thomas Ray, ed. *United States – Latin American Relations, 1800 – 1850: The Formative Generations* reviewed by Thomas Schoonover. *The Americas,* v. 49, no. 3 (Jan 93), pp. 405 – 407.

Wiarda, Howard J. *American Foreign Policy toward Latin America in the 80s and 90s: Issues and Controversies from Reagan to Bush* reviewed by Gordon Connell-Smith. *Journal of Latin American Studies,* v. 25, no. 3 (Oct 93), pp. 689 – 691.

Wilson, Michael. Hacia la próxima centuria americana: construyendo una nueva asociación con América Latina. *Relaciones Internacionales (Mexico),* v. 15, Nueva época, no. 57 (Jan – Mar 93), pp. 17 – 30. Bibl.

Zea, Leopoldo. América Latina: qué hacer con 500 años de historia. *Ibero-Amerikanisches Archiv,* v. 18, no. 3 – 4 (1992), pp. 445 – 453. Bibl.

Mexico

Andrews, Gregg. *Shoulder to Shoulder?: The American Federation of Labor, the United States, and the Mexican Revolution, 1910 – 1924* reviewed by Mark T. Gilderhus. *Hispanic American Historical Review,* v. 73, no. 1 (Feb 93), pp. 195 – 196.

Buchenau, Jürgen. Counter-Intervention against Uncle Sam: Mexico's Support for Nicaraguan Nationalism, 1903 – 1910. *The Americas,* v. 50, no. 2 (Oct 93), pp. 207 – 232. Bibl.

Caruso, Brooke A. *The Mexican Spy Company: United States Covert Actions in Mexico, 1845 – 1848* reviewed by Daniela Spenser. *Hispanic American Historical Review,* v. 73, no. 1 (Feb 93), p. 189.

Glennon, Michael J. Testimony before the Subcommittee on Civil and Constitutional Rights, Committee on the Judiciary, United States House of Representatives. *Mexican Studies,* v. 9, no. 1 (Winter 93), pp. 1 – 17.

Hernández Navarro, Luis. De Washington al Cerro de las Campanas: la exportación de la democracia a la hora del TLC. *El Cotidiano,* v. 9, no. 54 (May 93), pp. 101 – 107. Bibl.

Montaño, Jorge. Una visión desde Washington: México/Estados Unidos en los noventas. *Nexos,* v. 16, no. 187 (July 93), pp. 15 – 19.

Weintraub, Sidney. *A Marriage of Convenience: U.S. – Mexico Relations* reviewed by Lázaro Cárdenas Armenta (Review entitled "Las relaciones México – Estados Unidos: entre el conflicto y la cooperación"). *Relaciones Internacionales (Mexico),* v. 15, Nueva época, no. 57 (Jan – Mar 93), pp. 101 – 103.

Nicaragua

Buchenau, Jürgen. Counter-Intervention against Uncle Sam: Mexico's Support for Nicaraguan Nationalism, 1903 – 1910. *The Americas,* v. 50, no. 2 (Oct 93), pp. 207 – 232. Bibl.

Byrne, Malcolm and Peter R. Kornbluh. Iran – Contra: A Postmortem. *NACLA Report on the Americas,* v. 27, no. 3 (Nov – Dec 93), pp. 29 – 34 +. Il.

Dodd, Thomas Joseph. *Managing Democracy in Central America: A Case Study of United States Election Supervision in Nicaragua, 1927 – 1933* reviewed by Neill Macaulay. *Hispanic American Historical Review,* v. 73, no. 4 (Nov 93), pp. 730 – 731.

Robinson, William I. *A Faustian Bargain: U.S. Intervention in the Nicaraguan Elections and American Foreign Policy in the Post-Cold War Era* reviewed by Thomas P. Anderson. *Hispanic American Historical Review,* v. 73, no. 3 (Aug 93), pp. 541 – 542.

Stimson, Henry Lewis. *Henry L. Stimson's American Policy in Nicaragua: The Lasting Legacy* reviewed by Thomas W. Walker. *Hispanic American Historical Review,* v. 73, no. 3 (Aug 93), pp. 540 – 541.

Panama

Conniff, Michael L. *Panama and the United States: The Forced Alliance* reviewed by Walter Lafeber. *Hispanic American Historical Review,* v. 73, no. 1 (Feb 93), pp. 191 – 192.

Krosigk, Friedrich von. Panama und die Grenzen US-amerikanischer Hegemonie: Überlegungen zum Konzept der Gegenmacht. *Zeitschrift für Lateinamerika Wien,* no. 43 (1992), pp. 81 – 93. Bibl, tables.

Leis, Raúl. Panamá: desactivar la muerte. *Nueva Sociedad,* no. 123 (Jan – Feb 93), pp. 114 – 123.

Southern Cone of South America

Fifer, J. Valerie. *United States Perceptions of Latin America, 1850 – 1930: A "New West" South of Capricorn* reviewed by Thomas L. Whigham. *The Americas,* v. 49, no. 4 (Apr 93), pp. 559 – 561.

Spain

García B., Pantaleón. La adquisición de las Floridas por los Estados Unidos en 1819. *Revista Cultural Lotería,* v. 51, no. 387 (Feb 92), pp. 37 – 42. Bibl.

History

Sources

Schoonover, Ebba and Thomas David Schoonover, eds. *A Mexican View of America in the 1860s: A Foreign Diplomat Describes the Civil War and Reconstruction* reviewed by John A. Britton. *The Americas,* v. 49, no. 3 (Jan 93), pp. 407 – 409.

1898, War of

Offner, John L. *An Unwanted War: The Diplomacy of the United States and Spain over Cuba, 1895 – 1898* reviewed by Jules R. Benjamin. *Hispanic American Historical Review,* v. 73, no. 3 (Aug 93), pp. 539 – 540.

Robles Muñoz, Cristóbal. Triunfar en Washington: España ante Baire. *Anuario de Estudios Americanos,* v. 49 (1992), pp. 563 – 584. Bibl.

Politics and government

Pozzi, Pablo Alejandro. Estados Unidos entre la crisis y la legitimidad. *Realidad Económica,* no. 113 (Jan – Feb 93), pp. 103 – 121. Bibl, tables.

Race question

Massey, Douglas S. Latinos, Poverty, and the Underclass: A New Agenda for Research. *Hispanic Journal of Behavioral Sciences,* v. 15, no. 4 (Nov 93), pp. 449 – 475. Bibl.

Romero, Gloria Jean. "No se raje, chicanita": Some Thoughts on Race, Class, and Gender in the Classroom. *Aztlán,* v. 20, no. 1 – 2 (Spring – Fall 91), pp. 203 – 218. Bibl.

Rubin-Kurtzman, Jane R. La etnia en las políticas de población de la frontera norte: reflexiones sobre un tema poco explorado y una agenda de investigación. *Frontera Norte,* v. 4, no. 8 (July – Dec 92), pp. 111 – 123. Bibl.

Skidmore, Thomas E. Bi-Racial U.S.A. vs. Multi-Racial Brazil: Is the Contrast Still Valid? *Journal of Latin American Studies,* v. 25, no. 2 (May 93), pp. 373 – 386. Bibl.

Relations

Puerto Rico

Barreto Márquez, Amílcar A. The Debate over Puerto Rican Statehood: Language and the "Super-Majority." *Homines,* v. 15 – 16, no. 2 – 1 (Oct 91 – Dec 92), pp. 135 – 141. Bibl.

Berríos Martínez, Rubén. Independencia y plebiscito. *Homines,* v. 15 – 16, no. 2 – 1 (Oct 91 – Dec 92), pp. 118 – 125.

Corrada del Río, Baltasar. The Plebiscite: A Time for Change. *Hemisphere,* v. 5, no. 3 (Summer – Fall 93), pp. 44 – 46.

García-Passalacqua, Juan M. Negotiated Autonomy. *Hemisphere,* v. 5, no. 3 (Summer – Fall 93), pp. 38 – 41. Charts.

— El regreso de Babel. *Homines,* v. 15 – 16, no. 2 – 1 (Oct 91 – Dec 92), pp. 132 – 134.

Laguerre, Enrique Arturo. De espaldas a la historia. *Homines,* v. 15 – 16, no. 2 – 1 (Oct 91 – Dec 92), pp. 116 – 117.

Méndez, José Luis. Puerto Rico: ¿Español o inglés?; un debate sobre su identidad. *Cuadernos Americanos,* no. 40, Nueva época (July – Aug 93), pp. 84 – 96. Bibl.

Ostolaza Bey, Margarita. El bloque histórico colonial de Puerto Rico. *Homines,* v. 15 – 16, no. 2 – 1 (Oct 91 – Dec 92), pp. 152 – 178. Bibl, tables.

El plebiscito: una contestación a Rubén Berríos. *Homines,* v. 15 – 16, no. 2 – 1 (Oct 91 – Dec 92), pp. 126 – 131.

Rigau, Marco Antonio. Mutual Respect: Congress Must Act. *Hemisphere,* v. 5, no. 3 (Summer – Fall 93), pp. 47 – 49. Il.

Rodríguez-Orellana, Manuel. A Chance to Decolonize. *Hemisphere,* v. 5, no. 3 (Summer – Fall 93), pp. 42 – 43.

Weisman, Alan. El futuro de Puerto Rico. *Homines,* v. 15 – 16, no. 2 – 1 (Oct 91 – Dec 92), pp. 106 – 111.

Social policy

Murray, Charles. Política social y marginalidad: algunas lecciones de la experiencia norteamericana. *Estudios Públicos (Chile),* no. 52 (Spring 93), pp. 127 – 143.

UNITED STATES. AGENCY FOR INTERNATIONAL DEVELOPMENT

Cuenca, Breny. *El poder intangible: la AID y el estado salvadoreño en los años ochenta* reviewed by Rachel Sieder. *Journal of Latin American Studies,* v. 25, no. 3 (Oct 93), p. 670.

Curtis, Cynthia and Danielle Yariv. Después de la guerra: una mirada preliminar al papel de la ayuda militar de EE.UU. en la reconstrucción postguerra en El Salvador. *ECA; Estudios Centroamericanos,* v. 48, no. 531 – 532 (Jan – Feb 93), pp. 61 – 74. Il.

UNITED STATES. HOUSE OF REPRESENTATIVES

Glennon, Michael J. Testimony before the Subcommittee on Civil and Constitutional Rights, Committee on the Judiciary, United States House of Representatives. *Mexican Studies,* v. 9, no. 1 (Winter 93), pp. 1 – 17.

UNITED STATES IN LITERATURE

Leal, Luis. Sin fronteras: (des)mitificación en las letras norteamericanas y mexicanas. *Mexican Studies,* v. 9, no. 1 (Winter 93), pp. 95 – 118. Bibl.

UNITED STATES – MEXICO BORDER REGION

See

Mexican – American Border Region

UNIVERSIDAD AUTÓNOMA METROPOLITANA (MEXICO)

Bueno Rodríguez, Luis and Salvador T. Porras Duarte. Deshomologación salarial: ¿Cuánto por punto? *El Cotidiano,* v. 9, no. 55 (June 93), pp. 91 – 98. Tables, charts.

UNIVERSIDAD CATÓLICA DEL PERÚ

Chirinos Arrieta, Eduardo, ed. *Infame turba: poesía en la Universidad Católica, 1917 – 1992* reviewed by Abelardo Oquendo (Review entitled "Pero, ¿existe algo que pueda llarmarse un poeta de la Católica?"). *Debate (Peru),* v. 16, no. 72 (Mar – May 93), pp. 55 – 56. Il.

UNIVERSIDAD DE CHILE

Bravo Lira, Bernardino. Una de las universidades más antiguas del mundo. *Atenea (Chile),* no. 465 – 466 (1992), pp. 325 – 328.

Cruz-Coke Madrid, Ricardo. Desarrollo de las ciencias médicas en la U. de Chile. *Atenea (Chile),* no. 465 – 466 (1992), pp. 329 – 336. Bibl.

Dr. Jaime Lavados, el actual rector. *Atenea (Chile),* no. 465 – 466 (1992), pp. 349 – 351. Il.

Mellafe Rojas, Rolando. La importancia de la Universidad de Chile en la educación nacional. *Boletín de la Academia Chilena de la Historia,* v. 58 – 59, no. 102 (1991 – 1992), pp. 481 – 489.

Mellafe Rojas, Rolando and Antonia Rebolledo Hernández. La creación de la Universidad de Chile y el despertar de la identidad nacional. *Atenea (Chile),* no. 465 – 466 (1992), pp. 303 – 323. Bibl, il.

Osses Moya, Darío. La fundación de una literatura nacional y la Universidad de Chile. *Atenea (Chile),* no. 465 – 466 (1992), pp. 337 – 347. Bibl.

UNIVERSIDAD DE COSTA RICA

Chaves Salas, Ana Lupita. Reseña histórica de la regionalización de la Universidad de Costa Rica. *Revista de Ciencias Sociales (Costa Rica),* no. 60 (June 93), pp. 7 – 16. Bibl.

UNIVERSIDAD DE SAN CARLOS DE GUATEMALA

Alvarado Polanco, Romeo et al. Autonomía universitaria. *USAC,* no. 12 (Dec 90), pp. 49 – 59.

Fuentes Soria, Alfonso et al. Desarrollo de la Universidad de San Carlos de Guatemala en la década 1990 – 2000. *USAC,* no. 12 (Dec 90), pp. 36 – 48.

— Estado, universidad y sociedad: panel-foro. *USAC,* no. 13 (Mar 91), pp. 5 – 18.

García Laguardia, Jorge Mario. Antecedente y significado de la autonomía universitaria. *USAC,* no. 12 (Dec 90), pp. 60 – 65.

UNIVERSIDAD JAVERIANA

Rey Fajardo, José del. La presencia científica de la Universidad Javeriana en la Orinoquia. *Boletín de Historia y Antigüedades,* v. 79, no. 779 (Oct – Dec 92), pp. 925 – 952. Bibl.

UNIVERSIDAD NACIONAL AUTÓNOMA DE MÉXICO

Castrejón Diez, Jaime. *La universidad y el sistema* reviewed by Elías Margolis Schweber. *Revista Mexicana de Ciencias Políticas y Sociales,* v. 38, Nueva época, no. 153 (July – Sept 93), pp. 219 – 222.

— *La universidad y el sistema* reviewed by Margarita Jiménez Badillo. *El Cotidiano*, v. 8, no. 51ª (Nov – Dec 92), p. 115.

Holguín Quiñones, Fernando. Análisis comparativo de los egresados de las carreras de la FCPyS con otros similares. *Revista Mexicana de Ciencias Políticas y Sociales*, v. 37, Nueva época, no. 148 (Apr – June 92), pp. 143 – 184. Tables, charts.

— Encuesta a egresados de la Facultad de Ciencias Políticas y Sociales: I parte. *Revista Mexicana de Ciencias Políticas y Sociales*, v. 38, Nueva época, no. 153 (July – Sept 93), pp. 137 – 210. Tables, charts.

Suárez-Iñíguez, Enrique. El proyecto académico de la División de Estudios de Posgrado de la Facultad de Ciencias Políticas y Sociales de la UNAM. *Revista Mexicana de Ciencias Políticas y Sociales*, v. 38, Nueva época, no. 151 (Jan – Mar 93), pp. 187 – 193.

Vega Shiota, Gustavo de la. Reflexiones en torno al posgrado de sociología en la Facultad de Ciencias Políticas y Sociales de la UNAM. *Revista Mexicana de Ciencias Políticas y Sociales*, v. 38, Nueva época, no. 151 (Jan – Mar 93), pp. 195 – 203.

UNIVERSITIES AND COLLEGES

See also
Catholic universities and colleges
Education, Higher
Research institutes
Students

America

Arias Sánchez, Oscar. Las universidades y la mentalidad armamentista. *La Educación (USA)*, v. 36, no. 111 – 113 (1992), pp. 155 – 165.

Argentina

Romano Sued, Susana. Universidad Nacional de Córdoba: mirada a través de los últimos veinte años. *Cuadernos Hispanoamericanos*, no. 517 – 519 (July – Sept 93), pp. 92 – 104.

Sanguinetti, Horacio. Se abrió un período de tolerancia republicana. *Todo Es Historia*, v. 27, no. 317 (Dec 93), pp. 16 – 18. Il.

Administration

Barros, Enrique F. et al. 75 años de la reforma universitaria: manifiesto liminar de la reforma universitaria. *Realidad Económica*, no. 118 (Aug – Sept 93), pp. 117 – 122.

Brazil

Glezer, Raquel. São Paulo e a elite letrada brasileira no século XIX. *Siglo XIX: Revista*, no. 11, 2a época (Jan – June 92), pp. 149 – 160. Bibl.

Litto, Fredric M. A "escola do futuro" da Universidade de São Paulo: um laboratório de tecnologia-de-ponta para a educação. *Revista Brasileira de Estudos Pedagógicos*, v. 72, no. 172 (Sept – Dec 91), pp. 409 – 412.

Segismundo, Fernando. A filosofia no Colégio Pedro II. *Revista do Instituto Histórico e Geográfico Brasileiro*, no. 373 (Oct – Dec 91), pp. 948 – 953.

— Professores de história do Colégio Pedro II: esboço. *Revista do Instituto Histórico e Geográfico Brasileiro*, no. 370 (Jan – Mar 91), pp. 151 – 192.

Caribbean area

Nettleford, Rex and Philip Manderson Sherlock. *The University of the West Indies: A Caribbean Response to the Challenge of Change* reviewed by Rafael L. Ramírez. *Caribbean Studies*, v. 25, no. 1 – 2 (Jan – July 92), pp. 171 – 172.

— *The University of the West Indies: A Caribbean Response to the Challenge of Change* reviewed by Bruce King. *Journal of Caribbean Studies*, v. 9, no. 1 – 2 (Winter 92 – Spring 93), pp. 125 – 127.

Chile

Bravo Lira, Bernardino. Una de las universidades más antiguas del mundo. *Atenea (Chile)*, no. 465 – 466 (1992), pp. 325 – 328.

Cruz-Coke Madrid, Ricardo. Desarrollo de las ciencias médicas en la U. de Chile. *Atenea (Chile)*, no. 465 – 466 (1992), pp. 329 – 336. Bibl.

Dr. Jaime Lavados, el actual rector. *Atenea (Chile)*, no. 465 – 466 (1992), pp. 349 – 351. Il.

Mellafe Rojas, Rolando. La importancia de la Universidad de Chile en la educación nacional. *Boletín de la Academia Chilena de la Historia*, v. 58 – 59, no. 102 (1991 – 1992), pp. 481 – 489.

Mellafe Rojas, Rolando and Antonia Rebolledo Hernández. La creación de la Universidad de Chile y el despertar de la identidad nacional. *Atenea (Chile)*, no. 465 – 466 (1992), pp. 303 – 323. Bibl, il.

Osses Moya, Darío. La fundación de una literatura nacional y la Universidad de Chile. *Atenea (Chile)*, no. 465 – 466 (1992), pp. 337 – 347. Bibl.

Colombia

Administration

Bolaño Movilla, Rafael. Apuntes sobre la constitución colombiana de 1991. *Desarrollo Indoamericano*, v. 23, no. 91 (June 93), pp. 24 – 25. Il.

Vallejo M., César. Descentralización de la educación en Colombia: antecedentes históricos. *Planeación y Desarrollo*, v. 24, no. 1 (Jan – Apr 93), pp. 233 – 277. Bibl.

Costa Rica

Administration

Chaves Salas, Ana Lupita. Reseña histórica de la regionalización de la Universidad de Costa Rica. *Revista de Ciencias Sociales (Costa Rica)*, no. 60 (June 93), pp. 7 – 16. Bibl.

Guatemala

Fuentes Soria, Alfonso et al. Desarrollo de la Universidad de San Carlos de Guatemala en la década 1990 – 2000. *USAC*, no. 12 (Dec 90), pp. 36 – 48.

— Estado, universidad y sociedad: panel-foro. *USAC*, no. 13 (Mar 91), pp. 5 – 18.

Administration

Alvarado Polanco, Romeo et al. Autonomía universitaria. *USAC*, no. 12 (Dec 90), pp. 49 – 59.

García Laguardia, Jorge Mario. Antecedente y significado de la autonomía universitaria. *USAC*, no. 12 (Dec 90), pp. 60 – 65.

Latin America

Administration

Administración universitaria en América Latina: una perspectiva estratégica reviewed by Luisa Margarita Schweizer. *La Educación (USA)*, v. 37, no. 115 (1993), pp. 414 – 417.

Congresses

Casado Arboniés, Manuel. VI Jornadas sobre la Presencia Universitaria Española en América. *Anuario de Estudios Americanos*, v. 49, Suppl. 2 (1992), pp. 214 – 217.

International cooperation

García Guadilla, Carmen. Integración académica y nuevo valor del conocimiento. *Nueva Sociedad*, no. 126 (July – Aug 93), pp. 156 – 168. Bibl.

Mexico

Bueno Rodríguez, Luis and Salvador T. Porras Duarte. Deshomologación salarial: ¿Cuánto por punto? *El Cotidiano*, v. 9, no. 55 (June 93), pp. 91 – 98. Tables, charts.

Castrejón Diez, Jaime. *La universidad y el sistema* reviewed by Elías Margolis Schweber. *Revista Mexicana de Ciencias Políticas y Sociales*, v. 38, Nueva época, no. 153 (July – Sept 93), pp. 219 – 222.

— *La universidad y el sistema* reviewed by Margarita Jiménez Badillo. *El Cotidiano*, v. 8, no. 51 (Nov – Dec 92), p. 115.

Hernández Palacios, Aureliano. Orígenes de la formación docente en la Universidad Veracruzana. *La Palabra y el Hombre*, no. 81 (Jan – Mar 92), pp. 292 – 301. Il.

Ibarra Colado, Eduardo. El futuro de la universidad en México: los resortes de la diferenciación. *El Cotidiano*, v. 9, no. 55 (June 93), pp. 68 – 77. Tables, charts.

López Angel, Carlos. El sindicalismo universitario de hoy y su futuro. *El Cotidiano*, v. 9, no. 56 (July 93), pp. 75 – 85. Il.

Staples, Anne. Los últimos diez años de historia regional en el Colegio de México. *La Palabra y el Hombre*, no. 83 (July – Sept 92), pp. 299 – 303. Bibl.

Suárez-Iñíguez, Enrique. El proyecto académico de la División de Estudios de Posgrado de la Facultad de Ciencias Políticas y Sociales de la UNAM. *Revista Mexicana de Ciencias Políticas y Sociales*, v. 38, Nueva época, no. 151 (Jan – Mar 93), pp. 187 – 193.

Administration

Llinás Alvarez, Edgar. The Issue of Autonomy in the Royal and Pontifical University of Mexico. *Revista de Historia de América*, no. 112 (July – Dec 91), pp. 105 – 119. Bibl, charts.

Villaseñor García, Guillermo. El gobierno y la conducción en las universidades públicas: situación reciente y tendencias actuales. *El Cotidiano*, v. 9, no. 55 (June 93), pp. 85 – 90. Il.

Foreign influences

Abadie-Aicardi, Aníbal. La tradición institucional salmantina en los Libros de Claustros de la Universidad de México del renacimiento a la ilustración y la independencia, 1551 – 1821. *Jahrbuch für Geschichte von Staat, Wirtschaft und Gesellschaft Lateinamerikas*, v. 29 (1992), pp. 1 – 46. Bibl.

Peru

Céspedes Aguirre, Patricia. Universidad, deporte y agresividad juvenil: apuntes en torno a la Olimpiada UNSAAC, 1991. *Allpanchis*, v. 25, no. 41 (Jan – June 93), pp. 159 – 174.

Spain

Abadie-Aicardi, Aníbal. La tradición institucional salmantina en los Libros de Claustros de la Universidad de México del renacimiento a la ilustración y la independencia, 1551 – 1821. *Jahrbuch für Geschichte von Staat, Wirtschaft und Gesellschaft Lateinamerikas*, v. 29 (1992), pp. 1 – 46. Bibl.

UNIVERSITY AUTONOMY

See
> Subdivision *Administration* under *Universities and colleges*

UNIVERSITY OF THE WEST INDIES

Nettleford, Rex and Philip Manderson Sherlock. *The University of the West Indies: A Caribbean Response to the Challenge of Change* reviewed by Rafael L. Ramírez. *Caribbean Studies*, v. 25, no. 1 – 2 (Jan – July 92), pp. 171 – 172.

— *The University of the West Indies: A Caribbean Response to the Challenge of Change* reviewed by Bruce King. *Journal of Caribbean Studies*, v. 9, no. 1 – 2 (Winter 92 – Spring 93), pp. 125 – 127.

UPPER CLASSES

See
> Capitalists and financiers
> Elite (Social sciences)
> Oligarchy

URBAN PLANNING

See
> Regional planning
> Subdivision *Planning* under *Cities and towns*

URBANIZATION

See also
> Cities and towns
> Community centers
> Community development
> Ecology
> Housing
> Land use
> Local government
> Markets and merchants
> Migration, Internal
> Regional planning
> Slums
> Sociology, Urban
> Transportation
> Subdivision *Planning* under *Cities and towns*

Andean region

Kingman Garcés, Eduardo, ed. *Ciudades de los Andes: visión histórica y contemporánea* reviewed by Scarlett O'Phelan Godoy. *Anuario de Estudios Americanos*, v. 49, Suppl. 2 (1992), p. 244.

Argentina

Foschiatti dell'Orto, Ana María H. El desarrollo urbano y las particularidades demográficas del Chaco y su capital entre 1960 y 1990. *Revista Geográfica (Mexico)*, no. 115 (Jan – June 92), pp. 37 – 54. Bibl, tables, maps, charts.

Brazil

Davidovich, Fany Rachel. Brasil metropolitano e Brasil urbano não-metropolitano: algumas questões. *Revista Brasileira de Geografia*, v. 53, no. 2 (Apr – June 91), pp. 127 – 133. Bibl.

Chile

Mathematical models

Mozo, Rafael. Evolución de la primacia urbana y del aparato estatal chileno entre 1800 y 1980. *Estudios Sociales (Chile)*, no. 77 (July – Sept 93), pp. 61 – 72. Bibl, tables, charts.

Developing countries

Gilbert, Alan G. Ciudades del Tercer Mundo: la evolución del sistema nacional de asentamientos. *EURE*, v. 19, no. 57 (July 93), pp. 41 – 58. Tables.

Satterthwaite, David. Problemas sociales y medioambientales asociados a la urbanización acelerada. *EURE*, v. 19, no. 57 (July 93), pp. 7 – 30. Tables.

Latin America

Daher, Antonio and Guillermo Gisse. América Latina: ambiente y territorio en el cambio de modelo. *Revista Paraguaya de Sociología*, v. 29, no. 84 (May – Aug 92), pp. 25 – 40.

Mexico

Baños Ramírez, Othón. Reconfiguración rural – urbana en la zona henequenera de Yucatán. *Estudios Sociológicos*, v. 11, no. 32 (May – Aug 93), pp. 419 – 443. Tables, maps.

Cruz Rodríguez, María Soledad. La nueva ley agraria y su impacto en la periferia ejidal de la ciudad de México. *El Cotidiano*, v. 10, no. 57 (Aug – Sept 93), pp. 54 – 59. Bibl, il, tables.

González de Alba, Luis. La muerte del centro. *Nexos*, v. 16, no. 186 (June 93), pp. 19 – 20.

Ruiz Chiapetto, Crescencio. El desarrollo del México urbano: cambio de protagonista. *Comercio Exterior*, v. 43, no. 8 (Aug 93), pp. 708 – 716. Bibl, tables, maps.

Congresses

Aguilar, Adrián Guillermo. Relatoría de la mesa redonda "El Programa Nacional de Desarrollo Urbano, 1990 – 1994." *Estudios Demográficos y Urbanos*, v. 6, no. 3 (Sept – Dec 91), pp. 738 – 744.

Statistics

Garza Villarreal, Gustavo and Salvador Rivera. Desarrollo económico y distribución de la población urbana en México, 1960 – 1990. *Revista Mexicana de Sociología*, v. 55, no. 1 (Jan – Mar 93), pp. 177 – 212. Bibl, tables, charts.

URIBE-ECHEVARRÍA FREY, BÁRBARA

Obituaries

Parada Allende, Maritza. In memoriam. *Revista Musical Chilena*, v. 46, no. 178 (July – Dec 92), p. 131.

URUGUAY

See also
> Archaeology – Uruguay
> Architecture – Uruguay
> Artists – Uruguay
> Blacks – Uruguay
> Blacks in literature – Uruguay
> Books – Uruguay
> Canelones, Uruguay (Department)
> Catholic Church – Uruguay
> Cities and towns – Uruguay
> Composers – Uruguay
> Crime and criminals – Uruguay
> Democracy – Uruguay
> Education, Primary – Uruguay

Education and state – Uruguay
Elections – Uruguay
Electronics – Uruguay
Ethnobotany – Uruguay
Executive power – Uruguay
Folk festivals – Uruguay
Food industry and trade – Uruguay
Geography, Economic – Uruguay
Geography, Historical – Uruguay
Human rights – Uruguay
Industrial promotion – Uruguay
Inflation (Finance) – Uruguay
Lawyers – Uruguay
Legislative power – Uruguay
Literature and history – Uruguay
Local government – Uruguay
Medicine – Uruguay
Melo, Uruguay
Montevideo, Uruguay (City)
Musicians – Uruguay
Newspapers – Uruguay
Peasantry – Uruguay
Periodicals – Uruguay
Philosophy – Uruguay
Physicians – Uruguay
Political parties – Uruguay
Political sociology – Uruguay
Politics in literature – Uruguay
Population – Uruguay
Press and politics – Uruguay
Public administration – Uruguay
Research institutes – Uruguay
Scientific research – Uruguay
Sculpture – Uruguay
Sexism – Uruguay
Strikes and lockouts – Uruguay
Students – Uruguay
Theater – Uruguay
Trade unions – Uruguay
Wages – Uruguay
Women – Uruguay

Biography

Díaz de Guerra, María A. La zona de José Ignacio en el departamento de Maldonado y su incidencia en la evolución regional. *Hoy Es Historia,* v. 10, no. 58 (July – Aug 93), pp. 27 – 53. Bibl, il, facs.

Soiza Larrosa, Augusto. Un linaje carolino – minuano: Larrosa – Cortés, siglos XVIII – XIX. *Hoy Es Historia,* v. 10, no. 55 (Jan – Feb 93), pp. 62 – 71. Bibl, il.

Civilization

Achugar Ferrari, Hugo. *La balsa de la Medusa: ensayos sobre identidad, cultura y fin de siglo* reviewed by Fernando Errandonea. *Cuadernos del CLAEH,* v. 18, no. 65 – 66 (May 93), pp. 203 – 212. Bibl.

Barrán, José Pedro. *Historia de la sensibilidad en el Uruguay* reviewed by Alfonso Esponera. *Revista Andina,* v. 10, no. 2 (Dec 92), pp. 539 – 540.

Trigo, Abril. *Caudillo, estado, nación: literatura, historia e ideología en el Uruguay* reviewed by Gustavo Verdesio. *Nuevo Texto Crítico,* v. 6, no. 11 (1993), pp. 263 – 266.

— Un texto antropológico de Julio Herrera y Reissig (Includes a chapter from the text "Los nuevos charrúas" edited by Abril Trigo). *Escritura (Venezuela),* v. 17, no. 33 – 34 (Jan – Dec 92), pp. 127 – 142. Bibl.

Constitutional law

Riz, Liliana de and Catalina Smulovitz. Instauración democrática y reforma política en Argentina y Uruguay: un análisis comparado. *Ibero-Amerikanisches Archiv,* v. 18, no. 1 – 2 (1992), pp. 181 – 224. Bibl, tables.

Foreign economic relations

Brazil

Acuerdo de Complementación Económica concertado entre la república federativa del Brasil y la república oriental del Uruguay. *Integración Latinoamericana,* v. 18, no. 194 (Oct 93), pp. 64 – 65.

Southern Cone of South America

Achard, Diego et al. MERCOSUR: élites y política en Paraguay y Uruguay. *Integración Latinoamericana,* v. 18, no. 192 (Aug 93), pp. 59 – 61.

Berretta, Nora et al. *En el umbral de la integración* (Review). *Integración Latinoamericana,* v. 18, no. 191 (July 93), pp. 76 – 77.

Magariños, Gustavo. *Uruguay en el MERCOSUR* (Review). *Integración Latinoamericana,* v. 18, no. 192 (Aug 92), pp. 97 – 98.

Stolovich, Luis. Los empresarios, la apertura y los procesos de integración regional: contradicciones y estrategias; el caso de Uruguay en el MERCOSUR. *Revista Paraguaya de Sociología,* v. 29, no. 84 (May – Aug 92), pp. 53 – 90. Bibl, tables.

Historiography

Anastasia, Luis Víctor. Colón en la historiografía uruguaya. *Revista de Historia de América,* no. 113 (Jan – June 92), pp. 21 – 64.

History

Boggio de Harasymowicz, Adriana. Movimientos populares e independencia en México y Uruguay. *La Palabra y el Hombre,* no. 82 (Apr – June 92), pp. 107 – 142. Bibl.

Fernández Cabrelli, Alfonso. María Juárez, una desconocida luchadora artiguista. *Hoy Es Historia,* v. 10, no. 57 (Apr – May 93), pp. 76 – 77.

Oddone, Juan Antonio. *Uruguay entre la depresión y la guerra, 1929 – 1945* reviewed by Rosa Perla Raicher. *Estudios Interdisciplinarios de América Latina y el Caribe,* v. 3, no. 2 (July – Dec 92), pp. 129 – 133.

— *Uruguay entre la depresión y la guerra, 1929 – 1945* reviewed by Henry Finch. *Hispanic American Historical Review,* v. 73, no. 3 (Aug 93), p. 526.

Industries

Bértola, Luis. *The Manufacturing Industry of Uruguay, 1913 – 1961: A Sectoral Approach to Growth, Fluctuations, and Crisis* reviewed by Mario Zejan. *Ibero Americana (Sweden),* v. 22, no. 2 (Dec 92), pp. 82 – 85. Bibl.

Intellectual life

Michelena, Alejandro Daniel. Peñas y tertulias culturales en Montevideo. *Hoy Es Historia,* v. 10, no. 57 (Apr – May 93), pp. 33 – 39. Il.

— Valores notables de la cultura uruguaya. *Hoy Es Historia,* v. 10, no. 55 (Jan – Feb 93), pp. 24 – 31. Bibl.

Rocca, Pablo. 35 años en *Marcha:* escritura y ambiente literario en *Marcha* y en el Uruguay, 1939 – 1974. *Nuevo Texto Crítico,* v. 6, no. 11 (1993), pp. 3 – 151. Bibl, il.

Officials and public employees

Alvarez, Carmen R. Los cargos políticos y su incidencia en la estabilidad de los proyectos públicos: los casos de Uruguay y Japón. *Cuadernos del CLAEH,* v. 18, no. 65 – 66 (May 93), pp. 61 – 74. Bibl.

Bervejillo, Federico. El nuevo perfil del intendente: un cambio de curso. *Cuadernos del CLAEH,* v. 18, no. 67 (Nov 93), pp. 11 – 18.

Carminatti, Mario and Jorge Larrañaga. De intendentes a gobernadores: coloquio con los intendentes. *Cuadernos del CLAEH,* v. 18, no. 67 (Nov 93), pp. 19 – 34.

Politics and government

Achard, Diego. *La transición en Uruguay* reviewed by Fernando Errandonea. *Cuadernos del CLAEH,* v. 18, no. 67 (Nov 93), pp. 147 – 155.

Baeza, Cristina. Mauricio Rosencof: "Ni me bajo de este barco, ni cambio de capitán." *Casa de las Américas,* no. 191 (Apr – June 93), pp. 124 – 131.

Dutrénit, Silvia. Visiones de la crisis nacional que influyeron en el programa del movimiento obrero-popular uruguayo, 1958 – 1965. *Cuadernos Americanos,* no. 42, Nueva época (Nov – Dec 93), pp. 78 – 100. Bibl.

Gillespie, Charles Guy. *Negotiating Democracy: Politicians and Generals in Uruguay* reviewed by Howard Handelman. *Journal of Latin American Studies,* v. 25, no. 1 (Feb 93), pp. 218 – 219.

— *Negotiating Democracy: Politicians and Generals in Uruguay* reviewed by Silvia Dutrénit Bielous. *Revista Mexicana de Sociología,* v. 54, no. 1 (Jan – Mar 92), pp. 326 – 330.

Lanzaro, Jorge Luis. La "doble transición" en el Uruguay: gobierno de partidos y neo-presidencialismo. *Nueva Sociedad,* no. 128 (Nov – Dec 93), pp. 132 – 147.

Peixoto, Martín. Crisis de la deliberación. *Cuadernos del CLAEH,* v. 18, no. 67 (Nov 93), pp. 69 – 79.

Waksman, Guillermo. Uruguay: la gran derrota de Lacalle. *Nueva Sociedad,* no. 124 (Mar – Apr 93), pp. 17 – 21.

Bibliography

Sondrol, Paul C. Explaining and Reconceptualizing Underdevelopment: Paraguay and Uruguay (Review article). *Latin American Research Review,* v. 28, no. 3 (1993), pp. 235 – 250. Bibl.

Race question
Research

Sanz, Mónica et al. Blood Group Frequencies and the Question of Race Mixture in Uruguay. *Interciencia,* v. 18, no. 1 (Jan – Feb 93), pp. 29 – 32. Bibl, tables.

URUGUAYAN POETRY
Bibliography

Yáñez, Silvia. Poesía uruguaya (Review article). *Plural (Mexico),* v. 22, no. 258 (Mar 93), p. 79.

Black authors
Translations

Afro-Uruguayan Poetry (Poems by Juan Julio Arrascaeta, Cristina Rodríguez Cabral, José Emilio Cardoso, Manuel Angel Duarte López, Francisco Guatimí, and Beatriz Santos Arrascaeta). *Afro-Hispanic Review,* v. 12, no. 2 (Fall 93), pp. 37 – 47.

History and criticism

Trigo, Abril. Poesía uruguaya actual: los más jóvenes. *Hispamérica,* v. 22, no. 64 – 65 (Apr – Aug 93), pp. 121 – 124.

USIGLI, RODOLFO
Criticism and interpretation

Beardsell, Peter R. *A Theatre for Cannibals: Rodolfo Usigli and the Mexican Stage* reviewed by Frank Dauster. *Hispanic Review,* v. 61, no. 2 (Spring 93), pp. 306 – 308.

USLAR PIETRI, ARTURO
Biobibliography

Uslar Pietri, Arturo. Arturo Uslar Pietri: una biografía intelectual (Interview transcribed and edited by Rubén López Marroquín). *Cuadernos Americanos,* no. 40, Nueva época (July – Aug 93), pp. 146 – 163.

Criticism and interpretation

Ferreira de Cassone, Florencia. Arturo Uslar Pietri: historia y pasión de América. *Cuadernos Americanos,* no. 40, Nueva época (July – Aug 93), pp. 125 – 145. Bibl.

USSR
See
  Soviet Union

UTO-AZTECAN LANGUAGES
See
  Names of specific languages

UTOPIAS

Aínsa Amigues, Fernando. *Necesidad de la utopía* reviewed by Edgar Montiel (Review entitled "Fernando Aínsa: expedición a utopía"). *Plural (Mexico),* v. 22, no. 261 (June 93), pp. 91 – 92.

Baptiste, Victor N. *Bartolomé de las Casas and Thomas More's Utopia: Connections and Similarities; A Translation and Study* reviewed by Juan Durán Luzio. *Latin American Indian Literatures Journal,* v. 9, no. 1 (Spring 93), pp. 83 – 85.

Burgos, Nidia. Un documento inédito de Martínez Estrada: la creación de otra *Tierra purpúrea;* una república libertaria, federal y representativa. *Cuadernos Americanos,* no. 42, Nueva época (Nov – Dec 93), pp. 157 – 164. Bibl.

Cerutti Guldberg, Horacio V. Hacia la utopía de nuestra América. *Ibero-Amerikanisches Archiv,* v. 18, no. 3 – 4 (1992), pp. 455 – 465. Bibl.

Cró, Stelio. *The Noble Savage: Allegory of Freedom* reviewed by Dianne M. Bono. *Colonial Latin American Review,* v. 2, no. 1 – 2 (1993), pp. 288 – 290.

En todas partes la utopía. *La Palabra y el Hombre,* no. 81 (Jan – Mar 92), pp. 328 – 329.

Gómez Tabanera, José Manuel. Reencuentro desde la otra orilla: utopía europea, utopía indiana y utopía del Pacífico. *Boletín de la Academia Nacional de la Historia (Venezuela),* v. 75, no. 297 (Jan – Mar 92), pp. 5 – 20. Bibl.

Mestre, Juan Carlos. El discurso de la utopía en la poética de Gonzalo Rojas. *Chasqui,* v. 22, no. 1 (May 93), pp. 42 – 46.

Pastor, Beatriz. Utopía y conquista: dinámica utópica e identidad colonial. *Revista de Crítica Literaria Latinoamericana,* v. 19, no. 38 (July – Dec 93), pp. 105 – 113.

Pérez Villacampa, Gilberto. Utopía y marxismo: notas para un estudio. *Islas,* no. 96 (May – Aug 90), pp. 83 – 88.

Rotker, Susana. Simón Rodríguez: utopía y transgresión. *Casa de las Américas,* no. 191 (Apr – June 93), pp. 51 – 57. Bibl.

Sicard, Alain et al. Debate (on the third session of the symposium "Latinoamérica: Nuevas Direcciones en Teoría y Crítica Literarias, III"). *Revista de Crítica Literaria Latinoamericana,* v. 19, no. 38 (July – Dec 93), pp. 131 – 141.

Vidales, Raúl. Fin de la historia: "¿Fin de la utopía?"; frente a los 500 años. *Cristianismo y Sociedad,* v. 30, no. 113 (1992), pp. 53 – 84. Bibl.

Zea, Leopoldo. Vasconcelos y la utopía de la raza cósmica. *Cuadernos Americanos,* no. 37, Nueva época (Jan – Feb 93), pp. 23 – 36. Bibl.

Zemelman Merino, Hugo. Sobre bloqueo histórico y utopía en América Latina. *Estudios Sociológicos,* v. 10, no. 30 (Sept – Dec 92), pp. 809 – 817.

UZTÁRIZ Y TOVAR SUÁREZ DE LOREDA, GERÓNIMO ENRIQUE DE

Briceño Perozo, Mario. Un criollo de Caracas, asistente de Sevilla e intendente de Andalucia. *Boletín de la Academia Nacional de la Historia (Venezuela),* v. 76, no. 302 (Apr – June 93), pp. 35 – 40. Bibl.

Egea López, Antonio. El marqués de Uztáriz, asistente de Sevilla. *Boletín de la Academia Nacional de la Historia (Venezuela),* v. 76, no. 302 (Apr – June 93), pp. 142 – 144.

— El marqués de Uztáriz, un venezolano que gobernó Sevilla. *Boletín de la Academia Nacional de la Historia (Venezuela),* v. 75, no. 297 (Jan – Mar 92), pp. 113 – 116.

VAISMAN, MEYER

Amor E., Mónica. Meyer Vaisman, explorador de significados (Accompanied by an English translation). *Art Nexus,* no. 7 (Jan – Mar 93), pp. 129 – 131. Il.

VALADEZ, JOHN
Art reproductions

Valadez, John. Reproduction of *Revelations* by John Valadez. *The Americas Review,* v. 21, no. 1 (Spring 93), p. 39.

VALDÉS, HERNÁN
Criticism of specific works
Tejas verdes

Hunsaker, Steven V. The Problematics of the Representative Self: The Case of *Tejas verdes. Hispanic Journal,* v. 13, no. 2 (Fall 92), pp. 353 – 361. Bibl.

VALDIVIA, LUIS DE

Zapater Equioiz, Horacio. El padre Luis de Valdivia y la guerra defensiva. *Mensaje,* v. 42, no. 420 (July 93), pp. 220 – 223. Il.

VALDIVIESO, MERCEDES
Obituaries

Montecino Aguirre, Sonia. Mercedes Valdivieso: escritura y vida. *Mensaje,* v. 42, no. 422 (Sept 93), p. 463.

VALENCIA AVARIA, LUIS

Obituaries

Ramón Folch, Armando de. Don Luis Valencia Avaria. *Boletín de la Academia Chilena de la Historia,* v. 58 – 59, no. 102 (1991 – 1992), pp. 19 – 24.

VALENZUELA, LUISA

Criticism of specific works

Cambio de armas

Bilbija, Ksenija. "La palabra asesino" de Luisa Valenzuela: la entrada en la lengua. *Confluencia,* v. 8, no. 1 (Fall 92), pp. 159 – 164.

Magnarelli, Sharon Dishaw. El significante deseo en *Cambio de armas* de Luisa Valenzuela. *Escritura (Venezuela),* v. 16, no. 31 – 32 (Jan – Dec 91), pp. 161 – 169.

Rojas-Trempe, Lady. Apuntes sobre *Cambio de armas* de Luisa Valenzuela. *Letras Femeninas,* v. 19, no. 1 – 2 (Spring – Fall 93), pp. 74 – 83. Bibl.

Donde viven las águilas

Thompkins, Cynthia. La construcción del subalterno en *Homérica latina* de Marta Traba y *Libro que no muerde* y *Donde viven las águilas* de Luisa Valenzuela. *Confluencia,* v. 8, no. 1 (Fall 92), pp. 31 – 37. Bibl.

Libro que no muerde

Thompkins, Cynthia. La construcción del subalterno en *Homérica latina* de Marta Traba y *Libro que no muerde* y *Donde viven las águilas* de Luisa Valenzuela. *Confluencia,* v. 8, no. 1 (Fall 92), pp. 31 – 37. Bibl.

Realidad nacional desde la cama

Magnarelli, Sharon Dishaw. The Spectacle of Reality in Luisa Valenzuela's *Realidad nacional vista desde la cama. Letras Femeninas,* v. 19, no. 1 – 2 (Spring – Fall 93), pp. 65 – 73. Bibl.

Muñoz Cadima, Willy Oscar. Luisa Valenzuela: tautología lingüística y/o realidad nacional. *Revista Canadiense de Estudios Hispánicos,* v. 17, no. 2 (Winter 93), pp. 333 – 342. Bibl.

VALERO, ARIEL

Criticism and interpretation

Leyva, Daniel. Ariel Valero. *Nexos,* v. 16, no. 190 (Oct 93), p. 21.

VALLBONA, RIMA DE

Criticism and interpretation

Parham, Mary Helene. Men in the Short Stories of Rima de Vallbona. *Confluencia,* v. 8, no. 1 (Fall 92), pp. 39 – 49. Bibl.

Criticism of specific works

Cosecha de pecadores

Rosas, Yolanda. Hacia una identidad en *Cosecha de pecadores* de Rima de Vallbona. *The Americas Review,* v. 19, no. 3 – 4 (Winter 91), pp. 134 – 145. Bibl.

Noche en vela

Durán Cubillo, Ofelia. Rasgos del relato moderno en el orden temporal de *Noche en vela. Káñina,* v. 16, no. 2 (July – Dec 92), pp. 9 – 16. Tables, charts.

VALLE, RAFAEL HELIODORO

Correspondence, reminiscences, etc.

Valle, Rafael Heliodoro. Buzón de fantasmas: páginas de un diario. *Vuelta,* v. 17, no. 200 (July 93), p. 80.

VALLE-ARIZPE, ARTEMIO DE

Correspondence, reminiscences, etc.

Valle-Arizpe, Artemio de. Buzón de fantasmas: de Artemio de Valle-Arizpe a Ermilo Abreu Gómez. *Vuelta,* v. 17, no. 202 (Sept 93), pp. 71 – 72.

VALLE Y CAVIEDES, JUAN DEL

Criticism and interpretation

Costigan, Lúcia Helena Santiago. *A sátira e o intelectual criollo na colônia: Gregório de Matos e Juan del Valle y Caviedes* reviewed by Pedro Carlos L. Fonseca. *Colonial Latin American Review,* v. 2, no. 1 – 2 (1993), pp. 300 – 302.

López Estrada, Francisco. Los olvidados: Juan del Valle y Caviedes. *Insula,* no. 563 (Nov 93), p. 3. Il.

VALLEJO, CÉSAR ABRAHAM

Criticism and interpretation

Arévalo P., Milcíades. Coral para César Vallejo. *Plural (Mexico),* v. 22, no. 264 (Sept 93), pp. 88 – 92.

Canfield, Martha L. Muerte y redención en la poesía de César Vallejo. *Inti,* no. 36 (Fall 92), pp. 39 – 44. Bibl.

Chang-Rodríguez, Eugenio. Las crónicas posmodernistas de César Vallejo. *Inti,* no. 36 (Fall 92), pp. 11 – 22. Bibl.

Chisalita, Ruxandra. El tormentoso goce de la profanación en César Vallejo y Ramón López Velarde. *Casa de las Américas,* no. 189 (Oct – Dec 92), pp. 58 – 64.

Coddou Peebles, Marcelo. Proyección de Vallejo en la poesía de Gonzalo Rojas. *Revista Chilena de Literatura,* no. 41 (Apr 93), pp. 113 – 118. Bibl.

Delgado Molina, Teresa. Ideología de la expresión en la obra poética de César Vallejo: apuntes al pie de un siglo. *Casa de las Américas,* no. 189 (Oct – Dec 92), pp. 43 – 50.

Ferrari, Américo. La presencia del Perú. *Inti,* no. 36 (Fall 92), pp. 29 – 37.

Gazzolo, Ana María. El cubismo y la poética vallejiana. *Cuadernos Hispanoamericanos,* no. 510 (Dec 92), pp. 31 – 42. Il.

Gerendas, Judit. Imágenes y símbolos en algunos textos poéticos de César Vallejo. *Revista Nacional de Cultura (Venezuela),* v. 54, no. 287 (Oct – Dec 92), pp. 188 – 196. Il.

Gutiérrez Girardot, Rafael. César Vallejo y Walter Benjamin. *Cuadernos Hispanoamericanos,* no. 520 (Oct 93), pp. 55 – 72. Bibl, il.

León, Eleázar. Los días visionarios de Vallejo. *Revista Nacional de Cultura (Venezuela),* v. 54, no. 287 (Oct – Dec 92), pp. 217 – 220.

Llebot Cazalis, Amaya. César Vallejo y la guerra civil española. *Revista Nacional de Cultura (Venezuela),* v. 54, no. 287 (Oct – Dec 92), pp. 206 – 216. Bibl, il.

Martos, Marco. Imágenes paternas en la poesía de César Vallejo. *Casa de las Américas,* no. 189 (Oct – Dec 92), pp. 14 – 20.

Montaldo, Graciela R. Vallejo y las formas del pasado. *Revista Nacional de Cultura (Venezuela),* v. 54, no. 287 (Oct – Dec 92), pp. 178 – 187. Bibl, il.

Ortega, Julio. Cien años de Vallejo. *Inti,* no. 36 (Fall 92), pp. 3 – 10.

Osorio Tejeda, Nelson. Vallejo, autor teatral. *Revista Nacional de Cultura (Venezuela),* v. 54, no. 287 (Oct – Dec 92), pp. 197 – 205. Bibl, facs.

Ostria González, Mauricio. Gabriela Mistral y César Vallejo: la americanidad como desgarramiento. *Revista Chilena de Literatura,* no. 42 (Aug 93), pp. 193 – 199. Bibl.

Paoli, Roberto. Vallejo: herencia ideal y herencia creadora. *Inti,* no. 36 (Fall 92), pp. 51 – 57. Bibl.

Rodríguez Rivera, Guillermo. La elegía familiar de *Los heraldos negros* a *Trilce. Casa de las Américas,* no. 189 (Oct – Dec 92), pp. 51 – 56.

Sánchez Aguilera, Osmar. Del antetexto al texto: transición de normas y permanencia de Vallejo. *Casa de las Américas,* no. 189 (Oct – Dec 92), pp. 82 – 93.

Vélez, Julio. Estética del trabajo y la modernidad autóctona. *Casa de las Américas,* no. 189 (Oct – Dec 92), pp. 71 – 80.

Vitier, Cintio. Notas en el centenario de Vallejo. *Casa de las Américas,* no. 189 (Oct – Dec 92), pp. 7 – 13.

Yurkievich, Saúl. César Vallejo: la vigencia del rechazo. *Inti,* no. 36 (Fall 92), pp. 23 – 28.

Criticism of specific works
El acento me pende del zapato
Guzmán, Jorge. César Vallejo: "El acento me pende del zapato." *Inti,* no. 36 (Fall 92), pp. 45 – 50.

Considerando en frío, imparcialmente . . .
Reyero, Loló. Considerando . . . "Considerando en frío, imparcialmente . . . " (Includes the poem). *Inti,* no. 36 (Fall 92), pp. 81 – 88.

Hoy me gusta la vida mucho menos
Tono, Lucía. La pluralidad semántica en "Hoy me gusta la vida mucho menos" (Includes the poem). *Inti,* no. 36 (Fall 92), pp. 75 – 80.

Parado en una piedra . . .
Sacido Romero, Alberto. Dinámica paradójica en "Parado en una piedra . . . " (Includes the poem). *Inti,* no. 36 (Fall 92), pp. 89 – 96.

Quedéme a calentar la tinta
Santaballa, Sylvia R. El taller o el "abrecabezas" poético: análisis de "Quedéme a calentar la tinta" (Includes the poem). *Inti,* no. 36 (Fall 92), pp. 97 – 104.

Quisiera hoy ser feliz
Chorba, Carrie C. Coloquio y silencio en "Quisiera hoy ser feliz" (Includes the poem). *Inti,* no. 36 (Fall 92), pp. 105 – 110.

Trilce
Escalante, Evodio. Retornar a *Trilce:* hacia una lectura afirmativa de la poesía de César Vallejo. *Casa de las Américas,* no. 189 (Oct – Dec 92), pp. 65 – 70.

Hernández Novás, Raúl. El poema "preliminar" de *Trilce. Casa de las Américas,* no. 189 (Oct – Dec 92), pp. 21 – 28. Bibl.

Lemaître, Monique J. Análisis de *Trilce I* de César Vallejo: poema de la creación, del nacimiento del poeta y del Perú. *Casa de las Américas,* no. 189 (Oct – Dec 92), pp. 29 – 34. Bibl.

Suardíaz, Luis. Principalmente *Trilce. Casa de las Américas,* no. 189 (Oct – Dec 92), pp. 36 – 42.

El tungsteno
Díaz, Lisiak-Land. Jerarquía social y económica en *El tungsteno* de César Vallejo. *Inti,* no. 36 (Fall 92), pp. 59 – 71. Bibl, charts.

VALLENILLA LANZ, LAUREANO
Salcedo Picón, Jesús M. El pensamiento de Laureano Vallenilla Lanz. *Revista Nacional de Cultura (Venezuela),* v. 54, no. 287 (Oct – Dec 92), pp. 32 – 36. Bibl, il.

VALPARAÍSO, CHILE (CITY)
Ossandón Widow, María Eugenia. Proyecto para un plano de Valparaíso, 1675 – 1700. *Historia (Chile),* no. 26 (1991 – 1992), pp. 247 – 258. Bibl.

Salinas Meza, René. Una comunidad inmigrante: los alemanes en Valparaíso, 1860 – 1960; estudio demográfico. *Jahrbuch für Geschichte von Staat, Wirtschaft und Gesellschaft Lateinamerikas,* v. 29 (1992), pp. 309 – 342. Bibl, tables, charts.

VALUES
See
Ethics

VARELA, CARLOS MANUEL
Interviews
Bravo-Elizondo, Pedro. Teatro en el Cono Sur: Carlos Manuel Varela (Uruguay). *Latin American Theatre Review,* v. 26, no. 2 (Spring 93), pp. 143 – 150.

VARGAS, ANDRÉS
Interviews
Saavedra, Gonzalo. Para Andrés, la esperanza está en Bitkine. *Mensaje,* v. 42, no. 417 (Mar – Apr 93), pp. 104 – 105. Il.

VARGAS, DIEGO DE
Correspondence, reminiscences, etc.
Vargas, Diego de. *By Force of Arms: The Journals of Don Diego de Vargas, New Mexico, 1691 – 1693* edited and translated by John L. Kessell and Rick Hendricks. Reviewed by Timothy K. Perttula. *Colonial Latin American Historical Review,* v. 2, no. 3 (Summer 93), pp. 380 – 382.

— *By Force of Arms: The Journals of Don Diego de Vargas, New Mexico, 1691 – 1693* edited and translated by John L. Kessel and Rick Hendricks. Reviewed by Mark A. Burkholder. *Hispanic American Historical Review,* v. 73, no. 3 (Aug 93), pp. 510 – 511.

— *Letters from the New World: Selected Correspondence of Don Diego de Vargas to His Family, 1675 – 1706* edited and translated by John L. Kessell, Rick Hendricks, and Meredith D. Dodge. Reviewed by Jennifer L. Zimnoch. *The Americas Review,* v. 21, no. 1 (Spring 93), pp. 123 – 124.

— *Letters from the New World: Selected Correspondence of Don Diego de Vargas to His Family, 1675 – 1706* edited and translated by John L. Kessel, Rick Hendricks, and Meredith D. Dodge. Reviewed by Mark A. Burkholder. *Hispanic American Historical Review,* v. 73, no. 3 (Aug 93), pp. 510 – 511.

VARGAS, ENRIQUE
Interviews
Gutiérrez, Natalia. *El hilo de Ariadna:* laberinto de oscuridad (Accompanied by an English translation). *Art Nexus,* no. 8 (Apr – June 93), pp. 102 – 104. Il.

VARGAS, EUGENIA
Tejada, Roberto. Eugenia Vargas: el proscenio inevitable (Translated by Paloma Díaz Abreu). *Artes de México,* no. 21 (Fall 93), pp. 98 – 99. Il.

VARGAS, GETÚLIO
Nascimento, Benedicto Heloiz. Pensamento e atuação de Vargas. *Vozes,* v. 86, no. 4 (July – Aug 92), pp. 22 – 28.

VARGAS LLOSA, MARIO
Biography
Krauze, Enrique. Perú y Vargas Llosa: vidas variopintas. *Vuelta,* v. 17, no. 199 (June 93), pp. 17 – 20.

Correspondence, reminiscences, etc.
Vargas Llosa, Mario. *El pez en el agua* reviewed by Carlos Tello Díaz (Review entitled "Un pez fuera del agua"). *Nexos,* v. 16, no. 187 (July 93), pp. 81 – 83.

— *El pez en el agua* reviewed by Fabienne Bradu (Review entitled "Vida y biografía"). *Vuelta,* v. 17, no. 200 (July 93), pp. 54 – 55.

— *El pez en el agua* reviewed by Luis Pásara (Review entitled "Adiós al poder"). *Debate (Peru),* v. 16, no. 73 (June – Aug 93), pp. 64 – 67. Il.

— *El pez en el agua* reviewed by Marco Martos (Review entitled "Las memorias de tres novelistas peruanos"). *Debate (Peru),* v. 16, no. 73 (June – Aug 93), pp. 68 – 72. Il.

Criticism and interpretation
Compitello, Malcolm Alan. Reflexiones sobre el acto de narrar: Benet, Vargas Llosa y Euclides da Cunha. *Insula,* no. 559 – 560 (July – Aug 93), pp. 19 – 22.

Gutiérrez Mouat, Ricardo. Vargas Llosa's Poetics of the Novel and Camus' *Rebel. World Literature Today,* v. 67, no. 2 (Spring 93), pp. 283 – 290. Bibl, il.

Rivera-Rodas, Oscar. *El metateatro y la dramática de Vargas Llosa: hacia una poética del espectador* reviewed by Juan Villegas. *Revista Interamericana de Bibliografía,* v. 42, no. 4 (1992), pp. 661 – 662.

Standish, Peter. Contemplating Your Own Novel: The Case of Mario Vargas Llosa. *Hispanic Review,* v. 61, no. 1 (Winter 93), pp. 53 – 63. Bibl.

Criticism of specific works
Conversación en la catedral
Meneses, Carlos. Norwin y Carlitos, los periodistas de *Conversación en la catedral. La Palabra y el Hombre,* no. 84 (Oct – Dec 92), pp. 321 – 329. Il.

La guerra del fin del mundo

Bernucci, Leopoldo M. *Historia de un malentendido: un estudio transtextual de 'La guerra del fin del mundo' de Mario Vargas Llosa* reviewed by Sara Castro-Klarén. *Hispanic Review*, v. 61, no. 1 (Winter 93), pp. 133 – 134.

El hablador

Fornet, Jorge. Dos novelas peruanas: entre sapos y halcones. *Plural (Mexico)*, v. 22, no. 263 (Aug 93), pp. 57 – 62.

Historia de Mayta

Angvik, Birger. La risa que se vuelve mueca: el doble filo del humor y de la risa: *Historia de Mayta* frente a la crítica en Lima. *Káñina*, v. 16, no. 1 (Jan – June 92), pp. 91 – 109. Bibl.

Grandis, Rita de. La problemática del conocimiento histórico en *Historia de Mayta* de M. Vargas Llosa. *Revista de Crítica Literaria Latinoamericana*, v. 19, no. 38 (July – Dec 93), pp. 375 – 382. Bibl.

El pez en el agua

Sánchez Arnosi, Milagros. Vargas Llosa, en primera persona. *Cuadernos Hispanoamericanos*, no. 520 (Oct 93), pp. 102 – 105.

Interviews

Kushigian, Julia A. Mario Vargas Llosa. *Hispamérica*, v. 21, no. 63 (Dec 92), pp. 35 – 42.

VARGAS MARÍN, DENNIS

Interviews

Alvarez Rodrich, Augusto et al. Entrevista a Dennis Vargas Marín. *Debate (Peru)*, v. 16, no. 75 (Dec 93 – Jan 94), pp. 6 – 14. Il.

VARGAS MÉNDEZ, CARLOS ENRIQUE

Aguilar, Pilar. El maestro Carlos Enrique Vargas y su metodología en la enseñanza del piano. *Káñina*, v. 16, no. 1 (Jan – June 92), pp. 267 – 272. Il.

VARILLAS, ALBERTO

Interviews

Cisneros, Luis Jaime et al. La educación: ¿Reforma con futuro? *Debate (Peru)*, v. 16, no. 72 (Mar – May 93), pp. 20 – 27. Il, charts.

VARNHAGEN, FRANCISCO ADOLPHO DE

Lacombe, Américo Jacobina. A construção da historiografia brasileira: o IHGB e a obra de Varnhagen. *Revista do Instituto Histórico e Geográfico Brasileiro*, no. 370 (Jan – Mar 91), pp. 245 – 264.

VARON, BENNO WEISER

Correspondence, reminiscences, etc.

Varon, Benno Weiser. *Professions of a Lucky Jew* reviewed by Ignacio Klich. *Journal of Latin American Studies*, v. 25, no. 2 (May 93), pp. 430 – 431.

VASCONCELOS, JOSÉ

Gallegos, Carlos. Pensamiento y acción política de José Vasconcelos. *Revista Mexicana de Ciencias Políticas y Sociales*, v. 37, Nueva época, no. 149 (July – Sept 92), pp. 125 – 138. Bibl.

Pérez Priego, Rosalba. Las mujeres en Vasconcelos. *La Palabra y el Hombre*, no. 81 (Jan – Mar 92), pp. 341 – 348. Bibl.

Zea, Leopoldo. Vasconcelos y la utopía de la raza cósmica. *Cuadernos Americanos*, no. 37, Nueva época (Jan – Feb 93), pp. 23 – 36. Bibl.

VÁSQUEZ, ANA

Criticism and interpretation

Araújo, Helena. Las huellas del "propio camino" en los relatos de Ana Vásquez. *Escritura (Venezuela)*, v. 16, no. 31 – 32 (Jan – Dec 91), pp. 9 – 16. Bibl.

VAZ FERREIRA, CARLOS

Michelena, Alejandro Daniel. Vaz Ferreira, filósofo de cercanías. *Hoy Es Historia*, v. 10, no. 58 (July – Aug 93), pp. 4 – 9. Il.

Romero Baró, José María. Ciencia y filosofía en el pensador uruguayo Carlos Vaz Ferreira. *Hoy Es Historia*, v. 10, no. 58 (July – Aug 93), pp. 10 – 14. Bibl.

Wapnir, Salomón. Carlos Vaz Ferreira: entrevista en 1929. *Hoy Es Historia*, v. 10, no. 58 (July – Aug 93), pp. 15 – 18. Il.

VÁZQUEZ, TABARÉ

Klein, Darío and Fabián Lazovski. Tabaré Vázquez, un líder bien imaginado. *Cuadernos del CLAEH*, v. 18, no. 67 (Nov 93), pp. 37 – 52. Bibl.

VÁZQUEZ DE CORONADO, FRANCISCO

Mora Valcárcel, Carmen de. *Las siete ciudades de Cíbola: textos y testimonios sobre la expedición de Vázquez Coronado* reviewed by Francisco Noguerol Jiménez. *Anuario de Estudios Americanos*, v. 50, no. 1 (1993), pp. 323 – 324.

VEGA, ANA LYDIA

Criticism and interpretation

Captain-Hidalgo, Yvonne. El espíritu de la risa en el cuento de Ana Lydia Vega. *Revista Iberoamericana*, v. 59, no. 162 – 163 (Jan – June 93), pp. 301 – 308. Bibl.

Daroqui, María Julia. Palabra de mujer. *Escritura (Venezuela)*, v. 16, no. 31 – 32 (Jan – Dec 91), pp. 53 – 63. Bibl.

Gelpí, Juan G. Ana Lydia Vega: ante el debate de la cultura nacional de Puerto Rico. *Revista Chilena de Literatura*, no. 42 (Aug 93), pp. 95 – 99.

González, Aníbal. Ana Lydia Pluravega: unidad y multiplicidad caribeñas en la obra de Ana Lydia Vega. *Revista Iberoamericana*, v. 59, no. 162 – 163 (Jan – June 93), pp. 289 – 300. Bibl.

Interviews

Matibag, Eugenio D. Ana Lydia Vega. *Hispamérica*, v. 22, no. 64 – 65 (Apr – Aug 93), pp. 77 – 88.

VEGA CARPIO, LOPE FÉLIX DE

Criticism and interpretation

Shannon, Robert M. *Visions of the New World in the Drama of Lope de Vega* reviewed by James Mandrell. *Hispanic Review*, v. 61, no. 1 (Winter 93), pp. 100 – 102.

Criticism of specific works

El Nuevo Mundo descubierto por Cristóbal Colón

Berrettini, Célia. O teatro de Lope de Vega e o descobrimento da América. *Vozes*, v. 86, no. 4 (July – Aug 92), pp. 66 – 71. Il, facs.

VEGETABLES

See
> Botany
> Horticulture
> Names of specific vegetables

VEGETATION AND CLIMATE

See also
> Geographical distribution of plants and animals
> Subdivision *Climate* under names of specific countries

Latin America

Villagrán M., Carolina. Una interpretación climática del registro palinológico del último ciclo glacial – postglacial en Sudamérica. *Bulletin de l'Institut Français d'Etudes Andines*, v. 22, no. 1 (1993), pp. 243 – 258. Bibl, maps, charts.

Peru

Ferreyra, Ramón. Registros de la vegetación en la costa peruana en relación con el fenómeno El Niño. *Bulletin de l'Institut Français d'Etudes Andines*, v. 22, no. 1 (1993), pp. 259 – 266. Bibl, il, tables, maps.

Rodríguez, Rodolfo et al. Avances sobre estudios dendrocronológicos en la región costera norte del Perú para obtener un registro pasado del fenómeno El Niño. *Bulletin de l'Institut Français d'Etudes Andines*, v. 22, no. 1 (1993), pp. 267 – 281. Bibl, il, tables, maps, charts.

Sources

Morlon, Pierre. De las relaciones entre clima de altura y agricultura de la sierra del Perú en los textos de los siglos XVI y XVII. *Bulletin de l'Institut Français d'Etudes Andines,* v. 21, no. 3 (1992), pp. 929 – 959. Bibl, maps.

Venezuela

Cova, Maritza and Teresa Vegas Vilarrubia. Estudio sobre la distribución y ecología de macrofitos acuáticos en el embalse de Guri. *Interciencia,* v. 18, no. 2 (Mar – Apr 93), pp. 77 – 82. Bibl, tables, maps, charts.

VELASCO PIÑA, ANTONIO
Criticism of specific works
Regina

Mejía Madrid, Fabrizio. El nuevo retorno de los brujos. *Nexos,* v. 16, no. 190 (Oct 93), pp. 53 – 63.

VENEGAS, DANIEL
Criticism of specific works
Las aventuras de don Chipote o cuando los pericos mamen

Robles, Oscar. *Las aventuras de don Chipote o cuando los pericos mamen:* el retrato del hambre. *La Palabra y el Hombre,* no. 81 (Jan – Mar 92), pp. 332 – 338.

VENEREAL DISEASES

Agüero, Abel Luis. Desde Colón y la sífilis al hombre contemporáneo y el SIDA. *Todo Es Historia,* v. 26, no. 306 (Jan 93), pp. 74 – 85. Il.

Elias, Christopher. Enfermedades transmitidas sexualmente y la salud reproductiva de las mujeres en los países en vías de desarrollo. *Fem,* v. 17, no. 124 (June 93), pp. 26 – 29. Bibl.

VENEZUELA
See also
Actors and actresses – Venezuela
Agriculture – Venezuela
Agriculture, Cooperative – Venezuela
Agriculture and state – Venezuela
Amacuro, Venezuela
Architecture – Venezuela
Archives – Venezuela
Art – Venezuela
Artists – Venezuela
Augustinians – Venezuela
Barinas, Venezuela (State)
Biography (as a literary form) – Venezuela
Biotechnology – Venezuela
Blacks – Venezuela
Blacks in literature – Venezuela
Botany – Venezuela
Caciquism – Venezuela
Calabozo, Venezuela
Capuchins – Venezuela
Caracas, Venezuela
Carúpano, Venezuela
Catholic Church – Venezuela
Chocolate and cacao – Venezuela
Church and social problems – Venezuela
Church and state – Venezuela
Cities and towns – Venezuela
Coal mines and mining – Venezuela
Coasts – Venezuela
Conservatism – Venezuela
Corruption (in politics) – Venezuela
Crime and criminals – Venezuela
Criminal law – Venezuela
Dams and reservoirs – Venezuela
Diseases – Venezuela
Dissertations, Academic – Venezuela
Earthquakes – Venezuela
Ecology and development – Venezuela
Education – Venezuela
Education, Primary – Venezuela
Elite (Social sciences) – Venezuela
Emblems, National – Venezuela
Environmental policy – Venezuela
Europeans – Venezuela
Family – Venezuela
Finance, Public – Venezuela
Fishing – Venezuela
Folk dancing – Venezuela

Folk drama – Venezuela
Folk festivals – Venezuela
Food industry and trade – Venezuela
Food supply – Venezuela
Forestry – Venezuela
Forests – Venezuela
Freedom of the press – Venezuela
Gas, Natural – Venezuela
Geography – Venezuela
Guanare, Venezuela
Guerrillas – Venezuela
Haciendas – Venezuela
Highways – Venezuela
Human rights – Venezuela
Jesuits – Venezuela
Journalism – Venezuela
Labor laws and legislation – Venezuela
Labor relations – Venezuela
Land reform – Venezuela
Land tenure – Venezuela
Liberalism – Venezuela
Libraries and librarians – Venezuela
Literature and history – Venezuela
Literature and society – Venezuela
Local government – Venezuela
Maracaibo, Venezuela
Marriage – Venezuela
Martyrs – Venezuela
Medicine – Venezuela
Mérida, Venezuela (City)
Mérida, Venezuela (State)
Missions – Venezuela
Names, Geographical – Venezuela
Nationalism – Venezuela
Natural disasters – Venezuela
Natural resources – Venezuela
Oral tradition – Venezuela
Parks – Venezuela
Periodicals – Venezuela
Philosophy – Venezuela
Physicians – Venezuela
Physics – Venezuela
Political parties – Venezuela
Political sociology – Venezuela
Politics in literature – Venezuela
Pollution – Venezuela
Portuguese – Venezuela
Postmodernism – Venezuela
Poverty – Venezuela
Press and politics – Venezuela
Public health – Venezuela
Quality of life – Venezuela
Real property – Venezuela
Rivers – Venezuela
San Juan de Colón, Venezuela
San Sebastián de los Reyes, Venezuela
School management and organization – Venezuela
Scientific expeditions – Venezuela
Scientific research – Venezuela
Socialism – Venezuela
Spaniards – Venezuela
Spanish language – Venezuela
Spanish poetry – Venezuela
Subways – Venezuela
Táchira, Venezuela
Teaching and teachers – Venezuela
Technology and state – Venezuela
Theater – Venezuela
Transportation – Venezuela
Trujillo, Venezuela (State)
Vegetation and climate – Venezuela
Water – Venezuela
Wheat – Venezuela
Women – Venezuela
Women in literature – Venezuela

Biography

Pérez, Ana Mercedes. *Entre el cuento y la historia: 50 años del periodismo* reviewed by Pascual Venegas Filardo. *Revista Nacional de Cultura (Venezuela),* v. 53, no. 286 (July – Sept 92), p. 257.

Boundaries

Hernández Carstens, Eduardo. Conferencia del doctor Eduardo Hernández Carstens . . . , con motivo de conmemorar el 215° de la real cédula de Carlos III de 1777 . . . . *Boletín de la Academia Nacional de la Historia (Venezuela),* v. 75, no. 300 (Oct – Dec 92), pp. 21 – 27.

Civilization

Liscano Velutini, Juan. Venezuela: cultura y sociedad a fin de siglo. *Inti,* no. 37 – 38 (Spring – Fall 93), pp. 7 – 15.

Foreign influences

Pollak-Eltz, Angelina. Aportes españoles a la cultura popular venezolana. *Montalbán,* no. 24 (1992), pp. 167 – 219. Bibl.

Commerce

History

Lucena Salmoral, Manuel. *Características del comercio exterior de la provincia de Caracas durante el sexenio revolucionario, 1807 – 1812* reviewed by Adriana Rodríguez. *Revista de Historia de América,* no. 113 (Jan – June 92), pp. 173 – 174.

Constitutional law

Serrano Páez, J. Ezio. Estado, nación y patria en los debates constitucionales de 1830 y 1858: consideraciones historiográficas. *Montalbán,* no. 24 (1992), pp. 221 – 251. Bibl.

Description and travel

Sources

Brander, Laurs. Del diario de navegación del capitán Laurs Brander del bergantín *Fortuna* de Gotemburgo, 6/4 al 21/4 de 1732. *Boletín de la Academia Nacional de la Historia (Venezuela),* v. 75, no. 298 (Apr – June 92), pp. 146 – 150.

Castañón, Adolfo. Diario del delta. *Vuelta,* v. 17, no. 201 (Aug 93), pp. 35 – 42.

Discovery and exploration

Hernández Carstens, Eduardo. Conferencia del doctor Eduardo Hernández Carstens . . . , con motivo de conmemorar el 215º de la real cédula de Carlos III de 1777 . . . . *Boletín de la Academia Nacional de la Historia (Venezuela),* v. 75, no. 300 (Oct – Dec 92), pp. 21 – 27.

Salcedo-Bastardo, José Luis. En los comienzos de América. *Boletín de la Academia Nacional de la Historia (Venezuela),* v. 75, no. 300 (Oct – Dec 92), pp. 120 – 126.

Economic conditions

Egaña, Manuel R. *Obras y ensayos seleccionados* reviewed by Pascual Venegas Filardo. *Revista Nacional de Cultura (Venezuela),* v. 53, no. 286 (July – Sept 92), p. 256.

Economic policy

Egaña, Manuel R. *Obras y ensayos seleccionados* reviewed by Pascual Venegas Filardo. *Revista Nacional de Cultura (Venezuela),* v. 53, no. 286 (July – Sept 92), p. 256.

Jongkind, Coenraad Frederik. Venezuelan Industry under the New Conditions of the 1989 Economic Policy. *European Review of Latin American and Caribbean Studies,* no. 54 (June 93), pp. 65 – 93. Bibl, tables.

Emigration and immigration

Margalies de Gasparini, Luisa. Canarias – Venezuela – Canarias: proceso dinámico de migración y retorno en el siglo XX. *Montalbán,* no. 24 (1992), pp. 271 – 290. Bibl.

Foreign economic relations

Caribbean area

Comunidad del Caribe: Acuerdo sobre Comercio e Inversiones entre el Gobierno de la República de Venezuela y la Comunidad del Caribe (CARICOM). *Integración Latinoamericana,* v. 18, no. 186 (Jan – Feb 93), pp. 69 – 73.

Central America

Acuerdo sobre Comercio e Inversión entre las Repúblicas de Colombia y Venezuela y las Repúblicas de Costa Rica, El Salvador, Guatemala, Honduras y Nicaragua. *Integración Latinoamericana,* v. 18, no. 191 (July 93), pp. 67 – 71.

Foreign relations

Colombia

Bermúdez Merizalde, Jaime. Por la senda de la integración: balance. *Revista Javeriana,* v. 61, no. 594 (May 93), pp. 225 – 237.

Great Britain

Consalvi, Simón Alberto. *Grover Cleveland y la controversia Venezuela – Gran Bretaña* reviewed by H. Michael Tacver. *Hispanic American Historical Review,* v. 73, no. 4 (Nov 93), pp. 727 – 728.

Romania

Informe que envía al Ministerio de Relaciones Exteriores el excelentísimo señor Milos Alcalay, embajador de Venezuela en Rumania, acerca de la misión en Rumania del director de la Academia Nacional de la Historia, dr. Guillermo Morón. *Boletín de la Academia Nacional de la Historia (Venezuela),* v. 75, no. 299 (July – Sept 92), pp. 225 – 231.

History

Arends, Tulio. *Sir Gregor MacGregor, un escocés tras la aventura de América* reviewed by Juvenal López Ruiz. *Revista Nacional de Cultura (Venezuela),* v. 53, no. 286 (July – Sept 92), p. 263.

Arráiz, Antonio. *Los días de la ira: las guerras civiles en Venezuela, 1830 – 1903* reviewed by Raúl Agudo Freites. *Revista Nacional de Cultura (Venezuela),* v. 54, no. 287 (Oct – Dec 92), pp. 261 – 262.

Cipriano Castro y su época reviewed by Pascual Venegas Filardo. *Revista Nacional de Cultura (Venezuela),* v. 53, no. 286 (July – Sept 92), pp. 255 – 256.

Díaz, José Domingo. El terremoto del año de 1812 y nuestra independencia (Previously published in this journal vol. 1, no. 1, 1912). *Boletín de la Academia Nacional de la Historia (Venezuela),* v. 75, no. 300 (Oct – Dec 92), pp. 321 – 326.

Awards

Fuenmayor, Juan Bautista. Palabras del dr. Juan Bautista Fuenmayor, premio nacional de historia Francisco González Guinán, 1991. *Boletín de la Academia Nacional de la Historia (Venezuela),* v. 75, no. 299 (July – Sept 92), pp. 29 – 32.

Bibliography

Jiménez Emán, Gabriel. Notas bibliográficas del catálogo de publicaciones de la Academia Nacional de la Historia. *Boletín de la Academia Nacional de la Historia (Venezuela),* v. 75, no. 298 (Apr – June 92), pp. 99 – 107.

Sources

Acta en la cual Germán Vegas y Lucía Badaracco de Vegas donan a la Academia Nacional de la Historia trece (13) documentos relativos al general de división Lino de Clemente. *Boletín de la Academia Nacional de la Historia (Venezuela),* v. 75, no. 299 (July – Sept 92), pp. 235 – 239.

Jiménez Arraiz, Francisco. Antiguallas: orígenes caraqueños (Previously published in this journal vol. 1, no. 1, 1912). *Boletín de la Academia Nacional de la Historia (Venezuela),* v. 75, no. 300 (Oct – Dec 92), pp. 262 – 273.

Leal, Ildefonso. Palabras pronunciadas por el doctor Ildefonso Leal el día 6 de mayo de 1992, con motivo de la exposición de documentos Portugal – Venezuela en el Archivo Nacional de la Torre do Tombo, en la ciudad universitaria de Lisboa. *Boletín de la Academia Nacional de la Historia (Venezuela),* v. 76, no. 301 (Jan – Mar 93), pp. 41 – 43.

Mörner, Magnus. Breves apuntes sobre nuestro viaje a Ocumare de la costa, del 19 al 20 de julio de 1991. *Boletín de la Academia Nacional de la Historia (Venezuela),* v. 75, no. 298 (Apr – June 92), pp. 141 – 142.

Roscio, Juan Germán. Testamento del señor dr. Juan Germán Roscio (Previously published in this journal, vol. 1, no. 1, 1912). *Boletín de la Academia Nacional de la Historia (Venezuela),* v. 75, no. 300 (Oct – Dec 92), pp. 275 – 278.

Sosa Llanos, Pedro Vicente. Pleitos venezolanos en el Archivo Histórico Nacional de Madrid. *Boletín de la Academia Nacional de la Historia (Venezuela),* v. 75, no. 300 (Oct – Dec 92), pp. 223 – 247.

Industries

Jongkind, Coenraad Frederik. Venezuelan Industry under the New Conditions of the 1989 Economic Policy. *European Review of Latin American and Caribbean Studies,* no. 54 (June 93), pp. 65 – 93. Bibl, tables.

Intellectual life

Alcibíades, Mirla. De cómo una tabacalera devinó en revista cultural. *Revista Nacional de Cultura (Venezuela),* v. 53, no. 286 (July – Sept 92), pp. 167 – 174. Il.

Liscano Velutini, Juan. Polémica venezolana en México. *Vuelta,* v. 17, no. 203 (Oct 93), pp. 53 – 55.

Nuño Montes, Juan Antonio. ¿Qué pasa en Venezuela? *Vuelta,* v. 17, no. 203 (Oct 93), pp. 55 – 56.

Rivas Rivas, José. Una insólita misión cultural. *Revista Nacional de Cultura (Venezuela)*, v. 53, no. 286 (July – Sept 92), pp. 159 – 166. Il.

Segnini, Yolanda. *Los caballeros del postgomecismo* reviewed by Frédérique Langue. *Cahiers des Amériques Latines*, no. 13 (1992), pp. 185 – 186.

Sucre, Guillermo. Los cuadernos de la cordura. *Vuelta*, v. 17, no. 197 (Apr 93), pp. 16 – 18.

Maps

Solano y Pérez-Lila, Francisco de, ed. *Relaciones topográficas de Venezuela, 1815 – 1819* reviewed by María del Carmen Mena García. *Anuario de Estudios Americanos*, v. 49, Suppl. 1 (1992), pp. 258 – 260.

Bibliography

Donís Ríos, Manuel Alberto. Venezuela: topónimo afortunado en la cartografía auroral de América. *Montalbán*, no. 24 (1992), pp. 99 – 118. Bibl, maps.

Officials and public employees

Coromoto Nava Santana, Mayela. Un conflicto entre la Real Audiencia y el Ayuntamiento de Caracas: el nombramiento del Fiel Ejecutor, 1793 – 1797. *Boletín de la Academia Nacional de la Historia (Venezuela)*, v. 75, no. 298 (Apr – June 92), pp. 77 – 85.

Politics and government

Castro Leiva, Luis. The Dictatorship of Virtue or Opulence of Commerce. *Jahrbuch für Geschichte von Staat, Wirtschaft und Gesellschaft Lateinamerikas*, v. 29 (1992), pp. 195 – 240. Bibl.

1830 –

Dávila, Luis Ricardo. Rómulo Betancourt and the Development of Venezuelan Nationalism, 1930 – 1945. *Bulletin of Latin American Research*, v. 12, no. 1 (Jan 93), pp. 49 – 63. Bibl.

Pino Iturrieta, Elías. *Pensamiento conservador del siglo XIX* reviewed by Amaya Llebot Cazalis. *Revista Nacional de Cultura (Venezuela)*, v. 54, no. 287 (Oct – Dec 92), pp. 262 – 264. Il.

Quintero Montiel, Inés Mercedes. *Pensamiento liberal del siglo XIX* reviewed by Amaya Llebot Cazalis. *Revista Nacional de Cultura (Venezuela)*, v. 54, no. 287 (Oct – Dec 92), pp. 264 – 265.

Serrano Páez, J. Ezio. Estado, nación y patria en los debates constitucionales de 1830 y 1858: consideraciones historiográficas. *Montalbán*, no. 24 (1992), pp. 221 – 251. Bibl.

1935 –

Hellinger, Daniel Charles. *Venezuela: Tarnished Democracy* reviewed by Steve Ellner. *Journal of Developing Areas*, v. 28, no. 1 (Oct 93), pp. 142 – 143.

Malaver, Bernardo and Mario Peralta. Venezuela: el inicio de una nueva coyuntura política. *Revista Paraguaya de Sociología*, v. 29, no. 84 (May – Aug 92), pp. 41 – 51. Bibl.

Querales, Juandemaro. El Decreto 321: la iglesia como factor aglutinador de la oposición a los gobiernos de Betancourt y Gallegos. *Boletín de la Academia Nacional de la Historia (Venezuela)*, v. 75, no. 299 (July – Sept 92), pp. 180 – 183. Bibl.

Segnini, Yolanda. *Los caballeros del postgomecismo* reviewed by Frédérique Langue. *Cahiers des Amériques Latines*, no. 13 (1992), pp. 185 – 186.

1958 –

McCoy, Jennifer L. Venezuelan Alternatives. *Hemisphere*, v. 5, no. 2 (Winter – Spring 93), pp. 33 – 35. Tables.

Marta Sosa, Joaquín. Venezuela, 1989 – 1994: cambios, elecciones y balas. *Nueva Sociedad*, no. 124 (Mar – Apr 93), pp. 6 – 10.

Rural conditions

Paredes, Cándido A. Relaciones de la agricultura tradicional con el ausentismo y la deserción escolar: el referente empírico del piedemonte barinés. *Derecho y Reforma Agraria*, no. 24 (1993), pp. 63 – 71.

Wettstein, Germán. El mundo de Cristóbal Sánchez, campesino de los Andes. *Derecho y Reforma Agraria*, no. 24 (1993), pp. 95 – 113. Maps.

Statistics

Research

Mendoza, Héctor and Fabricio Vivas. Informe 1990 – 1991: estadísticas históricas de Venezuela; historia de las finanzas públicas en Venezuela. *Boletín de la Academia Nacional de la Historia (Venezuela)*, v. 75, no. 297 (Jan – Mar 92), pp. 169 – 176.

VENEZUELA IN LITERATURE

Freytez Arrieche, Gustavo A. *Palabreus:* una (re)visión del llano venezolano. *Revista Nacional de Cultura (Venezuela)*, v. 53, no. 286 (July – Sept 92), pp. 50 – 63. Bibl, il.

Guzmán, Patricia. El lugar como absoluto: Vicente Gerbasi, Ramón Palomares y Luis Alberto Crespo. *Inti*, no. 37 – 38 (Spring – Fall 93), pp. 107 – 115. Bibl.

VENEZUELAN LITERATURE

Barrera Linares, Luis, ed. *Memoria y cuento: 30 años de narrativa venezolana, 1960 – 1990* reviewed by Mercedes Franco. *Revista Nacional de Cultura (Venezuela)*, v. 53, no. 286 (July – Sept 92), pp. 262 – 263.

Black authors

Lewis, Marvin A. *Ethnicity and Identity in Contemporary Afro-Venezuelan Literature: A Culturalist Approach* reviewed by Jorge J. Rodríguez-Florido. *Hispania (USA)*, v. 76, no. 2 (May 93), p. 289.

History and criticism

Bermúdez, Manuel. El Orinoco literario: propuesta para una visión diferente de la literatura venezolana. *Revista Nacional de Cultura (Venezuela)*, v. 53, no. 286 (July – Sept 92), pp. 211 – 214.

Jaffé, Verónica. Anotaciones sobre la literatura venezolana. *Inti*, no. 37 – 38 (Spring – Fall 93), pp. 245 – 251.

Lasarte Valcárcel, Francisco Javier. Poéticas de la primera contemporaneidad y cambio intelectual en la narrativa venezolana. *Revista Chilena de Literatura*, no. 41 (Apr 93), pp. 79 – 97. Bibl.

Márquez Rodríguez, Alexis. *Historia y ficción en la novela venezolana* reviewed by R. J. Lovera De-Sola. *Revista Nacional de Cultura (Venezuela)*, v. 53, no. 286 (July – Sept 92), pp. 249 – 251.

Mata, Gonzalo Humberto. Flechas en la incertidumbre. *Inti*, no. 37 – 38 (Spring – Fall 93), pp. 57 – 60.

Mata Gil, Milagros. El espacio de la nostalgia en la escritura venezolana. *Inti*, no. 37 – 38 (Spring – Fall 93), pp. 23 – 28. Bibl.

Ríos, Alicia. La época de la independencia en la narrativa venezolana de los ochenta. *Hispamérica*, v. 22, no. 64 – 65 (Apr – Aug 93), pp. 48 – 54.

Rivera, Francisco. Sobre narrativa venezolana, 1970 – 1990. *Inti*, no. 37 – 38 (Spring – Fall 93), pp. 89 – 96. Bibl.

Rotker, Susana. La crónica venezolana de los '80: una lectura del caos. *Hispamérica*, v. 22, no. 64 – 65 (Apr – Aug 93), pp. 55 – 65. Bibl.

Sambrano Urdaneta, Oscar. Lo trascendental trujillano en sus letras. *Revista Nacional de Cultura (Venezuela)*, v. 53, no. 286 (July – Sept 92), pp. 39 – 49. Il.

Santaella, Juan Carlos. *Manifiestos literarios venezolanos* reviewed by Analy Lorenzo. *Revista Nacional de Cultura (Venezuela)*, v. 54, no. 287 (Oct – Dec 92), p. 269.

Silva Beauregard, Paulette. La narrativa venezolana de la época del modernismo. *Revista Chilena de Literatura*, no. 40 (Nov 92), pp. 41 – 56. Bibl.

Study and teaching

Varderi, Alejandro. Los talleres literarios en la formación de la literatura del fin de siglo. *Inti*, no. 37 – 38 (Spring – Fall 93), pp. 225 – 232.

VENEZUELAN POETRY

Mota, Luis Ramón, ed. *Recopilación de autores del folclor venezolano* reviewed by Antonio Bracho. *Revista Nacional de Cultura (Venezuela)*, v. 53, no. 286 (July – Sept 92), p. 267.

History and criticism

Castillo Zapata, Rafael. Palabras recuperadas: la poesía venezolana de los ochenta: rescate y transformación de las palabras de la tribu; el caso "Tráfico." *Hispamérica*, v. 22, no. 64 – 65 (Apr – Aug 93), pp. 67 – 75.

— Palabras recuperadas: la poesía venezolana de los ochenta: rescate y transformación de las palabras de la tribu; el caso "Tráfico." *Inti*, no. 37 – 38 (Spring – Fall 93), pp. 197 – 205.

Márquez Rodríguez, Alexis. J. A. Pérez Bonalde y la poesía venezolana del siglo XIX. *Revista Nacional de Cultura (Venezuela)*, v. 54, no. 287 (Oct – Dec 92), pp. 117 – 134. Bibl, il.

Romero León, Jorge. La sociedad de los poetas muertos. *Escritura (Venezuela)*, v. 17, no. 33 – 34 (Jan – Dec 92), pp. 101 – 113.

LA VENTA, MEXICO

González Lauck, Rebecca B. Algunas consideraciones sobre los monumentos 75 y 80 de La Venta, Tabasco. *Anales del Instituto de Investigaciones Estéticas*, v. 16, no. 62 (1991), pp. 163 – 174. Bibl, il.

VERA CRUZ, MEXICO (CITY)

Blázquez Domínguez, Carmen. Dos años críticos: la expulsión de los españoles en Xalapa y Veracruz, 1827 – 1828. *Siglo XIX: Cuadernos*, v. 2, no. 4 (Oct 92), pp. 31 – 58. Bibl.

Juárez Martínez, Abel. España, el Caribe y el puerto de Veracruz en tiempos del libre comercio, 1789 – 1821. *La Palabra y el Hombre*, no. 83 (July – Sept 92), pp. 93 – 108. Bibl.

Manrique, Jorge Alberto and Hipólito Rodríguez. *Veracruz: la ciudad hecha de mar, 1519 – 1821* (Review). *La Palabra y el Hombre*, no. 83 (July – Sept 92), pp. 347 – 349.

Widmer S., Rolf. La ciudad de Veracruz en el último siglo colonial, 1680 – 1820: algunos aspectos de la historia demográfica de una ciudad portuaria. *La Palabra y el Hombre*, no. 83 (July – Sept 92), pp. 121 – 134. Bibl, tables.

VERA CRUZ, MEXICO (STATE)

Arnold, Philip J., III et al. Intensive Ceramic Production and Classic-Period Political Economy in the Sierra de los Tuxtlas, Veracruz, Mexico. *Ancient Mesoamerica*, v. 4, no. 2 (Fall 93), pp. 175 – 191. Bibl, il, tables, maps.

Carroll, Patrick James. *Blacks in Colonial Veracruz: Race, Ethnicity, and Regional Development* reviewed by Linda A. Newson. *Journal of Latin American Studies*, v. 25, no. 1 (Feb 93), pp. 192 – 193.

Corzo Ramírez, Ricardo and Soledad García Morales. Políticas, instituciones públicas de salud y enfermedades en Veracruz: fines del siglo XIX y principios del siglo XX. *La Palabra y el Hombre*, no. 83 (July – Sept 92), pp. 275 – 298. Bibl, tables.

Franco, Miguel and Ana Mendoza. Integración clonal en una palma tropical. *Bulletin de l'Institut Français d'Etudes Andines*, v. 21, no. 2 (1992), pp. 623 – 635. Bibl, il, tables, charts.

García Morales, Soledad. Algunas consideraciones sobre la historiografía veracruzana del porfiriato y la revolución en Veracruz. *La Palabra y el Hombre*, no. 83 (July – Sept 92), pp. 304 – 313.

Gardner, David Skerritt. Colonización y modernización del campo en el centro de Veracruz, siglo XIX. *Siglo XIX: Cuadernos*, v. 2, no. 5 (Feb 93), pp. 39 – 57. Bibl, tables.

Grosso, Juan Carlos. El comercio interregional entre Puebla y Veracruz: de la etapa borbónica al México independiente. *La Palabra y el Hombre*, no. 83 (July – Sept 92), pp. 59 – 91. Bibl, tables, charts.

Hoffmann, Odile. Renovación de los actores sociales en el campo: un ejemplo en el sector cafetalero en Veracruz. *Estudios Sociológicos*, v. 10, no. 30 (Sept – Dec 92), pp. 523 – 554. Bibl, tables, maps.

— *Tierras y territorio en Xico, Veracruz* reviewed by Hipólito Rodríguez. *Estudios Sociológicos*, v. 11, no. 31 (Jan – Apr 93), pp. 274 – 276.

Ibarra-Manríquez, Guillermo. Fenología de las palmas de una selva cálido húmeda de México. *Bulletin de l'Institut Français d'Etudes Andines*, v. 21, no. 2 (1992), pp. 669 – 683. Bibl, tables, charts.

Johnson, Jessica. Whatever Happened to Laguna Verde? *Business Mexico*, v. 3, no. 5 (May 93), pp. 20 – 22. Il.

Marchal, Jean-Ives. Municipios vecinos, hermanos enemigos: esbozo de dos desarrollos divergentes; Tuxpan y Alamo, Veracruz. *Estudios Sociológicos*, v. 10, no. 30 (Sept – Dec 92), pp. 555 – 581. Bibl, maps.

Moncada Maya, J. Omar. Miguel Constanzó y el reconocimiento geográfico de la costa de Veracruz de 1797. *Anuario de Estudios Americanos*, v. 49, Suppl. 2 (1992), pp. 31 – 64. Bibl.

Skerritt, David A. Una historia dinámica entre la sierra y la costa. *La Palabra y el Hombre*, no. 83 (July – Sept 92), pp. 5 – 25. Bibl, tables, maps.

Téllez Guerrero, Francisco. La segregación de Tuxpan y Chicontepec en 1853. *La Palabra y el Hombre*, no. 83 (July – Sept 92), pp. 27 – 43. Bibl, tables, maps.

Zilli Mánica, José Benigno. *Frailes, curas y laicos* reviewed by Carmen Blázquez Domínguez. *La Palabra y el Hombre*, no. 83 (July – Sept 92), pp. 350 – 352.

VERACOECHEA DE CASTILLO, LUISA

Criticism of specific works

La huella del sabio

Veracoechea de Castillo, Luisa. Palabras de la profesora Luisa Veracoechea de Castillo en el acto de presentación de libro *La huella del sabio: el municipio foráneo Alejandro de Humboldt* con motivo de los 193 años de la visita del sabio a Caracas . . . . *Boletín de la Academia Nacional de la Historia (Venezuela)*, v. 76, no. 301 (Jan – Mar 93), pp. 27 – 31.

VESPUCCI, AMERIGO

Luigi Lemus, Juan de. Amerigo Vespucci (Includes reproductions of paintings by Enrique Boccaletti G. from his book entitled *América, el Nuevo Mundo y los navegantes italianos*, co-authored by Juan de Luigi Lemus). *Atenea (Chile)*, no. 465 – 466 (1992), pp. 177 – 186+. Il.

Pérez Tomás, Eduardo E. Nuevo aporte al esclarecimiento de un punto relativo a la "cuestión vespuciana." *Revista de Historia de América*, no. 113 (Jan – June 92), pp. 103 – 138. Bibl, tables, charts.

VIANNA, TYRTEU ROCHA DE

Criticism of specific works

Saco de viagem

Fischer, Luís Augusto. Um modernista extraviado. *Vozes*, v. 86, no. 6 (Nov – Dec 92), pp. 2 – 7.

VICTIMS OF CRIME

See
Child abuse
Crime and criminals
Crimes against women
Violence

VIDEO TAPE RECORDERS AND RECORDING

Argentina

Castrillón, Ernesto G. Panorama del audio y el video histórico en la Argentina. *Todo Es Historia*, v. 27, no. 315 (Oct 93), p. 61. Il.

Brazil

Tieppo, Marcelo. 9º Festival Internacional Videobrasil. *Vozes*, v. 86, no. 6 (Nov – Dec 92), p. 98.

VIEDMA, ARGENTINA

Brailovsky, Antonio Elio. Viedma: la capital inundable. *Todo Es Historia*, v. 26, no. 306 (Jan 93), pp. 60 – 71. Bibl, il.

VILLA-LOBOS, HEITOR

Peppercorn, Lisa M. *Villa-Lobos: The Music; An Analysis of His Style*, a translation of *Heitor Villa-Lobos: Leben und Werk des brasilianischen Komponist*, translated by Stefan de Haan (Review). *Inter-American Music Review*, v. 13, no. 2 (Spring – Summer 93), pp. 162 – 163. Bibl.

Toni, Flávia Camargo. Quatro concertos "progressistas" de Villa-Lobos. *Vozes*, v. 86, no. 6 (Nov – Dec 92), pp. 69 – 81. Il, facs.

Wright, Simon J. *Villa-Lobos* (Review). *Inter-American Music Review*, v. 13, no. 2 (Spring – Summer 93), p. 162.

— *Villa-Lobos* reviewed by E. Bradford Burns. *Hispanic American Historical Review*, v. 73, no. 4 (Nov 93), pp. 672 – 673.

— *Villa-Lobos* reviewed by Gerard Béhague. *Latin American Music Review*, v. 14, no. 2 (Fall – Winter 93), pp. 294 – 297.

VILLAHERMOSA, MEXICO

Martin, Christopher James. The "Shadow Economy" of Local School Management in Contemporary West Mexico. *Bulletin of Latin American Research*, v. 12, no. 2 (May 93), pp. 171 – 188. Bibl.

VILLALÓN-DAOIS, FERNANDO

Gutiérrez Revuelta, Pedro. Fernando Villalón, el amigo desconocido de Pablo Neruda. *Cuadernos Hispanoamericanos*, no. 514 – 515 (Apr – May 93), pp. 307 – 311.

VILLAPEDROSA, ROMUALDO

See
Irisarri, Antonio José de

VILLARREAL, JOSÉ ANTONIO

Criticism of specific works

The Fifth Horseman

Parotti, Phillip. Heroic Conventions in José Antonio Villarreal's *The Fifth Horseman*. *Bilingual Review/Revista Bilingüe*, v. 17, no. 3 (Sept – Dec 92), pp. 237 – 241.

VILLARRUTIA, XAVIER

See
Villaurrutia, Xavier

VILLAURRUTIA, XAVIER

Correspondence, reminiscences, etc.

Villaurrutia, Xavier. Buzón de fantasmas: de Xavier Villaurrutia a José Gorostiza. *Vuelta*, v. 17, no. 195 (Feb 93), p. 65.

— Taxco en Montenegro. *Vuelta*, v. 17, no. 198 (May 93), pp. 26 – 27.

Criticism and interpretation

Matamoro, Blas. Villaurrutia y Cernuda: Eros y cosmos. *Cuadernos Hispanoamericanos*, no. 514 – 515 (Apr – May 93), pp. 209 – 213. Il.

VILLAVERDE, CIRILO

Criticism of specific works

Cecilia Valdés

Sommer, Doris. Cecilia no sabe o los bloqueos que blanquean. *Revista de Crítica Literaria Latinoamericana*, v. 19, no. 38 (July – Dec 93), pp. 239 – 248. Bibl.

Williams, Lorna Valerie. The Representation of the Female Slave in Villaverde's *Cecilia Valdés*. *Hispanic Journal*, v. 14, no. 1 (Spring 93), pp. 73 – 89. Bibl.

VILLEGAIGNON, NICOLAS DURAND DE

Léry, Jean de. *History of a Voyage to the Land of Brazil, Otherwise Called America* translated by Janet Whatley. Reviewed by Maria Laura Bettencourt Pires. *Colonial Latin American Review*, v. 2, no. 1 – 2 (1993), pp. 279 – 281.

VIÑAS, DAVID

Criticism of specific works

Cuerpo a cuerpo

Jarkowski, Aníbal. Sobreviviente en una guerra: enviando tarjetas postales. *Hispamérica*, v. 21, no. 63 (Dec 92), pp. 15 – 24.

VIOLENCE

See also
Anarchism and anarchists
Guerrillas
Revolutions
Terrorism

Bonilla, Flory Stella. Orientación de poblaciones abusadas. *Revista de Ciencias Sociales (Costa Rica)*, no. 59 (Mar 93), pp. 53 – 62. Bibl.

Viera Gallo, José Antonio. Violencia y cultura política: un desafío para nuestro tiempo. *Mensaje*, v. 42, no. 417 (Mar – Apr 93), pp. 69 – 73. Il.

Andean region

Lauer, Mirko and Henrique-Osvaldo Urbano, eds. *Poder y violencia en los Andes* reviewed by Kenneth J. Andrien. *Hispanic American Historical Review*, v. 73, no. 1 (Feb 93), pp. 177 – 178.

— *Poder y violencia en los Andes* reviewed by Víctor Peralta Ruiz. *Revista de Indias*, v. 53, no. 197 (Jan – Apr 93), pp. 124 – 126.

Argentina

Abregú, Martín. Contra las apologías del "homocidio uniforme": la violencia policial en Argentina. *Nueva Sociedad*, no. 123 (Jan – Feb 93), pp. 68 – 83. Bibl.

Brazil

Linger, Daniel Touro. *Dangerous Encounters: Meanings of Violence in a Brazilian City* reviewed by David Cleary. *Bulletin of Latin American Research*, v. 12, no. 3 (Sept 93), pp. 344 – 345.

Sources

Soares, Gláucio Ary Dillon. Comentários adicionais (Response on commentaries to his article "A violência política na América Latina"). *Revista Brasileira de Ciências Sociais*, v. 8, no. 21 (Feb 93), pp. 48 – 51.

Colombia

Bergquist, Charles Wylie et al, eds. *Violence in Colombia: The Contemporary Crisis in Historical Perspective* reviewed by Mary Roldán. *The Americas*, v. 50, no. 1 (July 93), pp. 142 – 144.

— *Violence in Colombia: The Contemporary Crisis in Historical Perspective* reviewed by Víctor Peralta Ruiz. *Revista Andina*, v. 11, no. 1 (July 93), pp. 244 – 245.

Caballero, Antonio et al. Su lucha no propicia la justicia social (A reprinted letter signed by many Colombian intellectuals objecting to the use of violence and terrorism by the guerrillas). *Nueva Sociedad*, no. 125 (May – June 93), pp. 146 – 147.

Leal Buitrago, Francisco. La guerra y la paz en Colombia. *Nueva Sociedad*, no. 125 (May – June 93), pp. 157 – 161.

Marulanda V., Manuel et al. Estamos comprometidos en la solución política (A reply by members of the Coordinadora Guerrillera Simón Bolívar to the letter by Antonio Caballero et al.). *Nueva Sociedad*, no. 125 (May – June 93), pp. 147 – 148.

Samper Pizano, Ernesto. Democracia y paz (Previously published in this journal, no. 549, 1988). *Revista Javeriana*, v. 61, no. 596 (July 93), pp. 89 – 94.

El Salvador

Argueta, Manlio. An Exile's Return. *NACLA Report on the Americas*, v. 26, no. 5 (May 93), pp. 4 – 6. Il.

La cultura de la muerte. *ECA; Estudios Centroamericanos*, v. 48, no. 539 (Sept 93), pp. 886 – 889. Il.

Indicadores actuales de la violencia. *ECA; Estudios Centroamericanos*, v. 48, no. 536 (June 93), pp. 594 – 598. Il.

Guatemala

Carmack, Robert Marin, ed. *Guatemala: cosecha de violencias* reviewed by Manuel Angel Castillo G. *Revista Mexicana de Sociología*, v. 54, no. 1 (Jan – Mar 92), pp. 331 – 334.

Le Bot, Yvon. Le palimpseste maya: violence, communauté et territoire dans le conflit guatémaltèque. *Cahiers des Amériques Latines*, no. 13 (1992), pp. 87 – 105. Bibl, maps.

Morrison, Andrew R. Violence or Economics: What Drives Internal Migration in Guatemala? *Economic Development and Cultural Change*, v. 41, no. 4 (July 93), pp. 817 – 831. Bibl, tables.

Latin America

Rosenberg, Tina. *Children of Cain: Violence and the Violent in Latin America* reviewed by Troy M. Bollinger. *Journal of Inter-American Studies and World Affairs*, v. 35, no. 2 (Summer 93), pp. 159 – 163.

Sources

Adorno, Sérgio. Ciência, informação, verdade e universalidade: a propósito de "A violência política na América Latina." *Revista Brasileira de Ciências Sociais*, v. 8, no. 21 (Feb 93), pp. 40 – 43.

Caldeira, Teresa Pires do Rio. Comentários a partir do artigo "A violência política na América Latina." *Revista Brasileira de Ciências Sociais*, v. 8, no. 21 (Feb 93), pp. 44 – 47.

Soares, Gláucio Ary Dillon. A violência política na América Latina. *Revista Brasileira de Ciências Sociais*, v. 8, no. 21 (Feb 93), pp. 22 – 39. Bibl, tables, charts.

Mexico

Greenberg, James B. *Blood Ties: Life and Violence in Rural Mexico* reviewed by Richard N. Adams. *Mesoamérica (USA)*, v. 13, no. 23 (June 92), pp. 196 – 200.

Peru

Aguirre, Carlos and Charles Walker, eds. *Bandoleros, abigeos y montoneros: criminalidad y violencia en el Perú, siglos XVIII – XX* reviewed by Vincent Peloso. *The Americas*, v. 50, no. 2 (Oct 93), pp. 283 – 285.

— *Bandoleros, abigeos y montoneros: criminalidad y violencia en el Perú, siglos XVIII – XX* reviewed by Scarlett O'Phelan Godoy. *Anuario de Estudios Americanos*, v. 49, Suppl. 2 (1992), pp. 243 – 244.

Eyzaguirre, Graciela. Los escenarios de la guerra en la región Cáceres. *Allpanchis*, v. 23, no. 39 (Jan – June 92), pp. 155 – 180. Bibl, tables, maps.

Rodríguez G., Yolanda. Los actores sociales y la violencia política en Puno. *Allpanchis*, v. 23, no. 39 (Jan – June 92), pp. 131 – 154. Bibl.

VIOLENCE IN LITERATURE

Albuquerque, Severino João Medeiros. *Violent Acts: A Study of Contemporary Latin American Theatre* reviewed by Leslie Damasceno. *Latin American Theatre Review*, v. 26, no. 2 (Spring 93), pp. 210 – 212.

Hedi, Ben Abbes. A Variation on the Theme of Violence and Antagonism in V. S. Naipaul's Fiction. *Caribbean Studies*, v. 25, no. 1 – 2 (Jan – July 92), pp. 49 – 61. Bibl.

Noriega, Teobaldo A. *La mala hierba* de Juan Gossaín: consideraciones estéticas ante una escritura de la nueva violencia colombiana. *Revista Canadiense de Estudios Hispánicos*, v. 17, no. 3 (Spring 93), pp. 465 – 481. Bibl.

Reati, Fernando. *Nombrar lo innombrable: violencia política y novela argentina, 1975 – 1985* reviewed by David William Foster. *World Literature Today*, v. 67, no. 2 (Spring 93), pp. 341 – 342.

Tittler, Jonathan, ed. *Violencia y literatura en Colombia* reviewed by Hans Paschen. *Iberoamericana*, v. 17, no. 49 (1993), pp. 99 – 101.

VÍQUEZ JIMÉNEZ, ALÍ

Criticism of specific works

El maniaco

Víquez Jiménez, Alí. Texto y estrategia: análisis de la cooperación interpretativa en *El maniaco* por Alí Víquez. *Káñina*, v. 16, no. 2 (July – Dec 92), pp. 17 – 27. Bibl.

VIRGIN ISLANDS OF THE UNITED STATES

See
Slavery – Virgin Islands of the United States

VISION

Salzano, Francisco M. Color Vision in Four Brazilian Indian Tribes. *Interciencia*, v. 18, no. 4 (July – Aug 93), pp. 195 – 197. Bibl, tables.

VISUAL TEXT

Meyer-Minnemann, Klaus. Octavio Paz: "Topoemas"; elementos para una lectura. *Nueva Revista de Filología Hispánica*, v. 40, no. 2 (July – Dec 92), pp. 1113 – 1134. Bibl, charts.

VITIER, MEDARDO

García Machado, Xiomara. Medardo Vitier en la tradición humanista del pensamiento cubano: ¿Herencia o ruptura? *Islas*, no. 98 (Jan – Apr 91), pp. 119 – 127. Bibl.

VITORIA, FRANCISCO DE

Llera Esteban, Luis de. Recordando a Francisco de Vitoria en el V centenario. *Quaderni Ibero-Americani*, no. 72 (Dec 92), pp. 661 – 681. Bibl.

Salvat Monguillot, Manuel. Francisco de Vitoria y el nacimiento del capitalismo. *Boletín de la Academia Chilena de la Historia*, v. 58 – 59, no. 102 (1991 – 1992), pp. 329 – 347. Bibl.

VIZCARDO Y GUZMÁN, JUAN PABLO

Gandía, Enrique de. Prolegómenos a la independencia de la América Hispana: Francisco de Miranda y Juan Pablo de Vizcardo y Guzmán. *Investigaciones y Ensayos*, no. 41 (Jan – Dec 91), pp. 15 – 64.

VOCATIONAL EDUCATION

See also
Technical education

Congresses

Swope, John. Un foro internacional: educación media como estrategia de desarrollo con equidad. *Mensaje*, v. 42, no. 419 (June 93), pp. 208 – 210. Il.

Chile

Etcheberry, Blanca. Capacitación de presos: solidaridad entre rejas. *Mensaje*, v. 42, no. 421 (Aug 93), pp. 390 – 391. Il.

Soto Sandoval, Andrés. INFOCAP: en la senda de Ignacio y de Alberto Hurtado. *Mensaje*, v. 42, no. 420 (July 93), pp. 280 – 282. Il.

Latin America

Muñoz Izquierdo, Carlos. Tendencias observadas en las investigaciones y en las políticas relacionadas con el financiamiento de la educación técnica y vocacional en América Latina. *Revista Latinoamericana de Estudios Educativos*, v. 23, no. 1 (Jan – Mar 93), pp. 9 – 41. Bibl, tables.

Mexico

Coldwell, Pedro Joaquín. Service for Survival (Excerpt from a speech given by the Secretary of Tourism). *Business Mexico*, v. 3, no. 10 (Oct 93), pp. 16 – 17. Il.

United States

González, Ann. Teaching beyond the Classroom: Business Internships in Latin America; Issues in Cross-Cultural Adjustment. *Hispania (USA)*, v. 76, no. 4 (Dec 93), pp. 892 – 901.

VOLCANISM

Caribbean area

Carey, Steven and Haraldur Sigurdssen. *Caribbean Volcanoes: A Field Guide; Martinique, Dominica, and St. Vincent* reviewed by Trevor Jackson. *Caribbean Geography*, v. 3, no. 3 (Mar 92), pp. 211 – 212.

VOODOOISM

McAlister, Elizabeth. Sacred Stories from the Haitian Diaspora: A Collective Biography of Seven Vodou Priestesses in New York City. *Journal of Caribbean Studies*, v. 9, no. 1 – 2 (Winter 92 – Spring 93), pp. 11 – 27. Bibl.

Scalora, Sal. A Salute to the Spirits. *Américas*, v. 45, no. 2 (Mar – Apr 93), pp. 27 – 33. Il.

VOTING RESEARCH

See
Elections
Local elections

VUSKOVIC BRAVO, PEDRO

Ibarra Muñoz, David. Pedro Vuskovic, un socialista latinoamericano. *Problemas del Desarrollo,* v. 24, no. 94 (July – Sept 93), pp. 249 – 257.

Criticism of specific works

Pobreza y desigualdad en América Latina

Rey Romay, Benito. Comentarios al libro *Pobreza y desigualdad en América Latina* de Pedro Vuskovic. *Problemas del Desarrollo,* v. 24, no. 94 (July – Sept 93), pp. 258 – 263.

Obituaries

Ibarra Muñoz, David. Penurias de la modernidad. *Nexos,* v. 16, no. 191 (Nov 93), pp. 51 – 55.

WACQUEZ, MAURICIO

Criticism of specific works

Frente a un hombre armado

Santos, Danilo. Aproximación a una novela de Mauricio Wacquez: *Frente a un hombre armado;* una indagación del lenguaje en torno a la muerte y el erotismo. *Revista Chilena de Literatura,* no. 41 (Apr 93), pp. 119 – 122.

WAGES

Brazil

Amadeo Swaelen, Edward Joaquim. Restricciones institucionales a la política económica: negociación salarial y estabilización en el Brasil. *Desarrollo Económico (Argentina),* v. 33, no. 129 (Apr – June 93), pp. 29 – 47. Bibl, tables, charts.

Cacciamali, Maria Cristina and Paulo Springer de Freitas. Do capital humano ao salário-eficiência: uma aplicação para analisar os diferenciais de salários em cinco ramos manufatureiros da grande São Paulo. *Pesquisa e Planejamento Econômico,* v. 22, no. 2 (Aug 92), pp. 343 – 367. Bibl, tables.

Mattos, César Costa Alves de. O regime de expectativas e a política salarial: indexação x prefixação. *Revista de Economia Política (Brazil),* v. 13, no. 2 (Apr – June 93), pp. 137 – 143.

Telles, Edward E. Urban Labor Market Segmentation and Income in Brazil. *Economic Development and Cultural Change,* v. 41, no. 2 (Jan 93), pp. 231 – 249. Bibl, tables.

Mathematical models

Amadeo Swaelen, Edward Joaquim. Do Relative Wages Move Together with Relative Prices? *Revista Brasileira de Economia,* v. 47, no. 1 (Jan – Mar 93), pp. 33 – 52. Bibl, tables, charts.

Pero, Valéria Lúcia. A carteira de trabalho no mercado de trabalho metropolitano brasileiro. *Pesquisa e Planejamento Econômico,* v. 22, no. 2 (Aug 92), pp. 305 – 342. Bibl, tables, charts.

Chile

Bobenrieth H., Eugenio H. and Carlos Cáceres Sandoval. Determinantes del salario de los egresados de la enseñanza media técnico profesional en Chile. *Cuadernos de Economía (Chile),* v. 30, no. 89 (Apr 93), pp. 111 – 129. Bibl, tables.

Gómez Figueroa, Carlos. Situación de los profesores: un problema nacional. *Mensaje,* v. 42, no. 423 (Oct 93), pp. 491 – 494. Il, tables.

Colombia

Statistics

Colombia. Departamento Nacional de Planeación. Indicadores del sector rural. *Planeación y Desarrollo,* v. 24 (1993), All issues.

Costa Rica

Mathematical models

Gindling, T. H. Women's Wages and Economic Crisis in Costa Rica. *Economic Development and Cultural Change,* v. 41, no. 2 (Jan 93), pp. 277 – 297. Bibl, tables.

Mexico

Bueno Rodríguez, Luis and Salvador T. Porras Duarte. Deshomologación salarial: ¿Cuánto por punto? *El Cotidiano,* v. 9, no. 55 (June 93), pp. 91 – 98. Tables, charts.

Cohen, Joshua A. Productivity: A Jump Start to Better Wages. *Business Mexico,* v. 3, no. 6 (June 93), pp. 7 – 8.

Peña, Antonio. La ciencia y los salarios. *Nexos,* v. 16, no. 190 (Oct 93), pp. 12 – 16.

Rothstein, Richard. El desarrollo continental y el comercio entre México y Estados Unidos: ¿Por qué los trabajadores estadunidenses necesitan salarios más altos en México? *Relaciones Internacionales (Mexico),* v. 15, Nueva época, no. 57 (Jan – Mar 93), pp. 63 – 74.

Statistics

Rueda Peiró, Isabel. Deterioro y mayor desigualdad en el empleo y los salarios de los trabajadores mexicanos. *Momento Económico,* no. 69 (Sept – Oct 93), pp. 6 – 9. Tables.

Puerto Rico

Minimum wage

Santiago, Carlos Enrique. The Migratory Impact of Minimum Wage Legislation: Puerto Rico, 1970 – 1987. *International Migration Review,* v. 27, no. 4 (Winter 93), pp. 772 – 795. Bibl, tables, charts.

Statistics

Enchautegui, María E. The Value of U.S. Labor Market Experience in the Home Country: The Case of Puerto Rican Return Migrants. *Economic Development and Cultural Change,* v. 42, no. 1 (Oct 93), pp. 168 – 191. Bibl, tables, charts.

Río de la Plata region

Gelman, Jorge Daniel. Mundo rural y mercados: una estancia y las formas de circulación mercantil en la campaña rioplatense tardocolonial. *Revista de Indias,* v. 52, no. 195 – 196 (May – Dec 92), pp. 477 – 514. Bibl, tables.

United States

Borjas, George J. and Marta Tienda. The Employment and Wages of Legalized Immigrants. *International Migration Review,* v. 27, no. 4 (Winter 93), pp. 712 – 747. Bibl, tables.

Faux, Jeff and Thea Lee. Los efectos del Acuerdo de Libre Comercio de América del Norte en la fuerza de trabajo de Estados Unidos. *Relaciones Internacionales (Mexico),* v. 15, Nueva época, no. 57 (Jan – Mar 93), pp. 37 – 54.

Uruguay

Craven, Carolyn. Wage Determination and Inflation in Uruguay: Regime Changes. *Journal of Developing Areas,* v. 27, no. 4 (July 93), pp. 457 – 468. Bibl, tables, charts.

WALCOTT, DEREK

Addresses, essays, lectures

Walcott, Derek. The Antilles: Fragments of Epic Memory; The 1992 Nobel Lecture. *World Literature Today,* v. 67, no. 2 (Spring 93), pp. 260 – 267. Il.

Awards

González Villarroel, Oscar. Derek Walcott, premio Nobel de literatura 1992. *Atenea (Chile),* no. 465 – 466 (1992), pp. 357 – 359. Il.

Premios Nobel en el año del quinto centenario. *Casa de las Américas,* no. 190 (Jan – Mar 93), pp. 2 – 12.

Bibliography

Derek Walcott: Major Works. *Caribbean Quarterly,* v. 38, no. 4 (Dec 92), p. 142.

Criticism and interpretation

Baugh, Edward. Derek Walcott. *Caribbean Quarterly,* v. 38, no. 4 (Dec 92), pp. xiii – xv.

Breslow, Stephen P. Derek Walcott, 1992 Nobel Laureate in Literature. *World Literature Today,* v. 67, no. 2 (Spring 93), pp. 267 – 271. Bibl.

Sherlock, Philip Manderson. Yesterday Walks before Us with Esteem and Affection for Derek Walcott. *Caribbean Quarterly,* v. 38, no. 4 (Dec 92), pp. v – xii.

Criticism of specific works
Drums and Colours
Vaz, Noel. Original Foreword to *Drums and Colours. Caribbean Quarterly*, v. 38, no. 4 (Dec 92), pp. 22 – 23.

Omeros
Minkler, Julie A. Helen's Calibans: A Study of Gender Hierarchy in Derek Walcott's *Omeros. World Literature Today*, v. 67, no. 2 (Spring 93), pp. 272 – 276. Bibl.

Pantomime
Acosta Rabassa, Blanca. Viernes, ¿y por qué no jueves? *Conjunto*, no. 93 (Jan – June 93), pp. 44 – 45. Il.

Interviews
Scott, Dennis. Walcott on Walcott. *Caribbean Quarterly*, v. 38, no. 4 (Dec 92), pp. 136 – 141.

Translations
Walcott, Derek. Pantomima (Translated by Blanca Acosta Rabassa). *Conjunto*, no. 93 (Jan – June 93), pp. 46 – 71.

WALDEEN
Vázquez Hall, Patricia. Waldeen, pensadora y maestra de la danza. *Plural (Mexico)*, v. 22, no. 265 (Oct 93), p. 85.

WALKER, WILLIAM
Sagastume Fajardo, Alejandro S. El papel de la iglesia de Centroamérica en la guerra contra William Walker, 1856 – 1860. *Revista de Indias*, v. 53, no. 198 (May – Aug 93), pp. 529 – 544.

WALTER AGUILAR, SIGFRIDO
Samperio, Guillermo. Libertad y sujeción en Sigfrido Walter Aguilar. *Artes de México*, no. 20 (Summer 93), pp. 120 – 121. Il.

WAR
See also
Revolutions
Names of specific wars

Ferguson, R. Brian and Neil L. Whitehead, eds. *War in the Tribal Zone: Expanding States and Indigenous Warfare* reviewed by Elizabeth M. Brumfiel. *Hispanic American Historical Review*, v. 73, no. 3 (Aug 93), pp. 499 – 500.

WAR OF THE TRIPLE ALLIANCE
See
Paraguayan War, 1865 – 1870

WARI INDIANS
See
Huari culture, Peru

WARSAW PACT COUNTRIES
See
Europe, Eastern

WATER
See also
Dams and reservoirs
Erosion

Belize
Day, Michael J. The Geomorphology and Hydrology of the Blue Hole, Caves Branch. *Belizean Studies*, v. 20, no. 3 (Dec 92), pp. 3 – 10. Bibl, maps, charts.

Brazil
Brito, Maria Socorro. O Programa Nacional de Irrigação: uma avaliação prévia dos resultados. *Revista Brasileira de Geografia*, v. 53, no. 2 (Apr – June 91), pp. 113 – 125. Bibl, tables.

Cost
Guimarães, Paulo César Vaz. Instrumentos econômicos para gerenciamento ambiental: a cobrança pelo uso da água no estado de São Paulo. *RAE; Revista de Administração de Empresas*, v. 33, no. 5 (Sept – Oct 93), pp. 88 – 97.

Law and legislation
Machado, Rosa Maria de Oliveira and Ana Lúcia Magyar. A regulamentação da lei de recursos hídricos do estado de São Paulo: desafios e perspectivas. *RAE; Revista de Administração de Empresas*, v. 33, no. 6 (Nov – Dec 93), pp. 42 – 47. Bibl.

Chile
Guarda Geywitz, Gabriel. Obras hidráulicas en el reino de Chile. *Boletín de la Academia Chilena de la Historia*, v. 58 – 59, no. 102 (1991 – 1992), pp. 269 – 289. Bibl.

Latin America
Cost
Jouravlev, Andrei and Terence R. Lee. Self-Financing Water Supply and Sanitation Services. *CEPAL Review*, no. 48 (Dec 92), pp. 117 – 128. Bibl, tables, charts.

Mexican – American Border Region
Anguiano Téllez, María Eugenia. Irrigación y capital para transformar el desierto: la formación social del valle de Mexicali a principios del siglo XX. *Frontera Norte*, v. 4, no. 8 (July – Dec 92), pp. 125 – 147. Bibl.

Mexico
Blanco, José Luis et al. El tributo del campo a la ciudad: historias de chaneques y serpientes. *Revista Mexicana de Sociología*, v. 54, no. 3 (July – Sept 92), pp. 131 – 137. Bibl.

Doolittle, William Emery. *Canal Irrigation in Prehistoric Mexico: The Sequence of Technological Change* reviewed by Robert Kuhlken. *Mesoamérica (USA)*, v. 13, no. 24 (Dec 92), pp. 488 – 489.

Finn, Patrick J. Treating Water Industrially. *Business Mexico*, v. 3, no. 1 (Jan – Feb 93), pp. 83 – 84. Tables.

Geyer, Anne. Water on Schedule . . . and on Tap. *Business Mexico*, v. 3, no. 7 (July 93), pp. 16 – 19.

Lipsett-Rivera, Sonya. Water and Bureaucracy in Colonial Puebla de los Angeles. *Journal of Latin American Studies*, v. 25, no. 1 (Feb 93), pp. 25 – 44. Bibl, tables, maps.

Musset, Alain. *De l'eau vive à l'eau morte: enjeux techniques et culturels dans la vallée de Mexico, XVIᵉ – XIXᵉ siècles* reviewed by Marie-Danielle Démelas-Bohy. *Caravelle*, no. 59 (1992), p. 307.

Postel, Sandra L. Last Oasis (Excerpt from the book of the same title, part of the *Worldwatch Environmental Alert Series*). *Business Mexico*, v. 3, no. 1 (Jan – Feb 93), pp. 67 – 70. Il.

Law and legislation
Shedd, David. H$_2$0: Safe and Sound. *Business Mexico*, v. 3, no. 12 (Dec 93), pp. 40 – 42.

Peru
Junquera, Carlos. Antropología y paleotecnología: ayer y hoy de una situación agraria en Lambayeque (Perú). *Revista Española de Antropología Americana*, v. 23 (1993), pp. 165 – 187. Bibl.

Martínez, Héctor. Perú: la irrigación Jequetepeque – Zana; impacto de la presa de Gallito Ciego. *Estudios Rurales Latinoamericanos*, v. 15, no. 2 – 3 (May – Dec 92), pp. 3 – 27. Bibl, tables.

Venezuela
Cressa, Claudia et al. Aspectos generales de la limnología en Venezuela. *Interciencia*, v. 18, no. 5 (Sept – Oct 93), pp. 237 – 248. Bibl, tables, maps.

WATER POWER
See also
Electric power

Brazil
Almeida, Sérgio Barbosa de. O potencial hidrelétrico brasileiro. *Revista Brasileira de Geografia*, v. 53, no. 3 (July – Sept 91), pp. 183 – 203. Bibl, il, maps.

Latin America
Fontana Morialdo, Jorge et al. Aprovechamientos hidroeléctricos binacionales: aspectos relacionados con la integración latinoamericana. *Integración Latinoamericana*, v. 17, no. 184 (Nov 92), pp. 44 – 58.

WATER RIGHTS

Argentina

Supplee, Joan E. Vitivinicultura, recursos públicos y ganancias privadas en Mendoza, 1880 – 1914. *Siglo XIX: Cuadernos,* v. 2, no. 5 (Feb 93), pp. 81 – 94. Bibl.

Mexican – American Border Region

Waller, Thomas. Southern California Water Politics and U.S. – Mexican Relations: Lining the All-American Canal. *Journal of Borderlands Studies,* v. 7, no. 2 (Fall 92), pp. 1 – 32. Bibl, maps.

Mexico

Olvera Sandoval, José Antonio. Agricultura, riego y conflicto social en la región citrícola de Nuevo León, 1860 – 1910. *Siglo XIX: Cuadernos,* v. 2, no. 5 (Feb 93), pp. 59 – 78.

Peru

Guillet, David. *Covering Ground: Communal Water Management and the State in the Peruvian Highlands* reviewed by Evelyne Mesclier. *Revista Andina,* v. 11, no. 1 (July 93), pp. 247 – 249.

United States

Bauer, Carl J. Water Property Rights and the State: The United States Experience. *CEPAL Review,* no. 49 (Apr 93), pp. 75 – 89. Bibl.

WEAPONS SYSTEMS

See
 Armaments
 Atomic weapons and disarmament

WEATHER

See
 Subdivision *Climate* under names of specific countries

WEAVING

See
 Handicraft
 Textile industry and fabrics
 Subdivision *Textile industry and fabrics* under names of Indian groups

WELFARE

See
 Charities
 Social services
 Subdivision *Social policy* under names of specific countries

WEST INDIANS

Costa Rica

Harpelle, Ronald N. The Social and Political Integration of West Indians in Costa Rica, 1930 – 1950. *Journal of Latin American Studies,* v. 25, no. 1 (Feb 93), pp. 103 – 120. Bibl.

Great Britain

Western, John. *A Passage to England: Barbadian Londoners Speak of Home* reviewed by Thomas D. Anderson. *Geographical Review,* v. 83, no. 2 (Apr 93), pp. 219 – 220.

Puerto Rico

Funkhouser, Edward and Fernando A. Ramos. The Choice of Migration Destination: Dominican and Cuban Immigrants to the Mainland United States and Puerto Rico. *International Migration Review,* v. 27, no. 3 (Fall 93), pp. 537 – 556. Bibl, tables.

United States

Funkhouser, Edward and Fernando A. Ramos. The Choice of Migration Destination: Dominican and Cuban Immigrants to the Mainland United States and Puerto Rico. *International Migration Review,* v. 27, no. 3 (Fall 93), pp. 537 – 556. Bibl, tables.

WEST INDIES

See
 Caribbean area

WESTPHALEN, EMILIO ADOLFO

Criticism of specific works

Las ínsulas extrañas

Fernández Cozman, Camilo. *'Las ínsulas extrañas' de Emilio Adolfo Westphalen* reviewed by Javier Agreda S. *Revista de Crítica Literaria Latinoamericana,* v. 19, no. 38 (July – Dec 93), pp. 415 – 417.

WHEAT

Argentina

Caravaglia, Juan Carlos. Los labradores de San Isidro, siglos XVIII – XIX. *Desarrollo Económico (Argentina),* v. 32, no. 128 (Jan – Mar 93), pp. 513 – 542. Bibl, tables, charts.

Venezuela

Velázquez, Nelly. La implantación del cultivo del trigo en la cordillera de Mérida durante la dominación colonial. *Derecho y Reforma Agraria,* no. 24 (1993), pp. 115 – 138. Bibl.

WHITMAN, WALT

Criticism of specific works

Leaves of Grass

Paro, Maria Clara Bonetti. Ronald de Carvalho e Walt Whitman. *Revista de Letras (Brazil),* v. 32 (1992), pp. 141 – 151.

WINDWARD ISLANDS

See
 Banana trade – Windward Islands
 Capitalism – Windward Islands
 Peasantry – Windward Islands

WINE AND WINE MAKING

Argentina

Furlani de Civit, María Estela and María Josefina Gutiérrez de Manchón. Dinámica agraria en un oasis de especialización vitícola. *Revista Geográfica (Mexico),* no. 115 (Jan – June 92), pp. 85 – 137. Bibl, tables, maps.

Brazil

Stülp, Valter José and Bartholomeu E. Stein Neto. A vitivinicultura do Rio Grande do Sul e a integração econômica Brasil – Argentina. *Revista de Economia e Sociologia Rural,* v. 29, no. 4 (Oct – Dec 91), pp. 387 – 400. Bibl, tables.

WIT AND HUMOR

See also
 Caricatures and cartoons
 Comic books, strips, etc.
 Epigrams
 Irony in literature
 Satire

Zubieta, Ana María. El humor y el problema de narrar las diferencias. *Escritura (Venezuela),* v. 17, no. 33 – 34 (Jan – Dec 92), pp. 61 – 82.

Brazil

Wanderley Pinho, José. Humoristas no parlamento do império: notas esparsas. *Revista do Instituto Histórico e Geográfico Brasileiro,* no. 372 (July – Sept 91), pp. 908 – 929.

Mexico

Corral, Wilfrido Howard. ¿Dónde está el chiste en Monterroso? *Studi di Letteratura Ispano-Americana,* v. 24 (1993), pp. 83 – 93. Bibl.

Schmidt, Samuel. Humor y política en México. *Revista Mexicana de Sociología,* v. 54, no. 1 (Jan – Mar 92), pp. 225 – 250. Bibl.

Peru

Angvik, Birger. La risa que se vuelve mueca: el doble filo del humor y de la risa: *Historia de Mayta* frente a la crítica en Lima. *Káñina,* v. 16, no. 1 (Jan – June 92), pp. 91 – 109. Bibl.

Puerto Rico

Captain-Hidalgo, Yvonne. El espíritu de la risa en el cuento de Ana Lydia Vega. *Revista Iberoamericana,* v. 59, no. 162 – 163 (Jan – June 93), pp. 301 – 308. Bibl.

WITCHCRAFT

See also
Magic
Shamanism
Voodooism

Latin America

Rosenzvaig, Eduardo. Los hechiceros: una variante colonial americana de los brujos. *Cuadernos Hispanoamericanos,* no. 522 (Dec 93), pp. 47 – 66. Bibl, il.

Peru

Gareis, Iris. Brujos y brujas en el antiguo Perú: apariencia y realidad en las fuentes históricas. *Revista de Indias,* v. 53, no. 198 (May – Aug 93), pp. 583 – 613. Bibl, facs.

Millar Carvacho, René. Hechicería, marginalidad e inquisición en el distrito del tribunal de Lima. *Boletín de la Academia Chilena de la Historia,* v. 58 – 59, no. 102 (1991 – 1992), pp. 185 – 227.

WOJTYLA, KAROL

See
John Paul II, Pope

WOLFF, EGON

Criticism of specific works

Mansión de lechuzas

Helsper, Norma. The Ideology of Happy Endings: Wolff's *Mansión de lechuzas. Latin American Theatre Review,* v. 26, no. 2 (Spring 93), pp. 123 – 130.

Obituaries

Winz, Antônio Pimentel. In memoriam: Egon Wolff. *Revista do Instituto Histórico e Geográfico Brasileiro,* no. 370 (Jan – Mar 91), pp. 330 – 331.

WOMEN

See also
Abortion
Birth control
Crimes against women
Family
Fertility, Human
Hispanic American women (U.S.)
Mexican American women
Prostitution
Sex role
Sexism
Women's rights
Subdivision *Women* under names of Indian groups

Bibliography

Maura, Juan Francisco. En busca de la verdad: algunas mujeres excepcionales de la conquista. *Hispania (USA),* v. 76, no. 4 (Dec 93), pp. 904 – 910.

Congresses

Oliveira, Rosiska Darcy de. Memórias do Planeta Fêmea. *Estudos Feministas,* v. 0, no. 0 (1992), pp. 131 – 142.

Vasconcelos, Naumi A. de. Ecos femininos na Eco '92. *Estudos Feministas,* v. 0, no. 0 (1992), pp. 151 – 154.

Health and hygiene

Barbosa, Regina Helena Simões. AIDS, gênero e reprodução. *Estudos Feministas,* v. 1, no. 2 (1993), pp. 418 – 423. Bibl.

Mujer y SIDA reviewed by Beatriz Jiménez Carrillo. *El Cotidiano,* v. 9, no. 53 (Mar – Apr 93), p. 119.

Mujer y SIDA reviewed by Nelson Minello. *Estudios Sociológicos,* v. 10, no. 30 (Sept – Dec 92), pp. 825 – 830.

Rangel Martínez, Georgina M. Mujer, trabajo y medio ambiente. *Fem,* v. 17, no. 128 (Oct 93), pp. 22 – 25. Bibl.

History

Fraisse, Geneviève and Michelle Perrot, eds. *Historia de las mujeres en Occidente, tomo IV: El siglo XIX* reviewed by Lucía Solís Tolosa. *Todo Es Historia,* v. 27, no. 316 (Nov 93), p. 92. Il.

Political activity

Marx, Jutta. Construir el poder: entrevista con Anita Pérez Ferguson. *Feminaria,* v. 6, no. 11 (Nov 93), pp. 17 – 19.

Sampaolesi, Ana. Desvelos en el quehacer político. *Feminaria,* v. 6, no. 11 (Nov 93), pp. 8 – 11.

Psychology

Burin, Mabel. Algunos aportes al debate feminismo – posmodernismo. *Feminaria,* v. 6, no. 10 (Apr 93), pp. 21 – 23. Bibl.

Kane, Connie M. et al. Differences in the Manifest Dream Content of Mexican, Mexican American, and Anglo American College Women: A Research Note. *Hispanic Journal of Behavioral Sciences,* v. 15, no. 1 (Feb 93), pp. 134 – 139. Bibl, tables.

Maffia, Diana. Feminismo y epistemología: ¿Tiene sexo el sujeto de la ciencia? *Feminaria,* v. 6, no. 10 (Apr 93), pp. 13 – 15. Bibl.

Social conditions

Bonilla, Flory Stella. Orientación de poblaciones abusadas. *Revista de Ciencias Sociales (Costa Rica),* no. 59 (Mar 93), pp. 53 – 62. Bibl.

Solís, Bernarda. *Mi vida privada es del dominio público* reviewed by Friedhelm Schmidt. *Revista de Crítica Literaria Latinoamericana,* v. 19, no. 38 (July – Dec 93), pp. 428 – 429.

Velázquez, Carolina. "Soy optimista . . . ahora tenemos más opciones": Amparo Espinosa. *Fem,* v. 17, no. 130 (Dec 93), pp. 26 – 27. Il.

Argentina

History

Salessi, Jorge. La invasión de sirenas. *Feminaria,* v. 6, no. 10, Suppl. (Apr 93), pp. 2 – 7. Bibl.

Sweeney, Judith L. Las lavanderas de Buenos Aires en la segunda mitad del siglo XIX. *Todo Es Historia,* v. 27, no. 314 (Sept 93), pp. 46 – 48. Bibl, il.

Legal status, laws, etc.

Marx, Jutta and Ana Sampaolesi. Elecciones internas bajo el cupo: la primera aplicación de la Ley de Cuotas en la capital federal. *Feminaria,* v. 6, no. 11 (Nov 93), pp. 15 – 17.

Political activity

Bellucci, Mabel and Adriana Rofman. Una década de mujeres en movimiento. *Todo Es Historia,* v. 27, no. 317 (Dec 93), pp. 74 – 77. Il.

Lipszyc, Cecilia. Las mujeres y el poder: ¿Podemos las mujeres transformar el sistema de poder? *Feminaria,* v. 6, no. 11 (Nov 93), pp. 11 – 14. Bibl.

Marx, Jutta and Ana Sampaolesi. Elecciones internas bajo el cupo: la primera aplicación de la Ley de Cuotas en la capital federal. *Feminaria,* v. 6, no. 11 (Nov 93), pp. 15 – 17.

Social conditions

Guy, Donna Jane. *Sex and Danger in Buenos Aires: Prostitution, Family, and Nation in Argentina* reviewed by Sandra McGee Deutsch. *The Americas,* v. 49, no. 3 (Jan 93), pp. 411 – 412.

— *Sex and Danger in Buenos Aires: Prostitution, Family, and Nation in Argentina* reviewed by Kristin Ruggiero. *Hispanic American Historical Review,* v. 73, no. 1 (Feb 93), p. 165.

— *Sex and Danger in Buenos Aires: Prostitution, Family, and Nation in Argentina* reviewed by Paula Alonso. *Journal of Latin American Studies,* v. 25, no. 1 (Feb 93), pp. 198 – 200.

— *Sex and Danger in Buenos Aires: Prostitution, Family, and Nation in Argentina* reviewed by K. Lynn Stoner (Review entitled "Whores, Witches, and Unwed Mothers: Recent Scholarship on the Control of Sexuality"). *Studies in Latin American Popular Culture,* v. 12 (1993), pp. 207 – 214.

Bolivia

Economic conditions

Montoya, Víctor. La mujer entre el esclavismo y el capitalismo. *Signo,* no. 38, Nueva época (Jan – Apr 93), pp. 131 – 136. Bibl.

Brazil

Bibliography

Kuznesof, Elizabeth Anne. Sexuality, Gender, and the Family in Colonial Brazil (Review article). *Luso-Brazilian Review,* v. 30, no. 1 (Summer 93), pp. 119 – 132. Bibl.

Employment

Balção, Nilde and Maria Berenice Godinho Delgado. Mujer y trabajo. *Nueva Sociedad,* no. 124 (Mar – Apr 93), pp. 60 – 71.

Castro, Mary Garcia. Alquimia de categorias sociais na produção dos sujeitos políticos: gênero, raça e geração entre líderes do Sindicato de Trabalhadores Domésticos em Salvador. *Estudos Feministas, v.* 0, no. 0 (1992), pp. 57 – 73. Bibl.

Delgado, Maria Berenice Godinho and Maria Margareth Lopes. Mulheres trabalhadoras e meio ambiente: um olhar feminista no sindicalismo. *Estudos Feministas, v.* 0, no. 0 (1992), pp. 155 – 162.

Graham, Sandra Lauderdale. *House and Street: The Domestic World of Servants and Masters in Nineteenth-Century Rio de Janeiro* reviewed by Silvia Marina Arrom. *The Americas, v.* 49, no. 4 (Apr 93), pp. 553 – 555.

Health and hygiene

Araújo, Maria José de Oliveira. Aborto legal no hospital do Jabaquara. *Estudos Feministas, v.* 1, no. 2 (1993), pp. 424 – 428.

Arilha, Margareth and Regina Maria Barbosa. A experiência brasileira com o Cytotec. *Estudos Feministas, v.* 1, no. 2 (1993), pp. 408 – 417. Tables, charts.

Berquó, Elza Salvatori. Brasil: um caso exemplar; anticoncepção e parto cirúrgicos; à espera de uma ação exemplar (Accompanied by an English translation by Christopher Peterson). *Estudos Feministas, v.* 1, no. 2 (1993), pp. 366 – 381. Bibl, tables.

History

Bernardes, Maria Thereza Caiuby Crescenti. *Mulheres de ontem?* reviewed by José G. Bezerra Câmara. *Revista do Instituto Histórico e Geográfico Brasileiro,* no. 371 (Apr – June 91), pp. 610 – 611.

Bruschini, Cristina and Albertina de Oliveira Costa, eds. *Entre a virtude e o pecado* reviewed by Miriam Pillar Grossi (Review entitled "Enfoques de gênero na história social"). *Estudos Feministas, v.* 1, no. 1 (1993), pp. 215 – 216.

Del Priore, Mary. *Ao sul do corpo: condição feminina, maternidades e mentalidades no Brasil-colônia* reviewed by Maria Odila Silva Dias (Review entitled "A condição feminina e suas historicidades"). *Estudos Feministas, v.* 1, no. 2 (1993), pp. 481 – 485.

Deutsch, Sandra F. McGee. Afterword (to the issue entitled "Changing Images of the Brazilian Woman: Studies of Female Sexuality in Literature, Mass Media, and Criminal Trials, 1884 – 1992"). *Luso-Brazilian Review, v.* 30, no. 1 (Summer 93), pp. 107 – 117. Bibl.

Flores, Hilda Agnes Hübner. Participação da mulher na construção do Rio Grande do Sul. *Hoy Es Historia, v.* 10, no. 59 (Sept – Oct 93), pp. 67 – 74. Bibl.

Political activity

Mulher e políticas públicas reviewed by Helena Bocayuva Cunha (Review entitled "Gênero e planejamento"). *Estudos Feministas, v.* 1, no. 1 (1993), pp. 208 – 209.

Psychology

Massi, Marina. *Vida de mulheres: cotidiano e imaginário* reviewed by Lena Larinas (Review entitled "Ambivalências do desejo"). *Estudos Feministas, v.* 1, no. 1 (1993), pp. 206 – 207.

Social conditions

Fischer, Nilton Bueno. A história de Rose: classes populares, mulheres e cidadania. *Vozes, v.* 86, no. 6 (Nov – Dec 92), pp. 38 – 44.

Oliveira, Maria Coleta F. A. de. Condición femenina y alternativas de organización doméstica: las mujeres sin pareja en São Paulo. *Estudios Demográficos y Urbanos, v.* 7, no. 2 – 3 (May – Dec 92), pp. 511 – 537. Bibl, tables, charts.

Scheper-Hughes, Nancy. *Death without Weeping: The Violence of Everyday Life in Brazil* reviewed by Bernardo Kucinski. *Journal of Latin American Studies, v.* 25, no. 2 (May 93), pp. 419 – 420.

— *Death without Weeping: The Violence of Everyday Life in Brazil* reviewed by Glenn W. Erickson and Sandra S. Fernandes Erickson. *Luso-Brazilian Review, v.* 30, no. 1 (Summer 93), pp. 142 – 144.

Zaluar, Alba. Mulher de bandido: crônica de uma cidade menos musical (Accompanied by an English translation). *Estudos Feministas, v.* 1, no. 1 (1993), pp. 135 – 142. Bibl.

Caribbean area

Employment

Green, Cecilia. *The World Market Factory: A Study of Enclave Industrialization in the Eastern Caribbean and Its Impact on Women Workers* reviewed by Nan Wiegersma. *Journal of Developing Areas, v.* 27, no. 2 (Jan 93), pp. 269 – 270.

Central America

Employment

Rivera Bustamante, Tirza Emilia. Women Judges in Central America. *Hemisphere, v.* 5, no. 3 (Summer – Fall 93), pp. 18 – 19. Charts.

Political activity

Gargallo, Francesca. Los feminismos centroamericanos: sus surgimientos, sus negaciones, sus participaciones y sus perspectivas; un acercamiento a la política femenina. *Fem, v.* 17, no. 119 (Jan 93), pp. 13 – 21. Bibl.

Chile

Employment

Szasz, Ivonne. Trabajadoras inmigrantes en Santiago de Chile en los años ochenta. *Estudios Demográficos y Urbanos, v.* 7, no. 2 – 3 (May – Dec 92), pp. 539 – 553. Bibl, tables.

Societies, etc.

Etcheberry, Blanca. Las mujeres de La Pintana: conversar para vivir mejor. *Mensaje, v.* 42, no. 421 (Aug 93), p. 385. Il.

Colombia

Biography

Duque Gómez, Luis. Brillante trayectoria de la mujer en la Academia (Commentary on the speech by Carmen Ortega Ricaurte). *Boletín de Historia y Antigüedades, v.* 80, no. 781 (Apr – June 93), pp. 407 – 413.

History

Londoño, Patricia. Visual Images of Urban Colombian Women, 1800 to 1930. *SALALM Papers, v.* 34 (1989), pp. 99 – 114. Bibl.

Social conditions

Ewald, Wendy. *Magic Eyes: Scenes from an Andean Girlhood* reviewed by Barbara Mujica (Review entitled "A Coming of Age"). *Américas, v.* 45, no. 5 (Sept – Oct 93), pp. 60 – 61. Il.

Rodríguez Jiménez, Pablo. *Seducción, amancebamiento y abandono en la colonia* reviewed by Frédérique Langue. *Anuario de Estudios Americanos, v.* 49, Suppl. 2 (1992), pp. 261 – 262.

Costa Rica

Employment

Gindling, T. H. Women's Wages and Economic Crisis in Costa Rica. *Economic Development and Cultural Change, v.* 41, no. 2 (Jan 93), pp. 277 – 297. Bibl, tables.

Health and hygiene

Ramírez Quirós, Ileana. Mujer y SIDA: la exclusión de la mujer de las campañas comunicacionales. *Revista de Ciencias Sociales (Costa Rica),* no. 58 (Dec 92), pp. 11 – 22. Bibl.

Social conditions

Cerdas Bokhan, Dora. Matrimonio y vida cotidiana en el graven central costarricense, 1851 – 1890. *Revista de Historia (Costa Rica),* no. 26 (July – Dec 92), pp. 69 – 95. Bibl.

Cuba

Legal status, laws, etc.

Stoner, K. Lynn. *From the House to the Streets: The Cuban Woman's Movement for Legal Reform, 1898 – 1940* reviewed by Margarita Mergal (Review entitled "De domésticas a militantes: análisis de un processo transformador"). *Caribbean Studies, v.* 25, no. 1 – 2 (Jan – July 92), pp. 173 – 185. Bibl.

— *From the House to the Streets: The Cuban Woman's Movement for Legal Reform, 1898 – 1940* reviewed by Marifeli Pérez-Stable. *Cuban Studies/Estudios Cubanos, v.* 23 (1993), pp. 220 – 222.

— *From the House to the Streets: The Cuban Woman's Movement for Legal Reform, 1898 – 1940* reviewed by Jean Stubbs. *Journal of Latin American Studies,* v. 25, no. 2 (May 93), pp. 425 – 426.

Social conditions

Catasús Cervera, Sonia Isabel. La nupcialidad durante la década de los ochenta en Cuba. *Estudios Demográficos y Urbanos,* v. 7, no. 2 – 3 (May – Dec 92), pp. 465 – 477. Bibl, tables.

Developing countries

Health and hygiene

Elias, Christopher. Enfermedades transmitidas sexualmente y la salud reproductiva de las mujeres en los países en vías de desarrollo. *Fem,* v. 17, no. 124 (June 93), pp. 26 – 29. Bibl.

Dominican Republic

Employment

Guerrero, María Angustias. Costureras y producción mercantil en la sociedad dominicana: los orígenes. *Anuario de Estudios Americanos,* v. 49 (1992), pp. 601 – 614. Bibl, tables.

Safa, Helen Icken. The New Women Workers: Does Money Equal Power? *NACLA Report on the Americas,* v. 27, no. 1 (July – Aug 93), pp. 24 – 29 +. Bibl, il.

Guatemala

Social conditions

Brittin, Alice A. and Kenya C. Dworkin. Rigoberta Menchú: "Los indígenas no nos quedamos como bichos aislados, inmunes, desde hace 500 años. No, nosotros hemos sido protagonistas de la historia" (Includes Rigoberta Menchú's poem, "Patria abnegada"). *Nuevo Texto Crítico,* v. 6, no. 11 (1993), pp. 207 – 222.

Haiti

Legal status, laws, etc.

Szászdi León-Borja, István. Españolas en Haití: la condición jurídica de las primeras pobladoras europeas del Nuevo Mundo. *Revista de Indias,* v. 53, no. 198 (May – Aug 93), pp. 617 – 626. Bibl.

Latin America

Bitácora latinoamericana de FEMPRESS. *Fem,* v. 17, no. 119 – 130 (Jan – Dec 93), All issues.

Bibliography

Arrom, Silvia Marina. Historia de la mujer y de la familia latinoamericanas. *Historia Mexicana,* v. 42, no. 2 (Oct – Dec 92), pp. 379 – 418.

Caulfield, Sueann. Women of Vice, Virtue, and Rebellion: New Studies of Representation of the Female in Latin America (Review article). *Latin American Research Review,* v. 28, no. 2 (1993), pp. 163 – 174.

Nash, June. Estudios de género en Latinoamérica. *Mesoamérica (USA),* v. 13, no. 23 (June 92), pp. 1 – 22. Bibl.

Sección bibliográfica. *Feminaria,* v. 6, no. 10 – 11 (1993), All issues.

Education

Déleon Meléndez, Ofelia Columba. Problemas teóricos sobre la cultura popular tradicional, la educación y la mujer en América Latina. *Folklore Americano,* no. 52 (July – Dec 91), pp. 101 – 108.

Stromquist, Nelly P., ed. *Women and Education in Latin America: Knowledge, Power, and Change* reviewed by Rosemary G. Messick. *Revista Interamericana de Bibliografía,* v. 42, no. 2 (1992), pp. 288 – 289.

Employment

Candia, José Miguel. Tendencias recientes de la participación laboral femenina en América Latina. *Problemas del Desarrollo,* v. 24, no. 93 (Apr – June 93), pp. 195 – 209. Bibl, tables.

Filgueira, Nea. *Mujeres y trabajo en América Latina* (Review). *Revista Paraguaya de Sociología,* v. 30, no. 86 (Jan – Apr 93), pp. 208 – 209.

Sala, Mariella. Tecnologías invisibles: seis estudios de casos develan papel de la mujer latinoamericana como innovadora de tecnologías en procesos productivos. *Fem,* v. 17, no. 126 (Aug 93), pp. 32 – 33.

Wilson, Fiona. Industria informal, talleres y ámbito doméstico. *Revista Mexicana de Sociología,* v. 54, no. 4 (Oct – Dec 92), pp. 91 – 115. Bibl.

Health and hygiene

Chelala, César A. Prevención de la mortalidad materna en las Américas: perspectivas para los años noventa. *Fem,* v. 17, no. 123 (May 93), pp. 21 – 31. Bibl.

History

Lavrin, Asunción. La vida femenina como experiencia religiosa: biografía y hagiografía en Hispanoamérica colonial. *Colonial Latin American Review,* v. 2, no. 1 – 2 (1993), pp. 27 – 51. Bibl.

Maura, Juan Francisco. Esclavas españolas en el Nuevo Mundo. *Colonial Latin American Historical Review,* v. 2, no. 2 (Spring 93), pp. 185 – 194. Bibl.

Núñez Sánchez, Jorge, ed. *Historia de la mujer y la familia* reviewed by Gilma Mora de Tovar. *Anuario Colombiano de Historia Social y de la Cultura,* no. 20 (1992), pp. 164 – 167.

Legal status, laws, etc.

Pareja Ortiz, María del Carmen. Un aspecto de la vida cotidiana: la mujer ante el matrimonio en la legislación de Indias. *Hoy Es Historia,* v. 10, no. 60 (Nov – Dec 93), pp. 50 – 60. Il.

Political activity

Luna, Lola G. Movimientos de mujeres, estado y participación política en América Latina: una propuesta de análisis histórico. *Boletín Americanista,* v. 33, no. 42 – 43 (1992 – 1993), pp. 255 – 266. Bibl.

Miller, Francesca. *Latin American Women and the Search for Social Justice* reviewed by Trudy Yeager. *The Americas,* v. 49, no. 3 (Jan 93), pp. 412 – 414.

— *Latin American Women and the Search for Social Justice* reviewed by Asunción Horno-Delgado. *Letras Femeninas,* v. 19, no. 1 – 2 (Spring – Fall 93), pp. 139 – 140.

Radcliffe, Sarah A. and Sallie Westwood, eds. *"Viva": Women and Popular Protest in Latin America* reviewed by Tessa Cubitt. *Bulletin of Latin American Research,* v. 12, no. 2 (May 93), pp. 242 – 243.

Social conditions

Fernández Poncela, Anna M. Las latinoamericanas en el "decenio perdido para el desarrollo." *Fem,* v. 17, no. 122 (Apr 93), pp. 6 – 8.

Krawczyk, Miriam. Women in the Region: Major Changes. *CEPAL Review,* no. 49 (Apr 93), pp. 7 – 19. Bibl.

Statistics

Mulheres latino-americanas em dados (Review entitled "Estatísticas sobre as mulheres"). *Estudos Feministas,* v. 1, no. 2 (1993), pp. 502 – 503.

Mexican – American Border Region

History

Croston, Kendel. Women's Activities during the Prohibition Era along the U.S. – Mexico Border. *Journal of Borderlands Studies,* v. 8, no. 1 (Spring 93), pp. 99 – 113. Bibl.

Legal status, laws, etc.

Rock, Rosalind Z. "Mujeres de substancia": Case Studies of Women of Property in Northern New Spain. *Colonial Latin American Historical Review,* v. 2, no. 4 (Fall 93), pp. 425 – 440. Bibl, facs.

Mexico

Bain, Jennifer H. Mexican Rural Women's Knowledge of the Environment. *Mexican Studies,* v. 9, no. 2 (Summer 93), pp. 259 – 274. Bibl.

Bibliography

Ochoa Méndez, Jacqueline. Orientación bibliográfica sobre la mujer. *El Cotidiano,* v. 9, no. 53 (Mar – Apr 93), p. 120.

Biography

Hernández Carballido, Elvira Laura. En la vanguardia. *Fem,* v. 17, no. 119 – 130 (Jan – Dec 93), All issues.

Las mujeres en la revolución mexicana: biografías de mujeres revolucionarias reviewed by Martha Eva Rocha Islas (Review entitled "Más allá del estereotipo"). *Fem,* v. 17, no. 121 (Mar 93), pp. 46 – 48. Bibl.

Education

Morales Hernández, Liliana. Mujer que sabe latín: la mujer en la educación superior de México. *El Cotidiano,* v. 9, no. 53 (Mar – Apr 93), pp. 71 – 77. Il, tables.

Employment

Benería, Lourdes and Martha Roldán. *Las encrucijadas de clase y género: trabajo a domicilio; subcontratación y dinámica de la unidad doméstica en la ciudad de México* translated by Julio Colón Gómez. Reviewed by Norma Ilse Veloz Avila. *El Cotidiano,* v. 9, no. 53 (Mar – Apr 93), p. 118.

Chant, Sylvia H. *Women and Survival in Mexican Cities: Perspectives on Gender, Labour Markets, and Low-Income Households* reviewed by M. Patricia Fernández Kelly. *Economic Development and Cultural Change,* v. 41, no. 3 (Apr 93), pp. 671 – 673.

Donato, Katharine M. Current Trends and Patterns of Female Migration: Evidence from Mexico. *International Migration Review,* v. 27, no. 4 (Winter 93), pp. 748 – 771. Bibl, tables.

García Guzmán, Brígida. La ocupación en México en los años ochenta: hechos y datos. *Revista Mexicana de Sociología,* v. 55, no. 1 (Jan – Mar 93), pp. 137 – 153. Bibl, tables.

Gargallo, Francesca. Derechos humanos y trabajo doméstico asalariado. *Fem,* v. 17, no. 130 (Dec 93), pp. 4 – 6. Bibl.

Lezama, José Luis. Ciudad, mujer y conflicto: el comercio ambulante en el D.F. *Estudios Demográficos y Urbanos,* v. 6, no. 3 (Sept – Dec 91), pp. 649 – 675. Bibl, tables.

Macías V., María de la Luz. Mujeres e industria manufacturera en México. *El Cotidiano,* v. 9, no. 53 (Mar – Apr 93), pp. 33 – 39. Bibl, il, tables.

Martínez Morelos, Olivia. Las Trabajadoras del Servicio Doméstico: ¡Presentes! *Fem,* v. 17, no. 121 (Mar 93), pp. 34 – 35. Il.

— Trabajadoras del Servicio Doméstico: Sus Reivindicaciones en el Movimiento de Mujeres. *Fem,* v. 17, no. 130 (Dec 93), pp. 40 – 41.

Pérez, Emma Marie. "She Has Served Others in More Intimate Ways": The Domestic Servant Reform in Yucatán, 1915 – 1918. *Aztlán,* v. 20, no. 1 – 2 (Spring – Fall 91), pp. 11 – 37. Bibl.

Rendón, Teresa. El trabajo femenino en México: tendencias y cambios recientes. *El Cotidiano,* v. 9, no. 53 (Mar – Apr 93), pp. 3 – 9. Tables.

Rubin-Kurtzman, Jane R. Los determinantes de la oferta de trabajo femenino en la ciudad de México, 1970. *Estudios Demográficos y Urbanos,* v. 6, no. 3 (Sept – Dec 91), pp. 545 – 582. Bibl, tables.

Sandoval Flores, Etelvina. Maestras y modernización educativa. *El Cotidiano,* v. 9, no. 53 (Mar – Apr 93), pp. 78 – 82. Tables, charts.

Suárez López, Leticia. Trayectorias laborales y reproductivas: una comparación entre México y España. *Estudios Demográficos y Urbanos,* v. 7, no. 2 – 3 (May – Dec 92), pp. 359 – 375. Bibl, tables, charts.

Velázquez, Carolina. Las operadoras de TELMEX. *Fem,* v. 17, no. 128 (Oct 93), pp. 19 – 21.

Willis, Katie. Women's Work and Social Network Use in Oaxaca City. *Bulletin of Latin American Research,* v. 12, no. 1 (Jan 93), pp. 65 – 82. Bibl, tables.

Wilson, Fiona. *De la casa al taller: mujeres, trabajo y clase social en la industria textil y del vestido* reviewed by Soledad González Montes. *Estudios Sociológicos,* v. 11, no. 31 (Jan – Apr 93), pp. 288 – 290. Bibl.

— *Sweaters: Gender, Class, and Workshop-Based Industry in Mexico* reviewed by Tessa Cubitt. *Bulletin of Latin American Research,* v. 12, no. 1 (Jan 93), pp. 124 – 125.

Zabludovsky, Gina. Hacia un perfil de la mujer empresaria en México. *El Cotidiano,* v. 9, no. 53 (Mar – Apr 93), pp. 54 – 59 + . Tables.

Health and hygiene

Declaración de México para una maternidad sin riesgos: Cocoyoc, Morelos, 8 – 11 de febrero de 1993. *Fem,* v. 17, no. 122 (Apr 93), pp. 26 – 31. Il.

Pérez Gil, Sara Elena et al. La salud y la nutrición de las mujeres en México. *El Cotidiano,* v. 9, no. 53 (Mar – Apr 93), pp. 84 – 92. Il, tables.

Intellectual life

Franco, Jean. *Plotting Women: Gender and Representation in Mexico* reviewed by Ileana Rodríguez (Review entitled "Tramando y entramando una agenda feminista"). *Casa de las Américas,* no. 191 (Apr – June 93), pp. 133 – 137.

Political activity

Alonso, Claudio. La participación de las mujeres en el combate a la pobreza. *Fem,* v. 17, no. 120 (Feb 93), p. 44.

Carlsen, Laura. Reflexiones sobre un proyecto sindical feminista: el Sindicato "19 de Septiembre" siete años después del sismo. *El Cotidiano,* v. 9, no. 53 (Mar – Apr 93), pp. 93 – 98. Bibl, tables, charts.

Custodio, Isabel. Charla con René Juárez, presidente municipal de Acapulco. *Fem,* v. 17, no. 120 (Feb 93), p. 31.

Díaz Castellanos, Guadalupe. Patricia Mercado: feminismo sindical. *Fem,* v. 17, no. 129 (Nov 93), pp. 15 – 17. Il.

Espinosa Damián, Gisela. Feminismo y movimientos de mujeres: encuentros y desencuentros. *El Cotidiano,* v. 9, no. 53 (Mar – Apr 93), pp. 10 – 16. Il.

López García, Guadalupe. Bitácora de la mujer. *Fem,* v. 17, no. 119 – 130 (Jan – Dec 93), All issues.

Martínez F., Alicia. De poder, podemos: diferencias genéricas en la dinámica sociopolítica. *El Cotidiano,* v. 9, no. 53 (Mar – Apr 93), pp. 47 – 52. Tables.

Massolo, Alejandra. *Por amor y coraje: mujeres en movimientos urbanos de la ciudad de México* reviewed by Beatriz Almanza. *El Cotidiano,* v. 10, no. 57 (Aug – Sept 93), p. 109.

— *Por amor y coraje: mujeres en movimientos urbanos de la ciudad de México* reviewed by Elena Urrutia. *La Educación (USA),* v. 37, no. 114 (1993), pp. 164 – 165.

Massolo, Alejandra, ed. *Mujeres y ciudades* reviewed by Maribel Nicasio González. *El Cotidiano,* v. 10, no. 57 (Aug – Sept 93), p. 110.

Ravelo Blancas, Patricia. Breve balance del movimiento de costureras del Sindicato "19 de Septiembre." *El Cotidiano,* v. 9, no. 53 (Mar – Apr 93), pp. 99 – 104. Il, tables.

Psychology

Salgado de Snyder, V. Nelly. Family Life across the Border: Mexican Wives Left Behind. *Hispanic Journal of Behavioral Sciences,* v. 15, no. 3 (Aug 93), pp. 391 – 401. Bibl.

Social conditions

Barreda Solórzano, Luis de la. Las condiciones carcelarias de las mujeres. *Fem,* v. 17, no. 127 (Sept 93), pp. 13 – 16. Bibl.

— Mujeres en prisión. *Fem,* v. 17, no. 122 (Apr 93), pp. 20 – 21.

Garza Caligaris, Anna María and Juana María Ruiz Ortiz. Madres solteras indígenas. *Mesoamérica (USA),* v. 13, no. 23 (June 92), pp. 66 – 77. Bibl.

Martínez Vázquez, Griselda. La mujer en el proceso de modernización en México. *El Cotidiano,* v. 9, no. 53 (Mar – Apr 93), pp. 17 – 24. Bibl, tables.

Myers, Kathleen Ann. A Glimpse of Family Life in Colonial Mexico: A Nun's Account. *Latin American Research Review,* v. 28, no. 2 (1993), pp. 63 – 87. Bibl, il.

Pérez, Emma Marie. "She Has Served Others in More Intimate Ways": The Domestic Servant Reform in Yucatán, 1915 – 1918. *Aztlán,* v. 20, no. 1 – 2 (Spring – Fall 91), pp. 11 – 37. Bibl.

Robles B., Rosario et al. La mujer campesina en la época de la modernidad. *El Cotidiano,* v. 9, no. 53 (Mar – Apr 93), pp. 25 – 32. Bibl, il, tables.

Rus, Diane L. La vida y el trabajo en Ciudad Real: conversaciones con las "coletas." *Mesoamérica (USA),* v. 13, no. 23 (June 92), pp. 113 – 133. Il.

Societies, etc.

De Diego de Sousa, María Teresa de. Foro internacional sobre derechos humanos y filantropía. *Fem,* v. 17, no. 126 (Aug 93), pp. 8 – 9.

Saucedo, Irma. Las ONGs de mujeres en México. *Fem,* v. 17, no. 126 (Aug 93), pp. 10 – 13. Tables.

Nicaragua

Employment

Fernández Poncela, Anna M. La participación económica y política de las mujeres nicaragüenses. *Boletín Americanista*, v. 33, no. 42 – 43 (1992 – 1993), pp. 267 – 299. Bibl, tables, charts.

Political activity

Chinchilla, Norma Jean Stoltz. Classe, gênero e soberania na Nicarágua (A translation of "Revolutionary Popular Feminism in Nicaragua: Articulating Class, Gender, and National Sovereignty," translated by Vera Pereira. Originally published in *Gender and Society*, September 1990). *Estudos Feministas*, v. 1, no. 2 (1993), pp. 321 – 347. Bibl.

Fernández Poncela, Anna M. La participación económica y política de las mujeres nicaragüenses. *Boletín Americanista*, v. 33, no. 42 – 43 (1992 – 1993), pp. 267 – 299. Bibl, tables, charts.

Quandt, Midge. Nicaragua: Unbinding the Ties; Popular Movements and the FSLN. *Report on the Americas*, v. 26, no. 4 (Feb 93), pp. 11 – 14. Il.

Social conditions

Fernández Poncela, Anna M. El torbellino de la violencia alcanza a las mujeres nicaragüenses. *Fem*, v. 17, no. 119 (Jan 93), pp. 9 – 12.

Paraguay

Social conditions

Caballero Aquino, Olga and Marina Díaz de Vivar Prieto. *Mujer paraguaya: jefa de familia* (Review). *Revista Paraguaya de Sociología*, v. 29, no. 84 (May – Aug 92), p. 210. Il.

Ocampos, Genoveva. *Mujeres campesinas: estrategias de vida* reviewed by Sylvia Chant. *European Review of Latin American and Caribbean Studies*, no. 54 (June 93), pp. 137 – 138.

Peru

History

Villavicencio, Maritza. *Del silencio a la palabra: mujeres peruanas en los siglos XIX – XX* reviewed by Adriana Schaaf (Review entitled "El destape"). *Debate (Peru)*, v. 16, no. 74 (Sept – Oct 93), p. 66. Il.

Political activity

Pásara, Luis H. et al. *La otra cara de la luna: nuevos actores sociales en el Perú* reviewed by Romeo Grompone (Review entitled "Nuevos actores"). *Debate (Peru)*, v. 15, no. 70 (Sept – Oct 92), pp. 69 – 70.

Statistics

Sánchez León, Abelardo. Perfil del ama de casa limeña. *Debate (Peru)*, v. 16, no. 72 (Mar – May 93), pp. 32 – 38. Il, tables.

Puerto Rico

Employment

Safa, Helen Icken. The New Women Workers: Does Money Equal Power? *NACLA Report on the Americas*, v. 27, no. 1 (July – Aug 93), pp. 24 – 29 +. Bibl, il.

Southern Cone of South America

Political activity

Fisher, Jo. *Out of the Shadows: Women, Resistance, and Politics in South America* reviewed by Catherine Davies (Review entitled "Women and a Redefinition of Argentinian Nationhood"). *Bulletin of Latin American Research*, v. 12, no. 3 (Sept 93), pp. 333 – 341.

— Women and Democracy: For Home and Country. *NACLA Report on the Americas*, v. 27, no. 1 (July – Aug 93), pp. 30 – 36 +. Il.

Spain

Employment

Suárez López, Leticia. Trayectorias laborales y reproductivas: una comparación entre México y España. *Estudios Demográficos y Urbanos*, v. 7, no. 2 – 3 (May – Dec 92), pp. 359 – 375. Bibl, tables, charts.

United States

Social conditions

Chaffee, Sue. Haitian Women in Miami. *Hemisphere*, v. 5, no. 2 (Winter – Spring 93), pp. 22 – 23. Il.

Uruguay

History

Medina Ríos, Alba. El protagonismo femenino en la "redota": una lectura al padrón del éxodo del pueblo oriental. *Hoy Es Historia*, v. 10, no. 55 (Jan – Feb 93), pp. 58 – 61.

Ortiz de Terra, María del Carmen and Rosario Quijano. En busca de la memoria histórica de la mujer. *Hoy Es Historia*, v. 10, no. 55 (Jan – Feb 93), pp. 53 – 57.

Rodríguez Villamil, Silvia. Mujeres uruguayas a fines del siglo XIX: ¿Cómo hacer su historia? *Boletín Americanista*, v. 33, no. 42 – 43 (1992 – 1993), pp. 71 – 85. Bibl.

Political activity

Sapriza, Graciela. Valores notables de la cultura uruguaya: noticia biográfica sobre cuatro transgresoras. *Hoy Es Historia*, v. 10, no. 55 (Jan – Feb 93), pp. 48 – 52.

Social conditions

Filgueira, Nea. Otra vez las mujeres somos culpables: la procreación como una razón de estado. *Fem*, v. 17, no. 121 (Mar 93), pp. 11 – 13.

Venezuela

Education

Loreto Loreto, Blas. Decreto fundador de la Escuela de Artes y Oficios de Mujeres, hoy Ciclo Combinado "Teresa Carreño." *Boletín de la Academia Nacional de la Historia (Venezuela)*, v. 75, no. 297 (Jan – Mar 92), pp. 179 – 184.

WOMEN AND RELIGION

Aramoni Calderón, Dolores. De diosas y mujeres. *Mesoamérica (USA)*, v. 13, no. 23 (June 92), pp. 85 – 94. Bibl.

Chacón Echeverría, Laura. La mujer prostituta: cuerpo de suciedad, fermento de muerte; reflexiones en torno a algunos rituales de purificación. *Revista de Ciencias Sociales (Costa Rica)*, no. 58 (Dec 92), pp. 23 – 34. Bibl, il.

Iwasaki Cauti, Fernando A. Mujeres al borde de la perfección: Rosa de Santa María y las alumbradas de Lima. *Hispanic American Historical Review*, v. 73, no. 4 (Nov 93), pp. 581 – 613. Bibl.

Lavrin, Asunción. La vida femenina como experiencia religiosa: biografía y hagiografía en Hispanoamérica colonial. *Colonial Latin American Review*, v. 2, no. 1 – 2 (1993), pp. 27 – 51. Bibl.

McAlister, Elizabeth. Sacred Stories from the Haitian Diaspora: A Collective Biography of Seven Vodou Priestesses in New York City. *Journal of Caribbean Studies*, v. 9, no. 1 – 2 (Winter 92 – Spring 93), pp. 11 – 27. Bibl.

Nunes, Maria José Fontelas Rosado. De mulheres e de deuses. *Estudos Feministas*, v. 0, no. 0 (1992), pp. 5 – 30. Bibl.

Parentelli, Gladys. Teología feminista en América Latina. *Fem*, v. 17, no. 130 (Dec 93), pp. 7 – 12. Bibl.

Tamez, Elsa. Que la mujer no calle en la congregación: pautas hermenéuticas para comprender Gá. 3.28 y 1 Co. 14.23. *Cristianismo y Sociedad*, v. 30, no. 113 (1992), pp. 45 – 52. Bibl.

WOMEN ARTISTS

Argentina

Escallón, Ana María. Delia Cugat: la atmósfera de la condición humana (Accompanied by an English translation). *Art Nexus*, no. 9 (June – Aug 93), pp. 88 – 90. Il.

Brazil

Amaral, Aracy A. Tarsila: modernidade entre a racionalidade e o onírico. *Vozes*, v. 87, no. 4 (July – Aug 93), pp. 53 – 59. Il.

Iriarte, María Elvira. Mira Schendel (Accompanied by an English translation). *Art Nexus*, no. 8 (Apr – June 93), pp. 83 – 87. Il.

Chile

Madrid Letelier, Alberto. Roser Bru: iconografía de la memoria. *Cuadernos Hispanoamericanos*, no. 510 (Dec 92), pp. 7 – 12. Il.

Colombia

Merewether, Charles. Comunidad y continuidad: Doris Salcedo; nombrando la violencia (Accompanied by the English original, translated by Magdalena Holguín). *Art Nexus,* no. 9 (June – Aug 93), pp. 104 – 109. Bibl, il.

Costa Rica

Macaya T., Emilia. Lo inefable en Blanca Ruiz-Fontanorrosa (Includes reproductions of 12 paintings from her series "Puertas y ventanas"). *Káñina,* v. 16, no. 1 (Jan – June 92), pp. 229 – 241. Il.

Cuba

Damian, Carol. María Martínez Cañas: el viaje a casa (Accompanied by the English original, translated by Ignacio Zuleta Ll.). *Art Nexus,* no. 9 (June – Aug 93), pp. 114 – 117. Il.

Jamaica

Manley, Edna. *Edna Manley: The Diaries* edited by Rachel Manley. Reviewed by Adelaida de Juan (Review entitled "A Woman to Remember"). *Jamaica Journal,* v. 25, no. 1 (Oct 93), pp. 26 – 67. Il.

Mexican – American Border Region

Anzaldúa, Gloria. Chicana Artists: Exploring "nepantla; el lugar de la frontera." *NACLA Report on the Americas,* v. 27, no. 1 (July – Aug 93), pp. 37 – 42 +. Bibl, il.

Mexico

Ferrer, Elizabeth. Laura Cohen (Translated by Francisco Martínez Negrete). *Artes de México,* no. 19 (Spring 93), pp. 106 – 109. Il.

Gropp, Rose-Maria. ¡Contra el culto!: Frida Kahlo en Francfort (Translated by Gabriela Fonseca). *Humboldt,* no. 109 (1993), pp. 66 – 69. Il.

Herner de Larrea, Irene. Nahui Olin: años de gato. *Nexos,* v. 16, no. 185 (May 93), pp. 20 – 22. Il.

López, Gabriela. Irma Palacios: los elementos terrestres. *Nexos,* v. 16, no. 186 (June 93), pp. 89 – 90. Il.

Lozoya, Jorge Alberto and Jan M. William. María Sada: sonatina en gris mayor. *Artes de México,* no. 21 (Fall 93), p. 102. Il.

Martínez, Jesús. Olga Costa: "in memoriam." *Plural (Mexico),* v. 22, no. 263 (Aug 93), pp. 68 – 69.

Nieto, Margarita. Marie José Paz. *Latin American Art,* v. 5, no. 2 (Summer 93), pp. 53 – 54. Il.

Orellana, Margarita de. Eugenia Marcos: los frutos prohibidos. *Artes de México,* no. 19 (Spring 93), p. 110. Il.

Poniatowska, Elena. *Tinísima* reviewed by Carlos Monsiváis (Review entitled "Un cuarto de siglo"). *Nexos,* v. 16, no. 192 (Dec 93), p. 71.

Poniatowska, Elena and Carla Stellweg. *Frida Kahlo: la cámara seducida* reviewed by Andrés Salgado R. (Accompanied by an English translation). *Art Nexus,* no. 8 (Apr – June 93), p. 34. Il.

Ramírez, Fermín. María Eugenia Figueroa, pintora de luz y tierra (Includes reproductions of her paintings). *Plural (Mexico),* v. 22, no. 267 (Dec 93), pp. 41 – 48. Il.

Schaefer-Rodríguez, Claudia. *Textured Lives: Women, Art, and Representation in Modern Mexico* reviewed by Barbara Mujica (Review entitled "A Roundup of Stories"). *Américas,* v. 45, no. 1 (Jan – Feb 93), pp. 61 – 62.

— *Textured Lives: Women, Art, and Representation in Modern Mexico* reviewed by Susan Isabel Stein. *Hispania (USA),* v. 76, no. 2 (May 93), pp. 292 – 293.

— *Textured Lives: Women, Art, and Representation in Modern Mexico* reviewed by Kathleen Ross. *Hispanic American Historical Review,* v. 73, no. 2 (May 93), pp. 333 – 334.

Peru

Padurano, Dominique. Grimanesa Amorós: Mysteries and Metaphors. *Latin American Art,* v. 5, no. 1 (Spring 93), pp. 67 – 69. Il.

WOMEN AUTHORS

Hiriart, Berta. De mujeres y literatura. *Fem,* v. 17, no. 120 (Feb 93), pp. 15 – 17.

Núñez Miranda, Concepción S. La problemática de las mujeres escritoras (Speech given by the author to the Reunión de Mujeres Escritoras del Sureste, Villahermosa, Tabasco, 12 de noviembre, 1992). *Fem,* v. 17, no. 120 (Feb 93), pp. 10 – 11.

America

Study and teaching

Klein, Carol Ebersole. The Social Text in Writing by Hispanic Women: Critical Perspectives of Myriam Díaz-Diocaretz. *The Americas Review,* v. 21, no. 1 (Spring 93), pp. 79 – 90. Bibl.

Argentina

Gimbernat de González, Ester. *Aventuras del desacuerdo: novelistas argentinas de los '80* reviewed by David William Foster. *Chasqui,* v. 22, no. 1 (May 93), pp. 83 – 84.

Masiello, Francine Rose. *Between Civilization and Barbarism: Women, Nation, and Literary Culture in Modern Argentina* reviewed by Catherine Davies (Review entitled "Women and a Redefinition of Argentinian Nationhood"). *Bulletin of Latin American Research,* v. 12, no. 3 (Sept 93), pp. 333 – 341.

— *Between Civilization and Barbarism: Women, Nation, and Literary Culture in Modern Argentina* reviewed by Myron I. Lichtblau. *Hispania (USA),* v. 76, no. 3 (Sept 93), pp. 484 – 485.

— *Between Civilization and Barbarism: Women, Nation, and Literary Culture in Modern Argentina* reviewed by Verity Smith. *Journal of Latin American Studies,* v. 25, no. 3 (Oct 93), pp. 695 – 696.

— *Between Civilization and Barbarism: Women, Nation, and Literary Culture in Modern Argentina* reviewed by Naomi Lindstrom. *World Literature Today,* v. 67, no. 2 (Spring 93), p. 344.

Bolivia

Dávalos Arze, Gladys. La mujer poeta y la sociedad: cocinan tan bien como escriben. *Signo,* no. 38, Nueva época (Jan – Apr 93), pp. 105 – 111. Bibl.

Quiroga, Giancarla de. La mujer poeta en la sociedad. *Signo,* no. 38, Nueva época (Jan – Apr 93), pp. 123 – 130.

Congresses

Wiethüchter, Blanca. Primer Encuentro Nacional de Mujeres Poetas: surtidores de enigmas. *Signo,* no. 38, Nueva época (Jan – Apr 93), pp. 113 – 121.

Brazil

Sadlier, Darlene J., ed. *One Hundred Years after Tomorrow: Brazilian Women's Fiction in the 20th Century* translated by the editor. Reviewed by Candace Slater. *Letras Femeninas,* v. 19, no. 1 – 2 (Spring – Fall 93), pp. 163 – 164.

Caribbean area

Esteves, Carmen C. and Lizabeth Paravisini-Gebert. *Green Cane and Juicy Flotsam: Short Stories by Caribbean Women* reviewed by Ivette Romero. *Letras Femeninas,* v. 19, no. 1 – 2 (Spring – Fall 93), pp. 154 – 155.

Lent, John A. Mujeres periodistas en el Caribe (Translated by Jimmy Seale Collazo). *Homines,* v. 15 – 16, no. 2 – 1 (Oct 91 – Dec 92), pp. 262 – 272. Bibl.

Vicioso, Chiqui. *Algo que decir: ensayos sobre literatura femenina, 1981 – 1991* reviewed by Ester Gimbernat González. *Letras Femeninas,* v. 19, no. 1 – 2 (Spring – Fall 93), pp. 152 – 153.

Bibliography

Paravisini-Gebert, Lizabeth and Olga Torres-Seda. *Caribbean Women Novelists: An Annotated Bibliography* reviewed by David William Foster. *Chasqui,* v. 22, no. 2 (Nov 93), pp. 161 – 162.

Chile

Agosín, Marjorie. Un paisaje silencioso: las mujeres en la poesía chilena. *Fem,* v. 17, no. 125 (July 93), pp. 40 – 42.

Costa Rica

Berrón, Linda, ed. *Relatos de mujeres: antología de narradoras de Costa Rica* reviewed by Judy Berry-Bravo. *Chasqui,* v. 22, no. 2 (Nov 93), pp. 153 – 154.

Jaramillo Levi, Enrique, ed. *When New Flowers Bloomed: Short Stories by Women Writers from Costa Rica and Panama* reviewed by Cynthia Tompkins. *World Literature Today*, v. 67, no. 1 (Winter 93), pp. 164 – 165. II.

Dominican Republic

Bankay, Anne-Maria. Contemporary Women Poets of the Dominican Republic: Perspectives on Race and Other Social Issues. *Afro-Hispanic Review*, v. 12, no. 1 (Spring 93), pp. 34 – 41. Bibl.

Vicioso, Chiqui. *Algo que decir: ensayos sobre literatura femenina, 1981 – 1991* reviewed by Ester Gimbernat González. *Letras Femeninas*, v. 19, no. 1 – 2 (Spring – Fall 93), pp. 152 – 153.

Germany

Schmidt, Heide. La risa: etapas en la narrativa femenina en México y Alemania; una aproximación. *Escritura (Venezuela)*, v. 16, no. 31 – 32 (Jan – Dec 91), pp. 247 – 257. Bibl.

Great Britain

Ferguson, Moira. *Subject to Others: British Women Writers and Colonial Slavery, 1670 – 1834* reviewed by Karen Mead. *Hispanic American Historical Review*, v. 73, no. 4 (Nov 93), p. 675.

Latin America

Arenal, Electa and Stacey Schlau, eds. *Untold Sisters: Hispanic Nuns in Their Own Works* translated by Amanda Powell. Reviewed by Noël Valis. *Colonial Latin American Review*, v. 2, no. 1 – 2 (1993), pp. 304 – 308.

Bassnett, Susan, ed. *Knives and Angels: Women Writers in Latin America* reviewed by Beth E. Jörgensen. *Letras Femeninas*, v. 19, no. 1 – 2 (Spring – Fall 93), pp. 143 – 146.

Castillo, Debra A. *Talking Back: Toward a Latin American Feminist Literary Criticism* reviewed by Salvador A. Oropesa. *Chasqui*, v. 22, no. 1 (May 93), pp. 102 – 103.

— *Talking Back: Toward a Latin American Feminist Literary Criticism* reviewed by Vicente Cabrera. *Chasqui*, v. 22, no. 2 (Nov 93), pp. 155 – 156.

— *Talking Back: Toward a Latin American Feminist Literary Criticism* reviewed by Rosemary Geisdorfer Feal. *Hispania (USA)*, v. 76, no. 1 (Mar 93), pp. 82 – 83.

Castro-Klarén, Sara et al, eds. *Women's Writing in Latin America: An Anthology* reviewed by Lisa Jesse. *Bulletin of Latin American Research*, v. 12, no. 1 (Jan 93), pp. 128 – 129.

— *Women's Writing in Latin America: An Anthology* reviewed by Eva Paulino Bueno. *Revista de Crítica Literaria Latinoamericana*, v. 19, no. 37 (Jan – June 93), pp. 372 – 374.

Fernández Olmos, Margarite and Lizabeth Paravisini-Gebert. *El placer de la palabra: literatura erótica femenina de América Latina; antología crítica* reviewed by Mónica Zapata. *Canadian Journal of Latin American and Caribbean Studies*, v. 17, no. 34 (1992), pp. 135 – 138.

Granillo Vázquez, Lilia. Pensamiento indígena. *Fem*, v. 17, no. 125 (July 93), pp. 18 – 20.

Guerra-Cunningham, Lucía. Estrategias discursivas en la narrativa de la mujer latinoamericana. *Escritura (Venezuela)*, v. 16, no. 31 – 32 (Jan – Dec 91), pp. 115 – 122.

Maier, Carol and Noël Maureen Valis, eds. *In the Feminine Mode: Essays on Hispanic Women Writers* reviewed by Hazel Gold. *Hispanic Review*, v. 61, no. 4 (Fall 93), pp. 587 – 590.

Martínez, Elena M. Las "otras" voces de mujeres: narrativa y poesía. *Fem*, v. 17, no. 121 (Mar 93), pp. 36 – 37.

Oyarzún, Kemy. Género y etnia: acerca del dialogismo en América Latina. *Revista Chilena de Literatura*, no. 41 (Apr 93), pp. 33 – 45. Bibl.

Pratt, Mary Louise. Las mujeres y el imaginario nacional en el siglo XIX (Excerpt from a forthcoming book entitled *Latin American Narrative and Cultural Discourse* edited by Steve Bell et al.). *Revista de Crítica Literaria Latinoamericana*, v. 19, no. 38 (July – Dec 93), pp. 51 – 62. Bibl.

Trevizán, Liliana. Intersecciones: postmodernidad/feminismo/Latinoamérica. *Revista Chilena de Literatura*, no. 42 (Aug 93), pp. 265 – 273.

Bibliography

Cypess, Sandra Messinger et al. *Women Authors of Modern Hispanic South America: A Bibliography of Literary Criticism and Interpretation* reviewed by David William Foster. *Chasqui*, v. 22, no. 1 (May 93), pp. 87 – 88.

Sonntag-Grigera, María Gabriela. Lesser-Known Latin American Women Authors: A Bibliography. *Revista Interamericana de Bibliografía*, v. 42, no. 3 (1992), pp. 463 – 488.

Study and teaching

Feal, Rosemary Geisdorfer. Bordering Feminism in Afro-Hispanic Studies: Crossroads in the Field. *Latin American Literary Review*, v. 20, no. 40 (July – Dec 92), pp. 41 – 45. Bibl.

Mexico

Casas Chousal, Xolóxochitl and Sara Lovera. Razones y sinrazones de CIMAC y la población. *Fem*, v. 17, no. 128 (Oct 93), pp. 8 – 10.

Egan, Linda. Feminine Perspectives on Journalism: Conversations with Eight Mexican Women. *Studies in Latin American Popular Culture*, v. 12 (1993), pp. 175 – 187.

Franco, Jean. *Plotting Women: Gender and Representation in Mexico* reviewed by Ileana Rodríguez (Review entitled "Tramando y entramando una agenda feminista"). *Casa de las Américas*, no. 191 (Apr – June 93), pp. 133 – 137.

López González, Aralia et al, eds. *Mujer y literatura mexicana y chicana: culturas en contacto* reviewed by Pamela Murray. *Hispanic American Historical Review*, v. 73, no. 3 (Aug 93), p. 490.

Nieto-Cadena, Fernando. Mujer, literatura y sociedad en el sureste. *Fem*, v. 17, no. 120 (Feb 93), pp. 21 – 24.

Pardo Murray, Edmée. Las mil cabezas monstruosas sobre la literatura y las escritoras jóvenes en México. *Fem*, v. 17, no. 120 (Feb 93), pp. 12 – 13.

Ponce Jasso, Silvia. La problemática de las mujeres escritoras en el sureste. *Fem*, v. 17, no. 120 (Feb 93), pp. 4 – 6.

Schaefer-Rodríguez, Claudia. *Textured Lives: Women, Art, and Representation in Modern Mexico* reviewed by Barbara Mujica (Review entitled "A Roundup of Stories"). *Américas*, v. 45, no. 1 (Jan – Feb 93), pp. 61 – 62.

— *Textured Lives: Women, Art, and Representation in Modern Mexico* reviewed by Susan Isabel Stein. *Hispania (USA)*, v. 76, no. 2 (May 93), pp. 292 – 293.

— *Textured Lives: Women, Art, and Representation in Modern Mexico* reviewed by Kathleen Ross. *Hispanic American Historical Review*, v. 73, no. 2 (May 93), pp. 333 – 334.

Schmidt, Heide. La risa: etapas en la narrativa femenina en México y Alemania; una aproximación. *Escritura (Venezuela)*, v. 16, no. 31 – 32 (Jan – Dec 91), pp. 247 – 257. Bibl.

Valle, Norma. Ser periodista y sobrevivir en los '90. *Fem*, v. 17, no. 120 (Feb 93), p. 29.

Congresses

Alcalá, Aída Esmirna. Reunión de Mujeres Escritoras del Sureste, Villahermosa, Tabasco, jueves 12 de noviembre, 1992: "La provincia, casa de muñecas;" represión y extorsión vs. el abierto decir. *Fem*, v. 17, no. 120 (Feb 93), pp. 8 – 9.

López Lomas-Esali, Estela Alicia. Primer Encuentro Nacional de Mujeres Poetas: setenta voces de mujeres poetas para decir poesía. *Fem*, v. 17, no. 127 (Sept 93), pp. 36 – 38.

Interviews

Egan, Linda. Entrevistas con periodistas mujeres sobre la prensa mexicana. *Mexican Studies*, v. 9, no. 2 (Summer 93), pp. 275 – 294. Bibl.

— Feminine Perspectives on Journalism: Conversations with Eight Mexican Women. *Studies in Latin American Popular Culture*, v. 12 (1993), pp. 175 – 187.

Panama

Jaramillo Levi, Enrique, ed. *When New Flowers Bloomed: Short Stories by Women Writers from Costa Rica and Panama* reviewed by Cynthia Tompkins. *World Literature Today*, v. 67, no. 1 (Winter 93), pp. 164 – 165. II.

Paraguay

Fernández, Miguel Angel and Renée Ferrer de Arrellaga, eds. *Poetisas del Paraguay* reviewed by Claude Castro. *Caravelle*, no. 60 (1993), pp. 176 – 178.

Puerto Rico

Acosta Cruz, María Isabel. Historia y escritura femenina en Olga Nolla, Magali García Ramis, Rosario Ferré y Ana Lydia Vega. *Revista Iberoamericana*, v. 59, no. 162 – 163 (Jan – June 93), pp. 265 – 277. Bibl.

Daroqui, María Julia. Palabra de mujer. *Escritura (Venezuela)*, v. 16, no. 31 – 32 (Jan – Dec 91), pp. 53 – 63. Bibl.

Ferré, Rosario. *El coloquio de las perras* reviewed by Nara Araújo. *Iberoamericana*, v. 17, no. 49 (1993), pp. 103 – 104.

Solá Márquez, María Magdalena. *Aquí cuentan las mujeres: muestra y estudio de cinco narradoras puertorriqueñas* reviewed by Elena M. Martínez. *Revista Iberoamericana*, v. 59, no. 162 – 163 (Jan – June 93), p. 391.

Spain

Arenal, Electa and Stacey Schlau, eds. *Untold Sisters: Hispanic Nuns in Their Own Works* translated by Amanda Powell. Reviewed by Noël Valis. *Colonial Latin American Review*, v. 2, no. 1 – 2 (1993), pp. 304 – 308.

Maier, Carol and Noël Maureen Valis, eds. *In the Feminine Mode: Essays on Hispanic Women Writers* reviewed by Hazel Gold. *Hispanic Review*, v. 61, no. 4 (Fall 93), pp. 587 – 590.

United States

Horno Delgado, Asunción et al, eds. *Breaking Boundaries: Latina Writings and Critical Readings* reviewed by Miriam Bornstein. *Confluencia*, v. 8, no. 1 (Fall 92), pp. 177 – 179.

López González, Aralia et al, eds. *Mujer y literatura mexicana y chicana: culturas en contacto* reviewed by Pamela Murray. *Hispanic American Historical Review*, v. 73, no. 3 (Aug 93), p. 490.

WOMEN IN LITERATURE

Schmidt, Rita Terezinha. Un juego de máscaras: Nélida Piñon y Mary McCarthy (Translated by Eleonora Cróquer P.). *Escritura (Venezuela)*, v. 16, no. 31 – 32 (Jan – Dec 91), pp. 259 – 270.

Argentina

Fletcher, Lea. El desierto que no es tal: escritoras y escritura. *Feminaria*, v. 6, no. 11, Suppl. (Nov 93), pp. 7 – 13. Bibl.

Frankenthaler, Marilyn R. Agata Cruz, prototipo de la "heroína" existencialista. *La Palabra y el Hombre*, no. 84 (Oct – Dec 92), pp. 311 – 320. Bibl, il.

Frouman-Smith, Erica. Women on the Verge of a Breakthrough: Liliana Heker's *Zona de clivaje* as a Female "Bildungsroman." *Letras Femeninas*, v. 19, no. 1 – 2 (Spring – Fall 93), pp. 100 – 112. Bibl.

Masiello, Francine Rose. *Between Civilization and Barbarism: Women, Nation, and Literary Culture in Modern Argentina* reviewed by Catherine Davies (Review entitled "Women and a Redefinition of Argentinian Nationhood"). *Bulletin of Latin American Research*, v. 12, no. 3 (Sept 93), pp. 333 – 341.

— *Between Civilization and Barbarism: Women, Nation, and Literary Culture in Modern Argentina* reviewed by Myron I. Lichtblau. *Hispania (USA)*, v. 76, no. 3 (Sept 93), pp. 484 – 485.

— *Between Civilization and Barbarism: Women, Nation, and Literary Culture in Modern Argentina* reviewed by Verity Smith. *Journal of Latin American Studies*, v. 25, no. 3 (Oct 93), pp. 695 – 696.

— *Between Civilization and Barbarism: Women, Nation, and Literary Culture in Modern Argentina* reviewed by Naomi Lindstrom. *World Literature Today*, v. 67, no. 2 (Spring 93), p. 344.

Mizraje, Gabriela. El sexo despiadado: sobre Juana Manuela Gorriti. *Feminaria*, v. 6, no. 11, Suppl. (Nov 93), pp. 5 – 7.

Molinaro, Nina L. Resistance, Gender, and the Mediation of History in Pizarnik's *La condesa sangrienta* and Ortiz's *Urraca*. *Letras Femeninas*, v. 19, no. 1 – 2 (Spring – Fall 93), pp. 45 – 54. Bibl.

Monmany, Mercedes. Las mujeres imposibles en Bioy Casares. *Cuadernos Hispanoamericanos*, no. 513 (Mar 93), pp. 117 – 122.

Nari, Marcela M. Alejandra. Alejandra: maternidad e independencia femenina. *Feminaria*, v. 6, no. 10, Suppl. (Apr 93), pp. 7 – 9.

Seibel, Beatriz. *De ninfas a capitanas* reviewed by Ileana Azor. *Conjunto*, no. 92 (July – Dec 92), pp. 100 – 101.

— Mujer, teatro y sociedad en el siglo XIX. *Conjunto*, no. 92 (July – Dec 92), pp. 54 – 57. Bibl, il.

Brazil

Platt, Kamala. Race and Gender Representation in Clarice Lispector's "A menor mulher do mundo" and Carolina Maria de Jesus' *Quarto de despejo*. *Afro-Hispanic Review*, v. 11, no. 1 – 3 (1992), pp. 51 – 57. Bibl.

Ribeiro, Luís Filipe. O sexo e o poder no império: *Philomena Borges*. *Luso-Brazilian Review*, v. 30, no. 1 (Summer 93), pp. 7 – 20. Bibl.

Caribbean area

Demasy, Rose-Hélène. La femme et le pouvoir social dans *La rue Cases-Nègres*: roman de Joseph Zobel. *Caribbean Studies*, v. 25, no. 1 – 2 (Jan – July 92), pp. 11 – 26.

Dukats, Mara L. A Narrative of Violated Maternity: *Moi, Tituba, sorcière . . . noire de Salem*. *World Literature Today*, v. 67, no. 4 (Fall 93), pp. 745 – 750. Bibl.

Giacalone de Romero, Rita. Condicionamientos étnicos en la conformación de estereotipos femeninos en el Caribe hispánico y Caribe angloparlante. *Homines*, v. 15 – 16, no. 2 – 1 (Oct 91 – Dec 92), pp. 289 – 297. Bibl.

Manzor-Coats, Lillian. Of Witches and Other Things: Maryse Condé's Challenges to Feminist Discourse. *World Literature Today*, v. 67, no. 4 (Fall 93), pp. 737 – 744. Bibl, il.

Ndiaye, Christiane. Le réalisme merveilleux au féminin. *Canadian Journal of Latin American and Caribbean Studies*, v. 17, no. 34 (1992), pp. 115 – 117.

Williams, Claudette Rose-Green. The Myth of Black Female Sexuality in Spanish Caribbean Poetry: A Deconstructive Critical View. *Afro-Hispanic Review*, v. 12, no. 1 (Spring 93), pp. 16 – 23. Bibl.

Chile

Guerra-Cunningham, Lucía. La marginalidad subversiva del deseo en *La última niebla* de María Luisa Bombal. *Hispamérica*, v. 21, no. 62 (Aug 92), pp. 53 – 63.

Olea, Raquel. El cuerpo-mujer: un recorte de lectura en la narrativa de Diamela Eltit. *Revista Chilena de Literatura*, no. 42 (Aug 93), pp. 165 – 171. Bibl.

Costa Rica

Goff, Katrina. La imagen de la mujer en la *Obra poética* de Carlos de la Ossa. *Káñina*, v. 16, no. 1 (Jan – June 92), pp. 29 – 35. Bibl.

Cuba

Araújo, Nara. Raza y género en *Sab*. *Casa de las Américas*, no. 190 (Jan – Mar 93), pp. 42 – 49. Bibl.

Torres-Pou, Joan. La ambigüedad del mensaje feminista de *Sab* de Gertrudis Gómez de Avellaneda. *Letras Femeninas*, v. 19, no. 1 – 2 (Spring – Fall 93), pp. 55 – 64. Bibl.

El Salvador

McGowan, Marcia P. Mapping a New Territory: *Luisa in Realityland*. *Letras Femeninas*, v. 19, no. 1 – 2 (Spring – Fall 93), pp. 84 – 99. Bibl.

Latin America

Aronson, Stacey L. Parker and Cristina Enríquez de Salamanca. La textura del exilio: *Querido Diego, te abraza Quiela; Eva Luna; Crónica de una muerte anunciada*. *Chasqui*, v. 22, no. 2 (Nov 93), pp. 3 – 14. Bibl.

Bueno Chávez, Raúl et al. Debate (on the first session of the symposium "Latinoamérica: Nuevas Direcciones en Teoría y Crítica Literarias, III"). *Revista de Crítica Literaria Latinoamericana*, v. 19, no. 38 (July – Dec 93), pp. 63 – 69.

Castillo, Lidia E. La "mujer fatal" en la novela hispanoamericana contemporánea. *Revista Cultural Lotería*, v. 50, no. 384 (July – Aug 91), pp. 76 – 82.

Gutiérrez Estupiñán, Raquel. Sobre la crítica literaria femenina/feminista en Hispanoamérica. *Fem*, v. 17, no. 129 (Nov 93), pp. 42 – 46. Bibl.

Martínez, Elena M. Las "otras" voces de mujeres: narrativa y poesía. *Fem*, v. 17, no. 121 (Mar 93), pp. 36 – 37.

La mujer y la escena latinoamericana actual (A summary of four productions: *Medea húngara* by Arpad Göncz, *Naira Yawiña* by Isidora Aguirre, *O marinheiro* by Fernando Pessoa, and *Las ruinas circulares* by Raquel Carrió). *Conjunto*, no. 92 (July – Dec 92), pp. 58 – 62. Il.

Nigro, Kirsten F. Textualidad, historia y sujetividad: género y género. *Latin American Theatre Review*, v. 26, no. 2 (Spring 93), pp. 17 – 24.

Oyarzún, Kemy. Literaturas heterogéneas y dialogismo genérico – sexual. *Revista de Crítica Literaria Latinoamericana*, v. 19, no. 38 (July – Dec 93), pp. 37 – 50. Bibl.

Perilli de Garmendia, Carmen. *Imágenes de la mujer en Carpentier y García Márquez* reviewed by Rita Gnutzmann. *Revista Interamericana de Bibliografía*, v. 42, no. 3 (1992), p. 507.

Pieropan, María D. Alfonsina Storni y Clara Lair: de la mujer posmodernista a la mujer "moderna." *Hispania (USA)*, v. 76, no. 4 (Dec 93), pp. 672 – 682. Bibl.

Pratt, Mary Louise. Las mujeres y el imaginario nacional en el siglo XIX (Excerpt from a forthcoming book entitled *Latin American Narrative and Cultural Discourse* edited by Steve Bell et al.). *Revista de Crítica Literaria Latinoamericana*, v. 19, no. 38 (July – Dec 93), pp. 51 – 62. Bibl.

Queiroz Júnior, Teófilo de. Dois exemplos de mulher satânica na literatura latino-americana. *Vozes*, v. 87, no. 4 (July – Aug 93), pp. 20 – 29.

Russotto, Márgara. Pequeña diacronía: la heroína melodramática. *Escritura (Venezuela)*, v. 16, no. 31 – 32 (Jan – Dec 91), pp. 231 – 245. Bibl.

Mexico

Bilbija, Ksenija. Tiene los cabellos rojizos y se llama Sabina. *La Palabra y el Hombre*, no. 84 (Oct – Dec 92), pp. 228 – 239. Bibl.

Cypess, Sandra Messinger. *La Malinche in Mexican Literature: From History to Myth* reviewed by Salvador A. Oropesa. *Letras Femeninas*, v. 19, no. 1 – 2 (Spring – Fall 93), pp. 146 – 148.

— *La Malinche in Mexican Literature: From History to Myth* reviewed by Julie Greer Johnson. *Revista Interamericana de Bibliografía*, v. 42, no. 3 (1992), p. 502.

— Re-visión de la figura de la Malinche en la dramaturga mexicana contemporánea. *Cuadernos Americanos*, no. 40, Nueva época (July – Aug 93), pp. 208 – 222. Bibl.

Franco, Jean. La Malinche y el primer mundo. *Cuadernos Americanos*, no. 40, Nueva época (July – Aug 93), pp. 170 – 180.

Gartner, Bruce S. and Anita M. Hart. A Space of One's Own: Mexican Poets Kyra Galván and Perla Schwartz. *Confluencia*, v. 8, no. 1 (Fall 92), pp. 79 – 89. Bibl.

Pérez Priego, Rosalba. Las mujeres en Vasconcelos. *La Palabra y el Hombre*, no. 81 (Jan – Mar 92), pp. 341 – 348. Bibl.

Pratt, Dale J. Feminine Freedom/Metafictional Autonomy in *Los largos días. Chasqui*, v. 22, no. 2 (Nov 93), pp. 94 – 102. Bibl.

Valdés, María Elena de. La obra de Cristina Pacheco: ficción testimonial de la mujer mexicana. *Escritura (Venezuela)*, v. 16, no. 31 – 32 (Jan – Dec 91), pp. 271 – 279. Bibl.

Nicaragua

Moyano, Pilar. La transformación de la mujer y la nación en la poesía comprometida de Gioconda Belli. *Revista Canadiense de Estudios Hispánicos*, v. 17, no. 2 (Winter 93), pp. 319 – 331. Bibl.

Paraguay

Pompa Quiroz, María del Carmen. La mujer acerca de sí misma en el cuento y la novela del Paraguay. *Feminaria*, v. 6, no. 11, Suppl. (Nov 93), pp. 17 – 20. Bibl.

Puerto Rico

Roses, Lorraine Elena. Las esperanzas de Pandora: prototipos femeninos de la obra de Rosario Ferré. *Revista Iberoamericana*, v. 59, no. 162 – 163 (Jan – June 93), pp. 279 – 287.

United States

Gómez-Vega, Ibis. La mujer como artista en *Intaglio. Bilingual Review/Revista Bilingüe*, v. 18, no. 1 (Jan – Apr 93), pp. 14 – 22. Bibl.

Venezuela

Cunha-Giabbai, Gloria da. La problemática de la mujer hispanoamericana como reflejo del conflicto social: *No es tiempo para rosas* de Antonieta Madrid. *Inti*, no. 37 – 38 (Spring – Fall 93), pp. 145 – 153.

Ordóñez Vila, Montserrat. La loba insaciable de *La vorágine. Escritura (Venezuela)*, v. 16, no. 31 – 32 (Jan – Dec 91), pp. 205 – 213.

WOMEN IN MASS MEDIA

Avancini, Marta. Na era do ouro das cantoras do rádio. *Luso-Brazilian Review*, v. 30, no. 1 (Summer 93), pp. 85 – 93. Bibl.

Averbach, Márgara. Festival "Mujer y Cine": entrevista con Anamaría Muchnik. *Feminaria*, v. 6, no. 11 (Nov 93), pp. 23 – 24.

Bicalho, Maria Fernanda Baptista. The Art of Seduction: Representation of Women in Brazilian Silent Cinema (Fragment from *Entre a virtude e o pecado* edited by Albertina de Oliveira Costa and Cristina Bruschini, translated by Sueann Caulfield). *Luso-Brazilian Review*, v. 30, no. 1 (Summer 93), pp. 21 – 33. Bibl.

Bracho, Diana. La buena-buena y la mala-mala. *Fem*, v. 17, no. 130 (Dec 93), pp. 16 – 17.

Bustos Romero, Olga. Mujeres y telenovelas: audiencia cautiva; ¿Sumisa o crítica? *Fem*, v. 17, no. 130 (Dec 93), pp. 20 – 21.

Charles C., Mercedes. Modelo globalizador e imágenes femeninas. *Fem*, v. 17, no. 126 (Aug 93), pp. 29 – 30.

— Televisión y estereotipos sexuales. *Fem*, v. 17, no. 129 (Nov 93), pp. 20 – 21.

— Televisión y proyecto de mujer. *Fem*, v. 17, no. 127 (Sept 93), pp. 4 – 5.

Lauretis, Teresa de. Volver a pensar el cine de mujeres: estética y teoría feminista (Excerpt from *Technologies of Gender: Essays on Theory, Film, and Fiction* translated by Beatriz Olivier). *Feminaria*, v. 6, no. 10 (Apr 93), pp. 1 – 12. Bibl.

Lenharo, Alcir. Fascínio e solidão: as cantoras do rádio nas ondas sonoras do seu tempo. *Luso-Brazilian Review*, v. 30, no. 1 (Summer 93), pp. 75 – 84. Bibl.

Lepri, Jean-Pierre. *Images de la femme dans les annonces publicitaires des quotidiens au Mexique* reviewed by Héctor Ruiz Rivas. *Caravelle*, no. 59 (1992), pp. 313 – 314.

López García, Guadalupe. Las periodistas y el poder (y en los medios de comunicación). *Fem*, v. 17, no. 129 (Nov 93), pp. 24 – 25.

Millán Moncayo, Márgara. ¿Hacia una estética cinematográfica femenina? *Revista Mexicana de Ciencias Políticas y Sociales*, v. 37, Nueva época, no. 149 (July – Sept 92), pp. 177 – 188.

Morris, Barbara. Configuring Women: The Discourse of Empowerment in Latin American Cinema. *SALALM Papers*, v. 34 (1989), pp. 143 – 150. Bibl.

Simpson, Amelia S. Xuxa and the Politics of Gender. *Luso-Brazilian Review*, v. 30, no. 1 (Summer 93), pp. 95 – 106. Bibl.

Valle, Norma. Ser periodista y sobrevivir en los '90. *Fem*, v. 17, no. 120 (Feb 93), p. 29.

Zarattini, María. Las telenovelas y la imagen de la mujer. *Fem*, v. 17, no. 130 (Dec 93), pp. 18 – 19.

Catalogs

As cantoras do rádio: 50 anos de som e imagem da MPB reviewed by Irati Antonio. *Latin American Music Review*, v. 14, no. 2 (Fall – Winter 93), pp. 297 – 299.

Congresses

Los estereotipos y clichés en las telenovelas son un obstáculo para la credibilidad de las mujeres (Translated by Victoria E. Zamudio J.). *Fem*, v. 17, no. 130 (Dec 93), pp. 14 – 15.

Pennefather, Joan. La equidad en todas las etapas de la creación: ¡Eso es lo que cuenta! *Fem*, v. 17, no. 130 (Dec 93), pp. 24 – 25.

WOMEN'S RIGHTS

Barbieri, Teresita de. Mujeres y varones entre la libertad y la igualdad. *Fem*, v. 17, no. 129 (Nov 93), pp. 4 – 9. Bibl.

Bunch, Charlotte. Feminismo, democracia y derechos humanos (Paper presented at the congress "Mujer, Violencia y Derechos Humanos," Mexico, March 1993, translated by Victoria Zamudio Jasso). *Fem*, v. 17, no. 125 (July 93), pp. 6 – 10.

Declaración de las mujeres sobre políticas de población mundial (En preparación a la Conferencia Internacional de Población y Desarrollo de 1994). *Fem*, v. 17, no. 129 (Nov 93), pp. 36 – 39.

Fernández Poncela, Anna M. De la antropología de la mujer a la antropología feminista. *Fem*, v. 17, no. 128 (Oct 93), pp. 6 – 7.

Fischer, Amalia E. Feminismo: algo más que mujeres (Paper presented at the congress "Mujer, Violencia y Derechos Humanos," Mexico, March 1993). *Fem*, v. 17, no. 125 (July 93), pp. 11 – 13.

González, Lucero. Derechos humanos de las mujeres y la filantropía. *Fem*, v. 17, no. 126 (Aug 93), p. 4.

Hume, Patricia. ¿Por qué población, medio ambiente y desarrollo y no mujer, naturaleza y desarrollo? *Fem*, v. 17, no. 128 (Oct 93), pp. 26 – 29. Tables, charts.

Londoño E., María Ladi. Un asunto de mujeres: los derechos reproductivos; conciencia latinoamericana. *Fem*, v. 17, no. 121 (Mar 93), p. 20. Il.

Magaña Sánchez, Margarita Elena. Feminolecto y Masculinolecto: IIº Encuentro Feminista de la UAM, Unidad Xochimilco de la UAM, julio de 1992. *Fem*, v. 17, no. 125 (July 93), pp. 14 – 17. Bibl.

America

Congresses

Alberti Manzanares, Pilar. Mujer Indígena y II Encuentro Continental 500 Años de Resistencia Indígena, Negra y Popular, Guatemala, 1991. *Anuario de Estudios Americanos*, v. 49, Suppl. 1 (1992), pp. 186 – 193.

Argentina

Calvera, Leonor. *Mujeres y feminismo en la Argentina* reviewed by Eliana C. Hermann. *Hispanic Journal*, v. 14, no. 1 (Spring 93), pp. 175 – 176.

Marx, Jutta and Mónica Nosetto. ¿Las mujeres al poder?: la igualdad por decreto presidencial. *Feminaria*, v. 6, no. 10 (Apr 93), pp. 27 – 28.

Brazil

Avila, Maria Betânia. Modernidade e cidadania reprodutiva. *Estudos Feministas*, v. 1, no. 2 (1993), pp. 382 – 393.

Goldberg, Miriam and Moema Toscano. *A revolução das mulheres: uma balança do feminismo no Brasil* reviewed by Celi Regina Jardim Pinto (Review entitled "Falas de mulheres"). *Estudos Feministas*, v. 1, no. 1 (1993), pp. 219 – 221.

Hahner, June Edith. *Emancipating the Female Sex: The Struggle for Women's Rights in Brazil, 1850 – 1940* reviewed by Marianne Schmink. *Hispanic American Historical Review*, v. 73, no. 3 (Aug 93), pp. 514 – 515.

— *Emancipating the Female Sex: The Struggle for Women's Rights in Brazil, 1850 – 1940* reviewed by Kathleen J. Higgins. *Luso-Brazilian Review*, v. 30, no. 1 (Summer 93), pp. 145 – 146.

Manifesto das Mulheres: propostas de alteração do código penal brasileiro (Accompanied by an English translation). *Estudos Feministas*, v. 1, no. 1 (1993), pp. 159 – 161.

Ribeiro, Mariska. Direitos reprodutivos e políticas descartáveis. *Estudos Feministas*, v. 1, no. 2 (1993), pp. 400 – 407.

Schumaher, Maria Aparecida and Elisabeth Vargas. Lugar no governo: álibi ou conquista? (Accompanied by an English translation by Christopher Peterson). *Estudos Feministas*, v. 1, no. 2 (1993), pp. 348 – 364.

Teles, Maria Amélia de Almeida. *Breve história do feminismo no Brazil* reviewed by Joel Rufino dos Santos (Review entitled "Feministas fazendo história"). *Estudos Feministas*, v. 1, no. 2 (1993), pp. 499 – 501.

Central America

Congresses

Chinchilla, Norma Jean Stoltz. Women's Movements in the Americas: Feminism's Second Wave. *NACLA Report on the Americas*, v. 27, no. 1 (July – Aug 93), pp. 17 – 23 + . Bibl, il.

Chile

Societies, etc.

Cañadell, Rosa M. Chilean Women's Organizations: Their Potential for Change (Translated by John F. Uggen). *Latin American Perspectives*, v. 20, no. 4 (Fall 93), pp. 43 – 60. Bibl.

Cuba

Stoner, K. Lynn. *From the House to the Streets: The Cuban Woman's Movement for Legal Reform, 1898 – 1940* reviewed by Margarita Mergal (Review entitled "De domésticas a militantes: análisis de un processo transformador"). *Caribbean Studies*, v. 25, no. 1 – 2 (Jan – July 92), pp. 173 – 185. Bibl.

— *From the House to the Streets: The Cuban Woman's Movement for Legal Reform, 1898 – 1940* reviewed by Marifeli Pérez-Stable. *Cuban Studies/Estudios Cubanos*, v. 23 (1993), pp. 220 – 222.

— *From the House to the Streets: The Cuban Woman's Movement for Legal Reform, 1898 – 1940* reviewed by Jean Stubbs. *Journal of Latin American Studies*, v. 25, no. 2 (May 93), pp. 425 – 426.

Latin America

Azeredo, Sandra and Verena Stolcke, eds. *Direitos reprodutivos* (Review). *Estudos Feministas*, v. 0, no. 0 (1992), p. 230.

El movimiento feminista latinoamericano y del Caribe hacia la reunión de Beijing en 1995. *Fem*, v. 17, no. 130 (Dec 93), p. 39.

Congresses

Alvarez, Elizabeth. De brujas, lunas y aquelarres: VI Encuentro Feminista Latinoamericano y del Caribe. *Fem*, v. 17, no. 124 (June 93), pp. 33 – 34.

Gargallo, Francesca. El desencuentro de los encuentros feministas. *Fem*, v. 17, no. 130 (Dec 93), pp. 37 – 38.

— Rumbo a un primer foro sobre los derechos humanos de las mujeres. *Fem*, v. 17, no. 120 (Feb 93), pp. 32 – 33.

Mexico

Díaz Castellanos, Guadalupe. Elena Tapia . . . feminismo . . . Mujeres en Acción Sindical. *Fem*, v. 17, no. 128 (Oct 93), pp. 30 – 32.

Espinosa Damián, Gisela. Feminismo y movimientos de mujeres: encuentros y desencuentros. *El Cotidiano*, v. 9, no. 53 (Mar – Apr 93), pp. 10 – 16. Il.

Feminismo, vida cotidiana y política: una propuesta de acción positiva. *Fem*, v. 17, no. 123 (May 93), pp. 32 – 36.

Tarrés Barraza, María Luisa. El movimiento de mujeres y el sistema político mexicano: análisis de la lucha por la liberación del aborto, 1976 – 1990. *Estudios Sociológicos*, v. 11, no. 32 (May – Aug 93), pp. 365 – 397. Bibl, tables.

Torres Martínez, Lizandra. Feminismo popular en el México contemporáneo. *Homines*, v. 15 – 16, no. 2 – 1 (Oct 91 – Dec 92), pp. 283 – 288. Bibl.

Congresses

Bedregal S., Ximena. Discurso de inauguración del primer foro: "Mujer, Violencia y Derechos Humanos." *Fem*, v. 17, no. 122 (Apr 93), pp. 11 – 13.

López García, Guadalupe. Foro nacional: "Mujer, Violencia y Derechos Humanos." *Fem*, v. 17, no. 122 (Apr 93), pp. 9 – 10.

Martínez Morelos, Olivia. Trabajadoras del Servicio Doméstico: Sus Reivindicaciones en el Movimiento de Mujeres. *Fem,* v. 17, no. 130 (Dec 93), pp. 40 – 41.

Societies, etc.

Díaz Castellanos, Guadalupe. ¿Qué es la Sociedad Mexicana Pro-Derechos de la Mujer? *Fem,* v. 17, no. 126 (Aug 93), pp. 23 – 25.

Nicaragua

Chinchilla, Norma Jean Stoltz. Classe, gênero e soberania na Nicarágua (A translation of "Revolutionary Popular Feminism in Nicaragua: Articulating Class, Gender, and National Sovereignty," translated by Vera Pereira. Originally published in *Gender and Society,* September 1990). *Estudos Feministas,* v. 1, no. 2 (1993), pp. 321 – 347. Bibl.

United States

Friaz, Guadalupe Mendez. "I Want to Be Treated as an Equal": Testimony from a Latina Union Activist. *Aztlán,* v. 20, no. 1 – 2 (Spring – Fall 91), pp. 195 – 202.

WOOL INDUSTRY AND TRADE

See also
  Textile industry and fabrics

Argentina

Sábato, Hilda. *Agrarian Capitalism and the World Market: Buenos Aires in the Pastoral Age, 1840 – 1890* reviewed by Samuel Amaral. *Hispanic American Historical Review,* v. 73, no. 1 (Feb 93), pp. 161 – 162.

WORK FORCE

See
  Labor supply

WORKER SELF-MANAGEMENT

See
  Employees' representation in management

WORKING CONDITIONS

See
  Industrial sociology

WORLD HEALTH ORGANIZATION

Jablonska, Alejandra. La política de salud de la OMS: propuesta para los países en vías de desarrollo. *Revista Mexicana de Ciencias Políticas y Sociales,* v. 38, Nueva época, no. 153 (July – Sept 93), pp. 91 – 107.

WORLD POLITICS

See
  Geopolitics
  International relations

WORLD WAR, 1914 – 1918

Vinhosa, Francisco Luiz Teixeira. *O Brasil e a 1ª guerra mundial: a diplomacia brasileira e as grandes potências* reviewed by Claudio Moreira Bento. *Revista do Instituto Histórico e Geográfico Brasileiro,* no. 370 (Jan – Mar 91), pp. 338 – 339.

— Torre de Londres, 19 de outubro de 1915: as carabinas Mauser e o fuzilamento de Fernando Buschmann. *Revista do Instituto Histórico e Geográfico Brasileiro,* no. 371 (Apr – June 91), pp. 460 – 469. Bibl.

WORLD WAR, 1939 – 1945

Bento, Cláudio Moreira. Campo de prisioneiros de guerra em Pouso Alegre. *Revista do Instituto Histórico e Geográfico Brasileiro,* no. 373 (Oct – Dec 91), pp. 1052 – 1056.

— Participação das forças armadas e da marinha mercante do Brasil na segunda guerra mundial, 1942 – 1945. *Revista do Instituto Histórico e Geográfico Brasileiro,* no. 372 (July – Sept 91), pp. 685 – 745. Bibl, maps.

Carneiro, Maria Cecília Ribas. A política externa do Brasil e a segunda guerra mundial. *Revista do Instituto Histórico e Geográfico Brasileiro,* no. 373 (Oct – Dec 91), pp. 1032 – 1051. Bibl.

Moura, Gerson. Neutralidade dependente: o caso do Brasil, 1939 – 1942. *Estudos Históricos,* v. 6, no. 12 (July – Dec 93), pp. 177 – 189. Bibl.

Rolland, Denis. *Vichy et la France libre au Mexique: guerre, cultures et propagande pendant la deuxième guerre mondiale* reviewed by Thomas D. Schoonover. *Hispanic American Historical Review,* v. 73, no. 4 (Nov 93), pp. 726 – 727.

Waak, William. *As duas faces da glória* reviewed by Cláudio Moreira Bento. *Revista do Instituto Histórico e Geográfico Brasileiro,* no. 372 (July – Sept 91), pp. 930 – 932.

WRITING

Francis, Norbert and Rainer Enrique Hamel. La redacción en dos lenguas: escritura y narrativa en tres escuelas bilingües del valle del Mezquital. *Revista Latinoamericana de Estudios Educativos,* v. 22, no. 4 (Oct – Dec 92), pp. 11 – 35. Bibl, tables.

Muñoz Valenzuela, Josefina. Experiencia alfabetizadora del Taller de Acción Cultura, TAC: oralidad y escritura colectiva en Curacaví. *Revista Chilena de Literatura,* no. 42 (Aug 93), pp. 143 – 148. Bibl.

Ramírez Mercado, Sergio. Oficios compartidos. *Nuevo Texto Crítico,* v. 6, no. 11 (1993), pp. 245 – 252.

XOCHICALCO, MEXICO

Molina Montes, Augusto. Una visión de Xochicalco en el siglo XIX: Dupaix y Castañeda, 1805. *Anales del Instituto de Investigaciones Estéticas,* v. 16, no. 62 (1991), pp. 53 – 68. Bibl, il.

XOCHIMILCO, MEXICO

Cordero Espinosa, Sergio. Las flores en la arquitectura de Xochimilco (Accompanied by an English translation). *Artes de México,* no. 20 (Summer 93), pp. 74 – 79. Il.

Dufétel, Dominique. Pequeña historia de las chinampas y tres sueños (Accompanied by an English translation). *Artes de México,* no. 20 (Summer 93), pp. 37 – 47. Il.

Flores Marini, Carlos. El arte religioso de Xochimilco: un recorrido (Accompanied by an English translation). *Artes de México,* no. 20 (Summer 93), pp. 55 – 65. Il.

Hiriart, Hugo. Impresión de Xochimilco (Accompanied by an English translation). *Artes de México,* no. 20 (Summer 93), pp. 27 – 32.

Maza, Francisco de la. San Bernardino de Xochimilco: caciques domésticos (Accompanied by an English translation). *Artes de México,* no. 20 (Summer 93), pp. 67 – 73.

Salles, Vania and José Manuel Valenzuela Arce. Ambitos de relaciones sociales de naturaleza íntima e identidades culturales: notas sobre Xochimilco. *Revista Mexicana de Sociología,* v. 54, no. 3 (July – Sept 92), pp. 139 – 173. Bibl.

Bibliography

Bibliografía (to the articles on Xochimilco appearing in this issue). *Artes de México,* no. 20 (Summer 93), p. 93.

Fiction

Sarignana, Armando. Ebria bitácora (Accompanied by an English translation). *Artes de México,* no. 20 (Summer 93), pp. 81 – 92. Il.

Maps

Sánchez, Joaquín Ruy. Xochimilco. *Artes de México,* no. 20 (Summer 93), pp. 62 – 63.

Pictorial works

Sarignana, Armando. Ebria bitácora (Accompanied by an English translation). *Artes de México,* no. 20 (Summer 93), pp. 81 – 92. Il.

Stephan-Otto, Erwin. Xochimilco: fuente de historias (Accompanied by an English translation). *Artes de México,* no. 20 (Summer 93), pp. 33 – 35.

Poetry

González, Alejandro. Imágenes ("Haikú de abril," "Intrusa"), accompanied by an English translation. *Artes de México,* no. 20 (Summer 93), p. 51. Il.

Research

Martínez Salgado, Carolina. Métodos cualitativos para los estudios de población: un ejercicio en Xochimilco. *Revista Mexicana de Sociología,* v. 54, no. 3 (July – Sept 92), pp. 243 – 251. Bibl.

XUXA

See

Meneghel, Maria da Graça

YACONI, HUGO

Pérez Yoma, Marisi. Hugo Yaconi: solidaridad entre empresarios. *Mensaje*, v. 42, no. 421 (Aug 93), pp. 376 – 377. Il.

YACOPI, JOSÉ

Bach, Caleb. Where Sound Is Born (Photographs by Giancarlo Puppo). *Américas*, v. 45, no. 1 (Jan – Feb 93), pp. 24 – 29. Il.

YÁÑEZ, AGUSTÍN

Criticism of specific works

Al filo del agua

Pérez Zamora, Flor de María. *Al filo del agua:* la modificación de una estructura social. *Káñina*, v. 16, no. 2 (July – Dec 92), pp. 81 – 87.

— La religión: isotopía estructurante en *Al filo del agua*. *Káñina*, v. 16, no. 1 (Jan – June 92), pp. 69 – 77. Bibl.

YÁÑEZ, ALVARO

Criticism of specific works

Chuchezuma

Castillo de Berchenko, Adriana. Texto e intertexto en "Chuchezuma" de Juan Emar. *Revista Chilena de Literatura*, no. 40 (Nov 92), pp. 123 – 128.

YANOAMA INDIANS

Brasil: Protaria no. 580 que demarca o território da população indígena yanomami, 15 de novembro de 1991. *Anuario Indigenista*, v. 30 (Dec 91), pp. 461 – 471.

YAQUI INDIANS

Figueroa Valenzuela, Alejandro. Derechos políticos y organización social: el caso de los yaquis y los mayos. *Nueva Antropología*, v. 13, no. 44 (Aug 93), pp. 43 – 60. Bibl.

Velasco Toro, José. Autonomía y territorialidad entre los yaquis de Sonora, México. *La Palabra y el Hombre*, no. 82 (Apr – June 92), pp. 147 – 161. Bibl.

YAXCHILÁN, MEXICO

Beverido Pereau, Francisco. Estela 16 de Yaxchilán. *La Palabra y el Hombre*, no. 82 (Apr – June 92), pp. 291 – 293.

YOLI RAIMOND, GUADALUPE VICTORIA

Cabrera Infante, Guillermo. La Lupe cantaba: "Con el diablo en el cuerpo y un ángel en la voz." *Vuelta*, v. 17, no. 200 (July 93), pp. 19 – 20.

YOURCENAR, MARGUERITE

Fiction

Alvarez, María Auxiliadora. ¿Qué hace Marguerite Yourcenar en la eternidad? (Introduced by María Auxiliadora Alvarez. Article entitled "Voces o seres cercanos"). *Inti*, no. 37 – 38 (Spring – Fall 93), pp. 75 – 78.

YOUTH

See also

Adolescent psychology

Children

Hispanic American youth (U.S.)

Juvenile delinquency

Mexican American youth

Street children

Students

Argentina

Delfino, Silvia. Educación y democracia: una cultura joven en la Argentina. *La Educación (USA)*, v. 37, no. 114 (1993), pp. 47 – 58. Bibl.

Pujol, Sergio Alejandro. "Rock" y juventud: de las catacumbas al estrellato. *Todo Es Historia*, v. 27, no. 317 (Dec 93), pp. 70 – 73. Il.

Wortman, Ana. *Jóvenes desde la periferia* (Review). *Revista Paraguaya de Sociología*, v. 30, no. 86 (Jan – Apr 93), pp. 206 – 207.

Brazil

Costa, Marcia Regina da. "Skinheads": carecas do subúrbio. *Vozes*, v. 87, no. 2 (Mar – Apr 93), pp. 2 – 10.

Chile

Huneeus, Virginia. Comunidad terapéutica para jóvenes drogadictos. *Mensaje*, v. 42, no. 422 (Sept 93), pp. 465 – 466.

Mexico

Baird, Traci L. Mexican Adolescent Sexuality: Attitudes, Knowledge, and Sources of Information. *Hispanic Journal of Behavioral Sciences*, v. 15, no. 3 (Aug 93), pp. 402 – 417. Bibl, tables.

Urteaga Castro-Pozo, Maritza. Identidad y jóvenes urbanos. *Estudios Sociológicos*, v. 11, no. 32 (May – Aug 93), pp. 555 – 568. Bibl.

Peru

Béjar, Ana María. Cultura, utopía y percepción social: los festivales por la vida y por la paz y la práctica musical juvenil en Sicuani. *Allpanchis*, v. 25, no. 41 (Jan – June 93), pp. 109 – 141. Tables.

Cánepa, María Angela. Recuerdos, olvidos y desencuentros: aproximaciones a la subjetividad de los jóvenes andinos. *Allpanchis*, v. 25, no. 41 (Jan – June 93), pp. 11 – 37. Bibl.

Céspedes Aguirre, Patricia. Universidad, deporte y agresividad juvenil: apuntes en torno a la Olimpiada UNSAAC, 1991. *Allpanchis*, v. 25, no. 41 (Jan – June 93), pp. 159 – 174.

Cisneros, Luis Jaime and Arturo Ferrari. Del jardín a la calle: la juventud peruana de los '90s. *Debate (Peru)*, v. 16, no. 74 (Sept – Oct 93), pp. 19 – 25. Il, tables.

Cisneros C., Luis Fernán. Entre la ira y la paz: encuesta entre jóvenes. *Debate (Peru)*, v. 15, no. 70 (Sept – Oct 92), pp. 35 – 38. Il, tables.

Cosamalón, Ana Lucía. El lado oculto de lo cholo: presencia de rasgos culturales y afirmación de una identidad. *Allpanchis*, v. 25, no. 41 (Jan – June 93), pp. 211 – 226.

Degregori, Carlos Iván et al. Comentarios y réplica (to the article "Recuerdos, olvidos y desencuentros" by María Angela Cánepa). *Allpanchis*, v. 25, no. 41 (Jan – June 93), pp. 38 – 73.

Ochoa Rivero, Silvia. Algunas percepciones sobre lo femenino y lo masculino: hablan los jóvenes. *Allpanchis*, v. 25, no. 41 (Jan – June 93), pp. 143 – 158. Bibl.

Ollé, Carmen et al. Ni divino, ni tesoro (Three essays in which Carmen Ollé, Patricia Alba, and Beto Ortiz reminisce about their youth in Peru). *Debate (Peru)*, v. 16, no. 74 (Sept – Oct 93), pp. 27 – 30.

Trahtemberg Siederer, León. Juventud, educación, empleo y empresa. *Debate (Peru)*, v. 16, no. 74 (Sept – Oct 93), pp. 34 – 36. Il.

Valentín, Isidro. El gusto por la imagen: una vivencia de fotografía social. *Allpanchis*, v. 25, no. 41 (Jan – June 93), pp. 262 – 272. Il.

Vega-Centeno B., Imelda. Ser joven en el Perú: socialización, integración, corporalidad y cultura. *Allpanchis*, v. 25, no. 41 (Jan – June 93), pp. 177 – 210. Bibl, tables.

Pictorial works

Instantes que dejan huella. *Allpanchis*, v. 25, no. 41 (Jan – June 93), pp. 273 – 288. Il.

Political activity

Delpino, Nena. Jóvenes y política, ayer y hoy: carta a mi hija. *Debate (Peru)*, v. 15, no. 70 (Sept – Oct 92), pp. 39 – 44. Il.

Lindner, Bernardo. Nadie en quien confiar: actitud política de los jóvenes campesinos del altiplano puneño. *Allpanchis*, v. 25, no. 41 (Jan – June 93), pp. 77 – 108. Bibl, tables.

Rospigliosi, Fernando. La ausencia de los jóvenes en la política. *Debate (Peru)*, v. 16, no. 74 (Sept – Oct 93), pp. 32 – 33. Il.

Tanaka, Martín. Juventud y política en el cambio de una época. *Allpanchis*, v. 25, no. 41 (Jan – June 93), pp. 227 – 261. Bibl.

United States

Charles C., Mercedes. Violencia, televisión y niños. *Fem*, v. 17, no. 128 (Oct 93), pp. 4 – 5.

YRIGOYEN, HIPÓLITO

Solari Yrigoyen, Edelmiro M. Hipólito Yrigoyen, ¿hijo de Rosas? *Todo Es Historia,* v. 26, no. 308 (Mar 93), pp. 76 – 80. Bibl, il, facs.

YUCATÁN, MEXICO

Arnaiz Burne, Stella M. and Alfredo César Dachary. La frontera caribe de México en el XIX: una historia olvidada. *Siglo XIX: Cuadernos,* v. 3, no. 7 (Oct 93), pp. 33 – 62. Bibl, tables, maps.

Baños Ramírez, Othón. Reconfiguración rural – urbana en la zona henequenera de Yucatán. *Estudios Sociológicos,* v. 11, no. 32 (May – Aug 93), pp. 419 – 443. Tables, maps.

Brannon, Jeffery T. and Gilbert Michael Joseph, eds. *Land, Labor, and Capital in Modern Yucatán: Essays in Regional History and Political Economy* reviewed by Donald F. Stevens. *The Americas,* v. 49, no. 4 (Apr 93), pp. 558 – 559.

Castillo Peraza, Carlos. Viaje a Yucatán (sin Stephens). *Nexos,* v. 16, no. 182 (Feb 93), pp. 67 – 68.

Durán, Rafael and Miguel Franco. Estudio demográfico de "Pseudophoenix sargentii." *Bulletin de l'Institut Français d'Etudes Andines,* v. 21, no. 2 (1992), pp. 609 – 621. Bibl, maps, charts.

Franco Cáceres, Iván. Familias, oligarquía y empresarios en Yucatán, 1879 – 1906. *Siglo XIX: Cuadernos,* v. 3, no. 7 (Oct 93), pp. 9 – 31. Bibl, tables.

García Quintanilla, Alejandra. Salud y progreso en Yucatán en el XIX: Mérida; el sarampión de 1882. *Siglo XIX: Cuadernos,* v. 1, no. 3 (June 92), pp. 29 – 53. Bibl, tables.

Joseph, Gilbert Michael. *Revolución desde afuera: Yucatán, México y Estados Unidos, 1880 – 1924* translated by Eduardo L. Suárez. Reviewed by Othón Baños. *Estudios Sociológicos,* v. 11, no. 31 (Jan – Apr 93), pp. 265 – 270.

Keenan, Joe. Is There Life after Henequen? *Business Mexico,* v. 3, no. 4 (Apr 93), pp. 22 – 23. Il.

Millet Cámara, Luis et al. Tecoh, Izamal: nobleza indígena y conquista española. *Latin American Antiquity,* v. 4, no. 1 (Mar 93), pp. 48 – 58. Bibl, il, maps.

Orellana, Roger. Síndromes morfológicos y funcionales de las palmas de la península de Yucatán. *Bulletin de l'Institut Français d'Etudes Andines,* v. 21, no. 2 (1992), pp. 651 – 667. Bibl, tables, maps, charts.

Pérez, Emma Marie. "She Has Served Others in More Intimate Ways": The Domestic Servant Reform in Yucatán, 1915 – 1918. *Aztlán,* v. 20, no. 1 – 2 (Spring – Fall 91), pp. 11 – 37. Bibl.

Perry, Richard and Rosalind Perry. *Maya Missions: Exploring the Spanish Colonial Churches of Yucatán* reviewed by Miguel A. Bretos. *Hispanic American Historical Review,* v. 73, no. 1 (Feb 93), pp. 134 – 136.

Ramírez Carrillo, Luis Alfonso. El escenario de la industrialización en Yucatán. *Comercio Exterior,* v. 43, no. 2 (Feb 93), pp. 171 – 177. Bibl, tables.

Sarkisyanz, Manuel. *Vom Wirken und Sterben des Felipe Carrillo Puerto, des "Roten" Apostels der Maya-Indianer: Zur politischen Heiligenlegende im revolutionären Mexiko* reviewed by Jürgen Buchenau. *Hispanic American Historical Review,* v. 73, no. 2 (May 93), pp. 332 – 333.

Savage, Melissa. Ecological Disturbance and Nature Tourism. *Geographical Review,* v. 83, no. 3 (July 93), pp. 290 – 300. Bibl, il, maps.

Várguez Pasos, Luis A. Cultura obrera en crisis: el caso de los cordeleros de Yucatán. *Estudios Sociológicos,* v. 11, no. 31 (Jan – Apr 93), pp. 93 – 110. Bibl.

YUNGAS, BOLIVIA

Léons, Madeline Barbara. Risk and Opportunity in the Coca/Cocaine Economy of the Bolivian Yungas. *Journal of Latin American Studies,* v. 25, no. 1 (Feb 93), pp. 121 – 157. Bibl, charts.

YUPANQUI, TITU CUSI
Criticism of specific works
Relación

Jákfalvi-Leiva, Susana. De la voz a la escritura: la *Relación* de Titu Cusi, 1570. *Revista de Crítica Literaria Latinoamericana,* v. 19, no. 37 (Jan – June 93), pp. 259 – 277. Bibl.

YURA INDIANS

Rasnake, Roger Neil. *Autoridad y poder en los Andes: los kuraqkuna de Yura,* a translation of *Domination and Cultural Resistance: Authority and Power among an Andean People,* translated by Luis Brédow and Luis Huáscar Antezana. Reviewed by Pedro de Anasagasti. *Signo,* no. 35, Nueva época (Jan – Apr 92), pp. 243 – 244.

ZACATECAS, MEXICO (CITY)

García González, Francisco. Los muros de la vida privada y la familia: casa y tamaño familiar en Zacatecas; primeras décadas del siglo XIX. *Estudios Demográficos y Urbanos,* v. 7, no. 1 (Jan – Apr 92), pp. 35 – 52. Bibl, tables.

Klein, Herbert S. and Sonia Pérez Toledo. La población de la ciudad de Zacatecas en 1857. *Historia Mexicana,* v. 42, no. 1 (July – Sept 92), pp. 77 – 102. Bibl, tables, charts.

ZACATECAS, MEXICO (STATE)

Jiménez Pelayo, Agueda. *Haciendas y comunidades indígenas en el sur de Zacatecas* reviewed by Frédérique Langue. *Cahiers des Amériques Latines,* no. 13 (1992), pp. 182 – 183.

Langue, Frédérique. *Mines, terres et société à Zacatecas (Mexique) de la fin du XVIIe siècle a l'indépendance* reviewed by Manuel Castillo Martos. *Anuario de Estudios Americanos,* v. 50, no. 1 (1993), pp. 319 – 322.

ZAGO, ANGELA
Correspondence, reminiscences, etc.

Zago, Angela. Testimonio y verdad: un testimonio sobre la guerrilla. *Inti,* no. 37 – 38 (Spring – Fall 93), pp. 29 – 35.

ZAHLER, ROBERTO
Addresses, essays, lectures

Zahler, Roberto. Palabras de agradecimiento (for the "premio de la Asociación de Egresados de Ingeniería Comercial de la Universidad de Chile al ingeniero comercial más destacado del año 1992"). *Estudios Sociales (Chile),* no. 77 (July – Sept 93), pp. 197 – 202.

ZAMORA, RICARDO

Bartl, Johanna. Artistas latinoamericanos buscan mitos en Salzwedel. *Humboldt,* no. 110 (1993), p. 102. Il.

ZAMPA, JOSÉ

Torres, Angel. *José Zampa, pionero social – cristiano en Bolivia* reviewed by Pedro de Anasagasti. *Signo,* no. 35, Nueva época (Jan – Apr 92), pp. 250 – 252.

ZAPATA, EMILIANO

Brunk, Samuel. Zapata and the City Boys: In Search of a Piece of the Revolution. *Hispanic American Historical Review,* v. 73, no. 1 (Feb 93), pp. 33 – 65. Bibl.

ZAPATA OLIVELLA, JUAN
Interviews

La literatura y la medicina. *Desarrollo Indoamericano,* v. 23, no. 91 (June 93), pp. 20 – 21. Il.

ZAPOTEC INDIANS

Bustamante, Juan I. La princesa Donaji (Accompanied by an English translation). *Artes de México,* no. 21 (Fall 93), pp. 34 – 35.

Campbell, Howard B. Tradition and the New Social Movements: The Politics of Isthmus Zapotec Culture. *Latin American Perspectives,* v. 20, no. 3 (Summer 93), pp. 83 – 97. Bibl.

Hirabayashi, Lane Ryo. La politización de la cultura regional: zapotecos de la sierra Juárez en la ciudad de México. *América Indígena,* v. 51, no. 4 (Oct – Dec 91), pp. 185 – 218. Bibl.

Stephen, Lynn. *Zapotec Women* reviewed by Florence E. Babb. *The Americas,* v. 50, no. 2 (Oct 93), pp. 276 – 277.

Urcid Serrano, Javier. The Pacific Coast of Oaxaca and Guerrero: The Westernmost Extent of Zapotec Script. *Ancient Mesoamerica,* v. 4, no. 1 (Spring 93), pp. 141 – 165. Bibl, il, maps.

ZÉ, TOM

See
Martins, Antônio José Santana

ZEA, FRANCISCO ANTONIO

Beerman, Eric. Francisco Antonio Zea: su paso y matrimonio en España. *Boletín de Historia y Antigüedades,* v. 80, no. 780 (Jan – Mar 93), pp. 211 – 221. Bibl.

ZEA, LEOPOLDO

Casañas Díaz, Mirta. La recepción del marxismo en la obra de Leopoldo Zea. *Islas,* no. 96 (May – Aug 90), pp. 164 – 176. Bibl.

— Una variante del humanismo burgués en América Latina. *Islas,* no. 98 (Jan -- Apr 91), pp. 143 – 156. Bibl.

Casañas Díaz, Mirta and Rafael Plá León. La constancia de Leopoldo Zea en la búsqueda de un filosofar auténticamente americano. *Islas,* no. 99 (May – Aug 91), pp. 95 – 111. Bibl.

Dussel, Enrique D. El proyecto de una filosofía de la historia latinoamericana. *Hoy Es Historia,* v. 10, no. 57 (Apr – May 93), pp. 40 – 48. Bibl.

Guadarrama González, Pablo M. Urdimbres del pensamiento de Leopoldo Zea frente a la marginación y la barbarie. *Cuadernos Americanos,* no. 37, Nueva época (Jan – Feb 93), pp. 51 – 64. Bibl.

Vázquez, Susana. Leopoldo Zea y la conciencia latinoamericana. *Hoy Es Historia,* v. 10, no. 60 (Nov – Dec 93), pp. 4 – 13. Bibl, il.

Criticism of specific works

Filosofía de la historia americana

Plá León, Rafael. Marxismo: ¿Eurocentrismo o universidad? *Islas,* no. 96 (May – Aug 90), pp. 132 – 138. Bibl.

ZERPA, CARLOS

Sichel, Berta. Carlos Zerpa. *Latin American Art,* v. 5, no. 2 (Summer 93), pp. 33 – 35. Bibl, il.

ZOBEL, JOSEPH

Criticism of specific works

La rue Cases-Nègres

Demasy, Rose-Hélène. La femme et le pouvoir social dans *La rue Cases-Nègres:* roman de Joseph Zobel. *Caribbean Studies,* v. 25, no. 1 – 2 (Jan – July 92), pp. 11 – 26.

ZOOLOGY

See also
Animals
Birds
Entomology

Jamaica

Glimpses of Jamaica's Natural History: The Jamaican Crocodile (Crocodilus acutus). *Jamaica Journal,* v. 25, no. 1 (Oct 93), n.p.

ZORRILLA DE SAN MARTÍN, JUAN

Criticism of specific works

Tabaré

Torres, María Inés de. Ideología patriarcal e ideología estatal en el proceso modernizador uruguayo: una lectura de *Tabaré. Cuadernos del CLAEH,* v. 18, no. 65 – 66 (May 93), pp. 167 – 178. Bibl.

ZOTZIL INDIANS

See
Tzotzil Indians

ZUBELDIA, EMILIANA DE

Varela-Ruiz, Leticia T. *Zubeldia, maestra maitea* (Review). *Inter-American Music Review,* v. 13, no. 2 (Spring – Summer 93), pp. 163 – 164.

ZUM FELDE, ALBERTO

Michelena, Alejandro Daniel. Zum Felde, iniciador múltiple. *Hoy Es Historia,* v. 10, no. 55 (Jan – Feb 93), pp. 14 – 20. Bibl, il.

ZWEIG, STEFAN

Furtado Kestler, Izabela María. Stefan Zweig, Brasil e o holocausto. *Estudios Interdisciplinarios de América Latina y el Caribe,* v. 3, no. 2 (July – Dec 92), pp. 123 – 126. Bibl.

BOOK REVIEWS

BOOK REVIEWS

Abad Pérez, Antolín. *Las misiones de Apolobamba, Bolivia* reviewed by Pedro de Anasagasti. *Signo*, no. 35, Nueva época (Jan – Apr 92), pp. 199 – 200.

Achard, Diego. *La transición en Uruguay* reviewed by Fernando Errandonea. *Cuadernos del CLAEH*, v. 18, no. 67 (Nov 93), pp. 147 – 155.

Achugar Ferrari, Hugo. *La balsa de la Medusa: ensayos sobre identidad, cultura y fin de siglo* reviewed by Fernando Errandonea. *Cuadernos del CLAEH*, v. 18, no. 65 – 66 (May 93), pp. 203 – 212. Bibl.

Achugar Ferrari, Hugo, ed. *Cultura MERCOSUR: políticas e industrias culturales* (Review). *Integración Latinoamericana*, v. 18, no. 195 (Nov 93), pp. 58 – 59.

Actas del Cabildo de Santiago, 1795 – 1809 reviewed by Fernando Campos Harriet. *Boletín de la Academia Chilena de la Historia*, v. 58 – 59, no. 102 (1991 – 1992), pp. 531 – 533.

Acuña Casas, Ricardo and Tulio González Abuter. *Los Angeles durante la colonia* reviewed by Fernando Campos Harriet (Review entitled "Dos estudios sobre Los Angeles"). *Boletín de la Academia Chilena de la Historia*, v. 58 – 59, no. 102 (1991 – 1992), pp. 553 – 554.

Adam, Christopher et al. *Adjusting Privatization: Case Studies from Developing Countries* reviewed by Gladstone Hutchinson. *Social and Economic Studies*, v. 41, no. 4 (Dec 92), pp. 231 – 234.

Adams, Norman and Néstor Valdivia. *Los otros empresarios: ética de migrantes y formación de empresas en Lima* reviewed by Orazio A. Ciccarelli. *Hispanic American Historical Review*, v. 73, no. 4 (Nov 93), pp. 714 – 715.

Adán, Martín
See
Fuente Benavides, Rafael de la

Adelman, Jeremy, ed. *Essays in Argentine Labour History, 1870 – 1930* reviewed by Ronaldo Munck. *Bulletin of Latin American Research*, v. 12, no. 2 (May 93), pp. 229 – 230.

Administración universitaria en América Latina: una perspectiva estratégica reviewed by Luisa Margarita Schweizer. *La Educación (USA)*, v. 37, no. 115 (1993), pp. 414 – 417.

Adorno, Rolena and Kenneth James Andrien, eds. *Transatlantic Encounters: Europeans and Andeans in the Sixteenth Century* reviewed by Ann Zulawski. *Colonial Latin American Review*, v. 2, no. 1 – 2 (1993), pp. 273 – 275.

— *Transatlantic Encounters: Europeans and Andeans in the Sixteenth Century* reviewed by Patricia Seed. *Hispanic American Historical Review*, v. 73, no. 1 (Feb 93), pp. 156 – 157.

— *Transatlantic Encounters: Europeans and Andeans in the Sixteenth Century* reviewed by Gabriela Ramos and Natalia Majluf. *Revista Andina*, v. 11, no. 1 (July 93), pp. 239 – 243. Bibl.

Agier, Michel, ed. *Cantos e toques: etnografias do espaço negro na Bahia* reviewed by Fernando Costa Conceição. *Revista de Antropologia (Brazil)*, v. 34 (1991), pp. 223 – 227.

Agosín, Marjorie. *Sargazo* reviewed by Silvia Yáñez (Review entitled "Dos de poesía"). *Plural (Mexico)*, v. 22, no. 267 (Dec 93), pp. 83 – 84.

Agosín, Marjorie and Inés Dölz-Blackburn. *Violeta Parra o la expresión inefable: un análisis crítico de su poesía, prosa y pintura* reviewed by Beth Pollack. *Chasqui*, v. 22, no. 2 (Nov 93), pp. 179 – 180.

Aguerrondo, Inés. *El planeamiento educativo como instrumento de cambio* (Review). *La Educación (USA)*, v. 36, no. 111 – 113 (1992), pp. 277 – 279.

Aguilar, Luis Miguel. *Suerte con las mujeres* reviewed by José Ricardo Chaves. *Vuelta*, v. 17, no. 200 (July 93), pp. 59 – 60.

Aguilar, Rosario. *La niña blanca y los pájaros sin pies* reviewed by Edward Waters Hood. *World Literature Today*, v. 67, no. 4 (Fall 93), p. 780.

Aguilar Camín, Héctor. *Historias conversadas* reviewed by Alvaro Ruiz Abreu (Review entitled "Sueños que se cumplen tarde"). *Nexos*, v. 16, no. 188 (Aug 93), pp. 82 – 83.

— *Historias conversadas* reviewed by Fernando García Ramírez. *Vuelta*, v. 17, no. 194 (Jan 93), pp. 44 – 45.

Aguinis, Marcos. *La gesta del marrano* reviewed by José Schraibman. *Hispamérica*, v. 21, no. 63 (Dec 92), pp. 89 – 91.

Aguirre, Carlos and Charles Walker, eds. *Bandoleros, abigeos y montoneros: criminalidad y violencia en el Perú, siglos XVIII – XX* reviewed by Vincent Peloso. *The Americas*, v. 50, no. 2 (Oct 93), pp. 283 – 285.

— *Bandoleros, abigeos y montoneros: criminalidad y violencia en el Perú, siglos XVIII – XX* reviewed by Scarlett O'Phelan Godoy. *Anuario de Estudios Americanos*, v. 49, Suppl. 2 (1992), pp. 243 – 244.

Aguirre, Nataniel. *Juan de la Rosa: memorias del último hidalgo de la independencia* reviewed by Gaby Vallejo de Bolívar. *Signo*, no. 35, Nueva época (Jan – Apr 92), pp. 201 – 202.

Aguirre Rehbein, Edna and Sonia Riquelme, eds. *Critical Approaches to Isabel Allende's Novels* reviewed by Edward W. Hook. *World Literature Today*, v. 67, no. 1 (Winter 93), pp. 163 – 164.

Aínsa Amigues, Fernando. *Necesidad de la utopía* reviewed by Edgar Montiel (Review entitled "Fernando Aínsa: expedición a utopía"). *Plural (Mexico)*, v. 22, no. 261 (June 93), pp. 91 – 92.

Alatriste, Sealtiel. *En defensa de la envidia* reviewed by Christopher Domínquez (Review entitled "De envidia a envidia"). *Vuelta*, v. 17, no. 195 (Feb 93), pp. 40 – 41.

Alberro, Solange Behocaray de. *Del gachupín al criollo: o de cómo los españoles de México dejaron de serlo* reviewed by Patricia Schraer. *La Educación (USA)*, v. 37, no. 115 (1993), pp. 411 – 412.

— *Les espagnols dans le Mexique colonial: histoire d'une acculturation* reviewed by Frédérique Langue. *Caravelle*, no. 60 (1993), pp. 141 – 143.

Alberto, Eliseo. *La eternidad por fin comienza un lunes* reviewed by Fabrizio Mejía Madrid (Review entitled "Circo nutrido"). *Nexos*, v. 16, no. 181 (Jan 93), pp. 76 – 77. Il.

— *La eternidad por fin comienza un lunes* reviewed by Alvaro Enrigue. *Vuelta,* v. 17, no. 195 (Feb 93), pp. 38 – 39.

Albuquerque, Marcos Cintra Cavalcanti de, ed. *Imposto único sobre transações: prós e contras* reviewed by Eduardo Lundberg. *Revista de Economia Política (Brazil),* v. 13, no. 2 (Apr – June 93), pp. 153 – 154.

Albuquerque, Severino João Medeiros. *Violent Acts: A Study of Contemporary Latin American Theatre* reviewed by Leslie Damasceno. *Latin American Theatre Review,* v. 26, no. 2 (Spring 93), pp. 210 – 212.

Alchon, Suzanne Austin. *Native Society and Disease in Colonial Ecuador* reviewed by Linda A. Newson. *Bulletin of Latin American Research,* v. 12, no. 1 (Jan 93), pp. 112 – 113.

— *Native Society and Disease in Colonial Ecuador* reviewed by Robert H. Jackson. *Colonial Latin American Historical Review,* v. 2, no. 3 (Summer 93), pp. 375 – 377.

— *Native Society and Disease in Colonial Ecuador* reviewed by Susan M. Deeds. *Colonial Latin American Review,* v. 2, no. 1 – 2 (1993), pp. 284 – 285.

— *Native Society and Disease in Colonial Ecuador* reviewed by Karen M. Powers. *Hispanic American Historical Review,* v. 73, no. 4 (Nov 93), pp. 694 – 695.

Alcocer, Ernesto. *También se llamaba Lola* reviewed by Christopher Domínguez Michael (Review entitled "Dos heroínas"). *Vuelta,* v. 17, no. 204 (Nov 93), pp. 48 – 49.

Aldridge, Robert and John Connell. *France's Overseas Frontier: départements et territoires d'outremer* reviewed by W. Marvin Will. *Social and Economic Studies,* v. 41, no. 4 (Dec 92), pp. 243 – 246. Bibl.

Alegría, Fernando and Jorge Ruffinelli, eds. *Paradise Lost or Gained?: The Literature of Hispanic Exile* reviewed by Barbara Mujica (Review entitled "The Creative Subtext of Life"). *Américas,* v. 45, no. 3 (May – June 93), pp. 60 – 61.

— *Paradise Lost or Gained?: The Literature of Hispanic Exile* reviewed by Joseph F. Vélez. *Hispania (USA),* v. 76, no. 1 (Mar 93), pp. 80 – 82.

Alemán Alemán, Ricardo. *Guanajuato: espejismo electoral* reviewed by Pedro García Rodríguez. *El Cotidiano,* v. 10, no. 58 (Oct – Nov 93), pp. 117 – 118.

Alemany, Soline and Frédéric Mauro, eds. *Transport et commerce en Amérique Latine* reviewed by Rory Miller. *Journal of Latin American Studies,* v. 25, no. 1 (Feb 93), pp. 208 – 209.

Alexander, Robert Jackson. *Juscelino Kubitschek and the Development of Brazil* reviewed by Peter Flynn. *Bulletin of Latin American Research,* v. 12, no. 3 (Sept 93), pp. 348 – 349.

— *Juscelino Kubitschek and the Development of Brazil* reviewed by John W. F. Dulles. *Hispanic American Historical Review,* v. 73, no. 1 (Feb 93), pp. 168 – 169.

Allende, Isabel. *El plan infinito* reviewed by Barbara Loach. *Hispamérica,* v. 21, no. 62 (Aug 92), pp. 133 – 134.

— *El plan infinito* reviewed by Patricia Hart. *World Literature Today,* v. 67, no. 2 (Spring 93), pp. 335 – 336.

Alliende Luco, Joaquín. *Santo Domingo: una moción del espíritu para América Latina* reviewed by Alejandro Sifri. *Mensaje,* v. 42, no. 422 (Sept 93), p. 470.

Almeida, Paulo Guillerme de. *Aspectos jurídicos de reforma agraria no Brasil* reviewed by Arnaldo Gómez A. *Derecho y Reforma Agraria,* no. 23 (1992), p. 216.

Almoina de Carrera, Pilar. *El héroe en el relato oral venezolano* reviewed by Juvenal López Ruiz. *Revista Nacional de Cultura (Venezuela),* v. 53, no. 286 (July – Sept 92), pp. 263 – 264.

Alonso, Diana. *Memoria y olvido* reviewed by Rita Ceballos. *Todo Es Historia,* v. 26, no. 308 (Mar 93), p. 70. Il.

Alonso, Jorge et al, eds. *El nuevo estado mexicano, tomo I: Estado y economía* reviewed by Gonzalo Alejandre Ramos. *El Cotidiano,* v. 8, no. 52 (Jan – Feb 93), p. 114.

— *El nuevo estado mexicano, tomo II: Estado y política* reviewed by Teresa Rueda Lugo. *El Cotidiano,* v. 8, no. 52 (Jan – Feb 93), pp. 115 – 116.

— *El nuevo estado mexicano, tomo III: Estado, actores y movimientos sociales* reviewed by Griselda Martínez Vázquez. *El Cotidiano,* v. 8, no. 52 (Jan – Feb 93), p. 117.

— *El nuevo estado mexicano, tomo IV: Estado y sociedad* reviewed by Laura Franco Scherer. *El Cotidiano,* v. 8, no. 52 (Jan – Feb 93), pp. 118 – 119.

Alonso, Rodolfo. *El fondo del asunto* reviewed by Alfredo Veiravé (Review entitled "Justo en la frontera inasible"). *Revista Nacional de Cultura (Venezuela),* v. 53, no. 285 (Apr – June 92), pp. 256 – 257.

— *Jazmín del país* reviewed by Néstor Fenoglio (Review entitled "Hacia otra mirada"). *Revista Nacional de Cultura (Venezuela),* v. 53, no. 285 (Apr – June 92), pp. 257 – 259.

Altamirano, Ignacio Manuel. *Diarios: obras completas, XX* reviewed by Julián Andrade Jardí (Review entitled "Radiografía cotidiana"). *Nexos,* v. 16, no. 181 (Jan 93), p. 76. Il.

Altman, Ida and James J. Horn. *"To Make America": European Emigration in the Early Modern Period* reviewed by Alan L. Karras. *The Americas,* v. 49, no. 3 (Jan 93), pp. 402 – 404.

— *"To Make America": European Emigration in the Early Modern Period* reviewed by Magnus Mörner. *Hispanic American Historical Review,* v. 73, no. 1 (Feb 93), pp. 130 – 132.

Alvarez, Federico et al, eds. *Gramsci en América Latina: del silencio al olvido* reviewed by Mario Sznajder. *Estudios Interdisciplinarios de América Latina y el Caribe,* v. 3, no. 2 (July – Dec 92), pp. 133 – 137.

Alvarez, Jesús and Ascensión Martínez Riaza. *Historia de la prensa hispanoamericana* reviewed by Alfonso Braojos Garrido. *Anuario de Estudios Americanos,* v. 50, no. 1 (1993), pp. 307 – 308.

Alvarez, Julia. *How the García Girls Lost Their Accents* reviewed by Jason Zappe. *The Americas Review,* v. 19, no. 3 – 4 (Winter 91), pp. 150 – 152.

— *How the García Girls Lost Their Accents* reviewed by Luis Rebaza-Soraluz. *Hispanic Journal,* v. 14, no. 1 (Spring 93), pp. 173 – 175.

Alvarez Asomoza, Carlos and Luis Casasola García. *Las figurillas de Jonuta, Tabasco* reviewed by Françoise Milhorat. *Caravelle,* no. 59 (1992), pp. 253 – 256.

Alvarez de Castrillón, Anes and Guillermo Céspedes del Castillo. *El tabaco en Nueva España* reviewed by Dawn Keremitsis. *Hispanic American Historical Review,* v. 73, no. 2 (May 93), pp. 311 – 312.

Alzate Angel, Beatriz and María T. Ramírez V., eds. *Cinco lustros de actuación institucional nacional e internacional en Amazonia* reviewed by Olga Lucía Turbay. *La Educación (USA),* v. 36, no. 111 – 113 (1992), pp. 279 – 280.

Amado, Jorge. *The Golden Harvest,* a translation of *São Jorge dos Ilhéus,* translated by Clifford E. Landers. Reviewed by David T. Haberly. *Review,* no. 47 (Fall 93), pp. 90 – 92.

Aman, Kenneth and Christian Parker Gumucio, eds. *Popular Culture in Chile: Resistance and Survival* reviewed by Ton Salman. *European Review of Latin American and Caribbean Studies,* no. 53 (Dec 92), pp. 120 – 124.

Ambert, Alba Nydia. *Porque hay silencio* reviewed by Marina Catzaras. *Revista de Crítica Literaria Latinoamericana,* v. 19, no. 38 (July – Dec 93), pp. 424 – 426.

Americas Watch Committee. *Peru under Fire: Human Rights since the Return to Democracy* reviewed by Sarah A. Radcliffe. *Bulletin of Latin American Research,* v. 12, no. 1 (Jan 93), pp. 120 – 121.

— *Peru under Fire: Human Rights since the Return to Democracy* reviewed by Orazio A. Ciccarelli. *Revista Interamericana de Bibliografía,* v. 42, no. 2 (1992), p. 281.

Ampuero, Fernando. *Caramelo verde* reviewed by Rodrigo Quijano (Review entitled "Ocoña negro"). *Debate (Peru),* v. 16, no. 72 (Mar – May 93), p. 66.

Anales del I Seminario de Universidades por la Integración Brasil y Argentina (Review). *Integración Latinoamericana,* v. 18, no. 192 (Aug 92), p. 98.

Anasagasti, Iñaki, ed. *Homenaje al Comité Pro-Inmigación Vasca en la Argentina, 1940* reviewed by Oscar Alvarez Gila. *Revista de Indias,* v. 53, no. 197 (Jan – Apr 93), pp. 99 – 101.

Anasagasti, Pedro de. *Los franciscanos en Bolivia* reviewed by Lorenzo Calzavarini. *Signo,* no. 38, Nueva época (Jan – Apr 93), pp. 147 – 153.

Anaya, Héctor. *El sentido del amor* reviewed by Lazlo Moussong (Review entitled "Anaya: los embates del amor florido"). *Plural (Mexico),* v. 22, no. 265 (Oct 93), pp. 85 – 86.

Anaya, Rudolfo A., ed. *Voces: Anthology of New Mexican Writers* reviewed by Salvador Rodríguez del Pino. *The Americas Review,* v. 20, no. 1 (Spring 92), pp. 85 – 87.

Anaya, Rudolfo A. and Francisco A. Lomelí, eds. *Aztlán: Essays on the Chicano Homeland* reviewed by Kirsten F. Nigro (Review entitled "Looking Back to Aztlán from the 1990s"). *Bilingual Review/Revista Bilingüe,* v. 18, no. 1 (Jan – Apr 93), pp. 75 – 78.

Ancona, Alvaro. *La isla de los pelícanos* reviewed by Guillermo Fárber (Review entitled "La '68 al poder o la sangre del pelícano"). *Plural (Mexico),* v. 22, no. 267 (Dec 93), pp. 80 – 81.

Anders, Martha B. *Historia y etnografía: los mitmaq de Huanuco en las visitas de 1549, 1557 y 1562* translated by Rafael Varón. Reviewed by Nicanor Domínguez Faura. *Historia y Cultura (Peru),* no. 20 (1990), pp. 379 – 380.

Anderson, Anthony B., ed. *Alternatives to Deforestation: Steps toward Sustained Use of the Amazon Rain Forest* reviewed by David Cleary. *Journal of Latin American Studies,* v. 25, no. 2 (May 93), pp. 408 – 409.

Anderson, Anthony B. et al. *The Subsidy from Nature: Palm Forests, Peasantry, and Development on an Amazon Frontier* reviewed by Kathryn Smith Pyle. *Grassroots Development,* v. 17, no. 1 (1993), pp. 45 – 46. Il.

— *The Subsidy from Nature: Palm Forests, Peasantry, and Development on an Amazon Frontier* reviewed by Emilio F. Moran. *Journal of Developing Areas,* v. 28, no. 1 (Oct 93), pp. 116 – 117.

Andrade, Carlos Drummond de. *A amor natural* reviewed by Lídice Leaõ. *Vozes,* v. 86, no. 6 (Nov – Dec 92), pp. 100 – 101.

— *Itabira: antología* edited and translated by Pablo del Barco. Reviewed by Miguel Gomes. *Inti,* no. 36 (Fall 92), pp. 183 – 186.

Andradi, Esther. *Come, éste es mi cuerpo* reviewed by Angélica Gorodischer (Review entitled "Cuerpos enjaulados"). *Confluencia,* v. 8, no. 1 (Fall 92), pp. 183 – 184.

Andreo García, Juan. *La Intendencia en Venezuela: don Esteban Fernández de León, intendente de Caracas, 1791 – 1803* reviewed by Jean-Christian Tulet. *Caravelle,* no. 59 (1992), pp. 307 – 308.

Andrews, George Reid. *Blacks and Whites in São Paulo, Brazil, 1888 – 1988* reviewed by Michael Hanchard. *The Americas,* v. 50, no. 1 (July 93), pp. 134 – 136.

— *Blacks and Whites in São Paulo, Brazil, 1888 – 1988* reviewed by Joseph P. Love. *Hispanic American Historical Review,* v. 73, no. 1 (Feb 93), pp. 167 – 168.

— *Blacks and Whites in São Paulo, Brazil, 1888 – 1988* reviewed by Robert M. Levine. *Revista Interamericana de Bibliografía,* v. 42, no. 2 (1992), p. 282.

Andrews, Gregg. *Shoulder to Shoulder?: The American Federation of Labor, the United States, and the Mexican Revolution, 1910 – 1924* reviewed by Mark T. Gilderhus. *Hispanic American Historical Review,* v. 73, no. 1 (Feb 93), pp. 195 – 196.

Andrien, Kenneth James and Rolena Adorno, eds. *Transatlantic Encounters: Europeans and Andeans in the Sixteenth Century* reviewed by Ann Zulawski. *Colonial Latin American Review,* v. 2, no. 1 – 2 (1993), pp. 273 – 275.

— *Transatlantic Encounters: Europeans and Andeans in the Sixteenth Century* reviewed by Patricia Seed. *Hispanic American Historical Review,* v. 73, no. 1 (Feb 93), pp. 156 – 157.

— *Transatlantic Encounters: Europeans and Andeans in the Sixteenth Century* reviewed by Gabriela Ramos and Natalia Majluf. *Revista Andina,* v. 11, no. 1 (July 93), pp. 239 – 243. Bibl.

Anghiera, Pietro Martire d'. *De Orbe Novo Decades* reviewed by Keith Ellis. *Revista Canadiense de Estudios Hispánicos,* v. 17, no. 1 (Fall 92), pp. 221 – 223.

Anhalt, Nedda G. de et al. *La fiesta innombrable: trece poetas cubanos* reviewed by José Homero (Review entitled "Isla, historia y fiesta de la lengua"). *Vuelta,* v. 17, no. 194 (Jan 93), pp. 48 – 49.

Antichi libri d'America: censimento romano, 1493 – 1701 reviewed by Fernando I. Ortiz Crespo (Review entitled "Antiguos libros de America en Roma"). *Interciencia,* v. 18, no. 3 (May – June 93), pp. 164 – 165.

Antolín, Francisco, ed. *Los espacios en Juan Rulfo* reviewed by Susan Dennis. *Hispania (USA),* v. 76, no. 4 (Dec 93), pp. 733 – 734.

Aparicio, Carlos Hugo. *Trenes del sur* reviewed by Geneviève Despinoy. *Caravelle,* no. 59 (1992), pp. 320 – 322.

Aparicio, Frances R. *Versiones, interpretaciones y creaciones: instancias de la traducción literaria en Hispanoamérica en el siglo veinte* reviewed by László Scholz. *Revista de Crítica Literaria Latinoamericana,* v. 19, no. 37 (Jan – June 93), pp. 375 – 377.

Ara, Alejandro. *Cuentos para leer en los aviones* reviewed by Miguelángel Díaz Monges (Review entitled "Narrativa portatil"). *Nexos,* v. 16, no. 192 (Dec 93), p. 83.

Aragão, José Maria. *La armonización de políticas macroeconómicas en el MERCOSUR: la construcción de un mercado común* (Review). *Integración Latinoamericana,* v. 18, no. 191 (July 93), pp. 79 – 80.

Aragón, Luis E., ed. *A desordem ecológica na Amazônia* (Review). *La Educación (USA),* v. 37, no. 115 (1993), pp. 439 – 440.

Arana, Federico. *Comer insectos* reviewed by Susan N. Masuoka (Review entitled "Mexican Eating: The Work and the Haute Cuisine"). *Studies in Latin American Popular Culture,* v. 12 (1993), pp. 189 – 194. Bibl.

Araujo, Juan de. *Juan de Araujo: antología* compiled and transcribed by Carmen García Muñoz (Review). *Inter-American Music Review*, v. 13, no. 1 (Fall – Winter 92), pp. 119 – 120.

— *Juan de Araujo: antología* compiled and transcribed by Carmen García Muñoz (Review). *Inter-American Music Review*, v. 13, no. 2 (Spring – Summer 93), p. 155.

Archila Neira, Mauricio. *Cultura e identidad obrera: Colombia, 1910 – 1945* reviewed by Rocío Londoño B. *Anuario Colombiano de Historia Social y de la Cultura*, no. 20 (1992), pp. 174 – 180.

Ardao, Arturo. *España en el origen del nombre América Latina* reviewed by Alejandro Daniel Michelena. *Hoy Es Historia*, v. 10, no. 58 (July – Aug 93), p. 86.

Arduz Ruiz, Marcelo. *Hojas solares* reviewed by Jaime Martínez Salguero. *Signo*, no. 38, Nueva época (Jan – Apr 93), pp. 219 – 220.

Arellano, Jorge Eduardo. *Pablo Antonio Cuadra: aproximaciones a su vida y obra* reviewed by Amelia Mondragón. *Hispamérica*, v. 21, no. 63 (Dec 92), pp. 91 – 93.

Arellano Ayuso, Ignacio, ed. *Las Indias (América) en la literatura del siglo de oro* reviewed by Teodoro Hampe Martínez. *Anuario de Estudios Americanos*, v. 50, no. 1 (1993), pp. 308 – 310.

Arenal, Electa and Stacey Schlau, eds. *Untold Sisters: Hispanic Nuns in Their Own Works* translated by Amanda Powell. Reviewed by Noël Valis. *Colonial Latin American Review*, v. 2, no. 1 – 2 (1993), pp. 304 – 308.

Arenas, Reinaldo. *Antes que anochezca* reviewed by Daniel Zalacaín. *Hispania (USA)*, v. 76, no. 3 (Sept 93), pp. 490 – 491.

— *Antes que anochezca* reviewed by José Homero. *Vuelta*, v. 17, no. 195 (Feb 93), pp. 37 – 38.

— *El asalto* reviewed by Daniel Zalacaín. *Hispania (USA)*, v. 76, no. 1 (Mar 93), pp. 98 – 99.

— *El color del verano* reviewed by Daniel Zalacaín. *Hispania (USA)*, v. 76, no. 1 (Mar 93), pp. 98 – 99.

Arends, Tulio. *Sir Gregor MacGregor, un escocés tras la aventura de América* reviewed by Juvenal López Ruiz. *Revista Nacional de Cultura (Venezuela)*, v. 53, no. 286 (July – Sept 92), p. 263.

Aretz de Ramón y Rivera, Isabel. *Historia de la etnomusicología en América Latina: desde la época precolombina hasta nuestros días* reviewed by Irma Poletti. *La Educación (USA)*, v. 36, no. 111 – 113 (1992), pp. 280 – 281.

Argenti, Gisela et al. *Pequeños países en la integración: oportunidades y riesgos* (Review). *Integración Latinoamericana*, v. 18, no. 187 – 188 (Mar – Apr 93), pp. 69 – 70.

Arias, Arturo. *Los caminos de Paxil* reviewed by Dante Liano. *Hispamérica*, v. 21, no. 62 (Aug 92), pp. 134 – 136.

Aridjis, Homero. *La leyenda de los soles* reviewed by Víctor Manuel Mendiola. *Vuelta*, v. 17, no. 203 (Oct 93), pp. 51 – 52.

— *Memorias del Nuevo Mundo* reviewed by Encarna Ortega. *Anuario de Estudios Americanos*, v. 49, Suppl. 1 (1992), pp. 251 – 252.

Arizcurinaga, Olga V. de. *Poemario para todos* reviewed by Carlos Castañón Barrientos. *Signo*, no. 38, Nueva época (Jan – Apr 93), pp. 263 – 264.

Ariztía, Fernando. *25 años acompañando a su pueblo: testimonio vivo de una época dolorosa* reviewed by Mariano Arroyo. *Mensaje*, v. 42, no. 418 (May 93), p. 168. II.

Arnaud, Hélène and Alain Rouquié, eds. *Les forces politiques en Amérique Centrale* reviewed by Rodolfo Cerdas-Cruz. *Journal of Latin American Studies*, v. 25, no. 2 (May 93), pp. 416 – 417.

Arnold, Denise Y. et al. *Hacia un orden andino de las cosas: tres pistas de los Andes meridionales* reviewed by Jan Szeminski. *Estudios Interdisciplinarios de América Latina y el Caribe*, v. 4, no. 1 (Jan – June 93), pp. 175 – 176.

— *Hacia un orden andino de las cosas: tres pistas de los Andes meridionales* reviewed by Javier Albó. *Signo*, no. 38, Nueva época (Jan – Apr 93), pp. 220 – 224.

Arnold, Philip J., III. *Domestic Ceramic Production and Spatial Organization* reviewed by Dean E. Arnold. *Latin American Antiquity*, v. 4, no. 3 (Sept 93), pp. 297 – 299.

Arráiz, Antonio. *Los días de la ira: las guerras civiles en Venezuela, 1830 – 1903* reviewed by Raúl Agudo Freites. *Revista Nacional de Cultura (Venezuela)*, v. 54, no. 287 (Oct – Dec 92), pp. 261 – 262.

Arráiz Lucca, Rafael. *El abandono y la vigilía* reviewed by David Medina Portillo (Review entitled "Estar aquí"). *Vuelta*, v. 17, no. 197 (Apr 93), pp. 48 – 49.

Arrigoitia, Luis de. *Pensamiento y forma en la prosa de Gabriela Mistral* reviewed by Isabel Silva Aldrete. *Anuario de Letras (Mexico)*, v. 30 (1992), pp. 296 – 298.

Arrúe, Willie and Beatriz Kalinsky. *De "la médica" y el terapeuta: la gestión intercultural de la salud en el sur de la provincia del Neuquén* reviewed by P. Schraer. *La Educación (USA)*, v. 36, no. 111 – 113 (1992), pp. 281 – 282.

Artalejo, Lucrecia. *La máscara y el marañón: la identidad nacional cubana* reviewed by William L. Siemens. *World Literature Today*, v. 67, no. 1 (Winter 93), pp. 160 – 161.

Arteaga, Alfred. *Cantos* reviewed by Iliana Rodríguez (Review entitled "Alfred Arteaga: cantos chicanos"). *Plural (Mexico)*, v. 22, no. 260 (May 93), pp. 76 – 77.

Assies, Willem. *To Get out of the Mud: Neighborhood Associativism in Recife, 1964 – 1988* reviewed by Joe Foweraker. *Bulletin of Latin American Research*, v. 12, no. 3 (Sept 93), pp. 345 – 346.

— *To Get Out of the Mud: Neighborhood Associativism in Recife, 1964 – 1988* reviewed by Martine Droulers. *Cahiers des Amériques Latines*, no. 14 (1992), pp. 157 – 158.

— *To Get out of the Mud: Neighborhood Associativism in Recife, 1964 – 1988* reviewed by Vania Salles and João Francisco Souza. *Revista Mexicana de Sociología*, v. 54, no. 4 (Oct – Dec 92), pp. 251 – 257.

Assunção, Matthias Röhrig, ed. *A guerra dos bem-te-vis: a balaiada na memória oral* reviewed by Mary Karasch (Review entitled "A balaiada in Brazil"). *The Americas*, v. 49, no. 3 (Jan 93), pp. 392 – 394.

Aubert Cerda, Sergio. *Rescate de un sueño interrumpido* reviewed by Luis Merino Reyes. *Atenea (Chile)*, no. 467 (1993), pp. 271 – 272.

Aubry, Andrés. *San Cristóbal de las Casas: su historia urbana, demográfica y monumental, 1528 – 1990* reviewed by Sidney David Markman. *Mesoamérica (USA)*, v. 13, no. 23 (June 92), p. 183.

Aura, Alejandro. *Poeta en la mañana* reviewed by Terry O. Taylor. *World Literature Today*, v. 67, no. 1 (Winter 93), p. 160. II.

Aveni, Anthony F., ed. *The Lines of Nazca* reviewed by Katharina J. Schreiber. *Latin American Antiquity*, v. 4, no. 2 (June 93), pp. 202 – 203.

Avila, Elvio Arnoldo. *Cómo habla el santiagueño . . . y el argentino: diccionario de voces usuales que el 'Diccionario oficial' no registra; adhesión al V centenario del descubrimiento de América* reviewed by Félix Coluccio. *Folklore Americano*, no. 52 (July – Dec 91), pp. 167 – 168.

Avilés Fabila, René. *Réquiem por un suicida* reviewed by Alejandro Expósito (Review entitled "Avilés Fabila, un réquiem casi mozartiano"). *Plural (Mexico)*, v. 22, no. 267 (Dec 93), pp. 84 – 86.

Awoonor, Kofi Nyidevu. *The Latin American and Caribbean Notebook* reviewed by Tanure Ojaide. *World Literature Today*, v. 67, no. 4 (Fall 93), pp. 875 – 876.

Azeredo, Sandra and Verena Stolcke, eds. *Direitos reprodutivos* (Review). *Estudos Feministas*, v. 0, no. 0 (1992), p. 230.

Azpeitia Gómez, Hugo et al. *Los tiempos de la crisis, 1970 – 1982, partes 1 y 2: Historia de la cuestión agraria mexicana* reviewed by David W. Walker. *Hispanic American Historical Review*, v. 73, no. 3 (Aug 93), pp. 529 – 530.

Báez-Jorge, Félix. *Las voces del agua: el simbolismo de las sirenas y las mitologías americanas* reviewed by Mario M. Muñoz (Review entitled "Las seductoras macabras"). *La Palabra y el Hombre*, no. 84 (Oct – Dec 92), pp. 252 – 255. II.

Balán, Jorge. *Cuéntame tu vida: una biografía colectiva del psicoanálisis argentino* reviewed by Thomas F. Glick. *Hispanic American Historical Review*, v. 73, no. 1 (Feb 93), pp. 129 – 130.

Balderston, Daniel, ed. *The Latin American Short Story: An Annotated Guide to Anthologies and Criticism* reviewed by David William Foster. *Chasqui*, v. 22, no. 1 (May 93), pp. 86 – 87.

— *The Latin American Short Story: An Annotated Guide to Anthologies and Criticism* reviewed by Genaro J. Pérez. *Hispania (USA)*, v. 76, no. 3 (Sept 93), pp. 482 – 483.

— *The Latin American Short Story: An Annotated Guide to Anthologies and Criticism* reviewed by Enrique Pupo-Walker. *Revista Interamericana de Bibliografía*, v. 42, no. 3 (1992), p. 501.

— *The Latin American Short Story: An Annotated Guide to Anthologies and Criticism* reviewed by Melvin S. Arrington, Jr. *World Literature Today*, v. 67, no. 3 (Summer 93), pp. 593 – 594.

Balza, José. *Percusión* reviewed by Víctor R. Rivas. *World Literature Today*, v. 67, no. 1 (Winter 93), p. 154.

Banck, Geert A. and Kees den Boer, eds. *Sowing the Whirlwind: Soya Expansion and Social Change in Southern Brazil* reviewed by Martine Droulers. *Cahiers des Amériques Latines*, no. 14 (1992), pp. 158 – 159.

Bant A., Astrid. *Diagnóstico de la vocación de desarrollo y la intervención institucional en la región Loreto* reviewed by Claudia Rohrhirsch. *Apuntes (Peru)*, no. 29 (July – Dec 91), pp. 95 – 97.

Baptista Gumucio, Mariano. *Latinoamericanos y norteamericanos* reviewed by Aída Cometta Manzoni. *Revista Nacional de Cultura (Venezuela)*, v. 53, no. 285 (Apr – June 92), pp. 245 – 247.

Baptiste, Victor N. *Bartolomé de las Casas and Thomas More's Utopia: Connections and Similarities; A Translation and Study* reviewed by Juan Durán Luzio. *Latin American Indian Literatures Journal*, v. 9, no. 1 (Spring 93), pp. 83 – 85.

Baralt, Rafael María. *Antología* reviewed by Juvenal López Ruiz. *Revista Nacional de Cultura (Venezuela)*, v. 53, no. 285 (Apr – June 92), pp. 250 – 251.

Baratti, Abel and Eduardo Casali. *Del juego al deporte, I: Actividades para nivel primero* reviewed by Cora Céspedes. *La Educación (USA)*, v. 36, no. 111 – 113 (1992), pp. 282 – 283.

Barbano, Filippo et al, eds. *Sociologia, storia, positivismo: Messico, Brasile, Argentina e l'Italia* reviewed by Carlos Strasser (Review entitled "Sobre la formación y ciertas influencias en el desarrollo de las ciencias sociales latinoamericanas: una importante contribución italo-argentina"). *Desarrollo Económico (Argentina)*, v. 32, no. 128 (Jan – Mar 93), pp. 625 – 628.

— *Sociologia, storia, positivismo: Messico, Brasile, Argentina e l'Italia* reviewed by Giorgio Alberti. *Journal of Latin American Studies*, v. 25, no. 2 (May 93), pp. 417 – 418.

Barbeito, Alberto C. and Rubén M. Lo Vuolo. *La modernización excluyente: transformación económica y estado de bienestar en Argentina* reviewed by Mauricio Tenewicki. *Realidad Económica*, no. 118 (Aug – Sept 93), pp. 142 – 144.

Barbosa Estepa, Reinaldo. *Guadalupe y sus centauros: memorias de la insurrección llanera* reviewed by Hermes Tovar Pinzón. *Anuario Colombiano de Historia Social y de la Cultura*, no. 20 (1992), pp. 169 – 172.

Barboza, Mário Gibson. *Na diplomacia: o traço todo da vida* reviewed by Alexandra de Mello e Silva (Review entitled "História e histórias da política externa brasileira"). *Estudos Históricos*, v. 6, no. 12 (July – Dec 93), pp. 285 – 290.

Barclay, Federica et al. *Amazonía, 1940 – 1990* reviewed by Nicole Bernex. *Amazonía Peruana*, v. 11, no. 21 (Sept 92), pp. 240 – 242.

Barkin, David. *Distorted Development: Mexico in the World Economy* reviewed by Peter Gregory. *Economic Development and Cultural Change*, v. 42, no. 1 (Oct 93), pp. 210 – 215.

— *Distorted Development: Mexico in the World Economy* reviewed by Russell White (Review entitled "Postwar Mexican Development Policy: State and Class Contradictions"). *Latin American Perspectives*, v. 20, no. 3 (Summer 93), pp. 76 – 79.

Barnet, Miguel. *Rachel's Song*, a translation of *Canción de Rachel*, translated by W. Nick Hill. Reviewed by William L. Siemens. *World Literature Today*, v. 67, no. 1 (Winter 93), p. 164. II.

Barnstone, Willis. *With Borges on an Ordinary Evening in Buenos Aires: A Memoir* reviewed by Naomi Lindstrom. *World Literature Today*, v. 67, no. 4 (Fall 93), p. 787.

Barraclough, Solon Lovett. *An End to Hunger?: The Social Origins of Food Strategies* reviewed by Michaeline Crichlow. *Social and Economic Studies*, v. 41, no. 4 (Dec 92), pp. 234 – 239.

Barragán, Luis. *Barragán: Armando Salas Portugal Photographs of the Architecture of Luis Barragán*, essays by Ernest H. Brooks II et al. Reviewed by Max Underwood. *Latin American Art*, v. 4, no. 4 (Winter 92), pp. 94 – 95.

Barrán, José Pedro. *Historia de la sensibilidad en el Uruguay* reviewed by Alfonso Esponera. *Revista Andina*, v. 10, no. 2 (Dec 92), pp. 539 – 540.

Barreira, Irlys Alencar Firmo. *O reverso das vitrines: conflitos urbanos e cultura política em construção* reviewed by Glória Diógenes. *Revista Brasileira de Ciências Sociais*, v. 8, no. 23 (Oct 93), pp. 156 – 157.

Barrera Linares, Luis, ed. *Memoria y cuento: 30 años de narrativa venezolana, 1960 – 1990* reviewed by Mercedes Franco. *Revista Nacional de Cultura (Venezuela)*, v. 53, no. 286 (July – Sept 92), pp. 262 – 263.

Barreto, Mascarenhas. *The Portuguese Columbus: Secret Agent of King John II* translated by Reginald A. Brown. Reviewed by Robert Kern. *Colonial Latin American Historical Review*, v. 2, no. 1 (Winter 93), pp. 114 – 117.

— *The Portuguese Columbus: Secret Agent of King John II* reviewed by David Henige. *Hispanic American Historical Review*, v. 73, no. 3 (Aug 93), pp. 505 – 506.

Barrett, Rafael. *Sembrando ideas: antología de Rafael Barrett* edited by Vladimiro Muñoz and Roberto Lavín Bedia. Reviewed by Donald A. Randolph. *Chasqui*, v. 22, no. 2 (Nov 93), pp. 180 – 182.

Barry, Tom and Rachel Garst. *Feeding the Crisis: U.S. Food Aid and Farm Policy in Central America* reviewed by Melvin G. Blase. *Journal of Developing Areas*, v. 27, no. 4 (July 93), pp. 566 – 567.

Bartra, Roger. *Oficio mexicano* reviewed by Hugo Vargas (Review entitled "El radicalismo posible"). *Nexos*, v. 16, no. 190 (Oct 93), pp. 73 – 75.

Barzetti, Valerie and Yanina Rovinski, eds. *Towards a Green Central America: Integrating Conservation and Development*, a translation of *Hacia una Centroamérica verde*. Reviewed by L. Alan Eyre. *Caribbean Geography*, v. 3, no. 4 (Sept 92), pp. 277 – 278.

Basili D., Francisco. *Crisis y comercio sexual de menores en el Perú* (Review). *La Educación (USA)*, v. 36, no. 111 – 113 (1992), pp. 283 – 284.

Bass Werner de Ruiz, Zulema. *El drama de Margarita* reviewed by Pedro de Anasagasti. *Signo*, no. 35, Nueva época (Jan – Apr 92), pp. 202 – 204.

Bassnett, Susan, ed. *Knives and Angels: Women Writers in Latin America* reviewed by Beth E. Jörgensen. *Letras Femeninas*, v. 19, no. 1 – 2 (Spring – Fall 93), pp. 143 – 146.

Bassols Batalla, Angel et al, eds. *Zona metropolitana de la ciudad de México: complejo geográfico, socio-económico y político* reviewed by Alicia Ziccardi. *Problemas del Desarrollo*, v. 24, no. 94 (July – Sept 93), pp. 283 – 286.

Basualdo, Eduardo M. and Miguel Khavisse. *El nuevo poder terrateniente* reviewed by Horacio Giberti. *Realidad Económica*, no. 117 (July – Aug 93), pp. 30 – 32.

Bataillon, Claude et al. *Amérique Latine* reviewed by Evelyne Mesclier. *Bulletin de l'Institut Français d'Etudes Andines*, v. 21, no. 2 (1992), pp. 789 – 792.

— *Amérique Latine, vol. III: Géographie universelle* reviewed by Isabel Hurtado. *Revista Andina*, v. 11, no. 1 (July 93), pp. 243 – 244.

Batista Júnior, Paulo Nogueira and Luiz Gonzaga de Mello Belluzzo, eds. *A luta pela sobrevivência da moeda nacional: ensaios em homenagem a Dilson Funarol* reviewed by Eduardo Refinetti Guardia. *Revista de Economia Política (Brazil)*, v. 13, no. 3 (July – Sept 93), pp. 154 – 155.

Batou, Jean. *Cent ans de résistance au sous-développement: l'industrialisation de l'Amérique Latine et du Moyen-Orient face au défi européen, 1770 – 1870* reviewed by Hernán G. H. Taboada. *Cuadernos Americanos*, no. 40, Nueva época (July – Aug 93), pp. 238 – 242.

— *One Hundred Years of Resistance to Underdevelopment, 1770 – 1870* reviewed by Joseph L. Love. *Journal of Latin American Studies*, v. 25, no. 1 (Feb 93), pp. 206 – 208.

Batou, Jean, ed. *Between Development and Underdevelopment: The Precocious Attempts at Industrialization of the Periphery, 1800 – 1870/Entre développement et sous-développement: les tentatives précoces d'industrialisation de la périphérie, 1800 – 1870* reviewed by Colin M. Lewis. *Journal of Latin American Studies*, v. 25, no. 2 (May 93), pp. 395 – 396.

Baudez, Claude-François et al. *Papagayo: un hameau précolombien du Costa Rica* reviewed by Frederick W. Lange. *Latin American Antiquity*, v. 4, no. 4 (Dec 93), pp. 390 – 392.

Baudot, Georges and Tzvetan Todorov. *Récits aztèques de la conquête* reviewed by Guilhem Olivier. *Caravelle*, no. 59 (1992), pp. 241 – 249.

Bayón, Damián Carlos and Murillo Marx. *A History of South American Colonial Art and Architecture: Spanish South America and Brazil* translated by Jennifer A. Blankley, Angela P. Hall, and Richard L. Rees. Reviewed by Marcus B. Burke. *Latin American Art*, v. 5, no. 1 (Spring 93), pp. 94 – 95.

Bazán, Armando Raúl. *El noroeste y la Argentina contemporánea, 1853 – 1992* reviewed by Gastón Carranza. *Todo Es Historia*, v. 26, no. 308 (Mar 93), pp. 73 – 74. Il.

Bazán, Lucía. *Vivienda para los obreros: reproducción de clase y condiciones urbanas* reviewed by Margarita Estrada Iguíniz. *El Cotidiano*, v. 8, no. 52 (Jan – Feb 93), pp. 112 – 113.

Beardsell, Peter R. *A Theatre for Cannibals: Rodolfo Usigli and the Mexican Stage* reviewed by Frank Dauster. *Hispanic Review*, v. 61, no. 2 (Spring 93), pp. 306 – 308.

Becker, Bertha Koiffman and Claudio Antonio G. Egler. *Brasil: uma nova potência regional na economia-mundo* reviewed by Oscar D'Ambrosio (Review entitled "Uma potência regional"). *Problemas Brasileiros*, v. 30, no. 297 (May – June 93), pp. 54 – 55. Il.

Beckles, Hilary and Verene A. Sheperd, eds. *Caribbean Slave Society and Economy* reviewed by Paul Lachance. *Hispanic American Historical Review*, v. 73, no. 2 (May 93), pp. 315 – 316.

— *Caribbean Slave Society and Economy: A Student Reader* reviewed by Gert Oostindie. *European Review of Latin American and Caribbean Studies*, no. 54 (June 93), pp. 126 – 127.

Bedoya, Jaime. *Ay, qué rico: crónicas periodísticas* reviewed by Luis Jaime Cisneros V. (Review entitled "Oficio febril"). *Debate (Peru)*, v. 15, no. 70 (Sept – Oct 92), p. 70.

Befán, José. *Las supersticiones, conjuros, ritos, espíritus nefastos* reviewed by Félix Coluccio. *Folklore Americano*, no. 52 (July – Dec 91), pp. 165 – 166.

Behocaray Alberro, Solange
See
  Alberro, Solange Behocaray de

Bejel, Emilio F. *Escribir en Cuba: entrevistas con escritores cubanos, 1979 – 1989* reviewed by José Otero. *Chasqui*, v. 22, no. 1 (May 93), pp. 104 – 105.

— *Escribir en Cuba: entrevistas con escritores cubanos, 1979 – 1989* reviewed by William Luis. *Cuban Studies/ Estudios Cubanos*, v. 23 (1993), pp. 228 – 231.

— *Escribir en Cuba: entrevistas con escritores cubanos, 1979 – 1989* reviewed by Antonio Lobos. *Revista Chilena de Literatura*, no. 40 (Nov 92), pp. 161 – 162.

Bekerman, Marta, ed. *MERCOSUR: la oportunidad y el desafío* (Review). *Integración Latinoamericana*, v. 18, no. 194 (Oct 93), pp. 87 – 88.

Bell, C. Napier. *Tamgweera: Life and Adventures among Gentle Savages* reviewed by Elizabeth Kudin. *América Indígena*, v. 51, no. 2 – 3 (Apr – Sept 91), pp. 357 – 359.

Bellatín, Mario. *Canon perpetuo* reviewed by Giovanna Pollarolo (Review entitled "Más allá del realismo"). *Debate (Peru)*, v. 16, no. 75 (Dec 93 – Jan 94), pp. 79 – 80. Il.

Bellegarde-Smith, Patrick. *Haiti: The Breached Citadel* reviewed by Jorge Rodríguez Beruff. *Caribbean Studies*, v. 25, no. 1 – 2 (Jan – July 92), pp. 159 – 161.

Belluzzo, Luiz Gonzaga de Mello and Paulo Nogueira Batista Júnior, eds. *A luta pela sobrevivência da moeda nacional: ensaios em homenagem a Dilson Funarol* reviewed by Eduardo Refinetti Guardia. *Revista de Economia Política (Brazil)*, v. 13, no. 3 (July – Sept 93), pp. 154 – 155.

Beltrán Guerrero, Luis. *Candideces* reviewed by Raúl Agudo Freites. *Revista Nacional de Cultura (Venezuela)*, v. 54, no. 287 (Oct – Dec 92), pp. 260 – 261.

Benería, Lourdes and Martha Roldán. *Las encrucijadas de clase y género: trabajo a domicilio; subcontratación y dinámica de la unidad doméstica en la ciudad de México* translated by Julio Colón Gómez. Reviewed by Norma Ilse Veloz Avila. *El Cotidiano*, v. 9, no. 53 (Mar – Apr 93), p. 118.

Benítez, Fernando. *1992: ¿Qué celebramos, qué lamentamos?* reviewed by Alvaro Ruiz Abreu (Review entitled "En lengua propia"). *Nexos*, v. 16, no. 181 (Jan 93), pp. 70 – 72.

Benítez Rojo, Antonio. *The Repeating Island: The Caribbean and the Postmodern Perspective* reviewed by Klaus Müller-Bergh. *Cuban Studies/Estudios Cubanos*, v. 23 (1993), pp. 222 – 225.

— *The Repeating Island: The Caribbean and the Postmodern Perspective*, a translation of *Isla que se repite: el Caribe y la perspectiva posmoderna*, translated by James E. Maraniss. Reviewed by Edna Aizenberg. *Review*, no. 47 (Fall 93), pp. 93 – 95.

Bennassar, Lucile and Bartolomé Bennassar. *1492: un monde nouveau?* reviewed by Marie Cécile Bénassy-Berling (Review entitled "Notas sobre el quinto centenario en Francia"). *Colonial Latin American Review*, v. 2, no. 1 – 2 (1993), pp. 269 – 272.

Benson, Elizabeth P. and Gillett Good Griffin, eds. *Maya Iconography* reviewed by Martha J. Macri. *Mesoamérica (USA)*, v. 13, no. 24 (Dec 92), pp. 490 – 492.

Berbeglia, Carlos Enrique, ed. *Propuestas para una antropología argentina*, vol. II, reviewed by Gabriel Genise. *Todo Es Historia*, v. 26, no. 309 (Apr 93), p. 72. Il.

Bergad, Laird W. *Cuban Rural Society in the Nineteenth Century: The Social and Economic History of Monoculture in Matanzas* reviewed by Gert Oostindie. *European Review of Latin American and Caribbean Studies*, no. 53 (Dec 92), pp. 111 – 112.

Berger, Susan A. *Political and Agrarian Development in Guatemala* reviewed by Kenneth J. Grieb. *Hispanic American Historical Review*, v. 73, no. 3 (Aug 93), pp. 530 – 531.

Bergman, Roland W. *Economía amazónica* translated by Martha Beingolea. Reviewed by Jaime Regan, S.J. *Amazonía Peruana*, v. 11, no. 21 (Sept 92), pp. 243 – 244.

Bergquist, Charles Wylie et al, eds. *Violence in Colombia: The Contemporary Crisis in Historical Perspective* reviewed by Mary Roldán. *The Americas*, v. 50, no. 1 (July 93), pp. 142 – 144.

— *Violence in Colombia: The Contemporary Crisis in Historical Perspective* reviewed by Víctor Peralta Ruiz. *Revista Andina*, v. 11, no. 1 (July 93), pp. 244 – 245.

Bernardes, Maria Thereza Caiuby Crescenti. *Mulheres de ontem?* reviewed by José G. Bezerra Câmara. *Revista do Instituto Histórico e Geográfico Brasileiro*, no. 371 (Apr – June 91), pp. 610 – 611.

Bernucci, Leopoldo M. *Historia de un malentendido: un estudio transtextual de 'La guerra del fin del mundo' de Mario Vargas Llosa* reviewed by Sara Castro-Klarén. *Hispanic Review*, v. 61, no. 1 (Winter 93), pp. 133 – 134.

Berretta, Nora et al. *En el umbral de la integración* (Review). *Integración Latinoamericana*, v. 18, no. 191 (July 93), pp. 76 – 77.

Berrón, Linda, ed. *Relatos de mujeres: antología de narradoras de Costa Rica* reviewed by Judy Berry-Bravo. *Chasqui*, v. 22, no. 2 (Nov 93), pp. 153 – 154.

Bértola, Luis. *The Manufacturing Industry of Uruguay, 1913 – 1961: A Sectoral Approach to Growth, Fluctuations, and Crisis* reviewed by Mario Zejan. *Ibero Americana (Sweden)*, v. 22, no. 2 (Dec 92), pp. 82 – 85. Bibl.

Bethell, Leslie, ed. *The Cambridge History of Latin America, Vol. VIII: Latin America since 1930; Spanish South America* reviewed by Piero Gleijeses. *Journal of Latin American Studies*, v. 25, no. 1 (Feb 93), pp. 187 – 188.

— *Historia de América Latina* reviewed by Jorge F. Hernández (Review entitled "Para medir la distancia"). *Vuelta*, v. 17, no. 195 (Feb 93), pp. 44 – 45.

Beverley, John and Marc Zimmerman. *Literature and Politics in the Central American Revolutions* reviewed by Antony Higgins. *Revista de Crítica Literaria Latinoamericana*, v. 19, no. 37 (Jan – June 93), pp. 380 – 382.

Biagini, Hugo Edgardo. *Historia ideológica y poder social* reviewed by Daniel Omar de Lucia. *Todo Es Historia*, v. 27, no. 311 (June 93), pp. 56 – 58. Il.

Bianco, José. *La pérdida del reino* reviewed by Gabriel Ríos. *Plural (Mexico)*, v. 22, no. 263 (Aug 93), pp. 79 – 80.

Bibliowicz, Azriel. *El rumor del astracán* reviewed by William L. Siemens. *Chasqui*, v. 22, no. 2 (Nov 93), pp. 184 – 185.

Binford, Leigh and Scott Cook. *Obliging Need: Rural Petty Industry in Mexican Capitalism* reviewed by Peter Gregory. *Economic Development and Cultural Change*, v. 42, no. 1 (Oct 93), pp. 210 – 215.

Bioy Casares, Adolfo. *El lado de la sombra* reviewed by Ana María Hernández. *World Literature Today*, v. 67, no. 1 (Winter 93), pp. 154 – 155. Il.

Birmajer, Marcelo. *Historieta: la imaginación al cuadrado* reviewed by Carlos Salá. *La Educación (USA)*, v. 36, no. 111 – 113 (1992), pp. 284 – 285.

Birocco, Carlos María and Gabriela Gresores. *Arrendamientos, desalojos y subordinación campesina: Buenos Aires, siglo XVIII* reviewed by Carlos G. A. Bulcourf. *Todo Es Historia*, v. 27, no. 313 (Aug 93), p. 71. Il.

Bixio, Beatriz and Luis D. Heredia. *Distancia cultural y lingüística: el fracaso escolar en poblaciones rurales del oeste de la provincia de Córdoba* (Review). *La Educación (USA)*, v. 36, no. 111 – 113 (1992), pp. 296 – 298.

Bizarro Ujpán, Ignacio. *Ignacio: The Diary of a Maya Indian of Guatemala* edited and translated by James D. Sexton. Reviewed by Carol A. Smith. *Hispanic American Historical Review*, v. 73, no. 2 (May 93), pp. 340 – 341.

— *Ignacio: The Diary of a Maya Indian of Guatemala* edited and translated by James D. Sexton. Reviewed by Tracy Ulltveit-Moe. *Journal of Latin American Studies*, v. 25, no. 1 (Feb 93), pp. 221 – 222.

Blanchard, Enrique. *Desnudo de espectro* reviewed by Rodolfo Alonso (Review entitled "Un artista del hambre"). *Plural (Mexico)*, v. 22, no. 261 (June 93), p. 88.

Blanchard, Peter. *Slavery and Abolition in Early Republican Peru* reviewed by Charles Walker. *Bulletin of Latin American Research*, v. 12, no. 2 (May 93), pp. 227 – 228.

— *Slavery and Abolition in Early Republican Peru* reviewed by Sandra Lauderdale Graham. *Colonial Latin American Historical Review*, v. 2, no. 2 (Spring 93), pp. 230 – 231.

— *Slavery and Abolition in Early Republican Peru* reviewed by Christine Hunefeldt. *Hispanic American Historical Review*, v. 73, no. 4 (Nov 93), pp. 711 – 713.

— *Slavery and Abolition in Early Republican Peru* reviewed by Michael J. Gonzales. *Journal of Latin American Studies*, v. 25, no. 3 (Oct 93), pp. 657 – 658.

Blanco, José Joaquín. *Se visten novias* reviewed by Julián Andrade Jardí (Review entitled "Toda la ciudad"). *Nexos*, v. 16, no. 189 (Sept 93), pp. 68 – 69.

Blas Galindo, Carlos. *Enrique Guzmán, transformador y víctima* reviewed by José Manuel Springer (Accompanied by an English translation). *Art Nexus*, no. 10 (Sept – Dec 93), p. 41. Il.

Blomström, Magnus and Patricio Meller, eds. *Trayectorias divergentes* reviewed by Göran G. Lindahl (Review entitled "Commentary and Debate"). *Ibero Americana (Sweden)*, v. 22, no. 2 (Dec 92), pp. 67 – 76.

— *Trayectorias divergentes: comparación de un siglo de desarrollo económico latinoamericano y escandinavo* reviewed by Sérgio Savino Portugal. *Pesquisa e Planejamento Econômico*, v. 22, no. 1 (Apr 92), pp. 189 – 196.

Boccanera, Jorge Alejandro. *Sordomuda* reviewed by Francisco Rodríguez (Review entitled *"Sordomuda:* alambradas de la ficción"). *Plural (Mexico)*, v. 22, no. 260 (May 93), p. 68.

Boccia Paz, Alfredo et al. *Médicos, ética y tortura en el Paraguay* (Review). *Revista Paraguaya de Sociología*, v. 29, no. 84 (May – Aug 92), pp. 205 – 206. Il.

Bock Godard, Marie S. *Guayaquil: arquitectura, espacio y sociedad, 1900 – 1940* reviewed by Eduardo Figari Gold. *Bulletin de l'Institut Français d'Etudes Andines*, v. 21, no. 3 (1992), pp. 1082 – 1084.

Bodenheimer, Susanne Jonas

See
Jonas, Susanne Leilani

Boer, Kees den and Geert A. Banck, eds. *Sowing the Whirlwind: Soya Expansion and Social Change in Southern Brazil* reviewed by Martine Droulers. *Cahiers des Amériques Latines*, no. 14 (1992), pp. 158 – 159.

Boggs, Vernon W. *Salsiology: Afro-Cuban Music and the Evolution of Salsa in New York City* reviewed by Jerma Jackson. *Hispanic American Historical Review*, v. 73, no. 4 (Nov 93), pp. 673 – 674.

— *Salsiology: Afro-Cuban Music and the Evolution of Salsa in New York City* reviewed by Gerard Béhague. *Latin American Music Review*, v. 14, no. 1 (Spring – Summer 93), pp. 172 – 175.

Bohmann, Karin. *Medios de comunicación y sistemas informativos en México* reviewed by Susana González Reyna. *Revista Mexicana de Ciencias Políticas y Sociales*, v. 38, Nueva época, no. 154 (Oct – Dec 93), pp. 187 – 191.

Bokser de Liwerant, Judit, ed. *Imágenes de un encuentro: la presencia judía en México durante la primera mitad del siglo XX* reviewed by José María Pérez Gay (Review entitled "La ofrenda, el consuelo, el recuerdo, la admiración"). *Nexos*, v. 16, no. 190 (Oct 93), pp. 77 – 79.

Bonnett, Aubrey W. and G. Llewellyn Watson, eds. *Emerging Perspectives on the Black Diaspora* reviewed by Harry Goulbourne. *Caribbean Quarterly*, v. 38, no. 2 – 3 (June – Sept 92), pp. 115 – 116.

Bono, Diane M. *Cultural Diffusion of Spanish Humanism in New Spain: Francisco Cervantes de Salazar's 'Diálogo de la dignidad del hombre'* reviewed by William Mejías López. *Hispania (USA)*, v. 76, no. 2 (May 93), pp. 282 – 284.

Borello, Rodolfo A. *El peronismo (1943 – 1955) en la narrativa argentina* reviewed by Raúl Ianes. *Hispanic Review*, v. 61, no. 4 (Fall 93), pp. 590 – 592.

— *El peronismo (1943 – 1955) en la narrativa argentina* reviewed by Nicolas Shumway. *Revista Interamericana de Bibliografía*, v. 42, no. 2 (1992), pp. 282 – 283.

Borges, Dain Edward. *The Family in Bahia, Brazil, 1870 – 1945* reviewed by Sandra Lauderdale Graham. *Journal of Latin American Studies*, v. 25, no. 2 (May 93), pp. 399 – 401.

— *The Family in Bahia, Brazil, 1870 – 1945* reviewed by Robert M. Levine. *Luso-Brazilian Review*, v. 30, no. 1 (Summer 93), pp. 146 – 147.

Borjas, George J. and Richard B. Freeman, eds. *Immigration and the Work Force: Economic Consequences for the United States and Source Areas* reviewed by Jim Thomas. *Journal of Latin American Studies*, v. 25, no. 3 (Oct 93), pp. 683 – 684.

Bortolussi, Marisa. *El cuento infantil cubano: un estudio crítico* reviewed by Antonio Benítez-Rojo. *Hispanic Review*, v. 61, no. 4 (Fall 93), pp. 592 – 594.

Boucher, Philip Paul. *Cannibal Encounters: Europeans and Island Caribs, 1492 – 1763* reviewed by Irving Rouse. *Hispanic American Historical Review*, v. 73, no. 3 (Aug 93), pp. 495 – 496.

Boucher, Philip Paul and Patricia Galloway, eds. *Proceedings of the Fifteenth Meeting of the French Colonial Historical Society, Martinique and Guadeloupe, May 1989* reviewed by Paul Lachance. *Hispanic American Historical Review*, v. 73, no. 3 (Aug 93), pp. 502 – 503.

Boullosa, Carmen. *Llanto: novelas imposibles* reviewed by Cynthia Tompkins. *World Literature Today*, v. 67, no. 4 (Fall 93), pp. 780 – 781.

Bourguignon, François and Christian Morrisson, eds. *External Trade and Income Distribution* reviewed by Jaime de Melo. *Economic Development and Cultural Change*, v. 42, no. 1 (Oct 93), pp. 198 – 200.

Bouzas, Roberto and Nora Lustig, eds. *Liberalización comercial e integración regional: de NAFTA a MERCOSUR* (Review). *Integración Latinoamericana*, v. 18, no. 187 – 188 (Mar – Apr 93), p. 69.

Bove, Frederick Joseph and Lynette Heller, eds. *New Frontiers in the Archaeology of the Pacific Coast of Southern Mesoamerica* reviewed by Molly R. Mignon. *Latin American Antiquity*, v. 4, no. 1 (Mar 93), pp. 98 – 99.

Boyd-Bowman, Peter. *Indice y extractos del Archivo de Protocolos de Puebla de los Angeles, México, 1538 – 1556* reviewed by Linda Greenow. *Hispanic American Historical Review*, v. 73, no. 3 (Aug 93), pp. 486 – 487.

— *Léxico hispanoamericano del siglo XVI* reviewed by Linda Greenow. *Hispanic American Historical Review*, v. 73, no. 3 (Aug 93), pp. 486 – 487.

Bracho, Coral and Irma Palacios. *Tierra de entraña ardiente* reviewed by Jacobo Sefamí. *Vuelta*, v. 17, no. 200 (July 93), pp. 58 – 59.

Brading, David Anthony. *The First America: The Spanish Monarchy, Creole Patriots, and the Liberal State, 1492 – 1867* reviewed by Marie-Cécile Bénassy-Berling. *Caravelle*, no. 59 (1992), pp. 266 – 270.

— *The First America: The Spanish Monarchy, Creole Patriots, and the Liberal State, 1492 – 1867* reviewed by Eric Van Young. *Colonial Latin American Review*, v. 2, no. 1 – 2 (1993), pp. 291 – 296.

Bradley, Peter T. *Society, Economy, and Defence in Seventeenth-Century Peru: The Administration of the Count of Alba de Liste, 1655 – 1661* reviewed by Teodoro Hampe Martínez. *Colonial Latin American Review*, v. 2, no. 1 – 2 (1993), pp. 298 – 300.

— *Society, Economy, and Defence in Seventeenth-Century Peru: The Administration of the Count of Alba de Liste, 1655 – 1661* reviewed by Stephen J. Homick. *Hispanic American Historical Review*, v. 73, no. 2 (May 93), pp. 314 – 315.

— *Society, Economy, and Defence in Seventeenth-Century Peru: The Administration of the Count of Alba de Liste, 1655 – 1661* reviewed by Mark A. Burkholder. *Revista Interamericana de Bibliografía,* v. 42, no. 2 (1992), pp. 283 – 284.

Braga, Rubem. *Livro de versos* (Review). *Vozes,* v. 87, no. 2 (Mar – Apr 93), pp. 102 – 103.

Brailovsky, Antonio Elio. *Esta maldita lujuria* reviewed by Thomas E. Case. *World Literature Today,* v. 67, no. 1 (Winter 93), p. 155.

Brailovsky, Antonio Elio and Dina Foguelman. *Memoria verde: historia ecológica de la Argentina* reviewed by Adrián Gustavo Zarrilli. *Revista de Historia de América,* no. 113 (Jan – June 92), pp. 174 – 177.

Brannon, Jeffery T. and Gilbert Michael Joseph, eds. *Land, Labor, and Capital in Modern Yucatán: Essays in Regional History and Political Economy* reviewed by Donald F. Stevens. *The Americas,* v. 49, no. 4 (Apr 93), pp. 558 – 559.

Brash, Jorge. *Persistencia del agua* reviewed by José Homero. *Vuelta,* v. 17, no. 197 (Apr 93), pp. 49 – 50.

Brathwaite, Edward Kamau. *Middle Passages* reviewed by Cyril Dabydeen. *World Literature Today,* v. 67, no. 2 (Spring 93), pp. 425 – 426.

Brebbia, Fernando P. *Manual de derecho agrario* reviewed by Arnaldo Gómez A. *Derecho y Reforma Agraria,* no. 24 (1993), pp. 205 – 206.

Brenot, Anne-Marie. *Pouvoirs et profits au Pérou colonial au XVIIIᵉ siècle: gouverneurs, clientèles et ventes forcées* reviewed by Pierre Ragon. *Cahiers des Amériques Latines,* no. 14 (1992), pp. 152 – 153.

Breton, André et al, eds. *Vingt études sur le Mexique et le Guatemala réunies à la mémoire de Nicole Percheron* reviewed by Stephen Webre. *Hispanic American Historical Review,* v. 73, no. 2 (May 93), pp. 305 – 306.

Briceño Perozo, Mario. *Antonio Maceo, la voz del huracán* reviewed by José Manuel Castañón (Review entitled "El Antonio Maceo de Mario Briceño Perozo"). *Boletín de la Academia Nacional de la Historia (Venezuela),* v. 75, no. 298 (Apr – June 92), pp. 110 – 111.

Briceño Perozo, Mario, ed. *Sonetos a Bolívar* reviewed by Luis Gustavo Acuña Luco (Review entitled "Homenaje sonetístico a Simón Bolívar"). *Boletín de la Academia Nacional de la Historia (Venezuela),* v. 75, no. 298 (Apr – June 92), pp. 112 – 114.

Bricker, Victoria Reifler. *A Grammar of Mayan Hieroglyphs* reviewed by Barbara MacLeod. *Mesoamérica (USA),* v. 13, no. 23 (June 92), pp. 213 – 216.

Bricker, Victoria Reifler and Munro S. Edmonson, eds. *Supplement to 'The Handbook of Middle American Indians,' Vol. III: Literatures* reviewed by Jorge F. Travieso. *Mesoamérica (USA),* v. 13, no. 23 (June 92), pp. 205 – 209.

Briggs, Vernon M., Jr. *Mass Immigration and the National Interest* reviewed by Michael Ellis. *Journal of Borderlands Studies,* v. 7, no. 2 (Fall 92), pp. 109 – 111.

Brooks, Zelda Irene. *Carlos Alberto Trujillo, un poeta del sur de Sudamérica* reviewed by Alberto Gutiérrez de la Solana. *Chasqui,* v. 22, no. 2 (Nov 93), pp. 167 – 168.

Brown, Charles J. and Armando M. Lago. *The Politics of Psychiatry in Revolutionary Cuba* reviewed by Roberto Valero. *Cuban Studies/Estudios Cubanos,* v. 23 (1993), pp. 233 – 235.

Brown, Enid. *Suriname and the Netherlands Antilles: An Annotated English-Language Bibliography* reviewed by Gary Brana-Shute. *The Americas,* v. 50, no. 1 (July 93), pp. 123 – 124.

— *Suriname and the Netherlands Antilles: An Annotated English-Language Bibliography* reviewed by Rosemarijn Hoefte. *Hispanic American Historical Review,* v. 73, no. 4 (Nov 93), pp. 677 – 678.

Brown, Jonathan C. *Oil and Revolution in Mexico* reviewed by Rebeca de Gortari Rabiela. *Revista Mexicana de Sociología,* v. 55, no. 2 (Apr – June 93), pp. 389 – 395.

Brown, Michael F. *War of Shadows: The Struggle for Utopia in the Peruvian Amazon* reviewed by Oscar Espinoza. *Amazonía Peruana,* v. 11, no. 22 (Oct 92), pp. 278 – 284.

Bruno, Michael et al, eds. *Lessons of Economic Stabilization and Its Aftermath* reviewed by Peter Winglee. *Journal of Developing Areas,* v. 27, no. 2 (Jan 93), pp. 248 – 250.

Bruschini, Cristina and Albertina de Oliveira Costa, eds. *Entre a virtude e o pecado* reviewed by Miriam Pillar Grossi (Review entitled "Enfoques de gênero na história social"). *Estudos Feministas,* v. 1, no. 1 (1993), pp. 215 – 216.

Bryce Echenique, Alfredo. *Dos mujeres conversan* reviewed by Esther Martínez Luna (Review entitled "Nostalgia peruana"). *Nexos,* v. 16, no. 182 (Feb 93), p. 80.

— *Permiso para vivir* reviewed by Marco Martos (Review entitled "Las memorias de tres novelistas peruanos"). *Debate (Peru),* v. 16, no. 73 (June – Aug 93), pp. 68 – 72. Il.

— *A World for Julius,* a translation of *Un mundo para Julius,* translated by Dick Gerdes. Reviewed by César Ferreira. *Chasqui,* v. 22, no. 1 (May 93), pp. 76 – 78.

Bucher, Bernadette et al. *America: Bride of the Sun; 500 Years Latin America and the Low Countries* reviewed by Peter Mason. *European Review of Latin American and Caribbean Studies,* no. 53 (Dec 92), pp. 114 – 117.

Buenaño Rugel, Aminta. *La otra piel* reviewed by Peter N. Thomas. *Chasqui,* v. 22, no. 1 (May 93), pp. 107 – 110.

Bueno Chávez, Raúl. *Escribir en Hispanoamérica: ensayos sobre teoría y crítica literaria* reviewed by Miguel Angel Huamán. *Revista de Crítica Literaria Latinoamericana,* v. 19, no. 38 (July – Dec 93), pp. 397 – 399.

Burger, Richard Lewis. *Chavín and the Origins of Andean Civilization* reviewed by Thomas Pozorski and Shelia Pozorski. *Latin American Antiquity,* v. 4, no. 4 (Dec 93), pp. 389 – 390.

Burns, E. Bradford. *Patriarch and Folk: The Emergence of Nicaragua, 1798 – 1858* reviewed by Thomas M. Leonard. *The Americas,* v. 49, no. 4 (Apr 93), pp. 555 – 556.

— *Patriarch and Folk: The Emergence of Nicaragua, 1798 – 1858* reviewed by Elizabeth Dore. *Journal of Latin American Studies,* v. 25, no. 2 (May 93), pp. 403 – 404.

Bustamante, Jorge Agustín et al, eds. *U.S. – Mexico Relations: Labor Market Interdependence* reviewed by Sidney Weintraub. *International Migration Review,* v. 27, no. 3 (Fall 93), p. 646.

— *U.S. – Mexico Relations: Labor Market Interdependence* reviewed by Guillermo Arámburgo Vizcarra. *Journal of Latin American Studies,* v. 25, no. 2 (May 93), pp. 406 – 407.

Caballero Aquino, Olga and Marina Díaz de Vivar Prieto. *Mujer paraguaya: jefa de familia* (Review). *Revista Paraguaya de Sociología,* v. 29, no. 84 (May – Aug 92), p. 210. Il.

Cabrera Infante, Guillermo. *Mea Cuba* reviewed by Aurelio Asiaín. *Vuelta,* v. 17, no. 201 (Aug 93), pp. 43 – 45.

— *Mea Cuba* reviewed by Fabienne Bradu. *Vuelta,* v. 17, no. 198 (May 93), pp. 48 – 49.

— *Mea Cuba* reviewed by Juan Goytisolo (Review entitled "Una memoria de Cuba"). *Nexos,* v. 16, no. 184 (Apr 93), pp. 65 – 66.

— *Mea Cuba* reviewed by Will H. Corral. *World Literature Today*, v. 67, no. 2 (Spring 93), pp. 342 – 343.

Cacua Prada, Antonio. *Los hijos secretos de Bolívar* reviewed by Alfonso Gómez Gómez. *Boletín de Historia y Antigüedades*, v. 79, no. 779 (Oct – Dec 92), pp. 1071 – 1083.

— *Los hijos secretos de Bolívar* reviewed by Manuel Drezner (Review entitled "Tres nuevos libros del académico Cacua Prada"). *Boletín de Historia y Antigüedades*, v. 80, no. 781 (Apr – June 93), pp. 479 – 480.

Cadenas, Rafael. *Antología, 1958 – 1983* reviewed by Brian Evenson. *World Literature Today*, v. 67, no. 2 (Spring 93), pp. 337 – 338.

Cadogan, León. *Ayvu Rapytá: textos míticos de los mbyá-guaraní del Guairá* (Review). *Revista Paraguaya de Sociología*, v. 29, no. 85 (Sept – Dec 92), pp. 188 – 189.

Caetano, Gerardo, ed. *La alternativa parlamentarista* reviewed by Carlos Filgueira. *Cuadernos del CLAEH*, v. 18, no. 67 (Nov 93), pp. 135 – 140.

Calabi Abaroa, Guido. *Con la sed en los labios* reviewed by Raúl Rivadeneira Prada. *Signo*, no. 38, Nueva época (Jan – Apr 93), pp. 226 – 228.

Calavita, Kitty. *Inside the State: The Bracero Program, Immigration, and the I.N.S.* reviewed by Rodolfo O. de la Garza. *International Migration Review*, v. 27, no. 4 (Winter 93), pp. 895 – 896.

Calcagno, Alfredo Eric. *Estructura y funciones actuales de los organismos internacionales financieros y económicos* (Review). *Integración Latinoamericana*, v. 18, no. 195 (Nov 93), p. 57.

Calderón, Héctor and José David Saldívar, eds. *Criticism in the Borderlands: Studies in Chicano Literature, Culture, and Ideology* reviewed by Chuck Tatum (Review entitled "A New Standard for Chicano Literary Scholarship"). *Bilingual Review/Revista Bilingüe*, v. 18, no. 1 (Jan – Apr 93), pp. 64 – 74.

— *Criticism in the Borderlands: Studies in Chicano Literature, Culture, and Ideology* reviewed by Hanny Berkelmans (Review entitled "La literatura chicana de hoy en día"). *European Review of Latin American and Caribbean Studies*, no. 54 (June 93), pp. 111 – 115. Bibl.

— *Criticism in the Borderlands: Studies in Chicano Literature, Culture, and Ideology* reviewed by John Bruce-Novoa. *Hispania (USA)*, v. 76, no. 2 (May 93), pp. 280 – 281.

— *Criticism in the Borderlands: Studies in Chicano Literature, Culture, and Ideology* reviewed by Pedro Maligo. *Hispanic American Historical Review*, v. 73, no. 3 (Aug 93), pp. 489 – 490.

Calero, Fernando and Héctor Lucena R., eds. *Las relaciones de trabajo en los noventa: desafíos y propuestas* reviewed by T. M. van Hettema. *European Review of Latin American and Caribbean Studies*, no. 54 (June 93), pp. 139 – 140.

Calvera, Leonor. *Mujeres y feminismo en la Argentina* reviewed by Eliana C. Hermann. *Hispanic Journal*, v. 14, no. 1 (Spring 93), pp. 175 – 176.

Calvimontes de Rodríguez, Velia. *Abre la tapa y destapa un cuento: cuentos para niños* reviewed by Pepa Martínez de López. *Signo*, no. 35, Nueva época (Jan – Apr 92), pp. 204 – 206.

Calvo Pontón, Beatriz and Laura Donnadieu Aguado. *Una educación ¿indígena, bilingüe o bicultural?* reviewed by Salvador Martínez. *Revista Latinoamericana de Estudios Educativos*, v. 22, no. 4 (Oct – Dec 92), pp. 123 – 125.

Camacho, Georgette de. *Letra desleída* reviewed by Jaime Martínez Salguero. *Signo*, no. 38, Nueva época (Jan – Apr 93), pp. 229 – 230.

Camacho Guizado, Alvaro, ed. *La Colombia de hoy: sociología y sociedad* reviewed by Maurice P. Brungardt (Review entitled "Readings on Colombia?"). *Studies in Latin American Popular Culture*, v. 12 (1993), pp. 235 – 242.

Camp, Roderic Ai. *Generals in the Palacio: The Military in Modern Mexico* reviewed by Thomas M. Davies, Jr. *Hispanic American Historical Review*, v. 73, no. 2 (May 93), pp. 335 – 336.

Camp, Roderic Ai et al, eds. *Los intelectuales y el poder en México* reviewed by Carlos Alberto Torres. *Hispanic American Historical Review*, v. 73, no. 2 (May 93), pp. 336 – 337.

Campi, Daniel, ed. *Estudios sobre la historia de la industria azucarera argentina* reviewed by Federico Torres Quevedo. *Todo Es Historia*, v. 26, no. 306 (Jan 93), pp. 56 – 57.

Campos, Javier F. *Las cartas olvidadas del astronauta* reviewed by Grinor Rojo. *Hispamérica*, v. 22, no. 64 – 65 (Apr – Aug 93), pp. 187 – 191.

Campos, Mintaha Alcuri. *Turco pobre, sirio remediado, libanês rico* reviewed by Gabriel Bittencourt. *Revista do Instituto Histórico e Geográfico Brasileiro*, no. 373 (Oct – Dec 91), pp. 1207 – 1208.

Campos Ruiz Díaz, Daniel, ed. *Desarrollo en el Paraguay: contribuciones a una visión global* (Review). *Revista Paraguaya de Sociología*, v. 29, no. 85 (Sept – Dec 92), pp. 187 – 188.

Camprubí de Jiménez, Zenobia. *Diario, 1: Cuba, 1937 – 1939* introduced and translated by Graciela Palau de Nemes. Reviewed by Aleksandra Hadzelek. *Revista Iberoamericana*, v. 59, no. 162 – 163 (Jan – June 93), pp. 385 – 387.

Candelaria, Cordelia, ed. *Multiethnic Literature of the United States: Critical Introductions and Classroom Resources* reviewed by Genevieve M. Ramírez. *The Americas Review*, v. 19, no. 2 (Summer 91), pp. 107 – 109.

Cano Andrade, Daniel. *Pepe Ríos* reviewed by Gabriella de Beer (Review entitled "Coming of Age in the Mexican Revolution"). *Bilingual Review/Revista Bilingüe*, v. 17, no. 3 (Sept – Dec 92), pp. 285 – 286.

Cano Gaviria, Ricardo. *José Asunción Silva: una vida en clave de sombra* reviewed by José Ricardo Chaves. *Vuelta*, v. 17, no. 201 (Aug 93), pp. 53 – 54.

As cantoras do rádio: 50 anos de som e imagem da MPB reviewed by Irati Antonio. *Latin American Music Review*, v. 14, no. 2 (Fall – Winter 93), pp. 297 – 299.

Carbonell de Masy, Rafael et al. *Estrategias de desarrollo rural en los pueblos guaraníes, 1609 – 1767* reviewed by José Luis Mora Mérida. *Anuario de Estudios Americanos*, v. 50, no. 1 (1993), pp. 311 – 312.

Cardenal, Ernesto. *Cántico cósmico* reviewed by Juan Malpartida. *Vuelta*, v. 17, no. 196 (Mar 93), pp. 54 – 55.

— *Golden UFOs: The Indian Poems/Los ovnis de oro: poemas indios* edited by Russell O. Salmon, translated by Carlos and Monique Altschul. Reviewed by Marc Zimmerman. *Hispanic American Historical Review*, v. 73, no. 2 (May 93), pp. 295 – 296.

Cardoso, Eliana Anastasia and Ann Helwege. *Cuba after Communism* reviewed by Nicolás Sánchez. *Cuban Studies/Estudios Cubanos*, v. 23 (1993), pp. 210 – 213.

— *Latin America's Economy: Diversity, Trends, and Conflicts* reviewed by Antonio Jorge and Raúl Moncarz. *Journal of Developing Areas*, v. 27, no. 4 (July 93), pp. 552 – 553.

— *Latin America's Economy: Diversity, Trends, and Conflicts* reviewed by David Hojman. *Journal of Latin American Studies*, v. 25, no. 1 (Feb 93), pp. 209 – 211.

Cardoso, Fernando Henrique. *As idéias e seu lugar* (Review). *Vozes,* v. 87, no. 3 (May – June 93), pp. 91 – 92.

Cardozo Galué, Germán. *Maracaibo y su región histórica: el circuito agroexportador, 1830 – 1860* reviewed by Frédérique Langue. *Cahiers des Amériques Latines,* no. 13 (1992), pp. 184 – 185.

Cardozo Rodas, Victorino. *Lucha sindical y transición política en Paraguay* (Review). *Revista Paraguaya de Sociología,* v. 29, no. 84 (May – Aug 92), pp. 206 – 207. II.

Carey, Steven and Haraldur Sigurdssen. *Caribbean Volcanoes: A Field Guide; Martinique, Dominica, and St. Vincent* reviewed by Trevor Jackson. *Caribbean Geography,* v. 3, no. 3 (Mar 92), pp. 211 – 212.

Cariola, Cecilia, ed. *Sobrevivir en la pobreza: el fin de una ilusión* reviewed by María Elena Ducci. *EURE,* v. 19, no. 58 (Oct 93), pp. 86 – 87.

Cariola Sutter, Carmen and Osvaldo Sunkel. *Un siglo de historia económica de Chile, 1830 – 1930* reviewed by Juan Ricardo Couyoumdjian. *Boletín de la Academia Chilena de la Historia,* v. 58 – 59, no. 102 (1991 – 1992), pp. 561 – 562.

Carmack, Robert Marin, ed. *Guatemala: cosecha de violencias* reviewed by Manuel Angel Castillo G. *Revista Mexicana de Sociología,* v. 54, no. 1 (Jan – Mar 92), pp. 331 – 334.

Carmichael, Elizabeth and Chloë Sayer. *The Skeleton and the Feast: The Day of the Dead in Mexico* reviewed by Ward S. Albro III. *Hispanic American Historical Review,* v. 73, no. 1 (Feb 93), p. 127.

Carothers, Thomas H. *In the Name of Democracy: U.S. Policy toward Latin America in the Reagan Years* reviewed by Rubén M. Perina (Review entitled "La promoción de la democracia en América Latina"). *Estudios Internacionales (Chile),* v. 26, no. 102 (Apr – June 93), pp. 204 – 215.

— *In the Name of Democracy: U.S. Policy toward Latin America in the Reagan Years* reviewed by Dario Moreno. *Hispanic American Historical Review,* v. 73, no. 4 (Nov 93), pp. 729 – 730.

Carr, Barry. *Marxism and Communism in Twentieth-Century Mexico* reviewed by George Philip. *Bulletin of Latin American Research,* v. 12, no. 2 (May 93), pp. 230 – 231.

Carrasco, David, ed. *To Change Place: Aztec Ceremonial Landscapes* reviewed by Michael E. Smith. *Latin American Antiquity,* v. 4, no. 2 (June 93), p. 200.

Carrasco, David and Eduardo Matos Moctezuma. *Moctezuma's México: Visions of the Aztec World* reviewed by James N. Corbridge, Jr. *La Educación (USA),* v. 37, no. 115 (1993), pp. 413 – 414.

Carrera, Rodolfo Ricardo. *El problema de la tierra en el derecho agrario* reviewed by Arnaldo Gómez A. *Derecho y Reforma Agraria,* no. 24 (1993), pp. 203 – 204.

Carrera Damas, Germán. *El culto a Bolívar: esbozo para un estudio de la historia de las ideas en Venezuela* reviewed by Frédérique Langue. *Cahiers des Amériques Latines,* no. 13 (1992), p. 184.

Carril, Bonifacio del. *Los indios en la Argentina, 1536 – 1845, según la iconografía de la época* reviewed by María Sáenz Quesada. *Todo Es Historia,* v. 27, no. 315 (Oct 93), p. 63. II.

Carrillo Azpéitia, Rafael. *Posada y el grabado mexicano: desde el famoso grabador de temas populares hasta los artistas contemporáneos* reviewed by J. León Helguera (Review entitled "José Guadalupe Posada Yet Again"). *Studies in Latin American Popular Culture,* v. 12 (1993), pp. 203 – 206.

Carroll, Patrick James. *Blacks in Colonial Veracruz: Race, Ethnicity, and Regional Development* reviewed by Linda A. Newson. *Journal of Latin American Studies,* v. 25, no. 1 (Feb 93), pp. 192 – 193.

Carter, Miguel. *El papel de la iglesia en la caída de Stroessner* reviewed by Jerry W. Cooney. *The Americas,* v. 49, no. 3 (Jan 93), pp. 424 – 425.

— *El papel de la iglesia en la caída de Stroessner* reviewed by W. E. Hewitt. *Hispanic American Historical Review,* v. 73, no. 1 (Feb 93), p. 179.

Caruso, Brooke A. *The Mexican Spy Company: United States Covert Actions in Mexico, 1845 – 1848* reviewed by Daniela Spenser. *Hispanic American Historical Review,* v. 73, no. 1 (Feb 93), p. 189.

Casali, Eduardo and Abel Baratti. *Del juego al deporte, I: Actividades para nivel primero* reviewed by Cora Céspedes. *La Educación (USA),* v. 36, no. 111 – 113 (1992), pp. 282 – 283.

Casalla, Mario Carlos. *América en el pensamiento de Hegel: admiración y rechazo* reviewed by Daniel Toribio. *Todo Es Historia,* v. 27, no. 316 (Nov 93), p. 91. II.

Casanova, Ramón Vicente. *En las fronteras del viento: vivencias tachirenses* reviewed by Juvenal López Ruiz. *Revista Nacional de Cultura (Venezuela),* v. 53, no. 286 (July – Sept 92), pp. 264 – 265.

Casas Guerrero, Rosalba et al, eds. *La biotecnología y sus repercusiones socioeconómicas y políticas* reviewed by Eugenia J. Olguín. *Revista Mexicana de Sociología,* v. 55, no. 2 (Apr – June 93), pp. 397 – 404. Bibl.

Casasola García, Luis and Carlos Alvarez Asomoza. *Las figurillas de Jonuta, Tabasco* reviewed by Françoise Milhorat. *Caravelle,* no. 59 (1992), pp. 253 – 256.

Casaus Arzú, Marta Elena. *Guatemala: linaje y racismo* reviewed by Carlos M. Vilas. *Journal of Latin American Studies,* v. 25, no. 3 (Oct 93), pp. 662 – 663.

Casevitz, France-Marie
See
   Renard-Casevitz, France-Marie

Cassá, Roberto. *Los indios de las Antillas* reviewed by Genaro Rodríguez Morel. *Anuario de Estudios Americanos,* v. 50, no. 1 (1993), pp. 312 – 314.

Cassiolato, José Eduardo and Hubert Schmitz, eds. *Hi-tech for Industrial Development: Lessons from the Brazilian Experience in Electronics and Automation* reviewed by Rhys Jenkins. *Bulletin of Latin American Research,* v. 12, no. 3 (Sept 93), pp. 349 – 350.

Castañeda, Jorge G. *Utopia Unarmed: The Latin American Left after the Cold War* reviewed by Nicolás Shumway (Review entitled "La esperanza postdiluviana," translated by Pedro Garland). *Nexos,* v. 16, no. 192 (Dec 93), pp. 76 – 77.

Castañeda Delgado, Paulino and Pilar Hernández Aparicio. *La inquisición en Lima, tomo I: 1570 – 1635* reviewed by Hilda Raquel Zapico. *Revista de Historia de América,* no. 113 (Jan – June 92), pp. 161 – 165.

Castañón, Adolfo. *Alfonso Reyes, caballero de la voz errante* reviewed by Sam L. Slick. *World Literature Today,* v. 67, no. 1 (Winter 93), p. 162.

— *Arbitrario de literatura mexicana* reviewed by Christopher Domínguez Michael. *Vuelta,* v. 17, no. 203 (Oct 93), pp. 42 – 43.

Castelazo, José R. *Ciudad de México: reforma posible; escenarios en el porvenir* reviewed by Aída Escamilla Rubio. *El Cotidiano,* v. 9, no. 54 (May 93), p. 115. II.

Castellanos, Jorge and Isabel Mercedes Castellanos. *Cultura afrocubana, III: Las religiones y las lenguas* reviewed by Luis A. Jiménez. *Hispania (USA),* v. 76, no. 2 (May 93), pp. 281 – 282.

Castelló Yturbide, Teresa. *Presencia de la comida prehispánica* reviewed by Susan N. Masuoka (Review entitled "Mexican Eating: The Work and the Haute Cuisine"). *Studies in Latin American Popular Culture,* v. 12 (1993), pp. 189 – 194.

Castillo, Abelardo. *Crónica de un iniciado* reviewed by Jorge Timossi (Review entitled "La desacralización de la literatura"). *Casa de las Américas,* no. 190 (Jan – Mar 93), pp. 147 – 149.

Castillo, Debra A. *Talking Back: Toward a Latin American Feminist Literary Criticism* reviewed by Salvador A. Oropesa. *Chasqui,* v. 22, no. 1 (May 93), pp. 102 – 103.

— *Talking Back: Toward a Latin American Feminist Literary Criticism* reviewed by Vicente Cabrera. *Chasqui,* v. 22, no. 2 (Nov 93), pp. 155 – 156.

— *Talking Back: Toward a Latin American Feminist Literary Criticism* reviewed by Rosemary Geisdorfer Feal. *Hispania (USA),* v. 76, no. 1 (Mar 93), pp. 82 – 83.

Castillo de Berchenko, Adriana. *Alfredo Gangotena, poéte équatorien, 1904 – 1944, ou, l'écriture partagée* reviewed by Rogelio Arenas. *Caravelle,* no. 60 (1993), pp. 170 – 172.

Castrejón Diez, Jaime. *La universidad y el sistema* reviewed by Elías Margolis Schweber. *Revista Mexicana de Ciencias Políticas y Sociales,* v. 38, Nueva época, no. 153 (July – Sept 93), pp. 219 – 222.

— *La universidad y el sistema* reviewed by Margarita Jiménez Badillo. *El Cotidiano,* v. 8, no. 51 (Nov – Dec 92), p. 115.

Castro, Donald S. *The Development and Politics of Argentine Immigration Policy, 1852 – 1914: "To Govern Is to Populate"* reviewed by Samuel L. Baily. *International Migration Review,* v. 27, no. 1 (Spring 93), pp. 214 – 215.

Castro Gutiérrez, Felipe. *Movimientos populares en Nueva España: Michoacán, 1766 – 1797* reviewed by Frédérique Langue (Review entitled "Les soulèvements populaires de 1767 en Nouvell-Espagne: le point sur quelques publications récentes"). *Caravelle,* no. 60 (1993), pp. 152 – 154.

Castro-Klarén, Sara et al, eds. *Women's Writing in Latin America: An Anthology* reviewed by Lisa Jesse. *Bulletin of Latin American Research,* v. 12, no. 1 (Jan 93), pp. 128 – 129.

— *Women's Writing in Latin America: An Anthology* reviewed by Eva Paulino Bueno. *Revista de Crítica Literaria Latinoamericana,* v. 19, no. 37 (Jan – June 93), pp. 372 – 374.

Castro Morales, María Belén. *José E. Rodó, modernista: utopía y regeneración* reviewed by Julio Ricci. *Hispamérica,* v. 22, no. 64 – 65 (Apr – Aug 93), pp. 191 – 192.

Caunedo Madrigal, Silvia. *Las entrañas mágicas de América* reviewed by Paloma Lapuerta. *Cuadernos Hispanoamericanos,* no. 520 (Oct 93), pp. 127 – 128.

Caviedes L., César N. *Elections in Chile: The Road toward Redemocratization* reviewed by Paul E. Sigmund. *Hispanic American Historical Review,* v. 73, no. 3 (Aug 93), pp. 517 – 518.

— *Elections in Chile: The Road toward Redemocratization* reviewed by William W. Culver. *Revista Interamericana de Bibliografía,* v. 42, no. 4 (1992), p. 655.

Celorio, Gonzalo. *Amor propio* reviewed by Adriana Sandoval. *Caravelle,* no. 60 (1993), pp. 172 – 174.

— *Amor propio* reviewed by César Ferreira. *Chasqui,* v. 22, no. 2 (Nov 93), pp. 156 – 158.

Centeno, Israel. *Calletania* reviewed by R. J. Lovera De-Sola. *Revista Nacional de Cultura (Venezuela),* v. 53, no. 286 (July – Sept 92), pp. 252 – 253.

Centeno, Miguel Angel. *Mexico in the 1990s: Government and Opposition Speak Out* reviewed by Martin C. Needler (Review entitled "Economic Policy and Political Survival"). *Mexican Studies,* v. 9, no. 1 (Winter 93), pp. 139 – 143.

Cerda, Ictus-Carlos. *Morir en Berlín* reviewed by Antonio Avaria (Review entitled *"Morir en Berlín:* otra novela del exilio chileno"). *Mensaje,* v. 42, no. 423 (Oct 93), pp. 529 – 530. II.

Céspedes del Castillo, Guillermo and Anes Alvarez de Castrillón. *El tabaco en Nueva España* reviewed by Dawn Keremitsis. *Hispanic American Historical Review,* v. 73, no. 2 (May 93), pp. 311 – 312.

Cevallos Candau, Francisco Javier, ed. *Narraciones cortas de la América colonial* reviewed by Lee A. Daniel. *Hispania (USA),* v. 76, no. 3 (Sept 93), pp. 481 – 482.

Chamberlain, Bobby J. *Jorge Amado* reviewed by John Gledson. *Hispanic Review,* v. 61, no. 2 (Spring 93), pp. 308 – 310.

Chamberlain, Daniel Frank. *Narrative Perspective in Fiction: A Phenomenological Mediation of Reader, Text, and World* reviewed by Lois Parkinson Zamora. *Revista Canadiense de Estudios Hispánicos,* v. 17, no. 1 (Fall 92), pp. 211 – 213.

Chamoiseau, Patrick. *Texaco* reviewed by Juris Silenieks. *World Literature Today,* v. 67, no. 4 (Fall 93), pp. 877 – 878.

— *Texaco* reviewed by Nara Araújo (Review entitled "Texaco a la invasión de los márgenes"). *Casa de las Américas,* no. 191 (Apr – June 93), pp. 139 – 142.

Chandler, Dewitt Samuel. *Social Assistance and Bureaucratic Politics: The Montepíos of Colonial Mexico, 1767 – 1821* reviewed by Richard J. Salvucci. *The Americas,* v. 49, no. 4 (Apr 93), pp. 551 – 552.

— *Social Assistance and Bureaucratic Politics: The Montepíos of Colonial Mexico, 1767 – 1821* reviewed by Silvia Marina Arrom. *Hispanic American Historical Review,* v. 73, no. 1 (Feb 93), pp. 153 – 154.

— *Social Assistance and Bureaucratic Politics: The Montepíos of Colonial Mexico, 1767 – 1821* reviewed by Eric Van Young. *Journal of Latin American Studies,* v. 25, no. 3 (Oct 93), pp. 653 – 654.

Chant, Sylvia H. *Women and Survival in Mexican Cities: Perspectives on Gender, Labour Markets, and Low-Income Households* reviewed by M. Patricia Fernández Kelly. *Economic Development and Cultural Change,* v. 41, no. 3 (Apr 93), pp. 671 – 673.

Chao Ebergenyi, Guillermo. *De los altos* reviewed by Raymundo León (Review entitled *"De los altos:* la verdadera guerra cristera"). *La Palabra y el Hombre,* no. 81 (Jan – Mar 92), pp. 339 – 340.

Charnay, Désiré. *Le Mexique, 1858 – 1861: souvenirs et impressions de voyage* commentaries by Pascal Mongne. Reviewed by Françoise Milhorat. *Caravelle,* no. 59 (1992), pp. 273 – 277.

Chavez, Leo R. *Shadowed Lives: Undocumented Immigrants in American Society* reviewed by Susan González Baker. *International Migration Review,* v. 27, no. 1 (Spring 93), pp. 206 – 207.

Chávez, Linda. *Out of the Barrio: Toward a New Politics of Assimilation* reviewed by Cristóbal S. Berry-Cabán. *International Migration Review,* v. 27, no. 1 (Spring 93), pp. 208 – 210.

Chávez Candelaria, Cordelia

See
Candelaria, Cordelia

Checa Godoy, Antonio. *Historia de la prensa en Iberoamérica* reviewed by Alfonso Braojos Garrido. *Anuario de Estudios Americanos*, v. 50, no. 1 (1993), pp. 314 – 316.

Chiaramonte, José Carlos. *Mercaderes del litoral: economía y sociedad en la provincia de Corrientes, primera mitad del siglo XIX* reviewed by Jerry W. Cooney. *Hispanic American Historical Review*, v. 73, no. 2 (May 93), pp. 322 – 323.

Chinolope

See

López Junqué, Fernando

Chipman, Donald E. *Spanish Texas, 1519 – 1821* reviewed by E. A. Mares. *Colonial Latin American Historical Review*, v. 2, no. 4 (Fall 93), pp. 474 – 475.

Chipoco Cáceres, Carlos. *En defensa de la vida: ensayos sobre derechos humanos y derecho internacional humanitario* reviewed by Susana Villarán (Review entitled "Causa tomada"). *Debate (Peru)*, v. 15, no. 71 (Nov 92 – Jan 93), p. 80. Il.

Chirinos Arrieta, Eduardo, ed. *Infame turba: poesía en la Universidad Católica, 1917 – 1992* reviewed by Abelardo Oquendo (Review entitled "Pero, ¿existe algo que pueda llarmarse un poeta de la Católica?"). *Debate (Peru)*, v. 16, no. 72 (Mar – May 93), pp. 55 – 56. Il.

Choque Mata, Jaime. *Antología del ensueño: selección de poemas, 1966 a 1988* reviewed by Coral de la Zerda Hoffman. *Signo*, no. 38, Nueva época (Jan – Apr 93), p. 235.

Ciafardo, Eduardo O. *Los niños en la ciudad de Buenos Aires, 1850 – 1910* reviewed by Sergio A. Pujol. *Todo Es Historia*, v. 27, no. 311 (June 93), p. 58. Il.

Ciarnello, Nicolás. *Julio César Avanza: un homenaje demorado* reviewed by F. L. *Todo Es Historia*, v. 27, no. 311 (June 93), p. 60. Il.

Cintrón Mattos, Wilfredo

See

Mattos Cintrón, Wilfredo

Cipriano Castro y su época reviewed by Pascual Venegas Filardo. *Revista Nacional de Cultura (Venezuela)*, v. 53, no. 286 (July – Sept 92), pp. 255 – 256.

Ciria, Alberto. *Treinta años de política y cultura: recuerdos y ensayos* reviewed by Andrés Avellaneda. *Hispamérica*, v. 21, no. 62 (Aug 92), pp. 138 – 140.

Cisneros, Antonio. *Las inmensas preguntas celestes* reviewed by Patricia Alba (Review entitled "Poesía en blue"). *Debate (Peru)*, v. 15, no. 71 (Nov 92 – Jan 93), p. 79. Il.

Cisneros, Sandra. *Woman Hollering Creek and Other Stories* reviewed by Erlinda Gonzales-Berry. *The Americas Review*, v. 20, no. 1 (Spring 92), pp. 83 – 85.

Cleary, Edward L. and Hannah W. Stewart-Gambino, eds. *Conflict and Competition: The Latin American Church in a Changing Environment* reviewed by Michael LaRosa (Review entitled "Religion in a Changing Latin America: A Review"). *Journal of Inter-American Studies and World Affairs*, v. 34, no. 4 (Winter 92 – 93), pp. 245 – 255. Bibl.

— *Conflict and Competition: The Latin American Church in a Changing Environment* reviewed by Carl Elliott Meacham. *Revista Interamericana de Bibliografía*, v. 42, no. 2 (1992), pp. 284 – 285.

Clendinnen, Inga. *Aztecs: An Interpretation* reviewed by María J. Rodríguez Shadow. *Mesoamérica (USA)*, v. 13, no. 24 (Dec 92), pp. 480 – 487.

— *Aztecs: An Interpretation* reviewed by Sarah Cline. *The Americas*, v. 49, no. 3 (Jan 93), pp. 395 – 396.

Cobbs, Elizabeth Anne. *The Rich Neighbor Policy: Rockefeller and Kaiser in Brazil* reviewed by Joel Wolfe. *Hispanic American Historical Review*, v. 73, no. 3 (Aug 93), pp. 538 – 539.

Cobo Borda, Juan Gustavo. *Desde el tibio Caribe: antología poética* reviewed by Rodolfo Alonso. *Revista Nacional de Cultura (Venezuela)*, v. 53, no. 286 (July – Sept 92), pp. 265 – 266.

— *Poemas orientales y bogotanos* reviewed by David Medina Portillo (Review entitled "Estar aquí"). *Vuelta*, v. 17, no. 197 (Apr 93), pp. 48 – 49.

Coca: cronología; Bolivia, 1986 – 1992 reviewed by M. A. *Nueva Sociedad*, no. 124 (Mar – Apr 93), p. 173.

Coe, Michael D. *Breaking the Maya Code* reviewed by Aaron Segal (Review entitled "The Maya Code"). *Interciencia*, v. 18, no. 4 (July – Aug 93), p. 209.

Coke, Van Deren. *Secular and Sacred: Photographs of Mexico* reviewed by Diana Emery Hulick (Review entitled "Lo secular y lo sagrado: fotografías de México"). *Latin American Art*, v. 5, no. 2 (Summer 93), p. 104.

Colchie, Thomas, ed. *A Hammock beneath the Mangoes: Stories from Latin America* reviewed by Barbara Mujica (Review entitled " A Roundup of Stories"). *Américas*, v. 45, no. 1 (Jan – Feb 93), p. 60. Il.

Colecchia, Francesca and Luis F. González-Cruz, eds. *Cuban Theater in the United States: A Criticial Anthology* translated by the editors. Reviewed by Luis A. Jiménez. *Hispania (USA)*, v. 76, no. 4 (Dec 93), pp. 737 – 738.

Coleman, Kenneth M. and George C. Herring, eds. *Understanding the Central American Crisis: Sources of Conflict, U.S. Policy, and Options for Peace* reviewed by Orlando Peña. *Canadian Journal of Latin American and Caribbean Studies*, v. 17, no. 34 (1992), pp. 129 – 130.

Colina, José de la. *Viajes narrados* reviewed by Esther Martínez Luna (Review entitled "Elogio del movimiento"). *Nexos*, v. 16, no. 192 (Dec 93), p. 83.

Collazo Pérez, Enrique. *Cuba, banca y crédito, 1950 – 1958* reviewed by Jorge Salazar-Carrillo. *Hispanic American Historical Review*, v. 73, no. 4 (Nov 93), pp. 725 – 726.

Collazos Bascopé, Patricia. *Con la venda en los ojos* reviewed by Carlos Castañón Barrientos. *Signo*, no. 38, Nueva época (Jan – Apr 93), pp. 230 – 231.

Collier, Ruth Berins and David Collier. *Shaping the Political Arena: Critical Junctures, the Labor Movement, and Regime Dynamics in Latin America* reviewed by Francisco Zapata. *Foro Internacional*, v. 32, no. 5 (Oct – Dec 92), pp. 777 – 788.

— *Shaping the Political Arena: Critical Junctures, the Labor Movement, and Regime Dynamics in Latin America* reviewed by David Sowell. *Hispanic American Historical Review*, v. 73, no. 1 (Feb 93), pp. 194 – 195.

Columbus, Christopher. *The 'Diario' of Christopher Columbus' First Voyage to America, 1492 – 1493* abstracted by Fray Bartolomé de las Casas; transcribed and translated by Oliver Dunn and James E. Kelley, Jr. Reviewed by Aaron P. Mahr. *Colonial Latin American Historical Review*, v. 1, no. 1 (Fall 92), pp. 122 – 124.

Comajuncosa, Antonio. *Manifiesto histórico, geográfico, topográfico, apostólico y político de los misioneros franciscanos de Tarija* reviewed by Pedro de Anasagasti. *Signo*, no. 38, Nueva época (Jan – Apr 93), pp. 231 – 233.

Combès, Isabelle and Thierry Saignes. *Alter ego: naissance de l'identité chiriguano* reviewed by Marie-Danielle Demélas-Bohy. *Caravelle*, no. 60 (1993), pp. 166 – 170.

Comella, Beatriz, ed. *América, siglos XVIII – XX: III Simposio sobre el V Centenario del Descubrimiento de América celebrado en el Colegio Mayor Zurbarán, Madrid, 1989 – 1990* reviewed by Osvaldo Chiareno. *Quaderni Ibero-Americani,* no. 72 (Dec 92), pp. 751 – 755.

Compendio cartográfico de la región inka reviewed by Jean-Paul Deler. *Revista Andina,* v. 10, no. 2 (Dec 92), pp. 540 – 541.

Conciencia étnica y modernidad: etnias de Oriente y Occidente reviewed by Alberto Cheng Hurtado. *América Indígena,* v. 51, no. 2 – 3 (Apr – Sept 91), pp. 353 – 356.

Connell, John and Robert Aldridge. *France's Overseas Frontier: départements et territoires d'outremer* reviewed by W. Marvin Will. *Social and Economic Studies,* v. 41, no. 4 (Dec 92), pp. 243 – 246. Bibl.

Conniff, Michael L. *Panama and the United States: The Forced Alliance* reviewed by Walter Lafeber. *Hispanic American Historical Review,* v. 73, no. 1 (Feb 93), pp. 191 – 192.

Connolly, Priscilla et al. *"Cambiar de casa, pero no de barrio": estudios sobre la reconstrucción en la ciudad de México* reviewed by María Elena Ducci. *EURE,* v. 19, no. 57 (July 93), pp. 126 – 127. Il.

Consalvi, Simón Alberto. *Grover Cleveland y la controversia Venezuela – Gran Bretaña* reviewed by H. Michael Tacver. *Hispanic American Historical Review,* v. 73, no. 4 (Nov 93), pp. 727 – 728.

Contreras, Gonzalo. *La ciudad anterior* reviewed by Sergio Gómez M. *Atenea (Chile),* no. 465 – 466 (1992), pp. 376 – 377.

Cook, Alexandra Parma and Noble David Cook. *Good Faith and Truthful Ignorance: A Case of Transatlantic Bigamy* reviewed by Meredith Dodge. *Colonial Latin American Historical Review,* v. 1, no. 1 (Fall 92), pp. 124 – 125.

— *Good Faith and Truthful Ignorance: A Case of Transantlantic Bigamy* reviewed by Kenneth J. Andrien. *Colonial Latin American Review,* v. 2, no. 1 – 2 (1993), pp. 275 – 277.

Cook, Noble David and William George Lovell, eds. *"Secret Judgments of God": Old World Disease in Colonial Spanish America* reviewed by Ronn F. Pineo. *The Americas,* v. 50, no. 1 (July 93), pp. 126 – 127.

— *"Secret Judgments of God": Old World Disease in Colonial Spanish America* reviewed by Cynthia Radding. *Hispanic American Historical Review,* v. 73, no. 2 (May 93), pp. 309 – 311.

Cook, Scott and Leigh Binford. *Obliging Need: Rural Petty Industry in Mexican Capitalism* reviewed by Peter Gregory. *Economic Development and Cultural Change,* v. 42, no. 1 (Oct 93), pp. 210 – 215.

Cooney, Jerry Wilson. *Economía y sociedad en la Intendencia del Paraguay* reviewed by Edberto Oscar Acevedo. *Revista de Historia de América,* no. 112 (July – Dec 91), pp. 181 – 183.

Cordell, Linda S. and Nelson Foster, eds. *Chilies to Chocolate: Food the Americas Gave the World* reviewed by John C. Super. *Hispanic American Historical Review,* v. 73, no. 3 (Aug 93), p. 487.

Córdova, Gonzalo F. *Luis Sánchez Morales, servidor ejemplar* reviewed by Teresita Martínez-Vergne. *Hispanic American Historical Review,* v. 73, no. 2 (May 93), pp. 346 – 347.

Cornejo Polar, Antonio. *La formación de la tradición literaria en el Perú* reviewed by Javier Sanjinés C. *Hispamérica,* v. 21, no. 63 (Dec 92), pp. 93 – 96.

Corral, Wilfrido Howard and Norma Klahn, eds. *Los novelistas como críticos,* vol. I, reviewed by Sonia Mattalía. *Nuevo Texto Crítico,* v. 6, no. 11 (1993), pp. 259 – 261.

Correa Vázquez, Eugenia. *Los mercados financieros y la crisis en América Latina* reviewed by Rafael Bouchain Galicia. *Problemas del Desarrollo,* v. 24, no. 93 (Apr – June 93), pp. 236 – 239.

Correal Urrego, Gonzalo. *Aguazuque: evidencias de cazadores, recolectores y plantadores en la altaplanicie de la cordillera oriental* reviewed by Marianne Cardale de Schrimpff. *Revista Colombiana de Antropología,* v. 29 (1992), pp. 235 – 238.

Corro, Gaspar Pío del. *'Zama': zona de contacto* reviewed by Gloria Videla de Rivero. *Revista Chilena de Literatura,* no. 41 (Apr 93), pp. 134 – 135.

Cortázar, Julio. *Bestiario* reviewed by Ignacio Valente. *Atenea (Chile),* no. 465 – 466 (1992), pp. 363 – 365.

Cortés, Eladio, ed. *Dictionary of Mexican Literature* reviewed by David William Foster. *World Literature Today,* v. 67, no. 3 (Summer 93), p. 593.

Cortés C., Fernando and Oscar Cuéllar Saavedra, eds. *Crisis y reproducción social: los comerciantes del sector informal* reviewed by José Antonio Alonso. *Estudios Sociológicos,* v. 10, no. 30 (Sept – Dec 92), pp. 819 – 822.

Cortés Gumucio, José Simón. *Tu luz brillará como el amanecer* reviewed by Carlos Condarico Santillán. *Signo,* no. 38, Nueva época (Jan – Apr 93), pp. 234 – 235.

Cortina, Rodolfo J., ed. *Cuban American Theater* reviewed by José A. Escarpanter. *Latin American Theatre Review,* v. 26, no. 2 (Spring 93), pp. 203 – 204.

Costa, Albertina de Oliveira and Cristina Bruschini, eds. *Entre a virtude e o pecado* reviewed by Miriam Pillar Grossi (Review entitled "Enfoques de gênero na história social"). *Estudos Feministas,* v. 1, no. 1 (1993), pp. 215 – 216.

Costa, Iraci del Nero da. *Arraia-miúda: um estudo sobre os não-proprietários de escravos no Brasil* reviewed by José Flávio Motta. *Estudos Econômicos,* v. 22, no. 3 (Sept – Dec 92), pp. 485 – 487.

Costa, Marithelma and Alvin Joaquín Figueroa. *Kaligrafiando: conversaciones con Clemente Soto Vélez* reviewed by Evelyn Uhrhan Irving. *World Literature Today,* v. 67, no. 1 (Winter 93), p. 163.

Costa, Marithelma and Adelaida López. *Las dos caras de la escritura* reviewed by Gustavo Fares. *Revista Iberoamericana,* v. 59, no. 162 – 163 (Jan – June 93), pp. 380 – 382.

Costa, Octavio R. *El impacto creador de España sobre el Nuevo Mundo, 1492 – 1592* reviewed by William Mejías López. *Hispania (USA),* v. 76, no. 2 (May 93), pp. 282 – 284.

Costigan, Lúcia Helena Santiago. *A sátira e o intelectual criollo na colônia: Gregório de Matos e Juan del Valle y Caviedes* reviewed by Pedro Carlos L. Fonseca. *Colonial Latin American Review,* v. 2, no. 1 – 2 (1993), pp. 300 – 302.

Couffignal, Georges, ed. *Réinventer la démocratie: le défi latino-américain* reviewed by Giorgio Alberti. *Journal of Latin American Studies,* v. 25, no. 2 (May 93), pp. 409 – 410.

Covington, Paula Hattox, ed. *Latin America and the Caribbean: A Critical Guide to Research Sources* reviewed by Richard D. Woods. *Hispania (USA),* v. 76, no. 2 (May 93), pp. 284 – 285.

— *Latin America and the Caribbean: A Critical Guide to Research Sources* reviewed by Thomas L. Welch. *Revista Interamericana de Bibliografía,* v. 42, no. 2 (1992), pp. 285 – 286.

Crabtree, John. *Peru under García: An Opportunity Lost* reviewed by Alfonso W. Quiroz. *Hispanic American Historical Review,* v. 73, no. 4 (Nov 93), pp. 713 – 714.

— *Peru under García: An Opportunity Lost* reviewed by Carol Graham. *Journal of Latin American Studies,* v. 25, no. 2 (May 93), pp. 413 – 414.

Craig, Ann L. and Joseph W. Foweraker, eds. *Popular Movements and Political Change in Mexico* reviewed by Daniel C. Levy. *Studies in Comparative International Development,* v. 27, no. 3 (Fall 92), pp. 122 – 124.

Crandon-Malamud, Libbet. *From the Fat of Our Souls: Social Change, Political Process, and Medical Pluralism in Bolivia* reviewed by Marcos Cueto. *Hispanic American Historical Review,* v. 73, no. 1 (Feb 93), p. 172.

Craton, Michael and Gail Saunders. *Islanders in the Stream: A History of the Bahamian People* reviewed by William F. Keegan. *Hispanic American Historical Review,* v. 73, no. 4 (Nov 93), pp. 702 – 703.

Creedman, Theodore S. *Historical Dictionary of Costa Rica* reviewed by Kenneth J. Grieb. *The Americas,* v. 49, no. 3 (Jan 93), pp. 426 – 427.

— *Historical Dictionary of Costa Rica,* 2d edition, reviewed by Lowell Gudmundson. *Mesoamérica (USA),* v. 13, no. 23 (June 92), p. 178.

Cristi, Renato and Carlos Ruiz. *El pensamiento conservador en Chile* reviewed by Simon Collier. *Hispanic American Historical Review,* v. 73, no. 4 (Nov 93), pp. 708 – 709.

— *El pensamiento conservador en Chile* reviewed by Patricio Silva. *Journal of Latin American Studies,* v. 25, no. 2 (May 93), pp. 429 – 430.

Cristoffanini, Pablo Rolando. *Dominación y legitimidad política en Hispanoamérica: un estudio de la historia de las ideas políticas en la experiencia colonial y la formación del estado nacional en Chile* reviewed by Marcello Carmagnani. *Hispanic American Historical Review,* v. 73, no. 2 (May 93), pp. 328 – 329.

Cró, Stelio. *The Noble Savage: Allegory of Freedom* reviewed by Dianne M. Bono. *Colonial Latin American Review,* v. 2, no. 1 – 2 (1993), pp. 288 – 290.

Crumrine, N. Ross and E. Alan Morinis, eds. *Pilgrimage in Latin America* reviewed by María J. Rodríguez Shadow and Robert D. Shadow. *Mesoamérica (USA),* v. 13, no. 24 (Dec 92), pp. 473 – 480.

Cruz, Anne J. and Mary Elizabeth Perry, eds. *Cultural Encounters: The Impact of the Inquisition in Spain and the New World* reviewed by Teofilo F. Ruiz. *The Americas,* v. 50, no. 1 (July 93), pp. 121 – 123.

— *Cultural Encounters: The Impact of the Inquisition in Spain and the New World* reviewed by Henry Kamen. *Hispanic American Historical Review,* v. 73, no. 1 (Feb 93), p. 146.

Cruz, Victor Hernandez. *Red Beans* reviewed by Nicolás Kanellos. *The Americas Review,* v. 20, no. 1 (Spring 92), p. 87.

Cuba in Transition reviewed by Nicolás Sánchez. *Cuban Studies/Estudios Cubanos,* v. 23 (1993), pp. 210 – 213.

Cubena

See

Wilson, Carlos Guillermo

Cuéllar Saavedra, Oscar and Fernando Cortés C., eds. *Crisis y reproducción social: los comerciantes del sector informal* reviewed by José Antonio Alonso. *Estudios Sociológicos,* v. 10, no. 30 (Sept – Dec 92), pp. 819 – 822.

Cuenca, Breny. *El poder intangible: la AID y el estado salvadoreño en los años ochenta* reviewed by Rachel Sieder. *Journal of Latin American Studies,* v. 25, no. 3 (Oct 93), p. 670.

Cueto, Alonso. *Deseo de noche* reviewed by Abelardo Sánchez León (Review entitled "Las noches de Cueto"). *Debate (Peru),* v. 16, no. 73 (June – Aug 93), p. 73. Il.

— *Deseo de noche* reviewed by César Ferreira. *Chasqui,* v. 22, no. 2 (Nov 93), pp. 158 – 160.

Cueto, Marcos. *Excelencia científica en la periferia: actividades científicas e investigaciones biomédicas en el Perú, 1890 – 1950* reviewed by Ricardo Portocarrero Grados. *Historia y Cultura (Peru),* no. 20 (1990), pp. 373 – 377.

Cunningham, Ineke et al, eds. *El SIDA en Puerto Rico: acercamientos multidisciplinarios* reviewed by Víctor I. García Toro. *Caribbean Studies,* v. 25, no. 1 – 2 (Jan – July 92), pp. 162 – 163.

Cunningham, Lucía

See

Guerra-Cunningham, Lucía

Cussen, Antonio. *Bello and Bolívar: Poetry and Politics in the Spanish American Revolution* reviewed by Fernando Cervantes. *Bulletin of Latin American Research,* v. 12, no. 1 (Jan 93), pp. 114 – 115.

— *Bello and Bolívar: Poetry and Politics in the Spanish American Revolution* reviewed by Myron I. Lichtblau. *Hispania (USA),* v. 76, no. 2 (May 93), p. 285.

Cutter, Donald C., ed. *California in 1792: A Spanish Naval Visit* reviewed by Donald T. Garate. *Colonial Latin American Historical Review,* v. 2, no. 1 (Winter 93), pp. 117 – 118.

Cypess, Sandra Messinger. *La Malinche in Mexican Literature: From History to Myth* reviewed by Salvador A. Oropesa. *Letras Femeninas,* v. 19, no. 1 – 2 (Spring – Fall 93), pp. 146 – 148.

— *La Malinche in Mexican Literature: From History to Myth* reviewed by Julie Greer Johnson. *Revista Interamericana de Bibliografía,* v. 42, no. 3 (1992), p. 502.

Cypess, Sandra Messinger et al. *Women Authors of Modern Hispanic South America: A Bibliography of Literary Criticism and Interpretation* reviewed by David William Foster. *Chasqui,* v. 22, no. 1 (May 93), pp. 87 – 88.

Cypher, James Martin. *State and Capital in Mexico: Development Policy since 1940* reviewed by Russell White (Review entitled "Postwar Mexican Development Policy: State and Class Contradictions"). *Latin American Perspectives,* v. 20, no. 3 (Summer 93), pp. 76 – 79.

Dabène, Olivier. *Costa Rica: juicio a la democracia* reviewed by Manuel A. Solís. *Anuario de Estudios Centroamericanos,* v. 18, no. 2 (1992), pp. 117 – 121.

Dabydeen, David. *Disappearance* reivewed by Djelal Kadir. *World Literature Today,* v. 67, no. 3 (Summer 93), pp. 656 – 657.

— *The Intended* reviewed by Charles Ponnuthurai Sarvan. *World Literature Today,* v. 67, no. 1 (Winter 93), pp. 218 – 219.

Dacach, Solange and Giselle Israel. *As rotas do Norplant: desvios da contracepção* reviewed by Angela Regina Cunha (Review entitled "Risco de vida"). *Estudos Feministas,* v. 1, no. 2 (1993), pp. 489 – 491.

D'Altroy, Terence Norman. *Provincial Power in the Inka Empire* reviewed by Helaine Silverman. *The Americas,* v. 50, no. 1 (July 93), pp. 119 – 121.

Daniels, Anthony. *Sweet Waist of America: Travels around Guatemala* reviewed by Alan C. Hunsaker (Review entitled "Guatemala: Small Country, Big Problems"). *Hispanic Journal of Behavioral Sciences,* v. 15, no. 3 (Aug 93), pp. 418 – 423.

Dantas, Maria Teresa do Menino Jesus da Costa Pinto. *O Convento de Nossa Senhora das Mercês* reviewed by Raul Lima. *Revista do Instituto Histórico e Geográfico Brasileiro,* no. 373 (Oct – Dec 91), pp. 1208 – 1210.

Darío, Rubén. *Autobiografía; Ora de Mallorca* reviewed by Graciela Montaldo. *Revista de Crítica Literaria Latinoamericana,* v. 19, no. 38 (July – Dec 93), pp. 411 – 413.

— *Tierras solares* reviewed by Pilar Bellido Navarro. *Cuadernos Hispanoamericanos,* no. 520 (Oct 93), pp. 137 – 138.

Dávila Flores, Alejandro. *La apertura comercial y la frontera México – Texas* reviewed by David J. Molina. *Journal of Borderlands Studies,* v. 8, no. 1 (Spring 93), pp. 116 – 118. Bibl.

Dávila L. de Guevara, Carlos. *El empresariado colombiano: una perspectiva histórica* reviewed by Luis Aurelio Ordóñez B. (Review entitled "Un balance historiográfico exhaustivo y sugestivo"). *Anuario Colombiano de Historia Social y de la Cultura,* no. 20 (1992), pp. 147 – 152.

— *Historia empresarial de Colombia: estudios, problemas y perspectivas* reviewed by Luis Aurelio Ordóñez B. (Review entitled "Un balance historiográfico exhaustivo y sugestivo"). *Anuario Colombiano de Historia Social y de la Cultura,* no. 20 (1992), pp. 147 – 152.

Daza, Patricio. *Ethnies et révolution: Nicaragua, 1979 – 1987* reviewed by Maxime Haubert. *Tiers Monde,* v. 34, no. 134 (Apr – June 93), pp. 471 – 473.

Dealy, Glen Caudill. *The Latin Americans: Spirit and Ethos* reviewed by S. L. Andreski. *Journal of Latin American Studies,* v. 25, no. 3 (Oct 93), pp. 694 – 695.

Deans-Smith, Susan. *Bureaucrats, Planters, and Workers: The Making of the Tobacco Monopoly in Bourbon Mexico* reviewed by Michael P. Costeloe. *Bulletin of Latin American Research,* v. 12, no. 2 (May 93), pp. 221 – 222.

— *Bureaucrats, Planters, and Workers: The Making of the Tobacco Monopoly in Bourbon Mexico* reviewed by Mark A. Buckholder. *Colonial Latin American Historical Review,* v. 2, no. 2 (Spring 93), pp. 227 – 228.

La "découverte" de l'Amérique?: les regards sur l'autre à travers les manuels scolaires du monde reivewed by Pierre Ragon. *Cahiers des Amériques Latines,* no. 14 (1992), pp. 159 – 160.

Deere, Carmen Diana. *Household and Class Relations: Peasants and Landlords in Northern Peru* reviewed by William Roseberry. *Hispanic American Historical Review,* v. 73, no. 1 (Feb 93), pp. 174 – 175.

Deere, Carmen Diana et al. *In the Shadows of the Sun: Caribbean Development Alternatives and U.S. Policy* reviewed by Georges A. Fauriol. *Studies in Comparative International Development,* v. 27, no. 2 (Summer 92), pp. 110 – 112.

DeFreitas, Gregory. *Inequality at Work: Hispanics in the U.S. Labor Force* reviewed by Luis M. Falcón. *International Migration Review,* v. 27, no. 1 (Spring 93), pp. 207 – 208.

Dejoux, Claude and André Iltis, eds. *El lago Titicaca: síntesis del conocimiento limnológico actual* reviewed by Néstor Teves. *Bulletin de l'Institut Français d'Etudes Andines,* v. 21, no. 3 (1992), pp. 1075 – 1078.

De Lella Allevato, Cayetano and Carlos P. Krotsch, eds. *Congreso Pedagógico Nacional: evaluación y perspectivas* reviewed by Carlos Salá. *La Educación (USA),* v. 36, no. 111 – 113 (1992), pp. 285 – 291.

Delgado Martín, Jaime. *Historia general de España y América, vol. XVIII: Hispanoamérica en el siglo XX* reviewed by Luis Navarro García. *Anuario de Estudios Americanos,* v. 49, Suppl. 2 (1992), pp. 245 – 246.

Dellaferrera, Nelson C. *Catálogo de causas matrimoniales: obispado de Córdoba, 1688 – 1810* reviewed by Jesús María García Añoveros. *Revista de Indias,* v. 53, no. 197 (Jan – Apr 93), p. 101.

Del Priore, Mary. *Ao sul do corpo: condição feminina, maternidades e mentalidades no Brasil-colônia* reviewed by Maria Odila Silva Dias (Review entitled "A condição feminina e suas historicidades"). *Estudos Feministas,* v. 1, no. 2 (1993), pp. 481 – 485.

Demelas, Danièle and Yves Saint-Geours. *Jerusalén y Babilonia: religión y política en el Ecuador, 1780 – 1880* reviewed by Ana Luz Rodríguez González (Review entitled "Lo particular en el Ecuador del siglo XIX"). *Anuario Colombiano de Historia Social y de la Cultura,* no. 20 (1992), pp. 154 – 157.

Deniz, Gerardo. *Op. cit.* reviewed by Adriana Díaz Enciso. *Vuelta,* v. 17, no. 195 (Feb 93), p. 43.

Desmond, Lawrence Gustave and Phyllis Mauch Messenger. *A Dream of Maya: Augustus and Alice Le Plongeon in Nineteenth-Century Yucatán* reviewed by Kevin Gosner. *Hispanic American Historical Review,* v. 73, no. 3 (Aug 93), pp. 532 – 533.

Deutsch, Sandra F. McGee and Ronald H. Dolkart, eds. *The Argentine Right: Its History and Intellectual Origins, 1910 to the Present* reviewed by Alberto Spektorowski. *Estudios Interdisciplinarios de América Latina y el Caribe,* v. 4, no. 1 (Jan – June 93), pp. 166 – 170.

De Verteuil, Anthony. *Eight East Indian Immigrants* reviewed by F. Birbalsingh. *Caribbean Quarterly,* v. 38, no. 2 – 3 (June – Sept 92), pp. 119 – 122.

Dezotti, Maria Celeste Consolin, ed. *A tradição da fábula* reviewed by João Décio. *Revista de Letras (Brazil),* v. 32 (1992), pp. 268 – 270.

Diacon, Todd Alan. *Millenarian Vision, Capitalist Reality: Brazil's Contestado Rebellion, 1912 – 1916* reviewed by Cliff Welch. *The Americas,* v. 50, no. 2 (Oct 93), pp. 285 – 286.

— *Millenarian Vision, Capitalist Reality: Brazil's Contestado Rebellion, 1912 – 1916* reviewed by Anthony Pereira. *Canadian Journal of Latin American and Caribbean Studies,* v. 17, no. 34 (1992), pp. 132 – 135.

— *Millenarian Vision, Capitalist Reality: Brazil's Contestado Rebellion, 1912 – 1916* reviewed by Kees de Groot. *European Review of Latin American and Caribbean Studies,* no. 53 (Dec 92), pp. 112 – 114.

— *Millenarian Vision, Capitalist Reality: Brazil's Contestado Rebellion, 1912 – 1916* reviewed by Patricia R. Pessar. *Hispanic American Historical Review,* v. 73, no. 1 (Feb 93), pp. 166 – 167.

— *Millenarian Vision, Capitalist Reality: Brazil's Contestado Rebellion, 1912 – 1916* reviewed by Bernardo Kucinski. *Journal of Latin American Studies,* v. 25, no. 1 (Feb 93), pp. 201 – 202.

Diaz, Harry P. et al. *Forging Identities and Patterns of Development* reviewed by William A. Harris (Review entitled "Ethnicity and Development"). *Social and Economic Studies,* v. 41, no. 4 (Dec 92), pp. 225 – 230.

Díaz Covarrubias, José. *La instrucción pública en México: estado que guardan la instrucción primaria, la secundaria y la profesional en la república; progresos realizados, mejoras que deben introducirse* reviewed by Pablo Latapí. *Revista Latinoamericana de Estudios Educativos,* v. 23, no. 1 (Jan – Mar 93), pp. 129 – 133.

Díaz de Vivar Prieto, Marina and Olga Caballero Aquino. *Mujer paraguaya: jefa de familia* (Review). *Revista Paraguaya de Sociología,* v. 29, no. 84 (May – Aug 92), p. 210. II.

Díaz del Castillo Z., Emiliano. *Gutiérrez de Caviedes: una familia de próceres* reviewed by Hernán Díaz del Castillo Guerrero. *Boletín de Historia y Antigüedades,* v. 79, no. 779 (Oct – Dec 92), pp. 1065 – 1070.

Díaz Eterovic, Ramón. *Solo en la oscuridad* reviewed by Guillermo García Corales. *Hispania (USA),* v. 76, no. 2 (May 93), pp. 294 – 295.

Díaz-Jove Blanco, Santiago. *Gijoneses en Indias: notas sobre emigración e índice geobiográfico* reviewed by José Ramón García López. *Revista de Indias,* v. 53, no. 197 (Jan – Apr 93), pp. 102 – 103.

Díaz Rodríguez, Jesús. *Las palabras perdidas* reviewed by José B. Alvarez IV. *Chasqui,* v. 22, no. 2 (Nov 93), pp. 151 – 153.

Dietz, James L. and Dilmus D. James, eds. *Progress toward Development in Latin America: From Prebisch to Technological Autonomy* reviewed by Markos J. Mamalakis. *Studies in Comparative International Development,* v. 27, no. 2 (Summer 92), pp. 106 – 108.

Dietze, Rolando et al. *Los caminos de la diversidad: condiciones y potenciales para un desarrollo sostenible en el Paraguay* (Review). *Revista Paraguaya de Sociología,* v. 29, no. 85 (Sept – Dec 92), pp. 189 – 190.

Diez, Rolo. *Paso del tigre* reviewed by Alejandro Expósito (Review entitled "Un tigre, un gato"). *Plural (Mexico),* v. 22, no. 263 (Aug 93), pp. 76 – 77.

La diferencia es la excelencia sé gente CONALEP reviewed by Luis Miguel Bascones. *El Cotidiano,* v. 9, no. 55 (June 93), p. 118. II.

Dijkstra, Geske. *Industrialization in Sandinista Nicaragua: Policy and Practice in a Mixed Economy* reviewed by Claes Brundenius. *Hispanic American Historical Review,* v. 73, no. 4 (Nov 93), pp. 721 – 722.

Dimenstein, Gilberto. *Meninas da noite: a prostituição de meninas-escravas no Brasil* reviewed by Jenny K. Pilling. *Luso-Brazilian Review,* v. 30, no. 1 (Summer 93), pp. 148 – 149.

Din, Gilbert C. *Francisco Bouligny, a Bourbon Soldier in Spanish Louisiana* reviewed by Thomas E. Chávez. *Colonial Latin American Historical Review,* v. 2, no. 4 (Fall 93), pp. 477 – 478.

Diniz, Jaime C. *Mestres de Capela de Misericórdia da Bahía, 1647 – 1810* (Review). *Inter-American Music Review,* v. 13, no. 2 (Spring – Summer 93), pp. 159 – 160.

Di Tella, Torcuato S. *Historia de los partidos políticos en América Latina, siglo XX* (Review). *Revista Paraguaya de Sociología,* v. 30, no. 86 (Jan – Apr 93), pp. 205 – 206.

Dodd, Thomas Joseph. *Managing Democracy in Central America: A Case Study of United States Election Supervision in Nicaragua, 1927 – 1933* reviewed by Neill Macaulay. *Hispanic American Historical Review,* v. 73, no. 4 (Nov 93), pp. 730 – 731.

Dölz-Blackburn, Inés and Marjorie Agosín. *Violeta Parra o la expresión inefable: un análisis crítico de su poesía, prosa y pintura* reviewed by Beth Pollack. *Chasqui,* v. 22, no. 2 (Nov 93), pp. 179 – 180.

Dolkart, Ronald H. and Sandra F. McGee Deutsch, eds. *The Argentine Right: Its History and Intellectual Origins, 1910 to the Present* reviewed by Alberto Spektorowski. *Estudios Interdisciplinarios de América Latina y el Caribe,* v. 4, no. 1 (Jan – June 93), pp. 166 – 170.

Domenach, Hervé and Michel Picouet. *La dimension migratoire des Antilles* reviewed by Guy Caire. *Tiers Monde,* v. 34, no. 135 (July – Sept 93), pp. 716 – 718.

Domínguez Michael, Christopher. *La utopía de la hospitalidad* reviewed by Fabienne Bradu. *Vuelta,* v. 17, no. 202 (Sept 93), pp. 45 – 46.

Donnadieu Aguado, Laura and Beatriz Calvo Pontón. *Una educación ¿indígena, bilingüe o bicultural?* reviewed by Salvador Martínez. *Revista Latinoamericana de Estudios Educativos,* v. 22, no. 4 (Oct – Dec 92), pp. 123 – 125.

Donoso, José. *"Taratuta," "Naturaleza muerta con cachimba"* reviewed by Irene von Koerber. *Iberoamericana,* v. 16, no. 47 – 48 (1992), pp. 116 – 120.

— *Taratuta/Still Life with Pipe* reviewed by Barbara Mujica (Review entitled "Intriguing Family Histories"). *Américas,* v. 45, no. 4 (July – Aug 93), pp. 62 – 63.

Doolittle, William Emery. *Canal Irrigation in Prehistoric Mexico: The Sequence of Technological Change* reviewed by Robert Kuhlken. *Mesoamérica (USA),* v. 13, no. 24 (Dec 92), pp. 488 – 489.

Dorfman, Ariel. *Death and the Maiden* reviewed by Ilán Stavans. *World Literature Today,* v. 67, no. 3 (Summer 93), p. 596.

Dourado, Maria Cristina, ed. *Direito ambiental e a questão amazônica* (Review). *La Educación (USA),* v. 37, no. 115 (1993), pp. 439 – 440.

Dourojeanni, Marc J. *Amazonia: ¿Qué hacer?* reviewed by Richard Bustamante M. *Amazonía Peruana,* v. 11, no. 21 (Sept 92), pp. 238 – 239.

Dover, Robert V. H. *Andean Cosmologies through Time: Persistence and Emergence* reviewed by Jean-Jacques Decoster. *Latin American Indian Literatures Journal,* v. 9, no. 1 (Spring 93), pp. 73 – 78.

Dowdeswell, Jane. *La violación: hablan las mujeres* (Review). *Homines,* v. 15 – 16, no. 2 – 1 (Oct 91 – Dec 92), p. 383. II.

Drake, Paul Winter and Ivan Jaksic, eds. *The Struggle for Democracy in Chile, 1982 – 1990* reviewed by Tom Wright. *The Americas,* v. 49, no. 4 (Apr 93), pp. 568 – 569.

— *The Struggle for Democracy in Chile, 1982 – 1990* reviewed by Robert H. Dix. *Journal of Developing Areas,* v. 28, no. 1 (Oct 93), pp. 115 – 116.

Dresser, Denise. *Neopopulist Solutions to Neoliberal Problems: Mexico's National Solidarity Program* reviewed by Martin C. Needler (Review entitled "Economic Policy and Political Survival"). *Mexican Studies,* v. 9, no. 1 (Winter 93), pp. 139 – 143.

Dreyfus, Mariela. *Placer fantasma* reviewed by Rocío Silva-Santiesteban (Review entitled "Sufro y gozo"). *Debate (Peru),* v. 16, no. 75 (Dec 93 – Jan 94), p. 80. II.

Drummond, Roberto. *Hilda Furação* reviewed by Arsenio Cicero Sancristóbal (Review entitled *"Hilda Furação: '¿Adónde nos llevó el sueño?' "*). *Casa de las Américas,* no. 189 (Oct – Dec 92), pp. 146 – 148.

Dulles, John W. F. *Carlos Lacerda, Brazilian Crusader, Vol. I: The Years 1914 – 1960* reviewed by Thomas E. Skidmore. *The Americas,* v. 49, no. 3 (Jan 93), pp. 416 – 417.

Dunkerley, James. *Political Suicide in Latin America and Other Essays* reviewed by Walter Little. *Bulletin of Latin American Research,* v. 12, no. 1 (Jan 93), pp. 116 – 117.

Durán, Luis Horacio. *Songs of Love and Wind* translated by Diane Russell-Piñeda. Reviewed by José Otero. *Chasqui,* v. 22, no. 2 (Nov 93), pp. 174 – 177.

Durán Luzio, Juan. *Bartolomé de las Casas ante la conquista de América: las voces del historiador* reviewed by Juan Adolfo Vázquez. *Latin American Indian Literatures Journal,* v. 9, no. 1 (Spring 93), pp. 79 – 83.

— *Bartolomé de las Casas ante la conquista de América: las voces del historiador* reviewed by Lilian Uribe. *Revista de Crítica Literaria Latinoamericana,* v. 19, no. 37 (Jan – June 93), pp. 377 – 380.

— *Bartolomé de las Casas ante la conquista de América: las voces del historiador* reviewed by Danuta Teresa Mosejko. *Revista de Historia (Costa Rica),* no. 26 (July – Dec 92), pp. 209 – 216.

Echavarren Welker, Roberto. *Margen de ficción: poéticas de la narrativa hispanoamericana* reviewed by Thomas E. Case. *World Literature Today,* v. 67, no. 2 (Spring 93), p. 341.

Echeverría, Mónica. *Antihistoria de un luchador: Clotario Blest, 1823 – 1990* reviewed by G. A. C. *Mensaje,* v. 42, no. 424 (Nov 93), pp. 597 – 599. Il.

Edie, Carlene J. *Democracy by Default: Dependency and Clientelism in Jamaica* reviewed by Tony Thorndike. *Studies in Comparative International Development,* v. 27, no. 2 (Summer 92), pp. 108 – 110.

Edmonson, Munro S. and Victoria Reifler Bricker, eds. *Supplement to 'The Handbook of Middle American Indians,' Vol. III: Literatures* reviewed by Jorge F. Travieso. *Mesoamérica (USA),* v. 13, no. 23 (June 92), pp. 205 – 209.

Edwards, Jorge. *Fantasmas de carne y hueso* reviewed by Barbara Mujica (Review entitled "The Creative Subtext of Life"). *Américas,* v. 45, no. 3 (May – June 93), p. 60. Il.

— *El museo de cera* reviewed by Roberto González. *Atenea (Chile),* no. 465 – 466 (1992), pp. 377 – 379.

Egaña, Manuel R. *Obras y ensayos seleccionados* reviewed by Pascual Venegas Filardo. *Revista Nacional de Cultura (Venezuela),* v. 53, no. 286 (July – Sept 92), p. 256.

Egler, Claudio Antonio G. and Bertha Koiffman Becker. *Brasil: uma nova potência regional na economia-mundo* reviewed by Oscar D'Ambrosio (Review entitled "Uma potência regional"). *Problemas Brasileiros,* v. 30, no. 297 (May – June 93), pp. 54 – 55. Il.

Eguren, José María. *Antología* reviewed by Alfredo García Valdez. *Vuelta,* v. 17, no. 201 (Aug 93), pp. 52 – 53.

EL Arancel Externo Común (AEC) del MERCOSUR: los conflictos (Review). *Integración Latinoamericana,* v. 18, no. 187 – 188 (Mar – Apr 93), pp. 70 – 71.

Elías, Víctor Jorge. *Sources of Growth: A Study of Seven Latin American Economies* reviewed by David E. Hojman. *Journal of Latin American Studies,* v. 25, no. 3 (Oct 93), pp. 675 – 677.

Elichondo, Margarita. *La comida criolla* reviewed by Félix Coluccio. *Folklore Americano,* no. 53 (Jan – June 92), p. 180.

Elizondo, Sergio. *Suruma* reviewed by Víctor Hugo Vásquez Rentería. *La Palabra y el Hombre,* no. 81 (Jan – Mar 92), pp. 326 – 327.

Ellner, Steven B. *De la derrota guerrillera a la política innovadora: el Movimiento al Socialismo (MAS)* reviewed by Dick Parker. *Nueva Sociedad,* no. 124 (Mar – Apr 93), p. 174.

Elmore, Peter. *Los muros invisibles: Lima y la modernidad en la novela del siglo XX* reviewed by Rodrigo Quijano (Review entitled "Experiencia urbana"). *Debate (Peru),* v. 16, no. 73 (June – Aug 93), p. 74. Il.

Eltit, Diamela. *Vaca sagrada* reviewed by Gisela Norat. *Hispanic Journal,* v. 13, no. 2 (Fall 92), pp. 403 – 405.

— *Vaca sagrada* reviewed by Guillermo García-Corales. *Inti,* no. 36 (Fall 92), pp. 191 – 194.

Engel, Magali. *Meretrizes e doutores: saber médico e prostituição no Rio de Janeiro, 1840 – 1890* reviewed by Sandra Lauderdale Graham (Review entitled "Dangerous Fantasies: The Altered Vocabulary of Commercial Sex"). *Luso-Brazilian Review,* v. 30, no. 1 (Summer 93), pp. 133 – 139.

Enríquez, Laura Jean. *Harvesting Change: Labor and Agrarian Reform in Nicaragua, 1979 – 1990* reviewed by Elizabeth Dore. *Journal of Latin American Studies,* v. 25, no. 1 (Feb 93), pp. 211 – 212.

Epple, Juan Armando. *Patricio Manns: actas del cazador en movimiento* reviewed by Arturo C. Flores. *Chasqui,* v. 22, no. 1 (May 93), pp. 81 – 82.

Epstein, Edward C., ed. *The New Argentine Democracy: The Search for a Successful Formula* reviewed by David Rock. *Revista Interamericana de Bibliografía,* v. 42, no. 4 (1992), p. 656.

Eramy, Elio. *La cigüeña punzo* reviewed by Rodolfo Alonso. *Revista Nacional de Cultura (Venezuela),* v. 53, no. 285 (Apr – June 92), pp. 244 – 245.

Erisman, H. Michael. *Pursuing Postdependency Politics: South – South Relations in the Caribbean* reviewed by Thomas D. Anderson. *Revista Interamericana de Bibliografía,* v. 42, no. 4 (1992), p. 657.

Escalante Gonzalbo, Fernando. *Ciudadanos imaginarios* reviewed by Rafael Rojas (Review entitled "El riesgo de la imaginación liberal"). *Nexos,* v. 16, no. 187 (July 93), pp. 77 – 78.

Escudé, Carlos. *El fracaso del proyecto argentino: educación e ideología* reviewed by Aurora Ravina. *Revista de Historia de América,* no. 113 (Jan – June 92), pp. 177 – 179.

Espada, Joaquín. *Bolivia en la interamericanidad* reviewed by Pedro de Anasagasti. *Signo,* no. 38, Nueva época (Jan – Apr 93), pp. 236 – 237.

Esquivel, Laura. *Como agua para chocolate* reviewed by Alberto Farfán (Review entitled "Laura Esquivel: ¿La necesidad del malestar en la cultura?"). *Plural (Mexico),* v. 22, no. 259 (Apr 93), pp. 76 – 78.

— *Like Water for Chocolate* reviewed by Barbara Mujica (Review entitled "Intriguing Family Histories"). *Américas,* v. 45, no. 4 (July – Aug 93), pp. 60 – 61. Il.

Estay Reino, Jaime and Héctor Sotomayor, eds. *América Latina y México ante la Unión Europea de 1992* reviewed by Gilberto A. Cardoso Vargas. *Problemas del Desarrollo,* v. 24, no. 92 (Jan – Mar 93), pp. 236 – 238.

Esteves, Carmen C. and Lizabeth Paravisini-Gebert. *Green Cane and Juicy Flotsam: Short Stories by Caribbean Women* reviewed by Ivette Romero. *Letras Femeninas,* v. 19, no. 1 – 2 (Spring – Fall 93), pp. 154 – 155.

Estupiñán Bass, Nelson. *Curfew* translated by Henry J. Richards. Reviewed by Thomas E. Kooreman. *Afro-Hispanic Review,* v. 12, no. 1 (Spring 93), pp. 57 – 58.

Ette, Ottmar. *La escritura de la memoria: Reinaldo Arenas; textos, estudios y documentación* reviewed by Gudrun Wogatzke-Luckow. *Iberoamericana,* v. 16, no. 47 – 48 (1992), pp. 137 – 140.

— *José Martí, Teil I: Apostel, Dichter, Revolutinär; Eine Geschichte seiner Rezeption* reviewed by José Morales Saravia. *Revista de Crítica Literaria Latinoamericana,* v. 19, no. 38 (July – Dec 93), pp. 406 – 411.

Ewald, Wendy. *Magic Eyes: Scenes from an Andean Girlhood* reviewed by Barbara Mujica (Review entitled "A Coming of Age"). *Américas,* v. 45, no. 5 (Sept – Oct 93), pp. 60 – 61. Il.

Ezpeleta, Justa and Alfredo Furlan, eds. *La gestión pedagógica en la escuela* reviewed by Luis M. Flores. *La Educación (USA)*, v. 37, no. 115 (1993), p. 420.

Fabian, Stephen Michael. *Space – Time of the Bororo of Brazil* reviewed by Gary Urton. *Hispanic American Historical Review*, v. 73, no. 3 (Aug 93), pp. 496 – 498.

Faraco, Sérgio. *Noche de matar un hombre* translated by Julián Murguía. Reviewed by Manuel Márquez (Review entitled "Sérgio Faraco y las fronteras profundas"). *Plural (Mexico)*, v. 22, no. 258 (Mar 93), pp. 74 – 75.

Farage, Nádia. *As muralhas dos sertões: os povos indígenas no rio Branco e a colonização* reviewed by David Cleary. *Journal of Latin American Studies*, v. 25, no. 2 (May 93), pp. 394 – 395.

Faria, José Angelo Estrella. *O MERCOSUL: princípios, finalidade e alcance do Tratado de Assunção* (Review). *Integración Latinoamericana*, v. 18, no. 192 (Aug 92), pp. 96 – 97.

Farriss, Nancy Marguerite. *La sociedad maya bajo el dominio colonial*, a translation of *Maya Society under Colonial Rule* reviewed by Victoria González Muñoz. *Anuario de Estudios Americanos*, v. 49, Suppl. 1 (1992), pp. 252 – 254.

Fass, Simon M. *Political Economy in Haiti: The Drama of Survival* reviewed by Michael H. Allen (Review entitled "Rethinking Political Economy and Praxis in the Caribbean"). *Latin American Perspectives*, v. 20, no. 2 (Spring 93), pp. 111 – 119.

Feierstein, Ricardo. *We, the Generation in the Wilderness* translated by J. Kates and Stephen A. Sadow. Reviewed by James Graham. *Review*, no. 47 (Fall 93), pp. 101 – 103.

Fenwick, Mary Jane. *Writers of the Caribbean and Central America: A Bibliography* reviewed by Richard D. Woods. *Hispania (USA)*, v. 76, no. 4 (Dec 93), pp. 734 – 735.

Ferguson, Anne E. and Scott Whiteford, eds. *Harvest of Want: Hunger and Food Security in Central America and Mexico* reviewed by LaMond Tullis. *Journal of Developing Areas*, v. 27, no. 2 (Jan 93), pp. 253 – 254.

Ferguson, Moira. *Subject to Others: British Women Writers and Colonial Slavery, 1670 – 1834* reviewed by Karen Mead. *Hispanic American Historical Review*, v. 73, no. 4 (Nov 93), p. 675.

Ferguson, R. Brian and Neil L. Whitehead, eds. *War in the Tribal Zone: Expanding States and Indigenous Warfare* reviewed by Elizabeth M. Brumfiel. *Hispanic American Historical Review*, v. 73, no. 3 (Aug 93), pp. 499 – 500.

Fernandes, Ronaldo Costa. *Noticias del horto* reviewed by Amaya Llebot Cazalis. *Revista Nacional de Cultura (Venezuela)*, v. 54, no. 287 (Oct – Dec 92), pp. 266 – 267.

Fernández, Carole. *Sleep of the Innocents* reviewed by Dionne Espinoza. *Letras Femeninas*, v. 19, no. 1 – 2 (Spring – Fall 93), pp. 157 – 159.

Fernández, Damián J., ed. *Cuban Studies since the Revolution* reviewed by Martin Weinstein. *Hispanic American Historical Review*, v. 73, no. 3 (Aug 93), pp. 533 – 534.

— *Cuban Studies since the Revolution* reviewed by John M. Kirk. *Journal of Latin American Studies*, v. 25, no. 2 (May 93), p. 424.

Fernández, Fiz Antonio. *Antropología cultural, medicina indígena de América y arte rupestre argentino* reviewed by Hebe Clementi. *Todo Es Historia*, v. 26, no. 307 (Feb 93), pp. 75 – 76. Il.

Fernández, Miguel Angel and Renée Ferrer de Arrellaga, eds. *Poetisas del Paraguay* reviewed by Claude Castro. *Caravelle*, no. 60 (1993), pp. 176 – 178.

Fernández, Roberta. *Intaglio: A Novel in Six Stories* reviewed by Dionne Espinoza. *Letras Femeninas*, v. 19, no. 1 – 2 (Spring – Fall 93), pp. 157 – 159.

Fernández Christlieb, Fátima. *La radio mexicana: centro y regiones* reviewed by Guadalupe Cortés (Review entitled "Las desdeñadas fuentes de la radio mexicana"). *Plural (Mexico)*, v. 22, no. 258 (Mar 93), pp. 77 – 78.

Fernández Cozman, Camilo. *'Las ínsulas extrañas' de Emilio Adolfo Westphalen* reviewed by Javier Agreda S. *Revista de Crítica Literaria Latinoamericana*, v. 19, no. 38 (July – Dec 93), pp. 415 – 417.

Fernández de Carrasco, Rosa. *Caracola: cuentos para niños* reviewed by Jaime Martínez Salguero. *Signo*, no. 38, Nueva época (Jan – Apr 93), pp. 237 – 238.

Fernández de Lizardi, José Joaquín. *Obras, XII: Folletos, 1822 – 1824* edited and annotated by Irma Isabel Fernández Arias and María Rosa Palazón Mayoral. Reviewed by Roberto Bravo. *Hispania (USA)*, v. 76, no. 1 (Mar 93), pp. 83 – 84.

Fernández Olmos, Margarite and Lizabeth Paravisini-Gebert. *El placer de la palabra: literatura erótica femenina de América Latina; antología crítica* reviewed by Mónica Zapata. *Canadian Journal of Latin American and Caribbean Studies*, v. 17, no. 34 (1992), pp. 135 – 138.

Fernández Zayas, Marcelo. *La villa* reviewed by Barbara Mujica (Review entitled "The Creative Subtext of Life"). *Américas*, v. 45, no. 3 (May – June 93), pp. 61 – 62.

Ferraz, João Carlos et al. *Development, Technology, and Flexibility: Brazil Faces the Industrial Divide* reviewed by John Humphrey. *Journal of Latin American Studies*, v. 25, no. 3 (Oct 93), pp. 678 – 679.

Ferré, Rosario. *El coloquio de las perras* reviewed by Nara Araújo. *Iberoamericana*, v. 17, no. 49 (1993), pp. 103 – 104.

Ferrer de Arrellaga, Renée and Miguel Angel Fernández, eds. *Poetisas del Paraguay* reviewed by Claude Castro. *Caravelle*, no. 60 (1993), pp. 176 – 178.

Ferrero-Kellerhoff, Inés Cecilia. *Capacho: un pueblo de indios en la jurisdicción de la villa de San Cristóbal* reviewed by Carlos A. Mayo. *Hispanic American Historical Review*, v. 73, no. 1 (Feb 93), pp. 159 – 160.

Ferrez, Gilberto João Carlos. *Photography in Brazil, 1840 – 1900* translated by Stella de Sá Rêgo. Reviewed by Mary Karasch (Review entitled "Brazilian Photography"). *The Americas*, v. 49, no. 3 (Jan 93), pp. 391 – 392.

Ferry, Robert James. *The Colonial Elite of Early Caracas: Formation and Crisis, 1567 – 1767* reviewed by John Lynch. *Journal of Latin American Studies*, v. 25, no. 1 (Feb 93), pp. 191 – 192.

Fick, Carolyn E. *The Making of Haiti: The Saint Dominique Revolution from Below* reviewed by David Geggus. *Hispanic American Historical Review*, v. 73, no. 2 (May 93), pp. 343 – 345.

Fiedel, Stuart J. *Prehistory of the Americas*, 2d edition, reviewed by Gary M. Feinman. *Hispanic American Historical Review*, v. 73, no. 4 (Nov 93), pp. 679 – 680.

— *Prehistory of the Americas*, 2d edition, reviewed by Aaron Segal. *Interciencia*, v. 18, no. 3 (May – June 93), pp. 163 – 164.

Fields, Virginia M., ed. *Sixth Palenque Round Table, 1986* reviewed by Laura Finsten. *Latin American Antiquity*, v. 4, no. 2 (June 93), pp. 201 – 202.

Fifer, J. Valerie. *United States Perceptions of Latin America, 1850 – 1930: A "New West" South of Capricorn* reviewed by Thomas L. Whigham. *The Americas*, v. 49, no. 4 (Apr 93), pp. 559 – 561.

Figueroa, Alvin Joaquín. *La prosa de Luis Rafael Sánchez: texto y contexto* reviewed by Guada Martí-Peña. *Hispamérica,* v. 22, no. 64 – 65 (Apr – Aug 93), pp. 192 – 193.

Figueroa, Alvin Joaquín and Marithelma Costa. *Kaligrafiando: conversaciones con Clemente Soto Vélez* reviewed by Evelyn Uhrhan Irving. *World Literature Today,* v. 67, no. 1 (Winter 93), p. 163.

Figueroa, John J. *The Chase: A Collection of Poems, 1941 – 1989* reviewed by Andrew Salkey. *World Literature Today,* v. 67, no. 2 (Spring 93), p. 429.

Figueroa Navarro, Alfredo. *Testamento y sociedad en el Istmo de Panamá, siglos XVIII y XIX* reviewed by Christopher Ward. *Hispanic American Historical Review,* v. 73, no. 3 (Aug 93), pp. 509 – 510.

Filgueira, Nea. *Mujeres y trabajo en América Latina* (Review). *Revista Paraguaya de Sociología,* v. 30, no. 86 (Jan – Apr 93), pp. 208 – 209.

Finnegan-Smith, Pamela May. *The Tension of Paradox: José Donoso's 'The Obscene Bird of Night' as Spiritual Exercises* reviewed by George R. McMurray. *Chasqui,* v. 22, no. 1 (May 93), pp. 98 – 99.

— *The Tension of Paradox: José Donoso's 'The Obscene Bird of Night' as Spiritual Exercises* reviewed by Ricardo Gutiérrez Mouat. *World Literature Today,* v. 67, no. 2 (Spring 93), pp. 343 – 344.

Fisher, Jo. *Out of the Shadows: Women, Resistance, and Politics in South America* reviewed by Catherine Davies (Review entitled "Women and a Redefinition of Argentinian Nationhood"). *Bulletin of Latin American Research,* v. 12, no. 3 (Sept 93), pp. 333 – 341.

Fisher, John Robert. *Relaciones económicas entre España y América hasta la independencia* reviewed by Kendall W. Brown. *Hispanic American Historical Review,* v. 73, no. 3 (Aug 93), pp. 494 – 495.

— *Trade, War, and Revolution: Exports from Spain to Spanish America, 1797 – 1820* reviewed by James Schofield Saeger. *The Americas,* v. 50, no. 1 (July 93), pp. 127 – 128.

— *Trade, War, and Revolution: Exports from Spain to Spanish America, 1797 – 1820* reviewed by Richard Garner. *European Review of Latin American and Caribbean Studies,* no. 54 (June 93), pp. 138 – 139.

Fisher, John Robert et al, eds. *Reform and Insurrection in Bourbon New Granada and Peru* reviewed by Scarlett O'Phelan Godoy. *Anuario de Estudios Americanos,* v. 50, no. 1 (1993), pp. 316 – 317.

— *Reform and Insurrection in Bourbon New Granada and Peru* reviewed by Lawrence A. Clayton. *Colonial Latin American Historical Review,* v. 2, no. 4 (Fall 93), pp. 470 – 473.

— *Reform and Insurrection in Bourbon New Granada and Peru* reviewed by Caroline A. Williams. *Journal of Latin American Studies,* v. 25, no. 2 (May 93), pp. 392 – 394.

Fitz, Earl E. *Rediscovering the New World: Inter-American Literature in a Comparative Context* reviewed by Charles B. Moore. *Hispania (USA),* v. 76, no. 1 (Mar 93), pp. 84 – 85.

Fitzgerald, Frank T. *Managing Socialism: From Old Cadres to New Professionals in Revolutionary Cuba* reviewed by Linda Fuller (Review entitled "Cuba's 'Middle Class' "). *Latin American Perspectives,* v. 20, no. 1 (Winter 93), pp. 44 – 46.

Fitzmaurice, Sylvia. *Field Guide to the Plants of Inter American University of Puerto Rico, San Germán Campus* reviewed by Juan G. González Lagoa. *Homines,* v. 15 – 16, no. 2 – 1 (Oct 91 – Dec 92), p. 371. Il.

Fletcher, Valerie J., ed. *Crosscurrents of Modernism: Four Latin American Pioneers* reviewed by Carol Damian. *Hispanic American Historical Review,* v. 73, no. 4 (Nov 93), pp. 671 – 672.

Flores, Angel. *Spanish American Authors: The Twentieth Century* reviewed by Barbara Mujica (Review entitled "Wanderers and References"). *Américas,* v. 45, no. 2 (Mar – Apr 93), p. 63.

— *Spanish American Authors: The Twentieth Century* reviewed by Warren L. Meinhardt. *Chasqui,* v. 22, no. 1 (May 93), pp. 101 – 102.

— *Spanish American Authors: The Twentieth Century* reviewed by David William Foster. *Chasqui,* v. 22, no. 1 (May 93), pp. 82 – 83.

Flores Olea, Víctor Manuel. *Tiempos de olvido* reviewed by George R. Murray. *World Literature Today,* v. 67, no. 4 (Fall 93), p. 782.

Flores Saavedra, Mery. *Los silencios de Dios* reviewed by Carlos Castañón Barrientos. *Signo,* no. 35, Nueva época (Jan – Apr 92), pp. 212 – 213.

Flores Zúñiga, Juan Carlos, ed. *Magic and Realism: Central American Contemporary Art/Magia y realismo: arte contemporáneo centroamericano* reviewed by Ivonne Pini (Accompanied by an English translation). *Art Nexus,* no. 9 (June – Aug 93), p. 33. Il.

Florescano, Enrique. *El nuevo pasado mexicano* reviewed by Felícitas López-Portillo Tostado. *Cuadernos Americanos,* no. 38, Nueva época (Mar – Apr 93), pp. 239 – 243.

Florit, Eugenio. *Obras completas: versos nuevos y algunas prosas de ayer y de hoy,* vol. V, edited by Luis González del Valle and Roberto Esquenazi Mayo. Reviewed by James W. Robb. *Hispania (USA),* v. 76, no. 1 (Mar 93), pp. 85 – 86.

Fogel, Jean-François and Bertrand Rosenthal. *Fin de siècle à la Havane: les secrets du pouvoir cubain* reviewed by Ernesto Hernández Busto (Review entitled "Fin de siglo con Castro"). *Vuelta,* v. 17, no. 200 (July 93), pp. 55 – 56.

Foguelman, Dina and Antonio Elio Brailovsky. *Memoria verde: historia ecológica de la Argentina* reviewed by Adrián Gustavo Zarrilli. *Revista de Historia de América,* no. 113 (Jan – June 92), pp. 174 – 177.

Fonseca, Rubem. *Agosto* reviewed by José Woldenberg (Review entitled "¿Cuándo se perdió el Brasil?"). *Nexos,* v. 16, no. 191 (Nov 93), pp. 68 – 69.

Fonseca Corrales, Elizabeth. *Costa Rica colonial: la tierra y el hombre* reviewed by Marvín Barahona. *Mesoamérica (USA),* v. 13, no. 24 (Dec 92), pp. 454 – 457.

Fontaine Talavera, Arturo. *Oir su voz* reviewed by Ignacio Valente. *Atenea (Chile),* no. 467 (1993), pp. 261 – 263.

Fontes, Arivaldo Silveira. *Vultos do ensino militar* reviewed by Cláudio Moreira Bento. *Revista do Instituto Histórico e Geográfico Brasileiro,* no. 373 (Oct – Dec 91), pp. 1206 – 1207.

Forni, Floreal H. et al. *Empleo, estrategias de vida y reproducción: hogares rurales en Santiago del Estero* (Review). *La Educación (USA),* v. 37, no. 114 (1993), p. 156.

Fortique, José Rafael. *Crónicas médicas* reviewed by Juvenal López Ruiz. *Revista Nacional de Cultura (Venezuela),* v. 53, no. 286 (July – Sept 92), p. 265.

Foster, David William. *Gay and Lesbian Themes in Latin American Writing* reviewed by Donna J. Guy. *Hispanic American Historical Review,* v. 73, no. 1 (Feb 93), p. 137.

Foster, Nelson and Linda S. Cordell, eds. *Chilies to Chocolate: Food the Americas Gave the World* reviewed by John C. Super. *Hispanic American Historical Review,* v. 73, no. 3 (Aug 93), p. 487.

Foweraker, Joseph W. and Ann L. Craig, eds. *Popular Movements and Political Change in Mexico* reviewed by Daniel C. Levy. *Studies in Comparative International Development,* v. 27, no. 3 (Fall 92), pp. 122 – 124.

Fraga, Rosendo M. *El general Justo* reviewed by Félix Luna. *Todo Es Historia,* v. 27, no. 312 (July 93), p. 74. Il.

Fraisse, Geneviève and Michelle Perrot, eds. *Historia de las mujeres en Occidente, tomo IV: El siglo XIX* reviewed by Lucía Solís Tolosa. *Todo Es Historia,* v. 27, no. 316 (Nov 93), p. 92. Il.

Franco, Enrique, ed. *Imágenes de la música iberoamericana* (Review). *Inter-American Music Review,* v. 13, no. 1 (Fall – Winter 92), pp. 121 – 122.

Franco, Jean. *Plotting Women: Gender and Representation in Mexico* reviewed by Ileana Rodríguez (Review entitled "Tramando y entramando una agenda feminista"). *Casa de las Américas,* no. 191 (Apr – June 93), pp. 133 – 137.

Franco Marcano, Mercedes. *La capa roja* reviewed by Analy Lorenzo. *Revista Nacional de Cultura (Venezuela),* v. 54, no. 287 (Oct – Dec 92), pp. 269 – 270.

Freeman, Richard B. and George J. Borjas, eds. *Immigration and the Work Force: Economic Consequences for the United States and Source Areas* reviewed by Jim Thomas. *Journal of Latin American Studies,* v. 25, no. 3 (Oct 93), pp. 683 – 684.

Freire, Ana María Araújo. *Analfabetismo no Brasil* (Review). *La Educación (USA),* v. 37, no. 114 (1993), p. 151.

French, John David. *The Brazilian Workers' ABC: Class Conflict and Alliances in Modern São Paulo* reviewed by Peter Ranis. *Hispanic American Historical Review,* v. 73, no. 4 (Nov 93), pp. 707 – 708.

Frenk, Mariana. *Y mil aventuras* reviewed by Fabienne Bradu. *Vuelta,* v. 17, no. 195 (Feb 93), pp. 39 – 40.

Fresán, Rodrigo. *Historia argentina* reviewed by Silva G. Kurlat Ares. *Hispamérica,* v. 21, no. 62 (Aug 92), pp. 136 – 137.

Frías Núñez, Marcelo. *Enfermedad y sociedad en la crisis colonial del antiguo régimen: Nueva Granada en el tránsito del siglo XVIII al XIX; las epidemias de viruelas* reviewed by Juan A. Villamarín. *Hispanic American Historical Review,* v. 73, no. 4 (Nov 93), pp. 693 – 694.

Frieden, Jeffrey A. *Debt, Development, and Democracy: Modern Political Economy and Latin America* reviewed by Sidney Weintraub. *Studies in Comparative International Development,* v. 27, no. 2 (Summer 92), pp. 96 – 98.

Fuente Benavides, Rafael de la. *El más hermoso crepúsculo del mundo* selected and introduced by Jorge Aguilar Mora. Reviewed by Alfredo García Valdez. *Vuelta,* v. 17, no. 199 (June 93), pp. 44 – 45.

Fuentes, Carlos. *The Buried Mirror: Reflections on Spain and the New World* reviewed by John Lynch. *Hispanic American Historical Review,* v. 73, no. 3 (Aug 93), pp. 490 – 491.

— *La campaña* reviewed by Célica Cánovas Marmo (Review entitled "Carlos Fuentes: hacia el ser americano"). *Plural (Mexico),* v. 22, no. 259 (Apr 93), pp. 73 – 74.

— *La campaña* reviewed by Celina Márquez (Review entitled *"La campaña* de Fuentes: paralelismos del páramo aquél"). *La Palabra y el Hombre,* no. 81 (Jan – Mar 92), pp. 310 – 312.

— *'Constancia' y otras novelas para vírgenes* (Review entitled "La constancia del arte de escribir"). *La Palabra y el Hombre,* no. 81 (Jan – Mar 92), pp. 306 – 309.

— *Cristoph Ungeborn,* a translation of *Cristóbal Nonato,* introduced and translated by Maria Bamberg. Reviewed by Martina L. Caller. *Zeitschrift für Lateinamerika Wien,* no. 42 (1992), pp. 69 – 71.

— *El espejo enterrado* reviewed by Héctor Aguilar Camín (Review entitled "Por una historia patria para adultos"). *Nexos,* v. 16, no. 184 (Apr 93), pp. 59 – 63.

— *El espejo enterrado* reviewed by Marta Portal (Review entitled "Las tres hispanidades de España"). *Cuadernos Hispanoamericanos,* no. 522 (Dec 93), pp. 143 – 146.

— *El espejo enterrado/The Buried Mirror: Reflections on Spain and the New World* reviewed by John Incledon. *Hispania (USA),* v. 76, no. 4 (Dec 93), pp. 735 – 737.

— *El naranjo o los círculos del tiempo* reviewed by Julián Ríos (Review entitled *"El naranjo o los círculos del tiempo":* narrativo de Carlos Fuentes"). *Cuadernos Hispanoamericanos,* no. 522 (Dec 93), pp. 146 – 149.

— *El naranjo o los círculos del tiempo* reviewed by Julio Ortega (Review entitled "Nuevos relatos de Carlos Fuentes"). *Nexos,* v. 16, no. 188 (Aug 93), pp. 75 – 80.

— *El naranjo o los círculos del tiempo* reviewed by Iván Ríos Gascón (Review entitled "Carlos Fuentes y el tiempo circular"). *Plural (Mexico),* v. 22, no. 267 (Dec 93), pp. 79 – 80.

— *El naranjo y los círculos del tiempo* reviewed by José Homero. *Vuelta,* v. 17, no. 205 (Dec 93), pp. 40 – 41.

— *Le sourire d'Erasme: epopée, utopie et mythe dans le roman hispano-américain,* a translation of *Valiente mundo nuevo: épica, utopía y mito en la novela hispanoamericana.* Reviewed by John L. Brown. *World Literature Today,* v. 67, no. 4 (Fall 93), p. 790.

Fuguet, Alberto. *Mala onda* reviewed by Juan Gabriel Araya. *Atenea (Chile),* no. 467 (1993), pp. 270 – 271.

Fuller, Linda. *Work and Democracy in Socialist Cuba* reviewed by Samuel Farber. *Cuban Studies/Estudios Cubanos,* v. 23 (1993), pp. 238 – 240.

— *Work and Democracy in Socialist Cuba* reviewed by Jean Stubbs. *Journal of Latin American Studies,* v. 25, no. 2 (May 93), pp. 424 – 425.

— *Work and Democracy in Socialist Cuba* reviewed by Ronald H. Chilcote (Review entitled "Participation and the Workplace in Socialist Cuba"). *Latin American Perspectives,* v. 20, no. 1 (Winter 93), pp. 40 – 43.

Furlan, Alfredo and Justa Ezpeleta, eds. *La gestión pedagógica en la escuela* reviewed by Luis M. Flores. *La Educación (USA),* v. 37, no. 115 (1993), p. 420.

Furtado, Celso. *Brasil: a construção interrompida* reviewed by Rosa Maria Vieira. *RAE; Revista de Administração de Empresas,* v. 33, no. 1 (Jan – Feb 93), pp. 122 – 123.

Gajardo, Marcela. *La concientización en América Latina* reviewed by Orlando Fals Borda. *La Educación (USA),* v. 36, no. 111 – 113 (1992), pp. 291 – 294.

Galaz-Vivar Welden, Alicia

See

   Welden, Alicia Galaz-Vivar

Gallego, Ferran. *Ejército, nacionalismo y reformismo en América Latina: la gestión de Germán Busch en Bolivia* reviewed by Marta Irurozqui Victoriano. *Revista Andina,* v. 11, no. 1 (July 93), pp. 246 – 247.

— *Los orígenes del reformismo militar en América Latina: la gestión de David Toro en Bolivia* reviewed by Gary Prado. *Journal of Latin American Studies,* v. 25, no. 1 (Feb 93), pp. 205 – 206.

— *Los orígenes del reformismo militar en América Latina: la gestión de David Toro en Bolivia* reviewed by Marta Irurozqui Victoriano. *Revista Andina,* v. 11, no. 1 (July 93), pp. 246 – 247.

— *Los orígenes del reformismo militar en América Latina: la gestión de David Toro en Bolivia* reviewed by Marta Irurozqui Victoriano. *Revista de Indias,* v. 53, no. 197 (Jan – Apr 93), pp. 104 – 106.

Gallegos, Bernardo P. *Literacy, Education, and Society in New Mexico, 1693 – 1821* reviewed by B. Michael Miller. *Colonial Latin American Historical Review,* v. 1, no. 1 (Fall 92), pp. 118 – 119.

— *Literacy, Education, and Society in New Mexico, 1693 – 1821* reviewed by John E. Kicza. *Hispanic American Historical Review*, v. 73, no. 1 (Feb 93), pp. 150 – 151.

Gallo, Carmenza. *Taxes and State Power: Political Instability in Bolivia, 1900 – 1950* reviewed by Eduardo A. Gamarra. *Hispanic American Historical Review*, v. 73, no. 3 (Aug 93), pp. 523 – 526.

Galloway, Patricia and Philip Paul Boucher, eds. *Proceedings of the Fifteenth Meeting of the French Colonial Historical Society, Martinique and Guadeloupe, May 1989* reviewed by Paul Lachance. *Hispanic American Historical Review*, v. 73, no. 3 (Aug 93), pp. 502 – 503.

Galve, Gelvira de Toledo, condesa de. *Two Hearts, One Soul: The Correspondence of the Condesa de Galve, 1688 – 1696* edited, annotated, and translated by Meredith D. Dodge and Rick Hendricks. Reviewed by John E. Kicza. *Colonial Latin American Historical Review*, v. 2, no. 4 (Fall 93), pp. 475 – 477.

Gálvez, José de. *Informe sobre las rebeliones populares en 1767* reviewed by Frédérique Langue (Review entitled "Les soulèvements populaires de 1767 en Nouvell-Espagne: le point sur quelques publications récentes"). *Caravelle*, no. 60 (1993), pp. 152 – 154.

Gálvez, Manuel. *La maestra normal.* Critical edition by Myron Lichtblau. Reviewed by Lee A. Daniel. *Hispania (USA)*, v. 76, no. 2 (May 93), pp. 285 – 286.

Gambaro, Griselda. *The Impenetrable Madam X,* a translation of *Lo impenetrable,* translated by Evelyn Picon Garfield. Reviewed by Sandra Cypess. *Letras Femeninas,* v. 19, no. 1 – 2 (Spring – Fall 93), pp. 149 – 151.

Ganster, Paul and Eugenio O. Valenciano, eds. *The Mexican – U.S. Border Region and the Free Trade Agreement* reviewed by Christopher A. Erickson. *Journal of Borderlands Studies,* v. 7, no. 2 (Fall 92), pp. 103 – 105.

Garay Salamanca, Luis Jorge, ed. *Estrategia industrial e inserción internacional* reviewed by Horacio Osorio. *Planeación y Desarrollo,* v. 24, no. 2 (May – Aug 93), pp. 429 – 435.

Garcés Durán, Mario. *Crisis social y motines populares en el 1900* reviewed by Ricardo López (Review entitled "Buscar la historia y reconstruirla"). *Casa de las Américas,* no. 189 (Oct – Dec 92), pp. 142 – 145.

García, Mario T. *Mexican Americans: Leadership, Ideology, and Identity, 1930 – 1960* reviewed by Ramón D. Chacón. *Hispanic American Historical Review,* v. 73, no. 1 (Feb 93), pp. 139 – 140.

García, Nasario. *Abuelitos: Stories of the Río Puerco Valley* reviewed by Enrique R. Lamadrid. *Confluencia,* v. 8, no. 1 (Fall 92), p. 175.

Garcia, Richard A. *Rise of the Mexican American Middle Class: San Antonio, 1929 – 1941* reviewed by Francesco Cordasco. *International Migration Review,* v. 27, no. 2 (Summer 93), pp. 435 – 436.

García Aguilar, Eduardo. *Urbes luminosas* reviewed by José Ricardo Chaves. *Vuelta,* v. 17, no. 195 (Feb 93), p. 42.

García Alvarez, Alejandro. *La gran burguesía comercial en Cuba, 1899 – 1920* reviewed by Antonio Santamaría García. *Revista de Indias,* v. 53, no. 197 (Jan – Apr 93), pp. 106 – 107.

García Bergua, Ana. *El umbral: "Travels and Adventures"* reviewed by Christopher Domínguez. *Vuelta,* v. 17, no. 198 (May 93), p. 55.

García Blest, Fernando. *La familia Cerezos* reviewed by Baccio Salvo. *Atenea (Chile),* no. 465 – 466 (1992), pp. 367 – 369.

García Canclini, Néstor. *Culturas híbridas: estrategias para entrar y salir de la modernidad* reviewed by Ineke Phaf. *Hispamérica,* v. 22, no. 64 – 65 (Apr – Aug 93), pp. 193 – 197.

García Canclini, Néstor and Gilberto Guevara Niebla, eds. *La educación y la cultura ante el Tratado de Libre Comercio* reviewed by Fernando de Mateo (Review entitled "El jalón del TLC"). *Nexos,* v. 16, no. 189 (Sept 93), pp. 66 – 67.

García Cárcel, Ricardo. *La leyenda negra: historia y opinión* reviewed by Blas Matamoro. *Cuadernos Hispanoamericanos,* no. 511 (Jan 93), p. 137.

García Díaz, Bernardo. *Textiles del valle de Orizaba, 1880 – 1925* reviewed by Patricia Arias. *La Palabra y el Hombre,* no. 82 (Apr – June 92), pp. 310 – 312.

García Escobar, Carlos René. *La llama del retorno* reviewed by Amanda Castro-Mitchell. *Revista Iberoamericana,* v. 59, no. 162 – 163 (Jan – June 93), pp. 368 – 376.

García Godoy, Cristián. *Tomás Godoy Cruz: su tiempo, su vida, su drama* reviewed by Mario Luis Descotte. *Revista Interamericana de Bibliografía,* v. 42, no. 3 (1992), p. 503.

García Jordán, Pilar. *Iglesia y poder en el Perú contemporáneo, 1821 – 1919* reviewed by Patricia B. McRae. *The Americas,* v. 50, no. 1 (July 93), pp. 144 – 145.

— *Iglesia y poder en el Perú contemporáneo, 1821 – 1919* reviewed by Alfonso W. Quiroz. *Hispanic American Historical Review,* v. 73, no. 3 (Aug 93), pp. 522 – 523.

— *Iglesia y poder en el Perú contemporáneo, 1821 – 1919* reviewed by Nils Jacobsen. *Revista Andina,* v. 10, no. 2 (Dec 92), pp. 541 – 545.

García Márquez, Gabriel. *Doce cuentos peregrinos* reviewed by Barbara Mujica (Review entitled "Wanderers and References"). *Américas,* v. 45, no. 2 (Mar – Apr 93), pp. 62 – 63. II.

— *Doce cuentos peregrinos* reviewed by Edward Waters Hood. *Chasqui,* v. 22, no. 1 (May 93), pp. 95 – 98.

— *Doce cuentos peregrinos* reviewed by Edward Waters Hood. *World Literature Today,* v. 67, no. 4 (Fall 93), pp. 782 – 783.

— *Doce cuentos peregrinos* reviewed by Harley D. Oberhelman. *Hispania (USA),* v. 76, no. 3 (Sept 93), pp. 513 – 514.

— *Doce cuentos peregrinos* reviewed by Isabel Rodríguez-Vergara. *Revista Interamericana de Bibliografía,* v. 42, no. 4 (1992), pp. 651 – 653.

— *Doze contos peregrinos* translated by Eric Nepomuceno (Review). *Vozes,* v. 87, no. 2 (Mar – Apr 93), pp. 101 – 102.

García Martínez, Bernardo, ed. *Los pueblos de indios y las comunidades* reviewed by Woodrow Borah. *Hispanic American Historical Review,* v. 73, no. 3 (Aug 93), pp. 507 – 508.

García Ponce, Antonio. *La ilusión del miedo perenne* reviewed by Amaya Llebot Cazalis. *Revista Nacional de Cultura (Venezuela),* v. 53, no. 286 (July – Sept 92), pp. 258 – 260.

García Riera, Emilio. *Historia documental del cine mexicano* reviewed by Luis González y González (Review entitled "Una enciclopedia del cine mexicano"). *Nexos,* v. 16, no. 188 (Aug 93), pp. 85 – 87.

Garduño, Flor. *Witnesses of Time* reviewed by Jerald R. Green. *Latin American Art,* v. 5, no. 1 (Spring 93), p. 95.

Gargantini, Ricardo. *Paralelas divergentes* reviewed by Arnaldo Gómez A. *Derecho y Reforma Agraria,* no. 24 (1993), pp. 207 – 208.

Garibay, Ricardo. *Cómo se gana la vida* reviewed by Roberto Pliego (Review entitled "Garibay para sí mismo"). *Nexos,* v. 16, no. 185 (May 93), pp. 79 – 80.

Garré Copello, Belter. *Solución de controversias en el MERCOSUR* (Review). *Integración Latinoamericana*, v. 18, no. 194 (Oct 93), pp. 88 – 89.

— *Solución de controversias en el MERCOSUR: protocolo de Brasil* (Review). *Integración Latinoamericana*, v. 18, no. 194 (Oct 93), pp. 88 – 89.

Garro, Elena. *Memorias de España 1937* reviewed by Federico Alvarez. *Plural (Mexico)*, v. 22, no. 259 (Apr 93), pp. 69 – 71.

Garst, Rachel and Tom Barry. *Feeding the Crisis: U.S. Food Aid and Farm Policy in Central America* reviewed by Melvin G. Blase. *Journal of Developing Areas*, v. 27, no. 4 (July 93), pp. 566 – 567.

Garza Mercado, Ario. *Obras de consulta para estudiantes de ciencias sociales y humanidades* reviewed by Enrique Núñez. *La Educación (USA)*, v. 37, no. 114 (1993), pp. 157 – 158.

Garza Toledo, Enrique de la, ed. *Crisis y sujetos sociales en México*, 2 vols., reviewed by Alicia Inés Martínez. *El Cotidiano*, v. 9, no. 54 (May 93), pp. 116 – 117.

Garza Villarreal, Gustavo. *Desconcentración, tecnología y localización industrial en México: los parques y ciudades industriales, 1953 – 1988* reviewed by Carlos A. de Mattos. *EURE*, v. 19, no. 58 (Oct 93), pp. 88 – 89.

Garzón, Benito Carlos. *El presagio y otros cuentos* reviewed by Geneviève Despinoy. *Caravelle*, no. 60 (1993), pp. 178 – 179.

Garzón Céspedes, Francisco. *El arte escénico de contar cuentos* reviewed by Fernando Rodríguez Sosa (Review entitled "Sobre la narración oral escénica"). *Conjunto*, no. 90 – 91 (Jan – June 92), pp. 103 – 105. Il.

Gasparini, Marina, ed. *Obras de arte de la Ciudad Universitaria de Caracas* reviewed by Antonio Rodríguez (Accompanied by an English translation). *Art Nexus*, no. 8 (Apr – June 93), pp. 33 – 34. Il.

Gato Castaño, Purificación. *El informe del p. Gregorio de Bolívar a la Congregación de Propaganda Fide de 1623* reviewed by Pedro de Anasagasti. *Signo*, no. 35, Nueva época (Jan – Apr 92), pp. 214 – 216.

Gayoso, Milia. *Ronda en las olas* reviewed by Claude Castro. *Caravelle*, no. 59 (1992), pp. 315 – 317.

Gaytán Guzmán, Rosa Isabel. *Las relaciones comerciales entre México y Estados Unidos, 1867 – 1876* reviewed by Guadalupe González G. *Relaciones Internacionales (Mexico)*, v. 14, Nueva época, no. 55 (July – Sept 92), pp. 79 – 82.

Gazmuri Riveros, Cristián. *El "48" chileno: igualitarios, reformistas, radicales, masones y bomberos* reviewed by Ricardo Krebs. *Historia (Chile)*, no. 26 (1991 – 1992), pp. 464 – 469.

Geldof, Lynn. *Cubans: Voices of Change* reviewed by Rubén Berríos. *Cuban Studies/Estudios Cubanos*, v. 23 (1993), pp. 243 – 244.

Gelman, Juan. *En abierta oscuridad* reviewed by Alejandro Expósito (Review entitled "Juan Gelman redivivo: al menos para mí"). *Plural (Mexico)*, v. 22, no. 265 (Oct 93), pp. 80 – 81.

Gemert, Hans van. *Organos históricos del Perú* (Review). *Inter-American Music Review*, v. 13, no. 1 (Fall – Winter 92), pp. 114 – 115.

George, David. *The Modern Brazilian Stage* reviewed by Frank Dauster. *World Literature Today*, v. 67, no. 2 (Spring 93), p. 348.

Gerbi, Antonello. *Nature in the New World: From Christopher Columbus to Gonzalo Fernández de Oviedo* translated by Jeremy Moyle. Reviewed by Rick Hendricks. *Colonial Latin American Historical Review*, v. 1, no. 1 (Fall 92), pp. 120 – 121.

Gerdes, Claudia. *Eliten und Fortschritt: Zur Geschichte der Lebensstile in Venezuela, 1908 – 1915* reviewed by Nikita Harwich Vallenilla. *Iberoamericana*, v. 17, no. 49 (1993), pp. 96 – 97.

Gerhard, Peter. *Pirates in the Pacific, 1575 – 1742* reviewed by Patrick Bryan. *Caribbean Quarterly*, v. 38, no. 2 – 3 (June – Sept 92), pp. 117 – 118.

Gertz, René E. *O perigo alemão* reviewed by Jeff Lesser. *The Americas*, v. 50, no. 1 (July 93), pp. 141 – 142.

— *O perigo alemão* reviewed by Ronald C. Newton. *Hispanic American Historical Review*, v. 73, no. 2 (May 93), pp. 324 – 325.

Gestión ambiental en Chile: aportes del IV° Encuentro Científico sobre el Medio Ambiente reviewed by Ricardo Jordán Fuchs. *EURE*, v. 19, no. 56 (Mar 93), pp. 119 – 120.

Giardinelli, Mempo. *Santo oficio de la memoria* reviewed by Alicia Rolón. *Chasqui*, v. 22, no. 2 (Nov 93), pp. 182 – 184.

Giella, Miguel Angel. *Teatro Abierto, 1981: teatro argentino bajo vigilancia*, vol. I, reviewed by Claudia Ferman. *Latin American Theatre Review*, v. 26, no. 2 (Spring 93), pp. 212 – 214.

Giffords, Gloria Fraser, ed. *The Art of Private Devotion: Retablo Painting of Mexico* reviewed by Luis Cerda. *Hispanic American Historical Review*, v. 73, no. 1 (Feb 93), pp. 125 – 126.

Gikandi, Simon. *Writing in Limbo: Modernism and Caribbean Literature* reviewed by Bruce King. *World Literature Today*, v. 67, no. 2 (Spring 93), p. 426.

Gil, Carlos B., ed. *Hope and Frustration: Interviews with Leaders of Mexico's Political Opposition* reviewed by Denis L. Heyck. *Hispania (USA)*, v. 76, no. 1 (Mar 93), pp. 86 – 87.

Gil Antón, Manuel, ed. *Académicos: un botón de muestra* reviewed by Quetzalcóatl Gutiérrez Granados. *El Cotidiano*, v. 9, no. 55 (June 93), p. 119.

Gil Fernández, Juan. *Mitos y utopías del descubrimiento* reviewed by Fernando Aínsa. *Colonial Latin American Review*, v. 2, no. 1 – 2 (1993), pp. 286 – 288.

— *Mitos y utopías del descubrimiento*, vol. III, reviewed by Juha Pekka Helminen. *Ibero Americana (Sweden)*, v. 22, no. 2 (Dec 92), pp. 86 – 87.

Gilbert, Alan G. and Ann Varley. *Landlord and Tenant: Housing the Poor in Urban Mexico* reviewed by Nikki Craske. *Journal of Latin American Studies*, v. 25, no. 2 (May 93), pp. 418 – 419.

Gillespie, Charles Guy. *Negotiating Democracy: Politicians and Generals in Uruguay* reviewed by Howard Handelman. *Journal of Latin American Studies*, v. 25, no. 1 (Feb 93), pp. 218 – 219.

— *Negotiating Democracy: Politicians and Generals in Uruguay* reviewed by Silvia Dutrénit Bielous. *Revista Mexicana de Sociología*, v. 54, no. 1 (Jan – Mar 92), pp. 326 – 330.

Gillespie, Susan D. *The Aztec Kings: The Construction of Rulership in Mexica History* reviewed by Frances Karttunen. *Latin American Indian Literatures Journal*, v. 9, no. 1 (Spring 93), pp. 85 – 92.

Gilroy, Beryl. *Stedman and Joanna: A Love in Bondage* reviewed by A. S. Newson. *World Literature Today*, v. 67, no. 1 (Winter 93), p. 219.

Gimbernat de González, Ester. *Aventuras del desacuerdo: novelistas argentinas de los '80* reviewed by David William Foster. *Chasqui,* v. 22, no. 1 (May 93), pp. 83 – 84.

Gisbert de Mesa, Teresa. *Arte y desacralización* reviewed by María Elena Alzérreca Barbery (Review entitled "Resacralización del sincretismo cultural"). *Homines,* v. 15 – 16, no. 2 – 1 (Oct 91 – Dec 92), pp. 358 – 360.

Glave Testino, Luis Miguel. *Vida, símbolos y batallas: creación y recreación de la comunidad indígena, Cusco, siglo XVI – XX* reviewed by Manuel Burga (Review entitled "Los kanas en la historia"). *Debate (Peru),* v. 16, no. 72 (Mar – May 93), pp. 64 – 65. Il.

Gledhill, John. *"Casi nada": A Study of Agrarian Reform in the Homeland of Cardenismo* reviewed by Alan Knight. *Hispanic American Historical Review,* v. 73, no. 1 (Feb 93), pp. 181 – 182.

Gleijeses, Piero. *Shattered Hope: The Guatemalan Revolution and the United States, 1944 – 1954* reviewed by Jim Handy. *The Americas,* v. 49, no. 4 (Apr 93), pp. 562 – 564.

Glissant, Edouard. *The Indies/Les Indes* reviewed by Juris Silenieks. *World Literature Today,* v. 67, no. 4 (Fall 93), p. 878.

Godoy Gallardo, Eduardo. *La generación del '50 en Chile: historia de un movimiento literario* reviewed by Lon Pearson. *Chasqui,* v. 22, no. 2 (Nov 93), pp. 177 – 179.

Goldberg, Miriam and Moema Toscano. *A revolução das mulheres: uma balança do feminismo no Brasil* reviewed by Celi Regina Jardim Pinto (Review entitled "Falas de mulheres"). *Estudos Feministas,* v. 1, no. 1 (1993), pp. 219 – 221.

Gomes, Eustáquio. *Os rapazes d'"a Onda" e outros rapazes* reviewed by Elias Thomé Saliba. *Vozes,* v. 86, no. 6 (Nov – Dec 92), pp. 101 – 103.

Gomes, Miguel. *La cueva de Altamira* reviewed by R. J. Lovera De-Sola. *Revista Nacional de Cultura (Venezuela),* v. 53, no. 286 (July – Sept 92), pp. 253 – 254.

Gómez, Thomas. *L'invention de l'Amérique: rêve et réalités de la conquête* reviewed by Janny Chenu. *Caravelle,* no. 59 (1992), pp. 304 – 306.

Gómez Quezada, Rubén. *Crónicas pampinas: en busca del tiempo perdido* reviewed by Carlos Hallet C. *Mensaje,* v. 42, no. 424 (Nov 93), p. 599.

Gómez-Quiñones, Juan. *Chicano Politics: Reality and Promise, 1940 – 1990* reviewed by Javier Urbano Reyes (Review entitled "La gran realidad de los Estados Unidos: la comunidad chicana"). *Revista Mexicana de Ciencias Políticas y Sociales,* v. 38, Nueva época, no. 154 (Oct – Dec 93), pp. 193 – 196.

Gonzalbo Aizpuru, Pilar, ed. *Familias novohispanas, siglos XVI al XIX* reviewed by María Luisa Pérez-González. *Colonial Latin American Historical Review,* v. 2, no. 4 (Fall 93), pp. 479 – 480.

Gonzales, Laurence. *The Still Point* reviewed by Bruce-Novoa. *The Americas Review,* v. 20, no. 2 (Summer 92), pp. 115 – 116.

Gonzales, Odi. *Valle sagrado* reviewed by Patricia Alba (Review entitled "Qué oscuro era mi valle"). *Debate (Peru),* v. 16, no. 75 (Dec 93 – Jan 94), pp. 77 – 78. Il.

González, Alfonso. *Euphoria and Crisis: Essays on the Contemporary Mexican Novel* reviewed by George R. McMurray. *Chasqui,* v. 22, no. 2 (Nov 93), pp. 171 – 173.

González, Eduardo. *The Monstered Self: Narratives of Death and Performance in Latin American Fiction* reviewed by Ana Eire. *Hispania (USA),* v. 76, no. 2 (May 93), pp. 286 – 287.

González, Ester G. de

See
　　Gimbernat de González, Ester

González, Juan Gualbert. *Rompiendo cadenas* reviewed by José B. Alvarez IV. *Chasqui,* v. 22, no. 1 (May 93), pp. 73 – 74.

Gonzalez, Nancie L. Solien. *Dollar, Dove, and Eagle: One Hundred Years of Palestinian Migration to Honduras* reviewed by Caroline B. Brettell. *International Migration Review,* v. 27, no. 4 (Winter 93), pp. 899 – 900.

González, Otto-Raúl. *Luna mutilada* reviewed by Silvia Yáñez (Review entitled *"Luna mutilada:* poesía entera"). *Plural (Mexico),* v. 22, no. 259 (Apr 93), p. 73.

Gonzalez, Ray, ed. *After Aztlan: Latino Poets of the Nineties* reviewed by Charles Tatum. *World Literature Today,* v. 67, no. 2 (Spring 93), pp. 389 – 390.

González Abuter, Tulio and Ricardo Acuña Casas. *Los Angeles durante la colonia* reviewed by Fernando Campos Harriet (Review entitled "Dos estudios sobre los Angeles"). *Boletín de la Academia Chilena de la Historia,* v. 58 – 59, no. 102 (1991 – 1992), pp. 553 – 554.

González-Berry, Erlinda, ed. *"Pasó por aquí": Critical Essays on the New Mexican Literary Tradition, 1542 – 1988* reviewed by Arthur Brakel. *The Americas Review,* v. 19, no. 2 (Summer 91), pp. 105 – 107.

González Casanova, Pablo. *La literatura perseguida por la inquisición* reviewed by Solange Alberro (Review entitled "Regreso de un clásico"). *Nexos,* v. 16, no. 189 (Sept 93), pp. 59 – 61.

González-Crespo, Jorge L. *Memorias del almirante Isaac F. Rojas: conversaciones con Jorge González-Crespo* reviewed by Carmen Vrljicak-Espaín. *Todo Es Historia,* v. 27, no. 315 (Oct 93), p. 66. Il.

González-Cruz, Luis F. and Francesca Colecchia, eds. *Cuban Theater in the United States: A Criticial Anthology* translated by the editors. Reviewed by Luis A. Jiménez. *Hispania (USA),* v. 76, no. 4 (Dec 93), pp. 737 – 738.

González Echevarría, Roberto. *Myth and Archives: A Theory of Latin American Narrative* reviewed by Antonio Fama. *Revista Canadiense de Estudios Hispánicos,* v. 17, no. 2 (Winter 93), pp. 399 – 401.

González Miranda, Sergio. *Hombres y mujeres de la pampa: Tarapacá en el ciclo del salitre: primera parte* reviewed by Juan Ricardo Couyoumdjian. *Boletín de la Academia Chilena de la Historia,* v. 58 – 59, no. 102 (1991 – 1992), pp. 560 – 561.

— *Hombres y mujeres de la pampa: Tarapacá en el ciclo del salitre* reviewed by Carlos A. de Mattos. *EURE,* v. 19, no. 57 (July 93), pp. 129 – 130. Il.

González Pacheco, Cuauhtémoc and Felipe Torres Torres, eds. *Los retos de la soberanía alimentaria en México* reviewed by Argelia Salinas Ontiveros. *Problemas del Desarrollo,* v. 24, no. 93 (Apr – June 93), pp. 239 – 241.

González Pedrero, Enrique. *País de un sólo hombre: el México de Santa Anna* reviewed by Luis Villoro (Review entitled "Santa Anna o la nación sin estado"). *Nexos,* v. 16, no. 190 (Oct 93), pp. 69 – 72.

— *País de un sólo hombre: el México de Santa Anna, vol. I; La ronda de los contrarios* reviewed by Rafael Rojas. *Vuelta,* v. 17, no. 204 (Nov 93), pp. 34 – 36.

González Rodríguez, Sergio. *El centauro en el paisaje* reviewed by Alejandro de la Garza (Review entitled "El ensayo de arena"). *Nexos,* v. 16, no. 182 (Feb 93), pp. 81 – 85.

— *El centauro en el paisaje* reviewed by Christopher Domínguez. *Vuelta,* v. 17, no. 194 (Jan 93), pp. 43 – 44.

González Stephan, Beatriz et al. *Crítica y descolonización: el sujeto colonial en la cultura latinoamericana* reviewed by David William Foster. *Chasqui*, v. 22, no. 2 (Nov 93), pp. 162 – 163.

Goodison, Lorna. *Selected Poems* reviewed by Andrew Salkey. *World Literature Today*, v. 67, no. 4 (Fall 93), pp. 876 – 877. Il.

Goodman, David Edwin and Michael R. Redclift, eds. *Environment and Development in Latin America: The Politics of Sustainability* reviewed by Margaret E. Keck. *Studies in Comparative International Development*, v. 27, no. 3 (Fall 92), pp. 120 – 122.

Goodman, Louis Wolf et al, eds. *Political Parties and Democracy in Central America* reviewed by James Dunkerley. *Bulletin of Latin American Research*, v. 12, no. 2 (May 93), pp. 233 – 234.

Gorostiza, José and Carlos Pellicer. *Correspondencia, 1918 – 1928* edited and introduced by Guillermo Sheridan. Reviewed by David Medina Portillo. *Vuelta*, v. 17, no. 202 (Sept 93), pp. 44 – 45.

— *Correspondencia, 1918 – 1928* edited and introduced by Guillermo Sheridan. Reviewed by Rosa Beltrán. *Vuelta*, v. 17, no. 203 (Oct 93), pp. 44 – 45.

Gosner, Kevin. *Soldiers of the Virgin: The Moral Economy of a Colonial Maya Rebellion* reviewed by Robert M. Hill II. *The Americas*, v. 50, no. 2 (Oct 93), pp. 274 – 276.

— *Soldiers of the Virgin: The Moral Economy of a Colonial Maya Rebellion* reviewed by Kenneth Mills. *Bulletin of Latin American Research*, v. 12, no. 2 (May 93), pp. 223 – 224.

— *Soldiers of the Virgin: The Moral Economy of a Colonial Maya Rebellion* reviewed by Stephen Webre. *Colonial Latin American Historical Review*, v. 2, no. 1 (Winter 93), pp. 109 – 110.

— *Soldiers of the Virgin: The Moral Economy of a Colonial Maya Rebellion* reviewed by Linda A. Newson. *Journal of Latin American Studies*, v. 25, no. 3 (Oct 93), pp. 655 – 656.

Gottret Baldivieso, Augusto. *Imágenes y vivencias* reviewed by Raúl Rivadeneira Prada. *Signo*, no. 35, Nueva época (Jan – Apr 92), pp. 217 – 221.

Gould, Jeffrey L. *To Lead as Equals: Rural Protest and Political Consciousness in Chinandega, Nicaragua, 1912 – 1979* reviewed by Daniel Little. *Economic Development and Cultural Change*, v. 41, no. 4 (July 93), pp. 894 – 898.

— *To Lead as Equals: Rural Protest and Political Consciousness in Chinandega, Nicaragua, 1912 – 1979* reviewed by Michael F. Jiménez. *Hispanic American Historical Review*, v. 73, no. 1 (Feb 93), pp. 186 – 188.

Gow, Peter. *Of Mixed Blood: Kinship and History in Peruvian Amazonia* reviewed by Rodrigo Montoya. *Journal of Latin American Studies*, v. 25, no. 1 (Feb 93), pp. 222 – 224.

Graham, Carol. *Peru's APRA: Parties, Politics, and the Elusive Quest for Democracy* reviewed by Fredrick B. Pike. *Hispanic American Historical Review*, v. 73, no. 3 (Aug 93), pp. 518 – 519.

— *Peru's APRA: Parties, Politics, and the Elusive Quest for Democracy* reviewed by Giorgio Alberti. *Journal of Latin American Studies*, v. 25, no. 2 (May 93), pp. 414 – 415.

— *Peru's APRA: Parties, Politics, and the Elusive Quest for Democracy* reviewed by Henry Dietz. *Revista Interamericana de Bibliografía*, v. 42, no. 3 (1992), pp. 504 – 505.

Graham, Richard, ed. *Brazil and the World System* reviewed by Nancy Priscilla S. Naro. *The Americas*, v. 50, no. 2 (Oct 93), pp. 286 – 287.

— *Brazil and the World System* reviewed by Kees de Groot. *European Review of Latin American and Caribbean Studies*, no. 53 (Dec 92), pp. 117 – 118.

Graham, Sandra Lauderdale. *House and Street: The Domestic World of Servants and Masters in Nineteenth-Century Rio de Janeiro* reviewed by Silvia Marina Arrom. *The Americas*, v. 49, no. 4 (Apr 93), pp. 553 – 555.

Gramajo de Martínez Moreno, Amalia and Hugo N. Martínez Moreno. *Rasgos del folklore de Santiago del Estero* reviewed by Félix Coluccio. *Folklore Americano*, no. 53 (Jan – June 92), pp. 179 – 180.

Granado, Javier del. *Obras completas* reviewed by Pedro de Anasagasti. *Signo*, no. 35, Nueva época (Jan – Apr 92), pp. 209 – 211.

Granda, Germán de. *Sociedad, historia y lengua en el Paraguay* reviewed by Rafael Rodríguez Marín. *Anuario de Letras (Mexico)*, v. 30 (1992), pp. 265 – 269.

Graniela-Rodríguez, Magda. *El papel del lector en la novela mexicana contemporánea: José Emilio Pacheco y Salvador Elizondo* reviewed by Roberto Bravo. *Hispania (USA)*, v. 76, no. 2 (May 93), pp. 287 – 288.

Grasmuck, Sherri and Patricia R. Pessar. *Between Two Islands: Dominican International Migration* reviewed by André Corten. *Canadian Journal of Latin American and Caribbean Studies*, v. 17, no. 34 (1992), pp. 138 – 141.

Gratius, Susanne. *El MERCOSUR y la Comunidad Europea: una guía para la investigación* (Review). *Integración Latinoamericana*, v. 18, no. 195 (Nov 93), pp. 57 – 58.

Graulich, Michel. *Quetzalcóatl y el espejismo de Tollan* reviewed by Bernadette Alvarez-Ferrandiz. *Caravelle*, no. 59 (1992), pp. 295 – 297.

Graziano, Frank. *Divine Violence: Spectacle, Psychosexuality, and Radical Christianity in the Argentine "Dirty War"* reviewed by Ronaldo Munck. *Bulletin of Latin American Research*, v. 12, no. 1 (Jan 93), pp. 119 – 120.

— *Divine Violence: Spectacle, Psychosexuality, and Radical Christianity in the Argentine "Dirty War"* reviewed by Donald C. Hodges. *Hispanic American Historical Review*, v. 73, no. 3 (Aug 93), pp. 513 – 514.

— *Divine Violence: Spectacle, Psychosexuality, and Radical Christianity in the Argentine "Dirty War"* reviewed by Alberto Ciria. *Revista Interamericana de Bibliografía*, v. 42, no. 3 (1992), pp. 503 – 504.

Green, Cecilia. *The World Market Factory: A Study of Enclave Industrialization in the Eastern Caribbean and Its Impact on Women Workers* reviewed by Nan Wiegersma. *Journal of Developing Areas*, v. 27, no. 2 (Jan 93), pp. 269 – 270.

Greenberg, James B. *Blood Ties: Life and Violence in Rural Mexico* reviewed by Richard N. Adams. *Mesoamérica (USA)*, v. 13, no. 23 (June 92), pp. 196 – 200.

Greenblatt, Stephen Jay, ed. *New World Encounters* reviewed by Lee A. Daniel. *Hispania (USA)*, v. 76, no. 4 (Dec 93), pp. 738 – 739.

Greenleaf, Richard E. and Janin Benedict Warren. *Gonzalo Gómez, primer poblador español de Guayangareo (Morelia): proceso inquisitorial* translated by Alvaro Ochoa S. Reviewed by Frederick P. Bowser. *The Americas*, v. 49, no. 4 (Apr 93), pp. 544 – 545.

Gregori, Maria Filomena. *Cenas e queixas: um estudo sobre mulheres, relações violentas e a prática feminista* reviewed by Danielle Ardaillon (Review entitled "Facetas do feminino"). *Estudos Feministas*, v. 1, no. 2 (1993), pp. 487 – 489.

— *Cenas e queixas: um estudo sobre mulheres, relações violentas e a prática feminista* reviewed by Wânia Pasinato Izumino. *Revista Brasileira de Ciências Sociais*, v. 8, no. 22 (June 93), pp. 145 – 146.

— *Cenas e queixas: um estudo sobre mulheres, relações violentas e a prática feminista* (Review). *Vozes*, v. 87, no. 4 (July – Aug 93), p. 99.

Gregory, Desmond. *Brute New World: The Rediscovery of Latin America in the Early Nineteenth Century* reviewed by Jason Wilson. *Journal of Latin American Studies*, v. 25, no. 3 (Oct 93), pp. 656 – 657.

Gresores, Gabriela and Carlos María Birocco. *Arrendamientos, desalojos y subordinación campesina: Buenos Aires, siglo XVIII* reviewed by Carlos G. A. Bulcourf. *Todo Es Historia*, v. 27, no. 313 (Aug 93), p. 71. Il.

Griffin, Gillett Good and Elizabeth P. Benson, eds. *Maya Iconography* reviewed by Martha J. Macri. *Mesoamérica (USA)*, v. 13, no. 24 (Dec 92), pp. 490 – 492.

Griffin, Patricia C. *Mullet on the Beach: The Minorcans of Florida, 1768 – 1788* reviewed by Amy Turner Bushnell. *The Americas*, v. 49, no. 4 (Apr 93), pp. 550 – 551.

Griffith, James S. *Beliefs and Holy Places: A Spiritual Geography of the Pimería Alta* reviewed by Marth L. Henderson. *Geographical Review*, v. 83, no. 3 (July 93), pp. 334 – 336.

— *Beliefs and Holy Places: A Spiritual Geography of the Pimería Alta* reviewed by Martha L. Henderson (Review entitled "What Is Spiritual Geography?"). *Geographical Review*, v. 83, no. 4 (Oct 93), pp. 469 – 472.

Grizzolle Gómez, Juan. *La creación literaria en los niños: cómo estimular la creatividad* reviewed by Alberto Gómez Martínez. *La Educación (USA)*, v. 36, no. 111 – 113 (1992), pp. 294 – 295.

Grmek, Mirko Drazen. *Historia del SIDA* reviewed by Mario Bronfman and Héctor Gómez Dantés. *Plural (Mexico)*, v. 22, no. 265 (Oct 93), pp. 76 – 77.

Groof, Bard de and Thomas Werner, eds. *Rebelión y resistencia en el mundo hispánico del siglo XVII: actos del Coloquio Internacional Lovaina, 20 – 23 de noviembre de 1991* reviewed by Clara López Beltrán. *Hispanic American Historical Review*, v. 73, no. 4 (Nov 93), pp. 689 – 690.

Groot de Mahecha, Ana María and Eva María Hooykaas. *Intento de delimitación del territorio de los grupos étnicos pastos y quillacingas en el altiplano nariñense* reviewed by María Clemencia Ramírez de Jara. *Revista Colombiana de Antropología*, v. 29 (1992), pp. 242 – 246. Bibl.

Grove, David C. and Robert James Sharer, eds. *Regional Perspectives on the Olmec* reviewed by Michael Love. *Mesoamérica (USA)*, v. 13, no. 23 (June 92), pp. 209 – 213.

Gruzinski, Serge. *L'Amérique de la conquête peinte par les indiens de Mexique* reviewed by Marie Cécile Bénassy-Berling (Review entitled "Notas sobre el quinto centenario en Francia"). *Colonial Latin American Review*, v. 2, no. 1 – 2 (1993), pp. 269 – 272.

Guedes, Max Justo, ed. *História naval brasileira, vol. II: As guerras holandesas no mar* reviewed by Ramón Ezquerra Abadía. *Revista de Indias*, v. 53, no. 197 (Jan – Apr 93), pp. 110 – 111.

Guerra, Rubi. *El mar invisible* reviewed by Juvenal López Ruiz. *Revista Nacional de Cultura (Venezuela)*, v. 53, no. 285 (Apr – June 92), p. 248.

Guerra-Cunningham, Lucía. *Frutos extraños* reviewed by Ignacio Valente. *Atenea (Chile)*, no. 467 (1993), pp. 265 – 267.

— *Frutos extraños* reviewed by Lilianet Brintrup. *Letras Femeninas*, v. 19, no. 1 – 2 (Spring – Fall 93), pp. 148 – 149.

Guerreiro, Ramiro Elysio Saraiva. *Lembranças de um empregado do Itamaraty* reviewed by Alexandra de Mello e Silva (Review entitled "História e histórias da política externa brasileira"). *Estudos Históricos*, v. 6, no. 12 (July – Dec 93), pp. 285 – 290.

Guerrero, Juan Agustín. *La música ecuatoriana desde su origen hasta 1875* (Review of a reprint of the 1876 original). *Inter-American Music Review*, v. 13, no. 1 (Fall – Winter 92), pp. 109 – 111. Facs.

Guerrero Orozco, Omar. *El estado en la era de la modernización* reviewed by Gabriel Corona Armenta. *Revista Mexicana de Ciencias Políticas y Sociales*, v. 38, Nueva época, no. 153 (July – Sept 93), pp. 213 – 218.

Guest, Iain. *Behind the Disappearances: Argentina's Dirty War against Human Rights and the United Nations* reviewed by Erick Bridoux. *Journal of Inter-American Studies and World Affairs*, v. 34, no. 4 (Winter 92 – 93), pp. 257 – 262.

Guevara Niebla, Gilberto and Néstor García Canclini, eds. *La educación y la cultura ante el Tratado de Libre Comercio* reviewed by Fernando de Mateo (Review entitled "El jalón del TLC"). *Nexos*, v. 16, no. 189 (Sept 93), pp. 66 – 67.

Guicharnaud-Tollis, Michèle. *L'émergence du noir dans le roman cubain du XIXᵉ siècle* reviewed by Paul Estrade. *Caravelle*, no. 59 (1992), pp. 278 – 280.

— *L'émergence du noir dans le roman cubain du XIXᵉ siècle* reviewed by Paul Estrade. *Revista de Indias*, v. 53, no. 197 (Jan – Apr 93), pp. 108 – 109.

Guillén, Jorge and Pedro Salinas. *Pedro Salinas y Jorge Guillén: correspondencia, 1923 – 1951* edited by Andrés Soria Olmedo. Reviewed by Jean Cross Newman. *Revista Canadiense de Estudios Hispánicos*, v. 17, no. 3 (Spring 93), pp. 567 – 569.

Guillet, David. *Covering Ground: Communal Water Management and the State in the Peruvian Highlands* reviewed by Evelyne Mesclier. *Revista Andina*, v. 11, no. 1 (July 93), pp. 247 – 249.

Guimarães, Roberto Pereira. *The Ecopolitics of Development in the Third World: Politics and Environment in Brazil* reviewed by Margaret E. Keck. *Hispanic American Historical Review*, v. 73, no. 1 (Feb 93), p. 171.

Gunther, Richard and John Higley, eds. *Elites and Democratic Consolidation in Latin America and Southern Europe* reviewed by Richard Gillespie. *Bulletin of Latin American Research*, v. 12, no. 2 (May 93), pp. 235 – 236.

— *Elites and Democratic Consolidation in Latin America and Southern Europe* reviewed by Eric Hershberg. *Hispanic American Historical Review*, v. 73, no. 2 (May 93), pp. 298 – 299.

— *Elites and Democratic Consolidation in Latin America and Southern Europe* reviewed by Troy M. Bollinger. *Journal of Inter-American Studies and World Affairs*, v. 35, no. 1 (1993), pp. 158 – 166.

— *Elites and Democratic Consolidation in Latin America and Southern Europe* reviewed by Laura A. Hastings. *Journal of Latin American Studies*, v. 25, no. 1 (Feb 93), pp. 212 – 214.

Gutiérrez, Gustavo. *En busca de los pobres de Jesucristo* reviewed by Carlos Garatea Grau (Review entitled "Por la vida y la libertad"). *Debate (Peru)*, v. 16, no. 72 (Mar – May 93), p. 63. Il.

— *En busca de los pobres de Jesuscristo: el pensamiento de Bartolomé de las Casas* reviewed by Aníbal Edwards. *Mensaje*, v. 42, no. 417 (Mar – Apr 93), pp. 109 – 110.

Gutiérrez, Miguel. *La destrucción del reino* reviewed by Oscar Malca (Review entitled "La historia sin fin"). *Debate (Peru)*, v. 15, no. 71 (Nov 92 – Jan 93), pp. 76 – 77. Il.

Gutiérrez, Miguel Angel, ed. *Integración: experiencia en Europa y América Latina* (Review). *Integración Latinoamericana*, v. 18, no. 193 (Sept 93), p. 75.

Guy, Alain. *Panorama de la philosophie ibéro-américaine* reviewed by Solomon Lipp. *Revista Canadiense de Estudios Hispánicos,* v. 17, no. 1 (Fall 92), pp. 215 – 218.

Guy, Donna Jane. *Sex and Danger in Buenos Aires: Prostitution, Family, and Nation in Argentina* reviewed by Sandra McGee Deutsch. *The Americas,* v. 49, no. 3 (Jan 93), pp. 411 – 412.

— *Sex and Danger in Buenos Aires: Prostitution, Family, and Nation in Argentina* reviewed by Kristin Ruggiero. *Hispanic American Historical Review,* v. 73, no. 1 (Feb 93), p. 165.

— *Sex and Danger in Buenos Aires: Prostitution, Family, and Nation in Argentina* reviewed by Paula Alonso. *Journal of Latin American Studies,* v. 25, no. 1 (Feb 93), pp. 198 – 200.

— *Sex and Danger in Buenos Aires: Prostitution, Family, and Nation in Argentina* reviewed by K. Lynn Stoner (Review entitled "Whores, Witches, and Unwed Mothers: Recent Scholarship on the Control of Sexuality"). *Studies in Latin American Popular Culture,* v. 12 (1993), pp. 207 – 214.

Guzmán, Humberto. *Los buscadores de la dicha* reviewed by Ismael Pérez (Review entitled "La vigilia de la dicha"). *Plural (Mexico),* v. 22, no. 258 (Mar 93), pp. 75 – 76.

Guzmán, Luis Humberto. *Políticos en uniforme: un balance del poder del EPS* reviewed by Carlos M. Vilas. *Journal of Latin American Studies,* v. 25, no. 3 (Oct 93), pp. 672 – 674.

Haces, Carlos and Marco Antonio Pulido, eds. *José Guadalupe Posada y el amor: para iluminar* reviewed by J. León Helguera (Review entitled "José Guadalupe Posada Yet Again"). *Studies in Latin American Popular Culture,* v. 12 (1993), pp. 203 – 206.

Haggard, Stephan. *Pathways from the Periphery* reviewed by Henry J. Bruton. *Economic Development and Cultural Change,* v. 41, no. 4 (July 93), pp. 883 – 886.

Hahner, June Edith. *Emancipating the Female Sex: The Struggle for Women's Rights in Brazil, 1850 – 1940* reviewed by Marianne Schmink. *Hispanic American Historical Review,* v. 73, no. 3 (Aug 93), pp. 514 – 515.

— *Emancipating the Female Sex: The Struggle for Women's Rights in Brazil, 1850 – 1940* reviewed by Kathleen J. Higgins. *Luso-Brazilian Review,* v. 30, no. 1 (Summer 93), pp. 145 – 146.

Hale, Charles Adams. *La transformación del liberalismo en México a fines del siglo XIX* reviewed by David Aylett. *Vuelta,* v. 17, no. 204 (Nov 93), pp. 41 – 42.

Halebsky, Sandor and John M. Kirk, eds. *Cuba in Transition: Crisis and Transformation* reviewed by Nicolás Sánchez. *Cuban Studies/Estudios Cubanos,* v. 23 (1993), pp. 210 – 213.

— *Cuba in Transition: Crisis and Transformation* reviewed by Frank T. Fitzgerald. *Journal of Latin American Studies,* v. 25, no. 1 (Feb 93), pp. 219 – 220.

Hall, Neville A. T. *Slave Society in the Danish West Indies: St. Thomas, St. John, and St. Croix* edited by Barry W. Higman with a foreword by Kamau Brathwaite. Reviewed by Keith Mason. *Bulletin of Latin American Research,* v. 12, no. 2 (May 93), pp. 218 – 219.

— *Slave Society in the Danish West Indies: St. Thomas, St. John, and St. Croix* edited by Barry W. Higman with a foreword by Kamau Brathwaite. Reviewed by Bonham C. Richardson. *Caribbean Geography,* v. 3, no. 4 (Sept 92), pp. 275 – 276.

— *Slave Society in the Danish West Indies: St. Thomas, St. John, and St. Croix* reviewed by William A. Harris. *Social and Economic Studies,* v. 41, no. 3 (Sept 92), pp. 174 – 179.

Ham, Sam H. *Environmental Interpretation: A Practical Guide for People with Big Ideas and Small Budgets/Interpretación ambiental: una guía práctica . . .* reviewed by Martin Groebel. *La Educación (USA),* v. 37, no. 115 (1993), pp. 422 – 423.

Ham-Chande, Roberto and John R. Weeks, eds. *Demographic Dynamics of the U.S. – Mexico Border* reviewed by Ellwyn Stoddard. *Journal of Borderlands Studies,* v. 8, no. 1 (Spring 93), pp. 119 – 124. Bibl.

Hamill, Hugh M., Jr., ed. *Caudillos: Dictators in Spanish America,* revised edition. Reviewed by Stuart F. Voss. *Hispanic American Historical Review,* v. 73, no. 2 (May 93), pp. 321 – 322.

Hammond, Norman, ed. *Cuello: An Early Maya Community in Belize* reviewed by Paul F. Healy. *Latin American Antiquity,* v. 4, no. 3 (Sept 93), pp. 295 – 297.

Hándal, Schafik Jorge and Carlos María Vilas. *The Socialist Option in Central America: Two Reassessments* (Review). *NACLA Report on the Americas,* v. 27, no. 3 (Nov – Dec 93), p. 48.

Handelsman, Michael Howard. *Ideario de Benjamín Carrión* reviewed by José Otero. *Chasqui,* v. 22, no. 1 (May 93), p. 105.

Hanisch Espíndola, Walter. *El latín en Chile* reviewed by Sergio Martínez Baeza. *Boletín de la Academia Chilena de la Historia,* v. 58 – 59, no. 102 (1991 – 1992), pp. 559 – 560.

Hanks, William F. *Referential Practice: Language and Lived Space among the Maya* reviewed by John M. Watanabe. *Mesoamérica (USA),* v. 13, no. 23 (June 92), pp. 201 – 205. Charts.

Hanks, William F. and Don Stephen Rice, eds. *Word and Image in Maya Culture: Explorations in Language, Writing, and Representation* reviewed by Stephen D. Houston. *Mesoamérica (USA),* v. 13, no. 23 (June 92), pp. 191 – 193.

— *Word and Image in Maya Culture: Explorations in Language, Writing, and Representation* reviewed by Luis T. Sanz. *Revista Española de Antropología Americana,* v. 23 (1993), pp. 260 – 262.

Hann, John H., ed. *Missions to the Calusa* reviewed by Amy Turner Bushnell. *The Americas,* v. 49, no. 4 (Apr 93), pp. 548 – 549.

Harding, Richard. *Amphibious Warfare in the Eighteenth Century: The British Expedition to the West Indies, 1740 – 1742* reviewed by Christon I. Archer. *Hispanic American Historical Review,* v. 73, no. 2 (May 93), pp. 317 – 319.

Hardoy, Jorge Enrique. *Cartografía urbana colonial de América Latina y el Caribe* reviewed by María Elena Ducci. *EURE,* v. 19, no. 58 (Oct 93), pp. 87 – 88.

Hargreaves, Clare. *Snowfields: The War on Cocaine in the Andes* reviewed by Madeleine Barbara Léons. *Journal of Latin American Studies,* v. 25, no. 2 (May 93), pp. 422 – 423.

Harris, Claire. *Drawing Down a Daughter* reviewed by Andrew Salkey. *World Literature Today,* v. 67, no. 2 (Spring 93), pp. 435 – 436.

Harris, Olivia et al, eds. *La participación indígena en los mercados surandinos: estrategias y reproducción social, siglos XVI a XX* reviewed by Richard Warren. *Revista Andina,* v. 10, no. 2 (Dec 92), pp. 545 – 546.

Harris, Richard L. *Marxism, Socialism, and Democracy in Latin America* reviewed by Carlos M. Vilas. *Journal of Latin American Studies,* v. 25, no. 1 (Feb 93), p. 215.

Hart, Graham and Mike Morrissey. *Practical Skills in Caribbean Geography, Book 1: Grade 8 – Basic CXC and Book 2: Grade 10 – General CXC* reviewed by Laurence Neuville. *Caribbean Geography,* v. 3, no. 4 (Sept 92), pp. 279 – 280.

Hartlyn, Jonathan et al, eds. *The United States and Latin America in the 1990s: Beyond the Cold War* reviewed by David Ryan. *Journal of Latin American Studies,* v. 25, no. 3 (Oct 93), pp. 691 – 692.

Harvey, Edwin R. *Derecho cultural latinoamericano: Sudamérica y Panamá* reviewed by Juan Carlos Torchia Estrada. *La Educación (USA),* v. 37, no. 114 (1993), pp. 158 – 159.

Harvey, Herbert R., ed. *Land and Politics in the Valley of Mexico: A Two Thousand Year Perspective* reviewed by Wayne Osborn. *The Americas,* v. 49, no. 4 (Apr 93), pp. 542 – 544.

— *Land and Politics in the Valley of Mexico: A Two Thousand Year Perspective* reviewed by Jesús Monjarás-Ruiz. *Historia Mexicana,* v. 42, no. 1 (July – Sept 92), pp. 144 – 152.

— *Land and Politics in the Valley of Mexico: A Two Thousand Year Perspective* reviewed by Michael E. Smith. *Latin American Antiquity,* v. 4, no. 1 (Mar 93), pp. 97 – 98.

Harwich Vallenilla, Nikita. *Histoire du chocolat* reviewed by Teodoro Hampe Martínez. *Cuadernos Americanos,* no. 41, Nueva época (Sept – Oct 93), pp. 235 – 237.

Haskett, Robert Stephen. *Indigenous Rulers: An Ethnohistory of Town Government in Colonial Cuernavaca* reviewed by Eric Van Young. *Journal of Latin American Studies,* v. 25, no. 3 (Oct 93), pp. 653 – 654.

Hassler, Peter. *Menschenopfer bei den Azteken?: Eine quellen- und ideologiekritische Studie* reviewed by Norbert Rehrmann. *Iberoamericana,* v. 17, no. 49 (1993), pp. 95 – 96.

Hayashi Martínez, Laureano. *La educación mexicana en cifras* reviewed by Norma Ilse Veloz Avila. *El Cotidiano,* v. 8, no. 51 (Nov – Dec 92), pp. 115 – 116.

Heath, Roy Aubrey Kelvin. *From the Heat of the Day* reviewed by Cyril Dabydeen. *World Literature Today,* v. 67, no. 4 (Fall 93), p. 876.

— *The Murderer* reviewed by Cyril Dabydeen. *World Literature Today,* v. 67, no. 2 (Spring 93), pp. 427 – 428. II.

Heaven Born Mérida and Its Destiny: 'The Book of Chilam Balam of Chumayel' edited and translated by Munro S. Edmonson. Reviewed by Enrique Sam Colop. *Mesoamérica (USA),* v. 13, no. 23 (June 92), pp. 194 – 196.

Helguera, Luis Ignacio. *Minotauro* reviewed by David Medina Portillo. *Vuelta,* v. 17, no. 200 (July 93), p. 61.

Heller, Lynette and Frederick Joseph Bove, eds. *New Frontiers in the Archaeology of the Pacific Coast of Southern Mesoamerica* reviewed by Molly R. Mignon. *Latin American Antiquity,* v. 4, no. 1 (Mar 93), pp. 98 – 99.

Hellinger, Daniel Charles. *Venezuela: Tarnished Democracy* reviewed by Steve Ellner. *Journal of Developing Areas,* v. 28, no. 1 (Oct 93), pp. 142 – 143.

Helwege, Ann and Eliana Anastasia Cardoso. *Cuba after Communism* reviewed by Nicolás Sánchez. *Cuban Studies/Estudios Cubanos,* v. 23 (1993), pp. 210 – 213.

— *Latin America's Economy: Diversity, Trends, and Conflicts* reviewed by Antonio Jorge and Raúl Moncarz. *Journal of Developing Areas,* v. 27, no. 4 (July 93), pp. 552 – 553.

— *Latin America's Economy: Diversity, Trends, and Conflicts* reviewed by David Hojman. *Journal of Latin American Studies,* v. 25, no. 1 (Feb 93), pp. 209 – 211.

Henige, David P. *In Search of Columbus: The Sources for the First Voyage* reviewed by Rosalind Z. Rock. *Colonial Latin American Historical Review,* v. 1, no. 1 (Fall 92), pp. 117 – 118.

— *In Search of Columbus: The Sources for the First Voyage* reviewed by Margarita Zamora (Review entitled "Searching for Columbus in the Quincentennial: Three Recent Books on the Discovery"). *Colonial Latin American Review,* v. 2, no. 1 – 2 (1993), pp. 261 – 267.

Heredia, Luis D. and Beatriz Bixio. *Distancia cultural y lingüística: el fracaso escolar en poblaciones rurales del oeste de la provincia de Córdoba* (Review). *La Educación (USA),* v. 36, no. 111 – 113 (1992), pp. 296 – 298.

Herms, Dieter. *Die zeitgenössische Literatur der Chicanos, 1959 – 1988 (Contemporary Chicano Literature, 1959 – 1988)* reviewed by Horst Tonn. *The Americas Review,* v. 19, no. 3 – 4 (Winter 91), pp. 149 – 150.

Hernández, Guillermo E. *Chicano Satire: A Study in Literary Culture* reviewed by Chuck Tatum (Review entitled "A New Standard for Chicano Literary Scholarship"). *Bilingual Review/Revista Bilingüe,* v. 18, no. 1 (Jan – Apr 93), pp. 64 – 74.

Hernández, José M. *Cuba and the United States: Intervention and Militarism, 1868 – 1933* reviewed by Jules R. Benjamin. *Cuban Studies/Estudios Cubanos,* v. 23 (1993), pp. 213 – 215.

Hernández, Rafael and Joseph S. Tulchin, eds. *Cuba and the United States: Will the Cold War in the Caribbean End?* reviewed by Jorge I. Domínguez. *Cuban Studies/Estudios Cubanos,* v. 23 (1993), pp. 215 – 217.

Hernández Aparicio, Pilar and Paulino Castañeda Delgado. *La inquisición en Lima, tomo I: 1570 – 1635* reviewed by Hilda Raquel Zapico. *Revista de Historia de América,* no. 113 (Jan – June 92), pp. 161 – 165.

Hernández Chávez, Alicia and Manuel Miño Grijalva, eds. *Cincuenta años de historia en México,* vols. I y II, reviewed by Harold Dana Sims. *Hispanic American Historical Review,* v. 73, no. 4 (Nov 93), pp. 668 – 670.

Hernández Cruz, Víctor

See
  Cruz, Victor Hernandez

Hernández Rodríguez, Rogelio. *La formación del político mexicano: el caso de Carlos A. Madrazo* reviewed by Roderic Ai Camp. *Hispanic American Historical Review,* v. 73, no. 2 (May 93), pp. 334 – 335.

Hernández Sánchez-Barba, Mario et al, eds. *Reformismo y progreso en América, 1840 – 1905:* Vol. XV of *Historia general de España y América* reviewed by Antonio Santamaría García. *Anuario de Estudios Americanos,* v. 49, Suppl. 2 (1992), pp. 246 – 247.

Herrera Balharry, Eugenio. *Los alemanes y el estado cafetalero* reviewed by Gertrud Peters Solórzano (Review entitled "Café, familia y política"). *Revista de Historia (Costa Rica),* no. 25 (Jan – June 92), pp. 239 – 242.

Herrera y Ogazón, Alba. *El arte musical en México* (Review of a reprint of the 1917 original). *Inter-American Music Review,* v. 13, no. 1 (Fall – Winter 92), p. 111.

Herring, George C. and Kenneth M. Coleman, eds. *Understanding the Central American Crisis: Sources of Conflict, U.S. Policy, and Options for Peace* reviewed by Orlando Peña. *Canadian Journal of Latin American and Caribbean Studies,* v. 17, no. 34 (1992), pp. 129 – 130.

Herzog, Lawrence Arthur, ed. *Changing Boundaries in the Americas: New Perspectives on the U.S. – Mexican, Central American, and South American Borders* reviewed by Elizabeth Méndez Mungaray. *Frontera Norte,* v. 4, no. 8 (July – Dec 92), pp. 173 – 176.

— *Changing Boundaries in the Americas: New Perspectives on the U.S. – Mexican, Central American, and South American Borders* reviewed by Michael G. Ellis. *Journal of Borderlands Studies,* v. 8, no. 1 (Spring 93), pp. 125 – 127. Bibl.

Hewitt, Warren Edward. *Base Christian Communities and Social Change in Brazil* reviewed by Joan B. Anderson. *Journal of Developing Areas,* v. 27, no. 4 (July 93), pp. 573 – 574.

— *Base Christian Communities and Social Change in Brazil* reviewed by Michael LaRosa (Review entitled "Religion in a Changing Latin America: A Review"). *Journal of Inter-American Studies and World Affairs,* v. 34, no. 4 (Winter 92 – 93), pp. 245 – 255. Bibl.

Heyman, Josiah McConnell. *Life and Labor on the Border: Working People of Northeastern Sonora, Mexico, 1886 – 1986* reviewed by Miguel Tinker Salas. *The Americas,* v. 49, no. 4 (Apr 93), pp. 556 – 558.

— *Life and Labor on the Border: Working People of Northeastern Sonora, Mexico, 1886 – 1986* reviewed by Barry Carr. *Hispanic American Historical Review,* v. 73, no. 3 (Aug 93), pp. 526 – 528.

— *Life and Labor on the Border: Working People of Northeastern Sonora, Mexico, 1886 – 1986* reviewed by Evelyn Hu-Dehart. *International Migration Review,* v. 27, no. 3 (Fall 93), pp. 648 – 649.

Hicks, D. Emily. *Border Writing: The Multidimensional Text* reviewed by Kavita Panjabi. *Letras Femeninas,* v. 19, no. 1 – 2 (Spring – Fall 93), pp. 140 – 143.

— *Border Writing: The Multidimensional Text* reviewed by Rafael H. Mojica. *World Literature Today,* v. 67, no. 1 (Winter 93), pp. 243 – 244.

Higley, John and Richard Gunther, eds. *Elites and Democratic Consolidation in Latin America and Southern Europe* reviewed by Richard Gillespie. *Bulletin of Latin American Research,* v. 12, no. 2 (May 93), pp. 235 – 236.

— *Elites and Democratic Consolidation in Latin America and Southern Europe* reviewed by Eric Hershberg. *Hispanic American Historical Review,* v. 73, no. 2 (May 93), pp. 298 – 299.

— *Elites and Democratic Consolidation in Latin America and Southern Europe* reviewed by Troy M. Bollinger. *Journal of Inter-American Studies and World Affairs,* v. 35, no. 1 (1993), pp. 158 – 166.

— *Elites and Democratic Consolidation in Latin America and Southern Europe* reviewed by Laura A. Hastings. *Journal of Latin American Studies,* v. 25, no. 1 (Feb 93), pp. 212 – 214.

Hilbert, Klaus. *Aspectos de la arqueología en el Uruguay* reviewed by Arno Alvarez Kern (Review entitled "Coleções arqueológicas e aspectos de arqueologia no Uruguai"). *Estudos Ibero-Americanos,* v. 18, no. 1 (July 92), pp. 105 – 108. Bibl.

Hilton, Stanley Eon. *Brazil and the Soviet Union Challenge, 1917 – 1947* reviewed by John W. F. Dulles. *The Americas,* v. 49, no. 3 (Jan 93), pp. 417 – 418.

Himmerich y Valencia, Robert. *The Encomenderos of New Spain, 1521 – 1555* reviewed by J. Benedict Warren. *The Americas,* v. 50, no. 2 (Oct 93), pp. 272 – 273.

— *The Encomenderos of New Spain, 1521 – 1555* reviewed by Bernard Grunberg. *Caravelle,* no. 60 (1993), pp. 139 – 140.

— *The Encomenderos of New Spain, 1521 – 1555* reviewed by Robert McGeagh. *Colonial Latin American Historical Review,* v. 2, no. 1 (Winter 93), pp. 118 – 120.

— *The Encomenderos of New Spain, 1521 – 1555* reviewed by Murdo J. Macleod. *Hispanic American Historical Review,* v. 73, no. 1 (Feb 93), pp. 149 – 150.

Hinds, Harold E., Jr. and Charles M. Tatum. *Not Just for Children: The Mexican Comic Book in the Late 1960s and 1970s* reviewed by Helen Delpar. *Hispanic American Historical Review,* v. 73, no. 4 (Nov 93), pp. 670 – 671.

— *Not Just for Children: The Mexican Comic Book in the Late 1960s and 1970s* reviewed by Cornelia Butler Flora. *Revista Interamericana de Bibliografía,* v. 42, no. 4 (1992), pp. 657 – 658.

Hiriart, Hugo. *La destrucción de todas las cosas* reviewed by Roberto Pliego (Review entitled "La última carcajada"). *Nexos,* v. 16, no. 181 (Jan 93), p. 69.

— *El universo de Posada: estética de la obsolescencia* reviewed by J. León Helguera (Review entitled "José Guadalupe Posada Yet Again"). *Studies in Latin American Popular Culture,* v. 12 (1993), pp. 203 – 206.

History and Mythology of the Aztecs: The 'Codex Chimalpopoca' translated by John Bierhorst. Reviewed by David Johnson. *Colonial Latin American Historical Review,* v. 2, no. 1 (Winter 93), pp. 112 – 113.

Hoberman, Louisa Schell. *Mexico's Merchant Elite, 1590 – 1660: Silver, State, and Society* reviewed by Stanley J. Stein. *Hispanic American Historical Review,* v. 73, no. 1 (Feb 93), pp. 151 – 152.

— *Mexico's Merchant Elite, 1590 – 1660: Silver, State, and Society* reviewed by Gabriel Haslip-Viera. *Colonial Latin American Review,* v. 2, no. 1 – 2 (1993), pp. 296 – 298.

— *Mexico's Merchant Elite, 1590 – 1660: Silver, State, and Society* reviewed by Richard L. Garner. *Colonial Latin American Historical Review,* v. 2, no. 3 (Summer 93), pp. 369 – 371.

— *Mexico's Merchant Elite, 1590 – 1660: Silver, State, and Society* reviewed by Silvia C. Mallo. *Revista de Historia de América,* no. 113 (Jan – June 92), pp. 170 – 172.

Hoberman, Louisa Schell and Susan Migden Socolow, eds. *Cities and Society in Colonial Latin America* reviewed by Arij Ouweneel. *European Review of Latin American and Caribbean Studies,* no. 54 (June 93), pp. 125 – 126.

Hodges, Denise C. *Agricultural Intensification and Preshistoric Health in the Valley of Oaxaca, Mexico* reviewed by Dale L. Hutchinson. *Latin American Antiquity,* v. 4, no. 2 (June 93), pp. 200 – 201.

Hoffmann, Léon François. *Haïti: lettres et l'être* reviewed by Hal Wylie. *World Literature Today,* v. 67, no. 3 (Summer 93), pp. 657 – 658.

Hoffmann, Odile. *Tierras y territorio en Xico, Veracruz* reviewed by Hipólito Rodríguez. *Estudios Sociológicos,* v. 11, no. 31 (Jan – Apr 93), pp. 274 – 276.

Hofling, Charles Andrew. *Itza Maya Texts with a Grammatical Overview* reviewed by Barbara Edmonson. *Hispanic American Historical Review,* v. 73, no. 3 (Aug 93), pp. 498 – 499.

— *Itza Maya Texts with a Grammatical Overview* reviewed by Enrique Sam Colop. *Mesoamérica (USA),* v. 13, no. 24 (Dec 92), pp. 489 – 490.

Hojman A., David E., ed. *Change in the Chilean Countryside: From Pinochet to Aylwin and Beyond; The Proceedings of the 46th International Congress of Americanists, Amsterdam* reviewed by Walter Belik. *Journal of Latin American Studies,* v. 25, no. 3 (Oct 93), pp. 679 – 680.

Hollanda, Heloísa Buarque de, ed. *¿Y nosotras latinoamericanas?: estudos sobre gênero e raça* reviewed by Lena Lavinas (Review entitled "Contrapassos da latinidade"). *Estudos Feministas,* v. 1, no. 2 (1993), pp. 501 – 502.

Holt, Thomas C. *The Problem of Freedom: Race, Labor, and Politics in Jamaica and Britain, 1832 – 1938* reviewed by Alex Lichtenstein. *Hispanic American Historical Review,* v. 73, no. 2 (May 93), pp. 347 – 349.

Hooykaas, Eva María and Ana María Groot de Mahecha. *Intento de delimitación del territorio de los grupos étnicos pastos y quillacingas en el altiplano nariñense* reviewed by María Clemencia Ramírez de Jara. *Revista Colombiana de Antropología,* v. 29 (1992), pp. 242 – 246. Bibl.

Horn, James J. and Ida Altman. *"To Make America": European Emigration in the Early Modern Period* reviewed by Alan L. Karras. *The Americas,* v. 49, no. 3 (Jan 93), pp. 402 – 404.

— *"To Make America": European Emigration in the Early Modern Period* reviewed by Magnus Mörner. *Hispanic American Historical Review,* v. 73, no. 1 (Feb 93), pp. 130 – 132.

Horno Delgado, Asunción et al, eds. *Breaking Boundaries: Latina Writings and Critical Readings* reviewed by Miriam Bornstein. *Confluencia,* v. 8, no. 1 (Fall 92), pp. 177 – 179.

Horowitz, Joel. *Argentine Unions, the State, and the Rise of Perón* reviewed by Daniel J. Greenberg. *Hispanic American Historical Review,* v. 73, no. 1 (Feb 93), pp. 162 – 164.

Hourani, Albert and Nadim Shehadi, eds. *The Lebanese in the World: A Century of Emigration* reviewed by Jorge O. Bestene. *Journal of Latin American Studies,* v. 25, no. 3 (Oct 93), pp. 663 – 664.

Houtart, François and Geneviève Lemercinier. *El campesino como actor social: sociología de una comarca de Nicaragua* reviewed by Sergio Sarmiento Silva. *Revista Mexicana de Sociología,* v. 54, no. 3 (July – Sept 92), pp. 263 – 267.

Houwald, Götz Dieter, Freiherr von. *Mayangna = WIR: Zur Geschichte der Sumu-Indianer in Mittelamerika* reviewed by Wolfgang Haberland. *Mesoamérica (USA),* v. 13, no. 23 (June 92), pp. 217 – 218.

The Huarochiri Manuscript: A Testament of Ancient and Colonial Andean Religion translated by Frank Solomon and George L. Urioste. Reviewed by Karen Spalding. *The Americas,* v. 49, no. 3 (Jan 93), pp. 398 – 399.

Hünefeldt, Christine. *Lasmanuelos: vida cotidiana de una familia negra en la Lima del s. XIX* reviewed by Sara Mateos (Review entitled "Esclavitud urbana"). *Debate (Peru),* v. 15, no. 70 (Sept – Oct 92), pp. 67 – 68.

Huerta Martínez, Angel. *La enseñanza primaria en Cuba en el siglo XIX, 1812 – 1868* reviewed by Francisco Castillo Meléndez. *Anuario de Estudios Americanos,* v. 49, Suppl. 2 (1992), pp. 247 – 248.

Hulme, Peter and Neil L. Whitehead, eds. *Wild Majesty: Encounters with Caribs from Columbus to the Present Day; An Anthology* reviewed by Peter T. Bradley. *Bulletin of Latin American Research,* v. 12, no. 1 (Jan 93), pp. 111 – 112.

Hurtado, Liliana R. de. *La sucesión incaica: aproximación al mando y poder entre los incas a partir de la crónica de Betanzos* reviewed by Nicanor Domínguez Faura. *Revista Andina,* v. 11, no. 1 (July 93), pp. 250 – 251.

Husson, Patrick. *De la guerra a la rebelión: Huanta, siglo XIX* reviewed by Jaime Urrutia Ceruti. *Bulletin de l'Institut Français d'Etudes Andines,* v. 21, no. 3 (1992), pp. 1078 – 1082.

Ibáñez, Eduardo Alejandro. *Memorias de vértice* reviewed by Rodolfo Alonso. *Revista Nacional de Cultura (Venezuela),* v. 53, no. 285 (Apr – June 92), p. 242.

Ibáñez Montoya, María Victoria, ed. *La expedición Malaspina, 1789 – 1794, tomo IV: Trabajos científicos y correspondencia de Tadeo Haenke* reviewed by Oldrich Kaspar (Review translated by Eva Mánková). *Anuario de Estudios Americanos,* v. 50, no. 1 (1993), pp. 317 – 319. Bibl.

Ibargoyen Islas, Saúl. *Soñar la muerte* reviewed by Alejandro Expósito (Review entitled "Tal vez soñar"). *Plural (Mexico),* v. 22, no. 262 (July 93), pp. 78 – 79.

— *Soñar la muerte* reviewed by Marco T. Aguilera Garramuño. *Plural (Mexico),* v. 22, no. 267 (Dec 93), p. 86.

Ibargüengoitia, Jorge. *Autopsias rápidas* selected by Guillermo Sheridan. Reviewed by Elizabeth Corral Peña. *Caravelle,* no. 59 (1992), pp. 322 – 325.

Iglesias, Enrique V., ed. *El legado de Raúl Prebisch* (Review). *Integración Latinoamericana,* v. 18, no. 193 (Sept 93), pp. 77 – 79.

Iltis, André and Claude Dejoux, eds. *El lago Titicaca: síntesis del conocimiento limnológico actual* reviewed by Néstor Teves. *Bulletin de l'Institut Français d'Etudes Andines,* v. 21, no. 3 (1992), pp. 1075 – 1078.

Inda, Enrique S. *Los sobrevivientes del estrecho* reviewed by Carmen Vrljicak-Espaín. *Todo Es Historia,* v. 27, no. 312 (July 93), p. 75. Il.

Infante, Angel Gustavo. *Yo soy la rumba/I Am the Rumba* reviewed by Barbara Mujica (Review entitled "A Coming of Age"). *Américas,* v. 45, no. 5 (Sept – Oct 93), pp. 61 – 62. Il.

Informe sobre la situación económica de los países centroamericanos en 1992 (Review). *Integración Latinoamericana,* v. 18, no. 193 (Sept 93), p. 76.

Ireland, Rowan. *Kingdoms Come: Religion and Politics in Brazil* reviewed by Daniel H. Levine. *The Americas,* v. 49, no. 3 (Jan 93), pp. 419 – 421.

— *Kingdoms Come: Religion and Politics in Brazil* reviewed by David Lehmann. *Bulletin of Latin American Research,* v. 12, no. 3 (Sept 93), pp. 356 – 357.

— *Kingdoms Come: Religion and Politics in Brazil* reviewed by W. E. Hewitt. *Hispanic American Historical Review,* v. 73, no. 3 (Aug 93), pp. 516 – 517.

— *Kingdoms Come: Religion and Politics in Brazil* reviewed by Mark L. Grover. *Revista Interamericana de Bibliografía,* v. 42, no. 3 (1992), pp. 505 – 506.

Isbell, William Harris and Gordon Francis McEwan, ed. *Huari Administrative Structure: Prehistoric Monumental Architecture and State Government* reviewed by Mario A. Rivera. *Latin American Antiquity,* v. 4, no. 1 (Mar 93), pp. 95 – 96.

Israel, Giselle and Solange Dacach. *As rotas do Norplant: desvios da contracepção* reviewed by Angela Regina Cunha (Review entitled "Risco de vida"). *Estudos Feministas,* v. 1, no. 2 (1993), pp. 489 – 491.

Ita, Fernando de, ed. *Antología del teatro mexicano contemporáneo* reviewed by Hugo Gutiérrez Vega. *Cuadernos Hispanoamericanos,* no. 520 (Oct 93), pp. 113 – 118.

Jackson, Richard L. *The Afro-Spanish American Author, II: The 1980s; An Annotated Bibliography of Criticism* reviewed by Donald K. Gordon. *Revista Canadiense de Estudios Hispánicos,* v. 17, no. 2 (Winter 93), pp. 401 – 402.

Jaksic, Ivan and Paul Winter Drake, eds. *The Struggle for Democracy in Chile, 1982 – 1990* reviewed by Tom Wright. *The Americas,* v. 49, no. 4 (Apr 93), pp. 568 – 569.

— *The Struggle for Democracy in Chile, 1982 – 1990* reviewed by Robert H. Dix. *Journal of Developing Areas,* v. 28, no. 1 (Oct 93), pp. 115 – 116.

James, Dilmus D. and James L. Dietz, eds. *Progress toward Development in Latin America: From Prebisch to Technological Autonomy* reviewed by Markos J. Mamalakis. *Studies in Comparative International Development,* v. 27, no. 2 (Summer 92), pp. 106 – 108.

Jara, Alvaro and John Jay TePaske. *The Royal Treasuries of the Spanish Empire in America, Vol. IV: Eighteenth-Century Ecuador* reviewed by Franklin Pease G. Y. *Colonial Latin American Review*, v. 2, no. 1 – 2 (1993), pp. 311 – 312.

Jara, René and Nicholas Spadaccini, eds. *1492 – 1992: Re/Discovering Colonial Writing* reviewed by David A. Boruchoff. *Revista Canadiense de Estudios Hispánicos*, v. 17, no. 1 (Fall 92), pp. 207 – 209.

Jaramillo Buendía, Gladys et al, eds. *Indice de la narrativa ecuatoriana* reviewed by Carlos Orihuela. *Revista de Crítica Literaria Latinoamericana*, v. 19, no. 38 (July – Dec 93), pp. 413 – 415.

Jaramillo Levi, Enrique, ed. *When New Flowers Bloomed: Short Stories by Women Writers from Costa Rica and Panama* reviewed by Cynthia Tompkins. *World Literature Today*, v. 67, no. 1 (Winter 93), pp. 164 – 165. Il.

Jarquín Ortega, María Teresa. *Formación y desarrollo de un pueblo novohispano: Metepec en el valle de Toluca.* *Anuario de Estudios Americanos*, v. 49, Suppl. 1 (1992), pp. 254 – 256.

Jauberth, H. Rodrigo et al. *The Difficult Triangle: Mexico, Central America, and the United States*, a translation of *La triangulación Centroamérica – México – EUA.* Reviewed by Robert H. Holden. *Hispanic American Historical Review*, v. 73, no. 1 (Feb 93), pp. 192 – 194.

Jiménez de Báez, Yvette. *Juan Rulfo: del Páramo a la esperanza; una lectura crítica de su obra* reviewed by Luis Leal. *Hispanic Review*, v. 61, no. 2 (Spring 93), pp. 312 – 314.

Jiménez Pelayo, Agueda. *Haciendas y comunidades indígenas en el sur de Zacatecas* reviewed by Frédérique Langue. *Cahiers des Amériques Latines*, no. 13 (1992), pp. 182 – 183.

Jobet, Jorge. *Llueve sobre los poetas franceses y llueve en mi corazón* reviewed by Antonio Campaña. *Atenea (Chile)*, no. 465 – 466 (1992), pp. 384 – 386.

Johnson, John Randal, ed. *Tropical Paths: Essays on Modern Brazilian Literature* reviewed by Malcolm Silverman. *Hispania (USA)*, v. 76, no. 4 (Dec 93), pp. 739 – 740.

Johnson, Linton Kwesi. *Tings an Times* reviewed by Cyril Dabydeen. *World Literature Today*, v. 28, no. 2 (1993), pp. 219 – 220.

Johnson, Lyman L., ed. *The Problem of Order in Changing Societies: Essays on Crime and Policing in Argentina and Uruguay* reviewed by Carlos A. Mayo. *Revista de Indias*, v. 53, no. 197 (Jan – Apr 93), pp. 111 – 112.

Jonas, Susanne Leilani. *The Battle for Guatemala: Rebels, Death Squads, and U.S. Power* reviewed by B. H. Barlow. *Canadian Journal of Latin American and Caribbean Studies*, v. 17, no. 34 (1992), pp. 141 – 143.

— *The Battle for Guatemala: Rebels, Death Squads, and U.S. Power* reviewed by Alan C. Hunsaker (Review entitled "Guatemala: Small Country, Big Problems"). *Hispanic Journal of Behavioral Sciences*, v. 15, no. 3 (Aug 93), pp. 418 – 423.

Jonas, Susanne Leilani and Nancy Stein, eds. *Democracy in Latin America: Visions and Realities* reviewed by Eldon G. Kenworthy. *Hispanic American Historical Review*, v. 73, no. 2 (May 93), pp. 354 – 355.

Jones, Edwin. *Development Administration: Jamaican Adaptation* reviewed by Ian Boxill. *Social and Economic Studies*, v. 41, no. 3 (Sept 92), pp. 180 – 182.

Jones, Grant D. *Maya Resistance to Spanish Rule: Time and History on a Colonial Frontier* reviewed by J. C. Cambranes. *Mesoamérica (USA)*, v. 13, no. 23 (June 92), pp. 157 – 177. Bibl.

Jordan, Carl F., ed. *An Amazonian Rain Forest* reviewed by H. Tiessen (Review entitled "Amazonia"). *Interciencia*, v. 18, no. 4 (July – Aug 93), pp. 208 – 209.

Joseph, Gilbert Michael. *Revolución desde afuera: Yucatán, México y Estados Unidos, 1880 – 1924* translated by Eduardo L. Suárez. Reviewed by Othón Baños. *Estudios Sociológicos*, v. 11, no. 31 (Jan – Apr 93), pp. 265 – 270.

Joseph, Gilbert Michael and Jeffery T. Brannon, eds. *Land, Labor, and Capital in Modern Yucatán: Essays in Regional History and Political Economy* reviewed by Donald F. Stevens. *The Americas*, v. 49, no. 4 (Apr 93), pp. 558 – 559.

Juana Inés de la Cruz. *Antología poética* edited by Francisco Javier Cevallos. Reviewed by Georgina Sabat-Rivers. *Hispanic Review*, v. 61, no. 1 (Winter 93), pp. 124 – 125.

Juarroz, Roberto. *Poesía vertical: antología* edited and introduced by Francisco José Cruz Pérez. Reviewed by Alfredo García Valdez (Review entitled "La palabra vertical"). *Vuelta*, v. 17, no. 202 (Sept 93), pp. 49 – 50.

Julien, Catherine Jean. *Condesuyo: The Political Division of Territory under Inca and Spanish Rule* reviewed by Nicanor Domínguez. *Revista Andina*, v. 10, no. 2 (Dec 92), pp. 546 – 547.

Junquera, Carlos. *El chamanismo en el Amazonas* reviewed by Manuel Cerezo Lasne, Penélope Ranera Sánchez, and Javier Rubio Swift. *Revista Española de Antropología Americana*, v. 23 (1993), pp. 255 – 256.

Jurcich, Milenko Juan. *Lola Mora: el secreto de su sueño mineral* reviewed by Rodrigo Alcorta. *Todo Es Historia*, v. 26, no. 308 (Mar 93), p. 74. Il.

Kadir, Djelal. *Columbus and the Ends of the Earth: Europe's Prophetic Rhetoric as Conquering Ideology* reviewed by Margarita Zamora (Review entitled "Searching for Columbus in the Quincentennial: Three Recent Books on the Discovery"). *Colonial Latin American Review*, v. 2, no. 1 – 2 (1993), pp. 261 – 267.

— *Columbus and the Ends of the Earth: Europe's Prophetic Rhetoric as Conquering Ideology* reviewed by John Incledon. *Hispania (USA)*, v. 76, no. 2 (May 93), pp. 288 – 289.

— *Columbus and the Ends of the Earth: Europe's Prophetic Rhetoric as Conquering Ideology* reviewed by Martin Torodash. *Hispanic American Historical Review*, v. 73, no. 1 (Feb 93), p. 147.

Kalinsky, Beatriz and Willie Arrúe. *De "la médica" y el terapeuta: la gestión intercultural de la salud en el sur de la provincia del Neuquén* reviewed by P. Schraer. *La Educación (USA)*, v. 36, no. 111 – 113 (1992), pp. 281 – 282.

Kanellos, Nicholas Charles. *A History of Hispanic Theatre in the United States: Origins to 1940* reviewed by Joshua Al Mora. *Hispania (USA)*, v. 76, no. 1 (Mar 93), pp. 87 – 88.

Kappatos, Rigas and Pedro Lastra, eds. *Antología del cuento chileno* reviewed by Marina Catzaras. *Revista de Crítica Literaria Latinoamericana*, v. 19, no. 37 (Jan – June 93), pp. 392 – 396.

— *Antología del cuento peruano* reviewed by Marina Catzaras. *Revista de Crítica Literaria Latinoamericana*, v. 19, no. 37 (Jan – June 93), pp. 392 – 396.

Karlsson, Weine et al, eds. *Suecia – Latinoamérica: relaciones y cooperación* (Review). *Integración Latinoamericana*, v. 18, no. 195 (Nov 93), pp. 59 – 60.

Kay, Cristóbal and Patricio Silva, eds. *Development and Social Change in the Chilean Countryside: From the Pre-Land Reform Period to the Democratic Transition* reviewed by Chris Scott. *Journal of Latin American Studies*, v. 25, no. 2 (May 93), p. 407.

Keck, Margaret E. *The Workers' Party and Democratization in Brazil* reviewed by Thomas E. Skidmore. *Hispanic American Historical Review,* v. 73, no. 2 (May 93), pp. 325 – 326.

Kerr, Justin. *The Mayas Vase Book, Vol. III: A Corpus of Rollout Photographs of Maya Vases* reviewed by Alfonso Lacadena García-Gallo. *Revista Española de Antropología Americana,* v. 23 (1993), pp. 259 – 260.

Kerr, Lucille. *Reclaiming the Author: Figures and Fictions from Spanish America* reviewed by Nicolás Shumway. *Hispanic American Historical Review,* v. 73, no. 2 (May 93), pp. 297 – 298.

— *Reclaiming the Author: Figures and Fictions from Spanish America* reviewed by Pamela Bacarisse. *Revista Iberoamericana,* v. 59, no. 162 – 163 (Jan – June 93), pp. 365 – 368.

Khavisse, Miguel and Eduardo M. Basualdo. *El nuevo poder terrateniente* reviewed by Horacio Giberti. *Realidad Económica,* no. 117 (July – Aug 93), pp. 30 – 32.

King, Willard Fahrenkamp. *Juan Ruiz de Alarcón, letrado y dramaturgo: su mundo mexicano y español* reviewed by Charlotte Stein. *Hispanic Review,* v. 61, no. 2 (Spring 93), pp. 288 – 290.

Kingman Garcés, Eduardo, ed. *Ciudades de los Andes: visión histórica y contemporánea* reviewed by Scarlett O'Phelan Godoy. *Anuario de Estudios Americanos,* v. 49, Suppl. 2 (1992), p. 244.

Kirk, John M. *Politics and the Catholic Church in Nicaragua* reviewed by Daniel H. Levine. *Hispanic American Historical Review,* v. 73, no. 4 (Nov 93), pp. 722 – 724.

— *Politics and the Catholic Church in Nicaragua* reviewed by Laura Nuzzi O'Shaughnessy. *Journal of Latin American Studies,* v. 25, no. 3 (Oct 93), pp. 674 – 675.

Kirk, John M. and Sandor Halebsky, eds. *Cuba in Transition: Crisis and Transformation* reviewed by Nicolás Sánchez. *Cuban Studies/Estudios Cubanos,* v. 23 (1993), pp. 210 – 213.

— *Cuba in Transition: Crisis and Transformation* reviewed by Frank T. Fitzgerald. *Journal of Latin American Studies,* v. 25, no. 1 (Feb 93), pp. 219 – 220.

Klahn, Norma and Wilfrido Howard Corral, eds. *Los novelistas como críticos,* vol. I, reviewed by Sonia Mattalía. *Nuevo Texto Crítico,* v. 6, no. 11 (1993), pp. 259 – 261.

Kleinpenning, Jan M. G. *Rural Paraguay, 1870 – 1932* reviewed by Jerry W. Cooney. *Hispanic American Historical Review,* v. 73, no. 4 (Nov 93), pp. 710 – 711.

— *Rural Paraguay, 1870 – 1932* reviewed by R. Andrew Nickson. *Bulletin of Latin American Research,* v. 12, no. 2 (May 93), pp. 220 – 221.

— *Rural Paraguay, 1870 – 1932* reviewed by Vera Blinn Reber. *Journal of Latin American Studies,* v. 25, no. 2 (May 93), pp. 398 – 399.

Kliksberg, Bernardo, ed. *¿Cómo enfrentar la pobreza?: estrategias y experiencias organizacionales innovadoras* reviewed by Michel Mujica Ricardo. *Nueva Sociedad,* no. 124 (Mar – Apr 93), pp. 174 – 175.

Knapp, Gregory Walter. *Andean Ecology: Adaptive Dynamics in Ecuador* reviewed by Marie Price. *Geographical Review,* v. 83, no. 3 (July 93), pp. 341 – 343.

— *Andean Ecology: Adaptive Dynamics in Ecuador* reviewed by Arthur Morris. *Journal of Latin American Studies,* v. 25, no. 1 (Feb 93), p. 224.

Knouse, Stephen B. et al, eds. *Hispanics in the Workplace* reviewed by Peggy A. Lovell. *Hispanic American Historical Review,* v. 73, no. 2 (May 93), p. 301.

Kociancich, Vlady. *Los bajos del temor* reviewed by Christopher Domínguez. *Vuelta,* v. 17, no. 197 (Apr 93), p. 50.

— *Los bajos del temor* reviewed by David William Foster. *Chasqui,* v. 22, no. 1 (May 93), pp. 84 – 85.

Kofas, Jon V. *The Struggle for Legitimacy: Latin American Labor and the United States, 1930 – 1960* reviewed by Henry W. Berger. *Hispanic American Historical Review,* v. 73, no. 1 (Feb 93), pp. 196 – 197.

Kohut, Karl, ed. *De conquistadores y conquistados: realidad, justificación, representación* reviewed by Teodoro Hampe Martínez. *European Review of Latin American and Caribbean Studies,* no. 54 (June 93), pp. 116 – 118.

— *Der eroberte Kontinent: Historische Realität, Rechtfertigung und literarische Darstellung der Kolonisation Amerikas* reviewed by Gernot Stimmer. *Zeitschrift für Lateinamerika Wien,* no. 43 (1992), pp. 123 – 124.

Kozer, José. *Antología* reviewed by Víctor Sosa. *Vuelta,* v. 17, no. 204 (Nov 93), pp. 45 – 46.

Krotsch, Carlos P. and Cayetano De Lella Allevato, eds. *Congreso Pedagógico Nacional: evaluación y perspectivas* reviewed by Carlos Salá. *La Educación (USA),* v. 36, no. 111 – 113 (1992), pp. 285 – 291.

Kryzanek, Michael John. *Leaders, Leadership, and U.S. Policy in Latin America* reviewed by Johanna Mendelson-Forman. *Revista Interamericana de Bibliografía,* v. 42, no. 4 (1992), pp. 658 – 659.

Kübler, Manón. *Olympia* reviewed by Analy Lorenzo. *Revista Nacional de Cultura (Venezuela),* v. 53, no. 286 (July – Sept 92), pp. 261 – 262.

Kushigian, Julia A. *Orientalism in the Hispanic Tradition: In Dialogue with Borges, Paz, and Sarduy* reviewed by John Incledon. *Hispania (USA),* v. 76, no. 3 (Sept 93), pp. 483 – 484.

Lafourcade, Pedro D. *La autoevaluación institucional* reviewed by Luis O. Roggi. *La Educación (USA),* v. 37, no. 114 (1993), pp. 159 – 160.

Lago, Armando M. and Charles J. Brown. *The Politics of Psychiatry in Revolutionary Cuba* reviewed by Roberto Valero. *Cuban Studies/Estudios Cubanos,* v. 23 (1993), pp. 233 – 235.

Lagos-Pope, María-Inés. *H. A. Murena en sus ensayos y narraciones: de líder revisionista a marginado* reviewed by Fernando Reati. *Hispamérica,* v. 21, no. 63 (Dec 92), pp. 97 – 99.

Laguerre, Enrique Arturo. *Los gemelos* reviewed by Estelle Irizarry. *Hispania (USA),* v. 76, no. 1 (Mar 93), pp. 100 – 101.

Langer, Erick Detlef. *Economic Change and Rural Resistance in Southern Bolivia, 1880 – 1930* reviewed by Marie-Danielle Démelas-Bohy. *Caravelle,* no. 59 (1992), pp. 309 – 311.

Langue, Frédérique. *Mines, terres et société à Zacatecas (Mexique) de la fin du XVIIe siècle à l'indépendance* reviewed by Manuel Castillo Martos. *Anuario de Estudios Americanos,* v. 50, no. 1 (1993), pp. 319 – 322.

Laroche, Maximilien. *La découverte de l'Amérique par les américains* reviewed by Susanne Crosta. *Canadian Journal of Latin American and Caribbean Studies,* v. 17, no. 34 (1992), pp. 144 – 146.

Larraín B., Felipe and Marcelo Selowsky, eds. *The Public Sector and the Latin American Crisis* reviewed by Christian Anglade. *Journal of Latin American Studies,* v. 25, no. 2 (May 93), pp. 404 – 405.

Larsen, Neil. *Modernism and Hegemony: A Materialist Critique of Aesthetic Agencies* reviewed by Antony Higgins. *Revista de Crítica Literaria Latinoamericana,* v. 19, no. 37 (Jan – June 93), pp. 367 – 370.

Lastra, Pedro and Rigas Kappatos, eds. *Antología del cuento chileno* reviewed by Marina Catzaras. *Revista de Crítica Literaria Latinoamericana,* v. 19, no. 37 (Jan – June 93), pp. 392 – 396.

— *Antología del cuento peruano* reviewed by Marina Catzaras. *Revista de Crítica Literaria Latinoamericana,* v. 19, no. 37 (Jan – June 93), pp. 392 – 396.

Lastra de Suárez, Yolanda. *Sociolingüística para hispanoamericanos: una introducción* reviewed by John Baugh. *La Educación (USA),* v. 37, no. 114 (1993), pp. 160 – 161.

Lauderdale, Sandra

See

Graham, Sandra Lauderdale

Lauer, Mirko and Henrique-Osvaldo Urbano, eds. *Poder y violencia en los Andes* reviewed by Kenneth J. Andrien. *Hispanic American Historical Review,* v. 73, no. 1 (Feb 93), pp. 177 – 178.

— *Poder y violencia en los Andes* reviewed by Víctor Peralta Ruiz. *Revista de Indias,* v. 53, no. 197 (Jan – Apr 93), pp. 124 – 126.

Lausent Herrera, Isabelle. *Pasado y presente de la comunidad japonesa en el Perú* reviewed by Mariana Mould de Pease. *Bulletin de l'Institut Français d'Etudes Andines,* v. 21, no. 2 (1992), pp. 788 – 789.

Lavallé, Bernard. *Quito et la crise de l'alcabala, 1580 – 1600* reviewed by Michel Bertrand. *Caravelle,* no. 60 (1993), pp. 148 – 150.

Lavareda, José Antônio. *A democracia nas urnas* reviewed by Glória Diógenes. *Revista Brasileira de Ciências Sociais,* v. 8, no. 22 (June 93), pp. 156 – 157.

— *A democracia nas urnas: o processo partidário eleitoral brasileiro* reviewed by Stéphane Monclaire (Review entitled "Partis et représentations politiques au Brésil"). *Cahiers des Amériques Latines,* no. 13 (1992), pp. 173 – 177.

— *A democracia nas urnas: o processo partidário eleitoral brasileiro* reviewed by Paul Cammack. *Journal of Latin American Studies,* v. 25, no. 3 (Oct 93), pp. 665 – 666.

Lavaud, Jean-Pierre. *L'instabilité politique de l'Amérique Latine: le cas de la Bolivie* reviewed by Frédérique Langue. *Cahiers des Amériques Latines,* no. 13 (1992), pp. 179 – 180.

Lavrin, Asunción, ed. *Sexuality and Marriage in Colonial Latin America* reviewed by K. Lynn Stoner (Review entitled "Whores, Witches, and Unwed Mothers: Recent Scholarship on the Control of Sexuality"). *Studies in Latin American Popular Culture,* v. 12 (1993), pp. 207 – 214.

Lawless, Robert. *Haiti's Bad Press* reviewed by J. Michael Dash. *Social and Economic Studies,* v. 41, no. 4 (Dec 92), pp. 239 – 243.

— *Haiti's Bad Press: Origins, Development, and Consequences* reviewed by A. V. Catanese. *Journal of Developing Areas,* v. 28, no. 1 (Oct 93), pp. 141 – 142.

Leacock, Ruth. *Requiem for Revolution: The United States and Brazil, 1961 – 1969* reviewed by John W. F. Dulles. *The Americas,* v. 49, no. 4 (Apr 93), pp. 564 – 566.

Le Bot, Yvon. *La guerre en terre maya: communauté, violence et modernité au Guatemala, 1970 – 1992* reviewed by J. P. Pérez Sáinz. *Journal of Latin American Studies,* v. 25, no. 3 (Oct 93), pp. 670 – 672.

— *La guerre en terre maya: communauté, violence et modernité au Guatemala, 1970 – 1992* reviewed by Maxime Haubert. *Tiers Monde,* v. 34, no. 136 (Oct – Dec 93), pp. 952 – 953.

Lees, Francis A. et al. *Banking and Financial Deepening in Brazil* reviewed by Arnold W. Sametz. *Economic Development and Cultural Change,* v. 41, no. 3 (Apr 93), pp. 686 – 690.

Leff Zimmerman, Gloria. *Los pactos obreros y la institución presidencial en México, 1915 – 1938* reviewed by Mónica García Suárez. *El Cotidiano,* v. 9, no. 56 (July 93), p. 117.

Lehmann, David. *Democracy and Development in Latin America: Economics, Politics, and Religion in the Post-War Period* reviewed by Ricardo Grinspun and Sally Humphries. *Economic Development and Cultural Change,* v. 41, no. 4 (July 93), pp. 886 – 894. Bibl.

Leiria, Jerônimo Souto et al. *Terceirização passo à passo: o caminho para a administração pública e privada* reviewed by Michelle Montone. *RAE; Revista de Administração de Empresas,* v. 33, no. 2 (Mar – Apr 93), pp. 127 – 128.

Leite, Gabriela Silva. *Eu, mulher da vida* reviewed by Ana Arruda Callado (Review entitled "Ainda o poder da sedução"). *Estudos Feministas,* v. 0, no. 0 (1992), pp. 228 – 229.

Lemercinier, Geneviève and François Houtart. *El campesino como actor social: sociología de una comarca de Nicaragua* reviewed by Sergio Sarmiento Silva. *Revista Mexicana de Sociología,* v. 54, no. 3 (July – Sept 92), pp. 263 – 267.

Lempérière, Annick. *Intellectuels, état et société au Mexique, XXe siècle: les clercs de la nation* reviewed by Frédérique Langue. *Cahiers des Amériques Latines,* no. 13 (1992), pp. 181 – 182.

Lent, John A. *Mass Communication in the Caribbean* reviewed by Idsa E. Alegría-Ortega. *Caribbean Studies,* v. 25, no. 1 – 2 (Jan – July 92), pp. 164 – 166.

Lentz, Carola. *Buscando la vida: trabajadores temporales en una plantación de azúcar* reviewed by Alberto Cheng Hurtado. *América Indígena,* v. 51, no. 4 (Oct – Dec 91), pp. 219 – 222.

León-Portilla, Ascensión H. de, ed. *Bernardino de Sahagún: diez estudios acerca de su obra* reviewed by Pilar Maynez. *Estudios de Cultura Náhuatl,* v. 22 (1992), pp. 497 – 498.

León-Portilla, Miguel. *The Aztec Image of Self and Society: An Introduction to Nahua Culture* reviewed by Frances Karttunen. *Latin American Indian Literatures Journal,* v. 9, no. 1 (Spring 93), pp. 85 – 92.

— *The Aztec Image of Self and Society,* a translation of *Los antiguos mexicanos a través de sus crónicas y cantares* edited by José Jorge Klor de Alva. Reviewed by Inga Clendinnen. *Hispanic American Historical Review,* v. 73, no. 1 (Feb 93), pp. 142 – 143.

— *Endangered Cultures* reviewed by Susan Shattuck Benson. *La Educación (USA),* v. 37, no. 114 (1993), p. 162.

— *Fifteen Poets of the Aztec World* reviewed by Frances Karttunen. *Hispanic American Historical Review,* v. 73, no. 4 (Nov 93), pp. 681 – 682.

León-Portilla, Miguel, ed. *Poésie náhuatl d'amour et d'amitié* translated by Georges Baudot. Reviewed by Patrick Johansson. *Caravelle,* no. 60 (1993), pp. 135 – 138.

— *Visión de los vencidos: relaciones indígenas de la conquista* reviewed by Beatriz de la Fuente. *Estudios de Cultura Náhuatl,* v. 22 (1992), pp. 499 – 505.

Leonard, Irving Albert. *Books of the Brave: Being an Account of Books and of Men in the Spanish Conquest and Settlement of the Sixteenth-Century New World* introduced by Rolena Adorno. Reviewed by Kenneth Mills. *Bulletin of Latin American Research,* v. 12, no. 2 (May 93), pp. 224 – 227.

— *Viajeros por la América Latina colonial* reviewed by Luis Franco Ramos (Review entitled "Viajes sin guía de turistas"). *Nexos,* v. 16, no. 181 (Jan 93), pp. 75 – 76. Il.

Lepri, Jean-Pierre. *Images de la femme dans les annonces publicitaires des quotidiens au Mexique* reviewed by Héctor Ruiz Rivas. *Caravelle,* no. 59 (1992), pp. 313 – 314.

Lerner de Zunino, Delia and Alicia Palacios de Pizani. *El aprendizaje de la lengua escrita en la escuela: reflexiones sobre la propuesta pedagógica constructivista* reviewed by Magaly Muñoz de Pimentel. *La Educación (USA),* v. 37, no. 115 (1993), pp. 426 – 428.

Léry, Jean de. *History of a Voyage to the Land of Brazil, Otherwise Called America* translated by Janet Whatley. Reviewed by Maria Laura Bettencourt Pires. *Colonial Latin American Review,* v. 2, no. 1 – 2 (1993), pp. 279 – 281.

Leventhal, Paul L. and Sharon Tanzer, eds. *Averting a Latin American Nuclear Arms Race: New Prospects and Challenges for Argentine – Brazil Nuclear Cooperation* reviewed by Mónica Serrano. *Journal of Latin American Studies,* v. 25, no. 2 (May 93), pp. 426 – 429.

Levi, Darrell Erville. *Michael Manley: The Making of a Leader* reviewed by Herman McKenzie. *Jamaica Journal,* v. 24, no. 3 (Feb 93), pp. 55 – 57. Il.

Levin, Henry M. and Marlaine E. Lockheed, eds. *Effective Schools in Developing Countries* reviewed by Maria Valéria Junho Pena. *La Educación (USA),* v. 37, no. 115 (1993), pp. 437 – 439.

Levine, Barry B., ed. *El desafío neoliberal: el fin del tercermundismo en América Latina* reviewed by John W. F. Dulles. *Hispanic American Historical Review,* v. 73, no. 3 (Aug 93), pp. 542 – 543.

Levine, Daniel H. *Popular Voices in Latin American Catholicism* reviewed by John Hillman. *Bulletin of Latin American Research,* v. 12, no. 3 (Sept 93), pp. 354 – 355.

— *Popular Voices in Latin American Catholicism* reviewed by W. E. Hewitt. *Journal of Developing Areas,* v. 27, no. 4 (July 93), pp. 550 – 552.

Levine, Robert M. *Images of History: Nineteenth and Twentieth Century Latin American Photography as Documents* reviewed by William H. Beezley. *Hispanic American Historical Review,* v. 73, no. 1 (Feb 93), pp. 133 – 134.

— *Vale of Tears: Revisiting the Canudos Massacre in Northeastern Brazil, 1893 – 1897* reviewed by Francis Lambert. *Bulletin of Latin American Research,* v. 12, no. 3 (Sept 93), pp. 353 – 354.

— *Vale of Tears: Revisiting the Canudos Massacre in Northeastern Brazil, 1893 – 1897* reviewed by Dain Borges. *Hispanic American Historical Review,* v. 73, no. 3 (Aug 93), pp. 515 – 516.

— *Vale of Tears: Revisiting the Canudos Massacre in Northeastern Brazil, 1893 – 1897* reviewed by Jeff Lesser. *Journal of Latin American Studies,* v. 25, no. 2 (May 93), pp. 397 – 398.

— *Vale of Tears: Revisiting the Canudos Massacre in Northeastern Brazil, 1893 – 1897* reviewed by Steven C. Topik. *Luso-Brazilian Review,* v. 30, no. 2 (Winter 93), pp. 115 – 116.

Levine, Robert M., ed. *Windows on Latin America: Understanding Society through Photographs* reviewed by William H. Beezley. *Hispanic American Historical Review,* v. 73, no. 1 (Feb 93), pp. 133 – 134.

Lewis, James Allen. *The Final Campaign of the American Revolution: Rise and Fall of the Spanish Bahamas* reviewed by Francisco Castillo Meléndez. *Anuario de Estudios Americanos,* v. 49, Suppl. 2 (1992), pp. 249 – 250.

Lewis, Marvin A. *Ethnicity and Identity in Contemporary Afro-Venezuelan Literature: A Culturalist Approach* reviewed by Jorge J. Rodríguez-Florido. *Hispania (USA),* v. 76, no. 2 (May 93), p. 289.

Lezama Lima, José. *Paradiso* edited by Cintio Vitier. Reviewed by Samuel Gordon. *Revista de Crítica Literaria Latinoamericana,* v. 19, no. 37 (Jan – June 93), pp. 386 – 392.

Lezy, Emmanuel. *Guyane de l'autre côté des images* reviewed by Pierre Ragon. *Cahiers des Amériques Latines,* no. 14 (1992), pp. 151 – 152.

Libertella, Héctor. *Patografía: los juegos desviados de la literatura* reviewed by Jacobo Sefamí. *Revista Chilena de Literatura,* no. 41 (Apr 93), pp. 136 – 137.

Un libro sobre Guillermo Kuitca reviewed by Ivonne Pini (Accompanied by an English translation). *Art Nexus,* no. 9 (June – Aug 93), p. 32. Il.

Lienhard, Martín. *La voz y su huella: escritura y conflicto étnico – social en América Latina, 1492 – 1988* reviewed by Gustavo Fares. *Hispania (USA),* v. 76, no. 1 (Mar 93), pp. 88 – 89.

— *La voz y su huella: escritura y conflicto étnico – social en América Latina, 1492 – 1988* reviewed by José Prats Sariol. *Iberoamericana,* v. 16, no. 47 – 48 (1992), pp. 113 – 116.

— *La voz y su huella: escritura y conflicto étnico – social en América Latina, 1492 – 1988* reviewed by Antonio Cornejo Polar. *Revista de Crítica Literaria Latinoamericana,* v. 19, no. 38 (July – Dec 93), pp. 395 – 397.

Linares Pontón, María Eugenia, ed. *Del hecho al dicho hay menos trecho: ¿Qué hemos aprendido en los programas de apoyo a la familia para la crianza de los niños?* reviewed by María Bertha Fortoul O. *Revista Latinoamericana de Estudios Educativos,* v. 23, no. 1 (Jan – Mar 93), pp. 134 – 138. Il.

Lindo Fuentes, Héctor. *Weak Foundations: The Economy of El Salvador in the Nineteenth Century, 1821 – 1898* reviewed by E. Bradford Burns. *Mesoamérica (USA),* v. 13, no. 23 (June 92), pp. 184 – 186.

Lindstrom, Naomi. *Jorge Luis Borges: A Study of the Short Fiction* reviewed by Adriana J. Bergero. *Hispanic Review,* v. 61, no. 1 (Winter 93), pp. 131 – 133.

Linger, Daniel Touro. *Dangerous Encounters: Meanings of Violence in a Brazilian City* reviewed by David Cleary. *Bulletin of Latin American Research,* v. 12, no. 3 (Sept 93), pp. 344 – 345.

Lipp, Frank Joseph. *The Mixe of Oaxaca: Religion, Ritual, and Healing* reviewed by James Dow. *The Americas,* v. 49, no. 4 (Apr 93), pp. 545 – 547.

Lippy, Charles H. et al. *Christianity Comes to the Americas, 1492 – 1776* reviewed by Susan E. Ramírez. *The Americas,* v. 50, no. 1 (July 93), pp. 124 – 125.

Lo Vuolo, Rubén M. and Alberto C. Barbeito. *La modernización excluyente: transformación económica y estado de bienestar en Argentina* reviewed by Mauricio Tenewicki. *Realidad Económica,* no. 118 (Aug – Sept 93), pp. 142 – 144.

Lockhart, James Marvin. *The Nahuas after the Conquest: A Social and Cultural History of the Indians of Central Mexico, Sixteenth through Eighteenth Centuries* reviewed by Linda Hall. *Colonial Latin American Historical Review,* v. 2, no. 2 (Spring 93), pp. 233 – 234.

— *The Nahuas after the Conquest: A Social and Cultural History of the Indians of Central Mexico, Sixteenth through Eighteenth Centuries* reviewed by Rik Hoekstra. *European Review of Latin American and Caribbean Studies,* no. 54 (June 93), pp. 120 – 125.

— *The Nahuas after the Conquest: A Social and Cultural History of the Indians of Central Mexico, Sixteenth through Eighteenth Centuries* reviewed by Peter Gerhard. *Hispanic American Historical Review,* v. 73, no. 4 (Nov 93), pp. 697 – 698.

— *The Nahuas after the Conquest: A Social and Cultural History of the Indians of Central Mexico, Sixteenth through Eighteenth Centuries* reviewed by Fernando Cervantes. *Journal of Latin American Studies,* v. 25, no. 2 (May 93), pp. 389 – 391.

— *The Nahuas after the Conquest: A Social and Cultural History of the Indians of Central Mexico; Sixteenth through Eighteenth Centuries* reviewed by David Brading (Review entitled "Los nahuas después de la conquista," translated by Isabel Vericat). *Nexos*, v. 16, no. 186 (June 93), pp. 73 – 74.

— *Nahuas and Spaniards: Postconquest Central Mexican History and Philology* reviewed by Rik Hoekstra. *European Review of Latin American and Caribbean Studies*, no. 54 (June 93), pp. 120 – 125.

— *Nahuas and Spaniards: Postconquest Central Mexican History and Philology* reviewed by Fernando Cervantes. *Journal of Latin American Studies*, v. 25, no. 2 (May 93), pp. 389 – 391.

Lockheed, Marlaine E. and Henry M. Levin, eds. *Effective Schools in Developing Countries* reviewed by Maria Valéria Junho Pena. *La Educación (USA)*, v. 37, no. 115 (1993), pp. 437 – 439.

Löwy, Michael, ed. *Marxism in Latin America from 1909 to the Present: An Anthology* reviewed by Sheldon B. Liss. *Hispanic American Historical Review*, v. 73, no. 4 (Nov 93), pp. 728 – 729.

Lojo de Beuter, María Rosa. *Forma oculta del mundo* reviewed by Gustavo Fares and Eliana Hermann (Review entitled "¿Y ahora?: reflexiones acerca de la literatura femenina argentina actual"). *Letras Femeninas*, v. 19, no. 1 – 2 (Spring – Fall 93), pp. 121 – 134. Bibl.

Lomelí, Francisco A. and Rudolfo A. Anaya, eds. *Aztlán: Essays on the Chicano Homeland* reviewed by Kirsten F. Nigro (Review entitled "Looking Back to Aztlán from the 1990s"). *Bilingual Review/Revista Bilingüe*, v. 18, no. 1 (Jan – Apr 93), pp. 75 – 78.

Lope Blanch, Juan M. *El español hablado en el suroeste de los Estados Unidos: materiales para su estudio* reviewed by Jerry. R. Craddock. *Hispanic Review*, v. 61, no. 1 (Winter 93), pp. 88 – 90.

— *Investigaciones sobre dialectología mexicana*, 2d ed., reviewed by Isabel Silva Aldrete. *Anuario de Letras (Mexico)*, v. 30 (1992), pp. 262 – 265.

Lope Blanch, Juan M., ed. *Atlas lingüístico de México, vol. 1: Fonética* reviewed by Klaus Zimmermann. *Iberoamericana*, v. 16, no. 47 – 48 (1992), pp. 111 – 112.

Lopes, Luís Carlos and Mário José Maestri Filho. *Storia del Brasile* reviewed by Silvio Castro. *Quaderni Ibero-Americani*, no. 72 (Dec 92), pp. 745 – 746.

López, Adelaida and Marithelma Costa. *Las dos caras de la escritura* reviewed by Gustavo Fares. *Revista Iberoamericana*, v. 59, no. 162 – 163 (Jan – June 93), pp. 380 – 382.

López, Ricardo and Isidora Mena, eds. *Las ovejas y el infinito: contribución al estudio de la creatividad y la formulación de propuestas para el sistema educacional* reviewed by Luis Weinstein (Review entitled "Para saber y contar sobre *Las ovejas y el infinito*"). *Estudios Sociales (Chile)*, no. 78 (Oct – Dec 93), pp. 284 – 290.

López-Dóriga, Enrique. *Desarrollo humano: estudio general y aplicado al Perú* reviewed by Felipe E. MacGregor. *Apuntes (Peru)*, no. 31 (July – Dec 92), pp. 115 – 117.

López González, Aralia et al, eds. *Mujer y literatura mexicana y chicana: culturas en contacto* reviewed by Pamela Murray. *Hispanic American Historical Review*, v. 73, no. 3 (Aug 93), p. 490.

López Junqué, Fernando. *Temporada en el ingenio: ensayo fotográfico* introduced by José Lezama Lima. Reviewed by Antonio Santamaría García. *Anuario de Estudios Americanos*, v. 49, Suppl. 1 (1992), p. 256.

López Morales, Humberto. *Sociolingüística* reviewed by Dora Pellicer. *Anuario de Letras (Mexico)*, v. 30 (1992), pp. 251 – 262.

López Páez, Jorge. *Los cerros azules* reviewed by Esther Martínez Luna (Review entitled "Los pasos de López Páez"). *Nexos*, v. 16, no. 188 (Aug 93), p. 87.

Lorey, David E. *The Rise of the Professions in Twentieth-Century Mexico: University Graduates and Occupational Change since 1929* reviewed by Roderic A. Camp. *Journal of Latin American Studies*, v. 25, no. 2 (May 93), pp. 412 – 413.

Loubet, Jorgelina. *Metáforas y reflejos* reviewed by Gustavo Fares and Eliana Hermann (Review entitled "¿Y ahora?: reflexiones acerca de la literatura femenina argentina actual"). *Letras Femeninas*, v. 19, no. 1 – 2 (Spring – Fall 93), pp. 121 – 134. Bibl.

Lovell, William George. *Conquest and Survival in Colonial Guatemala: A Historical Geography of the Cuchumatán Highlands, 1500 – 1821* reviewed by Rob de Ridder. *European Review of Latin American and Caribbean Studies*, no. 54 (June 93), pp. 118 – 120. Bibl.

— *Conquest and Survival in Colonial Guatemala: A Historical Geography of the Cuchumatán Highlands, 1500 – 1821* reviewed by Raymond Buvé. *Journal of Latin American Studies*, v. 25, no. 1 (Feb 93), pp. 197 – 198.

— *Conquista y cambio cultural: la sierra de los Cuchumatanes de Guatemala, 1500 – 1821*, a translation of *Conquest and Survival in Colonial Guatemala*, translated by Eddy Gaytán. Reviewed by María Milagros Ciudad Suárez. *Anuario de Estudios Americanos*, v. 49, Suppl. 2 (1992), pp. 250 – 252.

Lovell, William George and Noble David Cook, eds. *"Secret Judgments of God": Old World Disease in Colonial Spanish America* reviewed by Ronn F. Pineo. *The Americas*, v. 50, no. 1 (July 93), pp. 126 – 127.

— *"Secret Judgments of God": Old World Disease in Colonial Spanish America* reviewed by Cynthia Radding. *Hispanic American Historical Review*, v. 73, no. 2 (May 93), pp. 309 – 311.

Lucena Giraldo, Manuel and Juan Pimentel Igea, eds. *Los "Axiomas políticos sobre la América" de Alejandro Malaspina* reviewed by O. Carlos Stoetzer. *Hispanic American Historical Review*, v. 73, no. 1 (Feb 93), pp. 160 – 161.

Lucena R., Héctor and Fernando Calero, eds. *Las relaciones de trabajo en los noventa: desafíos y propuestas* reviewed by T. M. van Hettema. *European Review of Latin American and Caribbean Studies*, no. 54 (June 93), pp. 139 – 140.

Lucena Salmoral, Manuel. *Características del comercio exterior de la provincia de Caracas durante el sexenio revolucionario, 1807 – 1812* reviewed by Adriana Rodríguez. *Revista de Historia de América*, no. 113 (Jan – June 92), pp. 173 – 174.

Luis, William. *Literary Bondage: Slavery in Cuban Narrative* reviewed by Antonio Benítez-Rojo. *Hispanic Review*, v. 61, no. 1 (Winter 93), pp. 125 – 127.

Lumsden, Ian. *Homosexualidad, sociedad y estado en México* reviewed by Leticia Santa María Gallegos (Review entitled "Ante todo, por la dignidad de ser humano"). *Fem*, v. 17, no. 119 (Jan 93), pp. 46 – 47.

Luque Alcaide, Elisa and José Ignacio Saranyana. *La iglesia católica y América* reviewed by Carmen J. Alejos-Grau. *Anuario de Estudios Americanos*, v. 50, no. 1 (1993), pp. 322 – 323.

Lustig, Nora. *Mexico: The Remaking of an Economy* reviewed by Luis Felipe Lagos M. *Cuadernos de Economía (Chile)*, v. 30, no. 90 (Aug 93), pp. 261 – 263.

— *Mexico: The Remaking of an Economy* reviewed by E. V. K. Fitzgerald. *Journal of Latin American Studies,* v. 25, no. 3 (Oct 93), pp. 680 – 681.

Lustig, Nora and Roberto Bouzas, eds. *Liberalización comercial e integración regional: de NAFTA a MERCOSUR* (Review). *Integración Latinoamericana,* v. 18, no 187 – 188 (Mar – Apr 93), p. 69.

Lustig, Nora et al. *North American Free Trade: Assessing the Impact* reviewed by Marlene Alcántara Domínguez (Review entitled "Costos y beneficios del Tratado de Libre Comercio de América del Norte"). *Relaciones Internacionales (Mexico),* v. 15, Nueva época, no. 58 (Apr – June 93), pp. 97 – 98.

Lynch, John. *Caudillos in Spanish America, 1800 – 1850* reviewed by Charles Walker. *Bulletin of Latin American Research,* v. 12, no. 1 (Jan 93), pp. 115 – 116.

— *Caudillos in Spanish America, 1800 – 1850* reviewed by Frank Safford. *Journal of Latin American Studies,* v. 25, no. 1 (Feb 93), pp. 188 – 190.

— *The Hispanic World in Crisis and Change, 1598 – 1700* reviewed by Richard L. Kagan. *Hispanic American Historical Review,* v. 73, no. 3 (Aug 93), pp. 492 – 494.

— *Spain, 1516 – 1598: From Nation State to World Empire* reviewed by Richard L. Kagan. *Hispanic American Historical Review,* v. 73, no. 3 (Aug 93), pp. 492 – 494.

McAfee, Kathy. *Storm Signals: Structural Adjustment and Development Alternatives in the Caribbean* reviewed by Peter Meel. *European Review of Latin American and Caribbean Studies,* no. 54 (June 93), pp. 128 – 131.

McClellan, James Edward, III. *Colonialism and Science: Saint Domingue in the Old Regime* reviewed by Michiel Baud. *European Review of Latin American and Caribbean Studies,* no. 53 (Dec 92), pp. 118 – 119.

MacCormack, Sabine G. *Religion in the Andes: Vision and Imagination in Early Colonial Peru* reviewed by Susan Ramírez. *The Americas,* v. 50, no. 2 (Oct 93), pp. 271 – 272.

— *Religion in the Andes: Vision and Imagination in Early Colonial Peru* reviewed by Frank Solomon. *Colonial Latin American Review,* v. 2, no. 1 – 2 (1993), pp. 281 – 284.

— *Religion in the Andes: Vision and Imagination in Early Colonial Peru* reviewed by Irene Silverblatt. *Hispanic American Historical Review,* v. 73, no. 1 (Feb 93), pp. 157 – 159.

Macera dall'Orso, Pablo. *La pintura mural andina, siglos XVI – XIX* reviewed by Carlos Rodríguez Saavedra (Review entitled "Arte mestizo"). *Debate (Peru),* v. 16, no. 75 (Dec 93 – Jan 94), p. 77. Il.

McEwan, Gordon Francis and William Harris Isbell, ed. *Huari Administrative Structure: Prehistoric Monumental Architecture and State Government* reviewed by Mario A. Rivera. *Latin American Antiquity,* v. 4, no. 1 (Mar 93), pp. 95 – 96.

McGowan, Chris and Ricardo Pessanha. *The Brazilian Sound: Samba, Bossa Nova, and the Popular Music of Brazil* reviewed by Randal Johnson. *Hispanic American Historical Review,* v. 73, no. 1 (Feb 93), p. 128.

Machado, Eduardo. *The Floating Island Plays* reviewed by Francisco Soto. *The Americas Review,* v. 21, no. 1 (Spring 93), pp. 121 – 123.

Machado de Assis, Joaquim Maria. *O velho senado* reviewed by Geraldo Menezes. *Revista do Instituto Histórico e Geográfico Brasileiro,* no. 370 (Jan – Mar 91), pp. 339 – 340.

McKenzie, Earl. *A Boy Named Ossie: A Jamaican Childhood* reviewed by Andrew Salkey. *World Literature Today,* v. 67, no. 1 (Winter 93), p. 220.

Madrid, Lelia M. *El estilo del deseo: la poética de Darío, Vallejo, Borges y Paz* reviewed by Martha J. Nandorfy. *Revista Canadiense de Estudios Hispánicos,* v. 17, no. 3 (Spring 93), pp. 562 – 565.

Maestri Filho, Mário José and Luís Carlos Lopes. *Storia del Brasile* reviewed by Silvio Castro. *Quaderni Ibero-Americani,* no. 72 (Dec 92), pp. 745 – 746.

Magariños, Gustavo. *Uruguay en el MERCOSUR* (Review). *Integración Latinoamericana,* v. 18, no. 192 (Aug 92), pp. 97 – 98.

Magnarelli, Sharon Dishaw. *Understanding José Donoso* reviewed by Pamela Finnegan. *World Literature Today,* v. 67, no. 3 (Summer 93), pp. 595 – 596.

Maier, Carol and Noël Maureen Valis, eds. *In the Feminine Mode: Essays on Hispanic Women Writers* reviewed by Hazel Gold. *Hispanic Review,* v. 61, no. 4 (Fall 93), pp. 587 – 590.

Malamud Goti, Jaime E. *Smoke and Mirrors: The Paradox of the Drug Wars* reviewed by Kevin Healy. *Journal of Latin American Studies,* v. 25, no. 3 (Oct 93), pp. 688 – 689.

Malavet Vega, Pedro. *Historia de la canción popular en Puerto Rico* reviewed by Donald Thompson. *Latin American Music Review,* v. 14, no. 2 (Fall – Winter 93), pp. 288 – 293.

Malca, Oscar. *Al final de la calle* reviewed by Oswaldo Chanove (Review entitled "Prosa impía"). *Debate (Peru),* v. 16, no. 74 (Sept – Oct 93), pp. 65 – 66.

Manley, Edna. *Edna Manley: The Diaries* edited by Rachel Manley. Reviewed by Adelaida de Juan (Review entitled "A Woman to Remember"). *Jamaica Journal,* v. 25, no. 1 (Oct 93), pp. 26 – 67. Il.

Mannarelli, María Emma. *Pecados públicos: la ilegitimidad en Lima, siglo XVII* reviewed by Arturo Ferrari (Review entitled "Un plancito cholifacio"). *Debate (Peru),* v. 16, no. 75 (Dec 93 – Jan 94), pp. 78 – 79. Il.

Manrique, Jorge Alberto and Hipólito Rodríguez. *Veracruz: la ciudad hecha de mar, 1519 – 1821* (Review). *La Palabra y el Hombre,* no. 83 (July – Sept 92), pp. 347 – 349.

Mansilla, Hugo Celso Felipe. *Consejeros de reyes* reviewed by Raúl Rivadeneira Prada. *Signo,* no. 38, Nueva época (Jan – Apr 93), pp. 239 – 241.

— *Opandamoiral* reviewed by Jaime Martínez Salguero. *Signo,* no. 38, Nueva época (Jan – Apr 93), pp. 241 – 243.

— *Opandamoiral* reviewed by Manuel Vargas. *Signo,* no. 35, Nueva época (Jan – Apr 92), pp. 221 – 223.

Mansour, Mónica. *En cuerpo y alma/In Body and Soul* reviewed by Barbara Mujica (Review entitled "A Coming of Age"). *Américas,* v. 45, no. 5 (Sept – Oct 93), p. 61. Il.

Manucy, Albert. *Menéndez: Pedro Menéndez de Avilés, Captain General of the Ocean Sea* reviewed by Paul E. Hoffman. *Hispanic American Historical Review,* v. 73, no. 2 (May 93), p. 321.

Manuel, Peter, ed. *Essays on Cuban Music: North American and Cuban Perspectives* reviewed by Lucy Durán. *Latin American Music Review,* v. 14, no. 2 (Fall – Winter 93), pp. 281 – 288.

Manzetti, Luigi and Peter G. Snow. *Political Forces in Argentina,* 3d edition, reviewed by Robert J. Alexander. *Hispanic American Historical Review,* v. 73, no. 4 (Nov 93), pp. 703 – 705.

Marco, Marcelo di. *El viento planea sobre la tierra* reviewed by Rodolfo Alonso. *Revista Nacional de Cultura (Venezuela),* v. 53, no. 285 (Apr – June 92), p. 241.

Marco, Miguel Angel de. *Carlos Casado de Alisal y el progreso argentino* reviewed by F. L. *Todo Es Historia,* v. 27, no. 311 (June 93), p. 60. Il.

Margolis, Mac. *The Last New World: The Conquest of the Amazon Frontier* reviewed by Gordon MacMillan. *Bulletin of Latin American Research,* v. 12, no. 3 (Sept 93), pp. 352 – 353.

Maril, Robert Lee. *Living on the Edge of America* reviewed by Matt S. Meier. *International Migration Review,* v. 27, no. 4 (Winter 93), pp. 897 – 898.

Marley, David F. *Pirates and Engineers* reviewed by Joel Russell (Review entitled "Swashbuckler's Paradise"). *Business Mexico,* v. 3, no. 4 (Apr 93), p. 52.

— *Pirates and Engineers: Dutch and Flemish Adventurers in New Spain, 1607 – 1697* reviewed by Peter T. Bradley. *Bulletin of Latin American Research,* v. 12, no. 2 (May 93), pp. 219 – 220.

Marmontel, Jean François. *Los incas o la destrucción del imperio del Perú,* a translation of *Les incas ou la destruction de l'empire du Pérou.* Reviewed by Carlos Garatea Grau (Review entitled "Conquista y fanatismo"). *Debate (Peru),* v. 15, no. 70 (Sept – Oct 92), p. 67. Il.

Marqués, Sarah. *La lengua que heredamos: curso de español para bilingües* reviewed by Jack B. Jelinski. *Hispania (USA),* v. 76, no. 4 (Dec 93), pp. 747 – 748.

Márquez Rodríguez, Alexis. *Historia y ficción en la novela venezolana* reviewed by R. J. Lovera De-Sola. *Revista Nacional de Cultura (Venezuela),* v. 53, no. 286 (July – Sept 92), pp. 249 – 251.

Marrone, Nila. *El habla de la ciudad de La Paz* reviewed by Carlos Coello Vila. *Signo,* no. 35, Nueva época (Jan – Apr 92), pp. 226 – 229.

Marshall, Jonathan and Peter Dale Scott. *Cocaine Politics: Drugs, Armies, and the CIA in Central America* reviewed by Donald J. Mabry. *Hispanic American Historical Review,* v. 73, no. 2 (May 93), p. 353.

Martin, Gerald. *Writers from Latin America* reviewed by Warren L. Meinhardt. *Chasqui,* v. 22, no. 1 (May 93), pp. 99 – 101.

Martin, Michel L. and Alain Yacou, eds. *Mourir pour les Antilles: indépendance nègre ou esclavage, 1802 – 1804* reviewed by Frédérique Langue. *Caravelle,* no. 60 (1993), pp. 157 – 159.

Martinell Gifre, Emma. *Aspectos lingüísticos del descubrimiento y de la conquista* reviewed by Ma. Angeles Soler Arechalde. *Estudios de Cultura Náhuatl,* v. 22 (1992), pp. 505 – 508.

Martínez, Gregorio. *Crónica de músicos y diablos* reviewed by Jesús Díaz-Caballero. *Hispamérica,* v. 22, no. 64 – 65 (Apr – Aug 93), pp. 197 – 200.

— *Crónica de músicos y diablos* reviewed by Ismael P. Márquez. *World Literature Today,* v. 67, no. 1 (Winter 93), pp. 155 – 156.

Martínez, Herminio. *Las puertas del mundo: una autobiografía hipócrita del Almirante* reviewed by Rafael H. Mojica. *World Literature Today,* v. 67, no. 2 (Spring 93), p. 336.

Martínez, José Luis. *Hernán Cortés* reviewed by Bernard Grunberg. *Caravelle,* no. 60 (1993), pp. 138 – 139.

— *Hernán Cortés* reviewed by María Justina Sarabia Viejo. *Anuario de Estudios Americanos,* v. 49, Suppl. 2 (1992), pp. 252 – 253.

— *El mundo privado de los emigrantes en Indias* reviewed by Antonio Saborit (Review entitled "Cartas de llamada"). *Nexos,* v. 16, no. 184 (Apr 93), pp. 67 – 68.

— *El mundo privado de los emigrantes en Indias* reviewed by Jorge F. Hernández (Review entitled "Correspondencias con el pasado"). *Vuelta,* v. 17, no. 198 (May 93), pp. 55 – 57.

Martínez-Assad, Carlos R. and Sergio Sarmiento, eds. *Nos queda la esperanza: el valle del Mezquital* reviewed by Marta Eugenia García Ugarte. *Revista Mexicana de Sociología,* v. 54, no. 2 (Apr – June 92), pp. 245 – 251.

Martínez Moreno, Hugo N. and Amalia Gramajo de Martínez Moreno. *Rasgos del folklore de Santiago del Estero* reviewed by Félix Coluccio. *Folklore Americano,* no. 53 (Jan – June 92), pp. 179 – 180.

Martínez Riaza, Ascensión and Jesús Alvarez. *Historia de la prensa hispanoamericana* reviewed by Alfonso Braojos Garrido. *Anuario de Estudios Americanos,* v. 50, no. 1 (1993), pp. 307 – 308.

Martínez Salguero, Jaime. *Tamayo, el hombre, la obra* reviewed by Rodolfo Salamanca L. *Signo,* no. 35, Nueva época (Jan – Apr 92), pp. 224 – 225.

Martínez Vergne, Teresita. *Capitalism in Colonial Puerto Rico: Central San Vicente in the Late Nineteenth Century* reviewed by Martin F. Murphy. *Hispanic American Historical Review,* v. 73, no. 2 (May 93), pp. 320 – 321.

Martins, Marlene Andrade. *O sentido comum das coisas* reviewed by Celso de Oliveira. *World Literature Today,* v. 67, no. 4 (Fall 93), p. 793.

Mártir, Pedro

See
Anghiera, Pietro Martire d'

Marx, Murillo and Damián Carlos Bayón. *A History of South American Colonial Art and Architecture: Spanish South America and Brazil* translated by Jennifer A. Blankley, Angela P. Hall, and Richard L. Rees. Reviewed by Marcus B. Burke. *Latin American Art,* v. 5, no. 1 (Spring 93), pp. 94 – 95.

Masiello, Francine Rose. *Between Civilization and Barbarism: Women, Nation, and Literary Culture in Modern Argentina* reviewed by Catherine Davies (Review entitled "Women and a Redefinition of Argentinian Nationhood"). *Bulletin of Latin American Research,* v. 12, no. 3 (Sept 93), pp. 333 – 341.

— *Between Civilization and Barbarism: Women, Nation, and Literary Culture in Modern Argentina* reviewed by Myron I. Lichtblau. *Hispania (USA),* v. 76, no. 3 (Sept 93), pp. 484 – 485.

— *Between Civilization and Barbarism: Women, Nation, and Literary Culture in Modern Argentina* reviewed by Verity Smith. *Journal of Latin American Studies,* v. 25, no. 3 (Oct 93), pp. 695 – 696.

— *Between Civilization and Barbarism: Women, Nation, and Literary Culture in Modern Argentina* reviewed by Naomi Lindstrom. *World Literature Today,* v. 67, no. 2 (Spring 93), p. 344.

Mason, Peter, ed. *Indianen en Nederlanders, 1492 – 1992* reviewed by Menno Oostra. *European Review of Latin American and Caribbean Studies,* no. 54 (June 93), pp. 145 – 147.

Massey, Douglas S. et al. *Los ausentes: el proceso social de la migración internacional en el occidente de México* reviewed by Janet E. Worrall. *Hispanic American Historical Review,* v. 73, no. 2 (May 93), pp. 337 – 338.

Massi, Marina. *Vida de mulheres: cotidiano e imaginário* reviewed by Lena Larinas (Review entitled "Ambivalências do desejo"). *Estudos Feministas,* v. 1, no. 1 (1993), pp. 206 – 207.

Massolo, Alejandra. *Por amor y coraje: mujeres en movimientos urbanos de la ciudad de México* reviewed by Beatriz Almanza. *El Cotidiano,* v. 10, no. 57 (Aug – Sept 93), p. 109.

— *Por amor y coraje: mujeres en movimientos urbanos de la ciudad de México* reviewed by Elena Urrutia. *La Educación (USA),* v. 37, no. 114 (1993), pp. 164 – 165.

Massolo, Alejandra, ed. *Mujeres y ciudades* reviewed by Maribel Nicasio González. *El Cotidiano,* v. 10, no. 57 (Aug – Sept 93), p. 110.

Masterson, Daniel M. *Militarism and Politics in Latin America: Peru from Sánchez Cerro to Sendero Luminoso* reviewed by Brian Loveman. *The Americas,* v. 49, no. 3 (Jan 93), pp. 422 – 424.

Mastretta, Angeles. *Arráncame la vida* reviewed by Nora Glickman. *World Literature Today,* v. 67, no. 4 (Fall 93), p. 785.

Matas, Julio. *El extravío; La crónica y el suceso; Aquí cruza el ciervo* reviewed by Guillermo Schmidhuber. *Revista Iberoamericana,* v. 59, no. 162 – 163 (Jan – June 93), pp. 392 – 394.

— *Juegos y rejuegos* reviewed by Matías Montes-Huidobro. *Latin American Theatre Review,* v. 26, no. 2 (Spring 93), pp. 205 – 206.

— *Juegos y rejuegos* reviewed by William L. Siemens. *World Literature Today,* v. 67, no. 4 (Fall 93), pp. 786 – 787. II.

Matos Moctezuma, Eduardo and David Carrasco. *Moctezuma's México: Visions of the Aztec World* reviewed by James N. Corbridge, Jr. *La Educación (USA),* v. 37, no. 115 (1993), pp. 413 – 414.

Matter, Robert Allen. *Pre-Seminole Florida: Spanish Soldiers, Friars, and Indian Missions, 1513 – 1763* reviewed by Amy Turner Bushnell. *The Americas,* v. 49, no. 4 (Apr 93), pp. 547 – 548.

Matthews, Marc. *A Season of Sometimes* reviewed by Andrew Salkey. *World Literature Today,* v. 67, no. 3 (Summer 93), p. 657.

Mattos, Carlos de Meira. *Geopolítica e teoria de fronteiras: fronteiras do Brasil* reviewed by Vicente Tapajós. *Revista do Instituto Histórico e Geográfico Brasileiro,* no. 370 (Jan – Mar 91), p. 340.

— *Geopolítica e trópicos* reviewed by Sydney Martins Gomes dos Santos. *Revista do Instituto Histórico e Geográfico Brasileiro,* no. 371 (Apr – June 91), pp. 605 – 609.

Mattos Cintrón, Wilfredo. *El cuerpo bajo el puente* reviewed by Carmen Dolores Trelles. *Homines,* v. 15 – 16, no. 2 – 1 (Oct 91 – Dec 92), pp. 381 – 382.

Mauro, Frédéric and Soline Alemany, eds. *Transport et commerce en Amérique Latine* reviewed by Rory Miller. *Journal of Latin American Studies,* v. 25, no. 1 (Feb 93), pp. 208 – 209.

Máynez Vidal, Pilar. *Religión y magia: un problema de transculturación lingüística en la obra de Bernardino de Sahagún* reviewed by María Angeles Soler Arechalde. *Anuario de Letras (Mexico),* v. 30 (1992), pp. 299 – 303.

Mayo, Carlos Alberto. *Los betlemitas en Buenos Aires: convento, economía y sociedad, 1748 – 1822* reviewed by Angela Fernández. *Todo Es Historia,* v. 26, no. 309 (Apr 93), pp. 70 – 71. II.

Medin, Tzvi. *El sexenio alemanista: ideología y praxis política de Miguel Alemán* reviewed by Errol D. Jones. *Hispanic American Historical Review,* v. 73, no. 1 (Feb 93), pp. 182 – 183.

Medina, Dante. *La dama de la gardenia* reviewed by Adolfo Castañón. *Vuelta,* v. 17, no. 194 (Jan 93), pp. 45 – 46.

Medina, Enrique. *Deuda de honor* reviewed by David William Foster. *World Literature Today,* v. 67, no. 2 (Spring 93), pp. 339 – 340.

— *Es Ud. muy femenina* reviewed by David William Foster. *World Literature Today,* v. 67, no. 3 (Summer 93), pp. 594 – 595.

Medina, José Toribio. *La imprenta en Lima, 1548 – 1824,* tomo IV, reviewed by Sergio Martínez Baeza. *Boletín de la Academia Chilena de la Historia,* v. 58 – 59, no. 102 (1991 – 1992), pp. 558 – 559.

Medina, Roberto Nicolás. *Bajo sospecha* reviewed by Rodolfo Alonso. *Revista Nacional de Cultura (Venezuela),* v. 53, no. 285 (Apr – June 92), pp. 244 – 245.

Medinaceli, Carlos. *La alegría de ayer* reviewed by Pedro de Anasagasti. *Signo,* no. 35, Nueva época (Jan – Apr 92), pp. 230 – 232.

Meier, Kenneth J. and Joseph Stewart, Jr. *The Politics of Hispanic Education: "un paso pa'lante y dos pa'tras"* reviewed by Francesco Cordasco. *International Migration Review,* v. 26, no. 4 (Winter 92), pp. 1464 – 1465.

Mejía, Myriam et al. *La biblioteca pública: manual para su organización y funcionamiento,* vols. I – II (Review). *La Educación (USA),* v. 36, no. 111 – 113 (1992), pp. 299 – 300.

Mejía Vallejo, Manuel. *La casa de las dos palmas* reviewed by Luis E. Restrepo. *Hispamérica,* v. 21, no. 63 (Dec 92), pp. 99 – 100.

Meller, Patricio and Magnus Blomström, eds. *Trayectorias divergentes* reviewed by Göran G. Lindahl (Review entitled "Commentary and Debate"). *Ibero Americana (Sweden),* v. 22, no. 2 (Dec 92), pp. 67 – 76.

— *Trayectorias divergentes: comparación de un siglo de desarrollo económico latinoamericano y escandinavo* reviewed by Sérgio Savino Portugal. *Pesquisa e Planejamento Econômico,* v. 22, no. 1 (Apr 92), pp. 189 – 196.

Mena, Isidora and Ricardo López, eds. *Las ovejas y el infinito: contribución al estudio de la creatividad y la formulación de propuestas para el sistema educacional* reviewed by Luis Weinstein (Review entitled "Para saber y contar sobre *Las ovejas y el infinito*"). *Estudios Sociales (Chile),* no. 78 (Oct – Dec 93), pp. 284 – 290.

Mena, Isidora and Mario Salazar, eds. *Para saber y contar: manual metodológico* reviewed by Luis Weinstein (Review entitled "Para saber y contar sobre *Las ovejas y el infinito*"). *Estudios Sociales (Chile),* no. 78 (Oct – Dec 93), pp. 284 – 290.

— *Para saber y contar: narraciones sobre niños, viejos y viejísimos* reviewed by Luis Weinstein (Review entitled "Para saber y contar sobre *Las ovejas y el infinito*"). *Estudios Sociales (Chile),* no. 78 (Oct – Dec 93), pp. 284 – 290.

Méndez Clark, Ronald. *Onetti y la (in)fidelidad a las reglas del juego* reviewed by Harley D. Oberhelman. *Hispania (USA),* v. 76, no. 4 (Dec 93), pp. 740 – 741.

Méndez M., Miguel. *Que no mueran los sueños* reviewed by Saúl Ibargoyen. *Plural (Mexico),* v. 22, no. 257 (Feb 93), p. 81.

Mendiola, Víctor Manuel. *Vuelo 294* reviewed by Adriana Díaz Enciso. *Vuelta,* v. 17, no. 197 (Apr 93), pp. 47 – 48.

Mendoza, José G. *Gramática castellana* reviewed by Carlos Coello Vila. *Signo,* no. 35, Nueva época (Jan – Apr 92), pp. 232 – 237.

Menegus Bornemann, Margarita. *Del señorío a la república de indios: el caso de Toluca, 1500 – 1600* reviewed by Michel Bertrand. *Caravelle,* no. 60 (1993), pp. 143 – 147.

Meneses, Georgina. *Tradición oral en el imperio de los incas: historia, religión y teatro* reviewed by Elizabeth Fonseca C. *Revista de Historia (Costa Rica),* no. 25 (Jan – June 92), pp. 235 – 237.

Meneses, Guillermo. *Diez cuentos* reviewed by Juvenal López Ruiz. *Revista Nacional de Cultura (Venezuela),* v. 53, no. 285 (Apr – June 92), pp. 249 – 250.

Menjívar Larín, Rafael and Juan Pablo Pérez Sáinz, eds. *Informalidad urbana en Centroamérica: entre la acumulación y la subsistencia* reviewed by Stephen Webre. *Hispanic American Historical Review,* v. 73, no. 2 (May 93), pp. 341 – 342.

Meo Zilio, Giovanni. *Estudios hispanoamericanos: temas lingüísticos* reviewed by Joel Rini. *Hispanic Review,* v. 61, no. 2 (Spring 93), pp. 271 – 273.

Mercado Jarrín, Edgardo et al. *Relaciones del Perú con Chile y Bolivia* (Review). *Integración Latinoamericana,* v. 18, no. 189 – 190 (May – June 93), p. 58.

El Mercado Unico Europeo y su impacto en América Latina reviewed by A. L. R. *Comercio Exterior,* v. 43, no. 11 (Nov 93), pp. 1095 – 1096.

MERCOSUL: sinopsis estatística/MERCOSUR: sinopsis estadística (Review). *Integración Latinoamericana,* v. 18, no. 194 (Oct 93), p. 89.

Merino, José María. *Las crónicas mestizas* reviewed by David Ross Gerling. *World Literature Today,* v. 67, no. 4 (Fall 93), pp. 785 – 786.

Merino Reyes, Luis. *Aurora y final del día* reviewed by Antonio Campaña. *Atenea (Chile),* no. 467 (1993), pp. 267 – 270.

Merrell, Floyd Fenly. *Unthinking Thinking: Jorge Luis Borges, Mathematics, and the New Physics* reviewed by Harley D. Oberhelman. *Hispania (USA),* v. 76, no. 2 (May 93), pp. 289 – 290.

Merrim, Stephanie, ed. *Feminist Perspectives on Sor Juana Inés de la Cruz* reviewed by Noël Valis. *Colonial Latin American Review,* v. 2, no. 1 – 2 (1993), pp. 304 – 308.

Messenger, Phyllis Mauch, ed. *The Ethics of Collecting Cultural Property: Whose Culture? Whose Property?* reviewed by Jorge Luján Muñoz. *Mesoamérica (USA),* v. 13, no. 24 (Dec 92), pp. 492 – 494.

Messenger, Phyllis Mauch and Lawrence Gustave Desmond. *A Dream of Maya: Augustus and Alice Le Plongeon in Nineteenth-Century Yucatán* reviewed by Kevin Gosner. *Hispanic American Historical Review,* v. 73, no. 3 (Aug 93), pp. 532 – 533.

Metcalf, Alida C. *Family and Frontier in Colonial Brazil: Santana de Parnaíba, 1580 – 1822* reviewed by Susan Migden Socolow. *The Americas,* v. 50, no. 2 (Oct 93), pp. 279 – 280.

México y el mundo: historia de sus relaciones exteriores reviewed by Marlene Alcántara Domínguez. *Relaciones Internacionales (Mexico),* v. 14, Nueva época, no. 55 (July – Sept 92), pp. 83 – 84.

Meyer, Jean A. *Los tambores de Calderón* reviewed by Alejandra Viveros (Review entitled "Adiós a los heroes"). *Nexos,* v. 16, no. 189 (Sept 93), p. 71.

— *Los tambores de Calderón* reviewed by Alvaro Enrique. *Vuelta,* v. 17, no. 201 (Aug 93), p. 47.

Meyer, Jean A., ed. *Egohistorias: el amor a Clío* reviewed by Jorge F. Hernández. *Vuelta,* v. 17, no. 204 (Nov 93), pp. 38 – 40.

Meyer, Karl Ernest. *El saqueo del pasado: historia del tráfico internacional ilegal de obras de arte* translated by Roberto Ramón Reyes Mazzoni. Reviewed by Jorge Luján Muñoz. *Mesoamérica (USA),* v. 13, no. 24 (Dec 92), pp. 492 – 494.

Meyer, Lorenzo. *La segunda muerte de la revolución mexicana* reviewed by Donald McCarthy (Review entitled "Critiquing the Critic"). *Business Mexico,* v. 3, no. 8 (Aug 93), p. 53.

— *Su majestad británica contra la revolución mexicana: el fin de un imperio informal* reviewed by Freidrich Katz. *Historia Mexicana,* v. 42, no. 1 (July – Sept 92), pp. 152 – 157.

Middlebrook, Kevin J., ed. *Unions, Workers, and the State in Mexico* reviewed by John A. Britton. *Hispanic American Historical Review,* v. 73, no. 1 (Feb 93), pp. 183 – 184.

Miguel, María Esther de. *Norah Lange* reviewed by Eliana C. Hermann. *Chasqui,* v. 22, no. 1 (May 93), pp. 92 – 94.

Milán, Eduardo. *Errar* reviewed by Juan Malpartida (Review entitled *"Errar* y acertar"). *Cuadernos Hispanoamericanos,* no. 516 (June 93), pp. 136 – 138.

— *La vida mantis* reviewed by David Medina Portillo. *Vuelta,* v. 17, no. 204 (Nov 93), p. 43.

— *La vida mantis* reviewed by Malva Flores. *Vuelta,* v. 17, no. 205 (Dec 93), pp. 51 – 52.

Miller, Errol L. *Jamaican Society and High Schooling* reviewed by J. Edward Greene. *La Educación (USA),* v. 36, no. 111 – 113 (1992), pp. 300 – 301.

— *Men at Risk* reviewed by Adam Jones. *Caribbean Studies,* v. 25, no. 1 – 2 (Jan – July 92), pp. 167 – 170.

— *Men at Risk* reviewed by Barry Chavannes. *Social and Economic Studies,* v. 41, no. 3 (Sept 92), pp. 186 – 192.

Miller, Francesca. *Latin American Women and the Search for Social Justice* reviewed by Trudy Yeager. *The Americas,* v. 49, no. 3 (Jan 93), pp. 412 – 414.

— *Latin American Women and the Search for Social Justice* reviewed by Asunción Horno-Delgado. *Letras Femeninas,* v. 19, no. 1 – 2 (Spring – Fall 93), pp. 139 – 140.

Miller, Ingrid Watson. *Afro-Hispanic Literature: An Anthology of Hispanic Writers of African Ancestry* reviewed by James J. Davis. *Afro-Hispanic Review,* v. 12, no. 1 (Spring 93), pp. 59 – 60.

Miller, Nicola. *Soviet Relations with Latin America, 1959 – 1987* reviewed by Marina Oborotova (Review entitled "Russian Policy in Latin America: Past, Present, and Future"). *Latin American Research Review,* v. 28, no. 3 (1993), pp. 183 – 188.

Miller, Simon and Arij Ouweneel, eds. *The Indian Community of Colonial Mexico: Fifteen Essays on Land Tenure, Corporate Organizations, Ideology, and Village Politics* reviewed by Margarita Menegus Bornemann. *Historia Mexicana,* v. 42, no. 1 (July – Sept 92), pp. 138 – 144.

Millones Santa Gadea, Luis and Hiroyasu Tomoeda. *500 años de mestizaje en los Andes* reviewed by Emma María Sordo. *Hispanic American Historical Review,* v. 73, no. 4 (Nov 93), p. 676.

Millones Santa Gadea, Luis et al, eds. *El retorno de las huacas: estudios y documentos sobre el Taki Onqoy, siglo XVI* reviewed by Javier Flores Espinoza. *Historia y Cultura (Peru),* no. 20 (1990), pp. 381 – 382.

Minaudier, Jean-Pierre. *Histoire de la Colombie: de la conquête à nos jours* reviewed by Scarlett O'Phelan Godoy. *Anuario de Estudios Americanos,* v. 49, Suppl. 1 (1992), p. 257.

— *Histoire de la Colombie: de la conquête à nos jours* reviewed by Frédérique Langue. *Caravelle,* no. 60 (1993), pp. 162 – 165.

Mingo de la Concepción, Manuel. *Historia de las misiones franciscanas de Tarija entre chiriguanos* reviewed by Pedro de Anasagasti. *Signo,* no. 35, Nueva época (Jan – Apr 92), pp. 237 – 239.

Miño Grijalva, Manuel and Alicia Hernández Chávez, eds. *Cincuenta años de historia en México,* vols. I y II, reviewed by Harold Dana Sims. *Hispanic American Historical Review,* v. 73, no. 4 (Nov 93), pp. 668 – 670.

Miranda, Ana María. *Bay of All Saints and Every Conceivable Sin,* a translation of *Boca do inferno,* translated by Giovanni Pontiero. Reviewed by Clifford E. Landers. *Review,* no. 47 (Fall 93), pp. 99 – 101.

— *Bocca d'inferno,* a translation of *Boca do inferno.* Reviewed by Silvio Castro. *Quaderni Ibero-Americani,* no. 72 (Dec 92), pp. 743 – 745.

Miranda, Julio E. *El guardián del museo* reviewed by Analy Lorenzo. *Revista Nacional de Cultura (Venezuela),* v. 53, no. 286 (July – Sept 92), pp. 260 – 261.

Miranda Bastidas, Haidée and David Ruiz Chataing. *El anti-imperialismo en la prensa de la época de Cipriano Castro, 1899 – 1908* reviewed by Julián Rodríguez Barazarte. *Boletín de la Academia Nacional de la Historia (Venezuela),* v. 76, no. 302 (Apr – June 93), pp. 152 – 153.

Mitchell, Christopher, ed. *Western Hemisphere Immigration and United States Foreign Policy* reviewed by Caroline Thomas. *Bulletin of Latin American Research,* v. 12, no. 2 (May 93), pp. 238 – 239.

Mitchell, William P. *Peasants on the Edge: Crop, Cult, and Crisis in the Andes* reviewed by Rodrigo Montoya. *Bulletin of Latin American Research,* v. 12, no. 1 (Jan 93), pp. 121 – 122.

— *Peasants on the Edge: Crop, Cult, and Crisis in the Andes* reviewed by Orin Starn. *Hispanic American Historical Review,* v. 73, no. 1 (Feb 93), pp. 175 – 76.

— *Peasants on the Edge: Crop, Cult, and Crisis in the Andes* reviewed by Thomas M. Davies, Jr. *Journal of Developing Areas,* v. 27, no. 3 (Apr 93), pp. 430 – 432.

Moisés, José Alvaro, ed. *O futuro do Brasil: a América Latina e o fim da guerra fria* reviewed by Bernardo Kucinski. *Journal of Latin American Studies,* v. 25, no. 2 (May 93), pp. 410 – 411.

Molina, Enrique. *Hacia una isla incierta* reviewed by Jacobo Sefamí. *Vuelta,* v. 17, no. 201 (Aug 93), pp. 49 – 51.

Molina, Silvia. *Un hombre cerca* reviewed by David Huerta (Review entitled "Las vías de pasión"). *Nexos,* v. 16, no. 186 (June 93), p. 75.

— *Un hombre cerca* reviewed by Esther Martínez Luna (Review entitled "Voz íntima"). *Nexos,* v. 16, no. 181 (Jan 93), p. 75. II.

Molina Cardona, Mauricio. *Tiempo lunar* reviewed by Christopher Domínguez Michael. *Vuelta,* v. 17, no. 201 (Aug 93), p. 48.

Molloy, Sylvia. *At Face Value: Autobiographical Writing in Spanish America* reviewed by Robert A. Parsons. *Hispania (USA),* v. 76, no. 2 (May 93), pp. 290 – 291.

— *At Face Value: Autobiographical Writing in Spanish America* reviewed by Kathleen Ross. *Hispanic Review,* v. 61, no. 4 (Fall 93), pp. 596 – 598.

— *At Face Value: Autobiographical Writing in Spanish America* reviewed by John Walker. *Revista Canadiense de Estudios Hispánicos,* v. 17, no. 2 (Winter 93), pp. 404 – 407.

Moncaut, Carlos Antonio. *Travesías de antaño: por caminos reales, postas y mensajerías* reviewed by Gregorio A. Caro Figueroa. *Todo Es Historia,* v. 27, no. 315 (Oct 93), pp. 62 – 63. II.

Monclaire, Stéphane, ed. *A constituição desejada: SAIC; as 72.719 sugestões enviadas pelos brasileiros à Assembléia Nacional Constituinte* reviewed by Carlos Schmidt Arturi. *Cahiers des Amériques Latines,* no. 14 (1992), pp. 153 – 156.

Monestier, Jaime. *El combate laico: bajorrelieve de la reforma valeriana* reviewed by Alfonso Fernández Cabrelli. *Hoy Es Historia,* v. 10, no. 57 (Apr – May 93), p. 80.

Monsalve, Alfonso. *Bogotanos* reviewed by Peter N. Thomas. *Chasqui,* v. 22, no. 1 (May 93), pp. 107 – 110.

Monsiváis, Carlos. *Nuevo catecismo para indios remisos* reviewed by Luis Miguel Aguilar (Review entitled "Nuevo Monsiváis para lectores indecisos"). *Nexos,* v. 16, no. 189 (Sept 93), pp. 63 – 65.

Montaner, Carlos Alberto. *Fidel Castro and the Cuban Revolution: Age, Position, Character, Destiny, Personality, and Ambition* reviewed by Rhoda P. Rabkin. *Cuban Studies/Estudios Cubanos,* v. 23 (1993), pp. 235 – 238.

Montello, Josué. *O baile da despedida* reviewed by Richard A. Preto-Rodas. *World Literature Today,* v. 67, no. 4 (Fall 93), pp. 791 – 792.

Montero, Mayra. *Del rojo de su sombra* reviewed by José Eduardo González. *Chasqui,* v. 22, no. 2 (Nov 93), pp. 165 – 167.

Monterroso, Augusto. *Los buscadores de oro* reviewed by Fabienne Bradu. *Vuelta,* v. 17, no. 205 (Dec 93), pp. 41 – 43.

— *Los buscadores de oro* reviewed by Horacio Ortiz González (Review entitled "Las armas de la memoria"). *Nexos,* v. 16, no. 191 (Nov 93), pp. 61 – 62. II.

Montes Brunet, Hugo. *De la vida de un profesor* reviewed by Gloria Videla de Rivero. *Revista Chilena de Literatura,* no. 40 (Nov 92), pp. 157 – 158.

— *Por nuestro idioma* reviewed by Julio Orlandi. *Revista Chilena de Literatura,* no. 41 (Apr 93), p. 140.

Montes Huidobro, Matías. *Funeral en Teruel* reviewed by Francisco Soto. *The Americas Review,* v. 21, no. 1 (Spring 93), pp. 120 – 121.

— *Qwert and the Wedding Gown* translated by John Mitchell and Ruth Mitchell de Aguilar. Reviewed by José B. Fernández. *The Americas Review,* v. 21, no. 1 (Spring 93), pp. 119 – 120.

Moore, Joan W. *Going Down to the Barrio: Homeboys and Homegirls in Change* reviewed by Kathleen Logan. *Hispanic American Historical Review,* v. 73, no. 3 (Aug 93), pp. 488 – 489.

Mora Camargo, Santiago et al. *Cultivars, Anthropic Soils, and Stability: A Preliminary Report of Archaeological Research in Araracuara, Colombian Amazonia* reviewed by Leonor Herrera Angel. *Revista Colombiana de Antropología,* v. 29 (1992), pp. 251 – 253.

Mora Valcárcel, Carmen de. *Las siete ciudades de Cíbola: textos y testimonios sobre la expedición de Vázquez Coronado* reviewed by Francisco Noguerol Jiménez. *Anuario de Estudios Americanos,* v. 50, no. 1 (1993), pp. 323 – 324.

Moraes, Dênis de. *A esquerda e o golpe de '64: vinte e cinco anos depois, as forças populares repensam seus mitos, sonhos, e ilusões* reviewed by Cliff Welch. *Hispanic American Historical Review,* v. 73, no. 1 (Feb 93), p. 170.

Morales, Andrés. *Verbo* reviewed by Vicente Mengod. *Atenea (Chile),* no. 465 – 466 (1992), pp. 370 – 372.

— *Vicio de belleza* reviewed by Jorge Rodríguez Padrón. *Revista Chilena de Literatura,* no. 41 (Apr 93), p. 139.

Morales, Jorge Luis. *Obelisco: diosa madre poesía* reviewed by Margarita Gardón. *Revista Iberoamericana,* v. 59, no. 162 – 163 (Jan – June 93), pp. 382 – 385.

Morales, Josefina, ed. *La reestructuración industrial en México: cinco aspectos fundamentales* reviewed by María Luisa González Marín. *Problemas del Desarrollo*, v. 24, no. 93 (Apr – June 93), pp. 235 – 236.

Morales, Waltraud Queiser. *Bolivia: Land of Struggle* reviewed by Christopher Mitchell. *Studies in Comparative International Development*, v. 27, no. 3 (Fall 92), pp. 124 – 125.

— *Bolivia: Land of Struggle* reviewed by Erick D. Langer. *Hispanic American Historical Review*, v. 73, no. 1 (Feb 93), p. 173.

— *Bolivia: Land of Struggle* reviewed by Robert H. Jackson. *The Americas*, v. 50, no. 1 (July 93), pp. 145 – 146.

Morand, Carlos. *Bienvenidos a Elsinor, profesor Freud* reviewed by Fernando Valenzuela Erazo. *Revista Chilena de Literatura*, no. 41 (Apr 93), pp. 131 – 133.

Moreira Neto, Carlos and Darcy Ribeiro. *A fundação do Brasil: testemunhos, 1500 – 1700* reviewed by José Carlos Sebe Bohn Meihy. *Vozes*, v. 87, no. 3 (May – June 93), pp. 90 – 91.

Moreno, Carlos. *Patrimonio de la producción rural en el antiguo partido de Cañuelas* reviewed by Silvina Ruiz Moreno de Bunge. *Todo Es Historia*, v. 26, no. 308 (Mar 93), p. 72. Il.

Moreno Ruffinelli, José A. *Régimen patrimonial del matrimonio: Ley no. 1/92 comentada* (Review). *Revista Paraguaya de Sociología*, v. 29, no. 85 (Sept – Dec 92), p. 190.

Moreno Sánchez, Manuel. *Notas desde Abraham Angel* reviewed by Hugo Hiriart (Review entitled "La flor de mil filosofías"). *Nexos*, v. 16, no. 190 (Oct 93), p. 81.

Morinis, E. Alan and N. Ross Crumrine, eds. *Pilgrimage in Latin America* reviewed by María J. Rodríguez Shadow and Robert D. Shadow. *Mesoamérica (USA)*, v. 13, no. 24 (Dec 92), pp. 473 – 480.

Morley, Morris H. and James F. Petras. *Latin America in the Time of Cholera: Electoral Politics, Market Economics, and Permanent Crisis* reviewed by Donald F. Stevens. *The Americas*, v. 50, no. 2 (Oct 93), pp. 291 – 292.

Morrison, Allen. *The Tramways of Brazil: A 130-Year Survey* reviewed by Carlos Wehrs. *Revista do Instituto Histórico e Geográfico Brasileiro*, no. 371 (Apr – June 91), pp. 609 – 610.

Morrissey, Mike and Graham Hart. *Practical Skills in Caribbean Geography, Book 1: Grade 8 – Basic CXC and Book 2: Grade 10 – General CXC* reviewed by Laurence Neuville. *Caribbean Geography*, v. 3, no. 4 (Sept 92), pp. 279 – 280.

Morrisson, Christian and François Bourguignon, eds. *External Trade and Income Distribution* reviewed by Jaime de Melo. *Economic Development and Cultural Change*, v. 42, no. 1 (Oct 93), pp. 198 – 200.

Moseley, Michael Edward. *The Incas and Their Ancestors: The Archaeology of Peru* reviewed by Richard L. Burger. *Hispanic American Historical Review*, v. 73, no. 4 (Nov 93), pp. 682 – 684.

— *The Incas and Their Ancestors: The Archaeology of Peru* reviewed by Monica Barnes. *Latin American Indian Literatures Journal*, v. 9, no. 1 (Spring 93), pp. 78 – 79.

Mota, Luis Ramón, ed. *Recopilación de autores del folclor venezolano* reviewed by Antonio Bracho. *Revista Nacional de Cultura (Venezuela)*, v. 53, no. 286 (July – Sept 92), p. 267.

Müller, Gabriele et al. *Pátzcuaro, Romantik und Kommerzialität* reviewed by Thomas D. Schoonover. *Hispanic American Historical Review*, v. 73, no. 2 (May 93), pp. 338 – 339.

Múgica de Fignoni, Nora and Zulema Solana. *La gramática modular* reviewed by Andrea Ostrov. *La Educación (USA)*, v. 37, no. 114 (1993), pp. 165 – 166.

Mujer y SIDA reviewed by Beatriz Jiménez Carrillo. *El Cotidiano*, v. 9, no. 53 (Mar – Apr 93), p. 119.

Mujer y SIDA reviewed by Nelson Minello. *Estudios Sociológicos*, v. 10, no. 30 (Sept – Dec 92), pp. 825 – 830.

Las mujeres en la revolución mexicana: biografías de mujeres revolucionarias reviewed by Martha Eva Rocha Islas (Review entitled "Más allá del estereotipo"). *Fem*, v. 17, no. 121 (Mar 93), pp. 46 – 48. Bibl.

Mulher e políticas públicas reviewed by Helena Bocayuva Cunha (Review entitled "Gênero e planejamento"). *Estudos Feministas*, v. 1, no. 1 (1993), pp. 208 – 209.

Mulheres latino-americanas em dados (Review entitled "Estatísticas sobre as mulheres"). *Estudos Feministas*, v. 1, no. 2 (1993), pp. 502 – 503.

Munford, Clarence J. *The Black Ordeal of Slavery and Slave Trading in the French West Indies, 1625 – 1715* reviewed by David Eltis. *Hispanic American Historical Review*, v. 73, no. 2 (May 93), pp. 316 – 317.

Muñoz Valenzuela, Heraldo, ed. *Environment and Diplomacy in the Americas* reviewed by Joan Martínez Alier. *Hispanic American Historical Review*, v. 73, no. 3 (Aug 93), pp. 536 – 537.

Murphy, Arthur D. and Alex Stepick. *Social Inequality in Oaxaca: A History of Resistance and Change* reviewed by John K. Chance. *The Americas*, v. 49, no. 4 (Apr 93), pp. 541 – 542.

Murphy, Martin Francis. *Dominican Sugar Plantations: Production and Foreign Labor Integration* reviewed by Michel-Rolph Trouillot. *Hispanic American Historical Review*, v. 73, no. 3 (Aug 93), pp. 535 – 536.

— *Dominican Sugar Plantations: Production and Foreign Labor Integration* reviewed by Tom Spencer-Walters. *Journal of Caribbean Studies*, v. 9, no. 1 – 2 (Winter 92 – Spring 93), pp. 140 – 142.

Música autóctona del norte de Potosí reviewed by Honoria Arredondo Calderón. *Revista Musical Chilena*, v. 46, no. 178 (July – Dec 92), pp. 127 – 128.

Musset, Alain. *De l'eau vive à l'eau morte: enjeux techniques et culturels dans la vallée de Mexico, XVIᵉ – XIXᵉ siècles* reviewed by Marie-Danielle Démelas-Bohy. *Caravelle*, no. 59 (1992), p. 307.

Mutis, Alvaro. *Tríptico de mar y tierra* reviewed by Esther Martínez Luna (Review entitled "Desde una gavia"). *Nexos*, v. 16, no. 189 (Sept 93), p. 71. Il.

— *La última escala del "tramp steamer"* reviewed by Nathalie Pauner. *Inti*, no. 36 (Fall 92), pp. 195 – 196.

Myers, Joan et al. *Santiago: Saint of Two Worlds.* Photographs by Joan Myers. Reviewed by Jeffrey Klaiber. *Hispanic American Historical Review*, v. 73, no. 3 (Aug 93), p. 492.

Nader, Gary. *Latin American Price Guide: Auction Records, May 1977 – May 1993* reviewed by Andrés Salgado R. (Accompanied by an English translation). *Art Nexus*, no. 10 (Sept – Dec 93), p. 42.

Nagy, Silvia. *Historia de la canción folkórica en los Andes* reviewed by Juan Zevallos Aguilar. *Revista de Crítica Literaria Latinoamericana*, v. 19, no. 37 (Jan – June 93), pp. 370 – 372.

Naharro-Calderón, José María, ed. *El exilio de las Españas de 1939 en las Américas: "¿Adónde fue la canción?"* reviewed by Nancy Vosburg. *Hispania (USA)*, v. 76, no. 2 (May 93), pp. 277 – 278.

Narváez, Jorge E., ed. *La invención de la memoria* reviewed by Domnita Dumitrescu. *Nuevo Texto Crítico,* v. 6, no. 11 (1993), pp. 268 – 270.

Navarro, Juan Carlos. *Descentralización: una alternativa de política educativa* reviewed by Emil Alvarado Vera. *La Educación (USA),* v. 36, no. 111 – 113 (1992), p. 301.

Navarro García, Luis, ed. *Historia de las Américas* reviewed by Ana María Cignetti. *Revista de Historia de América,* no. 113 (Jan – June 92), pp. 165 – 170.

Nawrot, Piotr. *Vespers Music in the Paraguay Reductions* reviewed by James Radomski. *Inter-American Music Review,* v. 13, no. 2 (Spring – Summer 93), pp. 157 – 159. Bibl.

Nazzari, Muriel. *Disappearance of the Dowry: Women, Families, and Social Change in São Paulo, Brazil, 1600 – 1900* reviewed by Susan M. Socolow. *The Americas,* v. 49, no. 3 (Jan 93), pp. 414 – 415.

— *Disappearance of the Dowry: Women, Families, and Social Change in São Paulo, Brazil, 1600 – 1900* reviewed by John E. Kicza. *Colonial Latin American Review,* v. 2, no. 1 – 2 (1993), pp. 308 – 311.

— *Disappearance of the Dowry: Women, Families, and Social Change in São Paulo, Brazil, 1600 – 1900* reviewed by Sandra Lauderdale Graham. *Journal of Latin American Studies,* v. 25, no. 1 (Feb 93), pp. 193 – 194.

— *Disappearance of the Dowry: Women, Families, and Social Change in São Paulo, Brazil, 1600 – 1900* reviewed by Dain Borges. *Luso-Brazilian Review,* v. 30, no. 1 (Summer 93), pp. 141 – 142.

Nebel, Richard. *Santa María Tonantzin, Virgen de Guadalupe: Religiöse Kontinuität und Transformation in Mexiko* reviewed by Teodoro Hampe Martínez. *Revista de Indias,* v. 53, no. 197 (Jan – Apr 93), pp. 114 – 116.

Negroni, María. *La jaula bajo el trapo* reviewed by Angélica Gorodischer (Review entitled "Cuerpos enjaulados"). *Confluencia,* v. 8, no. 1 (Fall 92), pp. 183 – 184.

Nelson, William Javier. *Almost a Territory: America's Attempt to Annex the Dominican Republic* reviewed by Mu-Kien Adriana Sang. *Afro-Hispanic Review,* v. 12, no. 1 (Spring 93), pp. 55 – 56.

Neruda, Pablo. *Maremoto* reviewed by Ignacio Valente. *Atenea (Chile),* no. 467 (1993), pp. 263 – 265.

Nettleford, Rex and Philip Manderson Sherlock. *The University of the West Indies: A Caribbean Response to the Challenge of Change* reviewed by Rafael L. Ramírez. *Caribbean Studies,* v. 25, no. 1 – 2 (Jan – July 92), pp. 171 – 172.

— *The University of the West Indies: A Caribbean Response to the Challenge of Change* reviewed by Bruce King. *Journal of Caribbean Studies,* v. 9, no. 1 – 2 (Winter 92 – Spring 93), pp. 125 – 127.

Newland, Carlos. *Buenos Aires no es pampa: la educación elemental porteña, 1820 – 1860* reviewed by Mariano Narodowski. *Todo Es Historia,* v. 26, no. 308 (Mar 93), pp. 72 – 73. Il.

Newman, Gray and Anna Szterenfeld. *Business International's Guide to Doing Business in Mexico* reviewed by Donald McCarthy (Review entitled "Help for Corporate Strategists"). *Business Mexico,* v. 3, no. 3 (Mar 93), p. 52.

Newton, Ronald C. *The "Nazi Menace" in Argentina, 1931 – 1947* reviewed by Joel Horowitz. *The Americas,* v. 50, no. 1 (July 93), pp. 140 – 141.

— *The "Nazi Menace" in Argentina, 1931 – 1947* reviewed by Walter Little. *Bulletin of Latin American Research,* v. 12, no. 1 (Jan 93), pp. 117 – 118.

— *The "Nazi Menace" in Argentina, 1931 – 1947* reviewed by Jeff Lesser. *European Review of Latin American and Caribbean Studies,* no. 54 (June 93), pp. 136 – 137.

— *The "Nazi Menace" in Argentina, 1931 – 1947* reviewed by Stanley E. Hilton. *Hispanic American Historical Review,* v. 73, no. 4 (Nov 93), pp. 706 – 707.

— *The "Nazi Menace" in Argentina, 1931 – 1947* reviewed by Celia Szusterman. *Journal of Latin American Studies,* v. 25, no. 1 (Feb 93), pp. 202 – 205.

— *The "Nazi Menace" in Argentina, 1931 – 1947* reviewed by Mario Rapoport. *Revista Interamericana de Bibliografía,* v. 42, no. 4 (1992), pp. 659 – 660.

Nguyen, Thai Hop, ed. *Evangelización y teología en el Perú* reviewed by Wilfredo Ardito Vega. *Amazonía Peruana,* v. 11, no. 22 (Oct 92), pp. 273 – 277.

Niess, Frank. *20mal Kuba* reviewed by Martin Franzbach. *Iberoamericana,* v. 16, no. 47 – 48 (1992), pp. 142 – 143.

Nieto Vélez, Armando. *Francisco del Castillo, el apóstol de Lima* reviewed by Pedro Guibovich. *Apuntes (Peru),* no. 30 (Jan – June 92), pp. 109 – 110.

Nisttahuz, Jaime. *La humedad es una sombra y otros poemas* reviewed by Jaime Martínez Salguero. *Signo,* no. 38, Nueva época (Jan – Apr 93), pp. 243 – 245.

Noé, Luis Felipe. *A Oriente por Occidente* reviewed by Ivonne Pini (Accompanied by an English translation). *Art Nexus,* no. 10 (Sept – Dec 93), pp. 41 – 42. Il.

Noemí Perilli, Carmen

See
Perilli de Garmendia, Carmen

Nostrand, Richard L. *The Hispano Homeland* reviewed by Carlos Brazil Ramírez. *Colonial Latin American Historical Review,* v. 2, no. 3 (Summer 93), pp. 379 – 380.

— *The Hispano Homeland* reviewed by Henry F. Dobyns. *Hispanic American Historical Review,* v. 73, no. 2 (May 93), pp. 302 – 303.

— *The Hispano Homeland* reviewed by Martha A. Works. *Geographical Review,* v. 83, no. 2 (Apr 93), pp. 224 – 226.

Novelo, Victoria. *La difícil democracia de los petroleros: historia de un proyecto sindical* reviewed by Aída Escamilla Rubio. *El Cotidiano,* v. 9, no. 56 (July 93), p. 117.

Nowak, Kerstin and Dagmar Schweitzer. *Die Inka und der Krieg* reviewed by Mónica Ricketts. *Revista Andina,* v. 11, no. 1 (July 93), pp. 249 – 250.

Núñez, Blanca. *El niño sordo y su familia: apontes desde la psicología clínica* reviewed by Aurora Pérez T. *La Educación (USA),* v. 37, no. 114 (1993), pp. 166 – 167.

Núñez González, Oscar. *Innovaciones democrático – culturales del movimiento urbano-popular* reviewed by José Javier Gutiérrez Rodríguez. *El Cotidiano,* v. 10, no. 57 (Aug – Sept 93), pp. 107 – 108.

Núñez Rebaza, Lucy. *Los dansaq* reviewed by Gérard Borras. *Caravelle,* no. 59 (1992), pp. 311 – 313.

Núñez Sánchez, Jorge, ed. *Historia de la mujer y la familia* reviewed by Gilma Mora de Tovar. *Anuario Colombiano de Historia Social y de la Cultura,* no. 20 (1992), pp. 164 – 167.

Nunn, Frederick M. *The Time of the Generals: Latin American Professional Militarism in World Perspective* reviewed by Daniel M. Masterson. *The Americas,* v. 50, no. 1 (July 93), pp. 137 – 139.

— *The Time of the Generals: Latin American Professional Militarism in World Perspective* reviewed by John D. Martz. *Revista Interamericana de Bibliografía,* v. 42, no. 3 (1992), p. 506.

Nuño Montes, Juan Antonio. *La escuela de la sospecha: nuevos ensayos polémicos* reviewed by Amaya Llebot Cazalis. *Revista Nacional de Cultura (Venezuela),* v. 54, no. 287 (Oct – Dec 92), pp. 267 – 268.

Oberhelman, Harley D. *Gabriel García Márquez: A Study of the Short Fiction* reviewed by R. A. Kerr. *Hispania (USA)*, v. 76, no. 2 (May 93), pp. 291 – 292.

Ocampos, Genoveva. *Mujeres campesinas: estrategias de vida* reviewed by Sylvia Chant. *European Review of Latin American and Caribbean Studies*, no. 54 (June 93), pp. 137 – 138.

Oddone, Juan Antonio. *Uruguay entre la depresión y la guerra, 1929 – 1945* reviewed by Rosa Perla Raicher. *Estudios Interdisciplinarios de América Latina y el Caribe*, v. 3, no. 2 (July – Dec 92), pp. 129 – 133.

— *Uruguay entre la depresión y la guerra, 1929 – 1945* reviewed by Henry Finch. *Hispanic American Historical Review*, v. 73, no. 3 (Aug 93), p. 526.

Offner, John L. *An Unwanted War: The Diplomacy of the United States and Spain over Cuba, 1895 – 1898* reviewed by Jules R. Benjamin. *Hispanic American Historical Review*, v. 73, no. 3 (Aug 93), pp. 539 – 540.

O'Hara Gonzales, Edgar. *Curtir las pieles* reviewed by Miguel Gomes. *Inti*, no. 36 (Fall 92), pp. 187 – 190.

— *Límites del criollismo* reviewed by Miguel Gomes. *Inti*, no. 36 (Fall 92), pp. 187 – 190.

Oliphant, David, ed. *Nahuatl to Rayuela: The Latin American Collection at Texas* reviewed by Deborah L. Jakubs. *Hispanic American Historical Review*, v. 73, no. 2 (May 93), pp. 293 – 294.

Olivar Jimenez, Martha Lucia et al. *O regime comum de origem no MERCOSUL* (Review). *Integración Latinoamericana*, v. 18, no. 192 (Aug 92), pp. 98 – 99.

Olivares, Enrique. *México: crisis y dependencia tecnológica* reviewed by Irma Portos. *Problemas del Desarrollo*, v. 24, no. 94 (July – Sept 93), pp. 290 – 292.

Oliveira, João Batista Araújo e and Greville Rumble, eds. *Educación a distancia en América Latina: análisis de costo-efectividad* reviewed by Aaron Segal. *Interciencia*, v. 18, no. 6 (Nov – Dec 93), pp. 327 – 328.

Oliveira, Vera Lúcia de. *Geografie d'ombra* reviewed by Raquel Villardi. *Quaderni Ibero-Americani*, no. 72 (Dec 92), pp. 746 – 747.

Olivero, Omar. *El tambor conga: un instrumento musical afroamericano; su función y transcendencia en la música latinoamerica* reviewed by Tulia Bonetti P. *La Educación (USA)*, v. 37, no. 115 (1993), pp. 428 – 429.

Ollé, Carmen. *¿Por qué hacen tanto ruido?* reviewed by Abelardo Sánchez León (Review entitled "Una voz en el caos"). *Debate (Peru)*, v. 15, no. 71 (Nov 92 – Jan 93), pp. 75 – 76. Il.

— *¿Por qué hacen tanto ruido?* reviewed by Antonio Cornejo Polar. *Revista de Crítica Literaria Latinoamericana*, v. 19, no. 38 (July – Dec 93), pp. 426 – 428.

Olmedo Jiménez, Manuel. *Jerónimo de Loaysa, O.P., pacificador de españoles y protector de indios* reviewed by Ximena Sosa-Buchholz. *Colonial Latin American Historical Review*, v. 2, no. 3 (Summer 93), pp. 371 – 372.

Olmos, Andrés de. *Tratado de hechicerías y sortilegios* edited and translated by Georges Baudot. Reviewed by Jacqueline de Durand-Forest. *Caravelle*, no. 59 (1992), pp. 300 – 302.

Olson, James Stuart, ed. *Historical Dictionary of the Spanish Empire, 1402 – 1975* reviewed by J. Benedict Warren. *Revista Interamericana de Bibliografía*, v. 42, no. 2 (1992), p. 286.

Onetti, Juan Carlos. *Cuando ya no importe* reviewed by Alvaro Enrigue. *Vuelta*, v. 17, no. 199 (June 93), p. 47.

— *Cuando ya no importe* reviewed by Milagros Sánchez Arnosi (Review entitled "Onetti: la literatura como pasión"). *Cuadernos Hispanoamericanos*, no. 522 (Dec 93), pp. 122 – 125.

— *Cuando ya no importe* reviewed by Sealtiel Alatriste (Review entitled "Sin final"). *Nexos*, v. 16, no. 185 (May 93), pp. 77 – 78.

Opatrny, Josef. *U.S. Expansionism and Cuban Annexationism in the 1850s* reviewed by Allan J. Kuethe. *Hispanic American Historical Review*, v. 73, no. 4 (Nov 93), pp. 724 – 725.

Oppenheimer, Andrés. *Castro's Final Hour: The Secret Story behind the Coming Downfall of Communist Cuba* reviewed by Harold Dana Sims. *Cuban Studies/Estudios Cubanos*, v. 23 (1993), pp. 240 – 242.

— *Castro's Final Hour: The Secret Story behind the Coming Downfall of Communist Cuba* reviewed by Damián Fernández (Review entitled "The Theater of Cuban Politics"). *Hemisphere*, v. 5, no. 2 (Winter – Spring 93), pp. 46 – 48.

— *La hora final de Castro* reviewed by Ernesto Hernández Busto (Review entitled "Fin del siglo con Castro"). *Vuelta*, v. 17, no. 200 (July 93), pp. 55 – 56.

Ormeño Ortíz, Eugenio et al. *Educación para los desarrollos locales: macrocomunas y sustrato material en la IX región de la Araucanía* (Review). *La Educación (USA)*, v. 36, no. 111 – 113 (1992), pp. 302 – 303.

Oropesa, Salvador A. *La obra de Ariel Dorfman: ficción y crítica* reviewed by Charles A. Piano. *World Literature Today*, v. 67, no. 3 (Summer 93), p. 592.

Orozco, Olga. *Mutaciones de la realidad* reviewed by Alfredo García Valdez. *Vuelta*, v. 17, no. 198 (May 93), pp. 51 – 52.

Ortega, Julio. *El discurso de la abundancia* reviewed by George R. McMurray. *Hispania (USA)*, v. 76, no. 3 (Sept 93), pp. 485 – 486.

— *Una poética del cambio* reviewed by George R. McMurray. *Hispania (USA)*, v. 76, no. 3 (Sept 93), pp. 485 – 486.

Ortiz de la Tabla Ducasse, Javier et al, eds. *Cartas de cabildos hispanoamericanos: Audiencia de Quito* reviewed by Frédérique Langue. *Caravelle*, no. 60 (1993), pp. 147 – 148.

Ortiz de Zevallos, Felipe. *A mitad de camino* reviewed by Alonso Cueto (Review entitled "La mitad del futuro"). *Debate (Peru)*, v. 16, no. 72 (Mar – May 93), pp. 63 – 64. Il.

— *A mitad de camino* reviewed by José Luis Sardón. *Apuntes (Peru)*, no. 31 (July – Dec 92), pp. 117 – 119.

Ortiz Pacheco, Nicolás. *Plenitud de plenitudes* reviewed by Carlos Castañón Barrientos. *Signo*, no. 35, Nueva época (Jan – Apr 92), pp. 239 – 243.

Osborn, Elizabeth M., ed. *On Common Ground: Contemporary Hispanic-American Plays* reviewed by Wilma Feliciano. *Latin American Theatre Review*, v. 26, no. 2 (Spring 93), pp. 206 – 208.

Oses, Darío. *Machos tristes* reviewed by Antonio Avaria (Review entitled "Darío Oses, un escritor joven contra la corriente"). *Mensaje*, v. 42, no. 416 (Jan – Feb 93), p. 52. Il.

Ospina, William. *El país del viento* reviewed by David Medina Portillo. *Vuelta*, v. 17, no. 203 (Oct 93), pp. 50 – 51.

Ossio Acuña, Juan M. *Parentesco, reciprocidad y jerarquía en los Andes: una aproximación a la organización social de la comunidad de Andamarca* reviewed by Penny Dransart. *Journal of Latin American Studies*, v. 25, no. 3 (Oct 93), pp. 684 – 686.

Oszlak, Oscar. *Merecer la ciudad: las pobres y el derecho al espacio urbano* reviewed by Gustavo de la Vega Shiota. *Revista Mexicana de Ciencias Políticas y Sociales*, v. 37, Nueva época, no. 148 (Apr – June 92), pp. 191 – 194.

Otazo, Antonio. *La fuente del universo: Pachamama* reviewed by José Roberto Arze. *Signo*, no. 38, Nueva época (Jan – Apr 93), pp. 245 – 247.

Otte, Enrique, ed. *Cartas privadas de emigrantes a Indias, 1540 – 1616* reviewed by Jorge F. Hernández (Review entitled "Correspondencias con el pasado"). *Vuelta*, v. 17, no. 198 (May 93), pp. 55 – 57.

Ouweneel, Arij and Simon Miller, eds. *The Indian Community of Colonial Mexico: Fifteen Essays on Land Tenure, Corporate Organizations, Ideology, and Village Politics* reviewed by Margarita Menegus Bornemann. *Historia Mexicana*, v. 42, no. 1 (July – Sept 92), pp. 138 – 144.

Padial Guerchoux, Anita Louise and Angel Manuel Vázquez-Bigi. *Quiche Vinak: tragedia; nueva versión española y estudio histórico – literario del llamado 'Rabinal-Achí'* reviewed by Enrique Sam Colop. *Mesoamérica (USA)*, v. 13, no. 24 (Dec 92), pp. 465 – 473.

Padilla, Lizbeth. *Ritual de juegos efímeros* reviewed by Silvia Yáñez (Review entitled "Dos de poesía"). *Plural (Mexico)*, v. 22, no. 267 (Dec 93), pp. 83 – 84.

Padilla, Mario. *Mar para Bolivia* reviewed by Raúl Rivadeneira Prada. *Signo*, no. 38, Nueva época (Jan – Apr 93), pp. 247 – 248.

Padoch, Christine and Kent H. Redford, eds. *Conservation of Neotropical Forests: Working from Traditional Resource Use* reviewed by Mahesh Rangarajan. *Journal of Latin American Studies*, v. 25, no. 3 (Oct 93), pp. 687 – 688.

Padrón, Justo Jorge

See

Rodríguez Padrón, Justo Jorge

Pagano, Mabel. *Los griegos no existen* reviewed by Gustavo Fares. *Hispamérica*, v. 22, no. 64 – 65 (Apr – Aug 93), pp. 200 – 202.

— *Lorenza Reinafé o Quiroga: la barranca de la tragedia* reviewed by Eliana C. Hermann. *Chasqui*, v. 22, no. 1 (May 93), pp. 91 – 92.

Palacios, Irma and Coral Bracho. *Tierra de entraña ardiente* reviewed by Jacobo Sefamí. *Vuelta*, v. 17, no. 200 (July 93), pp. 58 – 59.

Palacios de Pizani, Alicia and Delia Lerner de Zunino. *El aprendizaje de la lengua escrita en la escuela: reflexiones sobre la propuesta pedagógica constructivista* reviewed by Magaly Muñoz de Pimentel. *La Educación (USA)*, v. 37, no. 115 (1993), pp. 426 – 428.

Palerm Vich, Angel. *México prehispánico: evolución y ecología* reviewed by William R. Fowler, Jr. *Hispanic American Historical Review*, v. 73, no. 1 (Feb 93), pp. 145 – 146.

Palma de Feuillet, Milagros. *Bodas de cenizas* reviewed by David William Foster. *Chasqui*, v. 22, no. 2 (Nov 93), pp. 160 – 161.

Palmer, Bruce. *Intervention in the Caribbean: The Dominican Crisis of 1965* reviewed by G. Pope Atkins. *Hispanic American Historical Review*, v. 73, no. 1 (Feb 93), pp. 188 – 189.

Palmer, David Scott, ed. *The Shining Path of Peru* reviewed by Florencia E. Mallon. *Hispanic American Historical Review*, v. 73, no. 3 (Aug 93), pp. 520 – 522.

— *The Shining Path of Peru* reviewed by James Dunkerley. *Journal of Latin American Studies*, v. 25, no. 2 (May 93), pp. 421 – 422.

— *The Shining Path of Peru* reviewed by Peter F. Klarén. *The Americas*, v. 50, no. 2 (Oct 93), pp. 287 – 289.

Palmié, Stephan. *Das Exil der Götter: Geschichte und Vorstellungswelt einer afrokubanischen Religion* reviewed by Matthias Perl. *Iberoamericana*, v. 17, no. 49 (1993), pp. 101 – 102.

Palomino Thompson, Eduardo. *Educación peruana: historia, análisis y propuestas* reviewed by Marta Llames Murúa. *La Educación (USA)*, v. 37, no. 115 (1993), pp. 429 – 431.

Pang, Hildegard Delgado. *Pre-Columbian Art: Investigations and Insights* reviewed by John F. Scott. *Hispanic American Historical Review*, v. 73, no. 1 (Feb 93), pp. 140 – 141.

Paporov, Yuri. *Hemingway en Cuba* reviewed by Martí Soler (Review entitled "Ernest y Yuri"). *Plural (Mexico)*, v. 22, no. 263 (Aug 93), pp. 78 – 79.

Paravisini-Gebert, Lizabeth and Carmen C. Esteves. *Green Cane and Juicy Flotsam: Short Stories by Caribbean Women* reviewed by Ivette Romero. *Letras Femeninas*, v. 19, no. 1 – 2 (Spring – Fall 93), pp. 154 – 155.

Paravisini-Gebert, Lizabeth and Margarite Fernández Olmos. *El placer de la palabra: literatura erótica femenina de América Latina; antología crítica* reviewed by Mónica Zapata. *Canadian Journal of Latin American and Caribbean Studies*, v. 17, no. 34 (1992), pp. 135 – 138.

Paravisini-Gebert, Lizabeth and Olga Torres-Seda. *Caribbean Women Novelists: An Annotated Bibliography* reviewed by David William Foster. *Chasqui*, v. 22, no. 2 (Nov 93), pp. 161 – 162.

Paredes, Carlos and Jeffrey D. Sachs. *Estabilización y crecimiento en el Perú* reviewed by Martha Rodríguez. *Apuntes (Peru)*, no. 29 (July – Dec 91), pp. 91 – 94.

Parker, Andrew et al, eds. *Nationalisms and Sexualities* reviewed by Catherine Davies (Review entitled "Women and a Redefinition of Argentinian Nationhood"). *Bulletin of Latin American Research*, v. 12, no. 3 (Sept 93), pp. 333 – 341.

— *Nationalisms and Sexualities* reviewed by Raúl Rodríguez-Hernández. *Letras Femeninas*, v. 19, no. 1 – 2 (Spring – Fall 93), pp. 134 – 135.

Parker Gumucio, Christian and Kenneth Aman, eds. *Popular Culture in Chile: Resistance and Survival* reviewed by Ton Salman. *European Review of Latin American and Caribbean Studies*, no. 53 (Dec 92), pp. 120 – 124.

Parker Gumucio, Cristián. *Otra lógica en América Latina: religión popular y modernización capitalista* reviewed by G. A. C. (Review entitled "Religión popular y modernización en América Latina"). *Mensaje*, v. 42, no. 423 (Oct 93), p. 531. Il.

Parra, Teresa de la. *Obra escogida* reviewed by Amaya Llebot Cazalis. *Revista Nacional de Cultura (Venezuela)*, v. 54, no. 287 (Oct – Dec 92), pp. 268 – 269.

Parra Carrasco, Fredy Omar. *Pensamiento teológico en Chile: contribución a su estudio, tomo V: El reino que ha de venir; historia y esperanza en la obra de Manuel Lacunza* reviewed by José Arteaga. *Mensaje*, v. 42, no. 425 (Dec 93), p. 657. Il.

Partnoy, Alicia. *Revenge of the Apple/Venganza de la manzana* translated by Richard Schaaf, Regina Kreger, and Alicia Partnoy. Reviewed by Debra A. Castillo. *Letras Femeninas*, v. 19, no. 1 – 2 (Spring – Fall 93), pp. 153 – 154.

Pásara, Luis H. et al. *La otra cara de la luna: nuevos actores sociales en el Perú* reviewed by Romeo Grompone (Review entitled "Nuevos actores"). *Debate (Peru)*, v. 15, no. 70 (Sept – Oct 92), pp. 69 – 70.

Pascual Soto, Arturo. *Iconografía arqueológica de El Tajín* reviewed by Fernando Winfield Capitaine. *La Palabra y el Hombre*, no. 82 (Apr – June 92), pp. 313 – 314.

Paso, Fernando del. *Palinuro en la escalera* reviewed by George R. McMurray. *World Literature Today*, v. 67, no. 4 (Fall 93), pp. 781 – 782.

Passe-Smith, John T. and Edward J. Williams. *The Unionization of the Maquiladora Industry: The Tamaulipan Case in National Context* reviewed by Heather Fowler-Salamini. *Hispanic American Historical Review*, v. 73, no. 4 (Nov 93), pp. 718 – 719.

Pastor, Beatriz. *The Armature of Conquest: Spanish Accounts of the Discovery of America, 1492 – 1589* reviewed by Patricia Seed. *Journal of Latin American Studies*, v. 25, no. 2 (May 93), pp. 387 – 388.

Pastor, Robert A. *Integration with Mexico: Options for the U.S. Policy* reviewed by Robert Domínguez Rivera (Review entitled "Las relaciones México – Estados Unidos: viejos problemas, nuevas opciones"). *Relaciones Internacionales (Mexico)*, v. 15, Nueva época, no. 58 (Apr – June 93), pp. 99 – 100.

— *Whirlpool: U.S. Foreign Policy toward Latin America and the Caribbean* reviewed by Joseph S. Tulchin (Review entitled "A New Course in Foreign Affairs?"). *Hemisphere*, v. 5, no. 3 (Summer – Fall 93), pp. 50 – 52. Il.

— *Whirlpool: U.S. Foreign Policy toward Latin America and the Caribbean* reviewed by Javier Urbano Reyes (Review entitled "América Latina y el Caribe en la mira de Estados Unidos"). *Relaciones Internacionales (Mexico)*, v. 15, Nueva época, no. 57 (Jan – Mar 93), pp. 105 – 106.

Patán, Federico, ed. *Perfiles: ensayos sobre la literatura mexicana reciente* reviewed by Susan Dennis. *Hispania (USA)*, v. 76, no. 3 (Sept 93), pp. 486 – 487.

Patarra, Judith Lieblich. *Iara* reviewed by Marco Aurélio Garcia (Review entitled "Iara: história e cotidiano"). *Estudos Feministas*, v. 1, no. 1 (1993), pp. 210 – 212. Bibl.

Paternosto, César. *Piedra abstracta: la escultura inca; una visión contemporánea* reviewed by María Elvira Iriarte (Accompanied by an English translation). *Art Nexus*, no. 9 (June – Aug 93), pp. 32 – 33. Il.

Patterson, Thomas C. *The Inca Empire: The Formation and Disintegration of a Pre-Capitalist State* reviewed by Olivia Harris. *Bulletin of Latin American Research*, v. 12, no. 2 (May 93), pp. 217 – 218.

Pavan, Crodowaldo et al, eds. *Uma estratégia latino-americana para a Amazônia* reviewed by John Dickenson. *Bulletin of Latin American Research*, v. 12, no. 3 (Sept 93), pp. 351 – 352.

Paz, Octavio. *Al paso* reviewed by George R. McMurray. *World Literature Today*, v. 67, no. 2 (Spring 93), p. 340.

— *Al paso* reviewed by Guillermo Sheridan. *Vuelta*, v. 17, no. 197 (Apr 93), pp. 40 – 41.

— *Essays on Mexican Art* translated by Helen Lane. Reviewed by Margarita Nieto. *Latin American Art*, v. 5, no. 2 (Summer 93), p. 71.

— *Sor Juana Inés de la Cruz o las trampas de la fe* reviewed by Juan Malpartida (Review entitled "Sor Juana y Paz"). *Cuadernos Hispanoamericanos*, no. 516 (June 93), pp. 131 – 134.

Paz Martínez, Senel. *El lobo, el bosque y el hombre nuevo* reviewed by Emilio Bejel. *Hispamérica*, v. 22, no. 64 – 65 (Apr – Aug 93), pp. 202 – 204.

— *El lobo, el bosque y el hombre nuevo* reviewed by Antonio Marquet (Review entitled "El nombre de la fresa"). *Plural (Mexico)*, v. 22, no. 261 (June 93), pp. 86 – 87.

Paz Sánchez, Manuel de. *Wangüemert y Cuba*, vols. I y II, reviewed by Louis A. Pérez, Jr. *Journal of Latin American Studies*, v. 25, no. 3 (Oct 93), pp. 658 – 659.

Paz Zamora, Jaime et al. *Desarrollo social, democracia y crecimiento económico* (Review). *Integración Latinoamericana*, v. 18, no. 189 – 190 (May – June 93), pp. 56 – 57.

Pazos, Antón. *La iglesia en la América del IV centenario* reviewed by John Lynch. *Journal of Latin American Studies*, v. 25, no. 3 (Oct 93), pp. 659 – 660.

Pease G. Y., Franklin. *Curacas: reciprocidad y riqueza* reviewed by Thomas Abercrombie. *Hispanic American Historical Review*, v. 73, no. 4 (Nov 93), pp. 698 – 699.

— *Perú, hombre e historia: entre el siglo XVI y el XVIII* reviewed by Raúl Rivera Serna. *Anuario de Estudios Americanos*, v. 49, Suppl. 2 (1992), pp. 256 – 257.

— *Perú, hombre e historia: entre el siglo XVI y el XVIII* reviewed by Sara Mateos (Review entitled "Invasión y colonia"). *Debate (Peru)*, v. 15, no. 71 (Nov 92 – Jan 93), p. 77. Il.

Peavler, Terry J. *Julio Cortázar* reviewed by Alfred MacAdam. *Hispanic Review*, v. 61, no. 2 (Spring 93), pp. 310 – 312.

Pécaut, Daniel and Bernardo Sorj, eds. *Métamorphoses de la représentation politique au Brésil et en Europe* reviewed by Stéphane Monclaire (Review entitled "Partis et représentations politiques au Brésil"). *Cahiers des Amériques Latines*, no. 13 (1992), pp. 173 – 177.

Pellicer, Carlos and José Gorostiza. *Correspondencia, 1918 – 1928* edited and introduced by Guillermo Sheridan. Reviewed by David Medina Portillo. *Vuelta*, v. 17, no. 202 (Sept 93), pp. 44 – 45.

— *Correspondencia, 1918 – 1928* edited and introduced by Guillermo Sheridan. Reviewed by Rosa Beltrán. *Vuelta*, v. 17, no. 203 (Oct 93), pp. 44 – 45.

Pelosi, Carmen. *Historiografía y sociedad: las fuentes de 'Annales' y su recepción en la historiografía argentina* reviewed by Hebe Clementi. *Todo Es Historia*, v. 27, no. 311 (June 93), pp. 58 – 59. Il.

Peña León, Germán Alberto. *Exploraciones arqueológicas en la cuenca media del río Bogotá* reviewed by Mónika Therrien. *Revista Colombiana de Antropología*, v. 29 (1992), pp. 247 – 250. Bibl.

Penna, Maura. *O que faz ser nordestino?* reviewed by Rita Laura Segato (Review entitled "O que faz ser paulista?"). *Estudos Feministas*, v. 1, no. 1 (1993), pp. 213 – 214.

Pensar al Che reviewed by Luis Suárez Salazar (Review entitled "¿Cómo y para qué releer al Che?"). *Casa de las Américas*, no. 191 (Apr – June 93), pp. 144 – 147.

Peppercorn, Lisa M. *Villa-Lobos: The Music; An Analysis of His Style*, a translation of *Heitor Villa-Lobos: Leben und Werk des brasilianischen Komponist*, translated by Stefan de Haan (Review). *Inter-American Music Review*, v. 13, no. 2 (Spring – Summer 93), pp. 162 – 163. Bibl.

Peralta Ruiz, Víctor. *En pos del tributo: burocracia estatal, élite regional y comunidades indígenas en el Cusco rural, 1826 – 1854* reviewed by Paul Gootenberg. *Revista Andina*, v. 10, no. 2 (Dec 92), pp. 547 – 548.

— *En pos del tributo: burocracia estatal, élite regional y comunidades indígenas en el Cusco rural, 1826 – 1854* reviewed by Serena Fernández Alonso. *Revista de Indias*, v. 53, no. 197 (Jan – Apr 93), pp. 116 – 117.

Pereda, Carlos. *Conversar es humano* reviewed by Isabel Cabrera. *Vuelta*, v. 17, no. 196 (Mar 93), pp. 50 – 51.

Pereira de Queiroz, Maria Isaura

See
  Queiroz, Maria Isaura Pereira de

Perera, Víctor. *Unfinished Conquest: The Guatemalan Tragedy* (Review). *NACLA Report on the Americas*, v. 27, no. 3 (Nov – Dec 93), p. 48.

Pérez, Ana Mercedes. *Entre el cuento y la historia: 50 años del periodismo* reviewed by Pascual Venegas Filardo. *Revista Nacional de Cultura (Venezuela)*, v. 53, no. 286 (July – Sept 92), p. 257.

Pérez, Louis A., Jr. *Cuba and the United States: Ties of a Singular Intimacy* reviewed by Thomas Schoonover. *The Americas*, v. 50, no. 1 (July 93), pp. 130 – 131.

— *A Guide to Cuban Collections in the United States* reviewed by John M. Kirk. *Revista Interamericana de Bibliografía*, v. 42, no. 2 (1992), p. 287.

Pérez, Louis A., Jr., ed. *Slaves, Sugar, and Colonial Society: Travel Accounts of Cuba, 1801 – 1899* reviewed by Laurence A. Glasco. *Cuban Studies/Estudios Cubanos*, v. 23 (1993), pp. 219 – 220.

Pérez González, Benjamín et al. *Fundamentos para la escritura de las lenguas indígenas* reviewed by Rafael Rodríguez-Ponga. *Anuario de Letras (Mexico)*, v. 30 (1992), pp. 282 – 285.

Pérez Herrero, Pedro. *Comercio y mercados en América Latina colonial* reviewed by John Fisher. *Hispanic American Historical Review*, v. 73, no. 4 (Nov 93), pp. 688 – 689.

Pérez Herrero, Pedro, ed. *Región e historia en México, 1700 – 1850* reviewed by Margaret Chowning. *The Americas*, v. 50, no. 2 (Oct 93), pp. 280 – 282.

— *Región e historia en México, 1700 – 1850: métodos de análisis regional* reviewed by Donald F. Stevens. *Hispanic American Historical Review*, v. 73, no. 1 (Feb 93), pp. 154 – 155.

Pérez-López, Jorge F. *The Economics of Cuban Sugar* reviewed by Mieke Meurs. *Hispanic American Historical Review*, v. 73, no. 1 (Feb 93), p. 184.

Pérez-Mallaína Bueno, Pablo Emilio. *Los hombres del océano* reviewed by Benjamin Keen. *Hispanic American Historical Review*, v. 73, no. 3 (Aug 93), pp. 503 – 504.

Pérez Sáinz, Juan Pablo and Rafael Menjívar Larín, eds. *Informalidad urbana en Centroamérica: entre la acumulación y la subsistencia* reviewed by Stephen Webre. *Hispanic American Historical Review*, v. 73, no. 2 (May 93), pp. 341 – 342.

Pérez Tamayo, Ruy. *Ciencia, paciencia y conciencia* reviewed by Antonia González Barranco. *Revista Mexicana de Ciencias Políticas y Sociales*, v. 38, Nueva época, no. 151 (Jan – Mar 93), pp. 217 – 219.

Perilli de Garmendia, Carmen. *Imágenes de la mujer en Carpentier y García Márquez* reviewed by Rita Gnutzmann. *Revista Interamericana de Bibliografía*, v. 42, no. 3 (1992), p. 507.

Perlongher, Néstor, ed. *Caribe transplatino: poesía neobarroca cubana y rioplatense* reviewed by Bella Jozef. *Hispamérica*, v. 22, no. 64 – 65 (Apr – Aug 93), pp. 204 – 206.

Perrot, Michelle and Geneviève Fraisse, eds. *Historia de las mujeres en Occidente, tomo IV: El siglo XIX* reviewed by Lucía Solís Tolosa. *Todo Es Historia*, v. 27, no. 316 (Nov 93), p. 92. Il.

Perry, Mary Elizabeth and Anne J. Cruz, eds. *Cultural Encounters: The Impact of the Inquisition in Spain and the New World* reviewed by Teofilo F. Ruiz. *The Americas*, v. 50, no. 1 (July 93), pp. 121 – 123.

— *Cultural Encounters: The Impact of the Inquisition in Spain and the New World* reviewed by Henry Kamen. *Hispanic American Historical Review*, v. 73, no. 1 (Feb 93), p. 146.

Perry, Richard and Rosalind Perry. *Maya Missions: Exploring the Spanish Colonial Churches of Yucatán* reviewed by Miguel A. Bretos. *Hispanic American Historical Review*, v. 73, no. 1 (Feb 93), pp. 134 – 136.

Perry, Rosalind and Richard Perry. *Maya Missions: Exploring the Spanish Colonial Churches of Yucatán* reviewed by Miguel A. Bretos. *Hispanic American Historical Review*, v. 73, no. 1 (Feb 93), pp. 134 – 136.

Persaud, Sasenarine. *The Ghost of Bellow's Man* reviewed by Peter Nazareth. *World Literature Today*, v. 67, no. 2 (Spring 93), pp. 428 – 429.

Pescador C., Juan Javier. *De bautizados a fieles difuntos: familia y mentalidades en una parroquia urbana; Santa Catarina de México, 1568 – 1820* reviewed by Patricia Schraer. *La Educación (USA)*, v. 37, no. 115 (1993), pp. 431 – 433.

Pessanha, Ricardo and Chris McGowan. *The Brazilian Sound: Samba, Bossa Nova, and the Popular Music of Brazil* reviewed by Randal Johnson. *Hispanic American Historical Review*, v. 73, no. 1 (Feb 93), p. 128.

Pessar, Patricia R. and Sherri Grasmuck. *Between Two Islands: Dominican International Migration* reviewed by André Corten. *Canadian Journal of Latin American and Caribbean Studies*, v. 17, no. 34 (1992), pp. 138 – 141.

Petras, James F. and Morris H. Morley. *Latin America in the Time of Cholera: Electoral Politics, Market Economics, and Permanent Crisis* reviewed by Donald F. Stevens. *The Americas*, v. 50, no. 2 (Oct 93), pp. 291 – 292.

Philip, George D. E. *The Presidency in Mexican Politics* reviewed by Roderic Ai Camp. *The Americas*, v. 49, no. 3 (Jan 93), p. 425.

Phillips, William D., Jr. and Carla Rahn Phillips. *The Worlds of Christopher Columbus* reviewed by Peter T. Bradley. *Bulletin of Latin American Research*, v. 12, no. 1 (Jan 93), pp. 109 – 110.

Pianca, Marina. *El teatro de nuestra América: un proyecto continental, 1959 – 1989* reviewed by Pedro Bravo-Elizondo. *Latin American Theatre Review*, v. 26, no. 2 (Spring 93), pp. 214 – 216.

Pianzola, Maurice. *Des français à la conquête du Brésil, XVIIᵉ siècle: les perroquets jaunes* reviewed by Pierre Ragon. *Cahiers des Amériques Latines*, no. 14 (1992), pp. 156 – 157.

Picouet, Michel and Hervé Domenach. *La dimension migratoire des Antilles* reviewed by Guy Caire. *Tiers Monde*, v. 34, no. 135 (July – Sept 93), pp. 716 – 718.

Piel, Jean. *Sajcabajá: muerte y resurrección de un pueblo de Guatemala, 1500 – 1970* reviewed by David McCreery. *Mesoamérica (USA)*, v. 13, no. 24 (Dec 92), pp. 458 – 459.

Piglia, Ricardo. *La ciudad ausente* reviewed by Adriana Rodríguez Pérsico. *Hispamérica*, v. 21, no. 63 (Dec 92), pp. 100 – 106.

— *La ciudad ausente* reviewed by Naomi Lindstrom. *World Literature Today*, v. 67, no. 2 (Spring 93), pp. 336 – 337.

— *Cuentos con dos rostros* reviewed by José Ricardo Chaves (Review entitled "Respiración narrativa"). *Vuelta*, v. 17, no. 205 (Dec 93), pp. 53 – 54.

— *Respiración artificial* reviewed by José Ricardo Chaves (Review entitled "Respiración narrativa"). *Vuelta*, v. 17, no. 205 (Dec 93), pp. 53 – 54.

Pike, Fredrick B. *The United States and Latin America: Myths and Stereotypes of Civilization and Nature* reviewed by Peter Calvert. *Bulletin of Latin American Research*, v. 12, no. 2 (May 93), pp. 232 – 233.

— *The United States and Latin America: Myths and Stereotypes of Civilization and Nature* reviewed by Josef Opatrny. *Hispanic American Historical Review*, v. 73, no. 4 (Nov 93), pp. 667 – 668.

— *The United States and Latin America: Myths and Stereotypes of Civilization and Nature* reviewed by Gordon Connell-Smith. *Journal of Latin American Studies*, v. 25, no. 3 (Oct 93), pp. 689 – 691.

Pimentel Igea, Juan and Manuel Lucena Giraldo, eds. Los "Axiomas políticos sobre la América" de Alejandro Malaspina reviewed by O. Carlos Stoetzer. *Hispanic American Historical Review*, v. 73, no. 1 (Feb 93), pp. 160 – 161.

Piña, Juan Andrés. *Conversaciones con la narrativa chilena* reviewed by Guillermo García-Corales. *Chasqui*, v. 22, no. 2 (Nov 93), pp. 164 – 165.

— *Conversaciones con la poesía chilena* reviewed by Judy Berry-Bravo. *Chasqui*, v. 22, no. 1 (May 93), pp. 74 – 76.

Pinho, Wanderley

See

Wanderley Pinho, José

Pino Iturrieta, Elías. *Pensamiento conservador del siglo XIX* reviewed by Amaya Llebot Cazalis. *Revista Nacional de Cultura (Venezuela)*, v. 54, no. 287 (Oct – Dec 92), pp. 262 – 264. Il.

Piñon, Nélida. *Caetana's Sweet Song*, a translation of *A doce canção de Caetana*, translated by Helen Lane. Reviewed by Kevin S. Larsen. *Hispania (USA)*, v. 76, no. 1 (Mar 93), pp. 103 – 104.

— *Caetana's Sweet Song*, a translation of *A doce canção de Caetana*, translated by Helen Lane. Reviewed by Gregory Rabassa. *Review*, no. 47 (Fall 93), pp. 89 – 90. Il.

— *The Republic of Dreams* translated by Helen Lane. Reviewed by Kevin S. Larsen. *Hispania (USA)*, v. 76, no. 1 (Mar 93), pp. 103 – 104.

Piratininga Júnior, Luiz Gonzaga. *Dietário dos negros de São Bento* reviewed by Maria de Lourdes Beldi de Alcântara. *Revista de Antropologia (Brazil)*, v. 34 (1991), pp. 227 – 228.

Pistone, J. Catalina. *Estudio histórico de las artesanías en Santa Fe* reviewed by Félix Coluccio. *Folklore Americano*, no. 52 (July – Dec 91), pp. 166 – 167.

Pita, Edgar et al. *Informalidad urbana: dinámica y perspectiva en el Ecuador* reviewed by Jose A. Alonso H. *Problemas del Desarrollo*, v. 24, no. 92 (Jan – Mar 93), pp. 238 – 241.

Pizarnik, Flora Alejandra. *Alejandra Pizarnik: semblanza* edited by Frank Graziano. Reviewed by Adriana Díaz Enciso. *Vuelta*, v. 17, no. 198 (May 93), pp. 52 – 53.

Plummer, Brenda Gayle. *Haiti and the United States: The Psychological Moment* reviewed by Brian Weinstein. *Revista Interamericana de Bibliografía*, v. 42, no. 4 (1992), p. 661.

Policastro, Cristina. *La casa de las virtudes* reviewed by R. J. Lovera De-Sola. *Revista Nacional de Cultura (Venezuela)*, v. 53, no. 286 (July – Sept 92), pp. 254 – 255.

Politis, Gustavo, ed. *Arqueología en América Latina hoy* reviewed by Betty J. Meggars. *Latin American Antiquity*, v. 4, no. 4 (Dec 93), pp. 388 – 389.

Polzer, Charles W. et al, eds. *The Jesuit Missions of Northern Mexico* reviewed by Robert H. Jackson. *Hispanic American Historical Review*, v. 73, no. 2 (May 93), pp. 312 – 313.

Poniatowska, Elena. *Tinísima* reviewed by Carlos Monsiváis (Review entitled "Un cuarto de siglo"). *Nexos*, v. 16, no. 192 (Dec 93), p. 71.

Poniatowska, Elena and Carla Stellweg. *Frida Kahlo: la cámara seducida* reviewed by Andrés Salgado R. (Accompanied by an English translation). *Art Nexus*, no. 8 (Apr – June 93), p. 34. Il.

Poole, Deborah A. and Gerardo Rénique. *Peru: Time of Fear* reviewed by John Crabtree. *Bulletin of Latin American Research*, v. 12, no. 2 (May 93), pp. 243 – 244.

— *Peru: Time of Fear* reviewed by Lewis Taylor. *Journal of Latin American Studies*, v. 25, no. 3 (Oct 93), pp. 667 – 668.

Porchia, Antonio Stanley. *Voces abandonadas* reviewed by Alfredo García Valdez (Review entitled "La palabra vertical"). *Vuelta*, v. 17, no. 202 (Sept 93), pp. 49 – 50.

Porto Bucciarelli, Lucrecia. *Leopoldo Lugones de parte de los astros: el simbolismo hermético de 'Las montañas del oro'* reviewed by Estrella Ogden. *Hispanic Review*, v. 61, no. 1 (Winter 93), pp. 127 – 129.

Portocarrero Maisch, Javier. *Experiencia de la Comunidad Europea y perspectivas del Grupo Andino* (Review). *Integración Latinoamericana*, v. 18, no. 189 – 190 (May – June 93), pp. 57 – 58.

Posse, Abel. *El largo atardecer del caminante* reviewed by Lucía Gálvez. *Todo Es Historia*, v. 26, no. 308 (Mar 93), pp. 70 – 72. Il.

Pradilla Cobos, Emilio, ed. *Planeación urbana y bienestar social, vol. II: Democracia y desarrollo de la ciudad de México* reviewed by J. Verónica Ramírez Rangel. *El Cotidiano*, v. 9, no. 54 (May 93), p. 118. Il.

Prandi, José Reginaldo. *Os candomblés de São Paulo: a velha magia na metrópole nova* reviewed by Luciana Ferreira Moura Mendonça. *Revista de Antropologia (Brazil)*, v. 34 (1991), pp. 228 – 230.

Premdas, Ralph R. *Ethnic Conflict and Development: The Case of Guyana* reviewed by William A. Harris (Review entitled "Ethnicity and Development"). *Social and Economic Studies*, v. 41, no. 4 (Dec 92), pp. 225 – 230.

Prestes, Maria. *Meu companheiro: 40 anos ao lado de Luiz Carlos Prestes* reviewed by Maurício Tragtemberg. *Vozes*, v. 87, no. 2 (Mar – Apr 93), pp. 97 – 101.

Primera bienal del cuento ecuatoriano: obras premiadas reviewed by Barbara Mujica (Review entitled "A Roundup of Stories"). *Américas*, v. 45, no. 1 (Jan – Feb 93), pp. 60 – 61. Il.

Prizel, Ilya. *Latin America through Soviet Eyes: The Evolution of Soviet Perceptions during the Brezhnev Era* reviewed by Marina Oborotova (Review entitled "Russian Policy in Latin America: Past, Present, and Future"). *Latin American Research Review*, v. 28, no. 3 (1993), pp. 183 – 188.

Promis Ojeda, José M. *The Identity of Hispanoamerica: An Interpretation of Colonial Literature* reviewed by Eric Van Young. *Colonial Latin American Review*, v. 2, no. 1 – 2 (1993), pp. 291 – 296.

Prospects for the Processes of Sub-Regional Integration in Central and South America (Review). *Integración Latinoamericana*, v. 18, no. 189 – 190 (May – June 93), pp. 58 – 59.

Przeworski, Adam. *Democracy and the Market: Political and Economic Reforms in Eastern Europe and Latin America* reviewed by Carlos Maya Ambía. *El Trimestre Económico*, v. 60, no. 239 (July – Sept 93), pp. 733 – 744.

Puig, Juan Carlos. *Entre el río Perla y el Nazas: la China decimonónica y sus braceros emigrantes. Vuelta*, v. 17, no. 202 (Sept 93), p. 53.

Puig, Manuel. *Tropical Night Falling*, a translation of *Cae la noche tropical*, translated by Suzanne Jill Levine. Reviewed by Lucille Kerr. *Review*, no. 47 (Fall 93), pp. 92 – 93. Il.

Pulido, Marco Antonio and Carlos Haces, eds. *José Guadalupe Posada y el amor: para iluminar* reviewed by J. León Helguera (Review entitled "José Guadalupe Posada Yet Again"). *Studies in Latin American Popular Culture*, v. 12 (1993), pp. 203 – 206.

Queiroz, Maria Isaura Pereira de. *Carnaval brasileiro: o vivido e o mito* reviewed by Oscar D'Ambrosio (Review entitled "O mito do carnaval"). *Problemas Brasileiros*, v. 30, no. 296 (Mar – Apr 93), pp. 40 – 41. Il.

— *Carnaval brasileiro: o vivido e o mito* reviewed by Rita de Cássia Amaral. *Revista Brasileira de Ciências Sociais*, v. 8, no. 21 (Feb 93), pp. 118 – 119.

Quevedo, Hugo Orlando. *El partido peronista en La Rioja: crónica y personajes* reviewed by F. L. *Todo Es Historia*, v. 27, no. 311 (June 93), p. 60.

Quintero Montiel, Inés Mercedes. *Pensamiento liberal del siglo XIX* reviewed by Amaya Llebot Cazalis. *Revista Nacional de Cultura (Venezuela)*, v. 54, no. 287 (Oct – Dec 92), pp. 264 – 265.

Quiroga de Urquieta, Rosario. *De la palabra a las alas* reviewed by Gaby Vallejo de Bolívar. *Signo*, no. 38, Nueva época (Jan – Apr 93), pp. 250 – 251.

Quirós, Juan. *Fronteras movedizas* reviewed by Carlos Coello Vila (Review entitled *"Fronteras movedizas: 35 años de crítica literaria"*). *Signo*, no. 36 – 37, Nueva época (May – Dec 92), pp. 227 – 231.

Quiroz, Fernando. *"El reino que estaba para mí": conversaciones con Alvaro Mutis* reviewed by Fabienne Bradu (Review entitled "Vida y biografía"). *Vuelta*, v. 17, no. 200 (July 93), pp. 54 – 55.

Rabkin, Rhoda Pearl. *Cuban Politics: The Revolutionary Experiment* reviewed by H. Michael Erisman. *Cuban Studies/Estudios Cubanos*, v. 23 (1993), pp. 231 – 233.

— *Cuban Politics: The Revolutionary Experiment* reviewed by Damián Fernández (Review entitled "The Theater of Cuban Politics"). *Hemisphere*, v. 5, no. 2 (Winter – Spring 93), pp. 46 – 48.

Radcliffe, Sarah A. and Sallie Westwood, eds. *"Viva": Women and Popular Protest in Latin America* reviewed by Tessa Cubitt. *Bulletin of Latin American Research*, v. 12, no. 2 (May 93), pp. 242 – 243.

Raghavan, Chakravarthi. *Recolonization: GATT, the Uruguay Round, and the Third World* (Review entitled "Un libro para despertar al Tercer Mundo"). *Homines*, v. 15 – 16, no. 2 – 1 (Oct 91 – Dec 92), pp. 384 – 385.

Rago, Margareth. *Os prazeres da noite: prostituição e códigos da sexualidade feminina em São Paulo, 1890 – 1930* reviewed by Sandra Lauderdale Graham (Review entitled "Dangerous Fantasies: The Altered Vocabulary of Commercial Sex"). *Luso-Brazilian Review*, v. 30, no. 1 (Summer 93), pp. 133 – 139.

Ragon, Pierre. *Les amours indiennes ou l'imaginaire du conquistador* reviewed by Christian Satge. *Caravelle*, no. 59 (1992), pp. 297 – 300.

Rama, Angel. *La crítica de la cultura en América Latina* selected and introduced by Saúl Sosnowski and Tomás Eloy Martínez. Reviewed by Roy Hora. *Todo Es Historia*, v. 26, no. 307 (Feb 93), pp. 74 – 75. Il.

Ramírez, Sergio

See
Ramírez Mercado, Sergio

Ramírez Gatica, Soledad. *Estado de la docencia universitaria de pregrado en Chile* reviewed by Ricardo López P. *Estudios Sociales (Chile)*, no. 78 (Oct – Dec 93), pp. 227 – 231.

Ramírez-Horton, Susan Elizabeth. *Patriarcas provinciales: la tenencia de la tierra y la economía del poder en el Perú colonial* reviewed by Scarlett O'Phelan Godoy. *Anuario de Estudios Americanos*, v. 49, Suppl. 1 (1992), pp. 257 – 258.

Ramírez Mercado, Sergio. *Clave de sol* reviewed by Hermann Bellinghausen (Review entitled "Historias de un país pequeño donde la vida es ancha y transparente"). *Nexos*, v. 16, no. 186 (June 93), pp. 77 – 80.

Ramírez Sáiz, Juan Manuel. *¿Son políticos los movimientos urbano-populares?: un planteamiento teórico – metodológico* reviewed by Melchor Negrete Silva. *El Cotidiano*, v. 10, no. 57 (Aug – Sept 93), p. 107.

Ramírez V., María T. and Beatriz Alzate Angel, eds. *Cinco lustros de actuación institucional nacional e internacional en Amazonia* reviewed by Olga Lucía Turbay. *La Educación (USA)*, v. 36, no. 111 – 113 (1992), pp. 279 – 280.

Ramos, Agustín. *La gran cruzada* reviewed by Pablo Mora. *Hispamérica*, v. 21, no. 63 (Dec 92), pp. 106 – 108.

Ramos, Jorge Abelardo. *La aventura de La Pampa argentina: arquitectura, ambiente y cultura* reviewed by Alicia Novick. *Todo Es Historia*, v. 27, no. 312 (July 93), p. 77. Il.

Ramos, Luis Arturo. *La casa del ahorcado* reviewed by Christopher Domínguez Michael. *Vuelta*, v. 17, no. 202 (Sept 93), pp. 52 – 53.

— *La casa del ahorcado* reviewed by Miguelángel Díaz Monges (Review entitled "Cuatro generaciones"). *Nexos*, v. 16, no. 189 (Sept 93), p. 71. Il.

Ramos, María Elena. *Pistas para quedar mirando: fragmentos sobre arte* reviewed by Ivonne Pini (Accompanied by an English translation). *Art Nexus*, no. 8 (Apr – June 93), p. 33. Il.

Ramos Pérez, Demetrio. *Simón Bolívar, el Libertador* reviewed by R. J. Lovera De-Sola (Review entitled "El Bolívar de Demetrio Ramos Pérez"). *Boletín de la Academia Nacional de la Historia (Venezuela)*, v. 75, no. 298 (Apr – June 92), pp. 108 – 109.

Ramos Pérez, Demetrio et al. *Historia general de España y América. Vol. XIII: Emancipación y nacionalidades americanas* reviewed by Luis Navarro García. *Anuario de Estudios Americanos*, v. 49, Suppl. 2 (1992), pp. 257 – 259.

Ramsaran, Ramesh. *The Challenge of Structural Adjustment in the Commonwealth Caribbean* reviewed by Vicente Galbis. *Journal of Developing Areas*, v. 27, no. 4 (July 93), pp. 575 – 576.

Randall, Stephen J. *Colombia and the United States: Hegemony and Interdependence* reviewed by Frank Safford. *Hispanic American Historical Review*, v. 73, no. 1 (Feb 93), pp. 190 – 191.

— *Colombia and the United States: Hegemony and Interdependence* reviewed by Diana Pardo. *Journal of Inter-American Studies and World Affairs*, v. 35, no. 2 (Summer 93), pp. 163 – 166.

Randall, Stephen J. et al, eds. *North America without Borders?: Integrating Canada, the United States, and Mexico* reviewed by Benoit Brookens. *Journal of Inter-American Studies and World Affairs*, v. 35, no. 1 (1993), pp. 153 – 158.

Ranis, Peter. *Argentine Workers: Peronism and Contemporary Class Consciousness* reviewed by Joel Horowitz. *The Americas*, v. 50, no. 2 (Oct 93), pp. 289 – 290.

— *Argentine Workers: Peronism and Contemporary Class Consciousness* reviewed by Walter Little. *Bulletin of Latin American Research*, v. 12, no. 1 (Jan 93), pp. 118 – 119.

Rasnake, Roger Neil. *Autoridad y poder en los Andes: los kuraqkuna de Yura*, a translation of *Domination and Cultural Resistance: Authority and Power among an Andean People*, translated by Luis Brédow and Luis Huáscar Antezana. Reviewed by Pedro de Anasagasti. *Signo*, no. 35, Nueva época (Jan – Apr 92), pp. 243 – 244.

Raznovich, Diana. *Mater erótica* reviewed by David William Foster. *World Literature Today*, v. 67, no. 3 (Summer 93), p. 591.

Realidades y perspectivas del MERCOSUR (Review). *Integración Latinoamericana*, v. 18, no. 191 (July 93), pp. 75 – 76.

Reati, Fernando. *Nombrar lo innombrable: violencia política y novela argentina, 1975 – 1985* reviewed by David William Foster. *World Literature Today*, v. 67, no. 2 (Spring 93), pp. 341 – 342.

Redclift, Michael R. and David Edwin Goodman, eds. *Environment and Development in Latin America: The Politics of Sustainability* reviewed by Margaret E. Keck. *Studies in Comparative International Development*, v. 27, no. 3 (Fall 92), pp. 120 – 122.

Redford, Kent H. and Christine Padoch, eds. *Conservation of Neotropical Forests: Working from Traditional Resource Use* reviewed by Mahesh Rangarajan. *Journal of Latin American Studies*, v. 25, no. 3 (Oct 93), pp. 687 – 688.

Reed, Roger. *The Cultural Revolution in Cuba* reviewed by James Maraniss. *Cuban Studies/Estudios Cubanos*, v. 23 (1993), pp. 225 – 227.

Reff, Daniel T. *Disease, Depopulation, and Culture Change in Northwestern New Spain, 1518 – 1764* reviewed by Cynthia Radding. *The Americas*, v. 49, no. 3 (Jan 93), pp. 399 – 401.

Regaladas de Hurtado, Liliana
See
Hurtado, Liliana R. de

Regen, Jacobo. *Poemas reunidos* reviewed by Gustavo Fares. *Hispanic Journal*, v. 14, no. 1 (Spring 93), pp. 179 – 181.

Reichel-Dolmatoff, Gerardo. *Indios de Colombia: momentos vividos, mundos concebidos* reviewed by Jorge Morales Gómez. *Revista Colombiana de Antropología*, v. 29 (1992), pp. 239 – 241.

Reis, Roberto. *The Pearl Necklace: Toward an Archaeology of Brazilian Transition Discourse* translated by Aparecida de Godoy Johnson. Reviewed by Nelson H. Vieira. *Hispanic American Historical Review*, v. 73, no. 3 (Aug 93), pp. 484 – 485.

Reiss, Lilly. *Espacios encontrados* reviewed by Carmen Ollé (Review entitled "Las puertas del misterio"). *Debate (Peru)*, v. 16, no. 74 (Sept – Oct 93), pp. 64 – 65. II.

Remy S., Pilar and María Rostworowski Tovar de Diez Canseco, eds. *Las visitas a Cajamarca, 1571/72 – 1578* reviewed by Pedro Guibovich. *Apuntes (Peru)*, no. 31 (July – Dec 92), pp. 119 – 121.

— *Las visitas a Cajamarca, 1571/72 – 1578* reviewed by Jorge Montenegro. *Bulletin de l'Institut Français d'Etudes Andines*, v. 21, no. 3 (1992), pp. 1073 – 1074.

— *Las visitas a Cajamarca, 1571/72 – 1578* reviewed by Noble David Cook. *Hispanic American Historical Review*, v. 73, no. 2 (May 93), pp. 313 – 314.

— *Las visitas a Cajamarca, 1571/72 – 1578* reviewed by Carmen Beatriz Loza. *Revista Andina*, v. 10, no. 2 (Dec 92), pp. 548 – 550.

Renard-Casevitz, France-Marie. *Le banquet masqué: une mythologie de l'étranger chez les indiens matsiguenga* reviewed by Edmundo Magaña. *European Review of Latin American and Caribbean Studies*, no. 54 (June 93), pp. 139 – 145.

Rengifo V., Grimaldo and Marcos Sánchez. *Hacia una agricultura sostenible: el caso de Coronel Oviedo.* *Revista Paraguaya de Sociología*, v. 29, no. 85 (Sept – Dec 92), pp. 190 – 191.

Rénique, Gerardo and Deborah A. Poole. *Peru: Time of Fear* reviewed by John Crabtree. *Bulletin of Latin American Research*, v. 12, no. 2 (May 93), pp. 243 – 244.

— *Peru: Time of Fear* reviewed by Lewis Taylor. *Journal of Latin American Studies*, v. 25, no. 3 (Oct 93), pp. 667 – 668.

Reque Terán, Luis. *La campaña de Ñancahuazu* reviewed by René López Murillo. *Signo*, no. 35, Nueva época (Jan – Apr 92), pp. 245 – 247.

Retamal Favereau, Julio et al. *Familias fundadoras de Chile, 1540 – 1600* reviewed by Narciso Binayán Carmona. *Todo Es Historia*, v. 27, no. 312 (July 93), pp. 75 – 77. II.

Reyes Valerio, Constantino. *El pintor de conventos: los murales del siglo XVI en la Nueva España* reviewed by Rogelio Ruiz Gomar. *Anales del Instituto de Investigaciones Estéticas*, v. 16, no. 62 (1991), pp. 208 – 215.

Ribeiro, Darcy and Carlos Moreira Neto. *A fundação do Brasil: testemunhos, 1500 – 1700* reviewed by José Carlos Sebe Bohn Meihy. *Vozes*, v. 87, no. 3 (May – June 93), pp. 90 – 91.

Ribeyro, Julio Ramón. *La palabra del mudo IV* reviewed by César Ferreira. *Chasqui*, v. 22, no. 1 (May 93), pp. 79 – 81.

— *La tentación del fracaso* reviewed by Alonso Cueto (Review entitled "El tesoro escondido"). *Debate (Peru)*, v. 15, no. 70 (Sept – Oct 92), pp. 68 – 69. II.

— *La tentación del fracaso* reviewed by Marco Martos (Review entitled "Las memorias de tres novelistas peruanos"). *Debate (Peru)*, v. 16, no. 73 (June – Aug 93), pp. 68 – 72. II.

Rice, Don Stephen and William F. Hanks, eds. *Word and Image in Maya Culture: Explorations in Language, Writing, and Representation* reviewed by Stephen D. Houston. *Mesoamérica (USA)*, v. 13, no. 23 (June 92), pp. 191 – 193.

— *Word and Image in Maya Culture: Explorations in Language, Writing, and Representation* reviewed by Luis T. Sanz. *Revista Española de Antropología Americana*, v. 23 (1993), pp. 260 – 262.

Richard, Alfred Charles, Jr. *The Hispanic Image on the Silver Screen: An Interpretive Filmography from Silents into Sound, 1898 – 1935* reviewed by Paul J. Vanderwood. *Hispanic American Historical Review*, v. 73, no. 2 (May 93), pp. 294 – 295.

— *The Hispanic Image on the Silver Screen: An Interpretive Filmography from Silents into Sound, 1898 – 1935* reviewed by Ana M. Rodríguez-Vivaldi. *Revista Interamericana de Bibliografía*, v. 42, no. 3 (1992), pp. 507 – 508.

Richardson, Bonham C. *The Caribbean in the Wider World, 1492 – 1992: A Regional Geography* reviewed by Brian J. Hudson. *Caribbean Geography*, v. 3, no. 3 (Mar 92), pp. 209 – 210.

— *The Caribbean in the Wider World, 1492 – 1992: A Regional Geography* reviewed by David Barker. *Social and Economic Studies*, v. 41, no. 3 (Sept 92), pp. 183 – 186.

Ridley, Jasper Godwin. *Maximilian and Juárez* reviewed by Timothy E. Anna. *Hispanic American Historical Review*, v. 73, no. 4 (Nov 93), p. 717.

Rieu de Millán, Marie-Laure. *Los diputados americanos en las Cortes de Cádiz: igualdad o independencia* reviewed by María Lourdes Huarte Cambra. *Anuario de Estudios Americanos*, v. 49, Suppl. 2 (1992), pp. 259 – 261.

— *Los diputados americanos en las Cortes de Cádiz* reviewed by Michel Bertrand. *Caravelle*, no. 60 (1993), pp. 159 – 161.

Rigau, Jorge. *Puerto Rico, 1900: Turn of the Century Architecture in the Hispanic Caribbean, 1890 – 1930* reviewed by Max Underwood. *Latin American Art*, v. 4, no. 4 (Winter 92), p. 94.

Riley, Joan. *A Kindness to the Children* reviewed by Andrew Salkey. *World Literature Today*, v. 67, no. 3 (Summer 93), p. 658.

Riley, Sandra. *The Lucayans* reviewed by Veronica Salter. *Caribbean Quarterly*, v. 38, no. 2 – 3 (June – Sept 92), p. 118.

Ringrose, Basil. *A Buccaneer's Atlas: Basil Ringrose's South Seas Waggoner* edited by Derk Howse and Norman J. W. Thrower. Reviewed by Arnold J. Bauer. *Hispanic American Historical Review,* v. 73, no. 4 (Nov 93), pp. 691 – 693.

Río, Nela. *Las noches que desvisten otras noches* reviewed by Miriam Balboa Echeverría (Review entitled "La voz de las torturadas en el libro *Las noches que desvisten otras noches* de Nela Río"). *Confluencia,* v. 8, no. 1 (Fall 92), pp. 185 – 186.

Río Correa, Ana María del. *De golpe, Amalia en el umbral* reviewed by Maryvonne Rozenblat. *Caravelle,* no. 59 (1992), pp. 318 – 320.

Río Moreno, Justo L. del. *Los inicios de la agricultura europea en el Nuevo Mundo, 1492 – 1542* reviewed by María del Carmen Morales García. *Anuario de Estudios Americanos,* v. 49, Suppl. 1 (1992), pp. 260 – 261.

Ríos, Alberto Alvaro. *Teodoro Luna's Two Kisses* reviewed by Luz María Umpierre. *The Americas Review,* v. 19, no. 2 (Summer 91), pp. 104 – 105.

Ríos, Juan. *Sobre mi propia vida: diario, 1940 – 1991* reviewed by Carlos Garatea Grau (Review entitled "Tiempo de preguntas"). *Debate (Peru),* v. 16, no. 73 (June – Aug 93), pp. 73 – 74. Il.

Ríos-Bustamante, Antonio José. *Los Angeles: pueblo y región, 1781 – 1850* reviewed by Aurora Morcillo-Gómez. *Colonial Latin American Historical Review,* v. 2, no. 4 (Fall 93), pp. 473 – 474.

Riquelme, Sonia and Edna Aguirre Rehbein, eds. *Critical Approaches to Isabel Allende's Novels* reviewed by Edward W. Hook. *World Literature Today,* v. 67, no. 1 (Winter 93), pp. 163 – 164.

Rittershaussen, Silvia and Judith Scharager, eds. *Análisis y proyecciones en torno a la educación media y el trabajo* reviewed by María José Lemaitre. *Estudios Sociales (Chile),* no. 78 (Oct – Dec 93), pp. 279 – 283.

Rivadeneira Prada, Raúl. *Colección de vigilias: relatos* reviewed by Carlos Coello Vila. *Signo,* no. 38, Nueva época (Jan – Apr 93), pp. 251 – 256.

Rivarola, José Luis. *La formación lingüística de Hispanoamérica: diez estudios* reviewed by Klaus Zimmermann. *Iberoamericana,* v. 17, no. 49 (1993), pp. 90 – 94.

Rivas, José Luis. *Luz de mar abierto* reviewed by David Medina Portillo. *Vuelta,* v. 17, no. 199 (June 93), p. 41.

— *Raz de marea* reviewed by Guillermo Sheridan. *Vuelta,* v. 17, no. 203 (Oct 93), pp. 48 – 50.

— *Raz de marea* reviewed by Víctor Sosa. *Vuelta,* v. 17, no. 202 (Sept 93), pp. 51 – 52.

Rivera, Tomás. *The Complete Works* edited by Julián Olivares. Reviewed by Salvador C. Fernández. *Hispania (USA),* v. 76, no. 4 (Dec 93), p. 741.

— *The Harvest/La cosecha.* Bilingual edition, edited by Julián Olivares. Reviewed by Paul Guajaro (Review entitled "A Late Harvest: A Review of the Collected Stories of Tomás Rivera"). *Bilingual Review/Revista Bilingüe,* v. 17, no. 3 (Sept – Dec 92), pp. 279 – 284.

Rivera Martínez, J. Edgardo. *País de Jauja* reviewed by Luis Millones (Review entitled "La educación sentimental"). *Debate (Peru),* v. 16, no. 74 (Sept – Oct 93), p. 63. Il.

Rivera-Rodas, Oscar. *El metateatro y la dramática de Vargas Llosa: hacia una poética del espectador* reviewed by Juan Villegas. *Revista Interamericana de Bibliografía,* v. 42, no. 4 (1992), pp. 661 – 662.

Rivero Potter, Alicia. *Autor/lector: Huidobro, Borges, Fuentes y Sarduy* reviewed by R. A. Kerr. *Hispania (USA),* v. 76, no. 4 (Dec 93), pp. 741 – 742.

— *Autor/lector: Huidobro, Borges, Fuentes y Sarduy* reviewed by Gustavo Fares. *Revista Iberoamericana,* v. 59, no. 162 – 163 (Jan – June 93), pp. 376 – 379.

Roa Bastos, Augusto Antonio. *Vigilia del Almirante* reviewed by Diego F. Barros. *Todo Es Historia,* v. 26, no. 310 (May 93), p. 82. Il.

— *Vigilia del Almirante* reviewed by Fabrizio Mejía Madrid (Review entitled "Al deseo por mar"). *Nexos,* v. 16, no. 185 (May 93), p. 81. Il.

— *Vigilia del Almirante* reviewed by Milagros Ezquerro (Review entitled "Don Quijote de la mar oceana"). *Cuadernos Hispanoamericanos,* no. 522 (Dec 93), pp. 128 – 134.

— *Vigilia del Almirante* reviewed by Sealtiel Alatriste (Review entitled "El mercado literario"). *Nexos,* v. 16, no. 182 (Feb 93), pp. 78 – 79.

Robben, Antonius C. G. M. *Sons of the Sea Goddess: Economic Practice and Discursive Conflict in Brazil* reviewed by Paul Cammack. *Journal of Latin American Studies,* v. 25, no. 3 (Oct 93), pp. 686 – 687.

Robinson, David James, ed. *Migration in Colonial Spanish America* reviewed by Ida Altman. *The Americas,* v. 50, no. 2 (Oct 93), pp. 277 – 279.

— *Migration in Colonial Spanish America* reviewed by Martin W. Lewis. *Geographical Review,* v. 83, no. 1 (Jan 93), pp. 106 – 108.

Robinson, William I. *A Faustian Bargain: U.S. Intervention in the Nicaraguan Elections and American Foreign Policy in the Post-Cold War Era* reviewed by Thomas P. Anderson. *Hispanic American Historical Review,* v. 73, no. 3 (Aug 93), pp. 541 – 542.

Roca, Juan Manuel. *En la casa donde suceden milagros* reviewed by Manuel Ruano. *Revista Nacional de Cultura (Venezuela),* v. 53, no. 285 (Apr – June 92), pp. 254 – 256.

— *Pavana con el diablo* reviewed by Manuel Ruano. *Revista Nacional de Cultura (Venezuela),* v. 53, no. 285 (Apr – June 92), pp. 253 – 254.

Rocamora, Joan. *Catalanes en la Argentina: centenario del Casal de Catalunya* reviewed by Alicia Vidaurreta. *Revista de Indias,* v. 53, no. 197 (Jan – Apr 93), pp. 117 – 119.

Rocard, Marcienne. *The Children of the Sun: Mexican-Americans in the Literature of the United States* reviewed by Chuck Tatum. *The Americas Review,* v. 20, no. 2 (Summer 92), pp. 113 – 115.

Rock, David P. *La Argentina autoritaria: los nacionalistas; su historia y su influencia en la vida pública* reviewed by Rosana Guber (Review entitled "Bandos y trincheras"). *Desarrollo Económico (Argentina),* v. 33, no. 131 (Oct – Dec 93), pp. 453 – 456. Bibl.

— *Authoritarian Argentina: The Nationalist Movement; Its History, and Its Impact* reviewed by Jeremy Adelman. *Hispanic American Historical Review,* v. 73, no. 4 (Nov 93), pp. 705 – 706.

Rodríguez, Adriana C.
See
Rodríguez Pérsico, Adriana C.

Rodríguez, Aleida Anselma. *Arqueología de Omagua y Dorado* reviewed by Ligia Rodríguez. *Colonial Latin American Review,* v. 2, no. 1 – 2 (1993), pp. 277 – 279.

— *Arqueología de Omagua y Dorado* reviewed by Amelia Mondragón. *Revista de Crítica Literaria Latinoamericana,* v. 19, no. 37 (Jan – June 93), pp. 383 – 386.

Rodríguez, Hipólito and Jorge Alberto Manrique. *Veracruz: la ciudad hecha de mar, 1519 – 1821* (Review). *La Palabra y el Hombre,* no. 83 (July – Sept 92), pp. 347 – 349.

Rodríguez Feo, José. *Mi correspondencia con Lezama Lima* reviewed by Saïd Benabdelouahed. *Caravelle*, no. 59 (1992), pp. 289 – 293.

Rodríguez García, Rubén. *La Cámara Agrícola Nacional Jalisciense: una sociedad de terratenientes en la revolución mexicana* reviewed by Carlos Alba Vega. *Foro Internacional*, v. 32, no. 5 (Oct – Dec 92), pp. 788 – 793.

Rodríguez Jiménez, Pablo. *Seducción, amancebamiento y abandono en la colonia* reviewed by Frédérique Langue. *Anuario de Estudios Americanos*, v. 49, Suppl. 2 (1992), pp. 261 – 262.

Rodríguez-Luis, Julio. *The Contemporary Praxis of the Fantastic: Borges and Cortázar* reviewed by John Incledon. *Hispania (USA)*, v. 76, no. 1 (Mar 93), p. 89.

— *The Contemporary Praxis of the Fantastic: Borges and Cortázar* reviewed by John Incledon. *Revista de Crítica Literaria Latinoamericana*, v. 19, no. 38 (July – Dec 93), pp. 403 – 404.

Rodríguez O., Jaime E., ed. *The Independence of Mexico and the Creation of the New Nation* reviewed by Pilar Collado de De Bleser. *La Palabra y el Hombre*, no. 83 (July – Sept 92), pp. 353 – 361.

Rodríguez Padrón, Justo Jorge. *Del ocio sagrado: algunos poetas hispanoamericanos* reviewed by Jacobo Sefamí. *Revista Chilena de Literatura*, no. 41 (Apr 93), p. 138.

Rodríguez Pérsico, Adriana C. *Un huracán llamado progreso: utopía y autobiografía en Sarmiento y Alberdi* reviewed by Carlos E. Paldao. *La Educación (USA)*, v. 37, no. 115 (1993), pp. 435 – 437.

Rodríguez Rea, Miguel Angel. *El Perú y su literatura: guía bibliográfica* reviewed by M. Rozenblat. *Caravelle*, no. 60 (1993), pp. 179 – 180.

— *El Perú y su literatura: guía bibliográfica* reviewed by David William Foster. *Chasqui*, v. 22, no. 1 (May 93), pp. 86 – 87.

Rodríguez-Vergara, Isabel. *El mundo satírico de Gabriel García Márquez* reviewed by Francisca Noguerol Jiménez. *Anuario de Estudios Americanos*, v. 49, Suppl. 1 (1992), pp. 261 – 262.

Roggiano, Alfredo A. *Pedro Henríquez Ureña en México* reviewed by Gustavo Fares. *Nuevo Texto Crítico*, v. 6, no. 11 (1993), pp. 266 – 268.

Rohlehr, F. Gordon. *My Strangled City and Other Essays* reviewed by Rupert Lewis. *Social and Economic Studies*, v. 41, no. 3 (Sept 92), pp. 169 – 173.

Rojas, Elena M., ed. *Acerca de los relatos orales en la provincia de Tucumán* reviewed by Félix Coluccio. *Folklore Americano*, no. 53 (Jan – June 92), pp. 180 – 181.

Roldán, Martha and Lourdes Benería. *Las encrucijadas de clase y género: trabajo a domicilio; subcontratación y dinámica de la unidad doméstica en la ciudad de México* translated by Julio Colón Gómez. Reviewed by Norma Ilse Veloz Avila. *El Cotidiano*, v. 9, no. 53 (Mar – Apr 93), p. 118.

Rolland, Denis. *Vichy et la France libre au Mexique: guerre, cultures et propagande pendant la deuxième guerre mondiale* reviewed by Thomas D. Schoonover. *Hispanic American Historical Review*, v. 73, no. 4 (Nov 93), pp. 726 – 727.

Romero, Luis Alberto and Hilda Sábato. *Los trabajadores de Buenos Aires: la experiencia del mercado, 1850 – 1880* reviewed by María Cecilia Cangiano (Review entitled "¿Clase obrera o trabajadores?"). *Desarrollo Económico (Argentina)*, v. 33, no. 131 (Oct – Dec 93), pp. 445 – 448.

— *Los trabajadores de Buenos Aires: la experiencia del mercado, 1850 – 1880* reviewed by Susan Migden Socolow. *Hispanic American Historical Review*, v. 73, no. 2 (May 93), pp. 323 – 324.

— *Los trabajadores de Buenos Aires: la experiencia del mercado, 1850 – 1880* reviewed by Paula Alonso. *Journal of Latin American Studies*, v. 25, no. 2 (May 93), pp. 396 – 397.

— *Los trabajadores de Buenos Aires: la experiencia del mercado, 1850 – 1880* reviewed by Hobart A. Spalding. *Revista Interamericana de Bibliografía*, v. 42, no. 4 (1992), pp. 663 – 664.

Rondinelli, Dennis A. et al. *Planning Education Reforms in Developing Countries* reviewed by Maria Valéria Junho Pena. *La Educación (USA)*, v. 37, no. 115 (1993), pp. 437 – 439.

Rosenberg, Robin L. *Spain and Central America: Democracy and Foreign Policy* reviewed by Paul C. Sondrol. *Hispanic American Historical Review*, v. 73, no. 4 (Nov 93), pp. 731 – 732.

— *Spain and Central America: Democracy and Foreign Policy* reviewed by Joan Font. *Revista Interamericana de Bibliografía*, v. 42, no. 4 (1992), pp. 662 – 663.

Rosenberg, Tina. *Children of Cain: Violence and the Violent in Latin America* reviewed by Troy M. Bollinger. *Journal of Inter-American Studies and World Affairs*, v. 35, no. 2 (Summer 93), pp. 159 – 163.

Rosenthal, Bertrand and Jean-François Fogel. *Fin de siècle à la Havane: les secrets du pouvoir cubain* reviewed by Ernesto Hernández Busto (Review entitled "Fin de siglo con Castro"). *Vuelta*, v. 17, no. 200 (July 93), pp. 55 – 56.

Rosenzweig, Gabriel. *Autores mexicanos publicados en España, 1879 – 1936* reviewed by Jorge F. Hernández. *Vuelta*, v. 17, no. 196 (Mar 93), pp. 52 – 53.

Rossetti, José Paschoal. *Política e programação econômicas* reviewed by Anita Kon. *RAE; Revista de Administração de Empresas*, v. 33, no. 2 (Mar – Apr 93), pp. 124 – 126.

Rostworowski Tovar de Diez Canseco, María and Pilar Remy S., eds. *Las visitas a Cajamarca, 1571/72 – 1578* reviewed by Pedro Guibovich. *Apuntes (Peru)*, no. 31 (July – Dec 92), pp. 119 – 121.

— *Las visitas a Cajamarca, 1571/72 – 1578* reviewed by Jorge Montenegro. *Bulletin de l'Institut Français d'Etudes Andines*, v. 21, no. 3 (1992), pp. 1073 – 1074.

— *Las visitas a Cajamarca, 1571/72 – 1578* reviewed by Noble David Cook. *Hispanic American Historical Review*, v. 73, no. 2 (May 93), pp. 313 – 314.

— *Las visitas a Cajamarca, 1571/72 – 1578* reviewed by Carmen Beatriz Loza. *Revista Andina*, v. 10, no. 2 (Dec 92), pp. 548 – 550.

Rotker, Susana. *Fundación de una escritura: las crónicas de José Martí* reviewed by Richard B. Gray. *Hispanic American Historical Review*, v. 73, no. 3 (Aug 93), pp. 483 – 484.

Rouquié, Alain. *Guerres et paix en Amérique Centrale* reviewed by Edelberto Torres-Rivas. *Journal of Latin American Studies*, v. 25, no. 3 (Oct 93), pp. 668 – 669.

Rouquié, Alain and Hélène Arnaud, eds. *Les forces politiques en Amérique Centrale* reviewed by Rodolfo Cerdas-Cruz. *Journal of Latin American Studies*, v. 25, no. 2 (May 93), pp. 416 – 417.

Rouse, Irving. *The Tainos: Rise and Decline of the People Who Greeted Columbus* reviewed by Aaron Segal. *Interciencia*, v. 18, no. 1 (Jan – Feb 93), p. 46.

— *The Tainos: Rise and Decline of the People Who Greeted Columbus* reviewed by C. J. M. R. Gullick. *Journal of Latin American Studies*, v. 25, no. 2 (May 93), pp. 388 – 389.

Rovinski, Yanina and Valerie Barzetti, eds. *Towards a Green Central America: Integrating Conservation and Development,* a translation of *Hacia una Centroamérica verde.* Reviewed by L. Alan Eyre. *Caribbean Geography,* v. 3, no. 4 (Sept 92), pp. 277 – 278.

Rovner, Eduardo. *Volvió una noche* reviewed by Frank Dauster. *World Literature Today,* v. 67, no. 1 (Winter 93), pp. 159 – 160.

Rowe, William and Vivian Schelling. *Memory and Modernity: Popular Culture in Latin America* reviewed by Margaret Bullen. *Bulletin of Latin American Research,* v. 12, no. 1 (Jan 93), pp. 126 – 128.

— *Memory and Modernity: Popular Culture in Latin America* reviewed by Ineke Phaf. *Hispamérica,* v. 22, no. 64 – 65 (Apr – Aug 93), pp. 193 – 197.

— *Memory and Modernity: Popular Culture in Latin America* reviewed by David Lehmann. *Journal of Latin American Studies,* v. 25, no. 3 (Oct 93), pp. 692 – 694.

Ruano, Manuel. *Mirada de Brueghel* reviewed by R. H. Moreno-Durán. *Revista Nacional de Cultura (Venezuela),* v. 53, no. 285 (Apr – June 92), p. 245.

Rubio Correa, Marcial. *Constitución: qué ponerle y qué quitarle* reviewed by José Luis Sardón. *Apuntes (Peru),* no. 30 (Jan – June 92), pp. 105 – 107.

Rudman, Andrew I. and Joseph S. Tulchin, eds. *Economic Development and Environmental Protection in Latin America* reviewed by Steve Ellner. *Journal of Developing Areas,* v. 27, no. 3 (Apr 93), p. 441.

— *Economic Development and Environmental Protection in Latin America* reviewed by Margaret E. Keck. *Studies in Comparative International Development,* v. 27, no. 3 (Fall 92), pp. 120 – 122.

Rudolph, James D. *Peru: The Evolution of a Crisis* reviewed by David P. Werlich. *Hispanic American Historical Review,* v. 73, no. 3 (Aug 93), pp. 519 – 520.

Ruffinelli, Jorge and Fernando Alegría, eds. *Paradise Lost or Gained?: The Literature of Hispanic Exile* reviewed by Barbara Mujica (Review entitled "The Creative Subtext of Life"). *Américas,* v. 45, no. 3 (May – June 93), pp. 60 – 61.

— *Paradise Lost or Gained?: The Literature of Hispanic Exile* reviewed by Joseph F. Vélez. *Hispania (USA),* v. 76, no. 1 (Mar 93), pp. 80 – 82.

Ruiz, Carlos and Renato Cristi. *El pensamiento conservador en Chile* reviewed by Simon Collier. *Hispanic American Historical Review,* v. 73, no. 4 (Nov 93), pp. 708 – 709.

— *El pensamiento conservador en Chile* reviewed by Patricio Silva. *Journal of Latin American Studies,* v. 25, no. 2 (May 93), pp. 429 – 430.

Ruiz Abreu, Alvaro. *José Revueltas: los muros de la utopía* reviewed by Sergio González Rodríguez (Review entitled "El legado de José Revueltas"). *Nexos,* v. 16, no. 187 (July 93), pp. 73 – 75.

— *José Revueltas: los muros de la utopía* reviewed by Christopher Domínguez. *Vuelta,* v. 17, no. 196 (Mar 93), pp. 49 – 50.

Ruiz Chataing, David and Haidée Miranda Bastidas. *El anti-imperialismo en la prensa de la época de Cipriano Castro, 1899 – 1908* reviewed by Julián Rodríguez Barazarte. *Boletín de la Academia Nacional de la Historia (Venezuela),* v. 76, no. 302 (Apr – June 93), pp. 152 – 153.

Ruiz Churión, Jairo. *Mexa, Grameta, Metacuyá, el Meta: recopilación, cronistas e historiadores, 1530 – 1830* reviewed by Jorge Morales Gómez (Review entitled "Historia del Meta"). *Boletín de Historia y Antigüedades,* v. 80, no. 781 (Apr – June 93), pp. 481 – 482.

Ruiz Granados, Fernando. *Poemas de Brindisi* reviewed by Raúl Hernández Viveros (Review entitled "La escritura de Ruiz Granados"). *Plural (Mexico),* v. 22, no. 261 (June 93), pp. 92 – 94.

Ruiz Medrano, Ethelia. *Gobierno y sociedad en Nueva España: segunda Audiencia y Antonio de Mendoza* reviewed by Michel Bertrand. *Caravelle,* no. 59 (1992), pp. 270 – 273.

— *Gobierno y sociedad en Nueva España: segunda Audiencia y Antonio de Mendoza* reviewed by Brian R. Hamnett. *Hispanic American Historical Review,* v. 73, no. 3 (Aug 93), pp. 506 – 507.

Rulfo, Juan. *Toda la obra.* Critical edition by Claude Fell. Reviewed by Samuel Gordon. *Revista de Crítica Literaria Latinoamericana,* v. 19, no. 38 (July – Dec 93), pp. 417 – 423.

Rumble, Greville and João Batista Araújo e Oliveira, eds. *Educación a distancia en América Latina: análisis de costo-efectividad* reviewed by Aaron Segal. *Interciencia,* v. 18, no. 6 (Nov – Dec 93), pp. 327 – 328.

Rumeu de Armas, Antonio. *Libro copiador de Cristóbal Colón: correspondencia inédita con los reyes católicos sobre los viajes a América* reviewed by Margarita Zamora (Review entitled "Searching for Columbus in the Quincentennial: Three Recent Books on the Discovery"). *Colonial Latin American Review,* v. 2, no. 1 – 2 (1993), pp. 261 – 267.

Ruvalcaba, Eusebio. *Un hilito de sangre* reviewed by Barbara Mujica. *Hispania (USA),* v. 76, no. 2 (May 93), p. 298.

Saban, Mario Javier. *Los marranos y la economía en el Río de Plata* reviewed by José Federico Lima. *Todo Es Historia,* v. 27, no. 314 (Sept 93), pp. 71 – 72. Il.

Sábato, Ernesto R. *The Angel of Darkness,* a translation of *Abaddón, el exterminador,* translated by Andrew Hurley. Reviewed by James Polk. *Review,* no. 47 (Fall 93), pp. 96 – 97.

Sábato, Hilda. *Agrarian Capitalism and the World Market: Buenos Aires in the Pastoral Age, 1840 – 1890* reviewed by Samuel Amaral. *Hispanic American Historical Review,* v. 73, no. 1 (Feb 93), pp. 161 – 162.

Sábato, Hilda and Luis Alberto Romero. *Los trabajadores de Buenos Aires: la experiencia del mercado, 1850 – 1880* reviewed by María Cecilia Cangiano (Review entitled "¿Clase obrera o trabajadores?"). *Desarrollo Económico (Argentina),* v. 33, no. 131 (Oct – Dec 93), pp. 445 – 448.

— *Los trabajadores de Buenos Aires: la experiencia del mercado, 1850 – 1880* reviewed by Susan Migden Socolow. *Hispanic American Historical Review,* v. 73, no. 2 (May 93), pp. 323 – 324.

— *Los trabajadores de Buenos Aires: la experiencia del mercado, 1850 – 1880* reviewed by Paula Alonso. *Journal of Latin American Studies,* v. 25, no. 2 (May 93), pp. 396 – 397.

— *Los trabajadores de Buenos Aires: la experiencia del mercado, 1850 – 1880* reviewed by Hobart A. Spalding. *Revista Interamericana de Bibliografía,* v. 42, no. 4 (1992), pp. 663 – 664.

Sabines, Jaime. *Otro recuento de poemas, 1950 – 1991* reviewed by Enrique Saínz (Review entitled "Jaime Sabines entre la angustia y la palabra"). *Casa de las Américas,* no. 190 (Jan – Mar 93), pp. 150 – 155.

Sabrovsky, Eduardo, ed. *Tecnología y modernidad en Latinoamérica: ética, política y cultura* reviewed by Felipe Cabello (Review entitled "Don Andrés Bello: ¡Con cuánta nostalgia lo recordamos y cuánta falta nos hace!"). *Interciencia,* v. 18, no. 6 (Nov – Dec 93), pp. 329 – 333.

Sachs, Jeffrey D. and Carlos Paredes. *Estabilización y crecimiento en el Perú* reviewed by Martha Rodríguez. *Apuntes (Peru),* no. 29 (July – Dec 91), pp. 91 – 94.

Sacoto, Antonio. *El ensayo equatoriano* reviewed by Gerardo Sáenz. *Revista Interamericana de Bibliografía*, v. 42, no. 3 (1992), p. 508.

Sada, Daniel. *Registro de causantes* reviewed by Alvaro Enrique. *Vuelta*, v. 17, no. 204 (Nov 93), pp. 47 – 48.

Sader, Emir and Ken Silverstein. *Without Fear of Being Happy: Lula, the Workers Party, and Brazil* reviewed by Joel Wolfe. *The Americas*, v. 49, no. 4 (Apr 93), pp. 566 – 568.

— *Without Fear of Being Happy: Lula, the Workers Party, and Brazil* reviewed by John Humphrey. *Bulletin of Latin American Research*, v. 12, no. 3 (Sept 93), p. 347.

— *Without Fear of Being Happy: Lula, the Workers Party, and Brazil* reviewed by Paul Cammack. *Journal of Latin American Studies*, v. 25, no. 3 (Oct 93), pp. 666 – 667.

Sadlier, Darlene J., ed. *One Hundred Years after Tomorrow: Brazilian Women's Fiction in the 20th Century* translated by the editor. Reviewed by Candace Slater. *Letras Femeninas*, v. 19, no. 1 – 2 (Spring – Fall 93), pp. 163 – 164.

Saer, Juan José. *The Witness*, a translation of *El entenado*, translated by Margaret Jull Costa. Reviewed by Amy Fass Emery. *Review*, no. 47 (Fall 93), pp. 97 – 99.

Saignes, Thierry and Isabelle Combès. *Alter ego: naissance de l'identité chiriguano* reviewed by Marie-Danielle Demélas-Bohy. *Caravelle*, no. 60 (1993), pp. 166 – 170.

Saint-Geours, Yves and Danièle Demelas. *Jerusalén y Babilonia: religión y política en el Ecuador, 1780 – 1880* reviewed by Ana Luz Rodríguez González (Review entitled "Lo particular en el Ecuador del siglo XIX"). *Anuario Colombiano de Historia Social y de la Cultura*, no. 20 (1992), pp. 154 – 157.

Sáinz, Gustavo. *Retablo de inmoderaciones y heresiarcas* reviewed by Fabrizio Mejía Madrid (Review entitled "Una larga frase"). *Nexos*, v. 16, no. 185 (May 93), p. 81. Il.

— *Retablo de inmoderaciones y heresiarcas* reviewed by Salvador C. Fernández. *World Literature Today*, v. 67, no. 4 (Fall 93), p. 786.

Sáiz, Blanca. *Bibliografía sobre Alejandro Malaspina y acerca de la expedición Malaspina y de los marinos y científicos que en ella participaron* reviewed by Oldrich Kaspar (Review translated by Eva Máuková). *Anuario de Estudios Americanos*, v. 50, no. 1 (1993), p. 325.

Sala-Molins, Louis. *L'Afrique aux Amériques: le code noir espagnol* reviewed by Germán A. de la Raza. *Ibero Americana (Sweden)*, v. 22, no. 2 (Dec 92), pp. 77 – 81.

Salama, Pierre and Jacques Valier. *La economía gangrenada: ensayo sobre la hiperinflación* reviewed by Sebastián Katz and Pablo Sirlin (Review entitled "Las desventuras de un análisis francés sobre la desventura de América Latina"). *Desarrollo Económico (Argentina)*, v. 33, no. 131 (Oct – Dec 93), pp. 449 – 452.

Salazar, Mario and Isidora Mena, eds. *Para saber y contar: manual metodológico* reviewed by Luis Weinstein (Review entitled "Para saber y contar sobre Las ovejas y el infinito"). *Estudios Sociales (Chile)*, no. 78 (Oct – Dec 93), pp. 284 – 290.

— *Para saber y contar: narraciones sobre niños, viejos y viejísimos* reviewed by Luis Weinstein (Review entitled "Para saber y contar sobre Las ovejas y el infinito"). *Estudios Sociales (Chile)*, no. 78 (Oct – Dec 93), pp. 284 – 290.

Salazar M., Rafael. *Del joropo y sus andanzas* (Review). *Inter-American Music Review*, v. 13, no. 2 (Spring – Summer 93), p. 160.

Salazar Mora, Orlando. *El apogeo de la república liberal en Costa Rica, 1870 – 1914* reviewed by Fernando González Davidson. *Mesoamérica (USA)*, v. 13, no. 23 (June 92), pp. 179 – 182.

Salazar Mostajo, Carlos. *La "Taika": teoría y práctica de la escuela – ayllu* reviewed by Carlos Coello Vila. *Signo, no.* 38, Nueva época (Jan – Apr 93), pp. 256 – 257.

Saldívar, José David. *The Dialectics of Our America: Genealogy, Cultural Critique, and Literary History* reviewed by Stephen Minta. *Bulletin of Latin American Research*, v. 12, no. 1 (Jan 93), pp. 129 – 130.

— *The Dialectics of Our America: Genealogy, Cultural Critique, and Literary History* reviewed by John Bruce-Novoa. *Hispania (USA)*, v. 76, no. 2 (May 93), pp. 280 – 281.

Saldívar, José David and Héctor Calderón, eds. *Criticism in the Borderlands: Studies in Chicano Literature, Culture, and Ideology* reviewed by Chuck Tatum (Review entitled "A New Standard for Chicano Literary Scholarship"). *Bilingual Review/Revista Bilingüe*, v. 18, no. 1 (Jan – Apr 93), pp. 64 – 74.

— *Criticism in the Borderlands: Studies in Chicano Literature, Culture, and Ideology* reviewed by Hanny Berkelmans (Review entitled "La literatura chicana de hoy en día"). *European Review of Latin American and Caribbean Studies*, no. 54 (June 93), pp. 111 – 115. Bibl.

— *Criticism in the Borderlands: Studies in Chicano Literature, Culture, and Ideology* reviewed by John Bruce-Novoa. *Hispania (USA)*, v. 76, no. 2 (May 93), pp. 280 – 281.

— *Criticism in the Borderlands: Studies in Chicano Literature, Culture, and Ideology* reviewed by Pedro Maligo. *Hispanic American Historical Review*, v. 73, no. 3 (Aug 93), pp. 489 – 490.

Saldívar, Ramón David. *Chicano Narrative: The Dialectics of Difference* reviewed by Chuck Tatum (Review entitled "A New Standard for Chicano Literary Scholarship"). *Bilingual Review/Revista Bilingüe*, v. 18, no. 1 (Jan – Apr 93), pp. 64 – 74.

Saldívar y Silva, Gabriel. *Bibliografía mexicana de musicología y musicografía* (Review). *Inter-American Music Review*, v. 13, no. 1 (Fall – Winter 92), pp. 116 – 117.

— *Bibliografía mexicana de musicología y musicografía* (Review of a reprint of the 1876 original). *Inter-American Music Review*, v. 13, no. 2 (Spring – Summer 93), pp. 151 – 154.

Sale, Kirkpatrick. *The Conquest of Paradise: Christopher Columbus and the Columbian Legacy* reviewed by Stelio Cro. *Revista de Indias*, v. 53, no. 197 (Jan – Apr 93), pp. 119 – 121.

Salgado, Germánico and Rafael Urriola, eds. *El fin de las barreras: los empresarios y el Pacto Andino en la década de los '90* (Review). *Integración Latinoamericana*, v. 18, no. 189 – 190 (May – June 93), p. 57.

Salinas, Patricia Wilson
See
  Wilson, Patricia Ann

Salinas, Pedro and Jorge Guillén. *Pedro Salinas y Jorge Guillén: correspondencia, 1923 – 1951* edited by Andrés Soria Olmedo. Reviewed by Jean Cross Newman. *Revista Canadiense de Estudios Hispánicos*, v. 17, no. 3 (Spring 93), pp. 567 – 569.

Salkey, Andrew. *Anancy, Traveller* reviewed by Peter Nazareth. *World Literature Today*, v. 67, no. 2 (Spring 93), p. 429.

Sallmann, Jean-Michel, ed. *Visions indiennes, visions baroques: les métissages de l'inconscient* reviewed by Frédérique Langue. *Caravelle*, no. 60 (1993), pp. 154 – 157.

Salmón, Roberto Mario. *Indian Revolts in Northern New Spain: A Synthesis of Resistance, 1680 – 1786* reviewed by Luis Navarro García. *Hispanic American Historical Review*, v. 73, no. 3 (Aug 93), pp. 508 – 509.

Salmón Jordán, Jorge. *Entre la vanidad y el poder: memoria y testimonio* reviewed by Oscar Malca (Review entitled "Contra la corriente"). *Debate (Peru)*, v. 16, no. 72 (Mar – May 93), pp. 65 – 66. Il.

Sánchez, Ana. *Amancebados, hechiceros y rebeldes: Chancay, siglo XVII* reviewed by Irene Silverblatt. *Hispanic American Historical Review*, v. 73, no. 1 (Feb 93), pp. 157 – 159.

Sánchez, Marcos and Grimaldo Rengifo V. *Hacia una agricultura sostenible: el caso de Coronel Oviedo. Revista Paraguaya de Sociología*, v. 29, no. 85 (Sept – Dec 92), pp. 190 – 191.

Sánchez Agesta, Luis. *La democracia en Hispanoamérica: un balance histórico* reviewed by Frédérique Langue. *Cahiers des Amériques Latines*, no. 13 (1992), pp. 178 – 179.

Sánchez Alonso, Blanca. *La inmigración española en Argentina, siglos XIX y XX* reviewed by Hebe Clementi. *Todo Es Historia*, v. 26, no. 310 (May 93), p. 80. Il.

Sánchez Bella, Ismael. *Derecho indiano; estudios, vol. I: Las visitas generales en la América española, siglos XVI – XVII; vol. II: Fuentes; literatura jurídica, derecho público* reviewed by Benjamin Keen. *Hispanic American Historical Review*, v. 73, no. 1 (Feb 93), p. 148.

— *Iglesia y estado en la América española*, 2d ed., reviewed by Teodoro Hampe Martínez. *Revista Interamericana de Bibliografía*, v. 42, no. 4 (1992), p. 664.

Sánchez de Paz, Manuel

See

Paz Sánchez, Manuel de

Sánchez Durán, Fernando. *Narrativa chilena ultrarrealista* reviewed by Antonio Campaña. *Atenea (Chile)*, no. 465 – 466 (1992), pp. 382 – 384.

Sánchez Zúber, Leopoldo. *Qué más te da morir* reviewed by Guillermo Farber (Review entitled "Qué más te da escribir"). *Plural (Mexico)*, v. 22, no. 263 (Aug 93), pp. 74 – 75.

Sanciprián, Nancy. *B. Traven en México* reviewed by Fermín Ramírez. *Plural (Mexico)*, v. 22, no. 264 (Sept 93), pp. 123 – 124.

Sanderson, Steven E. *The Politics of Trade in Latin American Development* reviewed by S. P. Chakravarty. *Bulletin of Latin American Research*, v. 12, no. 2 (May 93), pp. 239 – 240.

Santaella, Juan Carlos. *Manifiestos literarios venezolanos* reviewed by Analy Lorenzo. *Revista Nacional de Cultura (Venezuela)*, v. 54, no. 287 (Oct – Dec 92), p. 269.

Santana, Roberto. *Les indiens d'Equateur: citoyens dans l'ethnicité?* reviewed by Maxime Haubert. *Tiers Monde*, v. 34, no. 134 (Apr – June 93), pp. 471 – 473.

Santiago, Carlos Enrique. *Labor in the Puerto Rican Economy: Postwar Development and Stagnation* reviewed by William D. Savedoff. *Hispanic American Historical Review*, v. 73, no. 3 (Aug 93), pp. 534 – 535.

Santiago, Silviano. *Uma história de família* reviewed by Malcolm Silverman. *World Literature Today*, v. 67, no. 2 (Spring 93), p. 346.

Santistevan, Miguel de. *Mil leguas por América: de Lima a Caracas, 1740 – 1741; diario de don Miguel de Santisteban* edited by David J. Robinson. Reviewed by Judith E. Villamarin. *Hispanic American Historical Review*, v. 73, no. 4 (Nov 93), pp. 701 – 702.

Santos, Murillo. *O caminho da profissionalização das forças armadas* reviewed by José Augusto Vaz Sampaio Neto. *Revista do Instituto Histórico e Geográfico Brasileiro*, no. 370 (Jan – Mar 91), pp. 333 – 335.

Santos, Wanderley Guilherme dos. *Razões da desordem* reviewed by Cláudio Gonçalves Couto. *Revista Brasileira de Ciências Sociais*, v. 8, no. 23 (Oct 93), pp. 153 – 155.

Santos Granero, Fernando. *The Power of Love: The Moral Use of Knowledge amongst the Amuesha of Central Peru* reviewed by Jaime Regan. *Amazonía Peruana*, v. 11, no. 22 (Oct 92), pp. 285 – 288.

— *The Power of Love: The Moral Use of Knowledge amongst the Amuesha of Central Peru* reviewed by Richard. C. Smith. *Bulletin de l'Institut Français d'Etudes Andines*, v. 21, no. 2 (1992), pp. 793 – 797. Bibl.

Saranyana, José Ignacio. *Teología profética americana: diez estudios sobre la evangelización fundante* reviewed by Pilar Gonzalbo Aizpuru. *Historia Mexicana*, v. 42, no. 1 (July – Sept 92), pp. 129 – 133.

Saranyana, José Ignacio and Elisa Luque Alcaide. *La iglesia católica y América* reviewed by Carmen J. Alejos-Grau. *Anuario de Estudios Americanos*, v. 50, no. 1 (1993), pp. 322 – 323.

Saravia, Enrique J. *Los sistemas de educación superior en los países del MERCOSUR: elementos fundamentales y bases para su integración* reviewed by Antônio Octávio Cintra. *La Educación (USA)*, v. 37, no. 114 (1993), pp. 168 – 169.

Saravia Quiroz, Leobardo, ed. *En la línea de fuego: relatos policíacos de frontera* (Review). *La Palabra y el Hombre*, no. 81 (Jan – Mar 92), pp. 324 – 325.

Sarkisyanz, Manuel. *Vom Wirken und Sterben des Felipe Carrillo Puerto, des "Roten" Apostels der Maya-Indianer: Zur politischen Heiligenlegende im revolutionären Mexiko* reviewed by Jürgen Buchenau. *Hispanic American Historical Review*, v. 73, no. 2 (May 93), pp. 332 – 333.

Sarmiento, Sergio and Carlos R. Martínez-Assad, eds. *Nos queda la esperanza: el valle del Mezquital* reviewed by Marta Eugenia García Ugarte. *Revista Mexicana de Sociología*, v. 54, no. 2 (Apr – June 92), pp. 245 – 251.

Sassone, Helena. *Palabras congeladas* reviewed by Juvenal López Ruiz. *Revista Nacional de Cultura (Venezuela)*, v. 53, no. 285 (Apr – June 92), p. 249.

Sater, William F. *Chile and the United States: Empires in Conflict* reviewed by David Sheinin. *The Americas*, v. 50, no. 1 (July 93), pp. 133 – 134.

— *Chile and the United States: Empires in Conflict* reviewed by Juan Ricardo Couyoumdijan. *Historia (Chile)*, no. 26 (1991 – 1992), pp. 461 – 464.

Sauer, Carl Ortwin. *The Early Spanish Main* reviewed by Peter T. Bradley. *Bulletin of Latin American Research*, v. 12, no. 1 (Jan 93), pp. 110 – 111.

Saunders, Gail and Michael Craton. *Islanders in the Stream: A History of the Bahamian People* reviewed by William F. Keegan. *Hispanic American Historical Review*, v. 73, no. 4 (Nov 93), pp. 702 – 703.

Sayer, Chloë and Elizabeth Carmichael. *The Skeleton and the Feast: The Day of the Dead in Mexico* reviewed by Ward S. Albro III. *Hispanic American Historical Review*, v. 73, no. 1 (Feb 93), p. 127.

Scarborough, Vernon Lee and David R. Wilcox, eds. *The Mesoamerican Ballgame* reviewed by Barbara J. Price. *Hispanic American Historical Review*, v. 73, no. 1 (Feb 93), pp. 144 – 145.

Schaefer-Rodríguez, Claudia. *Textured Lives: Women, Art, and Representation in Modern Mexico* reviewed by Barbara Mujica (Review entitled "A Roundup of Stories"). *Américas*, v. 45, no. 1 (Jan – Feb 93), pp. 61 – 62.

— *Textured Lives: Women, Art, and Representation in Modern Mexico* reviewed by Susan Isabel Stein. *Hispania (USA)*, v. 76, no. 2 (May 93), pp. 292 – 293.

— *Textured Lives: Women, Art, and Representation in Modern Mexico* reviewed by Kathleen Ross. *Hispanic American Historical Review*, v. 73, no. 2 (May 93), pp. 333 – 334.

Scharager, Judith and Silvia Rittershaussen, eds. *Análisis y proyecciones en torno a la educación media y el trabajo* reviewed by María José Lemaitre. *Estudios Sociales (Chile)*, no. 78 (Oct – Dec 93), pp. 279 – 283.

Schelling, Vivian and William Rowe. *Memory and Modernity: Popular Culture in Latin America* reviewed by Margaret Bullen. *Bulletin of Latin American Research*, v. 12, no. 1 (Jan 93), pp. 126 – 128.

— *Memory and Modernity: Popular Culture in Latin America* reviewed by Ineke Phaf. *Hispamérica*, v. 22, no. 64 – 65 (Apr – Aug 93), pp. 193 – 197.

— *Memory and Modernity: Popular Culture in Latin America* reviewed by David Lehmann. *Journal of Latin American Studies*, v. 25, no. 3 (Oct 93), pp. 692 – 694.

Scheper-Hughes, Nancy. *Death without Weeping: The Violence of Everyday Life in Brazil* reviewed by Bernardo Kucinski. *Journal of Latin American Studies*, v. 25, no. 2 (May 93), pp. 419 – 420.

— *Death without Weeping: The Violence of Everyday Life in Brazil* reviewed by Glenn W. Erickson and Sandra S. Fernandes Erickson. *Luso-Brazilian Review*, v. 30, no. 1 (Summer 93), pp. 142 – 144.

Schiefelbein, Ernesto. *En busca de la escuela del siglo XXI* reviewed by Marta Llames Murúa. *La Educación (USA)*, v. 37, no. 114 (1993), pp. 170 – 171.

Schlau, Stacey and Electa Arenal, eds. *Untold Sisters: Hispanic Nuns in Their Own Works* translated by Amanda Powell. Reviewed by Noël Valis. *Colonial Latin American Review*, v. 2, no. 1 – 2 (1993), pp. 304 – 308.

Schmidhuber de la Mora, Guillermo, ed. *'La segunda Celestina': una comedia perdida de sor Juana* reviewed by Francisco Javier Cevallos. *Colonial Latin American Review*, v. 2, no. 1 – 2 (1993), pp. 302 – 304.

Schmink, Marianne and Charles Howard Wood. *Contested Frontiers in Amazonia* reviewed by Philip A. Dennis. *Journal of Developing Areas*, v. 28, no. 1 (Oct 93), pp. 111 – 113.

Schmitz, Hubert and José Eduardo Cassiolato, eds. *Hi-tech for Industrial Development: Lessons from the Brazilian Experience in Electronics and Automation* reviewed by Rhys Jenkins. *Bulletin of Latin American Research*, v. 12, no. 3 (Sept 93), pp. 349 – 350.

Schneider, Ben Ross. *Politics within the State: Elite Bureaucrats and Industrial Policy in Authoritarian Brazil* reviewed by Sonny B. Davis. *Canadian Journal of Latin American and Caribbean Studies*, v. 17, no. 34 (1992), p. 131.

— *Politics within the State: Elite Bureaucrats and Industrial Policy in Authoritarian Brazil* reviewed by John W. Sloan. *Journal of Developing Areas*, v. 27, no. 3 (Apr 93), pp. 424 – 425.

Schneider, Ronald M. *"Order and Progress": A Political History of Brazil* reviewed by Neale J. Pearson. *Journal of Developing Areas*, v. 27, no. 4 (July 93), pp. 564 – 566.

Schoonover, Ebba and Thomas David Schoonover, eds. *A Mexican View of America in the 1860s: A Foreign Diplomat Describes the Civil War and Reconstruction* reviewed by John A. Britton. *The Americas*, v. 49, no. 3 (Jan 93), pp. 407 – 409.

Schoonover, Thomas David. *The United States in Central America, 1860 – 1911: Episodes of Social Imperialism and Imperial Rivalry in the World System* reviewed by Lester D. Langley. *The Americas*, v. 49, no. 4 (Apr 93), pp. 561 – 562.

— *The United States in Central America, 1860 – 1911: Episodes of Social Imperialism and Imperial Rivalry in the World System* reviewed by Rob van Vuurde. *European Review of Latin American and Caribbean Studies*, no. 54 (June 93), pp. 131 – 133.

— *The United States in Central America, 1860 – 1911: Episodes of Social Imperialism and Imperial Rivalry in the World System* reviewed by Lester D. Langley. *Journal of Latin American Studies*, v. 25, no. 1 (Feb 93), pp. 200 – 201.

Schoonover, Thomas David and Ebba Schoonover, eds. *A Mexican View of America in the 1860s: A Foreign Diplomat Describes the Civil War and Reconstruction* reviewed by John A. Britton. *The Americas*, v. 49, no. 3 (Jan 93), pp. 407 – 409.

Schroeder, Susan. *Chimalpahin and the Kingdoms of Chalco* reviewed by J. Benedict Warren. *The Americas*, v. 49, no. 3 (Jan 93), pp. 396 – 398.

Schteingart, Martha, ed. *Espacio y vivienda en la ciudad de México* reviewed by Richard Boyer. *Hispanic American Historical Review*, v. 73, no. 3 (Aug 93), pp. 528 – 529.

Schumm, Petra. *Exilerfahrung und Literatur: Lateinamerikanische Autoren in Spanien* reviewed by Monika Wehrheim-Peuker. *Iberoamericana*, v. 16, no. 47 – 48 (1992), pp. 135 – 137.

Schwartz, Jorge. *Las vanguardias latinoamericanas: textos programáticos y críticos* reviewed by Jacobo Sefamí. *Revista Chilena de Literatura*, no. 40 (Nov 92), pp. 159 – 160.

— *Las vanguardias latinoamericanas: textos programáticos y críticos* reviewed by Djelal Kadir. *World Literature Today*, v. 67, no. 1 (Winter 93), pp. 246 – 247.

Schwartzman, Simon. *A Space for Science: The Development of the Scientific Community in Brazil* reviewed by Marcos Cueto. *The Americas*, v. 49, no. 3 (Jan 93), pp. 418 – 419.

— *A Space for Science: The Development of the Scientific Community in Brazil* reviewed by Pedro Turina U. *La Educación (USA)*, v. 37, no. 114 (1993), p. 171.

Schwarz, Roberto. *Misplaced Ideas: Essays on Brazilian Culture* translated by John Gledson. Reviewed by Lisa Jesse. *Bulletin of Latin American Research*, v. 12, no. 3 (Sept 93), pp. 343 – 344.

— *Misplaced Ideas: Essays on Brazilian Culture* reviewed by T. F. Earle. *Journal of Latin American Studies*, v. 25, no. 3 (Oct 93), pp. 696 – 697.

Schweitzer, Dagmar and Kerstin Nowak. *Die Inka und der Krieg* reviewed by Mónica Ricketts. *Revista Andina*, v. 11, no. 1 (July 93), pp. 249 – 250.

Scobie, James Ralston. *Secondary Cities of Argentina: The Social History of Corrientes, Salta, and Mendoza, 1850 – 1910* completed and edited by Samuel L. Baily. Reviewed by Roy Hora. *Todo Es Historia*, v. 26, no. 309 (Apr 93), pp. 68 – 69. II.

Scott, Peter Dale and Jonathan Marshall. *Cocaine Politics: Drugs, Armies, and the CIA in Central America* reviewed by Donald J. Mabry. *Hispanic American Historical Review*, v. 73, no. 2 (May 93), p. 353.

Scully, Timothy R. *Rethinking the Center: Party Politics in Nineteenth- and Twentieth-Century Chile* reviewed by Iván Jaksic. *Hispanic American Historical Review*, v. 73, no. 2 (May 93), pp. 329 – 330.

— *Rethinking the Center: Party Politics in Nineteenth- and Twentieth-Century Chile* reviewed by Simon Collier. *Journal of Latin American Studies*, v. 25, no. 2 (May 93), pp. 411 – 412.

— *Rethinking the Center: Party Politics in Nineteenth- and Twentieth-Century Chile* reviewed by Peter Winn. *Revista Interamericana de Bibliografía*, v. 42, no. 4 (1992), p. 665.

Sefamí, Jacobo, ed. *Contemporary Spanish American Poets: A Bibliography of Primary and Secondary Sources* reviewed by David William Foster. *Chasqui,* v. 22, no. 1 (May 93), pp. 86 – 87.

— *Contemporary Spanish American Poets: A Bibliography of Primary and Secondary Sources* reviewed by Hensley C. Woodbridge. *Hispania (USA),* v. 76, no. 1 (Mar 93), pp. 89 – 90.

— *Contemporary Spanish American Poets: A Bibliography of Primary and Secondary Sources* reviewed by Miriam Bornstein. *Revista Interamericana de Bibliografía,* v. 42, no. 4 (1992), pp. 665 – 666.

Segal, Aaron and Brian Weinstein. *Haiti: The Failure of Politics* reviewed by Patrick Bellegarde-Smith. *Hispanic American Historical Review,* v. 73, no. 2 (May 93), p. 345.

Segnini, Yolanda. *Los caballeros del postgomecismo* reviewed by Frédérique Langue. *Cahiers des Amériques Latines,* no. 13 (1992), pp. 185 – 186.

Segovia, Tomás. *Casa del nómada* reviewed by José Homero. *Vuelta,* v. 17, no. 202 (Sept 93), pp. 50 – 51.

Segreti, Carlos S. A. *El unitarismo argentino: notas para su estudio en la etapa 1810 – 1819* reviewed by Aurora Ravina. *Revista de Historia de América,* no. 112 (July – Dec 91), pp. 183 – 185.

Seibel, Beatriz. *De ninfas a capitanas* reviewed by Ileana Azor. *Conjunto,* no. 92 (July – Dec 92), pp. 100 – 101.

— *Historia del circo* reviewed by María Rosa Figari. *Todo Es Historia,* v. 27, no. 313 (Aug 93), p. 73. Il.

Seixas, Jacy Alves de. *Mémoire et oubli: anarchisme et syndicalisme révolutionnaire au Brésil, 1890 – 1930* reviewed by Pierre Jarrige. *Cahiers des Amériques Latines,* no. 13 (1992), pp. 180 – 181.

Selowsky, Marcelo and Felipe Larraín B., eds. *The Public Sector and the Latin American Crisis* reviewed by Christian Anglade. *Journal of Latin American Studies,* v. 25, no. 2 (May 93), pp. 404 – 405.

Senkman, Leonardo. *Argentina, la segunda guerra mundial y los refugiados indeseables, 1933 – 1945* reviewed by Hebe Clementi. *Todo Es Historia,* v. 27, no. 316 (Nov 93), pp. 88 – 89. Il.

Senkman, Leonardo, ed. *El antisemitismo en la Argentina* reviewed by Marguerite Feitlowitz. *Estudios Interdisciplinarios de América Latina y el Caribe,* v. 4, no. 1 (Jan – June 93), pp. 170 – 174.

Sepúlveda, Luis. *Un viejo que leía novelas de amor* reviewed by Antonio Avaria (Review entitled "Chilenos leyendo novelas de amor"). *Mensaje,* v. 42, no. 419 (June 93), p. 217.

— *Un viejo que leía novelas de amor* reviewed by Fabienne Bradu. *Vuelta,* v. 17, no. 201 (Aug 93), p. 46.

Serna, Enrique. *Señorita México* reviewed by Christopher Domínguez Michael (Review entitled "Dos heroínas"). *Vuelta,* v. 17, no. 204 (Nov 93), pp. 48 – 49.

Servicio Paz y Justicia (Uruguay). *"Uruguay nunca más": Human Rights Violations, 1972 – 1985* translated by Elizabeth Hampsten. Reviewed by Marvin Alisky. *Hispanic American Historical Review,* v. 73, no. 4 (Nov 93), pp. 709 – 710.

Sevcenko, Nicolau. *Orfeu extático na metrópole: São Paulo; sociedade e cultura nos frementes anos '20* reviewed by Elias Thomé Saliba (Review entitled "Cultura modernista em São Paulo"). *Estudos Históricos,* v. 6, no. 11 (Jan – June 93), pp. 128 – 132.

— *Orfeu extático na metrópole: São Paulo; sociedade e cultura nos frementes anos '20* (Review). *Vozes,* v. 87, no. 1 (Jan – Feb 93), pp. 102 – 104.

Shannon, Robert M. *Visions of the New World in the Drama of Lope de Vega* reviewed by James Mandrell. *Hispanic Review,* v. 61, no. 1 (Winter 93), pp. 100 – 102.

Sharer, Robert James and David C. Grove, eds. *Regional Perspectives on the Olmec* reviewed by Michael Love. *Mesoamérica (USA),* v. 13, no. 23 (June 92), pp. 209 – 213.

Shavit, David. *The United States in Latin America: A Historical Dictionary* reviewed by Bruce Calder. *Revista Interamericana de Bibliografía,* v. 42, no. 3 (1992), p. 509.

Shaw, Donald Leslie. *Borges' Narrative Strategy* reviewed by Didier T. Jaén. *Revista Interamericana de Bibliografía,* v. 42, no. 3 (1992), pp. 509 – 510.

Sheahan, John. *Conflict and Change in Mexican Economic Strategy: Implications for Mexico and for Latin America* reviewed by Martin C. Needler (Review entitled "Economic Policy and Political Survival"). *Mexican Studies,* v. 9, no. 1 (Winter 93), pp. 139 – 143.

Shehadi, Nadim and Albert Hourani, eds. *The Lebanese in the World: A Century of Emigration* reviewed by Jorge O. Bestene. *Journal of Latin American Studies,* v. 25, no. 3 (Oct 93), pp. 663 – 664.

Sheperd, Verene A. and Hilary Beckles, eds. *Caribbean Slave Society and Economy* reviewed by Paul Lachance. *Hispanic American Historical Review,* v. 73, no. 2 (May 93), pp. 315 – 316.

— *Caribbean Slave Society and Economy: A Student Reader* reviewed by Gert Oostindie. *European Review of Latin American and Caribbean Studies,* no. 54 (June 93), pp. 126 – 127.

Sheridan, Thomas E. et al, eds. *The Franciscan Missions of Northern Mexico* reviewed by Robert H. Jackson. *Hispanic American Historical Review,* v. 73, no. 2 (May 93), pp. 312 – 313.

Sherlock, Philip Manderson and Rex Nettleford. *The University of the West Indies: A Caribbean Response to the Challenge of Change* reviewed by Rafael L. Ramírez. *Caribbean Studies,* v. 25, no. 1 – 2 (Jan – July 92), pp. 171 – 172.

— *The University of the West Indies: A Caribbean Response to the Challenge of Change* reviewed by Bruce King. *Journal of Caribbean Studies,* v. 9, no. 1 – 2 (Winter 92 – Spring 93), pp. 125 – 127.

Shua, Ana María. *El marido argentino promedio* reviewed by Beth Pollack. *Chasqui,* v. 22, no. 1 (May 93), pp. 105 – 107.

Shumway, Nicolás Standifird. *La invención de la Argentina: historia de una idea,* a translation of *The Invention of Argentina.* Reviewed by Alejandro Herrero. *Todo Es Historia,* v. 27, no. 315 (Oct 93), pp. 63 – 64. Il.

— *The Invention of Argentina* reviewed by Paula Alonso. *Bulletin of Latin American Research,* v. 12, no. 2 (May 93), pp. 231 – 232.

— *The Invention of Argentina* reviewed by Thomas L. Whigham. *The Americas,* v. 49, no. 3 (Jan 93), pp. 409 – 410.

Shurbutt, Thomas Ray, ed. *United States – Latin American Relations, 1800 – 1850: The Formative Generations* reviewed by Thomas Schoonover. *The Americas,* v. 49, no. 3 (Jan 93), pp. 405 – 407.

Sidicaro, Ricardo. *La política mirada desde arriba: las ideas del diario 'La Nación', 1909 – 1989* reviewed by Diego F. Barros. *Todo Es Historia,* v. 27, no. 315 (Oct 93), pp. 65 – 66. Il.

Siegrist de Gentile, Nora L. *Inmigración vasca en la ciudad de Buenos Aires, 1830 – 1855* reviewed by Oscar Alvarez Gila. *Revista de Indias,* v. 53, no. 197 (Jan – Apr 93), pp. 121 – 124.

Sierra, José Luis. *Sueña canarios, amor* reviewed by Perla Schwartz. *Plural (Mexico),* v. 22, no. 258 (Mar 93), pp. 76 – 77.

Sigurdssen, Haraldur and Steven Carey. *Caribbean Volcanoes: A Field Guide; Martinique, Dominica, and St. Vincent* reviewed by Trevor Jackson. *Caribbean Geography,* v. 3, no. 3 (Mar 92), pp. 211 – 212.

Sikkink, Kathryn. *Ideas and Institutions: Developmentalism in Brazil and Argentina* reviewed by Laura A. Hastings. *Journal of Latin American Studies,* v. 25, no. 1 (Feb 93), pp. 216 – 217.

Siles Salinas, María Eugenia de

See

Valle de Siles, María Eugenia del

Silva, Patricio and Cristóbal Kay, eds. *Development and Social Change in the Chilean Countryside: From the Pre-Land Reform Period to the Democratic Transition* reviewed by Chris Scott. *Journal of Latin American Studies,* v. 25, no. 2 (May 93), p. 407.

Silva Santisteban, Rocío. *Mariposa negra* reviewed by Oswaldo Chanove (Review entitled "Mortero de amor"). *Debate (Peru),* v. 16, no. 74 (Sept – Oct 93), p. 64. Il.

Silva Téllez, Armando. *Punto de vista ciudadano: focalización visual y puesta en escena del graffiti* reviewed by Maurice P. Brungardt (Review entitled "Readings on Colombia?"). *Studies in Latin American Popular Culture,* v. 12 (1993), pp. 235 – 242.

Silverstein, Ken and Emir Sader. *Without Fear of Being Happy: Lula, the Workers Party, and Brazil* reviewed by Joel Wolfe. *The Americas,* v. 49, no. 4 (Apr 93), pp. 566 – 568.

— *Without Fear of Being Happy: Lula, the Workers Party, and Brazil* reviewed by John Humphrey. *Bulletin of Latin American Research,* v. 12, no. 3 (Sept 93), p. 347.

— *Without Fear of Being Happy: Lula, the Workers Party, and Brazil* reviewed by Paul Cammack. *Journal of Latin American Studies,* v. 25, no. 3 (Oct 93), pp. 666 – 667.

Simmons, Marc. *The Last Conquistador: Juan de Oñate and the Settling of the Far Southwest* reviewed by Adrian Bustamante. *Colonial Latin American Historical Review,* v. 2, no. 2 (Spring 93), pp. 235 – 236.

Simões, Júlio Assis. *O dilema da participação popular: a etnografia de um caso* reviewed by Cláudio Novaes Pinto Coelho. *Revista Brasileira de Ciências Sociais,* v. 8, no. 22 (June 93), pp. 154 – 155.

Simpson, Amelia S., ed. *New Tales of Mystery and Crime from Latin America* reviewed by John Gledson. *Bulletin of Latin American Research,* v. 12, no. 1 (Jan 93), pp. 130 – 131.

Síntesis agro-regional reviewed by Fernando Riveros R. *EURE,* v. 19, no. 56 (Mar 93), p. 118.

Sklodowska, Elzbieta. *La parodia en la nueva novela hispanoamericana, 1960 – 1985* reviewed by Isabel Rodríguez-Vergara. *La Educación (USA),* v. 36, no. 111 – 113 (1992), pp. 304 – 305.

— *La parodia en la nueva novela hispanoamericana, 1960 – 1985* reviewed by George R. McMurray. *Hispania (USA),* v. 76, no. 2 (May 93), pp. 293 – 294.

— *La parodia en la nueva novela hispanoamericana, 1960 – 1985* reviewed by Donald L. Shaw. *Hispanic Review,* v. 61, no. 2 (Spring 93), pp. 316 – 317.

— *La parodia en la nueva novela hispanoamericana, 1960 – 1985* reviewed by Norman Cheadle. *Revista Canadiense de Estudios Hispánicos,* v. 17, no. 2 (Winter 93), pp. 413 – 414.

— *La parodia en la nueva novela hispanoamericana, 1960 – 1985* reviewed by Brian Evenson. *World Literature Today,* v. 67, no. 1 (Winter 93), p. 161.

Slater, Candace. *Trail of Miracles: Stories from a Pilgrimage in Northeast Brazil* reviewed by David T. Haberly. *Hispanic Review,* v. 61, no. 3 (Summer 93), pp. 449 – 451.

Slatta, Richard W. *Gauchos and the Vanishing Frontier* reviewed by Jeremy Adelman. *Journal of Latin American Studies,* v. 25, no. 2 (May 93), pp. 401 – 402.

Smart, Ian Isidore. *Nicolás Guillén, Popular Poet of the Caribbean* reviewed by José Quiroga. *Hispanic Review,* v. 61, no. 1 (Winter 93), pp. 129 – 131.

Smith, Carol A., ed. *Guatemalan Indians and the State, 1540 – 1988* reviewed by James Dunkerley. *Mesoamérica (USA),* v. 13, no. 23 (June 92), pp. 186 – 190.

Smith, Christian. *The Emergence of Liberation Theology: Radical Religion and Social Movement Theory* reviewed by Michael LaRosa. *Journal of Inter-American Studies and World Affairs,* v. 35, no. 2 (Summer 93), pp. 167 – 170.

Smith, Joseph. *Unequal Giants: Diplomatic Relations between the United States and Brazil, 1889 – 1930* reviewed by Stanley E. Hilton. *The Americas,* v. 50, no. 1 (July 93), pp. 131 – 133.

Smith, Nigel J. H. et al. *Tropical Forests and Their Crops* reviewed by David M. Kummer. *Geographical Review,* v. 83, no. 3 (July 93), pp. 339 – 341.

Smith, Patrick Bellegarde

See

Bellegarde-Smith, Patrick

Smith, Peter H., ed. *Drug Policy in the Americas* reviewed by Mariana Mould de Pease. *Hispanic American Historical Review,* v. 73, no. 4 (Nov 93), pp. 732 – 733.

Smith, Wayne S., ed. *The Russians Aren't Coming: New Soviet Policy in Latin America* reviewed by Lynn-Darrell Bender. *Cuban Studies/Estudios Cubanos,* v. 23 (1993), pp. 217 – 218.

— *The Russians Aren't Coming: New Soviet Policy in Latin America* reviewed by Marina Oborotova (Review entitled "Russian Policy in Latin America: Past, Present, and Future"). *Latin American Research Review,* v. 28, no. 3 (1993), pp. 183 – 188.

Snow, Peter G. and Luigi Manzetti. *Political Forces in Argentina,* 3d edition, reviewed by Robert J. Alexander. *Hispanic American Historical Review,* v. 73, no. 4 (Nov 93), pp. 703 – 705.

Soares, Luís Carlos. *Rameiras, ilhoas, polacas: a prostituição do Rio de Janeiro do século XIX* reviewed by Sandra Lauderdale Graham (Review entitled "Dangerous Fantasies: The Altered Vocabulary of Commercial Sex"). *Luso-Brazilian Review,* v. 30, no. 1 (Summer 93), pp. 133 – 139.

Socolow, Susan Migden and Louisa Schell Hoberman, eds. *Cities and Society in Colonial Latin America* reviewed by Arij Ouweneel. *European Review of Latin American and Caribbean Studies,* no. 54 (June 93), pp. 125 – 126.

Soderlund, Walter C. and Stuart H. Surlin. *Mass Media and the Caribbean* reviewed by Alan Frizzell. *Canadian Journal of Latin American and Caribbean Studies,* v. 17, no. 34 (1992), pp. 146 – 147.

Solá Márquez, María Magdalena. *Aquí cuentan las mujeres: muestra y estudio de cinco narradoras puertorriqueñas* reviewed by Elena M. Martínez. *Revista Iberoamericana,* v. 59, no. 162 – 163 (Jan – June 93), p. 391.

Solana, Zulema and Nora Múgica de Fignoni. *La gramática modular* reviewed by Andrea Ostrov. *La Educación (USA),* v. 37, no. 114 (1993), pp. 165 – 166.

Solano y Pérez-Lila, Francisco de, ed. *Relaciones topográficas de Venezuela, 1815 – 1819* reviewed by María del Carmen Mena García. *Anuario de Estudios Americanos,* v. 49, Suppl. 1 (1992), pp. 258 – 260.

Solares, Ignacio. *Delirium Tremens* reviewed by Roberto Pliego (Review entitled "El infierno como pretexto"). *Nexos,* v. 16, no. 182 (Feb 93), pp. 86 – 87.

— *La noche de Angeles* reviewed by Alfonso González. *Chasqui,* v. 22, no. 1 (May 93), pp. 89 – 91.

— *La noche de Angeles* reviewed by José Ricardo Chaves. *Vuelta,* v. 17, no. 198 (May 93), pp. 54 – 55.

Solares, Julio. *El gran elector* reviewed by Julio Ortega (Review entitled "El mundo como supermercado"). *Nexos,* v. 16, no. 191 (Nov 93), p. 63 +.

Solís, Bernarda. *Mi vida privada es del dominio público* reviewed by Friedhelm Schmidt. *Revista de Crítica Literaria Latinoamericana,* v. 19, no. 38 (July – Dec 93), pp. 428 – 429.

Solow, Barbara L., ed. *Slavery and the Rise of the Atlantic System* reviewed by Johannes M. Postma. *The Americas,* v. 49, no. 3 (Jan 93), pp. 404 – 405.

Sommer, Doris. *Foundational Fictions: The National Romances of Latin America* reviewed by Edgardo C. Krebs. *The Americas,* v. 50, no. 2 (Oct 93), pp. 282 – 283.

— *Foundational Fictions: The National Romances of Latin America* reviewed by Carlos L. Orihuela. *Revista de Crítica Literaria Latinoamericana,* v. 19, no. 38 (July – Dec 93), pp. 399 – 403.

Soria, Néstor. *Este país es mío* reviewed by Rodolfo Alonso. *Revista Nacional de Cultura (Venezuela),* v. 54, no. 287 (Oct – Dec 92), p. 260.

Soriano Badani, Armando, ed. *Antología del cuento boliviano,* 2d ed., reviewed by Melvin S. Arrington, Jr. *World Literature Today,* v. 67, no. 1 (Winter 93), pp. 161 – 162.

Sorj, Bernardo and Daniel Pécaut, eds. *Métamorphoses de la représentation politique au Brésil et en Europe* reviewed by Stéphane Monclaire (Review entitled "Partis et représentations politiques au Brésil"). *Cahiers des Amériques Latines,* no. 13 (1992), pp. 173 – 177.

Sorrentino, Fernando. *Siete conversaciones con Adolfo Bioy Casares* reviewed by Ted Lyon. *Chasqui,* v. 22, no. 2 (Nov 93), pp. 168 – 170.

— *Siete conversaciones con Adolfo Bioy Casares* reviewed by Ilán Stavans. *World Literature Today,* v. 67, no. 3 (Summer 93), pp. 592 – 593.

Soto, Francisco. *Conversación con Reinaldo Arenas* reviewed by Elena M. Martínez. *Revista Iberoamericana,* v. 59, no. 162 – 163 (Jan – June 93), pp. 389 – 390.

Soto, Pedro Juan. *Memoria de mi amnesia* reviewed by Elena M. Martínez. *Revista Iberoamericana,* v. 59, no. 162 – 163 (Jan – June 93), p. 388.

Sotomayor, Héctor and Jaime Estay Reino, eds. *América Latina y México ante la Unión Europea de 1992* reviewed by Gilberto A. Cardoso Vargas. *Problemas del Desarrollo,* v. 24, no. 92 (Jan – Mar 93), pp. 236 – 238.

Sowell, David Lee. *The Early Colombian Labor Movement: Artisans and Politics in Bogotá, 1832 – 1919* reviewed by Jane M. Rausch. *Hispanic American Historical Review,* v. 73, no. 4 (Nov 93), pp. 715 – 716.

Spadaccini, Nicholas and René Jara, eds. *1492 – 1992: Re/Discovering Colonial Writing* reviewed by David A. Boruchoff. *Revista Canadiense de Estudios Hispánicos,* v. 17, no. 1 (Fall 92), pp. 207 – 209.

Spiller, Roland, ed. *La novela argentina de los años ochenta* reviewed by Andrés Avellaneda. *Hispamérica,* v. 21, no. 63 (Dec 92), pp. 108 – 112.

Stabb, Martin S. *Borges Revisited* reviewed by Bruno Bosteels. *Hispanic Review,* v. 61, no. 4 (Fall 93), pp. 594 – 596.

Stanish, Charles. *Ancient Andean Political Economy* reviewed by Penny Dransart. *Journal of Latin American Studies,* v. 25, no. 2 (May 93), pp. 391 – 392.

— *Ancient Andean Political Economy* reviewed by Michael E. Moseley. *Revista Interamericana de Bibliografía,* v. 42, no. 2 (1992), pp. 287 – 288.

Stark, Barbara L., ed. *Settlement Archaelogy of Cerro de las Mesas, Veracruz, Mexico* reviewed by Ronald W. Webb. *Latin American Antiquity,* v. 4, no. 3 (Sept 93), pp. 299 – 300.

Staski, Edward and Livingston Delafield Sutro, eds. *The Ethnoarchaeology of Refuse Disposal* reviewed by María Josefa Iglesias Ponce de León. *Revista Española de Antropología Americana,* v. 23 (1993), pp. 256 – 258.

Stavans, Ilán. *Imagining Columbus: The Literary Voyage* reviewed by Elena M. Martínez. *Chasqui,* v. 22, no. 2 (Nov 93), pp. 170 – 171.

Stedman, John Gabriel. *Stedman's Surinam: Life in an Eighteenth-Century Slave Society* edited by Richard and Sally Price. Reviewed Jerry Gurulé. *Colonial Latin American Historical Review,* v. 1, no. 1 (Fall 92), pp. 121 – 122.

— *Stedman's Surinam: Life in an Eighteenth-Century Slave Society* edited by Richard and Sally Price. Reviewed by Michael Craton. *Hispanic American Historical Review,* v. 73, no. 3 (Aug 93), pp. 511 – 513.

Steen, Harold K. and Richard P. Tucker, eds. *Changing Tropical Forests: Historical Perspectives on Today's Challenges in Central and South America* reviewed by Rick B. Smith. *Colonial Latin American Historical Review,* v. 2, no. 3 (Summer 93), pp. 373 – 375.

Stein, Nancy and Susanne Leilani Jonas, eds. *Democracy in Latin America: Visions and Realities* reviewed by Eldon G. Kenworthy. *Hispanic American Historical Review,* v. 73, no. 2 (May 93), pp. 354 – 355.

Stellweg, Carla and Elena Poniatowska. *Frida Kahlo: la cámara seducida* reviewed by Andrés Salgado R. (Accompanied by an English translation). *Art Nexus,* no. 8 (Apr – June 93), p. 34. Il.

Stepan, Nancy Leys. *The Hour of Eugenics: Race, Gender, and Nation in Latin America* reviewed by Donna J. Guy. *The Americas,* v. 50, no. 1 (July 93), pp. 136 – 137.

— *The Hour of Eugenics: Race, Gender, and Nation in Latin America* reviewed by Aline Helg. *Hispanic American Historical Review,* v. 73, no. 1 (Feb 93), pp. 138 – 139.

— *The Hour of Eugenics: Race, Gender, and Nation in Latin America* reviewed by Francine Masiello. *Letras Femeninas,* v. 19, no. 1 – 2 (Spring – Fall 93), pp. 136 – 138.

Stephen, Lynn. *Zapotec Women* reviewed by Florence E. Babb. *The Americas,* v. 50, no. 2 (Oct 93), pp. 276 – 277.

Stepick, Alex and Arthur D. Murphy. *Social Inequality in Oaxaca: A History of Resistance and Change* reviewed by John K. Chance. *The Americas,* v. 49, no. 4 (Apr 93), pp. 541 – 542.

Stern, Steve J., ed. *Resistencia, rebelión y conciencia campesina de los Andes, siglos XVIII al XX* reviewed by Betford Betalleluz. *Historia y Cultura (Peru),* no. 20 (1990), pp. 369 – 371.

Stevens, Donald Fithian. *Origins of Instability in Early Republican Mexico* reviewed by Margaret Chowning. *The Americas,* v. 50, no. 1 (July 93), pp. 128 – 130.

— *Origins of Instability in Early Republican Mexico* reviewed by John Jay TePaske. *Hispanic American Historical Review,* v. 73, no. 1 (Feb 93), pp. 179 – 180.

Stewart, Joseph, Jr. and Kenneth J. Meier. *The Politics of Hispanic Education: "un paso pa'lante y dos pa'tras"* reviewed by Francesco Cordasco. *International Migration Review,* v. 26, no. 4 (Winter 92), pp. 1464 – 1465.

Stewart-Gambino, Hannah W. *The Church and Politics in the Chilean Countryside* reviewed by Daniel H. Levine. *Hispanic American Historical Review*, v. 73, no. 2 (May 93), pp. 326 – 328.

Stewart-Gambino, Hannah W. and Edward L. Cleary, eds. *Conflict and Competition: The Latin American Church in a Changing Environment* reviewed by Michael LaRosa (Review entitled "Religion in a Changing Latin America: A Review"). *Journal of Inter-American Studies and World Affairs*, v. 34, no. 4 (Winter 92 – 93), pp. 245 – 255. Bibl.

— *Conflict and Competition: The Latin American Church in a Changing Environment* reviewed by Carl Elliott Meacham. *Revista Interamericana de Bibliografía*, v. 42, no. 2 (1992), pp. 284 – 285.

Stimson, Henry Lewis. *Henry L. Stimson's American Policy in Nicaragua: The Lasting Legacy* reviewed by Thomas W. Walker. *Hispanic American Historical Review*, v. 73, no. 3 (Aug 93), pp. 540 – 541.

Stolcke, Verena and Sandra Azeredo, eds. *Direitos reprodutivos* (Review). *Estudos Feministas*, v. 0, no. 0 (1992), p. 230.

Stoll, David. *Is Latin America Turning Protestant?: The Politics of Evangelical Growth* reviewed by Michael LaRosa (Review entitled "Religion in a Changing Latin America: A Review"). *Journal of Inter-American Studies and World Affairs*, v. 34, no. 4 (Winter 92 – 93), pp. 245 – 255. Bibl.

Stone, Roger D. *The Nature of Development* reviewed by David Barton Bray. *Grassroots Development*, v. 17, no. 1 (1993), pp. 44 – 45. Il.

Stone, Samuel Z. *The Heritage of the Conquistadors: Ruling Classes in Central America from the Conquest to the Sandinistas* reviewed by Carlos M. Vilas. *Journal of Latin American Studies*, v. 25, no. 3 (Oct 93), pp. 660 – 662.

Stoner, K. Lynn. *From the House to the Streets: The Cuban Woman's Movement for Legal Reform, 1898 – 1940* reviewed by Margarita Mergal (Review entitled "De domésticas a militantes: análisis de un processo transformador"). *Caribbean Studies*, v. 25, no. 1 – 2 (Jan – July 92), pp. 173 – 185. Bibl.

— *From the House to the Streets: The Cuban Woman's Movement for Legal Reform, 1898 – 1940* reviewed by Marifeli Pérez-Stable. *Cuban Studies/Estudios Cubanos*, v. 23 (1993), pp. 220 – 222.

— *From the House to the Streets: The Cuban Woman's Movement for Legal Reform, 1898 – 1940* reviewed by Jean Stubbs. *Journal of Latin American Studies*, v. 25, no. 2 (May 93), pp. 425 – 426.

Stoopen, María. *El universo de la cocina mexicana* reviewed by Susan N. Masuoka (Review entitled "Mexican Eating: The Work and the Haute Cuisine"). *Studies in Latin American Popular Culture*, v. 12 (1993), pp. 189 – 194.

Stothert, Karen Elizabeth. *La prehistoria temprana de la península de Santa Elena: cultura Las Vegas* reviewed by Michael Malpass. *Latin American Antiquity*, v. 4, no. 4 (Dec 93), pp. 392 – 393.

Street, Susan L. *Maestros en movimiento: transformaciones en la burocracia estatal, 1978 – 1982* reviewed by Sylvia Schmelkes. *El Cotidiano*, v. 8, no. 51 (Nov – Dec 92), pp. 114 – 115.

Stromquist, Nelly P., ed. *Women and Education in Latin America: Knowledge, Power, and Change* reviewed by Rosemary G. Messick. *Revista Interamericana de Bibliografía*, v. 42, no. 2 (1992), pp. 288 – 289.

Strong, Simon. *Sendero Luminoso: el movimiento subversivo más letal del mundo* reviewed by Felipe Portocarrero S. *Apuntes (Peru)*, no. 29 (July – Dec 91), pp. 89 – 91.

— *Shining Path: The World's Deadliest Revolutionary Force* reviewed by Orin Starn. *Bulletin of Latin American Research*, v. 12, no. 2 (May 93), pp. 244 – 246.

— *Shining Path: The World's Deadliest Revolutionary Force* reviewed by James Dunkerley. *Journal of Latin American Studies*, v. 25, no. 2 (May 93), pp. 421 – 422.

Strosetzki, Christoph, ed. *Der Griff nach der Neuen Welt: Der Untergang der indianischen Kulturen im Spiegel zeitgenössischer Texte* reviewed by Augustín F. Seguí. *Iberoamericana*, v. 17, no. 49 (1993), pp. 87 – 89.

Suardíaz, Luis, ed. *No me dan pena los burgueses vencidos* reviewed by Silvia Yáñez (Review entitled "Poesía y lucha social"). *Plural (Mexico)*, v. 22, no. 260 (May 93), p. 70.

Suárez, Santiago Gerardo. *Las reales audiencias indianas: fuentes y bibliografía* reviewed by José María Mariluz Urquijo. *Boletín de la Academia Nacional de la Historia (Venezuela)*, v. 75, no. 297 (Jan – Mar 92), pp. 139 – 141.

Subercaseaux S., Bernardo. *Historia del libro en Chile: alma y cuerpo* reviewed by G. A. C. *Mensaje*, v. 42, no. 419 (June 93), p. 218.

Sullivan, Paul R. *Conversaciones inconclusas,* a translation of *Unfinished Conversations: Mayas and Foreigners between Two Wars* reviewed by Héctor Tejera Gaona (Review entitled "Antropólogos y mayas: el encuentro de expectativas"). *Nueva Antropología*, v. 13, no. 44 (Aug 93), pp. 147 – 150.

Suñé Blanco, Beatriz. *La documentación del cabildo secular de Guatemala, siglo XVI: estudio diplomático y valor etnográfico* reviewed by Olga Joya. *Mesoamérica (USA)*, v. 13, no. 24 (Dec 92), pp. 462 – 463.

Sunkel, Osvaldo and Carmen Cariola Sutter. *Un siglo de historia económica de Chile, 1830 – 1930* reviewed by Juan Ricardo Couyoumdjian. *Boletín de la Academia Chilena de la Historia*, v. 58 – 59, no. 102 (1991 – 1992), pp. 561 – 562.

Super, John Clay. *Food, Conquest, and Colonization in Sixteenth-Century Spanish America* reviewed by Jorge Luján Muñoz. *Mesoamérica (USA)*, v. 13, no. 24 (Dec 92), pp. 463 – 464.

Surlin, Stuart H. and Walter C. Soderlund. *Mass Media and the Caribbean* reviewed by Alan Frizzell. *Canadian Journal of Latin American and Caribbean Studies*, v. 17, no. 34 (1992), pp. 146 – 147.

Sutro, Livingston Delafield and Edward Staski, eds. *The Ethnoarchaeology of Refuse Disposal* reviewed by María Josefa Iglesias Ponce de León. *Revista Española de Antropología Americana*, v. 23 (1993), pp. 256 – 258.

Szlajfer, Henryk, ed. *Economic Nationalism in East-Central Europe and South America, 1918 – 1939* reviewed by Joseph L. Love. *Journal of Latin American Studies*, v. 25, no. 1 (Feb 93), pp. 206 – 208.

Szterenfeld, Anna and Gray Newman. *Business International's Guide to Doing Business in Mexico* reviewed by Donald McCarthy (Review entitled "Help for Corporate Strategists"). *Business Mexico*, v. 3, no. 3 (Mar 93), p. 52.

Tagle Domínguez, Matías. *La crisis de la democracia en Chile: antecendentes y causas* reviewed by Joaquín Fermandois. *Historia (Chile)*, no. 26 (1991 – 1992), pp. 469 – 477.

Taibo, Francisco Ignacio, II. *An Easy Thing,* a translation of *Cosa fácil,* translated by William I. Neuman. Reviewed by James Polk. *Review*, no. 47 (Fall 93), pp. 95 – 96.

— *The Shadow of the Shadow,* a translation of *Sombra de la sombra,* translated by William I. Neuman. Reviewed by James Polk. *Review*, no. 47 (Fall 93), pp. 95 – 96. Il.

— *Some Clouds,* a translation of *Algunas nubes,* translated by William I. Neuman. Reviewed by James Polk. *Review*, no. 47 (Fall 93), pp. 95 – 96.

Tandeter, Enrique. *Coacción y mercado: la minería de plata en el Potosí colonial, 1692 – 1826* reviewed by Margarita Suárez. *Revista Andina,* v. 11, no. 1 (July 93), pp. 251 – 254.

Tanzer, Sharon and Paul L. Leventhal, eds. *Averting a Latin American Nuclear Arms Race: New Prospects and Challenges for Argentine – Brazil Nuclear Cooperation* reviewed by Mónica Serrano. *Journal of Latin American Studies,* v. 25, no. 2 (May 93), pp. 426 – 429.

Tapia Anaya, Vilma. *Del deseo y la rosa: un nuevo rostro poético* reviewed by Rosario Q. de Urquieta. *Signo,* no. 35, Nueva época (Jan – Apr 92), pp. 248 – 249.

Taschner, Gisela. *Folhas ao vento: análise de um conglomerado jornalístico no Brasil* reviewed by Maria Luisa Nabinger de Almeida. *RAE; Revista de Administração de Empresas,* v. 33, no. 4 (July – Aug 93), pp. 106 – 107. Il.

Tatum, Charles M. and Harold E. Hinds, Jr. *Not Just for Children: The Mexican Comic Book in the Late 1960s and 1970s* reviewed by Helen Delpar. *Hispanic American Historical Review,* v. 73, no. 4 (Nov 93), pp. 670 – 671.

— *Not Just for Children: The Mexican Comic Book in the Late 1960s and 1970s* reviewed by Cornelia Butler Flora. *Revista Interamericana de Bibliografía,* v. 42, no. 4 (1992), pp. 657 – 658.

Tau Anzoátegui, Víctor. *Casuísmo y sistema: indagación histórica sobre el espíritu del derecho indiano* reviewed by Nelson Nogueira Saldanha. *Revista Brasileira de Estudos Políticos,* no. 76 (Jan 93), pp. 202 – 203.

— *La ley en América Hispana: del descubrimiento a la emancipación* reviewed by Rubén Darío Salas. *Revista de Historia de América,* no. 113 (Jan – June 92), pp. 179 – 182.

Tau Anzoátegui, Víctor et al, ed. *Libros registros – cedularios del Río de La Plata, 1534 – 1717: catálogo* reviewed by Sergio Martínez Baeza. *Boletín de la Academia Chilena de la Historia,* v. 58 – 59, no. 102 (1991 – 1992), pp. 557 – 558.

Taylor, Diana. *Theatre of Crisis: Drama and Politics in Latin America* reviewed by José Castro-Urioste. *Revista de Crítica Literaria Latinoamericana,* v. 19, no. 38 (July – Dec 93), pp. 405 – 406.

Taylor, Mervyn. *An Island of His Own* reviewed by Andrew Salkey. *World Literature Today,* v. 67, no. 1 (Winter 93), p. 224.

Teitelboim, Volodia. *Huidobro: la marcha infinita* reviewed by Antonio Avaria (Review entitled "Crónica de varia lección"). *Mensaje,* v. 42, no. 424 (Nov 93), pp. 596 – 597. Il.

— *Neruda: An Intimate Biography* translated by Beverly J. DeLong-Tonelli. Reviewed by Lucía Guerra Cunningham. *Revista Interamericana de Bibliografía,* v. 42, no. 2 (1992), pp. 289 – 290.

Teixidó, Raúl. *Autores y personajes* reviewed by Carlos Castañón Barrientos. *Signo,* no. 38, Nueva época (Jan – Apr 93), pp. 257 – 258.

Tejada, Roberto, ed. *En algún otro lado: México en la poesía de lengua inglesa* reviewed by Aurelio Major. *Vuelta,* v. 17, no. 194 (Jan 93), pp. 42 – 43.

Teles, Maria Amélia de Almeida. *Breve história do feminismo no Brazil* reviewed by Joel Rufino dos Santos (Review entitled "Feministas fazendo história"). *Estudos Feministas,* v. 1, no. 2 (1993), pp. 499 – 501.

Tello Díaz, Carlos. *El exilio: un relato de familia* reviewed by Adolfo Castañón. *Vuelta,* v. 17, no. 204 (Nov 93), pp. 36 – 38.

Tenorio Tagle, Fernando. *El control social de las drogas en México: una aproximación a las imágenes que han proyectado sus discursos* reviewed by Horacio Cerutti Guldberg. *Cuadernos Americanos,* no. 40, Nueva época (July – Aug 93), pp. 235 – 237.

TePaske, John Jay and Alvaro Jara. *The Royal Treasuries of the Spanish Empire in America, Vol. IV: Eighteenth-Century Ecuador* reviewed by Franklin Pease G. Y. *Colonial Latin American Review,* v. 2, no. 1 – 2 (1993), pp. 311 – 312.

Texera Arnal, Yolanda. *La exploración botánica en Venezuela, 1754 – 1950* reviewed by Stuart McCook. *Interciencia,* v. 18, no. 6 (Nov – Dec 93), pp. 328 – 329.

Thiercelin-Mejías, Raquel, ed. *Cultures et sociétés: Andes et Méso-Amérique; mélanges en homage à Pierre Duviols* reviewed by Gérard Borras. *Caravelle,* no. 59 (1992), pp. 285 – 289.

— *Cultures et sociétés: Andes et Méso-Amérique,* 2 vols., reviewed by Arnold J. Bauer. *Hispanic American Historical Review,* v. 73, no. 2 (May 93), pp. 306 – 307.

Thomas, Clive Yolande. *The Poor and Powerless: Economic Policy and Change in the Caribbean* reviewed by Michael H. Allen (Review entitled "Rethinking Political Economy and Praxis in the Caribbean"). *Latin American Perspectives,* v. 20, no. 2 (Spring 93), pp. 111 – 119.

Thomas, David Hurst, ed. *Columbian Consequences, III: The Spanish Borderlands in Pan-American Perspectives* reviewed by David Henige. *Hispanic Review,* v. 61, no. 3 (Summer 93), pp. 447 – 449.

— *Columbian Consequences, Vol. III: The Spanish Borderlands in Pan-American Perspective* reviewed by Linda A. Watson. *Journal of Latin American Studies,* v. 25, no. 1 (Feb 93), pp. 196 – 197.

— *Columbian Consequences, Vol. III: The Spanish Borderlands in Pan-American Perspective* reviewed by Winifred Creamer. *Latin American Antiquity,* v. 4, no. 1 (Mar 93), pp. 94 – 95.

Thomas, Elean. *The Last Room* reviewed by Robert P. Smith, Jr. *World Literature Today,* v. 67, no. 2 (Spring 93), p. 430.

Thompson, Donald. *Music and Dance in Puerto Rico from the Age of Columbus to Modern Times: An Annotated Bibliography* reviewed by Inés Grandela de Río. *Revista Musical Chilena,* v. 46, no. 178 (July – Dec 92), p. 127.

Thompson, George. *La guerra del Paraguay* (Review). *Revista Paraguaya de Sociología,* v. 29, no. 84 (May – Aug 92), p. 205. Il.

Thornton, John K. *Africa and the Africans in the Making of the Atlantic World, 1400 – 1680* reviewed by Stuart B. Schwartz. *Hispanic American Historical Review,* v. 73, no. 3 (Aug 93), pp. 500 – 502.

Thorp, Rosemary. *Economic Management and Economic Development in Peru and Colombia* reviewed by Eva A. Paus. *Hispanic American Historical Review,* v. 73, no. 1 (Feb 93), pp. 176 – 177.

Tironi B., Eugenio. *Autoritarismo, modernización y marginalidad: el caso de Chile* reviewed by Felipe Cabello (Review entitled "Don Andrés Bello: ¡Con cuánta nostalgia lo recordamos y cuánta falta nos hace!"). *Interciencia,* v. 18, no. 6 (Nov – Dec 93), pp. 329 – 333.

Tittler, Jonathan. *Manuel Puig* reviewed by Ilán Stavans. *World Literature Today,* v. 67, no. 4 (Fall 93), p. 789.

Tittler, Jonathan, ed. *Violencia y literatura en Colombia* reviewed by Hans Paschen. *Iberoamericana,* v. 17, no. 49 (1993), pp. 99 – 101.

Titu Cusi

See

Yupanqui, Titu Cusi

Todorov, Tzvetan and Georges Baudot. *Récits aztèques de la conquête* reviewed by Guilhem Olivier. *Caravelle,* no. 59 (1992), pp. 241 – 249.

Tomassini, Luciano et al. *La política internacional en un mundo post-moderno* (Review). *Integración Latinoamericana,* v. 18, no. 192 (Aug 92), pp. 95 – 96.

Tomoeda, Hiroyasu and Luis Millones Santa Gadea. *500 años de mestizaje en los Andes* reviewed by Emma María Sordo. *Hispanic American Historical Review,* v. 73, no. 4 (Nov 93), p. 676.

Torregrosa, José Luis. *Historia de la radio en Puerto Rico* reviewed by Pedro Zervigón (Review entitled "José Luis Torregrosa y su historia de la radio"). *Homines,* v. 15 – 16, no. 2 – 1 (Oct 91 – Dec 92), pp. 369 – 370. Il.

Torres, Ana Teresa. *Doña Inés contra el olvido* reviewed by Alexis Márquez Rodríguez. *Revista Nacional de Cultura (Venezuela),* v. 53, no. 286 (July – Sept 92), pp. 248 – 249.

— *Doña Inés contra el olvido* reviewed by Barbara Mujica (Review entitled "Intriguing Family Histories"). *Américas,* v. 45, no. 4 (July – Aug 93), pp. 61 – 62. Il.

— *Doña Inés contra el olvido* reviewed by Cynthia Tompkins. *World Literature Today,* v. 67, no. 2 (Spring 93), p. 337.

Torres, Angel. *José Zampa, pionero social – cristiano en Bolivia* reviewed by Pedro de Anasagasti. *Signo,* no. 35, Nueva época (Jan – Apr 92), pp. 250 – 252.

Torres, Antônio. *Um taxi para Viena d'Austria* reviewed by Dieter Messner. *Zeitschrift für Lateinamerika Wien,* no. 42 (1992), pp. 71 – 72.

Torres, Daniel. *José Emilio Pacheco: poética y poesía del prosaísmo* reviewed by Frank Dauster. *Hispanic Review,* v. 61, no. 2 (Spring 93), pp. 314 – 315.

Torres-Seda, Olga and Lizabeth Paravisini-Gebert. *Caribbean Women Novelists: An Annotated Bibliography* reviewed by David William Foster. *Chasqui,* v. 22, no. 2 (Nov 93), pp. 161 – 162.

Torres Torres, Felipe and Cuauhtémoc González Pacheco, eds. *Los retos de la soberanía alimentaria en México* reviewed by Argelia Salinas Ontiveros. *Problemas del Desarrollo,* v. 24, no. 93 (Apr – June 93), pp. 239 – 241.

Toscano, Guadalupe. *Testigos de piedra: las hornacinas del centro histórico de la ciudad de México* reviewed by Gustavo Curiel and Yolanda Bravo Saldaña. *Anales del Instituto de Investigaciones Estéticas,* v. 16, no. 62 (1991), pp. 203 – 208. Bibl.

Toscano, Moema and Miriam Goldberg. *A revolução das mulheres: uma balança do feminismo no Brasil* reviewed by Celi Regina Jardim Pinto (Review entitled "Falas de mulheres"). *Estudos Feministas,* v. 1, no. 1 (1993), pp. 219 – 221.

Townsend, Richard F. *The Aztecs* reviewed by Arturo Dell'Acqua. *Colonial Latin American Historical Review,* v. 1, no. 1 (Fall 92), pp. 127 – 128.

— *The Aztecs* reviewed by Susan Toby Evans. *Hispanic American Historical Review,* v. 73, no. 4 (Nov 93), pp. 680 – 681.

Trazegnies Granda, Fernando de. *Imágenes rotas* reviewed by Giovanna Pollarolo (Review entitled "Viaje al siglo XIX"). *Debate (Peru),* v. 15, no. 71 (Nov 92 – Jan 93), pp. 77 – 78. Il.

XXX años de jurisprudencia agraria en Venezuela reviewed by Arnaldo Gómez A. *Derecho y Reforma Agraria,* no. 23 (1992), p. 217.

Trejo Hernández, Raúl et al. *Perfil y semblanza política de la Asamblea de Representantes del Distrito Federal* reviewed by Felipe Solís Acero. *Revista Mexicana de Ciencias Políticas y Sociales,* v. 38, Nueva época, no. 151 (Jan – Mar 93), pp. 220 – 224.

Triana Martínez, Azucena, ed. *Sucesión presidencial y transición democrática* reviewed by Raúl Rodríguez Guillén. *El Cotidiano,* v. 10, no. 58 (Oct – Nov 93), p. 116.

Trigo, Abril. *Caudillo, estado, nación: literatura, historia e ideología en el Uruguay* reviewed by Gustavo Verdesio. *Nuevo Texto Crítico,* v. 6, no. 11 (1993), pp. 263 – 266.

Trindade, Antônio Augusto Cançado, ed. *A proteção dos direitos humanos nos planos nacional e internacional: perspectivas brasileiras* reviewed by José Filomeno de Morais Filho. *Revista Brasileira de Estudos Políticos,* no. 76 (Jan 93), pp. 197 – 202.

Triviños, Gilberto. *Ramón J. Sender: mito y contramito de Lope de Aguirre* reviewed by Berta López Morales. *Atenea (Chile),* no. 465 – 466 (1992), pp. 379 – 382.

Trombold, Charles D., ed. *Ancient Road Networks and Settlement Hierarchies in the New World* reviewed by David R. Ringrose. *Hispanic American Historical Review,* v. 73, no. 1 (Feb 93), pp. 141 – 142.

Trouillot, Michel-Rolph. *Peasants and Capital: Dominica in the World Economy* reviewed by Michael H. Allen (Review entitled "Rethinking Political Economy and Praxis in the Caribbean"). *Latin American Perspectives,* v. 20, no. 2 (Spring 93), pp. 111 – 119.

Trujillo, Carla, ed. *Chicana Lesbians: The Girls Our Mothers Warned Us About* reviewed by Tamara Parker. *Letras Femeninas,* v. 19, no. 1 – 2 (Spring – Fall 93), pp. 155 – 157.

Tuchman, Maurice. *Parallel Visions: Modern Artists and Outsider Art* reviewed by Andrés Salgado R. (Accompanied by an English translation). *Art Nexus,* no. 9 (June – Aug 93), p. 33. Il.

Tucker, Richard P. and Harold K. Steen, eds. *Changing Tropical Forests: Historical Perspectives on Today's Challenges in Central and South America* reviewed by Rick B. Smith. *Colonial Latin American Historical Review,* v. 2, no. 3 (Summer 93), pp. 373 – 375.

Tulchin, Joseph S. and Rafael Hernández, eds. *Cuba and the United States: Will the Cold War in the Caribbean End?* reviewed by Jorge I. Domínguez. *Cuban Studies/ Estudios Cubanos,* v. 23 (1993), pp. 215 – 217.

Tulchin, Joseph S. and Andrew I. Rudman, eds. *Economic Development and Environmental Protection in Latin America* reviewed by Steve Ellner. *Journal of Developing Areas,* v. 27, no. 3 (Apr 93), p. 441.

— *Economic Development and Environmental Protection in Latin America* reviewed by Margaret E. Keck. *Studies in Comparative International Development,* v. 27, no. 3 (Fall 92), pp. 120 – 122.

Tushnet, Mark V. *Central America and the Law: The Constitution, Civil Liberties, and the Courts* reviewed by Jorge Luján Muñoz. *Mesoamérica (USA),* v. 13, no. 24 (Dec 92), pp. 464 – 465.

Tyler, Joseph, ed. *Borges' Craft of Fiction: Selected Essays on His Writing* reviewed by Donald A. Yates. *World Literature Today,* v. 67, no. 2 (Spring 93), p. 343.

Ulchur Collazos, Iván. *Muerte profunda más allá de la ilusión* reviewed by Ester Gimbernat. *Chasqui,* v. 22, no. 1 (May 93), p. 89.

— *Muerte profunda más allá de la ilusión* reviewed by César Ferreira. *Chasqui,* v. 22, no. 1 (May 93), pp. 78 – 79.

Ulyses
See
Merino Reyes, Luis

Underwood, Leticia Iliana. *Octavio Paz and the Language of Poetry: A Psycholinguistic Approach* reviewed by Hugo J. Verani. *Revista Interamericana de Bibliografía,* v. 42, no. 4 (1992), pp. 666 – 667.

Undurraga, Antonio de. *Las mareas victoriosas* reviewed by Vicente Mengod. *Atenea (Chile),* no. 465 – 466 (1992), pp. 369 – 370.

United Nations. Economic Commission for Latin America and the Caribbean. *Caminos: un nuevo enfoque para la gestión y conservación de redes viales* (Review). *CEPAL Review,* no. 48 (Dec 92), pp. 169 – 171.

— *A Collection of Documents on Economic Relations between the United States and Central America, 1906 – 1956* (Review). *CEPAL Review,* no. 47 (Aug 92), p. 189.

— *Educación y conocimiento: eje de la transformación productiva con equidad* reviewed by Gloria González Salazar. *Problemas del Desarrollo,* v. 24, no. 94 (July – Sept 93), pp. 286 – 290.

— *Education and Knowledge: Basic Pillars of Changing Production Patterns with Social Equity* (Review). *CEPAL Review,* no. 47 (Aug 92), pp. 191 – 193.

— *Ensayos sobre coordinación de políticas macroeconómicas: inferencias para la integración latinoamericana* (Review). *Integración Latinoamericana,* v. 18, no. 194 (Oct 93), pp. 85 – 87.

— *Equidad y transformación productiva: un enfoque integrado* reviewed by Gloria González Salazar. *Problemas del Desarrollo,* v. 24, no. 92 (Jan – Mar 93), pp. 233 – 236.

— *Equity and Changing Production Patterns: An Integrated Approach* (Review). *CEPAL Review,* no. 47 (Aug 92), pp. 190 – 191.

— *La reestructuración de empresas públicas: el caso de los puertos de América Latina y el Caribe* (Review). *CEPAL Review,* no. 48 (Dec 92), pp. 171 – 172.

United Nations Educational, Scientific and Cultural Organization. *Situación educativa de América Latina y el Caribe, 1980 – 1990* reviewed by M. Dino Carelli. *Estudios Sociales (Chile),* no. 78 (Oct – Dec 93), pp. 232 – 234.

— *Situación educativa de América Latina y el Caribe, 1980 – 1990* reviewed by Dino Carelli. *Revista Latinoamericana de Estudios Educativos,* v. 23, no. 2 (Apr – June 93), pp. 127 – 129.

Urbano, Henrique-Osvaldo and Mirko Lauer, eds. *Poder y violencia en los Andes* reviewed by Kenneth J. Andrien. *Hispanic American Historical Review,* v. 73, no. 1 (Feb 93), pp. 177 – 178.

— *Poder y violencia en los Andes* reviewed by Víctor Peralta Ruiz. *Revista de Indias,* v. 53, no. 197 (Jan – Apr 93), pp. 124 – 126.

Urbanyi, Pablo. *Nacer de nuevo* reviewed by Jorge Aguilar Mora. *Hispamérica,* v. 22, no. 64 – 65 (Apr – Aug 93), pp. 206 – 208.

Urbina, Nicasio. *La significación del género: estudio semiótico de las novelas y ensayos de Ernesto Sábato* reviewed by Amelia Mondragón. *Chasqui,* v. 22, no. 2 (Nov 93), pp. 173 – 174.

Uribe Celis, Carlos. *La mentalidad del colombiano* reviewed by Gonzalo Serrano Escallón. *Anuario Colombiano de Historia Social y de la Cultura,* no. 20 (1992), pp. 159 – 162.

Urriola, Rafael and Germánico Salgado, eds. *El fin de las barreras: los empresarios y el Pacto Andino en la década de los '90* (Review). *Integración Latinoamericana,* v. 18, no. 189 – 190 (May – June 93), p. 57.

Urrutia Montoya, Miguel, ed. *Tendencias a largo plazo en el desarrollo económico de América Latina* (Review). *Integración Latinoamericana,* v. 18, no. 194 (Oct 93), pp. 89 – 91.

Urton, Gary. *The History of a Myth: Pacariqtambo and the Origin of the Inkas* reviewed by María Benavides. *Bulletin de l'Institut Français d'Etudes Andines,* v. 21, no. 2 (1992), pp. 785 – 787.

Urzagasti, Jesús. *De la ventana al parque* reviewed by Alberto Julián Pérez. *Signo,* no. 38, Nueva época (Jan – Apr 93), pp. 259 – 260.

Uslar Pietri, Arturo. *La creación del Nuevo Mundo* reviewed by Luis Franco Ramos (Review entitled "La región mestiza"). *Nexos,* v. 16, no. 181 (Jan 93), p. 77. Il.

— *Cuarenta cuentos* introduced by Víctor Bravo. Reviewed by Melvin S. Arrington. *World Literature Today,* v. 67, no. 1 (Winter 93), p. 165.

— *La visita en el tiempo* reviewed by George R. McMurray. *Hispania (USA),* v. 76, no. 1 (Mar 93), pp. 101 – 102.

Utting, Peter. *Economic Reform and Third-World Socialism* reviewed by S. P. Chakravarty. *Bulletin of Latin American Research,* v. 12, no. 1 (Jan 93), pp. 122 – 124.

— *Economic Reform and Third-World Socialism: A Political Economy of Food Policy in Post-Revolutionary Societies* reviewed by Kenneth P. Jameson. *Journal of Developing Areas,* v. 27, no. 4 (July 93), pp. 543 – 544.

Valcárcel Carnero, Rosina. *Una mujer canta en medio del caos: poesía, 1975 – 1990* reviewed by Esther Castañeda Vielakamen. *Revista de Crítica Literaria Latinoamericana,* v. 19, no. 38 (July – Dec 93), pp. 432 – 433.

Valdés, Adriana. *Roser Bru* reviewed by Ivonne Pini (Accompanied by an English translation). *Art Nexus,* no. 7 (Jan – Mar 93), p. 41. Il.

Valdez, Luis. *Zoot-Suit and Other Plays* reviewed by Arturo C. Flores. *Latin American Theatre Review,* v. 26, no. 2 (Spring 93), pp. 208 – 210.

— *Zoot Suit and Other Plays* reviewed by Charles Tatum. *World Literature Today,* v. 67, no. 2 (Spring 93), p. 384. Il.

Valdivia, Néstor and Norman Adams. *Los otros empresarios: ética de migrantes y formación de empresas en Lima* reviewed by Orazio A. Ciccarelli. *Hispanic American Historical Review,* v. 73, no. 4 (Nov 93), pp. 714 – 715.

Valdivieso, Jaime. *Voces de alarma* reviewed by Antonio Avaria (Review entitled "Una voz de alarma"). *Mensaje,* v. 42, no. 417 (Mar – Apr 93), p. 108.

Valencia, Richard R., ed. *Chicano School Failure and Success: Research and Policy Agendas for the 1990s* reviewed by Maryann Santos de Barona (Review entitled "Chicano Schooling: Ethnic Success or Societal Failure?"). *Bilingual Review/Revista Bilingüe,* v. 17, no. 3 (Sept – Dec 92), pp. 273 – 275.

Valencia Llano, Alonso. *Resistencia indígena a la colonización española: resistencia militar indígena en la gobernación de Popayán* reviewed by Joanne Rappaport. *Hispanic American Historical Review,* v. 73, no. 4 (Nov 93), pp. 690 – 691.

Valenciano, Eugenio O. *Disparidades regionales e integración económica* (Review). *Integración Latinoamericana,* v. 18, no. 189 – 190 (May – June 93), pp. 59 – 60.

Valenciano, Eugenio O. and Paul Ganster, eds. *The Mexican – U.S. Border Region and the Free Trade Agreement* reviewed by Christopher A. Erickson. *Journal of Borderlands Studies,* v. 7, no. 2 (Fall 92), pp. 103 – 105.

Valenzuela, Georgette José. *Legislación electoral mexicana, 1812 – 1921: cambios y continuidades* reviewed by Josefina MacGregor. *Revista Mexicana de Sociología,* v. 55, no. 1 (Jan – Mar 93), pp. 251 – 255.

Valenzuela, Luisa. *Black Novel (with Argentines),* a translation of *Novela negra con argentinos,* translated by Toby Talbot. Reviewed by Alan West. *Review,* no. 47 (Fall 93), pp. 103 – 104.

Valenzuela Arce, José Manuel. *Empapados de sereno: el movimiento urbano popular en Baja California, 1928 – 1988* reviewed by Miguel Angel Vite Pérez. *Estudios Sociológicos,* v. 11, no. 31 (Jan – Apr 93), pp. 285 – 288.

Valier, Jacques and Pierre Salama. *La economía gangrenada: ensayo sobre la hiperinflación* reviewed by Sebastián Katz and Pablo Sirlin (Review entitled "Las desventuras de un análisis francés sobre la desventura de América Latina"). *Desarrollo Económico (Argentina),* v. 33, no. 131 (Oct – Dec 93), pp. 449 – 452.

Valis, Noël Maureen and Carol Maier, eds. *In the Feminine Mode: Essays on Hispanic Women Writers* reviewed by Hazel Gold. *Hispanic Review,* v. 61, no. 4 (Fall 93), pp. 587 – 590.

Vallbona, Rima de. *Mundo, demonio y mujer* reviewed by Cida S. Chase. *Confluencia,* v. 8, no. 1 (Fall 92), pp. 181 – 182.

— *Mundo, demonio y mujer* reviewed by Cynthia Tompkins. *World Literature Today,* v. 67, no. 1 (Winter 93), pp. 158 – 159.

— *Mundo, demonio y mujer/World, Demon, and Woman* reviewed by Barbara Mujica (Review entitled "A Coming of Age"). *Américas,* v. 45, no. 5 (Sept – Oct 93), pp. 62 – 63. Il.

Valle de Siles, María Eugenia del. *Historia de la rebelión de Tupac Catari, 1781 – 1782* reviewed by Marie-Danielle Démelas-Bohy. *Caravelle,* no. 59 (1992), pp. 249 – 253.

Vallejo, Catharina Vanderplaats de. *Elementos para una semiótica del cuento hispanoamericano del siglo XX* reviewed by R. A. Kerr. *Hispania (USA),* v. 76, no. 3 (Sept 93), p. 482.

— *Teoría cuentística del siglo XX* reviewed by Marisa Bortolussi. *Revista Canadiense de Estudios Hispánicos,* v. 17, no. 1 (Fall 92), pp. 228 – 229.

Vallejo, César Abraham. *Obra poética* edited by Ricardo González Vigil. Reviewed by Raúl Hernández Novás (Review entitled "Una nueva edición crítica de la poesía de Vallejo"). *Casa de las Américas,* no. 189 (Oct – Dec 92), pp. 121 – 141. Bibl.

— *Trilce* edited by Julio Ortega. Reviewed by Jacobo Sefamí. *Revista Chilena de Literatura,* no. 40 (Nov 92), pp. 160 – 161.

Varas Bordeu, María Teresa. *Villa de Nuestra Señora de Los Angeles: época fundacional* reviewed by Fernando Campos Harriet (Review entitled "Dos estudios sobre Los Angeles"). *Boletín de la Academia Chilena de la Historia,* v. 58 – 59, no. 102 (1991 – 1992), pp. 553 – 554.

Varas Reyes, Víctor. *El castellano popular en Tarija* reviewed by Carlos Coello Vila. *Signo,* no. 38, Nueva época (Jan – Apr 93), pp. 260 – 262.

Varela, Beatriz. *El español cubano-americano* reviewed by Thomas M. Stephens. *Hispania (USA),* v. 76, no. 4 (Dec 93), pp. 745 – 746.

Varela, Blanca. *Poesía escogida, 1949 – 1991* reviewed by Ana Aridjis. *Vuelta,* v. 17, no. 205 (Dec 93), p. 49.

Varela, Leticia R.
See
  Varela-Ruiz, Leticia T.

Varela-Ruiz, Leticia T. *Zubeldia, maestra maitea* (Review). *Inter-American Music Review,* v. 13, no. 2 (Spring – Summer 93), pp. 163 – 164.

Vargas, Diego de. *By Force of Arms: The Journals of Don Diego de Vargas, New Mexico, 1691 – 1693* edited and translated by John L. Kessell and Rick Hendricks. Reviewed by Timothy K. Perttula. *Colonial Latin American Historical Review,* v. 2, no. 3 (Summer 93), pp. 380 – 382.

— *By Force of Arms: The Journals of Don Diego de Vargas, New Mexico, 1691 – 1693* edited and translated by John L. Kessel and Rick Hendricks. Reviewed by Mark A. Burkholder. *Hispanic American Historical Review,* v. 73, no. 3 (Aug 93), pp. 510 – 511.

— *Letters from the New World: Selected Correspondence of Don Diego de Vargas to His Family, 1675 – 1706* edited and translated by John L. Kessell, Rick Hendricks, and Meredith D. Dodge. Reviewed by Jennifer L. Zimnoch. *The Americas Review,* v. 21, no. 1 (Spring 93), pp. 123 – 124.

— *Letters from the New World: Selected Correspondence of Don Diego de Vargas to His Family, 1675 – 1706* edited and translated by John L. Kessell, Rick Hendricks, and Meredith D. Dodge. Reviewed by Mark A. Burkholder. *Hispanic American Historical Review,* v. 73, no. 3 (Aug 93), pp. 510 – 511.

Vargas, Manuel. *Estampas* reviewed by Julio de la Vega. *Signo,* no. 35, Nueva época (Jan – Apr 92), pp. 252 – 253.

Vargas Arias, Claudio Antonio. *El liberalismo, la iglesia y el estado en Costa Rica* reviewed by Miguel Picado G. *Revista de Historia (Costa Rica),* no. 26 (July – Dec 92), pp. 203 – 208.

Vargas de Saavedra, Alicia. *Hablemos con propiedad* reviewed by Raúl Rivadeneira Prada. *Signo,* no. 38, Nueva época (Jan – Apr 93), pp. 262 – 263.

Vargas Llosa, Mario. *El pez en el agua* reviewed by Carlos Tello Díaz (Review entitled "Un pez fuera del agua"). *Nexos,* v. 16, no. 187 (July 93), pp. 81 – 83.

— *El pez en el agua* reviewed by Fabienne Bradu (Review entitled "Vida y biografía"). *Vuelta,* v. 17, no. 200 (July 93), pp. 54 – 55.

— *El pez en el agua* reviewed by Luis Pásara (Review entitled "Adiós al poder"). *Debate (Peru),* v. 16, no. 73 (June – Aug 93), pp. 64 – 67. Il.

— *El pez en el agua* reviewed by Marco Martos (Review entitled "Las memorias de tres novelistas peruanos"). *Debate (Peru),* v. 16, no. 73 (June – Aug 93), pp. 68 – 72. Il.

— *A Writer's Reality* edited by Myron I. Lichtblau. Reviewed by Alfred MacAdam. *Hispanic Review,* v. 61, no. 3 (Summer 93), pp. 454 – 456.

— *A Writer's Reality* reviewed by Barbara Mujica (Review entitled "The Creative Subtext of Life"). *Américas,* v. 45, no. 3 (May – June 93), pp. 62 – 63. Il.

Varley, Ann and Alan G. Gilbert. *Landlord and Tenant: Housing the Poor in Urban Mexico* reviewed by Nikki Craske. *Journal of Latin American Studies,* v. 25, no. 2 (May 93), pp. 418 – 419.

Varon, Benno Weiser. *Professions of a Lucky Jew* reviewed by Ignacio Klich. *Journal of Latin American Studies,* v. 25, no. 2 (May 93), pp. 430 – 431.

Vásquez, María Esther
See
  Vázquez, María Esther

Vayssière, Pierre. *Les révolutions d'Amérique Latine* reviewed by Claire Pailler. *Caravelle,* no. 59 (1992), pp. 281 – 285.

— *Les révolutions d'Amérique Latine* reviewed by Frank MacDonald Spindler. *Hispanic American Historical Review,* v. 73, no. 2 (May 93), pp. 349 – 350.

— *Les révolutions d'Amérique Latine* reviewed by Pilar Domingo. *Journal of Latin American Studies,* v. 25, no. 1 (Feb 93), p. 214.

Vázquez, Josefina Zoraida, ed. *La educación en la historia de México* reviewed by Carlos Salá. *La Educación (USA)*, v. 37, no. 114 (1993), pp. 174 – 175.

Vázquez, María Esther. *Victoria Ocampo* reviewed by Eliana C. Hermann. *Chasqui*, v. 22, no. 1 (May 93), pp. 94 – 95.

— *Victoria Ocampo* reviewed by Gustavo Fares and Eliana Hermann (Review entitled "¿Y ahora?: reflexiones acerca de la literatura femenina argentina actual"). *Letras Femeninas*, v. 19, no. 1 – 2 (Spring – Fall 93), pp. 121 – 134. Bibl.

Vázquez-Bigi, Angel Manuel and Anita Louise Padial Guerchoux. *Quiche Vinak: tragedia; nueva versión española y estudio histórico – literario del llamado 'Rabinal-Achí'* reviewed by Enrique Sam Colop. *Mesoamérica (USA)*, v. 13, no. 24 (Dec 92), pp. 465 – 473.

Vázquez de Knauth, Josefina
See
    Vázquez, Josefina Zoraida

Vega, Ana Lydia. *Falsas crónicas del sur* reviewed by Seymour Menton. *World Literature Today*, v. 67, no. 1 (Winter 93), p. 159.

Vega Alfaro, Eduardo de la. *Arcady Boytler Rososbky, 1895 – 1965* reviewed by Sonia Hernández Briseño (Review entitled "Pioneros del cine sonoro II"). *Revista Mexicana de Ciencias Políticas y Sociales*, v. 37, Nueva época, no. 150 (Oct – Dec 92), pp. 189 – 190.

— *Gabriel Soria, 1903 – 1971* reviewed by Beatriz Valdés Lagunes (Review entitled "Pioneros del cine sonoro I"). *Revista Mexicana de Ciencias Políticas y Sociales*, v. 37, Nueva época, no. 150 (Oct – Dec 92), pp. 187 – 188.

— *Gabriel Soria, 1903 – 1971* reviewed by Juan Felipe Leal and Eduardo Barraza (Review entitled "Gabriel Soria y el cine sonoro mexicano"). *Revista Mexicana de Ciencias Políticas y Sociales*, v. 37, Nueva época, no. 150 (Oct – Dec 92), pp. 179 – 186.

— *José Bohr* reviewed by Beatriz Valdés Lagunes (Review entitled "Pioneros del cine sonoro III"). *Revista Mexicana de Ciencias Políticas y Sociales*, v. 37, Nueva época, no. 150 (Oct – Dec 92), pp. 191 – 192.

Vega Suñol, José. *Presencia norteamericana en el área nororiental de Cuba* reviewed by Lawrence A. Glasco. *Cuban Studies/Estudios Cubanos*, v. 23 (1993), pp. 227 – 228.

Vélez, Lydia. *Osadía de los soles truncos/Daring of the Brief Suns* translated by Angela McEwan. Reviewed by Yolanda Rosas. *The Americas Review*, v. 20, no. 2 (Summer 92), p. 112.

Velloso, João Paulo dos Reis, ed. *A ecologia e o novo patrão de desenvolvimento no Brasil* reviewed by Euridson de Sá Jr. *Revista de Economia Política (Brazil)*, v. 13, no. 2 (Apr – June 93), pp. 155 – 156.

Ventura, Roberto. *Estilo tropical: história cultural e polêmicas literárias no Brasil* reviewed by Geraldo de Menezes. *Revista do Instituto Histórico e Geográfico Brasileiro*, no. 372 (July – Sept 91), pp. 933 – 935.

Verne, Jules. *Les conquistadores* reviewed by Claude Castro. *Caravelle*, no. 60 (1993), pp. 175 – 176.

Vertovec, Steven. *Hindu Trinidad: Religion, Ethnicity, and Socio-Economic Change* reviewed by William A. Harris (Review entitled "Ethnicity and Development"). *Social and Economic Studies*, v. 41, no. 4 (Dec 92), pp. 225 – 230.

Vicioso, Chiqui. *Algo que decir: ensayos sobre literatura femenina, 1981 – 1991* reviewed by Ester Gimbernat González. *Letras Femeninas*, v. 19, no. 1 – 2 (Spring – Fall 93), pp. 152 – 153.

Vidal, Hernán. *Dictadura militar, trauma social e inauguración de la sociología del teatro en Chile* reviewed by Carlos Alberto Trujillo. *Hispanic Review*, v. 61, no. 3 (Summer 93), pp. 456 – 457.

— *Dictadura militar, trauma social e inauguración de la sociología del teatro en Chile* reviewed by Catherine M. Boyle. *Latin American Theatre Review*, v. 26, no. 2 (Spring 93), pp. 216 – 217.

Vidal, José Walter Bautista. *Soberania e dignidade: raízes da sobrevivência* (Review). *Vozes*, v. 86, no. 4 (July – Aug 92), pp. 89 – 90.

Vidal, Lux et al, eds. *Grafismo indígena: ensaios de antropologia estética* reviewed by Clarice Cohn. *Revista de Antropologia (Brazil)*, v. 34 (1991), pp. 230 – 232.

Videla de Rivero, Gloria. *Direcciones del vanguardismo hispanoamericano, tomo I: Estudios sobre poesía de vanguardia en la década del veinte; tomo II: Documentos* reviewed by Klaus Müller-Bergh. *Hispanic Review*, v. 61, no. 3 (Summer 93), pp. 451 – 454.

Vieira, Nelson H. *Brasil e Portugal: a imagem recíproca; o mito e a realidade na expressão literária* reviewed by Bobby J. Chamberlain. *Hispania (USA)*, v. 76, no. 1 (Mar 93), pp. 90 – 92.

Vila, Martinho da. *Kizombas, andanças e festanças* reviewed by Aroldo Souza Silva. *Américas*, v. 45, no. 1 (Jan – Feb 93), pp. 62 – 63.

Vilar, Juan Bautista. *Los murcianos y América* reviewed by José U. Martínez Carreras. *Revista de Indias*, v. 53, no. 197 (Jan – Apr 93), pp. 126 – 127.

Vilas, Carlos María and Schafik Jorge Hándal. *The Socialist Option in Central America: Two Reassessments* (Review). *NACLA Report on the Americas*, v. 27, no. 3 (Nov – Dec 93), p. 48.

Villaça, Aparecida Maria Neiva. *Comendo como gente: formas de canibalismo wari' (pakaa nova)* reviewed by Robin M. Wright. *Revista Brasileira de Ciências Sociais*, v. 8, no. 23 (Oct 93), pp. 146 – 148.

Villagrá, Gaspar Pérez de. *'Historia de la Nueva México, 1610' by Gaspar Pérez de Villagrá: A Critical and Annotated Spanish/English Edition* edited and translated by Miguel Encinias. Reviewed by Franklin G. Smith. *Colonial Latin American Historical Review*, v. 2, no. 3 (Summer 93), pp. 377 – 379.

— *Historia de Nuevo México.* Critical edition by Mercedes Junquera. Reviewed by Phil Jaramillo (Review entitled "Dispositio Textus: Paleographic or Semipaleographic Edition?"). *Bilingual Review/Revista Bilingüe*, v. 17, no. 3 (Sept – Dec 92), pp. 276 – 278. Bibl.

Villalba O., Marcelo. *Cotocollao: una aldea formativa del valle de Quito* reviewed by Tamara L. Bray. *Latin American Antiquity*, v. 4, no. 1 (Mar 93), pp. 96 – 97.

Villalón-Galdames, Alberto. *Thesauro de literatura infantil* (Review). *La Educación (USA)*, v. 36, no. 111 – 113 (1992), pp. 305 – 306.

Villarreal González, Diana R. *La política de vivienda del gobierno del estado de Nuevo León, 1970 – 1990* reviewed by Gustavo Garza. *Estudios Demográficos y Urbanos*, v. 6, no. 3 (Sept – Dec 91), pp. 773 – 778.

Villaseñor, Víctor. *Rain of Gold* reviewed by Verlene Kelsey (Review entitled "Mining for a Usable Past: Acts of Recovery, Resistance, and Continuity in Víctor Villaseñor's *Rain of Gold*"). *Bilingual Review/Revista Bilingüe*, v. 18, no. 1 (Jan – Apr 93), pp. 79 – 85.

Villavicencio, Maritza. *Del silencio a la palabra: mujeres peruanas en los siglos XIX – XX* reviewed by Adriana Schaaf (Review entitled "El destape"). *Debate (Peru)*, v. 16, no. 74 (Sept – Oct 93), p. 66. Il.

Villegas, Abelardo, ed. *Posgrado y desarrollo en América Latina* reviewed by Ana Lilia Delgadillo Ibarra. *Revista Mexicana de Ciencias Políticas y Sociales*, v. 38, Nueva época, no. 151 (Jan – Mar 93), pp. 213 – 216.

Villoro, Juan. *La alcoba dormida* reviewed by Alvaro Enrigue. *Vuelta*, v. 17, no. 197 (Apr 93), pp. 46 – 47.

Viloria Vera, Enrique. *Ender Cepeda: la recreación de una identidad* reviewed by María Clara Martínez R. (Accompanied by an English translation). *Art Nexus*, no. 8 (Apr – June 93), p. 33. Il.

Vincent, Bernard. *1492: l'année admirable* reviewed by Bernadette Alvarez-Ferrandiz. *Caravelle*, no. 59 (1992), pp. 302 – 304.

— *1492: l'année admirable* reviewed by Marie Cécile Bénassy-Berling (Review entitled "Notas sobre el quinto centenario en Francia"). *Colonial Latin American Review*, v. 2, no. 1 – 2 (1993), pp. 269 – 272.

Vinhosa, Francisco Luiz Teixeira. *O Brasil e a 1ª guerra mundial: a diplomacia brasileira e as grandes potências* reviewed by Claudio Moreira Bento. *Revista do Instituto Histórico e Geográfico Brasileiro*, no. 370 (Jan – Mar 91), pp. 338 – 339.

Vitale, Ida. *Obra poética* reviewed by Víctor Sosa (Review entitled "Jugando con fuego"). *Vuelta*, v. 17, no. 201 (Aug 93), pp. 51 – 52.

Vitale, Luis. *Introducción a una teoría de la historia para América Latina* reviewed by Carmen Urljicak-Espaín. *Todo Es Historia*, v. 26, no. 307 (Feb 93), p. 74. Il.

Vivanco Maldonado, Jorge. *La luz de los milagros* reviewed by Peter N. Thomas. *Chasqui*, v. 22, no. 1 (May 93), pp. 107 – 110.

Voces de ultramar: arte en América Latina y Canarias, 1910 – 1960 reviewed by Ivonne Pini (Accompanied by an English translation). *Art Nexus*, no. 7 (Jan – Mar 93), p. 40. Il.

Volpi Escalante, Jorge. *A pesar del oscuro silencio* reviewed by Christopher Domínguez (Review entitled "De envidia a envidia"). *Vuelta*, v. 17, no. 195 (Feb 93), pp. 40 – 41.

Vornefeld, Ruth M. *Spanische Geldpolitik in Hispanoamerica, 1750 – 1808: Konzepte und Massnahmen im Rahmen der bourbonischen Reformpolitik* reviewed by Teodoro Hampe Martínez. *Revista de Indias*, v. 53, no. 197 (Jan – Apr 93), pp. 127 – 129.

Vysokolán, Oleg. *La traición del Papa Rei* (Review). *Revista Paraguaya de Sociología*, v. 29, no. 84 (May – Aug 92), pp. 208 – 210. Il.

Waak, William. *As duas faces da glória* reviewed by Cláudio Moreira Bento. *Revista do Instituto Histórico e Geográfico Brasileiro*, no. 372 (July – Sept 91), pp. 930 – 932.

Walker, Charles and Carlos Aguirre, eds. *Bandoleros, abigeos y montoneros: criminalidad y violencia en el Perú, siglos XVIII – XX* reviewed by Vincent Peloso. *The Americas*, v. 50, no. 2 (Oct 93), pp. 283 – 285.

— *Bandoleros, abigeos y montoneros: criminalidad y violencia en el Perú, siglos XVIII – XX* reviewed by Scarlett O'Phelan Godoy. *Anuario de Estudios Americanos*, v. 49, Suppl. 2 (1992), pp. 243 – 244.

Walker, David Wayne. *Parentescos, negocios y política: la familia Martínez del Río en México, 1823 – 1867* reviewed by María del Carmen Collado Herrera. *Historia Mexicana*, v. 42, no. 1 (July – Sept 92), pp. 133 – 138.

Walker, Thomas W. *Nicaragua: The Land of Sandino*, 3d ed., reviewed by Roland Ebel. *Hispanic American Historical Review*, v. 73, no. 1 (Feb 93), pp. 185 – 186.

Walker, Thomas W., ed. *Revolution and Counterrevolution in Nicaragua* reviewed by Roland Ebel. *Hispanic American Historical Review*, v. 73, no. 1 (Feb 93), pp. 185 – 186.

— *Revolution and Counterrevolution in Nicaragua* reviewed by Elizabeth Dore. *Journal of Latin American Studies*, v. 25, no. 1 (Feb 93), pp. 220 – 221.

— *Revolution and Counterrevolution in Nicaragua* reviewed by D. Neil Snarr. *Revista Interamericana de Bibliografía*, v. 42, no. 2 (1992), pp. 290 – 291.

Wanderley Pinho, José. *Coletânea de textos históricos* reviewed by José Gomes Bezerra Câmara. *Revista do Instituto Histórico e Geográfico Brasileiro*, no. 372 (July – Sept 91), pp. 932 – 933.

Ward, Peter M. *México: una mega-ciudad; producción y reproducción de un medio ambiente urbano* reviewed by Eduardo Lozano Ortega. *El Cotidiano*, v. 9, no. 54 (May 93), p. 114.

Warren, Janin Benedict and Richard E. Greenleaf. *Gonzalo Gómez, primer poblador español de Guayangareo (Morelia): proceso inquisitorial* translated by Alvaro Ochoa S. Reviewed by Frederick P. Bowser. *The Americas*, v. 49, no. 4 (Apr 93), pp. 544 – 545.

Watanabe, John M. *Maya Saints and Souls in a Changing World* reviewed by John Managhan. *Hispanic American Historical Review*, v. 73, no. 4 (Nov 93), pp. 720 – 721.

Watson, G. Llewellyn and Aubrey W. Bonnett, eds. *Emerging Perspectives on the Black Diaspora* reviewed by Harry Goulbourne. *Caribbean Quarterly*, v. 38, no. 2 – 3 (June – Sept 92), pp. 115 – 116.

Weber, David J. *The Spanish Frontier in North America* reviewed by Timothy K. Perttula. *Colonial Latin American Historical Review*, v. 2, no. 1 (Winter 93), pp. 122 – 123.

Weddle, Robert S. *The French Thorn: Rival Explorers in the Spanish Sea, 1682 – 1762* reviewed by Gwendolyn Hall. *Hispanic American Historical Review*, v. 73, no. 2 (May 93), p. 319.

Weeks, John and Andrew S. Zimbalist. *Panama at the Crossroads: Economic Development and Political Change in the Twentieth Century* reviewed by George Irvin. *Bulletin of Latin American Research*, v. 12, no. 2 (May 93), pp. 236 – 238.

— *Panama at the Crossroads: Economic Development and Political Change in the Twentieth Century* reviewed by Robert Edward Looney. *Revista Interamericana de Bibliografía*, v. 42, no. 2 (1992), pp. 293 – 294.

Weeks, John R. and Roberto Ham-Chande, eds. *Demographic Dynamics of the U.S. – Mexico Border* reviewed by Ellwyn Stoddard. *Journal of Borderlands Studies*, v. 8, no. 1 (Spring 93), pp. 119 – 124. Bibl.

Weffort, Francisco Corrêa. *Qual democracia?* reviewed by José de Arimateia da Cruz (Review entitled "Review Essay: Democratic Consolidation and the Socio-Economic Crisis of Latin America"). *Journal of Inter-American Studies and World Affairs*, v. 35, no. 1 (1993), pp. 145 – 152. Bibl, tables.

Weinberg, Liliana Irene. *Ezequiel Martínez Estrada y la interpretación del 'Martín Fierro'* reviewed by María Andueza. *Cuadernos Americanos*, no. 40, Nueva época (July – Aug 93), pp. 229 – 234.

— *Ezequiel Martínez Estrada y la interpretación del 'Martín Fierro'* reviewed by Carmen Vrljicak-Espaín. *Todo Es Historia*, v. 26, no. 310 (May 93), p. 81. Il.

Weinberg, William J. *War on the Land: Ecology and Politics in Central America* reviewed by Anthony Bebbington. *Bulletin of Latin American Research*, v. 12, no. 2 (May 93), p. 242.

Weinstein, Brian and Aaron Segal. *Haiti: The Failure of Politics* reviewed by Patrick Bellegarde-Smith. *Hispanic American Historical Review,* v. 73, no. 2 (May 93), p. 345.

Weintraub, Sidney. *A Marriage of Convenience: U.S. – Mexico Relations* reviewed by Lázaro Cárdenas Armenta (Review entitled "Las relaciones México – Estados Unidos: entre el conflicto y la cooperación"). *Relaciones Internacionales (Mexico),* v. 15, Nueva época, no. 57 (Jan – Mar 93), pp. 101 – 103.

Weiss, Osvaldo and Eduardo Yurevich. *En la universidad del aire* reviewed by Pedro A. González Bofil. *Realidad Económica,* no. 113 (Jan – Feb 93), pp. 142 – 143.

Welch, John H. *Capital Markets in the Development Process: The Case of Brazil* reviewed by David E. Hojman. *Bulletin of Latin American Research,* v. 12, no. 3 (Sept 93), pp. 350 – 351.

— *Capital Markets in the Development Process: The Case of Brazil* reviewed by Tomás Bruginski de Paula. *Journal of Latin American Studies,* v. 25, no. 3 (Oct 93), pp. 677 – 678.

Welden, Alicia Galaz-Vivar. *Alta marea: introvisión crítica en ocho voces latinoamericanas; Belli, Fuentes, Lagos, Mistral, Neruda, Orrillo, Rojas, Villaurrutia* reviewed by Juvenal López Ruiz. *Revista Nacional de Cultura (Venezuela),* v. 53, no. 285 (Apr – June 92), pp. 252 – 253.

Wentzlaff-Eggebert, Harald. *Las literaturas hispánicas de vanguardia: orientación bibliográfica* reviewed by Hugo Verani (Review entitled "Las vanguardias latinoamericanas"). *Nuevo Texto Crítico,* v. 6, no. 11 (1993), pp. 262 – 263.

Wentzlaff-Eggebert, Harald, ed. *Europäische Avantgarde im lateinamerikanischen Kontext/La vanguardia europea en el contexto latinoamericano* reviewed by Hugo J. Verani (Review entitled "Las vanguardias latinoamericanas"). *Nuevo Texto Crítico,* v. 6, no. 11 (1993), pp. 262 – 263.

Werner, Thomas and Bard de Groof, eds. *Rebelión y resistencia en el mundo hispánico del siglo XVII: actos del Coloquio Internacional Lovaina, 20 – 23 de noviembre de 1991* reviewed by Clara López Beltrán. *Hispanic American Historical Review,* v. 73, no. 4 (Nov 93), pp. 689 – 690.

West, Donnamarie. *Between Two Worlds: The Human Side of Development* reviewed by Alan C. Hunsaker (Review entitled "Guatemala: Small Country, Big Problems"). *Hispanic Journal of Behavioral Sciences,* v. 15, no. 3 (Aug 93), pp. 418 – 423.

Western, John. *A Passage to England: Barbadian Londoners Speak of Home* reviewed by Thomas D. Anderson. *Geographical Review,* v. 83, no. 2 (Apr 93), pp. 219 – 220.

Westphal, Wilfried. *Die Mayaforschung: Geschichte, Methoden, Ergebnisse* reviewed by Andreas Koechert. *Iberoamericana,* v. 17, no. 49 (1993), pp. 89 – 90.

Westwood, Sallie and Sarah A. Radcliffe, eds. *"Viva": Women and Popular Protest in Latin America* reviewed by Tessa Cubitt. *Bulletin of Latin American Research,* v. 12, no. 2 (May 93), pp. 242 – 243.

Whigham, Thomas Lyle. *The Politics of River Trade: Tradition and Development in the Upper Plata, 1780 – 1870* reviewed by James Schofield Saeger. *The Americas,* v. 49, no. 4 (Apr 93), pp. 552 – 553.

— *The Politics of River Trade: Tradition and Development in the Upper Plata, 1780 – 1870* reviewed by Jeremy Adelman. *Journal of Latin American Studies,* v. 25, no. 1 (Feb 93), pp. 194 – 196.

— *La yerba mate del Paraguay, 1780 – 1870* reviewed by Jeremy Adelman. *Journal of Latin American Studies,* v. 25, no. 1 (Feb 93), pp. 194 – 196.

White, Russell N. *State, Class, and the Nationalization of the Mexican Banks* reviewed by Terry McKinley and Diana Alarcón (Review entitled "Mexican Bank Nationalization"). *Latin American Perspectives,* v. 20, no. 3 (Summer 93), pp. 80 – 82.

Whiteford, Scott and Anne E. Ferguson, eds. *Harvest of Want: Hunger and Food Security in Central America and Mexico* reviewed by LaMond Tullis. *Journal of Developing Areas,* v. 27, no. 2 (Jan 93), pp. 253 – 254.

Whitehead, Neil L. and R. Brian Ferguson, eds. *War in the Tribal Zone: Expanding States and Indigenous Warfare* reviewed by Elizabeth M. Brumfiel. *Hispanic American Historical Review,* v. 73, no. 3 (Aug 93), pp. 499 – 500.

Whitehead, Neil L. and Peter Hulme, eds. *Wild Majesty: Encounters with Caribs from Columbus to the Present Day; An Anthology* reviewed by Peter T. Bradley. *Bulletin of Latin American Research,* v. 12, no. 1 (Jan 93), pp. 111 – 112.

Whiting, Van R., Jr. *The Political Economy of Foreign Investment in Mexico: Nationalism, Liberalism, and Constraints on Choice* reviewed by Sylvia Maxfield. *Journal of Latin American Studies,* v. 25, no. 3 (Oct 93), pp. 682 – 683.

Whitmore, Thomas M. *Disease and Death in Early Colonial Mexico: Simulating Amerindian Depopulation* reviewed by Susan Austin Anchon. *Hispanic American Historical Review,* v. 73, no. 4 (Nov 93), pp. 695 – 696.

Wiarda, Howard J. *American Foreign Policy toward Latin America in the 80s and 90s: Issues and Controversies from Reagan to Bush* reviewed by Gordon Connell-Smith. *Journal of Latin American Studies,* v. 25, no. 3 (Oct 93), pp. 689 – 691.

Wickham-Crowley, Timothy P. *Guerrillas and Revolution in Latin America: A Comparative Study of Insurgents and Regimes since 1956* reviewed by Willem Assies. *European Review of Latin American and Caribbean Studies,* no. 54 (June 93), pp. 133 – 136.

— *Guerrillas and Revolution in Latin America: A Comparative Study of Insurgents and Regimes since 1956* reviewed by Brian Loveman. *Hispanic American Historical Review,* v. 73, no. 2 (May 93), pp. 350 – 352.

Wiesner Durán, Eduardo. *Colombia: descentralización y federalismo fiscal* reviewed by César Vargas. *Planeación y Desarrollo,* v. 24, no. 1 (Jan – Apr 93), pp. 465 – 471.

Wiethüchter, Blanca. *El verde en el ver de blanca* reviewed by Juan Quinteros Soria. *Signo,* no. 35, Nueva época (Jan – Apr 92), pp. 254 – 256.

Wilcox, David R. and Vernon Lee Scarborough, eds. *The Mesoamerican Ballgame* reviewed by Barbara J. Price. *Hispanic American Historical Review,* v. 73, no. 1 (Feb 93), pp. 144 – 145.

Wilk, Richard R. *Household Ecology: Economic Change and Domestic Life among the Kekchi Maya in Belize* reviewed by Joseph O. Palacio. *Belizean Studies,* v. 21, no. 1 (May 93), pp. 25 – 26.

— *Household Ecology: Economic Change and Domestic Life among the Kekchi Maya in Belize* reviewed by Laura Rival. *Bulletin of Latin American Research,* v. 12, no. 1 (Jan 93), pp. 125 – 126.

— *Household Ecology: Economic Change and Domestic Life among the Kekchi Maya in Belize* reviewed by Norman Ashcraft. *Journal of Developing Areas,* v. 27, no. 3 (Apr 93), pp. 422 – 424.

Williams, Eduardo. *Las piedras sagradas: escultura prehispánica del occidente de México* reviewed by Louise I. Paradis. *Latin American Antiquity,* v. 4, no. 4 (Dec 93), pp. 393 – 394.

Williams, Edward J. and John T. Passe-Smith. *The Unionization of the Maquiladora Industry: The Tamaulipan Case in National Context* reviewed by Heather Fowler-Salamini. *Hispanic American Historical Review*, v. 73, no. 4 (Nov 93), pp. 718 – 719.

Williams, Raymond Leslie. *The Colombian Novel, 1844 – 1987* reviewed by Gilberto Gómez Ocampo (Review entitled "Novela y poder en Colombia"). *La Palabra y el Hombre*, no. 81 (Jan – Mar 92), pp. 358 – 361.

Williams, Raymond Leslie, ed. *The Novel in the Americas* reviewed by Edward Waters Hood. *Hispania (USA)*, v. 76, no. 4 (Dec 93), pp. 742 – 743.

— *The Novel in the Americas* reviewed by John L. Brown. *World Literature Today*, v. 67, no. 4 (Fall 93), pp. 908 – 909.

Williamson, Edwin. *The Penguin History of Latin America* reviewed by Jorge F. Hernández (Review entitled "Para medir la distancia"). *Vuelta*, v. 17, no. 195 (Feb 93), pp. 44 – 45.

Wilson, Carlos Guillermo. *Los nietos de Felicidad Dolores* reviewed by David C. Alley. *Afro-Hispanic Review*, v. 12, no. 1 (Spring 93), pp. 53 – 54.

Wilson, Fiona. *De la casa al taller: mujeres, trabajo y clase social en la industria textil y del vestido* reviewed by Soledad González Montes. *Estudios Sociológicos*, v. 11, no. 31 (Jan – Apr 93), pp. 288 – 290. Bibl.

— *Sweaters: Gender, Class, and Workshop-Based Industry in Mexico* reviewed by Tessa Cubitt. *Bulletin of Latin American Research*, v. 12, no. 1 (Jan 93), pp. 124 – 125.

Wilson, Patricia Ann. *Exports and Local Development: Mexico's New Maquiladoras* reviewed by Alfredo Hualde. *Estudios Sociológicos*, v. 11, no. 32 (May – Aug 93), pp. 569 – 573.

— *Exports and Local Development: Mexico's New Maquiladoras* reviewed by Helen Icken Saja. *Hispanic American Historical Review*, v. 73, no. 4 (Nov 93), pp. 719 – 720.

— *Exports and Local Development: Mexico's New Maquiladoras* reviewed by David J. Molina. *Journal of Borderlands Studies*, v. 7, no. 2 (Fall 92), pp. 106 – 108.

Wilson-Bareau, Juliet. *Manet: 'The Execution of Maximilian'; Painting, Politics, and Censorship* reviewed by Paul J. Vanderwood. *Hispanic American Historical Review*, v. 73, no. 2 (May 93), p. 331.

Witzel de Ciudad, Renate, ed. *Más de cien años de movimiento obrero urbano en Guatemala, tomo I: Artesanos y obreros en el período liberal, 1877 – 1944* reviewed by Ana Lorena Carrillo. *Mesoamérica (USA)*, v. 13, no. 24 (Dec 92), pp. 459 – 462.

Wood, Charles Howard and Marianne Schmink. *Contested Frontiers in Amazonia* reviewed by Philip A. Dennis. *Journal of Developing Areas*, v. 28, no. 1 (Oct 93), pp. 111 – 113.

Wortman, Ana. *Jóvenes desde la periferia* (Review). *Revista Paraguaya de Sociología*, v. 30, no. 86 (Jan – Apr 93), pp. 206 – 207.

Wright, Simon J. *Villa-Lobos* (Review). *Inter-American Music Review*, v. 13, no. 2 (Spring – Summer 93), p. 162.

— *Villa-Lobos* reviewed by E. Bradford Burns. *Hispanic American Historical Review*, v. 73, no. 4 (Nov 93), pp. 672 – 673.

— *Villa-Lobos* reviewed by Gerard Béhague. *Latin American Music Review*, v. 14, no. 2 (Fall – Winter 93), pp. 294 – 297.

Wright, Thomas C. *Latin America in the Era of the Cuban Revolution* reviewed by Paul W. Drake. *The Americas*, v. 49, no. 3 (Jan 93), pp. 421 – 422.

— *Latin America in the Era of the Cuban Revolution* reviewed by Brian Loveman. *Hispanic American Historical Review*, v. 73, no. 2 (May 93), pp. 350 – 352.

Wu, Celia. *Generals and Diplomats: Great Britain and Peru, 1820 – 1840* reviewed by Betford Betalleluz. *Revista Andina*, v. 11, no. 1 (July 93), pp. 254 – 256.

Yacou, Alain and Michel L. Martin, eds. *Mourir pour les Antilles: indépendance nègre ou esclavage, 1802 – 1804* reviewed by Frédérique Langue. *Caravelle*, no. 60 (1993), pp. 157 – 159.

Yupanqui, Titu Cusi. *Instrucción al licenciado don Lope García de Castro, 1750* edited by Liliana Regalado de Hurtado. Reviewed by Raquel Chang-Rodríguez. *Hispanic American Historical Review*, v. 73, no. 4 (Nov 93), pp. 699 – 700.

Yurevich, Eduardo and Osvaldo Weiss. *En la universidad del aire* reviewed by Pedro A. González Bofil. *Realidad Económica*, no. 113 (Jan – Feb 93), pp. 142 – 143.

Yurkievich, Saúl. *A imagen y semejanza* reviewed by Víctor Sosa. *Vuelta*, v. 17, no. 198 (May 93), pp. 53 – 54.

Yuste, Carmen, ed. *Comerciantes mexicanos en el siglo XVIII* reviewed by Frédérique Langue. *Caravelle*, no. 60 (1993), pp. 151 – 152.

Zagorski, Paul W. *Democracy vs. National Security: Civil – Military Relations in Latin America* reviewed by Gamaliel Perruci. *Journal of Inter-American Studies and World Affairs*, v. 35, no. 1 (1993), pp. 167 – 170.

Zamarripa, Roberto. *Sonora '91: historia de políticos y policías* reviewed by Ana Ivonee Rivas García. *El Cotidiano*, v. 10, no. 58 (Oct – Nov 93), p. 117.

Zanetti Lecuona, Oscar. *Los cautivos de la reciprocidad: la burguesía cubana y la dependencia comercial* reviewed by Antonio Santamaría García. *Revista de Indias*, v. 53, no. 197 (Jan – Apr 93), pp. 129 – 132.

Zapata, Francisco. *Atacama: desierto de la discordia; minería y política internacional en Bolivia, Chile y Perú* reviewed by Andrea Ostrov. *La Educación (USA)*, v. 37, no. 114 (1993), pp. 175 – 176.

Zapata, Miguel Angel. *Poemas para violín y orquesta* reviewed by Carlos Germán Belli. *Hispamérica*, v. 21, no. 62 (Aug 92), pp. 140 – 141.

— *Poemas para violín y orquesta* reviewed by José A. Mazzotti. *Revista de Crítica Literaria Latinoamericana*, v. 19, no. 38 (July – Dec 93), pp. 430 – 432.

Zarur, George de Cerqueira Leite, ed. *A antropologia na América Latina* reviewed by Bernardo Berdichewsky. *Revista Interamericana de Bibliografía*, v. 42, no. 2 (1992), pp. 291 – 293.

Zavadivker, Ricardo Augusto. *Los primeros músicos en América* (Review). *Inter-American Music Review*, v. 13, no. 2 (Spring – Summer 93), pp. 154 – 155.

Zavala, Iris M. *Nocturna mas no funesta* reviewed by Mary Kathryn Addis. *Revista Iberoamericana*, v. 59, no. 162 – 163 (Jan – June 93), pp. 363 – 365.

Zea, Leopoldo. *The Role of the Americas in History*, a translation of *América en la historia* edited by Amy A. Oliver, translated by Sonja Karsen. Reviewed by Iván Jaksic. *Hispanic American Historical Review*, v. 73, no. 1 (Feb 93), pp. 132 – 133.

Zepeda, Rafael. *Horse Medicine and Other Stories* reviewed by Javier Rodríguez. *The Americas Review*, v. 19, no. 3 – 4 (Winter 91), pp. 147 – 148.

Ziccardi, Alicia. *Las obras públicas de la ciudad de México, 1976 – 1982: política urbana e industria de la construcción* reviewed by Matilde Luna. *Revista Mexicana de Sociología*, v. 54, no. 4 (Oct – Dec 92), pp. 259 – 261.

Zilio, Giovanni Meo

See
> Meo Zilio, Giovanni

Zilli Mánica, José Benigno. *Frailes, curas y laicos* reviewed by Carmen Blázquez Domínguez. *La Palabra y el Hombre*, no. 83 (July – Sept 92), pp. 350 – 352.

Zimbalist, Andrew S. and John Weeks. *Panama at the Crossroads: Economic Development and Political Change in the Twentieth Century* reviewed by George Irvin. *Bulletin of Latin American Research*, v. 12, no. 2 (May 93), pp. 236 – 238.

— *Panama at the Crossroads: Economic Development and Political Change in the Twentieth Century* reviewed by Robert Edward Looney. *Revista Interamericana de Bibliografía*, v. 42, no. 2 (1992), pp. 293 – 294.

Zimmerman, Marc and John Beverley. *Literature and Politics in the Central American Revolutions* reviewed by Antony Higgins. *Revista de Crítica Literaria Latinoamericana*, v. 19, no. 37 (Jan – June 93), pp. 380 – 382.

Zimmermann, Klaus. *Sprachkontakt, ethnische Identität und Identitätsbeschädigung: Aspekte der Assimilation der Otomí-Indianer an die hispanophone mexikanische Kultur* reviewed by Eva Gugenberger. *Iberoamericana*, v. 17, no. 49 (1993), pp. 84 – 86.

Zogbaum, Heidi. *B. Traven: A Vision of Mexico* reviewed by Frank Whitehead. *Journal of Latin American Studies*, v. 25, no. 1 (Feb 93), pp. 225 – 226.

Zovatto G., Daniel. *Los estados de excepción y los derechos humanos en la América Latina* reviewed by Natan Lerner. *Estudios Interdisciplinarios de América Latina y el Caribe*, v. 3, no. 2 (July – Dec 92), pp. 127 – 129.

Zuloaga, E. et al. *Prácticas de crianza* (Review). *Revista Paraguaya de Sociología*, v. 30, no. 86 (Jan – Apr 93), p. 209.

AUTHORS

AUTHORS

Abad Pérez, Antolín. Estadística franciscano – misionera en ultramar del siglo XVIII: un intento de aproximación. *Archivo Ibero-Americano,* v. 52, no. 205 – 208 (Jan – Dec 92), pp. 125 – 156. Bibl, tables.

Abadie-Aicardi, Aníbal. La tradición institucional salmantina en los Libros de Claustros de la Universidad de México del renacimiento a la ilustración y la independencia, 1551 – 1821. *Jahrbuch für Geschichte von Staat, Wirtschaft und Gesellschaft Lateinamerikas,* v. 29 (1992), pp. 1 – 46. Bibl.

Abdala Júnior, Benjamin. Do Brasil a Portugal: imagens na ação política. *Revista de Letras (Brazil),* v. 32 (1992), pp. 15 – 30. Bibl.

Abella Armengol, Gloria. La política exterior de México en el gobierno de Carlos Salinas de Gortari: ¿Una nueva concepción? *Revista Mexicana de Ciencias Políticas y Sociales,* v. 37, Nueva época, no. 148 (Apr – June 92), pp. 63 – 76.

Abella Rodríguez, Arturo. La muerte del padre Briceño Jáuregui. *Boletín de Historia y Antigüedades,* v. 80, no. 781 (Apr – June 93), pp. 323 – 325.

Abercrombie, Thomas Alan. La fiesta del carnaval postcolonial en Oruro: clase, etnicidad y nacionalismo en la danza folklórica (With commentaries by seven historians and a response by the author). *Revista Andina,* v. 10, no. 2 (Dec 92), pp. 279 – 352. Bibl, il.

Aboites, Hugo. Internacionalización de la educación superior: los probables beneficiarios en el marco de la integración económico. *El Cotidiano,* v. 8, no. 52 (Jan – Feb 93), pp. 84 – 91. Bibl, il, tables.

— La relación universidad – industria en el marco del Tratado de Libre Comercio. *El Cotidiano,* v. 9, no. 55 (June 93), pp. 78 – 84. Charts.

Aboites A., Jaime and Alenka Guzmán Chávez. Desempeño del sector manufacturero y relaciones laborales: la experiencia reciente de México. *El Cotidiano,* v. 10, no. 58 (Oct – Nov 93), pp. 103 – 111. Il, tables, charts.

— La industria textil mexicana y el Tratado de Libre Comercio. *El Cotidiano,* v. 8, no. 51 (Nov – Dec 92), pp. 102 – 109. Bibl, tables.

Aborampah, Osei-Mensah. Religious Sanction and Social Order in Traditional Akan Communities of Ghana and Jamaica. *Journal of Caribbean Studies,* v. 9, no. 1 – 2 (Winter 92 – Spring 93), pp. 41 – 58. Bibl, charts.

Abraham, Tomás. Operación ternura. *Cuadernos Hispanoamericanos,* no. 517 – 519 (July – Sept 93), pp. 27 – 40.

Abregú, Martín. Contra las apologías del "homocidio uniforme": la violencia policial en Argentina. *Nueva Sociedad,* no. 123 (Jan – Feb 93), pp. 68 – 83. Bibl.

Abundis Canales, Jaime. A Mansion in the City of Palaces. *Business Mexico,* v. 3, no. 12 (Dec 93), pp. 34 – 36. Il.

Accorsi O., Enrique et al. ¿Hacia qué sistema de salud?: debates. *Mensaje,* v. 42, no. 417 (Mar – Apr 93), pp. 86 – 92. Il.

Aceituno, Patricio and Aldo Montecinos. Análisis de la estabilidad de la relación entre la oscilación del sur y la precipitación en América del Sur. *Bulletin de l'Institut Français d'Etudes Andines,* v. 22, no. 1 (1993), pp. 53 – 64. Bibl, tables, maps, charts.

Acevedo, Edberto Oscar. San Martín y su ideario hacia 1810. *Investigaciones y Ensayos,* no. 41 (Jan – Dec 91), pp. 89 – 105. Bibl.

Acevedo, Ramón Luis. Rumbos de la narrativa centroamericana actual. *Káñina,* v. 16, no. 2 (July – Dec 92), pp. 39 – 51. Bibl.

Aceves, Patricia. La ilustración novohispana en el área farmacéutica, química y metalúrgica. *Cuadernos Americanos,* no. 38, Nueva época (Mar – Apr 93), pp. 92 – 120. Bibl.

Acha, Juan. El arte contemporáneo y la estética latinoamericana. *Plural (Mexico),* v. 22, no. 257 (Feb 93), pp. 60 – 67.

Achard, Diego et al. MERCOSUR: élites y política en Paraguay y Uruguay. *Integración Latinoamericana,* v. 18, no. 192 (Aug 93), pp. 59 – 61.

Achutti, Luiz Eduardo Robinson. Ensaio fotográfico: auto-retrato de Dina. *Vozes,* v. 86, no. 5 (Sept – Oct 92), pp. 95 – 98. Il.

Acosta, Ivonne. Hacia una historia de la persecución política en Puerto Rico. *Homines,* v. 15 – 16, no. 2 – 1 (Oct 91 – Dec 92), pp. 142 – 151.

Acosta, Mariclaire. Fabricación de culpables por discriminación de minorías: caso de Flor Melo. *Fem,* v. 17, no. 122 (Apr 93), pp. 18 – 19.

Acosta-Belén, Edna. Etnicidad, género y revitalización cultural en la literatura nuyorriqueña. *Homines,* v. 15 – 16, no. 2 – 1 (Oct 91 – Dec 92), pp. 338 – 357. Bibl.

Acosta Cruz, María Isabel. Historia y escritura femenina en Olga Nolla, Magali García Ramis, Rosario Ferré y Ana Lydia Vega. *Revista Iberoamericana,* v. 59, no. 162 – 163 (Jan – June 93), pp. 265 – 277. Bibl.

Acosta Rabassa, Blanca. Viernes, ¿y por qué no jueves? *Conjunto,* no. 93 (Jan – June 93), pp. 44 – 45. Il.

Acosta-Solís, Misael. Por la conservación de la Amazonia. *Revista Geográfica (Mexico),* no. 115 (Jan – June 92), pp. 77 – 84.

Acuña, Carlos H. Argentina: hacia un nuevo modelo. *Nueva Sociedad,* no. 126 (July – Aug 93), pp. 11 – 24.

Acuña, Marlene. La adopción: una alternativa de reubicación del menor abandonado. *Revista de Ciencias Sociales (Costa Rica),* no. 59 (Mar 93), pp. 37 – 46. Bibl, il.

Acuña Cañas, Alonso. Semblanza del maestro Acuña. *Boletín de Historia y Antigüedades,* v. 80, no. 781 (Apr – June 93), pp. 357 – 358.

Adams, John E. Fish Lovers of the Caribbean. *Caribbean Studies,* v. 25, no. 1 – 2 (Jan – July 92), pp. 1 – 10. Tables.

Adarve, Luz Helena. La importancia de las marcas en la industria de la confección: nuevo enfoque. *Revista Javeriana,* v. 61, no. 593 (Apr 93), pp. 156 – 158.

Adelman, Jeremy. State and Labour in Argentina: The Portworkers of Buenos Aires, 1910 – 1921. *Journal of Latin American Studies,* v. 25, no. 1 (Feb 93), pp. 73 – 102. Bibl, maps.

Adler, Ilya. Press – Government Relations in Mexico: A Study of Freedom of the Mexican Press and Press Criticism of Government Institutions. *Studies in Latin American Popular Culture,* v. 12 (1993), pp. 1 – 30. Bibl, tables.

Adorno, Rolena. The Genesis of Felipe Guamán Poma de Ayala's *Nueva corónica y buen gobierno. Colonial Latin American Review,* v. 2, no. 1 – 2 (1993), pp. 53 – 92. Bibl, il.

— Reconsidering Colonial Discourse for Sixteenth- and Seventeenth-Century Spanish America (Response to Patricia Seed's "Colonial and Postcolonial Discourse," *LARR,* v. 26, no. 3, 1991). *Latin American Research Review,* v. 28, no. 3 (1993), pp. 135 – 145.

Adorno, Sérgio. Ciência, informação, verdade e universalidade: a propósito de "A violência política na América Latina." *Revista Brasileira de Ciências Sociais,* v. 8, no. 21 (Feb 93), pp. 40 – 43.

Adorno, Sérgio and Túlio Kahn. Pena de morte: para que e para quem serve esse debate? *Vozes,* v. 87, no. 3 (May – June 93), pp. 14 – 30. Tables, charts.

Adoum, Jorge Enrique. Postales del trópico con mujeres. *Casa de las Américas,* no. 190 (Jan – Mar 93), pp. 106 – 111.

Adrogué, Gerardo. Los ex-militares en política: bases sociales y cambios en los patrones de representación política. *Desarrollo Económico (Argentina),* v. 33, no. 131 (Oct – Dec 93), pp. 425 – 442. Bibl, tables.

Aftalión, Marcelo E. Que diez años no es nada. *Todo Es Historia,* v. 27, no. 317 (Dec 93), pp. 58 – 60. Il.

Agosin, Manuel Roberto. Beneficios y costos potenciales para Chile de los acuerdos de libre comercio. *Estudios Públicos (Chile),* no. 52 (Spring 93), pp. 101 – 126. Bibl, tables.

— Política comercial en los países dinámicos de Asia: aplicaciones a América Latina. *Desarrollo Económico (Argentina),* v. 33, no. 131 (Oct – Dec 93), pp. 355 – 375. Bibl, tables.

Agosin, Manuel Roberto and Diana A. Tussie de Federman. Globalización, regionalización y nuevos dilemas en la política de comercio exterior para el desarrollo (Translated by Carlos Villegas). *El Trimestre Económico,* v. 60, no. 239 (July – Sept 93), pp. 559 – 599. Bibl, tables.

— Nuevos dilemas en la política comercial para el desarrollo (Excerpt from the introduction to the forthcoming book *Trading Places: New Dilemmas in Trade Policy for Development,* edited by Manuel R. Agosin and Diana Tussie, translated by Adriana Hierro). *Comercio Exterior,* v. 43, no. 10 (Oct 93), pp. 899 – 912. Bibl, tables.

Agosín, Marjorie. A Dreamy Oaxacan Fantasy (Translated by Ruth Morales). *Américas,* v. 45, no. 6 (Nov – Dec 93), pp. 44 – 45. Il.

— Gestos y rostros de mujeres: Gabriela Mistral y Violeta Parra. *Plural (Mexico),* v. 22, no. 260 (May 93), pp. 60 – 63.

— A horcajadas. *Fem,* v. 17, no. 127 (Sept 93), pp. 47 – 48.

— *La mujer desnuda* o el viaje decapitado: un texto de Armonía Somers. *Revista Interamericana de Bibliografía,* v. 42, no. 4 (1992), pp. 585 – 589.

— Un paisaje silencioso: las mujeres en la poesía chilena. *Fem,* v. 17, no. 125 (July 93), pp. 40 – 42.

Agostini, Claudio. Liberalización de la economía mexicana. *Estudios Sociales (Chile),* no. 76 (Apr – June 93), pp. 169 – 188. Bibl.

Agüero, Abel Luis. Desde Colón y la sífilis al hombre contemporáneo y el SIDA. *Todo Es Historia,* v. 26, no. 306 (Jan 93), pp. 74 – 85. Il.

Aguiar, Flávio. Cultura de contrabando: estudo sobre os contos de Simões Lopes Neto. *Vozes,* v. 86, no. 6 (Nov – Dec 92), pp. 13 – 20.

Aguiar, José Vangeliso de and José de Jesus Sousa Lemos. Produção do caupi irrigado em Bragança, Pará. *Revista de Economia e Sociologia Rural,* v. 30, no. 3 (July – Sept 92), pp. 239 – 252. Bibl, tables, charts.

Aguiar, Tereza Coni. O papel do poder público municipal e os desafios no criação de políticas para o desenvolvimento integral e harmónico da área rural. *Revista Geográfica (Mexico),* no. 114 (July – Dec 91), pp. 101 – 109.

Aguiar Estrada, Eliene. Cólera. *Revista Cultural Lotería,* v. 51, no. 390 (July – Aug 92), pp. 17 – 26. Bibl.

Aguila, Juan M. del. The Party, the Fourth Congress, and the Process of Counter-Reform. *Cuban Studies/Estudios Cubanos,* v. 23 (1993), pp. 71 – 90. Bibl, tables.

Aguila, Marcos Tonatiuh. Historia, revisionismo y educación: la nueva "revolución pasiva." *El Cotidiano,* v. 8, no. 51 (Nov – Dec 92), pp. 39 – 47. Bibl, il.

Aguilar, Adrián Guillermo. Las ciudades medias en México: hacia una diferenciación de sus atributos. *Revista Interamericana de Planificación,* v. 26, no. 101 – 102 (Jan – June 93), pp. 129 – 153. Bibl, tables, charts.

— Relatoría de la mesa redonda "El Programa Nacional de Desarrollo Urbano, 1990 – 1994." *Estudios Demográficos y Urbanos,* v. 6, no. 3 (Sept – Dec 91), pp. 738 – 744.

Aguilar, Edwin Eloy et al. Protestantism in El Salvador: Conventional Wisdom versus Survey Evidence. *Latin American Research Review,* v. 28, no. 2 (1993), pp. 119 – 140. Bibl, tables.

Aguilar, Luis Miguel. Cómo salvar al futbol mexicano. *Nexos,* v. 16, no. 185 (May 93), pp. 23 – 27.

— Tenga su festivaloti. *Nexos,* v. 16, no. 186 (June 93), pp. 31 – 33.

Aguilar, Pilar. El maestro Carlos Enrique Vargas y su metodología en la enseñanza del piano. *Káñina,* v. 16, no. 1 (Jan – June 92), pp. 267 – 272. Il.

Aguilar, Ricardo D.

See

Aguilar Melantzón, Ricardo D.

Aguilar Camín, Héctor. La invención de México. *Nexos,* v. 16, no. 187 (July 93), pp. 49 – 61.

Aguilar Gómez, J. Eduardo. Mexican Corporate Culture. *Business Mexico,* v. 3, no. 8 (Aug 93), pp. 8 – 9 + .

Aguilar Gómez, Javier de J. Cuba: comercialización de productos agrícolas. *Momento Económico,* no. 69 (Sept – Oct 93), pp. 24 – 28. Bibl.

Aguilar Hernández, Marielos. Costa Rica: democracia y libertades sindicales, 1980 – 1989. *Revista de Ciencias Sociales (Costa Rica),* no. 59 (Mar 93), pp. 71 – 80. Bibl, tables.

— Las libertades sindicales en los ochentas: el caso de las organizaciones bananeras costarricenses. *Revista de Ciencias Sociales (Costa Rica),* no. 58 (Dec 92), pp. 85 – 94. Bibl.

Aguilar Melantzón, Ricardo D. iGuache ése! *Plural (Mexico),* v. 22, no. 256 (Jan 93), pp. 40 – 45. Il.

Aguilar Monteverde, Alonso. Jesús Silva Herzog como economista. *Problemas del Desarrollo,* v. 24, no. 92 (Jan – Mar 93), pp. 209 – 217. Bibl.

Aguilar Ponce, Luis. Las influencias de la arquitectura española en el pensamiento del ser latinoamericano. *Revista Cultural Lotería,* v. 51, no. 391 (Sept – Oct 92), pp. 98 – 104.

Aguilera Garramuño, Marco Tulio. José Homero y *La construcción del amor. La Palabra y el Hombre,* no. 81 (Jan – Mar 92), pp. 265 – 268.

— Las noches de ventura. *Plural (Mexico),* v. 22, no. 258 (Mar 93), pp. 36 – 40.

— Revista *Literal. Plural (Mexico),* v. 22, no. 259 (Apr 93), pp. 75 – 76.

Aguilera Peralta, Gabriel Edgardo. Guatemala: transición sin llegar a ninguna parte. *Nueva Sociedad,* no. 123 (Jan – Feb 93), pp. 6 – 9.

Aguilú de Murphy, Raquel. Hacia un teorización del absurdo en el teatro de Myrna Casas. *Revista Iberoamericana,* v. 59, no. 162 – 163 (Jan – June 93), pp. 169 – 176. Bibl.

Aguirre, Carlos. Agentes de su propia emancipación: manumisión de esclavos en Lima, 1821 – 1854. *Apuntes (Peru),* no. 29 (July – Dec 91), pp. 35 – 56. Bibl, tables.

Aguirre, Mariano. Huidobro narrador. *Atenea (Chile),* no. 467 (1993), pp. 101 – 102.

Aguirre Anaya, Carmen. Industria y tecnología: motricidad en los textiles de algodón en el XIX. *Siglo XIX: Cuadernos,* v. 3, no. 6 (June 93), pp. 23 – 33. Bibl.

Aharonián, Coriún. Conversación con César Portillo de la Luz: "Y porque pienso vivo cuando canto." *Casa de las Américas,* no. 190 (Jan – Mar 93), pp. 141 – 146.

— Músicos uruguayos en el exterior (Segunda parte). *Hoy Es Historia,* v. 10, no. 59 (Sept – Oct 93), pp. 44 – 55. Bibl.

— Valores notables de la cultura uruguaya: músicos uruguayos en el exterior (Primera parte). *Hoy Es Historia,* v. 10, no. 55 (Jan – Feb 93), pp. 45 – 47.

Ahmed, Masood and Lawrence Summers. Informe sobre la crisis de la deuda en su décimo aniversario. *Comercio Exterior,* v. 43, no. 1 (Jan 93), pp. 74 – 78. Tables.

Ahmeduzzaman, Mohammad and Jaipaul L. Roopnarine. Puerto Rican Fathers' Involvement with Their Preschool-Age Children. *Hispanic Journal of Behavioral Sciences,* v. 15, no. 1 (Feb 93), pp. 96 – 107. Bibl, tables.

Ahumada Pacheco, Jaime. Descentralización, desarrollo local y municipios en América Latina. *Revista Paraguaya de Sociología,* v. 29, no. 85 (Sept – Dec 92), pp. 73 – 94. Bibl.

Ahumada Peña, Haydée. Apropiación del espacio americano en *Epitalamio del Prieto Trinidad. Revista Chilena de Literatura,* no. 42 (Aug 93), pp. 7 – 11.

Aínsa Amigues, Fernando. Nuestro Sur: fragmentos para una nueva geografía. *Plural (Mexico),* v. 22, no. 260 (May 93), pp. 16 – 22.

— La provocación como antiutopía en Roberto Arlt. *Cuadernos Hispanoamericanos,* no. Special issue, 11 (July 93), pp. 15 – 22.

Aja, Eliseo. El Proyecto de Ley colombiano visto por un español. *Planeación y Desarrollo,* v. 24, no. 1 (Jan – Apr 93), pp. 191 – 197.

Ajara, Cesar et al. O estado do Tocantins: reinterpretação de um espaço de fronteira. *Revista Brasileira de Geografia,* v. 53, no. 4 (Oct – Dec 91), pp. 5 – 48. Bibl, maps.

Akers, John C. From Translation to Rewriting: Rolando Hinojosa's *The Valley. The Americas Review,* v. 21, no. 1 (Spring 93), pp. 91 – 102. Bibl.

Akyüz, Yilmaz. Intervención del estado y crecimiento económico. *Pensamiento Iberoamericano,* no. 22 – 23, tomo II (July 92 – June 93), pp. 251 – 253.

Alarcón, Francisco X. Poems ("Cutting Wood," "To Earthworms before Fishing with a Hook," "Chicome-Coatl/Seven Snake," "For Planting Camotes," "To Undo Sleep Spell"). *The Americas Review,* v. 19, no. 3 – 4 (Winter 91), pp. 34 – 38.

Alarcón, Jorge A. and Maarten Dirk Cornelis Immink. Household Income, Food Availability, and Commercial Crop Production by Smallholder Farmers in the Western Highlands of Guatemala. *Economic Development and Cultural Change,* v. 41, no. 2 (Jan 93), pp. 319 – 342. Bibl, tables.

Alarcón Olguín, Víctor and César Cancino. La relación gobierno – partido en un régimen semi-competitivo: el caso de México. *Revista Mexicana de Ciencias Políticas y Sociales,* v. 38, Nueva época, no. 151 (Jan – Mar 93), pp. 9 – 33. Bibl.

Alba, Richard D. and John R. Logan. Assimilation and Stratification in the Homeownership Patterns of Racial and Ethnic Groups. *International Migration Review,* v. 26, no. 4 (Winter 92), pp. 1314 – 1341. Bibl, tables.

Alba-Hernández, Francisco. El Tratado de Libre Comercio y la emigración de mexicanos a Estados Unidos. *Comercio Exterior,* v. 43, no. 8 (Aug 93), pp. 743 – 749. Bibl.

Albero Vergara, Danilo. Estación Borges. *Cuadernos Hispanoamericanos,* no. 512 (Feb 93), pp. 91 – 94. Il.

Alberti Manzanares, Pilar. Mujer Indígena y II Encuentro Continental 500 Años de Resistencia Indígena, Negra y Popular, Guatemala, 1991. *Anuario de Estudios Americanos,* v. 49, Suppl. 1 (1992), pp. 186 – 193.

Albó, Xavier. Bolivia: La Paz/Chukiyawu; las dos caras de una ciudad. *América Indígena,* v. 51, no. 4 (Oct – Dec 91), pp. 107 – 158. Bibl, tables, maps.

Albó, Xavier and Matías Preiswerk. El Gran Poder: fiesta del aimara urbano. *América Indígena,* v. 51, no. 2 – 3 (Apr – Sept 91), pp. 293 – 352. Bibl, tables, maps.

Albónico, Aldo. Un' opera in difesa degli indi nella Milano del seicento: il *Llanto sagrado de la América meridional. Quaderni Ibero-Americani,* no. 72 (Dec 92), pp. 695 – 708. Bibl.

Alcalá, Aída Esmirna. Reunión de Mujeres Escritoras del Sureste, Villahermosa, Tabasco, jueves 12 de noviembre, 1992: "La provincia, casa de muñecas;" represión y extorsión vs. el abierto decir. *Fem,* v. 17, no. 120 (Feb 93), pp. 8 – 9.

Alcántar Flores, Arturo. Beserío. *Plural (Mexico),* v. 22, no. 257 (Feb 93), pp. 50 – 51.

Alcántara Sáez, Manuel. ¿Democracias inciertas o democracias consolidadas en América Latina? *Revista Mexicana de Sociología,* v. 54, no. 1 (Jan – Mar 92), pp. 205 – 223.

Alcibíades, Mirla. Bibliografía selecta sobre *El Cojo Ilustrado. Revista Nacional de Cultura (Venezuela),* v. 53, no. 286 (July – Sept 92), pp. 175 – 176.

— De cómo una tabacalera devinó en revista cultural. *Revista Nacional de Cultura (Venezuela),* v. 53, no. 286 (July – Sept 92), pp. 167 – 174. Il.

Alcina Franch, José. Las *Obras completas* de Las Casas. *Cuadernos Hispanoamericanos,* no. 520 (Oct 93), pp. 93 – 97. Bibl, il.

— Los orígenes del estado inca. *Revista de Indias,* v. 53, no. 197 (Jan – Apr 93), pp. 9 – 22. Bibl, charts.

Alcocer, Jorge. La tercera refundación del PRI. *Revista Mexicana de Sociología,* v. 55, no. 2 (Apr – June 93), pp. 119 – 131. Bibl.

Alcorta, Rodrigo. Artesanos del pan de Navidad. *Todo Es Historia,* v. 26, no. 305 (Dec 92), pp. 50 – 53. Il.

— Arturo Acevedo, un hombre de acero. *Todo Es Historia,* v. 26, no. 307 (Feb 93), pp. 50 – 53. Il.

— Con títulos de Nobleza: hacia un siglo de historia. *Todo Es Historia,* v. 27, no. 313 (Aug 93), pp. 50 – 53. Il.

— Del arte de producir el buen mate y el buen té. *Todo Es Historia,* v. 26, no. 309 (Apr 93), pp. 50 – 53. Il.

— La empresa de editar buenos libros. *Todo Es Historia,* v. 27, no. 311 (June 93), pp. 50 – 53. Il.

— "El Henry Ford argentino": Torquato di Tella; de los Apeninos a los Andes. *Todo Es Historia,* v. 26, no. 310 (May 93), pp. 64 – 67. Il.

— Una historia de película. *Todo Es Historia,* v. 26, no. 306 (Jan 93), pp. 50 – 53. Il.

— Juan Alfonso Carriza y medio siglo del Instituto Nacional de Antropología. *Todo Es Historia,* v. 27, no. 312 (July 93), pp. 62 – 65. Il.

Aldereguía Henriques, Jorge. Cuba: orientación humanista de su desarrollo económico – social. *Problemas del Desarrollo,* v. 24, no. 94 (July – Sept 93), pp. 191 – 207. Tables, charts.

Aldereguía Henriques, Jorge and Jorge Núñez Jover. Aproximaciones al marco conceptual de la sanología. *Interciencia,* v. 18, no. 2 (Mar – Apr 93), pp. 71 – 76. Bibl.

Aldunate L., José. Un "Informe Rettig" para El Salvador. *Mensaje,* v. 42, no. 418 (May 93), pp. 153 – 154.

Alegría, Claribel. Poems ("La abuela," "La Malinche"). *Casa de las Américas,* no. 190 (Jan – Mar 93), pp. 122 – 124.

Alegría, Fernando. La novela chilena del exilio interior. *Revista Chilena de Literatura,* no. 42 (Aug 93), pp. 13 – 17.

Alexander, Abel. La magia del daguerrotipo. *Todo Es Historia,* v. 27, no. 311 (June 93), pp. 74 – 77. Il.

Alexander, Philip N. John H. Rapier, Jr. and the Medical Profession in Jamaica, 1861 – 1862 (Part I). *Jamaica Journal,* v. 24, no. 3 (Feb 93), pp. 37 – 46. Bibl, il.

— John H. Rapier, Jr. and the Medical Profession in Jamaica, 1861 – 1862 (Part II). *Jamaica Journal,* v. 25, no. 1 (Oct 93), pp. 55 – 62. Bibl, il, facs.

Alexis Fils, Gerald. Haitian Art in the Twentieth Century. *SALALM Papers,* v. 34 (1989), pp. 40 – 47.

Alfaro, Alfonso. Elogio de la opulencia, la distancia y el cordero (Accompanied by an English translation). *Artes de México,* no. 19 (Spring 93), pp. 31 – 38. Il.

Alfaro Desentis, Samuel and Javier Salas Martín del Campo. Evolución de la balanza comercial del sector privado en México: evaluación con un modelo econométrico. *El Trimestre Económico,* v. 59, no. 236 (Oct – Dec 92), pp. 773 – 797. Bibl, tables, charts.

Alfie Cohen, Miriam. Las transformaciones de la política gubernamental en materia ecológica. *El Cotidiano,* v. 8, no. 52 (Jan – Feb 93), pp. 51 – 56. Il, tables, charts.

Alfie Cohen, Miriam and Godofredo Vidal de la Rosa. Hacia los acuerdos paralelos: el medio ambiente. *El Cotidiano,* v. 9, no. 56 (July 93), pp. 104 – 111. Bibl, il, tables.

Alford, Annika E. K. The Automation of Money. *Business Mexico,* v. 3, no. 9 (Sept 93), pp. 24 – 27. Il.

Alizal, Laura del. España en 1992: su integración a Europa y sus relaciones con México. *Revista Mexicana de Ciencias Políticas y Sociales,* v. 37, Nueva época, no. 149 (July – Sept 92), pp. 109 – 122.

Allende, Jorge E. Presentación del libro *La investigación universitaria en Chile: reflexiones críticas* de Manuel Krauskopf. *Estudios Sociales (Chile),* no. 75 (Jan – Mar 93), pp. 231 – 238.

Alleyne, Michael H. Approaches to Technical Education and the Evolving Role of the OAS. *La Educación (USA),* v. 36, no. 111 – 113 (1992), pp. 167 – 175.

Almada, Sergio. Chihuahua Redefines Success. *Business Mexico,* v. 3, no. 12 (Dec 93), pp. 22 – 23. Tables.

Almanza, Iraida América. 20 años de festival internacional de cine en Panamá: un evento que no debió acabarse, 1963 – 1983. *Revista Cultural Lotería,* v. 50, no. 386 (Nov – Dec 91), pp. 70 – 88.

Almaráz, Félix D., Jr. Franciscan Evangelization in Spanish Frontier Texas: Apex of Social Contact, Conflict, and Confluence, 1751 – 1761. *Colonial Latin American Historical Review,* v. 2, no. 3 (Summer 93), pp. 253 – 287. Bibl, il, maps.

Almeida, Maria Hermínia Tavares de
See
    Tavares de Almeida, Maria Hermínia

Almeida, Martinho Isnard Ribeiro et al. ¿Por qué administrar estrategicamente recursos humanos? *RAE; Revista de Administração de Empresas,* v. 33, no. 2 (Mar – Apr 93), pp. 12 – 24. Bibl, tables.

Almeida, Roberto Schmidt de and Miguel Angelo Campos Ribeiro. Análise da organização espacial da indústria nordestina através de uma tipologia de centros industriais. *Revista Brasileira de Geografia,* v. 53, no. 2 (Apr – June 91), pp. 5 – 31. Bibl, tables, maps.

— Os pequenos e medios estabelecimentos industriais nordestinos: padrões de distribuição e fatores condicionantes. *Revista Brasileira de Geografia,* v. 53, no. 1 (Jan – Mar 91), pp. 5 – 49. Bibl, tables, maps.

Almeida, Sérgio Barbosa de. O potencial hidrelétrico brasileiro. *Revista Brasileira de Geografia,* v. 53, no. 3 (July – Sept 91), pp. 183 – 203. Bibl, il, maps.

Almeida, Stela Borges de and Luiz Felippe Perret Serpa. Guia de fontes fotográficas para a história da educação. *Revista Brasileira de Estudos Pedagógicos,* v. 72, no. 172 (Sept – Dec 91), pp. 392 – 394.

Almeida, Yajaida. Estudio preliminar sobre la variabilidad del nivel del mar en las costas de Venezuela. *Revista Geográfica (Mexico),* no. 115 (Jan – June 92), pp. 5 – 26. Tables, maps, charts.

Almeyda Medina, Clodomiro et al. 20 años después: ¿Qué aprendimos del golpe militar?; debates (Introduced by G. Arroyo). *Mensaje,* v. 42, no. 422 (Sept 93), pp. 440 – 447.

Almonacid, Ruben Dario. Os dois pilares. *Problemas Brasileiros,* v. 30, no. 296 (Mar – Apr 93), pp. 13 – 14.

Alonso, Claudio. La participación de las mujeres en el combate a la pobreza. *Fem,* v. 17, no. 120 (Feb 93), p. 44.

Alonso, María Ernestina. 1983 – 1993: el nuevo poder político. *Realidad Económica,* no. 120 (Nov – Dec 93), pp. 61 – 68.

Alonso, Paula. Politics and Elections in Buenos Aires, 1890 – 1898: The Performance of the Radical Party. *Journal of Latin American Studies,* v. 25, no. 3 (Oct 93), pp. 465 – 487. Bibl, tables, charts.

Alonso, Rodolfo. Música concreta. *Plural (Mexico),* v. 22, no. 264 (Sept 93), pp. 19 – 22.

— Tres poemas en prosa. *Revista Nacional de Cultura (Venezuela),* v. 54, no. 287 (Oct – Dec 92), pp. 145 – 147.

Alonso de Jesús, Francisco. 1630 Memorial of Fray Francisco Alonso de Jesús on Spanish Florida's Missions and Natives (Introduced and translated by John H. Hann). *The Americas,* v. 50, no. 1 (July 93), pp. 85 – 105.

Alonso Martínez, María Nieves and Mario Rodríguez. Poesía chilena y española: Lihn y Gil de Biedma. *Atenea (Chile),* no. 467 (1993), pp. 197 – 219. Bibl.

Alonso Yodú, Odette. Poesía joven de Cuba. *La Palabra y el Hombre,* no. 84 (Oct – Dec 92), pp. 5 – 19.

Alpízar Quirós, Jorge Mario. Cuentos. *Káñina,* v. 16, no. 1 (Jan – June 92), pp. 275 – 276.

Alsina Gutiérrez, Rogelio. Filosofía de la liberación en Brasil: aproximación inicial al tema. *Islas,* no. 99 (May – Aug 91), pp. 30 – 37.

Alsina Gutiérrez, Rogelio and Xiomara García Machado. Un nuevo estilo de filosofar: polémica con Mario Casalla desde la alteridad. *Islas,* no. 96 (May – Aug 90), pp. 111 – 120. Bibl.

Altamirano Rúa, Teófilo. Pastores quechuas en el oeste norteamericano. *América Indígena,* v. 51, no. 2 – 3 (Apr – Sept 91), pp. 203 – 222. Maps.

— Un permanente reto. *Debate (Peru),* v. 15, no. 70 (Sept – Oct 92), pp. 31 – 32.

Altamirano Rúa, Teófilo and Lane Ryo Hirabayashi. Culturas regionales en ciudades de América Latina: un marco conceptual. *América Indígena,* v. 51, no. 4 (Oct – Dec 91), pp. 17 – 48. Bibl, il.

Altamirano Toledo, Carlos. Lecciones de una guerra. *Cuadernos Hispanoamericanos,* no. 517 – 519 (July – Sept 93), pp. 586 – 590.

Althusser, Louis. Louis Althusser: ante la muerte de Ernesto Che Guevara. *Casa de las Américas,* no. 190 (Jan – Mar 93), pp. 59 – 64.

Alvar, Jaime. Problemas metodológicos sobre el préstamo religioso. *Boletín de Antropología Americana,* no. 24 (Dec 91), pp. 123 – 142. Bibl, il.

Alvar López, Manuel. Alfonso Reyes y España. *Nueva Revista de Filología Hispánica,* v. 40, no. 2 (July – Dec 92), pp. 959 – 987. Bibl.

Alvarado, Lisandro. Ensayo sobre el caribe venezolano (Previously published in this journal vol. 1, no. 1, 1912). *Boletín de la Academia Nacional de la Historia (Venezuela),* v. 75, no. 300 (Oct – Dec 92), pp. 295 – 319.

Alvarado Mendoza, Arturo and Nelson Minello. Política y elecciones en Tamaulipas: la relación entre lo local y lo nacional. *Estudios Sociológicos,* v. 10, no. 30 (Sept – Dec 92), pp. 619 – 647. Charts.

Alvarado Polanco, Romeo et al. Autonomía universitaria. *USAC,* no. 12 (Dec 90), pp. 49 – 59.

Alvarez, Carmen R. Los cargos políticos y su incidencia en la estabilidad de los proyectos públicos: los casos de Uruguay y Japón. *Cuadernos del CLAEH,* v. 18, no. 65 – 66 (May 93), pp. 61 – 74. Bibl.

Alvarez, Cecilia. Poems ("Compañías," "Dictadura," "Maldición," "Puro cuento," "Garra charrúa"). *Hispamérica,* v. 22, no. 64 – 65 (Apr – Aug 93), pp. 125 – 126.

Alvarez, Elizabeth. De brujas, lunas y aquelarres: VI Encuentro Feminista Latinoamericano y del Caribe. *Fem,* v. 17, no. 124 (June 93), pp. 33 – 34.

Alvarez, Luis. Discurso pronunciado por el profesor Luis Alvarez con motivo de la presentación del libro *San Sebastián de los Reyes y sus ilustres próceres* en la Escuela de Música de San Sebastián de los Reyes, el 20 de enero de 1993. *Boletín de la Academia Nacional de la Historia (Venezuela),* v. 76, no. 301 (Jan – Mar 93), pp. 51 – 54.

Alvarez, María Auxiliadora. ¿Qué hace Marguerite Yourcenar en la eternidad? (Introduced by María Auxiliadora Alvarez. Article entitled "Voces o seres cercanos"). *Inti,* no. 37 – 38 (Spring – Fall 93), pp. 75 – 78.

Alvarez Bejar, Alejandro and Gabriel Mendoza Pichardo. Mexico, 1988 – 1991: A Successful Economic Adjustment Program? (Translated by John F. Uggen). *Latin American Perspectives,* v. 20, no. 3 (Summer 93), pp. 32 – 45. Bibl.

Alvarez-Borland, Isabel. The Task of the Historian in *El general en su laberinto. Hispania (USA),* v. 76, no. 3 (Sept 93), pp. 439 – 445. Bibl.

Alvarez C., Edwin. Criminalidad y abuso de poder: el caso argentino, 1976 – 1983. *Revista Cultural Lotería,* v. 51, no. 388 (Mar – Apr 92), pp. 5 – 33. Bibl.

Alvarez Gándara, Miguel. Santo Domingo: doloroso avance de la iglesia latinoamericana. *Cristianismo y Sociedad,* v. 30, no. 114 (1992), pp. 25 – 39.

Alvarez Icaza, Pablo. Marco teórico de la industria maquiladora de exportación. *Comercio Exterior,* v. 43, no. 5 (May 93), pp. 415 – 429. Bibl.

Alvarez Padilla, Alfredo. La cultura empresarial en el nuevo orden económico internacional. *El Cotidiano,* v. 10, no. 58 (Oct – Nov 93), pp. 112 – 115.

Alvarez Rodrich, Augusto and Pilar Dávila. Entrevista a Carlos Boloña. *Debate (Peru),* v. 15, no. 70 (Sept – Oct 92), pp. 8 – 14. Il.

Alvarez Rodrich, Augusto et al. Entrevista a Dennis Vargas Marín. *Debate (Peru),* v. 16, no. 75 (Dec 93 – Jan 94), pp. 6 – 14. Il.

Alvarez Santiago, Héctor and María Teresa Rodríguez. Estrategias productivas entre los nahuas de Zongolica. *La Palabra y el Hombre,* no. 84 (Oct – Dec 92), pp. 127 – 144. Tables.

Alzate Montoya, Rubelia. Por un reencuentro latinoamericano. *Estudios Rurales Latinoamericanos,* v. 15, no. 2 – 3 (May – Dec 92), pp. 113 – 120.

Alzugarat, Alfredo J. *Cien años de soleded:* veinticinco años de diálogo con América Latina. *Cuadernos del CLAEH,* v. 17, no. 63 – 64 (Oct 92), pp. 175 – 181. Bibl.

Amadeo Swaelen, Edward Joaquim. Do Relative Wages Move Together with Relative Prices? *Revista Brasileira de Economia,* v. 47, no. 1 (Jan – Mar 93), pp. 33 – 52. Bibl, tables, charts.

— Restricciones institucionales a la política económica: negociación salarial y estabilización en el Brasil. *Desarrollo Económico (Argentina),* v. 33, no. 129 (Apr – June 93), pp. 29 – 47. Bibl, tables, charts.

Amadeo Swaelen, Edward Joaquim and Tariq Banuri. Mundos dentro del Tercer Mundo: instituciones del mercado de trabajo en Asia y en América Latina (Translated by Carlos Villegas). *El Trimestre Económico,* v. 59, no. 236 (Oct – Dec 92), pp. 657 – 723. Bibl, tables.

Amadeo Swaelen, Edward Joaquim and José Márcio Camargo. Liberalização comercial, distribuição e emprego. *Revista de Economia Política (Brazil),* v. 13, no. 4 (Oct – Dec 93), pp. 58 – 76. Bibl, tables.

— Política comercial e distribuição funcional da renda. *Pesquisa e Planejamento Econômico,* v. 22, no. 1 (Apr 92), pp. 73 – 100. Bibl, tables, charts.

Amadeo Swaelen, Edward Joaquim and Elena Landau. Indexação e dispersão de preços relativos: análise do caso brasileiro, 1975 – 1991. *Revista de Economia Política (Brazil),* v. 13, no. 3 (July – Sept 93), pp. 130 – 138. Bibl, charts.

Amado, Jorge. Sailing the Shore: Notes for Memoirs I'll Never Write (Translated by Alfred MacAdam). *Review,* no. 47 (Fall 93), pp. 32 – 38.

Amado Aguirre, José. La primera década divorcista argentina. *Todo Es Historia*, v. 27, no. 317 (Dec 93), pp. 42 – 44. Il.

Amador Debernardi, Rocío and Laura González Hernández. Características de las familias y de los niños trabajadores de la calle. *Revista de Ciencias Sociales (Costa Rica)*, no. 59 (Mar 93), pp. 19 – 26. Bibl, tables, charts.

Amaral, Aracy A. Tarsila: modernidade entre a racionalidade e o onírico. *Vozes*, v. 87, no. 4 (July – Aug 93), pp. 53 – 59. Il.

Amaral, Roberto and Antônio Houaiss. A via partidária dos socialistas brasileiros. *Vozes*, v. 87, no. 1 (Jan – Feb 93), pp. 2 – 13. Il.

Amat y León, Carlos. La competitividad del sector agrícola. *Apuntes (Peru)*, no. 30 (Jan – June 92), pp. 3 – 11.

Amate Blanco, Juan José. El realismo mágico en la expedición amazónica de Orellana. *Cuadernos Hispanoamericanos*, no. 510 (Dec 92), pp. 61 – 72. Bibl.

Ambert, Alba Nydia. The Old Language. *The Americas Review*, v. 21, no. 1 (Spring 93), pp. 13 – 29.

Amodio, Emanuele. El otro americano: construcción y difusión de la iconografía del indio americano en Europa en el primer siglo de la conquista (Translated by Francesco Russo). *Montalbán*, no. 24 (1992), pp. 33 – 84. Bibl, il, maps, facs.

Amor E., Mónica. Meyer Vaisman, explorador de significados (Accompanied by an English translation). *Art Nexus*, no. 7 (Jan – Mar 93), pp. 129 – 131. Il.

Amor y Vázquez, José. Máscaras mexicanas en la poesía de Cernuda y Moreno Villa: Quetzalcóatl y Xochipilli (Includes the poem "Quetzalcóatl"). *Nueva Revista de Filología Hispánica*, v. 40, no. 2 (July – Dec 92), pp. 1057 – 1072.

Amoretti Hurtado, María. El discurso político y el discurso religioso en el apocalipsis de la modernidad. *Káñina*, v. 16, no. 1 (Jan – June 92), pp. 111 – 116.

Anasagasti, Pedro de. La angustia de Juan Quirós. *Signo*, no. 36 – 37, Nueva época (May – Dec 92), pp. 221 – 226.

— La labor humanizadora de los franciscanos en Bolivia. *Signo*, no. 36 – 37, Nueva época (May – Dec 92), pp. 89 – 108. Bibl.

— El mariscal Andrés de Santa Cruz, gran pacificador. *Signo*, no. 38, Nueva época (Jan – Apr 93), pp. 95 – 104. Bibl.

— Seis sonetos y tres poemas. *Signo*, no. 35, Nueva época (Jan – Apr 92), pp. 139 – 150.

Anastasia, Luis Víctor. Colón en la historiografía uruguaya. *Revista de Historia de América*, no. 113 (Jan – June 92), pp. 21 – 64.

Anawalt, Patricia Rieff. Reply to Helen Perlstein Pollard (On her comment on the article "Ancient Cultural Contacts between Ecuador, West Mexico, and the American Southwest" by Patricia Anawalt which appeared in this journal in 1992). *Latin American Antiquity*, v. 4, no. 4 (Dec 93), pp. 386 – 387. Bibl.

Andean Common Market. Armonización de políticas macroeconómicas en el Grupo Andino. *Integración Latinoamericana*, v. 18, no. 192 (Aug 93), pp. 41 – 52.

Ander-Egg, Ezequiel et al. El porvenir de América Latina (Question – answer forum by Latin American intellectuals on Latin America's economic future). *Desarrollo Indoamericano*, v. 23, no. 91 (June 93), pp. 7 – 16.

Anderle, Adám and Monika Kozári. Koloman von Kánya: Ein österreichisch-ungarischer Botschafter in Mexiko. *Zeitschrift für Lateinamerika Wien*, no. 43 (1992), pp. 63 – 80. Bibl.

Anderson, Danny J. Retórica de la legitimidad: las exigencias de la crónica en las "novelas sin ficción" de Vicente Leñero. *La Palabra y el Hombre*, no. 84 (Oct – Dec 92), pp. 63 – 80. Bibl.

Anderson, L. Susan. The Nature of Good Business. *Business Mexico*, v. 3, no. 1 (Jan – Feb 93), p. 66. Il.

Anderson, Leslie Elin. Bendiciones mezcladas: disrupción y organización entre uniones campesinas en Costa Rica. *Revista de Historia (Costa Rica)*, no. 25 (Jan – June 92), pp. 97 – 143. Bibl.

— Surprises and Secrets: Lessons from the 1990 Nicaragua Election. *Studies in Comparative International Development*, v. 27, no. 3 (Fall 92), pp. 93 – 119. Bibl, tables.

Andrade, Carlos Drummond de. El amor natural (Translated by Víctor Sosa). *Vuelta*, v. 17, no. 198 (May 93), pp. 24 – 25.

Andrade de Labadía, Gabriela. Una aproximación al estudio de la biblioteca privada de Mario Góngora del Campo. *Historia (Chile)*, no. 26 (1991 – 1992), pp. 5 – 60. Bibl.

Andrade Jardí, Julián. El milenio de Gloria Trevi. *Nexos*, v. 16, no. 183 (Mar 93), pp. 66 – 68.

Andrade Rives, Santiago. La mentira de Cristóbal Colón. *La Palabra y el Hombre*, no. 81 (Jan – Mar 92), pp. 23 – 44. Bibl.

Andréa, José. O marechal Soares Andréa nos relevos da história do Brasil. *Revista do Instituto Histórico e Geográfico Brasileiro*, no. 373 (Oct – Dec 91), pp. 1071 – 1084.

Andreas, Peter. Profits, Poverty, and Illegality: The Logic of Drug Corruption. *NACLA Report on the Americas*, v. 27, no. 3 (Nov – Dec 93), pp. 22 – 28 +. Bibl.

Andreu, Alicia G. Habla la ciudad: poética de la migración. *Revista Chilena de Literatura*, no. 42 (Aug 93), pp. 19 – 24.

Andrews, George Reid. Desigualdad racial en Brasil y en Estados Unidos: un estudio estadístico comparado. *Desarrollo Económico (Argentina)*, v. 33, no. 130 (July – Sept 93), pp. 185 – 216. Bibl, tables, charts.

Andrews, Jean. Diffusion of Mesoamerican Food Complex to Southeastern Europe. *Geographical Review*, v. 83, no. 2 (Apr 93), pp. 194 – 204. Bibl, maps.

Andrist, Debra D. Nature Imagery in Sylvia Puentes de Oyenard's *Rosa exigida*. *Letras Femeninas*, v. 19, no. 1 – 2 (Spring – Fall 93), pp. 117 – 119. Bibl.

Andueza, María. San Juan de la Cruz en México visto por Alfonso Méndez Plancarte. *Cuadernos Americanos*, no. 37, Nueva época (Jan – Feb 93), pp. 165 – 179. Bibl.

Aneiva I., Gonzalo. Poems ("Guitarra triste," "Flauta extraviada"). *Signo*, no. 38, Nueva época (Jan – Apr 93), pp. 187 – 190.

Angeles Rodríguez, María de los
See
Rodríguez, María de los Angeles

Angell, Alan. The Left in Latin America since 1930: A Bibliographical Essay. *Historia (Chile)*, no. 26 (1991 – 1992), pp. 61 – 70. Bibl.

Anglade, Roberto. Tiempo de no morir. *Cuadernos Hispanoamericanos*, no. 517 – 519 (July – Sept 93), pp. 474 – 477.

Anguiano, Arturo. Transición política: ¿Hacia dónde? *El Cotidiano*, v. 8, no. 52 (Jan – Feb 93), pp. 3 – 9. Bibl, il.

Anguiano Téllez, María Eugenia. Irrigación y capital para transformar el desierto: la formación social del valle de Mexicali a principios del siglo XX. *Frontera Norte*, v. 4, no. 8 (July – Dec 92), pp. 125 – 147. Bibl.

— Migración y derechos humanos: el caso de los mixtecos. *Estudios Fronterizos*, no. 26 (Sept – Dec 91), pp. 55 – 69. Bibl.

Anguita, Eduardo. Huidobro y Neruda: final. *Atenea (Chile)*, no. 467 (1993), pp. 145 – 147.

— Poems. *Inti*, no. 36 (Fall 92), pp. 130 – 138.

Angulo, Alejandro. Prólogo para una ética social. *Revista Javeriana*, v. 61, no. 599 (Oct 93), pp. 366 – 370.

Angulo, Federico. Lapis philosophorum. *Revista Cultural Lotería*, v. 51, no. 390 (July – Aug 92), pp. 85 – 93.

Angulo Barturén, Carmelo. La conmemoración de los 500 años: una visión constructiva. *Signo*, no. 36 – 37, Nueva época (May – Dec 92), pp. 279 – 298.

Angulo Carrera, Alejandro and Salvador Rodríguez y Rodríguez. Agricultura orgánica, desarrollo sustentable y comercio justo. *Problemas del Desarrollo*, v. 24, no. 94 (July – Sept 93), pp. 265 – 274.

Angvik, Birger. La risa que se vuelve mueca: el doble filo del humor y de la risa: *Historia de Mayta* frente a la crítica en Lima. *Káñina*, v. 16, no. 1 (Jan – June 92), pp. 91 – 109. Bibl.

Anhalt, Nedda G. de. A la sombra de una sombrilla: cronología de *Cine: la gran seducción*, a la manera de la cronología de *Caín*. *La Palabra y el Hombre*, no. 81 (Jan – Mar 92), pp. 372 – 382. Il.

Anna, Timothy E. Demystifying Early Nineteenth-Century Mexico (Review article). *Mexican Studies*, v. 9, no. 1 (Winter 93), pp. 119 – 137.

Ansaldi, Waldo. América, la cuestión de la alteridad y la hipótesis de la culpabilidad del caballo. *Cuadernos del CLAEH*, v. 17, no. 63 – 64 (Oct 92), pp. 53 – 66. Bibl.

Ansión, Juan. Acerca de un irritante debate entre antropólogos del norte: comentarios al artículo de O. Starn. *Allpanchis*, v. 23, no. 39 (Jan – June 92), pp. 113 – 122.

Antezana Villegas, Mauricio. Epilogo y prefacio. *Estado y Sociedad*, v. 8, no. 9 (Jan – June 92), pp. 99 – 105.

— La espectacularización de la política y las autoformaciones culturales. *Estado y Sociedad*, v. 8, no. 9 (Jan – June 92), pp. 53 – 68.

Antía, Fernando. El MERCOSUR dos años después. *Cuadernos del CLAEH*, v. 18, no. 65 – 66 (May 93), pp. 101 – 110. Bibl, tables.

Antoniazzi, Maria Regina Filgueiras. Guia de fontes literárias para o estudo da história da educação na Bahia. *Revista Brasileira de Estudos Pedagógicos*, v. 72, no. 172 (Sept – Dec 91), pp. 388 – 391.

Antônio, Iratí and Claudia Negrão Balby. Computer Training in Brazilian Library Schools. *SALALM Papers*, v. 36 (1991), pp. 347 – 368. Bibl, tables.

Antunes Filho. Confesiones de un fingidor. *Conjunto*, no. 93 (Jan – June 93), pp. 38 – 43. Il.

Anwandter P., Jorge. Una empresa de trabajadores para la economía solidaria. *Mensaje*, v. 42, no. 423 (Oct 93), pp. 504 – 505. Il.

Anzaldúa, Gloria. Chicana Artists: Exploring "nepantla; el lugar de la frontera." *NACLA Report on the Americas*, v. 27, no. 1 (July – Aug 93), pp. 37 – 42 +. Bibl, il.

Aparicio, Frances R. Entre la guaracha y el bolero: un ciclo de intertextos musicales en la nueva narrativa puertorriqueña. *Revista Iberoamericana*, v. 59, no. 162 – 163 (Jan – June 93), pp. 73 – 89. Bibl.

Aponte, Bárbara Bockus et al. Tributes to Peter G. Earle (A collection of 24 tributes in English and Spanish honoring Peter G. Earle). *Hispanic Review*, v. 61, no. 2 (Spring 93), pp. 149 – 165.

Apter Cragnolino, Aída

See

Cragnolino, Aída Apter

Aragão, José Maria. El Arancel Externo Común del MERCOSUR: reflexiones a partir de aspectos parciales de la realidad brasileña. *Integración Latinoamericana*, v. 18, no. 187 – 188 (Mar – Apr 93), pp. 3 – 12.

Aramoni Calderón, Dolores. De diosas y mujeres. *Mesoamérica (USA)*, v. 13, no. 23 (June 92), pp. 85 – 94. Bibl.

Arana, Auxiliadora and Philip C. Kloin. An Interview with Wolf Ruvinskis: The First Mexican Stanley Kowalski. *Latin American Theatre Review*, v. 26, no. 2 (Spring 93), pp. 158 – 165. Il.

Aranda Romero, José Luis and Agustín Grajales Porras. Perfil sociodemográfico de Tehuacán durante el virreinato. *Estudios Demográficos y Urbanos*, v. 7, no. 1 (Jan – Apr 92), pp. 53 – 76. Bibl, tables, maps, charts.

Arango de Maglio, Aída. Descentralización y tiempo y espacio newtonianos: un análisis de la descentralización "real" en la Argentina. *Realidad Económica*, no. 119 (Oct – Nov 93), pp. 73 – 102. Bibl.

Arango Londoño, Gilberto. Carlos Sanz de Santamaría, un colombiano de múltiples virtudes. *Boletín de Historia y Antigüedades*, v. 80, no. 781 (Apr – June 93), pp. 283 – 284.

Arango Montoya, Marta. La niñez y la juventud en riesgo: el gran desafío para América Latina y el Caribe. *La Educación (USA)*, v. 36, no. 111 – 113 (1992), pp. 1 – 24. Bibl.

Arango R., Sol Beatriz. La industria textil colombiana. *Revista Javeriana*, v. 61, no. 593 (Apr 93), pp. 143 – 146. Tables.

Araújo, Arturo Gouveia de. Literatura em cadeia. *Vozes*, v. 86, no. 5 (Sept – Oct 92), pp. 37 – 57.

Araújo, Helena. Las huellas del "propio camino" en los relatos de Ana Vásquez. *Escritura (Venezuela)*, v. 16, no. 31 – 32 (Jan – Dec 91), pp. 9 – 16. Bibl.

Araújo, Maria Celina d' and Angela Maria de Castro Gomes. Entrevista com Arnaldo Sussekind. *Estudos Históricos*, v. 6, no. 11 (Jan – June 93), pp. 113 – 127.

Araújo, Maria Celina d' and Gláucio Ary Dillon Soares. A imprensa, os mitos e os votos nas eleições de 1990. *Revista Brasileira de Estudos Políticos*, no. 76 (Jan 93), pp. 163 – 189. Tables, charts.

Araújo, Maria José de Oliveira. Aborto legal no hospital do Jabaquara. *Estudos Feministas*, v. 1, no. 2 (1993), pp. 424 – 428.

Araújo, Nara. La Avellaneda, la Merlin: una manera de ver y sentir. *Iberoamericana*, v. 17, no. 49 (1993), pp. 33 – 41. Bibl.

— Raza y género en *Sab. Casa de las Américas*, no. 190 (Jan – Mar 93), pp. 42 – 49. Bibl.

Araújo Júnior, José Tavares de. Reestruturação industrial e integração econômica: as perspectivas do MERCOSUL. *Revista Brasileira de Economia*, v. 47, no. 1 (Jan – Mar 93), pp. 97 – 113. Bibl, tables.

— The Scope for Industrial Policy in a Free Trade Environment. *Revista de Economia Política (Brazil)*, v. 13, no. 3 (July – Sept 93), pp. 102 – 113. Bibl, tables.

Araya G., Juan Gabriel. Conversaciones con Gonzalo Rojas. *Atenea (Chile)*, no. 465 – 466 (1992), pp. 269 – 280. Bibl, il.

Araya Guillén, Victorio. 1492 – 1992: una reflexión desde el reverso de la historia; las víctimas. *Revista de Historia (Costa Rica)*, no. 25 (Jan – June 92), pp. 151 – 156.

Araya P., Marilu et al. ?Cómo votarán los católicos?: debates (Introduced by G. Arroyo). *Mensaje*, v. 42, no. 424 (Nov 93), pp. 569 – 576. Il.

Arbea G., Antonio. El fromato centonario en la *Restauración de la imperial* de Juan de Barrenechea y Albis. *Revista Chilena de Literatura*, no. 42 (Aug 93), pp. 31 – 39.

Arce, Eric. El compadre. *Revista Cultural Lotería*, v. 51, no. 387 (Feb 92), pp. 76 – 79.

Arce, Manuel José. Arbenz, el coronel de la primavera. *USAC*, no. 13 (Mar 91), pp. 83 – 120.

Arcifa, Marlene Sofia and Adriana Jorge Meschiatti. Distribution and Feeding Ecology of Fishes in a Brazilian Reservoir: Lake Monte Alegre. *Interciencia*, v. 18, no. 6 (Nov – Dec 93), pp. 302 – 313. Bibl, tables, charts.

Arciniegas, Germán. El que no fue presidente. *Boletín de Historia y Antigüedades*, v. 80, no. 781 (Apr – June 93), pp. 277 – 278.

— Los 500 años de América. *Boletín de Historia y Antigüedades*, v. 79, no. 779 (Oct – Dec 92), pp. 865 – 870.

— Señora muerte que se va llevando. *Boletín de Historia y Antigüedades*, v. 80, no. 781 (Apr – June 93), pp. 273 – 275.

Arcondo, Aníbal B. Mortalidad general, mortalidad epidémica y comportamiento de la población de Córdoba durante el siglo XVIII. *Desarrollo Económico (Argentina)*, v. 33, no. 129 (Apr – June 93), pp. 67 – 85. Bibl, tables, charts.

Ardao, Arturo. El historicismo y la filosofía americana. *Hoy Es Historia*, v. 10, no. 59 (Sept – Oct 93), pp. 81 – 86. Bibl, il.

Ardito Vega, Wilfredo. La estructura de las reducciones de Maynas. *Amazonía Peruana*, v. 11, no. 22 (Oct 92), pp. 93 – 124. Bibl.

Arellanes Jiménez, Paulino E. Crisis capitalista e inversiones extranjeras directas: las norteamericanas en México. *Revista Mexicana de Ciencias Políticas y Sociales*, v. 38, Nueva época, no. 153 (July – Sept 93), pp. 61 – 90. Bibl, tables.

Arellano, Homero. La libertad de las libertades. *Revista Nacional de Cultura (Venezuela)*, v. 53, no. 286 (July – Sept 92), pp. 19 – 28.

Arellano Cadena, Rogelio. Relación de largo plazo del mercado bursátil mexicano con el estadunidense: un análisis de cointegración. *El Trimestre Económico*, v. 60, no. 237 (Jan – Mar 93), pp. 91 – 112. Bibl, tables, charts.

Arenas, Braulio. Vicente Huidobro y el creacionismo (A chapter from Braulio Arenas' book *Escritos y escritores chilenos* reproduced as the prologue to *Obras completas de Vicente Huidobro*). *Atenea (Chile)*, no. 467 (1993), pp. 23 – 63. Bibl, il, facs.

Arenas, José. El retorno de los jesuitas en el siglo XIX: el no-restablecimiento de la Compañía de Jesús en Chile. *Mensaje*, v. 42, no. 420 (July 93), pp. 253 – 258. Il, facs.

Arenas, Patricia and Elvira Inés Baffi. José Imbelloni: una lectura crítica. *Runa*, v. 20 (1991 – 1992), pp. 167 – 176. Bibl.

Arenas Frutos, Isabel. Expediciones franciscanas a Indias, 1700 – 1725. *Archivo Ibero-Americano*, v. 52, no. 205 – 208 (Jan – Dec 92), pp. 157 – 185. Tables.

Arenas Frutos, Isabel and Carmen Cebrián González. Situación de la provincia del Perú a finales del siglo XVI: *La crónica anónima de 1600. Anuario de Estudios Americanos*, v. 49, Suppl. 2 (1992), pp. 11 – 29. Tables.

Ares Queija, Berta. Representaciones dramáticas de la conquista: el pasado al servicio del presente. *Revista de Indias*, v. 52, no. 195 – 196 (May – Dec 92), pp. 231 – 250. Bibl.

Arévalo P., Milcíades. Coral para César Vallejo. *Plural (Mexico)*, v. 22, no. 264 (Sept 93), pp. 88 – 92.

Argentino Paoletti, Mario

See

    Paoletti, Mario Argentino

Argudo R., Jaime et al. Metodología para la reducción de la vulnerabilidad sísmica de escuelas y bibliotecas en Guayaquil (noviembre 1992). *La Educación (USA)*, v. 37, no. 115 (1993), pp. 333 – 352. Bibl, il, tables, charts.

Arguedas Chaverri, María Eugenia. Eva Luna: algunas de sus posibilidades significativas. *Káñina*, v. 16, no. 2 (July – Dec 92), pp. 105 – 108. Bibl.

— Week-end en Guatemala. *Káñina*, v. 16, no. 1 (Jan – June 92), pp. 53 – 59. Bibl.

Argüelles, Juan Domingo. Agua bajo los puentes. *Plural (Mexico)*, v. 22, no. 261 (June 93), pp. 34 – 38.

Argueta, Manlio. An Exile's Return. *NACLA Report on the Americas*, v. 26, no. 5 (May 93), pp. 4 – 6. Il.

Arias Sánchez, Oscar. Las universidades y la mentalidad armamentista. *La Educación (USA)*, v. 36, no. 111 – 113 (1992), pp. 155 – 165.

Arilha, Margareth and Regina Maria Barbosa. A experiência brasileira com o Cytotec. *Estudos Feministas*, v. 1, no. 2 (1993), pp. 408 – 417. Tables, charts.

Arizcorreta Buchholz, Luis. Interview: Luis Pazos. *Business Mexico*, v. 3, no. 3 (Mar 93), pp. 30 – 31. Il.

Arizpe Schlosser, Lourdes. Los desafíos intelectuales en las ciencias sociales. *Momento Económico*, no. 69 (Sept – Oct 93), pp. 29 – 30.

Ariztía, Fernando. La Compañía de Jesús en la nueva evangelización. *Mensaje*, v. 42, no. 420 (July 93), p. 329.

Arjona, Marina and Fernando Rodríguez Guerra. Las oraciones objetivas en el habla popular de la ciudad de México. *Anuario de Letras (Mexico)*, v. 30 (1992), pp. 61 – 74. Tables.

Armando Rojas, Rafael

See

    Rojas Guardia, Armando

Armas Vásquez, Antonio. Aspectos pragmáticos en la sociología contemporánea latinoamericana. *Islas*, no. 98 (Jan – Apr 91), pp. 177 – 187. Bibl.

Armendáriz de Aghion, Beatriz. El precio de los bonos, las razones deuda – exportación y las moratorias en el servicio de la deuda exterior de un país: el caso de México. *El Trimestre Económico*, v. 60, no. 237 (Jan – Mar 93), pp. 185 – 202. Bibl, tables, charts.

Arnaiz Burne, Stella M. and Alfredo César Dachary. La frontera caribe de México en el XIX: una historia olvidada. *Siglo XIX: Cuadernos*, v. 3, no. 7 (Oct 93), pp. 33 – 62. Bibl, tables, maps.

Arnault, Daniel. El personaje del pie amputado en la cultura mochica de Perú: un ensayo sobre la arqueología del poder. *Latin American Antiquity*, v. 4, no. 3 (Sept 93), pp. 225 – 245. Bibl, il.

Arnold, Albert James. The Novelist as Critic. *World Literature Today*, v. 67, no. 4 (Fall 93), pp. 711 – 716. Il.

Arnold, Denise Y. At the Heart of the Woven Dance-Floor: The Wayñu in Qaqachaka. *Iberoamericana*, v. 16, no. 47 – 48 (1992), pp. 21 – 66. Bibl, il, tables.

Arnold, Philip J., III et al. Intensive Ceramic Production and Classic-Period Political Economy in the Sierra de los Tuxtlas, Veracruz, Mexico. *Ancient Mesoamerica*, v. 4, no. 2 (Fall 93), pp. 175 – 191. Bibl, il, tables, maps.

Arnstein, Gustavo. El Quijote querrequerre. *Boletín de la Academia Nacional de la Historia (Venezuela)*, v. 76, no. 301 (Jan – Mar 93), pp. 113 – 114.

Arocha Vargas, Arnaldo. Acto de presentación de los libros *José Antonio Páez y Cristóbal Rojas, un pintor venezolano*, pertenecientes a la Biblioteca de Autores y Temas Mirandinos. *Boletín de la Academia Nacional de la Historia (Venezuela)*, v. 75, no. 299 (July – Sept 92), pp. 5 – 8.

Aronson, Stacey L. Parker and Cristina Enríquez de Salamanca. La textura del exilio: *Querido Diego, te abraza Quiela; Eva Luna; Crónica de una muerte anunciada*. *Chasqui*, v. 22, no. 2 (Nov 93), pp. 3 – 14. Bibl.

Arráiz Lucca, Rafael. Dos poemas. *Revista Nacional de Cultura (Venezuela)*, v. 54, no. 287 (Oct – Dec 92), pp. 140 – 141.

Arredondo, Arturo. La labor de *Scherezada* de Nedda G. de Anhalt. *La Palabra y el Hombre*, no. 81 (Jan – Mar 92), pp. 368 – 369.

Arriaga, Eduardo E. Comparación de la mortalidad en las Américas. *Estudios Demográficos y Urbanos*, v. 7, no. 2 – 3 (May – Dec 92), pp. 407 – 449. Tables, charts.

Arriaga de Lassel, Adriana. El viaje hacia América: la figura del inmigrante en algunos textos literarios. *Cuadernos Hispanoamericanos*, no. 513 (Mar 93), pp. 93 – 100. Bibl.

Arriagada, Eduardo. La política a la manera de Ignacio de Loyola. *Mensaje*, v. 42, no. 420 (July 93), pp. 317 – 321. Il.

Arrieta, María Stella. La conquista española cuestionada. *Hoy Es Historia*, v. 10, no. 57 (Apr – May 93), pp. 22 – 32. Bibl.

Arrieta Fernández, Pedro. Desarrollo social planificado en La Chontalpa, Tabasco. *La Palabra y el Hombre*, no. 81 (Jan – Mar 92), pp. 159 – 175.

— Identidades y culturas: su evolución y persistencia. *La Palabra y el Hombre*, no. 82 (Apr – June 92), pp. 163 – 179. Bibl.

Arriola Palomares, Joaquín and David Amílcar Mena. La transición: los proyectos en disputa. *ECA; Estudios Centroamericanos*, v. 48, no. 536 (June 93), pp. 527 – 544. Bibl, il, tables.

Arrivillaga Cortés, Alfonso. Marimbas, bandas y conjuntos orquestales de Petén. *La Tradición Popular*, no. 82 (1991), Issue. Bibl, il.

Arrom, Silvia Marina. Historia de la mujer y de la familia latinoamericanas. *Historia Mexicana*, v. 42, no. 2 (Oct – Dec 92), pp. 379 – 418.

Arroyo, Gonzalo. ?Es posible ser solidarios en un mundo competitivo? *Mensaje*, v. 42, no. 421 (Aug 93), pp. 368 – 373. Il.

— Fundación Rodelillo: profesionales se sensibilizan en la ayuda de familias de sectores populares. *Mensaje*, v. 42, no. 421 (Aug 93), pp. 387 – 388. Il.

— La justicia como camino para vivir la fe. *Mensaje*, v. 42, no. 420 (July 93), pp. 190 – 195. Il.

Arroyo, Gonzalo and Joaquín Silva Soler. Mesa redonda: educando para la solidaridad. *Mensaje*, v. 42, no. 421 (Aug 93), pp. 392 – 401. Il.

Arroyo, Rane. Poems (" . . . Angel . . . ," "Caribe Poems"). *The Americas Review*, v. 20, no. 2 (Summer 92), pp. 64 – 68.

— Poems ("Blonde as a Bat," "Columbus's Children"). *The Americas Review*, v. 20, no. 3 – 4 (Fall – Winter 92), pp. 248 – 252.

Arroyo Alejandre, Jesús and Stephen D. Morris. The Electoral Recovery of the PRI in Guadalajara, Mexico, 1988 – 1992. *Bulletin of Latin American Research*, v. 12, no. 1 (Jan 93), pp. 91 – 102. Bibl, tables.

Arroyo Alejandre, Jesús and Luis A. Velázquez Gutiérrez. La transición de los patrones migratorios y las ciudades medias. *Estudios Demográficos y Urbanos*, v. 7, no. 2 – 3 (May – Dec 92), pp. 555 – 574. Bibl, tables.

Arroyo Alvarez, Eduardo. Don Simón Rodríguez, el maestro. *Revista Nacional de Cultura (Venezuela)*, v. 53, no. 286 (July – Sept 92), pp. 142 – 147. Il.

Arroyo Pichardo, Graciela. Factores históricos y fuerzas mundiales en la interacción entre sistemas regionales: América Latina y Europa del Este. *Relaciones Internacionales (Mexico)*, v. 14, Nueva época, no. 56 (Oct – Dec 92), pp. 19 – 29. Bibl.

Arruda, Maria Cecília Coutinho de. A ética no "marketing" das indústrias de bens de consumo no Brasil. *RAE; Revista de Administração de Empresas*, v. 33, no. 1 (Jan – Feb 93), pp. 16 – 28. Bibl, tables, charts.

Arteaga, Agustín. Terra incognita. *Artes de México*, no. 18 (Winter 92), pp. 98 – 100.

Arteaga Llona, José. Marta Alvarez: "Estar cerca de Dios, estar cerca de los hombres." *Mensaje*, v. 42, no. 421 (Aug 93), pp. 359 – 360. Il.

Artiles, Freddy. Títeres en México. *Conjunto*, no. 89 (Oct – Dec 91), pp. 88 – 93. Il.

Arze, José Roberto. De Nebrija a Alonso: cinco siglos de gramática castellana. *Signo*, no. 36 – 37, Nueva época (May – Dec 92), pp. 443 – 452.

— *Signo* en el contexto de las revistas literarias de Bolivia. *Signo*, no. 36 – 37, Nueva época (May – Dec 93), pp. 11 – 14.

Ascarrunz, Eduardo. Ideología política y comunicación social en el proceso histórico de la colonia a la independencia. *Signo*, no. 35, Nueva época (Jan – Apr 92), pp. 59 – 76. Bibl.

Asdrúbal Silva, Hernán and Marcela V. Tejerina. De las Georgias del Sur a Cantón: los norteamericanos en la explotación y tráfico de pieles a fines del siglo XVIII y principios del siglos XIX. *Investigaciones y Ensayos*, no. 41 (Jan – Dec 91), pp. 315 – 327. Bibl.

Ashdown, Peter D. Alan Burns and Sidney Turton: Two Views of the Public Good. *Belizean Studies*, v. 21, no. 1 (May 93), pp. 21 – 24. Bibl.

Ashmore, Wendy. The Theme "Is" Variation: Recent Publications on the Archaeology of Southern Mesoamerica (Review article). *Latin American Research Review*, v. 28, no. 1 (1993), pp. 128 – 140. Bibl.

Asiaín, Aurelio. Jorge Hernández Campos. *Vuelta*, v. 17, no. 204 (Nov 93), pp. 58 – 59.

— El rumor. *Vuelta*, v. 17, no. 203 (Oct 93), p. 28.

Asís, Enrique and James N. Green. Gays and Lesbians: The Closet Door Swings Open. *Report on the Americas,* v. 26, no. 4 (Feb 93), pp. 4 – 7. Il.

Aspe Armella, Pedro and Gabriel Zaid. De la esquina. *Vuelta,* v. 17, no. 197 (Apr 93), pp. 82 – 84.

Aspell de Yanzi Ferreira, Marcela. La regulación jurídica de las formas del trabajo forzado (Segunda parte). *Investigaciones y Ensayos,* no. 41 (Jan – Dec 91), pp. 349 – 394. Bibl.

Assunção, Luiz Márcio and Ian Livingstone. Desenvolvimento inadequado: construção de açudes e secas no sertão do Nordeste. *Revista Brasileira de Economia,* v. 47, no. 3 (July – Sept 93), pp. 425 – 448. Bibl, tables, charts.

Astorga, Luz María. Rasgos humanos de un gran poeta. *Atenea (Chile),* no. 467 (1993), pp. 81 – 96. Il, facs.

Astudillo Moya, Marcela. La política fiscal en el IV Informe de Gobierno. *Momento Económico,* no. 65 (Jan – Feb 93), pp. 16 – 19. Tables.

Astudillo Moya, Marcela and Alejandro Méndez Rodríguez. Planes urbanos sin descentralización financiera en México. *Problemas del Desarrollo,* v. 24, no. 93 (Apr – June 93), pp. 153 – 174. Bibl, tables, charts.

Atria Benaprés, Raúl. Contribuciones para una discusión sobre la ruta de cambio de la sociedad chilena. *Estudios Sociales (Chile),* no. 75 (Jan – Mar 93), pp. 155 – 182.

— La educación superior desde el mundo de la vida. *Estudios Sociales (Chile),* no. 78 (Oct – Dec 93), pp. 159 – 177. Bibl.

Augras, Monique. A ordem na desordem: a regulamentação do desfile das escolas de samba e a exigência de "motivos nacionais." *Revista Brasileira de Ciências Sociais,* v. 8, no. 21 (Feb 93), pp. 90 – 103. Bibl.

Aura Palacios, María Elena. Los pasos lentos: drama en un acto. *Plural (Mexico),* v. 22, no. 259 (Apr 93), pp. 26 – 39.

Auty, Richard M. Intensified Dependence on a Maturing Mining Sector: The Jamaican Bauxite Levy. *Caribbean Geography,* v. 3, no. 3 (Mar 92), pp. 143 – 159. Bibl, tables.

Avancini, Marta. Na era do ouro das cantoras do rádio. *Luso-Brazilian Review,* v. 30, no. 1 (Summer 93), pp. 85 – 93. Bibl.

Avaria, Antonio. Nunca en punto muerto: la novela chilena. *Mensaje,* v. 42, no. 425 (Dec 93), pp. 654 – 655.

Averbach, Márgara. Festival "Mujer y Cine": entrevista con Anamaría Muchnik. *Feminaria,* v. 6, no. 11 (Nov 93), pp. 23 – 24.

Avila, Maria Betânia. Modernidade e cidadania reprodutiva. *Estudos Feministas,* v. 1, no. 2 (1993), pp. 382 – 393.

Avila, Raúl. La lengua española en América cinco siglos después. *Estudios Sociológicos,* v. 10, no. 30 (Sept – Dec 92), pp. 677 – 692. Bibl.

— Ortografía española: estratificación social y alternativas. *Nueva Revista de Filología Hispánica,* v. 40, no. 2 (July – Dec 92), pp. 649 – 672. Bibl, tables, charts.

Avila, Silvia Mercedes. Poems ("Piedra y ceniza," "Sol inútil," "Magoa"). *Signo,* no. 35, Nueva época (Jan – Apr 92), pp. 159 – 161.

Avilés Fabila, René. Réquiem por un suicida (Chapter from the novel of the same title). *Plural (Mexico),* v. 22, no. 261 (June 93), pp. 41 – 44.

Avritzer, Leonardo and Alberto Olvera. El concepto de sociedad civil en el estudio de la transición democrática. *Revista Mexicana de Sociología,* v. 54, no. 4 (Oct – Dec 92), pp. 227 – 248. Bibl.

Axer, Jersy. Una carta: correspondencia de Hernán Cortés con Jan Dantyszek (Includes the reproduction of one letter by Hernando Cortez). *Plural (Mexico),* v. 22, no. 266 (Nov 93), pp. 68 – 72. Bibl.

Ayala, Francisco J. and Rosaura Ruiz Gutiérrez. Darwinismo y sociedad en México. *Siglo XIX: Revista,* no. 12, 2a época (July – Dec 92), pp. 87 – 104. Bibl.

Ayala, Maries. Navegante. *Letras Femeninas,* v. 19, no. 1 – 2 (Spring – Fall 93), p. 177.

Ayala Diago, César Augusto. El Movimiento de Acción Nacional (MAN): movilización y confluencia de idearios políticos durante el gobierno de Gustavo Rojas Pinilla. *Anuario Colombiano de Historia Social y de la Cultura,* no. 20 (1992), pp. 44 – 70. Bibl.

Ayala F., Maricela and Linda Schele. De poesía e historia: el tablero de los glifos de Palenque. *Vuelta,* v. 17, no. 203 (Oct 93), pp. 25 – 27. Charts.

Ayre, Shirley. Bobbing for Apples. *Business Mexico,* v. 3, no. 9 (Sept 93), pp. 12 – 15. Il.

— A Rosier Image for the Zona Rosa. *Business Mexico,* v. 3, no. 10 (Oct 93), pp. 4 – 7. Il.

Azambuja, Marcos Castrioto de. O após-guerra no Golfo Pérsico: as lições de guerra e a construção da paz. *Revista do Instituto Histórico e Geográfico Brasileiro,* no. 371 (Apr – June 91), pp. 492 – 508.

Azcueta, Michel et al. ¿Por qué vivir en el Perú de hoy? (Testimonies of various people on why, in light of the present crisis, they choose to live in Peru). *Debate (Peru),* v. 15, no. 70 (Sept – Oct 92), pp. 29 – 34. Il.

Azparrén Giménez, Leonardo. El teatro en Venezuela: una historia para ser construida. *Revista Nacional de Cultura (Venezuela),* v. 53, no. 285 (Apr – June 92), pp. 179 – 198.

Azuela, Alicia. La presencia de Diego Rivera en los Estados Unidos: dos versiones de la historia. *Anales del Instituto de Investigaciones Estéticas,* v. 16, no. 62 (1991), pp. 175 – 180.

Azuela Herrera, Marina. Vértigo amoroso. *Plural (Mexico),* v. 22, no. 267 (Dec 93), pp. 56 – 57.

Azzoni, Carlos Roberto and João Yo Isai. Custo da proteção de áreas com interesse ambiental no estado de São Paulo. *Estudos Econômicos,* v. 22, no. 2 (May – Aug 92), pp. 253 – 271. Bibl, tables, charts.

Babini, Pablo. Los italianos en las letras argentinas. *Todo Es Historia,* v. 26, no. 305 (Dec 92), pp. 66 – 69. Bibl, il.

Baca, Jimmy-Santiago. Martín III. *The Americas Review,* v. 20, no. 3 – 4 (Fall – Winter 92), pp. 189 – 193.

Bacchi, Mirian Rumenos Piedade and Geraldo Sant'ana de Camargo Barros. Demanda de carne bovina no mercado brasileiro. *Revista de Economia e Sociologia Rural,* v. 30, no. 1 (Jan – Mar 92), pp. 83 – 96. Bibl, tables.

Baccino Ponce de León, Napoleón. Artigas: ¿Mi nombre suena todavía? *Casa de las Américas,* no. 190 (Jan – Mar 93), pp. 125 – 133.

Bach, Caleb. Chiseler of Timeless Forms. *Américas,* v. 45, no. 4 (July – Aug 93), pp. 26 – 33. Il.

— The Inventions of Adolfo Bioy Casares (Photographs by Lisl Steiner). *Américas,* v. 45, no. 6 (Nov – Dec 93), pp. 14 – 19. Il.

— Making Bricks Soar (Photographs by Oscar Bonilla). *Américas,* v. 45, no. 2 (Mar – Apr 93), pp. 38 – 45. Il.

— Where Sound Is Born (Photographs by Giancarlo Puppo). *Américas,* v. 45, no. 1 (Jan – Feb 93), pp. 24 – 29. Il.

Bacha, Carlos José Caetano. Alguns aspectos dos modelos de análise dos impactos de mudança tecnológica no comportamento do setor agrícola. *Revista de Economia e Sociologia Rural,* v. 30, no. 1 (Jan – Mar 92), pp. 41 – 62. Bibl, charts.

— As unidades de conservação do Brasil. *Revista de Economia e Sociologia Rural,* v. 30, no. 4 (Oct – Dec 92), pp. 339 – 358. Bibl, tables.

Badano G., Alondra. La poesía de Jorge Guillén. *Revista Cultural Lotería,* v. 50, no. 386 (Nov – Dec 91), pp. 89 – 93.

Badilla, Beatriz B. et al. Consumo de sustancias sicotrópicas en los estudiantes de la Facultad de Farmacia de la Universidad de Costa Rica. *Revista de Ciencias Sociales (Costa Rica),* no. 60 (June 93), pp. 63 – 72. Bibl, tables, charts.

Badilla, Crisanto. Suceso de fin de semana. *Káñina,* v. 16, no. 2 (July – Dec 92), p. 219.

— La xilografía (Examples by the author and his students illustrate the issue). *Káñina,* v. 16, no. 1 (Jan – June 92), pp. 221 – 223.

Baena Paz, Guillermina. Perspectivas de la comunicación en los noventa. *Revista Mexicana de Ciencias Políticas y Sociales,* v. 38, Nueva época, no. 154 (Oct – Dec 93), pp. 103 – 114.

Baer, James. Tenant Mobilization and the 1907 Rent Strike in Buenos Aires. *The Americas,* v. 49, no. 3 (Jan 93), pp. 343 – 368. Bibl, tables, maps.

Baer, Werner and Melissa H. Birch. La privatización y el rol cambiante del estado en América Latina. *Revista Paraguaya de Sociología,* v. 29, no. 85 (Sept – Dec 92), pp. 7 – 28. Bibl.

Báez, René. La quimera de la modernización. *Desarrollo Indoamericano,* v. 23, no. 91 (June 93), pp. 33 – 35. Il.

Báez Báez, Edith María. Versiones de la realidad en "Las babas del diablo" de Cortázar. *Hispanic Journal,* v. 14, no. 1 (Spring 93), pp. 47 – 61. Bibl.

Báez-Jorge, Félix. La afición arqueológica de Alejo Carpentier. *Plural (Mexico),* v. 22, no. 262 (July 93), pp. 46 – 50.

— Ignacio Bernal (1910 – 1992). *La Palabra y el Hombre,* no. 81 (Jan – Mar 92), pp. 258 – 259. Il.

— Mitla y el barroco: notas sobre la afición arqueológica de Alejo Carpentier. *La Palabra y el Hombre,* no. 82 (Apr – June 92), pp. 57 – 73. Il.

Baeza, Cristina. Mauricio Rosencof: "Ni me bajo de este barco, ni cambio de capitán." *Casa de las Américas,* no. 191 (Apr – June 93), pp. 124 – 131.

Baffi, Elvira Inés and Patricia Arenas. José Imbelloni: una lectura crítica. *Runa,* v. 20 (1991 – 1992), pp. 167 – 176. Bibl.

Bailey, Norman A. The No-NAFTA Scenario. *Business Mexico,* v. 3, no. 10 (Oct 93), pp. 29 – 32. Tables, charts.

Bain, Jennifer H. Mexican Rural Women's Knowledge of the Environment. *Mexican Studies,* v. 9, no. 2 (Summer 93), pp. 259 – 274. Bibl.

Baird, Traci L. Mexican Adolescent Sexuality: Attitudes, Knowledge, and Sources of Information. *Hispanic Journal of Behavioral Sciences,* v. 15, no. 3 (Aug 93), pp. 402 – 417. Bibl, tables.

Baker, George. Does Modernization at PEMEX Meet Consumer Needs? *Business Mexico,* v. 3, no. 5 (May 93), pp. 4 – 7 +. Il, tables.

— Know Your Vowels. *Business Mexico,* v. 3, no. 8 (Aug 93), pp. 20 – 22. Il.

Baker, George and Bart Van Aardenne. CNG: A Fuel for the Future. *Business Mexico,* v. 3, no. 1 (Jan – Feb 93), pp. 48 – 50.

Baker, Susan Gonzalez and Jacqueline Maria Hagan. Implementing the U.S. Legalization Program: The Influence of Immigrant Communities and Local Agencies on Immigration Policy Reform. *International Migration Review,* v. 27, no. 3 (Fall 93), pp. 513 – 536. Bibl.

Balán, Jorge. La proyección cultural del psicoanálisis argentino. *Cuadernos Hispanoamericanos,* no. 517 – 519 (July – Sept 93), pp. 105 – 119. Bibl.

Balbi, Carmen Rosa. Miseria del sindicalismo. *Debate (Peru),* v. 15, no. 71 (Nov 92 – Jan 93), pp. 37 – 39. Il.

Balby, Claudia Negrão. Bibliographic Control of Art Materials: The Experience of the Universidade de São Paulo. *SALALM Papers,* v. 34 (1989), pp. 401 – 413. Bibl.

Balby, Claudia Negrão and Iratí Antônio. Computer Training in Brazilian Library Schools. *SALALM Papers,* v. 36 (1991), pp. 347 – 368. Bibl, tables.

Balção, Nilde and Maria Berenice Godinho Delgado. Mujer y trabajo. *Nueva Sociedad,* no. 124 (Mar – Apr 93), pp. 60 – 71.

Baldeón Larrea, Eduardo. CEBs: vivir y luchar en común. *El Cotidiano,* v. 10, no. 57 (Aug – Sept 93), pp. 11 – 16. Il, tables.

Balderston, Daniel. Abel Posse y *Los demonios secretos:* ¿Otra vez el nazismo? *Nuevo Texto Crítico,* v. 6, no. 11 (1993), pp. 254 – 258. Bibl.

Baldinelli, Elvio. Políticas monetarias y fiscales en la integración regional. *Integración Latinoamericana,* v. 18, no. 189 – 190 (May – June 93), pp. 28 – 37. Bibl, tables.

— La protección contra el comercio desleal. *Integración Latinoamericana,* v. 17, no. 184 (Nov 92), pp. 26 – 35.

Ballester, Horacio P. Proyecciones geopolíticas hacia el tercer milenio: el dramático futuro latinoamericano caribeño (A chapter from Horacio P. Ballester's book of the same title, introduced by Fermín Chávez). *Realidad Económica,* no. 116 (May – June 93), pp. 137 – 141.

Ballesteros, Carlos. El concepto de seguridad ambiental y la integración del mercado norteamericano. *Relaciones Internacionales (Mexico),* v. 15, Nueva época, no. 58 (Apr – June 93), pp. 63 – 68.

— La política ambiental en América Latina después de la cumbre de Río. *Relaciones Internacionales (Mexico),* v. 14, Nueva época, no. 56 (Oct – Dec 92), pp. 103 – 106.

— El problema de la legitimidad democrática ante las transformaciones políticas. *Revista Mexicana de Ciencias Políticas y Sociales,* v. 38, Nueva época, no. 151 (Jan – Mar 93), pp. 103 – 116.

Ballesteros Gaibrois, Manuel. Ignacio Bernal: in memoriam. *Revista Española de Antropología Americana,* v. 23 (1993), pp. 242 – 243.

Balsas, Héctor. Una lengua favorable. *Cuadernos del CLAEH,* v. 17, no. 63 – 64 (Oct 92), pp. 131 – 135.

Balta Varillas, José. Derecho del trabajo y economía de mercado: ¿Términos compatibles? *Apuntes (Peru),* no. 29 (July – Dec 91), pp. 57 – 66.

Baltazar Muñoz, Silverio

See

Muñoz, Silverio Baltazar

Balza, José. El delta del relato: confesiones en Brown University. *Inti,* no. 37 – 38 (Spring – Fall 93), pp. 17 – 21.

Banck, Geert A. Cultura política brasileira: que tradição é esta? *Revista Brasileira de Estudos Políticos*, no. 76 (Jan 93), pp. 41 – 53. Bibl.

Banco de México. Evolución de la economía mexicana en 1992. *Comercio Exterior*, v. 43, no. 6 (June 93), pp. 585 – 593. Tables.

Bandieri, Susana O. Historia y planificación regional: un encuentro posible. *Revista Interamericana de Planificación*, v. 26, no. 101 – 102 (Jan – June 93), pp. 78 – 94. Bibl.

Bankay, Anne-Maria. Contemporary Women Poets of the Dominican Republic: Perspectives on Race and Other Social Issues. *Afro-Hispanic Review*, v. 12, no. 1 (Spring 93), pp. 34 – 41. Bibl.

Baños, Genoveva. La feminista. *Fem*, v. 17, no. 124 (June 93), pp. 45 – 46.

Baños Ramírez, Othón. Reconfiguración rural – urbana en la zona henequenera de Yucatán. *Estudios Sociológicos*, v. 11, no. 32 (May – Aug 93), pp. 419 – 443. Tables, maps.

Banuri, Tariq and Edward Joaquim Amadeo Swaelen. Mundos dentro del Tercer Mundo: instituciones del mercado de trabajo en Asia y en América Latina (Translated by Carlos Villegas). *El Trimestre Económico*, v. 59, no. 236 (Oct – Dec 92), pp. 657 – 723. Bibl, tables.

Baptista Gumucio, Fernando. Orígenes del pensamiento político hispanoamericano. *Signo*, no. 36 – 37, Nueva época (May – Dec 92), pp. 325 – 329.

Baptista Gumucio, Mariano. Una presencia insoslayable y otros derechos de los latinoamericanos. *Signo*, no. 38, Nueva época (Jan – Apr 93), pp. 91 – 93.

Baquerizo, Manuel J. La transición de la visión india a la visión mestiza en la poesía quechua oral. *Revista de Crítica Literaria Latinoamericana*, v. 19, no. 37 (Jan – June 93), pp. 117 – 124. Bibl.

Barata, Mário. 50 anos de museologia, I: Um fragmento pessoal. *Revista do Instituto Histórico e Geográfico Brasileiro*, no. 371 (Apr – June 91), pp. 554 – 561.

— Manuel Barata, republicano histórico. *Revista do Instituto Histórico e Geográfico Brasileiro*, no. 373 (Oct – Dec 91), pp. 1008 – 1021.

Barba, Fernando Enrique. El río Santa Ana. *Investigaciones y Ensayos*, no. 41 (Jan – Dec 91), pp. 261 – 268. Bibl.

Barberena Blásquez, Elsa. Investigación sobre arte latinoamericano: acceso a través de material publicado. *SALALM Papers*, v. 34 (1989), pp. 345 – 362. Bibl.

Barbieri, José Carlos and Walter Delazaro. Nova regulamentação da transferência de tecnologia no Brasil. *RAE; Revista de Administração de Empresas*, v. 33, no. 3 (May – June 93), pp. 6 – 19. Bibl, tables.

Barbieri, Teresita de. Mujeres y varones entre la libertad y la igualdad. *Fem*, v. 17, no. 129 (Nov 93), pp. 4 – 9. Bibl.

Barbosa, Fabio. Los retos del sindicalismo petrolero. *El Cotidiano*, v. 9, no. 56 (July 93), pp. 33 – 39. Il.

Barbosa, Fernando de Holanda. Hiperinflação e estabilização. *Revista de Economia Política (Brazil)*, v. 13, no. 4 (Oct – Dec 93), pp. 5 – 15. Bibl, charts.

— A indexação dos ativos financeiros: a experiência brasileira. *Revista Brasileira de Economia*, v. 47, no. 3 (July – Sept 93), pp. 373 – 397. Bibl, tables, charts.

Barbosa, Fernando de Holanda et al. A dinâmica da hiperinflação. *Revista de Economia Política (Brazil)*, v. 13, no. 1 (Jan – Mar 93), pp. 5 – 24. Bibl, tables, charts.

Barbosa, Ignez Costa

See

Ferreira, Ignez Costa Barbosa

Barbosa, Margareth L. and Rosa M. O. Fontes. Efeitos da integração econômica do MERCOSUL e da Europa na competitividade das exportações brasileiras de soja. *Revista de Economia e Sociologia Rural*, v. 29, no. 4 (Oct – Dec 91), pp. 335 – 351. Bibl, tables.

Barbosa, Maria José Somerlate. Nivelamento em *Morte e vida severina*. *Hispania (USA)*, v. 76, no. 1 (Mar 93), pp. 30 – 37. Bibl.

Barbosa, Regina Helena Simões. AIDS, gênero e reprodução. *Estudos Feministas*, v. 1, no. 2 (1993), pp. 418 – 423. Bibl.

Barbosa, Regina Maria and Margareth Arilha. A experiência brasileira com o Cytotec. *Estudos Feministas*, v. 1, no. 2 (1993), pp. 408 – 417. Tables, charts.

Barbosa, Rubens Antonio. Liberalização do comércio, integração regional e Mercado Comum do Sul: o papel do Brasil. *Revista de Economia Política (Brazil)*, v. 13, no. 1 (Jan – Mar 93), pp. 64 – 81.

Barbosa Estepa, Reinaldo. Clientelismo y antidemocracia: la acción política en la formación de la conciencia social. *Islas*, no. 96 (May – Aug 90), pp. 5 – 17. Bibl.

Barceló Aspeitia, Axel Arturo. Comics de amor y cohetes. *Nexos*, v. 16, no. 185 (May 93), pp. 88 – 89.

Bargellini, Clara. Frederic Edwin Church, Sor Pudenciana y Andrés López. *Anales del Instituto de Investigaciones Estéticas*, v. 16, no. 62 (1991), pp. 123 – 138. Bibl, il.

Barker, David. The UWI Scholarship Examination in Geography: An Analysis of the 1992 Results. *Caribbean Geography*, v. 3, no. 4 (Sept 92), pp. 270 – 274. Tables.

Barnes, Julian. El fusilamiento de Maximiliano (Translated by Ana Becerril). *Nexos*, v. 16, no. 187 (July 93), pp. 39 – 47. Il.

Barnes, Monica. Andean Religion (Review article). *Latin American Indian Literatures Journal*, v. 9, no. 1 (Spring 93), pp. 66 – 73.

Barnes, Monica and Daniel J. Slive. El puma de Cuzco: ¿Plano de la ciudad ynga o noción europea? *Revista Andina*, v. 11, no. 1 (July 93), pp. 70 – 102. Bibl, maps, facs.

Barnes, Susan J. Dallas Sheds New Light on Art Treasures. *Américas*, v. 45, no. 5 (Sept – Oct 93), pp. 50 – 53. Il.

Barnet, Miguel. La novela testimonio: alquimia de la memoria. *La Palabra y el Hombre*, no. 82 (Apr – June 92), pp. 75 – 78.

Barnhart, Katherine. Digging Up Mexico's Past. *Business Mexico*, v. 3, no. 11 (Nov 93), pp. 42 – 44. Il, maps.

— Pumping Out a New Image. *Business Mexico*, v. 3, no. 5 (May 93), pp. 8 – 12 +. Il, maps.

— Silver through the Centuries. *Business Mexico*, v. 3, no. 12 (Dec 93), pp. 12 – 14. Tables.

Barni, Euclides João and Sérgio Alberto Brandt. Descentralização, diversificação e tamanho de cooperativas agropecuárias. *Revista de Economia e Sociologia Rural*, v. 30, no. 1 (Jan – Mar 92), pp. 1 – 10. Bibl, tables.

Barquet, Jesús J. El grupo "Orígenes" y España. *Cuadernos Hispanoamericanos*, no. 513 (Mar 93), pp. 31 – 48. Bibl, il.

— Tres apuntes para el futuro: poesía cubana posterior a 1959. *Plural (Mexico)*, v. 22, no. 262 (July 93), pp. 51 – 56. Bibl.

Barradas, Efraín. 1493 también es 1492. *Latin American Literary Review*, v. 20, no. 40 (July – Dec 92), pp. 13 – 15.

Barragán, Juan Ignacio. Cemento, vidrio y explosivos: empresarios del norte e importación de tecnología a principios del siglo XX. *Siglo XIX: Cuadernos*, v. 3, no. 6 (June 93), pp. 9 – 21.

Barrancos, Dora. La modernidad redentora: difusión de las ciencias entre los trabajadores de Buenos Aires, 1890 – 1920. *Siglo XIX: Revista,* no. 12, 2a época (July – Dec 92), pp. 5 – 21. Bibl, tables.

Barrantes Alvarado, César A. Del sector informal urbano a la economía popular. *Revista de Ciencias Sociales (Costa Rica),* no. 57 (Sept 92), pp. 97 – 108. Bibl.

— Reflexiones sobre política social. *Revista de Ciencias Sociales (Costa Rica),* no. 58 (Dec 92), pp. 95 – 107. Bibl.

Barrantes Araya, Trino. Democracia y modernización en Costa Rica: proceso electoral y bipartidismo, 1983 – 1991. *Revista de Ciencias Sociales (Costa Rica),* no. 60 (June 93), pp. 17 – 26. Bibl, tables.

Barraza, Eduardo. La boda como objeto del deseo en cuentos orales de Osorno. *Revista Chilena de Literatura,* no. 42 (Aug 93), pp. 41 – 47.

Barraza, Eduardo and Juan Felipe Leal. Inicios de la reglamentación cinematográfica en la ciudad de México. *Revista Mexicana de Ciencias Políticas y Sociales,* v. 37, Nueva época, no. 150 (Oct – Dec 92), pp. 139 – 175. Bibl, charts.

Barreda Solórzano, Luis de la. Las condiciones carcelarias de las mujeres. *Fem,* v. 17, no. 127 (Sept 93), pp. 13 – 16. Bibl.

— Mujeres en prisión. *Fem,* v. 17, no. 122 (Apr 93), pp. 20 – 21.

Barredo, Lázaro et al. Cuban Responses to the Bishops (Edited excerpts of original statements gathered and translated by the Foreign Broadcast Information Service). *Hemisphere,* v. 5, no. 3 (Summer – Fall 93), pp. 5 – 6.

Barreiro Cavestany, Fernando. La cooperación española con Latinoamérica a la hora del quinto centenario. *Cuadernos del CLAEH,* v. 17, no. 63 – 64 (Oct 92), pp. 105 – 110. Bibl.

Barreiro Cavestany, Javier. Meditación oriental. *Hispamérica,* v. 22, no. 64 – 65 (Apr – Aug 93), p. 127.

Barrenechea, Ana María. Jorge Luis Borges y la ambivalente mitificación de su abuelo paterno. *Nueva Revista de Filología Hispánica,* v. 40, no. 2 (July – Dec 92), pp. 1005 – 1024. Bibl.

Barrera, José F. El centenario de Florentino V. Sanguinetti. *Todo Es Historia,* v. 27, no. 312 (July 93), pp. 20 – 26. Il.

Barrera, Pablo. Religiosidad y resistencia andina: la fe de los no creyentes. *Cristianismo y Sociedad,* v. 30, no. 113 (1992), pp. 15 – 34. Bibl.

Barrera Carranza, Estanislao. Los mayordomía entre los otomíes. *La Palabra y el Hombre,* no. 81 (Jan – Mar 92), pp. 97 – 119. Bibl, il.

— Prostitución y medios masivos de comunicación social. *La Palabra y el Hombre,* no. 84 (Oct – Dec 92), pp. 39 – 61. Bibl.

Barrera Linares, Luis. Julio Garmendia: mito y realidad/ ambigüedad e ironía. *Escritura (Venezuela),* v. 17, no. 33 – 34 (Jan – Dec 92), pp. 21 – 46. Bibl.

— La narrativa breve de Oswaldo Trejo: más allá del textualismo. *Inti,* no. 37 – 38 (Spring – Fall 93), pp. 97 – 106. Bibl.

Barreto, Dalmo Freire. Centenário de morte de Joaquim Norberto de Souza Silva. *Revista do Instituto Histórico e Geográfico Brasileiro,* no. 373 (Oct – Dec 91), pp. 937 – 941.

Barreto Márquez, Amílcar A. The Debate over Puerto Rican Statehood: Language and the "Super-Majority." *Homines,* v. 15 – 16, no. 2 – 1 (Oct 91 – Dec 92), pp. 135 – 141. Bibl.

Barretto, Vicente. Democracia, participação e cidadania. *Revista Brasileira de Estudos Políticos,* no. 76 (Jan 93), pp. 141 – 145.

Barrientos, Raúl. Domingo. *Revista Nacional de Cultura (Venezuela),* v. 54, no. 287 (Oct – Dec 92), pp. 142 – 144.

Barriga Calle, Irma. La experiencia de la muerte en Lima, siglo XVII. *Apuntes (Peru),* no. 31 (July – Dec 92), pp. 81 – 102. Bibl.

Barriga Villanueva, Rebeca. De "Cenicienta" a "Amor en silencio": un estudio sobre narraciones infantiles. *Nueva Revista de Filología Hispánica,* v. 40, no. 2 (July – Dec 92), pp. 673 – 697. Bibl.

— Tintes de subjetividad en las coplas de amor: *Cancionero folklórico de México. Caravelle,* no. 60 (1993), pp. 59 – 83.

Barrio Tosar, Adis. Algunas observaciones sobre las novelas de Piña. *Islas,* no. 98 (Jan – Apr 91), pp. 71 – 82. Bibl.

Barrios, Harald and Petra Bendel. Los sistemas políticos de América Latina: bibliografía comentada de obras recientes. *Ibero-Amerikanisches Archiv,* v. 18, no. 1 – 2 (1992), pp. 291 – 310. Bibl.

Barrios Morón, J. Raúl. La política contra las drogas en Bolivia: interdicción y guerra de baja intensidad. *Nueva Sociedad,* no. 123 (Jan – Feb 93), pp. 35 – 49. Bibl.

Barrios V., Marciano. Jesuitas en la Facultad de Teología de la Universidad Católica. *Mensaje,* v. 42, no. 420 (July 93), pp. 293 – 296. Il.

Barrios y Barrios, Catalina. Manifestaciones teatrales en Guatemala durante el siglo XIX. *USAC,* no. 12 (Dec 90), pp. 76 – 90. Bibl.

Barros, Alexandre Rands. A Periodization of the Business Cycles in the Brazilian Economy, 1856 – 1985. *Revista Brasileira de Economia,* v. 47, no. 1 (Jan – Mar 93), pp. 53 – 82. Bibl, tables, charts.

Barros, Enrique F. et al. 75 años de la reforma universitaria: manifiesto liminar de la reforma universitaria. *Realidad Económica,* no. 118 (Aug – Sept 93), pp. 117 – 122.

Barros, Geraldo Sant'Ana de Camargo and Mirian Rumenos Piedade Bacchi. Demanda de carne bovina no mercado brasileiro. *Revista de Economia e Sociologia Rural,* v. 30, no. 1 (Jan – Mar 92), pp. 83 – 96. Bibl, tables.

Barros, Henrique de. Just One Foot in the Market: Internal Strategies of Small Horticultural Farmers in Northeast Brazil. *Bulletin of Latin American Research,* v. 12, no. 3 (Sept 93), pp. 273 – 292. Bibl, tables.

Barros Charlín, Raymundo. Parámetros jurídico – institucionales de la integración latinoamericana. *Integración Latinoamericana,* v. 18, no. 193 (Sept 93), pp. 29 – 32.

Barros Franco, José Miguel. Rey Don Felipe: plano de una fundación hispana en el estrecho de Magallanes. *Boletín de la Academia Chilena de la Historia,* v. 58 – 59, no. 102 (1991 – 1992), pp. 387 – 401. Il, facs.

Barros Lezaeta, Carmen. Factores que intervienen en el bienestar de los adultos mayores. *Estudios Sociales (Chile),* no. 77 (July – Sept 93), pp. 31 – 47. Bibl, charts.

Barrubia, Lalo. Susuki 400: fragmentos. *Hispamérica,* v. 22, no. 64 – 65 (Apr – Aug 93), pp. 128 – 129.

Barsted, Leila de Andrade Linhares. Legalização e descriminalização do aborto no Brazil: 10 anos de luta feminista (Accompanied by an English translation by Christopher Peterson). *Estudos Feministas,* v. 0, no. 0 (1992), pp. 104 – 130. Bibl.

Bartl, Johanna. Artistas latinoamericanos buscan mitos en Salzwedel. *Humboldt,* no. 110 (1993), p. 102. Il.

Bartolomé, Miguel Alberto and Salomón Nahmad Sittón. Semblanza. *América Indígena*, v. 51, no. 2 – 3 (Apr – Sept 91), pp. 417 – 418.

Barzuna Pérez, Guillermo. Estructura y sentido en la crónica colonial. *Káñina*, v. 16, no. 2 (July – Dec 92), pp. 75 – 79. Bibl.

Basalisco, Lucio. Culture a confronto: guaraniés e yaros visti da un gesuito alla fine del seicento. *Quaderni Ibero-Americani*, no. 72 (Dec 92), pp. 709 – 720. Bibl.

Bascuñán, Carlos and Sol Serrano. La idea de América en los exiliados españoles en Chile (Excerpt from *El pensamiento español contemporáneo y la idea de América* edited by José Luis Abellán and Antonio Monclús Estella). *Atenea (Chile)*, no. 465 – 466 (1992), pp. 99 – 149. Bibl, tables.

Basile, María Teresa. La naturaleza como discurso sobre la identidad latinoamericana. *La Educación (USA)*, v. 36, no. 111 – 113 (1992), pp. 75 – 88. Bibl.

Bassols Ricárdez, Mario and Rocio Corona Martínez. Transición institucional y reforma política en el D.F. *El Cotidiano*, v. 10, no. 57 (Aug – Sept 93), pp. 28 – 37. Il, tables.

Bastardo Casañas, Antonio. A 50 años de una novela galleguiana: *El forastero;* sus dos versiones. *Revista Nacional de Cultura (Venezuela)*, v. 53, no. 286 (July – Sept 92), pp. 154 – 155.

Bastian, Jean-Pierre. The Metamorphosis of Latin American Protestant Groups: A Sociohistorical Perspective (Translated by Margaret Caffey-Moquin). *Latin American Research Review*, v. 28, no. 2 (1993), pp. 33 – 61. Bibl, tables.

Bastidas González, Pedro José and Damaris van der Dys. Programa de adaptación del Sistema de Información de la Planta Física Educativa (SIPFE) a los objetivos de reducción de la vulnerabilidad a las amenazas naturales en las escuelas. *La Educación (USA)*, v. 37, no. 115 (1993), pp. 365 – 377. Tables.

Bastos, Eni Santana Barretto et al. Guia de fontes de documentação para a história da educação na Bahia. *Revista Brasileira de Estudos Pedagógicos*, v. 72, no. 172 (Sept – Dec 91), pp. 385 – 387.

Bastos, Rafael José de Menezes. Musical Cognition and Structure: The Case of the Yawari of the Kamayurá Indians of Central Brazil, Xingu Indian Park, Mato Grosso. *La Educación (USA)*, v. 36, no. 111 – 113 (1992), pp. 227 – 233. Bibl.

Basualdo, Eduardo M. and Miguel Khavisse. El nuevo poder terrateniente (Excerpt from the forthcoming book of the same title). *Realidad Económica*, no. 113 (Jan – Feb 93), pp. 90 – 99.

Batalla Rosado, Juan José. Un nuevo códice para el estudio de las culturas mesoamericanas. *Revista Española de Antropología Americana*, v. 23 (1993), pp. 248 – 254. Bibl, il.

— La perspectiva planigráfica precolombina y el *Códice Borbónico:* página 31; escena central. *Revista Española de Antropología Americana*, v. 23 (1993), pp. 113 – 134. Bibl, il.

Batista, Marta Rossetti. Da passagem meteórica de Siqueiros pelo Brasil, 1933 (Includes reproductions of a text and an interview published in 1933 – 1934 after the artist's visit to Brazil). *Vozes*, v. 86, no. 5 (Sept – Oct 92), pp. 81 – 94. Il.

Batista Júnior, Paulo Nogueira. Dolarização, âncora cambial e reservas internacionais. *Revista de Economia Política (Brazil)*, v. 13, no. 3 (July – Sept 93), pp. 5 – 20. Bibl, tables.

Battista, Vicente. El difícil arte de volver. *Cuadernos Hispanoamericanos*, no. 517 – 519 (July – Sept 93), pp. 560 – 562.

Baud, Michiel. Una fortuna para cruzar: la sociedad rural a través de la frontera domínico – haitiana, 1870 – 1930 (Translated by Eugenio Rivas). *Estudios Sociales (Dominican Republic)*, v. 26, no. 94 (Oct – Dec 93), pp. 5 – 28. Bibl.

— Una frontera – refugio: dominicanos y haitianos contra el estado, 1870 – 1930 (Translated by Montserrat Planas Alberti). *Estudios Sociales (Dominican Republic)*, v. 26, no. 92 (Apr – June 93), pp. 39 – 64. Bibl.

Baudot, Georges. Chronologie pour l'émergence d'une organisation amérindienne, politique et culturelle, au Mexique. *Caravelle*, no. 59 (1992), pp. 7 – 17.

— Genaro Domínguez Maldonado: entrevista realizada el 15 de agosto de 1991 en la ciudad de México por Georges Baudot. *Caravelle*, no. 59 (1992), pp. 39 – 47.

— Malintzin, imagen y discurso de mujer en el primer México virreinal. *Cuadernos Americanos*, no. 40, Nueva época (July – Aug 93), pp. 181 – 207. Bibl.

Bauer, Carl J. Water Property Rights and the State: The United States Experience. *CEPAL Review*, no. 49 (Apr 93), pp. 75 – 89. Bibl.

Baugh, Edward. Derek Walcott. *Caribbean Quarterly*, v. 38, no. 4 (Dec 92), pp. xiii – xv.

Baumann Neves, Renato. An Appraisal of Recent Intra-Industry Trade for Latin America. *CEPAL Review*, no. 48 (Dec 92), pp. 83 – 94. Tables.

Bautista Romero, Jaime. Al aproximarse a su fin la venta de paraestatales, el gobierno subasta infraestructura y servicios. *Momento Económico*, no. 66 (Mar – Apr 93), pp. 2 – 6. Bibl.

Bava, Silvio Caccia and Laura Mullahy. Making Brazil's Cities Livable: NGOs and the Recycling of Human Waste (Adapted chapter from the forthcoming book *Joint Ventures in Urban Policy: NGO – Local Government Collaboration in Democratizing Latin America* edited by Charles A. Reilly). *Grassroots Development*, v. 17, no. 1 (1993), pp. 12 – 19. Bibl, il.

Bayardo, Rubens. Acerca de la cuestión postmoderna: una perspectiva antropológica. *Estudios Paraguayos*, v. 17, no. 1 – 2 (1989 – 1993), pp. 23 – 33. Bibl.

Bayón, Damián Carlos. Arte latinoamericano en el MOMA: una ocasión perdida. *Vuelta*, v. 17, no. 201 (Aug 93), pp. 60 – 62.

— Francis Bacon en Buenos Aires. *Cuadernos Hispanoamericanos*, no. 510 (Dec 92), pp. 97 – 100. Il.

— México, 1947. *Vuelta*, v. 17, no. 196 (Mar 93), pp. 75 – 76.

— Reencuentro con Oaxaca (Accompanied by an English translation). *Artes de México*, no. 21 (Fall 93), pp. 36 – 39. Il.

Bazán, Armando Raúl. Americanismo y nacionalismo en la emancipación sudamericana. *Revista de Historia de América*, no. 112 (July – Dec 91), pp. 5 – 19.

Bazán, Armando Raúl and Ricardo Zorraquín Becú. La historia y su divulgación (Two speeches on the occasion of Félix Luna's induction into the National Academy of History). *Todo Es Historia*, v. 27, no. 316 (Nov 93), pp. 43 – 49. Il.

Beane, Carol. Entrevista con Luz Argentina Chiriboga. *Afro-Hispanic Review*, v. 12, no. 2 (Fall 93), pp. 17 – 23.

Beaney, Peter W. The Irrigated Eldorado: State-Managed Rural Development, Redemocratisation and Popular Participation in the Brazilian Northeast. *Bulletin of Latin American Research*, v. 12, no. 3 (Sept 93), pp. 249 – 272. Bibl.

Beardsley, Theodore S. Necrology: Delos Lincoln Canfield (1903 – 1991). *Hispanic Review,* v. 61, no. 1 (Winter 93), pp. 135 – 137.

Bebbington, Anthony et al. From Protest to Productivity: The Evolution of Indigenous Federations in Ecuador. *Grassroots Development,* v. 16, no. 2 (1992), pp. 11 – 21. Il.

Beck, Heinrich. América Latina como encuentro cultural. *Cuadernos Americanos,* no. 41, Nueva época (Sept – Oct 93), pp. 158 – 166.

Becker, Bertha Koiffman. Geografia política e gestão do território no limiar do século XXI: uma representação a partir do Brasil. *Revista Brasileira de Geografia,* v. 53, no. 3 (July – Sept 91), pp. 169 – 182. Bibl.

Beckles, Hilary. Kalinago (Carib) Resistance to European Colonisation of the Caribbean. *Caribbean Quarterly,* v. 38, no. 2 – 3 (June – Sept 92), pp. 1 – 14. Bibl.

Bedê, Marco Aurélio. Evolução tecnológica na indústria de autopeças: resultados de estudos de caso. *Estudos Econômicos,* v. 22, no. 3 (Sept – Dec 92), pp. 409 – 428. Bibl, tables, charts.

Bedoya, Jaime. Cicatriz caribeña. *Debate (Peru),* v. 16, no. 72 (Mar – May 93), pp. 52 – 54.

Bedoya Ramírez, Josué. Fundación de la ciudad de "El Guamo," Tolima. *Boletín de Historia y Antigüedades,* v. 80, no. 780 (Jan – Mar 93), pp. 205 – 210.

Bedregal S., Ximena. Discurso de inauguración del primer foro: "Mujer, Violencia y Derechos Humanos." *Fem,* v. 17, no. 122 (Apr 93), pp. 11 – 13.

Beerman, Eric. Francisco Antonio Zea: su paso y matrimonio en España. *Boletín de Historia y Antigüedades,* v. 80, no. 780 (Jan – Mar 93), pp. 211 – 221. Bibl.

Begné, Patricia. El derecho a la salud y el aborto en el sistema legal mexicano. *Fem,* v. 17, no. 129 (Nov 93), pp. 12 – 14.

Béhague, Gerard. Luiz Heitor Corrêa de Azevedo (13 December 1905 – 10 November 1992). *Latin American Music Review,* v. 14, no. 1 (Spring – Summer 93), n.p. Il.

Béjar, Ana María. Cultura, utopía y percepción social: los festivales por la vida y por la paz y la práctica musical juvenil en Sicuani. *Allpanchis,* v. 25, no. 41 (Jan – June 93), pp. 109 – 141. Tables.

Béjar, Eduardo C. *Harlem todos los días:* el exilio del nombre/el nombre del exilio. *Revista Iberoamericana,* v. 59, no. 162 – 163 (Jan – June 93), pp. 329 – 343. Bibl.

Béjar, Héctor. Perú: el neoliberalismo realmente existente. *Nueva Sociedad,* no. 127 (Sept – Oct 93), pp. 13 – 18.

Bejarano Martínez, René. Los nexos de la historia. *El Cotidiano,* v. 8, no. 51 (Nov – Dec 92), pp. 48 – 53. Il.

Bejarano Orozco, Julio and Hannia Carvajal Morera. Abuso de drogas y conducta delictiva. *Revista de Ciencias Sociales (Costa Rica),* no. 60 (June 93), pp. 51 – 62. Bibl, tables, charts.

Bejel, Emilio F. La transferencia dialéctica en *El robo del cochino* de Estorino. *La Palabra y el Hombre,* no. 84 (Oct – Dec 92), pp. 291 – 295.

Bekerman, Marta. Apertura importadora e integración en el Cono Sur. *Comercio Exterior,* v. 43, no. 11 (Nov 93), pp. 1040 – 1045. Bibl.

— O setor petroquímico e a integração Argentina – Brasil. *Pesquisa e Planejamento Econômico,* v. 22, no. 2 (Aug 92), pp. 369 – 398. Bibl, tables.

Belanger, Alain and Andrei Rogers. The Internal Migration and Spatial Redistribution of the Foreign-Born Population in the United States: 1965 – 1970 and 1975 – 1980. *International Migration Review,* v. 26, no. 4 (Winter 92), pp. 1342 – 1369. Bibl, tables, charts.

Bell, Daniel. La corrupción y la política de la reforma (Translated by Rubén Gallo). *Vuelta,* v. 17, no. 202 (Sept 93), pp. 41 – 43.

Bell, John Patrick. La Asociación General de Agricultores frente a la reforma agraria en la Guatemala revolucionaria, 1944 – 1954. *Anuario de Estudios Centroamericanos,* v. 18, no. 1 (1992), pp. 17 – 28. Bibl.

Bell-Villada, Gene H. Our Own Miss Puerto Rico. *Chasqui,* v. 22, no. 2 (Nov 93), pp. 187 – 190.

Bellegarde-Smith, Patrick. "Pawol la pale": Reflections of an Initiate (Introduction to the special issue entitled "Traditional Spirituality in the African Diaspora"). *Journal of Caribbean Studies,* v. 9, no. 1 – 2 (Winter 92 – Spring 93), pp. 3 – 9. Bibl.

Bellessi, Diana. Lo propio y lo ajeno. *Feminaria,* v. 6, no. 11, Suppl. (Nov 93), p. 21.

Belli, Elena. Recordatorios, biografías y necrológicas: usos y sentidos en la historia de la antropología argentina. *Runa,* v. 20 (1991 – 1992), pp. 151 – 161. Bibl.

Bellinghausen, Hermann. Invitación a la pereza. *Nexos,* v. 16, no. 186 (June 93), p. 30.

Bellini, Giuseppe. Il dramma del mondo azteca e i "Dodici Apostoli." *Quaderni Ibero-Americani,* no. 72 (Dec 92), pp. 640 – 648. Bibl.

Bello, Daniel. La muerte en bicicleta: fragmentos. *Hispamérica,* v. 22, no. 64 – 65 (Apr – Aug 93), pp. 130 – 131.

Bellon, Mauricio R. and J. Edward Taylor. "Folk" Soil Taxonomy and the Partial Adoption of New Seed Varieties. *Economic Development and Cultural Change,* v. 41, no. 4 (July 93), pp. 763 – 786. Bibl, tables.

Bellotto, Manoel Lelo. A imigração espanhola no Brasil: estado do fluxo migratório para o estado de São Paulo, 1931 – 1936. *Estudios Interdisciplinarios de América Latina y el Caribe,* v. 3, no. 2 (July – Dec 92), pp. 59 – 73. Bibl, tables.

Bellucci, Mabel and Adriana Rofman. Una década de mujeres en movimiento. *Todo Es Historia,* v. 27, no. 317 (Dec 93), pp. 74 – 77. Il.

Beltrán Guerrero, Luis. Centenario de Casto Fulgencio López. *Boletín de la Academia Nacional de la Historia (Venezuela),* v. 76, no. 301 (Jan – Mar 93), pp. 114 – 116.

— La edición del *Quijote* de la Academia Nacional de la Historia. *Boletín de la Academia Nacional de la Historia (Venezuela),* v. 75, no. 299 (July – Sept 92), pp. 187 – 189.

— El gran Mariano. *Boletín de la Academia Nacional de la Historia (Venezuela),* v. 76, no. 301 (Jan – Mar 93), pp. 57 – 61.

— Un gran mestizo. *Boletín de la Academia Nacional de la Historia (Venezuela),* v. 76, no. 302 (Apr – June 93), pp. 139 – 140.

— Meritocracia: Federico Brito Figueroa. *Revista Nacional de Cultura (Venezuela),* v. 53, no. 286 (July – Sept 92), pp. 129 – 132.

— Varones: Julio Ramos. *Boletín de la Academia Nacional de la Historia (Venezuela),* v. 75, no. 297 (Jan – Mar 92), pp. 117 – 118.

— Vicente Gerbasi. *Boletín de la Academia Nacional de la Historia (Venezuela),* v. 76, no. 301 (Jan – Mar 93), pp. 112 – 113.

Beltrán Salmón, Ramiro. Ulíses Estrella, "peatón de Quito" y amigo de Bolivia. *Signo,* no. 38, Nueva época (Jan – Apr 93), pp. 143 – 145.

Beltrán-Vocal, María Antonia. Soledad, aislamiento y búsqueda de identidad en Nash Candelaria y Juan Goytisolo. *The Americas Review,* v. 21, no. 1 (Spring 93), pp. 103 – 111.

Beltrão, Maria da Conceição de M. C. A coleção egípcia do Museu Nacional (Speech given at the occasion of her induction into the Instituto Histórico e Geográfico Brasileiro). *Revista do Instituto Histórico e Geográfico Brasileiro,* no. 372 (July – Sept 91), pp. 806 – 811.

Benarós, León. El desván de Clío: personajes, hechos, anécdotas y curiosidades de la historia. *Todo Es Historia,* v. 26 – 27 (Dec 92 – Dec 93), All issues. Il.

Benavente, José Miguel and Peter J. West. Globalization and Convergence: Latin America in a Changing World. *CEPAL Review,* no. 47 (Aug 92), pp. 77 – 94. Bibl, charts.

Benavides, Pedro. "Declarándome por exento y libre de pagar la dicha alcabala." *Vuelta,* v. 17, no. 196 (Mar 93), pp. 38 – 39.

Benavides, Rosamel. Cuentos y cuentistas chicanos: perspectiva temática y producción histórica del género, 1947 – 1992. *Revista Chilena de Literatura,* no. 42 (Aug 93), pp. 49 – 56.

Benavides Montoya, Thelma et al. El menor deambulante en Costa Rica. *Revista de Ciencias Sociales (Costa Rica),* no. 59 (Mar 93), pp. 27 – 35. Bibl, charts.

Bencastro, Mario. Reviewing Barbara Mujica. *Américas,* v. 45, no. 2 (Mar – Apr 93), pp. 60 – 61. Il.

Bencomo Barrios, Héctor. El cuartel San Carlos de Caracas y la bandera nacional. *Boletín de la Academia Nacional de la Historia (Venezuela),* v. 76, no. 302 (Apr – June 93), pp. 140 – 141.

Bendel, Petra and Harald Barrios. Los sistemas políticos de América Latina: bibliografía comentada de obras recientes. *Ibero-Amerikanisches Archiv,* v. 18, no. 1 – 2 (1992), pp. 291 – 310. Bibl.

Bendezú Aybar, Edmundo. Los textos de D'Harcourt. *Revista de Crítica Literaria Latinoamericana,* v. 19, no. 37 (Jan – June 93), pp. 105 – 115.

Benedetti, Mario. Etica de amplio espectro. *Nexos,* v. 16, no. 187 (July 93), pp. 13 – 15.

Benencia, Roberto and Javier Souza Casadinho. Alimentos y salud: uso y abuso de pesticidas en la horticultura bonaerense. *Realidad Económica,* no. 114 – 115 (Feb – May 93), pp. 29 – 53. Bibl, tables.

Bengoa, José. Ley indígena: búsqueda de desarrollo con identidad. *Mensaje,* v. 42, no. 423 (Oct 93), pp. 501 – 503. Il.

— El país del censo. *Mensaje,* v. 42, no. 424 (Nov 93), pp. 543 – 546. Il, tables.

Benítez, Celeste. ¿Como votaron los caseríos de San Juan?: elecciones de 1988. *Homines,* v. 15 – 16, no. 2 – 1 (Oct 91 – Dec 92), pp. 102 – 105.

Benítez Burgos, Wilson Andrés. La presencia religiosa en la historia de Melo. *Hoy Es Historia,* v. 10, no. 57 (Apr – May 93), pp. 61 – 68.

Benítez Manaut, Raúl. El Salvador: paz conflictiva, democracia frágil. *Nueva Sociedad,* no. 126 (July – Aug 93), pp. 6 – 11.

— Identity Crisis: The Military in Changing Times (Translated by Kent Klineman). *NACLA Report on the Americas,* v. 27, no. 2 (Sept – Oct 93), pp. 15 – 19.

Benítez Pérez, María Elena. La familia cubana: principales rasgos sociodemográficos que han caracterizado su desarrollo y dinámica. *Estudios Demográficos y Urbanos,* v. 7, no. 2 – 3 (May – Dec 92), pp. 479 – 492. Bibl, tables.

Benítez Rojo, Antonio. La literatura caribeña y la teoría de caos. *Latin American Literary Review,* v. 20, no. 40 (July – Dec 92), pp. 16 – 18.

— Nacionalismo y nacionalización en la novela hispanoamericana del siglo XIX. *Revista de Crítica Literaria Latinoamericana,* v. 19, no. 38 (July – Dec 93), pp. 185 – 193.

Benítez Zenteno, Raúl. Visión latinoamericana de la transición demográfica. *Comercio Exterior,* v. 43, no. 7 (July 93), pp. 618 – 624. Bibl.

Benko, Susana. FIA '93: Caracas (Accompanied by an English translation). *Art Nexus,* no. 10 (Sept – Dec 93), pp. 110 – 112. Il.

Bennett, Karl M. Exchange Rate Management in a Balance of Payments Crisis: The Guyana and Jamaica Experience. *Social and Economic Studies,* v. 41, no. 4 (Dec 92), pp. 113 – 131. Bibl, tables.

Bensen, Robert. Columbus at the Abyss: The Genesis of New World Literature. *Jamaica Journal,* v. 24, no. 3 (Feb 93), pp. 48 – 54. Bibl, il.

Benso, Silvia. Il silenzio e la voce di Atahualpa. *Quaderni Ibero-Americani,* no. 72 (Dec 92), pp. 649 – 660. Bibl.

Benson, Elizabeth P. Bibliography (to the articles in this issue entitled "Sacred Space and Its Uses"). *Latin American Indian Literatures Journal,* v. 9, no. 1 (Spring 93), pp. 55 – 65.

Benson, LeGrace. Some Observations on West African Islamic Motifs and Haitian Religious Art. *Journal of Caribbean Studies,* v. 9, no. 1 – 2 (Winter 92 – Spring 93), pp. 59 – 66. Bibl.

Bento, Cláudio Moreira. Campo de prisioneiros de guerra em Pouso Alegre. *Revista do Instituto Histórico e Geográfico Brasileiro,* no. 373 (Oct – Dec 91), pp. 1052 – 1056.

— Participação das forças armadas e da marinha mercante do Brasil na segunda guerra mundial, 1942 – 1945. *Revista do Instituto Histórico e Geográfico Brasileiro,* no. 372 (July – Sept 91), pp. 685 – 745. Bibl, maps.

Beramendi Usera, Fernando. Intimate Openings through Prison Walls (Photographs by Oscar Bonilla). *Américas,* v. 45, no. 1 (Jan – Feb 93), pp. 30 – 35. Il.

Berástegui, Rafael. La Cuba de Fidel: algunas claves de interpretación. *Estudios Públicos (Chile),* no. 52 (Spring 93), pp. 309 – 328.

Berat, Lynn and Yossi Shain. Evening the Score: Layered Legacies of the Interregnum. *Estudios Interdisciplinarios de América Latina y el Caribe,* v. 4, no. 1 (Jan – June 93), pp. 57 – 91. Bibl.

Beraza, Luis Fernando. Perón, Braden y la guerra civil en el Paraguay, 1947. *Todo Es Historia,* v. 26, no. 307 (Feb 93), pp. 84 – 86. Bibl, il.

Berdan, Frances F. Economic Dimensions of Precious Metals, Stones, and Feathers: The Aztec State Society. *Estudios de Cultura Náhuatl,* v. 22 (1992), pp. 291 – 323. Bibl, tables, maps.

Berg, Egdardo H. Las poéticas narrativas actuales de la Argentina: líneas de reflexión crítica. *Escritura (Venezuela),* v. 17, no. 33 – 34 (Jan – Dec 92), pp. 115 – 125.

Berger, Mark T. Civilising the South: The U.S. Rise to Hegemony in the Americas and the Roots of "Latin American Studies," 1898 – 1945. *Bulletin of Latin American Research,* v. 12, no. 1 (Jan 93), pp. 1 – 48. Bibl.

Berger, Susan A. Guatemala: Coup and Countercoup. *NACLA Report on the Americas,* v. 27, no. 1 (July – Aug 93), pp. 4 – 7. Il.

Berglund, Susan. Las Migraciones en el Proceso de Integración de las Américas: Seminario Internacional/Migration in the Integration Process in the Americas: International Seminar. *International Migration Review,* v. 27, no. 1 (Spring 93), pp. 182 – 190.

Bermúdez, Manuel. Luis Beltrán Guerrero. *Boletín de la Academia Nacional de la Historia (Venezuela),* v. 76, no. 302 (Apr – June 93), pp. 151 – 152.

— El Orinoco literario: propuesta para una visión diferente de la literatura venezolana. *Revista Nacional de Cultura (Venezuela),* v. 53, no. 286 (July – Sept 92), pp. 211 – 214.

Bermúdez-Gallegos, Marta. Oralidad y escritura: Atahualpa; ¿Traidor or traicionado? *Revista de Crítica Literaria Latinoamericana,* v. 19, no. 38 (July – Dec 93), pp. 331 – 344. Bibl.

Bermúdez Merizalde, Jaime. Por la senda de la integración: balance. *Revista Javeriana,* v. 61, no. 594 (May 93), pp. 225 – 237.

Bermúdez Páez, Alvaro E. Etnohistoria de Subachoque, siglos XVI – XVIII. *Revista Colombiana de Antropología,* v. 29 (1992), pp. 81 – 117. Bibl, tables, maps.

— Reconstrucción de un conjunto funerario en el Alto de las Piedras (Isnos). *Revista Colombiana de Antropología,* v. 29 (1992), pp. 257 – 264. Bibl, il.

Bernabéu Albert, Salvador. El "virrey de California" Gaspar de Portolá y la problemática de la primera gobernación californiana, 1767 – 1769. *Revista de Indias,* v. 52, no. 195 – 196 (May – Dec 92), pp. 271 – 295. Bibl.

Bernal Leongómez, Jaime and José Joaquín Montes Giraldo. El verbo en el habla culta de Bogotá: frecuencia de categorías tradicionales y creación de otras nuevas. *Thesaurus,* v. 45, no. 3 (Sept – Dec 90), pp. 732 – 742. Bibl, tables.

Bernal Rodríguez, Manuel. Nota sobre el influjo de la espiritualidad renacentista en la reprobación moral de la emigración a Indias: el camino del infierno. *Anuario de Estudios Americanos,* v. 49, Suppl. 2 (1992), pp. 3 – 9. Bibl.

Bernal Sahagún, Víctor Manuel. La coyuntura económica semestral. *Momento Económico,* no. 68 (July – Aug 93), pp. 2 – 7. Bibl.

Bernard, Daniel Alberto. "Franchising" estratégico: como obter alavancagens e sinergias por meio da taxa inicial e dos "royalties." *RAE; Revista de Administração de Empresas,* v. 33, no. 4 (July – Aug 93), pp. 18 – 31. Tables.

Bernecker, Walther L. El aniversario del "descubrimiento" de América en el conflicto de opiniones (Translated by Verónica Jaffé). *Ibero-Amerikanisches Archiv,* v. 18, no. 3 – 4 (1992), pp. 501 – 520. Bibl.

Bernier F., Richard E. Cutting a New Cloth. *Business Mexico,* v. 3, no. 1 (Jan – Feb 93), pp. 27 – 28. Il.

Berquó, Elza Salvatori. Brasil: um caso exemplar; anticoncepção e parto cirúrgicos; à espera de uma ação exemplar (Accompanied by an English translation by Christopher Peterson). *Estudos Feministas,* v. 1, no. 2 (1993), pp. 366 – 381. Bibl, tables.

Berrettini, Célia. O teatro de Lope de Vega e o descobrimento da América. *Vozes,* v. 86, no. 4 (July – Aug 92), pp. 66 – 71. Il, facs.

Berrío-Lemm, Vladimir. En torno a los símbolos patrios tradicionales de Panamá. *Revista Cultural Lotería,* v. 51, no. 392 (Nov – Dec 93), pp. 55 – 77. Bibl, il.

Berríos Martínez, Rubén. Independencia y plebiscito. *Homines,* v. 15 – 16, no. 2 – 1 (Oct 91 – Dec 92), pp. 118 – 125.

Berrouët-Oriol, Robert and Robert Fournier. Créolophonie et francophonie nord – sud: transcontinuum. *Canadian Journal of Latin American and Caribbean Studies,* v. 17, no. 34 (1992), pp. 13 – 25. Bibl.

Bertrand, Michel. Un regard sur les publications françaises à l'occasion du Ve centenaire de la rencontre des deux mondes (Review article). *Caravelle,* no. 59 (1992), pp. 256 – 266.

Bertrand S., María. ¿Efímero vedetariado o auténtica preocupación?: reflexiones en torno a un aluvión anunciado. *EURE,* v. 19, no. 57 (July 93), pp. 134 – 135.

Bervejillo, Federico. El nuevo perfil del intendente: un cambio de curso. *Cuadernos del CLAEH,* v. 18, no. 67 (Nov 93), pp. 11 – 18.

Bespalova, Marina. Donde el polvo se posa. *Plural (Mexico),* v. 22, no. 267 (Dec 93), pp. 66 – 67.

Best, Lloyd. The Contribution of George Beckford. *Social and Economic Studies,* v. 41, no. 3 (Sept 92), pp. 5 – 23.

Betancourt Echeverry, Darío. Tendencias de las mafias colombianas de la cocaína y la amapola. *Nueva Sociedad,* no. 128 (Nov – Dec 93), pp. 38 – 47.

Beverido Duhalt, Francisco. Notas de un espectador en la XII Muestra Nacional de Teatro. *La Palabra y el Hombre,* no. 81 (Jan – Mar 92), pp. 362 – 367.

Beverido Pereau, Francisco. Estela 16 de Yaxchilán. *La Palabra y el Hombre,* no. 82 (Apr – June 92), pp. 291 – 293.

Beverido Pereau, Luis. Dos minificciones. *La Palabra y el Hombre,* no. 84 (Oct – Dec 92), p. 164.

Beverley, John. Cultural Studies. *Latin American Literary Review,* v. 20, no. 40 (July – Dec 92), pp. 19 – 22. Bibl.

— ¿Posliteratura?: sujeto subalterno e impasse de las humanidades. *Casa de las Américas,* no. 190 (Jan – Mar 93), pp. 13 – 24. Bibl.

Bevilacqua, Claudia. Transformaciones territoriales en el marco de las políticas del estado en la región metropolitana de Buenos Aires: el caso del municipio de Marcos Paz, 1945 – 1990. *Revista Interamericana de Planificación,* v. 26, no. 101 – 102 (Jan – June 93), pp. 154 – 182. Bibl, tables, maps.

Bey, Marguerite. La cinquième Séminaire Permanent de Recherche Agraire. *Tiers Monde,* v. 34, no. 136 (Oct – Dec 93), pp. 937 – 938.

Beyer, Bernd Fahmel. El empleo de una brújula en el diseño de los espacios arquitectónicos en Monte Albán, Oaxaca, México, 400 a.c. – 830 d.c. *Revista Española de Antropología Americana,* v. 23 (1993), pp. 29 – 40. Bibl, il, tables, charts.

Beyersdorff, Margot. La "puesta en texto" del primer drama indohispano en los Andes. *Revista de Crítica Literaria Latinoamericana,* v. 19, no. 37 (Jan – June 93), pp. 195 – 221. Bibl, il.

Biagini, Hugo Edgardo. La filosofía latinoamericana a partir de su historia. *Anuario de Estudios Americanos,* v. 49, Suppl. 1 (1992), pp. 3 – 45. Bibl.

Bianchi, Susana. Iglesia católica y peronismo: la cuestión de la enseñanza religiosa, 1946 – 1955. *Estudios Interdisciplinarios de América Latina y el Caribe,* v. 3, no. 2 (July – Dec 92), pp. 89 – 103. Bibl.

Bianciotti, Héctor. El vértigo de los carnavales (Translated by Aurelio Asiaín). *Vuelta,* v. 17, no. 201 (Aug 93), pp. 28 – 29.

Bianco, José. Páginas dispersas (A sampling of the author's writings on various topics). *Cuadernos Hispanoamericanos,* no. 516 (June 93), pp. 10 – 37.

Bicalho, Maria Fernanda Baptista. The Art of Seduction: Representation of Women in Brazilian Silent Cinema (Fragment from *Entre a virtude e o pecado* edited by Albertina de Oliveira Costa and Cristina Bruschini, translated by Sueann Caulfield). *Luso-Brazilian Review,* v. 30, no. 1 (Summer 93), pp. 21 – 33. Bibl.

Bieber, León Enrique. Las relaciones entre la Comunidad Europea y América Latina: problemas y perspectivas. *Homines,* v. 15 – 16, no. 2 – 1 (Oct 91 – Dec 92), pp. 13 – 30. Bibl.

Bifani, Patricia. Disponibilidad, derecho y gestión del espacio vital. *Nueva Sociedad,* no. 123 (Jan – Feb 93), pp. 84 – 93. Bibl.

Biggins, Alan. Libraries "sans frontières": REDIAL, European Bibliographic Cooperation, and 1992. *SALALM Papers,* v. 36 (1991), pp. 20 – 31.

Bilbao, María Josefina. La familia chilena hoy: ¿A qué conclusiones llegó la Comisión Nacional de la Familia? *Mensaje,* v. 42, no. 425 (Dec 93), pp. 626 – 628. Il, tables.

Bilbija, Ksenija. "La palabra asesino" de Luisa Valenzuela: la entrada en la lengua. *Confluencia,* v. 8, no. 1 (Fall 92), pp. 159 – 164.

— Tiene los cabellos rojizos y se llama Sabina. *La Palabra y el Hombre,* no. 84 (Oct – Dec 92), pp. 228 – 239. Bibl.

Bilder, Ernesto A. La demora. *Realidad Económica,* no. 118 (Aug – Sept 93), pp. 82 – 92. Bibl, tables.

Binková, Simona and Katerina Kozická. El dominio marítimo español en los materiales cartográficos y náuticos de Praga. *Anuario de Estudios Americanos,* v. 49, Suppl. 1 (1992), pp. 47 – 54. Bibl, maps.

Biord Castillo, Horacio. Organización social y resistencia a la conquista europea: los casos teque y cumanagoto. *Boletín de la Academia Nacional de la Historia (Venezuela),* v. 75, no. 297 (Jan – Mar 92), pp. 51 – 68. Bibl, maps.

Birbragher, Celia S. de. Chicago 1993 (Accompanied by an English translation). *Art Nexus,* no. 10 (Sept – Dec 93), pp. 108 – 109. Il.

Birch, Melissa H. and Werner Baer. La privatización y el rol cambiante del estado en América Latina. *Revista Paraguaya de Sociología,* v. 29, no. 85 (Sept – Dec 92), pp. 7 – 28. Bibl.

Birdsall, Nancy. Ajuste y reformas económicas: la necesidad de gestionar la transición al crecimiento. *Pensamiento Iberoamericano,* no. 22 – 23, tomo II (July 92 – June 93), pp. 255 – 258. Charts.

Bittencourt, Gabriel Augusto de Mello. A imprensa no Espírito Santo. *Revista do Instituto Histórico e Geográfico Brasileiro,* no. 373 (Oct – Dec 91), pp. 1022 – 1031.

Bizzozero, Lincoln J. La relación entre el MERCOSUR y la Comunidad Europa: ¿Un nuevo parametro de vinculación? *Estudios Internacionales (Chile),* v. 26, no. 101 (Jan – Mar 93), pp. 37 – 56. Bibl.

Blache, Martha Teresa. Folklore y nacionalismo en la Argentina: su vinculación de origen y su desvinculación actual. *Runa,* v. 20 (1991 – 1992), pp. 69 – 89. Bibl.

Black, David L. IICA Reaps the Seeds of a Half Century. *Américas,* v. 45, no. 4 (July – Aug 93), pp. 56 – 57. Il.

Black, Jan Knippers. Almost Free, Almost Fair: Paraguay's Ambiguous Election. *NACLA Report on the Americas,* v. 27, no. 2 (Sept – Oct 93), pp. 26 – 28. Il.

Blackman, Courtney N. An Analytical Framework for the Study of Caribbean Public Enterprise. *Social and Economic Studies,* v. 41, no. 4 (Dec 92), pp. 77 – 93. Bibl.

Blake, Vivian. In Pursuit of Excellence. *Jamaica Journal,* v. 25, no. 1 (Oct 93), pp. 2 – 8. Il.

Blanc, Giulio V. Art Miami '93 (Accompanied by the English original, translated by Andrés Salgado). *Art Nexus,* no. 8 (Apr – June 93), pp. 108 – 109. Il.

— Tomás Sánchez: obra reciente (Accompanied by the English original, translated by Magdalena Holguín). *Art Nexus,* no. 10 (Sept – Dec 93), pp. 51 – 53.

Blanco, Alberto. Arte contemporáneo de Oaxaca: la semilla de la visión. *Nexos,* v. 16, no. 186 (June 93), pp. 15 – 19.

— Arte de Oaxaca (Accompanied by an English translation). *Artes de México,* no. 21 (Fall 93), pp. 68 – 83. Il.

— Doce maestros latinoamericanos. *Artes de México,* no. 19 (Spring 93), pp. 100 – 101. Il.

— Los jardines flotantes de Brian Nissen (Accompanied by an English translation). *Artes de México,* no. 20 (Summer 93), pp. 52 – 53.

— Manual de sología fantástica de Rodolfo Nieto. *Vuelta,* v. 17, no. 200 (July 93), pp. 80 – 82.

— La música de la retina. *Nexos,* v. 16, no. 192 (Dec 93), pp. 9 – 15.

— Pintor de domingo (Accompanied by an English translation). *Artes de México,* no. 18 (Winter 92), p. 69. Il.

Blanco, Hugo Diego. La biblioteca sitiada. *Vuelta,* v. 17, no. 198 (May 93), pp. 67 – 71. Bibl, tables.

Blanco, José Luis et al. El tributo del campo a la ciudad: historias de chaneques y serpientes. *Revista Mexicana de Sociología,* v. 54, no. 3 (July – Sept 92), pp. 131 – 137. Bibl.

Blanco, Luciana. Herminia huye esta noche. *Letras Femeninas,* v. 19, no. 1 – 2 (Spring – Fall 93), pp. 184 – 187.

Blanco B., Gustavo. El movimiento: nuevos panoramas. *Nueva Sociedad,* no. 124 (Mar – Apr 93), pp. 134 – 145.

Blasco, María Concepción and Luis J. Ramos Gómez. Continuidad y cambio: interpretación de la decoración de una vasija nazca. *Revista Andina,* v. 10, no. 2 (Dec 92), pp. 457 – 471. Bibl, il.

Blasi Brambilla, Alberto. Ezeiza, veinte años después. *Todo Es Historia,* v. 27, no. 311 (June 93), pp. 79 – 83. Il.

Blasier, Cole. El fin de la asociación soviético – cubana. *Estudios Internacionales (Chile),* v. 26, no. 103 (July – Sept 93), pp. 296 – 340. Bibl, tables.

— The Impact of Perestroika on Soviet Latin Americanists. *SALALM Papers,* v. 36 (1991), pp. 10 – 14.

Blay, Eva Alterman. Projeto de lei sobre o aborto. *Estudos Feministas,* v. 1, no. 2 (1993), pp. 430 – 434.

Blázquez Domínguez, Carmen. Dos años críticos: la expulsión de los españoles en Xalapa y Veracruz, 1827 – 1828. *Siglo XIX: Cuadernos,* v. 2, no. 4 (Oct 92), pp. 31 – 58. Bibl.

— Proyectos de comunicación por el Istmo de Tehuantepec, 1842 – 1860. *La Palabra y el Hombre,* no. 83 (July – Sept 92), pp. 199 – 217. Bibl.

Blears, James. Getting Down to Bus-ness. *Business Mexico,* v. 3, no. 10 (Oct 93), pp. 23 – 26.

— Measuring Risk. *Business Mexico,* v. 3, no. 11 (Nov 93), pp. 15 – 16.

— Mexico in a No-NAFTA Future. *Business Mexico,* v. 3, no. 11 (Nov 93), pp. 32 – 35.

— The Show Goes On. *Business Mexico,* v. 3, no. 10 (Oct 93), pp. 8 – 11. Il.

— Star-Crossed Mexico. *Business Mexico*, v. 3, no. 12 (Dec 93), pp. 31 – 33. Il.

Bledel, Rodolfo. Epistemología económica y crisis de los sistemas. *Realidad Económica*, no. 116 (May – June 93), pp. 98 – 110. Bibl.

Bletzer, Keith V. Un análisis del rito de vigilia de las mujeres embarazadas entre los indígenas ngawbere, Panamá. *Vínculos*, v. 17, no. 1 – 2 (1991), pp. 53 – 74. Bibl, tables.

Bliss, Elaine. Adaptation to Agricultural Change among Garifuna Women in Hopkins, Belize. *Caribbean Geography*, v. 3, no. 3 (Mar 92), pp. 160 – 174. Bibl, tables, maps.

Block, David. Andean Textiles: Aesthetics, Iconography, and Political Symbolism. *SALALM Papers*, v. 34 (1989), pp. 223 – 231. Il.

— A Core Bibliography of Andean Weaving. *SALALM Papers*, v. 34 (1989), pp. 232 – 233.

— Latin American Book Prices: The Trends of Two Decades. *SALALM Papers*, v. 36 (1991), pp. 305 – 314. Tables, charts.

Blume, Jaime. 1992 y sus libros. *Mensaje*, v. 42, no. 416 (Jan – Feb 93), pp. 53 – 55.

Blym, Hugo. Mina. *Signo*, no. 38, Nueva época (Jan – Apr 93), pp. 211 – 215.

Boaventura, Edivaldo M. A contribuição de Pedro Calmon para a biografia de Castro Alves. *Revista do Instituto Histórico e Geográfico Brasileiro*, no. 370 (Jan – Mar 91), pp. 65 – 77. Bibl.

Bobenrieth H., Eugenio H. and Carlos Cáceres Sandoval. Determinantes del salario de los egresados de la enseñanza media técnico profesional en Chile. *Cuadernos de Economía (Chile)*, v. 30, no. 89 (Apr 93), pp. 111 – 129. Bibl, tables.

Boege, Eckart. Contradicciones en la identidad étnica mazateca: construyendo un objeto de estudio. *Nueva Antropología*, v. 13, no. 43 (Nov 92), pp. 61 – 81. Bibl.

Boero Rojo, Hugo. Orígenes de la polémica Franz Tamayo – Fernando Díez de Medina. *Signo*, no. 36 – 37, Nueva época (May – Dec 92), pp. 43 – 69.

Boggiano, Antonio. Justicia supranacional en América Latina y el Caribe: alternativas para la creación de un sistema. *Integración Latinoamericana*, v. 18, no. 189 – 190 (May – June 93), pp. 18 – 27. Bibl.

Boggio de Harasymowicz, Adriana. Movimientos populares e independencia en México y Uruguay. *La Palabra y el Hombre*, no. 82 (Apr – June 92), pp. 107 – 142. Bibl.

Bohemy, Helena. Novos talentos, vícios antigos: os renovadores e a política educacional. *Estudos Históricos*, v. 6, no. 11 (Jan – June 93), pp. 24 – 39. Bibl.

Bohon, Lisa M. et al. The Effects of Real-World Status and Manipulated Status on the Self-Esteem and Social Competition of Anglo-Americans and Mexican-Americans. *Hispanic Journal of Behavioral Sciences*, v. 15, no. 1 (Feb 93), pp. 63 – 79. Bibl, tables.

Bohórquez, Carmen L. Colonialismo escolar-izado. *Islas*, no. 96 (May – Aug 90), pp. 121 – 126.

Bohórquez R., Douglas. Re-escritura de lo oral y de lo rural en *Las memorias de Mamá Blanca*. *Escritura (Venezuela)*, v. 17, no. 33 – 34 (Jan – Dec 92), pp. 3 – 19.

Boisier E., Sergio. Las transformaciones en el pensamiento regionalista latinoamericano: escenas, discursos y actores. *Estudios Sociales (Chile)*, no. 78 (Oct – Dec 93), pp. 69 – 104. Bibl.

Bolaño Movilla, Rafael. Apuntes sobre la constitución colombiana de 1991. *Desarrollo Indoamericano*, v. 23, no. 91 (June 93), pp. 24 – 25. Il.

Bolaños Arquín, Margarita. Los indígenas y la conservación de la biodiversidad: 500 años de resistencia. *Revista de Historia (Costa Rica)*, no. 25 (Jan – June 92), pp. 165 – 180. Bibl, il, maps, charts.

Bolaños Cárdenas, Alvaro Félix. Panegírico y libelo del primer cronista de Indias, Gonzalo Fernández de Oviedo. *Thesaurus*, v. 45, no. 3 (Sept – Dec 90), pp. 577 – 649. Bibl.

Bolívar, Teolinda. Declaración de Caracas sobre la rehabilitación de los barrios del Tercer Mundo. *Revista Interamericana de Planificación*, v. 26, no. 101 – 102 (Jan – June 93), pp. 231 – 241.

Bolívar Espinoza, Augusto. TLCAN: ganadores y perdedores. *Nueva Sociedad*, no. 126 (July – Aug 93), pp. 110 – 121.

Bolívar Espinoza, Augusto et al. La competencia de partidos: el que siembra vientos cosecha tempestades. *El Cotidiano*, v. 9, no. 54 (May 93), pp. 60 – 71. Il.

— La debilidad de un estado fuerte. *El Cotidiano*, v. 9, no. 53 (Mar – Apr 93), pp. 60 – 68.

— Nuevos tiempos de coyuntura: consolidación del cambio y mucho desafío político. *El Cotidiano*, v. 8, no. 52 (Jan – Feb 93), pp. 60 – 66. Il.

— Partido sin competencia, luego competencia de partidos. *El Cotidiano*, v. 10, no. 57 (Aug – Sept 93), pp. 60 – 72. Il, tables.

— Se preparan tiempos de coyuntura, vísperas del cambio de gobierno. *El Cotidiano*, v. 9, no. 55 (June 93), pp. 60 – 67. Il.

— Los síntomas de la víspera. *El Cotidiano*, v. 9, no. 56 (July 93), pp. 60 – 68. Il.

Bolland, O. Nigel. "Indios Bravos" or "Gentle Savages": 19th Century Views of the "Indians" of Belize and the Miskito Coast. *Revista/Review Interamericana*, v. 22, no. 1 – 2 (Spring – Summer 92), pp. 36 – 54. Bibl.

Bolzman, Claudio. Los exiliados del Cono Sur: dos décadas más tarde. *Nueva Sociedad*, no. 127 (Sept – Oct 93), pp. 126 – 135. Bibl.

Bonano, Luis Marcos and Eduardo Rosenzvaig. Contrapunto azucarero entre relaciones de producción y tecnología: el perfil argentino. *Realidad Económica*, no. 113 (Jan – Feb 93), pp. 52 – 86. Il.

Bonaudo, Marta and Elida Sonzogni. Redes parentales y facciones en la política santafesina, 1850 – 1900. *Siglo XIX: Revista*, no. 11, 2a época (Jan – June 92), pp. 74 – 110. Bibl.

Bonaudo, Marta et al. Ferrocarriles y mercado de tierras en el centro-sur de Santa Fe, 1870 – 1900. *Siglo XIX: Cuadernos*, v. 3, no. 6 (June 93), pp. 37 – 64. Bibl, tables.

Bonavia, Duccio and John G. Jones. Análisis de coprolitos de llama (Lama glama) del precerámico tardío de la costa nor central del Perú. *Bulletin de l'Institut Français d'Etudes Andines*, v. 21, no. 3 (1992), pp. 835 – 852. Bibl, tables.

Bonelli, Regis. Crecimiento y productividad en las industrias brasileñas: efectos de la orientación del comercio exterior. *El Trimestre Económico*, v. 59, Special issue (Dec 92), pp. 109 – 140. Bibl, tables.

Bonelli, Regis and Lauro Roberto Albrecht Ramos. Distribuição de renda no Brasil: avaliação das tendências de longo prazo e mudanças na desigualdade desde meados dos anos '70. *Revista de Economía Política (Brazil)*, v. 13, no. 2 (Apr – June 93), pp. 76 – 97. Bibl, tables, charts.

Bonilla, Flory Stella. Orientación de poblaciones abusadas. *Revista de Ciencias Sociales (Costa Rica)*, no. 59 (Mar 93), pp. 53 – 62. Bibl.

— Sin sueños. *Káñina*, v. 16, no. 2 (July – Dec 92), pp. 215 – 217.

Bonilla Muñoz, Guillermo and Horacio Osorio Velosa. Estructura de mercado y prácticas comerciales en los sectores industrial, minero – energético y de servicios públicos en Colombia. *Planeación y Desarrollo*, v. 24, no. 2 (May – Aug 93), pp. 191 – 256. Tables, charts.

Borda, Dionisio. Empresariado y transición a la democracia en el Paraguay. *Revista Paraguaya de Sociología*, v. 30, no. 86 (Jan – Apr 93), pp. 31 – 66. Tables.

— La estatización de la economía y la privatización del estado en el Paraguay, 1954 – 1989. *Estudios Paraguayos*, v. 17, no. 1 – 2 (1989 – 1993), pp. 37 – 89. Bibl, tables.

Borello, Rodolfo A. Los diarios de Colón y el padre Las Casas. *Cuadernos Hispanoamericanos*, no. 512 (Feb 93), pp. 7 – 22. Bibl, il.

Borges, Dain Edward. "Puffy, Ugly, Slothful, and Inert": Degeneration in Brazilian Social Thought, 1880 – 1940. *Journal of Latin American Studies*, v. 25, no. 2 (May 93), pp. 235 – 256. Bibl.

— Salvador's 1890s: Paternalism and Its Discontents. *Luso-Brazilian Review*, v. 30, no. 2 (Winter 93), pp. 47 – 57. Bibl.

Borges Legrá, Félix. Las primeras manifestaciones del pensamiento filosófico en Cuba: la escolástica como teorización dominante en el período del criollismo. *Islas*, no. 96 (May – Aug 90), pp. 150 – 156.

Borgtaft Pederson, Henrick. Uses and Management of "Aphandra Natalia" (Palmae) in Ecuador. *Bulletin de l'Institut Français d'Etudes Andines*, v. 21, no. 2 (1992), pp. 741 – 753. Bibl, il, tables, maps.

Borinsky, Alicia. Donoso: perros y apuesta sexual. *Estudios Públicos (Chile)*, no. 49 (Summer 93), pp. 279 – 294.

Borja Ochoa, Roberto. La modernización política postergada. *Momento Económico*, no. 65 (Jan – Feb 93), pp. 24 – 25.

Borjas, George J. and Marta Tienda. The Employment and Wages of Legalized Immigrants. *International Migration Review*, v. 27, no. 4 (Winter 93), pp. 712 – 747. Bibl, tables.

Borrat, Héctor. Autocelebración de España: ¿Potenciación de Latinoamérica? *Cuadernos del CLAEH*, v. 17, no. 63 – 64 (Oct 92), pp. 117 – 123.

Borrero Garcés, Luis Enrique. Evaristo García Piedrahita, un varón epónimo. *Boletín de Historia y Antigüedades*, v. 80, no. 780 (Jan – Mar 93), pp. 223 – 231.

Boruchoff, David A. The Conflict of Natural History and Moral Philosophy in *De Antiquitatibus Novae Hispaniae* of Francisco Hernández. *Revista Canadiense de Estudios Hispánicos*, v. 17, no. 2 (Winter 93), pp. 241 – 258. Bibl.

Borzutzky, Silvia. Social Security and Health Policies in Latin America: The Changing Roles of the State and the Private Sector (Review article). *Latin American Research Review*, v. 28, no. 2 (1993), pp. 246 – 256.

Bos, Cornelio A. Wanted Now!: Direct Mail. *Business Mexico*, v. 3, no. 3 (Mar 93), pp. 20 – 23.

Bosch Vinelli, Julia Beatriz. Estudiantes norteños en el Colegio del Uruguay. *Investigaciones y Ensayos*, no. 41 (Jan – Dec 91), pp. 153 – 169. Bibl.

Boschi, Renato Raul and Eli Diniz. Lideranças empresariais e problemas da estratégia liberal no Brasil. *Revista Brasileira de Ciências Sociais*, v. 8, no. 23 (Oct 93), pp. 101 – 119. Bibl.

Boschín, María Teresa. Arqueología: categorías, conceptos, unidades de análisis. *Boletín de Antropología Americana*, no. 24 (Dec 91), pp. 79 – 110. Bibl, il.

— Historia de las investigaciones arqueológicas en Pampa y Patagonia. *Runa*, v. 20 (1991 – 1992), pp. 111 – 114. Bibl.

Bossio Penso, Bertalibia. Guía del Archivo Histórico de la Academia Nacional de la Historia. *Boletín de la Academia Nacional de la Historia (Venezuela)*, v. 75, no. 299 (July – Sept 92), pp. 150 – 156.

Botet, Violanda. Germany and Latin America. *Hemisphere*, v. 5, no. 2 (Winter – Spring 93), pp. 16 – 17.

Botey Sobrado, Ana María. Ferroviarios y portuarios frente al ajuste estructural. *Revista de Ciencias Sociales (Costa Rica)*, no. 60 (June 93), pp. 73 – 84. Bibl.

Bouchain Galicia, Rafael. Análisis sobre concentración y economías de escala en la industria bancaria dentro de la literatura económica: el caso de la banca mexicana. *Problemas del Desarrollo*, v. 24, no. 92 (Jan – Mar 93), pp. 171 – 196. Bibl, tables.

— La fortaleza del nuevo peso. *Momento Económico*, no. 66 (Mar – Apr 93), pp. 7 – 8.

Bouchard, Jean-François et al. Machu Picchu: problemas de conservación de un sitio inca de ceja de selva. *Bulletin de l'Institut Français d'Etudes Andines*, v. 21, no. 3 (1992), pp. 905 – 927. Bibl, il, maps.

Boudet, Rosa Ileana. Inventario de Cádiz. *Conjunto*, no. 93 (Jan – June 93), pp. 113 – 115. Il.

Bouysse-Cassagne, Thérèse. En souvenir de Thierry Saignes (27/09/1946 – 24/08/1992). *Bulletin de l'Institut Français d'Etudes Andines*, v. 21, no. 3 (1992), pp. 1085 – 1092. Il.

Bouzas, Roberto. Apertura comercial e integración en el Cono Sur. *Nueva Sociedad*, no. 125 (May – June 93), pp. 112 – 119.

— ¿Más allá de la estabilización y la reforma?: un ensayo sobre la economía argentina a comienzos de los '90. *Desarrollo Económico (Argentina)*, v. 33, no. 129 (Apr – June 93), pp. 3 – 28. Bibl, tables.

Bowen, Sally and Manuel Jesús Orbegozo. 1992: el año que vivimos al galope. *Debate (Peru)*, v. 15, no. 71 (Nov 92 – Jan 93), pp. 22 – 26. Il.

Boxer, Charles Ralph and José Honório Rodrigues. Correspondência de José Honório Rodrigues: a correspondência com Charles R. Boxer (Organized and annotated by Lêda Boechat Rodrigues). *Revista do Instituto Histórico e Geográfico Brasileiro*, no. 372 (July – Sept 91), pp. 828 – 907. Tables.

Boyd, Antonio Olliz. The Social and Ethnic Contexts of Machado de Assis' *Dom Casmurro*. *Afro-Hispanic Review*, v. 11, no. 1 – 3 (1992), pp. 34 – 41. Bibl.

Boza Dibós, Beatriz. Obstáculo a la inversión extranjera. *Debate (Peru)*, v. 16, no. 75 (Dec 93 – Jan 94), pp. 50 – 51.

Bra, Gerardo. ¿Nacionalismo, nazionalismo o nacionalismo frontal? *Todo Es Historia*, v. 26, no. 308 (Mar 93), pp. 82 – 91. Bibl, il, facs.

Bracho, Diana. La buena-buena y la mala-mala. *Fem*, v. 17, no. 130 (Dec 93), pp. 16 – 17.

Brack Egg, Antonio. La Amazonía: problemas y posibilidades. *Amazonía Peruana*, v. 11, no. 21 (Sept 92), pp. 9 – 22. Il.

Bradford, Colin I., Jr. Orientación y pertinencia de la política económica en América Latina. *Estudios Internacionales (Chile)*, v. 26, no. 102 (Apr – June 93), pp. 165 – 186. Bibl.

Bradley, Peter T. The Defence of Peru, 1648 – 1700. *Jahr-buch für Geschichte von Staat, Wirtschaft und Gesellschaft Lateinamerikas,* v. 29 (1992), pp. 90 – 120. Bibl, tables.

Bradu, Fabienne. Georges Simenon, el inclasificable. *Vuelta,* v. 17, no. 194 (Jan 93), pp. 52 – 55.

Braga, Ricardo Forin Lisboa and Luiz Góes-Filho. A vegetação do Brasil: desmatamento e queimadas. *Revista Brasileira de Geografia,* v. 53, no. 2 (Apr – June 91), pp. 135 – 141. Bibl, tables, maps.

Brailovsky, Antonio Elio. Viedma: la capital inundable. *Todo Es Historia,* v. 26, no. 306 (Jan 93), pp. 60 – 71. Bibl, il.

Brana-Shute, Gary. Guyana '92: It's About Time. *Hemisphere,* v. 5, no. 2 (Winter – Spring 93), pp. 40 – 44. Maps.

Brancato, Sandra Maria Lubisco. A conexão EUA/Brasil e a "questão argentina," 1943 – 1944. *Estudos Ibero-Americanos,* v. 18, no. 1 (July 92), pp. 89 – 101. Bibl.

Brandão, José Vieira. Curt Lange en Recife. *Revista Musical de Venezuela,* no. 28 (May – Dec 89), pp. 83 – 92.

Brander, Laurs. Del diario de navegación del capitán Laurs Brander del bergantín *Fortuna* de Gotemburgo, 6/4 al 21/4 de 1732. *Boletín de la Academia Nacional de la Historia (Venezuela),* v. 75, no. 298 (Apr – June 92), pp. 146 – 150.

Brandi, Carlos E. Poems ("Drama cautiva," "Amor geométrico"). *Hispamérica,* v. 22, no. 64 – 65 (Apr – Aug 93), pp. 132 – 133.

Brandt, Sérgio Alberto and Euclides João Barni. Descentralização, diversificação e tamanho de cooperativas agropecuárias. *Revista de Economia e Sociologia Rural,* v. 30, no. 1 (Jan – Mar 92), pp. 1 – 10. Bibl, tables.

Brash, Jorge. Muros. *Vuelta,* v. 17, no. 204 (Nov 93), p. 33.

Brathwaite, Edward Kamau. Yo, Cristóbal Colón. *Casa de las Américas,* no. 191 (Apr – June 93), pp. 67 – 69.

Bravo, Víctor. Poligrafía y consciencia de la escritura. *Boletín de la Academia Nacional de la Historia (Venezuela),* v. 76, no. 301 (Jan – Mar 93), pp. 106 – 108.

— La realidad del mundo invisible: la poesía de José Lezama Lima. *Revista Nacional de Cultura (Venezuela),* v. 53, no. 285 (Apr – June 92), pp. 22 – 39. Bibl.

— YPF S.A.: ¿Y ahora, qué? *Realidad Económica,* no. 117 (July – Aug 93), pp. 2 – 7.

Bravo-Elizondo, Pedro. Teatro en el Cono Sur: Carlos Manuel Varela (Uruguay). *Latin American Theatre Review,* v. 26, no. 2 (Spring 93), pp. 143 – 150.

Bravo Lira, Bernardino. Una de las universidades más antiguas del mundo. *Atenea (Chile),* no. 465 – 466 (1992), pp. 325 – 328.

— Democracia: ¿Antidoto frente a la corrupción? *Estudios Públicos (Chile),* no. 52 (Spring 93), pp. 299 – 308.

Brebbia, Fernando P. Tendencias de la doctrina agrarista. *Derecho y Reforma Agraria,* no. 23 (1992), pp. 17 – 32.

Breguêz, Sebastião Geraldo. Literatura de cordel em Minas Gerais, Brasil. *Folklore Americano,* no. 52 (July – Dec 91), pp. 145 – 148. Bibl.

Brenken, Anna. El artista Carybé de Salvador da Bahía (Translated by Mónica Perne). *Humboldt,* no. 109 (1993), pp. 70 – 75. Il.

Breslow, Stephen P. Derek Walcott, 1992 Nobel Laureate in Literature. *World Literature Today,* v. 67, no. 2 (Spring 93), pp. 267 – 271. Bibl.

Breton, André. El arte de México (Translated by Fabienne Bradu). *Vuelta,* v. 17, no. 205 (Dec 93), pp. 37 – 39.

Brett, Edward T. The Impact of Religion in Central America: A Bibliographical Essay. *The Americas,* v. 49, no. 3 (Jan 93), pp. 297 – 341. Bibl.

Brezzo, Liliana M. El general Guillermo Miller después de Ayacucho. *Investigaciones y Ensayos,* no. 41 (Jan – Dec 91), pp. 395 – 406. Bibl.

Briceño, José de and Pedro Vicente Sosa Llanos. El "Cólera morbus" en la Venezuela de 1854. *Boletín de la Academia Nacional de la Historia (Venezuela),* v. 76, no. 301 (Jan – Mar 93), pp. 197 – 208.

Briceño Ferrigni, Germán. La ciudad y el escritor. *Boletín de la Academia Nacional de la Historia (Venezuela),* v. 76, no. 301 (Jan – Mar 93), pp. 9 – 18.

Briceño Guerrero, José M. La situación cultural y la auto-consciencia de Latinoamérica y el Caribe. *Montalbán,* no. 24 (1992), pp. 25 – 31.

— La situación cultural y la autoconsciencia de Latinoamérica y el Caribe. *Revista Nacional de Cultura (Venezuela),* v. 53, no. 285 (Apr – June 92), pp. 13 – 21.

Briceño Perozo, Mario. Un criollo de Caracas, asistente de Sevilla e intendente de Andalucia. *Boletín de la Academia Nacional de la Historia (Venezuela),* v. 76, no. 302 (Apr – June 93), pp. 35 – 40. Bibl.

— Factores de diferenciación e instancias integradoras en la experiencia del mundo iberoamericano: Bolívar, arquitecto de la unión. *Boletín de la Academia Nacional de la Historia (Venezuela),* v. 76, no. 302 (Apr – June 93), pp. 21 – 33. Bibl.

— La hazaña de Colón. *Boletín de la Academia Nacional de la Historia (Venezuela),* v. 75, no. 300 (Oct – Dec 92), pp. 111 – 113.

— Isabel I de Castilla. *Boletín de la Academia Nacional de la Historia (Venezuela),* v. 75, no. 300 (Oct – Dec 92), pp. 113 – 115.

— Manuel Briceño Jáuregui, humanista de América. *Boletín de Historia y Antigüedades,* v. 80, no. 781 (Apr – June 93), pp. 327 – 330.

— Manuel Briceño Jáuregui, humanista de América. *Boletín de la Academia Nacional de la Historia (Venezuela),* v. 76, no. 301 (Jan – Mar 93), pp. 110 – 112.

Bridges, Christine M. E. El discurso oficial del Nuevo Mundo. *La Palabra y el Hombre,* no. 81 (Jan – Mar 92), pp. 61 – 69. Bibl.

Brigagão, Clóvis. Atlântico Sul: Zona de Paz e Cooperação. *Política e Estratégica,* v. 8, no. 2 – 4 (Apr – Dec 90), pp. 342 – 346. Bibl.

Brintrup H., Lillianet. El libro móvil: viaje y escritura en algunos viajeros chilenos del siglo XIX. *Revista Chilena de Literatura,* no. 42 (Aug 93), pp. 57 – 64.

Brioso Sánchez, Máximo and Héctor Brioso Santos. La picaresca y América en los siglos de oro. *Anuario de Estudios Americanos,* v. 49 (1992), pp. 207 – 232. Bibl.

Brito, Maria Socorro. O Programa Nacional de Irrigação: uma avaliação prévia dos resultados. *Revista Brasileira de Geografia,* v. 53, no. 2 (Apr – June 91), pp. 113 – 125. Bibl, tables.

Brittin, Alice A. and Kenya C. Dworkin. Rigoberta Menchú: "Los indígenas no nos quedamos como bichos aislados, inmunes, desde hace 500 años. No, nosotros hemos sido protagonistas de la historia" (Includes Rigoberta Menchú's poem, "Patria abnegada"). *Nuevo Texto Crítico,* v. 6, no. 11 (1993), pp. 207 – 222.

Broad, Dave. Revolution, Counterrevolution, and Imperialism: "¡La lucha continúa!" *Latin American Perspectives,* v. 20, no. 2 (Spring 93), pp. 6 – 20. Bibl.

Brocato, Carlos Alberto. Cultura y mitos argentinos. *Cuadernos Hispanoamericanos,* no. 517 – 519 (July – Sept 93), pp. 465 – 470.

Brochet, Michel. Les stratégies de lutte contre l'érosion et l'aménagement des bassins versants en Haïti. *Tiers Monde,* v. 34, no. 134 (Apr – June 93), pp. 423 – 436.

Brociner de Milewicz, Julia. José Rafael Arboleda, S.J. *Boletín de Historia y Antigüedades,* v. 80, no. 781 (Apr – June 93), pp. 287 – 288.

Brögger, Suzanne. El primer tango (Excerpt from *Kvaelstof* translated by Sergio Peña). *Plural (Mexico),* v. 22, no. 262 (July 93), pp. 10 – 13.

Bronner, Fred. Church, Crown, and Commerce in Seventeenth-Century Lima: A Synoptic Interpretation. *Jahrbuch für Geschichte von Staat, Wirtschaft und Gesellschaft Lateinamerikas,* v. 29 (1992), pp. 75 – 89. Bibl.

Brown, Janet Welsh and Arnoldo José Gabaldón. Moving the Americas toward Sustainable Development. *La Educación (USA),* v. 37, no. 115 (1993), pp. 273 – 288. Bibl.

Browne, David M. et al. A Cache of 48 Nasca Trophy Heads from Cerro Carapo, Peru. *Latin American Antiquity,* v. 4, no. 3 (Sept 93), pp. 274 – 294. Bibl, il, maps.

Browning, Richard L. La arquitectura de la memoria: los edificios y sus significados en *El obsceno pájaro de la noche* de José Donoso. *Chasqui,* v. 22, no. 2 (Nov 93), pp. 15 – 23. Bibl.

Bruce-Novoa, John D. Judith Ortiz Cofer's Rituals of Movement. *The Americas Review,* v. 19, no. 3 – 4 (Winter 91), pp. 88 – 99. Bibl.

— El pensamiento chicano. *Plural (Mexico),* v. 22, no. 256 (Jan 93), pp. 19 – 25. Bibl.

— Ritual in Judith Ortiz Cofer's *The Line of the Sun.* *Confluencia,* v. 8, no. 1 (Fall 92), pp. 61 – 69. Bibl.

Bruni Celli, Blas. García Bacca: dos discursos en su presencia. *Boletín de la Academia Nacional de la Historia (Venezuela),* v. 75, no. 299 (July – Sept 92), pp. 164 – 173. Bibl.

— Palabras pronuciadas por el doctor Blas Bruni Celli ante la estatua del Libertador Simón Bolívar en Lisboa el 6 de mayo de 1992, con motivo del I Encuentro de las Academias de Historia de Portugal y Venezuela. *Boletín de la Academia Nacional de la Historia (Venezuela),* v. 76, no. 301 (Jan – Mar 93), pp. 39 – 40.

Brunk, Samuel. Zapata and the City Boys: In Search of a Piece of the Revolution. *Hispanic American Historical Review,* v. 73, no. 1 (Feb 93), pp. 33 – 65. Bibl.

Bruno, Cayetano. La recia personalidad de fray Juan Capistrano Tissera, obispo de Córdoba. *Investigaciones y Ensayos,* no. 41 (Jan – Dec 91), pp. 107 – 137. Bibl.

Brushwood, John Stubbs. Writerly Novels/Readerly Responses. *Latin American Literary Review,* v. 20, no. 40 (July – Dec 92), pp. 23 – 25.

Bruzonic, Erika. Erythroxylum Coca L. *Signo,* no. 38, Nueva época (Jan – Apr 93), pp. 61 – 62.

Bryan, Patrick. Spanish Jamaica. *Caribbean Quarterly,* v. 38, no. 2 – 3 (June – Sept 92), pp. 21 – 31.

Bryce Echenique, Alfredo. Feliz viaje, hermano Antonio. *Debate (Peru),* v. 16, no. 75 (Dec 93 – Jan 94), pp. 74 – 76.

— Nuevas memorias de Adriano. *Nexos,* v. 16, no. 181 (Jan 93), pp. 7 – 9.

— Tiempo y contratiempo (Excerpt from a forthcoming book). *Debate (Peru),* v. 15, no. 71 (Nov 92 – Jan 93), pp. 68 – 74. Il.

Buarque de Hollanda Filho, Sérgio. A crise da indústria automobilística brasileira sob a perspectiva da evolução mundial do setor. *Estudos Econômicos,* v. 23, no. 1 (Jan – Apr 93), pp. 67 – 124. Bibl, tables.

Buccelato, Laura. Acentos y reseñas de los '90. *Cuadernos Hispanoamericanos,* no. 517 – 519 (July – Sept 93), pp. 383 – 387. Il.

Buchenau, Jürgen. Counter-Intervention against Uncle Sam: Mexico's Support for Nicaraguan Nationalism, 1903 – 1910. *The Americas,* v. 50, no. 2 (Oct 93), pp. 207 – 232. Bibl.

Büchi Buc, Hernán. Reactivación económica en tiempos de recesión. *Apuntes (Peru),* no. 30 (Jan – June 92), pp. 91 – 103.

Buenahora Febres-Cordero, Jaime. Reglamentación y desarrollo de la constitución del '91. *Revista Javeriana,* v. 61, no. 597 (Aug 93), pp. 183 – 189.

Bueno Chávez, Raúl et al. Debate (on the first session of the symposium "Latinoamérica: Nuevas Direcciones en Teoría y Crítica Literarias, III"). *Revista de Crítica Literaria Latinoamericana,* v. 19, no. 38 (July – Dec 93), pp. 63 – 69.

— Mesa redonda inicial: nuevas direcciones; estado de la cuestión y desarrollos recientes. *Revista de Crítica Literaria Latinoamericana,* v. 19, no. 38 (July – Dec 93), pp. 11 – 33.

Bueno Rodríguez, Luis and Salvador T. Porras Duarte. Deshomologación salarial: ¿Cuánto por punto? *El Cotidiano,* v. 9, no. 55 (June 93), pp. 91 – 98. Tables, charts.

Buffet, Jacky. Le Brésil: du "miracle" à la difficile gestion de l'"après-miracle." *Cahiers des Amériques Latines,* no. 14 (1992), pp. 67 – 93. Bibl.

Buffington, Robert. Revolutionary Reform: The Mexican Revolution and the Discourse on Prison Reform. *Mexican Studies,* v. 9, no. 1 (Winter 93), pp. 71 – 93. Bibl.

Buffon, Alain. La Banque de la Guadeloupe en 1895: le rapport Chaudie. *Revista/Review Interamericana,* v. 22, no. 1 – 2 (Spring – Summer 92), pp. 191 – 207. Bibl.

Buisseret, David and Arthur Holzheimer. The Enigma of the Jean Bellère Maps of the New World, 1554: A Historical Note. *Colonial Latin American Historical Review,* v. 2, no. 3 (Summer 93), pp. 363 – 367. Maps.

Bullard G., Alfredo. El juez peruano, ¿protagonista o extra? *Debate (Peru),* v. 16, no. 75 (Dec 93 – Jan 94), pp. 48 – 49.

Bumas, Ethan Shaskan. Metaphor's Exile: The Poets and Postmen of Antonio Skármeta. *Latin American Literary Review,* v. 21, no. 41 (Jan – June 93), pp. 9 – 20. Bibl.

Bunch, Charlotte. Feminismo, democracia y derechos humanos (Paper presented at the congress "Mujer, Violencia y Derechos Humanos," Mexico, March 1993, translated by Victoria Zamudio Jasso). *Fem,* v. 17, no. 125 (July 93), pp. 6 – 10.

Bunel, Jean. Sindicalismo, democracia y desarrollo (Translated by Francisco Zapata). *Estudios Sociológicos,* v. 11, no. 31 (Jan – Apr 93), pp. 133 – 153. Bibl.

Burbach, Roger. Clinton's Latin American Policy: A Look at Things to Come. *NACLA Report on the Americas,* v. 26, no. 5 (May 93), pp. 16 – 22 +. Bibl, il.

Burga, Manuel et al. ¿Por qué seguir discutiendo 1492? (A roundtable of six Peruvian intellectuals). *Hueso Húmero,* no. 29 (May 93), pp. 3 – 67.

Burgos, Nidia. Un documento inédito de Martínez Estrada: la creación de otra *Tierra purpúrea;* una república libertaria, federal y representativa. *Cuadernos Americanos,* no. 42, Nueva época (Nov – Dec 93), pp. 157 – 164. Bibl.

Burgueño Lomelí, Fausto. América Latina: el desarrollo del subdesarrollo. *Problemas del Desarrollo,* v. 24, no. 92 (Jan – Mar 93), pp. 103 – 115. Tables.

Burguera, Magaly. Macuro: vigía de boca de dragos. *Revista de Historia de América,* no. 113 (Jan – June 92), pp. 65 – 102. Bibl, il, charts.

Burin, Mabel. Algunos aportes al debate feminismo – posmodernismo. *Feminaria,* v. 6, no. 10 (Apr 93), pp. 21 – 23. Bibl.

Burkart, Rodolfo. Nuestros bosques norteños: desvaloración y deterioro. *Realidad Económica,* no. 114 – 115 (Feb – May 93), pp. 54 – 73. Bibl, tables, charts.

Burkhart, Louise M. Mujeres mexicas en "el frente" del hogar: trabajo doméstico y religión en el México azteca. *Mesoamérica (USA),* v. 13, no. 23 (June 92), pp. 23 – 54. Bibl, il.

Burt, Jo-Marie. The Dispossessed Look Homeward: Peru's Internal Refugees Organize for Return. *NACLA Report on the Americas,* v. 27, no. 1 (July – Aug 93), pp. 8 – 11. Il.

Burton, Richard D. E. Créolité, Négritude, and Metropolis. *Hemisphere,* v. 5, no. 3 (Summer – Fall 93), pp. 10 – 12. Il.

Busquet I., Jaime. INPROA: treinta años presente en el mundo rural. *Mensaje,* v. 42, no. 418 (May 93), pp. 154 – 156. Il.

Busquets, Loreto. Victoria Ocampo a través de su *Autobiografía. Cuadernos Hispanoamericanos,* no. 510 (Dec 92), pp. 121 – 133.

Bustamante, Jorge I. Optical Disk Possibilities in the Distribution of Information on Latin American Art. *SALALM Papers,* v. 34 (1989), pp. 316 – 322. Tables.

Bustamante, Juan I. La princesa Donaji (Accompanied by an English translation). *Artes de México,* no. 21 (Fall 93), pp. 34 – 35.

Bustamante Belaúnde, Alberto et al. Pensando en la reelección. *Debate (Peru),* v. 16, no. 72 (Mar – May 93), pp. 14 – 18. Il, charts.

Bustamante García, Jesús. De la naturaleza y los naturales americanos en el siglo XVI: algunas cuestiones críticas sobre la obra de Francisco Hernández. *Revista de Indias,* v. 52, no. 195 – 196 (May – Dec 92), pp. 297 – 328. Bibl.

Bustamante Ponce, Fernando. Ecuador: Putting an End to Ghosts of the Past? (Translated by Jane Marchi). *Journal of Inter-American Studies and World Affairs,* v. 34, no. 4 (Winter 92 – 93), pp. 195 – 224. Bibl.

Bustos Romero, Olga. Mujeres y telenovelas: audiencia cautiva; ¿Sumisa o crítica? *Fem,* v. 17, no. 130 (Dec 93), pp. 20 – 21.

Butler, Ron. The Colors between Earth and Sky. *Américas,* v. 45, no. 2 (Mar – Apr 93), pp. 14 – 21. Il.

Buvinich, Manuel J. Rojas. The Evaluation of Rural Development Projects Using the Social Accounting Matrix Approach. *Revista Brasileira de Economia,* v. 46, no. 4 (Oct – Dec 92), pp. 555 – 593. Bibl, tables.

Buye-Goyri Minter, Rafael. En torno a *Los demonios y los días. La Palabra y el Hombre,* no. 84 (Oct – Dec 92), pp. 240 – 245. Bibl.

Byé, Pascal and Jean-Pierre Frey. Le modèle chilien à la lumière de l'expérience des pays agro-exportateurs de l'ASEAN. *Cahiers des Amériques Latines,* no. 14 (1992), pp. 37 – 49. Bibl, tables.

Byrne, Malcolm and Peter R. Kornbluh. Iran – Contra: A Postmortem. *NACLA Report on the Americas,* v. 27, no. 3 (Nov – Dec 93), pp. 29 – 34 +. Il.

Caballero, Antonio et al. Su lucha no propicia la justicia social (A reprinted letter signed by many Colombian intellectuals objecting to the use of violence and terrorism by the guerrillas). *Nueva Sociedad,* no. 125 (May – June 93), pp. 146 – 147.

Caballero, Atilio J. Algo más que un teatro sin historia. *Conjunto,* no. 90 – 91 (Jan – June 92), pp. 92 – 96. Il.

Caballero, Claudia. Fin de milenio y el príncipe no llega. *Plural (Mexico),* v. 22, no. 267 (Dec 93), p. 55.

Caballero Wangüemert, María del Milagro. Discurso histórico y carnavalización de la historia: "El juramento" de René Marqués. *Revista Iberoamericana,* v. 59, no. 162 – 163 (Jan – June 93), pp. 145 – 156. Bibl.

Caballeros Otero, Rómulo. Reflexiones sobre la integración centroamericana en la década de 1990. *Integración Latinoamericana,* v. 17, no. 185 (Dec 92), pp. 17 – 22.

Cabanillas, Gilberto. Poems ("Poema," "El mar aparecía . . . "). *Plural (Mexico),* v. 22, no. 261 (June 93), pp. 23 – 24.

Cabello, Felipe C. La arqueología y la cultura maya: a propósito del premio Nobel de la paz, 1992 (Review article). *Interciencia,* v. 18, no. 5 (Sept – Oct 93), pp. 272 – 275.

Cabello Naranjo, Elena. El censo agropecuario de 1991: un retrato del campo mexicano. *Comercio Exterior,* v. 43, no. 4 (Apr 93), pp. 392 – 394. Tables, charts.

— La política presupuestaria para 1993. *Comercio Exterior,* v. 43, no. 1 (Jan 93), pp. 21 – 29. Tables.

— La siderurgia: ¿Una señal equivocada? *Comercio Exterior,* v. 43, no. 5 (May 93), pp. 463 – 469. Tables.

— III Cumbre Iberoamericana: hacia una agenda de desarrollo. *Comercio Exterior,* v. 43, no. 9 (Sept 93), pp. 836 – 839.

Cabezas Lacayo, Omar. Testimonio de mis testimonios: sobre preguntas de Edward Waters Hood. *Hispamérica,* v. 22, no. 64 – 65 (Apr – Aug 93), pp. 111 – 120.

Cabra Ybarra, José G. Las relaciones de México con Latinoamérica durante la última década: ¿Líder, intérprete o interlocutor? *Relaciones Internacionales (Mexico),* v. 14, Nueva época, no. 56 (Oct – Dec 92), pp. 117 – 122.

Cabrera, Ernesto. La cuestión de la proporcionalidad y las elecciones legislativas en la República Argentina. *Revista Mexicana de Sociología,* v. 54, no. 4 (Oct – Dec 92), pp. 153 – 182. Bibl.

— Magnitud de distrito y fórmula electoral en la representación proporcional. *Desarrollo Económico (Argentina),* v. 33, no. 130 (July – Sept 93), pp. 281 – 294. Bibl, tables.

Cabrera, Jorge René. Dos tiros de gracia. *Plural (Mexico),* v. 22, no. 267 (Dec 93), pp. 18 – 21.

Cabrera, Miguel. Las capitulaciones de una derrota. *Cuadernos Hispanoamericanos,* no. 513 (Mar 93), pp. 149 – 155. Bibl.

Cabrera, Napoleón. La música argentina entre 1970 y 1990. *Cuadernos Hispanoamericanos,* no. 517 – 519 (July – Sept 93), pp. 280 – 288. Il.

Cabrera, Vicente. Refracciones del cuerpo y la palabra de Eva Luna. *Revista Interamericana de Bibliografía,* v. 42, no. 4 (1992), pp. 591 – 615. Bibl.

Cabrera Acevedo, Gustavo. La población y la búsqueda de equilibrios. *Comercio Exterior,* v. 43, no. 7 (July 93), pp. 612 – 617. Bibl.

Cabrera Infante, Guillermo. Alice in Wondercontinent (Translated by Alfred MacAdam). *Review,* no. 47 (Fall 93), pp. 14 – 15.

— Guantanamerías: sobre un emblema musical de los años '60. *Vuelta,* v. 17, no. 203 (Oct 93), pp. 11 – 13.

— La Lupe cantaba: "Con el diablo en el cuerpo y un ángel en la voz." *Vuelta,* v. 17, no. 200 (July 93), pp. 19 – 20.

— Oh Bahia (Translated by Alfred MacAdam). *Review,* no. 47 (Fall 93), pp. 16 – 19.

— Sobre una tumba una rumba. *Vuelta,* v. 17, no. 201 (Aug 93), pp. 22 – 23.

Cacciamali, Maria Cristina and Paulo Springer de Freitas. Do capital humano ao salário-eficiência: uma aplicação para analisar os diferenciais de salários em cinco ramos manufatureiros da grande São Paulo. *Pesquisa e Planejamento Econômico,* v. 22, no. 2 (Aug 92), pp. 343 – 367. Bibl, tables.

Cacciatore, Julio. Dos décadas de arquitectura argentina: universalidad e identidad en la arquitectura argentina. *Cuadernos Hispanoamericanos,* no. 517 – 519 (July – Sept 93), pp. 207 – 230. Bibl, il.

Cáceres, Armando. 1994: el crecimiento debe llegar a todos. *Debate (Peru),* v. 16, no. 75 (Dec 93 – Jan 94), pp. 20 – 21. Il.

Cáceres, Luis René. Ecuador y la integración andina: experiencias y perspectivas. *Integración Latinoamericana,* v. 18, no. 195 (Nov 93), pp. 31 – 46. Bibl, tables, charts.

— Elementos para una estrategia centroamericana de renegociación de la deuda externa y captación de recursos. *ECA; Estudios Centroamericanos,* v. 48, no. 537 – 538 (July – Aug 93), pp. 693 – 709. Bibl, tables.

Cáceres Corrales, Pablo. La tutela: procesos, resultados, consecuencias y limitaciones. *Revista Javeriana,* v. 61, no. 598 (Sept 93), pp. 237 – 245.

Cáceres Romero, Adolfo. El "jukumari" en la literatura oral de Bolivia. *Revista de Crítica Literaria Latinoamericana,* v. 19, no. 37 (Jan – June 93), pp. 243 – 258.

Cáceres Sandoval, Carlos and Eugenio H. Bobenrieth H. Determinantes del salario de los egresados de la enseñanza media técnico profesional en Chile. *Cuadernos de Economía (Chile),* v. 30, no. 89 (Apr 93), pp. 111 – 129. Bibl, tables.

Cáceres Vega, Baldomero. Toros: balance ferial. *Debate (Peru),* v. 16, no. 75 (Dec 93 – Jan 94), p. 69. Il.

Cachan, Manuel. *En cuerpo de camisa* de Luis Rafael Sánchez: la antiliteratura alegórica del otro puertorriqueño. *Revista Iberoamericana,* v. 59, no. 162 – 163 (Jan – June 93), pp. 177 – 186. Bibl.

Cacua Prada, Antonio. Jorge Caro Copete. *Boletín de Historia y Antigüedades,* v. 80, no. 781 (Apr – June 93), pp. 373 – 375.

— 30 años del Instituto Universitario de Historia de Colombia. *Boletín de Historia y Antigüedades,* v. 80, no. 780 (Jan – Mar 93), pp. 121 – 203. Bibl.

Cadena, Agustín. *Farabeuf:* el espacio como metáforo del tiempo. *Plural (Mexico),* v. 22, no. 258 (Mar 93), pp. 50 – 56. Bibl.

Caetano, Mericy. Graciliano Ramos en la novela del '30. *Hoy Es Historia,* v. 10, no. 60 (Nov – Dec 93), pp. 39 – 42. Bibl.

Cagnin, Maria Aparecida H. The State of Scientific Research in Chemistry: A View from the Brazilian Community. *Interciencia,* v. 18, no. 3 (May – June 93), pp. 146 – 154. Bibl, tables.

Caiceo E., Jaime. El planteamiento filosófico – político de Maritain aplicado en Chile. *Estudios Sociales (Chile),* no. 76 (Apr – June 93), pp. 205 – 210. Bibl.

Caisso, Claudia. "El zumo del secreto se esfumara": algunas aventuras verbales en *Yo el Supremo. Escritura (Venezuela),* v. 17, no. 33 – 34 (Jan – Dec 92), pp. 143 – 148.

Cajamarca Castro, Orlando. Esquina Latina: dos décadas de teatro. *Latin American Theatre Review,* v. 26, no. 2 (Spring 93), pp. 167 – 170.

Cajero Vázquez, Antonio. En el crucero. *Plural (Mexico),* v. 22, no. 267 (Dec 93), pp. 36 – 37.

Calcagno, Alfredo Eric and Pedro Sáinz. In Search of Another Form of Development. *CEPAL Review,* no. 48 (Dec 92), pp. 7 – 38. Bibl, tables, charts.

Caldeira, Teresa Pires do Rio. Comentários a partir do artigo "A violência política na América Latina." *Revista Brasileira de Ciências Sociais,* v. 8, no. 21 (Feb 93), pp. 44 – 47.

Calderón, Enriqueta. Poems ("Pesadumbres," "Un instante para el infinito"). *Letras Femeninas,* v. 19, no. 1 – 2 (Spring – Fall 93), p. 176.

Calderón, Fina de. Repaso de la poesía boliviana: dos poetas en Madrid: Oscar Rivera-Rodas y Pedro Shimose. *Signo,* no. 35, Nueva época (Jan – Apr 92), pp. 5 – 13.

Calderón, Gabriela. Amor y tradición en la fiesta de la Virgen de las Peñas. *Mensaje,* v. 42, no. 425 (Dec 93), pp. 617 – 618. Il.

Calderón González, Arnoldo. El sector externo antes de la flotación del quetzal: capacidad de pagos internacionales de Guatemala, 1970 – 1988. *USAC,* no. 12 (Dec 90), pp. 66 – 75. Tables.

Calderón Gutiérrez, Fernando. The Trade Union System: Its Background and Future Prospects. *CEPAL Review,* no. 49 (Apr 93), pp. 103 – 115. Bibl.

Caldwell, Lynton Keith. Strategies in Hemispheric Cooperation for Environmentally Sustainable Development. *La Educación (USA),* v. 37, no. 115 (1993), pp. 257 – 272. Bibl.

Calla Ortega, Ricardo. Comentario (on the article by Roger Cortez). *Estado y Sociedad,* v. 8, no. 9 (Jan – June 92), pp. 91 – 98.

Calle Lombana, Humberto de la. Proyecto de reforma electoral (Previously published in this journal, no. 507, 1984). *Revista Javeriana,* v. 61, no. 596 (July 93), pp. 105 – 108.

Calligaris, Contardo. Brasil: país do futuro de quem? *Vozes,* v. 86, no. 6 (Nov – Dec 92), pp. 21 – 29.

Caloi

See
Loiseau, Carlos

Calva, José Luis. La reforma neoliberal del régimen agrario: en el cuarto año de gobierno de C. S. G. *Problemas del Desarrollo,* v. 24, no. 92 (Jan – Mar 93), pp. 31 – 39. Tables.

Calvi, Maria Vittoria. El diálogo entre españoles e indígenas en la *XIII relación* de Fernando de Alva Ixtlilxóchitl. *Quaderni Ibero-Americani,* no. 72 (Dec 92), pp. 621 – 639. Bibl.

Calvillo, Tomás. Una paradoja en el corazón de México (Accompanied by an English translation). *Artes de México,* no. 18 (Winter 92), pp. 26 – 27. Il.

Calviño Iglesias, Julio. Augusto Roa Bastos y la gran melopea de lo mismo. *Insula,* no. 562 (Oct 93), pp. 19 – 20. Il.

Calvo, Bernardino S. Nicolás Repetto y Juan B. Justo, pioneros de la educación rural. *Todo Es Historia,* v. 27, no. 315 (Oct 93), pp. 50 – 53. Il.

Calvo Buezas, Tomás. ¿Hacia una nueva identidad? (Commentary on the Latin American Conferences of Heads of State). *Cuadernos Americanos,* no. 41, Nueva época (Sept – Oct 93), pp. 14 – 75.

Calvo Coin, Luis Alberto. Las políticas económicas aplicadas en Costa Rica y los orígenes y bases de la política económica neoliberal o neoclásica. *Revista de Ciencias Sociales (Costa Rica),* no. 60 (June 93), pp. 101 – 115. Bibl.

Calzadilla, Juan. Angel Peña: el calmo y brillante acontecer del trópico. *Revista Nacional de Cultura (Venezuela),* v. 54, no. 287 (Oct – Dec 92), pp. 157 – 160.

— El Círculo de Bellas Artes y los paisajistas de la luz, 1912 – 1992. *Revista Nacional de Cultura (Venezuela),* v. 53, no. 286 (July – Sept 92), pp. 95 – 105. Il.

— Marcos Castillo o cómo rehacer la naturaleza en el taller. *Revista Nacional de Cultura (Venezuela),* v. 53, no. 285 (Apr – June 92), pp. 219 – 223. Il.

Camacho, Georgette de. Poesía mística de Juan Quirós. *Signo,* no. 36 – 37, Nueva época (May – Dec 92), pp. 211 – 213.

Camacho, Jorge Alejandro. Poems ("Del riego," "Historias del hombre," "Un día después del regreso de Odiseo"). *La Palabra y el Hombre,* no. 82 (Apr – June 92), pp. 186 – 187.

Camacho Naranjo, Luis A. Tradición, modernidad y tendencias contemporáneas en la cultura científica en Costa Rica. *Cuadernos Americanos,* no. 38, Nueva época (Mar – Apr 93), pp. 121 – 134. Bibl.

Câmara, Ibsen de Gusmão. Gestão do território: uma perspectiva conservacionista. *Revista Brasileira de Geografia,* v. 53, no. 3 (July – Sept 91), pp. 161 – 168. Bibl.

Câmara, Luís da

See
Cascudo, Luís da Câmara

Cámara, Madeline. La dama del jardín. *Plural (Mexico),* v. 22, no. 262 (July 93), pp. 23 – 24.

Camargo, José Márcio and Edward Joaquim Amadeo Swaelen. Liberalização comercial, distribuição e emprego. *Revista de Economia Política (Brazil),* v. 13, no. 4 (Oct – Dec 93), pp. 58 – 76. Bibl, tables.

— Política comercial e distribuição funcional da renda. *Pesquisa e Planejamento Econômico,* v. 22, no. 1 (Apr 92), pp. 73 – 100. Bibl, tables, charts.

Camargo Pérez, Gabriel. Los descubridores del Chocó. *Boletín de Historia y Antigüedades,* v. 79, no. 779 (Oct – Dec 92), pp. 1007 – 1018. Bibl.

Cameron, Maxwell A. and Ricardo Grinspun. Mexico: The Wages of Trade. *Report on the Americas,* v. 26, no. 4 (Feb 93), pp. 32 – 37 +. Bibl, il.

Camhi P., Rosa and Patricia Matte Larraín. Pobreza en la década de los '90 y desafíos futuros. *Estudios Sociales (Chile),* no. 75 (Jan – Mar 93), pp. 39 – 56. Tables.

Caminos, Hugo. Staying on Course with Law (Translated by Willem Daniels). *Américas,* v. 45, no. 5 (Sept – Oct 93), pp. 56 – 57.

Camnitzer, Luis. La 45ª Bienal de Venecia. *Art Nexus,* no. 10 (Sept – Dec 93), pp. 58 – 63. Il.

Camnitzer, Luis et al. XXXIV Salón Nacional de Artistas (Accompanied by an English translation). *Art Nexus,* no. 7 (Jan – Mar 93), pp. 140 – 144. Il.

Camou, Antonio N. Gobernabilidad y democracia en Mexico: avantares de una transición incierta. *Nueva Sociedad,* no. 128 (Nov – Dec 93), pp. 102 – 119.

Campbell, Howard B. Tradition and the New Social Movements: The Politics of Isthmus Zapotec Culture. *Latin American Perspectives,* v. 20, no. 3 (Summer 93), pp. 83 – 97. Bibl.

Campbell, Shirley. A Nicolás Guillén. *Afro-Hispanic Review,* v. 12, no. 1 (Spring 93), p. 48.

Campbell, Tim et al. Descentralización hacia los gobiernos locales en América Latina y el Caribe. *Planeación y Desarrollo,* v. 24, no. 1 (Jan – Apr 93), pp. 27 – 95. Tables, charts.

Campero, Ana María de. Comentario (on the article by Carlos D. Mesa Gisbert). *Estado y Sociedad,* v. 8, no. 9 (Jan – June 92), pp. 69 – 72.

Campo, Angel Esteban-P. del. Bécquer y Martí: una audiencia especial con el sentimiento. *Anuario de Letras (Mexico),* v. 30 (1992), pp. 177 – 189. Bibl.

Campo del Pozo, Fernando. Los mártires agustinos en la misión de Aricagua, Venezuela. *Boletín de la Academia Nacional de la Historia (Venezuela),* v. 76, no. 302 (Apr – June 93), pp. 119 – 129. Bibl.

Campos, José Carlos. Los primeros músicos españoles llegadas al Perú y los siguientes mestizajes musicales producidos en el Perú. *Revista Musical de Venezuela,* no. 28 (May – Dec 89), pp. 127 – 148. Bibl, facs.

Campos, José Carlos et al. Estado de la música en el Perú (An interview with five Peruvian composers). *Hueso Húmero,* no. 29 (May 93), pp. 93 – 104.

Campos, José Ribamar Silva and José de Jesus Sousa Lemos. Fundamentação dinâmica para a produção e comercialização de hortifrutigranjeiros. *Revista de Economia e Sociologia Rural,* v. 30, no. 1 (Jan – Mar 92), pp. 11 – 20. Bibl, tables.

Campos, Nauro and João Carlos Ferraz. Uma discussão sobre o padrão de concorrência no complexo eletrônico brasileiro. *Estudos Econômicos,* v. 23, no. 1 (Jan – Apr 93), pp. 125 – 147. Bibl, tables.

Campos Aragón, Leticia. Economía y humanismo: un modesto homenaje al maestro Jesús Silva Herzog. *Problemas del Desarrollo,* v. 24, no. 92 (Jan – Mar 93), pp. 221 – 225.

— El TLC y la nueva cultura laboral. *Momento Económico,* no. 65 (Jan – Feb 93), pp. 26 – 30.

Campos Castañeda, Jesús Martín del. El SNTE después del acuerdo. *El Cotidiano,* v. 8, no. 51 (Nov – Dec 92), pp. 71 – 75. Il.

Campos Flores, Nivia. Consideraciones para la evaluación de los estudiantes en la enseñanza superior. *Revista Cultural Lotería,* v. 51, no. 388 (Mar – Apr 92), pp. 48 – 61. Bibl.

Campos Harriet, Fernando. Dr. Edmundo Correas, historiador de Cuyo: réquiem para un gran señor. *Boletín de la Academia Chilena de la Historia,* v. 58 – 59, no. 102 (1991 – 1992), pp. 39 – 40.

— 1492 – 1992: la más gigantesca fusión vital. *Boletín de la Academia Chilena de la Historia,* v. 58 – 59, no. 102 (1991 – 1992), pp. 239 – 268. Bibl, il.

— La Real Audiencia de Concepción. *Atenea (Chile),* no. 465 – 466 (1992), pp. 151 – 156.

— La Real Audiencia de Concepción, 1565 – 1573. *Boletín de la Academia Chilena de la Historia,* v. 58 – 59, no. 102 (1991 – 1992), pp. 534 – 538.

Campos Mitjans, Gertrudis and Jesús Guanche Pérez. La antropología cultural en Cuba durante el presente siglo. *Interciencia,* v. 18, no. 4 (July – Aug 93), pp. 176 – 183. Bibl.

Camps Cruell, Carlos M. Fe, responsabilidad, democracia: desde una perspectiva de una historia de la creación; un desafío para América Latina hoy. *Cristianismo y Sociedad,* v. 30, no. 113 (1992), pp. 35 – 44.

Camuñas, Jaime. Dos letras a Rafael Hernández: in memoriam (Includes the poems "Lamento borincano," "Preciosa," "Mañanita campanera," "El cumbanchero," "El buen borincano," and "Mi guajirita"). *Homines,* v. 15 – 16, no. 2 – 1 (Oct 91 – Dec 92), pp. 327 – 337. Bibl.

Camuñas Madera, Ricardo R. El progreso material y las epidemias de 1856 en Puerto Rico. *Jahrbuch für Geschichte von Staat, Wirtschaft und Gesellschaft Lateinamerikas,* v. 29 (1992), pp. 241 – 277. Bibl.

Cañadell, Rosa M. Chilean Women's Organizations: Their Potential for Change (Translated by John F. Uggen). *Latin American Perspectives,* v. 20, no. 4 (Fall 93), pp. 43 – 60. Bibl.

Cancelada, Gregory D. et al. Market Moves. *Business Mexico,* v. 3 (1993), All issues.

Cancino, César and Víctor Alarcón Olguín. La relación gobierno – partido en un régimen semi-competitivo: el caso de México. *Revista Mexicana de Ciencias Políticas y Sociales,* v. 38, Nueva época, no. 151 (Jan – Mar 93), pp. 9 – 33. Bibl.

Candanedo, César A. Mamá – señora. *Revista Cultural Lotería,* v. 50, no. 383 (May – June 91), pp. 52 – 56.

Candelaria, Nash. Affirmative Action. *The Americas Review,* v. 20, no. 3 – 4 (Fall – Winter 92), pp. 39 – 46.

— The Dancing School. *Bilingual Review/Revista Bilingüe,* v. 17, no. 3 (Sept – Dec 92), pp. 256 – 263.

— Dear Rosita. *The Americas Review,* v. 19, no. 2 (Summer 91), pp. 5 – 11.

Candia, José Miguel. Tendencias recientes de la participación laboral femenina en América Latina. *Problemas del Desarrollo,* v. 24, no. 93 (Apr – June 93), pp. 195 – 209. Bibl, tables.

Candotti, Ennio. O sistema federal de ensino superior: problemas das alternativas (Comment on the article of the same title by Eunice Ribeiro Durham). *Revista Brasileira de Ciências Sociais,* v. 8, no. 23 (Oct 93), pp. 38 – 41.

Canelas, Jorge. Comentario (on the articles by Javier Protzel and Jorge Lazarte). *Estado y Sociedad,* v. 8, no. 9 (Jan – June 92), pp. 35 – 37.

Cánepa, María Angela. Recuerdos, olvidos y desencuentros: aproximaciones a la subjetividad de los jóvenes andinos. *Allpanchis,* v. 25, no. 41 (Jan – June 93), pp. 11 – 37. Bibl.

Canfield, Martha L. Muerte y redención en la poesía de César Vallejo. *Inti,* no. 36 (Fall 92), pp. 39 – 44. Bibl.

Cano, Lidia and Pablo M. Guadarrama González. Filosofía de la liberación en Colombia. *Islas,* no. 99 (May – Aug 91), pp. 51 – 74. Bibl.

Cañón Ortegón, Leonardo. La salud en el estado colombiano. *Revista Javeriana,* v. 61, no. 592 (Mar 93), pp. 76 – 80.

Canto Chac, Manuel. Elementos para una agenda de discusión sobre el futuro de la acción gubernamental. *El Cotidiano,* v. 10, no. 58 (Oct – Nov 93), pp. 39 – 46. Bibl.

Canziani Amico, José and Santiago Uceda C. Evidencias de grandes precipitaciones en diversas etapas constructivas de La Huaca de la Luna, costa norte del Perú. *Bulletin de l'Institut Français d'Etudes Andines,* v. 22, no. 1 (1993), pp. 313 – 343. Bibl, il.

Caparrós, Martín. Mientras *Babel. Cuadernos Hispanoamericanos,* no. 517 – 519 (July – Sept 93), pp. 525 – 528.

Capdevielle, Mario and Gabriela Dutrénit. El perfil tecnológico de la industria mexicana y su dinámica innovadora en la década de los ochenta. *El Trimestre Económico,* v. 60, no. 239 (July – Sept 93), pp. 643 – 674. Bibl, tables, charts.

Capdevila, Analía. Sobre la teatralidad en la narrativa de Arlt. *Cuadernos Hispanoamericanos,* no. Special issue, 11 (July 93), pp. 53 – 57. Facs.

Capdeville, Guy. O ensino superior agrícola no Brasil. *Revista Brasileira de Estudos Pedagógicos,* v. 72, no. 172 (Sept – Dec 91), pp. 229 – 261. Bibl, tables, charts.

Capetillo Hernández, Juan. Las voces del agua. *La Palabra y el Hombre,* no. 82 (Apr – June 92), pp. 301 – 305.

Cappelletti, Angel J. Pierre Clastres: la sociedad contra el estado. *Revista de Filosofía de la Universidad de Costa Rica,* v. 30, no. 72 (Dec 92), pp. 145 – 151.

Captain-Hidalgo, Yvonne. El espíritu de la risa en el cuento de Ana Lydia Vega. *Revista Iberoamericana,* v. 59, no. 162 – 163 (Jan – June 93), pp. 301 – 308. Bibl.

Caravaglia, Juan Carlos. Los labradores de San Isidro, siglos XVIII – XIX. *Desarrollo Económico (Argentina),* v. 32, no. 128 (Jan – Mar 93), pp. 513 – 542. Bibl, tables, charts.

Carbonell de Masy, Rafael. Análisis crítico de la ley vigente de cooperativas en el Paraguay. *Estudios Paraguayos,* v. 17, no. 1 – 2 (1989 – 1993), pp. 91 – 103.

Cardenal, Ernesto. Vénganos a la tierra la república de los cielos. *Cuadernos Americanos,* no. 40, Nueva época (July – Aug 93), pp. 35 – 52.

Cardenal Chamorro, Rodolfo. Las crisis del proceso de pacificación. *ECA; Estudios Centroamericanos,* v. 47, no. 529 – 530 (Nov – Dec 92), pp. 963 – 981. Il.

— La expansión imperial española en Centroamérica. *ECA; Estudios Centroamericanos,* v. 47, no. 528 (Oct 92), pp. 841 – 854. Il.

— El fracaso del estado salvadoreño. *ECA; Estudios Centroamericanos,* v. 48, no. 534 – 535 (Apr – May 93), pp. 351 – 375. Il.

Cárdenas, Fe Esperanza and Vincent Redonnet. Modernización de la empresa AHMSA en Monclova, Coahuila y su impacto sobre la población. *Estudios Demográficos y Urbanos,* v. 6, no. 3 (Sept – Dec 91), pp. 677 – 716. Bibl, tables.

Cárdenas, Manuel José. La integración andina: indicio de una nueva etapa. *Revista Javeriana,* v. 61, no. 594 (May 93), pp. 210 – 215.

Cárdenas Arroyo, Felipe. Pastos y quillacingas: dos grupos étnicos en busca de identidad arqueológica. *Revista Colombiana de Antropología,* v. 29 (1992), pp. 63 – 79. Bibl, il, tables.

Cárdenas de la Peña, Enrique. La política económica en la época de Cárdenas. *El Trimestre Económico,* v. 60, no. 239 (July – Sept 93), pp. 675 – 697. Bibl, tables.

Cárdenas Gueudinot, Mario. Grupos marginados en los inicios de la era republicana: vagabundos, mendigos e indigentes. *Cuadernos de Historia (Chile),* no. 11 (Dec 91), pp. 47 – 61. Bibl, tables.

Cardona Torrico, Alcira. Carta a Gustavo Medinaceli, porque los poetas nunca mueren. *Signo,* no. 36 – 37, Nueva época (May – Dec 92), pp. 3 – 12.

Cardoso, Eliana Anastasia. Cuba: un caso único de reforma anti-mercado; comentarios al artículo de Carmelo Mesa-Lago. *Pensamiento Iberoamericano,* no. 22 – 23, tomo II (July 92 – June 93), pp. 101 – 107. Tables.

— Cyclical Variations of Earnings Inequality in Brazil. *Revista de Economia Política (Brazil),* v. 13, no. 4 (Oct – Dec 93), pp. 112 – 124. Bibl, tables, charts.

— Private Investment in Latin America. *Economic Development and Cultural Change,* v. 41, no. 4 (July 93), pp. 833 – 848. Bibl, tables, charts.

Cardoso, Maria Francisca Thereza. Organização e reorganização do espaço no vale do Paraíba do sul: uma análise geográfica até 1940. *Revista Brasileira de Geografia,* v. 53, no. 1 (Jan – Mar 91), pp. 81 – 135. Bibl, maps.

Cardoso, Tereza Maria R. Fachada Levy. A *Gazeta do Rio de Janeiro:* subsídios para a história da cidade, 1808 – 1821. *Revista do Instituto Histórico e Geográfico Brasileiro,* no. 371 (Apr – June 91), pp. 341 – 436. Bibl, il, tables, maps.

Cardoso Frías, Joaquín. When the Inspector Calls . . . Be Prepared! *Business Mexico,* v. 3, no. 1 (Jan – Feb 93), p. 87.

Cardoso Vargas, Gilberto A. Iberoamérica ante la agenda internacional de fin de siglo. *Problemas del Desarrollo,* v. 24, no. 94 (July – Sept 93), pp. 275 – 281.

Cardozo-Freeman, Inez. José Inés Chávez García: Hero or Villain of the Mexican Revolution? (Includes the text of two corridos). *Bilingual Review/Revista Bilingüe,* v. 18, no. 1 (Jan – Apr 93), pp. 3 – 13. Bibl.

Cardozo Galué, Germán. El circuito agroexportador marabino a mediados del siglo XIX. *Boletín Americanista,* v. 33, no. 42 – 43 (1992 – 1993), pp. 367 – 393. Bibl, maps, charts.

Careaga, Gabriel. Gustavo Sáinz: una literatura incandescente. *Nexos,* v. 16, no. 184 (Apr 93), pp. 69 – 71.

Carlos, Ana Maria. De roca e fuso. *Revista de Letras (Brazil),* v. 32 (1992), pp. 101 – 107. Bibl.

Carlsen, Laura. A Failure to Educate. *Business Mexico,* v. 3, no. 6 (June 93), pp. 10 – 13. Il, tables, charts.

— Feeding Mexico. *Business Mexico,* v. 3, no. 7 (July 93), pp. 11 – 15. Il.

— Making Money in Difficult Times. *Business Mexico,* v. 3, no. 11 (Nov 93), pp. 4 – 7. Tables, charts.

— Reflexiones sobre un proyecto sindical feminista: el Sindicato "19 de Septiembre" siete años después del sismo. *El Cotidiano,* v. 9, no. 53 (Mar – Apr 93), pp. 93 – 98. Bibl, tables, charts.

— Worker Protection under NAFTA. *Business Mexico,* v. 3, no. 10 (Oct 93), pp. 38 – 39. Il.

Carminatti, Mario and Jorge Larrañaga. De intendentes a gobernadores: coloquio con los intendentes. *Cuadernos del CLAEH,* v. 18, no. 67 (Nov 93), pp. 19 – 34.

Carmona de la Peña, Fernando. IV Informe Presidencial: ¿Mayor transnacionalización y más soberanía? *Momento Económico,* no. 65 (Jan – Feb 93), pp. 2 – 7.

Carmona Estanga, Pedro. Políticas de convergencia y efectos del ajuste en la integración regional. *Integración Latinoamericana,* v. 18, no. 191 (July 93), pp. 30 – 36.

Carnegie, James Alexander. Sporting Hero and More. *Jamaica Journal,* v. 25, no. 1 (Oct 93), pp. 38 – 43. Il.

Carneiro, José Mário et al. Meio ambiente, empresário e governo: conflitos ou parceria? *RAE; Revista de Administração de Empresas,* v. 33, no. 3 (May – June 93), pp. 68 – 75. Bibl.

Carneiro, Maria Cecília Ribas. A política externa do Brasil e a segunda guerra mundial. *Revista do Instituto Histórico e Geográfico Brasileiro,* no. 373 (Oct – Dec 91), pp. 1032 – 1051. Bibl.

Carnese, Francisco R. et al. Análisis histórico y estado actual de la antropología biológica en la Argentina. *Runa,* v. 20 (1991 – 1992), pp. 35 – 67. Bibl.

Caro Copete, Jorge. Las Ciudades Amigas y Confederadas del Valle. *Boletín de Historia y Antigüedades,* v. 80, no. 781 (Apr – June 93), pp. 377 – 386.

Caro Figueroa, Gregorio A. Oleada democratizadora en el Cono Sur. *Todo Es Historia,* v. 27, no. 317 (Dec 93), pp. 78 – 81. Il.

Carpentier, Alejo. Prologue to *The Kingdom of This World* (Translated by Alfred MacAdam). *Review,* no. 47 (Fall 93), pp. 28 – 31.

Carpizo, Jorge. América Latina y sus problemas. *Cuadernos Americanos,* no. 42, Nueva época (Nov – Dec 93), pp. 28 – 42.

— Los derechos de la tercera generación: paz y desarrollo. *Cuadernos Americanos,* no. 39, Nueva época (May – June 93), pp. 27 – 33.

Carranza, Andrés. Poems ("Ganga Slanga," "Cruisin' the Boulevard"). *Bilingual Review/Revista Bilingüe,* v. 18, no. 1 (Jan – Apr 93), pp. 58 – 60.

Carranza Valdés, Julio. New Challenges for Cuban Policy toward Central America (Translated by Lucía Rayas). *Latin American Perspectives,* v. 20, no. 1 (Winter 93), pp. 58 – 63.

Carrasco, Hernán. Indígenas serranos en Quito y Guayaquil: relaciones interétnicas y urbanización de migrantes. *América Indígena,* v. 51, no. 4 (Oct – Dec 91), pp. 159 – 183. Bibl.

Carrasco, Sergio. Jugar en pared. *Debate (Peru),* v. 16, no. 72 (Mar – May 93), p. 57. Il.

Carrasco Muñoz, Iván. Literatura etnocultural en Hispanoamérica: concepto y precursores. *Revista Chilena de Literatura,* no. 42 (Aug 93), pp. 65 – 72. Bibl.

Carrazzoni, José Andrés. El caballo del indio del desierto. *Todo Es Historia,* v. 27, no. 315 (Oct 93), pp. 76 – 89. Bibl, il.

— De ganaderos y veterinarios. *Todo Es Historia,* v. 26, no. 306 (Jan 93), pp. 28 – 38. Bibl, il.

— Manuel José de Lavardén: poeta, ganadero y patriota. *Todo Es Historia,* v. 26, no. 310 (May 93), pp. 54 – 62. Bibl, il.

Carreño, Guillermina. Poesía ("Histectomía," "Melancolía," "Pasos"). *Plural (Mexico),* v. 22, no. 261 (June 93), pp. 55 – 57.

Carreño King, Tania and Angélica Vázquez del Mercado. Crítica de la historia pragmática: una entrevista con Luis González y González. *Nexos,* v. 16, no. 191 (Nov 93), pp. 35 – 39.

— La disputa por la historia patria: una entrevista con Lorenzo Meyer. *Nexos,* v. 16, no. 191 (Nov 93), pp. 41 – 49.

— La hija de la invención: una entrevista con Edmundo O'Gorman. *Nexos,* v. 16, no. 190 (Oct 93), pp. 45 – 51.

Carrera, Arturo. Qui sont les autres? *Vuelta,* v. 17, no. 205 (Dec 93), pp. 20 – 22.

Carretero, Andrés M. Las prostitutas en Buenos Aires. *Todo Es Historia,* v. 27, no. 315 (Oct 93), pp. 46 – 49.

Carriazo Moreno, George. Las relaciones económicas Cuba – Estados Unidos: una mirada al futuro. *Estudios Internacionales (Chile),* v. 26, no. 103 (July – Sept 93), pp. 480 – 499. Bibl, tables.

Carrillo, Mario Alejandro and Miguel Angel Romero Miranda. Un rostro nuevo en una vieja identidad: el Foro Doctrinario y Democrático en la formación de un nuevo partido político. *El Cotidiano,* v. 9, no. 53 (Mar – Apr 93), pp. 105 – 109. Bibl, il.

Carrillo, Mario Alejandro et al. Entre la contingencia y la permanencia: los municipios con alternancia del Partido Acción Nacional. *El Cotidiano,* v. 10, no. 58 (Oct – Nov 93), pp. 91 – 97. Il, maps.

Carrillo Castro, Alejandro and Miguel Angel Romero Miranda. Las preocupaciones públicas: el caso de Tamaulipas. *El Cotidiano,* v. 8, no. 51 (Nov – Dec 92), pp. 95 – 101. Tables.

Carrillo Viveros, Jorge and Oscar F. Contreras. Calificación en el trabajo: análisis de la industria maquiladora.
Frontera Norte, v. 4, no. 8 (July – Dec 92), pp. 49 – 78. Bibl,
tables, charts.

Carrington, Selwyn H. H. The American Revolution, British
Policy, and the West Indian Economy, 1775 – 1808.
Revista/Review Interamericana, v. 22, no. 1 – 2 (Spring –
Summer 92), pp. 72 – 108. Bibl, tables.

Cartón de Grammont, Hubert. Algunas reflexiones en
torno al mercado de trabajo en el campo latinoamericano.
Revista Mexicana de Sociología, v. 54, no. 1 (Jan – Mar
92), pp. 49 – 58. Bibl.

Carvajal Morera, Hannia and Julio Bejarano Orozco.
Abuso de drogas y conducta delictiva. *Revista de Ciencias
Sociales (Costa Rica),* no. 60 (June 93), pp. 51 – 62. Bibl,
tables, charts.

**Carvalhais, Jane Noronha and João Eustáquio da
Lima.** Distribuição dos ganhos com inovação tecnológica
na produção de milho entre categorias de pequenos produtores em Minas Gerais. *Revista de Economia e Sociologia Rural,* v. 29, no. 4 (Oct – Dec 91), pp. 373 – 385. Bibl.

Carvalho, Carlos Eduardo Vieira de. Brasil: la caída de
Collor. *Nueva Sociedad,* no. 124 (Mar – Apr 93), pp. 22 –
26.

— Liquidez dos haveres financeiros e zeragem automática
do mercado. *Revista de Economia Política (Brazil),* v. 13,
no. 1 (Jan – Mar 93), pp. 25 – 36.

Carvalho, Fernando. Egon Schaden: Aavanimondyiá
(1913 – 1991). *Revista de Antropologia (Brazil),* v. 34
(1991), pp. 239 – 240.

Carvalho, Flávio Condé de and Samira Aóun Marques.
Concentração municipal do beneficiamento de algodão no
estado do Paraná nos anos oitenta. *Revista de Economia e
Sociologia Rural,* v. 30, no. 2 (Apr – June 92), pp. 149 –
157. Bibl, tables.

Carvalho, José Geraldo Vidigal de. Atualidade de Jackson de Figueiredo. *Convivium,* v. 34, no. 2 (July – Dec 91),
pp. 150 – 153.

— A influencia da igreja na política social do Brasil: uma
visão histórica. *Convivium,* v. 34, no. 2 (July – Dec 91), pp.
138 – 145. Bibl.

Carvalho, José Jorge de. Aesthetics of Opacity and Transparence: Myth, Music, and Ritual in the Xangô Cult and in
the Western Art Tradition. *Latin American Music Review,* v.
14, no. 2 (Fall – Winter 93), pp. 202 – 231. Bibl, tables, facs.

— As duas faces da tradição: o clássico e o popular na
modernidade latinoamericana. *Dados,* v. 35, no. 3 (1992),
pp. 403 – 434.

**Carvalho, Maria Auxiliadora de and César Roberto
Leite da Silva.** Preços mínimos e estabilização de preços
agrícolas. *Revista de Economia Política (Brazil),* v. 13, no.
1 (Jan – Mar 93), pp. 52 – 63. Bibl, tables.

Carvalho, Martha de Ulhôa. Musical Style, Migration, and
Urbanization: Some Considerations on Brazilian "Música
Sertaneja" (Country Music). *Studies in Latin American Pop-
ular Culture,* v. 12 (1993), pp. 75 – 94. Bibl, tables.

Carvalho, Sílvia M. S. Miguel Angel Menéndez (1949 –
1991). *Revista de Antropologia (Brazil),* v. 34 (1991), pp.
240 – 242. Bibl.

Carvalho, Sônia Maria Rodrigues de. Inscrição e busca.
Revista de Letras (Brazil), v. 32 (1992), pp. 41 – 49.

Carvalho-Neto, Paulo de. Folklore extraterrestre II: los caminos y las bases. *Folklore Americano,* no. 53 (Jan – June
92), pp. 11 – 36. Bibl.

— La universalidad de Italia según la memoria popular: ensayo metódico sobre la confluencia tradicional entre Italia y
el Nuevo Mundo, basado en 294 hechos folklóricos. *Folklore Americano,* no. 53 (Jan – June 92), pp. 133 – 140. Bibl.

Casadinho, Javier Souza and Roberto Benencia. Alimentos y salud: uso y abuso de pesticidas en la horticultura
bonaerense. *Realidad Económica,* no. 114 – 115 (Feb –
May 93), pp. 29 – 53. Bibl, tables.

Casado, Miguel. Pistas para llegar a Gerardo Deniz. *Vuelta,*
v. 17, no. 198 (May 93), pp. 63 – 64.

Casado Arboniés, Manuel. VI Jornadas sobre la Presencia
Universitaria Española en América. *Anuario de Estudios
Americanos,* v. 49, Suppl. 2 (1992), pp. 214 – 217.

Casañas Díaz, Mirta. La recepción del marxismo en la obra
de Leopoldo Zea. *Islas,* no. 96 (May – Aug 90), pp. 164 –
176. Bibl.

— Una variante del humanismo burgués en América Latina.
Islas, no. 98 (Jan – Apr 91), pp. 143 – 156. Bibl.

Casañas Díaz, Mirta and Rafael Plá León. La constancia
de Leopoldo Zea en la búsqueda de un filosofar autenticamente americano. *Islas,* no. 99 (May – Aug 91), pp. 95 –
111. Bibl.

Casanova, Ramón Vicente. El derecho agrario iberoamericano: su vocación regional. *Derecho y Reforma Agraria,*
no. 24 (1993), pp. 11 – 26.

— Por qué la reforma agraria. *Derecho y Reforma Agraria,*
no. 23 (1992), pp. 11 – 16.

Casanova, Ramón Vicente et al. Consideraciones sobre
un proyecto vial: carretera Mérida – La Culata – Tucani. *Derecho y Reforma Agraria,* no. 23 (1992), pp. 163 – 183.

Casanueva Valencia, Fernando. Una peste de viruelas en
la región de la frontera de guerra hispano-indígena en el
reino de Chile, 1791. *Revista de Historia (Costa Rica),* no.
26 (July – Dec 92), pp. 31 – 65. Bibl, maps, charts.

Casar González, Eduardo. Imagen y semejanza. *Plural
(Mexico),* v. 22, no. 261 (June 93), pp. 25 – 31.

Casar Pérez, José I. La competitividad de la industria manufacturera mexicana, 1980 – 1990. *El Trimestre Económico,* v. 60, no. 237 (Jan – Mar 93), pp. 113 – 183. Bibl,
tables, charts.

Casaravilla, Diego. La cultura política uruguaya desde el
carnaval: heroísmo antimilitar, crisis del socialismo real y
MERCOSUR. *Cuadernos del CLAEH,* v. 18, no. 65 – 66
(May 93), pp. 151 – 165. Bibl.

Casas Castañeda, Fernando. Política exterior en el campo
de los recursos genéticos, el medio ambiente y la economía
internacional. *Revista Javeriana,* v. 61, no. 594 (May 93),
pp. 277 – 282. Bibl.

Casas Chousal, Xolóxochitl and Sara Lovera. Razones
y sinrazones de CIMAC y la población. *Fem,* v. 17, no. 128
(Oct 93), pp. 8 – 10.

Casaus Arzú, Marta Elena. La metamorfosis de las oligarquías centroamericanas. *Revista Mexicana de Sociología,*
v. 54, no. 3 (July – Sept 92), pp. 69 – 114. Bibl, tables,
charts.

Cascudo, Luís da Câmara. Jangada e carro de bois (Originally published in this journal in May 1941). *Vozes,* v. 87,
no. 4 (July – Aug 93), pp. 91 – 96.

Casevitz, France-Marie

See

Renard-Casevitz, France-Marie

Casimir de Brizuela, Gladys. Proyecto arqueológico Loma
Iguana. *La Palabra y el Hombre,* no. 81 (Jan – Mar 92), pp.
348 – 357. Bibl, il, maps, charts.

Cassá, Roberto and Genaro Rodríguez Morel. Consideraciones alternativas acerca de las rebeliones de esclavos en Santo Domingo. *Anuario de Estudios Americanos,* v. 50, no. 1 (1993), pp. 101 – 131. Bibl.

Cassaniga, Néstor J.

See

Cazzaniga, Néstor J.

Castaingts Teillery, Juan. Las olimpiadas . . . : nación, juego, rito y cultura. *Nueva Antropología,* v. 13, no. 44 (Aug 93), pp. 119 – 136. Bibl.

Castañeda, Gabriel et al. Antecedentes económicos para una ley federal de competencia económica. *El Trimestre Económico,* v. 60, no. 237 (Jan – Mar 93), pp. 230 – 268. Bibl.

Castañeda, Jorge G. La dinámica de las jerarquías y coaliciones. *Relaciones Internacionales (Mexico),* v. 15, Nueva época, no. 57 (Jan – Mar 93), pp. 95 – 96.

Castañeda, Jorge G. and Carlos Heredia. Hacia otro TLC. *Nexos,* v. 16, no. 181 (Jan 93), pp. 43 – 54.

Castañeda, Tarcisio. Descentralización de los sectores sociales: riesgos y oportunidades. *Planeación y Desarrollo,* v. 24, no. 1 (Jan – Apr 93), pp. 97 – 115. Tables, charts.

Castañeda Fuertes, Digna. Presencia africana en la identidad cultural de las sociedades caribeñas. *Boletín de la Academia Nacional de la Historia (Venezuela),* v. 75, no. 299 (July – Sept 92), pp. 77 – 90. Bibl.

Castañeda García, Carmen. Informe del simposio: "Las Elites Hispanoamericanas en el Período Colonial." *Anuario de Estudios Americanos,* v. 49, Suppl. 1 (1992), pp. 175 – 181.

Castañón, Adolfo. Aproximaciones a Rossi. *Vuelta,* v. 17, no. 200 (July 93), pp. 64 – 66.

— Diario del delta. *Vuelta,* v. 17, no. 201 (Aug 93), pp. 35 – 42.

— Dos voces mujeres. *Vuelta,* v. 17, no. 202 (Sept 93), pp. 60 – 63.

— Sergio Pitol o la metamorfosis del costumbrismo (Excerpt from the book *Arbitrario). Vuelta,* v. 17, no. 199 (June 93), pp. 22 – 23.

— El tesoro de Mutis. *Vuelta,* v. 17, no. 205 (Dec 93), pp. 60 – 63.

Castañón Barrientos, Carlos. La crítica literaria de Juan Quirós. *Signo,* no. 36 – 37, Nueva época (May – Dec 92), pp. 207 – 210.

— Escritores extranjeros en Bolivia (Segunda parte). *Signo,* no. 38, Nueva época (Jan – Apr 93), pp. 15 – 25.

Castellanos Guerrero, Alicia and Gilberto López y Rivas. Grupos étnicos y procesos nacionalitarios en el capitalismo neoliberal. *Nueva Antropología,* v. 13, no. 44 (Aug 93), pp. 27 – 41. Bibl.

Castello, Antonio Emilio. Entrevista: Eugenio Pucciarelli. *Todo Es Historia,* v. 26, no. 305 (Dec 92), pp. 58 – 64. Il.

— Entrevista al ex-vicepresidente de la república, dr. Víctor Martínez. *Todo Es Historia,* v. 27, no. 317 (Dec 93), pp. 84 – 95. Il.

— El porfiriato en México. *Todo Es Historia,* v. 26, no. 307 (Feb 93), pp. 9 – 34. Il.

Castilla Urbano, Francisco. Juan Ginés de Sepúlveda: en torno a una idea de civilización. *Revista de Indias,* v. 52, no. 195 – 196 (May – Dec 92), pp. 329 – 348. Bibl.

Castillo, Abelardo. La década vacía. *Cuadernos Hispanoamericanos,* no. 517 – 519 (July – Sept 93), pp. 604 – 611.

Castillo, Alejandro. The Challenge to Deliver (Translated by Richard Cadena). *Business Mexico,* v. 3, no. 7 (July 93), pp. 4 – 10. Maps, charts.

— Industrial Chambers: A Continuing Saga (Translated by Robert Brackney). *Business Mexico,* v. 3, no. 8 (Aug 93), pp. 10 – 13.

Castillo, Francisco A. and Zenaida Vizcaino Bravo. Observación del fitoplancton del Pacífico colombiano durante 1991 – 1992 en condiciones El Niño. *Bulletin de l'Institut Français d'Etudes Andines,* v. 22, no. 1 (1993), pp. 179 – 190. Bibl, il, maps.

Castillo, Jorge Luis. De la guerra a las sombras: sobre los pasos de *Peregrinación* de René Marqués. *Revista Iberoamericana,* v. 59, no. 162 – 163 (Jan – June 93), pp. 157 – 167. Bibl.

Castillo, José. Qué legitimidad para qué crisis: opciones de políticas. *Realidad Económica,* no. 114 – 115 (Feb – May 93), pp. 86 – 98. Bibl.

Castillo, José María. El nuevo catecismo y las cuestiones que plantea. *ECA; Estudios Centroamericanos,* v. 48, no. 536 (June 93), pp. 599 – 605. Il.

Castillo, Lidia E. La "mujer fatal" en la novela hispanoamericana contemporánea. *Revista Cultural Lotería,* v. 50, no. 384 (July – Aug 91), pp. 76 – 82.

Castillo, Tito. Gratos recuerdos de Vicente Huidobro y Jacques Lipchitz. *Atenea (Chile),* no. 467 (1993), pp. 149 – 154. Il, facs.

Castillo de Berchenko, Adriana. Texto e intertexto en "Chuchezuma" de Juan Emar. *Revista Chilena de Literatura,* no. 40 (Nov 92), pp. 123 – 128.

Castillo F., Dídimo. ¿Fin de las fronteras?: la migración indocumentada de México hacia Estados Unidos. *Problemas del Desarrollo,* v. 24, no. 93 (Apr – June 93), pp. 95 – 119. Bibl, tables.

Castillo G., Manuel Angel. La economía centroamericana y la inmigración a México. *Comercio Exterior,* v. 43, no. 8 (Aug 93), pp. 763 – 773. Bibl, tables.

Castillo Galástica, Adán. Cuestiones del desarrollo: la modernización en el agro-panameño. *Revista Cultural Lotería,* v. 50, no. 386 (Nov – Dec 91), pp. 25 – 46. Bibl.

Castillo Lara, Lucas Guillermo. San Juan Bautista de Colón, de Ayacucho y Sucre, Almirante de Lejanías, mariscal de voluntades. *Boletín de la Academia Nacional de la Historia (Venezuela),* v. 75, no. 300 (Oct – Dec 92), pp. 43 – 67. Bibl.

Castillo Martos, Manuel. III Congreso Latinoamericano de Historia de la Ciencia y la Tecnología. *Anuario de Estudios Americanos,* v. 49, Suppl. 1 (1992), pp. 196 – 201.

Castillo Peraza, Carlos. Viaje a Yucatán (sin Stephens). *Nexos,* v. 16, no. 182 (Feb 93), pp. 67 – 68.

Castillo Zapata, Rafael. Palabras recuperadas: la poesía venezolana de los ochenta: rescate y transformación de las palabras de la tribu; el caso "Tráfico." *Hispamérica,* v. 22, no. 64 – 65 (Apr – Aug 93), pp. 67 – 75.

— Palabras recuperadas: la poesía venezolana de los ochenta: rescate y transformación de las palabras de la tribu; el caso "Tráfico." *Inti,* no. 37 – 38 (Spring – Fall 93), pp. 197 – 205.

Castrillón, Ernesto G. Panorama del audio y el video histórico en la Argentina. *Todo Es Historia,* v. 27, no. 315 (Oct 93), p. 61. Il.

Castro, Adrian. Music and Guaracha When Stories Sound Too Tall. *Bilingual Review/Revista Bilingüe,* v. 18, no. 1 (Jan – Apr 93), pp. 53 – 55.

Castro, Carlo Antonio. Claudio. *La Palabra y el Hombre,* no. 84 (Oct – Dec 92), p. 62.

— ¡Totazqueh, Teicniuh Chuchotzin! *La Palabra y el Hombre,* no. 81 (Jan – Mar 92), p. 391.

— Wolferl. *La Palabra y el Hombre,* no. 81 (Jan – Mar 92), pp. 20 – 22.

Castro, Fernando. Luis González Palma: los iluminados (Accompanied by an English translation). *Art Nexus,* no. 7 (Jan – Mar 93), pp. 136 – 138. Il.

Castro, Mary Garcia. Alquimia de categorias sociais na produção dos sujeitos políticos: gênero, raça e geração entre líderes do Sindicato de Trabalhadores Domésticos em Salvador. *Estudos Feministas,* v. 0, no. 0 (1992), pp. 57 – 73. Bibl.

Castro, Nadya Araújo and Antônio Sérgio Alfredo Guimarães. Trabalhadores afluentes, indústrias recentes: revisitando a tese da aristocracia operária. *Dados,* v. 35, no. 2 (1992), pp. 173 – 191. Bibl.

Castro, Nils. Panamá: de movimientos sociales a partidos populares. *Nueva Sociedad,* no. 125 (May – June 93), pp. 15 – 19.

Castro, Sílvio. Europa America Americhe: la geometria asimmetrica. *Quaderni Ibero-Americani,* no. 72 (Dec 92), pp. 732 – 742. Bibl.

Castro Escudero, Alfredo. Deuda externa: avances y sinsabores del esfuerzo regional. *Comercio Exterior,* v. 43, no. 1 (Jan 93), pp. 58 – 66. Bibl, tables.

— Días de guardar en la industria editorial. *Comercio Exterior,* v. 43, no. 5 (May 93), pp. 430 – 437. Bibl.

— Días de temple para la siderurgia. *Comercio Exterior,* v. 43, no. 3 (Mar 93), pp. 201 – 206. Bibl, tables.

— Inflación en Argentina: ¿Un problema resuelto? *Comercio Exterior,* v. 43, no. 10 (Oct 93), pp. 954 – 964. Bibl.

— Productividad: el gran reto de la industria mexicana. *Comercio Exterior,* v. 43, no. 2 (Feb 93), pp. 125 – 128. Tables.

Castro Guerrero, Gustavo. Evolución de las relaciones colombo – ecuatorianas durante el gobierno del señor presidente César Gaviria. *Revista Javeriana,* v. 61, no. 594 (May 93), pp. 217 – 223. Tables, charts.

Castro-Klarén, Sara. Situations. *Latin American Literary Review,* v. 20, no. 40 (July – Dec 92), pp. 26 – 29.

Castro Leiva, Luis. The Dictatorship of Virtue or Opulence of Commerce. *Jahrbuch für Geschichte von Staat, Wirtschaft und Gesellschaft Lateinamerikas,* v. 29 (1992), pp. 195 – 240. Bibl.

Castro Martignoni, Jorge. México: estimación de la migración internacional en el período 1960 – 1980. *Estudios Fronterizos,* no. 26 (Sept – Dec 91), pp. 71 – 122. Bibl, tables.

Castro Martínez, Pedro Fernando. Comercio e inversiones México – Canadá: un asunto trilateral. *Comercio Exterior,* v. 43, no. 5 (May 93), pp. 498 – 506. Bibl, tables.

— Corporativismo y TLC: las viejas y nuevas alianzas del estado. *Plural (Mexico),* v. 22, no. 261 (June 93), pp. 63 – 73. Bibl.

Castro-Mitchell, Amanda. Autoridad y poder social de la mujer en Honduras: un estudio sociolingüístico de los pronombres de tratamiento. *Fem,* v. 17, no. 127 (Sept 93), pp. 42 – 45. Tables.

Castro S., Claudio de. El papel del estudiante universitario en el desarrollo científico y tecnológico. *Revista Cultural Lotería,* v. 50, no. 386 (Nov – Dec 91), pp. 58 – 66.

Castro Socarras, Alvaro. Pedro Castro Monsalvo. *Desarrollo Indoamericano,* v. 23, no. 91 (June 93), pp. 54 – 61. Il.

Castro Vega, Jorge. Poems ("Excalibur 7:30 a.m.," "Una copa con Hamlet"). *Hispamérica,* v. 22, no. 64 – 65 (Apr – Aug 93), pp. 134 – 135.

Castro y Castro, Manuel de. Lenguas indígenas americanas transmitidas por los franciscanos del siglo XVIII. *Archivo Ibero-Americano,* v. 52, no. 205 – 208 (Jan – Dec 92), pp. 585 – 628. Bibl.

Catalá, Rafael. La vanguardia atalayista y la obra de Clemente Soto Vélez. *Revista Iberoamericana,* v. 59, no. 162 – 163 (Jan – June 93), pp. 101 – 109. Bibl.

Cataño, Gonzalo. De la publicación oral a la publicación impresa: estrategias para desarrollar la producción intelectual en la universidad. *Revista Paraguaya de Sociología,* v. 29, no. 84 (May – Aug 92), pp. 7 – 23. Bibl.

Catão, Luís. A New Wholesale Price Index for Brazil during the Period 1870 – 1913. *Revista Brasileira de Economia,* v. 46, no. 4 (Oct – Dec 92), pp. 519 – 533. Bibl, tables, charts.

Catasús Cervera, Sonia Isabel. La nupcialidad durante la década de los ochenta en Cuba. *Estudios Demográficos y Urbanos,* v. 7, no. 2 – 3 (May – Dec 92), pp. 465 – 477. Bibl, tables.

Catatumbo, Pablo. La doctrina de la seguridad nacional: el principal obstáculo para la paz. *Revista Javeriana,* v. 60, no. 590 (Nov – Dec 92), pp. 303 – 315.

Caulfield, Carlota. Canción de la verdad sencilla: Julia de Burgos y su diálogo erótico – místico con la naturaleza. *Revista Iberoamericana,* v. 59, no. 162 – 163 (Jan – June 93), pp. 119 – 126. Bibl.

Caulfield, Sueann. Women of Vice, Virtue, and Rebellion: New Studies of Representation of the Female in Latin America (Review article). *Latin American Research Review,* v. 28, no. 2 (1993), pp. 163 – 174.

Caulfield, Sueann and Martha de Abreu Esteves. 50 Years of Virginity in Rio de Janeiro: Sexual Politics and Gender Roles in Juridical and Popular Discourse, 1890 – 1940. *Luso-Brazilian Review,* v. 30, no. 1 (Summer 93), pp. 47 – 74. Bibl, tables.

Causse, Cos. Vallejianas. *Casa de las Américas,* no. 191 (Apr – June 93), pp. 90 – 91.

Cavagnari Filho, Geraldo Lesbat. Introdução à estratégia brasileira. *Política e Estratégica,* v. 8, no. 2 – 4 (Apr – Dec 90), pp. 347 – 351.

Cayo Córdova, Percy. Santa Cruz y O'Higgins: dos efemérides de 1992. *Apuntes (Peru),* no. 31 (July – Dec 92), pp. 3 – 18.

Cazón, Sandra. Las fiestas populares en Hispanoamérica: el carnaval en la Argentina a principios del siglo XX. *Jahrbuch für Geschichte von Staat, Wirtschaft und Gesellschaft Lateinamerikas,* v. 29 (1992), pp. 343 – 367. Bibl.

Cazzaniga, Néstor J. Cecilia Grierson y las aves. *Todo Es Historia,* v. 26, no. 307 (Feb 93), pp. 46 – 47. Bibl, il.

— Historias de vampiros y hombres lobo. *Todo Es Historia,* v. 26, no. 309 (Apr 93), pp. 8 – 26. Bibl, il, maps.

Ceballos, Marta. Metodología cuantitativa para una caracterización diacrónica de recursos humanos desocupados. *Revista Paraguaya de Sociología,* v. 29, no. 85 (Sept – Dec 92), pp. 157 – 169. Bibl, tables, charts.

Ceballos Ramírez, Manuel and Lawrence D. Taylor. Síntesis histórica del poblamiento de la región fronteriza México – Estados Unidos. *Estudios Fronterizos,* no. 26 (Sept – Dec 91), pp. 9 – 37. Bibl.

Cebreros, Alfonso. La competitividad agropecuaria en condiciones de apertura económica. *Comercio Exterior,* v. 43, no. 10 (Oct 93), pp. 946 – 953. Bibl.

Cebreros, Alfonso and Carlos Pomareda. Mecanismos financieros para la modernización de la agricultura. *Comercio Exterior,* v. 43, no. 4 (Apr 93), pp. 328 – 335. Bibl, tables, charts.

Cebrián González, Carmen. Expediciones franciscanas a Indias, 1725 – 1750. *Archivo Ibero-Americano,* v. 52, no. 205 – 208 (Jan – Dec 92), pp. 187 – 207. Bibl, tables.

Cebrián González, Carmen and Isabel Arenas Frutos. Situación de la provincia del Perú a finales del siglo XVI: *La crónica anónima de 1600. Anuario de Estudios Americanos,* v. 49, Suppl. 2 (1992), pp. 11 – 29. Tables.

Cecereu Lagos, Luis Enrique. A propósito de Couve y Hagel, narradores. *Aisthesis,* no. 24 (1991), pp. 79 – 102. Bibl.

Cedeño Cenci, Diógenes F. Meditaciones sobre "Cartas de infancia:" poemario de Luis Carlos Jiménez Varela. *Revista Cultural Lotería,* v. 51, no. 392 (Nov – Dec 93), pp. 78 – 84.

Cedillo, Miguel Angel. La Comisión Nacional de Derechos Humanos: ¿Justicia para la democracia? *Revista Mexicana de Ciencias Políticas y Sociales,* v. 37, Nueva época, no. 149 (July – Sept 92), pp. 83 – 108.

Celedón, Carmen and Oscar Muñoz Gomá. La política económica durante la transición a la democracia en Chile, 1990 – 1992. *Estudios Sociales (Chile),* no. 75 (Jan – Mar 93), pp. 77 – 95. Bibl.

Centrangolo, Aníbal E. La musicología americanista en Europa. *Revista Musical de Venezuela,* no. 28 (May – Dec 89), pp. 112 – 117.

Centro de Espiritualidad Ignaciana. Decálogo de nuestra espiritualidad. *Mensaje,* v. 42, no. 420 (July 93), pp. 196 – 197. Il.

Cerdas Bokhan, Dora. Las fuentes eclesiásticas como develadoras de la vida cotidiana de los fieles. *Revista de Historia (Costa Rica),* no. 25 (Jan – June 92), pp. 251 – 259.

— Matrimonio y vida cotidiana en el graven central costarricense, 1851 – 1890. *Revista de Historia (Costa Rica),* no. 26 (July – Dec 92), pp. 69 – 95. Bibl.

Cerutti, Mario. Españoles, gran comercio y brote fabril en el norte de México, 1850 – 1910. *Siglo XIX: Cuadernos,* v. 1, no. 2 (Feb 92), pp. 49 – 93. Bibl, tables.

Cerutti Guldberg, Horacio V. Hacia la utopía de nuestra América. *Ibero-Amerikanisches Archiv,* v. 18, no. 3 – 4 (1992), pp. 455 – 465. Bibl.

Cervantes, Lorna Dee. Bajo de la sombra de la autopista (Translated by Sergio Elizondo and Ricardo Aguilar). *Plural (Mexico),* v. 22, no. 256 (Jan 93), pp. 5 – 7. Il.

— Poems ("The Poet Is Served Her Papers," "Blue Full Moon in Witch," "From the Cables of Genocide," "On Love and Hunger," "The Captive's Verses"). *The Americas Review,* v. 20, no. 3 – 4 (Fall – Winter 92), pp. 233 – 237.

Cervantes Gamboa, Laura. La función social de la música en el ritual fúnebre bribrí. *Káñina,* v. 16, no. 1 (Jan – June 92), pp. 245 – 265. Bibl, il, tables.

Cervantes Herrera, Joel and César Ramírez Miranda. México: del imperio del maíz al maíz del imperio. *Problemas del Desarrollo,* v. 24, no. 94 (July – Sept 93), pp. 97 – 112. Tables.

Cervera, Juan. Décimas a la muerte. *La Palabra y el Hombre,* no. 84 (Oct – Dec 92), p. 38.

Cervo, Amado Luiz. A historiografia brasileira das relações internacionais. *Revista Interamericana de Bibliografía,* v. 42, no. 3 (1992), pp. 393 – 409. Bibl.

César Dachary, Alfredo and Stella M. Arnaiz Burne. La frontera caribe de México en el XIX: una historia olvidada. *Siglo XIX: Cuadernos,* v. 3, no. 7 (Oct 93), pp. 33 – 62. Bibl, tables, maps.

Céspedes Aguirre, Patricia. Universidad, deporte y agresividad juvenil: apuntes en torno a la Olimpiada UNSAAC, 1991. *Allpanchis,* v. 25, no. 41 (Jan – June 93), pp. 159 – 174.

Céspedes Castro, Cristina and Sonia León Montoya. Terapia de grupo no directiva con pacientes seropositivos y con SIDA. *Revista de Ciencias Sociales (Costa Rica),* no. 58 (Dec 92), pp. 45 – 54. Bibl, charts.

Chababo, Rubén Alberto. Félix Pita Rodríguez o el elogio de la literatura. *Islas,* no. 98 (Jan – Apr 91), pp. 83 – 86.

Chacón, Alfredo. La experiencia de *Orígenes. Cuadernos Hispanoamericanos,* no. 511 (Jan 93), pp. 25 – 31.

— María Auxiliadora Alvarez: *Cuerpo y Ca(z)a* de palabras. *Inti,* no. 37 – 38 (Spring – Fall 93), pp. 207 – 214.

Chacón, Dulce. Poems. *Cuadernos Hispanoamericanos,* no. 520 (Oct 93), pp. 73 – 80.

Chacón, Katherine. Chillida: el cuerpo, el espacio. *Art Nexus,* no. 8 (Apr – June 93), pp. 80 – 81. Il.

Chacón, Vamireh. A civilização do planalto. *Revista do Instituto Histórico e Geográfico Brasileiro,* no. 372 (July – Sept 91), pp. 613 – 646. Bibl.

Chacón, Zully. Antropofagia y resistencia caribe: armas jurídicas de la corona española. *Boletín de la Academia Nacional de la Historia (Venezuela),* v. 75, no. 300 (Oct – Dec 92), pp. 89 – 107. Bibl, maps.

— Clío y Siquis o una visión del caudillismo en Venezuela. *Boletín de la Academia Nacional de la Historia (Venezuela),* v. 75, no. 299 (July – Sept 92), pp. 135 – 144. Bibl.

Chacón Echeverría, Laura. La mujer prostituta: cuerpo de suciedad, fermento de muerte; reflexiones en torno a algunos rituales de purificación. *Revista de Ciencias Sociales (Costa Rica),* no. 58 (Dec 92), pp. 23 – 34. Bibl, il.

Chacón Vargas, Ramón Vicente. La sociedad de consumo, 1945 – 1960. *Boletín de la Academia Nacional de la Historia (Venezuela),* v. 75, no. 299 (July – Sept 92), pp. 109 – 133. Bibl.

Chaffee, Sue. Haitian Women in Miami. *Hemisphere,* v. 5, no. 2 (Winter – Spring 93), pp. 22 – 23. Il.

Chalbaud, Román. Pequeño Chocrón ilustrado. *Conjunto,* no. 90 – 91 (Jan – June 92), p. 47. Il.

Chalhoub, Sidney. The Politics of Disease Control: Yellow Fever and Race in Nineteenth Century Rio de Janeiro. *Journal of Latin American Studies,* v. 25, no. 3 (Oct 93), pp. 441 – 463. Bibl.

Chamorro, Inés G. Dr. Daniel F. Rubín de la Borbolla: una visión de su obra latinoamericana. *Folklore Americano,* no. 53 (Jan – June 92), pp. 169 – 175.

Chamorro, Máximo. Retrato de una personalidad antisocial. *Revista Cultural Lotería,* v. 51, no. 392 (Nov – Dec 93), pp. 5 – 21.

Chanady, Amaryll. La ambivalencia del discurso indigenista en la nueva narrativa ecuatoriana. *Canadian Journal of Latin American and Caribbean Studies,* v. 17, no. 34 (1992), pp. 53 – 71. Bibl.

Chang-Rodríguez, Eugenio. Las crónicas posmodernistas de César Vallejo. *Inti,* no. 36 (Fall 92), pp. 11 – 22. Bibl.

Chang-Rodríguez, Raquel. Colonial Connections. *Latin American Literary Review,* v. 20, no. 40 (July – Dec 92), pp. 30 – 31.

Changmarín, Carlos Francisco. La tártara de Thomas Mann. *Revista Cultural Lotería,* v. 51, no. 392 (Nov – Dec 93), pp. 90 – 95.

Chapa, Jorge and Richard R. Valencia. Latino Population Growth, Demographic Characteristics, and Educational Stagnation: An Examination of Recent Trends. *Hispanic Journal of Behavioral Sciences,* v. 15, no. 2 (May 93), pp. 165 – 187. Bibl, tables.

Chapela, Francisco. ¿Podrá la nueva ley forestal detener la deforestación? *El Cotidiano,* v. 8, no. 52 (Jan – Feb 93), pp. 57 – 59 + . Bibl.

Chapin, Mac. The View from the Shore: Central America's Indians Encounter the Quincentenary. *Grassroots Development,* v. 16, no. 2 (1992), pp. 2 – 10. Bibl, il, maps.

Charles, Gérard-Pierre

See

Pierre-Charles, Gérard

Charles C., Mercedes. De la denuncia a la creación de alternativas. *Fem,* v. 17, no. 125 (July 93), pp. 4 – 5.

— Modelo globalizador e imágenes femeninas. *Fem,* v. 17, no. 126 (Aug 93), pp. 29 – 30.

— Televisión y estereotipos sexuales. *Fem,* v. 17, no. 129 (Nov 93), pp. 20 – 21.

— Televisión y proyecto de mujer. *Fem,* v. 17, no. 127 (Sept 93), pp. 4 – 5.

— Violencia, televisión y niños. *Fem,* v. 17, no. 128 (Oct 93), pp. 4 – 5.

Charlone, Silvana and Carlos Varela Nestier. Cuba: ¿Democratización y legitimidad?; los cambios en el sistema político cubano. *Hoy Es Historia,* v. 10, no. 59 (Sept – Oct 93), pp. 56 – 66. Il.

Chase, Alfonso. "Puertas abiertas": pasos a la pintura de José Luis López Escarré. *Káñina,* v. 16, no. 1 (Jan – June 92), pp. 225 – 227. Il.

Chassin, Joëlle. Protecteur d'indiens contre vice-roi: la lutte de Miguel de Eyzaguirre pour l'abolition du tribut au Pérou. *Cahiers des Amériques Latines,* no. 13 (1992), pp. 61 – 74. Bibl.

Chasteen, John Charles. Fighting Words: The Discourse of Insurgency in Latin American History. *Latin American Research Review,* v. 28, no. 3 (1993), pp. 83 – 111. Bibl, il.

Chatterji, Manas and Walter Isard. Ciencia regional: nuevo orden mundial y el desarrollo de México en la era del TLC. *Problemas del Desarrollo,* v. 24, no. 93 (Apr – June 93), pp. 39 – 54. Bibl, charts.

Chauchat, Claude and Jacques Pelegrin. Tecnología y función de las puntas de Paiján: el aporte de la experimentación. *Latin American Antiquity,* v. 4, no. 4 (Dec 93), pp. 367 – 382. Bibl, il, tables, charts.

Chauí, Marilena de Souza and Olgária Chaim Feres Mattos. Caio Graco Prado. *Vozes,* v. 86, no. 4 (July – Aug 92), pp. 79 – 82. Il.

Chauvet Sánchez, Michelle. Comida rápida contra comida corrida: repercusiones de la apertura comercial en la producción de cárnicos. *El Cotidiano,* v. 8, no. 52 (Jan – Feb 93), pp. 103 – 108. Bibl, il, tables, charts.

Chaverri, Amalia. Génesis y evolución de los títulos de la novelística costarricense. *Canadian Journal of Latin American and Caribbean Studies,* v. 17, no. 34 (1992), pp. 73 – 95. Bibl, tables.

Chaves, Celso Loureiro. Como uma placa de trânsito: a música brasileira no meio acadêmico internacional. *Vozes,* v. 86, no. 6 (Nov – Dec 92), pp. 8 – 12.

Chaves, Omar Emir. A Amazônia brasileira. *Revista do Instituto Histórico e Geográfico Brasileiro,* no. 370 (Jan – Mar 91), pp. 196 – 216.

Chaves Araya, Mariana. Impacto de los cursos de parto sin temor en el área de salud de San Ramón. *Revista de Ciencias Sociales (Costa Rica),* no. 60 (June 93), pp. 39 – 50. Bibl, tables, charts.

Chaves Salas, Ana Lupita. Reseña histórica de la regionalización de la Universidad de Costa Rica. *Revista de Ciencias Sociales (Costa Rica),* no. 60 (June 93), pp. 7 – 16. Bibl.

Chávez, Fermín. Un marxista alemán en San Luis. *Todo Es Historia,* v. 26, no. 310 (May 93), pp. 48 – 52. Il.

Chávez, Ignacio. In memoriam: Manuel Briceño Jáuregui, humanista integral. *Boletín de Historia y Antigüedades,* v. 80, no. 781 (Apr – June 93), pp. 321 – 322.

Chávez, Jorge Humberto. El poema jarocho. *La Palabra y el Hombre,* no. 82 (Apr – June 92), pp. 246 – 247.

Chávez, Martha and Francisco R. Sagasti. ¿Hacia un nuevo Perú? *Debate (Peru),* v. 16, no. 74 (Sept – Oct 93), pp. 10 – 12. Il.

Chávez G., Gerardo. Las ceremonias sincretas de San Juan Chamula. *Hoy Es Historia,* v. 10, no. 58 (July – Aug 93), pp. 77 – 79.

Chávez Martínez, Luis and Jorge E. Ordóñez. Fueling Industry. *Business Mexico,* v. 3, no. 12 (Dec 93), pp. 10 – 11.

Chávez O'Brien, Eliana. El sector informal urbano: estrategias de vida e identidad. *Nueva Sociedad,* no. 124 (Mar – Apr 93), pp. 82 – 93. Bibl, tables.

Chelala, César A. Prevención de la mortalidad materna en las Américas: perspectivas para los años noventa. *Fem,* v. 17, no. 123 (May 93), pp. 21 – 31. Bibl.

Chena R., Rodolfo. La población de una parroquia novohispana del siglo XVIII: Santa María de la Presentación de Chilapa. *Estudios Demográficos y Urbanos,* v. 7, no. 1 (Jan – Apr 92), pp. 169 – 192. Bibl, tables, charts.

Chenaut, Victoria and María Teresa Sierra. El campo de investigación de la antropología jurídica. *Nueva Antropología,* v. 13, no. 43 (Nov 92), pp. 101 – 109. Bibl.

Cheng Hurtado, Alberto. Informe sobre el XVI Curso Interamericano de Observación y Práctica Indigenista: "Lectoescritura computarizada del idioma quechua." *Anuario Indigenista,* v. 30 (Dec 91), pp. 425 – 435.

Cheng Hurtado, Alberto and José Matos Mar. Comas: lo andino en la modernidad urbana. *América Indígena,* v. 51, no. 2 – 3 (Apr – Sept 91), pp. 35 – 74. Il, tables, maps.

Cherchi, Grazia. Ponerse la sonrisa (Translated by Aurora Tejeda). *Nexos,* v. 16, no. 183 (Mar 93), p. 59.

Cheresky, Isidoro. Argentina: una democracia a la búsqueda de su institución. *European Review of Latin American and Caribbean Studies,* no. 53 (Dec 92), pp. 7 – 45.

Cherpak, Evelyn M. A Diplomat's Lady in Brazil: Selections from the Diary of Mary Robinson Hunter, 1834 – 1848. *Revista Interamericana de Bibliografía,* v. 42, no. 4 (1992), pp. 617 – 634. Bibl.

Chevalier, François. Los últimos adelantos en el campo de la historia (Originally published in *Cuadernos Americanos,* no. 1, 1955). *Hoy Es Historia,* v. 10, no. 60 (Nov – Dec 93), pp. 70 – 78. Bibl.

Cheveski, Ana. In memoriam. *Hispamérica,* v. 22, no. 64 – 65 (Apr – Aug 93), pp. 137 – 138.

Chiappo, Leopoldo. La concepción del hombre en Honorio Delgado. *Apuntes (Peru),* no. 31 (July – Dec 92), pp. 55 – 62.

Chiareno, Osvaldo. Altre postille linguistiche al testo del *Libro de la prima navegación. Quaderni Ibero-Americani,* no. 72 (Dec 92), pp. 564 – 570.

Chibnik, Michael and Wil de Jong. Organización de la mano de obra agrícola en las comunidades ribereñas de la Amazonía peruana. *Amazonía Peruana,* v. 11, no. 21 (Sept 92), pp. 181 – 215. Bibl.

Chiesa, Blanca and Ana María Reyes. El Congreso del Pueblo y su significación en el proceso de lucha, movilización y unificación sindical, años 1950 – 1966. *Hoy Es Historia,* v. 10, no. 56 (Mar – Apr 93), pp. 40 – 60. Bibl, il.

Chihuailaf Nahuelpan, Elicura and Pedro Marimán. Reflexions mapuches autour d'un voyage au Mexique et au Guatémala. *Caravelle,* no. 59 (1992), pp. 109 – 126. Il.

Chimal, Carlos. Mirar en el jardín mexicano: paisaje de la ciencia; entrevista con Elías Trabulse. *Vuelta,* v. 17, no. 194 (Jan 93), pp. 50 – 52.

Chinchilla, Norma Jean Stoltz. Classe, gênero e soberania na Nicarágua (A translation of "Revolutionary Popular Feminism in Nicaragua: Articulating Class, Gender, and National Sovereignty," translated by Vera Pereira. Originally published in *Gender and Society,* September 1990). *Estudos Feministas,* v. 1, no. 2 (1993), pp. 321 – 347. Bibl.

— Women's Movements in the Americas: Feminism's Second Wave. *NACLA Report on the Americas,* v. 27, no. 1 (July – Aug 93), pp. 17 – 23 +. Bibl, il.

Chinchilla Coto, José Carlos. Estado y democracia en la sociedad costarricense contemporánea. *Anuario de Estudios Centroamericanos,* v. 18, no. 2 (1992), pp. 101 – 114. Bibl.

Chinchilla Sánchez, Kattia. Mircea Eliade, una clave para la interpretación del pensamiento mítico. *Káñina,* v. 16, no. 1 (Jan – June 92), pp. 207 – 218. Bibl.

Chisalita, Ruxandra. El tormentoso goce de la profanación en César Vallejo y Ramón López Velarde. *Casa de las Américas,* no. 189 (Oct – Dec 92), pp. 58 – 64.

Chisholm, Patrick D. Steel Wars. *Business Mexico,* v. 3, no. 4 (Apr 93), pp. 34 – 37. Il.

Chitarroni, Luis. Narrativa: nuevas tendencias; relato de los márgenes. *Cuadernos Hispanoamericanos,* no. 517 – 519 (July – Sept 93), pp. 437 – 444. Il.

Chociay, Rogério. Três vertentes métricas na poesia de Manuel Botelho de Oliveira. *Revista de Letras (Brazil),* v. 32 (1992), pp. 207 – 221. Bibl.

Chocrón, Isaac. Solemán, el Magnífico. *Conjunto,* no. 90 – 91 (Jan – June 92), pp. 48 – 78. Il.

Choi, Dae Won. Globalização na era pacífico. *Vozes,* v. 87, no. 4 (July – Aug 93), pp. 13 – 19.

— Las nuevas relaciones económicas entre los "tigres" asiáticos y América Latina. *Comercio Exterior,* v. 43, no. 5 (May 93), pp. 457 – 462. Tables.

— The Pacific Basin and Latin America. *CEPAL Review,* no. 49 (Apr 93), pp. 21 – 40. Bibl, tables, charts.

Choque Mata, Jaime. Poems ("Fuego," "Valija de pena," "Manantial de ternura," "Manantial de fuego," "Anhelo"). *Signo,* no. 36 – 37, Nueva época (May – Dec 92), pp. 133 – 144.

Chorba, Carrie C. Coloquio y silencio en "Quisiera hoy ser feliz" (Includes the poem). *Inti,* no. 36 (Fall 92), pp. 105 – 110.

Christen, María. 1935. *La Palabra y el Hombre,* no. 82 (Apr – June 92), pp. 143 – 146.

Christian, Karen. Will the "Real Chicano" Please Stand Up?: The Challenge of John Rechy and Sheila Ortiz Taylor to Chicano Essentialism. *The Americas Review,* v. 20, no. 2 (Summer 92), pp. 89 – 104. Bibl.

Christie, John S. Fathers and Virgins: García Márquez's Faulknerian *Chronicle of a Death Foretold. Latin American Literary Review,* v. 21, no. 41 (Jan – June 93), pp. 21 – 29. Bibl.

Chudnovsky, Daniel. El futuro de la integración hemisférica: el MERCOSUR y la Iniciativa para las Américas. *Desarrollo Económico (Argentina),* v. 32, no. 128 (Jan – Mar 93), pp. 483 – 511. Bibl, tables.

Ciafardo, Eduardo O. and Daniel Espesir. Patología de la acción política anarquista: criminólogos, psiquiatras y conflicto social en Argentina, 1890 – 1910. *Siglo XIX: Revista,* no. 12, 2a época (July – Dec 92), pp. 23 – 40. Bibl.

Ciarnello, Nicolás. "La guerra del futbol": Honduras – El Salvador. *Todo Es Historia,* v. 26, no. 307 (Feb 93), pp. 36 – 45. Bibl, il, maps.

Cicerchia, Ricardo. "O inventamos o erramos": América Latina; ¿La política de la crisis o la crisis de la política? (Review article). *Nueva Sociedad,* no. 128 (Nov – Dec 93), pp. 166 – 171.

Cifuentes, María Cecilia. Impacto fiscal de la privatización en Chile, 1985 – 1990. *Estudios Públicos (Chile),* no. 51 (Winter 93), pp. 157 – 193. Bibl.

Cipriani, Juan Luis et al. ¿Qué quiere el peruano común y corriente? *Debate (Peru),* v. 16, no. 75 (Dec 93 – Jan 94), pp. 15 – 18. Il.

Ciria, Alberto. La historia argentina en el teatro de Roberto Cossa: a propósito de *Angelito. Revista Interamericana de Bibliografía,* v. 42, no. 4 (1992), pp. 577 – 583. Bibl.

Cirillo, Teresa. Colombo bifronte. *Quaderni Ibero-Americani,* no. 72 (Dec 92), pp. 571 – 594. Bibl.

Cisneros, Antonio. Homenaje a lo crudo: contra Claude Lévi-Strauss. *Debate (Peru),* v. 15, no. 71 (Nov 92 – Jan 93), pp. 58 – 59. Il.

Cisneros, Luis Jaime. De Atahualpa al Museo de la Nación: entrevista a Fernando de Szyszlo. *Debate (Peru),* v. 16, no. 75 (Dec 93 – Jan 94), pp. 70 – 73. Il.

— Entrevista a Enrique Chirinos Soto. *Debate (Peru),* v. 16, no. 73 (June – Aug 93), pp. 8 – 16. Il.

— Entrevista al general Luis Cisneros. *Debate (Peru),* v. 15, no. 71 (Nov 92 – Jan 93), pp. 8 – 16. Il.

— Nosequién y los Nosecuántos. *Debate (Peru),* v. 15, no. 71 (Nov 92 – Jan 93), p. 67. Il.

— El porvenir de la izquierda. *Debate (Peru),* v. 15, no. 71 (Nov 92 – Jan 93), pp. 40 – 43. Il.

Cisneros, Luis Jaime and Arturo Ferrari. Del jardín a la calle: la juventud peruana de los '90s. *Debate (Peru),* v. 16, no. 74 (Sept – Oct 93), pp. 19 – 25. Il, tables.

— Ni goles, ni milagros: entrevista a Francisco Lombardi. *Debate (Peru),* v. 16, no. 74 (Sept – Oct 93), pp. 14 – 18. Il.

Cisneros, Luis Jaime et al. La educación: ¿Reforma con futuro? *Debate (Peru),* v. 16, no. 72 (Mar – May 93), pp. 20 – 27. Il, charts.

Cisneros C., Luis Fernán. Entre la ira y la paz: encuesta entre jóvenes. *Debate (Peru),* v. 15, no. 70 (Sept – Oct 92), pp. 35 – 38. Il, tables.

Cisneros Vizquerra, Luis F. Perspectivas después de la detención. *Debate (Peru),* v. 15, no. 70 (Sept – Oct 92), pp. 21 – 22. Il.

Cixous, Hélène. Retratos: Clarice Lispector/Marina Tsvetaeva (Translated by Esther Levy). *Escritura (Venezuela),* v. 16, no. 31 – 32 (Jan – Dec 91), pp. 45 – 52.

Clarke, Christopher Martin. Unemployment Theory in the LDCs: A Test of the Generalized Segmentation Hypothesis. *Social and Economic Studies,* v. 41, no. 4 (Dec 92), pp. 25 – 51. Bibl.

Clavijo, Sergio. Variaciones en el criterio sobre necesidades básicas: aplicación al caso colombiano. *Planeación y Desarrollo,* v. 24, no. 1 (Jan – Apr 93), pp. 367 – 382. Bibl, tables.

Cleary, David. After the Frontier: Problems with Political Economy in the Modern Brazilian Amazon. *Journal of Latin American Studies,* v. 25, no. 2 (May 93), pp. 331 – 349. Bibl.

Clemente, Concepción. Ese Dios que se toca a manos plenas. *Letras Femeninas,* v. 19, no. 1 – 2 (Spring – Fall 93), p. 174.

Clemente B., Isabel. Un caso de conflicto cultural en el Caribe: de la imposición al reconocimiento. *Nueva Sociedad,* no. 127 (Sept – Oct 93), pp. 32 – 45. Bibl.

Clementi, Hebe. Homenaje a Las Marcas: el país de mis ancestros. *Todo Es Historia,* v. 26, no. 305 (Dec 92), pp. 70 – 80. Bibl, il.

Clements, Benedict J. and José W. Rossi. Ligações interindustriais e setores-chave na economia brasileira. *Pesquisa e Planejamento Econômico,* v. 22, no. 1 (Apr 92), pp. 101 – 123. Bibl, tables.

Cline, Sarah. The Spiritual Conquest Reexamined: Baptism and Christian Marriage in early Sixteenth-Century Mexico. *Hispanic American Historical Review,* v. 73, no. 3 (Aug 93), pp. 453 – 480. Bibl, tables.

Cluff, Russell M. El motivo del amor en la poesía de Gonzalo Rojas. *Chasqui,* v. 22, no. 1 (May 93), pp. 59 – 69.

Coatsworth, John Henry. Pax (norte) americana: América Latina después de la guerra fría (Translated by Marcela Pineda Camacho). *Revista Mexicana de Sociología,* v. 55, no. 2 (Apr – June 93), pp. 293 – 314. Bibl.

Cobo Borda, Juan Gustavo. *Cien años de soledad:* un cuarto de siglo; creación y crítica. *Revista Interamericana de Bibliografía,* v. 42, no. 3 (1992), pp. 411 – 420.

— Pablo Antonio Cuadra. *Cuadernos Hispanoamericanos,* no. 522 (Dec 93), pp. 7 – 17. Il.

— Páginas dispersas de José Bianco (1908 – 1986). *Cuadernos Hispanoamericanos,* no. 516 (June 93), pp. 7 – 9. Il.

— Poems. *Revista Nacional de Cultura (Venezuela),* v. 53, no. 285 (Apr – June 92), pp. 146 – 158.

— Poesía y novela colombiana: años '80. *Revista Nacional de Cultura (Venezuela),* v. 53, no. 285 (Apr – June 92), pp. 40 – 71. Bibl.

Cochet, Hubert. Agriculture sur brûlis, élevage extensif et dégradation de l'environnement en Amérique Latine: un exemple en Sierra Madre del Sur, au Mexique. *Tiers Monde,* v. 34, no. 134 (Apr – June 93), pp. 281 – 303. Maps, charts.

Cochrane, James D. The Troubled and Misunderstood Relationship: The United States and Latin America (Review article). *Latin American Research Review,* v. 28, no. 2 (1993), pp. 222 – 245.

Cockrell, Eddie. Seventh Heaven: The Americas Film Festival. *Américas,* v. 45, no. 6 (Nov – Dec 93), pp. 46 – 49. Il.

Coddou Peebles, Marcelo. Proyección de Vallejo en la poesía de Gonzalo Rojas. *Revista Chilena de Literatura,* no. 41 (Apr 93), pp. 113 – 118. Bibl.

Codina, Víctor. Crónica de Santo Domingo. *ECA; Estudios Centroamericanos,* v. 47, no. 529 – 530 (Nov – Dec 92), pp. 1057 – 1065.

Coelho, Nelly Novaes. A genealogia da palavra. *Convivium,* v. 34, no. 2 (July – Dec 91), pp. 98 – 104.

Coeli, Jaime Collier. A defesa da concorrência. *Problemas Brasileiros,* v. 30, no. 297 (May – June 93), pp. 41 – 53. Il.

— O desafio do abastecimento. *Problemas Brasileiros,* v. 30, no. 297 (May – June 93), pp. 15 – 24. Il.

— MP 312: iníqua e inócua. *Problemas Brasileiros,* v. 30, no. 296 (Mar – Apr 93), pp. 29 – 34. Il.

Coello Vila, Carlos. Caracterización del castellano boliviano. *Signo,* no. 35, Nueva época (Jan – Apr 92), pp. 47 – 57. Bibl.

— Nuestras lenguas nativas y los bolivianismos. *Signo,* no. 36 – 37, Nueva época (May – Dec 92), pp. 379 – 386. Bibl.

— *Signo; Cuadernos Bolivianos de Cultura,* 36 – 37. *Signo,* no. 38, Nueva época (Jan – Apr 93), pp. 7 – 10.

Coffey, Brian. Investment Incentives as a Means of Encouraging Tourism Development: The Case of Costa Rica. *Bulletin of Latin American Research,* v. 12, no. 1 (Jan 93), pp. 83 – 90. Bibl, tables, maps.

Cohen, Ernesto and Rolando Franco. Rationalizing Social Policy: Evaluation and Viability. *CEPAL Review,* no. 47 (Aug 92), pp. 163 – 172. Bibl, charts.

Cohen, Isaac. The Rise of the Hispanics. *Ibero Americana (Sweden),* v. 22, no. 2 (Dec 92), pp. 3 – 20. Bibl.

— El surgimiento de los hispanos. *Nueva Sociedad,* no. 127 (Sept – Oct 93), pp. 100 – 113. Bibl.

Cohen, Joshua A. Caught in the Squeeze. *Business Mexico,* v. 3, no. 9 (Sept 93), pp. 28 – 30. Charts.

— Filling the Basket. *Business Mexico,* v. 3, no. 12 (Dec 93), pp. 19 – 20. Tables, charts.

— The Myth of "Economical" Mexico. *Business Mexico,* v. 3, no. 7 (July 93), pp. 38 – 39. Tables.

— Productivity: A Jump Start to Better Wages. *Business Mexico,* v. 3, no. 6 (June 93), pp. 7 – 8.

— Productivity Goes into Labor. *Business Mexico,* v. 3, no. 11 (Nov 93), pp. 47 – 48.

— Reforming the Reforms. *Business Mexico,* v. 3, no. 10 (Oct 93), pp. 44 – 45. Tables.

— Requirements for Work Visas. *Business Mexico,* v. 3, no. 8 (Aug 93), pp. 14 – 15.

Cohen, Joshua A. and Joel Russell. A New Dynamic in the Americas. *Business Mexico,* v. 3, no. 12 (Dec 93), pp. 43 – 45. Il.

Cohn, Jeffrey P. Keeper of the Wild Side. *Américas,* v. 45, no. 2 (Mar – Apr 93), pp. 34 – 37. Il.

Colasanti, Marina. Ultima conversa com Otto. *Vozes,* v. 87, no. 2 (Mar – Apr 93), pp. 86 – 87.

Coldwell, Pedro Joaquín. Service for Survival (Excerpt from a speech given by the Secretary of Tourism). *Business Mexico,* v. 3, no. 10 (Oct 93), pp. 16 – 17. Il.

Colina, Nicolás. Poems ("El pueblo vive por amor," "Cortés y La Malinche en el pabellón de los condenados," "La máquina," "Escuadrón de las venganzas"). *The Americas Review,* v. 20, no. 2 (Summer 92), pp. 53 – 59.

Collins, Charles O. and Steven L. Scott. Air Pollution in the Valley of Mexico. *Geographical Review,* v. 83, no. 2 (Apr 93), pp. 119 – 133. Bibl, charts.

Colmenares, Hugo. El presidente de Hungría en Caracas: pocas veces los poetas han regido el destino del mundo. *Boletín de la Academia Nacional de la Historia (Venezuela),* v. 75, no. 297 (Jan – Mar 92), pp. 120 – 121.

Coloma C., Fernando and Viviana Fernández M. Los costos de despido: el efecto de las indemnizaciones por años de servicio. *Cuadernos de Economía (Chile)*, v. 30, no. 89 (Apr 93), pp. 77 – 109. Charts.

Colombia. Departamento Nacional de Planeación. Agregados monetarios. *Planeación y Desarrollo*, v. 24 (1993), All issues.

— Indicadores del sector rural. *Planeación y Desarrollo*, v. 24 (1993), All issues.

— Precios. *Planeación y Desarrollo*, v. 24 (1993), All issues.

— Sector externo. *Planeación y Desarrollo*, v. 24 (1993), All issues.

Colombo, Laura. Que todo suceda. *Plural (Mexico)*, v. 22, no. 264 (Sept 93), pp. 82 – 86.

Colombres, Diego and Jorge Gavilán. El daño ecológico y social que provocó La Forestal. *Todo Es Historia*, v. 26, no. 306 (Jan 93), pp. 42 – 47. Il.

Colomé, Delfín. Tres evocaciones de Agustín Lara. *Cuadernos Hispanoamericanos*, no. 521 (Nov 93), pp. 147 – 150. Il.

Coluccio, Félix. Augusto Raúl Cortázar a dieciocho años de su muerte. *Folklore Americano*, no. 53 (Jan – June 92), pp. 153 – 155.

— Creencias populares del nordeste argentino. *Folklore Americano*, no. 52 (July – Dec 91), pp. 149 – 161. Bibl.

Columbus, Claudette Kemper. "Pacha": Worlds in a Sacred Word. *Latin American Indian Literatures Journal*, v. 9, no. 1 (Spring 93), pp. 2 – 20.

Combes, André. Las logias del gran oriente de Francia en América Latina, 1842 – 1870. *Hoy Es Historia*, v. 10, no. 60 (Nov – Dec 93), pp. 14 – 21. Bibl, facs.

Compean, Guillermo and Rafael Girón Botello. La pesca en la cuenca del Pacífico: el caso del atún en México. *Comercio Exterior*, v. 43, no. 12 (Dec 93), pp. 1195 – 1201. Bibl, tables, charts.

Compitello, Malcolm Alan. Reflexiones sobre el acto de narrar: Benet, Vargas Llosa y Euclides da Cunha. *Insula*, no. 559 – 560 (July – Aug 93), pp. 19 – 22.

Compton, Nina H. and Garrett T. Newland. The Functional Border Equivalent. *Journal of Borderlands Studies*, v. 7, no. 2 (Fall 92), pp. 73 – 92. Bibl.

Concha, Edmundo. Neruda y Huidobro. *Atenea (Chile)*, no. 467 (1993), pp. 155 – 156.

Concha, Jaime. En el umbral del *Facundo*. *Hispamérica*, v. 21, no. 62 (Aug 92), pp. 21 – 31. Bibl.

Condé, Maryse. The Role of the Writer. *World Literature Today*, v. 67, no. 4 (Fall 93), pp. 697 – 699. Il.

— Vilma's Story (Excerpt from the forthcoming English translation of *Traversée de la mangrove*, translated by Richard Philcox). *World Literature Today*, v. 67, no. 4 (Fall 93), pp. 700 – 703. Il.

Conde, Teresa del. Diálogo con Roberto Parodi. *Plural (Mexico)*, v. 22, no. 257 (Feb 93), p. 45.

Conde Tudanca, Rodrigo. Un incidente olvidado del trienio adeco: la creación de la iglesia católica, apostólica, venezolana. *Boletín de la Academia Nacional de la Historia (Venezuela)*, v. 76, no. 302 (Apr – June 93), pp. 87 – 117. Bibl.

Conejeros A., Senén et al. ¿En qué fallan los periodistas y los medios de comunicación?: debates. *Mensaje*, v. 42, no. 419 (June 93), pp. 194 – 201. Il.

Connaughton, Brian F. América Latina, 1700 – 1850: entre el pacto colonial y el imperialismo moderno. *Cuadernos Americanos*, no. 38, Nueva época (Mar – Apr 93), pp. 38 – 66. Bibl.

Conner, Robert. Contingencia y realidad en la obra de Esther Seligson. *La Palabra y el Hombre*, no. 81 (Jan – Mar 92), pp. 279 – 284. Bibl, il.

Conrado, Regina Fátima de Almeida. Tradição e desvio: a rota do talento. *Revista de Letras (Brazil)*, v. 32 (1992), pp. 31 – 39. Bibl.

Conroy, Michael E. and Amy K. Glasmeier. Unprecedented Disparities, Unparalleled Adjustment Needs: Winners and Losers on the NAFTA "Fast Track." *Journal of Inter-American Studies and World Affairs*, v. 34, no. 4 (Winter 92 – 93), pp. 1 – 37. Bibl, tables, charts.

Consalvi, Simón Alberto. Una viuda no propiamente alegre. *Revista Nacional de Cultura (Venezuela)*, v. 53, no. 286 (July – Sept 92), pp. 87 – 91. Il.

Constantino, Mario and Rosalía Winocur. Cultura política y elecciones: algunas imágenes de la sucesión presidencial. *El Cotidiano*, v. 10, no. 58 (Oct – Nov 93), pp. 47 – 53. Bibl, tables.

Consuegra Higgins, José and Hernán Echavarría Olozaga. Tres cartas, dos opiniones. *Desarrollo Indoamericano*, v. 23, no. 91 (June 93), pp. 17 – 19. Il.

Contreras, Carlos. Mercado de tierras y sociedad campesina: el valle del Mantaro en el siglo XIX. *Historia y Cultura (Peru)*, no. 20 (1990), pp. 243 – 265. Bibl.

Contreras, Juan Pablo. Desde dentro. *Mensaje*, v. 42, no. 418 (May 93), p. 160.

— La formación de los jóvenes jesuitas hoy. *Mensaje*, v. 42, no. 420 (July 93), pp. 198 – 204. Il.

— Trabajos de Verano: formando en la solidaridad. *Mensaje*, v. 42, no. 421 (Aug 93), pp. 404 – 407.

Contreras, Oscar F. and Jorge Carrillo Viveros. Calificación en el trabajo: análisis de la industria maquiladora. *Frontera Norte*, v. 4, no. 8 (July – Dec 92), pp. 49 – 78. Bibl, tables, charts.

Contreras Cruz, Carlos. Ciudad y salud en el porfiriato: la política urbana y el saneamiento de Puebla, 1880 – 1906. *Siglo XIX: Cuadernos*, v. 1, no. 3 (June 92), pp. 55 – 76. Bibl, tables.

— Urbanización y modernidad en el porfiriato: el caso de la ciudad de Puebla. *La Palabra y el Hombre*, no. 83 (July – Sept 92), pp. 167 – 188. Bibl.

Cook, Jacqueline. Bibliography on Rosario Ferré. *Chasqui*, v. 22, no. 2 (Nov 93), pp. 129 – 149.

Cook, Noble David. Disease and the Depopulation of Hispaniola, 1492 – 1518. *Colonial Latin American Review*, v. 2, no. 1 – 2 (1993), pp. 213 – 245. Bibl, tables.

Cook, Scott. Toward a New Paradigm for Anthropology in Mexican Studies (Review article). *Mexican Studies*, v. 9, no. 2 (Summer 93), pp. 303 – 336. Bibl.

Cooney, Jerry Wilson. "La Dirección General de la Real Renta de Tabacos" and the Decline of the Royal Tobacco Monopoly in Paraguay, 1779 – 1800. *Colonial Latin American Historical Review*, v. 1, no. 1 (Fall 92), pp. 101 – 115. Bibl.

— Fraude y burócratas: tabaco y Paraguay, 1789 – 1790. *Revista Paraguaya de Sociología*, v. 29, no. 85 (Sept – Dec 92), pp. 29 – 40. Bibl.

Corbisier, Margarida. Drogas e educação. *Convivium*, v. 34, no. 2 (July – Dec 91), pp. 154 – 156.

Cordera Campos, Rolando. Guatemala: suave tierra; una entrevista con Rigoberta Menchú. *Nexos*, v. 16, no. 186 (June 93), pp. 9 – 15.

Cordero Espinosa, Sergio. Las flores en la arquitectura de Xochimilco (Accompanied by an English translation). *Artes de México*, no. 20 (Summer 93), pp. 74 – 79. Il.

Cordero Guzmán, Héctor R. Lessons from Operation Bootstrap. *NACLA Report on the Americas*, v. 27, no. 3 (Nov – Dec 93), pp. 7 – 10. Bibl, il.

Cordero López, Rodolfo. Leyenda de Ahuejote (Accompanied by an English translation). *Artes de México*, no. 20 (Summer 93), pp. 48 – 49. Il.

Cordero Michel, Emilio. Gregorio Luperón y Haití. *Anuario de Estudios Americanos*, v. 49 (1992), pp. 497 – 528. Bibl.

Cordones-Cook, Juanamaría. Contexto y proceso creador de *Maluco: la novela de los conquistadores*. *Chasqui*, v. 22, no. 2 (Nov 93), pp. 103 – 108.

— Una sombra donde sueña Camila O'Gorman: dimensión poética de la historia. *La Palabra y el Hombre*, no. 84 (Oct – Dec 92), pp. 271 – 276.

— Surgimiento y desaparición del Teatro Negro Uruguayo: entrevista con Andrés Castillo. *Afro-Hispanic Review*, v. 12, no. 2 (Fall 93), pp. 31 – 36.

Córdova, Arnaldo. El PAN: partido gobernante. *Revista Mexicana de Sociología*, v. 54, no. 3 (July – Sept 92), pp. 221 – 240. Bibl.

Corey, Jane. Solutions for the Throw-Away Society. *Business Mexico*, v. 3, no. 8 (Aug 93), pp. 44 – 45. Il.

Corfield M., Isabel. Constitucionalismo ilustrado en la experiencia poscolonial hispano-americana. *Todo Es Historia*, v. 26, no. 307 (Feb 93), pp. 79 – 83. Il.

— Hacia la creación intelectual del Nuevo Mundo. *Hoy Es Historia*, v. 10, no. 57 (Apr – May 93), pp. 69 – 75. Bibl.

Coriat R., Carola and Mario de Obaldía A. La influencia de la abuela en la percepción familiar del niño bajo su cuidado. *Revista Cultural Lotería*, v. 50, no. 383 (May – June 91), pp. 74 – 93. Bibl, tables.

Cornejo Guinassi, Pedro. Nosequién y los Nosecuántos: ¿Espejo de una generación? *Debate (Peru)*, v. 16, no. 74 (Sept – Oct 93), pp. 38 – 40. Il.

— La ruda sobriedad del realismo. *Debate (Peru)*, v. 15, no. 70 (Sept – Oct 92), pp. 45 – 47. Bibl, il.

Cornejo Oviedo, Alejandro and Emanuel Orozco. Relatoría del encuentro "Antropología Industrial: Avances de Investigación." *Nueva Antropología*, v. 13, no. 44 (Aug 93), pp. 143 – 145.

Cornejo Polar, Antonio. El discurso de la armonía imposible: el Inca Garcilaso de la Vega; discurso y recepción social. *Revista de Crítica Literaria Latinoamericana*, v. 19, no. 38 (July – Dec 93), pp. 73 – 80.

Cornelius, Wayne Armstrong and Philip L. Martin. The Uncertain Connection: Free Trade and Rural Mexican Migration to the United States. *International Migration Review*, v. 27, no. 3 (Fall 93), pp. 484 – 512. Bibl, tables, charts.

Coromoto Nava Santana, Mayela. Un conflicto entre la Real Audiencia y el Ayuntamiento de Caracas: el nombramiento del Fiel Ejecutor, 1793 – 1797. *Boletín de la Academia Nacional de la Historia (Venezuela)*, v. 75, no. 298 (Apr – June 92), pp. 77 – 85.

Corona Cuapio, Reina and José Rodolfo Luque González. Cambios recientes en los patrones migratorios a la zona metropolitana de la ciudad de México. *Estudios Demográficos y Urbanos*, v. 7, no. 2 – 3 (May – Dec 92), pp. 575 – 586. Bibl, tables, charts.

Corona Guzmán, Roberto. El entorno actual de la negociación comercial de América Latina. *Relaciones Internacionales (Mexico)*, v. 14, Nueva época, no. 56 (Oct – Dec 92), pp. 63 – 86. Tables.

Corona Martínez, Eduardo. Las insuficiencias del Acuerdo Nacional para la Modernización de la Educación Básica. *El Cotidiano*, v. 8, no. 51 (Nov – Dec 92), pp. 23 – 26. Il, tables.

Corona Martínez, Rocio and Mario Bassols Ricárdez. Transición institucional y reforma política en el D.F. *El Cotidiano*, v. 10, no. 57 (Aug – Sept 93), pp. 28 – 37. Il, tables.

Corona Vázquez, Rodolfo. La migración de mexicanos a los Estados Unidos: cambios en la década de 1980 – 1990. *Revista Mexicana de Sociología*, v. 55, no. 1 (Jan – Mar 93), pp. 213 – 233. Bibl, tables.

— Migración permanente interestatal e internacional, 1950 – 1990. *Comercio Exterior*, v. 43, no. 8 (Aug 93), pp. 750 – 762. Bibl, tables.

— Respuesta al comentario de Arturo Blancas Espejo: "Confiabilidad de la confiabilidad," *Estudios Demográficos y Urbanos*, vol. 6, núm. 2, 1991. *Estudios Demográficos y Urbanos*, v. 6, no. 3 (Sept – Dec 91), pp. 717 – 725.

Coronado Suzán, Gabriela. Entre la homogeneidad y la diferencia en los pueblos indohablantes de México. *Revista Latinoamericana de Estudios Educativos*, v. 22, no. 4 (Oct – Dec 92), pp. 37 – 62. Bibl, tables, charts.

Coronel Rivera, Juan. Héctor García. *Artes de México*, no. 19 (Spring 93), p. 116. Il.

Corpi, Lucha. Poems ("Invernario," "Fuga," "Canción de invierno"). *The Americas Review*, v. 20, no. 3 – 4 (Fall – Winter 92), pp. 209 – 212.

Corrada del Río, Baltasar. The Plebiscite: A Time for Change. *Hemisphere*, v. 5, no. 3 (Summer – Fall 93), pp. 44 – 46.

Corral, Wilfrido Howard. ¿Dónde está el chiste en Monterroso? *Studi di Letteratura Ispano-Americana*, v. 24 (1993), pp. 83 – 93. Bibl.

Corrales Ulloa, Francisco. Del oro al vidrio, de la piedra al hierro: la evidencia arqueológica y la desestructuración de la sociedad indígena. *Revista de Historia (Costa Rica)*, no. 25 (Jan – June 92), pp. 181 – 189. Bibl.

— Investigaciones arqueológicas en el Pacífico central de Costa Rica. *Vínculos*, v. 16, no. 1 – 2 (1990), pp. 1 – 29. Bibl, il, tables, maps.

Corrales Ulloa, Francisco and Ifigenia Quintanilla Jiménez. El Pacífico central de Costa Rica y el intercambio regional. *Vínculos*, v. 16, no. 1 – 2 (1990), pp. 111 – 126. Bibl, tables, maps.

Correa, Alejandra. La pasión según los Sábato. *Todo Es Historia*, v. 26, no. 305 (Dec 92), pp. 85 – 94. Bibl, il.

Corrêa, Henrique Luiz. Flexibilidade nos sistemas de produção. *RAE; Revista de Administração de Empresas*, v. 33, no. 3 (May – June 93), pp. 22 – 35. Bibl.

Corrêa, Roberto Lobato. Corporação e organização espacial: um estudo de caso. *Revista Brasileira de Geografia*, v. 53, no. 3 (July – Sept 91), pp. 33 – 66. Bibl, il, tables, maps.

Correa Díaz, Luis. Rosario de actos de habla (Fragmentos). *Inti*, no. 36 (Fall 92), pp. 139 – 142.

Correa Vásquez, Pedro Francisco. Cuadros de palabra. *Revista Cultural Lotería*, v. 51, no. 388 (Mar – Apr 92), pp. 78 – 84.

— Cuando se enferma el amor: a propósito de los cuentos de Gloria Guardia. *Revista Cultural Lotería*, v. 51, no. 387 (Feb 92), pp. 69 – 71.

Cortázar, Julio. Llama el teléfono, Delia (Introduced by Nicolás Cócoro. Article entitled "El primer cuento de Julio Cortázar"). *Confluencia,* v. 8, no. 1 (Fall 92), pp. 3 – 8.

Cortázar, Julio and Liliana Heker. Polémica sobre el exilio (Debate between Julio Cortázar and Liliana Heker on the subject of exiles). *Cuadernos Hispanoamericanos,* no. 517 – 519 (July – Sept 93), pp. 590 – 604.

Cortelesse, Claudio. Competitividad de los sistemas productivos y las empresas pequeñas y medianas: campo para la cooperación internacional. *Comercio Exterior,* v. 43, no. 6 (June 93), pp. 519 – 524.

Cortés, Carlos E. Chicanos y medios masivos de comunicación (Translated by Leticia García Cortés). *Plural (Mexico),* v. 22, no. 256 (Jan 93), pp. 50 – 59.

Cortés, Laia. Paloma La Hoz: Made in Perú. *Debate (Peru),* v. 16, no. 75 (Dec 93 – Jan 94), pp. 57 – 58. Il.

Cortés C., Fernando and Rosa María Rubalcava. Algunas determinantes de la inserción laboral en la industria maquiladora de exportación de Matamoros. *Estudios Sociológicos,* v. 11, no. 31 (Jan – Apr 93), pp. 59 – 91. Bibl, tables.

Cortés Conde, Roberto. El crecimiento de las economías latinoamericanas, 1880 – 1930. *Historia Mexicana,* v. 42, no. 3 (Jan – Mar 93), pp. 633 – 648. Tables.

Cortez, Roger. El impacto de los medios en la política. *Estado y Sociedad,* v. 8, no. 9 (Jan – June 92), pp. 81 – 90.

Cortez Ruiz, Carlos. El sector forestal mexicano: ¿Entre la economía y la ecología? *Comercio Exterior,* v. 43, no. 4 (Apr 93), pp. 370 – 377. Bibl.

Cortínez, Verónica. "Yo, Bernal Díaz del Castillo": ¿Soldado de a pie o idiota sin letras? *Revista Chilena de Literatura,* no. 41 (Apr 93), pp. 59 – 69. Bibl.

Corzo Ramírez, Ricardo. Catálogo de la Biblioteca Quinto Centenario y comentario al libro *Iberoamérica: una comunidad. La Palabra y el Hombre,* no. 83 (July – Sept 92), pp. 322 – 346. Bibl.

Corzo Ramírez, Ricardo and Soledad García Morales. Políticas, instituciones públicas de salud y enfermedades en Veracruz: fines del siglo XIX y principios del siglo XX. *La Palabra y el Hombre,* no. 83 (July – Sept 92), pp. 275 – 298. Bibl, tables.

Cosamalón, Ana Lucía. El lado oculto de lo cholo: presencia de rasgos culturales y afirmación de una identidad. *Allpanchis,* v. 25, no. 41 (Jan – June 93), pp. 211 – 226.

Cosío, María Eugenia. Los antecedentes de la transición demográfica en México. *Historia Mexicana,* v. 42, no. 1 (July – Sept 92), pp. 103 – 128. Bibl, tables, charts.

Cossa, Roberto M. Teatro Abierto: un fenómeno antifascista. *Cuadernos Hispanoamericanos,* no. 517 – 519 (July – Sept 93), pp. 529 – 532.

Cossío Lagarde, Francisco Javier. Notas de un arquitecto (Accompanied by an English translation). *Artes de México,* no. 18 (Winter 92), pp. 37 – 43. Il.

Costa, Cláudia de Lima. Rigoberta Menchú: a história de um depoimento. *Estudos Feministas,* v. 1, no. 2 (1993), pp. 306 – 320.

Costa, Iraci del Nero da and José Flávio Motta. Vila Rica: inconfidência e crise demográfica. *Estudos Econômicos,* v. 22, no. 2 (May – Aug 92), pp. 321 – 346. Bibl, tables, charts.

Costa, Lygia Martins. 50 anos de museologia, II: Significado da homenagem. *Revista do Instituto Histórico e Geográfico Brasileiro,* no. 371 (Apr – June 91), pp. 562 – 567.

Costa, Marcia Regina da. "Skinheads": carecas do subúrbio. *Vozes,* v. 87, no. 2 (Mar – Apr 93), pp. 2 – 10.

Costa, Nadja Maria Castilho da and Cláudia Rodrigues Segond. Plano de manejo ecológico da reserva particular de Bodoquena. *Revista Geográfica (Mexico),* no. 114 (July – Dec 91), pp. 91 – 100. Bibl, tables, maps.

Costa, Thomaz Guedes da. Cooperação e conflito nas interações estratégicas do Brasil: os desafios da nova década. *Política e Estratégia,* v. 8, no. 2 – 4 (Apr – Dec 90), pp. 141 – 152. Bibl.

Cotler, Julio C. Golpe a golpe . . . . *Debate (Peru),* v. 15, no. 71 (Nov 92 – Jan 93), pp. 18 – 19. Il.

Cott, Donna Lee van
See
Van Cott, Donna Lee

Cotto Medina, Celestino. La cuenta regresiva. *The Americas Review,* v. 19, no. 2 (Summer 91), pp. 32 – 35.

Courtoisie, Rafael. Poems ("La curva terrestre," "El hilo de voz," "El axioma del gato"). *Hispamérica,* v. 22, no. 64 – 65 (Apr – Aug 93), p. 136.

Couturier, Guy and Francis Kahn. Notes on the Insect Fauna of Two Species of "Astrocaryum" (Palmae, Cocoeae, Bactridinae) in Peruvian Amazonia, with Emphasis on Potential Pests of Cultivated Palms. *Bulletin de l'Institut Français d'Etudes Andines,* v. 21, no. 2 (1992), pp. 715 – 725. Bibl, il, tables, maps.

Couyoumdjian Bergamil, Juan Ricardo. Fichero bibliográfico, 1989 – 1991. *Historia (Chile),* no. 26 (1991 – 1992), pp. 385 – 459. Bibl.

Cova, Maritza and Teresa Vegas Vilarrubia. Estudio sobre la distribución y ecología de macrofitos acuáticos en el embalse de Guri. *Interciencia,* v. 18, no. 2 (Mar – Apr 93), pp. 77 – 82. Bibl, tables, maps, charts.

Covarrubias, Javier. La tecnología del sacrificio: la idea del "calor" y otros mitos encontrados. *Plural (Mexico),* v. 22, no. 258 (Mar 93), pp. 18 – 28. Bibl.

Covarrubias M., Isaías. Reflexiones acerca del porqué de la reforma agraria. *Derecho y Reforma Agraria,* no. 23 (1992), pp. 135 – 140.

Covo, Jacqueline. La prensa en la historiografía mexicana: problemas y perspectivas. *Historia Mexicana,* v. 42, no. 3 (Jan – Mar 93), pp. 689 – 710. Bibl.

Cowgill, George L. Comments on Andrew Sluyter: "Long Distance Staple Transport in Western Mesoamerica; Insights through Quantitative Modeling." *Ancient Mesoamerica,* v. 4, no. 2 (Fall 93), pp. 201 – 203. Bibl.

Coyula, Mario. El veril entre dos siglos: tradición e innovación para un desarrollo sustentable. *Casa de las Américas,* no. 189 (Oct – Dec 92), pp. 94 – 101.

Cragnolino, Aída Apter. De sitios y asedios: la escritura de Rosario Ferré. *Revista Chilena de Literatura,* no. 42 (Aug 93), pp. 25 – 30. Bibl.

Craipeau, Carine. El café en Nicaragua. *Anuario de Estudios Centroamericanos,* v. 18, no. 2 (1992), pp. 41 – 69. Bibl, tables, maps, charts.

Craven, Carolyn. Wage Determination and Inflation in Uruguay: Regime Changes. *Journal of Developing Areas,* v. 27, no. 4 (July 93), pp. 457 – 468. Bibl, tables, charts.

Crespo, José Antonio. Democratización: el esfuerzo ciudadano. *El Cotidiano,* v. 8, no. 52 (Jan – Feb 93), pp. 13 – 18. Il.

Crespo, Leila. Nivel de razonamiento cognoscitivo en una muestra de estudiantes universitarios: sus implicaciones para la docencia. *Homines,* v. 15 – 16, no. 2 – 1 (Oct 91 – Dec 92), pp. 95 – 101. Bibl, tables.

Crespo Martínez, Ismael and Antonia Martínez Rodríguez. Discurso político y realidad económica: las relaciones entre España y la comunidad iberoamericana. *Cuadernos del CLAEH,* v. 17, no. 63 – 64 (Oct 92), pp. 99 – 103. Bibl.

Crespo R., Alberto. Gustavo Adolfo Otero: sus años en Quito. *Signo,* no. 38, Nueva época (Jan – Apr 93), pp. 81 – 89.

Cressa, Claudia et al. Aspectos generales de la limnología en Venezuela. *Interciencia,* v. 18, no. 5 (Sept – Oct 93), pp. 237 – 248. Bibl, tables, maps.

Cresswell, Peter. Insiders and Outsiders: The Annual National Exhibition 1991 and "Homage to John Dunkley." *Jamaica Journal,* v. 24, no. 3 (Feb 93), pp. 29 – 35. Il.

Criado Boado, Felipe. Construcción social del espacio y reconstrucción arqueológica del paisaje. *Boletín de Antropología Americana,* no. 24 (Dec 91), pp. 5 – 30. Bibl, il.

Crisafio, Raúl. Roberto Arlt: el lenguaje negado. *Cuadernos Hispanoamericanos,* no. Special issue, 11 (July 93), pp. 37 – 46. Bibl.

Cross, Elsa. Dos poemas (From the unpublished book *Moira). Vuelta,* v. 17, no. 194 (Jan 93), p. 17.

Cross, Esther. El salto mortal. *Plural (Mexico),* v. 22, no. 258 (Mar 93), pp. 14 – 17.

Croston, Kendel. Women's Activities during the Prohibition Era along the U.S. – Mexico Border. *Journal of Borderlands Studies,* v. 8, no. 1 (Spring 93), pp. 99 – 113. Bibl.

Crovi Druetta, Delia María. Libre comercio en TV . . . : fantasía de diversidad. *Revista Mexicana de Ciencias Políticas y Sociales,* v. 38, Nueva época, no. 154 (Oct – Dec 93), pp. 91 – 102.

Crumlish, Rebecca. Stepping into the Picture with Raimundo Rubio. *Américas,* v. 45, no. 1 (Jan – Feb 93), pp. 52 – 53. Il.

Cruz, Arnaldo. Para virar al macho: la autobiografía como subversión en la cuentística de Manuel Ramos Otero. *Revista Iberoamericana,* v. 59, no. 162 – 163 (Jan – June 93), pp. 239 – 263. Bibl.

Cruz, Jacqueline. Reflexiones y reflejos: *Rayuela* como una novela de espejos. *Chasqui,* v. 22, no. 2 (Nov 93), pp. 24 – 33. Bibl.

Cruz, Justino de la. Integración económica del hemisferio occidental. *Integración Latinoamericana,* v. 18, no. 193 (Sept 93), pp. 53 – 54. Charts.

Cruz Barrera, Nydia E. La higiene y la política sanitaria en el porfiriato: su difusión y ejercicio en Puebla. *La Palabra y el Hombre,* no. 83 (July – Sept 92), pp. 255 – 273. Bibl, maps.

— Reclusión, control social y penitenciaria en Puebla en el siglo XIX. *Siglo XIX: Revista,* no. 12, 2a época (July – Dec 92), pp. 119 – 146.

Cruz Castellanos, Federico. Economía cañero – azucarera: neoliberalismo y crisis. *Momento Económico,* no. 67 (May – June 93), pp. 19 – 22. Tables.

Cruz-Coke Madrid, Ricardo. Desarrollo de las ciencias médicas en la U. de Chile. *Atenea (Chile),* no. 465 – 466 (1992), pp. 329 – 336. Bibl.

Cruz Cruz, Petrona and Isabel Juárez Ch'ix. *La desconfiada:* diálogo dramático. *Mesoamérica (USA),* v. 13, no. 23 (June 92), pp. 135 – 141.

Cruz Júnior, Ademar Seabra de et al. Brazil's Foreign Policy under Collor. *Journal of Inter-American Studies and World Affairs,* v. 35, no. 1 (1993), pp. 119 – 144. Bibl.

Cruz Ovalle de Amenábar, Isabel. Arte jesuita en Chile: la huella del barroco bávaro. *Mensaje,* v. 42, no. 420 (July 93), pp. 234 – 238. Il.

— Reseña de una sonrisa: los comienzos de la caricatura en Chile decimonónico, 1858 – 1868. *Boletín de la Academia Chilena de la Historia,* v. 58 – 59, no. 102 (1991 – 1992), pp. 107 – 138. Bibl, il.

Cruz Pérez, Francisco José. Alejandra Pizarnik: el extravío en el ser. *Cuadernos Hispanoamericanos,* no. 520 (Oct 93), pp. 105 – 109.

— Eugenio Montejo: el viaje hacia atrás. *Revista Nacional de Cultura (Venezuela),* v. 54, no. 287 (Oct – Dec 92), pp. 55 – 71. Bibl, il.

— García Márquez: la realidad sin mediaciones. *Cuadernos Hispanoamericanos,* no. 512 (Feb 93), pp. 115 – 120.

Cruz Rodríguez, María Soledad. La nueva ley agraria y su impacto en la periferia ejidal de la ciudad de México. *El Cotidiano,* v. 10, no. 57 (Aug – Sept 93), pp. 54 – 59. Bibl, il, tables.

Cruz Vergara, Eliseo. Comentarios generales sobre los aspectos metodológicos de la historia como ciencia sociológica en la obra de Eugenio María de Hostos y Bonilla. *Diálogos (Puerto Rico),* no. 62 (July 93), pp. 87 – 129.

Cuadra, Angel. El tema de lo cubano en el escritor exiliado. *Plural (Mexico),* v. 22, no. 262 (July 93), pp. 32 – 39.

Cuadra, Héctor. La cuenca del Pacífico en los albores del siglo XXI. *Comercio Exterior,* v. 43, no. 12 (Dec 93), pp. 1107 – 1110. Bibl, tables.

Cuadra, Pablo Antonio. Memorias/La tribu. *Vuelta,* v. 17, no. 199 (June 93), pp. 13 – 16.

Cuartas, Juan Manuel. En torno al concepto de "koiné" o interdialecto. *Thesaurus,* v. 45, no. 3 (Sept – Dec 90), pp. 743 – 746. Bibl.

Cuattromo, Oscar Julio et al. Argentina en crecimiento, 1993 – 1995: proyecciones oficiales. *Realidad Económica,* no. 117 (July – Aug 93), pp. 8 – 23. Charts.

Cubano Iguina, Astrid Teresa. La emigración mallorquina a Puerto Rico en el siglo XIX: el caso de los sollerenses. *Op. Cit.,* no. 7 (1992), pp. 229 – 253. Bibl, il, tables, charts.

Cuervo de Jaramillo, Elvira. Premio Jiménez de Quesada 1992 al doctor Germán Arciniegas. *Boletín de Historia y Antigüedades,* v. 79, no. 779 (Oct – Dec 92), pp. 1053 – 1059.

Cuesta Domingo, Mariano. Descubrimientos geográficos durante el siglo XVIII: acción franciscana en la ampliación de fronteras. *Archivo Ibero-Americano,* v. 52, no. 205 – 208 (Jan – Dec 92), pp. 293 – 342. Bibl, il, maps.

Cueva, Agustín. Falacias y coartadas del quinto centenario. *Boletín de Antropología Americana,* no. 23 (July 91), pp. 5 – 12. Bibl, il.

Cueva Jaramillo, Juan. Aquí entre nos: madame Paul Rivet. *Cahiers des Amériques Latines,* no. 13 (1992), pp. 161 – 162.

Cuevas, José Luis. Roberto Parodi, transvanguardista. *Plural (Mexico),* v. 22, no. 257 (Feb 93), pp. 41 – 44. Il.

Cuevas, Roberto. Comentario (on the article by Carlos D. Mesa Gisbert). *Estado y Sociedad,* v. 8, no. 9 (Jan – June 92), pp. 73 – 75.

Cuevas Molina, Rafael. Estado y cultura en Guatemala y Costa Rica. *Anuario de Estudios Centroamericanos,* v. 18, no. 2 (1992), pp. 25 – 39. Bibl.

Cummins, Alissandra. Exhibiting Culture: Museums and National Identity in the Caribbean. *Caribbean Quarterly,* v. 38, no. 2 – 3 (June – Sept 92), pp. 33 – 53. Bibl.

Cúneo, Dardo. Sarmiento y Unamuno: Sarmiento, el hombre de carne y hueso de Unamuno. *Hoy Es Historia,* v. 10, no. 56 (Mar – Apr 93), pp. 75 – 86. Il.

Cúneo Macchiavello, Ana María. La oralidad como primero elemento de formación de la poética mistraliana. *Revista Chilena de Literatura,* no. 41 (Apr 93), pp. 5 – 13. Bibl.

Cunha, José Marcos Pinto de. Caraterístics de la movilidad intrametropolitana en el estado de São Paulo, Brasil, 1970 – 1980. *Estudios Demográficos y Urbanos,* v. 7, no. 2 – 3 (May – Dec 92), pp. 587 – 602. Bibl, tables, maps.

Cunha, Olívia Maria Gomes da. Fazendo a "coisa certa": reggae, rastas e pentecostais em Salvador. *Revista Brasileira de Ciências Sociais,* v. 8, no. 23 (Oct 93), pp. 120 – 137. Bibl.

Cunha-Giabbai, Gloria da. La problemática de la mujer hispanoamericana como reflejo del conflicto social: *No es tiempo para rosas* de Antonieta Madrid. *Inti,* no. 37 – 38 (Spring – Fall 93), pp. 145 – 153.

Cunningham, Lucía

See
Guerra-Cunningham, Lucía

Curbelo Ranero, José Luis. Positive Adjustment in Latin America: On Decentralization and Development Planning. *European Review of Latin American and Caribbean Studies,* no. 54 (June 93), pp. 25 – 44. Bibl.

Curtis, Cynthia and Danielle Yariv. Después de la guerra: una mirada preliminar al papel de la ayuda militar de EE.UU. en la reconstrucción postguerra en El Salvador. *ECA; Estudios Centroamericanos,* v. 48, no. 531 – 532 (Jan – Feb 93), pp. 61 – 74. Il.

Curtis, James R. Central Business Districts of the Two Laredos. *Geographical Review,* v. 83, no. 1 (Jan 93), pp. 54 – 65. Bibl, tables, charts.

Cury, Maria Zilda Ferreira. O olhar do Papa e o navegador: Leão XIII descobre a América. *Cuadernos del CLAEH,* v. 17, no. 63 – 64 (Oct 92), pp. 35 – 42. Bibl.

Custodio, Isabel. Charla con René Juárez, presidente municipal de Acapulco. *Fem,* v. 17, no. 120 (Feb 93), p. 31.

Cypess, Sandra Messinger. Los géneros re/velados en *Los empeños de una casa* de sor Juana Inés de la Cruz. *Hispamérica,* v. 22, no. 64 – 65 (Apr – Aug 93), pp. 177 – 185. Bibl.

— Otro monólogo más (D'après Oscar Villegas' *Un señor y una señora*). *Latin American Theatre Review,* v. 26, no. 2 (Spring 93), pp. 89 – 92.

— Re-visión de la figura de la Malinche en la dramaturga mexicana contemporánea. *Cuadernos Americanos,* no. 40, Nueva época (July – Aug 93), pp. 208 – 222. Bibl.

Cysne, Rubens Penha. Reforma financeira: aspectos gerais e análise do projeto de lei complementar. *Revista de Economia Política (Brazil),* v. 13, no. 3 (July – Sept 93), pp. 21 – 40. Bibl.

Czar de Zalduendo, Susana. Empresas binacionales: el estatuto argentino – brasileño. *Integración Latinoamericana,* v. 17, no. 184 (Nov 92), pp. 16 – 25. Bibl.

Dacanal, José Hildebrando. A alternativa socialdemocrata. *Vozes,* v. 86, no. 6 (Nov – Dec 92), pp. 45 – 52.

Dagnino, Renato Peixoto. A indústria de armamentos brasileira e a segurança comum na América do Sul. *Política e Estratégica,* v. 8, no. 2 – 4 (Apr – Dec 90), pp. 383 – 399. Charts.

Daher, Antonio. Infraestructuras: regiones estatales y privadas en Chile. *Estudios Públicos (Chile),* no. 49 (Summer 93), pp. 137 – 173. Bibl, tables.

— Santiago estatal, Chile liberal. *Revista Interamericana de Planificación,* v. 26, no. 101 – 102 (Jan – June 93), pp. 43 – 62. Bibl, tables.

Daher, Antonio and Guillermo Gisse. América Latina: ambiente y territorio en el cambio de modelo. *Revista Paraguaya de Sociología,* v. 29, no. 84 (May – Aug 92), pp. 25 – 40.

Dahse, Fernando. Elementos de una metodología participativa para el desarrollo rural. *Estudios Sociales (Chile),* no. 78 (Oct – Dec 93), pp. 185 – 201. Bibl.

Dall'igna, Maria Antonieta. Políticas públicas de educação: a (des)articulação entre a união, o estado e os municípios. *Revista Brasileira de Estudos Pedagógicos,* v. 72, no. 172 (Sept – Dec 91), pp. 394 – 397.

D'Ambrosio, Oscar. Claquete quebrada. *Problemas Brasileiros,* v. 30, no. 295 (Jan – Feb 93), pp. 62 – 64. Il.

— Décadas produtivas. *Problemas Brasileiros,* v. 30, no. 295 (Jan – Feb 93), pp. 59 – 61.

Damián, Araceli. La investigación urbana en México, 1980 – 1990. *Estudios Demográficos y Urbanos,* v. 6, no. 3 (Sept – Dec 91), pp. 613 – 648. Bibl.

Damian, Carol. Art Miami '93. *Latin American Art,* v. 5, no. 1 (Spring 93), pp. 82 – 84. Il.

— The Latin American Art Scene in South Florida. *Latin American Art,* v. 4, no. 4 (Winter 92), pp. 65 – 68. Il.

— María Martínez Cañas: el viaje a casa (Accompanied by the English original, translated by Ignacio Zuleta Ll.). *Art Nexus,* no. 9 (June – Aug 93), pp. 114 – 117. Il.

Damill, Mario et al. Crecimiento económico en América Latina: experiencia reciente y perspectivas (Translated by Leandro Wolfson). *Desarrollo Económico (Argentina),* v. 33, no. 130 (July – Sept 93), pp. 237 – 264. Bibl, tables.

Damm Arnal, Arturo. Del porqué de la desaceleración. *Problemas del Desarrollo,* v. 24, no. 94 (July – Sept 93), pp. 32 – 38.

Daniel, Mary L. Coelho Neto revisitado. *Luso-Brazilian Review,* v. 30, no. 1 (Summer 93), pp. 175 – 180.

D'Aquino, Alfonso. El día (From the book *Naranja verde*). *Vuelta,* v. 17, no. 194 (Jan 93), p. 23.

Darío Murrieta, Rubén and María Rosa Palazón Mayoral. Las verdaderas leyendas de Joaquín Murrieta. *Casa de las Américas,* no. 191 (Apr – June 93), pp. 37 – 49. Bibl.

Darling, J. Andrew. Notes on Obsidian Sources of the Southern Sierra Madre Occidental. *Ancient Mesoamerica,* v. 4, no. 2 (Fall 93), pp. 245 – 253. Bibl, il, maps.

Daroqui, María Julia. Palabra de mujer. *Escritura (Venezuela),* v. 16, no. 31 – 32 (Jan – Dec 91), pp. 53 – 63. Bibl.

D'Artagnan. Academias sin un pe$$o: su importancia se subestima, ante la falta de prensa y de apoyo oficial. *Boletín de Historia y Antigüedades,* v. 79, no. 779 (Oct – Dec 92), pp. 1097 – 1099.

Dary Fuentes, Claudia. Los artesanos de la Nueva Guatemala de la Asunción, 1871 – 1898 (Photographs by Jorge Estuardo Molina L.). *La Tradición Popular,* no. 78 – 79 (1990), Issue. Bibl, il, tables, facs.

Dary Fuentes, Claudia and Aracely Esquivel. Los artesanos de la piedra: estudio sobre la cantería de San Luis Jilotepeque. *La Tradición Popular,* no. 85 (1991), Issue. Bibl, il.

Dassori, Albana M. et al. Ethnic and Gender Differences in the Diagnostic Profiles of Substance Abusers. *Hispanic Journal of Behavioral Sciences,* v. 15, no. 3 (Aug 93), pp. 382 – 390. Bibl.

Dauster, Frank N. Hacia la historia del teatro hispanoamericano. *Latin American Theatre Review,* v. 26, no. 2 (Spring 93), pp. 9 – 15. Il.

Dauzier, Martine. Comment affronter les 500 ans à venir?: mémoire et projet des indiens du Mexique. *Caravelle,* no. 59 (1992), pp. 87 – 98.

— Tous des indiens?: la "réindianisation"; force ou fiction: débats autour des essais de Guillermo Bonfil Batalla. *Cahiers des Amériques Latines,* no. 13 (1992), pp. 147 – 158. Bibl.

Dávalos Arze, Gladys. La mujer poeta y la sociedad: cocinan tan bien como escriben. *Signo,* no. 38, Nueva época (Jan – Apr 93), pp. 105 – 111. Bibl.

David, León. Tito Cánepa. *Latin American Art,* v. 4, no. 4 (Winter 92), pp. 69 – 71. Bibl, il.

Davidovich, Fany Rachel. Brasil metropolitano e Brasil urbano não-metropolitano: algumas questões. *Revista Brasileira de Geografia,* v. 53, no. 2 (Apr – June 91), pp. 127 – 133. Bibl.

— Gestão do território: um tema em questão. *Revista Brasileira de Geografia,* v. 53, no. 3 (July – Sept 91), pp. 7 – 31. Bibl.

— Poder local e município: algumas considerações. *Revista Geográfica (Mexico),* no. 115 (Jan – June 92), pp. 27 – 36. Bibl.

Davidson, Martha R. A Bibliography on Photography. *SALALM Papers,* v. 34 (1989), pp. 130 – 134.

Davies, Thomas M., Jr. Disintegration of a Culture: Peru into the 1990s. *SALALM Papers,* v. 36 (1991), pp. 42 – 48.

Dávila, Alberto E. and Rogelio Sáenz. Chicano Return Migration to the Southwest: An Integrated Human Capital Approach. *International Migration Review,* v. 26, no. 4 (Winter 92), pp. 1248 – 1266. Bibl, tables.

Dávila, Luis Ricardo. Rómulo Betancourt and the Development of Venezuelan Nationalism, 1930 – 1945. *Bulletin of Latin American Research,* v. 12, no. 1 (Jan 93), pp. 49 – 63. Bibl.

Dávila, Pilar and Augusto Alvarez Rodrich. Entrevista a Carlos Boloña. *Debate (Peru),* v. 15, no. 70 (Sept – Oct 92), pp. 8 – 14. Il.

Dávila Aldás, Francisco Rafael. La revolución científica – técnica, la globalización industrial, la formación de bloques y los nuevos cambios mundiales. *Relaciones Internacionales (Mexico),* v. 15, Nueva época, no. 58 (Apr – June 93), pp. 15 – 23.

Dávila Aldás, Francisco Rafael and Edgar Ortiz. Del antagonismo a la cooperación entre el Este y el Oeste para la búsqueda de un mundo más humano. *Revista Mexicana de Ciencias Políticas y Sociales,* v. 37, Nueva época, no. 149 (July – Sept 92), pp. 49 – 81.

Dávila Diez, Enrique. Estos fueron los cines. *Nexos,* v. 16, no. 187 (July 93), pp. 87 – 89. Il.

Dávila-López, Grace. Entrevista a Roberto Ramos-Perea. *Latin American Theatre Review,* v. 26, no. 2 (Spring 93), pp. 151 – 157.

Dávila Pérez, María del Consuelo. El modelo mexicano: ¿El ejemplo para la región? *Relaciones Internacionales (Mexico),* v. 14, Nueva época, no. 56 (Oct – Dec 92), pp. 123 – 127. Bibl.

— La política exterior en la revolución mexicana: bases histórico – jurídicas. *Relaciones Internacionales (Mexico),* v. 14, Nueva época, no. 55 (July – Sept 92), pp. 65 – 73. Bibl.

Dávila Ruiz, Emma A. Apuntes sobre el comercio entre Puerto Rico y Gran Bretaña durante el siglo XIX. *Op. Cit.,* no. 7 (1992), pp. 255 – 292. Bibl, il, tables, charts.

Dávila Santiago, Rubén and Jorge Rodríguez Beruff. Puerto Rico: frente a la nueva época. *Nueva Sociedad,* no. 127 (Sept – Oct 93), pp. 6 – 12.

Davis, Diane E. The Dialectic of Autonomy: State, Class, and Economic Crisis in Mexico, 1958 – 1982. *Latin American Perspectives,* v. 20, no. 3 (Summer 93), pp. 46 – 75. Bibl, tables, charts.

Davis, James J. Index of *Afro-Hispanic Review,* Volumes 8 – 12. *Afro-Hispanic Review,* v. 12, no. 2 (Fall 93), pp. 48 – 53.

Davis, Shelton H. Guillermo Bonfil Batalla y el movimiento indio latinoamericano (Translated by Alvaro González R.). *América Indígena,* v. 51, no. 2 – 3 (Apr – Sept 91), pp. 411 – 416.

Day, Douglas. Humboldt and the Casiquiare: Modes of Travel Writing. *Review,* no. 47 (Fall 93), pp. 4 – 8. Il.

Day, Michael J. The Geomorphology and Hydrology of the Blue Hole, Caves Branch. *Belizean Studies,* v. 20, no. 3 (Dec 92), pp. 3 – 10. Bibl, maps, charts.

Deal, Carl W. A Survey of Latin American Collections. *SALALM Papers,* v. 36 (1991), pp. 315 – 324. Tables.

Dean, Carolyn Sue. Ethnic Conflict and Corpus Christi in Colonial Cuzco. *Colonial Latin American Review,* v. 2, no. 1 – 2 (1993), pp. 93 – 120. Bibl, il.

Deans-Smith, Susan. Compromise and Conflict: The Tobacco Workers of Mexico City and the Colonial State, 1770 – 1810. *Anuario de Estudios Americanos,* v. 49 (1992), pp. 271 – 309. Bibl.

Deaver, William O., Jr. *Raining Backwards:* Colonization and the Death of a Culture. *The Americas Review,* v. 21, no. 1 (Spring 93), pp. 112 – 118.

De Beer, Gabriella. Entre la aventura y el litigio: una entrevista con Angela Mastretta. *Nexos,* v. 16, no. 184 (Apr 93), pp. 33 – 39.

— Narrativa y periodismo en *Morir en el golfo* de Héctor Aguilar Camín. *Revista Interamericana de Bibliografía,* v. 42, no. 2 (1992), pp. 215 – 221. Bibl.

Decierdo, Margarita Arce. A Mexican Migrant Family in North Carolina. *Aztlán,* v. 20, no. 1 – 2 (Spring – Fall 91), pp. 183 – 193.

Deckers, Daniel. La justicia de la conquista de América: consideraciones en torno a la cronología y a los protagonistas de una controversia del siglo XVI muy actual. *Ibero-Amerikanisches Archiv,* v. 18, no. 3 – 4 (1992), pp. 331 – 366. Bibl.

De Diego de Sousa, María Teresa de. Foro internacional sobre derechos humanos y filantropía. *Fem,* v. 17, no. 126 (Aug 93), pp. 8 – 9.

Degregori, Carlos Iván. Guzmán y Sendero: después de la caída. *Nueva Sociedad,* no. 124 (Mar – Apr 93), pp. 53 – 58.

Degregori, Carlos Iván et al. Comentarios y réplica (to the article "Recuerdos, olvidos y desencuentros" by María Angela Cánepa). *Allpanchis,* v. 25, no. 41 (Jan – June 93), pp. 38 – 73.

Dehouve, Danièle. El discípulo de Silo: un aspecto de la literatura náhuatl de los jesuitas del siglo XVIII. *Estudios de Cultura Náhuatl,* v. 22 (1992), pp. 345 – 379. Bibl.

De Hoyos, Angela. Poems ("Ten Dry Summers Ago," "How to Eat Crow on a Cold Sunday Morning," "Ramillete para Elena Poniatowska," "When Conventional Methods Fail"). *The Americas Review,* v. 20, no. 3 – 4 (Fall – Winter 92), pp. 149 – 152.

Delahaye, Olivier. Reforma agraria, renta y mercadeo de la tierra agrícola: una reflexión a partir de los casos venezolano y chileno. *Estudios Rurales Latinoamericanos,* v. 15, no. 2 – 3 (May – Dec 92), pp. 29 – 63. Bibl, tables.

De la Rosa Salazar, Denise and Sonia M. Pérez. Economic, Labor Force, and Social Implications of Latino Educational and Population Trends. *Hispanic Journal of Behavioral Sciences,* v. 15, no. 2 (May 93), pp. 188 – 229. Bibl, tables, charts.

Delazaro, Walter and José Carlos Barbieri. Nova regulamentação da transferência de tecnologia no Brasil. *RAE; Revista de Administração de Empresas,* v. 33, no. 3 (May – June 93), pp. 6 – 19. Bibl, tables.

De Leon, Brunilda. Sex Role Identity among College Students: A Cross-Cultural Analysis. *Hispanic Journal of Behavioral Sciences,* v. 15, no. 4 (Nov 93), pp. 476 – 489. Bibl, tables.

Déleon Meléndez, Ofelia Columba. Problemas teóricos sobre la cultura popular tradicional, la educación y la mujer en América Latina. *Folklore Americano,* no. 52 (July – Dec 91), pp. 101 – 108.

Déleon Meléndez, Ofelia Columba and Brenda Ninette Mayol Baños. Aproximación a la cultura popular tradicional de los municipios de Ciudad Flores, San José y la aldea Santa Eleana del departamento de Petén, Guatemala. *La Tradición Popular,* no. 76 – 77 (1990), Issue. II, facs.

— Una muestra de juguetes populares de la ciudad de Guatemala. *La Tradición Popular,* no. 86 – 87 (1992), Issue. II. Bibl, il.

Delfau, Antonio. Benito Baranda y Lorena Cornejo: una vida solidaria. *Mensaje,* v. 42, no. 421 (Aug 93), pp. 374 – 375. II.

Delfino, Silvia. Educación y democracia: una cultura joven en la Argentina. *La Educación (USA),* v. 37, no. 114 (1993), pp. 47 – 58. Bibl.

Delgadillo Macías, Javier. Economía y migración: la nueva geografía de la movilidad poblacional en México. *Problemas del Desarrollo,* v. 24, no. 94 (July – Sept 93), pp. 113 – 132. Bibl, tables, charts.

Delgado, Dora. A New "Look" for Your Money. *Business Mexico,* v. 3, no. 12 (Dec 93), p. 18.

— Resolving Conflicts Out of Court. *Business Mexico,* v. 3, no. 12 (Dec 93), p. 30.

— The Search for Capital. *Business Mexico,* v. 3, no. 11 (Nov 93), pp. 12 – 14.

— Taking a Bite Out of Competition. *Business Mexico,* v. 3, no. 11 (Nov 93), pp. 23 – 26. II.

Delgado, Josefina. Andrés Rivera y el sueño eterno de Castelli. *Todo Es Historia,* v. 27, no. 315 (Oct 93), pp. 56 – 59. II.

Delgado, Maria Berenice Godinho and Nilde Balção. Mujer y trabajo. *Nueva Sociedad,* no. 124 (Mar – Apr 93), pp. 60 – 71.

Delgado, Maria Berenice Godinho and Maria Margareth Lopes. Mulheres trabalhadoras e meio ambiente: um olhar feminista no sindicalismo. *Estudos Feministas,* v. 0, no. 0 (1992), pp. 155 – 162.

Delgado Aparicio, Vielka R. La perspectiva en la novela *El cabecilla* de José Agustín Cajar Escala. *Revista Cultural Lotería,* v. 50, no. 385 (Sept – Oct 91), pp. 83 – 87.

Delgado Aparicio, Vielka R. and Jézer González Picado. Introducción al estudio de *Huasipungo* y de *Los perros hambrientos. Revista Cultural Lotería,* v. 51, no. 392 (Nov – Dec 93), pp. 41 – 54. Bibl.

Delgado Chinchilla, Carmen. Environment: A Key Factor in Second Language Acquisition. *Káñina,* v. 16, no. 1 (Jan – June 92), pp. 185 – 193. Bibl.

Delgado Cintrón, Carmelo. La culminación de la lucha por el idioma: el caso de Puerto Rico. *Homines,* v. 15 – 16, no. 2 – 1 (Oct 91 – Dec 92), pp. 179 – 184.

Delgado Martínez, Irma. XII Seminario de Economía Agrícola del Tercer Mundo. *Problemas del Desarrollo,* v. 24, no. 93 (Apr – June 93), pp. 221 – 226.

Delgado Molina, Teresa. Ideología de la expresión en la obra poética de César Vallejo: apuntes al pie de un siglo. *Casa de las Américas,* no. 189 (Oct – Dec 92), pp. 43 – 50.

Delgado Ocando, José Manuel. Relectura posmodernista de Jesús Enrique Lossada. *Revista Nacional de Cultura (Venezuela),* v. 54, no. 287 (Oct – Dec 92), pp. 37 – 54. II.

Delhumeau Arrecillas, Antonio. El maestro: dignidad y deterioro. *Revista Mexicana de Ciencias Políticas y Sociales,* v. 38, Nueva época, no. 151 (Jan – Mar 93), pp. 205 – 210.

Della Cava, Ralph. Thinking about Current Vatican Policy in Central and East Europe and the Utility of the "Brazilian Paradigm." *Journal of Latin American Studies,* v. 25, no. 2 (May 93), pp. 257 – 281. Bibl.

De Looze, Laurence and Martha Gil-Montero. On the Tucumán Trail (Photographs by Jorge Provenza). *Américas,* v. 45, no. 5 (Sept – Oct 93), pp. 22 – 33. II, maps.

Delpar, Helen. Art in Latin America: Recent Writings (Review article). *Studies in Latin American Popular Culture,* v. 12 (1993), pp. 229 – 234. Bibl.

Delpino, Nena. Jóvenes y política, ayer y hoy: carta a mi hija. *Debate (Peru),* v. 15, no. 70 (Sept – Oct 92), pp. 39 – 44. II.

Deltoro, Antonio. La costumbre de lo oculto. *Vuelta,* v. 17, no. 197 (Apr 93), p. 19.

— Lluvia nocturna. *Vuelta,* v. 17, no. 203 (Oct 93), p. 14.

DeMar, Margaretta. Constraints on Constrainers: Limits on External Economic Policy Affecting Nutritional Vulnerability in the Caribbean. *Latin American Perspectives,* v. 20, no. 2 (Spring 93), pp. 54 – 73. Bibl.

Demasy, Rose-Hélène. La femme et le pouvoir social dans *La rue Cases-Nègres:* roman de Joseph Zobel. *Caribbean Studies,* v. 25, no. 1 – 2 (Jan – July 92), pp. 11 – 26.

Dembicz, Andrzej. Estudios latinoamericanos en Polonia: retos y proyecciones. *Cuadernos Americanos,* no. 42, Nueva época (Nov – Dec 93), pp. 43 – 47.

Demelas, Danièle and François-Xavier Guerra. Un processus révolutionnaire méconnu: l'adoption des formes representatives modernes en Espagne et en Amérique Latine, 1808 – 1810. *Caravelle,* no. 60 (1993), pp. 5 – 57. Bibl.

De Mello, George. "-Ra" vs. "-se" Subjunctive: A New Look at an Old Topic. *Hispania (USA),* v. 76, no. 2 (May 93), pp. 235 – 244. Bibl, tables.

— "Hasta = no hasta/hasta no = hasta" en el español hablado de once ciudades. *Anuario de Letras (Mexico),* v. 30 (1992), pp. 5 – 28. Bibl, tables.

Denevan, William M. The 1931 Shippee – Johnson Aerial Photography Expedition to Peru. *Geographical Review,* v. 83, no. 3 (July 93), pp. 238 – 251. Bibl, il, maps.

Denis, Paul-Yves and José Ismael Jaspe Alvarez. Estudio de la distribución espacial del sistema cooperativo de "Ferias de Consumo Familiar" (FCF) y de su papel en el abastecimiento alimentario en la región centro-occidental de Venezuela. *Revista Geográfica (Mexico)*, no. 114 (July – Dec 91), pp. 5 – 36. Bibl, maps, charts.

Deniz, Gerardo. Fiesta de guardar. *Vuelta*, v. 17, no. 197 (Apr 93), p. 15.

Dennis, Philip Adams. The Miskito – Sandinista Conflict in Nicaragua in the 1980s (Review article). *Latin American Research Review*, v. 28, no. 3 (1993), pp. 214 – 234.

Denton, Dan. Acapulco Renaissance. *Business Mexico*, v. 3, no. 3 (Mar 93), pp. 15 – 16. Il.

Derby, Robin L. H. and Richard Turits. Historias de terror y los terrores de la historia: la masacre haitiana de 1937 en la República Dominicana (Translated by Eugenio Rivas and Mario Alberto Torres). *Estudios Sociales (Dominican Republic)*, v. 26, no. 92 (Apr – June 93), pp. 65 – 76. Bibl.

Derné, Marie-Claude et al. Business Opportunities in Caribbean Cooperation. *Social and Economic Studies*, v. 41, no. 3 (Sept 92), pp. 65 – 100. Bibl, tables.

Desch, T. J. Capoeira: Martial Art as Spiritual Discipline. *Journal of Caribbean Studies*, v. 9, no. 1 – 2 (Winter 92 – Spring 93), pp. 87 – 98. Bibl.

Desroches, Monique. Créolisation musicale et identité culturelle aux Antilles françaises. *Canadian Journal of Latin American and Caribbean Studies*, v. 17, no. 34 (1992), pp. 41 – 51. Bibl.

Destéfani, Laurio Hedelvio. La Argentina y Colón. *Revista de Historia de América*, no. 113 (Jan – June 92), pp. 7 – 19. Bibl.

Deutsch, Sandra F. McGee. Afterword (to the issue entitled "Changing Images of the Brazilian Woman: Studies of Female Sexuality in Literature, Mass Media, and Criminal Trials, 1884 – 1992"). *Luso-Brazilian Review*, v. 30, no. 1 (Summer 93), pp. 107 – 117. Bibl.

Deveny, John J., Jr. and Peter C. Rollins, eds. *Culture and Development in Colombia: Study of Changes in Social Roles, Religion, Literature* . . . Special issue of *Journal of Popular Culture*, 22:1 (Summer 88), reviewed by Maurice P. Brungardt (Review entitled "Readings on Colombia?"). *Studies in Latin American Popular Culture*, v. 12 (1993), pp. 235 – 242.

Devincenzi, Roberto Marcos. Los estribos de la conquista. *Todo Es Historia*, v. 26, no. 309 (Apr 93), pp. 85 – 95. Bibl, il, tables.

Devlin, Robert T. Canje de deuda por naturaleza: la necesidad de una nueva agenda. *Revista de Economia Política (Brazil)*, v. 13, no. 3 (July – Sept 93), pp. 69 – 81. Tables.

— Privatizations and Social Welfare. *CEPAL Review*, no. 49 (Apr 93), pp. 155 – 180. Bibl, tables.

Devlin, Robert T. and Ricardo Ffrench-Davis. Diez años de crisis de la deuda latinoamericana. *Comercio Exterior*, v. 43, no. 1 (Jan 93), pp. 4 – 20. Bibl, tables.

Devoto, Daniel. La lengua de las tribus: de Guéret Chaminadour a Santa María de los Buenos Aires. *Nueva Revista de Filología Hispánica*, v. 40, no. 2 (July – Dec 92), pp. 921 – 958.

Dew, Edward. Caribbean Paths in the Dark (Review article). *Latin American Research Review*, v. 28, no. 1 (1993), pp. 162 – 173. Bibl.

Díaz, Amanda and Luc Ortlieb. El fenómeno El Niño y los moluscos de la costa peruana. *Bulletin de l'Institut Français d'Etudes Andines*, v. 22, no. 1 (1993), pp. 159 – 177. Bibl, tables, maps.

Díaz, Eduardo Alberto. Estrategias empresariales para la integración: el papel de la universidad en su determinación. *Integración Latinoamericana*, v. 18, no. 194 (Oct 93), pp. 15 – 22. Bibl, charts.

Díaz, Jairo et al. Determinantes del precio de los inmuebles en Bogotá. *Planeación y Desarrollo*, v. 24, no. 2 (May – Aug 93), pp. 315 – 327. Tables, charts.

— Dinámica de la construcción entre 1950 y 1991. *Planeación y Desarrollo*, v. 24, no. 2 (May – Aug 93), pp. 263 – 313. Tables, charts.

— Elementos del mercado del suelo urbano. *Planeación y Desarrollo*, v. 24, no. 2 (May – Aug 93), pp. 329 – 338. Tables.

Díaz, José Domingo. El terremoto del año de 1812 y nuestra independencia (Previously published in this journal vol. 1, no. 1, 1912). *Boletín de la Academia Nacional de la Historia (Venezuela)*, v. 75, no. 300 (Oct – Dec 92), pp. 321 – 326.

Díaz, José Enrique. Los descendientes de africanos en el Uruguay. *Afro-Hispanic Review*, v. 12, no. 2 (Fall 93), pp. 24 – 25.

Díaz, Lisiak-Land. Jerarquía social y económica en *El tungsteno* de César Vallejo. *Intí*, no. 36 (Fall 92), pp. 59 – 71. Bibl, charts.

Díaz, Luis Felipe. "En el fondo del caño hay un negrito" de José Luis González: estructura y discurso narcisistas. *Revista Iberoamericana*, v. 59, no. 162 – 163 (Jan – June 93), pp. 127 – 143. Bibl.

Díaz, María Eugenia. Liberación en las luchas latinoamericanas. *Islas*, no. 98 (Jan – Apr 91), pp. 167 – 176. Charts.

Díaz Alvarez, Manuel. In memoriam: Basilio de Barral, misionero y antropólogo. *Montalbán*, no. 24 (1992), pp. 21 – 24.

— Palabras del r.p. Manuel Díaz Alvarez con motivo de los 100 años del reingreso a Venezuela de los rr.pp. capuchinos. *Boletín de la Academia Nacional de la Historia (Venezuela)*, v. 76, no. 302 (Apr – June 93), pp. 15 – 19.

Díaz Barriga, Angel. Investigación en la formación de profesores: relaciones particulares y contradictorias. *Revista Latinoamericana de Estudios Educativos*, v. 23, no. 2 (Apr – June 93), pp. 105 – 116. Bibl, tables.

Díaz-Briquets, Sergio. Collision Course: Labor Force and Educational Trends in Cuba. *Cuban Studies/Estudios Cubanos*, v. 23 (1993), pp. 91 – 112. Bibl, tables.

— "Dollarization": Castro's Latest Economic Miracle? *Hemisphere*, v. 5, no. 3 (Summer – Fall 93), pp. 8 – 9.

Díaz Castellanos, Guadalupe. Desde su cotidianidad . . . : Benita Galeana y su lucha (Part I). *Fem*, v. 17, no. 124 (June 93), pp. 18 – 20. Il.

— Desde su cotidianidad . . . : Benita Galeana y su lucha (Part II). *Fem*, v. 17, no. 125 (July 93), pp. 21 – 23. Il.

— Elena Tapia . . . feminismo . . . Mujeres en Acción Sindical. *Fem*, v. 17, no. 128 (Oct 93), pp. 30 – 32.

— Graciela Hierro y la filosofía feminista. *Fem*, v. 17, no. 127 (Sept 93), pp. 17 – 19.

— Patricia Mercado: feminismo sindical. *Fem*, v. 17, no. 129 (Nov 93), pp. 15 – 17. Il.

— ¿Qué es la Sociedad Mexicana Pro-Derechos de la Mujer? *Fem*, v. 17, no. 126 (Aug 93), pp. 23 – 25.

Díaz Corvalán, Eugenio. Nuevo sindicalismo, viejos problemas: la concertación en Chile. *Nueva Sociedad*, no. 124 (Mar – Apr 93), pp. 114 – 121.

Díaz de Alpirez, Magali M. La familia como unidad de atención de la enfermera a través de la visita domiciliaria. *Revista Cultural Lotería*, v. 51, no. 390 (July – Aug 92), pp. 53 – 57.

Díaz de Guerra, María A. La zona de José Ignacio en el departamento de Maldonado y su incidencia en la evolución regional. *Hoy Es Historia,* v. 10, no. 58 (July – Aug 93), pp. 27 – 53. Bibl, il, facs.

Díaz del Castillo Z., Emiliano. La cultura en la evangelización del Nuevo Reino de Granada. *Boletín de Historia y Antigüedades,* v. 80, no. 781 (Apr – June 93), pp. 415 – 434.

Díaz Gómez, Floriberto. Las celebraciones de los 500 años. *Caravelle,* no. 59 (1992), pp. 33 – 37.

Díaz Granados, José Luis. Los míos. *Boletín de Historia y Antigüedades,* v. 80, no. 780 (Jan – Mar 93), pp. 243 – 246.

Díaz I., Gloria. La celebración del quinto centenario del descubrimiento de América. *Revista Cultural Lotería,* v. 51, no. 391 (Sept – Oct 92), pp. 7 – 12.

Díaz Infante, Fernando. Las voces del agua. *La Palabra y el Hombre,* no. 81 (Jan – Mar 92), pp. 388 – 390.

Díaz-Jove Blanco, Santiago. Alonso Carrió de Lavandera, "Concoloncorvo": el contexto migratorio de su época y lugar de origen. *Revista de Indias,* v. 53, no. 198 (May – Aug 93), pp. 639 – 649.

Díaz Martínez, Manuel. La generación del '27 e Hispanoamérica. *Cuadernos Hispanoamericanos,* no. 514 – 515 (Apr – May 93), pp. 143 – 154. Il.

Díaz Polanco, Héctor. El quinto centenario y los pueblos indios. *Boletín de Antropología Americana,* no. 23 (July 91), pp. 13 – 29. Bibl, il.

Díaz Polanco, Héctor and Consuelo Sánchez. Cronología de los hechos históricos de la costa atlántica de Nicaragua: primera parte. *Boletín de Antropología Americana,* no. 23 (July 91), pp. 171 – 184. Bibl.

— Cronología de los hechos históricos de la costa atlántica de Nicaragua: segunda parte. *Boletín de Antropología Americana,* no. 24 (Dec 91), pp. 151 – 178. Bibl, il.

Díaz Quiñones, Arcadio. El enemigo íntimo: cultura nacional y autoridad en Ramiro Guerra y Sánchez y Antonio S. Pedreira. *Op. Cit.,* no. 7 (1992), pp. 9 – 65. Bibl.

— *El entenado:* las palabras de la tribu. *Hispamérica,* v. 21, no. 63 (Dec 92), pp. 3 – 14.

Díaz Ruiz, Ignacio. El recurso de la historia: a propósito de Carpentier. *Nueva Revista de Filología Hispánica,* v. 40, no. 2 (July – Dec 92), pp. 1073 – 1086. Bibl.

Díaz-Salazar, Rafael. La crítica cristiana a la civilización del capital: aportaciones de la doctrina social de la iglesia a la construcción de un nuevo socialismo. *ECA; Estudios Centroamericanos,* v. 47, no. 529 – 530 (Nov – Dec 92), pp. 999 – 1014. Bibl, il.

— Izquierda y cristianismo en América Latina. *ECA; Estudios Centroamericanos,* v. 48, no. 536 (June 93), pp. 563 – 576.

Díaz Sosa, Rafael Angel
See
Pineda, Rafael

Díaz Sustaeta, Federico and Sumie Prado Arai. Estudio de las actitudes de los estudiantes de posgrado de la Universidad Iberoamericana ante las metas de la institución. *Revista Latinoamericana de Estudios Educativos,* v. 23, no. 2 (Apr – June 93), pp. 71 – 85. Bibl, tables.

Dicker, Susan J. Examining the Myths of Language and Cultural Diversity: A Response to Rosalie Pedalino Porter's *Forked Tongue: The Politics of Bilingual Education. Bilingual Review/Revista Bilingüe,* v. 17, no. 3 (Sept – Dec 92), pp. 210 – 230. Bibl.

Diego Ortega, Roberto
See
Ortega, Roberto Diego

Dietz, James L. Reviewing and Renewing Puerto Rican and Caribbean Studies: From Dependency to What? *Caribbean Studies,* v. 25, no. 1 – 2 (Jan – July 92), pp. 27 – 48. Bibl.

Díez Hochleitner, Ricardo. Iberoamérica ante el siglo XXI. *Cuadernos Americanos,* no. 39, Nueva época (May – June 93), pp. 42 – 52. Bibl.

Diez Hurtado, Alejandro. El poder de las varas: los cabildos en Piura a fines de la colonia. *Apuntes (Peru),* no. 30 (Jan – June 92), pp. 81 – 90. Bibl, tables.

Di Girólamo, Claudio. Festival Mundial Teatro de las Naciones: saliendo de la isla. *Mensaje,* v. 42, no. 418 (May 93), pp. 164 – 165. Il.

Di Girólamo, Giovanni. The World Agricultural Outlook in the 1990s. *CEPAL Review,* no. 47 (Aug 92), pp. 95 – 114. Bibl, tables, charts.

Dijck, Pitou van. The Empty Box Syndrome. *CEPAL Review,* no. 47 (Aug 92), pp. 21 – 36. Bibl, tables, charts.

Dijk, Meine Pieter van. Guyana: Economic Recession and Transition. *European Review of Latin American and Caribbean Studies,* no. 53 (Dec 92), pp. 95 – 110. Bibl, tables.

Dimo, Edith. Una voz nacida del silencio: conversación con Juan Gelman. *Chasqui,* v. 22, no. 2 (Nov 93), pp. 109 – 113.

Dinechin, Olivier de. SIDA: educar, acompañar . . . . *Mensaje,* v. 42, no. 422 (Sept 93), pp. 427 – 431.

Dinerstein, Ana Cecilia. Privatizaciones y legitimidad: la lógica de la coerción. *Realidad Económica,* no. 113 (Jan – Feb 93), pp. 18 – 30.

Diniz, Eli and Renato Raul Boschi. Lideranças empresariais e problemas da estratégia liberal no Brasil. *Revista Brasileira de Ciências Sociais,* v. 8, no. 23 (Oct 93), pp. 101 – 119. Bibl.

Di Tella, Torcuato S. La unión obrera textil, 1930 – 1945. *Desarrollo Económico (Argentina),* v. 33, no. 129 (Apr – June 93), pp. 109 – 136. Bibl, tables.

Divinsky, Daniel. Acerca de la inexistencia de América Latina como uno de los inconvenientes para adquirir material literario a su respecto. *SALALM Papers,* v. 36 (1991), pp. 165 – 170.

— Vicios públicos, virtudes privadas: editar en la Argentina; memorias abreviadas. *Cuadernos Hispanoamericanos,* no. 517 – 519 (July – Sept 93), pp. 516 – 520.

Dixon, David and Richard Dixon. Culturas e identidades populares y el surgimiento de los evangélicos en América Latina. *Cristianismo y Sociedad,* v. 30, no. 114 (1992), pp. 61 – 74. Bibl.

Dobrian, Walter A. The Dialog of Genres: Hispanic Literature to Film. *Hispania (USA),* v. 76, no. 1 (Mar 93), pp. 140 – 146. Bibl.

Docampo, César. Iniciativas estadounidenses de la política económica: consecuencias hemisféricas. *Realidad Económica,* no. 119 (Oct – Nov 93), pp. 117 – 132. Bibl.

Dockall, John Edward and Harry J. Shafer. Testing the Producer – Consumer Model for Santa Rita Corozal, Belize. *Latin American Antiquity,* v. 4, no. 2 (June 93), pp. 158 – 179. Bibl, il, maps.

Dodds, Klaus-John. Geography, Identity, and the Creation of the Argentine State. *Bulletin of Latin American Research,* v. 12, no. 3 (Sept 93), pp. 311 – 331. Bibl.

Dodson, Michael. The Changing Spectrum of Religious Activism in Latin America (Review article). *Latin American Perspectives*, v. 20, no. 4 (Fall 93), pp. 61 – 74. Bibl.

Dodsworth, Mark. Susan Rocyn-Jones (1940 – 1992): An Appreciation. *Bulletin of Latin American Research*, v. 12, no. 2 (May 93), pp. 215 – 216.

Dölz-Blackburn, Inés and Violeta Sulsona. Isabel Allende a través de sus entrevistas. *Revista Interamericana de Bibliografía*, v. 42, no. 3 (1992), pp. 421 – 430. Bibl.

Doerflinger, Enrique Ricardo et al. La realidad sociolingüística del pueblo quechua. *Anuario Indigenista*, v. 30 (Dec 91), pp. 267 – 288.

Domingo Acebrón, María Dolores. La participación de españoles en el ejército libertador en Cuba, 1895 – 1898. *Revista de Indias*, v. 52, no. 195 – 196 (May – Dec 92), pp. 349 – 363. Bibl, tables.

Domingues, José Maurício. A América: intelectuais, interpretações e indentidades. *Dados*, v. 35, no. 2 (1992), pp. 267 – 289. Bibl, charts.

Domínguez Díaz, Marta Silvia. Arte chileno: una contribución bibliográfica. *SALALM Papers*, v. 34 (1989), pp. 369 – 388.

— El arte popular chileno. *SALALM Papers*, v. 34 (1989), pp. 9 – 16. Bibl.

— El medio ambiente en Chile hoy: informe y bibliografía. *SALALM Papers*, v. 36 (1991), pp. 130 – 156.

— Transición política en Chile: documentación y fuentes. *SALALM Papers*, v. 34 (1989), pp. 459 – 474. Bibl.

Domínguez Faura, Nicanor. La conformación de la imagen del espacio andino: geografía e historia en el Perú colonial, 1530 – 1820; crónica bibliográfica. *Revista Andina*, v. 11, no. 1 (July 93), pp. 201 – 237. Bibl.

Domínguez I., Manuel F. El Colegio Franciscano de Propaganda Fide de Moquegua, 1775 – 1825. *Archivo Ibero-Americano*, v. 52, no. 205 – 208 (Jan – Dec 92), pp. 221 – 254. Bibl.

Domínguez Michael, Christopher. Altamirano íntimo y sentimental (Review article). *Vuelta*, v. 17, no. 200 (July 93), pp. 60 – 61.

— Jorge Cuesta o la crítica del demonio (Chapter from the book *Tiros en el concierto*). *Vuelta*, v. 17, no. 194 (Jan 93), pp. 28 – 36. Bibl.

— Lepra y utopía (Chapter from the book *Tiros en el concierto*). *Vuelta*, v. 17, no. 199 (June 93), pp. 24 – 31. Bibl.

Domínguez Miranda, Manuel. Ignacio Ellacuría, filósofo de la realidad latinoamericana. *ECA; Estudios Centroamericanos*, v. 47, no. 529 – 530 (Nov – Dec 92), pp. 983 – 998.

Domnick, Heinz-Joachim. América, 1492 – 1992: nuevos mundos, nuevas realidades (Translated by Ricardo Barra). *Humboldt*, no. 109 (1993), pp. 76 – 83. Il.

Doñán, Juan José et al. Carta de Guadalajara (Regular feature appearing in most issues). *Vuelta*, v. 17 (1993), All issues.

Donato, Katharine M. Current Trends and Patterns of Female Migration: Evidence from Mexico. *International Migration Review*, v. 27, no. 4 (Winter 93), pp. 748 – 771. Bibl, tables.

Donís Ríos, Manuel Alberto. Venezuela: topónimo afortunado en la cartografía auroral de América. *Montalbán*, no. 24 (1992), pp. 99 – 118. Bibl, maps.

Donoso Letelier, Crescente. Libro copiador de telegramas del presidente Carlos Ibáñez, 1928 – 1931. *Historia (Chile)*, no. 26 (1991 – 1992), pp. 297 – 383. Bibl.

Dorfman, Ariel. Comments (on the panel "Liberty and Justice for All: Human Rights and Democratization in Latin America"). *SALALM Papers*, v. 36 (1991), pp. 209 – 212.

Dossar, Kenneth. Capoeira Angola: Dancing between Two Worlds. *Afro-Hispanic Review*, v. 11, no. 1 – 3 (1992), pp. 5 – 10. Bibl.

Doudoroff, Michael J. Nuevo mundo Orinoco de Juan Liscano: reflexiones sobre sus contextos. *Inti*, no. 37 – 38 (Spring – Fall 93), pp. 81 – 87.

Doughty, Paul L. Perú: . . . y la vida continúa. *América Indígena*, v. 51, no. 4 (Oct – Dec 91), pp. 49 – 79. Bibl, tables, maps.

Dougnac Rodríguez, Antonio. Algunas manifestaciones del regalismo borbónico a fines del siglo XVIII. *Boletín de la Academia Chilena de la Historia*, v. 58 – 59, no. 102 (1991 – 1992), pp. 43 – 94. Bibl.

Dourado, Anísio Brasileiro de Freitas. Relaciones contractuales entre los poderes públicos y las empresas privadas de autobuses urbanos en Brasil (Translated by Martín Figueroa). *EURE*, v. 19, no. 56 (Mar 93), pp. 29 – 39. Bibl.

Douzant Rosenfeld, Denise and Laura Faxas. Equipements urbains et services de remplacement: le cas de Santo Domingo, République Dominicaine. *Tiers Monde*, v. 34, no. 133 (Jan – Mar 93), pp. 139 – 151.

Doyle, Kate. Drug War: A Quietly Escalating Failure. *NACLA Report on the Americas*, v. 26, no. 5 (May 93), pp. 29 – 34 + . Bibl, il.

Dragún, Osvaldo. Cómo lo hicimos. *Cuadernos Hispanoamericanos*, no. 517 – 519 (July – Sept 93), pp. 532 – 535.

— El delirio. *Conjunto*, no. 89 (Oct – Dec 91), pp. 40 – 83.

Dreiss, Meredith L. et al. Expanding the Role of Trace-Element Studies: Obsidian Use in the Late and Terminal Classic Periods at the Lowland Maya Site of Colha, Belize. *Ancient Mesoamerica*, v. 4, no. 2 (Fall 93), pp. 271 – 283. Bibl, il, maps, charts.

Dror, Yehezkel. Conducción del estado hacia la integración. *Integración Latinoamericana*, v. 18, no. 189 – 190 (May – June 93), pp. 3 – 9.

Drouvot, Hubert. Libéralisme et politique nationale de développement technologique: l'industrie aéronautique au Brésil. *Cahiers des Amériques Latines*, no. 14 (1992), pp. 95 – 118. Bibl, tables, charts.

Duany, Jorge. Más allá de la válvula de escape: tendencias recientes en la migración caribeña. *Nueva Sociedad*, no. 127 (Sept – Oct 93), pp. 80 – 99. Bibl.

— Neither Golden Exile Nor Dirty Worm: Ethnic Identity in Recent Cuban-American Novels. *Cuban Studies/Estudios Cubanos*, v. 23 (1993), pp. 167 – 183. Bibl.

Duarte, Luiz Fernando Dias et al. Vicissitudes e limites da conversão à cidadania nas classes populares brasileiras. *Revista Brasileira de Ciências Sociais*, v. 8, no. 22 (June 93), pp. 5 – 19. Bibl.

Duarte, María Amalia. La ley de amnistía de 1875 y el proceder del jordanismo. *Investigaciones y Ensayos*, no. 41 (Jan – Dec 91), pp. 171 – 213. Bibl.

Dubatti, Jorge A. El nuevo teatro de Buenos Aires, 1983 – 1992. *Cuadernos Hispanoamericanos*, no. 517 – 519 (July – Sept 93), pp. 445 – 462. Bibl.

Duchesne, Juan Ramón. Multitud y tradición en "El entierro de Cortijo" de Edgardo Rodríguez Juliá. *Revista Iberoamericana*, v. 59, no. 162 – 163 (Jan – June 93), pp. 221 – 237. Bibl.

Dueñas Vargas, Guiomar. Algunas hipótesis para el estudio de la resistencia campesina en la región central de Colombia, siglo XIX. *Anuario Colombiano de Historia Social y de la Cultura,* no. 20 (1992), pp. 90 – 106. Bibl.

Dufétel, Dominique. La otra vida en Monte Albán (Accompanied by an English translation). *Artes de México,* no. 21 (Fall 93), pp. 60 – 65. Il.

— Pequeña historia de las chinampas y tres sueños (Accompanied by an English translation). *Artes de México,* no. 20 (Summer 93), pp. 37 – 47. Il.

Duff, Ernest A. Attack and Counterattack: Dynamics of Transculturation in the Caribbean (Review article). *Studies in Latin American Popular Culture,* v. 12 (1993), pp. 195 – 202.

Duhau, Emilio and Alejandro Suárez Pareyón. Sistemas de planeación y política de desarrollo urbano en la ciudad de México. *El Cotidiano,* v. 9, no. 54 (May 93), pp. 3 – 9. Bibl, il.

Dukats, Mara L. A Narrative of Violated Maternity: *Moi, Tituba, sorcière . . . noire de Salem. World Literature Today,* v. 67, no. 4 (Fall 93), pp. 745 – 750. Bibl.

Dumont, Jean-François. Rasgos morfoestructurales de la llanura amazónica del Perú: efecto de la neotectónica sobre los cambios fluviales y la delimitación de las provincias morfológicas. *Bulletin de l'Institut Français d'Etudes Andines,* v. 21, no. 3 (1992), pp. 801 – 833. Bibl, il, maps.

Dunn, Christopher. Afro-Bahian Carnival: A Stage for Protest. *Afro-Hispanic Review,* v. 11, no. 1 – 3 (1992), pp. 11 – 20. Bibl.

— It's Forbidden to Forbid. *Américas,* v. 45, no. 5 (Sept – Oct 93), pp. 14 – 21. Il.

Duque, Job
See
Gutiérrez Nájera, Manuel

Duque Corredor, Ramón José. El derecho agrario y su vocación regional: sentido y principios funcionales. *Derecho y Reforma Agraria,* no. 24 (1993), pp. 27 – 31.

Duque Escobar, Iván. Carlos Sanz de Santamaría. *Boletín de Historia y Antigüedades,* v. 80, no. 781 (Apr – June 93), pp. 281 – 282.

Duque Gómez, Luis. Brillante trayectoria de la mujer en la Academia (Commentary on the speech by Carmen Ortega Ricaurte). *Boletín de Historia y Antigüedades,* v. 80, no. 781 (Apr – June 93), pp. 407 – 413.

— La orden seráfica en América y en Colombia. *Boletín de Historia y Antigüedades,* v. 79, no. 779 (Oct – Dec 92), pp. 919 – 923.

Duque Mesa, Fernando. *Maravilla estar* en el laberinto de la postmodernidad. *Conjunto,* no. 93 (Jan – June 93), pp. 84 – 90. Bibl.

Durán, Ana María and María Concepción Huerta Trujillo. Cambios de usos del suelo y despoblamiento en la colonia Roma. *El Cotidiano,* v. 10, no. 57 (Aug – Sept 93), pp. 73 – 77. Il, tables.

Durán, Diana. El desarrollo sustentable: ¿Un nuevo modelo? (Excerpts from *Convivir en la tierra* by Diana Durán and Albina L. Lara). *Realidad Económica,* no. 113 (Jan – Feb 93), pp. 31 – 39. Bibl.

Durán, Rafael and Miguel Franco. Estudio demográfico de "Pseudophoenix sargentii." *Bulletin de l'Institut Français d'Etudes Andines,* v. 21, no. 2 (1992), pp. 609 – 621. Bibl, maps, charts.

Durán Cubillo, Ofelia. Rasgos del relato moderno en el orden temporal de *Noche en vela. Káñina,* v. 16, no. 2 (July – Dec 92), pp. 9 – 16. Tables, charts.

Durán Luzio, Juan. Modos de relación en historia y literatura hispanoamericana durante el siglo XIX. *Escritura (Venezuela),* v. 17, no. 33 – 34 (Jan – Dec 92), pp. 83 – 100.

Durán Montero, María Antonia. Lima en 1613: aspectos urbanos. *Anuario de Estudios Americanos,* v. 49 (1992), pp. 171 – 188. Bibl, maps.

Durand Alcántara, Carlos Humberto. Las reformas y adicionales al Artículo 27 constitucional, 1857 – 1992. *Derecho y Reforma Agraria,* no. 24 (1993), pp. 139 – 157. Bibl.

Durand Ponte, Víctor Manuel. La cultura política en nueve ciudades mexicanas. *Revista Mexicana de Sociología,* v. 54, no. 1 (Jan – Mar 92), pp. 289 – 322. Tables, charts.

Durbin, Pamela. Transcultural Steps with a Flair. *Américas,* v. 45, no. 3 (May – June 93), pp. 18 – 23. Il.

Durham, Carolyn Richardson. Sônia Fátima da Conceição's Literature for Social Change. *Afro-Hispanic Review,* v. 11, no. 1 – 3 (1992), pp. 21 – 25. Bibl.

Durham, Eunice Ribeiro. O sistema federal de ensino superior: problemas e alternativas. *Revista Brasileira de Ciências Sociais,* v. 8, no. 23 (Oct 93), pp. 5 – 37. Bibl, tables.

Dussel, Enrique D. El proyecto de una filosofía de la historia latinoamericana. *Hoy Es Historia,* v. 10, no. 57 (Apr – May 93), pp. 40 – 48. Bibl.

Dutrénit, Gabriela. Las agroindustrias exportadoras: su penetración en Estados Unidos. *Comercio Exterior,* v. 43, no. 4 (Apr 93), pp. 336 – 343. Tables.

Dutrénit, Gabriela and Mario Capdevielle. El perfil tecnológico de la industria mexicana y su dinámica innovadora en la década de los ochenta. *El Trimestre Económico,* v. 60, no. 239 (July – Sept 93), pp. 643 – 674. Bibl, tables, charts.

Dutrénit, Silvia. Visiones de la crisis nacional que influyeron en el programa del movimiento obrero-popular uruguayo, 1958 – 1965. *Cuadernos Americanos,* no. 42, Nueva época (Nov – Dec 93), pp. 78 – 100. Bibl.

Dutton, John C., Jr. and Orlando Monteiro da Silva. O mercado internacional de suco de laranja concentrado congelado: um modelo com produtos diferenciados. *Revista de Economia e Sociologia Rural,* v. 29, no. 4 (Oct – Dec 91), pp. 353 – 371. Bibl, tables.

Dworkin, Kenya C. and Alice A. Brittin. Rigoberta Menchú: "Los indígenas no nos quedamos como bichos aislados, inmunes, desde hace 500 años. No, nosotros hemos sido protagonistas de la historia" (Includes Rigoberta Menchú's poem, "Patria abnegada"). *Nuevo Texto Crítico,* v. 6, no. 11 (1993), pp. 207 – 222.

Dys, Damaris van der and Pedro José Bastidas González. Programa de adaptación del Sistema de Información de la Planta Física Educativa (SIPFE) a los objetivos de reducción de la vulnerabilidad a las amenazas naturales en las escuelas. *La Educación (USA),* v. 37, no. 115 (1993), pp. 365 – 377. Tables.

Earle, Peter G. Octavio Paz: poesía e historia. *Nueva Revista de Filología Hispánica,* v. 40, no. 2 (July – Dec 92), pp. 1101 – 1112. Bibl.

— On Culture and Critical Hangovers. *Latin American Literary Review,* v. 20, no. 40 (July – Dec 92), pp. 32 – 33.

— Las soledades de Martínez Estrada. *Cuadernos Americanos,* no. 42, Nueva época (Nov – Dec 93), pp. 148 – 156.

Eaton, William W. and Roberta Garrison. Mental Health in Mariel Cubans and Haitian Boat People. *International Migration Review,* v. 26, no. 4 (Winter 92), pp. 1395 – 1415. Bibl, tables.

Echanove Huacuja, Flavia. El mercado del algodón: políticas de Estados Unidos y México y el Tratado de Libre Comercio. *Comercio Exterior*, v. 43, no. 11 (Nov 93), pp. 1046 – 1051. Bibl, tables.

Echavarría, Fernando R. Cuantificación de la deforestación en el valle del Huallaga, Perú. *Revista Geográfica (Mexico)*, no. 114 (July – Dec 91), pp. 37 – 53. Bibl, tables, maps, charts.

Echavarría, Rogelio. Poems. *Revista Nacional de Cultura (Venezuela)*, v. 53, no. 286 (July – Sept 92), pp. 116 – 119.

Echavarría Olozaga, Hernán and José Consuegra Higgins. Tres cartas, dos opiniones. *Desarrollo Indoamericano*, v. 23, no. 91 (June 93), pp. 17 – 19. Il.

Echazú, Roberto. La sal de la tierra (Fragmentos). *Casa de las Américas*, no. 190 (Jan – Mar 93), pp. 112 – 115.

Echegaray, Fabián. Elecciones y partidos provinciales en la Argentina. *Nueva Sociedad*, no. 124 (Mar – Apr 93), pp. 46 – 52. Tables.

Echegollen Guzmán, Mayleth. Destino humano. *Fem*, v. 17, no. 119 (Jan 93), p. 29.

Echevarría, Evelio A. La novela histórica de Chile: deslinde y bibliografía, 1852 – 1990. *Revista Interamericana de Bibliografía*, v. 42, no. 4 (1992), pp. 643 – 650. Bibl.

Echeverri, Clara. Maquila o diseño. *Revista Javeriana*, v. 61, no. 593 (Apr 93), pp. 160 – 162.

Edelman, Marc and Rodolfo Monge Oviedo. Costa Rica: The Non-Market Roots of Market Success. *Report on the Americas*, v. 26, no. 4 (Feb 93), pp. 22 – 29 + . Bibl, il.

Edwards, Beatrice. Interview with Errol Miller. *La Educación (USA)*, v. 37, no. 114 (1993), pp. 125 – 134.

— Linking the Social and Natural Worlds: Environmental Education in the Hemisphere. *La Educación (USA)*, v. 37, no. 115 (1993), pp. 231 – 256. Bibl.

Edwards, Jack E. et al. Willingness to Relocate for Employment: A Survey of Hispanics, Non-Hispanic Whites, and Blacks. *Hispanic Journal of Behavioral Sciences*, v. 15, no. 1 (Feb 93), pp. 121 – 133. Bibl, tables.

Edwards, Jorge. El encuentro y el desencuentro. *Atenea (Chile)*, no. 465 – 466 (1992), pp. 35 – 37.

— El otro Occidente. *Estudios Públicos (Chile)*, no. 50 (Fall 93), pp. 345 – 351.

— Una vida cubana. *Vuelta*, v. 17, no. 201 (Aug 93), pp. 26 – 27.

Edwards, Marta. Percepción de la familia y de la formación de los hijos. *Estudios Públicos (Chile)*, no. 52 (Spring 93), pp. 191 – 214. Tables, charts.

Edwards, Sebastián. Orientación del comercio exterior, deformaciones y crecimiento en los países en desarrollo. *El Trimestre Económico*, v. 59, Special issue (Dec 92), pp. 41 – 74. Bibl, tables.

Eeckhout, Peter. Le créateur et le devin: à propos de Pachacamac, dieu précolombien de la côte centrale du Pérou. *Revista Española de Antropología Americana*, v. 23 (1993), pp. 135 – 152. Bibl, tables.

Egan, Linda. Entrevistas con periodistas mujeres sobre la prensa mexicana. *Mexican Studies*, v. 9, no. 2 (Summer 93), pp. 275 – 294. Bibl.

— Feminine Perspectives on Journalism: Conversations with Eight Mexican Women. *Studies in Latin American Popular Culture*, v. 12 (1993), pp. 175 – 187.

Egaña, María José. De las ollas comunes a microempresarias. *Mensaje*, v. 42, no. 425 (Dec 93), pp. 650 – 653. Il.

Egea López, Antonio. El marqués de Uztáriz, asistente de Sevilla. *Boletín de la Academia Nacional de la Historia (Venezuela)*, v. 76, no. 302 (Apr – June 93), pp. 142 – 144.

— El marqués de Uztáriz, un venezolano que gobernó Sevilla. *Boletín de la Academia Nacional de la Historia (Venezuela)*, v. 75, no. 297 (Jan – Mar 92), pp. 113 – 116.

Eger, Ernestina N. Poems ("Oración agnóstica: respuesta a Quevedo," "Aniversario"). *Bilingual Review/Revista Bilingüe*, v. 18, no. 1 (Jan – Apr 93), pp. 61 – 63.

Egler, Claudio Antonio G. As escalas de economia: uma introdução à dimensão territorial da crise. *Revista Brasileira de Geografia*, v. 53, no. 3 (July – Sept 91), pp. 229 – 245.

Eguizábal, Cristina. De Contadora a Esquipulas: Washington y Centroamérica en un mundo cambiante. *Anuario de Estudios Centroamericanos*, v. 18, no. 1 (1992), pp. 5 – 15. Bibl.

Eidelberg, Nora. El teatro en Lima en 1991 y 1992. *Latin American Theatre Review*, v. 26, no. 2 (Spring 93), pp. 191 – 195.

Eielson, Jorge Eduardo. Arte poética III. *Vuelta*, v. 17, no. 194 (Jan 93), p. 10.

Eisenstadt, Todd. Nuevo estilo diplomático: cabildeo y relaciones públicas, 1986 – 1991 (Translated by Martha Elena Venier). *Foro Internacional*, v. 32, no. 5 (Oct – Dec 92), pp. 667 – 702. Bibl, tables, charts.

Eizykovicz, José. Los peones rurales después de la revolución, 1815 – 1823. *Todo Es Historia*, v. 27, no. 312 (July 93), pp. 28 – 42. Bibl, il, facs.

Elbanowski, Adam. El espacio y lo fantástico en la cuentística de Cortázar. *La Palabra y el Hombre*, no. 81 (Jan – Mar 92), pp. 273 – 278. Bibl.

Elias, Christopher. Enfermedades transmitidas sexualmente y la salud reproductiva de las mujeres en los países en vías de desarrollo. *Fem*, v. 17, no. 124 (June 93), pp. 26 – 29. Bibl.

Elizondo, Salvador. Juan Rulfo. *Vuelta*, v. 17, no. 203 (Oct 93), pp. 8 – 9.

Elizondo, Sergio. Quién le manda. *Plural (Mexico)*, v. 22, no. 256 (Jan 93), pp. 70 – 73.

Eljuri, José Ramón. Campañas libertadoras suramericanas del general de brigada Héctor Bencomo Barrios. *Boletín de la Academia Nacional de la Historia (Venezuela)*, v. 76, no. 301 (Jan – Mar 93), pp. 130 – 131.

Elliott, Enrique. El bibliotecario profesional. *Revista Cultural Lotería*, v. 50, no. 384 (July – Aug 91), pp. 45 – 55. Bibl.

Ellner, Steven B. A Tolerance Worn Thin: Corruption in the Age of Austerity. *NACLA Report on the Americas*, v. 27, no. 3 (Nov – Dec 93), pp. 13 – 16 + . Bibl, il.

Elmendorf, George F. and Joan A. Quillen. Mexico's Environmental and Ecological Organizations and Movements. *SALALM Papers*, v. 36 (1991), pp. 123 – 129.

— Serials and Government Documents from the States of Mexico. *SALALM Papers*, v. 36 (1991), pp. 425 – 431.

Elmore, Peter. Sobre el volcán: seis novelas peruanas de los '90 (Review article). *Hueso Húmero*, no. 29 (May 93), pp. 125 – 143.

Encarnación, Filomeno. Conservación en la Amazonía. *Amazonía Peruana*, v. 11, no. 21 (Sept 92), pp. 49 – 72. Bibl.

Enchautegui, María E. Geographical Differentials in the Socioeconomic Status of Puerto Ricans: Human Capital Variations and Labor Market Characteristics. *International Migration Review*, v. 26, no. 4 (Winter 92), pp. 1267 – 1290. Bibl, tables.

— The Value of U.S. Labor Market Experience in the Home Country: The Case of Puerto Rican Return Migrants. *Economic Development and Cultural Change,* v. 42, no. 1 (Oct 93), pp. 168 – 191. Bibl, tables, charts.

Encinas Cueto, Ives and Wigberto Rivero Pinto. La presencia aimara en la ciudad de La Paz: Chuquiyawu Marka; entre la participación y la sobrevivencia. *América Indígena,* v. 51, no. 2 – 3 (Apr – Sept 91), pp. 273 – 292.

Engle, Robert F. and João Victor Issler. Common Trends and Common Cycles in Latin America. *Revista Brasileira de Economia,* v. 47, no. 2 (Apr – June 93), pp. 149 – 176. Bibl, tables, charts.

Enríquez, Manuel. Blas Galindo Dimas (1910 – 1993). *Inter-American Music Review,* v. 13, no. 2 (Spring – Summer 93), pp. 171 – 172.

Enríquez de Salamanca, Cristina and Stacey L. Parker Aronson. La textura del exilio: *Querido Diego, te abraza Quiela; Eva Luna; Crónica de una muerte anunciada. Chasqui,* v. 22, no. 2 (Nov 93), pp. 3 – 14. Bibl.

Epple, Juan Armando. Post-modernismo: una poética desde el Tercer Mundo; conversación con Patricio Manns. *Confluencia,* v. 8, no. 1 (Fall 92), pp. 123 – 135.

Ergood, Bruce. Belize as Presented in Her Literature. *Belizean Studies,* v. 21, no. 2 (Oct 93), pp. 3 – 14. Bibl, tables.

Erlich, Marc I. Making Sense of the Bicultural Workplace. *Business Mexico,* v. 3, no. 8 (Aug 93), pp. 16 – 19.

Ermida Uriarte, Oscar. La intervención estatal en las relaciones colectivas de trabajo latinoamericanas. *Nueva Sociedad,* no. 128 (Nov – Dec 93), pp. 29 – 37.

Erosa, Daniel. Poema. *Hispamérica,* v. 22, no. 64 – 65 (Apr – Aug 93), p. 139.

Errázuriz Edwards, Aníbal. Juan Francisco Fresno: una eclesiología cordial. *Mensaje,* v. 42, no. 419 (June 93), p. 182. Il.

Escalante, Evodio. Retornar a *Trilce:* hacia una lectura afirmativa de la poesía de César Vallejo. *Casa de las Américas,* no. 189 (Oct – Dec 92), pp. 65 – 70.

Escalante Gonzalbo, Pablo. El llanto de los antiguos nahuas. *Nexos,* v. 16, no. 186 (June 93), pp. 88 – 91. Bibl.

Escalante Gutiérrez, Carmen and Ricardo Valderrama Fernández. Canciones de imploración y de amor en los Andes: literatura oral de los quechuas del siglo XX. *Revista de Crítica Literaria Latinoamericana,* v. 19, no. 37 (Jan – June 93), pp. 11 – 39.

Escallón, Ana María. Delia Cugat: la atmósfera de la condición humana (Accompanied by an English translation). *Art Nexus,* no. 9 (June – Aug 93), pp. 88 – 90. Il.

Escamilla, Kathy Cogburn and Marcello Medina. English and Spanish Acquisition by Limited-Language-Proficient Mexican Americans in a Three-Year Maintenance Bilingual Program. *Hispanic Journal of Behavioral Sciences,* v. 15, no. 1 (Feb 93), pp. 108 – 120. Bibl, tables.

Escandón, Patricia. Los problemas de la administración franciscana en las misiones sonorenses, 1768 – 1800. *Archivo Ibero-Americano,* v. 52, no. 205 – 208 (Jan – Dec 92), pp. 277 – 291.

Escardó, Florencio. Florencio Escardó. *Realidad Económica,* no. 119 (Oct – Nov 93), pp. 69 – 72.

Escarreola Palacio, Rommel. El conquistador Nuñez de Balboa. *Revista Cultural Lotería,* v. 51, no. 391 (Sept – Oct 92), pp. 22 – 46. Bibl.

Escobar, Francisco Andrés. Rigoberta entre nosotros. *ECA; Estudios Centroamericanos,* v. 48, no. 531 – 532 (Jan – Feb 93), pp. 105 – 108. Il.

Escobar Herrán, Guillermo León. Participación, legitimidad y gobernabilidad. *Cuadernos Americanos,* no. 39, Nueva época (May – June 93), pp. 53 – 56.

— Tres años de confusión social. *Revista Javeriana,* v. 61, no. 597 (Aug 93), pp. 166 – 168.

Escobar Navarro, Marcos Eligio and Manuel Martínez Santana. Características geoquímicas y petrográficas de los principales yacimientos carboníferos venezolanos. *Interciencia,* v. 18, no. 2 (Mar – Apr 93), pp. 62 – 70. Bibl, tables, maps, charts.

— Los depósitos de carbón en Venezuela. *Interciencia,* v. 18, no. 5 (Sept – Oct 93), pp. 224 – 229. Bibl, tables, maps, charts.

Escobar Sepúlveda, Santiago. La política de la integración. *Nueva Sociedad,* no. 126 (July – Aug 93), pp. 62 – 71.

Escorza, Cecilia. Suplemento a la bibliografía sobre Manuel Scorza. *Revista de Crítica Literaria Latinoamericana,* v. 19, no. 37 (Jan – June 93), pp. 361 – 364.

Escudero de Paz, Angel. Participación de Colombia en el sistema de las Naciones Unidas. *Revista Javeriana,* v. 61, no. 594 (May 93), pp. 238 – 245.

Esenwein, George and William Ratliff. Latin American Posters at the Hoover Institution: The Lexicons of State and Society. *SALALM Papers,* v. 34 (1989), pp. 214 – 220.

Espada, Martín. Poems ("David Leaves the Saints for Paterson," "Colibrí," "The Words of the Mute Are Like Silver Dollars," "Shaking Hands with Mongo"). *The Americas Review,* v. 20, no. 3 – 4 (Fall – Winter 92), pp. 177 – 181.

Espejo, Beatriz. Sólo era una broma. *Plural (Mexico),* v. 22, no. 261 (June 93), pp. 8 – 11.

Espesir, Daniel and Eduardo O. Ciafardo. Patología de la acción política anarquista: criminólogos, psiquiatras y conflicto social en Argentina, 1890 – 1910. *Siglo XIX: Revista,* no. 12, 2a época (July – Dec 92), pp. 23 – 40. Bibl.

Espina, Eduardo. Poems ("La novia de Hitler," "Más felices que en Vietnam," "Decir de dudas del filántropo"). *Inti,* no. 36 (Fall 92), pp. 143 – 146.

Espino, María Dolores. Tourism in Cuba: A Development Strategy for the 1990s? *Cuban Studies/Estudios Cubanos,* v. 23 (1993), pp. 49 – 69. Bibl, tables.

Espínola, Blanca Rosa Humberto de. El rol de las universidades regionales en el contexto del MERCOSUR: la educación superior del nordeste argentino y áreas de fronteras de países limítrofes. *Revista Paraguaya de Sociología,* v. 30, no. 86 (Jan – Apr 93), pp. 83 – 112. Bibl, tables, charts.

Espínola, Julio César. La inmigración brasileña en el este misionero argentino: nuevo examen de un antiguo problema. *Revista Paraguaya de Sociología,* v. 29, no. 85 (Sept – Dec 92), pp. 133 – 155. Bibl, tables, maps, charts.

Espinosa Damián, Gisela. Feminismo y movimientos de mujeres: encuentros y desencuentros. *El Cotidiano,* v. 9, no. 53 (Mar – Apr 93), pp. 10 – 16. Il.

Espinosa López, Elia. Gramática y lenguaje del orden y el caos. *Anales del Instituto de Investigaciones Estéticas,* v. 16, no. 62 (1991), pp. 139 – 150. Bibl, il.

Espinosa V., Ismael. Las ediciones originales de Vicente Huidobro: ensayo de una bio-bibliografía. *Atenea (Chile),* no. 467 (1993), pp. 103 – 122. Il.

— Significado de *Altazor. Atenea (Chile),* no. 467 (1993), pp. 123 – 125.

Espinosa y Pitman, Alejandro. Huellas de plata (Accompanied by an English translation). *Artes de México,* no. 18 (Winter 92), pp. 63 – 67. Il.

Espinoza, Malva and Manuel Antonio Garretón Merino. ¿Reforma del estado o cambio en la matriz sociopolítica? *Estudios Sociales (Chile),* no. 74 (Oct – Dec 92), pp. 7 – 37. Bibl.

Espinoza Orellana, Manuel. Los signos en rotación de Octavio Paz. *Revista Nacional de Cultura (Venezuela),* v. 53, no. 285 (Apr – June 92), pp. 104 – 114.

Espinoza Valle, Víctor Alejandro. Las transformaciones del corporativismo regional: relaciones estado – sindicato en el sector público de Baja California. *Frontera Norte,* v. 4, no. 8 (July – Dec 92), pp. 79 – 110.

Espinoza Valle, Víctor Alejandro and Tania Hernández Vicencio. Tendencias de cambio en la estructura corporativa mexicana: Baja California, 1989 – 1992. *El Cotidiano,* v. 8, no. 52 (Jan – Feb 93), pp. 25 – 29.

Espriella, Andrés de la. Hacia una integración comercial con los Estados Unidos. *Revista Javeriana,* v. 61, no. 593 (Apr 93), pp. 148 – 154. Tables.

Esquinca Azcárate, Jorge. Cuatro poemas ("Casa de salud," "Belerofonte," "Malagua," "Tindarapo"). *Vuelta,* v. 17, no. 195 (Feb 93), p. 25.

Esquivel, Aracely and Claudia Dary Fuentes. Los artesanos de la piedra: estudio sobre la cantería de San Luis Jilotepeque. *La Tradición Popular,* no. 85 (1991), Issue. Bibl, il.

Esquivel Hernández, María Teresa et al. La zona metropolitana de la ciudad de México: dinámica demográfica y estructura poblacional, 1970 – 1990. *El Cotidiano,* v. 9, no. 54 (May 93), pp. 10 – 17. Bibl, il, tables, charts.

Esser, Klaus. América Latina: industrialización sin visión (Translated by Friedrich Welsch). *Nueva Sociedad,* no. 125 (May – June 93), pp. 27 – 46. Bibl.

Estenssoro Fuchs, Juan Carlos. Los bailes de los indios y el proyecto colonial (With commentaries by T. Abercrombie, J. Flores Espinoza, C. Itier, and S. E. Ramírez and a response by the author). *Revista Andina,* v. 10, no. 2 (Dec 92), pp. 353 – 404. Bibl.

— El mulato José Onofre de la Cadena: didáctica, estética musical y modernismo en el Perú del siglo XVIII. *Historia y Cultura (Peru),* no. 20 (1990), pp. 201 – 220.

Estevão, Marcello. Employment Level, Hours of Work, and Labor Adjustment Cost in the Brazilian Industry. *Revista Brasileira de Economia,* v. 47, no. 2 (Apr – June 93), pp. 205 – 242. Bibl, tables, charts.

Esteves, Antônio Roberto. Em torno de uma "Conversa de bois": alguns elementos de teoria da narrativa. *Revista de Letras (Brazil),* v. 32 (1992), pp. 109 – 117.

Esteves, Juan. Ensaio fotográfico: portraits. *Vozes,* v. 87, no. 2 (Mar – Apr 93), pp. 76 – 83. Il.

Esteves, Martha de Abreu and Sueann Caulfield. 50 Years of Virginity in Rio de Janeiro: Sexual Politics and Gender Roles in Juridical and Popular Discourse, 1890 – 1940. *Luso-Brazilian Review,* v. 30, no. 1 (Summer 93), pp. 47 – 74. Bibl, tables.

Esteves, Sandra María. Poems ("Amor negro," "Portraits for Shamsul Alam," "Transference"). *The Americas Review,* v. 20, no. 3 – 4 (Fall – Winter 92), pp. 144 – 148.

Estorino, Abelardo. Vagos rumores. *Conjunto,* no. 92 (July – Dec 92), pp. 66 – 94. Il.

Estrada Vásquez, Luis Everardo. La industria maquiladora en Guatemala. *USAC,* no. 13 (Mar 91), pp. 53 – 60. Bibl.

Estrella Valenzuela, Gabriel. Dinámica de los componentes demográficos de Baja California durante el período 1985 – 1990. *Estudios Fronterizos,* no. 26 (Sept – Dec 91), pp. 39 – 53.

Etcheberry, Blanca. Capacitación de presos: solidaridad entre rejas. *Mensaje,* v. 42, no. 421 (Aug 93), pp. 390 – 391. Il.

— Empresarios formados por la Compañía de Jesús: un acercamiento de este último tiempo. *Mensaje,* v. 42, no. 420 (July 93), pp. 322 – 325. Il.

— Las mujeres de La Pintana: conversar para vivir mejor. *Mensaje,* v. 42, no. 421 (Aug 93), p. 385. Il.

Etcheverry, Jorge. Dream with Guaracha (Translated by Sharon Khan and Jorge Etcheverry). *The Americas Review,* v. 19, no. 2 (Summer 91), pp. 15 – 17.

— Twin Beds. *The Americas Review,* v. 19, no. 2 (Summer 91), pp. 12 – 14.

Eyzaguirre, Graciela. Los escenarios de la guerra en la región Cáceres. *Allpanchis,* v. 23, no. 39 (Jan – June 92), pp. 155 – 180. Bibl, tables, maps.

Eyzaguirre, Luis B. Eugenio Montejo, poeta de fin de siglo. *Inti,* no. 37 – 38 (Spring – Fall 93), pp. 123 – 132. Bibl.

— Rito y sacrificio en *Crónica de una muerte anunciada. Revista Chilena de Literatura,* no. 42 (Aug 93), pp. 81 – 87.

Eyzaguirre, Nicolás and Rodrigo Vergara M. Reflexiones en torno a la experiencia de autonomía del Banco Central de Chile. *Cuadernos de Economía (Chile),* v. 30, no. 91 (Dec 93), pp. 327 – 347. Bibl, tables.

Fábregas Puig, Andrés A. Acerca de las relaciones entre sociedad y política. *Nueva Antropología,* v. 13, no. 43 (Nov 92), pp. 53 – 59.

— El textil como resistencia cultural (Accompanied by an English translation). *Artes de México,* no. 19 (Spring 93), pp. 25 – 27. Il.

Façanha, Luís Otávio de Figueiredo and Denise A. Rodrigues. Indústria brasileira na década de '70: interpretação de resultados de estatística multivariada e de aspectos da dinâmica concorrencial. *Revista Brasileira de Economia,* v. 46, no. 4 (Oct – Dec 92), pp. 447 – 476. Bibl, tables.

Facciolo, Osvaldo Adolfo. Los 50 años de la "Orden del Libertador General San Martín." *Todo Es Historia,* v. 27, no. 315 (Oct 93), pp. 90 – 94. Il.

Facio, Sara. Fotografía: la memoria cuestionada. *Cuadernos Hispanoamericanos,* no. 517 – 519 (July – Sept 93), pp. 269 – 279. Il.

Fagundes, Umberto Peregrino Seabra
See
　　Peregrino, Umberto

Fairlie Reinoso, Alan. Crisis, integración y desarrollo en América Latina: la dinámica del Grupo Andino con el MERCOSUR en la década de 1980. *Integración Latinoamericana,* v. 18, no. 192 (Aug 93), pp. 11 – 40. Bibl, tables, charts.

Fajnzylber, Fernando. Education and Changing Production Patterns with Social Equity. *CEPAL Review,* no. 47 (Aug 92), pp. 7 – 19. Tables, charts.

Falquet, France-Jules. Les femmes indiennes et la reproduction culturelle: réalités, mythes, enjeux; le cas des femmes indiennes au Chiapas, Mexique. *Cahiers des Amériques Latines,* no. 13 (1992), pp. 135 – 146. Bibl.

Fals Borda, Orlando and Lorenzo Muelas Hurtado. Pueblos indígenas y grupos étnicos. *Anuario Indigenista,* v. 30 (Dec 91), pp. 185 – 212.

Fandiño, Mario. Land Titling and Peasant Differentiation in Honduras. *Latin American Perspectives,* v. 20, no. 2 (Spring 93), pp. 45 – 53. Bibl.

Fanesi, Pietro Rinaldo. El exilio antifascista en América Latina: el caso mexicano; Mario Montagnana y la "Garibaldi," 1941 – 1945. *Estudios Interdisciplinarios de América Latina y el Caribe,* v. 3, no. 2 (July – Dec 92), pp. 39 – 57. Bibl.

Faria, José Eduardo. O Brasil no MERCOSUL. *Problemas Brasileiros,* v. 30, no. 297 (May – June 93), pp. 30 – 35. Il.

Farquharson, Mary. Is It Safe to Breathe? *Business Mexico,* v. 3, no. 3 (Mar 93), pp. 32 – 35.

Farr, Thomas H. and Elaine Fisher. A Tribute to C. Bernard Lewis, OBE (1913 – 1992). *Jamaica Journal,* v. 24, no. 3 (Feb 93), pp. 25 – 26. Il.

Farver, Deena. Franchising Frenzy. *Business Mexico,* v. 3, no. 8 (Aug 93), pp. 34 – 36.

Faure, Guy Olivier. Teoría de la negociación: el giro interdisciplinario. *Revista Mexicana de Sociología,* v. 54, no. 2 (Apr – June 92), pp. 233 – 242. Bibl.

Faux, Jeff and Thea Lee. Los efectos del Acuerdo de Libre Comercio de América del Norte en la fuerza de trabajo de Estados Unidos. *Relaciones Internacionales (Mexico),* v. 15, Nueva época, no. 57 (Jan – Mar 93), pp. 37 – 54.

Favaro, Orietta et al. El Neuquén: límites estructurales de una estrategia de distribución, 1958 – 1980. *Realidad Económica,* no. 118 (Aug – Sept 93), pp. 123 – 138. Bibl.

Favi, Gloria. Las acciones de habla en un texto de Enrique Lihn: *El paseo ahumada. Revista Chilena de Literatura,* no. 40 (Nov 92), pp. 91 – 96.

Favre, Henri. Contra-revolución en México (Translated by Jorge Padín Videla). *Cuadernos Americanos,* no. 39, Nueva época (May – June 93), pp. 101 – 113.

— La contrarrevolución mexicana (Translated by Laia Cortés). *Debate (Peru),* v. 16, no. 74 (Sept – Oct 93), pp. 49 – 52. Il.

— Informe de consultoría. *Anuario Indigenista,* v. 30 (Dec 91), pp. 385 – 403.

Faxas, Laura and Denise Douzant Rosenfeld. Equipements urbains et services de remplacement: le cas de Santo Domingo, République Dominicaine. *Tiers Monde,* v. 34, no. 133 (Jan – Mar 93), pp. 139 – 151.

Feal, Rosemary Geisdorfer. Bordering Feminism in Afro-Hispanic Studies: Crossroads in the Field. *Latin American Literary Review,* v. 20, no. 40 (July – Dec 92), pp. 41 – 45. Bibl.

— Entrevista con Luz Argentina Chiriboga (Followed by poems from her *La contraportada del deseo* translated by Rosemary Geisforfer Feal). *Afro-Hispanic Review,* v. 12, no. 2 (Fall 93), pp. 12 – 16.

Febles, Jorge M. En torno al personaje degradado en *La montaña rusa:* vigencia del doble paródico dentro de un espacio carnavalesco. *The Americas Review,* v. 19, no. 3 – 4 (Winter 91), pp. 101 – 115. Bibl.

— "Un pueblo": *Menosprecio de corte y alabanza de aldea* en la poesía de Agustín Acosta. *Anuario de Letras (Mexico),* v. 30 (1992), pp. 133 – 152. Bibl.

Febres, Laura M. Fragmentos para la comprensión de América, 1880 a 1900. *Montalbán,* no. 24 (1992), pp. 253 – 269. Bibl.

Febres, Xavier. Primera aproximación a la habanera en Cataluña. *Boletín Americanista,* v. 33, no. 42 – 43 (1992 – 1993), pp. 349 – 365.

Feijóo Seguín, María Luisa. El polémico fray Bartolomé de las Casas. *Hoy Es Historia,* v. 10, no. 60 (Nov – Dec 93), pp. 22 – 33. Il.

Feinman, Gary M. and Linda M. Nicholas. Shell-Ornament Production in Ejutla: Implications for Highland – Coastal Interaction in Ancient Oaxaca. *Ancient Mesoamerica,* v. 4, no. 1 (Spring 93), pp. 103 – 119. Bibl, il, tables, maps, charts.

Feinsilver, Julie M. Can Biotechnology Save the Revolution? *NACLA Report on the Americas,* v. 26, no. 5 (May 93), pp. 7 – 10. Il.

Feldman, Lila María et al. Tres poetas jóvenes (Lila María Feldman, Verónica Parcellis, Gisela K. Szneiberg). *Feminaria,* v. 6, no. 10, Suppl. (Apr 93), p. 18.

Fellay, Jean-Blaise. SIDA, preservativos y continencia. *Mensaje,* v. 42, no. 419 (June 93), pp. 211 – 212.

Feria H., Eduardo. Situación actual potencial a nivel nacional e internacional: informe de prensa. *Revista Javeriana,* v. 61, no. 593 (Apr 93), pp. 168 – 169.

Fermandois Huerta, Joaquín. Del unilateralismo a la negociación: Chile, Estados Unidos y la deuda de largo plazo, 1934 – 1938. *Historia (Chile),* no. 26 (1991 – 1992), pp. 71 – 115. Bibl.

Fernandes, Rosângela. A informática nas relações internacionais. *Revista Brasileira de Estudos Políticos,* no. 76 (Jan 93), pp. 147 – 162. Bibl.

Fernandez, Adolfo and Melanie Treviño. The Maquiladora Industry, Adverse Environmental Impact, and Proposed Solutions. *Journal of Borderlands Studies,* v. 7, no. 2 (Fall 92), pp. 53 – 72. Bibl.

Fernández, Nancy P. Violencia, risa y parodia: "El niño proletario" de O. Lamborghini y *Sin rumbo* de E. Cambacérès. *Escritura (Venezuela),* v. 17, no. 33 – 34 (Jan – Dec 92), pp. 159 – 164.

Fernández, Roberta. Andrea. *The Americas Review,* v. 20, no. 3 – 4 (Fall – Winter 92), pp. 66 – 83.

Fernández, Roberto G. Raining Backwards. *The Americas Review,* v. 20, no. 3 – 4 (Fall – Winter 92), pp. 33 – 38.

Fernández Alonso, Serena. Las montoneras como expresión política armada en el camino hacia la constitucionalidad del Perú republicano, siglo XIX. *Anuario de Estudios Americanos,* v. 50, no. 1 (1993), pp. 163 – 180. Bibl.

— Perfil biográfico y acción de gobierno de don Jorge Escobedo y Alarcón. *Revista de Indias,* v. 52, no. 195 – 196 (May – Dec 92), pp. 365 – 383. Bibl.

— Selección bibliográfica sobre el Perú virreinal durante el período reformista borbónico. *Anuario de Estudios Americanos,* v. 49, Suppl. 2 (1992), pp. 153 – 205.

Fernández Ariza, María Guadalupe. Los *Comentarios reales* del Inca Garcilaso y el humanismo renacentista. *Studi di Letteratura Ispano-Americana,* v. 24 (1993), pp. 23 – 35.

Fernández-Baca, Jorge. La importancia de la democracia para los economistas. *Apuntes (Peru),* no. 29 (July – Dec 91), pp. 9 – 16. Bibl, charts.

— Rol judicial en una economía de mercado. *Debate (Peru),* v. 16, no. 75 (Dec 93 – Jan 94), pp. 51 – 52. Il.

Fernández Buey, Francisco. La controversia entre Ginés de Sepúlveda y Bartolomé de las Casas: una revisión. *Boletín Americanista,* v. 33, no. 42 – 43 (1992 – 1993), pp. 301 – 347. Bibl.

Fernández Cabrelli, Alfonso. Institucionalización y desarrollo de la masonería uruguaya, 1830 – 1885. *Hoy Es Historia,* v. 10, no. 56 (Mar – Apr 93), pp. 20 – 32. Bibl, facs.

— María Juárez, una desconocida luchadora artiguista. *Hoy Es Historia,* v. 10, no. 57 (Apr – May 93), pp. 76 – 77.

— Las panaderías montevideanas en 1774. *Hoy Es Historia,* v. 10, no. 60 (Nov – Dec 93), pp. 84 – 85. Facs.

— El pueblo de Cuba: entre el drama y la esperanza. *Hoy Es Historia,* v. 9, no. 54 (Nov – Dec 92), pp. 69 – 76.

— El trato al indio en la colonización ibérica y en la anglosajona. *Hoy Es Historia,* v. 9, no. 54 (Nov – Dec 92), pp. 39 – 43. Il.

Fernández de Mata, Ignacio. La imagen de América. *Revista Española de Antropología Americana,* v. 23 (1993), pp. 243 – 248. Bibl.

Fernández González, Alvaro. Todo empezó en el '53: historia oral de un distrito liberacionista. *Revista de Historia (Costa Rica),* no. 26 (July – Dec 92), pp. 97 – 142. Bibl.

Fernández Hernández, Bernabé. Crisis de la minería de Honduras a fines de la época colonial. *Mesoamérica (USA),* v. 13, no. 24 (Dec 92), pp. 365 – 383. Bibl, maps, facs.

Fernández Herrero, Beatriz. El "otro" descubrimiento: la imagen del español en el indio americano. *Cuadernos Hispanoamericanos,* no. 520 (Oct 93), pp. 7 – 35. Bibl.

Fernández Koprich, Daniel. Vías elevadas para Santiago: ¿Una opción válida? (With commentaries by Jorge Heine, Oscar Figueroa, Juan de Dios Ortúzar, Víctor Basauri, and Daniel Fernández). *EURE,* v. 19, no. 56 (Mar 93), pp. 95 – 115. Charts.

Fernández M., Viviana and Fernando Coloma C. Los costos de despido: el efecto de las indemnizaciones por años de servicio. *Cuadernos de Economía (Chile),* v. 30, no. 89 (Apr 93), pp. 77 – 109. Charts.

Fernández Marquínez, María Yolanda and Alfonso Muñoz Cosme. Estilos arquitectónicos y estadios constructivos en el Grupo May, Oxkintok, Yucatán. *Revista Española de Antropología Americana,* v. 23 (1993), pp. 67 – 82. Bibl, il.

Fernández Menéndez, Jorge. Las elecciones en Guerrero. *Nexos,* v. 16, no. 182 (Feb 93), pp. 59 – 62.

— San Luis Potosí: ¿Lejos de la estabilidad? *Nexos,* v. 16, no. 184 (Apr 93), pp. 49 – 52.

Fernández Molina, José Antonio. Producción indígena y mercado urbano a finales del período colonial: la provisión de alimentos a la ciudad de Guatemala, 1787 – 1822. *Revista de Historia (Costa Rica),* no. 26 (July – Dec 92), pp. 9 – 30. Bibl, tables, maps, charts.

Fernández Poncela, Anna M. De la antropología de la mujer a la antropología feminista. *Fem,* v. 17, no. 128 (Oct 93), pp. 6 – 7.

— Un delito social: la violencia contra la mujer. *Fem,* v. 17, no. 126 (Aug 93), pp. 34 – 35.

— Una lacra mundial: la violencia contra la mujer. *Fem,* v. 17, no. 125 (July 93), pp. 27 – 29.

— Las latinoamericanas en el "decenio perdido para el desarrollo." *Fem,* v. 17, no. 122 (Apr 93), pp. 6 – 8.

— La participación económica y política de las mujeres nicaragüenses. *Boletín Americanista,* v. 33, no. 42 – 43 (1992 – 1993), pp. 267 – 299. Bibl, tables, charts.

— El torbellino de la violencia alcanza a las mujeres nicaragüenses. *Fem,* v. 17, no. 119 (Jan 93), pp. 9 – 12.

— Yo juego, tú estudias, ellos sobreviven: ser niño en América Latina. *Fem,* v. 17, no. 121 (Mar 93), pp. 25 – 27.

Fernández Retamar, Roberto. Adiós a Calibán. *Casa de las Américas,* no. 191 (Apr – June 93), pp. 116 – 122. Bibl.

— *Calibán:* quinientos años más tarde. *Nuevo Texto Crítico,* v. 6, no. 11 (1993), pp. 223 – 244. Bibl.

— Desde el Martí de Ezequiel Martínez Estrada. *Cuadernos Americanos,* no. 42, Nueva época (Nov – Dec 93), pp. 131 – 147.

— Duerme, sueña, haz. *Inti,* no. 36 (Fall 92), pp. 147 – 148.

— En la Casa de América, hacia la casa del futuro. *Casa de las Américas,* no. 190 (Jan – Mar 93), pp. 75 – 81.

— El Golfo y el Caribe a la mesa del mundo. *La Palabra y el Hombre,* no. 82 (Apr – June 92), pp. 5 – 19.

— Más de cien años de previsión: algunas reflexiones sobre el concepto martiano de *Nuestra América. Cuadernos Americanos,* no. 40, Nueva época (July – Aug 93), pp. 65 – 77.

— *Nuestra América:* cien años. *Nueva Revista de Filología Hispánica,* v. 40, no. 2 (July – Dec 92), pp. 791 – 806.

— Sobre la edición cubana de *Martí, el apóstol. Revista de Crítica Literaria Latinoamericana,* v. 19, no. 37 (Jan – June 93), pp. 345 – 351.

Fernández Santillán, José F. Democracia y liberalismo: ensayo de filosofía política. *Revista Mexicana de Ciencias Políticas y Sociales,* v. 38, Nueva época, no. 151 (Jan – Mar 93), pp. 157 – 183. Bibl.

Fernández-Shaw, Félix. Cinco quintos centenarios: entre pasado y futuro. *Cuadernos del CLAEH,* v. 17, no. 63 – 64 (Oct 92), pp. 21 – 33. Bibl.

Fernández Vilches, Antonio. Guayasamín y su visión del Nuevo Mundo. *Atenea (Chile),* no. 467 (1993), pp. 237 – 258. Il.

Fernández Villegas, Oswaldo. La desestructuración de los curacazgos andinos: conflictos por la residencia del curaca de Colán, costa norte. *Allpanchis,* v. 23, no. 40 (July – Dec 92), pp. 97 – 115. Bibl.

Ferpozzi, Luis Humberto and José María Suriano. Los cambios climáticos en la pampa también son historia. *Todo Es Historia,* v. 26, no. 306 (Jan 93), pp. 8 – 25. Bibl, il, maps.

Ferrari, Américo. La presencia del Perú. *Inti,* no. 36 (Fall 92), pp. 29 – 37.

Ferrari, Arturo and Luis Jaime Cisneros. Del jardín a la calle: la juventud peruana de los '90s. *Debate (Peru),* v. 16, no. 74 (Sept – Oct 93), pp. 19 – 25. Il, tables.

— Ni goles, ni milagros: entrevista a Francisco Lombardi. *Debate (Peru),* v. 16, no. 74 (Sept – Oct 93), pp. 14 – 18. Il.

Ferrari Etcheberry, Alberto. Sindicalistas en la bancada conservadora. *Todo Es Historia,* v. 27, no. 314 (Sept 93), pp. 74 – 83. Il.

Ferraz, João Carlos and Nauro Campos. Uma discussão sobre o padrão de concorrência no complexo eletrônico brasileiro. *Estudos Econômicos,* v. 23, no. 1 (Jan – Apr 93), pp. 125 – 147. Bibl, tables.

Ferreira, Afonso Henriques Borges. Testes de cointegração e um modelo de correção de erro para a balança comercial brasileira. *Estudos Econômicos,* v. 23, no. 1 (Jan – Apr 93), pp. 35 – 65. Bibl, tables.

— Testes de Granger-causalidade a balança comercial brasileira. *Revista Brasileira de Economia,* v. 47, no. 1 (Jan – Mar 93), pp. 83 – 95. Bibl, tables.

Ferreira, César. Bryce Echenique y la novela del posboom: lectura de *La última mudanza de Felipe Carrillo. Chasqui,* v. 22, no. 2 (Nov 93), pp. 34 – 48. Bibl.

Ferreira, Ignez Costa Barbosa. Gestão do espaço agrário. *Revista Brasileira de Geografia,* v. 53, no. 3 (July – Sept 91), pp. 149 – 159. Bibl, tables, maps.

Ferreira, Marieta de Moraes. A reação republicana e a crise política dos anos '20. *Estudos Históricos,* v. 6, no. 11 (Jan – June 93), pp. 9 – 23. Bibl.

Ferreira de Cassone, Florencia. Arturo Uslar Pietri: historia y pasión de América. *Cuadernos Americanos,* no. 40, Nueva época (July – Aug 93), pp. 125 – 145. Bibl.

Ferrer, Aldo. Iberoamérica: una nueva sociedad. *Cuadernos Americanos,* no. 39, Nueva época (May – June 93), pp. 57 – 64.

— Nuevos paradigmas tecnológicos y desarrollo sostenible: perspectiva latinoamericana. *Comercio Exterior,* v. 43, no. 9 (Sept 93), pp. 807 – 813. Bibl.

Ferrer, Elizabeth. Laura Cohen (Translated by Francisco Martínez Negrete). *Artes de México,* no. 19 (Spring 93), pp. 106 – 109. Il.

— Manos poderosas: The Photography of Graciela Iturbide. *Review,* no. 47 (Fall 93), pp. 69 – 78. Il.

Ferreyra, Ramón. Registros de la vegetación en la costa peruana en relación con el fenómeno El Niño. *Bulletin de l'Institut Français d'Etudes Andines,* v. 22, no. 1 (1993), pp. 259 – 266. Bibl, il, tables, maps.

Ferri, Olga. La danza y el Teatro Colón: mi pasión y mi vida. *Cuadernos Hispanoamericanos,* no. 517 – 519 (July – Sept 93), pp. 541 – 543.

Ferrufino Coqueugniot, Claudio. Apuntes para dos soledades. *Signo,* no. 36 – 37, Nueva época (May – Dec 92), pp. 13 – 22.

— Ayopaya: el mundo perdido. *Signo,* no. 35, Nueva época (Jan – Apr 92), pp. 3 – 4.

Fèvre, Fermín. Una mirada al arte argentino. *Cuadernos Hispanoamericanos,* no. 517 – 519 (July – Sept 93), pp. 230 – 244. Il.

Feyder, Linda. Marta del Angel. *The Americas Review,* v. 19, no. 3 – 4 (Winter 91), pp. 29 – 33.

Ffrench-Davis, Ricardo. Los desafíos de la deuda externa y el desarrollo: a diez años del inicio de la crisis. *Estudios Internacionales (Chile),* v. 26, no. 102 (Apr – June 93), pp. 155 – 156. Tables.

Ffrench-Davis, Ricardo and Robert T. Devlin. Diez años de crisis de la deuda latinoamericana. *Comercio Exterior,* v. 43, no. 1 (Jan 93), pp. 4 – 20. Bibl, tables.

Field, Christopher B. and Carlos Vázquez-Yanes. Species of the Genus "Piper" Provide a Model to Study How Plants Can Grow in Different Kinds of Rainforest Habitats. *Interciencia,* v. 18, no. 5 (Sept – Oct 93), pp. 230 – 236. Bibl, il.

Fierro, Enrique. Travestia (I). *Vuelta,* v. 17, no. 198 (May 93), p. 32.

Fierro, Gabriel and Pablo J. Serra. Un modelo de estimación del costo de falla: el caso de Chile. *Cuadernos de Economía (Chile),* v. 30, no. 90 (Aug 93), pp. 247 – 259. Bibl, tables.

Fifer, J. Valerie. South of Capricorn: A Review Revisited (Rebuttal of a review of her *United States' Perceptions of Latin America, 1850 – 1930: A "New West" South of Capricorn?). Bulletin of Latin American Research,* v. 12, no. 1 (Jan 93), pp. 103 – 107.

Figallo, Beatriz J. Yrigoyen y su segundo gobierno vistos por Ramiro de Maeztu. *Todo Es Historia,* v. 27, no. 312 (July 93), pp. 80 – 93. Bibl, il.

Figueroa, Francisco. Opinión política y post-guerra. *ECA; Estudios Centroamericanos,* v. 48, no. 534 – 535 (Apr – May 93), pp. 430 – 436. Il.

Figueroa, Sílvia Fernanda de Mendonça. Las ciencias geológicas en Brasil en el siglo XIX (Translated by Hernán G. H. Taboada). *Cuadernos Americanos,* no. 38, Nueva época (Mar – Apr 93), pp. 180 – 204. Bibl.

Figueroa, Víctor et al. Un modelo de bienestar social. *Estudios Sociales (Chile),* no. 77 (July – Sept 93), pp. 139 – 147. Bibl.

Figueroa Casas, Vilma and Israel López Pino. Hacia una filosofía de la liberación uruguaya. *Islas,* no. 99 (May – Aug 91), pp. 38 – 44.

— Rodney Arismendi: su posición político – ideológica. *Islas,* no. 96 (May – Aug 90), pp. 71 – 77.

Figueroa Sala, Jonas. Las ciudades lineales chilenas, 1910 – 1930. *Revista de Indias,* v. 53, no. 198 (May – Aug 93), pp. 651 – 662. Il, maps.

Figueroa Valenzuela, Alejandro. Derechos políticos y organización social: el caso de los yaquis y los mayos. *Nueva Antropología,* v. 13, no. 44 (Aug 93), pp. 43 – 60. Bibl.

Filgueira, Nea. Otra vez las mujeres somos culpables: la procreación como una razón de estado. *Fem,* v. 17, no. 121 (Mar 93), pp. 11 – 12.

Finisterre, Alejandro. El premio León Felipe 1993. *Cuadernos Americanos,* no. 41, Nueva época (Sept – Oct 93), pp. 183 – 186.

Finn, Patrick J. Treating Water Industrially. *Business Mexico,* v. 3, no. 1 (Jan – Feb 93), pp. 83 – 84. Tables.

Finol Urdaneta, Hermán. Propuesta de nueva estrategia para la producción agropecuaria y forestal sobre una base ecológica. *Derecho y Reforma Agraria,* no. 23 (1992), pp. 73 – 82.

Fiori, José Luís. The Political Economy of the Developmentalist State in Brazil. *CEPAL Review,* no. 47 (Aug 92), pp. 173 – 186. Bibl.

Fischer, Amalia E. Feminismo: algo más que mujeres (Paper presented at the congress "Mujer, Violencia y Derechos Humanos," Mexico, March 1993). *Fem,* v. 17, no. 125 (July 93), pp. 11 – 13.

Fischer, Luís Augusto. Um modernista extraviado. *Vozes,* v. 86, no. 6 (Nov – Dec 92), pp. 2 – 7.

— As sete razões do sucesso de Paulo Coelho. *Vozes,* v. 86, no. 5 (Sept – Oct 92), pp. 58 – 61.

Fischer, Nilton Bueno. A história de Rose: classes populares, mulheres e cidadania. *Vozes,* v. 86, no. 6 (Nov – Dec 92), pp. 38 – 44.

Fischer, Tânia et al. Olodum: a arte e o negócio. *RAE; Revista de Administração de Empresas,* v. 33, no. 2 (Mar – Apr 93), pp. 90 – 99. Bibl.

Fisher, Elaine and Thomas H. Farr. A Tribute to C. Bernard Lewis, OBE (1913 – 1992). *Jamaica Journal,* v. 24, no. 3 (Feb 93), pp. 25 – 26. Il.

Fisher, Jo. Women and Democracy: For Home and Country. *NACLA Report on the Americas,* v. 27, no. 1 (July – Aug 93), pp. 30 – 36 +. Il.

Fitch, John Samuel. The Decline of U.S. Military Influence on Latin America. *Journal of Inter-American Studies and World Affairs,* v. 35, no. 2 (Summer 93), pp. 1 – 49. Bibl, tables, charts.

El Flaco
See
Maldonado, Jesús María

Fleischman, Cristopher and Joel Russell. The Company You Keep. *Business Mexico,* v. 3, no. 5 (May 93), pp. 42 – 43. Charts.

Fleites-Lear, Marisela and Enrique Patterson. Teoría y praxis de la revolución cubana: apuntes críticos. *Nueva Sociedad,* no. 123 (Jan – Feb 93), pp. 50 – 64.

Fletcher, G. Richard and Robert A. Pastor. El Caribe en el siglo XXI. *Integración Latinoamericana,* v. 18, no. 187 – 188 (Mar – Apr 93), pp. 13 – 22. Bibl.

Fletcher, Lea. El desierto que no es tal: escritoras y escritura. *Feminaria,* v. 6, no. 11, Suppl. (Nov 93), pp. 7 – 13. Bibl.

Fleury, Maria Tereza Leme. Cultura da qualidade e mudança organizacional. *RAE; Revista de Administração de Empresas,* v. 33, no. 2 (Mar – Apr 93), pp. 26 – 34.

Flores, Arturo C. Chile: acerca de la relación teatro – sociedad. *La Palabra y el Hombre,* no. 81 (Jan – Mar 92), pp. 73 – 84. Bibl.

Flores, Hilda Agnes Hübner. Participação da mulher na construção do Rio Grande do Sul. *Hoy Es Historia,* v. 10, no. 59 (Sept – Oct 93), pp. 67 – 74. Bibl.

Flores, Marco Antonio. El bastón. *Plural (Mexico),* v. 22, no. 265 (Oct 93), pp. 16 – 19.

Flores, María Antonieta. La inevitable visión sombría. *Inti,* no. 37 – 38 (Spring – Fall 93), pp. 253 – 255.

Flores, Mercedes and Roxana Hidalgo Xirinachs. El autoritarismo en la vida cotidiana: SIDA, homofobia y moral sexual. *Revista de Ciencias Sociales (Costa Rica),* no. 58 (Dec 92), pp. 35 – 44. Bibl.

Flores Andino, Francisco A. Medicina tradicional, magia y mitos entre los miskitos de Honduras. *Folklore Americano,* no. 52 (July – Dec 91), pp. 131 – 144.

Flores Clair, Eduardo. Trabajo, salud y muerte: Real del Monte, 1874. *Siglo XIX: Cuadernos,* v. 1, no. 3 (June 92), pp. 9 – 28. Bibl, charts.

Flores López, Domingo. Conversaciones sobre el destino de Bolivia. *Signo,* no. 36 – 37, Nueva época (May – Dec 92), pp. 147 – 167.

Flores Marini, Carlos. El arte religioso de Xochimilco: un recorrido (Accompanied by an English translation). *Artes de México,* no. 20 (Summer 93), pp. 55 – 65. Il.

Flores Olea, Víctor Manuel. Los sistemas políticos y su crisis, parte II: La articulación democrática y el caso de México. *Revista Mexicana de Ciencias Políticas y Sociales,* v. 38, Nueva época, no. 152 (Apr – June 93), pp. 143 – 160.

Flores-Ortiz, Yvette G. Levels of Acculturation, Marital Satisfaction, and Depression among Chicana Workers: A Psychological Perspective. *Aztlán,* v. 20, no. 1 – 2 (Spring – Fall 91), pp. 151 – 175. Bibl, tables.

Flores Santamaría, Dunia et al. Reflexiones en torno a la adopción. *Revista de Ciencias Sociales (Costa Rica),* no. 59 (Mar 93), pp. 47 – 51.

Florescano, Enrique. El mito de Quetzalcóatl. *Allpanchis,* v. 23, no. 40 (July – Dec 92), pp. 11 – 93. Bibl, il.

— Muerte y resurrección del dios del maíz. *Nexos,* v. 16, no. 184 (Apr 93), pp. 21 – 31. Bibl, il.

Florescano Mayet, Sergio. Xalapa y su región durante el siglo XIX: las principales vertientes de su desarrollo económico, social y político. *La Palabra y el Hombre,* no. 83 (July – Sept 92), pp. 135 – 165. Bibl, tables.

Flórez Gallego, Lenín. Historias nacionales, historias de los trabajadores y el problema de la democracia en la obra de Charles Bergquist. *Anuario Colombiano de Historia Social y de la Cultura,* no. 20 (1992), pp. 73 – 88. Bibl, tables.

Flynn, Peter. Collor, Corruption, and Crisis: Time for Reflection. *Journal of Latin American Studies,* v. 25, no. 2 (May 93), pp. 351 – 371. Bibl.

Fonseca, Rubem. El campeonato (Translated by Marco Tulio Aguilera Garramuño). *La Palabra y el Hombre,* no. 82 (Apr – June 93), pp. 239 – 245.

Font, Mauricio A. City and the Countryside in the Onset of Brazilian Industrialization. *Studies in Comparative International Development,* v. 27, no. 3 (Fall 92), pp. 26 – 56. Bibl, tables, charts.

Fontaine Aldunate, Arturo. La historia reciente de Chile a través de "La semana política" (Part IV, introduced by Miguel González Pino). *Estudios Públicos (Chile),* no. 49 (Summer 93), pp. 305 – 419.

Fontaine T., Juan Andrés. Transición económica y política en Chile, 1970 – 1990. *Estudios Públicos (Chile),* no. 50 (Fall 93), pp. 230 – 279. Bibl, tables.

Fontana, Bernard L. Pál Kelemen (1894 – 1993). *Hispanic American Historical Review,* v. 73, no. 3 (Aug 93), pp. 481 – 482.

Fontana Morialdo, Jorge et al. Aprovechamientos hidroeléctricos binacionales: aspectos relacionados con la integración latinoamericana. *Integración Latinoamericana,* v. 17, no. 184 (Nov 92), pp. 44 – 58.

Fontanarrosa, Roberto. Nos tocó hacer reír. *Cuadernos Hispanoamericanos,* no. 517 – 519 (July – Sept 93), pp. 353 – 360. Il.

Fontes, Rosa M. O. and Margareth L. Barbosa. Efeitos da integração econômica do MERCOSUL e da Europa na competitividade das exportações brasileiras de soja. *Revista de Economia e Sociologia Rural,* v. 29, no. 4 (Oct – Dec 91), pp. 335 – 351. Bibl, tables.

Forde, D. H. One Market for All? *Américas,* v. 45, no. 5 (Sept – Oct 93), pp. 34 – 39. Il, charts.

Forde, Penelope and Kelvin Sergeant. The State Sector and Divestment in Trinidad and Tobago: Some Preliminary Findings. *Social and Economic Studies,* v. 41, no. 4 (Dec 92), pp. 173 – 204. Bibl, tables.

Forjaz, Maria Cecília Spina. Os exilados da década de '80: imigrantes brasileiros nos Estados Unidos. *RAE; Revista de Administração de Empresas,* v. 33, no. 1 (Jan – Feb 93), pp. 66 – 83. Bibl.

Forlán Lamarque, Raúl. (vallejo). *Hispamérica,* v. 22, no. 64 – 65 (Apr – Aug 93), p. 140.

Fornet, Ambrosio. Las máscaras del tiempo en la novela de la revolución cubana. *Casa de las Américas,* no. 191 (Apr – June 93), pp. 12 – 24. Bibl.

Fornet, Jorge. Dos novelas peruanas: entre sapos y halcones. *Plural (Mexico),* v. 22, no. 263 (Aug 93), pp. 57 – 62.

Fornetti, Marco et al. Desenvolvimento e uso de modelos computacionais no planejamento da produção em indústrias laticinistas de pequeno porte: um estudo de caso. *Revista de Economia e Sociologia Rural,* v. 29, no. 4 (Oct – Dec 91), pp. 401 – 410. Bibl, charts.

Forster, Merlin H. El concepto del "Ars Poética" en la poesía de Gonzalo Rojas. *Chasqui,* v. 22, no. 1 (May 93), pp. 51 – 58.

Forsyth, Donald W. The Ceramic Sequence at Nakbe, Guatemala. *Ancient Mesoamerica,* v. 4, no. 1 (Spring 93), pp. 31 – 53. Bibl, il, maps.

Fort, Alfredo L. Fecundidad y comportamiento reproductivo en la sierra y selva del Perú. *Estudios Demográficos y Urbanos,* v. 7, no. 2 – 3 (May – Dec 92), pp. 327 – 357. Bibl, tables, maps, charts.

Fortique, José Rafael. El primer obispo de Maracaibo y su médico personal. *Boletín de la Academia Nacional de la Historia (Venezuela),* v. 76, no. 302 (Apr – June 93), pp. 133 – 139.

Fortoul V., Freddy. Satisfacción comunitaria: indicador social subjetivo de bienestar. *Estudios Sociales (Chile),* no. 74 (Oct – Dec 92), pp. 119 – 148. Bibl.

Foschiatti de dell'Orto, Ana María H. El desarrollo urbano y las particularidades demográficas del Chaco y su capital entre 1960 y 1990. *Revista Geográfica (Mexico),* no. 115 (Jan – June 92), pp. 37 – 54. Bibl, tables, maps, charts.

Foster, David William. Consideraciones en torno a la sensibilidad "gay" en la narrativa de Reinaldo Arenas. *Revista Chilena de Literatura,* no. 42 (Aug 93), pp. 89 – 94. Bibl.

— On Expanding the Base of Latin American Studies. *Latin American Literary Review,* v. 20, no. 40 (July – Dec 92), pp. 34 – 37.

Fournier, Robert and Robert Berrouët-Oriol. Créolophonie et francophonie nord – sud: transcontinuum. *Canadian Journal of Latin American and Caribbean Studies,* v. 17, no. 34 (1992), pp. 13 – 25. Bibl.

Fournier G., Patricia and Andrea K. L. Freeman. El razonamiento analógico en etnoarqueología: el caso de la tradición alfarera de Mata Ortiz, Chihuahua, México. *Boletín de Antropología Americana,* no. 23 (July 91), pp. 109 – 118. Bibl, il.

Fowler-Salamini, Heather
See
Salamini, Heather Fowler

Fox, John Gerard. The Ballcourt Markers of Tenam Rosario, Chiapas, Mexico. *Ancient Mesoamerica,* v. 4, no. 1 (Spring 93), pp. 55 – 64. Bibl, il.

Fox, Lorna Scott. Zona: nuevo espacio plástico. *Artes de México,* no. 20 (Summer 93), p. 116. Il.

Foxley, Carmen. Enrique Lihn y los juegos excéntricos de la imaginación. *Revista Chilena de Literatura,* no. 41 (Apr 93), pp. 15 – 24. Bibl.

Foxley R., Alejandro. Entrando a una nueva fase. *Mensaje,* v. 42, no. 422 (Sept 93), pp. 448 – 451.

Fraga, Rosendo M. Las fuerzas armadas y los diez años de democracia. *Todo Es Historia,* v. 27, no. 317 (Dec 93), pp. 20 – 25. Il.

Fragoso, José Manoel. O Atlântico e o mundo de língua portuguesa. *Revista do Instituto Histórico e Geográfico Brasileiro,* no. 373 (Oct – Dec 91), pp. 1107 – 1114.

Frajman, Mauricio. Aspectos sociales de SIDA. *Revista de Ciencias Sociales (Costa Rica),* no. 58 (Dec 92), pp. 7 – 10. Bibl.

Frambes-Buxeda, Aline. Bolivia: eje vital de la integración económica andina y latinoamericana. *Homines,* v. 15 – 16, no. 2 – 1 (Oct 91 – Dec 92), pp. 187 – 248. Bibl, tables.

Francis, Norbert and Rainer Enrique Hamel. La redacción en dos lenguas: escritura y narrativa en tres escuelas bilingües del valle del Mezquital. *Revista Latinoamericana de Estudios Educativos,* v. 22, no. 4 (Oct – Dec 92), pp. 11 – 35. Bibl, tables.

Franco, Albano. Towards a Common Frontier for Trade (Translated by Barbara Meza). *Américas,* v. 45, no. 1 (Jan – Feb 93), pp. 56 – 57. Il.

Franco, Carlos. Visión de la democracia y crisis del régimen. *Nueva Sociedad,* no. 128 (Nov – Dec 93), pp. 50 – 61.

Franco, Gustavo Henrique Barroso. Alternativas de estabilização: gradualismo, dolarização e populismo. *Revista de Economia Política (Brazil),* v. 13, no. 2 (Apr – June 93), pp. 28 – 45. Bibl, tables, charts.

Franco, Jean. La Malinche y el primer mundo. *Cuadernos Americanos,* no. 40, Nueva época (July – Aug 93), pp. 170 – 180.

— Remapping Culture. *Latin American Literary Review,* v. 20, no. 40 (July – Dec 92), pp. 38 – 40.

Franco, Miguel and Rafael Durán. Estudio demográfico de "Pseudophoenix sargentii." *Bulletin de l'Institut Français d'Etudes Andines,* v. 21, no. 2 (1992), pp. 609 – 621. Bibl, maps, charts.

Franco, Miguel and Ana Mendoza. Integración clonal en una palma tropical. *Bulletin de l'Institut Français d'Etudes Andines,* v. 21, no. 2 (1992), pp. 623 – 635. Bibl, il, tables, charts.

Franco, Rolando and Ernesto Cohen. Rationalizing Social Policy: Evaluation and Viability. *CEPAL Review,* no. 47 (Aug 92), pp. 163 – 172. Bibl, charts.

Franco Cáceres, Iván. Familias, oligarquía y empresarios en Yucatán, 1879 – 1906. *Siglo XIX: Cuadernos,* v. 3, no. 7 (Oct 93), pp. 9 – 31. Bibl, tables.

Franco Marcano, Mercedes. In memoriam: Juvenal López Ruiz. *Revista Nacional de Cultura (Venezuela),* v. 53, no. 286 (July – Sept 92), pp. 206 – 207.

Franconi, Rodolfo A. The Fictionalization of a Diary (Translated by Barbara Meza). *Américas,* v. 45, no. 6 (Nov – Dec 93), pp. 60 – 63. Il.

Frank, André Gunder. América Latina al margen de la historia del sistema mundial (Translated by Hernán G. H. Taboada). *Cuadernos Americanos,* no. 39, Nueva época (May – June 93), pp. 114 – 133. Bibl, tables.

— América Latina al margen del sistema mundial: historia y presente. *Nueva Sociedad,* no. 123 (Jan – Feb 93), pp. 23 – 34. Bibl, tables.

Frankenthaler, Marilyn R. Agata Cruz, prototipo de la "heroína" existencialista. *La Palabra y el Hombre,* no. 84 (Oct – Dec 92), pp. 311 – 320. Bibl, il.

Franzbach, Martin. Die beiden Deutschlands auf Kuba: Ein Beitrag zur Geschichte der Auslandsdeutschen in der Karibik. *Iberoamericana,* v. 17, no. 50 (1993), pp. 5 – 15. Bibl.

Franzé, Javier. El peronismo según Sebreli. *Cuadernos Hispanoamericanos,* no. 512 (Feb 93), pp. 127 – 129.

Fraser, Howard M. Dissertations, 1992. *Hispania (USA),* v. 76, no. 2 (May 93), pp. 324 – 348.

— La Edad de Oro and José Martí's Modernist Ideology for Children. *Revista Interamericana de Bibliografía,* v. 42, no. 2 (1992), pp. 223 – 232. Bibl.

Freebairn, Donald K. Posibles pérdidas y ganancias en el sector agrícola bajo un Tratado de Libre Comercio entre Estados Unidos y México. *Revista Mexicana de Sociología,* v. 54, no. 1 (Jan – Mar 92), pp. 3 – 28. Bibl, tables.

Freeman, Andrea K. L. and Patricia Fournier G. El razonamiento analógico en etnoarqueología: el caso de la tradición alfarera de Mata Ortiz, Chihuahua, México. *Boletín de Antropología Americana,* no. 23 (July 91), pp. 109 – 118. Bibl, il.

Freidel, David A. and Linda Schele. Un bosque de reyes: la historia no narrada de los antiguos mayas. *La Palabra y el Hombre,* no. 82 (Apr – June 92), pp. 79 – 94. Tables.

Freidemberg, Daniel. Poesía argentina de los años '70 y '80: la palabra a prueba. *Cuadernos Hispanoamericanos,* no. 517 – 519 (July – Sept 93), pp. 139 – 160.

Freitas, Paulo Springer de and Maria Cristina Cacciamali. Do capital humano ao salário-eficiência: uma aplicação para analisar os diferenciais de salários em cinco ramos manufatureiros da grande São Paulo. *Pesquisa e Planejamento Econômico,* v. 22, no. 2 (Aug 92), pp. 343 – 367. Bibl, tables.

Freites, Yajaira. Ciencia y honor en Venezuela: concepciones y cambios. *Cuadernos Americanos,* no. 38, Nueva época (Mar – Apr 93), pp. 135 – 154. Bibl, tables.

Frenkel, Roberto. Ajuste y reformas económicas en América Latina: problemas y experiencias recientes; comentarios al artículo de Patricio Meller. *Pensamiento Iberoamericano,* no. 22 – 23, tomo II (July 92 – June 93), pp. 59 – 63.

Freter, Ann Corinne. Obsidian-Hydration Data: Its Past, Present, and Future Application in Mesoamerica. *Ancient Mesoamerica,* v. 4, no. 2 (Fall 93), pp. 285 – 303. Bibl, tables, charts.

Frey, Jean-Pierre and Pascal Byé. Le modèle chilien à la lumière de l'expérience des pays agro-exportateurs de l'ASEAN. *Cahiers des Amériques Latines,* no. 14 (1992), pp. 37 – 49. Bibl, tables.

Freytez Arrieche, Gustavo A. *Palabreus:* una (re)visión del llano venezolano. *Revista Nacional de Cultura (Venezuela),* v. 53, no. 286 (July – Sept 92), pp. 50 – 63. Bibl, il.

Friaz, Guadalupe Mendez. "I Want to Be Treated as an Equal": Testimony from a Latina Union Activist. *Aztlán,* v. 20, no. 1 – 2 (Spring – Fall 91), pp. 195 – 202.

Frischtak, Claudio R. Automação bancária e mudança na produtividade: a experiência brasileira. *Pesquisa e Planejamento Econômico,* v. 22, no. 2 (Aug 92), pp. 197 – 239. Bibl, tables.

Friszman, Marcos. Globalidad de los derechos humanos. *Realidad Económica,* no. 113 (Jan – Feb 93), pp. 40 – 44. Il.

Fritsch, Winston. 1922: a crise econômica. *Estudos Históricos,* v. 6, no. 11 (Jan – June 93), pp. 3 – 8.

Fritsch, Winston and João Roberto Teixeira. Fatores determinantes das exportações brasileiras para a CE: uma análise prospectiva dos impactos da ampliação do espaço econômico. *Revista de Economia Política (Brazil),* v. 13, no. 3 (July – Sept 93), pp. 82 – 101. Bibl, tables, charts.

Frohmann, Alicia. Hacia una integración comercial hemisférica? (Review article). *Pensamiento Iberoamericano,* no. 22 – 23, tomo I (July 92 – June 93), pp. 347 – 356. Tables, charts.

Froldi, Walter. La llegada de los cangaceiros (Translated by Saúl Ibargoyen). *Plural (Mexico),* v. 22, no. 265 (Oct 93), pp. 39 – 41.

Frouman-Smith, Erica. Women on the Verge of a Breakthrough: Liliana Heker's *Zona de clivaje* as a Female "Bildungsroman." *Letras Femeninas,* v. 19, no. 1 – 2 (Spring – Fall 93), pp. 100 – 112. Bibl.

Fuchslocher Arancibia, Luz María. Indice: *Cuadernos de Historia,* desde no. 1 (diciembre, 1981) al no. 10 (diciembre, 1990). *Cuadernos de Historia (Chile),* no. 11 (Dec 91), pp. 211 – 226.

Fuenmayor, Juan Bautista. Palabras del dr. Juan Bautista Fuenmayor, premio nacional de historia Francisco González Guinán, 1991. *Boletín de la Academia Nacional de la Historia (Venezuela),* v. 75, no. 299 (July – Sept 92), pp. 29 – 32.

Fuente, Juan Ramón de la. Medical Education in Mexico. *Mexican Studies,* v. 9, no. 2 (Summer 93), pp. 295 – 302. Bibl.

Fuentes, Carlos. Los hijos del conquistador (Excerpt from *El naranjo o los círculos del tiempo* with illustrations by the author). *Nexos,* v. 16, no. 185 (May 93), pp. 33 – 41. Il.

— Lectura derridiana de Juan Rulfo. *Nexos,* v. 16, no. 188 (Aug 93), pp. 7 – 8.

Fuentes, José Lorenzo. Cortázar habla de las manos en la máquina de escribir. *Plural (Mexico),* v. 22, no. 258 (Mar 93), pp. 48 – 49.

Fuentes, José María. La alternativa proporcional con barreras de entrada: un sistema electoral adecuado para Chile. *Estudios Públicos (Chile),* no. 51 (Winter 93), pp. 269 – 301. Bibl, tables.

Fuentes, Juan Alberto. European Investment in Latin America: An Overview. *CEPAL Review,* no. 48 (Dec 92), pp. 61 – 81. Bibl, tables, charts.

Fuentes, Napoleón. Espacio mutilado. *Plural (Mexico),* v. 22, no. 257 (Feb 93), pp. 46 – 47.

Fuentes Aguilar, Luis and Consuelo Soto Mora. El control institucional en el Plan Nacional de Desarrollo en México. *Revista Interamericana de Planificación,* v. 26, no. 101 – 102 (Jan – June 93), pp. 183 – 195. Bibl.

— La industria del aluminio en el Tratado de Libre Comercio. *Problemas del Desarrollo,* v. 24, no. 93 (Apr – June 93), pp. 75 – 93. Bibl, tables, maps.

Fuentes Aguilar, Luis and Juan Vargas González. La articulación espacial de la ciudad colonial de Puebla, México. *Revista de Historia de América,* no. 112 (July – Dec 91), pp. 43 – 62. Bibl, il, maps.

Fuentes Bajo, María Dolores. Amor y desamor en la Venezuela hispánica: Caracas, 1701 – 1791. *Boletín de la Academia Nacional de la Historia (Venezuela),* v. 75, no. 298 (Apr – June 92), pp. 49 – 62. Bibl.

Fuentes Soria, Alfonso et al. Desarrollo de la Universidad de San Carlos de Guatemala en la década 1990 – 2000. *USAC,* no. 12 (Dec 90), pp. 36 – 48.

— Estado, universidad y sociedad: panel-foro. *USAC,* no. 13 (Mar 91), pp. 5 – 18.

Fuenzalida, Edmundo F.
See
   Fuenzalida Faivovich, Edmundo

Fuenzalida F., Valerio. La TV infantil vista desde la televisión. *Estudios Sociales (Chile),* no. 76 (Apr – June 93), pp. 95 – 110. Bibl.

Fuenzalida Faivovich, Edmundo. Internacionalización de la educación superior en América Latina. *Estudios Sociales (Chile),* no. 74 (Oct – Dec 92), pp. 39 – 73. Bibl.

Fujii Gambero, Gerardo and Noemí Levy. Composición de las exportaciones de Brasil, Corea, España y México. *Comercio Exterior,* v. 43, no. 9 (Sept 93), pp. 844 – 851. Tables.

Fukuyama, Francis. El futuro después del fin de la historia (Introduced by Arturo Fontaine Talavera). *Estudios Públicos (Chile),* no. 52 (Spring 93), pp. 5 – 24.

Fulk, Randal C. The Spanish of Mexico: A Partially Annotated Bibliography for 1970 – 1990 (Part I). *Hispania (USA),* v. 76, no. 2 (May 93), pp. 245 – 270.

— The Spanish of Mexico: A Partially Annotated Bibliography for 1970 – 1990 (Part II). *Hispania (USA),* v. 76, no. 3 (Sept 93), pp. 446 – 468.

Fumarola, Eduardo V. 1992: hechos que han hecho historia. *Todo Es Historia,* v. 26, no. 306 (Jan 93), pp. 86 – 98. Il.

Funari, Pedro Paulo Abreu. El mito candeirante: élite brasileña, cultura material e identidad. *Boletín de Antropología Americana,* no. 24 (Dec 91), pp. 111 – 122. Bibl, il.

Funes, Patricia. Del "Mundus Novus" al novomundismo: algunas reflexiones sobre el nombre de América Latina. *Cuadernos del CLAEH,* v. 17, no. 63 – 64 (Oct 92), pp. 67 – 79. Bibl.

Funkhouser, Edward and Fernando A. Ramos. The Choice of Migration Destination: Dominican and Cuban Immigrants to the Mainland United States and Puerto Rico. *International Migration Review,* v. 27, no. 3 (Fall 93), pp. 537 – 556. Bibl, tables.

Furlani de Civit, María Estela and María Josefina Gutiérrez de Manchón. Dinámica agraria en un oasis de especialización vitícola. *Revista Geográfica (Mexico),* no. 115 (Jan – June 92), pp. 85 – 137. Bibl, tables, maps.

Furlong, William Leon. Panama: The Difficult Transition towards Democracy. *Journal of Inter-American Studies and World Affairs,* v. 35, no. 3 (Fall 93), pp. 19 – 64. Bibl, tables, charts.

Furtado, Celso. La cosmovisión de Prebisch: una visión actual. *Estudios Internacionales (Chile),* v. 26, no. 101 (Jan – Mar 93), pp. 89 – 97. Bibl.

— A ordem mundial emergente e o Brasil. *Vozes,* v. 86, no. 5 (Sept – Oct 92), pp. 21 – 25.

Furtado Kestler, Izabela María. Stefan Zweig, Brasil e o holocausto. *Estudios Interdisciplinarios de América Latina y el Caribe,* v. 3, no. 2 (July – Dec 92), pp. 123 – 126. Bibl.

Futoransky, Luisa. Poems ("Crema catalana," "Mantua," "Cama camera," "Castillón de Fougères," "Aire libre"). *Hispamérica,* v. 21, no. 63 (Dec 92), pp. 49 – 51.

Gabaldón, Arnoldo José and Janet Welsh Brown. Moving the Americas toward Sustainable Development. *La Educación (USA),* v. 37, no. 115 (1993), pp. 273 – 288. Bibl.

Gaiso, Pisco del. Ensaio fotográfico: subjetivismo visual. *Vozes,* v. 87, no. 3 (May – June 93), pp. 73 – 75. Il.

Gajardo, Marcela. Recent Literacy Development in Chilean Society. *La Educación (USA),* v. 36, no. 111 – 113 (1992), pp. 89 – 95.

Galarza, Elsa and Roberto Urrunaga. La economía de los recursos naturales: políticas extractivas y ambientales. *Apuntes (Peru),* no. 30 (Jan – June 92), pp. 45 – 61. Bibl.

Galdemar, Edith. Peintures faciales de la femme mexica: système chromatique des cosmétiques. *Estudios de Cultura Náhuatl,* v. 22 (1992), pp. 143 – 165. Bibl, tables.

Galeano, Eduardo H. The Corruption of Memory (Translated by Mark Fried). *NACLA Report on the Americas,* v. 27, no. 3 (Nov – Dec 93), pp. 35 – 38.

— Historia de la justiciera y el arcángel en el palacio de las pecadoras. *Casa de las Américas,* no. 191 (Apr – June 93), pp. 59 – 62.

Galeano Garcés, Gloria. Patrones de distribución de las palmas de Colombia. *Bulletin de l'Institut Français d'Etudes Andines,* v. 21, no. 2 (1992), pp. 599 – 607. Bibl, maps, charts.

Galecio, Jorge. El trabajo de los jesuitas en la educación. *Mensaje,* v. 42, no. 420 (July 93), pp. 275 – 279. Il.

Galindo Blanco, Adán. Tourism in a Trap. *Business Mexico,* v. 3, no. 10 (Oct 93), pp. 18 – 19. Il.

Galindo López, Olga. La filosofía inculturada: ¿Una alternativa social para la América Latina? *Islas,* no. 99 (May – Aug 91), pp. 5 – 14. Bibl.

Gallego, Ferran. La política económica del "socialismo militar" boliviano. *Anuario de Estudios Americanos,* v. 50, no. 1 (1993), pp. 213 – 234. Bibl, tables.

Gallegos, Carlos. Pensamiento y acción política de José Vasconcelos. *Revista Mexicana de Ciencias Políticas y Sociales,* v. 37, Nueva época, no. 149 (July – Sept 92), pp. 125 – 138. Bibl.

Gallisá, Carlos. Análisis electoral, 1988: apuntes preliminares. *Homines,* v. 15 – 16, no. 2 – 1 (Oct 91 – Dec 92), pp. 112 – 115.

Gallo, Lylia. Evocación de Luis Alberto Acuña (1904 – 1993). *Boletín de Historia y Antigüedades,* v. 80, no. 781 (Apr – June 93), pp. 365 – 367.

Galloway, Jonathan F. ¿Industrias globales? *Revista Mexicana de Sociología,* v. 54, no. 2 (Apr – June 92), pp. 75 – 100. Bibl, tables, charts.

Galve-Peritore, Ana Karina and N. Patrick Peritore. Cleavage and Polarization in Mexico's Ruling Party: A Field Study of the 1988 Presidential Election. *Journal of Developing Areas,* v. 28, no. 1 (Oct 93), pp. 67 – 88. Bibl, tables.

Gálvez Cancino, Alejandro. Arnaldo Orfila Reynal, un difundidor cultural. *Plural (Mexico),* v. 22, no. 263 (Aug 93), pp. 32 – 39.

Gama, Elizabeth Maria Pinheiro. As percepções sobre a causalidade do fracasso escolar no discurso descontente do magistério. *Revista Brasileira de Estudos Pedagógicos,* v. 72, no. 172 (Sept – Dec 91), pp. 356 – 384. Bibl, tables.

Gamarra, Jefrey. Estado, modernidad y sociedad regional: Ayacucho, 1920 – 1940. *Apuntes (Peru),* no. 31 (July – Dec 92), pp. 103 – 114. Bibl.

Gamarra Durana, Alfonso. La economía realista como provocadora de rebeldías. *Signo,* no. 36 – 37, Nueva época (May – Dec 92), pp. 361 – 378. Bibl.

— No sirven escudos ni banderas. *Signo,* no. 35, Nueva época (Jan – Apr 92), pp. 35 – 36.

Gamboa, Aldo Horacio. The "Brasiguayos": People in Search of a Country (Translated by NACLA). *NACLA Report on the Americas,* v. 27, no. 3 (Nov – Dec 93), pp. 4 – 6. Il, maps.

Gamboa Ojeda, Leticia. Historia de una pequeña empresa: la Compañía Petrolera de Puebla en Pánuco, 1916 – 1924. *La Palabra y el Hombre,* no. 83 (July – Sept 92), pp. 219 – 253. Bibl, tables, maps.

— Mercado de fuerza de trabajo e industria textil: el centro-oriente de México durante el porfiriato. *Siglo XIX: Cuadernos,* v. 1, no. 1 (Oct 91), pp. 9 – 36. Bibl.

Games, Alison F. Survival Strategies in Early Bermuda and Barbados. *Revista/Review Interamericana,* v. 22, no. 1 – 2 (Spring – Summer 92), pp. 55 – 71. Bibl, tables.

Gana, Víctor. Jesuitas en la región de Antofagasta. *Mensaje,* v. 42, no. 420 (July 93), p. 297.

Gandásegui, Marco A., Jr. The Military Regimes of Panama. *Journal of Inter-American Studies and World Affairs,* v. 35, no. 3 (Fall 93), pp. 1 – 17.

Gandía, Enrique de. Prolegómenos a la independencia de la América Hispana: Francisco de Miranda y Juan Pablo de Vizcardo y Guzmán. *Investigaciones y Ensayos,* no. 41 (Jan – Dec 91), pp. 15 – 64.

Gandolfo, Carlos. El régimen parlamentario y la estabilidad democrática. *Apuntes (Peru),* no. 29 (July – Dec 91), pp. 17 – 25.

Gandolfo, Elvio E. El legado de una lengua plena. *Cuadernos del CLAEH,* v. 17, no. 63 – 64 (Oct 92), pp. 137 – 139.

Ganga, Sharda. Suriname: testimonio teatral de una práctica. *Conjunto,* no. 90 – 91 (Jan – June 92), pp. 97 – 100. Il.

Gannon, Michael. Primeros encuentros en el Nuevo Mundo. *Atenea (Chile),* no. 465 – 466 (1992), pp. 45 – 52.

Gantiva Silva, Jorge. El conflicto de la identidad en la cultura. *Islas,* no. 97 (Sept – Dec 90), pp. 3 – 6.

Garabano, Sandra and Guillermo García-Corales. Diamela Eltit. *Hispamérica*, v. 21, no. 62 (Aug 92), pp. 65 – 75.

Garabedian, Martha Ann. Visión fantástica de la muerte en algunos poemas de Oscar Hahn. *Revista Chilena de Literatura*, no. 41 (Apr 93), pp. 71 – 78. Bibl.

Garate, Donald T. Basque Names, Nobility, and Ethnicity on the Spanish Frontier. *Colonial Latin American Historical Review*, v. 2, no. 1 (Winter 93), pp. 77 – 104. Bibl, facs.

Gárate, Miriam Viviana. El diario de Helena Morley o de la vida de las mujeres en la Diamantina finisecular. *Escritura (Venezuela)*, v. 16, no. 31 – 32 (Jan – Dec 91), pp. 65 – 80. Bibl.

Garbulsky, Edgardo O. La antropología social en la Argentina. *Runa*, v. 20 (1991 – 1992), pp. 11 – 33. Bibl.

García, Alfredo T. Las transformaciones del sector financiero en los últimos diez años. *Realidad Económica*, no. 120 (Nov – Dec 93), pp. 41 – 60. Tables, charts.

García, Arturo. Reality in the "Campo." *Business Mexico*, v. 3, no. 8 (Aug 93), pp. 30 – 31. Il.

García, Erica C. Por qué "como" o "porque." *Nueva Revista de Filología Hispánica*, v. 40, no. 2 (July – Dec 92), pp. 599 – 621. Bibl.

García, José Hermenegildo. La muerte de Ricuarte (Previously published in this journal vol. 1, no. 1, 1912). *Boletín de la Academia Nacional de la Historia (Venezuela)*, v. 75, no. 300 (Oct – Dec 92), pp. 327 – 330.

García, José Z. Migración y posmodernidad: efectos culturales; ¿Una nueva ciencia social fronteriza? *Nueva Sociedad*, no. 127 (Sept – Oct 93), pp. 148 – 157. Bibl.

García, Lionel G. The Day They Took My Uncle. *The Americas Review*, v. 20, no. 3 – 4 (Fall – Winter 92), pp. 57 – 65.

García, Marcela A. and Aníbal Iturrieta. Perón en el exilio español: la búsqueda de la legitimidad. *Todo Es Historia*, v. 27, no. 313 (Aug 93), pp. 8 – 25. Bibl, il.

García, Mario T. Working for the Union. *Mexican Studies*, v. 9, no. 2 (Summer 93), pp. 241 – 257. Il.

García, Pío. Asia y el Pacífico: la dimensión promisoria. *Revista Javeriana*, v. 61, no. 594 (May 93), pp. 271 – 276. Bibl.

García, Sebastián. América en la legislación general de la orden franciscana, siglo XVIII. *Archivo Ibero-Americano*, v. 52, no. 205 – 208 (Jan – Dec 92), pp. 629 – 689. Bibl, facs.

García, Soledad

See
García Morales, Soledad

García Ahumada, Enrique. Crecimiento hacia la santidad en Teresa de los Andes. *Mensaje*, v. 42, no. 417 (Mar – Apr 93), pp. 64 – 68. Il.

— La promoción humana en la Conferencia de Santo Domingo. *Estudios Sociales (Chile)*, no. 78 (Oct – Dec 93), pp. 245 – 257.

García Añoveros, Jesús María. Discrepancias del obispo y de los doctrineros con la Audiencia y los indígenas de Guatemala, 1687. *Revista de Indias*, v. 52, no. 195 – 196 (May – Dec 92), pp. 385 – 441.

García B., Pantaleón. La adquisición de las Floridas por los Estados Unidos en 1819. *Revista Cultural Lotería*, v. 51, no. 387 (Feb 92), pp. 37 – 42. Bibl.

— La política del buen vecino y Latinoamérica. *Revista Cultural Lotería*, v. 51, no. 388 (Mar – Apr 92), pp. 62 – 77. Bibl.

— Resistencia y rebelión durante el siglo XVIII en la región andina (Review article). *Revista Cultural Lotería*, v. 51, no. 391 (Sept – Oct 92), pp. 80 – 97. Bibl.

García Belaúnde, José Antonio. El Perú y la América Latina en los '90. *Debate (Peru)*, v. 15, no. 71 (Nov 92 – Jan 93), pp. 52 – 57. Il.

— Promoción, imagen, diplomacia. *Debate (Peru)*, v. 16, no. 72 (Mar – May 93), pp. 46 – 48. Il.

García Blanco, Rolando. Perspectivas de la historia regional en Cuba. *Islas*, no. 98 (Jan – Apr 91), pp. 3 – 12. Bibl.

García Cambeiro, Marcelo. LATBOOK en CD-ROM: una respuesta profesional de libreros latinoamericanos a las necesidades bibliográficas. *SALALM Papers*, v. 36 (1991), pp. 432 – 434.

García Canclini, Néstor. La cultura visual en la época del posnacionalismo: ¿Quién nos va a contar la identidad? *Nueva Sociedad*, no. 127 (Sept – Oct 93), pp. 23 – 31.

García Capote, Emilio and Tirso W. Sáenz. El desarrollo de la ciencia y la tecnología en Cuba: algunas cuestiones actuales. *Interciencia*, v. 18, no. 6 (Nov – Dec 93), pp. 289 – 294. Bibl, tables.

García-Corales, Guillermo. Entrevista con Antonio Skármeta: de *El entusiasmo* a *Match ball*. *Chasqui*, v. 22, no. 2 (Nov 93), pp. 114 – 119.

García-Corales, Guillermo and Sandra Garabano. Diamela Eltit. *Hispamérica*, v. 21, no. 62 (Aug 92), pp. 65 – 75.

García Costa, Víctor O. Como viví estos diez años de democracia. *Todo Es Historia*, v. 27, no. 317 (Dec 93), pp. 30 – 37. Il.

García de Fuentes, Ana. Comercio, modernización y procesos territoriales: el caso de Mérida, Yucatán. *Problemas del Desarrollo*, v. 24, no. 94 (July – Sept 93), pp. 133 – 163. Bibl, tables, maps, charts.

García del Toro, Antonio. La jerga teatral puertorriqueña (Includes a basic glossary). *Homines*, v. 15 – 16, no. 2 – 1 (Oct 91 – Dec 92), pp. 298 – 308.

García Duarte, Ricardo. La paz esquiva: negociaciones, desencuentros y rediseño de estrategias. *Revista Javeriana*, v. 60, no. 590 (Nov – Dec 92), pp. 316 – 322.

García Echeverría, Luis. La economía durante el gobierno Gaviria. *Revista Javeriana*, v. 61, no. 597 (Aug 93), pp. 143 – 152. Charts.

García Escobar, Carlos René. Historia antigua: historia y etnografía del *Rabinal Achí*. *La Tradición Popular*, no. 81 (1991), Issue. Bibl, il.

García Fernández, Irsa Teresa. Aproximaciones para un estudio del trotskismo en Bolivia. *Islas*, no. 96 (May – Aug 90), pp. 78 – 82. Bibl.

— El pensamiento boliviano: ¿Hacia una filosofía de la liberación? *Islas*, no. 99 (May – Aug 91), pp. 45 – 50. Bibl.

García-García, José Manuel. Poema para caminar junto a Adriana. *Plural (Mexico)*, v. 22, no. 256 (Jan 93), pp. 60 – 62.

— Poesía de la interzona. *Plural (Mexico)*, v. 22, no. 265 (Oct 93), pp. 6 – 14.

García Godoy, Cristián. A 500 años del descubrimiento de un nuevo mundo: Colón en Estados Unidos. *Revista de Historia de América*, no. 112 (July – Dec 91), pp. 63 – 84. Bibl, il.

García González, Francisco. Los muros de la vida privada y la familia: casa y tamaño familiar en Zacatecas; primeras décadas del siglo XIX. *Estudios Demográficos y Urbanos*, v. 7, no. 1 (Jan – Apr 92), pp. 35 – 52. Bibl, tables.

García González, José. Iteración léxico – semántica en las metáforas de José Martí sobre la patria cubana. *Islas,* no. 96 (May – Aug 90), pp. 139 – 149. Bibl.

García Guadilla, Carmen. Integración académica y nuevo valor del conocimiento. *Nueva Sociedad,* no. 126 (July – Aug 93), pp. 156 – 168. Bibl.

García Gutiérrez, Georgina. *Terra nostra:* crónica universal del orbe; apuntes sobre intertextualidad. *Nueva Revista de Filología Hispánica,* v. 40, no. 2 (July – Dec 92), pp. 1135 – 1148.

García Guzmán, Brígida. La ocupación en México en los años ochenta: hechos y datos. *Revista Mexicana de Sociología,* v. 55, no. 1 (Jan – Mar 93), pp. 137 – 153. Bibl, tables.

García Hurtado, Jorge. La acción de la Veeduría del Tesoro. *Revista Javeriana,* v. 61, no. 598 (Sept 93), pp. 259 – 268.

García Jordán, Pilar. Reflexiones sobre el darwinismo social: inmigración y colonización; mitos de los grupos modernizadores peruanos, 1821 – 1919. *Bulletin de l'Institut Français d'Etudes Andines,* v. 21, no. 3 (1992), pp. 961 – 975. Bibl.

García Laguardia, Jorge Mario. Antecedente y significado de la autonomía universitaria. *USAC,* no. 12 (Dec 90), pp. 60 – 65.

García Machado, Xiomara. Medardo Vitier en la tradición humanista del pensamiento cubano: ¿Herencia o ruptura? *Islas,* no. 98 (Jan – Apr 91), pp. 119 – 127. Bibl.

— Notas críticas para la "transcendencia" de un proyecto liberador: Mario Casalla y Silvio Maresca. *Islas,* no. 99 (May – Aug 91), pp. 15 – 20. Bibl.

García Machado, Xiomara and Rogelio Alsina Gutiérrez. Un nuevo estilo de filosofar: polémica con Mario Casalla desde la alteridad. *Islas,* no. 96 (May – Aug 90), pp. 111 – 120. Bibl.

García Martínez, Bernardo. Jurisdicción y propiedad: una distinción fundamental en la historia de los pueblos de indios del México colonial. *European Review of Latin American and Caribbean Studies,* no. 53 (Dec 92), pp. 47 – 60. Bibl.

García Medrano, Renward. Década perdida y planes de ajuste: crecimiento económico y pobreza. *Relaciones Internacionales (Mexico),* v. 14, Nueva época, no. 56 (Oct – Dec 92), pp. 45 – 48.

García Mora, Luis Miguel. Un cubano en la corte de la restauración: la labor intelectual de Rafael Montoro, 1875 – 1878. *Revista de Indias,* v. 52, no. 195 – 196 (May – Dec 92), pp. 443 – 475. Bibl.

García Morales, Soledad. Algunas consideraciones sobre la historiografía veracruzana del porfiriato y la revolución en Veracruz. *La Palabra y el Hombre,* no. 83 (July – Sept 92), pp. 304 – 313.

García Morales, Soledad and Ricardo Corzo Ramírez. Políticas, instituciones públicas de salud y enfermedades en Veracruz: fines del siglo XIX y principios del siglo XX. *La Palabra y el Hombre,* no. 83 (July – Sept 92), pp. 275 – 298. Bibl, tables.

García Muñiz, Humberto. "Los últimos treinta años, 1898 – 1928": un manuscripto inédito de Frank Tannenbaum sobre Puerto Rico; ensayo introductorio. *Op. Cit.,* no. 7 (1992), pp. 145 – 164. Bibl, il.

García Negrete, Gloria. Problemas de la regionalización económica de Cuba en la primera mitad del siglo XIX. *Islas,* no. 98 (Jan – Apr 91), pp. 28 – 39. Tables.

García Pabón, Leonardo. Comunicación, escritura e imaginario social en la *Tragedia del fin de Atahuallpa. Caravelle,* no. 59 (1992), pp. 225 – 240. Bibl.

García-Passalacqua, Juan M. Negotiated Autonomy. *Hemisphere,* v. 5, no. 3 (Summer – Fall 93), pp. 38 – 41. Charts.

— El regreso de Babel. *Homines,* v. 15 – 16, no. 2 – 1 (Oct 91 – Dec 92), pp. 132 – 134.

García Pombo, Pablo. Alemania y Colombia: trayectoria de una larga amistad. *Boletín de Historia y Antigüedades,* v. 80, no. 780 (Jan – Mar 93), pp. 79 – 108.

García Ponce, Antonio. Bajando por la Santa Capilla. *Revista Nacional de Cultura (Venezuela),* v. 54, no. 287 (Oct – Dec 92), pp. 109 – 116. Il.

García Quiñones, Rolando. Análisis comparativo de un tipo singular de retorno: el caso de los mexicanos indocumentados devueltos. *Problemas del Desarrollo,* v. 24, no. 93 (Apr – June 93), pp. 121 – 151. Bibl, tables.

García Quintanilla, Alejandra. Salud y progreso en Yucatán en el XIX: Mérida; el sarampión de 1882. *Siglo XIX: Cuadernos,* v. 1, no. 3 (June 92), pp. 29 – 53. Bibl, tables.

García Reyes, Miguel. El pueblo de Cuba: entre el drama y la esperanza, V; La crisis económica en Cuba. *Hoy Es Historia,* v. 10, no. 58 (July – Aug 93), pp. 54 – 58. Il, tables.

García Ríos, José María and Giulia Tamayo. El escenario como dictador: configuración metropolitana y experiencia cotidiana. *Nueva Sociedad,* no. 123 (Jan – Feb 93), pp. 94 – 103. Bibl.

García Rivadeneira, Edgar Allan. En la madrugada. *Plural (Mexico),* v. 22, no. 267 (Dec 93), p. 40.

García Ruiz, Jesús F. De la identidad aceptada a la identidad elegida: el papel de lo religioso en la politización de las identificaciones étnicas en Guatemala. *Estudios Sociológicos,* v. 10, no. 30 (Sept – Dec 92), pp. 713 – 733. Bibl.

— El misionero, las lenguas mayas y la traducción de los conceptos del catolicismo ibérico en Guatemala. *Folklore Americano,* no. 53 (Jan – June 92), pp. 103 – 131. Bibl.

García Sánchez, Franklin B. El dionisismo paródico – grotesco de *La loma del ángel* de Reinaldo Arenas. *Revista Canadiense de Estudios Hispánicos,* v. 17, no. 2 (Winter 93), pp. 271 – 279. Bibl.

García Targa, Juan. Unidades habitacionales en el área maya. *Boletín Americanista,* v. 33, no. 42 – 43 (1992 – 1993), pp. 231 – 254. Bibl, il.

García Ugarte, Marta Eugenia. El estado y la iglesia católica: balance y perspectivas de una relación. *Revista Mexicana de Sociología,* v. 55, no. 2 (Apr – June 93), pp. 225 – 242. Bibl.

García Zambrano, Angel Julián. El poblamiento de México en la época del contacto, 1520 – 1540. *Mesoamérica (USA),* v. 13, no. 24 (Dec 92), pp. 239 – 296. Bibl, il, facs, charts.

Garciga Garciga, Orestes. El estudio de la conquista castellana de las Antillas en un libro inédito de Fernando Ortiz. *Anuario de Estudios Americanos,* v. 49, Suppl. 2 (1992), pp. 253 – 256.

Gardner, David Skerritt. Colonización y modernización del campo en el centro de Veracruz, siglo XIX. *Siglo XIX: Cuadernos,* v. 2, no. 5 (Feb 93), pp. 39 – 57. Bibl, tables.

Gardner, Jeffrey J. Scholarship, Research Libraries, and Foreign Publishing in the 1990s. *SALALM Papers,* v. 36 (1991), pp. 277 – 293.

Garduño E., León and Magdalena Lorandi T. Desarrollo y evaluación del proyecto educativo Ixtliyollotl. *Revista Latinoamericana de Estudios Educativos,* v. 22, no. 3 (July – Sept 92), pp. 109 – 121. Bibl, tables.

Gardy, Alison. Emerging from the Shadows: A Visit to an Old Jewish Community. *NACLA Report on the Americas,* v. 27, no. 2 (Sept – Oct 93), pp. 10 – 13. Il.

Gareis, Iris. Brujos y brujas en el antiguo Perú: apariencia y realidad en las fuentes históricas. *Revista de Indias,* v. 53, no. 198 (May – Aug 93), pp. 583 – 613. Bibl, facs.

— Religión popular y etnicidad: la población indígena de Lima colonial. *Allpanchis,* v. 23, no. 40 (July – Dec 92), pp. 117 – 143. Bibl.

Gargallo, Francesca. ¿Las calles también son nuestras? *Fem,* v. 17, no. 122 (Apr 93), pp. 4 – 5. Il.

— Derechos humanos y trabajo doméstico asalariado. *Fem,* v. 17, no. 130 (Dec 92), pp. 4 – 6. Bibl.

— El desencuentro de los encuentros feministas. *Fem,* v. 17, no. 130 (Dec 93), pp. 37 – 38.

— Los feminismos centroamericanos: sus surgimientos, sus negaciones, sus participaciones y sus perspectivas; un acercamiento a la política femenina. *Fem,* v. 17, no. 119 (Jan 93), pp. 13 – 21. Bibl.

— Rumbo a un primer foro sobre los derechos humanos de las mujeres. *Fem,* v. 17, no. 120 (Feb 93), pp. 32 – 33.

Garín, Richard. Poema. *Hispamérica,* v. 22, no. 64 – 65 (Apr – Aug 93), p. 141.

Garma Navarro, Carlos. Enfoques teóricos en la antropología mexicana reciente: tercera reunión anual de *Nueva Antropología. Nueva Antropología,* v. 13, no. 43 (Nov 92), pp. 139 – 141.

Garmendia, Salvador. Por qué escribo. *Inti,* no. 37 – 38 (Spring – Fall 93), pp. 263 – 272.

Garrels, Elizabeth. Traducir a América: Sarmiento y el proyecto de una literatura nacional. *Revista de Crítica Literaria Latinoamericana,* v. 19, no. 38 (July – Dec 93), pp. 269 – 278. Bibl.

— Ver y ser vista: la mirada fálica en *La última niebla. Escritura (Venezuela),* v. 16, no. 31 – 32 (Jan – Dec 91), pp. 81 – 90. Bibl.

Garretón, Oscar Guillermo. Seis comentarios sobre la empresa del siglo XXI. *Mensaje,* v. 42, no. 422 (Sept 93), pp. 432 – 439. Il.

Garretón Merino, Manuel Antonio. Aprendizaje y gobernabilidad en la redemocratización chilena. *Nueva Sociedad,* no. 128 (Nov – Dec 93), pp. 148 – 157.

— Avances, límites y perspectivas de una política cultural. *Estudios Sociales (Chile),* no. 75 (Jan – Mar 93), pp. 113 – 128.

— El Festival Mundial de Teatro y Política. *Mensaje,* v. 42, no. 419 (June 93), pp. 175 – 177. Il.

— Los jesuitas y el pensamiento social de los sesenta en Chile. *Mensaje,* v. 42, no. 420 (July 93), pp. 298 – 303. Il.

— La redemocratización política en Chile: transición, inauguración y evolución. *Estudios Interdisciplinarios de América Latina y el Caribe,* v. 4, no. 1 (Jan – June 93), pp. 5 – 25. Bibl.

— El tupido velo. *Mensaje,* v. 42, no. 425 (Dec 93), pp. 619 – 625. Il.

Garretón Merino, Manuel Antonio and Malva Espinoza. ¿Reforma del estado o cambio en la matriz sociopolítica? *Estudios Sociales (Chile),* no. 74 (Oct – Dec 92), pp. 7 – 37. Bibl.

Garrido, Consuelo. Mi querido Tom Mix. *Nexos,* v. 16, no. 189 (Sept 93), pp. 75 – 76.

Garrigus, John D. Blue and Brown: Contraband Indigo and the Rise of a Free Colored Planter Class in French Saint-Domingue. *The Americas,* v. 50, no. 2 (Oct 93), pp. 233 – 263. Bibl, tables, maps, charts.

— Catalyst or Catastrophe?: Saint-Domingue's Free Men of Color and the Battle of Savannah, 1779 – 1782. *Revista/Review Interamericana,* v. 22, no. 1 – 2 (Spring – Summer 92), pp. 109 – 125. Bibl.

Garrison, John W., II. UNCED and the Greening of Brazilian NGOs. *Grassroots Development,* v. 17, no. 1 (1993), pp. 2 – 11. Bibl, il.

Garrison, Roberta and William W. Eaton. Mental Health in Mariel Cubans and Haitian Boat People. *International Migration Review,* v. 26, no. 4 (Winter 92), pp. 1395 – 1415. Bibl, tables.

Garrocho, Carlos. De la casa al hospital: un enfoque espacio – temporal. *Estudios Sociológicos,* v. 11, no. 32 (May – Aug 93), pp. 547 – 554. Bibl, charts.

Garscha, Karsten. Das Leben, nur eine kurze Reise: Der mexikanische Totenkult. *Iberoamericana,* v. 17, no. 50 (1993), pp. 16 – 37. Bibl.

Garsd, Marta S. The Broken Mirror: Argentine Art in the 1980s. *SALALM Papers,* v. 34 (1989), pp. 33 – 39. Bibl.

Gartner, Bruce S. and Anita M. Hart. A Space of One's Own: Mexican Poets Kyra Galván and Perla Schwartz. *Confluencia,* v. 8, no. 1 (Fall 92), pp. 79 – 89. Bibl.

Garza, Alejandro de la. Cinco minutos de sexo al milenio. *Nexos,* v. 16, no. 185 (May 93), pp. 83 – 85.

Garza Caligaris, Anna María and Juana María Ruiz Ortiz. Madres solteras indígenas. *Mesoamérica (USA),* v. 13, no. 23 (June 92), pp. 66 – 77. Bibl.

Garza Cuarón, Beatriz. La poética de José Gorostiza y "el grupo sin grupo" de la revista *Contemporáneos. Nueva Revista de Filología Hispánica,* v. 40, no. 2 (July – Dec 92), pp. 891 – 907. Bibl.

Garza Toledo, Enrique de la. Reestructuración del corporativismo en México: siete tesis. *El Cotidiano,* v. 9, no. 56 (July 93), pp. 47 – 53. Il.

Garza Villarreal, Gustavo and Salvador Rivera. Desarrollo económico y distribución de la población urbana en México, 1960 – 1990. *Revista Mexicana de Sociología,* v. 55, no. 1 (Jan – Mar 93), pp. 177 – 212. Bibl, tables, charts.

Gas, Gelsen. El grupo Tlalpuente. *Plural (Mexico),* v. 22, no. 258 (Mar 93), pp. 41 – 44. Il.

Gascón, Margarita. The Military of Santo Domingo, 1720 – 1764. *Hispanic American Historical Review,* v. 73, no. 3 (Aug 93), pp. 431 – 452. Bibl.

Gates, Thomas P. Meadows Museum of Spanish Art Book Collection: An Overview. *SALALM Papers,* v. 34 (1989), pp. 439 – 451. Bibl.

Gavilán, Jorge and Diego Colombres. El daño ecológico y social que provocó La Forestal. *Todo Es Historia,* v. 26, no. 306 (Jan 93), pp. 42 – 47. Il.

Gaviria Trujillo, César. Palabras del presidente de la república, César Gaviria Trujillo, en el acto de instalación. *Planeación y Desarrollo,* v. 24, no. 1 (Jan – Apr 93), pp. 17 – 25.

— La política y la crisis fiscal (Previously published in this journal, no. 508, 1984). *Revista Javeriana,* v. 61, no. 596 (July 93), pp. 111 – 113.

Gaytán Guzmán, Rosa Isabel. La política exterior mexicana en el marco de los procesos mundiales de integración comercial. *Relaciones Internacionales (Mexico),* v. 15, Nueva época, no. 58 (Apr – June 93), pp. 25 – 37. Bibl, tables.

Gazzolo, Ana María. El cubismo y la poética vallejiana. *Cuadernos Hispanoamericanos,* no. 510 (Dec 92), pp. 31 – 42. Il.

Geiger, Pedro Pinchas. In memoriam: Nilo e Lysia Bernardes. *Revista Geográfica (Mexico),* no. 114 (July – Dec 91), pp. 111 – 118.

Geirola, Gustavo. Juan Gabriel: cultura popular y sexo de los ángeles. *Latin American Music Review,* v. 14, no. 2 (Fall – Winter 93), pp. 232 – 267. Bibl.

Gelman, Jorge Daniel. Los caminos del mercado: campesinos, estancieros y pulperos en una región del Río de la Plata colonial. *Latin American Research Review,* v. 28, no. 2 (1993), pp. 89 – 118. Bibl, tables.

— Mundo rural y mercados: una estancia y las formas de circulación mercantil en la campaña rioplatense tardocolonial. *Revista de Indias,* v. 52, no. 195 – 196 (May – Dec 92), pp. 477 – 514. Bibl, tables.

Gelman, Juan. Lo judío y la literatura en castellano. *Hispamérica,* v. 21, no. 62 (Aug 92), pp. 83 – 90.

Gelpí, Juan G. Ana Lydia Vega: ante el debate de la cultura nacional de Puerto Rico. *Revista Chilena de Literatura,* no. 42 (Aug 93), pp. 95 – 99.

— El clásico y la reescritura: "Insularismo" en las páginas de *La guaracha del macho Camacho. Revista Iberoamericana,* v. 59, no. 162 – 163 (Jan – June 93), pp. 55 – 71. Bibl.

Gelsi Bidart, Adolfo. Individualización del derecho agrario. *Derecho y Reforma Agraria,* no. 24 (1993), pp. 53 – 62.

Gené, Juan Carlos. Atavismos y teatro. *Conjunto,* no. 93 (Jan – June 93), pp. 116 – 117. Il.

Genzano, Alicia. A la muerte. *Feminaria,* v. 6, no. 10, Suppl. (Apr 93), p. 16.

George, David. Socio-Criticism and Brazilian Literature: Changing Perspectives. *Chasqui,* v. 22, no. 2 (Nov 93), pp. 49 – 56.

Gerardi Conedera, Juan et al. La alternativa para el desarrollo democrático de Guatemala: panel-foro. *USAC,* no. 14 (June 91), pp. 24 – 43.

Gerendas, Judit. Hacia una problematización de la escritura femenina. *Escritura (Venezuela),* v. 16, no. 31 – 32 (Jan – Dec 91), pp. 91 – 101.

— Imágenes y símbolos en algunos textos poéticos de César Vallejo. *Revista Nacional de Cultura (Venezuela),* v. 54, no. 287 (Oct – Dec 92), pp. 188 – 196. Il.

Gervitz, Gloria. Pythia (From the unpublished book of the same title). *Vuelta,* v. 17, no. 197 (Apr 93), pp. 25 – 26.

Gewecke, Frauke. "El corte" oder "Les vêpres dominicaines": Trujillos "dominicanización de la frontera" und ihr Reflex in der dominikanischen und haitianischen Literatur. *Iberoamericana,* v. 17, no. 50 (1993), pp. 38 – 62. Bibl.

Geyer, Anne. Challenges for the Modern Metropolis. *Business Mexico,* v. 3, no. 10 (Oct 93), pp. 48 – 49.

— Chronicles of Success. *Business Mexico,* v. 3, no. 5 (May 93), pp. 32 – 35. Il.

— Jet-Set Capitalism. *Business Mexico,* v. 3, no. 9 (Sept 93), pp. 20 – 22. Il.

— Water on Schedule . . . and on Tap. *Business Mexico,* v. 3, no. 7 (July 93), pp. 16 – 19.

Ghersi, Enrique. La ecuación Manuel Prado. *Debate (Peru),* v. 16, no. 73 (June – Aug 93), pp. 24 – 25. Il.

Giacalone de Romero, Rita. Condicionamientos étnicos en la conformación de estereotipos femeninos en el Caribe hispánico y Caribe angloparlante. *Homines,* v. 15 – 16, no. 2 – 1 (Oct 91 – Dec 92), pp. 289 – 297. Bibl.

Giambiagi, Fábio. Financiamento do governo através de senhoriagem em condições de equilíbrio: algumas simulações. *Revista Brasileira de Economia,* v. 47, no. 2 (Apr – June 93), pp. 265 – 279. Bibl, tables.

Giambiagi, Fábio and Armando Castelar Pinheiro. As empresas estatais e o programa de privatização do governo Collor. *Pesquisa e Planejamento Econômico,* v. 22, no. 2 (Aug 92), pp. 241 – 288. Bibl, tables.

Giambiagi, Fábio and Alvaro Antônio Zini Júnior. Renegociação da dívida interna mobiliária: uma proposta. *Revista de Economia Política (Brazil),* v. 13, no. 2 (Apr – June 93), pp. 5 – 27. Bibl, tables, charts.

Giandalia, Paulo. Ensaio fotográfico: Paris, 1991. *Vozes,* v. 87, no. 4 (July – Aug 93), pp. 70 – 76. Il.

Giannini, Isabelle Vidal. Os domínios cósmicos: um dos aspectos da construção da categoria humana kayapó – xikrin. *Revista de Antropologia (Brazil),* v. 34 (1991), pp. 35 – 58. Bibl.

Giarracca, Norma. Campesinos y agroindustrias en los tiempos del "ajuste": algunas reflexiones para pensar la relación, con especial referencia a México y la Argentina. *Realidad Económica,* no. 114 – 115 (Feb – May 93), pp. 13 – 28. Bibl.

Giarracca, Norma and Miguel Teubal. El día en que la Plaza de Mayo se vistió de campo (Includes interviews with six agricultural producers). *Realidad Económica,* no. 118 (Aug – Sept 93), pp. 5 – 17. Tables.

Gibson, Kean. An African Work: The Guyanese Comfa Dance. *Journal of Caribbean Studies,* v. 9, no. 1 – 2 (Winter 92 – Spring 93), pp. 99 – 111. Bibl.

Giddings, Lorrain Eugene. Visión por satélite de las inundaciones extraordinarias de la cuenca del Río de la Plata. *Interciencia,* v. 18, no. 1 (Jan – Feb 93), pp. 16 – 23. Bibl, il, tables, charts.

Giella, Miguel Angel. Inmigración y exilio: el limbo del lenguaje. *Latin American Theatre Review,* v. 26, no. 2 (Spring 93), pp. 111 – 121. Bibl.

Gierhake, Klaus-Ulrich. La inversión pública como instrumento de evaluación del proceso de planificación regional en Bolivia, 1987 – 1990. *Revista Interamericana de Planificación,* v. 26, no. 101 – 102 (Jan – June 93), pp. 112 – 128. Bibl, tables, maps, charts.

Gil, Francisco Javier. Ponderar mejor la enseñanza media: una experiencia de la Universidad de Chile. *Mensaje,* v. 42, no. 425 (Dec 93), pp. 637 – 639. Il.

Gil-Montero, Martha. The Liberator's Noble Match (Photographs by Jorge Provenza). *Américas,* v. 45, no. 3 (May – June 93), pp. 6 – 17. Il.

Gil-Montero, Martha and Laurence De Looze. On the Tucumán Trail (Photographs by Jorge Provenza). *Américas,* v. 45, no. 5 (Sept – Oct 93), pp. 22 – 33. Il, maps.

Gil Olivo, Ramón. Nuevo cine latinoamericano, 1955 – 1973: fuentes para un lenguaje. *Plural (Mexico),* v. 22, no. 263 (Aug 93), pp. 50 – 56. Bibl.

Gil Zúñiga, José Daniel. Nuestra historia: un intento de popularizar la historia. *Revista de Historia (Costa Rica),* no. 25 (Jan – June 92), pp. 229 – 233.

Gilard, Jacques. *La huella de abril* de Alicia Miranda. *Káñina,* v. 16, no. 1 (Jan – June 92), pp. 19 – 21.

Gilbert, Alan G. Ciudades del Tercer Mundo: la evolución del sistema nacional de asentamientos. *EURE,* v. 19, no. 57 (July 93), pp. 41 – 58. Tables.

Gilberti, Horacio. Cambios en las estructuras agrarias. *Realidad Económica,* no. 113 (Jan – Feb 93), pp. 87 – 89.

Gill, Henry S. The Caribbean in a World of Economic Blocks. *Social and Economic Studies,* v. 41, no. 3 (Sept 92), pp. 25 – 36.

— CARICOM: origen, objetivos y perspectivas de integración en el Caribe. *Integración Latinoamericana,* v. 18, no. 191 (July 93), pp. 37 – 44. Bibl, tables.

Gilly, Adolfo. ¿Dónde pintar la raya del socialismo? *Nexos,* v. 16, no. 183 (Mar 93), pp. 39 – 46.

— 1968: la ruptura en los bordes. *Nexos,* v. 16, no. 191 (Nov 93), pp. 25 – 33.

Gilman, Claudia. Política y cultura: *Marcha* a partir de los años '60. *Nuevo Texto Crítico,* v. 6, no. 11 (1993), pp. 153 – 186. Bibl.

— *Los siete locos:* novela sospechosa de Roberto Arlt. *Cuadernos Hispanoamericanos,* no. Special issue, 11 (July 93), pp. 77 – 94. Il.

Giménez, Carlos. Homenaje a Pepe Tejera: palabras del director de Rajatabla a su actor galardonado. *Conjunto,* no. 90 – 91 (Jan – June 92), pp. 40 – 42. Il.

Gimferrer, Pedro. *La cuarentena* de Juan Goytisolo. *Vuelta,* v. 17, no. 197 (Apr 93), pp. 11 – 12.

Gindling, T. H. Women's Wages and Economic Crisis in Costa Rica. *Economic Development and Cultural Change,* v. 41, no. 2 (Jan 93), pp. 277 – 297. Bibl, tables.

Giordano, Jaime. Más allá de las palabras: Gonzalo Rojas. *Atenea (Chile),* no. 467 (1993), pp. 187 – 196.

— Más allá de las palabras: Gonzalo Rojas. *Chasqui,* v. 22, no. 1 (May 93), pp. 31 – 37.

Girarte, Luis. Lo que soy está aquí. *Plural (Mexico),* v. 22, no. 267 (Dec 93), pp. 25 – 26.

Girbal de Blacha, Noemí M. Azúcar, cambio político y acción empresaria en la Argentina, 1916 – 1930. *Investigaciones y Ensayos,* no. 41 (Jan – Dec 91), pp. 269 – 314. Bibl, tables.

— Tradición y modernización en la agricultura cerealera argentina, 1910 – 1930: comportamiento y propuestas de los ingenieros agrónomos. *Jahrbuch für Geschichte von Staat, Wirtschaft und Gesellschaft Lateinamerikas,* v. 29 (1992), pp. 369 – 395. Bibl.

Girón, Nicole. Altamirano, diplomático. *Mexican Studies,* v. 9, no. 2 (Summer 93), pp. 161 – 185.

Girón Botello, Rafael and Guillermo Compean. La pesca en la cuenca del Pacífico: el caso del atún en México. *Comercio Exterior,* v. 43, no. 12 (Dec 93), pp. 1195 – 1201. Bibl, tables, charts.

Girón González, Alicia. Sociología entre dos mundos. *Problemas del Desarrollo,* v. 24, no. 92 (Jan – Mar 93), pp. 227 – 231.

Girón Mena, Manuel Antonio. Meditaciones frente al quetzal. *USAC,* no. 14 (June 91), pp. 74 – 82. Bibl, il.

Girot, Pascal-Olivier. Parcs nationaux et développement rural au Costa Rica: mythes et réalités. *Tiers Monde,* v. 34, no. 134 (Apr – June 93), pp. 405 – 421. Bibl, tables, maps, charts.

Gisse, Guillermo and Antonio Daher. América Latina: ambiente y territorio en el cambio de modelo. *Revista Paraguaya de Sociología,* v. 29, no. 84 (May – Aug 92), pp. 25 – 40.

Gladhart, Amalia. Narrative Foregrounding in the Plays of Osvaldo Dragún. *Latin American Theatre Review,* v. 26, no. 2 (Spring 93), pp. 93 – 109. Bibl.

Glantz, Margo. La Malinche, sus padres y sus hijos. *Cuadernos Americanos,* no. 40, Nueva época (July – Aug 93), pp. 167 – 169.

Glasmeier, Amy K. and Michael E. Conroy. Unprecedented Disparities, Unparalleled Adjustment Needs: Winners and Losers on the NAFTA "Fast Track." *Journal of Inter-American Studies and World Affairs,* v. 34, no. 4 (Winter 92 – 93), pp. 1 – 37. Bibl, tables, charts.

Glassman, Steve. The Sinners' Bossanova: Its Caribbean Roots. *Belizean Studies,* v. 21, no. 2 (Oct 93), pp. 23 – 27.

Glave Testino, Luis Miguel. La sociedad campesina andina a mediados del siglo XVII: estructura social y tendencias de cambio. *Historia y Cultura (Peru),* no. 20 (1990), pp. 81 – 132. Bibl, tables.

Gleijeses, Piero. La muerte de Francisco Arana. *Mesoamérica (USA),* v. 13, no. 24 (Dec 92), pp. 385 – 412. Bibl, il.

Glennon, Michael J. Testimony before the Subcommittee on Civil and Constitutional Rights, Committee on the Judiciary, United States House of Representatives. *Mexican Studies,* v. 9, no. 1 (Winter 93), pp. 1 – 17.

Glezer, Raquel. São Paulo e a elite letrada brasileira no século XIX. *Siglo XIX: Revista,* no. 11, 2a época (Jan – June 92), pp. 149 – 160. Bibl.

Glick, Curtis R. Parámetros sociales para la planificación en Colombia. *Revista Interamericana de Planificación,* v. 26, no. 101 – 102 (Jan – June 93), pp. 95 – 111. Bibl.

Gliksberg, Isaac. El laboratorio tecnológico de Uruguay: entrevista a su presidente ing. Ruperto M. Long. *Interciencia,* v. 18, no. 6 (Nov – Dec 93), pp. 314 – 316. Il.

Godfrey, Brian J. Regional Depiction in Contemporary Film. *Geographical Review,* v. 83, no. 4 (Oct 93), pp. 428 – 440. Bibl, il.

Godio, Julio Félix. Reestructuración del mercado laboral y estrategia sindical. *Nueva Sociedad,* no. 124 (Mar – Apr 93), pp. 104 – 113.

Godoy, Scarlett O'Phelan
See
   O'Phelan Godoy, Scarlett

Godoy Arcaya, Oscar. Un año electoral. *Mensaje,* v. 42, no. 416 (Jan – Feb 93), pp. 5 – 7.

— A veinte años de la crisis de la democracia chilena. *Mensaje,* v. 42, no. 422 (Sept 93), pp. 415 – 418.

Godoy Urzúa, Hernán. La hegemonía cultural jesuita y el barroco. *Mensaje,* v. 42, no. 420 (July 93), pp. 228 – 233. Il.

Goebel, J. Martin. Mexico: The Natural Factory. *Business Mexico,* v. 3, no. 1 (Jan – Feb 93), pp. 6 – 8. Il, tables, charts.

Góes-Filho, Luiz and Ricardo Forin Lisboa Braga. A vegetação do Brasil: desmatamento e queimadas. *Revista Brasileira de Geografia,* v. 53, no. 2 (Apr – June 91), pp. 135 – 141. Bibl, tables, maps.

Goff, Katrina. La imagen de la mujer en la *Obra poética* de Carlos de la Ossa. *Káñina,* v. 16, no. 1 (Jan – June 92), pp. 29 – 35. Bibl.

Gold-Biss, Michael. Colombia: Understanding Recent Democratic Transformations in a Violent Polity (Review article). *Latin American Research Review,* v. 28, no. 1 (1993), pp. 215 – 234. Bibl.

Goldberg, Jacqueline. Dos notas ("El desconocido confiesa," "El caleidoscopio de enfrente"). *Inti,* no. 37 – 38 (Spring – Fall 93), pp. 259 – 261.

Goldman, Shifra M. Artistas latinoamericanos del siglo XX: MOMA (Accompanied by the English original, translated by Magalena Holguín). *Art Nexus,* no. 10 (Sept – Dec 93), pp. 84 – 89. Il.

— La década crítica de la vanguardia cubana (Accompanied by the English original, translated by Ignacio Zuleta Lleras). *Art Nexus*, no. 7 (Jan – Mar 93), pp. 52 – 57. Bibl, il.

— Voz pública: quince años de carteles chicanos (Translated by Margarita Martínez Duarte). *Plural (Mexico)*, v. 22, no. 256 (Jan 93), pp. 28 – 37. Bibl.

Goldstein, Paul. Tiwanaku Temples and State Expansion: A Tiwanaku Sunken-Court Temple in Moquequa, Peru. *Latin American Antiquity*, v. 4, no. 1 (Mar 93), pp. 22 – 47. Bibl, il, tables, maps.

Goloboff, Gerardo Mario. Algunos antecedentes de la narrativa arltiana. *Cuadernos Hispanoamericanos*, no. Special issue, 11 (July 93), pp. 47 – 51.

Gomes, Angela Maria de Castro. Essa gente do Rio . . . : os intelectuais cariocas e o modernismo. *Estudos Históricos*, v. 6, no. 11 (Jan – June 93), pp. 62 – 77.

Gomes, Angela Maria de Castro and Maria Celina d'Araújo. Entrevista com Arnaldo Sussekind. *Estudos Históricos*, v. 6, no. 11 (Jan – June 93), pp. 113 – 127.

Gomes, Miguel. El lenguaje de las destrucciones: Caracas y la novela urbana. *Inti*, no. 37 – 38 (Spring – Fall 93), pp. 217 – 224. Bibl.

Gómez, Magdalena. Hacia una definición del espacio de lo consuetudinario en el medio indígena y de sus posibilidades de ejercicio en el marco de la nueva legalidad. *Nueva Antropología*, v. 13, no. 44 (Aug 93), pp. 9 – 15.

Gómez, Marcelo Flavio. Los problemas de la reproducción cultural en el capitalismo argentino: el caso de la anomia disciplinaria en las escuelas de sectores marginados. *La Educación (USA)*, v. 36, no. 111 – 113 (1992), pp. 195 – 225. Bibl.

Gómez, Miguel. Sueños de paraíso y de luz: la poesía de Pedro Lastra. *Revista Chilena de Literatura*, no. 40 (Nov 92), pp. 105 – 113.

Gómez, Robert P. Hacia tí. *The Americas Review*, v. 21, no. 1 (Spring 93), pp. 69 – 70.

Gómez, Sergio. ¿Cosas nuevas en la agricultura? *Estudios Sociales (Chile)*, no. 75 (Jan – Mar 93), pp. 141 – 153. Tables.

— Grupos sociales, organizaciones representativas y movilizaciones políticas: las dos caras de la modernización de la agricultura chilena. *Estudios Sociales (Chile)*, no. 76 (Apr – June 93), pp. 9 – 66. Tables.

Gómez Betancur, Rafael. En que quedamos por fin: ¿Concordato sí o concordato no?; ¿De qué y para qué sirven los pactos si no hay voluntad previa de cumplirlos? *Revista Javeriana*, v. 61, no. 599 (Oct 93), pp. 354 – 356.

Gómez Cruz, Filiberta. La Sociedad de Fomento en el puerto de Tuxpan, 1841. *La Palabra y el Hombre*, no. 83 (July – Sept 92), pp. 189 – 197. Bibl, tables.

Gómez de León, José and Virgilio Partida Bush. Niveles de mortalidad infantil y fecundidad en México, por entidad federativa, 1990. *Revista Mexicana de Sociología*, v. 55, no. 1 (Jan – Mar 93), pp. 97 – 135. Bibl, tables, charts.

Gómez Díez, Francisco Javier. El reformismo jesuítico en Centroamérica: La revista ECA en los años de la guerra fría, 1946 – 1965. *Anuario de Estudios Americanos*, v. 49, Suppl. 1 (1992), pp. 85 – 105. Tables.

Gómez Figueroa, Carlos. Situación de los profesores: un problema nacional. *Mensaje*, v. 42, no. 423 (Oct 93), pp. 491 – 494. Il, tables.

Gómez García, Pedro. Moros y cristianos, indios y españoles: esquema de la conquista del otro. *Allpanchis*, v. 23, no. 39 (Jan – June 92), pp. 221 – 261. Bibl.

Gómez García, Zoila. El folklore: antes y ahora. *Plural (Mexico)*, v. 22, no. 264 (Sept 93), pp. 119 – 120.

— ¿Música y aspiraciones humanas? *Plural (Mexico)*, v. 22, no. 262 (July 93), p. 75.

— ¿Sale de la calle o viene de la academia? *Plural (Mexico)*, v. 22, no. 265 (Oct 93), pp. 81 – 82.

— Siempre el bolero. *Plural (Mexico)*, v. 22, no. 263 (Aug 93), pp. 71 – 72.

Gómez Grillo, Elio. Sucedió en Barinas. *Boletín de la Academia Nacional de la Historia (Venezuela)*, v. 76, no. 301 (Jan – Mar 93), pp. 127 – 128.

Gómez Haco, Claudia. El "mysterium maximum" en la obra de Alejandro Colunga. *Artes de México*, no. 20 (Summer 93), pp. 117 – 119. Il.

Gómez Haro, Germaine. Krzysztof Augustín: la pintura; poesía silenciosa. *Artes de México*, no. 19 (Spring 93), pp. 98 – 99. Il.

Gómez Jiménez, Alcides. Seguridad alimentaria: problemas grandes y políticas pobres. *Revista Javeriana*, v. 61, no. 591 (Jan – Feb 93), pp. 26 – 33. Bibl, tables.

Gómez Latorre, Armando. Réquiem por cuatro académicos. *Boletín de Historia y Antigüedades*, v. 80, no. 781 (Apr – June 93), pp. 339 – 340.

Gómez López, Hugo. Los goznes del tiempo. *Plural (Mexico)*, v. 22, no. 267 (Dec 93), pp. 58 – 59.

Gómez-Martínez, José Luis. El pensamiento de la liberación: hacia una posición dialógica. *Cuadernos Americanos*, no. 40, Nueva época (July – Aug 93), pp. 53 – 61. Bibl.

Gómez Morín, Manuel. Buzón de fantasmas: de Manuel Gómez Morín al abate González de Mendoza. *Vuelta*, v. 17, no. 194 (Jan 93), pp. 62 – 64.

Gómez Otero, Julieta. The Function of Small Rock Shelters in the Magallanes IV Phase Settlement System, South Patagonia. *Latin American Antiquity*, v. 4, no. 4 (Dec 93), pp. 325 – 345. Bibl, il, tables, maps, charts.

Gómez Parham, Mary
See
 Parham, Mary Helene

Gómez Rivas, León. Don Francisco de Toledo, comendador de Alcántara, virrey del Perú: guía de fuentes (I). *Anuario de Estudios Americanos*, v. 49, Suppl. 1 (1992), pp. 123 – 171.

— Don Francisco de Toledo, comendador de Alcántara, virrey del Perú: guía de fuentes (II). *Anuario de Estudios Americanos*, v. 49, Suppl. 2 (1992), pp. 95 – 152.

Gómez Rogers, Jaime. El litoral de los poetas (Includes a poem about Vicente Huidobro). *Atenea (Chile)*, no. 467 (1993), pp. 157 – 159.

Gómez Rosa, Alexis. Salutación a don Pedro Mir. *Plural (Mexico)*, v. 22, no. 264 (Sept 93), pp. 43 – 45.

Gómez Tabanera, José Manuel. Reencuentro desde la otra orilla: utopía europea, utopía indiana y utopía del Pacífico. *Boletín de la Academia Nacional de la Historia (Venezuela)*, v. 75, no. 297 (Jan – Mar 92), pp. 5 – 20. Bibl.

Gómez Tagle, Silvia. Balance de las elecciones de 1991 en México. *Revista Mexicana de Sociología*, v. 54, no. 1 (Jan – Mar 92), pp. 253 – 287. Charts.

Gómez-Vega, Ibis. La mujer como artista en *Intaglio*. *Bilingual Review/Revista Bilingüe*, v. 18, no. 1 (Jan – Apr 93), pp. 14 – 22. Bibl.

Gonçalves, Aguinaldo et al. Avaliação e perspectivas de ciência e tecnologia nas endemias infecciosas brasileiras. *Interciencia*, v. 18, no. 3 (May – June 93), pp. 142 – 145. Bibl.

Gonçalves, João Francisco Franklin. Mário de Andrade e o avô presidente: dois projetos para o Brasil. *Vozes*, v. 87, no. 4 (July – Aug 93), pp. 65 – 69. Il.

Gonçalves, Williams da Silva and Shiguenoli Miyamoto. Os militares na política externa brasileira, 1964 – 1984. *Estudos Históricos*, v. 6, no. 12 (July – Dec 93), pp. 211 – 246. Bibl.

Góngora Soberanes, Janette. ¿Carrera magisterial emergente? o el magisterio a la carrera. *El Cotidiano*, v. 8, no. 51 (Nov – Dec 92), pp. 31 – 33.

Goñi, Alejandro. Palabras del r.p. Alejandro Goñi, S.J. *Boletín de la Academia Nacional de la Historia (Venezuela)*, v. 75, no. 299 (July – Sept 92), pp. 19 – 24.

Gonzalbo Aizpuru, Pilar. "La familia" y las familias en el México colonial. *Estudios Sociológicos*, v. 10, no. 30 (Sept – Dec 92), pp. 693 – 711. Bibl.

— Las fiestas novohispanas: espectáculo y ejemplo. *Mexican Studies*, v. 9, no. 1 (Winter 93), pp. 19 – 45. Bibl.

— Hacia una historia de la vida privada en la Nueva España. *Historia Mexicana*, v. 42, no. 2 (Oct – Dec 92), pp. 353 – 377.

Gonzales de Olarte, Efraín. Economic Stabilization and Structural Adjustment under Fujimori. *Journal of Inter-American Studies and World Affairs*, v. 35, no. 2 (Summer 93), pp. 51 – 80. Bibl, tables.

Gonzales de Olarte, Efraín and Julio Velarde F. ¿Es posible el liberalismo en el Perú? *Debate (Peru)*, v. 15, no. 70 (Sept – Oct 92), pp. 15 – 18. Il.

González, Alberto Rex. A cuatro décadas del comienzo de una etapa: apuntes marginales para la historia de la antropología argentina. *Runa*, v. 20 (1991 – 1992), pp. 91 – 110. Bibl.

González, Alejandro. Imágenes ("Haikú de abril," "Intrusa"), accompanied by an English translation. *Artes de México*, no. 20 (Summer 93), p. 51. Il.

González, Anabel. Comercio internacional y medio ambiente. *Comercio Exterior*, v. 43, no. 9 (Sept 93), pp. 827 – 835. Bibl.

González, Aníbal. After 1992: A Latin Americanist Wish List. *Latin American Literary Review*, v. 20, no. 40 (July – Dec 92), pp. 46 – 50.

— Ana Lydia Pluravega: unidad y multiplicidad caribeñas en la obra de Ana Lydia Vega. *Revista Iberoamericana*, v. 59, no. 162 – 163 (Jan – June 93), pp. 289 – 300. Bibl.

González, Ann. Teaching beyond the Classroom: Business Internships in Latin America; Issues in Cross-Cultural Adjustment. *Hispania (USA)*, v. 76, no. 4 (Dec 93), pp. 892 – 901.

González, Flora M. Masking History in Donoso's *Taratuta*. *Revista Canadiense de Estudios Hispánicos*, v. 17, no. 1 (Fall 92), pp. 47 – 62. Bibl.

González, Florencia. Solución de conflictos en un sistema de integración: los casos del MERCOSUR y la CEE. *Integración Latinoamericana*, v. 17, no. 185 (Dec 92), pp. 33 – 44. Bibl.

González, Humberto. La industria de confecciones o la competitividad amenazada. *Revista Javeriana*, v. 61, no. 593 (Apr 93), pp. 163 – 166.

González, José R. La cultura de ser y la cultura de tener. *Homines*, v. 15 – 16, no. 2 – 1 (Oct 91 – Dec 92), pp. 185 – 186.

González, Lucero. Derechos humanos de las mujeres y la filantropía. *Fem*, v. 17, no. 126 (Aug 93), p. 4.

González, Nelly S. Images from Inca Lands: An Index of Photographic Slides from the OAS. *SALALM Papers*, v. 34 (1989), pp. 115 – 122.

— Stretching the Budget: Developing Latin American and Caribbean Serial Collections for University Libraries. *SALALM Papers*, v. 36 (1991), pp. 325 – 334. Bibl.

González, Nelson Simón. Con la misma levedad de un náufrago. *Plural (Mexico)*, v. 22, no. 259 (Apr 93), pp. 8 – 13.

Gonzalez, Ray. Poems ("Walk," "Two Wolf Poems"). *The Americas Review*, v. 20, no. 3 – 4 (Fall – Winter 92), pp. 200 – 202.

González Acosta, Alejandro. Carta abierta a Dulce María Loynaz. *Plural (Mexico)*, v. 22, no. 262 (July 93), pp. 18 – 22.

González Aguayo, Leopoldo Augusto. La geopolítica de América Latina. *Relaciones Internacionales (Mexico)*, v. 14, Nueva época, no. 56 (Oct – Dec 92), pp. 97 – 102. Bibl.

— Notas sobre la geopolítica de las fronteras. *Relaciones Internacionales (Mexico)*, v. 14, Nueva época, no. 55 (July – Sept 92), pp. 23 – 30. Bibl.

González Amer, Edgardo. Sobre bolsas de escombros. *Cuadernos Hispanoamericanos*, no. 517 – 519 (July – Sept 93), pp. 503 – 505.

González Ascencio, Gerardo. Políticas públicas y hostigamiento sexual. *Nueva Sociedad*, no. 123 (Jan – Feb 93), pp. 104 – 113.

González Block, Miguel A. and Ana Luisa Liguori. El SIDA en los de abajo. *Nexos*, v. 16, no. 185 (May 93), pp. 15 – 20.

González Bolaños, Aimée. El arte narrativo de Lino Novás Calvo en *El negrero*. *Islas*, no. 98 (Jan – Apr 91), pp. 87 – 97.

González Cajiao, Fernando. El teatro precolombino siempre fue callejero. *Conjunto*, no. 92 (July – Dec 92), pp. 7 – 11. Il.

González Casasnovas, Ignacio and Guillermo Mira Delli-Zotti. Reflexiones y sugerencias a propósito de la minería colonial. *Historia Mexicana*, v. 42, no. 2 (Oct – Dec 92), pp. 309 – 332.

González Chávez, Gerardo. Monclova: algunos efectos del neoliberalismo. *Momento Económico*, no. 66 (Mar – Apr 93), pp. 18 – 22.

González Cruchaga, Carlos. La Compañía de Jesús y el futuro. *Mensaje*, v. 42, no. 420 (July 93), pp. 330 – 331.

González de Alba, Luis. 1968: la fiesta y la tragedia. *Nexos*, v. 16, no. 189 (Sept 93), pp. 23 – 31.

— La muerte del centro. *Nexos*, v. 16, no. 186 (June 93), pp. 19 – 20.

— El sueño y la vigilia. *Nexos*, v. 16, no. 181 (Jan 93), pp. 13 – 14.

González de Guebara, Ruby Cecilia. El mito y su influencia en la sociedad actual. *Revista Cultural Lotería*, v. 51, no. 388 (Mar – Apr 92), pp. 85 – 92.

González de León, Teodoro. Mario Pani. *Vuelta*, v. 17, no. 199 (June 93), pp. 58 – 59.

González de León, Ulalume. Una página de *El diario rojo*, año V. *Vuelta*, v. 17, no. 204 (Nov 93), p. 20.

González Dueñas, Daniel. Una voz en "off": *Cine: la gran seducción*. *La Palabra y el Hombre*, no. 81 (Jan – Mar 92), pp. 370 – 371.

González Echenique, Javier. Discurso de recepción de don René Millar Carvacho. *Boletín de la Academia Chilena de la Historia*, v. 58 – 59, no. 102 (1991 – 1992), pp. 229 – 233.

— Discurso de recepción de doña Isabel Cruz Ovalle de Amenábar. *Boletín de la Academia Chilena de la Historia*, v. 58 – 59, no. 102 (1991 – 1992), pp. 139 – 144.

González Echevarría, Roberto. Reflections on My Crystal Ball. *Latin American Literary Review*, v. 20, no. 40 (July – Dec 92), pp. 51 – 53.

González Encinar, José Juan et al. El proceso constituyente: enseñanzas a partir de cuatro casos recientes: España, Portugal, Brasil y Chile. *Ibero-Amerikanisches Archiv*, v. 18, no. 1 – 2 (1992), pp. 151 – 179. Tables.

González García, Juan Francisco. El desafío de la banca mexicana frente a la cuenca del Pacífico. *Comercio Exterior*, v. 43, no. 12 (Dec 93), pp. 1173 – 1180. Bibl, tables.

— Matanzas: su historia, 1868 – 1878. *Islas*, no. 97 (Sept – Dec 90), pp. 64 – 78. Bibl.

— Matanzas: su historia; los tiempos de tregua, 1878 – 1895. *Islas*, no. 98 (Jan – Apr 91), pp. 47 – 57. Bibl.

González Hernández, Laura and Rocío Amador Debernardi. Características de las familias y de los niños trabajadores de la calle. *Revista de Ciencias Sociales (Costa Rica)*, no. 59 (Mar 93), pp. 19 – 26. Bibl, tables, charts.

González Herrera, Carlos. La agricultura en el proyecto económico de Chihuahua durante el porfiriato. *Siglo XIX: Cuadernos*, v. 2, no. 5 (Feb 93), pp. 9 – 37. Bibl, tables, maps.

González Izquierdo, Jorge. Prioridades y opciones para la integración latinoamericana. *Integración Latinoamericana*, v. 18, no. 193 (Sept 93), pp. 13 – 19. Bibl.

González Lauck, Rebecca B. Algunas consideraciones sobre los monumentos 75 y 80 de La Venta, Tabasco. *Anales del Instituto de Investigaciones Estéticas*, v. 16, no. 62 (1991), pp. 163 – 174. Bibl, il.

González León, Adriano. Cántico de Jajó. *Plural (Mexico)*, v. 22, no. 262 (July 93), pp. 4 – 9.

González López, Waldo. Testimonio de Lionel Méndez D'Avila. *Conjunto*, no. 92 (July – Dec 92), pp. 98 – 99. Il.

González Martínez, Elda Evangelina. Los españoles en un país más allá del océano: Brasil; notas acerca de las etapas de la emigración. *Revista de Indias*, v. 52, no. 195 – 196 (May – Dec 92), pp. 515 – 527. Bibl, tables, charts.

González P., María Teresa and Rolando Mellafe Rojas. La Ley Orgánica de Instrucción Secundaria y Superior de 1879. *Cuadernos de Historia (Chile)*, no. 11 (Dec 91), pp. 63 – 69. Bibl.

González Padilla, María Enriqueta. La traducción de Shakespeare: comentario de una experiencia. *Plural (Mexico)*, v. 22, no. 259 (Apr 93), pp. 56 – 63. Bibl.

González Pedrero, Enrique. Santa Anna antes de Santa Anna (A chapter from the book *País de un sólo hombre: el México de Santa Anna*). *Vuelta*, v. 17, no. 198 (May 93), pp. 42 – 47. Bibl, tables.

González Pérez, Armando. Magia, mito y literatura en *La navaja de Olofé*. *Revista Interamericana de Bibliografía*, v. 42, no. 4 (1992), pp. 635 – 641. Bibl.

González Picado, Jézer and Vielka R. Delgado Aparicio. Introducción al estudio de *Huasipungo* y de *Los perros hambrientos*. *Revista Cultural Lotería*, v. 51, no. 392 (Nov – Dec 93), pp. 41 – 54. Bibl.

González Pizarro, José Antonio. Imagen e impresiones de América de los integrantes de la armada y de la Comisión de Naturalistas Españoles, 1862 – 1866. *Jahrbuch für Geschichte von Staat, Wirtschaft und Gesellschaft Lateinamerikas*, v. 29 (1992), pp. 279 – 307. Bibl.

González Quiroga, Miguel. La puerta de México: los comerciantes texanos y el noreste mexicano, 1850 – 1880. *Estudios Sociológicos*, v. 11, no. 31 (Jan – Apr 93), pp. 209 – 236. Bibl, tables, maps.

González Rodrigo, José. Manejo de recursos naturales renovables en una comunidad indígena náhuatl. *Estudios de Cultura Náhuatl*, v. 22 (1992), pp. 445 – 459. Bibl, maps.

González Rodrigo, José and Regina Leal. Manejo de resursos naturales y derecho consuetudinario. *Nueva Antropología*, v. 13, no. 44 (Aug 93), pp. 61 – 70. Bibl.

González Rodríguez, Adolfo Luis. II Congreso Internacional de Etnohistoria. *Anuario de Estudios Americanos*, v. 49, Suppl. 1 (1992), pp. 181 – 185.

González Rodríguez, Jaime. La cátedra de Escoto en México en el siglo XVIII. *Archivo Ibero-Americano*, v. 52, no. 205 – 208 (Jan – Dec 92), pp. 561 – 584. Bibl, tables.

González Rodríguez, Sergio. Lola Alvarez Bravo: la luz en el espejo. *Nexos*, v. 16, no. 190 (Oct 93), pp. 16 – 20.

González Rubí, Rafael. América Latina y las barreras no arancelarias de los gigantes económicos. *Comercio Exterior*, v. 43, no. 3 (Mar 93), pp. 248 – 253. Bibl.

— Panorama de la exportación de manufacturas de América Latina. *Comercio Exterior*, v. 43, no. 2 (Feb 93), pp. 141 – 146. Tables.

González Ruiz, José Enrique and Francisco Navarrete González. México: educación superior y nación hacia el siglo XXI. *Problemas del Desarrollo*, v. 24, no. 93 (Apr – June 93), pp. 175 – 194.

González-Souza, Luis F. Estados Unidos ante el nuevo milenio: consensos y grilletes bipartidistas. *Relaciones Internacionales (Mexico)*, v. 15, Nueva época, no. 57 (Jan – Mar 93), pp. 7 – 12.

González Stephan, Beatriz. No sólo para mujeres: el sexismo en los estudios literarios. *Escritura (Venezuela)*, v. 16, no. 31 – 32 (Jan – Dec 91), pp. 103 – 113.

González Vigil, Fernando. Crisis andina e integración. *Debate (Peru)*, v. 16, no. 72 (Mar – May 93), pp. 49 – 51. Il.

González Villarroel, Oscar. Derek Walcott, premio Nobel de literatura 1992. *Atenea (Chile)*, no. 465 – 466 (1992), pp. 357 – 359. Il.

Gordillo, Elba Esther. El SNTE ante la modernización de la educación básica. *El Cotidiano*, v. 8, no. 51 (Nov – Dec 92), pp. 12 – 16. Il.

Gordillo, Gustavo. Ayudando a la mano invisible: el compromiso democrático. *Nexos*, v. 16, no. 189 (Sept 93), pp. 41 – 43.

Gordon Rapoport, Sara. La política social y el Programa Nacional de Solidaridad. *Revista Mexicana de Sociología*, v. 55, no. 2 (Apr – June 93), pp. 351 – 366. Bibl, tables.

Gorenstein, Silvia. El complejo petroquímico Bahía Blanca: algunas reflexiones sobre sus implicancias especiales. *Desarrollo Económico (Argentina)*, v. 32, no. 128 (Jan – Mar 93), pp. 575 – 601. Bibl, tables, charts.

Gorlier, Juan Carlos. Democratización en América del Sur: una reflexión sobre el potencial de los movimientos sociales en Argentina y Brasil. *Revista Mexicana de Sociología*, v. 54, no. 4 (Oct – Dec 92), pp. 119 – 151. Bibl.

Gorodischer, Angélica. Borges y los judíos. *Confluencia*, v. 8, no. 1 (Fall 92), pp. 9 – 18.

— Quién es Shan Coctó. *Hispamérica*, v. 21, no. 63 (Dec 92), pp. 53 – 60.

Górski, Eugeniusz. Filosofía y sociedad en el pensamiento europeo oriental y latinoamericano (Translated by Jorge Radín Videla). *Cuadernos Americanos*, no. 41, Nueva época (Sept – Oct 93), pp. 76 – 92. Bibl.

Goslinga, Marian. Guyana. *Hemisphere*, v. 5, no. 2 (Winter – Spring 93), pp. 50 – 52.

— The US, Cuba, and Puerto Rico. *Hemisphere*, v. 5, no. 3 (Summer – Fall 93), pp. 54 – 56.

Gotlib, Nádia Battella. Las mujeres y "el otro": tres narradoras brasileñas. *Escritura (Venezuela)*, v. 16, no. 31 – 32 (Jan – Dec 91), pp. 123 – 136. Bibl.

Gouëset, Vincent. L'impact du "narcotrafic" à Médellin. *Cahiers des Amériques Latines*, no. 13 (1992), pp. 27 – 52. Bibl, tables.

Gouëset, Vincent and Fabio Zambrano Pantoja. Géopolitique du district spécial de Bogotá et du Haut-Sumapaz, 1900 – 1990. *Bulletin de l'Institut Français d'Etudes Andines*, v. 21, no. 3 (1992), pp. 1053 – 1071. Bibl, maps.

Gould, Jeffrey L. "¡Vana ilusión!": The Highlands Indians and the Myth of Nicaragua Mestiza, 1880 – 1925. *Hispanic American Historical Review*, v. 73, no. 3 (Aug 93), pp. 393 – 429. Bibl, maps.

Gouvêa, Fernando da Cruz. Notas sobre a influência dos senhores rurais na vida política brasileira. *Revista do Instituto Histórico e Geográfico Brasileiro*, no. 372 (July – Sept 91), pp. 815 – 827.

Gouvea Neto, Raul de and Geraldo M. Vasconcellos. La diversificación de las exportaciones y la eficiencia de la cartera de exportación: estudio comparativo de los países del sureste de Asia y de la América Latina (Translated by Carlos Villegas). *El Trimestre Económico*, v. 60, no. 237 (Jan – Mar 93), pp. 29 – 52. Bibl, tables, charts.

Goytisolo, Juan. La cuarentena (A chapter from the novel of the same title). *Vuelta*, v. 17, no. 197 (Apr 93), pp. 13 – 14.

— Severo Sarduy: "in memoriam." *Vuelta*, v. 17, no. 201 (Aug 93), pp. 24 – 25.

— Si no existiera Sarduy. *Vuelta*, v. 17, no. 201 (Aug 93), p. 25.

Grabendorff, Wolf. La integración europea: consequencias para América Latina. *Nueva Sociedad*, no. 126 (July – Aug 93), pp. 122 – 143. Bibl.

Grabois, José and Mauro José da Silva. O breja de Natuba: estudo da organização de um espaço periférico. *Revista Brasileira de Geografia*, v. 53, no. 2 (Apr – June 91), pp. 33 – 62. Bibl, il, tables, maps.

Grabois, José et al. A organização do espaço no baixo vale do Taperoá: uma ocupação extensiva em mudança. *Revista Brasileira de Geografia*, v. 53, no. 4 (Oct – Dec 91), pp. 81 – 114. Bibl, il, tables, maps.

Graham, Crystal. Microform Cataloging: Current Issues and Selected Bibliography. *SALALM Papers*, v. 36 (1991), pp. 393 – 407.

Graizbord, Boris. Estructura y posibilidades de crecimiento de 22 ciudades industriales mexicanas. *Comercio Exterior*, v. 43, no. 2 (Feb 93), pp. 149 – 158. Bibl, tables.

— Geografías electorales: cambio y participación en el voto de diputados federales de 1988 y 1991. *Estudios Sociológicos*, v. 11, no. 32 (May – Aug 93), pp. 497 – 514. Bibl, tables, maps.

Grajales Porras, Agustín and José Luis Aranda Romero. Perfil sociodemográfico de Tehuacán durante el virreinato. *Estudios Demográficos y Urbanos*, v. 7, no. 1 (Jan – Apr 92), pp. 53 – 76. Bibl, tables, maps, charts.

Gramuglio, María Teresa. Literatura y nacionalismo: Leopoldo Lugones y la construcción de imágenes de escritor. *Hispamérica*, v. 22, no. 64 – 65 (Apr – Aug 93), pp. 5 – 22. Bibl.

Granda, Germán de. Estudios lingüísticos sobre el español paraguayo. *Estudios Paraguayos*, v. 17, no. 1 – 2 (1989 – 1993), pp. 169 – 319. Bibl.

Grande, Félix. Con octubre en los hombros. *Cuadernos Hispanoamericanos*, no. 517 – 519 (July – Sept 93), pp. 562 – 568.

Grande, Guadalupe. La claridad de la vida antes de la niebla. *Cuadernos Hispanoamericanos*, no. 516 (June 93), pp. 61 – 68.

Grandi, Rodolfo and Marcelo Resende. Inflação e variabilidade dos preços relativos no Brasil: a questão da causalidade. *Revista Brasileira de Economia*, v. 46, no. 4 (Oct – Dec 92), pp. 595 – 604. Bibl, tables.

Grandis, Rita de. La cita como estrategia narrativa en *Respiración artificial*. *Revista Canadiense de Estudios Hispánicos*, v. 17, no. 2 (Winter 93), pp. 259 – 269. Bibl.

— The First Colonial Encounter in *El entenado* by Juan José Saer: Paratextuality and History in Postmodern Fiction. *Latin American Literary Review*, v. 21, no. 41 (Jan – June 93), pp. 30 – 38. Bibl.

— La problemática del conocimiento histórico en *Historia de Mayta* de M. Vargas Llosa. *Revista de Crítica Literaria Latinoamericana*, v. 19, no. 38 (July – Dec 93), pp. 375 – 382. Bibl.

Granillo Vázquez, Lilia. Pensamiento indígena. *Fem*, v. 17, no. 125 (July 93), pp. 18 – 20.

Granville, Jean-Jacques de. Life Forms and Growth Strategies of Guianan Palms as Related to Their Ecology. *Bulletin de l'Institut Français d'Etudes Andines*, v. 21, no. 2 (1992), pp. 533 – 548. Bibl, il, tables.

Grass, Günter Wilhelm. Compasión hacia Cuba (Translated by Julio Colón Gómez). *Nexos*, v. 16, no. 188 (Aug 93), pp. 10 – 13.

Graulich, Michel. Las brujas de las peregrinaciones aztecas. *Estudios de Cultura Náhuatl*, v. 22 (1992), pp. 87 – 98. Bibl.

Gravina Telechea, María. Filosofía. *Casa de las Américas*, no. 191 (Apr – June 93), pp. 83 – 84.

Grebe López, Horst. La industrialización latinoamericana: ¿Sólo un recuento de frustraciones? *Nueva Sociedad*, no. 125 (May – June 93), pp. 47 – 57. Bibl.

Green, James N. and Enrique Asís. Gays and Lesbians: The Closet Door Swings Open. *Report on the Americas*, v. 26, no. 4 (Feb 93), pp. 4 – 7. Il.

Green, Raúl H. Economía industrial alimentaria: reflexiones en torno de América Latina. *Realidad Económica*, no. 119 (Oct – Nov 93), pp. 15 – 33.

Greenfield, Gerald Michael. "Sertão" and "Sertanejo": An Interpretive Context for Canudos. *Luso-Brazilian Review*, v. 30, no. 2 (Winter 93), pp. 35 – 46. Bibl.

Gregori, Maria Filomena. As desventuras do vitimismo (Accompanied by an English translation). *Estudos Feministas*, v. 1, no. 1 (1993), pp. 143 – 149. Bibl.

Gregorio, José de. El crecimiento económico en la América Latina. *El Trimestre Económico*, v. 59, Special issue (Dec 92), pp. 75 – 107. Bibl, tables, charts.

Griffith-Jones, Stephany et al. El retorno de capital a América Latina. *Comercio Exterior*, v. 43, no. 1 (Jan 93), pp. 37 – 50. Bibl, tables.

Grinberg, Samuel. Cuatro grabadores judíos en la confederación argentina. *Todo Es Historia,* v. 27, no. 314 (Sept 93), pp. 50 – 53. Il.

Grindle, Merilee Serrill. Agrarian Class Structures and State Policies: Past, Present, and Future (Review article). *Latin American Research Review,* v. 28, no. 1 (1993), pp. 174 – 187.

Grinspun, Ricardo and Maxwell A. Cameron. Mexico: The Wages of Trade. *Report on the Americas,* v. 26, no. 4 (Feb 93), pp. 32 – 37 +. Bibl, il.

Grizzard, Mary Faith Mitchell. The "Retablos Mayores" of the Cantuña Chapel of San Francisco in Quito, Ecuador. *Anales del Instituto de Investigaciones Estéticas,* v. 16, no. 62 (1991), pp. 103 – 110. Bibl.

Gronk

See

Nicandro, Glugio Gronk

Gropp, Rose-Maria. ¡Contra el culto!: Frida Kahlo en Francfort (Translated by Gabriela Fonseca). *Humboldt,* no. 109 (1993), pp. 66 – 69. Il.

Gros, Christian. Attention!: un indien peut en cacher un autre; droits indigènes et nouvelle constitution en Colombie. *Caravelle,* no. 59 (1992), pp. 139 – 160. Bibl.

— Fondamentalisme protestant et populations indiennes: quelques hypothèses. *Cahiers des Amériques Latines,* no. 13 (1992), pp. 119 – 134.

— El futuro de la reforma agraria en Brasil. *Revista Mexicana de Sociología,* v. 54, no. 1 (Jan – Mar 92), pp. 59 – 73. Tables.

Gross, Liza. Humble Art of Life. *Américas,* v. 45, no. 1 (Jan – Feb 93), pp. 14 – 23. Il.

— Pupusas and Potpourri (Includes recipes). *Américas,* v. 45, no. 5 (Sept – Oct 93), p. 49. Il.

Gross Fuentes, Patricio. Bases para una futura planificación de la ciudad chilena. *EURE,* v. 19, no. 57 (July 93), pp. 117 – 123.

Grossi, Miriam Pillar. De Angela Diniz a Daniela Perez: a trajetória da impunidade. *Estudos Feministas,* v. 1, no. 1 (1993), pp. 166 – 168.

Grossman, Lawrence S. Pesticides, People, and the Environment in St. Vincent. *Caribbean Geography,* v. 3, no. 3 (Mar 92), pp. 175 – 186. Bibl, tables, maps.

Grosso, Juan Carlos. El comercio interregional entre Puebla y Veracruz: de la etapa borbónica al México independiente. *La Palabra y el Hombre,* no. 83 (July – Sept 92), pp. 59 – 91. Bibl, tables, charts.

Grün, Roberto. Sindicalismo e anti-sindicalismo e a gênese das novas classes médias brasileiras. *Dados,* v. 35, no. 3 (1992), pp. 435 – 471. Bibl.

Grützmacher, Thomas. Salve-se quem souber: lembrando Smetak. *Vozes,* v. 87, no. 1 (Jan – Feb 93), pp. 77 – 83. Il.

Grunwald, Joseph. El escabroso camino hacia la integración económica hemisférica: análisis regional de antecedentes orientado al futuro (Chapter from the book *The Enterprise for the Americas Initiative* translated by Carlos Villegas). *El Trimestre Económico,* v. 60, no. 239 (July – Sept 93), pp. 713 – 732. Bibl, tables.

Guadarrama González, Pablo M. Las alternativas sociales en América Latina y la filosofía de la liberación. *Islas,* no. 96 (May – Aug 90), pp. 89 – 102. Bibl.

— Balance y perspectivas del marxismo y el antimarxismo en América Latina. *Islas,* no. 98 (Jan – Apr 91), pp. 188 – 200. Bibl.

— La identidad conflictiva de la cultura. *Islas,* no. 97 (Sept – Dec 90), pp. 7 – 9.

— Urdimbres del pensamiento de Leopoldo Zea frente a la marginación y la barbarie. *Cuadernos Americanos,* no. 37, Nueva época (Jan – Feb 93), pp. 51 – 64. Bibl.

Guadarrama González, Pablo M. and Lidia Cano. Filosofía de la liberación en Colombia. *Islas,* no. 99 (May – Aug 91), pp. 51 – 74. Bibl.

Guadarrama González, Pablo M. et al. El humanismo en la filosofía latinoamericana de la liberación. *Islas,* no. 99 (May – Aug 91), pp. 173 – 199. Bibl.

Guajardo Soto, Guillermo. Tecnología y trabajo en Chile, 1850 – 1930. *Cuadernos Americanos,* no. 38, Nueva época (Mar – Apr 93), pp. 155 – 179. Bibl, tables.

Guanche Pérez, Jesús. Proyección contemporánea de la artesanía popular en Cuba: su investigación y perspectivas. *Folklore Americano,* no. 52 (July – Dec 91), pp. 93 – 99. Bibl.

Guanche Pérez, Jesús and Gertrudis Campos Mitjans. La antropología cultural en Cuba durante el presente siglo. *Interciencia,* v. 18, no. 4 (July – Aug 93), pp. 176 – 183. Bibl.

Guarda Geywitz, Gabriel. Las misiones de la Compañía de Jesús en el período español. *Mensaje,* v. 42, no. 420 (July 93), pp. 215 – 219. Il, facs.

— Obras hidráulicas en el reino de Chile. *Boletín de la Academia Chilena de la Historia,* v. 58 – 59, no. 102 (1991 – 1992), pp. 269 – 289. Bibl.

Guardado de del Cid, Helen. La carrera de bibliotecología en El Salvador: su nueva orientación curricular. *SALALM Papers,* v. 36 (1991), pp. 441 – 454. Tables.

Guedea, Virginia. La sociedad secreta de los Guadalupes: una nueva forma de organización política. *Siglo XIX: Revista,* no. 11, 2a época (Jan – June 92), pp. 28 – 45. Bibl.

Güenaga de Silva, Rosario and Adriana C. Rodríguez Pérsico. El interés de la diplomacia española por los problemas argentino – chilenos en el seno de Ultima Esperanza. *Revista de Historia de América,* no. 112 (July – Dec 91), pp. 85 – 103. Bibl.

Guerra, Francisco. A problemática floresta amazônica. *Revista Brasileira de Geografia,* v. 53, no. 3 (July – Sept 91), pp. 125 – 132.

Guerra, François-Xavier and Danièle Demelas. Un processus révolutionnaire méconnu: l'adoption des formes representatives modernes en Espagne et en Amérique Latine, 1808 – 1810. *Caravelle,* no. 60 (1993), pp. 5 – 57. Bibl.

Guerra, Javier and David Robinson. The 6 Million Ton Question. *Business Mexico,* v. 3, no. 9 (Sept 93), pp. 36 – 38. Charts.

Guerra, Silvia. Poema. *Hispamérica,* v. 22, no. 64 – 65 (Apr – Aug 93), p. 142.

Guerra, Sinclair Mallet-Guy et al. Perspectivas y estrategias para el gas natural en la América Latina: Brasil y Venezuela. *Interciencia,* v. 18, no. 1 (Jan – Feb 93), pp. 24 – 28. Bibl, tables, maps.

Guerra Borges, Alfredo. Integración centroamericana en los noventa: de la crisis a las perspectivas. *Revista Mexicana de Sociología,* v. 54, no. 3 (July – Sept 92), pp. 115 – 127.

— Nuevo contexto mundial para América Latina. *Integración Latinoamericana,* v. 18, no. 192 (Aug 93), pp. 3 – 10. Bibl.

— La reestructuración del Mercado Común Centroamericano: notas para una evaluación crítica. *Integración Latinoamericana,* v. 18, no. 195 (Nov 93), pp. 3 – 9. Bibl.

Guerra-Cunningham, Lucía. Estrategias discursivas en la narrativa de la mujer latinoamericana. *Escritura (Venezuela),* v. 16, no. 31 – 32 (Jan – Dec 91), pp. 115 – 122.

— La marginalidad subversiva del deseo en *La última niebla* de María Luisa Bombal. *Hispamérica,* v. 21, no. 62 (Aug 92), pp. 53 – 63.

Guerra E., Guillermo A. América Latina: la empresa agropecuaria ante la modernización. *Comercio Exterior,* v. 43, no. 4 (Apr 93), pp. 344 – 352. Bibl, tables, charts.

Guerra García, Francisco. Crisis nacional y crisis de la izquierda. *Debate (Peru),* v. 16, no. 75 (Dec 93 – Jan 94), pp. 23 – 24. Il.

Guerrero, María Angustias. Costureras y producción mercantil en la sociedad dominicana: los orígenes. *Anuario de Estudios Americanos,* v. 49 (1992), pp. 601 – 614. Bibl, tables.

Guerrero del Río, Eduardo. Teatro chileno contemporáneo: una visión panorámica de las dos últimas décadas. *Aisthesis,* no. 24 (1991), pp. 55 – 63. Bibl.

— El teatro chileno contemporáneo: una visión panorámica de las dos últimas décadas. *Conjunto,* no. 89 (Oct – Dec 91), pp. 33 – 39. Il.

Guerrero Guerrero, Raúl. Cantos populares mexicanos de Navidad en el estado de Hidalgo. *Revista Musical de Venezuela,* no. 28 (May – Dec 89), pp. 148 – 165. Facs.

Guerrero Miranda, Juan Vicente et al. Entierros secundarios y restos orgánicos de ca. 500 a.c. preservados en una área de inundación marina, golfo de Nicoya, Costa Rica. *Vínculos,* v. 17, no. 1 – 2 (1991), pp. 17 – 51. Bibl, il, tables, maps.

Guerrero Rincón, Amado A. La provincia de Muzo en 1754: informe presentado al rey. *Anuario Colombiano de Historia Social y de la Cultura,* no. 20 (1992), pp. 133 – 145.

Guerrero Yoacham, Cristián. Carlos Ruiz-Tagle Gandarillas (1932 – 1991). *Cuadernos de Historia (Chile),* no. 11 (Dec 91), pp. 13 – 25. Il.

Guevara, Nancy. Fábricas de bebés: ¿Fantasía o profecía? (Translated by Victoria Zamudio Jasso). *Fem,* v. 17, no. 121 (Mar 93), pp. 4 – 8. Bibl.

Guevara, Roberto. Manuel Hernández: el espacio otro en la pintura. *Art Nexus,* no. 10 (Sept – Dec 93), pp. 92 – 95. Il.

Guevara Niebla, Gilberto. Volver al '68 (Interview transcribed and edited by Luis Miguel Aguilar and Rafael Pérez Gay). *Nexos,* v. 16, no. 190 (Oct 93), pp. 31 – 43.

Guevara Reyes, Olimpia. Literatura chicana: el sentido de una respuesta histórica. *Plural (Mexico),* v. 22, no. 256 (Jan 93), pp. 46 – 49. Bibl.

Guibovich Pérez, Pedro. La cultura libresca de un converso procesado por la inquisición de Lima. *Historia y Cultura (Peru),* no. 20 (1990), pp. 133 – 160 +. Bibl.

Guichón, Víctor. Poemas. *Hispamérica,* v. 22, no. 64 – 65 (Apr – Aug 93), p. 143.

Guido, Margarita. Poems ("Cuando los perros no ladraron," "Poema 17"). *The Americas Review,* v. 20, no. 2 (Summer 92), pp. 69 – 71.

Guijosa, Marcela. Querido diario . . . . *Fem,* v. 17, no. 119 – 130 (Jan – Dec 93), All issues.

Guilbault, Jocelyne. Sociopolitical, Cultural, and Economic Development through Music: Zouk in the French Antilles. *Canadian Journal of Latin American and Caribbean Studies,* v. 17, no. 34 (1992), pp. 27 – 40. Bibl.

Guillén, Ann Cyphers. Women, Rituals, and Social Dynamics at Ancient Chalcatzingo. *Latin American Antiquity,* v. 4, no. 3 (Sept 93), pp. 209 – 224. Bibl, il.

Guillén López, Tonatiuh. Relatoría de la mesa redonda "La Estadística Electoral, el Nuevo Patrón y la Dinámica Demográfica en Mexico." *Estudios Demográficos y Urbanos,* v. 6, no. 3 (Sept – Dec 91), pp. 745 – 755.

Guillén López, Tonatiuh and Gerardo M. Ordóñez B. La marginalidad social en la frontera norte: discrepancias empíricas al concepto de la marginalidad. *Frontera Norte,* v. 4, no. 8 (July – Dec 92), pp. 149 – 163. Tables.

Guillén Romo, Arturo. La desaceleración de la economía mexicana: causas y perspectivas; las dificultades de la actual estrategia del desarrollo. *Problemas del Desarrollo,* v. 24, no. 94 (July – Sept 93), pp. 15 – 19.

Guimarães, Antônio Sérgio Alfredo. Operários e mobilidade social na Bahia: análise de uma trajetória individual. *Revista Brasileira de Ciências Sociais,* v. 8, no. 22 (June 93), pp. 81 – 97. Bibl, tables.

Guimarães, Antônio Sérgio Alfredo and Nadya Araújo Castro. Trabalhadores afluentes, indústrias recentes: revisitando a tese da aristocracia operária. *Dados,* v. 35, no. 2 (1992), pp. 173 – 191. Bibl.

Guimarães, Eduardo Augusto de Almeida. Terra de Vera Cruz, Brasil. *Vozes,* v. 86, no. 4 (July – Aug 92), pp. 16 – 21.

Guimarães, Jorge A. Perspectivas para as instituições federais de ensino superior (Comment on the article "O sistema federal de ensino superior: problemas e alternativas" by Eunice Ribeiro Durham). *Revista Brasileira de Ciências Sociais,* v. 8, no. 23 (Oct 93), pp. 42 – 47. Bibl.

Guimarães, Manoel Luiz Lima Salgado. A historiografia brasileira do século XX: os anos '30. *Revista do Instituto Histórico e Geográfico Brasileiro,* no. 370 (Jan – Mar 91), pp. 275 – 288.

Guimarães, Paulo César Vaz. Instrumentos econômicos para gerenciamento ambiental: a cobrança pelo uso da água no estado de São Paulo. *RAE; Revista de Administração de Empresas,* v. 33, no. 5 (Sept – Oct 93), pp. 88 – 97.

Guimarães, Paulo César Vaz and Elio Jardanovski. O desafio da eqüidade no setor saúde. *RAE; Revista de Administração de Empresas,* v. 33, no. 3 (May – June 93), pp. 38 – 51.

Guimarães, Roberto Pereira. Deuda externa y desarrollo sustentable en América Latina: una perspectiva sociopolítica. *Revista Interamericana de Planificación,* v. 26, no. 101 – 102 (Jan – June 93), pp. 7 – 42. Bibl.

— Development Pattern and Environment in Brazil. *CEPAL Review,* no. 47 (Aug 92), pp. 47 – 62. Bibl.

Guitarte, Guillermo L. Sobre la generalidad del yeísmo porteño en el siglo XIX. *Nueva Revista de Filología Hispánica,* v. 40, no. 2 (July – Dec 92), pp. 547 – 574. Bibl.

Gullón Abao, Alberto José. Las reducciones del este de la provincia del Tucumán en la segunda mitad del siglo XVIII bajo la administración franciscana. *Archivo Ibero-Americano,* v. 52, no. 205 – 208 (Jan – Dec 92), pp. 255 – 276. Bibl, tables, maps, charts.

Gunder Frank, André

See

Frank, André Gunder

Gussinyer i Alfonso, Jordi. Notas para el concepto de espacio en la arquitectura precolombina de Mesoamérica. *Boletín Americanista,* v. 33, no. 42 – 43 (1992 – 1993), pp. 183 – 230. Bibl, il.

Gutiérrez, Héctor and Dieter Wunder. Determinantes del precio de mercado de los terrenos en el área urbana de Santiago: comentario (on the article by Figueroa and Lever in *Cuadernos de Economía,* v. 29, no. 86). *Cuadernos de Economía (Chile),* v. 30, no. 89 (Apr 93), pp. 131 – 138. Bibl, tables.

Gutiérrez, José Luis. Aguascalientes: A Model of Development. *Business Mexico,* v. 3, no. 5 (May 93), pp. 26 – 28. Tables.

Gutiérrez, Natalia. Cambio de foco (Accompanied by an English translation). *Art Nexus,* no. 9 (June – Aug 93), pp. 96 – 99. Il.

— *El hilo de Ariadna:* laberinto de oscuridad (Accompanied by an English translation). *Art Nexus,* no. 8 (Apr – June 93), pp. 102 – 104. Il.

Gutiérrez de Manchón, María Josefina and María Estela Furlani de Civit. Dinámica agraria en un oasis de especialización vitícola. *Revista Geográfica (Mexico),* no. 115 (Jan – June 92), pp. 85 – 137. Bibl, tables, maps.

Gutiérrez Escudero, Antonio. X Coloquio de Historia Canaria – Americana. *Anuario de Estudios Americanos,* v. 49, Suppl. 2 (1992), pp. 217 – 221.

Gutiérrez Estupiñán, Raquel. Sobre la crítica literaria femenina/feminista en Hispanoamérica. *Fem,* v. 17, no. 129 (Nov 93), pp. 42 – 46. Bibl.

Gutiérrez Girardot, Rafael. César Vallejo y Walter Benjamin. *Cuadernos Hispanoamericanos,* no. 520 (Oct 93), pp. 55 – 72. Bibl, il.

— La tierra prometida: la trilogía novelística de Gerardo Mario Goloboff. *Hispamérica,* v. 21, no. 62 (Aug 92), pp. 111 – 126.

Gutiérrez Lara, Abelardo Aníbal and Luis Rodríguez Medellín. La economía mexicana en la búsqueda de su modernización. *El Cotidiano,* v. 9, no. 55 (June 93), pp. 103 – 110. Tables, charts.

Gutiérrez M., Alejandro and Raúl León Palencia P. Lineamientos de política científica y tecnológica para el estado Mérida: área agrícola agroalimentaria; ideas para la discusión. *Derecho y Reforma Agraria,* no. 23 (1992), pp. 141 – 160. Bibl.

Gutiérrez Mouat, Ricardo. Travesía y regresos de Alfredo Bryce: *La última mudanza de Felipe Carrillo. Hispamérica,* v. 21, no. 63 (Dec 92), pp. 73 – 79.

— Vargas Llosa's Poetics of the Novel and Camus' *Rebel. World Literature Today,* v. 67, no. 2 (Spring 93), pp. 283 – 290. Bibl, il.

Gutiérrez Nájera, Manuel. Para el álbum de Amalia Paz. *Vuelta,* v. 17, no. 201 (Aug 93), p. 12.

Gutiérrez Revuelta, Pedro. Fernando Villalón, el amigo desconocido de Pablo Neruda. *Cuadernos Hispanoamericanos,* no. 514 – 515 (Apr – May 93), pp. 307 – 311.

Gutiérrez Rodríguez, Javier and Miguel Angel Romero Miranda. Síndrome de fin de sexenio. *El Cotidiano,* v. 10, no. 58 (Oct – Nov 93), pp. 8 – 21. Il, tables.

Gutiérrez Romero, Elizabeth. El dilema del acero mexicano: apertura o proteccionismo. *Momento Económico,* no. 67 (May – June 93), pp. 15 – 18. Bibl.

Gutiérrez Vega, Hugo. Noche en Sinaia. *Nexos,* v. 16, no. 191 (Nov 93), p. 15.

— Pensando en Musil. *Cuadernos Hispanoamericanos,* no. 511 (Jan 93), pp. 71 – 76.

Gutman, Pablo. La Habana y Seul: ejemplos de metropolización. *EURE,* v. 19, no. 57 (July 93), pp. 103 – 115. Bibl, tables.

Gutmann, Matthew C. Rejoinder (to James C. Scott's commentaries in "Reply" on Gutmann's original article entitled "Rituals of Resistance"). *Latin American Perspectives,* v. 20, no. 2 (Spring 93), pp. 95 – 96.

— Rituals of Resistance: A Critique of the Theory of Everyday Forms of Resistance. *Latin American Perspectives,* v. 20, no. 2 (Spring 93), pp. 74 – 92. Bibl.

Gutmann, Myron P. et al. Matrimonio y migración en la frontera: patrones de nupcialidad en Texas, 1850 – 1910. *Historia Mexicana,* v. 42, no. 1 (July – Sept 92), pp. 45 – 76. Bibl, tables, charts.

Guttentag Tichauer, Werner. El arte pictórico en la bibliografía boliviana. *SALALM Papers,* v. 34 (1989), pp. 261 – 268. Bibl.

Guy, Donna Jane. "Oro Blanco": Cotton, Technology, and Family Labor in Nineteenth-Century Argentina. *The Americas,* v. 49, no. 4 (Apr 93), pp. 457 – 478. Bibl.

Guzik, Alberto. Un ejercicio de la memoria: dramaturgia de los '80. *Conjunto,* no. 93 (Jan – June 93), pp. 8 – 12. Il.

Guzmán, Jorge. César Vallejo: "El acento me pende del zapato." *Inti,* no. 36 (Fall 92), pp. 45 – 50.

Guzmán, Patricia. Ese viejo y muerto amor a la muerte (Introduced by María Auxiliadora Alvarez. Article entitled "Voces o seres cercanos"). *Inti,* no. 37 – 38 (Spring – Fall 93), pp. 70 – 72.

— El lugar como absoluto: Vicente Gerbasi, Ramón Palomares y Luis Alberto Crespo. *Inti,* no. 37 – 38 (Spring – Fall 93), pp. 107 – 115. Bibl.

Guzmán A., Eugenio. Reflexiones sobre el sistema binomial. *Estudios Públicos (Chile),* no. 51 (Winter 93), pp. 303 – 324. Bibl, charts.

Guzmán Betancourt, Ignacio. La lengua: ¿Compañera del imperio?; destino de un "presagio" nebrisense en la Nueva España. *Cuadernos Americanos,* no. 37, Nueva época (Jan – Feb 93), pp. 148 – 164. Bibl.

— Primeros empleos de la palabra "lingüística" en México. *Plural (Mexico),* v. 22, no. 257 (Feb 93), pp. 52 – 57.

Guzmán Brito, Alejandro. Don Alamiro de Avila Martel. *Boletín de la Academia Chilena de la Historia,* v. 58 – 59, no. 102 (1991 – 1992), pp. 25 – 32.

Guzmán Chávez, Alenka and Jaime Aboites A. Desempeño del sector manufacturero y relaciones laborales: la experiencia reciente de México. *El Cotidiano,* v. 10, no. 58 (Oct – Nov 93), pp. 103 – 111. Il, tables, charts.

— La industria textil mexicana y el Tratado de Libre Comercio. *El Cotidiano,* v. 8, no. 51 (Nov – Dec 92), pp. 102 – 109. Bibl, tables.

Guzmán Pineda, Jesús Ignacio. Industria automotriz y medio ambiente. *El Cotidiano,* v. 8, no. 52 (Jan – Feb 93), pp. 70 – 75. Il.

Gwynne, Robert N. Non-Traditional Export Growth and Economic Development: The Chilean Forestry Sector since 1974. *Bulletin of Latin American Research,* v. 12, no. 2 (May 93), pp. 147 – 169. Bibl, maps, charts.

Gyarmati, Gabriel. Notas para una estrategia de participación, II. *Estudios Sociales (Chile),* no. 78 (Oct – Dec 93), pp. 145 – 158. Charts.

Haagen, Victor. The Abaco Cays: Anchors of Tradition. *Américas,* v. 45, no. 1 (Jan – Feb 93), pp. 36 – 43. Il, maps.

Haase, Amine. La magia colorista de un continente: la mayor muestra de arte latinoamericana en el siglo XX. *Humboldt,* no. 109 (1993), pp. 60 – 65. Il.

Haber, Alicia. Carlos Capelán: una formulación antropológica (Accompanied by an English translation). *Art Nexus,* no. 7 (Jan – Mar 93), pp. 92 – 96. Bibl, il.

Haber, Stephen H. La industrialización de México: historiografía y análisis (Translated by Laura Elena Pulido Varela). *Historia Mexicana,* v. 42, no. 3 (Jan – Mar 93), pp. 649 – 688.

Hachette, Dominique. Estrategias de globalización del comercio. *Estudios Públicos (Chile),* no. 51 (Winter 93), pp. 45 – 85. Bibl, tables, charts.

Hadzelek, Aleksandra. Imagen de América en la poesía de la generación del '27. *Cuadernos Hispanoamericanos,* no. 514 – 515 (Apr – May 93), pp. 155 – 183. Il.

Haensch, Günther. La lexicografía del español de América en el umbral del siglo XXI. *Signo,* no. 36 – 37, Nueva época (May – Dec 92), pp. 331 – 360. Bibl.

Hagan, Jacqueline Maria and Susan Gonzalez Baker. Implementing the U.S. Legalization Program: The Influence of Immigrant Communities and Local Agencies on Immigration Policy Reform. *International Migration Review,* v. 27, no. 3 (Fall 93), pp. 513 – 536. Bibl.

Hahn, Oscar Arturo. Huidobro, un niño de cien años. *Atenea (Chile),* no. 467 (1993), pp. 67 – 74. Il.

— Vicente Huidobro o las metamorfosis del ruiseñor. *Revista Chilena de Literatura,* no. 40 (Nov 92), pp. 97 – 103.

Haidar de Maríñez, Julieta. La música como cultura y como poesía: Juan Luis Guerra y el Grupo 4:40. *Homines,* v. 15 – 16, no. 2 – 1 (Oct 91 – Dec 92), pp. 316 – 326. Bibl.

Hakim, Peter. La empresa para la Iniciativa de las Américas. *Relaciones Internacionales (Mexico),* v. 15, Nueva época, no. 57 (Jan – Mar 93), pp. 31 – 35.

Halperín, Marcelo. Discriminación y no discriminación en los esquemas de integración económica: el caso de MERCOSUR. *Integración Latinoamericana,* v. 18, no. 195 (Nov 93), pp. 23 – 29.

— Lealtad competitiva y dilemas de la integración: el caso del MERCOSUR. *Integración Latinoamericana,* v. 17, no. 184 (Nov 92), pp. 36 – 43.

Halperin, Maurice. Return to Havana: Portrait of a Loyalist. *Cuban Studies/Estudios Cubanos,* v. 23 (1993), pp. 187 – 193.

Halperín Donghi, Tulio. Hispanoamérica en el espejo: reflexiones hispanoamericanas sobre Hispanoamérica, de Simón Bolívar a Hernando de Soto. *Historia Mexicana,* v. 42, no. 3 (Jan – Mar 93), pp. 745 – 787. Bibl.

Ham, Sam H. and Richard A. Meganck. The Transferability of U.S. Environmental Education Programs in Rural Central America: A Case Study from Honduras. *La Educación (USA),* v. 37, no. 115 (1993), pp. 289 – 301. Bibl, tables.

Ham-Chande, Roberto. México: país en proceso de envejecimiento. *Comercio Exterior,* v. 43, no. 7 (July 93), pp. 688 – 696. Bibl, tables.

Hamed Franco, Alejandro. La cultura árabe en el Paraguay. *Plural (Mexico),* v. 22, no. 264 (Sept 93), pp. 115 – 117.

Hamel, Rainer Enrique. Derechos lingüísticos. *Nueva Antropología,* v. 13, no. 44 (Aug 93), p. 71 +.

Hamel, Rainer Enrique and Norbert Francis. La redacción en dos lenguas: escritura y narrativa en tres escuelas bilingües del valle del Mezquital. *Revista Latinoamericana de Estudios Educativos,* v. 22, no. 4 (Oct – Dec 92), pp. 11 – 35. Bibl, tables.

Hamer, Thurston R. The Hunt for Local Talent. *Business Mexico,* v. 3, no. 6 (June 93), pp. 4 – 6.

Hamm, Lyta. Archipelago Lessons: AIDS in the Islands; A Comparative Study of Cuba, Haiti, and Hawaii. *Interciencia,* v. 18, no. 4 (July – Aug 93), pp. 184 – 189. Bibl, tables.

Hampe Martínez, Teodoro. Apuntes documentales sobre inmigrantes europeos y norteamericanos en Lima, siglo XIX. *Revista de Indias,* v. 53, no. 198 (May – Aug 93), pp. 459 – 491. Bibl.

— The Diffusion of Books and Ideas in Colonial Peru: A Study of Private Libraries in the Sixteenth and Seventeenth Centuries. *Hispanic American Historical Review,* v. 73, no. 2 (May 93), pp. 211 – 233. Bibl, tables.

— Los funcionarios de la monarquía española en América: notas para una caracterización política, económica y social. *Revista Interamericana de Bibliografía,* v. 42, no. 3 (1992), pp. 431 – 452. Bibl.

— Hacia una nueva periodificación de la historia del Perú colonial: factores económicos, políticos y sociales. *Jahrbuch für Geschichte von Staat, Wirtschaft und Gesellschaft Lateinamerikas,* v. 29 (1992), pp. 47 – 74. Bibl.

— La recepción del Nuevo Mundo: temas y personajes indianos ante la corte imperial de los Habsburgo, 1530 – 1670. *Revista de Historia de América,* no. 113 (Jan – June 92), pp. 139 – 160. Bibl.

— VII Simposio Hispano – Austriaco "España, Austria e Iberoamérica, 1492 – 1992." *Anuario de Estudios Americanos,* v. 49, Suppl. 1 (1992), pp. 209 – 213.

Handelsman, Michael Howard. Ubicando la literatura afroecuatoriana en el contexto nacional: ¿Ilusión o realidad? *Afro-Hispanic Review,* v. 12, no. 1 (Spring 93), pp. 42 – 47. Bibl.

Hanisch Espíndola, Walter. Los jesuitas en La Serena, 1672 – 1767. *Boletín de la Academia Chilena de la Historia,* v. 58 – 59, no. 102 (1991 – 1992), pp. 291 – 328. Bibl, tables.

Hank González, Carlos. El Procampo: estrategia de apoyos al productor del agro. *Comercio Exterior,* v. 43, no. 10 (Oct 93), pp. 982 – 984.

Haq, Mahbubul and Jan Pronk. Desarrollo sostenible: del concepto a la acción. *El Trimestre Económico,* v. 59, no. 236 (Oct – Dec 92), pp. 799 – 815.

Harker, Trevor. Caribbean Economic Performance: An Overview. *Social and Economic Studies,* v. 41, no. 3 (Sept 92), pp. 101 – 143. Tables.

Harms, Mike. Nurturing Conservation Naturally in the Twin Isles (Photographs by Michael Ventura). *Américas,* v. 45, no. 2 (Mar – Apr 93), pp. 22 – 25. Il, maps.

Harpelle, Ronald N. The Social and Political Integration of West Indians in Costa Rica, 1930 – 1950. *Journal of Latin American Studies,* v. 25, no. 1 (Feb 93), pp. 103 – 120. Bibl.

Harris, Patricia and David Lyon. Memory's Persistence: The Living Art. *Américas,* v. 45, no. 6 (Nov – Dec 93), pp. 26 – 37. Il.

Harris, Richard L. The Nicaraguan Revolution: A Postmortem (Review article). *Latin American Research Review,* v. 28, no. 3 (1993), pp. 197 – 213.

Harrison, Regina. Confesando el pecado en los Andes: del siglo XVI hacia nuestros días. *Revista de Crítica Literaria Latinoamericana,* v. 19, no. 37 (Jan – June 93), pp. 169 – 184. Bibl.

Harrison Flores, Joseph. ¿Caos de preservación histórica o preservación histórica del caos?: el caso de Puerto Rico. *Homines,* v. 15 – 16, no. 2 – 1 (Oct 91 – Dec 92), pp. 262 – 264.

Hart, Anita M. and Bruce S. Gartner. A Space of One's Own: Mexican Poets Kyra Galván and Perla Schwartz. *Confluencia,* v. 8, no. 1 (Fall 92), pp. 79 – 89. Bibl.

Hart, Pansy Rae. Out to Build a New Jamaica. *Jamaica Journal,* v. 25, no. 1 (Oct 93), pp. 29 – 37. Il.

Hart, Richard. Federation: An Ill-Fated Design. *Jamaica Journal*, v. 25, no. 1 (Oct 93), pp. 10 – 16. Bibl, il.

Harto de Vera, Fernando. La resolución del proceso de negociaciones de paz. *ECA; Estudios Centroamericanos*, v. 48, no. 531 – 532 (Jan – Feb 93), pp. 27 – 38. Bibl, il.

Hartup, Cheryl. Early Twentieth Century Peruvian Photography. *Latin American Art*, v. 5, no. 2 (Summer 93), pp. 60 – 62. Bibl, il.

Haskett, Robert Stephen. Visions of Municipal Glory Undimmed: The Nahuatl Town Histories of Colonial Cuernavaca. *Colonial Latin American Historical Review*, v. 1, no. 1 (Fall 92), pp. 1 – 36. Bibl, il.

Haubrich, Walter. Un vate de la noche tropical con motivo del fallecimiento del escritor cubano Severo Sarduy (Translated by José Luis Gómez y Patiño). *Humboldt*, no. 110 (1993), p. 98. Il.

Haupt, Gerhard. Latinoamérica y el surrealismo en Bochum (Includes several pages of colored art reproductions, translated by José García). *Humboldt*, no. 110 (1993), pp. 82 – 89. Il.

Hausberger, Bernd. Movimientos estacionales en los registros de oro y plata en las cajas de la Real Hacienda de la Nueva España, 1761 – 1767. *Anuario de Estudios Americanos*, v. 49 (1992), pp. 335 – 369. Bibl, tables, charts.

Hauser, Rex. Settings and Connections: Darío's Poetic "Engarce." *Revista Canadiense de Estudios Hispánicos*, v. 17, no. 3 (Spring 93), pp. 437 – 451. Bibl.

— Two New World Dreamers: Manzano and Sor Juana. *Afro-Hispanic Review*, v. 12, no. 2 (Fall 93), pp. 3 – 11. Bibl.

Hayes, Joy Elizabeth. Early Mexican Radio Broadcasting: Media Imperialism, State Paternalism, or Mexican Nationalism? *Studies in Latin American Popular Culture*, v. 12 (1993), pp. 31 – 55. Bibl.

Hayes-Bautista, David E. et al. Latinos and the 1992 Los Angeles Riots: A Behavioral Sciences Perspective. *Hispanic Journal of Behavioral Sciences*, v. 15, no. 4 (Nov 93), pp. 427 – 448. Bibl, charts.

Hazen, Dan C. The Latin American Conspectus: Panacea or Pig in a Poke? *SALALM Papers*, v. 36 (1991), pp. 235 – 247. Bibl.

— Latin American Studies, Information Resources, and Library Collections: The Contexts of Crisis. *SALALM Papers*, v. 36 (1991), pp. 267 – 271.

Healy, Kevin. Back to the Future: Ethnodevelopment among the Jalq'a of Bolivia. *Grassroots Development*, v. 16, no. 2 (1992), pp. 22 – 34. Il.

Heath, Hilarie J. British Merchant Houses in Mexico, 1821 – 1860: Conforming Business Practices and Ethics. *Hispanic American Historical Review*, v. 73, no. 2 (May 93), pp. 261 – 290. Bibl.

Héau de Giménez, Catherine and Enrique Rajchenberg. La leyenda negra y la leyenda rosa en la nueva historiografía de la revolución mexicana. *Revista Mexicana de Sociología*, v. 54, no. 3 (July – Sept 92), pp. 175 – 188. Bibl.

— Región y nación: una antigua polémica resucitada. *Revista Mexicana de Ciencias Políticas y Sociales*, v. 38, Nueva época, no. 154 (Oct – Dec 93), pp. 19 – 34. Bibl.

Hebrón, Aurelio del
See
Zum Felde, Alberto

Heckadon Moreno, Stanley. Impact of Development on the Panama Canal Environment (Translated by Jane Marchi). *Journal of Inter-American Studies and World Affairs*, v. 35, no. 3 (Fall 93), pp. 129 – 149. Bibl.

Hedi, Ben Abbes. A Variation on the Theme of Violence and Antagonism in V. S. Naipaul's Fiction. *Caribbean Studies*, v. 25, no. 1 – 2 (Jan – July 92), pp. 49 – 61. Bibl.

Heine, Jorge. En defensa de Santiago: la ciudad que queremos. *EURE*, v. 19, no. 56 (Mar 93), pp. 127 – 128.

Heker, Liliana. Los talleres literarios. *Cuadernos Hispanoamericanos*, no. 517 – 519 (July – Sept 93), pp. 187 – 194.

Heker, Liliana and Julio Cortázar. Polémica sobre el exilio (Debate between Julio Cortázar and Liliana Heker on the subject of exiles). *Cuadernos Hispanoamericanos*, no. 517 – 519 (July – Sept 93), pp. 590 – 604.

Helguera, Luis Ignacio. Astor Piazzolla. *Vuelta*, v. 17, no. 204 (Nov 93), pp. 64 – 65.

— Ginastera a diez años de su muerte. *Vuelta*, v. 17, no. 202 (Sept 93), pp. 67 – 69.

— Nuestra música. *Vuelta*, v. 17, no. 197 (Apr 93), pp. 70 – 73.

Helminen, Juha Pekka. Las Casas, los judíos, los moros y los negros. *Cuadernos Hispanoamericanos*, no. 512 (Feb 93), pp. 23 – 28. Bibl.

Helsper, Norma. The Ideology of Happy Endings: Wolff's *Mansión de lechuzas*. *Latin American Theatre Review*, v. 26, no. 2 (Spring 93), pp. 123 – 130.

Henderson, Peter V. N. Modernization and Change in Mexico: La Zacualpa Rubber Plantation, 1890 – 1920. *Hispanic American Historical Review*, v. 73, no. 2 (May 93), pp. 235 – 260. Bibl, tables.

Henestrosa, Andrés. Hechicera Oaxaca (Accompanied by an English translation). *Artes de México*, no. 21 (Fall 93), p. 43. Il.

Henige, David P. Counting the Encounter: The Pernicious Appeal of Verisimilitude. *Colonial Latin American Historical Review*, v. 2, no. 3 (Summer 93), pp. 325 – 361. Bibl, tables, charts.

Henríquez Amestoy, Lysette. Chile: experiencia exportadora de las empresas pequeñas y medianas. *Comercio Exterior*, v. 43, no. 6 (June 93), pp. 547 – 552.

Henry, Etienne. Autotransporte urbano colectivo en desarrollo: el abanico de las empresas. *EURE*, v. 19, no. 56 (Mar 93), pp. 71 – 78.

Hentschke, Jens. Alternativas del desarrollo histórico en el Brasil en los años veinte: contribución a la discusión. *Islas*, no. 97 (Sept – Dec 90), pp. 26 – 31. Bibl.

Henwood, Doug. Impeccable Logic: Trade, Development, and Free Markets in the Clinton Era. *NACLA Report on the Americas*, v. 26, no. 5 (May 93), pp. 23 – 28 +. Bibl, il.

Heras, Julián. Significado y extensión de la obra misionera de Ocopa en el siglo XVIII. *Archivo Ibero-Americano*, v. 52, no. 205 – 208 (Jan – Dec 92), pp. 209 – 220. Bibl, il.

Heras León, Eduardo. La visita. *Casa de las Américas*, no. 191 (Apr – June 93), pp. 73 – 78.

Herbort, Heinz Josef. "Jungla de silencio": una semblanza de la compositora Silvia Fómina (Translated by Carlos Caramés). *Humboldt*, no. 110 (1993), pp. 56 – 59. Il, facs.

Heredia, Carlos and Jorge G. Castañeda. Hacia otro TLC. *Nexos*, v. 16, no. 181 (Jan 93), pp. 43 – 54.

Heredia, Jorge. Avatares de la obra del fotógrafo peruano Martín Chambi (1891 – 1973) y reseña de dos monografías recientes. *Hueso Húmero*, no. 29 (May 93), pp. 144 – 173. Bibl.

Heredia Correa, Roberto. Fray Juan Agustín Morfi, humanista y crítico de su tiempo. *Archivo Ibero-Americano*, v. 52, no. 205 – 208 (Jan – Dec 92), pp. 107 – 124. Bibl.

Hermes, Bernard A. Adiciones tipológicas a los complejos Eb, Tzec y Manik de Tikal, Guatemala. *Revista Española de Antropología Americana,* v. 23 (1993), pp. 9 – 27. Bibl, il.

Hernández, Consuelo. La arquitectura poética de Eugenio Montejo. *Inti,* no. 37 – 38 (Spring – Fall 93), pp. 133 – 143. Bibl.

Hernandez, Deborah Pacini

See

    Pacini Hernandez, Deborah

Hernández, Esther María. Machurrucutu en seis tiempos: crónica de septiembre. *Conjunto,* no. 90 – 91 (Jan – June 92), pp. 79 – 84. Il.

Hernández, Max. La piel dura. *Debate (Peru),* v. 15, no. 71 (Nov 92 – Jan 93), pp. 20 – 21. Il.

Hernández, Max and Francisco R. Sagasti. La crisis de gobernabilidad democrática en el Perú. *Debate (Peru),* v. 16, no. 75 (Dec 93 – Jan 94), pp. 24 – 28. Il.

Hernández, Prisco. "Décima," "Seis," and the Art of the Puertorican "Trovador" within the Modern Social Context. *Latin American Music Review,* v. 14, no. 1 (Spring – Summer 93), pp. 20 – 51. Bibl, il, facs.

Hernández, Raúl Augusto. Correlación y correspondencia en la acción social. *Revista Paraguaya de Sociología,* v. 29, no. 84 (May – Aug 92), pp. 171 – 185. Bibl.

  — Indecisión social o crisis de conciencia: los cardinales de la desolación. *Estudios Interdisciplinarios de América Latina y el Caribe,* v. 4, no. 1 (Jan – June 93), pp. 141 – 163. Bibl, tables, charts.

Hernández Agosto, Miguel A. Mensaje del presidente de la Comisión Puertorriqueña para la Celebración del Quinto Centenario del Descubrimiento de América y Puerto Rico, en ocasión de la presentación del libro – periódico *Desde el tuétano,* de don Salvador Tió. *Homines,* v. 15 – 16, no. 2 – 1 (Oct 91 – Dec 92), pp. 372 – 373.

Hernández Aparicio, Pilar. Las reducciones jesuíticas de los llanos que pasaron a los franciscanos. *Archivo Ibero-Americano,* v. 52, no. 205 – 208 (Jan – Dec 92), pp. 445 – 463. Bibl, tables.

Hernández Campos, Jorge. Sed lux. *Vuelta,* v. 17, no. 204 (Nov 93), p. 26.

Hernández Carballido, Elvira Laura. En la vanguardia. *Fem,* v. 17, no. 119 – 130 (Jan – Dec 93), All issues.

Hernández Carstens, Eduardo. Conferencia del doctor Eduardo Hernández Carstens . . . , con motivo de conmemorar el 215° de la real cédula de Carlos III de 1777 . . . . *Boletín de la Academia Nacional de la Historia (Venezuela),* v. 75, no. 300 (Oct – Dec 92), pp. 21 – 27.

  — Discurso de orden pronunciado por el doctor Eduardo Hernández Carstens, cronista oficial de la ciudad de Achaguas, . . . en el acto conmemorativo de los 200 años del nacimiento del general en jefe José Antonio Páez . . . . *Boletín de la Academia Nacional de la Historia (Venezuela),* v. 76, no. 302 (Apr – June 93), pp. 41 – 45.

Hernández Castellón, Raúl. El envejecimiento de la población en Cuba. *Estudios Demográficos y Urbanos,* v. 7, no. 2 – 3 (May – Dec 92), pp. 603 – 617. Bibl, tables.

Hernández Cruz, Omar. Historias de vida e identidades étnicas: la visión de los maestros del Atlántico costarricense. *Revista de Ciencias Sociales (Costa Rica),* no. 58 (Dec 92), pp. 75 – 83. Bibl.

Hernández Díaz, Rosha and María Pérez Tzu. Mujer florida (Translated by Ambar Past). *Artes de México,* no. 19 (Spring 93), p. 60. Il.

Hernández García, Lissette. Entrevista con Ramiro Guerra. *La Palabra y el Hombre,* no. 82 (Apr – June 92), pp. 285 – 290.

Hernández González, Pablo J. La comarca de Vuelta Abajo, isla de Cuba, en 1755: recuento de un obispo ilustrado. *Anuario de Estudios Americanos,* v. 50, no. 1 (1993), pp. 251 – 268. Bibl, maps.

Hernández Hernández, Natalio. Más allá de los 500 años. *Caravelle,* no. 59 (1992), pp. 25 – 31.

Hernández Navarro, Luis. De Washington al Cerro de las Campanas: la exportación de la democracia a la hora del TLC. *El Cotidiano,* v. 9, no. 54 (May 93), pp. 101 – 107. Bibl.

  — SNTE: la transición difícil. *El Cotidiano,* v. 8, no. 51 (Nov – Dec 92), pp. 54 – 59 +. Bibl, il.

Hernández Novás, Raúl. El poema "preliminar" de *Trilce. Casa de las Américas,* no. 189 (Oct – Dec 92), pp. 21 – 28. Bibl.

Hernández Palacios, Aureliano. Orígenes de la formación docente en la Universidad Veracruzana. *La Palabra y el Hombre,* no. 81 (Jan – Mar 92), pp. 292 – 301. Il.

Hernández Pico, Juan. Guatemala: ¿Fructificará la democracia? *ECA; Estudios Centroamericanos,* v. 48, no. 536 (June 93), pp. 545 – 562. Il.

  — Significado ético – político del informe de la verdad: "La verdad nos hará libres." *ECA; Estudios Centroamericanos,* v. 48, no. 534 – 535 (Apr – May 93), pp. 377 – 387. Il.

Hernández Rodríguez, Rogelio. La administración al servicio de la política: la Secretaría de Programación y Presupuesto. *Foro Internacional,* v. 33, no. 1 (Jan – Mar 93), pp. 145 – 173. Bibl, tables.

  — Preparación y movilidad de los funcionarios de la administración pública mexicana. *Estudios Sociológicos,* v. 11, no. 32 (May – Aug 93), pp. 445 – 473. Bibl, tables.

Hernández Sánchez, José Luis. El cuento de nunca empezar. *La Palabra y el Hombre,* no. 84 (Oct – Dec 92), pp. 160 – 164.

Hernández T., Leonardo and Eduardo Walker H. Estructura de financiamiento corporativo en Chile, 1978 – 1990: evidencia a partir de datos contables. *Estudios Públicos (Chile),* no. 51 (Winter 93), pp. 87 – 156. Bibl, tables, charts.

Hernández Téllez, Josefina. "Año con año se ha consolidado el trabajo": lic. Fernando Portilla, director gral. de la Supervisión General de Servicios a la Comunidad de la PGJDF. *Fem,* v. 17, no. 125 (July 93), p. 39.

  — ¿Cómo funciona y para qué sirve la participacíon en la Procuraduría General de Justicia del D.F.? *Fem,* v. 17, no. 123 (May 93), p. 43.

  — Dirección de Atención a Víctimas de la SGSC – PGJDF. *Fem,* v. 17, no. 121 (Mar 93), p. 38.

  — Servicios a la comunidad de la PGJDF: por el trato humano en la impartición de justicia. *Fem,* v. 17, no. 119 (Jan 93), p. 30.

  — 24 horas captando quejas . . . . *Fem,* v. 17, no. 122 (Apr 93), p. 40.

Hernández Vela Salgado, Edmundo. La política exterior en México en el umbral del tercer milenio. *Revista Mexicana de Ciencias Políticas y Sociales,* v. 37, Nueva época, no. 148 (Apr – June 92), pp. 77 – 86.

  — El Sistema Interamericano ante los cambios mundiales. *Relaciones Internacionales (Mexico),* v. 14, Nueva época, no. 56 (Oct – Dec 92), pp. 31 – 34. Bibl.

Hernández Vicencio, Tania and Víctor Alejandro Espinoza Valle. Tendencias de cambio en la estructura corporativa mexicana: Baja California, 1989 – 1992. *El Cotidiano,* v. 8, no. 52 (Jan – Feb 93), pp. 25 – 29.

Herndon, Gerise. Gender Construction and Neocolonialism. *World Literature Today,* v. 67, no. 4 (Fall 93), pp. 731 – 736. Bibl, il.

Herner de Larrea, Irene. Carlos Mérida y la realidad auténtica. *Nexos,* v. 16, no. 182 (Feb 93), pp. 13 – 15. Il.

— Erika Billeter y el arte mexicano en Europa. *Nexos,* v. 16, no. 183 (Mar 93), pp. 10 – 12. Il.

— Nahui Olin: años de gato. *Nexos,* v. 16, no. 185 (May 93), pp. 20 – 22. Il.

Herr Solé, Alberto. El Archivo Angel María Garibay Kintana de la Biblioteca Nacional. *Estudios de Cultura Náhuatl,* v. 22 (1992), pp. 181 – 222.

Herra, Mayra. *Vigilia en pie de muerte:* una lectura. *Káñina,* v. 16, no. 1 (Jan – June 92), pp. 23 – 28. Bibl.

Herranz Gómez, Yolanda. Latinoamericanos en Madrid: integración en la sociedad española. *Revista Española de Antropología Americana,* v. 23 (1993), pp. 189 – 211. Bibl, tables, charts.

Herrasti Aguirre, María Emilia. La promoción inmobiliaria popular autogestiva: ¿Tendrá futuro? *El Cotidiano,* v. 10, no. 57 (Aug – Sept 93), pp. 17 – 22. Il.

Herrera, Alejandra. The Privatization of the Argentine Telephone System. *CEPAL Review,* no. 47 (Aug 92), pp. 149 – 161. Bibl.

Herrera, Fabio. Reproductions of *Humanidad, Mujer, Cardinal, Cristo de Monimbo, Luz, La india,* and *Tres botes. Káñina,* v. 16, no. 2 (July – Dec 92), pp. 179 – 185. Il.

— Reproductions of *Silla, Ventana al futuro, El grabador, Mario, Madre, Arturo, Francisco, Miss Daisy,* and *Alajuelita. Káñina,* v. 16, no. 2 (July – Dec 92), Issue.

Herrera, Luis. SALALM and the Public Library. *SALALM Papers,* v. 36 (1991), pp. 224 – 227.

Herrera Angel, Marta. El corregidor de naturales y el control económico de las comunidades: cambios y permanencias en la provincia de Santafé siglo XVIII. *Anuario Colombiano de Historia Social y de la Cultura,* no. 20 (1992), pp. 7 – 25. Bibl.

Herrera C., J. Noé. Colombia: ¿Atenas suramericana . . . o apenas suramericana? *SALALM Papers,* v. 34 (1989), pp. 275 – 306. Bibl.

Herrera Lima, Fernando Francisco. Dina: del enfrentamiento a la negociación. *El Cotidiano,* v. 9, no. 56 (July 93), pp. 69 – 73. Il.

Herrera Toledano, Salvador. Secondary Petrochemicals: Risks and Rewards (Translated by Robert Brackney). *Business Mexico,* v. 3, no. 7 (July 93), pp. 34 – 36. Tables.

— Strategies for a Dynamic Market. *Business Mexico,* v. 3, no. 4 (Apr 93), pp. 11 – 14. Il.

Herrera Vial, Felipe. Viento abracadabra del oeste. *Revista Nacional de Cultura (Venezuela),* v. 53, no. 286 (July – Sept 92), pp. 109 – 110.

Herrera Villalobos, Anaysy and Felipe Solís del Vecchio. Lomas Entierros: un centro político prehispánico en la cuenca baja del Río Grande de Tárcoles. *Vínculos,* v. 16, no. 1 – 2 (1990), pp. 85 – 110. Bibl, il, tables, maps.

Herrero, Fabián and Alejandro Herrero Rubio. A propósito de la prensa española en Buenos Aires: el estudio de un caso: *El Correo Español,* 1872 – 1875. *Anuario de Estudios Americanos,* v. 49, Suppl. 1 (1992), pp. 107 – 120.

Herrero, Ramiro. Machurrucutu. *Conjunto,* no. 90 – 91 (Jan – June 92), pp. 85 – 91. Il.

Herrero Díaz, Luis F. Desarrollo urbano y estrategias de supervivencia en la periferia de la ciudad de México: Chalco; una aproximación antropológica. *Revista Española de Antropología Americana,* v. 23 (1993), pp. 213 – 232. Bibl, tables.

Herrero-Olaizola, Alejandro. Condenados por leer: lectura y lectores de Puig en *Maldición eterna a quien lea estas páginas. Hispanic Review,* v. 61, no. 4 (Fall 93), pp. 483 – 500. Bibl.

Herrero Rubio, Alejandro and Fabián Herrero. A propósito de la prensa española en Buenos Aires: el estudio de un caso: *El Correo Español,* 1872 – 1875. *Anuario de Estudios Americanos,* v. 49, Suppl. 1 (1992), pp. 107 – 120.

Hers, Marie-Aretti. Chicomóztoc o el noroeste mesoamericano. *Anales del Instituto de Investigaciones Estéticas,* v. 16, no. 62 (1991), pp. 1 – 22. Bibl.

Heuzé de Icaza, Patricia. La Coalición de Ejidos Colectivos de los valles de Yaqui y Mayo: una experiencia de autonomía campesina en México. *Estudios Rurales Latinoamericanos,* v. 15, no. 2 – 3 (May – Dec 92), pp. 65 – 77. Bibl.

Hevia, Renato. El milagro del padre Hurtado. *Mensaje,* v. 42, no. 424 (Nov 93), pp. 552 – 554. Il.

Hey, Jeanne A. K. Foreign Policy Options under Dependence: A Theoretical Evaluation with Evidence from Ecuador. *Journal of Latin American Studies,* v. 25, no. 3 (Oct 93), pp. 543 – 574. Bibl.

Hibon, Albéric et al. El maíz de temporal en México: tendencias, restricciones y retos. *Comercio Exterior,* v. 43, no. 4 (Apr 93), pp. 311 – 327. Bibl, tables, charts.

Hidalgo, Alvaro Barrantes. O intercâmbio comercial brasileiro intra-indústria: uma análise entre indústrias e entre países. *Revista Brasileira de Economia,* v. 47, no. 2 (Apr – June 93), pp. 243 – 264. Bibl, tables.

Hidalgo de Jesús, Amarilis. *Abrapalabra:* el discurso desmitificador de la historia colonial venezolana. *Inti,* no. 37 – 38 (Spring – Fall 93), pp. 163 – 169. Bibl.

Hidalgo Xirinachs, Roxana and Mercedes Flores. El autoritarismo en la vida cotidiana: SIDA, homofobia y moral sexual. *Revista de Ciencias Sociales (Costa Rica),* no. 58 (Dec 92), pp. 35 – 44. Bibl.

Hierro de Matte, Graciela. Historia del PUEG. *Fem,* v. 17, no. 121 (Mar 93), p. 32.

Higa, Jorge. La Argentina vista con ojos oblicuos. *Todo Es Historia,* v. 27, no. 316 (Nov 93), pp. 60 – 80. Il, maps.

Higinio, Egbert and Ian Munt. Belize: Eco Tourism Gone Awry. *Report on the Americas,* v. 26, no. 4 (Feb 93), pp. 8 – 10. Il.

Hilbert, Pia. Politically Correct Coverage. *Business Mexico,* v. 3, no. 11 (Nov 93), pp. 18 – 19. Tables.

— Refining Mexican Metal Production. *Business Mexico,* v. 3, no. 12 (Dec 93), pp. 4 – 8. Charts.

Hill, Nick. Poems ("Un Altar for the Abuelitos," "Transfer Points"). *Bilingual Review/Revista Bilingüe,* v. 17, no. 3 (Sept – Dec 92), pp. 268 – 272.

Hilton, Sylvia-Lyn and Amancio Labandeira Fernández. El americanismo en España, 1991 – 1992. *Revista de Indias,* v. 53, no. 197 (Jan – Apr 93), pp. 133 – 409.

— La sensibilidad cromática y estética del Inca Garcilaso. *Revista de Indias,* v. 52, no. 195 – 196 (May – Dec 92), pp. 529 – 558. Bibl.

Himelfarb, Célia. Convertibilité, stabilisation et dérégulation en Argentine. *Cahiers des Amériques Latines,* no. 14 (1992), pp. 51 – 66. Bibl, tables.

Himmerich y Valencia, Robert. Historical Objectivity and the Persistence of Fray Bartolomé de las Casas: A Commentary. *Colonial Latin American Historical Review,* v. 2, no. 1 (Winter 93), pp. 105 – 108. Il.

Hinds, Harold E., Jr. Boundaries and Popular Culture Theory: Recent Works on Folklore and Mexican Folkways (Review article). *Studies in Latin American Popular Culture,* v. 12 (1993), pp. 243 – 249.

Hirabayashi, Lane Ryo. La politización de la cultura regional: zapotecos de la sierra Juárez en la ciudad de México. *América Indígena,* v. 51, no. 4 (Oct – Dec 91), pp. 185 – 218. Bibl.

Hirabayashi, Lane Ryo and Teófilo Altamirano Rúa. Culturas regionales en ciudades de América Latina: un marco conceptual. *América Indígena,* v. 51, no. 4 (Oct – Dec 91), pp. 17 – 48. Bibl, il.

Hiriart, Berta. De mujeres y literatura. *Fem,* v. 17, no. 120 (Feb 93), pp. 15 – 17.

Hiriart, Hugo. Felipe Leal, arquitecto. *Artes de México,* no. 20 (Summer 93), pp. 114 – 115. Il.

— Impresión de Xochimilco (Accompanied by an English translation). *Artes de México,* no. 20 (Summer 93), pp. 27 – 32.

Hirst, Mónica. Brasil en el MERCOSUR: costos y beneficios. *Integración Latinoamericana,* v. 18, no. 186 (Jan – Feb 93), pp. 3 – 11. Bibl.

Hochman, Gilberto. Os cardeais da previdência social: gênese e consolidação de uma elite burocrática. *Dados,* v. 35, no. 3 (1992), pp. 371 – 401. Bibl.

— Regulando os efeitos da interdependência: sobre as relações entre saúde pública e construção do estado; Brasil, 1910 – 1930. *Estudos Históricos,* v. 6, no. 11 (Jan – June 93), pp. 40 – 61. Bibl.

Hodel, Donald R. "Chamaedorea": Diverse Species in Diverse Habitats. *Bulletin de l'Institut Français d'Etudes Andines,* v. 21, no. 2 (1992), pp. 433 – 458. Bibl, il.

Hodge, Mary G. et al. Black-on-Orange Ceramic Production in the Aztec Empire's Heartland. *Latin American Antiquity,* v. 4, no. 2 (June 93), pp. 130 – 157. Bibl, il, tables, maps.

Hodgman, Suzanne. SALALM Membership, 1956 – 1990: A Brief Overview. *SALALM Papers,* v. 36 (1991), pp. 215 – 223. Tables.

Hodgson, Michael E. and Risa Palm. Natural Hazards in Puerto Rico. *Geographical Review,* v. 83, no. 3 (July 93), pp. 280 – 289. Bibl, tables.

Hoffmann, Odile. Renovación de los actores sociales en el campo: un ejemplo en el sector cafetalero en Veracruz. *Estudios Sociológicos,* v. 10, no. 30 (Sept – Dec 92), pp. 523 – 554. Bibl, tables, maps.

Hoffmann, Rodolfo. A dinâmica da modernização da agricultura em 157 microrregiões homogêneas do Brasil. *Revista de Economia e Sociologia Rural,* v. 30, no. 4 (Oct – Dec 92), pp. 271 – 290. Bibl, tables, charts.

— Sensibilidade das medidas de desigualdade a transferências regressivas. *Pesquisa e Planejamento Econômico,* v. 22, no. 2 (Aug 92), pp. 289 – 304. Bibl, tables, charts.

— Vinte anos de desigualdade e pobreza na agricultura brasileira. *Revista de Economia e Sociologia Rural,* v. 30, no. 2 (Apr – June 92), pp. 97 – 113. Bibl, tables, charts.

Hogue, W. Lawrence. An Unresolved Modern Experience: Richard Rodríguez's *Hunger of Memory. The Americas Review,* v. 20, no. 1 (Spring 92), pp. 52 – 64. Bibl.

Hohmann B., Claudio. La encrucijada del transporte urbano de Santiago. *EURE,* v. 19, no. 56 (Mar 93), pp. 9 – 27.

Hojman A., David E. Non-Governmental Organisations (NGOs) and the Chilean Transition to Democracy. *European Review of Latin American and Caribbean Studies,* no. 54 (June 93), pp. 7 – 24. Bibl.

Holanda Filho, Sérgio Buarque de
See
Buarque de Hollanda Filho, Sérgio

Holdsworth, Carole A. Two Contemporary Versions of the Persephone Myth. *Revista Interamericana de Bibliografía,* v. 42, no. 4 (1992), pp. 571 – 576. Bibl.

Holguín Quiñones, Fernando. Análisis comparativo de los egresados de las carreras de la FCPyS con otros similares. *Revista Mexicana de Ciencias Políticas y Sociales,* v. 37, Nueva época, no. 148 (Apr – June 92), pp. 143 – 184. Tables, charts.

— Encuesta a egresados de la Facultad de Ciencias Políticas y Sociales: I parte. *Revista Mexicana de Ciencias Políticas y Sociales,* v. 38, Nueva época, no. 153 (July – Sept 93), pp. 137 – 210. Tables, charts.

Holiday, David and William Deane Stanley. La construcción de la paz: las lecciones preliminares de El Salvador. *ECA; Estudios Centroamericanos,* v. 48, no. 531 – 532 (Jan – Feb 93), pp. 39 – 59. Il.

Hollanda, Heloísa Buarque de. A roupa da Rachel: um estudo sem importância (Accompanied by an English translation by Christopher Peterson). *Estudos Feministas,* v. 0, no. 0 (1992), pp. 74 – 96.

Hollanda Filho, Sérgio Buarque de
See
Buarque de Hollanda Filho, Sérgio

Holston, James. Legalizando o ilegal: propriedade e usurpação no Brasil (A translation of "The Misrule of Law: Land and Usurpation in Brazil," translated by João Vargas. Reprinted from *Comparative Studies in Society and History,* vol. 33, num. 4, 1991). *Revista Brasileira de Ciências Sociais,* v. 8, no. 21 (Feb 93), pp. 68 – 89. Bibl.

Holston, Mark. The Composer's Muse as Master. *Américas,* v. 45, no. 3 (May – June 93), pp. 56 – 57. Il.

— Everything Old Is New Again. *Américas,* v. 45, no. 6 (Nov – Dec 93), pp. 56 – 57. Il.

— Old Bits, New Beats. *Américas,* v. 45, no. 2 (Mar – Apr 93), pp. 52 – 53. Il.

— Playing the Heartstrings. *Américas,* v. 45, no. 5 (Sept – Oct 93), pp. 58 – 59. Il.

— Tom Zé: The Conscience of Brazil's Tropicalismo. *Américas,* v. 45, no. 1 (Jan – Feb 93), pp. 58 – 59. Il.

— Variations on Themes. *Américas,* v. 45, no. 4 (July – Aug 93), pp. 52 – 53. Il.

Holt, Douglas. Aftershocks in Guadalajara. *Business Mexico,* v. 3, no. 5 (May 93), pp. 39 – 40. Il.

— Guadalajara Gambles with Expansion. *Business Mexico,* v. 3, no. 6 (June 93), pp. 30 – 31. Il.

Holzheimer, Arthur and David Buisseret. The Enigma of the Jean Bellère Maps of the New World, 1554: A Historical Note. *Colonial Latin American Historical Review,* v. 2, no. 3 (Summer 93), pp. 363 – 367. Maps.

Homem de Melo, Fernando Bento. Café brasileiro: não a um novo acordo internacional. *Revista de Economia Política (Brazil),* v. 13, no. 4 (Oct – Dec 93), pp. 37 – 46. Bibl, tables, charts.

Hopenhayn, Martín. The Social Sciences without Planning or Revolution? *CEPAL Review,* no. 48 (Dec 92), pp. 129 – 140. Bibl.

Hora, Roy and Javier A. Trimboli. Entrevista al historiador Daniel James. *Todo Es Historia,* v. 27, no. 314 (Sept 93), pp. 24 – 30. Il.

Horch, Rosemarie Erika. Os primeiros mapas do Brasil. *Vozes,* v. 86, no. 4 (July – Aug 92), pp. 8 – 15. Il.

Horton, Anne. Conversation with Curator Waldo Rasmussen. *Latin American Art,* v. 5, no. 1 (Spring 93), pp. 40 – 41. Il.

Hospital, Carolina. Poems ("Dear Tía," "Papa"). *The Americas Review,* v. 20, no. 3 – 4 (Fall – Winter 92), pp. 223 – 224.

Houaiss, Antônio and Roberto Amaral. A via partidária dos socialistas brasileiros. *Vozes,* v. 87, no. 1 (Jan – Feb 93), pp. 2 – 13. Il.

Howard, Philip A. The Spanish Colonial Government's Responses to the Pan-Nationalist Agenda of the Afro-Cuban Mutual Aid Societies, 1868 – 1895. *Revista/Review Interamericana,* v. 22, no. 1 – 2 (Spring – Summer 92), pp. 151 – 167. Bibl.

Howell, Calvin A. Trends in Environmental Education in the English-Speaking Caribbean. *La Educación (USA),* v. 37, no. 115 (1993), pp. 303 – 316. Bibl.

Hoyos, Angela

See

De Hoyos, Angela

Hoyt, Edward. Countdown to NAFTA. *Business Mexico,* v. 3, no. 10 (Oct 93), pp. 33 – 34.

Hudson, Brian J. The Landscapes of Cayuna: Jamaica through the Senses of John Hearne. *Caribbean Geography,* v. 3, no. 3 (Mar 92), pp. 187 – 199. Bibl.

Huerta, Alberto. Un adiós no significa olvido. *Plural (Mexico),* v. 22, no. 267 (Dec 93), pp. 14 – 15.

— La que se fue. *Plural (Mexico),* v. 22, no. 261 (June 93), pp. 39 – 40.

Huerta, David. La novela órfica del escultor Juan Soriano. *Nexos,* v. 16, no. 181 (Jan 93), pp. 35 – 38. Il.

Huerta, Efraín. El vapuleado *Cuadrante. Nexos,* v. 16, no. 183 (Mar 93), pp. 55 – 56.

Huerta, Héctor. El reptil y la monja. *Plural (Mexico),* v. 22, no. 267 (Dec 93), pp. 38 – 39.

Huerta, Joel. Poems ("La Smiley," "El Big Man," "Las Chrome Doors of Heaven"). *The Americas Review,* v. 19, no. 3 – 4 (Winter 91), pp. 55 – 62.

Huerta G., Arturo. Los cambios estructurales de la política salinista: su inviabilidad de alcanzar un crecimiento sostenido. *Problemas del Desarrollo,* v. 24, no. 92 (Jan – Mar 93), pp. 15 – 23.

Huerta-Nava, Raquel. La tercera región. *Plural (Mexico),* v. 22, no. 257 (Feb 93), p. 48.

Huerta Trujillo, María Concepción and Ana María Durán. Cambios de usos del suelo y despoblamiento en la colonia Roma. *El Cotidiano,* v. 10, no. 57 (Aug – Sept 93), pp. 73 – 77. Il, tables.

Huertas Bartolomé, Tebelia. Análisis crítico de la legislación laboral en El Salvador. *ECA; Estudios Centroamericanos,* v. 47, no. 529 – 530 (Nov – Dec 92), pp. 1021 – 1027. Il.

— Libertad sindical, tratados internacionales y constitución. *ECA; Estudios Centroamericanos,* v. 48, no. 537 – 538 (July – Aug 93), pp. 657 – 675. Bibl, il.

Huertas Vallejos, Lorenzo. Anomalías cíclicas de la naturaleza y su impacto en la sociedad: el fenómeno El Niño. *Bulletin de l'Institut Français d'Etudes Andines,* v. 22, no. 1 (1993), pp. 345 – 393. Bibl, il, tables, maps, facs, charts.

— Los chancas: proceso disturbativo en los Andes. *Historia y Cultura (Peru),* no. 20 (1990), pp. 11 – 48. Bibl, maps.

Huhle, Rainer. El V centenario a través de los libros en Alemania. *Ibero-Amerikanisches Archiv,* v. 18, no. 3 – 4 (1992), pp. 543 – 557. Bibl.

— El terremoto de Cajamarca: la derrota del Inca en la memoria colectiva; elementos para un análisis de la resistencia cultural de los pueblos andinos. *Ibero-Amerikanisches Archiv,* v. 18, no. 3 – 4 (1992), pp. 387 – 426. Il, facs.

Huidobro, Vicente. Defendamos la revolución de Cuba: los Estados Unidos no tienen ningún derecho para meterse en los asuntos de Cuba. *Casa de las Américas,* no. 191 (Apr – June 93), pp. 10 – 11.

— Greguerías y paradojas (Excerpt from the book *Vientos contrarios*). *Atenea (Chile),* no. 467 (1993), pp. 143 – 144.

— Jimena (Fragment from the novel *Mío Cid Campeador*). *Atenea (Chile),* no. 467 (1993), pp. 97 – 99.

— Selección de poemas de Vicente Huidobro ("Arte poética," "Canto II," "Noche y día," "El paso del retorno"). *Atenea (Chile),* no. 467 (1993), pp. 75 – 79.

Hulick, Diana Emery. Modernism in Latin America: Fact, Fiction, or Fabrication? *Latin American Art,* v. 5, no. 2 (Summer 93), pp. 64 – 65.

Hume, Patricia. ¿Por qué población, medio ambiente y desarrollo y no mujer, naturaleza y desarrollo? *Fem,* v. 17, no. 128 (Oct 93), pp. 26 – 29. Tables, charts.

Humphreys, Francis. Afro-Belizean Cultural Heritage: Its Role in Combating Recolonization. *Belizean Studies,* v. 20, no. 3 (Dec 92), pp. 11 – 16. Bibl.

Huneeus, Francisco et al. El libro y la irrupción de los medios audiovisuales: debates. *Mensaje,* v. 42, no. 416 (Jan – Feb 93), pp. 29 – 36.

Huneeus, Virginia. Un auténtico poeta popular. *Mensaje,* v. 42, no. 416 (Jan – Feb 93), pp. 49 – 50. Il.

— Comunidad terapéutica para jóvenes drogadictos. *Mensaje,* v. 42, no. 422 (Sept 93), pp. 465 – 466.

Hunsaker, Steven V. The Problematics of the Representative Self: The Case of *Tejas verdes. Hispanic Journal,* v. 13, no. 2 (Fall 92), pp. 353 – 361. Bibl.

Hurrell, Andrew. Os blocos regionais nas Américas (Translated by João Roberto Martins Filho). *Revista Brasileira de Ciências Sociais,* v. 8, no. 22 (June 93), pp. 98 – 118. Bibl.

Hurtado, Isabel. Importancia del empleo estatal en los mercados de trabajo regionales: el caso del sur peruano entre 1961 y 1981. *Revista Andina,* v. 11, no. 1 (July 93), pp. 55 – 78. Bibl, tables, maps, charts.

Hurtado, Liliana R. de. Santiago entre los chiriguanos: una caso de aculturación y resistencia. *Amazonía Peruana,* v. 11, no. 22 (Oct 92), pp. 147 – 173. Bibl.

Huseby, Gerardo Víctor, ed. Bibliografía musicológica latinoamericana: no. 1, segunda parte (7/01 a 12/04), 1987, 1988, 1989. *Revista Musical Chilena,* v. 46, no. 178 (July – Dec 92), pp. 7 – 89.

Husson, Jean-Phillipe. La poesía quechua prehispánica: sus reglas, sus categorías, sus temas; através de los poemas transcritos por Wamán Puma de Ayala. *Revista de Crítica Literaria Latinoamericana,* v. 19, no. 37 (Jan – June 93), pp. 63 – 85. Bibl, il.

Hvalkof, Sören. La naturaleza del desarrollo: perspectivas de los nativos y de los colonos en el gran pajonal. *Amazonía Peruana,* v. 11, no. 21 (Sept 92), pp. 145 – 173. Bibl.

Ianni, Octávio. El laberinto latinoamericano (Translated by Ramón Martínez Escamilla). *Problemas del Desarrollo,* v. 24, no. 92 (Jan – Mar 93), pp. 81 – 101. Bibl.

— O labirinto latino-americano. *Vozes,* v. 87, no. 1 (Jan – Feb 93), pp. 14 – 29. Bibl, il.

Iannone, Carlos Alberto. Variações sobre um conto de Vergílio Ferreira. *Revista de Letras (Brazil),* v. 32 (1992), pp. 185 – 189.

Ibargoyen Islas, Saúl. Cuba: crisis editorial, alternativas y esperanzas. *Plural (Mexico),* v. 22, no. 263 (Aug 93), pp. 69 – 70.

— Encuentros y desencuentros con la revolución cubana. *Plural (Mexico),* v. 22, no. 256 (Jan 93), pp. 77 – 78.

— Graffiti 2000. *Plural (Mexico),* v. 22, no. 264 (Sept 93), pp. 8 – 15.

— Plurales hacia afuera, plurales hacia adentro. *Plural (Mexico),* v. 22, no. 262 (July 93), p. 79.

— Soñar la muerte (Excerpt from the forthcoming novel of the same title). *Plural (Mexico),* v. 22, no. 258 (Mar 93), pp. 45 – 47.

Ibarra Colado, Eduardo. El futuro de la universidad en México: los resortes de la diferenciación. *El Cotidiano,* v. 9, no. 55 (June 93), pp. 68 – 77. Tables, charts.

Ibarra-Manríquez, Guillermo. Fenología de las palmas de una selva cálido húmeda de México. *Bulletin de l'Institut Français d'Etudes Andines,* v. 21, no. 2 (1992), pp. 669 – 683. Bibl, tables, charts.

Ibarra Muñoz, David. Equidad y desarrollo. *Nexos,* v. 16, no. 184 (Apr 93), pp. 41 – 46.

— Interdependencia y desarrollo (Excerpt from a forthcoming book). *Comercio Exterior,* v. 43, no. 11 (Nov 93), pp. 991 – 1000.

— Pedro Vuskovic, un socialista latinoamericano. *Problemas del Desarrollo,* v. 24, no. 94 (July – Sept 93), pp. 249 – 257.

— Penurias de la modernidad. *Nexos,* v. 16, no. 191 (Nov 93), pp. 51 – 55.

Ibarra Pardo, Gabriel. Políticas de competencia en la integración en América Latina. *Integración Latinoamericana,* v. 18, no. 193 (Sept 93), pp. 45 – 51. Bibl.

Ibarra Rojas, Eugenia. Documentos para el estudio de la participación indígena en la campaña nacional de 1856. *Revista de Historia (Costa Rica),* no. 25 (Jan – June 92), pp. 245 – 250. Bibl, tables.

Igel, Regina. Reavaliação de estudos sobre o negro brasileiro. *Iberoamericana,* v. 17, no. 49 (1993), pp. 16 – 32. Bibl.

Iglesias, Enrique V. América Latina: un decenio dramático. *Mensaje,* v. 42, no. 417 (Mar – Apr 93), pp. 74 – 76. Il.

Ignácio, Sebastião Expedito. Dois aspectos da obra de Graciliano Ramos atestados pela tipologia oracional. *Revista de Letras (Brazil),* v. 32 (1992), pp. 69 – 78.

Ilarrequi, Gladys. Poems ("Zonas prohibidas," "Textos ficticios"). *Letras Femeninas,* v. 19, no. 1 – 2 (Spring – Fall 93), p. 170.

Illueca Sibauste, Aníbal. El congreso anfictiónico de 1826 como contribución de América al derecho internacional. *Revista Cultural Lotería,* v. 51, no. 388 (Mar – Apr 92), pp. 34 – 47.

Imaz, José Luis de. MERCOSUR y matrícula primaria para el año 2000. *Integración Latinoamericana,* v. 18, no. 194 (Oct 93), pp. 35 – 36.

Immink, Maarten Dirk Cornelis and Jorge A. Alarcón. Household Income, Food Availability, and Commercial Crop Production by Smallholder Farmers in the Western Highlands of Guatemala. *Economic Development and Cultural Change,* v. 41, no. 2 (Jan 93), pp. 319 – 342. Bibl, tables.

Infante Caffi, María Teresa and Manfred Wilhelmy von Wolff. La política exterior chilena en los años '90: el gobierno del presidente Aylwin y algunas proyecciones. *Estudios Sociales (Chile),* no. 75 (Jan – Mar 93), pp. 97 – 112.

Infesta, María Elena and Marla Valencia. Los criterios legales en la revisión de la política rosista de tierras públicas: Buenos Aires, 1852 – 1864. *Investigaciones y Ensayos,* no. 41 (Jan – Dec 91), pp. 407 – 421. Bibl.

Infiesta, Jesús. Al humanismo, a la ternura y a la caridad por el humor (Originally published in *Ecclesia*). *Mensaje,* v. 42, no. 423 (Oct 93), pp. 499 – 500. Il.

Iñiguez A., Ignacio. A Stage for International Fraternity (Translated by Kathleen Forrester, photographs by Claudio Pérez R.). *Américas,* v. 45, no. 4 (July – Aug 93), pp. 48 – 51. Il.

Inoa, Orlando. El arroz como ejemplo de la producción campesina para el mercado interno en la era de Trujillo. *Estudios Sociales (Dominican Republic),* v. 26, no. 92 (Apr – June 93), pp. 21 – 38. Bibl, tables.

Insulza, José Miguel. El Salvador: el más exitoso proceso de paz. *Mensaje,* v. 42, no. 416 (Jan – Feb 93), p. 48.

Inter-American Development Bank. Las maquiladoras en México en vísperas del TLC (Adapted from the text published in *Progreso Económico y Social en América Latina*). *Comercio Exterior,* v. 43, no. 2 (Feb 93), pp. 159 – 161. Tables.

Iokoi, Zilda Márcia Gricoli. Questão agrária e meio ambiente: 500 anos de destruição. *Vozes,* v. 86, no. 5 (Sept – Oct 92), pp. 12 – 20.

Ipanema, Marcello Moreira de and Cybelle Moreira de Ipanema. Indicador bioemerográfico brasileiro: Rio Grande do Norte, 1832 – 1908. *Revista do Instituto Histórico e Geográfico Brasileiro,* no. 371 (Apr – June 91), pp. 437 – 459.

— Pedro Calmon no cinqüentenário e no centenário dos cursos jurídicos no Rio de Janeiro. *Revista do Instituto Histórico e Geográfico Brasileiro,* no. 370 (Jan – Mar 91), pp. 78 – 81.

Ipola, Emilio de. La democracia en el amanecer de la sociología. *Revista Mexicana de Sociología,* v. 54, no. 2 (Apr – June 92), pp. 215 – 232. Bibl.

Irarrázaval Llona, Ignacio. Autonomía municipal: un proyecto político perdiente. *EURE,* v. 19, no. 57 (July 93), pp. 79 – 94. Bibl, tables.

Irarrázaval Llona, Ignacio and Juan Pablo Valenzuela. La ilegitimidad en Chile: ¿Hacia un cambio en la conformación de la familia? *Estudios Públicos (Chile),* no. 52 (Spring 93), pp. 145 – 190. Bibl, tables, charts.

Irausquin, Rossi and Barbara Younoszai. Not Establishing Limits: The Writing of Isaac Chocrón. *Inti,* no. 37 – 38 (Spring – Fall 93), pp. 155 – 161. Bibl.

Iriarte, María Elvira. Fernando Botero: la corrida (Accompanied by an English translation). *Art Nexus,* no. 9 (June – Aug 93), pp. 92 – 93. Il.

— Mira Schendel (Accompanied by an English translation). *Art Nexus,* no. 8 (Apr – June 93), pp. 83 – 87. Il.

Irías, Jorge et al. De la pobreza a la abundancia o la abundancia de la pobreza. *Revista de Ciencias Sociales (Costa Rica),* no. 57 (Sept 92), pp. 79 – 86. Bibl.

Irurozqui Victoriano, Marta. La guerra de razas en Bolivia: la (re)invención de una tradición. *Revista Andina,* v. 11, no. 1 (July 93), pp. 163 – 200. Bibl.

— ¿Qué hacer con el indio?: un análisis de las obras de Franz Tamayo y Alcides Arguedas. *Revista de Indias,* v. 52, no. 195 – 196 (May – Dec 92), pp. 559 – 587.

Isai, João Yo and Carlos Roberto Azzoni. Custo da proteção de áreas com interesse ambiental no estado de São Paulo. *Estudos Econômicos,* v. 22, no. 2 (May – Aug 92), pp. 253 – 271. Bibl, tables, charts.

Isaia, Artur Cesar. Catolicismo, regeneração social e castilhismo na república velha gaúcha. *Estudos Ibero-Americanos,* v. 18, no. 1 (July 92), pp. 5 – 18. Bibl.

Isard, Walter and Manas Chatterji. Ciencia regional: nuevo orden mundial y el desarrollo de México en la era del TLC. *Problemas del Desarrollo,* v. 24, no. 93 (Apr – June 93), pp. 39 – 54. Bibl, charts.

Isava, Luis Miguel. La escritura, la lectura, lo fantástico: análisis de "Continuidad de los parques" de Julio Cortázar. *Revista Nacional de Cultura (Venezuela),* v. 54, no. 287 (Oct – Dec 92), pp. 72 – 82. Bibl, il.

Issa, Richard. Port Royal Dockyard Repairs in 1789. *Jamaica Journal,* v. 24, no. 3 (Feb 93), pp. 11 – 14. Il, tables, facs.

Issler, João Victor and Robert F. Engle. Common Trends and Common Cycles in Latin America. *Revista Brasileira de Economia,* v. 47, no. 2 (Apr – June 93), pp. 149 – 176. Bibl, tables, charts.

Itier, César. La tradición oral quechua antigua en los procesos de idolatrías de Cajatambo. *Bulletin de l'Institut Français d'Etudes Andines,* v. 21, no. 3 (1992), pp. 1009 – 1051. Bibl.

Iturrieta, Aníbal and Marcela A. García. Perón en el exilio español: la búsqueda de la legitimidad. *Todo Es Historia,* v. 27, no. 313 (Aug 93), pp. 8 – 25. Bibl, il.

Iwasaki Cauti, Fernando A. Mujeres al borde de la perfección: Rosa de Santa María y las alumbradas de Lima. *Hispanic American Historical Review,* v. 73, no. 4 (Nov 93), pp. 581 – 613. Bibl.

— Toros y sociedad en Lima colonial. *Anuario de Estudios Americanos,* v. 49 (1992), pp. 311 – 333. Bibl.

Izard, Miquel. Elegir lo posible y escoger lo mejor. *Boletín Americanista,* v. 33, no. 42 – 43 (1992 – 1993), pp. 141 – 182. Bibl.

— Poca subordinación y menos ambición. *Boletín Americanista,* v. 33, no. 42 – 43 (1992 – 1993), pp. 159 – 182. Bibl.

Jablonska, Alejandra. La política de salud de la OMS: propuesta para los países en vías de desarrollo. *Revista Mexicana de Ciencias Políticas y Sociales,* v. 38, Nueva época, no. 153 (July – Sept 93), pp. 91 – 107.

Jackson, Robert H. The Impact of Liberal Policy on Mexico's Northern Frontier: Mission Secularization and the Development of Alta California, 1812 – 1846. *Colonial Latin American Historical Review,* v. 2, no. 2 (Spring 93), pp. 195 – 225. Bibl, tables.

Jaffé, Verónica. Anotaciones sobre la literatura venezolana. *Inti,* no. 37 – 38 (Spring – Fall 93), pp. 245 – 251.

Jákfalvi-Leiva, Susana. De la voz a la escritura: la *Relación* de Titu Cusi, 1570. *Revista de Crítica Literaria Latinoamericana,* v. 19, no. 37 (Jan – June 93), pp. 259 – 277. Bibl.

Jaksic, Ivan. The Legacies of Military Rule in Chile (Review article). *Latin American Research Review,* v. 28, no. 1 (1993), pp. 258 – 269.

— Sarmiento y la prensa chilena del siglo XIX. *Historia (Chile),* no. 26 (1991 – 1992), pp. 117 – 144. Bibl.

James, Dilmus D. Technology Policy and Technological Change: A Latin American Emphasis (Review article). *Latin American Research Review,* v. 28, no. 1 (1993), pp. 89 – 101. Bibl.

Jamieson Villiers, Martín. Africanismos en el español de Panamá. *Revista Cultural Lotería,* v. 50, no. 384 (July – Aug 91), pp. 5 – 31. Bibl.

Janssen, Willem et al. Adoção de cultivares melhoradas de feijão em estados selecionados no Brasil. *Revista de Economia e Sociologia Rural,* v. 30, no. 4 (Oct – Dec 92), pp. 321 – 338. Bibl, tables, charts.

Jara, Umberto. Entrevista a Guillermo Thorndike. *Debate (Peru),* v. 16, no. 72 (Mar – May 93), pp. 6 – 12. Il.

Jaramillo, Diego. El hombre latinoamericano y la transformación social. *Islas,* no. 96 (May – Aug 90), pp. 18 – 26.

Jaramillo de Velasco, María Mercedes. Por la insubordinación: Albalucía Angel y Fanny Buitrago. *Conjunto,* no. 92 (July – Dec 92), pp. 46 – 54. Bibl.

Jaramillo Gómez, William. Legislación de prensa a la luz de la nueva constitución. *Revista Javeriana,* v. 61, no. 595 (June 93), pp. 292 – 297.

Jaramillo Lyon, Armando. Don Andrés Bello en Santiago. *Boletín de Historia y Antigüedades,* v. 79, no. 779 (Oct – Dec 92), pp. 1037 – 1051.

Jardanovski, Elio and Paulo César Vaz Guimarães. O desafio da eqüidade no setor saúde. *RAE; Revista de Administração de Empresas,* v. 33, no. 3 (May – June 93), pp. 38 – 51.

Jarkowski, Aníbal. La colección Arlt: modelos para cada temporada. *Cuadernos Hispanoamericanos,* no. Special issue, 11 (July 93), pp. 23 – 36. Bibl, il.

— Sobreviviente en una guerra: enviando tarjetas postales. *Hispamérica,* v. 21, no. 63 (Dec 92), pp. 15 – 24.

Jarque, Carlos M. La población de México en el último decenio del siglo XX. *Comercio Exterior,* v. 43, no. 7 (July 93), pp. 642 – 651. Tables, charts.

Jarque, Fietta and Mauricio Vicent. La poetisa cubana Dulce María Loynaz gana el premio Cervantes. *Humboldt,* no. 108 (1993), p. 104.

Jaspe Alvarez, José Ismael and Paul-Yves Denis. Estudio de la distribución espacial del sistema cooperativo de "Ferias de Consumo Familiar" (FCF) y de su papel en el abastecimiento alimentario en la región centro-occidental de Venezuela. *Revista Geográfica (Mexico),* no. 114 (July – Dec 91), pp. 5 – 36. Bibl, maps, charts.

Jáuregui, Eloy. Vorágine de la caja negra. *Debate (Peru),* v. 16, no. 75 (Dec 93 – Jan 94), pp. 65 – 66. Il.

Jáuregui Moreno, Jesús Manuel. El rancho de Mariachi en 1837. *Plural (Mexico),* v. 22, no. 261 (June 93), pp. 85 – 93. Bibl.

Jiménez, Agustín. Minerva Song. *Plural (Mexico),* v. 22, no. 260 (May 93), pp. 49 – 53.

Jiménez, Carlos. ARCO '93 (Accompanied by an English translation). *Art Nexus,* no. 8 (Apr – June 93), pp. 110 – 111. Il.

— Bienal de Venecia. *Art Nexus,* no. 10 (Sept – Dec 93), pp. 56 – 58.

— Guillermo Kuitca, un pintor teatral (Accompanied by an English translation). *Art Nexus,* no. 9 (June – Aug 93), pp. 48 – 51. Il.

— Indian Summer (Accompanied by an English translation). *Art Nexus,* no. 7 (Jan – Mar 93), pp. 48 – 51. Il.

— Voces de ultramar: arte en América Latina y Canarias, 1910 – 1960 (Accompanied by an English translation). *Art Nexus,* no. 8 (Apr – June 93), pp. 48 – 49. Il.

Jiménez, Juan Ramón. Buzón de fantasmas: de Juan Ramón Jiménez a Ermilo Abreu Gómez. *Vuelta,* v. 17, no. 205 (Dec 93), pp. 87 – 88.

Jiménez Arce, Ana Cecilia et al. La agricultura de cambio en el contexto del ajuste estructural. *Revista de Ciencias Sociales (Costa Rica),* no. 60 (June 93), pp. 27 – 38. Bibl, tables.

Jiménez Arraiz, Francisco. Antiguallas: orígenes caraqueños (Previously published in this journal vol. 1, no. 1, 1912). *Boletín de la Academia Nacional de la Historia (Venezuela),* v. 75, no. 300 (Oct – Dec 92), pp. 262 – 273.

Jiménez de Báez, Yvette. Los de abajo de Mariano Azuela: escritura y punto de partida. *Nueva Revista de Filología Hispánica,* v. 40, no. 2 (July – Dec 92), pp. 843 – 874. Bibl.

Jiménez de la Jara, Jorge. Cambio y salud: adaptaciones de los sistemas de salud al cambio epidemiológico, socioeconómico y políticocultural. *Estudios Sociales (Chile),* no. 77 (July – Sept 93), pp. 49 – 59.

Jiménez Emán, Ennio. Tres temas de Octavio Paz en *El arco y la lira. Revista Nacional de Cultura (Venezuela),* v. 54, no. 287 (Oct – Dec 92), pp. 83 – 91. Bibl, il.

Jiménez Emán, Gabriel. Notas bibliográficas del catálogo de publicaciones de la Academia Nacional de la Historia. *Boletín de la Academia Nacional de la Historia (Venezuela),* v. 75, no. 298 (Apr – June 92), pp. 99 – 107.

— Octavio Paz: las voces de lo poético. *Revista Nacional de Cultura (Venezuela),* v. 53, no. 285 (Apr – June 92), pp. 233 – 236.

Jiménez López, Lexa. "Como la luna nos enseñó a tejer" (Translated by Ambar Past). *Artes de México,* no. 19 (Spring 93), pp. 40 – 41. Il.

Jiménez Varela, Luis Carlos. Memorias del olvido. *Revista Cultural Lotería,* v. 51, no. 392 (Nov – Dec 93), pp. 85 – 86.

Jiménez Vázquez, Miguel A. La reforma monetaria de México a la luz de la teoría monetarista. *Momento Económico,* no. 65 (Jan – Feb 93), pp. 11 – 15. Tables.

Johansson, Patrick. Yaocuicatl: cantos de guerra y guerra de cantos. *Estudios de Cultura Náhuatl,* v. 22 (1992), pp. 29 – 43.

John Paul II, Pope. "Si quieres la paz, sal al encuentro del pobre": mensaje de su santidad Juan Pablo II para la celebración de la Jornada Mundial de la Paz, 1 de enero de 1993. *ECA; Estudios Centroamericanos,* v. 48, no. 531 – 532 (Jan – Feb 93), pp. 18 – 26.

Johnson, David E. Face Value: An Essay on Cecile Pineda's *Face. The Americas Review,* v. 19, no. 2 (Summer 91), pp. 73 – 93. Bibl.

Johnson, Jessica. Whatever Happened to Laguna Verde? *Business Mexico,* v. 3, no. 5 (May 93), pp. 20 – 22. Il.

Johnson, Peter T. Guidelines for Collecting Documentation on Marginalized Peoples and Ideas in Latin America. *SALALM Papers,* v. 34 (1989), pp. 455 – 458.

Johnstone, Nick. Comparative Advantage, Transfrontier Pollution, and the Environmental Degradation of a Border Region: The Case of the Californias. *Journal of Borderlands Studies,* v. 7, no. 2 (Fall 92), pp. 33 – 52. Bibl.

Jones, Errol D. Ríus: Still a Thorn in the Side of the Mexican Establishment (Review article). *Studies in Latin American Popular Culture,* v. 12 (1993), pp. 221 – 227. Bibl.

Jones, John G. and Duccio Bonavia. Análisis de coprolitos de llama (Lama glama) del precerámico tardío de la costa nor central del Perú. *Bulletin de l'Institut Français d'Etudes Andines,* v. 21, no. 3 (1992), pp. 835 – 852. Bibl, tables.

Jones, Robert S. and David Robinson. Protection + Environment = Future Growth. *Business Mexico,* v. 3, no. 1 (Jan – Feb 93), pp. 37 – 39. Il.

Jones, Robert W. A Content Comparison of Daily Newspapers in the El Paso – Juárez Circulation Area. *Journal of Borderlands Studies,* v. 7, no. 2 (Fall 92), pp. 93 – 100. Bibl, tables.

Jong, Wil de and Michael Chibnik. Organización de la mano de obra agrícola en las comunidades ribereñas de la Amazonía peruana. *Amazonía Peruana,* v. 11, no. 21 (Sept 92), pp. 181 – 215. Bibl.

Jongkind, Coenraad Frederik. Venezuelan Industry under the New Conditions of the 1989 Economic Policy. *European Review of Latin American and Caribbean Studies,* no. 54 (June 93), pp. 65 – 93. Bibl, tables.

Joralemon, Peter David. Treasures of the New World. *Latin American Art,* v. 4, no. 4 (Winter 92), pp. 40 – 43. Il.

Jordán, Alberto R. Cámpora: siete semanas de gobierno. *Todo Es Historia,* v. 26, no. 310 (May 93), pp. 8 – 36. Bibl, il.

Jordán Sandoval, Santiago. Coincidentes y respuestas alarmantes a una pregunta sobre *Bolivia y el equilibrio del Cono Sur. Signo,* no. 35, Nueva época (Jan – Apr 92), pp. 37 – 41. Bibl.

Jou, Maite. Gabriel García y Tassara: del nacionalismo romántico al concepto de raza hispana. *Anuario de Estudios Americanos,* v. 49 (1992), pp. 529 – 562. Bibl.

Jouravlev, Andrei and Terence R. Lee. Self-Financing Water Supply and Sanitation Services. *CEPAL Review,* no. 48 (Dec 92), pp. 117 – 128. Bibl, tables, charts.

Joy-Karno, Beverly. Latin American Government Documents on the Arts: Introductory Guide. *SALALM Papers,* v. 34 (1989), pp. 239 – 260. Bibl.

Joyce, Arthur A. Interregional Interaction and Social Development on the Oaxaca Coast. *Ancient Mesoamerica,* v. 4, no. 1 (Spring 93), pp. 67 – 84. Bibl, il, maps.

Juan, Adelaida de. José Martí y el arte mexicano. *La Palabra y el Hombre,* no. 82 (Apr – June 92), pp. 45 – 56. Bibl.

— Pintar sobre piedra. *Casa de las Américas,* no. 189 (Oct – Dec 92), pp. 102 – 106.

Juan-Navarro, Santiago. 79 ó 99/modelos para desarmar: claves para una lectura morelliana de "Continuidad de los parques" de Julio Cortázar. *Hispanic Journal,* v. 13, no. 2 (Fall 92), pp. 241 – 249. Bibl.

Juárez, Fátima. Intervención de las instituciones en la reducción de la fecundidad y la mortalidad infantil. *Estudios Demográficos y Urbanos,* v. 7, no. 2 – 3 (May – Dec 92), pp. 377 – 405. Bibl, tables, charts.

Juárez Ch'ix, Isabel and Petrona Cruz Cruz. La desconfiada: diálogo dramático. *Mesoamérica (USA),* v. 13, no. 23 (June 92), pp. 135 – 141.

Juárez Martínez, Abel. España, el Caribe y el puerto de Veracruz en tiempos del libre comercio, 1789 – 1821. *La Palabra y el Hombre,* no. 83 (July – Sept 92), pp. 93 – 108. Bibl.

Jürth, Max. Plegarias incaicas. *Revista de Crítica Literaria Latinoamericana,* v. 19, no. 37 (Jan – June 93), pp. 159 – 168.

Julien, Daniel G. Late Pre-Inkaic Ethnic Groups in Highland Peru: An Archaeological – Ethnohistorical Model of the Political Geography of the Cajamarca Region. *Latin American Antiquity,* v. 4, no. 3 (Sept 93), pp. 246 – 273. Bibl, il, tables, maps, charts.

Junio, Juan Carlos. Participación democrática. *Realidad Económica,* no. 116 (May – June 93), pp. 29 – 31.

Junquera, Carlos. Antropología y paleotecnología: ayer y hoy de una situación agraria en Lambayeque (Perú). *Revista Española de Antropología Americana,* v. 23 (1993), pp. 165 – 187. Bibl.

Kage, Hedda. Carlos Giménez ha muerto (Translated by José Luis Gómez y Patiño). *Humboldt,* no. 109 (1993), p. 99.

Kahn, Francis and Guy Couturier. Notes on the Insect Fauna of Two Species of "Astrocaryum" (Palmae, Cocoeae, Bactridinae) in Peruvian Amazonia, with Emphasis on Potential Pests of Cultivated Palms. *Bulletin de l'Institut Français d'Etudes Andines,* v. 21, no. 2 (1992), pp. 715 – 725. Bibl, il, tables, maps.

Kahn, Francis and Betty Millán. "Astrocaryum" (Palmae) in Amazonia: A Preliminary Treatment. *Bulletin de l'Institut Français d'Etudes Andines,* v. 21, no. 2 (1992), pp. 459 – 531. Bibl, il, tables.

Kahn, Francis et al. Datos preliminares a la actualización de la flora de palamae del Perú: intensidad de herborización y riqueza de las colecciones. *Bulletin de l'Institut Français d'Etudes Andines,* v. 21, no. 2 (1992), pp. 549 – 563. Bibl, tables, maps.

Kahn, Túlio and Sérgio Adorno. Pena de morte: para que e para quem serve esse debate? *Vozes,* v. 87, no. 3 (May – June 93), pp. 14 – 30. Tables, charts.

Kaliman, Ricardo J. Sobre la construcción del objeto en la crítica literaria latinoamericana. *Revista de Crítica Literaria Latinoamericana,* v. 19, no. 37 (Jan – June 93), pp. 307 – 317. Bibl.

Kalman L., Judith. En búsqueda de una palabra nueva: la complejidad conceptual y las dimensiones sociales de la alfabetización. *Revista Latinoamericana de Estudios Educativos,* v. 23, no. 1 (Jan – Mar 93), pp. 87 – 95. Bibl.

Kamp, Dick. Mexico's Mines: Source of Wealth or Woe? *Business Mexico,* v. 3, no. 1 (Jan – Feb 93), pp. 29 – 30. Il.

Kane, Connie M. et al. Differences in the Manifest Dream Content of Mexican, Mexican American, and Anglo American College Women: A Research Note. *Hispanic Journal of Behavioral Sciences,* v. 15, no. 1 (Feb 93), pp. 134 – 139. Bibl, tables.

Kanter, Deborah E. Viudas y vecinos, milpas y magueyes: el impacto del auge de la población en el valle de Toluca; el caso de Tenango del Valle en el siglo XVIII. *Estudios Demográficos y Urbanos,* v. 7, no. 1 (Jan – Apr 92), pp. 19 – 33. Bibl, tables.

Kaplan, Joanna Overing. A estética da produção: o senso de comunidade entre os cubeo e os piaroa. *Revista de Antropologia (Brazil),* v. 34 (1991), pp. 7 – 33. Bibl.

Kaplan, Marcos. Crisis del estado latinoamericano: decadencia o palingenesia? *Relaciones Internacionales (Mexico),* v. 14, Nueva época, no. 56 (Oct – Dec 92), pp. 35 – 44.

— La crisis del estado y el narcotráfico latinoamericano. *Cuadernos Americanos,* no. 40, Nueva época (July – Aug 93), pp. 11 – 34. Bibl.

— La internacionalización del narcotráfico latinoamericano y Estados Unidos. *Relaciones Internacionales (Mexico),* v. 15, Nueva época, no. 57 (Jan – Mar 93), pp. 75 – 86. Bibl.

Kaplan, Marina E. *La reina del Plata:* pastiche postmoderno. *Chasqui,* v. 22, no. 2 (Nov 93), pp. 57 – 72. Bibl.

Karlsson, Weine. Un estudio sueco sobre Francisco de Miranda. *Boletín de la Academia Nacional de la Historia (Venezuela),* v. 75, no. 299 (July – Sept 92), pp. 189 – 190.

Kartun, Mauricio O. Los ciclos del final. *Cuadernos Hispanoamericanos,* no. 517 – 519 (July – Sept 93), pp. 535 – 538.

Kaulicke, Peter. Evidencias paleoclimáticas en asentamientos del alto Piura durante el período intermedio temprano. *Bulletin de l'Institut Français d'Etudes Andines,* v. 22, no. 1 (1993), pp. 283 – 311. Bibl, il, maps.

— Moche, Vicús moche y el mochica temprano. *Bulletin de l'Institut Français d'Etudes Andines,* v. 21, no. 3 (1992), pp. 853 – 903. Bibl, il, tables, maps, charts.

Kaye, Susan. A Living Venue for Cultural Crossroads. *Américas,* v. 45, no. 3 (May – June 93), pp. 48 – 51. Il.

Keen, Benjamin. Lewis Hanke (1905 – 1993). *Hispanic American Historical Review,* v. 73, no. 4 (Nov 93), pp. 663 – 665.

Keenan, Joe. Corporate Mexico Goes for the Green. *Business Mexico,* v. 3, no. 1 (Jan – Feb 93), pp. 31 – 32. Il.

— Is There Life after Henequen? *Business Mexico,* v. 3, no. 4 (Apr 93), pp. 22 – 23. Il.

Keinert, Tania Margarete Mezzomo. Reforma administrativa nos anos '90: o caso da prefeitura municipal de São Paulo. *RAE; Revista de Administração de Empresas,* v. 33, no. 4 (July – Aug 93), pp. 66 – 81. Tables, maps, charts.

Kelly, Thomas C. Preceramic Projectile-Point Typology in Belize. *Ancient Mesoamerica,* v. 4, no. 2 (Fall 93), pp. 205 – 227. Bibl, il, tables, maps.

Kelso, Laura. Mission NAFTA. *Business Mexico,* v. 3, no. 7 (July 93), p. 20+. Il.

Kendall, Jonathan. The Thirteen Volatiles: Representation and Symbolism. *Estudios de Cultura Náhuatl,* v. 22 (1992), pp. 99 – 131. Bibl.

Kent, Robert B. Geographical Dimensions of the Shining Path Insurgency in Peru. *Geographical Review,* v. 83, no. 4 (Oct 93), pp. 441 – 454. Bibl, maps.

Keoseyán, Nelly. Los paisajes del sueño: metáforas para inventar un paraíso. *La Palabra y el Hombre,* no. 81 (Jan – Mar 92), p. 392.

Kerdel Vegas, Francisco. El inspector general doctor James Barry. *Boletín de la Academia Nacional de la Historia (Venezuela),* v. 75, no. 299 (July – Sept 92), pp. 157 – 162.

Kerr, Lucille. Frames for the Future: Some Thoughts on Latin American Literary Studies. *Latin American Literary Review,* v. 20, no. 40 (July – Dec 92), pp. 54 – 57.

Kessel, Juan J. M. M. van. El pago a la tierra: porque el desarrollo lo exige. *Allpanchis,* v. 23, no. 40 (July – Dec 92), pp. 201 – 217. Bibl.

Khan, Ahmad Saeed and Lúcia Maria Ramos Silva. Características sócio-econômicas de produtores rurais, conservação do solo e produtividade agrícola. *Revista de Economia e Sociologia Rural,* v. 30, no. 3 (July – Sept 92), pp. 225 – 237. Bibl, tables.

Khan, Ahmad Saeed and José da Silva Souza. Taxa de retorno social do investimento em pesquisa na cultura da mandioca no Nordeste. *Revista de Economia e Sociologia Rural,* v. 29, no. 4 (Oct – Dec 91), pp. 411 – 426. Bibl, tables, charts.

Khavisse, Miguel and Eduardo M. Basualdo. El nuevo poder terrateniente (Excerpt from the forthcoming book of the same title). *Realidad Económica,* no. 113 (Jan – Feb 93), pp. 90 – 99.

Kinzo, Maria d'Alva Gil. The 1989 Presidential Election: Electoral Behaviour in a Brazilian City. *Journal of Latin American Studies,* v. 25, no. 2 (May 93), pp. 313 – 330. Bibl, tables.

Kirbus, Federico B. Técnicas y trucos de nuestros fotógrafos. *Todo Es Historia,* v. 26, no. 309 (Apr 93), pp. 74 – 78. Il.

Kit, Wade. The Unionist Experiment in Guatemala, 1920 – 1921: Conciliation, Disintegration, and the Liberal Junta. *The Americas,* v. 50, no. 1 (July 93), pp. 31 – 64.

Klaveren, Alberto van. América Latina: entre la crisis y la esperanza. *Mensaje,* v. 42, no. 423 (Oct 93), pp. 481 – 483. II.

— Europa – Lateinamerika: Zwischen Illusion und Realismus, auch nach 1992. *Zeitschrift für Lateinamerika Wien,* no. 43 (1992), pp. 95 – 119. Bibl.

Klein, Carol Ebersole. The Social Text in Writing by Hispanic Women: Critical Perspectives of Myriam Díaz-Diocaretz. *The Americas Review,* v. 21, no. 1 (Spring 93), pp. 79 – 90. Bibl.

Klein, Darío and Fabían Lazovski. Tabaré Vázquez, un líder bien imaginado. *Cuadernos del CLAEH,* v. 18, no. 67 (Nov 93), pp. 37 – 52. Bibl.

Klein, Emilio. El mundo de trabajo rural. *Nueva Sociedad,* no. 124 (Mar – Apr 93), pp. 72 – 81. Bibl, tables.

Klein, Herbert S. Historia fiscal colonial: resultados y perspectivas (Translated by Laura Elena Pulido Varela). *Historia Mexicana,* v. 42, no. 2 (Oct – Dec 92), pp. 261 – 307.

Klein, Herbert S. and Sonia Pérez Toledo. La población de la ciudad de Zacatecas en 1857. *Historia Mexicana,* v. 42, no. 1 (July – Sept 92), pp. 77 – 102. Bibl, tables, charts.

Klesner, Joseph L. Modernization, Economic Crisis, and Electoral Realignment in Mexico. *Mexican Studies,* v. 9, no. 2 (Summer 93), pp. 187 – 223. Bibl, tables.

Klich, Ignacio. Argentine – Ottoman Relations and Their Impact on Immigrants from the Middle East: A History of Unfulfilled Expectations, 1910 – 1915. *The Americas,* v. 50, no. 2 (Oct 93), pp. 177 – 205. Bibl, tables.

Klintowitz, Jacob. Multiplicidade de estilos. *Problemas Brasileiros,* v. 30, no. 295 (Jan – Feb 93), pp. 57 – 58. II.

Klitenik, Carlos Espartaco. La pintura de los ochenta: el eclecticismo como estilo. *Cuadernos Hispanoamericanos,* no. 517 – 519 (July – Sept 93), pp. 371 – 381. II.

Kloin, Philip C. and Auxiliadora Arana. An Interview with Wolf Ruvinskis: The First Mexican Stanley Kowalski. *Latin American Theatre Review,* v. 26, no. 2 (Spring 93), pp. 158 – 165. II.

Kluback, William. Our Gentile Guides: Jorge Luis Borges and Franz Kafka. *Confluencia,* v. 8, no. 1 (Fall 92), pp. 19 – 27.

Klüppelholz, Heinz. Alejo Carpentiers orphische Beschwörung. *Zeitschrift für Lateinamerika Wien,* no. 42 (1992), pp. 17 – 25. Bibl.

Knight, Franklin W. Columbus and Slavery in the New World and Africa. *Revista/Review Interamericana,* v. 22, no. 1 – 2 (Spring – Summer 92), pp. 18 – 35. Bibl.

Knight, George Preston et al. The Socialization of Cooperative, Competitive, and Individualistic Preferences among Mexican American Children: The Mediating Role of Ethnic Identity. *Hispanic Journal of Behavioral Sciences,* v. 15, no. 3 (Aug 93), pp. 291 – 309. Bibl, tables, charts.

Knorozov, Yuri V. Los códices jeroglíficos mayas (Translated by Francisco Beverido Pereau). *La Palabra y el Hombre,* no. 82 (Apr – June 92), pp. 189 – 195.

Koegel, John. Calendar of Southern California Amusements (1852 – 1897) Designed for the Spanish-Speaking Public. *Inter-American Music Review,* v. 13, no. 2 (Spring – Summer 93), pp. 115 – 143. Bibl, il.

— Mexican and Mexican-American Musical Life in Southern California, 1850 – 1900. *Inter-American Music Review,* v. 13, no. 2 (Spring – Summer 93), pp. 111 – 114. Bibl.

Kohlhepp, Gerd. Mudanças estruturais na agropecuária e mobilidade da população rural no norte do Paraná (Brasil). *Revista Brasileira de Geografia,* v. 53, no. 2 (Apr – June 91), pp. 79 – 94. Bibl, il, tables, maps.

Kolesov, Mijail. El pensamiento filosófico de América Latina en la búsqueda de su autenticidad. *Islas,* no. 96 (May – Aug 90), pp. 42 – 52.

Korn, Francis. Il popolo minuto: La Boca, 1895. *Todo Es Historia,* v. 26, no. 305 (Dec 92), pp. 46 – 49. II.

Kornbluh, Peter R. and Malcolm Byrne. Iran – Contra: A Postmortem. *NACLA Report on the Americas,* v. 27, no. 3 (Nov – Dec 93), pp. 29 – 34 + . II.

Korzeniewicz, Roberto P. Contested Arenas: Recent Studies on Politics and Labor (Review article). *Latin American Research Review,* v. 28, no. 2 (1993), pp. 206 – 220.

— The Labor Politics of Radicalism: The Santa Fe Crisis of 1928. *Hispanic American Historical Review,* v. 73, no. 1 (Feb 93), pp. 1 – 32.

— Labor Unrest in Argentina, 1930 – 1943. *Latin American Research Review,* v. 28, no. 1 (1993), pp. 7 – 40. Bibl, tables.

— Las vísperas del peronismo: los conflictos laborales entre 1930 y 1943. *Desarrollo Económico (Argentina),* v. 33, no. 131 (Oct – Dec 93), pp. 323 – 354. Bibl, tables.

Kothe, Flávio R. Heine, Nerval, Castro Alves: "o negreiro." *Iberoamericana,* v. 17, no. 49 (1993), pp. 42 – 63.

Kovadloff, Santiago. Un oscuro país. *Cuadernos Hispanoamericanos,* no. 517 – 519 (July – Sept 93), pp. 575 – 581.

Kozári, Monika and Adám Anderle. Koloman von Kánya: Ein österreichisch-ungarischer Botschafter in Mexiko. *Zeitschrift für Lateinamerika Wien,* no. 43 (1992), pp. 63 – 80. Bibl.

Kozická, Katerina and Simona Binková. El dominio marítimo español en los materiales cartográficos y náuticos de Praga. *Anuario de Estudios Americanos,* v. 49, Suppl. 1 (1992), pp. 47 – 54. Bibl, maps.

Kozik, K. K. Julio Larraz: Exile and Reality. *Latin American Art,* v. 4, no. 4 (Winter 92), pp. 35 – 37. Bibl, il.

Krantzer, Guillermo and Jorge Sánchez. Regulaciones en el transporte urbano: el caso de Buenos Aires. *EURE,* v. 19, no. 56 (Mar 93), pp. 41 – 53. Bibl.

Krauze, Enrique. Madero vivo. *Vuelta,* v. 17, no. 196 (Mar 93), pp. 11 – 14.

— México en dos abuelos. *Vuelta,* v. 17, no. 202 (Sept 93), pp. 26 – 28.

— Perú y Vargas Llosa: vidas variopintas. *Vuelta,* v. 17, no. 199 (June 93), pp. 17 – 20.

— Zonas de Rossi. *Vuelta,* v. 17, no. 200 (July 93), pp. 62 – 63.

Krawczyk, Miriam. Women in the Region: Major Changes. *CEPAL Review,* no. 49 (Apr 93), pp. 7 – 19. Bibl.

Krebs, Brenda. Festival Iberoamericano de Teatro, Santiago de Compostela. *Latin American Theatre Review,* v. 26, no. 2 (Spring 93), pp. 183 – 186.

Krebs Wilckens, Ricardo. Discurso de recepción de don Julio Retamal Favereau. *Boletín de la Academia Chilena de la Historia,* v. 58 – 59, no. 102 (1991 – 1992), pp. 173 – 180.

— Don Gonzalo Izquierdo Fernández. *Boletín de la Academia Chilena de la Historia,* v. 58 – 59, no. 102 (1991 – 1992), pp. 33 – 38.

Kremlicka, Raimund. Zwei Frauen: Eva Peron und Marie Langer. *Zeitschrift für Lateinamerika Wien,* no. 42 (1992), pp. 53 – 65. Bibl.

Krennerich, Michael. Die Kompetitivität der Wahlen in Nicaragua, El salvador und Guatemala in historisch – vergleichender Perspektive. *Ibero-Amerikanisches Archiv,* v. 18, no. 1 – 2 (1992), pp. 245 – 290. Bibl.

Kristan-Graham, Cynthia. The Business of Narrative at Tula: An Analysis of the Vestibule Frieze, Trade, and Ritual. *Latin American Antiquity,* v. 4, no. 1 (Mar 93), pp. 3 – 21. Bibl, il.

Kronik, John W. Invasions from Outer Space: Narration and Dramatic Art in Spanish America. *Latin American Theatre Review,* v. 26, no. 2 (Spring 93), pp. 25 – 47. Bibl.

Krosigk, Friedrich von. Panama und die Grenzen US-amerikanischer Hegemonie: Überlegungen zum Konzept der Gegenmacht. *Zeitschrift für Lateinamerika Wien,* no. 43 (1992), pp. 81 – 93. Bibl, tables.

Krotz, Esteban. Aspectos de la discusión antropológica. *Nueva Antropología,* v. 13, no. 43 (Nov 92), pp. 9 – 22. Bibl.

Krüggeler, Thomas. Los artesanos del Cusco, la crisis regional y el régimen republicano, 1824 – 1869. *Siglo XIX: Revista,* no. 11, 2a época (Jan – June 92), pp. 111 – 148. Bibl, tables.

Kuschick, Murilo. Sucesión presidencial: sondeo de opinión. *El Cotidiano,* v. 10, no. 58 (Oct – Nov 93), pp. 54 – 58. Il, charts.

Kushigian, Julia A. Mario Vargas Llosa. *Hispamérica,* v. 21, no. 63 (Dec 92), pp. 35 – 42.

Kuwayama, Mikio. Nuevas formas de inversión en el comercio entre América Latina y Estados Unidos (Translated by Adriana Hierro). *Comercio Exterior,* v. 43, no. 5 (May 93), pp. 478 – 497. Bibl.

Kuznesof, Elizabeth Anne. Sexuality, Gender, and the Family in Colonial Brazil (Review article). *Luso-Brazilian Review,* v. 30, no. 1 (Summer 93), pp. 119 – 132. Bibl.

Labaki, Aimar. Nueve comentarios sobre los directores teatrales. *Conjunto,* no. 93 (Jan – June 93), pp. 13 – 17. Il.

Labandeira Fernández, Amancio and Sylvia-Lyn Hilton. El americanismo en España, 1991 – 1992. *Revista de Indias,* v. 53, no. 197 (Jan – Apr 93), pp. 133 – 409.

— La sensibilidad cromática y estética del Inca Garcilaso. *Revista de Indias,* v. 52, no. 195 – 196 (May – Dec 92), pp. 529 – 558. Bibl.

Labariega Villanueva, Pedro Gabriel. La adopción internacional de menores y sus repercusiones en las relaciones internacionales. *Relaciones Internacionales (Mexico),* v. 14, Nueva época, no. 55 (July – Sept 92), pp. 61 – 64. Charts.

Labastida, Jaime. De la serenidad (Includes reproductions of *Chalma, La bruma, Tlalmanalco, Iztaccíhuatl, Xilitla, San Luis Potosí,* and *La recua, Xochitlán, Puebla*). *Plural (Mexico),* v. 22, no. 262 (July 93), pp. 40 – 45. Il.

— El México que quiero. *Plural (Mexico),* v. 22, no. 264 (Sept 93), pp. 23 – 29.

Lacombe, Américo Jacobina. A construção da historiografia brasileira: o IHGB e a obra de Varnhagen. *Revista do Instituto Histórico e Geográfico Brasileiro,* no. 370 (Jan – Mar 91), pp. 245 – 264.

— Estudos cariocas. *Revista do Instituto Histórico e Geográfico Brasileiro,* no. 370 (Jan – Mar 91), pp. 310 – 329.

— Papéis velhos. *Revista do Instituto Histórico e Geográfico Brasileiro,* no. 371 (Apr – June 91), pp. 596 – 604.

Lacombe, Lourenço Luís. Dom Pedro II no centenário de sua morte. *Revista do Instituto Histórico e Geográfico Brasileiro,* no. 373 (Oct – Dec 91), pp. 1176 – 1182. Bibl.

Lacoste, Pablo Alberto. Lucha de élites en Argentina: la Unión Cívica Radical en Mendoza, 1890 – 1905. *Anuario de Estudios Americanos,* v. 50, no. 1 (1993), pp. 181 – 212. Bibl, tables.

La France, David G. Politics, Violence, and the Press in Mexico (Review article). *Studies in Latin American Popular Culture,* v. 12 (1993), pp. 215 – 220.

Lagmanovich, David. Nueva lectura de *Nuestra América. Casa de las Américas,* no. 191 (Apr – June 93), pp. 107 – 110.

Lagos, María L. The Politics of Representation: Class and Ethnic Identities in Cochabamba, Bolivia. *Boletín de Antropología Americana,* no. 24 (Dec 91), pp. 143 – 150. Bibl, il.

Lagos, María Soledad. El teatro chileno de creación colectiva desde sus orígenes hasta fines de la década de los '80: algunas reflexiones. *Aisthesis,* no. 24 (1991), pp. 45 – 53. Bibl.

Laguerre, Enrique Arturo. De espaldas a la historia. *Homines,* v. 15 – 16, no. 2 – 1 (Oct 91 – Dec 92), pp. 116 – 117.

Laguna, Justo. La iglesia y diez años de democracia. *Todo Es Historia,* v. 27, no. 317 (Dec 93), pp. 8 – 9. Il.

Lahera, Eugenio. Dinámica, restricciones y políticas de la integración. *Integración Latinoamericana,* v. 17, no. 184 (Nov 92), pp. 3 – 15. Bibl.

— Integration Today: Bases and Options. *CEPAL Review,* no. 47 (Aug 92), pp. 63 – 76. Bibl.

Laks, Jacobo. La banca cooperativa en períodos de ajuste. *Realidad Económica,* no. 116 (May – June 93), pp. 21 – 29.

Lamborghini, Leónidas C. Digresiones, 1976 – 1993. *Cuadernos Hispanoamericanos,* no. 517 – 519 (July – Sept 93), pp. 498 – 502.

Lamego, Valéria. A desonra de uma sociedade patriarcal. *Estudos Feministas,* v. 1, no. 1 (1993), pp. 152 – 154.

Lamming, George. Coming, Coming, Coming Home. *Casa de las Américas,* no. 190 (Jan – Mar 93), pp. 65 – 74.

Lamounier, Bolivar. Empresarios, partidos y democratización en Brasil, 1974 – 1990. *Revista Mexicana de Sociología,* v. 54, no. 1 (Jan – Mar 92), pp. 77 – 97. Bibl.

— O modelo institucional brasileiro: a presente crise e propostas de reforma. *Ibero-Amerikanisches Archiv,* v. 18, no. 1 – 2 (1992), pp. 225 – 244. Bibl, tables.

Landau, Elena and Edward Joaquim Amadeo Swaelen. Indexação e dispersão de preços relativos: análise do caso brasileiro, 1975 – 1991. *Revista de Economia Política (Brazil),* v. 13, no. 3 (July – Sept 93), pp. 130 – 138. Bibl, charts.

Landau, Elena and Suzana S. Peixoto. Inflação, indexação e preços relativos: novas evidências para o Brasil. *Pesquisa e Planejamento Econômico,* v. 22, no. 1 (Apr 92), pp. 125 – 167. Bibl, tables, charts.

Landau, Saul. Clinton's Cuba Policy: A Low-Priority Dilemma. *NACLA Report on the Americas,* v. 26, no. 5 (May 93), pp. 35 – 37 +.

Lande, Stephen. Think Globally, Trade Locally. *Business Mexico,* v. 3, no. 11 (Nov 93), pp. 8 – 11.

Landeo, Liliam. Bibliografía sobre ecología. *Amazonía Peruana,* v. 11, no. 21 (Sept 92), pp. 223 – 237.

Landim, Leilah. Can NGOs Help Stitch Together a Safety Net for Brazil's Poor? *Grassroots Development,* v. 17, no. 1 (1993), pp. 36 – 37. Il.

Langebaek, Andrés. Colombia y los flujos de capital privado a América Latina, 1970 – 1991. *Planeación y Desarrollo,* v. 24, no. 2 (May – Aug 93), pp. 401 – 425. Bibl, tables, charts.

Langebaek, Carl Henrik. Competencia por prestigio político y momificación en el norte de Suramérica y el Istmo de Panamá. *Revista Colombiana de Antropología,* v. 29 (1992), pp. 7 – 26. Bibl.

Langevin, André. Las zampoñas del conjunto de kantu y el debate sobre la función de la segunda hilera de tubos: datos etnográficos y análisis semiótico. *Revista Andina,* v. 10, no. 2 (Dec 92), pp. 405 – 440. Bibl, tables.

Langue, Frédérique. Antagonismos y solidaridades en un cabildo colonial: Caracas, 1750 – 1810. *Anuario de Estudios Americanos,* v. 49 (1992), pp. 371 – 393. Bibl.

— El arbitrismo en el gremio minero novohispano o la representación de J. de la Borda y J. L. Lazaga, 1767: documentos. *Anuario de Estudios Americanos,* v. 50, no. 1 (1993), pp. 269 – 302. Bibl.

— De moralista a arbitrista: don Francisco de Ibarra, obispo de Venezuela, 1798 – 1806; recopilación documental. *Anuario de Estudios Americanos,* v. 49, Suppl. 1 (1992), pp. 55 – 84. Bibl.

— Las élites en América Española: actitudes y mentalidades. *Boletín Americanista,* v. 33, no. 42 – 43 (1992 – 1993), pp. 123 – 139. Bibl.

— Simposio "El Nuevo Mundo – Mundos Nuevos: La Experiencia Americana." *Anuario de Estudios Americanos,* v. 49, Suppl. 1 (1992), pp. 220 – 222.

Lanzana, Antonio. A realidade dos salários. *Problemas Brasileiros,* v. 30, no. 296 (Mar – Apr 93), pp. 15 – 16. Tables, charts.

Lanzaro, Jorge Luis. La "doble transición" en el Uruguay: gobierno de partidos y neo-presidencialismo. *Nueva Sociedad,* no. 128 (Nov – Dec 93), pp. 132 – 147.

Laporte, Jean Pierre. Los sitios arqueológicos del valle de Dolores en las montañas mayas de Guatemala. *Mesoamérica (USA),* v. 13, no. 24 (Dec 92), pp. 413 – 439. Bibl, il, tables, maps.

Lapuente, Felipe-Antonio. Cervantes en la perspectiva de Fuentes. *Cuadernos Americanos,* no. 39, Nueva época (May – June 93), pp. 228 – 242. Bibl.

Lara, Luis Fernando. Para la historia lingüística del pachuco. *Anuario de Letras (Mexico),* v. 30 (1992), pp. 75 – 88. Bibl.

Lara de la Fuente, Leonor. Arturo Rivera: una pasión renacentista. *Artes de México,* no. 21 (Fall 93), pp. 100 – 101.

Lara Figueroa, Celso A. El cuento popular de raíz europea en el oriente de Guatemala. *Folklore Americano,* no. 53 (Jan – June 92), pp. 37 – 53.

— Cuentos maravillosos de tradición oral del oriente guatemalteco. *La Tradición Popular,* no. 83 – 84 (1991), Issue. II, maps.

— Cuentos populares del "Aprendiz de brujo" en Guatemala. *La Tradición Popular,* no. 80 (1990), Issue. Bibl, il, maps.

— Presencia del cuento popular en Guatemala: estudio histórico – etnográfico del tipo AT 325. *Folklore Americano,* no. 52 (July – Dec 91), pp. 7 – 37. Bibl, maps.

Lara Flores, Sara María. La flexibilidad del mercado de trabajo rural: una propuesta que involucra a las mujeres. *Revista Mexicana de Sociología,* v. 54, no. 1 (Jan – Mar 92), pp. 29 – 48. Bibl.

Lara M., Carlos. Mexicans outside Mexico. *Business Mexico,* v. 3, no. 7 (July 93), pp. 24 – 26. Il, tables.

Lara Zavala, Hernán. El cantar del pecador (Text read by the author upon presentation of the newly published book). *Plural (Mexico),* v. 22, no. 265 (Oct 93), pp. 78 – 79.

Laroche, Rose Claire. Ecossistemas e impactos ambientais da modernização agrícola do vale São Francisco. *Revista Brasileira de Geografia,* v. 53, no. 2 (Apr – June 91), pp. 63 – 77. Bibl, il, charts.

La Rosa, Pablo. Chronicle of the Argonaut Polypus. *The Americas Review,* v. 20, no. 3 – 4 (Fall – Winter 92), pp. 124 – 129.

Larraín Arroyo, Luis et al. ¿Un neoliberalismo en declinación?: debates. *Mensaje,* v. 42, no. 418 (May 93), pp. 142 – 151. Il.

Larraín Barros, Horacio. Identidad cultural indígena tras quinientos años de aculturación: desafío y destino. *Estudios Sociales (Chile),* no. 76 (Apr – June 93), pp. 135 – 148. Bibl.

Larraín Mira, Paz and René Millar Carvacho. Notas para la historia de la cultura en el período indiano: la biblioteca del obispo de Santiago, Juan Bravo del Rivero y Correa, 1685 – 1752. *Historia (Chile),* no. 26 (1991 – 1992), pp. 173 – 211. Bibl.

Larrañaga, Jorge and Mario Carminatti. De intendentes a gobernadores: coloquio con los intendentes. *Cuadernos del CLAEH,* v. 18, no. 67 (Nov 93), pp. 19 – 34.

Larriqueta, Daniel E. El "pacto social" como yo lo viví. *Todo Es Historia,* v. 26, no. 310 (May 93), pp. 38 – 42. Il.

Larsen, Neil. En contra de la des-estetización del "discurso" colonial. *Revista de Crítica Literaria Latinoamericana,* v. 19, no. 37 (Jan – June 93), pp. 335 – 342. Bibl.

— Latin America and "Cultural Studies." *Latin American Literary Review,* v. 20, no. 40 (July – Dec 92), pp. 58 – 62.

Lartigue, François. México '92: les amérindiens dans la ville. *Caravelle,* no. 59 (1992), pp. 99 – 108.

Larue, J. William. Some Observations on a Model 1799 Infantry Officer's Short Saber. *Colonial Latin American Historical Review,* v. 2, no. 4 (Fall 93), pp. 441 – 448. Bibl, il.

Lasaga, Ignacio. La eticidad del pobre. *Estudios Sociales (Dominican Republic),* v. 26, no. 91 (Jan – Mar 93), pp. 61 – 76.

Lasarte Valcárcel, Francisco Javier. Poéticas de la primera contemporaneidad y cambio intelectual en la narrativa venezolana. *Revista Chilena de Literatura,* no. 41 (Apr 93), pp. 79 – 97. Bibl.

Laserna, Roberto. Integración y gobernabilidad: los nuevos desafíos de la democracia en Bolivia. *Nueva Sociedad,* no. 128 (Nov – Dec 93), pp. 120 – 131.

Lasso de Paulis, Marixa. La mentalidad en la sociedad colonial: la importancia de la etiqueta y de la ceremonia en los conflictos políticos del siglo XVII panameño. *Revista Cultural Lotería,* v. 51, no. 391 (Sept – Oct 92), pp. 105 – 111. Bibl.

Lastra, Pedro. Eduardo Anguita. *Inti,* no. 36 (Fall 92), p. 129.

— Imágenes de José María Arguedas. *Escritura (Venezuela),* v. 17, no. 33 – 34 (Jan – Dec 92), pp. 47 – 59.

— Noticias de maestro Ricardo Latcham, muerto en La Habana. *Casa de las Américas,* no. 191 (Apr – June 93), pp. 79 – 81.

Latapí, Pablo. El pensamiento educativo de Torres Bodet: una apreciación crítica. *Revista Latinoamericana de Estudios Educativos,* v. 22, no. 3 (July – Sept 92), pp. 13 – 44. Bibl.

— Reflexiones sobre la justicia en la educación. *Revista Latinoamericana de Estudios Educativos,* v. 23, no. 2 (Apr – June 93), pp. 9 – 41. Bibl.

Laudanna, Mayra. Ernesto de Fiori. *Vozes,* v. 86, no. 4 (July – Aug 92), pp. 59 – 65. Il.

Lauer, Mirko. Un escándalo en bohemia (Three poems). *Hueso Húmero,* no. 29 (May 93), pp. 105 – 114.

— La mentira cordial. *Debate (Peru),* v. 16, no. 74 (Sept – Oct 93), pp. 41 – 45. Bibl.

Lauretis, Teresa de. Volver a pensar el cine de mujeres: estética y teoría feminista (Excerpt from *Technologies of Gender: Essays on Theory, Film, and Fiction* translated by Beatriz Olivier). *Feminaria,* v. 6, no. 10 (Apr 93), pp. 1 – 12. Bibl.

Lausent Herrera, Isabelle. La cristianización de los chinos en el Perú: integración, sumisión y resistencia. *Bulletin de l'Institut Français d'Etudes Andines,* v. 21, no. 3 (1992), pp. 977 – 1007. Bibl, il.

Lautier, Bruno. Les Nouvelles Politiques d'Ajustement en Amérique Latine: Guadalajara, Mexique, 24 – 27 février 1992. *Cahiers des Amériques Latines,* no. 13 (1992), pp. 171 – 172.

Lavados Montes, Iván and Juan Enrique Vargas. La gestión judicial. *Estudios Sociales (Chile),* no. 78 (Oct – Dec 93), pp. 203 – 225.

Lavell Thomas, Allan. Ciencias sociales y desastres naturales en América Latina: un encuentro inconcluso (Chapter from the book entitled *Desastres naturales, sociedad y protección civil).* *EURE,* v. 19, no. 58 (Oct 93), pp. 73 – 84. Bibl.

Lavergne, Néstor. Argentina, 1993: estabilidad económica, democracia y estado-nación. *Realidad Económica,* no. 116 (May – June 93), pp. 5 – 20.

— Democracia, estado-nación y socialismo en América Latina. *Realidad Económica,* no. 119 (Oct – Nov 93), pp. 47 – 68. Bibl.

Laviera, Tato. Poems ("Latero Story," "Viejo," "Melao," "Bochinche bilingüe"). *The Americas Review,* v. 20, no. 3 – 4 (Fall – Winter 92), pp. 203 – 208.

Laviery, Ricardo. La añorada trampa del estímulo para el escritor. *Revista Cultural Lotería,* v. 50, no. 383 (May – June 91), pp. 43 – 51.

Lavín Infante, Joaquín. Las Condes: un nuevo plan regulador. *EURE,* v. 19, no. 57 (July 93), pp. 132 – 133.

Lavou, Victorien. El juego de los programas narrativos en *Oficio de tinieblas* de Rosario Castellanos. *Revista de Crítica Literaria Latinoamericana,* v. 19, no. 37 (Jan – June 93), pp. 319 – 332.

Lavrin, Asunción. La vida femenina como experiencia religiosa: biografía y hagiografía en Hispanoamérica colonial. *Colonial Latin American Review,* v. 2, no. 1 – 2 (1993), pp. 27 – 51. Bibl.

Lázaro Avila, Carlos. Un freno a la conquista: la resistencia de los cacicazgos indígenas americanos en la bibliografía histórico – antropológica. *Revista de Indias,* v. 52, no. 195 – 196 (May – Dec 92), pp. 589 – 609. Bibl.

Lazaroff, León. Auto Workers Seek Quality Wages. *Business Mexico,* v. 3, no. 4 (Apr 93), pp. 20 – 21 +. Il.

— Border Blues. *Business Mexico,* v. 3, no. 4 (Apr 93), pp. 24 – 26.

— A Tight Squeeze in Sonora. *Business Mexico,* v. 3, no. 3 (Mar 93), pp. 8 – 9.

Lazarte Rojas, Jorge. Democracia y problemas de representación política. *Estado y Sociedad,* v. 8, no. 9 (Jan – June 92), pp. 13 – 26.

Lazo M., José Francisco. El Salvador: de la locura a la esperanza. *Nueva Sociedad,* no. 127 (Sept – Oct 93), pp. 158 – 162.

Lazovski, Fabían and Darío Klein. Tabaré Vázquez, un líder bien imaginado. *Cuadernos del CLAEH,* v. 18, no. 67 (Nov 93), pp. 37 – 52. Bibl.

Leal, Henry. Alejandro Ibarra: primer tratadista de física experimental en la UCV, 1834 – 1874. *Revista Nacional de Cultura (Venezuela),* v. 54, no. 287 (Oct – Dec 92), pp. 238 – 258. Bibl, il.

Leal, Ildefonso. Bajo los auspicios de la Universidad Pedagógica Nacional de Bogotá, Colombia, se celebró el I Congreso Iberoamericano de Docentes e Investigadores en Historia de la Educación Latinoamericana, del 2 al 5 de septiembre del año 1992. *Boletín de la Academia Nacional de la Historia (Venezuela),* v. 76, no. 302 (Apr – June 93), pp. 179 – 180.

— Palabras pronunciadas por el doctor Ildefonso Leal el día 6 de mayo de 1992, con motivo de la exposición de documentos Portugal – Venezuela en el Archivo Nacional de la Torre do Tombo, en la ciudad universitaria de Lisboa. *Boletín de la Academia Nacional de la Historia (Venezuela),* v. 76, no. 301 (Jan – Mar 93), pp. 41 – 43.

Leal, Juan Felipe. Regímenes políticos en el proceso de estructuración del nuevo estado, 1915 – 1928. *Revista Mexicana de Ciencias Políticas y Sociales,* v. 37, Nueva época, no. 148 (Apr – June 92), pp. 11 – 61.

— Vistas que no se ven: el cine mexicano anterior a la revolución. *Revista Mexicana de Ciencias Políticas y Sociales,* v. 38, Nueva época, no. 153 (July – Sept 93), pp. 111 – 133.

Leal, Juan Felipe and Eduardo Barraza. Inicios de la reglamentación cinematográfica en la ciudad de México. *Revista Mexicana de Ciencias Políticas y Sociales,* v. 37, Nueva época, no. 150 (Oct – Dec 92), pp. 139 – 175. Bibl, charts.

Leal, Luis. Sin fronteras: (des)mitificación en las letras norteamericanas y mexicanas. *Mexican Studies,* v. 9, no. 1 (Winter 93), pp. 95 – 118. Bibl.

Leal, Luisa María. Pocas perspectivas de despenalización del aborto (Excerpt from *Estrategias en salud y derechos reproductivos: la legalización del aborto en América Latina).* *Fem,* v. 17, no. 129 (Nov 93), pp. 10 – 11.

Leal, Regina and José González Rodrigo. Manejo de resursos naturales y derecho consuetudinario. *Nueva Antropología,* v. 13, no. 44 (Aug 93), pp. 61 – 70. Bibl.

Leal Buitrago, Francisco. La guerra y la paz en Colombia. *Nueva Sociedad,* no. 125 (May – June 93), pp. 157 – 161.

Leal F., Gustavo and Martha Singer S. Gobernando desde la oposición: ayuntamiento de Durango, 1992 – 1995. *El Cotidiano,* v. 9, no. 54 (May 93), pp. 90 – 100. Bibl, il, tables.

Le Bot, Yvon. Le palimpseste maya: violence, communauté et territoire dans le conflit guatémaltèque. *Cahiers des Amériques Latines,* no. 13 (1992), pp. 87 – 105. Bibl, maps.

Lecomte, Sergio. Muerto de no conocerse. *Afro-Hispanic Review,* v. 12, no. 1 (Spring 93), p. 50.

Lee, Terence R. and Andrei Jouravlev. Self-Financing Water Supply and Sanitation Services. *CEPAL Review,* no. 48 (Dec 92), pp. 117 – 128. Bibl, tables, charts.

Lee, Thea and Jeff Faux. Los efectos del Acuerdo de Libre Comercio de América del Norte en la fuerza de trabajo de Estados Unidos. *Relaciones Internacionales (Mexico),* v. 15, Nueva época, no. 57 (Jan – Mar 93), pp. 37 – 54.

Leguizamón, Martiniano. La república de Entre Ríos. *Hoy Es Historia,* v. 10, no. 60 (Nov – Dec 93), pp. 82 – 83.

Lehoucq, Fabrice Edouard. Conflicto de clases, crisis política y destrucción de las prácticas democráticas en Costa Rica: reevaluando los orígenes de la guerra civil de 1948. *Revista de Historia (Costa Rica),* no. 25 (Jan – June 92), pp. 65 – 96. Bibl.

Leis, Raúl. Panamá: desactivar la muerte. *Nueva Sociedad,* no. 123 (Jan – Feb 93), pp. 114 – 123.

Leite, Cristina Maria Costa. Uma análise sobre o processo de organização do território: o caso do zoneamento ecológico – econômico. *Revista Brasileira de Geografia,* v. 53, no. 3 (July – Sept 91), pp. 67 – 90. Bibl.

Leite, Márcia de Paula. Organización del trabajo y relaciones industriales en el Brasil. *Nueva Sociedad,* no. 124 (Mar – Apr 93), pp. 94 – 103. Bibl.

Leite, Milu. Antenas diabólicas. *Problemas Brasileiros,* v. 30, no. 295 (Jan – Feb 93), pp. 54 – 56. Il.

Leite, Miriam Lifchitz Moreira. Fontes históricas e estilo acadêmico. *Estudos Feministas,* v. 1, no. 1 (1993), pp. 83 – 95. Bibl.

Lemaître, Monique J. Análisis de *Trilce I* de César Vallejo: poema de la creación, del nacimiento del poeta y del Perú. *Casa de las Américas,* no. 189 (Oct – Dec 92), pp. 29 – 34. Bibl.

Lemmon, Alfred E. Colonial Discography. *The Americas,* v. 49, no. 3 (Jan 93), pp. 388 – 390.

Lemogodeuc, Jean-Marie. Las máscaras y las marcas de la autobiografía: la cuestión del narrador en *El jardín de al lado* de José Donoso. *Revista de Crítica Literaria Latinoamericana,* v. 19, no. 38 (July – Dec 93), pp. 383 – 392. Bibl.

Lemos, José de Jesus Sousa and José Vangeliso de Aguiar. Produção do caupi irrigado em Bragança, Pará. *Revista de Economia e Sociologia Rural,* v. 30, no. 3 (July – Sept 92), pp. 239 – 252. Bibl, tables, charts.

Lemos, José de Jesus Sousa and José Ribamar Silva Campos. Fundamentação dinâmica para a produção e comercialização de hortifrutigranjeiros. *Revista de Economia e Sociologia Rural,* v. 30, no. 1 (Jan – Mar 92), pp. 11 – 20. Bibl, tables.

Lemos, José de Jesus Sousa and Pedro F. Adeodato de Paula Pessoa. Mercado de exportação e estabilização de preços externos para amêndoas de castanha de caju. *Revista de Economia e Sociologia Rural,* v. 30, no. 2 (Apr – June 92), pp. 171 – 187. Bibl, tables, charts.

Lemus, Silvia. El barco donde estaba el paraíso: una entrevista con Gabriel García Márquez. *Nexos,* v. 16, no. 192 (Dec 93), pp. 32 – 39. Il.

Lencioni, Vincent. The Chinese Tariff Tactic. *Business Mexico,* v. 3, no. 7 (July 93), p. 22. Tables.

— The Pro Sports Money Game. *Business Mexico,* v. 3, no. 7 (July 93), p. 32.

Lenharo, Alcir. Fascínio e solidão: as cantoras do rádio nas ondas sonoras do seu tempo. *Luso-Brazilian Review,* v. 30, no. 1 (Summer 93), pp. 75 – 84. Bibl.

Lent, John A. Mujeres periodistas en el Caribe (Translated by Jimmy Seale Collazo). *Homines,* v. 15 – 16, no. 2 – 1 (Oct 91 – Dec 92), pp. 262 – 272. Bibl.

Lenti, Paul. Latin America Takes on Hollywood. *NACLA Report on the Americas,* v. 27, no. 2 (Sept – Oct 93), pp. 4 – 9. Il.

Lentini, Javier. Poems ("La cenicienta," "Petra Pan"). *Inti,* no. 36 (Fall 92), pp. 149 – 151.

Leo, Mariella. Problemática del parque nacional Río Abiseo. *Amazonia Peruana,* v. 11, no. 21 (Sept 92), pp. 109 – 144. Bibl, il, tables, maps, charts.

León, Aracely de. Doctrinas económicas en el contexto de la expansión europea. *Revista Cultural Lotería,* v. 51, no. 391 (Sept – Oct 92), pp. 47 – 57. Bibl.

León, Carlos A. El desarrollo agrario de Tucumán en el período de transición de la economía de capitalismo incipiente a la expansión azucarera. *Desarrollo Económico (Argentina),* v. 33, no. 130 (July – Sept 93), pp. 217 – 236. Bibl, tables.

León, Eleázar. Los días visionarios de Vallejo. *Revista Nacional de Cultura (Venezuela),* v. 54, no. 287 (Oct – Dec 92), pp. 217 – 220.

León, Fidel de. Repertorio y estrategias narrativas en *Las muertas. La Palabra y el Hombre,* no. 81 (Jan – Mar 92), pp. 316 – 323. Bibl.

León, Idalia de. Abrirse paso ante lo adverso: el teatro universitario en Venezuela. *Conjunto,* no. 89 (Oct – Dec 91), pp. 105 – 111. Il.

León, Jesús Alberto. La narrativa de la adolescencia: ¿Signo de crisis social? *Inti,* no. 37 – 38 (Spring – Fall 93), pp. 117 – 122.

León de D'Empaire, Arleny. El gran viaje de descubrimiento: las crónicas americanas. *Montalbán,* no. 24 (1992), pp. 85 – 97. Bibl.

León del Río, Yohanka. La historia de las ideas como una de las problemáticas de la filosofía de la liberación en el Ecuador. *Islas,* no. 99 (May – Aug 91), pp. 75 – 86. Bibl.

León Femat, Socorro. Detrás de la nada. *Plural (Mexico),* v. 22, no. 267 (Dec 93), pp. 29 – 31.

León G., Ricardo. La banca chihuahuense durante el porfiriato. *Siglo XIX: Cuadernos,* v. 1, no. 2 (Feb 92), pp. 9 – 47. Bibl, tables, maps.

León Gómez, Miguel. El testamento del licenciado Diego Alvarez. *Historia y Cultura (Peru),* no. 20 (1990), pp. 319 – 350.

León González, Francisco. Entrevista con Juan Soriano. *Artes de México,* no. 19 (Spring 93), pp. 104 – 105. Il.

León M., José Luis. Propuestas, retos y alternativas hacia el futuro. *Relaciones Internacionales (Mexico),* v. 14, Nueva época, no. 56 (Oct – Dec 92), pp. 107 – 116. Bibl.

León Montoya, Sonia and Cristina Céspedes Castro. Terapia de grupo no directiva con pacientes seropositivos y con SIDA. *Revista de Ciencias Sociales (Costa Rica),* no. 58 (Dec 92), pp. 45 – 54. Bibl, charts.

León-Portilla, Ascensión H. de. Algunas publicaciones sobre lengua y literatura nahuas. *Estudios de Cultura Náhuatl,* v. 22 (1992), pp. 468 – 493.

— Nebrija y las lenguas compañeras del imperio. *Cuadernos Americanos,* no. 37, Nueva época (Jan – Feb 93), pp. 135 – 147. Bibl.

— Las primeras biografías de Bernardino de Sahagún. *Estudios de Cultura Náhuatl,* v. 22 (1992), pp. 235 – 252.

León-Portilla, Miguel. Angel Ma. Garibay K. (1892 – 1992): en el centenario de su nacimiento. *Estudios de Cultura Náhuatl,* v. 22 (1992), pp. 167 – 180.

— Encuentro de dos mundos. *Estudios de Cultura Náhuatl,* v. 22 (1992), pp. 15 – 27.

— A modo de comentario (Response to Amos Segala's commentary on Miguel León-Portilla's review of *Histoire de la littérature náhuatl: sources, identités, répresentations*). *Caravelle,* no. 59 (1992), pp. 221 – 223.

— Naturaleza y cultura. *Cuadernos Americanos,* no. 39, Nueva época (May – June 93), pp. 65 – 71.

— Por qué los escribanos y pintores prehispánicos estaban exentos de pagar tributo. *Vuelta,* v. 17, no. 196 (Mar 93), pp. 36 – 37. Il.

León Tejera, Francisco. Crisis Challenges Social Researchers. *Hemisphere*, v. 5, no. 3 (Summer – Fall 93), pp. 36 – 37.

Leonard, Thomas Michael. Central America and the United States: Overlooked Foreign Policy Objectives. *The Americas*, v. 50, no. 1 (July 93), pp. 1 – 30. Bibl.

Léons, Madeline Barbara. Risk and Opportunity in the Coca/Cocaine Economy of the Bolivian Yungas. *Journal of Latin American Studies*, v. 25, no. 1 (Feb 93), pp. 121 – 157. Bibl, charts.

Leriche, Christian E. La propuesta cepalina del desarrollo sustentable latinoamericano y medio ambiente. *El Cotidiano*, v. 8, no. 52 (Jan – Feb 93), pp. 109 – 111. Il.

Leriche, Christian E. and Sandra Navarrete R. América Latina: problemas actuales en el estilo de crecimiento de la región. *El Cotidiano*, v. 9, no. 54 (May 93), pp. 108 – 113. Il, tables.

Lerner, Jaime. La ciudad optimista. *Nexos*, v. 16, no. 189 (Sept 93), pp. 13 – 15.

Lescano, Oscar et al. Las centrales sindicales frente al MERCOSUR. *Nueva Sociedad*, no. 126 (July – Aug 93), pp. 176 – 178.

Lesser, Ricardo. El cuerpo de la democracia: la crónica de las condiciones de vida de los sectores populares en esta democracia renovada . . . . *Todo Es Historia*, v. 27, no. 317 (Dec 93), pp. 50 – 56. Il.

Letelier S., Leonardo. La teoría del federalismo fiscal y su relevancia en el caso municipal chileno. *Cuadernos de Economía (Chile)*, v. 30, no. 90 (Aug 93), pp. 199 – 224. Bibl, tables.

Letelier Sotomayor, Mario. Posibilidades efectivas de innovación en la docencia universitaria chilena: problemas y perspectivas. *Estudios Sociales (Chile)*, no. 74 (Oct – Dec 92), pp. 191 – 199.

Leturia M., Juan Miguel. Hacer teología es como escribir una "carta de amor." *Mensaje*, v. 42, no. 424 (Nov 93), pp. 555 – 558. Il.

— Información: derecho y dignidad. *Mensaje*, v. 42, no. 419 (June 93), pp. 210 – 211.

— 1993 - 1593 = 400: itinerario de una aventura. *Mensaje*, v. 42, no. 420 (July 93), pp. 209 – 214. Il.

Levaggi, Abelardo. Muerte y resurrección del derecho indiano sobre el aborigen en la Argentina del siglo XIX. *Jahrbuch für Geschichte von Staat, Wirtschaft und Gesellschaft Lateinamerikas*, v. 29 (1992), pp. 179 – 193. Bibl.

Levine, Elaine. Significado del programa de Bill Clinton para México y América Latina. *Problemas del Desarrollo*, v. 24, no. 93 (Apr – June 93), pp. 22 – 26.

Levine, Robert M. The Singular Brazilian City of Salvador. *Luso-Brazilian Review*, v. 30, no. 2 (Winter 93), pp. 59 – 69. Bibl.

Levine, Ruth E. and Rebeca Wong. Estructura del hogar como respuesta a los ajustes económicos: evidencia del México urbano de los ochenta. *Estudios Demográficos y Urbanos*, v. 7, no. 2 – 3 (May – Dec 92), pp. 493 – 509. Bibl, tables, charts.

Levine, Suzanne Jill. El traductor en la guarida del escritor: entrevista con Guillermo Cabrera Infante (Translated by Mario Ojeda Revah). *Vuelta*, v. 17, no. 198 (May 93), pp. 59 – 63.

Levinson, Brett. La responsabilidad de Lezama. *Revista Chilena de Literatura*, no. 42 (Aug 93), pp. 101 – 105.

Levy, David L. Use and Reproduction of Photographs: Copyright Issues. *SALALM Papers*, v. 34 (1989), pp. 135 – 140.

Levy, Janice. Feliciano's Wife Wants Her Tooth Back. *The Americas Review*, v. 21, no. 1 (Spring 93), pp. 30 – 38.

Levy, Noemí and Gerardo Fujii Gambero. Composición de las exportaciones de Brasil, Corea, España y México. *Comercio Exterior*, v. 43, no. 9 (Sept 93), pp. 844 – 851. Tables.

Levy, Santiago and Sweder van Wijnbergen. Mercados de trabajo, migración y bienestar: la agricultura en el Tratado de Libre Comercio entre México y los Estados Unidos (Translated by Carlos Villegas). *El Trimestre Económico*, v. 60, no. 238 (Apr – June 93), pp. 371 – 411. Bibl, tables.

Lewis, Maureen A. User Fees in Public Hospitals: Comparison of Three Country Case Studies. *Economic Development and Cultural Change*, v. 41, no. 3 (Apr 93), pp. 513 – 532. Bibl, tables.

Lewis, Rupert. The Contemporary Significance of the African Diaspora in the Americas. *Caribbean Quarterly*, v. 38, no. 2 – 3 (June – Sept 92), pp. 73 – 80. Bibl.

Leytón Ovando, Rubén and Juan Carlos Reyes Garza. Cuyutlán: una cultura salinera. *La Palabra y el Hombre*, no. 81 (Jan – Mar 92), pp. 120 – 146. Bibl, il.

Leyva, Daniel. Ariel Valero. *Nexos*, v. 16, no. 190 (Oct 93), p. 21.

Leyva, María. The Museum of Modern Art of Latin America: A Guide to Its Resources. *SALALM Papers*, v. 34 (1989), pp. 417 – 427.

Lezama, José Luis. Ciudad, mujer y conflicto: el comercio ambulante en el D.F. *Estudios Demográficos y Urbanos*, v. 6, no. 3 (Sept – Dec 91), pp. 649 – 675. Bibl, tables.

— Trabajo, familia e infancia en la ciudad de México: convergencias y divergencias. *Comercio Exterior*, v. 43, no. 7 (July 93), pp. 677 – 687. Bibl, tables.

Lezama Lima, José. Diarios. *Vuelta*, v. 17, no. 198 (May 93), pp. 16 – 23.

Li Kam, Sui Moy. Costa Rica ante la internacionalización de la agricultura. *Revista de Ciencias Sociales (Costa Rica)*, no. 57 (Sept 92), pp. 87 – 96. Bibl.

Liberman, Arnoldo. Rememoración del exilio. *Cuadernos Hispanoamericanos*, no. 517 – 519 (July – Sept 93), pp. 544 – 552.

Licandro, José Antonio. Análisis de la zona objetivo para el tipo de cambio en Chile. *Cuadernos de Economía (Chile)*, v. 30, no. 90 (Aug 93), pp. 179 – 198. Bibl, tables, charts.

Lienhard, Martín. La cosmología poética en los waynos quechuas tradicionales. *Revista de Crítica Literaria Latinoamericana*, v. 19, no. 37 (Jan – June 93), pp. 87 – 103. Bibl.

— Kulturelle Heterogenität und Literatur in Lateinamerika. *Iberoamericana*, v. 16, no. 47 – 48 (1992), pp. 95 – 110. Bibl.

— "Nosotros hemos resuelto y mandamos . . . ": textos indígenas destinados a los extraños, siglos XVIII y XIX. *Revista de Crítica Literaria Latinoamericana*, v. 19, no. 38 (July – Dec 93), pp. 173 – 184. Bibl.

Liev, Daniel. Cine nacional durante el Proceso. *Cuadernos Hispanoamericanos*, no. 517 – 519 (July – Sept 93), pp. 305 – 312.

Ligorred, Francesc. "Yaax indios yoko cab": pronosticar; una práctica estimulante y poética entre los mayas. *Iberoamericana*, v. 16, no. 47 – 48 (1992), pp. 6 – 20. Bibl, il.

Liguori, Ana Luisa and Miguel A. González Block. El SIDA en los de abajo. *Nexos*, v. 16, no. 185 (May 93), pp. 15 – 20.

Lillo, Armando. La expulsión de los jesuitas. *Mensaje*, v. 42, no. 420 (July 93), pp. 247 – 252. Il, facs.

Lima, Elcyon Caiado Rocha et al. Efeitos dinâmicos dos choques de oferta e demanda agregadas sobre o nível de atividade econômica do Brasil. *Revista Brasileira de Economia,* v. 47, no. 2 (Apr – June 93), pp. 177 – 204. Bibl, tables, charts.

Lima, João Eustáquio da and Jane Noronha Carvalhais. Distribuição dos ganhos com inovação tecnológica na produção de milho entre categorias de pequenos produtores em Minas Gerais. *Revista de Economia e Sociologia Rural,* v. 29, no. 4 (Oct – Dec 91), pp. 373 – 385. Bibl.

Lima, Magali Alonso de and Roberto Kant de Lima. Capoeira e cidadania: negritude e identidade no Brasil republicano. *Revista de Antropologia (Brazil),* v. 34 (1991), pp. 143 – 182. Bibl.

Lima, Mariângela Alves de. Teatro brasileño de hoy: tendencias actuales de la puesta en escena. *Conjunto,* no. 93 (Jan – June 93), pp. 3 – 7. Il.

Lima, Robert. Xangô and Other Yoruba Deities in the Plays of Zora Seljan. *Afro-Hispanic Review,* v. 11, no. 1 – 3 (1992), pp. 26 – 33. Bibl.

Lima, Roberto Kant de and Magali Alonso de Lima. Capoeira e cidadania: negritude e identidade no Brasil republicano. *Revista de Antropologia (Brazil),* v. 34 (1991), pp. 143 – 182. Bibl.

Lima Júnior, Olavo Brasil de. A reforma das instituições políticas: a experiência brasileira e o aperfeiçoamento democrático. *Dados,* v. 36, no. 1 (1993), pp. 89 – 117. Bibl, tables.

Lima Sobrinho, Alexandre José Barbosa. No centenário do *Jornal do Brasil. Revista do Instituto Histórico e Geográfico Brasileiro,* no. 372 (July – Sept 91), pp. 746 – 761.

Linares, Julio E. Política y moral. *Revista Cultural Lotería,* v. 50, no. 383 (May – June 91), pp. 33 – 42. Bibl.

Linares Zapata, Luis. El plebiscito: un fracaso bien hecho. *El Cotidiano,* v. 9, no. 54 (May 93), pp. 30 – 36. Il, tables.

Lince, Ricardo A. and Roberto Núñez Escobar. Aporte para una legislación de prensa. *Revista Cultural Lotería,* v. 50, no. 386 (Nov – Dec 91), pp. 5 – 24.

Lindenberg, Gail. The Labor Union in the Cuban Workplace. *Latin American Perspectives,* v. 20, no. 1 (Winter 93), pp. 28 – 39.

Lindner, Bernardo. Nadie en quien confiar: actitud política de los jóvenes campesinos del altiplano puneño. *Allpanchis,* v. 25, no. 41 (Jan – June 93), pp. 77 – 108. Bibl, tables.

Linhares, Célia Frazão. A ANPEd e a cooperação latino-americana em pesquisa educacional. *Revista Brasileira de Estudos Pedagógicos,* v. 72, no. 172 (Sept – Dec 91), pp. 405 – 408.

Linkohr, Rolf. Los procedimientos institucionales de decisión de la Comunidad Europea (Translated by Sandra Carreras). *Cuadernos del CLAEH,* v. 18, no. 65 – 66 (May 93), pp. 111 – 121.

Lins Ribeiro, Gustavo. Ambientalismo e desenvolvimento sustentado: nova ideologia/utopia do desenvolvimento. *Revista de Antropologia (Brazil),* v. 34 (1991), pp. 59 – 101. Bibl, tables.

Lipsett-Rivera, Sonya. Water and Bureaucracy in Colonial Puebla de los Angeles. *Journal of Latin American Studies,* v. 25, no. 1 (Feb 93), pp. 25 – 44. Bibl, tables, maps.

Lipszyc, Cecilia. Las mujeres y el poder: ¿Podemos las mujeres transformar el sistema de poder? *Feminaria,* v. 6, no. 11 (Nov 93), pp. 11 – 14. Bibl.

Lira Montt, Luis. La fundación de mayorazgos en Indias: estudio histórico – jurídico. *Boletín de la Academia Chilena de la Historia,* v. 58 – 59, no. 102 (1991 – 1992), pp. 349 – 386. Bibl, il, tables.

Liscano, Alirio. El adelantado Mariano Picón Salas. *Boletín de la Academia Nacional de la Historia (Venezuela),* v. 76, no. 301 (Jan – Mar 93), pp. 108 – 109.

Liscano Velutini, Juan. Polémica venezolana en México. *Vuelta,* v. 17, no. 203 (Oct 93), pp. 53 – 55.

— Venezuela: cultura y sociedad a fin de siglo. *Inti,* no. 37 – 38 (Spring – Fall 93), pp. 7 – 15.

Listabarth, Christian. A Survey of Pollination Strategies in the "Bactridinae" (Palmae). *Bulletin de l'Institut Français d'Etudes Andines,* v. 21, no. 2 (1992), pp. 699 – 714. Bibl, il, tables.

Litto, Fredric M. A "escola do futuro" da Universidade de São Paulo: um laboratório de tecnologia-de-ponta para a educação. *Revista Brasileira de Estudos Pedagógicos,* v. 72, no. 172 (Sept – Dec 91), pp. 409 – 412.

Livingstone, Ian and Luiz Márcio Assunção. Desenvolvimento inadequado: construção de açudes e secas no sertão do Nordeste. *Revista Brasileira de Economia,* v. 47, no. 3 (July – Sept 93), pp. 425 – 448. Bibl, tables, charts.

Lizalde, Eduardo. Severo Sarduy (1937 – 1993). *Vuelta,* v. 17, no. 201 (Aug 93), p. 30.

— La sucesión ministral. *Vuelta,* v. 17, no. 197 (Apr 93), pp. 65 – 67.

Lizardo, Pedro Francisco. La pasión biográfica en Tomás Polanco Alcántara. *Revista Nacional de Cultura (Venezuela),* v. 53, no. 286 (July – Sept 92), pp. 188 – 202. Il.

— Raúl Agudo Freites: periodismo y novela como afirmación y destino. *Revista Nacional de Cultura (Venezuela),* v. 54, no. 287 (Oct – Dec 92), pp. 162 – 176. Il.

— Vicente Gerbasi en Canoabo. *Revista Nacional de Cultura (Venezuela),* v. 54, no. 287 (Oct – Dec 92), pp. 14 – 15.

Llano, Aymara de. El lector: ¿Un lector que elige o que es elegido? *Escritura (Venezuela),* v. 17, no. 33 – 34 (Jan – Dec 92), pp. 149 – 157.

Llanos Melussa, Eduardo. Jorge Teillier, poeta fronterizo. *Casa de las Américas,* no. 191 (Apr – June 93), pp. 112 – 115.

Llanos Zuloaga, Martha. Programas de intervención temprana en América Latina: modelo Portage con base en el hogar; una experiencia peruana. *Revista Latinoamericana de Estudios Educativos,* v. 22, no. 3 (July – Sept 92), pp. 89 – 107. Bibl, tables.

Llebot Cazalis, Amaya. César Vallejo y la guerra civil española. *Revista Nacional de Cultura (Venezuela),* v. 54, no. 287 (Oct – Dec 92), pp. 206 – 216. Bibl, il.

Llera Esteban, Luis de. Recordando a Francisco de Vitoria en el V centenario. *Quaderni Ibero-Americani,* no. 72 (Dec 92), pp. 661 – 681. Bibl.

Llinás Alvarez, Edgar. The Issue of Autonomy in the Royal and Pontifical University of Mexico. *Revista de Historia de América,* no. 112 (July – Dec 91), pp. 105 – 119. Bibl, charts.

Lloreda, Waldo César. La transformación de Rubén Darío en Chile. *La Palabra y el Hombre,* no. 84 (Oct – Dec 92), pp. 93 – 109. Bibl.

Lloreda Caicedo, Rodrigo. La acción de tutela. *Revista Javeriana,* v. 61, no. 595 (June 93), pp. 299 – 305.

Llorente Martínez, Rodrigo. El maestro Arciniegas y su visión de América. *Boletín de Historia y Antigüedades,* v. 79, no. 779 (Oct – Dec 92), pp. 1061 – 1064.

Lloyd, Paul M. Peter Guyon Earle. *Hispanic Review,* v. 61, no. 2 (Spring 93), pp. 145 – 148.

Loaeza, Soledad. La incertidumbre política mexicana. *Nexos,* v. 16, no. 186 (June 93), pp. 47 – 59. Bibl.

Loáiciga G., María Elena. Condiciones psicosociales vinculadas a la atención institucional de los ancianos. *Revista de Ciencias Sociales (Costa Rica),* no. 60 (June 93), pp. 135 – 141.

Loáiciga G., María Elena and Rosa Rosales O. La población anciana de Liberia: condición socioeconómica precaria. *Revista de Ciencias Sociales (Costa Rica),* no. 59 (Mar 93), pp. 95 – 106. Bibl, tables.

Loayza, Luis. El estilo: arma del conocimiento. *Hueso Húmero,* no. 29 (May 93), pp. 115 – 119.

Lobillo, Jorge. El amor, el agua. *Plural (Mexico),* v. 22, no. 264 (Sept 93), pp. 112 – 113.

Lobo, Isaura et al. Televisión: ideología y socialización. *Revista de Ciencias Sociales (Costa Rica),* no. 57 (Sept 92), pp. 57 – 66. Bibl.

Loete, Sylvia K. Aspects of Modernization on a Mexican Hacienda: Labour on San Nicolás del Moral (Chalco) at the End of the Nineteenth Century. *European Review of Latin American and Caribbean Studies,* no. 54 (June 93), pp. 45 – 64. Bibl, charts.

Löwy, Michael. Los intelectuales latinoamericanos y la crítica social de la modernidad. *Casa de las Américas,* no. 191 (Apr – June 93), pp. 100 – 105. Bibl.

— Marxism and Christianity in Latin America (Translated by Claudia Pompan). *Latin American Perspectives,* v. 20, no. 4 (Fall 93), pp. 28 – 42. Bibl.

Logan, John R. and Richard D. Alba. Assimilation and Stratification in the Homeownership Patterns of Racial and Ethnic Groups. *International Migration Review,* v. 26, no. 4 (Winter 92), pp. 1314 – 1341. Bibl, tables.

Loiseau, Carlos. A través de la ventana. *Cuadernos Hispanoamericanos,* no. 517 – 519 (July – Sept 93), pp. 361 – 368. Il.

Loker, William M. et al. Identification of Areas of Land Degradation in the Peruvian Amazon Using a Geographic Information System. *Interciencia,* v. 18, no. 3 (May – June 93), pp. 133 – 141. Bibl, tables, maps, charts.

Lomelí, Francisco A. Artes y letras chicanas en la actualidad: más allá del barrio y las fronteras. *La Palabra y el Hombre,* no. 84 (Oct – Dec 92), pp. 220 – 227. Il.

Lomnitz, Cinna. La ciencia al paso. *Nexos,* v. 16, no. 187 (July 93), pp. 24 – 26.

— De pilones y poemas. *Nexos,* v. 16, no. 192 (Dec 93), pp. 15 – 16.

— Gloria y el TLC. *Nexos,* v. 16, no. 189 (Sept 93), pp. 8 – 13.

— Violines y sismos de otoño. *Nexos,* v. 16, no. 191 (Nov 93), pp. 12 – 14.

Lomnitz-Adler, Claudio. Hacia una antropología de la nacionalidad mexicana. *Revista Mexicana de Sociología,* v. 55, no. 2 (Apr – June 93), pp. 169 – 195. Bibl.

Londero, Renata. La scrittura della marginalità: *Extraño oficio* di Syria Poletti. *Studi di Letteratura Ispano-Americana,* v. 24 (1993), pp. 47 – 65.

Londoño, Patricia. Visual Images of Urban Colombian Women, 1800 to 1930. *SALALM Papers,* v. 34 (1989), pp. 99 – 114. Bibl.

Londoño E., María Ladi. Un asunto de mujeres: los derechos reproductivos; conciencia latinoamericana. *Fem,* v. 17, no. 121 (Mar 93), p. 20. Il.

Long, Veronica H. Monkey Business: Mixing Tourism with Ecology. *Business Mexico,* v. 3, no. 1 (Jan – Feb 93), pp. 23 – 26. Il.

Longley, Kyle. Peaceful Costa Rica: The First Battleground; The United States and the Costa Rican Revolution of 1948. *The Americas,* v. 50, no. 2 (Oct 93), pp. 149 – 175. Bibl.

Longo, Carlos Alberto. A tributação da renda no sistema federativo. *Estudos Econômicos,* v. 22, no. 2 (May – Aug 92), pp. 157 – 219. Bibl, tables, charts.

Longoni, Ana. Vanguardia artística y vanguardia política en la Argentina de los sesenta: una primera aproximación. *Revista Chilena de Literatura,* no. 42 (Aug 93), pp. 107 – 114.

Lope Blanch, Juan M. Mex. "-che, -i(n)che": ¿Nahuatlismo? *Nueva Revista de Filología Hispánica,* v. 40, no. 2 (July – Dec 92), pp. 623 – 636. Bibl.

Lopes, Maria Margareth and Maria Berenice Godinho Delgado. Mulheres trabalhadoras e meio ambiente: um olhar feminista no sindicalismo. *Estudos Feministas,* v. 0, no. 0 (1992), pp. 155 – 162.

López, Gabriela. Irma Palacios: los elementos terrestres. *Nexos,* v. 16, no. 186 (June 93), pp. 89 – 90. Il.

López, L. Luis. Poems ("Encounter with La Llorona," "For Old Men"). *The Americas Review,* v. 20, no. 2 (Summer 92), pp. 60 – 63.

Lopez, Linda C. Mexican-American and Anglo-American Parental Involvement with a Public Elementary School: An Exploratory Study. *Hispanic Journal of Behavioral Sciences,* v. 15, no. 1 (Feb 93), pp. 150 – 155. Bibl, tables.

Lopez, Luiz Roberto. Brasil: o federalismo mal costurado. *Vozes,* v. 87, no. 3 (May – June 93), pp. 79 – 82.

— Neonazismo, estilo tropical. *Vozes,* v. 87, no. 1 (Jan – Feb 93), pp. 97 – 101.

— A quem serviu o mito do gaúcho. *Vozes,* v. 86, no. 5 (Sept – Oct 92), pp. 99 – 101.

— As transfigurações da cidadania no Brasil. *Vozes,* v. 86, no. 6 (Nov – Dec 92), pp. 92 – 95.

López, Santos. Dialecto fogaje. *Revista Nacional de Cultura (Venezuela),* v. 54, no. 287 (Oct – Dec 92), pp. 137 – 139.

Lopez, Telê Porto Ancona. Mário de Andrade: um bailado em prosa. *Vozes,* v. 87, no. 1 (Jan – Feb 93), pp. 84 – 91. Il.

López, Verónica. La penúltima pregunta. *Nexos,* v. 16, no. 184 (Apr 93), pp. 34 – 37.

López Acuña, Daniel. Para reformar la salud en México. *Nexos,* v. 16, no. 186 (June 93), pp. 20 – 24.

López-Adorno, Pedro. Poems ("Bodywriting," "Skirmish," "Unfinished Journey," "On Becoming Calibans," "Within the Mist"). *The Americas Review,* v. 20, no. 1 (Spring 92), pp. 45 – 49.

López Angel, Carlos. El sindicalismo universitario de hoy y su futuro. *El Cotidiano,* v. 9, no. 56 (July 93), pp. 75 – 85. Il.

López Austin, Alfredo et al. El templo de Quetzalcóatl en Teotihuacán: su posible significado ideológico. *Anales del Instituto de Investigaciones Estéticas,* v. 16, no. 62 (1991), pp. 35 – 52. Bibl, il.

López-Baralt, Mercedes. Is There Life after 1992?: On the Future of Colonial Studies. *Latin American Literary Review,* v. 20, no. 40 (July – Dec 92), pp. 63 – 65.

López Bohórquez, Alí Enrique. El descubrimiento de América en el *Boletín de la Academia Nacional de la Historia. Boletín de la Academia Nacional de la Historia (Venezuela),* v. 75, no. 300 (Oct – Dec 92), pp. 166 – 171.

López Bohórquez, Alí Enrique and Alberto Rodríguez C. Visión americanista de la conquista española: el reverso del descubrimiento. *Boletín de la Academia Nacional de la Historia (Venezuela),* v. 75, no. 300 (Oct – Dec 92), pp. 69 – 77. Bibl.

López Estrada, Francisco. Los olvidados: Juan del Valle y Caviedes. *Insula,* no. 563 (Nov 93), p. 3. Il.

López Gallardo, Julio. The Potential of Mexican Agriculture and Options for the Future. *CEPAL Review,* no. 47 (Aug 92), pp. 137 – 148. Tables.

López García, Guadalupe. Los ángeles que habitan el claustro. *Fem,* v. 17, no. 122 (Apr 93), p. 43.

— Bitácora de la mujer. *Fem,* v. 17, no. 119 – 130 (Jan – Dec 93), All issues.

— *Fem* y sus colaboradoras. *Fem,* v. 17, no. 119 (Jan 93), p. 26. Il.

— Foro nacional: "Mujer, Violencia y Derechos Humanos." *Fem,* v. 17, no. 122 (Apr 93), pp. 9 – 10.

— Las periodistas y el poder (y en los medios de comunicación). *Fem,* v. 17, no. 129 (Nov 93), pp. 24 – 25.

López González, Eneyda. Sinonimia y antonimia en unidades fraseológicas usadas por estudiantes de Santa Clara. *Islas,* no. 97 (Sept – Dec 90), pp. 79 – 84. Bibl.

López Lomas-Esali, Estela Alicia. Primer Encuentro Nacional de Mujeres Poetas: setenta voces de mujeres poetas para decir poesía. *Fem,* v. 17, no. 127 (Sept 93), pp. 36 – 38.

López Mejía, Alejandro. La teoría del ingreso permanente en un mercado de capitales imperfecto: el caso colombiano. *Planeación y Desarrollo,* v. 24, no. 1 (Jan – Apr 93), pp. 385 – 423. Bibl, tables.

López Michelsen, Alfonso. El gran ciudadano Carlos Sanz de Santamaría. *Boletín de Historia y Antigüedades,* v. 80, no. 781 (Apr – June 93), pp. 269 – 272.

López-Ocón Cabrera, Leoncio. Texto y contexto en la obra de Jiménez de la Espada: un modelo interpretativo. *Revista de Indias,* v. 52, no. 195 – 196 (May – Dec 92), pp. 611 – 625. Bibl, charts.

López Ojeda, Florencio. El prefecto del mar. *Plural (Mexico),* v. 22, no. 267 (Dec 93), pp. 60 – 65.

López Pino, Israel and Vilma Figueroa Casas. Hacia una filosofía de la liberación uruguaya. *Islas,* no. 99 (May – Aug 91), pp. 38 – 44.

— Rodney Arismendi: su posición político – ideológica. *Islas,* no. 96 (May – Aug 90), pp. 71 – 77.

López Rodríguez, Ramón. A Different Solution. *Business Mexico,* v. 3, no. 6 (June 93), pp. 16 – 18. Il.

López Subirós, Marta Eugenia. Costa Rica: la opinión pública y el SIDA, 1989 – 1991. *Revista de Ciencias Sociales (Costa Rica),* no. 58 (Dec 92), pp. 55 – 64. Bibl, tables.

López Villafañe, Víctor. La integración económica en la cuenca del Pacífico: el reto de la América del Norte. *Comercio Exterior,* v. 43, no. 12 (Dec 93), pp. 1145 – 1152. Bibl, tables.

López y Rivas, Gilberto and Alicia Castellanos Guerrero. Grupos étnicos y procesos nacionalitarios en el capitalismo neoliberal. *Nueva Antropología,* v. 13, no. 44 (Aug 93), pp. 27 – 41. Bibl.

López y Sebastián, Lorenzo Eladio and Justo L. del Río Moreno. Comercio y transporte en la economía del azúcar antillano durante el siglo XVI. *Anuario de Estudios Americanos,* v. 49 (1992), pp. 55 – 87. Bibl, maps.

Lorandi T., Magdalena and León Garduño E. Desarrollo y evaluación del proyecto educativo Ixtliyollotl. *Revista Latinoamericana de Estudios Educativos,* v. 22, no. 3 (July – Sept 92), pp. 109 – 121. Bibl, tables.

Lorca A., Carlos. Presentación del libro: *Los estudios de postgrado y el desarrollo universitario en Chile. Estudios Sociales (Chile),* no. 74 (Oct – Dec 92), pp. 201 – 211. Tables.

Lorente-Murphy, Silvia. Las voces no-oficiales en *Todo eso oyes* de Luisa Peluffo. *Confluencia,* v. 8, no. 1 (Fall 92), pp. 149 – 153. Bibl.

Lorenzo Alcalá, May. El utopismo en Brasil: una experiencia fourierista. *Todo Es Historia,* v. 27, no. 313 (Aug 93), pp. 56 – 68. Bibl, il.

Lorenzo Fuentes, José. García Márquez: un concepto obrero de la inspiración. *Plural (Mexico),* v. 22, no. 259 (Apr 93), pp. 52 – 55.

Lorenzo Schiaffino, Santiago. Las estancias de Puchacay, según un catastro predial del año 1779. *Boletín de la Academia Chilena de la Historia,* v. 58 – 59, no. 102 (1991 – 1992), pp. 491 – 504.

Loreti, Miguel. Cronología social y política de la Argentina, 1970 – 1990. *Cuadernos Hispanoamericanos,* no. 517 – 519 (July – Sept 93), pp. 15 – 24.

Loreto Loreto, Blas. Decreto fundador de la Escuela de Artes y Oficios de Mujeres, hoy Ciclo Combinado "Teresa Carreño." *Boletín de la Academia Nacional de la Historia (Venezuela),* v. 75, no. 297 (Jan – Mar 92), pp. 179 – 184.

Loría Díaz, Eduardo. La recuperación económica mundial y los ciclos de largo plazo. *Comercio Exterior,* v. 43, no. 10 (Oct 93), pp. 933 – 939. Bibl, tables.

Losada Lora, Rodrigo. La evolución del orden público. *Revista Javeriana,* v. 61, no. 597 (Aug 93), pp. 159 – 165.

Lottman, Maryrica. Victoria Falls. *Bilingual Review/Revista Bilingüe,* v. 17, no. 3 (Sept – Dec 92), pp. 242 – 246.

Love, Michael W. Ceramic Chronology and Chronometric Dating: Stratigraphy and Seriation at La Blanca, Guatemala. *Ancient Mesoamerica,* v. 4, no. 1 (Spring 93), pp. 17 – 29. Bibl, il, tables, maps, charts.

Lovell, William George. Los registros parroquiales de Jacaltenango, Guatemala. *Mesoamérica (USA),* v. 13, no. 24 (Dec 92), pp. 441 – 453.

Lovera, Sara and Xolóxochitl Casas Chousal. Razones y sinrazones de CIMAC y la población. *Fem,* v. 17, no. 128 (Oct 93), pp. 8 – 10.

Lovera De-Sola, Roberto J. Mariano Picón Salas: sus rasgos vitales. *Boletín de la Academia Nacional de la Historia (Venezuela),* v. 76, no. 301 (Jan – Mar 93), pp. 89 – 92. Bibl.

— Tomás Polanco Alcántara, el biógrafo. *Boletín de la Academia Nacional de la Historia (Venezuela),* v. 75, no. 299 (July – Sept 92), pp. 191 – 196. Bibl.

Lovera De-Sola, Roberto J. et al. El Gómez de Tomás Polanco Alcántara (Reprints from Venezuelan newspapers of fifteen reviews of the book *Juan Vicente Gómez* by Tomás Polanco Alcántara). *Boletín de la Academia Nacional de la Historia (Venezuela),* v. 75, no. 298 (Apr – June 92), pp. 116 – 138.

Low, Ann M. Bolstering the "Bolsa." *Business Mexico,* v. 3, no. 6 (June 93), pp. 24 – 26. Tables.

Lowden, Pamela. The Ecumenical Committee for Peace in Chile, 1973 – 1975: The Foundation of Moral Opposition to Authoritarian Rule in Chile. *Bulletin of Latin American Research,* v. 12, no. 2 (May 93), pp. 189 – 203. Bibl.

Lowenthal, Abraham F. El hemisferio interdoméstico. *Relaciones Internacionales (Mexico),* v. 15, Nueva época, no. 57 (Jan – Mar 93), pp. 13 – 15.

Loynaz, Dulce María. Autógrafos de bestiarium. *Plural (Mexico),* v. 22, no. 262 (July 93), pp. 14 – 15.

— Imágenes de Raimundo Lazo. *Plural (Mexico),* v. 22, no. 262 (July 93), pp. 16 – 17.

Loyo Brambila, Aurora. Actores y tiempos políticos en la modernización educativa. *El Cotidiano,* v. 8, no. 51 (Nov – Dec 92), pp. 17 – 22. Bibl, il.

— ¿Modernización educativa o modernización del aparato educativo? *Revista Mexicana de Sociología,* v. 55, no. 2 (Apr – June 93), pp. 339 – 349. Bibl.

Loyola, Alberto. Los jesuitas y la cuestión social. *Mensaje,* v. 42, no. 420 (July 93), pp. 304 – 307. Il.

Loyola Campos, Alicia. El mercado mundial del banano: nuevas realidades e incertidumbres. *Comercio Exterior,* v. 43, no. 2 (Feb 93), pp. 163 – 170. Tables.

Loyola Goich, Lorena. Las sociedades campesinas: un retrato de cambios y permanencias a través de la literatura criollista chilena, 1920 – 1950. *Cuadernos de Historia (Chile),* no. 11 (Dec 91), pp. 127 – 148. Bibl.

Loyola Guerra, Hernán. Neruda 1923: el año de la encrucijada. *Revista Chilena de Literatura,* no. 40 (Nov 92), pp. 5 – 16.

Lozada, Salvador María. Dos dictámenes contra la concentración del poder. *Realidad Económica,* no. 113 (Jan – Feb 93), pp. 45 – 51.

Lozano, Claudio. La reforma previsional. *Realidad Económica,* no. 113 (Jan – Feb 93), pp. 6 – 11. Tables.

Lozano García, Lucrecia. La Iniciativa para las Américas: el comercio hecho estrategia. *Nueva Sociedad,* no. 125 (May – June 93), pp. 98 – 111. Tables.

Lozoya, Jorge Alberto and Jan M. William. María Sada: sonatina en gris mayor. *Artes de México,* no. 21 (Fall 93), p. 102. Il.

Lucena Giraldo, Manuel. ¿Filántropos u oportunistas?: ciencia y política en los proyectos de obras públicas del Consulado de Cartagena de Indias, 1795 – 1810. *Revista de Indias,* v. 52, no. 195 – 196 (May – Dec 92), pp. 627 – 646. Bibl, maps.

Luciani, Frederick William. The *Comedia de San Francisco de Borja* (1640): The Mexican Jesuits and the "Education of the Prince." *Colonial Latin American Review,* v. 2, no. 1 – 2 (1993), pp. 121 – 141. Bibl.

Ludmer, Josefina. El delito: ficciones de exclusión y sueños de justicia. *Revista de Crítica Literaria Latinoamericana,* v. 19, no. 38 (July – Dec 93), pp. 145 – 153.

Lugo, Kenneth. Informe académico del Centro de Historia Oral. *Homines,* v. 15 – 16, no. 2 – 1 (Oct 91 – Dec 92), pp. 361 – 363.

Luigi Lemus, Juan de. Amerigo Vespucci (Includes reproductions of paintings by Enrique Boccaletti G. from his book entitled *América, el Nuevo Mundo y los navegantes italianos,* co-authored by Juan de Luigi Lemus). *Atenea (Chile),* no. 465 – 466 (1992), pp. 177 – 186 +. Il.

Lula
See
Silva, Luís Inácio da

Luna, Felicitas. A ciento cincuenta años de la fotografía: Segundo Congreso de la Fotografía Argentina, 1839 – 1939. *Todo Es Historia,* v. 27, no. 313 (Aug 93), p. 92. Il.

— La fotohistoria del mes (A regular feature that presents historical photographs along with a brief biography or description). *Todo Es Historia,* v. 26 – 27 (Dec 92 – Dec 93), All issues.

Luna, Félix. Discurso del doctor Félix Luna (On the occasion of his induction into the National Academy of History). *Todo Es Historia,* v. 27, no. 316 (Nov 93), pp. 50 – 58. Il.

Luna, Francisco Vidal. Características demográficas dos escravos de São Paulo, 1777 – 1829. *Estudos Econômicos,* v. 22, no. 3 (Sept – Dec 92), pp. 443 – 483. Bibl, tables.

Luna, Lola G. Movimientos de mujeres, estado y participación política en América Latina: una propuesta de análisis histórico. *Boletín Americanista,* v. 33, no. 42 – 43 (1992 – 1993), pp. 255 – 266. Bibl.

Luna, Matilde and Cristina Puga. Modernización en México: la propuesta empresarial. *Revista Mexicana de Ciencias Políticas y Sociales,* v. 38, Nueva época, no. 151 (Jan – Mar 93), pp. 35 – 49. Bibl.

Luna, Matilde and Ricardo Tirado. Los empresarios en el escenario del cambio: trayectoria y tendencias de sus estrategias de acción colectiva. *Revista Mexicana de Sociología,* v. 55, no. 2 (Apr – June 93), pp. 243 – 271. Bibl, tables, charts.

Luna Moreno, Carmen de. Alternativa en el siglo XVIII: franciscanos de la provincia del Santo Evangelio de México. *Archivo Ibero-Americano,* v. 52, no. 205 – 208 (Jan – Dec 92), pp. 343 – 371.

Luque, Carlos António. Observações sobre o processo inflacionário brasileiro, 1986 – 1991. *Revista de Economia Política (Brazil),* v. 13, no. 2 (Apr – June 93), pp. 46 – 60. Bibl, charts.

Luque, Mónica G. The Idea of the University in Newman, Ortega y Gasset, and Jaspers: A Point of Departure for Analyses of the Current Problems Facing Latin American Universities. *La Educación (USA),* v. 37, no. 114 (1993), pp. 115 – 118.

Luque González, José Rodolfo and Reina Corona Cuapio. Cambios recientes en los patrones migratorios a la zona metropolitana de la ciudad de México. *Estudios Demográficos y Urbanos,* v. 7, no. 2 – 3 (May – Dec 92), pp. 575 – 586. Bibl, tables, charts.

Luque Muñoz, Henry. Poems ("La casa," "Hazaña," "Urbe," "Carta de navegación"). *Revista Nacional de Cultura (Venezuela),* v. 53, no. 285 (Apr – June 92), pp. 159 – 164.

Lustig, Nora. La medición de la pobreza en México (Translated by Carlos Villegas). *El Trimestre Económico,* v. 59, no. 236 (Oct – Dec 92), pp. 725 – 749. Bibl, tables, charts.

Luza, Mónica and Ricardo Zamora. Exposición de arte contemporáneo de artistas latinoamericanos en Berlín. *Humboldt,* no. 108 (1993), pp. 100 – 101. Il.

Lyon, David and Patricia Harris. Memory's Persistence: The Living Art. *Américas,* v. 45, no. 6 (Nov – Dec 93), pp. 26 – 37. Il.

Mabres, Antonio and Ronald F. Woodman. Formación de un cordón litoral en Máncora, Perú, a raíz de El Niño de 1983. *Bulletin de l'Institut Français d'Etudes Andines,* v. 22, no. 1 (1993), pp. 213 – 226. Bibl, il, maps.

Mabres, Antonio et al. Algunos apuntes históricos adicionales sobre la cronología de El Niño. *Bulletin de l'Institut Français d'Etudes Andines,* v. 22, no. 1 (1993), pp. 395 – 406. Bibl, tables, charts.

MacAdam, Alfred J. Daniel Thomas Egerton, the Unfortunate Traveler. *Review,* no. 47 (Fall 93), pp. 9 – 13. Il.

McAlister, Elizabeth. Sacred Stories from the Haitian Diaspora: A Collective Biography of Seven Vodou Priestesses in New York City. *Journal of Caribbean Studies,* v. 9, no. 1 – 2 (Winter 92 – Spring 93), pp. 11 – 27. Bibl.

Macaya T., Emilia. Discurso de la decana dra. Emilia Macaya, con motivo de la inauguración del mural de la Facultad de Letras. *Revista de Filosofía de la Universidad de Costa Rica,* v. 34, no. 74 (July 93), pp. 93 – 94.

— Lo inefable en Blanca Ruiz-Fontanorrosa (Includes reproductions of 12 paintings from her series "Puertas y ventanas"). *Káñina,* v. 16, no. 1 (Jan – June 92), pp. 229 – 241. Il.

McCarthy, Cavan Michael. Recent Political Events in Brazil as Reflected in Popular Poetry Pamphlets: "Literatura de Cordel." *SALALM Papers,* v. 34 (1989), pp. 491 – 513. Bibl.

— A Regional Database for the Brazilian Northeast. *SALALM Papers,* v. 36 (1991), pp. 369 – 386. Bibl, tables.

McCarthy, William J. Between Policy and Prerogative: Malfeasance in the Inspection of the Manila Galleons at Acapulco, 1637. *Colonial Latin American Historical Review,* v. 2, no. 2 (Spring 93), pp. 163 – 183. Bibl, maps.

McCaughan, Edward J. Mexico's Long Crisis: Toward New Regimes of Accumulation and Domination. *Latin American Perspectives,* v. 20, no. 3 (Summer 93), pp. 6 – 31. Bibl.

McConnell, Shelley. Rules of the Game: Nicaragua's Contentious Constitutional Debate. *NACLA Report on the Americas,* v. 27, no. 2 (Sept – Oct 93), pp. 20 – 25. Il.

MacCormack, Sabine G. Myth, History, and Language in the Andes (Review article). *Colonial Latin American Review,* v. 2, no. 1 – 2 (1993), pp. 247 – 260. Bibl.

McCoy, Jennifer L. Venezuelan Alternatives. *Hemisphere,* v. 5, no. 2 (Winter – Spring 93), pp. 33 – 35. Tables.

McCreery, David J. and Doug Munro. The Cargo of the *Montserrat:* Gilbertese Labor in Guatemalan Coffee, 1890 – 1908. *The Americas,* v. 49, no. 3 (Jan 93), pp. 271 – 295. Bibl, tables.

McCurry, Patrick. Starting at the Top. *Business Mexico,* v. 3, no. 1 (Jan – Feb 93), pp. 80 – 82. Il.

MacDonald, Christine. Artists against Taxes. *Business Mexico,* v. 3, no. 4 (Apr 93), p. 44.

— Customs' Unsung Hero? *Business Mexico,* v. 3, no. 4 (Apr 93), pp. 27 – 29. Il.

— Duel of the Desk-Top Computers. *Business Mexico,* v. 3, no. 9 (Sept 93), pp. 4 – 6. Il.

McDonald, M. A. et al. The Effects of Forest Clearance on Soil Conservation: Preliminary Findings from the Yallahs Valley, Jamaican Blue Mountains. *Caribbean Geography,* v. 3, no. 4 (Sept 92), pp. 253 – 260. Bibl.

McDonald, Robert. An Incredible Graph: Sor Juana's *Respuesta. Revista Canadiense de Estudios Hispánicos,* v. 17, no. 2 (Winter 93), pp. 297 – 318. Bibl.

Mace, Gordon et al. Regionalism in the Americas and the Hierarchy of Power. *Journal of Inter-American Studies and World Affairs,* v. 35, no. 2 (Summer 93), pp. 115 – 157. Bibl, tables, maps.

Macedo, Ubiratan Borges de. Presença de Miguel Reale na cultura brasileira. *Convivium,* v. 34, no. 2 (July – Dec 91), pp. 127 – 137.

Macera dall'Orso, Pablo. Los acuerdos Perú – Chile. *Debate (Peru),* v. 16, no. 73 (June – Aug 93), pp. 49 – 51. Il.

— Locos, titiriteros y poetas: las opciones limeñas, 1828 – 1840. *Debate (Peru),* v. 16, no. 72 (Mar – May 93), pp. 42 – 45. Il.

— Los verdaderos ambulantes. *Debate (Peru),* v. 16, no. 72 (Mar – May 93), pp. 43 – 44. Il.

McFadyen, Deidre. Invigorating the Public Debate: Popular Media in the Age of Mass Communications. *NACLA Report on the Americas,* v. 27, no. 2 (Sept – Oct 93), pp. 35 – 37 + . Bibl, il.

McGeagh, Robert. Thomas Fields and the Precursor of the Guaraní "Reducciones." *Colonial Latin American Historical Review,* v. 2, no. 1 (Winter 93), pp. 35 – 55. Bibl.

McGee, Sandra F.
See
Deutsch, Sandra F. McGee

McGlone, Mary H. The King's Surprise: The Mission Methodology of Toribio de Mogrovejo. *The Americas,* v. 50, no. 1 (July 93), pp. 65 – 83. Bibl.

McGowan, Marcia P. Mapping a New Territory: *Luisa in Realityland. Letras Femeninas,* v. 19, no. 1 – 2 (Spring – Fall 93), pp. 84 – 99. Bibl.

McGraw, Sarah A. and Kevin W. Smith. Smoking Behavior of Puerto Rican Women: Evidence from Caretakers of Adolescents in Two Urban Areas. *Hispanic Journal of Behavioral Sciences,* v. 15, no. 1 (Feb 93), pp. 140 – 149. Bibl, tables.

MacGregor, Felipe E. La ética periodística ante la información de la violencia. *Apuntes (Peru),* no. 29 (July – Dec 91), pp. 27 – 34. Tables.

Machado, Rosa Maria de Oliveira and Ana Lúcia Magyar. A regulamentação da lei de recursos hídricos do estado de São Paulo: desafios e perspectivas. *RAE; Revista de Administração de Empresas,* v. 33, no. 6 (Nov – Dec 93), pp. 42 – 47. Bibl.

Macharé, José and Luc Ortlieb. Registros del fenómeno El Niño en el Perú. *Bulletin de l'Institut Français d'Etudes Andines,* v. 22, no. 1 (1993), pp. 35 – 52. Bibl, tables, charts.

Macías, Elva. Ciudad prohibida. *Plural (Mexico),* v. 22, no. 261 (June 93), pp. 6 – 7.

Macías, Jesús Manuel. Significado de la vulnerabilidad social frente a los desastres. *Revista Mexicana de Sociología,* v. 54, no. 4 (Oct – Dec 92), pp. 3 – 10.

Macías, Reynaldo F. Language and Ethnic Classification of Language Minorities: Chicano and Latino Students in the 1990s. *Hispanic Journal of Behavioral Sciences,* v. 15, no. 2 (May 93), pp. 230 – 257. Bibl, tables, charts.

Macías V., María de la Luz. Mujeres e industria manufacturera en México. *El Cotidiano,* v. 9, no. 53 (Mar – Apr 93), pp. 33 – 39. Bibl, il, tables.

McIntyre, Loren A. Rapture of the Heights (Photographs by the author). *Américas,* v. 45, no. 6 (Nov – Dec 93), pp. 7 – 13. Il.

McKenna, Peter. Canada – OAS Relations during the Trudeau Years. *Revista Interamericana de Bibliografía,* v. 42, no. 3 (1992), pp. 373 – 391. Bibl.

McNeill, Anthony. Summer Maid. *Jamaica Journal,* v. 24, no. 3 (Feb 93), pp. 58 – 59.

McQuade, Frank. *Mundo Nuevo:* el discurso político en una revista intelectual de los sesenta. *Revista Chilena de Literatura,* no. 42 (Aug 93), pp. 123 – 130.

Madden, Lori. The Canudos War in History. *Luso-Brazilian Review,* v. 30, no. 2 (Winter 93), pp. 5 – 22. Bibl.

Maddox, Brent F. Visual Research Cataloging at the Getty Center for the History of Art and the Humanities. *SALALM Papers,* v. 34 (1989), pp. 391 – 400. Bibl.

Madeira, Marcos Almir. Rememorando Delso Renault. *Revista do Instituto Histórico e Geográfico Brasileiro,* no. 370 (Jan – Mar 91), pp. 217 – 222.

— Uma senhora em sua casa (Speech given in honor of Maria Beltrão's induction into the Instituto Histórico e Geográfico Brasileiro). *Revista do Instituto Histórico e Geográfico Brasileiro,* no. 372 (July – Sept 91), pp. 800 – 805.

Madrazo Miranda, María. Literatura y vida en el testimonio: *Tuzamapan; el poder viene de las cañas. Fem,* v. 17, no. 120 (Feb 93), pp. 18 – 20. Il.

Madrid Hurtado, Miguel de la. Notas sobre democracia y cultura. *Cuadernos Americanos,* no. 39, Nueva época (May – June 93), pp. 34 – 41.

Madrid Letelier, Alberto. Roser Bru: iconografía de la memoria. *Cuadernos Hispanoamericanos,* no. 510 (Dec 92), pp. 7 – 12. Il.

Madueño, Amalio. Poems ("Alambristas," "The Bato Prepares for Winter"). *The Americas Review,* v. 20, no. 3 – 4 (Fall – Winter 92), pp. 255 – 256.

— Poems. *The Americas Review,* v. 20, no. 2 (Summer 92), pp. 36 – 45.

Maeder, Ernesto J. A. La segunda evangelización del Chaco: las misiones franciscanas de Propaganda Fide, 1854 – 1900. *Investigaciones y Ensayos,* no. 41 (Jan – Dec 91), pp. 227 – 247. Bibl.

Maffia, Diana. Feminismo y epistemología: ¿Tiene sexo el sujeto de la ciencia? *Feminaria,* v. 6, no. 10 (Apr 93), pp. 13 – 15. Bibl.

Mafra, Antônio. Festival de Inverno de Campos do Jordão. *Vozes,* v. 86, no. 4 (July – Aug 92), pp. 86 – 87. Il.

Magaldi, Cristina. Mozart Camargo Guarnieri (1907 – 1993). *Inter-American Music Review,* v. 13, no. 2 (Spring – Summer 93), pp. 168 – 170.

Magaldi, Sábato. Atos heróicos. *Problemas Brasileiros,* v. 30, no. 295 (Jan – Feb 93), p. 64.

Magaloni de Bustamante, Ana María. El papel del gobierno mexicano en apoyo del desarrollo cultural. *SALALM Papers,* v. 34 (1989), pp. 3 – 8.

Magaña Sánchez, Margarita Elena. Clasismo, racismo y sexismo en el discurso escolar de México. *Fem,* v. 17, no. 123 (May 93), pp. 13 – 15.

— Feminolecto y Masculinolecto: II° Encuentro Feminista de la UAM, Unidad Xochimilco de la UAM, julio de 1992. *Fem,* v. 17, no. 125 (July 93), pp. 14 – 17. Bibl.

Magnabosco, Ana. Viejo smoking. *Conjunto,* no. 92 (July – Dec 92), pp. 35 – 45. Il.

Magnarelli, Sharon Dishaw. El significante deseo en *Cambio de armas* de Luisa Valenzuela. *Escritura (Venezuela),* v. 16, no. 31 – 32 (Jan – Dec 91), pp. 161 – 169.

— The Spectacle of Reality in Luisa Valenzuela's *Realidad nacional vista desde la cama.* Letras Femeninas, v. 19, no. 1 – 2 (Spring – Fall 93), pp. 65 – 73. Bibl.

Maguire, Robert et al. Food Security and Development in Haiti. *Grassroots Development,* v. 16, no. 2 (1992), pp. 35 – 39. Il.

Magyar, Ana Lúcia and Rosa Maria de Oliveira Machado. A regulamentação da lei de recursos hídricos do estado de São Paulo: desafios e perspectivas. *RAE; Revista de Administração de Empresas,* v. 33, no. 6 (Nov – Dec 93), pp. 42 – 47. Bibl.

Mahieu, José Agustín. Cine argentino: las nuevas fronteras. *Cuadernos Hispanoamericanos,* no. 517 – 519 (July – Sept 93), pp. 289 – 304.

— Cine en tres tiempos. *Cuadernos Hispanoamericanos,* no. 511 (Jan 93), pp. 125 – 133. Il.

Maingot, Anthony Peter. Cheddi Jagan and Democracy: An Interview. *Hemisphere,* v. 5, no. 2 (Winter – Spring 93), pp. 36 – 39. Il.

— Quid Pro Quo with Cuba. *Hemisphere,* v. 5, no. 3 (Summer – Fall 93), pp. 22 – 25.

Maio, Marcos Chor. "A nação no microscópio": intelectuais médicos e ordem social no Brasil. *Siglo XIX: Revista,* no. 12, 2a época (July – Dec 92), pp. 41 – 62. Bibl.

Majchrzak, Irena. El nombre propio, enlace natural entre un ser iletrado y el universo de la escritura. *Revista Latinoamericana de Estudios Educativos,* v. 22, no. 4 (Oct – Dec 92), pp. 77 – 87.

Makuch, Andrew L. From Zarabanda to Salsa: An Overview of Reference Sources on Latin American Music. *SALALM Papers,* v. 34 (1989), pp. 363 – 368.

Malamud, Carlos D. Encuentro de Americanistas Españoles: América Latina; Pasado y Presente. *Anuario de Estudios Americanos,* v. 49, Suppl. 1 (1992), pp. 194 – 195.

Malatesta, Parisina. Mega Shoppings: Playgrounds for Today's Porteños (Translated by Ruth Morales, photographs by Jorge Provenza). *Américas,* v. 45, no. 4 (July – Aug 93), pp. 14 – 19. Il.

— Tracing Evolution in the Land of the Sand (Translated by Barbara Meza, photographs by Jorge Provenza). *Américas,* v. 45, no. 4 (July – Aug 93), pp. 6 – 13. Il, maps.

Malaver, Bernardo and Mario Peralta. Venezuela: el inicio de una nueva coyuntura política. *Revista Paraguaya de Sociología,* v. 29, no. 84 (May – Aug 92), pp. 41 – 51. Bibl.

Maldonado, Jesús María. Poems ("Pesadilla no soñada," "Buñuelitos," "Cuando yo crezca," "Respeto y amor sincero"). *The Americas Review,* v. 21, no. 1 (Spring 93), pp. 71 – 76.

Maldonado Cárdenas, Rubén. Las pinturas de Sodzil, Yucatán, México. *Revista Española de Antropología Americana,* v. 23 (1993), pp. 101 – 111. Bibl, il.

Maldonado Jiménez, Rubén. Algunas reflexiones sobre la historiografía cubana y puertorriqueña en torno a la abolición de la esclavitud. *Homines,* v. 15 – 16, no. 2 – 1 (Oct 91 – Dec 92), pp. 31 – 38. Bibl.

Maldonado Toro, Francisco Armando. Expediente de órdenes del seminario interdiocesano de Caracas, 1613 – 1923, obispado y después arzobispado de Caracas. *Boletín de la Academia Nacional de la Historia (Venezuela),* v. 76, no. 302 (Apr – June 93), pp. 185 – 216.

Malfavón, Carlos David. Retorno. *Plural (Mexico),* v. 22, no. 264 (Sept 93), pp. 77 – 79.

Mallarino Botero, Gonzalo. In memoriam C. S. de S. *Boletín de Historia y Antigüedades,* v. 80, no. 781 (Apr – June 93), pp. 279 – 280.

Mallo, Silvia. La libertad en el discurso del estado, de amos y esclavos, 1780 – 1830. *Revista de Historia de América,* no. 112 (July – Dec 91), pp. 121 – 146. Bibl.

Mallon, Florencia E. Entre la utopía y la marginalidad: comunidades indígenas y culturas políticas en México y los Andes, 1780 – 1990. *Historia Mexicana,* v. 42, no. 2 (Oct – Dec 92), pp. 473 – 504.

Malo, Salvador. Las nuevas políticas y las estrategias en materia de ciencia y tecnología. *Revista Latinoamericana de Estudios Educativos,* v. 22, no. 3 (July – Sept 92), pp. 133 – 139.

Malpartida Ortega, Juan. El bosque vacío (First chapter of the novel of the same title). *Cuadernos Hispanoamericanos,* no. 511 (Jan 93), pp. 43 – 70.

— La poesía en Hispanoamérica: algunos ejemplos. *Cuadernos Hispanoamericanos,* no. 513 (Mar 93), pp. 73 – 84.

Mancera Aguayo, Miguel. Discurso de Miguel Mancera en la recepción del premio de economía rey Juan Carlos (Introduced by Luis Angel Rojo). *El Trimestre Económico*, v. 60, no. 237 (Jan – Mar 93), pp. 212 – 229.

Mandelli, Luiz Carlos. Cambios geopolíticos e integración. *Nueva Sociedad*, no. 126 (July – Aug 93), pp. 178 – 180.

Manfredo, Fernando. The Future of the Panama Canal. *Journal of Inter-American Studies and World Affairs*, v. 35, no. 3 (Fall 93), pp. 103 – 128.

Manley, Rachel. Poems ("N.W.M.," "Memory," "Regardless"). *Jamaica Journal*, v. 25, no. 1 (Oct 93), p. 44.

Manrique Campos, María Irma. La reforma monetaria en el IV Informe Presidencial. *Momento Económico*, no. 65 (Jan – Feb 93), pp. 8 – 10.

Manríquez, Miguel. El cuerpo. *Plural (Mexico)*, v. 22, no. 265 (Oct 93), pp. 49 – 54.

Manríquez S., Germán. Las relaciones entre literatura y ciencias en el ejemplo de la obra fisiológica de Alejandro Lipschütz y parte de la obra literaria de Thomas Mann (Accompanied by an appendix of texts by the authors). *Revista Chilena de Literatura*, no. 42 (Aug 93), pp. 115 – 121.

Mansilla, Hugo Celso Felipe. Comentario (on the topic "Industria electoral y comunicación política"). *Estado y Sociedad*, v. 8, no. 9 (Jan – June 92), pp. 77 – 79.

— La crisis de la modernidad en América Latina y lo razonable de la cultura premoderna. *Signo*, no. 36 – 37, Nueva época (May – Dec 92), pp. 299 – 323. Bibl.

— La economía informal y las modificaciones del movimiento sindical en Bolivia. *Revista Paraguaya de Sociología*, v. 30, no. 86 (Jan – Apr 93), pp. 113 – 126. Bibl.

Manso, Leonor. Los actores en las décadas del '70 y del '80. *Cuadernos Hispanoamericanos*, no. 517 – 519 (July – Sept 93), pp. 538 – 540.

Mantecón, Arturo. The Cardinal Virtues of Demetrio Huerta. *The Americas Review*, v. 20, no. 3 – 4 (Fall – Winter 92), pp. 84 – 93.

Manthorne, Katherine Emma. Up the Andes and Down the Amazon: 19th Century North American Views of South America. *Review*, no. 47 (Fall 93), pp. 39 – 44. Il.

Mantilla Ruiz, Luis Carlos. La búsqueda de la verdad (Commentary on the speech by Alfonso María Pinilla Cote). *Boletín de Historia y Antigüedades*, v. 80, no. 780 (Jan – Mar 93), pp. 23 – 30.

— In memoriam: fray Alberto Lee López, O.F.M. (1927 – 1992). *Boletín de Historia y Antigüedades*, v. 80, no. 781 (Apr – June 93), pp. 333 – 337.

— Las últimas expediciones de franciscanos españoles que vinieron a Colombia, 1759 y 1784. *Archivo Ibero-Americano*, v. 52, no. 205 – 208 (Jan – Dec 92), pp. 403 – 443. Bibl.

— El último cronista franciscano de la época colonial en el Nuevo Reino de Granada: fray Juan de Santa Gertrudis Serra. *Boletín de Historia y Antigüedades*, v. 79, no. 779 (Oct – Dec 92), pp. 889 – 917. Bibl.

Manwaring, Max G. The Security of Panama and the Canal: Now and for the Future. *Journal of Inter-American Studies and World Affairs*, v. 35, no. 3 (Fall 93), pp. 151 – 170.

Manz, Beatriz. Elections without Change: The Human Rights Record of Guatemala. *SALALM Papers*, v. 36 (1991), pp. 191 – 200. Bibl.

Manzino, Leonardo. La música uruguaya en los festejos de 1892 con motivo del IV centenario del encuentro de dos mundos. *Latin American Music Review*, v. 14, no. 1 (Spring – Summer 93), pp. 102 – 130. Bibl, facs.

Manzoni, Celina. Vanguardia y nacionalismo: itinerario de la *Revista de Avance*. *Iberoamericana*, v. 17, no. 49 (1993), pp. 5 – 15. Bibl.

Manzor-Coats, Lillian. Of Witches and Other Things: Maryse Condé's Challenges to Feminist Discourse. *World Literature Today*, v. 67, no. 4 (Fall 93), pp. 737 – 744. Bibl, il.

Manzotti, Vilma. Del Barco Centenera y su poema como justicia en una hazaña desventurada. *Revista Interamericana de Bibliografía*, v. 42, no. 3 (1992), pp. 453 – 462. Bibl.

Marcelo Pérez, Carmen. *En ciudad semejante* de Lisandro Otero. *Islas*, no. 97 (Sept – Dec 90), pp. 32 – 43. Bibl.

March, Ignacio J. and Rosa María Vidal. The Road to Success. *Business Mexico*, v. 3, no. 1 (Jan – Feb 93), pp. 10 – 12. Il, maps.

Marchal, Jean-Ives. Municipios vecinos, hermanos enemigos: esbozo de dos desarrollos divergentes; Tuxpan y Alamo, Veracruz. *Estudios Sociológicos*, v. 10, no. 30 (Sept – Dec 92), pp. 555 – 581. Bibl, maps.

Marchena Fernández, Juan. De franciscanos, apaches y ministros ilustrados en los pasos perdidos del norte de Nueva España. *Archivo Ibero-Americano*, v. 52, no. 205 – 208 (Jan – Dec 92), pp. 513 – 559. Bibl, tables.

Marco, Miguel Angel de. Pellegrini contra la langosta, 1891 – 1892. *Todo Es Historia*, v. 27, no. 311 (June 93), pp. 62 – 73. Il.

— Repercusiones del invento y construcción del submarino *Peral* en la Argentina. *Investigaciones y Ensayos*, no. 41 (Jan – Dec 91), pp. 215 – 225. Bibl.

Marcos, Juan Manuel. Jorge Luis Borges y el museo imaginario: en torno al debate conceptual sobre postboom y post modernidad. *Estudios Paraguayos*, v. 17, no. 1 – 2 (1989 – 1993), pp. 151 – 166. Bibl.

Maresca, Silvio Juan. Por qué Nietzsche en la Argentina no es (solamente) posmoderno. *Cuadernos Hispanoamericanos*, no. 517 – 519 (July – Sept 93), pp. 477 – 483.

Margalies de Gasparini, Luisa. Canarias – Venezuela – Canarias: proceso dinámico de migración y retorno en el siglo XX. *Montalbán*, no. 24 (1992), pp. 271 – 290. Bibl.

Margulis, Mario. Población y sociedad en la España imperial. *Estudios Demográficos y Urbanos*, v. 7, no. 1 (Jan – Apr 92), pp. 223 – 272. Bibl, tables.

Mariluz Urquijo, José María. Roma y su derecho en el Río de la Plata durante la década liberal, 1820 – 1829. *Investigaciones y Ensayos*, no. 41 (Jan – Dec 91), pp. 77 – 88. Bibl. ·

Marimán, José. Cuestión mapuche, descentralización del estado y autonomía regional. *Caravelle*, no. 59 (1992), pp. 189 – 205. Bibl.

Marimán, Pedro and Elicura Chihuailaf Nahuelpan. Reflexions mapuches autour d'un voyage au Mexique et au Guatémala. *Caravelle*, no. 59 (1992), pp. 109 – 126. Il.

Marín, Gerardo et al. Alcohol Expectancies among Hispanic and Non-Hispanic Whites: Role of Drinking Status and Acculturation. *Hispanic Journal of Behavioral Sciences*, v. 15, no. 3 (Aug 93), pp. 373 – 381. Bibl, tables.

Marín, Jonier. La última carta del almirante. *Plural (Mexico)*, v. 22, no. 264 (Sept 93), pp. 56 – 65.

Mariñez, Pablo A. Democracia y descolonización en el Caribe. *Estudios Sociales (Dominican Republic)*, v. 26, no. 92 (Apr – June 93), pp. 5 – 20. Bibl, tables.

— Entrevista con Nicomedes Santa Cruz, poeta afroamericano. *Cuadernos Americanos*, no. 40, Nueva época (July – Aug 93), pp. 110 – 124.

— El proceso democrático en República Dominicana: algunos rasgos fundamentales. *Estudios Sociales (Dominican Republic),* v. 26, no. 93 (July – Sept 93), pp. 27 – 39. Bibl.

— Procesos de integración e identidad cultural en el Caribe. *Integración Latinoamericana,* v. 17, no. 185 (Dec 92), pp. 23 – 32. Bibl.

Marinho, Mara de Andrade et al. Bibliografia brasileira de levantamento e de interpretação de levantamento de solos para fins agrícolas (com mapa-índice). *Revista Brasileira de Geografia,* v. 53, no. 1 (Jan – Mar 91), pp. 147 – 172. Bibl, maps.

Marino, Ruggiero. Innocenzo VIII, il papa di Cristoforo Colombo. *Quaderni Ibero-Americani,* no. 72 (Dec 92), pp. 595 – 602. Bibl.

Mariscal, Beatriz. Mujer y literatura oral. *Escritura (Venezuela),* v. 16, no. 31 – 32 (Jan – Dec 91), pp. 171 – 178.

Mariz, Vasco. Perigrinação a Clavadel. *Revista do Instituto Histórico e Geográfico Brasileiro,* no. 370 (Jan – Mar 91), pp. 140 – 150.

Marques, Pedro V. Integração vertical da avicultura de corte no estado de São Paulo. *Revista de Economia e Sociologia Rural,* v. 30, no. 3 (July – Sept 92), pp. 189 – 202. Bibl, tables.

Marques, Samira Aóun and Flávio Condé de Carvalho. Concentração municipal do beneficiamento de algodão no estado do Paraná nos anos oitenta. *Revista de Economia e Sociologia Rural,* v. 30, no. 2 (Apr – June 92), pp. 149 – 157. Bibl, tables.

Marquet, Antonio and Eduardo Ramírez Lozano. El inestable equilibrio del caos. *Plural (Mexico),* v. 22, no. 262 (July 93), pp. 57 – 62.

Márquez, Celina. La nostalgia por la cursilería: a un año yo te recuerdo. *La Palabra y el Hombre,* no. 84 (Oct – Dec 92), pp. 206 – 212.

Márquez, Viviane Brachet de and Margaret Sherraden. Austeridad fiscal, el estado de bienestar y el cambio político: los casos de la salud y la alimentación en México, 1970 – 1990 (Translated by Armando Castellanos). *Estudios Sociológicos,* v. 11, no. 32 (May – Aug 93), pp. 331 – 364. Bibl, tables.

Márquez Morfín, Lourdes. El cólera en la ciudad de México en el siglo XIX. *Estudios Demográficos y Urbanos,* v. 7, no. 1 (Jan – Apr 92), pp. 77 – 93. Bibl, tables, maps, charts.

Márquez Rodríguez, Alexis. Historia y ficción en la novela histórica. *Boletín de la Academia Nacional de la Historia (Venezuela),* v. 75, no. 300 (Oct – Dec 92), pp. 29 – 39. Bibl.

— J. A. Pérez Bonalde y la poesía venezolana del siglo XIX. *Revista Nacional de Cultura (Venezuela),* v. 54, no. 287 (Oct – Dec 92), pp. 117 – 134. Bibl, il.

— Mariano Picón Salas: teoria y práctica del estilo. *Boletín de la Academia Nacional de la Historia (Venezuela),* v. 76, no. 301 (Jan – Mar 93), pp. 79 – 88. Bibl.

— La obra ensayística de Mariano Picón Salas. *Boletín de la Academia Nacional de la Historia (Venezuela),* v. 76, no. 301 (Jan – Mar 93), pp. 63 – 78. Bibl.

Marras, Sergio. América en plural y en singular, I: El baile de los enmascarados; entrevista con Octavio Paz (Fragment from the book *América Latina: marca registrada). Vuelta,* v. 17, no. 194 (Jan 93), pp. 11 – 16.

— América en plural y en singular, II: Los nacionalismos y otros bemoles; entrevista con Octavio Paz (Fragment from the book *América Latina: marca registrada). Vuelta,* v. 17, no. 195 (Feb 93), pp. 26 – 30.

Marrero Fente, Raúl and Mirta Yordi. El tema de la democracia en pensadores políticos argentinos. *Islas,* no. 96 (May – Aug 90), pp. 67 – 70. Bibl.

Marshall, Santiago. Una misión de la Santa Sede: Arica. *Mensaje,* v. 42, no. 420 (July 93), pp. 287 – 289.

Marshall, Thomas H. OCLC and the Bibliographic Control of Preservation Microform Masters. *SALALM Papers,* v. 36 (1991), pp. 418 – 421.

Marshall, Timon L. and William E. Perry. Defending Antidumping Actions. *Business Mexico,* v. 3, no. 8 (Aug 93), pp. 26 – 28.

Marshall S., Guillermo. Carta del provincial a los jesuitas de Chile. *Mensaje,* v. 42, no. 420 (July 93), pp. 183 – 185. II.

Marta Sosa, Joaquín. Venezuela, 1989 – 1994: cambios, elecciones y balas. *Nueva Sociedad,* no. 124 (Mar – Apr 93), pp. 6 – 10.

Martha, Alice Aurea Penteado. Policarpo Quaresma: a história carnavalizada. *Revista de Letras (Brazil),* v. 32 (1992), pp. 119 – 125.

Martin, Christopher James. The Dynamics of School Relations on the Urban Periphery of Guadalajara, Western Mexico. *European Review of Latin American and Caribbean Studies,* no. 53 (Dec 92), pp. 61 – 81.

— The "Shadow Economy" of Local School Management in Contemporary West Mexico. *Bulletin of Latin American Research,* v. 12, no. 2 (May 93), pp. 171 – 188. Bibl.

Martin, Frederick. A *Dresden Codex* Eclipse Sequence: Projections for the Years 1970 – 1992. *Latin American Antiquity,* v. 4, no. 1 (Mar 93), pp. 74 – 93. Bibl, il, tables.

Martin, Philip L. and Wayne Armstrong Cornelius. The Uncertain Connection: Free Trade and Rural Mexican Migration to the United States. *International Migration Review,* v. 27, no. 3 (Fall 93), pp. 484 – 512. Bibl, tables, charts.

Martín P., Juan and Arturo Núñez del Prado Benavente. Strategic Management, Planning, and Budgets. *CEPAL Review,* no. 49 (Apr 93), pp. 41 – 54. Bibl.

Martín Rubio, María del Carmen. El Cuzco incaico, según Juan de Betanzos. *Cuadernos Hispanoamericanos,* no. 511 (Jan 93), pp. 7 – 23. Bibl, il.

Martinell Gifre, Emma. El uso de las formas "un," "uno," "una," "unos," "unas," en español y de sus equivalentes en inglés. *Anuario de Letras (Mexico),* v. 30 (1992), pp. 29 – 45. Bibl.

Martinengo, Alessandro. La utopía de Cristóbal Colón. *Quaderni Ibero-Americani,* no. 72 (Dec 92), pp. 554 – 563. Bibl.

Martínez, Elena M. Conversación con Magali Alabau. *Fem,* v. 17, no. 119 (Jan 93), pp. 22 – 23.

— El discurso patriarcal y el discurso feminista en *Excepto la muerte* de Carmen Elvira Moreno. *Fem,* v. 17, no. 127 (Sept 93), pp. 6 – 10. Bibl.

— Entrevista con Carmen Lugo Filippi. *Fem,* v. 17, no. 122 (Apr 93), pp. 41 – 42.

— Las "otras" voces de mujeres: narrativa y poesía. *Fem,* v. 17, no. 121 (Mar 93), pp. 36 – 37.

— Two Poetry Books of Magali Alabau. *Confluencia,* v. 8, no. 1 (Fall 92), pp. 155 – 158.

Martínez, Guillermo. Consideraciones de un ex-político. *Cuadernos Hispanoamericanos,* no. 517 – 519 (July – Sept 93), pp. 495 – 498.

Martínez, Gustavo. Lo real-maravilloso o el redescubrimiento de América. *Plural (Mexico),* v. 22, no. 265 (Oct 93), pp. 60 – 69.

Martínez, Héctor. Perú: la irrigación Jequetepeque – Zana; impacto de la presa de Gallito Ciego. *Estudios Rurales Latinoamericanos,* v. 15, no. 2 – 3 (May – Dec 92), pp. 3 – 27. Bibl, tables.

Martínez, Jesús. Don Antonio Rodríguez. *Plural (Mexico),* v. 22, no. 267 (Dec 93), pp. 74 – 75.

— Olga Costa: "in memoriam." *Plural (Mexico),* v. 22, no. 263 (Aug 93), pp. 68 – 69.

Martínez, Juan A. Cuban Vanguardia Painting in the 1930s. *Latin American Art,* v. 5, no. 2 (Summer 93), pp. 36 – 38. Bibl, il.

Martínez, Julia Evelyn. Neoliberalismo y derechos humanos. *ECA; Estudios Centroamericanos,* v. 47, no. 529 – 530 (Nov – Dec 92), pp. 1028 – 1036. Il.

Martínez, María Eugenia and Cirila Quintero Ramírez. Sindicalismo y contratación colectiva en las maquiladoras fronterizas: los casos de Tijuana, Ciudad Juárez y Matamoros. *Frontera Norte,* v. 4, no. 8 (July – Dec 92), pp. 7 – 47. Bibl, tables.

Martínez, Osvaldo. Debt and Foreign Capital: The Origin of the Crisis (Translated by Luis Fierro). *Latin American Perspectives,* v. 20, no. 1 (Winter 93), pp. 64 – 82. Bibl, tables.

Martínez, Ronald. La posición horizontal. *Signo,* no. 38, Nueva época (Jan – Apr 93), pp. 177 – 179.

Martínez Anaya, Efraín. San Miguel Teotongo: a contrapelo del neoliberalismo. *El Cotidiano,* v. 10, no. 57 (Aug – Sept 93), pp. 23 – 27. Tables.

Martínez Aparicio, Jorge. La tenencia de la tierra, luego de un año de la reforma al 27: nuevos cambios, fenómenos viejos; la tierra caliente. *El Cotidiano,* v. 10, no. 57 (Aug – Sept 93), pp. 86 – 92. Il.

Martínez Baeza, Sergio. El general don Orozimbo Barbosa y la revolución de 1891. *Boletín de la Academia Chilena de la Historia,* v. 58 – 59, no. 102 (1991 – 1992), pp. 459 – 479. Il.

Martínez Duarte, Margarita. *Biombo Negro:* lo que nos faltaba. *Plural (Mexico),* v. 22, no. 265 (Oct 93), pp. 86 – 87.

— Los hombres – instrumento de "Guardaos de los ídolos." *Plural (Mexico),* v. 22, no. 263 (Aug 93), p. 68.

Martínez Escamilla, Ramón. El estado en América Latina: teoría y práctica. *Problemas del Desarrollo,* v. 24, no. 93 (Apr – June 93), pp. 227 – 233.

— El estado mexicano y la economía en la década 1983 – 1993. *Momento Económico,* no. 68 (July – Aug 93), pp. 16 – 18. Bibl.

Martínez F., Alicia. De poder, podemos: diferencias genéricas en la dinámica sociopolítica. *El Cotidiano,* v. 9, no. 53 (Mar – Apr 93), pp. 47 – 52. Tables.

Martínez Fernández, Luis N. El anexionismo dominicano y la lucha entre imperios durante la primera republica, 1844 – 1861. *Revista/Review Interamericana,* v. 22, no. 1 – 2 (Spring – Summer 92), pp. 168 – 190. Bibl.

Martínez G., Miguel A. Ayacucho. *Boletín de la Academia Nacional de la Historia (Venezuela),* v. 75, no. 298 (Apr – June 92), pp. 90 – 93.

— Recursos tecno-científicos que se conjugan en el descubrimiento de América. *Boletín de la Academia Nacional de la Historia (Venezuela),* v. 75, no. 300 (Oct – Dec 92), pp. 79 – 88.

Martínez Heredia, Fernando. El Che y el socialismo de hoy. *Casa de las Américas,* no. 189 (Oct – Dec 92), pp. 111 – 120.

Martínez K., Marcelo. Calidad de la educación y redefinición del rol del estado en Chile, en el contexto de los proyectos de modernización. *Estudios Sociales (Chile),* no. 77 (July – Sept 93), pp. 171 – 196. Bibl.

— Calidad de la educación y redefinición del rol del estado en Chile, en el contexto de los proyectos de modernización. *Revista Paraguaya de Sociología,* v. 30, no. 86 (Jan – Apr 93), pp. 139 – 159. Bibl, tables.

Martínez Martín, Jaime J. La defensa del indio americano en un diálogo del renacimiento: *Los coloquios de la verdad* de Pedro Quiroga. *Studi di Letteratura Ispano-Americana,* v. 24 (1993), pp. 7 – 24.

Martínez Morales, Manuel. Entropía y complejidad en *La biblioteca de Babel. La Palabra y el Hombre,* no. 82 (Apr – June 92), pp. 249 – 257. Bibl.

Martínez Morelos, Olivia. Las Trabajadoras del Servicio Doméstico: ¡Presentes! *Fem,* v. 17, no. 121 (Mar 93), pp. 34 – 35. Il.

— Trabajadoras del Servicio Doméstico: Sus Reivindicaciones en el Movimiento de Mujeres. *Fem,* v. 17, no. 130 (Dec 93), pp. 40 – 41.

Martínez Quijano, Ana. El mítico mural de Siqueiros en la Argentina (Accompanied by an English translation). *Art Nexus,* no. 9 (June – Aug 93), pp. 110 – 112. Il.

Martínez Riaza, Ascensión. Las diputaciones provinciales americanas en el sistema liberal español. *Revista de Indias,* v. 52, no. 195 – 196 (May – Dec 92), pp. 647 – 691. Bibl.

Martínez Rizo, Felipe. Las desigualdades de la oferta y la demanda educativa: pasado, presente y futuro de las políticas compensatorias. *Revista Latinoamericana de Estudios Educativos,* v. 23, no. 2 (Apr – June 93), pp. 55 – 70. Bibl.

Martínez Rodríguez, Antonia and Ismael Crespo Martínez. Discurso político y realidad económica: las relaciones entre España y la comunidad iberoamericana. *Cuadernos del CLAEH,* v. 17, no. 63 – 64 (Oct 92), pp. 99 – 103. Bibl.

Martínez Ruiz, Florencio. Diván de Mangana. *Cuadernos Hispanoamericanos,* no. 510 (Dec 92), pp. 57 – 59.

Martínez Saldaña, Jesús. Los Tigres del Norte en Silicon Valley. *Nexos,* v. 16, no. 191 (Nov 93), pp. 77 – 83. Il.

Martínez Salgado, Carolina. Métodos cualitativos para los estudios de población: un ejercicio en Xochimilco. *Revista Mexicana de Sociología,* v. 54, no. 3 (July – Sept 92), pp. 243 – 251. Bibl.

— Recursos sociodemográficos y daños a la salud en unidades domésticas campesinas del estado de México. *Estudios Demográficos y Urbanos,* v. 7, no. 2 – 3 (May – Dec 92), pp. 451 – 463. Bibl, tables.

— Relatoría de la mesa redonda El Programa Nacional de Salud, 1990 – 1994. *Estudios Demográficos y Urbanos,* v. 6, no. 3 (Sept – Dec 91), pp. 756 – 772.

Martínez Salgado, Homero and José Romero Keith. La educación nutricional en el medio rural: una propuesta pedagógica. *Revista Latinoamericana de Estudios Educativos,* v. 23, no. 1 (Jan – Mar 93), pp. 75 – 86.

Martínez Salguero, Jaime. Juan Quirós, crítico literario. *Signo,* no. 36 – 37, Nueva época (May – Dec 92), pp. 215 – 219.

— Por culpa de la imagen. *Signo,* no. 35, Nueva época (Jan – Apr 92), pp. 99 – 109.

— Sociedad y folklore. *Signo,* no. 38, Nueva época (Jan – Apr 93), pp. 137 – 142.

Martínez Santana, Manuel and Marcos Eligio Escobar Navarro. Características geoquímicas y petrográficas de los principales yacimientos carboníferos venezolanos. *Interciencia,* v. 18, no. 2 (Mar – Apr 93), pp. 62 – 70. Bibl, tables, maps, charts.

— Los depósitos de carbón en Venezuela. *Interciencia,* v. 18, no. 5 (Sept – Oct 93), pp. 224 – 229. Bibl, tables, maps, charts.

Martínez Tabares, Vivian. *Vagos rumores:* reafirmación de cubanía. *Conjunto,* no. 92 (July – Dec 92), pp. 63 – 66. Il.

Martínez Valle, Luciano. Cambios en la fuerza de trabajo y conflicto social en el agro ecuatoriano. *Revista Paraguaya de Sociología*, v. 29, no. 84 (May – Aug 92), pp. 101 – 113. Bibl.

— El empleo en economías campesinas productoras para el mercardo interno: el caso de la sierra ecuatoriana. *European Review of Latin American and Caribbean Studies*, no. 53 (Dec 92), pp. 83 – 93. Bibl, tables.

Martínez Vara, Gerardo. México y el Caribe: un encuentro necesario en la problemática regional. *Relaciones Internacionales (Mexico)*, v. 14, Nueva época, no. 56 (Oct – Dec 92), pp. 129 – 132.

Martínez Vázquez, Griselda. La mujer en el proceso de modernización en México. *El Cotidiano*, v. 9, no. 53 (Mar – Apr 93), pp. 17 – 24. Bibl, tables.

Martini, Juan Carlos. Naturaleza del exilio. *Cuadernos Hispanoamericanos*, no. 517 – 519 (July – Sept 93), pp. 552 – 555.

Martini, Mónica Patricia and Daisy Rípodas Ardanaz. Aportes sobre el voseo en Córdoba a horcajadas de los siglos XVIII y XIX: sus modalidades en la obra de Cristóbal de Aguilar. *Investigaciones y Ensayos*, no. 41 (Jan – Dec 91), pp. 139 – 151. Bibl.

Martinic Drpic, Zvonimir. El tribunal arbitral italo – chileno y las reclamaciones italianas de los poseedores de certificados salitreros: evolución histórica de la problemática. *Cuadernos de Historia (Chile)*, no. 11 (Dec 91), pp. 71 – 104. Bibl, tables.

Martinière, Guy. A propos de l'histoire de l'historiographie brésilienne. *Cahiers des Amériques Latines*, no. 14 (1992), pp. 119 – 148. Bibl.

Martins, Carlos Benedito. Caminhos e descaminhos das universidades federais (Comment on the article "O sistema federal de ensino superior: problemas e alternativas" by Eunice Ribeiro Durham). *Revista Brasileira de Ciências Sociais*, v. 8, no. 23 (Oct 93), pp. 48 – 54. Bibl.

Martins-Zurhorst, Ida. Restauración y preservación de la historia del cine latinoamericano (Translated by Gabriela Fonseca). *Humboldt*, no. 108 (1993), p. 103. Il.

Martner Fanta, Ricardo. Efeitos macroeconômicos de uma desvalorização cambial: análise de simulações para o Brasil. *Pesquisa e Planejamento Econômico*, v. 22, no. 1 (Apr 92), pp. 35 – 72. Bibl, tables, charts.

Martner Fanta, Ricardo and Daniel Titelman Kardonsky. Un análisis de cointegración de las funciones de demanda de dinero: el caso de Chile. *El Trimestre Económico*, v. 60, no. 238 (Apr – June 93), pp. 413 – 446. Bibl, tables, charts.

Martos, Laura Helena. Short Stories ("El diluvio y otros cuentos," "Génesis," "El enigma," "Auto de fe"). *La Palabra y el Hombre*, no. 81 (Jan – Mar 92), pp. 70 – 72.

Martos, Marco. Imágenes paternas en la poesía de César Vallejo. *Casa de las Américas*, no. 189 (Oct – Dec 92), pp. 14 – 20.

Marulanda V., Manuel et al. Estamos comprometidos en la solución política (A reply by members of the Coordinadora Guerrillera Simón Bolívar to the letter by Antonio Caballero et al.). *Nueva Sociedad*, no. 125 (May – June 93), pp. 147 – 148.

Marx, Jutta. Construir el poder: entrevista con Anita Pérez Ferguson. *Feminaria*, v. 6, no. 11 (Nov 93), pp. 17 – 19.

Marx, Jutta and Mónica Nosetto. ¿Las mujeres al poder?: la igualdad por decreto presidencial. *Feminaria*, v. 6, no. 10 (Apr 93), pp. 27 – 28.

Marx, Jutta and Ana Sampaolesi. Elecciones internas bajo el cupo: la primera aplicación de la Ley de Cuotas en la capital federal. *Feminaria*, v. 6, no. 11 (Nov 93), pp. 15 – 17.

Masiello, Francine Rose. Rethinking Neocolonial Esthetics: Literature, Politics, and Intellectual Community in Cuba's *Revista de Avance*. *Latin American Research Review*, v. 28, no. 2 (1993), pp. 3 – 31. Bibl, facs.

Masoliver Ródenas, Juan Antonio. Paisaje de la narrativa mexicana. *Vuelta*, v. 17, no. 197 (Apr 93), pp. 58 – 62.

— Poemas. *Vuelta*, v. 17, no. 203 (Oct 93), pp. 19 – 20.

Massey, Douglas S. Latinos, Poverty, and the Underclass: A New Agenda for Research. *Hispanic Journal of Behavioral Sciences*, v. 15, no. 4 (Nov 93), pp. 449 – 475. Bibl.

Massolo, Alejandra. Descentralización y reforma municipal: ¿Fracaso anunciado y sorpresas inesperadas? *Revista Interamericana de Planificación*, v. 26, no. 101 – 102 (Jan – June 93), pp. 196 – 230. Bibl, tables.

Mastretta, Angeles. Fuentes: la edad de su tiempo. *Nexos*, v. 16, no. 186 (June 93), pp. 27 – 28.

— La tía Elena: mujeres de ojos grandes. *Fem*, v. 17, no. 123 (May 93), pp. 44 – 45.

— La tía Mónica: mujeres de ojos grandes. *Fem*, v. 17, no. 122 (Apr 93), p. 46.

Mastretta, Angeles and Rafael Pérez Gay. Días de parque, futbol y confesiones. *Nexos*, v. 16, no. 181 (Jan 93), pp. 17 – 20.

Mata, Gonzalo Humberto. Flechas en la incertidumbre. *Inti*, no. 37 – 38 (Spring – Fall 93), pp. 57 – 60.

Mata Gil, Milagros. El espacio de la nostalgia en la escritura venezolana. *Inti*, no. 37 – 38 (Spring – Fall 93), pp. 23 – 28. Bibl.

Matamoro, Blas. El Astrólogo y la muerte. *Cuadernos Hispanoamericanos*, no. Special issue, 11 (July 93), pp. 95 – 102. Il.

— Villaurrutia y Cernuda: Eros y cosmos. *Cuadernos Hispanoamericanos*, no. 514 – 515 (Apr – May 93), pp. 209 – 213. Il.

Matarrita M., Estébana. La polifuncionalidad en *El general en su laberinto*. *Káñina*, v. 16, no. 2 (July – Dec 92), pp. 109 – 113. Bibl.

Mateo y Sousa, Eligio de. De la geopolítica a la geoeconomía: una lectura del siglo XX. *Comercio Exterior*, v. 43, no. 10 (Oct 93), pp. 974 – 978.

Mateos Fernández-Maquieira, B. Sara. Juan Santos Atahualpa: un movimiento milenarista en la selva. *Amazonía Peruana*, v. 11, no. 22 (Oct 92), pp. 47 – 60. Bibl.

Mathews, Juan Carlos and Carlos Parodi Zevallos. El comercio exterior del Perú con la Comunidad Económica Europea. *Apuntes (Peru)*, no. 31 (July – Dec 92), pp. 29 – 39. Tables.

Mathias, Herculano Gomes. O primeiro decênio da república no Brasil, 1889 – 1899. *Revista do Instituto Histórico e Geográfico Brasileiro*, no. 370 (Jan – Mar 91), pp. 7 – 64. Bibl.

Mathurin B., José Antonio. Filosofía, ciencia y tecnología. *Revista Cultural Lotería*, v. 50, no. 384 (July – Aug 91), pp. 32 – 37.

Matibag, Eugenio D. Ana Lydia Vega. *Hispamérica*, v. 22, no. 64 – 65 (Apr – Aug 93), pp. 77 – 88.

Matorell, Antonio. Imalabra. *Conjunto*, no. 92 (July – Dec 92), pp. 95 – 97. Il.

Matos, Francisco Gomes de. Amar a Deus e à língua portuguesa. *Vozes*, v. 87, no. 2 (Mar – Apr 93), p. 92.

Matos Mar, José. La experiencia popular en Comas: 10 casos. *América Indígena*, v. 51, no. 2 – 3 (Apr – Sept 91), pp. 75 – 105. Tables.

— Informe de actividades, 1991. *Anuario Indigenista*, v. 30 (Dec 91), pp. 347 – 384.

— El nuevo rostro de la cultura urbana del Perú. *América Indígena*, v. 51, no. 2 – 3 (Apr – Sept 91), pp. 11 – 34. Tables, maps.

— Taquileños, quechuas del lago Titicaca, en Lima. *América Indígena*, v. 51, no. 2 – 3 (Apr – Sept 91), pp. 107 – 166. Il, maps.

Matos Mar, José and Alberto Cheng Hurtado. Comas: lo andino en la modernidad urbana. *América Indígena*, v. 51, no. 2 – 3 (Apr – Sept 91), pp. 35 – 74. Il, tables, maps.

Matos Moctezuma, Eduardo. Arqueología urbana en el centro de la ciudad de México. *Estudios de Cultura Náhuatl*, v. 22 (1992), pp. 133 – 141.

Matos Rodríguez, Félix and Marta Villaizán. "Para que vayan y produzcan frutos y ese fruto permanezca": descripción de los fondos documentales del Archivo Eclesiástico de San Juan de Puerto Rico. *Op. Cit.*, no. 7 (1992), pp. 208 – 228. Bibl, il, facs.

Matrajt, Miguel. Prevenção de "stress" ocupacional em linha de montagem: um estudo de caso mexicano (Translated by Geni Goldschmidt). *RAE; Revista de Administração de Empresas*, v. 33, no. 5 (Sept – Oct 93), pp. 98 – 108.

Mattalía Alonso, Sonia. El canto del "aura": autonomía y mercado literario en los cuentos de *Azul . . . . Revista de Crítica Literaria Latinoamericana*, v. 19, no. 38 (July – Dec 93), pp. 279 – 292.

Máttar, Jorge and Claudia Schatan. El comercio intraindustrial e intrafirme México – Estados Unidos: autopartes, electrónicos y petroquímicos (Translated by Adriana Hierro). *Comercio Exterior*, v. 43, no. 2 (Feb 93), pp. 103 – 124. Bibl, tables.

Mattarollo, Rodolfo. Proceso a la impunidad de crímenes de lesa humanidad en América Latina, 1989 – 1991. *ECA; Estudios Centroamericanos*, v. 47, no. 528 (Oct 92), pp. 867 – 882. Bibl, il.

Matte Larraín, Patricia and Rosa Camhi P. Pobreza en la década de los '90 y desafíos futuros. *Estudios Sociales (Chile)*, no. 75 (Jan – Mar 93), pp. 39 – 56. Tables.

Mattie, Mailer and Dorothea Melcher. Interpretaciones teóricas al sector informal urbano. *Derecho y Reforma Agraria*, no. 23 (1992), pp. 83 – 103. Bibl.

Mattos, Carlos António de. Modernización y reestructuración global en Chile: de la génesis autoritaria a la consolidación democrática. *Revista Paraguaya de Sociología*, v. 30, no. 86 (Jan – Apr 93), pp. 7 – 30. Bibl, tables.

— Nuevas estrategias empresariales y mutaciones territoriales en los procesos de reestructuración en América Latina. *Revista Paraguaya de Sociología*, v. 29, no. 84 (May – Aug 92), pp. 145 – 170. Bibl.

Mattos, Carlos de Meira. Geopolítica do Paraguai. *Política e Estratégica*, v. 8, no. 2 – 4 (Apr – Dec 90), pp. 400 – 404.

Mattos, César Costa Alves de. Prefixação, expectativas e inflação. *Revista Brasileira de Economia*, v. 47, no. 1 (Jan – Mar 93), pp. 131 – 144. Bibl.

— O regime de expectativas e a política salarial: indexação x prefixação. *Revista de Economia Política (Brazil)*, v. 13, no. 2 (Apr – June 93), pp. 137 – 143.

Mattos, Olgária Chaim Feres and Marilena de Souza Chauí. Caio Graco Prado. *Vozes*, v. 86, no. 4 (July – Aug 92), pp. 79 – 82. Il.

Mattos, Tomás de. Alonso de Sandoval (1576 – 1652), jesuita de esclavos. *Cuadernos del CLAEH*, v. 17, no. 63 – 64 (Oct 92), pp. 141 – 147.

Matus, Macario. Poema XXX. *Plural (Mexico)*, v. 22, no. 264 (Sept 93), pp. 108 – 109.

Matute, Mario René. Rigoberta Menchú, premio Nobel de la paz 1992 (Introduced by Alfonso Fernández Cabrelli). *Hoy Es Historia*, v. 10, no. 55 (Jan – Feb 93), pp. 97 – 101. Il.

Maura, Juan Francisco. En busca de la verdad: algunas mujeres excepcionales de la conquista. *Hispania (USA)*, v. 76, no. 4 (Dec 93), pp. 904 – 910.

— Esclavas españolas en el Nuevo Mundo. *Colonial Latin American Historical Review*, v. 2, no. 2 (Spring 93), pp. 185 – 194. Bibl.

May, Hilda R. El tiempo como kairós en la poética de Gonzalo Rojas. *Chasqui*, v. 22, no. 1 (May 93), pp. 37 – 41.

Máynez Vidal, Pilar. Documentos de Tezcoco: consideraciones sobre tres manuscritos en mexicano del ramo "Tierras." *Estudios de Cultura Náhuatl*, v. 22 (1992), pp. 325 – 343.

Mayo, Carlos Alberto and Jaime Antonio Peire. Iglesia y crédito colonial: la política crediticia de los conventos de Buenos Aires, 1767 – 1810. *Revista de Historia de América*, no. 112 (July – Dec 91), pp. 147 – 157. Bibl.

Mayo, John K. British Merchants in Chile and on Mexico's West Coast in the Mid-Nineteenth Century: The Age of Isolation. *Historia (Chile)*, no. 26 (1991 – 1992), pp. 144 – 171. Bibl.

Mayol Baños, Brenda Ninette and Ofelia Columba Déleon Meléndez. Aproximación a la cultura popular tradicional de los municipios de Ciudad Flores, San José y la aldea Santa Eleana del departamento de Petén, Guatemala. *La Tradición Popular*, no. 76 – 77 (1990), Issue. Il, facs.

— Una muestra de juguetes populares de la ciudad de Guatemala. *La Tradición Popular*, no. 86 – 87 (1992), Issue. Bibl, il.

Mayor Zaragoza, Federico. Las aportaciones de Iberoamérica a la nueva comunidad internacional. *Cuadernos Americanos*, no. 39, Nueva época (May – June 93), pp. 13 – 26.

Mayrink, Paulo Tarcísio. School Libraries in Brazil Facing the Twenty-First Century: New Formats. *SALALM Papers*, v. 36 (1991), pp. 357 – 390.

Maza, Francisco de la. San Bernardino de Xochimilco: caciques domésticos (Accompanied by an English translation). *Artes de México*, no. 20 (Summer 93), pp. 67 – 73.

Maza Miquel, Manuel P. Desiderio Mesnier (1852 – 1913): un sacerdote y patriota cubano para todos los tiempos. *Estudios Sociales (Dominican Republic)*, v. 26, no. 92 (Apr – June 93), pp. 77 – 92. Bibl.

Mazariegos, Rita. Poemas. *Káñina*, v. 16, no. 2 (July – Dec 92), pp. 213 – 214.

Mazzali, Leonel. A crise do estado. *Revista de Economia Política (Brazil)*, v. 13, no. 3 (July – Sept 93), pp. 139 – 143. Bibl.

Mazzone, Daniel. Tango y bandoneón: encuentros y tristezas de un doble A. *Cuadernos del CLAEH*, v. 17, no. 63 – 64 (Oct 92), pp. 167 – 173. Bibl.

Mazzucchelli, Aldo. Poems ("La casa", "Epitafio"). *Hispamérica*, v. 22, no. 64 – 65 (Apr – Aug 93), p. 144.

Mazzuchi, Silvia and Héctor Sambuceti. Santos Pérez: alegato y ejecución. *Todo Es Historia*, v. 26, no. 308 (Mar 93), pp. 26 – 35. Il.

Meade, Joaquín. Breve descripción del templo de Carmen. *Artes de México*, no. 18 (Winter 92), pp. 53 – 61. Il.

Medina, Alvaro. Milton Becerra: piedras atadas y geometría desatada (Accompanied by an English translation). *Art Nexus*, no. 8 (Apr – June 93), pp. 64 – 68. Il.

— Quien mucho abarca poco aprieta (Accompanied by an English translation). *Art Nexus*, no. 9 (June – Aug 93), pp. 62 – 64. Il.

Medina, Marcello and Kathy Cogburn Escamilla. English and Spanish Acquisition by Limited-Language-Proficient Mexican Americans in a Three-Year Maintenance Bilingual Program. *Hispanic Journal of Behavioral Sciences*, v. 15, no. 1 (Feb 93), pp. 108 – 120. Bibl, tables.

Medina, Pablo. Poems ("Madame America," "The Apostate"). *The Americas Review*, v. 20, no. 3 – 4 (Fall – Winter 92), pp. 229 – 232.

Medina A., Gilberto Javier. Exploraciones entre Chagres a Panamá: cartografía de la ciudad. *Revista Cultural Lotería*, v. 50, no. 385 (Sept – Oct 91), pp. 5 – 45. Bibl, tables, maps.

— La realidad del descubrimiento de las Indias occidentales. *Revista Cultural Lotería*, v. 51, no. 391 (Sept – Oct 92), pp. 58 – 79. Bibl, maps.

Medina Cárdenas, Eduardo. El modelo "región de refugio" de Aguirre Beltrán: teoría, aplicaciones y perspectivas. *Siglo XIX: Cuadernos*, v. 2, no. 4 (Oct 92), pp. 61 – 82. Bibl.

Medina Flórez, Enrique. Ante el féretro del maestro Acuña. *Boletín de Historia y Antigüedades*, v. 80, no. 781 (Apr – June 93), pp. 355 – 356.

Medina López, Javier. Esbozo de una guía bibliográfica del tratamiento. *Anuario de Letras (Mexico)*, v. 30 (1992), pp. 233 – 248.

Medina Perdomo, Alvaro. El segundo matrimonio: matrimonio de segunda. *Revista Javeriana*, v. 61, no. 599 (Oct 93), pp. 349 – 350.

Medina Ríos, Alba. El protagonismo femenino en la "redota": una lectura al padrón del éxodo del pueblo oriental. *Hoy Es Historia*, v. 10, no. 55 (Jan – Feb 93), pp. 58 – 61.

Meding, Holger M. German Emigration to Argentina and the Illegal Brain Drain to the Plate, 1945 – 1955. *Jahrbuch für Geschichte von Staat, Wirtschaft und Gesellschaft Lateinamerikas*, v. 29 (1992), pp. 397 – 419. Bibl, tables.

Medrano, Carmen. Ana Beker. *Todo Es Historia*, v. 27, no. 313 (Aug 93), pp. 48 – 49. Il.

— Syria Poletti. *Todo Es Historia*, v. 26, no. 305 (Dec 92), pp. 34 – 36. Il.

Medrano Puyol, Juan A. Dr. José María Núñez Quintero. *Revista Cultural Lotería*, v. 50, no. 383 (May – June 91), pp. 57 – 62.

Meganck, Richard A. and Sam H. Ham. The Transferability of U.S. Environmental Education Programs in Rural Central America: A Case Study from Honduras. *La Educación (USA)*, v. 37, no. 115 (1993), pp. 289 – 301. Bibl, tables.

Meihy, José Carlos Sebe Bom. "Meu empenho foi ser o tradutor do universo sertanejo": entrevista com José Calazans (Interviewed and transcribed by José Carlos Sebe Bom Meihy). *Luso-Brazilian Review*, v. 30, no. 2 (Winter 93), pp. 23 – 33.

Meikle, Paulette. Spatio-Temporal Trends in Root Crop Production and Marketing in Jamaica. *Caribbean Geography*, v. 3, no. 4 (Sept 92), pp. 223 – 235. Bibl, tables, maps, charts.

Meira, Alcyr Boris de Souza. Amazônia: gestão do território. *Revista Brasileira de Geografia*, v. 53, no. 3 (July – Sept 91), pp. 133 – 147.

Meira, Sílvio Augusto de Bastos. Um parecer inédito de Rui Barbosa (Includes Rui Barbosa's text regarding the rejection by the city of Belém, Pará, of an electrical transportation contract in the late 19th century). *Revista do Instituto Histórico e Geográfico Brasileiro*, no. 372 (July – Sept 91), pp. 647 – 658.

— Relacionamento histórico entre o Brasil e o Chile. *Revista do Instituto Histórico e Geográfico Brasileiro*, no. 370 (Jan – Mar 91), pp. 102 – 126.

Meirinho, Jali. O governo federalista em Santa Catarina. *Hoy Es Historia*, v. 10, no. 60 (Nov – Dec 93), pp. 43 – 49. Bibl.

Mejía, Kember. Las palmeras en los mercados de Iquitos. *Bulletin de l'Institut Français d'Etudes Andines*, v. 21, no. 2 (1992), pp. 755 – 769. Bibl, il, tables, maps.

Mejía, Manuel Zacarías and Edmundo Morel. Los impactos de los desalojos: la constitución o reconstitución de las identidades. *Estudios Sociales (Dominican Republic)*, v. 26, no. 94 (Oct – Dec 93), pp. 45 – 74. Bibl.

Mejía, Marco Raúl. Educación popular: una fuerza creativa desde los sectores populares. *Estudios Sociales (Dominican Republic)*, v. 26, no. 93 (July – Sept 93), pp. 61 – 82.

Mejía Gutiérrez, Carlos. Esbozos para un estudio psicológico del Libertador. *Boletín de Historia y Antigüedades*, v. 80, no. 781 (Apr – June 93), pp. 443 – 462. Bibl.

Mejía Madrid, Fabrizio. Con el corazón en la mano. *Nexos*, v. 16, no. 192 (Dec 93), pp. 21 – 22.

— El nuevo retorno de los brujos. *Nexos*, v. 16, no. 190 (Oct 93), pp. 53 – 63.

Mejías Alvarez, María Jesús. Muerte regia en cuatro ciudades peruanas del barroco. *Anuario de Estudios Americanos*, v. 49 (1992), pp. 189 – 205. Bibl, il.

Melcher, Dorothea and Mailer Mattie. Interpretaciones teóricas al sector informal urbano. *Derecho y Reforma Agraria*, no. 23 (1992), pp. 83 – 103. Bibl.

Melchior, José Carlos de Araújo. Financiamento da educação: gestão democrática dos recursos financeiros públicos em educação. *Revista Brasileira de Estudos Pedagógicos*, v. 72, no. 172 (Sept – Dec 91), pp. 262 – 290. Bibl.

Meléndez, Gabriel. Carrying the Magic of His People's Heart: An Interview with Jimmy Santiago Baca. *The Americas Review*, v. 19, no. 3 – 4 (Winter 91), pp. 64 – 86.

Meléndez, Priscilla. Leñero's *Los albañiles:* Assembling the Stage/Dismantling the Theatre. *Latin American Literary Review*, v. 21, no. 41 (Jan – June 93), pp. 39 – 52. Bibl.

Meléndez Chaverri, Carlos. El verdadero Morazán. *Revista de Historia (Costa Rica)*, no. 26 (July – Dec 92), pp. 219 – 240.

Melgar Bao, Ricardo. Militancia aprista en el Caribe: la sección cubana. *Cuadernos Americanos*, no. 37, Nueva época (Jan – Feb 93), pp. 208 – 226. Bibl.

— Nuevo Mundo y área mediterránea en confrontación: sistemas político – culturales en los siglos XV – XIX. *Boletín de Antropología Americana*, no. 23 (July 91), pp. 99 – 108. Bibl, il.

Melis, Antonio. Poesía y política en *Las uvas y el viento*. *Revista de Crítica Literaria Latinoamericana*, v. 19, no. 38 (July – Dec 93), pp. 123 – 130.

Melis, Antonio et al. Debate (on the second session of the symposium "Latinoamérica: Nuevas Direcciones en Teoría y Crítica Literarias, III"). *Revista de Crítica Literaria Latinoamericana*, v. 19, no. 38 (July – Dec 93), pp. 91 – 101.

— Debate (on the sixth session of the symposium "Latinoamérica: Nuevas Direcciones en Teoría y Crítica Literarias, III"). *Revista de Crítica Literaria Latinoamericana*, v. 19, no. 38 (July – Dec 93), pp. 261 – 266.

Mellafe Rojas, Rolando. La importancia de la Universidad de Chile en la educación nacional. *Boletín de la Academia Chilena de la Historia*, v. 58 – 59, no. 102 (1991 – 1992), pp. 481 – 489.

Mellafe Rojas, Rolando and María Teresa González P. La Ley Orgánica de Instrucción Secundaria y Superior de 1879. *Cuadernos de Historia (Chile)*, no. 11 (Dec 91), pp. 63 – 69. Bibl.

Mellafe Rojas, Rolando and Antonia Rebolledo Hernández. La creación de la Universidad de Chile y el despertar de la identidad nacional. *Atenea (Chile)*, no. 465 – 466 (1992), pp. 303 – 323. Bibl, il.

Meller, Patricio. Ajuste y reformas económicas en América Latina: problemas y experiencias recientes. *Pensamiento Iberoamericano*, no. 22 – 23, tomo II (July 92 – June 93), pp. 15 – 58. Bibl, tables, charts.

Mello, Celso Duvivier de Albuquerque. O Brasil e o direito internacional na nova ordem mundial. *Revista Brasileira de Estudos Políticos*, no. 76 (Jan 93), pp. 7 – 26. Bibl.

Melo, Fernando Bento Homem de

See

Homem de Melo, Fernando Bento

Melo, Marcus André Barreto Campelo de. Anatomia do fracasso: intermediação de interesses e a reforma das políticas sociais na nova república. *Dados*, v. 36, no. 1 (1993), pp. 119 – 163. Bibl, tables.

— Municipalismo, "Nation-Building" e a modernização do estado no Brasil. *Revista Brasileira de Ciências Sociais*, v. 8, no. 23 (Oct 93), pp. 85 – 100. Bibl.

Mena, David Amílcar and Joaquín Arriola Palomares. La transición: los proyectos en disputa. *ECA; Estudios Centroamericanos*, v. 48, no. 536 (June 93), pp. 527 – 544. Bibl, il, tables.

Menchú, Rigoberta. Un homenaje a los pueblos indígenas. *Realidad Económica*, no. 114 – 115 (Feb – May 93), pp. 74 – 85. Il.

— Mensaje de Rigoberta Menchú Tum, premio Nobel de la paz 1992. *Cuadernos Americanos*, no. 39, Nueva época (May – June 93), pp. 96 – 97.

— ¿Por qué se discrimina al indígena? *Hoy Es Historia*, v. 10, no. 58 (July – Aug 93), pp. 80 – 83. Il.

Méndez, Angel. Obonobu y el viento. *Revista Nacional de Cultura (Venezuela)*, v. 54, no. 287 (Oct – Dec 92), pp. 103 – 108. Il.

Méndez, Cecilia. ¿Economía moral versus determinismo económico?: dos aproximaciones a la historia colonial hispanoamericana. *Historia y Cultura (Peru)*, no. 20 (1990), pp. 361 – 366.

Méndez, José Luis. Puerto Rico: ¿Español o inglés?; un debate sobre su identidad. *Cuadernos Americanos*, no. 40, Nueva época (July – Aug 93), pp. 84 – 96. Bibl.

Méndez, Luis and José Othón Quiroz Trejo. El conflicto de la Volkswagen: crónica de una muerte inesperada. *El Cotidiano*, v. 8, no. 51 (Nov – Dec 92), pp. 81 – 94. Bibl, il, tables, charts.

— Productividad, respuesta obrera y sucesión presidencial. *El Cotidiano*, v. 10, no. 58 (Oct – Nov 93), pp. 71 – 78.

— El proyecto cetemista y la modernidad laboral. *El Cotidiano*, v. 9, no. 56 (July 93), pp. 8 – 17. Il.

— El sindicalismo mexicano en los noventas: los sectores y las perspectivas. *El Cotidiano*, v. 9, no. 56 (July 93), pp. 3 – 7. Il.

Méndez, Luis et al. Historia y poder. *El Cotidiano*, v. 8, no. 51 (Nov – Dec 92), pp. 60 – 69. Il, tables.

Méndez Avellaneda, Juan María. La vida privada de Trinidad Guevara. *Todo Es Historia*, v. 27, no. 311 (June 93), pp. 26 – 40. Il, facs.

Méndez Dávila, Lionel. Acerca del público latrocinio de las "lumpen burguesías" y las tropelías del poder bajo las clases residuales. *USAC*, no. 12 (Dec 90), pp. 31 – 35.

Méndez de Gamboa, Irene. Logro académico estudiantil en el área de salud. *Revista de Ciencias Sociales (Costa Rica)*, no. 60 (June 93), pp. 117 – 133. Bibl, tables.

Méndez G., Juan Carlos. Análisis de las fuentes de financiamiento de CODELCO. *Estudios Públicos (Chile)*, no. 50 (Fall 93), pp. 281 – 343. Bibl, tables, charts.

Méndez M., José Luis. La política pública como variable dependiente: hacia un análisis más integral de las políticas públicas. *Foro Internacional*, v. 33, no. 1 (Jan – Mar 93), pp. 111 – 144. Bibl, tables, charts.

Méndez Rodríguez, Alejandro and Marcela Astudillo Moya. Planes urbanos sin descentralización financiera en México. *Problemas del Desarrollo*, v. 24, no. 93 (Apr – June 93), pp. 153 – 174. Bibl, tables, charts.

Méndez Rojas, Conny. Algunas reflexiones sobre lo que SALALM podría ofrecer a los bibliotecarios nicaragüenses. *SALALM Papers*, v. 36 (1991), pp. 228 – 232.

— La situación de la producción bibliográfica nicaragüense. *SALALM Papers*, v. 36 (1991), pp. 171 – 183. Bibl.

Mendoza, Ana and Miguel Franco. Integración clonal en una palma tropical. *Bulletin de l'Institut Français d'Etudes Andines*, v. 21, no. 2 (1992), pp. 623 – 635. Bibl, il, tables, charts.

Mendoza, Héctor and Fabricio Vivas. Informe 1990 – 1991: estadísticas históricas de Venezuela; historia de las finanzas públicas en Venezuela. *Boletín de la Academia Nacional de la Historia (Venezuela)*, v. 75, no. 297 (Jan – Mar 92), pp. 169 – 176.

Mendoza, José G. Bello y los verbos abstractos en el análisis de los modos. *Signo*, no. 35, Nueva época (Jan – Apr 92), pp. 83 – 97. Bibl.

— El castellano del siglo XVI en el Alto Perú, hoy Bolivia. *Signo*, no. 36 – 37, Nueva época (May – Dec 92), pp. 409 – 432. Bibl.

Mendoza, Plinio Apuleyo. La guerra que nunca quisimos ver. *Nueva Sociedad*, no. 125 (May – June 93), pp. 149 – 153.

Mendoza Pichardo, Gabriel and Alejandro Alvarez Bejar. Mexico, 1988 – 1991: A Successful Economic Adjustment Program? (Translated by John F. Uggen). *Latin American Perspectives*, v. 20, no. 3 (Summer 93), pp. 32 – 45. Bibl.

Menéndez, Eduardo L. Investigación antropológica, biografía y controles artesanales. *Nueva Antropología*, v. 13, no. 43 (Nov 92), pp. 23 – 37. Bibl.

Menéndez Alarcón, Antonio V. Television Culture: The Dominican Case. *Studies in Latin American Popular Culture*, v. 12 (1993), pp. 95 – 112. Bibl.

Menéndez Martínez, Otto R. Alimentación – nutrición y salud – enfermedad estomatológica: revisión de literatura. *USAC*, no. 13 (Mar 91), pp. 61 – 75. Bibl, charts.

Menéndez Martínez, Otto R. et al. ¿Salud para todos en el año 2000?: panel-foro. *USAC*, no. 14 (June 91), pp. 3 – 23. Bibl.

Menéndez Menéndez, Libertad. Investigación y evaluación en pedagogía. *Revista Mexicana de Ciencias Políticas y Sociales*, v. 37, Nueva época, no. 149 (July – Sept 92), pp. 139 – 152. Bibl.

Meneses, Carlos. Norwin y Carlitos, los periodistas de *Conversación en la catedral. La Palabra y el Hombre*, no. 84 (Oct – Dec 92), pp. 321 – 329. Il.

Menezes, Flávio Marques. Leilões de privatização: uma análise de equilíbrio. *Revista Brasileira de Economia*, v. 47, no. 3 (July – Sept 93), pp. 317 – 348. Bibl.

Menezes, Geraldo Bezerra de. A presença dos intelectuais brasileiros na campanha abolicionista. *Revista do Instituto Histórico e Geográfico Brasileiro*, no. 370 (Jan – Mar 91), pp. 226 – 230.

Mentz de Boege, Brígida M. von. La desigualdad social en México: revisión bibliográfica y propuesta de una visión global. *Historia Mexicana*, v. 42, no. 2 (Oct – Dec 92), pp. 505 – 561.

Meo Zilio, Giovanni. A propósito de ecos petrarquistas en el argentino Enrique Banchs. *Nueva Revista de Filología Hispánica*, v. 40, no. 2 (July – Dec 92), pp. 909 – 920.

Mercado Celis, Alejandro. El déficit, los impuestos, solidaridad y Clinton. *Problemas del Desarrollo*, v. 24, no. 93 (Apr – June 93), pp. 27 – 33. Bibl.

Mercado Jarrín, Edgardo. Fuerzas armadas: constitución y reconversión. *Debate (Peru)*, v. 16, no. 75 (Dec 93 – Jan 94), pp. 31 – 34. Il.

Mercieca, Eddie. Jesuitas en parroquias. *Mensaje*, v. 42, no. 420 (July 93), pp. 285 – 286. Il.

Merewether, Charles. Comunidad y continuidad: Doris Salcedo; nombrando la violencia (Accompanied by the English original, translated by Magdalena Holguín). *Art Nexus*, no. 9 (June – Aug 93), pp. 104 – 109. Bibl, il.

Mérida, Gladys A. De virtudes y de hombres. *Letras Femeninas*, v. 19, no. 1 – 2 (Spring – Fall 93), pp. 193 – 194.

Merino, Carolina. Entre la cohesión y la diáspora: 25 años de poesía chilena. *Aisthesis*, no. 24 (1991), pp. 9 – 19. Bibl.

Merino Huerta, Mauricio. Democracia, después. *Nexos*, v. 16, no. 185 (May 93), pp. 51 – 60. Bibl.

Merkx, Gilbert W. The Progress of Alliance: Confronting the Crisis in Resources for Foreign Area Studies in the United States. *SALALM Papers*, v. 36 (1991), pp. 294 – 302. Bibl.

Merlino, Rodolfo J. and Mario A. Rabey. Resistencia y hegemonía: cultos locales y religión centralizada en los Andes del sur. *Allpanchis*, v. 23, no. 40 (July – Dec 92), pp. 173 – 200. Bibl.

Merten, Luiz Carlos. A agonia do cinema nacional. *Vozes*, v. 87, no. 3 (May – June 93), pp. 64 – 66.

Mesa Gisbert, Carlos D. Televisión y elecciones: ¿El poder total? *Estado y Sociedad*, v. 8, no. 9 (Jan – June 92), pp. 39 – 52.

Mesa-Lago, Carmelo. Cuba: un caso único de reforma antimercado; retrospectiva y perspectivas. *Pensamiento Iberoamericano*, no. 22 – 23, tomo II (July 92 – June 93), pp. 65 – 100. Bibl, tables.

— Efectos económicos en Cuba del derrumbe del socialismo en la Unión Soviética y Europa Oriental. *Estudios Internacionales (Chile)*, v. 26, no. 103 (July – Sept 93), pp. 341 – 414. Bibl, tables.

— The Social Safety Net Unravels. *Hemisphere*, v. 5, no. 3 (Summer – Fall 93), pp. 26 – 30. Charts.

Meschiatti, Adriana Jorge and Marlene Sofia Arcifa. Distribution and Feeding Ecology of Fishes in a Brazilian Reservoir: Lake Monte Alegre. *Interciencia*, v. 18, no. 6 (Nov – Dec 93), pp. 302 – 313. Bibl, tables, charts.

Mesclier, Evelyne. Cusco: espacios campesinos en un contexto de inestabilidad económica y retracción del estado (With several commentaries and a response by the authoress). *Revista Andina*, v. 11, no. 1 (July 93), pp. 7 – 53. Bibl, maps.

Messner, Dirk. Shaping Competitiveness in the Chilean Wood-Processing Industry. *CEPAL Review*, no. 49 (Apr 93), pp. 117 – 137. Bibl, charts.

Mestre, Juan Carlos. El discurso de la utopía en la poética de Gonzalo Rojas. *Chasqui*, v. 22, no. 1 (May 93), pp. 42 – 46.

Methol Ferré, Alberto. El fracaso del V centenario. *Cuadernos del CLAEH*, v. 17, no. 63 – 64 (Oct 92), pp. 11 – 20. Bibl.

Metz, Allan Sheldon. Cuban – Israeli Relations: From the Cuban Revolution to the New World Order. *Cuban Studies/Estudios Cubanos*, v. 23 (1993), pp. 113 – 134. Bibl.

— Israeli Military Assistance to Latin America (Review article). *Latin American Research Review*, v. 28, no. 2 (1993), pp. 257 – 263.

Mexico. Secretaría de Comercio y Fomento Industrial. Ley de Comercio Exterior. *Comercio Exterior*, v. 43, no. 9 (Sept 93), pp. 870 – 884.

Meyemberg Léycegui, Yolanda. Jesús Reyes Heroles. *Revista Mexicana de Ciencias Políticas y Sociales*, v. 38, Nueva época, no. 151 (Jan – Mar 93), pp. 81 – 99. Bibl.

Meyer, Arno. Apoio financeiro externo e estabilização econômica. *Revista de Economia Política (Brazil)*, v. 13, no. 1 (Jan – Mar 93), pp. 135 – 148. Tables.

Meyer, Carrie A. Environmental NGOs in Ecuador: An Economic Analysis of Institutional Change. *Journal of Developing Areas*, v. 27, no. 2 (Jan 93), pp. 191 – 210. Bibl.

Meyer, Doris L. Letters and Lines of Correspondence in the Essays of Victoria Ocampo. *Revista Interamericana de Bibliografía*, v. 42, no. 2 (1992), pp. 233 – 240. Bibl.

Meyer, Jean A. Una historia política de la religión en el México contemporáneo. *Historia Mexicana*, v. 42, no. 3 (Jan – Mar 93), pp. 714 – 744. Bibl.

Meyer, Lorenzo. El presidencialismo: del populismo al neoliberalismo. *Revista Mexicana de Sociología*, v. 55, no. 2 (Apr – June 93), pp. 57 – 81. Bibl.

Meyer-Minnemann, Klaus. Apropiaciones de realidad en las novelas de José Joaquín Fernández de Lizardi. *Iberoamericana*, v. 17, no. 50 (1993), pp. 63 – 78. Bibl.

— Octavio Paz: "Topoemas"; elementos para una lectura. *Nueva Revista de Filología Hispánica*, v. 40, no. 2 (July – Dec 92), pp. 1113 – 1134. Bibl, charts.

Meza, Robinzon. Bandos de buen gobierno para Mérida durante la colonia y su continuidad en los diversos instrumentos jurídicos del gobierno local de la república. *Boletín de la Academia Nacional de la Historia (Venezuela)*, v. 75, no. 299 (July – Sept 92), pp. 174 – 180. Bibl.

Miaja, María Teresa. Salvador Reyes Nevares en mi autobiografía. *Cuadernos Americanos*, no. 41, Nueva época (Sept – Oct 93), pp. 222 – 225.

Michelena, Alejandro Daniel. Peñas y tertulias culturales en Montevideo. *Hoy Es Historia*, v. 10, no. 57 (Apr – May 93), pp. 33 – 39. Il.

— El pueblo de Cuba, entre el drama y la esperanza, III; Cuba: las auténticas "permanencias." *Hoy Es Historia*, v. 10, no. 56 (Mar – Apr 93), pp. 69 – 74.

— Tercer indice trianual: autores y materias, 1990 – 1992. *Hoy Es Historia,* v. 10, no. 55 (Jan – Feb 93), Insert.

— Valores notables de la cultura uruguaya. *Hoy Es Historia,* v. 10, no. 55 (Jan – Feb 93), pp. 24 – 31. Bibl.

— Vaz Ferreira, filósofo de cercanías. *Hoy Es Historia,* v. 10, no. 58 (July – Aug 93), pp. 4 – 9. Il.

— Zum Felde, iniciador múltiple. *Hoy Es Historia,* v. 10, no. 55 (Jan – Feb 93), pp. 14 – 20. Bibl, il.

Micheli, Alfredo de. Un mexicano en la Italia del siglo de las luces. *La Palabra y el Hombre,* no. 81 (Jan – Mar 92), pp. 85 – 93. Bibl, il.

Middlebrook, Kevin J. Estructuras del estado y política de registro sindical en el México posrevolucionario. *Revista Mexicana de Sociología,* v. 54, no. 4 (Oct – Dec 92), pp. 65 – 90.

Mier y Terán, Marta and Cecilia Andrea Rabell Romero. Inicio de la transición de la fecundidad en México: descendencias de mujeres nacidas en la primera mitad del siglo XX. *Revista Mexicana de Sociología,* v. 55, no. 1 (Jan – Mar 93), pp. 41 – 81. Bibl, tables, charts.

Mieres, Pablo. Canelones, 1989: el fin del bipartidismo. *Cuadernos del CLAEH,* v. 18, no. 67 (Nov 93), pp. 121 – 131. Tables.

Mifsud, Tony. Juan Pablo II: "Si quieres la paz, sal al encuentro del pobre." *Mensaje,* v. 42, no. 417 (Mar – Apr 93), pp. 96 – 98.

Mignolo, Walter D. "Colonial and Postcolonial Discourse": Cultural Critique or Academic Colonialism? (Response to Patricia Seed's "Colonial and Postcolonial Discourse," *LARR,* v. 26, no. 3, 1991). *Latin American Research Review,* v. 28, no. 3 (1993), pp. 121 – 134. Bibl.

— Second Thoughts on Canon and Corpus. *Latin American Literary Review,* v. 20, no. 40 (July – Dec 92), pp. 66 – 69. Bibl.

Milán, Eduardo. Algo de Huidobro ahora. *Vuelta,* v. 17, no. 204 (Nov 93), pp. 59 – 62.

— Sarduy. *Vuelta,* v. 17, no. 201 (Aug 93), pp. 31 – 32.

— Tres poemas. *Vuelta,* v. 17, no. 200 (July 93), p. 16.

Milaré, Sebastião. Las estaciones poéticas de Antunes Filho. *Conjunto,* no. 93 (Jan – June 93), pp. 26 – 37. Il.

Millán, Betty and Francis Kahn. "Astrocaryum" (Palmae) in Amazonia: A Preliminary Treatment. *Bulletin de l'Institut Français d'Etudes Andines,* v. 21, no. 2 (1992), pp. 459 – 531. Bibl, il, tables.

Millán, René. Orden y cultura política en México. *Revista Mexicana de Sociología,* v. 55, no. 2 (Apr – June 93), pp. 155 – 168.

Millán Bojalil, Julio Alfonso. La cuenca del Pacífico: mito o realidad. *Comercio Exterior,* v. 43, no. 12 (Dec 93), pp. 1121 – 1127. Bibl.

Millán Moncayo, Márgara. ¿Hacia una estética cinematográfica femenina? *Revista Mexicana de Ciencias Políticas y Sociales,* v. 37, Nueva época, no. 149 (July – Sept 92), pp. 177 – 188.

Millar Carvacho, René. Hechicería, marginalidad e inquisición en el distrito del tribunal de Lima. *Boletín de la Academia Chilena de la Historia,* v. 58 – 59, no. 102 (1991 – 1992), pp. 185 – 227.

Millar Carvacho, René and Paz Larraín Mira. Notas para la historia de la cultura en el período indiano: la biblioteca del obispo de Santiago, Juan Bravo del Rivero y Correa, 1685 – 1752. *Historia (Chile),* no. 26 (1991 – 1992), pp. 173 – 211. Bibl.

Miller, Eugene D. Labour and the War-Time Alliance in Costa Rica, 1943 – 1948. *Journal of Latin American Studies,* v. 25, no. 3 (Oct 93), pp. 515 – 541. Bibl, tables.

Miller, Learie A. A Preliminary Assessment of the Economic Cost of Land Degradation: The Hermitage Catchment, Jamaica. *Caribbean Geography,* v. 3, no. 4 (Sept 92), pp. 244 – 252. Bibl, tables, maps.

Miller, Rory M. Transferencia de técnicas: la construcción y administración de ferrocarriles en la costa occidental de Sudamérica (Translated by Isabel Cristina Mata Velázquez). *Siglo XIX: Cuadernos,* v. 3, no. 7 (Oct 93), pp. 65 – 102. Bibl, maps.

Millet Cámara, Luis et al. Tecoh, Izamal: nobleza indígena y conquista española. *Latin American Antiquity,* v. 4, no. 1 (Mar 93), pp. 48 – 58. Bibl, il, maps.

Millett, Richard L. Review Essay: Looking beyond the Invasion; A Review of Recent Books on Panama. *Journal of Inter-American Studies and World Affairs,* v. 35, no. 3 (Fall 93), pp. 173 – 180. Bibl.

Millones Santa Gadea, Luis. Poemas y canciones en honor de Santa Rosa: profecías del pasado, voces del presente. *Revista de Crítica Literaria Latinoamericana,* v. 19, no. 37 (Jan – June 93), pp. 185 – 194. Bibl.

Milstein, Renée and Richard A. Raschio. Bibliografía anotada de logicales, videodiscos y discos compactos para la enseñanza del español o para el uso en cursos bilingües. *Hispania (USA),* v. 76, no. 4 (Dec 93), pp. 683 – 720.

Milton, Heloisa Costa. O *Diário* de Cristóvão Colombo: discurso da "maravilha" americana. *Revista de Letras (Brazil),* v. 32 (1992), pp. 169 – 183.

Minard, Evelyne. Un example d'utilisation de l'histoire par Ernesto Cardenal: *El estrecho dudoso. Caravelle,* no. 60 (1993), pp. 101 – 121. Bibl.

Minello, Nelson. Entrevistas a Rodolfo Stavenhagen, José Luis Reyna y Claudio Stern. *Estudios Sociológicos,* v. 11, no. 31 (Jan – Apr 93), pp. 19 – 31.

Minello, Nelson and Arturo Alvarado Mendoza. Política y elecciones en Tamaulipas: la relación entre lo local y lo nacional. *Estudios Sociológicos,* v. 10, no. 30 (Sept – Dec 92), pp. 619 – 647. Charts.

Minkler, Julie A. Helen's Calibans: A Study of Gender Hierarchy in Derek Walcott's *Omeros. World Literature Today,* v. 67, no. 2 (Spring 93), pp. 272 – 276. Bibl.

Miño Grijalva, Manuel. Estructura económica y crecimiento: la historiografía económica colonial mexicana. *Historia Mexicana,* v. 42, no. 2 (Oct – Dec 92), pp. 221 – 260.

Minsburg, Naúm. Política privatizadora en América Latina. *Comercio Exterior,* v. 43, no. 11 (Nov 93), pp. 1060 – 1067. Bibl, tables.

— Privatizaciones y reestructuración económica en América Latina. *Realidad Económica,* no. 116 (May – June 93), pp. 76 – 97. Bibl, tables.

Mira Delli-Zotti, Guillermo and Ignacio González Casasnovas. Reflexiones y sugerencias a propósito de la minería colonial. *Historia Mexicana,* v. 42, no. 2 (Oct – Dec 92), pp. 309 – 332.

Mira Delli-Zotti, Guillermo and Julio C. Sánchez. III Curso de Historia de la Técnica: Procesos de Industrialización en América y la Península Ibérica. *Anuario de Estudios Americanos,* v. 49, Suppl. 1 (1992), pp. 215 – 216.

Miranda, Danilo Santos de. Descobertas em tom de aventura. *Problemas Brasileiros,* v. 30, no. 297 (May – June 93), pp. 26 – 29.

— No ritmo da mudança. *Problemas Brasileiros,* v. 30, no. 295 (Jan – Feb 93), pp. 69 – 70. Il.

Miranda, Evaristo Eduardo de. Variabilidad espacio-temporal de las quemas en el Brasil. *Interciencia,* v. 18, no. 6 (Nov – Dec 93), pp. 300 – 301. Tables.

Miranda, Julio E. Miguel Hernández en la literatura venezolana. *Cuadernos Hispanoamericanos,* no. 510 (Dec 92), pp. 23 – 29.

Miranda López, Francisco. Descentralización educativa y modernización del estado. *Revista Mexicana de Sociología,* v. 54, no. 2 (Apr – June 92), pp. 19 – 44. Bibl, tables.

Mitchell, William P. Producción campesina y cultura regional. *América Indígena,* v. 51, no. 4 (Oct – Dec 91), pp. 81 – 106. Bibl, tables.

Mitre, Eduardo. Líneas de otoño. *Vuelta,* v. 17, no. 195 (Feb 93), p. 21.

— Poemas ("Al pie de la letra," "Húmeda llama"). *Vuelta,* v. 17, no. 202 (Sept 93), pp. 33 – 34.

Miyamoto, Shiguenoli and Williams da Silva Gonçalves. Os militares na política externa brasileira, 1964 – 1984. *Estudos Históricos,* v. 6, no. 12 (July – Dec 93), pp. 211 – 246. Bibl.

Miyazaki, Silvio Yoshiro Mizuguchi. Economias do Pacífico asiático: "tigres e dragões" (Includes a bibliography compiled by Heraldo Vasconcellos). *RAE; Revista de Administração de Empresas,* v. 33, no. 2 (Mar – Apr 93), pp. 112 – 123. Bibl, tables, charts.

Mizrahi, Yemile. La nueva oposición conservadora en México: la radicalización política de los empresarios norteños. *Foro Internacional,* v. 32, no. 5 (Oct – Dec 92), pp. 744 – 771. Bibl, tables.

Mizraje, Gabriela. El sexo despiadado: sobre Juana Manuela Gorriti. *Feminaria,* v. 6, no. 11, Suppl. (Nov 93), pp. 5 – 7.

Moctezuma Barragán, Pedro. Del movimiento urbano popular a los movimientos comunitarios: el espejo desenterrado. *El Cotidiano,* v. 10, no. 57 (Aug – Sept 93), pp. 3 – 10. Il.

— El espejo desenterrado. *El Cotidiano,* v. 9, no. 54 (May 93), pp. 49 – 54. Il.

Mörner, Magnus. Breves apuntes sobre nuestro viaje a Ocumare de la costa, del 19 al 20 de julio de 1991. *Boletín de la Academia Nacional de la Historia (Venezuela),* v. 75, no. 298 (Apr – June 92), pp. 141 – 142.

— Historia social hispanoamericana de los siglos XVIII y XIX: algunas reflexiones en torno a la historiografía reciente. *Historia Mexicana,* v. 42, no. 2 (Oct – Dec 92), pp. 419 – 471.

Mogollón, José Luis et al. Uso de los parámetros físico – químicos de las aguas fluviales como indicadores de influencias naturales y antrópicas. *Interciencia,* v. 18, no. 5 (Sept – Oct 93), pp. 249 – 254. Bibl, tables, maps.

Mohr, Nicholasa. An Awakening . . . Summer 1956. *The Americas Review,* v. 20, no. 3 – 4 (Fall – Winter 92), pp. 14 – 19.

Moisés, José Alvaro. Democratización y cultura política de masas en Brasil. *Revista Mexicana de Sociología,* v. 54, no. 1 (Jan – Mar 92), pp. 167 – 203. Bibl, tables.

— Elections, Political Parties, and Political Culture in Brazil: Changes and Continuities. *Journal of Latin American Studies,* v. 25, no. 3 (Oct 93), pp. 575 – 611. Bibl, tables, charts.

Moissén, Xavier

See

Moyssén Echeverría, Xavier

Molina, Eduardo. El diario. *Plural (Mexico),* v. 22, no. 267 (Dec 93), pp. 32 – 35.

Molina, Silvia. El discurso escéptico: su expresión en la caricatura política. *Revista Mexicana de Ciencias Políticas y Sociales,* v. 38, Nueva época, no. 154 (Oct – Dec 93), pp. 79 – 89. Bibl.

Molina Cardona, Mauricio. Mantis religiosa. *Vuelta,* v. 17, no. 194 (Jan 93), pp. 37 – 39.

Molina Chocano, Guillermo. Honduras: ¿Del ajuste neoliberal al liberalismo social? *Nueva Sociedad,* no. 128 (Nov – Dec 93), pp. 18 – 23.

Molina Jiménez, Iván and Arnaldo Moya Gutiérrez. Leyendo "lecturas": documentos para la historia del libro en Costa Rica a comienzos del siglo XIX. *Revista de Historia (Costa Rica),* no. 26 (July – Dec 92), pp. 241 – 262.

Molina Jiménez, Iván and Eugenia Rodríguez Sáenz. Compraventas de cafetales y haciendas de café en el valle central de Costa Rica, 1834 – 1850. *Anuario de Estudios Centroamericanos,* v. 18, no. 1 (1992), pp. 29 – 50. Bibl, tables, maps, charts.

Molina Montes, Augusto. Una visión de Xochicalco en el siglo XIX: Dupaix y Castañeda, 1805. *Anales del Instituto de Investigaciones Estéticas,* v. 16, no. 62 (1991), pp. 53 – 68. Bibl, il.

Molinar Horcasitas, Juan. Escuelas de interpretación del sistema político mexicano. *Revista Mexicana de Sociología,* v. 55, no. 2 (Apr – June 93), pp. 3 – 56. Bibl, tables.

Molinaro, Nina L. Resistance, Gender, and the Mediation of History in Pizarnik's *La condesa sangrienta* and Ortiz's *Urraca. Letras Femeninas,* v. 19, no. 1 – 2 (Spring – Fall 93), pp. 45 – 54. Bibl.

Mollis, Marcela. Evaluación de la calidad universitaria: elementos para su discusión. *Realidad Económica,* no. 118 (Aug – Sept 93), pp. 97 – 116. Bibl, tables.

Moncada Maya, J. Omar. Miguel Constanzó y el reconocimiento geográfico de la costa de Veracruz de 1797. *Anuario de Estudios Americanos,* v. 49, Suppl. 2 (1992), pp. 31 – 64. Bibl.

Mond, Rebecca Earle. Indian Rebellion and Bourbon Reform in New Granada: Riots in Pasto, 1780 – 1800. *Hispanic American Historical Review,* v. 73, no. 1 (Feb 93), pp. 99 – 124. Bibl.

Mondragón, Ana Laura. Contratos-ley y sindicatos: huleros y textileros. *El Cotidiano,* v. 9, no. 56 (July 93), pp. 18 – 22. Il, tables.

Moneta, Carlos Juan. Alternativas de la integración en el contexto de la globalización. *Nueva Sociedad,* no. 125 (May – June 93), pp. 80 – 97. Bibl, tables.

— As forças armadas latino-americanas nos anos '90. *Política e Estratégica,* v. 8, no. 2 – 4 (Apr – Dec 90), pp. 153 – 167. Bibl.

Monge Oviedo, Rodolfo and Marc Edelman. Costa Rica: The Non-Market Roots of Market Success. *Report on the Americas,* v. 26, no. 4 (Feb 93), pp. 22 – 29 + . Bibl, il.

Monjarás-Ruiz, Jesús. La antigua Sinaloa y Pérez de Ribas. *Plural (Mexico),* v. 22, no. 265 (Oct 93), pp. 70 – 72.

Monmany, Mercedes. Las mujeres imposibles en Bioy Casares. *Cuadernos Hispanoamericanos,* no. 513 (Mar 93), pp. 117 – 122.

Monreal, David. Short Stories ("Abuelo," "Wrath"). *The Americas Review,* v. 19, no. 2 (Summer 91), pp. 18 – 31.

Monreal González, Pedro. Cuba y América Latina y el Caribe: apuntes sobre un caso de inserción económica. *Estudios Internacionales (Chile),* v. 26, no. 103 (July – Sept 93), pp. 500 – 536. Bibl, tables.

Monroy, María Isabel. La minería: aventura entrañable (Accompanied by an English translation). *Artes de México,* no. 18 (Winter 92), pp. 71 – 77. Il.

Monroy de Gómez, Carlota. Serología en una población centroamericana infectada con "Trypanosoma Cruzi," "T. Rangeli" y "Leishmania Ssp." *USAC,* no. 13 (Mar 91), pp. 76 – 80. Bibl, tables.

Montalbetti Solari, Mario. El paso del norte. *Hueso Húmero,* no. 29 (May 93), pp. 88 – 92.

Montaldo, Graciela R. Imaginación e historia en América Latina (Review article). *Nueva Sociedad,* no. 127 (Sept – Oct 93), pp. 163 – 167.

— Vallejo y las formas del pasado. *Revista Nacional de Cultura (Venezuela),* v. 54, no. 287 (Oct – Dec 92), pp. 178 – 187. Bibl, il.

Montalvo Arriete, Luis F. Biotecnología en Cuba como una ventana de oportunidad. *Interciencia,* v. 18, no. 6 (Nov – Dec 93), pp. 295 – 299. Bibl.

Montaner, Carlos Alberto. La revolución cubana y sus últimos alabarderos. *Vuelta,* v. 17, no. 205 (Dec 93), pp. 74 – 80.

Montaño, Jorge. Una visión desde Washington: México/ Estados Unidos en los noventas. *Nexos,* v. 16, no. 187 (July 93), pp. 15 – 19.

Montecino, Marcelo. Signs That Sell (Photographs by the author). *Américas,* v. 45, no. 5 (Sept – Oct 93), pp. 40 – 41. Il.

Montecino Aguirre, Sonia. Mercedes Valdivieso: escritura y vida. *Mensaje,* v. 42, no. 422 (Sept 93), p. 463.

Montecinos, Aldo and Patricio Aceituno. Análisis de la estabilidad de la relación entre la oscilación del sur y la precipitación en América del Sur. *Bulletin de l'Institut Français d'Etudes Andines,* v. 22, no. 1 (1993), pp. 53 – 64. Bibl, tables, maps, charts.

Montecinos, Verónica. Economic Policy Elites and Democratization. *Studies in Comparative International Development,* v. 28, no. 1 (Spring 93), pp. 25 – 53. Bibl.

Monteiro, Mário Ypiranga. Da capacidade ociosa do escravo negro libertado. *Revista do Instituto Histórico e Geográfico Brasileiro,* no. 370 (Jan – Mar 91), pp. 223 – 225.

Montejano y Aguiñaga, Rafael. Orígenes de San Luis Potosí (Accompanied by an English translation). *Artes de México,* no. 18 (Winter 92), pp. 29 – 35. Il, facs.

Montejo, Víctor Dionicio. Sirviendo al pueblo: la vida ejemplar de madre Rosa Cordis. *Mesoamérica (USA),* v. 13, no. 23 (June 92), pp. 219 – 220.

Monteleone, Jorge J. Cuerpo constelado: sobre la poesía de "rock" argentino. *Cuadernos Hispanoamericanos,* no. 517 – 519 (July – Sept 93), pp. 401 – 420.

Montenegro Trujillo, Armando. Descentralización en Colombia: una perspectiva internacional. *Planeación y Desarrollo,* v. 24, no. 1 (Jan – Apr 93), pp. 279 – 307. Bibl.

Montero, Ignacio and Carmen Varela Torrecilla. Cuantificación y representación gráfica de los materiales cerámicos mayas: una propuesta metodológica. *Revista Española de Antropología Americana,* v. 23 (1993), pp. 83 – 100. Bibl, tables, charts.

Montero Mallo, Benicio. Diario de la campaña del Chaco. *Signo,* no. 36 – 37, Nueva época (May – Dec 92), pp. 171 – 195.

Montero Tirado, María del Carmen. La industria de la loza y la cerámica: el ascenso de la CROC. *El Cotidiano,* v. 9, no. 56 (July 93), pp. 86 – 88.

Montes Brunet, Hugo. Un discurso inédito de Vicente Huidobro (Includes the transcription of "Discurso leído en Madrid en el Segundo Congreso Internacional de Escritores para la Defensa de la Cultura"). *Revista Chilena de Literatura,* no. 41 (Apr 93), pp. 123 – 129.

— Evocación de Marta Brunet. *Atenea (Chile),* no. 465 – 466 (1992), pp. 291 – 297. Facs.

— La maestría de Huidobro. *Atenea (Chile),* no. 467 (1993), pp. 137 – 141. Il.

— Poesía chilena de hoy. *Aisthesis,* no. 24 (1991), pp. 21 – 27. Bibl.

Montes de Oca, Marco Antonio. Cuatro poemas. *Vuelta,* v. 17, no. 204 (Nov 93), p. 17.

— Cuatro poemas. *Vuelta,* v. 17, no. 205 (Dec 93), p. 27.

Montes Giraldo, José Joaquín and Jaime Bernal Leongómez. El verbo en el habla culta de Bogotá: frecuencia de categorías tradicionales y creación de otras nuevas. *Thesaurus,* v. 45, no. 3 (Sept – Dec 90), pp. 732 – 742. Bibl, tables.

Montes Huidobro, Matías. Fetuses. *The Americas Review,* v. 19, no. 2 (Summer 91), pp. 37 – 41.

Montes M., Fernando. Alberto Hurtado, signo y apóstol de la solidaridad. *Mensaje,* v. 42, no. 421 (Aug 93), pp. 353 – 357. Il.

— Calera de Tango: evocación de nuestra historia. *Mensaje,* v. 42, no. 420 (July 93), pp. 239 – 242. Il.

— ¿La Compañía de Jesús sigue siendo la misma? *Mensaje,* v. 42, no. 420 (July 93), pp. 186 – 189. Il, tables.

— El documento final de Santo Domingo. *Mensaje,* v. 42, no. 416 (Jan – Feb 93), pp. 8 – 13. Il.

— Iglesia en Chile, 1973 – 1993: veinte años anunciando el evangelio. *Mensaje,* v. 42, no. 422 (Sept 93), pp. 419 – 424.

Monti, Ricardo. Asunción. *Hispamérica,* v. 22, no. 64 – 65 (Apr – Aug 93), pp. 149 – 165.

Montiel, Edgar. Perú: la construcción política de la nación. *Plural (Mexico),* v. 22, no. 263 (Aug 93), pp. 16 – 24.

Montoya, Aquiles. ¿Qué cabría esperar en materia económica y social, si un gobierno "progresista" accediera al poder en el '94? *ECA; Estudios Centroamericanos,* v. 48, no. 536 (June 93), pp. 582 – 587. Il.

— El sector cooperativo: elemento clave para una estrategia de desarrollo popular. *ECA; Estudios Centroamericanos,* v. 48, no. 539 (Sept 93), pp. 855 – 873. Bibl, il, tables.

Montoya, Rodrigo. El teatro quechua como lugar de reflexión sobre la historia y la política. *Revista de Crítica Literaria Latinoamericana,* v. 19, no. 37 (Jan – June 93), pp. 223 – 241. Bibl.

Montoya, Víctor. La mujer entre el esclavismo y el capitalismo. *Signo,* no. 38, Nueva época (Jan – Apr 93), pp. 131 – 136. Bibl.

Montserrat, Marcelo. La influencia italiana en el desarrollo científico argentino. *Todo Es Historia,* v. 26, no. 305 (Dec 92), pp. 8 – 19. Bibl, il.

Moore, Charles B. Las influencias clásicas en la descripción del desierto en el canto XXXV de *La araucana. Confluencia,* v. 8, no. 1 (Fall 92), pp. 99 – 107. Bibl.

Moore, Daniel. Latinoamericanos en Suecia. *Cuadernos Americanos,* no. 41, Nueva época (Sept – Oct 93), pp. 131 – 157. Bibl, tables.

Moore, Robin. Directory of Latin American and Caribbean Music Theses and Dissertations since 1988. *Latin American Music Review,* v. 14, no. 1 (Spring – Summer 93), pp. 145 – 171.

Mora, Gabriela. Notas teóricas en torno a las colecciones de cuentos integrados (a veces cíclicos). *Revista Chilena de Literatura,* no. 42 (Aug 93), pp. 131 – 137. Bibl.

— La prosa política de Gabriela Mistral. *Escritura (Venezuela),* v. 16, no. 31 – 32 (Jan – Dec 91), pp. 193 – 203.

— Tununa Mercado. *Hispamérica,* v. 21, no. 62 (Aug 92), pp. 77 – 81.

Mora, Pat. Poems ("Bailando," "Elena"). *The Americas Review,* v. 20, no. 3 – 4 (Fall – Winter 92), pp. 175 – 176.

Mora Chinchilla, Carolina. Los Estados Unidos: una imagen modelo para Costa Rica, 1880 – 1903. *Anuario de Estudios Centroamericanos,* v. 18, no. 2 (1992), pp. 91 – 101. Bibl.

Mora de Tovar, Gilma Lucía. El deber de vivir ordenadamente para obedecer al rey. *Anuario Colombiano de Historia Social y de la Cultura,* no. 20 (1992), pp. 109 – 131.

Mora Gaitán, Alvaro. Lo que usted debe saber sobre la personería jurídica eclesiástica y su tratamiento legal en Colombia. *Revista Javeriana,* v. 61, no. 599 (Oct 93), pp. 357 – 364.

Mora Heredia, Juan. Educación y política: un acercamiento al ANMEB. *El Cotidiano,* v. 8, no. 52 (Jan – Feb 93), pp. 76 – 83. Il, tables.

Mora Heredia, Juan and Raúl Rodríguez Guillén. El agotamiento del autoritarismo con legitimidad y la sucesión presidencial. *El Cotidiano,* v. 10, no. 58 (Oct – Nov 93), pp. 22 – 28. Il, tables.

Morábito, Fabio. El escritor en busca de una lengua. *Vuelta,* v. 17, no. 195 (Feb 93), pp. 22 – 24.

Moraes, José Geraldo Vinci de. Sonoridades urbanas. *Vozes,* v. 87, no. 3 (May – June 93), pp. 48 – 58. Il.

Moraes, Marcos Antônio. Cromos, vilegiatura: cartõespostais de Mário de Andrade. *Vozes,* v. 87, no. 2 (Mar – Apr 93), pp. 63 – 75. Il, facs.

Moraes, Maria Célia Marcondes de. Francisco Campos: o caminho de uma definição ideológica; anos '20 e '30. *Dados,* v. 35, no. 2 (1992), pp. 239 – 265. Bibl.

Moraes R., Mónica and Jaime Sarmiento. Contribución al estudio de biología reproductiva de una especia de "Bactris" (Palmae) en el bosque de galería, depto. Beni, Bolivia. *Bulletin de l'Institut Français d'Etudes Andines,* v. 21, no. 2 (1992), pp. 685 – 698. Bibl, il, tables, maps.

Moraga-Rojel, Jubel R. et al. La biotecnología agrícola y la privatización del conocimiento en la transferencia tecnológica universidad – empresa. *Estudios Sociales (Chile),* no. 77 (July – Sept 93), pp. 117 – 137. Bibl.

Morales, Adolfo de. Tratados de límites de las posesiones americanas entre España y Portugal. *Signo,* no. 36 – 37, Nueva época (May – Dec 92), pp. 387 – 407.

Morales, Alejandro. Cara de caballo. *The Americas Review,* v. 20, no. 3 – 4 (Fall – Winter 92), pp. 29 – 32.

Morales, Andrés. Poesía chilena y poesía española: convergencias y divergencias. *Revista Chilena de Literatura,* no. 42 (Aug 93), pp. 139 – 141.

Morales, Francisco. Antonine Tibesar, O.F.M. (1901 – 1992): in memoriam. *Estudios de Cultura Náhuatl,* v. 22 (1992), pp. 495 – 496.

— Secularización de doctrinas: ¿Fin de un modelo evangelizador en la Nueva España? *Archivo Ibero-Americano,* v. 52, no. 205 – 208 (Jan – Dec 92), pp. 465 – 495. Bibl.

Morales, Josefina. Cuba '93. *Problemas del Desarrollo,* v. 24, no. 93 (Apr – June 93), pp. 211 – 220. Bibl.

Morales, Orlando M. Participación sobre derechos ecológicos. *Cuadernos Americanos,* no. 39, Nueva época (May – June 93), pp. 72 – 73.

Morales, Salvador. El reto de la historia regional en la enseñanza de la historia. *Islas,* no. 98 (Jan – Apr 91), pp. 22 – 27.

Morales Baranda, Francisco. In Xochitlahtolcuicapihqui Ilnamiquiliz: Carlos López Avila (1922 – 1991). *Estudios de Cultura Náhuatl,* v. 22 (1992), pp. 462 – 465.

Morales Bocardo, Rafael. El Convento de San Francisco (Accompanied by an English translation). *Artes de México,* no. 18 (Winter 92), pp. 45 – 51. Il.

Morales Cavero, Hugo. Apuntes para un estudio de la poesía revolucionaria. *Signo,* no. 35, Nueva época (Jan – Apr 92), pp. 163 – 195. Bibl.

Morales Gómez, Jorge. Alvaro Chaves Mendoza (1930 – 1992). *Revista Colombiana de Antropología,* v. 29 (1992), pp. 265 – 266.

— Cuerpo humano y contexto cultural en el Golfo de Morrosquillo. *Revista Colombiana de Antropología,* v. 29 (1992), pp. 191 – 205. Bibl.

Morales Hernández, Liliana. Mujer que sabe latín: la mujer en la educación superior de México. *El Cotidiano,* v. 9, no. 53 (Mar – Apr 93), pp. 71 – 77. Il, tables.

Morales Hernández, Xiomara et al. Gaspar Jorge García Galló y su labor de divulgación de la filosofía marxista – leninista. *Islas,* no. 98 (Jan – Apr 91), pp. 128 – 134. Bibl.

Morales Saviñón, Héctor. Otra vez el amor (Excerpt from the novel of the same title). *Plural (Mexico),* v. 22, no. 261 (June 93), pp. 58 – 62.

Morales Toro, Leonidas. Misiones y las macrofiguras narrativas hispanoamericanas. *Hispamérica,* v. 21, no. 63 (Dec 92), pp. 25 – 34.

Morán, Carlos Roberto. Adolfo Bioy Casares o la aventura de imaginar. *Revista Nacional de Cultura (Venezuela),* v. 54, no. 287 (Oct – Dec 92), pp. 222 – 230. Il.

— El envoltorio. *Plural (Mexico),* v. 22, no. 267 (Dec 93), pp. 22 – 24.

— La máquina. *La Palabra y el Hombre,* no. 84 (Oct – Dec 92), pp. 110 – 114.

Morandé Lavín, Felipe Guillermo. La dinámica de los precios de los activos reales y el tipo de cambio real: las reformas al comercio exterior y las entradas de capital extranjero; Chile, 1976 – 1989. *El Trimestre Económico,* v. 59, Special issue (Dec 92), pp. 141 – 186. Bibl, tables, charts.

Moreira, Ajax Reynaldo Bello et al. Um modelo macroeconômico para o nível de atividade: previsões e projeções condicionais. *Revista Brasileira de Economia,* v. 47, no. 3 (July – Sept 93), pp. 349 – 371. Bibl, tables, charts.

Moreiras, Alberto. The Secret Agency of Disillusionment. *Latin American Literary Review,* v. 20, no. 40 (July – Dec 92), pp. 70 – 74.

Morejón, Nancy. Ana Mendieta. *Casa de las Américas,* no. 190 (Jan – Mar 93), pp. 116 – 118.

— Pierrot y la luna. *Homines,* v. 15 – 16, no. 2 – 1 (Oct 91 – Dec 92), pp. 309 – 315.

Morel, Edmundo and Manuel Zacarías Mejía. Los impactos de los desalojos: la constitución o reconstitución de las identidades. *Estudios Sociales (Dominican Republic),* v. 26, no. 94 (Oct – Dec 93), pp. 45 – 74. Bibl.

Morelos, José B. Una mirada a la demografía de los países de la cuenca del Pacífico. *Comercio Exterior,* v. 43, no. 8 (Aug 93), pp. 774 – 786. Bibl, tables.

Morelos García, Noel. Consideraciones teóricas sobre el proceso de urbanización en Mesoamérica. *Boletín de Antropología Americana*, no. 23 (July 91), pp. 137 – 160.

Moreno, Gean. Poems ("Reinaldo Arenas," "Years of Apocalypse," "Gonzalo Arango," "The Painter Pedro Moreno"). *The Americas Review*, v. 21, no. 1 (Spring 93), pp. 62 – 68.

Moreno, Mariano. Sobre el servicio personal de los indios, en general, y sobre el particular de yanaconas y mitayos. *Signo*, no. 36 – 37, Nueva época (May – Dec 92), pp. 455 – 474.

Moreno Alonso, Manuel. Las cosas de España y la política americana de Carlos III en Inglaterra. *Hoy Es Historia*, v. 9, no. 54 (Nov – Dec 92), pp. 44 – 59. Il.

Moreno Armella, Florita. Representación vecinal y gestión urbana en el D.F. *El Cotidiano*, v. 10, no. 57 (Aug – Sept 93), pp. 38 – 45. Il.

Moreno Casamitjana, Antonio. Descubrimiento y evangelización de América. *Atenea (Chile)*, no. 465 – 466 (1992), pp. 53 – 66. Bibl.

Moreno Davis, Julio César. Diego Domínguez Caballero, o las facetas de un educador. *Revista Cultural Lotería*, v. 51, no. 392 (Nov – Dec 93), pp. 31 – 40.

— El estro poético de Isaías García Aponte: filosofía y poesía. *Revista Cultural Lotería*, v. 50, no. 385 (Sept – Oct 91), pp. 46 – 72. Bibl.

Moreno de Alba, José G. Léxico de las capitales hispanoamericanas: propuesta de zonas dialectales. *Nueva Revista de Filología Hispánica*, v. 40, no. 2 (July – Dec 92), pp. 575 – 597. Bibl.

— Revisión de mexicanismos en el *Diccionario* de la Academia. *Anuario de Letras (Mexico)*, v. 30 (1992), pp. 165 – 172. Bibl.

Moreno Gómez, Luis. Desarrollo latinoamericano y periodismo científico. *Revista Nacional de Cultura (Venezuela)*, v. 53, no. 286 (July – Sept 92), pp. 215 – 244. Bibl, il, tables.

Moreno Mejía, Luis Alberto. La apertura en el sector textil. *Revista Javeriana*, v. 61, no. 593 (Apr 93), pp. 141 – 142.

Moreno Pascal, Francisco. Poems ("Tus ojos," "Meditaciones," "Viaje a la isla centinela"). *Revista Cultural Lotería*, v. 50, no. 386 (Nov – Dec 91), pp. 67 – 69.

Moreno Toscano, Alejandra. López Castro y la función del sol. *Nexos*, v. 16, no. 188 (Aug 93), pp. 8 – 10.

Moreno Uscanga, Ivonne. Juan García Ponce: la bifurcación del amor. *La Palabra y el Hombre*, no. 81 (Jan – Mar 92), pp. 313 – 315.

Moreno Villarreal, Jaime. La mujer de Lima. *Vuelta*, v. 17, no. 204 (Nov 93), pp. 56 – 57.

Morera, Carlos Manuel. Justificación de una tez. *Afro-Hispanic Review*, v. 12, no. 1 (Spring 93), pp. 51 – 52.

Morera Pérez, Marcial. La preposición española "contra": su evolución semántica. *Thesaurus*, v. 45, no. 3 (Sept – Dec 90), pp. 650 – 689. Bibl.

Morgner, Fred G. Cracks in the Mirror: The Nicaraguan War and Human Rights in Honduras. *SALALM Papers*, v. 34 (1989), pp. 475 – 490. Bibl, il, tables.

— Poisoning the Garden: Costa Rica's Ecological Crisis. *SALALM Papers*, v. 36 (1991), pp. 77 – 87. Bibl.

— Posters and the Sandinista Revolution (Accompanied by a descriptive list of posters). *SALALM Papers*, v. 34 (1989), pp. 183 – 213. Il.

Morin, Françoise. Evaristo Nugkuag Ikanana, presidente de la Coordinadora de las Organizaciones Indígenas de la Cuenca Amazónica (COICA), Perú: entrevista realizada el 7 de julio de 1992 en Lima por Françoise Morin. *Caravelle*, no. 59 (1992), pp. 67 – 70.

— Le mythe du 500ème: convergences et divergences. *Caravelle*, no. 59 (1992), pp. 75 – 85. Bibl.

— Revendications et stratégies politiques des organisations indigènes amazoniennes. *Cahiers des Amériques Latines*, no. 13 (1992), pp. 75 – 85. Bibl.

Morino, Angelo. Hernán Cortés e la regina Calafia. *Quaderni Ibero-Americani*, no. 72 (Dec 92), pp. 603 – 620. Bibl.

Morley, Morris H. and James F. Petras. Latin America: Poverty and the Democracy of Poverty. *Homines*, v. 15 – 16, no. 2 – 1 (Oct 91 – Dec 92), pp. 75 – 94. Bibl.

Morlon, Pierre. De las relaciones entre clima de altura y agricultura de la sierra del Perú en los textos de los siglos XVI y XVII. *Bulletin de l'Institut Français d'Etudes Andines*, v. 21, no. 3 (1992), pp. 929 – 959. Bibl, maps.

Morón Montero, Guillermo. Un acercamiento a la *Historia general de América. Boletín de la Academia Nacional de la Historia (Venezuela)*, v. 75, no. 300 (Oct – Dec 92), pp. 155 – 166.

— El catálogo de las mujeres. *Revista Nacional de Cultura (Venezuela)*, v. 54, no. 287 (Oct – Dec 92), pp. 95 – 102. Il.

— Palabras del director de la Academia Nacional de la Historia, dr. Guillermo Morón. *Boletín de la Academia Nacional de la Historia (Venezuela)*, v. 75, no. 300 (Oct – Dec 92), pp. 11 – 16.

— Los portugueses en Venezuela: I Encuentro de las Academias de Historia de Portugal y Venezuela en Lisboa, Portugal, mayo de 1992. *Boletín de la Academia Nacional de la Historia (Venezuela)*, v. 76, no. 301 (Jan – Mar 93), pp. 33 – 37. Bibl.

— Sesión especial con motivo de los quinientos años del nacimiento de San Ignacio de Loyola: Ignacio de Loyola, 1491 – 1991. *Boletín de la Academia Nacional de la Historia (Venezuela)*, v. 75, no. 299 (July – Sept 92), pp. 9 – 17.

Morosini, Francisco. Y seguirán siendo hombres verdaderos. *La Palabra y el Hombre*, no. 81 (Jan – Mar 92), pp. 383 – 385.

Morris, Barbara. Configuring Women: The Discourse of Empowerment in Latin American Cinema. *SALALM Papers*, v. 34 (1989), pp. 143 – 150. Bibl.

Morris, Robert J. Sol de la guacamaya de fuego: novela pionera maya por Joaquín Bestard Vázquez. *Confluencia*, v. 8, no. 1 (Fall 92), pp. 165 – 171. Bibl.

Morris, Stephen D. Political Reformism in Mexico: Past and Present (Review article). *Latin American Research Review*, v. 28, no. 2 (1993), pp. 191 – 205. Bibl.

Morris, Stephen D. and Jesús Arroyo Alejandre. The Electoral Recovery of the PRI in Guadalajara, Mexico, 1988 – 1992. *Bulletin of Latin American Research*, v. 12, no. 1 (Jan 93), pp. 91 – 102. Bibl, tables.

Morris, Walter F., Jr. Simbolismo de un huipil ceremonial (Accompanied by the English original, translated by Ana Rosa González Matute). *Artes de México*, no. 19 (Spring 93), pp. 65 – 71. Il.

Morrison, Andrew R. Violence or Economics: What Drives Internal Migration in Guatemala? *Economic Development and Cultural Change*, v. 41, no. 4 (July 93), pp. 817 – 831. Bibl, tables.

Morrissey, Laverne and Amado M. Padilla. Place of Last Drink by Repeat DUI Offenders: A Retrospective Study of Gender and Ethnic Group Differences. *Hispanic Journal of Behavioral Sciences*, v. 15, no. 3 (Aug 93), pp. 357 – 372. Bibl, tables.

Mortimer, Mildred P. A Sense of Place and Space in Maryse Condé's *Les derniers rois mages. World Literature Today,* v. 67, no. 4 (Fall 93), pp. 757 – 762. Bibl.

Mortimore, Michael D. A New International Industrial Order. *CEPAL Review,* no. 48 (Dec 92), pp. 39 – 59. Bibl, tables, charts.

Morton, Carlos. Rewriting Southwestern History: A Playwright's Perspective. *Mexican Studies,* v. 9, no. 2 (Summer 93), pp. 225 – 239. Il.

Morton, Colleen S. Economic Instruments Protect the Earth. *Business Mexico,* v. 3, no. 1 (Jan – Feb 93), pp. 40 – 43. Il.

Moscona, Myriam. Sueños con Rainer Maria. *Hispamérica,* v. 21, no. 63 (Dec 92), pp. 43 – 45.

Moscoso, Francisco. Encomendero y esclavista: Francisco Manuel de Lando. *Anuario de Estudios Americanos,* v. 49 (1992), pp. 119 – 142. Bibl.

Mosquera, Gerardo. Encuentros/Desplazamientos: arte conceptual y política; Luis Caminitzer, Alfredo Jaar y Cildo Meireles (Accompanied by an English translation). *Art Nexus,* no. 8 (Apr – June 93), pp. 88 – 91. Il.

— Plástico afroamericana (Accompanied by an English translation). *Art Nexus,* no. 9 (June – Aug 93), pp. 100 – 102. Il.

— Tomás Sánchez: mística del paisaje (Accompanied by an English translation). *Art Nexus,* no. 10 (Sept – Dec 93), pp. 48 – 51. Il.

Mosquera, Marta. La casa de "El silencio." *Revista Nacional de Cultura (Venezuela),* v. 53, no. 286 (July – Sept 92), pp. 71 – 80.

Mosquera Aguilar, Antonio. Pop Wuj: el libro de los testimonios y de las tradiciones como recreación popular. *Folklore Americano,* no. 52 (July – Dec 91), pp. 123 – 129. Bibl.

Moss, Alan. Art Publishing in the Contemporary Caribbean. *SALALM Papers,* v. 34 (1989), pp. 269 – 274. Bibl.

Mossbrucker, Harald. El proceso de migración en el Perú: la revolución clandestina. *América Indígena,* v. 51, no. 2 – 3 (Apr – Sept 91), pp. 167 – 201. Bibl, charts.

Mota Murillo, Rafael. Fuentes para la historia franciscano – americana del siglo XVIII: esbozo de bibliografía. *Archivo Ibero-Americano,* v. 52, no. 205 – 208 (Jan – Dec 92), pp. 1 – 80.

Motta, José Flávio and Iraci del Nero da Costa. Vila Rica: inconfidência e crise demográfica. *Estudos Econômicos,* v. 22, no. 2 (May – Aug 92), pp. 321 – 346. Bibl, tables, charts.

Motta, Roberto M. C. Transe, sacrifício, comunhão e poder no xangô de Pernambuco. *Revista de Antropologia (Brazil),* v. 34 (1991), pp. 131 – 142.

Motta, Sérgio Vicente. Ser/tão . . . somente linguagem. *Revista de Letras (Brazil),* v. 32 (1992), pp. 81 – 99. Bibl.

Moura, Demócrito. Problema vital. *Problemas Brasileiros,* v. 30, no. 295 (Jan – Feb 93), pp. 48 – 49. Il.

— A revolução da mandioca. *Problemas Brasileiros,* v. 30, no. 296 (Mar – Apr 93), pp. 24 – 25. Il.

Moura, Gerson. Neutralidade dependente: o caso do Brasil, 1939 – 1942. *Estudos Históricos,* v. 6, no. 12 (July – Dec 93), pp. 177 – 189. Bibl.

Mourão, Fernando Augusto Albuquerque. O Atlântico Sul e os novos vetores do sistema internacional. *Política e Estratégica,* v. 8, no. 2 – 4 (Apr – Dec 90), pp. 333 – 341.

Mouriño, Jorge. Poems ("Desamorado," "Primavera no es," "Redundancias," "Irremediablemente curvo"). *Plural (Mexico),* v. 22, no. 261 (June 93), pp. 74 – 75.

Moussa, Farana et al. Las palmeras en los valles principales de la Amazonia peruana. *Bulletin de l'Institut Français d'Etudes Andines,* v. 21, no. 2 (1992), pp. 565 – 597. Maps.

Moussong, Lazlo. La crítica: ¿Objetiva o subjetiva? *Plural (Mexico),* v. 22, no. 261 (June 93), pp. 12 – 15.

— Revolución y libre expresión. *Plural (Mexico),* v. 22, no. 259 (Apr 93), p. 68.

Moya Gutiérrez, Arnaldo and Iván Molina Jiménez. Leyendo "lecturas": documentos para la historia del libro en Costa Rica a comienzos del siglo XIX. *Revista de Historia (Costa Rica),* no. 26 (July – Dec 92), pp. 241 – 262.

Moyano, Pilar. La transformación de la mujer y la nación en la poesía comprometida de Gioconda Belli. *Revista Canadiense de Estudios Hispánicos,* v. 17, no. 2 (Winter 93), pp. 319 – 331. Bibl.

Moyano Bazzani, Eduardo L. Aportaciones de la historiografía portuguesa a la problemática fronteriza luso – española en América meridional, 1750 – 1778. *Revista de Indias,* v. 52, no. 195 – 196 (May – Dec 92), pp. 723 – 747. Bibl, maps.

Moyario, Daniel. En la atmósfera. *Casa de las Américas,* no. 190 (Jan – Mar 93), pp. 82 – 105.

Moyssén Echeverría, Xavier. Bibliografía mexicana de arte, 1990. *Anales del Instituto de Investigaciones Estéticas,* v. 16, no. 62 (1991), pp. 223 – 229. Bibl.

Mozo, Rafael. Evolución de la primacia urbana y del aparato estatal chileno entre 1800 y 1980. *Estudios Sociales (Chile),* no. 77 (July – Sept 93), pp. 61 – 72. Bibl, tables, charts.

Mudimbé-Boyi, Elizabeth. Giving Voice to Tituba: The Death of the Author? *World Literature Today,* v. 67, no. 4 (Fall 93), pp. 751 – 756. Il.

Mudrovcic, María Eugenia. *Mundo Nuevo:* hacia la definición de un modelo discursivo. *Nuevo Texto Crítico,* v. 6, no. 11 (1993), pp. 187 – 206. Bibl.

Muelas Hurtado, Lorenzo and Orlando Fals Borda. Pueblos indígenas y grupos étnicos. *Anuario Indigenista,* v. 30 (Dec 91), pp. 185 – 212.

Müller, Jürgen. Hitler, Lateinamerika und die Weltherrschaft. *Ibero-Amerikanisches Archiv,* v. 18, no. 1 – 2 (1992), pp. 67 – 101. Bibl.

Mueller, RoseAnna M. Teaching beyond the Quincentennial. *Hispania (USA),* v. 76, no. 3 (Sept 93), pp. 586 – 592.

Mueses de Molina, Carolina. Educación popular en salud y nutrición: revisión de bibliografía. *Estudios Sociales (Dominican Republic),* v. 26, no. 93 (July – Sept 93), pp. 83 – 108. Bibl.

Mujica, Barbara Kaminar de. Marjorie Agosín Weaves Magic with Social Vision (Photographs by Ted Polumbaum). *Américas,* v. 45, no. 1 (Jan – Feb 93), pp. 44 – 49. Il.

— Persona Gratissima. *Américas,* v. 45, no. 3 (May – June 93), pp. 24 – 29. Il.

Mujica Ateaga, Rodrigo. El desempeño del sector agrícola entre 1991 y 1993. *Estudios Sociales (Chile),* no. 75 (Jan – Mar 93), pp. 129 – 139. Tables.

Mullahy, Laura and Silvio Caccia Bava. Making Brazil's Cities Livable: NGOs and the Recycling of Human Waste (Adapted chapter from the forthcoming book *Joint Ventures in Urban Policy: NGO – Local Government Collaboration in Democratizing Latin America* edited by Charles A. Reilly). *Grassroots Development,* v. 17, no. 1 (1993), pp. 12 – 19. Bibl, il.

Mullen, Edward James. Langston Hughes in Mexico and Cuba. *Review,* no. 47 (Fall 93), pp. 23 – 27. Il.

Múnera, Leopoldo. La cabecera de la mesa. *Fem,* v. 17, no. 126 (Aug 93), p. 26.

Muñoz, Cecilia. Immigration Policy: A Tricky Business. *NACLA Report on the Americas,* v. 26, no. 5 (May 93), pp. 38 – 41 +. Bibl, il.

Muñoz, Elías Miguel. Carta de Julio. *The Americas Review,* v. 20, no. 3 – 4 (Fall – Winter 92), pp. 130 – 136.

— Of Small Conquests and Big Victories: Gender Constructs in *The Modern Ladies of Guanabacoa. The Americas Review,* v. 20, no. 2 (Summer 92), pp. 105 – 111. Bibl.

— Short Stories ("Carta de Julio," "El hombre de piedra"). *The Americas Review,* v. 19, no. 3 – 4 (Winter 91), pp. 20 – 28.

Muñoz, Silverio Baltazar. Vivir y escribir en los Estados Unidos: sobre la novela *Peralillo: desde USA con amor* de Juan Torres. *Revista Chilena de Literatura,* no. 42 (Aug 93), pp. 149 – 156.

Muñoz, Víctor Manuel. El liberalismo social: propuesta ideológica del salinismo. *Revista Mexicana de Ciencias Políticas y Sociales,* v. 37, Nueva época, no. 149 (July – Sept 92), pp. 29 – 47. Bibl.

Muñoz Cadima, Willy Oscar. Joaquín Aguirre Lavayén: la escatología política en *Guano maldito. Latin American Theatre Review,* v. 26, no. 2 (Spring 93), pp. 131 – 142. Bibl.

— Luisa Valenzuela: tautología lingüística y/o realidad nacional. *Revista Canadiense de Estudios Hispánicos,* v. 17, no. 2 (Winter 93), pp. 333 – 342. Bibl.

Muñoz Cosme, Alfonso and María Yolanda Fernández Marquínez. Estilos arquitectónicos y estadios constructivos en el Grupo May, Oxkintok, Yucatán. *Revista Española de Antropología Americana,* v. 23 (1993), pp. 67 – 82. Bibl, il.

Muñoz García, Humberto. Los valores educativos en México. *Revista Mexicana de Ciencias Políticas y Sociales,* v. 38, Nueva época, no. 154 (Oct – Dec 93), pp. 159 – 184. Bibl, tables.

Muñoz García, Ileana and Claudio Antonio Vargas Arias. La producción de fertilizantes en Costa Rica y el modelo estatal costarricense: el caso Fertica. *Anuario de Estudios Centroamericanos,* v. 18, no. 1 (1992), pp. 61 – 83. Bibl, tables, charts.

Muñoz Gomá, Oscar and Carmen Celedón. La política económica durante la transición a la democracia en Chile, 1990 – 1992. *Estudios Sociales (Chile),* no. 75 (Jan – Mar 93), pp. 77 – 95. Bibl.

Muñoz González, Luis. Noticias de Miguel Hernández en Chile. *Cuadernos Hispanoamericanos,* no. 510 (Dec 92), pp. 13 – 22.

Muñoz Izquierdo, Carlos. Comentarios a la propuesta que hace el dr. Pablo Latapí en el artículo "Reflexiones sobre la justicia en la educación." *Revista Latinoamericana de Estudios Educativos,* v. 23, no. 2 (Apr – June 93), pp. 43 – 53.

— Tendencias observadas en las investigaciones y en las políticas relacionadas con el financiamiento de la educación técnica y vocacional en América Latina. *Revista Latinoamericana de Estudios Educativos,* v. 23, no. 1 (Jan – Mar 93), pp. 9 – 41. Bibl, tables.

Muñoz M., Mario. En torno a la narrativa mexicana de tema homosexual. *La Palabra y el Hombre,* no. 84 (Oct – Dec 92), pp. 21 – 37. Bibl.

Muñoz Portugal, Ismael. Ajuste y desarrollo en América Latina: el contexto de los países andinos. *Cristianismo y Sociedad,* v. 30, no. 113 (1992), pp. 7 – 14. Bibl.

Muñoz Valenzuela, Josefina. Experiencia alfabetizadora del Taller de Acción Cultura, TAC: oralidad y escritura colectiva en Curacaví. *Revista Chilena de Literatura,* no. 42 (Aug 93), pp. 143 – 148. Bibl.

Munro, Doug and David J. McCreery. The Cargo of the *Montserrat:* Gilbertese Labor in Guatemalan Coffee, 1890 – 1908. *The Americas,* v. 49, no. 3 (Jan 93), pp. 271 – 295. Bibl, tables.

Munt, Ian and Egbert Higinio. Belize: Eco Tourism Gone Awry. *Report on the Americas,* v. 26, no. 4 (Feb 93), pp. 8 – 10. Il.

Muricy, Carmen Meurer. Environment in Brazil: A Checklist of Current Serials. *SALALM Papers,* v. 36 (1991), pp. 88 – 104.

Murphy, Douglas. Teeing Off: Dwight, JFK, and Fidel. *Hemisphere,* v. 5, no. 2 (Winter – Spring 93), pp. 18 – 21. Il.

Murray, Charles. Política social y marginalidad: algunas lecciones de la experiencia norteamericana. *Estudios Públicos (Chile),* no. 52 (Spring 93), pp. 127 – 143.

Murray, David R. Slavery and the Slave Trade: New Comparative Approaches (Review article). *Latin American Research Review,* v. 28, no. 1 (1993), pp. 150 – 161.

Muschietti, Delfina. Poems ("armonías," "desligadas," "desiertos," "orillas," "sueltas"). *Feminaria,* v. 6, no. 10, Suppl. (Apr 93), pp. 17 – 18.

Muschkin, Clara G. Consequences of Return Migrant Status for Employment in Puerto Rico. *International Migration Review,* v. 27, no. 1 (Spring 93), pp. 79 – 102. Bibl, tables, charts.

Mutis Durán, Santiago. Francisco Toledo. *Revista Nacional de Cultura (Venezuela),* v. 53, no. 285 (Apr – June 92), pp. 165 – 175.

Myers, Kathleen Ann. A Glimpse of Family Life in Colonial Mexico: A Nun's Account. *Latin American Research Review,* v. 28, no. 2 (1993), pp. 63 – 87. Bibl, il.

Nabão, Márcia. Os efeitos de variações cambiais sobre o déficit público. *Revista de Economia Política (Brazil),* v. 13, no. 1 (Jan – Mar 93), pp. 37 – 51. Bibl, tables.

Nabers, Mary Scott. A Growing Love Affair. *Business Mexico,* v. 3, no. 5 (May 93), pp. 13 – 14. Charts.

Nahmad Sittón, Salomón. Guillermo Bonfil, un visionario de la sociedad multiétnica mexicana. *América Indígena,* v. 51, no. 2 – 3 (Apr – Sept 91), pp. 403 – 409. Il.

— Los quinientos años de dominación y colonialismo y los pueblos étnicos de México. *Estudios Sociológicos,* v. 10, no. 30 (Sept – Dec 92), pp. 651 – 675. Bibl, tables.

Nahmad Sittón, Salomón and Miguel Alberto Bartolomé. Semblanza. *América Indígena,* v. 51, no. 2 – 3 (Apr – Sept 91), pp. 417 – 418.

Nallim, Carlos Orlando. Borges y Cervantes: *Don Quijote* y "Alonso Quijano." *Nueva Revista de Filología Hispánica,* v. 40, no. 2 (July – Dec 92), pp. 1047 – 1056. Bibl.

Náñez, José E. and Raymond V. Padilla. Processing of Simple and Choice Reaction Time Tasks by Chicano Adolescents. *Hispanic Journal of Behavioral Sciences,* v. 15, no. 4 (Nov 93), pp. 498 – 508. Bibl, tables.

Nanfito, Jacqueline C. Time as Space in Sor Juana's *El sueño. Hispanic Journal,* v. 13, no. 2 (Fall 92), pp. 345 – 352.

Nanita-Kennett, Milagros. Industrial Free Zones in the Dominican Republic. *Caribbean Geography,* v. 3, no. 3 (Mar 92), pp. 200 – 204. Tables.

Nansen Díaz, Eréndira. Las lenguas americanas y la teoría del tipo lingüístico en Wilhelm von Humboldt. *Estudios de Cultura Náhuatl,* v. 22 (1992), pp. 223 – 233. Bibl.

Naranjo, Marcelo F. Convidados de piedra: los indios en el proceso urbano de Quito. *América Indígena,* v. 51, no. 2 – 3 (Apr – Sept 91), pp. 251 – 272. Bibl.

Naranjo Orovio, V. Consuelo. Trabajo libre e inmigración española en Cuba, 1880 – 1930. *Revista de Indias,* v. 52, no. 195 – 196 (May – Dec 92), pp. 749 – 794. Bibl, charts.

Nari, Marcela M. Alejandra. Alejandra: maternidad e independencia femenina. *Feminaria,* v. 6, no. 10, Suppl. (Apr 93), pp. 7 – 9.

— Milagros y Juana. *Todo Es Historia,* v. 27, no. 312 (July 93), pp. 44 – 45.

Narváez, Jorge E. El estatuto de los textos coloniales y el canon literario: algunos antecedentes en el sistema literario del Brasil-colonia, s. XVI y XVII. *Revista Chilena de Literatura,* no. 40 (Nov 92), pp. 17 – 33. Bibl.

Nascimbene, Mario C. G. and Mauricio Isaac Neuman. El nacionalismo católico, el fascismo y la inmigración en la Argentina, 1927 – 1943: una aproximación teórica. *Estudios Interdisciplinarios de América Latina y el Caribe,* v. 4, no. 1 (Jan – June 93), pp. 116 – 140. Bibl.

Nascimento, Benedicto Heloiz. Pensamento e atuação de Vargas. *Vozes,* v. 86, no. 4 (July – Aug 92), pp. 22 – 28.

Nash, June. Estudios de género en Latinoamérica. *Mesoamérica (USA),* v. 13, no. 23 (June 92), pp. 1 – 22. Bibl.

Nastase, Adrián. Titulescu y América Latina. *Boletín de la Academia Nacional de la Historia (Venezuela),* v. 75, no. 298 (Apr – June 92), pp. 9 – 14.

Naudón de la Sotta, Carlos. Haití: ¿Muros o puentes? *Mensaje,* v. 42, no. 418 (May 93), pp. 156 – 157. Il.

Nava L., E. Fernando and Judith Orozco. El "Sistema de Cristóbal Colón" y la "Biografía de Colón": una muestra de poesía popular mexicana (Includes the two texts). *Cuadernos Americanos,* no. 42, Nueva época (Nov – Dec 93), pp. 203 – 241.

Navarrete González, Francisco and José Enrique González Ruiz. México: educación superior y nación hacia el siglo XXI. *Problemas del Desarrollo,* v. 24, no. 93 (Apr – June 93), pp. 175 – 194.

Navarrete R., Sandra and Christian E. Leriche. América Latina: problemas actuales en el estilo de crecimiento de la región. *El Cotidiano,* v. 9, no. 54 (May 93), pp. 108 – 113. Il, tables.

Navarro, Jorge. Poverty and Adjustment: The Case of Honduras. *CEPAL Review,* no. 49 (Apr 93), pp. 91 – 101. Bibl, tables.

Navarro, Zander. Reclaiming the Land: Rural Poverty and the Promise of Small Farmers in Brazil (Photographs by Jofre Masceno from his book *Imagem reflexa). Grassroots Development,* v. 17, no. 1 (1993), pp. 20 – 24. Il.

Navarro Benítez, Bernardo. La ciudad y sus transportes, la metrópoli y sus transportes. *El Cotidiano,* v. 9, no. 54 (May 93), pp. 18 – 23. Il.

Navarro García, Jesús Raúl. Grupos de poder y tensiones sociales en Puerto Rico durante la crisis del imperio, 1815 – 1837: un intento de síntesis. *Anuario de Estudios Americanos,* v. 50, no. 1 (1993), pp. 133 – 162. Bibl.

Navarro García, Luis. Presentación de la *Historia de las Américas. Anuario de Estudios Americanos,* v. 49, Suppl. 1 (1992), pp. 242 – 247.

Navascués, Javier de. *El sueño de los héroes:* un conflicto trágico entre dos lealtades. *Revista Canadiense de Estudios Hispánicos,* v. 17, no. 3 (Spring 93), pp. 453 – 463. Bibl.

Naveda Chávez-Hita, Adriana. Consideraciones sobre comercio y crédito en la villa de Córdoba, siglo XVIII. *La Palabra y el Hombre,* no. 83 (July – Sept 92), pp. 109 – 120. Bibl.

Ndiaye, Christiane. Le réalisme merveilleux au féminin. *Canadian Journal of Latin American and Caribbean Studies,* v. 17, no. 34 (1992), pp. 115 – 117.

Nedel, João Carlos. Florestas nacionais. *Revista Brasileira de Geografia,* v. 53, no. 3 (July – Sept 91), pp. 205 – 227. Bibl, il.

Neghme Echeverría, Lidia. Análisis comparado de *Imagen* de Gerardo Diego y de *Poemas árticos* de Vicente Huidobro. *Revista Chilena de Literatura,* no. 41 (Apr 93), pp. 99 – 112. Bibl.

— Lo fantástico y algunos datos intertextuales en *Poema de Chile* de Gabriela Mistral. *Revista Interamericana de Bibliografía,* v. 42, no. 2 (1992), pp. 241 – 250. Bibl.

— Poems ("Encuentro," "Desarraigada"). *Letras Femeninas,* v. 19, no. 1 – 2 (Spring – Fall 93), pp. 171 – 173.

Neglia, Erminio G. El teatro modernista de Leopoldo Lugones. *Revista Canadiense de Estudios Hispánicos,* v. 17, no. 3 (Spring 93), pp. 549 – 556. Bibl.

Negrín Fajardo, Olegario. Krausismo, positivismo y currículum científico en el bachillerato costarricense. *Siglo XIX: Revista,* no. 12, 2a época (July – Dec 92), pp. 105 – 118. Bibl.

Negrón-Muntaner, Frances. Magali García Ramis. *Hispamérica,* v. 22, no. 64 – 65 (Apr – Aug 93), pp. 89 – 104.

Negroni, María. La dama de estas ruinas: sobre Alejandra Pizarnik. *Feminaria,* v. 6, no. 11, Suppl. (Nov 93), pp. 14 – 17. Bibl.

— Islandia. *Hispamérica,* v. 21, no. 63 (Dec 92), pp. 47 – 48.

Nepomuceno, Eric. Coisas da vida (Translated by Francisco Hernández Avilés). *Plural (Mexico),* v. 22, no. 259 (Apr 93), pp. 14 – 25.

Neruda, Pablo. Discurso de las liras. *Vuelta,* v. 17, no. 202 (Sept 93), p. 9.

— Soy un poeta de utilidad pública. *Hispamérica,* v. 22, no. 64 – 65 (Apr – Aug 93), pp. 105 – 109.

Nettleford, Rex. Fifty Years of the Jamaican Pantomime, 1941 – 1991. *Jamaica Journal,* v. 24, no. 3 (Feb 93), pp. 2 – 9. Il.

— Surviving Columbus: Caribbean Achievements in the Encounter of Worlds, 1492 – 1992. *Caribbean Quarterly,* v. 38, no. 2 – 3 (June – Sept 92), pp. 97 – 112. Bibl.

Neugebauer, Rhonda L. Videos and Films Shown at the Conference. *SALALM Papers,* v. 34 (1989), pp. 172 – 174.

Neuman, Mauricio Isaac and Mario C. G. Nascimbene. El nacionalismo católico, el fascismo y la inmigración en la Argentina, 1927 – 1943: una aproximación teórica. *Estudios Interdisciplinarios de América Latina y el Caribe,* v. 4, no. 1 (Jan – June 93), pp. 116 – 140. Bibl.

Neumann, Holly. From Pigs to Pesticides. *Business Mexico,* v. 3, no. 1 (Jan – Feb 93), pp. 19 – 22. Il, tables.

— Tales from the Deep. *Business Mexico,* v. 3, no. 6 (June 93), p. 28 +. Il, tables, maps.

Neves, Renato Baumann

See
  Baumann Neves, Renato

Newland, Garrett T. and Nina H. Compton. The Functional Border Equivalent. *Journal of Borderlands Studies,* v. 7, no. 2 (Fall 92), pp. 73 – 92. Bibl.

Newman, Gray. Laying Down the Law. *Business Mexico,* v. 3, no. 1 (Jan – Feb 93), pp. 75 – 77.

Newson, Linda A. Variaciones regionales en el impacto del dominio colonial español en las poblaciones indígenas de Honduras y Nicaragua. *Mesoamérica (USA)*, v. 13, no. 24 (Dec 92), pp. 297 – 312. Bibl, tables, maps.

Nicandro, Glugio Gronk. Reproduction of *Invasion of Dixie(Cup)Series – Hot Vessel* by Gronk. *The Americas Review*, v. 21, no. 1 (Spring 93), p. 77.

Nicastro, Laura. Jaguares. *Letras Femeninas*, v. 19, no. 1 – 2 (Spring – Fall 93), pp. 195 – 197.

Nicholas, Linda M. and Gary M. Feinman. Shell-Ornament Production in Ejutla: Implications for Highland – Coastal Interaction in Ancient Oaxaca. *Ancient Mesoamerica*, v. 4, no. 1 (Spring 93), pp. 103 – 119. Bibl, il, tables, maps, charts.

Nicolás, Juan Antonio. ¿Por qué una nueva ley federal de educación? *Plural (Mexico)*, v. 22, no. 262 (July 93), pp. 81 – 83.

Nicoliello, Nelson. Valores notables de la cultura uruguaya: algunos abogados ilustres del Uruguay. *Hoy Es Historia*, v. 10, no. 55 (Jan – Feb 93), pp. 31 – 34.

Nieto, Margarita. Carlos Almaraz: Genesis of a Chicano Painter. *Latin American Art*, v. 5, no. 1 (Spring 93), pp. 37 – 39. Bibl, il.

— Marie José Paz. *Latin American Art*, v. 5, no. 2 (Summer 93), pp. 53 – 54. Il.

— Vladimir Cora. *Latin American Art*, v. 4, no. 4 (Winter 92), pp. 80 – 81. Il.

Nieto-Cadena, Fernando. Mujer, literatura y sociedad en el sureste. *Fem*, v. 17, no. 120 (Feb 93), pp. 21 – 24.

Nieto Degregori, Luis. Buscando un inca. *Debate (Peru)*, v. 16, no. 73 (June – Aug 93), pp. 61 – 63. Il.

Nigro, Kirsten F. Textualidad, historia y sujetividad: género y género. *Latin American Theatre Review*, v. 26, no. 2 (Spring 93), pp. 17 – 24.

Niño de Guzmán, Guillermo. El desnudo latinoamericano. *Debate (Peru)*, v. 15, no. 71 (Nov 92 – Jan 93), pp. 60 – 63. Il.

Niño Guarín, Juan Enrique. El Plan Especial de Cooperación (P.E.C.) de la CE: balance satisfactorio pero no suficiente. *Revista Javeriana*, v. 61, no. 594 (May 93), pp. 263 – 269. Bibl, tables.

Nishida, Mieko. Manumission and Ethnicity in Urban Slavery: Salvador, Brazil, 1808 – 1888. *Hispanic American Historical Review*, v. 73, no. 3 (Aug 93), pp. 361 – 391. Bibl, tables, charts.

Nítolo, Miguel Roberto. Um grande laboratório. *Problemas Brasileiros*, v. 30, no. 295 (Jan – Feb 93), pp. 19 – 21. Il.

— Retrato áspero. *Problemas Brasileiros*, v. 30, no. 296 (Mar – Apr 93), pp. 7 – 12. Il.

— A riqueza vem do lixo. *Problemas Brasileiros*, v. 30, no. 297 (May – June 93), pp. 10 – 14. Il.

Noble, Patricia E. Collection Evaluation Techniques: A British Pilot Study. *SALALM Papers*, v. 36 (1991), pp. 248 – 257. Tables.

Noble Martínez, Guadalupe. Búsqueda. *Letras Femeninas*, v. 19, no. 1 – 2 (Spring – Fall 93), p. 175.

Nocton, Amy. Fragmentos. *Inti*, no. 36 (Fall 92), pp. 165 – 168.

Nodal, Roberto. The Concept of "Ebbo" (Sacrifice) as a Healing Mechanism in Santería. *Journal of Caribbean Studies*, v. 9, no. 1 – 2 (Winter 92 – Spring 93), pp. 113 – 124. Bibl.

Noé, Luis Felipe. Artes Plásticas Argentinas, Sociedad Anónima. *Cuadernos Hispanoamericanos*, no. 517 – 519 (July – Sept 93), pp. 245 – 268. Il.

Noelle, Louise. Nueve libros sobre arquitectura latinoamericana (Review article). *Anales del Instituto de Investigaciones Estéticas*, v. 16, no. 62 (1991), pp. 218 – 222.

Nofal, Rossana. *Biografía de un cimarrón* de Miguel Barnet: "la construcción de una voz." *Revista Chilena de Literatura*, no. 40 (Nov 92), pp. 35 – 39. Bibl.

Noguera, Carlos. La convergencia múltiple: una aproximación a la narrativa de José Balza. *Inti*, no. 37 – 38 (Spring – Fall 93), pp. 179 – 185. Bibl.

Nómez, Naín. Literatura, cultura y sociedad: el modernismo y la génesis de la poesía chilena contemporánea. *Revista Chilena de Literatura*, no. 42 (Aug 93), pp. 157 – 164. Bibl.

Norambuena Carrasco, Carmen. Inmigración, agricultura y ciudades intermedias, 1880 – 1930. *Cuadernos de Historia (Chile)*, no. 11 (Dec 91), pp. 105 – 123. Bibl, tables.

Nordenflycht, Adolfo. Historización literaria y architextualidad: el cuento chileno (1888 – 1938); formaciones y transformaciones. *Revista Chilena de Literatura*, no. 42 (Aug 93), pp. 73 – 80.

Noriega, Carlos Augusto. Las innovaciones políticas del gobierno Gaviria. *Revista Javeriana*, v. 61, no. 597 (Aug 93), pp. 129 – 142.

Noriega, Julio E. El quechua: voz y letra en el mundo andino. *Revista de Crítica Literaria Latinoamericana*, v. 19, no. 37 (Jan – June 93), pp. 279 – 301. Bibl.

Noriega, Margarita. La descentralización educativa: los casos de Francia y México. *Revista Latinoamericana de Estudios Educativos*, v. 23, no. 1 (Jan – Mar 93), pp. 43 – 74. Bibl, tables.

— La equidad y el financiamiento educativo: problemas clave de la federalización. *El Cotidiano*, v. 8, no. 51 (Nov – Dec 92), pp. 34 – 38. Il, tables.

Noriega, Teobaldo A. *La mala hierba* de Juan Gossaín: consideraciones estéticas ante una escritura de la nueva violencia colombiana. *Revista Canadiense de Estudios Hispánicos*, v. 17, no. 3 (Spring 93), pp. 465 – 481. Bibl.

Nosetto, Mónica and Jutta Marx. ¿Las mujeres al poder?: la igualdad por decreto presidencial. *Feminaria*, v. 6, no. 10 (Apr 93), pp. 27 – 28.

Novaes, Ana Dolores and David Rosenblatt. O poder regional no Congresso: uma atualização. *Revista Brasileira de Economia*, v. 47, no. 2 (Apr – June 93), pp. 305 – 312. Bibl, tables.

Novelo, Victoria. Las tentaciones de doña Victoria. *Nueva Antropología*, v. 13, no. 43 (Nov 92), pp. 45 – 51.

Novoa, Bruce

See
Bruce-Novoa, John D.

Nun, José. Democracy and Modernization Thirty Years Later. *Latin American Perspectives*, v. 20, no. 4 (Fall 93), pp. 7 – 27. Bibl.

Nunes, Antonietta de Aguiar. O processo brasileiro da independência. *Revista do Instituto Histórico e Geográfico Brasileiro*, no. 373 (Oct – Dec 91), pp. 942 – 947.

Nunes, Maria José Fontelas Rosado. De mulheres e de deuses. *Estudos Feministas*, v. 0, no. 0 (1992), pp. 5 – 30. Bibl.

Núñez, Charo. Poems ("Cuarto propio," "Son los astros," "Vida continúa," "Me pongo . . . "). *Feminaria*, v. 6, no. 11, Suppl. (Nov 93), p. 20.

Núñez, Luis V. Anthony. Disposable People. *The Americas Review*, v. 20, no. 1 (Spring 92), pp. 25 – 31.

Núñez del Prado Benavente, Arturo and Juan Martín P. Strategic Management, Planning, and Budgets. *CEPAL Review*, no. 49 (Apr 93), pp. 41 – 54. Bibl.

Núñez Domingo, Pedro Pablo. Realidad y simbolismo de la privatización (Review article). *Pensamiento Iberoamericano*, no. 22 – 23, tomo I (July 92 – June 93), pp. 357 – 385. Charts.

Núñez Escobar, Roberto and Ricardo A. Lince. Aporte para una legislación de prensa. *Revista Cultural Lotería*, v. 50, no. 386 (Nov – Dec 91), pp. 5 – 24.

Núñez Florencio, Rafael. Los republicanos españoles ante el problema colonial: la cuestión cubana. *Revista de Indias*, v. 53, no. 198 (May – Aug 93), pp. 545 – 561.

Núñez Jover, Jorge and Jorge Alderegía Henriques. Aproximaciones al marco conceptual de la sanología. *Interciencia*, v. 18, no. 2 (Mar – Apr 93), pp. 71 – 76. Bibl.

Núñez Miranda, Concepción S. La problemática de las mujeres escritoras (Speech given by the author to the Reunión de Mujeres Escritoras del Sureste, Villahermosa, Tabasco, 12 de noviembre, 1992). *Fem*, v. 17, no. 120 (Feb 93), pp. 10 – 11.

— Rosa Ceniza. *Fem*, v. 17, no. 120 (Feb 93), p. 14.

Núñez Seixas, Xosé M. Inmigración y galleguismo en Cuba, 1879 – 1930. *Revista de Indias*, v. 53, no. 197 (Jan – Apr 93), pp. 53 – 95. Bibl.

Nuño Montes, Juan Antonio. ¿Qué pasa en Venezuela? *Vuelta*, v. 17, no. 203 (Oct 93), pp. 55 – 56.

Nylen, William R. Selling Neoliberalism: Brazil's Instituto Liberal. *Journal of Latin American Studies*, v. 25, no. 2 (May 93), pp. 301 – 311. Bibl.

Obaldía A., Mario de and Carola Coriat R. La influencia de la abuela en la percepción familiar del niño bajo su cuidado. *Revista Cultural Lotería*, v. 50, no. 383 (May – June 91), pp. 74 – 93. Bibl, tables.

Obando Arboleda, María Cecilia. Una propuesta de reforma pensional: ¿Qué falló? *Revista Javeriana*, v. 61, no. 592 (Mar 93), pp. 91 – 96.

Obando Arbulú, Enrique. Situación de la subversión: después de la caída de Abimael Guzmán. *Debate (Peru)*, v. 15, no. 70 (Sept – Oct 92), pp. 19 – 22. Il.

— Unas fuerzas armadas para el siglo XXI. *Debate (Peru)*, v. 15, no. 71 (Nov 92 – Jan 93), pp. 32 – 36. Il.

Obando Hidalgo, Iris María and Ana Isabel Ruiz Rojas. Epidemiología del abuso físico y sexual en niños atendidos en el Hospital de Niños, 1988 – 1990. *Revista de Ciencias Sociales (Costa Rica)*, no. 59 (Mar 93), pp. 63 – 70. Bibl, tables, charts.

Obando Obando, William. Repercusiones sociológicas de las exploraciones petroleras en los pueblos shiroles y suretka – talamanca. *Revista de Ciencias Sociales (Costa Rica)*, no. 57 (Sept 92), pp. 109 – 119. Bibl, tables.

Obejas, Achy. Poems ("Kimberle," "Sugarcane"). *The Americas Review*, v. 20, no. 3 – 4 (Fall – Winter 92), pp. 158 – 160.

O'Brian, Robin. Un mercado indígena de artesanías en los altos de Chiapas: persistencia y cambio en las vidas de las vendedoras mayas. *Mesoamérica (USA)*, v. 13, no. 23 (June 92), pp. 79 – 84. Bibl.

Ocampo, Orlando. Interpretando el pasado histórico: el acto referencial en *Una sombra donde sueña Camila O'Gorman*. *Revista Chilena de Literatura*, no. 40 (Nov 92), pp. 83 – 89. Bibl.

Ocampo López, Javier. El maestro Luis Alberto Acuña y el nacionalismo artístico. *Boletín de Historia y Antigüedades*, v. 80, no. 781 (Apr – June 93), pp. 343 – 354.

— El padre Manuel Briceño Jáuregui, S.J. y el humanismo clásico. *Boletín de Historia y Antigüedades*, v. 80, no. 781 (Apr – June 93), pp. 293 – 318. Bibl.

— La rebelión de las alcabalas. *Boletín de Historia y Antigüedades*, v. 79, no. 779 (Oct – Dec 92), pp. 993 – 1005. Bibl.

Ocampo Sigüenza, Daniel. Los puertos y las ciudades costeras ante la apertura comercial de México. *Comercio Exterior*, v. 43, no. 8 (Aug 93), pp. 731 – 742. Bibl, tables.

Ocasio, Rafael. "Babalú Ayé": Santería and Contemporary Cuban Literature. *Journal of Caribbean Studies*, v. 9, no. 1 – 2 (Winter 92 – Spring 93), pp. 29 – 40. Bibl.

Ochagavía Larraín, Juan. La Compañía de Jesús y la formación de los laicos. *Mensaje*, v. 42, no. 420 (July 93), pp. 311 – 316.

Ocharán, Leticia. Las artes plásticas frente al TLC. *Plural (Mexico)*, v. 22, no. 258 (Mar 93), pp. 72 – 73.

Ochoa, Enriqueta. Un hilo de neblina y luz. *Plural (Mexico)*, v. 22, no. 267 (Dec 93), pp. 12 – 13.

Ochoa, Rosa Margot. Haikú. *Letras Femeninas*, v. 19, no. 1 – 2 (Spring – Fall 93), pp. 178 – 180.

Ochoa Antich, Fernando. Sesión solemne de las academias nacionales con motivo de la conmemoración del V centenario del descubrimiento de América: palabras del ministro de relaciones exteriores, general Fernando Ochoa Antich. *Boletín de la Academia Nacional de la Historia (Venezuela)*, v. 75, no. 300 (Oct – Dec 92), pp. 5 – 9.

Ochoa Méndez, Jacqueline. Orientación bibliográfica sobre educación básica. *El Cotidiano*, v. 8, no. 51 (Nov – Dec 92), p. 117.

— Orientación bibliográfica sobre educación superior en Canadá, E.U.A. y México. *El Cotidiano*, v. 9, no. 55 (June 93), p. 120.

— Orientación bibliográfica sobre el Distrito Federal. *El Cotidiano*, v. 9, no. 54 (May 93), pp. 119 – 120.

— Orientación bibliográfica sobre el movimiento urbano popular en la ciudad de México. *El Cotidiano*, v. 10, no. 57 (Aug – Sept 93), pp. 111 – 112.

— Orientación bibliográfica sobre la mujer. *El Cotidiano*, v. 9, no. 53 (Mar – Apr 93), p. 120.

— Orientación bibliográfica sobre narcotráfico. *El Cotidiano*, v. 8, no. 52 (Jan – Feb 93), p. 120.

— Orientación bibliográfica sobre sindicalismo en México. *El Cotidiano*, v. 9, no. 56 (July 93), pp. 119 – 120.

— Orientación bibliográfica sobre sucesión presidencial y partidos políticos. *El Cotidiano*, v. 10, no. 58 (Oct – Nov 93), pp. 119 – 120.

Ochoa Rivero, Silvia. Algunas percepciones sobre lo femenino y lo masculino: hablan los jóvenes. *Allpanchis*, v. 25, no. 41 (Jan – June 93), pp. 143 – 158. Bibl.

Odio Orozco, Eduardo. La Pochota: un complejo cerámico temprano en las tierras bajas del Guanacaste, Costa Rica. *Vínculos*, v. 17, no. 1 – 2 (1991), pp. 1 – 16. Bibl, il, tables, maps.

O'Donnell, Guillermo A. Acerca del estado, la democratización y algunos problemas conceptuales: una perspectiva latinoamericana con referencias a países poscomunistas (Translated by Leandro Wolfson). *Desarrollo Económico (Argentina)*, v. 33, no. 130 (July – Sept 93), pp. 163 – 184. Bibl.

— Estado, democratización y ciudadanía. *Nueva Sociedad*, no. 128 (Nov – Dec 93), pp. 62 – 87.

O'Donnell, Madalene T. El Salvador: The Electoral Test. *Hemisphere,* v. 5, no. 3 (Summer – Fall 93), pp. 13 – 15.

Oelrich, Amy. Marching to the Beat of the Market. *Business Mexico,* v. 3, no. 11 (Nov 93), p. 30. II.

Offutt, Leslie S. Levels of Acculturation in Northeastern New Spain: San Esteban Testaments of the Seventeenth and Eighteenth Centuries. *Estudios de Cultura Náhuatl,* v. 22 (1992), pp. 409 – 443.

Ogaz Pierce, Héctor. La función de Gompertz – Makeham en la descripción y proyección de fenómenos demográficos. *Estudios Demográficos y Urbanos,* v. 6, no. 3 (Sept – Dec 91), pp. 485 – 520. Bibl, tables, charts.

Ogno, Lía. Augusto Monterroso, la oveja negra de la literatura hispanoamericana. *Cuadernos Hispanoamericanos,* no. 511 (Jan 93), pp. 33 – 42. Bibl.

O'Gorman, Pamela. Music: A Personal Memoir. *Jamaica Journal,* v. 25, no. 1 (Oct 93), pp. 18 – 24. Bibl, il, facs.

Ojeda, Alvaro. Poemas. *Hispamérica,* v. 22, no. 64 – 65 (Apr – Aug 93), p. 145.

Olea, Raquel. El cuerpo-mujer: un recorte de lectura en la narrativa de Diamela Eltit. *Revista Chilena de Literatura,* no. 42 (Aug 93), pp. 165 – 171. Bibl.

Oleszkiewicz, Malgorzata. El ciclo de la muerte de Atahualpa: de la fiesta popular a la representación teatral. *Allpanchis,* v. 23, no. 39 (Jan – June 92), pp. 185 – 220. Bibl.

Olguín, David. La mano ausente: una entrevista con Luis de Tavira. *Nexos,* v. 16, no. 186 (June 93), pp. 86 – 88.

— Tradición y novedad. *Nexos,* v. 16, no. 187 (July 93), pp. 90 – 91.

Olguín Pérez, Palmira. Las reglas del juego: moralidad y moraleja en la telenovela. *Fem,* v. 17, no. 130 (Dec 93), pp. 22 – 23.

Olivar Jimenez, Martha Lucia. Integración en el Cono Sur: realidad y perspectivas. *Vozes,* v. 86, no. 6 (Nov – Dec 92), pp. 62 – 68.

Olivares, Julián. Russell Lee, Photographer *The Americas Review,* v. 19, no. 3 – 4 (Winter 91), pp. 17 – 19 +. II.

Oliveira, Ana Maria Domingues de. A temática da morte em Cecília Meireles e Gabriela Mistral. *Revista de Letras (Brazil),* v. 32 (1992), pp. 127 – 139. Bibl.

Oliveira, Eleonora Menicucci de and Lucila Amaral Carneiro Vianna. Violência conjugal na gravidez. *Estudos Feministas,* v. 1, no. 1 (1993), pp. 162 – 165.

Oliveira, Henrique Altemani de. Política externa independente: fundamentos da política africana do Brasil. *Política e Estratégica,* v. 8, no. 2 – 4 (Apr – Dec 90), pp. 268 – 284. Bibl, tables.

Oliveira, José Aparecido de et al. Homenaje al doctor Francisco Curt Lange. *Revista Musical de Venezuela,* no. 28 (May – Dec 89), Issue. Bibl, il, facs.

Oliveira, Maria Coleta F. A. de. Condición femenina y alternativas de organización doméstica: las mujeres sin pareja en São Paulo. *Estudios Demográficos y Urbanos,* v. 7, no. 2 – 3 (May – Dec 92), pp. 511 – 537. Bibl, tables, charts.

Oliveira, Orlandina de and Bryan R. Roberts. La informalidad urbana en años de expansión, crisis y restructuración económica (Translated by Laura Elena Pulido). *Estudios Sociológicos,* v. 11, no. 31 (Jan – Apr 93), pp. 33 – 58. Bibl, tables.

Oliveira, Renato José de. Análise epistemológica da visão de ciência dos professores de química e física do município do Rio de Janeiro. *Revista Brasileira de Estudos Pedagógicos,* v. 72, no. 172 (Sept – Dec 91), pp. 335 – 355. Bibl, tables.

Oliveira, Rosiska Darcy de. Memórias do Planeta Fêmea. *Estudos Feministas,* v. 0, no. 0 (1992), pp. 131 – 142.

Olivera, María Elena. Pecado original. *Fem,* v. 17, no. 129 (Nov 93), p. 40.

Olivera, Mauricio. El costo de uso del capital en Colombia: una nueva estimación. *Planeación y Desarrollo,* v. 24, no. 2 (May – Aug 93), pp. 373 – 400. Bibl, tables, charts.

Olivera Lozano, Guillermo. Movilidad residencial y expansión física reciente en la ciudad de México. *Revista Geográfica (Mexico),* no. 115 (Jan – June 92), pp. 55 – 76. Bibl, tables, maps.

Olivera-Williams, María Rosa. El derrumbamiento de Armonía Somers y El ángel caído de Cristina Peri-Rossi: dos manifestaciones de la narrativa imaginaria. *Revista Chilena de Literatura,* no. 42 (Aug 93), pp. 173 – 181. Bibl.

Olivier, Michele. Global Finance for Mexican Corporations. *Business Mexico,* v. 3, no. 7 (July 93), p. 27 +. Tables.

— Shared Responsibility. *Business Mexico,* v. 3, no. 6 (June 93), pp. 43 – 45. Tables, charts.

Ollé, Carmen et al. Ni divino, ni tesoro (Three essays in which Carmen Ollé, Patricia Alba, and Beto Ortiz reminisce about their youth in Peru). *Debate (Peru),* v. 16, no. 74 (Sept – Oct 93), pp. 27 – 30.

Olliz-Boyd, Antonio

See
Boyd, Antonio Olliz

Olmedo Carranza, Bernardo. Crisis de la seguridad social: el caso de México. *Momento Económico,* no. 69 (Sept – Oct 93), pp. 13 – 15.

— Ofensiva proteccionista norteamericana: el acero. *Relaciones Internacionales (Mexico),* v. 15, Nueva época, no. 58 (Apr – June 93), pp. 89 – 91.

Olmo Pintado, Margarita del. La historia natural en la *Historia del Nuevo Mundo* del p. Cobo. *Revista de Indias,* v. 52, no. 195 – 196 (May – Dec 92), pp. 795 – 823. Maps, charts.

Olveda, Jaime. Las viejas oligarquías y la reforma liberal: el caso de Guadalajara. *Siglo XIX: Cuadernos,* v. 2, no. 4 (Oct 92), pp. 9 – 30. Bibl.

Olvera, Alberto and Leonardo Avritzer. El concepto de sociedad civil en el estudio de la transición democrática. *Revista Mexicana de Sociología,* v. 54, no. 4 (Oct – Dec 92), pp. 227 – 248. Bibl.

Olvera Pomar, Daniel. The Information Trade. *Business Mexico,* v. 3, no. 11 (Nov 93), p. 38.

Olvera Sandoval, José Antonio. Agricultura, riego y conflicto social en la región citrícola de Nuevo León, 1860 – 1910. *Siglo XIX: Cuadernos,* v. 2, no. 5 (Feb 93), pp. 59 – 78.

Olza Zubiri, Jesús. Homenaje a Nebrija: el genitivo subjectivo determinado con predicativo. *Montalbán,* no. 24 (1992), pp. 11 – 19.

Onetti, Juan Carlos. Cuando nada importe (Excerpt from the novel entitled *Cuando ya no importe*). *Nexos,* v. 16, no. 181 (Jan 93), pp. 39 – 41.

— Cuando ya no importe. *Hispamérica,* v. 21, no. 62 (Aug 92), pp. 105 – 110.

Opazo, José Luis et al. El descontrol del sistema de buses de Santiago: síntesis de un diagnóstico técnico – institucional. *EURE*, v. 19, no. 56 (Mar 93), pp. 79 – 91. Bibl, tables.

O'Phelan Godoy, Scarlett. Rebeliones andinas anticoloniales: Nueva Granada, Perú y Charcas entre el siglo XVIII y el XIX. *Anuario de Estudios Americanos*, v. 49 (1992), pp. 395 – 440. Bibl, maps.

Orbegozo, Manuel Jesús and Sally Bowen. 1992: el año que vivimos al galope. *Debate (Peru)*, v. 15, no. 71 (Nov 92 – Jan 93), pp. 22 – 26. Il.

Ordenes Lavadenz, Jorge. Los principios de Norman. *Signo*, no. 38, Nueva época (Jan – Apr 93), pp. 203 – 205.

Ordóñez, Andrés. El fin de una historia: la comunicación intercultural y el nuevo orden internacional en formación. *Cuadernos Americanos*, no. 42, Nueva época (Nov – Dec 93), pp. 101 – 111. Bibl.

Ordóñez, Jorge E. and Luis Chávez Martínez. Fueling Industry. *Business Mexico*, v. 3, no. 12 (Dec 93), pp. 10 – 11.

Ordóñez B., Gerardo M. and Tonatiuh Guillén López. La marginalidad social en la frontera norte: discrepancias empíricas al concepto de la marginalidad. *Frontera Norte*, v. 4, no. 8 (July – Dec 92), pp. 149 – 163. Tables.

Ordóñez Vila, Montserrat. La loba insaciable de *La vorágine*. *Escritura (Venezuela)*, v. 16, no. 31 – 32 (Jan – Dec 91), pp. 205 – 213.

Ordorica Mellado, Manuel. Desarrollo y aplicación de una función expológistica para el análisis de congruencia de las fuentes demográficas entre 1940 y 1990: el caso de México. *Revista Mexicana de Sociología*, v. 55, no. 1 (Jan – Mar 93), pp. 3 – 16. Tables, charts.

— La población de México en los albores del siglo XXI: ¿Predicción o proyección? *Comercio Exterior*, v. 43, no. 7 (July 93), pp. 634 – 641. Bibl, tables, charts.

Oreillard, Bernard. Approche sociologique de la presse à Porto Rico et en Guadeloupe/Martinique. *Caribbean Studies*, v. 25, no. 1 – 2 (Jan – July 92), pp. 63 – 73.

Orellana, Margarita de. Eugenia Marcos: los frutos prohibidos. *Artes de México*, no. 19 (Spring 93), p. 110. Il.

— Voces entretejidas: testimonios del arte textil (Accompanied by an English translation). *Artes de México*, no. 19 (Spring 93), pp. 43 – 59. Il.

Orellana, Roger. Síndromes morfológicos y funcionales de las palmas de la península de Yucatán. *Bulletin de l'Institut Français d'Etudes Andines*, v. 21, no. 2 (1992), pp. 651 – 667. Bibl, tables, maps, charts.

Orenstein, Catherine. An Interview with Ben Dupuy. *NACLA Report on the Americas*, v. 27, no. 1 (July – Aug 93), pp. 12 – 15. Il.

Organization of American States. Resolución sobre el Instituto Indigenista Interamericano. *Anuario Indigenista*, v. 30 (Dec 91), pp. 345 – 346.

Orlandi, Eni Pulcinelli. O discurso dos naturalistas. *Vozes*, v. 87, no. 1 (Jan – Feb 93), pp. 62 – 76.

Ormeño O., Alejandro. Las universidades pedagógicas y el desafío de la formación de profesores. *Estudios Sociales (Chile)*, no. 75 (Jan – Mar 93), pp. 225 – 230.

Orozco, Claudia. Marco legal para la promoción de la competencia en derecho comparado y en Colombia. *Planeación y Desarrollo*, v. 24, no. 2 (May – Aug 93), pp. 95 – 144. Bibl.

Orozco, Emanuel and Alejandro Cornejo Oviedo. Relatoría del encuentro "Antropología Industrial: Avances de Investigación." *Nueva Antropología*, v. 13, no. 44 (Aug 93), pp. 143 – 145.

Orozco, Judith and E. Fernando Nava L. El "Sistema de Cristóbal Colón" y la "Biografía de Colón": una muestra de poesía popular mexicana (Includes the two texts). *Cuadernos Americanos*, no. 42, Nueva época (Nov – Dec 93), pp. 203 – 241.

Orozco H., María Angélica. Los franciscanos y el caso del Real Colegio Seminario de México, 1749. *Archivo Ibero-Americano*, v. 52, no. 205 – 208 (Jan – Dec 92), pp. 497 – 512.

Orrego Larraín, Claudio. ¿Corrupción en Chile? *Mensaje*, v. 42, no. 418 (May 93), p. 159.

Ortega, Eliana. Travesías bellessianas. *Revista Chilena de Literatura*, no. 42 (Aug 93), pp. 183 – 191.

Ortega, Emiliano. Evolution of the Rural Dimension in Latin America and the Caribbean. *CEPAL Review*, no. 47 (Aug 92), pp. 115 – 136. Bibl, tables.

Ortega, José. Las Casas, un reformador social "por abajo." *Cuadernos Hispanoamericanos*, no. 512 (Feb 93), pp. 29 – 38. Bibl, il.

— Conmemoración del genocidio de las Indias. *La Palabra y el Hombre*, no. 81 (Jan – Mar 92), pp. 11 – 19. Bibl.

— Verdad poética e histórica en *Vigilia del Almirante*. *Cuadernos Hispanoamericanos*, no. 513 (Mar 93), pp. 108 – 111.

— La visión del mundo de Arlt: *Los siete locos/Los lanzallamas*. *Cuadernos Hispanoamericanos*, no. Special issue, 11 (July 93), pp. 71 – 76. Il.

Ortega, Julio. Alfredo Bryce Echenique y la estética de la exageración. *Cuadernos Hispanoamericanos*, no. 521 (Nov 93), pp. 71 – 86. Il.

— El arte de la lectura: encuentros con Borges. *Nexos*, v. 16, no. 182 (Feb 93), pp. 41 – 50.

— Cien años de Vallejo. *Inti*, no. 36 (Fall 92), pp. 3 – 10.

Ortega, Julio et al. Las dos orillas: una intervención de Julio Ortega. *Inti*, no. 36 (Fall 92), pp. 113 – 125.

Ortega, Luis. El proceso de industrialización en Chile, 1850 – 1930. *Historia (Chile)*, no. 26 (1991 – 1992), pp. 213 – 246. Bibl.

Ortega, Roberto Diego. Rapsodia. *Nexos*, v. 16, no. 183 (Mar 93), pp. 13 – 14.

Ortega Escalona, Fernando. El recurso madera desde la conquista hasta principios del siglo XX. *La Palabra y el Hombre*, no. 81 (Jan – Mar 92), pp. 45 – 60. Bibl, il.

Ortega Ricaurte, Carmen. Semblanza de don José González Llorente. *Boletín de Historia y Antigüedades*, v. 80, no. 781 (Apr – June 93), pp. 389 – 405. Il.

Ortiz, Edgar. TLC e inversión extranjera en México. *Comercio Exterior*, v. 43, no. 10 (Oct 93), pp. 967 – 973. Bibl.

Ortiz, Edgar and Francisco Rafael Dávila Aldás. Del antagonismo a la cooperación entre el Este y el Oeste para la búsqueda de un mundo más humano. *Revista Mexicana de Ciencias Políticas y Sociales*, v. 37, Nueva época, no. 149 (July – Sept 92), pp. 49 – 81.

Ortiz, Isidro D. Gloria Molina, líder popular chicana (Translated by Leticia García Cortés). *Plural (Mexico)*, v. 22, no. 256 (Jan 93), pp. 63 – 69. Bibl.

Ortiz, Renato. Cultura, modernidade e identidades. *Vozes*, v. 87, no. 2 (Mar – Apr 93), pp. 24 – 30. Bibl.

Ortiz Cofer, Judith. The Black Virgin. *The Americas Review*, v. 20, no. 3 – 4 (Fall – Winter 92), pp. 94 – 99.

— Monologue of the Spanish Gentleman. *The Americas Review*, v. 20, no. 2 (Summer 92), pp. 31 – 35.

— Poems ("La fe," "El olvido, según las madres," "So Much for Mañana," "The Latin Deli"). *The Americas Review,* v. 20, no. 3 – 4 (Fall – Winter 92), pp. 153 – 157.

Ortiz de Montellano, Bernardo R. Buzón de fantasmas: de Bernardo Ortiz de Montellano a Emilio Portes Gil. *Vuelta,* v. 17, no. 199 (June 93), pp. 74 – 75.

— Buzón de fantasmas: de Ortiz de Montellano a Torres Bodet. *Vuelta,* v. 17, no. 198 (May 93), pp. 78 – 79.

Ortiz de Terra, María del Carmen and Rosario Quijano. En busca de la memoria histórica de la mujer. *Hoy Es Historia,* v. 10, no. 55 (Jan – Feb 93), pp. 53 – 57.

Ortiz de Zevallos, Augusto. Carta sobre (o debajo de) Lima. *Debate (Peru),* v. 15, no. 70 (Sept – Oct 92), pp. 48 – 52. Il.

Ortiz de Zevallos, Felipe. El optimismo es frágil. *Debate (Peru),* v. 16, no. 73 (June – Aug 93), pp. 18 – 21. Il.

Ortiz Flores, Carlos Iván. Efraín Castro: "Revisión de lo invisible." *Nexos,* v. 16, no. 185 (May 93), pp. 86 – 87. Il.

Ortiz Mesa, Luis Javier. Elites en Antioquia, Colombia, en los inicios de la regeneración, 1886 – 1896. *Anuario Colombiano de Historia Social y de la Cultura,* no. 20 (1992), pp. 27 – 42. Bibl.

— Procesos de descentralización en Colombia durante el período federal, 1850 – 1886. *Planeación y Desarrollo,* v. 24, no. 1 (Jan – Apr 93), pp. 199 – 231. Bibl, tables.

Ortiz O., María Salvadora. Mamita Yunai: novela de la plantación bananera. *Káñina,* v. 16, no. 1 (Jan – June 92), pp. 9 – 17. Bibl.

Ortiz Sotelo, Jorge. Embarcaciones aborígenes en el área andina. *Historia y Cultura (Peru),* no. 20 (1990), pp. 49 – 79. Bibl.

Ortiz Wadgymar, Arturo. El desequilibrio externo: talón de Aquiles del salinismo. *Problemas del Desarrollo,* v. 24, no. 92 (Jan – Mar 93), pp. 24 – 30. Tables.

— La pequeña y mediana industrias ante la apertura comercial y el Tratado de Libre Comercio: los costos de la desprotección industrial en México, 1985 – 1992. *Problemas del Desarrollo,* v. 24, no. 93 (Apr – June 93), pp. 55 – 74. Bibl, tables.

— La política económica de México, 1988 – 1992: hacia una evaluación preliminar. *Relaciones Internacionales (Mexico),* v. 14, Nueva época, no. 56 (Oct – Dec 92), pp. 133 – 141. Bibl, tables, charts.

— La recesión del '93: neoliberalismo en entredicho. *Momento Económico,* no. 69 (Sept – Oct 93), pp. 2 – 5.

Ortlieb, Luc and Amanda Díaz. El fenómeno El Niño y los moluscos de la costa peruana. *Bulletin de l'Institut Français d'Etudes Andines,* v. 22, no. 1 (1993), pp. 159 – 177. Bibl, tables, maps.

Ortlieb, Luc and José Macharé. Registros del fenómeno El Niño en el Perú. *Bulletin de l'Institut Français d'Etudes Andines,* v. 22, no. 1 (1993), pp. 35 – 52. Bibl, tables, charts.

Ortlieb, Luc et al. Beach-Ridge Series in Northern Peru: Chronology, Correlation, and Relationship with Major Late Holocene El Niño Events. *Bulletin de l'Institut Français d'Etudes Andines,* v. 22, no. 1 (1993), pp. 191 – 212. Bibl, il, tables, maps, charts.

Ortúzar S., Juan de Dios. Congestión y transporte público: una relación mal entendida. *EURE,* v. 19, no. 56 (Mar 93), pp. 124 – 126. Tables.

Osorio, Alejandra. Una interpretación sobre la extirpación de idolatrías en el Perú: Otuco, Cajatambo, siglo XVII. *Historia y Cultura (Peru),* no. 20 (1990), pp. 161 – 199. Bibl.

Osorio, Jaime. Bloque comercial sí, tratados comerciales tal vez. *El Cotidiano,* v. 9, no. 56 (July 93), pp. 113 – 116. Il, tables.

Osorio, Manuel. Conversación con Roa Bastos: *Yo el Supremo;* la contrahistoria. *Plural (Mexico),* v. 22, no. 263 (Aug 93), pp. 29 – 31.

Osorio Osorio, Alberto. Natá de los caballeros, madre de pueblos. *Revista Cultural Lotería,* v. 51, no. 387 (Feb 92), pp. 26 – 30.

Osorio Paz, Saúl. ¿Está resuelta el problema de la deuda? *Momento Económico,* no. 66 (Mar – Apr 93), pp. 28 – 30.

— Golpe de estado y situación socioeconómica en Guatemala. *Momento Económico,* no. 69 (Sept – Oct 93), pp. 20 – 23.

Osorio Tejeda, Nelson. La alucinación del petróleo en una obra de César Rengifo. *Hispamérica,* v. 21, no. 63 (Dec 92), pp. 81 – 87.

— La historia y las clases en la narrativa de Miguel Otero Silva. *Casa de las Américas,* no. 190 (Jan – Mar 93), pp. 34 – 41. Bibl.

— Vallejo, autor teatral. *Revista Nacional de Cultura (Venezuela),* v. 54, no. 287 (Oct – Dec 92), pp. 197 – 205. Bibl, facs.

Osorio Urbina, Jaime. La democracia ordenada: análisis crítico de la nueva sociología del Cono Sur latinoamericano. *Estudios Sociológicos,* v. 11, no. 31 (Jan – Apr 93), pp. 111 – 132. Bibl.

Osorio Velosa, Horacio and Guillermo Bonilla Muñoz. Estructura de mercado y prácticas comerciales en los sectores industrial, minero – energético y de servicios públicos en Colombia. *Planeación y Desarrollo,* v. 24, no. 2 (May – Aug 93), pp. 191 – 256. Tables, charts.

Ossandón Buljevic, Carlos A. Una historia de la filosofía en Chile: modernidad e institucionalidad. *Estudios Sociales (Chile),* no. 77 (July – Sept 93), pp. 9 – 15.

Ossandón Widow, María Eugenia. Proyecto para un plano de Valparaíso, 1675 – 1700. *Historia (Chile),* no. 26 (1991 – 1992), pp. 247 – 258. Bibl.

Osses Moya, Darío. La fundación de una literatura nacional y la Universidad de Chile. *Atenea (Chile),* no. 465 – 466 (1992), pp. 337 – 347. Bibl.

Osterroth, María de Jesús. "Radio Alicia": el espíritu de los '60. *Plural (Mexico),* v. 22, no. 263 (Aug 93), pp. 73 – 74.

— "XX – XXI": música entre los siglos. *Plural (Mexico),* v. 22, no. 265 (Oct 93), pp. 83 – 84.

Ostleitner, Elena. Europas Musik zwischen Mambo und Tango: Musikalische Einflüsse Lateinamerikas auf Europa. *Zeitschrift für Lateinamerika Wien,* no. 42 (1992), pp. 7 – 15. Bibl.

Ostolaza Bey, Margarita. El bloque histórico colonial de Puerto Rico. *Homines,* v. 15 – 16, no. 2 – 1 (Oct 91 – Dec 92), pp. 152 – 178. Bibl, tables.

Ostria González, Mauricio. Gabriela Mistral y César Vallejo: la americanidad como desgarramiento. *Revista Chilena de Literatura,* no. 42 (Aug 93), pp. 193 – 199. Bibl.

Osuna, William. Viajes a través de Vicente Gerbasi. *Revista Nacional de Cultura (Venezuela),* v. 54, no. 287 (Oct – Dec 92), pp. 16 – 17. Il.

Othón Quiroz Trejo, José and Luis Méndez. El conflicto de la Volkswagen: crónica de una muerte inesperada. *El Cotidiano,* v. 8, no. 51 (Nov – Dec 92), pp. 81 – 94. Bibl, il, tables, charts.

— Productividad, respuesta obrera y sucesión presidencial. *El Cotidiano,* v. 10, no. 58 (Oct – Nov 93), pp. 71 – 78.

— El proyecto cetemista y la modernidad laboral. *El Cotidiano*, v. 9, no. 56 (July 93), pp. 8 – 17. Il.

— El sindicalismo mexicano en los noventas: los sectores y las perspectivas. *El Cotidiano*, v. 9, no. 56 (July 93), pp. 3 – 7. Il.

Otis Charlton, Cynthia L. Obsidian as Jewelry: Lapidary Production in Aztec Otumba, Mexico. *Ancient Mesoamerica*, v. 4, no. 2 (Fall 93), pp. 231 – 243. Bibl, il, tables, maps.

Otten, Alexandre H. A influência do ideário religioso na construção da comunidade de Belo Monte. *Luso-Brazilian Review*, v. 30, no. 2 (Winter 93), pp. 71 – 95. Bibl.

Ottone, Ernesto. CEPAL: un planteamiento renovado frente a los nuevos desafíos del desarrollo (Review article). *Pensamiento Iberoamericano*, no. 22 – 23, tomo I (July 92 – June 93), pp. 386 – 392. Bibl.

Otzoy, Irma. Identidad y trajes mayas. *Mesoamérica (USA)*, v. 13, no. 23 (June 92), pp. 95 – 112. Bibl, tables.

Ouellette, Roger. Democracia y reformas administrativas: los casos de Argentina y Uruguay. *Cuadernos del CLAEH*, v. 18, no. 65 – 66 (May 93), pp. 75 – 85. Bibl.

Ouimette, Victor. Azorín y la América española. *Insula*, no. 556 (Apr 93), pp. 14 – 15.

Ovalles, Caupolicán. Poems ("Arden de cadáveres las funerarias," "Guardo la guadaña solitaria de la infancia," "Juego mi vida al azar," "Olvídate por mi de un aire sonriente"). *Revista Nacional de Cultura (Venezuela)*, v. 53, no. 286 (July – Sept 92), pp. 120 – 125.

Overing, Joanna
See
Kaplan, Joanna Overing

Oviedo, Cecilia. Identidad nacional y desarrollo: entrevista a Jürgen Golte. *Debate (Peru)*, v. 16, no. 72 (Mar – May 93), pp. 40 – 41. Il.

Oviedo, José Miguel. La crítica y sus riesgos, hoy. *Latin American Literary Review*, v. 20, no. 40 (July – Dec 92), pp. 75 – 79.

— El mundo vertiginoso de Rubem Fonseca. *Cuadernos Hispanoamericanos*, no. 512 (Feb 93), pp. 143 – 145.

Oviedo Cavada, Carlos. Cuatro siglos de la Compañía de Jesús en Chile. *Mensaje*, v. 42, no. 420 (July 93), pp. 264 – 269. Il.

Oyarzún, Kemy. Género y etnia: acerca del dialogismo en América Latina. *Revista Chilena de Literatura*, no. 41 (Apr 93), pp. 33 – 45. Bibl.

— Literaturas heterogéneas y dialogismo genérico – sexual. *Revista de Crítica Literaria Latinoamericana*, v. 19, no. 38 (July – Dec 93), pp. 37 – 50. Bibl.

Ozler, Sule and Dani Rodrik. Los choques externos, la política y la inversión privada: algo de teoría y evidencia empírica. *El Trimestre Económico*, v. 59, Special issue (Dec 92), pp. 187 – 212. Bibl, tables, charts.

P-Miñambres, Matías. *Tun tun de pasa y grifería*: perpetuación de estereotipos euroetnologocéntricos en el discurso poético afroantillano de Palés Matos. *Chasqui*, v. 22, no. 2 (Nov 93), pp. 73 – 84. Bibl.

Paatz, Annette. Reflexiones acerca de la traducción de obras teatrales: un simposio de autores latinoamericanos y traductores (Translated by Gabriela Fonseca). *Humboldt*, no. 108 (1993), pp. 102 – 103.

Pacheco, Gumersindo. En su propia trampa. *Casa de las Américas*, no. 191 (Apr – June 93), pp. 93 – 98.

Pacheco, José Emilio. Circo de noche. *Hispamérica*, v. 21, no. 62 (Aug 92), pp. 91 – 104.

Pacheco, Juan Manuel. 15 años más (Previously published in this journal, no. 400, 1973). *Revista Javeriana*, v. 61, no. 596 (July 93), pp. 37 – 40.

Pacheco, Paco. Gorgona. *Plural (Mexico)*, v. 22, no. 267 (Dec 93), pp. 68 – 69.

Pacheco O., Gilda. Migraciones forzadas en Centroamérica: evolución psicosocial. *Nueva Sociedad*, no. 127 (Sept – Oct 93), pp. 114 – 125. Bibl.

Pachón, Efraín. Los invitados del mes. *Revista Javeriana*, v. 61, no. 593 (Apr 93), pp. 170 – 178. Il.

Pacini Hernandez, Deborah. Dominican Popular Music under the Trujillo Regime. *Studies in Latin American Popular Culture*, v. 12 (1993), pp. 127 – 140. Bibl.

Padilla, Amado M. and Laverne Morrissey. Place of Last Drink by Repeat DUI Offenders: A Retrospective Study of Gender and Ethnic Group Differences. *Hispanic Journal of Behavioral Sciences*, v. 15, no. 3 (Aug 93), pp. 357 – 372. Bibl, tables.

Padilla, Raymond V. and José E. Náñez. Processing of Simple and Choice Reaction Time Tasks by Chicano Adolescents. *Hispanic Journal of Behavioral Sciences*, v. 15, no. 4 (Nov 93), pp. 498 – 508. Bibl, tables.

Padrón, Justo Jorge
See
Rodríguez Padrón, Justo Jorge

Padrón, Leonardo. El heroe derrotado de la noche occidental (Introduced by María Auxiliadora Alvarez. Article entitled "Voces o seres cercanos"). *Inti*, no. 37 – 38 (Spring – Fall 93), pp. 72 – 75.

Padula Perkins, Jorge Eduardo. Ulrico Schmidel: un periodismo sin periódico. *Todo Es Historia*, v. 27, no. 313 (Aug 93), pp. 88 – 91. Bibl, il.

— Los valesanos tras la esperanza americana: de Suiza a la Confederación Argentina. *Todo Es Historia*, v. 27, no. 316 (Nov 93), pp. 82 – 85. Il.

Padurano, Dominique. Grimanesa Amorós: Mysteries and Metaphors. *Latin American Art*, v. 5, no. 1 (Spring 93), pp. 67 – 69. Il.

Páez Escobar, Gustavo. Germán Pardo García: el ocaso del héroe. *Boletín de Historia y Antigüedades*, v. 79, no. 779 (Oct – Dec 92), pp. 1085 – 1091.

Páez Monzón, Charles R. Discursos y senderos de Briceño Guerrero. *Revista Nacional de Cultura (Venezuela)*, v. 53, no. 285 (Apr – June 92), pp. 115 – 129. Il.

Page, Carlos A. Los cien años del Teatro Mayor de Córdoba. *Todo Es Historia*, v. 26, no. 308 (Mar 93), pp. 56 – 59. Bibl, il.

Page, Joseph A. Brazil's Daredevil of the Air. *Américas*, v. 45, no. 2 (Mar – Apr 93), pp. 6 – 13. Il.

— A Leap for Life. *Américas*, v. 45, no. 4 (July – Aug 93), pp. 34 – 41. Il.

Paige, Jeffrey M. Coffee and Power in El Salvador. *Latin American Research Review*, v. 28, no. 3 (1993), pp. 7 – 40. Bibl.

Pailler, Claire. Avatares del tiempo histórico en dos poetas nicaragüenses de hoy: Ernesto Cardenal y Pablo Antonio Cuadra. *Caravelle*, no. 60 (1993), pp. 85 – 99. Bibl.

— Les indigènes du Costa Rica: éveil d'une conscience? *Caravelle*, no. 59 (1992), pp. 127 – 137. Bibl.

— El reportaje del guerillero: una narrativa ambigua. *Studi di Letteratura Ispano-Americana*, v. 24 (1993), pp. 67 – 82. Tables.

— Severiano Fernández, pueblo bribrí: "el rescate de ser indígena"; entretien réalisé le 16 avril 1992 à San José, par Claire Pailler. *Caravelle,* no. 59 (1992), pp. 49 – 58.

Paim, Antônio. Perspectivas do capitalismo no Brasil. *Convivium,* v. 34, no. 2 (July – Dec 91), pp. 34 – 40.

Palacio, Joseph O. Garifuna Immigrants in Los Angeles: Attempts at Self-Improvements. *Belizean Studies,* v. 20, no. 3 (Dec 92), pp. 17 – 26. Bibl.

— Social and Cultural Implications of Recent Demographic Changes in Belize (The Fourth Annual Signa L. Yorke Memorial Lecture). *Belizean Studies,* v. 21, no. 1 (May 93), pp. 3 – 12. Bibl, tables.

— The Sojourn toward Self Discovery among Indigenous Peoples. *Caribbean Quarterly,* v. 38, no. 2 – 3 (June – Sept 92), pp. 55 – 72.

Palacios, Conny. Acercamiento al "Canto temporal" de Pablo Antonio Cuadra. *Confluencia,* v. 8, no. 1 (Fall 92), pp. 51 – 59.

Palacios L., Juan José. Inversión e integración regional en el Pacífico: entre los acuerdos y los procesos "naturales." *Comercio Exterior,* v. 43, no. 12 (Dec 93), pp. 1128 – 1138. Bibl, tables.

Palacios Maldonado, Carlos. Confusión en el Grupo Andino. *Integración Latinoamericana,* v. 18, no. 194 (Oct 93), pp. 23 – 33.

Palazón Mayoral, María Rosa and Rubén Darío Murrieta. Las verdaderas leyendas de Joaquín Murrieta. *Casa de las Américas,* no. 191 (Apr – June 93), pp. 37 – 49. Bibl.

Paldao, Carlos E. Spreading the Word on Education. *Américas,* v. 45, no. 3 (May – June 93), pp. 54 – 55. Il.

Palencia P., Raúl León and Alejandro Gutiérrez M. Lineamientos de política científica y tecnológica para el estado Mérida: área agrícola agroalimentaria; ideas para la discusión. *Derecho y Reforma Agraria,* no. 23 (1992), pp. 141 – 160. Bibl.

Palermo, Miguel Angel. La etnohistoria en la Argentina: antecedentes y estado actual. *Runa,* v. 20 (1991 – 1992), pp. 145 – 150.

Paley de Francescato, Martha. Elena Poniatowska: convergencias en *La "flor de lis". Hispamérica,* v. 21, no. 62 (Aug 92), pp. 127 – 132.

Pallares, Eugenia. Lacandonia: el último refugio. *Artes de México,* no. 19 (Spring 93), pp. 114 – 115. Il.

Pallottini, Michele. Meditación del mestizo: la otra cara del hispanismo. *Cuadernos Americanos,* no. 39, Nueva época (May – June 93), pp. 167 – 214. Bibl.

Pallottini, Renata. Cuba: os artistas estão vivos. *Vozes,* v. 86, no. 5 (Sept – Oct 92), pp. 32 – 36.

Palm, Risa and Michael E. Hodgson. Natural Hazards in Puerto Rico. *Geographical Review,* v. 83, no. 3 (July 93), pp. 280 – 289. Bibl, tables.

Palma, Eduardo and Dolores María Rufián Lizana. La descentralización de los servicios sociales. *Estudios Sociales (Chile),* no. 77 (July – Sept 93), pp. 73 – 116. Bibl.

Palmer, Steven. Central American Union or Guatemalan Republic?: The National Question in Liberal Guatemala, 1871 – 1885. *The Americas,* v. 49, no. 4 (Apr 93), pp. 513 – 530. Bibl.

— El consumo de heroína entre los artesanos de San José y el pánico moral de 1929. *Revista de Historia (Costa Rica),* no. 25 (Jan – June 92), pp. 29 – 63. Bibl.

— Getting to Know the Unknown Soldier: Offical Nationalism in Liberal Costa Rica, 1880 – 1900. *Journal of Latin American Studies,* v. 25, no. 1 (Feb 93), pp. 45 – 72. Bibl, maps.

Palomero, Federica. Ignacio Iturria (Accompanied by an English translation). *Art Nexus,* no. 7 (Jan – Mar 93), pp. 88 – 90. Il.

Panesi, Jorge. Banquetes en el living: Tamara Kamenszain. *Hispamérica,* v. 22, no. 64 – 65 (Apr – Aug 93), pp. 167 – 175.

Paniagua Pérez, Jesús. Congreso Internacional de Monacato Femenino en España, Portugal y América, 1492 – 1992. *Anuario de Estudios Americanos,* v. 49, Suppl. 1 (1992), pp. 213 – 215.

Panizza, Francisco E. Democracy's Lost Treasure (Review article). *Latin American Research Review,* v. 28, no. 3 (1993), pp. 251 – 266.

— Human Rights: Global Culture and Social Fragmentation. *Bulletin of Latin American Research,* v. 12, no. 2 (May 93), pp. 205 – 214. Bibl.

Pantín, Yolanda. De *Casa o lobo* al *Cielo de París:* el futuro imposible. *Inti,* no. 37 – 38 (Spring – Fall 93), pp. 47 – 55.

Paoletti, Mario Argentino. Tiempo de desprecio. *Cuadernos Hispanoamericanos,* no. 517 – 519 (July – Sept 93), pp. 581 – 586.

Paoli, Roberto. Vallejo: herencia ideal y herencia creadora. *Inti,* no. 36 (Fall 92), pp. 51 – 57. Bibl.

Parada Allende, Maritza. In memoriam. *Revista Musical Chilena,* v. 46, no. 178 (July – Dec 92), p. 131.

Pardo, María del Carmen. La administración pública en México: su desarrollo como disciplina. *Foro Internacional,* v. 33, no. 1 (Jan – Mar 93), pp. 12 – 29. Bibl.

Pardo, Mary Santoli. Creating Community: Mexican American Women in Eastside Los Angeles. *Aztlán,* v. 20, no. 1 – 2 (Spring – Fall 91), pp. 39 – 71. Bibl.

Pardo Murray, Edmée. Las mil cabezas monstruosas sobre la literatura y las escritoras jóvenes en México. *Fem,* v. 17, no. 120 (Feb 93), pp. 12 – 13.

— El reloj de pared. *Plural (Mexico),* v. 22, no. 267 (Dec 93), pp. 71 – 73.

Pardo Pérez, Gastón. Deficiencias de la memoria histórica. *Plural (Mexico),* v. 22, no. 257 (Feb 93), pp. 73 – 75.

Paredes, Cándido A. Relaciones de la agricultura tradicional con el ausentismo y la deserción escolar: el referente empírico del piedemonte barinés. *Derecho y Reforma Agraria,* no. 24 (1993), pp. 63 – 71.

Paredes, Pedro. Etnicidad, clases sociales, resistencia y participación social en los procesos de cambio en Guatemala. *USAC,* no. 13 (Mar 91), pp. 37 – 52. Bibl.

Paredes, Pedro Pablo. Lucas Guillermo Castillo Lara. *Boletín de la Academia Nacional de la Historia (Venezuela),* v. 76, no. 301 (Jan – Mar 93), pp. 128 – 130.

Pareja, Carlos and Romeo Pérez Antón. América y Europa: asimetrías e inmadurez. *Cuadernos del CLAEH,* v. 17, no. 63 – 64 (Oct 92), pp. 81 – 98.

Pareja Ortiz, María del Carmen. Un aspecto de la vida cotidiana: la mujer ante el matrimonio en la legislación de Indias. *Hoy Es Historia,* v. 10, no. 60 (Nov – Dec 93), pp. 50 – 60. Il.

Parejo, Antonio. Historia de Colombia (Previously published in this journal vol. 1, no. 1, 1912). *Boletín de la Academia Nacional de la Historia (Venezuela),* v. 75, no. 300 (Oct – Dec 92), pp. 335 – 348.

Parentelli, Gladys. Teología feminista en América Latina. *Fem,* v. 17, no. 130 (Dec 93), pp. 7 – 12. Bibl.

Parham, Mary Helene. Men in the Short Stories of Rima de Vallbona. *Confluencia,* v. 8, no. 1 (Fall 92), pp. 39 – 49. Bibl.

— Why Toycie Bruk Down: A Study of Zee Edgell's *Beka Lamb. Belizean Studies,* v. 21, no. 2 (Oct 93), pp. 15 – 22. Bibl.

Parker Gumucio, Christián. Primera santa chilena. *Mensaje,* v. 42, no. 418 (May 93), pp. 158 – 159.

Paro, Maria Clara Bonetti. Ronald de Carvalho e Walt Whitman. *Revista de Letras (Brazil),* v. 32 (1992), pp. 141 – 151.

Parodi Zevallos, Carlos and Juan Carlos Mathews. El comercio exterior del Perú con la Comunidad Económica Europea. *Apuntes (Peru),* no. 31 (July – Dec 92), pp. 29 – 39. Tables.

Parotti, Phillip. Heroic Conventions in José Antonio Villarreal's *The Fifth Horseman. Bilingual Review/Revista Bilingüe,* v. 17, no. 3 (Sept – Dec 92), pp. 237 – 241.

Parra Luzardo, Gastón. ¿Hacia dónde nos conduce la política neoliberal? *Desarrollo Indoamericano,* v. 23, no. 91 (June 93), pp. 36 – 40. Il.

Parra M., Augusto. La universidad en un contexto de cambio. *Estudios Sociales (Chile),* no. 75 (Jan – Mar 93), pp. 211 – 223.

Partida Bush, Virgilio. Niveles y tendencias de la migración interna en México a partir de las cifras censales, 1970 – 1990. *Revista Mexicana de Sociología,* v. 55, no. 1 (Jan – Mar 93), pp. 155 – 176. Bibl, tables, charts.

Partida Bush, Virgilio and José Gómez de León. Niveles de mortalidad infantil y fecundidad en México, por entidad federativa, 1990. *Revista Mexicana de Sociología,* v. 55, no. 1 (Jan – Mar 93), pp. 97 – 135. Bibl, tables, charts.

Partida Tayzán, Armando. El año editorial de Hugo Argüelles. *Plural (Mexico),* v. 22, no. 260 (May 93), pp. 69 – 70.

— ¡Jaque al peón! *Plural (Mexico),* v. 22, no. 257 (Feb 93), p. 80.

Pásara, Luis H. El país imprevisible. *Debate (Peru),* v. 16, no. 74 (Sept – Oct 93), pp. 6 – 9. Il.

— Peru: Into a Black Hole. *Hemisphere,* v. 5, no. 2 (Winter – Spring 93), pp. 26 – 30. Tables, charts.

— Rafael Rabinovich. *Debate (Peru),* v. 15, no. 70 (Sept – Oct 92), p. 55. Il.

— El rol del parlamento: Argentina y Perú. *Desarrollo Económico (Argentina),* v. 32, no. 128 (Jan – Mar 93), pp. 603 – 624. Bibl.

Pascual, Liliana. Exitos y fracasos de una innovación educativa en el marco de las instituciones escolares. *Revista Latinoamericana de Estudios Educativos,* v. 23, no. 2 (Apr – June 93), pp. 87 – 104. Bibl.

Pascual Soto, Arturo. Jacques Soustelle (1912 – 1990). *Anales del Instituto de Investigaciones Estéticas,* v. 16, no. 62 (1991), pp. 200 – 202.

Passafari de Gutiérrez, Clara. El dominio del fuego y la noche en San Juan: tradiciones populares de la Argentina. *Folklore Americano,* no. 53 (Jan – June 92), pp. 141 – 150.

Pastor, Beatriz. Utopía y conquista: dinámica utópica e identidad colonial. *Revista de Crítica Literaria Latinoamericana,* v. 19, no. 38 (July – Dec 93), pp. 105 – 113.

Pastor, Beatriz et al. Debate (on the fourth session of the symposium "Latinoamérica: Nuevas Direcciones en Teoría y Crítica Literarias, III"). *Revista de Crítica Literaria Latinoamericana,* v. 19, no. 38 (July – Dec 93), pp. 163 – 169.

Pastor, Robert A. and G. Richard Fletcher. El Caribe en el siglo XXI. *Integración Latinoamericana,* v. 18, no. 187 – 188 (Mar – Apr 93), pp. 13 – 22. Bibl.

Pastor Núñez, Aníbal. Los centros comunales urbanos: una alternativa de extensión educativa y recreación social. *Revista Cultural Lotería,* v. 51, no. 390 (July – Aug 92), pp. 44 – 52. Bibl, il.

— Medicina popular y creencias mágico – religiosas de la población negra del Darién. *Revista Cultural Lotería,* v. 51, no. 387 (Feb 92), pp. 61 – 68. Bibl.

Pastor Poppe, Ricardo. *El tiempo de lo cotidiano* de Raúl Rivadeneira Prada. *Signo,* no. 35, Nueva época (Jan – Apr 92), pp. 77 – 81. Bibl.

Pastori, Luis. Palabras del presidente de la Academia Venezolana de la Lengua, correspondiente de la Real Española, dr. Luis Pastori. *Boletín de la Academia Nacional de la Historia (Venezuela),* v. 75, no. 300 (Oct – Dec 92), pp. 17 – 19.

Pastoriza, Elisa. Dirigentes obreros y política en el marco de la gestación de un peronismo periférico: Mar del Plata, 1935 – 1948. *Todo Es Historia,* v. 27, no. 314 (Sept 93), pp. 32 – 43. Il, tables.

Pastrana Arango, Andrés. En busca de una Bogotá más humana (Previously published in this journal, no. 566, 1990). *Revista Javeriana,* v. 61, no. 596 (July 93), pp. 95 – 101.

Pastrana Borrero, Misael. Memorial de agravios a la constituyente y a la constitución. *Revista Javeriana,* v. 61, no. 598 (Sept 93), pp. 215 – 225.

Patán Tobío, Julio. Ripstein entre nosotros. *Nexos,* v. 16, no. 191 (Nov 93), pp. 73 – 74.

Patiño Castaño, Diógenes. Arqueología del Bajo Patía: fases y correlaciones en la costa pacífica de Colombia y Ecuador. *Latin American Antiquity,* v. 4, no. 2 (June 93), pp. 180 – 199. Bibl, il, tables, maps.

Patrinos, Harry Anthony and George Psacharopoulos. The Cost of Being Indigenous in Bolivia: An Empirical Analysis of Educational Attainments and Outcomes. *Bulletin of Latin American Research,* v. 12, no. 3 (Sept 93), pp. 293 – 309. Bibl, tables, charts.

Patterson, Enrique and Marisela Fleites-Lear. Teoría y praxis de la revolución cubana: apuntes críticos. *Nueva Sociedad,* no. 123 (Jan – Feb 93), pp. 50 – 64.

Pau-Llosa, Ricardo. Conversation with Art Dealer César Segnini. *Latin American Art,* v. 5, no. 2 (Summer 93), pp. 31 – 32. Il.

Pauls, Alan. La retrospectiva intermitente. *Cuadernos Hispanoamericanos,* no. 517 – 519 (July – Sept 93), pp. 470 – 474.

Paupério, Artur Machado. Centenario de *Rerum Novarum. Revista do Instituto Histórico e Geográfico Brasileiro,* no. 372 (July – Sept 91), pp. 766 – 774.

Paxman, Andrew. Art for Sale's Sake. *Business Mexico,* v. 3, no. 3 (Mar 93), pp. 17 – 19. Il.

— The New TV Azteca. *Business Mexico,* v. 3, no. 11 (Nov 93), pp. 39 – 41. Il, tables.

— Selling in a Second Language. *Business Mexico,* v. 3, no. 6 (June 93), pp. 36 – 37.

— Truck Market Picks Up. *Business Mexico,* v. 3, no. 4 (Apr 93), pp. 8 – 10. Tables.

Payán, Humberto. Aviso clasificado: casas. *Plural (Mexico),* v. 22, no. 256 (Jan 93), pp. 26 – 27.

Payne, Anthony John and Paul K. Sutton. The Commonwealth Caribbean in the New World Order: Between Europe and North America? *Journal of Inter-American Studies and World Affairs,* v. 34, no. 4 (Winter 92 – 93), pp. 39 – 75. Bibl.

Paz, Octavio. Buzón entre dos mundos: de Octavio Paz a Luis Buñuel. *Vuelta*, v. 17, no. 201 (Aug 93), pp. 72 – 73.

— La casa de la presencia (Prologue to Volume I of Paz's *Obras completas*). *Vuelta*, v. 17, no. 198 (May 93), pp. 10 – 15.

— Excursiones a incursiones (Prologue to Volume II of Paz's *Obras completas*). *Vuelta*, v. 17, no. 199 (June 93), pp. 8 – 12.

— Instantáneas. *Vuelta*, v. 17, no. 205 (Dec 93), p. 8.

— Pablo Neruda (1904 – 1973). *Vuelta*, v. 17, no. 202 (Sept 93), p. 8.

— Respiro. *Vuelta*, v. 17, no. 197 (Apr 93), p. 10.

— Tránsito y permanencia (Prologue to Volume IV of *Obras completas*). *Vuelta*, v. 17, no. 201 (Aug 93), pp. 8 – 12.

— Unidad, modernidad, tradición (Prologue to Volume III of Paz's *Obras completas*). *Vuelta*, v. 17, no. 200 (July 93), pp. 10 – 13.

Paz Ballivián, Danilo. Cuestión agraria y campesina en Bolivia. *Revista Paraguaya de Sociología*, v. 29, no. 84 (May – Aug 92), pp. 115 – 133.

Paz Zamora, Jaime. La diplomacia de la coca. *Nueva Sociedad*, no. 124 (Mar – Apr 93), pp. 168 – 172.

Pearson, Barbara Z. Predictive Validity of the Scholastic Aptitude Test (SAT) for Hispanic Bilingual Students. *Hispanic Journal of Behavioral Sciences*, v. 15, no. 3 (Aug 93), pp. 342 – 356. Bibl, tables.

Peavler, Terry J. After the Boom: The Coming of Age of Latin American Literary Criticism (Review article). *Latin American Research Review*, v. 28, no. 2 (1993), pp. 221 – 231.

Pedoja Riet, Eduardo. Algunas causas que determinaron la derrota del Partido Nacional en 1966. *Hoy Es Historia*, v. 10, no. 60 (Nov – Dec 93), pp. 34 – 38. Il.

— El caudillaje en Hispanoamérica. *Hoy Es Historia*, v. 10, no. 56 (Mar – Apr 93), pp. 61 – 68.

— Monseñor Escrivá y el Opus Dei. *Hoy Es Historia*, v. 9, no. 54 (Nov – Dec 92), pp. 6 – 10.

Pedraglio, Santiago. De Merlín a Popovic. *Debate (Peru)*, v. 16, no. 73 (June – Aug 93), pp. 22 – 24. Il.

Peire, Jaime Antonio. La manipulación de los capítulos provinciales, las élites y el imaginario socio-político colonial tardío. *Anuario de Estudios Americanos*, v. 50, no. 1 (1993), pp. 13 – 54.

Peire, Jaime Antonio and Carlos Alberto Mayo. Iglesia y crédito colonial: la política crediticia de los conventos de Buenos Aires, 1767 – 1810. *Revista de Historia de América*, no. 112 (July – Dec 91), pp. 147 – 157. Bibl.

Peixoto, Martín. Crisis de la deliberación. *Cuadernos del CLAEH*, v. 18, no. 67 (Nov 93), pp. 69 – 79.

Peixoto, Suzana S. and Elena Landau. Inflação, indexação e preços relativos: novas evidências para o Brasil. *Pesquisa e Planejamento Econômico*, v. 22, no. 1 (Apr 92), pp. 125 – 167. Bibl, tables, charts.

Peláez, Jorge Humberto. El invitado del mes: interrogantes éticos de la reproducción asistida. *Revista Javeriana*, v. 61, no. 595 (June 93), pp. 337 – 344. Il.

Pelegrí Pedrosa, Luis Vicente. XI Jornadas de Andalucía y América: "Huelva y América." *Anuario de Estudios Americanos*, v. 49, Suppl. I (1992), pp. 204 – 209.

Pelegrin, Jacques and Claude Chauchat. Tecnología y función de las puntas de Paiján: el aporte de la experimentación. *Latin American Antiquity*, v. 4, no. 4 (Dec 93), pp. 367 – 382. Bibl, il, tables, charts.

Pelkmans, Jacques. Comparando las integraciones económicas: prerrequisitos, opciones e implicaciones. *Integración Latinoamericana*, v. 18, no. 191 (July 93), pp. 3 – 17. Tables.

Pell, George. *Rerum Novarum:* cien años después. *Estudios Públicos (Chile)*, no. 50 (Fall 93), pp. 177 – 200. Bibl.

Pellegrini, Josué Alfredo. As funções do Banco Central do Brasil e o contrôle monetário. *Estudos Econômicos*, v. 22, no. 2 (May – Aug 92), pp. 221 – 252. Bibl, tables.

Pellettieri, Osvaldo. Actualidad del sainete en el teatro argentino. *Cuadernos Hispanoamericanos*, no. 517 – 519 (July – Sept 93), pp. 421 – 436. Bibl, il.

— Los '80: el teatro porteño entre la dictadura y la democracia. *Cuadernos Hispanoamericanos*, no. 517 – 519 (July – Sept 93), pp. 313 – 322.

— El teatro argentino en su período finisecular, 1700 – 1930: un sistema teatral y sus intertextos. *Conjunto*, no. 89 (Oct – Dec 91), pp. 2 – 6. Bibl.

Pellizzi, Francesco. La colección Pellizzi de textiles de Chiapas (Accompanied by an English translation). *Artes de México*, no. 19 (Spring 93), pp. 75 – 79. Il.

Pellón, Gustavo. The Canon, the Boom, and Literary Theory. *Latin American Literary Review*, v. 20, no. 40 (July – Dec 92), pp. 80 – 82.

Peluso, Daniela. Conservation and Indigenismo. *Hemisphere*, v. 5, no. 2 (Winter – Spring 93), pp. 6 – 8.

Peña, Antonio. La ciencia y los salarios. *Nexos*, v. 16, no. 190 (Oct 93), pp. 12 – 16.

Pena, Maria Valéria Junho. O surgimento do imposto de renda: um estudo sobre a relação entre estado e mercado no Brasil. *Dados*, v. 35, no. 3 (1992), pp. 337 – 370. Bibl.

Peña Guerrero, Roberto. Los proyectos latinoamericanos: ¿Libre comercio o integración fragmentada? *Relaciones Internacionales (Mexico)*, v. 14, Nueva época, no. 56 (Oct – Dec 92), pp. 55 – 61.

Peñalosa, Fernando. El cuento popular: patrimonio del pueblo maya del sur de Mesoamérica. *Folklore Americano*, no. 52 (July – Dec 91), pp. 39 – 92. Bibl.

Peñalosa, Raúl. Evaluating Management Seminars. *Business Mexico*, v. 3, no. 7 (July 93), pp. 42 – 43. Il.

Pendergast, David Michael et al. Locating Maya Lowlands Spanish Colonial Towns: A Case Study from Belize. *Latin American Antiquity*, v. 4, no. 1 (Mar 93), pp. 59 – 73. Bibl, il, maps.

Pennefather, Joan. La equidad en todas las etapas de la creación: ¡Eso es lo que cuenta! *Fem*, v. 17, no. 130 (Dec 93), pp. 24 – 25.

Pepin Lehalleur, Marielle. Regiones y poder local en el Golfo de México: los andamios de un programa de investigación. *Estudios Sociológicos*, v. 10, no. 30 (Sept – Dec 92), pp. 517 – 522. Maps.

Pepin Lehalleur, Marielle and Marie-France Prévôt-Schapira. Cuclillos en un nido de gorrión: espacio municipal y poder local en Altamira, Tamaulipas. *Estudios Sociológicos*, v. 10, no. 30 (Sept – Dec 92), pp. 583 – 617. Bibl, maps.

Pera, Cristóbal. Alienación (europeización) o introversión (incesto): Latinoamérica y Europa en *Cien años de soledad*. *Chasqui*, v. 22, no. 2 (Nov 93), pp. 85 – 93. Bibl.

Peralta, Mario and Bernardo Malaver. Venezuela: el inicio de una nueva coyuntura política. *Revista Paraguaya de Sociología*, v. 29, no. 84 (May – Aug 92), pp. 41 – 51. Bibl.

Peraza Martell, Elina and Tomás Amadeo Vasconi B. Social Democracy and Latin America (Translated by Fred Murphy). *Latin American Perspectives,* v. 20, no. 1 (Winter 93), pp. 99 – 113. Bibl.

Perazzo, Nelly. Xul Solar: la imaginación desenfrenada (Accompanied by an English translation). *Art Nexus,* no. 8 (Apr – June 93), pp. 96 – 100. Il.

Perea, Héctor. Arte escondido de Oaxaca (Accompanied by an English translation). *Artes de México,* no. 21 (Fall 93), pp. 48 – 53. Il.

Perea Dallos, Margarita. Biotecnología y agricultura. *Revista Javeriana,* v. 61, no. 591 (Jan – Feb 93), pp. 35 – 40. Bibl, charts.

Peregrino, Umberto. Discurso do sócio-benemérito general Umberto Peregrino Seabra Fagundes, na inauguração do Museu de Arte Popular, em 23 de outubro de 1991. *Revista do Instituto Histórico e Geográfico Brasileiro,* no. 373 (Oct – Dec 91), pp. 1201 – 1203.

Pereira, Antônio Carlos. As transformações na Europa e o Brasil. *Política e Estratégica,* v. 8, no. 2 – 4 (Apr – Dec 90), pp. 168 – 191.

Pereira, José Maria. Os trinta anos de *A inflação brasileira* de Ignácio Rangel. *Revista de Economia Política (Brazil),* v. 13, no. 3 (July – Sept 93), pp. 144 – 149. Bibl.

Pereira, Laércio Barbosa. O estado e o desempenho da agricultura paranaense no período de 1975 – 1985. *Revista de Economia e Sociologia Rural,* v. 30, no. 2 (Apr – June 92), pp. 115 – 133. Bibl, tables.

Pereira, Luiz Carlos Bresser. Estabilização em um ambiente adverso: a experiência brasileira de 1987. *Revista de Economia Política (Brazil),* v. 13, no. 4 (Oct – Dec 93), pp. 16 – 36. Bibl.

Pereira, Luiz Carlos Bresser and José Márcio Rego. Um mestre da economia brasileira: Ignácio Rangel. *Revista de Economia Política (Brazil),* v. 13, no. 2 (Apr – June 93), pp. 98 – 119.

Perelli, Carina. Corruption and Democracy. *Hemisphere,* v. 5, no. 2 (Winter – Spring 93), pp. 31 – 32. Il.

Perelman Fajardo, Juan Adolfo. Altiplano. *Signo,* no. 38, Nueva época (Jan – Apr 93), pp. 183 – 186.

Peres Núñez, Wilson. The Internationalization of Latin American Industrial Firms. *CEPAL Review,* no. 49 (Apr 93), pp. 55 – 74. Bibl, tables.

Pérez, Alberto Julián. La poesía de Eduardo Mitre en el contexto de la poesía latinoamericana contemporánea. *Signo,* no. 36 – 37, Nueva época (May – Dec 92), pp. 23 – 42. Bibl.

Pérez, Benito. El minero. *Signo,* no. 38, Nueva época (Jan – Apr 93), p. 201.

Pérez, Carlos Andrés. Venezuela: Decreto 1633 que crea la reserva de biosfera Delta del Orinoco. *Anuario Indigenista,* v. 30 (Dec 91), pp. 497 – 502.

— Venezuela: Decreto 1635 que declara reserva de biosfera el sector sureste del territorio federal Amazonas. *Anuario Indigenista,* v. 30 (Dec 91), pp. 503 – 508.

— Venezuela: Decreto 1636 que crea el parque nacional Parima – Tapirapeco en el alto Orinoco. *Anuario Indigenista,* v. 30 (Dec 91), pp. 509 – 512.

Pérez, Emma Marie. "She Has Served Others in More Intimate Ways": The Domestic Servant Reform in Yucatán, 1915 – 1918. *Aztlán,* v. 20, no. 1 – 2 (Spring – Fall 91), pp. 11 – 37. Bibl.

Pérez, Félix. Félix Pérez: medio siglo de memoria sindical (A chapter from his autobiography entitled *Hicimos patria trabajando). Todo Es Historia,* v. 27, no. 314 (Sept 93), pp. 84 – 92. Il.

Pérez, Hildebrando. Poems ("María Fénix, tahona feliz, María Capulí," "Guy"). *Casa de las Américas,* no. 191 (Apr – June 93), pp. 88 – 89.

Pérez, Sonia M. and Denise De la Rosa Salazar. Economic, Labor Force, and Social Implications of Latino Educational and Population Trends. *Hispanic Journal of Behavioral Sciences,* v. 15, no. 2 (May 93), pp. 188 – 229. Bibl, tables, charts.

Pérez, Tibisay and Eugenio Sanhueza. Concentraciones atmosféricas y estimación de las emisiones H2S en la saba de Trachypogon, Calabozo, estado Guárico, Venezuela. *Interciencia,* v. 18, no. 2 (Mar – Apr 93), pp. 83 – 87. Bibl, il, tables, maps, charts.

Pérez Alencart, Alfredo. Todas las historias de Guillermo Morón, un venezolano en Salamanca. *Boletín de la Academia Nacional de la Historia (Venezuela),* v. 75, no. 299 (July – Sept 92), pp. 163 – 164.

Pérez Antón, Romeo. Glosario para la reforma política. *Cuadernos del CLAEH,* v. 18, no. 67 (Nov 93), pp. 113 – 119.

Pérez Antón, Romeo and Carlos Pareja. América y Europa: asimetrías e inmadurez. *Cuadernos del CLAEH,* v. 17, no. 63 – 64 (Oct 92), pp. 81 – 98.

Pérez Calderón, Luis Jorge. Medio ambiente y desarrollo: el Decenio Internacional para la Reducción de los Desastres Naturales. *Amazonía Peruana,* v. 11, no. 21 (Sept 92), pp. 175 – 180.

Pérez Celis. Through the Eyes of the Heart. *Américas,* v. 45, no. 2 (Mar – Apr 93), pp. 56 – 59. Il.

Pérez de Tudela y Bueso, Juan. El descubrimiento: historia de secretos y de secretismos rigurosos. *Boletín de Historia y Antigüedades,* v. 80, no. 780 (Jan – Mar 93), pp. 31 – 70. Bibl.

Pérez Firmat, Gustavo. My Critical Condition. *Latin American Literary Review,* v. 20, no. 40 (July – Dec 92), pp. 83 – 84.

— Poems ("Lime Cure," "The Poet's Mother Gives Him a Birthday Present"). *The Americas Review,* v. 20, no. 3 – 4 (Fall – Winter 92), pp. 253 – 254.

— Poems. *The Americas Review,* v. 20, no. 1 (Spring 92), pp. 38 – 44.

Pérez Gay, Rafael. Benito Juárez perdido en el norte de México. *Nexos,* v. 16, no. 182 (Feb 93), pp. 21 – 22.

Pérez Gay, Rafael and Angeles Mastretta. Días de parque, futbol y confesiones. *Nexos,* v. 16, no. 181 (Jan 93), pp. 17 – 20.

Pérez Gil, Sara Elena et al. La salud y la nutrición de las mujeres en México. *El Cotidiano,* v. 9, no. 53 (Mar – Apr 93), pp. 84 – 92. Il, tables.

Pérez González, María Luisa. La organización sociopolítica del grupo chol – manché en Guatemala durante el siglo XVII: estudio preliminar. *Colonial Latin American Historical Review,* v. 2, no. 1 (Winter 93), pp. 57 – 75. Bibl.

Pérez González-Rubio, Jesús. Casi no reconozco la constitución que aprobé. *Revista Javeriana,* v. 61, no. 597 (Aug 93), pp. 175 – 181.

Pérez Hernández, Francisco Javier. Cinco siglos de lexicografía del español en Venezuela. *Montalbán,* no. 24 (1992), pp. 119 – 166. Bibl.

Pérez Jérez, Cristóbal. Políticas de ajuste estructural y reforma del estado. *USAC,* no. 14 (June 91), pp. 56 – 70. Bibl.

Pérez Leyva, Leonardo. Algunas consideraciones sobre la filosofía existencialista de Ernesto Mayz Vallenilla. *Islas,* no. 96 (May – Aug 90), pp. 27 – 33.

— Arturo Andrés Roig: algunas consideraciones sobre su pensamiento filosófico. *Islas,* no. 99 (May – Aug 91), pp. 87 – 94. Bibl.

Pérez-López, René. Recent Work in Cuban Studies. *Cuban Studies/Estudios Cubanos,* v. 23 (1993), pp. 245 – 275.

Pérez Maldonado, Alberto. La reforma agraria: un proceso de transformación social y una política del estado; base de un desarrollo integral del país. *Derecho y Reforma Agraria,* no. 23 (1992), pp. 123 – 133. Bibl.

Pérez Marchelli, Héctor. Bibliografía sobre Vicente Marcano, 1848 – 1891. *Boletín de la Academia Nacional de la Historia (Venezuela),* v. 75, no. 299 (July – Sept 92), pp. 207 – 212.

Pérez Molina de Lara, Olga. Cultura y sociedad: la empresa del V centenario: su significancia para el reino de España y el gobierno de Guatemala. *Folklore Americano,* no. 53 (Jan – June 92), pp. 81 – 90.

Pérez Morales, Constantino Alberto. Fortalecimiento municipal para el desarrollo regional en Oaxaca. *Problemas del Desarrollo,* v. 24, no. 92 (Jan – Mar 93), pp. 137 – 169. Tables.

Pérez Ochoa, Eduardo. El problema de guerra irregular referido en los congresos del Instituto Histórico y Geográfico del Brasil, IHGB. *Estudos Ibero-Americanos,* v. 18, no. 1 (July 92), pp. 71 – 88. Bibl.

Pérez Oramas, Luis. Cuadros en una exposición (Accompanied by an English translation). *Art Nexus,* no. 9 (June – Aug 93), pp. 59 – 61. Il.

— José Gamarra: después del Edén (Accompanied by an English translation). *Art Nexus,* no. 8 (Apr – June 93), pp. 92 – 94. Il.

Pérez Pérez, Gabriel. El SME ante el reto de la modernización del sector eléctrico. *El Cotidiano,* v. 10, no. 58 (Oct – Nov 93), pp. 98 – 102. Il.

Pérez Piera, Adolfo. Reforma del estado: otra vuelta de tuerca. *Cuadernos del CLAEH,* v. 18, no. 65 – 66 (May 93), pp. 87 – 96.

Pérez Priego, Rosalba. Las mujeres en Vasconcelos. *La Palabra y el Hombre,* no. 81 (Jan – Mar 92), pp. 341 – 348. Bibl.

Pérez-Rayón, Nora. Iglesia y estado ante el desafío de la credibilidad. *El Cotidiano,* v. 10, no. 58 (Oct – Nov 93), pp. 79 – 85. Bibl, il.

Pérez Sáinz, Juan Pablo et al. Trayectorias laborales y constitución de identidades: los trabajadores indígenas en la ciudad de Guatemala. *Estudios Sociológicos,* v. 11, no. 32 (May – Aug 93), pp. 515 – 545. Bibl, tables.

Pérez Tenreiro, Tomás. 12 de octubre de 1492 – 12 de octubre de 1992. *Boletín de la Academia Nacional de la Historia (Venezuela),* v. 75, no. 300 (Oct – Dec 92), pp. 116 – 117.

— Presentación del libro *Vida del general Carlos Soublette, 1789 – 1870,* escrito por el académico profesor J. A. Armas Chitty y editado por la Comisión Nacional Bicentenario general en jefe, Carlos Soublette. *Boletín de la Academia Nacional de la Historia (Venezuela),* v. 75, no. 299 (July – Sept 92), pp. 27 – 28.

Pérez Toledo, Sonia and Herbert S. Klein. La población de la ciudad de Zacatecas en 1857. *Historia Mexicana,* v. 42, no. 1 (July – Sept 92), pp. 77 – 102. Bibl, tables, charts.

Pérez Tomás, Eduardo E. Nuevo aporte al esclarecimiento de un punto relativo a la "cuestión vespuciana." *Revista de Historia de América,* no. 113 (Jan – June 92), pp. 103 – 138. Bibl, tables, charts.

Pérez Tzu, María and Rosha Hernández Díaz. Mujer florida (Translated by Ambar Past). *Artes de México,* no. 19 (Spring 93), p. 60. Il.

Pérez V., Carlos. América Latina: marca registrada. *Mensaje,* v. 42, no. 416 (Jan – Feb 93), pp. 20 – 21.

Pérez Villacampa, Gilberto. Enjuiciamiento advertido de la sombra de Colón. *Islas,* no. 98 (Jan – Apr 91), pp. 98 – 118.

— Enrique Dussel: ¿De la metafísica de la alteridad al humanismo real? *Islas,* no. 99 (May – Aug 91), pp. 160 – 167.

— *Filosofía de la liberación* de Enrique Dussel: apuntes sobre un diario íntimo. *Islas,* no. 97 (Sept – Dec 90), pp. 52 – 63. Bibl.

— Horacio Cerutti y el problema del fin de la filosofía clásica de la liberación. *Islas,* no. 99 (May – Aug 91), pp. 168 – 172.

— Utopía y marxismo: notas para un estudio. *Islas,* no. 96 (May – Aug 90), pp. 83 – 88.

Pérez-Yglesias, María. Entre lo escolar y los medios informativos: políticas neoliberales y educación. *Revista de Ciencias Sociales (Costa Rica),* no. 57 (Sept 92), pp. 41 – 55. Bibl.

Pérez Yoma, Marisi. Hugo Yaconi: solidaridad entre empresarios. *Mensaje,* v. 42, no. 421 (Aug 93), pp. 376 – 377. Il.

Pérez Zamora, Flor de María. *Al filo del agua:* la modificación de una estructura social. *Káñina,* v. 16, no. 2 (July – Dec 92), pp. 81 – 87.

— La religión: isotopía estructurante en *Al filo del agua. Káñina,* v. 16, no. 1 (Jan – June 92), pp. 69 – 77. Bibl.

Pereznieto Castro, Leonel. Algunos aspectos del sistema de solución de controversias en el Tratado Norteamericano de Libre Comercio. *Relaciones Internacionales (Mexico),* v. 15, Nueva época, no. 58 (Apr – June 93), pp. 69 – 77. Bibl.

Perfetti, Mauricio. Algunas precisiones en cuanto a la reforma de la seguridad social. *Revista Javeriana,* v. 61, no. 592 (Mar 93), pp. 102 – 100. Bibl, tables.

Peri Rossi, Cristina. La última romántica. *Nuevo Texto Crítico,* v. 6, no. 11 (1993), pp. 253 – 254.

Peritore, N. Patrick. El surgimiento del cártel biotecnológico. *Revista Mexicana de Sociología,* v. 54, no. 2 (Apr – June 92), pp. 101 – 131. Bibl, tables.

Peritore, N. Patrick and Ana Karina Galve-Peritore. Cleavage and Polarization in Mexico's Ruling Party: A Field Study of the 1988 Presidential Election. *Journal of Developing Areas,* v. 28, no. 1 (Oct 93), pp. 67 – 88. Bibl, tables.

Perlongher, Néstor. Introducción a la poesía neobarroca cubana y rioplatense. *Revista Chilena de Literatura,* no. 41 (Apr 93), pp. 47 – 57. Bibl.

Pero, Valéria Lúcia. A carteira de trabalho no mercado de trabalho metropolitano brasileiro. *Pesquisa e Planejamento Econômico,* v. 22, no. 2 (Aug 92), pp. 305 – 342. Bibl, tables, charts.

Perrone, Charles A. *Axé, Ijexá, Olodum:* The Rise of Afro- and African Currents in Brazilian Popular Music. *Afro-Hispanic Review,* v. 11, no. 1 – 3 (1992), pp. 42 – 50. Bibl.

Perry, William E. and Timon L. Marshall. Defending Anti-dumping Actions. *Business Mexico,* v. 3, no. 8 (Aug 93), pp. 26 – 28.

Persia, Jorge de. Aspectos de la vida y obra de músicos españoles emigrados a Argentina en los años de la guerra civil. *Revista Musical de Venezuela,* no. 28 (May – Dec 89), pp. 165 – 182.

Peruyero Sánchez, Alfredo. *Los recuerdos del tiempo* de Carlos Juan Islas. *La Palabra y el Hombre*, no. 84 (Oct – Dec 92), pp. 259 – 267. Il.

Pesavento, Sandra Jatahy. Exposições universais: palcos de exibição do mundo burguês; em cena: Brasil e Estados Unidos. *Siglo XIX: Revista*, no. 12, 2a época (July – Dec 92), pp. 63 – 85. Bibl.

Pescador, Alejandro. Un mambo con sabor a bolero. *La Palabra y el Hombre*, no. 81 (Jan – Mar 92), pp. 269 – 272. Il.

Pescador C., Juan Javier. La demografía histórica mexicana. *Estudios Demográficos y Urbanos*, v. 7, no. 1 (Jan – Apr 92), pp. 7 – 17.

— La nupcialidad urbana preindustrial y los límites del mestizaje: características y evolución de los patrones de nupcialidad en la ciudad de México, 1700 – 1850. *Estudios Demográficos y Urbanos*, v. 7, no. 1 (Jan – Apr 92), pp. 137 – 168. Bibl, tables.

Pescador Osuna, José Angel. Acuerdo Nacional para la Modernización de la Educación Básica: una visión integral. *El Cotidiano*, v. 8, no. 51 (Nov – Dec 92), pp. 3 – 11. Il, tables.

Peschard, Jacqueline. Entre lo nuevo y lo viejo: la sucesión de 1994. *El Cotidiano*, v. 10, no. 58 (Oct – Nov 93), pp. 3 – 7. Il.

— El fin del sistema de partido hegemónico. *Revista Mexicana de Sociología*, v. 55, no. 2 (Apr – June 93), pp. 97 – 117. Bibl, tables.

— Una reforma para la ciudad capital. *El Cotidiano*, v. 9, no. 54 (May 93), pp. 37 – 40. Il.

Pesquera, Beatriz Margarita. "Work Gave Me a Lot of Confianza": Chicanas' Work Commitment and Work Identity. *Aztlán*, v. 20, no. 1 – 2 (Spring – Fall 91), pp. 97 – 118. Bibl.

Pessoa, Pedro F. Adeodato de Paula and José de Jesus Sousa Lemos. Mercado de exportação e estabilização de preços externos para amêndoas de castanha de caju. *Revista de Economia e Sociologia Rural*, v. 30, no. 2 (Apr – June 92), pp. 171 – 187. Bibl, tables, charts.

Peterson, Gabriela and Víctor Valembois. Los epígrafes en *El siglo de las luces*: su interpretación; de Goya a Carpentier. *Káñina*, v. 16, no. 2 (July – Dec 92), pp. 89 – 100. Bibl, il, tables.

— Los epígrafes en *El siglo de las luces*: su ubicación; de Goya a Carpentier. *Káñina*, v. 16, no. 1 (Jan – June 92), pp. 79 – 89. Bibl, il.

Petras, James F. Una pequeña parte de la lucha (Response to the article "Between Skepticism and Protocol" by Carlos María Vilas). *Nueva Sociedad*, no. 123 (Jan – Feb 93), pp. 165 – 170.

— Reply (to the article "Between Skepticism and Protocol" by Carlos María Vilas). *Latin American Perspectives*, v. 20, no. 2 (Spring 93), pp. 107 – 110.

Petras, James F. and Morris H. Morley. Latin America: Poverty and the Democracy of Poverty. *Homines*, v. 15 – 16, no. 2 – 1 (Oct 91 – Dec 92), pp. 75 – 94. Bibl.

Pfeiffer, Wolfgang. Exvotos en Brasil (Translated by Ricardo Barda). *Humboldt*, no. 110 (1993), pp. 90 – 93. Il.

Pfromm Netto, Samuel. Caminhamos para trás. *Problemas Brasileiros*, v. 30, no. 295 (Jan – Feb 93), pp. 45 – 47. Il.

Phaf, Ineke. La introducción emblemática de la nación mulata: el contrapunteo híbrido en las culturas de Suriname y Cuba. *Revista de Crítica Literaria Latinoamericana*, v. 19, no. 38 (July – Dec 93), pp. 195 – 215. Bibl.

Phillips, Fred P., IV and Steven M. Rubin. Debt for Nature: Swap Meet for the '90s. *Business Mexico*, v. 3, no. 1 (Jan – Feb 93), pp. 46 – 47.

Phillips, Graciela. Para una pianista. *Plural (Mexico)*, v. 22, no. 263 (Aug 93), pp. 72 – 73.

Piaggio, Laura Raquel. Fotos, historia, indios y antropólogos. *Runa*, v. 20 (1991 – 1992), pp. 163 – 166. Bibl.

Pichón Rivière, Marcelo. La irrealidad de una literatura y el despertar del mercado. *Cuadernos Hispanoamericanos*, no. 517 – 519 (July – Sept 93), pp. 511 – 513.

Pichs Madruga, Ramón. Problemas y opciones del sector energético cubano. *Problemas del Desarrollo*, v. 24, no. 92 (Jan – Mar 93), pp. 197 – 208. Bibl.

Pieropan, María D. Alfonsina Storni y Clara Lair: de la mujer posmodernista a la mujer "moderna." *Hispania (USA)*, v. 76, no. 4 (Dec 93), pp. 672 – 682. Bibl.

Pierre-Charles, Gérard. El Caribe en el mundo. *Cuadernos Americanos*, no. 40, Nueva época (July – Aug 93), pp. 78 – 83.

Pierro, Maria Inês Valente and Sílvia Pimentel. Proposta de lei contra a violência familiar. *Estudos Feministas*, v. 1, no. 1 (1993), pp. 169 – 175.

Pietschmann, Horst. Entstehung und innere Auswirkungen der lateinamerikanischen Schuldenkrise. *Jahrbuch für Geschichte von Staat, Wirtschaft und Gesellschaft Lateinamerikas*, v. 29 (1992), pp. 421 – 444. Bibl, tables.

Pieza, Ramón. Análisis coyuntural de la industria textil mexicana. *Momento Económico*, no. 65 (Jan – Feb 93), pp. 31 – 34. Tables.

— Análisis cuantitativo de la evolución del proceso industrial de septiembre de 1989 a junio de 1992 con datos trimestrales. *Problemas del Desarrollo*, v. 24, no. 92 (Jan – Mar 93), pp. 40 – 48. Tables.

— PEMEX frente a la nación mexicana: su integración al proceso de desarrollo nacional. *Momento Económico*, no. 68 (July – Aug 93), pp. 23 – 28. Tables.

Piga T., Domingo. Homenaje al medio siglo de TEUCH. *Latin American Theatre Review*, v. 26, no. 2 (Spring 93), pp. 197 – 198.

Piglia, Ricardo. The Absent City (Translated by Alfred MacAdam). *Review*, no. 47 (Fall 93), pp. 83 – 86.

— Ficción y política en la literatura argentina. *Cuadernos Hispanoamericanos*, no. 517 – 519 (July – Sept 93), pp. 514 – 516.

Pijning, Ernst. Conflicts in the Portuguese Colonial Administration: Trials and Errors of Luís Lopes Pegado e Serpa, "provedor-mor da fazenda real" in Salvador, Brazil, 1718 – 1721. *Colonial Latin American Historical Review*, v. 2, no. 4 (Fall 93), pp. 403 – 423. Bibl, maps.

Pimentel, Sílvia and Maria Inês Valente Pierro. Proposta de lei contra a violência familiar. *Estudos Feministas*, v. 1, no. 1 (1993), pp. 169 – 175.

Piña, Cristina. La narrativa argentina de los años setenta y ochenta. *Cuadernos Hispanoamericanos*, no. 517 – 519 (July – Sept 93), pp. 121 – 138. Bibl.

Piña, Juan Andrés. Estética del "mall." *Mensaje*, v. 42, no. 424 (Nov 93), pp. 567 – 568. Il.

— Modos y temas del teatro chileno: la voz de los ochenta. *Conjunto*, no. 89 (Oct – Dec 91), pp. 28 – 32. Il.

Pineda, Rafael. Poems ("Vicente Gerbasi y los talismanes," "Jonathan Swift y Aquiles Nazoa se visitan"). *Revista Nacional de Cultura (Venezuela)*, v. 53, no. 286 (July – Sept 92), pp. 111 – 115.

Piñero, Eugenio. Accounting Practices in a Colonial Economy: A Case Study of Cacao Haciendas in Venezuela, 1700 – 1770. *Colonial Latin American Historical Review*, v. 1, no. 1 (Fall 92), pp. 37 – 66. Bibl, tables.

Pinheiro, Armando Castelar and Fábio Giambiagi. As empresas estatais e o programa de privatização do governo Collor. *Pesquisa e Planejamento Econômico*, v. 22, no. 2 (Aug 92), pp. 241 – 288. Bibl, tables.

Pinheiro, Letícia. Restabelecimento de relações diplomáticas com a República Popular da China: uma análise do processo de tomada de decisão. *Estudos Históricos*, v. 6, no. 12 (July – Dec 93), pp. 247 – 270. Bibl.

Pinho, Wanderley

See

Wanderley Pinho, José

Pini, Ivonne. Ante América (Accompanied by an English translation). *Art Nexus*, no. 7 (Jan – Mar 93), pp. 60 – 64. Il.

Pinilla Cote, Alfonso María. ¿La historia: alabanza o diatriba? *Boletín de Historia y Antigüedades*, v. 80, no. 780 (Jan – Mar 93), pp. 11 – 21.

Pino, Diego A. del. El barrio porteño de Boedo. *Todo Es Historia*, v. 26, no. 310 (May 93), pp. 84 – 94. Il.

— José González Castillo y el mundo literario de Boedo. *Todo Es Historia*, v. 27, no. 311 (June 93), pp. 84 – 92. Bibl, il, maps.

Pino Díaz, Fermín del. Indianismo, hispanismo y antropología: acerca de la identidad autóctona de los indios de América. *Revista de Indias*, v. 52, no. 195 – 196 (May – Dec 92), pp. 825 – 838.

Pinochet de la Barra, Oscar. Recuerdos de la Conferencia del Tratado Antártico de 1959. *Estudios Internacionales (Chile)*, v. 26, no. 102 (Apr – June 93), pp. 268 – 274.

Piñón, Francisco José. Educación y procesos de integración económica: el caso del MERCOSUR. *La Educación (USA)*, v. 37, no. 114 (1993), pp. 19 – 32. Bibl, tables.

Piñón A., Rosa María. América Latina y el Caribe en el nuevo orden capitalista mundial: Estados Unidos, Japón y Comunidad Europea. *Relaciones Internacionales (Mexico)*, v. 14, Nueva época, no. 56 (Oct – Dec 92), pp. 7 – 18. Tables.

Pinto, Márnio Teixeira. Corpo, morte e sociedade: um ensaio a partir da forma e da razão de se esquartejar um inimigo. *Revista Brasileira de Ciências Sociais*, v. 8, no. 21 (Feb 93), pp. 52 – 67. Bibl, charts.

Pinto Santa Cruz, Aníbal. Notas sobre estilos de desarrollo: origen, naturaleza y esquema conceptual. *Revista Paraguaya de Sociología*, v. 29, no. 84 (May – Aug 92), pp. 91 – 99. Bibl.

Piotti Núñez, Diosma Elena. La escuela primaria como generadora y reproductora de contenidos sexistas en la sociedad uruguaya. *La Educación (USA)*, v. 36, no. 111 – 113 (1992), pp. 97 – 110.

Piqueras Céspedes, Ricardo. Alfínger y Portolá: dos modelos de frontera. *Boletín Americanista*, v. 33, no. 42 – 43 (1992 – 1993), pp. 107 – 121. Bibl.

Pires, Nielsen de Paula. Brasil: transición, crisis y triunfo de la democracia. *Mensaje*, v. 42, no. 417 (Mar – Apr 93), pp. 79 – 81. Il.

— Escollos a la democracia: Haití y Perú. *Mensaje*, v. 42, no. 425 (Dec 93), pp. 646 – 648. Il.

Pitanguy, Jacqueline. Um estudo americano sobre violência no Brazil. *Estudos Feministas*, v. 1, no. 1 (1993), pp. 150 – 151.

Pites, Silvia. Entrevista con Abel Posse. *Chasqui*, v. 22, no. 2 (Nov 93), pp. 120 – 128. Bibl.

Pitol, Sergio. Julio Galán: la lección del sí y el no. *Vuelta*, v. 17, no. 204 (Nov 93), pp. 21 – 25.

Pizarro, Ana. Gabriela Mistral en el discurso cultural. *Escritura (Venezuela)*, v. 16, no. 31 – 32 (Jan – Dec 91), pp. 215 – 221. Bibl.

— Para ser jóvenes en cien años más. *Casa de las Américas*, no. 191 (Apr – June 93), pp. 5 – 7.

Pizarro, Roberto. Las negociaciones comerciales Chile – Bolivia: vacilaciones chilenas y sensibilidades bolivianas. *Mensaje*, v. 42, no. 417 (Mar – Apr 93), pp. 99 – 100.

Plá León, Rafael. La idea del mestizaje en representantes del positivismo en Argentina y México en el siglo XIX. *Islas*, no. 98 (Jan – Apr 91), pp. 135 – 142. Bibl.

— Marxismo: ¿Eurocentrismo o universidad? *Islas*, no. 96 (May – Aug 90), pp. 132 – 138. Bibl.

Plá León, Rafael and Mirta Casañas Díaz. La constancia de Leopoldo Zea en la búsqueda de un filosofar auténticamente americano. *Islas*, no. 99 (May – Aug 91), pp. 95 – 111. Bibl.

Planchart, Alfredo. Bases científicas del descubrimiento de América. *Boletín de la Academia Nacional de la Historia (Venezuela)*, v. 75, no. 297 (Jan – Mar 92), pp. 97 – 109. Bibl.

Planells, Antonio. Borges y Narciso: dos espejos enfrentados. *Hispanic Journal*, v. 13, no. 2 (Fall 92), pp. 213 – 239. Bibl.

Platt, Kamala. Race and Gender Representation in Clarice Lispector's "A menor mulher do mundo" and Carolina Maria de Jesus' *Quarto de despejo*. *Afro-Hispanic Review*, v. 11, no. 1 – 3 (1992), pp. 51 – 57. Bibl.

Platt, Tristán. Simón Bolívar, the Sun of Justice, and the Amerindian Virgin: Andean Conceptions of the "Patria" in Nineteenth-Century Potosí. *Journal of Latin American Studies*, v. 25, no. 1 (Feb 93), pp. 159 – 185. Bibl.

Plaza Martínez, Pedro. Tendencias sociolingüísticas en Bolivia. *Signo*, no. 35, Nueva época (Jan – Apr 92), pp. 117 – 138. Bibl, tables.

Plentz, Leopoldo. Ensaio fotográfico: a miséria estética (Includes poems by Nei Duclós, Henrique do Valle, and João Angelo Salvadori). *Vozes*, v. 86, no. 6 (Nov – Dec 92), pp. 82 – 91. Il.

Pliego, Roberto. Don Juan en calzoncillos: una entrevista a Carlos Cuarón. *Nexos*, v. 16, no. 183 (Mar 93), pp. 62 – 63.

— Los emblemas del metal: una entrevista con Guillermo del Toro. *Nexos*, v. 16, no. 186 (June 93), pp. 85 – 86.

Pliego Carrasco, Fernando. Estrategias de desarrollo social en situaciones de desastre. *Revista Mexicana de Sociología*, v. 54, no. 4 (Oct – Dec 92), pp. 11 – 24.

Poblete B., Renato. El Hogar de Cristo. *Mensaje*, v. 42, no. 420 (July 93), pp. 290 – 291. Il, tables.

Podalsky, Laura. Disjointed Frames: Melodrama, Nationalism, and Representation in 1940s Mexico. *Studies in Latin American Popular Culture*, v. 12 (1993), pp. 57 – 53. Bibl.

Polanco Alcántara, Tomás. Palabras del dr. Tomás Polanco Alcántara en la Biblioteca Nacional de Lisboa, 7 de mayo de 1992. *Boletín de la Academia Nacional de la Historia (Venezuela)*, v. 76, no. 301 (Jan – Mar 93), pp. 47 – 49.

— Palabras leídas por Tomás Polanco Alcántara. *Boletín de la Academia Nacional de la Historia (Venezuela)*, v. 75, no. 298 (Apr – June 92), pp. 35 – 37.

Poli, Beatriz Trois Cunha and Jairo Laser Procianoy. A política de dividendos como geradora de economia fiscal e do desenvolvimento do mercado de capitais: uma proposta criativa. *RAE; Revista de Administração de Empresas*, v. 33, no. 4 (July – Aug 93), pp. 6 – 15. Bibl, tables.

Pollak-Eltz, Angelina. Aportes españoles a la cultura popular venezolana. *Montalbán,* no. 24 (1992), pp. 167 – 219. Bibl.

Pollard, Helen Perlstein. Merchant Colonies, Semi-Mesoamericans, and the Study of Cultural Contact: A Comment on Anawalt (Comment on the article "Ancient Cultural Contacts between Ecuador, West Mexico, and the American Southwest" by Patricia Anawalt which appeared in this journal in 1992). *Latin American Antiquity,* v. 4, no. 4 (Dec 93), pp. 383 – 385. Bibl.

Pollard, Velma. Drake's Straight Revisited (from Virgin Island's Suite). *Caribbean Quarterly,* v. 38, no. 2 – 3 (June – Sept 92), p. 32.

— Drake's Strait (from Virgin Island's Suite). *Caribbean Quarterly,* v. 38, no. 2 – 3 (June – Sept 92), pp. vi – vii.

— Drake's Strait Remembered (from Virgin Island's Suite). *Caribbean Quarterly,* v. 38, no. 2 – 3 (June – Sept 92), p. 113.

Pollarolo, Giovanna. Catalina y sus hermanas. *Debate (Peru),* v. 16, no. 74 (Sept – Oct 93), pp. 61 – 62. Il.

Pomareda, Carlos and Alfonso Cebreros. Mecanismos financieros para la modernización de la agricultura. *Comercio Exterior,* v. 43, no. 4 (Apr 93), pp. 328 – 335. Bibl, tables, charts.

Pomer, León. El animal que imagina. *Revista de Letras (Brazil),* v. 32 (1992), pp. 153 – 167. Bibl.

Pompa Quiroz, María del Carmen. La mujer acerca de sí misma en el cuento y la novela del Paraguay. *Feminaria,* v. 6, no. 11, Suppl. (Nov 93), pp. 17 – 20. Bibl.

Pompeu, Paulo de Tarso. Nas malhas da rodovia. *Problemas Brasileiros,* v. 30, no. 295 (Jan – Feb 93), pp. 37 – 39. Il.

Ponce, Gilberto. *Turandot* en el Municipal. *Mensaje,* v. 42, no. 424 (Nov 93), pp. 594 – 595. Il.

Ponce, Mary Helen. Three Stories ("Campesinas," "Onions," "Granma's Apron"). *Aztlán,* v. 20, no. 1 – 2 (Spring – Fall 91), pp. 177 – 182.

Ponce de León, Ernesto Zedillo

See

Zedillo Ponce de León, Ernesto

Ponce Jasso, Silvia. La problemática de las mujeres escritoras en el sureste. *Fem,* v. 17, no. 120 (Feb 93), pp. 4 – 6.

Ponce Leiva, Pilar. Un espacio para la controversia: la Audiencia de Quito en el siglo XVIII. *Revista de Indias,* v. 52, no. 195 – 196 (May – Dec 92), pp. 839 – 865. Bibl.

Poniatowska, Elena. El otro gran arte. *Nexos,* v. 16, no. 183 (Mar 93), pp. 31 – 38. Il.

Pons, María Cristina. Compromiso político y ficción en "Segunda vez" y "Apocalipsis de Solentiname" de Julio Cortázar. *Revista Mexicana de Sociología,* v. 54, no. 4 (Oct – Dec 92), pp. 183 – 203. Bibl.

Poo, Jorge. Los signos de la barbarie: la búsqueda de culpables en épocas de crisis. *Hoy Es Historia,* v. 10, no. 58 (July – Aug 93), pp. 84 – 85.

Poole, Deborah A. Adaptación y resistencia en la danza ritual andina. *Conjunto,* no. 89 (Oct – Dec 91), pp. 13 – 27. Bibl, il.

Poole, Deborah A. and Gerardo Rénique. Perdiendo de vista al Perú: réplica a Orin Starn. *Allpanchis,* v. 23, no. 39 (Jan – June 92), pp. 73 – 92. Bibl.

Poole, Linda J. CIM: Making Women's Rights Human Rights. *Américas,* v. 45, no. 2 (Mar – Apr 93), pp. 48 – 49.

Poot Herrera, Sara. *La hija del judío:* entre la inquisición y la imprenta. *Nueva Revista de Filología Hispánica,* v. 40, no. 2 (July – Dec 92), pp. 761 – 777. Bibl.

Porras Cardozo, Baltazar Enrique. Discurso de orden en la sesión solemne de la Academia Nacional de la Historia en homenaje al bicentenario de la muerte de fray Juan Ramos de Lora, Aula Magna de la Universidad de los Andes, 30 de marzo de 1990. *Boletín de la Academia Nacional de la Historia (Venezuela),* v. 76, no. 302 (Apr – June 93), pp. 7 – 14.

Porras Duarte, Salvador T. and Luis Bueno Rodríguez. Deshomologación salarial: ¿Cuánto por punto? *El Cotidiano,* v. 9, no. 55 (June 93), pp. 91 – 98. Tables, charts.

Porrini Beracochea, Rodolfo. ¿Mitin contra la dictadura o huelga contra la burguesía? *Hoy Es Historia,* v. 10, no. 58 (July – Aug 93), pp. 19 – 26. Bibl, il.

Portal, Marta. *Gringo viejo:* diálogo de culturas. *Cuadernos Americanos,* no. 39, Nueva época (May – June 93), pp. 217 – 227. Bibl.

Portella, Eduardo. La reconstrucción de la ciudad hacia la nueva sociedad. *Cuadernos Americanos,* no. 39, Nueva época (May – June 93), pp. 74 – 76.

Portillo, Luis. El Convenio Internacional de Café y la crisis del mercado. *Comercio Exterior,* v. 43, no. 4 (Apr 93), pp. 378 – 391. Bibl, tables.

Portocarrero de Guzmán, Blancanieve. El derecho agrario iberoamericano: su vocación regional. *Derecho y Reforma Agraria,* no. 24 (1993), pp. 43 – 52. Bibl.

Portos, Irma. Notas sobre textiles en Estados Unidos y México. *Momento Económico,* no. 69 (Sept – Oct 93), pp. 10 – 12. Tables.

Portuondo Zúñiga, Olga. Criollidad y patria local en campo geométrico. *Islas,* no. 98 (Jan – Apr 91), pp. 40 – 46.

Posada, Jaime. Don Antonio Nariño, ideólogo de la emancipación. *Boletín de Historia y Antigüedades,* v. 80, no. 781 (Apr – June 93), pp. 435 – 442.

Posada, Marcelo Germán. La conformación del perfil del empresariado pecuario: el caso del partido de Mercedes (Buenos Aires, Argentina), 1850 – 1890. *Revista de Historia de América,* no. 112 (July – Dec 91), pp. 159 – 177. Bibl, tables, charts.

— Crisis estatal y nuevo entramado social: la emergencia de las organizaciones no gubernamentales; el rol de las ONGs en el agro argentino. *Revista Paraguaya de Sociología,* v. 29, no. 85 (Sept – Dec 92), pp. 99 – 131. Bibl.

Possuelo, Sydney Ferreira. Brasil: Decreto 828/91 que crea la Comisión de Defensa de los Derechos Indígenas. *Anuario Indigenista,* v. 30 (Dec 91), pp. 457 – 459.

Postel, Sandra L. Last Oasis (Excerpt from the book of the same title, part of the *Worldwatch Environmental Alert Series*). *Business Mexico,* v. 3, no. 1 (Jan – Feb 93), pp. 67 – 70. Il.

Potter, Robert B. Caribbean Views on Environment and Development: A Cognitive Perspective. *Caribbean Geography,* v. 3, no. 4 (Sept 92), pp. 236 – 243. Bibl, tables.

Pou, Francis. Inmigración de agricultores españoles a la República Dominicana en el período Franco – Trujillo, 1939 – 1961. *Revista de Indias,* v. 53, no. 198 (May – Aug 93), pp. 563 – 582. Bibl, tables, charts.

Poujade, Ruth. Poblamiento prehistórico y colonial de Misiones. *Estudos Ibero-Americanos,* v. 18, no. 1 (July 92), pp. 29 – 70. Bibl, maps.

Pourrut, Pierre. L'effet "ENSO" sur les précipitations et les écoulements au XXème siècle: exemple de l'Equateur. *Bulletin de l'Institut Français d'Etudes Andines*, v. 22, no. 1 (1993), pp. 85 – 98. Bibl, tables, maps, charts.

Pozas Horcasitas, Ricardo. El desarrollo de la seguridad social en México. *Revista Mexicana de Sociología*, v. 54, no. 4 (Oct – Dec 92), pp. 27 – 63.

Pozzi, Pablo Alejandro. Estados Unidos entre la crisis y la legitimidad. *Realidad Económica*, no. 113 (Jan – Feb 93), pp. 103 – 121. Bibl, tables.

Prada Oropeza, Renato. Los condenados de la tierra. *Plural (Mexico)*, v. 22, no. 262 (July 93), pp. 63 – 70.

— *Dominio de la tarde:* el verbo grave. *Plural (Mexico)*, v. 22, no. 258 (Mar 93), pp. 57 – 63. Bibl.

Prado, Gustavo and Manuel E. Tron. Tri-lateral Taxation. *Business Mexico*, v. 3, no. 3 (Mar 93), pp. 40 – 45.

Prado Arai, Sumie and Federico Díaz Sustaeta. Estudio de las actitudes de los estudiantes de posgrado de la Universidad Iberoamericana ante las metas de la institución. *Revista Latinoamericana de Estudios Educativos*, v. 23, no. 2 (Apr – June 93), pp. 71 – 85. Bibl, tables.

Pratt, Dale J. Feminine Freedom/Metafictional Autonomy in *Los largos días. Chasqui*, v. 22, no. 2 (Nov 93), pp. 94 – 102. Bibl.

Pratt, Mary Louise. La liberación de los márgenes: literaturas canadiense y latinoamericana en el contexto de la dependencia. *Casa de las Américas*, no. 190 (Jan – Mar 93), pp. 25 – 33. Bibl.

— Las mujeres y el imaginario nacional en el siglo XIX (Excerpt from a forthcoming book entitled *Latin American Narrative and Cultural Discourse* edited by Steve Bell et al.). *Revista de Crítica Literaria Latinoamericana*, v. 19, no. 38 (July – Dec 93), pp. 51 – 62. Bibl.

Pratts, Alexandra. Poems ("Orfandad de la memoria," "Improvisación no. 2"). *Letras Femeninas*, v. 19, no. 1 – 2 (Spring – Fall 93), pp. 167 – 169.

Preble-Niemi, Oralia. *Pedro Páramo* and the Anima Archetype. *Hispanic Journal*, v. 13, no. 2 (Fall 92), pp. 363 – 373. Bibl.

Precht B., Cristián. Mirando el futuro. *Mensaje*, v. 42, no. 420 (July 93), p. 333.

Preiswerk, Matías and Xavier Albó. El Gran Poder: fiesta del aimara urbano. *América Indígena*, v. 51, no. 2 – 3 (Apr – Sept 91), pp. 293 – 352. Bibl, tables, maps.

Premazzi, Javier. La España de la conquista y la América indígena. *Hoy Es Historia*, v. 9, no. 54 (Nov – Dec 92), pp. 27 – 38.

Prescott, Laurence E. "Negro nací": Authorship and Voice in Verses Attributed to Candelario Obeso. *Afro-Hispanic Review*, v. 12, no. 1 (Spring 93), pp. 3 – 15. Bibl.

Prestes, Anita Leocadia. Luiz Carlos Prestes e a revolução socialista. *Vozes*, v. 87, no. 2 (Mar – Apr 93), pp. 11 – 17. Il.

Prévôt-Schapira, Marie-France. Argentine: fédéralisme et territoires. *Cahiers des Amériques Latines*, no. 14 (1992), pp. 4 – 32. Bibl, tables, maps.

Prévôt-Schapira, Marie-France and Marielle Pepin Lehalleur. Cuclillos en un nido de gorrión: espacio municipal y poder local en Altamira, Tamaulipas. *Estudios Sociológicos*, v. 10, no. 30 (Sept – Dec 92), pp. 583 – 617. Bibl, maps.

Pries, Ludger. Aspectos del mercado de trabajo en Puebla: la relación entre trabajo asalariado y por cuenta propia. *El Cotidiano*, v. 8, no. 52 (Jan – Feb 93), pp. 31 – 37. Bibl, il, charts.

— Movilidad en el empleo: una comparación de trabajo asalariado y por cuenta propia en Puebla. *Estudios Sociológicos*, v. 11, no. 32 (May – Aug 93), pp. 475 – 496. Bibl, charts.

Prieto Taboada, Antonio. El caso de las pistas culturales en *Partners in Crime. The Americas Review*, v. 19, no. 3 – 4 (Winter 91), pp. 117 – 132. Bibl.

Procianoy, Jairo Laser and Beatriz Trois Cunha Poli. A política de dividendos como geradora de economia fiscal e do desenvolvimento do mercado de capitais: uma proposta criativa. *RAE; Revista de Administração de Empresas*, v. 33, no. 4 (July – Aug 93), pp. 6 – 15. Bibl, tables.

Pronk, Jan and Mahbubul Haq. Desarrollo sostenible: del concepto a la acción. *El Trimestre Económico*, v. 59, no. 236 (Oct – Dec 92), pp. 799 – 815.

Protzel, Javier. Industrias electorales y culturas políticas. *Estado y Sociedad*, v. 8, no. 9 (Jan – June 92), pp. 1 – 12.

Proust, Marcel. El eclipse (Introduced and translated by Javier García Méndez). *Plural (Mexico)*, v. 22, no. 264 (Sept 93), pp. 40 – 42.

Psacharopoulos, George and Harry Anthony Patrinos. The Cost of Being Indigenous in Bolivia: An Empirical Analysis of Educational Attainments and Outcomes. *Bulletin of Latin American Research*, v. 12, no. 3 (Sept 93), pp. 293 – 309. Bibl, tables, charts.

Puchet Anyul, Martín. La economía durante los '80: notas para un debate sobre sus cambios analíticos y profesionales. *Desarrollo Económico (Argentina)*, v. 33, no. 129 (Apr – June 93), pp. 49 – 65. Bibl.

Puente Lafoy, Patricio de la et al. Familia, vecindario y comunidad: un modelo sistémico para la interpretación del desarrollo progresivo. *Estudios Sociales (Chile)*, no. 76 (Apr – June 93), pp. 149 – 167. Bibl.

Puga, Cristina and Matilde Luna. Modernización en México: la propuesta empresarial. *Revista Mexicana de Ciencias Políticas y Sociales*, v. 38, Nueva época, no. 151 (Jan – Mar 93), pp. 35 – 49. Bibl.

Puga, Mariano. ¡Corran el riesgo! *Mensaje*, v. 42, no. 420 (July 93), p. 334.

Puglia, Sergio. El choque y la mezcla de los sabores (Excerpts from a transcribed interview by Elvio E. Gandolfo). *Cuadernos del CLAEH*, v. 17, no. 63 – 64 (Oct 92), pp. 155 – 160.

Pujol, Sergio Alejandro. Canto y contracanto. *Cuadernos Hispanoamericanos*, no. 517 – 519 (July – Sept 93), pp. 389 – 399. Bibl, il.

— Un estilo italiano. *Todo Es Historia*, v. 26, no. 305 (Dec 92), pp. 28 – 33. Bibl, il.

— "Rock" y juventud: de las catacumbas al estrellato. *Todo Es Historia*, v. 27, no. 317 (Dec 93), pp. 70 – 73. Il.

Pulido Jiménez, Juan José. El humor satírico en *El eterno femenino* de Rosario Castellanos. *Revista Canadiense de Estudios Hispánicos*, v. 17, no. 3 (Spring 93), pp. 483 – 494. Bibl.

Pursifull, Carmen M. Poems ("Tourist," "The Bed," "Nineteen Sixty Nine in Jacksonville Beach," "Mourning in a Parallel Universe," "To You on Wave No. Negative 4"). *The Americas Review*, v. 19, no. 2 (Summer 91), pp. 42 – 59.

Pusineri Scala, Carlos Alberto. Oratorio de San Carlos en la estancia de Olivares. *Estudios Paraguayos*, v. 17, no. 1 – 2 (1989 – 1993), pp. 121 – 147. Il, tables.

Puwainchir, Miguel. The Voice of the Ecuadorian Amazon. *Grassroots Development*, v. 16, no. 2 (1992), p. 40.

Quackenbush, Louis Howard. La realidad detrás de la realidad: Gonzalo Rojas y lo numinoso. *Chasqui,* v. 22, no. 1 (May 93), pp. 23 – 30.

Quandt, Midge. Nicaragua: Unbinding the Ties; Popular Movements and the FSLN. *Report on the Americas,* v. 26, no. 4 (Feb 93), pp. 11 – 14. Il.

Queiroz Júnior, Teófilo de. Dois exemplos de mulher satânica na literatura latino-americana. *Vozes,* v. 87, no. 4 (July – Aug 93), pp. 20 – 29.

Quer Antich, Santiago. Conspiremos por la democracia o la democracia "a la Maturana." *Estudios Sociales (Chile),* no. 76 (Apr – June 93), pp. 197 – 203.

Querales, Juan Bautista. Relaciones de Venezuela con la Santa Sede, 1830 – 1835. *Boletín de la Academia Nacional de la Historia (Venezuela),* v. 75, no. 298 (Apr – June 92), pp. 93 – 95.

Querales, Juandemaro. El Decreto 321: la iglesia como factor aglutinador de la oposición a los gobiernos de Betancourt y Gallegos. *Boletín de la Academia Nacional de la Historia (Venezuela),* v. 75, no. 299 (July – Sept 92), pp. 180 – 183. Bibl.

Quesada, Uriel. El juego de la ruta definitiva. *La Palabra y el Hombre,* no. 82 (Apr – June 92), pp. 258 – 259.

Quesada Lastiri, Patricia. Con mi Señor. *Letras Femeninas,* v. 19, no. 1 – 2 (Spring – Fall 93), pp. 188 – 189.

Quesada Monge, Rodrigo. El paraíso perdido: nueva historia y utopía en Costa Rica. *Revista de Historia (Costa Rica),* no. 26 (July – Dec 92), pp. 187 – 200. Bibl.

— Quinto centenario y ciencias sociales. *Revista de Historia (Costa Rica),* no. 25 (Jan – June 92), pp. 221 – 226.

Quesada Pacheco, Jorge Arturo. La neutralización fonética: más acá del Caribe. *Káñina,* v. 16, no. 1 (Jan – June 92), pp. 165 – 169. Bibl.

Quesada Pacheco, Miguel Angel. Correspondencia de Carlos Gagini con Rufino José Cuervo y Ricardo Palma. *Káñina,* v. 16, no. 1 (Jan – June 92), pp. 197 – 206.

Quesada Soto, Alvaro. Identidad nacional y literatura nacional en Costa Rica: la "generación del Olimpo." *Canadian Journal of Latin American and Caribbean Studies,* v. 17, no. 34 (1992), pp. 97 – 113. Bibl.

Quetzal

See

Girón Mena, Manuel Antonio

Quevedo, Raul. Realidade e mitos do Rio Grande antigo. *Vozes,* v. 87, no. 4 (July – Aug 93), pp. 86 – 90. Il.

Quezada, Freddy. Nicaragua: en busca de un nuevo rumbo. *Nueva Sociedad,* no. 123 (Jan – Feb 93), pp. 18 – 22.

Quijada Mauriño, Mónica. De Perón a Alberdi: selectividad étnica y construcción nacional en la política inmigratoria argentina. *Revista de Indias,* v. 52, no. 195 – 196 (May – Dec 92), pp. 867 – 888. Bibl.

Quijano, José Manuel. Integración competitiva para los nuevos países industrializados en América Latina. *Integración Latinoamericana,* v. 18, no. 193 (Sept 93), pp. 3 – 11. Bibl, tables.

Quijano, Rosario and María del Carmen Ortiz de Terra. En busca de la memoria histórica de la mujer. *Hoy Es Historia,* v. 10, no. 55 (Jan – Feb 93), pp. 53 – 57.

Quijano Guerrero, Alberto. Dos caciques legendarios. *Boletín de Historia y Antigüedades,* v. 80, no. 780 (Jan – Mar 93), pp. 71 – 77.

Quillen, Joan A. and George F. Elmendorf. Mexico's Environmental and Ecological Organizations and Movements. *SALALM Papers,* v. 36 (1991), pp. 123 – 129.

— Serials and Government Documents from the States of Mexico. *SALALM Papers,* v. 36 (1991), pp. 425 – 431.

Quilodrán de Aguirre, Julieta. Cambios y permanencias de la nupcialidad en México. *Revista Mexicana de Sociología,* v. 55, no. 1 (Jan – Mar 93), pp. 17 – 40. Bibl, tables, maps, charts.

Quintanilla, Víctor G. Problemas y consecuencias ambientales sobre el bosque de Alerce, "Fitzroya Cupressoides (Mol) Johnst," debido a la explotación de la cordillera costera de Chile austral. *Revista Geográfica (Mexico),* no. 114 (July – Dec 91), pp. 54 – 72. Bibl, il, maps, charts.

Quintanilla Jiménez, Ifigenia. La Malla: un sitio arqueológico asociado con el uso de recursos del Manglar de Tivives, Pacífico central de Costa Rica. *Vínculos,* v. 16, no. 1 – 2 (1990), pp. 57 – 83. Bibl, il, tables, maps.

Quintanilla Jiménez, Ifigenia and Francisco Corrales Ulloa. El Pacífico central de Costa Rica y el intercambio regional. *Vínculos,* v. 16, no. 1 – 2 (1990), pp. 111 – 126. Bibl, tables, maps.

Quintero, Alfredo E. Dos poemas ("Memoria de yerba y sexo," "El canta con las manos"). *Plural (Mexico),* v. 22, no. 261 (June 93), pp. 45 – 47.

Quintero, Fernando. Cesantías y pensiones: el reordenamiento laboral. *Revista Javeriana,* v. 61, no. 592 (Mar 93), pp. 81 – 85. Tables.

Quintero Esquivel, Jorge Eliécer. Ergotismo, ilustración y utilitarismo en Colombia: siglos XVIII y XIX. *Islas,* no. 96 (May – Aug 90), pp. 53 – 66. Bibl, tables, charts.

Quintero Herencia, Juan Carlos. Los poetas en La Pampa o las "cantidades poéticas" en el *Facundo. Hispamérica,* v. 21, no. 62 (Aug 92), pp. 33 – 52.

Quintero Ramírez, Cirila. Flexibilidad sindical en las maquiladoras: el caso de Agapito González Cavazos. *El Cotidiano,* v. 8, no. 52 (Jan – Feb 93), pp. 92 – 96.

— Tendencias sindicales en la frontera norte de México. *El Cotidiano,* v. 9, no. 56 (July 93), pp. 41 – 46.

Quintero Ramírez, Cirila and María Eugenia Martínez. Sindicalismo y contratación colectiva en las maquiladoras fronterizas: los casos de Tijuana, Ciudad Juárez y Matamoros. *Frontera Norte,* v. 4, no. 8 (July – Dec 92), pp. 7 – 47. Bibl, tables.

Quintero Rivera, Angel Guillermo. El tambor oculto en el cuatro: la melodización de ritmos y la etnicidad cimarroneada en la caribeña cultura de la contraplantación. *Boletín Americanista,* v. 33, no. 42 – 43 (1992 – 1993), pp. 87 – 106. Bibl, facs.

Quiroga, Giancarla de. La mujer poeta en la sociedad. *Signo,* no. 38, Nueva época (Jan – Apr 93), pp. 123 – 130.

Quiroga, Hugo. Los derechos humanos en la Argentina: entre el realismo político y la ética. *Cuadernos Hispanoamericanos,* no. 517 – 519 (July – Sept 93), pp. 77 – 92. Bibl.

Quiroga Micheo, Ernesto. El hermano Bernardo, el gran pecador. *Todo Es Historia,* v. 27, no. 312 (July 93), pp. 48 – 59. Bibl, il, facs.

— Los mazorqueros: ¿Gente decente o asesinos? *Todo Es Historia,* v. 26, no. 308 (Mar 93), pp. 38 – 55. Bibl, il, facs.

Quirós, Juan. La lengua de Cervantes y la nuestra. *Signo,* no. 36 – 37, Nueva época (May – Dec 92), pp. 275 – 277.

Quirós, Oscar E. Values and Aesthetics in Cuban Arts and Cinema. *SALALM Papers,* v. 34 (1989), pp. 151 – 171. Bibl.

Quispe Arce, Juan. Variaciones de la temperatura superficial del mar en Puerto Chicama y del índice de oscilación del sur, 1925 – 1992. *Bulletin de l'Institut Français d'Etudes Andines,* v. 22, no. 1 (1993), pp. 111 – 124. Bibl, tables, charts.

Rabanal, Rodolfo. Reflexiones sobre una realidad objetable. *Todo Es Historia,* v. 27, no. 317 (Dec 93), pp. 62 – 65. Il.

Rabell, Carmen R. Cervantes y Borges: relaciones intertextuales en "Pierre Ménard, autor del Quijote." *Revista Chilena de Literatura,* no. 42 (Aug 93), pp. 201 – 207. Bibl.

Rabell Romero, Cecilia Andrea. Matrimonio y raza en una parroquia rural: San Luis de la Paz, Guanajuato, 1715 – 1810. *Historia Mexicana,* v. 42, no. 1 (July – Sept 92), pp. 3 – 44. Bibl, tables, charts.

Rabell Romero, Cecilia Andrea and Marta Mier y Terán. Inicio de la transición de la fecundidad en México: descendencias de mujeres nacidas en la primera mitad del siglo XX. *Revista Mexicana de Sociología,* v. 55, no. 1 (Jan – Mar 93), pp. 41 – 81. Bibl, tables, charts.

Rabey, Mario A. and Rodolfo J. Merlino. Resistencia y hegemonía: cultos locales y religión centralizada en los Andes del sur. *Allpanchis,* v. 23, no. 40 (July – Dec 92), pp. 173 – 200. Bibl.

Rabkin, Rhoda Pearl. The Aylwin Government and "Tutelary" Democracy: A Concept in Search of a Case? *Journal of Inter-American Studies and World Affairs,* v. 34, no. 4 (Winter 92 – 93), pp. 119 – 194. Bibl, tables.

Rabow, Jerome and Kathleen A. Rodriguez. Socialization toward Money in Latino Families: An Exploratory Study of Gender Differences. *Hispanic Journal of Behavioral Sciences,* v. 15, no. 3 (Aug 93), pp. 324 – 341. Bibl.

Rachum, Ilan. Intellectuals and the Emergence of the Latin American Political Right, 1917 – 1936. *European Review of Latin American and Caribbean Studies,* no. 54 (June 93), pp. 95 – 110. Bibl.

Radomski, James. Manuel García in Mexico: Part II. *Inter-American Music Review,* v. 13, no. 1 (Fall – Winter 92), pp. 15 – 20. Facs.

Rago, Margareth. Prazer e sociabilidade no mundo da prostituição em São Paulo, 1890 – 1930. *Luso-Brazilian Review,* v. 30, no. 1 (Summer 93), pp. 35 – 46. Bibl.

Raine, Philip. Rebeliones de los comuneros paraguayos. *Hoy Es Historia,* v. 10, no. 57 (Apr – May 93), pp. 54 – 60.

Rajchenberg, Enrique and Catherine Héau de Giménez. La leyenda negra y la leyenda rosa en la nueva historiografía de la revolución mexicana. *Revista Mexicana de Sociología,* v. 54, no. 3 (July – Sept 92), pp. 175 – 188. Bibl.

— Región y nación: una antigua polémica resucitada. *Revista Mexicana de Ciencias Políticas y Sociales,* v. 38, Nueva época, no. 154 (Oct – Dec 93), pp. 19 – 34. Bibl.

Ramharack, Baytoram. Consociational Democracy: A Democratic Option for Guyana. *Caribbean Studies,* v. 25, no. 1 – 2 (Jan – July 92), pp. 75 – 101. Bibl.

Ramires, Julio Cesar Lima. As grandes corporações e a dinâmica socioespacial: a ação da PETROBRAS em Macaé. *Revista Brasileira de Geografia,* v. 53, no. 4 (Oct – Dec 91), pp. 115 – 151. Bibl, tables, maps.

Ramírez, Fermín. Daniel Chavarría: al mundo clásico vía Macondo. *Plural (Mexico),* v. 22, no. 260 (May 93), pp. 23 – 26.

— Elías Nandino: con el hervor del fuego en llamas. *Plural (Mexico),* v. 22, no. 266 (Nov 93), pp. 78 – 80.

— Jaime Labastida, poeta en la hora del saber. *Plural (Mexico),* v. 22, no. 261 (June 93), pp. 16 – 22.

— José Luis Cuevas, ave de tempestades. *Plural (Mexico),* v. 22, no. 265 (Oct 93), pp. 42 – 48. Il.

— María Eugenia Figueroa, pintora de luz y tierra (Includes reproductions of her paintings). *Plural (Mexico),* v. 22, no. 267 (Dec 93), pp. 41 – 48. Il.

— Moreno Capdevila, un boceto vespertino (Includes reproductions by the artist). *Plural (Mexico),* v. 22, no. 264 (Sept 93), pp. 66 – 75. Il.

— El paisaje de Jesús Martínez. *Plural (Mexico),* v. 22, no. 261 (June 93), pp. 48 – 54. Il.

— Un poeta de luz: Eliseo Diego. *Plural (Mexico),* v. 22, no. 263 (Aug 93), pp. 66 – 67.

Ramírez, Jorge Enrique. ¿Qué haces por la paz? *Revista Javeriana,* v. 61, no. 595 (June 93), pp. 346 – 347.

Ramírez, Miguel D. Stabilization and Trade Reform in Mexico, 1983 – 1989. *Journal of Developing Areas,* v. 27, no. 2 (Jan 93), pp. 173 – 190. Bibl, tables, charts.

Ramírez, Pablo A. La extraordinaria popularidad de Boca Juniors. *Todo Es Historia,* v. 26, no. 310 (May 93), pp. 74 – 78. Il.

Ramírez, Sergio

See
    Ramírez Mercado, Sergio

Ramírez, Socorro. Sujetos y no objetos de las políticas de población. *Fem,* v. 17, no. 121 (Mar 93), pp. 13 – 14.

Ramírez Acuña, Luis Fernando. Privatización en las administraciones tributarias. *Planeación y Desarrollo,* v. 24, no. 2 (May – Aug 93), pp. 341 – 372.

Ramírez Bonilla, Juan José. ¿Hacia la creación de la comunidad del Pacífico? *Comercio Exterior,* v. 43, no. 12 (Dec 93), pp. 1139 – 1144. Tables.

Ramírez Carrillo, Luis Alfonso. El escenario de la industrialización en Yucatán. *Comercio Exterior,* v. 43, no. 2 (Feb 93), pp. 171 – 177. Bibl, tables.

— Estratificación, clase y parentesco: empresarios libaneses en el sureste de México. *Nueva Antropología,* v. 13, no. 43 (Nov 92), pp. 123 – 137. Bibl.

Ramírez Castilla, Gustavo A. En torno a la restauración de monumentos arqueológicos en México. *La Palabra y el Hombre,* no. 84 (Oct – Dec 92), pp. 165 – 178. Bibl.

Ramírez Cuellar, Alfonso. La reforma necesaria. *El Cotidiano,* v. 9, no. 54 (May 93), pp. 24 – 29. Il, tables.

Ramírez de Jara, María Clemencia. Los quillacinga y su posible relación con grupos prehispánicos del oriente ecuatoriano. *Revista Colombiana de Antropología,* v. 29 (1992), pp. 27 – 61. Bibl, maps.

Ramírez-Horton, Susan Elizabeth. Recent Writing on the Peoples of the Andes (Review article). *Latin American Research Review,* v. 28, no. 3 (1993), pp. 174 – 182. Bibl.

Ramírez León, José Luis. La OEA en su laberinto. *Revista Javeriana,* v. 61, no. 594 (May 93), pp. 247 – 255. Bibl.

Ramírez López, Berenice Patricia. El desempeño de la economía latinoamericana durante 1992. *Momento Económico,* no. 66 (Mar – Apr 93), pp. 23 – 27.

Ramírez Lozano, Eduardo and Antonio Marquet. El inestable equilibrio del caos. *Plural (Mexico),* v. 22, no. 262 (July 93), pp. 57 – 62.

Ramírez Mercado, Sergio. Oficios compartidos. *Nuevo Texto Crítico,* v. 6, no. 11 (1993), pp. 245 – 252.

Ramírez Miranda, César and Joel Cervantes Herrera. México: del imperio del maíz al maíz del imperio. *Problemas del Desarrollo,* v. 24, no. 94 (July – Sept 93), pp. 97 – 112. Tables.

Ramírez Montes, Mina. Un ensamblador poblano en Querétaro: Luis Ramos Franco. *Anales del Instituto de Investigaciones Estéticas,* v. 16, no. 62 (1991), pp. 151 – 161. Bibl.

Ramírez Morales, Fernando. Apuntes para una historia ecológica de Chile. *Cuadernos de Historia (Chile),* no. 11 (Dec 91), pp. 149 – 196. Bibl, tables.

Ramírez Murzi, Marco. Palabras de Marco Ramírez Murzi en la entrega del premio Círculo de Escritores, 1991. *Boletín de la Academia Nacional de la Historia (Venezuela),* v. 75, no. 298 (Apr – June 92), p. 33.

Ramírez Quintero, Gonzalo. La poesía venezolana actual: tres ejemplos. *Inti,* no. 37 – 38 (Spring – Fall 93), pp. 187 – 195.

Ramírez Quirós, Ileana. Mujer y SIDA: la exclusión de la mujer de las campañas comunicacionales. *Revista de Ciencias Sociales (Costa Rica),* no. 58 (Dec 92), pp. 11 – 22. Bibl.

Ramírez Rancaño, Mario. La organización obrera y campesina en Tlaxcala durante el cardenismo. *Revista Mexicana de Sociología,* v. 54, no. 3 (July – Sept 92), pp. 189 – 219. Bibl, tables.

Ramírez Vallejo, Jorge. Una nueva mirada a la reforma agraria colombiana. *Planeación y Desarrollo,* v. 24, no. 1 (Jan – Apr 93), pp. 425 – 461. Bibl, tables, charts.

Ramón Folch, Armando de. Don Luis Valencia Avaria. *Boletín de la Academia Chilena de la Historia,* v. 58 – 59, no. 102 (1991 – 1992), pp. 19 – 24.

Ramón Folch, Armando de et al. En recuerdo de Jorge Enrique Hardoy. *EURE,* v. 19, no. 58 (Oct 93), pp. 92 – 94.

Ramos, Antonio. "Infinito": Giacomo Leopardi. *Vozes,* v. 87, no. 3 (May – June 93), pp. 59 – 63. Il.

Ramos, Domingo. Poemas. *Káñina,* v. 16, no. 2 (July – Dec 92), pp. 221 – 222.

Ramos, Donald. From Minho to Minas: The Portuguese Roots of the Mineiro Family. *Hispanic American Historical Review,* v. 73, no. 4 (Nov 93), pp. 639 – 662. Bibl, tables.

Ramos, Fernando A. and Edward Funkhouser. The Choice of Migration Destination: Dominican and Cuban Immigrants to the Mainland United States and Puerto Rico. *International Migration Review,* v. 27, no. 3 (Fall 93), pp. 537 – 556. Bibl, tables.

Ramos, Graciliano. Discurso de Graciliano Ramos (Excerpt from *Homenagem a Graciliano Ramos* introduced by Yêdda Dias Lima). *Vozes,* v. 86, no. 4 (July – Aug 92), pp. 72 – 77. Il.

Ramos, Joseph R. Reformas económicas en América Latina: lecciones para Europa oriental: comentarios a los artículos de Patricio Meller y Carmelo Mesa-Lago. *Pensamiento Iberoamericano,* no. 22 – 23, tomo II (July 92 – June 93), pp. 109 – 118.

Ramos, Julio. Cuerpo, lengua, subjetividad. *Revista de Crítica Literaria Latinoamericana,* v. 19, no. 38 (July – Dec 93), pp. 225 – 237. Bibl.

Ramos, Julio et al. Debate (on the fifth session of the symposium "Latinoamérica: Nuevas Direcciones en Teoría y Crítica Literarias, III"). *Revista de Crítica Literaria Latinoamericana,* v. 19, no. 38 (July – Dec 93), pp. 217 – 221.

— Debate (on the seventh session of the symposium "Latinoamérica: Nuevas Direcciones en Teoría y Crítica Literarias, III"). *Revista de Crítica Literaria Latinoamericana,* v. 19, no. 38 (July – Dec 93), pp. 293 – 296.

Ramos, Lauro Roberto Albrecht and Regis Bonelli. Distribuição de renda no Brasil: avaliação das tendências de longo prazo e mudanças na desigualdade desde meados dos anos '70. *Revista de Economia Política (Brazil),* v. 13, no. 2 (Apr – June 93), pp. 76 – 97. Bibl, tables, charts.

Ramos, Luis Arturo. El agua y su lenguaje. *La Palabra y el Hombre,* no. 82 (Apr – June 92), pp. 306 – 309.

Ramos Gómez, Luis J. and María Concepción Blasco. Continuidad y cambio: interpretación de la decoración de una vasija nazca. *Revista Andina,* v. 10, no. 2 (Dec 92), pp. 457 – 471. Bibl, il.

Ramos Serpa, Gerardo. Gramsci: salvación o desacierto del marxismo latinoamericano. *Islas,* no. 98 (Jan – Apr 91), pp. 157 – 166. Bibl.

Ramsaran, Ramesh. Factors Affecting the Income Velocity of Money in the Commonwealth Caribbean. *Social and Economic Studies,* v. 41, no. 4 (Dec 92), pp. 205 – 223. Bibl, tables.

— Growth, Employment, and the Standard of Living in Selected Commonwealth Caribbean Countries. *Caribbean Studies,* v. 25, no. 1 – 2 (Jan – July 92), pp. 103 – 122. Tables.

Randall, Laura Regina Rosenbaum. Petróleo, economía y medio ambiente en Brasil. *Revista Mexicana de Sociología,* v. 54, no. 2 (Apr – June 92), pp. 185 – 211. Tables.

Rangel, Armênio de Souza. A economia do município de Taubaté, 1798 a 1835. *Estudos Econômicos,* v. 23, no. 1 (Jan – Apr 93), pp. 149 – 179. Bibl, tables, charts.

Rangel Díaz, José. La "Clintonomics": ¿Nuevas señales para la economía mundial? *Problemas del Desarrollo,* v. 24, no. 93 (Apr – June 93), pp. 15 – 21.

Rangel Martínez, Georgina M. Mujer, trabajo y medio ambiente. *Fem,* v. 17, no. 128 (Oct 93), pp. 22 – 25. Bibl.

Ranger, Edward M., Jr. A Compliance Checklist. *Business Mexico,* v. 3, no. 1 (Jan – Feb 93), p. 86.

— The Environment and NAFTA. *Business Mexico,* v. 3, no. 1 (Jan – Feb 93), pp. 78 – 79.

— The High Cost of Noncompliance. *Business Mexico,* v. 3, no. 7 (July 93), p. 44 +.

Rappaport, Joanne. Textos legales e interpretación histórica: una etnografía andina de la lectura. *Iberoamericana,* v. 16, no. 47 – 48 (1992), pp. 67 – 81. Bibl.

Raschio, Richard A. and Renée Milstein. Bibliografía anotada de logicales, videodiscos y discos compactos para la enseñanza del español o para el uso en cursos bilingües. *Hispania (USA),* v. 76, no. 4 (Dec 93), pp. 683 – 720.

Rashford, John H. Arawak, Spanish, and African Contributions to Jamaica's Settlement Vegetation. *Jamaica Journal,* v. 24, no. 3 (Feb 93), pp. 17 – 23. Bibl, il.

Ratliff, William and George Esenwein. Latin American Posters at the Hoover Institution: The Lexicons of State and Society. *SALALM Papers,* v. 34 (1989), pp. 214 – 220.

Ravelo Blancas, Patricia. Breve balance del movimiento de costureras del Sindicato "19 de Septiembre." *El Cotidiano,* v. 9, no. 53 (Mar – Apr 93), pp. 99 – 104. Il, tables.

Ravina, Arturo Octavio. Algunos aspectos críticos del Acuerdo de Transporte Fluvial por la Hidrovía Paraguay – Paraná (Puerto Cáceres – Nueva Palmira). *Integración Latinoamericana,* v. 17, no. 185 (Dec 92), pp. 45 – 50.

Ravines Pérez, Eudocio. El indigenismo como instrumento político: un problema artificial (Excerpt from *La gran promesa*). *Atenea (Chile),* no. 465 – 466 (1992), pp. 157 – 172. Il.

Rebaza Soraluz, Luis. Mariano Isolda y mosquera. *Inti,* no. 36 (Fall 92), pp. 169 – 174.

Rebollar, Juan L. Jorge Rosano: una aseveración plástica sin alardes. *Artes de México*, no. 19 (Spring 93), p. 117. Il.

Rebolledo Hernández, Antonia and Rolando Mellafe Rojas. La creación de la Universidad de Chile y el despertar de la identidad nacional. *Atenea (Chile)*, no. 465 – 466 (1992), pp. 303 – 323. Bibl, il.

Rebollo, Eduardo. 500 años de historia universal: con Guido Castillo en Barcelona. *Cuadernos del CLAEH*, v. 17, no. 63 – 64 (Oct 92), pp. 43 – 52.

— 500 años de incomunicación. *Cuadernos del CLAEH*, v. 17, no. 63 – 64 (Oct 92), pp. 125 – 129.

Rébora Togno, Alberto. Los planificadores urbanos ante el cambio. *EURE*, v. 19, no. 57 (July 93), pp. 31 – 40.

Recio Adrados, Juan Luis. Incidencia política de las sectas religiosas: el caso de Centroamérica (Previously published in *Rábida*, no. 12, 1992). *ECA; Estudios Centroamericanos*, v. 48, no. 531 – 532 (Jan – Feb 93), pp. 75 – 91. Bibl, il.

Recio Ferreras, Eloy. Diario inédito escrito por un soldado español en la guerra de Cuba, 1896 – 1899. *Revista de Historia de América*, no. 112 (July – Dec 91), pp. 21 – 42. Facs.

Redonnet, Vincent and Fe Esperanza Cárdenas. Modernización de la empresa AHMSA en Monclova, Coahuila y su impacto sobre la población. *Estudios Demográficos y Urbanos*, v. 6, no. 3 (Sept – Dec 91), pp. 677 – 716. Bibl, tables.

Regaladas de Hurtado, Liliana

See
    Hurtado, Liliana R. de

Regan, Jaime. En torno a la entrevista de los jesuitas con Juan Santos Atahualpa. *Amazonía Peruana*, v. 11, no. 22 (Oct 92), pp. 61 – 92. Bibl, maps.

Regis, Humphrey A. Three Caribbean Islands' Interest in Popularity of Caribbean Music. *Caribbean Studies*, v. 25, no. 1 – 2 (Jan – July 92), pp. 123 – 132. Bibl, tables.

Rego, José Márcio and Luiz Carlos Bresser Pereira. Um mestre da economia brasileira: Ignácio Rangel. *Revista de Economia Política (Brazil)*, v. 13, no. 2 (Apr – June 93), pp. 98 – 119.

Rêgo, Stella M. de Sá. Access to Photograph Collections. *SALALM Papers*, v. 34 (1989), pp. 123 – 129. Bibl.

Rehren, Alfredo J. La presidencia en el gobierno de la concertación. *Estudios Sociales (Chile)*, no. 75 (Jan – Mar 93), pp. 15 – 38. Bibl.

Reichardt, Dieter. *Humano ardor* por Alberto Ghiraldo: la novela autobiográfica de un anarquista argentino. *Iberoamericana*, v. 17, no. 50 (1993), pp. 79 – 88. Bibl.

Reid, Basil. Arawak Archaeology in Jamaica: New Approaches, New Perspectives. *Caribbean Quarterly*, v. 38, no. 2 – 3 (June – Sept 92), pp. 15 – 20.

Reilly, Charles A. The Road from Rio: NGO Policy Makers and the Social Ecology of Development. *Grassroots Development*, v. 17, no. 1 (1993), pp. 25 – 35. Bibl, il.

Reimel de Carrasquel, Sharon. La calidad de vida del profesorado de la Universidad Simón Bolívar: resultados de una prueba piloto. *La Educación (USA)*, v. 36, no. 111 – 113 (1992), pp. 25 – 45. Bibl, tables, charts.

Reimers A., Fernando. Fe y Alegría: una innovación educativa para proporcionar educación básica con calidad y equidad. *Revista Paraguaya de Sociología*, v. 29, no. 85 (Sept – Dec 92), pp. 41 – 58. Bibl, tables.

Rein, Raanan. El antifranquismo durante el régimen peronista. *Cuadernos Americanos*, no. 37, Nueva época (Jan – Feb 93), pp. 90 – 114. Bibl.

Reinert, Kenneth A. Discriminatory Export Taxation in Costa Rica: A Counterfactual History. *Journal of Developing Areas*, v. 28, no. 1 (Oct 93), pp. 39 – 48. Bibl, tables, charts.

Reinhard, Johan. Llullaillaco: An Investigation of the World's Highest Archaelogical Site. *Latin American Indian Literatures Journal*, v. 9, no. 1 (Spring 93), pp. 31 – 54. Il, maps.

Reinstein A., Andrés and Rodrigo Vergara M. Hacia una regulación y supervisión más eficiente del sistema bancario. *Estudios Públicos (Chile)*, no. 49 (Summer 93), pp. 99 – 136. Bibl, tables.

Reis, Arthur Cézar Ferreira. O conde dos Arcos na Amazônia. *Revista do Instituto Histórico e Geográfico Brasileiro*, no. 370 (Jan – Mar 91), pp. 134 – 139. Bibl.

Reis, Sandra Loureiro de Freitas. A *Opera Tiradentes* de Manuel Joaquim de Macedo e Augusto de Lima. *Latin American Music Review*, v. 14, no. 1 (Spring – Summer 93), pp. 131 – 144. Bibl.

Remmer, Karen L. The Process of Democratization in Latin America. *Studies in Comparative International Development*, v. 27, no. 4 (Winter 92 – 93), pp. 3 – 24. Bibl.

Remus Araico, José. La angustia social y el nacimiento de dos mitos modernos. *Revista Mexicana de Ciencias Políticas y Sociales*, v. 38, Nueva época, no. 154 (Oct – Dec 93), pp. 65 – 78.

Renard-Casevitz, France-Marie. Les guerriers du sel: chronique '92. *Cahiers des Amériques Latines*, no. 13 (1992), pp. 107 – 118.

Rendón, José. Poems ("Bad Memory," "To Maribel on Her Engagement to a Long Time Boyfriend," "Letter from Laredo"). *The Americas Review*, v. 19, no. 2 (Summer 91), pp. 67 – 72.

Rendón, Teresa. El trabajo femenino en México: tendencias y cambios recientes. *El Cotidiano*, v. 9, no. 53 (Mar – Apr 93), pp. 3 – 9. Tables.

Rendón, Teresa and Carlos Salas Páez. El empleo en México en los ochenta: tendencias y cambios. *Comercio Exterior*, v. 43, no. 8 (Aug 93), pp. 717 – 730. Bibl, tables, charts.

Rendón Monzón, Juan José. Apuntes en torno a la alfabetización en lenguas indígenas. *Revista Latinoamericana de Estudios Educativos*, v. 22, no. 4 (Oct – Dec 92), pp. 63 – 76.

Rénique, Gerardo and Deborah A. Poole. Perdiendo de vista al Perú: réplica a Orin Starn. *Allpanchis*, v. 23, no. 39 (Jan – June 92), pp. 73 – 92. Bibl.

Renshaw, John and Daniel Rivas. Un programa integrado para combatir el mal de Chagas: el Proyecto Boliviano – Británico "Cardenal Maurer." *Estudios Paraguayos*, v. 17, no. 1 – 2 (1989 – 1993), pp. 323 – 344.

Repetto, Fabián. La construcción de un nuevo orden, o el final de una época . . . . *Realidad Económica*, no. 120 (Nov – Dec 93), pp. 18 – 40. Bibl, tables.

Resende, Marcelo and Rodolfo Grandi. Inflação e variabilidade dos preços relativos no Brasil: a questão da causalidade. *Revista Brasileira de Economia*, v. 46, no. 4 (Oct – Dec 92), pp. 595 – 604. Bibl, tables.

Reséndiz García, Ramón. Reforma educativa y conflicto interburocrático en México, 1978 – 1988. *Revista Mexicana de Sociología*, v. 54, no. 2 (Apr – June 92), pp. 3 – 18. Bibl.

Restrepo, Félix. Bajo la insignia de Javier: veinticinco años de historia (Previously published in this journal, no. 51, 1959). *Revista Javeriana*, v. 61, no. 596 (July 93), pp. 17 – 36.

Retta, Luis A. Publicaciones uruguayas incluidas en LATBOOK. *SALALM Papers*, v. 36 (1991), pp. 435 – 437.

Revel-Mouroz, Jean François. Thierry Saignes (27 septembre 1946 – 24 ao + Aot 1992). *Cahiers des Amériques Latines*, no. 13 (1992), pp. 5 – 6.

Reverte Bernal, Concepción. VII Festival Iberoamericano de Teatro de Cádiz, 1992. *Latin American Theatre Review*, v. 26, no. 2 (Spring 93), pp. 171 – 182. Il.

Revilla Vergara, Ana Teresa. La justicia informal. *Debate (Peru)*, v. 16, no. 75 (Dec 93 – Jan 94), pp. 49 – 50.

Rey Fajardo, José del. La misión del Airico, 1695 – 1704. *Boletín de la Academia Nacional de la Historia (Venezuela)*, v. 76, no. 302 (Apr – June 93), pp. 49 – 68. Bibl.

— Palabras pronunciadas por el r.p. José del Rey Fajardo, S.J. en la presentación de la obra *La pedagogía jesuítica en Venezuela, 1628 – 1767. Boletín de la Academia Nacional de la Historia (Venezuela)*, v. 75, no. 299 (July – Sept 92), pp. 25 – 26.

— La presencia científica de la Universidad Javeriana en la Orinoquia. *Boletín de Historia y Antigüedades*, v. 79, no. 779 (Oct – Dec 92), pp. 925 – 952. Bibl.

Rey Romay, Benito. Comentarios al libro *Pobreza y desigualdad en América Latina* de Pedro Vuskovic. *Problemas del Desarrollo*, v. 24, no. 94 (July – Sept 93), pp. 258 – 263.

Reyero, Loló. Considerando . . . "Considerando en frío, imparcialmente . . . " (Includes the poem). *Inti*, no. 36 (Fall 92), pp. 81 – 88.

Reyes, Alfonso. Buzón de fantasmas: de Alfonso Reyes a Genaro Estrada. *Vuelta*, v. 17, no. 196 (Mar 93), pp. 76 – 77.

Reyes, Ana María and Blanca Chiesa. El Congreso del Pueblo y su significación en el proceso de lucha, movilización y unificación sindical, años 1950 – 1966. *Hoy Es Historia*, v. 10, no. 56 (Mar – Apr 93), pp. 40 – 60. Bibl, il.

Reyes, Carmen et al. Matrimonios: la ardua búsqueda de felicidad; debates (Introduced by G. Arroyo). *Mensaje*, v. 42, no. 425 (Dec 93), pp. 629 – 636.

Reyes, Guillermo A. Miss Consuelo. *The Americas Review*, v. 20, no. 3 – 4 (Fall – Winter 92), pp. 100 – 115.

— Pinochet in Hollywood. *The Americas Review*, v. 20, no. 2 (Summer 92), pp. 5 – 14.

Reyes, Juan José. Salvador Reyes Nevares, el mejor amigo. *Cuadernos Americanos*, no. 41, Nueva época (Sept – Oct 93), pp. 218 – 221.

Reyes, Pedro and Richard R. Valencia. Educational Policy and the Growing Latino Student Population: Problems and Prospects. *Hispanic Journal of Behavioral Sciences*, v. 15, no. 2 (May 93), pp. 258 – 283. Bibl.

Reyes del Campillo, Juan. La legitimidad de la sucesión presidencial. *El Cotidiano*, v. 10, no. 58 (Oct – Nov 93), pp. 34 – 38. Il.

— El PRI, el sistema de partidos y la sucesión presidencial. *El Cotidiano*, v. 8, no. 52 (Jan – Feb 93), pp. 10 – 12.

Reyes del Campillo, Juan and Verónica Vázquez Mantecón. ¿Ciudadanos en ciernes?: la cultura política en el distrito XXVII del D.F. *El Cotidiano*, v. 9, no. 54 (May 93), pp. 41 – 48. Il, tables, charts.

Reyes Garza, Juan Carlos and Rubén Leytón Ovando. Cuyutlán: una cultura salinera. *La Palabra y el Hombre*, no. 81 (Jan – Mar 92), pp. 120 – 146. Bibl, il.

Reyes Larios, Sandra. Tiempos difíciles en la industria del juguete. *Comercio Exterior*, v. 43, no. 10 (Oct 93), pp. 913 – 916. Bibl, tables.

Reyes Nevares, Beatriz. Salvador Reyes Nevares. *Cuadernos Americanos*, no. 41, Nueva época (Sept – Oct 93), pp. 212 – 217.

Reyes Ramírez, Rocío de los. Expediciones y viajes de franciscanos en los libros registros del Archivo General de Indias, siglo XVIII. *Archivo Ibero-Americano*, v. 52, no. 205 – 208 (Jan – Dec 92), pp. 811 – 832.

Reyes Ramos, Manuel. Descubramos a Carlos Pellicer Cámara. *La Palabra y el Hombre*, no. 81 (Jan – Mar 92), pp. 177 – 192. Bibl.

— Juárez a través de su epistolario. *La Palabra y el Hombre*, no. 82 (Apr – June 92), pp. 294 – 300.

Reyna Bernal, Angélica. Políticas de migración y distribución de población en México: ejecución e impactos regionales. *Estudios Demográficos y Urbanos*, v. 6, no. 3 (Sept – Dec 91), pp. 583 – 611. Bibl, tables, charts.

Reynales, Trish. The Looting of the Royal Tombs of Sipán. *Latin American Art*, v. 5, no. 2 (Summer 93), pp. 50 – 52. Il.

Reynoso, Víctor Manuel. El Partido Acción Nacional: ¿La oposición hará gobierno? *Revista Mexicana de Sociología*, v. 55, no. 2 (Apr – June 93), pp. 133 – 151.

Ribeiro, Carlos A. C. A responsabilidade social da empresa: uma nova vantagem competitiva. *RAE; Revista de Administração de Empresas*, v. 33, no. 1 (Jan – Feb 93), p. 46.

Ribeiro, Darcy. A Amazônia. *Vozes*, v. 86, no. 4 (July – Aug 92), pp. 42 – 52.

Ribeiro, Eliane. "Dose unitária": sistema de distribuição de medicamentos em hospitais. *RAE; Revista de Administração de Empresas*, v. 33, no. 6 (Nov – Dec 93), pp. 62 – 73. Tables, charts.

Ribeiro, Gustavo Lins

See

Lins Ribeiro, Gustavo

Ribeiro, João Roberto Inácio. O gongorismo na poesia latina de Manuel Botelho de Oliveira. *Revista de Letras (Brazil)*, v. 32 (1992), pp. 199 – 206. Bibl.

Ribeiro, Lourival. Conselheiro Jaoquim Vicente de Torres Homem. *Revista do Instituto Histórico e Geográfico Brasileiro*, no. 370 (Jan – Mar 91), pp. 94 – 101. Bibl, facs.

Ribeiro, Luís Filipe. O sexo e o poder no império: *Philomena Borges*. *Luso-Brazilian Review*, v. 30, no. 1 (Summer 93), pp. 7 – 20. Bibl.

Ribeiro, Mariska. Direitos reprodutivos e políticas descartáveis. *Estudos Feministas*, v. 1, no. 2 (1993), pp. 400 – 407.

Ribeiro, Miguel Angelo Campos and Roberto Schmidt de Almeida. Análise da organização espacial da indústria nordestina através de uma tipologia de centros industriais. *Revista Brasileira de Geografia*, v. 53, no. 2 (Apr – June 91), pp. 5 – 31. Bibl, tables, maps.

— Os pequenos e medios estabelecimentos industriais nordestinos: padrões de distribuição e fatores condicionantes. *Revista Brasileira de Geografia*, v. 53, no. 1 (Jan – Mar 91), pp. 5 – 49. Bibl, tables, maps.

Ribeiro, Simone. A Casa de Jorge Amado. *Vozes*, v. 87, no. 3 (May – June 93), pp. 41 – 47. Il.

Ribeyro, Julio Ramón. La estación del diablo. *Debate (Peru)*, v. 16, no. 72 (Mar – May 93), pp. 58 – 62. Il.

— La tentación de la memoria. *Debate (Peru)*, v. 15, no. 70 (Sept – Oct 92), pp. 56 – 59. Il.

Ricci, Maria Lúcia de Souza Rangel. A problemática do negro no Brasil. *Hoy Es Historia*, v. 10, no. 55 (Jan – Feb 93), pp. 82 – 87.

Riccio, Alessandra. Eros y poder en *Informe bajo llave* de Marta Lynch. *Escritura (Venezuela)*, v. 16, no. 31 – 32 (Jan – Dec 91), pp. 223 – 229. Bibl.

Richard, Nelly. Alteridad y descentramiento culturales. *Revista Chilena de Literatura,* no. 42 (Aug 93), pp. 209 – 215.

Richers, Raimar. A emancipação do executivo de "marketing." *RAE; Revista de Administração de Empresas,* v. 33, no. 1 (Jan – Feb 93), pp. 52 – 65. Bibl.

Rienner, Lynne. Is the Sky Falling?: Scholarly Publishing in the 1990s. *SALALM Papers,* v. 36 (1991), pp. 159 – 164.

Rieser, Leonard M. James W. Rowe (1929 – 1993). *Interciencia,* v. 18, no. 4 (July – Aug 93), p. 202.

Rigau, Marco Antonio. Mutual Respect: Congress Must Act. *Hemisphere,* v. 5, no. 3 (Summer – Fall 93), pp. 47 – 49. Il.

Riner, Deborah L. Is Maxi-Devaluation upon the Peso? *Business Mexico,* v. 3, no. 6 (June 93), pp. 22 – 23 +. Tables.

— A Pact for All Seasons. *Business Mexico,* v. 3, no. 11 (Nov 93), p. 20. Charts.

— A Third-Quarter Perspective. *Business Mexico,* v. 3, no. 9 (Sept 93), pp. 32 – 35. Charts.

Ring, Ano. La narrativa brasileña después de 1964: escribir como alternativa. *Islas,* no. 97 (Sept – Dec 90), pp. 20 – 25.

Río Correa, Ana María del. Jahuel: valores versus "rating." *Mensaje,* v. 42, no. 419 (June 93), pp. 205 – 207.

Río Moreno, Justo L. del and Lorenzo Eladio López y Sebastián. Comercio y transporte en la economía del azúcar antillano durante el siglo XVI. *Anuario de Estudios Americanos,* v. 49 (1992), pp. 55 – 87. Bibl, maps.

Río Reynaga, Julio del. Desarrollo y tendencias de la enseñanza en comunicación colectiva. *Revista Mexicana de Ciencias Políticas y Sociales,* v. 37, Nueva época, no. 149 (July – Sept 92), pp. 153 – 176. Bibl.

Rionda, Jorge I. La industria maquiladora de exportación en Guanajuato. *Comercio Exterior,* v. 43, no. 2 (Feb 93), pp. 132 – 134. Tables.

Ríos, Alberto Alvaro. The Birthday of Mrs. Piñeda. *The Americas Review,* v. 20, no. 3 – 4 (Fall – Winter 92), pp. 20 – 28.

— Poems ("Five Indiscretions, or," "On January 5, 1984, El Santo the Wrestler Died, Possibly"). *The Americas Review,* v. 20, no. 3 – 4 (Fall – Winter 92), pp. 182 – 188.

Ríos, Alicia. La época de la independencia en la narrativa venezolana de los ochenta. *Hispamérica,* v. 22, no. 64 – 65 (Apr – Aug 93), pp. 48 – 54.

Ríos, Francisco Armando. Poems ("El aborto," "A Caín"). *The Americas Review,* v. 19, no. 2 (Summer 91), pp. 60 – 63.

Ríos, Javier Enrique de los. La huelga de Campana de 1915: conflicto olvido. *Todo Es Historia,* v. 27, no. 314 (Sept 93), pp. 56 – 69. Bibl, il.

Rios, José Arthur. Jackson de Figueiredo: perfil e formação de um pensador. *Revista do Instituto Histórico e Geográfico Brasileiro,* no. 373 (Oct – Dec 91), pp. 1085 – 1106. Bibl.

Ríos-Avila, Rubén. La invención de un autor: escritura y poder en Edgardo Rodríguez Juliá. *Revista Iberoamericana,* v. 59, no. 162 – 163 (Jan – June 93), pp. 203 – 219. Bibl.

Rípodas Ardanaz, Daisy and Mónica Patricia Martini. Aportes sobre el voseo en Córdoba a horcajadas de los siglos XVIII y XIX: sus modalidades en la obra de Cristóbal de Aguilar. *Investigaciones y Ensayos,* no. 41 (Jan – Dec 91), pp. 139 – 151. Bibl.

Ritchey-Vance, Marion. Grassroots Development Results: Widening the Lens. *Grassroots Development,* v. 17, no. 1 (1993), pp. 42 – 43. Charts.

Ritter, Archibald R. M. Cuba en los noventa: reorientación económica y reintegración internacional. *Estudios Internacionales (Chile),* v. 26, no. 103 (July – Sept 93), pp. 454 – 479. Bibl, tables.

— Exploring Cuba's Alternate Economic Futures. *Cuban Studies/Estudios Cubanos,* v. 23 (1993), pp. 3 – 31. Bibl, tables.

— Seized Properties vs. Embargo Losses. *Hemisphere,* v. 5, no. 3 (Summer – Fall 93), pp. 31 – 35. Tables.

Rivadeneira Prada, Raúl. El cine alternativo en Bolivia. *Signo,* no. 38, Nueva época (Jan – Apr 93), pp. 47 – 60. Bibl.

— Un fragmento para la historia de la Asociación de Periodistas. *Signo,* no. 35, Nueva época (Jan – Apr 92), pp. 15 – 33.

— La gran elección. *Signo,* no. 35, Nueva época (Jan – Apr 92), pp. 111 – 112.

— Juan Quirós, periodista. *Signo,* no. 36 – 37, Nueva época (May – Dec 92), pp. 201 – 206.

— La venganza de Julia Irene. *Signo,* no. 35, Nueva época (Jan – Apr 92), pp. 113 – 115.

Rivadeneira Vargas, Antonio José. El pensamiento integrador de Carlos Sanz de Santamaría. *Boletín de Historia y Antigüedades,* v. 79, no. 779 (Oct – Dec 92), pp. 953 – 973. Bibl.

Rivas, Daniel and John Renshaw. Un programa integrado para combatir el mal de Chagas: el Proyecto Boliviano – Británico "Cardenal Maurer." *Estudios Paraguayos,* v. 17, no. 1 – 2 (1989 – 1993), pp. 323 – 344.

Rivas, Juan Antonio. Estructura de mercado, innovación y crecimiento. *Planeación y Desarrollo,* v. 24, no. 2 (May – Aug 93), pp. 73 – 93. Bibl.

Rivas Dugarte, Rafael Angel. Cronología de Mariano Picón Salas. *Boletín de la Academia Nacional de la Historia (Venezuela),* v. 76, no. 301 (Jan – Mar 93), pp. 93 – 100.

Rivas Mira, Fernando Alonso. Transporte, telecomunicaciones y turismo: el Proyecto Triple T. *Comercio Exterior,* v. 43, no. 12 (Dec 93), pp. 1188 – 1194.

Rivas Rivas, José. Una insólita misión cultural. *Revista Nacional de Cultura (Venezuela),* v. 53, no. 286 (July – Sept 92), pp. 159 – 166. Il.

Rivera, Angel A. *La peregrinación de Bayoán* de Eugenio María de Hostos: viaje de retorno al caos. *Revista Canadiense de Estudios Hispánicos,* v. 17, no. 3 (Spring 93), pp. 525 – 535. Bibl.

Rivera, Beatriz. Paloma. *The Americas Review,* v. 20, no. 2 (Summer 92), pp. 15 – 30.

Rivera, Diana. Learning to Speak. *The Americas Review,* v. 20, no. 3 – 4 (Fall – Winter 92), pp. 225 – 228.

Rivera, Francisco. Sobre narrativa venezolana, 1970 – 1990. *Inti,* no. 37 – 38 (Spring – Fall 93), pp. 89 – 96. Bibl.

Rivera, Jorge B. "Dameros": la utopía urbanística de la ciudad de Indias. *Cuadernos del CLAEH,* v. 17, no. 63 – 64 (Oct 92), pp. 149 – 154. Bibl.

— Periodismo y transición: de la recuperación pluralista al "shopping" comunicacional. *Cuadernos Hispanoamericanos,* no. 517 – 519 (July – Sept 93), pp. 337 – 351. Bibl.

Rivera, José María. Aarón Cruz: el laberinto en el universo. *Plural (Mexico),* v. 22, no. 263 (Aug 93), pp. 40 – 45. Il.

Rivera, Juan Manuel. Champ: vídeo para el tercer milenio. *Revista Nacional de Cultura (Venezuela),* v. 53, no. 286 (July – Sept 92), pp. 81 – 86.

Rivera, Rolando and David Smith. Organización, movilización popular y desarrollo regional en el Atlántico costarricense. *Estudios Rurales Latinoamericanos,* v. 15, no. 2 – 3 (May – Dec 92), pp. 79 – 110. Tables.

Rivera, Salvador and Gustavo Garza Villarreal. Desarrollo económico y distribución de la población urbana en México, 1960 – 1990. *Revista Mexicana de Sociología,* v. 55, no. 1 (Jan – Mar 93), pp. 177 – 212. Bibl, tables, charts.

Rivera, Tomás. Era muy llorón. *The Americas Review,* v. 19, no. 2 (Summer 91), p. 36.

Rivera Bustamante, Tirza Emilia. Women Judges in Central America. *Hemisphere,* v. 5, no. 3 (Summer – Fall 93), pp. 18 – 19. Charts.

Rivera de los Reyes, Julio M. Plant Shutdown?: Here's What to Do. *Business Mexico,* v. 3, no. 1 (Jan – Feb 93), p. 88.

Rivera Domínguez, Juan Antonio. Relato de un viaje a San Blas. *Revista Cultural Lotería,* v. 50, no. 385 (Sept – Oct 91), pp. 88 – 92.

Rivera Dorado, Miguel et al. Trabajos arqueológicos en Oxkintok durante el verano de 1991. *Revista Española de Antropología Americana,* v. 23 (1993), pp. 41 – 65. Bibl, il, tables, maps.

Rivera Martínez, J. Edgardo. Singularidad y carácter de los *Naufragios* de Alvar Núñez Cabeza de Vaca. *Revista de Crítica Literaria Latinoamericana,* v. 19, no. 38 (July – Dec 93), pp. 301 – 315.

Rivera Ramos, José Antonio. El descubrimiento de América. *Revista Cultural Lotería,* v. 51, no. 391 (Sept – Oct 92), pp. 13 – 21. Bibl.

Rivera-Rodas, Oscar. La modernidad en el lenguaje poético hispánico. *Signo,* no. 36 – 37, Nueva época (May – Dec 92), pp. 109 – 123.

Rivero Pinto, Wigberto and Ives Encinas Cueto. La presencia aimara en la ciudad de La Paz: Chuquiyawu Marka; entre la participación y la sobrevivencia. *América Indígena,* v. 51, no. 2 – 3 (Apr – Sept 91), pp. 273 – 292.

Riz, Liliana de and Catalina Smulovitz. Instauración democrática y reforma política en Argentina y Uruguay: un análisis comparado. *Ibero-Amerikanisches Archiv,* v. 18, no. 1 – 2 (1992), pp. 181 – 224. Bibl, tables.

Rizk, Beatriz J. TENAZ XVI: la muestra de un teatro en transición. *Latin American Theatre Review,* v. 26, no. 2 (Spring 93), pp. 187 – 190.

Rizzi, Milton. De héroes a encargados: la traqueotomía en el Uruguay. *Hoy Es Historia,* v. 10, no. 58 (July – Aug 93), pp. 71 – 76. Bibl.

Roa, Natalia. Vicente Huidobro: la luna era mi tierra. *Mensaje,* v. 42, no. 417 (Mar – Apr 93), pp. 77 – 78. Il.

Roa Bastos, Augusto Antonio. Augusto Roa Bastos: dos cartas. *Casa de las Américas,* no. 190 (Jan – Mar 93), pp. 134 – 135.

— Vigilia del Almirante (Excerpt from the novel of the same title). *Nexos,* v. 16, no. 182 (Feb 93), pp. 53 – 58.

Roa de la Carrera, Cristián. El discurso de la guerra en los textos chilenos del siglo XVI. *Revista Chilena de Literatura,* no. 42 (Aug 93), pp. 217 – 221.

Roa Kourí, Raúl. Gobierno, legitimidad y participación democrática. *Cuadernos Americanos,* no. 39, Nueva época (May – June 93), pp. 77 – 80.

Roazzi, Antonio et al. A arte do repente e as habilidades lingüísticas. *Revista Brasileira de Estudos Pedagógicos,* v. 72, no. 172 (Sept – Dec 91), pp. 291 – 317. Bibl, tables, charts.

Robertiello, Jack. Dominican Chutzpah: The Story of Sosua. *Américas,* v. 45, no. 4 (July – Aug 93), pp. 20 – 25. Il, maps.

— It's Mealtime in Santo Domingo (Includes recipes). *Américas,* v. 45, no. 6 (Nov – Dec 93), pp. 58 – 59. Il.

— Pecan/Pacana/Nogueira Americana (Includes recipes). *Américas,* v. 45, no. 2 (Mar – Apr 93), pp. 54 – 55. Il.

— The Quest for Maya Meals (Includes recipes). *Américas,* v. 45, no. 3 (May – June 93), pp. 58 – 59. Il.

Roberts, Bryan R. and Orlandina de Oliveira. La informalidad urbana en años de expansión, crisis y restructuración económica (Translated by Laura Elena Pulido). *Estudios Sociológicos,* v. 11, no. 31 (Jan – Apr 93), pp. 33 – 58. Bibl, tables.

Robertson, Jack S. and Margarita Jerabek Wuellner. A Computer Search on Latin American Architecture: Results and Implications. *SALALM Papers,* v. 34 (1989), pp. 92 – 96.

Robinson, David and Javier Guerra. The 6 Million Ton Question. *Business Mexico,* v. 3, no. 9 (Sept 93), pp. 36 – 38. Charts.

Robinson, David and Robert S. Jones. Protection + Environment = Future Growth. *Business Mexico,* v. 3, no. 1 (Jan – Feb 93), pp. 37 – 39. Il.

Robinson, Sherman et al. Las políticas agrícolas y la migración en un área de libre comercio de los Estados Unidos y México: un análisis de equilibrio general computable (Translated by Carlos Villegas). *El Trimestre Económico,* v. 60, no. 237 (Jan – Mar 93), pp. 53 – 89. Bibl, tables, charts.

Robledo Quijano, Fernando and Germán Sánchez Franco. El doble carácter de las administradoras. *Revista Javeriana,* v. 61, no. 592 (Mar 93), pp. 112 – 116.

Robles, Oscar. Las aventuras de don Chipote o cuando los pericos mamen: el retrato del hambre. *La Palabra y el Hombre,* no. 81 (Jan – Mar 92), pp. 332 – 338.

— Por tu culpa, por mi gran culpa. *Plural (Mexico),* v. 22, no. 256 (Jan 93), pp. 8 – 9.

Robles B., Rosario et al. La mujer campesina en la época de la modernidad. *El Cotidiano,* v. 9, no. 53 (Mar – Apr 93), pp. 25 – 32. Bibl, il, tables.

Robles Muñoz, Cristóbal. Negociar la paz en Cuba, 1896 – 1897. *Revista de Indias,* v. 53, no. 198 (May – Aug 93), pp. 493 – 527. Bibl.

— Triunfar en Washington: España ante Baire. *Anuario de Estudios Americanos,* v. 49 (1992), pp. 563 – 584. Bibl.

Robles Robles, J. Amando. La evangelización imposible. *Revista de Historia (Costa Rica),* no. 25 (Jan – June 92), pp. 207 – 219. Bibl.

Roca, Juan Manuel. Poems. *Revista Nacional de Cultura (Venezuela),* v. 53, no. 285 (Apr – June 92), pp. 133 – 145.

Roca, Sergio G. A Critical Review of *Economía y Desarrollo. Cuban Studies/Estudios Cubanos,* v. 23 (1993), pp. 205 – 210. Bibl, tables.

— Evolución del pensamiento cubano sobre Cuba y la economía mundial a través de las revistas económicas. *Estudios Internacionales (Chile),* v. 26, no. 103 (July – Sept 93), pp. 537 – 564. Bibl, tables.

Rocca, Pablo. 35 años en *Marcha:* escritura y ambiente literario en *Marcha* y en el Uruguay, 1939 – 1974. *Nuevo Texto Crítico,* v. 6, no. 11 (1993), pp. 3 – 151. Bibl, il.

Rocha, Antônio Penalves. A difusão da economia política no Brasil entre os fins do século XVIII e início do XIX. *Revista de Economia Política (Brazil),* v. 13, no. 4 (Oct – Dec 93), pp. 47 – 57. Bibl.

Rocha, Carlos Henrique. Sobre a reforma fiscal. *Revista de Economia Política (Brazil),* v. 13, no. 2 (Apr – June 93), pp. 144 – 145.

Rocha, Paulina. Huellas del humo: Gerardo Lartigue. *Artes de México,* no. 18 (Winter 92), p. 97. Il.

Rocha Campos, Adolfo. El patrimonio de Perón. *Todo Es Historia,* v. 27, no. 313 (Aug 93), pp. 26 – 42. Bibl, il.

Rock, Rosalind Z. "Mujeres de substancia": Case Studies of Women of Property in Northern New Spain. *Colonial Latin American Historical Review,* v. 2, no. 4 (Fall 93), pp. 425 – 440. Bibl, facs.

Rodino Pierri, Ana María. Language Rights and Education for the Afro-Caribbean, English-Speaking Minorities in Central America: Contributions to the Discussion on Bilingual Education in Costa Rica. *La Educación (USA),* v. 36, no. 111 – 113 (1992), pp. 137 – 154. Bibl.

Rodowska, Krystyna. Poems ("Razón del juego," "La creación de Adán," "Transparencias"). *La Palabra y el Hombre,* no. 82 (Apr – June 92), pp. 196 – 198.

Rodrigues, Denise A. and Luís Otávio de Figueiredo Façanha. Indústria brasileira na década de '70: interpretação de resultados de estatística multivariada e de aspectos da dinâmica concorrencial. *Revista Brasileira de Economia,* v. 46, no. 4 (Oct – Dec 92), pp. 447 – 476. Bibl, tables.

Rodrigues, José Honório and Charles Ralph Boxer. Correspondência de José Honório Rodrigues: a corrspondência com Charles R. Boxer (Organized and annotated by Lêda Boechat Rodrigues). *Revista do Instituto Histórico e Geográfico Brasileiro,* no. 372 (July – Sept 91), pp. 828 – 907. Tables.

Rodríguez, Adriana C.

See

Rodríguez Pérsico, Adriana C.

Rodríguez, Alfonso. La tía Delia. *Confluencia,* v. 8, no. 1 (Fall 92), pp. 191 – 197.

Rodríguez, Antonio. Milton Becerra, la voz milenaria del hombre (Accompanied by an English translation). *Art Nexus,* no. 8 (Apr – June 93), pp. 68 – 70. Il.

Rodríguez, Bélgica. Un re-descubrimiento (Accompanied by an English translation). *Art Nexus,* no. 9 (June – Aug 93), pp. 56 – 58. Il.

Rodríguez, Flavia. The Mexican Privatization Programme: An Economic Analysis. *Social and Economic Studies,* v. 41, no. 4 (Dec 92), pp. 149 – 171. Bibl, tables, charts.

Rodríguez, Francisco. Luis Cardoza y Aragón: las paradojas de la escritura. *Plural (Mexico),* v. 22, no. 264 (Sept 93), pp. 52 – 55. Bibl.

Rodríguez, Hipólito. La antropología urbana y los estudios sobre migración. *La Palabra y el Hombre,* no. 84 (Oct – Dec 92), pp. 145 – 159. Bibl.

Rodríguez, José Carlos. Paraguay: mansa transición democrática. *Nueva Sociedad,* no. 127 (Sept – Oct 93), pp. 18 – 22.

Rodríguez, José Luis. Cuba en la economía internacional: nuevos mercados y desafíos de los años noventa. *Estudios Internacionales (Chile),* v. 26, no. 103 (July – Sept 93), pp. 415 – 453. Bibl, tables.

— The Cuban Economy in a Changing International Environment. *Cuban Studies/Estudios Cubanos,* v. 23 (1993), pp. 33 – 47. Bibl, tables.

Rodríguez, Juan Manuel. El movimiento sindical ante los procesos de integración. *Nueva Sociedad,* no. 126 (July – Aug 93), pp. 144 – 155.

Rodríguez, Julia. El cazador de vampiros. *Plural (Mexico),* v. 22, no. 261 (June 93), pp. 76 – 78.

Rodríguez, Julio P. Evolución de la medicina familiar y comunitaria en la Facultad de Medicina. *Revista Cultural Lotería,* v. 50, no. 383 (May – June 91), pp. 63 – 73. Bibl.

Rodríguez, Kathleen A. and Jerome Rabow. Socialization toward Money in Latino Families: An Exploratory Study of Gender Differences. *Hispanic Journal of Behavioral Sciences,* v. 15, no. 3 (Aug 93), pp. 324 – 341. Bibl.

Rodríguez, Lola. Conguero. *Afro-Hispanic Review,* v. 12, no. 1 (Spring 93), p. 49.

Rodríguez, Manuel Alfredo. Los pardos libres en la colonia y la independencia. *Boletín de la Academia Nacional de la Historia (Venezuela),* v. 75, no. 299 (July – Sept 92), pp. 33 – 62. Bibl.

Rodríguez, María de los Angeles. Las frutas y legumbres en el comercio exterior de México. *La Palabra y el Hombre,* no. 82 (Apr – June 92), pp. 199 – 227. Bibl, tables.

Rodríguez, María Teresa and Héctor Alvarez Santiago. Estrategias productivas entre los nahuas de Zongolica. *La Palabra y el Hombre,* no. 84 (Oct – Dec 92), pp. 127 – 144. Tables.

Rodríguez, Mario and María Nieves Alonso Martínez. Poesía chilena y española: Lihn y Gil de Biedma. *Atenea (Chile),* no. 467 (1993), pp. 197 – 219. Bibl.

Rodríguez, Orlando

See

Rodríguez B., Orlando

Rodríguez, Pilar. Living the Spanglish Way: A Conversation with Jim Sagel. *Confluencia,* v. 8, no. 1 (Fall 92), pp. 137 – 146.

— Poems ("Autodefinición," "Triángulo prohibido"). *The Americas Review,* v. 19, no. 2 (Summer 91), pp. 64 – 66.

— Poems ("La mala del cuento," "Geometría emocional"). *Bilingual Review/Revista Bilingüe,* v. 18, no. 1 (Jan – Apr 93), pp. 56 – 57.

Rodríguez, Reina María. Violet Island (Fragment). *Casa de las Américas,* no. 191 (Apr – June 93), pp. 85 – 87.

Rodríguez, Rodolfo et al. Avances sobre estudios dendrocronológicos en la región costera norte del Perú para obtener un registro pasado del fenómeno El Niño. *Bulletin de l'Institut Français d'Etudes Andines,* v. 22, no. 1 (1993), pp. 267 – 281. Bibl, il, tables, maps, charts.

Rodríguez, Victoria Elizabeth. The Politics of Decentralisation in Mexico: From "Municipio Libre" to "Solidaridad." *Bulletin of Latin American Research,* v. 12, no. 2 (May 93), pp. 133 – 145. Bibl.

Rodríguez B., Orlando. Venezuela: mestizaje y teatro. *Conjunto,* no. 92 (July – Dec 92), pp. 2 – 6. Il.

Rodríguez Beruff, Jorge and Rubén Dávila Santiago. Puerto Rico: frente a la nueva época. *Nueva Sociedad,* no. 127 (Sept – Oct 93), pp. 6 – 12.

Rodríguez C., Alberto and Alí Enrique López Bohórquez. Visión americanista de la conquista española: el reverso del descubrimiento. *Boletín de la Academia Nacional de la Historia (Venezuela),* v. 75, no. 300 (Oct – Dec 92), pp. 69 – 77. Bibl.

Rodríguez-Camilloni, Humberto. The "Retablo-Façade" as Transparency: A Study of the Frontispiece of San Francisco, Lima. *Anales del Instituto de Investigaciones Estéticas,* v. 16, no. 62 (1991), pp. 111 – 122. Bibl, il.

Rodríguez Castro, María Elena. Las casas del porvenir: nación y narración en el ensayo puertorriqueño. *Revista Iberoamericana,* v. 59, no. 162 – 163 (Jan – June 93), pp. 33 – 54. Bibl.

Rodríguez del Pino, Salvador. Realidad y mito en las relaciones chicano – mexicanas. *Bilingual Review/Revista Bilingüe*, v. 17, no. 3 (Sept – Dec 92), pp. 231 – 236. Bibl.

Rodríguez Elizondo, José. Salvador Allende: el tabú y el mito. *Debate (Peru)*, v. 16, no. 74 (Sept – Oct 93), pp. 53 – 56. Il.

— Salvador Allende: el tabú y el mito. *Nueva Sociedad*, no. 128 (Nov – Dec 93), pp. 24 – 28.

Rodríguez Fernández, Mario. De Neruda a Lihn: tres oposiciones complementarias en la poesía chilena contemporánea. *Atenea (Chile)*, no. 465 – 466 (1992), pp. 261 – 268.

Rodríguez Fernández, Mario et al. Opinan profesores de la Universidad de Concepción. *Atenea (Chile)*, no. 465 – 466 (1992), pp. 39 – 44.

Rodríguez G., Yolanda. Los actores sociales y la violencia política en Puno. *Allpanchis*, v. 23, no. 39 (Jan – June 92), pp. 131 – 154. Bibl.

Rodríguez Guerra, Fernando and Marina Arjona. Las oraciones objetivas en el habla popular de la ciudad de México. *Anuario de Letras (Mexico)*, v. 30 (1992), pp. 61 – 74. Tables.

Rodríguez Guillén, Raúl and Juan Mora Heredia. El agotamiento del autoritarismo con legitimidad y la sucesión presidencial. *El Cotidiano*, v. 10, no. 58 (Oct – Nov 93), pp. 22 – 28. Il, tables.

Rodríguez H., María Elia. Intertextualidad y dialogismo: el funcionamiento paródico del texto poético; análisis de dos series poéticas del *Canto general*. *Káñina*, v. 16, no. 1 (Jan – June 92), pp. 61 – 67.

Rodríguez-Izquierdo y Gavala, Fernando. Aspectos de la personalidad de Rufino José Cuervo. *Thesaurus*, v. 45, no. 3 (Sept – Dec 90), pp. 747 – 757.

Rodríguez-Luis, Julio. Los borradores de Pierre Ménard. *Nueva Revista de Filología Hispánica*, v. 40, no. 2 (July – Dec 92), pp. 1025 – 1045. Bibl.

— On the Criticism of Latin American Literature. *Latin American Literary Review*, v. 20, no. 40 (July – Dec 92), pp. 85 – 87.

Rodríguez Mansilla, Darío. Salud, enfermedad y rol del enfermo. *Estudios Sociales (Chile)*, no. 74 (Oct – Dec 92), pp. 75 – 95. Bibl.

Rodríguez Medellín, Luis and Abelardo Aníbal Gutiérrez Lara. La economía mexicana en la búsqueda de su modernización. *El Cotidiano*, v. 9, no. 55 (June 93), pp. 103 – 110. Tables, charts.

Rodríguez Morel, Genaro. Esclavitud y vida rural en las plantaciones azucareras de Santo Domingo, siglo XVI. *Anuario de Estudios Americanos*, v. 49 (1992), pp. 89 – 117. Bibl.

Rodríguez Morel, Genaro and Roberto Cassá. Consideraciones alternativas acerca de las rebeliones de esclavos en Santo Domingo. *Anuario de Estudios Americanos*, v. 50, no. 1 (1993), pp. 101 – 131. Bibl.

Rodríguez O., Jaime E. La independencia de la América española: una reinterpretación. *Historia Mexicana*, v. 42, no. 3 (Jan – Mar 93), pp. 571 – 620. Bibl.

Rodríguez Ochoa, Patricia. Del arte a la escritura, de la visión al desciframiento. *Vuelta*, v. 17, no. 203 (Oct 93), pp. 23 – 24. Il.

— El desciframiento de la escritura maya: una historia. *Vuelta*, v. 17, no. 203 (Oct 93), pp. 21 – 22.

Rodríguez-Orellana, Manuel. A Chance to Decolonize. *Hemisphere*, v. 5, no. 3 (Summer – Fall 93), pp. 42 – 43.

Rodríguez Ozán, María Elena. Las ideologías de los inmigrantes europeos en América Latina. *Cuadernos Americanos*, no. 41, Nueva época (Sept – Oct 93), pp. 122 – 130. Bibl.

— La inmigración europea en Latinoamérica. *Cuadernos Americanos*, no. 37, Nueva época (Jan – Feb 93), pp. 37 – 47. Bibl.

Rodríguez Padrón, Justo Jorge. La palabra en Atacama. *Chasqui*, v. 22, no. 1 (May 93), pp. 19 – 22.

Rodríguez-Peralta, Phyllis White. The Modernist Nocturno and the Nocturne in Music. *Hispanic Journal*, v. 14, no. 1 (Spring 93), pp. 143 – 155.

Rodríguez Pérsico, Adriana C. Arlt: sacar las palabras de todos los ángulos. *Cuadernos Hispanoamericanos*, no. Special issue, 11 (July 93), pp. 5 – 14. Bibl, il.

— Entrevista con Ana María Barrenechea. *La Educación (USA)*, v. 36, no. 111 – 113 (1992), pp. 237 – 243. Il.

— Las fronteras de la identidad: la pregunta por la identidad nacional. *Hispamérica*, v. 22, no. 64 – 65 (Apr – Aug 93), pp. 23 – 48. Bibl.

— Sarmiento y Alberdi: una práctica legitimante. *La Educación (USA)*, v. 36, no. 111 – 113 (1992), pp. 177 – 192. Bibl.

Rodríguez Pérsico, Adriana C. and Rosario Güenaga de Silva. El interés de la diplomacia española por los problemas argentino – chilenos en el seno de Ultima Esperanza. *Revista de Historia de América*, no. 112 (July – Dec 91), pp. 85 – 103. Bibl.

Rodríguez Rabanal, César. La cultura del diálogo. *Debate (Peru)*, v. 16, no. 73 (June – Aug 93), pp. 27 – 30. Il.

— Momento de escozor. *Debate (Peru)*, v. 16, no. 72 (Mar – May 93), p. 29.

Rodríguez Rivera, Guillermo. La elegía familiar de *Los heraldos negros* a *Trilce*. *Casa de las Américas*, no. 189 (Oct – Dec 92), pp. 51 – 56.

Rodríguez Rivera, Oscar. Derechos políticos y autonomía regional. *Nueva Antropología*, v. 13, no. 44 (Aug 93), pp. 137 – 141.

Rodríguez Sáenz, Eugenia. Historia de la familia en América Latina: balance de las principales tendencias. *Revista de Historia (Costa Rica)*, no. 26 (July – Dec 92), pp. 145 – 183. Bibl.

Rodríguez Sáenz, Eugenia and Iván Molina Jiménez. Compraventas de cafetales y haciendas de café en el valle central de Costa Rica, 1834 – 1850. *Anuario de Estudios Centroamericanos*, v. 18, no. 1 (1992), pp. 29 – 50. Bibl, tables, maps, charts.

Rodríguez Solera, Carlos Rafael. Problemas y perspectivas de la sociología costarricense contemporánea. *Anuario de Estudios Centroamericanos*, v. 18, no. 1 (1992), pp. 51 – 59. Bibl.

Rodríguez Villamil, Silvia. Mujeres uruguayas a fines del siglo XIX: ¿Cómo hacer su historia? *Boletín Americanista*, v. 33, no. 42 – 43 (1992 – 1993), pp. 71 – 85. Bibl.

Rodríguez y Rodríguez, Salvador and Alejandro Angulo Carrera. Agricultura orgánica, desarrollo sustentable y comercio justo. *Problemas del Desarrollo*, v. 24, no. 94 (July – Sept 93), pp. 265 – 274.

Rodrik, Dani and Sule Ozler. Los choques externos, la política y la inversión privada: algo de teoría y evidencia empírica. *El Trimestre Económico*, v. 59, Special issue (Dec 92), pp. 187 – 212. Bibl, tables, charts.

Rofman, Adriana and Mabel Bellucci. Una década de mujeres en movimiento. *Todo Es Historia*, v. 27, no. 317 (Dec 93), pp. 74 – 77. Il.

Rofman, Alejandro Boris. Estrategias frente al desafío MERCOSUR. *Realidad Económica,* no. 114 – 115 (Feb – May 93), pp. 130 – 189. Bibl, il, tables.

Rogachevesky, Jorge R. When Does It Snow in Cuba?: Nicolás Guillén and the Poetry of *Cerebro y corazón. Afro-Hispanic Review,* v. 12, no. 1 (Spring 93), pp. 24 – 33. Bibl.

Rogers, Andrei and Alain Belanger. The Internal Migration and Spatial Redistribution of the Foreign-Born Population in the United States: 1965 – 1970 and 1975 – 1980. *International Migration Review,* v. 26, no. 4 (Winter 92), pp. 1342 – 1369. Bibl, tables, charts.

Rogers, John E. NAFTA Dispute Settlement for the Finance Sector. *Business Mexico,* v. 3, no. 6 (June 93), pp. 40 – 42.

Roitman Rosenmann, Marcos. Democracia y estado multiétnico en América Latina. *Boletín de Antropología Americana,* no. 24 (Dec 91), pp. 63 – 78. Bibl, il.

— España y América Latina en el contexto del quinto centenario. *Boletín de Antropología Americana,* no. 23 (July 91), pp. 83 – 98. Bibl, il.

— Gregorio Selser: "Maestro artesano del pensamiento latinoamericano." *Revista Española de Antropología Americana,* v. 23 (1993), pp. 233 – 242.

Rojas, Gonzalo. Breve antología poética de Gonzalo Rojas. *Atenea (Chile),* no. 465 – 466 (1992), pp. 281 – 290.

— Carta a Huidobro y otros poemas. *Vuelta,* v. 17, no. 202 (Sept 93), pp. 10 – 12. Il.

— Discurso de aceptación del premio Reina Sofía de Poesía Iberoamericana, 1993. *Chasqui,* v. 22, no. 1 (May 93), pp. 4 – 11. Il.

— Huidobro de repente. *Atenea (Chile),* no. 467 (1993), pp. 65 – 66. Il.

— Poems ("Cítara por el muerto," "Pasto del verano," "Arco y tensión," "Orquídea en el gentío," "Enigma de la deseosa"). *Casa de las Américas,* no. 191 (Apr – June 93), pp. 64 – 66.

Rojas, Rafael. La memoria de un patricio. *Op. Cit.,* no. 7 (1992), pp. 121 – 144. Il.

Rojas, Rafael Armando

See
    Rojas Guardia, Armando

Rojas, Waldo. Motivos, prevenciones y algunas reservas para entrar en materia: o preámbulo evitable a una lectura de poemas. *Revista Chilena de Literatura,* no. 42 (Aug 93), pp. 223 – 236.

Rojas Aravena, Francisco. América Latina: el difícil camino de la concertación y la integración. *Nueva Sociedad,* no. 125 (May – June 93), pp. 60 – 69. Bibl.

— El Cono Sur latinoamericano y la Iniciativa para las Américas. *Estudios Internacionales (Chile),* v. 26, no. 101 (Jan – Mar 93), pp. 98 – 122. Bibl.

Rojas Beltrán, Fabio Augusto. El divorcio. *Revista Javeriana,* v. 61, no. 599 (Oct 93), pp. 351 – 353.

Rojas Flores, Gonzalo. La casa comercial Gibbs y Co. y sus inversiones en Chile entre las décadas de 1920 y 1940. *Historia (Chile),* no. 26 (1991 – 1992), pp. 259 – 295. Bibl.

Rojas Gil, Rogelio. Eloy Febres Cordero. *Boletín de la Academia Nacional de la Historia (Venezuela),* v. 76, no. 302 (Apr – June 93), pp. 144 – 145.

Rojas Gómez, Miguel. Alejandro Serrano Caldera: una nueva filosofía de la conciencia y la libertad. *Islas,* no. 99 (May – Aug 91), pp. 130 – 154. Bibl.

— Del exilio de la razón a la razón de la libertad en Osvaldo Ardiles. *Islas,* no. 99 (May – Aug 91), pp. 112 – 129. Bibl.

— Identidad cultural y liberación en la filosofía latinoamericana de la liberación. *Islas,* no. 96 (May – Aug 90), pp. 103 – 110.

Rojas Guardia, Armando. El deslumbramiento del Almirante. *Boletín de la Academia Nacional de la Historia (Venezuela),* v. 75, no. 300 (Oct – Dec 92), pp. 118 – 120.

— El deslumbramiento del Almirante. *Revista Nacional de Cultura (Venezuela),* v. 54, no. 287 (Oct – Dec 92), pp. 234 – 236.

— Palabras pronunciadas en el acto de inauguración de un busto del dr. Alberto Adriani en Caracas el día 14 de junio de 1991. *Boletín de la Academia Nacional de la Historia (Venezuela),* v. 75, no. 297 (Jan – Mar 92), pp. 43 – 46.

Rojas Orozco, Rodrigo. Reinserción y educación: el programa piloto-experimental de pedagogía para la paz y la reconciliación nacional. *Revista Javeriana,* v. 60, no. 590 (Nov – Dec 92), pp. 325 – 329.

Rojas Osorio, Carlos. Hostos y la identidad caribeña. *Caribbean Studies,* v. 25, no. 1 – 2 (Jan – July 92), pp. 133 – 145. Bibl.

Rojas Ramos, Patricio. El dinero como un objetivo intermedio de política monetaria en Chile: un análisis empírico. *Cuadernos de Economía (Chile),* v. 30, no. 90 (Aug 93), pp. 139 – 178. Bibl, tables, charts.

Rojas-Trempe, Lady. Apuntes sobre *Cambio de armas* de Luisa Valenzuela. *Letras Femeninas,* v. 19, no. 1 – 2 (Spring – Fall 93), pp. 74 – 83. Bibl.

Rojas y Gutiérrez de Gandarilla, José Luis de. La sociedad indígena novohispana en el siglo XVI a través del tributo. *Revista Española de Antropología Americana,* v. 23 (1993), pp. 153 – 164. Bibl.

Rojas Zolezzi, Enrique Carlos. Concepciones sobre la relación entre géneros: mitos, ritual y organización del trabajo en la unidad doméstica campa – asháninka. *Amazonía Peruana,* v. 11, no. 22 (Oct 92), pp. 175 – 220. Bibl.

Rojo, Daniel. Trades. *The Americas Review,* v. 20, no. 1 (Spring 92), pp. 50 – 51.

Rojo, Grínor. El teatro latinoamericano moderno: notas para una nueva historia, primer movimiento. *Conjunto,* no. 90 – 91 (Jan – June 92), pp. 2 – 9. Bibl.

Roldán Fernández de Soldevilla, Francisco. Al señor Marqués de Menahermosa (dn. Joseph de Llamas), brigadier de los Reales Exércitos de S.M. Cabo Principal del Callao, teniente de capitán general de S.E. comandante general de las fronteras de la provincia de Tarma D.O.C. (1751). *Amazonía Peruana,* v. 11, no. 22 (Oct 92), pp. 221 – 254.

Rollins, Peter C. and John J. Deveny, Jr., eds. *Culture and Development in Colombia: Study of Changes in Social Roles, Religion, Literature* . . . Special issue of *Journal of Popular Culture,* 22:1 (Summer 88), reviewed by Maurice P. Brungardt (Review entitled "Readings on Colombia?"). *Studies in Latin American Popular Culture,* v. 12 (1993), pp. 235 – 242.

Roman, Peter. Representative Government in Socialist Cuba. *Latin American Perspectives,* v. 20, no. 1 (Winter 93), pp. 7 – 27.

Román de Dios, Eurídice. Luna eclipsada. *Plural (Mexico),* v. 22, no. 267 (Dec 93), pp. 49 – 50.

Román Delgado, Samuel. El atalayismo: innovación y renovación en la literatura puertorriqueña. *Revista Iberoamericana,* v. 59, no. 162 – 163 (Jan – June 93), pp. 93 – 100. Bibl.

Romaña, José María de. 1994, ¿decisión o incertidumbre? *Debate (Peru),* v. 16, no. 75 (Dec 93 – Jan 94), p. 19. Il.

Romano, Eduardo. Parodia televisiva y sobre otros géneros discursivos populares. *Cuadernos Hispanoamericanos,* no. 517 – 519 (July – Sept 93), pp. 323 – 335. Bibl.

Romano Sued, Susana. Universidad Nacional de Córdoba: mirada a través de los últimos veinte años. *Cuadernos Hispanoamericanos,* no. 517 – 519 (July – Sept 93), pp. 92 – 104.

Romany, Celina. Hacia una crítica feminista del derecho internacional en materia de derechos humanos. *Fem,* v. 17, no. 126 (Aug 93), pp. 19 – 22.

— Poems ("Personales," "Plegaria en Bahía," "en nueva york," "a la cama, niños," "ábrete sésamo," "oda a la muerte"). *The Americas Review,* v. 21, no. 1 (Spring 93), pp. 41 – 48.

Romay, Benito Rey

See

Rey Romay, Benito

Romero, Armando. Historia de dos en el cenobio. *Inti,* no. 36 (Fall 92), pp. 175 – 179.

Romero, Gloria Jean. "No se raje, chicanita": Some Thoughts on Race, Class, and Gender in the Classroom. *Aztlán,* v. 20, no. 1 – 2 (Spring – Fall 91), pp. 203 – 218. Bibl.

Romero, Jorge Javier. La política de mañana: la futura forma institucional. *Nexos,* v. 16, no. 192 (Dec 93), pp. 53 – 67. Bibl.

Romero, José and Leslie Young. Crecimiento constante y transición en un modelo dinámico dual del Acuerdo de Libre Comercio de la América del Norte (Translated by Carlos Villegas). *El Trimestre Económico,* v. 60, no. 238 (Apr – June 93), pp. 353 – 370. Bibl.

Romero, José Luis. La ciudad latinoamericana y los movimientos políticos. *Siglo XIX: Revista,* no. 11, 2a época (Jan – June 92), pp. 15 – 27.

Romero, Leo. Poems ("I Bring Twins over to Meet Pito," "How Did I Land up in This City," "Pito Had a Dream That," "Diane's Knocking," "When Pito Tried to Kill"). *The Americas Review,* v. 20, no. 3 – 4 (Fall – Winter 92), pp. 238 – 247.

— Rita and Los Angeles. *Bilingual Review/Revista Bilingüe,* v. 18, no. 1 (Jan – Apr 93), pp. 23 – 47.

— Short Stories ("Lucinda," "Lucinda at Home," "When Women Go to Sleep," "Besides Wasting Electricity, It's Dangerous"). *The Americas Review,* v. 19, no. 3 – 4 (Winter 91), pp. 7 – 16.

Romero, Rita Giacalone de

See

Giacalone de Romero, Rita

Romero Baró, José María. Ciencia y filosofía en el pensador uruguayo Carlos Vaz Ferreira. *Hoy Es Historia,* v. 10, no. 58 (July – Aug 93), pp. 10 – 14. Bibl.

Romero C., Paulino. Pedagogía experimental y política. *Revista Cultural Lotería,* v. 50, no. 384 (July – Aug 91), pp. 68 – 75.

— La planificación de la educación superior. *Revista Cultural Lotería,* v. 51, no. 387 (Feb 92), pp. 52 – 60.

— Vida familiar y adolescencia. *Revista Cultural Lotería,* v. 50, no. 385 (Sept – Oct 91), pp. 73 – 82. Bibl.

Romero de Nohra, Flor. El espíritu del volcán. *Caravelle,* no. 60 (1993), pp. 123 – 134.

Romero Gil, Juan Manuel. Minería y sociedad en el noroeste porfirista. *Siglo XIX: Cuadernos,* v. 1, no. 1 (Oct 91), pp. 37 – 73. Bibl, tables.

Romero Keith, José and Homero Martínez Salgado. La educación nutricional en el medio rural: una propuesta pedagógica. *Revista Latinoamericana de Estudios Educativos,* v. 23, no. 1 (Jan – Mar 93), pp. 75 – 86.

Romero León, Jorge. La sociedad de los poetas muertos. *Escritura (Venezuela),* v. 17, no. 33 – 34 (Jan – Dec 92), pp. 101 – 113.

Romero Miranda, Miguel Angel. PRD: futuro inmediato. *El Cotidiano,* v. 9, no. 55 (June 93), pp. 99 – 102. Il.

Romero Miranda, Miguel Angel and Mario Alejandro Carrillo. Un rostro nuevo en una vieja identidad: el Foro Doctrinario y Democrático en la formación de un nuevo partido político. *El Cotidiano,* v. 9, no. 53 (Mar – Apr 93), pp. 105 – 109. Bibl, il.

Romero Miranda, Miguel Angel and Alejandro Carrillo Castro. Las preocupaciones públicas: el caso de Tamaulipas. *El Cotidiano,* v. 8, no. 51 (Nov – Dec 92), pp. 95 – 101. Tables.

Romero Miranda, Miguel Angel and Javier Gutiérrez Rodríguez. Síndrome de fin de sexenio. *El Cotidiano,* v. 10, no. 58 (Oct – Nov 93), pp. 8 – 21. Il, tables.

Romero Miranda, Miguel Angel and Arturo Venegas. Acción Nacional: consolidar espacios de poder regional. *El Cotidiano,* v. 10, no. 57 (Aug – Sept 93), pp. 79 – 85. Il.

Romero Miranda, Miguel Angel et al. Muchos cambios legales que agitan las aguas políticas. *El Cotidiano,* v. 10, no. 58 (Oct – Nov 93), pp. 60 – 70. Il, tables.

Romero Ortiz, María Elena. Energía y desarrollo económico en la cuenca del Pacífico. *Comercio Exterior,* v. 43, no. 12 (Dec 93), pp. 1181 – 1187.

Romero Pittari, Salvador. Movimientos regionales en Bolivia. *Homines,* v. 15 – 16, no. 2 – 1 (Oct 91 – Dec 92), pp. 61 – 74. Bibl, tables.

Romero Polanco, Emilio. Comercialización del café y el sector social en México. *Momento Económico,* no. 66 (Mar – Apr 93), pp. 14 – 17. Tables.

— Crisis internacional del café: impactos y perspectivas. *Problemas del Desarrollo,* v. 24, no. 94 (July – Sept 93), pp. 75 – 95. Bibl, tables.

Romero Romero, Catalina. Tres bibliotecas jesuitas en pueblos de misión: Buenavista, Paila y Santa Rosa en la región de Moxos. *Revista de Indias,* v. 52, no. 195 – 196 (May – Dec 92), pp. 889 – 921.

Rondón de Sansó, Hildegard. Tomás Polanco Alcántara o el hombre que venció los tabúes impuestos al biógrafo contemporáneo. *Boletín de la Academia Nacional de la Historia (Venezuela),* v. 75, no. 298 (Apr – June 92), pp. 29 – 31.

Roopnarine, Jaipaul L. and Mohammad Ahmeduzzaman. Puerto Rican Fathers' Involvement with Their Preschool-Age Children. *Hispanic Journal of Behavioral Sciences,* v. 15, no. 1 (Feb 93), pp. 96 – 107. Bibl, tables.

Ropp, Steve C. What Have We Learned from the Noriega Crisis? (Review article). *Latin American Research Review,* v. 28, no. 3 (1993), pp. 189 – 196.

Rosa, Nicolás. Veinte años después o la "novela familiar" de la crítica literaria. *Cuadernos Hispanoamericanos,* no. 517 – 519 (July – Sept 93), pp. 161 – 186.

Rosa, William. Ciencia y literatura en Alfredo Collado Martell: un primer caso de inseminación artificial. *Revista Iberoamericana,* v. 59, no. 162 – 163 (Jan – June 93), pp. 111 – 118. Bibl.

Rosales, Osvaldo. La segunda fase exportadora en Chile. *Comercio Exterior,* v. 43, no. 9 (Sept 93), pp. 859 – 864.

Rosales O., Rosa and María Elena Loáiciga G. La población anciana de Liberia: condición socioeconómica precaria. *Revista de Ciencias Sociales (Costa Rica),* no. 59 (Mar 93), pp. 95 – 106. Bibl, tables.

Rosas, Alan L. et al. NAFTA's Environmental Issues and Opportunities. *Business Mexico,* v. 3, no. 9 (Sept 93), pp. 42 – 45.

Rosas, Yolanda. Hacia una identidad en *Cosecha de pecadores* de Rima de Vallbona. *The Americas Review,* v. 19, no. 3 – 4 (Winter 91), pp. 134 – 145. Bibl.

Rosas González, María Cristina. El TLC entre México, Estados Unidos y Canadá: semejanzas y diferencias con el ALC entre Canadá y Estados Unidos. *Relaciones Internacionales (Mexico),* v. 15, Nueva época, no. 57 (Jan – Mar 93), pp. 55 – 62. Charts.

Roscio, Juan Germán. Testamento del señor dr. Juan Germán Roscio (Previously published in this journal, vol. 1, no. 1, 1912). *Boletín de la Academia Nacional de la Historia (Venezuela),* v. 75, no. 300 (Oct – Dec 92), pp. 275 – 278.

Rosell Gómez, Eunice et al. Dussel: dependencia y liberación en los marcos de la teoría económica. *Islas,* no. 99 (May – Aug 91), pp. 155 – 159.

Rosemberg, Fernando. La aventura chaqueña de Horacio Quiroga. *Todo Es Historia,* v. 27, no. 312 (July 93), pp. 66 – 72. Il, facs.

Rosenberg, Mark B. Whither the Caribbean?: Whither Florida? *Hemisphere,* v. 5, no. 2 (Winter – Spring 93), pp. 9 – 11.

Rosenberg, Mirta. Poems (Excerpt from the forthcoming book entitled *Teoría sentimental). Feminaria,* v. 6, no. 11, Suppl. (Nov 93), p. 22.

Rosenblatt, David and Ana Dolores Novaes. O poder regional no Congresso: uma atualização. *Revista Brasileira de Economia,* v. 47, no. 2 (Apr – June 93), pp. 305 – 312. Bibl, tables.

Rosende Ramírez, Francisco. La autonomía del Banco Central de Chile: una evaluación preliminar. *Cuadernos de Economía (Chile),* v. 30, no. 91 (Dec 93), pp. 293 – 326. Bibl, tables.

— La economía chilena en el gobierno de la concertación: una evaluación preliminar. *Estudios Sociales (Chile),* no. 75 (Jan – Mar 93), pp. 57 – 76. Tables.

Rosenfeld, Stephanie. Comunero Democracy Endures in Chile. *NACLA Report on the Americas,* v. 27, no. 2 (Sept – Oct 93), pp. 29 – 34.

Rosenhek, Zeev. "Desarrollo controlado": la economía política del desarrollo en la región atlántica de Costa Rica. *Ibero Americana (Sweden),* v. 22, no. 2 (Dec 92), pp. 21 – 46. Bibl, tables.

Rosenthal, Gert. Balance preliminar de la economía de América Latina y el Caribe, 1992. *Comercio Exterior,* v. 43, no. 3 (Mar 93), pp. 276 – 298. Tables.

— Treinta años de integración en América Latina: un examen crítico. *Estudios Internacionales (Chile),* v. 26, no. 101 (Jan – Mar 93), pp. 74 – 88.

Rosenzvaig, Eduardo. Los hechiceros: una variante colonial americana de los brujos. *Cuadernos Hispanoamericanos,* no. 522 (Dec 93), pp. 47 – 66. Bibl, il.

Rosenzvaig, Eduardo and Luis Marcos Bonano. Contrapunto azucarero entre relaciones de producción y tecnología: el perfil argentino. *Realidad Económica,* no. 113 (Jan – Feb 93), pp. 52 – 86. Il.

Roses, Lorraine Elena. Las esperanzas de Pandora: prototipos femeninos de la obra de Rosario Ferré. *Revista Iberoamericana,* v. 59, no. 162 – 163 (Jan – June 93), pp. 279 – 287.

Rospigliosi, Fernando. La ausencia de los jóvenes en la política. *Debate (Peru),* v. 16, no. 74 (Sept – Oct 93), pp. 32 – 33. Il.

Rossi, José W. and Benedict J. Clements. Ligações interindustriais e setores-chave na economia brasileira. *Pesquisa e Planejamento Econômico,* v. 22, no. 1 (Apr 92), pp. 101 – 123. Bibl, tables.

Rosso, Walter Betbeder. Alberto Schunk: A Canvas for Contemplation (Translated by Kathleen Forrester). *Américas,* v. 45, no. 4 (July – Aug 93), pp. 54 – 55. Il.

Rostworowski Tovar de Diez Canseco, María. El Dios Con y el misterio de la pampa de Nasca. *Latin American Indian Literatures Journal,* v. 9, no. 1 (Spring 93), pp. 21 – 30.

— La visita de Urcos de 1652: un kipu pueblerino. *Historia y Cultura (Peru),* no. 20 (1990), pp. 295 – 317. Bibl, tables.

Rothstein, Richard. El desarrollo continental y el comercio entre México y Estados Unidos: ¿Por qué los trabajadores estadunidenses necesitan salarios más altos en México? *Relaciones Internacionales (Mexico),* v. 15, Nueva época, no. 57 (Jan – Mar 93), pp. 63 – 74.

Rotker, Susana. La crónica venezolana de los '80: una lectura del caos. *Hispamérica,* v. 22, no. 64 – 65 (Apr – Aug 93), pp. 55 – 65. Bibl.

— Crónica y cultura urbana: Caracas, la última década. *Inti,* no. 37 – 38 (Spring – Fall 93), pp. 233 – 242. Bibl.

— Simón Rodríguez: utopía y transgresión. *Casa de las Américas,* no. 191 (Apr – June 93), pp. 51 – 57. Bibl.

Rovira, José Carlos. Dos novelas de Alcides Arguedas. *Cuadernos Hispanoamericanos,* no. 512 (Feb 93), pp. 103 – 106.

Rowe, William. Dimensiones históricas de la poesía quechua: el caso de las danzas guerreras de Toqroyoq y su relación con la producción poética andina. *Revista de Crítica Literaria Latinoamericana,* v. 19, no. 37 (Jan – June 93), pp. 41 – 62. Bibl.

Royle, Stephen A. The Small Island as Colony. *Caribbean Geography,* v. 3, no. 4 (Sept 92), pp. 261 – 269. Bibl, tables, maps.

Rozitchner, León. Marxismo, crisis e intelectuales. *Cuadernos Hispanoamericanos,* no. 517 – 519 (July – Sept 93), pp. 483 – 494.

Rubalcava, Rosa María and Fernando Cortés C. Algunas determinantes de la inserción laboral en la industria maquiladora de exportación de Matamoros. *Estudios Sociológicos,* v. 11, no. 31 (Jan – Apr 93), pp. 59 – 91. Bibl, tables.

Rubalcava, Rosa María and Vania Salles. Hogares de trabajadoras y percepciones femeninas. *El Cotidiano,* v. 9, no. 53 (Mar – Apr 93), pp. 40 – 46. Tables.

Rubial García, Antonio. Un mercader de plata andaluz en Nueva España: Diego del Castillo, 161? – 1683. *Anuario de Estudios Americanos,* v. 49 (1992), pp. 143 – 170. Bibl, il.

Rubiano Caballero, Germán. I Bienal de Pintura del Caribe y Centroamérica (Accompanied by an English translation). *Art Nexus,* no. 7 (Jan – Mar 93), pp. 81 – 82. Il.

Rubin, Steven M. and Fred P. Phillips IV. Debt for Nature: Swap Meet for the '90s. *Business Mexico,* v. 3, no. 1 (Jan – Feb 93), pp. 46 – 47.

Rubin-Kurtzman, Jane R. Los determinantes de la oferta de trabajo femenino en la ciudad de México, 1970. *Estudios Demográficos y Urbanos,* v. 6, no. 3 (Sept – Dec 91), pp. 545 – 582. Bibl, tables.

— La etnia en las políticas de población de la frontera norte: reflexiones sobre un tema poco explorado y una agenda de investigación. *Frontera Norte*, v. 4, no. 8 (July – Dec 92), pp. 111 – 123. Bibl.

Rubio del Valle, Ximena. Minuto de cambio. *Letras Femeninas*, v. 19, no. 1 – 2 (Spring – Fall 93), p. 181.

Rubio F., Luis. Los límites del cambio político. *Nexos*, v. 16, no. 187 (July 93), pp. 63 – 68.

— El talón de Aquiles de la reforma económica. *Vuelta*, v. 17, no. 200 (July 93), pp. 36 – 39.

— El TLC y la democracia (Response to the article entitled "Hacia otro TLC" by Jorge G. Castañeda and Carlos Heredia). *Nexos*, v. 16, no. 182 (Feb 93), pp. 63 – 66.

Ruccio, David F. The Hidden Successes of Failed Economic Policies. *Report on the Americas*, v. 26, no. 4 (Feb 93), pp. 38 – 43 + . Bibl, il, tables.

Rueda Iturrate, Carlos José de. Financiación de la Orden de San Francisco en los cedularios del Archivo General de Indias. *Archivo Ibero-Americano*, v. 52, no. 205 – 208 (Jan – Dec 92), pp. 833 – 848.

Rueda Peiró, Isabel. Deterioro y mayor desigualdad en el empleo y los salarios de los trabajadores mexicanos. *Momento Económico*, no. 69 (Sept – Oct 93), pp. 6 – 9. Tables.

Rufián Lizana, Dolores María. Una nueva administración municipal. *Revista Paraguaya de Sociología*, v. 29, no. 85 (Sept – Dec 92), pp. 59 – 71. Charts.

Rufián Lizana, Dolores María and Eduardo Palma. La descentralización de los servicios sociales. *Estudios Sociales (Chile)*, no. 77 (July – Sept 93), pp. 73 – 116. Bibl.

Ruge S., Tiahoga. It's Not Nice to Fool Mother Nature. *Business Mexico*, v. 3, no. 1 (Jan – Feb 93), pp. 63 – 64. Il.

Ruiloba C., Rafael. Consuelo Tomás o la nueva mirada. *Revista Cultural Lotería*, v. 51, no. 390 (July – Aug 92), pp. 27 – 32.

— "No me resigno a que el lenguaje pierda su capacidad de alucinar": entrevista con Lionel Méndez D'Avila. *USAC*, no. 12 (Dec 90), pp. 28 – 30.

— Viviane Nathan o la profecía de la ternura. *Revista Cultural Lotería*, v. 51, no. 387 (Feb 92), pp. 43 – 51.

Ruiz, Bernardo. José Juan Tablada escribe un poema. *Nexos*, v. 16, no. 192 (Dec 93), pp. 89 – 90.

Ruiz, David. Belize's Literary Heritage: A 500-Year Perspective. *Belizean Studies*, v. 21, no. 2 (Oct 93), pp. 28 – 33.

Ruiz, Gabriela. To Go or Not to Go. *Business Mexico*, v. 3, no. 10 (Oct 93), pp. 20 – 22.

Ruiz, Irma. Un proyecto trunco. *Revista Musical de Venezuela*, no. 28 (May – Dec 89), pp. 98 – 105. Charts.

Ruiz, Marta. Migración entre Haití y la República Dominicana. *Cuadernos Hispanoamericanos*, no. 522 (Dec 93), pp. 77 – 86.

Ruiz, Rosa. El aporte de la cultura negra en el departamento de Cerro Largo. *Hoy Es Historia*, v. 10, no. 55 (Jan – Feb 93), pp. 72 – 75.

Ruiz Abreu, Alvaro. Revueltas o la fidelidad eterna. *Nexos*, v. 16, no. 183 (Mar 93), pp. 53 – 55.

— Sergio Galindo: las letras solitarias. *Nexos*, v. 16, no. 182 (Feb 93), pp. 11 – 13.

Ruiz Barrionuevo, Carmen. *Cinco visiones* de Gonzalo Rojas. *Chasqui*, v. 22, no. 1 (May 93), pp. 12 – 18.

Ruiz Chataing, David. Novedades bibliográficas en la Biblioteca Nacional. *Boletín de la Academia Nacional de la Historia (Venezuela)*, no. 297, 299 – 302 (Jan 92 – June 93), All issues.

— La revista *El Cojo Ilustrado* y el antiimperialismo. *Revista Nacional de Cultura (Venezuela)*, v. 53, no. 286 (July – Sept 92), pp. 177 – 186. Bibl, il.

Ruiz Chiapetto, Crescencio. El desarrollo del México urbano: cambio de protagonista. *Comercio Exterior*, v. 43, no. 8 (Aug 93), pp. 708 – 716. Bibl, tables, maps.

— Migración interna y desarrollo económico: tres etapas. *Estudios Demográficos y Urbanos*, v. 6, no. 3 (Sept – Dec 91), pp. 727 – 736.

Ruiz Durán, Clemente. México: crecimiento e innovación en las micro y pequeñas empresas. *Comercio Exterior*, v. 43, no. 6 (June 93), pp. 525 – 529.

Ruiz-Giménez, Guadalupe. Un nuevo orden internacional para el desarrollo sostenible. *Cuadernos Americanos*, no. 39, Nueva época (May – June 93), pp. 81 – 87.

Ruiz Granados, Fernando. Agua de piedra. *Plural (Mexico)*, v. 22, no. 258 (Mar 93), pp. 4 – 13.

Ruiz Gutiérrez, Rosaura and Francisco J. Ayala. Darwinismo y sociedad en México. *Siglo XIX: Revista*, no. 12, 2a época (July – Dec 92), pp. 87 – 104. Bibl.

Ruiz Martínez, Eduardo. ¿Qué es la "Sociedad Nariñista de Colombia"? *Boletín de Historia y Antigüedades*, v. 80, no. 780 (Jan – Mar 93), pp. 247 – 249.

Ruiz Ortiz, Juana María and Anna María Garza Caligaris. Madres solteras indígenas. *Mesoamérica (USA)*, v. 13, no. 23 (June 92), pp. 66 – 77. Bibl.

Ruiz Rivera, Julián Bautista. Congreso internacional: 500 Años de Hispanoamérica; Descubrimiento y Formación de un Mundo Nuevo. *Anuario de Estudios Americanos*, v. 49, Suppl. 2 (1992), pp. 209 – 210.

— V Congreso de la Asociación Española de Americanistas. *Anuario de Estudios Americanos*, v. 49, Suppl. 1 (1992), pp. 216 – 219.

Ruiz Rojas, Ana Isabel and Iris María Obando Hidalgo. Epidemiología del abuso físico y sexual en niños atendidos en el Hospital de Niños, 1988 – 1990. *Revista de Ciencias Sociales (Costa Rica)*, no. 59 (Mar 93), pp. 63 – 70. Bibl, tables, charts.

Ruiz-Tagle P., Jaime. La CUT acepta el modelo exportador. *Mensaje*, v. 42, no. 418 (May 93), pp. 117 – 119. Tables.

— ONG y políticas públicas: nuevas formas de solidaridad institucionalizada. *Mensaje*, v. 42, no. 421 (Aug 93), pp. 378 – 381. Il, tables.

— Reducción de la pobreza y distribución de los ingresos en Chile: tareas pendientes. *Mensaje*, v. 42, no. 425 (Dec 93), pp. 640 – 643. Il, tables.

Rus, Diane L. La vida y el trabajo en Ciudad Real: conversaciones con las "coletas." *Mesoamérica (USA)*, v. 13, no. 23 (June 92), pp. 113 – 133. Il.

Russell, Craig H. Musical Life in Baroque Mexico: Rowdy Musicians, Confraternities, and the Holy Office. *Inter-American Music Review*, v. 13, no. 1 (Fall – Winter 92), pp. 11 – 14. Bibl, facs.

— Newly Discovered Treasures from Colonial California: The Masses at San Fernando. *Inter-American Music Review*, v. 13, no. 1 (Fall – Winter 92), pp. 5 – 9. Bibl.

Russell, Joel. Advice for Insurance Shoppers. *Business Mexico*, v. 3, no. 11 (Nov 93), pp. 27 – 28.

— A Better Neighborhood. *Business Mexico*, v. 3, no. 3 (Mar 93), pp. 46 – 47. Il.

— Governing for Growth. *Business Mexico*, v. 3, no. 5 (May 93), pp. 29 – 30. Il.

— Pass the Chips. *Business Mexico,* v. 3, no. 8 (Aug 93), pp. 39 – 41. Il.

— Quiet Revolution. *Business Mexico,* v. 3, no. 6 (June 93), p. 27. Il.

— Stating Their Case. *Business Mexico,* v. 3, no. 12 (Dec 93), pp. 24 – 28.

— A Worldwide Brand Name. *Business Mexico,* v. 3, no. 10 (Oct 93), pp. 12 – 14. Il.

Russell, Joel and Joshua A. Cohen. A New Dynamic in the Americas. *Business Mexico,* v. 3, no. 12 (Dec 93), pp. 43 – 45. Il.

Russell, Joel and Cristopher Fleischman. The Company You Keep. *Business Mexico,* v. 3, no. 5 (May 93), pp. 42 – 43. Charts.

Russell, Roberto G. Reflexiones sobre lo "nuevo" del "nuevo orden mundial." *Estudios Internacionales (Chile),* v. 26, no. 102 (Apr – June 93), pp. 134 – 154. Bibl.

Russotto, Márgara. Pequeña diacronía: la heroína melodramática. *Escritura (Venezuela),* v. 16, no. 31 – 32 (Jan – Dec 91), pp. 231 – 245. Bibl.

Ruz, Mario Humberto. Sebastiana de la Cruz, alias "La Polilla": mulata de Petapa y madre del hijo de Dios. *Mesoamérica (USA),* v. 13, no. 23 (June 92), pp. 55 – 66. Bibl.

Ruz Ruz, Juan D. Lo instrumental y lo valórico en la educación chilena: aportes para la discusión sobre los objetivos fundamentales y los contenidos mínimos de la educación. *Estudios Sociales (Chile),* no. 74 (Oct – Dec 92), pp. 167 – 175.

Saavedra, Gonzalo. La familia grande de Rosario y Manuel. *Mensaje,* v. 42, no. 419 (June 93), pp. 214 – 215. Il.

— Mercedes Echeñique: la tía Pin tocó "la verdad de Chile." *Mensaje,* v. 42, no. 421 (Aug 93), pp. 361 – 362. Il.

— Para Andrés, la esperanza está en Bitkine. *Mensaje,* v. 42, no. 417 (Mar – Apr 93), pp. 104 – 105. Il.

Saavedra Pinochet, Rafael. Los rivadeneiros relatos de Rivadeneira Prada. *Signo,* no. 38, Nueva época (Jan – Apr 93), pp. 155 – 160.

Saba, Raúl P. Peru's Informal Sector: Hope in the Midst of Crisis. *SALALM Papers,* v. 36 (1991), pp. 35 – 41. Bibl.

Sabalette, Delfor. Nunca más una sombra. *Plural (Mexico),* v. 22, no. 263 (Aug 93), pp. 63 – 65.

Sábato, Ernesto R. Críticas al bloqueo norteamericano a Cuba. *Realidad Económica,* no. 117 (July – Aug 93), pp. 33 – 34.

— Nunca más (Prologue to the book of the same title). *Cuadernos Hispanoamericanos,* no. 517 – 519 (July – Sept 93), pp. 571 – 573.

Sábato, Hilda. Ciudadanía, participación política y formación en una esfera pública en Buenos Aires, 1850 – 1880. *Siglo XIX: Revista,* no. 11, 2a época (Jan – June 92), pp. 46 – 73. Bibl.

Sabines, Jaime. Poems ("Preocupación de Job," "El que se quedó sin dientes," "¿Cómo puede decirse un amanecer en Comitán?"). *Casa de las Américas,* no. 191 (Apr – June 93), pp. 70 – 71.

Saborit, Antonio. Tomóchic (Excerpt from the forthcoming book entitled *Los doblados de Tomóchic*). *Nexos,* v. 16, no. 185 (May 93), pp. 69 – 75.

Sabugo Abril, Amancio. Descenso a la cotidianidad. *Insula,* no. 564 (Dec 93), pp. 21 – 23. Il.

— Historia, biografía, ficción en *Yo el Supremo. Hoy Es Historia,* v. 10, no. 57 (Apr – May 93), pp. 5 – 14. Bibl, il.

Sacido Romero, Alberto. Dinámica paradójica en "Parado en una piedra . . . " (Includes the poem). *Inti,* no. 36 (Fall 92), pp. 89 – 96.

Sada, Daniel. Obra de roedores. *Vuelta,* v. 17, no. 196 (Mar 93), pp. 27 – 33.

Sáenz, Benjamín Alire. Quiero escribir un poema americano: cómo ser un poeta chicano en la América poscolombina (Translated by Aída Espinosa). *Plural (Mexico),* v. 22, no. 256 (Jan 93), pp. 10 – 18.

Sáenz, Carmen María and María Elena Vinueza. El aporte africano en la formación de la cultura musical cubana. *Folklore Americano,* no. 53 (Jan – June 92), pp. 55 – 80. Bibl.

Sáenz, Josué. Diálogo con Adam Smith. *Vuelta,* v. 17, no. 197 (Apr 93), pp. 27 – 31.

Sáenz, Rogelio and Alberto E. Dávila. Chicano Return Migration to the Southwest: An Integrated Human Capital Approach. *International Migration Review,* v. 26, no. 4 (Winter 92), pp. 1248 – 1266. Bibl, tables.

Sáenz, Tirso W. and Emilio García Capote. El desarrollo de la ciencia y la tecnología en Cuba: algunas cuestiones actuales. *Interciencia,* v. 18, no. 6 (Nov – Dec 93), pp. 289 – 294. Bibl, tables.

Sáenz Quesada, María. Agustina Palacio de Libarona, heroína del amor conyugal. *Todo Es Historia,* v. 26, no. 310 (May 93), pp. 70 – 72. Il.

— Los 25 años de *Todo Es Historia. Revista Interamericana de Bibliografía,* v. 42, no. 4 (1992), pp. 561 – 569. Bibl, il.

Safa, Helen Icken. The New Women Workers: Does Money Equal Power? *NACLA Report on the Americas,* v. 27, no. 1 (July – Aug 93), pp. 24 – 29 +. Bibl, il.

Saffioti, Heleieth Iara Bongiovani. Reminiscências, releituras, reconceituações. *Estudos Feministas,* v. 0, no. 0 (1992), pp. 97 – 103. Bibl.

Sagasti, Francisco R. and Martha Chávez. ¿Hacia un nuevo Perú? *Debate (Peru),* v. 16, no. 74 (Sept – Oct 93), pp. 10 – 12. Il.

Sagasti, Francisco R. and Max Hernández. La crisis de gobernabilidad democrática en el Perú. *Debate (Peru),* v. 16, no. 75 (Dec 93 – Jan 94), pp. 24 – 28. Il.

Sagastume Fajardo, Alejandro S. El papel de la iglesia de Centroamérica en la guerra contra William Walker, 1856 – 1860. *Revista de Indias,* v. 53, no. 198 (May – Aug 93), pp. 529 – 544.

Saguier, Eduardo Ricardo. La corrupción de la burocracia colonial borbónica y los orígenes del federalismo: el caso del virreinato del Río de la Plata. *Jahrbuch für Geschichte von Staat, Wirtschaft und Gesellschaft Lateinamerikas,* v. 29 (1992), pp. 149 – 177. Bibl.

— La crisis de un estado colonial: balance de la cuestión rioplatense. *Anuario de Estudios Americanos,* v. 49, Suppl. 2 (1992), pp. 65 – 91. Bibl.

— La crisis minera en el Alto Perú en su fase extractiva: la producción de plata del cerro de Potosí en la luz de ocho visitas ignoradas de minas, 1778 – 1803. *Colonial Latin American Historical Review,* v. 1, no. 1 (Fall 92), pp. 67 – 100. Bibl, tables.

Sahakián, Carlos. Plástica y poética. *Plural (Mexico),* v. 22, no. 260 (May 93), pp. 40 – 48.

Sahni, Varun. Not Quite British: A Study of External Influences on the Argentine Navy. *Journal of Latin American Studies,* v. 25, no. 3 (Oct 93), pp. 489 – 513. Bibl, tables, charts.

Saignes, Thierry. Pierre Chaunu, l'Amérique et nous: essai d'égo-histoire. *Cahiers des Amériques Latines,* no. 13 (1992), pp. 7 – 24. Bibl.

St. Cyr, Eric B. A. Money in Caribbean Economy: A Theoretical Perspective. *Social and Economic Studies,* v. 41, no. 4 (Dec 92), pp. 95 – 111. Bibl, tables, charts.

Sáinz, Pedro and Alfredo Eric Calcagno. In Search of Another Form of Development. *CEPAL Review,* no. 48 (Dec 92), pp. 7 – 38. Bibl, tables, charts.

Sáinz de Medrano Arce, Luis. *Materia de testamento* como etopeya. *Chasqui,* v. 22, no. 1 (May 93), pp. 47 – 51.

Saítta, Sylvia. Roberto Arlt y las nuevas formas periodísticas. *Cuadernos Hispanoamericanos,* no. Special issue, 11 (July 93), pp. 59 – 69. Bibl.

Sala, Mariella. Tecnologías invisibles: seis estudios de casos develan papel de la mujer latinoamericana como innovadora de tecnologías en procesos productivos. *Fem,* v. 17, no. 126 (Aug 93), pp. 32 – 33.

Sala i Vila, Nuria. Alianzas y enfrentamientos regionales: consideraciones sobre la represión de un ritual andino en Lircay, 1794 – 1814. *Historia y Cultura (Peru),* no. 20 (1990), pp. 221 – 242. Bibl.

— La constitución de Cádiz y su impacto en el gobierno de las comunidades indígenas en el Virreinato del Perú. *Boletín Americanista,* v. 33, no. 42 – 43 (1992 – 1993), pp. 51 – 70. Bibl.

— Gobierno colonial, iglesia y poder en Perú, 1784 – 1814. *Revista Andina,* v. 11, no. 1 (July 93), pp. 133 – 161. Bibl.

Saladino García, Alberto. Función modernizadora de las sociedades económicas de Amigos del País en el Nuevo Mundo. *Cuadernos Americanos,* no. 38, Nueva época (Mar – Apr 93), pp. 225 – 236. Bibl.

Salamanca Lafuente, Rodolfo. Juan Quirós, caudal de cultura. *Signo,* no. 36 – 37, Nueva época (May – Dec 92), pp. 197 – 200.

— Memoria de la Asociación de Periodistas de La Paz. *Signo,* no. 38, Nueva época (Jan – Apr 93), pp. 27 – 46.

Salamini, Heather Fowler. The Boom in Regional Studies of the Mexican Revolution: Where Is It Leading? (Review article). *Latin American Research Review,* v. 28, no. 2 (1993), pp. 175 – 190. Bibl.

Salas, Alberto Mario. Armas de la conquista: venenos y gases. *Hoy Es Historia,* v. 10, no. 59 (Sept – Oct 93), pp. 87 – 97. Il.

Salas, Andrés Alberto. La carreta. *Todo Es Historia,* v. 27, no. 315 (Oct 93), pp. 30 – 43. Il.

Salas, Horacio. Duro oficio el exilio. *Cuadernos Hispanoamericanos,* no. 517 – 519 (July – Sept 93), pp. 555 – 559.

Salas Martín del Campo, Javier and Samuel Alfaro Desentis. Evolución de la balanza comercial del sector privado en México: evaluacíon con un modelo economé-trico. *El Trimestre Económico,* v. 59, no. 236 (Oct – Dec 92), pp. 773 – 797. Bibl, tables, charts.

Salas Páez, Carlos and Teresa Rendón. El empleo en México en los ochenta: tendencias y cambios. *Comercio Exterior,* v. 43, no. 8 (Aug 93), pp. 717 – 730. Bibl, tables, charts.

Salas Porras Soule, Alejandra. Globalización y proceso corporativo de los grandes grupos económicos en México. *Revista Mexicana de Sociología,* v. 54, no. 2 (Apr – June 92), pp. 133 – 162. Bibl, tables.

Salas Santana, Adalberto. Lingüística mapuche: guía bibliográfica. *Revista Andina,* v. 10, no. 2 (Dec 92), pp. 473 – 537. Bibl.

Salazar, Boris. Fat Boy (Translated by Boris Salazar and Jonathan Tittler). *The Americas Review,* v. 20, no. 1 (Spring 92), pp. 18 – 24.

Salazar, Jorge. La coartada del gobierno: homosexualidad y sociedad. *Debate (Peru),* v. 16, no. 72 (Mar – May 93), pp. 28 – 30.

Salazar Ramírez, Hilda. Mujer y medio ambiente. *Fem,* v. 17, no. 128 (Oct 93), pp. 11 – 15.

Salcedo, Salomón et al. Política agrícola y maíz en México: hacia el libre comercio norteamericano. *Comercio Exterior,* v. 43, no. 4 (Apr 93), pp. 302 – 310. Bibl, tables, charts.

Salcedo-Bastardo, José Luis. Día de la Humanidad. *Boletín de la Academia Nacional de la Historia (Venezuela),* v. 75, no. 298 (Apr – June 92), pp. 89 – 90.

— En el 170° aniversario de la municipalidad de Carúpano. *Boletín de la Academia Nacional de la Historia (Venezuela),* v. 75, no. 297 (Jan – Mar 92), pp. 33 – 42.

— En los comienzos de América. *Boletín de la Academia Nacional de la Historia (Venezuela),* v. 75, no. 300 (Oct – Dec 92), pp. 120 – 126.

— Palabras pronunciadas por el dr. José Luis Salcedo Bastardo en el banquete ofrecido por el consejo académico en el Hotel Mundial, Lisboa, 8 de mayo de 1992. *Boletín de la Academia Nacional de la Historia (Venezuela),* v. 76, no. 301 (Jan – Mar 93), pp. 45 – 46.

— Sobre el civismo y la solidaridad: por Montalvo de Venezuela a Ecuador. *Revista Nacional de Cultura (Venezuela),* v. 53, no. 286 (July – Sept 92), pp. 11 – 18.

Salcedo Picón, Jesús M. El pensamiento de Laureano Vallenilla Lanz. *Revista Nacional de Cultura (Venezuela),* v. 54, no. 287 (Oct – Dec 92), pp. 32 – 36. Bibl, il.

Saldaña, Juan José. Nuevas tendencias en la historia latinoamericana de las ciencias. *Cuadernos Americanos,* no. 38, Nueva época (Mar – Apr 93), pp. 69 – 91. Bibl.

Saldes Báez, Sergio. Narrativa chilena, 1966 – 1991: en busca de continuidad e integración. *Aisthesis,* no. 24 (1991), pp. 67 – 78. Bibl.

Sales, Fernando. Uma visão do folclore nacional. *Convivium,* v. 34, no. 2 (July – Dec 91), pp. 75 – 90. Bibl.

Salessi, Jorge. La invasión de sirenas. *Feminaria,* v. 6, no. 10, Suppl. (Apr 93), pp. 2 – 7. Bibl.

Salgado, Germánico. Integración andina y apertura externa: las nuevas tendencias. *Nueva Sociedad,* no. 125 (May – June 93), pp. 130 – 137.

— Modelo y políticas de integración. *Integración Latinoamericana,* v. 18, no. 186 (Jan – Feb 93), pp. 12 – 19. Bibl.

Salgado, Luiz Francisco de Assis. Em dia com o futuro. *Problemas Brasileiros,* v. 30, no. 295 (Jan – Feb 93), pp. 71 – 72.

Salgado de Snyder, V. Nelly. Family Life across the Border: Mexican Wives Left Behind. *Hispanic Journal of Behavioral Sciences,* v. 15, no. 3 (Aug 93), pp. 391 – 401. Bibl.

Saliba, Elias Thomé. A dimensão cômica do dilema brasileiro. *Vozes,* v. 87, no. 1 (Jan – Feb 93), pp. 46 – 54. Bibl.

Salinas, Augusto. La primera década de FONDECYT: un balance positivo. *Estudios Sociales (Chile),* no. 74 (Oct – Dec 92), pp. 177 – 189. Bibl.

Salinas, Luis Omar. Poems ("Cancer," "Poem," "Women in My Youth," "Sweet Drama," "Poem for Ernesto Trejo"). *The Americas Review,* v. 20, no. 1 (Spring 92), pp. 32 – 37.

— Poems ("What Is My Name?" "Nights in Fresno," "When the Evening Is Quiet," "Middle Age," "Sweet Drama," "Poem for Ernesto Trejo"). *The Americas Review,* v. 20, no. 3 – 4 (Fall – Winter 92), pp. 194 – 199.

Salinas Amescua, Bertha. Descripción de cinco modelos de "pedagogía de la organización" prevalecientes en el movimiento de educación popular en América Latina. *Revista Latinoamericana de Estudios Educativos,* v. 22, no. 3 (July – Sept 92), pp. 45 – 87. Bibl.

Salinas Campos, Maximiliano A. Don Enrique Alvear: la solidaridad como unión mística entre Jesús y los pobres. *Mensaje,* v. 42, no. 421 (Aug 93), pp. 350 – 352. Il.

Salinas Chávez, Antonio. El cambio estructural de PEMEX: más empresa, menos política económica. *Comercio Exterior,* v. 43, no. 11 (Nov 93), pp. 1001 – 1009. Bibl, charts.

Salinas de Gortari, Carlos. Iniciativa para la reforma del Artículo Cuarto de la constitución mexicana. *Anuario Indigenista,* v. 30 (Dec 91), pp. 145 – 154.

— Iniciativa para la reforma del régimen ejidal: Artículo 27 de la constitución mexicana. *Anuario Indigenista,* v. 30 (Dec 91), pp. 155 – 184.

— El libre comercio en Norteamérica: oportunidad de progreso y bienestar. *Comercio Exterior,* v. 43, no. 1 (Jan 93), pp. 32 – 33.

— México: decreto por el que se reforma el Artículo 4 de la constitución política de los Estados Unidos Mexicanos. *Anuario Indigenista,* v. 30 (Dec 91), pp. 487 – 488.

— México: decreto por el que se reforma el Artículo 27 de la constitución política de los Estados Unidos Mexicanos. *Anuario Indigenista,* v. 30 (Dec 91), pp. 489 – 496.

— Quinto Informe de Gobierno. *Comercio Exterior,* v. 43, no. 11 (Nov 93), pp. 1068 – 1094.

— Quinto Informe de Gobierno. *Nexos,* v. 16, no. 192 (Dec 93), Insert.

— V Informe de Gobierno del presidente Carlos Salinas de Gortari. *Fem,* v. 17, no. 129 (Nov 93), p. 41. Il.

Salinas Meza, René. Una comunidad inmigrante: los alemanes en Valparaíso, 1860 – 1960; estudio demográfico. *Jahrbuch für Geschichte von Staat, Wirtschaft und Gesellschaft Lateinamerikas,* v. 29 (1992), pp. 309 – 342. Bibl, tables, charts.

Salles, Vania and Rosa María Rubalcava. Hogares de trabajadoras y percepciones femeninas. *El Cotidiano,* v. 9, no. 53 (Mar – Apr 93), pp. 40 – 46. Tables.

Salles, Vania and José Manuel Valenzuela Arce. Ambitos de relaciones sociales de naturaleza íntima e identidades culturales: notas sobre Xochimilco. *Revista Mexicana de Sociología,* v. 54, no. 3 (July – Sept 92), pp. 139 – 173. Bibl.

Salles Filho, Sérgio L. M. et al. Estratégias empresariais em agrobiotecnologia no Brasil: um estudo de casos relevantes. *Revista de Economia e Sociologia Rural,* v. 30, no. 3 (July – Sept 92), pp. 203 – 224. Bibl, tables.

Salmon, Russell. El proceso poético: entrevista con Ernesto Cardenal. *Cuadernos Americanos,* no. 40, Nueva época (July – Aug 93), pp. 99 – 109.

Salmones M., María de Lourdes. Isabel. *Fem,* v. 17, no. 123 (May 93), p. 18.

Salomon, Frank. "Una polémica de once años de antigüedad": comentarios al artículo de Stern. *Allpanchis,* v. 23, no. 39 (Jan – June 92), pp. 109 – 112.

Saltz, Joanne. *Pánico o peligro* de María Luisa Puga: reescribiendo la familia. *Káñina,* v. 16, no. 2 (July – Dec 92), pp. 101 – 104. Bibl.

Salvat Monguillot, Manuel. Discurso de recepción de don Antonio Dougnac Rodríguez. *Boletín de la Academia Chilena de la Historia,* v. 58 – 59, no. 102 (1991 – 1992), pp. 95 – 99.

— Francisco de Vitoria y el nacimiento del capitalismo. *Boletín de la Academia Chilena de la Historia,* v. 58 – 59, no. 102 (1991 – 1992), pp. 329 – 347. Bibl.

Salvatore, Ricardo Donato. Los viajeros y sus miradas. *Todo Es Historia,* v. 27, no. 315 (Oct 93), pp. 8 – 23. Bibl, il.

Salvucci, Richard J. "La parte más difícil": Recent Works on Nineteenth-Century Mexican History (Review article). *Latin American Research Review,* v. 28, no. 1 (1993), pp. 102 – 110.

Salwen, Michael Brian. "Eddie" Chibás, the "Magic Bullet" of Radio. *Studies in Latin American Popular Culture,* v. 12 (1993), pp. 113 – 126. Bibl.

Salzano, Francisco M. Color Vision in Four Brazilian Indian Tribes. *Interciencia,* v. 18, no. 4 (July – Aug 93), pp. 195 – 197. Bibl, tables.

Sambrano Urdaneta, Oscar. Lo trascendental trujillano en sus letras. *Revista Nacional de Cultura (Venezuela),* v. 53, no. 286 (July – Sept 92), pp. 39 – 49. Il.

Sambuceti, Héctor and Silvia Mazzuchi. Santos Pérez: alegato y ejecución. *Todo Es Historia,* v. 26, no. 308 (Mar 93), pp. 26 – 35. Il.

Samour, Héctor. Universidad y derechos humanos. *ECA; Estudios Centroamericanos,* v. 47, no. 528 (Oct 92), pp. 894 – 900. Bibl, il.

Sampaio, Consuelo Novais. Repensando Canudos: o jogo das oligarquias. *Luso-Brazilian Review,* v. 30, no. 2 (Winter 93), pp. 97 – 113. Bibl, tables.

Sampaio Neto, José Augusto Vaz. O ensino na corte e na província. *Revista do Instituto Histórico e Geográfico Brasileiro,* no. 373 (Oct – Dec 91), pp. 1115 – 1144. Bibl.

Sampaolesi, Ana. Desvelos en el quehacer político. *Feminaria,* v. 6, no. 11 (Nov 93), pp. 8 – 11.

Sampaolesi, Ana and Jutta Marx. Elecciones internas bajo el cupo: la primera aplicación de la Ley de Cuotas en la capital federal. *Feminaria,* v. 6, no. 11 (Nov 93), pp. 15 – 17.

Samper Pizano, Ernesto. Balance de actividades de la embajada de Colombia en España durante el año de 1992 y primer trimestre de 1993. *Revista Javeriana,* v. 61, no. 594 (May 93), pp. 256 – 262.

— Democracia y paz (Previously published in this journal, no. 549, 1988). *Revista Javeriana,* v. 61, no. 596 (July 93), pp. 89 – 94.

Samperio, Guillermo. Libertad y sujeción en Sigfrido Walter Aguilar. *Artes de México,* no. 20 (Summer 93), pp. 120 – 121. Il.

— Los poetas malditos de la subsecretaría. *Nexos,* v. 16, no. 183 (Mar 93), pp. 9 – 10.

San Cristóbal, Antonio. Reconversión de la iglesia del Convento de Santo Domingo (Lima) durante el siglo XVII. *Anuario de Estudios Americanos,* v. 49 (1992), pp. 233 – 270. Bibl.

San Miguel, Pedro Luis. Discurso racial e identidad nacional en la República Dominicana. *Op. Cit.,* no. 7 (1992), pp. 67 – 120. Bibl, il.

Sanabria, Carolina. *El cristiano errante:* ¿Novela que tiene mucho de historia o historia que contiene mucho de novela?; consideraciones teóricas sobre el discurso crítico contemporáneo. *Káñina,* v. 16, no. 2 (July – Dec 92), pp. 31 – 38. Bibl.

Sanches, Marcos Guimarães. História e desenvolvimento: um problema na historiografia brasileira nos anos '50. *Revista do Instituto Histórico e Geográfico Brasileiro,* no. 370 (Jan – Mar 91), pp. 289 – 299. Bibl.

Sánchez, Alexander. La patria es el recuerdo. *Revista Cultural Lotería,* v. 50, no. 384 (July – Aug 91), pp. 91 – 93.

Sánchez, Antulio. El pueblo de Cuba: entre el drama y la esperanza, IV: Cuba en la opción cero; situación actual de la economía cubana. *Hoy Es Historia,* v. 10, no. 57 (Apr – May 93), pp. 49 – 53.

Sánchez, Consuelo and Héctor Díaz Polanco. Cronología de los hechos históricos de la costa atlántica de Nicaragua: primera parte. *Boletín de Antropología Americana,* no. 23 (July 91), pp. 171 – 184. Bibl.

— Cronología de los hechos históricos de la costa atlántica de Nicaragua: segunda parte. *Boletín de Antropología Americana,* no. 24 (Dec 91), pp. 151 – 178. Bibl, il.

Sánchez, Joaquín Ruy. Oaxaca, Oax. *Artes de México,* no. 21 (Fall 93), pp. 32 – 33. Il.

— San Luis Potosí. *Artes de México,* no. 18 (Winter 92), pp. 78 – 79. Il.

— Xochimilco. *Artes de México,* no. 20 (Summer 93), pp. 62 – 63.

Sánchez, Jorge and Guillermo Krantzer. Regulaciones en el transporte urbano: el caso de Buenos Aires. *EURE,* v. 19, no. 56 (Mar 93), pp. 41 – 53. Bibl.

Sánchez, Joseph P. In Memoriam: Albert H. Schroeder (1914 – 1993). *Colonial Latin American Historical Review,* v. 2, no. 4 (Fall 93), pp. 401 – 402. Il.

Sánchez, Julio C. and Guillermo Mira Delli-Zotti. III Curso de Historia de la Técnica: Procesos de Industrialización en América y la Península Ibérica. *Anuario de Estudios Americanos,* v. 49, Suppl. 1 (1992), pp. 215 – 216.

Sánchez, Luis Rafael. Voyage to Caribbean Identity: The Caribbean Sounds, the Caribbean Resounds (Translated by Alfred MacAdam). *Review,* no. 47 (Fall 93), pp. 20 – 22.

Sánchez, Marcelo and Pablo Sirlin. Elementos de una propuesta transformadora para el desarrollo económico argentino. *Realidad Económica,* no. 117 (July – Aug 93), pp. 36 – 160. Bibl.

Sánchez, Miguel Alberto. Privatizaciones y extranjerización de la economía argentina. *Realidad Económica,* no. 116 (May – June 93), pp. 33 – 45.

Sánchez, Ricardo. Constitución y vida social. *Revista Javeriana,* v. 61, no. 597 (Aug 93), pp. 169 – 173.

Sánchez, Ricardo R. Poems ("En-ojitos: canto a Piñero," "Notas a Federico García Lorca, con disculpas y festejos"). *The Americas Review,* v. 20, no. 3 – 4 (Fall – Winter 92), pp. 213 – 222.

Sánchez, Robert A. Maquila Masquerade. *Business Mexico,* v. 3, no. 1 (Jan – Feb 93), pp. 13 – 15. Il, charts.

Sánchez, Rosaura. Discourses of Gender, Ethnicity, and Class in Chicano Literature. *The Americas Review,* v. 20, no. 2 (Summer 92), pp. 72 – 88. Bibl.

— Tres generaciones. *The Americas Review,* v. 20, no. 1 (Spring 92), pp. 5 – 11.

— Tres generaciones. *The Americas Review,* v. 20, no. 3 – 4 (Fall – Winter 92), pp. 137 – 143.

Sánchez Aguilera, Osmar. Del antetexto al texto: transición de normas y permanencia de Vallejo. *Casa de las Américas,* no. 189 (Oct – Dec 92), pp. 82 – 93.

Sánchez Almanza, Adolfo and Manuel Urbina Fuentes. Distribución de la población y desarrollo en México. *Comercio Exterior,* v. 43, no. 7 (July 93), pp. 652 – 661. Bibl, tables, maps, charts.

Sánchez Arnosi, Milagros. Vargas Llosa, en primera persona. *Cuadernos Hispanoamericanos,* no. 520 (Oct 93), pp. 102 – 105.

Sánchez Arteche, Alfonso. Letras del estado de México. *Plural (Mexico),* v. 22, no. 258 (Mar 93), pp. 76 – 77.

Sánchez-Concha B., Rafael. Las expediciones descubridoras: la entrada al país de los chunchos, 1538 – 1539. *Amazonía Peruana,* v. 11, no. 22 (Oct 92), pp. 125 – 145. Bibl.

Sánchez de Irarrázabal, Elena. Manuel y Carolina, anfitriones del choque entre dos mundos. *Mensaje,* v. 42, no. 418 (May 93), pp. 161 – 162. Il.

Sánchez Franco, Germán. Antecedentes de la reforma laboral acerca del tema de las cesantías. *Revista Javeriana,* v. 61, no. 592 (Mar 93), pp. 86 – 89.

Sánchez Franco, Germán and Fernando Robledo Quijano. El doble carácter de las administradoras. *Revista Javeriana,* v. 61, no. 592 (Mar 93), pp. 112 – 116.

Sánchez Fuentes, Porfirio. Martina Andrión, ruiseñor coclesano. *Revista Cultural Lotería,* v. 51, no. 390 (July – Aug 92), pp. 58 – 64.

— Recordando a José Avila. *Revista Cultural Lotería,* v. 51, no. 387 (Feb 92), pp. 72 – 75.

Sánchez Fuertes, Cayetano. México: puente franciscano entre España y Filipinas. *Archivo Ibero-Americano,* v. 52, no. 205 – 208 (Jan – Dec 92), pp. 373 – 401. Bibl.

Sánchez Gamboa, Silvio Ancísar. La concepción del hombre en la investigación educativa: algunas consideraciones. *Islas,* no. 96 (May – Aug 90), pp. 34 – 41. Bibl.

Sánchez-Gey Venegas, Juana. El modernismo filosófico en América. *Cuadernos Americanos,* no. 41, Nueva época (Sept – Oct 93), pp. 109 – 121. Bibl.

Sánchez León, Abelardo. Perfil del ama de casa limeña. *Debate (Peru),* v. 16, no. 72 (Mar – May 93), pp. 32 – 38. Il, tables.

Sánchez-Mejorada F., María Cristina. Las clases medias en la gestión y el gobierno de la ciudad. *El Cotidiano,* v. 10, no. 57 (Aug – Sept 93), pp. 46 – 53. Il, maps.

Sánchez Munguía, Vicente. Matamoros-sur de Texas: el tránsito de los migrantes de América Central por la frontera México – Estados Unidos. *Estudios Sociológicos,* v. 11, no. 31 (Jan – Apr 93), pp. 183 – 207. Bibl, tables.

Sánchez Noguera, Abdón. La reforma agraria: vigencia o caducidad. *Derecho y Reforma Agraria,* no. 23 (1992), pp. 115 – 122.

Sánchez Otero, Germán. Neoliberalism and Its Discontents. *Report on the Americas,* v. 26, no. 4 (Feb 93), pp. 18 – 21. Il.

Sánchez Parga, José. Ecuador: en el engranaje neoliberal. *Nueva Sociedad,* no. 123 (Jan – Feb 93), pp. 12 – 17. Tables.

Sánchez Rebolledo, Adolfo. La herencia de la revolución mexicana: una entrevista con François-Xavier Guerra. *Nexos,* v. 16, no. 182 (Feb 93), pp. 7 – 9.

Sánchez Robayna, Andrés. A Thomas Tallis. *Vuelta,* v. 17, no. 201 (Aug 93), p. 13.

Sánchez Ruiz, Jorge Ernesto. Privatização de estradas no Brasil: comentário sobre a viabilidade financeira. *Revista de Economia Política (Brazil),* v. 13, no. 3 (July – Sept 93), pp. 41 – 53. Bibl, tables.

Sánchez Susarrey, Jaime. La escena política (Regular feature appearing in most issues). *Vuelta,* v. 17 (1993), n.p.

Sánchez-Ugarte, Fernando J. Acciones en favor de las micro, pequeñas y medianas industrias en México. *Comercio Exterior,* v. 43, no. 6 (June 93), pp. 539 – 543.

Sánchez Vaca, María Luisa. Hace cincuenta años: una mujer al volante. *Fem,* v. 17, no. 127 (Sept 93), p. 22.

Sánchez Vázquez, Adolfo. Prólogo a *Obra estética. Casa de las Américas,* no. 190 (Jan – Mar 93), pp. 136 – 140.

Sánchez Zúber, Leopoldo. Short Stories ("La lobina," "En fila"). *Plural (Mexico),* v. 22, no. 261 (June 93), pp. 79 – 81.

Sanchiz Ochoa, Pilar. Poder y conflictos de autoridad en Santiago de Guatemala durante el siglo XVI. *Anuario de Estudios Americanos,* v. 49 (1992), pp. 21 – 54. Bibl.

Sandoval, José-Luis. Poems ("Mexicans and Others," "When Eye Was a Child," "Before Eye Could Tell Time," "Street Gangs"). *The Americas Review,* v. 21, no. 1 (Spring 93), pp. 55 – 61.

Sandoval Flores, Etelvina. La educación básica y la posibilidad de cambios. *El Cotidiano,* v. 8, no. 51 (Nov – Dec 92), pp. 27 – 30.

— Maestras y modernización educativa. *El Cotidiano,* v. 9, no. 53 (Mar – Apr 93), pp. 78 – 82. Tables, charts.

Sandoval García, Carlos. Programas de ajuste estructural e industria de la publicidad en Costa Rica. *Revista de Ciencias Sociales (Costa Rica),* no. 57 (Sept 92), pp. 17 – 29. Bibl, tables.

Sandoval Sánchez, Alberto. La puesta en escena de la familia inmigrante puertorriqueña. *Revista Iberoamericana,* v. 59, no. 162 – 163 (Jan – June 93), pp. 345 – 359. Bibl.

Sands, Benjamin. Financing Compliance. *Business Mexico,* v. 3, no. 1 (Jan – Feb 93), pp. 34 – 35 +.

Sanguinetti, Horacio. Se abrió un período de tolerancia republicana. *Todo Es Historia,* v. 27, no. 317 (Dec 93), pp. 16 – 18. Il.

Sanguinetti, Jorge. Conferencia sobre aspectos sociopolíticos y económicos de la hidrovía. *Revista Geográfica (Mexico),* no. 114 (July – Dec 91), pp. 73 – 90. Tables.

Sanhueza, Eugenio and Tibisay Pérez. Concentraciones atmosféricas y estimación de las emisiones H2S en la saba de Trachypogon, Calabozo, estado Guárico, Venezuela. *Interciencia,* v. 18, no. 2 (Mar – Apr 93), pp. 83 – 87. Bibl, il, tables, maps, charts.

Sanicky, Cristina Aurora. Los usos y las formas del verbo en Misiones, Argentina. *Hispanic Journal,* v. 14, no. 1 (Spring 93), pp. 25 – 36. Bibl.

Sanín, Javier. La década ganada. *Revista Javeriana,* v. 61, no. 596 (July 93), pp. 45 – 48.

— Editorial: Noemí en el torbellino mundial. *Revista Javeriana,* v. 61, no. 594 (May 93), pp. 199 – 200.

Sanín, Noemí. Discurso de la señora ministro de relaciones exteriores de Colombia en la Universidad de Sofía. *Revista Javeriana,* v. 60, no. 590 (Nov – Dec 92), pp. 339 – 343.

Sanjinés C., Javier. Pedro Shimose, poeta rebelde e intelectual letrado. *Signo,* no. 36 – 37, Nueva época (May – Dec 92), pp. 75 – 88. Bibl.

Sanjurjo de Casciero, Annick. The Sterling Legacy of Peru. *Américas,* v. 45, no. 1 (Jan – Feb 93), pp. 50 – 51. Il.

Santa, Eduardo. Honda: ciudad clave en la historia de Colombia. *Boletín de Historia y Antigüedades,* v. 79, no. 779 (Oct – Dec 92), pp. 975 – 991. Bibl.

— Luis Alberto Acuña, pintor de América. *Boletín de Historia y Antigüedades,* v. 80, no. 781 (Apr – June 93), pp. 359 – 363.

Santa Ana A., Otto. Chicano English and the Nature of the Chicano Language Setting. *Hispanic Journal of Behavioral Sciences,* v. 15, no. 1 (Feb 93), pp. 3 – 35. Bibl, tables, charts.

Santa María Gallegos, Leticia E. Charlas en la cocina. *Fem,* v. 17, no. 130 (Dec 93), p. 30.

— De soledades. *Fem,* v. 17, no. 122 (Apr 93), pp. 44 – 45.

Santaballa, Sylvia R. El taller o el "abrecabezas" poético: análisis de "Quédeme a calentar la tinta" (Includes the poem). *Inti,* no. 36 (Fall 92), pp. 97 – 104.

Santamaría, Daniel J. La guerra Guaykurú: expansión colonial y conflicto interétnico en la cuenca del alto Paraguay, siglo XVIII. *Jahrbuch für Geschichte von Staat, Wirtschaft und Gesellschaft Lateinamerikas,* v. 29 (1992), pp. 121 – 148. Bibl.

Santamaría Tavera, Fanny. La reforma de ISS: los colombianos tienen la palabra. *Revista Javeriana,* v. 61, no. 592 (Mar 93), pp. 69 – 75. Il.

Santana, Adalberto. Los nacionalismos de México, Cuba y Centroamérica frente a los de Europa Oriental. *Cuadernos Americanos,* no. 41, Nueva época (Sept – Oct 93), pp. 167 – 174.

— Visiones del área del litoral mediterráneo latinoamericano continental. *Cuadernos Americanos,* no. 37, Nueva época (Jan – Feb 93), pp. 65 – 75. Bibl.

Santana, Antônio Cordeiro de. Análise econômica da produção agrícola sob condições de risco numa comunidade amazônica. *Revista de Economia e Sociologia Rural,* v. 30, no. 2 (Apr – June 92), pp. 159 – 170. Bibl, tables.

— Custo social da depredação florestal no Pará: o caso da castanha-do-Brasil. *Revista de Economia e Sociologia Rural,* v. 30, no. 3 (July – Sept 92), pp. 253 – 269. Bibl, tables, charts.

— Estrutura de oferta de carne suína sob condições de risco no Brasil. *Revista de Economia e Sociologia Rural,* v. 30, no. 1 (Jan – Mar 92), pp. 21 – 39. Bibl, tables.

Santana, Jorge A. La adivinanza a través de quinientos años de cultura hispánica: antología histórica. *Explicación de Textos Literarios,* v. 21, no. 1 – 2 (1992), Issue. Bibl.

Santana, Roberto. Actores y escenarios étnicos en Ecuador: el levantamiento de 1990. *Caravelle,* no. 59 (1992), pp. 161 – 188. Bibl.

— Jacinto Guamán, ex-vice-presidente de la Confederación de las Nacionalidades Indígenas del Ecuador (CONAIE): entrevista realizada el 23 de noviembre de 1988, por Roberto Santana. *Caravelle,* no. 59 (1992), pp. 59 – 65.

— Trois ans de chronologie indianiste en Equateur. *Caravelle,* no. 59 (1992), pp. 19 – 24.

Sant'Anna, Affonso Romano de. Otto, um moleque adorável (Reprinted from *Jornal do Brasil,* December 30, 1992). *Vozes,* v. 87, no. 2 (Mar – Apr 93), pp. 84 – 86.

Santí, Enrico-Mario. Latinamericanism and Restitution. *Latin American Literary Review,* v. 20, no. 40 (July – Dec 92), pp. 88 – 96.

— El tronco y la rama: literatura cubana y legado español. *Vuelta,* v. 17, no. 195 (Feb 93), pp. 53 – 55.

— Ultima postal para Severo. *Vuelta,* v. 17, no. 201 (Aug 93), p. 32.

Santiago, Carlos Enrique. The Migratory Impact of Minimum Wage Legislation: Puerto Rico, 1970 – 1987. *International Migration Review,* v. 27, no. 4 (Winter 93), pp. 772 – 795. Bibl, tables, charts.

Santiago, Chiori. Conversation with Art Collector Robert Marcus. *Latin American Art,* v. 4, no. 4 (Winter 92), pp. 38 – 39. Il.

Santiago Castillo, Javier. Las elecciones locales en 1992. *El Cotidiano,* v. 8, no. 52 (Jan – Feb 93), pp. 19 – 24. Il, tables.

Santos, Danilo. Aproximación a una novela de Mauricio Wacquez: *Frente a un hombre armado;* una indagación del lenguaje en torno a la muerte y el erotismo. *Revista Chilena de Literatura,* no. 41 (Apr 93), pp. 119 – 122.

Santos, Gilberto de los and Vern Vincent. Tex-Mex Tourism (Excerpt from *Mexican Tourism Market in the Rio Grande Valley of Texas*). *Business Mexico,* v. 3, no. 3 (Mar 93), pp. 27 – 29. Tables.

Santos, Lucíola Licínio de C. P. Problemas e alternativas no campo da formação de professores. *Revista Brasileira de Estudos Pedagógicos,* v. 72, no. 172 (Sept – Dec 91), pp. 318 – 334. Bibl.

Santos, Maria Madalena Rodrigues dos. The Challenge of Educational Reforms in Brazil. *La Educación (USA),* v. 37, no. 114 (1993), pp. 59 – 75. Bibl.

Santos, Milton. Imigração e movimento. *Vozes,* v. 87, no. 3 (May – June 93), pp. 2 – 6.

Santos, Myrian S. Objetos, memória e história: observação e análise de um museu histórico brasileiro. *Dados,* v. 35, no. 2 (1992), pp. 217 – 237. Bibl.

Santos, Theotonio dos. Brazil's Controlled Purge: The Impeachment of Fernando Collor (Translated by Phillip Berryman). *NACLA Report on the Americas,* v. 27, no. 3 (Nov – Dec 93), pp. 17 – 21. Il.

— Globalización financiera y estrategias de desarrollo. *Nueva Sociedad,* no. 126 (July – Aug 93), pp. 98 – 109.

Santos Ascarza, José Manuel. ?Qué espero de los jesuitas? *Mensaje,* v. 42, no. 420 (July 93), p. 332.

Santos Pires, Manuel. El IV° centenario en Mercedes. *Hoy Es Historia,* v. 9, no. 54 (Nov – Dec 92), pp. 60 – 68. Il.

Santos Urriola, José. Discurso de orden pronunciado por el profesor José Santos Urriola, el día 16 de enero de 1992, en la sesión especial con que la Academia Nacional de la Historia conmemoró los cuatrocientos años de la fundación de Guanare. *Boletín de la Academia Nacional de la Historia (Venezuela),* v. 76, no. 301 (Jan – Mar 93), pp. 19 – 26.

Sanz, Mónica et al. Blood Group Frequencies and the Question of Race Mixture in Uruguay. *Interciencia,* v. 18, no. 1 (Jan – Feb 93), pp. 29 – 32. Bibl, tables.

Sanzana Fuentes, Eva. Indice: *Revista Chilena de Literatura,* desde el n° 1 (otoño 1970) al n° 39 (abril 1992). *Revista Chilena de Literatura,* no. 40 (Nov 92), pp. 139 – 155.

Sapia, Yvonne. Poems ("Del medio del sueño," "La Mujer, Her Back to the Spectator," "La desconocida," "Define the Grateful Gesture," "Aquí"). *The Americas Review,* v. 20, no. 3 – 4 (Fall – Winter 92), pp. 169 – 174.

Sapriza, Graciela. Valores notables de la cultura uruguaya: noticia biográfica sobre cuatro transgresoras. *Hoy Es Historia,* v. 10, no. 55 (Jan – Feb 93), pp. 48 – 52.

Sarabia, Rosa. Raúl González Tuñón: poesía ciudadana y tono conversacional. *Hispanic Journal,* v. 13, no. 2 (Fall 92), pp. 323 – 344. Bibl.

Sarabia Viejo, María Justina. Primer Congreso Internacional de Historia: "El Mundo Colonial; Examen de una Historia." *Anuario de Estudios Americanos,* v. 49, Suppl. 2 (1992), pp. 210 – 212.

— I Simposio Internacional "España y Nueva España: La Vida Cotidiana." *Anuario de Estudios Americanos,* v. 49, Suppl. 1 (1992), pp. 201 – 203.

Sarduy, Severo. Epitafios. *Vuelta,* v. 17, no. 201 (Aug 93), p. 29.

— El hombre que parecía un caballo (Chapter IV from the forthcoming novel entitled *Pájaros en la playa*). *Vuelta,* v. 17, no. 201 (Aug 93), pp. 33 – 34.

— Imágenes del tiempo inmóvil. *Vuelta,* v. 17, no. 200 (July 93), pp. 21 – 22.

— Para los pájaros de la playa (Excerpts from the last chapter of the forthcoming novel entitled *Pájaros en la playa*). *Vuelta,* v. 17, no. 201 (Aug 93), pp. 20 – 21.

— Prólogo para leer como un epílogo. *Hispamérica,* v. 21, no. 63 (Dec 92), pp. 69 – 71.

Sarignana, Armando. Ebria bitácora (Accompanied by an English translation). *Artes de México,* no. 20 (Summer 93), pp. 81 – 92. Il.

— La Soledad (Accompanied by an English translation). *Artes de México,* no. 21 (Fall 93), pp. 44 – 47. Il.

Sarlo Sabajanes, Beatriz. Notas sobre política y cultura. *Cuadernos Hispanoamericanos,* no. 517 – 519 (July – Sept 93), pp. 51 – 64.

Sarmento, Walney Moraes. Política externa no contexto do subdesenvolvimento: o exemplo do Brasil. *Política e Estratégica,* v. 8, no. 2 – 4 (Apr – Dec 90), pp. 241 – 267. Bibl, tables.

Sarmiento, Jaime and Mónica Moraes R. Contribución al estudio de biología reproductiva de una especie de "Bactris" (Palmae) en el bosque de galería, depto. Beni, Bolivia. *Bulletin de l'Institut Français d'Etudes Andines,* v. 21, no. 2 (1992), pp. 685 – 698. Bibl, il, tables, maps.

Sarmiento, Oscar D. La desconstrucción del autor: Enrique Lihn y Jorge Teillier. *Revista Chilena de Literatura,* no. 42 (Aug 93), pp. 237 – 244.

Sarmiento Palacio, Eduardo. Growth and Income Distribution in Countries at Intermediate Stages of Development. *CEPAL Review,* no. 48 (Dec 92), pp. 141 – 155. Tables, charts.

Sarquís, David J. 10 de diciembre de 1992: 44° aniversario de la Declaración Universal de los Derechos Humanos. *Relaciones Internacionales (Mexico),* v. 15, Nueva época, no. 57 (Jan – Mar 93), pp. 97 – 100.

Sartelli, Eduardo. Barcos en la pradera: los carreros pampeanos; de la colonia al "granero del mundo." *Todo Es Historia,* v. 27, no. 315 (Oct 93), pp. 68 – 75. Bibl, il, tables.

Sarukhán Kermez, José. Intervención del dr. José Sarukhán, rector de la UNAM, en la clausura del acto de homenaje al maestro Jesús Silva Herzog en su centenario. *Problemas del Desarrollo,* v. 24, no. 92 (Jan – Mar 93), pp. 218 – 220.

— A Wealth of Life. *Business Mexico,* v. 3, no. 1 (Jan – Feb 93), pp. 60 – 62. Il, tables.

Sasso, Javier. Arturo Ardao, historiador de las ideas. *Hoy Es Historia,* v. 10, no. 59 (Sept – Oct 93), pp. 4 – 12. Bibl, il.

Satas, Hugo Raúl. El pensamiento italiano del siglo XIX en la sociedad argentina. *Todo Es Historia,* v. 26, no. 305 (Dec 92), pp. 40 – 44. Il.

Satterthwaite, David. Problemas sociales y medioambientales asociados a la urbanización acelerada. *EURE,* v. 19, no. 57 (July 93), pp. 7 – 30. Tables.

Saucedo, Irma. Las ONGs de mujeres en México. *Fem,* v. 17, no. 126 (Aug 93), pp. 10 – 13. Tables.

— Violencia doméstica: hecho y espacio de desestructuración de la subordinación de la mujer. *Fem,* v. 17, no. 122 (Apr 93), pp. 16 – 17. Il.

Sauve, John. Suggestions for a Jamaican Theology of Psycho-Social Emancipation. *Caribbean Quarterly,* v. 38, no. 2 – 3 (June – Sept 92), pp. 81 – 95. Bibl.

Savage, Melissa. Ecological Disturbance and Nature Tourism. *Geographical Review,* v. 83, no. 3 (July 93), pp. 290 – 300. Bibl, il, maps.

Saviñón Díez de Sollano, Adalberto. México: identidad y cultura. *Comercio Exterior,* v. 43, no. 10 (Oct 93), pp. 940 – 945. Bibl.

Saxe-Fernández, John. América Latina – Estados Unidos: ¿Hacia una nueva era? *Nueva Sociedad,* no. 125 (May – June 93), pp. 6 – 15. Bibl.

Sayago, Luis Rodrigo. Biotecnología, agricultura y ecología: un dilema para el futuro. *Derecho y Reforma Agraria,* no. 24 (1993), pp. 159 – 165.

Saylor-Javaherian, Cheryll. Nietzschean Antagonism, Self-Sacrifice, and Redemption in Enrique Larreta's *La gloria de don Ramiro. Hispanic Journal,* v. 14, no. 1 (Spring 93), pp. 7 – 23. Bibl.

Scalora, Sal. A Salute to the Spirits. *Américas,* v. 45, no. 2 (Mar – Apr 93), pp. 27 – 33. Il.

Scarabôtolo, Hélio Antônio. Rio Branco, Euclides da Cunha e o tratado de limites com o Peru. *Revista do Instituto Histórico e Geográfico Brasileiro,* no. 370 (Jan – Mar 91), pp. 82 – 93.

— Saudação ao honorário Marcos Castrioto de Azambuja (Speech given in honor of Marcos Azambuja's induction into the Instituto Histórico e Geográfico Brasileiro). *Revista do Instituto Histórico e Geográfico Brasileiro,* no. 371 (Apr – June 91), pp. 489 – 491.

Scaramuzza Vidoni, Mariarosa. La ritrattistica nella *Nueva corónica* de Guamán Poma de Ayala. *Quaderni Ibero-Americani,* no. 72 (Dec 92), pp. 682 – 694. Bibl.

Schaefer, Stacy. Huichol Indian Costumes: A Transforming Tradition. *Latin American Art,* v. 5, no. 1 (Spring 93), pp. 70 – 73. Bibl, il.

Schaffenburg, Carlos A. El títere. *Plural (Mexico),* v. 22, no. 267 (Dec 93), p. 70.

Schaposnik, Eduardo Carlos. La integración en una etapa de confusión. *Desarrollo Indoamericano,* v. 23, no. 91 (June 93), pp. 41 – 46. Il.

Schatan, Claudia and Jorge Máttar. El comercio intraindustrial e intrafirme México – Estados Unidos: autopartes, electrónicos y petroquímicos (Translated by Adriana Hierro). *Comercio Exterior,* v. 43, no. 2 (Feb 93), pp. 103 – 124. Bibl, tables.

Schávelzon, Daniel. La arqueología como ciencia o como ficción. *Todo Es Historia,* v. 26, no. 309 (Apr 93), pp. 32 – 49. Bibl, il.

Scheerer, Thomas M. Congreso de los hispanistas alemanes en Augsburgo, 1993 (Translated by José Luis Gómez y Patiño). *Humboldt,* no. 109 (1993), p. 97.

Schele, Linda and Maricela Ayala F. De poesía e historia: el tablero de los glifos de Palenque. *Vuelta,* v. 17, no. 203 (Oct 93), pp. 25 – 27. Charts.

Schele, Linda and David A. Freidel. *Un bosque de reyes:* la historia no narrada de los antiguos mayas. *La Palabra y el Hombre,* no. 82 (Apr – June 92), pp. 79 – 94. Tables.

Schenkolewski-Kroll, Silvia. Los archivos de S.I.A.M. Di Tella S.A.: primera organización de fuentes en la historia de las empresas argentinas. *Estudios Interdisciplinarios de América Latina y el Caribe,* v. 3, no. 2 (July – Dec 92), pp. 105 – 122. Bibl.

Schers, David. Inmigrantes y política: los primeros pasos del Partido Sionista Socialista Poalei Sion en la Argentina, 1910 – 1916. *Estudios Interdisciplinarios de América Latina y el Caribe,* v. 3, no. 2 (July – Dec 92), pp. 75 – 88.

Schiavini, Adrián. Los lobos marinos como recurso para cazadores-recolectores marinos: el caso de Tierra del Fuego. *Latin American Antiquity,* v. 4, no. 4 (Dec 93), pp. 346 – 366. Bibl, tables, maps.

Schiefelbein, Ernesto. La calidad de la enseñanza media chilena en el contexto internacional: VI Jornadas del Seminario de Evaluación, Universidad de Playa Ancha. *Estudios Sociales (Chile),* no. 78 (Oct – Dec 93), pp. 291 – 299.

Schillat, Monika. Los gigantes patagónicos: historia de una leyenda. *Todo Es Historia,* v. 26, no. 309 (Apr 93), pp. 60 – 66. Bibl, il.

Schmidhuber de la Mora, Guillermo. Hallazgo y significación de un texto en prosa perteneciente a los últimos años de sor Juana Inés de la Cruz. *Hispania (USA),* v. 76, no. 2 (May 93), pp. 189 – 196. Bibl.

Schmidt, Friedhelm. Bibliografía de y sobre Manuel Scorza: nuevas aportaciones. *Revista de Crítica Literaria Latinoamericana,* v. 19, no. 37 (Jan – June 93), pp. 355 – 359.

Schmidt, Heide. La risa: etapas en la narrativa femenina en México y Alemania; una aproximación. *Escritura (Venezuela),* v. 16, no. 31 – 32 (Jan – Dec 91), pp. 247 – 257. Bibl.

Schmidt, Rita Terezinha. Un juego de máscaras: Nélida Piñon y Mary McCarthy (Translated by Eleonora Cróquer P.). *Escritura (Venezuela),* v. 16, no. 31 – 32 (Jan – Dec 91), pp. 259 – 270.

Schmidt, Samuel. Humor y política en México. *Revista Mexicana de Sociología,* v. 54, no. 1 (Jan – Mar 92), pp. 225 – 250. Bibl.

— Lo tortuoso de la democratización mexicana. *Estudios Interdisciplinarios de América Latina y el Caribe,* v. 4, no. 1 (Jan – June 93), pp. 93 – 114. Bibl.

— Migración o refugio económico: el caso mexicano. *Nueva Sociedad,* no. 127 (Sept – Oct 93), pp. 136 – 147. Bibl.

Schneider, Cathy. Chile: The Underside of the Miracle. *Report on the Americas,* v. 26, no. 4 (Feb 93), pp. 30 – 31 +. Bibl, il.

Schreiter, Robert J. Inculturación: opción por el otro. *Amazonía Peruana,* v. 11, no. 22 (Oct 92), pp. 9 – 46.

Schroeder, Susan. The Noblewomen of Chalco. *Estudios de Cultura Náhuatl,* v. 22 (1992), pp. 45 – 86. Tables, maps, facs.

Schubert, Guilherme. Homilia pronunciada pelo sócio monsenhor Guilherme Schubert na missa pelo centenário da morte de dom Pedro II. *Revista do Instituto Histórico e Geográfico Brasileiro,* no. 373 (Oct – Dec 91), pp. 1183 – 1187.

Schulman, Iván A. Critical Crossroads. *Latin American Literary Review,* v. 20, no. 40 (July – Dec 92), pp. 97 – 99.

— ¿Más allá de la literatura?: un álbum de Cayo Hueso, 1891 – 1892. *Casa de las Américas,* no. 190 (Jan – Mar 93), pp. 50 – 55. Bibl.

— *La vorágine:* contrapuntos y textualizaciones de la modernidad. *Nueva Revista de Filología Hispánica,* v. 40, no. 2 (July – Dec 92), pp. 875 – 890. Bibl.

Schulz, Donald E. Can Castro Survive? *Journal of Inter-American Studies and World Affairs,* v. 35, no. 1 (1993), pp. 89 – 117. Bibl.

— The United States and Cuba: From a Strategy of Conflict to Constructive Engagement. *Journal of Inter-American Studies and World Affairs,* v. 35, no. 2 (Summer 93), pp. 81 – 102. Bibl.

Schulze Arana, Beatriz. Arte. *Signo,* no. 36 – 37, Nueva época (May – Dec 92), pp. 71 – 73.

Schumaher, Maria Aparecida and Elisabeth Vargas. Lugar no governo: álibi ou conquista? (Accompanied by an English translation by Christopher Peterson). *Estudos Feministas,* v. 1, no. 2 (1993), pp. 348 – 364.

Schvarzer, Jorge. Expansión, maduración y perspectivas de las ramas básicas de procesos en la industria argentina: una mirada "ex post" desde la economía política. *Desarrollo Económico (Argentina),* v. 33, no. 131 (Oct – Dec 93), pp. 377 – 402. Bibl, tables, charts.

— El MERCOSUR: la geografía a la espera de actores. *Nueva Sociedad,* no. 126 (July – Aug 93), pp. 72 – 83.

— El proceso de privatizaciones en la Argentina: implicaciones preliminares sobre sus efectos en la gobernabilidad del sistema. *Realidad Económica,* no. 120 (Nov – Dec 93), pp. 79 – 143. Bibl.

Schwartz, Jorge. ¡Abajo Tordesillas! *Casa de las Américas,* no. 191 (Apr – June 93), pp. 26 – 35. Bibl.

Schwartz, Stuart B. Panic in the Indies: The Portuguese Threat to the Spanish Empire, 1640 – 1650. *Colonial Latin American Review,* v. 2, no. 1 – 2 (1993), pp. 165 – 187. Bibl.

Schwegler, Armin. "Abrakabraka," "suebbesuebbe" y otras voces palenqueras: sus orígenes e importancia para el estudio de dialectos afrohispanocaribeños. *Thesaurus,* v. 45, no. 3 (Sept – Dec 90), pp. 690 – 731. Bibl.

Scott, Dennis. Walcott on Walcott. *Caribbean Quarterly,* v. 38, no. 4 (Dec 92), pp. 136 – 141.

Scott, James C. Reply (to the article "Rituals of Resistance" by Matthew C. Gutmann). *Latin American Perspectives,* v. 20, no. 2 (Spring 93), pp. 93 – 94.

Scott, Nadine Althea Theda. 1992: The Annual National Exhibition, National Gallery of Jamaica. *Jamaica Journal,* v. 25, no. 1 (Oct 93), pp. 45 – 53. Il.

Scott, Steven L. and Charles O. Collins. Air Pollution in the Valley of Mexico. *Geographical Review,* v. 83, no. 2 (Apr 93), pp. 119 – 133. Bibl, charts.

Scranton, Margaret E. Consolidation after Imposition: Panama's 1992 Referendum. *Journal of Inter-American Studies and World Affairs,* v. 35, no. 3 (Fall 93), pp. 65 – 102. Bibl, tables.

Scully, Timothy R. and J. Samuel Valenzuela. De la democracia a la democracia: continuidad y variaciones en las preferencias del electorado y en el sistema de partidos en Chile. *Estudios Públicos (Chile),* no. 51 (Winter 93), pp. 195 – 228. Bibl, tables.

Sebreli, Juan José. La dolorosa transición. *Todo Es Historia,* v. 27, no. 317 (Dec 93), pp. 26 – 29. Il.

Secchi, Carlo. Europe et Amérique Latine: Quelles relations pour les années '90? *Tiers Monde,* v. 34, no. 136 (Oct – Dec 93), pp. 781 – 806. Bibl, tables.

Seed, Patricia Pauline. "Are These Not Also Men?": The Indians' Humanity and Capacity for Spanish Civilisation. *Journal of Latin American Studies,* v. 25, no. 3 (Oct 93), pp. 629 – 652. Bibl.

— More Colonial and Postcolonial Discourses (Response to previous three responses). *Latin American Research Review,* v. 28, no. 3 (1993), pp. 146 – 152.

Segal, Aaron. Opciones comerciales del Caribe: las cartas de Europa, América del Norte y América Latina. *Comercio Exterior,* v. 43, no. 11 (Nov 93), pp. 1019 – 1030. Bibl, tables, charts.

Segala, Amos. La literatura náhuatl: ¿Un coto privado? (Response to Miguel León-Portilla's review of Amos Segala's *Histoire de la littérature náhuatl: sources, identités, représentations). Caravelle,* no. 59 (1992), pp. 209 – 219. Bibl.

Segato, Rita Laura. Okarilé: Yemoja's Icon Tune. *Latin American Music Review,* v. 14, no. 1 (Spring – Summer 93), pp. 1 – 19. Bibl, facs.

Seggerman, Helen-Louise. Arte latinoamericano en Christie's y Sotheby's (Accompanied by the English original, translated by Magdalena Holguín). *Art Nexus,* no. 10 (Sept – Dec 93), pp. 104 – 106. Il.

Segismundo, Fernando. A filosofia no Colégio Pedro II. *Revista do Instituto Histórico e Geográfico Brasileiro,* no. 373 (Oct – Dec 91), pp. 948 – 953.

— Professores de história de Colégio Pedro II: esboço. *Revista do Instituto Histórico e Geográfico Brasileiro,* no. 370 (Jan – Mar 91), pp. 151 – 192.

Segond, Cláudia Rodrigues and Nadja Maria Castilho da Costa. Plano de manejo ecológico da reserva particular de Bodoquena. *Revista Geográfica (Mexico),* no. 114 (July – Dec 91), pp. 91 – 100. Bibl, tables, maps.

Segovia, Francisco. Juan Pascoe y Cornelio Adrián César, impresores de México. *Artes de México,* no. 19 (Spring 93), pp. 111 – 113. Il.

Segovia, Tomás. Amigo taurófilo. *Vuelta,* v. 17, no. 204 (Nov 93), pp. 27 – 32.

Segre, Roberto. La poesía ambiental como proyecto de vida: la obra de Fernando Salinas (1930 – 1992). *Casa de las Américas,* no. 189 (Oct – Dec 92), pp. 107 – 108.

Segura, Denise Anne. Ambivalence or Continuity?: Motherhood and Employment among Chicanas and Mexican Immigrant Women Workers. *Aztlán,* v. 20, no. 1 – 2 (Spring – Fall 91), pp. 119 – 150. Bibl, charts.

Seibel, Beatriz. Mujer, teatro y sociedad en el siglo XIX. *Conjunto,* no. 92 (July – Dec 92), pp. 54 – 57. Bibl, il.

Selbert, Pamela. Pooling Forces on a Belizean Caye. *Américas,* v. 45, no. 6 (Nov – Dec 93), pp. 20 – 25. Il, maps.

Self, Robert. Intimidate First, Ask Questions Later: The INS and Immigration Rights. *NACLA Report on the Americas,* v. 26, no. 5 (May 93), pp. 11 – 14. Il.

Seligman, Linda Jane. "Es más fácil destruir que crear": comentarios y respuesta. *Allpanchis,* v. 23, no. 39 (Jan – June 92), pp. 93 – 101.

Seminiski, Jan. Manqu Qhapaq Inka: ¿Un poeta religioso? *Revista de Crítica Literaria Latinoamericana,* v. 19, no. 37 (Jan – June 93), pp. 131 – 158. Bibl.

Semo, Ilán. El cardenismo revisado: la tercera vía y otras utopías inciertas. *Revista Mexicana de Sociología,* v. 55, no. 2 (Apr – June 93), pp. 197 – 223. Bibl.

Sen, Amartya Kumar. A economia da vida e da morte (Translated by Heloisa Jahn). *Revista Brasileira de Ciências Sociais,* v. 8, no. 23 (Oct 93), pp. 138 – 145.

Sena, Consuelo Pondé de. A condessa de Barral, a grande dama do segundo reinado. *Revista do Instituto Histórico e Geográfico Brasileiro,* no. 372 (July – Sept 91), pp. 677 – 684. Bibl.

Sena, Davis Ribeiro de. A guerra das caatingas. *Revista do Instituto Histórico e Geográfico Brasileiro,* no. 373 (Oct – Dec 91), pp. 954 – 1007. Bibl, il.

Senén González, Santiago. Diez años de sindicalismo en democracia. *Todo Es Historia,* v. 27, no. 317 (Dec 93), pp. 66 – 69. Il.

— José Ignacio Rucci, "el soldado de Perón." *Todo Es Historia,* v. 27, no. 314 (Sept 93), pp. 8 – 22. Bibl, il, facs.

Senkman, Leonardo. Etnicidad e inmigración durante el primer peronismo. *Estudios Interdisciplinarios de América Latina y el Caribe,* v. 3, no. 2 (July – Dec 92), pp. 5 – 38. Bibl.

Sepúlveda Garza, Manola. El este de Guanajuato, 1760 – 1900: microhistoria de alianzas sociales. *Cuadernos Americanos*, no. 37, Nueva época (Jan – Feb 93), pp. 76 – 89. Bibl, tables.

Sepúlveda Llanos, Fidel. Nicanor, Violeta, Roberto Parra: encuentro de tradición y vanguardia. *Aisthesis*, no. 24 (1991), pp. 29 – 42. Bibl.

Sequeira, José. The Duty. *The Americas Review*, v. 20, no. 1 (Spring 92), pp. 12 – 17.

Sequera Tamayo, Isbelia. Rumania en Venezuela: en las academia nacionales. *Boletín de la Academia Nacional de la Historia (Venezuela)*, v. 75, no. 298 (Apr – June 92), pp. 5 – 7.

Serafino, Nina M. et al. Latin American Indigenous Peoples and Considerations for U.S. Assistance. *Anuario Indigenista*, v. 30 (Dec 91), pp. 11 – 144. Bibl.

Serbín, Andrés. El Grupo de los Tres y el proceso de regionalización en la cuenca del Caribe. *Nueva Sociedad*, no. 125 (May – June 93), pp. 120 – 129. Bibl.

Sercan, Cecilia S. Preservation Microforms in an RLIN Environment. *SALALM Papers*, v. 36 (1991), pp. 408 – 417.

Sergeant, Kelvin and Penelope Forde. The State Sector and Divestment in Trinidad and Tobago: Some Preliminary Findings. *Social and Economic Studies*, v. 41, no. 4 (Dec 92), pp. 173 – 204. Bibl, tables.

Serna Arnáiz, Mercedes. Algunas dilucidaciones sobre el krausismo en José Martí. *Cuadernos Hispanoamericanos*, no. 521 (Nov 93), pp. 137 – 145.

Serpa, Luiz Felippe Perret and Stela Borges de Almeida. Guia de fontes fotográficas para a história da educação. *Revista Brasileira de Estudos Pedagógicos*, v. 72, no. 172 (Sept – Dec 91), pp. 392 – 394.

Serpa Uribe, Horacio. La paz primero que la guerra. *Nueva Sociedad*, no. 125 (May – June 93), pp. 153 – 156.

Serra, José. As vicissitudes do orçamento. *Revista de Economia Política (Brazil)*, v. 13, no. 4 (Oct – Dec 93), pp. 143 – 149.

Serra, Luis. Democracy in Times of War and Socialist Crisis: Reflections Stemming from the Sandinista Revolution. *Latin American Perspectives*, v. 20, no. 2 (Spring 93), pp. 21 – 44. Bibl.

Serra, Pablo J. and Gabriel Fierro. Un modelo de estimación del costo de falla: el caso de Chile. *Cuadernos de Economía (Chile)*, v. 30, no. 90 (Aug 93), pp. 247 – 259. Bibl, tables.

Serrano, Eduardo. Acuña y el nacionalismo. *Boletín de Historia y Antigüedades*, v. 80, no. 781 (Apr – June 93), pp. 369 – 372.

Serrano, Juan F. Computer Acquisition Policy. *Business Mexico*, v. 3, no. 9 (Sept 93), pp. 7 – 8.

Serrano, Sol and Carlos Bascuñán. La idea de América en los exiliados españoles en Chile (Excerpt from *El pensamiento español contemporáneo y la idea de América* edited by José Luis Abellán and Antonio Monclús Estella). *Atenea (Chile)*, no. 465 – 466 (1992), pp. 99 – 149. Bibl, tables.

Serrano Páez, J. Ezio. Estado, nación y patria en los debates constitucionales de 1830 y 1858: consideraciones historiográficas. *Montalbán*, no. 24 (1992), pp. 221 – 251. Bibl.

Serva, Maurício. O fenômeno das organizações substantivas. *RAE; Revista de Administração de Empresas*, v. 33, no. 2 (Mar – Apr 93), pp. 36 – 43. Bibl.

Sevcenko, Nicolau. Transformações da linguagem e advento da cultura modernista no Brasil (Translated by Dora Rocha). *Estudos Históricos*, v. 6, no. 11 (Jan – June 93), pp. 78 – 88.

Severino, Francisca E. S. O candomblé visto de fora. *Vozes*, v. 87, no. 4 (July – Aug 93), pp. 41 – 45. Il.

Sevilla Soler, María Rosario. Capital y mercado interno en Colombia, 1880 – 1930. *Anuario de Estudios Americanos*, v. 49 (1992), pp. 585 – 599. Bibl.

Shady Solís, Ruth. Del arcaico al formativo en los Andes centrales. *Revista Andina*, v. 11, no. 1 (July 93), pp. 103 – 132. Bibl, tables, maps.

Shafer, Harry J. and John Edward Dockall. Testing the Producer – Consumer Model for Santa Rita Corozal, Belize. *Latin American Antiquity*, v. 4, no. 2 (June 93), pp. 158 – 179. Bibl, il, maps.

Shain, Yossi and Lynn Berat. Evening the Score: Layered Legacies of the Interregnum. *Estudios Interdisciplinarios de América Latina y el Caribe*, v. 4, no. 1 (Jan – June 93), pp. 57 – 91. Bibl.

Shedd, David. H_2O: Safe and Sound. *Business Mexico*, v. 3, no. 12 (Dec 93), pp. 40 – 42.

Sheinbaum Pardo, Claudia. Políticas de conservación de electricidad en México: costos sociales y alternativos. *Momento Económico*, no. 67 (May – June 93), pp. 7 – 14. Bibl, tables, charts.

Shelton, Marie-Denise. Condé: The Politics of Gender and Identity. *World Literature Today*, v. 67, no. 4 (Fall 93), pp. 717 – 722. Bibl, il.

Shen, Glen T. Reconstruction of El Niño History from Reef Corals. *Bulletin de l'Institut Français d'Etudes Andines*, v. 22, no. 1 (1993), pp. 125 – 158. Bibl, tables, maps, charts.

Sheridan, Guillermo. "Los Contemporáneos" y la generación del '27: documentando un desencuentro. *Cuadernos Hispanoamericanos*, no. 514 – 515 (Apr – May 93), pp. 185 – 194.

— José Juan Tablada en su *Diario*. *Vuelta*, v. 17, no. 198 (May 93), pp. 28 – 31.

Sherlock, Philip Manderson. Yesterday Walks before Us with Esteem and Affection for Derek Walcott. *Caribbean Quarterly*, v. 38, no. 4 (Dec 92), pp. v – xii.

Sherraden, Margaret and Viviane Brachet de Márquez. Austeridad fiscal, el estado de bienestar y el cambio político: los casos de la salud y la alimentación en México, 1970 – 1990 (Translated by Armando Castellanos). *Estudios Sociológicos*, v. 11, no. 32 (May – Aug 93), pp. 331 – 364. Bibl, tables.

Shifter, Michael. Un brindis por Lima. *Debate (Peru)*, v. 15, no. 71 (Nov 92 – Jan 93), pp. 49 – 51. Il.

Shimose Kawamura, Pedro. Homenaje a un cubano universal. *Signo*, no. 38, Nueva época (Jan – Apr 93), pp. 193 – 197.

Shipp, Adriana. Poems ("La chanteuse de jazz," "La pachanga," "Boca oficial"). *The Americas Review*, v. 19, no. 3 – 4 (Winter 91), pp. 51 – 54.

Siavelis, Peter. Nuevos argumentos y viejos supuestos: simulaciones de sistemas electorales alternativos para las elecciones parlamentarias chilenas. *Estudios Públicos (Chile)*, no. 51 (Winter 93), pp. 229 – 267. Tables, charts.

Sicard, Alain. Poder de la escritura: ¿El crepúsculo de los chamanes? *Revista de Crítica Literaria Latinoamericana*, v. 19, no. 38 (July – Dec 93), pp. 155 – 162.

Sicard, Alain et al. Debate (on the third session of the symposium "Latinoamérica: Nuevas Direcciones en Teoría y Crítica Literarias, III"). *Revista de Crítica Literaria Latinoamericana,* v. 19, no. 38 (July – Dec 93), pp. 131 – 141.

Sichel, Berta. Artistas latinoamericanos del siglo XX (Accompanied by an English translation). *Art Nexus,* no. 9 (June – Aug 93), pp. 52 – 56. Il.

— Carlos Zerpa. *Latin American Art,* v. 5, no. 2 (Summer 93), pp. 33 – 35. Bibl, il.

Sidicaro, Ricardo. Reflexiones sobre la accidentada trayectoria de la sociología en la Argentina. *Cuadernos Hispanoamericanos,* no. 517 – 519 (July – Sept 93), pp. 65 – 76. Bibl.

Sierra, María Teresa. Usos y desusos del derecho consuetudinario indígena. *Nueva Antropología,* v. 13, no. 44 (Aug 93), pp. 17 – 26. Bibl.

Sierra, María Teresa and Victoria Chenaut. El campo de investigación de la antropología jurídica. *Nueva Antropología,* v. 13, no. 43 (Nov 92), pp. 101 – 109. Bibl.

Sievernich, Michael. Visiones teológicas en torno al quinto centenario. *Ibero-Amerikanisches Archiv,* v. 18, no. 3 – 4 (1992), pp. 367 – 385. Bibl.

Sigal, Víctor. El acceso a la educación superior: el ingreso irrestricto; ¿Una falacia? *Desarrollo Económico (Argentina),* v. 33, no. 130 (July – Sept 93), pp. 265 – 280. Bibl, tables.

Sikkink, Kathryn. Las capacidades y la autonomía del estado en Brasil y la Argentina: un enfoque neoinstitucionalista (Translated by Leandro Wolfson). *Desarrollo Económico (Argentina),* v. 32, no. 128 (Jan – Mar 93), pp. 543 – 574. Bibl, charts.

Silberfeld, Jean-Claude. O fator regional. *Problemas Brasileiros,* v. 30, no. 296 (Mar – Apr 93), pp. 35 – 37. Il.

Silenzi de Stagni, Adolfo et al. La privatización de YPF. *Realidad Económica,* no. 118 (Aug – Sept 93), pp. 18 – 67. Tables, charts.

Siles Salinas, María Eugenia de

See

Valle de Siles, María Eugenia del

Sili, Marcelo Enrique. Desarrollo local: entre la realidad y la utopía. *Revista Interamericana de Planificación,* v. 26, no. 101 – 102 (Jan – June 93), pp. 63 – 77. Bibl, charts.

Silva, Alberto Martins da. Um inédito de João Severiano da Fonseca: *Serafim Moreira da Silva Júnior, um herói de Diamantina, 1850 – 1868* (Includes the previously unpublished text). *Revista do Instituto Histórico e Geográfico Brasileiro,* no. 371 (Apr – June 91), pp. 518 – 532. Bibl.

Silva, Alexandra de Mello e and Paulo S. Wrobel. Entrevista com Celso Lafer. *Estudos Históricos,* v. 6, no. 12 (July – Dec 93), pp. 271 – 284.

Silva, Barbara-Christine Nentwig. Análise comparativa da posição de Salvador e do estado da Bahia no cenário nacional. *Revista Brasileira de Geografia,* v. 53, no. 4 (Oct – Dec 91), pp. 49 – 79. Bibl, tables, maps, charts.

Silva, Carlos da. A narrativa como expressão e conhecimento do ser: *Insônia* de Graciliano Ramos. *Revista de Letras (Brazil),* v. 32 (1992), pp. 51 – 67. Bibl.

Silva, César Roberto Leite da and Maria Auxiliadora de Carvalho. Preços mínimos e estabilização de preços agrícolas. *Revista de Economia Política (Brazil),* v. 13, no. 1 (Jan – Mar 93), pp. 52 – 63. Bibl, tables.

Silva, Eduardo. Capitalist Regime Loyalties and Redemocratization in Chile. *Journal of Inter-American Studies and World Affairs,* v. 34, no. 4 (Winter 92 – 93), pp. 77 – 117. Bibl.

Silva, Gabriel Luiz Seraphico Peixoto da et al. Mudança tecnológica e produtividade do milho e da soja no Brasil. *Revista Brasileira de Economia,* v. 47, no. 2 (Apr – June 93), pp. 281 – 303. Bibl, tables.

Silva, Geraldo Eulálio do Nascimento e. As relações diplomáticas entre o Brasil e a Austria. *Revista do Instituto Histórico e Geográfico Brasileiro,* no. 372 (July – Sept 91), pp. 665 – 676.

Silva, Jorge Xavier da. Um banco de dados ambientais para a Amazônia. *Revista Brasileira de Geografia,* v. 53, no. 3 (July – Sept 91), pp. 91 – 124. Bibl, il, tables, maps.

Silva, José David. Entrega o recuperación de la reserva forestal de Ticoporo. *Derecho y Reforma Agraria,* no. 24 (1993), pp. 183 – 193. Tables.

Silva, Lúcia Maria Ramos and Ahmad Saeed Khan. Características sócio-econômicas de produtores rurais, conservação do solo e produtividade agrícola. *Revista de Economia e Sociologia Rural,* v. 30, no. 3 (July – Sept 92), pp. 225 – 237. Bibl, tables.

Silva, Luís Inácio da. Discurso de Luís Inácio "Lula" da Silva (given at the IV Encuentro del Foro de São Paulo). *Nueva Sociedad,* no. 128 (Nov – Dec 93), pp. 162 – 165.

Silva, Maurício Corrêa da et al. Rentabilidade e risco no produção de leite numa região de Santa Catarina. *Revista de Economia e Sociologia Rural,* v. 30, no. 1 (Jan – Mar 92), pp. 63 – 81. Bibl, tables.

Silva, Mauro José da and José Grabois. O breja de Natuba: estudo da organização de um espaço periférico. *Revista Brasileira de Geografia,* v. 53, no. 2 (Apr – June 91), pp. 33 – 62. Bibl, il, tables, maps.

Silva, Orlando Monteiro da. Elasticidade de substituição para o suco de laranja no mercado internacional. *Revista de Economia e Sociologia Rural,* v. 30, no. 2 (Apr – June 92), pp. 135 – 147. Bibl, tables.

Silva, Orlando Monteiro da and John C. Dutton, Jr. O mercado internacional de suco de laranja concentrado congelado: um modelo com produtos diferenciados. *Revista de Economia e Sociologia Rural,* v. 29, no. 4 (Oct – Dec 91), pp. 353 – 371. Bibl, tables.

Silva, Patricio. La historia, la política y el futuro. *Mensaje,* v. 42, no. 423 (Oct 93), pp. 495 – 499.

— Intelectuales, tecnócratas y cambio social en Chile: pasado, presente y perspectivas futuras. *Revista Mexicana de Sociología,* v. 54, no. 1 (Jan – Mar 92), pp. 130 – 166. Bibl.

Silva, Rebeca de Souza e. Cegonhas indesejadas: aborto provocado. *Estudos Feministas,* v. 1, no. 1 (1993), pp. 123 – 134. Bibl.

Silva, Sonia T. Dias Gonçalves da. A colonização italiana no sul do Brasil em "posters." *SALALM Papers,* v. 34 (1989), pp. 177 – 182. Bibl.

Silva, Sylvio Carlos Bandeira de Mello e and Jaimeval Caetano de Souza. Análise da hierarquia urbana do estado da Bahia. *Revista Brasileira de Geografia,* v. 53, no. 1 (Jan – Mar 91), pp. 51 – 79. Bibl, tables, maps, charts.

Silva, Vera Alice Cardoso. A política externa brasileira na década de '90: possibilidades de acomodação à nova fase do capitalismo internacional. *Política e Estratégia,* v. 8, no. 2 – 4 (Apr – Dec 90), pp. 224 – 240. Bibl.

Silva Beauregard, Paulette. La narrativa venezolana de la época del modernismo. *Revista Chilena de Literatura,* no. 40 (Nov 92), pp. 41 – 56. Bibl.

Silva C., Alberto. Una "nueva frontera": el Pacífico. *Mensaje,* v. 42, no. 416 (Jan – Feb 93), pp. 41 – 42.

Silva G., Sergio. La iglesia interpelada. *Mensaje,* v. 42, no. 417 (Mar – Apr 93), pp. 100 – 102.

Silva Galdames, Osvaldo. Acerca de los capitanes de amigos: un documento y un comentario. *Cuadernos de Historia (Chile),* no. 11 (Dec 91), pp. 29 – 45. Bibl.

— Gonzalo Izquierdo Fernández (1932 – 1990). *Cuadernos de Historia (Chile),* no. 11 (Dec 91), pp. 7 – 12. Il.

Silva Galdames, Osvaldo et al. Junta de los pehuenches de Malargüe con el comandante general de armas y frontera de Mendoza, don Francisco José de Amigorena. *Cuadernos de Historia (Chile),* no. 11 (Dec 91), pp. 199 – 209. Bibl, facs.

Silva Galeana, Librado. Cozcacuauhco: en el lugar de las águilas reales. *Estudios de Cultura Náhuatl,* v. 22 (1992), pp. 253 – 289.

Silva Herzog, Jesús. Crisis humana y post-guerra. *Hoy Es Historia,* v. 10, no. 58 (July – Aug 93), pp. 59 – 70. Il.

Silva Soler, Joaquín and Gonzalo Arroyo. Mesa redonda: educando para la solidaridad. *Mensaje,* v. 42, no. 421 (Aug 93), pp. 392 – 401. Il.

Silveira, Helder Gordim da. A ofensiva política dos EUA sobre a América Latina na visão alemã: uma face do confronto interimperialista, 1938. *Estudos Ibero-Americanos,* v. 18, no. 1 (July 92), pp. 19 – 27. Bibl.

Silveira, Maria Dutra da. Mauá e a revolução farroupilha. *Hoy Es Historia,* v. 10, no. 59 (Sept – Oct 93), pp. 75 – 81. Il.

Silverstein, Jeffrey. Banking on the Future. *Business Mexico,* v. 3, no. 3 (Mar 93), pp. 10 – 11.

— Wave of the Future. *Business Mexico,* v. 3, no. 4 (Apr 93), pp. 38 – 39. Il.

Simons Chirinos, Andrés. La teoría de las uniones aduaneras y el Pacto Andino. *Apuntes (Peru),* no. 31 (July – Dec 92), pp. 41 – 54.

Simpson, Amelia S. Xuxa and the Politics of Gender. *Luso-Brazilian Review,* v. 30, no. 1 (Summer 93), pp. 95 – 106. Bibl.

Singelmann, Peter Marius. The Sugar Industry in Postrevolutionary Mexico: State Intervention and Private Capital. *Latin American Research Review,* v. 28, no. 1 (1993), pp. 61 – 88. Bibl, tables.

Singer S., Martha and Gustavo Leal F. Gobernando desde la oposición: ayuntamiento de Durango, 1992 – 1995. *El Cotidiano,* v. 9, no. 54 (May 93), pp. 90 – 100. Bibl, il, tables.

Singh, Naresh Charan. Sustainable Development: Its Meaning for the Caribbean. *Social and Economic Studies,* v. 41, no. 3 (Sept 92), pp. 145 – 167. Bibl.

Sintura, Francisco José. La Fiscalía General de la Nación desde la Fiscalía. *Revista Javeriana,* v. 61, no. 598 (Sept 93), pp. 227 – 235.

Siqueira, Baptista. Características de la música brasileña. *Revista Musical de Venezuela,* no. 28 (May – Dec 89), pp. 197 – 206. Facs.

Sirlin, Pablo and Marcelo Sánchez. Elementos de una propuesta transformadora para el desarrollo económico argentino. *Realidad Económica,* no. 117 (July – Aug 93), pp. 36 – 160. Bibl.

Siscar, Cristina. Prose Poems ("Diccionario enciclopédico," "Peine con incrustaciones," "Corazones flechados," "Cuaderno y bloc de cartas"). *Inti,* no. 36 (Fall 92), pp. 153 – 156.

Skerritt, David A. Una historia dinámica entre la sierra y la costa. *La Palabra y el Hombre,* no. 83 (July – Sept 92), pp. 5 – 25. Bibl, tables, maps.

Skidmore, Thomas E. Bi-Racial U.S.A. vs. Multi-Racial Brazil: Is the Contrast Still Valid? *Journal of Latin American Studies,* v. 25, no. 2 (May 93), pp. 373 – 386. Bibl.

Sklair, Leslie. Las maquilas en México: una perspectiva global. *Revista Mexicana de Sociología,* v. 54, no. 2 (Apr – June 92), pp. 163 – 183. Bibl.

Sklodowska, Elzbieta. Testimonio mediatizado: ¿Ventriloquia o heteroglosia?; Barnet/Montejo; Burgos/Menchú. *Revista de Crítica Literaria Latinoamericana,* v. 19, no. 38 (July – Dec 93), pp. 81 – 90. Bibl.

Skolnik, Howard B. A Different Drum. *Business Mexico,* v. 3, no. 5 (May 93), pp. 36 – 38. Il.

Slater, Candace. New Directions in Latin American Oral Traditions. *Latin American Literary Review,* v. 20, no. 40 (July – Dec 92), pp. 100 – 103.

Sletto, Bjorn. Crosscurrents to the Mainland (Photographs by the author). *Américas,* v. 45, no. 5 (Sept – Oct 93), pp. 6 – 13. Il, maps.

Slive, Daniel J. and Monica Barnes. El puma de Cuzco: ¿Plano de la ciudad ynga o noción europea? *Revista Andina,* v. 11, no. 1 (July 93), pp. 70 – 102. Bibl, maps, facs.

Sluyter, Andrew. Long-Distance Staple Transport in Western Mesoamerica: Insights through Quantitative Modeling. *Ancient Mesoamerica,* v. 4, no. 2 (Fall 93), pp. 193 – 199. Bibl, tables, maps, charts.

Smith, David and Rolando Rivera. Organización, movilización popular y desarrollo regional en el Atlántico costarricense. *Estudios Rurales Latinoamericanos,* v. 15, no. 2 – 3 (May – Dec 92), pp. 79 – 110. Tables.

Smith, E. Valerie. The Sisterhood of Nossa Senhora da Boa Morte and the Brotherhood of Nossa Senhora do Rosario: African-Brazilian Cultural Adaptations to Antebellum Restrictions. *Afro-Hispanic Review,* v. 11, no. 1 – 3 (1992), pp. 58 – 69. Bibl, tables.

Smith, Kevin W. and Sarah A. McGraw. Smoking Behavior of Puerto Rican Women: Evidence from Caretakers of Adolescents in Two Urban Areas. *Hispanic Journal of Behavioral Sciences,* v. 15, no. 1 (Feb 93), pp. 140 – 149. Bibl, tables.

Smith, Morgan. Lifting the "Brown Cloud." *Business Mexico,* v. 3, no. 9 (Sept 93), pp. 39 – 40.

Smith, Patrick Bellegarde

See
Bellegarde-Smith, Patrick

Smith, Peter H. Latin America and the New World Order. *SALALM Papers,* v. 36 (1991), pp. 3 – 9.

Smith, William C. Reestructuración neoliberal y escenarios políticos en América Latina. *Nueva Sociedad,* no. 126 (July – Aug 93), pp. 25 – 39. Bibl.

Smulovitz, Catalina. La eficacia como crítica y utopía: notas sobre la caída de Illia. *Desarrollo Económico (Argentina),* v. 33, no. 131 (Oct – Dec 93), pp. 403 – 423. Bibl.

Smulovitz, Catalina and Liliana de Riz. Instauración democrática y reforma política en Argentina y Uruguay: un análisis comparado. *Ibero-Amerikanisches Archiv,* v. 18, no. 1 – 2 (1992), pp. 181 – 224. Bibl, tables.

Snoeck, Michele et al. Tecnología de punta en un pequeño país subdesarrollado: la industria electrónica en el Uruguay. *Desarrollo Económico (Argentina),* v. 33, no. 129 (Apr – June 93), pp. 87 – 107. Bibl, tables.

Soares, Gláucio Ary Dillon. Comentários adicionais (Response on commentaries to his article "A violência política na América Latina"). *Revista Brasileira de Ciências Sociais,* v. 8, no. 21 (Feb 93), pp. 48 – 51.

— A violência política na América Latina. *Revista Brasileira de Ciências Sociais*, v. 8, no. 21 (Feb 93), pp. 22 – 39. Bibl, tables, charts.

Soares, Gláucio Ary Dillon and Maria Celina d'Araújo. A imprensa, os mitos e os votos nas eleições de 1990. *Revista Brasileira de Estudos Políticos*, no. 76 (Jan 93), pp. 163 – 189. Tables, charts.

Sobral, Fernanda Antônia da Fonseca. La politique scientifique et technologique du Brésil et la conception du développement national. *Cahiers des Amériques Latines*, no. 13 (1992), pp. 163 – 170. Bibl, tables.

Sobrino, Jon. Reflexiones teológicas sobre el informe de la Comisión de la Verdad. *ECA; Estudios Centroamericanos*, v. 48, no. 534 – 535 (Apr – May 93), pp. 389 – 408. Il.

— Relectura cristiana del quinto centenario. *ECA; Estudios Centroamericanos*, v. 47, no. 528 (Oct 92), pp. 855 – 866. Il.

Socarrás, José Francisco. Las academias al borde del cierre. *Boletín de Historia y Antigüedades*, v. 79, no. 779 (Oct – Dec 92), pp. 1093 – 1095.

— Manuel Briceño Jáuregui, S.J. *Boletín de Historia y Antigüedades*, v. 80, no. 781 (Apr – June 93), pp. 319 – 320.

Sodré, Muniz. Por que uma escola de comunicação? (Originally published in this journal in October 1972). *Vozes*, v. 87, no. 3 (May – June 93), pp. 85 – 89.

Soete, George J. Resource Sharing: The Only Reasonable Whither. *SALALM Papers*, v. 36 (1991), pp. 272 – 276.

Soiza Larrosa, Augusto. Un linaje carolino – minuano: Larrosa – Cortés, siglos XVIII – XIX. *Hoy Es Historia*, v. 10, no. 55 (Jan – Feb 93), pp. 62 – 71. Bibl, il.

— Medicina popular. *Hoy Es Historia*, v. 10, no. 59 (Sept – Oct 93), pp. 98 – 99.

— Valores notables de la cultura uruguaya: algunos aportes médicos uruguayos a la comunidad científica mundial. *Hoy Es Historia*, v. 10, no. 55 (Jan – Feb 93), pp. 35 – 44. Bibl.

Sokoloff Gutiérrez, Ana. El arte latinoamericano en Christie's y Sotheby's (Accompanied by an English translation). *Art Nexus*, no. 8 (Apr – June 93), pp. 105 – 107. Tables.

Sol, Ricardo. Nuevo orden planetario: comunicación y neoliberalismo. *Revista de Ciencias Sociales (Costa Rica)*, no. 57 (Sept 92), pp. 31 – 39.

Solano Jiménez, Ronald. Crítica literaria en Costa Rica: de las *Historias de Tata Mundo. Anuario de Estudios Centroamericanos*, v. 18, no. 1 (1992), pp. 85 – 95. Bibl.

Solano y Pérez-Lila, Francisco de. Inmigración latinoamericana a Puerto Rico, 1800 – 1898. *Revista de Indias*, v. 52, no. 195 – 196 (May – Dec 92), pp. 923 – 957. Tables.

Solari Yrigoyen, Edelmiro M. Hipólito Yrigoyen, ¿hijo de Rosas? *Todo Es Historia*, v. 26, no. 308 (Mar 93), pp. 76 – 80. Bibl, il, facs.

Solberg, V. Scott et al. Development of the College Stress Inventory for Use with Hispanic Populations: A Confirmatory Analytic Approach. *Hispanic Journal of Behavioral Sciences*, v. 15, no. 4 (Nov 93), pp. 490 – 497. Bibl, tables, charts.

— Self-Efficacy and Hispanic College Students: Validation of the College Self-Efficacy Instrument. *Hispanic Journal of Behavioral Sciences*, v. 15, no. 1 (Feb 93), pp. 80 – 95. Bibl, tables.

Soldatenko, Maria Angelina. Organizing Latina Garment Workers in Los Angeles. *Aztlán*, v. 20, no. 1 – 2 (Spring – Fall 91), pp. 73 – 96. Bibl.

Solimano, Andrés. Diversidad en la reforma económica: experiencias recientes en economías de mercado y economías socialistas. *Pensamiento Iberoamericano*, no. 22 – 23, tomo I (July 92 – June 93), pp. 59 – 100. Bibl, tables, charts.

Solís Alpízar, Olman E. Jesús María: un sitio con actividad doméstica en el Pacífico central, Costa Rica. *Vínculos*, v. 16, no. 1 – 2 (1990), pp. 31 – 56. Bibl, il.

Solís Avendaño, Manuel. El ascenso de la ideología de la producción en Costa Rica: el Partido Liberación Nacional. *Revista de Ciencias Sociales (Costa Rica)*, no. 60 (June 93), pp. 85 – 100. Bibl.

Solís del Vecchio, Felipe and Anaysy Herrera Villalobos. Lomas Entierros: un centro político prehispánico en la cuenca baja del Río Grande de Tárcoles. *Vínculos*, v. 16, no. 1 – 2 (1990), pp. 85 – 110. Bibl, il, tables, maps.

Solís Tolosa, Lucía S. María Bertolozzi: de la narración histórica a la historia social. *Todo Es Historia*, v. 26, no. 309 (Apr 93), pp. 56 – 59. Il.

Solla Olivera, Horacio. Cultos afrobrasileños: un templo de umbanda en la ciudad de Montevideo. *Hoy Es Historia*, v. 10, no. 56 (Mar – Apr 93), pp. 33 – 39. Bibl.

Solleiro, José Luis et al. La innovación tecnológica en la agricultura mexicana. *Comercio Exterior*, v. 43, no. 4 (Apr 93), pp. 353 – 369. Bibl, charts.

Solórzano Fonseca, Juan Carlos. La búsqueda de oro y la resistencia indígena: campañas de exploración y conquista de Costa Rica, 1502 – 1610. *Mesoamérica (USA)*, v. 13, no. 24 (Dec 92), pp. 313 – 363. Bibl.

— Conquista, colonización y resistencia indígena en Costa Rica. *Revista de Historia (Costa Rica)*, no. 25 (Jan – June 92), pp. 191 – 205. Bibl.

Solotorevsky, Myrna. La tetralogía de Martini o la obsesión de la historia. *Hispamérica*, v. 21, no. 62 (Aug 92), pp. 3 – 19. Bibl.

Sommer, Doris. Cecilia no sabe o los bloqueos que blanquean. *Revista de Crítica Literaria Latinoamericana*, v. 19, no. 38 (July – Dec 93), pp. 239 – 248. Bibl.

— Resistant Texts and Incompetent Readers. *Latin American Literary Review*, v. 20, no. 40 (July – Dec 92), pp. 104 – 108.

Sommers, Ira et al. Sociocultural Influences on the Explanation of Delinquency for Puerto Rican Youths. *Hispanic Journal of Behavioral Sciences*, v. 15, no. 1 (Feb 93), pp. 36 – 62. Bibl, tables.

Sondrol, Paul C. Explaining and Reconceptualizing Underdevelopment: Paraguay and Uruguay (Review article). *Latin American Research Review*, v. 28, no. 3 (1993), pp. 235 – 250. Bibl.

Sonntag-Grigera, María Gabriela. Lesser-Known Latin American Women Authors: A Bibliography. *Revista Interamericana de Bibliografía*, v. 42, no. 3 (1992), pp. 463 – 488.

Sonzogni, Elida and Marta Bonaudo. Redes parentales y facciones en la política santafesina, 1850 – 1900. *Siglo XIX: Revista*, no. 11, 2a época (Jan – June 92), pp. 74 – 110. Bibl.

Sorensen, Lee R. Art Reference: Visual Information and Sources for Latin America. *SALALM Papers*, v. 34 (1989), pp. 325 – 333. Bibl.

Soria, Giuliano Oreste. Echi della conquista nella Torino del '600: Valerio Fulvio Savoiano e Bartolomé de Las Casas. *Quaderni Ibero-Americani*, no. 72 (Dec 92), pp. 721 – 731. Bibl.

Soria, Víctor M. Nouvelles politiques d'ajustement et de re-légitimation de l'état au Mexique: le rôle du PRONASOL et de la privatisation des entreprises publiques. *Tiers Monde,* v. 34, no. 135 (July – Sept 93), pp. 603 – 623. Bibl, tables.

Soriano, Osvaldo. The Eye of the Fatherland (Translated by Alfred MacAdam). *Review,* no. 47 (Fall 93), pp. 79 – 82.

Sosa, Víctor. Poesía y antología (Review article). *Vuelta,* v. 17, no. 199 (June 93), pp. 42 – 44.

Sosa de Newton, Lily. César Duayen, una mujer que se adelantó a su tiempo. *Todo Es Historia,* v. 27, no. 311 (June 93), pp. 46 – 48. Bibl, il.

Sosa Llanos, Pedro Vicente. Pleitos venezolanos en el Archivo Histórico Nacional de Madrid. *Boletín de la Academia Nacional de la Historia (Venezuela),* v. 75, no. 300 (Oct – Dec 92), pp. 223 – 247.

Sosa Llanos, Pedro Vicente and José de Briceño. El "Cólera morbus" en la Venezuela de 1854. *Boletín de la Academia Nacional de la Historia (Venezuela),* v. 76, no. 301 (Jan – Mar 93), pp. 197 – 208.

Sosamontes Herreramoro, Ramón. El reclamo de la seguridad. *El Cotidiano,* v. 9, no. 54 (May 93), pp. 76 – 80. Il.

Sotelo Valencia, Adrián. La crisis estructural en México. *El Cotidiano,* v. 9, no. 53 (Mar – Apr 93), pp. 110 – 117. Bibl, tables.

Sotelo Vázquez, Adolfo. Leopoldo Alas "Clarín" en Nueva York, 1894 – 1897: las novedades de Hispanoamérica. *Cuadernos Hispanoamericanos,* no. 511 (Jan 93), pp. 115 – 123. Bibl, il.

Soto, Francisco. Reinaldo Arenas: The Pentagonia and the Cuban Documentary Novel. *Cuban Studies/Estudios Cubanos,* v. 23 (1993), pp. 135 – 166. Bibl.

— La transfiguración del poder en *La vieja Rosa* y *Arturo, la estrella más brillante. Confluencia,* v. 8, no. 1 (Fall 92), pp. 71 – 78. Bibl.

Soto, Oscar David. (Letter from Oscar David Soto, Ex-President of the IAN, to the Agricultural Commission of the Chamber of Deputies). *Derecho y Reforma Agraria,* no. 24 (1993), pp. 197 – 200.

— Propiedad agraria y desafectación. *Derecho y Reforma Agraria,* no. 23 (1992), pp. 33 – 50.

Soto Mora, Consuelo and Luis Fuentes Aguilar. El control institucional en el Plan Nacional de Desarrollo en México. *Revista Interamericana de Planificación,* v. 26, no. 101 – 102 (Jan – June 93), pp. 183 – 195. Bibl.

— La industria del aluminio en el Tratado de Libre Comercio. *Problemas del Desarrollo,* v. 24, no. 93 (Apr – June 93), pp. 75 – 93. Bibl, tables, maps.

Soto Pérez, José Luis. Fuentes documentales para la historia de la provincia franciscana de Michoacán en el siglo XVIII. *Archivo Ibero-Americano,* v. 52, no. 205 – 208 (Jan – Dec 92), pp. 81 – 106. Facs.

Soto Sandoval, Andrés. La candidatura de Eugenio Pizarro. *Mensaje,* v. 42, no. 417 (Mar – Apr 93), pp. 102 – 103.

— INFOCAP: en la senda de Ignacio y de Alberto Hurtado. *Mensaje,* v. 42, no. 420 (July 93), pp. 280 – 282. Il.

Sotomayor, María Lucía. Organización socio-política de las cofradías. *Revista Colombiana de Antropología,* v. 29 (1992), pp. 155 – 189. Bibl, tables.

Sotomayor Miletti, Aurea María. Si un nombre convoca un mundo . . . : *Felices días, tío Sergio* en la narrativa puertorriqueña contemporánea. *Revista Iberoamericana,* v. 59, no. 162 – 163 (Jan – June 93), pp. 317 – 327. Bibl.

Sotomayor Yalán, Maritza. La producción automotriz en México y el Tratado de Libre Comercio México – Estados Unidos – Canadá. *Frontera Norte,* v. 4, no. 8 (July – Dec 92), pp. 165 – 172.

Sousa, Maria da Conceição Sampaio de. Reforma tarifária no Brasil: uma abordagem de "second best." *Revista Brasileira de Economia,* v. 47, no. 1 (Jan – Mar 93), pp. 3 – 31. Bibl, tables.

Sousa Vidal, Alejandro. Desaceleración económica: causas y perspectivas. *Problemas del Desarrollo,* v. 24, no. 94 (July – Sept 93), pp. 20 – 24.

Souza, Herbert José de. IBASE e os desafios colocados pela situação política. *Vozes,* v. 87, no. 4 (July – Aug 93), pp. 77 – 85.

Souza, Jaimeval Caetano de and Sylvio Carlos Bandeira de Mello e Silva. Análise da hierarquia urbana do estado da Bahia. *Revista Brasileira de Geografia,* v. 53, no. 1 (Jan – Mar 91), pp. 51 – 79. Bibl, tables, maps, charts.

Souza, Jaimeval Caetano de et al. Combinações agrícolas no estado da Bahia, 1970 – 1980: uma contribuição metodológica. *Revista Brasileira de Geografia,* v. 53, no. 2 (Apr – June 91), pp. 95 – 112. Bibl, tables, maps.

Souza, José da Silva and Ahmad Saeed Khan. Taxa de retorno social do investimento em pesquisa na cultura da mandioca no Nordeste. *Revista de Economia e Sociologia Rural,* v. 29, no. 4 (Oct – Dec 91), pp. 411 – 426. Bibl, tables, charts.

Souza, Luís de Castro. Saudação a Fernando da Cruz Gouvêa. *Revista do Instituto Histórico e Geográfico Brasileiro,* no. 372 (July – Sept 91), pp. 812 – 814.

— Saudação ao sócio honorário Alberto Martins da Silva: os médicos militares no Instituto Histórico e Geográfico Brasileiro (Speech given in honor of Dr. Silva's induction into the Instituto Histórico e Geográfico Brasileiro). *Revista do Instituto Histórico e Geográfico Brasileiro,* no. 371 (Apr – June 91), pp. 509 – 517. Bibl.

Souza, Maria Tereza Saraiva de. Uma estratégia de "marketing" para cooperativas de artesanato: o caso do Rio Grande do Norte. *RAE; Revista de Administração de Empresas,* v. 33, no. 1 (Jan – Feb 93), pp. 30 – 38. Bibl, tables, charts.

— Rumo à prática empresarial sustentável. *RAE; Revista de Administração de Empresas,* v. 33, no. 4 (July – Aug 93), pp. 40 – 52. Bibl.

Souza, Washington Peluso Albino de. Constituição e direito cultural: uma "revisita" aos conceitos básicos. *Revista Brasileira de Estudos Políticos,* no. 76 (Jan 93), pp. 117 – 130.

Sowell, David Lee. La Caja de Ahorros de Bogotá, 1846 – 1865: Artisans, Credit, Development, and Savings in Early National Colombia. *Hispanic American Historical Review,* v. 73, no. 4 (Nov 93), pp. 615 – 638. Bibl, tables.

Spalding, Hobart A., Jr. New Directions and Themes in Latin American Labor and Working-Class History: A Sampler (Review article). *Latin American Research Review,* v. 28, no. 1 (1993), pp. 202 – 214. Bibl.

Sparks, David Hatfield. Gilberto Gil, Praise Singer of the Gods. *Afro-Hispanic Review,* v. 11, no. 1 – 3 (1992), pp. 70 – 75. Bibl.

Spear, Thomas C. Individual Quests and Collective History. *World Literature Today,* v. 67, no. 4 (Fall 93), pp. 723 – 730. Il.

Spicer, Juan Pablo. *Don Segundo Sombra:* en busca del "otro." *Revista de Crítica Literaria Latinoamericana,* v. 19, no. 38 (July – Dec 93), pp. 361 – 373. Bibl.

Spinetto, Horacio Julio. Abelardo Arias: de *Alamos talados* a *El, Juan Facundo. Todo Es Historia,* v. 27, no. 313 (Aug 93), pp. 74 – 87. Il.

Spitta, Silvia. Chamanismo y cristiandad: una lectura de los *Naufragios* de Cabeza de Vaca. *Revista de Crítica Literaria Latinoamericana,* v. 19, no. 38 (July – Dec 93), pp. 317 – 330. Bibl.

Spoor, Max. La política de precios agrícolas en Nicaragua durante el régimen sandinista, 1979 – 1990 (Translated by Carlos Villegas). *El Trimestre Económico,* v. 60, no. 239 (July – Sept 93), pp. 601 – 641. Bibl, tables, charts.

Spores, Ronald. Tututepec: A Postclassic-Period Mixtec Conquest State. *Ancient Mesoamerica,* v. 4, no. 1 (Spring 93), pp. 167 – 174. Bibl, tables, maps, charts.

Sprout, Ronald V. A. La economía política de Prebisch. *Pensamiento Iberoamericano,* no. 22 – 23, tomo I (July 92 – June 93), pp. 315 – 343. Bibl, tables.

Squirra, S. Boris Casoy, o âncora brasileiro e o modelo norte-americano. *Vozes,* v. 87, no. 4 (July – Aug 93), pp. 3 – 12. Bibl, il.

Stam, Juan. La *Biblia* en la teología colonialista de Juan Ginés de Sepúlveda. *Revista de Historia (Costa Rica),* no. 25 (Jan – June 92), pp. 157 – 164. Bibl.

Standish, Peter. Contemplating Your Own Novel: The Case of Mario Vargas Llosa. *Hispanic Review,* v. 61, no. 1 (Winter 93), pp. 53 – 63. Bibl.

Stanford, Lois. The "Organization" of Mexican Agriculture: Conflicts and Compromises (Review article). *Latin American Research Review,* v. 28, no. 1 (1993), pp. 188 – 201. Bibl.

Stanley, William Deane and David Holiday. La construcción de la paz: las lecciones preliminares de El Salvador. *ECA; Estudios Centroamericanos,* v. 48, no. 531 – 532 (Jan – Feb 93), pp. 39 – 59. Il.

Stanton, Anthony. Octavio Paz, Alfonso Reyes y el análisis del fenómeno poético. *Hispanic Review,* v. 61, no. 3 (Summer 93), pp. 363 – 378. Bibl.

Staples, Anne. Los últimos diez años de historia regional en el Colegio de México. *La Palabra y el Hombre,* no. 83 (July – Sept 92), pp. 299 – 303. Bibl.

Starn, Orin. Algunas palabras finales. *Allpanchis,* v. 23, no. 39 (Jan – June 92), pp. 123 – 129. Bibl.

— Antropología andina, "andinismo" y Sendero Luminoso. *Allpanchis,* v. 23, no. 39 (Jan – June 92), pp. 15 – 71. Bibl.

Statland de López, Rhona. Cross Over Dreams. *Business Mexico,* v. 3, no. 5 (May 93), pp. 23 – 24 +. Il.

— Profile of an Entrepreneur. *Business Mexico,* v. 3, no. 3 (Mar 93), pp. 12 – 14.

Staudacher, Cornelia. Autores de Río de la Plata en la Casa de Culturas del Mundo (Translated by José Luis Gómez y Patiño). *Humboldt,* no. 110 (1993), p. 96. Il.

Stavans, Ilán. El arte de la memoria. *La Palabra y el Hombre,* no. 81 (Jan – Mar 92), pp. 241 – 253. Bibl.

Stavenhagen, Rodolfo. Democracia, modernización y cambio social en México. *Nueva Sociedad,* no. 124 (Mar – Apr 93), pp. 27 – 45. Bibl.

— Los derechos de los indígenas: algunos problemas conceptuales. *Nueva Antropología,* v. 13, no. 43 (Nov 92), pp. 83 – 99. Bibl.

Stawicka, Bárbara. La selva en flor: Alejo Carpentier y el diálogo entre las vanguardias europeas del siglo XX y el barroco latinoamericano. *La Palabra y el Hombre,* no. 81 (Jan – Mar 92), pp. 193 – 199. Bibl.

Stecher, Gerta. Un muchacho y otro. *La Palabra y el Hombre,* no. 82 (Apr – June 92), pp. 181 – 185.

Steele, Cynthia. Indigenismo y posmodernidad: narrativa indigenista, testimonio, teatro campesino y video en el Chiapas finisecular. *Iberoamericana,* v. 16, no. 47 – 48 (1992), pp. 82 – 94. Bibl.

— Indigenismo y posmodernidad: narrativa indigenista, testimonio, teatro campesino y video en el Chiapas finisecular. *Revista de Crítica Literaria Latinoamericana,* v. 19, no. 38 (July – Dec 93), pp. 249 – 260. Bibl.

Stefanich Irala, Juan. Alberdi, Latinoamérica y el Paraguay. *Estudios Paraguayos,* v. 17, no. 1 – 2 (1989 – 1993), pp. 107 – 119.

Steger, Hanns Albert. Antropología cultural histórica (Translated by Elsa Cecilia Frost). *Cuadernos Americanos,* no. 39, Nueva época (May – June 93), pp. 134 – 166. Bibl.

Stegmann, Wilhelm. Artistic Representation of German Book Collections and Picture Archives. *SALALM Papers,* v. 34 (1989), pp. 428 – 438.

Stein Neto, Bartholomeu E. and Valter José Stülp. A vitivinicultura do Rio Grande do Sul e a integração econômica Brasil – Argentina. *Revista de Economia e Sociologia Rural,* v. 29, no. 4 (Oct – Dec 91), pp. 387 – 400. Bibl, tables.

Steinitz-Kannan, Miriam et al. The Fossil Diatoms of Lake Yambo, Ecuador: A Possible Record of El Niño Events. *Bulletin de l'Institut Français d'Etudes Andines,* v. 22, no. 1 (1993), pp. 227 – 241. Bibl, il, maps, charts.

Steinmetz, Klauss. El Caribe en Santo Domingo (Accompanied by an English translation). *Art Nexus,* no. 7 (Jan – Mar 93), pp. 83 – 85. Il.

Stella, Aldo. ¿Padre, puedo casarme de nuevo? *Revista Javeriana,* v. 61, no. 599 (Oct 93), pp. 305 – 318.

Sten, María. Cristóbal Colón en Polonia. *Plural (Mexico),* v. 22, no. 266 (Nov 93), pp. 63 – 67.

Stephan-Otto, Erwin. Xochimilco: fuente de historias (Accompanied by an English translation). *Artes de México,* no. 20 (Summer 93), pp. 33 – 35.

Stephens, Evelyne Huber and John D. Stephens. Changing Development Models in Small Economies: The Case of Jamaica from the 1950s to the 1990s. *Studies in Comparative International Development,* v. 27, no. 3 (Fall 92), pp. 57 – 92. Bibl, tables.

Stern, Marc A. A Critique of Eco-Strategies. *Business Mexico,* v. 3, no. 10 (Oct 93), pp. 40 – 43.

Stern, Peter A. Art and the State in Post-Revolutionary Mexico and Cuba. *SALALM Papers,* v. 34 (1989), pp. 17 – 32. Bibl.

— Origins and Trajectory of the Shining Path. *SALALM Papers,* v. 36 (1991), pp. 49 – 74. Bibl.

Stewart, Hamish. El Acuerdo de Libre Comercio entre Estados Unidos y Canadá: algunas lecciones. *Estudios Internacionales (Chile),* v. 26, no. 102 (Apr – June 93), pp. 187 – 203. Bibl, tables.

Stier, Haya and Marta Tienda. Family, Work, and Women: The Labor Supply of Hispanic Immigrant Wives. *International Migration Review,* v. 26, no. 4 (Winter 92), pp. 1291 – 1313. Bibl, tables, charts.

Stoddard, Ellwyn R. Teen-Age Pregnancy in the Texas Borderlands. *Journal of Borderlands Studies,* v. 8, no. 1 (Spring 93), pp. 77 – 98. Bibl, tables, maps.

Stoetzer, Otto Carlos. Tradition and Progress in the Late Eighteenth-Century Jesuit Rediscovery of America: Francisco Javier Clavijero's Philosophy and History. *Colonial Latin American Historical Review,* v. 2, no. 3 (Summer 93), pp. 289 – 324. Bibl.

Stolley, Karen. Sins of the Father: Hernando Colón's *Life of the Admiral. Latin American Literary Review,* v. 21, no. 41 (Jan – June 93), pp. 53 – 64. Bibl.

Stolovich, Luis. Los empresarios, la apertura y los procesos de integración regional: contradicciones y estrategias; el caso de Uruguay en el MERCOSUR. *Revista Paraguaya de Sociología,* v. 29, no. 84 (May – Aug 92), pp. 53 – 90. Bibl, tables.

Stone, Jeff. The Dating Game. *Business Mexico,* v. 3, no. 9 (Sept 93), p. 46.

Stoub, Jeffrey. De-Fossilizing the Fuel Industry. *Business Mexico,* v. 3, no. 1 (Jan – Feb 93), pp. 16 – 18. Il.

— NAFTA's "Green" Thumb. *Business Mexico,* v. 3, no. 10 (Oct 93), pp. 35 – 36.

— Sustainable Policies. *Business Mexico,* v. 3, no. 8 (Aug 93), pp. 46 – 47. Il.

Stragier, Julio. Hogar de Cristo Viviendas. *Mensaje,* v. 42, no. 420 (July 93), p. 292. Il.

Street, Susan L. SNTE: ¿Proyecto de quién? *El Cotidiano,* v. 9, no. 56 (July 93), pp. 54 – 59. Il.

— El SNTE Y la política educativa, 1970 – 1990. *Revista Mexicana de Sociología,* v. 54, no. 2 (Apr – June 92), pp. 45 – 72. Bibl.

Strepponi, Blanca. El mal, los verdugos y sus víctimas: acerca de una escritura compartida en *El diario de John Robertson. Inti,* no. 37 – 38 (Spring – Fall 93), pp. 61 – 68.

— Poems ("Ars Moriendi," "Sueño," "Azteca," "Palabras de Gregorio Magno (590)," "El jardín del verdugo"). *Inti,* no. 36 (Fall 92), pp. 157 – 162.

Ströbele-Gregor, Juliana. Las comunidades religiosas fundamentalistas en Bolivia: sobre el éxito misionero de los Adventistas del Séptimo Día. *Allpanchis,* v. 23, no. 40 (July – Dec 92), pp. 219 – 253. Bibl.

Stroud, Matthew D. The Desiring Subject and the Promise of Salvation: A Lacanian Study of Sor Juana's *El divino Narciso. Hispania (USA),* v. 76, no. 2 (May 93), pp. 204 – 212. Bibl.

Stülp, Valter José and Bartholomeu E. Stein Neto. A vitivinicultura do Rio Grande do Sul e a integração econômica Brasil – Argentina. *Revista de Economia e Sociologia Rural,* v. 29, no. 4 (Oct – Dec 91), pp. 387 – 400. Bibl, tables.

Sturm, Russell and Michael Totten. Bright Ideas. *Business Mexico,* v. 3, no. 1 (Jan – Feb 93), pp. 55 – 57. Il.

— Delivering the Goods. *Business Mexico,* v. 3, no. 5 (May 93), pp. 15 – 18. Il.

Sturzenegger, Adolfo C. Encuesta a empresas industriales exportadoras latinoamericanas sobre el proceso de integración regional: informe de resultados. *Nueva Sociedad,* no. 126 (July – Aug 93), pp. 169 – 176.

Suardíaz, Luis. Principalmente *Trilce. Casa de las Américas,* no. 189 (Oct – Dec 92), pp. 36 – 42.

Suárez, Santiago Gerardo. Informe 1990 – 1991 del Departamento de Investigaciones Históricas de la Academia Nacional de la Historia. *Boletín de la Academia Nacional de la Historia (Venezuela),* v. 75, no. 297 (Jan – Mar 92), pp. 147 – 168.

— Informe 1991 – 1992 del Departamento de Investigaciones Históricas de la Academia Nacional de la Historia. *Boletín de la Academia Nacional de la Historia (Venezuela),* v. 75, no. 300 (Oct – Dec 92), pp. 197 – 222.

Suárez Durán, Esther. El teatro: un mundo para el hombre. *Conjunto,* no. 93 (Jan – June 93), pp. 119 – 125. Il.

Suárez Farías, Francisco. Familias y dinastías políticas de los presidentes del PNR – PRM – PRI. *Revista Mexicana de Ciencias Políticas y Sociales,* v. 38, Nueva época, no. 151 (Jan – Mar 93), pp. 51 – 79. Bibl.

Suárez Guevara, Sergio. A 55 de la expropiación petrolera: nuevas y profundas luchas. *Momento Económico,* no. 67 (May – June 93), pp. 2 – 6.

Suárez-Iñíguez, Enrique. El proyecto académico de la División de Estudios de Posgrado de la Facultad de Ciencias Políticas y Sociales de la UNAM. *Revista Mexicana de Ciencias Políticas y Sociales,* v. 38, Nueva época, no. 151 (Jan – Mar 93), pp. 187 – 193.

Suárez López, Leticia. Trayectorias laborales y reproductivas: una comparación entre México y España. *Estudios Demográficos y Urbanos,* v. 7, no. 2 – 3 (May – Dec 92), pp. 359 – 375. Bibl, tables, charts.

Suárez Pareyón, Alejandro and Emilio Duhau. Sistemas de planeación y política de desarrollo urbano en la ciudad de México. *El Cotidiano,* v. 9, no. 54 (May 93), pp. 3 – 9. Bibl, il.

Suárez Salazar, Luis. "Drug Trafficking" and Social and Political Conflicts in Latin America: Some Hypotheses (Translated by Luis Fierro). *Latin American Perspectives,* v. 20, no. 1 (Winter 93), pp. 83 – 98. Bibl, tables.

Suárez Zozaya, María Herlinda. Equidad en una sociedad desigual: reto de la modernización educativa. *Revista Mexicana de Ciencias Políticas y Sociales,* v. 38, Nueva época, no. 154 (Oct – Dec 93), pp. 137 – 158. Bibl, tables.

Subercaseaux, Benjamín. Lo masculino y lo femenino en el imaginario colectivo de comienzos de siglo. *Revista Chilena de Literatura,* no. 42 (Aug 93), pp. 245 – 249.

Subercaseaux S., Bernardo. Las industrias culturales: desafíos para una política cultural. *Cuadernos Hispanoamericanos,* no. 510 (Dec 92), pp. 100 – 104. Bibl.

Subervi-Vélez, Federico A. et al. Los medios de comunicación masiva en Puerto Rico. *Homines,* v. 15 – 16, no. 2 – 1 (Oct 91 – Dec 92), pp. 39 – 60. Bibl.

Suchlicki, Jaime. Myths and Realities in US – Cuban Relations. *Journal of Inter-American Studies and World Affairs,* v. 35, no. 2 (Summer 93), pp. 103 – 113.

Sucre, Guillermo. Los cuadernos de la cordura. *Vuelta,* v. 17, no. 197 (Apr 93), pp. 16 – 18.

— La polvareda y la falacia (Response to the Venezuelan press's reaction to his two earlier articles published in *Vuelta). Vuelta,* v. 17, no. 202 (Sept 93), pp. 54 – 55.

Sucre Figarella, José Francisco. El español: la palabra solidaria; permanencia y transformación. *Revista Nacional de Cultura (Venezuela),* v. 54, no. 287 (Oct – Dec 92), pp. 21 – 31.

Sudarev, Vladimir P. Russia and Latin America. *Hemisphere,* v. 5, no. 2 (Winter – Spring 93), pp. 12 – 14.

Suescún Mutis, Fabio. Intervención ante la Comisión II de la Honorable Cámara de Representantes. *Revista Javeriana,* v. 61, no. 599 (Oct 93), pp. 293 – 303.

Süssekind, Maria Flora. La imaginación monológica: Gerald Thomas y Bia Lessa. *Conjunto,* no. 93 (Jan – June 93), pp. 18 – 25. Bibl, il.

Sugiyama, Saburo. Worldview Materialized in Teotihuacán, Mexico. *Latin American Antiquity,* v. 4, no. 2 (June 93), pp. 103 – 129. Bibl, il, maps, charts.

Sulsona, Violeta and Inés Dölz-Blackburn. Isabel Allende a través de sus entrevistas. *Revista Interamericana de Bibliografía,* v. 42, no. 3 (1992), pp. 421 – 430. Bibl.

Summerer, Stefan. La política ambiental de la Comunidad Europea: ¿Un ejemplo para otros hemisferios? (Translated by Raquel García de Sanjurjo). *Cuadernos del CLAEH,* v. 18, no. 65 – 66 (May 93), pp. 123 – 134.

Summers, Lawrence and Masood Ahmed. Informe sobre la crisis de la deuda en su décimo aniversario. *Comercio Exterior,* v. 43, no. 1 (Jan 93), pp. 74 – 78. Tables.

Sung, Jung Mo. Crisis de las ideologías: utopías seculari- zadas versus reino de Dios (Translated by Juan Michel). *Realidad Económica,* no. 118 (Aug – Sept 93), pp. 68 – 81. Bibl.

Sunkel, Guillermo and Eugenio Tironi B. Modernización de las comunicaciones y democratización de la política: los medios en la transición a la democracia en Chile. *Estudios Públicos (Chile),* no. 52 (Spring 93), pp. 215 – 246. Bibl, tables.

Sunkel, Osvaldo. La consolidación de la democracia y del desarrollo en Chile: desafíos y tareas. *El Trimestre Econó- mico,* v. 59, no. 236 (Oct – Dec 92), pp. 816 – 830.

— Consolidating Democracy and Development in Chile. *CEPAL Review,* no. 47 (Aug 92), pp. 37 – 46.

Supplee, Joan E. Vitivinicultura, recursos públicos y ganan- cias privadas en Mendoza, 1880 – 1914. *Siglo XIX: Cua- dernos,* v. 2, no. 5 (Feb 93), pp. 81 – 94. Bibl.

Suriano, José María and Luis Humberto Ferpozzi. Los cambios climáticos en la pampa también son historia. *Todo Es Historia,* v. 26, no. 306 (Jan 93), pp. 8 – 25. Bibl, il, maps.

Sutton, Paul K. and Anthony John Payne. The Com- monwealth Caribbean in the New World Order: Between Europe and North America? *Journal of Inter-American Stud- ies and World Affairs,* v. 34, no. 4 (Winter 92 – 93), pp. 39 – 75. Bibl.

Sutz, Judith. Innovación e integración en América Latina. *Nueva Sociedad,* no. 126 (July – Aug 93), pp. 84 – 97. Bibl.

Sweeney, Judith L. Las lavanderas de Buenos Aires en la segunda mitad del siglo XIX. *Todo Es Historia,* v. 27, no. 314 (Sept 93), pp. 46 – 48. Bibl, il.

Swope, John. Anita Goossens: "Llorar con los que lloran y gozar con los que gozan." *Mensaje,* v. 42, no. 424 (Nov 93), pp. 590 – 591. Il.

— Un foro internacional: educación media como estrategia de desarrollo con equidad. *Mensaje,* v. 42, no. 419 (June 93), pp. 208 – 210. Il.

Szasz, Ivonne. Trabajadoras inmigrantes en Santiago de Chile en los años ochenta. *Estudios Demográficos y Urba- nos,* v. 7, no. 2 – 3 (May – Dec 92), pp. 539 – 553. Bibl, tables.

Szászdi León-Borja, István. Españolas en Haití: la condi- ción jurídica de las primeras pobladoras europeas del Nuevo Mundo. *Revista de Indias,* v. 53, no. 198 (May – Aug 93), pp. 617 – 626. Bibl.

— Un tabú de la muerte: la innominación de los vivos y los difuntos como norma jurídica prehispánica. *Anuario de Es- tudios Americanos,* v. 49 (1992), pp. 3 – 20. Bibl.

Székely, Gabriel. California Sunrise. *Nexos,* v. 16, no. 185 (May 93), pp. 13 – 15.

Szeminski, Jan. Manqu Qhapaq Inka según Anello Oliva, S.J., 1631. *Historia y Cultura (Peru),* no. 20 (1990), pp. 269 – 280.

Sznajder, Mario. Legitimidad y poder políticos frente a las herencias autoritarias: transición y consolidación democrá- tica en América Latina. *Estudios Interdisciplinarios de Amé- rica Latina y el Caribe,* v. 4, no. 1 (Jan – June 93), pp. 27 – 55. Bibl.

Tablada, José Juan. Buzón de fantasmas: de José Juan Tablada a Genaro Estrada. *Vuelta,* v. 17, no. 197 (Apr 93), pp. 76 – 77.

— Buzón de fantasmas: de José Juan Tablada a Julio Torri. *Vuelta,* v. 17, no. 203 (Oct 93), pp. 73 – 74.

Tablante Garrido, Pedro Nicolás. Vuelta a Mérida de don Mariano Picón Salas. *Boletín de la Academia Nacional de la Historia (Venezuela),* v. 76, no. 301 (Jan – Mar 93), pp. 103 – 105.

Taggart, Kenneth M. *Eva Luna:* la culminación del neo- feminismo de Isabel Allende. *Fem,* v. 17, no. 126 (Aug 93), pp. 43 – 45. Bibl.

Tagle, Andrés. Comentario en torno a los trabajos de José María Fuentes y Peter Siavelis. *Estudios Públicos (Chile),* no. 51 (Winter 93), pp. 325 – 330.

Tamayo, Giulia and José María García Ríos. El esce- nario como dictador: configuración metropolitana y expe- riencia cotidiana. *Nueva Sociedad,* no. 123 (Jan – Feb 93), pp. 94 – 103. Bibl.

Tamayo, Jesús. The Maquila Industry in Perspective. *Jour- nal of Borderlands Studies,* v. 8, no. 1 (Spring 93), pp. 67 – 76. Bibl, tables.

Tamer, Norma Liliana. Possibilities and Conditions of Inte- gral Education for Older Citizens: Pedagogic Proposal. *La Educación (USA),* v. 37, no. 114 (1993), pp. 119 – 122.

Tamez, Elsa. Que la mujer no calle en la congregación: pau- tas hermenéuticas para comprender *Gá.* 3.28 y 1 *Co.* 14.23. *Cristianismo y Sociedad,* v. 30, no. 113 (1992), pp. 45 – 52. Bibl.

Tampe, Eduardo. Chiloé: misión circular. *Mensaje,* v. 42, no. 420 (July 93), pp. 224 – 227. Il.

— Jesuitas alemanes y la colonización del sur. *Mensaje,* v. 42, no. 420 (July 93), pp. 259 – 263. Il.

Tanaka, Martín. Juventud y política en el cambio de una época. *Allpanchis,* v. 25, no. 41 (Jan – June 93), pp. 227 – 261. Bibl.

Tandeter, Enrique. El período colonial en la historiografía argentina reciente. *Historia Mexicana,* v. 42, no. 3 (Jan – Mar 93), pp. 789 – 819.

Tannenbaum, Frank. Los últimos treinta años, 1898 – 1928 (Translated by Sara Irizarry). *Op. Cit.,* no. 7 (1992), pp. 165 – 207. Il, tables.

Tapajós, Vicente Costa Santos. Cristovão Colombo: o ho- mem e o mito. *Revista do Instituto Histórico e Geográfico Brasileiro,* no. 371 (Apr – June 91), pp. 470 – 488. Bibl.

— A historiografia colonial. *Revista do Instituto Histórico e Geográfico Brasileiro,* no. 370 (Jan – Mar 91), pp. 232 – 244.

— O homem que Colombo encontrou nas Indias Ocidentais (I). *Revista do Instituto Histórico e Geográfico Brasileiro,* no. 372 (July – Sept 91), pp. 785 – 799. Bibl.

Tapia de la Puente, Daniel. Experiencia del Banco Central autónomo. *Cuadernos de Economía (Chile),* v. 30, no. 91 (Dec 93), pp. 349 – 355. Tables.

Taracena Arriola, Arturo. El APRA, Haya de la Torre y la crisis del liberalismo guatemalteco en 1928 – 1929. *Cua- dernos Americanos,* no. 37, Nueva época (Jan – Feb 93), pp. 183 – 197. Bibl.

— El APRA, Haya de La Torre y la crisis del liberalismo guatemalteco en 1928 – 1929. *Revista de Historia (Costa Rica),* no. 25 (Jan – June 92), pp. 9 – 25. Bibl.

— *Sábado de gloria:* fuente literaria de *El señor presidente. Studi di Letteratura Ispano-Americana,* v. 24 (1993), pp. 37 – 46.

— Un testimonio francés del triunfo liberal de 1829: el papel del doctor Mariano Gálvez. *Mesoamérica (USA)*, v. 13, no. 23 (June 92), pp. 143 – 156. Bibl.

Tardieu, Jean-Pierre. Los jesuitas y la "lengua de Angola" en Perú, siglo XVII. *Revista de Indias*, v. 53, no. 198 (May – Aug 93), pp. 627 – 637. Bibl.

— Las vistas de un arbitrista sobre la aparición de un hombre nuevo en las Indias Occidentales, mitad del siglo XVII. *Anuario de Estudios Americanos*, v. 50, no. 1 (1993), pp. 235 – 249. Bibl.

Tarn, Nathaniel. Santo Domingo de Guzmán, Oaxaca: origen del orden (Accompanied by the English original, translated by Osvaldo Sánchez and Roberto Tejada). *Artes de México*, no. 21 (Fall 93), pp. 40 – 41.

Tarrés Barraza, María Luisa. El movimiento de mujeres y el sistema político mexicano: análisis de la lucha por la liberación del aborto, 1976 – 1990. *Estudios Sociológicos*, v. 11, no. 32 (May – Aug 93), pp. 365 – 397. Bibl, tables.

Tattay, Pablo. La reinserción desde la perspectiva indígena. *Revista Javeriana*, v. 60, no. 590 (Nov – Dec 92), pp. 331 – 337.

Taube, Karl Andreas. The Bilimek Pulque Vessel: Starlore, Calendrics, and Cosmology of Late Postclassic Central Mexico. *Ancient Mesoamerica*, v. 4, no. 1 (Spring 93), pp. 1 – 15. Bibl, il.

Tavares, Luís Henrique Dias. In memoriam: Pinto de Aguiar, Alagoinhas (7.3.1910 – Rio de Janeiro, 24.11.1991). *Revista do Instituto Histórico e Geográfico Brasileiro*, no. 373 (Oct – Dec 91), pp. 1204 – 1205.

Tavares de Almeida, Maria Hermínia. Sindicatos, crisis económica y alta inflación en Brasil y Argentina. *Revista Mexicana de Sociología*, v. 54, no. 1 (Jan – Mar 92), pp. 99 – 137. Bibl, tables, charts.

Taviani, Paolo Emilio. Fecha inolvidable: 12 de octubre de 1492; lugar: isla Guanahaní. *Atenea (Chile)*, no. 465 – 466 (1992), pp. 23 – 34. Il.

— Programas conmemorativos del quinto centenario en Italia. *Atenea (Chile)*, no. 467 (1993), pp. 223 – 236. Bibl.

Taylor, Diana. Negotiating Performance. *Latin American Theatre Review*, v. 26, no. 2 (Spring 93), pp. 49 – 57. Bibl.

Taylor, J. Edward and Mauricio R. Bellon. "Folk" Soil Taxonomy and the Partial Adoption of New Seed Varieties. *Economic Development and Cultural Change*, v. 41, no. 4 (July 93), pp. 763 – 786. Bibl, tables.

Taylor, Lawrence D. and Manuel Ceballos Ramírez. Síntesis histórica del poblamiento de la región fronteriza México – Estados Unidos. *Estudios Fronterizos*, no. 26 (Sept – Dec 91), pp. 9 – 37. Bibl.

Techeira, Diego. Poema. *Hispamérica*, v. 22, no. 64 – 65 (Apr – Aug 93), p. 146.

Tedlock, Barbara. Mayans and Mayan Studies from 2000 B.C. to A.D. 1992 (Review article). *Latin American Research Review*, v. 28, no. 3 (1993), pp. 153 – 173. Bibl.

Tegart, Peter F. A Ton of Dirt, a Trickle of Gold. *Business Mexico*, v. 3, no. 12 (Dec 93), pp. 15 – 16.

Teitelboim, Volodia. Sobre la antología del '35 y la generación del '38. *Revista Chilena de Literatura*, no. 42 (Aug 93), pp. 251 – 263.

Teixeira, Erly Cardoso et al. A política de investimentos agrícolas e seu efeito sobre a distribuição de renda. *Revista de Economia e Sociologia Rural*, v. 30, no. 4 (Oct – Dec 92), pp. 291 – 303. Bibl, tables, charts.

Teixeira, João Roberto and Winston Fritsch. Fatores determinantes das exportações brasileiras para a CE: uma análise prospectiva dos impactos da ampliação do espaço econômico. *Revista de Economia Política (Brazil)*, v. 13, no. 3 (July – Sept 93), pp. 82 – 101. Bibl, tables, charts.

Teixeira, Jorge Leão. Da queda de Jango à renúncia de Collor. *Problemas Brasileiros*, v. 30, no. 295 (Jan – Feb 93), pp. 10 – 16. Il.

— O país do desperdício. *Problemas Brasileiros*, v. 30, no. 297 (May – June 93), pp. 6 – 9. Il.

— Relíquias diplomáticas. *Problemas Brasileiros*, v. 30, no. 296 (Mar – Apr 93), pp. 17 – 23. Il.

— Tudo nos une, muito nos separa. *Problemas Brasileiros*, v. 30, no. 297 (May – June 93), pp. 36 – 40. Il.

Teixidó, Raúl. Prójimos. *Signo*, no. 36 – 37, Nueva época (May – Dec 92), pp. 125 – 132.

Tejada, Roberto. Carlos Arias: delirios de la figura. *Artes de México*, no. 20 (Summer 93), pp. 122 – 124. Il.

— Eugenia Vargas: el proscenio inevitable (Translated by Paloma Díaz Abreu). *Artes de México*, no. 21 (Fall 93), pp. 98 – 99. Il.

Tejada de Rivero, David. Informe de consultoría. *Anuario Indigenista*, v. 30 (Dec 91), pp. 405 – 423.

Tejera, María Josefina. Venezolano y caraqueño: el nacimiento de los gentilicios y la nacionalidad. *Boletín de la Academia Nacional de la Historia (Venezuela)*, v. 75, no. 299 (July – Sept 92), pp. 69 – 76. Bibl.

Tejerina, Marcela V. and Hernán Asdrúbal Silva. De las Georgias del Sur a Cantón: los norteamericanos en la explotación y tráfico de pieles a fines del siglo XVIII y principios del siglos XIX. *Investigaciones y Ensayos*, no. 41 (Jan – Dec 91), pp. 315 – 327. Bibl.

Telles, Edward E. Racial Distance and Region in Brazil: Intermarriage in Brazilian Urban Areas. *Latin American Research Review*, v. 28, no. 2 (1993), pp. 141 – 162. Bibl, tables.

— Urban Labor Market Segmentation and Income in Brazil. *Economic Development and Cultural Change*, v. 41, no. 2 (Jan 93), pp. 231 – 249. Bibl, tables.

Téllez, Rafael Adolfo. La hora infinita. *Cuadernos Hispanoamericanos*, no. 516 (June 93), pp. 93 – 98.

Téllez A., Isabel. Colegio San Lorenzo: cuando la solidaridad es contagiosa. *Mensaje*, v. 42, no. 421 (Aug 93), pp. 402 – 403. Il.

— Fernando Castillo Velasco: la solidaridad implica confianza. *Mensaje*, v. 42, no. 421 (Aug 93), pp. 383 – 384. Il.

— ILADES: instituto de postgrado con acento en lo social. *Mensaje*, v. 42, no. 420 (July 93), pp. 283 – 284. Il.

Téllez Guerrero, Francisco. La segregación de Tuxpan y Chicontepec en 1853. *La Palabra y el Hombre*, no. 83 (July – Sept 92), pp. 27 – 43. Bibl, tables, maps.

Tello, Ana Laura. Esperanza fallida. *Confluencia*, v. 8, no. 1 (Fall 92), pp. 189 – 190.

Tello Díaz, Carlos. Porfirio Díaz: álbum de familia. *Nexos*, v. 16, no. 182 (Feb 93), pp. 69 – 74. Il, facs.

Tello Villagrán, Pedro. 1993: el cuadro productivo. *Problemas del Desarrollo*, v. 24, no. 94 (July – Sept 93), pp. 25 – 31.

Tenenbaum, León. Los dientes de Rosas. *Todo Es Historia*, v. 26, no. 308 (Mar 93), pp. 8 – 21. Il, facs.

TePaske, John Jay. The Costs of Empire: Spending Patterns and Priorities in Colonial Peru, 1581 – 1820. *Colonial Latin American Historical Review*, v. 2, no. 1 (Winter 93), pp. 1 – 33. Tables, charts.

Terán, Matilde. Violencia intrafamiliar: trabajo con hombres agresores. *Fem,* v. 17, no. 126 (Aug 93), p. 42.

Terán, Oscar. El fin de siglo argentino: democracia y nación. *Cuadernos Hispanoamericanos,* no. 517 – 519 (July – Sept 93), pp. 41 – 50. Bibl.

— Representaciones intelectuales de la nación. *Realidad Económica,* no. 118 (Aug – Sept 93), pp. 94 – 96.

Terbeck, C. Augusto. La promoción minera intentada por Rivadavia: las minas de Cuyo y "The River Plate Mining Association." *Investigaciones y Ensayos,* no. 41 (Jan – Dec 91), pp. 423 – 455. Bibl.

Terena, Marcos. La resistencia indígena: 500 años después. *Nueva Sociedad,* no. 123 (Jan – Feb 93), pp. 156 – 159.

Terra, J. Evangelista Martins. Motivação religiosa dos descobrimentos. *Revista do Instituto Histórico e Geográfico Brasileiro,* no. 373 (Oct – Dec 91), pp. 1145 – 1175.

Terrón de Bellomo, Herminia. Literatura fantástica y denuncia social: Juana Manuela Gorriti. *Letras Femeninas,* v. 19, no. 1 – 2 (Spring – Fall 93), pp. 113 – 116. Bibl.

Terrones López, Víctor Manuel. Las micro, pequeñas y medianas empresas en el proceso de globalización. *Comercio Exterior,* v. 43, no. 6 (June 93), pp. 544 – 546.

Testa, Julio C. La incidencia del "contexto organizacional" en el análisis de los procesos de incorporación de las nuevas tecnologías informatizadas: acerca de la constitución de los "espacios de aprendizaje." *Revista Paraguaya de Sociología,* v. 30, no. 86 (Jan – Apr 93), pp. 161 – 183. Bibl.

Teubal, Miguel and Norma Giarracca. El día en que la Plaza de Mayo se vistió de campo (Includes interviews with six agricultural producers). *Realidad Económica,* no. 118 (Aug – Sept 93), pp. 5 – 17. Tables.

Teves Rivas, Néstor. Erosion and Accretion Processes during El Niño Phenomenon of 1982 – 1983 and Its Relation to Previous Events. *Bulletin de l'Institut Français d'Etudes Andines,* v. 22, no. 1 (1993), pp. 99 – 110. Bibl, tables, maps, charts.

Tezanos, Sabela de. Poemas ("XXIV," "XXV"). *Hispamérica,* v. 22, no. 64 – 65 (Apr – Aug 93), p. 147.

Theodore, Karl. Privatization: Conditions for Success and Fiscal Policy Implications. *Social and Economic Studies,* v. 41, no. 4 (Dec 92), pp. 133 – 148. Bibl.

Théret, Bruno. Hyperinflation de producteurs et hyperinflation de rentiers: le cas du Brésil. *Tiers Monde,* v. 34, no. 133 (Jan – Mar 93), pp. 37 – 67. Bibl, charts.

Thibaut, Bernhard. Präsidentialismus, Parlamentarismus und das Problem der Konsolidierung der Demokratie in Lateinamerika. *Ibero-Amerikanisches Archiv,* no. 18, no. 1 – 2 (1992), pp. 107 – 150. Bibl.

— Presidencialismo, parlamentarismo y el problema de la consolidación democrática en América Latina. *Estudios Internacionales (Chile),* v. 26, no. 102 (Apr – June 93), pp. 216 – 252. Bibl.

Thiemer-Sachse, Ursula. Un autógrafo de Cristóbal Colón (Cristóforo Colombo) en la colección especial de la biblioteca de la Universidad de Rostock. *Ibero-Amerikanisches Archiv,* v. 18, no. 3 – 4 (1992), pp. 523 – 541. Bibl, facs.

Thomas, Luis. La crisis social del pueblo. *Cristianismo y Sociedad,* v. 30, no. 114 (1992), pp. 47 – 48.

Thompkins, Cynthia. La construcción del subalterno en *Homérica latina* de Marta Traba y *Libro que no muerde* y *Donde viven las águilas* de Luisa Valenzuela. *Confluencia,* v. 8, no. 1 (Fall 92), pp. 31 – 37. Bibl.

Thompson, Angela T. To Save the Children: Smallpox Inoculation, Vaccination, and Public Health in Guanajuato, Mexico, 1797 – 1840. *The Americas,* v. 49, no. 4 (Apr 93), pp. 431 – 455. Bibl, tables.

Thompson, Donald. The "Cronistas de Indias" Revisited: Historical Reports, Archaeological Evidence, and Literary and Artistic Traces of Indigenous Music and Dance in the Greater Antilles at the Time of the "Conquista." *Latin American Music Review,* v. 14, no. 2 (Fall – Winter 93), pp. 181 – 201. Bibl.

Thompson, Gary D. and Paul N. Wilson. Common Property and Uncertainty: Compensating Coalitions by Mexico's Pastoral "Ejidatarios." *Economic Development and Cultural Change,* v. 41, no. 2 (Jan 93), pp. 301 – 318. Bibl, tables, charts.

Thompson, John Eric Sidney. El papel de las cuevas en la cultura maya (A translation of "The Role of Caves in Maya Culture," originally published in 1959. Introduced, translated, and annotated by Juan Luis Bonon Villarejo and Carolina Martínez Klemm). *Boletín Americanista,* v. 33, no. 42 – 43 (1992 – 1993), pp. 395 – 424. Bibl.

Thompson, Lonnie G. Reconstructing the Paleo ENSO Records from Tropical and Subtropical Ice Cores. *Bulletin de l'Institut Français d'Etudes Andines,* v. 22, no. 1 (1993), pp. 65 – 83. Bibl, il, maps, charts.

Thomson, Ian. Un análisis de la institucionalidad del transporte colectivo urbano latinoamericano: reformas para mejorarla. *EURE,* v. 19, no. 56 (Mar 93), pp. 55 – 70. Tables, charts.

— Improving Urban Transport for the Poor. *CEPAL Review,* no. 49 (Apr 93), pp. 139 – 153. Bibl, tables.

Thoumi, Francisco E. Estrategias de desarrollo, convergencias de políticas, integración económica. *Nueva Sociedad,* no. 125 (May – June 93), pp. 70 – 79. Bibl.

Thurner, Mark. ¿Una conclusión resulta prematura?: comentario a propósito del artículo de O. Starn. *Allpanchis,* v. 23, no. 39 (Jan – June 92), pp. 103 – 108.

— Peasant Politics and Andean Haciendas in the Transition to Capitalism: An Ethnographic History. *Latin American Research Review,* v. 28, no. 3 (1993), pp. 41 – 82. Bibl, charts.

Thurow, Lester C. Estados Unidos y la economía mundial (Translated by Isabel Vericat). *Nexos,* v. 16, no. 187 (July 93), pp. 22 – 24.

Thwaites, Jeanne. The Use of Irony in Oscar Zeta Acosta's *Autobiography of a Brown Buffalo. The Americas Review,* v. 20, no. 1 (Spring 92), pp. 73 – 82. Bibl.

Thwaites Rey, Mabel. La política de privatizaciones en la Argentina: consideraciones a partir del caso de Aerolíneas. *Realidad Económica,* no. 116 (May – June 93), pp. 46 – 75. Bibl, tables.

Tiburcio Robles, Armando. La FSTSE en el esquema del sindicalismo moderno. *El Cotidiano,* v. 9, no. 56 (July 93), pp. 23 – 32. Il, charts.

Tienda, Marta and George J. Borjas. The Employment and Wages of Legalized Immigrants. *International Migration Review,* v. 27, no. 4 (Winter 93), pp. 712 – 747. Bibl, tables.

Tienda, Marta and Haya Stier. Family, Work, and Women: The Labor Supply of Hispanic Immigrant Wives. *International Migration Review,* v. 26, no. 4 (Winter 92), pp. 1291 – 1313. Bibl, tables, charts.

Tieppo, Marcelo. Caderno de artista. *Vozes,* v. 87, no. 3 (May – June 93), pp. 83 – 84. Facs.

— 9° Festival Internacional Videobrasil. *Vozes,* v. 86, no. 6 (Nov – Dec 92), p. 98.

Tirado, Ricardo and Matilde Luna. Los empresarios en el escenario del cambio: trayectoria y tendencias de sus estrategias de acción colectiva. *Revista Mexicana de Sociología,* v. 55, no. 2 (Apr – June 93), pp. 243 – 271. Bibl, tables, charts.

Tironi B., Eugenio. Las vueltas de la historia. *Mensaje,* v. 42, no. 424 (Nov 93), pp. 563 – 566. Il.

Tironi B., Eugenio and Guillermo Sunkel. Modernización de las comunicaciones y democratización de la política: los medios en la transición a la democracia en Chile. *Estudios Públicos (Chile),* no. 52 (Spring 93), pp. 215 – 246. Bibl, tables.

Tisnés Jiménez, Roberto María. Bibliografía (Reviews of books on Latin American history written between 1989 and 1992). *Boletín de Historia y Antigüedades,* v. 80, no. 781 (Apr – June 93), pp. 465 – 475.

— La "leyenda negra" de los criminales descubridores. *Boletín de Historia y Antigüedades,* v. 79, no. 779 (Oct – Dec 92), pp. 1019 – 1035. Bibl.

Tísoc Lindley, Hilda. De los orígenes del APRA en Cuba: el testimonio de Enrique de la Osa. *Cuadernos Americanos,* no. 37, Nueva época (Jan – Feb 93), pp. 198 – 207. Bibl.

Tissera, Ramón. Una alucinante fiesta guaraní: el Tata-Yehesá. *Todo Es Historia,* v. 26, no. 308 (Mar 93), pp. 95 – 96. Il.

Titelman Kardonsky, Daniel and Ricardo Martner Fanta. Un análisis de cointegración de las funciones de demanda de dinero: el caso de Chile. *El Trimestre Económico,* v. 60, no. 238 (Apr – June 93), pp. 413 – 446. Bibl, tables, charts.

Tizón, Héctor. Las palabras que narran. *Cuadernos Hispanoamericanos,* no. 517 – 519 (July – Sept 93), pp. 506 – 511.

Tjarks, Alicia V.
See
Vidaurreta de Tjarks, Alicia

Tojeira, José María. Tercer aniversario de los mártires de la UCA: homilía. *ECA; Estudios Centroamericanos,* v. 47, no. 529 – 530 (Nov – Dec 92), pp. 951 – 953.

Tokman, Marcelo and Andrés Velasco. Opciones para la política comercial chilena en los '90. *Estudios Públicos (Chile),* no. 52 (Spring 93), pp. 53 – 99. Bibl, tables.

Tolentino Tapia, Lorenzo. Perfil para un balance jurídico de la reforma agraria peruana. *Derecho y Reforma Agraria,* no. 24 (1993), pp. 33 – 41.

Tolliver, Joyce. "Otro modo de ver": The Gaze in *La última niebla. Revista Canadiense de Estudios Hispánicos,* v. 17, no. 1 (Fall 92), pp. 105 – 121. Bibl.

Tolosa, Fernando. El sistema financiero, el financiamiento del desarrollo y la reforma previsional. *Realidad Económica,* no. 113 (Jan – Feb 93), pp. 13 – 17.

Tomasa Rivera, Silvia. En memoria del águila. *Nexos,* v. 16, no. 182 (Feb 93), p. 16.

Tomassini, Luciano. Decidiendo el futuro. *Mensaje,* v. 42, no. 417 (Mar – Apr 93), pp. 61 – 63.

Tomic, Tonci. Participation and the Environment. *CEPAL Review,* no. 48 (Dec 92), pp. 107 – 115. Bibl.

Ton, Giel and Gerda Zijm. Matrimonio conflictivo: cooperativas en un proyecto agroindustrial; el caso de Sébaco, Nicaragua. *Estudios Rurales Latinoamericanos,* v. 15, no. 2 – 3 (May – Dec 92), pp. 121 – 138. Bibl, tables.

Toni, Flávia Camargo. Memória: Mário de Andrade escreve para as crianças. *Vozes,* v. 87, no. 3 (May – June 93), pp. 67 – 72. Facs.

— Quatro concertos "progressistas" de Villa-Lobos. *Vozes,* v. 86, no. 6 (Nov – Dec 92), pp. 69 – 81. Il, facs.

Tono, Lucía. La pluralidad semántica en "Hoy me gusta la vida mucho menos" (Includes the poem). *Inti,* no. 36 (Fall 92), pp. 75 – 80.

Tonooka, Eduardo Kiyoshi. Política nacional de informática: vinte anos de intervenção governamental. *Estudos Econômicos,* v. 22, no. 2 (May – Aug 92), pp. 273 – 297. Bibl.

Torales Pacheco, María Cristina. Consideraciones generales sobre los comerciantes de Veracruz en la segunda mitad del s. XVIII. *La Palabra y el Hombre,* no. 83 (July – Sept 92), pp. 314 – 321. Bibl.

Toranzo Roca, Carlos F. Bolivia: tedios, desafíos y sorpresas. *Nueva Sociedad,* no. 124 (Mar – Apr 93), pp. 11 – 16. Bibl.

— Comentario (on the articles by Javier Protzel and Jorge Lazarte). *Estado y Sociedad,* v. 8, no. 9 (Jan – June 92), pp. 27 – 34.

Toro, Antonio del
See
Deltoro, Antonio

Toro Dávila, Agustín. El espacio en la perspectiva de un nuevo orden político – estratégico internacional. *Estudios Internacionales (Chile),* v. 26, no. 102 (Apr – June 93), pp. 253 – 267. Bibl.

Toro González, Aída Julia de. Pablo de la Torriente Brau: bibliografía pasiva. *Islas,* no. 97 (Sept – Dec 90), pp. 44 – 51.

Torre, Luis Alberto de la. Una experiencia educativa bilingüe en el Ecuador. *Revista Latinoamericana de Estudios Educativos,* v. 22, no. 4 (Oct – Dec 92), pp. 89 – 110. Bibl.

Torre Villar, Ernesto de la. Discurso del dr. Ernesto de la Torre Villar sobre fray Vicente de Santa María. *Archivo Ibero-Americano,* v. 52, no. 205 – 208 (Jan – Dec 92), pp. 849 – 856.

Torrealba Lossi, Mario et al. Bibliográficas. *Boletín de la Academia Nacional de la Historia (Venezuela),* v. 76, no. 301 (Jan – Mar 93), pp. 121 – 127.

Torres, Ana Teresa. El escritor ante la realidad política venezolana. *Inti,* no. 37 – 38 (Spring – Fall 93), pp. 37 – 45. Bibl.

Torres, Angel. Aldana, un capitán de la conquista. *Signo,* no. 38, Nueva época (Jan – Apr 93), pp. 63 – 72.

Torres, Daniel. Indagación sobre la técnica escritural "diferente" en la lírica barroca colonial. *Hispanic Journal,* v. 13, no. 2 (Fall 92), pp. 281 – 287. Bibl.

Torres, Graciela. Poems ("Presencia," "Génesis II," "Ciudad absurda"). *Revista Nacional de Cultura (Venezuela),* v. 54, no. 287 (Oct – Dec 92), pp. 148 – 154.

Torres, María Inés de. Ideología patriarcal e ideología estatal en el proceso modernizador uruguayo: una lectura de *Tabaré. Cuadernos del CLAEH,* v. 18, no. 65 – 66 (May 93), pp. 167 – 178. Bibl.

Torres, Víctor. Perspectivas de la Iniciativa para las Américas. *Apuntes (Peru),* no. 30 (Jan – June 92), pp. 63 – 79. Bibl, tables.

Torres Bodet, Jaime. Buzón de fantasmas: de Jaime Torres Bodet a Ermilo Abreu Gómez. *Vuelta,* v. 17, no. 204 (Nov 93), pp. 68 – 69.

Torres Carrasco, Maritza. Colombia: dimensión ambiental en la escuela y la formación docente. *La Educación (USA),* v. 37, no. 115 (1993), pp. 317 – 330. Bibl, charts.

Torres Díaz, Jorge H. Dimensión gerencial del trabajo social laboral. *Desarrollo Indoamericano*, v. 23, no. 91 (June 93), pp. 47 – 53. Il.

Torres Fierro, Danubio. El "apartheid" cubano: entrevista con Guillermo Cabrera Infante. *Vuelta*, v. 17, no. 198 (May 93), pp. 58 – 59.

— La fortaleza latinoamericana: conversación con Carlos Fuentes. *Cuadernos Hispanoamericanos*, no. 510 (Dec 92), pp. 104 – 107.

— Memoria, historia, desmemoria. *Vuelta*, v. 17, no. 201 (Aug 93), pp. 55 – 56.

— Verdades de ayer y verdades de hoy: entrevista con Reinaldo Arenas. *Vuelta*, v. 17, no. 195 (Feb 93), pp. 49 – 52.

Torres García, Joaquín. (Reproduction of an untitled graphic text by Joaquín Torres García). *Nexos*, v. 16, no. 183 (Mar 93), pp. 66 – 69.

Torres-Guzmán, Esteban. Poems ("Texcalapan, at the Stream Surrounded by Rocks," "Cosmogony," "Corn"). *The Americas Review*, v. 20, no. 2 (Summer 92), pp. 46 – 52.

Torres Hansen, Arnaldo. La avioneta IN-23 y los buscadores de metales. *Todo Es Historia*, v. 26, no. 309 (Apr 93), pp. 80 – 84. Il.

Torres Marín, Manuel. Los dos imperios: la doble herencia de Carlos V. *Boletín de la Academia Chilena de la Historia*, v. 58 – 59, no. 102 (1991 – 1992), pp. 505 – 527. Bibl, il, facs.

Torres Martínez, Lizandra. Feminismo popular en el México contemporáneo. *Homines*, v. 15 – 16, no. 2 – 1 (Oct 91 – Dec 92), pp. 283 – 288. Bibl.

Torres Ortiz, Víctor F. El teatro de René Marqués: bibliografía anotada. *Revista Interamericana de Bibliografía*, v. 42, no. 2 (1992), pp. 251 – 257.

Torres-Pou, Joan. La ambigüedad del mensaje feminista de *Sab* de Gertrudis Gómez de Avellaneda. *Letras Femeninas*, v. 19, no. 1 – 2 (Spring – Fall 93), pp. 55 – 64. Bibl.

Torres-Rivas, Edelberto. América Latina: gobernabilidad y democracia en sociedades en crisis. *Nueva Sociedad*, no. 128 (Nov – Dec 93), pp. 88 – 101.

— Escenarios y lecciones de las elecciones centroamericanas, 1980 – 1991. *Revista Mexicana de Sociología*, v. 54, no. 3 (July – Sept 92), pp. 45 – 67. Tables.

Torres Salcido, Gerardo. Pobreza y organización social: acceso a programas sociales de abasto. *Momento Económico*, no. 68 (July – Aug 93), pp. 19 – 22. Bibl.

Torres Torres, Felipe. Los desequilibrios de la balanza comercial agropecuaria. *Momento Económico*, no. 66 (Mar – Apr 93), pp. 9 – 13. Tables.

Torrico Calvimontes, Sissy. Por la gracia de Dios. *Signo*, no. 36 – 37, Nueva época (May – Dec 92), pp. 241 – 273.

Tosta, Virgilio. Huella y presencia de médicos europeos en el estado Barinas. *Boletín de la Academia Nacional de la Historia (Venezuela)*, v. 75, no. 297 (Jan – Mar 92), pp. 69 – 95.

Totten, Michael and Russell Sturm. Bright Ideas. *Business Mexico*, v. 3, no. 1 (Jan – Feb 93), pp. 55 – 57. Il.

— Delivering the Goods. *Business Mexico*, v. 3, no. 5 (May 93), pp. 15 – 18. Il.

Tovar de Teresa, Guillermo. México entre el fundamentalismo y la globalización. *Vuelta*, v. 17, no. 198 (May 93), pp. 33 – 40.

Tovar López, Ramón Adolfo. Contestación al discurso de incorporación a la Academia Nacional de la Historia del dr. Manuel Alfredo Rodríguez . . . . *Boletín de la Academia Nacional de la Historia (Venezuela)*, v. 75, no. 299 (July – Sept 92), pp. 63 – 65.

— Proposición para una organización de la función social: educación en una sociedad masificada. *Boletín de la Academia Nacional de la Historia (Venezuela)*, v. 76, no. 302 (Apr – June 93), pp. 226 – 234.

Townsend, John W. Mexico and Its Baby Boom. *Business Mexico*, v. 3, no. 1 (Jan – Feb 93), pp. 58 – 59. Il.

Tozzer, Alfred M. Una evaluación de los trabajos referentes al lenguaje maya. *La Palabra y el Hombre*, no. 82 (Apr – June 92), pp. 95 – 106. Bibl, maps.

Trahtemberg Siederer, León. Juventud, educación, empleo y empresa. *Debate (Peru)*, v. 16, no. 74 (Sept – Oct 93), pp. 34 – 36. Il.

Trein, Franklin. A Europa '92 e a América Latina. *Política e Estratégica*, v. 8, no. 2 – 4 (Apr – Dec 90), pp. 213 – 223. Bibl, tables.

Trejo, Oswaldo. El pozo (From the collection *Mientras octubre afuera*). *Revista Nacional de Cultura (Venezuela)*, v. 53, no. 286 (July – Sept 92), pp. 67 – 70. Il.

Trejos Montero, Elisa. Conversación con Rigoberta Menchú. *Káñina*, v. 16, no. 2 (July – Dec 92), pp. 65 – 71.

— Me llamo Rigoberta Menchú y así me nació la conciencia: un texto de literatura testimonial. *Káñina*, v. 16, no. 2 (July – Dec 92), pp. 53 – 63. Bibl.

Trelles Aréstegui, Efraín. La química de Popovic. *Debate (Peru)*, v. 15, no. 71 (Nov 92 – Jan 93), pp. 64 – 66. Il.

Treviño, Melanie and Adolfo Fernandez. The Maquiladora Industry, Adverse Environmental Impact, and Proposed Solutions. *Journal of Borderlands Studies*, v. 7, no. 2 (Fall 92), pp. 53 – 72. Bibl.

Trevizán, Liliana. Intersecciones: postmodernidad/feminismo/Latinoamérica. *Revista Chilena de Literatura*, no. 42 (Aug 93), pp. 265 – 273.

Triana, José. *Cruzando el puente*: obra en un acto. *Latin American Theatre Review*, v. 26, no. 2 (Spring 93), pp. 59 – 87.

Triana Antorveza, Adolfo. Contribución a la historia de la provincia de Neiva: el caso del Caguán. *Revista Colombiana de Antropología*, v. 29 (1992), pp. 119 – 154. Bibl, tables, maps.

Trigo, Abril. Poesía uruguaya actual: los más jóvenes. *Hispamérica*, v. 22, no. 64 – 65 (Apr – Aug 93), pp. 121 – 124.

— Un texto antropológico de Julio Herrera y Reissig (Includes a chapter from the text "Los nuevos charrúas" edited by Abril Trigo). *Escritura (Venezuela)*, v. 17, no. 33 – 34 (Jan – Dec 92), pp. 127 – 142. Bibl.

Trigueros Legarreta, Ignacio. Programas de estabilización sin credibilidad e intermediación financiera. *El Trimestre Económico*, v. 59, no. 236 (Oct – Dec 92), pp. 641 – 655. Bibl, tables, charts.

Trimboli, Javier A. and Roy Hora. Entrevista al historiador Daniel James. *Todo Es Historia*, v. 27, no. 314 (Sept 93), pp. 24 – 30. Il.

Triviño Anzola, Consuelo. América en los libros (Short book reviews). *Cuadernos Hispanoamericanos*, no. 516, 520 (1993), All issues.

— La escritura errante. *Cuadernos Hispanoamericanos*, no. 513 (Mar 93), pp. 140 – 144. Bibl.

Triviños, Gilberto. La sombra de los héroes. *Atenea (Chile)*, no. 465 – 466 (1992), pp. 67 – 97. Bibl, il.

Troconis de Veracoechea, Ermila. Josefa Camejo, una mujer en la historia. *Boletín de la Academia Nacional de la Historia (Venezuela)*, v. 75, no. 297 (Jan – Mar 92), pp. 21 – 31. Bibl.

Trombold, Charles D. et al. Chemical Characteristics of Obsidian from Archaeological Sites in Western Mexico and the Tequila Source Area: Implications for Regional and Pan-Regional Interaction within the Northern Mesoamerican Periphery. *Ancient Mesoamerica*, v. 4, no. 2 (Fall 93), pp. 255 – 270. Bibl, tables, maps, charts.

Tron, Manuel E. and Gustavo Prado. Tri-lateral Taxation. *Business Mexico*, v. 3, no. 3 (Mar 93), pp. 40 – 45.

Trudeau, Robert H. Understanding Transitions to Democracy: Recent Work on Guatemala (Review article). *Latin American Research Review*, v. 28, no. 1 (1993), pp. 235 – 247.

Trueba Lara, José Luis. La biblioteca de Minos. *Plural (Mexico)*, v. 22, no. 267 (Dec 93), pp. 51 – 54.

Trujillo Muñoz, Gabriel. La alquimia de la voz. *La Palabra y el Hombre*, no. 81 (Jan – Mar 92), pp. 330 – 331.

— La ciencia ficción que llegó quedarse. *La Palabra y el Hombre*, no. 84 (Oct – Dec 92), pp. 303 – 304.

— Dos guerras paralelas, dos novelas complementarias. *La Palabra y el Hombre*, no. 84 (Oct – Dec 92), pp. 296 – 298. Il.

— Historias de la guerra menor. *La Palabra y el Hombre*, no. 84 (Oct – Dec 92), pp. 305 – 306.

Tudela, Fernando. Población y sustentabilidad del desarrollo: los desafíos de la complejidad. *Comercio Exterior*, v. 43, no. 8 (Aug 93), pp. 698 – 707. Bibl, charts.

Tuirán Gutiérrez, Rodolfo A. Algunos hallazgos recientes de la demografía histórica mexicana. *Estudios Demográficos y Urbanos*, v. 7, no. 1 (Jan – Apr 92), pp. 273 – 312. Bibl, tables.

— Vivir en familias: hogares y estructura familiar en México, 1976 – 1987. *Comercio Exterior*, v. 43, no. 7 (July 93), pp. 662 – 676. Bibl, tables, charts.

Tuñón Pablos, Julia. Between the Nation and Utopia: The Image of Mexico in the Films of Emilio "Indio" Fernández. *Studies in Latin American Popular Culture*, v. 12 (1993), pp. 159 – 174. Bibl.

Tur Donati, Carlos M. Crisis social, xenofobia y nacionalismo en Argentina, 1919. *Cuadernos Americanos*, no. 42, Nueva época (Nov – Dec 93), pp. 48 – 77. Bibl.

Turbay Ayala, Julio César. La misión del liberalismo como partido moderno (Previously published in this journal, no. 382, 1972). *Revista Javeriana*, v. 61, no. 596 (July 93), pp. 85 – 87.

Turcotte, Richard E. Tracing the Pipeline. *Business Mexico*, v. 3, no. 3 (Mar 93), pp. 24 – 26.

Turino, Thomas. Del esencialismo a lo esencial: pragmática y significado de la interpretación de los sikuri puneños en Lima. *Revista Andina*, v. 10, no. 2 (Dec 92), pp. 441 – 456. Bibl.

Turits, Richard and Robin L. H. Derby. Historias de terror y los terrores de la historia: la masacre haitiana de 1937 en la República Dominicana (Translated by Eugenio Rivas and Mario Alberto Torres). *Estudios Sociales (Dominican Republic)*, v. 26, no. 92 (Apr – June 93), pp. 65 – 76. Bibl.

Turner, Doris J. The "Teatro Experimental do Negro" and Its Black Beauty Contests. *Afro-Hispanic Review*, v. 11, no. 1 – 3 (1992), pp. 76 – 81. Bibl.

Turner, Elisa. María Martínez Cañas. *Latin American Art*, v. 5, no. 1 (Spring 93), pp. 85 – 86. Il.

Tussie de Federman, Diana A. and Manuel Roberto Agosin. Globalización, regionalización y nuevos dilemas en la política de comercio exterior para el desarrollo (Translated by Carlos Villegas). *El Trimestre Económico*, v. 60, no. 239 (July – Sept 93), pp. 559 – 599. Bibl, tables.

— Nuevos dilemas en la política comercial para el desarrollo (Excerpt from the introduction to the forthcoming book *Trading Places: New Dilemmas in Trade Policy for Development*, edited by Manuel R. Agosin and Diana Tussie, translated by Adriana Hierro). *Comercio Exterior*, v. 43, no. 10 (Oct 93), pp. 899 – 912. Bibl, tables.

Tutino, John. Historias del México agrario (Translated by Mario A. Zamudio Vega). *Historia Mexicana*, v. 42, no. 2 (Oct – Dec 92), pp. 177 – 220.

Uceda C., Santiago and José Canziani Amico. Evidencias de grandes precipitaciones en diversas etapas constructivas de La Huaca de la Luna, costa norte del Perú. *Bulletin de l'Institut Français d'Etudes Andines*, v. 22, no. 1 (1993), pp. 313 – 343. Bibl, il.

Ugarteche, Oscar. Bonjour tristesse (Illustrated by Piero Quijano). *Debate (Peru)*, v. 15, no. 70 (Sept – Oct 92), pp. 63 – 66.

Uhart, Hebe. Mi nuevo amor. *Confluencia*, v. 8, no. 1 (Fall 92), p. 199.

Ulive, Ugo. Solimán, el Magnífico en la obra de Chocrón. *Conjunto*, no. 90 – 91 (Jan – June 92), pp. 43 – 45. Il.

Umaña Chaverri, José Otilio. Una opción teórico – metodológica para la enseñanza de la literatura en programas de aprendizaje de lenguas extranjeras y segundas lenguas. *Káñina*, v. 16, no. 1 (Jan – June 92), pp. 171 – 183. Bibl.

Umpierre Herrera, Luz María. Incitaciones lesbianas en "Milagros, calle Mercurio" de Carmen Lugo Filippi. *Revista Iberoamericana*, v. 59, no. 162 – 163 (Jan – June 93), pp. 309 – 316.

— Poems ("Bella ilusión que fugaz/To a Beautiful Illusion, Fleeting," "Para Ellen/For Ellen," "Poema para Elliot Gilbert/Elliot's Sunset") translated by Patsy Boyer and Ellen J. Stekert. *The Americas Review*, v. 19, no. 3 – 4 (Winter 91), pp. 39 – 50.

Unamuno, Miguel. El acuerdo político: una asignatura pendiente. *Todo Es Historia*, v. 27, no. 317 (Dec 93), pp. 10 – 15. Il.

United Nations. Commission on Human Rights. Proyecto de Declaración Universal sobre los Derechos de los Pueblos Indígenas. *Anuario Indigenista*, v. 30 (Dec 91), pp. 513 – 524.

United Nations. Conference on Environment and Development. Propuestas para la Conferencia de Naciones Unidas sobre el Medio Ambiente y el Desarrollo. *Anuario Indigenista*, v. 30 (Dec 91), pp. 331 – 333.

United Nations. Working Group of Indigenous Populations. Declaración Universal sobre los Derechos de los Pueblos Indígenas. *Revista Latinoamericana de Estudios Educativos*, v. 22, no. 4 (Oct – Dec 92), pp. 111 – 121.

Unruh, Vicky Wolff. Art's "Disorderly Humanity" in Torres Bodet's *La educación sentimental*. *Revista Canadiense de Estudios Hispánicos*, v. 17, no. 1 (Fall 92), pp. 123 – 136. Bibl.

— Cultural Enactments: Recent Books on Latin American Theatre (Review article). *Latin American Research Review*, v. 28, no. 1 (1993), pp. 141 – 149.

Unruh, Vicky Wolff and George W. Woodyard. Latin American Theatre Today: A 1992 Conference in Kansas. *Latin American Theatre Review*, v. 26, no. 2 (Spring 93), pp. 6 – 8. Il.

Urbani Patat, Franco. Bibliografía de Vicente Marcano, 1848 – 1891. *Boletín de la Academia Nacional de la Historia (Venezuela)*, v. 75, no. 299 (July – Sept 92), pp. 196 – 207.

Urbano, Henrique-Osvaldo. Huayna Cápac y sus enanos: huellas de un ciclo mítico andino prehispano. *Historia y Cultura (Peru)*, no. 20 (1990), pp. 281 – 293. Bibl.

Urbanyi, Pablo. El robot de acero inoxidable. *Hispamérica,* v. 21, no. 63 (Dec 92), pp. 61 – 68.

Urbina, Nicasio. *Cien años de soledad:* un texto lúdico con implicaciones muy serias. *Revista Canadiense de Estudios Hispánicos,* v. 17, no. 1 (Fall 92), pp. 137 – 152. Bibl.

— La risa como representación del horror en la obra de Reinaldo Arenas. *The Americas Review,* v. 19, no. 2 (Summer 91), pp. 94 – 103.

Urbina Fuentes, Manuel and Adolfo Sánchez Almanza. Distribución de la población y desarrollo en México. *Comercio Exterior,* v. 43, no. 7 (July 93), pp. 652 – 661. Bibl, tables, maps, charts.

Urcid Serrano, Javier. The Pacific Coast of Oaxaca and Guerrero: The Westernmost Extent of Zapotec Script. *Ancient Mesoamerica,* v. 4, no. 1 (Spring 93), pp. 141 – 165. Bibl, il, maps.

Uriarte Ayo, R. The Hispanic American Market and Iron Production in the Basque Country, 1700 – 1825. *Ibero Americana (Sweden),* v. 22, no. 2 (Dec 92), pp. 47 – 65. Bibl, tables, charts.

Urías, Homero. La ofensiva comercial de la diplomacia mexicana. *Comercio Exterior,* v. 43, no. 12 (Dec 93), pp. 1099 – 1106.

Uribe, Armando. Eduardo Anguita (1914 – 1992). *Estudios Públicos (Chile),* no. 49 (Summer 93), pp. 259 – 260.

Uribe-Echeverría, J. Francisco. Problemas regionales en las economías abiertas del Tercer Mundo. *EURE,* v. 19, no. 58 (Oct 93), pp. 7 – 17. Bibl.

Urquidi, Víctor L. La educación: eje para el futuro desarrollo de la potencialidad latinoamericana. *Revista Latinoamericana de Estudios Educativos,* v. 22, no. 3 (July – Sept 92), pp. 123 – 131.

Urquiza, Fernando Carlos. Etiquetas y conflictos: el obispo, el virrey y el cabildo en el Río de la Plata en la segunda mitad del siglo XVIII. *Anuario de Estudios Americanos,* v. 50, no. 1 (1993), pp. 55 – 100. Bibl.

— Iglesia y revolución: un estudio acerca de la actuación política del clero porteño en la década 1810 – 1820. *Anuario de Estudios Americanos,* v. 49 (1992), pp. 441 – 495. Bibl, tables.

Urquiza Almandoz, Oscar F. El traslado de la capital entrerriana, 1883. *Investigaciones y Ensayos,* no. 41 (Jan – Dec 91), pp. 329 – 347. Bibl.

Urraca, Beatriz. Wor(l)ds through the Looking-Glass: Borges' Mirrors and Contemporary Theory. *Revista Canadiense de Estudios Hispánicos,* v. 17, no. 1 (Fall 92), pp. 153 – 176. Bibl.

Urrea Giraldo, Fernando and Diego Zapata Ortega. El síndrome de los nervios en el imaginario popular en una población urbana de Cali. *Revista Colombiana de Antropología,* v. 29 (1992), pp. 207 – 232. Bibl.

Urriola, José Santos
See
Santos Urriola, José

Urruela V. de Quezada, María. El indio en la literatura hispanoamericana: un esbozo. *Boletín de la Academia Nacional de la Historia (Venezuela),* v. 75, no. 299 (July – Sept 92), pp. 91 – 108. Bibl.

Urrunaga, Roberto and Elsa Galarza. La economía de los recursos naturales: políticas extractivas y ambientales. *Apuntes (Peru),* no. 30 (Jan – June 92), pp. 45 – 61. Bibl.

Urrutia Montoya, Miguel. Competencia y desarrollo económico. *Planeación y Desarrollo,* v. 24, no. 2 (May – Aug 93), pp. 49 – 72. Bibl, charts.

— El Consejo Nacional de Política Económica y Social y la planeación en Colombia. *Planeación y Desarrollo,* v. 24, no. 1 (Jan – Apr 93), pp. 349 – 364.

Urteaga Castro-Pozo, Maritza. Identidad y jóvenes urbanos. *Estudios Sociológicos,* v. 11, no. 32 (May – Aug 93), pp. 555 – 568. Bibl.

Uslar Pietri, Arturo. Arturo Uslar Pietri: una biografía intelectual (Interview transcribed and edited by Rubén López Marroquín). *Cuadernos Americanos,* no. 40, Nueva época (July – Aug 93), pp. 146 – 163.

Vacchino, Juan Mario. La dimensión institucional en la integración latinoamericana. *Integración Latinoamericana,* v. 17, no. 185 (Dec 92), pp. 3 – 16. Bibl.

Vachon, Michael. Onchocerciasis in Chiapas, Mexico. *Geographical Review,* v. 83, no. 2 (Apr 93), pp. 141 – 149. Bibl, il, maps.

Valadez, John. Reproduction of *Revelations* by John Valadez. *The Americas Review,* v. 21, no. 1 (Spring 93), p. 39.

Valcárcel Esparza, Carlos Daniel. Histórica contribución integracionista (Introduction to three works on the history of Bolivia, Canada, and Peru published by the Academia Nacional de la Historia de Venezuela within the series "El libro menor"). *Boletín de la Academia Nacional de la Historia (Venezuela),* v. 76, no. 302 (Apr – June 93), pp. 154 – 155.

Valdeavellano Valle, Marcela. Declaración conjunta. *USAC,* no. 13 (Mar 91), p. 81.

Valderrama Fernández, Ricardo and Carmen Escalante Gutiérrez. Canciones de imploración y de amor en los Andes: literatura oral de las quechuas del siglo XX. *Revista de Crítica Literaria Latinoamericana,* v. 19, no. 37 (Jan – June 93), pp. 11 – 39.

Valdés, Gina. Poems ("English con salsa," "Los Angeles," "Changing the World"). *The Americas Review,* v. 21, no. 1 (Spring 93), pp. 49 – 54.

Valdés, María Elena de. La obra de Cristina Pacheco: ficción testimonial de la mujer mexicana. *Escritura (Venezuela),* v. 16, no. 31 – 32 (Jan – Dec 91), pp. 271 – 279. Bibl.

Valdés Bunster, Gustavo. Las riquezas de los antiguos jesuitas de Chile. *Mensaje,* v. 42, no. 420 (July 93), pp. 243 – 246. Charts.

Valdés de Zamora, María Ester. El último recurso. *Letras Femeninas,* v. 19, no. 1 – 2 (Spring – Fall 93), pp. 182 – 183.

Valdés García, Félix and María Teresa Vila Bormey. La filosofía de la liberación en Perú: de Augusto Salazar Bondy a Francisco Miró Quesada. *Islas,* no. 99 (May – Aug 91), pp. 21 – 29. Bibl.

Valdés Ugalde, Francisco. Concepto y estrategia de la "reforma del estado." *Revista Mexicana de Sociología,* v. 55, no. 2 (Apr – June 93), pp. 315 – 338. Bibl, tables.

Valdés Zurita, Leonardo. La sucesión presidencial: "Back to the Basics." *El Cotidiano,* v. 10, no. 58 (Oct – Nov 93), pp. 29 – 33. Il.

Valdivia Dounce, Teresa. ¿Por que hoy una antropología jurídica en México? *Nueva Antropología,* v. 13, no. 43 (Nov 92), pp. 111 – 122. Bibl.

Valdivieso, Jaime. Poesía, lenguaje y universo: una conversación. *Estudios Públicos (Chile),* no. 52 (Spring 93), pp. 343 – 466.

Valdivieso Belaunde, Felipe. Un acuerdo mezquino. *Debate (Peru),* v. 16, no. 73 (June – Aug 93), pp. 51 – 56. Il.

Valdovinos, Hernán. Vicente Huidobro y *Altazor* (Includes the author's illustrations for Huidobro's book *Altazor*). *Atenea (Chile),* no. 467 (1993), pp. 127 – 136. Il.

Vale, Vanda Arantes do. Pintores estrangeiros no Brasil: Museu Mariano Procópio. *Vozes,* v. 87, no. 2 (Mar – Apr 93), pp. 55 – 62. Bibl, il.

Valembois, Víctor and Gabriela Peterson. Los epígrafes en *El siglo de las luces:* su interpretación; de Goya a Carpentier. *Káñina,* v. 16, no. 2 (July – Dec 92), pp. 89 – 100. Bibl, il, tables.

— Los epígrafes en *El siglo de las luces:* su ubicación; de Goya a Carpentier. *Káñina,* v. 16, no. 1 (Jan – June 92), pp. 79 – 89. Bibl, il.

Valencia, Marla and María Elena Infesta. Los criterios legales en la revisión de la política rosista de tierras públicas: Buenos Aires, 1852 – 1864. *Investigaciones y Ensayos,* no. 41 (Jan – Dec 91), pp. 407 – 421. Bibl.

Valencia, Richard R. and Jorge Chapa. Latino Population Growth, Demographic Characteristics, and Educational Stagnation: An Examination of Recent Trends. *Hispanic Journal of Behavioral Sciences,* v. 15, no. 2 (May 93), pp. 165 – 187. Bibl, tables.

Valencia, Richard R. and Pedro Reyes. Educational Policy and the Growing Latino Student Population: Problems and Prospects. *Hispanic Journal of Behavioral Sciences,* v. 15, no. 2 (May 93), pp. 258 – 283. Bibl.

Valender, James. Emilio Prados y la guerra civil española: dos prosas olvidadas. *Nueva Revista de Filología Hispánica,* v. 40, no. 2 (July – Dec 92), pp. 989 – 1003. Bibl.

Valente, Edna Fátima Barros. Os filhos pródigos da educação pública: um estudo sobre os evadidos da escola pública num bairro periférico do município de Santarém. *Revista Brasileira de Estudos Pedagógicos,* v. 72, no. 172 (Sept – Dec 91), pp. 397 – 400.

Valente, José Angel. Poema. *Vuelta,* v. 17, no. 200 (July 93), p. 14.

Valente, Luiz Fernando. Fiction as History: The Case of João Ubaldo Ribeiro. *Latin American Research Review,* v. 28, no. 1 (1993), pp. 41 – 60. Bibl.

— Paulo Leminski e a poética do inútil. *Hispania (USA),* v. 76, no. 3 (Sept 93), pp. 419 – 427. Bibl.

Valentín, Isidro. El gusto por la imagen: una vivencia de fotografía social. *Allpanchis,* v. 25, no. 41 (Jan – June 93), pp. 262 – 272. Il.

Valenzuela, Angela. Liberal Gender Role Attitudes and Academic Achievement among Mexican-Origin Adolescents in Two Houston Inner-City Catholic Schools. *Hispanic Journal of Behavioral Sciences,* v. 15, no. 3 (Aug 93), pp. 310 – 323. Bibl, tables.

Valenzuela, J. Samuel and Timothy R. Scully. De la democracia a la democracia: continuidad y variaciones en las preferencias del electorado y en el sistema de partidos en Chile. *Estudios Públicos (Chile),* no. 51 (Winter 93), pp. 195 – 228. Bibl, tables.

Valenzuela, Juan Pablo and Ignacio Irarrázaval Llona. La ilegitimidad en Chile: ¿Hacia un cambio en la conformación de la familia? *Estudios Públicos (Chile),* no. 52 (Spring 93), pp. 145 – 190. Bibl, tables, charts.

Valenzuela, Lucia. Cultural Ecology. *Business Mexico,* v. 3, no. 3 (Mar 93), p. 36.

Valenzuela Arce, José Manuel and Vania Salles. Ambitos de relaciones sociales de naturaleza íntima e identidades culturales: notas sobre Xochimilco. *Revista Mexicana de Sociología,* v. 54, no. 3 (July – Sept 92), pp. 139 – 173. Bibl.

Valenzuela Fuenzalida, Rafael. Pérdida y degradación de suelos en América Latina y el Caribe. *EURE,* v. 19, no. 58 (Oct 93), pp. 61 – 72. Bibl.

Vallbona, Rima de. La tejedora de palabras. *The Americas Review,* v. 20, no. 3 – 4 (Fall – Winter 92), pp. 116 – 123.

Valle, Norma. Ser periodista y sobrevivir en los '90. *Fem,* v. 17, no. 120 (Feb 93), p. 29.

Valle, Rafael Heliodoro. Buzón de fantasmas: páginas de un diario. *Vuelta,* v. 17, no. 200 (July 93), p. 80.

Valle-Arizpe, Artemio de. Buzón de fantasmas: de Artemio de Valle-Arizpe a Ermilo Abreu Gómez. *Vuelta,* v. 17, no. 202 (Sept 93), pp. 71 – 72.

Valle de Siles, María Eugenia del. Gregorio Francisco de Campos, un obispo ilustrado que presiente la independencia. *Boletín de la Academia Nacional de la Historia (Venezuela),* v. 76, no. 302 (Apr – June 93), pp. 71 – 86. Il.

Vallejo, Catharina Vanderplaats de. La noche boca arriba de Julio Cortázar: la estética como síntesis entre dos cosmovisiones. *Káñina,* v. 16, no. 2 (July – Dec 92), pp. 115 – 120. Bibl.

Vallejo M., César. Descentralización de la educación en Colombia: antecedentes históricos. *Planeación y Desarrollo,* v. 24, no. 1 (Jan – Apr 93), pp. 233 – 277. Bibl.

Vallejo Mejía, Jesús. Responsabilidad social del periodista frente a los nuevos derechos que ha consagrado la constitución: fundamentalmente el derecho a la vida privada. *Revista Javeriana,* v. 61, no. 595 (June 93), pp. 307 – 316.

Vallejos, Marcelo. Los crímenes del Petiso Orejudo. *Todo Es Historia,* v. 27, no. 312 (July 93), pp. 8 – 19. Bibl, il.

Vallejos de Llobet, Patricia. El vocabulario científico en la prensa iluminista porteña, 1800 – 1825. *Cuadernos Americanos,* no. 38, Nueva época (Mar – Apr 93), pp. 205 – 224. Bibl.

Valverde, Clara. Poems ("Otra noche en la frontera," "Campaña de alfabetización," "Diálogo sobre la invasión europea a cuarenta grados bajo cero"). *Casa de las Américas,* no. 190 (Jan – Mar 93), pp. 119 – 121.

Valverde Obando, Luis Alberto. La sociedad y los niños de la calle. *Revista de Ciencias Sociales (Costa Rica),* no. 59 (Mar 93), pp. 9 – 17. Bibl.

Van Aardenne, Bart and George Baker. CNG: A Fuel for the Future. *Business Mexico,* v. 3, no. 1 (Jan – Feb 93), pp. 48 – 50.

Van Cott, Donna Lee. Ecuador: Is Modernization Enough? *Hemisphere,* v. 5, no. 3 (Summer – Fall 93), pp. 16 – 17. Il.

Van Jacob, Scott. Basic Reference Sources for Latin American Dramatic Arts. *SALALM Papers,* v. 34 (1989), pp. 334 – 344. Bibl.

— Latin American Periodicals Prices Revisited. *SALALM Papers,* v. 36 (1991), pp. 335 – 344. Tables.

Van Kessel, Juan J. M. M.

See
  Kessel, Juan J. M. M. van

Vanossi, Jorge Reinaldo. Las reformas de la constitución. *Todo Es Historia,* v. 27, no. 316 (Nov 93), pp. 8 – 32. Bibl, il.

Van Young, Eric. The Cuautla Lazarus: Double Subjectives in Reading Texts on Popular Collective Action. *Colonial Latin American Review,* v. 2, no. 1 – 2 (1993), pp. 3 – 26. Bibl.

Varas Reyes, Víctor. América en tres momentos de la lírica rubendariana: miscelánea. *Signo,* no. 36 – 37, Nueva época (May – Dec 92), pp. 433 – 442.

Varderi, Alejandro. Los talleres literarios en la formación de la literatura del fin de siglo. *Inti,* no. 37 – 38 (Spring – Fall 93), pp. 225 – 232.

Varela, Blanca. Crónica. *Hueso Húmero,* no. 29 (May 93), pp. 68 – 70.

Varela, José R. El tema de la alienación en *La rosa separada* de Pablo Neruda. *Revista Canadiense de Estudios Hispánicos,* v. 17, no. 1 (Fall 92), pp. 177 – 206. Bibl.

Varela, Roberto. Reflexiones sobre la expansión de sistemas y las relaciones de poder. *Nueva Antropología,* v. 13, no. 43 (Nov 92), pp. 39 – 43.

Varela Barraza, Hilda. Nuevos temas de investigación en relaciones internacionales: la ecología. *Relaciones Internacionales (Mexico),* v. 14, Nueva época, no. 55 (July – Sept 92), pp. 31 – 41. Bibl.

Varela Nestier, Carlos and Silvana Charlone. Cuba: ¿Democratización y legitimidad?; los cambios en el sistema político cubano. *Hoy Es Historia,* v. 10, no. 59 (Sept – Oct 93), pp. 56 – 66. Il.

Varela Torrecilla, Carmen and Ignacio Montero. Cuantificación y representación gráfica de los materiales cerámicos mayas: una propuesta metodológica. *Revista Española de Antropología Americana,* v. 23 (1993), pp. 83 – 100. Bibl, tables, charts.

Varga, Gyorgy. Estratégias de proteção no mercado futuro do dólar. *Revista Brasileira de Economia,* v. 47, no. 3 (July – Sept 93), pp. 449 – 466. Bibl, tables.

Vargas, César et al. Financiamiento del desarrollo regional: situación actual y perspectivas. *Planeación y Desarrollo,* v. 24, no. 1 (Jan – Apr 93), pp. 311 – 346. Tables, charts.

Vargas, Elisabeth and Maria Aparecida Schumaher. Lugar no governo: álibi ou conquista? (Accompanied by an English translation by Christopher Peterson). *Estudos Feministas,* v. 1, no. 2 (1993), pp. 348 – 364.

Vargas, Juan Enrique and Iván Lavados Montes. La gestión judicial. *Estudios Sociales (Chile),* no. 78 (Oct – Dec 93), pp. 203 – 225.

Vargas, Rocío. El proyecto económico de Clinton: posibles repercusiones para México y América Latina. *Problemas del Desarrollo,* v. 24, no. 93 (Apr – June 93), pp. 34 – 38.

Vargas Arias, Claudio Antonio and Ileana Muñoz García. La producción de fertilizantes en Costa Rica y el modelo estatal costarricense: el caso Fertica. *Anuario de Estudios Centroamericanos,* v. 18, no. 1 (1992), pp. 61 – 83. Bibl, tables, charts.

Vargas Cariola, Juan Eduardo. Estilo de vida en el ejército de Chile durante el siglo XVII. *Revista de Indias,* v. 53, no. 198 (May – Aug 93), pp. 425 – 457. Bibl.

Vargas Castaño, Alfredo. La suerte de caracol: expatriados, expropiados, desterrados y desplazados en Colombia. *Nueva Sociedad,* no. 123 (Jan – Feb 93), pp. 144 – 155.

Vargas González, Juan and Luis Fuentes Aguilar. La articulación espacial de la ciudad colonial de Puebla, México. *Revista de Historia de América,* no. 112 (July – Dec 91), pp. 43 – 62. Bibl, il, maps.

Vargas Llosa, Mario. La trompeta de Deyá. *Vuelta,* v. 17, no. 195 (Feb 93), pp. 10 – 14.

Vargas Lozano, Gabriel. Cuba, el socialismo y la crisis de nuestro tiempo (Response to articles on Cuba in *Plural,* no. 250). *Plural (Mexico),* v. 22, no. 259 (Apr 93), pp. 66 – 68.

— La filosofía mexicana del siglo XX en una nuez. *Plural (Mexico),* v. 22, no. 257 (Feb 93), pp. 78 – 79.

— Función actual de la filosofía en México. *Plural (Mexico),* v. 22, no. 265 (Oct 93), pp. 36 – 38.

Vargas Lugo, Elisa. Comentarios acerca de la construcción de retablos en México, 1687 – 1713. *Anales del Instituto de Investigaciones Estéticas,* v. 16, no. 62 (1991), pp. 93 – 101. Bibl.

— Un retablo de encaje (Accompanied by an English translation). *Artes de México,* no. 21 (Fall 93), pp. 54 – 59. Il.

Vargas Montero, Guadalupe. Espacio físico y espacio sagrado: la territorialidad en una comunidad mixteca, Oaxaca, México. *La Palabra y el Hombre,* no. 84 (Oct – Dec 92), pp. 179 – 189. Bibl.

— Migraciones mixtecas y relaciones regionales a fines del siglo XIX. *La Palabra y el Hombre,* no. 83 (July – Sept 92), pp. 47 – 57. Bibl.

Vargas Ulate, Gilberto. Estudio del uso actual y capacidad de uso de la tierra en América Central. *Anuario de Estudios Centroamericanos,* v. 18, no. 2 (1992), pp. 7 – 23. Bibl, maps.

— La protección de los recursos naturales en un país subdesarrollado: caso de Costa Rica. *Revista de Ciencias Sociales (Costa Rica),* no. 59 (Mar 93), pp. 81 – 93. Bibl, maps.

Vargas Uribe, Guillermo. Geografía histórica de la ciudad de Morelia, Michoacán, México: su evolución demográfica. *Islas,* no. 98 (Jan – Apr 91), pp. 58 – 70. Bibl, tables, maps, charts.

— Geografía histórica de la población de Michoacán, siglo XVIII. *Estudios Demográficos y Urbanos,* v. 7, no. 1 (Jan – Apr 92), pp. 193 – 222. Bibl, tables, maps, charts.

— Michoacán en la red internacional del narcotráfico. *El Cotidiano,* v. 8, no. 52 (Jan – Feb 93), pp. 38 – 50. Tables, maps, charts.

Várguez Pasos, Luis A. Cultura obrera en crisis: el caso de los cordeleros de Yucatán. *Estudios Sociológicos,* v. 11, no. 31 (Jan – Apr 93), pp. 93 – 110. Bibl.

Varón Gabai, Rafael. El Archivo Arzobispal de Lima: apuntes históricos y archivísticos. *Historia y Cultura (Peru),* no. 20 (1990), pp. 351 – 360. Bibl.

Vasco, Justo E. El caso arcoíris. *Plural (Mexico),* v. 22, no. 262 (July 93), pp. 25 – 31.

Vasconcellos, Geraldo M. and Raul de Gouvea Neto. La diversificación de las exportaciones y la eficiencia de la cartera de exportación: estudio comparativo de los países del sureste de Asia y de la América Latina (Translated by Carlos Villegas). *El Trimestre Económico,* v. 60, no. 237 (Jan – Mar 93), pp. 29 – 52. Bibl, tables, charts.

Vasconcelos, Isabela Francisca Freitas Gouvêa de. IBM: o desafio da mudança. *RAE; Revista de Administração de Empresas,* v. 33, no. 3 (May – June 93), pp. 84 – 97. Bibl.

Vasconcelos, Naumi A. de. Ecos femininos na Eco '92. *Estudos Feministas,* v. 0, no. 0 (1992), pp. 151 – 154.

Vasconi B., Tomás Amadeo and Elina Peraza Martell. Social Democracy and Latin America (Translated by Fred Murphy). *Latin American Perspectives,* v. 20, no. 1 (Winter 93), pp. 99 – 113. Bibl.

Vásquez, Magdalena. Adela Ferreto: un sujeto histórico particular en una época de transición. *Káñina,* v. 16, no. 1 (Jan – June 92), pp. 37 – 49. Bibl.

Vásquez Rodríguez, Raúl. Petróleo y gas en el gobierno Gaviria. *Revista Javeriana,* v. 61, no. 597 (Aug 93), pp. 153 – 158.

Vassallo, Marta. Identidad nacional y chivos expiatorios. *Feminaria,* v. 6, no. 10, Suppl. (Apr 93), pp. 9 – 12. Bibl.

Vaz, Noel. Original Foreword to *Drums and Colours. Caribbean Quarterly,* v. 38, no. 4 (Dec 92), pp. 22 – 23.

Vázquez, Josefina Zoraida. El dilema de la enseñanza de la historia de México. *La Educación (USA)*, v. 37, no. 114 (1993), pp. 77 – 89.

— Un viejo tema: el federalismo y el centralismo. *Historia Mexicana*, v. 42, no. 3 (Jan – Mar 93), pp. 621 – 631.

Vázquez, Patricia

See
   Vázquez Hall, Patricia

Vázquez, Susana. Leopoldo Zea y la conciencia latinoamericana. *Hoy Es Historia*, v. 10, no. 60 (Nov – Dec 93), pp. 4 – 13. Bibl, il.

— El "redescubrimiento," 1492 – 1992. *Hoy Es Historia*, v. 9, no. 54 (Nov – Dec 92), pp. 11 – 26. Bibl, il.

Vázquez Arce, Carmen. Los desastres de la guerra: sobre la articulación de la ironía en los cuentos "La recién nacida sangre," de Luis Rafael Sánchez y "El momento divino de Caruso Llompart," de Félix Córdova Iturregui. *Revista Iberoamericana*, v. 59, no. 162 – 163 (Jan – June 93), pp. 187 – 201. Bibl.

Vázquez Carrizosa, Alfredo. La política internacional de Colombia hasta la época neoliberal. *Revista Javeriana*, v. 61, no. 594 (May 93), pp. 202 – 208.

Vázquez de Acuña, Isidoro. Evolución de la población de Chiloé, siglos XVI – XX. *Boletín de la Academia Chilena de la Historia*, v. 58 – 59, no. 102 (1991 – 1992), pp. 403 – 457. Bibl, tables.

Vázquez de Knauth, Josefina

See
   Vázquez, Josefina Zoraida

Vázquez del Mercado, Angélica and Tania Carreño King. Crítica de la historia pragmática: una entrevista con Luis González y González. *Nexos*, v. 16, no. 191 (Nov 93), pp. 35 – 39.

— La disputa por la historia patria: una entrevista con Lorenzo Meyer. *Nexos*, v. 16, no. 191 (Nov 93), pp. 41 – 49.

— La hija de la invención: una entrevista con Edmundo O'Gorman. *Nexos*, v. 16, no. 190 (Oct 93), pp. 45 – 51.

Vázquez Hall, Patricia. Concurso de INBA: premios inexplicables. *Plural (Mexico)*, v. 22, no. 261 (June 93), pp. 88 – 89.

— Danza: de todo en un día. *Plural (Mexico)*, v. 22, no. 263 (Aug 93), p. 80.

— Danza folklórica hoy. *Plural (Mexico)*, v. 22, no. 259 (Apr 93), pp. 72 – 73.

— Palabras con Rodolfo Lastra. *Plural (Mexico)*, v. 22, no. 257 (Feb 93), pp. 75 – 76.

— Pilar Medina, un águila mestiza. *Plural (Mexico)*, v. 22, no. 258 (Mar 93), p. 72.

— Waldeen, pensadora y maestra de la danza. *Plural (Mexico)*, v. 22, no. 265 (Oct 93), p. 85.

Vázquez Janeiro, Isaac. Documentación americana en el Pontificio Ateneo Antoniano de Roma. *Archivo Ibero-Americano*, v. 52, no. 205 – 208 (Jan – Dec 92), pp. 767 – 809.

Vázquez Mantecón, Carmen. Espacio social y crisis política: la Sierra Gorda, 1850 – 1855. *Mexican Studies*, v. 9, no. 1 (Winter 93), pp. 47 – 70. Bibl, maps.

Vázquez Mantecón, Verónica and Juan Reyes del Campillo. ¿Ciudadanos en ciernes?: la cultura política en el distrito XXVII del D.F. *El Cotidiano*, v. 9, no. 54 (May 93), pp. 41 – 48. Il, tables, charts.

Vázquez Trejo, Adela. Consideraciones sobre el proceso de privatización en Brasil y México. *Relaciones Internacionales (Mexico)*, v. 14, Nueva época, no. 55 (July – Sept 92), pp. 75 – 78.

Vázquez-Yanes, Carlos and Christopher B. Field. Species of the Genus "Piper" Provide a Model to Study How Plants Can Grow in Different Kinds of Rainforest Habitats. *Interciencia*, v. 18, no. 5 (Sept – Oct 93), pp. 230 – 236. Bibl, il.

Vega, Bernardo. Etnicidad y el futuro de las relaciones domínico – haitianas. *Estudios Sociales (Dominican Republic)*, v. 26, no. 94 (Oct – Dec 93), pp. 29 – 43.

Vega, Ed. Mayonesa Peralta. *The Americas Review*, v. 20, no. 3 – 4 (Fall – Winter 92), pp. 47 – 56.

Vega-Centeno B., Imelda. Ser joven en el Perú: socialización, integración, corporalidad y cultura. *Allpanchis*, v. 25, no. 41 (Jan – June 93), pp. 177 – 210. Bibl, tables.

Vega Jiménez, Patricia. Nacimiento y consolidación de la Escuela de Ciencias de la Comunicación Colectiva. *Revista de Ciencias Sociales (Costa Rica)*, no. 57 (Sept 92), pp. 67 – 78. Tables, charts.

Vega Martínez, Mylena. Cultura política y legitimidad: encuesta de opinión entre estudiantes avanzados de la sede central de la Universidad de Costa Rica. *Anuario de Estudios Centroamericanos*, v. 18, no. 2 (1992), pp. 71 – 90. Bibl, tables.

Vega Shiota, Gustavo de la. Reflexiones en torno al posgrado de sociología en la Facultad de Ciencias Políticas y Sociales de la UNAM. *Revista Mexicana de Ciencias Políticas y Sociales*, v. 38, Nueva época, no. 151 (Jan – Mar 93), pp. 195 – 203.

Vega Yunqué, Edgardo

See
   Vega, Ed

Vegas Vilarrubia, Teresa and Maritza Cova. Estudio sobre la distribución y ecología de macrofitos acuáticos en el embalse de Guri. *Interciencia*, v. 18, no. 2 (Mar – Apr 93), pp. 77 – 82. Bibl, tables, maps, charts.

Veiga, Alberto. Agricultura e processo político: o caso brasileiro. *Revista de Economia e Sociologia Rural*, v. 29, no. 4 (Oct – Dec 91), pp. 285 – 334. Bibl, tables.

Velandia, Roberto. El Batallón Guarda Presidencial. *Boletín de Historia y Antigüedades*, v. 80, no. 780 (Jan – Mar 93), pp. 109 – 120. Bibl.

— Informe de labores. *Boletín de Historia y Antigüedades*, v. 79, no. 779 (Oct – Dec 92), pp. 871 – 886.

Velarde F., Julio and Efraín Gonzales de Olarte. ¿Es posible el liberalismo en el Perú? *Debate (Peru)*, v. 15, no. 70 (Sept – Oct 92), pp. 15 – 18. Il.

Velasco, Andrés and Marcelo Tokman. Opciones para la política comercial chilena en los '90. *Estudios Públicos (Chile)*, no. 52 (Spring 93), pp. 53 – 99. Bibl, tables.

Velasco M. L., María del Pilar. La epidemia de cólera de 1833 y la mortalidad en la ciudad de México. *Estudios Demográficos y Urbanos*, v. 7, no. 1 (Jan – Apr 92), pp. 95 – 135. Bibl, tables, charts.

Velasco Toro, José. América: voz de múltiples raíces. *La Palabra y el Hombre*, no. 84 (Oct – Dec 92), pp. 256 – 258.

— Autonomía y territorialidad entre los yaquis de Sonora, México. *La Palabra y el Hombre*, no. 82 (Apr – June 92), pp. 147 – 161. Bibl.

Velazco, Jorge. La confluencia intelectual y académica en la formación escolástica y la obra de investigación de Francisco Curt Lange. *Revista Musical de Venezuela*, no. 28 (May – Dec 89), pp. 207 – 223.

Velázquez, Carolina. Las operadoras de TELMEX. *Fem*, v. 17, no. 128 (Oct 93), pp. 19 – 21.

— "Soy optimista . . . ahora tenemos más opciones": Amparo Espinosa. *Fem*, v. 17, no. 130 (Dec 93), pp. 26 – 27. II.

Velázquez, Nelly. La implantación del cultivo del trigo en la cordillera de Mérida durante la dominación colonial. *Derecho y Reforma Agraria*, no. 24 (1993), pp. 115 – 138. Bibl.

Velázquez Gutiérrez, Luis A. and Jesús Arroyo Alejandre. La transición de los patrones migratorios y las ciudades medias. *Estudios Demográficos y Urbanos*, v. 7, no. 2 – 3 (May – Dec 92), pp. 555 – 574. Bibl, tables.

Velázquez Zárate, Enrique. La contaminación atmosférica en la ciudad de México. *El Cotidiano*, v. 9, no. 54 (May 93), pp. 55 – 59. II.

Vélez, José Roberto. Nefasta aventura de amor. *Bilingual Review/Revista Bilingüe*, v. 17, no. 3 (Sept – Dec 92), pp. 247 – 255.

Vélez, Julio. Estética del trabajo y la modernidad autóctona. *Casa de las Américas*, no. 189 (Oct – Dec 92), pp. 71 – 80.

— Revistas hispánicas de vanguardia. *Cuadernos Hispanoamericanos*, no. 514 – 515 (Apr – May 93), pp. 343 – 344.

Vélez Boza, Fermín. Introducción al trabajo *Expediente de órdenes, 1613 – 1923* de monseñor dr. F. Maldonado Toro. *Boletín de la Academia Nacional de la Historia (Venezuela)*, v. 76, no. 302 (Apr – June 93), pp. 183 – 185.

Vélez Correa, Jaime. Ultimo decenio de *Revista Javeriana* (Previously published in this journal, no. 500, 1983). *Revista Javeriana*, v. 61, no. 596 (July 93), pp. 41 – 43.

Velloso, Mônica Pimenta. A brasilidade verde – amarela: nacionalismo e regionalismo paulista. *Estudos Históricos*, v. 6, no. 11 (Jan – June 93), pp. 89 – 112. Bibl.

Veloz Avila, Norma Ilse. Conflictos y concertación obrero – patronal. *El Cotidiano*, v. 8, no. 51 (Nov – Dec 92), pp. 76 – 80. II, tables.

— Conflictos y negociación obrero – patronal: septiembre – noviembre de 1992. *El Cotidiano*, v. 8, no. 52 (Jan – Feb 93), pp. 97 – 102. Tables.

— Diecisiete meses de respuesta obrera: conflictos obrero – patronales, 1992 – 1993. *El Cotidiano*, v. 9, no. 56 (July 93), pp. 89 – 103. II, tables.

— Entre la productividad y el salario: conflictos y concertación obrero – patronal, enero – marzo 1993. *El Cotidiano*, v. 9, no. 54 (May 93), pp. 81 – 89. II, tables.

Venâncio Filho, Alberto. Lembrança de Afonso Arinos. *Revista do Instituto Histórico e Geográfico Brasileiro*, no. 372 (July – Sept 91), pp. 762 – 765.

Venegas, Arturo and Miguel Angel Romero Miranda. Acción Nacional: consolidar espacios de poder regional. *El Cotidiano*, v. 10, no. 57 (Aug – Sept 93), pp. 79 – 85. II.

Venegas Delgado, Hernán. Acerca del concepto de región histórica. *Islas*, no. 98 (Jan – Apr 91), pp. 13 – 21. Bibl.

Ventosa del Campo, Andrés. Hacia una zona continental de libre comercio. *Relaciones Internacionales (Mexico)*, v. 14, Nueva época, no. 56 (Oct – Dec 92), pp. 87 – 96. Bibl, tables, maps.

— La política exterior de Canadá y la América Latina. *Relaciones Internacionales (Mexico)*, v. 14, Nueva época, no. 55 (July – Sept 92), pp. 51 – 59. Bibl.

Vera, Pedro Jorge. La cuarta tentación. *Plural (Mexico)*, v. 22, no. 267 (Dec 93), pp. 16 – 17.

Vera Ferrer, Oscar. Tendencias de la productividad en México: la concepción de las empresas. *Comercio Exterior*, v. 43, no. 11 (Nov 93), pp. 1052 – 1056. Bibl, tables.

Vera-León, Antonio. Jesús Díaz: Politics of Self-Narration in Revolutionary Cuba. *Latin American Literary Review*, v. 21, no. 41 (Jan – June 93), pp. 65 – 78. Bibl.

Vera-Meiggs, David. Cine en Viña del Mar. *Mensaje*, v. 42, no. 424 (Nov 93), pp. 592 – 593. II.

Veracoechea, Ermila de

See

    Troconis de Veracoechea, Ermila

Veracoechea de Castillo, Luisa. Palabras de la profesora Luisa Veracoechea de Castillo en el acto de presentación de libro *La huella del sabio: el municipio foráneo Alejandro de Humboldt* con motivo de los 193 años de la visita del sabio a Caracas . . . . *Boletín de la Academia Nacional de la Historia (Venezuela)*, v. 76, no. 301 (Jan – Mar 93), pp. 27 – 31.

Verba, Ericka Kim. "Las hojas sueltas" (Broadsides): Nineteenth-Century Chilean Popular Poetry as a Source for the Historian. *Studies in Latin American Popular Culture*, v. 12 (1993), pp. 141 – 158. Bibl.

Verdesio, Gustavo. La *Argentina*: tipología textual y construcción de los referentes. *Revista de Crítica Literaria Latinoamericana*, v. 19, no. 38 (July – Dec 93), pp. 345 – 360. Bibl.

Verdicchio, Gastón Pablo. Fondas, hoteles y otras formas de hospedaje en el viejo Buenos Aires. *Todo Es Historia*, v. 27, no. 315 (Oct 93), pp. 24 – 28. II.

Verdugo, Patricia. Andrés Aylwin: "Hay situaciones que claman a Dios." *Mensaje*, v. 42, no. 421 (Aug 93), pp. 382 – 383. II.

Vergara, Pilar. Ruptura y continuidad en la política social del gobierno democrático. *Estudios Sociales (Chile)*, no. 78 (Oct – Dec 93), pp. 105 – 144. Bibl, tables.

Vergara Figueroa, César Abilio. La educación, el trabajo y lo lícito en un relato oral. *Folklore Americano*, no. 52 (July – Dec 91), pp. 109 – 121. Bibl.

Vergara M., Rodrigo and Nicolás Eyzaguirre. Reflexiones en torno a la experiencia de autonomía del Banco Central de Chile. *Cuadernos de Economía (Chile)*, v. 30, no. 91 (Dec 93), pp. 327 – 347. Bibl, tables.

Vergara M., Rodrigo and Andrés Reinstein A. Hacia una regulación y supervisión más eficiente del sistema bancario. *Estudios Públicos (Chile)*, no. 49 (Summer 93), pp. 99 – 136. Bibl, tables.

Versiani, Flávio Rabelo. Imigrantes, trabalho qualificado e industrialização: Rio e São Paulo no início do século. *Revista de Economia Política (Brazil)*, v. 13, no. 4 (Oct – Dec 93), pp. 77 – 96. Bibl, tables.

Vetancourt Vigas, F. C. El pendón español en el ayuntamiento de Cumaná (Previously published in this journal vol. 1, no. 1, 1912). *Boletín de la Academia Nacional de la Historia (Venezuela)*, v. 75, no. 300 (Oct – Dec 92), pp. 279 – 293.

Vetter, Ulrich. La "nueva metafísica" latinoamericana y las "filosofías para la liberación": dimensiones del término "liberación." *Islas*, no. 96 (May – Aug 90), pp. 127 – 131.

Vial Correa, Juan de Dios. Cincuenta números de revista *Estudios Públicos*. *Estudios Públicos (Chile)*, no. 51 (Winter 93), pp. 331 – 335.

Vianna, Lucila Amaral Carneiro and Eleonora Menicucci de Oliveira. Violência conjugal na gravidez. *Estudos Feministas*, v. 1, no. 1 (1993), pp. 162 – 165.

Vicent, Mauricio and Fietta Jarque. La poetisa cubana Dulce María Loynaz gana el premio Cervantes. *Humboldt*, no. 108 (1993), p. 104.

Vicente, José R. Modelos estruturais para previsão das produções brasileiras de carne de frango e ovos. *Revista de Economia e Sociologia Rural*, v. 30, no. 4 (Oct – Dec 92), pp. 305 – 319. Bibl, tables, charts.

Vickers, William T. The Anthropology of Amazonia (Review article). *Latin American Research Review*, v. 28, no. 1 (1993), pp. 111 – 127. Bibl.

Victoria, José Guadalupe. Noticias sobre la antigua plaza y el Mercado del Volador de la ciudad de México. *Anales del Instituto de Investigaciones Estéticas*, v. 16, no. 62 (1991), pp. 69 – 91. Bibl, il.

Vidal, Hernán. The Concept of Colonial and Postcolonial Discourse: A Perspective from Literary Criticism (Response to Patricia Seed's article "Colonial and Postcolonial Discourse," *LARR*, v. 26, no 3, 1991), translated by Sharon Kellum. *Latin American Research Review*, v. 28, no. 3 (1993), pp. 113 – 119.

Vidal, Lux. As pesquisas mais freqüentes em etnologia e historia indígena na Amazônia: uma abordagem musical. *Revista de Antropologia (Brazil)*, v. 34 (1991), pp. 183 – 196.

Vidal, Rosa María and Ignacio J. March. The Road to Success. *Business Mexico*, v. 3, no. 1 (Jan – Feb 93), pp. 10 – 12. Il, maps.

Vidal Buzzi, Fernando. De pizzas y ravioles. *Todo Es Historia*, v. 26, no. 305 (Dec 92), pp. 22 – 26. Il.

Vidal de la Rosa, Godofredo and Miriam Alfie Cohen. Hacia los acuerdos paralelos: el medio ambiente. *El Cotidiano*, v. 9, no. 56 (July 93), pp. 104 – 111. Bibl, il, tables.

Vidal Ramírez, Fernando. El camino del porvenir. *Debate (Peru)*, v. 16, no. 73 (June – Aug 93), pp. 56 – 60. Il.

Vidales, Raúl. Fin de la historia: "¿Fin de la utopía?"; frente a los 500 años. *Cristianismo y Sociedad*, v. 30, no. 113 (1992), pp. 53 – 84. Bibl.

Vidaurreta de Tjarks, Alicia. Vicente Gregorio Quesada. *Investigaciones y Ensayos*, no. 41 (Jan – Dec 91), pp. 457 – 496. Bibl.

Videla, Horacio. La evangelización del Nuevo Mundo. *Investigaciones y Ensayos*, no. 41 (Jan – Dec 91), pp. 65 – 75. Bibl.

Vieira, Nelson H. "Closing the Gap" between High and Low: Intimation on the Brazilian Novel of the Future. *Latin American Literary Review*, v. 20, no. 40 (July – Dec 92), pp. 109 – 119. Bibl.

— Simulation and Dissimulation: An Expression of Crypto-Judaism in the Literature of Colonial Brazil. *Colonial Latin American Review*, v. 2, no. 1 – 2 (1993), pp. 143 – 164. Bibl.

Vieira, Oldegar Franco. Dom Pedro II e o parlamentarismo. *Convivium*, v. 34, no. 2 (July – Dec 91), pp. 120 – 126.

Vieira Posada, Edgar. Promoción de exportaciones: reflexiones para una nueva política. *Integración Latinoamericana*, v. 18, no. 189 – 190 (May – June 93), pp. 35 – 37.

— Una unión aduanera para América Latina. *Integración Latinoamericana*, v. 18, no. 187 – 188 (Mar – Apr 93), pp. 23 – 34. Bibl.

Viera Gallo, José Antonio. Violencia y cultura política: un desafío para nuestro tiempo. *Mensaje*, v. 42, no. 417 (Mar – Apr 93), pp. 69 – 73. Il.

Viereck, Roberto. De la tradición a las formas de la experiencia: entrevista a Ricardo Piglia. *Revista Chilena de Literatura*, no. 40 (Nov 92), pp. 129 – 138.

Vigil Piñón, Evangelina. Poems ("The Bridge People," "Dumb Broad!," "Telephone Line"). *The Americas Review*, v. 20, no. 3 – 4 (Fall – Winter 92), pp. 161 – 168.

Viglione de Arrastía, Hebe. Población e inmigración: producción historiográfica en la provincia de Santa Fe, Argentina. *Revista Interamericana de Bibliografía*, v. 42, no. 3 (1992), pp. 489 – 500. Bibl.

Vijil, Alfonso. Central American Art Publications, 1986 – 1989: A Brief Survey and Bibliography. *SALALM Papers*, v. 34 (1989), pp. 307 – 315. Bibl.

Vila Bormey, María Teresa and Félix Valdés García. La filosofía de la liberación en Perú: de Augusto Salazar Bondy a Francisco Miró Quesada. *Islas*, no. 99 (May – Aug 91), pp. 21 – 29. Bibl.

Vilanova, Angel. Motivo clásico y novela latinoamericana. *Nueva Revista de Filología Hispánica*, v. 40, no. 2 (July – Dec 92), pp. 1087 – 1099. Bibl.

Vilas, Carlos María. América Latina: la hora de la sociedad civil (Originally published in *NACLA: Report on the Americas*, Sept – Oct 93). *Realidad Económica*, no. 120 (Nov – Dec 93), pp. 7 – 17. Bibl.

— Between Skepticism and Protocol: The Defection of the "Critical Intellectuals" (Translated by Sarah Stookey). *Latin American Perspectives*, v. 20, no. 2 (Spring 93), pp. 97 – 106. Bibl.

— Contra el sectarismo (Response to James Petras' article "Los intelectuales en retirada" in *Nueva Sociedad*, no. 107). *Nueva Sociedad*, no. 123 (Jan – Feb 93), pp. 165 – 170.

— Después de la revolución: democratización y cambio social en Centroamérica. *Revista Mexicana de Sociología*, v. 54, no. 3 (July – Sept 92), pp. 3 – 44. Bibl.

— The Hour of Civil Society (Translated by Mark Fried). *NACLA Report on the Americas*, v. 27, no. 2 (Sept – Oct 93), pp. 38 – 42 +. Bibl, il.

— Sociedad civil y pueblo. *Revista Paraguaya de Sociología*, v. 30, no. 86 (Jan – Apr 93), pp. 71 – 82. Bibl.

Villa Pelayo, José Jesús. Nota crítica sobre la novela *El amor y el interés* de Gerónimo Pérez Rescanière. *Revista Nacional de Cultura (Venezuela)*, v. 53, no. 286 (July – Sept 92), pp. 148 – 150.

Villagrán Kramer, Francisco. La integración económica y la justicia. *Integración Latinoamericana*, v. 18, no. 187 – 188 (Mar – Apr 93), pp. 35 – 47. Bibl.

Villagrán M., Carolina. Una interpretación climática del registro palinológico del último ciclo glacial – postglacial en Sudamérica. *Bulletin de l'Institut Français d'Etudes Andines*, v. 22, no. 1 (1993), pp. 243 – 258. Bibl, maps, charts.

Villaizán, Marta and Félix Matos Rodríguez. "Para que vayan y produzcan frutos y ese fruto permanezca": descripción de los fondos documentales del Archivo Eclesiástico de San Juan de Puerto Rico. *Op. Cit.*, no. 7 (1992), pp. 208 – 228. Bibl, il, facs.

Villalba, Miguel Angel. La revolución radical de 1933 en paso de los libres. *Todo Es Historia*, v. 27, no. 311 (June 93), pp. 8 – 24. Bibl, il, maps.

Villamán P., Marcos J. Religión y pobreza: una aproximación a los nuevos movimientos religiosos. *Estudios Sociales (Dominican Republic)*, v. 26, no. 94 (Oct – Dec 93), pp. 75 – 96. Bibl, tables.

Villaneuva Villanueva, Nancy Beatriz. La práctica docente en la educación preescolar: ¿Autonomía o control? *Nueva Antropología*, v. 13, no. 44 (Aug 93), pp. 103 – 117. Bibl.

Villanueva, Tino. Tierras prometidas. *Plural (Mexico)*, v. 22, no. 256 (Jan 93), pp. 38 – 39.

Villanueva Collado, Alfredo. Eugenio María de Hostos ante el conflicto modernismo/modernidad. *Caribbean Studies*, v. 25, no. 1 – 2 (Jan – July 92), pp. 147 – 158.

— Eugenio María de Hostos ante el conflicto modernismo/modernidad. *Revista Iberoamericana,* v. 59, no. 162 – 163 (Jan – June 93), pp. 21 – 32. Bibl.

Villar, Samuel I. del. El programa económico del PRD. *Nexos,* v. 16, no. 192 (Dec 93), pp. 41 – 45.

Villarreal, José B. La danza de los diablos cucúas. *Revista Cultural Lotería,* v. 51, no. 387 (Feb 92), pp. 7 – 25. Bibl.

Villarreal, Martín. El hombre de los árboles. *Plural (Mexico),* v. 22, no. 264 (Sept 93), pp. 80 – 81.

Villarrutia, Xavier

See
 Villaurrutia, Xavier

Villaseñor García, Guillermo. El gobierno y la conducción en las universidades públicas: situación reciente y tendencias actuales. *El Cotidiano,* v. 9, no. 55 (June 93), pp. 85 – 90. Il.

Villaurrutia, Xavier. Buzón de fantasmas: de Xavier Villaurrutia a José Gorostiza. *Vuelta,* v. 17, no. 195 (Feb 93), p. 65.

— Taxco en Montenegro. *Vuelta,* v. 17, no. 198 (May 93), pp. 26 – 27.

Villavicencio de Mencías, Gladys. Indígenas en Quito. *América Indígena,* v. 51, no. 2 – 3 (Apr – Sept 91), pp. 223 – 250. Bibl.

Villela, Luis. Sistema tributario y relaciones financieras intergubernamentales: la experiencia brasileña. *Planeación y Desarrollo,* v. 24, no. 1 (Jan – Apr 93), pp. 171 – 188. Tables.

Viñas, Angel. La política exterior española frente a Iberoamérica: pasado y presente. *Ibero-Amerikanisches Archiv,* v. 18, no. 3 – 4 (1992), pp. 469 – 500. Bibl.

Viñas, David. Nueve apuntes para conjurar el olvido de indios y genocidas (Interview transcribed by Jean Andreu and Claude Castro). *Caravelle,* no. 59 (1992), pp. 71 – 73.

Vincent, Vern and Gilberto de los Santos. Tex-Mex Tourism (Excerpt from *Mexican Tourism Market in the Rio Grande Valley of Texas). Business Mexico,* v. 3, no. 3 (Mar 93), pp. 27 – 29. Tables.

Vinderman, Paulina. Poems ("Simbad en la taza," "Pasillos de hospital," "Campo quemado"). *Feminaria,* v. 6, no. 10, Suppl. (Apr 93), p. 17.

Vinhosa, Francisco Luiz Teixeira. Torre de Londres, 19 de outubro de 1915: as carabinas Mauser e o fuzilamento de Fernando Buschmann. *Revista do Instituto Histórico e Geográfico Brasileiro,* no. 371 (Apr – June 91), pp. 460 – 469. Bibl.

Vinueza, María Elena and Carmen María Sáenz. El aporte africano en la formación de la cultura musical cubana. *Folklore Americano,* no. 53 (Jan – June 92), pp. 55 – 80. Bibl.

Vio, Fernando. La salud está enferma: ¿Es posible su recuperación? *Mensaje,* v. 42, no. 425 (Dec 93), pp. 607 – 611. Il.

Viola Recasens, Andreu. La cara oculta de los Andes: notas para una redefinición de la relación histórica entre sierra y selva. *Boletín Americanista,* v. 33, no. 42 – 43 (1992 – 1993), pp. 7 – 22. Bibl, charts.

Víquez Jiménez, Alí. Texto y estrategia: análisis de la cooperación interpretativa en *El maniaco* por Alí Víquez. *Káñina,* v. 16, no. 2 (July – Dec 92), pp. 17 – 27. Bibl.

Viramontes, Helena María. Miss Clairol. *The Americas Review,* v. 20, no. 3 – 4 (Fall – Winter 92), pp. 9 – 13.

Visbal Martelo, Jorge. Producción y política ganadera en Colombia. *Revista Javeriana,* v. 61, no. 591 (Jan – Feb 93), pp. 20 – 24.

Vitale, Ida. La voz cantante. *Vuelta,* v. 17, no. 199 (June 93), pp. 32 – 33.

Vitier, Cintio. Latinoamérica: integración y utopía. *Cuadernos Americanos,* no. 42, Nueva época (Nov – Dec 93), pp. 112 – 128.

— Notas en el centenario de Vallejo. *Casa de las Américas,* no. 189 (Oct – Dec 92), pp. 7 – 13.

— La tierra adivinada. *Cuadernos Americanos,* no. 39, Nueva época (May – June 93), pp. 88 – 90.

Vivas, Fabricio and Héctor Mendoza. Informe 1990 – 1991: estadísticas históricas de Venezuela; historia de las finanzas públicas en Venezuela. *Boletín de la Academia Nacional de la Historia (Venezuela),* v. 75, no. 297 (Jan – Mar 92), pp. 169 – 176.

Vives Pérez-Cotapos, Cristián. Iglesia y pastoral social: un camino de solidaridad. *Mensaje,* v. 42, no. 421 (Aug 93), pp. 363 – 366. Il.

Vizcaino Bravo, Zenaida and Francisco A. Castillo. Observación del fitoplancton del Pacífico colombiano durante 1991 – 1992 en condiciones El Niño. *Bulletin de l'Institut Français d'Etudes Andines,* v. 22, no. 1 (1993), pp. 179 – 190. Bibl, il, maps.

Voeks, Robert. African Medicine and Magic in the Americas. *Geographical Review,* v. 83, no. 1 (Jan 93), pp. 66 – 78. Bibl, maps.

Vogeley, Nancy J. Colonial Discourse in a Postcolonial Context: Nineteenth-Century Mexico. *Colonial Latin American Review,* v. 2, no. 1 – 2 (1993), pp. 189 – 212. Bibl.

Volek, Emil. Cartas de amor de la Avellaneda. *Cuadernos Hispanoamericanos,* no. 511 (Jan 93), pp. 103 – 113. Bibl.

Volk, Steven S. Mine Owners, Money Lenders, and the State in Mid-Nineteenth Century Chile: Transitions and Conflicts. *Hispanic American Historical Review,* v. 73, no. 1 (Feb 93), pp. 67 – 98. Bibl, tables.

Volkow, Verónica. Dos poemas ("Arcano XXII," "Arcano V"). *Vuelta,* v. 17, no. 198 (May 93), p. 41.

Von Baer, Heinrich. Extensión universitaria: reflexiones para la acción. *Estudios Sociales (Chile),* no. 74 (Oct – Dec 92), pp. 159 – 166.

Von Barghahn, Barbara. The Colonial Paintings of Leonardo Flores. *Latin American Art,* v. 5, no. 2 (Summer 93), pp. 47 – 49. Bibl, il.

— Colonial Statuary of New Spain. *Latin American Art,* v. 4, no. 4 (Winter 92), pp. 77 – 79. Bibl, il.

Wade, Ann E. European Approaches to the Conspectus. *SALALM Papers,* v. 36 (1991), pp. 258 – 264.

Waitling, John. Small Businesses in a Big-Time Economy. *Business Mexico,* v. 3, no. 3 (Mar 93), pp. 4 – 7. Tables.

Waksman, Guillermo. Uruguay: la gran derrota de Lacalle. *Nueva Sociedad,* no. 124 (Mar – Apr 93), pp. 17 – 21.

Walcott, Derek. The Antilles: Fragments of Epic Memory; The 1992 Nobel Lecture. *World Literature Today,* v. 67, no. 2 (Spring 93), pp. 260 – 267. Il.

— Drums and Colours. *Caribbean Quarterly,* v. 38, no. 4 (Dec 92), pp. 23 – 135.

— Pantomima (Translated by Blanca Acosta Rabassa). *Conjunto,* no. 93 (Jan – June 93), pp. 46 – 71.

— Poems ("Against My Holy Rage," "Gib Hall Revisited," "Self Portrait"). *Caribbean Quarterly,* v. 38, no. 4 (Dec 92), pp. 18 – 21.

— Poems ("The Yellow Cemetery," "Soles Occidere et Redire Possunt," "Choc Bay," "Words for Rent," "As John to Patmos"). *Caribbean Quarterly*, v. 38, no. 4 (Dec 92), pp. 1 – 14.

— Poems ("Two Hieroglyphs in the Passing of Empires," "A City's Death by Fire," "A Lesson for This Sunday"). *Caribbean Quarterly*, v. 38, no. 4 (Dec 92), pp. 15 – 17.

Waldmann, Peter. "Was ich mache, ist Justicialismus, nicht Liberalismus": Menems Peronismus und Peróns Peronismus; Ein vorläufiger Vergleich. *Ibero-Amerikanisches Archiv*, v. 18, no. 1 – 2 (1992), pp. 5 – 29. Bibl.

Walger, Christian. "Nova música baiana": Musikszene Bahia; Kultursoziologische Betrachtungen zur schwarzen Musik Brasiliens. *Zeitschrift für Lateinamerika Wien*, no. 42 (1992), pp. 27 – 51. Bibl.

Walker H., Eduardo. Desempeño financiero de las carteras accionarias de los fondos de pensiones en Chile: ¿Ha tenido desventajas ser grandes? *Cuadernos de Economía (Chile)*, v. 30, no. 89 (Apr 93), pp. 33 – 75. Bibl, tables, charts.

— Desempeño financiero de las carteras de "renta fija" de los fondos de pensiones de Chile: ¿Ha tenido desventajas ser grandes? *Cuadernos de Economía (Chile)*, v. 30, no. 89 (Apr 93), pp. 1 – 33. Bibl, tables.

Walker H., Eduardo and Leonardo Hernández T. Estructura de financiamiento corporativo en Chile, 1978 – 1990: evidencia a partir de datos contables. *Estudios Públicos (Chile)*, no. 51 (Winter 93), pp. 87 – 156. Bibl, tables, charts.

Wall, David L. Spatial Inequalities in Sandinista Nicaragua. *Geographical Review*, v. 83, no. 1 (Jan 93), pp. 1 – 13. Bibl, maps.

Waller, Thomas. Southern California Water Politics and U.S. – Mexican Relations: Lining the All-American Canal. *Journal of Borderlands Studies*, v. 7, no. 2 (Fall 92), pp. 1 – 32. Bibl, maps.

Walter, Knut and Philip J. Williams. El ejército y la democratización en El Salvador. *ECA; Estudios Centroamericanos*, v. 48, no. 539 (Sept 93), pp. 813 – 839. Bibl, il, tables.

— The Military and Democratization in El Salvador. *Journal of Inter-American Studies and World Affairs*, v. 35, no. 1 (1993), pp. 39 – 88. Bibl, tables.

Walters, Keith. Waste Not, Want Not. *Business Mexico*, v. 3, no. 12 (Dec 93), pp. 38 – 39. Charts.

Walvin, James. Selling the Sun: Tourism and Material Consumption. *Revista/Review Interamericana*, v. 22, no. 1 – 2 (Spring – Summer 92), pp. 208 – 225. Bibl.

Wanderley Pinho, José. Humoristas no parlamento do império: notas esparsas. *Revista do Instituto Histórico e Geográfico Brasileiro*, no. 372 (July – Sept 91), pp. 908 – 929.

Wapnir, Salomón. Carlos Vaz Ferreira: entrevista en 1929. *Hoy Es Historia*, v. 10, no. 58 (July – Aug 93), pp. 15 – 18. Il.

Wara Céspedes, Gilka. "Huayño," "Saya," and "Chuntunqui": Bolivan Identity in the Music of "Los Kjarkas." *Latin American Music Review*, v. 14, no. 1 (Spring – Summer 93), pp. 52 – 101. Bibl, il, facs.

Ward, Peter M. Social Welfare Policy and Political Opening in Mexico. *Journal of Latin American Studies*, v. 25, no. 3 (Oct 93), pp. 613 – 628. Bibl, tables.

Ward, Thomas Butler. Toward a Concept of Unnatural Slavery during the Renaissance: A Review of Primary and Secondary Sources. *Revista Interamericana de Bibliografía*, v. 42, no. 2 (1992), pp. 259 – 279. Bibl.

Warley, Jorge. Revistas culturales de dos décadas, 1970 – 1990. *Cuadernos Hispanoamericanos*, no. 517 – 519 (July – Sept 93), pp. 195 – 207. Bibl.

Warnken, Cristián. Eduardo Anguita en la generación del '38. *Estudios Públicos (Chile)*, no. 52 (Spring 93), pp. 329 – 342.

Warren, Patrizio. Mercado, escuelas y proteínas: aspectos históricos, ecológicos y económicos del cambio de modelo de asentamiento entre los achuar meridionales. *Amazonía Peruana*, v. 11, no. 21 (Sept 92), pp. 73 – 107. Bibl, tables.

Watkins, Kevin. El GATT y el Tercer Mundo: como establecer las normas (Excerpt from *Fixing the Rules: North – South Issues in International Trade and the GATT Uruguay Round*, translated by Cecilia M. Mata). *Realidad Económica*, no. 113 (Jan – Feb 93), pp. 122 – 141.

Watson, Hilbourne Alban. The U.S. – Canada Free Trade Agreement and the Caribbean, with a Case Study of Electronics Assembly in Barbados. *Social and Economic Studies*, v. 41, no. 3 (Sept 92), pp. 37 – 64. Bibl.

Watson, Patrick Kent. Savings, the Rate of Interest, and Growth in a Small Open Economy: The Trinidad and Tobago Experience. *Social and Economic Studies*, v. 41, no. 4 (Dec 92), pp. 1 – 23. Tables, charts.

Weaver, David B. Model of Urban Tourism for Small Caribbean Islands. *Geographical Review*, v. 83, no. 2 (Apr 93), pp. 134 – 140. Bibl, charts.

Weaver, Dion. The History of Television in Belize, 1980 – Present. *Belizean Studies*, v. 21, no. 1 (May 93), pp. 13 – 20. Bibl.

Webster, David et al. The Obsidian Hydration Dating Project at Copán: A Regional Approach and Why It Works. *Latin American Antiquity*, v. 4, no. 4 (Dec 93), pp. 303 – 324. Bibl, tables, charts.

Wehling, Arno. Capistrano de Abreu e Sílvio Romero: um paralelo cientificista. *Revista do Instituto Histórico e Geográfico Brasileiro*, no. 370 (Jan – Mar 91), pp. 265 – 274.

Wehrs, Carlos. Machado de Assis e a música. *Revista do Instituto Histórico e Geográfico Brasileiro*, no. 373 (Oct – Dec 91), pp. 1057 – 1070. Bibl, il.

— Pelo centenário de morte de Antônio da Silva Jardim, 1891 – 1991. *Revista do Instituto Histórico e Geográfico Brasileiro*, no. 372 (July – Sept 91), pp. 775 – 784. Bibl.

— Vida e morte do general Fonseca Ramos: escorço biográfico. *Revista do Instituto Histórico e Geográfico Brasileiro*, no. 371 (Apr – June 91), pp. 533 – 553. Bibl, il.

Weigand, Phil C. Teuchitlán and Central Mexico: Geometry and Cultural Distance. *Anales del Instituto de Investigaciones Estéticas*, v. 16, no. 62 (1991), pp. 23 – 34. Bibl, il, maps.

Weinberg, Gregorio. Viejo y nuevo humanismo. *Cuadernos Americanos*, no. 38, Nueva época (Mar – Apr 93), pp. 13 – 16.

Weinberg, Liliana Irene. Diálogo sobre España y América. *Nueva Revista de Filología Hispánica*, v. 40, no. 2 (July – Dec 92), pp. 807 – 821. Bibl.

— Ezequiel Martínez Estrada y el universo de la paradoja. *Cuadernos Americanos*, no. 42, Nueva época (Nov – Dec 93), pp. 165 – 199. Bibl.

— León Felipe y *Cuadernos Americanos. Cuadernos Americanos*, no. 41, Nueva época (Sept – Oct 93), pp. 187 – 189.

— Lo mexicano en el México moderno. *Cuadernos Americanos*, no. 41, Nueva época (Sept – Oct 93), pp. 204 – 211. Bibl.

Weinberger, Eliot. El zócalo: centro del universo (Accompanied by the English original, translated by Magali Tercero). *Artes de México*, no. 21 (Fall 93), pp. 26 – 31. Il, maps.

Weiskopf, Jimmy. Healing Secrets in a Shaman's Garden. *Américas*, v. 45, no. 4 (July – Aug 93), pp. 42 – 47. Il.

— The Little House of Muses. *Américas*, v. 45, no. 2 (Mar – Apr 93), pp. 50 – 51. Il.

Weisman, Alan. El futuro de Puerto Rico. *Homines*, v. 15 – 16, no. 2 – 1 (Oct 91 – Dec 92), pp. 106 – 111.

Weiss, Raquel. Los colores unidos del Whitney (Accompanied by the English original, translated by Magdalena Holguín). *Art Nexus*, no. 10 (Sept – Dec 93), pp. 98 – 102. Il.

Welch, John H. The New Face of Latin America: Financial Flows, Markets, and Institutions in the 1990s. *Journal of Latin American Studies*, v. 25, no. 1 (Feb 93), pp. 1 – 24. Bibl, tables.

Welti Chanes, Carlos. Políticas públicas de población: un tema en debate permanente. *Fem*, v. 17, no. 128 (Oct 93), pp. 16 – 18.

Werner, Johannes. Plastics Mold into Auto Boom. *Business Mexico*, v. 3, no. 4 (Apr 93), pp. 16 – 19.

— Return of the Gas Crisis Jitters. *Business Mexico*, v. 3, no. 6 (June 93), pp. 32 – 34 +. Tables.

Werner, Martín. La solvencia del sector público: el caso de México in 1988 (Translated by Carlos Villegas). *El Trimestre Económico*, v. 59, no. 236 (Oct – Dec 92), pp. 751 – 772. Bibl, tables, charts.

Werz, Nikolaus. Aspectos del pensamiento político y cultural en Latinoamérica (Translated by Irma Lorini). *Ibero-Amerikanisches Archiv*, v. 18, no. 3 – 4 (1992), pp. 429 – 443. Bibl.

Weschler, Lawrence. A Miracle, a Universe: Settling Accounts with Torturers. *SALALM Papers*, v. 36 (1991), pp. 201 – 208.

West, Peter J. and José Miguel Benavente. Globalization and Convergence: Latin America in a Changing World. *CEPAL Review*, no. 47 (Aug 92), pp. 77 – 94. Bibl, charts.

Westbrook, Leslie A. "Cambios": The Spirit of Transformation in Spanish Colonial Art. *Latin American Art*, v. 5, no. 1 (Spring 93), pp. 54 – 57. Il.

Wettstein, Germán. El mundo de Cristóbal Sánchez, campesino de los Andes. *Derecho y Reforma Agraria*, no. 24 (1993), pp. 95 – 113. Maps.

— La producción y valorización del espacio en un país estancado: interpretación geográfica del caso uruguayo. *Derecho y Reforma Agraria*, no. 23 (1992), pp. 51 – 72. Bibl.

Wey, Valquiria. La Malinche, sus padres y sus hijos. *Cuadernos Americanos*, no. 40, Nueva época (July – Aug 93), pp. 223 – 226.

Weyland, Kurt. The Rise and Fall of President Collor and Its Impact on Brazilian Democracy. *Journal of Inter-American Studies and World Affairs*, v. 35, no. 1 (1993), pp. 1 – 37. Bibl.

Whigham, Thomas Lyle. La transformación económica del Paraguay: una perspectiva oficial de 1863. *Revista Paraguaya de Sociología*, v. 29, no. 85 (Sept – Dec 92), pp. 95 – 98.

— La transformación económica del Paraguay: una perspectiva oficial de 1863. *Revista Paraguaya de Sociología*, v. 30, no. 86 (Jan – Apr 93), pp. 67 – 70.

White, Steven F. La traducción y la poesía chilena de postgolpe: historicidad e identidad de género. *Revista Chilena de Literatura*, no. 42 (Aug 93), pp. 275 – 279.

White Navarro, Gladys. El drama americano de Calderón: mesianismo oficial y estrategias de dominación. *Revista de Crítica Literaria Latinoamericana*, v. 19, no. 38 (July – Dec 93), pp. 115 – 122.

Widmer S., Rolf. La ciudad de Veracruz en el último siglo colonial, 1680 – 1820: algunos aspectos de la historia demográfica de una ciudad portuaria. *La Palabra y el Hombre*, no. 83 (July – Sept 92), pp. 121 – 134. Bibl, tables.

Wiethüchter, Blanca. Primer Encuentro Nacional de Mujeres Poetas: surtidores de enigmas. *Signo*, no. 38, Nueva época (Jan – Apr 93), pp. 113 – 121.

Wijnbergen, Sweder van and Santiago Levy. Mercados de trabajo, migración y bienestar: la agricultura en el Tratado de Libre Comercio entre México y los Estados Unidos (Translated by Carlos Villegas). *El Trimestre Económico*, v. 60, no. 238 (Apr – June 93), pp. 371 – 411. Bibl, tables.

Wilcox, Robert. Paraguayans and the Making of the Brazilian Far West, 1870 – 1935. *The Americas*, v. 49, no. 4 (Apr 93), pp. 479 – 512. Bibl, tables, maps.

Wilde, Alexander. Do Human Rights Exist in Latin American Democracies? *SALALM Papers*, v. 36 (1991), pp. 187 – 190.

Wildes, Kevin. Tecnología médica y el surgimiento de la bioética. *Mensaje*, v. 42, no. 418 (May 93), pp. 129 – 132. Il.

Wilhelmy von Wolff, Manfred and María Teresa Infante Caffi. La política exterior chilena en los años '90: el gobierno del presidente Aylwin y algunas proyecciones. *Estudios Sociales (Chile)*, no. 75 (Jan – Mar 93), pp. 97 – 112.

Wilken, Gene C. Future Caribbean Donor Landscapes: A Geographic Interpretation of Contemporary Trends. *Caribbean Geography*, v. 3, no. 4 (Sept 92), pp. 215 – 222. Bibl.

William, Jan M. and Jorge Alberto Lozoya. María Sada: sonatina en gris mayor. *Artes de México*, no. 21 (Fall 93), p. 102. Il.

Williams, Claudette Rose-Green. The Myth of Black Female Sexuality in Spanish Caribbean Poetry: A Deconstructive Critical View. *Afro-Hispanic Review*, v. 12, no. 1 (Spring 93), pp. 16 – 23. Bibl.

Williams, Gareth. Translation and Mourning: The Cultural Challenge of Latin American Testimonial Autobiography. *Latin American Literary Review*, v. 21, no. 41 (Jan – June 93), pp. 79 – 99. Bibl.

Williams, Lorna Valerie. The Representation of the Female Slave in Villaverde's *Cecilia Valdés*. *Hispanic Journal*, v. 14, no. 1 (Spring 93), pp. 73 – 89. Bibl.

Williams, Philip J. and Knut Walter. El ejército y la democratización en El Salvador. *ECA; Estudios Centroamericanos*, v. 48, no. 539 (Sept 93), pp. 813 – 839. Bibl, il, tables.

— The Military and Democratization in El Salvador. *Journal of Inter-American Studies and World Affairs*, v. 35, no. 1 (1993), pp. 39 – 88. Bibl, tables.

Williams, Raymond Leslie. After Foucault: On the Future of Indo-Afro-Iberoamerican Studies. *Latin American Literary Review*, v. 20, no. 40 (July – Dec 92), pp. 120 – 124.

Williams García, Roberto. Las voces del agua. *La Palabra y el Hombre*, no. 81 (Jan – Mar 92), pp. 386 – 387.

Willis, Katie. Women's Work and Social Network Use in Oaxaca City, Mexico. *Bulletin of Latin American Research*, v. 12, no. 1 (Jan 93), pp. 65 – 82. Bibl, tables.

Willmore, Larry N. Industrial Policy in Central America. *CEPAL Review*, no. 48 (Dec 92), pp. 95 – 105. Bibl, tables.

Wilson, Fiona. Industria informal, talleres y ámbito doméstico. *Revista Mexicana de Sociología,* v. 54, no. 4 (Oct – Dec 92), pp. 91 – 115. Bibl.

Wilson, Michael. Hacia la próxima centuria americana: construyendo una nueva asociación con América Latina. *Relaciones Internacionales (Mexico),* v. 15, Nueva época, no. 57 (Jan – Mar 93), pp. 17 – 30. Bibl.

Wilson, Paul N. and Gary D. Thompson. Common Property and Uncertainty: Compensating Coalitions by Mexico's Pastoral "Ejidatarios." *Economic Development and Cultural Change,* v. 41, no. 2 (Jan 93), pp. 301 – 318. Bibl, tables, charts.

Wilson, Tamar Diana. Theoretical Approaches to Mexican Wage Labor Migration. *Latin American Perspectives,* v. 20, no. 3 (Summer 93), pp. 98 – 129. Bibl.

Winkelbauer, Waltraud. Osterreich-Ungarns Handelsvertragsprojekte mit Lateinamerika nach 1870. *Zeitschrift für Lateinamerika Wien,* no. 43 (1992), pp. 7 – 62. Bibl.

Winocur, Rosalía and Mario Constantino. Cultura política y elecciones: algunas imágenes de la sucesión presidencial. *El Cotidiano,* v. 10, no. 58 (Oct – Nov 93), pp. 47 – 53. Bibl, tables.

Winograd, Alejandro. Areas naturales protegidas y desarrollo: perspectivas y restricciones para el manejo de parques y reservas en la Argentina. *SALALM Papers,* v. 36 (1991), pp. 105 – 122. Bibl.

Winz, Antônio Pimentel. In memoriam: Egon Wolff. *Revista do Instituto Histórico e Geográfico Brasileiro,* no. 370 (Jan – Mar 91), pp. 330 – 331.

Witoshynsky, Mary. A Builder of Bridges. *Business Mexico,* v. 3, no. 4 (Apr 93), p. 42. Charts.

— Changing of the Guard. *Business Mexico,* v. 3, no. 8 (Aug 93), pp. 42 – 43. Il.

— The Essence of Partnership. *Business Mexico,* v. 3, no. 7 (July 93), pp. 28 – 31. Il.

— "An Extraordinary Visit." *Business Mexico,* v. 3, no. 4 (Apr 93), pp. 40 – 41. Il.

— "The Final Steps." *Business Mexico,* v. 3, no. 10 (Oct 93), p. 47. Il.

— Florida Governor Puts Trade Focus on Mexico. *Business Mexico,* v. 3, no. 7 (July 93), p. 50. Il.

— The New Politics of NAFTA. *Business Mexico,* v. 3, no. 3 (Mar 93), p. 48. Il.

Wojtyla, Karol
See
John Paul II, Pope

Woldenberg, José. Estado y partidos: una periodización. *Revista Mexicana de Sociología,* v. 55, no. 2 (Apr – June 93), pp. 83 – 95. Bibl.

— ¿Un nuevo animal? *Nexos,* v. 16, no. 185 (May 93), pp. 61 – 65.

Wolfe, Joel. Social Movements and the State in Brazil (Review article). *Latin American Research Review,* v. 28, no. 1 (1993), pp. 248 – 257. Bibl.

Wolter, Matilde. Chile renueva su democracia. *Nueva Sociedad,* no. 128 (Nov – Dec 93), pp. 6 – 11.

Womack, James P. Awaiting NAFTA. *Business Mexico,* v. 3, no. 4 (Apr 93), pp. 4 – 7. Il.

Wong, David. La bolsa de valores de Lima, 1980 a 1990: un análisis de liquidez, rentabilidad y riesgo. *Apuntes (Peru),* no. 29 (July – Dec 91), pp. 67 – 87. Bibl, tables.

Wong, Oscar. Ritual de la mujer amada. *La Palabra y el Hombre,* no. 81 (Jan – Mar 92), pp. 94 – 96.

Wong, Rebeca and Ruth E. Levine. Estructura del hogar como respuesta a los ajustes económicos: evidencia del México urbano de los ochenta. *Estudios Demográficos y Urbanos,* v. 7, no. 2 – 3 (May – Dec 92), pp. 493 – 509. Bibl, tables, charts.

Wong González, Pablo. La región norte de México en la triangulación comercial y productiva del Pacífico. *Comercio Exterior,* v. 43, no. 12 (Dec 93), pp. 1153 – 1163. Bibl, tables.

Woo Morales, Ofelia. La migración internacional desde una perspectiva regional: el caso de Tijuana y Ciudad Juárez. *Relaciones Internacionales (Mexico),* v. 15, Nueva época, no. 57 (Jan – Mar 93), pp. 87 – 94. Charts.

Wood, Stephanie. The Evolution of the Indian Corporation of the Toluca Region, 1550 – 1810. *Estudios de Cultura Náhuatl,* v. 22 (1992), pp. 381 – 407. Bibl, maps.

Woodman, Ronald F. and Antonio Mabres. Formación de un cordón litoral en Máncora, Perú, a raíz de El Niño de 1983. *Bulletin de l'Institut Français d'Etudes Andines,* v. 22, no. 1 (1993), pp. 213 – 226. Bibl, il, maps.

Woodyard, George W. El teatro hispánico en Estados Unidos: ¿Cruce o choque de culturas? *Conjunto,* no. 89 (Oct – Dec 91), pp. 7 – 12. Bibl, il.

Woodyard, George W. and Vicky Wolff Unruh. Latin American Theatre Today: A 1992 Conference in Kansas. *Latin American Theatre Review,* v. 26, no. 2 (Spring 93), pp. 6 – 8. Il.

World Bank. Directiva operacional concerniente a pueblos indígenas. *Anuario Indigenista,* v. 30 (Dec 91), pp. 255 – 266. Bibl.

World Council of Indigenous Peoples. Declaración universal de las primeras naciones. *Anuario Indigenista,* v. 30 (Dec 91), pp. 317 – 319.

— Resoluciones del Quinto Encuentro del Parlamento Indígena de América. *Anuario Indigenista,* v. 30 (Dec 91), pp. 321 – 330.

Woss W., Herfreid. Calculating Customs Valuation. *Business Mexico,* v. 3, no. 6 (June 93), pp. 38 – 39.

Wrobel, Paulo S. Aspectos da política externa independente: a questão do desarmamento e o caso de Cuba (Translated by Dora Rocha). *Estudos Históricos,* v. 6, no. 12 (July – Dec 93), pp. 191 – 209. Bibl.

Wrobel, Paulo S. and Alexandra de Mello e Silva. Entrevista com Celso Lafer. *Estudos Históricos,* v. 6, no. 12 (July – Dec 93), pp. 271 – 284.

Wuellner, Margarita Jerabek. Argentine Architect Julián García Núñez, 1875 – 1944. *SALALM Papers,* v. 34 (1989), pp. 53 – 91. Bibl, il.

Wuellner, Margarita Jerabek and Jack S. Robertson. A Computer Search on Latin American Architecture: Results and Implications. *SALALM Papers,* v. 34 (1989), pp. 92 – 96.

Wunder, Dieter and Héctor Gutiérrez. Determinantes del precio de mercado de los terrenos en el área urbana de Santiago: comentario (on the article by Figueroa and Lever in *Cuadernos de Economía,* v. 29, no. 86). *Cuadernos de Economía (Chile),* v. 30, no. 89 (Apr 93), pp. 131 – 138. Bibl, tables.

Wylie, Harold A. The Cosmopolitan Condé, or, Unscrambling the Worlds. *World Literature Today,* v. 674, no. 4 (Fall 93), pp. 763 – 768. Il.

Xirau, Ramón. Dos poemas ("Nosotros, vosotros," "Muertos del '39"). *Vuelta,* v. 17, no. 199 (June 93), p. 21.

— Variación. *Vuelta,* v. 17, no. 196 (Mar 93), p. 15.

Xu, Wenyuan. El enfoque chino sobre los estudios latinoamericanos. *SALALM Papers,* v. 36 (1991), pp. 15 – 19.

Yacou, Alain. La insurgencia negra en la isla de Cuba en la primera mitad del siglo XIX. *Revista de Indias,* v. 53, no. 197 (Jan – Apr 93), pp. 23 – 51. Bibl.

Yáñez, Silvia. Poesía uruguaya (Review article). *Plural (Mexico),* v. 22, no. 258 (Mar 93), p. 79.

Yánover, Héctor. La librería: escenas domésticas. *Cuadernos Hispanoamericanos,* no. 517 – 519 (July – Sept 93), pp. 521 – 524.

Yarbro-Bejarano, Ivonne. The Multiple Subject in the Writing of Ana Castillo. *The Americas Review,* v. 20, no. 1 (Spring 92), pp. 65 – 72. Bibl.

Yariv, Danielle and Cynthia Curtis. Después de la guerra: una mirada preliminar al papel de la ayuda militar de EE.UU. en la reconstrucción postguerra en El Salvador. *ECA; Estudios Centroamericanos,* v. 48, no. 531 – 532 (Jan – Feb 93), pp. 61 – 74. Il.

Yarza, Pálmenes. Otros comentarios acerca de *Multitud secreta. Revista Nacional de Cultura (Venezuela),* v. 53, no. 285 (Apr – June 92), pp. 227 – 232.

Yep, Virginia. El vals peruano. *Latin American Music Review,* v. 14, no. 2 (Fall – Winter 93), pp. 268 – 280. Bibl, facs.

Yepes Arcila, Hernando. La independencia del poder judicial. *Revista Javeriana,* v. 61, no. 598 (Sept 93), pp. 247 – 257.

Yepes del Castillo, Ernesto. Un balance 500 años después: ciencia, biodiversidad y futuro. *Debate (Peru),* v. 16, no. 74 (Sept – Oct 93), pp. 57 – 60.

Yglesia Martínez, Teresita. The History of Cuba and Its Interpreters, 1898 – 1935 (Translated by Néstor Capote). *The Americas,* v. 49, no. 3 (Jan 93), pp. 369 – 385. Bibl.

Yordi, Mirta and Raúl Marrero Fente. El tema de la democracia en pensadores políticos argentinos. *Islas,* no. 96 (May – Aug 90), pp. 67 – 70. Bibl.

Young, Caroll Mills. Virginia Brindis de Salas vs. Julio Guadalupe: A Question of Authorship. *Afro-Hispanic Review,* v. 12, no. 2 (Fall 93), pp. 26 – 30. Bibl.

Young, George F. W. German Banking and German Imperialism in Latin America in the Wilhelmine Era. *Ibero-Amerikanisches Archiv,* v. 18, no. 1 – 2 (1992), pp. 31 – 66. Bibl, tables.

Young, Leslie and José Romero. Crecimiento constante y transición en un modelo dinámico dual del Acuerdo de Libre Comercio de la América del Norte (Translated by Carlos Villegas). *El Trimestre Económico,* v. 60, no. 238 (Apr – June 93), pp. 353 – 370. Bibl.

Young, Richard A. "Verano" de Julio Cortázar, *The Nightmare* de John Henry Fuseli y "the judicious adoption of figures in art." *Revista Canadiense de Estudios Hispánicos,* v. 17, no. 2 (Winter 93), pp. 373 – 382. Bibl.

Younoszai, Barbara and Rossi Irausquin. Not Establishing Limits: The Writing of Isaac Chocrón. *Inti,* no. 37 – 38 (Spring – Fall 93), pp. 155 – 161. Bibl.

Yunén, Rafael Emilio. André Corten y la debilidad del estado. *Estudios Sociales (Dominican Republic),* v. 26, no. 93 (July – Sept 93), pp. 41 – 60.

Yurkievich, Saúl. César Vallejo: la vigencia del rechazo. *Inti,* no. 36 (Fall 92), pp. 23 – 28.

Zabludovsky, Gina. Hacia un perfil de la mujer empresaria en México. *El Cotidiano,* v. 9, no. 53 (Mar – Apr 93), pp. 54 – 59 +. Tables.

Zachrisson, Boris A. Navidad de oro. *Revista Cultural Lotería,* v. 51, no. 392 (Nov – Dec 93), pp. 87 – 89.

Zacklin, Lyda. Escritura, exactitud y fascinación en la narrativa de José Balza. *Inti,* no. 37 – 38 (Spring – Fall 93), pp. 171 – 177. Bibl.

Zaglul, Jesús M. Documento: *Estudios Sociales;* 25 años de reflexión y análisis. *Estudios Sociales (Dominican Republic),* v. 26, no. 92 (Apr – June 93), pp. 93 – 99.

Zago, Angela. Testimonio y verdad: un testimonio sobre la guerrilla. *Inti,* no. 37 – 38 (Spring – Fall 93), pp. 29 – 35.

Zahler, Roberto. Monetary Policy and an Open Capital Account. *CEPAL Review,* no. 48 (Dec 92), pp. 157 – 166. Bibl.

— Palabras de agradecimiento (for the "premio de la Asociación de Egresados de Ingeniería Comercial de la Universidad de Chile al ingeniero comercial más destacado del año 1992"). *Estudios Sociales (Chile),* no. 77 (July – Sept 93), pp. 197 – 202.

Zaid, Gabriel. La Jeune Belgique y la poesía mexicana. *Vuelta,* v. 17, no. 200 (July 93), pp. 17 – 18.

— Razones para la exención. *Vuelta,* v. 17, no. 196 (Mar 93), pp. 43 – 47.

Zaid, Gabriel and Pedro Aspe Armella. De la esquina. *Vuelta,* v. 17, no. 197 (Apr 93), pp. 82 – 84.

Zaitzeff, Serge Ivan. Cartas de Gabriela Mistral a Genaro Estrada (Includes four letters). *Cuadernos Americanos,* no. 37, Nueva época (Jan – Feb 93), pp. 115 – 131.

Zalduendo, Susana C. de
See
Czar de Zalduendo, Susana

Zaluar, Alba. Mulher de bandido: crônica de uma cidade menos musical (Accompanied by an English translation). *Estudos Feministas,* v. 1, no. 1 (1993), pp. 135 – 142. Bibl.

Zambrano Pantoja, Fabio and Vincent Gouëset. Géopolitique du district spécial de Bogotá et du Haut-Sumapaz, 1900 – 1990. *Bulletin de l'Institut Français d'Etudes Andines,* v. 21, no. 3 (1992), pp. 1053 – 1071. Bibl, maps.

Zamora, Ricardo and Mónica Luza. Exposición de arte contemporáneo de artistas latinoamericanos en Berlín. *Humboldt,* no. 108 (1993), pp. 100 – 101. Il.

Zamora Jambrina, Hermenegildo. Escritos franciscanos americanos del siglo XVIII. *Archivo Ibero-Americano,* v. 52, no. 205 – 208 (Jan – Dec 92), pp. 691 – 766.

Zanotti de Medrano, Lilia Inés. Rio Grande do Sul: una provincia brasileña vinculada comercialmente al Plata en el siglo XIX. *Todo Es Historia,* v. 26, no. 307 (Feb 93), pp. 60 – 72. Bibl, il, maps.

Zapata, Francisco. Transición democrática y sindicalismo en Chile. *Foro Internacional,* v. 32, no. 5 (Oct – Dec 92), pp. 703 – 721. Bibl, tables.

Zapata, Sonia. La mendicidad y su mundo. *Estudios Sociales (Chile),* no. 76 (Apr – June 93), pp. 67 – 94. Bibl.

Zapata Ortega, Diego and Fernando Urrea Giraldo. El síndrome de los nervios en el imaginario popular en una población urbana de Cali. *Revista Colombiana de Antropología,* v. 29 (1992), pp. 207 – 232. Bibl.

Zapata Prill, Norah. Venezia sin tí. *Signo,* no. 36 – 37, Nueva época (May – Dec 92), pp. 233 – 237.

Zapata Saldaña, Eduardo E. El personaje que se le olvidó a Ribeyro: Roberto Challe. *Debate (Peru),* v. 15, no. 70 (Sept – Oct 92), pp. 60 – 62. Il.

Zapater Equioiz, Horacio. El padre Luis de Valdivia y la guerra defensiva. *Mensaje,* v. 42, no. 420 (July 93), pp. 220 – 223. Il.

Zapiola, Guillermo. Indios y españoles en pantalla grande. *Cuadernos del CLAEH,* v. 17, no. 63 – 64 (Oct 92), pp. 161 – 166.

Zarattini, María. Las telenovelas y la imagen de la mujer. *Fem,* v. 17, no. 130 (Dec 93), pp. 18 – 19.

Zavala, Ricardo I. The Prayer. *Bilingual Review/Revista Bilingüe,* v. 18, no. 1 (Jan – Apr 93), pp. 48 – 52.

Zavala, Silvio Arturo. Justo Sierra Méndez, educador. *Hoy Es Historia,* v. 10, no. 55 (Jan – Feb 93), pp. 76 – 81. Il.

Zaverucha, Jorge. The Degree of Military Political Autonomy during the Spanish, Argentine, and Brazilian Transitions. *Journal of Latin American Studies,* v. 25, no. 2 (May 93), pp. 283 – 299. Bibl, tables.

Zayas de Lille, Gabriela. Los sermones políticos de José Mariano Beristáin de Souza. *Nueva Revista de Filología Hispánica,* v. 40, no. 2 (July – Dec 92), pp. 719 – 759. Bibl.

Zea, Leopoldo. América Latina: qué hacer con 500 años de historia. *Ibero-Amerikanisches Archiv,* v. 18, no. 3 – 4 (1992), pp. 445 – 453. Bibl.

— Conciencia de América (Excerpt from his book entitled *La esencia de lo americano). Hoy Es Historia,* v. 10, no. 60 (Nov – Dec 93), pp. 61 – 69. Bibl.

— Emigración igual a conquista y ocupación. *Cuadernos Americanos,* no. 37, Nueva época (Jan – Feb 93), pp. 13 – 22.

— Filosofía de las relaciones de América Latina con el mundo. *Cuadernos Americanos,* no. 41, Nueva época (Sept – Oct 93), pp. 93 – 100.

— Historia de dos ciudades. *Cuadernos Americanos,* no. 41, Nueva época (Sept – Oct 93), pp. 175 – 179.

— Lo mexicano en la universalidad. *Cuadernos Americanos,* no. 41, Nueva época (Sept – Oct 93), pp. 193 – 203.

— Naturaleza y cultura. *Cuadernos Americanos,* no. 39, Nueva época (May – June 93), pp. 91 – 95.

— Vasconcelos y la utopía de la raza cósmica. *Cuadernos Americanos,* no. 37, Nueva época (Jan – Feb 93), pp. 23 – 36. Bibl.

Zea Prado, Irene. El reto de la integración de América Latina: entre Bolívar y Monroe. *Relaciones Internacionales (Mexico),* v. 14, Nueva época, no. 56 (Oct – Dec 92), pp. 49 – 53.

Zeballos, Carlos A. El protocolo de Brasilia. *Integración Latinoamericana,* v. 17, no. 185 (Dec 92), pp. 51 – 54.

Zecenarro Villalobos, Bernardino. De fiestas, ritos y batallas: algunos comportamientos folk de la sociedad andina de los k'anas y ch'umpiwillcas. *Allpanchis,* v. 23, no. 40 (July – Dec 92), pp. 147 – 172. Bibl.

Zedillo Ponce de León, Ernesto. Palabras de Ernesto Zedillo Ponce de León, secretario de educación pública, en la inauguración de la reunión "La Reforma del Estado y las Nuevas Aristas de la Democracia en Iberoamérica," organizada por El Colegio de México, el 17 de marzo de 1992. *Foro Internacional,* v. 32, no. 5 (Oct – Dec 92), pp. 772 – 776.

Zegers A., Cristián. El carisma de San Ignacio está vigente. *Mensaje,* v. 42, no. 420 (July 93), pp. 335 – 336. Il.

Zeitlin, Judith Francis. The Politics of Classic-Period Ritual Interaction: Iconography of the Ballgame Cult in Coastal Oaxaca. *Ancient Mesoamerica,* v. 4, no. 1 (Spring 93), pp. 121 – 140. Bibl, il, maps.

Zeitlin, Robert Norman. Pacific Coastal Laguna Zope: A Regional Center in the Terminal Formative Hinterlands of Monte Albán. *Ancient Mesoamerica,* v. 4, no. 1 (Spring 93), pp. 85 – 101. Bibl, il, maps.

Zeledón Cambronero, Mario. Periodismo, historia y democracia. *Revista de Ciencias Sociales (Costa Rica),* no. 57 (Sept 92), pp. 7 – 16. Bibl.

Zeller, Ludwig. Tejedor zapoteco (Accompanied by an English translation). *Artes de México,* no. 21 (Fall 93), pp. 66 – 67.

Zemelman Merino, Hugo. Sobre bloqueo histórico y utopía en América Latina. *Estudios Sociológicos,* v. 10, no. 30 (Sept – Dec 92), pp. 809 – 817.

Zepeda Martínez, Mario Joaquín. La hora de sobreajuste: de la desaceleración hacia . . . ¿la recesión? *Momento Económico,* no. 68 (July – Aug 93), pp. 8 – 15. Tables, charts.

Zermeño García, Sergio. La derrota de la sociedad: modernización y modernidad en el México de Norteamérica. *Revista Mexicana de Sociología,* v. 55, no. 2 (Apr – June 93), pp. 273 – 290. Bibl.

Zherdinovskaya, Margarita. Colón en la polémica. *Plural (Mexico),* v. 22, no. 262 (July 93), pp. 77 – 78.

Ziccardi, Alicia. Los organismos de vivienda de los asalariados y la política social. *EURE,* v. 19, no. 57 (July 93), pp. 95 – 102. Bibl, tables.

Zijm, Gerda and Giel Ton. Matrimonio conflictivo: cooperativas en un proyecto agroindustrial; el caso de Sébaco, Nicaragua. *Estudios Rurales Latinoamericanos,* v. 15, no. 2 – 3 (May – Dec 92), pp. 121 – 138. Bibl, tables.

Zilio, Giovanni Meo

See

    Meo Zilio, Giovanni

Zilli Mánica, José Benigno. Una reflexión sobre la religiosidad mexicana. *La Palabra y el Hombre,* no. 81 (Jan – Mar 92), pp. 147 – 158. Bibl.

Zimbalist, Andrew S. Cuba in the Age of "Perestroika" (Review article). *Latin American Perspectives,* v. 20, no. 1 (Winter 93), pp. 47 – 57. Bibl.

Zimmermann, Klaus. Zur Sprache der afrohispanischen Bevölkerung im Mexiko der Kolonialzeit. *Iberoamericana,* v. 17, no. 50 (1993), pp. 89 – 111. Bibl.

Zimmermann Martí, María. Estudio paralelo de *Azul* y *Versos sencillos. Revista Cultural Lotería,* v. 51, no. 390 (July – Aug 92), pp. 65 – 84. Bibl.

Zini Júnior, Alvaro Antônio and Fábio Giambiagi. Renegociação da dívida interna mobiliária: uma proposta. *Revista de Economia Política (Brazil),* v. 13, no. 2 (Apr – June 93), pp. 5 – 27. Bibl, tables, charts.

Zinkant, Annette. Fotos mexicanas en la Casa de las Culturas (Translated by José Luis Gómez y Patiño). *Humboldt,* no. 109 (1993), p. 96. Il.

Zlotchew, Clark M. Literatura israelí en español: entrevista con Leonardo Senkman. *Confluencia,* v. 8, no. 1 (Fall 92), pp. 111 – 121. Bibl.

Zlotnik, Hania. América Latina y México ante el panorama de la población mundial. *Comercio Exterior,* v. 43, no. 7 (July 93), pp. 625 – 633. Tables.

Zonana, Víctor Gustavo. Geografía ocular: elementos para una poética de la visión en la poesía de vanguardia hispanoamericana: Huidobro y Marechal. *Revista Chilena de Literatura,* no. 40 (Nov 92), pp. 57 – 67. Bibl.

Zorraquín Becú, Ricardo and Armando Raúl Bazán. La historia y su divulgación (Two speeches on the occasion of Félix Luna's induction into the National Academy of History). *Todo Es Historia,* v. 27, no. 316 (Nov 93), pp. 43 – 49. Il.

Zubieta, Ana María. El humor y el problema de narrar las diferencias. *Escritura (Venezuela),* v. 17, no. 33 – 34 (Jan – Dec 92), pp. 61 – 82.

Zubieta Castillo, Gustavo. Una belleza que da pánico. *Signo,* no. 38, Nueva época (Jan – Apr 93), pp. 207 – 208.

Zubiri Olza, Jesús

See

Olza Zubiri, Jesús

Zuccotti, Liliana. Juana Manso: contar historias. *Feminaria,* v. 6, no. 11, Suppl. (Nov 93), pp. 2 – 4.

Zum Felde, Alberto. Torres de marfil: Aurelio del Hebrón explica su actitud en política; juzga que todo ciudadano debe interesarse por la marcha de la sociedad en que vive. *Hoy Es Historia,* v. 10, no. 55 (Jan – Feb 93), pp. 21 – 23. Il.

— La tragedia del indio en Suramérica. *Hoy Es Historia,* v. 10, no. 55 (Jan – Feb 93), pp. 102 – 113. Il.

Zúñiga, Víctor. Promover el arte en una ciudad del norte de México: los proyectos artísticos en Monterrey, 1940 – 1960. *Estudios Sociológicos,* v. 11, no. 31 (Jan – Apr 93), pp. 155 – 181. Bibl, tables.

Zúñiga Herrera, Elena. Cambios en el nivel de fecundidad deseada en las mujeres mexicanas, 1976 – 1986. *Revista Mexicana de Sociología,* v. 55, no. 1 (Jan – Mar 93), pp. 83 – 96. Bibl, tables, charts.

Zúñiga Molina, Leonel. Entrevista con Margarita Gómez-Palacio Muñoz. *La Educación (USA),* v. 37, no. 115 (1993), pp. 381 – 394.